Contents

VARIETY'S®
FILM
REVIEWS
1989-1990

VOLUME 21

R.R. Bowker

Volume 21, 1989-1990 of Variety's Film Reviews
was prepared by R.R. Bowker's Database Publishing Division

Peter Simon, Vice President, Database Publishing Group
Albert Simmonds, Editorial Director, Bibliographies

Doreen Gravesande, Senior Managing Editor
George Tibbetts, Senior Editor
Gene Gold, Senior Associate Editor

Published by R. R. Bowker, a division of Reed Publishing (USA) Inc.
121 Chanlon Road, New Providence, NJ 07974

Volume Twenty-One, 1989-1990

PRINTED AND BOUND IN THE UNITED STATES OF AMERICA

Library of Congress Serial Data

Variety's Film Reviews, 1989-1990
Volume 21

ISSN 0897-4373

ISBN 0-8352-3089-9

Manufactured in the United States of America

ISBN 0-8352-3089-9

9 780835 230896

Preface

The reviews contained in this volume are complete and comprehensive reproductions of the original reviews printed in *Variety*. Only full-length feature films are included. Short subjects and made for television films are not included.

User's Guide

The reviews in this collection are published in chronological order, by the date on which the original review appeared. The date of each issue appears at the top of the column where the reviews for that issue begin. The reviews continue through that column and all following columns, until a new date appears at the top of the page. Where blank spaces occur at the end of a column, this indicates the end of that particular week's reviews. An index to film titles for the years 1989-1990 is published in this volume.

1989

Camille Claudel
(FRENCH)

Paris A Gaumont release of a Films Christian Fechner/Lilith Films/Gaumont/A2 T.V. France/Films A2/D.D. Prods. coproduction. Produced by Christian Fechner. Directed by Bruno Nuytten. Screenplay, Nuytten, Marilyn Goldin, from the biography by Reine-Marie Paris; camera (Eastmancolor and Fujicolor), Pierre Lhomme; editor, Joelle Hache, Jeanne Kef; music, Gabriel Yared; art direction, Bernard Vezat; sound, Guillaume Sciama; costumes, Dominique Borg; makeup, Thi Loan N'Cuyen; production manager, Yvonn Crenn; casting, Shula Siegfried. Reviewed at Club Gaumont, Matignon, Paris, Nov. 29, 1988. Running time: **173 MIN.**

Camille Claudel . . . . Isabelle Adjani
Auguste Rodin . . . . Gérard Depardieu
Paul Claudel . . . . Laurent Crevill
Mr. Claudel . . . . Alain Cuny
Madame Claudel . . . . . Madeleine Robinson
Jessie . . . . Katrine Boorman
Rose Beuret . . . . Danièle Lebrun
Louise Claudel . . . . Aurelle Doazan
Victoire . . . . Madeleine Marie
Claude Debussy . . . . Maxime Leroux
Blot . . . . Philippe Clevenot
Morhardt . . . . Roger Planchon

■**France's two top stars Isabelle Adjani and Gérard Depardieu find roles tailored to their considerable talents in this conscientious but dramatically conventional biopic about the gifted sculptress Camille Claudel, who was the muse and mistress of Auguste Rodin.**

Commercial and cultural credentials for this unusually long but slickly produced film should ensure overseas sales.

Made in closed-set circumstances on a $16-million budget (cofinanced by pubcaster Antenne 2, which will get a longer miniseries version), film has become the must-see, year-end domestic attraction.

Though nominal producer and director are Christian Fechner and ace lenser Bruno Nuytten, in his scripting-helming debut, "Camille Claudel" is very much Adjani's picture. She bought the rights to a recent official biography, won the exclusive blessings of the Claudel estate (which effectively sank two rival film projects, including one by Claude Chabrol with Isabelle Huppert) and developed the project over a 5-year period.

The screenplay by Nuytten and Marilyn Goldin (and presumably Adjani) attempts to reestablish Camille Claudel as an artist and woman in her own right, fighting for control of her artistic and emtional destiny and losing in the end.

The film (in its theatrical cut anyway) tends to define Claudel essentially in her tumultuous 15-year relationship with Rodin, who at the beginning of the picture is sufficiently impressed with her work (and her ambitious temperament) to take her on as assistant in his public works atelier.

As exclusive in her romantic needs as she is exacting in her artistic standards, Claudel pushes the complex liaison toward its breaking point. In the process her own mind begins to go. The film wisely ends with her being committed by her family to a mental institution to wretchedly spent the last 30 years of her life.

Treatment glosses over her family's responsibility in Camille's drift toward madness. As her brother, Paul Claudel, rises to celebrity as Catholic poet and dramatist, Camille declines. Her situation between Rodin and Paul, both overbearing and pompous artists, never is seriously dramatized. Scenes with the parents (played by Madeleine Robinson and Alain Cuny, 80-year-old veteran of Paul Claudel's theater) are not the most convincing.

Film's dramatic interest is sustained for much of its length and Nuytten, using his lenser's eye to stylish effect, molds a number of well-textured sequences, notably those involving Rodin and Claudel amid their creative trances.

Adjani throws herself into a role worthy of her abilities, giving intense relief, if not enough pathos, to a strong-willed femme artist in a male-dominated society and art form.

There's no question that the titanic Rodin was destined to be played by Depardieu, who has the stature, style and feeling for such a role. Sporting a thick beard, he "sculpts" a massive portrait of the artist as man, lover and creator.

What's missing between the two performances, however, is the evolution of feelings complicated by professional and private jealousies. When, in one of the film's big scenes, Adjani vents her anger and frustration on Rodin, one is given (somewhat too theatrically) information that has not been adquately communicated earlier.

Period feeling is superbly caught in Pierre Lhomme's subdued lensing, Bernard Vezat's art direction and Dominique Borg's costumes. Editors Joelle Hache and Jeanne Kef manage to avoid the digest feeling that plagues most cinema/tv hybrids.—*Len.*

War Requiem
(BRITISH)

London An Anglo Intl. Films production for the BBC in association with Liberty Films. Executive producer, John Kelleher. Produced by Don Boyd. Directed by Derek Jarman. Camera (color), Richard Greatrex; editor, Rick Elgood; production design, Lucy Morahan; costumes, Linda Alderson. The recording: Composed by Benjamin Britten; Latin text from Missa pro defunctis; poems by Wilfred Owen. With, Galina Vishnevskaya (soprano), Peter Pears (tenor), Dietrich Fischer-Dieskau (baritone), the Bach Choir & London Symphony Chorus, Highgate School Choir, Simon Preston (organ), Orgel Melos Ensemble, London Symphony, conducted by Benjamin Britten. Reviewed at Century Preview theater, London, Dec. 19, 1988. Running time: **85 MIN.**

Wilfred Owen . . . . Nathaniel Parker
The Nurse . . . . Tilda Swinton
Old Soldier . . . . Laurence Olivier
Mother . . . . Patricia Hayes
Enemy Mother . . . . Rohan McCullough
Abraham . . . . Nigel Terry
Unknown Soldier . . . . Owen Teale
German Soldier . . . . Sean Bean

■**As well as being a stunning visual and serious music treat, "War Requiem" is probably avant garde British director Derek Jarman's most mature effort and will certainly attract interest on the festival circuit.**

It will never be a boxoffice bang, but is intelligent art cinema.

Pic is a visualization of Benjamin Britten's oratorio and was financed through the BBC's Independent Planning Unit on a budget of just £650,000 (about $1.2-million). It was shot and released in the U.K. within a staggeringly short 3-month period.

"War Requiem" has no dialog, though it opens with Laurence Olivier reciting Wilfred Owen's poem "Strange Meeting." Olivier — in a welcome return to the screen — also appears in cameo as an old solider tended by a young nurse, Tilda Swinton.

The live-action footage is intercut with documentary footage from the Imperial War Museum.

Pic uses the story of Wilfred Owen's experiences in World War I, up to his death by a sniper bullet one week before the war ended), as its structure, while a nurse and unknown soldier are introduced to supplement Britten's musical scenarios.

Nathaniel Parker as tortured poet Owen and Swinton (a Jarman regular) as the nurse are excellent and made all the better by compassionate direction plus evocative camerawork by Richard Greatrex.

Jarman and his producer, Don Boyd, have constructed a moving and highly original cinematic visualization of Britten's impressive choral work, featuring excellent technical and acting qualities.

The soundtrack is the original recording of the work — composed for the re-opening of Coventry Cathedral in 1962 — with the voices of Peter Pears, Dietrich Fischer-Dieskau and Galina Vishnevskaya, conducted by Britten himself. —*Adam.*

Le Palanquin des larmes
(The Palanquin Of Tears)
(FRENCH-CANADIAN-CHINESE)

Paris An AAA release of an Eiffel Productions/Belstar Prods./Antenne 2 TV France/Films A2/Filmline Intl./Compagnie de Films des Nouveaux Territories Ltd./Canadian Broadcasting Corp./Radio Canada/Shanghai Film Studios/China Film Corp. coproduction, with the participation of the French Ministry of Culture. Produced and directed by Jacques Dorfmann. Screenplay, Dorfmann, Zhang Nuanxin, Max Fischer, David Milhaud, from the autobiography of Chow Ching Lie (with Georges Walter); camera (color), Jean-Claude Larrieu; editor, Françoise Bonnot, Yves Langlois; music, Maurice Jarre; art direction, Quranxin; sound, Bernard Rochut; costumes, Chao Yi Pin; assistant director, Pierre Magny; production manager, Gérard Martin; coproducers, Nicolas Clermont, Pieter Kroonenburg; associate producers, Claude Leger, Chi Xi Dao. Reviewed at the Marignan-Concorde cinema, Paris, Nov. 3, 1988. Running time: **114 MIN.**

Chow Ching Lie (adult) . . . . Quing Yi
   (teen) . . . . Tu Huai Qinq
   (child) . . . . Chen Jie
Wei Hi . . . . Jiang Wen
Yu Wang . . . . Zhou Yiemang
Judy Wang . . . . Huang Zhong Yin
Uncle King . . . . Jiang Xi Ren
Tsou Hon . . . . Huang Fei
Tsong Hai . . . . Elisabeth Sung

■**Classical pianist Chow Ching Lie's bestselling memoir about her painful childhood in China before and after the Communist Revolution of 1949 has been made into an unsatisfactory theatrical film along with a tv miniseries.**

A French-Canadian coprod with China that was some five years in the making, film is hurt by the unskilled direction of its producer, Jacques Dorfmann, and a trite English-dialog track that ruins Dorfmann's search for historical and psychological authenticity (it was shot on location in Shanghai with Chinese actors). Theatrical cut also suffers as an obvious digest of the miniseries which may work better on the basic tearjerking level.

Chow Ching Lie suffered the final outrages of an antiquated feudal system when her financially straitened family married her at age 13 into a wealthy Shanghai family in order to provide latter with an heir.

Ironically, the marriage took place as the Red Chinese Army liberated Shanghai. Chow Ching Lie's marriage to her Chinese noodle of a husband, however, was consummated.

Plucky youngster clung to her passion for the piano and managed to introduce the instrument into her unhappy household, despite a tyrannical mother-in-law.

Film (in its theatrical cut) begins toward the end of the Japanese occupation of Shanghai and concludes when the protagonist goes off to Hong Kong to visit her dying husband, though she knows she will be walking back into the claws of her suffocating, domineering mother-in-law.

How she frees herself from domestic bondage seems to have been saved for the miniseries. That's cheating the paying moviegoer.

Material is bookended by a contemporary frame in which Chow Ching Lie, now the celebrated pianist, is going onstage for a Paris recital. She anxiously is awaiting her father, whom she has not seen since leaving Shanghai decades earlier. At the end of the film he arrives, late: reunion, smiles, tears & curtain.

As producer, Dorfmann no doubt deserves kudos for bringing off what must have been an often frustratingly complicated coproduction. As neophyte helmer he is unable to mold his material convincingly, either on an intimate or grand scale (the sequences of the Red Army's occupation of Shanghai are flat).

Protagonist is portrayed by three actresses, of whom the teen Tu Huai Qinq has the most screen time. She has an immediate visual credibility, as does Jiang Wen as the weak-willed father, and Zhou Yiemang as the kind sickly husband whom Chow Ching Lie eventually learns to appreciate. The accented voices and banal dialog reduce whatever value the performances have.

Tech credits are good, but Maurice Jarre's score is obvious and intrusive. —*Len.*

Les Maris, les femmes, les amants
(Husbands, Wives, Lovers)
(FRENCH)

Paris An MK2 release of a Téléma/Cine 5/Les Films Français coproduction. Produced by Charles Gassot. Directed by Pascal Thomas. Screenplay, Thomas, François Caviglio-li; camera (Eastmancolor), Renan Polles; editor, Nathalie Lataurie; music, Marine Rosier; art direction, Christian Vallerin; sound, Michel Vionnet, Jacques Thomas Gérard, Michel Kharate; assistant director, Patrick Cartoux; production manager, Nicole Firm; casting, Romain Brémond. Reviewed at the Marignan-Concorde cinema, Paris, Dec. 13, 1988. Running time: **117 MIN.**

Martin	Jean-François Stevenin
Dora	Susan Moneur
Emilie	Emilie Thomas
Clément	Clément Thomas
Olga	Olga Vincent
Tocanier	Michel Robin
Marie-Françoise	Catherine Jacob
Jacques	Daniel Ceccaldi
Jacqueline	Anne Guinou
Odette	Hélène Vincent
Bruno	Guy Marchand
Michel	Pierre Jean
Widow Pichard	Isabelle Petit-Jacques
Annette	Catherine Bidaut

■**Overlong, familiar Gallic comic musings on marital couplings, uncouplings, sex and the rest, "Husbands, Wives, Lovers" marks the theatrical return of Pascal Thomas.**

A specialist in gentle sentimental comedies of manners, his previous film dates from 1981. New one's a very French mix of social comedy, farce and armchair sociology that lacks comic edge and control.

Screenplay superficially recalls the inverted structure of the more mordant Canadian sex comedy "Decline Of The American Empire," where its males puttered about the kitchen while the complacent womenfolk worked out at the gym before joining up later for some unsettling revelations.

Here an assortment of men, married, remarried, cuckolded or abandoned, head out for their vacation homes on the Atlantic coast (with the kids) while the ladies stay in Paris and work. Late in the film both sexes are united on holiday, but Thomas and coscripter François Caviglioli just let things ride in an unsatisfying finale.

Dramatic interest is dispersed among a large cast, with standout comic performances by Hélène Vincent as a sniveling, frumpy divorcee who despairs of finding a new mate, and Michel Robin, as an eccentric publisher hounded by a chronically jealous wife. Other players are adequate but often poorly served by falsely epigrammatic dialog. Tech credits are good. —*Len.*

Plaff!
(CUBAN)

Havana An Icaic (Instituto Cubano de Artes e Indústrias Cinematográficas) production. Directed by Juan Carlos Tablo. Screenplay, Daniel Chavarría Reynoso; sound, Raúl García. Reviewed at Havana Film Festival, Dec. 6, 1988. Running time: **90 MIN.**

Concha	Daisy Granados
Clarita	Thais Valdés
Tomás	Raúl Pomares
José Ramón	Luis Alberto García
Asunción	Alicia Bustamante
Contreras	Jorge Cao.

■**From the minute the projector rolls, it is obvious "Plaff!" is an original venture. Using satire, cinema in-jokes and a running gag à la "Murder On The Orient Express," it's the best Cuban film this decade and should be bullish worldwide.**

Starting in the second reel, story finds us deeply involved in the quotidian problems of Concha (admirably played by veteran thesp Daisy Granados). Her life was fine until son José Ramón married Clarita and brought her home to live. Now Concha can't seem to get along with anyone — family, neighbors or friends.

At pic's core is a mystery: Who is tossing eggs at Concha's house? (Film's onomatopoeic title refers to the sound of an egg hitting the house.)

Movie lampoons "santería" (Cuba's unofficial Afro-based religion), daily Cuban problems such as the housing shortage, family relations and bureaucracy in a light-handed fashion, while also calling mocking attention to the filmmaking process. Glitches, sloppy editing, missed cues, end-of-reel overexposed film, clapboards and other filmmaking in-jokes all figure into the jumpy narrative making for humorous results.

At times the in-jokes wear thin, but the overall effect is unexpected and snaps the viewer in and out of the storyline.

"Plaff!" calls to mind the bold celluloid efforts that launched Cuba's entry into world cinema in the early '60s, and is a breath of fresh air after many of the heavy-handed ventures that have characterized recent production. —*Lent.*

Itinéraire d'un enfant gaté
(Itinerary Of A Spoiled Child)
(FRENCH-WEST GERMAN)

Paris An AFMD release of a Films 13/-Cerito Films/TFI Films/Stallion Film/-Gerhard Schmidt Film coproduction. Produced by Claude Lelouch, Jean-Paul Belmondo. Written and directed by Claude Lelouch. Camera (Eastmancolor, 70m), Jean-Yves Le Mener; editor, Sophie Bhaud; music, Francis Lai; art direction, Jacques Bufnoir; sound, Harald Maury; costumes, Mic Cheminal; makeup, Charley Koubesserian; assistant director, Paul Gueu; production managers, Tania Zazulinsky, Claude Albouze; casting, Arlette Gordon. Reviewed at Gaumont Ambassade cinema, Paris, Nov. 30, 1988. Running time: **125 MIN.**

Sam Lion	Jean-Paul Belmondo
Albert Duvivier	Richard Anconina
Victoria Lion	Marie-Sophie L.
Pierre Duvivier	Daniel Gélin
Jean-Philippe Lion	Jean-Philippe Chatrier
First wife	Lio
Second wife	Béatrice Agenin
Lawyer	Michel Beaune
Priest	Pierre Vernier

■**Filmmaker Claude Lelouch and screen star Jean-Paul Belmondo join forces for this long-winded yarn about a world-weary industrialist who sets off on his boat for solitary musings, until he's brought home by news of his collapsing commercial empire.**

Typical globe-trotting, time-tripping Lelouch romance has Belmondo ending a 2-year screen hiatus but failing to renew himself.

First half of this overlong tale is a virtuoso jigsaw of flashbacks and flashforwards as the sea-bound Belmondo remembers his past and present; abandoned by a desperate mother at age three, he is adopted by a circus family and becomes an adolescent bigtop prodigy until he is maimed in a trapeze accident. He finally finds his fortune as an innovative sanitation equipment manufacturer.

Exactly what his belated midlife crisis is about is never pinned down, though it's clear he never wants to return — thus he arranges a phony death at sea. Insensitive to the obvious pain he's inflicting on his kin, Belmondo changes identity and wanders the globe until he meets young Richard Anconina (a former employee of his firm) in Zimbabwe.

This is where a semblance of plot (developed rather indifferently) begins and where the film starts to seem interesting. Belmondo learns that his business is tottering and decides to groom the shy, naive Anconina to infiltrate the company. Anconina sets the account books straight, asserts his new personality (a carbon copy of his Pygmalion) and even marries the boss' daughter (played by Lelouch's teary-eyed new spouse, Marie Sophie L.).

Belmondo, who has wallowed lazily through a long string of commercial vehicles, is still taking it easy there though his charm functions when Lelouch gives him the chance. His long dialog scenes with the intimidated Anconina, who takes film's real acting honors, are comically brisk and entertaining.

Tech credits are lush in the usual Lelouch manner. Overloaded soundtrack has Francis Lai music and songs and a couple of lyrics by the late Jacques Brel, to whom film is dedicated (like story's hero, the songwriter abandoned his career at the height of fame for a solitary life at sea). —*Len.*

Fourteen Days In May
(BRITISH-DOCU)

Florence A BBC-TV release of a Paul Hamann production. Executive producer, Jenny Barraclough. Directed by Hamann. Camera (color, 16m), Patrick O'Shea; editor, Andrew Willsmore; sound, Ron Brown. Reviewed at Festival dei Popoli, Florence, Italy, Dec. 2, 1988. Running time: **80 MIN.**

■This chilling docu, entirely shot in a Mississippi penitentiary by Brit helmer-producer Paul Hamann, portrays the last two weeks in the life of 26-year-old Edward Earl Johnson, convicted of murdering a white town marshal.

Its impact is all the greater because neither filmmakers nor most prison guards and officials believed Johnson is guilty.

Film won top honors at the Festival dei Popoli docu meet in the film category, though its natural outlet is tv. Funded by the BBC, it has been sold to 22 countries. It ran in the U.S. on HBO in a cut 48-minute version, which the director disowns as a "vulgar, insensitive piece of shlock."

In its full version, "Fourteen Days In May" provokes thought and anger over the use of the death penalty, statistically much higher for blacks convicted of murdering whites than vice versa. The quiet, modest Johnson never loses hope for a last-minute reprieve as he waits on death row.

Since his idealistic young ACLU lawyers say reprieves usually are granted up to an hour before the trip to the gas chamber, there is plenty of suspense on the filmmakers' part.

The reaction of prison authorities is surprisingly humane, and in general pic succeeds in holding onto a human dimension that makes the bureaucratic machinery of capital punishment and stays of execution a macabre game. The testing of the electric chair prior to use is an example. As believable as it is maddening, Johnson's story of how a confession was scared out of him on a deserted road makes a strong indictment against racism, as well as capital punishment.

Only jarring note in this well-filmed docu is the fact filmmaker is not American but British, and his emotional involvement with the condemned man too naively evident — where pic's greatest power comes from an objective recounting of the facts. —*Yung.*

Miss Right
(ITALIAN)

Hollywood An Ibrahim Moussa presentation. Produced by Moussa. Executive producer, Michael Janczarek. Directed by Paul Williams. Screenplay, William Tepper, story by Williams, Tepper; camera (Widescreen, color), Franco Di Giacomo; editor, Alessandro Lucidi, Pete Kameron, Alan Stern; music, Michael Small; art direction, Francesco Chianese; costume design, Annalisa Nassali Rocca; sound, Carlo Palmieri; assistant director, Gianni Cozzo; casting, Paola Rolli. Reviewed on Sony vidcassette, L.A., Dec. 17, 1988. MPAA Rating: R. Running time: **100 MIN.**

Amy	Karen Black
Juliet	Margot Kidder
Anna	Virna Lisi
BB	Marie-France Pisier
Terry Bartell	William Tepper

■"Miss Right" is a dismal study of a ladies' man trying to clean up his act. Shot in Rome in 1980, first exhibited at Mifed that year but never released in the U.S., claustrophobic pic is out now on vidcassette.

Written as a vanity vehicle for himself by William Tepper, the lead in Jack Nicholson's 1972 "Drive, He Said," this is the most recent film directed by Paul Williams, who in the late 1960s and '70s was responsible for "Out Of It," the interesting "The Revolutionary" and "Dealing," as well as "Nunzio." Result here reveals no sign of his earlier talent, and bears the earmarks of extensive, if futile, postproduction cut-and-paste work.

Ibrahim Moussa presentation has Tepper as an Italian-based American reporter who, in one evening, intends to "clean out the emotional part of my brain," as he puts it, by ending all his crazy love affairs and devoting himself henceforth to the search for Miss Right.

Boring setup has Tepper scheduling kiss-off dinners with three different women at 2-hour intervals. First up is impossibly neurotic model Marie-France Pisier, who attempts suicide when she hears the news. Next is an elegant, older married woman, Virna Lisi, with whom things go relatively smoothly. Finally, Karen Black arrives by jet from America for a midnight rendezvous, and she is dispatched as well.

Next morning, Tepper picks up Margot Kidder, loses her, then rediscovers her, starting the cycle all over again and leaving the viewer distinctly unrewarded for the time expended on this uninsightful, unamusing drivel.

Although all the actresses save Lisi briefly appear topless, there is no sex at all, and Tepper's abysmal, unconversational dialog consists mainly of defensive maneuvers on his part and mindless babble for the women. Except for a couple of excursions through the streets, entire picture unfolds within Tepper's apartment, suggesting both a highly cramped budget and a 3-act, 1-set play format.

The actresses uniformly come across as overly mannered, and Tepper proves unappealing and quickly tiresome as the manic Romeo who allows his glands to rule his life.

Providing evidence of rumored attempts at editorial doctoring is the total absence from the screen of then-ingenue sexpot Clio Goldsmith despite sixth billing in the credits. Conversely, Jenny Agutter, who was mentioned among the cast members during production but receives no credit herein, can be glimpsed fleetingly getting her purse snatched in the opening minute.

Tech contributions are okay under the circumstances. —*Cart.*

Philippines, My Philippines
(AUSTRALIAN-DOCU)

Sydney A Stoney Desert production. Produced by Maree Delofski, Chris Nash. Directed by Nash. Camera (color), John Whitteron; editor, Ruth Cullen; sound, Bronwyn Murphy. Reviewed at Mosman screening room, Sydney, Nov. 27, 1988. Running time: **73 MIN.**

■This is a hard-hitting docu about life in the Philippines today, almost three years after "People Power" ousted the Marcos regime and restored democracy. Film suggests that, if anything, the troubled country is going downhill faster than before.

Director Chris Nash and his crew filmed in many parts of the country, including villages in which resistance groups, such as the Communist New People's Army, are in control and maintain grassroots popularity. Unending poverty, undiminished since the election of President Aquino, is seen as the country's ongoing problem, with an upsurge in the violent activities of heavily armed vigilantes, openly supported by the military, a factor in the increasing bloodshed.

There are the expected horrific scenes of urban slumdwellers, including some who live solely by recycling garbage. Peasants struggle to survive in the most primitive conditions. Meanwhile, an American serviceman refers to Manila as "the sexual Disneyland of the world" and, at a bicentennial bash, overweight Aussies hold beer-drinking contests and shamelessly humiliate local girls.

America's deputy ambassador takes a positive note on Aquino's achievements, while brushing off the point that the U.S. is flouting the Philippines' non-nuclear constitution. Meanwhile, a Filipino officer, who admits he's been charged with torture by the Human Rights Commission, gives his men a violent pep-talk. Back in the provinces, the nun sadly notes that, under the democratic government, human rights violations continue undiminished, and the actions of vigilantes are on the increase.

In all, it's a depressing picture of a beautiful and vibrant country in very deep trouble. Documentary is expertly made, with top-quality lensing and sound recording. Director Nash and editor Ruth Cullen have done a fine job in assembling the disparate material to obtain maximum impact.

In Australian cities, where docus of this type can have successful runs in arthouse theaters, this one shapes up as a must-see item.
— *Strat.*

White Ghost

New York A Gibraltar Releasing Organization presentation of a White Ghost production. Executive producer, Joel Levine. Produced by Jay Davidson, William Fay. Directed by B.J. Davis. Screenplay, Gary Thompson; camera (Kodak color), Hans Kühle; editor, Ettie Feldman; music, Parmer Fuller; sound, John Bergman; art direction, Dankert Guillaume; assistant director, Raymond Bark; production manager-associate producer, Barrie Saint Clair; fight choreography, Mike Stone; stunt coordinator, Paul Siebert; associate producer, Karl Johnson. Reviewed on TWE vidcassette, Dec. 6, 1988. MPAA Rating: R. Running time: **93 MIN.**

Steve Shepard	William Katt
Thi Hau	Rosalind Chao
Waco	Martin Hewitt
Capt. Walker	Wayne Crawford
Major Cross	Reb Brown
Camp commander	Raymond Ma
Brownie	Karl Johnson
Doc	Graham Clark
Gen. Stafford	Joe Stewardson

■"White Ghost" is a competently made war film looking at the legacy of the Vietnam War from a fable-like viewpoint: the legendary titular U.S. soldier still over there avenging his comrades 15 years later.

William Katt assumes the

Tarzan-type central role, sending a signal back to Washington (in vintage code) while fighting on solo (with spooky white kabuki makeup) in what is now a Vietnam/Cambodia border war. Major Cross (burly Reb Brown) sends in Wayne Crawford and a band of mercenaries to find Katt; wrinkle is that Crawford and Katt previously were at odds when serving together as Green Berets.

Film succeeds in capturing the morbid spirit attending the un-resolved conflict, culminating in a Pyrrhic victory here as Katt hands over scores of collected dogtags to Brown in the finale.

Pic was lensed on Zimbabwe locations, ably doubling for Southeast Asia, and has good action footage directed by B.J. Davis, a graduate from the stunt director ranks. Film originally was planned for release by American Distribution Group, but that firm merged with Spectrafilm and pic ended up direct-to-video via TWE. —*Lor.*

ARCHIVE REVIEW

Manon des sources
(Manon Of The Spring)
(FRENCH-B&W-1953)

Paris   A Franfilmdis release of a Films Marcel Pagnol production. Written, produced and directed by Marcel Pagnol. Camera (b&w), Willy Faktorovitch; editor, Raymonde, Jacques Bianchi; music, Raymond Legrand; art direction, Eugène Delfau; sound, Marcel Royne; makeup, Paul Ralph; production manager, Charles Pons. First released by Gaumont January 16, 1953. Reviewed at the Champo theater, Paris, Oct. 25, 1988. Running time: **222 MIN.**

Manon Cadoret	Jacqueline Pagnol
The Schoolmaster	Raymond Pellegrin
Ugolin	Rellys
Le Papet	Henri Poupon
M. Belloiseau	Robert Vattier
Philoxene, the mayor	Fernand Sardou
The priest	Henri Vilbert
Anatole, the baker	André Bervil
Pamphile, the carpenter	Charles Blavette
The brigadier	René Sarvil
Anglade	Edouard Delmont
Claudius, the butcher	Arius

■ **The Marcel Pagnol novel that inspired Claude Berri's 1986 twin features, "Jean de Florette" and "Manon des sources," was itself a literary reworking of Pagnol's penultimate theatrical feature in 1953.**

Gaumont released the original only after getting Pagnol to make cuts in the nearly 4-hour rural opus (reviewed in truncated form in VARIETY, Feb. 18, 1953).

Recently the major (via affiliate Franfilmdis) had the good idea to revive the film for the first time in its uncut version. Though Pagnol's postwar films generally have been downgraded by critics, "Manon" merits renewed consideration, including for foreign repertory markets, though proper subtitling will be a daunting obstacle.

Action of the 1953 film corresponds roughly to that of the Berri "Manon," with much of the past history of "Jean de Florette" retraced in Pagnol's favorite medium — dialog. Unlike Berri, who had to cram the story into two hours, Pagnol leisurely unfolds his tale, taking the time to sketch a gallery of colorful types familiar from many of the writer-director's earlier classics (e.g., "The Baker's Wife").

"Manon" contains the best and worst of Pagnol. On the debit side notably is the mediocre technical quality, the indifference to classical notions of direction, and a major miscasting, that of Manon, the wild solitary shepherdess who cuts off a village's water supply as vengeance for her father's death. She is played by Jacqueline Pagnol, the filmmaker's lovely wife, whose artificial manner and diction never suggest an orphan who's grown up in the Provençal hills. Emmanuelle Béart is even less convincing in the Berri film.

Yet the film is buoyed by its other vivid characterizations and the nonstop verve of Pagnol's dialog. Though story is plotted in mostly static sequences, there's an enchanting quality in many scenes that is simply not reproduceable on a stage.

Pagnol didn't have Berri's technical polish and basic filmmaking knowhow, but his unselfconscious feeling for his people and his sly manner in exposing their foibles and petty-mindedness gives the b&w film a large edge on its glossy color successor.

Most of the cast is drawn from among Pagnol's regular troupers, including Henri Poupon, as the village elder Le Papet, which Pagnol (in his novel) and Berri expanded as a more central role. Ugolin, the ignorant peasant who is most directly responsible for the death of Jean de Florette and has the misfortune of desperately loving Manon, is unforgettably played by Rellys, a Marselles comic who proved he could shoul-der a dramatic role and generate pathos.

Village types are played to the hilt by naturals such as Robert Vattier, Fernand Sardou (as the fatuous mayor), Henri Vilbert (the priest, who delivers a Sunday sermon lasting some 15 minutes of screen time) and Edouard Delmont. The young Raymond Pellegrin is the condescending but sympathetic school teacher who defends and finally marries Manon.
—*Len.*

FLORENCE FILM FESTIVAL REVIEWS

Comedy's Dirtiest Dozen
(DOCU)

Florence   A 4th & Broadway release of an Intl. Harmony production. Produced by Stuart S. Shapiro. Directed by Lenny Wong. In color. Reviewed at Florence Film Festival, Dec. 9, 1988. Running time: **88 MIN.**

With: Ben Creed, Chris Rock, Jackie (The Jokeman) Martling, Tim Allen, John Fox, Joey Gaynor, Bill Hicks, Stephanie Hodge, Monty Hoffman, Otto Petersen and George, Steven Pearl, Larry Scarano, Thea Vidale.

■ **After "Mondo New York," producer Stuart S. Shapiro has found another entertaining bit of scandal that should do brisk business among uninhibited audiences.**

"Comedy's Dirtiest Dozen" presents 12 American masters and mistresses of barroom and bathroom humor, in 7-minute stand-up routines. It is a compulsively watchable idea (filmed live by Lenny Wong) at New York's Minetta Lane Theater in July 1988) with some real gems, and should be a sure hit on the college circuit.

Lensed with minimum camera movement (some shots of the audience reaction in the theater, but mostly straight filming of the acts), "Comedy's Dirtiest" is a fast-moving hour and a half that looks like a tv variety show, except for the X-rated language. The dirty dozen includes two women comics, two blacks, several New Yorkers and even a ventriloquist's dummy. Humor obviously tends to be ribald, vulgar and deliberately offensive, though some of the comedians sneak in political material, too. The audience eats it up, even when mercilessly provoked.

According to the filmmakers, many of the comedians are regional legends on the comedy circuit, and many have been censored from standard cable tv and talk shows. It isn't hard to see why. For mature viewers, however, film is a well-packaged anthology with filmmakers' and host's interventions kept to a minimum.
—*Yung.*

Astonished

Florence   A Dream Bird Prods. production. Produced by Sydney and Herman Kahn. Directed by Jeff Kahn, Travis Preston. Screenplay, Jeff Kahn; camera (color), Peter Fernberger, Rob Draper; editor, Peter Friedman, Bill Daughton; music, Michael Urbaniak; art direction, Chris Barreca. Reviewed at Florence Film Festival, Dec. 8, 1988. Running time: **103 MIN.**

Sonia	Liliana Komorowski
Detective Jonah Wylee	Ken Ryan

Also with: Rock Dutton, Theresa Merritt, Fred Neuman, Tommy Hollis.

■ **Despite its many amateurish qualities, "Astonished" becomes curiously engrossing in a number of scenes, thanks mostly to the hypnotic powers of actress Liliana Komorowski and a very offbeat storyline that keeps the audience guessing what's coming next.**

The idea of basing film on Dostoevski's "Crime And Punishment" is overdone in the extreme, but directors Jeff Kahn and Travis Preston astutely mix clubs on New York's Lower East Side, yuppies, pimps, detectives and black rock in a hip modern medley aimed at the young crowd. It looks like more of a cult item than mainstream fare.

Film is framed with a crime-pays scene in Brazil, where heroine Sonia Ivanovna (Komorowski) relaxes on the beach and sings to calypso rhythms. Main story takes place in a cold New York winter. Sonia, a spacy resident of a cold water flat who doesn't have money to pay the rent, is propositioned by her heavy-set, middle-aged black landlord, also a pimp.

After refusing cash from a good friend (pride?), and watching the unsavory landlord beat up one of his girls in a bar, Sonia goes to his apartment and stabs him to death, along with a woman who stumbles onto the scene.

Film runs the gamut in tone, from eerie special effects during the murder to parodistic comedy to mellow rhythm and blues clubs (a great music score is pic's main asset), without much rhyme, reason, or control. Film comes closest to Dostoevski in Sonia's bizarre meetings with police detective Ken Ryan, who knows she did it and plays a cat and mouse game with erotic undertones.

Sonia may not be the screen's most coherent character, but Komorowski bears an unusual face capable of some intensity. Exhibitionistic and rebellious, Sonia carries on an affair with a Harry Belafonte-style singer until film's end, when she ends up in Brazil with an obsessed detective. So much for punishment.

It's technically acceptable.
— *Yung.*

Tin Star Void

Florence A Six-Shooter Films production. Intl. sales, Double Helix Films. Produced by Jean Bodon, Paul Falcone, Tom Gniazdowski, Leopold Wurm. Directed by Gniazdowski. Camera (color), Adam Goldfine; editor, Michael Lang; music, Sound X; art direction, David Perlman. Reviewed at Florence Film Festival, Dec. 9, 1988. Running time: **95 MIN.**

Wade Holt	Daniel Chapman
Annie	Ruth Collins
Hawk	Loren Blackwell
Star	Karen Rizzo

Also with: Phillip Nutman (Tough), John Pierce (Kid).

■ "Tin Star Void," a self-consciously post-modern Western-comedy-sci-fi actioner, comes from Tom Gniazdowski, producer of indies like "Sid And Nancy." It is a work whose only chance is to make it as a cult film, since it's so far out from normal schemes and conventions.

Its 2-D comic strip characters aren't likely to inspire much intense identification, but their violent adventures, adorned with guns and black stockings, could interest younger viewers. Pic is titled "Death Collector" for foreign release.

The place is an imaginary Hartford City, sparsely populated by cowboys in '50s roadsters and criminals who live in luxury in Greek-urned hotels. In this apocalyptic landscape, lone cowboy Wade Holt (lanky, muscular Daniel Chapman, always grinning infectiously) arrives with his guitar. Recklessly taking the crime lord's girlfriend Annie (B-movie queen Ruth Collins) to bed, Wade gets his brother the Sheriff killed.

His quest for revenge lands him in a surrealist Southern prison for many years, until a nationwide disaster, the collapse of the economy, closes the prison down and sets Wade and a black sidekick free. Together with Annie they stage a raid on Hawk's (Loren Blackwell) hotel, mowing down his space-suited network of guards till they each the Boss.

This tongue-in-cheek punk Western is professionally lensed. Thesps are called on only to pose, which Chapman in particular is quite skilled at. There is a lot of shooting and kittenish women in their underwear. Collins is barely there as the female lead; Karen Rizzo plays a tough saloon owner with more style. Nonsense plot is strictly for the kiddies. — *Yung.*

Street Story

Florence A Films Around the World release of a Three Wise Monkeys Filmworks production, in association with the Picker Film Group. Written and produced and directed by Joseph B. Vasquez. Camera (color), editor, Vasquez; music, Edward W. Burrows. Reviewed at Florence Film Festival, Dec. 8, 1988. Running time: **90 MIN.**

Junior	Angelo Lopez
Joey	Cookie
Cecilia	Lydia Ramirez
T.C.	Melvin Muza
Rosa	Soraya Andrade

Also with: Zerocks (Willie), Rena Zentner (Nadia), Edward W. Burrows (father).

■ One of the standouts at the American indie fest in Florence, "Street Story" manages to make the South Bronx an almost human neighborhood, countering its innate violence with appealing characters and humor.

Despite its conventional story of two brothers, personal tragedy and the mafia, "Street Story" shines with a memorable realism, both in its depiction of the slum and an astonishingly good non-pro cast. It could make the leap to theatrical release with the right distribbery.

Made on the tiniest of shoestrings, pic was written, directed, produced, lensed and cut by South Bronx resident Joseph B. Vasquez, a film cutter whose directing talent is obvious. The two brothers are Junior (Angelo Lopez), a muscle-bound, good-hearted neighborhood hero, and Joey (Cookie), who dreams of finishing college and moving out of the area's bleak poverty and violence. Their father owns a barber shop and is resigned to paying the local mafia protection money each month.

Though poor, Junior and Joey are full of life, affection, and humor. Lopez' Junior is a particularly convincing portrait of a strongman who defends abandoned mother Soraya Andrade and fights Joey's decision to marry his pregnant girlfriend and leave school (as he did). Dialog is often improvised and Joey's clowning around with his black pals is as believable as Junior's strained relations with his young wife.

Film falls into melodramatic cliché around the time Joey's girlfriend is knifed to death by drug addicts, and storywise never quite recovers its initial force. Joey's shooting rampage of the mafia collectors ends in arbitrary bloodshed and takes film down to the level of an actioner. Its bitter conclusion, barely lightened by a little boy's defiant anger, makes a trite ending to a sensitive story.

Naturalness of setting and thesps more than makes up for a shortage of production coin. A pathetic music score is the weak point of good technical credits. — *Yung.*

Severance

Florence A Fox/Lorber Films release of a Euphoria Film production. Produced by Ann Bohrer, David Max Steinberg. Directed by Steinberg. Screenplay, Steinberg, Cynthia Hochman; camera (color), Steinberg; editor, Steinberg, Thomas R. Rodinella, Cecilia Zanuso; music, Daniel May. Reviewed at Florence Film Festival, Dec. 10, 1988. Running time: **95 MIN.**

Ray Ponti	Lou Liotta
Cly Ponti	Lisa Nicole Wolpe
P.J.	Linda Christian-Jones

Also with: Carl Pistilli (Marty), Sandra Soehngen (Sonia), Martin Haber (Lyle), Lou Bonaki (Georgie).

■ Pro cinematographer David Max Steinberg makes a dignified directing debut with "Severance," an indie production whose excellent technical work belies its shoestring budget.

Tale of a New York drifter trying to win back his daughter's affection banks on the sensitive performances of the two principals. Film is human to the point of being over-emotional at times, and ought to find sizable audiences with the right handling.

Ray (Lou Liotta) has sunk from Air Force officer to alcoholic bum after a car accident in which his wife was killed. He says his daughter Cly (Lisa Nicole Wolpe), who was a child at the time of the accident, is away at college. Actually she has been estranged from her father for years, and works as a go-go dancer in a sleazy bar.

Ray has a strange idealistic streak that puts him on the wrong side of some underworld drug pushers. In danger of his life, he borrows a car from friend P.J. (fine performance from Linda Christian-Jones, even if we never know what she sees in Ray) and goes to see Cly in their old family home, which she has just bought back. Their reconcilation is handled effectively, thanks to Liotta and Wolpe's restrained performances.

Script is in a classic mode without too many surprises, but works emotionally most of the time. Its weak point is redundant dialog and some scenes of unmotivated violence from down-and-outer Ray. This shouldn't bother most audiences. Lensing (by Steinberg), score (by Daniel May) and soundtrack are atmospheric and lovingly worked on. — *Yung.*

Office Party
(CANADIAN)

Florence An SC Entertainment production. Produced by George Flak. Executive producers, Nicolas Stiliadis, Syd Cappe. Directed by George Mihalka. Screenplay, Stephen Zoller, Michael A. Gilbert, based on Gilbert's novel; camera (color), Ludek Bogner; editor, Stan Cole; music, Billy Bryans. Reviewed at Florence Film Festival, Dec. 10, 1988. Running time: **95 MIN.**

Eugene Brackin	David Warner
Larry Gaylord	Michael Ironside
Sally Laird	Kate Vernon
Joan Talmage	Jayne Eastwood
Police chief	Will Lyman
Sergeant	Graeme Campbell

■ An unassuming accountant snaps and takes his office hostage in George Mihalka's black comedy-drama "Office Party." This professionally lensed Canadian indie was warmly received at the closing of the Florence Film Festival.

Its slightly demented sense of humor and ironic reading of the hostage film genre should appeal to young audiences especially, while a top-notch cast injects a subtle note of melancholy under the gags.

Virtually the whole film unfolds at a bleak hydroelectric plant where mild-mannered, reliable employee Eugene Brackin (played with gentlemanly containment by David Warner) works in a quiet office. One day, for no apparent reason, he brings a machine gun to work and at closing time orders boss Michael Ironside, office manager Sally Laird, and prim secretary Jayne Eastwood to handcuff themselves to their swivel chairs.

The fun of "Office Party" is its keeps-you-guessing tone that ranges from the deadly serious to the totally absurd. The plant is, in the best tradition of the genre, immediately surrounded by police cars, sheriffs, politicians, helicopters, powerful searchlights and walkie talkies. Level-headed police chief Will Lyman feverishly struggles to reason with the berserk employee who has no demands to make other than dinner, while fighting off a trigger-happy squad of sharpshooters sent in by the nervous mayor. The big shootout and technical fireworks are kept for the final scene.

Inside the office, the drama of Eugene and his three hostages crescendos as the captives try to persuade him to surrender. Based on a novel by Michael A. Gilbert, script has its highest moments in the absurd psychological dynamics betwen the characters — the alluring office manager sympathizes with Eugene and uses the occasion to humiliate her smug supervisor who got the job she wanted, while the stiff elderly secretary reveals an unsuspected human side.

For some reason the director winds T.S. Eliot and "The Love Song Of J. Alfred Prufrock" into Eugene's twisted psyche as a kind of philosophical support for the film, causing him to speak in literary riddles that make little sense. His lack of rational explanation for his actions is what gives "Office Party" its offbeat humor. —*Yung.*

The January Man

New York   An MGM/UA Distribution. Co. release from MGM of a Norman Jewison production. Produced by Jewison, Ezra Swerdlow. Directed by Pat O'Connor. Screenplay, John Patrick Shanley; camera (Duart and Medallion color, Deluxe prints), Jerzy Zielinski; editor, Lou Lombardo; music, Marvin Hamlisch; sound (Dolby), Bruce Carwardine; production design, Philip Rosenberg; costumes, Ann Roth, Neil Spisak; assistant director, Martin Walters; associate producer, Christopher Cook; casting, Risa Bramon, Billy Hopkins. Reviewed at MGM screening room, N.Y., Dec. 29, 1988. MPAA Rating: R. Running time: **97 MIN.**

Nick Starkey	Kevin Kline
Christine Starkey	Susan Sarandon
Bernadette Flynn	Mary Elizabeth Mastrantonio
Frank Starkey	Harvey Keitel
Vincent Alcoa	Danny Aiello
Eamon Flynn	Rod Steiger
Ed	Alan Rickman
Alison Hawkins	Faye Grant

Also with: Ken Walsh, Jayne Haynes, Brian Tarantina, Bruce Macvittie, Bill Cobbs, Greg Walker, Tandy Cronyn, Gerard Parkes, Erol Slue.

■**An improbable, Gotham-set romantic** *policier***, "The January Man" may capture some post-holiday business by default, but will need exceptional critical goodwill to last beyond February.**

Kevin Kline as an unorthodox but indispensable detective tracking a serial strangler infuses the film with personality. But the character of sensitive supersleuth Nick Starkey ultimately is as unconvincing as the scenario's plot mechanics and its superficial evocation of political New York's ingrained corruption and cynicism.

Screenwriter John Patrick Shanley's ear for the ragged rhythms of New York speech and bent for fevered off-kilter lyricism lit up "Moonstruck" and fired his underappreciated Bronx period piece, "Five Corners," with originality. In "The January Man," the writer's droll, tennis-volley dialog serves a premise that seems disconcertingly familiar: A disgraced cop who can't get along with the establishment is summoned from exile to crack an unsolvable crime.

Kline has been hung out to dry on dubious allegations of graft by his mean-spirited brother, Police Commissioner Frank Starkey (Harvey Keitel), and brutish Mayor Eamon Flynn (Rod Steiger). He's transferred to the Fire Department, implication being that there's no other recourse for a working-class lunatic Gotham Irishman addicted to danger. But Kline is no ordinary outer-borough habitué of bowling alleys and Blarney Stone bars. He lives in Greenwich Village, loves to cook and pals around with neighbor Ed (Alan Rickman), a struggling artist from somewhere in the British Isles. To his antagonist, police Captain Vincent Alcoa (Danny Aiello) Kline is "a f ... 'n beatnik!"

Apparently he's also the only investigative genius in the entire NYPD, which Kline agrees to rejoin if he's allowed to cook dinner for Keitel's haughty, social climbing wife Christine (Susan Sarandon). These in-laws were once lovers, a situation that's supposed to spice their scenes with bristling erotic tension but doesn't. Kline does strike sexual sparks with the mayor's daughter Bernadette (Mary Elizabeth Mastrantonio) whose friend was murdered by the break-and-enter strangler.

Credit the filmmakers for disdaining safe-sex voguishness. Kline and Mastrantonio take a hotel room 10 minutes after meeting, with the Shanley-esque rationale that, after all, "in a hundred years we'll all be dead."

The strangler of young women has struck for the 11th time in 11 months on New Year's Eve. Shanley's Sherlock is convinced he'll make it a symmetrical 12 in January on a date that's a prime number — elementary. Using inspired intuition and some ultra high-tech computer imaging software (a blatant product placement plug for NEC degrades the dialog), Kline preposterously zeroes in on the precise apartment in the exact building targeted next by the ingenious psychopath.

There's a false ending that does little to make up for the picture's dearth of dry-throat suspense, and only leads to a morally ambiguous albeit happy resolution. Steiger has some volcanic moments in this comeback turn, while the other supporting actors provide serviceable foils for Kline's quirky cop.

Ireland's Pat O'Connor ("Cal") directs like a tourist in a New York that's so bereft of grit and character that it could be Toronto — which it often is. With the exception of the Times Square opening, cinematographer Jerzy Zielinski's pick-up shots of Gotham's rivers, bridges and chic apartment buildings are closer to picture postcards than combat photos. —*Rich.*

The Adventures Of Baron Munchausen (BRITISH)

Hollywood   A Columbia release of a Prominent Features & Laura Film production in association with Allied Filmmakers. Produced by Thomas Schühly. Executive producer, Jake Eberts. Line producer, David Tomblin. Supervising producer, Stratton Leopold. Coproducer, Ray Cooper. Directed by Terry Gilliam. Screenplay, Charles McKeown, Gilliam; camera (Rank color), Giuseppe Rotunno; editor, Peter Hollywood; music, Michael Kamen; sound (Dolby), Frank Jahn; production design, Dante Ferretti; supervising art director, Massimo Razzi; art direction, Teresa Barbasso, Giorgio Giovannini, Nazzareno Piana; set decoration, Francesca Lo Schiavo; costume design, Gabriella Pescucci; makeup, hair design, Maggie Weston; special effects, Richard Conway; optical effects, Peerless Camera Co. Ltd.; assistant directors, John Cozzo, Lee Cleary; second unit director, Michele Soavi; second unit camera, Gianni Fiore Coltellaci; model unit camera, Roger Pratt; casting, Irene Lamb, Margery Simkin, Francesco Cinieri. Reviewed at The Burbank Studios, Burbank, Calif., Jan. 13, 1989. Running time: **125 MIN.**

Baron Munchausen	John Neville
Desmond/Berthold	Eric Idle
Sally Salt	Sarah Polley
Vulcan	Oliver Reed
Rupert/Adolphus	Charles McKeown
Bill/Albrecht	Winston Dennis
Jeremy/Gustavus	Jack Purvis
Queen Ariadne/Violet	Valentina Cortese
Horatio Jackson	Jonathan Pryce
Henry Salt	Bill Paterson
The Sultan	Peter Jeffrey
Venus/Rose	Uma Thurman
Daisy	Alison Steadman
Functionary	Ray Cooper
Commander	Don Henderson
Colonel	Andrew Maclachlan
Executioner	Mohamed Badrsalem
Executioner's Assistant	Kiran Shah
First General	Ettore Martini
Heroic Officer	Sting
Dr. Death	Jose Lifante
King Of The Moon	Ray D. Tutto (Robin Williams)

■**A fitting final installment in Terry Gilliam's trilogy begun with "Time Bandits" and continued with "Brazil," "The Adventures Of Baron Munchausen" shares many of those films' strengths and weaknesses, but doesn't possess the visionary qualities of the latter that made it a cause célèbre with some critics.**

While sustaining interest thanks to its fantastically imaginative conceptual and visual aspects, film falls short in wit, and its entertainment values would seem to lack a certain relevance to current audience tastes and concerns.

Already notorious because of its enormous production problems, alleged position as the crown jewel on David Puttnam's Columbia slate and outrageous cost, said to be about $50-million, pic has no chance of even approaching breakeven, and seems destined to appeal to a specialized, rather than wide, public when it opens domestically in March. A dubbed version did only fair business as a Christmas attraction in West Germany.

A celebration of fantasy and an adventurous spirit in the face of dull reason and logic, "Baron Munchausen" represents a Quixotic undertaking for both its hero and maker; much probably will be made, as it was in the case of Francis Coppola's "Tucker," of the undoubted parallels between fiction and reality.

But looked at squarely on its own terms, the film offers a continual feast for the eyes, rather an overload for the ears, and not enough for the funnybone or the heart. Set in Europe in the 18th century, tale begins with a city under intense siege by the Turks. In true showbiz tradition, the Henry Salt Players are carrying on with an entertainment about the fabulous Baron Munchausen, but the performance in the bombed-out theater is interrupted by an elderly gent who purports to be the Baron himself and begins relating the true story of how he caused the war.

With this, Gilliam takes the viewer into the exquisite palace of the Sultan, whose ferocity is aroused when he loses a bet to the visiting Baron (John Neville). With the help of his variously and superhumanly gifted gang of four, which consists of the fastest runner in the world, a dwarf who can exhale with hurricane force, an expert sharpshooter and an immeasurably strong black man, the Baron makes off with the Sultan's entire treasure, but his city is left to suffer the consequences.

Promising to save the city from the renewed attack, the Baron escapes, with Salt's little daughter in tow, in a gigantic hot-air balloon fashioned out of ladies' underwear, and goes in search of his four comrades.

This journey takes the unlikely pair to some unlikely places. First is the moon, which is presided over by a nutty king (Robin Williams in an uncredited cameo) and queen (Valentina Cortese) whose heads and bodies are detachable.

Next comes the underworld domain of Vulcan (Oliver Reed), a beast whose impossibly lovely young wife (Uma Thurman) surprisingly becomes enamored of the craggy Baron. The enraged Vulcan tosses the old soldier and his motley crew into a forbidding vortex, through which they pass only to emerge into an open sea and thereupon into the mouth of an all-

consuming sea monster, in whose belly the entire unit is finally reunited.

The group's return home occasions a massive, quite goofy battle that results in the city's liberation from the Turks, but that is hardly the end, as the specter of death that has been pursuing the Baron must pay a final visit. But even that does not finish off the film, since Gilliam, in the final analysis, seems willing to give hope and the forces of good the edge over despair and evil.

Physically, the film is opulent on every level, beginning with Dante Ferretti's stupendous production design. The number of sets seems countless, and every one has been conceived on a grand scale but also endowed with endlessly clever detail. The same could be said of Gabriella Pescucci's costumes and Maggie Weston's makeup and hair creations.

Special effects man Richard Conway's ingenuity has been tested at each step of the way, and the film's hallmark may well be its incredibly elaborate fantastical set-pieces, which include the Baron shooting through the night over Turkish troops clinging to a cannonball, the old man and Thurman dancing high above the ground, an island transforming itself into a giant fish, the enemy army being laid waste by otherworldly powers. The effects are generally so successful that these events nearly appear normal.

Unfortunately, the spectacular occurrences sparkle as ornamented vignettes upon a relative skeleton of a plot, one which creates little involvement on its own terms. The Baron himself is rather vain, impatient and not exceptionally lovable as a leading man, and one goes along for the ride with him more out of curiosity about the sights to be seen along the way rather than any sense of excitement about his mission.

Although Gilliam's nimble direction, Giuseppe Rotunno's mobile camerawork, Peter Hollywood's high-gear editing and Michael Kamen's propellent score keep things moving, and the work from the lively cast is uniformly enthusiastic, there is a certain heaviness about the proceedings that no doubt stems from the period trappings and, even more, from the sheer weight of the production. Unlike the case with the best adventures and fantasies, the viewer never becomes swept up in the ex-

citement here, but sort of judges it, admiringly at times, more severely at others, from outside.—*Cart.*

Deepstar Six

Hollywood   A Tri-Star release of a Carolco production. Executive producers, Mario Kassar, Andrew Vajina. Produced by Sean S. Cunningham, Patrick Markey. Directed by Cunningham. Screenplay, Lewis Abernathy, Geof Miller, based on story by Abernathy; camera (Metrocolor), Mac Ahlberg; editor, David Handman; music, Harry Manfredini; sound (Dolby), Hans Roland; production design, John Reinhart; art direction, Larry Fulton, Don Diers; set design, Scott Herbertson; set decoration, Christina Volz; costume design, Amy Endries; underwater camera, Pete Romano; creature design, Shagamauw Prods., creature effects, Mark Shostrom; stunt coordinator, Kane Hodder; assistant director, Peter Gries; casting, Melissa Skoff. Reviewed at UA Coronet Theater, Westwod, Calif., Jan. 10;, 1989. MPAA Rating: R. Running time: **100 MIN.**
Laidlaw . . . . Taurean Blacque
Joyce Collins . . . . Nancy Everhard
McBride . . . . Greg Evigan
Snyder . . . . Miguel Ferrer
Scarpelli . . . . Nia Peeples
Richardson . . . . Matt McCoy
Diane Norris . . . . Cindy Pickett
Van Gelder . . . . Marius Weyers
   Also with: Elya Baskin, Thom Bray, Ronn Carroll.

■ Not for nothing is Tri-Star launching this water-logged suspenser in January, when a dearth of new films gives it a shot at bobbing to the surface. Pic might float initial weekend, but word of mouth will soon deep-six it.

Director-producer Sean Cunningham ("Friday The 13th," "House") molds this tale of a sea monster attacking an ocean-bottom research team.

Crew, while trying to create a level launch site for some ocean-floor Navy missiles, blows up a cavern in which the creature has been dwelling for eons. Enraged, it attacks their craft, manages to get inside, and more or less picks them off one by one. Situation, with surviving crewmen trapped far below the surface in damaged craft that's going to blow up unless they can get past the creature to repair some valves, creates a few good segments of shock and suspense.

But effect is diluted by implausibility, as creature never seems real — more like a goof on a '50s horror movie monster than a true threat. Likewise, tone of the pic vacillates between a realistic suspenser à la "Alien" or "Jaws" to a campy, groan-including gore-fest. In one scene, a panicked crewman hightails it for the surface in a craft that hasn't been depressurized, and is shown bloodily crumpling like a baked apple as

the pressure crushes him. Other crewmen also meet gruesome ends.

One gets the impression that more time was spent conceiving the special effects than the script, but both are murky.

Ditto the underwater photography, as ocean bottom, created and shot in a specially built tank, looks blurry, gloomy and bleak.

Creature is withheld from sight for much of the film, and when it's shown in brief bursts, looks too much like an overgrown lobster. But it is pretty spectacular when it finally gets screen time.

Pic's cast is a grab-bag ensemble with no real center (toplined Taurean Blacque is killed early on). It eventually finds its emotional core in an affair between crewmen Greg Evigan and Nancy Everhard.

A sharp performance by Miguel Ferrer as a punchy, smart-mouthed crewman is diluted when character goes campily berserk. Marius Weyers ("The Gods Must Be Crazy") is buried in a role as preoccupied, stressed-out crew supervisor.

And dialog penned by scripters Lewis Abernathy and Geof Miller wastes time on weak banter and choppy techno-gibberish.

Robust score by Harry Manfredini injects some bouyancy in an otherwise soggy effort.
—*Daws.*

Farewell To The Channel (TAIWANESE)

London   A Long Shong Motion Picture Co. production. Executive producer, Wang Ying-hsiang. Produced by Chang Tui-shu. Written and directed by Wan Jen. Camera (color), Lin Tsan-t'ing; editor, Liao Ch'ing-sung; music, Chang Hung-yi; sound, Tu Tu-chin; art direction, Lai Ming-t'ang; costumes, Chu Mei-yu. Reviewed at London Film Festival, Nov. 22, 1988. Running time: **89 MIN.**
Ah-ch'eng . . . . Yu An-shun
Yeh Hsiao-hui . . . . Yuan Chieh-ying
Her father . . . . Wang Yu
Ah-ch'eng's mother . . . . Mei Fung

■ "Farewell To The Channel" is a wistful tale of doomed young love, played out against the backcloth of a modern Taiwan torn by separation from the Chinese mainland and unsure of its future.

Despite impressive performances from its two photogenic young leads, pic is unlikely to stray far beyond the fest circuit and some Chinese theaters.

Story concerns a young innocent who arrives in Taipei and works as a waiter. He picks up an attractive girl sitting alone in the restaurant, and gallantly offers to escort her home. She accepts, but turns out to be a hooker.

She's a whore with a heart of gold, however, who plies her trade in order to support her aged and sick father. His memory is disintegrating, but he still dreams vividly of inheriting a plot of land on the mainland.

Although love blossoms between the waiter and the reformed prostitute, harmony is threatened by a series of mishaps which leads to an accidental killing and forces the pair on the run from both the police and the underworld.

Pic grinds to its inevitable tragic conclusion of a double suicide, the two lovers resigned to a short life with no future. Director-scripter Wan Jen seems to question whether that may be the fate of Taiwan itself.

Pic is capably shot, offering occasional fascinating glimpses of the seedier parts of capital Taipei and the Taiwan countryside. Outstanding performances from the leads sustain momentum even when the plot seems likely to collapse under sheer weight of pathos. —*Coop.*

Compagni di scuola
(Schoolmates)
(ITALIAN)

Rome   A Columbia Tri-Star Films Italia release of a Cecchi Gori Group Tiger Cinematografica production. Produced by Mario and Vittorio Cecchi Gori. Directed by Carlo Verdone. Screenplay, Leo Benvenuti, Piero De Bernardi, Verdone; camera (color), Danilo Desideri; editor, Antonio Siciliano; music, Fabio Liberatori; art direction, Giovanni Natalucci. Reviewed at Europa Cinema, Rome, Jan. 6, 1989. Running time: **110 MIN.**
Piero (Potato) . . . . Carlo Verdone
Federica . . . . Nancy Brilli
Maria Rita . . . . Athina Cenci
Tony . . . . Christian De Sica
Valeria . . . . Eleonora Giorgi
Cristina . . . . Natasha Hovey
    Also with: Fabio Traversa (Fabris), Alessandro Benvenuti (Gino), Piero Natoli (Luca), Luisa Maneri (Gloria), Angelo Bernabucci, Giusi Cataldo, Maurizio Ferrini, Isa Gallinelli, Massimo Ghini, Luigi Petrucci, Silvio Vannucci, Giovanni Vettorazzo, Carmela Vincenti.

■**Director-comic Carlo Verdone scores a merited Xmas hit with "Schoolmates," a winning look at a class reunion featuring sparkling dialog and fine ensemble acting from a big cast.**

A good example of current Italo comedy, "Schoolmates" is a pro piece of work that could make it abroad with special handling.

The melancholy balance sheet drawn up by these 35-year-olds could be made anywhere in the world, though Verdone is savvy enough to tell his tale in an Italian idiom. From the minute the ex-classmates arrive at the deluxe villa of blond bombshell Nancy Brilli (a self-confessed kept woman), their poses and mannerisms reveal more than they hide about their post-high school lives.

Verdone is a frustrated high school teacher, henpecked by his wife and carrying on a precarious relationship with pretty student Natasha Hovey. In the course of the evening he loses both women. Christian De Sica plays his usual sleazy entertainer down on his luck; Eleonora Giorgi a traumatized ex-wife whose hubby Piero Natoli wins her back during the evening; Luisa Maneri a happy unwed mother; Athina Cenci a psychologist forced to listen to everybody's problems.

A rich meat packer cuts the company down to size with hilariously down-to-earth 1-liners.

Verdone adds a healthy dose of irony to this cross-section of Italian citizens, creating believable characters even out of stereotypes. Most of cast rises far above the mean in comic thesping.

Steering clear of the saccarine and the pathetic, film hits the bull's-eye time and time again. Second half is less inventive than the beginning, and pic lacks a dazzling finale to make it a classic. It remains a finely scripted and lensed offering from one of Italy's top comic talents whose audience appeal extends across age lines.

Film is obtrusively lensed by Danilo Desideri set in an eye-catching villa (which in the end turns out to be another illusion, when Brilli announces she's been tossed out) by art director Giovanni Natalucci. —*Yung.*

Una botta di vita
(A Taste Of Life)
(ITALIAN-FRENCH)

Rome   An Italian Intl. Film release of an Intl. Dean Film/Italian Intl. Film coproduction. Produced by Fulvio Lucisano, Pio Angeletti, Adriano De Micheli. Associate producer, Antonio Passaglia. Directed by Enrico Oldoini. Screenplay, Age, Oldoini, Liliana Betti; camera (color), Giuseppe Ruzzolini; editor, Raimondo Crociani; music, Manuel De Sica; art direction, Luciano Sagoni. Reviewed at Fiamma Cinema, Rome, Dec. 4, 1989. Running time: **106 MIN.**
Battistini . . . . Alberto Sordi
Mondardini . . . . Bernard Blier
Germaine . . . . Andréa Ferréol
Cook . . . . Vittorio Caprioli

■**"A Taste Of Life," an Italian comedy neatly balanced with its French partners in stars and locations, entertains thanks to the lively performances of Alberto Sordi and Bernard Blier, two pensioners who take a vacation together on the Côte d'Azur.**

The oldtimers' theme is dealt with superficially; helmer Enrico Oldoini gets most of his results out of the contrast between Blier's refinement and Sordi's earthiness, plus a good dose of sentimentality. Italo boxoffice has been satisfying, without taking the lead over other Christmas releases.

It's a relief to find Sordi (as Battistini) finally an honest gray — and limping, as he has a wooden leg in the film. As mid-August approaches, he finds himself deserted by his holiday-bound family in a tiny town. Almost the only other inhabitant who hasn't left for vacation is Mondardini (Blier), an elderly gentleman who's dissipated his fortune on women and lives alone. Together they decide to take off in Mondardini's ancient car and experience "a taste of life."

Much against Sordi's will, they end up in St. Tropez and spend the night on the beach (all hotels are full). When they wake up the next morning, they're surrounded by nude sunbathers — to Blier's delight.

Always the ladies' man, Blier strikes up a gallant friendship with Germaine, a down-on-her-luck gambler (Andréa Ferréol). Sordi, instead, bumps into the man who stole his wife from him (Vittorio Caprioli); now penitent, Caprioli offers to give her back, but Sordi brushes him off disconsolately.

The two pals fight, make up and compare life views. This lightweight entry carefully steers clear of unpleasantness like illness and death except to immediately exorcise them. On the other hand, pic achieves a comic balance between the hammy, ever-Roman Sordi and more refined Blier (who makes an admirable Italian snob). Dialog is witty and cast well up to it. Especially appealing are the splendid views of Cannes, St. Tropez and Portofino. Technical work is topnotch. —*Yung.*

Black Eagle

New York   A Taurus Entertainment release of a Rotecon/Magus Prods. presentation of a Shah/Arama production. Executive producer, Sunil R. Shah. Produced by Shimon Arama. Directed by Eric Karson. Screenplay, A.E. Peters, Michael Gonzales, from story by Arama; camera (Rank color), George Koblasa; editor, Michael Kelly; music, Terry Plumeri; sound, Shlomo Freiman; assistant director, Sharon Shamir; fight choreography, Sho Kosugi; associate producers, Ash R. Shah, Jonathan Lurie; casting, Penny Perry. Reviewed on Imperial Entertainment vidcassette, N.Y., Jan. 9, 1989. MPAA Rating: R. Running time: **94 MIN.**
Ken Tani . . . . Sho Kosugi
Andrei . . . . Jean-Claude Van Damme
Patricia Parker . . . . Doran Clark
Father Joseph Bedelia . . . . . . Bruce French
Vladimir Klimenko . . . . Vladimir
                                   Skontarovsky
Dean Richert . . . . William H. Bassett
Brian Tani . . . . Kane Kosugi
Denny Tani . . . . Shane Kosugi
    Also with: Dorota Puzio, Jan Triska, Gene Davis, Alfred Mallia, Julie Rudolph, Eric Karson.

■**"Black Eagle" is an above-average action pic (boasting two of the top names in the genre), released last spring in the South and reviewed on the occasion of its video launch.**

Sho Kosugi toplines as our government's top freelance secret agent, called away from his mission in Afghanistan to travel to Malta and retrieve a crashed F-111 jet that was carrying a secret laser guidance system.

Rather dubious twist is that he's scheduled for a high-priority vacation with his cute (real-life) kids, who are dragged to Malta by pretty blond CIA babysitter/hitlady Doran Clark to be with daddy while he saves the free world. It's fun seeing Kane and Shane Kosugi horsing around with their dad, but such a breach of spy protocol plays off as silly.

Pic is standard spy stuff but enhanced by solid fight scenes choreographed by the elder Kosugi, attractive Malta locations and a most impressive villain, Brussels heartthrob Jean-Claude Van Damme. One the basis of this appearance, Van Damme, who rocketed to good-guy stardom in Cannon's "Bloodsport," would make the perfect James Bond villain with his combo of glamor and physical menace.

Pic suffers from anticlimax after the inevitable Kosugi/Van Damme hand-to-hand battle and lacks a socko finish to round off the action. It's a pleasant enough picture but missing that freshness and audience identification needed for theatrical success. —*Lor.*

SOS — En segelsäll
skapsresa
(SOS — Swedes At Sea)
(SWEDISH)

Malmö   An SF release of a Viking Film production with SF (Svensk Filmindustri), Cinema Art Prods. and Smart Egg Pictures.

Produced by Bo Jonsson. Associate producer, Christer Abrahamsen. Directed by Lasse Aberg. Screenplay, Aberg, with Jonsson; camera (Eastmancolor), Rune Ericson; editor, Sylvia Ingemarsson; music, Bengt Palmers; production design, Styrbjörn Engström; costumes, Hedvig Ander; production management, Britt Ohlsson, Bamse Ulfung; assistant director, Peter Hald. Reviewed at the Palladium, Malmö, Dec. 21, 1988. Running time: **94 MIN.**

Stig-Helmer	Lasse Aberg
Ole	Jon Skolmen
Stig-Helmer's mother	Barbro Hjorth af Ornäs
Arne	Anders Ahlbom
Aelskling	Lena-Pia Bernhardsson

Also with: Tor Isedal, Birgitte Söndergaard, Susanne Barklund, Per Eggers, Ewa Fröling, Johan Rabaeus, Cecilia Haglund, Ulla-Britt Norrman, Björn Wallde.

■ **"SOS — Swedes At Sea" is sure to sail into major boxoffice status in Sweden and neighboring Norway.**

Writer-director-actor Lasse Aberg reunites his fictional creation Stig-Helmer with brash, brassy Norwegian ad man Ole, (played by Norway's comedy favorite Jon Skolmen, in a farcical portrayal of Aberg's countrymen out of their natural element).

A bit of the energy and surprise fun has petered out since Aberg and producer-cowriter Bo Jonsson sent their Nordic city-dwellers to Mallorca in "The Package Tour" and to the Alps in "The Package Tour 2." Lots of chuckles will still follow in the wake of "SOS — Swedes At Sea," in which the foibles of the Swedes, indulging in sailing and other water sports during their brief midsummer holiday in Stockholm's grandiose archipelago, are regarded with as much sympathy as satire.

Stig-Helmer, still mother-dominated and goofy-looking, can neither swim nor sail. His friend Ole would never admit to not being a latterday viking in all respects. They both get ducked at lot, but they also have more luck with a variety of goodlooking young women than all the yuppies, millionaires or other male swashbucklers setting sail around them.

Even when Aberg sees his Swedes at their most ridiculous, he obviously loves them. As for his own Stig-Helmer character, latter is given far too little to do this time around. Wet or dry, he is allowed to remain more an observer than the reluctant participant of the earlier films. To make up for it, Skolmen's Ole is all over the place even if his role also is of diminished substance.

All thesps seem happy and natural in their roles but tread water a lot of the time. —*Kell.*

Dracula's Widow

New York A De Laurentiis Entertainment Group presentation. Produced by Stephen Traxler. Directed by Christopher Coppola. Screenplay, Kathryn Ann Thomas, Coppola; camera (Technicolor), Giuseppe Macari; editor, Tom Siiter; music, James Campbell; sound (Ultra-Stereo), Alan Selk; production design, Alexandra Kicenik; production manager-assistant director, Traxler; special effects unit director, Todd Masters; special makeup effects, Dean Gates; additional editor, Phillip Linson. Reviewed on HBO Video vidcassette, N.Y., Dec. 30, 1988. MPAA Rating: R. Running time: **86 MIN.**

Vanessa	Sylvia Kristel
Lt. Lannon	Josef Sommer
Raymond Everett	Lenny Von Dohlen
Brad	Marc Coppola
Helsing	Stefan Schnabel
Jenny	Rachel Jones

Also with: Traber Burns, Rick Warner, Candice Sims.

■ **"Dracula's Widow" suffers from tired blood. Very minor would-be horror spoof was completed in 1987 but recently sent direct-to-video following the De Laurentiis Entertainment Group's financial collapse.**

As the most oft-filmed character in screen history, Count Dracula was spoofed successfully in a spate of films made a decade ago, notably the George Hamilton-starrer "Love At First Bite." New offering unfolds in flat, unfunny fashion as Vanessa (Sylvia Kristel), Dracula's spouse, shows up in L.A. at Lenny Von Dohlen's Hollywood House of Wax museum and starts putting the bite on people.

He informs her the Count is dead, having been killed by the legendary Von Helsing, whose grandson (Stefan Schnabel) soon is out to get her and her minions. Von Dohlen becomes one of Kristel's slaves after she bites him in a friendly way.

Besides the miscasting of character actor Josef Sommer as the hardboiled detective on the case, filmmaker Christopher Coppola never creates the proper atmosphere for either horror or sendup. Kristel's walkthrough is a bore and even her fans will be disappointed at erstwhile "Emmanuelle's" latterday prudishness regarding sex or nudity (left here to starlets Rachel Jones and Candice Sims). Von Dohlen's affected vocal style doesn't come off either. —*Lor.*

Escape—World Safari III
(AUSTRALIAN)

Sydney An Adventure Bound Prods. presentation. Produced and directed by Alby Mangels. Screenplay, Esben Storm; camera (color, 16m), Graham Dimmitt, Rick Snell,

Evan Ham, Chris Strewe, Graeme Gillies, Rhys Shepherd, Pierre Van Heerden, Reinhold Thaumuller, Alby Mangels; editor, Rod Hay, Tim Jordon. In Dolby. stereo. Reviewed at Hoyts Center, Sydney, Jan. 3, 1989. Running time: **109 MIN.**

With: Alby Mangels, Michelle Els, Lucinda Dunn, Rick Snell, Judy Groon.

■ **Third installment in self-styled adventurer Alby Mangels' semi-dramatized exploits is more of the same although slicker in look.**

Formula has clicked well here and elsewhere to date; indeed, few filmmakers in Oz would have an offering they'd be confident enough with to self-finance, then roadshow around the country under their own banner as Mangels does.

Bronzed and bare-chested, Mangels this time treks around West Africa, some of New Zealand and various regions of Australia. Along the way he effortlessly picks up vehicles and an assortment of animals for transport, has various close calls with danger and suffers the occasional personal loss.

Rough story outline in this strange mixture of fact and the contrived is pursuing the prophecy of a Zulu witchdoctor, but that's more a device to allow Mangels' restlessness to take him hither and thither.

With him, apart from the everfaithful dog, are the usual assortment of scantily clad gorgeous companions he finds on the way who unexplainedly disappear. In a more developed presence, however, Michelle Els returns from "World Safari II" to cause about the same amount of restlessness in Mangels as the witchdoctor.

Much of the dialog and homespun philosophy is awkward. Humor plays a stronger role this time, and Mangels, slowly, is becoming more comfortable in front of the cameras.

Pic is too long. However, "Escape" is more stylish this time around with some good lensing from a bevy of contributors translating well via the 16m blowup, plus a crisp Dolby soundtrack. Whether it'll do as well as its predecessors remains to be seen; more is at stake because of a higher budget, but it has an audience base as a headstart.—*Doch.*

Milan noir
(Black Milan)
(FRENCH-SWISS)

Paris A Capital Cinéma release of a Baccara Prods./Palmyre Productions/CFC/La

Sept/Cofici (Genéva)/Films du Camélias coproduction. Executive producers, Chantal Perrin, Antoine Gannage. Directed by Ronald Chammah. Screenplay, Chammah, Catherine Breillat, Michel Butel, Simon Michael; camera (Eastmancolor), Willy Kurant; editor, Genevieve Winding; music, Michel Portal; sound, Alain Curvelier; production manager, Eric Dussart. Reviewed at Elysées Lincoln theater, Paris, Jan. 3, 1989. Running time: **80 MIN.**

Sarah	Isabelle Huppert
Tremaine	Joaquim de Almeida
Molan	David Warrilow
Hardy	Hanns Zischler
De Giorgi	Jean Benguigui

■ **"Milan noir" is a tedious, incoherent romantic thriller which puts Isabelle Huppert in Milan as the former lover of a long-vanished terrorist.**

The man's imminent return to Italy activates a convoluted mechanism of police and underworld snares.

An international cast, inexplicably bearing Anglo-Saxon character names, sinks into the murk of a talky scenario concocted by four (credited) scripters and turgidly executed by newcomer Ronald Chammah (responsible for the original story).

Lack of suspense, action or logic commercially dooms this pretentious effort. Willy Kurant's lensing is a plus, but Michel Portal's score is not among his best. —*Len.*

Purgatory

New York A New Star Entertainment release and production, in association with Intl. Media Exchange, Filmco and Kingsway Communications. Executive producers, Dimitri Villard, Robby Wald. Produced and directed by Ami Artzi. Screenplay, Felix Kroll, Paul Aratow; camera (color), Tom Fraser; editor, Ettie Feldman; executive editor, Skip Schollnik; music, Julian Laxton; sound, Philip Key; production design, Robert van der Coolwijk; set decoration, Eva Strack; assistant director, Howard Rennie; production manager, Peter Smook; stunt coordinator, Mark Myron; second unit camera, Jerry Lotter; associate producers, Patricia Shorten, Elizabeth Rowley, Smook; casting, Pat Cordes. Reviewed at Criterion 3 theater, N.Y., Jan. 6, 1989. MPAA Rating: R. Running time: **93 MIN.**

Carly Arnold	Tanya Roberts
Melanie	Julie Pop
Bledsoe	Hal Orlandini
Paul Cricks	Rufus Swart
Janine	Adrienne Pearce
Kirsten	Marie Human
Stern	David Sherwood
Ruth Arnold	Clare Marshall
Rivers	Hugh Rouse
Ambassador Whitney	John Newland

■ **Tanya Roberts, erstwhile "Sheena" (Queen of the Jungle), returns to Africa for desultory women-in-stir opus "Purgatory," more embarrassing than her earlier flop.**

One of scores of recent pics lensed in South Africa and environs, pic is less fun than a similar S.A. direct-to-video captive women feature, "Captive Rage," but has received theatrical exposure.

Roberts is undeniably sexy as a Peace Corps worker in a fictional African country who's locked up with pal Julie Pop on a trumped-up drugs charge. Despite her mom Clare Marshall's bribes, the gals get 11-year sentences in a run-down prison known as Purgatory.

Twist is that the evil warden Bledsoe (Hal Orlandini playing a sleazeball with posh accent, similar to Paul Freeman in "Raiders Of The Lost Ark") has his prettier inmates serve their time as prostitutes. Roberts whines and squeals as she's put through the wringer including discreetly filmed but sleazy scenes of simulated fellatio, while Pop is gangraped by the black prison guards, leading to her suicide.

Poorly lit pic limps listlessly to a tired escape-from-stir climax, with time out for typical political content. The American Ambassador (played by uncredited John Newland, a helmer familiar from his "One Step Beyond" tv hosting stint) is a heavy more interested in covering up the fracas than helping U.S. citizens. Unlike the film's numerous Filipino-lensed forebears of 15-plus years back which often featured Pam Grier and Juanita Brown, there are no strong black femme roles among the prisoners, giving the film an unfortunate racist undertone.

Roberts tries hard but the acting is miserable. Though the script was cowritten by her "Sheena" mentor Paul Aratow, she nonetheless gets stuck with an unflattering role. Filmmaker Ami Artzi's direction is leaden and he doesn't know how to have fun with an exploitation subject.—*Lor.*

Glitch

New York   An Omega Pictures production. Produced and directed by Nico Mastorakis. Screenplay, Mastorakis; camera (CFI color), Peter Jensen; editor, Mastorakis, George Rosenberg; music, Tom Maroida; sound (Dolby), Blake Wilcox; production design, Gary New; production manager, Bill Berry; assistant director-associate producer, Perry Husman. Reviewed on Academy Entertainment vidcassette, N.Y., Dec. 17, 1988. MPAA Rating: R. Running time: **90 MIN.**

Todd	Will Egan
Bo	Steve Donmyer
Michelle	Julia Nickson
Julius Lazar	Dick Gautier
DuBois	Ted Lange
Lydia	Teri Weigel
Brucie	Dan Speaker

Also with: Dallas Cole, Ji-Tu Kumbuka, Fernando Carzon, John Kreng, Lindsay Carr, Susan Youngbluth, Bunty Bailey, Joy Rinal-

di, Lisa Erickson, Caroldean Ross, Penny Wiggins, Christina Cardan, Kahlena Marie, Laura Albert, Debra Lamb, Bridget Boland.

■ Action filmmaker Nico Mastorakis switches to comedy with okay results in "Glitch," an insider look at casting a Hollywood movie that's being released direct-to-video.

After a very slow 2-reel opening to laboriously set up the situation of two young goofballs (Will Egan and Steve Donmyer) breaking into Dick Gautier's mansion, pic warms up with the appearance of 100 beauties in bathing suits to audition for Gautier's new film "Sex & Violence."

Egan and Donmyer pose as producer and director of the epic and have fun testing the babes, except for uppity Julia Nickson, who stands up against their sexist behavior. Comedy complications ensue, including a visit from mafia enforcer Ted Lange.

Pic is fun until a namedropping finale in which Mastorakis turns rather preachy, defending the world of low-budget filmmaking (like his "Glitch") against Hollywood's penchant for overly costly blockbusters.

Gimmick of "all those girls" in the cast is pretty much a waste, while leads Nickson and former Playboy mag model Teri Weigel are quite appealing on their own. Donmyer's routine of shifting from dullard to smart guy every time a sound occurs (after being hypnotized) is well done as are physical comedy shticks. Comical end credits are funny, including mention of a "bra wrangler" among crew members. —*Lor.*

Een ongeshreven geschiedenis
(An Unwritten History)
(DUTCH-DOCU)

Amsterdam   A Cinemien release of a DD Filmprodukties production. Produced by Phil van der Linden. Directed by Jeanne Wikler. Camera (color, 16m), Cees Samson; editor, Jack van Doornik; sound, Lukas Boeke, Jac Bol; interviewers, Wikler, Diana Lebacs. Reviewed at Desmet theater, Amsterdam, Oct. 27, 1988. Running time: **110 MIN.**

■ "An Unwritten History" is a 2-part report about the situation of women in the Dutch West Indies by American-born Jeanne Wikler, who has been working in the Netherlands, chiefly in tv, for the past dozen years.

First part, subtitled "Mama Grandi," is an often funny reportage on macho behavior in Cura-

çao. Part two, "Money In The Pocket," deals with money fever on the furiously developing island of Saint Martin, where the less than 20,000 inhabitants discover how to make money without emigrating.

"Mama Grandi" is structured around a day in the life of Elsa: wife, mother, social worker and committee woman. The second half is more like a travelog and dry.

Both chapters are engaging, however, because the director and her subjects clearly have taken a liking to each other. The interviewees wear their best dresses and finest jewelry; everything in their homes is dusted and polished, even the kids. Everybody gives his or her best, so much so that the spontaneity often tends to take a seat in the corner. —*Wall.*

Witchcraft

New York   A Vista Street Prods. presentation of a Feifer/Miller production. Executive producers, Jerry Feifer, Tony Miller. Produced by Megan Barnett, Yoram Barzilai. Directed by Robert Spera. Screenplay, Jody Savin; camera (color), Jens Sturup; editor, Tony Miller; music, Randy Miller; sound, Chris Baker; production design, Ray Lorenz; assistant director, Joe Calk; supervising producer, James Hanson; special makeup effects, Angela Levin; stunt coordinator, Bob Ivy. Reviewed on Academy Entertainment vidcassette, N.Y., Jan. 4, 1989. No MPAA Rating. Running time: **86 MIN.**

Grace	Anat Topol-Barzilai
John	Gary Sloan
Elizabeth	Mary Shelley
Linda	Deborah Scott
Priest	Alexander Kirkwood
Ellsworth	Lee Kisman

■ "Witchcraft" is an underwhelming supernatural horror piece, released direct to video (with video postproduction and credits).

Unrelated to another new (Italian-backed) scream pic named "Witchcraft" and toplining Linda Blair, this film adds a dash of "Rosemary's Baby" to the hoary formula of a new mother's fears and the oppressive move to a gothic mansion.

Pretty Anat Topol-Barzilai is the new mother of a bouncing baby boy who haplessly finds herself moved in with a decidedly evil-seeming mother-in-law (Mary Shelley is the actress' gothic stage name) in an ancient house. She starts seeing visions, particularly in mirrors, and wisely fears for her newborn's safety. Following a burn-at-the-stake prolog, it's finally revealed that Shelley and Anat's husband Gary Sloan are reincar-

nated witches and they're definitely after the kid.

Pert Deborah Scott adds some life as the heroine's best pal, but pic is mainly a string of genre clichés executed by helmer Robert Spera with very little imagination. Pace slows to a crawl in the second half.

Topol-Barzilai is pleasant to look at, with her ample figure kept under wraps here even in scenes (such as human sacrifice climax) when a bit bolder approach is in order. Shelley, despite her apt name, fails at achieving a transition from menacing to out-and-out evil. —*Lor.*

Black Roses

New York   A Shapiro Glickenhaus Entertainment presentation of a Rayvan production. Executive producer, Leonard Shapiro. Produced by John Fasano, Ray Van Doorn. Directed by Fasano. Screenplay, Cindy Sorrell; camera (Medallion color), Paul Mitchnick; editor, Fasano, Van Doorn, James K. Ruxin; music, Elliot Solomon; sound, Robert Vollum; art direction, Nick White; assistant director, Allan Levine; production manager, Sorrell; creature effects, Richard Alonzo, Anthony C. Bua, Arnold Gargiulo 2d; additional camera, Mark MacKay; associate producer, Jerry Landesman. Reviewed on Imperial Entertainment vidcassette, N.Y., Jan. 3, 1989. MPAA Rating: R. Running time: **83 MIN.**

Matthew Moorhouse	John Martin
Mayor Farnsworth	Ken Swofford
Damian	Sal Viviano
Mrs. Miller	Julia Adams
Johnny	Frank Dietz
Priscilla Farnsworth	Carla Ferrigno
Vinny Apache	Carmine Appice
Tony Ames	Anthony C. Bua
Julie	Karen Planden

Also with David Crichton, Jesse D'Angelo, Robin Stewart, Pat Streloff.

■ Made by the team who produced "The Edge Of Hell," "Black Roses" is another direct-to-video monster film uniting rock 'n' roll with satanic horror.

Though played straight, pic covers the same thematic ground as the spoof "Hardrock Zombies," with title band Black Roses coming to the small town of Mill Basin against the city fathers' wishes to delight local teens with heavy metal sounds. It turns out the old fogeys were on the mark, however, since the band led by aptly named Damian (Sal Viviano), is really from hell, bent on leading the teens astray Pied Piper-style.

The kids' English teacher John Martin figures this out and leads an uprising to save the youngsters' souls, achieving same when he burns up Damian (literally) at a climactic concert. Typical tag scene has the group back in action in New York six months later.

Interesting makeup effects are the film's highlight, with rock verisimilitude helped by casting ex-Vanilla Fudge stalwart Carmine Appice as the band's drummer. There are some sexy scenes, but "Creature From The Black Lagoon" alumna Julia Adams has little to do here.—*Lor.*

En el Aire
(On The Air)
(CUBAN)

Havana An Icaic (Instituto Cubano del Arte e Industria Cinematográfica) production. Produced by José R. Pérez. Directed by Pastor Vega. Screenplay, Aida Bahr, Vega, with additional dialog by Julio García Espinosa; camera (color), Julio Valdés; editor, Justo Vega; music, Carlos Fariñas; sound, Germinal Hernández. Reviewed at 10th Havana Film Fest (out of competition), Dec. 13, 1988. Running time: **85 MIN.**
Ans....................Susana Tejera
Daniel................Omar Moynello
Also with Raúl Pomares, Justo Vega.

■ In "En el Aire" (On the Air) Cuban helmer Pastor Vega manages to insert a few brief moments of fresh air into an uneven love story that never becomes airborne.

Storyline involves two young radio journalists — he a local hotshot, she a city girl still green from school — working in the provincial town of Barocoa. Pic deals with their work, their ambitions, their relationship with the community they serve and ultimately, their mismatched love life which eventually comes together through a predictable and promised happy ending.

Young newcomer thesps Susana Tejera and Omar Moynella are sprightly and well-intentioned but hampered by plodding script and heavy-handed direction. Periodic man-on-the-street interviews with locals pepper the plot and provide humor and occasional glimpses of self criticism. Not everything works and some of the jackhammer dialectical commentary comes off as absolutely risible to those familiar with revolutionary propaganda.

On the technical side, pic is lazy and utilizes many extended shots that merely allow the narrative to unravel in the most functional and unimaginative manner possible.

"On The Air" never quite makes it on the screen, and global b.o. appeal rates a mere ho-hum.
—*Lent.*

El Espectro de la Guerra
(The Ghost Of War)
(NICARAGUAN-CUBAN-SPANISH-MEXICAN)

Havana An Incine (Instituto Nicaragüense de Cine) release of an Incine-Televisión Española-Icaic (Cuba)-Imevisión (Instituto Mexicano de Televisión) production. Executive producer, Carlos Alvarez. Produced by Julio Torres. Directed by Ramiro Lacayo Deshón. Screenplay, Lacayo Deshón, Franco Reggiani; camera (color), Livio Delgado; editor, Michael Bloecher; music, Randall Watson; sound, Luis Fuentes; choreography, Alberto Méndez. Reviewed at Havana Film Festival, Cuba, Dec. 10, 1988. Running time: **124 MIN.**
Reynaldo................Elmer Macfield
María...................Alenka Díaz
Miguel...............Manuel Poveda
Grandmother.............Pilar Aguirre
Don Teofilo.....Carlos Alemán Ocampo

■ Boasting slick Hollywood-style production values, the Nicaraguan feature "El Espectro de la Guerra" (The Ghost Of War) comes across as a bizarre hybrid of "Flashdance" meets "Platoon."

Pic may get some international play as a curiosity item, but advocates of New Latino Cinema will come away disappointed. Like the ghost in the title, film is neither fish or fowl.

Film recounts a surface-deep tale of a young dancer from the Bluefields on Nicaragua's Caribbean coast, who goes off to fight the Contras at the price of his own career. For those who aren't interested in politics there are plenty of glossy hoofing sequences — including a breakdance section at a Managua disco — to perk up the plot.

Fast-paced editing keeps the film moving at a rapid clip, too often at the price of the storyline. Dialog is also kept to a minimum: main romantic moments and key exposition scenes are mostly relegated to pretty images set to music.

Pic was dubbed in Spain, which accounts for the Nicaraguan actors using a mixed bag of Argentine, Spanish and other distinctive accents that seem out of place in Central America. —*Lent.*

Juliana
(PERUVIAN)

Havana A Grupo Chaski production. Produced by Stefán Kaspar. Directed by Fernando Espinoza, Alejandro Legaspi. Screenplay, René Weber, Oswaldo Carpio, Kaspar, Espinoza, Legaspi; camera (color), Dany Gavidia; editor, Roberto Aponte; music, José Bárcenas; sound, Mario Rivas, Daniel Padilla. Reviewed at Havana Film Festival, Cuba, Dec. 6, 1988. Running time: **97 MIN.**
Juliana............Rosa Isabel Morfino

Don Pedro..................Julio Vega
Stepfather.........Guillermo Esqueche
Clavito...............Edwar Centeno
Cobra..................David Zúñiga

■ The Peruvian feature "Juliana," produced, written and directed by the 5-member cooperative Grupo Chaski, is a sensitive portrait of street kids living in modern-day Lima. Socially relevant film should find keen interest on arthouse circuit.

Thematically, pic follows on the heels of Chaski's 1984 feature "Gregorio" — about a kid from the countryside and the problems he encounters in the big city. "Juliana" is broader in scope than that film, using fully developed characterizations, humor and poetic moments.

Pic concerns a poor adolescent girl, abused by her layabout stepfather, who finds it better to strike out on her own than endure a miserable life at home. Disguising herself as a boy, she and her younger brother join up with a group of young street thieves à la "Oliver Twist."

In avoiding genre clichés, the duo director team (Fernando Espinoza, Alejandro Legaspi) delves into the protagonist's inner life and studies the complex relationships between characters. In a moving sequence lit only by a solitary candle, Juliana discusses her dreams with her brother, addressing the camera directly in closeup.

Thesping by young actors is well handled, especially Rosa Isabel Morfino in the title role, who gives a moving performance.
—*Lent.*

Murphy's Fault
(BRITISH)

Hollywood A Triax Entertainment release of an Anglo Pacific Films production. Executive producers, David Barrett, Don L. Parker. Produced by Chris Davies, Lionel A. Ephraim. Written and directed by Rogert J. Smawley. Camera (color), Rod Stewart; editor, Simon Grimley. Reviewed at Hollywood Pacific theater, L.A., Jan. 6, 1989. MPAA Rating: PG-13. Running time: **96 MIN.**
David Wayne.........Patrick Dollaghan
Spider...................Stack Pierce
Samantha.................Anne Curry
Also with: Matthew Stewardson.

■ "Murphy's Fault" has some bright spots for being such unsophisticated comedic fluff, especially when considering its main storyline concerns a would-be author whose greatest ambition in life is to own and keep a van.

Actual title on the screen is "It's Murphy's Fault," taking its theme from the old Murphy's Law adage

— what can go wrong will — as it pertains to a certain nightwatchman (Patrick Dollaghan) desperate to move beyond his menial job rut into a writing career. Instead he finds himself down on his luck at every turn.

In the space of a couple of days, he loses two jobs but finds some immediate solace in the news that he's finally sold a story, the money for which goes immediately towards a van that is stolen less than an hour later.

In the context of this thin and poorly developed scenario which roams all over the place in terms of tone, degrees of unoriginality and level of acting, are found at least a handful of funny, clever bits that would make decent sketches on a tv variety hour.

Dollaghan and femme interest Anne Curry, playing a single mother cop, play tag on an emotional and physical level for the duration of this quasi-comedic adventure. Oftentimes, they are expected to exchange ridiculous dialog — like how she's afraid he's too eager for a commitment when they're out on their *first* date — while other lines obviously intended to be light banter come off rather flat.

Not for a second does it seem that Dollaghan's character could possibly be an author — let alone that he even reads — but forgetting that, the actor is convincing as a strong average-Joe type.

His scheme to revenge the coke addict boyfriend of his little sister by substituting the drug with a granular epoxy glue, which he carries out with longtime buddy Spider (Stack Pierce), is particularly funny. —*Brit.*

Les Tisserands du Pouvoir
(Mills Of Power, Part II)
(CANADIAN-FRENCH)

Montreal A Malofilm Distribution release of a Malofilm Group production. Produced by René Malo, Marie-José Raymond. Directed by Claude Fournier. Screenplay, Monique Champange; camera (color), John Berrie; editor, Yurij Luhovy, Fournier; music, Martin Fournier. Reviewed at Cineplex Odeon St. Denis cinema, Montreal, Jan. 4, 1989. Running time: **116 MIN.**
Jean-Baptiste Lambert....Gratien Gélinas
Valmore Lambert.........Michel Forget
Simone Fontaine........Gabrielle Lazure
Jacques Roussel........Aurélien Recoing
Fidélia..............Anne Létourneau
Henriette Fontaine.....Dominique Michel

■ Part two of this power, politics and romance bonanza inexpediently culminates in the beleaguered Quebec pet peeve of language rights.

It is a rich and colorful romp through the American roots of the Quebecois, but its boxoffice appeal beyond rustic boundaries is questionable.

Principally staged in Rhode Island at the turn of the century, the follow-up to "The Mills Of Power, Part I" testifies that fighting for the right to speak French on English turf is an age-old Quebecois tradition.

As in Part I, Quebec history unfolds via the fatigued flashback formula using Gratien Gélinas (playing Jean-Baptiste Lambert) as a vehicle to the past. Gélinas shines as a crotchety old man holed up in 1988 in an abandoned factory threatening to dynamite the place sky high. He wants an American tv network to reinstate his favorite French tv programs. He feels he's paid his dues to the U.S. and they owe him primetime French soaps in his golden years.

Part II further unravels the retrospective tale of Lambert's family who moved to the States to work for French industrialists which then controlled the textile mills. He was one of many toddlers subjected to child labor and lost his arm in the process.

The Catholic church is attacked for its indifference to the plight of its immigrant congregation who sacrificed all for workers rights. The French are attacked for their willingness to unabashedly marry the American capitalist system.

Speckled with modest romance and nudity, this indigenous feature will fare better on the small screen. A 6-part miniseries is set to follow. —*Suze.*

Ghosthouse
(ITALIAN)

New York   A Filmirage production. (Intl. sales. Filmexport Group.) Produced by (uncredited) Aristide Massaccesi, Donatella Donati. Directed by "Humphrey Humbert" (Umberto Lenzi). Screenplay, Cinthia McGavin, from story by "Humbert," dialog, Sheila Goldberg; camera (Telecolor), Franco Delli Colli; editor, Kathleen Stratton; music, Piero Montanari; sound (Dolby), Hubrecht Nijhuis, David Lee; art direction, Alexander Colby; production manager, Tony Hood. Reviewed on Imperial Entertainment vidcassette, N.Y., Dec. 31, 1988. Running time: **94 MIN.**

Martha . . . . Lara Wendel
Paul . . . . Greg Scott
Susan . . . . Mary Sellers
Tina . . . . Kate Silver
Mark . . . . Ron Houck
Jim . . . . Martin Jay
Henrietta . . . . Kristen Fougerousse
Pepe . . . . Willy H. Moon
Valkos . . . . Donald O'Brien
(English soundtrack)

■Umberto Lenzi's supernatural horror pic "Ghosthouse" covers well-trod territory in dull fashion, its main novelty being an Italo film shot on location in Boston.

Lara Wendel, young vet of several Bernardo Bertolucci films, is topcast as a nervous teen who accompanies boyfriend Greg Scott to a spooky mansion from whence he has picked up odd radio messages. These turn out to be screams and warnings from the future, as killings begin to occur at the haunted site caused by violence 20 years before (as shown in a prolog featuring a spooky little girl — Kristen Fougerousse).

Though pic aims for the uppercase status of a Dario Argento shrieker (particularly via its above-average rock score), it degenerates into perfunctory horror not aided by stiff acting (with Wendel a bit stymied by English lingo). Supernatural elements are mainly explained away at the end, but a stupid tag sequence tries to leave matters up in the air.

Tech credits are acceptable.
—*Lor.*

Jacoba
(DUTCH-DOCU)

Amsterdam   A René Scholten production. Written and directed by Joram Ten Brink. Camera (color, 16m), Goert Giltaij; editor, Ton de Graaf; sound, Lukas Boeke, Pjotr van Dijk, Jan van Sandwijk. Reviewed at Nederland Filmmuseum, Amsterdam, Sept. 12, 1988. Running time: **65 MIN.**

■"Jacoba" is an absorbing report from the backwaters of history, and an ode to decency. Joram Ten Brink's documentary recounts the intertwined destinies of two provincial families in Nazi-occupied Holland during the war.

They are the Ten Brinks, Jews established in the area for some 250 years, and the Omvlees, who were millers.

Though Jacoba Omvlees, the miller's widow, had been no particular friend of the Ten Brinks, she risked her life and that of her family to hide the four Ten Brinks for more than two years in a room of a house next to the mill. Jacoba and her eight children kept their dangerous secret with an unselfconscious decency bordering on the heroic.

The director, who is the son of the youngest Ten Brink, and who was born and raised in Israel, has told this story with sympathy and restraint. The only dramatic recreations involve the Ten Brinks' flight to Jacoba's house, and life in their clandestine room, where the Jews are portrayed by members of the Omvlees family. Jacoba is never shown, except for a portrait, but her presence is always felt.
—*Wall.*

Mangeclous
(FRENCH)

Paris   An AAA release of a Mod Film/Initiale Groupe/Initiale Creation/FR3 Films production. Produced by Jacques Kirsner. Written and directed by Moshe Mizrahi, from the novel by Albert Cohen; camera (Eastmancolor), Patrick Blossier; editor, Emmanuelle Castro; music, Philippe Sarde; sound, Daniel Brisseau; art direction, Guy Claude François; costumes, Olga Berluti; makeup, Charly Koubesserian; production manager, Gérard Gaultier. Reviewed at Marignan-Concorde cinema, Paris, Dec. 8, 1988. Running time: **120 MIN.**

Mangeclous . . . . Pierre Richard
Saltiel . . . . Bernard Blier
Salomon . . . . Jacques Villeret
Mattathias . . . . Jacques Dufilho
Michael . . . . Jean-Luc Bideau
Scipion . . . . Jean Carmet
Jeremie . . . . Charles Aznavour
De Surville . . . . Jean-Pierre Cassel
Also the voice of: Bernard Pivot.

■Moshe Mizrahi returns to France with a tame all-star adaptation of "Mangeclous," Albert Cohen's extravagant comic novel about five Mediterranean Jews who in 1938 lay blustering siege to the League of Nations as self-appointed ambassadors of a projected Zionist state in Palestine.

Cohen's novel is a long, rambling ethnic odyssey that moves from a Greek island to Geneva with a Pagnol-like stopover in Marseille. Plot is thin and unconvincing, but is carried along by brilliant flights of comic oratory, topical satire and wild farce in the Marx Bros. vein.

Alas, Mizrahi, a filmmaker firmly entrenched in romanticized realism ("Madame Rosa"), lacks the stylistic panache to recreate Cohen's fantastical universe. Instead he banks on his actors to carry the cut-and-paste screenplay. Rhythm is thus theatrically sluggish, dragging from one verbose setpiece to another.

Cohen's five eccentric Jewish naifs (French-speaking Greek-domiciled Jews who descend from an itinerant clan of French Jews) are portrayed by Bernard Blier, Jacques Villeret, Jacques Dufilho, Jean-Luc Bideau and Pierre Richard, in the role of Mangeclous, the rapacious braggart who gives the story most of its dramatic impetus.

Blier's rotund pious bonhomie is closest to the spirit of the book; Richard's attempt to break away from his stereotyped comic simpletons is an honorable failure. The others are silhouettes that have little more than chorus-like functions.

Jean Carmet has an amusing secondary role as their gentile Marseille friend, and Charles Aznavour is a cowered Polish Jewish immigrant who winds up in Geneva, where he is pressed into a diplomatic imposture by Carmet. Both drop out of the film (and the book) with disconcerting suddenness.

Tech credits are passable. Philippe Sarde's score has a flavor the film lacks. —*Len.*

Iced

New York   A Mikon Releasing Corp. presentation. Executive producer, Michael Biber. Produced by Robert Seibert. Directed by Jeff Kwitny. Screenplay, Joseph Alan Johnson; camera (color), Eugene Shlugleit; editor, Carol Oblath; music, Dan Milner; sound, Fred Aldous; production design, Tim Boxell; production manager-assistant director, Tom Stevenson; special makeup effects, Mike Klint. Reviewed on Academy Entertainment vidcassette, N.Y., Dec. 14, 1988. No MPAA Rating. Running time: **85 MIN.**

Tina . . . . Debra DeLiso
Cory . . . . Doug Stevenson
Carl . . . . Ron Kologie
Diane . . . . Elizabeth Gorcey
John . . . . John C. Cooke
Alex . . . . Joseph Alan Johnson
Jeff . . . . Dan Smith
Eddie . . . . Michael Picardi
Jeanette . . . . Lisa Loring
Suzanne . . . . Sharon Bingham

■Familiar horror scheme of a group of young people invited to a remote spot and killed sequentially is utilized for "Iced," a mild, direct-to-video thriller.

Pic was lensed in Utah in 1987 with the title "Blizzard Of Blood."

Tale is set four years after a fatal skiing accident, when the folks held responsible (by a nutcase) are invited for a free weekend at Snow Peak resort.

Identity of the killer is quite predictable, while the linkup and reason for revenge turn out to be pretty flimsy. Cast is slightly older than the usual teen format but their interrrlationships and problems are no less trivial and boring.

Wintry locations photographed by Eugene Shlugleit are atmospheric, but pic fails to grab one's interest. Gore content is minimal. —*Lor.*

No More Boomerang
(DUTCH-DOCU)

Amsterdam A NFI release of a Yuca Film production. Produced by Suzanne van Voorst. Written and directed by Tom d'Angremond. Camera (color, 16m), Bernd Wouthysen; editor, Jan Dop; music, Maarten Altena; sound, Paul Bolger, D'Angremond; production manager, Gerard d'Olivat. Reviewed at Demset theater, Amsterdam, Nov. 25, 1988. Running time: **83 MIN.**

■ "No More Boomerang" is a reminder that the bicentennial of the discovery of Australia is no cause for celebration for the original inhabitants of the continent, the Aborigines.

Film starts with some lively, well-shot and edited footage but soon gets bogged down in inert interviews with Aborigines in Sydney's Redfern ghetto, and in the Gibson desert in Western Australia, which is studded with "Aboriginal reserves." The Abos, who today number only some 110,000, exist in an "apartheid" all their own, with little chance for decent work and lodging, without hope for cultural, economic and political self-determination. —*Wall.*

Milagro en Roma
(Miracle In Rome)
(COLOMBIAN-SPANISH)

Havana A Televisión Española (TVE) release of a TVE-International Network Group (ING)-Para Elisa Cinematográfica (Colombia) production, under the auspices of the New Latin American Cinema Foundation (Havana). Executive producer, Max Marambio. Produced by Luis Reneses (Spain), Gloria Zea (Colombia). Directed by Lisandro Duque Naranjo. Screenplay, Duque Naranjo, Gabriel García Márquez; camera (color), Mario García Joya; editor, Gabriel González; music, Blas Emilio Atehortua; sound, Heriberto García. Reviewed at Havana Film Festival, Cuba, Dec. 9, 1988. Running time: **80 MIN.**
Margarito Duarte . . . . Frank Ramírez
Tenor . . . . Gerardo Arellano
Evilia Duarte . . . . Amalia Duque García
Bishop of Armenia . . . . . . Santiago García
Ambassador's Secretary . . Lisandro Duque

■ Based on the short story "The Long Happy Life Of Margarito Duarte," the Colombian feature "Miracle In Rome" is the most successful film in the 6-pic series based on stories by Nobel Prize-winning author Gabriel García Márquez under the collective title "Difficult Loves."
Fellow countryman Lisandro Duque brings this fantastic tale to life with a great deal of pathos and charm.

Story begins with the sudden death of young girl Evilia Duarte (Amalia Duque García) and her subsequent interment. Action picks up around a decade later when her father Margarito joins other relatives at the town cemetery who must move family members' remains to a new resting place.

Margarito receives a shock when he opens the coffin: although the box is rotted and falls apart, the girl looks as fresh as the day she died. For all practical purposes, she is merely asleep.

Townsfolk fall to their knees and proclaim her a saint, but the local bishop wants none of it. According to him, the child must be reburied and put to rest along with any superstitious speculations. So, the good townspeople chip in and soon Margarito is off to Rome, toting his daughter as carry-on luggage.

Moral story is told with a great deal of charm. Humor emerges, such as in the scene when Margarito's luggage must be x-rayed by Vatican security.

Acting credits are strong (notably Frank Ramírez as Margarito, and his tenor friend played by Gerardo Arellano). Camerawork, by Cuban cinematographer Mario García Joya, is imaginative and crisp utilizing many complicated dolly shots.

Pic should find interest on the arthouse circuit, especially due to its sense of human interest, magic and innate humor that all combine to lend "Miracle In Rome" the charm of a present-day fairy tale. —*Lent.*

Pleure pas my love
(Don't Cry, My Love)
(FRENCH)

Paris A K.G. production and release. Produced by Michèle Ray-Gavras. Directed by Tony Gatlif. Screenplay, Gatlif, Marie-Hélène Rudel. Camera (Fujicolor), Jacques Loiseleux; editor, Claudine Bouché; music, Raymond Alessandrini; sound, Jean-Pierre Duret; art direction, Denis Mercier; production managers, Pierre Tati, Michèle Ray-Gavras. Reviewed at the Club Gaumont Matignon, Paris, Jan. 3, 1989. Running time: **90 MIN.**
Roxane . . . . Fanny Ardant
Baronski . . . . Jean Pierre Sentier
Fred Lary . . . . Rémi Martin
Olive . . . . Laszlo Szabo
Jules . . . . Fred Personne
Anna Eschenbrenner . . . . Ysabelle Lacamp

■ "Don't Cry, My Love" is an unconvincing romantic drama about the orphaned son of a '50s starlet and an idle contemporary

actress.
Pic is latest entry by Tony Gatlif, Algerian-born helmer whose reputation stands on his 1982 "Les Princes," a flawed but powerful tale of gypsy life. His subsequent feature, "Rue de départ," was a melodrama of marginals inspired more by movie stereotypes than real life.

Newest film brings Gatlif into the realm of bourgeois soul-searching and the results are strained. Rémi Martin is the flighty son of a has-been actress who has committed suicide. Martin visits the film director (Jean-Pierre Sentier) who directed his mother's only screen success and announces her death, then reveals that he's the helmer's son. Sentier welcomes the news but then withdraws into his idiosyncratic creative solitude to mull over a pretentious new film project.

This leaves Martin alone with the helmer's bored wife, Fanny Ardant, a successful thesp who has not worked for some time. The youth falls for her but Ardant (obviously a sub for his dead mom) keeps her distance though feels a kindred attachment to Martin's volatile nature. Martin's desperation peaks when Ardant finally agrees to do a film. He nearly kills himself in a motorcycle accident because of her, though there is a tacit reconciliation between them.

Gatlif's sincerity and relatively low-keyed treatment provides some moments of warmth in the Martin-Ardant relationship but many of the key elements (notably those involving the self-absorbed Sentier) never jell. Ardant, well-photographed by Jacques Loiseleux, is superior to her partners, who are essentially artificial characterizations.

Good tech credits belie film's troubled production history: shooting was interrupted due to bankruptcy of original producer Jacques Le Glou, then bailed out and completed by Michèle Ray-Gavras.—*Len.*

Un Domingo Feliz
(A Happy Sunday)
(VENEZUELAN-SPANISH)

Havana A Televisión Española (TVE) release of a TVE-Intl. Network Group (ING) production, under the auspices of the New Latin American Cinema Foundation (Havana). Executive producer, Max Marambio. Produced by Luis Reneses. Directed by Olegario Barrera. Screenplay, Eliseo Alberto Diego, Barrera, Gabriel García Márquez; camera (color), Juan Andrés Valledares; editor, Armando Silva; music, Maurice Reyna.

Reviewed at Havana Film Festival, Cuba, Dec. 11, 1988. Running time: **90 MIN.**
Silvino . . . . Víctor Cuica
Carlitos . . . . Anthony Sauce
Carlos Arismendi . . . . Daniel López
Laura Arismendi . . . . Marilda Vera
Inspector Carrasco . . . . Alejo Felipe
Also with: Abril Méndez, Carlos Sánchez, Olga Marina Irausquin, Johan Andrade.

■ Part of the 6-pic film series based on Gabriel García Márquez works, "A Happy Sunday" is a predictable tale of a rich kid who pretends to be kidnapped in order to teach his family a lesson. Needless to say, he is the one who learns the lesson.

Venezuelan filmmaker Olegario Barrera offers no surprises and writer García Márquez manages to leave no visible contribution to the production either in theme or style.

Series originally was filmed for Spanish tv, and entire production has the labored feel of a formula-ridden made-for-tv throwaway entertainment. When the story turns predictably into a cop show, pic follows the formula to its eventual conclusion without skipping a beat.

Film attempts to explore the nightlife of Caracas, as the kid (Anthony Sauce) teams up with jazz saxophonist Víctor Ciuca while he goes from club to club performing. Kid meets scantily clad showgirls and demimondaines, all barely discernible from tired, clichéd characterizations. Kid's too-busy-to-care parents also receive functional stock treatment.

Tech credits, nightlife atmosphere and acting are okay, but any b.o. interest in "A Happy Sunday" comes merely from its inclusion in the series. On its own merits, pic rates a resounding zero. —*Lent.*

David Or Goliath
(DANISH-DOCU)

Copenhagen A Hanne Höyberg Film-produktion production and release. Produced by Hanne Höyberg. Conceived and directed by Anne Wivel. Camera (Eastmancolor, 16m), Dan Lausten; editor, Ghita Leavens Beckendorff; sound, Morten Degnböl; production management, Louis Kjär; Danish Film Institute consultant producer, Georg Metz; State Film Central consultant producer, Niels Jensen. Reviewed at the Delta Bio, Copenhagen, Dec. 12, 1988. Running time: **110 MIN.**
With: Murbarak Awad, David Bedein, Zeev Chavets, Mike Elkins, Ilya Gerol, Rafi Horowitz, Daniel Rubinstein, Elias Zananiri, Steve Weizman, Keith Graves, Robert Slater, Ola Andreasen, Geoffrey Bartholet, Gerald Butt, Mary Curtius.

■ With her long docu "David Or Goliath," Denmark's Anne Wivel zeroes in calmly on the moral dilemmas created or enhanced by the Palestinians vs. the Israeli occupiers.

She does so by juxtaposing quotes from prominent members of the foreign press corps and spokesmen for Israeli government press or other media representatives.

Most of "David Or Goliath" was filmed in March in Jerusalem's Beit Agron building, the foreign press headquarters. From outside the building, Reuters' Steve Weizman is heard and seen just before his credentials are revoked (for bypassing the censors), and a visit is paid to Elias Zananiri just as the latter's Palestinian Press Service was closed down by the Israeli authorities.

Main focus, however, is on the Israeli Government Press Office spokesman Rafi Horowitz; Daniel Rubinstein of the Israeli Labor Party daily D'War; Mike Elkins, the ex-BBC correspondent who actually sued the Israeli government all the way to its superior court after its first refusal to allow the foreign press to visit any occupied territory; Ilya Gerol, the Russian-Canadian-Jewish journalist and political analyst; and David Bedein of Israel's Media Relations Agency.

Only one thing seems certain: There is no longer one Goliath and one David in the Israeli-Palestinian confrontation. The film is a credit to the documentary form. —Kell.

The Carrier

New York   A Swan production. Executive producer, Nathan J. White. Produced by Jeffrey Dougherty. Written and directed by White. Camera (color), Peter Deming; editor, White; music, Joseph LoDuca; sound, William Shaffer; assistant director, Michael Sowle; associate producer, Michael Jarema. Reviewed on Magnum Entertainment vidcassette, Dec. 7, 1988. MPAA Rating: R. Running time: **99 MIN.**
Jake . . . . .Gregory Fortescue
Dr. Anthony King . . . . .Steve Dixon
The Reverend . . . . .N. Paul Silverman
Joshua . . . . .Paul Urbanski
Tim . . . . .Patrick Butler
Treva . . . . .Stevie Lee

■ Shot about four years ago in Michigan, "The Carrier" is an amateurish horror film that treats a serious subject — contagion — in ludicrous fashion.

Yet another of the recent horror allegories about the AIDS epidemic, Nathan J. White's indie feature unconvincingly posits the spread of an unknown, fatal disease in a small community, just when it's been cut off from civilization by a rainstorm flooding a nearby gorge.

One touch of a contaminated object or by a person carrying the disease causes the victim to sizzle away as if by acid (though special effects here are chintzy, lacking the goopiness of "The Devil's Rain"). Paranoia quickly takes hold on the community, as a single human carrier (who survives without being consumed) is sought for extermination.

Young hero Jake (Gregory Fortescue) is early on shown to be the carrier, robbing film of much suspense. The whole farrago turns self-destructively into low camp when everyone in town wraps himself up in plastic (as if artist Christo had visited the set) to prevent accidental contamination. A wise guy yells "Go out there and get me cats!" and everyone scurries around trying to catch the critters to be used (rather distastefully) to test objects

Veneer of civilization wears off fast, with film aping horror expert George A. Romero in a showdown between two rival groups at a barricaded house. A subplot attempting to link the murder of Jake's parents to some of the rowdies is extraneous.

Silly treatment submerges some okay ideas in a backyard film. Acting is weak, with poorest performance by heroine Stevie Lee as Treva. —Lor.

Phantom Of Death
(ITALIAN)

New York   A Globe Films/Tandem Cinematografica production, in association with Reteitalia. Produced by Pietro Innocenzi. Directed by Ruggero Deodato. Screenplay, Gigliola Battagnini, Vincenzo Mannino, Gianfranco Clerici, from story by Mannino, Clerici; camera (color), Giorgio Di Battista; editor, Daniele Alabiso; music, Pino Donaggio; set design, Paola Innocenzi; production manager, Giuliano Permarioli. Reviewed on Vidmark vidcassette, N.Y., Dec. 7, 1988. No MPAA Rating. Running time: **91 MIN.**
Robert Domenici . . . . .Michael York
Inspector Downey . . . . . .Donald Pleasence
Elaine Martel . . . . .Edwige Fenech
   Also with: Mapi Galan, Fabio Sartor, Renato Cortesi, Antonella Ponziani, Carola Stagnaro, Daniele Brado, Caterina Boratto.

■ Michael York gives an impressive interpretation as a prematurely aging hero in the otherwise undistinguished Italian horror pic "Phantom Of Death," a direct-to-video release in the U.S.

Previously titled "House On Rubens St.," "Off Balance" and "An Unusual Crime," pic has York as a concert pianist who's contracted a rare disease that's turning him rapidly into a wizened old man. With little suspense, he goes on a killing spree shot on attractive locations including Venice at festival time, while slow-on-the-uptake Donald Pleasence (in a bored walk-through) dogs his trail.

Besides York's solid thesping which engenders some pathos for the central figure, pic benefits from a lush musical score by Pino Donaggio. English dialog track is highly variable in quality, giving beautiful local star Edwige Fenech an opportunity to fracture the language with a sexy but thick French accent. —Lor.

Daisy And Simon
(HONG KONG-AUSTRALIAN)

Las Vegas   An Executive Producers (Hong Kong) Ltd. production, in association with Falcon Films-Barron Films (Perth). Produced by Pamela Borain, Paul Barron. Executive producer, Charles E. Wolnizer. Directed by Stasch Radwanski Jr. Screenplay, Anthony Wheeler; camera (color), John McLean; editor, Mark Norfolk; music, Andrew Hagan, Morton Wilson; sound, Les McKenzie; production design, Kelvin Sexton; production manager, Bill Hughes; assistant director, Steve Jodrell; casting, Frog Promotions. Reviewed at Cinetex Film Festival, Las Vegas, Sept. 29, 1988. Running time: **106 MIN.**
Daisy . . . . .Jan Adele
Simon .Sean Scully
Vince . . . . .Colin McEwan
Susie . . . . .Loith Taylor
Joan . . . . .Shaunna O'Grady
Cuthbert . . . . .Tony Wager

■ "Daisy And Simon" is a decent, audience-pleasing low comedy with a kicker of pathos.

Vet Australian musical comedy star Jan Adele gives a full-throttle performance of Falstaffian proportions as an eccentric old hag figuratively brought back to life by a drifter, and her sometimes explosive humor, much appreciated by the festival viewers here, could give pic some commercial potential, although her accent will pose a problem for the general American public.

Pic was originally titled "Where The Outback Ends."

When first seen, 70-year-old Daisy is a living portrait of rotten filth and self-loathing. Residing on a run-down farm in the middle of nowhere, she spends most of her time in bed, rarely bathes or does the dishes and hasn't been to town since her beloved husband Harry died, years ago.

It's a standoff when mysterious stranger Simon arrives from Perth and camps out on her land, but he quickly begins shaming her into cleaning up her act, as well as helping her around the farm.

Daisy's gruffness, rude insults and cranky stubbornness quickly become lovable as well as amusingly predictable. The pair's interplay may be the stuff of standard situation comedy, but some of it is undeniably funny and deftly played under Stasch Radwanski Jr.'s amiable direction.

Trouble arrives in the form of Daisy's officious daughter, Joan, who becomes more determined than ever to put her batty old mother in a home now that she has shacked up with a man half her age. Joan manages to discover that, contrary to his own stories, Simon is a fugitive from justice.

None of this fazes good old Daisy, however, who is the life of the party at a local dance, makes the farm productive again and tries to get Simon to take her to Cottesloe Beach in distant Perth, where she took her honeymoon with Harry.

Sean Scully as Simon makes an ideal low-key foil for the exuberantly irrepressible Adele, as he successfully keeps everyone guessing about his background and present motives. Supporting actors are fine, and pic is simple from a production p.o.v. It's really Adele's show, and she walks away with it. —Cart.

Dangerous Curves

New York   A Lightning Pictures presentation of a Mark Borde production. Executive producers, Larry Kasanoff, Ellen Steloff. Produced by Mark Borde, Kenneth Raich. Directed by David Lewis. Screenplay, Michael Dugan, Michael Zand, Paul Brown; camera (Deluxe color), Lewis; editor, Bob Bring; music, John D'Andrea; sound (Ultra-Stereo), Bill Dager; production design, Elliot Gilbert; production manager, Shayne Sawyer; assistant director, Steven F. Pomeroy; second unit director, Raich; stunt coordinator, Eddie Braun; casting, Joyce Robinson, Penny Ellers. Reviewed on Vestron vidcassette, N.Y., Dec. 10, 1988. MPAA Rating: PG. Running time **93 MIN.**
Chuck . . . . .Tate Donovan
Michelle West . . . . .Danielle Von Zerneck
Wally . . . . .Grant Heslov
Blake Courtland . . . . .Valeri Breiman
Shawn Brooks . . . . .Karen Lee Scott
   Also with: Leslie Nielsen, Elizabeth Ashley, Robert Stack, Robert Klein, Michael J. Rosenberg, Eva La Rue, Marie Cheatham, Armin Shimerman, Freeman King, Robert Romanus, Martha Quinn, Theresa Ring.

■ "Dangerous Curves" is a squeaky-clean youth comedy about two guys, a Porsche and a beauty contest. Vestron wisely is sending this out direct-to-video.

Tate Donovan and Grant Heslov are the pleasant-enough nerds headed for a weekend aventure driving a new red Porsche, a birthday gift from industrialist Robert Stack to his daughter in Lake Tahoe.

The car is stolen and they're diverted to San Diego and a beauty pageant where the hot vehicle is being offered as main prize.

Predictable hijinks benefit from the two leads' personable thesping, with a bevy of pretty girls on display (but tastefully covered for that PG rating). Guest star "Airplane" alumni Robert Stack and Leslie Nielsen aren't funny here, nor is Robert Klein as an aging surfer. —*Lor.*

Dr. Hackenstein

New York   A Vista Street Prods. presentation of a Feifer/Miller production. Executive producers, Jerry Feifer, Tony Miller. Produced by Reza Mizbani, Megan Barnett. Supervising producer, James Hanson. Directed by Richard Clark. Screenplay, Clark; camera (color), Jens Sturup; editor, Tony Miller; music, Randy Miller; sound, Steve Evans; production design, Leon King; art direction, Craig Voigt; production manager, Joe Calk; casting, Catherine Davis Cox. Reviewed on Forum Home Video vidcassette, N.Y., Dec. 10, 1988. MPAA Rating: R. Running time: **88 MIN.**

Dr. Elliot Hackenstein . . . . David Muir
Melanie Victor . . . . Stacey Travis
Leslie . . . . Catherine Davis Cox
Wendy . . . . Dyanne DiRosario
Alex . . . . John Alexis
Yolanda . . . . Catherine Cahn

   Also with: William Schreiner, Sylvia Lee Baker, Jeff Rector, Anne Ramsey, Logan Ramsey, Phyllis Diller, Michael Ensign.

■**Even with a new name, you can't keep the Frankenstein monster down for long as "Dr. Hackenstein" presents a pleasant sex-switch comedy spoof in the vein of Mel Brooks' "Young Frankenstein."**

Pic is set in 1909 with David Muir as the good doctor, intent on bringing his wife (Sylvia Lee Baker) back to life with the aid of spare body parts. Chief victims are a trio of comely girls who stay the night at Hackenstein Manor after their car crashes.

With topless footage (a bit incongruous concerning the femme monster) and gore added, pic is still quaint with okay period atmosphere and plenty of black humor. Muir is effective, playing the role straight, while in the supporting cast the late Anne Ramsey acts opposite hubby Logan Ramsey as a pair of grotesque graverobbers.

Color scheme here is rather drab and film probably would have been more effective (though less saleable) in black & white à la Brooks' classic homage. —*Lor.*

Skeleton Coast

New York   A Silvertree Pictures presentation, in association with the Walanar Group and Breton Film Prods. Ltd. Executive producers, Gerald Milton, Michelle Marshall, Barry Wood. Produced by Harry Alan Towers. Directed by John (Bud) Cardos. Screenplay, Nadia Calliou, from story by "Peter Welbeck" (Towers); camera (color), Hanro Möhr; editor, Allan Morrison, Mac Errington; music, Colin Shapiro, Barry Bekker; sound, Conrad Kühne; production design, Leonardo Coen Cagli; production manager, Roger Orpen; assistant director, Richard Green; second unit director, Cedric Sundström; stunt coordinator, Reo Ruiters; associate producers, Keith Rosenbaum, John Stodel; casting, Don Pembrich (U.S.), Gianna Pisanello & Associates (Africa). Reviewed on Nelson Entertainment vidcassette, N.Y., Dec. 24, 1988. MPAA Rating: R. Running time: **98 MIN.**

Col. Smith . . . . Ernest Borgnine
Col. Schneider . . . . Robert Vaughn
Capt. Simpson . . . . Oliver Reed
Elia . . . . Herbert Lom
Rick Weston . . . . Daniel Greene
Chuck . . . . Leon Isaac Kennedy
Gen. Sekatri . . . . Simon Sabela
Sam . . . . Nancy Mulford

   Also with: Peter Kwong, Robin Townsend, Arnold Vosloo, Larry Taylor.

■**Attractive visuals of the Namibian desert highlight this actioner from producer Harry Alan Towers, returning to the locale of his 1965 Edgar Wallace tale "Coast Of Skeletons" with a new story.**

Bad guys this time are safe targets, the Cubans and East Germans, involved in a border war in Angola. Ernest Borgnine toplines as a worried daddy, who organizes his own cutrate "Dirty Dozen" (actually only seven) commando unit to crossover into Angola and rescue his son, a CIA agent who's been captured and is being tortured for info by evil East German commandant Robert Vaughn.

Along the way Borgnine & crew also have a run-in with evil South African diamond security chief Oliver Reed. There are numerous escapes and recaptures before the ragtag mob, aided by rebel general Simon Sabela, head to safety with a horde of stolen diamonds as booty.

There are solid action scenes and largescale explosions to punctuate the cornball story with Borgnine especially giving his all to breathe life into a stet character. Vaughn, who played the good-guy daddy in another recent Towers production about kidnaping, "Captive Rage," wisely uses his normal accent as the Germanic baddie here.

Among the commandos, statuesque blond pinup Nancy Mulford looks out of place but acquits herself well in hand-to-hand combat with the guys. In one of seven

---

southern African-lensed pics he's made in a row, Herbert Lom makes a token appearance delivering exposition as Borgnine's local contact.—*Lor.*

Ne reveillez pas un flic qui dort
(Let Sleeping Cops Lie)
(FRENCH)

Paris   A Capital-Cinéma release of a Leda Prods./TF1 Films coproduction. Produced by Alain Delon, Daniel Champagnon. Directed by Jose Pinheiro. Screenplay, Delon, Pinheiro, Fréderic H. Fajardie, based on Fajardie's novel, "Claude de style;" camera (Eastmancolor), Raoul Coutard; editor, Jennifer Auge; music, Pino Marchese; art direction, Theo Meurisse; sound, Louis Gimel, Jean-Paul Loublier; production managers, Bernard Marescot, Michel Nicolini; associate producer, Jacques Bar (Cité-Film). Reviewed at Marignan-Concorde theater, Paris, Dec. 16, 1988. Running time: **98 MIN.**

Grindel . . . . Alain Delon
Scatti . . . . Michel Serrault
Lutz . . . . Xavier Deluc
Peret . . . . Patrick Catalifo
Spiero . . . . Stéphane Jobert

   Also with: Bernard Farcy, Raymond Gerome, Roxan Gould, Consuelo de Haviland, Feodor Atkine, Serge Reggiani.

■**Alain Delon returns to the screen with his first theatrical feature in three years, but "Let Sleeping Cops Lie" is a nonevent. Delon has fallen back on his routine lone-cop role in a film distinguished only by its periodic outbursts of gruesome violence.**

Delon plays a police inspector on a campaign to crush neo-fascism in the French police force. Special death squads of extreme right-wing cops are exacting extralegal justice of their own on untouchable underworld figures. When killings begin to target fellow police of orthodox integrity, Delon gets real mad.

Michel Serrault, who shares top billing with Delon, overacts as a mad-dog killer cop, who in fact is only a secondary figure in the action and has few scenes opposite Delon.

Film seems to preach against vigilante justice but negates the message in the climactic scene when Delon, after having exposed the network kingpins, cold-bloodedly puts a bullet in Serrault's head for having summarily executed his defenseless partner.

Jose Pinheiro, who alternates commercial assignments with more personal projects, directed without subtlety. Tech credits, including lensing by ace Raoul Coutard, are merely workmanlike.

—*Len.*

Fantozzi va in pensione
(Fantozzi Retires)
(ITALIAN)

Rome   A Columbia Tri-Star Films release of a Maura Intl. Film/Cecchi Gori Group Tiger Cinematografica/Reteitalia coproduction. Produced by Mario and Vittorio Cecchi Gori, with Bruno Altissimi, Claudio Saraceni. Directed by Neri Parenti. Screenplay, Leo Bonvenuti, Piero De Bernardi, Parenti, Alessandro Bencivenni, Saverni; camera (color), Sergio D'Offizi; editor, Sergio Montanari; music, Bruno Zambrini; art direction, Giovanni Licheri. Reviewed at Supercinema, Rome, Jan. 4, 1989. Running time: **100 MIN.**

Ugo Fantozzi . . . . Paolo Villaggio
Pina . . . . Milena Vukotíc
Mariangela/Baby . . . . Plinio Fernando
Also with: Gigi Reder, Anna Mazzamauro.

■**Latest in the Fantozzi film series about a luckless little office worker is "Fantozzi Retires," with the gags getting tireder and more predictable.**

Film has lagged behind other Xmas offerings domestically, attracting younger and matinee audiences with its clean humor.

The tireless Paolo Villaggio, who has impersonated Fantozzi for years, receives his gold watch (with his name inscribed wrong) during a funeral company retirement ceremony. Among the slew of retirees are other familiar faces — Gigi Reder, his myopic coworker, and Anna Mazzamauro, Fantozzi's eternally unrequited passion.

Their brave talk of "a new life" is immediately deflated when, after his first hour of freedom, Fantozzi begins to go stir-crazy at home. Long-suffering wife Pina (fine comic Milena Vukotíc) tries everything to keep him busy, from taking him shopping to going to a hardcore porn film (accidentally) with him.

At last she takes a back-breaking job as a hotel maid to pay for a fake "job" her boss pays hubby to do. When that fails, Fantozzi crawls back to his old employer and agrees to give up his pension and go on working for free, in a hellish basement peopled with all the other office oldtimers.

Giving the characters more room to be human than before, series helmer Neri Parenti lets a pathetic tone creep into the story, where once only deadpan irony was to be found.

The theme is universal, but some barbed social humor needs the Italo context to be appreciated, e.g., the thieves on motorcycles who swipe Fantozzi's pension week after week. Plinio Fernando, the boy who always plays Ugo and Pina's monkey-faced daughter

Mariangela, now has a double role as mother and baby. Special effects work is strong as usual; technical credits okay. —*Yung.*

La Mémoire tatouée
(Secret Obsession)
(FRENCH-TUNISIAN)

New York A Paris Pro-Motion (Paris)/Jugurtha Intl. Prods. (Tunis) coproduction. Executive producer, Lofti Layouni. Produced by Jalel Saada, Ridha Behi. Written and directed by Behi. Camera (Eclair color), Pierre Lhomme; editor, Eric Pluet, Kahena Attia Riveill, Catherine Kelber; music, George Garvarentz; sound (Dolby), Louis Gimel; production design, Andrea Crisante; production manager, Henri Vart; associate producer, Jan Olivier. Reviewed on Vidmark vidcassette, N.Y., Nov. 27, 1988. MPAA Rating: PG. Running time: **84 MIN.**

Betty	Julie Christie
Paul	Ben Gazzara
Wanis	Patrick Bruel
Zigou	Jean Carmet
Mariam	Ida De Benedetto
Slim	Amidou
Wanis as child	Sofiane Aouissi

(English soundtrack)

■ **This variously titled 1986 production filmed in Tunisia makes its belated bow direct to video as an engrossing period drama giving Julie Christie and Ben Gazzara rather oddball roles.**

Julie's a saloon singer (with Liverpudlian accent when speaking) married to Gazzara, but both must flee from their North African homestead in 1955 on the eve of independence. Gazzara's illegitimate son Wanis has a crush on Christie that's fortunately not consummated, even when as an adult (played by handsome star Patrick Bruel) Wanis meets up with her again in a nightclub.

Pic meanders with various metaphorical subplots, particularly young Wanis' preoccupation with cars (and Gazzara/Christie's vintage Buick) leading to an unexciting stock car race. Supporting cast is dubbed while leads speak direct-sound English in an unhappy mixture.

Cassette packaging credits direction to Henri Vart, who was production manager on the film, while Tunisian filmmaker Ridha Behi (whose "Les Anges" was a Directors Fortnight selection at the 1985 Cannes film fest) receives proper credit on screen. Another oddity is that Christie's singing voice is dubbed in the jazz mode by no less than Chan Parker and Kim Parker. —*Lor.*

De Bruit et de fureur
(The Sound And The Fury)
(FRENCH)

London A Films du Losange production. Produced by Margaret Menegoz. Written and directed by Jean-Claude Brisseau. Camera (color), Romain Winding; editor, Laria-Louisa Garcia, Jean-Claude Brisseau, Annick Hurst; sound, Louis Gimel; costume design, Lisa Garcia. Reviewed at London Film Festival, Nov. 23, 1988. Running time: **95 MIN.**

Bruno	Vincent Gasperitsch
Jean-Roger	François Negret
Marcel	Bruno Cremer
Thierry	Thierry Helaine
Teacher	Fabienne Babe
Headmaster	Antoine Fontaine
The apparition	Lisa Heredia

Also with: Sandrine Arnault, Victoire Buff, Françoise Vatel, Albert Montais, Luc Ponette, Isabelle Hurtin, Fejria Deliba.

■ **"The Sound And The Fury" is about lost youth and the savageness of urban life, but helmer/writer Jean-Claude Brisseau has overplayed his hand with the pic, bordering on the pretentious and exploitative.**

Characters and scenes are exaggerated to emphasize the tragic situations faced by the youngsters, and while the pic condemns an uncaring society it is simplistic.

Young Vincent Gasperitsch (Bruno) goes to live with his mother (who is always working) in a high-rise block of flats where violence is the order of the day. He is befriended by Jean-Roger (François Negret), whose pranks include stealing motorcycles, setting fire to tramps and attacking teachers.

Negret is cruel but adores his father, who has a shooting gallery in his front room. Gasperitsch, a quiet daydreamer, is helped at school by attractive teacher Fabiene Babe, while Negret takes to carrying one of his father's guns. All spirals to a bloody climax. Brisseau directs with committed energy, but is at times a little ham-fisted. Gasperitsch is suitably mouselike, but Negret sometimes goes over the top in his acting. Babe is fine as the caring teacher.

"The Sound And The Fury" is full of symbols and deeper meanings, which sometimes are hard to reconcile in what pretends to be a brutal, realistic movie. —*Adam.*

ARCHIVE REVIEWS

Way Down East
(B&W/TINTED-1920)

Pordenone A MoMA Film Department reconstruction and presentation of a D. W. Griffith Inc. production. Produced and directed by D. W. Griffith. Screenplay, Griffith, Anthony Paul Kelly, from the play by Lottie Blair Parker, William Brady, Joseph R. Grismer; camera (b&w, tinted); G. W. Bitzer, Hendrik Sartov; sets, Charles O. Seessel, Clifford Pember; music (1920), Louis Silvers, William F. Peters. Reconstruction editor, Peter Wiliamson; music, reconstruction, Gillian B. Anderson. Premiered at 44th St. Theater, N.Y. Sept. 3, 1920. General release by United Artists, Aug. 21, 1921. Reviewed at Pordenone Film Festival, Italy, Oct. 8, 1988. Length (MoMA version): 11,100 ft. Running time (at 18 frames per second): **165 MIN.**

Anna Moore	Lillian Gish
David Bartlett	Richard Barthelmess
Lennox Sanderson	Lowell Sherman
Squire Bartlett	Burr McIntosh

Also with: Creighton Hale, Vivia Ogden, Kate Bruce, Mary Hay, Mrs. David Landau, Josephine Bernard, Mrs. Morgan Belmont, Patricia Fiden, Florence Short, Porter Strong, George Neville, Edgar Nelson, Mary Hay, Emily Fitzroy.

■ **"Way Down East" ranks way up high on the list of major film archive achievements. Reconstruction by New York's Museum of Modern Art of D. W. Griffith's 1920 classic took four years and $80,000 and every dollar was worth it.**

To this exemplary work has been added the resurrection of the original musical score by Louis Silvers and William F. Peters, which served as editorial blueprint for the reconstitution. Both film and music (unearthed and conducted by Library of Congress music specialist Gillian Anderson) closed 1988's Silent Film Festival of Pordenone in rousing style.

Griffith's exciting cinematic transfiguration of a dated legit potboiler about a seduced and abandoned country girl who seeks regeneration and happiness with a puritanical New England farming family needs no introduction.

Yet the MoMA print will be a revelation to those who think they know the film in its circulating b&w versions (usually in mediocre 16m prints).

Restorers have reintegrated many of the secondary scenes and comic episodes Griffith himself later cut for subsequent reissues (undoubtedly reacting to increasing criticism that he was as old-fashioned as the theatrical property for which he nearly ruined himself to film).

Griffith's great star, Lillian Gish, was critical of MoMA's restoration zeal. Yet these sequences, essential to the rhythm if not the plot, fully reveal Griffith's sense of narrative construction and delimit his deep attachment to the 19th century Americana which inspired his best work.

Several sequences and shots are still missing, but are indicated by extant stills and title cards. Few film reconstitutions go this far in respecting the intelligence and curiosity of the audience.

The most important aspect of MoMA's work is the restoration of film's pictorial splendors, complete with the beautiful, nuanced tints and tones.

The camerawork by G. W. Bitzer and Hendrik Sartov recovers much of its clarity and relief, which in turn reinforces the poignancy and drama. Gish's performance seems suddenly to acquire new depths, and the breathtaking finale on the ice floes reveals the full extent of Griffith's virtuosity. The crisp photo quality also vindicates Griffith's often-criticized sense of lyricism.

The reconstructed musical score still goes well with the film. Adapting many Yank standards (from "No Place Like Home" to "The Old Grey Mare") and occasionally mixing in classical extracts, it is typical of the mostly compiled orchestral scores of the silent period and a perfect support for the period imagery Griffith so brilliantly fixed on film. —*Len.*

Visages d'enfants
(Children's Faces)
(SWISS-FRENCH-B&W)

Brussels A Zoubaloff and Porchat/Mundus Film/Grands Films Indépendants production (1923-25), reconstructed by the Royal Belgian Film Archive, with the participation of the Cinémathèque Française. Written and directed by Jacques Feyder. Camera (b&w), Léonce Henri Burel, Paul Parguel; assistant directors, Françoise Rosay, Charles Barrois, Arthur Porchat. First presented in Paris, Jan. 24, 1925, by Jean de Merly. Reviewed at Royal Belgian Film Archive, Brussels, Sept. 21, 1988. Running time (at 18 frames per second): **111 MIN.**

Jean Amsler	Jean Forest
Jeanne Dutois	Rachel Devirys
Pierre Amsler	Victor Vina
Arlette Dutois	Arlette Peyran
Pierrette Amsler	Pierrette Houyez
Canon Taillier	Herni Duval
The mother	Suzy Vernon
Neighbor	Jean Marie Laurent

■An early masterpiece by the great (and shamefully neglected) Jacques Feyder, "Visages d'enfants" perhaps is the cinema's first mature, realistic study of children.

Shot in 1923 in the magnificent mountain ranges of Switzerland's upper Valais, it's a film for which few excuses need be made for contemporary audiences. Delicately observed and deeply poignant, it remains one of the screen's best depictions of childhood despair, loneliness and jealousy.

Ahead of its time, "Visages d'enfants" was a complete commercial failure in 1925, and its negative subsequently disappeared. Two prints, both incomplete, were preserved by the Cinémathèque Française and the Royal Belgian Film Archive. It was one of the last major reconstructions of the late Jacques Ledoux, curator of the Brussels archive, who put together a composite montage now lasting nearly two hours. It's the most complete version we are likely to have and the pictorial quality is variable. After more than 60 years of limbo, the film at last recovers its dramatic integrity.

Feyder's original script (undoubtedly coauthored by Françoise Rosay, his wife, but not yet the brilliant actress) deals with a 10-year-old boy in a mountain village who is deeply affected by the death of his mother. When his father, the president of the community, decides to remarry, the child is further shaken. He sees his new mom, a widow with a daughter his age, as a usurper.

With compassionate lucidity, Feyder dramatizes the growing enmity between the two children. The boy's hatred and resentment become so strong that he sends his step-sister out one winter night in a vain search for a lost doll, during which she is trapped by an avalanche.

A village search party saves her, but the boy, horrified by his act and alienated from his family, throws himself into the river. His stepmother, alerted in time, saves him from certain death in the rapids. When the boy comes to and realizes what has happened he addresses her, for the first time, as "mamma."

Though melodramatic climaxes (the latter certainly influenced by D.W. Griffith's "Way Down East," released in France in 1922) and the happy ending may seem concessions to public taste, they have been subtly prepared and masterfully executed by Feyder.

The film's most vibrant triumph is the acting by the children. Jean Forest, later to become a well-known radio personality, is unforgettable as the hypersensitive orphan who worships the memory of his mother. Arlette Peyran is a perfect foil as the step-sister. Forest's kid sister, too young to understand the emotional storm that has burst around her, is played irresistibly by Pierrette Houyez. The adults, notably Rachel Devirys as the new mother, are still fine by modern standards.

This evergreen film still is plagued by bad luck. A live orchestral presentation at the recent Ghent Film Festival in Belgium was a technical and artistic fiasco: a specially commissioned score by a young Flemish composer proved to be a hopeless musical mishmash, insensitive to the film's nuances and inner force. "Visages d'enfants" still awaits a proper rebirth. —*Len.*

Parents

Hollywood A Vestron Pictures release, produced in association with Great American Films Limited Partnership. Produced by Bonnie Palef. Executive producers, Mitchell Cannold, Steven Reuther. Directed by Bob Balaban. Screenplay, Christopher Hawthorne; camera (Filmhouse color), Ernest Day, Robin Vidgeon; editor, Bill Pankow; music, Jonathan Elias; art direction, Andris Hausmanis; set decoration, Michael Harris; costume design, Arthur Rowsell; sound (Dolby), Douglas Thane Stewart; assistant director, Gary Flanagan; casting, Risa Bramon, Billy Hopkins. Reviewed at Warner Hollywood Studios, L.A., Jan. 17, 1989. MPAA Rating: R. Running time: **82 MIN.**
Nick Laemle ....Randy Quaid
Lily Laemle ....Mary Beth Hurt
Millie Dew ....Sandy Dennis
Michael Laemle ....Bryan Madorsky
Sheila Zellner ....Juno Mills-Cockell
Miss Baxter ....Kathryn Grody
Mrs. Zellner ....Deborah Rush
Mr. Zellner ....Graham Jarvis

■"Parents" is your typical anthropological analysis of cannibalism in 1950s suburbia. In other words, this represents a real oddball entry, one whose central idea is weird enough to attract some, but the writing and execution of which proves much too thin.

Already test run in Buffalo, pic is destined for marginal theatrical release before landing in videoland.

First feature from actor Bob Balaban, who has worked behind the camera on shorts and in tv, delights in its evocation of plastic suburbia, highlighting the bad-taste clothes and furniture that look vaguely fashionable today.

Most of the action takes place in the home of the Laemles, where Dad (Randy Quaid) lords it over little Michael (Bryan Madorsky) while Mom (Mary Beth Hurt) mostly busies herself in the kitchen. Michael, who's a real shrimp, suffers from recurring nightmares, and at school paints a picture of family life so disturbing that he is sent to see the in-house psychologist-social worker, played by, of all people, Sandy Dennis.

It's pretty clear to the viewer early on that Mom and Dad are up to something very nasty, so it's only a matter of time, quite laboriously spent, considering the brief running time, until the folks attempt to indoctrinate little Michael in their peculiar tastes. Conclusion is a bloody, violent mess, but leaves room for a sequel best never made.

Sprightly survey of suburban motifs in the opening moments encourages one to hope for some nifty satire on the "Leave It To Beaver" lifestyle along the lines of John Waters' films or Paul Bartel's "Eating Raoul," which pioneered in the area of middle-class cannibalism. The laughs never come, as Balaban chooses to direct Christopher Hawthorne's strange script with grim portentiousness.

Unfortunately, there is not enough weight or complexity to the material to justify the serious approach, and while the potential for considerable black comedy exists, Balaban only scratches the surface.

Another problem is the remoteness of the picture's lead and victim, Michael. Kid is so traumatized and terrorized by his father that he says virtually nothing, creating a cipher at the film's center. A different sort of character or actor could have gotten across the central dilemma of being the offspring of people-eaters, but still been a lot more lively and interesting; some private voiceover might have helped.

Shot in Toronto, pic conveys the desired look, but a repeated distraction is the presence of scenes in which dialog is delivered off-screen or with the character's back to the camera, a bad sign no matter what the reason. —*Cart.*

Gleaming The Cube

Hollywood A 20th Century Fox release of a Gladden Entertainment film. Produced by Lawrence Turman, David Foster. Directed by Graeme Clifford. Screenplay, Michael Tolkin; camera (Deluxe color), Reed Smoot; editor, John Wright; music, Jay Ferguson; sound, Donald B. Summer; production design, John Muto; art direction, Dan Webster; set decoration, Susan Emshwiller; costumes, Ann Somers Major; assistant director, Dennis White; assistant camera, Brian Sullivan; casting, Elisabeth Leustig. Reviewed at Avco Center theater, L.A., Jan. 12, 1988. MPAA Rating: PG-13. Running time: **105 MIN.**
Brian Kelly ....Christian Slater
Al Lucero ....Steven Bauer
Tina Trac ....Min Luong
Vinh Kelly ....Art Chudabala
Colonel Trac ....Le Tuan

■Of all the stories that could have been set around skateboarding, "Gleaming The Cube" is about the most off-the-wall concept that could be conceived. Pic ought to skate right into video.

The term "gleaming the cube" isn't even a real skateboarding term; it was just made up to sell the concept to audiences. Well, the dudes miscalculated by a whole bunch.

A skateboarding-obsessed suburban kid (Christian Slater) goes about solving — exploitation style

— the death of his adopted Vietnamese brother (Art Chudabala), who Slater knows in his heart was too smart to commit suicide.

Slater skateboards all over Little Saigon, going in and out of minimalls skillfully enough to elude Vietnamese hoods on his trail while conducting some Chuck Norris-inspired sleuthing.

It's laudable that the filmmakers attempted to work up a teenage "thriller" (the studio's description) around a timely crosscultural theme, but this mix doesn't work.

Slater, who sounds as if he is trying to imitate Jack Nicholson, is the only character who has a shading of personality. His skateboarding buddies are funny, considering one needs a glossary to translate their dialog, while the Vietnamese are mostly sleazy cardboard figures. The police are inept and the mastermind villain (Richard Herd) seems to be right out of the Method acting school.

A good opportunity to launch or promote the careers of Asian actors is wasted in this formula. Also questionable is the understanding that it's okay for underagers to break into warehouses and otherwise go outside the law.

The music subs Vietnamese lyrics for English ones in otherwise imitative versions of such American tunes as "Nowhere To Run."

After the opening scene, best aerials and minicam shots come near the end when Slater (actually a number of w.k. skaters like Mike McGill, Mark (Gator) Rogowski, Rodney Mullen and others) do 180-degree turns above drained swimming pools and more breathtaking stunts. The freeway scenes in which Slater holds onto a speeding Corvette and then cuts across lanes and skates under a trailer truck to hook up with his pal's pizza delivery vehicle on the other side is pretty impressive.

Editor John Wright deserves special credit for seamlessly cutting in the skater doubles with head and body shots of Slater. Otherwise, tech credits are undistinguished. —*Brit.*

Physical Evidence

Hollywood Columbia Pictures release of a Martin Ransohoff production. Produced by Ransohoff. Executive producer, Don Carmody. Directed by Michael Crichton. Screenplay, Bill Phillips; story, Steve Ransohoff, Phillips; camera (Medallion color), John A. Alonzo; editor, Glenn Farr; music, Henry Mancini; production design, Dan Yarhi; art direction, Dennis Davenport; set decoration, Jacques Bradette; costume design, Betsy Cox; sound (Dolby), Alan Geldart; assistant directors, Don Granbery, Bill Bannerman; second unit camera, Joe Vitagliano; casting, Lynn Stalmaster & Associates. Reviewed at Directors Guild of America, Hollywood, Jan. 20, 1989. MPAA Rating: R. Running time: **99 MIN.**

Joe Paris	Burt Reynolds
Jenny Hudson	Theresa Russell
James Nicks	Ned Beatty
Deborah Quinn	Kay Lenz
Kyle	Ted McGinley
Matt Farley	Tom O'Brien
Harry Norton	Kenneth Walsh
Strickler	Ray Baker

■Evidence of this pic's inevitable boxoffice bellyflop should be its presence in videostores shortly. **Even Burt Reynolds' marquee value will do little to help, since his role is all but indistinguishable from the myriad tough-as-nails cop parts he's essayed in recent years, and most of those have fired blanks as well.**

A courtroom-oriented drama, "Physical Evidence" is wanting in several areas, but its biggest liability stems from deadly slow pacing that limps along at roughly the rate of the real judicial system. Alas, that's about the only vague resemblance to reality.

Reynolds plays Joe Paris, a suspended detective who wakes up from a drunken binge to find himself the lead suspect in a murder investigation. His case is given to an assertive debutante (Theresa Russell) working in the public defender's office, whose obsession with the case begins to wreak havoc on her relationship with her yuppie, hot-tubbing fiancé stockbroker (Ted McGinley).

Beyond that it's really anybody's guess as to what's going on, since the film is so choppily assembled none of the various clues and innumerable suspects ever seem to lead anywhere. Much of the problem lies in the editing and the script, though there are one or two inspired moments — particularly the opening, where an inept suicide attempt yields darkly comic results.

Another major shortcoming is the woeful miscasting of Russell as the young attorney. Even with her hair tightly pulled back into an unflattering bun (to be literally and symbolically let down in quieter moments), Russell's uncommon onscreen beauty proves a distraction.

Adding to the problem, Russell sounds uncomfortable with her tongue-twisting courtroom dialog and ends up being completely unconvincing in efforts to project the brains and tenacity her character keeps bragging about.

The film is loaded with oddities to make legal purists cringe, such as the prosecutor (Ned Beatty) participating in a latenight raid with the police, or the numerous revelations made during the trial — a contrived effort to heighten the drama.

That aside, Beatty deftly underplays the prosecutor, and McGinley is appropriately repugnant as the preppie boyfriend. Angelo Rizacos also has a screen-stealing turn as a slimy contract killer.

Reynolds postures and scowls well enough as the hardened cop, though there's little else for him to do. His screentime actually is quite limited, with Russell most often in the center of cameraman John A. Alonzo's squandered spotlight.

Director Michael Crichton certainly used to be able to tell a pretty good suspense yarn ("Westworld" and "Coma" attest to that), but muddled storytelling here leaves loose ends not only as to whodunit but why. By the time the film reaches that point, tangible evidence of an audience may have removed itself from the theater. —*Bril.*

Double Exposure

New York A United Film Distribution Co. release (in 1987) of an Omega Entertainment production. Executive producer, Isabel Mastorakis. Produced and directed by Nico Mastorakis. Screenplay, Nico Mastorakis, Kirk Ellis, from story by Nico Mastorakis; camera (United color; Technicolor prints), Cliff D. Ralke; editor, Nico Mastorakis, Roger Tweten; music, Hans Zimmer; additional music, Mel Wesson, Roger Bolton; sound (Dolby), Jock Putnam; production design, Patricia Hall; set decoration, Joe Garcia; assistant director, Kelly Schroeder; production manager, Aladdin Pojhan; associate producer, Ellis. Reviewed on HBO, Jan. 13, 1989. MPAA Rating: R. Running time: **103 MIN.**

Lenny	Mark Hennessy
Bruce	Scott King
Christie	Hope Marie Carlton
Skip	Steve Donmyer
Fantastic	Ted Lange
Karrothers	John Vernon
Eskanazy	Joe Phelan

■Nico Mastorakis' "Double Exposure" is an oddball comedy-thriller focusing on the a in "t&a." Pic had a brief theatrical run in Miami in fall 1987 and is now cablecast by HBO.

Mark Hennessy and Scott King portray two aimless guys in Venice Beach, Calif., who decide to take photos of the lovely derrières paraded daily by beach bunnies in order to come up with a salable photo montage or calendar (film originally was titled "Terminal Exposure"). In homage to the classic film "Blow-Up" they accidentally photograph a murder, with the clue being a rose tattoo on the posterior of a woman holding a gun.

Antics of the duo trying to solve the murder involve mafia hitmen, a wild bachelor party and endless rearend-themed puns. The emphasis is towards comedy rather than thrills, but it's okay (if a bit fetishistic) light entertainment. Amoral attitude is emphasized, especially in the film's payoff.

Two lead players are pleasant, abetted by Playboy magazine model Hope Marie Carlton as their beautiful prime suspect. Joe Phelan as a hitman in a black van bears strong facial and vocal resemblance to his brother Martin Sheen. —*Lor.*

Caruso Pascoski-Di Padre Polacco

(Caruso Pascoski — Of Polish Origin) (ITALIAN)

Rome A Columbia Tri-Star Films Italia release of a Unione Cinematografica/Cecchi Gori Group/Tiger Cinematografica coproduction. Produced by Gianfranco Piccioli, Giorgio Leopardi, Mario and Vittorio Cecchi Gori. Directed by Francesco Nuti. Screenplay, Giovanni Veronesi, David Grieco, Nuti; camera (Luciano Vittori color), Gianlorenzo Battaglia; editor, Sergio Montanari; music, Giovanni Nuti. Reviewed at Barbarini Cinema, Rome, Jan. 2, 1989. Running time: **102 MIN.**

Caruso	Francesco Nuti
Ciulia	Clarissa Burt
Boyfriend	Ricky Tognazzi

Also with: Antonio Petrocelli, Novello Novelli, Giovanni Nannini, Maurizio Frittelli, Lorenzo Ariani, Umberto Angelucci, Gianni Sammaroo, Margherita Nuti, Carlo Nonni, Narcisa Bonati, Giovanni Veronesi, Luigi Frosali, Carlo Monni.

■Likable young comic Francesco Nuti's latest "Caruso Pascoski — Of Polish Origin" has led the pack of native Christmas releases at the boxoffice.

It is arguably the best-directed of Nuti's solo work since he took over helming his own films. In addition to the actor's undeniable personal charm, first half of pic boasts some very fine sight gags, which peter out as story moves to a messy conclusion.

Offshore play will be limited probably to related markets, though some sequences feel like Nuti is approaching a level of more universal entertainment.

Opening sequence is one of pic's best, as hero Caruso Pascoski (whose father is barely glimpsed) recalls his sex-obsessed childhood, beginning with his fatal attraction to a naked 2-year-old — his future wife Giulia. Now he's a grownup and a psychoanalyst with a bevy of wacky patients he calls "monsters" (who pass in review in a wordless series of sight gags).

Caruso himself goes over the edge when Giulia (attractive newcomer Clarissa Burt) leaves him without a word of explanation. At length it turns out she's fallen for one of his patients, Ricky Tognazzi, diagnosed by Caruso as a latent homosexual. Caruso buys a gun and goes after them.

At this point pic loses its steam. Giulia, also sex-obsessed, tires of her gentle lover and makes appointments in the ladies' room of a film theater with her ex-husband. Caruso begins dressing as a woman to meet her; at last he convinces Tognazzi to give back his wife and take up men. His patient's one condition is that Caruso initiate him — a scene that is luckily left out of a dissatisfying ending.

Florence makes a picturesque backdrop for the action. Editing (by Sergio Montanari) is surprisingly snappy, giving pic an upbeat pace overall. Giovanni Nuti's score includes a hit song and some lively pieces. —*Yung.*

La Petite voleuse
(The Little Thief)
(FRENCH)

Paris An AMLF release of an Orly Films/Renn Prods./Ciné-Cinq/Films du Carrosse/SEDIF coproduction, with the participation of the CNC. Executive producer, Orly Films. Produced by Jean-José Richer. Directed by Claude Miller. Screenplay, Claude and Annie Miller, Luc Béraud, from an original scenario by François Truffaut, Claude de Givray; camera (Fujicolor), Dominique Chapuis; editor, Albert Jurgenson; music, Alain Jomy; sound, Paul Laine, Gérard Lamps; art direction, Jean-Pierre Kohut-Svelko; assistant director, Valérie Othnin-Girard; production manager, Daniel Chevalier. Reviewed at Gaumont Ambassade, Paris, Dec. 29, 1988. Running time: **109 MIN.**
Janine Castang . . . . . . Charlotte Gainsbourg
Michel Davenne . . . . Didier Bezace
Raoul . . . . Simon de la Brosse
André Rouleau . . . . Raoul Billery
Aunt Lea . . . . Chantal Banlier
Mauricette . . . . Nathalie Cardone
Severine Longuet . . . . . . Clotilde de Bayser
Jacques Longuet . . . . . . Philippe Deplanche
Kebadian . . . . Marion Grimault
Raymond . . . . Erick Deshors
Pascouette . . . . Remy Kirch
Mother Busato . . . . Renée Faure

Young priest . . . . Claude Guyonnet

■**François Truffaut died before he could direct this period drama about a teenage girl's antisocial behavior in post World War II France, but Claude Miller, who was his longtime assistant, has done the job with style and keen sensitivity.**

Adapting Truffaut's (and Claude de Givray's) original 30-page treatment, Miller has paid the ultimate homage to Truffaut and has deepened his own thematic interests. Miller dealt perceptively with troubled adolescence in his films "The Best Way" (1976) and especially "L'Effrontée" (1985), and has made Truffaut's story his own. It stands fine odds to score in offshore situations.

Truffaut's tale of female juvenile delinquency in fact dates back to the start of his career, when he imagined a feminine counterpart to Antoine Doinel in his New Wave classic "The 400 Blows." Truffaut had to sacrifice his antiheroine, but never abandoned the idea of giving her a film of her own. Before his death, Truffaut gave his script to producer-director Claude Berri, asking that it be filmed some day.

Charlotte Gainsbourg, the gawky wallflower of "L'Effrontée," is Truffaut/Miller's little thief, an unloved 16-year-old whose mother, "purged" after World War II for consorting with the Germans, has abandoned her to the care of a weakwilled uncle and spiteful aunt.

Kleptomania is Gainsbourg's instinctive form of rebellion, but her exploits in the small town where she's being brought up are quickly exposed. She soon gets legal employ as the maid of a young bourgeois couple and (like Truffaut) haunts the movie theaters in her spare time.

The skillfully articulated script, which sets the action in 1950, blocks out Gainsbourg's emotional and social growth in three distinct situations: her first romance with a 40ish and married intellectual, her subsequent footloose passion for a beguiling young ne'er-do-well, and her time in a reform institution, from which she escapes in the company of another girl.

Gainsbourg's moviegoing is not a perfunctory buff wink to Truffaut, but an integral part of film's texture and dramatic scheme. Newsreels serve not only to describe the period, but also drive personal realities home when Gainsbourg searches for her boy-

friend thief and identifies him in a docu report on young recruits embarking for the nascent Indochinese War. She also meets her first lover at the movies, innocently falling asleep on his shoulder.

The entire cast is perfect. Gainsbourg's gaucheness, moping vulnerability and desperate provocations take her dramatically farther than her fetching adolescent role in "L'Effrontée." Didier Bezace is a touching screen newcomer as the considerate first love, and Simon de la Brosse is winning as the blithely asocial good-for-nothing who takes her to the seaside (a central Truffaut image), where ironically they are separated by police.

Superb supporting cast includes Raoul Billery and Chantal Banlier as girl's neglectful wards, Nathalie

Cardone as the delinquent she befriends in imprisonment, and Clotilde de Bayser as the bourgeoise who hires Gainsbourg as a maid.

Despite the seriousness of subject, situations and dialog are laced with humor and irony that keep film from becoming sordid or gratuitous. Miller owes much to his habitual script collaborators, Annie Miller (his wife) and Luc Béraud (himself a director).

Tech credits are excellent. Alain Jomy's music and arragements of inane French boy scout marching songs deliberately evoke Jean Vigo's screen classic of tonic disrespect "Zero For Conduct" (which Truffaut quoted in a scene in "400 Blows"). —*Len.*

U.S. FESTIVAL REVIEWS

84 Charlie Mopic

Hollywood A New Century/Vista release of a Charlie Mopic Co. production. Produced by Michael Nolin. Coproducer, Jill Griffith. Written and directed by Patrick Duncan. Camera (Duart color), Alan Caso; editor, Stephen Purvis; songs, Donovan; art direction, Douglas Dick; costume design, Lyn Paolo; sound, Michael Moore, Craig Woods; technical advisor, Capt. Russ (Gunny) Thurman; makeup design, Ron Wild; special effects coordinator, Eric Rylander; assistant director, Benita Allen; associate producer, Stephen Flick. Reviewed at the American Film Institute, L.A. (in competition, U.S. Film Festival), Jan. 10, 1989. MPAA Rating: R. Running time: **95 MIN.**
LT . . . . Jonathan Emerson
Easy . . . . Nicholas Cascone
Pretty Boy . . . . Jason Tomlins
Hammer . . . . Christoper Burgard
Cracker . . . . Glenn Morshower
OD . . . . Richard Brooks
Mopic . . . . Byron Thomas
   Also with: Russ Thurman, Joseph Hieu, Don Schiff.

■ **"84 Charlie Mopic" is a bracingly original and intimate look at the Vietnam combat experience. Low-budget indie effort should attract some critical attention, paving the way for reasonable theatrical b.o. possibilities.**

Similar to "Platoon" and especially "Hamburger Hill" in that it focuses squarely on the intense experiences of a few men in a single unit, Patrick Duncan's first feature diverges from any other fictional war film in memory on its stylistic daring, as it is presented exclusively from the point-of-view of a documentary camaraman following the soldiers. Approach has its pluses and minuses, but lends the picture a close-up distinction that

is quite novel.

A Vietnam war vet who has supervised and written much of the acclaimed HBO series "Vietnam War Story," Duncan establishes a simple premise, that of a 7-man Army unit on a reconnaisance mission, and lends it distinction through the moment-by-moment dissection of human experience involved. One of the men is "Mopic," a military motion picture lenser whose eventual film is designed to be used to expose and instruct newcomers in the ways of the war.

LT, who is unfamiliar with the others, is officially in command of the brief recon assignment, but the tough, experienced OD, the only black in the group, is the natural leader, the only one to instill total confidence even under crisis conditions.

Inevitably, things begin to heat up, as booby traps and snipers take their toll on the Americans. They move into a enemy encampment after a jet and artillery attack, begin arguing among themselves about how to deal with wounded Viet Cong and their own dead, and finally stumble upon a devastated village, from which they must make a desperate escape. Ending is surprisingly and startlingly ironic.

Downside of presenting dramatic material in extended takes and real time is that the valuable tool of creative film editing is removed, to the detriment of tension and excitement. Without normal cutting, first hour does feel dialog-heavy, even if Duncan has written a great deal of colorful Army lingo.

On the other hand, prolonged exposure brings the viewer very close to the men, and each of them emerges sharply with his own idiosyncracies, strengths and vulnerabilities. Described as "a walking razor blade" by one of the guys, Richard Brooks' OD is a fascinating character, extremely private, harsh but ultimately inspiring.

Nicholas Cascone's Easy is a self-deprecating goofball, Christopher Burgard's Hammer is a gung-ho, lower-class recruit, Glenn Morshower's Cracker is a Carolina family man, Jason Tom-'lins' Pretty Boy is an easy-going tough luck case, and Jonathan Emerson's LT is an outsider made insecure by this status. Byron Thames' Mopic is often heard but rarely seen, and all the young actors are impressive, performing capably as a unit.

Shot in Southern California, pic mostly makes a virtue of its budget limitations and small scale, which in any case are appropriate for the hand-held tactics. Pic is, in fact, edited in the sense of jumping from one unit of time to another, but not in the usual dramatic, cross-cutting manner.

Alan Caso's mobile lensing is crucial to the film's effectiveness, and blowup from Super 16m is outstanding. Only musical accompaniment consists of a couple of 1960s Donovan songs. —*Cart.*

Heathers

Hollywood   A New World Pictures release, produced in association with Cinemarque Entertainment (USA) Ltd. Produced by Denise Di Novi. Executive producer, Christopher Webster. Directed by Michael Lehmann. Screenplay, Daniel Waters; camera (Deluxe color; Technicolor prints), Francis Kenney; editor, Norman Hollyn; music, David Newman; production design, Jon Hutman; art direction, Kara Lindstrom; costume design, Rudy Dillon; sound, Douglas Axtell; assistant director, Mary Ellen Woods; associate producer, Iya Labunka; casting, Sally Dennison, Julie Selzer. Reviewed at New World Pictures screening room, L.A., Jan. 19, 1989 (at U.S. Film Festival). MPAA Rating: R. Running time: **102 MIN.**

Veronica Sawyer . . . . .Winona Ryder
J.D. . . . . .Christian Slater
Heather Duke . . . . .Shannen Doherty
Heather McNamara . . . . .Lisanne Falk
Heather Chandler . . . . .Kim Walker
Pauline Fleming . . . . .Penelope Milford
Father Ripper . . . . .Glenn Shadix
Kurt Kelly . . . . .Lance Fenton
Ram . . . . .Patrick Labyorteaux
Peter Dawson . . . . .Jeremy Applegate
Rodney . . . . .Jon Matthews
Martha Dunnstock/Dumptruck Carrie Lynn

■ "Heathers" is a super-smart black comedy about high school politics and teenage suicide that showcases a host of promising young talents and should garner nifty b.o. results.

Inventive and entertaining nearly every step of the way, pic possesses the sort of edge and hipness about teen life that will make youthful audiences adopt it as their own. Best film made at New World Pictures since Roger Corman sold the company premiered at the U.S. Film Festival in Park City, Utah.

Daniel Waters' enormously clever screenplay blazes a trail of originality through the dead wood of the teen comedy genre by focusing on the "Heathers," the four prettiest and most popular girls at Westerburg High, three of whom are named Heather.

Setting the tone for the group is founder and queen bitch Heather No. 1, who has a devastating putdown or comeback for every occasion and could freeze even a heat-seeking missile in its tracks with her icy stare.

Heathers No. 2 and 3 get off their own zingers once in a while, while the fourth nubile beauty, Veronica (Winona Ryder), goes along for the ride but seems to have a mind of her own. She also has eyes for a rebellious-looking school newcomer named J.D. (Christian Slater).

Opening couple of reels are jammed with brilliantly insolent and irreverent insights into school-age caste systems, power structures and social rituals, many of them conveyed through Waters' spiky, up-to-the-minute dialog. The consistently witty production, costume design, musical choices and casting picks indicate how completely on-target Michael Lehmann is in his directorial debut.

Goaded by the seductive J.D., Veronica half-heartedly goes along with an attempt to murder Heather No. 1, who has become irritating beyond endurance. J.D. makes sure the effort succeeds, but makes the deed look like a suicide, which throws the school into a dither.

Before long, the school's leading jocks are lured into a similar fateful trap, and once again the locals are stunned that such seemingly popular kids would be driven to take their own lives. Events spin on from there, as J.D. and Veronica break up and the seriousness of what they've done settles in.

Entire cast sparkles under Lehmann. Winona Ryder is utterly fetching and winning as an intelligent but seriously divided young lady.

Oozing an insinuating sarcasm reminiscent of Jack Nicholson, Christian Slater has what it takes to make J.D. both alluring and dangerous. The three Heathers (Shannen Doherty, Lisanne Falk and Kim Walker) look like they've spent their lives practicing putdowns, which is the the highest compliment under the circumstances.

Some adults might feel insulted that such grim issues are sent up so devilishly, but the filmmakers override such objections by vividly delineating the extent of teen cruelty and attacking the way teenage angst is treated in the mass media. The film's sword has many edges, all of them razor sharp. —*Cart.*

Lean On Me

New York   A Warner Bros. Pictures release. Executive produced, directed by John Avildsen. Produced by Norman Twain. Screenplay, Michael Schiffer; camera (Technicolor), Victor Hammer; editor, John Carter, Avildsen; music, Bill Conti; production design, Doug Kraner; art direction, Tim Galvin; set decoration, Caryl Heller; costume design, Jennifer Von Mayrthauper; casting, Mary Colquhoun. Reviewed at the Mann 9 Theaters, San Diego, Jan. 21, 1989. MPAA Rating: PG-13. Running time: **104 MIN.**

Joe Clark . . . . .Morgan Freeman
Dr. Frank Napier . . . . . .Robert Guillaume
Ms. Levias . . . . .Beverly Todd
Leona Barrett . . . . .Lynne Thigpen
Thomas Sams . . . . .Jermaine Hopkins
Keneesha Carter . . . . .Karen Malina White

■ Morgan Freeman's inspired performance as Joe Clark, the New Jersey principal who uses controversial methods to clean up a drug- and crime-ridden high school, makes it easier to forgive John Avildsen's rather glossy and simplistic treatment of a serious dilemma in the public school system.

Nevertheless, Avildsen's enthusiastic direction gives "Lean On Me" a heartwarming, feel-good tone that is accessible beyond the environs of its subject.

Clark's efforts to return Eastside High in Paterson, N.J., to an institution of learning rather than a chaotic meeting place for mayhem and maliciousness earned him kudos in some circles. Others questioned his severity — even megalomania — in dealing with what appears to have been an out-of-control student population and a staff unable to deal with it.

Freeman embodies all the purported strengths of the real-life Clark and gives an uncompromising and oftentimes not very sympathetic portrayal of an individual that few ever could get close to but many could admire.

He bullies, threatens, throws his weight around as chief administrator of a huge, largely black school. But he gets the job done. He reclaims the school by expelling the drug pushers and other delinquents, putting the near-bad to work painting over graffiti and making the entire student body learn the school song — ostensibly to instill a sense of spirit and unity in Eastsiders — all the while knowing he has to answer to his superiors at the mayor's office who have given him one year to get the students to pass a basic skills test.

Scripter Michael Schiffer has seemingly successfully captured the voice and mannerisms of an unyielding taskmaster, which is a wonderful role for Freeman and one he's wonderful in. Short shrift is given to those around him who have little or no shading, with the one exception being that of vulnerable and good student Keneesha Carter (Karen Malina White).

Surely, things were much more complex and wearisome for the real Joe Clark, who ran up against opposition from parents and politicians for his quasi-unlawful practices (he locks all but one entrance to the school, which is a violation of the fire code, and fires a teacher without having authority to do so).

Through his dealings with only a handful of individuals, each representing a different faction of his limited school environment, Freeman triumphs. But the feeling remains that his glory is one of discipline, not of education.

As sanitized a treatment as this is, filmmakers deserve credit for bringing to the screen a slice of Americana not usually experienced by most movie audiences.

Avildsen knows how to pull the right strings in any regard, his greatest strengths mixing humor and pathos into a narrowly focused melodrama. Here, best renderings are Freeman's encounters with the comical pudgy student Thomas Sams (Jermaine Hopkins) and with Robert Guillaume, the school superintendent.

Bill Conti's scoring pales next to the fine rap and other tunes that are on the soundtrack.

Bill Withers' "Lean On Me" is actually the weakest number, however, even though it is the title track. A school assembly where the students break out to sing this song following the music teacher's gospel-like lead strains credibility.

Other tech credits are fine.
—*Brit.*

Three Fugitives

Hollywood   A Buena Vista release of a Touchstone Pictures presentation in association with Silver Screen Partners IV. Produced by Lauren Shuler Donner. Executive producer, Francis Veber. Written and directed by Veber. Camera (Metrocolor), Haskell Wexler; editor, Bruce Green; music, David McHugh; production design, Rick Carter; art direction, Marjorie Stone McShirley; set design, Lauren Cory; set decoration, Richard C. Goddard; costume design, April Ferry; sound (Dolby), C. Darin Knight; assistant director, Van Wyck; second unit camera, Dan Lerner; associate producers, Karen Kovacevich, Duncan Henderson, James R. Van Wyck; casting, Carrie Frazier, Shani Ginsberg. Reviewed at Avco Cinema Center, Westwood, Calif., Jan. 24, 1989. MPAA Rating: PG-13. Running time: 96 MIN.
Lucas . . . . Nick Nolte
Perry . . . . Martin Short
Meg . . . . Sarah Rowland Doroff
Dugan . . . . James Earl Jones
Tener . . . . Alan Ruck
Horvath . . . . Kenneth McMillan

■ **Light pastry and light comedy are two things the French do best. This remade French crime caper comes out half-baked on the American side, even with the same sweet "tough guys and a baby" Disney recipe going for it. Boxoffice prospects look mild.**

"Three Fugitives" marks the Hollywood helming debut of bankable French director Francis Veber, remaking his own 1986 comedy "Les Fugitifs" American-style. Clever premise starts pic off on a roll, as master bankrobber Lucas (Nick Nolte) gets out of the slammer determined to go straight, only to get involved in another heist in the very first bank he enters.

This time, he's an innocent bystander taken hostage by a hysterically inept gunman (Martin Short). But who's going to believe that? Even worse, he was driven to the bank in a squad car by a cop (James Earl Jones) who bet him he'd pull another job in no time. Now the cops are really on his tail.

Short, once he figures out Nolte's predicament, blackmails him into aiding and abetting his es-

Original Film
Les Fugitifs
(FRENCH)

A Gaumont release of a Fideline Films/D. D. Prods./Efve Films/Orly Films coproduction. Produced by Jean-José Richer. Written and directed by Francis Veber. Stars Gérard Depardieu, Pierre Richard. Camera (Eastmancolor), Luciano Tovoli; editor, Marie-Sophie Dubus; music, Vladimir Costma; art director, Gérard Daoudal; sound, Jean-Pierre Ruh; assistant director, Xavier Castano; François Menidrey; production manager, Jean-Claude Bourlat. Reviewed at the Gaumont Ambassade cinema, Paris, Dec. 19, 1986. Running time: 87 MIN.
Jean Lucas . . . . Gérard Depardieu
François Pignon . . . . Pierre Richard
Mr. Martin . . . . Jean Carmet
Dr. Bourdarias . . . . Michel Blanc
Commissioner Duroc . . . . . Maurice Barrier
Labib . . . . Jean Benguigui
Idriss . . . . Roland Blanche
Jeanne . . . . Anais Bret

cape from the country. To make things even stickier, Short's got an emotionally withdrawn little girl (Sarah Rowland Doroff) who latches onto Nolte like a stray kitten.

Unfortunately, the plot begins to flatten after about 20 minutes and unlikely elements are introduced to keep the comedy flowing.

Short has shot Nolte in the leg; for treatment he takes him to an addled old veterinarian (the late Kenneth McMillan, in his last screen appearance) who offers him dog food to eat (shades of "Down And Out In Beverly Hills," Nolte's previous comedy, in which he ate the stuff).

In exchange for a signed confession from Short, Nolte helps them cross the border, which involves dressing Short in drag to confuse the police.

Director Veber uses abundant slapstick to keep the story pumped up, with crash, stumble and bump the order of the day, and stunts aplenty.

Even location is incidental, with L.A. streets often subbing for overall Northwest locale (though it does include some fetching roadside scenery near the Canadian border).

As for the Nolte-Short pairing, it'll do, but it's no chemical marvel. Nolte, not really a comic natural, gruffs and grumbles his way through as hunky straight man to Short's calamitous comedian. Short runs with the slapstick style and certainly gets his showcase, getting to play both a devoted father and an expectant mother (in a hilarious hospital scene).

Pic has numerous good laughs, but is a cream puff overall. Haskell Wexler's cinematography makes distinctive the look of some gritty scenes in an underlit underworld bar, but is otherwise wasted on this genre.

Score by David McHugh is a bit too sweet and stale. —*Daws.*

Kinjite
(Forbidden Subjects)

New York   A Cannon Entertainment release of a Golan-Globus production. Executive producers, Menahem Golan, Yoram Globus. Produced by Pancho Kohner. Directed by J. Lee-Thompson. Screenplay, Harold Nebenzal; camera (TVC color), Gideon Porath; editor, Peter Lee-Thompson, Mary E. Jochem; music, Greg DeBelles; sound (Ultra-Stereo), Craig Felburg; art direction, W. Brooke Wheeler; set decoration, Margaret C. Fischer; assistant director, Robert C. Ortwin Jr.; production manager, Sheridan (Dar) Reid; additional camera, Ronald Vidor; stunt coordinator, Ernie Orsatti; associate producer, Patricia G. Payro; casting, Nancy Lara, Perry Bullington. Reviewed at Broadway screening room, N.Y., Jan. 4, 1989. MPAA Rating: R. Running time: 97 MIN.
Lt. Crowe . . . . Charles Bronson
Eddie Rios . . . . Perry Lopez
Duke . . . . Juan Fernandez
Kathleen Crowe . . . . Peggy Lipton
Hiroshi Hada . . . . James Pax
Lavonne . . . . Sy Richardson
 Also with: Marion Kodama Yue, Bill McKinney, Gerald Castillo, Nicole Eggert, Amy Hathaway, Kumiko Hayakawa, Michelle Wong, Alex Hyde-White, Richard Egan Jr.

■ **"Kinjite (Forbidden Subjects)" is a lackluster Cannon vehicle for Charles Bronson, destined to test the patience of his most loyal fans during its probable brief run.**

Title, pronounced kin-ja-tay, refers to taboo subjects that the Japanese repress. Inept screenplay by Harold Nebenzal fails to mesh two parallel storylines into a convincing or even vaguely interesting whole.

First plot thread, reminiscent of Hiroto Yokoyama's 1979 pic "Jun," has Tokyo businessman James Pax highly impressed at the sight of a man molesting a woman on a crowded subway and eliciting no project from the femme (subject is kinjite). After being transferred to L.A., Pax is sleeping on a bus when beautiful young blond teen Amy Hathaway stands next to him; he fondles her under her skirt, provoking a furor and police chase.

Though he escapes, Pax was most unfortunate to have molested Charles Bronson's daughter. Very coincidentally (and impossible for the viewer to believe), vice cop Bronson is soon assigned to the case of retrieving Pax' young daughter Kumiko Hayakawa, who's been kidnaped by evil ethnic heavies Juan Fernandez and Sy Richardson and forced into their underage stable of prostitutes.

Pic unravels at a tortuously slow pace, with poor dialog and several howler scenes that ultimately turn it into low camp. Capper is when Bronson and his partner Perry Lopez dangle Richardson off a balcony to get info and accidentally drop him (to his death), police procedure that is meant to be cute in context.

Given the tastelessness of the subject matter, helmer J. Lee-Thompson manages to shoot the pic with a tv look and feel, which will require only brief pruning of nudity from a shooting of a lesbian-porntape sequence to meet network standards. An energetic score by Greg DeBelles fails to hide the film's lack of forward momentum.

Cast is unexceptional, with Bronson playing it by the numbers, tv ingenue Nicole Eggert beautifying the proceedings as a hardened young prostie and Peggy Lipton making a welcome return in the underwritten role of Bronson's wife.

Scene of Bronson's daughter recognizing her assailant is poorly staged and has no impact, rendering the film as pure shaggy-dog. Offensive coda scene trashes Bronson's screen image, as he metes out "justice" to pimp Fernandez by sending him to a prison block of oversized, aggressively homosexual inmates. —*Lor.*

Escape From Safehaven

New York An SVS Films release of an Avalon production. Produced by Steven Mackler. Line producer, Robert Zimmerman. Directed by Brian Thomas Jones, James McCalmont. Screenplay, Jones, McCalmont, from story by Mark Bishop, Ethan Reiff; additional material, William Milling; camera (Technicolor), McCalmont; editor-2d unit director, Brian O'Hara; music, Taj; sound, Pawel Wdowczak; production design, Mikhail Fishgoyt; assistant director, Joe Derrig; production manager, Philip Dolin; special makeup effects, James Chai; second unit camera, Bob Rudis; associate producer, Bernard E. Goldberg; casting, Nancy Winter Cook, Dennis M. Lee. Reviewed at Westside Cinema 2, N.Y., Jan. 28, 1989. MPAA Rating: R. Running time: **85 MIN.**

Pierce	Rick Gianasi
Jeff Colt	John Wittenbauer
Preacher	Roy MacArthur
Ben Colt	William Beckwith
Janet Colt	Sammi Gavich
Natalie	Mollie O'Mara
Mayor McGee	Marcus Powell

Also with: Jessica Dublin, Sharon Shahinian, Damon Clarke, Tere Malson, Ric Siler.

■ **"Escape From Safehaven" is an impoverished sci-fi film, offering little interest for exploitation audiences.**

Set in the future after a world collapse and shot on decrepit locations in the Bronx, pic looks more like a backyard movie than a pro effort as thesps familiar from local B pictures huddle in a refuge or safehaven from the marauding scavengers (not shown) outside.

A stranger (Rick Gianasi) returns to help the bedraggled Colt family that's being persecuted by Safehaven 186 evil leaders Marcus Powell and Roy MacArthur (both baddie roles are cast with Brits). Uninvolving action has an uprising of rebels vs. the status quo within the housing project locale, nearly everyone styled with punk garb. There's nothing that's the slightest bit futuristic on view.

Sole diversion here is statuesque Tere Malson, cast as a blond dominatrix wielding a mean whip who has the good sense to carefully remove her top while torturing Gianasi. Otherwise pic is drab, ugly and in need of a storyline. Many of the principals behind and in front of the camera made the fun horror flick "The Rejuvenator" but strike out this time. —*Lor.*

No Retreat, No Surrender II
(HONG KONG)

Hollywood A Shapiro Glickenhaus Entertainment release of a Seasonal Films (Hong Kong) production. Produced by Roy Horan. Executive producer, Ng See Yuen. Directed by Corey Yuen. Screenplay, Horan, Keith W. Strandberg, Maria Elene Cellino; camera (CFI color), Nicholas Von Sternberg, Ma Kam Cheung; music, David Spear. Reviewed at Hollywood Pacific theater, L.A., Jan. 27, 1989. MPAA Rating: R. Running time: **92 MIN.**

Scott	Loren Avedon
Mac	Max Thayer
Terri	Cynthia Rothrock
Yuri	Matthias Hues

■ **The spirit of glasnost apparently hasn't influenced the action genre yet as attested by "No Retreat, No Surrender II" where an all-purpose seditious Soviet plot to overthrow governments in Southeast Asia serves as a backdrop for a lot of martial arts fighting. Pic has little to nyet b.o. potential.**

What this has in common with the 1986 release "No Release, No Surrender" is the same crude direction by Corey Yuen and skimpy plotting whereby a seemingly unstoppable and doltish Russkie (Matthias Hues) comes to a violent end only when his dim wits are matched by the quicker moves of a blond, blue-eyed Bruce Lee stand-in (Loren Avedon).

Action opens up on Avedon who has chosen the cheesiest section of Bangkok in which to rendezvous with his Vietnamese g.f. After a too-brief interlude, she is kidnapped from their filthy hotel room by enemies of her wealthy expatriate merchant father and transported across the Thai-Cambodian border to be held hostage in various female bondage apparatuses by Hues. It seems her father is behind a coup scheme with some of his other expatriate cronies.

Before one can say Khmer Rouge, Avedon rounds up old American buddy Mac (Max Thayer) of the import-export (that is, arms) business and the two of them set out to rescue the damsel in distress.

Lunchtime Bangkok becomes the setting for some fantastical martial arts encounters as Avedon kicks, jumps and fells handfuls of Asian goons while sidekick Thayer has to resort to the more mundane techniques of punching and stabbing.

After a quick stop by Thayer's warehouse to stock up on bazookas, grenades and other useful items of self-defense, the boys are transported by chopper into the jungle with macha kid-sister-acting Terri (Cynthia Rothrock) as pilot and aide-de-camp.

A pool filled with snapping alligators, a horde of faceless Asians and a couple dozen Soviet soldiers led by the steroid-pumped Hues compose the obstacles this troika has to overcome to be able to say "mission accomplished."

For those only interested in impressive demonstrations of karate and kung fu "No Retreat II" is marginally entertaining (if totally implausible) storytelling. The principals are adequate, delivering what male posturing is required of them in limited roles.

Tech credits are skimpy and it shows. —*Brit.*

U.S. FESTIVAL REVIEWS

Lobster Man From Mars

Park City An Electric Pictures presentation of a Filmrullen Prod. Produced by Eyal Rimmon, Steven S. Greene. Executive producers, Nicole Seguin, Staffan Ahrenberg, Tom Eliasson. Line producer, Gary M. Bettman. Directed by Stanley Sheff. Screenplay, Bob Greenberg; camera (Foto-Kem color), Gerry Lively; editor, Sheff, Joan Peterson; music, Sasha Matson; production design, Daniel White; sound, Robert Janiger; assistant director, Richard Oswald; casting, William Ackerman. Reviewed at the U.S. Film Festival, Park City, Utah (in competition), Jan. 22, 1989. Running time: **93 MIN.**

J.P. Sheildrake	Tony Curtis
Mary	Deborah Foreman
Professor Piccostomos	Patrick Macnee
Throckmorton	Billy Barty
John	Anthony Hickox
Tommy Sledge	Himself
Stevie Horowitz	Dean Jacobsen
Colonel Ankrum	Fred Holiday
King of Mars/The Astrologer	Bobby Pickett
The Dreaded Lobster Man	S.D. Nemeth
Narrator	Dr. Demento

■ **Despite plenty of amiable good cheer, "Lobster Man From Mars" falls into the trap of self-consciously resurrecting all the clichés of low-budget 1950s monster quickies while only mildly sending them up.**

Not wild and audacious enough to satisfy adults, this may amuse young teens, but looks more likely as a video attraction than a solid theatrical bet.

Lifting a page from "The Producers," motion picture mogul Tony Curtis is told he desperately needs a flop for tax purposes, and sets out to find the worst film he can. What should find its way onto his screening room projector but "Lobster Man From Mars," a homemade item from a barely pubescent nerd.

The film-within-the-film occupies nearly the entire running time. Intentionally inane plot has the dreaded title creature venturing to Earth in order to return some urgently needed air to its native planet. Once it arrives, however, the beast devotes itself entirely to snacking on whatever inhabitants it can find in the Southwestern American desert, a task in which it is aided by two little flying offspring that resembly furry green bats with lobster tails.

Among the characters on the trail of the monster are a clean-cut young couple played by Deborah Foreman and Anthony Hickox; Professor Patrick Macnee, who delights that his original prediction that Martians would take the form of giant clams was so close to the mark; Tommy Sledge, a tough-talking private eye, and a shoot-first, ask-questions-later military man, Fred Holiday.

As usual in such concoctions, the monster can only be eliminated by an obscure but perfectly logical means, and at long last the screening comes to an end. Curtis gleefully snatches up the flabbergasted boy's picture and — surprise, surprise — it turns out to be an all-time smash, which can only be wishful thinking on the filmmakers' parts.

The late screenwriter Bob Greenberg clearly knew his way around the genre, and numerous individual bits are clever and so tacky as to be amusing. Director Stanley Sheff lets it all go on too long, as no such pic should run more than 80-85 minutes, and the level of inspiration simply isn't high enough to put this on the "Airplane!"-"The Naked Gun" level of parody.

Performances are all enthusiastic, and tech credits are just right — cheap, but effective where they count. —*Cart.*

Motel
(DOCU)

Park City A Caligari Film production. Executive producer, Gabriele Walther. Produced, directed and camera (color, 16m), by Christian Blackwood. Editor, sound, Monika Abstacher; music, Alwin Nikolais. Reviewed at the U.S. Film Festival, Park City, Utah (in competition), Jan. 23, 1989. Running time: **86**

MIN.

■ **Minor-key documentary doesn't possess the kind of biog subject that might offer a theatrical life, but festival and international television audiences could take to this indiosyncratic work.**

Avoiding the interstates and driving down the backroads of American culture, Christian Blackwood stumbles across some genuine curios in "Motel," a good-natured, sometimes fascinating look at a substratum of American life that has thus far held out against the pressures of homogenization and corporatism.

Traversing the American Southwest, Blackwood has focused upon three privately run motels, each of which has a very distinct identity. First is the Silver Saddle in Santa Fe, N.M., a presentable establishment operated by three middle-aged women, two of whom are sisters.

Second episode is utterly mesmerizing. The Blue Mist Motel is located across the road from the state prison in Florence Arizona, and counts among its primary visitors the wives who come in to visit their incarcerated husbands.

Just as the first episode looked at three women who run a motel, this one features three ladies who are remarkable in their own ways, in that their love for their mates prevails over all more mundane matters and the inconvenience that the men's imprisonment carries with it.

Final chapter, which is equally curious if less compelling, relates the rate of the Amargosa Hotel and Opera in Death Valley Junction, which is operated by the ghost town's only inhabitants, the aging ballerina Marta Becket and her husband.

Interspersed between the episodes are vignettes about some other oddities of the overnight stay, such as the fabled Wigwam teepee motels, a dilapidated converted whorehouse and the unique Movie Manor, where motel patrons look out picture windows to the drive-in screen across the parking lot. —*Cart.*

Sex, Lies And Videotape

Park City   An Outlaw production. Produced by Robert Newmyer, John Hardy. Executive producers, Nancy Tenenbaum, Nick Wechsler, Morgan Mason. Written and directed by Steven Soderbergh. Camera (CFI col-

or), Walt Lloyd; music, Cliff Martinez; art direction, Joanne Schmidt; set decoration, Victoria Spader; costumes, James Ryder; sound, Paul Ledford; assistant director, Michael Dempsey; casting, Deborah Aquila. Reviewed at the U.S. Film Festival, Park City, Utah (in competition), Jan. 25, 1989. No MPAA Rating. Running time: **101 MIN.**
Graham Dalton . . . . James Spader
Ann Millaney . . . . Andie MacDowell
John Millaney . . . . Peter Gallagher
Cynthia Bishop . . . . Laura San Giacomo
Therapist . . . . Ron Vawter
Barfly . . . . Steven Brill

■ **"Sex, Lies And Videotape" is one of the best American independent films in quite a long while, a sexy, nuanced, beautifully controlled examination of how a quartet of people are defined by their erotic impulses and inhibitions.**

Steven Soderbergh's highly impressive directorial debut is owned in the domestic homevideo market by RCA/Columbia, while Virgin has foreign territories. Despite the limited rights available, theatrical distribs should be competing avidly for the film due to its promising potential on the upscale baby boomer circuit.

Imaginatively presented opening intercuts the embarrassed therapy confessions of young wife Andie MacDowell with the impending arrival in town of James Spader, a mysterious stranger type who was a college chum of MacDowell's handsome husband, Peter Gallagher.

Given MacDowell's admissions that she and Gallagher are no longer having sex, it would seem that Spader is walking into a potentially provocative situation, all the more so because he no longer has anything in common with his old buddy, who is now a yuppie lawyer, and feels drawn to the needy MacDowell.

He drops a bombshell by revealing that he is impotent, seemingly scratching any developments on that end.

Gallagher has been conducting a secret affair with his wife's wild sister, Laura San Giacomo. Latter is incredibly sexy but a real handful, as she persists in demanding that he break up his busy work day for quickies.

Pic is absorbing and titillating because nearly every conversation is about sex and aspects of these attractive people's relationships. Several steamy scenes between Gallagher and San Giacomo, and some extremely frank videotapes featuring women speaking about their sex lives, turn the temperature up even more.

What's really impressive about

Soderbergh's work here is the cool precision with which he both unfolds the unusual story, and probes ever further into the private recesses of the characters' sexual makeups. Few American films attempt this sort of ambitious psychological analysis, and this new writer-director has succeeded memorably.

Gallagher and MacDowell very accurately convey the upwardly mobile preoccupations of their class. Former is also called upon to be shallow and evasive, which he does well, while the latter is spookily convincing in her uptightness and insecurity about the realities of sex.

Spader does very well developing the character of what was undoubtedly once a nice, bright, normal young man made into a handicapped weirdo by troubles in love.

The star of the film whenever she's on is San Giacomo. Fiery, caustic and devastatingly erotic, she's the hottest thing to turn up onscreen recently and sure to soon be a busy young actress.

Lensed on location in Baton Rogue, La., for $1.2-million, production looks splendid thanks to the standout cinematography of Walt Lloyd, and Joanne Schmidt's perceptive art direction. Cliff Martinez' electronic score is eerily effective. —*Cart.*

Clownhouse

Park City   A Commercial Pictures production. Produced by Michael Danty, Robin Mortarotti, Victor Salva. Written and directed by Salva. Camera (Deluxe color), Mortarotti; editors, Roy Anthony Cox, Sabrina Plisco-Morris; music, Michael Becker, Thomas Richardson; sound, Plisco-Morris; production design, Cox; art direction, Tom Rubalcava; associate producer, Sara Strom; assistant director, Laura Marks. Reviewed at U.S. Film Festival, Park City, Utah (in competition), Jan. 23, 1989. Running time: **84 MIN.**
Casey . . . . Nathan Forrest Winters
Geoffrey . . . . Brian McHugh
Randy . . . . Sam Rockwell
Cheezo . . . . Tree
Also with: Byron Weible, David C. Reinecker.

■ **Project: to make an effective but virtually bloodless scare pic for less than $1-million. Result: "Clownhouse," a serviceable but formulaic old-dark-house opus that could flush out a little theatrical business with kids before finding its appropriate resting place in homevid stores.**

Pic represents first effort from the frankly named Commercial

Pictures, a hitherto low-profile off-shoot of Zoetrope Studios in San Francisco.

Company subsequently has produced a Western and a rock 'n' roll comedy on similarly tight budgets and with fresh talents. Zoetrope link is tipped by the company logo, which, in a design somewhat reminiscent of the old RKO logo, has lightning hitting the tower atop the Zoetrope Building on Kearney Street in San Francisco.

Playing on the not unusual fear of clowns held by many youngsters, story has three brothers heading for an evening at the Jolly Bros. Circus.

Youngest of the trio, Casey, still has nightmares because of his traumatic experience with the clowns the year before, but he's dragged along anyway, to a similar result.

Much of the early going is devoted to interplay among the boys. The oldest, Randy, is cocky and foul-mouthed, a teenager embarrassed to be hanging out with his still immature kid brothers. Geoffrey, in the middle, seems to be the most intelligent of the bunch, but is not physically up to challenging Randy's constant bullying.

Primary focus, however, falls upon little Casey, who's scared to go anywhere alone and, predictably, has no success convincing Randy that the clowns are following them.

And, of course, they are, since three escaped lunatics have killed the circus clowns and are now galavanting around the small town murdering anyone they can get their hands on.

Protracted climax finds the boys alone late at night in their absent parents' rambling old house. Naturally, the sinister clowns invade the premises, the lights go out, and wits are matched until four of the six combatants lie dead.

Given the restricted conditions of the genre, writer-director Victor Salva's plotting is reasonably resourceful, and numerous moments provoke nervous laughter from the audience. On the chintzy budget, pic looks sharp and is technically impressive.

Only problem is that this has been done a thousand times before. —*Cart.*

Tap

Hollywood   A Tri-Star Pictures release. Produced by Gary Adelson, Richard Vane. Executive producer, Francine Saperstein. Written and directed by Nick Castle. Camera (CFI color), David Gribble; editor, Patrick Kennedy; music, James Newton Howard; executive music producer, Joel Sill; production design, costume design, Patricia Norris; set decoration, Leslie Morales; sound (Dolby), Stephan Von Hase; choreography, Henry Le-Tang; improvography, Gregory Hines; Tap-Tronics concept and development, Alfred Desio; assistant directors, Dennis White, Emmit-Leon (Kip) O'Neil. Reviewed at UA Coronet, Westwood, Calif., Jan. 30, 1989. MPAA Rating: PG-13. Running time: **110 MIN.**

Max	Gregory Hines
Amy	Suzzanne Douglas
Little Mo	Sammy Davis Jr.
Louis	Savion Glover
Nicky	Joe Morton
Francis	Dick Anthony Williams
Bob	Terrence McNally
Sandman	Sandman Sims
Bunny	Bunny Briggs
Steve	Steve Condos
Slim	Jimmy Slyde
Spats	Pat Rico
Arthur	Arthur Duncan
Harold	Harold Nicholas

■ "Tap" is a surprisingly rich and affecting blend of dance and story that transcends its respectful deference toward the great hoofers of a bygone era to deliver plenty of glowing contemporary entertainment.

Impassioned by the twin personal commitments of writer-director Nick Castle (whose father choreographed for Fred Astaire and Gene Kelly) and star Gregory Hines (whose tap career began at five at Harlem's Apollo Theater), project benefits from a dream cast and crew and is sure to dance away with a sizeable slab of the boxoffice once the word gets out.

Hines plays Max, an ex-con torn between the high style and fast money of his former career as a jewel thief and the more deeply felt pleasures of tap dance, a form he'd learned from his dead father, Sonny Washington, who'd been a legendary hoofer.

Trying to spark up an old romance with a dance teacher (Suzzanne Douglas), whose father, Lil Mo (Sammy Davis Jr.), was his dad's pal, Max gets pulled unwillingly into the world of the oldtime hoofers, who occupy the exalted third floor of Sonny's, a dance studio and shabby shrine to the all-but-forgotten form.

Writer-director Castle proves himself extraordinarily sensitive to the subject matter from the first frame, a striking nighttime scene in which the imprisoned Hines, provoked by the torturous rhythm of dripping water, performs a dance that expresses both his anger and the reawakening of a dormant force inside him.

Particularly valuable about "Tap" is the way it makes a clear distinction between the glib, glamorous top 'n tails variety of tap dancing that film and audiences are most familiar with and the tougher, more soulful and athletic style of the hoofers.

Much like blues music, the dancing in this pic seems a heartfelt and exuberant response to urban struggle.

Pic brims with treasures, like the third-floor "challenge" contest at Sonny's, featuring greats Sandman Sims, Bunny Briggs, Jimmy Slyde, Steve Condos, Pat Rico, Arthur Duncan and Harold Nicholas, in an astounding display in which each dancer's turn is as diverse and expressive as those of soloists in a great jazz band.

Another big asset is pic's introduction in final dance seg of Tap-Tronics, a blend of tap and electric rock in which dancer's taps are connected with synthesizers that allow him to make both rhythmic and melodic music. Enough cannot be said about the exhaustive, precise sound and lighting work required to pull off the Tap-Tronics seg.

In large part, its Hines' performance that makes pic work, as he balances the occasionally broad, storybook style of its musical-genre direction with an understated but deeply felt portrayal of conflicted Max.

Role of Lil Mo, a bandanna-ed survivor who won't give up on tap, fits Davis like a glove, though Douglas, lovely as she is, makes choices a bit too strident and obvious as Max' girlfriend.

Among supporting players, Joe Morton gives a cutting, focused perf as the wound-up Nicky.

David Gribble contributes burnished, glowing photography that emphasizes nostalgia and sentiment of the piece, and James Newton Howard's canny score is an essential element in success of the era-hopping dances. —*Daws*.

True Believer

New York   A Columbia Pictures release of a Lasker/Parkes production. Executive producer, Peter Rosten. Produced by Walter F. Parkes, Lawrence Lasker. Coproducer, Patrick Crowley. Directed by Joseph Ruben. Screenplay, Wesley Strick; camera (Deluxe color), John W. Lindley; editor, George Bowers; music, Brad Fiedel; production design, Lawrence Miller; costumes, Erica Edell Phillips; production manager, Whitney Green; assistant director, Michael Steele; sound, Larry Kemp, Lon E. Nader; stunts, Rocky Capella; casting, Karen Rea. Reviewed at Columbia Pictures screening room, N.Y., Jan. 17, 1989. MPAA Rating: R. Running time: 103 **MIN.**

Eddie Dodd	James Woods
Roger Baron	Robert Downey Jr.
Shu Kai Kim	Yuji Okumoto
Kitty Greer	Margaret Colin
Robert Reynard	Kurtwood Smith
Cecil Skell	Tom Bower
Art Esparza	Miguel Ferenandes
Vincent Dennehy	Charles Hallahan

Also with: Sully Diaz, Misan Kim, John Snyder, Luis Guzman, Graham Beckel, Tony Haney, Joel Polis, Will Marchetti.

■In "True Believer" James Woods drives still another self-possessed character to the precipice, but the spectacle of drug lawyer Eddie Dodd's frenetic fight for self-redemption doesn't redeem the dubious boxoffice prospects of this overheated crime melodrama.

Recently, Hollywood has inclined to depict the firebrand youth of the 1960s as burnouts or sellouts in the 1980s. "True Believer" presents Woods as a former radical idealist lawyer and media star who has degenerated into a directionless but effective defender of drug dealers. He sleeps in his Greenwich Village tenement office, smokes pot to unwind and isn't picky about where his clients get their cash.

When wide-eyed tyro attorney Roger Baron (Robert Downey Jr.) arrives in Gotham to clerk for Woods he's shocked by the cynical dissipation and low-life clientele of his scruffy legal hero. Woods passionately contends that while his clients are surely guilty, they deserve the same constitutional protections accorded others. Otherwise headline-seeking prosecutors like Woods' antagonist, district attorney Robert Reynard (bitingly played by Kurtwood Smith) will be free to trample on everybody's civil liberties.

One day Woods is asked to represent an Asian prisoner who has killed a racist convict in defending himself from a jailhouse assassination attempt. Goaded by Downey, Woods investigates the case of Shu Kai Kim (Yuji Okumoto) and decides that he's been framed on his original conviction eight years previously for killing a rival gang member in Chinatown. If he can prove this, the bumpy script reasons, Woods can obtain Kim's release and salvage his own self-respect.

In a patented speed-rapping turn bristling with overdriven agitation, Woods propels Eddie Dodd in reckless pursuit of the truth through a netherworld populated by crypto-fascist ex-cons, corrupt cops and unscrupulous prosecutors. Woods' diffuse intensity virtually obliterates bland performances by Downey and by Margaret Colin who plays private eye Kitty Greer. Her purported investigative wizardry and platonic relationship with Woods are unconvincingly written and rendered.

Director Joseph Ruben pushes the narrative headlong to its whodunit and why denouement, but the real story is Woods' self-confrontational quest to recover the lost promise of his past. The film's conceit of the '60s as a brief shining time whose ideals have been dashed on the shoals of Reagan-era reality is underscored through the elegiac use of fragments from period rock classics.

Cinematographer John W. Lindley drenches the film in a sea-green darkness appropriate to Woods' nightcrawling existence. For obvious production exigencies on a Gotham-set film shot mainly in California, the lawyer invariably returns to his office/pad on Seventh Avenue and Christopher Street at an hour so late that even the hustlers have gone to sleep. The courtroom showdown payoff of "True Believer" is not worth staying up for either. —*Rich*.

Cousins

Hollywood   A Paramount Picture's release. Produced by William Allyn. Executive producer, George Goodman. Directed by Joel Schumacher. Screenplay, Stephen Metcalfe based on 1975 film "Cousin, Cousine" written by Jean-Charles Tacchella; camera (Technicolor), Ralf D. Bode; editor, Robert Brown; music, Angelo Badalamenti; production design, Mark S. Freeborn; set decoration, Linda Vipond; costume design, Michael Kaplan; sound, Larry Sutton, Rob Young; assistant director, David W. Rose; casting, Marci Liroff. Reviewed at Paramount Studios, L.A, Feb. 2, 1989. MPAA Rating: PG-13. Running time: **110 MIN.**

Larry	Ted Danson
Maria	Isabella Rossellini
Tish	Sean Young
Tom	William Petersen
Vince	Lloyd Bridges
Edie	Norma Aleandro
Mitch	Keith Coogan
Aunt Sofia	Gina de Angelis

■As derivative as it is, "Cousins" still is a hugely entertaining Americanized version of the French film "Cousin, Cousine." If love really does conquer all, so too will "Cousins" at the b.o.

This has nearly the same insouciant tone as the Jean-Charles Tac-

Original Film
Cousin, Cousine
(FRENCH)

Paris   A Gaumont release of Les Films Pomereau (Bertrand Javal)-Gaumont production. Features entire cast. Written and directed by Jean-Charles Tacchella. Camera (Eastmancolor), Georges Lendi; editor, Agnes Guillemot; music, Gerard Anfasso. Reviewed at Publicis, Paris, Nov. 9, 1975. Running time: **95 MIN.**
Marthe . . . . .Marie-Christine Barrault
Ludovic . . . . .Victor Lanoux
Karine . . . . .Marie-France Pisier
Pascal . . . . .Guy Marchand
Biju . . . . .Ginette Garcin
Diane . . . . .Sybil Maas
Sacy . . . . .Jean Herbert
Gobert . . . . .Pierre Plessis

chella comedy of 1975. It's been spiced with a dash of '80s social commentary and a dollop of Italian ethnic flavoring, which clearly seems lifted from the much more charming "Moonstruck."

It is the gushy story of two new cousins (Isabella Rossellini, Ted Danson), now related when her mother marries his uncle. They fall in love as their respective spouses (Sean Young and William Petersen) fall in lust.

The least colorful characters also are the central once, those being the odds-on pair of Rossellini and Danson, but their sappy, overly sentimental series of rendezvous are well compensated by their relatives' caustic comments, irreverent asides and other antics at the three weddings, one funeral and other functions all attend during the course of the picture.

Noisy scenes of assimilating first- and second-generation types into suburban culture make for predictable situations, though scripter Stephen Metcalfe has the good sense to mix them up with an equal number of loose, bawdy and silly ones from the white-bread folks.

Object of most of the ridicule is Petersen, the unctuous BMW car salesman and Don Juan pretender who starts everything off in the opening wedding scene drooling at Danson's flamboyantly dressed wife (Young).

It's obvious enough that Rossellini, the martyred Madonna type who knows of her husband's philandering, represents prudishness and purity as much as Young, dressed in outlandish high-fashion ruffles of red and black, represents the opposite.

What's most fun is to get everyone else's thoughts on the matter. There's Rossellini's mother Edie (Norma Aleandro), wealthy after inheriting her first husband's garbage fortune, cranky old Aunt Sofia (Gina De Angelis, patterned after the dotty grandfather in

"Moonstruck") and Danson's son Mitchell (Keith Coogan), who has a penchant for videotaping family gatherings.

Best of all is Lloyd Bridges, Danson's irascible, sporting uncle, who has as much pep in his step and gleam in his eye for Aleandro as the two main couples have combined.

Joel Schumacher's direction captures well enough the playfulness of family assemblies in the backyard and in reception halls, allowing the actors space enough to laugh at themselves. He doesn't yet have a feel for lightening up for the serious encounters, as is apparent in the too-lushly scored and shot getting-to-know-you scenes with Rossellini and Danson.

Overall, it's enjoyable and diversionary. Tech credits are rich, maybe too much so. —*Brit.*

Siddheswari
(INDIAN — COLOR/B&W)

New Delhi   A Films Division release of an Infrakino Film Production Private Ltd. production. Produced by Mani Kaul, Lalitha Krishna. Written and directed by Mani Kaul. Camera (color), Riyush Shah; editor, Krishna; music, Siddheswari Devi; art direction, Kamal Swaroop. Reviewed at the French Embassy, New Delhi, Jan. 23, 1989. Running time: **86 MIN.**
With: Mita Vasisth
(Soundtrack in Hindi)

■ **Likely to be mistaken for a documentary, "Siddheswari" is actually an ambitious attempt to create a visual correlative for the extraordinary music of one of the century's greatest Thumri singers, Siddheswari Devi.**

Filmmaker Mani Kaul brushes over the lady's life (1908-1977) very lightly. The languid poetry of her music is film's real subject, most in focus in the first half. This difficult experiment is bound to attract serious attention abroad, though viewers need imagination and good will to follow it.

Kaul and cinematographer Riyush Shah capture the plaintive sensuality of India's holy city Benares in superb image. The disturbing rhythms of Siddheswari's songs are captured in images of mysterious beauty — boats poised on the river, a bejeweled girl kneeling before a sultan in a terraced garden.

Film is in color with some black and white to change the pace. The long succession of hypnotic shots gets a little tedious by the end, partly because of deliberate ambiguities. Multiple incarnations of

the singer (from actress Mita Vasisth, to an apt final video of the aged Siddheswari herself) make it even harder to follow her story, though some sketchy notes at the beginning help.

Sensual sets are by Kamal Swaroop, who directed "Om Dar-B-Dar." —*Yung.*

The Expendables

New York   A Concorde Pictures release of a Premiere Prods. Intl. presentation. Produced by Anna Roth, Christopher Santiago. Directed by Cirio H. Santiago. Screenplay, Phillip Alderton; camera (color), Ricardo Remias; editor, Edgar Viner; music director, Jaime Fabregas; sound, Do Bulotano, Vic Dona; production design, Joe Mari Avellana; assistant director, Jose Torres; second unit director, Bobby Santiago; casting, Enrique Reyes. Reviewed on Media Home Entertainment vidcassette, N.Y., Jan. 18, 1989. MPAA Rating: R. Running time: **95 MIN.**
Capt. Rosello . . . . .Anthony Finetti
Sterling . . . . .Peter Nelson
Lord . . . . .Loren Haynes
Jackson . . . . .Kevin Duffis
Col. Ridamann . . . . .William Steis
Col. Tran Um Phi . . . . .Vic Diaz
Cabrini . . . . .David Light
Phu Ling . . . . .Leah Navarro
   Also with: Janet Price, Jeff Griffith, Jim Moss.

■ **Filipino action specialist Cirio H. Santiago comes up with a well-made but ho-hum Vietnam War saga in "The Expendables," which played off theatrically last year.**

His excellent handling of English dialog makes this indistinguishable from all-American films, as gung-ho Capt. Rosello (Anthony Finetti) leads his band of misfits on various missions, notably to capture a Vietnamese colonel (the ubiquitous Vic Diaz) for interrogation.

With its usual quota of explosions and battles, film is enjoyable on a mindless action level, but bogs down in some rather pretentious verbal exchanges as Philip Alderton's script tries lamely for significance.

Cast is adequate in executing stereotypes (the religious fanatic nicknamed Lord, a bitter black soldier, a racist in the platoon, etc.). Glum ending is overly downbeat. —*Lor.*

Her Alibi

Hollywood   A Warner Bros. release. Executive producer, Martin Elfand. Produced by Keith Barish. Directed by Bruce Beresford. Screenplay, Charlie Peters; camera (Technicolor), Freddie Francis; editor, Anne Goursaud; music, Georges Delerue; sound (Dolby), Bruce Bisenz; production design, Henry Bumstead; art direction, Steve Walker; set decoration, James W. Payne; costume design, Ann Roth; associate producer, Daniel Franklin;

assistance director, Richard Luke Rothschild; second unit director, Ron Rondell; casting, Ken Carlson. Reviewed at Warner Bros. Studios, Burbank, Calif., Jan. 27, 1989. MPAA Rating: PG. Running time: **94 MIN.**
Phil Blackwood . . . . .Tom Selleck
Nina . . . . .Paulina Porizkova
Sam . . . . .William Daniels
Frank Polito . . . . .James Farentino
Troppa . . . . .Hurd Hatfield
"Lucy" Comanescu . . . . .Ronald Guttman
Avram . . . . .Victor Argo
Gary Blackwood . . . . .Patrick Wayne
Sally Blackwood . . . . .Tess Harper

■ **He's a mystery writer; she's a mystery, and it's also a mystery how tv fodder like this manages to get the high-gloss, top-talent treatment at studios.**

It's an ideal vehicle for the great-looking duo of Tom Selleck and model Paulina Porizkova, since they get to play essentially themselves, while the only stretching is left to director Bruce Beresford, who adds this offbeat gossamer frolic to his formerly substantive repertoire. Easy appeal of stars should guarantee a glowing b.o. reception, but don't expect this one to show legs — except, of course, his and hers.

Visually, pic gets off to a sharp, edgy start, with a montage of retro detective novel covers whetting the appetite for a good, stylized yarn.

Beresford's textured, brightly composed opening shots and Anne Goursaud's alert editing set a very promising tone, as do some fine character scenes with the plainfolks courtroom regulars with whom bestselling writer Phil Blackwood (Selleck) huddles for ideas.

Relationship with his anxious publisher Sam (William Daniels, in a well-pitched performance) also is well-handled.

As soon as Selleck, out of stories and under pressure for his next book, decides to rescue drop-dead beautiful Porizkova from court custody as a murder suspect, things begin to turn the corner.

He gives her an alibi by telling the canny D.A. (rigorously played in a welcome appearance by James Farentino) that they're having an affair and were together during the time of the alleged murder.

Farentino suspects the obvious motive, but what can he do? To maintain the facade, Selleck has to take the aloof Rumanian beauty out to his lush country estate to live while he pecks away at his new novel — about her, naturally, and his feverishly imagined version of their relationship. Meanwhile, they chastely close the bedroom doors between them each night.

Porizkova has the disconcerting habit of hurling kitchen knives at the wall and otherwise inviting Selleck's demise. He soon begins to suspect she is a murderer, and that to preserve her mock alibi, she intends to kill him. Before long, he's barricading his bedroom door at night rather than trying to lure her through it.

Mix of sexual tension, physical danger and quirky black humor has a certain appealing bouyancy, but ultimately it's deflated by general lack of credibility. At no point are we tempted to suspend disbelief, and therefore, level of involvement remains light.

This pic is not without charms, like the mock-macho voiceover of Selleck's debonair detective novelhero Peter Swift "writing" events in marked contrast to the calamitous way they're unfolding.

Czech-born Porizkova, last seen onscreen in the artsy "Anna," has a bemused sparkle that serves her well in the light comic interchanges with Selleck, though the declarations of love between them must be taken on faith, as scripter Charlie Peters offers no logical support. Meanwhile, onscreen lust is nearly absent, though given amusing lip service.

Selleck, who has bigscreen presence to spare, continues to amiably play against type, in this role going so far as to absorb such unmanly indignations as an arrow in his flanks and a crazed female driver.

Georges Delerue contributes a witty score. —Daws.

L.A. Heat

New York A PM Entertainment Group presentation of a Pepin/Merhi production. Produced by Joseph Merhi, Richard Pepin. Directed by Merhi. Screenplay, Charles T. Kanganis; additional dialog, Lawrence-Hilton Jacobs; camera (color), Pepin; editor, Paul Volk; music, John Gonzalez; sound, Mike Hall; second unit director, Red Horton; special makeup effects, Judy Yonemoto; coproducers, Charla Driver, Addison Randall; associate producer, Jacobs. Reviewed on Raedon Entertainment Group videocassette, N.Y., Jan. 23, 1989. No MPAA Rating. Running time: **85 MIN.**

Jon Chance ......Lawrence-Hilton Jacobs
Captain ....Jim Brown
Clarence ....Kevin Benton
Spyder ....Myles Thoroughgood
Jane ....Pat Johnson
Boris....................Jay Richardson
   Also with: Raymond Martino, Robert Gallo, Joe Vance, Gretchen Becker, Jamie Baker, Pamela Dixon, Jacqueline Jade, Marisa Wade, Renny Stroud.

■ **Jim Brown fans will be happy to see him back in straight-ahead fashion — after the self-spoofing of "I'm Gonna Git You Sucka"** — in "L.A. Heat," an okay made-for-video feature.

Pic benefits from an earnest performance by Lawrence-Hilton Jacobs as cop Jon Chance, who's having plenty of trouble with his captain (Brown) over a drug case.

Actually Chance dreams of being a Wild West gunfighter (illustrated in fantasy inserts), but Brown keeps giving him deadlines to catch the violent dealer (Kevin Benton) who's making fools out of the L.A. police.

Trademark exploding bloodpacks (by Judy Yonemoto) punctuate Joseph Merhi's B-picture. Tech credits are acceptable, though the sound recording is a bit rough and ready. —Lor.

Who's Harry Crumb?

Hollywood A Tri-Star Picture release of a Tri-Star and NBC Prods. presentation of an Arnon Milchan/Frostbacks production. Produced by Milchan. Executive producer, John Candy. Directed by Paul Flaherty. Screenplay, Robert Conte, Peter Martin Wortmann; camera (Alpha Cine color, Technicolor prints), Stephen M. Katz; editor, Danford B. Greene; music, Michel Colombier; production design, Trevor Williams; art direction, Stephen Geaghan; set decoration, Elizabeth Wilcox; costume design, Jerry R. Allen; sound (Dolby), Rick Patton; stunt coordinator, Bill Ferguson; associate producer, Les Kimber; assistant director, Tom Rowe; second unit director & camera, Curtis Peterson; casting, Susan Bluestein. Reviewed at Cineplex Odeon Century Plaza theater, L.A., Jan. 31, 1989. MPAA Rating: PG-13. Running time: **98 MIN.**

Harry Crumb...............John Candy
Eliot Draisen..............Jeffrey Jones
Helen Downing.............Annie Potts
Vince Barnes ....Tim Thomerson
P.J. Downing ....Barry Corbin
Nikki Downing ....Shawnee Smith
Det. Casey ....Valri Bromfield
Dwayne ....Doug Steckler
Jennifer Downing ....Renee Coleman
Tim....................Wesley Mann
Receptionist ....Fiona Roeske
   Also with: Joe Flaherty, Lyle Alzado, Jim Belushi, Stephen Young.

■ **Foolishness in the right hands can be sublimely funny, and combo of star John Candy and director Paul Flaherty (former SCTV cohorts) puts the perfect spin on "Who's Harry Crumb?," a "Naked Gun"-style farce about a bumbling private eye who succeeds in spite of himself.**

Tri-Star will no doubt benefit at the b.o. from the ready-made audience for this vein of goofball humor and pic's obvious potential for a sequel.

Candy plays Crumb, a complete idiot who remains appealing because he's too tough to admit it. Luckily, he's related by birth to a line of crack detectives, and finally gets assigned to a lucrative kidnaping case — but only because his beady-eyed boss (Jeffrey Jones), who's the kidnaper, doesn't want it solved.

At stake is Jone's lust for the golddigging newlywed wife (maliciously and deliciously played by Annie Potts) of a benign, trusting multimillionaire (Barry Corbin). The plot is to get $10-million ransom for the return of Corbin's slinky daughter (Renee Coleman), and use the riches to pry Potts away from her main meal-ticket.

Candy finds a fertile vehicle in this, easily carrying every scene and getting laughs in a bizarre array of disguises and plenty of wild physical stunts made funnier by his ample girth.

He seems to have picked up some tricks from Dan Aykroyd and Steve Martin (both former costars) that he applies to good effect to achieve the attitude of a winning but moronic wiseguy in this pic. Scripters Robert Conte and Peter Martin Wortmann provide lines so dumb only Candy could pull them off, as well as ridiculous non sequiturs and some pretty snappy retorts.

A butchy, spiteful police detective (Valri Bromfield) to Candy: "When this is all over, I'm gonna rip your face off and eat it for breakfast." Candy: "Take a number."

On the other hand, his unthreatening teddy-bear quality is played off to good effect in a charming sidekick relationship with the kidnapee's kid sister, keenly played by Shawnee Smith.

Director Flaherty peppers the action with goofy business, like a sick orange tree that drops fruit onto Candy's desk while he's interviewing clients, and stretches to comic book extremes a stunt in which Candy takes a wild ride down an air conditioner shaft.

Good character bits abound, like Joe Flaherty's performance as a punchy doorman.

Plot sometimes gets sloppy, like some murky business with kidnapee and her sadistic captor, and one can't deny that the basic elements have all been seen before.

Still, foolery pulled off with a wink and a flourish is hard to argue with.

Action throughout is vigorously punched up by Michael Colombier's robust score. —Daws.

Wicked Stepmother

San Rafael An MGM/UA Distribution release of an MGM picture. Produced by Robert Littman. Executive producer, Larry Cohen. Written and directed by Cohen. Camera (Deluxe color), Bryan England; editor, David Kern; music, Robert Folk; sound, Kim Ornitz, art direction, Gene Abel; assistant director, Sanford Hampton. Reviewed at the Rafael theater, San Rafael, Calif., Feb. 4, 1989. MPAA Rating: PG-13. Running time: **92 MIN.**

Miranda ....Bette Davis
Priscilla ....Barbara Carrera
Jenny ....Colleen Camp
Steve ....David Rasche
Sam ....Lionel Stander
Lt. MacIntosh ....Tom Bosley
Mike ....Shawn Donahue
Nat ....Richard Moll
Witch mistress ....Evelyn Keyes
Nandy ....Susie Garrett
Vanilla ....Laurene Landon

■ **It's a kindness to all concerned that "Wicked Stepmother" will apparently be allowed to play off in the backwaters, away from prying eyes and cruel questions.**

As was publicized, writer-director Larry Cohen and Bette Davis had their disagreements over this one and her character disappears from the film about half way through. She may or may not have been replaced by Barbara Carrera; it's hard to tell and who cares.

Colleen Camp and David Rasche — a couple of otherwise able performers who seem thunderstruck in the midst of this mess — come home from vacation to find that dad (Lionel Stander) has taken a new wife (Davis).

The kids don't know (and it wouldn't make any difference if they did) that Davis is also a witch being pursued by detective Tom Bosley because she shrinks people. Before anything else interesting happens, Davis has made a quiet exit and Carrera is hanging around the house saying she's Davis' daughter.

There are an awful lot of bad process shots of Carrera. Whether this is witch stuff or just trying to force her into some previously shot footage is not evident. But it doesn't upset the story since there is no story. In fact, all of the special effects shots are exquisitely terrible throughout.

At the end, Bosley suggests there may be a sequel. He doesn't say that as if he's anxious to take part. —Har.

Piravi
(INDIAN)

New Delhi A Film Folk production. Directed by Shaji Story, S. Jayachandran Nair; camera (color), Sunny Joseph; music, Aravindan. Reviewed at Taj Palace screening room, New Delhi, Jan. 18, 1989. Running

time: **110 MIN.**
With: Premji, Archana, C.V. Sreeraman.
(Soundtrack in Malayam)

■ **"Piravi,"** the first film directed by Aravindan's cinematographer Shaji, is very much in the Aravindan tradition: a sensual, slow, thoughtful tale with a beginning but no end, achieving moving closeness to its characters.

Because so little happens, film has some very long stretches, especially at the beginning. Its portrait of a father and daughter in the rain-drenched greenery of Kerala ultimately grabs hold of the viewer, however, making it a film hard to forget.

Story examines the almost mystical bond between a father and son, although the son, who is probably dead when film begins, never appears. The aged father goes to a distant bus stop to meet Raghu, an engineering student in the state captial coming home on vacation. Gradually his eagerness turns to disappointment.

He continues making a daily trip to the bus stop, despite the reproaches of his sick wife and schoolteacher daughter Malathi (played by India's fine new actress Archana).

Film picks up when first the father, then the daughter make trips to the capital to inquire about Raghu. The father's visit to a minister of his acqaintance and the chief of police proves a cruel deception.

Malathi's meeting with Raghu's schoolmates is more agonizing still, when they tell her they think her brother was tortured to death by the police. The father prays to his temple gods in desperation, and finally (mercifully) goes mad, happy in the belief his son has returned.

Cast is outstanding. Camera concentrates on their sensitive faces to convey the full poignancy of the human dilemma. The film's social criticism hovers just below the surface. Lensing by Sunny Joseph is a remarkable play of black and color. —*Yung.*

All's Fair

Hollywood A Moviestore Entertainment release of a Midwood production. Executive producer, David G. Stern. Produced by Jon Gordon. Directed by Rocky Lane. Screenplay, Randee Russel, John Finegan, Tom Rondinella, William Pace, story by Finegan and Watt Tyler; camera (color), Peter Lyons Collister; editor, Maryann Brandon; music, Bill Myers; line producer, Claude Lawrence, Jr.; associate producer, Tricia Gordon. Reviewed at the UA Coronet theater, Westwood, Calif., Feb. 4, 1989. MPAA Rating: PG-13. Running time: **89 MIN.**

Colonel	George Segal
Florence	Sally Kellerman
Mark	Robert Carradine
Ann	Jennifer Edwards
Linda	Jane Kaczmarek
Eddie	John Kapelos
Klaus	Lou Ferrigno

■ **Four people get screenplay credit on this atrocious comedy, which means the writing crew could well outnumber the ranks of those who'll see it during its theatrical run. Even homevideo prospects seem grim.**

The story, such as it is, involves a trigger-happy candy bar magnate (George Segal) obsessed with those weekend war games where morons tromp out into the woods and shoot each other with paint pellets. Robert Carradine is the fair-haired boy in the company because of his wargame prowess, a source of constant frustration to the hardworking Ann (Jennifer Edwards) who's locked out of the good ol' boy network.

In order to earn her promotion, Ann forms her own wargame team by enlisting the wives of the men in the company — including Segal's (Sally Kellerman), in the midst of divorcing him and out to seize control of the company. The ladies hire a humongous mercenary (Lou Ferrigno) to train them and end up in an extended battle with the menfolk that's as tedious as it is stupid.

Rarely has a script been as flat as this one. There isn't a legitimate laugh in the entire film.

The performances prove equally embarrassing — devoid of any direction or subtlety. Segal sputters ridiculously, Kellerman's predatory wife has no spark whatsoever, and Carradine's inevitable attraction to Ann (Edwards) is built on nothing but the convenience of formula. Ferrigno has a nice moment or two as the mercenary, but one can't help hoping he'll turn green, smash a wall and escape from the film.

Tech credits are equally lame, as the pic feels as if it were shot over the weekend in a neighbor's yard. From the first opening frame to its silly "American Graffiti"-style postscripts (few will see those), "All's Fair" is all foul. —*Bril.*

Rage To Kill

New York An Action Intl. Pictures production. Executive producer, Hope Holiday. Produced and directed by David Winters. Screenplay, Winters, Ian Yule; camera (Irene color), Vincent Cox; editor, Bill Asher; music, Tim James, Steven McClintock, Mark Mancina; sound, Neil Thain; assistant director, Neal Sundstrom; production manager, Debi Nethersole; associate producer, Jonathan Vanger. Reviewed on AIP Home Video vidcassette, N.Y., Jan. 21, 1989. MPAA Rating: R. Running time: **92 MIN.**

Blaine Striker	James Ryan
Gen. Turner	Oliver Reed
Miller	Cameron Mitchell
Trishia Baker	Maxine John
Wally Arn	Henry Cele
Slade	Ian Yule

Also with: Sydney Chama, Liam Cundill, Lionel Newton, Michael Clark, Beverly McLeish, John Hussey.

■ **South Africa and environs double adequately for fictionalized Grenada in the oddball actioner "Rage To Kill," a mishmash politically somewhere to the right of Clint Eastwood's "Heartbreak Ridge" but typical of today's homevideo fare.**

James Ryan, South Africa's answer to Alain Delon, stars rather unconvincingly (amidst a welter of incorrect accents) as a U.S. racing driver hero who heads to the Caribbean island of St. Heron to see how his medical student brother (Liam Cundill) is doing now that meanie Oliver Reed has seized control.

Ryan is taken hostage and organizes the students, with the aid of CIA undercover man Cameron Mitchell, to escape captivity and team up with the good-guy rebels, led by Henry Cele.

Filmmaker David Winters manages to mix in several genres, what with torture and sadism scenes, sexy coeds in the shower and his trademark aerobics class footage. Unfortunately, most of the excitement is in the opening reels and stagings purporting to be Washington, D.C., cabinet meetings are poorly cast and silly.
— *Lor.*

Cross Fire

New York A Silvertree Pictures presentation, in association with the Walanar Group and Cari-Phil Pictures. Executive producer, Gerald Milton. Produced by Anthony Maharaj. Coproduced by Michelle Marshall. Line producer, Ursula Marquez. Directed by Maharaj. Screenplay, Maharaj, Noah Blough; camera (Motion Pictures color), Johnny Araojo; editor, Bass Santos; music, Ron Jones; sound, Bing Santos; art direction, Gents Inarda; assistant director, Bill Baldridge; production manager, Arnold Go Jr.; stunt coordinator, Glen Ruehland. Reviewed on Nelson Entertainment/Orion Home Video vidcassette, N.Y., Jan. 28, 1989. MPAA Rating: R. Running time: **104 MIN.**

Richard Straker	Richard Norton
Soleri	Michael Meyer
Pappas	Daniel Dietrich
Varela	Eric Hahn
Brown	Wren T. Brown

■ **Filipino producer Anthony Maharaj directs a war film in strictly routine fashion in** "Cross Fire," an adventure about MIAs in Laos that originally was titled more colorfully "Not Another Mistake," i.e., "NAM."

Vidcassette box calls hero Richard Norton "Striker" (a name used interchangeably on numerous recent action pics), but he really is named Straker, an Aussie 'Nam veteran sent back with a squad to bring back his captured commander (Paul Holmes).

Film is as filled with postwar bitterness as most 1940s films noirs, plus the usual quota of explosions and platoonmate stereotypes. Genre champ Sylvester Stallone even gets a verbal homage, when midway through a gung ho soldier yells "I'm your worst nightmare" at the enemy.

Minor plot twist has Holmes found to be suffering from leprosy, but pic ends cornily with the usual double-dealing, in the name of expediency, by the heroes' superiors. Glum finale has Holmes shot down just as they're escaping in a helicopter.

Tech credits and acting are fair, but a certain degree of carelessness is shown by the music running out before the end credits are over.
—*Lor.*

The Iron Triangle

New York A Scotti Bros. Pictures release of a Eurobrothers production, in association with Intl. Video Entertainment. Executive producers, Ben Scotti, Fred Scotti. Produced by Tony Scotti, Angela P. Schapiro. Directed by Eric Weston. Screenplay, Weston, John Bushelman, Larry Hilbrand; narration written by Marshall Drazen; camera (Metrocolor), Irv Goodnoff; editor, Roy Watts; music, Michael Lloyd, John D'Andrea, Nick Strimple; sound (Dolby), Douglas Jackson, Jeff Okun; production design, Errol Kelly; assistant director, Bill Westley; second unit director, Watts; special effects supervisor, Yves De Bono; casting, Stacy Adams. Reviewed at Magno Preview 4 screening room, N.Y., Jan. 24, 1989. MPAA Rating: R. Running time: **91 MIN.**

Capt. Keene	Beau Bridges
Capt. Tuong	Haing S. Ngor
Jacques	Johnny Hallyday
Ho	Liem Whatley
Khoi	James Ishida
Pham	Ping Wu
Khan Ly	Iilana B'Tiste

■ **"The Iron Triangle" does a switcheroo by presenting (sympathetically) the point-of-view of a 17-year-old Vietcong soldier during the war. Novelty grabs audience's attention, but weak scripting and execution mark this one for mild b.o.**

Eric Weston's film argues for an equal-time look at the conflict in 1969, with two good men on opposite sides singled out for attention and ultimate bonding in adversity.

Beau Bridges narrates the tale as an army captain who gets to know his enemy when young Ho (a persuasive performance by newcomer Liem Whatley) captures him and protects him against a fellow Vietcong meanie, Khoi (hissable James Ishida).

The reason for the kinship between Bridges and his black pajamas counterpart is rather flimsy, but film develops some emotion in sentimental terms. At first disconcerting, the Vietcong speaking in unaccented English works to the film's advantage. Main trick here is that pic's political stance is mushy; there are bad apples on all sides with the two heroes INDIVIDUALS, and the Vietnamese' nationalistic wish to boot out all outsiders (Chinese, French and Americans) endorsed.

Acting is fine, with Oscar-winner Haing S. Ngor as a communist captain playing it straight in a smaller role. Tech credits are good. —Lor.

La Vouivre
(FRENCH)

Paris   A Gaumont release of a Gaumont/Gaumont Prod./Cameras Continentales/Nymphea France Films/Films A2 coproduction. Produced by Alain Poiré, Jean-Pierre Gallo. Written and directed by Georges Wilson, based on Marcel Aymé's novel; camera (Eastmancolor), André Neau; editor, Françoise Berger-Garnault; music, Vladimir Cosma; sound, Eric Devulder; art direction, Jacques Dugied; production managers, Marc Goldstaub, Guy Azzi; assistant director, Jean-Claude Ventura. Reviewed at Gaumont Ambassade theater, Paris, Jan. 11, 1989. Running time: 92 MIN.
Arsene . . . . .Lambert Wilson
Requiem . . . . .Jean Carmet
Louise . . . . .Suzanne Flon
Urbain. . . . . .Jacques Dufilho
Germaine . . . . .Kathie Kriegel
Robidet . . . . .Macha Meril
Victor . . . . .Jean-Jacques Moreau
Belette . . . . .Paola Lanzi
The Vouivre . . . . .Laurence Treil

■ Stage actor-director Georges Wilson makes his theatrical filmmaking debut with his well-acted but timid adaptation of Marcel Aymé's brilliant novel of peasant mores.

His son, Lambert Wilson, stars as a young rube who meets and has a fling with a demonic wood nymph (the Vouivre), who wears only a priceless jewel and is attended by deadly serpents.

Wilson has wrought some important changes on the story, notably in making the central character, a taciturn young farmer, a homecoming soldier in 1919, who has been thought dead by family and neighbors. Wilson also gives

him a war wound (a piece of shrapnel lodged in his head) which apparently provokes hallucinations (hence, the Vouivre may be part of his tormented imagination, though for Aymé the creature's reality is not questioned).

Director has deftly cast his film with excellent thesps and the first part of the film neatly situates its rural milieu and types. Yet Wilson lacks the audacity to fulfill Aymé's design, with its superb blend of realism, farce and the supernatural. Wilson especially misses one of the book's main points; that the Vouivre, for all her immortality and eternal beauty, is a banal creature next to her peasant lover, who embodies the mysteries of human nature.

Fine in supporting roles are Suzanne Flon as Lambert Wilson's mother, Jean Carmet as an alcoholic gravedigger abandoned by a slatternly mate (Macha Meril), Jacques Dufilho, as an aging family retainer (one of the most touching moments is between Flon and Dufilho), and Kathie Kriegel as the local nymphomaniac. Newcomer Laurent Treil is adequate as the otherworldly nymph contemptuous of mortal humanity. —Len.

Trishagni
(Sandstorm)
(INDIAN)

New Delhi   A Nebendu Ghosh Prods. film. Produced, written and directed by Nabendu Ghosh. Executive producer, Subhankar Ghosh. Screenplay, based on a story by Saradindu Banarjee; camera (color), Moloy Dasgupta; editor, Afaque Husein; music, Salil Chowdhury; art direction, Gautam Sen. Reviewed at the Intl. Film Festival of India (Panorama), New Delhi, Jan. 15, 1989. Running time: 130 MIN.
Monk. . . . . .Nana Patekar
Nirvana . . . . .Nitish Bharadwaj
Also with: Aloke Nath, Pallavi Joshi
(Soundtrack in Hindi)

■ Though the plot sounds racy and exotic, "Sandstorm" falls short of the authenticity, thesping, and lensing needed to pull off this tale of Freudian passion in a Buddhist monastery.

Best thing about film is its screenplay, written by director Nabendu Ghosh, an award-winning scripter making his directing debut. Setting is a Central Asian desert in 100 B.C., where a small group of Buddhist monks live happily in the town of Sariput.

A savage sandstorm soon wipes Sariput off the map. The two surviving monks miraculously find two children alive, and decide to raise them.

Some 20 years later, Nirvana (the boy) and Iti (the girl) have grown up. While the kindly old monk would like to see them marry, his sexually repressed disciple convinces Nirvana, who is a bit of a dolt, to shave his head and join the order.

Pretty Iti has no inhibitions — she's been forbidden a religious education because of her sex — and seduces Nirvana anyway. Banished, the two youngsters are overtaken by another sandstorm, while the old monk anguishes at Buddha's feet and the troublemaker, now repentant, braves the elements to search for them.

Story's simplicity has a primordial appeal, but all four actors are miscast and lensing is heavyhanded. Some nice insights into monastic life are thrown in (such as rigorous confession of sins called "patimoksha"). —Yung.

Sanshiro Sugata Zoku
(Sanshiro, Sugata, Part 2)
(JAPANESE-B&W)

New York   An R5/S8 release of a Toho production. Produced by Motohiko Ito. Directed by Akira Kurosawa. Screenplay, Kurosawa, from novel by Tsuneo Tomita; camera (b&w), Takeo Ito; music, Seichi Suzuki; art direction, Kazuo Kubo. Reviewed at Film Forum, N.Y., Jan. 29, 1989. Running time: 83 MIN.
Shanshiro Sugata. . . . . .Susumu Fujita
Shogoro Yano . . . . .Denjiro Okochi
Sayo . . . . .Yukiko Todoriki
Gennosuke &
    Tesshin Higaki . . . .Ryunosuke Tsukigata
Genzaburo Higaki . . . . .Akitake Kono
Yoshima Dan . . . . .Masayuki Mori
The Priest . . . . .Kuninori Kodo

■ "Sanshiro Sugata, Part 2" premiered in wartime Japan in May 1945, just before the Hiroshima and Nagasaki atomic bombings and subsequent Japanese surrender. This is early Akira Kurosawa that impressively displays his full mature powers as screenwriter and director.

The film now receives its first New York showing 44 years later, in a somewhat cut version that was subtitled in 1981.

Print quality is fair. The film screened at Film Forum in tandem with the earlier (1943) and better "Sanshiro Sugata, Part One."

Period is the 1880s, as Japan undergoes unwanted changes per westernization. Film's theme of judo discipline and skill, based upon ancient traditions, connects with wartime Japanese propaganda promoting indirectly such virtues as heroic patriotism and cou-

rageous militarism. However, film has segued almost a half century later into an engrossing drama of martial arts training and combat, with some love interest. Both pictures are must-see for Kurosawa fans and for students of Japanese culture.

Susumu Fujita, star of wartime military films, plays Sanshiro Sugata, a young, shy judo expert, handsome and built like a tank, who is unbeatable in combat but gets into trouble through his innocence and pride — a variant of the familiar reluctant warrior.

In their apprentice-master relationship, Sugata is trained in body and soul by wise judo founder Yano (Denjiro Okochi). Renowned for his strength and moral purity, Sugata is challenged repeatedly, accepts regretfully, disables his opponents neatly, and suffers with them as they endure humiliation and crippled retirement.

Romance accrues as Sayo (Yukiko Todoriki), daughter of a venerated martial arts opponent who Sugata dispatches mercifully, sews garments for Sugata and follows him meekly through both films. Her father is played by longtime Kurosawa character actor Takashi Shimura — the woodsman in "Rashomon" and Samurai leader in "Seven Samurai."

Of special interest as propaganda are two scenes of an American boxer named "Killer" in the ring against judo experts. The the first, "Killer" slaughters his puzzled Japanese adversary, who cannot cope with flying fists; in the second bout, Sugata sends the boxer on a flight that puts him out of action, whereupon Sugata gives the prize money to his defeated judo colleague.

Whites at the match, both men and women, are depicted as gross, ugly, vulgar and blood-thirsty. Their behavior contrasts with the decorous behavior of Japanese spectators at martial-arts events — in short, the enemy consists of barbarians. Earlier, a scene shows a huge Yank sailor beating a tiny rickshaw youth, until Sugata tosses the sailor off a pier.

In the film's showdown Sugata fights on a snow-covered mountain-top against a ju-jitsu master and his insane brother, who have stalked him for both films. Despite treachery, Sugata is again victorious and generously cooks soup for them. Last shot has Sugata smiling at the sun — dawn of another day. —Hitch.

Things And Other Stuff
(AUSTRALIAN)

Sydney A Lynchpin & Tosh presentation, in association with the Australian Film Commission. Produced by Michael Lynch. Written and directed by Tony Wellington. Camera (color), Kim Batterham; editor, Marcus D'Arcy; music, Dale Barlow; production designer, Judith Harvey; production manager, Dixi Betts; associate producer, Richard Harper. Reviewed at the Hoyts Theaterette, Sydney, Jan. 23, 1989. Running time: **88 MIN.**
David . . . . Kelly Dingwall
Michelle . . . . Rebecca Rigg
Billy . . . . John Polson
Also with: Barry Leane, Jan Ringrose, Kate Reid, Sylvia Coleman.

■This modest but satisfying Aussie offering attempts in a "Breakfast Club" fashion to examine three teenagers from various walks of life.

Trigger of what becomes a warts and all examination is a burglary: Kelly Dingwall and, reluctantly, Rebecca Rigg, break into a plush house ostensibly for quick cash, Dingwall claiming he's an old hand at such mischief. They're tailed by Dingwall's friend, played by John Polson, who disrupts the orderly break-in and runs riot in the lavish settings.

What follows is a complex interaction between the three as the class distinctions and emotional barriers between them are torn down in sometimes almost violent encounters. Gulf between each player becomes painfully wide towards the end until each is drawn together again when the deepest hurts of each is drawn out, triggered by Dingwall's revelation as to why he's chosen this particularly to ransack.

Scenario is generally credible (although a bit slow to take off), but it is a concentrated portrayal which makes for excess intensity. Nevertheless the trio, all relative newcomers, handle the range of rising emotions well. Polson is particularly good as the belligerent Billy from the wrong side of town.

Pic, funded by the Australian Film Commission, succeeds overall as a small glimpse into what on the outside are normal lives, and could garner some interest outside Oz. Tech credits are fine. —*Doch.*

U.S. FEST REVIEWS
The Big Picture

Park City A Columbia release of an Aspen Film Society production. Produced by Michael Varhol. Executive producers, William E. McEuen, Richard Gilbert Abramson. Directed by Christopher Guest. Screenplay, Varhol, Guest, Michael McKean, story by Varhol, Guest; camera (Deluxe color), Jeff Jur; editor, Marty Nicholson; music, David Nichtern; production design, Joseph Garrity; art direction, Patrick Tagliaferro; set decoration, Jerie Kelter; costume design, Karen Patch; sound (Ultra-Stereo), Jon Huck; associate producers, Valen Watson, Richard Luke Rothschild; assistant director, Paul Deason; casting, Nina Axelrod. Reviewed at the U.S. Film Festival, Park City Utah (out of competition), Jan. 28, 1989. No MPAA Rating. Running time: **99 MIN.**
Nick Chapman . . . . Kevin Bacon
Susan Rawlings . . . . Emily Longstreth
Allen Habel . . . . J.T. Walsh
Lydia Johnson . . . . . . Jennifer Jason Leigh
Neil Sussman . . . . Martin Short
Emmet Sumner . . . . Michael McKean
Jenny Sumner . . . . Kim Miyori
Gretchen . . . . Teri Hatcher
Jonathan Tristan-Bennet . . . . Dan Schneider
Carl Manknik . . . . Jason Gould
Lori Pressman . . . . . . Tracy Brooks Swope
Also with: Don Franklin, Fran Drescher, Eddie Albert, June Lockhart, Stephen Collins, Roddy McDowall, John Cleese, Elliott Gould.

■"The Big Picture" is a surprisingly genial, good-natured satire on contemporary Hollywood mores. One of the last pics made under the David Puttnam regime at Columbia, film faces an uncertain future at the distrib; studio logo was conspicuously absent at the start of the world premiere showing here.

Aside from obvious appeal to the very limited buff audience, pic has enough heart and insight into the downside of upward mobility to possibly break through to the wider young adult market given a marketing push.

Although many of the countless in-jokes land squarely on target, the thrusts don't cut very deep, and it eventually becomes clear that the filmmakers' primary aim was to portray the dehumanizing side effects of the showbiz rat race.

Christopher Guest's debut feature as helmer is loaded with the kind of detail that will make it a hot party chatter item if it is ever shown around. Industryites will want to see the scene in which on-the-rise director Kevin Bacon makes his best friend get out of his Porsche while he takes a call on his car phone. They'll want to decide for themselves whether the spider woman studio executive is really a nasty portrait of Dawn Steel, delight in the devastating sight gags about colorization, and roar at

Martin Short's merciless impersonation of a flaky agent.

Befitting two of the co-authors of "This Is Spinal Tap," Guest and Michael McKean, "The Big Picture" displays a keen eye for the silliness of film biz customs, lingo and attitudes.

Pic also makes the point that success in Hollywood bears only a coincidental relationship to talent and can't rationally be explained. More conventional themes stress the importance of sticking by one's friends and remaining ever-watchful of the glitzy temptations that can so easily lead people astray and into the many traps in the jungle.

Pic is consistently amusing, but not devastatingly funny à la "Spinal Tap" except, perhaps, when an unbilled Martin Short takes centerstage with his flamboyant characterization as Bacon's crass, hopelessly neurotic agent. Bewigged with a ridiculous mop, facially weird as if victimized by a botched facelift and vaguely cross-eyed, Short may not be anyone in particular, but still savagely conveys many of the short-sighted characteristics of the species. Pic in general could have used more of the indelible strokes of the sort Short provides.

Bacon and Emily Longstreth are appealing enough in the leads, but it is in the supporting roles that things come alive, thanks also to Jennifer Jason Leigh, almost unrecognizable as an avant-garde hip-hoppy dancer, J.T. Walsh as the super-cool but shallow studio boss and Teri Hatcher as the starlet with a perfect body. Cameos by the likes of John Cleese, Elliott Gould, Eddie Albert, June Lockhart, Roddy McDowall and Stephen Collins help root the picture in its setting. Tracy Brooks Swope's icy blond studio chief appears only briefly and would seem to have little to do with Columbia's current boss.

Tech credits are fine, notably Joseph Garrity's production design, which hilariously sends up the office decorating tastes of production executives. —*Cart.*

For All Mankind
(DOCU)

Park City An Apollo Associates release. Executive producers, Fred Miller, Ben Y. Mason. Produced and directed by Al Reinert; co-producer, Betsy Broyles Breier; editor, Susan C. Korda, Goran Milutinovic, Eric Jenkins, Chuck Weiss; music, Brian Eno; associate producer-technical director, David Leitner. In

color. Reviewed at U.S. Film Festival, Park City, Utah (in competition), Jan. 25, 1989. No MPAA Rating. Running time: **90 MIN.**

■Frame for frame, "For All Mankind" probably ranks among the most expensive documentaries ever filmed, put together entirely from official space-agency footage of the awesome Apollo VIII mission that first landed men on the moon.

Though that's 20 years ago now and much has happened to the space program since to take the new away, the earth and its mysterious companion really haven't changed much in that flicker of time, making "Mankind" as compelling as ever.

You'd have to be jaded, indeed, not to get caught up in the magnitude of these images. With such material, producer-director Al Reinert could hardly fail. Nonetheless, he and his crew have done a terrific job in assembling a cohesive vision from what must have been literally miles of footage shot from countless angles.

Blown up to 35m and enhanced by Brian Eno's avant-garde score, the film ranges from imposingly powerful close-ups literally captured within the flames on takeoff to the serenely beautiful lunar landscapes and all the exotically odd views of Earth from afar.

Using off-screen recollections by a score of astronauts who've made the first journey and eight more that followed, Reinert constructs a composite of emotional memories that stretch for the poetic, sometimes coming close, but are often mundane when matched against the visual record of what they did. —*Har.*

Zadar! Cow From Hell

Park City A Stone Peach production. Produced and directed by Robert C. Hughes. Executive producer, Scott Smith. Screenplay, Merle Kessler, from a story by Duck's Breath Mystery Theater; camera (color), James Mathers; editor, Michael Ruscio; music, Greg Brown; art direction, Ginni Barr; associate producers, Steve Baker, Tom Higgins; assistant director, Oak O'Connor. Reviewed at the U.S. Film Festival, Park City, Utah, Jan. 24, 1989. Running time: **87 MIN.**
Mr. Nifty . . . . Bill Allard
Rex . . . . Dan Coffey
Sleepless Walker . . . . Merle Kessler
Dan Tension . . . . Leon Martell
Max . . . . Jim Turner
Amy Walker . . . . Deborah Gwinn
Ralph Jr. . . . . Eric Topham
Chip . . . . Ned Holbrook
Clerk . . . . Toby Huss
Ralph Walker . . . . J.R. Walker
Grandma . . . . Lucinda Matlock
Gloria . . . . Kate Kelleher
Old Man Benson . . . . Lee Roberts

■This bigscreen debut for the

Duck's Breath Mystery Theater comedy troupe is an excruciatingly thin conceit that represents an embarrassing return to their native Iowa. Offering only the most meager of laughs, pic has no conceivable market of any size.

After a faintly promising opening, film proceeds straight down from whence the eponymous cow came and stays there. In this instance, that means Iowa, where a rag-tag team of bumbling filmmakers goes to produce a horror picture about an enormous radioactive cow.

Location happens to be the home town of the director, so all sorts of meaningless family dramas intervene at incredible length. Citizenry is pressed into service as extras and just about the only vaguely funny idea has dozens of the locals left with large cow horns irremovably stuck to their foreheads, thanks to some industrial strength adhesive.

This is one of those films where it's easy to tell after 20 minutes that it will never improve, and it doesn't — it only gets longer. For a comedy outfit of some renown, the schtick throughout is remarkably unimaginative, and the ultimate joke — that the Iowans know better than the Hollywood types how to make the picture — hardly comes as a surprise.

Technically, the film is handsome and Greg Brown's most appealing score is the one standout element here. —*Cart.*

Of Men And Angels

Park City A William Farley Film Group production, in association with Champion Films. Produced by Simon Edery, Farley. Executive producers, Ann Hatch, Farley. Directed by Farley. Screenplay, Deborah Rogin, Farley, Marjorie Berger; camera (Monaco color), Kathleen Beeler; editor, Ian Turner, Farley; music, Eric Muhler; production design, Jack Wright; art direction, costumes, Megan Eymann; sound, Zeca Araujo; assistant director, Jack Gallagher; associate producer, Mark Yellin; casting, Annette Perrone, Dorothy Desrosiers. Reviewed at the U.S. Film Festival, Park City, Utah (in competition), Jan. 24, 1989. No MPAA Rating. Running time: **91 MIN.**

Mike O'Donahue	Jack Byrne
Padric Reilly	John Molloy
Maria Montoya	Theresa Saldana
Danny	Paul Finocchiaro
Roy	Nicky C. O'Brien
Dolly	Regina Waldon
Dorothy	Larallee Westaway
Moriarty	James McCann

■ A good idea goes unrealized in "Of Men And Angels," a portrait of transplanted Irish angst that just doesn't cut it dramatically. A steep hill looms com-

mercially.

Beguiling notion has San Francisco cabbie and self-styled writer Mike O'Donahue (Jack Byrne) happening to pick up his literary hero, the aging Irishman Padric Reilly (John Molloy). A total sucker for lost causes and a bighearted life saver, Mike takes the drunken scribe home and puts him up on the couch, to the annoyance of his live-in, El Salvadorian lady Maria (Theresa Saldana).

Naturally, the old man settles in for an extended stay and makes a celebrity of himself at the local Irish pub while awaiting the return of his latest manuscript from his estranged female companion.

In the meantime, Maria becomes pregnant, which depresses Mike, but not nearly as much as the fact that the venerable Reilly has made fun of his short stories down at the saloon. A bit of Irish politics is dragged in toward the end via an assassination attempt, and everyone grows quite fed up with everyone else by the time the climax rolls around.

Unfortunately, this attitude also applies to the audience, as the characters, like Reilly, overstay their welcome. A pretty obvious loser, Mike becomes irritating with his immature attitude concerning his unborn child and his unwillingness to face life's realities.

Similarly, Reilly's charm wears thin rather quickly, and Maria seems increasingly bewildering for her ability to put up with these grown-up Irish children.

Known mainly for his work in the documentary field, director William Farley displays little feel for strong visuals or propulsive storytelling. Dramatic approach is flat, as every scene exists to address one issue, such as Mike's soft touch, his artistic aspirations, Reilly's equivocation and so on.

Furthermore, one never senses anything strong or real between Mike and Maria, and each scene featuring the two of them seems to begin with a confrontation and end with a kiss and making up. It's dullsville.

Farley and lenser Kathleen Beeler capture some nice Bay Area color, but the picture laboriously plays out its themes and never comes to believable life. —*Cart.*

God's Will

San Francisco A Power and Light production. Produced, written and directed by

Julia Cameron. Coproducer, Pam Moore. Camera (color, 16m), William Nusbaum; music, Christopher (Hambone) Cameron; sound, Ric Coken; assistant director, Phillip Halprin. Reviewed at Kabuki theatre, San Francisco, Jan. 5, 1989. No MPAA Rating. Running time: **100 MIN.**

God	Marge Kotlisky
Peter Potter	Daniel Region
Gillian Potter	Laura Margolis
Victoria Potter	Domenica Cameron-Scorsese
Gwyneth	Linda Edmond
Mitchell	Mitchell Canoff
Hedy	Holly Fulger
Giles	Tim Hopper

■ Veteran Hollywood screenwriter Julia Cameron moved home to Chicago to produce and direct her first feature, "God's Will," and discovered first-hand one of a filmmaker's worst nightmares: the production soundtrack was stolen after shooting wrapped.

As a consequence, the awkwardly dubbed result which opened the "On Screen" women's film festival in San Francisco is probably fatally injured for commercial release of the comedy in its present state. The scenes, delicate at best under normal low-budget conditions, simply don't play right.

Still, it's promisingly written and Cameron deserves credit for persevering under the conditions. With luck, what she has on screen now might even bring forth the wherewithal to redo the project on a bigger budget under better conditions.

Another plus for the Cameron family is an outstanding debut by preteen daughter Domenica Cameron-Scorsese (whose father is director Martin Scorsese). In a pivotal part, she was obviously at ease in front of the camera and also seems less troubled with the difficulties of recapturing her dialog.

Cameron's intent, obviously, was to create a lighthearted effort at family fun in which a divorced, self-centered show-business couple (Daniel Region and Laura Margolis) meet an untimely demise and wind up in heaven squabbling over what will happen now to their daughter.

The little girl has fallen into the custody of the couple's new spouses (Linda Edmond and Mitchell Canoff) and from their new vantage point the parents realize how much they still prefer each other to the other two.

Some ghostly haunting is therefore required to free Domenica into the hands of another couple preferred by the parents and the result is a romp. Throughout, they get an assist from the female God,

amusingly played by Marge Kotlisky, who's always around with some mildly feminist views on the world She created.

The ear aside, the eye sees a quality look about the film and Cameron will doubtlessly be at work again behind the camera.
—*Har.*

Morgan's Cake
(B&W/COLOR)

Park City An L.L. production. Executive producers, Jim Newman, Judy Newman, Lura Janda. Produced, written, directed and edited by Rick Schmidt. Additional writing, Morgan Schmidt-Feng, Aaron Leon Kenin, Willie Boy Walker. Camera (b&w, color, 16m), Kathleen Beeler; music, Gary Thorp; sound, Nick Bertoni, John Claudio; video by Schmidt, Schmidt-Feng; associate producer, Schmidt-Feng. Reviewed at the U.S. Film Festival, Park City, Utah (in competition), Jan. 21, 1989. Running time: **83 MIN.**

Morgan	Morgan Schmidt-Feng
Morgan's Dad	Willie Boy Walker
Morgan's Mother	M. Louise Stanley
Rachel	Rachel Pond
Leon	Aaron Leon Kenin
Leon's Dad	Ellot Kenin
John	John Claudio
Painter	Lee Chapman
Nick	Nick Bertoni

■ Rick Schmidt, author of the low-budget primer "Feature Filmmaking At Used Car Prices," has practiced what he preaches in "Morgan's Cake," a 16m, mostly black-and-white effort brought in on nine days at a total cost of $15,000.

Such an accomplishment generates considerable good will, as does the family atmosphere permeating the project. Amiable as it is, however, pic proves amusing or convincing only in snatches, and would have trouble generating audience interest outside the fest circuit, where it is now making the rounds, or in video distribution, where Schmidt is already offering it up in specialized locales.

This look at teenage angst and confusion is a long way from the Hollywood designer version. Morgan, 17, whose mother cutely named him after Karel Reisz' wild 1960s British comedy bearing that title, lives in cramped quarters in the San Francisco Bay Area with his impoverished, divorced father.

With his mother headed for New York, it becomes clear that Morgan is going to be left pretty much to his own devices in life, but he remains relatively cheerful in the face of his numerous immediate crises, which include impending draft registration, his firing from his job as a delivery man, and his girlfriend's pregnancy.

Presumably as much for budget as artistic reasons, Schmidt has filmed most of his vignette-like scenes in long takes using partially impovised dialog, with mixed results. Approach has resulted in at least one priceless sequence, in which Morgan's father hilariously recounts how he acted crazy at his draft board appearance in order to avoid military service back in the 1960s.

Morgan is played, sweetly enough, by Schmidt's son, Morgan Schmidt-Feng. Rachel Pond is the adolescent's girlfriend in both the film and real life, and all the other cast members are non-pros except for Willie Boy Walker, who so engagingly plays Dad.

Pic does offer encouragement by showing that something presentable can still be put on the screen for what amounts to lunch money on studio productions, but the inspiration is lacking to make this into a real audience picture.
—*Cart.*

Farewell To The King

Paris   An Ariane Distribution release (Orion Pictures in U.S.) of a Vestron presentation of a Ruddy and Morgan production. Produced by Albert S. Ruddy, Andre Morgan. Written and directed by John Milius, from novel by Pierre Schoendoerffer; camera (Technicolor), Dean Semler; editor, C. Timothy O'Meara, Anne V. Coates; music, Basil Poledouris; art direction, Bernard Hides, Gil Parrondo; stunts, Terry Leonard; casting, Mike Fenton. Reviewed at the UGC Biarritz Theater, Paris, Feb. 7, 1989. MPAA Rating: PG-13. Running time: **117 MIN.**

Learoyd	Nick Nolte
Capt. Fairbourne	Nigel Havers
Col. Ferguson	James Fox
Yoo	Marily Tokuda
Sgt. Tenga	Frank MacRae
Col. Mitamura	Aki Aleong
Dynamite Dave	William Wise
Gwai	Gerry Lopez
Sgt. Conklin	Marius Weyers
Vivienne	Elan Oberon
Lian	Choy Chan Wing

■ **The clichés are as thick as the foliage in "Farewell To The King," John Milius' adaptation of a novel by French author-filmmaker Pierre Schoendoerffer. Pic recycles familiar situations and stock characters in an overlong actioner that never builds to a spiritual climax.**

Perfunctorily staged battle scenes in the bush may satisfy the action crowd but commercial chances of survival are limited. Pic, in a world premiere in France, has opened weakly.

Ostensibly drawing on numerous film and literary sources (such as Joseph Conrad's "Lord Jim"), pic looks something like an inversion of "Apocalypse Now," Francis Coppola's Vietnam variation on Conrad's "Heart Of Darkness" (which Milius coscripted).

Here two British army officers (Nigel Havers and Frank MacRae) are parachuted into the Borneo jungle to rally the tribes against imminent Japanese invasion in the latter days of World War II. Instead of finding a gross Marlon Brando sinking into a small moral vacuum, they come across a virile and fulfilled Nick Nolte, playing a freedom-loving white man who's anxious to protect his natives from the barbarities of civilization.

The barbarism is shared between Japanese, who sink to cannibalism as they ravage native settlements, and the Allied forces, who cynically provide Nolte with a treaty guaranteeing his people's independence while having no intention of respecting their word.

Nolte, however, needs no further prompting to fight when the Japanese slaughter his own family. Hitting the Rambo warpath, the ex-Yank sergeant (who deserted after General MacArthur's defeat at Corregidor) performs a ruthless clean-up operation and even bags the "Phantom" equestrian Japanese who evades his bullets throughout the action.

The Allies hang the Japanese colonel and ship off Nolte to Manila for a court-martial, but Havers springs him when the military ship runs aground.

Milius splatters the familiar set-pieces with hokey, pretentions dialog which strains for philosophical and historical resonance. The actors succumb under the crushing weight of the hollow phrasing.

Nolte, in a purely exterior performance, never rises to the nobility and tragic majesty the at-first skeptical British officers finally see in him. Havers is a sympathetic presence in an equally empty role (he is even given a fiancée to situate his innate decency). Other performers, including James Fox as Havers' commanding officer, are treated as trite thumbnail portraits.

Dean Semler's jungle photography is excellent. Other tech credits are good. —*Len.*

Out Cold

New York   A Hemdale release of a Braunstein/Hamady production. Executive producers, John Daly, Derek Gibson. Produced by George G. Braunstein, Ron Hamady. Directed by Malcolm Mowbray. Screenplay, Howard Glasser, George Malko, from Glasser's story; camera (CFI color), Tony Pierce-Roberts; editor, Dennis M. Hill; music, Michel Colombier; sound (Dolby), Robert Eber; production design, Linda Pearl; art direction, Lisa Fischer; costume design, Linda Bass; assistant director, Scott Easton; production manager-associate producer, Chris Coles; Ernie dummy and special makeup effects, Andy Schoneberg; casting, Nan Dutton. Reviewed at Magno Preview 4 screening room, N.Y. Feb. 9, 1989. MPAA Rating: R. Running time: **91 MIN.**

Dave	John Lithgow
Sunny Cannald	Teri Garr
Lester Atlas	Randy Quaid
Ernie Cannald	Bruce McGill

Also with: Lisa Blount, Alan Blumenfeld, Morgan Paull, Barbara Rhoades, Tom Blyrd, Frederick Coffin, Fran Ryan.

■**Talented performers are trapped in a pointless, unfunny attempt at black comedy in "Out Cold," a shelved Hemdale pic originally titled more appropriately "Stiffs" and finally unfrozen for public consumption.**

George Malko and Leonard Glasser's leaden script contrives an intrigue among butchers: Bruce McGill is the hissable creep who's cheating on wife Teri Garr, while partner at his butcher shop John Lithgow is a lonely nerd. After McGill beats her up, Garr goes to klutzy private eye Randy Quaid to get the goods on hubbie. Quaid is so incompetent he photographs the other woman — Garr in a black wig — and doesn't even recognize her. Why Garr dresses up in unbecoming wigs is the first of many indigestible plot pegs.

Contrived plot heats up in the butcher shop freezer with its conveniently faulty lock: After an argument Lithgow nearly locks McGill in there by accident and then Garr visits to lock him in on purpose. With McGill dead, Garr and Lithgow team up romantically, leading to several double crosses and an ironic payoff. The black humor is supposed to derive from duo's difficulties in disposing of McGill's body, handled in tired fashion.

Without a single witty line to utter, the leads are left stumbling around in stillborn situation comedy, not helped by Malcolm Mowbray's flat direction. A scene at a topless bar in hunting country is meant to condescendingly satirize Middle American folkways but looks like random footage spliced in from a '70s exploitation film.

For Quaid, this marks with "Parents" two (dissimilar) "red meat" films in a row, in which closeups of ambiguous cold cuts are the most lasting image. He, Garr and Lithgow give it a college try but are a bit embarrassing in failed slapstick. Tech credits are perfunctory. —*Lor.*

The Mighty Quinn

New York   An MGM/UA Distribution release from MGM Pictures of an A&M Films production. Executive producers, Dale Pollock, Gil Friesen. Produced by Sandy Lieberson, Marion Hunt, Ed Elbert. Directed by Carl Schenkel. Screenplay, Hampton Fancher, from A.H.Z. Carr's novel "Finding Maubee;" camera (Continental color), Jacques Steyn; editor, John Jympson; music, Anne Dudley; music supervision, David Anderle; sound (Dolby), John Pritchett; production design, Roger Murray-Leach; costume design, Dana Lyman; assistant director, J. Stephen Buck; production manager, Matthew Binns; second unit camera, Karl Kases; associate producer, Jack Cummins; casting, Wallis Nicita. Reviewed at Bruno Walter Auditorium, N.Y., Feb. 10, 1989. MPAA Rating: R. Running time: **98 MIN.**

Xavier Quinn	Denzel Washington
Maubee	Robert Townsend
Elgin	James Fox
Hadley	Mimi Rogers
Miller	M. Emmet Walsh
Lola	Sheryl Lee Ralph
Jump	Art Evans
Ubu Pearl	Esther Rolle
Gov. Chalk	Norman Beaton
Patina	Alex Colon

Also with: Tyra Ferrell, Keye Luke, Carl Bradshaw, Maria McDonald.

■ "The Mighty Quinn" is an ill-conceived, poorly executed mystery film. It's set in an exotic clime but is strictly routine. It shapes as another off-season flop from MGM.

Denzel Washington, trying too hard to become the '80s Sidney Poitier, toplines as Quinn, a police chief on a Caribbean island (shot in Jamaica but left unnamed in story) tracking the killer of a white businessman. Powerful figures like resort owner James Fox and island governor Norman Beaton want the case closed. Ne'er-do-well Maubee (Robert Townsend in a juicy but brief role) is targeted as the fall guy.

In cornball fashion, Washington and Townsend turn out to have been boyhood friends, former taking the high road and latter becoming a legendary local criminal. Washington's film-long hunt for the outlaw is peppered with boring subplots: They involve a lusty white woman (Mimi Rogers looking marvelous in a nothing role); voodoo-style witch (Esther Rolle out of place), and an unconvincing gimmick of covert U.S. aid to rebels via archaic $10,000 bills, hardly suitable for laundering.

Hampton Fancher's script, adapted from novel "Finding Maubee" (which was pic's shooting title), is relentlessly pointless. Such films as Basil Dearden's "Sapphire" and Norman Jewison's "In The Heat Of The Night" have presented taut detective stories with underlying social comment on race relations, but "Quinn" avoids all such opportunities.

Direction by Swiss-born Carl Schenkel doesn't help. Overly flashy individual shots don't cut well together and sluggish pacing fails to build scene by scene. Frequent timeouts for musical interludes involving Washington and wife Sheryl Lee Ralph also destroy the narrative flow.

Cast is barely adequate and decision to use mainly American thesps fitted with variable West Indies accents destroys credibility. Washington's thesping is strictly on the surface while Townsend does little more than smile and provide comic relief. Villains Fox and M. Emmet Walsh are transparent. Reggae soundtrack, with several reprises of the Bob Dylan-penned title standard, is pic's main asset.—*Lor.*

Slipstream
(BRITISH)

London   An Entertainment Film production. Executive producers, Nigel Green, William Braunstein, Arthur Maslansky. Produced by Gary Kurtz. Coproducer, Steve Lanning. Directed by Steven Lisberger. Screenplay, Tony Kayden, based on story by Sam Clemens; camera (Eastmancolor), Frank Tidy; editor, Terry Rawlings; music, Elmer Bernstein; production design, Andrew McAlpine; visual effects, Brian Johnson; art direction, Malcolm Stone; costumes, Catherine Cook; casting, Marilyn Johnson. Reviewed at Century Preview Theater, London, Jan. 19, 1989. Running time: **101 MIN.**

Tasker	Mark Hamill
Byron	Bob Peck
Matt	Bill Paxton
Belitski	Kitty Aldridge
Ariel	Eleanor David
Avatar	Ben Kingsley
Cornelius	F. Murray Abraham
Montclaire	Robbie Coltrane

■ British-made sci-fi adventure romp "Slipstream" is one of those films that had potential, but unfortunately it doesn't make the grade. Pic was made as a deliberate attempt to crack the U.S. market but sadly it crushes mid-Atlantic.

Production and casting are fine, but Tony Kayden's ponderous and unexciting script combined with a few scenes that should have been left on the cutting room floor make "Slipstream" an also-ran.

Pic reunites "Star Wars" producer Gary Kurtz and actor Mark Hamill. While the film lacks the exuberance of their original, a mature Hamill is excellent as the bearded baddie — a far cry from his freshfaced Luke Skywalker days.

"Slipstream" seems to be making some kind of ecological message; the film's version of Earth is a place ruined by pollution with the planet washed clean by a river of wind called the "Slipstream."

Lawman Hamill and his partner Kitty Aldridge capture Bob Peck, who's wanted for murder. When adventurer Bill Paxton discovers there is a price on Peck's head he snatches him and makes his escape down the Slipstream.

They come across a cult of religious fanatics who worship the wind, led by Ben Kingsley. One of the cult (Eleanor David) falls for Peck — even though it turns out he is an android.

In one unfortunate scene, Peck, in evening dress, dances around a room à la Fred Astaire while Paxton beds the nearest blond floozy, despite having previously expressed more than a passing interest in the beautiful Aldridge.

Pic climaxes with the obligatory gunfight with Eleanor David getting shot and Peck pursuing Hamill into the Slipstream for the final showdown.

Strong points of "Slipstream" are the stunning locations (Turkey and the Yorkshire moors), the performances by Hamill and Aldridge, plus impresive aircraft and technical effects. Paxton gives his part all he's worth but the character and dialog are not up to his acting. Bob Peck, fine actor though he is, looks totally unsure what sort of movie he is in.

Ben Kingsley and F. Murray Abraham have virtual walk-on parts. Kingsley redoes his Gandhi routine as leader of the wind worshippers, while Abraham, in a smart suit, at least makes an impact as the diplomatic head of an academic community.

Helmer Steven Lisberger handles the technical and action scenes well enough, but seems out of his element when the human touch is needed. The love affair between Paxton and Aldridge occurs so quickly maybe the editing is to blame.

Entertainment Film Prods. is to be applauded for a brave attempt to make a feature with international appeal, but will have to chalk the $12-million "Slipstream" up to experience. —*Adam.*

The Fly II

Hollywood   A 20th Century Fox release of a Brooksfilms presentation. Produced by Steven-Charles Jaffe. Executive producer, Stuart Cornfeld. Directed by Chris Walas. Screenplay, Mick Garris, Jim and Ken Wheat, Frank Darabont, based on a story by Garris and characters created by George Langelaan; camera (Deluxe color), Robin Vidgeon; editor, Sean Barton; music, Christopher Young; production design, Michael S. Bolton; art direction, Sandy Cochrane; set decoration, Rose Mary McSherry; costume design, Christopher Ryan; sound (Dolby), Rob Young; sound design, Leslie Shatz; effects created, designed by Chris Walas Inc.; creature effects supervisor, Jon Berg; special makeup effects supervisor, Stephen Dupuis; assistant director, Peter D. Marshall; associate producer, Gillian Richardson; casting, Deborah Lucchesi. Reviewed at 20th Century Fox Studios, L.A., Feb. 9, 1989. MPAA Rating: R. Running time: **105 MIN.**

Martin Brundle	Eric Stoltz
Beth Logan	Daphne Zuniga
Anton Bartok	Lee Richardson
Stathis Borans	John Getz
Dr. Shepard	Frank Turner
Dr. Jainway	Ann Marie Lee
Scorby	Gary Chalk
Ronnie	Saffron Henderson
10-year-old Martin	Harley Cross
4-year-old Martin	Matthew Moore

■ "The Fly II" is an expectedly gory and gooey but mostly plodding sequel to the 1986 hit that was a remake of the 1958 sci-fier that itself spawned two sequels.

Teenage boys with a taste for the gruesome could provide enough of an audience to keep this going for a few weeks.

After a shock opening in which the late man-fly's son is born within a horrible insect-like encasement, resulting in the death of the mother (*not* played by Geena Davis), slickly produced pic generates some interest and promise as little Martin Brundle is raised in laboratory conditions provided by scientific tycoon Anton Bartok (Lee Richardson).

Afflicted with a dramatically accelerated lifecycle, Martin quickly demonstrates genius, and by the age of five emerges fully grown in the person of Eric Stoltz. Given his own apartment in Bartok's industrial park, Martin becomes determined to perfect his father's teleportation machine, which Bartok controls, and also takes an interest in researcher Beth Logan (Daphne Zuniga). Original film's star Jeff Goldblum appears briefly here via videotape recording.

Martin gradually becomes aware that Bartok's motives are far from benign, and simultaneously begins mutating into a hideous beast while retaining his human sensibility.

Things bog down as soon as Stoltz and Zuniga start checking each other out, largely because one expects something more than a typical teen-type first romance from these characters.

The romantic paces the couple goes through are utterly conventional, and these two science nuts never speak in an impassioned way about the subject that fascinates them most. It also says something about how far off the mark the film is emotionally when the greatest sentiment is generated for a golden retriever that is genetically scrambled by the teleporter to resemble a canine version of the Hunchback of Notre Dame.

By the climax, the film more closely comes to resemble "Aliens" than the previous "Fly," as the transformed Martin hides behind walls and in the ceiling before pouncing on Bartok's goons, spitting on them, chewing them up and spitting them out. The gore becomes very vivid during this stretch, undoubtedly to the delight of some and the disgust of others.

First-time director Chris Walas handled the special effects on David Cronenberg's "Fly," as well as on such other pics as "Gremlins" and "Enemy Mine," and his heart is still clearly with that specialty. Technically, enough goods are delivered for genre fans, but it's ponderous going most of the way. —*Cart.*

The Big Dis
(B&W)

Park City An Olympia Pictures presentation. Produced, written, directed and edited by Gordon Eriksen, John O'Brien. Camera (b&w), O'Brien; music, Kev Ses & Harry B, with Dr. Cranium and The Big Dis Crew; sound, Eriksen; associate producer, Heather Johnston. Reviewed at the U.S. Film Festival, Park City, Utah (in competition), Jan. 26, 1989. No MPAA Rating. Running time: **84 MIN.**
JD . . . . James Haig
    Also with: Kevin Haig, Monica Sparrow, Lisa Rivers, Aratha Johnston, Allysunn Walker, Gordon Eriksen, Heather Johnson.

■ **"The Big Dis" is fresh and vibrant, worth a look by adventurous viewers interested in work coming up from the streets. Pic deserves exposure at fests and specialized venues, although it is undoubtedly not of high enough professional standards to find mainstream bookings.**

If the late John Cassavetes were 18 years old today, he might make a film resembling "The Big Dis." Like Cassavetes' first film, "Shadows," this $10,000 black-and-white debut feature from Harvard graduates Gordon Eriksen and John O'Brien is technically rough, visually awkward and sometimes incoherent dramatically.

In his first weekend pass home from military training, young JD returns to his Hempstead, Long Island neighborhood with just one thing on his mind. With barely a moment wasted on his family, the black youth sets out to find himself a woman, and the picture documents his humorously aggravating confrontation with *dis,* meaning disrespect or affront.

Pic unfolds in long, real-time scenes, creating longueurs in some instances but also gives full play to the colorful local language and improvisational give-and-take among the mostly very young cast. Using a hand-held style with 20-year-old camera equipment, directors have clearly reacted against any impulse toward slickness to achieve a style that recalls not only Cassavetes but the early French New Wave.

A strong measure of interest also stems from the racial mix that appears to prevail in the community in question. Area looks like a picture book white, middle-class suburb from the 1950s, but seems populated mostly by blacks, with a smattering of Hispanics, whites and Asians. Some of the black women speak with typical Brooklyn accents, while others betray roots closer to the ghetto. Through it all, none of this is commented upon, making the film one of the more fascinating presentations of the American melting pot in recent memory.

Because that dramatic line is so weak, pic lives and dies on a moment-by-moment basis. Comparisons, largely misleading, will no doubt be made to "She's Gotta Have It," due to the black, sexual and low-budget angles. Overall, this stands as a commendable, if limited, accomplishment, the equivalent of a garage band's album, a signal of the cultural expression that can be achieved on a practically nonexistent budget.
    —*Cart.*

True Love

Park City A Forward Films production. Produced by Richard Guay, Shelley Houis. Directed by Nancy Svoca. Screenplay, Savoca, Guay; camera (Duart color), Lisa Rinzler; editor, John Tintori; sound, Mathew Price; production design. Lester W. Cohen; art direction, Pamela Woodbridge; assistant director, Richard Guay; associate producer, Jeffrey Kimball; casting, Breanna Benjamin. Reviewed at the U.S. Film Festival, Park City, Utah (in competition), Jan. 27, 1989. No MPAA Rating. Running time: **104 MIN.**
Donna . . . . Annabella Sciorra
Michael . . . . Ron Eldard
J.C. . . . . Star Jasper
Grace . . . . Aida Turturro
Dom . . . . Roger Rignack
Brian . . . . Michael J. Wolfe
Yvonne . . . . Kelly Cinnante
Kevin . . . . Rick Shapiro
Fran . . . . Suzanne Costallos
Angelo . . . . Vinny Pastore
Carmella . . . . Marianne Leone
Benny . . . . John Nacco
Barbara . . . . Ann Tucker
Chickie . . . . Marie Michaels

■ **"True Love" is almost certain to round out some company's distribution schedule, probably pocketing a lot of profit on its very low budget.**

It might even break out into big bucks if a smart marketer can overcome its unknown cast and hook into young people's increasing interest in traditional matters like matrimony. It won the grand prize in the dramatic competition here at the U.S. Film Festival.

The film is anything but traditional, however, even though it's solidly rooted in the Bronx working-class Italian community. The bride (wonderfully played by newcomer Annabella Sciorra) and her bridesmaids know enough 4-letter words to easily supply all the "something blue" needed for the wedding preparations.

In addition, like most young women in films made by women these days, Sciorra and her friends aren't too starry-eyed about the men available for matrimony. Certainly, her fiancé (well-acted by Ron Eldard in his feature debut) is no bargain, except perhaps in bed. For most of the picture, Sciorra frets about why she's marrying the immature, self-centered lout and never comes up with a good reason, except he's good-looking and says he loves her even though he doesn't act like it.

"True Love" is very much a story about family and neighborhood and Nancy Savoca obviously has an eye for the several generations. This is Savoca's first feature and first-rate performances out of neophytes.

Forgetting the men, which Savoca often does except on the surface, "True Love" delves superbly into the emotions of the women, young and old, as one of them once more approaches the frightening milestone of a first marriage. —*Har.*

Embrasse-moi
(Kiss Me)
(FRENCH)

Paris A SECAE release of a Go Films/La Sept coproduction. Written and directed by Michèle Rosier. Camera (Eastmancolor), Darius Khondji; editor, Andrée Davanture; sound, Jean-Jacques Ferran; music, Aldo Romano; art direction, Raul Gimenez; costumes, Marie-Claude Altot; production manager, Joey Fare. Reviewed at Cannon screening room, Paris, Jan. 9, 1989. Running time: **92 MIN.**
Louise . . . . Sophie Rochut
Mother . . . . Dominique Valadié
Father . . . . Patrick Chesnais
Helmut . . . . Thomas Nock
Photographer . . . . Yann Collete
Grandmother . . . . Isabelle Sadoyan
Piano tuner . . . . Philippe Clevenot
Therese . . . . Muriel Jolly

■ **"Kiss Me" is the yearning request of an 11-year-old girl to the adults in her life, notably her divorced mother, a successful concert pianist, who is self-absorbed with her career and love life.**

This third feature film by Michele Rosier is a low-key, affecting portrait of a neglected childhood. It's fine for fests and arthouse play.

Acting is restrained to the point of deadpan — Rosier rejects emotive pathos and melodramatics, but strikes home with deceptively simple scripting and direction.

Sophie Rochut is credibly appealing as a lonely child, fighting for attention and love, but without tears or tantrums. When her mom (Dominique Valadié) brings home a lover musician (much younger than she), Rochut seeks response from others. Her father, a preoccupied businessman, and grandmother are equally absent.

In one of the best sequences, Rochut meets a 1-eyed photojournalist who specializes in war coverage. They become friends for a day, but in the evening he boards a train for his hometown. He has left neither name nor address, but the child (in a non-represented sequence) runs away in hopes of finding him. When she returns, she throws herself into the river. The suicide attempt superficially brings mother and daughter together, but in the final scene the child is once again (as in opening sequence) playacting before her mirror.

Rosier, who previously directed two theatrical features (one about George Sand) and several tv docus, directs with a casual manner that is always attentive to the essential. Camerawork (by newcomer Darius Khondji) and other credits are solid. —*Len.*

Kärlighed uden stop
(Love On The Rails)
(DANISH)

Copenhagen A Nordisk Film release of Nordisk Film production, with the Danish Film Institute. Produced by Bo Christensen. DFI consultant producer, Peter Poulsen. Written and directed by Hans Kristensen; camera (Eastmancolor), Peter Roos; editor, Jörgen Kastrup; music, Anders Kopple; saxophone solos, Jens Haack; production design, Bent Kielberg, Leif Stoltze; sound, Henrik Jörgensen; costumes, Ole Gläsner; assistant director, Birger Larsen; second unit director, Tom Hedegaard; production management, Gerd Roos. Reviewed at the Palads, Copenhagen, Jan. 31, 1989. Running time: **78 MIN.**
Peter . . . . Otto Brandenburg
Eva . . . . Ann-Mari Max Hansen
Bent . . . . Benny Hansen
Train conductor . . . . Bent Warburg
Peter & Bent's mother . . . Lise Henningsen
Their stepfather . . . . Lars Lunöe
    Also with: Susanne Lundberg, Gyda Hansen, Sandra Day, Jesper Tue Bonde, Daniel Deutsch, Gösta Engström, Hugo Herrestrup, Dag Hollerup, John Martinus, William Kissum, Rikke Sölvhöj.

■ **Writer-director Hans Kristensen's "Love On The Rails" takes a quick, cool look at a rarely explored phenomenon, wife-beating, allows itself an unlikely happy ending and may come away with good business both at home and in offshore sales.**

Kristensen actually took over the production when its was faltering in its early stages. Frank Lauridsen, assigned to take his helmer bow, resigned on the day set for shooting's start. Jes Oernsbo, a noted novelist-playwright, withdrew his screenplay. Kristensen then stepped in and soon turned the project into his very own.

Assorted low-life characters creep in and out of the frames of "Love On The Rails," but essentially the picture is a love triangle in which middle-aged Benny slaps his wife Eva around plenty without her doing too much to get away from the punishment, although she is in love with Benny's slightly younger brother Peter. Peter loves her, too, even to distraction. Unfortunately, Peter is an alcoholic who cannot make up his mind to be brave and decisive.

Probably even the brute husband wants something better out of life, but he, like Eva and Peter, lacks the ability to break away from the rut they are mired in. When Benny's brutality escalates, so does Eva's mute submission. Peter's feeble efforts to save her are soon dissolved in alcoholic binges.

The production itself is crude in its execution of practically all credits, the colors are gaudy and lots of the 35m footage looks like it has been blown up from 16m.

Ann-Mari Max Hansen has a broad, big-boned Slavic face that lends itself efficiently to mirroring of passive pain. Chubby Benny Hansen slyly avoids caricature even when he has his quavering lips and fat jowls literally drooling with vicious lust. You really feel that this man is dangerous, even to himself.

The truly shining performance, something akin to Jack Nicholson in "Ironweed," is put in by Otto Brandenburg. As weak but benevolent Peter, he is angelic in his squalor, devilish in his cunning, the optimist in extremis even when down and out. There may not be much of the lover left in him, but as a loving and giving spirit, he reflects the true survivor in every minutely controlled bodily gesture and facial nuance. —Kell.

Il Frullo del Passero
(The Sparrow's Fluttering)
(ITALIAN-FRENCH)

Rome   A Medusa Distribuzione release of a BASICinematografica (Rome)/Candice Prod. (Paris)/Initial Group (Paris) coproduction, in association with Reteitalia. Produced by Amedeo Pagani. Directed by Gianfranco Mingozzi. Screenplay, Tonino Guerra, Mingozzi, with Roberto Roversi; camera (Telecolor),

Luigi Verga; editor, Alfredo Muschietti; music, Lucio Dalla, Mauro Malavasi; art direction, Giancarlo Nasili. Reviewed at Politecnico Cinema, Rome, Dec. 13, 1988. Running time: **95 MIN.**
Gabriele Battistini . . . . .Philippe Noiret
Silvana . . . . .Ornella Muti
Young man . . . . .Nicola Farron
  Also with: Claudine Auger (widow), Peppe Chierici, Claudio Del Falco, Mariam Axa, Giuseppe Mauro Cruciano, Claudio Rosini.

■ **A May-December love story somewhere between Scheherazade's 1,001 nights and a bedtime sex fable, "The Sparrow's Fluttering" is an art film hard to classify.**

Toplining Philippe Noiret as the erotic-impotent storyteller and Ornella Muti as his paid listener, pic's main interest lies in dignified performances from two watchable thesps and an attractive offbeat quality. A handful of awkward sex scenes are more likely to confuse viewers than attract them in droves, however. Boxoffice looks muddled.

Noiret plays Italians well, and his Gabriele Battistini, a restlessly retired businessman, comes across as modest and charming. He's reached an age in which pleasure comes only from memories, and he seeks out Silvana (Muti) to hear his erotic recollections.

The girl is at loose ends after the death of the man who was keeping her, and she agrees to be kept by Gabriele in a splendid country house.

All this takes a lot of screen time to set up, and when the hot stories get started they're something of an anticlimax. Helmer Gianfranco Mingozzi, a serious director lacking in prurient interests, has everyone make love with their clothes on; there is no nudity in the film, and the erotic content is feeble, often awkward.

Film picks up steam when Gabriele makes Silvana go to the city to buy new clothes. Her fling on the beach with a handsome shoe salesman (Nicola Farron) is mysteriously retold to her by Gabriele as his own story, and the line between storytelling and reality becomes difficult to make sense of. It seems the young man is really (magically) Gabriele, who loves Silvana as she loves him.

Based on a short story by top Italian scripter Tonino Guerra, film has a strangely literary quality. The ending, at least, is happy.

Music by Lucio Dalla and Mauro Malavasi is okay but not exceptional, which may be said of all technical credits. —Yung.

BERLIN FEST REVIEWS

Resurrected
(BRITISH)

London   A Film Four Intl. and British Screen presentation of a St. Pancras Film. Produced by Adrian Hughes, Tara Prem. Directed by Paul Greengrass. Screenplay, Martin Allen; camera (color), Ivan Strasburg; editor, Dan Rea; sound, Mike McDuffie; production design, Christopher Burke; costumes, Tudor George; casting, Gail Stevens. Reviewed at Chelsea Cinema, London, Nov. 6, 1988. (In Berlin Film Festival — main competition). Running time: **96 MIN.**
Kevin Deakin . . . . .David Thewlis
Mr. Deakin . . . . .Tom Bell
Mrs. Deakin . . . . .Rita Tushingham
Gregory Deakin . . . . .Michael Pollitt
Julie . . . . .Rudi Davies
Captain Sinclair . . . . .William Hoyland
Cpl. Byker . . . . .Ewan Stewart
Slaven . . . . .Christopher Fulford

■ **"Resurrected" makes for powerful and sometimes harrowing viewing. It takes a relatively unemotional look at the effects of war on a very ordinary family, featuring solid topline performances but with a slight tendency to be predictable.**

Pic could work well in the U.K. due to its controversial nature, though will need some work to have impact offshore.

First-time helmer Paul Greengrass gained a certain notoriety in the U.K. as co-author, with former MI5 man Peter Wright, of the book "Spycatcher" which was banned in Britain for some time.

He displays a restrained, even sensible, directorial style, but with a nice eye for location and detail. "Resurrected" comes at a time when the Falklands campaign is being re-evaluated (the BBC's "Tumbledown" caused a stir and Argentine/British co-production "Veronico Cruz" ("The Debt") helmed by Miguel Pereira, looked at the war from the Argentine side) and will certainly cause a rumpus in the U.K. when a release is settled.

Lost in a battle during the Falklands war, David Thewlis is officially pronounced dead. Seven weeks later, when the war is long over, he staggers to an isolated farmhouse apparently suffering from amnesia.

When he returns to England to be met by his relieved family and girlfriend the press interpret official army dissatisfaction with his story as a hint that he deserted. His homecoming turns sour as newspapers start carrying the "coward" smear.

Relationships get more and more strained within his family and when Thewlis finally returns to barracks he finds his fellow soldiers have turned against him. They hold a vicious court martial, find him guilty and "punish" him with a brutal beating. Pic ends with Thewlis admitted to a military hospital, broken both physically and mentally.

Before the final credits pic carries the line "Inspired by the story of one soldier's war. This film is a work of imagination." Producers are trying to play down the fact that one British soldier did vanish then reappear during the conflict and much of pic is based on his story. Even though "Resurrected" is not pretending to be a biopic its strength is that it looks compassionately, and sometimes ironically, at real people coping as best they can in an "unreal" situation.

David Thewlis is excellent as the bemused and disturbed Private Deakin, essentially a smalltown lad unable to cope with the realities of war. As his parents Tom Bell and Rita Tushingham are fine, if slightly underused, while Rudi Davies is an actress for the future, giving a nice performance as gentle but confused girlfriend Julie.

Much of the storyline is telegraphed and repetitive use of shorts involving television set's showing clips from the Falklands conflict are a little naive, but helmer Greengrass displays an intelligent style, with the opening scenes in the Falklands especially good. Other technical credits are fine, while nice use of locations enhance the pic. —Adam.

Fallada — letztes Kapitel
(Fallada — The Last Chapter)
(EAST GERMAN)

Berlin   A Defa (foreign sales) presentation of a Defa Studio/Roter Kreis Group production. Produced by Herbert Ehler. Directed by Roland Gräf. Screenplay, Roland Gräf, Christel Gräf, Helga Schütz; camera (Orwocolor), Roland Dressel; editor, Monika Schindler; music, quotes from Sibelius' "Valse triste," Robert Stoltz' "Fragt nicht, warum;" sound, Werner Krehbiel; production design, Georg Wratsch; costumes, Christianne Dorst; production management, Andrea Hoffman. Reviewed at Berlin Film Festival (competing) Feb. 11, 1989. Running time: **99**

MIN.

Hans Fallada . . . . .Jörg Gudzuhn
Anna, his wife . . . . .Jutta Wachowiak
Ursula Losch . . . . .Katrin Sass
Elsa-Marie Bukonje . . . .Corinna Harfouch
Anneliese . . . . .Ulrike Krumbiegel
  Also with: Kirsten Arland, Sabrina Mende, Robert Schulz, Christine Siebert.

■ **This story of the sordid decline of German novelist Hans Fallada is told with fine attention to authentic detail by East Germany's Roland Gräf. A plus for wider audiences (mostly via tv sales) is the lead performance by Jörg Gudzuhn.**

Without striking a false note, Gudzuhn plays it to the hilt as an artist as well as a man trapped by forces surrounding him. There are his tough but patiently loving wife, sweet children, the protected but suffocating life in a remote village, the adulation bestowed on a famous writer (of such novels as ''When You Once Have Eaten From A Tin Plate'' and ''Little Man, What Now?'') and the persistent nudging of the Nazis to have him write ''The Great Anti-Jewish Novel.''

Screenplay allows Gudzuhn the rare opportunity to demonstrate in a film what actual writing is all about. During a brief jail stint, he solves the problem of being rationed only a few sheets of paper by using minuscule calligraphy and filling out the space between lines with new, tinier letters.

As his wife, Jutta Wachowiak makes both her long-suffering patience and her final breakup entirely plausible. Corinna Harfouch, who runs errands on behalf of the Gestapo, is the old-fashioned movie vamp. Katrin Sass as Ursula Losch (the writer's Evil Angel, complete with hypodermic needle at the ready and displays of cheap sexual allure) is given short shrift by both the writer-director and herself as just a dumb baddie.

Fine production gloss notwithstanding, ''Fallada'' becomes repetitive in its delving into the psychology of decline. It never regains the momentum of its early scenes. Focusing on Fallada's final decade, pic is missing any hint at the pre-1937 events that lay behind his greatness as a writer in the socialist mold.—*Kell.*

Wan Zhong
(Evening Bells)
(CHINESE)

Berlin   An August 1st Filmstudio, China Film, production. Directed by Wu Ziniu. Screenplay, Wu Ziniu, Wang Yifei; camera (Widescreen, color), Hou Yong; editor, Zong Lijiang; music, Ma Jianping; production design, Na Shufeng; production manager, Yan Rirong. Reviewed at Berlin Film Festival (competing), Feb. 12, 1989. Running time **89 MIN.**
  With: Tao Zeru, Liu Ruolei, Ge Yaming, Ye Nanqin, Zhao Qi, Sun Min, Cong Peipei, Xiang Zongi.

■ **A commanding use of widescreen and barren, mountainous locations give distinction to this often powerful drama about the immediate aftermath of World War II. It's another quality film from China.**

In 1945, following the Japanese surrender, a small unit of five members of China's Eighth Army is on a mopping-up operation to bury the dead and dispose of unexploded bombs and shells.

The area has been devastated by the Japanese, with homes and villages destroyed, women raped and murdered, thousands killed and homeless.

Against this background, the unit stumbles across a semidelirious Japanese soldier who's unaware the war is over. He leads them to a cave concealing an arms dump and a unit of 32 Japanese soldiers, all heavily armed, who far outnumber the little squad of Chinese. What follows is a tense stand-off between the two sides, with the Chinese trying to persuade their starving foes to lay down their arms.

Director Wu Ziniu tells his story with minimal dialog (there are long stretches of only natural sound) and with a striking visual feel that, allied to use of landscape, is sometimes reminiscent of a Western. Indeed, the drama could almost be transposed to the West, with the Japanese as an outlaw gang and the Chinese as a posse.

Though early scenes make no bones about the brutality of the Japanese, the film takes pains to treat them with respect now that the war's over. Produced by China's Army-controlled film studio, August 1st, ''Evening Bells'' was completed three years ago and its release delayed, possibly because of its attitude towards the conquered Japanese.

There are indications that it may also have been tampered with, since a sequence of a roll-call of Japanese POWs, which a printed synopsis places at the end of the film, is now its opening sequence: this is followed by what appears to be the destruction of the POWs by fire.

The director shows great flair throughout this finely made film, though a grim moment in which a German Shepard dog is gunned down, and seen in its death throes, is gratuitous (and looks unfaked).
—*Strat.*

The 'Burbs

Hollywood   A Universal Pictures release, presented by Imagine Entertainment, of a Rollins-Morra-Brezner production. Produced by Larry Brezner, Michael Finnell. Directed by Joe Dante. Screenplay, Dana Olsen. Camera (Deluxe color), Robert Stevens; editor. Marshall Harvey; music. Jerry Goldsmith; production design. James Spencer; sound (Dolby), Michael J. Benavente, Warren Hamilton Jr.; associate producer, Pat Kehoe; costumes, Rosanna Norton; coproducer, Olsen; casting, Mike Fenton, Judy Taylor. Reviewed at Cineplex Odeon Cinemas, Universal City, Calif., Feb. 15, 1989. MPAA Rating: PG. Running time: **103 MIN.**
Ray Peterson . . . . .Tom Hanks
Mark Rumsfield . . . . .Bruce Dern
Carol Peterson . . . . .Carrie Fisher
Art Weingartner . . . . .Rick Ducommun
Ricky Butler . . . . .Corey Feldman
Bonnie Rumsefield . . . . .Wendy Schaal
Dr. Werner Klopek . . . . .Brother Theodore
Hans Klopek . . . . .Courtney Gains
Walter . . . . .Gale Gordon
Garbagemen . .Dick Miller, Robert Picardo
Dave . . . . .Dave Peterson
Detectives .Franklyn Ajaye, Rance Howard

■ **Director Joe Dante funnels his decidedly cracked view of suburban life through dark humor in ''The 'Burbs,'' which starts brilliantly but lacks the inventiveness to sustain its last third.**

Tom Hanks' marquee value and many early bellylaughs should roll out the b.o. red carpet during its first few weeks, but the aftertaste of a flat finale will likely muffle longterm b.o. prospects, prompting many to wait and see it on tape in the safety of their own 'burb.

As in ''Gremlins,'' Dante displays an uncanny knack for taking tv sitcom-style family life and turning it on its ear.

It's actually impressive that ''The 'Burbs'' holds up as well as it does, since it never strays beyond the cozy confines of the nightmarish block everyman Ray (Hanks) inhabits along with an uproarious assemblage of wacky neighbors.

Unfortunately, the central device used to spur the action along — a new, unseen and by-all-indications sinister family that moves in next door — eventually forces the audience to become preoccupied with the payoff rather than just the fun of getting there. Like Dante's ''Explorers,'' the revelation is hardly worth the wait and proves anticlimatic.

Poor Ray has a week off and just wants to spend it quietly at home with his wife Carol (Carrie Fisher). Instead, he's drawn into an increasingly elaborate sleuthing game involving the mysterious Klopeks, who reside in a ''Munsters''-esque house rife with indications of foul play.

Ray's more familiar neighbors are equally bizarre: the corpulent Art (Rick Ducommun), convinced the Klopeks are performing satanic sacrifices; Rumsfield (Bruce Dern), a shell-shocked ex-G.I.; Walter (Gale Gordon), who delights in letting his dog relieve himself on Rumsfield's lawn; and Ricky (Corey Feldman), a teenager seemingly transferred from "Fast Times At Ridgemont High," who sees all the strange goings-on as viewing fodder for parties with his friends.

Dana Olsen's script is peppered with gems, and Dante includes the usual array of in-jokes and sight gags, both subtle and not-so-subtle.

Technical credits help mightily in sustaining the film's farcical nature, from Robert Stevens' brilliant camerawork to Jerry Goldsmith's portentous score, which would do Bernard Herrmann proud.

Despite similar heroics from the cast, however, Dante can't keep the rollercoaster on track through to the end and finally runs out of momentum.

Hanks does a fine impersonation of a regular guy on the verge of a nervous breakdown, while Dern adds another memorable psychotic to his résumé.

The big breakthroughs, however, are Ducommun, superb in a role that would have well-suited John Candy; and Wendy Schaal as Dern's airhead wife. —*Bril.*

Bill & Ted's Excellent Adventure

Hollywood An Orion Pictures release of a Nelson Entertainment presentation of an Interscope Communications production, in association with Soisson/Murphey Prods. Produced by Scott Kroopf, Michael S. Murphey, Joel Soisson. Executive producers, Ted Field, Robert W. Cort. Directed by Stephen Herek. Screenplay, Chris Matheson, Ed Solomon; camera (Technicolor), Timothy Suhrsedt; editor, Larry Bock, Patrick Rand; music, David Newman; production design, Ray Forge Smith; art direction, Gordon White, set decoration, Jennifer Williams; costume design, Jill Ohanneson; sound (Dolby), Ed White; visual effects supervisor, Barry Nolan; co-executive producer, Stephen Deutsch; assistant director, Kristine Peterson; casting, Stanzi Stokes. Reviewed at Orion Pictures screening room, L.A., Feb. 14, 1989. MPAA Rating: PG. Running time: **90 MIN.**

Ted Logan ....Keanu Reeves
Bill S. Preston ....Alex Winter
Rufus ....George Carlin
Napoleon ....Terry Camilleri
Billy The Kid ....Dan Shor
Socrates ....Tony Steedman
Freud ....Rod Loomis
Genghis Khan ....Al Leong
Joan of Arc ....Jane Wiedlin
Abraham Lincoln ....Robert V. Barron
Beethoven ....Clifford Davis

Captain Logan ....Hal Landon Jr.
Mr. Ryan ....Bernie Casey
Missy/Mom ....Amy Stock-Poynton
Mr. Preston ....J. Patrick McNamara

■ Not since Sean Penn's send-up of an airhead California high-schooler in "Fast Times At Ridgemont High" has the screen seen young characters as witlessly appealing as this pic's Bill and Ted. The excellence of their inspired chemistry doesn't extend to the rest of this overcrowded, dismally shallow adventure. Boxoffice report card will likely be average.

Keanu Reeves (Ted) and Alex Winter (Bill) play San Dimas "dudes" so close they seem wired together. In fact when they look at each other and play air guitar, it's the same imaginary chord.

Preoccupied with plans for "a most triumphant video" to launch their 2-man rock band, The Wyld Stallyns, they're suddenly, as Bill puts it, "in danger of flunking most heinously" out of history. That would mean Ted has a ticket to military school, definitely "bogus."

George Carlin appears as a cosmic benefactor who offers them a chance to travel back through history and gather up the speakers they need for an awesome presentation.

Through brief, perilous stops here and there, they end up jamming Napoleon, Billy The Kid, Sigmund Freud, Socrates, Joan of Arc, Genghis Khan, Abraham Lincoln and Mozart into their time-traveling phone booth.

Each encounter is so brief and utterly cliched that history has little chance to contribute anything to this pic's two dimensions, nor do the overtaxed director (Stephen Herek) and designers manage to find a coherent style or tone.

Reeves, with his beguilingly blank face and loose-limbed, happy-go-lucky physical vocabulary, and Winter, with his golden curls, gleefully good vibes and "bodacious" vocabulary, propel this adventure as long as they can.

Even the fast-forward scenes reflect little imagination, with tin-foil covered geometric shapes and modified Star Trek costumes reflecting the usual implausible vision of the future.

On the plus side, there's a strong and savvy soundtrack, mostly performed by newcomers, and now and then some "savory" dialog penned by writers Chris Matheson and Ed Solomon, who reportedly created Bill and Ted in an improv

routine.

Bernie Casey gives a commendable performance as the history teacher. —*Daws.*

Under The Gun

New York A Marquis Pictures release and production. Executive producer, Steven J. Shotz. Produced by Warren Stein. Directed by James Sbardellati. Screenplay, Almer John Davis, James Devney, Sbardellati, from Devney's story; camera (United color), Gary Thieltges; editor, George Copanas; music, John Sterling; sound (Ultra-Stereo), Peter Bentley; production design, James Shumaker; set decoration, Dian Perryman; assistant director, Perry Husman; production manager, Kelly A. Oram; stunt coordinator, Harry Wowchuk; associate producers, Copanas, Arthur J. Marion, Burton Satzberg, Myron Miller; casting, Cathy Henderson, Barbra Hanley. Reviewed on Magnum Entertainment vidcassette, N.Y., Feb. 11, 1989. MPAA Rating: R. Running time: **89 MIN.**

Mike Braxton ....Sam Jones
Samantha Richards .....Vanessa Williams
Simon Stone ....John Russell
Frank ....Michael Halsey
Tony ....Nick Cassavetes
Gallagher ....Steven Williams
Miller ....Bill McKinney
Also with: Rockne Tarkington, Don Stark, Chris Mulkey, Michelle Russell, Steve Geray.

■ Vanessa Williams makes an impressive feature film starring debut in "Under The Gun." Competent actioner was shot in 1986, before her current singing career.

Sam Jones ("Flash Gordon") toplines as a folksy St. Louis cop who heads to L.A. to help his younger brother (Nick Cassavetes). He'd phoned for help just before being killed by henchmen of corrupt arms dealer John Russell.

Jones attempts revenge against Russell by teaming with innocent bystander Williams, cast as Russell's new lawyer. She has access to the records which can put him away for good.

Helmer James Sbardellati stages fine action sequences as everyone scurries around trying to get their hands on some stolen plutonium.

Cast does a good job, particularly Williams who's both glamorous and feisty. Producer Warren Stein and his fellow filmmakers are to be congratulated for casting her in a nonexploitive role which never identifies or pigeonholes the character on the basis of race. —*Lor.*

Future Hunters

New York A Lightning Pictures presentation of a Maharaj/Santiago production. Produced by Anthony Maharaj. Directed by Cirio H. Santiago. Screenplay, J.L. Thompson, from story by Maharaj; camera (CFI color), Ricardo Remias; editor, Bass Santos; mu-

sic, Ron Jones; production design, Joe Mari Avellana; second unit director, Maharaj; second unit camera, Johnny Araojo. Reviewed on Vestron Video vidcassette, N.Y., Jan. 28, 1989. MPAA Rating: R. Running time: **100 MIN.**

Slade ....Robert Patrick
Michelle ....Linda Carol
Fielding ....Ed Crick
Bauer ....Bob Schott
Matthew ....Richard Norton
Amazon queen ....Ursula Marquez
Also with: Elizabeth Oropesa, Bruce Li, Wang Chang Lee, David Light, Peter Shilton, Paul Holmes.

■ From the rash of lookalike adventure features on video emerges a winner: "Future Hunters," in which prolific Filipino helmer Cirio H. Santiago outdoes himself in fresh and entertaining fashion.

Lengthy pic unfolds as a virtual homage to the high adventure motifs of George Lucas yet moves beyond mere imitation into its own successful territory.

Prolog is set in the year 2025 with regular Santiago hero Richard Norton chased around by baddies in "Mad Max"-style cars and outfits. In a remote temple in the desert he finds the head of a spear, said by legend to have pierced the body of Christ on the cross and to hold spectacular powers.

Back in present time (1986, when pic was shot under the moniker "The Spear (Of Destiny)"), statuesque blond Linda Carol plays a college anthropology student who, with boyfriend Robert Patrick, visits the same temple. Norton, who has traveled back in time via the spear's power, helps the duo fight off a gang of mean bikers (who at first think futuristic Norton is a kindred biker, given his "Mad Max" leather garb).

Complicated plot, punctuated constantly by action sequences, has Norton expiring but setting the young couple on his mission, to unite the spearhead with its lost shaft, and use resulting object's power to head off an imminent world holocaust and thus change the future from whence he came.

Elements of both "Indiana Jones" films plus a healthy sprinkling of "Romancing The Stone" are pleasantly arranged, with pic steadily put across by heroine Carol, an American beauty closely resembling Greta Scacchi. Her willingness to get her hair mussed and enter enthusiastically into the action is a big plus.

Patrick is merely okay as the hero and the villains are nondescript; more upscale casting might have earned this laudable little film some theatrical attention. —*Lor.*

Funny
(DOCU)

Park City An Associates and Ferren production. Produced, directed and photographed by Bran Ferren. In color. Reviewed at the U.S. Film Festival, Park City, Utah (in competition), Jan. 20, 1989. No MPAA Rating. Running time: **60 MIN.**

■ Academy Award-winning technical wizard Bran Ferren made "Funny" more or less as an off-hours amusement, conceding the cinematic effort was almost totally limited to pointing a camera at people telling jokes, That's it, more a curio than a viable commercial enterprise.

Ferren obviously knows a lot of celebrities and it's kind of interesting to see what their favorite joke might be. Often, they're no better telling a gag than the amateurs Ferren also has captured. Bartender John Iulo beats the best of the pros and one machinist, A.J. Garmon, is just hilarious to watch long before he reaches his punchlines.

Ferren's professional expertise shows in the crisp editing, sometimes intercutting three or four people for continuous renditions of the same familiar yarn.

Nobody was censored and the jokes cover all kinds, from funny to flat. —*Har.*

Emerald City
(AUSTRALIAN)

Sydney A Greater Union (Australia) release of a Limelight production, in association with the New South Wales Film Corp. Produced by Joan Long. Directed by Michael Jenkins. Screenplay, David Williamson, based on his play; camera (Eastmancolor), Paul Murphy; editor, Neil Thumpston; music, Chris Neal; production design, Owen Williams; costumes, Anthony James; sound, Ben Osmo; production manager, Brenda Pam; assistant director, Chris Webb; casting, Alison Barrett. Reviewed at Village-Roadshow screening room, Sydney, Nov. 18, 1988. Running time: **93 MIN.**

Colin Rogers	John Hargreaves
Kate Rogers	Robyn Nevin
Mike McCord	Chris Haywood
Helen Davey	Nicole Kidman
Elaine Ross	Ruth Cracknell
Malcolm Bennett	Dennis Miller
Penny Rogers	Ella Scott
Sam Rogers	Hayden Samuels
Kath Mitchell	Michelle Torres

Also with: Bruce Venables, Rebel Penfold-Russell, Robert Rosen, Wenanty Nosul, Philip Dodd, Aki Taninaka, Jan Ringrose.

■ Following on from the local success of "Travelling North," "Emerald City" is the latest of David Williamson's hit plays to reach the screen. Handsome production has a prestige feel about it, but the rather insular nature of the material may make this one a tough boxoffice sell.

Subject here is the Australian film industry and reasons for its apparent decline in recent years. Protagonist Colin Rogers (John Hargreaves) is a highly successful writer (evidently based on Williamson himself) torn between the need to make money and a desire to keep his projects "serious" and Australian.

He's contrasted to a cheerfully ruthless hustler, Mike McCord (Chris Haywood), a small-time writer with a pretty young mistress (Nicole Kidman) and high ambitions: McCord will do anything to make a buck, and winds up in partnership with money man Dennis Mitchell to produce Americanized versions of Aussie screenplays for the "international" (read American) market.

Rogers' wife Kate (Robyn Nevin) works for a publisher and treats her work very seriously: her great ambition is to have a radical book by an aboriginal woman activist (Michelle Torres) published; ironically, it's only after the intervention of McCord, via a threatening phone call to Kate's boss, that the book *is* published.

Later, the successful book is bought by McCord for filming in the American South with a black American cast, an act of cultural vandalism supposed to represent an extreme instance of the Americanization of the Aussie film industry.

Unlike "Travelling North," "Emerald City" can't hide its legit origins. It's a very talky piece, and director Michael Jenkins (whose first pic, "Rebel," misfired a couple of years ago) has tried to keep things moving by having his actors deliver their often very witty lines at rapid-fire rate, akin to an early Frank Capra pic. Modern ears aren't as attuned to this kind of delivery, and audiences may have trouble keeping up.

Chris Haywood steals the film as the enjoyably dreadful McCord, seen as the type who's destroying the film industry for financial gain. John Hargreaves and Robyn Nevin are solid as the central characters who vacillate between seeking money and power, or settling for critically acclaimed, but modestly rewarded, efforts.

Nicole Kidman has little to do but look beautiful as McCord's live-in girlfriend, and Ruth Cracknell is waspish, but a touch theatrical, as world-weary film producer.

Internationally, pic will register among film communities in such countries as Britain and Canada, but is likely to be seen as insular by Americans.

Producer Joan Long has done her usual impeccable job of putting all the elements together: subject matter reflects her interest in cinema (she produced "The Picture Show Man" as well as a trio of docus tracing the history of the Aussie film industry).

"Emerald City" was the final film made in association with the now shuttered New South Wales Film Corp. —*Strat.*

Les Cigognes n'en font qu'à leur tête
(The Storks Are Capricious)
(FRENCH)

Paris AAA release of a Hugo Films/Labbefilms/AAA Prods./TFI Films coproduction. Produced by Xavier and Evelyne Gélin. Written and directed by Didier Kaminka. Camera (Eastmancolor), Martial Thury; sound, Jean-Louis Ughetto, Claude Villand; art direction, Dominique André; assistant director, Christophe Vassort; production manager, Claude Parnet. Reviewed at the Marignan-Concorde theater, Paris, Feb. 3, 1989. Running time: **82 MIN.**

Marie	Marlène Jobert
Jeremie	Patrick Chesnais
Sam	Claude Rich
Valerie	Virginia Demians
Joanna	Ariane Lorent
Helene Parnet	Zabou
Anselme	Roland Giraud

■ Screenwriter Didier Kaminka tries his hand once again at directing his own script in this romantic comedy about a middle-aged couple trying to adopt a baby.

They first go through an official adoption agency, then via a pregnant young girl who doesn't want to keep the kid. Both plans don't work and neither does pic, which is weak in both writing and directing.

Comedy marks screen comeback of Marlène Jobert, topbilled opposite Patrick Chensnais. Kaminka ribs the absurdities of adoption bureaucracies, using café-theater and screen funnyman Gérard Jugnot, Christian Clavier and Romain Bouteille in cameo caricatures, while Roland Giraud, veteran of baby boom comedies ("Three Men And A Cradle") plays an agency inspector.

Subplot involving Chesnais, playing a restaurateur menaced by racketeers demanding protection money, is dropped rather suddenly. —*Len.*

The Lawless Land

New York A Concorde Pictures release. Executive producers, Roger Corman, Juan Forch. Produced by Tony Cinciripini, Larry Leahy. Directed by Jon Hess. Screenplay, Cinciripini, Leahy, from story by Cinciripini; camera (Foto-Kem color, Filmhouse prints), Makoto Watanabe; editor, Bernard Caputo; music, Lucia Hwong; sound, Felipe Zabala; production design, Rafael Sanudo; art direction, Roberto di Girolamo; production manager, Maria Sanchez; additional camera, Teddy Chu; additional editor, Stephen Mark. Reviewed on MGM/UA Home Video vidcassette, N.Y., Jan. 18, 1989. MPAA Rating: R. Running time: **80 MIN.**

Falco	Nick Corri
Road Kill	Leon
EZ Andy	Xander Berkeley
Diana	Amanda Peterson
Don Enrique	Patricio Bunster
Chairman	Walter Kliche
Billy	Alejandro Heinrich
Venus	Ann-Marie Peterson

■ Minor sci-fi effort "The Lawless Land" serves to introduce some new talent. Pic played briefly theatrically last year ahead of homevideo release.

Helmer Jon Hess, who went on to shoot Carolco's "Watchers" for Universal release, shows technical know-how in this "Mad Max" genre tale set in "the Southern continent after the collapse" (lensed in Chile). Nick Corri portrays Falco, who runs afoul of the chairman (Walter Kliche), an industrial magnate, when he elopes with his pretty daughter (Amanda Peterson).

In road movie fashion, much of film is taken up by the chairman's goons, led by Road Kill (played by laconic Leon), chasing after the lovers. Odd casting has a tramp-styled beauty hitchhiking and getting mixed up in the violence, played by Peterson lookalike Ann-Marie Peterson, evidently the actress' sister.

Corri exudes an engaging personality in the undemanding lead role, and went on to a subsequent toplined part in "Slaves Of New York." Rest of cast is fine, with some scene-stealing by Xander Berkeley as a folksy guy who always seems to turn up when the good guys need an assist.

Tech credits are acceptable, with an excellent out-theme ballad, "We Found Our Way," sung by Gary Stockdale. —*Lor.*

Amors Bilar
(Cupid's Cars)
(SWEDISH-DOCU)

Berlin A Lystra production of the Swedish Film Institute, Swedish TV/Channel 1. Produced by Lisbet Gabrielsson, Ylva Floreman. Written and directed by Ylva Floreman.

Camera (color), Hans-Ake Lerin; editor, Lisskulla Moltke-Hoff; music, Gudrun Hauksdottir, Erland Mauritzon, Jan Sjoberg, Johan Valentin; production managers, Annika Hedman, Anja Floreman; sound, Peter Holthausen; coordinator, Lena Enquist. Reviewed at Berlin Film Festival (Panorama), Feb. 11, 1989. Running time: **65 MIN.**

With: Jan Broberg, Lars Broberg, Tony Broberg, Kenneth Dahlberg, Jan Fridh, Tommy Granath, Petra Andersson, Yvonne Granath, Ann-Louis Hensson, Camilla Herman.

■ **"Cupid's Cars," journalist Ylva Floreman's first solo docu, is a study of a working-class subculture, the "hotrodders." Skillful handling of the topic gives it a wide scope and should ensure it a place in documentary sections of festivals and in offshore tv programming.**

The three main characters, brothers Jan, Lars and Tony Broberg, are part of a circle of friends preoccupied with rebuilding old cars. For them a car is much more than a vehicle. It is both a symbol of manhood and an expression of the owner's personality, a mobile rec room.

Floreman's viewpoint is neither condescending nor critical. The pic gives a sense of the hard work that goes into rehabbing an old wreck and conveys the feeling it is a creative endeavor.

The playful camaraderie of several segments, including one showing the guys getting drunk and discussing their love lives, is remarkably unselfconscious. The close camerawork in interiors is good and a pleasant rock score accents the car rides. —*Sam.*

Dr. Alien

New York A Phantom Prods. presentation. Produced by Dave DeCoteau, John Schouweiler. Directed by DeCoteau. Screenplay, Kenneth J. Hall; camera (Deluxe color) Nicholas Von Sternberg; editor, Tony Malanowski; music, Reg Purcell, Sam Winans; sound (Ultra-Stereo), Christopher Endicott; production design, Royce Mathew; assistant director, Will Clark; production manager, Ellen Cabot; special makeup effects, Greg Cannom Creations — supervisor, John Vulich; 2d unit director-stunt coordinator, Chuck Borden; associate producer, Hall; casting, Clair Sinnett. Reviewed on Paramount/Phantom Video vidcassette, N.Y., Feb. 11, 1989. MPAA Rating: R. Running time: **87 MIN.**
Wesley Littlejohn . . . . Billy Jacoby
Ms. Xenobia . . . . Judy Landers
Leeanne . . . . Olivia Barash
Marvin . . . . Stuart Fratkin
Drax . . . . Raymond O'Connor
Mom . . . . Arlene Golonka
Dad . . . . Jim Hackett
Bradford Littlejohn . . . . Bobby Jacoby
Karla . . . . Julie Gray
Dirk . . . . Scott Morris
Dr. Ackerman . . . . Troy Donahue
Also with: Tom De Franco, Geno Andrews, Russell Hines, Ginger Lynn Allen, Linnea Quigley, Laura Albert, Michelle Bauer, Karen Russell, Edy Williams, Elizabeth Kaitan.

■ **Sci-fi meets teen sex comedy in "Dr. Alien," a campy direct-to-video film. It was more colorfully (and accurately) titled "I Was A Teenage Sex Mutant" when presold by Charles Band's organization years ago.**

Tone recalls the Scott Baio-starrer "Zapped," and new pic is likely to establish its own healthy following in ancillary media. Billy Jacoby is a nerdish college freshman selected by new biology teacher Judy Landers for an experiment. She's an alien from planet Altaria, who's killed biology prof Troy Donahue and is testing a formula on Jacoby in support of repopulating her world, whose males are dying out.

Filmmaker David DeCoteau juggles numerous staples of the various teen genres: Jacoby is converted into a hip dude after the first injection (and sexual initiation) by Landers; he joins rock band The Sex Mutants, and his best pal Stuart Fratkin ogles the girls' gym class for voyeur action. Girls can't resist Jacoby, including zoftig Julie Gray, g.f. of school bully Scott Morris.

Harmless fun is easy to take, the excellent makeup effects by John Vulich include a tentacle growing out of the top of Jacoby's head and a huge blue head for Landers' real self that allows the comedienne to inject her own personality into her monster-masked scenes. Landers is quite funny, ably matched by Jacoby.

Dark Tower

New York A Spectrafilm and Sandy Howard presentation. (Intl. sales, Fries Distribution.) Executive producers, Tom Fox, Ken Wiederhorn. Produced by John R. Bowey, David M. Witz. Directed by "Ken Barnett" (Freddie Francis). Screenplay, Robert J. Avrech, Wiederhorn, Ken Blackwell, from Avrech's story; camera (color), Gordon Hayman; editor, Tom Merchant; music, Stacy Widelitz; sound, Jaume Puig, Margaret Duke; art direction, Jose Maria Espada; 2d unit director, Dan Bradley; 2d unit camera, Chris Tufty; special makeup effects, Steve Neill; coproducer, Paco Poch; associate producers, Merchant, Michael Masciarelli; casting, Paul Bengston, David Cohn. Reviewed on Forum Home Video vidcassette, N.Y., Feb. 11, 1989. MPAA Rating: R. Running time: **91 MIN.**
Dennis Randall . . . . Michael Moriarty
Carolyn Page . . . . Jenny Agutter
Tilly Ambrose . . . . Carol Lynley
Dr. Max Gold . . . . Theodore Bikel
Elaine . . . . Anne Lockhart
Sergie . . . . Kevin McCarthy
Maria . . . . Patch Mackenzie
Williams . . . . Robert Sherman
Charlie . . . . Rick Azulay
Joseph . . . . Radmiro Oliveros

■ **"Dark Tower" is a perfuncto-**ry horror thriller going direct to video in the U.S. after being sold internationally for the last two years. Spectrafilm had domestic theatrical plans but abandoned them.

Pic's director credit is a pseudonym; originally planned to be helmed by Ken Wiederhorn, it was directed by ace lenser and horror vet Freddie Francis but his name is missing on screen.

Reason may be that "Tower" plays like a bloated segment (usually 1-reel long) from one of Francis' horror anthologies, such as "Tales From The Crypt."

Roughly resembling "Poltergeist III" (but actually lensed a year earlier), "Tower" is about a rash of murders in an under-construction Barcelona skyscraper. Company security chief Michael Moriarty is called in to investigate and prime suspect soon turns out to be the ghost (!) of skyscraper architect Jenny Agutter's late husband.

Parapsychologist Theodore Bikel and exorcist Kevin McCarthy are hired to battle the demon, leading to an underwhelming climactic battle and cheaply ironic finish. Film's special effects are decidedly chintzy.

Cast is stuck with nondimensional roles and Bikel is forced to play several embarrassing scenes trying to talk to the invisible presence. Spanish supporting cast's dialog is haphazardly looped. —*Lor.*

Space Mutiny

New York An Action Intl. Pictures presentation of a Winters/Holiday production. Executive producers, Hope Holiday, John DeKock. Produced and directed by David Winters. Codirector, Neal Sundstrom. Screenplay, Maria Dante; camera (Image Transform color), Vincent Cox; editor, Bill Asher, Charlotte Konrad, Catherine Meyburgh; music, Tim James, Steve McClintock, Mark Mancina; sound (Ultra-Stereo), Konrad Khune; production design, Geoff Hill; assistant director, Mark West; production manager-associate producer, Debi Nethersole; camera — Bellerian sequences, Andrew Parke; special optical effects, Jerry Kitz. Reviewed on AIP Home Video Vidcassette, N.Y., Jan. 28, 1989. No MPAA Rating. Running time: **91 MIN.**
Dave Ryder . . . . Reb Brown
Kalgan . . . . John Phillip Law
MacPhearson . . . . James Ryan
Alex Jansen . . . . Cameron Mitchell
Lea Jansen . . . . Cissy Cameron
Scott Dyers . . . . Graham Clark
Also with: Billy Second, Rufus Swart, Chip Mitchell, Madyelene Reynel.

■ **An okay space saga for homevideo fans, "Space Mutiny" probably is the first such picture made in South Africa,** featuring a cast of genre stalwarts.

Reb Brown, looking a bit silly bulging out of a Flash Gordon-type costume plays a space jockey helping Cameron Mitchell and his zoftig daughter Cissy Cameron fight off a mutiny led by such evildoers as John Phillip Law and S.A. star James Ryan. Plotline injects motifs from such early '70s sci-fi sources as "Silent Running" and tv's "The Starlost" series, as main problem is folks going stir crazy aboard the huge Southern Sun spaceship taking generations to transport Earth migrants to a new home in a distant star system.

Cute model shots provide a patina of space opera action, though the special effects are decidedly chintzy. A frequently emphasized subplot involving a group of telepathic femmes known as Bellerians aboard the ship is clumsily inserted, appearing to be an afterthought and mere padding.

Campy acting and dialog climaxes in an absurd final chase/battle featuring what look like vehicles left over from a Dodgem arcade ride. —*Lor.*

Nayakan
(Hero)
(INDIAN)

New Delhi A Sujatha Film Ltd. production. Produced by G. Venkataswaran. Written and directed by Mani Rathnam. Camera (Eastmancolor), P.C. Sriram; editor, Lenin and Vijayan; music, Ilayaraja (additional lyrics Pulamai Pithan); art direction, Thotta Tharani. Reviewed at the Intl. Film Festival of India (Panorama), New Delhi, Jan. 20, 1989. Running time: **145 MIN.**
Shakthivelu Nayakan . . . . . . Kamal Haasan
Neela . . . . Saranya
Also with: Janakaraj, Kartika.
(Soundtrack in Tamil)

■ **Anyone looking for a rollicking, splashy Indian production with violence, love, populist politics, song and dance will find it in "Nayakan" (Hero).**

Plot is more engrossing than most Indian entertainment, containing notable similarities to "The Godfather," not least a hero who is made up to look like Al Pacino as a young man and Marlo Brando (complete with mumbled rasp) as an oldster.

Film was a hit in spite of being in Tamil (not the better-known Hindi language) and even got picked as India's Oscar hope last year. Its recent Hindi remake was a flop.

Son of assassinated trade union leader, Velu (the personable giant Kamal Hasan) commits a murder as a young boy and runs off to Bombay. He is brought up by a kindly fisherman-smuggler in a Tamil slum. The old man's innocent belief that nothing done for a good cause is bad becomes Velu's credo, too.

When the friendly young giant bashes in the head of a cruel policeman (police brutality comes in for savage attacks throughout pic), Velu becomes the hero of the oppressed. As time goes on Robin Hood imperceptibly merges into the kingpin of Bombay's mafia. He marries fallen woman Neela (Saranya), which occasions some sentimental song and dance numbers, but she is brutally murdered by a rival gang.

As an old man, Velu lives to see his son killed and daughter estranged. Though acquitted by a court of law, Velu is gunned down by one of his most trusted man.

Locals claim "Nayakan" has too many serious underpinnings to qualify as typical mainstream cinema, but offshore audiences are not likely to take it for more than exotic fun. Flashy lighting and fine lensing give a quality look. Performances are so-so. It is helmer Mani Rathnam's sixth film.
—*Yung.*

17 Op
(17 Up)
(DANISH)

Copenhagen A Scala Film release of a Danish Film Studio and Obel Film production. Produced by Jörgen Hinsch, Gunnar Obel. Directed by Brita Wielopolska. Screenplay, Dorthea Birkedal Andersen; camera (Eastmancolor), Morten Bruus; editor, Kasper Schyberg; music, Oyvind Ougard, James R. Crabb; sound, Leif Jensen; production design, Peter Höimark; costumes, Pia Myrdal, Merete Engbäk; production management, Peter Aalbäk Jensen; assistant director, Tove Berg; casting, Jette Termann; Danish Film Institute consultant producer, Ida Zeruneith. Reviewed at Palads, Copenhagen, Jan. 26, 1989. Running time: **72 MIN.**

Sally . . . . Jane Eggertsen
Zuhal . . . . Mia El Mousti
Leo . . . . Jonathan Grumme
Sally's father . . . . Torben Jensen
The janitor . . Flemming (Bamse) Jörgensen
Also with: Ulla Henningsen, Birgitte Bruun, Ole Meyer, Jörn Fauerschou, Jarl Forsman, Jens del Place Björn, Lilly Holmer, Musa Harmanci, Bekir Demir Bas, Denis Küzük Avci, Davut Küzük Avci, Renée Laumann, Jens Bo Jörgensen.

■ **A quick descent into oblivion is predicted for this picture of good intentions but otherwise almost totally failing both as narrative and in all technical departments.**

The title of "17 Up" refers to the top floor terrace, "closer to heaven," where young teenager Sally of Brita Wielopolska's third kiddie & youth comedy feature seeks refuge from the general hustle of the high-rise slum of her daily life.

Okay story has quick-witted Sally seen as a survivor-scavenger who sets up an almost regular business with empty bottles, etc. All the other kids parade emptily and dangerously in their various gang costumes and makeup.

Sally, bred to become a racist, is won over by a Turkish guestworker girl of equal sharpness plus a real talent for playing the accordion.

Sally and the girl musician soon make a profit via street performances but both the fun and the profits are spoiled by the forces of prejudice: the Turkish parents take their daughter away to a marriage with an unknown.

Wielopolska parades cliché-ridden dialog side-by-side with clichéd characters, while she loses her grip on any and all technique almost completely. No narrative sequence is followed through.

Jane Eggertsen has the right gamin qualities for the lead, while Mia El Mousti as the Turkish girl is solemnly beautiful and retains her dignity through all the cinematic wreckage surrounding her.
—*Kell.*

The Luckiest Man In The World

New York A Second Effort Co. release of a McLaughlin, Piven, Vogel Inc. presentation. Produced by Norman I. Cohen. Written and directed by Frank D. Gilroy. Camera (TVC color), Jeri Sopanen; editor, John Gilroy; music, Warren Vaché, Jack Gale; sound, Lee Orloff; production design, Nick Romanec; production manager, Lois Hartwick; assistant director, Cohen; associate producers, Scott Hancock, John Gilroy; casting, Abigail McGrath. Reviewed at Magno Preview 9 screening room, N.Y., Feb. 7, 1989. No MPAA Rating. Running time: **82 MIN.**

Sam Posner . . . . Philip Bosco
Mrs. Posner . . . . Doris Belack
Laura . . . . Joanne Camp
Sheldon . . . . Matthew Gottlieb
Cleveland . . . . Arthur French
Schwartz . . . . Stan Lachow
Mrs. Gonzalez . . . . Yamil Borges
Robert Whitley . . . . J.D. Clarke
Voice . . . . Moses Gunn

■ **"The Luckiest Man In The World" is a Capraesque film from playwright Frank D. Gilroy. Like his previous indie pic "The Gig," it should find an appreciative audience in ancillary markets following a modest theatrical run.**

Philip Bosco toplines as a mean-spirited N.Y. garment center businessman who decides to make amends to everyone in his life after narrowly missing death in a plane crash. Money is the bribe he offers them all, starting with the chauffeur (Arthur French, delightful in deadpan role). Bosco browbeats the driver into rushing him to the airport, only to arrive too late to catch the doomed aircraft. Rewarded with the gift of Bosco's Rolls-Royce, French immediately boots out his boss/benefactor.

Bosco's uncharacteristic kindliness brings ironic results throughout: Both wife and mistress can't bear Mr. Nice Guy rocking the boat; his gay son feels cheated by loss of a solid icon to hate, and even a bum begging for a buck for a drink responds to Bosco's proffering a $20 bill, "What ya tryin' to do, kill me?"

Moses Gunn is fun as an unseen (except for shoes and trouser cuffs) presence in a bathroom stall who serves as comical deus ex machina for Bosco.

Gilroy nimbly extracts black humor out of the situation, notably when Bosco visits a dying partner in the hospital and at the climax when he visits the widow of the standby passenger who took his seat on the death plane. It all adds up to a slight but entertaining picture.

Bosco is excellent in staying true to central character, ably fleshing out the kind of broad role once a screen staple for George Arliss. Supporting cast, several of whom appeared in "The Gig," is fine. Technical credits are strictly functional as Gilroy emphasizes performance and dialog rather than cinematic effects.—*Lor.*

Cannibal Women In The Avocado Jungle Of Death

New York A Guacamole Films presentation of a Gary W. Goldstein production. Produced by Goldstein. Line producer, Jeanne Stack. Written and directed by J.D. Athens. Camera (Deluxe color), Robert G. Knouse; editor, King Louis; music, Carl Dante; sound, Jerry Wolfe, art direction, Kimberly Charles Rees; costume design, Barbara Anne Klein; assistant director, Michael Snyder; production manager, Thomas Calabrese; casting, Dorian Dunas. Reviewed on Paramount/Phantom Video vidcassette, N.Y., Feb. 8, 1989. MPAA Rating: PG-13. Running time: **89 MIN.**

Dr. Margo Hunt . . . . Shannon Tweed
Dr. Kurtz . . . . Adrienne Barbeau
Jim . . . . Bill Maher
Bunny . . . . Karen Mistal
Jean-Pierre . . . . Brett Stimely
Ford Maddox . . . . Barry Primus
College Dean Stockwell . . . James MacKrell
Col. Mattel . . . . Paul Ross

■ **This off-the-wall satire, originally titled "Piranha Women . . . ," packs some good laughs (and bad puns) but is unfortunately underproduced, giving Paramount Video an okay rental item.**

Filmmaker J.D. Athens shows promise, but is over-reliant upon endless dialog to make his comic points. A budget allowing Landis- or Zuckers & Abrahams-style sight gags would have created theatrical possibilities.

Shannon Tween stars as the no-nonsense ethno-historian prof at a college's Feminist Studies Dept., recruited by the government to mount an expedition into the jungle near San Bernardino to find missing Dr. Kurtz (Adrienne Barbeau) who's been lost there. Government hacks claim a commie plot to destroy America's avocado crop, but it turns out the feds actually are out to destroy the ancient tribe of militant feminists (the Piranha Women) who live there, preying off a clan of neighboring wimpy males called the Donnahews. (Puns include Tweed's college dean being named Stockwell.)

With cute, buxom valley girl Bunny (Karen Mistal) tagging along, Tweed treks with the aid of bumbling guide Bill Maher. Feminist ideology is relentlessly parodied as Tweed verbally (and with ⌐rds) battles Barbeau for ⌐premacy, ultimately uniting the Piranha Women with their rival tribe the Barracuda Women, separated long ago due to a schism over which type of dip to use when they eat their male victims.

Cute satirical ideas keep the film afloat, ranging from spoof of the "2001" bonetossing Dawn Of Intelligence scene (better done in John Landis' debut pic "Schlock") to Barbeau as Kurtz contemplating "The horror! The horror!" of having to go on the David Letterman show and get insulted while plugging a feminist book.

Tweed is impressive handling rapidfire dialog and leaving the pulchritude assignment to newcomer Mistal, a very attractive young performer. Barbeau's role is tailormade and supporting cast is adequate. If only they could have afforded some action . —*Lor.*

Ginger Ale Afternoon

Park City A NeoPictures Ltd. production. Produced by Susan Hillary Shapiro, Rafal Zielenski. Executive producer, Alexander Sachs. Directed by Zielinski. Screenplay, Gina Wendkos, based on her play; camera (color),

Yuri Neyman; editor-associate producer, Lorenzo De Stefano; music, Willie Dixon; coproducer, James Zatolokin; production design, Michael Helmy; art direction, Vally Mestroni; costumes, Marlene Stewart. Reviewed at U.S. Film Festival, Park City, Utah (in competition), Jan. 26, 1989. No MPAA Rating. Running time: **94 MIN.**

Jesse Mickers . . . . Dana Andersen
Hank Mickers . . . . John M. Jackson
Bonnie . . . . Yeardly Smith

■ **"Ginger Ale Afternoon" was adapted by Gina Wendkos from her own stage play, but director Rafal Zielinski failed to open up the 2-hander for the screen.**

Pic holds out the promise that unattractive, unpleasant and unintelligent people can find love, too. All they have to do is find a mate as unattractive, unpleasant and unintelligent as they are.

Jesse and Hank Mickers (Dana Andersen and John M. Jackson) reside in a trashy trailer court, cozily encased in an aluminum shell that looks like a septic tank tipped on its side. Thanks to production designer Michael Helmy, it's even worse on the inside, junked and cramped, the perfect cage for what the Mickers do best: The Mickers bicker.

With absolutely no charm and only flashes of humor, they fight constantly, especially about whether they really love or hate each other. On the afternoon in question, Andersen is trying to enjoy her one day off from her cashier's job, sunning by their 6-inch rubber wading pool in a chaise lounge with a ripped cover.

They fight a lot about the impending birth of Guy Wayne, who must surely ranks as one of the most unfortunate fetuses in recent film history. Jackson hates him because he's already stealing Andersen's attention, although why he would want more of her attention remains amazing.

Ultimately, the quarrels disclose that Jackson is having an affair with a pudgy young neighbor, Yeardly Smith, who lures him to her converted school bus with low self-esteem.

Andersen is forgiving, however, and she and Jackson retreat to their tiny bedroom to make up, raising a multitude of fears that the audience may actually be required to watch. Fortunately, before this can progress too far, little Guy Wayne rides to the rescue. —*Har.*

El Verano de la Señora Forbes
(The Summer Of Ms. Forbes)
(MEXICAN-SPANISH)

Havana   A Televisión Española (TVE) release of a TVE-Intl. Network Group (ING)-ICAIC production, under the auspices of the New Latin American Cinema Foundation (Havana). Executive producer, Max Marambio. Produced by Luis Reneses. Directed by Jaime Humberto Hermosillo. Screenplay, Hermosillo, Gabriel García Márquez; camera (color), Rodrigo García; editor, Nelson Rodríguez; music, Sergio Vitier; sound, Carlos Fernández. Reviewed at Havana Film Festival, Cuba, Dec. 12, 1988. Running time: **88 MIN.**

Governess . . . . Hanna Schygulla
Aquiles . . . . Francisco Gattorno
Child #1 . . . . Alexis Castañares
Child #2 . . . . Víctor César Villalobos
Mother . . . . Guadalupe Sandoval
Father . . . . Fernando Balzaretti
Maid . . . . Yuriria Munguía

■ **As part of the 6-pic series "Difficult Loves," based on works by Nobel Prize-winning Colombian author Gabriel García Márquez, "The Summer Of Ms. Forbes" is an amusing albeit minor work by Mexican helmer Jaime Humberto Hermosillo.**

Black comedy stands a chance on the arthouse circuit, aided by b.o. draw of Hanna Schygulla in the title role.

Various themes, developed by Hermosillo in earlier works — such as underwater fantasies and homosexuality — are present here in a rehashed form that give a dream-like or disturbing quality to the narrative.

Story begins with the coming of Ms. Forbes, a nanny hired to take charge of two small boys while their parents are off on a 6-week cruise. The boys (well played by Alexis Castañares and Víctor César Villalobos) are Caribbean versions of the Katzenjammer Kids, out for lots of mischief and fun. Things change, of course, when nanny begins to impose military-style discipline and revenge is a logical answer.

During the day, Ms. Forbes is like a field marshal, but at night her Prussian rigidity falls away. The boys are awakened by nightly binges: dressed in a slip she drinks copious amounts of tequila, mutters verses from Kleist and hankers after the boys' muscular scuba instructor, Aquiles.

Production values are high, especially underwater photography.

Artsy ending seems tacked on deliberately to confuse the audience and provide a depth that frankly isn't there. Black-humored vehicle follows mildly in the vein of director's 1985 comedy "Doña Herlinda And Her Son" and should find international reception promising but not enduring. —*Lent.*

Two To Tango
(U.S.-ARGENTINE)

New York   A Concorde Pictures release of a New Horizons Picture-Aries Films Intl. coproduction. Produced by Roger Corman, Alex Sessa. Directed by Hector Olivera. Screenplay, Yolande Finch, Jose Pablo Feinman, based on Feinman's novel "Last Days Of The Victim;" camera (color), Leo Solis; editor, Ed Lowe; music, Cardozo Ocampo, with additional tangos by Raúl Garello; art direction, Al Guglielmoni. Reviewed on Virgin Vision vidcassette, N.Y., Jan. 19, 1989. MPAA Rating: R. Running time: **87 MIN.**

James Conrad . . . . Don Stroud
Cecilia Lorca . . . . Adrienne Sachs
Paulino Velasco . . . . Duilio Marzio
Dean Boyle . . . . Michael Cavanaugh
Lorenzo (Lucky) Lara . . . . . Alberto Segado
Carlos Pino . . . . Francisco Cocuzza
(English soundtrack)

■ **This uneven, spiced-up English-lingo remake of Adolfo Aristarain's gaucho thriller "Last Days Of The Victim," helmed by veteran Argentine director Hector Olivera (who produced the 1982 version), has gone direct to homevid.**

"Tango" plot concerns a professional killer (Stroud) afflicted with weltschmerz. As an agent of death, life has lost its meaning and his sleep is haunted by nightmares. His dream is to escape to Nepal ("the top of the world") to start a new life.

Instead, antihero goes to "the bottom of the world," with an assignment to kill a powerful and heavily guarded man in Buenos Aires. This is to be his final murder-for-hire. En route, he falls

---

ORIGINAL FILM
Los Ultimos Dias
de la Victima
(ARGENTINE)

Aries release of own production. Produced by Hector Olivera and Luis Osvaldo Repetto. Directed by Adolfo Aristarain. Features entire cast. Screenplay, Aristarain, Jose Pablo Feinman, based on latter's novel; camera (Eastmancolor), Horacio Maira; art direction, Abel Facello; costumes, Trini Munoz Ibanez; assistant director, Jorge Gundin. Reviewed at the Normandie Theater, Buenos Aires, April 8, 1982. Running time: **91 MIN.**

With: Federico Luppi, Soledad Silveyra, Ulises Dumont, China Zorrilla, Elena Tasisto, Julio de Grazia.

---

in love with a beautiful N.Y.-born tango dancer (Adrienne Sachs), who happens to be his target's lover.

Voyeuristic gameplan includes extended spying on his target, bugging the house and watching surreptitiously while he makes love to the dancer. Everywhere sex abounds, hot and steamy, heightened by torrid dance scenes at a

club run by an old friend.

Whereas the original dealt with moral sense (the killer is the only moral man in an immoral world), this remake concerns a man over his head in an infernal machine out of control and is almost existential in design. Love gives life new meaning, as does the promise of imminent escape from his current life.

Pic suggests a Colombian international cocaine connection, although the killer never knows who he is working for. Also, his rooming house is run by former Nazis, which is meant to add to film's sinister tone, but comes off merely as a gratuitous element.

Stroud puts in a good performance. Tech credits are fine, with lots of tension, but pacing is quirky. Hoofing sequences are enjoyable, yet narrative makes several unbelievable leaps — such as the dancer's ready acceptance of him as a paid killer. —*Lent.*

Das Sonntagskind
(Sunday's Child)
(WEST GERMAN)

San Francisco   A Nour Film production. Written and directed by Marianne Rosenbaum, based on book by Gudrun Mebs. Camera (color), Alexander Opp; editor, Helga Endler; music, Konstantin Wecker. Reviewed at On Screen Film Festival, S.F., Jan. 15, 1989. Running time: **89 MIN.**

Anna . . . . Gudrun Mebs
Barbara . . . . Nurith-Hayat Samaan
Wolfgang . . . . Hans Peter Korff
Also with: Mirjam Niemeier, Wenzel Heubeck, Timm Schnabbe, Udo Weinberger, Johannes Wilbrink, Dietrich von Watzdorf, Luca Lombardi.

■ **A less ambiguous ending might have broadened the American appeal of "Sunday's Child," but the West German film by Marianne Rosenbaum nonetheless deals deftly with the conflicts women have between maternity and the marketplace.**

Based on her own book adapted by Rosenbaum, Gudrun Mebs is very good as a single-minded unmarried writer totally involved in the novels she grinds out in her smoke-filled, messy apartment.

Inspired to write about an orphan, Mebs turns on her tape recorder and becomes a "Sunday mother" to a 10-year-old (Eurith-Hayat Samaan). Initially, the little girl is just one more subject for research.

Like most screen orphans, however, Samaan is emotionally irresistible and Mebs is soon up to her carbon paper in maternal feelings. None of this is maudlin, however, and Rosenbaum sketches the growing attachment between the two with a satisfying blend of humor and sweetness.

Once hooked, Mebs wants to become an adoptive mother and it's obvious she would be a benefit to the lonely, needy Samaan.

Unfortunately, Mebs and motherhood don't mesh within the rules for adoption. Though published, her novels aren't the source of a steady income and she can't think of abandoning her art for a regular job.

The authorities suggest marriage as another acceptable solution. A sometimes boyfriend (Hans Peter Korff) offers his hand, but he's a philanderer.

Both the would-be mother and daughter are touchingly torn by the seeming impossibility of their legal union. Unfortunately, Rosenbaum seems unsure whether she wants to solve their problem or be content with a denunciation of the bureaucracy.

At the end, it's unclear whether the woman and child actually end up together or are just left with their fantasies of being together. Nothing terribly wrong with that, of course, except for those who would have liked to know for sure.
—*Har.*

Slipping Into Darkness

New York An MCEG release of a Jonathan D. Krane production. Produced by Krane. Executive producer, William J. Rouhana Jr. Coproducers, Don Schain, Simon R. Lewis; line producer, Lydia Pilcher. Written and directed by Eleanor Gaver. Camera (Foto-Kem color), Loren Bivens; editor, Barbara Pokras; music, Joey Rand; sound, Dennis Carr; production design, Patricia Woodbridge; assistant director, Heidi Gutman; additional camera, Bobby Bukowski; associate producer, Judith Ann Friend. Reviewed on Virgin Vision vidcassette, N.Y., Jan. 14, 1989. MPAA Rating: R. Running time: **87 MIN.**

Carlyle . . . . Michelle Johnson
Fritz . . . . John DiAquino
Ebin . . . . Neil! Barry
Genevieve . . . . Anastasia Fielding
Alex . . . . Cristen Kauffman
Otis . . . . Vyto Ruginis
Also with: David Sherrill, Terrence Markovich, Adam Roarke.

■A youth-themed film noir in the new genre initiated by "River's Edge," "Slipping Into Darkness" is an interesting near-miss that ultimately becomes too cute for its own good.

Picture opened theatrically in limited fashion last November and is en route to videostores.

Michelle Johnson, Anastasia

Fielding and Cristen Kauffman portray three spoiled, rich college girls in Nebraska who run afoul of hero John DiAquino when they kid around with his retarded brother (Neill Barry in a small but telling role). Johnson (whose dad is the college's dean) accidentally hit the kid's dog with her Mercedes and when Barry is found dead at the railroad tracks, DiAquino sets out with the aid of his biker pals (Vyto Ruginis and David Sherrill) for revenge.

Filmmaker Eleanor Gaver bears down accurately on social class resentment and small-town provincialism well in pic's first half, but it trails off into kinky bondage motifs as the have-nots kidnap the heroines to punish them. Final reel is loaded with unconvincing revelations (flashbacks providing alternate information on the boy's death) and dubious plot twists ranging from incest to a surprising homicidal maniac.

Johnson is an effective anti-heroine and contrasting newcomers Fielding (extremely tall) and Kauffman also make distinctive impressions. Of the male protagonists, Vyto Ruginis' mannered performance is tough to take.
—*Lor.*

Marratam
(Masquerade)
(INDIAN)

New Delhi A Doordharshan India production. Directed by G. Aravindan. Screenplay, Aravindan, based on a play by Kavalam Narayana Panicker; camera (color). Shaji; editor, Bose; narrative poetry and choreography, Panicker; singers, Panicker, Kavalam, Sreekumar, Pulluvan Narayanan and wife, Velayudhan Asan and Group. Reviewed at Films Division Auditorium, New Delhi, Jan. 24, 1989. Running time: **90 MIN.**

With: Urmila Unni, Sadhanam Krishnan Kutty, Kalamandalam Kesavan, Thiruvarangu.

(Soundtrack in Malayam)

■"Masquerade," latest effort by Keralan director Aravindan, is a complex experimental film blending a traditional Kathakali play with an exploration of the actor's identity and questions about reality and illusion in art.

Produced by India's state television Doordarshan, "Masquerade" is sure to make fest rounds and find takers abroad in the more refined realms of art cinema.

With the help of only a few explanatory titles scattered throughout the film, Aravindan gets the essence of the complicated K.N. Panicker play across. In the last scene of a highly stylized Kathaka-

li play, the villain Keechaka is slain by Bhima, disguised as Valalan. A modern "audience" enacts three versions of the murder, each set to a different style of folk singing.

In the first, the feudal lord takes responsibility for the killing, because Keechaka made advances to his wife. In the second, his wife says she killed the ugly actor Kelu who played Keechaka, because she was so disappointed that he wasn't the embodiment of male charm, like the character he played. In the third, Kelu's acting students say they are the real killers; they murdered neither Keechaka nor Kelu, but feelings in the minds of the people.

A master of striking images, Aravindan alternates his colorful stage set with sunrise over the forest and shots from nature. Music and lensing are as hypnotic as the actors' Kathakali costumes.

Like a multi-media performance on film, "Masquerade" puts Aravindan in the forefront of India's experimental filmmakers, as well as showing off his gifts as a refined practitioner of Keralan folk music and dance.

A potentially mystical element in the film is corrected by the sensual-intellectual staging. Intertitles are suggestive and thought-provoking, skillfully woven into the images. —*Yung.*

That's Adequate
(COLOR/B&W)

Park City A Vidmark release of a That's Adequate Co. production. Produced by Irving Schwartz, Harry Hurwitz. Executive producer, John Manocherian. Written and directed by Hurwitz. Camera, (color, b&w), João Fernandes. No other credits available. Reviewed at the U.S. Film Festival, Park City, Utah (in competition), Jan. 27, 1989. No MPAA rating. Running time: **80 MIN.**

With: Tony Randall, James Coco, Jerry Stiller, Anne Meara, Ina Balin, Anne Bloom, Irwin Corey, Susan Dey, Robert Downey Jr., Richard Lewis, Chuck McCann, Stuart Pankin, Peter Riegert, Robert Staats, Brother Theodore, Robert Townsend, Robert Vaughn, Marshall Brickman, Martha Coolidge, Joe Franklin, Renée Taylor, Bruce Willis.

■For understandable reasons, those in the motion picture business are often drawn inexorably to participate in a satire of same and "That's Adequate" has a load of them. The cast obviously had a good time and hopefully everybody will get a videocassette to amuse their friends.

Though funny in fits, "Adequate" is little more than that, rarely original and sometimes surprisingly imitative of what's al-

ready been done.

Narrator Tony Randall is kind of wonderfully pompous as he recalls the history of Adequate Studios founded by a B-budget mogul (the late James Coco). Segment on the early years, when the studio was cranking out such hits as "Sluts Of The South" and "Singing In The Synagogue," provides this pic's best stuff, hardly able to miss given the material.

Some of the subsequent concepts are outrageous enough (unable to compete with the majors for prewar financing; Adequate takes money from the Nazis to do a sympathetic "Young Adolf"), but the payoff is usually weak unless you're bowled over by Robert Vaughn as an hysterical Hitler.

From time to time, there are amusing ideas: Unable to afford full color, Adequate offers one film in a different color each month, illustrated by an awful clip "from one of our red months."

When stumped for anything else, writer-director Harry Hurwitz falls back on simple vulgarity. Some of it is vulgar, indeed, unfortunately with no justifying humor.

Except for those involved, the world will little note nor long remember what they did here, which they will probably be very grateful for later. —*Har.*

Prisoners Of Inertia

Park City A Northwinds Entertainment production, in association with Magnus Films. Produced by Zanne Devine, Deirdre Gainor. Executive producer, Julie Kemper. Written and directed by J. Noyes Scher. Camera (TVC color), James McCalmont; editor, Chip Cronkite, Darren Kloomok, Juliet Weber; music, William Swindler; sound, William Sarokin; production design, Bill Groom; art direction, Betsy Klompus; assistant director, Stephen Apicella; casting, Deborah Brown, Allison Jones. Reviewed at the U.S. Film Festival Park City, Utah (in competition), Jan. 28, 1989. No MPAA Rating. Running time: **95 MIN.**

Sam . . . . Amanda Plummer
Dave . . . . Christopher Rich
Weed . . . . Mark Boone Jr.
Ogden . . . . John C. McGinley
Charlotte . . . . Melinda Mullins
Birney . . . . Gary Keats
Raul . . . . Raul Aranas

■A lot more seems to happen in "Prisoners Of Inertia" than ever really does. Amanda Plummer and Christopher Rich create some very funny moments in their highly improbable odyssey from Manhattan to Hoboken, a journey of little distance but considerable daffiness.

Writer-director J. Noyes Scher risks it all in the first 10 minutes or so with newlyweds Plummer and Rich squeezed into their tiny apartment, she in the bathtub, he in the bed.

By the time the couple have their day planned — or unplanned — the audience is either anxious to spend the rest of Sunday with the pair or the picture is in deep trouble. Scher won't have it any other way.

Fortunately, Plummer is delightfully oddball, almost militantly indecisive. She has a lot to be undecided about, including her marriage. Boyishly charming, Rich is playing at wedlock and a writing career, self-centered about both and anything else that comes up. (He is handsome and likable, his feature debut establishing him as a potential matinee idol. He can act, besides.)

They have a briefly hilarious encounter with a worthless boring acquaintance, John C. McGinley, who's too soon departed. It's a shame Scher had no way to bring him back into the story again.

Very little of first reel's characterization and relationships come into play later. Given her earlier feistiness, Plummer is disappointingly accepting and calm about old girlfriends and fresh disasters.

She's still likable and so is Rich. So it's a likable picture, made more so by William Swindler's pseudo-Parisian accordion score, which has a point to it. —Har.

Striker
(ITALIAN)

New York   A Panther Entertainment presentation of a Filmustang production, in association with Key West Prods. Produced by Giorgio Salvioni. Directed by "Stephen M. Andrews" (Enzo G. Castellari). Screenplay, Tito Carpi, Umberto Lenzi; camera (Fotocinema color), Sandro Mancori; editor, Gianfranco Amicucci; music, Detto Mariano; sound (Dolby), Luciano Muratori; assistant director, Stefania Girolami; production manager, Giuseppe Pedersoli; special effects, Paolo Ricci; special action supervisor, Jeff Moldovan. Reviewed on AIP Home Video videassette, N.Y., Jan. 16, 1989. MPAA Rating: R. Running time: 89 MIN.

John Slade . . . . Frank Zagarino
Marta . . . . Melonee Rodgers
Frank Morris . . . . John Phillip Law
Kayatzin . . . . John Steiner
Dutchman . . . . Werner Pochat
Gen. Rosen . . . . Frank Zagarino Sr.
    Also with: Peter Gold, Mike Kirton, Daniel Greene.

(English soundtrack)

■ Bearing the generic title "Striker" (used for numerous '80s action pics), this above-average Italian actioner actually is a 1987 production called "Combat Force" introducing a pair of impressive gung-ho stars.

Frank Zagarino is the blond commando blackmailed (on a trumped-up charge) to go to Nicaragua on behalf of the Patriotic Freedom Organization to rescue a journalist (John Phillip Law) being held by the Sandinistas and their evil Soviet leader (John Steiner). Accompanying him on his mission is beautiful black commando Marta (Melonee Rodgers) who proves to be able to hold her own and then some in both hand-to-hand combat and wielding automatic weaponry.

Pic, attractively lensed on location in Santo Domingo, is a series of battles, captures and escapes that's well-executed by Enzo G. Castellari, here credited with a new pseudonym: Stephen M. Andrews. Zagarino is physically right for the role and has some okay emotional scenes later on after being introed as a monotone "Rambo" clone. Costar Rodgers is a find; her combination of statuesque beauty and convincing physical prowess mark a logical successor to Pam Grier.

Weird touch has Zagarino's real-life dad (who bears a close family resemblance to the star) cast as the evil general in charge of the rightwing PFO. Their final confrontation carries some added bite.

The Italian filmmakers take potshots at both superpowers meddling in Latin America, with Steiner a heinous torturer for the Russkies while the PFO is revealed to be shipping arms to both the contras and Sandinistas as part of a drug-trafficking ring.

Tech credits are fine. —Lor.

Klassezämekunft
(Class Meeting)
(SWISS)

Zurich   A Monopole Pathé Films release of a Condor Features production. Executive producer, Peter-Christian Fueter. Written and directed by Walter Deuber, Peter Stierlin. Camera (Eastman color), Edwin Horak; editor, Daniela Roderer; music, Jonas C. Haefeli; sound, Hans Künzi; art direction, Franz Maurer; production manager, Rose-Marie Schneider. Reviewed at Corso 1, Zurich, Dec. 27, 1988. Running time: 87 MIN.

    With: Anne-Marie Blanc, Paul Hubschmid, Stephanie Glaser, Lukas Ammann, Eva Langraf, Hannes Schmidhauser, Inigo Gallo, Peter W. Staub, Ruedi Walter, Ursula Andress, Mathias Gnädinger, Hans Leutenegger, François Meienberg, Irene Schiesser, Sabina Ritzmann, Gerardo Zanetti.

■ An Agatha Christie-type Swiss meller unites for the first time nine of Switzerland's most popular vet players, plus Swiss-born Ursula Andress in her first homemade film. Script and direction do not quite live up to total b.o. expectations and the high-caliber cast.

Patterned after the "Ten Little Indians" scheme, the story by Walter Deuber and Peter Stierlin (who also directed) concerns an invitation by the owner of an off-the-road mansion to eight of her former classmates 50 years after their graduation. During an excursion way back when to the Rhine Falls, one of them (disliked by most) "accidentally" fell into the waterfalls. It had never been revealed nor proven that he was actually pushed.

The hostess' intention to settle the old account (the dead boy was her lover and she was pregnant at the time) leads to a series of deaths during the evening — some plotted, some accidental — as well as a "surprise" ending.

Script doesn't seem quite logic-proof and the directing team's lack of feature film experience (both did mostly tv and documentary work up to now) shows. The music score is too obtrusive.

Assets include the excellent, atmospheric camerawork by Edwin Horak. More important where boxoffice is concerned is the handpicked cast, each a local name. Anne-Marie Blanc, playing the hostess, is one of Switzerland's "great ladies" of stage and screen. Paul Hubschmid may be known to an older generation overseas from his Hollywood days as Paul Christian.

Ursula Andress looks as decorative as ever in a relatively small role. The others are all in top form, with a special nod for characterization to Ruedi Walter and Stephanie Glaser. —Mezo.

El Día Que Me Quieras
(The Day You Love Me)
(COLOMBIAN-VENEZUELAN)

San Juan   A Warner Bros release of a Focine-Productora Colombian de Peliculas-Publicidad Ténica (Venezuela) production. Directed by Sergio Dow. Screenplay, José Ignacio Cabrujas, Dow, Olinto Taverna, Jorge Goldenberg, based on the play by Cabrujas; camera (color), Edward Lachman; editor, Sabine Mamou, Taverna; music, Luis María Serra; sound, Victor José Luckert; art direction, Miguel González. Reviewed at San Juan (Puerto Rico) Film Festival, Oct. 3, 1988. Running time: 76 MIN.

    With: Graciela Duffau, Fausto Verdial, María Eugenia Dávila, Ulises Dumont, Claudio Berge, Adriana Herrán, Juan Leyrado, Omar Sánchez.

■ Based on the legit work of Venezuelan playwright José Ignacio Cabrujas, "El Día Que Me Quieras" is a complex film that deals with illusions and lies cloaked within Latin myths.

Story is set in 1935 Caracas, last stop of gaucho tango singer Carlos Gardel before the fatal plane crash on his triumphant return to his homeland. Pic shares the same title as Gardel's final Hollywood effort.

Argentine actor Claudio Berge is amazing in his recreation here of Gardel, whose mythlike presence permeates the entire pic, whether crooning tangos (dubbed from real Gardel recordings) or being the charming Latin caballero. Rather than portrayed as a real man, Gardel is always depicted in character as if he just emerged from one of his film roles.

Pic's timeframe also encompasses the last year of Venezuela's dictator Juan Vicente Gómez when the political climate was rife with activity. In contrast to Gardel is militant Marxist Pio Miranda (Fausto Verdial), whose longrange plans include moving with his girlfriend of 10 years to a blissful life in the Ukraine.

The two myths (romantic vs. political) overlap and clash, exposing the lies, hopes and false dreams of an era on the eve of change. Intelligent script uses humor and occasional caricature to make its point.

Dreamy photography by N.Y.-based lenser Ed Lachman and able art direction capture the period, while thesping pinpoints differing social attitudes of the principals.

Pic should do well in Latino markets, especially Argentina, where Gardel has achieved a near god-like stature. —Lent.

Arhus By Night
(DANISH)

Copenhagen   A Karne Film release of a Per Holst Film production. Produced by Per Holst. Written and directed by Nils Malmros. Camera (Eastmancolor), Jan Weincke; editor, Birger Möller Jensen; music, Gunnar Möllar Pedersen; production design, Sören Kragh Sörensen; sound, Niels Arild; costumes, Pia Myrdal, Francoise Nicolet; assistant director, Sören Kjär Nielsen; production manager, Ib Tardini; camera for exteriors, Dirk Brüel; Danish Film Institute producer-consultants, Peter Poulsen, Kirsten Rask. Reviewed at the Dagmar, Copenhagen, Jan. 20, 1989. Running time: 98 MIN.

Frederik . . . . Thomas Schindel
Ronnie . . . . Tom McEwan
Flemming . . . . Michael Caröe

Delcuran . . . . Sören Oestergaard
Anton . . . . Lars H.U.G.
Lisa . . . . Line Arlien-Söborg
Pernille . . . . Vibeke Borberg
Frederik's mother . . . . Ghita Norby
    Also with: Thomas Howalt Olsen, Steen

Lommer, Robert Gellin, Dennis Otto Hansen, Niels Henrik Markvad, Henrik Tolboe, Carsten Gjörtz, Mads Jacob Poulsen, Thomas Rasmus Sörensen, Sören Bärentzen, Jörgen Kristian Schindel, Suzette Kempf, Eva Maria Zacho, Linda Andersen, Vibeke Andkjär Axvärd.

■ **"Arhus By Night" is Nils Malmros' very personal memoir of the shooting of his first feature, which is seen as having its own two parallel storylines, one about the helmer's early boyhood, the other about his first adolescent love.**

Thrown in are sequences of dreams and nightmares, and what works for a while as charming self-indulgency eventually turns into silly and tedious repetition.

Malmros is just fine when telling in the film-within-the-film, of his pranks, fears and wishful (sexual) thinking as a doctor's small son exploring the women's sun parlors, the underground passageways and even the morgue of a large hospital. In describing his more memorable experiences as an adolescent, he is also true to his well-tried formula form.

Broader and more traditional, although still affectionate, fun & games are conjured up by Malmros when he tells of the arrival and work in provincial Arhus of the professional Copenhagen film crew that is to help him through his first major helmer effort. Individual crew members' vignettes are given spirit and polish by veteran actor Tom McEwan and by relatively untried talent such as Michael Caröe and Sören Oestergaard. Thomas Schindel in the role of Malmros himself combines tenacious strength with shyness in the face of all the surrounding cynicism and locker-room hilarity.
—*Kell.*

Jydekompagniet
(The Jut-Nuts)
(DANISH)

Copenhagen   A Nordisk Film release of a Nordisk Film production, with the Danish Film Institute. Produced by Michael Obel. DFI consultant producer, Georg Metz. Written and directed by Finn Henriksen, based on story by Finn Nörbygaard, Jacob Haugaard, Steen Herdel. Lasse Spang Olsen; camera (Eastmancolor), Lasse Spang Olsen; editor, Finn Henriksen, Karen Margrethe Nielsen; music, Jesper Ranum; sound, Jörgen Lyd Nielsen; costumes, Bente Ranning; assistant director, Sanni Sylvester Petersen; production management, Jens Arnoldus. Reviewed at the Palads, Copenhagen, Dec. 14, 1988. Running time: **91 MIN.**
Finn . . . . Finn Nörbygaard
Jacob . . . . Jacob Haugaard
Social worker . . . . Kirsten Lehfeldt
Jacob's brother . . . . Sören Oestergaard

Mrs. Bang-Bendix . . . . Ellen Winther
                                  Lembourn
The guru . . . . Hans Henrik Bärentzen
His manager . . . . Poul Hüttel
Disciple Maibritt . . . . Michelle Björn
                                  Andersen
Also with: Pia Koch, Ulla Asbjörn Andersen, Sören Hauch-Fausböll, Birthe Kjär, Surya Mistry, Bendt Reiner.

■ **Danish tv stars Finn Nörbygaard and Jacob Haugaard bring their act to the big screen with "The Jut-Nuts," a venture that may pay off via fast local saturation booking but not an inch further.**

Where the pair's original tv skits were fast, funny and thrown at an unsuspecting audience, journeyman writer-director Finn Henriksen has not been able to fashion the ideas supplied by the Nörbygaard-Haugaard duo into a feature of sustained energy and movement. In the development of a story about the Jutlanders' attempt at making the grade as private eyes, all the fun is delivered like one long walk on sore feet.

The clown detectives must invade an Oriental guru's headquarters in a moat-surrounded castle to free the deluded Flower Child daughter of a wealthy family. One of them falls in love with the girl, the other seems about to fall into the moat.

A social worker (Kirsten Lehfeldt) serves as a target for some satirical darts thrown at Welfare State excesses. Sweet anarchy is represented by Jacob's auto mechanic-cum-hustler brother (Sören Oestergaard).

The cast contributes with bits and pieces of fairly intelligent fun that never is allowed to fuse into a sustaining context. Out of context is veteran pop singer Birthe Kjär, but she belts out a song with the professionalism absent elsewhere in the film. —*Kell.*

ARCHIVE REVIEW

La Torre de los Siete Jorobados
(The Tower Of The Seven Hunchbacks)
(SPANISH-B&W)

New York   A Producciones Luis Judes-Germán López España Films production. Directed by Edgar Neville. Screenplay, José Santagini, Neville, based on the book by Emilio Carrère; camera (b&w), Enrique Barkelby; editor, Sara Ontañon; music, Azana. Reviewed in series "Images in the Shadows," Museum of Modern Art, N.Y., Jan. 5, 1989. Running time: **81 MIN.**
Basilio Beltrán . . . . Antonio Casal
Doña Inés . . . . Isabel de Pomes
Dr. Sabatino . . . . Guillermo Marín

Also with: Julia Lajos, Manolita Moran, Julio Panelo, Félix de Pomes.

■ **The 1944 Spanish pic "The Tower Of The Seven Hunchbacks," based on the book by Emilio Carrère, is a Gothic oddity which, although cited from time to time in books dealing with horror and fantasy genres, is seldom seen.**

Filmmaker-writer-diplomat Edgar Neville, also known as the Count of Berlanga de Duero, has mixed elements of horror, comedy, crime and expressionist-inspired sets to relate a mystery tale that revolves around an ancient upside-down tower burrowing deep into the earth under contemporary Madrid.

Subterranean labyrinth was built by Jews who preferred to live underground than leave Spain during the 1492 Inquisition, and it currently serves as hideout for a gang of hunchbacks involved in counterfeiting.

Like "Hamlet," tale begins with an unquiet ghost. A sinister-looking, lanky, 1-eyed anthropologist, murdered for his discovery of the secret lair, wishes to protect his lovely young niece who is currently in danger. He uses his power to enlist the aid of the impressionable but sympathetic hero Basilio Beltrán (Antonio Casal).

Representing the forces of evil, tale's villain (Guillermo Marín) has an unexplained hypnotic power that he uses on the girl — à la Dr. Caligari — as he plots his murderous intent.

Comic bits throughout, such as a phantom Napoleon who can't find the right seance, bring macabre humor to the disturbing tale.

Story has enough bizarre elements to intrigue contemporary viewers. Renewed interest may spark more frequent screenings of this seldom-seen curiosity. —*Lent.*

BERLIN FEST REVIEWS

Esquilache
(SPANISH)

Madrid   A Sabre Films production. Produced by José Sámano. Directed by Josefina Molina. Screenplay, Molina, Joaquin Oristrell, José Sámano, based on play "Un Soñador Para Un Pueblo" by Antonio Buero Vallejo; camera (Eastmancolor), Juan Amorós; editor, Pablo G. del Amo; music, José Nieto; sets. Ramior Gómez, Javier Artiñano. Reviewed at Cine Paz, Madrid, Jan. 26, 1989. (In Berlin Film Festival — competing.) Running time: **105 MIN.**
Marqués de Esquilache . . Fernando Fernán
                                  Gómez
Antonio Campos . . . . José Luis
                                  López Vázquez
Fernanda . . . . Angela Molina
Pastora Paterno . . . . Concha Velasco
King Carlos III . . . . Adolfo Marsillach
Isabel de Farnesio . . . . Amparo Rivelles
Duque de Villasanta . . . . Alberto Closas

■ **Berlin fest entry is a handsomely produced period piece about a minor footnote of Spanish 18th century history during the reign of King Carlos III when his minister, the Marqués de Esquilache (also a Bourbon of Italian upbringing), tried to bring reforms to the country but succeeded only in triggering a mutiny for his troubles.**

Pic is less a critique of Spain's backwardness and obtuseness at that time than a study of the aged Esquilache (well played by Fernando Fernán Gómez), the unhappy Italian who vainly strove to bring a spark of enlightenment to Spaniards.

Despite the distinguished cast of thesps and a high budget (by local standards), pic drags along due to weak scripting and use of constant flashbacks within a flashback, that lasts the whole film.

The few action sequences are wooden and unconvincing and we know little more of Esquilache at the end of the film than we did at the beginning. His seeming romance with an ignorant palace maid remains sketchy and of scant interest.

Sidestepped is the real hero of the story (historically speaking), Carlos III, who did succeed in "illuminating" a city and a country wallowing in ignorance and brutality. The talents of Spanish thesps Adolfo Marsillach, Concha Velasco and José Vázquez are never given a chance to shine through.

Local subject matter of pic, dispassionate directing and a meandering script will make item a hard sell outside Spain. —*Besa.*

Naga Bonar
(INDONESIAN)

Berlin   A Pt. Prasidi Teta Film presentation and production. Directed by M.T. Risyaf. Screenplay, Asrul Sani; camera (Cinemascope, color), Sri Atmo; editor, Karsono Hadi; music, Franky Haden; production design, Radjul Kahfi. Reviewed at Berlin Film Festival (Forum of Young Film), Feb. 12, 1989. Running time: **100 MIN.**
Nagar Bonar . . . . Deddy Mizwar
Kirana . . . . Nurul Arifin
Also with: Roldiah Matulessi. Wawan Sarwani.

■ "Naga Bonar" is an impressively produced farce about a pickpocket's self-promotion to the rank of general in the Freedom Forces that won the Indonesians their independence after Japanese occupation and Dutch colonial rule in 1945.

Mildly funny at best, M.T. Risyaf's film conveys its jokes and emotional points too indulgently to stand much of a chance with Western audiences beyond the international festival circuit.

Deddy Mizwar, a rotund, popular comedy actor in Indonesia, plays Naga Bonar mostly as a Sancho Panza suddenly finding himself in Don Quixote's armor. Emboldened by his new rank, he pushes his men around quite roughly. However, when one of them steals his insignia to conduct war in a different way and is killed by Dutch bullets, Bonar bawls like a child.

It is never clear how Bonar could lead Indonesia to victory, but that is how the film ends. He seems better at playing the guitar to woo Kirana, the beautiful woman (played wittily by Nurul Arifin) he is sent to protect.

There is good acting in secondary roles and episodes of human folly in war and peace come across successfully. —*Kell.*

Celia
(AUSTRALIAN)

Sydney   A Hoyts (Australia) release of a Seon Films production. Produced by Timothy White, Gordon Glenn. Executive producer, Bryce Menzies. Directed by Ann Turner. Screenplay, Turner; camera (color), Geoffrey Simpson; editor, Ken Sallows; music, Chris Neal; production design, Peta Lawson; sound, Lloyd Carrick; production manager, Lynda House; assistant director, Phil Jones; casting, Liz Mullinar; associate producer, Ian Pringle. Reviewed at Hoyts Center, Sydney, Nov. 20, 1988. (At Berlin Film Festival — Panorama.) Running time: **102 MIN.**
Celia . . . . Rebecca Smart
Ray . . . . Nicholas Eadie
Pat . . . . Maryanne Fahey
Alice . . . . Victoria Longley
Uncle John . . . . William Zappa
Teacher . . . . Deborra-Lee Furness

 "Celia" starts out as a likeable family pic about the traumas of a sensitive 9-year-old girl growing up in a Melbourne suburb in the conservative late '50s. It winds up as something quite different, with the filmmakers implicitly endorsing a violent act of defiance which results in the murder of a policeman.

Whether audiences will accept this premise or not will be a key factor in the film's eventual commercial career. Pic participates in Panorama section of the Berlin Film Festival.

Firsttime director Ann Turner won an award for her screenplay of "Celia" from the Australian Writers' Guild in 1984; production was made possible thanks to the innovative Seon Films production company of helmer Ian Pringle, with support from the Australian Film Commission and Film Victoria.

Celia, 9, played by Rebecca Smart (who was the sprig in Dusan Makavejev's "The Coca-Cola Kid") is an only child; she loves her old grandmother more than her rather distant parents, and when she discovers her grandmother's body, in the film's opening scene, it's the first of several traumas. Troubled by nightmares featuring monsters from a book read to her at school, Celia is delighted when newcomers, with three children, come to live next door; and finds Alice (Victoria Longley) far more sympathetic than her own mother. Trouble is, Alice and her husband are active members of the Communist Party, and before long Celia is forbidden to see her new friends.

The child's other obsession is her pet rabbit, but she is faced with more drama when a national plague of rabbits results in the Victorian state government calling for the handing over of all domestic bunnies. She blames her uncle, the local policeman, for enforcing the law, and when her beloved rabbit dies in Melbourne Zoo, she takes a surprisingly violent revenge.

Despite intimations of horror in the nightmares that plague Celia throughout the film, and the occasional brutality of the children's games, there's little preparation for Celia's lethal act of rebellion against her hated uncle, an act for which she receives no retribution. Indeed, at fadeout, she's seen still playing her fantasy games, though now they're more macabre than before.

Some will doubtless be startled by this turn of events, but it certainly makes for an interesting, if not totally realized, concept. Turner's direction is competent, but the film runs much too long, and a harsher mood was required. Much of the time, the film plays as an amusing look at the world of children, with allusions to adult intolerance, via the rabbit ban and the anti-Communist mood of the times.

Rebecca Smart, on-screen throughout, is effective as the ultimately scary Celia, but the film's best performance comes from Victoria Longley as the warm-hearted neighbor; her departure from the film two-thirds of the way in leaves a palpable void.

Geoffrey Simpson's camerawork is tops, though the geography of the area around Celia's house remains vague, as do the family relationships at first. It looms as a tricky prospect which will have to rely on good notices to find a receptive audience.
—*Strat.*

Fun Down There

Berlin   An Angelina production. Produced and directed by Roger Stigliano. Screenplay, production design, Stigliano; camera (color), Peggy Ahwesh, Eric Saks; editor, Stigliano; Keith Sanborn; music, James Baker, Wayne Hammond; sound, Karin Litzmann. Carolyn Skaife; production manager, Peggy Ahwesh. Reviewed at Berlin Film Festival (Panorama), Feb. 12, 1989. Running time: **85 MIN.**
Buddy Fields . . . . Michael Waite
Joseph . . . . Nickolas B. Nagourney
Angelo . . . . Martin Goldin
Judy Fields . . . . Jeanne Smith
Mrs. Fields . . . . Betty Waite
Mr. Fields . . . . Harold Waite
Sandy . . . . Yvonne Fisher
    Also with: Gretschen Somerville (Greta), Gary Onsum (Cary), Paul Saindon (Singer), Kenneth R. Clarke (Kent), Judy Joseph (Woman in Red), Kayla Serotti (Kayla), Caroline Paddock (Catherine), Howard Roxs (Simon), Richard Hailey (Ricky).

■ A low-budget U.S. indie first feature from Roger Stigliano, "Fun Down There" is an uneven comedy-drama about a gay youth from the sticks who finds love in the Big Apple. Pic's pretentious elements outweigh its occasional charms.

Buddy (Michael Waite) leaves a job on the farm and life with his folks in upstate New York. In Manhattan he's soon picked up by Joseph, a photographer from Brooklyn, and initiated into sex.

Before long he has a job washing dishes, a second lover, Angelo, and a lot of new friends. Film is subtitled "A Week In The Life," and seven days is all it takes for this eager virgin to get started on a new lifestyle.

Early scenes with mom and dad and knowing sister are quite amusing, as is a party sequence peopled with various eccentrics. Too often, however, the film is burdened with uninteresting talk. Every so often it grinds to a halt for some wholly extraneous, home-movie-ish footage of city streets, often without sound.

Sex scenes are explicit enough to alert censors in some parts of the world, but the film takes a responsible attitude toward AIDS, with Buddy's first lover instructing him on safe sex. Performances are on the amateurish side, in keeping with the slapdash mood.

Though well received in Berlin, "Fun Down There" will have a tough time in the outside world, though screenings in gay areas could turn it into a cult item. Technical credits are below par.
—*Strat.*

Mielott befejezi roptét
a denever
(Before The Bat's Flight Is Done)
(HUNGARIAN)

Budapest   A Hungarofilm presentation. A Dialog Film production. Written and directed by Péter Timár. Camera (Eastmancolor), Sándor Kardos; editor, Timár; music, Zoltán Farkas; sound, Tamás Márkus; sets, László Gárdonyi; costumes, Zsuzsa Pártényi. Reviewed at Hungarian Film Week, Budapest. Feb. 5, 1989. (In Berlin Film Festival — competing). Running time: **94 MIN.**
Robi . . . . Robert Csontos
Mother . . . . Erika Bodnár
Lover . . . . Gábor Máté

■ Péter Timár's record as a special effects artist and cameraman and his fascination for videoclips show in this picture, selected for the Berlin competition. The subject is kinky enough and so is the treatment.

The story basically is the classical romantic triangle with a perverse twist. It starts as a sort of comedy, goes into a family drama and comes very close to a horror movie before it is over.

A divorced middle-aged woman takes home an ardent suitor, only to discover that he prefers her teenage son. The mother is an overworked coffeeshop attendant, the suitor turns out to be a plainclothes cop and the boy is a frustrated flutist. The proletarian background is stressed, lending picture a dimension of social criticism as well.

Timár seems to have difficulties deciding how far to go with his commentary on Hungarian life, relations between parents and children and sexual frustrations. The irony quickly turns bitter and psychological family drama resorts too easily to the gothic.

The film has its entertaining moments during the mother's early courtship and when the boy plots his revenge on the lover.

Robert Csontos and Erika Bodnár are reliable performers as son and mother. Gábor is amusing when he doesn't take himself too seriously. That is the problem with the rest of the film as well.

—*Edna.*

Heavy Petting
(DOCU-COLOR/B&W)

Park City A Fossil Films production. Produced and directed by Obie Benz. Codirector, Josh Waletzky. Camera (color), Sandi Sissel; editor, Waletzky, Judith Sobol; coproducer, Carol Noblitt. Reviewed at the U.S. Film Festival Park City, Utah (in competition), Jan. 27, 1989. (In Berlin Film Festival — Panorama.) No MPAA Rating. Running time: **80 MIN.**

With: David Byrne, Sandra Bernhard, Allen Ginsberg, William Burroughs, Judith Malina, Josh Mostel, Abbie Hoffman, John Oates, Spalding Gray, Paula Longendyke, Ann Magnuson, Elizabeth Lahey, Duka, Zoe Tamerlaine, Marshall Turner, Wayne Johson, Laurie Anderson, Barry Bartkowski, Jim Dyer, Jacki Ochs, Frederic Lahey, Frances Fisher, Sandi Sissel.

■ The essential silliness of sex and America's often completely addled attitudes toward bodily functions are sorted through once again in "Heavy Petting," an unavoidably amusing effort distinguished more by the sheer volume of its research than anything new it uncovers.

Producer-director Obie Benz spent years culling the archives, looking at the familiarly quaint scenes from old films, particularly from the '50s, plus a treasure of sex-instruction films done for schools and the military.

It's all laughable now, just as today's seemingly more sophisticated sex programs doubtless will set the next century to guffawing.

Benz also has assembled some knowns and unknowns to recall their early sexual memories. Best by far is Josh Mostel, obviously a late bloomer. Also amusing are David Byrne, Spalding Gray and Abbie Hoffman, whose later triumphs in life were not foreshadowed by early sexual success.

Oddly, two writers whose erotic outpouring upset so many censors of yore — Allen Ginsberg and William Burroughs — have little to say on the subject here, awkwardly presented sitting side by side. Ginsberg tries to get into the spirit of the fun, but Burroughs is almost moribund.

Overall, the subject has never been done better. Unfortunately, it has been done before, over and over again. —*Har.*

Chilsu oa Mansu
(Chilsu And Mansu)
(SOUTH KOREAN)

Berlin A Dong-A presentation and production. Produced by Lee-U-Sok. Directed by Park Kwang-Su. Screenplay, Choi In-Sok, based on an idea by Oh Chong-Wo; camera (color), Yu Young-Gil; editor, Kim Hyon; music, Kim Su-Chol; sound, Lee Young-Gil; assistant directors, Hwang Kyu-Dok, Kim Dong-Bin, Lee Hyon-Seung, Shin Han-Sop. Reviewed at Berlin Film Festival (Forum of Young Film), Feb. 13, 1989. Running time: **109 MIN.**
Chilsu . . . . Park Djung-Hun
Mansu . . . . Ahn Song-Gi
Chin-A . . . . Bae Chong-Ok
Also with: Na Han-Il, Dju Ho-Song.

■ "Chilsu And Mansu" is Seoul Film Collective activist Park Kwang-Su's celebration of the newly achieved artistic freedom in South Korean filmmaking. His picture is a delightful, if overlong, comedy with a downbeat ending.

It also is a classic buddy story, fashioned à la Italian neorealism. It should find easy acceptance with modern audiences everywhere.

The buddies of the title are hanging by ropes in all respects. They paint the exteriors of city highrises and giant billboards, while low pay and personal trouble threaten their humble but cozy existence in a makeshift garage-like home.

Chilsu is young and in love and daydreams of joining relatives in Miami. Mansu, in his 30s, is hiding from family responsibilities by doing nothing to help his father who has been a political prisoner for 27 years.

Chilsu (played with exuberant charm and innocent tricker's mien by Park Djung-Hun) and Mansu (a muted, austere performance by Ahn Song-Gi) manage to have a lot of fun at work and at home or going to discos with pretty Chin-A, a waitress.

One day, Chin-A announces she is going to marry another man chosen for her by her parents, while Mansu is informed by letter that his father has been denied a leave from prison on his 60th birthday.

The two friends climb to the top of the billboard on the top of a high-rise and start yelling and posing as protesters. They are spotted by some kids on the sidewalk. Within an hour, the area is swarming with police, ambulances and tv crews.

Helmer Kwang-Su, working from a screenplay by Choi In-Sok, has opted for a logical denouement, which avoids a maudlin extreme. Production credits are first-rate. —*Kell.*

El Vuelo De La Paloma
(The Flight Of The Dove)
(SPANISH)

Berlin An Ion production, in association with Television Española. Directed by José Luis Garcia Sanchez. Screenplay, Garcia Sanchez, Rafael Azcona; camera (Widescreen, Eastmancolor), Fernando Arribas; editor, Pablo G. Del Amo; music, Mariano Diaz; sound, Gilles Ortion; production design, Luis Valles; production manager, Andres Santana; assistant director, Manuel Gomez Pereira. Reviewed at Berlin Film Festival. (Panorama), Feb. 11, 1989. Running time: **88 MIN.**
Paloma . . . . Ana Belen
Pepe . . . . José Sacristan
Juancho . . . . Juan Echanove
Luis Doncel . . . . Juan Luis Galiardo
Toñito . . . . Antonio Resines
Cañete . . . . José Maria Cañete
Also with: Miguel Angel Rellan (Miguel), Manolo Huete (Ciri), Luis Ciges (Columbia).

■ "The Flight Of The Dove" is a spirited comedy which cheerfully lampoons just about every aspect of contemporary Spanish life. It could travel internationally to fests and should play well in Latino-language areas where its references will be appreciated.

Action unfolds during a single day in a quarter of Madrid (an elaborate studio set). A film unit is shooting yet another Civil War epic, while at the same time the city is paralyzed by strikes. Focus is on bored housewife Paloma (means "dove"), played by Ana Belen. Her lazy husband Pepe (José Sacristan) is an ardent communist who won't work for fear of being exploited.

Paloma is pursued by an overweight fishmonger (Juan Echanove) who has vain hopes she'll leave her husband and marry him. On an upper floor of the same building lives an unregenerate fascist, lampooned as a flamboyant homosexual whose live-in lover is more attracted to Paloma's pubescent daughter.

Filming is at a standstill because the director hasn't shown up (he's embroiled in a violent domestic fight with his wife, and never appears). The lead actor (Juan Luis Galiardo), an aging lothario with phony chest hair, decides to relieve his boredom by seducing Paloma, and she hardly resists.

Smartly paced film is filled with gags and amusing characters, though specific references to the Franco period may make it less comprehensible for audiences without some idea of recent Spanish history.

Director José Luis Garcia San-chez, who won the Golden Bear at Berlin in 1977 with his comedy "The Trouts," keeps the laughs coming, though his style may be too broad for some. Actors do their stuff with enthusiasm. The widescreen camerawork of Fernando Arribas is distinguished.

—*Strat.*

Lain ulkopuolella
(Beyond The Law)
(FINNISH)

Lübeck A Finnkino release of Filminor production. Produced by Heikki Takkinen. Directed by Ville Mäkelä. Screenplay, Olli-Pekka Parviainen; camera (Fujicolor), Olli Varja; editor, Timo Linnasalo; sound, Matti Kuortti; production design, Juha Tuura; casting and assistant director, Nadja Pykkö. Reviewed at Nordic Film Days (official entry), Lübeck, W. Germany, Nov. 4, 1988. (In Berlin Film Festival — market.) Running time: **86 MIN.**
The Husband . . . . Taneli Mäkelä
The Wife . . . . Pirjo Luoma-aho
The Brother-In-Law . . . . . . Kari Heiskanen
The Rapist . . . . Antti Litja
Also with: Juoko Klementtilä, Leena Uotila, Eina Rinne, Tauno Lehtihalmes, Heikki Nousiainen, Antti Virmavirta, Kalevi Kahra, Ake Lindman, Kari Sorvali, lasse Pöysti, Juha Muje, Hillevi Lagerstam.

■ "Beyond The Law" is a no-frills thriller about rape & consequences by first-time helmer Ville Mäkelä.

Along with writer Olli-Pekka Parviainen, Mäkelä displays fine psychological insights in telling the story of a victim suffering from the niceties of a legal system that seems mostly preoccupied with protecting the rights of whoever is accused.

Item may well find some offshore theatrical exposure before finding its more substantial rewards via tv pickups. Told alternately as a courtroom drama and a psychological suspenser with action, "Beyond The Law" relies on a calm, near-documentary style in its accounting for events that have led up to the charging of two men with assault and assorted other crimes.

They are the husband and brother of a young woman, seen being pursued and then raped by an errant but otherwise solid citizen. There were no witnesses to the brutal rape and authorities tend to be skeptical of the victim's testimony, especially when the rapist's wife lets herself be bullied into supplying her husband with an alibi for the fateful evening.

At long last, the victim's husband is taunted and coached into joining his brother-in-law in going on a vengeance-is-mine spree. The violence soon escalates and the would-be avengers wind up in the dock themselves, while the true culprit is made to look innocent in the eyes of the law and the public.

All this adds to the agonies of the raped woman who gradually finds herself turned into a suspect. Her inner turmoil is described with harrowing precision by actress Pirjo Luoma-aho.

Most of the way, Mäkelä keeps story development and actors in a tight rein for maximum verisimilitude. A few instances of veering into propaganda excess do not significantly detract from the picture's strong indictment of the forces of the law as being callous and careless in dealing with the crime of rape. —*Kell.*

Joyriders
(BRITISH)

Berlin   A Granada Film Prods., in association with British screen, presentation of a Little Bird production, in association with Walsh Smith. (World Sales: The Sales Co.) Produced by Emma Hayter. Directed by Aisling Walsh. Screenplay, Andy Smith, from a story by Walsh, Smith; camera (Technicolor), Gabriel Beristain; editor, Tom Schwalm; music, Tony Britten; associate producer, Jonathan Cavendish; production design, Leigh Malone; production manager, Gemma Fallon; assistant director, David Brown; casting, Di Carling. Reviewed at Berlin Film Festival (Market), Feb. 13, 1989. Running time: **94 MIN.**
Mary . . . . Patricia Kerrigan
Perky . . . . Andrew Connolly
Tammy . . . . Billie Whitelaw
Daniel . . . . David Kelly
Manager . . . . John Kavanagh
Dolores . . . . Deirdre Donoghue
Finbar . . . . Tracey Peacock
Also with: Rolf Saxon, Otto Jarman (U.S. sailors).

■ **There isn't too much joy in "Joyriders" which, for most of its length, is a downbeat movie about a couple of life's losers. Confidently made first feature looks more suited to tv than theatrical release.**

Originally developed by the now defunct Irish Film Board, drama revolves around Mary (Patricia Kerrigan), who's forced to abandon her two small children after being beaten and ejected from her home by her husband (a character never shown).

Without money or a place to stay, she's befriended by Perky (Andrew Connolly) who has troubles of his own, both with the law and with his mates. He steals a car and together with Mary heads off for the coastal town where she'd honeymooned years before.

Mary's determined not to let a man use or abuse her again, and is forever fighting with Perky. When he finally drops her off, she manages to get a job at a dance hall, where she meets Tammy

(Billie Whitelaw), a former singer, now a pathetic drunk. Since she'd idolized Tammy when she was young, Mary sees another illusion shattered; and the dance hall manager makes unwanted sexual advances to boot.

Happily, Perky turns up to take her away, and they find peace for a while on a desolate farm occupied by a lonely widower (David Kelly); this character, with his tart sense of humor, provides the film's liveliest moments.

Femme director Aisling Walsh makes a confident debut with thin material. The character of Perky remains ill-defined, and the film has an aimless central section. Things pick up before the end, with the rescue of Mary's daughters from a Dublin orphanage, but there are lots of key questions unanswered at fadeout.

Players do what they can with often sparsely written characters. The film is fine in all technical departments, with Dublin coming across as a nightmare place of violence and misery, while the bleak, desolate countryside at least offers peace of a sort. —*Strat.*

Fordringsägare
(Creditors)
(SWEDISH)

Berlin   A Swedish Film Institute release of a Boomerangfilm production, in association with Sverige TV 1 and Film Teknik. Produced by Lars Johansson. Directed by Stefan Böhm, Keve Hjelm, John O. Olsson. Screenplay, uncredited, based on August Strindberg's play; camera (Eastmancolor), Olsson; editor, Solveig Nordlund; production design, Anders Barréus; sound, Björn Thisell, Mats Lindskog; production manager, Pelle Norén; assistant director, Nina Carlsson. Reviewed at Berlin Film Festival (Market), Feb. 11, 1989. Running time: **118 MIN.**
Tekla . . . . Bibi Andersson
Adolf . . . . Tomas Bolme
Gustav . . . . Keve Hjelm

■ **Lovers of the great Swedish theater tradition, and the work of August Strindberg in particular, will relish this straightforward film record of "Creditors" in which three fine actors handle the intricate, waspish dialog with grace.**

Film lovers, on the other hand, will find little to excite them in this single-set transposition to the screen, in which the filmmakers largely fail to make the drama cinematic.

Strindberg wrote "Creditors" in 1888, soon after "Miss Julie," and it's a lesser play. Set in what appears to be an almost deserted

hotel, drama plays out between three people. Adolf (Tomas Bolme) is a crippled artist. Tekla (Bibi Andersson), his wife, a writer whom Adolf devoutly loves, has attitudes that are ambivalent. Smooth-talking Gustav (Keve Hjelm), Tekla's ex-husband, bears a grudge against her (she referred to him disparingly in a novel) and sets about destroying the marriage. He knows Adolph isn't aware that Gustav is Tekla's ex.

First 50 minutes of the film/play are occupied by the two men alone. With the wife's belated appearance, Gustav retires to spy on them. The pattern shifts again allowing for a duolog between Tekla and Gustav with an anguished Adolf watching them unseen.

The 1-act drama is mainly a stream of dialog, much of it riveting and beautifully spoken. Production is vaguely modern-dress. Waiters and hotel staff drift in and out of the background from time to time.

As a record of a play by a major writer, "Creditors" will find its niche in colleges and should play better on home screens than in cinemas. It won't achieve the classic status of Alf Sjöberg's film of "Miss Julie." —*Strat.*

Gekitotsu
(Shogun's Shadow)
(JAPANESE)

Berlin   A Toei Co. presentation and production. Produced by Shigeru Oakada. Directed by Yasuo Furuhata. Screenplay, Sadao Nakajima; camera (color), Hiroo Matsuda; editor, Eifu Tamakj; music, Masaru Satu; director of fight sequences, Shinichi (Sonny) Chiba; production design, Norimichi Igawa; sound, Yoshio Horiike. Reviewed at Berlin Film Festival (Panorama), Feb. 11, 1989.
Running time: **114 MIN.**
Igo Gyobu . . . . Ken Ogata
Hotta Masamori . . . . Tetsuro Tamba
Shishi Jingoemon . . . . Hu Chien Chiang
Abe Shigeji . . . . Hiroki Matsukata
Iba Shoemon . . . . . . Shinichi (Sonny) Chiba

■ **"Shogun's Shadow" is grand-scale fun, furious action, lusty gore, outrageous adventure and brazen satire. Whether placed in art or action houses, this one should go over big everywhere.**

Director Yasuo Furuhata, a skilled hand with many genres, and writer Sadao Nakajima have their bodyguard and seven samurai crossing deserts, high-diving into roaring rivers and climbing snowy mountains, all with entire armies in hot pursuit. Their assignment is to transport the title brat to safety. Fight scenes have been choreographed with tongue-in-cheek exaggeration by Shinichi (Sonny) Chiba.

Much court intrigue and sly toying with the theme of women's role in the Shogun era find their way into this tall tale. Ken Igata ("Mishima," "Ballad Of Narayama") is bland as the hero-bodyguard, but other actors are allowed more fun with their roles.

At one point, helmer Furuhata lets loose a joyous rock score to accompany a major battle scene. The suspense throbs along with the fun all the way to an ending that winds up in the shogun's palace. The boy emerges from all the rough experience as a true little man, more fit for power than his father ever was.

A little editing down plus a few censorial cuts ought not to spoil anybody's fun with this genre extravagnza. —*Kell.*

HUNGARIAN FILM WEEK REVIEWS

Jezus Krisztus Horoszkopiä
(Jesus Christ's Horoscope)
(HUNGARIAN)

Budapest   A Budapest Studio, Mafilm, production. Directed by Miklos Jancso. Screenplay, Gyula Hernadi; camera (Eastmancolor), Janos Kende; editor, Zsuzsa Csakany; music, Group 13 + 1, Group Kommando; production design, Tamas Danovich; sound, György Pinter; assistant director, Andras Böhm. Reviewed at Hungarian Film Week, Budapest, Feb. 8, 1989. Running time: **90 MINS.**
With: Juli Basti, György Cserhalmi, Ildiko Bansagi, Dorottya Udvaros, Andras Balint, Laszlo Galffi, Andras Kozak, Zoltan Papp, Ottilia Barbath, Istvan Marton, Tamas Andor.

■ **Miklos Jancso's latest pic is a** visually brilliant, dramatically challenging film that is more for fests and specialist screenings than for regular theatrical or tube outlets.

Even Hungarians seem to have trouble understanding the film, which has nothing to do with Jesus Christ but seems to center on the anguished lives of intellectuals who remained silent while the country went through a recent series of crisis.

Film is extremely stylized, and lacks an easily comprehensible narrative. It develops into a kind of existential thriller, with shootings, betrayals, doomed relationships and suicide.

Difficult as the film undoubtedly is, it's dazzling to watch. Janos Kende's sinuous camera weaves around the characters in complicated, lengthy takes. Much use is made of multiple video images, which comment on the main action. There are the usual naked girls, and even horsemen (and police cars) whose movements are choreographed like a ballet.

A superb cast of top Magyar actors have followed Jancso's directions, and often are effective even if motivations remain obscure.

In all, a difficult but perversely enjoyable film, definitely not for everyone, but essential viewing for Jancso fans and viewers open to new directions in cinema. A superb music track, including many rousing songs, is a plus.

—*Strat.*

Piroska és a farkas
(Bye Bye Red Riding Hood)
(HUNGARIAN-CANADIAN)

Budapest A Hungarofilm presentation. A Prod. de la Fête (Canada), Budapest Studio (Hungary) production. Produced by Rock Demers. Directed by Márta Mészáros. Screenplay, Mészáros, Eva Pataki, Jan Nowicki; camera (Eastmancolor), Nyika Jancsó, Tamás Vámos; editor, Louise Cote. Eva Kármento; music, Zsolt Döme; sound, István Sipos; art director, Violette Deneau; sets, László Rajk; costumes, Eva Kemenes. Reviewed at Hungarian Film Week, Feb. 7, 1989. Running time: **96 MIN.**
With: Fanny Lauzier, Pamela Collier, Jan Nowicki, Teri Tordai, Margit Makai, David Vermes, Ann Blazeiczak.

■ **Neither a fairytale nor a feminist statement, this version of the kiddie classic, part of Rock Demers' series "Tales For All," may find itself snubbed in both potential markets.**

A meteorologist, abandoned by her husband, takes her little daughter and moves into a forest dwelling, not far from the home of her mother and grandmother. The story skips several years and the little girl (Fanny Lauzier), now in her early teens and a true child of nature, revels in the beauty of her forest. She frequently crosses the forest to visit granny, whose relations with her mother are less than friendly.

In the woods, she variously meets a talking wolf, an ornithologist always dressed in grey and a boy from the city. All marvel at a magic tree whose flowers project images. In a way, she meets three wolves instead of one, and the point of the tale seems to be that all

men are finally wolves and that growing up means losing the magic sight of childhood.

That's all right, except that the story doesn't make any sense and isn't sufficiently fantastic or charming.

None of the characters is more than a shadow. Acting isn't very good, and the dialog is often embarrassing. There's beautiful photography of the Canadian landscape. A grey wolf is far more enticing than the humans.

—*Edna.*

Tusztörtenet
(Stand Off)
(HUNGARIAN)

Budapest An Objektiv Studio, Mafilm, production. Directed by Gyula Gazdag. Screenplay, Gazdag, Antal Vegh; camera (Eastmancolor), Elemer Ragalyi; editor, Julia Sivo; music, Istvan Martha; production design, Jozsef Romvari; sound, Tamas Markus; assistant director, Mara Luttor. Reviewed at Hungarian Film Week, Budapest, Feb. 4, 1989. Running time: **104 MIN.**

Zoltan	Ary Beri
Istvan	Gabor Svidrony
Police chief	Zbigniew Zapasiewicz
Dr. Kalman	Istvan Szabo
Mother	Judit Pogany
Father	Tibor Bitskey
Bea	Denissa Dor
Ilona	Veronika Adam Molnar
Klari	Barbara Krisztics

■ **A gripping drama about a pair of youthful gunmen who invade a girls' dormitory and hold 18 of them hostage, "Stand Off" is an unusually "Westernized" Hungarian film.**

Inspired by an actual case, drama takes place in a border town where Zoltan and his younger brother Ari, sons of a border guard, decide to escape the violent way. Zoltan, a gun freak (first seen shooting at birds near the barbed-wire border fence) has his head shaved before he and his brother invade the dorm. Five of the girls escape through the washroom window and alert the police, and the 5-day siege begins.

Claustrophobic scenes inside the dorm are well handled, with the girls alternating between hysteria and acceptance. A couple even cozy up to the young hoods. Shortage of water and toilet facilities becomes acute as the siege drags on.

Meanwhile, outside, parents await news and the cop in charge (Polish actor Zbigniew Zapasiewicz) decides to wait until the boys make a mistake. He has marksmen at the ready and assault teams standing by. The only outsider allowed in to the dorm is a doctor, excellently played by Istvan Szabo, director of "Mephisto,"

"Hanussen" and other pics. His edgy performance is one of the pic's highlights.

Politics are referred to only obliquely here (things must be desperate if these kids take such drastic action to flee the country) and the pic should be accessible to audiences worldwide. Fest exposure also is indicated. It's a change of pace for director Gyula Gazdag, best known for his political docus and occasional fantasies ("Hungarian Fairy Tale").

—*Strat.*

Az En XX. Szazadom
(My 20th Century)
(HUNGARIAN-W.GERMAN - B&W)

Budapest A Budapest Studio, Mafilm-Friedlander Filmproduktion coproduction. Produced by Norbert Friedlander. Directed by Ildiko Enyedi. Screenplay, Enyedi; camera (b&w), Tibor Mathé; editor, Maria Rigo; music, Laszlo Vidovszky; production design, Zoltan Labas; sound, Istvan Sipos; costumes, Agnes Gyarmathy; assistant director, Janos Tamasi. Reviewed at Hungarian Film Week, Budapest, Feb. 4, 1989. Running time: **98 MIN.**

Dora/Lili	Dorotha Segda
Z	Oleg Jankowski
Thomas Alva Edison	Peter Andorai
X	Gabor Mate

Also with: Paulus Manker, Gyula Kery, Andrei Schwartz, Sandor Tery, Sandor Czvetko, Endre Koronszi, Agnes Kovacs, Eszter Kovacs.

■ **A playful, charming first feature, "My 20th Century" looks like a good bet for fest exposure later this year and may attract specialist distribs with its offbeat, winning style.**

Femme director Ildiko Enyedi's story is set at the turn of the century and uses standard aspect ratio, black & white camerawork and iris editing to enhance the mood. Pic actually opens in New York City in 1880 with a brilliant demonstration of electricity, staged by Thomas Edison (Peter Andorai). Meanwhile, in far-off Budapest, twin girls are born, but soon are orphaned and reduced to begging in the snow. Benefactors separate them, and by 1900 Dora has become a femme fatale while Lili is working as a bomb-toting anarchist.

Unknown to each other, both girls become involved with the mysterious Z (elegantly played by Russian actor Oleg Jankowski) with amusing results. Film is pitched on a disarmingly playful level, with titles, mystic visions and songs to punctuate the story.

As the twin sisters (and, briefly, their mother), Dorotha Segda is a

delight, and her lovemaking scenes with Jankowski are both funny and sexy. Narrative isn't always clear, but the cheerful mood and nods to famous pics will have buffs entranced.

Locations are extremely varied, taking in the Burmese jungle and the wastes of Siberia. Standout scene has a chauvinist prof lecturing a class of women who become more and more insulted at his myopic approach.

Certainly one of the better Magyar pics around, it's one that, with care, could find audiences internationally. —*Strat.*

Ehes Ingovany
(Hungry Swamp)
(HUNGARIAN)

Budapest An Outsider Film production. Written, directed, camera (color) by Miklos Acs. Sound, Tamas Markus. Reviewed at Hungarian Film Week, Budapest, Feb. 6, 1989. Running time: **60 MIN.**
With: Peto Aranka, Juli Sandor.

■ **Miklos Acs is a maverick on the Hungarian film scene who makes Super-8m features outside the studio system. This is his second pic, even less structured than his first.**

Images of huge apartment blocks, bored girls talking to the camera, foul language, plenty of nudity (with clips from porno films), wild rock songs (by the Dead Kennedys group), razors cutting into flesh — it all adds up to a cry of protest from disaffected youth. "Who Gives A Damn?" is the title of one song, and "If Only War Would Start" another.

This is strictly amateur stuff, but Ac's out-on-a-limb approach may favor with fests looking for really offbeat material — except that these experiments were the type fashionable in the west 20 years ago. Technically, it's very poor.

—*Strat.*

Titania, Titania
(HUNGARIAN)

Budapest A Hungarofilm presentation of a Dialog Studio production. Written and directed by Péter Bacsó. Camera (Eastmancolor), Tamás Andor; editor, Mihály Morell; music, György Vukán; sound, Károly Peller; sets, Tamás Banovich; costumes, Erzsbét Mialkovszky. Reviewed at Hungarian Film Week, Budapest, Feb. 6, 1989. Running time: **138 MIN.**

Grand Titan	Gyula Bodrogyi
Grand Titan's wife	Dorottya Udvaros
Ban Teller	Eva Igó
Village Commander	Andrea Kiss
General	Attila Kaszás

■ **Director Péter Bacsó returns**

to political satire with a vengeance. Hungary's next-door neighbor Rumania isn't going to like this picture much, as its barbs are clearly pointed across the border.

Imaginary country Titania is ruled by the Grand Titan, an unscrupulous and capricious tyrant married to a younger wife who is even worse.

City blocks are scrapped to make room for some new palaces for the leader. As far as Titanians are concerned, the poor get poorer and the rich are extinct; no Jews are left to take the blame for all the evils, the intelligentsia volunteer to dig trenches or else, and the people eat grass because it's good for them.

The Grand Titan can't be everywhere at the same time, but likes to give the impression he can. He has three doubles — a peasant, bank robber and actor — chosen for their uncanny resemblance to the great man. Once he is dead, however, their usefulness is gone.

Second part of the film follows their escape, as each tries to regain, not very successfully, his own home ground.

Bacsó, never a subtle filmmaker, doesn't mince words. He cheerfully punches away, painting a picture of decadent tyranny that would even put Caligula to shame.

Technical credits are of a high order throughout. Nothing has been spared in making Titania as realistic as possible. The actors lustily ham it up, with Gyula Bodrogyi playing the tyrant and his three doubles in the spirit of a vaudeville sketch, and Dorottya Udvaros, a Bacsó regular, doing same as the Grant Titan's wife and heir apparent.

This extended political parody would be fine on a cabaret stage, but at over two hours outstays its screen welcome. —Edna.

Hat Bagatell
(Six Bagatelles)
(HUNGARIAN-B&W)

Budapest A Hungarofilm presentation. A Társulás Studio production. Written and directed by Andrá Jeles (The Audition); Gábor Bódy (A Bagatelle); Bela Tarr (Hotel Magnezit); Pia Pál Wilt (Ságpuszta); György Fehér (The Old Ones); István Dárday (Just To Be On The Safe Side). In black & white. Reviewed at Hungarian Film Week, Budapest, Feb. 5, 1989. Running time: **85 MIN.**

■ **Reviewed for the record, this collection of six shorts made between 1969-80 by different direc-**tors who at the time were film school students, was put together by one of them, Grörgy Fehér, as an introduction to what is generally known as the Budapest School.

Each of these directors has since moved on to key positions in Hungarian cinema, and each episode points to the direction they were later to adopt.

"The Audition," reminiscent of early Milos Forman, is a sketch on youthful dreams of fame, a realistic basis on which director András Jeles later embroidered his fantasy fabrics.

"One Bagatelle" by the late Gábor Bódy is a sarcastic portrait of society approaching its evils the wrong way.

Pál Wilt's film on the destruction of an ancient village to make room for an international youth center is typical of the outspoken social consciousness developed by documentaries in this country.

György Fehér adds a bitter ironical touch, describing the fate of old people living under the poverty line; István Dárday adds a sardonic touch.

Finally, hostility and despair as the basis of human relations, a trademark of Béla Tarr's later films, are mulled in "Hotel Magnezit."

All six episodes are shot in black and white, often favored by these directors in their later films as well. They all tend to cross the border between documentary and fiction. Techniques vary from experimental (Bódy) to straightforward documentary (Wilt).

Film archives, clubs and organizers of film events may find this item useful. —Edna.

K
(A Film About Prostitution)
(HUNGARIAN-DOCU)

Budapest A Hungarofilm presentation. A Hunnia Studio, Helikon Film production. Directed by György Dobray; camera (Eastmancolor, video), Tamás Andor; editor, Zsuzsa Pósán; music, László Dés; sound, András Vámosi. Reviewed at Hungarian Film Week, Budapest, Feb. 6, 1989. Running time: **89 MIN.**

■ **Compared to some Western documentaries on this subject, György Dobray's look at the Hungarian version of the oldest profession in the world is almost cheerful.**

Smiling girls ply their trade in a central Budapest square where even the weather is nice. The money is certainly fabulous, one average day producing much more than the monthly income from any legitimate job.

The most interesting aspect of the film is the easy, almost undisturbed acceptance of prostitution by a socialist state. All the girls are attracted by the easy money and convenient hours, and none seems overly concerned with the moral aspects involved.

As long as Dobray stays within the boundaries of traditional documentary, his film proceeds on predictable lines. The trouble starts once he tries to go beyond that, and penetrate the intimacy of the relations between a young hooker and her man. Conscious of the film crew's presence and their request to act real, the couple delivers an awkward, watered-down parody, breaking now and then into barely concealed guffaws. The same goes for a sequence showing a client being serviced by the girl.

Deft camerawork and lively editing, combined with the shock value of this subject (taboo until now in Hungary, as prostitution is officially forbidden), have helped the picture score on the home market. Outside it, however, its appeal is less evident. —Edna.

Soha, Sehol, Senkinek
(Never, Nowhere, To No One)
(HUNGARIAN)

Budapest A Budapest Studio, Mafilm production. Directed by Ferenc Teglasy. Screenplay, Teglasy; camera (Eastmancolor), Ferenc Pap; editor, Margit Galamo; production design, Zsolt Czengery; sound, György Kovacs; assistant director, Janos Rekasi. Reviewed at Hungarian Film Week, Budapest, Feb. 4, 1989. Running time: **93 MIN.**
Imre Vendel . . . . Andras Kozak
Vali Vendel . . . . Jolanta Grusznic
Lamas Vendel . . . . Tibor Antai
Bandi Vendel . . . . Peter Kurdi
Also with: Lazslo Horvath.

■ **A fresh look at the infamous Stalinist period in Hungary, this autobiographical first feature already has won prizes at Mannheim and Turin, and deserves its accolades.**

Set in 1951, pic concerns the forcible relocation of people accused by the Communist regime of any of a number of crimes. In this case, Imre Vendel, his pregnant wife Vali and their two sons are forced to leave their Budapest apartment and are taken by train to a remote spot on the Ungarian Plain where they've been allocated an abandoned farmhouse.

Vendel has to find farm work to feed his family, and gamely sets about brooking horses (a gripping sequence) and ingratiating himself to hostile locals. Meanwhile, the family is harassed by the police, who even interrupt the couple's lovemaking by flashing torches at them.

Vendel has been arrested temporarily for no good reason when his wife's baby is due and, in a harrowing sequence, her two small sons have to assist her in the birth.

First-time director Ferenc Teglasy has done a fine job, aided by solid thesping and superior camerawork (Ferenc Pap). He's dedicated the pic "To my parents and sons," and concludes with a sad note that this family — presumably his own, as this smacks of autobiography — broke up as a result of their bitter experiences. —Strat.

A dokumentátor
(The Documentator)
(HUNGARIAN)

Budapest A Hungarofilm presentation of a Hunnia Film production. Written and directed by István Dárday, György Szalai; camera (Eastmancolor), video, Péter Timár, Sándor Csukás; editors, Klára Majoros, Hajnal Veil; music, József Czencz, János Molnár, Péter Kaszás; sound, Gábor Erdélyi, István Fehér; sets, László Gárdonyi; costumes, Tamás Nágy. Reviewed at Hungarian Film Week, Feb. 4, 1989. Running time: **215 MIN.**
Raffael . . . . Mihály Dés
Chip . . . . Lilla Pászti
Rambo . . . . János Agoston

■ **István Dárday and György Szalai indulge themselves way beyond need in another long-winded, unconventional foray into the social conditions of Hungary.**

Many interesting points are raised and some of the visual ideas work out nicely, but there doesn't seem to be any real distinction between relevant and obvious.

The sketchy plot, an excuse to hang on the filmmakers' countless observations, refers to a video merchant who peddles sex and violence for a nice profit, while on the side he is an obsessive documentarist.

Film shows Hungary invaded by Western cultural values. Things are not seen unless perceived by the camera, and video invades private lives. Profit is the only accepted morality, and socialist ideals are put to sleep.

All this is conveyed via film footage and video material. Every element is shown from several angles at the same time. The fact that it all happens in Hungary 1987 is stressed strongly with all the political and social implications of such a statement.

In all this epic visual orgy, however, characters and relations between them remain schematic. The actors can't contribute much, since they are only present to enforce the impact of the objects around them.

Camerawork is superior and sets are functional. The editing, which often employs repeat action and inserts of brief fantasy sequences, might have been more effective had various elements been trimmed to manageable length. At this pace, the picture, as eye-catching as it is, stands little chance of moving outside the specialized art-club circuit. —*Edna.*

Alombrigád
(Dream Brigade)
(HUNGARIAN)

Budapest   A Hungarofilm presentation. A Tarsulas Studio production. Written and directed by András Jeles. Camera (Eastmancolor), Sándor Kardos; editor, Zsuzsa Pósán; music, Ferenc Darvas, László Melis; sound, Péter Lackovics, Tamás Márkus; sets, Attila Kovács; costumes, Gyula Pauer. Reviewed at Hungarian Film Week, Budapest, Feb. 4, 1989. In Berlin Film Festival — Panorama. Running time: **107 MIN.**
Narrator . . . . Robert Rátonyi
Oláh . . . . Tibor Láng
Duba . . . . István Patai

■ **Finished in 1983 and first screened here unofficially two years ago, András Jeles' film is a hodge-podge of insufficiently developed ideas.**

It addresses the gross commercialization of film and the conditioning of film audiences, combined with remarks about the nature of democracy, art and entertainment in a socialist state.

This is too much for a single movie. Jeles distracts his audience by jumping from one topic to another and indulging in side issues.

Pic tells the story of a worker's brigade attempting to produce a play by a Soviet writer. The discussions around this effort — clear hints about censorship and brutal law enforcement — quite possibly had something to do with its delayed release.

Complex visuals and a particularly rich soundtrack are a constant challenge to the viewer. Use of a narrator doesn't always help. Whether foreign audiences will be able to unravel Jeles' intentions is questionable. —*Edna.*

Ismeretien Ismerös
(The Little Alien)
(HUNGARIAN)

Budapest   An Objektiv Studio, Mafilm, production. Directed by Janos Rozsa. Screenplay, Istvan Kardos; camera (Eastmancolor), Andras Szalai; editor, Zsuzsa Csakany; music and lyrics, Janus Brody; production design, Laszlo Szekely, Attila Köves, Sandor Katona; sound, György Fek; assistant director, Gabor Ferenczi. Reviewed at Hungarian Film Week, Budapest, Feb. 4, 1989. Running time: **104 MIN.**
The Actress . . . . Judit Halasz
The Boy . . . . Dani Szabo
The Husband . . . . Karoly Eperjes
The Father . . . . Dezsö Garas
    Also with: Erika Bodnar, Eva Olsavszky, Frigyes Hollosi, Erzsebet Gaal, Laszlo Szacsvay, Tamas Puskas.

■ **A musical for children, "The Little Alien" is undemanding fare which makes little of its basic premise.**

A youngster, about eight, lands in Budapest in his primitive spacecraft, actually an old suitcase with rotor blade to propel it. He's taken to an orphanage where he's spotted by a lonely actress who takes him in.

Pic is basically an excuse for numerous songs, pleasantly put across by popular warbler Judit Halasz, best known outside Hungary as the femme lead of early Istvan Szabo pics. For the uninitiated, the songs become repetitive.

Comedy is simple, with best scene being the total demolition of a supermarket after the lad removes just one can from a display. Little is done with the idea of the alien — the boy is simply a cute kid with no home. Director Janes Rozsa, who's made more distinguished pics in the past, is marking time with this one. It is, however, well produced.

Offshore chances are remote, though with some trimming pic could work as moppet tv programming. —*Strat.*

Az Uj Földesur
(The New Landlord)
(HUNGARIAN)

Budapest   A Hunnia Studio, Mafilm, production. Directed by Andras Lanyi. Screenplay, Lanyi, based on novel by Mor Jokai; camera (Eastmancolor), Gabor Halasz; editor, Maria Nagy; music, Zoltan Papp; production design, Andras Gyürky; costumes, Klara Konkoly-Thege; sound, György Kovacs; assistant director, Istvan Mag. Reviewed at Hungarian Film Week, Budapest, Feb. 6, 1989. Running time: **108 MIN.**
Knight Ankerschmidt . . . . . . Imre Sinkovits
Aladar Garanvölgyi . . . . Joszef Szarvas
Hermine . . . . Aniko Für
Adam Garanvölgyi . . . . Laszlo Sinko
Corinna . . . . Katalin Takacs
Grisak . . . . Peter Vallai

■ **A handsome, stately adaptation of a famous 19th century Magyar novel, "The New Landlord" covers familiar territory but misses its target.**

Mor Jokai was the most popular Hungarian writer of his time, and managed to romanticize the turmoil that followed the defeat of his country by Austria in the mid-1800s. In "The New Landlord" he created the character of a former Austrian general, Knight Ankerschmidt (based on a real-life Austrian officer) who supervised the bloody aftermath of the Hungarian revolt and settled in an estate once owned by a rebellious nobleman.

All of this would seem to be fruitful material for a film, but "The New Landlord" is just an average period romance in which the Austrian tries to make peace with the Hungarians by offering his daughter, Hermine, in marriage to the son of the man whose estate he's usurped. The daughter will have none of it, since she has her own lover. The son has, in any case, lost his memory as a result of war wounds.

Handsome production values and solid thesping make this pic watchable, but it's never as enthralling as it might have been. In consequence, international possibilities look bleak, except in situations where the original book is known. —*Strat.*

Vadon
(Wild)
(HUNGARIAN)

Budapest   A Dialog Studio, Mafilm, production. Directed by Ferenc Andras. Screenplay, Andras, from novel by Peter Dobai; camera (Eastmancolor), Gabor Szabo; music, Istvan Martha; assistant director, Istvan Albrecht. Reviewed at Hungarian Film Week, Budapest, Feb. 5, 1989. Running time: **132 MIN.**
Kristof Batiszy . . . . Sandor Oszter
Amadea Zsablyay . . . . . Maria Gladkowska
Laszlo Görgenyi . . . . Gabor Reviczky
Denes Nevedy . . . . Lajos Kovacs
Gyula Krizsan . . . . Peter Andorai
Greti . . . . Barbara Hegyi
General Kayatz . . . . Anatol Konstantin

■ **A lavishly filmed costume drama about a doomed attempt to free Hungary from Austrian rule in the mid-19th century, "Wild" is visually splendid but too long and conventional to make much international impact.**

In 1859 a Hungarian regiment is formed in a vain attempt to drive out the Austrian forces (who are simultaneously in conflict with the French and Italians). Pic's protagonist is the Magyar leader, a brave officer who winds up on an Austrian scaffold and buried in an unmarked grave.

There are well-staged battle scenes in leafy forest glades, and, thanks to the camerawork of Gabor Szabo, the film's often breathtakingly beautiful. Lovely too is Polish actress Maria Gladkowska, playing a lonely widow who dallies with the Hungarian leader.

Director Ferenc Andras ("Rain And Shine Together," "The Great Generation") fills the pic with superb vistas, but the drama is muted. "Wild" might get fest exposure on the basis of its classical handling of a great, tragic theme. —*Strat.*

Isten akaratábol
(By The Will Of God)
(HUNGARIAN-DOCU)

Budapest   A Hungarofilm presentation of a Budapest Studio, Hungarian TV, MOKEP Budapest, Videothek of Historical interviews, Soros Collection production. Directed by Péter Bokor. Screenplay, Bokor, Gábor Hanák; camera (Eastmancolor), Sándor Kurucz, László Marczali; editor, Valéria Somogyi; music, László Dés; sound, Mariann Takács. Reviewed at Hungarian Film Week, Budapest, Feb. 6, 1989. Running time: **83 MIN.**

■ **The most significant fact about this film on Otto von Habsburg is that a socialist state finds it necessary to devote an admiring, sympathetic picture to its own crown prince.**

The scion of the dynasty that ruled the Austro-Hungarian Empire for centuries never attempted to ascend to the throne. He was a student in Berlin during the early '30s, but left the day Hitler became the German chancellor. He tried to persuade Austria to resist the Nazis, and later became a journalist. For several years he has been a delegate to the European Parliament for Bavaria.

His outlook on and version of this century's political events offer interesting insights into history and his character.

A believer in a united Europe, he has tried to promote a Danube political entity, to include most of the central European nations. He considers Hungary his homeland and speaks the language fluently, although he left the country when he was four.

As if not to disturb the flow of his interviewee's discourse, director Péter Bokor uses mostly one camera angle, intercutting the monolog with archive material. It is almost radio technique in its simplicity, a respectful tribute to a lively elder statesman. —*Edna.*

Rock Térito
(The Rock Convert)
(HUNGARIAN)

Budapest A Mozgokep production. Directed by Janos Xantus. Screenplay, Xantus. Mihaly Vig; camera (Eastmancolor), Tibor Klöpfler; editor, Klara Major; music, Tamas Pajor, Neurotic; sound, Istvan Sipos. Reviewed at Hungarian Film Week, Budapest, Feb. 6, 1989. Running time: **104 MIN.**

With: Tamas Pajor, Mariann Urban, Laszlo Bojki, Henrik Pauer, Janos (Dixi) Gemes, Sarah Frucht, Adalbert Vacz, Ildiko Molnar.

■Director Janos Xantus was making a video study of Hungarian rock star Tamas Pajor when Pajor became converted to Christianity. This roughly made pic records that transformation, with some fictional embellishments.

Pajor was into sex, drugs and rock 'n' roll before his conversion. He also had a wild temper, and Xantus filmed him going nuts and smashing his fist through a plate-glass window (a heavily bandaged Pajor is filmed watching the footage of himself on the rampage).

Once he becomes a born-again Christian, though, the formerly ragged rocker becomes a clean-cut, clean-living youth who socks over songs like "The Lord Is Alive."

Pajor's conversion is interesting enough without the fictional bits Xantus has added; they merely pad the running time to little effect.

Transfer from video to film makes for some striking images at times, though all-too-often pic looks murky. It's an unusual item and fests specializing in music pics could be interested. —*Strat.*

Tanmesek A Szexröl
(Moral Stories About Sex)
(HUNGARIAN)

Budapest A Dialog Studio, Mafilm, production. Directed and written by Szilveszter Siklosi. Camera (Eastmancolor), Nyika Jancso; editor, Gabriella Koncz; music, Zoltan Mericske; sound, Peter Laczkovich; assistant director, Maria Eperjes. Reviewed at Hungarian Film Week, Budapest, Feb. 5, 1989. Running time: **84 MIN.**

Teacher/Ildiko	Enikö Eszenyi
Waiter/Peter	Peter Rudolf
Headmaster/Fidler	Adam Rajhona
Tamas	Janos Ban
Mrs. Schneider	Ida Turay

■Two medium-length stories, sharing cast members and a theme about the link between living accommodations and sexual frustration, are to be found in this minor exercise.

In Part 1, "Saturday Off" (45 minutes), a pretty schoolteacher and her boyfriend can't earn enough to get an apartment. On a solo visit to a Budapest hotel, she's mistaken by a German for a prostie, and spends a drunken night with him, earning 100 marks the next day. She continues to earn foreign money the same way each Saturday, until unexpectedly confronted by the school's headmaster.

Enikö Eszenyi is pretty and charming as the novice prostie. This is the better of the two stories, though basically slight.

Eszenyi also plays the lead in story two, "The Council Story" (39 minutes). She and her fiancee can't find a place to make love, so they do it under the table in a restaurant or he smuggles her into his room disguised as a man. When the couple finally get a place of their own, they find they can no longer perform.

Both tales are predictable and lightweight, though agreeably acted. Despite the title, there are no sex scenes on display: It's all extremely discreet. Offshore chances are minimal for such slender material. —*Strat.*

New York Stories

Hollywood A Buena Vista release of a Touchstone presentation of a Jack Rollins and Charles H. Joffe production. Film in three episodes, produced by Robert Greenhut.

Life Lessons

Produced by Barbara DeFina. Directed by Martin Scorsese. Screenplay, Richard Price; camera (Duart color; Metrocolor prints), Nestor Almendros; editor, Thelma Schoonmaker; production design, Kristi Zea; art direction, Wray Steven Graham; set decoration, Nina F. Ramsey; costume design, John Dunn; sound, James Sabat; assistant director, Joseph Reidy; casting, Ellen Lewis.

Life Without Zoe

Produced by Fred Roos, Fred Fuchs. Directed by Francis Coppola. Screenplay, Francis Coppola, Sofia Coppola; camera (color), Vittorio Storaro; editor, Barry Malkin; music, Carmine Coppola, Kid Creole and the Coconuts; production design, Dean Tavoularis; art direction, Speed Hopkins; set decoration, George DeTitta Jr.; costume design, Sofia Coppola; sound, James Sabat; assistant director, Joseph Reidy; casting, Aleta Chappelle.

Oedipus Wrecks

Produced by Robert Greenhut. Executive producers, Jack Rollins, Charles H. Joffe. Written and directed by Woody Allen. Camera (color), Sven Nykvist; editor, Susan E. Morse; production design, Santo Loquasto; art direction, Speed Hopkins; set decoration, Susan Bode; costume design, Jeffrey Kurland; sound, James Sabat; assistant director, Thomas Reilly; casting Juliet Taylor. Reviewed at the Walt Disney Studios, Burbank, Calif., Feb. 22, 1989. MPAA Rating: PG. Running time: **123 MIN.**

Lionel Dobie	Nick Nolte
Paulette	Rosanna Arquette
Phillip Fowler	Patrick O'Neal
Reuben Toro	Jesse Borrego
Gregory Stark	Steve Buscemi
Peter Gabriel	Himself
Paulette's Friend	Illeana Douglas

Zoe	Heather McComb
Charlotte	Talia Shire
Claudio	Giancarlo Giannini
Clifford, The Doorman	Paul Herman
Jimmy	James Keane
Hector	Don Novello
Abu	Selim Tlili
Street Musician	Carmine Coppola
Princess Soroya	Carole Bouquet

Sheldon Mills	Woody Allen
Lisa	Mia Farrow
Treva	Julie Kavner
Mother	Mae Questel
Psychiatrist	Marvin Chatinover
Aunt Ceil	Jessie Keosian
Shandu, The Magician	George Schindler
Rita	Bridgit Ryan
Mayor Edward I. Koch	Himself

■"New York Stories" showcases the talents of three of the modern American cinema's foremost auteurs, Martin Scorsese, Francis Coppola and Woody Allen. As seems always to be the case with multi-episode projects, not all the segments turn out well, and the ratio here is two winners to one clinker.

Picture will obviously draw a limited buff crowd automatically interested in the directors, but prospects beyond that look dicey because each installment is pitched to a different audience. Scorsese's is aimed at serious-minded adults, Coppola's to children, and Allen's to a more general public looking for laughs. Making this into a commercial success would represent a true victory for Disney.

Filmmakers were given carte blanche to develop subjects that dealt in some way with life in Gotham and might not fit a normal running time. With just a couple of exceptions, they reassembled top collaborators from previous pictures, and main thing works have in common is their setting among different segments of New York's privileged, elite class.

Scorsese's "Life Lessons" gets things off to a pulsating start, as Nestor Almendros' camera darts, swoops and circles around Nick Nolte and Rosanna Arquette as they face the end of an intense romantic entanglement. Looking not unlike his parasitic hobo of "Down And Out In Beverly Hills," the leonine Nolte plays a leading light of the downtown art scene, an abstract painter unprepared for a major gallery opening three weeks away.

Announcing that she's had a fling, Arquette, Nolte's lover and artistic protege, agrees to stay on in his loft as long as she no longer has to sleep with him but doesn't make life easy for him, as she's continually creating a scene and even brings a pickup back to their bed for a night.

Through all the domestic adversity, the agitated Nolte, to the accompaniment of Procol Harum's "Whiter Shade Of Pale," Dylan's "Like A Rolling Stone" and a host of other tunes, furiously works on his enormous canvases.

Sometimes conjuring up memories of his first film, "Who's That Knocking At My Door?," Scorsese cogently works out his theme of how art can thrive on emotional turmoil. While one can wonder at Nolte so patiently tolerating Arquette's tantrums and abuse, it becomes clear that he actually needs it to egg him on in his work.

Working from a deft script by Richard Price, who penned "The Color Of Money," for him, Scorsese and his team use every camera, editing, optical, music and sound effects trick in the book to make this a dynamic display of almost off-hand mastery.

Nolte is at his most appealing here, and sidetrips out of the loft provide a voyeuristic tour of the club, gallery and bar scene, with such in-crowd types as performance artist Steve Buscemi, Peter Gabriel, Deborah Harry, Price and Scorsese himself putting in brief appearances. At 45 minutes, this is the longest of the episodes.

At 33 minutes, Francis Coppola's "Life Without Zoe" is the shortest of the three, but that is still not nearly short enough, as the director and his daughter Sofia have concocted the flimsiest of conceits for their contribution.

Vignette is a wispy urban fairy tale about a 12-year-old girl who, because her parents are on the road most of the time, basically lives alone at the ritzy Sherry Netherland Hotel while attending a private school populated by kids of some of the world's richest people.

This milieu of privileged children is a fresh one with plenty of potential in numerous directions, and during the course of the pretty, fanciful nothingness that occupies the half-hour, the mind wanders to what might have been. On the one hand, Coppola, himself a resident of the Sherry Netherland, could have made a very personal film about his own family's life in such a rarified environment. Alternatively, the offspring of diplomats, Arab Sheiks and world famous artists throwing elaborate parties and prematurely assuming the airs of their parents provides plenty of material for delicious satire.

As it stands, this whimsy goes nowhere, as little Zoe floats through the lush wonderland of production designer Dean Tavoularis and lenser Vittorio Storaro on her way to a preposterous reunion with her folks in front of the Parthenon. Given the chance to say anything he wanted, it comes as a staggering disappointment that Coppola chose to say nothing, or worse, had nothing on his mind.

Happily, Woody Allen salvages matters rather nicely with "Oedipus Wrecks." As soon as he commences complaining about his mother to his psychiatrist, the viewer breathes a welcome sigh of relief that Allen, absent as an actor from the screen since "Hannah And Her Sisters" three years ago, is back with jokes up his sleeve.

As the title suggests, subject here is the Jewish mother syndrome, of which Allen moans he is still a victim at age 50. When Allen takes shiksa girlfriend Mia Farrow home for dinner, he winces as Mama assails him for

choosing a blond with three kids.

In a hilarious sequence, Allen's fondest wish — that his mother just disappear — comes true when a magician literally loses her in the course of a trick. To relate the upshot of this would spoil the fun, but Allen comes to suffer the ultimate in mother domination via a conception that calls to mind the rampaging giant breast of "Everything You Always Wanted To Know About Sex."

Much of the humor is of the Catskills circuit variety, and while several of the jokes detonate belly laughs, others are admittedly on the feeble side. About five minutes could profitably have been shaved from the 40-minute running time, and there are those who will assert that this simply represents a vehicle for Allen's uncomfortable squirming about his own Jewishness. In this vein, "Oedipus" marks the first time Allen has ended up with a Jewish woman since the earliest days of his screen career.

Pic concludes with five minutes of credits, certainly the longest end credit roll since "Who Framed Roger Rabbit." —Cart.

Dream A Little Dream

Hollywood   A Vestron Pictures release. Produced by D.E. Eisenberg, Marc Rocco. Executive producers, Lawrence Kasanoff, Ellen Steloff. Directed by Rocco. Screenplay, Daniel Jay Franklin, Rocco, D.E. Eisenberg; camera (Foto-Kem color), King Baggot; editor, Russell Livingstone; music, John William Dexter; production design, Matthew C. Jacobs; costume design, Kristine Brown; sound, Blake Wilcox; assistant director, Patrick Leyba; casting, Jane Feinberg, Mike Fenton. Reviewed at Warner Hollywood screening room, Jan. 25, 1989. MPAA Rating: PG-13. Running time: **99 MIN.**
Bobby Keller . . . . Corey Feldman
Lainie Diamond . . . . . . Meredith Salenger
Coleman Ettinger . . . . Jason Robards
Gene Ettinger . . . . Piper Laurie
Ike Baker . . . . Harry Dean Stanton
Joel . . . . William McNamara
    Also with: Corey Haim.

■ **"Dream A Little Dream" makes the case for a film that is better heard than seen. Its role-reversal theme is tired, the veteran actors wasted and the overall tempo amateurish, although the soundtrack is great.**

For all the money already spent to secure the music rights, Vestron may want to put out a CD and skip theatrical and video altogether.

As if there weren't enough features made along the man-trapped-in-boy's-body storyline, "Dream A Little Dream" is the fifth such release in the last 18 months and the least well conceived and ex-

ecuted of the bunch.

Unlike the others, which are played mostly for laughs, this effort is more an adolescent drama that centers on the minor puppy-love traumas of gawky Corey Feldman as he tries to win over h.s. femme fatale Meredith Salenger.

As the result of a bike accident when Feldman slams into Jason Robards, who's out in the backyard doing Tai Chi with wife Piper Laurie, their personalities are exchanged.

Fault lies both with Marc Rocco and Danny Eisenberg's poorly developed script. Writing only elliptically alludes to the fact that something wonderfully strange should have caused these two to reassess who they are. Rocco's muddy direction probably seems worse than it actually is because of the uneven editing of murky footage that looks bright one minute and dark the next.

Robards has little to do or work with, but gives his best in a limited role as a quiet thinker type who draws inspiration from homilies he writes to himself on a blackboard and love from his devoted companion, Laurie. She too is effective in an even more restrictive part, even as she does little else than say "I love you" several different times and ways.

Mostly the film trails Feldman around in his dogged pursuit of Salenger in scenes that more often than not are set to pop tunes than dialog. Clearly, they are targeted for the MTV crowd, but don't come off half as polished or visually compelling.

There is the usual teenage melodramatic material about whether to be rebellious of one's parents, loyal to one's chums and how much it's worth to get the girl in the end. Feldman pleads with Salenger's b.f. (William McNamara) not too shoot him—which is supposed to seem extraordinary considering the circumstances, though the result is the opposite.

Harry Dean Stanton and Corey Haim get feature billing though both really have only bit parts. It's never explained who Stanton is supposed to be, other than some sort of odd mentor of gruff manner and kindly intentions. Haim, at least, knows what he's supposed to be doing as Feldman's closest buddy, meaning at least one character doesn't seem confused.—Brit.

Ivan I Aleksandra
(Ivan And Alexandra)
(BULGARIAN)

Berlin   A Bojana Filmstudio, Bulgariafilm, production. Directed by Ivan Nichev. Screenplay, Nichev; camera (color), Georgi Nikolov; editor, Ani Cerneva; music, Bozidar Petkov; sound, Christo Cristov; production design, Ana Makarova, Angel Adreev. Reviewed at Berlin Film Festival (competing), Feb. 20, 1989. Running time: **79 MIN.**
Ivan . . . . Kliment Corbadziev
Alexandra . . . . Monika Budjonova
    Also with: Filip Trifonov, Marija Statulova, Kalin Arsov, Mariana Krumova, Christo Gyrbov, Simeon Savov, Galina Lazova.

■ **Bulgaria has its glasnost breakthrough with "Ivan And Alexandra," a film about the Stalinist '50s and the way children were used to denounce their parents. It was one of the best entries in Berlin's competition this year.**

It's 1952, and 11-year-old Ivan is filled with puppy love for classmate Alexandra (a whole head taller than he), daughter of a famous wartime partisan.

The Party decides the ex-hero is now an enemy of the people and he's arrested. At school, Alexandra, bewildered and ashamed, is stripped of membership in the Young Pioneers and ostracized by her classmates, save for the loyal Ivan. Even he tries to get her to go along with the authorities and publicly denounce her father, which she refuses to do.

Within a commendably tight running time, director Ivan Nichev has made a fully rounded picture of a grim era. The kids listen to western music, sneak into cinemas by the back door and take part in patriotic plays. The horror of the Stalinist purges eventually envelops them, and it's made tougher because they don't really understand what's going on.

As things get worse, police roam the Sofia streets and grab hold of youths to cut their long hair or slice open their trendy tight pants. Meanwhile, the schoolteacher who forced the humiliation of Alexandra in class is seen silently weeping in the empty schoolroom.

It's strong stuff, beautifully acted by Kliment Corbadziev and Monika Budjonova as the children and with, presumably, more than a touch of autobiography. —Strat.

Kronvittnet
(Experiment In Murder)
(SWEDISH)

Berlin   A Swedish Film Institute presentation (and foreign sales) of a Nordisk Tonefilm Intl. with the Swedish Film Institute and Sonet Media production. Produced by Ingemar Ejve. Directed by Jon Lindström. Screenplay, Rita Holst, Lindström, based on novel by Maarten t'Hart; camera (color). Esa Vuorinen; editor, Darek Hodor; music, Wlodek Gulgowski; production design, Niklas Ejve; costumes, Lena Söderström; production management, Kaj Larsen; assistant director, Daniel Bergman. Reviewed at Berlin Film Festival (Market), Feb. 13, 1989. Running time: **105 MIN.**

Thomas	Per Mattsson
Leoni, his wife	Marika Lagercrantz
Chief of Detectives Lambert	Gösta Ekman
Jenny	Emma Norbeck
Verner	Patrik Ersgard
Arianne	Jessica Zandén
Robert	Stefan Sauk

Also with: Mimi Pollak, Janne Carlsson, Janos Hersko, Allan Svensson, Lotta Krook.

■ **"Experiment In Murder"** **suffers from blurry plot development and a confusing whodunit denouement. Jon Lindström's thriller has a glossy look and some psycho-erotic impact.**

Fine acting in strongly written roles plus unusual settings helps the bewildering story of a scientist who stands accused of the murder of Jenny, a sexy wench who chanced into his lab.

Lambert, the policeman who investigates the case, fails to produce Jenny's body, but evidence turns up that Thomas' laboratory has been a front for big-scale dope dealing.

The ending has everybody looking and feeling guilty without any among those present having actually committed the murder.

—*Kell.*

Jacknife

New York A Cineplex Odeon Films release of a Kings Road Entertainment presentation of a Sandollar-Schaffel production. Produced by Robert Schaffel, Carol Baum. Directed by David Jones. Screenplay, Stephen Metcalfe, from his play "Strange Snow;" camera (Technicolor; Filmhouse prints), Brian West; editor, John Bloom; music, Bruce Broughton; sound (Dolby), Gary Alper, Patrick Rousseau; production design, Edward Pisoni; production manager-associate producer, Bruce S. Pustin; assistant director, Robert Shapiro; stunt coordinator/2d unit director, Everett Creach; casting, Judy Courtney, D.L. Newton. Reviewed at Broadway screening room, N.Y., Feb. 1, 1989. MPAA Rating: R. Running time: **102 MIN.**

Joseph (Megs) Megessey	Robert De Niro
Dave	Ed Harris
Martha	Kathy Baker
Jake	Charles Dutton
Ferretti	Loudon Wainwright 3d

■ **Robert De Niro's tour de force turn as a feisty Vietnam vet fails to save "Jacknife," a poorly scripted 3-hander drama. Cineplex Odeon will have to work hard to get any mileage out of this dinky Kings Road picture.**

De Niro is Megs (alternately nicknamed Jacknife by his war buddy Bobby, who was killed in action), a burnout working as a car repairman. He decides to get another war buddy, Dave (Ed Harris), to break out of his shell by forcing him to have a good time and remember those blocked-out adventures the trio had in 'Nam.

Scripter Stephen Metcalfe, who also adapted Par's recent "Cousins" feature, fails to establish why De Niro suddenly pounces on Harris, living in the same Connecticut small town together. Brittle opening has Harris' high school teacher sister (Kathy Baker) frightened by the noisy De Niro who invades their house to take Harris fishing.

A romance eventually blossoms between Baker and De Niro (with Harris opposing the alliance), leading to a prom night where she is the chaperone with De Niro her date; Harris violently disrupts the event. Script arbitrarily has De Niro leaving Baker once he's brought Harris back to reality, a gimmick seemingly designed by Metcalfe just so a corny reconciliation scene can be inserted as wrapup.

Besides its romance of "little people," film's central treatment of the Vietnam hangover that hamstrings Harris' return to normal living proves to be flat and uninvolving, a subject better treated head-on in Par's recent flop "Distant Thunder" which had John Lithgow in that role.

Three Method acting leads are interesting to watch, though Harris' 1-note performance is offputting and his crying jag in the climactic scene is self-defeating. Baker grows in her plain-Jane part after initially wrestling with non-colloquial dialog.

De Niro is spectacular, bringing life to every scene he's in, including a cute homage to Jack Nicholson's classic diner encounter in "Five Easy Pieces."

Unfortunately, helmer David Jones, who had better luck with the Harold Pinter 3-hander "Betrayal," fails to generate much interest in the material and early on has his camera too close up, causing De Niro's gesticulations to leave the frame in one scene.

Elsewhere, Brian West's photography of Connecticut locations is nondescript, while flashbacks of Vietnam battles are chintzy and unconvincing. —*Lor.*

American Ninja 3: Blood Hunt

Hollywood A Cannon release of a Breton Film Prods. Ltd. production. Produced by Harry Alan Towers. Executive producer, Avi Lerner. Written and directed by Cedric Sundström. Story by Gary Conway, based on characters created by Avi Kleinberger, Gideon Amir; camera (Rank color), George Bartels; editor, Michael J. Duthie; music, George S. Clinton; production design, Ruth Strimling; sound (Ultra-Stereo), Colin MacFarlane; assistant director, Sally Ann Caro; martial arts choreographer-second unit director, Mike Stone; second unit camera, Rene Smith; associate producer, John Stodel; casting, Gianna Pisanello & Associates. Reviewed at the AMC Century 14, L.A., Feb. 24, 1989. MPAA Rating: R. Running time: **90 MIN.**

Sean	David Bradley
Curtis Jackson	Steve James
Cobra	Marjoe Gortner
Chan Lee	Michele Chan
Andreas	Yehuda Efroni
Izumo	Calvin Jung
Minister's Secretary	Adrienne Pearce
Dexter	Evan J. Klisser
Minister of Interior	Grant Preston

■ **At the conclusion of "American Ninja 3: Blood Hunt," Steve James, the only actor to have appeared in all three series installments, says that he's tired of fighting ninjas. He could easily be speaking for the audience.**

By the end of this fatigued actioner, one feels like taking an extended vacation from black hooded warriors. Theatrical welcome will be worn out after a couple of weekends.

With karate expert David Bradley replacing Michael Dudikoff in the leading role, 4-year-old series continues with a rehash of the enjoyable second entry, as top international martial arts combatants gather on a tropical isle for a tournament.

As before, the island plays host to an evil entrepreneur, portrayed in this case by Marjoe Gortner, who is on the verge of perfecting a virus that will become the ultimate terrorist weapon. Ridiculously, he is looking for the perfect specimen on whom to test the germ, and finds him in the hunky Bradley, who is prepared for a "designer death."

For his part, Bradley is determined to rescue his Japanese master, whom he believes has been kidnapped by the baddies. This provokes him and his fearless partners into an assault on the fortress-like laboratory, in which three good guys and a gal neatly dispatch dozens of anonymous hooded ones before Marjoe gets his.

Even for this level of by-the-numbers action filmmaking, Cedric Sundström script is incredibly lame, and his staging of chop-socky violence is little better. Nor are matters helped by George Bartel's muddy lensing or George S. Clinton's irritating score.

Cheap-looking pic was produced in South Africa by the irrepressible Harry Alan Towers, who henceforth ought to seek new national and genre horizons for his cinematic attentions. —*Cart.*

Die Jungfrauenmaschine (Virgin Machine) (WEST GERMAN-B&W)

Berlin A First Run Features release (U.S.) of a Hyänc Film 1/11 production. Produced and directed by Monika Treut. Screenplay, Treut; camera (b&w), Elfi Mikesch; editor, Renate Merck; music, Mona Mur; sound, Alf Olbrisch; production manager, Anita Horz; assistant director, Greta Schiller. Reviewed at Berlin Film Festival (New German Cinema), Feb. 16, 1989. Running time: **85 MIN.**

Dorothee Müller	Ina Blum
Dominique	Dominique Caspar
Ramona	Shelly Mars
Bruno	Marcelo Uriona
Heinz	Gad Klein
Hormone Specialist	Peter Kern
Stripper	Fanny Fatal
Susie Sexpert	Susie (Sexpert) Bright

Also with: H-C Blumenberg, Mona Mur, Erica Marcus, Pearl Harbor.

■ **An uneven effort about a young Hamburg femme journalist who leaves behind unsatisfactory male relationships at home and heads for San Francisco and the lesbian scene; this is a good bet for gay venues, with crossover action doubtful.**

Pic recently opened at a Greenwich Village theater.

Ina Blum is perky as the wide-eyed heroine, Dorothee, but her early adventures in Germany, involving boring boyfriend and a brother for whom she has incestuous yearings, are strictly ho-hum.

Things pick up when she lands in Frisco searching for her long-lost mother. Here she meets Susie Sexpert, who urges her to check out femme only strip clubs, and the domineering Dominique, who speaks German and comes from Uruguay. Most importantly, Dorothee has a roll in the hay with the fetching Ramona, but is alarmed to get a $500 bill when it's all over.

Gay audiences should respond to Dorothee's adventures, but director Monika Treut's touch is too heavy to give the film a consistent lift that might have made it a bet for wider acceptance. Film is shot in high-contrast black and white (only the credit titles are printed in red). It's technically very good, with some bouncy music in the second half. —*Strat.*

La Noche Oscura
(The Dark Night)
(SPANISH)

Berlin A Iberoamericana presentation of an Iberoamericana Generale de'Images, TV Española production. Produced by Andres Vincent Gomes. Written and directed by Carlos Saura. Camera (Fotofilm color), Teo Escamilla; editor, Pedro del Rey; music, J.S. Bach; sound, Carlos Faruolo, Gilles Orthion; art direction, Gerardo Vera. Reviewed at Berlin Film Festival (competing), Feb. 12, 1989. Running time: **93 MIN.**

St. John of the Cross . . . . Juan Diego
Ana, de Jesus/Virgin Mary . . . . Julie Delpy
Vailer . . . . Fernando Guillen
Prior . . . . Manuel de Blas
   Also with: Fermi Reixach (Friar Jerome), Adolfo Thous (Friar Maria), Abel Viton (Friar Jacinto), Francisco Casares (Friar Joseph), Marilena Flores (Mother Superior).

■It's a radical change of pace for Carlos Saura from the oversize dimensions of his recent "El Dorado," to this intimate study of a monk grappling with faith and temptation.

St. John of the Cross was a 16th century mystic poet, imprisoned by his Carmelite brethren. He was threatened with damnation and tortured to give up his attempts of reforming the order and his vows of poverty.

For nine months he remained unrepentant.

Saura, who has used quotes by St. John of the Cross several times in his previous films, concedes this is very close to a philosophical tale, dealing with the nature of faith, not the most evident material for film drama. Not quite as ascetic as a Bresson or Dreyer to appeal to film buffs and art houses, nor as spectacular as "The Name Of The Rose," which dealt with similar theological conflicts but in a more extensive manner, Saur fails to put real passion into his picture.

With no strong emotions or characters to grab attention, his picture looks remote and theatrical.

Performances aren't much help, since Juan Diego, constantly on screen, wears the same painted expression throughout, while his inquisitors, except the kind-hearted Vailer, are typical bigots from whom nothing but grim stares can be expected.

Teo Escamilla, Saura's regular cameraman, used period paintings for inspiration with impressive results, and the choice of Bach's music for the soundtrack is most welcome.

However, Saura's admirers, who have been expecting him for some years to choose a new direction for his pictures will evidently have to wait some more.
—*Edna.*

Schweinegeld, Ein Märchen der Gebrüder Nimm
(Cash, A Political Fairytale)
(WEST GERMAN)

Berlin A FFAT Film and Maran-Film/B A Film Produktion/Pro-ject Filmproduktion/Kairos Film Alexander Kluge coproduction. Executive producer, Michael Boheme. Directed by Norbert Kückelmann. Screenplay, Kückelmann, Michael Juncker, Dagmar Kekule; camera (color), Frank Brühne; editor, Nani Schumann; music, Hanno Rinne, Gabriela di Rosa; sets, Olaf Schiefner; sound, Wolf-Dietrich Peters-Vallerius. Reviewed at Berlin Film Festival (competing), Feb. 17, 1989. Running time: **102 MIN.**

Maxwell . . . . Armin Mueller-Stahl
Wally . . . . Claudia Messner
Harry . . . . Rolf Zacher
Ferdinand Liebkind . . . . Stefan Suske
   Also with: Hans-Michael Rehberg, Günter Grävert, Manfred Rendl, Alfred Edel, Georg Tryphon, Christine Prober.

■This is a droll, lighthearted comedy about an impecunious trio who set up a charity organization and decide to buck a shady group of businessmen whose "charity" fundraising is designed to fill their own coffers. Pic has numerous amusing episodes, but interest is probably limited to its own domestic market.

One of the conniving trio is a tramp, Maxwell, with the gastronomic tastes of a gourmet. The second is a film producer, pursued by creditors, who is trying to make a pic called "Limping Dogs," and for which he goes in for a bit of dognaping. Third of the triumvirate is a girl, Wally, who's an out-of-work actress working on her part in "Joan Of Arc."

Entering into the scene is a low-echelon tax investigator who becomes aware of the illegal manipulations of the Tattenbach Corporation, and joins forces with the trio, who have set up their "Bit 'O Luck" company. The four of them storm the corporate headquarters of the Tattenbach operation and confiscate incriminating documents that will prove their fraudulent operations.

There's especially fine thesping by Armin Mueller-Stahl as the tramp turned businessman, with other performances and helming effective. —*Besa.*

Ja Milujem, Ty Milujes
(I Love, You Love)
(CZECH)

Berlin A Slovenska Filmova studio production. (Intl. sales, Ceskoslovensky Fil-mexport.) Produced by Karol Bakos. Directed by Dušan Hanák. Screenplay, Hanak, Dušan Dusek; camera (color), Jozef Ort-Snep, Alojz Hanusek; editor, Alfred Bencic; music, Miroslav Korinek; production design, Milos Kalina; sound, Ondrej Polomsky. Reviewed at Berlin Film Festival (competing), Feb. 19, 1989. Running time: **95 MIN.**

Pista . . . . Roman Klosowski
Vinco . . . . Milan Jelic
Viera . . . . Iva Janzurova
Albinko . . . . Vaclav Babka
Aunt Sida . . . . Marie Motlova
Pista's mother . . . . Milada Jezkova

■Shelved for almost 10 years, this Slovak item emerges as a quite typical Czechoslovak comedy, bittersweet in mood, relaxed in pacing, universal in theme. However, it's not up to the best work of past Czech masters Milos Forman or Jiri Menzel.

Plump, nerdish Pista (Roman Klosowski) and tall, maladroit Vinco (Milan Jelic) live in a village backwater and work for the postoffice. Vinco has constant success with the girls, whereas Pista is one of life's complete failures. Both drink schnapps and beer in quite incredible amounts.

On one drunken binge, Vinco lights the gas to make coffee, then passes out. Pista finds his friend dead next morning, leaving behind his pregnant girlfriend, the much cheated-on Viera (Iva Janzurova). Pista decides to sober up and accept the responsibility of his old friend's girl and child.

The film is simple stuff, filled with chuckles even though its protagonists are hardly likeable types. The bitter humor is often pleasing, and the acting is first-rate, with a winning performance from Milada Jezkova (remembered from past Czech comedy classics) as Pista's senile old mother.

Presumably the pic was banned because the Prague bureaucrats objected to the slothful lifestyle, with ultra-heavy boozing, plus the rundown houses and uncared-for public buildings on display. Pic was worth resurrecting, and may play the fest circuit after its Berlin debut. —*Strat.*

Bert Rigby, You're A Fool

Hollywood A Warner Bros. Pictures release of a Lorimar Film Entertainment presentation of a Clear production. Produced by George Shapiro. Written and directed by Carl Reiner. Camera (Metrocolor), Jan de Bont; editor, Bud Molin; music, Ralph Burns; production design, Terrence Marsh; art direction, Dianne Wager; set decoration, John Franco Jr.; costume design, Ruth Myers; choreography, Larry Hyman; sound (Dolby), Joe Kenworthy; assistant director, Marty Ewing; production manager (U.K.), Hugh O'Donnell; casting, Penny Perry, Rose Tobias Shaw. Reviewed at Glen Glenn Sound screening room, L.A., Feb. 16, 1989. MPAA Rating: R. Running time: **94 MIN.**

Bert Rigby . . . . Robert Lindsay
Laurel Pennington . . . . . Cathryn Bradshaw
Sid Trample . . . . Robbie Coltrane
Meredith Perlestein . . . . Anne Bancroft
Jim Shirley . . . . Corbin Bernsen
I.I. Perlestein . . . . Jackie Gayle
Elvis impersonator . . . . . . Liberty Mounten
   Also with: Bruno Kirby, Liz Smith, Lila Kaye.

■Watching Robert Lindsay sing and dance his way through "Bert Rigby, You're A Fool" is like eating English trifle. It's sweet, mushy, looks good and is pleasurable — but not worth the calories. Warner Bros. will eat profits on this one.

Carl Reiner wrote and directed this homage to '30s and '40s musical comedies as a vehicle for Lindsay, a Tony Award winner for "Me And My Girl," who clearly is a much more talented and versatile performer than this pedestrian material allows him to demonstrate.

Bert Rigby (Lindsay) is a striking coal miner who's got a certain talent recreating unforgettable screen moments of the likes of Fred Astaire, Gene Kelly and Buster Keaton, which mildly amuses his pub chums.

The film plays like one long-forgettable vaudeville act. That's consistent with the kinds of skits that make up the majority of the storyline that follows Lindsay from depressed, industrial Northern England to a paid talent plant in a traveling "Amateur Show," to naive, exploited aspiring Hollywood actor.

There is little to laugh at or be caught up in here, though Lindsay's hoofing is impressive and his energy and enthusiasm are laudable. Unfortunately his best routines are weighed down by the completely banal voiceover narration he has to deliver in between.

Exchanges with his next-door neighbor and barmaid sweetheart Laurel (Cathryn Bradshaw) are appropriately cute and relatively authentic sounding for ordinary, everyday lovers. His encounters with kewpie-doll sounding producer's wife Anne Bancroft are embarrassing.

Lindsay finds himself taking odd jobs as a gardener, pizza delivery man and butler in Los Angeles. Being a butler places him in the one amusing sequence — as Cockney voice coach to heartthrob film star Jim Shirley (Corbin Bernsen), who's as oily a personality as Lindsay is squeaky clean and virtuous.

Reiner has created as many smarmy and 1-dimensional Limey characters as American ones, with at least one inbetweener, an English Elvis impersonator whose name is Liberty Mouten.

Tech credits are fine. The musical numbers are well orchestrated and the English countryside is lovely to look at. —*Brit.*

La Bande des quatre
(Band Of Four)
(FRENCH-SWISS)

Paris   A films du Losange release of a Pierre Grise Prods./Limbo Film/La Sept coproduction. Produced by Martine Marignac. Directed by Jacques Rivette. Screenplay, Rivette, Pascal Bonitzer, Christine Laurent. Camera (Eastmancolor), Caroline Champetier; editor, Catherine Quesemand; music, Monteverdi; sound, Florian Eidenbenz; art direction, Emmanuel de Chauvigny; assistant director, Lorraine Groleau. Reviewed at the 3 Balzac Theater, Paris, Feb. 15, 1989. Running time: **160 MIN.**

Constance	Bulle Ogier
Thomas	Benoit Régent
Claude	Laurence Cote
Anna	Fejria Deliba
Joyce	Bernadette Giraud
Lucia	Inès de Medeiros
Cecile	Nathalie Richard

■Jacques Rivette returns to some favorite themes in this long, monotonous tale about a group of acting students pursuing courses while trying to help out a girlfriend in mysterious distress. Competing at Berlin, pic will obviously divide fest and art house goers into two warring camps.

That hoary dialectic favorite, the interplay of Theater and Life, is again at the heart of Rivette's new film. One of the two principal settings is the Paris studio theater where no-nonsense acting prof (and former legit star) Bulle Ogier conducts an all-female group of theatrical hopefuls into the secrets of acting truth.

In typical Rivette style, the theatricals alternate with extramural scenes in the real world where four classmate-roommates learn their girl friend (and former roommate) has fallen into dangerous company with a new boyfriend.

Events take a more alarming turn when a stranger begins to importune each of the girls and finally seduces one of them, gains entry to the house and begins a vain search for a mysterious key. The girls finally band together to dispose of the intruder.

Even though the plot leads to a surprise arrest and the murder of the cop by the four girls, suspense is not Rivette's concern or talent.

Script by Rivette, Pascal Bonitzer (a Cahiers du Cinema scribe-turned-screenwriter) and designer-filmmaker Christine Laurent is a basically humorless intellectual blueprint upon which Rivette constructs a cold, artificial edifice of a film.

New actresses Laurence Cote, Fejria Deliba, Bernadette Giraud and Inès de Medeiros are good, but their personal warmth and spontaneity suffer under Rivette's bloodless directives. Ogier is icily forbidding as the apparently all-for-art acting teacher.

Ironically Benoit Regent turns in the most appealing performance as the "villain," a morally ambiguous cop fascinated by chance but driven by a need for order. Tech credits are okay. —*Len.*

Histoires D'Amerique
(American Stories)
(FRENCH-BELGIAN)

Berlin   A Mallia Films (Paris)-Paradise Films (Brussels) coproduction, with La Sept, The Pompidou Center, R.T.B.F., in cooperation with the Ministry of Culture (France) and the Ministry of French Culture (Belgium). (World sales: Metropolis Films, Zurich). Executive producers, Bertrand van Effenterre, Marilyn Watelet. Written and directed by Chantal Akerman. Camera (color), Luc Ben Hamou; editor, Patrick Mimouni; music, Sonia Wieder Atherton; production design costumes, Marily Watelet; sound, Alix Comte; production manager, Edwin Baily; assistant director, Ellen M. Kuras; casting, Marcia Muraskin Shulman. Reviewed at Berlin Film Festival (competing), Feb. 14, 1989. Running time: **99 MIN.**

With: Mark Amitin, Eszter Balint, Stefan Balint, Kirk Baltz, George Bartenieff, Bill Bastiani, Isha Manna Beck, Jacob Becker, Max Brandt, Maurice Brenner, David Buntzman, Marilyn Chris, Sharon Diskin, Carl Don, Pierre Esptein, Michael Grodenchik, Ben Hammer, Dean Jackson, Robert Katims, Mordecai Lawner, Boris Leskin, Elliot Levine, Justine Lichtman, Judith Malina, Jerry Matz, Charles Mayer, Roy Nathanson, Bruce Nozik, Deborah Offner, Irina Pasmur, Herschel Rosen, Joan Rosenfels, Herbert Rubens, Claudia Silver, Arthur Tracy, Victor Talmadge.

(English soundtrack)

■A film consisting entirely of stories and anecdotes, some tragic, some wryly funny, some simply human, told mostly straight to camera by a wonderful cast of New York Jewish actors, "American Stories" is a very special pic whose appeal may be limited but should score well in special situations.

These stories were written by Belgium director Chantal Akerman, but are evidently culled from the memories of Jews throughout this century, so that though the setting is contemporary, some of the stories told deal with pogroms of more than 70 years ago.

There are tragic stories: a girl who, at 13, was sole survivor of a pogrom and, having been raped, felt she could never be married; a girl who left Poland at 16, instructed by her parents to marry a man she didn't know; a woman with several children who lived in poverty until helped by a rich couple who then demanded as payment one of the children.

Then there are more amusing stories, such as that told by a woman in love with two men, or the monolog of a cynical athiest who becomes hooked on the Talmud.

All these stories are told by a superb cast of Jewish actors and actresses (whose contributions aren't individually indentified). Akerman has filmed near the illuminated Williamsburg Bridge, making the real setting appear like an artifical set.

This is obviously special fare, and won't appeal to wide audiences. It's a must for lovers of Jewish culture and humor, and could have long runs in special locations. It's a bit on the long side at 99 minutes, but it would be a pity to drop any of the material.

It's technically fine, with a plaintive music score that's sparsely used.

The film is subtitled "Food, Family And Philosophy," and is dedicated to the late Jacques Ledoux (of the Brussels Film Archive) —*Strat.*

Paris By Night
(BRITISH)

Berlin   A Cineplex Odeon Films release (in U.S.) of a British Screen, in association with Zenith and Film Four Intl., presentation of a Greenpoint-Pressman production. (Intl. Sales: The Sales Co.) Executive producer, Edward R. Pressman. Produced by Patrick Cassavetti. Written and directed by David Hare. Camera (Technicolor), Roger Pratt; editor, George Akers; music, Georges Delerue; production design, Anthony Pratt; sound, Clive Winter; production managers, Linda Bruce (U.K.), Françoise Leherissey (France); assistant director, Chris Hall; casting, Mary Selway. Reviewed at Berlin Film Festival (Market), Feb. 13, 1989. Running time: **101 MIN.**

Clara Paige	Charlotte Rampling
Gerald Paige	Michael Gambon
Adam Gillvray	Robert Hardy
Wallace Sharp	Iain Glen
Michael Swanton	Andrew Ray
Pauline	Jane Asher
Janet Swanton	Linda Bassett
Jenny Swanton	Niamh Cusack

Also with: Robert Flemyng (Jack Sidmouth), Sandi Toksvig (Sandra), Jonathan White (Simon), Juliet Harmer (Delia), Melissa Stribling (Lady Boeing), Brian Cobby (Foreign Secretary).

■David Hare's second feature as a director (his first, "Wetherby," won the Golden Bear at Berlin in 1985) is a handsomely produced, rather cold drama abut the fall of a femme politician.

Hare's clever screenplay and formal, crisp direction, allied to a strong performance from Charlotte Rampling, should give the picture a career in limited, top-class locations.

Although Clara Paige is at the top of the ladder, a high-profile, pro-Thatcher, Tory politico and member of the European parliament, she still finds other people's lives more attractive than her own. Her husband, Gerald (an M.P.) is a drunk she's come to despise. She has little time to spend with their son.

When not hobnobbing with influential Tories, or meeting with constituents, Clara is full of private troubles. An anonymous caller is making vague threats, and she feels she's being blackmailed by Gerald's former business partner, Michael.

On a high-level trip to Paris to haggle with the French over farm prices she meets with a young British businessman, Wallace, and starts an affair with him. Late at night, by the Seine, she's walking along when she sees Michael. Certain he's followed her, and that he's the anonymous caller, she tips him into the river, where he drowns.

What follows involves Clara's attempts to cover up her crime and her gradual realization that Michael, after all, was neither a blackmailer nor her telephone caller. Pic ends with an act of savage violence.

Hare handles it all with dry, often witty, precision, but with a slightly academic style. Most of the characters are cleverly written and powerfully acted. The screenplay bristles with sharp lines (a Foreign Office types notes, wryly, that Britain used to have "a special relationship" with America; now it's with American Express) and the direction proves Hare is a born filmmaker.

Roger Pratt's camerawork is outstanding, and Georges Delerue contributes one of his more effective scores.

Hare falters, however, in the central love story. Iain Glen is miscast as the lover, and hardly comes across as a candidate for a passionate love affair. Not enough is made of his political opposition to Clara (though he notes she's his first naked Tory) and their scenes together are flat.

Michael Gambon is fine as Clara's pathetic husband. Andrew Ray is moving as the desperate murder victim, while Robert Hardy makes his odious Tory politico effortlessly smug and sinister.

As Clara, Charlotte Rampling catches the coldness of this Thatcherite woman who believes that, for the privileged, doing whatever you want is the very basis of freedom — but who finds her world collapsing around her.

''Paris By Night'' will be a tricky film to handle, but should find an appreciative audience. Hare already has completed a third feature, 'Strapless.'' —*Strat.*

A Mulher Do Proximo
(Your Neighbor's Wife)
(PORTUGUESE)

Berlin Produced by MGN, Filmes e Espectaculos, R.T.C. and Radiotelevisao Commercial. Directed by Jose Fonseca e Costa. Screenplay, Fonseca e Costa, Miguel Esteves Cardoso; camera (color), Eduardo Serra; editor, Fonseca e Costa, Jose Alves Pereira; music, Antonio Emiliano; sound, Carlos Alberto Lopes. Reviewed at Berlin Film Festival (Market), Feb. 12, 1989. Running time: **84 MIN.**

Cristina	Carmen Dolores
Antonio	Vergilio Teixeira
Isabel	Fernanda Torres
Henrique	Mario Viegas
Manuel	Vitor Norte

■ ''Your Neighbor's Wife'' is **described as a black comedy yet its plot and treatment rely heavily on stereotypical melodrama, à la the ''telenovela'' romances imported from Brazilian tv. Prospects look brightest for offshore tv and video.**

The dinner of the wealthy Castro Silva family is interrupted by a phone call announcing the death of the father Mario. When the mother, Cristina, daughter Isabel and son-in-law Henrique go to the morgue to identify him, they discover the body of a young woman, apparently his lover, who was killed with him.

Cristina pines away for her dead husband while Isabel overcomes her grief through afternoon trysts with the butler Manuel. Longing for true love, she announces her intentions to divorce her childish and dissolute conductor husband although he does not seem to take the threat seriously.

It is difficult to empathize with any of the family members. Fernanda Torres, the Brazilian cast as Isabel, is comely and lively. Vitor Norte is perfect as the macho but-

ler Manuel.

The mainly interior cinematography is conventional and other tech credits are adequate. Scenes of fortresses outside Lisbon and picturesque parts of its old town provide a visual tribute to Portugal's beauty. —*Sam.*

Pestalozzis Berg
(Pestalozzi's Mountain)
(WEST GERMAN)

Berlin A Stella-Film, Praesens-Film. Ellepi Film coproduction with DEFA-Studio für Spielfilme, in conjunction with SRG DRS-ZDF. Directed by Peter von Gunten. Screenplay, von Gunten, Peter Schneider, Lukas Hartmann, based on novel by Hartmann; camera (Eastmancolor), Jürgen Lenz; music, Heinz Ruber. Reviewed at Berlin Film Festival (competing), Feb. 14, 1989. Running time: **120 MIN.**

With: Gian Maria Volonté, Rolf Hoppe, Heidi Züger, Christian Grashof, Michael Gwisdek, Corinna Harfouch, Silvia Jost, Angelica Ippolito, Peter Wyssbrod, Käthe Reichel, Isolde Barth, Mathias Gnädinger, Roger Jendly.

■ **This is a slow-paced, introspective period piece set in 1798 Switzerland, chronicling the tribualations of Swiss educational pioneer Johann Heinrich Pestalozzi and told mostly in flashback as the educator rests in a friend's spa hotel.**

Beautifully photographed and handsomely produced, pic nonetheless lacks any internal rhythm or drama as scenes and flashbacks succeed each other without building up. Most of the pic concerns Pestalozzi's efforts in a mountain convent where he undertakes to provide shelter and food plus a dose of education to the village children, whose parents are willing to put them in his care.

Story is set against the Napoleonic wars, though the only time we see French troops is near the end, when they evict the educator and his two dozen charges, when the site is needed by the French as a refuge.

Considered an outcast and dangerous innovator, Pestalozzi nonetheless manages to find some people sympathetic to his cause, and is given succor by the village authorities. Overcoming the initial suspicion of the ragged children, he proceeds to care for them as best he can.

Gian Maria Volonté puts in a fine performance as the bedraggled and struggling educator, and technical credits are fine, but pic will be too slow for theatrical release. It may prove okay for European or educational tv. —*Besa.*

Odpadnik
(Maverick)
(YUGOSLAV)

Berlin A Viba Film production. Directed by Bozo Sprajc. Screenplay, Sprajc; camera (Eastmancolor), Goran Trbuljak; editor, Vesna Kreber; music, Jani Golob; production design, Janez Kovic; production manager, Iztok Preinfalk; sound, Matjaz Janezic. Reviewed at Berlin Film Festival (Panorama), Feb. 20, 1989. Running time: **95 MIN.**

Oto Kern	Ivo Ban
Silvo Hren	Radko Polic
Nina	Sasa Pavcek
Emma	Savina Gersak
Ida Kern	Alenka Vipotnik
Hugo Ropar	Janez Hocevar
Vili	Cojmir Lesnjak
Luka Kern	Matjaz Tribuson

■ **A hard-hitting melodrama about corruption within Yugoslavia's large business corporations, this Slovenian pic ultimately degenerates into fanciful melodrama, but notches up a few plus points along the way.**

Oto Kern is an electro-technician in a Ljubljana factory, but he's unpopular with his superiors when he accuses them of accepting bribes from western companies for raw materials which could have been obtained locally, thus wasting vital hard currency.

His anger increases when he's by-passed for a top lab job. He takes his accusations both to the police and the union, but with no success. Eventually, he takes a gun and metes out his own justice against the corrupt businessmen before committing suicide. It ends the pic on an overblown note.

Until then, though, the pic has made some interesting points about corruption in Yugoslavia (Kern refers to Mafia, while urging the workers to strike in protest). The corruption extends to the private lives of these execs, who relish western porn (on two occasions they're seen enjoying hardcore videos) and enjoy dalliances with their employees.

Kern himself is no angel in this respect, since he neglects his bitter wife in favor of a pretty secretary, who, however, cheats on him with one of his enemies. An extraneous sub-plot has Kern infatuated with a blond dream woman (Savina Gersak), with whom he eventually goes off on an idyllic spree, complete with nude bathing.

Ivo Ban makes Kern too macho and single-minded to be a very interesting hero, and it's a pity that writer-director Bozo Sprajc couldn't have made more of his important subject than this flashy but ultimately rather silly, thriller.
—*Strat.*

Stagefright

Berlin An Autumn production. Executive producer, Barbie Cox. Produced by Bradford Mays, Loretto Gubernatis. Directed by Mays. Screenplay, Stanley Keyes from story by Mays; additional dialog, Mays; camera (color), John Van Strien; editor, Mays; production manager, Leslie Resnick; sound, James Gouldthorpe. Reviewed at Berlin Film Festival (Market), Feb. 14, 1989. Running time: **88 MIN.**

Grayson Osterman	Rick Hammontree
Lori Glenn	Susan Rome
Broderick Kands	Greg McClure
Zip Marris	Willie Brookes
Chuck Pines	David Caltrider
Frannie Goodman	Marcy Emmer
Crazy Otto	Arthur Laupus
Dereck Soriven	Derek Neal

■ **A low-cost debut feature, ''Stagefright'' concerns the backstage quarrels, love intrigues and artistic frustrations among a hard-working acting troupe within an avant garde storefront theater in Baltimore.**

Time is 1971, but pic ''Stagefright'' does not comment in original or interesting fashion on the mores of that time. It is stylistically conventional, with nonstop small talk by narcissistic characters (the performers of the theater company) who do not inspire concern or respect.

Greg McClure as Brod, the theater director, has a certain flair. Susan Rome is Lori, the one character of spirit, who leaves Baltimore to follow her star and become one in Hollywood.

Marcy Emmer as Frannie scores as an eccentric, hyperactive bisexual. Others in the cast do their best with shallow characterizations provided by the script. —*Hitch.*

Der Bruch
(The Break)
(EAST GERMAN)

Berlin A DEFA Studio production of the Babelsberg Group, with production support from Allianz Filmproduktion of West Berlin. Produced by Gerrit List. Directed by Frank Beyer. Screenplay, Wolfgang Kohlhaase; dramaturgy, Dieter Wolf, camera (Orwocolor), Peter Ziesche; editor, Rita Hiller; music, Günther Fischer, ''Tango For Paul'' sung by Jürgen Walter, lyrics by Kohlhaase; sound, Hans-Henning Thölert; art direction, Dieter Adam. Reviewed as official selection at Berlin Film Festival (out of competition), Feb. 15, 1989. Running time: **119 MIN.**

Graf	Götz George
Markward	Rolf Hoppe
Lubowitz	Otto Sander
Kollmorgen	Hermann Beyer
Biegel	Jens-Uwe Bogadtke
Lotz	Gerhard Hähndel
Pinske	Reiner Heisc
Tina	Ulrike Krumbiegel
Julian	Volker Rainisch
Bubi	Thomas Rudnick
Frau Markward	Franziska Troegner
Anita	Angelika Waller
Müller	Jürgen Walter

■ **Good screenplay, top notch**

acting by a mixed team of East German and West German thesps, and solid directing come together to produce a bank heist pic with mass appeal.

This picture could become the year's big hit in the German-lingo market and turn handsome coin in specialty houses elsewhere.

In war devastated 1946 Berlin, a quirky band of small time crooks crack a bank vault. From the opening sequence in a ratty postwar movie house, Peter Ziesche's fluid camerawork establishes the film's bittersweet nostalgic mood. There are food shortages, black market swindlers, tattered pin-striped suits — everything in flux.

Dialog is crisp and full of delightful word plays and puns which will have foreign subtitling teams tearing their hair. There's not a single superfluous line in this pic's screenplay by veteran DEFA director and scriptwriter Wolfgang Kohlhaase.

West German tv police action series star Götz George gets top billing and turns in a relatively subdued performance.

Director Frank Beyer, who has been making films and tv shows in East Germany for 35 years now, has a firm grip throughout this film, resulting in fine ensemble acting.

Rolf Hoppe handles his role as a retired safecracker who is talked into taking on one last job with a skill and charm that has the audience rooting for the "bad guys."

Politics in wartorn Berlin are ever present, and the "good guys" are bumbling rookie postwar policemen who have replaced ousted Nazis. In one moving scene, Hoppe's safecracker is interrogated by a detective (Gerhard Hähndel) who was once incarcerated at the same Nazi prison as the safecracker. The detective, a communist, had been branded a political criminal.

That vignette is typical of Beyer's attenton to detail and his ability to reach inside characters to show what makes them tick.

Technical credits are superb, fleshing out a bombed-out city and making it come to life through rich color and sound. —*Gill.*

Slaves Of New York

New York   A Tri-Star Pictures release of a Hendler/Merchant Ivory production. Produced by Ismail Merchant, Gary Hendler. Directed by James Ivory. Screenplay, Tama Janowitz, based on her stories; camera (Technicolor), Tony Pierce-Roberts; editor, Kather-ine Wenning; music, Richard Robbins; production design, David Gropman; art direction, Karen Schultz; costumes, Carol Ramsey; production manager, Mary Kane; assistant director, Richard Hawley; sound (Dolby), Tom Nelson; associate producers, Fred Hughes, Vincent Fremont; casting, Howard Feuer. Reviewed at Columbia Pictures screening room, N.Y., Feb. 23, 1989. MPAA Rating: R. Running time: **121 MIN.**
Eleanor . . . . .Bernadette Peters
Stash . . . . .Adam Coleman Howard
Marley . . . . .Nick Corri
Daria . . . . .Madeleine Potter
Sherman . . . . .Charles McCaughan
Victor Okrent . . . . .Chris Sarandon
Ginger Booth . . . . .Mary Beth Hurt
Samantha . . . . .Mercedes Ruehl
Chuck Dade Dolger . . . . . . .John Harkins
Mooshka . . . . .Anna Katarina
Mikell . . . . .Bruce Peter Young
Jan . . . . .Michael Schoeffling
Wilfredo . . . . .Steve Buscemi
B . . . . .Christine Dunford
Also with: Betty Comden, Tammy Grimes, Tama Janowitz, Joe Leeway, Michael Butler, Johann Carlo, Philip Lenkowsky, Harsh Nayyar, Stanley Tucci, Louis Guss, Maura Moynihan, Kim Larese, Ken Kensei, Kevin John Gee, Rick Hara, Francine Hunter.

■Adapted by Tama Janowitz from her book of interlinked stories about young strivers on Manhattan's downtown art scene, "Slaves Of New York" mutes the fiction's mordant, ironic voice and accentuates its contemporary trappings. To succeed, "Slaves" will need the support of the hip audience it so assiduously courts.

The bestselling book's high profile as a hot property undoubtedly boosted its transition to the screen. Because the author was closely involved with the picture (as screenwriter and in a supporting role) comparisons between the fiction and the film are apropos.

Director James Ivory unfolds this ensemble narrative with characteristic fluidity, staying true to the off-kilter hyper-reality of Janowitz' mise-en-scène. The novel's subcultural atmospherics and bent discourse are dutifully grafted to the screen. But the film's self-possessed creative misfits — slaves to Gotham's crushing indifference — lack the revealing focus of the fiction's first-person point of view. Their motivating obsessions are constantly evoked, but never truly animated.

An insecure aspiring designer of outré hats, Eleanor (Bernadette Peters), is held in emotional and economic thrall by her thoughtless, moderately talented painter boyfriend Stash (Adam Coleman Howard). Peters is beguiling as the pliable, dizzy Eleanor, who longs for a "normal" life but desperately seeks social acceptance in the cruel concrete bohemia of mid-'80s Manhattan.

The film follows Eleanor as she embarks on a tenuous evolution toward independence and self-realization. She exists in a hermetic milieu of ramshackle studios, avant-garde performance clubs and trendy boutiques inhabited by the cliquish players on the downtown scene: backbiting artists, craven gallery owners, ruthless agents, crude patrons and trash-talking parasites. Eleanor is surrounded by artistic dropouts who have been thoroughly corrupted by the go-go material success ethics of Reagan-era New York.

Except for Peters' plucky heroine, the performances in "Slaves" tend to be perfunctory. Screenplay reduces the characters to quick-sketch concepts — worse than unsympathetic, they are uninteresting. There are Marley Mantello (Nick Corri), who is leader of the pack of hustling painters; Marley's best friend Sherman (Charles McCaughan), an embittered struggling artist, and his scheming sculptress girlfriend Daria (Madeleine Potter), who's two-timing with Marley. Maximizing a secondary role is Steve Buscemi as Wilfredo, the punk-couture king who becomes Eleanor's angel.

Marley wants Eleanor to model for his dream project: a fantastical chapel in Rome, dedicated to "Jesus Christ As A Woman." His flights of fancy greatly distress Marley's yupped-out agent (Mary Beth Hurt) and self-interested gallery owner (Chris Sarandon). In the book, Marley is a high-strung maverick, processing the bombardment of exterior perceptions with a wild interiorized logic that lends a weird credibility to his fixations. In the film, Corri's Marley carries on like a swaggering jock with an outsized ego, devoid of esthetic, intellectual and emotional depth.

Janowitz' screenplay is nothing but faithful to her book's time/-place locus, impeccably served by the first-rate design and production values that are standard in Merchant Ivory offerings. Ivory employs split screens and superimpositions to suggest the intersection of the episodic vignettes. A soundtrack peppered with contempo sounds ranging from speed-metal to house music may bear too much responsibility for sustaining dramatic momentum as the film shuttles betwixt its various closed-in locations.

Missing are the dark psychological backfill, graffiti-like detail and twisty rueful humor that gave the book idiosyncratic personality. It also misses by a few beats the au courant immediacy that gave the book pop-fave cachet.

There are laughs, but they are either tossed-off or painful situational laughs squeezed dry of the book's satirical juices. In the end, however, the film is more optimistic than the book by seeming to offer marginal hope in the redeeming power of relationships.—*Rich.*

Chances Are

Hollywood   A Tri-Star Pictures release of a Lobell/Bergman production. Produced by Mike Lobell. Executive producers, Andrew Bergman, Neil A. Machlis. Directed by Emile Ardolino. Screenplay, Perry Howze, Randy Howze; camera (Metrocolor), William A. Fraker; editor, Harry Keramidas; music, Maurice Jarre; production design, Dennis Washington; sound (Dolby), Charles L. Campbell, Richard C. Franklin; costume design, Albert Wolsky; makeup, Cheri Minns; associate producer, Leslie Benziger; casting, Mike Fenton, Judy Taylor. Reviewed at AMC Century 14 Theaters, L.A., Feb. 18, 1989. MPAA Rating: PG. Running time: **108 MIN.**
Corinne Jeffries . . . . .Cybill Shepherd
Alex Finch . . . . .Robert Downey Jr.
Philip Train . . . . .Ryan O'Neal
Miranda Jeffries . . .Mary Stuart Masterson
Louie Jeffries . . . . .Christopher McDonald
Judge Fenwick . . . . .Josef Sommer
Omar . . . . .Joe Grifasi
Woman in bookstore . . . . .Susan Ruttan
Mavis Talmadge . . . . .Fran Ryan
Dr. Bailey . . . . .James Noble

■Here comes "Chances Are" and there goes Mr. Jordan, no doubt in a huff. While this new pic hinges on the same cloud-carpeted conception of heaven as a way station for earth-bound souls, the similarity ends there, and a potentially charming premise yields only a handful of chuckles.

Boxoffice prospects look as wispy as those clouds, unless an unusual number of filmgoers are willing to suspend disbelief and buy into this silliness.

Almost everything that happens in "Chances Are" occurs as a convenience to advance the story toward some crowd-pleasing finale, with little regard to logic or consistency.

Cybill Shepherd is expected to look twentysomething at the outset and mid-to-late 40s (with a 22-year-old daughter) during the bulk of the action. Falling in the middle she's convincing as neither.

The plot hangs on the death of Shepherd's husband, who flees heaven to be reincarnated before being "innoculated" to prevent a return of past-life memory.

He comes back 23 years later as Robert Downey Jr. and stumbles into the life of Corinne (Shepherd), as well as that of her daughter Miranda (Mary Stuart Masterson) and former best friend Philip (Ryan O'Neal). Philip harbors a long-suffering adoration for Corinne, who has kept him at arm's length while turning the house into a veritable shrine to her husband.

There's a nice scene when Alex (Downey) first comes to dinner and starts to remember his past life, but from then on Perry and Randy Howze's screenplay is patently predictable.

Downey sparkles at times simply with his stunned expressions. Beyond that, the rest of the characters are at best absurd: Masterson throws herself at him instantaneously. O'Neal and Shepherd have both supposedly been pining the past 23 years until the hubby's return spurs them to action.

It's difficult to accept that any of these characters existed a moment before the credits come up, making it hard to swallow nearly everything that ensues. Director Emile Ardolino ("Dirty Dancing") keeps the pace moving and tone light but can't sidestep all the ludicrous situations strewn before him.

The depiction of heaven is almost unforgivably cliched. Cameraman William Fraker certainly knows his way around the neighborhood, having previously shot "Heaven Can Wait."

Maurice Jarre contributes yet another fine score, and Johnny Mathis' vocal on the title track remains as warming as a blanket on a chilly night. Unfortunately, even with back-breaking efforts to neatly tie up all the loose ends, "Chances Are" doesn't come close to equalling those dulcet tones. —*Bril.*

La Soule
(FRENCH)

Paris An AMLF release of an Agepro Cinéma/MF Productions/TF1 Films coproduction. Produced by Marie-Christine de Montbrial, Michel Frichet. Directed by Michel Sibra. Screenplay, Sibra, Jacques Emond, from original story idea by Emond; camera (Agfa color), Jean-Jacques Bouhon; editor, Elisabeth Couque; music, Nicola Piovani; art direction, Jacques Rouxel; sound, Daniel Ollivier, Laurent Quaglio, Dominique Hennequin, Francois Groult; costumes, Mic Cheminal; production manager, Eric Dussart; assistant director, Gérard Pujolar; casting, Françoise Menidrey. Reviewed at Marignan-Concorde theater. Paris, Feb. 15, 1989. Running time: **98 MIN.**
Francois Lemercier . . . . Richard Bohringer
Pierre Cursey . . . . Christophe Malavoy
Marion . . . . Marianne Basler
Gauberlin . . . . Roland Blanche
Priest . . . . Jean-Pierre Sentier
Col. Valbert . . . . . . Jean-Francois Stévenin
Marie-Joseph Granier . . . . Eric Marion

■Newcomer Michel Sibra has found an unusual subject in this period drama about a brutal popular sport that anticipated modern rugby football. The script he and Jacques Emond have imaged to set out the game is weak in characterization and stale in dialog.

Sport was called La Soule (which was an oblong ball of leather filled with bran). Dating back to the Middle Ages, it remained popular into the 19th century in certain provinces. Its scrimmage resembled war games and frequently left players maimed or dead.

Sibra's pretext for a reconstitution of one deadly match is the vengeance sought by a Napoleonic officer (Christophe Malavoy) against a French soldier (Richard Bohringer) whose cowardice on the battlefield led to former's capture and humiliating imprisonment by the English. The time is 1813-1815, after the defeat of the French army in Spain and Napoleon's first exile to Elba.

Malavoy tracks down his man to a village in southwestern France, where Bohringer is now a cobbler and proud captain of a champion Soule team. Malavoy decides that the best revenge would be to beat him at the game in which Bohringer has invested most of his masculine honor.

Tech credits are smart. Music is unmistakably by Nicola Piovani.
—*Len.*

See You In The Morning

Hollywood A Warner Bros. release of a Lorimar Film Entertainment production. Produced, written and directed by Alan J. Pakula. Camera (Metrocolor), Donald McAlpine; editor, Evan Lottman; sound, Michael Steinfield, Louis Berfini; production design, George Jenkins; art direction, Bob Guerra; costume design, John Boxer; casting, Alixe Gordin. Reviewed at The Burbank Studios, Burbank, Calif. March 3, 1989. MPAA Rating: PG-13. Running time: **119 MIN.**
Larry Livingston . . . . Jeff Bridges
Beth Goodwin . . . . Alice Krige
Jo Livingston . . . . Farrah Fawcett
Cathy Goodwin . . . . Drew Barrymore
Petey Goodwin . . . . Lukas Haas
Peter Goodwin . . . . David Dukes
Neenie . . . . Frances Sternhagen
Robin Livingston . . . . Heather Lilly

■ "See You In The Morning" is a bad dream for those who've admired Alan J. Pakula's best work. For the sake of him and the mostly fine talent involved, it can be be hoped the film won't be seen by anyone. Theatrical and video prospects look equally dismal.

This angst-filled melodrama could best be described as a "late-thirtysomething."

Pakula produced, wrote and directed "See You In The Morning" as a semi-autobiographical story of a man torn between two families and two marriages. Jeff Bridges is a Manhattan psychiatrist who tries earnestly to fit in with his new life with second wife Beth (Alice Krige) and her two kids, while remaining the most decent of dads to his own two kids. Their mother is played by Farrah Fawcett.

As dull as this sounds, it's even more boring to watch. At just under two hours, it seems nearly interminable.

Not only does Pakula announce what is upcoming, with titles to introduce the Livingstones and the Goodwins, he makes sure the viewer doesn't confuse them by going over their biographies repeatedly.

Pakula tried too hard to make this into a romantic comedy. Bridges' character jokes to avoid talking about his feelings (some shrink!) while Krige is the guilt-ridden martyr type.

Given the seemingly endless dialog, the lack of real communication among Bridges, Krige and their children seems incredible. Add to this the near non-existence of physical passion between the duo and you wonder how they ever fell in love.

Drew Barrymore and Lukas Haas are fine as Krige's troubled kids, the former shoplifting to get attention and the latter playing the cello to escape. Bridges' own daughter, Robin (Heather Lilly) comes off as if she were a better therapist than her father.

About the only redeeming quality of this effort is that Nat Cole's great rendition of "Our Love Is Here To Stay" opens and closes the picture and production designer George Jenkins' sense of place is as fine as ever. —*Brit.*

Skin Deep

Hollywood A 20th Century Fox release of a Morgan Creek Prods. presentation of a BECO production. Produced by Tony Adams. Executive producers, Joe Roth, James G. Robinson. Written and directed by Blake Edwards. Camera (Panavision, Deluxe color), Isidore Mankofsky; editor, Robert Pergament; production design, Rodger Maus; set decoration, Marvin March; set design, Bob Beall; costume design, Nolan Miller; sound (Dolby), Milton C. Burrow; special effects, Industrial Light & Magic; assistant director, David C. Anderson; associate producer, Trish Caroselli; casting, Jackie Burch. Reviewed at the Cary Grant theater, Culver City, Calif., Feb. 25, 1989. MPAA Rating: R. Running time: **101 MIN.**
Zach .John Ritter
Barney . . . . Vincent Gardenia
Alex . . . . .Alyson Reed
Jake . . . . .Joel Brooks
Molly . . . . .Julianne Phillips
Lonnie . . . . .Raye Hollit
Dr. Westford . . . . .Michael Kidd
Amy . . . . .Chelsea Field

■Blake Edwards' "Skin Deep" finds the director centering again on the trials and tribulations of his favorite kind of character — the charming, womanizing sot. Fortunately, he freshens up his trademark formula by satirizing the most contemporary of current social practices: safe sex.

If for one hysterically funny scene alone (that the networks have censored from the pic's trailers for being too anatomically obvious for general audiences), "Skin Deep" probably will do better than it would without all this fuss. Fox should score well with this entry.

John Ritter is a dissipated writer with writer's block who is always to be found with a drink in his hand and an eye on a potential sexual conquest.

Like many other drunks in Edwards' films, Ritter is set up well financially and never is without enough money to pay the bar tab. He's also very lucky to have as a confidant (and pushover) Vincent Gardenia, proprietor of his favorite watering hole who indulges Ritter's fantasies to be a torch singer-pianist.

While most of their dialog is unprintable, suffice it to say Gardenia and Ritter have great "man talk" that turns out to be more cathartic therapy for the patient than he gets from his shrink (Michael Kidd).

Ritter is married to a pretty (and pretty dull) newscaster (Alyson Reed) who is smart enough, however, to boot her husband out when she finds him in bed with her hairdresser (Julianne Phillips). No matter, Ritter moves in with her at another elegant home and tries half-heartedly to remain faithful. Of course, he can't, whereby she nastily plays the first of her two outrageous tricks on him, the latter in her role as an herbal wrap masseuse who uses electrical impulses as part of her technique.

With neither a sophisticated nor particularly distinctive plotline, film still is enjoyable as Ritter suffers a series of humiliations while sloshed or hungover — for which he grows increasingly remorseful — even as he can't seem to restrain himself as soon as another opportunity to score comes along.

The funniest of these slapstick setups has Ritter asked to use a condom that, unbeknownst to either him or his rather easy target (Chelsea Field), glows in the dark.

She's the battered girlfriend of a played-to-type low-class British rocker who, like Ritter, is hot to trot. As Ritter scurries into the closet, the boyfriend returns to his hotel room and emerges from the bathroom similarly protected.

The inevitable and technically very convincing fight between the two guys follows, set against a completely black screen — a priapic duel, as the ancient Romans might say. Clearly, the very fertile minds of the special effects wizards at Industrial Light & Magic had a good time with this assignment, and the visual treat is just as much a hoot for the film's audiences. —

Revenge is sweet and Ritter gets his due in any number of silly and embarrassing situations which he handles with nearly perfect comic timing. Those cast to play off him are (mostly) equally wonderful, especially Joel Brooks as his cynical and competent lawyer (and fellow ladies' man) and intimidating bodybuilder Raye Hollit, who wreaks a kind of sexual havoc of her own on Ritter.

This is not an R film in the usual sense. Some of the language is as descriptive as the footage and may offend those who don't appreciate such frank treatment of man's favorite topic (other than sports).

For everyone else, it's a romp, a real roll in the hay. —*Brit.*

Scandal
(BRITISH)

London A Miramax Films release of a Palace Pictures production, in association with British Screen and Miramax. Produced by Stephen Woolley. Executive producers, Nik Powell, Joe Boyd. Co-executive producers, Harvey Weinstein, Bob Weinstein. Directed by Michael Caton-Jones. Screenplay, Michael Thomas; camera (Technicolor), Mike Molloy; editor, Angus Newton; music, Carl Davis; production design, Simon Holland; art direction, Chris Townsend; casting, Susie Figgis; associate producer, Redmond Morris. Reviewed at Century preview theater, London, Feb. 2, 1989. Running time: **114 MIN.**
Stephen Ward . . . . John Hurt
Christine Keeler . . . Joanne Whalley-Kilmer
Mandy Rice-Davies . . . . Bridget Fonda
John Profumo . . . . Ian McKellen
Lord Astor . . . . Leslie Phillips
Mariella Novotny . . . . Britt Ekland
Johnnie Edgecombe . . . . Roland Gift
Eugene Ivanov . . . . Jeroen Krabbé

◼ **In 1963 the sensational revelations that a good-time girl had** been having affairs with a British cabinet minister and a Soviet naval attaché shocked the U.K. and helped bring down the conservative government. "Scandal" reexamines the controversy and looks to be a hit in the U.K. Film could click offshore if handled properly.

"Scandal" has been garnering mucho publicity locally in both serious and lightweight media with its combination of political wrangling and sexual dalliances. Pic is given extra credibility by strong acting talent, some of which is underused.

The film's problem is Michael Thomas' busy script, which hasn't quite made the transition from its intended tv miniseries format to the strictures of a feature film. Some major characters slip in and out of the pic, and for an audience unaware of the background (unlike the Brits) there may be unanswered questions.

"Scandal" is an intriguing examination of the darker side of the swinging '60s, but it is at its strongest when it comes down to the basic story of Christine Keeler and Stephen Ward — the tragic characters of the movie.

Man-about-town Ward (John Hurt) meets young showgirl Keeler (Joanne Whalley-Kilmer) and decides to transform her into a glamorous sophisticate.

He also takes in hand (though touches neither girl sexually) 16-year-old Mandy Rice-Davies (Bridget Fonda). Ward is delighted when Soviet naval attaché Ivanov (Jeroen Krabbé) takes a shine to Whalley-Kilmer, though at the same time Cabinet Minister John Profumo (Ian McKellen), the secretary of state for war, falls for her.

At one point she is sleeping with both men, and though Krabbé is sent home and the affair with McKellen soon ends, the minister foolishly gives her presents and sends notes. A year later she has left Hurt's flat and taken up with a series of West Indian lovers.

When she is fought over by two lovers, she returns to Hurt's flat. One of the men (Roland Gift) follows her and starts shooting at the building when she refuses to appear. After a spell in the police station, a vulnerable Whalley-Kilmer talks to a seemingly sympathetic reporter who smells a story when Profumo's and Ivanov's names are mentioned.

As the story breaks, McKellen is forced to resign and Hurt's influential friends abandon him and he is eventually arrested and charged with living on the earnings of prostitutes.

Hurt is excellent as the charming but shallow Ward, and portrays him as a sad man who wanted powerful and beautiful friends around him and who suffers the worst possible sentence for him — social ostracism.

Joanne Whalley-Kilmer looks the part, but seems happier with the humorous and ironic parts of the script than with the more serious and sexual elements. American Bridget Fonda — with an admirable British accent — is perfect, though unfortunately her character disappears for chunks of the film.

First-time feature helmer Michael Caton-Jones handles the film well and obviously was not over-awed by his subject or cast. He is a stylish director and the strong cast responds well. Other technical credits are fine and a smooth soundtrack should help market the pic.

Since the film is set less than three decades ago, many characters involved are still alive and there is a slight sense that "Scandal" is not the film it could be because it is forced to tread a safe path. —*Adam.*

Dan le ventre du dragon
(In The Belly Of The Dragon)
(CANADIAN)

Montreal An Alliance Vivafilm release of a Prods. Québec/Amérique production. Produced by Michel Gauthier; Executive producers, Monique H. Messier, Lorraine Richard. Directed by Yves Simoneau. Screenplay, Simoneau, Pierre Revelin, Marcel Beaulieu; camera (color), Alain Dostie; editor, André Corriveau; sound (Dolby), Michel Charron, Paul Dion. Reviewed at Cineplex Odeon's Cinema Le Berri, Montreal, Feb. 21, 1989. Running time: **102 MIN.**
Lou . . . . David La Hayne
Steve . . . . Rémy Girard
Bozo . . . . Michel Côté
Le Boss . . . . Pierre Curzi
Mireille . . . . Monique Mercure
Doctor Lucas . . . . Marie Tifo
Madame Cote . . . . Andrée Lachapelle

◼ **In a seemingly impossible task, Yves Simoneau has magically blended two almost completely unrelated stories using an all-star Quebec cast. What results is an entertaining psycho/comedy with a well-camouflaged social message and a dash of animation.**

There's a humorous tale about a happy-go-lucky trio and their boss who deliver department store flyers.

The youngest of the three, Lou (played smoothly by debutant actor, La Haye), clearly needs a new pair of boots, and flyers paying 3¢ a crack won't do the trick.

Enter Story B. Lou sees an ad in the classified section promising "fast cash."

In a "castle" — complete with a moat — Lou gets a job as a human guinea pig for a giant pharmaceutical firm.

For $250 per week, Lou could be injected with the common cold and take experimental cold pills. He wants super "fast" cash, so he opts for the $1,500 per week salary which involves a high-risk experiment.

Marie Tifo, shines as the mad scientist running the experiment. At any price, she wants to find a way to allow the average human being to use more than 12% of his brain.

In a Frankenstein-style experiment, Tifo succeeds in increasing brain capacity to 80%. The unfortunate side effect of her experiment is that patients become 100 years old overnight. Minor detail, Lucas will just have to use babies.

A happy ending superbly entwines Simoneau's bizarre mixture of fantasy and reality without compromising the moral of the story: "Cut off the head of the dragon before it eats you."

Riddled with homegrown humor and dialect, "In The Belly Of The Dragon" may prove a very difficult time to subtitle or dub. However, an English version will be ready for the Cannes Film Festival in May. —*Suze.*

Hit List

Hollywood A New Line Cinema release of a Cinetel Films production. Produced by Paul Hertzberg. Executive producer, Lisa M. Hansen. Coproducer, Jef Richard. Directed by William Lustig. Screenplay, John Goff, Peter ——era (Foto-Kem color), James Lemmo; editor, David Kern; music, Garry Schyman; art direction, Pamela Marcotte; set decoration, Michael Warga; costume design, Elizabeth Gower-Grudzinski; stunt coordinator, Spiro Razatos. Reviewed at Mann Theater, Hollywood, March 3, 1989. MPAA Rating: R. Running time: **87 MIN.**
Jack Collins . . . . Jan-Michael Vincent
Frank DeSalvo . . . . Leo Rossi
Chris Caleek . . . . Lance Henriksen
Tom Mitchum . . . . Charles Napier
Vic Luca . . . . Rip Torn
Jared Riley . . . . Jere Burns
Gravenstein . . . . Ken Lerner
Sandi Collins . . . . Harriet Hall
Kenny Collins . . . . Junior Richard
Abe Fazio . . . . Jack Andreozzi
Brian Armstrong . . . . Harold Sylvester

◼ **"Hit List" won't be on many.**

A gritty look and nearly non-stop action pace could generate sparse b.o. among the very, very undemanding, but things get drawn out and silly down the stretch.

The film at first has the makings of a pleasant surprise, as director William Lustig — veteran of three such action yarns — brings a real flair to the early scenes, particularly some well-choreographed fight sequences featuring a ninja-like assassin (Lance Henriksen).

Once the plot begins to coalesce, however, it's apparent that no one cared if anything made sense scriptwise as long as it provided a flimsy excuse for shootouts, chases and righteous indignation.

A mafia kingpin (Rip Torn) hires hitman Caleek (Henriksen) to kill witnesses who can testify against him. Unfortunately, Caleek unwittingly (and he's not alone in that regard) hits the house across the street, where Jack Collins (Jan-Michael Vincent) and his family live.

With his child abducted by the assassin, Jack ends up teaming up with one of the mobsters scheduled to testify, nicely played by Leo Rossi.

Aside from the absurd plot (killers apparently aren't schooled about the segregation of "evens" and "odds" on street addresses), writers John Goff and Peter Brosnan shoot themselves in the feet with much of the dialog, and the performances don't help matters.

With the exception of Rossi's slimy mobster and Henriksen's killer, nearly everyone chews the scenery when not shooting holes through it. Vincent, last seen piloting "Airwolf" on tv, gives an unbearably wooden performance as the supposedly distraught dad, while Torn blusters pathetically as the overfed mobster.

Tech credits are really topnotch in light of the material, most notably James Lemmo's camerawork and some excellent stuntwork, as Caleek flits about like a murderous Spiderman. —Bril.

BERLIN FEST REVIEWS

Restrisiko — Oder Die Arroganz Der Macht
(An Act Of God)
(WEST GERMAN)

Berlin A Denkmal Film production. Written and directed by Bertram Verhaag, Claus Strigel. Camera (color), Strigel, Waldemar Hauschild, Friedrich Klütsch, Thomas Willke; editor, Matthias Bauer; music, V. Bassenge, W. Neumann; sound, Liane Grimm. Reviewed at Berlin Film Festival (Panorama), Feb. 12, 1989. Running time: 95 MIN.

■ German leftwing documentary directors Bertram Verhaag and Claus Strigel have now made a second film about a controversial nuclear fuel rod reprocessing plant. Unfortunately, it's no more watchable than the first.

Last time around, with "Spalt-Prozesse," the directors focused on demonstrations at the plant site. This time they set their cameras up at a public hearing on the plant's construction plans. The result is 95 minutes of sweaty-faced people yelling at each other in German about points of order.

The uninitiated viewer is never given any background on the controversy. Proponents and opponents are never identified by more than name and obscure title.

The filmmakers' goal of seeking to inform a mass audience about a hearing where officials clearly attempted to put one over on local residents is thwarted by the dullness of presentation. —Gill.

RobbyKallePaul
(WEST GERMAN-SWISS)

Berlin A Metropolis Film release, produced by Luna Film (Berlin), Gudrun Ruzickova with Fool Film (Berlin), Levy/Koschnick & Atlas Saskia (Duisberg), Hanns Eckelkamp & Fama Film (Bern), Rolf Schmid, with grants from DRS-TV (Zurich), Federal Department of the Interior (Bern) and the Cantons of Basel-City and Basel-Country. Directed by Dani Levy. Screenplay, Levy, Maria Schrader, Anja Franke, Holger Franke; camera (color), Carl F. Koschnick; editor, Uwe Lauterhorn; music, Niki Reiser; song "Damn Child" composed and sung by Nina Schultz; sound, Christian Moldt; art direction, Edwin Wengoborski; costumes, Mona Kuschel; production manager, Gudrun Ruzickova. Reviewed at Berlin Film Festival (New German Films), Feb. 15, 1989. Running time: 95 MIN.

Robby . . . . .Dani Levy
Kalle . . . . .Frank Beilicke
Paul . . . . .Josef Hofmann
Henny . . . . .Anja Franke
Malu . . . . .Maria Schrader
Tilla . . . . .Nina Schultz
Kalle's mother . . . . .Helma Fehrmann
Also with: Martin Walz, Li Hensel, Holger Franke, Thomas Wolff, Gerd Hunger.

■ "RobbyKallePaul" is a fast-paced comedy about three roommates seeking romance. It should do especially well with viewers in their late teens through late 20s but could draw a wider audience by capitalizing on the success of Doris Dörrie's likeminded German comedy "Men."

When Robby returns from a trip to Japan, he discovers his girlfriend Henny has taken up with his roommate Kalle. Robby is shattered; Henny moves out, and Robby begins to mediate and declares, "Sex is a waste of time."

Paul, a successful but sexually frustrated factory supervisor, moves in. When his attempt to seduce Tilla (one of his employees) fails and she becomes enamored with Kalle, the three roommates begin a hostile battle of wills.

The conversations among the three provide self-parodying insight into the male psyche. Especially funny are sight gags revolving around lanky Kalle moving all the fixtures to a height unsuitable for his two shorter roommates and Kalle's attempt to produce tears to splash on a letter to Henny.

The humor is fresh, the acting natural. An unfortunate tendency to play to and with the camera could have been tempered. A scintillating jazz score by Niki Reiser adds a lot of spark. —Sam.

Tag till himlen/El tren al cielo
(Train To Heaven)
(SWEDISH-ECUADORIAN)

Berlin An Exat (Stockholm) presentation (and world sales) of a Filmstallet. Exat coproduction with Condor Film, Cinemateca Ecuador. Produced by Anders Birkeland, Hans Lönnerheden. Directed by Torgny Anderberg. Screenplay, Anderberg, based on his novel; camera (Eastmancolor), Tony Forsberg; editor, Susanne Linnman; music, Gunnar Edander; sound, Kurt Holmberg; production design, Julio Garcia; costumes, Lenamari Wallström; production management, Jill Devell. Reviewed at Berlin Film Festival (Children's Film Festival, in competition), Feb. 16, 1989. Running time: 95 MIN.

Nino . . . . .Carlos Lopez
Gregorios . . . . .James Coburn
Train Conductor . . . . .Hugo Alvarez
Padre Juan . . . . .Teodor de la Torre

■ Filmed on location in Ecuador and with Spanish dialog, "Train To Heaven" by Swedish writer Torgny Anderberg overflows with the sweetness of its intentions.

It chugs its way erratically through its simple plot: 10-year-old orphan Nino runs away from the Catholic strictness of Padre Juan's school and sets off in search of his parents. They are said to be "in heaven," and since heaven is also where the mountain city of Quito supposedly lies, Nino and his dog stow themselves away on a quaint old train bearing them upward.

En route, Nino and the dog are pursued by Padre Juan, the police and sundry other evil-minded persons of all ages. They are also befriended by an old Gringo hobo (James Coburn, still grinning hugely but moving a mite more stiffly than before) and by a train conductor (Hugo Alvarez, the Brazilian actor-director who now runs a Latin-American stage in Sweden).

Nino is played by quietly charming Carlos Lopez, who was discovered while shining shoes in Guayaquil by director Anderberg.

"Train To Heaven" could find its way into homevid and tv situations, where items of guaranteed innocence and upbeat sentiment are in demand. For wider audiences, this film is too condescending, too talkative and, in its few bursts of real action, too afraid to go beyond merely hinting of danger. —Kell.

Pol
(WEST GERMAN)

Berlin A CAM Film production. Directed by Aribert Weis. Screenplay, Weis, Peter Gocolin; camera (color), Michael Riebl; editor, Klaus Basler; music, Willi Siebert. Reviewed at Berlin Film Festival (Market), Feb. 12, 1989. Running time: 85 MIN.
With: Angelika Bartsch, Walter Sachers, Jürgen Schornagel.

■ Pol is the name of a popular female singer in this odd little story about the German music scene. Though the story seemed implausible at the screening, there was a similar story in the local press a few days later.

A singer returns unannounced to the loft of an ex-lover, a popular composer who has done successful material for her. Unbeknownst to her, she is being stalked by a deranged fan who seems bent on killing the composer because he thinks they are still involved. The film documents the couple during an evening that is by turns loving and antagonistic.

For some reason not made clear, she discovers the crazed fan with his highpowered rifle in position in the opposite loft across the courtyard. She seems undisturbed by the gun, but the fan (apparently so overwhelmed by her presence) flees.

Angelika Bartsch is terrific as Pol. Gorgeous to look at, she has incredible vocal skills and is given ample opportunity to display them. It's just that this vehicle

doesn't seem to have much point.
—*Owl.*

Fifty Fifty
(WEST GERMAN)

Berlin A Filmverlag release of a Markus Trebitsch production, coproduced by Aspekt Telefilm/Ottokar Runze Filmproduktion/ZDF Mainz. Directed by Peter Timm. Screenplay, Detlef Michel; camera (color), Fritz Seemann; music, City; sound, Ernst-Hermann Marell; art direction, Frank Geuer; costumes, Regina Troester; makeup, Erich Lothar Schmekel, Jutta Krollpfeifer; production manager, Boris Riaskov. Reviewed at Berlin Film Festival (New German Films), Feb. 15, 1989. Running time: **88 MIN.**
Schröder . . . . .Heinz Hönig
Willi . . . . .Dominique Horwitz
Regina . . . . .Suzanne von Borsody
Lopitz . . . . .Siegfried Kernen
Kniepel . . . . .Karl Friedrich
Vater Kranich . . . . .Gert Haucke
Mutter Kranich . . . . .Katharina Matz
Also with: Peter-Heinrich Brix, Kurt Ackermann, Holger Mahlich, Jörg Gillner.

■ "Fifty Fifty," a light caper pic about a bank robbery, sustains interest through its amusing variations on familiar themes. It could do well in theaters at home but prospects loom brighter offshore for video sales.

Willi, the hapless son of a wealthy businessman, holds up his father's bank in an attempt to prove to the family he is not a complete failure. He bungles the job, however, and the police are tipped off by a safety alarm. Willi is saved from arrest by Regina and Schröder, an estranged couple who volunteer to be taken hostage.

Schröder advises Willi on how to make demands of the police and how to get away in one of their cars. He is a suspended policeman who wants to get revenge. He easily masterminds their getaway with the loot until tough police commissioner Lopitz catches on to what is happening.

The unconventional cast has good comic timing, which along with the lively pop-rock score accents the upbeat tempo of the script. Other tech credits are good.—*Sam.*

Die Drei Unteroffiziere
(The Three Junior Officers)
(GERMAN-B&W)

Berlin A Universum-Film (Ufa) production and release. Producers, Hans Herbert Ulrich, Ernst Martin. Directed by Werner Hochbaum. Screenplay, Jacob Geis, Fred Hildenbrandt, from an idea by Werner Schoknecht; camera (b&w), Werner Krien; music, Hansom Milde-Meissner; sound, Williband Zunft; art direction, Willy Schiller. Premiered March 31, 1939, at the Ufa Palast am Zoo in Berlin. Reviewed at Berlin Film Festival (Europe 1939 retrospective), Feb. 13, 1989. Running time: **94 MIN.**
With: Albert Hehn, Fritz Genschow, Wilhelm H. König, Wilhelm Althaus, Heinz Englemann, Wolfgang Staudte, Ruth Hellberg, Ingeborg von Kusserow, Hilde Schneider, members of the German Wehrmacht's Berlin Regiment and Infantry Training Regiment and the Luftwaffe.

■ This remarkable film, as timely now as it was when it was released half a century ago, was intended to be a blatant glorification of the Nazi military buildup. Director Werner Hochbaum gave this pic a touchingly tragic love story which ultimately sours military enthusiasm.

In hindsight, it is little wonder that Hochbaum was banned from filmmaking in June 1939, just weeks after the film preemed in Berlin amid martial hoopla.

Plot involves three junior officers (the film's title in German) who head companies in the same regiment and are best buddies. When one of them (Albert Hehn) falls for a legit stage actress (Ruth Hellberg), the other two cover up for his increasing dereliction of duty. The climax comes when the lovers decide to run off together.

Military officials put tanks, aircraft and hundreds of men at Hochbaum's disposal for realistic scenes of maneuvers which have an uncanny effect on today's viewer. The strutting, barking officers work like caricatures from some postwar spoof of German officers.

Best scene is when the two lovers stroll down a foggy Berlin street discussing their hopes for the future. The fog closes in, obscuring the outside world from the pair until they pass by a construction site where a welder's torch emits a shower of sparks reminiscent of artillery fire.

Hochbaum enlisted in the German army after war broke out and made military newsreels until he contracted TB. Before his death in 1946 he issued a caustic condemnation of the Nazi film industry, saying, "One of the most repulsive things about Nazism was the pairing of brutality and sadistic atrocities with sentimentality. That really made you gag from time to time." —*Gill.*

Rok
(Rock)
(SOVIET-DOCU-
COLOR/B&W)

Berlin A Leningrad Documentary Film Studio production. Directed by Alexei Utschitel. Written by Juri Filinow; camera (color, b&w), Dmitri Mass; editor, Valentina Torgajewa; music & lyrics, Boris Grebentschikow; sound, Sergei Litwjakow; production manager, Maja Schtschatkowa. Reviewed at Berlin Film Festival (Forum), Feb. 14, 1989. Running time: **84 MIN.**
With: Boris Grebentschikow & Aquarium, Viktor Zoi & Kino, Anton Adassinski & AWIA, Juri Schewtschuk & DDT, Oleg Garkuscha & Auktion.

■ The power of music is universal even when lyrics are in an unfamiliar tongue, as is illustrated nicely in this docu about Soviet rock music. This interestingly shot pic is sure to do well at fests and special screenings.

The workaday lives of five lead singers are contrasted with footage of them in performance with their bands. One works as a movie projectionist, another at manual labor. At night or on weekends when they don their performance drag, they become the swirling golden boys of the Soviet rock scene.

The music sequences are effectively photographed in black & white to emphasize the nuances of each performance. Presentation is similar to what Western rock audiences experience, but because these musicians aren't working with major budgets, production values are not as elaborate.

The unglamorous side of backstage life is also depicted: the seedy dressing rooms, dingy toilets and makeshift greenrooms. We get to see their relationships to their families, friends, fans and colleagues. One band even plays before a group of Soviet prisoners.

For those interested in the international rock music scene, docu is a good bet. —*Owl.*

Sluga
(The Servant)
(SOVIET)

Berlin A Mosfilm production. Directed by Vadim Abdrashitov. Screenplay, Alexander Mindadze; camera (Sovcolor), Denis Evstigneev; editor, R. Rogatkina; music, Vladimir Daskevic; production design, Alexander Tolkacov, Oleg Potanin; sound, Lilija Terechovskaya. Reviewed at Berlin Film Festival (competing), Feb. 15, 1989. Running time: **138 MIN.**
Pavel Kljuev . . . . .Yuri Beljaev
Andrei Gudionov . . . . .Oleg Borisov
Maria . . . . .Irina Rozanova
Roman Bryzgin . . . . .Alexei Petrenko
Valery . . . . .Alexander Teresko

■ "Sluga" is a long, challenging drama about shifting relationships between a powerful government man and his driver (his servant) over many years. It's not an easy film experience, but a clear indication that challenging themes are continuing to be tackled in the new Soviet cinema.

Drama opens in the present with Gudionov, an insignificant-looking man, arriving at the country home of famous orchestra conductor Kljuev and making contact with him. Seems that years before Gudionov was a powerful government man who appointed the young Kljuev as his driver, at the same time insisting absolute loyalty to him and to his sometimes eccentric ways. In time, he even insisted his driver marry Maria, Gudionov's discarded mistress.

Over the years, the positions have shifted, and now it's Kljuev who's the VIP with a driver of his own. That's when Gudionov, now retired, returns from the past to persuade his old servant to help rid him of an old political enemy who's still causing him trouble.

Director Vadim Abdrashitov, best known for "Planets On Parade," handles this relatively simple story in exceedingly complex style, cutting back and forth in time with only the physical appearance of the characters to differentiate the eras.

The theme of the master-servant relationship is evidently a tricky one for a communist society, and scenes in which the master forces his servant to obey his strange whims carry considerable impact.

Problem for the non-Soviet viewer will be sorting out all the references that are clearly in the film — they're not easy to identify on one viewing. What is very clear, though, is the talent of the director and his two principal actors, Oleg Borisov as the deceptively charming, utterly ruthless Gudionov and Yuri Beljaev as the former servant who feels compelled to remain loyal to his former master, despite the changed circumstances.

Since this is a less accessible film internationally than "Commissar" or "The Theme," it's not likely to set art house boxoffices on fire, but followers of the current changes in the USSR should go out of their way to see this one.
—*Strat.*

Kafr Qar'a — Israel
(FRENCH-DOCU)

Berlin A coproduction of Cineteve, ZDF and La Sept. Produced by Denis Leroy. Directed by Nurith Aviv. Written by Eglai Errera, Aviv; camera (color, 16m), Aviv; music, Pedro Elias; sound, Daniel Olivieri. Editor, Sabine Mamou. Reviewed at Berlin Film Festival (Forum), Feb. 14, 1989. Running time: **66 MIN.**

■ Pic makes a powerful statement by letting the Palestinian inhabitants, old and young, of an

Israeli-occupied village tell stories about their lives filtered through over 40 years of occupation.

Pic is an excellent document for those looking for another view of the events and circumstances that continually propel this part of the world into the international headlines.

Director Nurith Aviv's camera never seems to be intruding as we share reflections and experiences that have confronted the Arab population since Israel annexed their village-city in 1948. An old man tells how he lost his teaching position because he was not respectful enough to the military authorities.

An Arab woman who had Jewish friends when she was a teenager notes, not without a certain irony, that she grew up hearing repeatedly the word ''Akhva'' which is Hebrew for brotherhood. A young doctor remembers helping a badly injured man, who thanked him profusely for saving his life, only to return the next day and have the man refuse to let him come near because overnight he had learned his angel of mercy was an Arab.

Shot as a day in the life of the village, Aviv returns to some of her subjects long after they have already made very effective points. Tighter editing would enhance the docu's impact. —Owl.

Der Sommer Des Falken
(Summer Of The Falcon)
(WEST GERMAN)

Berlin A Topas Film production, with Atlas Sashia, WDR. (Intl. sales, Filmverlag der Autoren, Munich.) Produced by Ulrich Ströhle, Horst Burkhard. Directed by Arend Agthe. Screenplay, Monika Seck-Agthe, Arend Agthe; camera (color), Jürgen Jürges; editor, Yvonne Kölsch; music, Matthias Raue, Martin Cyrus; production design, Ulrich Bergfelder; stunts, John Delbridge. Reviewed at Berlin Film Festival (New German Cinema), Feb. 17, 1989. Running time: **103 MIN.**
Marie . . . . Andrea Lösch
Rick . . . . Janos Crecelius
Herbert . . . . Hermann Lause
Marck . . . . Rolf Zacher
Rick's father . . . . Volker Brandt

■ Seemingly aimed at a young teen audience, "Summer Of The Falcon" combines simple adventure and comedy, with spectacular mountain scenery. It's probably a better prospect for teenage girls than boys.

Marie, who lives on a mountain farm, saves a falcon which broke its wing. Rick, a city boy who effects a punk hairstyle and facial makeup, comes with his father to the mountains for a hang-gliding holiday. When Marie's falcon is killed by a poacher after valuable falcon eggs for Arab buyers, Rick teams up with her to foil the baddie.

Comic relief is supplied by Hermann Lause as a pigeon fancier whose top bird was consumed by the falcon. He comes searching for it and his car is sabotaged by the villain, resulting in an extended stunt sequence that's familiar but fun.

The whole film is pretty familiar stuff, right down to the English-

Die Feuerprobe
(Ordeal By Fire)
(WEST GERMAN-DOCU-COLOR/B&W)

Berlin An EML Film & TV production. Written, narrated and directed by Erwin Leiser, in collaboration with Vera Leiser. Camera (color, b&w), Peter Werneke; editor, Eva Schlensag, Wolfgang Gessat; sound, Klaus Klingler; research, Monika Handschuch; production manager, Elke Peters. Reviewed at Berlin Film Festival (New German Films), Feb. 20, 1989. Running time: **80 MIN.**

■ In another docu about the Holocaust, director Erwin Leiser, who survived Kristalnacht as a youngster in Berlin, has spliced together eyewitness accounts, archival footage and unpublished photos taken secretly by amateurs, to focus on Nov. 9-10, 1938.

Heartfelt and with absorbing recollections, docu was made for German tv. It should move abroad with relative ease.

Perhaps the most disturbing interview is with a woman who was unsympathetic to the Jewish plight under the Nazis and seemed to feel that what happened, if not exactly justified, was acceptable.

Subject continues to fascinate and outrage. Docu fits nicely into efforts to make certain the world never forgets. —Owl.

Tillbaka Till Ararat
(Back To Ararat)
(SWEDISH-DOCU-B&W/COLOR)

Berlin A First Run Features and Icarus release of a Swedish TV and Swedish Film Institute production. Directed by PeA Holmquist. Camera, (b&w, color), Holmquist. Collaborators, Goran Gunner, Jim Downing, Suzanne Khardalian. Reviewed at Berlin Film Festival (Market), Feb. 14, 1989. Running time: **100 MIN.**

■ A well-made docu about the genocide of 1.5-million Armenians in 1915 makes its point without resorting to sentimentality.

It could attract notice on its own merits in specialty theatrical screenings and on tv.

Pic likely will provoke controversy, especially in the U.S., Canada and France, which have large Armenian populations.

''Back To Ararat'' combines footage of contemporary Armenian communities, stills from Armenia before the tragedy and interviews with survivors. A brief historical background of the ''forgotten genocide'' is an essential feature.

Survivors recount their experiences calmly. Several interviews took place in the Los Angeles-Fresno area, home to over 300,000 Armenians. One witness related how he had been forced as a child to participate in the stoning of other Armenian children who were swimming across a river. Another elderly man on welfare gives a chilling account of surviving in a cave in Der el Zor with 15 others by eating the charred flesh of victims of a fire.

To director PeA Holmquist's credit, he touches upon the fanatic element present among Armenian nationalists. A sequence with an Armenian who shot a Turkish diplomat in Yugoslavia and was sentenced to 20 years ends with him proclaiming he is ready to sacrifice everything until the goal of re-establishing the nation is achieved. —Sam.

La Fille De Quinze Ans
(The 15-Year-Old Girl)
(FRENCH)

Berlin A Lola Films-Odessa Films production. (Intl. sales, Motion Media, Paris.) Produced by Jacques Doillon, Yannick Bernard. Written and directed by Doillon. Camera (Fujicolor), Caroline Champetier de Ribes; editor, Catherine Quesemand; sound, Jean-Claude Laureux. Reviewed at Berlin Film Festival (Market), Feb. 15, 1989. Running time: **84 MIN.**
Juliette . . . . Judith Godrèche
Willy . . . . Jacques Doillon
Thomas . . . . Melvil Poupaud

■ Jacques Doillon's latest exploration into sexual relationships is a 3-hander idyllically set in a Spanish seaside villa. Doillon creates some emotional and sexual suspense, but pic has more talk than action, and the talk is on the empty side.

Juliette, the eponymous 15-year-old, is a ''modern'' girl: she sleeps with her boyfriends once only, to get sex out of the way, then refuses. With her latest friend, Thomas, a year younger than she, the relationship has remained platonic, though the lad is

seriously smitten.

Willy (played by Doillon himself), Thomas' rather remote father, takes the two youngsters off to a rented villa on Ibiza, and even before they leave Paris the sexual sparring between middle-aged man and pert teenager has begun. Thomas rightly suspects the worst, though at first Juliette sleeps (chastely) with him at night and frolics topless in the sea when Willy isn't around.

Eventually, though, the inevitable seduction takes place, though in its aftermath Juliette remains true to her usual form.

Atmosphere here is calmer than usual for a Doillon film, though there's a genuinely moving moment when the tormented Thomas breaks down and cries with pain and humiliation.

As usual, Doillon fills his pic with rather cerebral talk, the kind more appreciated by French intellectuals than anyone else. The three actors are good, with young Judith Godrèche a find as the teasing Juliette.

The sun-splashed location settings are a positive factor in a film that never reaches the heights of Doillon's ''Touched In The Head'' or ''The Crying Woman.''
—Strat.

Risk-II
(SOVIET-U.S.-DOCU-B&W/COLOR)

Berlin A Sovexport presentation of a Gorki Filmstudio (Moscow) with Hollywood Film Co. (L.A.) production. Directed by Dimitri Barschevski. Sequence planning, Natalja Violina; camera (b&w, color), Oleg Voinov, Alexander Kulidshanov; editor, Tatjana Odnorobova; music, Anatoli Vajnstein; narration, Igor Kostolevski. Reviewed at Berlin Film Festival (Panorama), Feb. 16, 1989. Running time: **170 MIN.**

■ With "Risk II," history buffs may enjoy another feast of World War II-and-after docu footage, with the accent on the development of the atom bomb in Russia, the U.S. and elsewhere.

The Klaus Fuchs spy affair is given a large play in this 3-hour-long sequel by compilation planner Natalja Violina and director Dimitri Barschevski. They also aim at closeup portraiture of Hitler, Stalin, John F. Kennedy and all the other major (and some minor) men of power.

One should consult regular historians before believing everything put on display in "Risk-II." Some juggling has obviously been done with archive material to make the Russians come out looking better than anybody else in every context, and U.S. coproducer Hollywood Film Co. remains an unidentified entity.

Unidentified are also many of the archive sources of newsreel, official and private footage. Some has never been seen publicly before, including material only made accessible from the KGB vaults after glasnost. —*Kell.*

Brun Bitter
(Hair Of The Dog)
(NORWEGIAN)

Berlin A Filmeffekt production, with Viking Film, Norsk Film. Produced by Dag Alveberg. Directed by Solve Skagen. Screenplay, Skagen; camera (Eastmancolor), Erling Thurmann-Andersen; editor, Malte Wadman; music, Geir Bohren, Bent Aserud; production manager, Aage Aaberge; assistant director, Finn Krogvig. Reviewed at Berlin Film Festival (Market), Feb. 19, 1989. Running time: **82 MIN.**
Lex Larsen . . . . Frank Krog
Vigdis Wang . . . . Kristin Kajander
Liv Bredesen . . . . Anne Krigsvoll
Jocken Bredesen . . . . Rolf Skoien
Jens (Falcon) Pedersen . . . . . Vidar Sandem
Asbjorn Wang . . . . Svein Erik Brodal

■ **Writer-director Solve Skagen's followup to his hit "Hard Asphalt" is a flashy, gritty whodunit which is well executed but rather small beer.**

The scruffy, less-than-charming hero is lawyer Lex Larsen, who gets involved when he tries to help a small boy find his stolen bike, and instead saves the moppet's attractive mother, Vigdis, from a nasty gang rape by a bunch of punks.

Vigdis asks Lex to help her get a divorce from her estranged husband who in short time winds up dead on Vigdis' apartment floor. If she didn't do it, who did?

Suspects include the punk leader, Vigdis' unctuous boss (and possible secret lover) and her lifelong friend, a crippled former sportsman. As the suspects start getting knocked off one by one, it isn't hard to guess the killer(s).

Skagen handles all this with confident economy and a smart, surface style. Efforts at humor fall flat and Frank Krog is a boorish hero. As in many private eye/whodunit movies, it's the peripheral characters who're most interesting here, such as the charming Vigdis' ultrareligious sister and brother-in-law.

There are plenty of moments of well-constructed suspense and editor Malte Wadman has kept the action zipping along. Though not as good as his first outing, "Hair Of

The Dog" confirms Skagen as one of Norway's better current directors. Original title means brown bitter, the drink the hero slurps down every so often during the picture. —*Strat.*

Shuttlecock

Berlin A Edery Films production. Produced by Simon Edery. Written and directed by Jerry R. Barrish. Camera (color, 16m, Hiro Narita; editor, Barrish, Rhian Miller; music, Richard Secrist; songs, performed by Liane Hielscher, Willie K.; art direction, Jack Gallagher; costumes, Miller, Kincaid Jones. Reviewed at Berlin Film Festival (Forum of Young Cinema), Feb. 18, 1989. Running time: **85 MIN.**
Mona . . . . Ann Block
Jack . . . . Will Durst
Christie . . . . Maria Isaacs
Lina . . . . Liane Hielscher
Psychiatrist . . . . Christian Phillips
Also with: Jim Bowyer, Billy Richardson, Richard Pastor, Alois Hessling, Richard Secrist, Willie K., Simon Edery, Aarin Burch, Verner Hoefner, Cynthia van Every, Claudia Gauster.

■ **This romantic comedy, California style with the Pacific Ocean always in the background, seems for a while to be quite earnestly concerned with emotions, then it steps up the irony as it goes along. By the end social satire has taken over from personal drama.**

The shrink is in love with his patient, an insecure art teacher. She loves a stand-up comic, but he lives with a winsome stripper. A nightclub performer next door observes the proceedings and offers her comments in the songs she performs on stage.

Jerry Barrish describes a typical bunch of artistic Californians, obsessed by sex and going through analysis to discover its meaning. They bare their souls in front of their friends at the drop of a hat and use their art to relieve their emotional hang-ups. One of the funniest moments shows the analyst himself being analyzed, after having pretended to offer wise advice to his client.

Ann Block offers a soulful, sincere performance as the art teacher, the most developed of the film's characters. Will Durst wrote himself a sequence or two of biting stand-up comedy and Liane Hiescher lends an old world charm to the musical commentary.

The film's main problem is whether it wants to take itself seriously or not. As it is now, somewhere in the middle, it may appeal to some, while others will argue it is neither funny nor moving enough to touch them. —*Edna.*

Illusion In Moll
(Illusion In A Minor Key)
(WEST GERMAN-B&W)

Berlin An Intercontinental production, released by Deutsche-Kosmopol. Original release, 1952. Produced by Erich Pommer. Directed by Rudolph Jugert. Screenplay, Fritz Rotter; camera (b&w), Vaclav Vich; music, Friedrich Meyer. Reviewed at Berlin Film Festival (Pommer Retrospective), Feb. 13, 1989. Running time: **90 MIN.**
With: Hildegard Knef, Sybille Schmitz, Hardy Krüger, Maurice Teynac, Albrecht Schoenhals.

■ **This slow-paced melodrama about the fragility of human relationships received little notice when released in 1952, but now stands out as a turning point in German film history.**

"Illusion In A Minor Key" (roughly translated) was the last minor film featuring the Third Reich's sultry film siren Sybille Schmitz. With her looks fading and her Crawfordesque portrayals no longer in demand, she turned to drugs and alcohol and died at her own hand in 1955.

The following year her longtime female companion and physician was tried in connection with the death. Her demise was the inspiration for Rainer Werner Fassbinder's "Veronika Voss."

Blond young costars Hardy Krüger and Hildegard Knef (a.k.a. Hildegarde Neff) were on their way up. "Illusion" was one of six films 27-year-old Knef made in 1952, including Henry Hathaway's "Diplomatic Courier" and Henry King's "The Snows Of Kilimanjaro."

The pic helped solidify Krüger's image as what the Germans call a "sunnyboy" type — the big blond, blue-eyed, kid-next-door kind of guy. His international breakthrough came in 1953 with Otto Preminger's "The Moon Is Blue."

In "Illusion" wealthy young widow (Schmitz) falls for a womanizing band leader over the objections of her ever-pouting son (Krüger), whose terminally ill fiancée (Knef) puts her life on the line to unmask the gigolo for what he is.

Schmitz has little to do in this film but look matronly and gaze adoringly at her lover. Knef has difficulties delivering some of the cornier lines dealing with her character's scarcely discernible illness. She's at her best in tender scenes with Krüger.

"Illusion" opens with Schmitz at the center of her screen family. Befitting its watershed nature, it

ends with Schmitz alone and dejected as Krüger and Knef walk away arm-in-arm to face the future. —*Gill.*

Lei Chang Xian Si Shu
(The Lives They Left Behind)
(CHINESE)

Berlin An August First Filmstudio production. Produced by Zhao Xuehua. Written and directed by Wei Lian, based on novel by Jiang Qitao. Camera (Eastmancolor), Xu Lianqin, Xu Jiunsheng; editor, Lu Chongzhen; music, Qu Xiaoshong, Liao Shoula. Reviewed at Berlin Film Festival (Panorama), Feb. 16, 1989. Running time: **110 MIN.**
With Wu Gang, Zhao Jun, Zhang Jianming.

■ **Set during the Chinese-Vietnamese war, Wei Lian's film chronicles the war experiences of five soldiers right out of military school, with occasional short flashbacks to their former lives. Pic never develops a plot, and even the few short action scenes are padded in endless chatter.**

Spectator never penetrates into the character of the five cadets who are flimsily treated in a script that is totally unrevealing. Film soon becomes tedious due to lack of any dramatic structure. Even the war sequences are dull and emotionless.

Technical credits and direction are okay but item is a loser from the start and never generates an iota of interest, nor gives any insight into modern China. —*Besa.*

Salut Victor!
(Bye Bye Victor!)
(CANADIAN)

Berlin A National Film Board of Canada-Les Producteurs TV Films Associes production, with Telefilm Canada. (Intl. sales, Films Transit, Montreal.) Produced by Monique Létourneau. Directed by Anne Claire Poirier. Screenplay, Marthe Blackburn, from the book "Matthew And Chauncy" by Edward O. Phillips; camera (Eastmancolor), Michel Brault; editor, Suzanne Allard; music, Joël Vincent Bienvenue; sound, Richard Besse; production manager, Michelle Marcil; assistant director, Mireille Goulet. Reviewed at Berlin Film Festival (Market), Feb. 16, 1989. Running time: **84 MIN.**
Philippe Lanctot . . . . Jean-Louis Roux
Victor Laprade . . . . Jacques Godin

■ **This is a simple, pleasant, predictable tale of two old men who meet in an old people's home and form a close friendship. It's more for the small screen than theatrical outings, but still a modest charmer.**

Philippe Lanctot (Jean-Louis Roux), a lifelong bachelor and a wealthy man, moves to the home after the death of his sister. At first he's irritated by the compulsively friendly, talkative Victor, who latches on to him. Gradually a close bond is formed between the two, with the title giving away the inevitable conclusion.

What's different here is that both men are gay. The apparently macho Victor was in love with a pilot and left his wife and family for him. They were happy until the pilot died in a light plane crash. The uptight Lanctot then reveals he's had a brief, passionate affair with a Mexican employee, which ended when the youth was deported.

Homosexual theme gives an added edge to an otherwise familiar tale. Both thesps are excellent, and director Anne Claire Poirier has done a sensitive job on an obviously restricted budget. —*Strat.*

Fletch Lives

Hollywood A Universal Pictures release of a Douglas/Greisman prdouction. Produced by Alan Greisman, Peter Douglas. Executive producers, Bruce Bodner, Bob Larson. Directed by Michael Ritchie. Screenplay, Leon Capetanos, based on characters created by Gregory McDonald; camera (Deluxe color), John McPherson; editor, Richard A. Harris; music, Harold Faltermeyer; art direction, Cameron Birnie, Jimmie Bly, W. Steven Graham, Donald B. Woodruff; set decoration, Garry Fettis, Susan Bode; costume design, Anna Hill Johnstone; sound (Dolby), Jim Alexander; assistant director, James Sbardellati; second unit director, Peter Norman; visual effects, Boss Film Corp.; casting, Patricia Mock. Reviewed at Cineplex Odeon Universal City Cinema, Universal City, Calif., March 9, 1989. MPAA Rating: PG. Running time: **95 MIN.**

Fletch	Chevy Chase
Ham Johnson	Hal Holbrook
Becky Culpepper	Julianne Phillips
Calculus	Cleavon Little
Jimmy Lee Farnsworth	R. Lee Ermey
Amanda	Patricia Kalember

Also with: Richard Libertini, Randall (Tex) Cobb, George Wyner, Geoffrey Lewis, Richard Belzer.

■ **Chevy Chase is perfectly suited to playing a smirking, wisecracking, multiple-identitied reporter in "Fletch Lives," a sillier and more satirical chapter that may offend Southern sensibilities but otherwised is lensed for broad appeal.**

Outside of those who watch and believe televangelists, film should do well in wide release.

Ridiculous and anecdotal plot that transports Chase from his beloved L.A. base to Louisiana's bayou country to take over his dead aunt's crumbling plantation works for the simple reason that Chase's sly, glib persona is in sync with Michael Ritchie's equally breezy direction.

Constant stream of 1-liners under Chase's various identities are consistently funny, even as they are often incredibly stupid and acted so shamelessly coarse.

Working from Gregory McDonald's popular novel, scripter Leon Capetanos has worked out an excessive and cliché-ridden portrait of a Southern, insular town. Dimwits abound as if inbreeding has been going on since the days of slavery.

The night Chase arrives, he beds the sexy executor/lawyer of his aunt's estate (Patricia Kalember as a convincing belle), who is then murdered while they're slumbering. The task is handled so deftly (chloroform?), Chase doesn't wake up. It also doesn't seem to disturb him much the next morning that she's dead — just as long as he has something to keep his easily distracted mind busy for the

ensuing 95 minutes of the film.

Chase tracks the murderer through some inane sequences as only he could do — and some Southerners might want to lynch him for it.

He dances out on his overgrown lawn with a sad assemblage of Ku Klux Klanners, some hired for the staging; goes 'coon hunting with a miner's hat on; steps on some stinky stuff that later becomes a clue, and sports a blond wig and wimpy mustache while trying to pass himself off in a biker bar as the Harley-Davidson heir.

Film's saving grace is Capetanos' scathing satirical sketches of fictional televangelist preacher Jimmy Lee Farnsworth, an obvious takeoff on other Jim-named, unabashedly money-grubbing ministers.

Farnsworth (R. Lee Ermey is perfect casting) wants to buy up Chase's property so he can expand his Disneyland-inspired, biblically themed empire. There's a Noah's Ark ride that washes away one of the villains in a particularly hysterical scene.

Most supporting characters are thinly drawn — notably Cleavon Little as the patronizing plantation hand — or badly acted, especially by Julianne Phillips, whose accent roams over practically every American region but the South.

Brisk editing by original "Fletch" cutter Richard A. Harris, reunited with other alums, producers Alan Greisman and Peter Douglas and scorer Harold Faltermeyer, adds to the snappy tenor of the proceedings.

Boss Film deserves special mention for its clever, effective and convincing integration of cartoon characters with a lavish live-action '40s musical parody of "Song Of The South" — a dream sequence in which Chase lords over his real-life nemesis and has a cast of (seemingly) thousands supporting him. —*Brit.*

Gabriela
(DUTCH-DOCU)

Amsterdam A Cinemien release. Produced, written and directed by Trix Betlem. Camera (color, 16m), Steve Carscallen; editor, Mario Steenbergen; sound, Jose Guarosma. Reviewed at Desmet theater, Amsterdam, Feb. 27, 1989. Running time: **67 MIN.**

■ **This docu about the situation of women in the Phillippines is effective because it doesn't shout, but just states facts, soberly, without facile exhibition**

of suffering. It should generate international interest.

"Gabriela" is the name of a national organization comprising diverse groups of women — nuns, farm workers, students, factory workers, artists, prostitutes and housewives.

It was founded four years ago, when Marcos decamped and Cory entered the scene. Initial enthusiasm has waned. There has been little improvement in conditions, though the women have grown more self-reliant.

"We'll band together, stand together, fight together now; we'll win in the end" — that's the gist of the film via its numerous interviews. A drawback is that commentary takes over when interviews end, and the continuous flow of words may numb foreign audiences. —*Wall.*

Police Academy 6:
City Under Siege

Hollywood A Warner Bros. release of a Paul Maslansky production. Produced by Paul Maslansky. Directed by Peter Bonerz. Screenplay, Stephen J. Curwick, based on characters created by Neal Israel, Pat Proft; camera (Panavision, Technicolor), Charles Rosher Jr.; editor, Hubert De La Bouillerie; music, Robert Folk; production design, Tho E. Azzari; costume design, Peter Flaherty; coproducer, Don West; casting, Glenn Daniels. Reviewed at Mann Chinese theater, Hollywood, March 10, 1989. MPAA Rating: PG. Running time: **83 MIN.**

Hightower	Bubba Smith
Tackleberry	David Graf
Jones	Michael Winslow
Callahan	Leslie Easterbrook
Hooks	Marion Ramsey
Proctor	Lance Kinsey
Nick	Matt McCoy
Fackler	Bruce Mahler
Harris	G.W. Bailey
Lassard	George Gaynes
Mayor	Kenneth Mars
Ace	Gerrit Graham
Hurst	George R. Robertson

■ **The "Police Academy" series has now reached 6-pack status, and it's doubtful even an installment as dreadful as this one can prevent them from beginning work on another case. Unless they've locked up the undemanding hordes that saw the first handful, boxoffice should be inexplicably arresting.**

The 6-pack analogy is appropriate, since Warner Bros. has churned these films out since 1984 like clockwork, with all the precision of a softdrink manufacturer. Unlike Coke, however, they know better than to tamper with the formula.

Commandant Lassard (George Gaynes) and his crack team are assigned to stop a wave of robberies, much to the chagrin of the cartoonish Captain Harris (G.W. Bailey). The crimes are committed by a trio with circus-like skills, keyed by a not-so-mysterious Mr. Big.

Director Peter Bonerz and writer Stephen J. Curwick (the latter taking his second "Academy" shift) both cut their teeth on tv sitcoms, and it shows. Rarely has a film cried out so desperately for a laughtrack.

That's exactly what "Police Academy" has become: an hour-plus sitcom with a predictable cast who recycle the same jokes. It's just that the shows come out annually, or about as often as a new "Moonlighting" episode.

Michael Winslow still has the funniest shtick with his seemingly limitless ability to perform vocal gymnastics — the film's only truly amusing moment coming when he nails one of the bad guys, first as a badly dubbed ninja, then a herky-jerky robot.

Aside from that, there are some decent stunts, an okay score by Robert Folk and nothing really to offend anyone unless they resent paying money to see it. Let the buyer beware. —*Bril.*

The Errors Of Youth
(SOVIET)

New York   A Lenfilm Studio production. Produced by Evgeny Volkov. Directed by Boris Frumin. Screenplay, Edward Topol, Frumin; camera (color), Alexi Gambarian; editor, Tamara Denisova; music, Victor Lebedev; production design, Yuri Pugatch; sound, Galina Lukina. Reviewed at Museum of Modern Art, N.Y. (in New Directors/New Films), March 2, 1989. Running time: **87 MIN.**
Dimitri Gurianov . . . . . Stanislav Zhadanko
Polina . . . . Marina Neyelova
Zina . . . . Natalia Varley
Burkov . . . . Michail Vaskov
Also with: Nikolai Karatchetsov, Nicolai Penkov, Marina Maltseva, Bella Tchirina, A. Kotchetkov, N. Mamayeva, V. Marenkov, A. Garitchev, A. Gorin and A. Vedenskaya.

■**Of interest as a portrait of contemporary Russian life and as a demonstration of artistic flexibility under glasnost, "The Errors Of Youth" is as directionless as its self-searching protagonist and is best suited for special programs on modern Soviet cinema.**

Dimitri (Stanislav Zhadanko) and Burkov (Mikhail Vaskov) are Red Army conscripts eagerly anticipating their imminent demobilization. Although they have cushy duty in the Black Sea resort region, they're anxious to trade the petty tyrannies of army life for high-paying construction jobs in

Siberia.

Buddies, girlfriends and the affection of his elders come easily to the handsome, laconic hero who turns down opportunities in the army and in his pastoral hometown because he's driven "to see life." Wanderlust leads Dimitri from the home of his loving parents to the Great White North, where he quickly loses his pal Burkov to marriage.

The hero has his own loving affair with a beautiful, enigmatic coworker (Marina Neyelova), but they split up over the question of parenthood. Shaken up, Dimitri moves on to Leningrad, where he drifts into a marriage of expediency. Having seen some of life, Dimitri resigns himself to a life of circumscribed possibilities. The filmmakers seem to suggest the blame lies more with the becalmed stasis of Soviet society rather than with Dimitri.

From a Western point of view there is nothing incendiary about "The Errors Of Youth," but Soviet authorities deemed it sufficiently subversive to ban it in 1979. Its "critical realism" is subtle to the point of documentary flatness, and its characters' gripes, unless severely glossed in the occasionally awkward subtitles, are existential rather than political. Vodka-lubricated party scenes provide a pretext for a jaunty soundtrack of homegrown folk rock.

Cinematography is sharp and impressive. Director Boris Frumin and cameraman Alexi Gambarian tend to overdo wide-angle shots of Mother Russia's curving horizons but the technique does evoke the topographical grandeur and sweeping vastness of the land. This sense of limitless space contrasts poignantly with the darkened, closed-in corridors of the Leningrad housing project where Dimitri finally makes his stand. —*Rich.*

Cavalli Si Nasce
(Born Dumb)
(ITALIAN)

Rome   A CDI release of a Reteitalia/Yarno Cinematografica coproduction. Produced by Mauro Berardi. Written and directed by Sergio Staino. Camera (color), Camillo Bazzoni; editor, Nino Baragli; music, Eugenio Bennato, Carlo Angiò; art direction, Franco Velchi. Reviewed at Ariston 2 Cinema, Rome, Feb. 5, 1989. Running time: **102 MIN.**
Paolo . . . . Paolo Hendel
Ottavio . . . . David Riondino
Baroness . . . . Delia Boccardo
Priest . . . . Giacomo Marramao
Carola . . . . Pietra Montecorvino
Also with: Franca D'Amato, Vincent Gardenia, Michele Placido, Bonvi, Paco Reconte, Riccardo Pangallo, Robert Murolo.

(old singer).

■**Debut effort by political satirist Sergio Staino is a simple-hearted yet sophisticated comedy set in the Naples of 1832.**

Setting, style of hour, and star Paolo Hendel all recall last season's surprise hit "It'll Happen Tomorrow," and "Horse" suffers somewhat in comparison. However, local boxoffice has been good, and film retains enough originality to merit a look from offshore markets for the offbeat.

With tongue-in-cheek wit, quasi-gentleman Paolo (played by Paolo Hendel with the same amiable nonchalance as his previous film) accompanies young Duke Ottavio (David Riondino) on his travels to the uncivilized regions of southern Italy.

Paolo makes friends with a nutty painter and a revolutionary stable hand, who espouse the new egalitarian ideas sweeping the country. Though for one dark moment the forces of repression seem to have our heroes cornered, a surprise ending puts things right again.

A sunny, intelligent film with moments of genuine humor, "Born Dumb" sketches a detailed canvas (with the aid of Franco Velchi's fine art direction) of mid-19th century life, from its lustiness and chaos to currents of thought then in vogue.

Hendel and supporting cast (Delia Boccardo as an ethereal German Baroness, Giacomo Marramao as a hypocritical Jesuit) inject color into the proceedings, which tend to bog down in a lurching rhythm.

Robert Murolo, one of the top Neapolitan traditional singers, performs in a cameo treat. —*Yung.*

The Toxic Avenger, Part II

Detroit   A Troma release of a Lloyd Kaufman/Michael Herz production, in association with Lorimar. Produced and directed by Lloyd Kaufman, Michael Herz. Screenplay, Gay Partington Terry, from an original story by Kaufman; camera (TVC Color), James London; editor, Michael Schweitzer; music, Barrie Guard; art director, Alex Grey; special effects coordinator, Pericles Lewnes; sound, Sekou Shepard; casting, Phil Rivo. Reviewed at Main theater, Royal Oak, Mich., March 4, 1989. MPAA Rating: R. Running time: **95 MIN.**
The Toxic
Avenger . . . . . Ron Fazio, John Altamura
Claire . . . . Phoebe Legere
Apocalypse Inc.
  Chairman . . . . Rick Collins
Big Mac . . . . Rikiya Yasouka
Announcer . . . . Tsutomu Sekine
Masami . . . . Mayako Katsuragi
Shockikuyama . . . . Shinoburyu
Malfaire . . . . Lisa Gaye
Mrs. Junko . . . . Jessica Dublin
Mr. Junko . . . . Jack Cooper
Psychiatrist . . . . Erika Schickel

■**Even die-hard Troma fans will have a hard time stomaching "The Toxic Avenger, Part II." A weak script and sluggish direction turn this sequel to the 1985 spoof into a seemingly endless, stultifying mess.**

Troma's usual limited theatrical success may well be followed by a limited homevideo run as word of mouth leaks out.

Sure, the acting here is mediocre; the special effects are rank, and the situations often volley between rude and boorish, but this is Troma, and fans have come to expect that as part of the enjoyment of fare from the company, whose titles include "Surf Nazis Must Die," "War" and "Nuke 'Em High."

Planned mediocrity as a spoof of the slasher/superhero genre can generate chuckles only so long, and in "Toxic II" these elements wear thin quickly.

What's left is an anemic script peppered with uninspired sight gags and a somnambulistic directorial pace that makes its 95-minute running time seem an eternity.

"Toxic II" finds 90-pound weakling Melvin — who last time out fell into a vat of toxic waste and emerged the super powerful and super ugly Toxic Avenger — suffering from emotional problems.

It seems he was unable to save a home for the blind from an evil drug magnate who razed the center and killed its inhabitants in his march to conquer Tromaville.

Toxi's shrink tells him the only thing that will help his depression is a trip to Japan to find his father, Big Mac, who turns out to be a fish peddler who is really an underworld coke peddler.

"I am Big Mac," he tells his son in the confrontation sequence between son and underworld king. "I am the big cheese. You might say I am the Big Mac with cheese." The jokes don't get any better. And the visual gags this time out lack the spunk of the original.

"Toxic II" plays like the "Three Stooges From Hell." When he knocks two thugs' heads together, the heads explode in a bloody mess. When he finally chases down a rotund street gang member in a Japanese bath house, Toxi throws him into a tub, turns up the heat beyond boiling, throws in some fish and vegetables and kills him in a lethal legume soup.

If the jokes, such as they are, came fast and furiously, like in "Airplane!" or "The Naked Gun," there might be enough humor to carry the film to its predictable conclusion. Because each limited spoof is telegraphed and laboriously executed, this toxic sequel can be hazardous to your health. —*Advo.*

La Salle de bain
(The Bathroom)
(FRENCH-B&W)

Paris A Bac Film release of a Paradis Films/Générale d'Images/La Sept coproduction. Produced by Eric Heumann, Stéphane Soriat. Directed by John Lvoff. Screenplay, Lvoff, Jean-Philippe Toussaint, from Toussaint's novel; camera (b&w), Jean-Claude Larrieu; editor, Annick Rousset-Rouard; music, Charlelie Couture; art direction, Thérése Ripaud; sound, Jérôme Thiault; costumes, Christine Chauvey; production manager, Christophe Vallette; assistant director, Catherine Charlot; casting, Marie-Christine Lafosse. Reviewed at Cannon screening room, Paris, Feb. 24, 1989. Running time: **93 MIN.**
The man .... Tom Novembre
Edmonsson .... Gunilla Karlzen
Kabrowinski .... Jiri Stanislav
Kowalskazinski ...... Jerzy Piwowarczyk
Former tenant .... Roland Bertin
Brigitte .... Charlotte de Turkheim
Mother .... Anouk Ferjac
Family friend .... Philippe Morier-Genoud

■ **Dramas of alienation are especially perilous ventures for a debutant director. John Lvoff, a Franco-American assistant director tackles the question with professionalism but draws a cinematic blank.**

Shot in black and white (by the excellent Jean-Claude Larrieu), "La Salle de bain" was originally a literary exercise by Jean-Philippe Toussaint, who collaborated with Lvoff on the screenplay.

Initial premise is piquant and deals with a young man who decides to live in his bathroom, meditating, reading or just starring at the walls in his tub (fully clothed).

This Becket-style image is promising, but the film leaves the bathroom rather quickly never to return.

The protagonist flees to avoid his pretty blond girlfriend, a couple of Polish artists hired as house painters and assorted irksome friends, family and other pests.

We next find him in a nondescript hotel room which turns out to be in Venice, though the man prefers playing darts in his room to exploring the picturesque canal city. His girlfriend comes to join him and he gratuitously wounds her in the forehead with a dart. After some more wandering he returns to Paris, his apartment and an apparent reconciliation with his mate.

Despite his technical care, Lvoff only intermittently communicates the book's dry, philosophical humor, which remains essentially literary.

Film's principal plus is Tom Novembre as the protagonist, whose Buster Keaton-like deadpan and rich speaking voice give the "action" an appealing offbeat accent. —*Len.*

Luigi's Ladies
(AUSTRALIAN)

Sydney A Hoyts Distribution release of a Tra La La Films production. Executive producer, Wendy Hughes. Produced by Patric Juillet. Directed by Judy Morris. Screenplay, Jennifer Claire, Ronald Allan, Hughes, Morris; camera (color), Steve Mason; editor, Pamela Barnetta; music, Sharon Calcraft; sound, Ken Hammond, Joe Spinelli, Andrew Plain; associate producer, Rachel Symes. Reviewed at the Hoyts Cinema Center, Sydney, Feb. 20, 1989. Running time: **95 MIN.**
Sara .... Wendy Hughes
Cee .... Sandy Gore
Jane .... Anne Tenney
Luigi .... David Rappaport
Steve .... John Walton
Trev .... Serge Lazaroff
Lance .... Ray Meagher
Also with: Joe Spano, Maggie Dence, Max Cullen.

■ **Australian feature comedies don't come along very often, so it's a shame "Luigi's Ladies" misfires on several levels, despite its potentially humorous premise.**

It's a relationship piece, set against the 1987 stock crash. Core characters are three friends (Wendy Hughes, Anne Tenney and Sandy Gore), who literally wake up one morning to find themselves, to differing degrees, substantially out of pocket because of the crash.

Three subplots are triggered as the relationships of the three then unfold only to coalesce — after such goings on as attempted murder by poisoning with frangipani jam, an affair with a playboy, and an excursion into macrobiotic cooking and new age "rebirthing."

Set against all this is pint-sized David Rappaport as Luigi, a cockney-speaking (thinly disguised by an Italian accent when on the job) maitre'd of a ritzy harbor-view restaurant. As the women's confidante and neutral friend, however, his role is surprisingly peripheral — it's the relationships that propel the film — and his character is barely dealt with in any depth.

While technically proficient and sporting some genuinely funny moments, pic lacks consistency in its humor and grabs too much at the ridiculous for laughs at the expense of characters. Its best moments are some of the repartee between couples. Its worst are some awkward scenes that helmer Judy Morris (a talented thesp making her directing debut here) has lingered over excessively. Some 15 minutes have been cut to date; more could go.

Best portrayal comes from Tenney, whose character is the most balanced, as befits her role. There are nice comic performances from John Walton, Hughes' husband, playing a lawyer who's drunk for most of the film, and Ray Meagher, Gore's partner, playing an ex-cop embroiled in new age thinking who's told he was Genghis Khan in a former life. Max Cullen wastes his talent playing a psychotic chef whose wildly exaggerated French utterings are mainly unintelligible for most of the film.

Pic should find business in Oz but its patchy nature makes theatrical life internationally unlikely; cable and homevid seem more likely. —*Doch.*

Malarek: A Street Kid Who Made It
(CANADIAN)

Toronto A Malofilms release of a Telescene Films production. Executive producers, Neil Leger, Paul Painter. Produced by Jamie Brown, Robin Spry. Directed by Roger Cardinal. Screenplay, Avrum Jacobson, based on novel "Hey, Malarek" by Victor Malarek; camera (color), Karol Ike; editor, Yves Langlois; music, Alexandre Stank; art direction, Claude Pare; sound, Richard Nichol; assistant director, Pierre Plante. Reviewed at Canada Square Cinema, Toronto, March 3, 1988. Running time: **100 MIN.**
Victor Malarek .... Elias Koteas
Claire .... Kerrie Keane
Gray .... Kahlil Karn
Stern .... Al Waxman
Moorcraft .... Michael Sarrazin
Max Middleton .... Daniel Pilon
Mom .... Claire Rodger

■ **Inspired by the real-life exploits of a Montreal street kid turned crack investigative journalist, "Malarek" has an energy and appeal supplied largely by the buoyant star turn by Elias Koteas in the title role.**

While subject matter is fiery and socially important, pic's lensing and direction make it far less appealing as a theatrical entry and better suited to video and tv.

Malarek, a mail sorter at a Montreal newspaper, has a professional passion for wanting to get to the heart of a story. After he crashes his fancy boss' (Michael Sarrazin) party, he manages to nab a job as a cub reporter under the tutelage of almost-flirtatious city editor Kerrie Keane.

Malarek's first journalistic coup is witnessing a cop kill a teen who escapes from a juvenile detention center. When he investigates the details, he discovers that the inmates are killing themselves with embarrassing frequency due to the abhorrent conditions in the facilities.

Through a series of awkward flashbacks, director Roger Cardinal brings in Malarek's obsessive interest in the story — he, too, was the victim of an abusive father and spent time in a horrific boys' home.

Koteas infuses Malarek with an innate forcefulness, perseverance, and quest for social rights in uncovering the brilliant exposé of the juvenile detention center. He's charming, raw and rough around the edges, sexy with a sense of humor.

He brings the role as much depth as he can, although he's forced to play off stereotypical newsroom types.

Al Waxman as a no-nonsense social worker is the only other character with meat, and helps bring an element of gutsy realism to the pic. Production values are weak, but Koteas is able to transcend his cinematic surroundings to pack a punch with his screen persona. —*Devo.*

'O Re
(The King Of Naples)
(ITALIAN)

Rome A CDI release of a Clemi Cinematografica production, in association with Titanus Produzioni. Produced by Giovanni Di Clementi. Written and directed by Luigi Magni. Camera (color), Franco Di Giacomo; editor, Ruggero Mastroianni; music, Nicola Piovani; art direction, Lucia Mirisola. Reviewed at Etoile Cinema, Rome, Feb. 6, 1989. Running time: **103 MIN.**
Francesco .... Giancarlo Giannini
Maria Sofia .... Ornella Muti
Actress .... Christina Marsillach
Also with: Carlo Croccolo, Corrado Panni, Luc Merenda, Sergio Solli.

■ **Luigi Magni, a helmer specializing in offbeat historical films, looks at the period of Italy's Unification in " 'O Re" (The King Of Naples). Story lacks the breadth that might have made it work on a wider scale.**

It settles instead for the difficult conjugal relations between the last Bourbon king, Francesco, and his firebrand young wife. Casting Giancarlo Giannini as the deposed king and Ornella Muti as his consort gives the characters famous faces but has not made pic a b.o. breadwinner. Offshore life looks spotty.

A year after fleeing Naples and the Kingdom of the Two Sicilies, Francesco has retired to eccentric isolation in Rome. His bloodless surrender to Garibaldi doesn't go down well with his wife Maria Sofia, who rides around in men's clothing planning to reconquer the kingdom. Francesco, a resigned realist, knows there's no hope of a popular uprising in his favor, and spends his time trying to get his mother cannonized.

Maria Sofia would settle for having a baby, but Francesco has taken a vow never to have an heir, in homage to his mother's presumed saintliness. Ignoring the warnings of his comic manservant, the seduction attempts of his wife (aided by a jovial troupe of Neopolitan actors) and later her threats to get pregnant without him, Francesco retreats into his world of penniless luxury.

In its favor is Lucia Mirisola's glorious princely interiors and pleasure gardens, enriching visuals in every scene. Despite their airs, Giannini and Muti come through as unreal royalty, playing for easy laughs and sympathy. Cristina Marsillach is a mysterious would-be regicide, in a sketchy role. —*Yung.*

Comment faire l'amour avec un nègre sans se fatiguer
(How To Make Love To A Negro Without Getting Tired) (CANADIAN-FRENCH)

Montreal An Aska Film Intl. release of a Stock Intl. (Montreal) production in association with Molecule (Paris). Produced by Richard Sadler, Ann Burke, Henry Lange. Directed by Jacques W. Benoit. Screenplay, Dany Laferrière, Sadler, from Dany Laferrière's novel; camera (color), John Berrie; editor, Dominique Roy (France); music, Manu Dibango (France); sound, Claude Langlois. Reviewed at Famous Players' Le Parisien Theater, Montreal, Feb. 22, 1989. Running time: **97 MIN.**

Man	Issach de Bankolé
Bouba	Maka Kotto
Miz Literature	Roberta Bizeau
Miz Suicide	Miriam Cyr
Miz Mystic	Marie-Josée Gauthier
Miz Duras	Susan Almgren
Miz Oh My God	Alexandra Innes
Miz Disillusioned	Nathalie Coupal
Miz Redhead	Isabelle L'Écuyer
Miz Feminist	Patricia Tulasne

■ **The title is an eye-grabber. Based on a best-selling first novel** by Haitian-born Dany Laferrière, the story is an autobiographical comedy about getting rich white university girls between the sheets.

Playing on every possible stereotype that whites may harbor about blacks, Lafarrière turns the tables, and the cameras, to the "black" perspective.

In the reverse-stereotype vein, the film resembles "My Beautiful Laundrette." Neither film attempts to break down stereotypes; both films champion non-whites exploiting whites.

The female nudity and several somewhat graphic sex scenes in "How To . . ." will make or break the film. However, these racier elements will brand it as a "fast times at high school" flick rather than as a profound political exposé. This may have been intentional on the part of first-time feature director, Jacques W. Benoit.

Sensibilities of such humor will determine which foreign markets will appreciate and therefore prosper with such a graphic and offbeat film. An English version is forthcoming. —*Suze.*

Helmut Newton: Frames From The Edge (W. GERMAN-FRENCH-DOCU)

Montreal An RM Associates release of an RM ARTS, ORF, WDR coproduction. Written, directed and narrated by Adrian Maben. Camera (color, 16m), Claude Agostini, Michel Bazille, Jean-Philippe Agnan; editor, Maben; sound, Bela Bartok, Franz Schubert. Reviewed at Festival Intl. du film sur l'art, Montreal, March 7, 1989. Running time: **104 MIN.**

With: Catherine Deneuve, Sigourney Weaver, Charlotte Rampling, Faye Dunaway, Karl Lagerfeld.

■ **Masquerading as an art film, "Helmut Newton: Frames From The Edge" is a hard-sell promotional docu glorifying a photographer who revolutionized the cover of Vogue magazine in the 1950s and '60s with wacky fashion pics.**

Newton is also renowned for his stark black and white stills of female nudes, including a bevy of Hollywood and internationally acclaimed actresses.

A candid interview with Charlotte Rampling — who claims to be Newton's first nude subject — begins a series of confession-like observations heralding Newton's penetrating eye.

Catherine Deneuve — who did not pose nude but appears on the cover of his new book at gun point — said Newton is the only photographer she ever invited to her home for a session.

Sigourney Weaver says he won her over when she realized "his ego was bigger and more important" than her own.

Interviews with the rich and famous are what give both the film and Newton the credibility that debutant director Adrian Maben is clearly trying to achieve. Otherwise, the docu style is amateurish. The film is long and often repetitive during interviews with unknown models.

Extensive nudity will limit its television play.

The film wraps in the tax haven of Monaco where Newton has retired. He says simply: "I like the light here." —*Suze.*

Je suis le seigneur de chateau (I'm The King Of The Castle) (FRENCH)

Paris An AAA release of an Odessa Films/AAA Prods. coproduction. Produced by Yannick Bernard. Directed by Régis Wargnier. Screenplay, Wargnier, Alain Le Henry, based freely on novel "I'm The King Of The Castle" by Susan Hill; camera (color), François Catonné; editor, Genevieve Winding; music, Sergei Prokofiev; art direction, Jean-Jacques Caziot; sound, Guillaume Sciama, Dominique Hennequin; assistant director, Pascal Chaumeil; production manager, Ilya Claisse. Reviewed at Pathé Marignan-Concorde theater, Paris, Feb. 20, 1989. Running time: **88 MIN.**

M. Bread	Jean Rochefort
Mme. Vernet	Dominique Blanc
Thomas	Régis Arpin
Charles	David Behar

■ **Régis Wargnier, whose debut feature in 1987, "La Femme de ma vie" heralded an interesting new talent, fumbles pretentiously in his second film, "I'm The King Of The Castle."**

Freely adapted from a British novel, it is a laboriously baroque tale of the dangerous games played by two children of different social stations in and around a Brittany castle.

Wargnier's script, elaborated with Alain Le Henry, resets the story to the early 1950s, with the Indochinese War in the psychological background.

The two protagonists are both 10 years old. One lives with his recently widowed father (Jean Rochefort) in a vast Renaissance chateau. The other is a prole, the son of a governess (Dominique Blanc) whom Rochefort brings in to look after the house and to provide his boy with a companion.

Rochefort's blond, blue-eyed darling doesn't see the situation in the same way. He declares war on the low-born newcomers. His scare tactics, aimed at the boy, include putting a dead raven in his bed. His antagonist gets his revenge by luring the castle-bound young master out into the forest for a nocturnal hike that nearly veers to tragedy.

The childhood class warfare is complicated when the adults start getting romantically involved. This despite the fact that Blanc's husband has been reported missing in action in Indochina. If she seems unconcerned, her son is obsessed by his missing father, and in the film's bizarre climax decides to do something about it.

Wargnier attempts a manner meant to be grand but finally most portentous. He goes in for underlined symbols and effects (a blood-stained bedsheet floating down a castle stairwell) and theatrical set-pieces (a popular ball where Blanc and her son spin around the floor with increasing frenzy).

Most of this is heavily larded with music of Prokofiev, which the themes and scale of Wargnier's script rarely justify.

The two youngsters, Régis Arpin and David Behar, are adequate. Rochefort and Blanc, in clumsily directed roles, are unconvincing.

François Catonné's images of castle and forest are majestic. Other tech credits are solid. —*Len.*

S.F. FEST REVIEWS

How To Get Ahead In Advertising
(BRITISH)

San Francisco   A Warner Bros. release of a Handmade Films production. Produced by David Wimbury. Executive producers, George Harrison, Denis O'Brien. Written and directed by Bruce Robinson. Camera (Fujicolor), Peter Hannan; editor, Alan Strachan; music, David Dundas, Rick Wentworth; production design, Michael Pickwoad; sound, Clive Winter; art direction, Henry Harris; assistant director, Peter Kohn; coproducer, Ray Cooper; casting, Lucy Boulting. Reviewed at San Francisco Film Festival, March 10, 1989. No MPAA Rating. Running time: **95 MIN.**

Bagley . . . . Richard E. Grant
Julia . . . . Rachel Ward
Bristol . . . . Richard Wilson
Penny . . . . Jacqueline Tong
Psychiatrist . . . . John Shrapnel
Monica . . . . Susan Wooldridge
Richard . . . . Mick Ford
Maud . . . . Jacqueline Pearce
Dr. Gatty . . . . Roddy Maude-Roxby

■ **Although its target already has been shelled to shreds, "How To Get Ahead In Advertising" joins the attack with a truly weird weapon that generates enough dark humor to give the film a commercial shot in special situations.**

Getting its world preem at the Frisco fest, "Advertising" is writer-director Bruce Robinson's second feature following his successful "Withnail And I" and the picture would be genuinely hilarious were the subject matter not so overworked.

As a hotshot go-getter in the British equivalent of Madison Avenue, Richard E. Grant is pricelessly cynical and his opening observations to his cronies about salesmanship amount to an amusingly neat summary of how to exploit cravings and insecurity.

Grant is having a problem coming up with an original campaign for a pimple cream and the pressure is on from the client and his boss (wonderfully droll Richard Wilson). As dutiful wives do, Rachel Ward tries to assure him that something in his genius will come forward, but he's floundering with an idea to make pimples popular.

Rapidly, the pressure propels an obsession until Grant can think of nothing but skin disorders. When a small boil breaks out on his own neck, Grant realizes the stress has become too much and it's time to quit the business.

It's too late. The boil begins to grow — and starts to talk, giving form to all that's vile and venal in his nature.

In the film's funniest scene, as Grant awaits surgery to remove his companion, it takes on all his features and persuades the doctors to lance the original. They don't get all of him and now Grant becomes the wart on the devious ambitions displayed by his new-headed body.

Ward is quite good at reacting to all this lunacy, assisted by her friend Jacqueline Tong and psychiatrist John Shrapnel. True to the tradition of British comedy, Robinson makes entertaining use of a number of diverting bit players as well.

Ultimately, Robinson believes materialism will ever shelter its disciples, no matter how crazed they become in its service. For those who find news in that, "Advertising" will seem a lot more outrageous. Others will just have to enjoy what fresh folly they can find. —*Har.*

Joe Leahy's Neighbors
(AUSTRALIAN-DOCU)

San Francisco   An Arundell production. Directed by Robin Anderson, Bob Connolly. Camera (color), Connolly; editor, Ray Thomas, Connolly. Reviewed at San Francisco Film Festival, March 10, 1989. No MPAA Rating. Running time: **90 MIN.**

■ **The coming of cash and capitalism to a previously primitive closed economic system is fairly esoteric stuff for film, but "Joe Leahy's Neighbors" makes it interesting by reducing the conflicts to simple human terms.**

Before the arrival of white men, the Ganiga tribe of Papua New Guinea enjoyed a rather charming concept of wealth. Once a man acquired an excess of pigs and similar property, he was judged among his peers by how generously he gave portions away.

Even for the poor, prosperity had nothing to do with getting or keeping. Seemingly without an excess of hard labor, the tribe prospered collectively off the land, largely spending their days enjoying themselves.

This began to change when Joe Leahy, himself a half-breed sired by a white, saved his wages from working on a coffee plantation and persuaded one of the Gingas to sell him some land for $600. Working like a Westerner, Leahy built his holdings into a successful plantation grossing $1-million a year.

Still owning the land around him, the Gingas don't work for Leahy. They only harvest enough coffee to keep themselves in cigarets and other outside items like "Iron Maiden" t-shirts. What cash comes into the community is still readily shared according to tribal custom.

Nonetheless, the Gingas — the younger ones particularly — are hardly oblivious to Leahy's prosperity, his big house, his Mercedes and many trucks, his children being educated abroad. They would like to have such things, too, but really haven't the foggiest idea how to get them.

As filmmakers Robin Anderson and Bob Connolly join up with the tribe, the discontent is spreading, fueled by talk that Leahy somehow cheated them in the first place. Now he wants more land and they are determined this time to share whatever wealth he earns from it.

For his part, Leahy candidly discusses his view that the natives are hardly more than children when it comes to "business," ready enough to covet quick dividends but lacking any concept of the longterm efforts needed to reach a payoff.

Leahy, however, is quite willing to exploit the situation, painting grand pictures for the Gingas of all the cars and other goodies they will enjoy once they sign over the additional land.

The film culminates in an illuminating confrontation between Leahy and his neighbors over terms of the lease. They think he's agreed to a 50-50 deal, but it's now 60-40 in his favor and they would like to know why.

Of course, the simple Gingas don't understand any of his explanations about banks and lending requirements, which may or may not be double-talk on his part. It's clear from the beginning that Leahy will have his way.

This isn't all as bad as it may appear. Leahy still retains enough of his own native blood, it seems, to genuinely care about the tribesmen, even though there's no doubt he will work the deal to his advantage. Throughout it all, the old ways surface engagingly with members of the tribe coming forth to hand Leahy little offerings of cash and bags of sugar to show their respect and affection.

A hard nosed assessment might be that "Neighbors" is a solid journalistic examination of economic exploitation. That's undermined by a clear feeling that the Gingas probably were better off with their old ways and there are no real riches ahead in whatever wealth they win. —*Har.*

BERLIN FEST REVIEWS

Seoul Jesu
(Jesus Christ In Seoul)
(SOUTH KOREAN)

Berlin   A Hyun Jin Films production. Written and directed by Wan Son-U, Chang Son-U. Camera (color), Suh Chong-Min; editor, Hyon Dong-Chun; sound, Kim Song-Chan. Reviewed at Berlin Film Festival (Forum of Young Cinema), Feb. 11, 1989. Running time: **102 MIN.**
With: Kim Myong-Kon, Oh Su-Mi, Ahn Yong-Nam, Na Han-Il, Kang Sok-Ran, Park Sang-Cho.

■ **South Korean censorship rejected the current title of this picture when it was shot in 1985-86 and for a long time it was known under its working title, "The King Of Seoul." Premiered in October 1988 outside Seoul, it has no national distribution deal as yet.**

This modern story of faith and redemption sees Seoul as a new version of Sodom, a doomed nest of iniquity and sin, awaiting a beautiful woman to redeem it with her tears.

So says the inmate of a lunatic asylum who escapes his guardians and roams barefoot through the South Korean capital, introducing himself as Jesus Christ and looking for a new version of Mary Magdalene. On the way, he picks himself an assistant, a lively street urchin who becomes his personal angel.

When they encounter the subject of their search, she turns out to be a beautiful, hardboiled, kept young lady, who is annoyed by their insistent appeals to her conscience.

Pleasantly naive morality tale hints that Jesus would be given as hard a time today as he had 2,000 years ago. The picture combines melodramatic social criticism with slapstick comedy and refuses to spell out human relations or define characters beyond their symbolic status.

There are some moments of zany surrealism and some moving

sequences involving the woman's mysterious personality. The mood is uneven and pace drops off after a while. —*Edna.*

Rosa De Areia
(The Sand Rose)
(PORTUGUESE)

Berlin An Inforfilmes production. Produced by Acácio de Almeida, Fernando Nero, José Mazeda. Written, directed and edited by Margarida Cordeiro, Antonio Reis. Adapted from texts by Kafka, Montaigne, Saint John Perse, Carl Sagan, Atharvaveda, Zen stories, medieval documents; camera (color), Acácio de Almeida; music, Cesar Frank; sound, Jean Paul Mugel; art direction, Cordeiro, Reis; costumes, Susana Carvalho. Reviewed at Berlin Film Festival (Forum of Young Cinema), Feb. 18, 1989. Running time: **87 MIN.**
With: Ana Umbelina, Balbina Ferro, Cristina de Jesus, Lia Nascimento, Maria Olinda, Alberto Mendes, Antonio Reis, Artur Semedo, Carlos Alberto Comes, Francisco Nascimento, Frederico Robalo, Roxana, Ilda Pais, Luis Silva, Rodolfo Silva.

■ **"The Sand Rose" contains a flow of handsome images unburdened by any narrative continuity, accompanied by a selection of texts ranging from Kafka to medieval tales. Picture will appeal only to audiences exclusively concerned with film language and poetry.**

Decorously clad figures, mostly women, are arranged around breathtaking landscapes, their expressions denoting a state of constant angst.

Film is mostly about the abject conditions of human existence, with historical episodes such as the 15th century trial of a sow. The exact significance of all these images is far from evident, but it seems the point is to create moods, rhythms and images.

The film contains its own criticism when it says that these have already been seen before: they are senseless, but also beautiful.

It's strictly arthouse experimental fare. —*Edna.*

Amor America
(ARGENTINE-
WEST GERMAN-DOCU)

Berlin A Wolfgang Pfeiffer Films production. Written, directed and camera (color, 16m), Ciro Capellari; editor, Regine Heuser; sound, Didi Danquart; production manager, Corny Rosenthal; narration, Osvaldo Bayer; narrators, Jorge Honig (Spanish), Moe Thyssen (German); historical research, Jorge Luis Ubertalli. Reviewed at Berlin Film Festival (Forum of Young Cinema), Feb. 13, 1989. Running time: **107 MIN.**
With: Luisa Calcumil.

■ **A typical Forum selection, this documentary on genocide of the Mapuche Indians (the original** inhabitants of South Argentina) **was shot in Patagonia by a Latin American filmmaker based in West Germany.**

Combining historical data with verbal traditions and stories of the Mapuches, the film leaves little doubt about the crime against this people. Those who stole their land at the end of the last century are still heroes in Argentina's history.

Actress Luisa Calcumil put on in the last sequence a 1-woman show in open air for the benefit of an improvised audience, which sums up quite succinctly the woes and tragedy of the Mapuches.

The first determined efforts of this nation to assume its rights after years of dejected submission can't fail to appeal to a liberal audience. The nagging doubts about future prospects are intelligently presented, but there is a tendency to drown everything in long monologs which sound too familiar, from many other films dealing with similar subjects. —*Edna.*

A Rustling Of Leaves
(CANADIAN-BRITISH-
DOCU)

Berlin A Kalasikas Prod./Channel Four production. Written, produced and directed by Nettie Wild. Camera (color, 16m), Kirk Tougas; editor, Peter Wintonick; music, Joey Ayala, Salvador Ferreras, Rob Porter, David Byrne, The Talking Heads; sound, Gary Marcuse, Paul Moralis, Jean-Marie Hallessey. Reviewed at Berlin Film Festival (Forum of Young Cinema), Feb. 16, 1989. Running time: **110 MINS.**
With: Father Frank Navaro, Bernabe Buscayno (alias Commander Dante), Jun Pala, Father Ed de la Torre, members of the Alsa Masa.

■ **In trying to explore the legality of the Philippines' revolutionary leftwing factions, Nettie Wild makes no claim to objectivity; It is perfectly clear from the very first moment she is siding with the guerrillas and their struggle.**

Her main effort is to substantiate her position by bringing in a wealth of material proving that the Aquino regime still has a long way to go before the Phillippines can reach a state remotely akin to democracy.

Interviews with leaders of the revolutionaries, like Father Navaro and Commander Dante, carry their own weight. Images of the fascist Alsa Masa movement and more particularly the cool, murderous opinions delivered by disk jockey Jun Pala (whose propaganda on the air will remind WW2 veterans of Lord Haw Haw and Tokyo Rose) are responsible for the film's real shock effect.

Pala professes to be a Hitler admirer, promises to follow his example and says that whatever has been going on is nothing compared to what he prepares for the future.

Given the conditions under which pic was shot, quality of image is remarkable and cutting effective. —*Edna.*

Luk Erosa
(Cupid's Bow)
(POLISH)

Berlin A Perspektywa Unit, Polish Film Corp. production. Directed by Jerzy Domaradzki. Screenplay, Domaradzki, Jacek Kondracki; camera (color), Jacek Blawut; editor, Miroslawa Garlicka; music, Michal Lorenc; production design, Andrzej Przedworski; sound, Piotr Knop; production manager, Pawel Rakowski. Reviewed at Berlin Film Festival (Market), Feb. 18, 1989. Running time: **112 MIN.**
Maryska . . . . .Grazyna Trela
Prof. Stanislaw Ciaglewicz . . . .Jerzy Stuhr
Adam Korowski . . . . .Henryk Bista
Also with: Olaf Lubaszenko, Janusz Michalowski, Piotr Machalica, Anna Majcher, Ewa Isajewicz-Telega, Elzbieta Karkoszka. Kazimierz Kaczor.

■ **Jerzy Domaradzki's "Cupid's Bow," is a more conventional effort which explores the hedonistic lives of aristocrats on the home front during World War I.**

Behind the opening credits, naked lovers writhe in slow motion, setting the scene for what's to come. Maryska's (Grazyna Trela) husband is off to the war. Before long he's reported missing, and soon she's making little protest when seduced by the husband's friend, a seedy professor (Jerzy Stuhr) with sickly wife and other mistresses on the side.

However, the love of Maryska's life turns out to be a shy 17-year-old youth, Adam (Henryk Bista), son of friends with whom she goes to stay. She initiates the boy, and falls in love with him, at least for a while.

Based on a novel, "Cupid's Bow" is a lavish romantic melodrama almost obsessively concerned with sex. Grazyna Trela gamely disrobes at the drop of a hat, and almost every sexual position imaginable is employed during the film.

Despite, or because, of this obsession with depicting scenes of lovemaking, the pic remains on the surface, with the viewer never very interested in the heroine or her plight.

Production is top class, with sumptuous settings and costumes — when the actors happen to wear them. Pic could be trimmed from its overlong 112-minute running time. It bears a 1987 date. —*Strat.*

Qi Lian Shan De
Hul Sheng
(The Echo Of Qi
Lian Mountain)
(CHINESE)

Berlin A Beijing August First Studio production, released by China Film Import and Export Corp. Produced by Ba Yi Dian Ying, Zhi Pian Chang. Directed by Zhang Yongshou. Screenplay, Li Maolin, Zhang Yongshou, Zhang Fengchu. Camera (color), Ding Shanfa. Reviewed at Berlin Film Festival (Panorama), Feb. 15, 1989. Running time: **100 MIN.**
With: Ni Ping, Wang Baokun, Zhang Chao.

■ **This, the third feature film by 54-year-old Zhang Yongshou, is a war story with a difference. It depicts an all-woman company of soldiers with the doomed task of holding off advancing enemy forces at a mountain pass long enough to permit their male troops to retreat to safety.**

From the start it's clear there's no way out for the stalwart heroines of this battle actioner set in the remote Gobi region of western China in 1936. Pic is a downer, but is worth the depressing ride because of its touching insights into the response of people who know they have to die in order that others might live.

The women's lives flash before their eyes in bittersweet flashbacks which add depth to an already deeply textured and well-acted film.

Tech credits are good and top-drawer lensing makes good use of the story's moonscape location setting. —*Gill.*

The Stupid Years

Berlin Produced by Alyson Mead, Macall Polay. Written, directed and edited by Mead. Camera (color, 16m), Lisa Bruce; sound, Stephanie Beroes, Eli Veitzer, Alexander Markowski, Kevin Bill; production managers, Polay, Carol Schwartz. Reviewed at Berlin Film Festival (Market), Feb. 14, 1989. Running time: **78 MIN.**
Ted . . . . .Douglas Gibson
Carol . . . . .Sarah Newhouse
Bob . . . . .Edward Weiss
Alice . . . . .Diane Gaidry
Game Show Host . . . . .Sam Samuels
Interviewer . . . . .John Natale
Peter . . . . .Milo Kevin Floeter

■ **Aptly titled, "The Stupid Years" concerns a young quartet — Bob and Carol and Ted and Alice — whose names recall an earlier and far better film.**

It's a road movie full of potholes and also a rites of passage film. Plot is minimal, concerning how the young travelers cross the country toward some measure of mature self-knowledge.

Produced for $30,000, plus deferrals, edited at a 3-to-1 ratio, "The Stupid Years" is so clumsily incompetent as to have almost no redeeming qualities. —*Hitch.*

Bankomatt
(SWISS-ITALIAN)

Berlin An Imago Films, Lugano and AB-Cinema Rome production, with RTTSI/SSR. Produced by Villi Hermann, Enzo Porcelli. Directed by Villi Hermann. Screenplay, Giovanni Pascutto; camera (color), Carlo Varini; editor, Fernanda Indoni; music, Franco Piersanti; costumes, Lia Morandini; sound, Felix Singer; production manager, Bruno Moll. Reviewed at Berlin Film Festival (competing), Feb. 18, 1989. Running time: **88 MIN.**
Bruno . . . . Bruno Ganz
Stefano . . . . Giovanni Guidelli
Maria . . . . Francesca Neri
Bank Director . . . . Omero Antonutti
Also with: Pier Paolo Capponi, Roberto De Francesco, Andrea Novicov, Fabrizio Cerusico, Mauro Guidelli.

(Italian soundtrack)

■Though director Villi Hermann's hero has robbed a bank and is apparently going to get away with it, it doesn't seem likely this pic will hit the financial jackpot. Even though stylishly photographed and with first-rate performances, pic never quite jells.

Things get off to a good start. Four perfectly unlikable punks get caught up in a police chase after one casually robs a gas station and kills the attendant. Trying to avoid a roadblock, they drive into the lake.

The authorities aren't certain how many were in the car, but only three bodies are found. The fourth has survived unbeknownst to them, rescued by a reclusive gardener played by Bruno Ganz.

The gardener encourages his charge not to turn himself in and it soon becomes clear that he wants an accomplice for a little job he plans to pull off. Soon the young fugitive's girlfriend gets involved, a little bit too eagerly for credibility, and the big heist is underway.

From here on out we've seen it all before, and better done. Pic offers an upbeat message to would-be young crooks, though: Sometimes you can get away with it and fly off to your island paradise. The big question is, what was this film doing in the Berlin fest competition? —*Owl.*

Der Philosoph
(The Philosopher)
(WEST GERMAN)

Berlin A Filmverlag der Autoren release of a Moana Film production. Produced and directed by Rudolf Thome. Screenplay, Thome; camera (color), Reinhold Vorschneider; editor, Dörte Völz-Mammarella; music, Hanno Rinne; production design, Eve Schaenen; sound, Frank Behnke; production manager, Joan Spiekermann; assistant director, Irmela Baumert. Reviewed at Berlin Film Festival (New German Cinema), Feb. 15, 1989. Running time: **83 MIN.**
Georg Hermes . . . . . Johannes Herrschmann
Franziska . . . . Adriana Altaras
Beate . . . . Friederike Tiefenbacher
Marthe . . . . Claudia Matschulla

■Here's an amiable fantasy about a serious, hermit-like young man, who's spent years alone writing, and who's taken up by three attractive young women. The menage-à-quatre theme might give the pic some international play.

Franziska, Beate and Marthe share a large Berlin apartment and run a men's clothes store. Bored with fleeting relationships and 1-night stands, they latch on to the naive, gangly, virginal Georg when he comes to buy a new suit.

Franziska (Adriana Altaras) seduces Georg on a boating trip, and persuades him to move into the girls' apartment, whereupon the other two shower him with gifts and attention. For a while Georg resists, but when Franziska okays the arrangement, he winds up in an enviable 4-in-a-bed situation.

Feminists will probably blanch at this male wish-fulfillment fantasy, but the pic has a certain charm and naiveté all its own. Writer-director Rudolf Thome handles it all with a brisk sense of humor.

The actors enter into the spirit of the fun, disrobing regularly for the numerous bed scenes. —*Strat.*

Dni Satmenyia
(Day Of Darkness)
(SOVIET)

Berlin A Sovexportfilm presentation of a Lenfilm Studios production. Directed by Alexander Sokurov. Screenplay, Yuri Arabov, Arkadi Strugatzky, Boris Strugatzky, Piotr Kadochnikov, based on story by Arkadi and Boris Strugatzky; camera (Widescreen, color), Serghei Jurisditzky; editor, Leda Semionova; music, Yuri Chanin; sound, Vladimir Persov; art direction, Yelena Amshinskaya; costumes, Lydia Kryukova. Reviewed at Berlin Film Festival (Forum of Young Cinema), Feb. 19, 1989. Running time: **139 MIN.**
Malyanov . . . . Alexei Ananishov
Vecherovsky . . . . Eskender Umarov
Malyanov's sister . . . . Irina Sokolova
Snegovoy . . . . Vladimir Samansky
Gluchov . . . . Kyril Dudkin
Also with: Vikto Belovolsky (Gubar), Alexei Yankovsky (Snegovoy's father), Serioja

Krylov (little boy).

■Alexander Sokurov seems determined never to use conventional cinema narrative and to persist in reinventing film language. The visual impact of his latest picture is such that it may well carry the audience over many a mystifying patch.

The story of a young doctor, who, after finishing his studies in Moscow, is sent to a far corner of Turkmenia, on the Caspian Sea, the film is a series of disconnected episodes. All of them lead to the same pessimistic conclusions: Man's lot is bleak and his future unpromising.

Cultures and traditions clash in this Tower of Babel. Uprooted people live in a vacuum; unhappy, paranoid and desperately seeking a way out, even at the cost of their own lives.

The focus is on strangers from all corners of the Soviet Union thrown together arbitrarily in this meeting point of East and West. This is a clear reference to the policy of forcibly displacing entire nations, in an attempt to wipe out their identity.

Spectacular use of widescreen photography is accompanied by uncanny choice of camera angles. The image is drained in yellowish tinges, to strengthen the effect of heat and outlandish landscape.

Sokurov's handling of actors and his visual conception show he is an adept follower of his late master, Andrei Tarkovsky, but with a strong personal style of his own. His films may not be easy fare, but are bound to appeal to movie buffs. —*Edna.*

Martha Jellneck
(WEST GERMAN)

Berlin A Basis Film release of an Ottakar Runze Film production. (Intl. Sales, Unimedia Intl., Munich.) Directed by Kai Wessel. Screenplay, Beate Langmaack; camera (color), Achim Poulheim; editor, Sabine Jagiella; music, Michael Haase; production design, Beata Langmaack; sound, Gerard Rueff; production manager, Michael Beier; assistant director, Kerstin Schwarzburg. Reviewed at Berlin Film Festival (New German Cinema), Feb. 14, 1989. Running time: **94 MIN.**
Martha Jellneck . . . . . Heidemarie Hatheyer
Thomas . . . . Dominique Horwitz
Hanne Schmitz . . . . Angelika Thomas
Franz Laub . . . . Ulrich Matschoss
Hayati . . . . Hayati Yesikaya
Monika . . . . Sylvia Anders

■This is a tautly written and directed first feature which, despite the apparent disadvantages of restricted location and cast, emerges as a gripping, polished drama with some arthouse prospects.

The 72-year-old Martha Jellneck lives with only her dog as company in a small apartment she can't leave because of her arthritis. Her only contacts with the outside world are a cheerful youth who brings her a hot meal a day, a woman neighbor who covets the apartment and a Turkish boy who walks her dog.

With these basic elements, and a fine performance from Heidemarie Hatheyer as the old lady, writer Beate Langmaack and director Kai Wessel have crafted a drama in which Martha gradually realizes that her beloved half-brother Franz, who died in France during the war, was actually murdered by his superior officer. The officer has assumed Franz' identity and lives nearby.

Martha invites the old man to her place for coffee and cakes while she tries to check her suspicions, then listens, horrified, as the former SS man admits his crimes, showing no remorse. Ulrich Matschoss is tops as the old murderer.

Film's resolution is satisfying, though the implications of Martha's revenge for her brother's killer are disturbing.

Pic should play at festivals later this year and might spark specialized release interest. Print caught, probably a blow-up from 16m, was on the grainy side. —*Strat.*

Ayahku
(My Father)
(INDONESIAN)

Berlin A Pt. Prasidi Teta Films production. Produced by Bustal Nawawi. Directed by Aguy Elias. Screenplay, H. Misbach Yusa Biran; camera (color), Sri Atmo; editor, Arturo GP. (No further credits available.) Reviewed at Berlin Film Festival (Forum of Young Cinema), Feb. 13, 1989. Running time: **90 MIN.**
With: WD Mochtar, Deddy Mizwar, Rima Melati.

■Film concerns a man who abandoned his wife and kids, went to live with another woman and repents 20 years later. It develops into a surprisingly honest and committed family drama.

The rough edges, and there are many throughout the film, lend a degree of authenticity to the proceedings and add to pic's effectiveness.

The older son, who was 11 when the father left and who kept the family going, refuses to see the old man. His younger brother and sister are less sanguine about it, and the mother evidently still has some affection for the man who had betrayed her.

Divided neatly into sequences — each one locked into a single set and sticking to the basic long shot, medium shot, closeup sequence — the pic actually gains by its unpretentious simplicity.

Subplots concerning the younger brother's marriage to a rich and authoritative woman, or the younger sister's preparation to marry which involve further sacrifice from her older brother, are neatly introduced and treated.

The one technical sopohistication is the use of deep focus, which only stresses the tense stage-effect of each dramatic set-up.

No stunning cinematic achievement, this thoughtful treatment of a universal conflict is deeply rooted in local background. This is a sincere and touching effort.

—*Edna.*

L'Enfant de l'Hiver
(Winter Child)
(FRENCH)

Berlin   A Gemini Films, GPFI Production. Written and directed by Olivier Assayas. Camera (color), Denis Lenoir; editor, Luc Barnier; music, Jorge Arriagada; sound, Oliver Schwob; art direction, François-Renaud Labarthe; costumes, Françoise Clavel. Reviewed at Berlin Film Festival (Forum of Young Cinema), Feb. 15, 1989. Running time: **85 MIN.**

Stéphane . . . . Michel Feller
Sabine . . . . Clotilde de Bayser
Natalia . . . . Marie Matheron
Bruno . . . . Jean-Philippe Ecoffey
Father. . . . . Gerard Blain
     Also with: Anouk Grinberg (Agnès), Inès de Medeiros (Ana), Nathalie Richard (Leni).

■**This tale of obsessive love complicated by immaturity, generation gaps and general unhappiness, goes well with the romantic traditions of the French cinema.**

Stéphane leaves Natalia in her last month of pregnancy and embarks on a new romance with stage designer Sabine. She leaves him because she is still in love with stage actor Bruno who is fed up with her and prefers his regular relationship with Maryse.

The plot ties and unties these relations, as each character desperately looks for happiness and ends at best in compromise, at worst in utter despair.

Director Olivier Assayas focuses on two central characters, the immature Stéphane, who refuses responsibility, and confused Sabine, torn between passion and affection. Natalia and Bruno also have important roles in the proceedings. Since his first film,

"Disorder," dealt with the end of youth, this could be taken as a sequel about the first crisis of adult life.

Soulful performances by Marie Matheron and Clotilde de Bayser, confident direction and smooth technical credits will help this romantic merry-go-round find its admirers beyond the French film buff audience, which has already adopted Assayas as one of their own. —*Edna.*

Polizei
(TURKISH)

Berlin   A Penta Film production. Produced by Turgay Aksoy. Directed by Serif Gören. Screenplay, Huseyin Kuzu; camera (color), Erdal Kahraman; editor, Mevlut Kocak; music, Timur Selcuk. Reviewed at the Berlin Film Festival (Panorama), Feb. 14, 1989. Running time: **96 MIN.**

     With: Kemal Sunai; Babett Jutte; Yalcin Guzelce, Kaya Gurei, Nilufur Usku, Nuri Sezer, Atilla Cansever, Levent Beceren, Matthias Drawe, Claudie Hackermesser.

■**This is a would-be love story that promises more than it ultimately delivers. For undemanding audiences looking for an easy laugh, this could very well be the ticket.**

A street cleaner has a crush on a waitress who works at a snack bar on his route. He enlists the aide of a friend, something of a Casanova, who instead of helping puts the make on her himself.

When our hero gets the part of a policeman in a local play, he takes to wearing the uniform after performances. He not only fools his friends and neighborhood business people but the real cop on the beat.

Though the film gets better with the cop inpersonation and all the anticipated jokes are there, the humor dissipates. Naturally, after a twist or two, he ends up getting the girl, but the proceedings all go on a bit too long.

Cameraman Erdal Kahraman has beautifully captured a summertime Berlin. —*Owl.*

Herbstmilch
(Autumn Milk)
(WEST GERMAN)

Berlin   A Perathon Film-ZDF production. (Intl. sales, Cine Intl., Munich.) Produced and directed by Joseph Vilsmaier. Screenplay, Peter Steinbach, from the book by Anna Wimschneider; camera (Eastmancolor), Vilsmaier; editor, Ingrid Broszat; music, Norbert Jürgen Schneider; production design, Wolfgang Hundhammer; sound, Jochen Schwarzat, Milan Bor; assistant director, Helga Asenbaum. Reviewed at Berlin Film Festival (New German Cinema), Feb. 18, 1989. Running time: **111 MIN.**

Anna . . . . Dana Vavrova

Albert . . . . Werner Stocker
Photographer . . . . Eva Mattes
Resl . . . . Ilona Meyer
Mother-in-law . . . . Renate Grosser
     Also with: Claude Oliver Rudolph, Hertha Schwarz, Julius Mitterer, Albert Wimschneider, Marie Bardischewski, Werner Schnitzer.

■**A lovingly made recollection of the life of a teenage girl on a Bavarian farm in the Nazi era, "Autumn Milk" is a fine debut for cameraman Joseph Vilsmaier and could spark international fest and arthouse attention.**

Anna Wimschneider published her acclaimed autobiography in 1984, when she was 64. Tome was snapped up by Vilsmaier, who hails from the part of Germany where the tale is set, and the film was made over a 4-year period.

Dana Vavrova is luminous as 18-year-old Anna, eldest daughter of a widowed farmer, forced to cook and clean for her father and numerous brothers. Uninterested in the increasingly alarming political developments, she wants to be a nurse, but falls in love with a neighboring farmer, Albert.

They marry, but almost immediately Albert is drafted and Anna becomes pregnant. Now, she has to run her husband's new farm, facing the undisguised hostility of her mother-in-law and the wonderment of a clutch of aged aunts and uncles. In a nice touch, one of the uncles is played by the real Albert Wimschneider.

Film is principally a study of a young woman forced to carry a workload that would break many a man, and Dana Vavrova convincingly matures from shy young girl to tough, resourceful farmer during the course of the drama. Vilsmaier, who doubles as cameraman on the film, captures the seasons on the farm with all their beauty. He also shows the devastatingly hard work of farming in that era, with antiquated equipment and rigid sexual and social structures to boot.

Entire cast, with quite a few villagers from the neighborhood, is fine, with Eva Mattes a standout as a sympathetic photographer for whom the young couple poses for a post-wedding portrait. Always, the political events are there as a grim background.

The real Anna is seen as an old lady trudging along a country road at the beginning of this simple, but enormously effective, pic. —*Strat.*

Voices From The Attic
(DOCU)

Berlin   A Jane Balfour presentation of a Siren Pictures production. Executive producers, Julio Caro, Stephen Klein. Produced and directed by Debbie Goodstein. Screenplay, Goodstein, Jim Butler; camera (Duart color, 16m), Oren Rudavsky; editor, Toby Shimins; music, Ken Mazur, Russ Landau; sound, David Leitner. Reviewed at Berlin Film Festival (Forum of Young Cinema), Feb. 12, 1989. Running time: **60 MIN.**

■**This is basically a home movie in which director Debbie Goodstein goes with some members of her family back to the Polish village of their origins, to exorcise memories of the Holocaust experiences there.**

Documentary offers some disturbing insights not only into the past but also the present.

Ostensibly, this should be an uplifting story about a non-Jew who saved his neighbors from the gas chambers, but as the truth gradually emerges, the purity of the motives behind the noble deed is slightly tarnished. The Jews had to give all their valuables to the farmer's wife before she agreed to take them in to her attic.

One of the mysteries unravelled under the circumstances, to Goodstein's horror, is the story of her mother's baby sister who had to be abandoned on the church steps, since there was no way to keep a newborn child in the attic.

What strikes most, however, is that nothing much has really changed since. Immediately after the war, Polish patriots visited the Jewish survivors, as they came out of hiding, told them they were not wanted in their country and should leave immediately, which they did.

Now, when they visit the village as American tourists, swastika graffiti are painted once again on the walls, accompanied by typical anti-Semitic threats. If only for this sequence, this is a movie that had to be done. —*Edna.*

Banana Shoot
(JAPANESE)

Berlin   A Banana Shoot Committee, Japan Academy of Visual Arts production. Produced by Hironori Miyagawa, Masaki Ito. Directed by Tosuke Sato. Screenplay, Sato, Nobuaki Ito; camera (color, 16m), Tomotoshi Hamaguchi, Tamio Hayashi, Motot Takeda; editor, Toshihide Fukano, Yasuko Monji; music, Shuichi Toshima; sound, Hiroshi Ishigai; art direction, Shinji Furuya; costumes, Miyuki Sato. Reviewed at Berlin Film Festival (Forum of Young Cinema), Feb. 15, 1989. Running time: **102 MIN.**

Sojiro . . . . Masayuki Yui
Fukuo . . . . Hiroyuki Hara

Hiromi . . . . Makiko Kono
Kazuhiko . . . . Tatsuya Irie
Also with: Yoshihiro Mine, Yasuo Kawakami, Yoshinori Oishi, Kazunari Tajima, Hiroshi Kinoshita.

■ **A first film by a director who was barely 23 when he finished it, "Banana Shoot" deals with a subject he is obviously very familiar with, the crisis of the average Japanese high school graduate, facing a future of constant rat races.**

Two such graduates who are also close friends, Fukuo and Kazuhiko, let off steam on a soccer field, playing with an imaginary ball, when an older man, Sojiro, joins them in the game and soon becomes their bosom pal. He inspires the two friends, and a girl schoolmate, Hiromi, to dreams of freedom in exotic wide spaces where everything is possible.

For them, this stranger is a romantic figure who dares to break rules and conventions by which they have to abide. They're moved to tears when he says goodbye in a railway station before leaving to fulfill his dreams. They remain behind to join the long line of anxiety-stricken applicants to universities which reject 90% of the candidates.

In the second part of the film, most of the illusions turn out to be just that, and it is not by accident that the two friends are seen walking out together from a stage performance of Don Quixote. Yet, the picture seems to say, the ability to dream is essential to survive in the over-organized, rigid framework of the Japanese society.

Director Sato, a student of Shohei Imamura, still lacks control and confidence in pacing the film and his camera is at times unnecessarily nervous. He has the right feeling for the moods of his generation and puts them across in a clear manner. He also manages to get sympathetic performances from his cast, with Makiko Kono lending much warmth to the character of Hiromi.—*Edna.*

Johanna d'Arc Of Mongolia
(Joan Of Arc Of Mongolia)
(WEST GERMAN)

Berlin A NEF 2 Filmverleih release (in German-speaking territories) of an Ulrike Ottinger Film production with Popular Film (Hans H. Kaden), ZDF Mainz. Produced, written, directed, edited and camera (color) by Ulrike Ottinger; music arrangements, Wilhelm Dieter Siebert; sound, Margit Eschenbach; production design, Ottinger, Peter Bausch; costumes, Gisela Storch; production management, Renée Gundelach, Hanna Rogge, Harald Muchametow, Erica Marcus; production management (China), China Central TV, CITV Beijing, Ren Da Hui, Weng Dao Cai, Lian Zhen Hua. Reviewed at Berlin Film Festival (competing), Feb. 14, 1989. Running time: **165 MIN.**
```
Lady Windermere . . . . . . . Delphine Seyrig
Ulun Iga . . . . . . . . . . . . . . . . . . Xu Re Huar
Frau Müller-Vohwinkel . . . . . Irm Hermann
Fanny Ziegfeld . . . . . . . . . . . Gillian Scalici
Giovanna . . . . . . . . . . . . . . . . . Inès Sastre
Mickey Katz . . . . . . . . . . . . . . Peter Kern
Colonel Muravjev . . . . . . . . Nougzar Sharia
Alyosha . . . . . . . . . . . . . Christoph Eichhorn
```
Also with: Jacinta, Else Nabu, Sevembike Elibay (The Kalinka Sisters), Lydia Billiet, Marek Szmelkin, Amadeus Flössner, Dong Zihao, Kunio Sato, Alfredo Cocozza, Badema, Jan Deckers, Xu Ren Hu, Tu Hai, Yi Tuo Ya.

■ **Since the fiction of "Johanna d'Arc" lacks narrative cohesion, while its mock documentary aspects appear awfully rigged, it seems unlikely that Berlin's Ulrike Ottinger will find many media windows accessible for her lengthy hybrid.**

There is no character even remotely akin to the Orléans Maiden fighting a Holy War for King and Nation in "Johanna d'Arc Of Mongolia." There is, instead, a fictional story of a group of waylaid Western women travellers being abducted from the Trans-Mongolian Express by a tribe of mostly female locals, led by a sweetly persuasive Mongolian princess.

The fiction turns out to be a joke device to move things into documentary territory with a recording of the culture clash arising when the Western women try to adapt to the tribal customs of their Mongolian sisters. Then this documentation turns out at the end to have been a hoax.

The women travellers are first seen aboard the famed Trans-Siberian Express (an opulent studio reconstruction). They are characters right out of an old-style Berliner cabaret: Delphine Seyrig as Lady Windermere, a refined word-gusher; Irm Hermann as Frau Müller-Vohwinkel, a German botanist; Gillian Scalici as Broadway musical star Fanny Ziegfeld; Peter Kern as a Jewish opera tenor and Inès Sastre as Giovanna, a young back-packer in jeans.

A couple of Russian officers are present too. The men disappear as all the women transfer to the more austere Trans-Mongolian. They have hardly settled here before swarms of romantically clad Mongolian women stop the train to take their hostages away for what is to become a month in a moving summer camp.

Lady Windermere spouts anthropological comment in a condescending tour-guide way. The other Western women seem to come out of the culture clash with no other newly achieved knowledge than adhering to a rule of not washing their clothes. The Mongolians, constantly decked out in their folkloristic Sunday best and never for a second seen at weekday work, are rewarded with the gift of a set of cheap camp cutlery.

When the other women are finally escorted back to their train, Giovanna stays behind. She soon catches up with the train anyway, and here she joins Lady Windermere in conversation (in French) with an elegant Mongolian lady, wearing Parisian haute-couture, who gives the whole show away: it seems that many Mongolians spend a summer holiday in such camps, just to keep in touch with their old traditions. —*Kell.*

Der Kuss Des Tigers
(The Kiss Of The Tiger)
(WEST GERMAN-FRENCH)

Berlin A Futura Film production, with Filmedis (Paris) and Balance Film (Munich). (Intl. sales, Filmverlag der Autoren, Munich.) Produced by Theo Hinz. Directed by Petra Haffter. Screenplay, Haffter, Gerd Weiss, Peter Reinholz, from novel "Come Die With Me," by Francis Ryck; camera (color), Wolfgang Simon, Gerard Vandenberg; editor, Barbara von Weitershausen; music, Inga Humpe, Thomas Fehlmann; sound, Jean-Philippe LeRoux; production design, Georg von Kieseritzky; assistant director, Sabine Eckhard; production manager, Jean Lara. Reviewed at Berlin Film Festival (New German Cinema), Feb. 18, 1989. Running time: **103 MIN.**
```
Peter . . . . . . . . . . . . . . . . Stephane Ferrara
Michele . . . . . . . . . . . . . . . . Beate Jensen
Jacques . . . . . . . . . . . . . . . . Yves Beneyton
Mme. Monestier . . . . . . . Kristina van Eyck
Frank . . . . . . . . . . . . . . . . Dimitri Rougeuil
Mme. Morey . . . . . . . . . . . . Caroline Berg
```

■ **Obscure motivations drag down this brooding thriller in which a lonely German girl in Paris becomes infatuated with a self-confessed murderer.**

Beate Jensen is good as the boyish heroine, Michele, who meets handsome stranger Peter (Stephane Ferrara) in the Tuileries. Right out, he confesses he's killed women purely for pleasure (as we saw, disturbingly, in the film's credit sequence). Michele only half believes him, but soon they're involved in a passionate (and quite graphically depicted) love affair.

It's never made clear why the girl goes along with this dangerous stranger, or why she stays by when he kills a woman who's befriended the couple and invited them to her home. At fadeout, Michele takes action to protect herself from Peter, but the film's final scene suggests she hasn't learned her lesson — indeed, she may even have enjoyed being on a killing spree.

Femme director Petra Haffter handles her material briskly, and the sex and the killings with frankness. We never know what compels Peter, apparently a Canadian tourist, to act the way he does, or why Michele goes along.

A crippling blow to authenticity is the German fetish for having everyone speak German: This film's entirely set in France, and when a Paris cop or taxi driver starts speaking Deutsch, credibility flies out the window. Maybe the pic will work better in its French version.

This said, Jensen and Ferrara make an exciting team. —*Strat.*

Akira
(JAPANESE-ANIMATED)

Berlin An Akira Committee production. Directed by Katsuhiro Otomo. Screenplay, Otomo, Izo Hashimoto; camera (Widescreen, color), Katsuji Misawa; music, Shoji Yamashiro; art direction, Toshiharu Mizutani; trick effects, Takashi Nakamura; in Dolby stereo. Reviewed at Berlin Film Festival (Forum of Young Cinema), Feb. 17, 1989. Running time: **124 MIN.**
With the voices of: Mitsuo Iwara, Nozomu Sasaki, Mami Koyama, Taro Ishida.

■ **A lavish animation extravaganza produced at a cost of $8-million, this futuristic exploration is a followup by author-director Katsuhiro Otomo to his tremendously popular comic books.**

The action takes place 30 years from now, in neo-Tokyo, the reconstructed version of the Japanese capital, previously destroyed in a 1988 nuclear war.

The shape of the city has changed but not its problems, as the social fabric is falling to pieces, students organize demonstrations, unemployment generates constant unrest and terrorists conspire to overthrow the government.

The military is developing a new and more powerful source of energy, ESP. The problem is that they don't quite know how to control it, and when a young biker with natural talents refuses to cooperate, the entire world is in a lot of trouble.

A remarkable technical achievement in every respect, from the imaginative and detailed design of tomorrow to the booming Dolby effects on the soundtrack, pic's only drawback is the slight stiffness in the drawing of human movement.

Videogame buffs are the obvious audience of this item, with territories familiar with Otomo's comic books bound to give it high priority. —*Edna.*

Soloveckaya Vlast
(The Power Of Solovki)
(SOVIET-DOCU-COLOR/B&W)

Berlin A Sovexportfilm presentation of a Mosfilm production. Directed by Marina Goldovskaya. Written by Viktor Listov, Dimitri Cukovsky; camera (color, b&w), Goldovskaya; music, Nikolai Karetnikov, Marina Krutoyarskaya. Reviewed at Berlin Film Festival (out of competition), Feb. 20, 1989. Running time: **93 MIN.**

■**Solovki, a small nordic island in the White Sea, is entitled to claim the title of Patriarch Gulag. It's the first of its kind established by the Soviet regime and the infamous example for the countless ones erected later, as this film states in no uncertain manner.**

Once a monastery and a center of learning for all Russia, it was first used as a prison by Ivan the Terrible. From 1923-39, the place was known as SLON, converted into a special camp, advertised officially as a re-education center for dissenting elements.

Moscow was so confident of the definition it even sponsored a film about Solovki, shot in 1927-28 but unreleased until recently. It is around this footage, presenting the establishment in the best constructive tradition of socialist cinema, that director Marina Goldovskaya structured her own film. She counterpoints the images of old propaganda film with the tales of horror unfolded by the octogenarians still alive, who had gone through that valley of tears.

Many of the inmates, as it turns out, were intellectuals thrown into jail arbitrarily, sometimes only because they had refused to cooperate with secret police. The beatings and the tortures are described in detail and, typically, the criminals and the prostitutes there had an easier time than all the rest.

One sarcastic episode refers to the visit of author Maxim Gorki, through whose eyes the world was supposed to be convinced of the usefulness and probity of the place. Gorki let himself be deceived without any effort and went away, singing Solovki's praise.

A state in its own right — with

its own airplanes, ships, trains, theaters and shops — it was often said the law there was not Soviet law, but Solovki law, and the two were not necessarily identical.

The facts, as described by Goldovskaya's witnesses, are predictable after all the publications on the Russian gulags. What is surprising is that Moscow is assuming full responsibility. It clears a film which compares Stalin to Nero and the GPU to the Spanish Inquisition, allows it to introduce evidence showing how the sick and feeble were put on boats and drowned in the sea, and to tell its audience they have no right to forget it. Indeed, they don't. —*Edna.*

Boulevards d'Afrique
(FRENCH)

Berlin A Philippe Dussart, INA, FEMIS, Comité du Film Ethnographique, La Sept production. Directed by Jean Rouch, Tam-Sir 'Doueb. Screenplay, Gérard Noyer, based on musical comedy "Tali Bu Mag" (Boulevards d'Afrique) by Doueb, from idea by Djibril Tam-Sir Niane; camera (color, 16m), Philippe Constantini, Rouch; editor, Françoise Beloux; music, Irène Tassembedo; sound, Jean-Claude Brisson, Patrick Genet. Reviewed at Berlin Film Festival (Forum of Young Cinema), Feb. 15, 1989. Running time: **70 MIN.**
Sukey . . . . Mouna Ndiaye
Sukey's mother . . . . Irène Tassembedo
Sukey's father . . . . . . Dante Alou Badara
Prospective bridegroom . . . Sotigui Kouyaté
 Also with: Ndeye Meissa Diop, Mbaye Dramé.
 Dancers: Manuella Morvan, Stephane Mensah, Issa Djomandé, Emanuelle Lamon, Tony Bomba and Dakar's Manhattan School Dance.

■**This film is another lively African trip for French ethnograph-cineaste Jean Rouch, based on a Senegalese musical and dealing, in a cheerful mood, with the generation gap.**

Young Sukey has just graduated from high school and wants to go on studying. Her parents, however, have promised to marry her off to a rich merchant, an older man who already has two wives. Sukey balks, the parents are scandalized by her impertinence and Sukey's friends promise to lend a hand and deliver her from the annoying predicament.

The brief story intercuts with energetic dance scenes not really incorporated into the plot. Rouch, who codirects the film with the author of the original musical, Tam-Sir Doueb, evidently has a lot of affection for his characters and understanding for both the parents and the kids. His sympathy for both sides comes out loud and clear.

Neatly shot and edited, this is pleasant addition to the rich

documentation of the African continent, a field in which Rouch is one of the leading contributors. —*Edna.*

Ban
(The House)
(THAI)

Berlin A Pholsiam production. Produced by Amphol Polsayam. Written and directed by Egalag and Chat Gobjitti, from novel "Jon Trog" by Gobjitti. Camera (color), Bunyong Mongkolmuang; music, Mongkol Utok, Tonggrau Tana; production manager, Mana Limpipolbaibul. Reviewed at Berlin Film Festival (Forum), Feb. 15, 1989. Running time: **120 MIN.**
Boonma, the husband . . . . Sorapong Chatri
Pin, his wife . . . . Piathip Khumwong
Boonma's father . . . . . Somchai Asanajinda
Sida, the daughter . . Somrudee Numampan
Odd, the son . . . . Padej Tiamsawje
Dum, younger son . . . Chalermde Tiamsawej

■**This is a disturbing saga of people at the bottom of Thai society, leaving one with no sense of hope about their fate.**

Whether there is a large audience for this glimpse into the Third World remains uncertain, but it gives a good taste of the region's high level of film production and performances.

A young father moves his family to the city to find work. With the help of a friend he succeeds and is soon able to arrange a loan with his employer to build a modest house.

He loses the first job during a layoff, but this former employer arranges for him to ship out as a fisherman and his new boss takes on the loan note. While he is at sea, his teenage daughter is gradually lured into prostitution.

The wife, who the hero has not slept with for sometime, fearful she'd become pregnant, admits that she has been unfaithful and is with child. He beats her and turns her out.

The hero ends up in an island prison camp because the boat's captain has taken them fishing in illegal waters. While serving his 6-month stretch, things at home continue to spiral downward.

The father returns to find his house empty, his father dead, his oldest son doing time, and his youngest son living with neighbors. Completely broken, the father decides there is no point in going on. He poisons himself and his young son, but ironically manages to survive and gets life imprisonment for murder.

This very realistic depiction of a Thai family's decline is pretty heavy stuff, but pic is beautifully produced, acted and edited.
—*Owl.*

Tiger, Löwe, Panther
(Tiger, Lion, Panther)
(WEST GERMAN)

Berlin A Bavaria Film production commissioned by SDR tv, Stuttgart. Produced by Michael Hild. Directed by Dominik Graf. Screenplay, Sherry Hormann; camera (color, 16m), Klaus Eichhammer; editor, Christel Suckow; music, Andreas Koebner, Dominik Graf; sound, Günther Blumenhagen. Reviewed at Berlin Film Festival, (New German Films), Feb. 11, 1989. Running time: **93 MIN.**
 With: Natja Brunckhorst, Sabine Kaack, Martina Gedek, Thomas Winkler, Oliver Stokowski, Peter Lohmeyer, Hinrich Schafmeister, Michael Maertens, Heinz Hönig, Ursula Dirichs, Charles Brauer.

■**Dominik Graf's attempt at a sophisticated comedy does not live up to the standards of his earlier work. This story of three madcap young women quickly loses itself in trivialities.**

The idea was good, though: Three woman draw on their youthful friendship with one another to come to terms with adult problems. The intricacies of Sherry Hormann's screenplay are too daunting to give any of the thesps a chance to establish a clearly defined character.

By the time boyfriends, husbands, ex-boyfriends, coworkers, parents and even a dentist are thrown in, the viewer is faced with a formidable task remembering who's who.

Klaus Eichhammer's camera brings mundane settings to life and expands the limitations of 16m.
—*Gill.*

Maicol
(ITALIAN)

Berlin A Sacis presentation (and foreign sales) of an Ipotesa Cinema/Istituto Paolo Valmarana production, in collaboration with Raiuno. Executive producer, Toni di Gregorio. Directed by Mario Brenta. Screenplay, Angela Cervi, with Francesca Marciano, Robert Mazzoni; camera (color), Fabricio Borelli; editor, Maurizio Zaccaro; no music credit; production design, Caterina Gatti; sound, Franco Borni. Reviewed at Berlin Film Festival (Forum of Young Film), Feb. 17, 1989. Running time: **90 MIN.**
Maicol . . . . Simone Tessarolo
Anita . . . . Sabina Regazzi
 Also with: Giovanni Crespi, Maria Teresa Oldani, Monica Saccomandi, Sergio Colomba.

■**After a 15-year hiatus with docu and tv work, Venice's Mario Brenta is back with another spare and unsentimental feature. Too austere to attract general audiences, "Maicol" seems sure to make its mark, albeit quietly, on the international fest and arthouse circuit.**

It is a harsh close-up of the loneliness of big city people. Anita and Maicol, an unmarried mother and her 5-year-old son, face their frustrations silently.

Anita works at a factory's assembly line and lies to get off from work early to keep a rendezvous with Giulio, her off-and-on lover.

Maicol has seen the film ''Dune'' several times and lives inside the images and characters of its story. He has hardly a word to spare on any other subject, and his mother would not listen anyway.

Anita spends her night distractedly looking for Giulio who never showed up for the rendezvous. Maicol walks in and out of subway trains, looking at people without offering them answers to their queries as to where his parents are. Found sleeping at daybreak and turned over to police, he does nothing to help bring about his eventual reunion with his mother.

—*Kell.*

Sa Gar Ett Ar;
Teden I Sjöbo
(A Year Goes By)
(SWEDISH-DOCU)

Berlin   A Mexfilm production by the Swedish Film Institute Foundation and Swedish TV Malmö. Produced by Lisbet Gabrielsson, Lena Hansson. Written and directed by Ebbe Gilbe, Gunnar Källström, Kjell Tunegärd. Collaborators, Anna Eriksson, Mats Erixon, Mats Dalunde, John Gilbe. In color. Reviewed at Berlin Film Festival (Panorama), Feb. 11, 1989. Running time: **173 MIN.**

With: Carl Andersson, Ove Andersson, Ruth Andersson, Joel Eriksson, Mikael Franzen, Lief Larsson, Astrid Skov, Madeleine Ramel, Sven-Olle Olsson.

■ ''A Year Goes By'' is a sensitive docu about Sjöbo, a small town near Malmö which became embroiled in a controversy over allowing Middle Eastern refugees to emigrate to their community. The pic's 3-hour length will be a deterent to theatrical release but it could fare better in tv exposure.

Various sectors of Sjöbo are glimpsed. The overall impression is of a wholesome and warmhearted social climate.

This image is dispelled when the various factions for and against the relocation of refugees to Sjöbo are introduced. Tv coverage of speeches given by Sven-Olle Olsson, leader of the conservative Center Party, are revealing. He laments the uncertain fate of Sweden's younger generation which, if the emigration of the outsiders is allowed, ''will have neither blond hair nor blue eyes.''

The film has caused a furor. Two days after its release in Sept., 1988, the citizens of Sjöbo went to the polls. A referendum vote as to whether they should take in 15 refugees in a camp showed 32% were in favor of sheltering the refugees and 65% were against it.

—*Sam.*

Leviathan

Hollywood   An MGM/UA from MGM Pictures release of a Luigi and Aurelio De Laurentiis presentation of a Gordon Co. production. Produced by Luigi De Laurentiis, Aurelio De Laurentiis. Executive producers, Lawrence Gordon, Charles Gordon. Directed by George Pan Cosmates. Screenplay, David Peoples, Jeb Stuart, from story by Peoples; camera (J-D-C widescreen, Technicolor), Alex Thomson; editor, Roberto Silvi, John F. Burnett; music, Jerry Goldsmith; production design, Ron Cobb; supervising art directors, William Ladd Skinner, Pier Luigi Basile; art direction, David Klassen, Franco Ceraolo; set design, Craig Edgar, Jim Teegarden, Maria Teresa Barbasso, Alessandro Alberti, Daniela Giovannoni; set decoration, Robert Gould, Bruno Cesari; costume design, April Ferry; sound (Dolby), Robin Gregory; creature effects, Stan Winston; mechanical effects, Nick Allder; visual effects, Barry Nolan; additional visual effects, Industrial Light & Magic; assistant directors, Juan Carlos Lopez Rodero, Matt Earl Beesley; additional camera Giuseppe Maccari; underwater camera, Mike Valentine, Ramon Bravo; casting, Mike Fenton; Jane Feinberg, Lynda Gordon. Reviewed at Cary Grant Theater, Culver City (Calif.), March 13, 1989. MPAA Rating: R. Running time: **98 MIN.**

Beck	Peter Weller
Doc	Richard Crenna
Willie	Amanda Pays
Sixpack	Daniel Stern
Jones	Ernie Hudson
DeJesus	Michael Carmine
Bowman	Lisa Eilbacher
Cobb	Hector Elizondo
Martin	Meg Foster

■ **Breed an ''Alien'' with a ''Thing,'' marinate in salt water, and you get a ''Leviathan.'' It's a soggy recycling of gruesome monster attacks unleashed upon a crew of macho men and women confined within a far-flung scientific outpost.**

This second entry in the underwater sci-fi cycle will not doubt do better than ''Deepstar Six,'' but displeasure with the film's bottomless derivativeness should quickly dampen whatever initial b.o. is generated.

Because the format is so familiar by now, some suspense is built up over the course of the first hour through recognition that something truly awful lurks in store. A stock team of six ethnically mixed men and two alluring women is working out of a mining camp 16,-000 feet down on the Atlantic floor, and only has a short time to go until heading back to the surface.

As usual per the formula for these films, the ruthless capitalists in charge of the operation have their own devious agenda, and in due course announce to the staff that a hurricane up top will delay their ascent for awhile.

In the meantime, one of the crew, the randy Daniel Stern takes

ill after investigating the sunken remains of a Russian ship named Leviathan, dies, and begins transforming into a grotesque, eel-like creature.

The same fate awaits Lisa Eilbacher, and medic Richard Crenna quickly deduces that some genetic transferal is going on. Remainder of the action sees crew members Peter Weller, Amanda Pays, Ernie Hudson, Michael Carmine and Hector Elizondo doing fierce battle with the ever-growing creature and being horrifically eliminated one by one.

Director George Pan Cosmates supplies a fair number of shock moments up to this point, and there is enough going on to tolerably distract an escapist-minded viewer. Climax is entirely botched, however, with so much visual cheating and/or inadequate coverage on display that one feels initially bewildered, then incensed.

Key action moments are rushed through in perfunctory, even messy, fashion, to the extent that one can't really tell what 's happening. When the three survivors implausibly manage to reach the ocean's surface after escaping the exploding mining camp, by far the most sympathetic character in the film is senselessly killed off, resulting in total audience alienation. Feeling at fadeout is one of resentment for having been brought so far and left with so little.

Shot on elaborate sets in Rome, pic boasts impressive production design by Ron Cobb, quite believable monster effects by Stan Winston, mobile widescreen lensing by Alex Thomson and a fine score by Jerry Goldsmith. The real genetic problem here has to do with genre inbreeding, resulting in a feeble younger sibling to some imposing older relatives. —*Cart.*

Rooftops

Hollywood   A New Visions Pictures release. Produced by Howard W. Koch Jr. Executive producers, Taylor Hackford, Stuart Benjamin. Directed by Robert Wise. Screenplay, Terence Brennan, based on story by Allan Goldstein, Tony Mark. Camera (Deluxe color; Duart prints), Theo Van de Sande; editor, William Reynolds; music, David A. Stewart, Michel Kamen; production designer, Jeannine C. Oppewall; art director, John Wright Stevens; set decorator, Gretchen Rau; costume designer, Kathleen Detoro; capoeira choreographer, Jelon Vieira; choreographer, John Carrafa; sound (Dolby), Tom Nelson; casting, Paula Herold. Reviewed at the New Vision screening room, L.A., March 13, 1989. MPAA Rating: R. Running time: **95 MIN.**

T	Jason Gedrick

Elena ....Troy Beyer
Lobo ....Eddie Velez
Squeak ....Alexis Cruz
Amber ....Tisha Campbell
Kadim ....Allen Payne

■ "Rooftops" zooms in on life atop Manhattan's drug-overrun ghetto, Alphabet City, where kids live like pigeons, venturing streetside mostly to engage in a literal combat dance to vent their frustrations. As visually interesting as this setting is, "Rooftops" never soars beyond its too-familiar teen drama beat. Box-office looks limited for indie producer/distrib New Visions Pictures.

After an 8-year absence, Robert Wise directs what appears to be an '80s update of "West Side Story."

Despite its sanitized view of urban conflict, that musical, which earned Wise and codirector Jerome Robbins an Oscar in 1961, was compelling entertainment. Its stunning choreography, clever libretto and engaging characters equaled their Shakespearean roots.

"Rooftops" sadly is lacking in these categories, the weakest element being the story itself.

Scripter Terence Brennan chooses for his protagonists a handful of youths from broken homes who live in makeshift shelters on the roofs of abandoned tenements. They earn cash from plundering copper piping from other buildings or stripping cars for parts.

Mentor of what Jesse Jackson would call a "rainbow coalition" of okay-behaving teens is T (Jason Gedrick), muscular and fit from pumping iron outside his water-tower abode.

His obsession is to be the best combat dancer at the nighttime mixers held at a vacant lot, where reps from the neighborhood factions hang out, drink, flirt and otherwise work off energy "fighting" each other in dance competition.

There he meets Elena (Troy Beyer, known to tv audiences as Diahann Carroll's daughter in "Dynasty"), the cousin to crack king Lobo (Eddie Velez).

With the help of an unmerciful band of cast-to-type thugs, the sharkskin-suited Velez moves in to convert Gedrick's airy pad to a rock house.

This forces Beyer to chose between working for Velez as a lookout (for cops) — something she'd rather not do, although she realizes it's more lucrative than waitressing — and heartthrob Gedrick, who's a delinquent perhaps, but not a felon.

Time, place and dialog ring true in this production, lensed with gritty realism by Theo Van de Sande and appropriately scored by the Eurythmics' David A. Stewart and Pink Floyd producer Michael Kamen, even as the tone swings from sentimental yarn to gangster-genre filmmaking.

What is curious is how it fails as a dance-oriented picture despite every obvious effort to integrate into the action Gedrick's capoeira, a karate-choppy Brazilian step, to pounding rock and rap songs by Grace Jones, Jeffrey Osborne and others.

Film, about a subject better suited to a vidpic than cinematic treatment, instead evolves as a cement and brick turf war pitting coked-out bully Velez against soft-spoken Gedrick, neither of them particularly interesting characters. What would have vastly improved watchability is a central figure with a personality to match his talent.

Gedrick, Beyer and rooftop chums Tisha Campbell and Allen Payne are as sympathetic and likable a troupe as one might find on the Lower East Side — maybe too much so.

Collectively, they are less colorful than the little squirt who is always trailing them around, Squeak (Alexis Cruz), an energetic and feisty Artful Dodger-type with a certain skill as a graffiti artist.

Instead, he's relegated to a role as comic relief — not that the picture doesn't need it — even as he's the one most worth rooting for.
—*Brit.*

Used Innocence

New York   A First Run Features release. Produced, directed, camera (color, 16m), and edited by James Benning. Reviewed at Film Forum, N.Y., March 3, 1989. No MPAA Rating. Running time: **95 MIN.**

■ **Experimental filmmaker James Benning approaches the sensational 1981 murder case in Wisconsin, when Laurie Bembenek was convicted of shooting her husband's ex-wife, as his own personal spiritual odyssey.**

Denying that he is a professional detective or traditional documentarian — and we believe him — Benning instead subjectively examines the puzzling murder case using re-enactments, the trial transcript and fragments of newspaper articles and photographs.

"Used Innocence" expresses Benning's judgment that Bembenek — the beautiful, blond 22-year-old ex-cop and former Playboy bunny — was misused and abused and is innocent. Meanwhile, Laurie continues in Taycheeday Correctional Institution, a mandatory lifer, convicted of first degree murder.

Benning visits Laurie in prison and is fascinated by her. She had been a militant feminist within the Milwaukee police force of almost entirely white males. She antagonized some cops as a self-taught Marxist. Defending her, Benning presents options, rehashes facts and speculates.

"Used Innocence" deals with the important topic of our occasional miscarriages of justice, but likely will not inspire the ripples of Errol Morris' "Thin Blue Line."

Benning's irksome mannerisms make his film look amateurish and labored. For example, a stand-in for Laurie in prison performs a monotonous task taking perhaps 15 seconds — we have to look at the task repeated ad nauseum, perhaps 20 times in five minutes.

Similarly, when Benning goes to visit Laurie's prison in the countryside, he sticks his camera out the car window and shoots all those cow pastures, used-car lots and shopping malls.

Screened with the market at the recent Berlin film festival, "Used Innocence" doubtlessly will find its own small loyal audiences in specialized screenings and perhaps on public tv. —*Hitch.*

Wild Man

New York   An Allan Nadohl Films presentation. Executive producer, Rand Capp. Produced by Nadohl. Directed by Fred J. Lincoln. Screenplay, Marc Jonathan, from story by Nadohl, Jonathan; camera (Foto-Kem color), Jacob Eleasari; editor. Lincoln, Steve Fuiten; music, Gary Lionelli; sound, John Kopchak; assistant director, Patti Tessel; associate producer, Marc Sachnoff. Reviewed on Celebrity Home Entertainment vidcassette. N.Y., March 4, 1989. No MPAA Rating. Running time: **117 MIN.**
Eric Wilde ....Don Scribner
Trisha Collins ....Michelle Bauer
Jessica Wilde ....Kathleen Middleton
Brad ....Travis Silver
Dawn Hall ....Ginger Lynn Allen
Tommy Lee ....James L. Newman
Nick ....Tom Green
Old Indian ....Fred J. Lincoln

■ **Direct-to-video feature "Wild Man" curiously mixes mystical elements in a standard he-man adventure. Overlong effort plays** like a tv action pilot for an uncensored network.

Don Scribner is rather unconvincing as Eric Wilde, a casino manager in Las Vegas called in by the government to go after an old adversary, drug kingpin Tommy Lee Smith (played hammily by James L. Newman).

As a destitute man's James Bond, Wilde beds every woman in sight, including a lovely tv newshen played by ubiquitous starlet Michelle Bauer. Complicating the plot is Tommy Lee's latest girlfriend, Jessica (Kathleen Middleton), who's Wilde's ex-wife.

Pic derails via its heavy emphasis on Wilde's magic ring, with director Fred J. Lincoln cameoing in flashback as an Indian medicine man who makes Wilde invulnerable. With the ring he's able to come back to life twice after being killed, a bit of hokum that combines self-destructively with pic's unjustified 2-hour running time.

Action scenes are awkwardly staged and worst thesping is turned in by Tom Green as one of Tommy Lee's henchman.

Former porn star Ginger Lynn Allen (whose mainstream career was derailed a bit by her omission from the final cut of Blake Edwards' "Skin Deep") is okay here doing what comes naturally. Since she's assistant to a government spook, her character name of "Dawn Hall" is mildly amusing.
—*Lor.*

1999 - Nen No Natsu Yasumi
(Summer Vacation: 1999)
(JAPANESE)

Hollywood   A New Yorker Films (U.S.) release of a New Century Producers & CBS/Sony Group production. Produced by Naoya Narita, Mitsuhisa Hida. Executive producers, Yutaka Okada, Eiji Kishi. Directed by Shusuke Kaneko. Screenplay, Michiyo Kishida. Camera (color), Kenji Takama; lighting, Hiroyuki Yasukochi; editor, Isao Temita; music, Yuriko Nakamura; art direction, Shu Yamaguchi; sound, Koshiro Jimbo. Reviewed in Los Angeles, March 12, 1989. Also in New Directors/New Films series at Museum Of Modern Art.) Running time: **90 MIN.**
Yu/Kaeru ....Eri Miyajima
Kazuhike ....Temeke Otakara
Naeto ....Miyuki Nakano
Nerie ....Rie Misuhara

■ **In an era of sparse, quality independent production in Japan, "Summer Vacation: 1999" arrives as on a jetstream of warm, heady, intoxicating wind.**

A film of extreme poetic beauty that intensely evokes the adolescent birth pangs of romantic love, sexual awareness and jealousy, feature debut by Shusuke Kaneko received limited play in its native country last year and showed at the Telluride Film Festival in advance of its current date at the New Directors/New Films series and forthcoming domestic release by New Yorker Films. Art film audiences should take heed.

The pubescent characters possess an androgynous quality that is fascinating and sometimes even unnerving, the reason being that these boys are actually played by girls. This decision was no less daring for falling in the Japanese tradition of Takurazuka, and pays off brilliantly.

Incisively and rigorously written by Michiyo Kishida, who was formerly associated with the late director Shuji Torayama, haunting tale begins with the apparent suicide of a schoolboy named Yu. Left behind at the impeccable country boarding school are three other boys in their early teens who are studying on their own through the summer at the otherwise abandoned institution.

Emotionally formulated but physically unrealized love has awakened among the boys. Yu has evidently taken his own life due to his unrequited passion for the beautiful looking Kazuhike, who is also doted upon by the even more exquisite Naeto. Watching all this with a degree of detachment is the younger, more innocent Nerie.

Just as the threesome resumes its studious routine, in walks a lad named Kaeru who is a dead ringer for the late Yu. So complete is the resemblance that the boys can't decide whether this is actually Yu come back to play a joke on them, truly a different fellow, or perhaps a ghost of some kind.

Set against a languid summer ripe with the longings of budding youth and the full blossoming of nature, the drama slowly plays itself out as it observes its emotional ramifications, finally evolving into a cyclical story pregnant with metaphysical possibilities.

Throughout, director Kaneko, who heretofore has only made softcore Nikkatsu sex pics, displays an unusually disciplined, delicate hand as he fuses beauty and mystery in equal measure to forge a seductive yet measured style that is exceptionally impressive for a first-timer.

Combining superbly to create a work of seamless beauty are Shu Yamaguchi's astute art direction,

Kenji Takama's very alert camerawork and Yuriko Nakamura's gorgeous score. In all ways, this represents a most auspicious debut. —*Cart.*

Coupe franche
(Clean Cut)
(FRENCH)

Paris   A CDF Film-Films Arpège release of a Film Arpège production. Produced by Jean-Pierre Sauné, Jean-Noël Bert. Directed by Sauné. Screenplay, Sauné, Marcel Carlou; camera (Eastmancolor), Philippe Théaudière; editor, Marie-Castro Bréchignac; music, Georges Baux; art direction, Michel Lagrange; sound, Bruno Charier, Jean-Paul Loublier; assistant director, Yves-Noël François. Reviewed at the Gaumont Ambassade theater, Paris, Feb. 21, 1989. Running time: **100 MIN.**
Mathieu	Serge Reggiani
Marie	Julie Jezequel
Cyuri	Wojtek Pszoniak
Favier	Guy Marchand
François	Pierre-Loup Rajot
Yvon	Jean-Quentin Chatelain
Dédé	Laszlo Szabo

■Features newcomer Jean-Pierre Sauné, a former cameraman and editor, displays directorial skill and a sympathy with actors in "Coupe franche," a realistic drama set in a lumber mill in the Pyrenees.

Sauné found regional funding for the film, which he coproduced, and rounded up a good cast of name actors.

Sauné also coscripted (with Marcel Carlou), which is another matter. Themes of provincial boredom, frustration and sexual discontent are over-familiar and don't get much new insight here. Actors bring sincerity and feeling to their roles.

Story begins with the arrival of a young stranger (Pierre-Loup Rajot) at a mountain mill owned by proud but grizzled artisan Serge Reggiani and now run by his son-in-law (Guy Marchand), whose management notions have not lifted the enterprise out of its rut. Marchand is married to Reggiani's young daughter, Julie Jezequel, who feels excluded from the masculine world of the mill and wants out.

Thanks to one of the workers, Wojtek Pszoniak, who turns out to be the ex-lover of Rajot's mother, the newcomer is quickly integrated into the mill and almost just as quickly becomes Jezequel's lover. This excites the ineffectual jealousies of Marchand and his younger loser brother, Jean-Quentin Chatelain.

Action builds predictably to a conclusion in which all the char-

acters are immobilized in an emotional stalemate, which is nicely visualized in film's final shot.

Sauné is especially good in creating the ambience of the lumber mill, the feeling of hard work and pride in craftsmanship, and the sense of camaraderie. —*Len.*

Romuald et Juliette
(Romuald And Juliette)
(FRENCH)

Paris   A UGC release of a Cinéa/Eniloc Films/FR3 Films coproduction. Produced by Philippe Carcassonne, Jean-Louis Piel. Written and directed by Coline Serreau. Camera (Eastmancolor), Jean-Noël Ferragut; editor, Catherine Renault; sound, Philippe Lioret, Gérard Lamps; art direction, Jean-Marc Stehle; assistant director, Elisabeth Parnière; production manager, Michéle Plaa; casting, Evy Figliolini. Reviewed at Club Gaumont Matignon, Paris, March 8, 1989. Running time: **111 MIN.**
Juliette Bonaventure	Firmine Richard
Blache	Pierre Vernier
Cloquet	Maxime Leroux
Paulin	Gilles Privat
Nicole	Muriel Combeau
Françoise	Catherine Salviat

  Also with: Alexandre Basse, Aissatou Bah, Mamadou Bah, Marina M'Boa Ngong, Sambou Tati, Isabelle Carre, Jean-Christophe Itier, Caroline Jaquin, Jacques Poitrenaud, Gilles Cohen.

■Nearly four years after "Three Men And A Cradle," Coline Serreau has come up with a new comedy, "Romuald And Juliette," about a hardnosed business exec who falls in love with his office's black cleaning lady. It's breezy enough but lacks the sitcom charms and laughter of her monster success.

Business however should be good at home and sales abroad healthy.

Serreau as usual scripted and it's an ill-balanced affair, too concerned with a labored plot that smothers the theme. The crux of the matter is late in coming and only after an intrigue lacking in novelty.

Daniel Auteuil is the self-centered head of a dairy products company who is being framed in a food poisoning and stock speculation scandal by a couple of ruthless associates preparing a boardroom coup.

Struggling vainly to clear his name, he finds an unexpected ally in the stocky West Indian cleaning lady who comes in at night and whose existence he previously never suspected.

She's overheard some of the underhanded plotting during her cleaning rounds and has collected some of the evidence that eventually turns the tables on Auteuil's

adversaries.

Hiding from the police, Auteuil moves into the woman's cramped low-income apartment, where she lives with her five children (each from different mates who gather once a year for "Husbands Day").

All of this is a lot of social and psychological exposition for the final section of the film in which Auteuil, his reputation and position now restored, realizes his life is founded on illusions and that he's really in love with the cleaning lady, whose generosity and strength have quietly seduced him.

Pic on the whole may disappoint those who expect a laugh riot. Most of the humor is generated by Auteuil's contact with a different social station he normally wouldn't give a second thought to. Serreau's direction is brisk but it's only in the last half-hour or so that the comedy and feeling begin to jell.

Auteuil is fine, though the role is a variation on the part he played only recently in Claude Sautet's "Quelques jours avec moi," where he was a businessman who falls for maid Sandrine Bonnaire. Nonprofessional newcomer Firmine Richard gives a fresh, full-blooded performance as Juliette, the husky, independent cleaning lady who finally succumbs to the advances of her yuppie Romeo.

Tech credits are okay.—*Len.*

I Ragazzi di Via Panisperna
(The Panisperna Street Boys)
(ITALIAN)

Rome   A BIM Distribuzione release of a Urania Film/Beta Film/RAI-1 coproduction. Produced by Concita Airoli, Dino Di Dionisio, Giovanna Genoesi. Directed by Gianni Amelio. Screenplay, Amelio, Alessandro Sermoneta; camera (color), Tonino Nardi; editor, Roberto Perpignano; music, Riz Ortolani; art direction, Franco Velchi. Reviewed at Mignon Cinema, Rome, March 5, 1989. Running time: **125 MIN.**
Ettore Maiorana	Andrea Prodan
Enrico Fermi	Ennio Fantastichini
Laura Fermi	Laura Morante

  Also with: Virna Lisi (Ettore's mother), Mario Adorf, Michele Melega, Giovanni Romani, Alberto Gimignani, Giorgio Dall'-Piaz.

■The private lives of nuclear physicists Enrico Fermi and Ettore Maiorana make a surprisingly suspenseful, engrossing film in "The Panisperna Street Boys."

Helmer Gianni Amelio's treatment is as offbeat as the characters, whose tormented relationship takes place against the background of the race to split the atom and the approaching world war. Film has had limited release on home territory, but should attract tv bids.

At Rome U. in the 1930s, famed physicist Enrico Fermi (Ennio Fantastichini) gathers a group of bright young scientists around him. The standout is aloof Ettore Maiorana (Andrea Prodan), a handsome young genius from Sicily, whose mathematical brilliance surpasses Fermi's.

Despite his complex, unstable personality, Ettore grows close to Fermi and his sensitive wife Laura Morante. The Fermis offer him shelter for a while, but lose his trust when Enrico tells the boy's mother (Virna Lisi) where he is.

The breakdown of Maiorana's personality is painfully emotional. A revealing flashback to his boyhood in Sicily shows how his mother cruelly forced the child prodigy to perform math feats to amuse her friends.

More than Fermi, Ettore seems to sense the dangers of the scientist's use of his knowledge and intellect. He retreats from the world, living like a bum on his family's abandoned estate, finally disappearing altogether. His death (suicide? hiding? transfer to Russia?) remains a mystery to this day.

Fermi is last glimpsed brooding on a boat for America, where he will win a Nobel in 1938 for his work on radioactivity and nuclear chain reactions.

Newcomers Andrea Prodan and Ennio Fantaschini, fresh and convincing, provide a crisp contrast between the two scientists. Morante's fans will appreciate her elegant understatement as Fermi's Jewish wife.

Tonino Nardi's cinematography and Franco Velchi's sets recreate the '30s simply, without mannerisms. The Riz Ortolani period score is intrusive —*Yung.*

M'Agapas?
(Love Me Not?)
(GREEK)

Athens   An A.G. Panoussopoulou/Greek Film Center/Home Video Hellas production. Directed by George Panoussopoulos. Screenplay, Panoussopoulos, Vassilis Alexikis, Sotiris Kakisis; camera (color), Panoussopoulos; editor, Giorgos Mavropsaridis; music, Winter Swimmers; art direction, Marilena Mouschouti; sound, Marinos Athanassopoulos, Christos Patas; production manager, Stamatis Athanassoulas. Reviewed at Opera Cinema, Athens, Feb. 3, 1989. Running time: **98 MIN.**
Giorgos . . . . Andreas Barcoulis
Wife (Thespina) . . . . Betty Livanou
Heart recipient . . . . Giorgos Constas

Also with: Antonis Theodorakopoulos, Myrto Paraschi, Vana Barba, Sophia Aliberti.

■ **"Love Me Not?" feature cements helmer George Panoussopoulos' reputation as an ace cameraman and inventive visual stylist. Pic could hook an audience on eye appeal alone but rapid changes of cast and settings deprive it of adequate character development.**

Giorgos, happily married with a family, climbs up on a rooftop to get a better look at a topless lass reciting lines on a balcony. He is startled by his wife and friends calling to him, slips off the roof and plummets to the ground.

At the hospital, his condition is declared hopeless but his heart continues to function. A doctor proposes it be donated to a stranger for a transplant and Giorgos' wife eventually agrees.

The thrust of the main plot rests on the inevitable meeting of Giorgos' wife and the recipient. A series of sketches revolving around the themes of pubescent coming of age and actualization of amorous male fantasies are initially entertaining but become repetitive.

Panoussopoulos' lensing lovingly scans the supple naked woman and more full-frontal male nudity is seen than in any other mainstream Greek film.

The underlying message seems to be casual sex is jolly good fun but only true love lasts. The emphasis of the film is on the former so that the final scene is without sufficient emotional power.

Barcoulis and Livanou (helmer's wife) are effective as the leads although their screen exposure is limited. The eclectic score, featuring the talented group "Winter Swimmers," is appropriate and other tech credits are good.

A 10-minute short, "Cup Of Coffee," preceeded the Athens' screenings and is considered an integral introduction to the film. Based on an idea by "Love Me Not?" coscripter Alexakis and directed by Panoussopoulos, it contains the germ of the feature's scenario. In it, 19 different actors play the same couple in a montage series, all during a seduction scene, illustrating the idea that no matter who the players are, the game's the same. —*Sam.*

Mes meilleurs copains
(My Best Pals)
(FRENCH-COLOR/B&W)

Paris   A Gaumont release of a Christian Fechner production. Coproducers, Films A2, Amigo Prods., Alpille Prods. Produced by Bernard Artigues. Directed by Jean-Marie Poiré. Screenplay, Poiré, Christian Clavier; camera (Fuji color, b&w), Claude Agostini; editor, Catherine Kelber, Adeline Yoyotte-Husson; music, Michel Goglat; art direction, Hugues Tissandier; sound, Jean-Bernard Thomasson; makeup, Muriel Baurens; assistant director, Michel Such; production manager, Philippe Desmoulins; casting, Françoise Menidrey. Reviewed at Gaumont Ambassade theater, Paris, March 2, 1989. Running time: **110 MIN.**
Bernadette Legranbois . . . . . . Louise Portal
Richard Chappoteaux . . . . . . Gérard Lanvin
Jean-Michel Thuilliet . . . . Christian Clavier
Eric Guidolini . . . . Jean-Pierre Bacri
Antoine Jobert . . . . Philippe Khorsand
Daniel Pequou . . . . Jean-Pierre Darroussin
Anne . . . . Marie-Anne Chazel
Monique . . . . Elizabeth Margoni
Mr. Thuilliet . . . . Jacques François

■ **"Mes meilleurs copains" is a superficial but moderately entertaining variation on the theme of a group of buddies confronting their youth and past dreams and (sex) fantasies.**

Script by director Jean-Marie Poiré and actor Christian Clavier is a departure from the tandem's previous café-theater inspired comedies. It skims surfaces briskly but without mordancy.

Clavier, Gérard Lanvin, Jean-Pierre Bacri, Philippe Khorsand and Jean-Pierre Darroussin are old pals who were part of the post-May 1968 generation and are now pushing 40 as today's Gallic yuppies.

Though still in touch, they are brought together for a weekend for a reunion with Louise Portal, the sexy, liberated distaff member of the rock group they once formed. The band split up when Portal left for Canada with a new boyfriend-manager and becomes a pop star there.

She's in Paris for a concert engagement and her presence reignites some old sores and carnal desires.

Action shuttles conventionally between today and (sometimes in black-and-white) yesterday, when the gang was young, freewheeling and horny.

Portal serviced some of them without qualms, but Clavier, pic's narrator, never managed to make it with her, a fact which still obsesses him.

Sextet of players is fine. Lanvin is the hypocritical family man, Khorsand the permanent cuckold, and Bacri, the forlorn gay who's sworn off sex but feels new stirrings.

Most touching of the guys is Darroussin.

Poiré directed with a light touch absent from his earlier efforts. Tech credits are good. —*Len.*

Uaka
(Sky)
(BRAZILIAN-DOCU)

San Francisco   A Grupo Novo de Cinema/Embrafilme production. Produced by Tarcisio Vidigal. Written and directed by Paula Gaitan. Camera (color), Johnny Haward; editor, Aida Marquez; music, Kamauira. Reviewed at San Francisco Film Festival, March 9, 1989. Running time: **90 MIN.**

■ **A sleep-inducing San Francisco fest entry, "Sky" deals with a tribe called the Xingu, discovered in the Amazon jungle by outsiders only a couple of decades ago. They may have been discovered much earlier, but nobody bothered to mention it because they are such a boring bunch.**

The Xingus have a legend about the great god Mavutsinim who had an idea for bringing the dead back to life by decorating tree trunks. It didn't work, but Xingus still try.

Apparently documentarian Paula Gaitan thought her camera might help, but the tree trunks never come to life and neither, unfortunately, do the Xingus. They're content to paint each other, shake rattles, wrestle, grunt and smile at the camera.

Oddly, director Gaitan also takes a writing credit, but it's not clear what she's written. There are only a handful of subtitles to explain what's going on, none remotely helpful, and the native dialect seems largely ad-libbed.

From time to time, Gaitan edits in, for no apparent reason, brief clips from Georges Méliès 1902 classic "A Trip To The Moon." They are at least a relief from the locals. —*Har.*

Der Lindenbaum
(The Linden Tree)
(JAPANESE)

Hollywood   A Toei presentation. Directed by Kashuhiko Yamaguchi. Screenplay, Makoto Naito, Chiho Katsura, from original story by Kasunori Yamato; camera (color), Masahiro Okumura; music, Kasuhiko Kato; art direction, Akira Takahasi. Reviewed at Little Tokyo Cinema, L.A. (Japan Film Week), March 6, 1989. Running time: **90 MIN.**
With: Yoko Minsino (Asami), Hasaki Kanda, Shingo Yasagisawa, Chiaki Matsubara, Shigeru Kohyama.

■ **"Der Lindenbaum" (or "Bodaiju" in Japanese) is a high-minded Japanese soap opera about life, love and death among medical students. Done with a straight face and great seriousness, this tale of youthful angst possesses no artistic merits** to warrant the attention of viewers outside Japan.

The linden tree is described herein as the tree of medicine, but also has strong romantic connotations in German literature and myth. Director Kashuhiko Yamaguchi clearly aspires to a heightened, even epic, romanticism in relating the story of one young woman's search for her true calling, but lacks the inspiration to raise the film above hackneyed banalities.

Primly attractive, incoming freshman Asami was orphaned as a child but continues to be subsidized in her studies by an unknown benefactor she calls "Daddy-Long-Legs."

As the high-melodrama unfolds, it turns out that her supporter has been none other than the alluring Dr. Hayasaka, who was responsible for Asami's parents' deaths in an auto accident and has been paying ever since out of guilt and the hope that Asami would become a doctor, like her father was.

Pic's best achievement lies in its relatively successful attainment of an innocent girl's point-of-view. A highly romantic score contributes more to the desired mood than does the modulation of the storytelling.

Asami's cloistered approach to life becomes tiresome long before the slow hour-and-a-half is up. Older-but-wiser lesson delivered at wrap-up is consistent with the thoroughly coventional thinking on display throughout. —Cart.

Tsuri Baka Nisshi
(Free & Easy)
(JAPANESE)

Hollywood A Shochiku release. Executive producer, Shisue Yamanouchi. Directed by Tomio Kuriyama. Screenplay, Yoji Yamada, Akira Momei, based on a comic book series by Juse Yamasaki, Kenichi Kitami; camera (color), Kosuko Yasuda; art direction, Shigemori Shigota. Reviewed at the Little Tokyo Cinema, L.A., March 5, 1989. Running time: **93 MIN.**

Densuke . . . . Toshiyuki Nishidin
Michiko . . . . Eri Ishida
Suzuki . . . . Rentaro Mikuni
Suzuki's wife . . . . Yatsuko Tanami
Section chief . . . . Kei Tani

■ **As a determined audience-pleaser that pricks a tiny comic pin into the self-seriousness of the Japanese corporate world, "Free & Easy" may go over well in its native country, but to Western eyes plays like a feature-length sitcom. Pic's good naturedness is not enough to make it exportable.**

The contented life of middle-aged construction company clerk Densuke is disrupted when he is transferred from Southern Shikoku to Tokyo h.q. Worst aspect of the move is that it will halt his morning ritual of fishing, which is all he cares about.

By chance, the affable fellow meets the elderly Suzuki, whom Densuke does not recognize as the president of his firm and instead takes only as a lonely old man. To cheer him up, he invites the beleaguered gentleman on a fishing expedition, where the guest enjoys extreme beginner's luck, and a fine friendship is forged.

Suzuki soon learns that Densuke is his employee but decides to keep it a secret to preserve the relationship. Climax arrives when Densuke discovers his angling buddy's true identity, and resolution has a neat symmetrical quality.

Cowritten by Yoji Yamada, creator of Tora-san, film betrays its comic book origins through its brightly-lit look and broad acting style. Director Tomio Kuriyama sustains the interest with just enough laughs and minor plot complications, but result can't help but be minor with such mild material. —Cart.

L'Appassionata
(ITALIAN)

Rome An Istituto Luce-Italnoleggio release of an ABCinema production, in association with RAI-TV Channel 2 and Pegaso productions. Produced by Enzo Porcelli. Directed by Gianfranco Mingozzi. Screenplay, Lucia Drudi Demby, Mingozzi; camera (Luciano Vittori color), Luigi Verga; editor, Fernanda Indoni; music, Nicola Piovani; art direction, Leonardo Scarpa, Giancarlo Basili. Reviewed at Politecnico Cinema, Rome, Feb. 3, 1989. Running time: **97 MIN.**

Gilberta . . . . Piera Degli Esposti
Toni . . . . Nicola Farron
Enzo . . . . Federico Provvedi
Also with: Ornella Marcucci (Ileana), Daniela Morelli (Toni's mother), Paolo Bacchi, Gaetano Naccarato, Guido Luigi Cavalleri, Massimo Madrigali, Zeno Pezzoli, Alberto Bartolani.

■ **A homey psychodrama of three characters set in Bologna of the 1950's, "L'Appassionata" ("The Impassioned Woman," literally) isn't likely to set local theaters on fire. Intentions are serious, cast is mostly good, but this tragic May-December love affair remains more on paper than on the screen.**

It is Gianfranco Mingozzi's second feature this season (the other is "The Sparrow's Flutter," doing okay business with Ornella Muti and Philippe Noiret). Main off-shore market should be tv ready to pick up sensitve, rather offbeat product.

Stage thesp Piera Degli Esposti headlines as "L'Appassionata," a widow in her 40s with a 16-year-old son who, unknown to her, supports them by selling family knick-knacks and cleaning the public swimming pool.

The arrival of a handsome young lodger, Toni (Nicola Farron), momentarily brings life and joy to the house. Mama Gilberta, a warm woman of precarious mental balance, embarks on an intense, guiltless love affair with the boy, while Son Enzo (Federico Provvedi) treats him as a big brother, though with misgivings. These prove to be justified. Toni leaves Gilberta for one of her piano pupils, a pretty girl closer to his own age.

Gilberta, guileless and vulnerable, takes Toni's betrayal so hard she loses her reason. In and out of mental hospitals, she has one last painful meeting with Toni, then begs her son to put an end to her suffering, which he does with an overdose of medicine.

Very much an actors' story, "L'Appassionata" benefits from Degli Esposti's daft but always appealing mother-lover, a totally natural woman. Also impressive is Provvedi's screen debut as her loving, anxious offspring. Farron lacks range in the key role of Toni, settling for being just likable and ordinary. —Yung.

Deux
(Two)
(FRENCH)

Paris An AMLF release of a Films 17/DD Prods./Orly Films/SEDIF/TF1 Films Prods. coproduction. Produced and directed by Claude Zidi. Screenplay, Zidi, Catherine Rihoit; camera (Eastmancolor), Jean-Jacques Tarbes; editor, Nicole Saunier; music, Jean-Claude Petit; art direction, Michel de Broin; sound, Jean-Louis Ughetto, William Flageollet; costumes, Hortense Guillemard; assistant director, Denis Seurat; production manager, Pierre Gauchet; casting, Mamade. Reviewed at the UGC Normandie theater, Paris, Feb. 27, 1989. Running time: **113 MIN.**

Marc Lambert . . . . Gérard Depardieu
Hélène Muller . . . . Maruschka Detmers
Juliette . . . . Michele Goddet
Louis . . . . François Cluzet
Walkowicz . . . . Wojtek Pszoniak
Mr. Muller . . . . . . Philippe Leroy-Beaulieu
Mrs. Muller . . . . Beata Tyskiewicz

■ **Getting "serious," the occupational hazard of comedy masters from Molière to Woody Allen, has now infected Claude Zidi, one of the French screen's erstwhile artisans of low comedy.**

He has conceived, cowritten, produced and directed "Deux," a basically humorless love story about an ill-assorted upwardly-mobile couple, played by Gérard Depardieu and Maruschka Detmers. Fairly well made and acted, it's nonetheless a disconcertingly glum affair that will prove a hard sell.

Zidi's shift from the nonsensical to the no-nonsense is not as sudden as it seems. A turning point in his career was the 1984 hit "Les Reipoux," a dramatic comedy about crooked cops on the make, which had plenty of humor, but also a more serious attempt at characterization. The failure of his subsequent "Les Rois des gags," a farce in his earlier manner, convinced Zidi he could not turn back.

What surprises most in "Deux" is that Zidi has gone straight-faced with a vengeance. Though there are some moments of humor and detente, the general mood is somber, almost oppressive, with Jean-Claude Petit's symphonic score swelling moodily at regular intervals.

To make sure there'd be no backsliding into funny stuff, Zidi hired Catherine Rihoit, a well-known if diversely appreciated Serious Novelist to script with him. Together these strange bedfellows have concocted a story that seems less a dramatic screenplay than a psycho-sociological report on today's attractive, rich Parisian couple and their rapport with sex, money, marriage, divorce, babies, in-laws, fidelity, ambition, and mortality.

Depardieu plays a successful contemporary music concert promoter with suppressed artistic ambitions and unsuppressed sexual appetite, who has his sights set on a dream house in Montmartre. Detmers is a beautiful real estate agent who sets her sights on Depardieu. In the course of their apartment visiting they inevitably end up in the sack.

Their attraction, at first sexual, soon takes a turn that alarms yet fixates both. They decide to marry, but the engagement period is plagued by Depardieu's obvious terror of convention, and Detmers' covert anxieties about commitment.

A split is imminent but a traumatic accident binds the couple together again indissolubly. The film ends with Depardieu taking the now pregnant and in labor Detmers to the hospital and being obliged to deliver the baby himself in a roadside ravine. They have not transcended their final barriers to happiness — end of report.

Depardieu and Detmers both succeed in wringing some moments of true emotion out of this over-wrought, self-conscious script. Some of the supporting roles, such as Wojtek Pszoniak's pompous Eastern European composer, are less happy. Tech credits are slick down the line. —*Len.*

After School

New York   A Moviestore Entertainment release of a Hugh Parks production. Produced by Parks. Coproduced and directed by William Olsen. Screenplay, Parks, John Linde, Rod McBrien, Joe Tankersley; camera (TVC color), Austin McKinney; editor, John David Allen; music, David C. Williams; sound, Lee Strosnider; art direction, David Meo; second unit director-associate producer, Tankersley; assistant director, Gus Holzer; production manager, Jan Thompson. Reviewed on Academy Entertainment vidcassette, N.Y., Feb. 20, 1989. MPAA Rating: R. Running time: **89 MIN.**
Father Michael McCarren . . . Sam Bottoms
September Lane . . . . Renée Coleman
Monsignor Barrett . . . . Edward Binns
First leader . . . . James Farkas
Annie . . . . Page Hannah
Nathan . . . . Don Harvey
C.A. Thomas . . . . Robert Lansing
Dick Cavett . . . . Himself
    Also with: Holt McCallany, Catherine Williams, John Perkins, Jacqueline Rodriguez, Alison Woodward, Tony Cucci.

■ **Intriguing but disappointing, "After School" attempts to mix exploitation elements with the traditional morality tale. Pic received a modest regional release last year ahead of video.**

Format of present-day moral crisis mirrored by intercutting with primitive man's behavior thousands of years ago is a throwback to silent cinema, especially the work of Cecil B. DeMille. Confusion of content is reflected in pic's title changes, ranging from "Before God" and "Return To Eden" to distrib's racier "Private Tutor" and finally "After School."

Sam Bottoms toplines as a young priest teaching at St. Joseph's Catholic College in Florida who is selected to defend the faith on the Dick Cavett tv talkshow against ex-priest Robert Lansing's book "Before God," which claims man created God in his own image.

While prepping for the debate, Bottoms falls in love with beautiful student Renée Coleman, whose own perceptive classroom questioning of church dogma adds to his doubts and ultimately forces Bottoms to go his own way, leaving Lansing victorious.

Pic's use of primitive man footage is a bit suspect, since it includes lots of topless scenes of beautiful cavewomen Alison Woodward, Jacqueline Rodriguez and Catherine Williams that are extraneous to the main action. Director William Olsen managed to juggle the commercial realities of exploitation filmmaking and thoughtful themes far more convincingly in his 1983 feature "Getting It On."

Bottoms is earnest in an old-fashioned style and the film drags on repetitively rather than developing its religious ideas. Coleman as his love interest is a fresh new actress worth watching (also seen to good effect as the kidnapped beauty in recent release "Who's Harry Crumb?").

Tech credits are fine, with colorful lensing in the Orlando, Fla., area. —*Lor.*

The Siege Of Firebase Gloria
(AUSTRALIAN)

New York   A Fries Entertainment release of an Eastern Film Management Corp. production, in association with Bancannia Entertainment. Executive producers, Antony I. Ginnane, Marilyn G. Ong. Produced by Howard Grigsby, Rudolfos S.M. Confessor. Directed by Brian Trenchard-Smith. Screenplay, William Nagle, Tony Johnston; additional dialog, R. Lee Ermey, Trenchard-Smith; camera (color), Kevan Lind; editor-2d unit director, Andrew Prowse; music, Paul Shutze; sound, Phil Judd; production design, Toto Castillo; art direction, Armando Raysag; production manager, Jessie Cuneta; 2d unit camera, Joe Batac Jr.; associate producers, Mike Fuller, Ana Maria Dans. Reviewed on Fries Home Video vidcassette, N.Y., March 8, 1988. MPAA Rating: R. Running time: **100 MIN.**
DiNardo . . . . Wings Hauser
Hafner . . . . R. Lee Ermey
Sgt. Jones . . . . Albert Popwell
Cao Van . . . . Robert Arevalo
Murphy . . . . Mark Neely
    Also with: Gary Hershberger, Clyde R. Jones, Margi Gerard, Richard Kuhlman.

■ **Solid performances by R. Lee Ermey and Wings Hauser distinguish this otherwise routine Vietnam War pic. In regional release since January, it's headed for vidstores in April.**

Ermey delivers extensive voice-over narration shaping this tale of the heroes who held out at the forward outpost Gloria during the 1968 Tet Offensive. Essentially humorless approach lightens up a bit in the later reels. It's built around the character of a sadistic marine, played by Hauser, whose ruthless approach is condemned by the script but shown to be understandable considering the circumstances he's in. Hauser makes the guy both believable and scary.

Ermey's no-nonsense thesping is excellent, providing a different approach than his superlative but one-note turn as the d.i. in "Full Metal Jacket." Capably helmed by Aussie Brian Trenchard-Smith, film turns a bit soggy in the final reel with an unconvincing euthanasia scene and lameduck equal time afforded the enemy's point of view. Tech credits are fine. —*Lor.*

Desert Warrior
(FILIPINO)

New York   A Silver Star Film Co. production. Produced by (uncredited) Kimmy Lim. Directed by Jim Goldman. Screenplay, Bob Davies, Carl Kuntze; camera (Hong Kong color), Fred Conrad; editor, Rene Tucker; music, Marita A. Manuel; sound, John Thomas; art direction, Vic Davies; assistant director, Sonny Sanders; production manager, Kim Lane. Reviewed on Prism Entertainment vidcassette, N.Y., March 9, 1989. MPAA Rating: PG-13. Running time: **88 MIN.**
Zerak . . . . Lou Ferrigno
Racela . . . . Shari Shattuck
Baktar . . . . Kenneth Peer
Cortaz . . . . Anthony East
Dr. Creo . . . . Mike Monty

■ **This Filipino-lensed action pic is something of a fiasco, providing unintentional humor and inept filmmaking technique to video fans.**

Shot in 1987 under the title "Sand Wars," pic has been retitled "Desert Warrior," but is unrelated to Cirio Santiago's 1985 Filipino film of that title.

Lou Ferrigno plays the beefy hero of a post-nuclear society whose corrupt bossman (Kenneth Peer) needs uncontaminated women for mating purposes. Shari Shattuck is just the ticket, and most of pic consists of Lou, clad in a Roman gladiator outfit, trying to help her escape from the bad guys' clutches.

Film unfolds like a bad parody of this overworked genre, with a very poor sound mix and ridiculously cheap-looking vehicles for the "Mad Max" fans to ogle. Poor Ferrigno, dubbed in his "Hercules" epics, uses his own voice here with embarrassing results.
—*Lor.*

Deadly Embrace

New York   A Gerardfilm Ltd. presentation of an Arcade production. Executive producer, Anthony Ferrari. Produced by David DeCoteau, Richard Gabai. Directed by Ellen Cabot. Screenplay, Gabai; additional dialog, Tony Malanowski; camera (color), Thomas Callaway; editor, Malanowski; music, Del Casher; sound, D.J. Ritchie; production design, Royce Mathew; additional camera, Stephen Ashley Blake; associate producer, Dwayne Murakami. Reviewed on Prism En-
tertainment vidcassette, N.Y., Feb. 11, 1989. No MPAA Rating. Running time: **83 MIN.**
Stewart Morland . . . . Jan-Michael Vincent
Charlotte Morland . . . . Ty Randolph
Michelle Arno . . . . Linnea Quigley
Chris Thompson . . . . Ken Abraham
Evan Weiss . . . . Jack Carter
Female spirit of sex . . . . . . Michelle Bauer
Dede Magnolia . . . . Ruth Collins

■ **"Deadly Embrace" is an offbeat film noir, going direct to video. More care and a bigger budget would have helped.**

Framed by an awkward and irritating flashback structure, pic has Ken Abraham as a hapless young stud hired (rather suspiciously) to work as a houseman at rich businessman Jan-Michael Vincent's Beverly Hills estate.

Vincent only has time for weekends at home, leaving his beautiful wife (Ty Randolph) alone and lonely. Her affair with Abraham starts on cue, but is disrupted when Abraham has his cute young girlfriend (perky Linnea Quigley) visit and shack up with him.

Blackmailing and doublecrossing ensue, with a surprise ending. The flashback structure, with abstract shots of the hands of two guys, smoking, across a table while they voiceover the plot, doesn't pay off.

Despite top billing Vincent merely walks through this assignment. This focuses attention on Randolph, who is an impressive presence as the neglected wife. She previously used the monikers Tylor Windsor Randolph and Mindi Miller for screen credits in "Amazons" and "Body Double."

Tech credits are okay but on the cheap side. —*Lor.*

Dead End City

New York   An Action Intl. production. Executive producers, David Winters, Bruce Lewin. Produced and directed by Peter Yuval. Screenplay, Yuval, Michael Bogert; camera (United color), Paul Maibaum; editor, David Khachatorian; music, Brian Bennett; sound, Ken Segal; art direction, Eric Warren; assistant director, Alec Griffith; production manager-associate producer, Bogert; special effects, Chuck Whitton. Reviewed on AIP Home Video, March 5, 1989. No MPAA rating. Running time: **85 MIN.**
Chief Felker . . . . Dennis Cole
Jack Murphy . . . . Greg Cummins
Opal Brand . . . . Christine Lunde
Max . . . . Robert Zdar
Brett . . . . Durrell Nelson
Nancy . . . . Aleana Downs
Paul . . . . Johnny Venocur
    Also with: Ingrid Vold, Kelly Dixon, Tammy Carrera.

■ **Los Angeles' trouble with gang warfare takes on a sci-fi slant in "Dead End City," an okay direct-to-video actioner.**

Greg Cummins plays a rugged individualist who decides to stay and fight to protect his family factory when the government orders an evacuation of the area. He teams up with various friends and an uppity tv newshen (beautiful Christine Lunde) to battle against the Ratts gang, led by burly Robert Zdar.

Predictably, the government (personified by police chief Dennis Cole) is behind everyone's problems, with a scheme to use gangs to level sections of the city as part of a warped urban renewal project.

Helmer Peter Yuval handles the action well, Cummins is an effective hero defending his turf and Lunde provides visual appeal.

—*Lor.*

Plan Delta
(DUTCH)

Rotterdam A Bob Visser production. Produced by Karin Spiegel, Petra Deelen. Written and directed by Bob Visser. Camera (color, 16m), Dick Verdult, Paul Hosek; editor, Wim Louwrier; music, Tuxedomoon; sound, Mark Glynne; art direction, Jan de Winter, Ton Scheerder. Reviewed at Rotterdam Film Festival, Jan. 31, 1989. Running time: **90 MIN.**
With: Bruce Geduldig, Hans Man in't Veld, Ralph Wingens, Anna Visser, Aram.

■ **A few years ago Bob Visser filmed these gigantic futuristic edifices that disappeared shortly after under the waters of the North Sea according to Plan Delta, meant to secure the lowlands of Holland for another 250 years.**

Visser wanted to use the footage of the $250-million worth of concrete and steel as sci-fi-like background for a feature film. He searched hard for a story angle or fascinating fable, but unfortunately found neither.

In the 23d century or so there are two cities: one for the wealthy elite, the other for the nearly enslaved poor. The flabby elite lose their fertility, but the poor remain potent. The rich take a low-caste beauty into their precincts.

The story is fuzzy and uninteresting. Actors and tech credits just barely scrape by. The band Tuxedomoon contributes some good music. Their leader, Bruce Geduldig, plays one of the leads, but he says it better with music.

Pic ranked low in opinion polls during the Rotterdam Film Festival. It's unlikely to travel far.

—*Wall.*

Cinq jours en juin
(Five Days In June)
(FRENCH)

Paris An AAA release of a CFC/PML/-Films A2 coproduction. Executive producers, Cyril de Rouvre, Isabelle Rondon, Christian Charret. Directed by Michel Legrand. Screenplay, Michel Legrand, Pierre Uytterhoeven, Benjamin Legrand; camera (color), Jean-Yves Le Mener; editor, Jean Ravel; music, Michel Legrand; sound, Jean-Pierre Ruh; art direction, Bernard Léonard; technical advisor, Bernard Toublanc-Michel; assistant director, Patrick Jaquillard; production manager, Philippe Modave; casting, Anita Benoist. Reviewed at Club de l'Etoile, Paris, Feb. 20, 1989. Running time: **100 MIN.**
Marcelle . . . . Annie Girardot
Yvette . . . . Sabine Azéma
Michel . . . . Mathieu Rozé
Also with: Jean-Jacques Moreau, Bernard Lavalette, André Weber, Nathalie Nerval, Christophe Moosbrugger.

■ **For his first filmmaking effort, renowned film composer Michel Legrand has chosen the autobiographical mode, to tell the story of his D-Day, when at age 14 he discovered his musical honors (at the Paris Conservatoire), the war, and first love (and heartbreak) in the arms of a free-spirited and impetuous woman twice his age.**

If one's to believe Legrand's scenario, he lost his innocence in a Normandy bush as a corpse-strewn German convoy burned a few yards away.

Oh what a lovely war it was in 1944 when the Allies landed on the beaches of Normandy and young Michel Legrand, his mom and a brash, attractive young woman stole three bicycles in a Paris train station and pedaled out to the Norman city of Saint-Lô.

Like many neophyte helmers, Legrand tries to make up in technical gloss what he lacks in such elementary areas as credible scripting, fresh dialog and truthful acting. He allows Annie Girardot and Sabine Azéma to fall back on their recognizable tics (frenzied overacting in Azéma's case).

Next to them, newcomer Mathieu Rozé, as the young Legrand, is refreshingly unaffected.

Reconstruction of the period is also unconvincing, with Normandy in full pastoral summer glory, its countryside and people rarely troubled by the devastation wrought by Allies invasion. Black American soldiers are stereotypes who shoot craps and give young Legrand some piano lessons in playing the blues. —*Len.*

BERLIN FEST REVIEWS

Ponedelnik Soutrin
(Monday Morning)
(BULGARIAN-B&W)

Berlin Produced by Sofia Feature Film Studios. Directed by Irina Aktasheva, Hristo Piskov. Screenplay, Nikola Tiholov; camera (b&w), Dimo Kolarov; music, Milcho Leviev; art direction, Violeta Yovcheva. Reviewed at Berlin Film Festival (Panorama), Feb. 17, 1989. Running time: **99 MIN.**
With: Pepa Nikolova, Assen Kisimov, Peter Slabakov, Kiril Gospodinov, Roussi Chanev, Stefan Danailov.

■ **"Monday Morning," made in 1965 but banned until 1988, is particularly bold and advanced, especially in its social implications. Although it may seem dated technically, the issues it deals with are as relevant today as they were 24 years ago.**

Pepa Nikolova is well cast as a wayward girl who is sent to a communist construction brigade to be reformed. Instead, she exposes the hypocrisy and double standards of the workers.

Ironically, her ethics seem sounder than those of the role models she is supposed to emulate, whose main concern is achieving material rewards.

The plot is representative of the socially conscious films of well-respected directors Irina Aktasheva and Hristo Piskov.

Naturally, the film will arouse interest simply on the basis of coming off the shelf. It is worthy on its own merits as well, and will fill a gap in retrospectives of its creators. —*Sam.*

Singles
(WEST GERMAN)

Berlin An Apollo-Film release. Produced by Frankfurter Filmproduktion, with ZDF, Mainz. Written and directed by Ecki Ziedrich. Camera (color), Egon Werdin; editor, Thomas Balkenhol, Brigitte Lippmann; music, Lothar Krell, Thomas Lohr; sound, Peter Dick; art direction, Brigit Meewes. Reviewed at Berlin Film Festival (New German Films), Feb. 19, 1989. Running time: **81 MIN.**
Mickey . . . . Helmut Zierl
Archer . . . . Leonard Lansink
Gilla . . . . Claudia Demarmels
Sabrina . . . . Nina Hoger
Stefan . . . . Jan Fedder
Dietmar . . . . Franz Nagler
Angelika . . . . Nikola Kress
Also with: Michael Quast, Dieter Brandecker, Cornelia Nemann, Andreas Mannkopf, Gerd Knebel, Gerhard Klarner, Phillip Mosetter, Ulrich Moller.

■ **"Singles" is a well-conceived social comedy providing both funny and melancholy views of the dating game. Pic should cap-** ture the fancy of domestic audiences and travel easily.

Mickey falls apart when his girlfriend Gilla wants him to move out because she is involved with another man. After a long search, he finds a depressing flat and attempts to cope on his own. His only hope is that Gilla will return to him.

His best friend and colleague Archer, cynical but supportive, cannot understand why he is so shattered. Mickey is further disheartened by attempts to make new contacts in a singles bar in which the other patrons ignore him.

A scene in which Mickey listens as the members of a support group pour their hearts out to a therapist who cools soothing clichés is incisive and humorous in a bittersweet way. The dialog captures the flavor of exchanges in trendy bars from both the male and female end.

The technique of characters relating their personal experiences followed by flashbacks showing what really happened is clever but overused. Tech standards are high and the attractive thesps look as though they are having a good time. —*Sam.*

Vlastne Se Nic Nestalo
(Killing With Kindness)
(CZECH)

Berlin A Barrandov Studio, Ceskoslovensky Film production. Directed by Evald Schorm. Screenplay, Jaroslava Moserova-Davidova; camera (color), Jiri Macak; editor, Petr Sitar; music, Jan Klusak; production design, Jiri Hlupy. Reviewed at Berlin Film Festival (Market), Feb. 16, 1989. Running time: **86 MIN.**
Blanka Halerova . . . . Jana Brejchova
Otakar Nyvlt . . . . Jan Kacer
Sarka . . . . Tereza Brodska
Vojta . . . . Jan Potmesil
Frantisek . . . . Marek Vasut
Petr . . . . Zdenek Zak

■ **All those with fond memories of the golden days of pre-1968 Czech cinema will be touched by "Killing With Kindness," a comeback and, sadly, a valedictory, for Evald Schorm (who died suddenly from a heart attacks a couple of months ago).**

Back in 1966, Schorm directed "Courage For Every Day," a biting film about Czech youth at the time: pic toplined Jana Brejchova (then married to Milos Forman) and Jan Kacer; the pair are reunited for Schorm's final film.

Brejchova has matured gracefully into a Gena Rowlands type and is highly appealing as Blanka, a widow troubled by her teenage children. She feels guilty because, years before, she accidentally spilled boiling water on daughter Sarka, who has severe bodily scars as a result.

Sarka has accepted the situation and resents her mother's constant attempts to "kill her with kindness." Without telling her mother, she's enrolled in a nighttime college course (on the history of Czech film!) and has started dating a boy who isn't worried about the scars.

Since politics is the game in Central Europe, the scarred girl could be seen as the legacy of the generation of the '60s, now trying to cope with the past and start anew, while the radicals of 20 years ago drift into defeated middle age.

Blanka's son, Vojta, is involved in shady black market deals in a society where, as he says, everyone's out for what they can get.

Hacer plays Otakar, Blanka's lover, lawyer friend of her dead husband. He lives with his aged mother.

On the surface, a simple tale of suffocating mother love; beneath the surface, perhaps quite a lot more. "Killing With Kindness" should rep Czechoslovakia at fests later in the year. —*Strat.*

Xu Mao He Ta De Nüermen
(Xu Mao And His Daughters) (CHINESE)

Berlin A Beijing August First Studio production, released by China Film Import and Export Corp. Produced by By Yi Dian Ying, Zhi Pian Chang. Directed by Li Jun. Screenplay, Zhou Keqin, Xiao Mu from novel by Zhou Keqin; camera (color), Yang Guangyuan, Ye Nai Jun; editor, Zou Ting; music, Yan Ke; sound, Zhen Ming Zhe; art direction, Li Jian. Reviewed at the Berlin Film Festival (Panorama), Feb. 14, 1989. Running time: **94 MIN.**
With: Jia Liu, Wang Fuli, Siqin Gaowa, Zhao Na, Tian Hua.

■This 1981 film by veteran Chinese director Li Jun uses the metaphor of family strife to illustrate Chinese communism's developmental problems. Beyond that it offers a fascinating look at rural village life in modern day China, and is a good choice for festival programs.

Xu Mao is an aging farmer with nine daughters who has scrimped to make ends meet since his wife's death. Preoccupied with worries, he loses touch with his maturing daughters. It takes the stubborn but

kindly intervention of a woman making a governmental inspection tour to cause father and daughters to appreciate their loving family.

Atmospheric photography in foggy Szechuan locations gives this pic the feel of a Chinese tapestry. Intense acting bordering on melodrama helps the viewer distinguish the many characters in this large cast. The father's transformation from careworn curmudgeon to loving father is the key to film's success. —*Gill.*

Play Me Something
(BRITISH-COLOR/B&W)

Berlin A British Film Institute presentation of a BFI production with Film Four Intl., the Scottish Film Prod. Fund and Grampian TV. Produced by Kate Swan. Executive producer, Colin McCabe. Directed by Timothy Neat. Screenplay, Neat, John Berger, from Berger's short story; camera (Eastmancolor, b&w), Chris Cox; interpolated stills & 16m footage, Jean Mohr; editor, Russell Fenton; music, Jim Sutherland; casting and production management, Lee Leckie; production design, Annette Gillies; assistant director, Darryl Collins. Reviewed at Berlin Film Festival (Panorama), Feb. 18, 1989. Running time: **80 MINS.**
The Stranger . . . . John Berger
TV repairman . . . . Hamish Henderson
Hairdresser . . . . Tilda Swinton
Motorcyclist . . . . Stewart Ennis
Schoolteacher . . . . Margaret Bennett
Marietta . . . . Lucia Lanzarini
Bruno . . . . Charlie Barron
Also with: Liz Lochhead, John Louis Mansi, Harry Glass, Ann-Louise Ross, Alison Carruthers.

■This finely honed British item by Scottish helmer Timothy Neat, written by and starring John Berger, has the look of a film school graduation work. It has every conceivable technique on display and the flimsiest of subject matter. Its distribution history is likely to be confined to the educational circuit.

It tells the story-within-the-story about a group of passengers in the waiting room of a tiny Scottish Outer Hebrides airport listening to (and soon participating in) a stranger's dramatic tale. He recounts a short, politically tinged love affair between a musical Italian peasant and a pretty secretary.

The story is droned out with lip-smacking gusto by Berger himself. The waiting passengers are seen becoming increasingly engrossed in the tale, illustrated with 16m shots emulating a tourist's recordings of sights plus black & white stills of the two lovers. At the end, the Venice Affair lives on, shown on the screen of a broken-down tv set being carted away by an elderly repairman.

Poetic, political and philosophi-

cal platitudes abound in Berger's tale-spinning. They're easily forgotten when he pulls a disappearing act as the plane lands to take the passengers back to British mainland reality.

For audiences, only the textbook-technical fireworks will linger, along with the soft guitar-strumming and jazzy trombone wailing of the soundtrack. —*Kell.*

Vatanyolu-Die Heimreise
(Vatanyolu — The Journey Home) (WEST GERMAN)

Berlin Produced by Pro-ject Filmproduktion, Heissischer Föderung with Berlin Senate funding. Written and directed by Enis Günay, Rasim Konyar. Camera (color), Egon Werdin; editor, Beate Gotschall; music, Timur Selcuk; sound, Horst Zinsmeister; art direction, Jürgen Troster; production manager, Elvira Bolz. Reviewed at Berlin Film Festival (New German Films), Feb. 16, 1989. Running time: **97 MIN.**
Jusuf . . . . Yaman Okay
Havva . . . . Füsun Sen
Temel . . . . Yavuz Güzelce
Omer . . . . Baris Cetinkaya
Stolze . . . . Hans Hamacher
Also with: Yale Arikan, Andrej Diamanstein, Heinz Diesing, Dieter Dost, Felix Schneider-Henninger, Robert Fleischer, Hans-Jurgen Martin.

■"Vatanyolu — The Journey Home" is a good-natured comedy about a Turkish family, long-time residents of West Germany, who plan to resettle in their homeland. It could provide a welcome contrast at festivals to the somber dramas usually exported from Turkey and it should travel well.

Jusuf is offered a cash bonus from the factory he has worked at for years if he will return to Turkey. He feels he will be able to fulfill his dream of opening a grocery in his village. Other family members are not as enthusiastic about the move.

After much arguing and cajoling, Jusuf starts off for Turkey with his family and their possessions squeezed into their car. The car breaks down in a pastoral setting in the country and Jusuf has difficulty finding a new axle.

Some interesting observations about human psychology lie beneath the entertaining scenario. Jusuf's nostalgia for his birthplace dims as he and the family adapt to their new surroundings and begin to cultivate the land.

Tech credits are fine and the acting is believable. Powerful thesp Yaman Okay is especially good as Jusuf. —*Sam.*

Schlachtenbummel
(Battlefield Tour) (WEST GERMAN)

Berlin An HE Film production. Written, directed and edited by Thomas Frickel. Camera (color, 16m), Kerstin Dechering, Horst Gössl, Wolfram Dormann, Michael Busch, Fritz Mettal, Jens Jensen. Editing consultant, Regine Heuser. Reviewed at Berlin Film Festival (New German Films), Feb. 14, 1989. Running time: **152 MIN.**

■Documentary filmmaker Thomas Frickel has combined rare old footage, interviews with war veterans, tv commercials and many other sources to come up with a sometimes moving and always impressive history of German soldiery in this century.

At 2½ hours film is far too long and becomes tedious despite generally fast pacing. Judicious cutting at the hands of a merciless editor could sharpen it into a memorable antiwar piece.

Frickel has a good feel for his subject. Instead of deriding aging German war veterans who trot out their medals and uniforms once a year, he takes his audience on an odyssey of battlefields to rediscover the intense emotions which every frontline solider experiences.

His playful intermingling of old and new advertisements and commercials works surprisingly well and helps make the point that business goes on as usual, war or no war. His interviews are short and moving, particularly one with an elderly Belgian farmer who inspects a now-peaceful field and recalls the moans of the dying.
—*Gill.*

Ressisim
(Burning Memory) (ISRAELI)

Berlin A Compact Film presentation (intl. sales, Mutual Reception, London) of an Ami Amir production. Produced by Ami Amir. Directed by Yossi Somer. Screenplay, Amir, Somer; camera (Eastmancolor), Yoav Kosh; editor, Ya'akov Dagan, Rifka Yogev; music, Jan Gabarek; production design, Robert Bassal; sound, David Liss; production management, Mickey Rabinovitz; assistant director, Izidor Musalem. Reviewed at Berlin Film Festival (Panorama), Feb. 15, 1989. Running time: **93 MIN.**
Gary . . . . Danny Roth
Tzvika . . . . Shmuel Edelman
Alex . . . . Pauli Reshef
Ruth . . . . Etty Ankri
Rubi . . . . Alon Oliarchick
Avram . . . . Yossef El-Dror
Nissim . . . . Renven Dayan
Ronen . . . . Yahli Bergman
Tzukerman . . . . Koby Hagoel
Amos . . . . Avi Gilor

■"Burning Memory" is based on personal experiences of

debuting filmmaker Yossi Somer during and in the wake of Israel's Lebanon invasion.

He offers a few flashback combat shots but otherwise sticks to his highly dramatic, convincing story of a group of so-called shell-shocked men undergoing three weeks of therapy in a Haifa military hospital.

Although "Burning Memory" neatly avoids the politically controversial subject of mental wounds induced by fighting in this particular war, it remains strong meat as a portrayal of mental casualties of what could be any war at any time. The device of the patients being granted a maximum of three weeks to get well is ironic since "get well" means well enough to perform further military duty.

Alex (Pauli Reshef) is the army psychiatrist who in turn despairs and remains patient in dealing with a group of men whose primary defense is that they don't want the therapy at all. Especially not handsome, strong and silent Gary (Danny Roth), who has violent breakdowns following his realistic nightmares about seeing a buddy die horribly without being able to help him.

The individual group members are given fine and nuanced character delineations.

Only one man, Gary, is seen leaving the hospital with his sanity restored. He rejoins his wife, who has had as little patience with the army therapy methods as she has had with the war in general. She (Etty Ankri) is the cast's only civilian, and director Somer has reduced her to a mere cliché.

"Burning Memory" has fine production credits down the line, and Norwegian jazzman Jan Gabarek's wailing dirge makes the soundtrack swell with all the desperation we know to be suffered by everyone in the group.

Beyond obvious tv sales, quite a few theatrical pickups were already looming at film's world preem in Berlin. —Kell.

Abschied Von Falschen Paradies
(Farewell To False Paradise)
(WEST GERMAN)

Berlin   An Impuls-Film release of a Studio Hamburg/ZDF production. Produced by Ottokar Runze Filmproduktion. Production director, Michael Beier. Written and directed by Tevfik Baser, based on the novel "Women Who Died Without Having Lived" by Salina Scheinhardt. Camera (color), Izzet Akay; editor, Klaus Bassiner; music, Claus Bantzer; sound, Ernest-Hermann Marell; costumes, Gabriele Friedrich; makeup, Bothilla Bergschmidt. Reviewed at Berlin Film Festival, official program (out of competition), Feb. 13, 1989. Running time: 92 MIN.
Elif . . . . Zuhal Olcay
Marianne . . . . Brigitte Janner
Gabriella . . . . Ruth Olafsdottir
Nora . . . . Barbara Morawiecz
Gulizar . . . . Ayse Altan
Hatice . . . . Serpil Inanc
Isolde . . . . Karin Klugmann
Hasan . . . . Celik Bilge

■In "Farewell To False Paradise" — about a Turkish woman who kills her husband and is given a 6-year jail sentence in Germany — Tevfik Baser focuses on the uplifting aspects of her development of an identity. Film should do well in European arthouses and in video releases.

Elif arrives in prison frightened and feeling isolated. She moved from a Turkish village to Hamburg with her brutish husband and doesn't know any German. She has had all of her decisions made by the males in her family and never exercised a sense of autonomy.

Most films set in prison, including those of Turkish directors such as Yilmaz Guney's "The Wall," emphasize the grim conditions and physical abuse suffered by the inmates. Baser chose to focus on the interaction of Elif with the other women. He doesn't idealize a prison setting but shows what the women have done to make the best of their environment.

Elif's growing camaraderie with the other prisoners, well-cast with German and Turkish character actors, and a budding romance, give her the strength to confront her bullying brother when he comes to visit. Unfortunately, an ironic twist shatters her newfound happiness when she discovers she must stand trial in Turkey and will be deported. The freedom she as acquired behind bars will be impossible for her to maintain in her homeland. She must decide if suicide is the only solution to the dilemma.

Zuhal Olcay, star of a number of popular Turkish films, is photogenic and gives a remarkably expressive performance that helps to sustain interest. The lensing is adept and other tech credits are fine. —Sam.

Georgette Menuier
(WEST GERMAN)

Berlin   Produced by Deutsche Film und Fernsehnakademie Berlin. Written and directed by Tania Stöcklin. Cyrille Rey-Coquais. Camera (color), Ciro Cappellari, Anka Schmid; music, Nikolaus Utermöhlien; sound, Magarethe Heitmüller, Chris Suglyama. Reviewed at Berlin Film Festival (Forum), Feb. 12, 1989. Running time: 80 MIN.
With: Tiziana Jelmini, Diana Stöcklin, Thomas Schunke, Martin Peter, Giles Dommann, Heinz Rathsack.

■This is a hard to categorize film, made in luscious color with good performances and a weird enough plot line to sustain interest.

A beautiful woman has been in love with her brother since childhood. She marries after he disappears during battle. She accidentally kills her husband but is tried for murder and made to serve time. In prison she shares a cell with a mad woman

Released, Georgette, who is a trained pharmacist, goes on a killing spree that makes Lizzie Borden look like a wimp. Of course, the deaths are very suspicious in this not too large town and there are all sorts of speculation about the cause.

Being a good pharmacist, Georgette has been able to cover her tracks well. After first experimenting with a potion slipped into unsuspecting victims' drinks, she hits on a more foolproof method, putting the poison in batches of chocolate truffles.

Beautifully photographed and produced "Georgette Menuier" may be able to win a cult following if the screening audience's enthusiasm is any indication of its overall appeal. —Owl.

Prokurorut
(The Prosecutor)
(BULGARIAN-B&W)

Berlin   Produced by Sofia Feature Film Studios. Directed by Lyubomir Sharlandjiev. Screenplay, Budimir Metalnikov, based on play by Georgi Ojagarov; camera (b&w), Borislav Pounchev; music, Ivan Halechev; art direction, Petko Bonchev. Reviewed at Berlin Film Festival (Panorama), Feb. 20, 1989. Running time: 72 MIN.
With: Georgi Georgiev-Getz, Yordan Matev, Olga Kircheva, Stefan Peichev, Dorotea Toncheva and Vassil Popiliev.

■"The Prosecutor," had its international bow at the Berlin film fest. It is a gripping psychological drama which has appeal that extends beyond what was once a daring and timely topic.

"The Prosecutor" is based on a play of the same title considered a classic of Bulgarian theater and has become a mainstay of many European theater troupes. A humane prosecutor faces a moral dilemma when he is asked to sign the warrant for the arrest of a friend, one of the victims of the political trials of the repressive Stalinist era. When he hesitates, a determined investigation urges him to carry out his duty.

The excellent acting by the leads, Georgi Georgiev-Getz and Yordan Matev, brings life to the well-written but conventional dialog and courtroom sequences.

The black and white lensing is outstanding. The fantasy sequences of the prosecutor observing the reactions of his friend, his friend's mother and his own father are creatively integrated into the ongoing action. —Sam.

Anni tahtoo äidin
(Mother Wanted)
(FINNISH)

Berlin   A Petra Tarjanne/Reppu Filmi presentation and production. Produced by Petra Tarjanne. Written and directed by Anssi Määntäri. Camera (color), Heikki Katajisto; editor, Marjo Valve; music, Asko Mänttäri; production design, Risto Karhula; sound, Timo Linnasalo; assistant director, Marjo Valve. Reviewed at Berlin Film Festival (Market), Feb. 12, 1989. Running time: 65 MIN.
Anni . . . . Kirsikka Tykkyläinen
Timppa, her dad . . . . Kari Heiskinen
Leena . . . . Susanna Haavisto
Also with: Outi Mäenpää, Ritva Valkama, Miitta Sorvali, Antti Mäkelä, and singers Rea Mauranen, Ulla Tapaninen, Eija Ahvo, Petri Johansson, Kosti Kotiranta.

■With "Mother Wanted," which he styles a musical comedy, writer-helmer Anssi Määntäri has turned from adult psychology dramas to kiddie fare. Cleanly executed, pic should find sales into age group 5-to-10 programming on offshore tv services.

Story's widowed father is shy, nice and a lousy cook. The candidates to replace little Anni's mother are mostly brash and unmindful of Anni's sensitivities. Anni is a persistent matchmaker; her daddy is elusive, but a redhead hairdresser teams up with Anni, and "Here Comes The Bride" is heard anew.

Pic is padded with a few Greek Chorus musical numbers with spectators to the action breaking out in moralistic lyrics.

Kirsikka Tykkyläinen has the glint of devilish fun in her otherwise somber eyes and avoids overt cuteness most of the time.

As the father, Kari Heiskinen is suitably befuddled while retaining some measure of male dignity and attraction. As the redhead, Susanna Haavisto puts in a laid-back performance of gentle feminine charm and fun. —Kell.

Aufruhr in Damaskus
(Uprising In Damascus)
(GERMAN-B&W)

Berlin A Terra Filmkunst production. Produced by Otto Lehmann. Directed by Gustav Ucicky. Screenplay, Philipp Lothar Mayring, Jacob Greis, from a manuscript by Herbert Tjadens; camera (b&w), Oskar Schnirch, Paul Rischke; editor, Gertrud Hinz; sound, Walter Rühland; art direction, Erich Czerwonski, Carl Böhm. Premiered Feb. 24, 1939, in Leipzig. Berlin premiere, March 8, 1939. Film banned by Allied Military Command in 1945. Reviewed at Berlin Film Festival (Europe 1939 Retrospective), Feb. 13, 1989. Running time: **105 MIN.**

With: Brigitte Horney, Joachim Gottschalk, Hans Nielsen, Ernst von Klipstein, Paul Otto, Ingolf Kuntze, Paul Westermeier, Gerhard Bienert, Friedrich Gnaas.

■Here's the Nazi propaganda machine's version of "Lawrence Of Arabia" — from the German side, of course. Prominent Nazi-era director Gustav Ucicky neatly put together a Howard Hawks-style yarn about young soldiers far from home, in this case in Syria in 1918.

There's even a love element between a volunteer nurse (Brigitte Horney) and a square-jawed officer (Joachim Gottschalk). The officer manages to elude Col. T.E. Lawrence and lead 14 surviving soldiers to safety through the burning sands.

"Aufruhr in Damaskus," which roughly translated means "Uprising In Damascus," was shot in 1939 outside Tripoli, with interior shooting done at Berlin's Babelsberg studios. War broke out before the film could be released abroad. After the war, the Allied victors banned it as Nazi propaganda.

Half a century later, one is surprised by the lack of vehement anti-British sentiment in the film. It is a standard actioner suited to Gottschalk's talents.

Gottschalk made seven films between 1938 and 1941, and was considered Germany's answer to Clark Gable. He was well-suited to play the wiry officer who keeps his head in times of peril while wiping a tear from his girl's eye.

As with many Nazi-era celebrities, his own story was full of more peril and intrigue than any role he every played. His wife was Jewish, and as he rose to stardom, pressures mounted for him to rid himself of her and their young son.

In 1941 at the height of his career, an order was issued for the death camp deportation of his wife and the 7-year-old boy. Gottschalk's request to accompany them to the camp was rejected.

On Nov. 7, 1941, the day the deportations were to take place, the bodies of all three family members were found in their Berlin home. Circumstances surrounding the suicides were hushed up, and Gottschalk's money-making films continued to play. —*Gill.*

Privurzaniyet Balon
(The Attached Balloon)
(BULGARIAN-B&W)

Berlin Produced by the Sofia Feature Film Studios. Directed by Binka Zhelyazkova. Screenplay, Yordan Radichkov; camera (b&w), Emil Wagenstein; music, Simeon Pironkov. Reviewed at Berlin Film Festival (Panorama), Feb. 18, 1989. Running time: **98 MIN.**

With: Grigor Vachkov, Georgi Kaloyanchev, Ivan Bratanov, Georgi Partsalev, Tsvyatko Nikolov, Georgi Georgiev, Peter Slabakov, Zhanet Miteva, Stoyanka Moutafova, Konstantin Kotsev.

■Made in 1967, "The Attached Balloon" had a brief run in cinemas before being shelved by censors. A simple parable, it is proof that a large budget is not necessary to make a visually appealing, interesting picture.

A huge zeppelin lands in the middle of nowhere, i.e., the interior of Bulgaria. At first it inspires awe in the inhabitants of two villages. It doesn't take long before they are scheming about how it can be used for their own purposes. A battle breaks out between the two factions and a young girl witnesses the whole spectacle.

The ambivalent nature of the peasants provokes both laughter and anxiety. The acting is pleasantly unaffected.

The eventual fate of the lofty balloon is symbolic of the destructive political and social climate of the era in which the film was made. For this reason and because it was forbidden for over two decades, pic will attract attention at home and in fests and specialty screenings, particularly at film archives. —*Sam.*

L'home de neó
(Man Of Neon)
(SPANISH)

Berlin A Virginia Film (Barcelona) release and world sales of a Barcelonafilm and Virginia Film producton, with TV3/Televisió de Catalunia. Produced by Paco Poch. Written and directed by Albert Abril. Camera (Agfacolor), Lorenc Soler; editor, Emili Rodriguez; music, Toti Soler; production design, Rosa Espanol. Reviewed at Berlin Film Festival (Panorama) Feb. 15, 1989. Running time: **100 MIN.**

David . . . . Feodor Atkine
Lynda . . . . Assumpta Serna
Jordi . . . . Lluis Homar
Rosa . . . . Viviane Vives

Also with: Moises Torner, Victor Israel, Jordi Torras.

■"Man Of Neon" is a stylish Catalan-Spanish thriller that has enough metaphysical aspects plus satirical jabs to make it a likely small winner on the international theatrical circuit. Film is Albert Abril's first feature.

David (Feodor Atkine) makes a modest living repairing neon signs atop Barcelona high-rises. In a world of poverty and violence, he still likes the beat of the big city and enlivens his bachelor existence with recording, often on the sly, what goes on around him with his video camera.

David is lured by Lynda (Assumpta Serna), a beautiful radio reporter, into accepting a secret mission: he is to bring a parcel to a seaside hotel and wait there until somebody comes to pick it up.

David winds up being shot at and nearly killed. He loses the use of his right arm. Bitter but stubborn, he goes back to and literally hangs on to his real job anyway. Linda turns up with another job proposal and bigger money as reward and recompense.

Soon David is back in hospital, hit and beaten once more, with fate hard at this otherwise nearly organized man's heels.

There is quietly convincing playing in all roles, and every frame is full of eerie atmosphere. The dialog is heavy with menace but it has wit, too. The entertainment is on a high level throughout. —*Kell.*

Himmelsheim
(WEST GERMAN)

Berlin A Journal Film-Maran Film production. Produced by Klaus Volkenborn. Directed by Manfred Stelzer. Screenplay, Fitzgerald Kusz; camera (color), Frans Bromet; editor, Dagmar Hirtz; music, Rio Reiser; production design, Maciej Maria Putowski; sound, Hans Zinsmeister; production manager, Nani Mahlo. Reviewed at Berlin Film Festival (New German Cinema), Feb. 17, 1989. Running time: **89 MIN.**

Helga . . . . Elke Sommer
Toni . . . . Siggi Zimmerschied
Ehrenfried . . . . Hanns Zischler
Maria . . . . Elisabeth Welz
Erich . . . . Theo Massingschlager
Mrs. Pokorny . . . . Tilly Lauenstein
Franzi . . . . Dietmar Mössmer

■A comedy along the lines of director Manfred Stelzer's 1987 pic "The Chinese Are Coming," "Himmelsheim" takes a serious theme — the destruction of the environment — and has mild fun with it.

The title refers to a cute little village, the kind of place where even cats and dogs are friends. All that is about to change since a tunnel for a new fast express train line is to be built through the place.

The impact of "progress" on a little backwater is good material for comedy, but Stelzer doesn't make the most of it here. Laughs come only intermittently. Basically, the subject is just too painful to be very amusing.

Production is excellent, though, and a fine cast of troupers play along the broad lines called for. Dagmar Hirtz edited to a crisp 89 minutes. —*Strat.*

Im Jahr Der Schildkröte
(Year Of The Turtle)
(WEST GERMAN)

Berlin A Geissendörfer Film, WDR coproduction. Produced by Hans W. Geissendörfer. Written and produced by Ute Wieland. Camera (color), Karl-Walter Lindenlaub; editor, Helga Borsche; sound, Hardy Hardt; art direction, Günther Naumann. Reviewed at Berlin Film Festival (Market), Feb. 13, 1989. Running time: **97 MIN.**

With: Heinz Bennent, Karina Fallenstein, Anke Tegtmeyer, Arpad Kraupa.

■Like the turtle of the title, Ute Wieland's touching made-for-tv film about a May-December love affair gets off to a slow start but gains momentum to cross the finish line in style.

Pic shows promise for the European tv market, though it is too downbeat and slow-paced for the U.S.

Heinz Bennent has a tough role here, playing a 60ish, unemployed accountant who against his better judgment falls in love with a 21-year-old punk rocker (Karina Fallenstein).

That the premise is at all credible is a tribute to Bennent's skill in transforming his mousy accountant into a man no longer afraid to take a risk. Fallenstein's role is no easier, but she handles it less adeptly.

Tech credits are of a high standard. —*Gill.*

Zabij Mnie, Glino
(Kill Me, Cop)
(POLISH)

Berlin A Perspektywa Unit, Polish Film Corp. production. Directed by Jacek Bromski. Screenplay, Bromski; camera (color), Jacek Mieroslawski; editor, Jadwiga Zajicek; music, Henri Seroka; production design, Jerzy Sajko; sound, Jerzy Szawlowski; production manager, Dorota Ostrowska-Orlinska. Reviewed at Berlin Film Festival (Market), Feb. 17, 1989. Running time: **122 MIN.**

Malik . . . . Boguslaw Linda
Capt. Popczyk . . . . Piotr Machalica

Dorothy . . . . Maria Pakulnis
Also with: Anna Romantowska, Jadwiga Jankowska-Cieslak.

■ **"Kill Me Cop" is a routine Polish crime thriller, laced with sex and violence that seems to be aping Hollywood prototypes. Most filmgoers would rather see the original than this pale imitation.**

Central situation involves a duel between criminal-on-the-run, Malik, and the cop who put him behind bars in the first place, Popczyk. First-time director Jacek Bromski borrows freely from staples of *film noir*, such as a double-crossing Mr. Big and a daring escape from court-room at knifepoint. There's even a Hitchcock-inspired sequence in which the hero/villain meets a femme fatale on a train.

Despite all the shoot-outs and intrigue, plus a solid performance from Boguslaw Linda as the fugitive criminal, the picture remains obstinately uninvolving, and at over two hours is far too long. Technical credits are all fine.
—*Strat.*

Split

Berlin   A Starker Film production. Produced by Barbara Horscraft. Written, directed, camera (color), edited by Chris Shaw. Music, Chris Shaw, Robert Shaw, Ugi Tojo; sound, Shaw, Robert Galpren; computer effects, Robert Shaw. Reviewed at Berlin Film Festival (Market), Feb. 14, 1989. Running time: **85 MIN.**
    With: Chris Shaw, Tim Dwight, Joan Bechtel, John Flynn.

■ **"Split" moves so fast and with such high-tech confusion and sensation, that the eye is engaged even as the brain is puzzled. It's merely a provocative rough draft for a futuristic chase-thriller, a notepad of jottings and computer effects, not a completed, satisfying film.**

Insofar as one can discern a plot in "Split," it takes place in the future and deals with Starker (Tim Dwight), prophet of peace, sanity and order. He wishes to liberate humankind oppressed by media and junk ideas.

Deified by the public, Starker realizes that omniscient Big Brother has him targeted as its rival for power. Kept under electronic surveillance, Starker must stay on the run, seeking shelter where he can, at times changing his appearance.

When hit men follow Starker, he escapes in drag and blackface. An evil genius whose face peels off in layers (filmmaker Chris Shaw) masterminds the treachery against

Starker. In a strange final scene, he attempts to pull Starker below the surface of a magic pond.

"Split" achieved some following at the Denver and Telluride festivals. Its net effect is closer to chaos than coherence. —*Hitch.*

Circus On The Moon
(W. GERMAN-SRI LANKAN)

Berlin   A Satellit Film production, in coproduction with ZDF, Novotrade Ltd. Produced by Barna Kabay. Directed by Imre Gyöngyössy. Kabay. Screenplay, Gyöngyössy, Katalin Petényi; camera (color), Michael Teutsch; music, Glenn Morrow, Ian (Koko) Kojima. Reviewed at Berlin Film Festival (Market), Feb. 12, 1989. Running time: **100 MIN.**
    With Ishrat Ismail, Hannelore Elsner, Harshana Jayawardene, Johann Cooke, Neil Karunaratine, Finbarr Madden, Réka Gyöngyössy.

■ **This amateurish production in badly dubbed English is a turkey from start to finish. Best performers in this circus are Gogo the apple-eating bear and Dudi the beefsteak-eating elephant.**

An 8-year-old Sri Lankan boy flees the island's civil war by hiding in a traveling circus run by his mother. She's a white woman who survived a Nazi death camp and miraculously doesn't look a day over 35.

The circus is run by a young Jewish fellow from New York. There's also a teenaged dwarf.

The whole troupe is joined by a white German and a dark-skinned Sinhalese who are supposed to be brothers fighting on opposite sides. These addlepated black-and-white metaphors don't work — not with a screenplay like this.

Inexplicably, Dire Straits rock musician Ian (Koko) Kojima and Glenn Morrow are in this film. They compose the circus combo that plays blues tunes while armed guerrillas are held at bay in the ring by the eight-year-old's mother. —*Gill.*

Vienna Is Different
(DOCU)

Berlin   A Leitmotif Films production. Written, produced and directed by Susan Korda, David Leitner. Camera (color, 16m), Leitner; editor & sound, Korda. Reviewed at Berlin Film Festival (Forum of Young Cinema), Feb. 11, 1989. Running time: **73 MIN.**

■ **This portrait of Austria, 50 years after it was taken over by Nazis, is one more by-product of the worldwide anti-Waldheim protests and the discussions generated as a result.**

Opening premise is that Austria should accept its share of the guilt in World War II crimes, with various witnesses pointing out not one shot was fired to prevent Hitler's invasion, and stating that Austria ceased to exist as a nation from 1938 until 1945.

Featured are interviews with historians, journalists and various other public figures, public discussions on national responsibility and a piece of Waldheim's address to the nation plus some footage shot after the broadcast. Susan Korda and David Leitner paint an unflattering image of a country which was only too glad to adopt officially the conqueror's racist dictates, showing at times more enthusiasm than their tutors. Now, they prefer to argue that being themselves victims of Nazi aggression, they had no other choice of conduct.

The film's centerpieces are an interview with a Neo-Nazi who denies the existence of gas chambers and actor-director Maximilian Schell trying to persuade a young student that the past has to be assumed. Also a street argument between a man maintaining Waldheim is Austria's popular choice and an older woman trying to convince him that choosing Waldheim was a mistake.

The construction and the organization of the material is rather haphazard, but it still delivers relevant insights. —*Edna.*

Stek
(Bit Part)
(CZECH)

Berlin   A Slovak Film Studios production (Intl. sales, Ceskoslovensky Filmexport). Directed by Miloslav Luther. Screenplay, Jan Fleischer, Ondrej Sulav, Bolek Polivka; camera (color), Vladimir Hollos; music, Jiri Bulis; production design, Petr Canecky; sound, Csaba Torok; production manager, Villam Richter; assistant director, Eva Vadikova. Reviewed at Berlin Film Festival (Czech Day), Feb. 15, 1989. Running time: **90 MIN.**
Perda . . . . Bolek Polivka
Heda . . . . Ivana Chylkova
Director . . . . Ivan Petrovicky
Manager . . . . Frantise Rehak
Laborec . . . . Andrej Hryc

■ **A comedy with a slight political tinge, "Bit Part" centers around a provincial theater company about to perform a local play thought to have a few barbs in it.**

Perda, a lowly member of the troupe, is given the chance to play the lead in this production but, troubled by the break-up of his marriage and aware that Ministry heavies are in the audience, he

goes dry on opening night and simply walks off the stage.

Demoted to the humble role of a waiter with one line, he hams it up next night and is further demoted, this time to stage manager, in which role he causes chaos by tampering with the props.

By this time he's turned a serious play into a farce, but everyone agrees it works better that way.

After an abrupt start, pic hits its stride and turns into a pleasant, if low-key, experience. Scenes of the members of the theater troup arguing about their production are fun.

Bolek Polivka, who co-scripted, is fine as the nervous, yet resourceful, actor. —*Strat.*

Eden Is Burning

Berlin   An Ocean Pictures production. Produced by Curt Rosen, Richard Connors. Directed by Connors. Screenplay, Connors, Rosen, from story by Connors; additional dialog, Henry Roth, Jan Schmidt; camera (color), Rosen; editing and design, Rosen, Connors; music, Cebello Morales; sound, Linda Wissmath. Reviewed at Berlin Film Festival (Market), Feb. 14, 1989. Running time: **81 MIN.**
Alyssa (age six) . . . . Alexandra Lee
Alyssa (young adult) . . . . . . Andrea Istvan
Father . . . . John MacKay
Mother . . . . Tara Tyson
Doctor Ridley . . . . George Vlachos
Jesse Valentine . . . . Richard Gitlin

■ **Highly stylized, intelligent and crafted with great care on a low budget, "Eden Is Burning" shows originality and personality.**

A somber tale of mental illness and pyromania, it's fated to specialized distribution at arthouses that will take a risk with an offbeat U.S. feature lacking stars.

As an adult in a mental hospital, Alyssa (Andrea Istvan) relives the moments of her father's death by suicide. Seeking to help Alyssa work through the horror of witnessing her father perish by fire, her psychiatrist (George Vlachos) investigates the mysterious event.

His investigative work is advanced, and impeded, by a naive young hospital attendant, Jesse (Richard Gitlin), whom Alyssa finds appealing, uncharacteristically opening herself and showing affection. The doctor gambles that he can gain insight into Alyssa's illness by using Jesse's generous and simple nature. Both Jesse and the doctor, however, fail to reckon with Alyssa, who gains access to a can of gasoline.

Gothic and melodramatic, "Eden Is Burning" shifts variously among delusions, dreams, memories and reality.

Music and mood are skillfully controlled, but performances, especially of secondary characters, are wooden. Despite its contradictions, "Eden Is Burning" is an auspicious debut for filmmakers Richard Connors and Curt Rosen. —*Hitch.*

Ariel
(FINNISH)

Berlin A Christa Saredi presentation of a Vilealfa Films production. Produced, written and directed by Aki Kaurismäki. Camera (color), Timo Salminen; editor, Raija Talvio; music, Olavi Virta, Rauli Somejoki, Melrose, Bill Casey, Esko Rahkonen. Tchaikovsky, Taisio Tammi, Shostakovich; sound (Dolby), Jouko Lumme; art direction, Risto Karhula; costumes, Tuula Hilkamo. Reviewed at Berlin Film Festival (Forum of Young Cinema), Feb. 16, 1989. Running time: **74 MIN.**
Taisto . . . . Turo Pajala
Irmeli . . . . Susanna Haavisto
Mikonnen . . . . Matti Pellonpää
   Also with: Eetu Hilkamo, Erkki Pajala, Matti Jaaranen, Hannu Viholainen, Jorma Markkula.

◼ **Aki Kaurismäki confirms his reputation as the dark humorist of the north in this sarcastically grim tale of an unemployed Lap miner hiking through the underbelly of Finland, before fleeing for his life to the other end of the globe.**

Kaurismäki's special type of humor is there from the onset, when the hero's father shoots himself in the lavatories of a diner, after the mine is closed down, while the jukebox is playing a carefree tango.

Kaurismäki looks at life with a jaundiced eye, lending a hangman's sense of humor to the most desperate scenes. He is almost shy when he has to elicit emotions, but does it very effectively because he rarely indulges them.

His sympathy for his characters is evident and persistent, whatever they are forced to do. Any and all blame is carried here by society, which practically forces the Finns into desperate acts. Unemployment, corruption and constant police surveillance, are some of the features the film exposes at length.

Delivered at a staccato pace with actors playing as if there were no camera around, a soundtrack which stresses the use of Dolby effects and camera which never tries to impose itself, this is one of Kaurismäki's best efforts to date. It represents a companion piece, if a grimmer one, to his earlier "Shadows In Paradise." —*Edna.*

Die Weissen Zwerge
(The White Dwarfs)
(WEST GERMAN-B&W)

Berlin A ZDF, Mainz and Tara-Film, Berlin coproduction. Produced by Karin Scheuven, Susann Gartell, Rudi Teichmann. Directed by Dirk Schäfer. Screenplay, Schäfer, Patricia Kalmar; camera (b&w), Ernst Kubitza; editor, Patricia Rommel; sound, Arno Wilms; settings, Alexander Manasse, Michael Kölker; costumes, Petra Rospert. Reviewed at Berlin Film Festival (New German Films), Feb. 13, 1989. Running time: **75 MIN.**
   With: Nirit Sommerfeld, Michael Schech.

◼ **Pic follows the increasingly monotonous life of a mixed German-Turkish relationship in contemporary Berlin. A prize winner at the Max Ophüls film competition late last year, this modest undertaking, shot in black and white, might be a good bet for fests and other specialized screening venues.**

Director Dirk Schäfer meticulously demonstrates that even couples that take ethnic and religious risks aren't always able to work things out. Both are employed in low-level jobs; he an institutional cook, she a department store cashier.

There are problems in their sex life and even in their lifestyles. He'd like to move to a larger place that's about to become available and all she can think about is the work of refurbishing and cleaning that will face them after the move.

Nirit Sommerfeld and Michael Schech are attractive actors who make their skillful performances as the couple seem effortless. There is some effective but unobtrusive camerawork by Ernst Kubitza. It's low-budget, nicely handled pic showing promise. —*Owl.*

Flüstern & Schreien — Ein Rockreport
(Whispers And Outcry: A Rock Report)
(EAST GERMAN-DOCU)

Berlin A VEB DEFA Documentary Studios production. Directed by Dieter Schumann. Screenplay, Schumann, Jochen Wisotzky; camera (color), Michael Lösche, Christian Lehmann, Bernd Schadewald, Sebastian Richter, Steffen Sebastian, Udo Bress; editor, Karin Schöning, Manuela Bothe, Inge Marszulek; sound, Henner Golz, Jochen Huschenbett; music, Feeling B. Chicoree, Silly Sandow, Pop Generation, Andre & Firma; production managers, Roland K.G. Gernhard, Heinz Arnold. Reviewed at Berlin Film Festival (Forum of Young Cinema), Feb. 15, 1989. Running time: **120 MIN.**

◼ **The obvious appeal of this documentary is the revelation of** a rock world teeming in East Germany, and the evident political connotations carried by their concerts and the lyrics they sing.

For German-speaking audiences it carries the additional bonus of using an almost extinct Berlinese slang, which delighted the SRO crowds at the Forum midnight screening.

More than a musical statement, East German rock is an act defying the conformism imposed by the regime. Lyrics constantly refer to wider horizons and open skies, satirically mention the need to be well-behaved in order to be accepted and demand the right to be different.

This is reinforced in interviews with the artists and their fans, for whom punk attire expresses their personal declaration of independence. The camera follows the musicians into their homes

The first such documentary made in East Germany, it had to surmount numerous difficulties on the production level, not least because necessary equipment to shoot and record live performances was not available and had to be improvised. Results are technically gratifying. —*Edna.*

Gekauftes Glück
(Bride Of The Orient)
(WEST GERMAN-SWISS)

Berlin A Balanco Film, Munich and Cinefilm, Zurich coproduction. Produced by Walter Saxer, Christoph Locher. Written and directed by Urs Odermatt. Camera (color), Rainer Klausmann; editor, Ulrike Pahl, Anne Wagner; sound, Chris Price, Günther Knon; costumes, Silvia Grabowski. Reviewed at Berlin Film Festival (Market), Feb. 13, 1989. Running time: **96 MIN.**
   With: Wolfram Berger, Arunotai Jitreekan, Werner Herzog, Mathias Gnädinger, Marie-Therese Mäder, Annamirl Bierbichler.

◼ **This low-key offering from director Urs Odermatt examines the inherent racism of small, close-knit communities. Film might enjoy modest success beyond the German-speaking territories.**

Farmer Windleter (Wolfram Berger), in the Swiss Alps, is in the market for a bride but the local girls are either a trifle fast for his comprehension or just not interested. After paying a visit to a girlie bar in Zurich that features Asian girls, he orders a Thai farmer's daughter and several weeks later she arrives.

A man not given to many demands, he and his accommodating bride live a relatively chaste life as they go about the chores of farming. Even when she wearies of waiting for him to make the first move and tries to seduce him, she doesn't have much luck.

The locals are a bit put out about him taking a "slit-eyed thingemabob" as she is referred to, and there is a lot of talk both in the local pub and church pews, even some open hostility. The minister pays a none-too-subtle social call to investigate the situation.

Unfortunate complications arise when a hostile neighbor tries to take advantage of the girl and all ends rather tragically for the hapless farmer.

This serviceably scripted film is well shot and has some nice performances form Berger and Arunotai Jitreekan as the Thai bride. There's even a slightly overdone turn by director Werner Herzog as the jealous neighbor. —*Owl.*

Troop Beverly Hills

Hollywood   A Weintraub Entertainment Group release through Columbia Pictures of a Fries Entertainment and Avanti production. Produced by Ava Ostern Fries. Executive producer, Charles Fries. Directed by Jeff Kanew; William B. Screenplay, Pamela Norris, Margaret Grieco Oberman, based on story by Ava Ostern Fries; camera (Metrocolor), Donald E. Thorin; editor, Mark Melnick; production design, Robert F. Boyle; art direction, Jack G. Taylor Jr.; set decoration, Anne McCulley-Reynolds; costume design, Theodora Van Runkle; sound (Dolby), William B. Kaplan; assistant director, Jack F. Sanders; casting, Fern Champion, Pamela Basker. Reviewed at Mann Bruin Theater, Westwood, Calif., March 21, 1989. MPAA Rating: PG. Running time: 105 MIN.

Phyllis Nefler	Shelley Long
Freddy Nefler	Craig T. Nelson
Velda Plendor	Betty Thomas
Annie Herman	Mary Gross
Vicki Sprantz	Stephanie Beacham
Frances Temple	Audra Lindley
Ross Coleman	Edd Byrnes
Hannah Nefler	Jenny Lewis
Jasmine	Tasha Scott
Claire	Ami Foster
Chica	Carla Gugino
Tessa	Heather Hopper
Lily	Aquilina Soriano

■Exploits of a Rodeo Drive shop 'n' lunch queen who decides to bolster her wobbly self-esteem by leading a scout troop makes for amusing light comedy in this Weintraub Entertainment Group/Columbia release.

Pitched toward kids and teens, and more likely to appeal to females than males, pic may struggle to catch on, but could generate reasonable b.o. returns.

Shelley Long stars as Phyllis Nefler, whose marriage is on the rocks and whose skills are limited to acquiring new costumes and tossing lavish catered parties.

Accused by her husband (Craig T. Nelson) of having lost her spark, she offers herself up to Wilderness Girls of America as the unlikely candidate to revitalize the faltering, scorned Beverly Hills troop, of which her daughter (Jenny Lewis) is a dissatisfied member.

This is thankfully, no nuts, berries 'n' bears saga, as Troop B.H. develops a scouting style all its own. Merit patches are awarded for sushi appreciation, community service consists of "describing the fall fashions to the blind," and chocolate fondue replaces marshmallows around the campfire — all of which earn razzberries from the other troops.

Pic would not likely have flown without Long, whose airy, whimsical charm builds a winning momentum that prevails over a decidedly flat beginning and implausible story.

Long's pitted against fellow Second City comedy alum Betty Thomas as the gung-ho, around-the-bend troop sergeant ("I love the smell of cookies in the morning") who wants to see her fail at any cost. Pair generates enough comedic energy to keep things afloat, as do bright flashes from a script that's more often as airily unconcerned with reality as its pampered protagonist.

Eventually, pic is about the few things that B.H. money can't buy — self esteem, team spirit, family harmony and merit patches — a fitting theme for young viewers, since film is otherwise awash in the glitzy flotsam of wealth.

Several of the young scouts shine, particularly Jenny Lewis as Long's daughter Hannah and Tasha Scott as Jasmine, daughter of a black boxing champion, who does a mean Tina Turner imitation in a talent show.

There's wit in the editing — which folds vidclips of the Pee-wee Herman tv show and Jane Fonda's workout into the comedy fabric — and in Randy Edelman's airy, synthesized arrangement of campfire standby "Kumbaya" and other soundtrack goodies.

Shelley Morrison also is an asset as the Hispanic ("We don't need no stinkin' patches") maid.

Endless parade of costumes for Long — 47 in all, by Theodora Van Runkle — contribute plenty of character. —Daws.

Papa est parti, maman aussi
(Daddy's Gone, And Mom Too)
(FRENCH-SWISS)

Paris   A UGC release of a Films de l'Ecluse (Paris)/SFPC (Geneva) coproduction. Produced by Yves Gasser. Directed by Christine Lipinska. Screenplay, Lipinska, Rémo Forlani, from Forlani's novel; camera (Eastmancolor), Alain Derobe; editor, Marie-Claude Lacambre; music, Jean-Marie Senia; art direction, Jean-Pierre Clech; sound, Henri Roux; production manager, Bernard Lorain; assistant director, Gabriel Julien-Laferriere; casting, Marie-Claude Schwartz. Reviewed at UGC Ermitage theater, Paris, Feb. 26, 1989. Running time: 99 MIN.

Laurette	Sophie Aubry
Lucien	Jérôme Kirchner
Jérôme	Benoit Magimel
Pamela	Anasi Subra
Manu	Nicolas Neuhuys
Mother	Marie Rivière
Father	Stéphane Bouy

■A cast of children, teens and animals inject some facile charm into this well-made but routine comedy-drama about a family left on its own when mom and dad both bolt in separate directions after a stormy marital quarrel.

Christine Lipinska directed from a screenplay she wrote with Rémo Forlani, a well-known French journalist and author, based on his novel.

Family, and the film, is held together by Sophie Aubry, a 16-year-old newcomer with talent and temperament. She plays the oldest of four kids, including two brothers and a sister, who together provide a hyperactive handful (not to mention two housecats and a pet white mouse).

Aubry won't brook the selfish attitudes of her parents who seek a divorce and won't accept anything less than a reunited family. In the meantime she uses the two weeks of domestic disorder to experience her first romance with a young would-be writer who picks her up in a fast food joint.

In the end, the family is brought together again (ironically not through Aubry's efforts) and Aubrey ends up a teen mother in New York to join her boyfriend.
—Len.

Dead-Bang

Hollywood   A Warner Bros. release of a Lorimar Film Entertainment presentation of a Steve Roth production. Produced by Roth. Executive producer, Robert L. Rosen. Co-executive producer, Robert Foster. Directed by John Frankenheimer. Screenplay, Foster; camera (Alpha Cine color, Metrocolor prints), Gerry Fisher; editor, Robert F. Shugrue; music, Gary Chang; additional music, Michael Kamen; production design, Ken Adam; art direction, Richard Hudolin, Alan Manzer; set decoration, Art Parker; costume design, Jodie Tillen; sound (Dolby), Claude Hazanavicious, Charles Wilborn; assistant director, James R. Dyer; production manager, Grace Gilroy. Reviewed at Mann's Chinese theater, Hollywood, March 24, 1989. MPAA Rating: R. Running time: 105 MIN.

Jerry Beck	Don Johnson
Linda	Penelope Ann Miller
Arthur Kressler	William Forsythe
Elliot Webly	Bob Balaban
Bobby Burns	Frank Military
John Burns	Tate Donovan
Chief Dixon	Tim Reid

■Though there's little to suggest it in "Dead-Bang's" off-hand title and marketing, there's actually a pretty good film here, enriched by John Frankenheimer's potent imagination and rich character work.

Don Johnson clicks as an obsessed L.A. detective on a cop-killer's trail; he may be on the trail of a string of similar roles, likely to be big crowdpleasers.

Johnson plays a lonely, frustrated cop separated from his kids by a hostile ex-wife, and enduring the cheap, sad reality of a grungy apartment assaulted by the noise of the Burbank airport. On the brink of losing it, he dives into a homicide case that leads to a cross-country crime trail and a national conspiracy of zealous white supremacists.

A charismatic young ex-con, Bobby Burns (Frank Military) with a Manson-like hold on his biker disciples has a little problem — he doesn't like anyone whose skin isn't white and he doesn't mind expressing his displeasure through bullets.

When a cop gets in his way after a convenience store slaying, Burns pumps a round of lead into his stomach — pissing Beck off enough to make him lay aside his nonexistent Christmas Eve plans and go after him.

Trail of crime leads to a small-town Oklahoma church that's h.q. for a web of Hitler-worshipping extremists plotting to change the U.S. Pic ends in about 20 minutes of gunfire in a grimy labyrinth of tunnels within the group's survival bunker.

Plot design is fairly standard and outcome predictable — save one small twist — but there's much to savor in Frankenheimer's rich treatment of Robert Foster's script. Frankenheimer enriches each scene and character with telling detail and a wily, sardonic sense of humor.

Key to Johnson's success here the way pic's gritty, unadorned realism strips away the gloss of his "Miami Vice" image — in this no-frills milieu, it's character, not surfaces, that emerges in sharp relief, and the role fits Johnson like a worn glove.

One of pic's best aspects is its humor — in a hilarious scene, hungover Beck becomes probably the first cop in movie history to get information from a suspect by threatening to puke on him — again.

Casting is also savvy — with nerdy Bob Balaban as Beck's fiercely reluctant accomplice and Woody Allen lookalike (well, not quite) Michael Jeter as a hostile, paranoid psychiatrist.

Yet casting the instantly likable Tim Reid as the black cop who helps Johnson close in on the zealots seems too calculated to win sympathy in a plot where the villains already are a bit cartoonish.

Penelope Ann Miller as Beck's Christmas Eve roll-in-the-hay is a welcome presence with her wide-open, wheat-field fresh face, but her brief role — never returned to — amounts to a puzzling glitch in the script. Viewer is as unsettled as Beck when he learns her relationship to the freshly deceased cop — she was his wife.

Flaws aside, pic has the ripe texture and pace of a great pulp novel. Story came from veteran L.A. sheriff's detective Jerry Beck, who served as technical adviser. If he has more stories to tell, it's a good bet Johnson will star in them.
—*Daws.*

Confession: A Chronicle Of Alienation
(SOVIET-DOCU-COLOR/B&W)

San Francisco   A Mosfilm/VGIF/Goskino production. Directed by Georgi Gavrilov. Written by Gavrilov, Yu Kotliar; camera (color, b&w), A. Koulik, G. Larine; editor, I. Tsekavaia, V. Nekiforova. Reviewed at the San Francisco Film Festival, March 11, 1989. Running time: **90 MIN.**

■ Since the Soviet government heretofore has not been anxious to discuss the country's drug problems, "Confession: A Chronicle Of Alienation" tears away some of the veil with an intense portrait of a Moscow heroin addict.

The portrait will seem familiar, almost tiresomely so, to those already acquainted with the ravages of drug abuse.

To whatever degree he shakes up Soviet complacency, of course, director Georgi Gavrilov certainly meets his duty as a documentarian. In any such effort, however, a filmmaker always skirts dangerously close to exploitation. Are we looking for answers here or just gasping at another well-photographed freak show?

No doubt, the long-term answers to the alcohol and drug problems are as elusive in the USSR as they are in this country and many others. No one can be immune to the human suffering involved in any language.

That said, however, "Confession" remains another 90 minutes with junkies who show no real desire to come to grips with their problems. If nothing else, the film demonstrates that the underlying characteristics of addicts don't vary much universally.

The 23-year-old, long-haired rebel examined here could qualify for a flophouse in any tenderloin district anywhere. Mad at the world, down on himself, cynical and distrustful, he has opted for "out" and whatever it takes to get there. The same goes for his girl-

friend and others around him.

As a filmmaker, Gavrilov gets in admiringly close on his subject, following the lad through various shabby living quarters and into equally grim hospitals and recovery units. There, the Soviet authorities sometimes seem brutally unsympathetic toward the addict, but that's often true elsewhere.

Because it rings so real, "Confession" is a harsh film. Like most efforts of its kind, however, it's content to record the shock value and step aside. Fair enough, but that's of limited value. Thousands of similar films could be made about thousands of addicts who remain beyond reach.

When solutions are sorely needed, uncovering more of the same problem is no big deal, even if it's found in faraway places. —*Har.*

La nuit de l'éclusier
(The Night Of The Sluice Guard) (SWISS-W. GERMAN-FRENCH)

Zurich   An Odyssee Film Zurich release and coproduction with Bayerischer Rundfunk, Munich, Swiss TV DRS, Zurich, and Paris Classics Production, Paris. Written, produced and directed by Franz Rickenbach. Camera (color), Pio Corradi; editor, Elisabeth Waelchli, Jürgen Böttcher; music, Mario Beretta; sound, Jürg von Allmen, Florian Eidenbenz; assistant producer, Rolf Schleitzer; assistant director, Claudia Sontheim. Reviewed at Corso 3, Zurich, March 15, 1989. Running time: **93 MIN.**

With: Magali Noël, Michel Robin, Alain Cuny, Sigfrit Steiner, Mathias Gnädinger, Johanna Lier, Stéphanie Noël, Voli Geiler.

■ This is a curious, offbeat Swiss comedy-drama with a French flair, spoken in French with three excellent Gallic actors in the leads. Not easy to sell and with a weak title, poetic film has a feeling for cinematic expression.

Filmed in the town of Biel-Bienne, story concerns a middle-age, stolid official working for the city administration. Instead of a hoped-for promotion, he is merely set to take over the job of an old archivist who refuses to retire.

One night the building floods. It's actually an act of sabotage, presumably by the vindictive anarchist. Event sets off a complete change of mind in the younger official, whose long-slumbering frustrations come to light. His hour of truth comes when he folds, together with the archivist, hundreds of official forms ruined in the flood into little paper boats

and sets them on the river.

The title is insignificant and not very attractive. The film's qualities — not very commercial ones, to be sure — are its almost dreamlike atmosphere, a sort of wry poetic humor and its cast. Helmer Franz Rickenbach deserves credit for coaxing such name thesps as Magali Noël, and Alain Cuny to work in this modest-budgeted film. All three turn in excellent performances.

Especially noteworthy are Pio Corradi's striking atmospheric lensing and Mario Beretta's unobtrusive but affecting music. —*Mezo.*

A Sinful Life

Hollywood   A New Line Cinema release of an IRS World Media production. Produced by Daniel Raskov. Executive producers, Miles A. Copeland 3d, Paul Colichman. Directed by William Schreiner. Screenplay, Melanie Graham, based on her play "Just Like The Pom Pom Girls;" camera (Foto-Kem color, Metrocolor prints), Jonathan West; editor, Jeffrey Reiner; music, Todd Hayden; production design, Robert Zentis; costume design, Sylvia Moss; casting, Lynn Stalmaster, Debra Rubinstein. Reviewed at Filmcorp screening room, Culver City, Calif., March 16, 1989. MPAA Rating: R. Running time: **90 MIN.**

Claire	Anita Morris
Janitor	Rick Overton
Nathan Flowers	Dennis Christopher
Baby	Blair Tefkin
Teresa	Mark Rolston
Mrs. Crow	Cynthia Szigeti

■ "A Sinful Life" represents strike two for adaptations of The Groundlings productions to the screen, the other being Universal's "Casual Sex?" last summer.

William Schreiner's disastrous direction of Melanie Graham's legit work "Just Like The Pom Pom Girls" is duplicated here, which is to say "A Sinful Life" is a failed attempt at dark comedy.

Picture not only looks like it was lensed on a soundstage, it sounds like it also. For added authenticity, it appears as if production designer Robert Zentis and costume designer Sylvia Moss raided the prop department at the Groundling Theater for the walls, furnishings and doo-dads that clutter the living space of alcoholic floozy Claire (Anita Morris) and her squealing child Baby (played by adult actress and Groundling Blair Tefkin).

Because Morris is such an awful mother — so self-absorbed and usually blotto she can't remember her own daughter's birthday — the authorities (actually Tefkin's elementary school teacher acting

on behalf of them) threaten to yank the kid from her mom and place her in a foster home.

This sets Morris on a course to straighten up and fly right before Saturday when the corpulent teacher (Cynthia Szigeti) returns for the child.

Morris uses subterfuge to engage the neighbors' help in her self-improvement scam. Dressed most often in a drooping leopard-patterned negligee and see-through pink peignoir robe, she traps her janitor (Rick Overton) as a sex-starved slave and makes holy-roller Dennis Christopher, a Sears credit manager, her savior. She'll get one of them to marry her and act as frontman for domestic stability.

Add to these transvestite Teresa (Mark Rolston) and the cast of oddball characters is complete — without much interesting to do but act broadly in a seedy parlor room show that badly needs clowns for comic relief.

There are hints that Graham has an eye for the humorously absurd as little gems are to be found amid the many vulgar scenes.

When Morris manipulates her baby-talking third-grader into picking out a peach loveseat in the Sears catalog for her birthday that Morris herself wants, one senses there could have been a riotously funny setup here instead of another one that just falls flat.

The actors do all right, though even the talented Morris can't' overcome the material.

Tefkin is convincing in as much as she becomes so irritatingly pathetic. As well as she manages playing a doll-toting, 4-eyed geek, the actress surely is worthy of better parts.

Unhappy ending (unhappy because poor Baby gets stuck living with maudlin Claire) doesn't come soon enough. —*Brit.*

976-EVIL

Hollywood   A New Line Cinema release of a Cinetel Films presentation. Produced by Lisa M. Hansen. Executive producer, Paul Hertzberg. Directed by Robert Englund. Screenplay, Rhet Topham, Brian Helgeland; camera (Foto-Kem color), Paul Elliot; editor, Stephen Myers; music, Thomas Chase, Steve Rucker; art direction, David Brian Miller; set decoration, Nancy Booth; costume design, Elizabeth Gower-Gruzinski; sound (Ultra-Stereo), Beau Franklin; visual effects director, Bill Mesa; special effects makeup, Kevin Yagher; assistant director, R.B. Graham; second unit camera, Greg Gardiner. Reviewed on vidcassette, L.A., March 25, 1989. MPAA Rating R. Running time: **93 MIN.**

Hoax	Stephen Geoffreys
Aunt Lucy	Sandy Dennis

Spike	Patrick O'Bryan
Marty	Jim Metzler
Angella	Maria Rubell
Suzie	Lezlie Deane
Rags	Jim Thiebaud
Airhead	Gunther Jensen
Jeff	Darren Burrows
Mark Dark	Robert Picardo

■ On the basis of "976-EVIL," Robert (Freddy Krueger) Englund had best stick to acting for the foreseeable future, since his directorial debut here is more likely to bore than scare viewers to death.

Catchy title and Englund's name indicate a measure of business for this New Line release from Cinetel, but watching this wrong number is no more pleasurable than listening to a busy signal for an hour and a half.

Almost nothing of any importance happens during the first interminable hour. Undersized teenager Stephen Geoffreys lives with his religious zealot of a mother (Sandy Dennis) while his chopper-riding cousin (Patrick O'Bryan) holes up next door.

Dennis is thrown into a tizzy when some fish come raining down from the sky one night, while Geoffreys spends most of his time either getting roughed up by some local punks or imitating his cousin by calling the eponymous phone number to hear his "horrorscope."

At long last, special effects makeup artist Kevin Yagher is given something to do, as little Stephen begins transforming into the Devil and proceeds to claw to shreds everyone who's ever given him a hard time. Effects are bloody, but hardly enough to make gore fans raise an eyebrow.

Too long by at least 20 minutes, pic is mostly devoted to meaningless chatter and lame attempts to concoct a sinister atmosphere by placing the action at night, laying on threatening music, and using as settings a horror film grind house and a cafe called Dante's. Call it "976-FEEBLE." —*Cart.*

Screwball Hotel
(U.S.-BRITISH)

New York A Universal Pictures release of a Maurice Smith production, in association with Avatar Film. Produced by Smith. Executive producers, Joe Garofolo, Robert Patterson, Jon Gansel Brewer. Directed by Rafal Zielinski. Screenplay, B.K. Roderick, Phil Kueber, Charles Wiener, Nick Holeris; additional material, Sam Kaufman; camera (Continental & Foto-Kem color), Thomas F. Denove; editor, Joseph Tornatore; music, Nathan Wang; sound (Ultra-Stereo), Tom Colucci, Michael Eric Fowler; production design, Naomi Shohan; assistant director, James R. Van Voris; production manager, Gregory Cararito; associate producers, Terrea Smith, Debi Davis; casting, Dennis Gallegos. Reviewed on MCA vidcassette, N.Y., March 22, 1989. MPAA Rating: R. Running time: 101 MIN.

Mike	Michael C. Bendetti
Herbie	Andrew Zeller
Norman	Jeff Greenman
Mr. Ebbel	Kelly Monteith
Cherry Amour	Corinne Alphen
Stoner	Charles Ballinger
Miss Walsh	Laurah Guillen
Candy	Lori Deann Pallet

Also with: Theresa Bell, Jack L. Dillard, Tina Bayne, Richard Norton, Gianna Amore, Laura Lewis, Reneé Shugart, Andi Bruce.

■ "Screwball Hotel" is a painless but overly familiar sex comedy. Universal briefly released it last December in Florida (where pic was lensed), with ancillary markets likely to provide effective returns commencing with May vid release.

Well-worn formula, familiar from endless Cannon releases, has three young guys on the loose amidst beautiful women in an idyllic resort setting. Jeff Greenman plays the stereotypical fat boy, kicked out of a Massachusetts military school with mates Michael C. Bendetti and Andrew Zeller.

Trio heads to Florida to work at the Rochester Hotel whose staff has quit over back pay. They unite with pretty staffer Lori Deann Pallet to try and save the hotel from corrupt schemer Charles Ballinger by organizing weird fundraising efforts, including illegal casino gambling and an oil wrestling contest.

Loosely directed by Rafal Zielinski, whose "Screwballs" is a forerunner in the same genre, pic features relatively little nudity but plenty of tease. Former Penthouse models Corinne Alphen (a vet of the similar "Spring Break" feature), Lori Deann Pallet and Andi Bruce add to the pulchritude, with fellow looker Laurah Guillen also handling okay slapstick comedy bits.

With British backing from London-based Avatar, pic seems tailored for the U.K. market and has popular Yank-in-Blighty comedian Kelly Monteith prominently featured. He does tv-type skits, dressing up as Indiana Jones or Bogey in "Casablanca," as part of his varied sex games with Guillen.

Problem is that script (credited to five writers) isn't very funny, especially the old-fashioned spoofing of drugs and silly satire of prudish, hypocritical televangelists (much better handled in U's recent "Fletch Lives" release). Tech credits are fine and pic boasts a bouncy out-theme sung by Fire On Blonde. —*Lor.*

Union sacrée
(Holy Alliance)
(FRENCH)

Paris A Films Number One (U.S. rights, Nelson Entertainment Intl.) release of an Alexandre Films/SGGC/FR3 Films coproduction. Executive producer, Alexandre Films. Produced by Robert Benmussa, associate producer, Jean-Bernard Fetoux. Directed by Alexandre Arcady. Screenplay, Daniel Saint-Hamont, Arcady, Pierre Aknine; camera (Eastmancolor), Robert Alazraki; editor, Joëlle van Effenterre; music, Jean-Jacques Goldman, Roland Romanelli; art direction, Gérard Daoudal; sound, Alain Sempé, Jean Paul Loublier; production manager, Philippe Lièvre. Reviewed at Club Gaumont Matignon, Paris, March 2, 1989. Running time: 125 MIN.

Karim Hamida	Richard Berry
Simon Atlan	Patrick Bruel
Radjani	Said Amadis
Lisa	Corinne Dacla
Joulin	Bruno Cremer
Revers	Claude Brasseur
Blanche Atlan	Marthe Villalonga
Dealer	Hammou Graia
Kabyle racketeer	Amidou

■ "Holy Alliance" is a long and unlikely thriller in which a Jewish cop and an Arab undercover agent overcome ethnic animosities to fight Islamic terrorism.

Algerian-born Alexandre Arcady has paved his screenplay with good intentions but not enough story sense or sustained tension.

Nelson Entertainment Intl. bought up worldwide all-media rights for the film last September as pic went into production. It certainly has gained topicality, though current nervousness about Islamic fundamentalist threats could work against the pic, which lacks star force for off-shore play.

Patrick Bruel is a young impetuous *flic* in the French anti-drug brigade who finds himself paired with French Arab government man Richard Berry to bust a drug operation peddling pure heroin to high school kids.

They make an odd law enforcement couple, but momentarily bury the hatchet when they get on the track of a fanatical terrorist who poses as an embassy attaché and director of an Islamic cultural center, which is a front for a terrorist training ground.

Bruel and Berry infiltrate the center and just barely get away with their lives. Their antagonist, Said Amadis, swears vengeance for the death of his associate, and pursues the pair with deadly perseverance.

Arcady and his longtime script collaborator Daniel Saint-Hamont don't shy away from overt references to real terrorist horror. A climactic scene, marred by Arcady's affection for slow-motion effects, involves a terrorist machine gun attack on a delicatessen run by Bruel's family. The sequence was shot at the famous Goldenberg's Parisian deli which was victimized by a similar assault.

Overexplicit script makes a sentimental plea for Jewish-Arab brotherhood and sees to it that there's no ambiguity about Arcady-Saint Hamont's stand on religion. Berry is, despite his metier, an observant Muslim who also has a sense of conventional morality; he backs away from romancing Bruel's estranged gentile wife (Corinne Dacla), whom the Jewish cop still loves deeply.

The unmistakeable evil is intolerance as personified by Amadis' rabid fundamentalist, who seems to be heading a 1-man war on the wicked West.

Arcady's direction is effectively streamlined when he's not delivering messages on brotherhood or playing the tear ducts. He handles the Berry-Bruel rapport with a fair dose of humor and good sense of contrast, exploiting Bruel's kinetic energy and Berry's big brother restraint.

Supporting cast, including Bruno Cremer as Bruel's boss and Claude Brasseur in a cameo as a military intelligence chief, is sound, Marthe Villalonga, an Arcady faithful, gives her 4-matzohball performance as Bruel's mom.

Jean-Jacques Goldman's English-lingo theme song obviously targets the international record charts. —*Len.*

Grandmother's House

New York An Omega Pictures presentation of a Nico Mastorakis production. Produced by Mastorakis. Executive producers, Peter Rader, Peter Jensen. Directed by Rader. Screenplay, Jensen, from story by Gayle Jensen, Peter Jensen; camera (CFI color, Technicolor prints), Peter Jensen; editor, Barry Zetlin; music, Nigel Holton. Clive Wright; sound (Ultra-Stereo), George Mahlberg; art direction, Steven Michael Casey; set decoration, Janet Laick; assistant director, Perry Husman, production manager, Shelley Mills; associate producers, Husman, Aladdin Pojhan; casting, Jon Samsel. Reviewed on Academy Entertainment vidcassette, N.Y., March 19, 1989. MPAA Rating: R. Running time: 89 MIN.

David	Eric Foster
Lynn	Kim Valentine
Woman	Brinke Stevens
Grandmother	Ida Lee
Grandfather	Len Lesser

Also with: David Donham, Michael Robinson, Craig Yerman, Joan-Carol Bensen, Angela O'Neill, R. J. Walker, Furley Lumpkin.

■ "Grandmother's House" (alternately "Grandma's House") is a clever nailbiter, providing suspenseful variations on gothic thriller themes. Pic should get a good reaction in the video rental market, bypassing theatrical release.

When attractive youngsters Eric Foster and Kim Valentine go to live with their grandparents following their dad's funeral, Foster immediately becomes suspicious of the old folks' behavior.

He's soon convinced that kindly looking Ida Lee and Len Lesser are murderous crazies preying on passers-by. Cinematographer Peter Jensen's script takes an excellent turn midway when Foster frees a mystery woman (Brinke Stevens) seemingly held in bondage by his grandfolks and she immediately tries to kill him. She turns out to be the kids' long-gone mom (they thought she was dead) whom grandfolks were hiding.

Hectic final reel is loaded with switcheroos, including a surprise incest subplot and morbid final twist. Tightly directed by Peter Rader, pic definitely will keep the viewer guessing.

Both Foster and Nastassja Kinski-esque Valentine score in the lead roles, while Len Lesser is properly ambiguous as granddad. Usually a decorative beauty, Brinke Stevens is scary in the character role of mom.—*Lor.*

So Howato
(So What)
(JAPANESE)

San Francisco   A CCJ production. Produced by Shuhei Nozu. Directed by Naoto Yamakawa. Screenplay, Yasushi Hirano, Toshiyuki Mizutani, Yamakawa, based on comic book by Katsuhiro Ohtomo; camera (color), Noboru Shinoda; editor, Kan Suzuki; music, Yasuhiko Terajima; sound, Yutaka Tsurumaki; art direction, Terumi Hosoishi; assistant director, Yoshiko Fukuoka; coproducers, Akira Morishige, Hiromichi Tanaka, Hirohiko Sueyoshi, Tadaaki Motomura. Reviewed at the San Francisco Film Festival, March 12, 1989. Running time: **90 MIN.**

With: Kazuki Minibuchi, Mikihisa Azu-Taiji Yano, Shinya Kawagishi, Reiko Yasuhara, Yumeko Kitaoka, Shigeru Moroi, Masayuki Shionoya, Naoto Takenaka, Rokko Toura, Kouen Okumura, Akiyuki Ohba, Lisa Honda, Sho Ryuzanji, Hakuseki Shin, Koji Yamaguchi, Osamu Yagihashi.

■ There's a major difference between American teenage rock & roll films and Japanese teenage rock & roll films like "So What?" In Japan, the adults win.

It may or may not be a compliment to describe young (22) director Naoto Yamakawa as a Japanese John Hughes, but he's assuredly close to his generation and those right behind.

Like the teens the world over, Japanese youngsters are often insecure, uncertain and frustrated. In the rigid, academically disciplined society they live in, there's not much room for rebellion.

Only a generation or two removed from peasantry, the rural high-school seniors of "So What" appreciate parental and school pressure to knuckle down and pass the college-entrance exams that will set them on an approved career path. The life of a rock star seems ever so much more appealing.

Typical of Yamakawa's neat satirical touches, the film opens with four boys tuning their instruments intently. Just as they strike the first heavy chords, what seems to be a spotlight falls upon them — illuminating their talent for the crowd that must be waiting. It's only granddad opening the barn door to let the cow back in.

Though the boys would all like to be professional musicians, they are equally intimidated by the dismal job prospects if they allow themselves to become too distracted and fail to advance academically. Even more discouraging, their peers often regard them more as a distraction to their own studies than teen idols.

Determined to have at least one moment on stage, the group promotes a concert and this time, there really is an anxious crowd awaiting. Unfortunately, just as they hit the first harmony again, members of the Board of Education pull the plug on the concert.

If this were the U.S., there might have been a riot under the circumstances. If this were a U.S. film, there would have at least been a food fight. Alas, the kids here retreat meekly and it's obvious the boys' "Rolling Rock" band is destined for yearbook memories and nothing more. Yamakawa bids farewell with a nice scene of them playing alone at night to an empty parking lot.

Unfortunately, the director adds a footnote about the leader of the band leaving friends and family behind to take a train toward an uncertain future, a corny bit that over-punctuates the points Yamakawa has already made. It's a youthful excess that doesn't detract from the fact that Japan now has another major new director to keep an eye on. —*Har.*

Isolde
(DANISH)

Copenhagen   A Camera Film release of Nordisk Film production, in association with the Danish Film Institute and DR/TV. Produced by Christian Braad Thomsen. Directed by Jytte Rex. Screenplay, Rex, Christian Braad Thomsen, Henrik Jul Hansen; camera (Eastmancolor), Manuel Sellner; editor, Grete Möldrup; music, quotes from Vivaldi, Bach, Brian Eno, others; production design, Tove Robert Rasmussen; costumes, Ole Gläsner; sound, Morten Degnböl, Lars Lund; assistant director, Annemarie Aaes; production management, Sanne Arnt Torp, Per Arman; Danish Film Institute consultant producer, Kirsten Bonnén Rask. Reviewed at the Grand, Copenhagen, March 15, 1989. Running time: **96 MIN.**

Isolde	Pia With
The Warrior	Kim Jansson
The Husband	Claus Flygare

Aso with: Kirsten Bröndum, Bodil Lassen, Britta Lillesöe, Claus Nissen, Peter Boesen, Aase Hansen, Thomas Mörk, Anne Wedege, Carsten Bang, Preben Lerdorff Rye, Tove Maes, Gerda Gilboe, Christine Crone.

■ Young love, doomed by being pitted against the dark forces of whatever current power establishment, is given a contemporary whirl by Denmark's Jytte Rex in a neatly controlled mixture of mainstream action and metaphysical depth-probings. Audiences are likely to be found mainly on the minor fest circuit.

Rex' protagonists are a young librarian (darkly handsome and brightly intelligent looking Pia Vieth as Isolde), her ex-husband and her new lover. The ex is a politician, mentally locked in power manipulations, the lover is a mercenary soldier wanted for murder in Marseilles. He is also a gentle lover, but the politician blackmails him into committing one more murder.

The suspense element is rudimentary at best. What really has the interest of helmer Rex is her cinematic sliding back and forth between dream and reality.

"Isolde" abounds with literary illusions and cinematographer Manuel Sellner works congenially with the helmer in setting up montage shots and other technical fireworks that call to mind vintage Alain Resnais.

With nothing new to say neither in psychology nor in visual artistry, "Isolde" stays mired from beginning to end in old-hat modernist posturing. Still, the entire production looks stunning enough to merit whatever Prix Technique kudos that may well come its way.

While Pia With obviously has talent to go with her beauty, Kim Jansson as The Warrior succeeds impressively in giving quiet life and mute hurt to his stony-faced Action Man stereotype. —*Kell.*

BERLIN FEST REVIEWS

Erebos
(WEST GERMAN)

Berlin   A Von Vietinghoff Filmproduktion production. Directed by Nicos Ligouris. Screenplay, Ligouris, Claus Wilbrandt; camera (color), Sabri Ozaydin; editor, Galip Iyanier; music, Nicoss Drelas; sound, Horst Zinsmeister; set decoration, Barbara Golombek, Gonda Hinrichs, Maria Dimler; makeup, Eberhard Neufink; production manager, Gilbert Funke. Reviewed at the Berlin Film Festival (New German Films), Feb. 17, 1989. Running time: **89 MIN.**

Manos	Dimitri Poulikakos
Maria	Chrissoula Diaavati
Xeni	Pia Podgornik
Jurgen	Bernd Vollbrecht
Andromache	Dora Volanaki

Also with: Orhan Guner, Rosemarie Fendel, Christiane Maybach.

■ In "Erebos," a greek tailor makes his family labor away at his tailoring & dry cleaning business so that he can stow away money to realize his dream of opening a tourist resort in Crete. Travel beyond special venues seems unlikely.

Foreigners living in Berlin make for a timely subject, especially after the recent election, which saw the emergence of a party that has voiced strong anti-foreigner sentiments. It is this aspect of the film that makes it of more than passing interest.

The daughter becomes involved with a German taxi driver and tries to sabotage her father's plans. Feeling betrayed, the father makes a hasty deal with another foreign national to sell his business. Just as the family is all packed, a call comes from the airport; the tailor's mother has sold the family property in Greece and has arrived in Berlin.

There's nice camerawork, which opens up an essentially 1-set film, and decent performances, but pic is ultimately unsatisfying.

In Greek mythology the word "erebos" means the place of deepest darkness in the underworld, and also the abyss of the human soul. —*Owl.*

Oh Babylon
(GREEK)

Berlin A George Zervoulakos production through Andromada 2 Ltd., in association with Greek Film Center. Written and directed by Costas Ferris, based on Euripides' play "The Bacchae." Camera (color) Takis Zervoulakos; editor, Ferris; music, Thesia Panagiotou; costume design, Paul Kyriakides; set decoration, Taesos Zografos. Reviewed at Berlin Film Festival (market), Feb. 18, 1989. Running time: **90 MIN.**

Pentheus . . . . Alkis Panayiotidis
Agave . . . . Sotiria Leonardou
Cadmus . . . . George Moschidia
 Also with: Elena Mirchofska, Konstandinos, Palietearas, Maxi Priest.

■ **"Oh Babylon" is best described as an inventive visual exercise. The plot, based on Euripides' play "The Bacchae" is muddled and the total affect is a hodgepodge of ideas and influences that do not mesh into one cohesive whole.**

Pentheus, the ethical king of Thebes who resisted the worship of Dionysus, has been transformed into a stuffy intellectual in this version. He labors over the book he is trying to write while the "grown-ups" are engaged in bacchanalian pleasures upstairs. His grandfather Cadmus, the former king and mom Ageve pop in now and then to mock him for his uptight attitude.

Pentheus pads about in pajamas while struggling to preserve his virtue and virginity. The commendable camerawork of Takis Zervoulakos adeptly takes in Salvador Dali-inspired landscapes and surrealistic vignettes in the villa. The compelling score is highlighted by interludes with Rastafarians led by singer Maxi Priest, providing a rousing if incongruous diversion.

Attempts by a schizophrenic nymphette and her nubile companions to seduce Pentheus never get beyond the titillation stage. Pentheus' continually dour expression, even at his surprise birthday party, may be due to anxiety over an impending deadline.

"Oh Babylon" presents a case for subtitling as the dubbing, in proper British English, does not suit the cast nor the scenario.
—*Sam.*

Schön War Die Zeit
(The Good Old Days)
(WEST GERMAN)

Berlin A Westallgäuer Filmproduktion prod., with Maran Filmproduktion and B.A.-Filmproduktion. Executive producer, George Viet. Directed by Klaus Gietinger,

Leo Hiemer. Screenplay, Gietinger, with Marian Czura, Hiemer; camera (color), Czura; editor, Ilona Bruver; music, Klaus Roggors; sound, Kurt Eggmann; art direction, Anna Prankl; costumes, Beate Bonk. Reviewed at Berlin Film Festival (Market), Feb. 11, 1989. Running time: **109 MIN.**

Franz Bauer . . . . Gottfried John
Helmut Hartmeyer . . . . Edgar Selge
Eva Kramer . . . . Ewa Blaszczyk
Otto Brettschneider . . . . . Jochim Bernhard
Anna Waschmitzius . . . . . . Jessica Kosmala
Schnufel . . . . Dietmar Mössmer
Müller . . . . Ottfried Fischer
Jockel . . . . Jockel Thiersch

■ **This pic attempts to tell the story of the German film industry's revival after World War II. Beautifully photographed and well conceived, some judicious editing might give this overlong pic legs outside of German-speaking territories.**

Pic tells two parallel stories. A popular pre-war director and his cameraman have buried their camera equipment in the hopes that after the war they can resume their careers. Less idealistic than his cameraman the director is willing to go along with the public taste for frivolous films that do not confront issues.

The cameraman has written a script that does attempt to come to terms with the war but though the studio boss thinks its a terrific idea he tells him there's no chance of it being produced. The two friends finally come to a parting of the ways over their love for the same woman (the production manager).

In the other tale, a young soldier has returned to his little town where he had been the projectionist in the local cinema. He goes back to work while Moroccan soldiers, part of the French occupying forces, are causing local tensions. He gets his old job back, but as the occupying army leaves many of the village's residents are quietly reverting to their old Nazi ways.

Period re-creations are fairly successful and the color photography is outstanding. —*Owl.*

My Name Is Bertolt Brecht -Exile in U.S.A.
(WEST GERMAN-COLOR/B&W)

Berlin Produced by Norman Bunge. Written and directed by Bunge, Christine Fischer-Defoy. Camera (Eastmancolor), Bunge; editor, Ron Orders, Arpad Bondy; music, Hanna Eisler; sound, Caroline Goldie; production manager, Wolfgang Pfeiffer; narrator, Otto Sander. Reviewed at Berlin Film Festival (New German Films), Feb. 20, 1989. Running time: **95 MIN.**

With: Gene Fowler, Anna Lee, Hans and Salka Viertel, Ricky Pecker, Hans Sahl, Hilda Waldo, Mordecai Bauman, Naomi Raplan-

sky, Ron Sossi, Frank Concon, Morton Wurtele, Francs Heflin, David Clarke, Ring Lardner Jr.

■ **This docu provides insight into the relatively unknown exile of Bertolt Brecht in the U.S. from 1941-47. Confirmed Brechtians will be enthralled and it should find a niche at Fests, in educational tv and institutional screenings.**

The well-researched docu uses Brecht's diary, letters and writing to convey his reflections during the period he lived as a refugee from Nazi Germany in the U.S. Other insights into his character are revealed through interviews with colleagues and friends from those years.

Brecht became discouraged when his idealistic expectations of life in the U.S. were not fulfilled. His disillusionment peaked when he was summoned to appear at the HUAC hearings in 1947.

Footage from the hearings of Ring Lardner Jr. and others of the "Hollywood Ten" enliven the verbal recollections. As an alien, Brecht was placed in a precarious position when he came to the stand. For this reason, he answered in the negative when asked if he had ever been or now was a member of the Communist Party, instead of refusing to answer. Because of his status, the other defendants accepted his action.

Brecht returned to Germany via Switzerland the day after testifying. Archival clips from "Galileo Galilei" written in collaboration with and starring Charles Laughton prove that Brecht was still productive under adverse conditions during his exile. They also illustrate the point stressed by several of the directors: Brecht was so far ahead of his time even today he is considered daringly "avant-garde." —*Sam.*

The Dream Team

Hollywood A Universal release of an Imagine Entertainment presentation of a Christopher W. Knight production. Produced by Knight. Executive producer, Joseph M. Caracciolo. Supervising producer, Terry Spazek. Directed by Howard Zieff. Screenplay-coproducers, Jon Connolly, David Loucka; camera (Deluxe color), Adam Holender; editor, C. Timothy O'Meara; music, David McHugh; production design, Todd Hallowell; art direction, Christopher Nowak (U.S.), Greg Keem (Toronto); set decoration, John Alan Hicks (U.S.), Mike Harris, Robert James, Jaro Dick, Elena Kenney, Dan Conley (Toronto); costume design, Ruth Morley; sound (Dolby), Gary Parker (U.S.), Bruce Carwardine, Glenn Gauthier (Toronto); associate producer, Michael Sheehy; assistant director, Joe Napolitano; casting, Ilene Starger. Reviewed at Avco Cinema, L.A., March 30, 1989. MPAA Rating: PG-13. Running time: **113 MIN.**

Billy Caulfield . . . . Michael Keaton
Henry Sikorsky . . . . Christopher Lloyd
Jack McDermott . . . . Peter Boyle
Albert Ianuzzi . . . . Stephen Furst
Dr. Weitzman . . . . Dennis Boutsikaris
Riley . . . . Lorraine Bracco
Dr. Newald . . . . Milo O'Shea
O'Malley . . . . Philip Bosco
Gianelli . . . . James Remar
Dr. Talmer . . . . Jack Gilpin
Dr. Verboven . . . . Macintyre Dixon
Ed . . . . Michael Lembeck

■ **"The Dream Team" is a hokey comedy that basically reduces mental illness to a grab bag of quirky schtick. Yet with a quartet of gifted comic actors having a field day playing loonies on the loose in Manhattan, much of that schtick is awfully funny, so Universal looks to have a springtime winner on its hands.**

While still incarcerated in a New Jersey psychiatric hospital, volatile patient Michael Keaton proclaims, "It's great to be young and insane." This could just about serve as the overriding motto of the picture — during the course of which the four stooges wreak havoc on New York's medical and religious communities, exact revenge on assorted big city bullies, triumph over some corrupt cops and achieve improved prognoses and a measure of self-respect in the bargain.

Premise serves as an illustrative example of liberal teaching methods gone awry. In an attempt to give his patients a taste of the real world, hospital doctor Dennis Boutsikaris decides to treat four of his charges to a day game at Yankee Stadium.

Going along for the ride are the certified oddballs: Keaton, who seems to have his wits about him but periodically displays extreme delusions of grandeur, as well as a mean violent streak; Christopher Lloyd, a prissy fuss-budget who enjoys posing as a member of the hospital staff; Peter Boyle, a man with a heavy Jesus complex given to undressing at moments of intense spirituality, and Stephen Furst, an uncommunicative simpleton who speaks mainly in baseball jargon.

As soon as they hit the Big Apple, however, the good doctor is seriously injured after witnessing a killing, and the boys are left to their own devices. One by one, they scatter: Keaton to look up his old girlfriend Lorraine Bracco, Lloyd to compulsively pick up every scrap of litter in the city, and Boyle, in a riotous scene, to enact his unsolicited striptease while witnessing at a black revival meeting.

Furst just sits tight, and the foursome finally reunites to try to locate Boutsikaris, who is now targeted by the murderers — who happen to be cops. As an aggressive antisocial type, Keaton proves particularly adept at working the streets until they all land, first, on the tv news and, second, in jail. Further unexpected smarts produce an escape and an ultimate victory over all baddies on the horizon.

The way in which the mentally handicapped characters are used in essentially artificial situations for comic reasons is occasionally off-putting and unsettling. The overall thrust, which has the patients representing eternal underdogs and have-nots who must outwit those in power to survive, will be enormously appealing to audiences.

The many scenes of confrontation that go the boys' way possess a frequently convulsive impact, and if one can accept this at its own level of burlesque with a screw loose, the laughs fly freely.

As the one closest to normalcy, Keaton must hold the group together, and relishes the opportunities to display his dangerous side. Bracco's continued interest in this ne'er-do-well is hard to take, and the actress' role never blossoms beyond being a plot device.

Keaton is at his manic best, Christopher Lloyd prompts numerous guffaws with his impersonation of a self-serious tidiness freak, and Stephen Furst quietly impresses as the sickest and most helpless of the lot.

Given the impressive company, it is even more impressive how Peter Boyle manages to steal the picture. One never knows what this king-sized religious fanatic might do, and his outbursts upon deciding whether to bless someone or

play a very dirty trick are often uproarious. Boyle's work here is the definition of a career revivifier.

Howard Zieff's direction of the lively Jon Connolly-David Loucka script is straightforward, and tightening by a few minutes might have helped. Although Gotham locations were employed, Toronto was the main base of shooting and served adequately. David McHugh's score is varied and helpful.
—*Cart.*

Dead Calm
(AUSTRALIAN)

Sydney   A Warner Bros. release (Roadshow in Australia) of a Kennedy Miller production. Produced by Terry Hayes, Doug Mitchell, George Miller. Directed by Phillip Noyce. Screenplay, Hayes, from the novel by Charles Williams; camera (Panavision, Eastmancolor), Dean Semler; editor, Richard Francis-Bruce; music, Graeme Revill; production design, Graham (Grace) Walker; sound, Ben Osmo, sound design, Lee Smith; 2d unit directors, George Miller, Vincent Monton; assistant directors, Colin Fletcher, Tony Wellington; production managers, Narelle Barsby, Barbara Gibbs; casting, Liz Mullinar, Wally Nicita. Reviewed at Film Australia screening room, Sydney, March 2, 1989. MPAA Rating: R. Running time: **96 MIN.**
John Ingram . . . . Sam Neill
Rae Ingram . . . . Nicole Kidman
Hughie . . . . Billy Zane

■**Though not always entirely credible, "Dead Calm" is a nail-biting suspense pic, handsomely produced and inventively directed. It has all the elements to be a solid b.o. success, packing enough of a wallop to ensure enthusiastic word of mouth.**

It's basically a 3-hander: a happily married couple John and Rae Ingram, (Sam Neill and Nicole Kidman), have found peace alone on the Pacific on their well-equipped yacht after the trauma of the death of their baby son in a car accident when they're threatened by a vicious, unstable young killer, Hughie (Billy Zane).

They come to Hughie's aid initially, when he seeks help, but Ingram doesn't believe his story that the passengers and crew on the decrepit yacht he's abandoned all died from food poisoning. Leaving Hughie asleep, Ingram goes across to the delapidated vessel to discover dead bodies in the bilges and a video tape indicating that a deranged Hughie killed them.

While he's away, Hughie awakens, overpowers Rae, and sets sail in the opposite direction, abandoning Ingram. Rest of the film intercuts between Ingram trying to get the old boat restarted, then struggling to survive as he's trapped below decks in the sinking

vessel; and Rae trying to find a way to return to find her husband, while reluctant, at first, to use physical violence against the brutal Hughie.

In one of the film's powerful scenes, Rae even submits to Hughie's lovemaking: it's not exactly rape, but the horror of the woman's situation is unflinchingly presented. In this scene, and throughout the film, Nicole Kidman is excellent. This is the role this talented young actress has been waiting for, and it will bring her international attention. She gives the character of Rae real tenacity and energy.

Sam Neill is good, too, as the husband who spends most of the film unable to contact his wife, and Yank newcomer Billy Zane is suitably manic and evil as the deranged Hughie.

An opening sequence, set in Sydney, and depicting the accident that killed the couple's child, looks a bit like an afterthought, but gets the film off to a strong start. Similarly, the final sequence, in which the hateful Hughie returns unexpectedly for one final attack on Rae, smacks a bit of overkill but will probably have audiences cheering when he finally gets his comeuppance.

Coproducer Terry Hayes has fashioned a lean screenplay based on the Charles Williams novel which was the basis for the never-completed Orson Welles film "The Deep" (which was filmed off the coast of Yugoslavia between 1967 and 1969, with Welles, Jeanne Moreau and Laurence Harvey in the principal roles.).

Director Phillip Noyce has done a great job maintaining the suspense with only three actors, two boats, a dog and an ocean at his disposal.

He fits well into the Kennedy Miller house style (KM produced the "Mad Max" movies, and their director, George Miller, was coproducer and 2d unit director on this one).

"Dead Calm" is handsomely produced, with top camerawork by Dean Semler, tight editing by Richard Francis-Bruce, a great soundtrack and an inventive music score by first-timer Graeme Revell. Use of choral motifs for this kind of thriller is a bit unusual, but it works.

Occasional over-the-top moments, such as Rae atop the yacht's highest mast as she searches for her missing spouse in

the dusk, may cause a snicker, but overall "Dead Calm" should generate enough visceral excitement to keep audiences around the world in a state of suspense.
—*Strat.*

Hei Tai Yang 731
(Black Sun 731)
(HONG KONG)

New York   A Grand Essex Enterprises release of a Sil-Metropole Organisation presentation. Executive producer, Chu Hung. Produced by Fu Chi. Directed by T. F. Mous. Screenplay, Mou Wen Yuan, Teng Dun Jing. Liu Mei Fei; in color. No other credits provided. Reviewed at Essex theater, N.Y., April 1, 1989. (Also in Berlin Film Festival — Panorama.) No MPAA Rating. Running time: **103 MIN.**
With: Wang Gang, Mei Zhao Hua, Jin Tie Long, Quan Zhe, Wu Dai Yao, Wang Run Shen, Tian Jie Fu, Li Bo Lin, Chen Jian Xin, Min Chiang.

(Japanese soundtrack)

■**Exposé pic "Black Sun 731" (a.k.a. "Men Behind The Sun") is a lowbrow exploitationer treating a serious subject, Japanese war atrocities. Though screened in the Panorama section of this year's Berlin film fest, pic's main audience is devotees of the "Ilsa, She Wolf Of The SS" school of shlock.**

Filmed in China with a mainly Chinese cast dubbed into Japanese, pic is heavy on the gore in limning sadistic Lt. Col. Ishii who leads a corps in experimenting on Chinese (and a few Russian) prisoners in Manchuko early in 1945. Bacteriological warfare, including raising billions of fleas carrying an intensified strain of bubonic plague, is pegged to turnaround Japan's failing war effort.

Explosive material is dramatically potent and could have been handled tastefully, as with Kon Ichikawa's classic films like "Fires On The Plain." However, helmer T. F. Mous resorts to nauseating sensationalism, with butcher-shop depiction of autopsies on live subjects, a disgusting "decompression" experiment spewing intestines out of a victim and a horrendously realistic scene of a pussycat bloodily mauled by a room full of rats.

Yucky content is matched with sickly sentimentality, as the adults' mayhem is mirrored by a youth corps of adolescent soldiers who have been brutally trained to think of the Chinese not as humans but "maruta" (wooden logs). These kids befriending a mute Chinese boy is milked for bathos climaxing with the cute fellow delivered over as a live organ donor. Pic ends in heavyhanded fashion with the Japanese flag covered in blood as a Chinese prisoner is mowed down escaping during the Japanese retreat.

Postscript in credits states that these Japanese war criminals were not tried in exchange for giving their research material to the American Occupation force and that bacteriological warfare subsequently was used in the Korean War (presumably by both sides). That accusation might make for a dramatized, hardhitting film (à la "The Wannsee Conference"), but there's no easy gore and titillation for filmmakers like Mous & company to be found in such a tale of behind-closed-doors command decisions. —*Lor.*

Cyborg

Hollywood   A Cannon Entertainment release of a Golan-Globus production. Produced by Menahem Golan, Yoram Globus; line producer, Tom Karnowski. Directed by Albert Pyun. Screenplay, Kitty Chalmers; camera (TVC color), Philip Alan Waters; additional photography, Phillip Dillon; editor, Rozanne Zingale, Scott Stevenson; music, Kevin Bassinson; production design, Douglas Leonard; set decoration, Yvonne Hegney; costume design, Heidi Kaczenski; sound (Ultra-Stereo), Alan J. Selk, Gary Dowling; visual effects, Fantasy II Film Effects; special effects supervisors, Joey DiGaetano, R.J. Hohman; makeup effects, Greg Cannom, Thom Floutz; assistant directors, Michael Katleman, Jonathan P. Pare; casting, Nancy Lara, Beth Anne Bowen. Reviewed at Cannon Films theater, L.A., March 16, 1989. MPAA Rating: R. Running time: **85 MIN.**
Gibson Rickenbacker . . . . Jean-Claude Van Damme
Nady Simmons . . . . Deborah Richter
Fender Tremolo . . . . Vincent Klyn
Marshall Strat . . . . Alex Daniels
Pearl Prophet . . . . Dayle Haddon
Furman Vox . . . . Blaise Loong
Brick Bardo . . . . Rolf Muller
Haley . . . . Haley Peterson
Mary . . . . Terri Batson

■ **Aimed squarely at the most undiscriminating yahoo trade, "Cyborg" is a virtually nonstop series of noisy and brutal futuristic fight scenes featuring the martial arts talents of Jean-Claude Van Damme.**

The Cannon release has some kinetic action direction by Albert Pyun, and line producer Tom Karnowski makes the most of the modest budget, but the unimaginative pic covers terrain overly familiar from dozens of more substantial forerunners.

Kitty Chalmer's dimwitted script, which consists largely of curses, grunts and screams, plants the Belgian muscleman Van Damme (star of Cannon's "Blood-sport") in the usual garbage-strewn post-apocalyptic landscape, locked in mortal combat with superthug Vincent Klyn.

At first it seems Van Damme might be persuaded to search for a cure for the AIDS-like plague that is wiping out the remnants of the already devastated society, but that promising element is soon discarded as the plot follows a numbingly predictable revenge pattern.

Van Damme manages to transcend his monosyllabic killing-machine role by exuding a certain sensitivity as he suffers through recurrent traumatic flashbacks while tracking down Klyn for sadistically murdering his family. Thesp has little space for dramatic interaction, but he handles all of the knife fights, gun battles, and chopsocky exploits with the requisite flair.

Klyn, a model making his screen debut as the embodiment of evil, is the most imposing presence on screen, even if his dialog makes him sound like Fred Flintstone with a terrible hangover.

Director Pyun uses slow-motion and telephoto lenses to stylize the action, but is undercut by the lack of plot and characterization, which renders his rapid pacing monotonous.

Philip Alan Waters, previously active in music videos, makes an impressive feature lensing debut, enriching the mood of the film by casting a restrained sunset glow over the relentlessly ugly terrain.

Production designer Douglas Leonard and set decorator Yvonne Hegney add nothing fresh to the conventions of the genre, but they keep the eye stimulated with their energetic scavenging and their adroit redressing of sets at the DEG Film Studios in Wilmington, N.C.

Kevin Bassinson's lively score also helps the film lift itself ever so slightly above the level of pure shlock. —*Mac.*

Sing

Hollywood   A Tri-Star Pictures release of a Craig Zadan production from Storyline Prods. Produced by Zadan. Coproducer, Neil Meron. Executive producer, Wolfgang Glattes. Directed by Richard Baskin. Screenplay, Dean Pitchford; camera (Technicolor), Peter Sova; editor, Bud Smith, Jere Huggins, Scott Smith; music adapted, composed by Jay Gruska; music supervision, Maureen Crowe; production design, Carol Spier; art direction, James McAteer; set decoration, Michael Harris; costume design, John Hay; sound (Dolby), David Lee; choreography, Otis Sallid, John Carrafa; assistant director, Bill Spahic; casting, Donna Isaacson, John Lyons. Reviewed at Coronet theater, L.A., March 27, 1989.
MPAA Rating: PG-13. Running time: **97 MIN.**
Miss Lombardo . . . . Lorraine Bracco
Dominic . . . . Peter Dobson
Hannah. . . . . Jessica Steen
Rosie . . . . Louise Lasser
Mr. Marowitz . . . . George DiCenzo
Mrs. DeVere . . . . Patti LaBelle
Mrs. Tucci . . . . Susan Peretz
Zena . . . . Laurnea Wilkerson
Cecelia . . . . Rachel Sweet

■ **"Sing" needs voice lessons. A weak addition to the predictable "let's-put-on-a-show" genre, pic doesn't contain a move, sound or attitude that hasn't been tried out a hundred times before.**

The target audience of "Fame," "Flashdance" and "Footloose" fans will lose interest fast, resulting in unspirited b.o.

If you're going to make an up-to-the-minute teen musical with unknowns, it helps to have music with an edge and performers with some charisma. Although the music surges along adequately, little of great potential leaps off the soundtrack, and the young actors, by and large, are unfortunately all too believable as high school amateurs.

It's easy to chart the entire story within the first 10 minutes. Brooklyn Central High, now in a deteriorating neighborhood, is putting on its annual musical talent extravaganza, "Sing." In classic fashion, teach Lorraine Bracco, who has a heavy missionary complex, appoints street tough Peter Dobson to help put on the show with goody-goody Jessica Steen.

Dobson, who sports an ubiquitous black leather jacket and whose brother is a smalltime hood, can't be bothered with such playschool stuff, but finally comes around when his talent for dancing and choreography surfaces.

When the board of education announces the closing of Central, the gang bands together to put on the show anyway for a final celebration of school and community pride. It's easy to guess the rest.

Acting consists entirely of striking stock attitudes — Dobson's superior gruffness, Steen's oversensitivity, Bracco's intelligent street smarts and the supporting cast's clichéd ethnicity vary little throughout.

Main new motif to the dancing here is a repetitive swirling of the arms that resembles airplane propellers, and the manner in which first-time director Richard Baskin shoots the musical numbers often recalls "Footloose," which was written by present screenwriter Dean Pitchford.

There's no freshness here, only an impression of recycled ideas from a bunch of livelier previous films. —*Cart.*

Riding The Edge

New York   A Trans World Entertainment release of a Kodiak Films production. Produced by Wolf Schmidt. Directed by James Fargo. Screenplay, Ronald A. Suppa; camera (color), Bernard Salzmann; supervising editor, James Ruxin; music, Michael Gibbs; production design, James Shanahan; casting, Fenton-Taylor; in Dolby stereo. Reviewed at Essex theater, N.Y., April 1, 1989. MPAA Rating: R. Running time: **95 MIN.**
Matt Harman . . . . Raphael Sbarge
Maggie Kemp . . . . Catherine Mary Stewart
Dean Stradling . . . . Peter Haskell
Dr. Harman . . . . Lyman Ward
Moussa . . . . Asher Sarfati
Boy . . . . Benny Bruchim
Kroll . . . . Michael Sarne
Karima . . . . Nili Zomer
Tarek . . . . James Fargo
Mrs. Harman . . . . Brooke Bundy

■ **"Riding The Edge" is a weak entry in the current cycle of youth wish-fulfillment films wherein a boy ventures overseas to rescue his dad. Its soft-R rating aims it mainly for homevid and pay-tv usage.**

Raphael Sbarge is a young motocross enthusiast whose chopper skills come in handy when terrorists kidnap his scientist dad (Lyman Ward) in North Africa and demand that the boy act as courier. Rather dubious plot peg has a little arguing against putting the kid in danger (mostly by Sbarge's mom Brooke Bundy), followed by Sbarge heading to the Mideast with full government and corporate approval.

He's delivering a secret microprocessor to the terrorists in exchange for springing daddy. Along the way he teams up with a beautiful U.S. not-so-secret agent (Catherine Mary Stewart, a bit young for an older woman role) and a cute Arab princeling (Benny Bruchim).

Pale adventure in the vein of "Iron Eagle" and "The Rescue" mixes Israeli and California locations atmospherically but is sunk by dumb dialog and flat direction. Climax set at a vast dam (looking more like Hoover than Aswan) is rousing, however.

Acting is so-so, with Sbarge overly emphatic and Stewart once against wasted. Erstwhile director Michael Sarne ("Myra Breckinridge") is unconvincing with fake German accent as an Eastern European baddie and pic's helmer James Fargo pops us as the leader of the terrorists. Tech credits are adequate. —*Lor.*

Laura Ley
(DUTCH)

Amsterdam A Hungry Eye release of an Allarts production. Produced by Kees Kasander, Denis Wigman. Written and directed by Jenne Sipman. Dialog, Willem Jan Ottem; camera (color), Tom Dicillo; lighting, Reinier van Brummelen; editor, Menno Boerema; music, Henk Hofstede; art direction, Ben van Os, Jan Roelfs; sound, Arno Hagers; production manager, Gerrit Martijn. Reviewed at Uitkijk, Amsterdam, March 20, 1989. Running time: **94 MIN.**

With: Hilde van Mieghem, Tom Jansen, Miguel Stigter, Maurits Martijn, Martin Lüttge.

■ Jenne Sipman's feature debut confirms her gift for beautiful photography, stunning colors and intriguing pictures. As soon as the story proper begins the film flaps, then flops. Only the visual credits stand up till the end.

Laura Ley, divorced, works as chambermaid in a motel. In the evenings, having tucked in her intelligent, slightly precocious son, she makes up most carefully, dons very sumptuous evening gowns and enters a locked room where she operates an illegal radio transmitter.

Her velvety voice whispers, her alluring laughter titillates as she converses with men who drive their cars and trucks through the night. Some are casual listeners in, others come back every night for an exciting aural tryst. These sequences should be sizzling with sensualiity and eroticism, but never rise above room temperature.

Subplots involving politics, jealousy, stealthy stalking, violence and death don't create any involvement. Allusions to the old myth of Lorelei, the maiden who by her singing from a high rock above the river Rhine lures the boatmen to their death, are blatantly intentional.

The pity is that all the time a very good film remains submerged. Difficult to say where the blame lies: with the script, in which coincidence too often replaces logic; wrong casting nearly throughout, or the final cut. What remains is a valiant try gone astray. —*Wall.*

Jorge um Brasileiro
(Jorge, A Brazilian)
(BRAZILIAN)

Rio de Janeiro An Embrafilme release of an Embrafilme/Encontro Producoes production. Produced by Claudia Camargos. Executive producer, Carlos Moletta. Directed by Paulo Thiago. Screenplay, Thiago, Alcione Araujo, based on novel by Oswaldo Franca Jr.; camera (color), Antonio Meliande; editor, Gilberto Santeiro; music, Tulio Mourao; song "Jorge, um Brasileiro" by Mourao and Ronaldo Bastos, sung by Millton Nascimento; sound (Dolby), Jose Luis Sasso, Carlos dos Santos, Helio Lemos; production design, Clovis Bueno; costumes, Isabel Paranhos; production mangement, Caique Martins Ferreira; special effects, Edu von Paungarten; associate producers, Transvideo, Skylight. Reviewed at Barra 2 Theatre, Rio de Janeiro, Feb. 9, 1989. Running time: **130 MIN.**
Jorge . . . . Carlos Alberto Riccelli
Mario . . . . Dean Stockwell
Sandra . . . . Gloria Pires
Fernanda . . . . Denise Dummont
Helena . . . . Imara Reia
Olga . . . . Denise Bandeira
Altair . . . . Roberto Bonfim
Toledo . . . . Paulo Castelli
Fefeu . . . . Antonio Grassi
Oliveira . . . . Jackson de Souza
Also with: Rodrigo Santiago, Flabio Sao Thiago, Fabio Sabag, Fabio Junqueira, Waldir Onofre, Vinicius Salvatori, Rui Polanah, Ricardo Batista, Eduardo Rodrigues, Antonio Nadeo, Elisa Santana, Romulo Duque, Toninho Lobo, José Roberto, Dalmy Veiga, Paulina Galinkin.

■ "Jorge, A Brazilian" relates a fine story about the working relations among employers and employees, taking a truck driver as a starting point. Presence of Dean Stockwell in the cast is part of the effort for an international release.

Production is the star of this $1.5-million pic directed by Paulo Thiago, known as a producer and activist of Brazilian cinema. This is by far the most articulate of Thiago's films. He concentrated on the production efforts, in the technical efficiency (Dolby sound was processed in the U.S.) and in an international star for the cast.

Original script by writer Oswaldo Franca Jr. tells the story of two truck drivers who started together (Carlos Alberto Riccelli and Stockwell) and later became boss and employee. Jorge, the employee, believes in the true friendship of his former colleague and accomplishes impossible missions to help him.

Action is concentrated in one of these missions, where Jorge is determined to take several trucks through roads severely jeopardized by permanent rains so his friend will gain a good government contract. He finds out that such friendship was only in his mind, and that there can be no such friendship between the worker and the boss.

Acting is fine, especially by male characters (Stockwell is dubbed in Portuguese by Odilon Wagner, but an English version was prepared for international release). Denise Dummont, in a leading female role, was seen as the Latin night club singer in Woody Allen's "Radio Days."

Thiago's carefully constructed images attract the viewer's attention. Editing helps to keep the narrative on track when danger is imminent.

Technical credits are otherwise good and pic may actually gain with English dubbing for some of its major weaknesses lie in the Portuguese dialog.

A promising career can be forecasted in some markets eager for a Brazilian product efficient in telling universal story with strong local elements. —*Hoin.*

Ochlim Lokshim
(Crazy Camera)
(ISRAELI-SOUTH AFRICAN)

Tel Aviv A Crazy Camera presentation of a Boaz Davidson, Zwi Shissel procuction. Executive producer, Avi Lerner. Produced by Danny Lerner. Written and directed by Davidson, Shissel; camera (color, 16m), Joseph Wein; editor, David Tur; associate producers, Morris Yosselevsky, Philip Jaffe. Reviewed at Hod Cinema, Tel Aviv, March 12, 1989. Running time: **87 MIN.**
With: Davidson, Shissel, Allen B. Wolf, Nadia Bilchick. Guest star: Yehuda Barkan.
(English-language version)

■ This substandard candid camera caper was shot in South Africa by an Israeli crew. Ploy has misfired and even in these territories where exploitative humor has scored in the past, prospects are dim.

Never a very subtle or refined kind of cinema, in this case candid camera isn't even funny. The gimmicks used are both tried and tired, perfunctorily performed and gracelessly enacted.

Both the unsuspecting victims on screen and the audience in the theater are taken for granted, and neither side seems to enjoy it very much. Boaz Davidson and Zwi Shissel, who have been associated with similar projects at various times in the past, are obviously too exhausted to invent fresh material yet again.

English dialog is not the only reason for poor local boxoffice returns. —*Edna.*

Radio corbeau
(Radio Raven)
(FRENCH)

Paris An AAA release of a Sara Films/SARIS/Ciné coproduction. Produced by Alain Sarde. Directed by Yves Boisset. Screenplay, Alain Scoff, Boisset, from novel by Yves Ellena; camera (Eastmancolor), Jacques Loiseleux; editor, Laurence Leininger; sound, Jean-Pierre Duret; art direction, Claude Bouvard; assistant director, Frédérique Noiret; production manager, Christine Gozlan. Reviewed at AMLF screening room, Paris, Jan. 23, 1989. Running time: **99 MIN.**
Paul Maurier . . . . Claude Brasseur
Julien Duval . . . . Pierre Arditi
Agnes . . . . Christine Boisson
Françoise . . . . Evelyne Bouix
Faber . . . . Roger Planchon
Briand . . . . Julien Bukowski
Bouthier . . . . Jean-Pierre Bisson
Gerfaut . . . . Bernard Bloch

■ Though nominally based on a contemporary print mystery, the obvious inspiration for "Radio corbeau" is Hènri-Georges Clouzot's 1943 masterpiece, "Le Corbeau" (The Raven), about poison pen letters in a seemingly typical French provincial town.

Director Yves Boisset and coscripter Alain Scoff, adapting Yves Ellena's novel, update the tale to media-mad France, with a clandestine pirate radio station providing the medium for the venom against town notables.

Not a bad idea, but Boisset and his collaborators provide only obvious variations on the theme and a cast of stock characters. There are the usual corrupt politicians, seemingly upright cop (Pierre Arditi) and embittered journalist (Claude Brasseur), whose bum leg and laconic disdain set him up as prime suspect. Evelyne Bouix and Christine Boisson are injected for pointless romantic interest.

Boisset as usual sacrifices style and coherence to rhythm à l'americaine, but the whodunit suspense evaporates before the final ironic climax in the town church, a flagrant paraphrasing of a key scene in Clouzot's original film.

Tech credits okay. —*Len.*

Splendor
(ITALIAN-FRENCH)

Rome A Warner Bros. Italia release of a Tiger Group Cinematografica/Studio E.L. coproduction. Produced by Mario & Vittorio Cecchi Gori. Written and directed by Ettore Scola. Camera (Cinecittà color), Luciano Tovoli; editor, Franco Malvestito; music, Armando Trovajoli; art direction, Luciano Ricceri. Reviewed at Barberini Cinema, Rome, March 20, 1989. Running time: **125 MIN.**
Jordan . . . . Marcello Mastroianni
Luigi . . . . Massimo Troisi
Chantal . . . . Marina Vlady
Also with: Paolo Panelli, Pamela Villoresi.

■ "Splendor" is Ettore Scola's hymn to the Bijou of yesteryear. It strikes a particularly poignant chord in Italy, where viewers are notoriously on the wane and whose hardtops close every week. Local boxoffice has been only fair.

Abroad, a thin plot and scant emotion could outweigh pic's

good intentions and respectable cast.

Remarkably similar to Titanus' "New Paradise Cinema," released a few months earlier, "Splendor" wisely sidesteps the maudlin, melodramatic approach to the end of an epoch, but finds no convincing emotion to take its place.

As pic opens, Jordan (Marcello Mastroianni), aging owner of the Splendor theater, has been forced to sell out to a furniture store. Flashbacks summon up memories of his father's traveling film shows when Jordan was a boy, and the post-war years when he took over management and police kept mobs in order at packed shows.

French showgirl Chantal (Marina Vlady) is swept away by the dashing exhib and leaves the stage to become the Splendor's usherette. Her disappointing relationship with Jordan, a bachelor used to his mother's cooking, is sketched too lightly to have an impact.

In time, curly haired young Luigi (Neapolitan comic Massimo Troisi) arrives to partner Chantal, briefly, but his mind is on the movies more than love, and he becomes the Splendor's faithful projectionist. All three are lonely oddballs with a singular passion for films, which sets them apart from the indifferent townsfolk who gradually desert the cinema.

After a few hopeless attempts to draw in audiences with B-movies and go-go girls, Jordan finds his debts have caught up with him. Finalé is a dubious fantasy sequence inspired by Frank Capra, in which the townspeople occupy the premises and prevent its sale.

For a film saluting the cinema, "Splendor" curiously lacks fireworks. Lensing is ho-hum, flashbacks hard to read due to muddy time clues, and cast is given few chances to shine — apart from a scene of Mastroianni weeping at "It's A Wonderful Life," and Troisi berating the town loafers for their cinematic ignorance.

Most splendid thing about the film is its 15-odd excerpts from film classics (mainly Italian) sprinkled liberally throughout, next to which today's films look pallid, indeed. —*Yung*.

Baxter
(FRENCH)

Paris   A UGC release of a Partner's Prod./PCC Prod./Christian Bourgois Prod./Gérard Mital Prod./ISSA/Aliceleo coproduc-

tion. Produced by Ariel Zeitoun, Patrick Godeau. Directed by Jérôme Boivin. Screenplay, Boivin, Jacques Audiard, from Ken Greenhall's novel "Hell Hound;" camera (color), Yves Angelo; editor, Marie-Jo Audiard; music, Marc Hillman, Patrick Roffé; sound, François Waledisch, Joël Beldent; art direction, Dominique Maleret; production manager, Daniel Deschamps. Reviewed at UGC Biarritz theater, Paris, Jan. 20, 1988. Running time: **82 MIN.**

Mme. Deville	Lise Delamare
M. Cuzzo	Jean Mercure
Michel Ferrer	Jacques Spiesser
Florence Morel	Catherine Ferran
Joseph Barsky	Jean-Paul Roussillon
Noëlle	Sabrina Leurquin
Jean	Daniel Rialet
Marie Cuzzo	Evelyne Didi
Charles	François Liancourt
Veronique	Eve Ziberlin

Also with the voice of Maxime Leroux (Baxter).

■ This fable about a thinking dog and his successive masters competed at the recent Avoriaz Fantasy Film Festival. Beyond its central gimmick it has few conventional attributes of a genre film.

Feature debutant Jérôme Boivin and scripter Jacques Audiard, adapting an Anglo-Saxon novel "Hell Hound," aim more for a moral tale than a thriller, but fall short on both counts.

"Baxter" is the name of an unprepossessing bull-terrier (more porcine than canine) who takes a philosophical bent as he ponders the specimens of suburban humanity into whose lives he waddles. These include a morbid old lady on the edge of senility, a banal young couple, and an insensitive boy with a cult fixation on Adolph Hitler and Eva Braun.

One of the script's chief faults is a lack of consistent viewpoint. Though at first beginning from Baxter's subjective vision, action wanders to a series of varied and often superfluous scenes with the human characters, to which the dog is not witness. Scenes, for instance, linger for futile poignancy on an old lady and an elderly suitor, who eventually joins her in the grave.

Boivin fails to instill a feeling of strangeness, a sense of life seen by a lowly creature who can think but is still a dumb mutt. Though Baxter is responsible for the old lady's "accidental" death and tries (out of jealousy) to drown the baby of the young couple, he is not a "hell hound" but a beast on the defensive.

When his final master, the neofascist boy, tries to train him to kill, Baxter refuses and is dispatched to animal heaven.—*Len*.

Vechir Na Ivana Kupala
(The Eve Of Ivan Kupalo)
(SOVIET)

San Francisco   A Dovzhenko Film Studio production. Written and directed by Yuri Ilienko, based on stories by N.V. Gogol. Camera (color), Vadim Illyenko; editor, Y. Parkhomenko; music, L. Hrabovsky; art direction, M. Tereschenko; sound, L. Vachy. Reviewed at San Francisco Film Festival, March 11, 1989. Running time: **71 MIN.**

With: Larisa Kadochnikova, Boris Khmelnitsky, B. Friedman, D. Franko, B. Brandukov, M. Ilienko, V. Panchenko, K. Yershov, D. Yanover, D. Mikosha, S. Pidlisna, M. Sylis, Sashko Sergienko.

■ The reels were out of order for the Frisco film festival's screening of "The Eve Of Ivan Kupalo," but the audience took no overt notice until the opening titles appeared close to the end.

Then, with the prospect of a ticket refund at hand, many in the crowd began complaining that Yuri Ilienko's "poetic" nonlinear short feature had been ruined for them.

Others walked away muttering it probably made just as much sense one way as the other.

In truth, it would be hard going in any sequence as Ilienko glides from one surrealistically symbolic scene to another in this folk tale of a young peasant falling into the grips of evil in an effort to win the hand of a rich man's daughter.

With barely adequate subtitles as an additional complication, Ilienko's thoughts are hard to follow. There's no question his imagery is astounding and imaginative; he was an active cinematographer before turning to directing.

Even at the edge of incomprehension, it's interesting to see where the director heads next visually. Given the subject matter, the mood of the film is mostly dark, although the likes of a blue cow may appear at any point, and the acting is properly, peasantly wrought.

Shot in 1968, the Ukranian film "Ivan" is only now being released by Soviet film authorities. Some have detected political overtones in this, though it's hard to see what's on screen that could be so threatening.

Others have guessed the film has been ignored because it's too far out of the mainstream for audiences in the USSR. That seems reasonable. —*Har*.

Blueberry Hill
(BELGIAN)

Berlin   A Blueberry Hill production, with the Ministries of Flemish and French Culture,

Brussels. Produced by Marc Punt Jan Verheyen. Directed by Robbe de Hert. Screenplay, Walter van den Broeck, Noël Degelin, De Hert; camera (Fujicolor), Jean Claude Neckelbrouck; editor, Ludo Troch; music, Jan Leyers; sound, Ricardo Castro; production design, Hubert Pouille; costumes, Kristin van Passel; assistant director, Stijn Coninx; production manager, Dirk Impens. Reviewed at Berlin Film Festival (Panorama), Feb. 20, 1989. Running time: **90 MIN.**

Robin de Hert	Michael Pas
Cathy	Babette van Veen
Jeanine	Hilde Heijnen
Verbist	Frank Aendenboom
Suzanne Claessens	Myriam Meszieres
Valère	Ronny Coutteure
Priest	Bernard Faure

Also with: Frank Dingenen (Stier), Oliver Windross (Rudy), Gert Nevens (Eddy), Bart Siegers (Felix), Eric Clerckx (Stafke), Aimé Ntibanoboka (Leo), Patje de Neve (Perre), Stijn Meuris (Bernard).

■ Subtitled "A Love Story From The Fifties," "Blueberry Hill" is familiar, autobiographical nostalgia of the "American Graffiti" type, charmingly handled by one of Belgian's most experienced filmmakers, Robbe de Hert.

Set in a Catholic school in 1958, pic has all the elements of this kind of coming-of-age drama. Basic story involves hero Robin's rejection of nice, sweater-knitting, chaste girlfriend Jeaniné in favor of impossibly beautiful Cathy, a sophisticated blond whom the boy does, finally, get to bed.

Subplot involves the school's fanatical headmaster, who's indirectly responsible for the suicide of a sensitive kid, prompting a rebellion of the students.

It smacks of contrivance at times and is far more European in feel than its Yank counterparts would be. Overall it's a pleasant, if unremarkable, nostalgia trip, with the usual clutch of memory-tugging songs on the soundtrack.

Michael Pas is adequate as the director's alter ego, while Babette van Veen shines as his alluring dream girl. Technical credits are all good. —*Strat*.

Tekno Love
(DANISH)

Copenhagen   A Cinnamon Film release of Metropol Film production. Produced by Kim Toftum, Birger Möller Jensen. Written and directed by Kim Toftum. Camera (Eastmancolor), Christina Voight, Marcel Berga; editor, Birger Möller Jensen; music, Lars Muhl, Pete Repete. Reviewed at Scala-1, Copenhagen, March 20, 1989. Running time: **80 MIN.**

Robert	Andy Dauscha
Sasja	Rikke Christiansen
Computer Engineer	Jörn Faurschou
Robert's mother	Liselotte Norup

Also with: Janni Faurschou, Thorkil Lodahl, Bent Hildebrandt, Camilla Lehde Pedersen, Peter Krogstrup, Alexis Ellgard.

■ "Tekno Love" is a quick-witted kiddie & youth comedy-suspenser about a 13-year-old computer freak who hacks his way into a girl's heart while at the same time thwarting a big-scale scheme to divert the city's welfare coin to the wrong pockets.

Although clearly the work of semi-amateurs working with a mostly amateur cast of kids, "Tekno Love" writer-director Kim Toftum has come up with an item meriting its initial theatrical release via eight prints. A bright future in offshore tv (late afternoon slotting) looks likely for this one.

Background sketches of old-line office staffers puzzlement over their new life in front of computer screens and of young teenagers at their party-games are worked deftly into the plot development.

In the lead role, Andy Dauscha shines with mischievous charm. —Kell.

War Birds

New York A Vidmark Entertainment and Hess Kallberg Associates presentation of a Skyhawk Enterprises production. Executive producers, Kevin M. Kallberg, Suzanna Love. Produced by Kurt Eggert, Joanne Watkins. Directed by Ulli Lommel. Screenplay, Clifford B. Wellman, Lommel; camera (Foto-Kem color), Deland Nuse; editor, Joe Negron; music, Jerry Lambert; sound, Bob Gitzen; production design, Angela Allaire, Lou Ann Quast; assistant director, Charles Jung; associate producers. Cookie Amerson, Morton J. Kennedy. Reviewed on Vidmark vidcassette, N.Y., March 4, 1989. MPAA Rating: R. Running time: **88 MIN.**
Billy Hawkins . . . . Jim Eldert
Jim Harris . . . . .Timothy Hicks
Lt. Col. Ronson . . . . .Bill Brinsfield
Vince Costello . . . . .Cully Holland
Van Dam . . . . .David Schroeder
Jeff Rinks . . . . .Stephen Quadros
Carolyn . . . . .Joanne Watkins
Salim . . . . .Rick Anthony Monroe
Also with: Tina Carlisi, Don Hibdon, Camille Marie, Taunie Vrenon.

■ German helmer Ulli Lommel displays scant affinity for the "Top Gun"/"Iron Eagle" genre with "War Birds," a low-budget exercise headed direct to vidstores.

A rather bland cast goes through the motions in a tired tale of Middle Eastern derring-do. U.S. government has Lt. Col. Ronson organize a squad of mercenaries to fly into El Alahaim, a U.S. ally, and aid the pro-American sheik against some feisty rebels.

Among the mercenaries are two graduates from the "Top Gun" school, one of whom is killed when the mission goes awry due to treachery. Several missions later, the Yanks have wupped some rather stereotyped Arab bad guys.

Problem is that the aerial dog-fights here are unexciting, relying on stock footage and minimal action. Otherwise, tech credits are okay.

Pic is dedicated to "Charlie Varrick, last of the independents," evidently Lommel's homage to ace action film director Don Siegel. —Lor.

Moitié-moitié
(Fifty-Fifty)
(FRENCH)

Paris An AFMD release of a Joseph Prods./Générales d'Images coproduction. Executive producer, Joseph Prods. Produced by Bob Zaremba. Directed by Paul Boujenah. Screenplay, Boujenah, Victor Lanoux; camera (Eastmancolor), Yves Dahan; editor, Luce Crunewaldt; music, Gérard Presgurvic; art direction, Dan Weil; sound, Bernard Rochut; assistant director, Yann Michel; production manager, Jean-Marc Isy; casting, Marie-Christine Lafosse. Reviewed at Pathé Marignan-Concorde theater, Paris, Feb. 26, 1989. Running time: **81 MIN.**
Arthur . . . . .Michel Boujenah
Sarah . . . . .Zabou
Sarah's boss . . . . .Jean-Pierre Bisson
Xavier . . . . .Antoine Dulery
Notary . . . . .Ged Marlon
Helena . . . . .Janine Darcey
Julie . . . . .Anais Jeanneret

■ Innocuous local romantic comedy for basically home playoffs, "Fifty-Fifty" pairs comedian Michel Boujenah and vivacious actress Zabou in a story conceived and directed by Paul Boujenah, brother of Michel.

Plot confronts the two temperamentally opposed stars in an inheritance battle for a country house where both were brought up by Zabou's warm-hearted granny. When latter dies, they find themselves equal owners of the property. Sentimental Boujenah wants to preserve it but the businesslike Zabou, a professional architect, intends to raze it for a real estate deal.

Unexceptional comedy situations are intended to play up Boujenah's genial Mediterranean clowning. The Tunisian-Jewish comic, popular for his 1-man-shows, is familiar to overseas audiences as one of the "Three Men And A Cradle."

A special mention goes to Ged Marlon, who temporarily steals the show as a hilariously fidgety notary.—Len.

Fists Of Blood
(AUSTRALIAN)

New York A Virgo Prods. and TVM Studios production, in association with the Mandemar Group. Executive producers, Judith West, Grahame Jennings. Produced by Damien Parer. Directed by Brian Trenchard-Smith. Screenplay, Peter West; additional dialog, Ronald Allan, Trenchard-Smith; camera (Eastmancolor), Simon Akkerman; editor, Kerry Regan, David Jaeger; music, Garry Hardman, Brian Beamish; sound, David Glasser; assistant director-2d unit director, Stuart Wood; production manager, Deb Copland; fight coordinators, Edward John Stazak, Jim Richards. Reviewed on Celebrity Home Entertainment vidcassette, N.Y., March 8, 1989. No MPAA Rating. Running time: **84 MIN.**
Jason Blade . . . . .Edward John Stazak
William Anderson . . . . .John Stanton
Lucy Andrews . . . . .Rowena Wallace
Jim Baxter . . . . .Jim Richards
Gemma Anderson. . . . . . . .Paris Jefferson
Colin . . . . .Zale Daniel
Constable Lambert . .Mathew Quartermaine

■ This sequel to "Day Of The Panther" is an uninteresting Aussie adventure pic. Two films were shot back to back in 1987, but one would have been plenty.

Opening 10 minutes of "Fists Of Blood" are devoted to recapitulating the events in "Day" by reusing the old footage. Sequel has stalwart martial arts hero Jason Blade (Edward John Stazak, his acting still wooden) trying to rescue his girlfriend (pretty redhead Paris Jefferson) from the clutches of heavy Jim Richards, who has escaped from jail since part 1.

Other than for the appearance of tough cop Rowena Wallace, a striking platinum blond, nonstory exists as an undiverting series of comic book climaxes. Any hope of making the Blade character into a longrunning phenomenon is dashed by the absence of suitable challenges with which to prove his mettle.

Helming is under par for the usually reliable Brian Trenchard-Smith. Repetitive music score is another minus. —Lor.

Lost In Amsterdam
(DUTCH-B&W)

Rotterdam A Cor Koppies Film Distribution release of a Commercial Artists 1988 production. Produced by Fransjoris de Graaf. Directed by Pim de la Parra. Screenplay De la Parra, Paul Ruven; camera (b&w), Dirk Teenstra, Jan Wich, Nils Post; editor, Herman P. Koerts; music, Patrick Sedoc; sound, Wim Nelissen, Bert Flantua; art direction, Rebecca Geskus. Reviewed at Venster theater, Rotterdam, Jan. 31, 1989. Running time: **115 MIN.**
Max Binger . . . . .Kenneth Herdigein
Rebecca . . . . .Sabine van den Eynden
Scotty . . . . .Ira Goldwasser
Laura Binger . . . . .Manouk van der Meulen
Bonnie . . . . .Bonnie Williams
Carmen . . . . .Barbara Martijn
Mr. Johnny . . . . .Ralph Wingens
(English soundtrack)

■ Pim de la Parra's latest super-quickie — made in 50 days from first shot to first showing — should bring in some nice box-office from a good number of markets, pending some stern trimming.

"Lost In Amsterdam" works in the B-picture tradition with an honest, wily and wisecracking detective, powerful villains, sleek sexy dames, etc. It's fast, black and white, and speaks English. There are also subplots in the best genre manner, as well as some titillating near-porn.

Pic was made with $40,000 in cash, much enthusiasm and the promise of shares in any profits by an unpaid cast and crew. Six days of shooting relied on lots of improvisation in the organization and the acting. Oddly enough, it works.

Nearly two hours of B entertainment is too much. Judicious trimming and some wholesale cuts might be painful but would be finally beneficial. —Wall.

Tiger Shark

New York A Chappell production. (Intl. sales, Manson Intl.) Executive producer, C.A. Chappell. Produced by Lana Lee Jones. Directed by Emmet Alston. Screenplay, Mike Stone, Ivan Rogers; camera (Foto-Kem color), Robert Ebinger; editor, uncredited; music, Quito Colayco; sound, Bill Fiege; art direction, Lito Nicdao; assistant director, Boy Sequerata; production manager, Sammy Interno; fight choreography, Stone; associate producer, Fred Pierson; casting, Tim Bismark. Reviewed on Diamond Entertainment vidcassette, N.Y., Feb. 20, 1989. MPAA Rating: R. Running time: **99 MIN.**
Tava, Tiger Shark . . . . .Mike Stone
Dave, Cowboy . . . . .John Quade
Karen . . . . .Pamela Bryant
Col. Barro . . . . .Vic Silayan
Tony . . . . .Roy Alvarez
Ponsok . . . . .Roland Dantes
Vladimir . . . . .Jimmy Fabrigas
Jan Carter . . . . .Lana Lee Jones

■ "Tiger Shark" is a Filipino-lensed action pic that rarely rises above the routine but functions adequately as a throwback to the soldier of fortune pics popular in the '50s.

Mike Stone toplines (and collaborates behind the camera too) as Tava, nicknamed Tiger Shark, called from his Hawaiian martial arts academy to help war buddy John Quade rescue Stone's kidnapped girlfriend Pamela Bryant.

A subplot involving a Soviet communist leader (played as a lecherous caricature by Jimmy Fabrigas) providing military aid to rebels goes nowhere. Pic climaxes in a well-staged, to-the-death kickboxing contest, the combatants joined with a steel chain.

Acting is weak except for a very entertaining, salt-of-the-earth performance by Quade, a familiar good ol' boy character actor who rarely gets such a meaty role as here. —Lor.

HONG KONG FEST REVIEWS

Huanle Yingxiong
(The Joyous Heroes)
(CHINESE)

Hong Kong A Fujian Film Studio production. Directed by Wu Ziniu. Screenplay, Sima Xiaojia, from the novel "Storm On The Tong River," by Sima Wensen; camera (Widescreen, color), Yang Wei, Liu Junyun; editor, Zheng Rongyun; music, Shi Wanchun; production design, Tang Peijun, Zhao Shaoping. Reviewed at Hong Kong Film Festival, March 27, 1989. Running time: **96 MIN.**

With: Tao Zeru, Xu Shouli, Jin Hua, Shen Junyl, Jun Yi, Jin Di, Xu Men, Yang Zhaoquan.

■ **Western admirers of quality Chinese cinema over the last few years may wonder, on the strength of "The Joyous Heroes" and its sequel, "Realm Between The Living And The Dead," if Chinese filmmakers are going Hollywood. Both films are lavishly staged, widescreen action epics, with more action than characterization.**

Director Wu Ziniu, winner of the runner-up prize at Berlin last month with his "Evening Bell," collaborated with his wife, Sima Xiaojia, on adapting her father's novel, "Storm On The Tong River," to the screen. The book was written in 1964, when Sima Wensen was working at the Chinese Embassy in Indonesia. Later, the writer became a victim of the Cultural Revolution, and died in 1968.

The two films based on the book have been released in separate parts. "The Joyous Heroes" is set in Fujian in the early '30s. Three well-armed bandit gangs vie for supremacy over the region. A Nationalist officer is sent from Beijing to restore order, and he decides to ally himself to one gang leader, Wu, to eradicate the other two.

Meanwhile Liu, a Communist, returns home after seven years abroad; he's discomfited to discover that his wife, Yusuan, has a 5-year-old daughter and also that his father is a hopeless opium addict (and, unknown to Liu, a police informer). One gang leader, Sanduo, meanwhile tries tentatively to ally himself with members of another gang led by an old man, his son, Datu, and daughter, Dagu. A further subplot involves a schoolteacher who has a secret love affair with the daughter-in-law of a rich merchant.

There are battles galore, and plenty of intrigue, all of it expertly staged by Wu who (as he did in "Evening Bell") shows a bold command of wide screen and use of landscape that evokes the Hollywood western. Unusual, too, for a Chinese film is the fact that the Communist hero is so human, and by no means a glorified figure. It's part of a campaign to bring people back to cinemas to see popular adventure-epics.

Though the film ends in tragedy, it sets the stage for the sequel. Robust and entertaining, the film won't please more serious devotees of Chinese cinema, but because it has more the feel of a film from Hong Kong than a film from China, will probably mop up right across Asia, creating want-to-see audiences for the sequel when it's released. —*Strat.*

Yingyang Jie
(Realm Between The Living And The Dead)
(CHINESE)

Hong Kong A Fujian Film Studio production. Directed by Wu Ziniu. Screenplay, Sima Xiaojia, from the novel "Storm On The Tong River," by Sima Wensen; camera (Widescreen/color), Yang Wei, Liu Junyun; editor, Zheng Rongyun; music, Shi Wanchun; production design, Tang Peijun, Zhao Shaoping. Reviewed at Hong Kong Film Festival, March 27, 1989. Running time: **93 MIN.**

With: Jun Yi, Jin Di, Yang Zhaoquan, Xu Men.

■ **This is the sequel to Wu Ziniu's "The Joyous Heroes," with both pics based on a novel, "Storm On The Tong River," by the director's father-in-law. It has even more action and mayhem than the first film, and is solid entertainment, even if it's not exactly a thought-provoking drama of gang warfare in Fujian in the '30s.**

Since Liu, the hero of the first film, was killed off at fadeout, the mantle now falls on Sanduo, leader of Lower Wood gang, who's presented as the most moderate of the three gang leaders who control the area. The Nationalist government, anxious to stamp out not only the gangs but, more importantly, local communists, has allied itself to the most brutal gang leader, Wu.

When not romancing his widowed sister-in-law, Kucha, Sandou is attempting to ally his gang with the Flying Tigers, led by the unpredictable Datu and his sister, Dagu. It all ends in betrayal, as allegiances shift and savage gun-battles destroy peace talks. Comparisons with Hollywood westerns are, once again, inescapable, and once again director Wu Ziniu demonstrates his skill at staging action scenes against impressively photographed backdrops.

Climax is bloody, with most of the characters eliminated, but the suggestion is that the remnants of these bandit gangs, wiser for their bitter experiences, may form a grassroots movement against the Nationalists.

A subplot from the earlier film, concerning the affair between a schoolteacher and a woman married to the son of a local merchant, is also resolved in "Realm," again by violent means.

The same technical crew worked on both films, which were shot back to back and are just commencing China-wide release. They should prove popular, not only at home but throughout Southeast Asia — wherever Hong Kong action films are played. They're not so much for western festivals, though, where more "serious" product from China will usually be preferred. —*Strat.*

Ji Tong Ya Jiang
(Chicken And Duck Talk)
(HONG KONG)

Hong Kong A Hui's Film Co. production. Produced by Ronny Yu. Executive producer, Michael Hui. Directed by Clifton Ko. Screenplay, Hui, Ko; camera (color), Derek Wan; editor, Wong Yee-shun; music, Richard Yuen; production design, Yeo Chung-man, Ben Lau; associate producer, Paul Lai; assistant director, Terrence Yung. Reviewed at Hong Kong Film Festival, March 28, 1989. Running time: **99 MIN.**

Ah Hui . . . . .Michael Hui
Cuttlefish . . . . .Ricky Hui
Ah Hui's wife . . . . .Sylvia Chang
Also with: Lowell Lo.

■ **Confirming his position as Hong Kong's top screen comic, after a couple of years in the wilderness Michael Hui is in top form in "Chicken And Duck Talk." A fine example of local comedy, it has already proved a hit here.**

He plays Ah Hui, owner of a small restaurant where the house specialty is barbecued duck, made to the owner's secret recipe. Though the food is good, the place is a mess. The chef smokes constantly, dropping ash in the soup; cockroaches get into the food; tablecloths get dirty and worn; plates and cups are chipped and broken, and the head waiter, Cuttlefish (Ricky Hui) is a disaster.

Early scenes have fun with this chaotic situation, which is exacerbated by the fact that Ah Hui is almost as mean as Jack Benny, refusing to pay his staff the bonuses and allowances due to them. He lives above the restaurant in an old-fashioned apartment (no air conditioning, black and white tv) with his long-suffering wife (the charming Sylvia Chang) and son, and is nervously preparing for a visit from his predatory mother-in-law, who lives abroad.

Disaster looms when an American-style fast-food outlet, Danny's Fried Chicken, opens right across the street, with lots of hoopla, advertising and giveaways. Ah Hui's customers defect, and so does Cuttlefish, who gets a job parading up the street in a giant yellow chicken outfit. Ah Hui decides to fight back and modernize his operation, with hilarious results.

The film, funny as it is, has a serious message, about the need to maintain Chinese traditions in a world where everything's becoming international, and also the need to become more efficient in a competitive world. These points are rightly submerged beneath the rapid-fire comedy, which is practically non-stop from start to finish.

Pic is technically excellent, though composer Richard Yuen has borrowed his main theme from the Alain Romans/Frank Barcellini score for Jacques Tati's "My Uncle." The comedic timing is precise, and Michael Hui, especially, is a joy to watch.

His pop-singer brother, Sam Hui, does an unbilled cameo as the VIP who comes to open the rival restaurant, and director Clifton Ko does a walk-on and a classic doubletake.

Fests looking for comedy might try this one, though the English subtitles are, as usual, poor.*Strat.*

Jixu Taiowu
(Carry On Dancing)
(HONG KONG)

Hong Kong A D&B Films production. Executive producers, Winnie Yu, Kam Kwok-leung. Produced by Dickson Poon. Directed by Po-chih Leong, Kam Kwok-leung. Screenplay, Kam Kwok-leung, Winnie Yu; camera (color), Wong Po-man; production design, Robert Luk, William Cheung. Reviewed at Hong Kong Film Festival, March 29, 1989. Running time: **89 MIN.**

With: Cora Miao, Lam Kin-ming, Richard Ng, Lo Hoi-pang, Michael Chow, John Lee.

■ **"Carry On Dancing" is a comedy about twin sisters, one** of whom has been placed in a mental home by her husband. They swap places, with predictable results.

In the outside world, the "mad" sister is able to humiliate her beastly husband, foil a couple of hit men, bring happiness into the lonely life of a rich old man and fall in love with an eager postman. Meanwhile, in the mental home, the "sane" sister falls for a sympathetic doctor none of the other staff understands.

The pic, dated 1987, had a troubled production history. Director Po-chih Leong (who made "Ping Pong" in London's Chinatown in 1985 for Film Four) started shooting but after a while was replaced by screenwriter Kam Kwok-leung, apparently because Po-chih wasn't capturing the subtleties of the original dialog. If there are, indeed, subtleties, they're lost in the usual slapdash English subtitles habitually imposed on Hong Kong pictures.

Cora Miao saves the picture with a winning performance as the twins, while Richard Ng makes the doctor a sympathetic character. The slapstick scenes are labored.
—*Strat.*

Telesm
(The Spell)
(IRANIAN)

Hong Kong A Farabi Cinema Foundation release of an Institute of Cinematic Affairs (Mostazafan Foundation) production. Directed by Dariush Farhang. Screenplay, Farhang; camera (color), Ali-Reza Zarrindast; editor, Ruhollah Emami; music, Babad Bayat. Reviewed at Hong Kong Film Festival, March 26, 1989. Running time: **94 MIN.**

With: Jamshid Mashayekhi, Susan Taslimi, Parviz Poorhosseini, Attila Pessyani, S. Rahmani.

■ Iranian filmmakers continue to produce fascinating films which find their way to international festivals. "The Spell" is a gothic melodrama which seemingly harks back to the Roger Corman/Edgar Allan Poe cycle of films for inspiration.

Period drama opens with the marriage of a young woman to a man from an enemy clan. The union is a business arrangement and the couple despise one another. Custom has it that the bride may not speak to strangers for a year.

As they ride off on their honeymoon, the pair run into a violent storm and are attacked by a savage wolf. They seek shelter in a mysterious palace, home of a lonely aristocrat and his unctuous servant. The Prince still grieves over

the loss of his wife, who disappeared on their wedding day, five years previously.

Before long, the new bride has vanished too, through a secret door leading from a mirrored room into labyrinthine passageways. Here she finds the missing bride, ghostly white, but alive and still eager to escape.

Villain of the piece turns out to be the servant, who wants the house for himself and has been tormenting and slowly poisoning his master for years. It ends with the women (significantly) triumphant, the overthrow of the evil servant, the destruction of the palace, and a fresh future for the young couple.

Apart from echoes of Poe, there are direct references here to Charles Dickens' "Great Expectations." The Prince is a kind of Miss Havisham, with a cobwebbed banquet table still awaiting his missing bride.

The film can also be seen as a rather daring political allegory, with references to the Iran/Iraq war and the stranglehold the Ayatollah Khomeini has on all aspects of life in Iran. These allusions may or may not have been intended by writer-director Dariush Farhang in his stylish first feature.

Handsomely photographed sets and a rich soundtrack (with the sinister sound of rats prevailing near the end) are assets to this well made yarn, which could find favor with selected foreign audiences based on its exotic treatment of classical themes. Those in search of symbols will have a field day.
—*Strat.*

Ashita
(Tomorrow)
(JAPANESE)

Hong Kong A Right Vision Co. production. Produced by Hisao Nabeshima. Directed by Kazuo Kuroki. Screenplay, Masako Inoue, Juichiro Takeuchi, Kazuo Kuroki, from a story by Mitsuharu Inoue; camera (color), Tatsuo Suzuki; editor, Masaru Iizuka; music, Teizo Matsumura; production design, Akira Naito. Reviewed at Hong Kong Film Festival, March 28, 1989. Running time: **101 MIN.**

With: Kaori Momoi, Kaho Minami, Nobuko Sendo, Arther Kuroda.

■ This is a sincere but ultimately emotionless drama about the last day in the lives of a group of people living in the Urakami district of Nagasaki.

The day is Aug. 8, 1945, and next day, at 11:02 a.m., Urakami was the epicenter of the atom bomb explosion.

Since we're aware at the outset that the characters whose lives we're watching are doomed, the film carries surprisingly little impact. In the main, that's because these are hardly flesh and blood people, but stock characters from fiction.

Yae, a young nurse, is marrying Shoji, who's unfit for military service. Family and friends gather for a simple wedding ceremony, including Yae's pregnant sister Tsuruko, whose husband is at the front.

There's also the groom's friend, Tsuguo, medical orderly at a POW camp. This character is unbelievably saintly, speaks perfect English, and has befriended Yank POWs — one of whom dies that day from starvation despite Tsuguo's protests to the authorities. He spends his last night in a brothel with one of those lovely, sweet, understanding prostitutes beloved by some filmmakers.

There are a handful of other characters too, including a girl whose sweetheart has just been drafted and another who finds herself pregnant; kindly mother and inquisitive little brother round out the main cast.

Tsuruko's baby son is born as dawn breaks, and the bomb drops a few hours later, ending the film in a flash of light. The result should be devastating, but isn't. We haven't come to care for these characters, and the pic seems manipulative. An insistent, sentimental music score doesn't help.

Statistics, printed at the start of the film, are more sobering than the film itself: 75,000 people died in Nagasaki, and 74,000 were injured, many of them still suffering from after-effects today. This is a tragedy with which "Tomorrow" never really comes to grips.
—*Strat.*

Shot Down
(SOUTH AFRICAN)

Hong Kong A Weekend Theater production. Produced by Jeremy Nathan. Directed by Andrew Worsdale. Screenplay, Rick Shaw; camera (color), Matthys Mocke, Guilio Biccari; music, The Cherry-Faced Lurchers, Kalahari Surfers, Bernoldus Niemand, Corporal Punishment; production manager, Ami Wright; production design, Dave Barkham. Reviewed at Hong Kong Film Festival, March 28, 1989. Running time: **98 MIN.**
Paul Gillett . . . . Robert Colman
Caesar . . . . Robert Whitehead
  Also with: Megan Kruskal, Mavuso Tshabalala.

■ An anti-apartheid film from white South Africa will be of immediate interest to fest programmers and specialized distributors, but "Shot Down" (currently banned on its home turf) is a film which presumably means a lot more to South Africans than it ever could to outsiders. For much of its length, it's pretty near incomprehensible.

Pic appears to be about a police spy, Paul Gillett, posing as a film director and seeking an interview with a black radical activist who's in hiding. Gillett starts out as an unregenerate villain, but somehow gets converted by the end of the film (the hows and the whys are none too clear) so that he turns the tables on his police contact.

There's a great deal of footage involving a political cabaret in Johannesburg which is filled with local references. There's also a relentless, constant use of 4-letter dialog, which gets tedious after a while.

One sequence, which apparently gave South African censors particular cause for concern, apparently involves interracial sex — apparently because, again, it's none too clear.

There are a couple of moments when a powerful theme starts to emerge: Police raid on interracial party late at night, ordering everyone home, and the nature of the society is chillingly conveyed. Scenes in which black representatives of the activist meet secretly with Gillett also carry a charge.

Overall this is a disappointing effort which won't travel far. In fairness, projection at the fest screening caught was appalling, and it's hard to know whether the murky camerawork was actually caused by insufficient light on the screen. —*Strat.*

Francesco
(ITALIAN-W. GERMAN)

Rome   An Istituto Luce/Italnoleggio release of a RAI-TV Channel 1/Istituto Luce/Italnoleggio Cinematografico/Karol Film/Royal Film (Munich) coproduction. (Intl. Sales, Sacis.) Directed by Liliana Cavani. Screenplay, Cavani, Roberta Mazzoni, based on "Francis Of Assisi" by Herman Hesse;. camera (color), Giuseppe Lanci, Ennio Guarnieri; editor, Gabriella Cristiani; music, Vangelis; art direction and costumes, Danilo Donati. Reviewed at Adriano Cinema, Rome, March 7, 1989. Running time: 155 MIN.
Francesco . . . . Mickey Rourke
Clare . . . . Helena Bonham Carter
Father . . . . :Paolo Bonacelli
Mother . . . . Andréa Ferréol
Pope Innocence III . . . . Hanns Zischler
Bishop . . . . Peter Berling
Also with: Mario Adorf, Fabio Bussotti, Riccardo Di Torrebruna, Alekander Duin, Edward Farrelly, Paolo Proietti, Paco Reconti, Diego Ribon, Maurizio Schmidt, Nikolaus Dutsch, Stanko Molnar.

■Liliana Cavani's "Francesco," her second film portrait of Francis Of Assisi, wanders from episode to episode like a homeless friar, finding its center only in its forceful final scenes. Mickey Rourke gives a likable if at times too contemporary performance as a mystical loner in search of God, and is pic's main audience draw.

Film has the look of a classy tv production of pious intent (albeit with a good deal of nudity), and got off to a good start over Easter at local wickets. Sacis has already sold it to many territories.

The problem is mainly Cavani and Rourke's lack of a clearcut idea of their hero, who oscillates between saint, visionary, and psycho. The lack of definition begins to tell in a 2-½ hour marathon.

Cavani — purportedly not a religious person — tackled Francis 23 years ago in "Francesco d'Assisi," in which a rebellious Lou Castel took on the social forces of 13th century Italy. Current film bristles with modern themes — church politics, the horror of war, poverty as an outlaw's choice in a rich man's world — though main focus is Francis' religious vocation.

Francesco's life is recounted in episodes by Clare and his disciples after his death. He begins life as the rich, pampered son of cloth merchants (finely cast are both Paolo Bonacelli and Andréa Ferréol). A year of imprisonment following Assisi's gory war with Perugia introduces him to suffering, privation, and the gospel.

Ransomed by his father, Francesco returns home a changed man. He's put on the path of charity by Clare, played by Madonna-faced Helena Bonham Carter as an active young lady of courage and sense. He scandalizes good Assisi society by renouncing his inheritance, stripping naked in public, and giving his father the clothes on his back.

Though living in abject poverty with lepers and the poor, derided by the townsfolk as a beggar, Francesco is joined by other well-to-do lads. Film offers no reason for these conversions from riches to rags, choosing to skip over the historical Middle Ages with its violent reform movements, where Francis was a natural focus for disillusioned young people.

Equally sketchy is Francesco's meeting with Pope Innocence III (Hanns Zischler), resulting in the birth of the Franciscan order. Its abrupt growth (suddenly there are thousands of brown-robed extras) goes unexplained while the angry insistence of many new members to stop being barefoot mendicants and "go official" has the ring of an ill-defined metaphor.

Drama makes a strong return in film's closing scenes, when Francesco, a physical wreck, covered with sores and light years away from the concerns of his followers, retreats to the woods with the faithful Brother Leone to write a program for his order.

Desperately alone and consumed with a need for God to speak to him, Francesco isolates himself from the world and, in a moving finale where Rourke comes into his own, receives Christ's stigmata.

Pro work behind the scenes gives pic its $13,000,000 budget's worth, from Danilo Donati's simple costumes and art direction to Ennio Guarnieri and Giuseppe Lanci's humbly dark-hued lensing. (Guarnieri also shot Franco Zeffirelli's film on the subject, "Brother Sun, Sister Moon." — Ed.) —Yung.

Outlaw of Gor

New York   A Cannon Intl. presentation of a Breton Film Prods. Ltd. production. Produced by Harry Alan Towers, Avi Lerner. Directed by John (Bud) Cardos. Screenplay, Rick Marx, "Peter Welbeck" (Towers), based on John Norman's novel; camera (Rank color), Johan van de Vyfer; editor, Mac Errington; sound, Conrad Kuhne; art direction, Geoffrey Hill; assistant director, Neal Sundström; 2d unit director, Cedric Sundström; stunt coordinator, Reo Ruiters; additional editing, Ken Bornstein; casting, Don Pemrick. Reviewed on Warner Home Video vidcassette, N.Y., March 28, 1989. MPAA Rating: PG-13. Running time: 89 MIN.
Tarl Cabot . . . . Urbano Barberini
Talena . . . . Rebecca Ferrati
Lara . . . . Donna Denton
Xenos . . . . Jack Palance
Watney . . . . Russel Savadier
Hup . . . . Nigel Chipps
Elder . . . . Alex Heyns
Marlenus . . . . Larry Taylor
Vera . . . . Michelle Clarke

■This followup shot in 1987 in southern Africa back-to-back with Cannon's "Gor" is a puerile adventure film. It's headed direct to video in the U.S. from Warners.

Handsome Italian star Urbano Barberini encores as the hero of John Norman's endless series of pulp novels, transported hokily to the planet of Gor in what plays like a daydream. With nerdy sidekick Russel Savadier and a helpful dwarf (Nigel Chipps) he battles gladiator-style against evil high priest Jack Palance, attempting to free the planet from slavery.

Ho-hum plot goes nowhere and beautiful heroine Rebecca Ferrati (a Playboy mag graduate) is wasted. With no sci-fi or fantasy trappings, pic has only pretty views of the Namib desert to offer. —Lor.

Say Anything

Hollywood   A 20th Century Fox release of a Gracie Films production. Produced by Polly Platt. Executive producer, James L. Brooks. Coproducer-editor, Richard Marks. Written and directed by Cameron Crowe; camera (Deluxe color), Laszlo Kovacs; music, Richard Gibbs, Anne Dudley; additional music, Nancy Wilson; production design, Mark Mansbridge; set decoration, Joe Mitchell; costume design, Jane Ruhm; sound (Dolby), Art Rochester; associate producer, Paul Germain; assistant directors, Jerry Ziesmer, Herb Adelman (Seattle); casting, Randy Stone, Patti Kalles (Seattle). Reviewed at 20th Century Fox Studios, L.A., April 6, 1989. MPAA Rating: PG-13. Running time: 100 MIN.
Lloyd Dobler . . . . John Cusack
Diane Court . . . . Ione Skye
James Court . . . . John Mahoney
Corey Flood . . . . Lili Taylor
D.C. . . . . Amy Brooks
Rebecca . . . . Pamela Segall
Mike Cameron . . . . Jason Gould
Joe . . . . Loren Dean
Constance . . . . Joan Cusack
Also with: Lois Chiles, Eric Stoltz.

■"Say Anything" is a half-baked love story, full of good intentions but uneven in the telling. Appealing tale of an undirected Army brat proving himself worthy of the most exceptional girl in high school elicits a few laughs, plenty of smiles and some genuine feeling.

At the same time, first-time director Cameron Crowe still has plenty to learn about filmmaking, resulting in a pic that could have sleeper potential but will likely generate no more than decent b.o.

On the eve of high school graduation, bright but unremarkable student John Cusack decides he's just got to go out with "Miss Priss," Ione Skye. The class valedictorian and academic leader in every subject, Skye is doted upon by her divorced father, John Mahoney, and is headed for studies in England on a fellowship.

Cusack, who bunks with his nephew and sister (the latter played in an unbilled appearance by his real-life sister Joan Cusack) screws up the courage to ask his dream girl out, and lays on enough nervous charm to get her to agree. Skye takes an instant liking to the fellow's gentlemanliness, and they start a friendship that slowly grows into something more.

Conflict rears its head in a conventional way when Skye becomes torn between leaving for England at Summer's end and staying with her boyfriend and, in a less conventional way, when her father (who up to now has really been Superdad) is accused by the Feds of running a scam at his nursing home for old folks. Pic's final stretch is heavily devoted to the repercussions of this subplot which is odd and somewhat off-putting.

At the same time, film is unusual for a teenpic in that it treats this parent figure seriously and sympathetically. Mahoney displays his boundless affection for and generosity to his daughter with engaging glee.

Cusack and Skye's relationship develops nicely and believably, but Crowe has not written an entirely convincing character for the latter to play.

Pic also has considerable structural problems, as many scenes feel unachieved, severely truncated, awkwardly modulated, abruptly concluded or some combination of the above.

Playing a far from fully formed young man, Cusack is winning as he convinces both Skye and the viewer that he's a very solid guy who will develop a sense of personal responsibility despite his uncertainties.

Crowe's direction is as erratic as his writing, as he communicates the story's basic qualities while clearly not achieving many of his desired effects. Tech contributions are serviceable. Lois Chiles (unbilled) plays a scene as Skye's mother, and Eric Stoltz pops up briefly at a teen party. —Cart.

Jinye Xingguang Canlan
(Starry Is The Night)
(HONG KONG)

Hong Kong A Shaw Bros. release of a Shaw Bros.-Tomson Films Co. production. Executive producer, Virginia Lok. Produced by Mona Fong, Hsu Feng. Directed by Ann Hui. Screenplay, Katy Leung; camera (color), Henry Chan; editor, Wong Yee Shun; music, Danny Chung; production design, Daniel Lee; production manager, Jessinta Liu; assistant director, Anthony Wong. Reviewed at City Hall, Hong Kong, March 29, 1989. Running time: **94 MIN.**

To Choi Mei	Lin Ching Hsia
Professor Cheung Yin-Chuen	George Lam
Cheung Tin-On	David Wu
Poon Chung Long	Yee Tung Shing

Also with: Yip Sun, Ann-Marie, Jade Hsu, John Woo.

■ **Ann Hui, Hong Kong's most prolific femme director, comes up with a subpar romantic drama with political overtones this time around.**

Cutting back and forth between events in 1968, year of pro-Mao riots in Hong Kong (which coincided with the climax of the Cultural Revolution across the border) and the present, when the Colony is facing more political upheavals (return to Chinese rule in 1997), Hui tells a generation-gap love story which teeters on the edge of banality.

In 1968, Choi-Mei is a university student having a secret affair with one of her professors, Dr. Cheung. In 1988, she is approaching forty and working as a social worker when she embarks on a passionate affair with a teenage boy, Tin-On, to whom she's been assigned.

The romance triggers off memories of her previous grand amour, which ended when the prof's pregnant wife discovered his infidelity. Only belatedly does she discover what the audience had guessed from the start — that her teen lover is the son of her ex.

If the screenplay sounds a bit corny, Hui's direction is accomplished enough to just about carry it off. Lin Ching Hsia looks too old in the 1968 scenes and too young to be 40 in the present-day scenes, but the actress is accomplished enough to get away with it. George Lam is suitably dissolute as the academic with an eye for the ladies.

The fact that Choi-Mei's longtime best friend, Poon, is fighting a political campaign in 1988 (which he loses) gives the political elements of 20 years ago added weight. One point is given special emphasis: Told she shouldn't be so selfish, Choi-Mei

replies that Hong Kong wouldn't be where it is today if people hadn't been selfish.

Underlying the soapie melodrama is a subtext about Hong Kong itself in these nervous times, when the heroine's school friends are heading off overseas, to Canada or Australia.

Though it flounders towards the end, the film has a few sharp barbs about modern society. When Choi-Mei and her teenager first go to bed, he rejects the use of a condom, and instead produces a certificate to show that he's AIDS-free; so much for romance. —*Strat.*

Major League

Hollywood A Paramount Pictures release of a Morgan Creek/Mirage production. Produced by Chris Chesser, Irby Smith. Executive producer, Mark Rosenberg. Coproducer, Julie Bergman. Written and directed by David S. Ward. Camera (Astro color; Technicolor prints), Reynaldo Villalobos; editor, Dennis M. Hill; music, James Newton Howard; production design, Jeffrey Howard; art direction, John Krenz Reinhart Jr.; set design, Bill Rea; set decoration, Celeste Lee; costume design, Erica Edell Phillips; sound (Dolby), Susumu Tokunow; assistant director, Jerry Grandey, Louis D'Esposito; second unit director, Irby Smith; second unit camera, James Pergola. Reviewed at Mann National theater, Westwood, Calif., April 4, 1989. MPAA Rating: R. Running time: **107 MIN.**

Jake Taylor	Tom Berenger
Ricky Vaughn	Charlie Sheen
Roger Dorn	Corbin Bernsen
Rachel Phelps	Margaret Whitton
Lou Brown	James Gammon
Lynn Wells	Rene Russo
Willie Mays Hayes	Wesley Snipes
Charlie Donovan	Charles Cyphers
Eddie Harris	Chelcie Ross
Pedro Cerrano	Dennis Haysbert
Pepper Leach	Andy Romano
Harry Doyle	Bob Uecker

■ **"Major League" lacks the subtlety of "Bull Durham" or the drama of "Eight Men Out," but for sheer crowd-pleasing fun it belts one high into the left-field bleachers.**

Writer-director David S. Ward creates an adult version of "The Bad News Bears" in this R-rated baseball comedy about a squad of misfits who rally together to bring the pennant back to Cleveland. The Paramount release is a sunny entry in the spring b.o. parade.

Though the plot turns are mostly predictable, they are executed with wit and style. There's a lot of rooting interest for the audience in the sad sacks cynically assembled by new Indians owner Margaret Whitton with the secret hope that they'll draw so poorly that she'll be able to break the stadium lease and head for Miami.

Naturally, when the guys get wind of this maneuver, they recover their lost pride and bring off the pennant miracle.

The cast is a fine ensemble, leading off with Tom Berenger as the battered, world-weary catcher and Charlie Sheen as the juve delinquent pitcher with punk hairdo who fully merits his nickname of "Wild Thing."

Smart comic turns are taken by the rest of the lineup, including the endearing young hot dog (Wesley Snipes), the voodoo-practicing slugger (Dennis Haysbert), the gravel-voiced manager (James Gammon), the Jesus freak pitcher with a weakness for Hustler magazine (Chelcie Ross), the veteran whose mind is on his investments rather than on the game (Corbin Bernsen), and the tippling broadcaster who keeps afloat by maintaining a healthy sense of the absurd (Bob Uecker, in an uproarious film debut).

As long as it sticks to the field and the clubhouse, the script doesn't falter, but there's time to go out for popcorn during the cliched love scenes of Berenger trying to jumpstart his broken-down romance with yuppie librarian Rene Russo. The characters are too reminiscent of Kevin Costner and Susan Sarandon in "Bull Durham."

Reynaldo Villalobos' lensing captures the tingle of ballpark atmosphere. Since Ward is from Cleveland, and the Indians have one of the longest streaks of futility in the majors, he set the film in that rustbelt city, but he filmed it in Milwaukee for economic reasons. Milwaukee County Stadium fills in for the much larger (and contrastingly circular) Cleveland ballpark, which is unconvincingly used for establishing shots.—*Mac.*

Necromancer

New York A Bonnaire Films and Spectrum Entertainment presentation. Executive producer, Michael A.P. Scording. Produced by Roy McAree. Line producer, William J. Males. Directed by Dusty Nelson. Screenplay, Bill Naud; camera (Foto-Kem color), Richard Clabaugh, Eric Cayla; editor, Carole A. Kenneally; music, Gary Stockdale, Kevin Klingler, Bob Mamet; sound, Scott Smith; art direction, Scott Harrison; assistant director, Eric Brown, Bob Swain; special makeup effects, William J. Males & Associates; casting, Daniel Travis. Reviewed on Forum Home Video vidcassette, N.Y., March 25, 1989. MPAA Rating: R. Running time: **88 MIN.**

Julie	Elizabeth Kaitan
Prof. Charles DeLonge	Russ Tamblyn
Eric	John Tyler
Freda	Rhonda Durton
Paul	Stan Hurwitz
Carl	Edward Wright
Allan	Shawn Eisner

Ernest	Waide A. Riddle
Lisa, necromancer	Lois Masten

■ **Modest horror pic uses the ever-popular revenge motif for this supernatural tale bowing domestically in videostores.**

Attractive, round-faced Elizabeth Kaitan toplines (in her biggest role to date) as an acting student who's gang-raped by classmates but blackmailed to avoid reporting it.

Her roommate talks her into answering a "revenge" ad in the paper.

Lois Masten is the gypsy-styled necromancer who places these ads. She's in touch with the devil and uses a client's revenge request as license to go hog wild killing people, with the hapless instigator unable to stop her. In Kaitan's case, she demonically assumes Kaitan's form, seduces the rapists and then offs them (with minimal makeup and gore effects).

Okay acting saves this low-budgeter, which spotlights Kaitan's beauty in a multiple role. Russ Tamblyn has fun as her lecherous, Shakespeare-spouting acting prof. —*Lor.*

Cameron's Closet

New York An SVS Films release of a Smart Egg Pictures presentation of a Luigi Cingolani production. Produced by Cingolani. Executive producer, George Zecevic. Line producer, John S. Curran. Directed by Armand Mastroianni. Screenplay, Gary Brandner, based on his novel; camera (United color), Russell Carpenter; music, Harry Manfredini; sound (Ultra-Stereo), Bob Gravenor; assistant director-production manager, Kelly Van Horn; special creature effects, Carlo Rambaldi; associate producer, Frank Caggiano. Reviewed at 57th St. Playhouse, N.Y., April 8, 1989. MPAA Rating: R. Running time: **86 MIN.**

Det. Sam Talliaferro	Cotter Smith
Nora Haley	Mel Harris
Cameron Lansing	Scott Curtis
Ben Majors	Chuck McCann
Det. Pete Groom	Leigh McCloskey
Dory Lansing	Kim Lankford
Bob	Gary Hudson
Owen Lansing	Tab Hunter

■ **"Cameron's Closet" is an ambitious but very disappointing horror film. Pic arrived tardily in Manhattan theaters months after its poster went up in subway displays, just in time for its appearance in vidstores.**

Attempt at a minor league "Exorcist" on a puny budget is a mistake. Levitation and other effects are merely okay and pic lacks the scope of a horror epic. Gary ("The Howling") Brandner merely has fashioned a convoluted tale of a monster in the closet of little boy Cameron (Scott Curtis).

The kid has been experimented upon (à la Michael Powell's "Peeping Tom") by his dad Tab Hunter, combining psychokinesis with demonology to unleash a monster (a demon worshipped by the Mayans, no less).

Hunter exits early, killed by the demon, and main story psychically (and unconvincingly) links Cameron with the police detective (Cotter Smith) assigned coincidentally to the serial murders caused by the hellish critter. Smith's real-life mate, Mel Harris of tv's "thirtysomething," is cast as a psychiatrist treating both Curtis and Smith (!), latter suffering from blackouts caused by the demon.

Not helped by flat lighting of interiors and dullish Armand Mastroianni direction, pic plods to several confrontations with the monster, poorly executed by Carlo Rambaldi to look like Batman wearing his cowl. An extraneous near-incest scene is pointlessly thrown in near the end like an audience wakeup call.

Harris adds plenty of class to the proceedings, while Smith is bland and little Curtis merely competent. Chuck McCann scores in a noncomedic role as a boozing ex-scientist. —Lor.

The Perfect Model

Chicago A Chicago Cinema Entertainment release of a Darryl Roberts production. Executive producers, Theresa McDade, Kari A. Coken, Darryl Roberts. Produced and directed by Roberts. Screenplay, Roberts, McDade, Ivory Ocean; camera (color), Sheldon Lane; editor, Tom Miller; music, Joe Thomas, Steve Grissette; production design, Phillipé, Roberts; art direction, Simmie Williams; set decoration, Phillipé; costume design; Wilson Harris; sound, Jerome Williams, Dejunius Hughes, James Harris; choreography, Rosemary Barnes; production manager, Yvette Culver, Barbara Falkenburg. Reviewed at Cinecenter screening room, Chicago, April 4, 1989. MPAA Rating: R. Running time: **89 MIN.**
Stedman Austin . . . . Stoney Jackson
Mario Sims . . . . . Anthony Norman McKay
Linda Johnson . . . . Liza Cruzat
Crystal Jennings . . . . Tatiana Tumbtzen
David Johnson . . . . Catero Colbert
Dexter Sims . . . . Reggie Theus
Robert Darryls . . . . Darryl Roberts

■**Latest in a series of low-budget indie features by black filmmakers, "The Perfect Model" may pick up some coin initially by following in the wake of Robert Townsend and Spike Lee, but pic's many flaws, both narrative and technical, make it unlikely to receive the word-of-mouth support necessary for sustained success.**

"The Perfect Model" benefits from a certain amount of goodwill going in because of its obviously tyro status (it was lensed under trying conditions with very little money and with a largely nonprofessional cast), but even the most generous handicap is eventually eroded by the film's flat lighting, hollow sound, bland dialog, tiresome characters, lethargic pacing and anticlimatic ending.

Familiar story concerns the romance between a Hollywood movie star and a girl from the ghetto, who the actor tries to elevate through participation in a high-stakes modeling pageant to make her more acceptable to his high-class friends. Plot is set up as Cinderella story complicated by the moral issue of material success vs. personal integrity, but the payoff never comes because, in this case, Cinderella doesn't even go to the ball.

On the plus side, "The Perfect Model" is graced by a surprisingly good original score by Joe Thomas and Steve Grissette. Most of the acting in the picture is self-conscious and ineffective but there are some standout performances, notably: Stoney Jackson, suitably sleazy as the pageant promoter; Liza Cruzat, very appealing as the girl from the wrong side of the tracks; and Catero Colbert, provider of much-needed comic relief as the girl's wisecracking little brother.

As for Darryl Roberts, producer, director and co-scripter of this opus, his outstanding achievement is the fact that the film was actually completed. Despite its many shortcomings, pic is realized at a remarkably ambitious level, indicating that Roberts' greatest skill, at this point, is probably on the production side. —Brin.

Intruder

New York A Phantom production. Produced by Lawrence Bender. Directed by Scott Spiegel. Screenplay, Spiegel, from story by Bender, Spiegel; camera (Deluxe color), Fernando Arguelles; editor, King Wilder; music, courtesy of APM; sound, Sara Oldfield; production design, Wendy Guidery; art direction, Mara Massey; assistant director, Eddie Ziv; production manager-coproducer, Douglas Hessler; special makeup effects, Greg Nicotero, Robert Kurtzman, Howard Berger. Reviewed on Paramount Video/Phantom Video vidcassette, N.Y., April 5, 1989. MPAA Rating: R. Running time: **83 MIN.**
Jennifer . . . . Elizabeth Cox
Linda . . . . Renée Estevez
Bill . . . . Danny Hicks
Craig. . . . . David Byrnes
Randy . . . . Sam Raimi
Danny . . . . Eugene Glazer
   Also with: Billy Marti, Burr Steers, Craig

Stark, Ted Raimi, Alvy Moore, Tom Lester, Emil Sitka, Bruce Campbell.

■**Stylish direction can't save "Intruder," another leftover Charles Band pic going direct-to-vid via Paramount.**

Lensed under the catchy title "Night Crew: The Final Checkout," pic comes off closer to a student experiment than a commercial feature. Claustrophobic premise has all the action taking place, almost real-time, at a grocery story after hours.

Elizabeth Cox is the lovely checkout cashier, whose ex-boyfriend Craig (David Byrnes, a Micky Rourke type) pops up fresh from the slammer to harass her. After a big fight with other employees, he hides out, becoming the chief suspect as one by one the cast is wiped out in grisly fashion.

After half an hour of prep, murders start happening like clockwork every two or three minutes. Pic benefits from an okay twist as to who the real killer is and a clever, nasty ending.

Keeping things pepped up is director Scott Spiegel's affection for comically goofy camera angles, silliest of which are point-of-view shots from inside a telephone (!) and cash register. He displays technical expertise, but needs to come up with a more interesting script next time out.

Cast is effective, especially Cox, while helmer Sam Raimi is okay in front of the camera as one of the hapless employees. Uncredited musical score is annoyingly overdone. Lor.

Jan Rap en z'n maat
(Tough)
(DUTCH)

Amsterdam A United International Pictures (Netherlands) release of an Elsevier-Vendex-NOS coproduction. Produced by Gys Versluys. Executive producer, Remmelt Remmelts. Directed by Ine Schenkkan. Screenplay, Yvonne Keuls, Schenkkan, based on novel by Keuls; camera (color), Goert Giltay; editor, Ton Ruys; music, Henny Vrienten; sound, Peter Flamman; art direction, Harry Ammerlaan; production manager, Eric Hadkamp; casting, Frank Krom. Reviewed at Tuschinski theater, Amsterdam, Feb. 18, 1989. Running time: **116 MIN.**
Elly . . . . Jasperina de Jong
Gemma . . . . Heidi Arts
Doctor Jo . . . . Dora van der Groen
Klass . . . . John Leddy
Tymen . . . . Edwin de Vries
Derek . . . . Paul de Leeuw
   Also with: Jack Spijkerman, Jan Pontier, Eric Arens, Erna Bos, Jaloe Maat, Marc Hazewinkel, Celia Nufaar.

■**Ine Schenkkan's second feature film (after the award-winning "Bygone") is fuzzy,**

fussy and shapeless. It doesn't really flop because it never takes off.

"Tough" is based on a bestselling novel by Yvonne Keuls who later adapted it for the stage in the 1970s. She also collaborated on the screenplay, which fails to define itself purposefully; is it melodrama, sitcom, social comment or teen romp?

Story is set in a large house transformed into a youth center where kids in trouble can find refuge for a maximum of 30 days. Only junkies and nut cases are excluded. The center has funding from the city and a devoted, if overworked, staff. The inmates include runaways, rape victims, thieves and other assorted problem youths.

Much work went into the production, but to no avail: tech credits remain under par. The large cast of young players give enthusiastically of their best (which is quite good), the more experienced thesps bring their routines — but it never jells. —Wall.

The Tall Guy
(BRITISH)

Hollywood A Vestron Pictures release of an LWT & Virgin Vision presentation of a Working Title production. Produced by Paul Webster. Executive producer, Tim Bevan. Directed by Mel Smith. Screenplay, Richard Curtis; camera (color), Adrian Biddle; editor, Dan Rae; music, Peter Brewis; production design, Grant Hicks; art direction, Andrew Rothschild; sound (Dolby), Peter Glossop; assistant director, Waldo Roeg; casting, Sheila Trezise. Reviewed at the Beverly Center Cineplex, L.A. (American Film Market), March 1, 1989. No MPAA Rating. Running time: **92 MIN.**
Dexter King . . . . Jeff Goldblum
Kate Lemon . . . . Emma Thompson
Ron Anderson . . . . Rowan Atkinson
Cyprus Charlie . . . . Emil Wolk
Carmen . . . . Geraldine James
Cheryl . . . . Kim Thomson
Dr. Freud . . . . Susan Field
Karabekian . . . . Hugh Thomas

■**"The Tall Guy" is a cheery, ingratiating romantic comedy that should be greeted by audiences with open arms. Jeff Goldblum puts in a stellar performance as a bumbling American actor in London whose career and romantic tribulations are suddenly transformed into triumphs.**

Prospects for this guy look bright on the upper-middle brow circuit on both sides of the Atlantic.

Intimate and small in scope, film has the measure of an exceptionally well written, directed and acted tv sitcom, with its snappy dialog, agonizing comic complications, appealingly broad performances and send-'em-home-happy resolution. Throw in a dash of heightened sexual frankness and the commercial recipe looks complete.

At the outset, Yank thesp Goldblum has been performing in the West End for several years as straight man to popular comic Rowan Atkinson. The insecure goofball is earning a living but going nowhere fast when he comes under the care of hospital nurse Emma Thompson.

Immediately smitten, Goldblum spends the time between weekly visits for injections desperately concocting ways to ask her out, but the nurse is so primly efficient that the shots are over with before he can open his mouth.

When the two finally connect, instant result is a riotous sex scene that does more bedroom damage than the jilted Orson Welles did in "Citizen Kane." Throughout the entire film, the relationship evolves winningly, with so much believable give-and-take, mutual ribbing and support that one roots for it heavily.

As soon as he has discovered domestic bliss, however, Goldblum is sacked by Atkinson, who resents anyone else in his show getting a laugh, and is thrust into the forbidding world of the unemployed actor.

By happy accident, he is cast in the title role of "Elephant," a musical version of "The Elephant Man." Along with romantic entanglements, the final third of the picture is devoted to seeing the production through casting and rehearsals to its smash opening night in what cumulatively amounts to a devastatingly accurate send-up of the Andrew Lloyd Webber cycle of dramatic musicals.

The fresh, alert performances add enormously to the polished sparkle of Richard Curtis' script. Goldblum is in splendid form as the eternally naive American abroad, careening about with expert timing as events send him up and down the emotional ladder.

Emma Thompson makes a wonderfully poised foil for her leading man's volubility, and in her own quiet way is hilarious as she bluntly informs her partner that she fully expects sex on the first date.

British favorite Rowan Atkinson has a great time enacting the most vain and mean-spirited of stars, and Hugh Thomas elicits quite a few laughs in his brief appearance as a wild-eyed medic.

Director Mel Smith, better known as a comic actor, orchestrates all the elements adeptly, and behind-the-scenes contributions are solid.—*Cart.*

Edge Of Sanity
(BRITISH)

Hollywood   A Millimeter Films release of an Allied Vision presentation. Produced by Edward Simons, Harry Alan Towers. Executive producer, Peter A. McRae. Directed by Gérard Kikoïne. Screenplay, J. P. Felix, Ron Raley, based on novel "Dr. Jekyll And Mr. Hyde" by Robert Louis Stevenson (uncredited); camera (Eastmancolor), Tony Spratling; editor, Malcolm Cooke; music, Frederic Talgorn; production design, Jean Charles Dedieu; art direction, Fred Carter, Tivadar Bertalan; costume design, Valerie Lanee; sound (Dolby), Paul Sharkey; makeup supervisor, Gordon Kaye; assistant directors, Vic Smith, Gabor Varadi; associate producers, James Swann, Maria Rohm. Reviewed at The Burbank Studios, Calif., April 3, 1989. MPAA Rating: R. Running time: **90 MIN.**
Dr. Jekyll/Mr. Hyde.....Anthony Perkins
Elisabeth Jekyll...........Glynis Barber
Susannah ....Sarah Maur-Thorp
Underwood ....David Lodge
Johnny ....Ben Cole
Newcomen ....Ray Jewers
Flora ....Jill Melford
Maria ....Lisa Davis
Egglestone ....Noel Coleman
   Also with: Briony McRoberts, Claudia Udy.

■ Neither Anthony Perkins, in a too-obvious outing as Dr. Jekyll and Mr. Hyde, nor Robert Louis Stevenson, whose source novel is both uncredited and luridly travestied, is well served by this shlocky Edward Simons-Harry Alan Towers production, lensed mostly in Hungary.

Limited b.o. mileage can be wrung from the Perkins name for this R-rated release by Millimeter Films, an affiliate of Miramax.

Someone had the not-so-bright idea of turning Mr. Hyde into Jack the Ripper, which is basically nothing more than an excuse for extended gore and adds nothing to the literature of Ripper speculation.

In a misguided attempt at trendiness, the character's rampages in 1895 London are blamed on his experiments with cocaine and the accidental invention of freebasing by his pet monkey. The net effect of these changes is to rob the character of complexity and turn the film into an extended drug freakout with mostly unintentional comic overtones.

Eschewing heavy makeup, Perkins effectively relies mostly on demented facial expressions to convey the evil of Mr. Hyde, as Spencer Tracy did in the 1941 version of this oft-filmed tale. He appears almost as demented while playing Dr. Jekyll, a mistaken notion that quickly makes the character monotonous and strains credibility past the breaking point.

Director Gérard Kikoïne, despite having graduated from softcore and hardcore porno pics, still retains some of his old predilections, dwelling lasciviously on kinky sex scenes as Mr. Hyde prowls the brothels and back alleys of Victorian London. The garishly staged and lensed film resembles a porno film with the hardcore inserts excised, and the ghoulish mingling of sex and violence is not only a revolting turnoff, but boringly predictable as the Ripper's mayhem unspools.

Screenwriters J. P. Felix and Ron Raley trot out some cheapjack Freudianisms in the repeated evocations of a childhood sexual trauma to explain the character's sadomasochistic urges. Since they make Jekyll/Hyde such a 1-note monster, there's little room to explore Stevenson's theme of the beast underlying the surface of civilized man.

Glynis Barber has the thankless role of Jeklyll's beautiful but numbingly normal wife, whose blithe innocence of his nocturnal life makes her seem a ninny and provides some of the film's choicest moments of inadvertent hilarity.

When she finally confides her suspicions to his barrister — only 13 minutes from the fadeout — the old gentleman notes gravely, "Yes, you're quite right, Eliza. His behavior is very strange." Not half as strange as hers.

Perhaps this film could have worked if it had been played more for black comedy (Perkins toys with that notion at times), but its uncertain vacillation between heavy melodrama and tongue-in-cheek horror does not work at all. Tech credits are okay.—*Mac.*

Blood Reincarnation
(HONG KONG)

Hong Kong   A Fong Ming Co. production. Executive producers, Yang Chun. Produced by Yu Feng-Chih. Directed by Ding Shan-Hsi. Screenplay, Shan-Hsi; camera (Widescreen, color), Chen Chung-Chu; editor, Hu Kuo-Chuan; music, Chou Fu-Liang; production design, Yang Shih-Cheng; costumes, Ma Chia-Hua; production managers, Kao Fei, Ma Fei, Lin Hung-Ying; assistant director, Peter Pan. Reviewed at Hong Kong Film Festival, March 24, 1989. Running time: **99 MIN.**
The Treasure
Ah Tak ....Shih Tien
Ah Heung ....Shirley Huang
Gan Niang...............Chi Shih-Ying
The Wanton
Chang Fa ....Chiang Nan
Mrs. Chang ....Meng Li
Lover ....Yu Yang
Lau Tin Sok
Dr. Lau Tin-Sok ....Yang Chun
Wife ....Tang Pao-Yun
Chiu Hung ....Chi Lien-Kui
Nobleman ....Li Yun-Chung
Nobleman's fourth wife.......Wang Ting
Her lover (Luk Tse-Chuen) Chang Pei-Shan

■ "Blood Reincarnation" was made in 1974 and played at the London film fest the following year. As a good example of Hong Kong cinema of the macabre, it was included in the recent Hong Kong film fest retro of "phantom" films, and is reviewed here for the record.

Pic consists of three stories; the first two about 15 minutes each, the third lasting an hour. The kickoff is, in many ways, the best of the trio. It's a wild little tale about a young husband and his pregnant wife who help an old woman recover a buried pot containing, supposedly, buried treasure. The young husband kills the old woman before discovering the pot contains only bones.

During labor, the wife drips blood on the old woman's corpse, and the baby boy, when delivered, bites off his father's finger and then kills him. Edited with quick dissolves and rapid cutting, plus exaggerated soundtrack, this is an object lesson in short-film storytelling.

·Story two has a merchant discover his wife in bed with another man. The couple overpower the husband, nail him into a wooden box and dump him in the sea, but their troubles are only just beginning. This is a comic tale, involving a bottomless bathtub and an agile bed, but though sometimes amusing the segment lacks the right macabre touch.

Part three stars the film's executive producer, Yang Chun, as a revered doctor unjustly accused of killing the wife of a nobleman. By invoking an ancient spell at the moment of his execution, he lives on for a few days as a ghost, able to return home and finish writing his life's work before disintegrating in a pool of blood. Apart from some minor miscalculations, this is a finely wrought suspense piece, nobly acted by Yang.

The film overall is something of a mixed bag, but indicates writer-director Ding Shan-Hsi was, at least at this period, a more than competent purveyor of classy horror pics. Comparisons with Roger Corman aren't too far off the mark. —*Strat.*

Vice Academy

New York   A Rick Sloane production. Written, produced, directed and edited by Sloane. Camera (color), Stephen Ashley Blake; music, Alan der Marderosian; sound, Diana Flores; assistant director, Pamela Reese; production manager, Steve Crawford; associate producer, Kathleen Vandale. Reviewed on Prism Entertainment vidcassette, N.Y., March 31, 1989. MPAA Rating: R. Running time: **90 MIN.**

Didi	Linnea Quigley
Holly	Ginger Lynn Allen
Shawnee	Karen Russell
Devonshire	Jayne Hamil
Dwayne	Ken Abraham
Chucky	Stephen Steward

Also with: Jeannie Carol, Tami Bakke, Jo Brewer, Manny Serrano, Cliff Corder, Christian Barr, Mark Richardson, Stephanie Bishop.

■It takes a quickie, direct-to-video pic like "Vice Academy" to make the latterday "Police Academy" series look good.

Former porn star Ginger Lynn Allen teams up with current softcore star Linnea Quigley as warring police cadets studying to join the L.A. vice squad. Pic limns their unfunny (not for lack of trying) misadventures as whores, porn stars, etc. to entrap unsuspecting sleazeballs.

The two blond leads are nice to look at, while newcomer Karen Russell amply fills the tease genre gap left by her namesake Betsy Russell. Filmmaker Rick Sloane's most daring motif is spoofing another ex-porn starlet Traci Lords, but effort is generally puerile.
—*Lor.*

Obsession: A Taste For Fear
(Pathos)
(ITALIAN)

New York   A Titanus Produzione presentation, in association with Reteitalia, of an Exordia production. Produced by Jacques L. Goyard. Directed by Piccio Raffanini. Screenplay, Raffanini, Lidia Ravera, from story by Goyard; camera (Luciano Vittori color), Romano Albani; editor, Mario Morra; music, Gabriele Ducros; art direction, Paolo Biagetti; costume design, Vera Cozzolino; production manager, Vincenzo Cartuccia; in Dolby stereo. Reviewed on Imperial Entertainment vidcassette, N.Y., March 25, 1989. MPAA Rating: R. Running time: **89 MIN.**

Diane	Virginia Hey
Georges	Gérard Darmon
Valerie	Gioia Scola
Paul	Carlo Mucari
Lt. Arnold	Dario Parisini
Kim	Carin McDonald
Teagan Morrison	Teagan Clive
Pearl	Eva Grimaldi
Bookmaker	August Darnell

■This thriller is an excellent example of a recent Italian genre little-known Stateside: the glamorous horror/fashion pic. Direct-to-video release should generate interest in other pasta couture shriekers.

Pic aroused interest in Europe last year (and was featured in photo spreads in "Lui" and other mags) under the title "Pathos." Helmer Piccio Raffanini has adapted the style of Jean-Jacques Beineix' "Diva" (and cast Beineix' regular thesp Gérard Darmon) to this tale of decadent photographers using high-tech equipment to stylize erotic fashion photos.

Virginia Hey is the antiheroine, whose sexy models are being murdered. Identity of the assailant is possible to figure out, and getting to the bottom of the mystery is made exciting by an excellent musical score, vivid pastel-lit photography by Romano Albani and a very attractive cast (frequently nude).

Hey, an Aussie thesp in tv series "Dolphin Cove," is solid as the shutterbug with a sadistic streak, while Teagan Clive and Carin McDonald offer diverting beauty as muscular femme models. August Darnell, Kid Creole of the vocal group, pops up in a small role.

Gabriele Ducros' hypnotic background score is augmented by well-chosen songs, including Chrissie Hynde's "Private Life," sung by Grace Jones. Tech credits, including English postsynch, are way above average.—*Lor.*

Brothers In Arms

New York   An Ablo presentation, in association with Jel A.S, Produced by Mark R. Gordon, Christopher Meledandri. Executive producers, André Boissier, Jan Erik Lunde. Directed by George Jay Bloom 3d. Screenplay, D. Shone Kirkpatrick; camera (FotoKem color), Kim Haun; editor, Chuck Weiss; music, Alan Howarth; sound, Rick Waddell; production design, Kirk D. Phillips; assistant director-production manager, Bob Hurrie; second unit camera, Kenneth Wiatrak; casting, Billy DaMota. Reviewed on Republic Pictures vidcassette, N.Y., March 7, 1989. MPAA Rating: R. Running time: **94 MIN.**

Joey	Todd Allen
Dallas	Charles Grant
Father	Jack Starrett
Stevie	DeDee Pfeiffer
Caleb	Mitch Pileggi

Also with: Dan Bell, Shannon Norfleet, Jay Richardson.

■A standard revenge/survival tale, "Brothers In Arms" is chiefly of interest to video fans based on scenic views of wilderness lensed in the Big Bear region of California.

Charles Grant is the intentionally dislikable "hero" Dallas, who drags along his unknowing younger brother (Todd Allen) on a quest for vengeance up in the mountains. A family of religious nuts (led by the late director Jack Starrett) killed his pal Cody and literally crucified him.

Pic features plenty of violence but fails to create any interesting opposition between Dallas and either the religious creeps or city slicker types who illegally kill does in what passes for weekend hunting. Sole femme in cast, DeDee Pfeiffer, is saddled with an underwritten, contradictory role as the damsel rescued by the brothers.

Tech credits are okay. —*Lor.*

Deadly Obsession

New York   A Distant Horizon presentation. Produced by Anant Singh. Line producer, Charles Brown. Directed by Jeno Hodi. Screenplay, Hodi, Paul Wolansky, Brian Cox, from story by Hodi, Wolansky; camera (Technicolor), Zoltan David; editor, Wolansky; music, Marty Dunayer; sound, Darris Meehan; production design, Kimberly von Brandenstein; production manager, Cox; stunt coordinator, Jeffrey R. Iorio; second unit camera, Brown; associate producer, Sarjeev Singh. Reviewed on Republic Pictures vidcassette, N.Y., March 25, 1989. MPA Rating: R. Running time: **95 MIN.**

Dino Andretti	Jeffrey R. Iorio
John Doe	Joe Paradise
Denise	Darnell Martin
Lt. Walsh	Martin Haber
Pamela	Monica Breckenridge

■Gotham-lensed thriller is an okay lowbudget entry dealing with a contemporary fear similar to the Tylenol scare a while back. Item from South Africa-based Indian producer Anant Singh went direct to video Stateside.

Nonactress Darnell Martin is the pretty heroine in jeopardy, barely saved from death when she ingests some ice cream dosed with rat poison. Baddie Joe Paradise is poisoning the dessert on store shelves to protest a company's mistreating of animals.

Hungarian-born debuting helmer Jeno Hodi keeps the pic suspenseful, though a sci-fi premise (e.g., involving experimental drugs) would have been more intresting than a kook with rat poison. Martin is a winning presence; ditto her protector/leading man Jeffrey R. Iorio.

Pic makes good use of its locale. Shot on the campus of Columbia U. (called "Gotham College" in the story), pic's best scene is an extended homage to Val Lewton set after hours at the school's indoor pool. —*Lor.*

I, Madman

New York   A Trans World Entertainment release of a Sarlui/Diamant production. Executive producers, Paul Mason, Helen Sarlui-Tucker. Produced by Rafael Eisenman. Directed by Tibor Takacs. Screenplay, David Chaskin; camera (color), Bryan England; editor, Marcus Manton; music, Michael Hoenig; sound (Ultra-Stereo), Robert Janiger; production design, Ron Wilson, Matthew Jacobs; production manager, Bob Manning; special visual effects, Randall William Cook; postproduction supervisor, Fima Noveck; associate producer, Patti Meade; casting, Ed Mitchell, Robert Litvak. Reviewed at Warner theater, N.Y., April 8, 1989. MPAA Rating: R. Running time: **89 MIN.**

Virginia/Anna	Jenny Wright
Richard	Clayton Rohner
Malcolm Brand	Randall William Cook
Lenny	Steven Memel
Mona	Stephanie Hodge
Pianist	Bruce Wagner

■"I, Madman," originally titled "Hardcover," is an inept horror opus, paying too much attention to in-jokes and homages than to its storytelling craft. Current theatrical prospects are nil; video not much better.

Helmer Tibor Tikacs (of "The Gate") and writer David Chaskin nostalgically pay allegiance to a dizzying number of topics here, ranging from Tod Browning films ("The Unknown" and "Freaks" in particular) to pulp novels and creature features. On a TWE poverty row budget, results are embarrassing.

Jenny Wright, looking ultrasexy and smashing at the outset in both '50s nightgown and '80s teddy (and unaccountably dowdy for the rest of the pic), plays a dual role. She's an acting student working with pal Stephanie Hodge in an antiquarian bookstore, while also portraying (in illustrated fantasy footage) the heroine of one Malcolm Brand's '50s pulp novels.

Ridiculous storyline has Wright's horrific imaginings from reading the novels come to life and a series of murders/mutilations occurring. Or course, Wright's boyfriend Clayton Rohner also is the cop on the case and predictably he and his superiors refuse to believe Wright's explanation since it smacks of the super natural.

Grainy, ugly-looking pic confuses backlighting and fog with film noir styling. There's no credibility to the proceedings and the '50s milieu is not even campy. Pic's only redeeming element (for the kiddies) is a stopmotion animation monster executed by Randall Cook. Cook also costars to little effect as the Lon Chaney Senioresque villain, sporting quite variable makeup effects as he kills folks to obtain body parts to sew back on his mutilated face.

Wright, as always, is basically appealing but wasted here in a preposterous role. Rohner is miscast and the unfamiliar supporting players merely adequate. Ace film doctor Fima Noveck fails to shore up the loose ends. —Lor.

Hell On The Battleground

New York   An Action Intl. Pictures production. Executive producers, David Winters, Marc Winters. Produced by Fritz Matthews. Written and directed by David A. Prior. Camera (United color), Stephen Ashley Blake; editor, Todd Felker; music, Tim James, Steve McClintock, Mark Mancina; sound, Timothy J. Garrity; assistant director-second unit director, Kimberley Casey; production manager, Frank James; stunt coordinator, Bob Ivy. Reviewed on AIP Home Video vidcassette, N.Y., March 29, 1989. No MPAA Rating. Running time: **86 MIN.**

Col. Meredith	William Smith
Casey	Fritz Matthews
Lance	Ted Prior
Lt. Hayes	Chet Hood
Kelly	David Campbell
Johnson	Johnnie Johnson
Johnny Boy	Sean Holton
Karen	Ingrid Vold
Donna	Alyson Davis

■Formerly titled "Battle-ground," this utterly routine war actioner is another Action Intl. pic lensed in Riverside by prolific but styleless helmer David Prior; it's a direct-to-vid-stores release.

Producer Fritz Matthews doubles as pic's lead, Rambo-esque Casey, a gung-ho soldier faced with green troops in endless infantry and tank battles with the Russkies. (Pic is abstracted to the extent that time, place and occasion of a U.S./USSR faceoff are left blank.)

Perfunctory staging of the battles and cornball sentimentality (a lucky crucifix is handed off, soldier to soldier) make this one a chore to watch. Little sense of reality is engendered as Matthews and fellow hero Ted Prior head back to base camp from time to time for r&r with their pretty blond nurses/girlfriends. —Lor.

Thomas Hart Benton
(DOCU)

St. Louis   A Florentine Films release of a Ken Burns film. Produced by Ken Burns, Julie Dunfey. Directed by Ken Burns. Written by Geoffrey C. Ward; camera (color), Burns, Buddy Squires; editor, Donna Marino; musical director, John Colby, narrator, Jason Robards; sound, Peter Agoos, Alex Griswold, Tom Nelson, Roger Sherman; animation photography, Ed Joyce, Ed Searles. Reviewed at Webster University, St. Louis, Mo., March 30, 1989. No MPAA Rating. Running time: **85 MIN.**

■Documentary filmmaker Ken Burns turns to the American art scene for "Thomas Hart Benton," another of his rich, insightful views of the history and the people of the United States.

In Benton's centennial year, the film should score in museums and art houses, with a PBS tv date of May 1.

Benton was a controversial figure throughout his career and remains so 14 years after his death. Born in Neosho, Mo., Benton was a newspaper cartoonist and artist in his youth who studied in Paris, moved to New York in the 1920s, finally returned to the Midwest and scored as a painter of vibrant, larger-than-life, passionate scenes of America.

Burns has rounded up a variety of experts to testify about Benton's skills. Hilton Kramer is the most outspoken of those who damn the painter, though Kramer praises Benton's 1938 autobiography and adds, not unexpectedly, "He really should have been a writer rather than a painter."

Henry Adams, curator of the Nelson-Atkins Museum in Kansas City, speaks strongly in defense of Benton, as do artists like Raphael Soyer and Vincent Campanella.

The contemporary interviews are generally excellent, with Benton's wife (who died a few months after him) and daughter showing the artist as a man of stubbornness and strength who would not yield to the Eastern establishment.

At the same time, his homophobic attitude toward the art community did not help him make friends. Narrator Jason Robards discusses the relationship between Benton and Jackson Pollock, one of his students. Home movies from summers on Martha's Vineyard brighten the film.

Benton's paintings are shown to their best advantage as Burns' camera focuses on both details and the wider sweep. —Jopo.

Nash Dvor
(Our Courtyard)
(SOVIET-B&W)

Hong Kong   A Gruziafilm (1956) production. Directed by Rezo Chkheidze. Screenplay, Georgi Medivani; camera (b&w), G. Chelidze; music, L. Kereselidze; production design, G. Gigauri; sound, R. Kezeli. Reviewed at Hong Kong Film Festival, March 25, 1989. Running time: **89 MIN.**

Tsitsino	Sofiko Tchiaurelli
Dato	Georgi Shengelaya
Manana	Leila Abachidze

■Director Rezo Chkheidze, co-director with Tengiz Abuladze of the Cannes prizewinner "Magdana's Donkey" (1955), produced "Our Courtyard," his first solo feature, apparently under the influence of such Italian films as "Sunday In August."

Tale is a simple one involving a group of teenagers all of whom live in apartments overlooking the same Tbilisi courtyard.

The film is peopled with stock characters, like the nosy concierge and the elderly bore, but the teenagers themselves are freshly observed. Much of the film's interest today centers on the casting of young Georgi Shengelaya as the hero, Dato. At the time, Shengelaya would have been known chiefly as the son of veteran director Nikolai Shengelaya, but today he's a director in his own right, with such films as "Pirosmani" and "Journey Of A Young Composer." He gives a fresh, unaffected performance as the lovelorn Dato who wrongly thinks his girl Tsitsino (Sofiko Tchiaurelli) is in love with someone else.

Pic explores such problems as whether to go on to university from high school or enter the workforce (no shortage of jobs, apparently). One youth is castigated for his laziness; son of a famous singer, he becomes a drifter who turns to drink and emerges as the villain of the piece.

There's a touching innocence about the film and an affection for the city of Tbilisi itself (which is crisply photographed), but the scripting never elevates the drama above the level of innocuous teen problems. Despite that, the film has a freshness that sets it apart from other Soviet films of the early '50s. —Strat.

Sol Dla Svanetia
(Salt For Svanetia)
(SOVIET-B&W)

Hong Kong   A Goskinprom (1930) production. Directed by Mikhail Kalatazov. Screenplay, Sergei Tretjakov; camera (b&w), Kalatazov, Salva Gegelasvili. Reviewed at Hong Kong Film Festival, March 27, 1989. Running time (at 24 frames per second): **61 MIN.**

■Celebrated as a classic example of silent Soviet documentary, "Salt For Svanetia" would by today's standards be considered *dramatized* documentary, since it was filmed according to a screenplay, and, though it uses non-professional actors, is filled with stage scenes.

Svanetia is a valley in Georgia, 6,000 ft. up, where the Greater and Lesser ranges of the Caucasus meet. Access to the area is blocked by snow for most of the year; even in July (as we see) there are snow storms. The people who live here struggle to survive, growing bar-

ley, and building homes from slate chipped from the mountains.

What they lack most is salt: To obtain it, animals lap up human urine or lick the sweat from a man; a newborn baby is devoured by a wolf seeking the salt in its blood.

According to the film, Svanetia's chief problem is its religion and age-old customs, which only exacerbate the difficulties of living in the region. Thus, a woman is left to give birth to a child alone, since she goes into labor during a funeral ceremony, which is considered blasphemy.

This was the first film made by director Mikhail Kalatazov, who also co-photographed. In 1957, he directed the Cannes prizewinner "The Cranes Are Flying." Here, Kalatazov is concerned with getting across the message that communism will help modernize Svanetia, so that its age-old problems will be overcome. The film ends in a triumphant note, since a new road is being built up to the mountain valley.

With its lovingly shot images of poverty and hardship, "Salt For Svanetia" has, understandably, been compared to Luis Buñuel's "Land Without Bread," which was made a few years later. "Salt" still impresses for the sheer beauty of its images and for its illumination of an almost unknown world. Despite its contrivances, these qualities endure. —Strat.

Stripped To Kill 2

Hollywood   A Concorde Pictures release. Produced by Andy Ruben. Executive producer, Roger Corman. Written and directed by Katt Shea Ruben. Camera (Foto-Kem color), Phedon Papamichael; editor, Stephen Mark; music, Gary Stockdale; production design, Virginia Lee; art direction, Greg Maher; set decoration, John Shapiro; costume design, Ellen Gross; sound, Michael Clark; choreography, Ted Lin; associate producer, Rodman Flender; assistant director, Adam Shapiro; second unit director, Carole Kravatz; second unit camera, Geza Sinkovics. Reviewed at Academy theater, Pasadena, Calif., April 1, 1989. MPAA Rating: R. Running time: **82 MIN.**

Shady	Maria Ford
Decker	Eb Lottimer
Cassandra	Karen Mayo Chandler
Dazzle	Birke Tan
Something Else	Marjean Holden
Montra	Debra Lamb
Victoria	Lisa Glaser
Ike	Tommy Ruben
Shirl	Virginia Peters

■Sequel to Katt Shea Ruben's "Stripped To Kill" is a fairly engaging low-key thriller that achieves more than the usual within its budget constraints.

Aficionados of shoe-string filmmaking, along with soft-porn fans, should make the video market lucrative after this limited theatrical release.

Pic may be about strippers, and rife with imaginative topless dancing routines and sleek, barely clad bodies, but thanks to distaff direction, its effect is less exploitative than "Flashdance."

Strippers aren't romanticized — nor are they humiliated. They're just a bunch of whiny, catty girls with great bodies, making a late-night living. Unexpectedly good choreography, costumes, vivid cinematography by Phedon Papamichael, some nice moments among the actors and a few witty lines and characters are what makes this pic stand out in its genre.

Pic tells the story of Sandy (Maria Ford), a stripper tormented by violent dreams in which she slashes the throats of other dancers via a razor blade held in her teeth.

When the dancers turn up dead and Shady wakes up with blood dribbling from her lips, things sure look bad for her. Yet she's too kittenish and vulnerable for us to believe she's a killer — even if she was once stuck in a psycho ward for a violent attack on her boyfriend.

Hunky Sgt. Decker (Eb Lottimer) doesn't believe she's guilty either — nor does her protective roommate, fellow stripper Cassandra (Karen Mayo Chandler) who's weirdly unconcerned about living with an apparent psycho killer.

Plot drags somewhat after first hour, but final twist is fairly satisfying, disregarding numerous implausibilities in plot.

Ruben and Papamichael make pic more visually engrossing than one has a right to expect, with imaginative angles, garish lighting that inflames the constant dressing room bickering, and some eerie touches — like the mannequins (or are they bodies?) sprawled atop a skylight in Shady and Cassandra's apartment.

Ruben, who also scripted, takes the trouble to build some compassion and humor into the characters. Decker, beneath his smooth good looks, has a wooden leg that makes him afraid of female rejection. In one scene, while he's trying to impress Shady with his familiarity with the low-lifes in a sleazy hotdog joint, she interrupts to point out that he's wearing a woman's trenchcoat.

Casting of Virginia Peters as a bullish, dryly witty police detective is an appealing touch.

Nonetheless, for much of audience, stripper's routines will be pic's drawing card, and they're well conceived and well shot.

Sound quality, though, fell far below standard in print viewed for review, with levels uneven and voices sometimes inaudible.

—*Daws.*

Dance Of The Damned

New York A Concorde Pictures presentation of a New Classics production. Produced by Andy Ruben. Directed by Katt Shea Ruben. Screenplay, Andy and Katt Shea Ruben; camera (Foto-Kem color), Phedon Papamichael; editor, Carole Kravetz; music, Gary Stockdale; sound, Michael Clark; production design, Stephen Greenberg; assistant director, Albert T. Dickerson 3d; production manager, Reid Shane; special effects, Steve Neill; choreography, Ted Lin; coproducers, Shane, Anna Rock. Reviewed on Virgin Vision vidcassette, N.Y., March 29, 1989. (In AFI Festival, L.A.) MPAA Rating: R. Running time: **83 MIN.**

Jodi Kurtz	Starr Andreeff
Vampire	Cyril O'Reilly
La Donna	Deborah Ann Nassar
Teacher	Maria Ford
Ray gun girl	Athena Worthy
Cabby	Tom Ruben

■This morbid but engrossing vampire drama is skedded for direct-to-video release this month, but gets brief big-screen exposure at the AFI Festival in Los Angeles.

Filmed back-to-back last year with same filmmakers' "Stripped To Kill 2," pic shares that sequel's strippers milieu. Starr Andreeff is a suicidal peeler, distraught at having a court order barring her from visiting her young son.

A handsome vampire, Cyril O'Reilly, is in the Paradise Cafe and senses Andreeff's despair, propositioning her after hours to spend the night with him for a quick g-note; he even promises to kill her at dawn after their confab.

Despite that claustrophobic premise, reminiscent of the launching point of Anne Rice's novel "Interview With The Vampire," pic covers much ground, with an especially atmospheric latenight visit to the beach. Helmer Katt Shea Ruben bears down effectively on the various philosophical questions of the genre: emptiness of immortality, search for meaning in existence, etc.

Punching it across is an uninhibited performance by brunet Andreeff, whose unusual beauty and on-the-edge thesping command sympathy and interest. O'Reilly also is impressive, rising above obvious James Dean mannerisms

to create his own persona as the brooding, shoulder-length-hair night creature.

Special effects are modest but fresh. Climax is predictable and undercut by an unintelligible final line of dialog. —*Lor.*

Return To The River Kwai (BRITISH)

London Rank Film Distributors release (U.K.), Tri-Star Pictures (tentative, in U.S.) of a Braveworld presentation of a Kurt Unger production. Executive producer, Daniel Unger. Directed by Andrew V. McLaglen. Screenplay, Sargon Tamimi, Paul Mayersberg, based on the book by Joan and Clay Blair Jr.; camera, Arthur Wooster; editor, Alan Strachan; music, Lalo Schifrin; production design, Michael Stringer; art direction, Cesar Hernando; costume design, Wynn Arenas; sound, Paul Le Mare; casting, Warren Maclean. Reviewed at Odeon Marble Arch, London, March 1, 1989. Running time: **98 MIN.**

Hunt	Nick Tate
Miller	Timothy Bottoms
Tanaka	George Takei
Benford	Edward Fox
Crawford	Christopher Penn
Perry	Richard Graham
Harada	Tatsuya Nakadai
Grayson	Denholm Elliott
Yamashita	Masato Nagamori
Ozawa	Etsushi Takahashi
Davidson	Michael Dante

■ "Return To The River Kwai" is artless World War II action whose only hope is that its resonating title will pull business via fast playoff on the circuits.

The Kurt Unger production picks up where Columbia's classic 1957 "Bridge On The River Kwai" more or less left off, namely with the blowing up of a POW-built bridge in enemy-occupied Thailand. After which, in the sequel, the mostly Australian prisoners are brutally herded by rail and sea to be deployed in Japan as slave labor.

The incident-rich, harrowing journey is based on an exhaustively-researched and absorbing book by Joan & Clay Blair Jr. that crackles with what the screen version doesn't — gripping narrative tension and logistical interest.

Instead, with a Sunday supplement treatment routinely directed by action specialist Andrew V. McLaglen, pic only flickers to suspenseful life in the waning minutes when the prisoner-laden ship, now with the POWs in control, is sunk by torpedoes from a U.S. sub in the South China Sea. By then it's a lost cause as compelling docudrama.

As for characterization, recall the old double-feature days when the military types were instantly recognizable for the clichés they were and you'll get the idea. Given those shallow dimensions, the cast performs competently enough. Denholm Elliott, in what amounts to little more than a cameo as a Brit commando, and Edward Fox as a prison compound medic, are both too good to waste on an epic story that could and should have been more than a sowhat.

"Return" was shot entirely in the Philippines. All tech credits are good, including Arthur Wooster's crisp lensing, aerial footage by Kevan Ross Lind and Lalo Schifrin's score.

Film opened April 7 in London, but U.S. preem via Tri-Star is delayed at least to the fall by a legal dispute between producer and distrib. —*Pit.*

LATE FILM REVIEW

Winter People

Hollywood A Columbia release of a Nelson Entertainment presentation of a Robert H. Solo production. Produced by Solo. Directed by Ted Kotcheff. Screenplay, Carol Sobieski, based on the novel by John E ...e; camera (Deluxe color; Panavision), François Protat; editor, Thom Noble; music, John Scott; sound (Dolby), Robert Gravenor; production design, Ron Foreman; art direction, Chas. Butcher; set decoration, Leslie Morales; costume design, Ruth Morley; assistant directors, Craig Huston, Bruce Moriarty; casting, Lynn Stalmaster. Reviewed at Coronet theater, L.A., April 7, 1989. MPAA Rating: PG-13. Running time: **110 MIN.**

Wayland Jackson	Kurt Russell
Collie Wright	Kelly McGillis
William Wright	Lloyd Bridges
Drury Campbell	Mitchell Ryan
Paula Jackson	Amelia Burnette
Annie Wright	Eileen Ryan
Gudger Wright	Lanny Flaherty
Young Wright	Don Michael Paul
Milton Wright	David Dwyer
Cole Campbell	Jeffrey Meek

■The wages of sin are forever up in the old North Carolina hills, especially when they concern clans carrying on a blood feud. That's the backdrop for "Winter People," a grimly unappetizing melodrama that forwards themes and concerns as remote as its time and place.

Set for its world premiere April 13 as the opening-night attraction of the American Film Institute Los Angeles Intl. Film Festival, pic has little to offer artistically or commercially.

By delving into the nasty, unforgiving ways of some people that time forgot, this thoroughly misfired romance recalls any number of earlier films, but few that have been made in the last 50 years. One thought that the "Tol'able David" genre of backwoods sagas virtually died off with silent pictures, and this isn't about to bring it back.

Adaptation of John Ehle's novel is set around the time such rural fare was popular, back in 1934. Widower Kurt Russell decamps form his native town with little daughter in tow and alights at the remote cabin of Kelly McGillis, who has an illegitimate baby son.

An old-fashioned, unassertive type, Russell has to prove himself to McGills' three brothers by joining them on a bear hunt, and wins the approval of her pa, Lloyd Bridges, by designing and building a clock tower for the little community.

But the demented Campbell clan lives across the river, and McGillis' dark secret turns out to be that the father of her child actually is the meanest of the Campbell boys.

After a vicious confrontation with the aborning lovebirds, this tomcat meets a sorry end, whereupon the Campbell clan descends with all its wrath. An eye for an eye, they say, and Bridges' family must decide who will be sacrificed to restore order.

However much one might want to pull for such determinedly unfashionable material, the filmmakers just won't permit it. Despite the tension of the numerous dramatic confrontations, some of the scenes are way over the top and invite derision, while others are just flat and stagey. Along with this, director Ted Kotcheff's constantly moving camera is forever calling attention to itself.

Nor are the actors in a position to help themselves. Continual histrionic demands are placed upon McGillis, who is not necessarily always up to them, and Russell is stuck with the Richard Barthlemess role of the earnest dogooder forced to lower himself to the occasion of taking on brutal thugs.

Bridges lends some dignity to the proceedings as the thoughtful patriarch, while Mitchell Ryan and Jeffrey Meek, as the most prominent Campbells, exude pure evil.

Wintery North Carolina locations are refreshing, although a sense of place is not sustained by the variable accents sported by the cast. —*Cart.*

Miss Firecracker

New York　A Corsair Pictures production and release. Executive producers, Lewis Allen, Ross E. Milloy. Produced by Fred Berner. Directed by Thomas Schlamme. Screenplay, Beth Henley, based on her play "The Miss Firecracker Contest;" camera (Duart color), Arthur Albert; editor, Peter C. Frank; music, David Mansfield; additional music, Homer Denison; sound (Dolby), Glenn Berkovitz; production design, Kristi Zea; art direction, Maher Ahmad; set decoration, Debra Schutt; costume design, Molly Maginnis; production manager, Berner; coproducer, Richard Coll; associate producer, Helen Pollak; casting, Avy Kaufman, Mindy Marin. Reviewed at Corsair screening room, N.Y., March 9, 1989. MPAA Rating: PG. Running time: **102 MIN.**

Carnelle Scott . . . . Holly Hunter
Elain Rutledge . . . . Mary Steenburgen
Delmount Williams . . . . Tim Robbins
Popeye Jackson . . . . Alfre Woodard
Mac Sam . . . . Scott Glenn
Tessy Mahoney . . . . Veanne Cox
Miss Blue . . . . Ann Wedgeworth
Benjamin Drapper . . . . Trey Wilson
Missy Mahoney . . . . Amy Wright
　Also with: Bert Remsen, Christine Lahti.

■ Some of the best acting around is on display in "Miss Firecracker," stage-to-screen adaptation bound to please Beth Henley fans. Precious nature of material and treatment probably will limit general audience acceptance, however.

Holly Hunter reprises her stage role as Carnelle, a former goodtime girl whose dream is to win the local Miss Firecracker contest in her hometown of Yazoo City, Miss. (where film was atmospher-

ORIGINAL PLAY
The Miss Firecracker Contest

A Manhattan Theater Club presentation of a play in two acts by Beth Henley. Staged by Stephen Tobolowsky; scenery, John Lee Beatty; costumes, Jennifer Von Mayrhauser; lighting, Dennis Parichy; sound, Stan Metelits; general manager, Connie L. Alexis; stage managers, Wendy Chapin, Daniel Kanter; publicity, Virginia P. Louloudes. Opened May 27, 1984, at the Manhattan Theater Club, N.Y.; $20 top.
Cast: Holly Hunter, Mark Linn-Baker, Margo Martindale, Belita Moreno, Patricia Richardson, Budge Threlkeld.

ically lensed). Her cousin (Mary Steenburgen) is a role model having won the crown over a decade earlier, and against all odds Carnelle makes it to the finals as an alternate.

Typical of "Crimes Of The Heart" and Henley's coscripted (with helmer David Byrne) "True Stories," "Miss Firecracker" is peopled with oddball characters, notably Tim Robbins as Steenburgen's free spirit brother and Alfre Woodard as the black seamstress assigned to fabricate Carnelle's contest costume.

Henley's faith in the capacity of her characters to aspire to self-improvement comes through winningly, reaching a most optimistic expression in film's post-contest coda of a Fourth of July fireworks display that illuminates the connections between the myriad cast-members.

Henley and first-feature director Thomas Schlamme have adopted a fragmented approach, featuring numerous fadeouts between individual scenes, that (à la Byrne's "True Stories") tends to block viewer involvement in the material. A more seamless approach, emphasizing unity of time and place on the big day of the contest, might have helped. Another drawback is David Mansfield's overly cutesy musical score, which in opening reels is too close to '50s library music for comfort.

Putting the show over with a bang is Hunter, the epitome of energy in a tailormade feisty role. She very accurately judges the line between high and low camp in her climactic tapdance for the talent contest, entertaining but just klutzy enough to be authentic.

Surprise is that "Firecracker" emerges not as a Hunter vehicle to follow up her scoring in "Broadcast News" but a nearly equal-time showcase for her costars. Steenburgen and Woodard are consistent scene-stealers here, former dead-on as a Southern belle putting on airs and latter revivifying ethnic stereotypes such as bugged-out eyes into a hilarious, original character.

Robbins gives a bravura performance capturing the crazy elements of his role. Scott Glenn makes little impact as Hunter's tubercular former lover, a part underwritten and evidently watered down from the stage version.

Small roles tend toward caricature, but the late Trey Wilson ("Bull Durham" costar to whom "Firecracker" is dedicated) is delightful as the contest emcee, Amy Wright is the ultimate plain-Jane contestant and Veanne Cox is incredibly hyper as Wright's sister. Director's wife Christine Lahti pops in for a brief cameo as a neighbor.

Tech credits are fine. Pic is an auspicious debut production for Gotham-based distrib Corsair Pictures. —*Lor.*

Signs Of Life

Hollywood　An Avenue Pictures release of an American Playhouse Theatrical Film pro-

duction. Produced by Marcus Viscidi, Andrew Reichman. Executive producers, Cary Brokaw, Lindsay Law. Directed by John David Coles. Screenplay, Mark Malone; camera (Technicolor), Elliot Davis; editor, William A. Anderson, Angelo Corrao; music, Howard Stone; production design, Howard Cummings; art direction, Beth Rubino; set decoration, Jeanette Scott; sound, Rick Waddell; assistant director, Matthew Carlisle; casting, Doug Aibel. Reviewed at the Burbank (Calif.) Studios, March 30, 1989. MPAA Rating: PG-13. Running time: **91 MIN.**

Owen Coughlin . . . . Arthur Kennedy
Eddie Johnson . . . . Kevin J. O'Connor
Daryl Monahan . . Vincent Philip D'Onofrio
Joey Monahan . . . . Michael Lewis
John Alder . . . . Beau Bridges
Mrs. Wrangway . . . . Kate Reid
Charlotte . . . . Mary Louise Parker
Betty . . . . Georgia Engel

■ "Signs Of Life" is a heartwarming, magical gem of a film from first-time feature director John Coles. Centering on the unique dilemmas facing small town characters, Avenue Pictures release could become a nice little hit given a chance to breathe and grow with strong word of mouth.

The story is simple enough, nearest an ensemble piece that tells how the closing of the last wooden fishing boat builder in tiny, declining Easthasset, Maine affects its handful of employees and the people who depend on them.

In the small space of 24 hours, everyone's future is thrown into disarray and each asks themselves whether to stay and find unrelated work none really wants to do or move away.

First unexpected notion that is dispelled is that it appears — at least initially — that everyone except crotchety boatyard owner Arthur Kennedy is resigned to leaving Easthasset.

His pragmatic housekeeper (Kate Reid) is trying to get him to settle down and his men to work up some enthusiasm for a farewell party.

As it happens, three of them — rivals Eddie (Kevin J. O'Connor) and Daryl (Vincent Philip D'Onofrio) and the latter's retarded brother Joey (Michael Lewis) can't even manage to successfully carry the elaborately decorated going-away cake five feet from the car inside to the table.

The minor traumas of everyday life are celebrated here as well as the major ones — like birth, death and especially rebirth. (Film was originally titled "One For Sorrow, Two For Joy.")

Kathy Bates harangues husband Beau Bridges about responsibility to his growing family while being wheeled into the operating room to deliver another baby — setting him out on a short, desperately funny crime spree at the hardware store.

O'Connor is as wonderful here as he was the bad high school poet in "Peggy Sue Got Married." Playing well off him is D'Onofrio and to more comic ends, smitten g.f. Charlotte (Mary Louis Parker), who'll try anything to keep her man close by.

A real find is Michael Lewis, a stage actor in his 20s who is convincing and compelling as the mentally impaired teenager Joey.

For what presumably is a small-budgeted venture cofunded by Avenue Pictures and PBS' American Playhouse, film looks at all times rich. While Davis' cinematography is particularly stunning, kudos also go to production designer Howard Cummings, art director Beth Rubino and set decorator Jeanette Scott for capturing a small slice of Americana that is fading fast — the tiny Yankee fishing town with a craggy shoreline and a seemingly crazy collection of inhabitants. —Brit.

Young Nurses In Love

New York   A Platinum Pictures presentation. Produced and directed by Chuck Vincent. Screenplay, Vincent, Craig Horrall; camera (color), Larry Revene; editor, "Marc Ubell" (Vincent), James Davalos; music supervision, Bill Heller; sound, Peter Penguin; art direction, D. Gary Phelps; assistant director, Bill Slobodian; production manager-associate producer, Bill Tasgal; casting, Lem Amero. Reviewed on Vestron Video vidcassette, N.Y., April 12, 1989. MPAA Rating: R. Running time: **76 MIN.**
Nurse Ellis . . . . .Jeanne Marie
Dr. Reilly . . . . .Alan Fisler
Francesca . . . . .Jane Hamilton
Dr. Spencer . . . . .Jamie Gillis
Dr. Young . . . . .Harv Siegel
    Also with: James Davies, Barbra Robb, Jennifer Delora, Beth Broderick, Annie Sprinkle, Sharon Moran, John Altamura, Daniel Chapman.

■ Arriving a bit belatedly, "Young Nurses In Love" is an inoffensive sex comedy going direct to video. Pic's main audience probably will consist of paycable viewers into mild titillation.

Evidently a low-budget response to the 1982 Fox release "Young Doctors In Love," pic was made in New Jersey at the end of 1986 by prolific helmer Chuck Vincent, who's completed 10 films since.

Jeanne Marie toplines as a Soviet spy who infiltrates Hoover General Hospital as an all-American nurse. Her mission: steal the deposits by such geniuses as Einstein and Edison from the hospital's sperm bank to enable the next

generation of Russkies to be brainier than us.

Okay slapstick antics are handled by a motley cast which includes good-natured former porn stars Jamie Gillis, Jane Hamilton and Annie Sprinkle. Unfortunately, there aren't enough laughs to distinguish this entry from the pack of similar comedies. —Lor.

Marrakesh Express
(ITALIAN)

Rome   A Columbia Tri-Star Films Italia release of an AMA Film production. Produced by Gianni Minervini. Directed by Gabriele Salvatores. Screenplay, Carlo Mazzcurati, Umberto Contarello, Vincenzo Monteleone; camera (Eastmancolor), Italo Petriccione; editor, Nino Baragli; music, Roberto Ciotti; art direction, Gabriele Serra. Reviewed at Columbia screening room, Rome, April 6, 1989. Running time: **111 MIN.**
Ponchia . . . . .Diego Abatantuono
Marco . . . . .Fabrizio Bentivoglio
Teresa . . . . .Cristina Marsillach
Paolino . . . . .Giuseppe Cederna

■ An Italian road movie with an intriguing premise, "Marrakesh Express" boasts a spirit that is young and comic, plus a good cast, but story is a little too dated and predictable to qualify as offbeat or new.

It should find mainstream audiences onshore and some takers abroad.

A Spanish girl, Teresa (Cristina Marsillach), turns up on Marco's (Fabrizio Bentivoglio) doorstep one day, asking for $20,000 to pay off a judge and get her pot-smoking boyfriend Rudy out of jail in Morocco. Though he hasn't seen Rudy since college 10 years before, Marco lets himself be persuaded to track down the old gang. The money is collected and the four set off with the girl to find the long-lost Rudy.

By jeep from Milan to St. Tropez, Spain to Marrakesh, the trip is full of comic ups and downs. The boys get reacquainted, open old wounds, goof off, smoke dope and generally have a ball. Trouble starts in Marrakesh, where the innocent Teresa disappears with the cash. The boys set off across the Sahara on bicycles to track her and false friend Rudy down.

Thesps are a likable crew, particularly Diego Abatantuono in his transformation as a stuffy car salesman.

Scripting is very loose, a plus for spontaneity but a minus for tension. Though it seems like a story where anything could happen, what does happen — running out of gas, shoplifting in a supermar-

ket, reviving old grudges and making peace again — isn't hard to guess.

"Marrakesh" marks the third feature for Gabriele Salvatores. His attention to performances is a strong plus. Lensing by Italo Petriccione nicely gets across a feeling for a land of broiling sun.
                                —Yung.

Disorganized Crime

Hollywood   A Buena Vista release of a Touchstone Pictures presentation, in association with Silver Screen Partners IV. Produced by Lynn Bigelow. Executive producers, Rob Cohen, John Badham. Written and directed by Jim Kouf. Camera (Metrocolor), Ron Garcia; editor, Frank Morriss, Dallas Puett; music, David Newman; production design, Waldemar Kalinowski; art direction, David Lubin; set design, Florence Fellman; costume design, Stephanie Maslansky; sound (Dolby), Doug Axtell; assistant director, John R. Woodward; additional camera, Yuri Neyman, Sean Doyle; second unit director, Dan Bradley; associate producer, Marie Butler Kouf; casting, Lora Kennedy. Reviewed at the Avco Cinema, L.A. April 11, 1989. MPAA Rating: R. Running time: **101 MIN.**
Sheriff Henault . . . . .Hoyt Axton
Frank Salazar . . . . .Corbin Bernsen
Carlos Barrios . . . . .Rubén Blades
Max Green . . . . .Fred Gwynne
George Denver . . . . .Ed O'Neill
Ray Forgy . . . . .Lou Diamond Phillips
Bill Lonigan . . . . .Daniel Roebuck
Nick Bartkowski . . . . .William Russ

■ As innocuous as its title, "Disorganized Crime" is a heist comedy of the most modest possible dimensions in both suspense and humor. Disney probably can milk this for some decent returns over the short term, but this reps a minor league entry for the company.

Lensed in Montana as "Waiting For Salazar," this second feature as director from Jim Kouf possesses more action than the original title would indicate. Four former cohorts of Salazar (Corbin Bernsen) do, in fact, spend the entire film waiting for their convict friend to turn up at a rural house in order to pull a job. In the meantime, however, they manage to stir up plenty of trouble for the local authorities and themselves.

Body of the film consists of intercutting among three sections of a chase. Rubén Blades, Fred Gwynne, Lou Diamond Phillips and William Russ argue among themselves and play a sort of hide-and-seek until the first three feel obliged to commit two robberies in order to raise bail money for Russ, who's been picked up on stolen vehicle and drunk driving charges.

At the same time, bumbling detectives Ed O'Neill and Daniel Roebuck slog through the wilder-

ness trying to track down Bernsen, who has escaped from their care while being escorted back to New Jersey and is having trouble of his own.

For most of his attempts at humor, Kouf resorts to coarse exchanges among the 2-bit criminals or slapstick, going to the well of manure-covered comedy on more than one occasion.

Pic's uninsistent charms lie mainly in the realm of character comedy. Once again, Gwynne comes off exceedingly well as a likable heavy. Just watching him weakens one's resistence to the routine surroundings he inhabits.

A seeming cross between Peter Falk and Mickey Rourke, William Russ brings a tart intensity to his unpredictable character, and Rubén Blades has a few good moments of amusing irritability. Lou Diamond Phillips can't do much with his underwritten role as the youngest collaborator.

Corbin Bernsen spends his brief stretch of running time looking pained and exhausted from his travails, while Ed O'Neill and Daniel Roebuck as the hapless cops try out every possible expression to convey exasperation.

Tech credits are very average with the exception of David Newman's excellent and varied score.
                                —Cart.

Field Of Dreams

New York   A Universal Pictures release of a Gordon Co. production. Produced by Lawrence Gordon, Charles Gordon. Executive producer, Brian Frankish. Directed by Phil Alden Robinson. Screenplay, Robinson, based on the book "Shoeless Joe," by W.P. Kinsella; camera (Deluxe color), John Lindley; editor, Ian Crafford; music, James Horner; sound (Dolby), Russell Williams 2d; production design, Dennis Gassner; costumes, Linda Bass; assistant director, William M. Elvin; special visual effects, Industrial Light & Music — supervisor Bruce Nicholson; associate producer, Lloyd Levin; casting, Margery Simkin. Reviewed at Fifth Avenue screening room, N.Y., April 6, 1989. MPAA Rating: PG. Running time: **106 MIN.**
Ray Kinsella . . . . .Kevin Costner
Annie Kinsella . . . . .Amy Madigan
Karin Kinsella . . . . .Gaby Hoffman
Shoeless Joe Jackson . . . . .Ray Liotta
Mark . . . . .Timothy Busfield
Terence Mann . . . . .James Earl Jones
Dr. "Moonlight" Graham . .Burt Lancaster
Archie Graham . . . . .Frank Whaley
John Kinsella . . . . .Dwier Brown

■ Alternately affecting and affected, "Field Of Dreams" is a fable about redemption and reconciliation that uses the mythos of baseball as an organizing metaphor. Its quixotic nature makes the film a hard-to-figure box-office prospect, but its fine cast could attract an audience if enticed by favorable reviews.

Kevin Costner plays Ray Kinsella, a new-age farmer who has come to Iowa's cornfields by way of a nomadic childhood, the ferment of the '60s and a stabilizing marriage with his college sweetheart, Amy Madigan. Together with their cute daughter (Gaby Hoffman), the couple scrapes out a don't-worry-be-happy life on the land.

In the fields one day Costner hears a celestial voice that cryptically advises: "If you build it, he will come." Once he convinces himself and his family that he's not going crazy, Costner — whose dead father imbued him with baseball lore but kept him at an emotional distance — sets out to sculpt a beautiful baseball diamond from his precious cornfield. This costs the family their entire savings. The whole town thinks the outsider has gone bonkers, but one night Costner's faith is rewarded: the spirit of Shoeless Joe Jackson, the most precipitously fallen off the disgraced World Series fixers, the 1919 Chicago White Sox, materializes on his ballfield.

Shoeless Joe, rendered with appropriately disembodied detachment by Ray Liotta, soon assembles other uniformed spirits on the cornfield basepaths. In keeping with the fairytale motif, this ghostly team is visible only to true believers. Materialistic cynics like brother-in-law Timothy Busfield ("thirtysomething"), who's trying to persuade Costner to sell his failing farm, are blind to the heavenly hardball.

Fully in the grip of supernatural forces and blessed with an exceptionally understanding wife, Costner leaves the farm on a cross-country pilgrimage to find the Boston home of America's best-known reclusive writer — a cultural demigod depicted as a cross between J.D. Salinger and Bob Dylan. James Earl Jones, in a very likable turn, plays the dried-up novelist Terence Mann as a bitter sage disenchanted with the engagement politics of the '60s and disgusted with the me-first ethos of the '80s.

Through sheer persistence, Costner convinces the hermit genius Jones to take in a game at Fenway Park. Here the major leagues get metaphysical as both men receive a subliminal message to im-

mediately head out west in search of one Dr. "Moonlight" Graham, a country doctor who half a century earlier appeared in one big league game, but never got to bat. Although his character is dead and buried, his spirit turns up in the person of an avuncular Burt Lancaster.

Costner, Shoeless Joe, Jones and Lancaster are all haunted by regrets over failed relationships, life-shattering mistakes and missed opportunities. All yearn for a collective second chance at inner peace. In spite of a script hobbled with cloying aphorisms and shameless sentimentality, "Field Of Dreams" sustains a dreamy mood in which the idea of baseball is distilled to its purest essence: a game that stands for unsullied innocence in a cruel, imperfect world. —Rich.

She's Out Of Control

Hollywood A Columbia Pictures release of a Weintraub Entertainment Group presentation. Produced by Stephen Deutsch. Executive producer, Robert Kaufman. Coproducer, John G. Wilson. Directed by Stan Dragoti. Screenplay, Seth Winston, Michael J. Nathanson; camera (CFI color, Film House prints), Donald Peterman; editor, Dov Hoenig; music, Alan Silvestri; music supervisor, Tim Sexton; production design, David L. Snyder; art direction, Joe Wood; set design, Daniel Maltese, John O. Warnke; set decoration, Bruce Gibeson; costume design, Marie France; sound (Dolby), Ronald Cogswell; assistant director, Tom Mack; second unit director, Bill Wilson. Reviewed at Samuel Goldwyn theater, Beverly Hills, Calif., April 11, 1989. MPAA Rating: PG. Running time: **95 MIN.**

Doug Simpson . . . . Tony Danza
Janet Pearson . . . . Catherine Hicks
Katie Simpson . . . . Ami Dolenz
Dr. Fishbinder . . . . Wallace Shawn
Mr. Pearson . . . . Dick O'Neill
Bonnie Simpson . . . . Laura Mooney
Jeff . . . . Derek McGrath
Joey . . . . Dana Ashbrook
Timothy . . . . Matthew L. Perry

■Somewhere lurking behind the scenes of "She's Out Of Control" is the germ of a good idea. Despite some funny scenes, the sitcomish treatment of a father's anxiety over his teenage daughter's budding sexuality is mostly shallow and uneven.

The innocuous PG-rated Tony Danza-starrer should do okay in the teenage market.

Danza makes an uncertain transition to the big screen under Stan Dragoti's direction, trying to shake some of the mannerisms of his "Who's The Boss?" tv character in playing a supposedly mature man. He plays too many scenes on a one-note level rather than weaving his character's changes into the stuff of more complex comedy. Danza has a likable persona, and

his fans will not be disappointed.

The widowed g.m. of an L.A. rock radio station, Danza is no square, but he freaks out when his g.f. Catherine Hicks decides to transform his daughter Ami Dolenz from a studious wallflower into an airheaded sexpot. Though teenage girls often do seem to grow up overnight, their emotions don't develop as quickly as their bodies, a point this film doesn't grasp in painting Dolenz as an instant heartbreaker.

After the shaky opening, film picks up some wit and steam when Danza begins consulting a shrink played with his customary sly intelligence by Wallace Shawn.

Naturally, everything Shawn tells Danza to do backfires. When Dolenz appears with punker Dana Ashbrook, Shawn advises the appalled Danza to "befriend the enemy." It's not long before the daughter dumps the punker and he begins clinging to Danza as the dad he's never had.

There's also some good fun in the parade of eager boys Danza has to keep turning away from the door, Laura Mooney is terrif as Danza's precocious younger daughter, and the episode of Dolenz' attempted seduction by Matthew L. Perry is also a standout.

For too much of its 95-minute running time, though, the film is loud, broad and panders to the filmmakers' condescending conception of teenage tastes.

Technically, pic has a rather cold look and feel. —Mac.

Roselyne et les lions
(Roselyne And The Lions)
(FRENCH)

Paris A Gaumont release of a Cargo Films/Gaumont coproduction. Produced and directed by Jean-Jacques Beineix. Screenplay, Beineix, Jacques Forgeas, with technical collaboration of Thierry Le Portier; camera (color), Jean-François Robin; editor, Marie Castro-Brechignac; music, Reinhardt Wagner; art direction, Carlos Conti; sound, Pierre Befve, Dominique Hennequin; assistant director, Jérome Chalou; production manager, Catherine Mazières; casting, Gérard Moulevrier; animal advisor, Thierry Le Portier. Reviewed at Gaumont Ambassade theater, Paris, April 13, 1889. Running time: **127 MIN.**

Boselyne . . . . Isabelle Pasco
Thierry . . . . Gérard Sandoz
Bracquard . . . . Philippe Clevenot
Klint . . . . Gunter Meisner
Koenig . . . . Wolf Harnish
Frazier . . . . Gabriel Monnet
Markovitch . . . . Jacques Le Carpentier
Little Prince . . . . Carlos Pavlidis

■Jean-Jacques Beineix' "Betty Blue" had animal heat. His new film, "Roselyne And The Lions," has animals but no

heat.

This tale of two youths who climb the ladder of success as lion tamers in the big top is almost as tepid and empty a tale of initiation and mystical self-fulfillment at Luc Besson's "The Big Blue," another Gaumont-produced spectacular. Beineix has merely replaced the dolphins with lions and tigers.

Industry mavens were wrong about "Blue" (for France anyway), so it may be presumptuous to say Beineix has caged himself in commercially. With no stars and a two hours-plus running time, its overseas chances will depend largely on helmer's reputation.

The title is unfair billing. Roselyne, played by Isabelle Pasco, forms a tandem with Gérard Sandoz, who's as nuts about the lions as she. A zero in school, Sandoz spends his free hours at the local (Marseilles) zoo working with an aging lion tamer. Pasco, who lives with her mother and has no other visible employ, avidly watches. They're young and in love, but mostly with the animals.

When Sandoz is bounced out of his zoo job he takes to the road with Pasco. They find work in a small provincial circus, but a muscle-bound macho animal trainer limits them to menial labors.

The couple get lucky when they get a break from a famous German big top. In Munich, they begin their real apprenticeship. Despite some antagonism from a mysterious veteran with a tiger act (who's dark secret is that he once was a famous lion tamer but was traumatically mauled by his beasts), the youths find few major obstacles on their way to the big time. The film climaxes with a public apotheosis in their big kitsch debut, complete with a lion that snatches a rose from the breast of the prostrate Pasco.

Unlike the couple in "Betty Blue," Beineix' new lovers are devoid of personal charm or depth. Their only psychological trait is their passion for beasts and their will to succeed. They don't seem to mind the commercialism and glitz of the professional circus as long as they are left a margin of "style" (the unorthodox climax of their act is a surprise to their employer, who has prepared their show with canny media hyperbole).

Beineix and his lenser Jean-

François Robin (who once studied at the Fratellini circus school) film the many training scenes with feline swoops and bounds of virtuoso mobile camera. The presence of immediate physical danger gives the scenes some dramatic meat, though their repetitiveness soon wears away any suspense.

Pasco and Sandoz don't add up to much as characters though they display obvious courage in accepting to go into the lion cage time and again with some pretty fierce-looking cats.

Philippe Clevenot, a fine stage actor, is wasted in an inane supporting role as a language teacher who gives the youths their first real moral support. Jacques Le Carpentier is the hulking macho trainer who tries to bridle the couple, and Carlos Pavlidis is a midget ally.

German actors Gunter Meisner, as the psychologically maimed tiger trainer, and Wolf Harnish, as the German circus mogul, are Teutonic monoliths who cast troubled shadows over the innocent youth Gauls.

Tech credits are slick. —Len.

Lo Que Importa Es Vivir
(What's Important Is To Live)
(MEXICAN)

Mexico City   A Películas Mexicanas release of an Imcine (Mexican Film Institute) production. Produced by Héctor López Lechuga. Written and directed by Luis Alcoriza. Camera (color), Miguel Garzón; editor, Federico Landero; music, Pedro Plascenia Salinas; sets, José López Hernández. Reviewed at National Cinémathèque screening room, Mexico City, Feb. 11, 1989. Running time: 102 MIN.

Candelario . . . . Gonzalo Vega
Don Lázaro . . . . Ernesto Gómez Cruz
Chabela . . . . Marla Rojo
    Also with: Alejandro Parodi, Lolo Navarro, Justo Martínez, Eduardo Borja.

■ In an attempt to criticize hypocritical macho values, former Luis Buñuel collaborator Luis Alcoriza misses the mark entirely and instead presents a rambling, risibly distorted picture about the mores of rural Mexico.

Excessively long pic begins with the arrival of an uncompromising drifter (Gonzalo Vega) vaguely en route to the sea. He stops by a hacienda asking for work in exchange for room and board, and is soon running the farm. He is treated like a son by rancho honcho Don Lázaro (Ernesto Gómez Cruz).

Bucolic tranquility does not last long. Don Lázaro's faithful wife (María Rojo) gets a hankering for the ranch's new stud and the two are soon involved in a too-hot-to-handle relationship.

When seeking revenge, the jealous rancher suffers a fall that leaves him with the intelligence of a 5-year-old and roles are reversed: Our drifter now runs both the hacienda and hausfrau, while the rancher turns raunchy. He rolls his eyes, lollygags and calls Vega daddy. He is soon joined by a baby brother, the illegitimate son of his wife and the drifter.

The plot complicates insufferably. The townsfolk have not only accepted Vega's outrage to the community but hail him as a local leader. He finds himself trapped into country bourgeois life, and in the end he bolts.

Script flaunts misunderstood view of Mexican country life. As the drama turns to melodrama, the production flounders through inconsistency. Actor Vega loses touch with his characterization, and Gómez Cruz offers a simplistic parody as rancher-cum-cucumber.

Obviously Alcoriza's intention is to shock the audience, but he accomplishes this task at the expense of the story. —Lent.

Ladri di saponette
(Soap Thieves)
(ITALIAN-COLOR/B&W)

Rome   A Warner Bros. Italia release of a Bambù Cinema e TV production. (Intl. sales, Italtoons.) Produced by Ernesto Sarrù. Directed by Maurizio Nichetti. Screenplay, Nichetti, Mauro Monti; camera (color, b&w), Mario Battistoni; editor, Rita Rossi, Anna Missoni; music, Manuel De Sica. Reviewed at Madonna di Campiglio, Rome, March 18, 1989. Running time: 93 MIN.

Film director/Antonio . . . Maurizio Nichetti
Maria . . . . Caterina Sylos Labini
Priest . . . . Renato Scarpa
Model . . . . Heidi Komarek
    Also with: Federico Rizzo, Matteo Auguardi, Carlina Torta, Massimo Sacilotto, Lella Costa, Claudio G. Fava.

■ Comic Maurizio Nichetti directs an affectionate send-up of Italian neorealism in "Soap Thieves." An act of love towards the black & white social dramas of the post-war years, "Soap" is no less a declaration of hatred towards tv commercials, especially the ones that interrupt feature films on tv.

Proclaiming itself "the first film that interrupts commercials," "Soap" is a witty spoof that gets tangled up in its own meandering plot — if plot it can be called. Box-office has been only so-so locally, where Nichetti's fans are many.

The director plays the two main roles himself. In one he's a fuzzy-haired film director present in the tv studio where his film "Soap Thieves" — supposedly a remake of a neorealist film — is being aired. Not only does the host (RAI-TV's programmer Claudio G. Fava in a good-humored spoof of tv critics) hog the microphone and not let him talk, but his film is cut to pieces with constant commercial interruptions.

Nichetti (whose familiar face is all but unrecognizable clean-shaven) also plays Antonio, his film's poor unemployed hero, who finds a job at a glass factory but immediately runs away with an enormous chandelier for his wife Maria (Caterina Sylos Labini). Before he can get home, however, a 6-foot blond model in a skimpy bikini pops up out of a tv commercial. Antonio takes her home, outraging his wife until, by another electronic mix-up, Maria gets transferred to soap commercials.

Nichetti the director goes into his film to rescue the plot, but only succeeds in confusing it further. From a tv set's point of view, we see a middle-class family tuning in and out of "Soap Thieves" with typical distraction.

This Babel of run-on images has moments of great fun. More than the protest message behind the story, however, Nichetti's humor comes across best in throwaway details (a baby miraculously saved from one lethal danger after another; the little son's casual exploitation by family and parish priest).

As inventive as "Soap Thieves" is, and as cinematically erudite, it lacks the popular appeal of Nichetti's best work. Stepping out of the amiable mute character he created in earlier pics, his double incarnations are abstractions.

Special effects are worth watching, like the injection of color into black-and-white images. Technical work is generally top-notch.
—Yung.

ARCHIVE REVIEWS

Ya, Babushka, Illiko & Illarion
(I, Grandmother, Illiko & Illarion)
(SOVIET-B&W)

Hong Kong   A Gruziafilm (1963) production. Directed by Tengiz Abuladze. Screenplay, Abuladze; camera (b&w), Georgi Kalatozhivili; music, N. Vatsadze; sound, R. Kezel. Reviewed at Hong Kong Film Festival March 25, 1989. Running time: 86 MIN.
    With Zurab Ordzhonikidze, C. Takayshuili, A. Zhorzheliani.

■ An early film from the director of the prize-winning "Repentance," Tengiz Abuladze, this charmer is blessed both with a quirky sense of humor and a typically Georgian feeling for the rocky landscape of small towns and villages.

The story spans a number of years, from pre-World War II until some time after the conflict, but the war is seen only as it affects this isolated part of the world. A parade is held as men leave to join the army, reports come of casualties and a parade welcomes the survivors home again.

Focus is on the "I" of the title — Zuriko, a gangly youth who lives with his feisty old grandmother. She accompanies him on his trips to school, since she also wants to be educated. They have two close friends, the nearsighted hunter Illarion (who accidentally kills Zuriko's dog, mistaking it for a rabbit) and the 1-eyed Illiko. After the war, they sell their communal cow to pay for Zuriko's college education in Tbilisi.

Pic has a simple theme, but handles it with a style and humor that's most appealing. Visually, it's outstanding, both in the crisp black & white images and in the placing of characters against landscapes. As in many Georgian films, there's a love of the country that suffuses the drama and the wide streets of Tbilisi are as beautiful as the snowscapes of the countryside. One sequence, shot entirely in silhouettes, is a standout.

When Zuriko is about to kiss Mary, his sweetheart, for the first time, the camera pans tactfully away from them. Though he dallies with another girl at college, the magic of the countryside eventually draws the young man back to Mary and his dying grandmother.

The film's ending seems almost a nod to "The Grapes Of Wrath." "There'll never be an end to us," says Zuriko, after grandmother's death. And Abuladze has drawn us so close to these funny, sweet characters that we believe him.
—Strat.

Moya Babushka
(My Grandmother)
(SOVIET-B&W)

Hong Kong   A Goskinprom production (1929), restored by Gruziafilm (1976). Directed by Kote Mikaberidze. Screenplay, Georgi Mdivani, Semion Dolidze, Mikaberidze; camera (b&w), Anton Polikevic, Vladimir Poznan; production design, T. Gamrekeli, Valerian Sidamon-Eristavi. Reviewed at Hong Kong Film Festival, March 26, 1989. Running time: (at 24 frames per second): **60 MIN.**
The Bureaucrat . . . . .A. Takaishvili
His Wife . . . . .B. Chepnova
The Doorman . . . . .E. Ovanov

■ This silent film, made in Soviet Georgia in 1929, was such a frontal attack on communist bureaucracy that the authorities in Moscow promptly banned it. It was released only in 1976, when Gruziafilm, the Georgian production house, added a music score and sound effects. In this version, it unspooled at the 1977 New York Film Festival.

Director Kote (Konstantine) Mikaberidze (1896-1973) was an actor and cartoonist, but "My Grandmother" was, apparently, by far his most successful attempt at feature film direction. The very stylized film mocks a Kafkaesque state corporation where most of the bureaucrats are either asleep on the job, or are occupied with non-essentials (one man, responsible for saving paper, instead whiles away his time sending love notes to a secretary and, when rejected, shoots himself).

The outfit's boss (amusingly played by A. Takaishvili rather in the style of Harold Lloyd) is grossly incompetent and is eventually fired, to the alarm of his exuberant, charleston-loving wife (a very funny performance from B. Chepnova). Of her, an intertitle remarks: "She bought from speculators everything she ever wanted."

The out-of-work bureaucrat quickly discovers that a "grandmother" (influence or privilege) is required to find a new job, and he sets about getting a recommendation, which he eventually extracts from an unwilling executive. A representative of the workers, a Lenin-like figure (shot so that he looks enormous) rejects this "grandmother," and the film ends with titles which demand "Death To Red Tape! Death To Slovenliness! Death To Bureaucrats!" No wonder the censors in Moscow got cold feet.

The film's themes probably are as relevant today as they ever were, and its style is a consistently funny mixture of slapstick and surrealism — the latter exemplified by a scene in which the "hero's wife kicks him out of their apartment window, but he lands on the sidewalk below unhurt. There's also a naked male statue that comes to life, and other, less successful attempts at animation.

In all, it's a delightful film, full of invention, smartly paced, cleverly acted. —*Strat.*

Eliso
(SOVIET-B&W)

Hong Kong A Gruziafilm production (1928). Directed by Nikolai Shengelaya. Screenplay, Shengelaya, Sergei Tretjakov, from a story by Alexander Qazbegi; camera (b&w), Vladimir Kereselidze; art direction, Dimitri Sevarnadze. Reviewed at Hong Kong Film Festival, March 25, 1989. Running time (at 24 frames per second): **75 MIN.**
Eliso . . . . .Kira Andronikashvili
Vazho . . . . .Kokta Karalahvili
Astamir . . . . .Alexander Imedashvili
Seidulla . . . . .I. Mamporia
Seidulla's wife . . . . .Tu. Tsutsunava

■ Nikolai Shengelaya (1901-1943) was a leading figure in Georgian cinema from 1927 on. He tackled a legendary epic theme in "Eliso," made in 1928.

The drama is set in 1864, when the Czarist regime in far-off St. Petersburg is using its cossack forces to deport Muslim Georgians from their villages and arable land and send them into neighboring Turkey, also a Muslim country (according to the film, Russian motives were simply to steal the land).

One such village is Verdi where Eliso, daughter of the village chief, is in love with Vazho, who hails from a Christian village nearby. Little is made of this Romeo/Juliet theme, however.

The cossacks, needing an excuse to deport the peaceful villagers, send men to rustle their cattle, and it's Vazho who comes to the rescue, saving the cattle but — by killing a couple of cossacks — unwittingly providing the Russians with the excuse they need to oust the villagers.

Pic climaxes with the exodus of the Verdi people, though Eliso slips back to the village to set it alight, destroying what the Russians have seized. When a woman dies during the trek towards Turkey, the furious villagers are calmed when Eliso's father encourages the playing of (presumably) traditional Georgian music.

The most striking element here is the glorious camerawork by Vladimir Kereselidze, which lovingly captures the mountain-top village and the rugged terrain surrounding it. From the beginning, it seems, Georgian films have evoked a passion for the landscape and traditions of a people whose land straddles Europe and Asia.

In two key sequences, Shengelaya employs Eisensteinian montage to powerful effect, especially at the end with the death of the woman and the commencement of a mood of national fervor, brought about by the (unheard) music and dance.

Kira Andronikashvili makes Eliso a strong, passionate heroine, but Kokta Karalahvili is rather a wan hero, and a scene in which he single-handedly fights off saber-wielding cossacks is laughable today. It's the kind of scene at which Doug Fairbanks excelled, but the actor in this case in no Doug.

Otherwise, "Eliso" survives as a major example of early Georgian cinema. —*Strat.*

Pet Sematary

Hollywood   A Paramount Pictures release of a Richard P. Rubinstein production. Executive producer, Tim Zinnemann. Produced by Rubinstein. Directed by Mary Lambert. Screenplay, Stephen King, based upon his novel; Camera (Technicolor), Peter Stein; editor, Michael Hill, Daniel Hanley; music, Elliot Goldenthal; production design, Michael Z. Hanan; costume design, M. Stewart; art direction, Dins Danielson; set decoration, Katharin Briggs; coproducer, Mitchell Galin; associate producer, Ralph S. Singleton; casting, Fern Champion, Pamela Basker; in Dolby stereo. Reviewed at Village theater, Westwood, Calif., April 18, 1989. MPAA Rating: R. Running time: **102 MIN.**
Louis Creed . . . . .Dale Midkiff
Jud Crandall . . . . .Fred Gwynne
Rachel Creed . . . . .Denise Crosby
Victor Pascow . . . . .Brad Greenquist
Irwin Goldman . . . . .Michael Lombard
Ellie Creed . . . . .Blaze Berdahl
Gage Creed . . . . .Miko Hughes
Missy Dandridge . . . . . . .Susan Blommaert

■ If Stephen King (rightly) feels that most of his novels have been botched in their translation to film, at least this time he has to point a finger at himself. "Pet Sematary" marks the first time King has adapted his own book for the screen, and the result is undead schlock dulled by a slasher-film mentality — squandering its chilling and fertile source material.

Paramount should exhume early riches from the teen crowd that enjoys watching someone walk down a foreboding hallway over and over again, but word of mouth should send the film to the great beyond within a matter of weeks.

Director Mary Lambert cut her teeth on rock videos before her first feature, "Siesta," and "Pet Sematary" exhibits some of those sensibilities: Most of the action from the novel makes its way to the screen but all the necessary exposition and setups have been omitted, leaving a mess of images that any vet or script doctor would be hard-pressed to revive.

The story hinges on a small family that comes to New England, moving into a vintage Americana house alongside a truck route. When Louis Creed (Dale Midkiff) finds his daughter's cat dead along the road, his elderly neighbor Jud (Fred Gwynne) takes him to a hidden Indian burial ground that brings the beast back to life.

The quiet madness that gradually leads Louis to try and bring a person back via the same process — despite the repeated warnings of a friendly ghost — isn't apparent in Lambert's hastily assembled narrative.

King appears in a cameo as a minister presiding over a funeral.

He has also introduced some wan, recurrent humor in the form of the reappearing and grisly ghost (Brad Greenquist) similar to Griffin Dunne's chatty, decaying corpse in "An American Werewolf In London."

With the exception of Midkiff, an appealing if ill-developed lead, the cast endures tortures reserved for the living. Absent motivation, Gwynne and Denise Crosby (as Louis' wife) are utterly two-dimensional, and the former's Pepperidge Farm acccent makes him sound as if he needs oral surgery.

Blaze Berdahl emerges as one of the most annoying child actors in memory as the six-year-old daughter, though Miko Hughes should be the envy of the two-year-old set with his role as Gage. Even the cat overacts.

The distressing thing is that the filmmakers chose to take the easy route of gore and cheap thrills and steered clear of the much harder yet rewarding task of building genuine terror. Even then, some of the choices are staggeringly odd — including shooting many of the fright scenes in broad daylight.

Tech credits are generally okay — especially Peter Stein's cinematography, properly unnerving in some scenes — but clearly look to have been done under a limited budget. —Bril.

The Freeway Maniac

New York   A Cannon Intl. presentation of a Wintertree production. Produced by Paul Winters, Loren Winters. Directed by Paul Winters. Screenplay, Paul Winters, Gahan Wilson; camera (United color), Ronald Vidor; editor, David Marsh; music, Greg Stewart; songs, Robby Krieger; sound, Daniel Monahan; assistant director, Linda Stewart; production manager, Tony Brewster; sand clam design, Wilson; associate producer, Jeff Van Der Pol. Reviewed on Media Home Entertainment vidcassette, N.Y., Jan. 21, 1989. MPAA Rating: R. Running time: 93 MIN.
Linda . . . . Loren Winters
Arthur . . . . James Courtney
Burt Overman . . . . Shepard Sanders
Steven Day . . . . Donald Hotton
Ray . . . . Jeff Morris
Terry . . . . Robert Bruce
Mannie . . . . Frank Jasper

■ Previously known as "Breakdown," this threadbare horror pickup from Cannon boasts a couple of unusual names in the credits but flunks out in execution, accounting for its direct-to-video release.

Coproducer Loren Winters toplines as a model who gets a job starring in low-budget sci-fi flick, "Astronette." She also has a run-in with an escaped looney (James Courtney), who slashed folks in the pic's prolog and keeps getting loose to wreak havoc on or near the freeway.

Filmmaker Paul Winters includes some heavyhanded spoofing of low-budget genre lensing, while his own work is a substandard example of same. Renowned horror cartoonist Gahan Wilson contributed to the ho-hum script and also fashioned a large clam monster for the film-within-a-film that resembles his magazine drawings. Lead guitarist for The Doors, Robby Krieger, delivers some forgettable songs, and such heavyweights as Robert Bloch and Stan Lee figure in thank-you credits.

It's all a lost cause with amateurish acting, cheapo technical work and little imagination.—Lor.

Misplaced

Washington, D.C.   A Subway Films production. Produced by Lisa Zwerling. Directed by Louis Yansen. Screenplay, Yansen, Thomas DeWolfe; camera (color) Igor Sunara; editor, Michael Berenbaum; music, Michael Urbaniak; production design, Beth Kukn; costume design, Linda-Lee Cocuzzo; assistant directors, Steve Apicella, Richard Murray; casting, Robin Monroe. Reviewed at American Film Institute theater, Washington, D.C., April 2. 1989. No MPAA Rating. Running time: 95 MIN.
Jacek Nowak . . . . . John Cameron Mitchell
Zofia . . . . Viveca Lindfors
Halina Nowak . . . . Elzbieta Czyzewska
Bill . . . . Drew Snyder
Ela . . . . Deirdre O'Connell

■ Trials of a Polish mother and her son in assimilating into U.S. culture are given sensitive treatment in "Misplaced." Sturdy performances by principals make this intriguing tale believable.

Writer-director Louis Yansen pens a largely autobiographical yarn about his eye-opening experiences as a young immigrant. Film follows the duo from Warsaw, where they are escaping the 1981 Solidarity uprising, to Washington, D.C., and a new life with family.

Mother (Elzbieta Czyzewska) sweeps floors until landing a job as an announcer with Voice of America, while teenage son (John Cameron Mitchell) copes with adolescence and assorted pressures. He tackles the role with wide-eyed ingenuousness. Another strong performance is turned in by Viveca Lindfors as the opinionated grandmother.

Initial scenes are shot in Polish with subtitles, possibly limiting the film's commercial appeal. Pic, which debuted at the Women Make Movies film festival here, received funding from the American Film Institute. —Paul.

Lords Of The Deep

Hollywood   A Concorde Pictures release. Produced by Roger Corman. Associate producer, Rodman Flender. Directed by Mary Ann Fisher. Screenplay, Howard Cohen, Daryl Haney; camera (Foto-Kem color), Austin McKinney; editor, Nina Gilberti; music, Jim Berenholtz; art direction, Troy Myers; set decoration, Ildiko Toth; sound, Michael Clark; visual effects coordinator, Ray Greer; assistant director, Jonathan Allen Winfrey; second unit director, Tom Campbell. Reviewed at Aidikoff screening room, L.A., April 19, 1989. MPAA Rating: PG-13. Running time: 82 MIN.
Dobler . . . . Bradford Dillman
Claire . . . . Priscilla Barnes
Barbara . . . . Melody Ryane
O'Neill . . . . Daryl Haney
Seaver . . . . Eb Lottimer
Engel . . . . Greg Sobeck
Chadwick . . . . Richard Young
Fernandez . . . . Stephen Davies

■ Concorde's ultra low-budget "Lords of The Deep" is a meek, unsuspenseful little submarine saga with a mawkish New Age twist. In a year that has launched a fleet of underwater vehicles, "Lords" makes it three too many so far.

It presents the instantly familiar shipboard scenario — a crew of research scientists in the employ of an unfeeling corporation encounter a strange life form, and are instructed to suppress, rather than explore, their findings.

A feisty researcher stands up to the commander in the name of science. The commander turns out to be a psychopath who starts to kill his crew as he feels control slipping away.

A strange life form metamorphasizes into some threatening shape and invades ship's air vents or water supply. Crew members seize weapons and seek it out. They die, one by one. The survivors confront the beast.

That's where "Lords Of The Deep" abandons ship — because the monsters (appearing as foaming goop, mantra rays with evil red eyes, and a benign E.T.-like thing) turn out to be friendly aliens from the future who've come to warn Earthlings to stop poisoning their planet before it's too late.

Pic behaves like a sprung spring flopping around. Even at a scant 82 minutes, it has scenes that drop their pacing to an embarrassing degree.

Bradford Dillman is an irritating and too-abundant presence as the deteriorating commander, but Stephen Davies manages to build some low-key comic appeal into his role as crewman Fernandez.

Priscilla Barnes, with her goofy flower-child grins, seems miscast until you realize that she's just the one the aliens could use as a spokesperson.

Camerawork and musical score are bottom-grade, but underwater models and some aspects of the production design are actually quite handsome.

—Daws.

Red Scorpion

New York   A Shapiro Glickenhaus Entertainment release of an Abramoff production. Executive producers, Robert Abramoff, Daniel Sklar, Paul Erickson. Produced by Jack Abramoff. Directed by Joseph Zito. Screenplay, Arne Olsen, from story by Robert and Jack Abramoff, Olsen; camera (Deluxe color), Joao Fernandes; editor, Daniel Loewenthal; music, Jay Chattaway; sound (Dolby), Gary Rich; production design, Ladislav Wilheim; 2d unit directors, Newt Arnold, Eddie Stacey; stunt coordinators, Stacey, Peter Diamond; special makeup effects, Tom Savini; special effects supervisor, John Evans. Reviewed at Criterion 2, N.Y., April 19, 1989. MPAA Rating: R. Running time: 102 MIN.
Lt. Nikolai . . . . Dolph Lundgren
Dewey Ferguson . . . . M. Emmet Walsh
Kallunda . . . . Al White
Gen. Vortek . . . . T.P. McKenna
Zayas . . . . Carmen Argenziano
Mendez . . . . Alex Colon
Krasnov . . . . Brion James
Gao, bushman . . . . Regopstaan

■ "Red Scorpion" is a dull, below-average action pic doomed to poor word-of-mouth domestically. Foreign chances are better for this Dolph Lundgren vehicle.

Pic goes out independently after Warner Bros. backed out of a negative pickup deal (following bad publicity relating to production services coming out of South Africa on the Swaziland-lensed feature).

Out-of-date screenplay by Arne Olsen has the Scandinavian star playing a Russian special services officer ordered by his nasty commander (Irish thesp T.P. McKenna) to kill the rebel leader of a fictional African country. Lundgren fails in his mission and is tortured by Cubans.

Under the guidance of a knowing, mystical bushman (Regopstaan, obviously patterned on the hero of "The Gods Must Be Crazy") who tattoos a scorpion on Dolph's chest, Lundgren realizes the commies are oppressing the Africans. Anticlimax has this Nordic giant leading the otherwise defeated rebels to defeat the combined Russian/Cuban might.

Jospeh Zito's sluggish direction lingers on nonessentials, giving the film a tediousness that could have been alleviated by dropping at least a reel's worth of trekking across the African desert.

Lundgren's nonacting cancels out any empathy that might have been earned by his character. He provides little more than sustained beefcake, with a very weak, virtually all-male supporting cast on hand.

Stunts and explosions are okay, but battle scenes remain unexciting. Pic's highlight undoubtedly is provided by Tom Savini's very convincing make-up effects when Lundgren is tortured with an extreme form of Cuban acupuncture. —Lor.

Checking Out

New York   Warner Bros. release of a Handmade Films presentation. Produced by Ben Myron. Executive producers, George Harrison, Denis O'Brien. Directed by David Leland. Screenplay, Joe Eszterhas; camera (color), Ian Wilson; editor, Lee Percy; music, Carter Burwell; production design, Barbara Ling; coproducer, Garth Thomas; costumes, Adele Lutz; in Dolby stereo. Reviewed at Review 2 screening room, N.Y., April 17, 1989. MPAA Rating: R. Running time: 93 MIN.
Ray Macklin . . . . .Jeff Daniels
Jenny Macklin . . . . .Melanie Mayron
Harry Lardener . . . . .Michael Tucker
Diana . . . . .Kathleen York
Pat Hagen . . . . .Allan Havey
Connie Hagen . . . . .Ann Magnuson
Barbara . . . . .Jo Harvey Allen
Dr. Duffin . . . . .Felton Perry
Mr. D'Amato . . . . .Ian Wolfe
Spenser Gittinger . . . . .John Durbin

■A dreadfully unfunny 1-joke black comedy about hypochondria and mortality, "Checking Out" should die quickly and leave no mourners at the box-office. Warner Bros. is advised to bury this stiff as quickly as decency allows.

"Checking Out" depends almost entirely for suspense on Jeff Daniels' quest for the puchline to one joke: "Why don't Italians have barbecues?" Sadly, some 90

minutes elapse before he finds out.

In the interim Daniels, as budget airline executive Ray Macklin witnesses the death by coronary of his irreverent best buddy Allan Havey. This trauma triggers the onset of a hysterical, fetishistic hypochondria that possesses the hero and propels him, in a state of ever-accelerating mental disintegration, through a series of discombobulating misadventures.

Daniels live in a tacky California suburb with wife Melanie Mayron and two kids. The blue-sky normalcy of his middle-class life-style is clearly intended by director David Leland and scripter Joe Eszterhas to set up a big soft target for satirical demolition. Potshots also are misfired at American big business funeral homes, medicine and sexual hypocrisy.

Leland fails to control a helter-skelter jumble of gags and painfully forced situations that are meant to outrage but tend to clunk embarrassingly. Daniels gamely contorts himself to fit the twisting parameters of a scenario in which his libido, career and home life take a constant situational beating.

Sturdy supporting players Melanie Mayron and Michael Tucker (as Daniels' exasperated boss) don't seem to know what to make of their roles, while Havey does his expansive best to upstage everyone during his limited screen time.

Seeds of a more interesting film are scattered here and there, especially in a dazzlingly photographed dream sequence that imagines heaven as a cloyingly hellish redneck cabana club in a desert oasis. Like everything else in "Checking Out," however, this adds up to a whole lot of nothing.

Incidentally, the punchline is ... "Because the spaghetti falls through the grill." Better 1-liners are available on tv. —Rich.

1980s.

The filmmakers are completely incapable of offering any insight into or analysis of the self-styled radicals or the political context that spawned them, resulting in a virtually worthless picture. There's no b.o. potential here.

Title refers to an actual group of violent anarchists responsible for some attacks against industrial targets between 1981-1983. In a dry, thoroughly unbelievable manner, pic details how a naive young punkette named Julie is intimidated into getting into a "heavy-duty direct action trip" by a bunch of hippies playing at revolution, and how nearly all of the group's efforts go awry.

Certainly without intending to, the filmmakers make their subjects look like complete imbeciles at all times, the result of their having no discernable point-of-view about the events being chronicled. Why they feel these screwed-up kids are worthy of serious attention is anybody's guess given the lack of illumination offered here.

Pic has a plain visual look, and is generally overacted by a cast urgently searching for reality, man. —Cart.

Warm Summer Rain

Hollywood   A Cinema Corp. of America presentation of an Elwes/Wigram production for Smoking Gun Prods. Produced by Cassian Elwes, Lionel Wigram. Written and directed by Joe Gayton. Camera (color), Fernando Arguelles; editor, Ed Rothkowitz, Robin Katz; music, Roger Eno; production design, Richard Helo; art direction, Patricia Ellis; sound, Tom Cunliffe; assistant director, Eddie Ziv. Reviewed at AFI/L.A. Fest, L.A., April 18, 1989. No MPAA Rating. Running time: 82 MIN.
Kate . . . . .Kelly Lynch
Guy . . . . .Barry Tubb
Andy . . . . .Ron Sloan

■Little theater comes to the big screen in "Warm Summer Rain." For the most part a 1-set, 2-character piece, this first feature from screenwriter Joe Gayton offers sex, pseudo-poetic speechifying and unintentional laughs in roughly equal measures, which is not a combination designed to line folks up at the b.o.

Video release aimed at male viewers hot to see model Kelly Lynch in a frequent state of undress will prove more viable than theatrical playoff.

After a self-consciously cinematic opening impressionistically sketching Lynch's erotic memories and subsequent suicide attempt, pic settles into the limited

confines of a seedy, abandoned house in the desert where Lynch wakes one morning next to stranger Barry Tubb.

The young lady has to ask if anything happened between them the night before, and the spunky guy assures her that plenty did. Remainder of the first hour alternates between nude simulated sex scenes, some raunchy pillow talk and confessional monologs, in which Gayton's penchant for high-falutin' verbosity gets the better of him and the worse of the film.

In what comes off like classroom acting exercises, Lynch gets to go on (and on) about her suicide, while Tubb wallows in having allegedly killed his fiancée after she stood him up at the altar.

It's an ideal match, at least for awhile, until the two head out into the real world, where Lynch implausibly bumps into her former lover at a gas station and Tubb turns out to be rather less than he claimed.

Thesps give it the old college try, but the conviction just isn't there in the material, which doesn't amount to much. Sexual interludes offer plenty of skin but no eroticism. Roger Eno's musical score achieves some good effects. —Cart.

Hellbent
(Los Angeles Is Hellbent)

Hollywood   A Hellbent production. (Intl. sales, Double Helix Films.) Produced by Louise Jaffe. Executive producer, Phil Casella. Written and directed by Richard Casey. Camera (Foto-Kem color), Jim Gillie; editor, Matthew Harrison, Casey; music, Greg Burk, Mark Wheaton, Trotsky Icepick; additional music, Angry Samoans, Drowning Pool, Angst, Gone, Love Supremes; sound, George Hampton; art direction, Fred Wasser, Richard Scully; costume design, Mary Cheung; associate producer, Randy Polk; assistant director, Richard Eyler; casting, Steven P. Deworkin. Reviewed at American Film Institute (AFI/L.A. Fest), March 23, 1989. No MPAA Rating. Running time: 87 MIN.
Lemmy . . . . .Phil Ward
Angel . . . . .Lyn Levand
Sally . . . . .Cheryl Slean
Tanas . . . . .David Marciano
Spike . . . . .James Orr
Duke . . . . .Phil Therrien
Willie . . . . .Paul Greenstein
Jane . . . . .Leigh Decio
Mr. Jones . . . . .Stanley Wells
Jimmy Jones . . . . .Daniel W. Devorkin
Mel . . . . .Steve Devorkin

■Populated by a dungeonful of musictrash, this tale of an L.A. garage band, Faust, and a Mephistophelian manager is repellent in every detail. And destined for quick oblivion in the remainder bin after possible midnight screenings.

Even adherents of the zoned-out

AFI/L.A. FEST

The Squamish Five
(CANADIAN)

Hollywood   A CBC Film production. Produced by Bernard Zukerman. Coproducer, Harris Verge. Directed by Paul Donovan. Screenplay, Ken Gass, Terence McKenna; camera (color), Richard Leiterman; editor, Gordon McClellan; music, Marty Simon; sound, Gerry King; assistant director, Phil Mead; art direction, Margin Wihak; associate producer, Gail Carn; casting, Doug Barnes. Reviewed at American Film Institute (AFI/L.A. Fest), March 15, 1989. Running time:

96 MIN.
Julie Belmas . . . . .Robyn Stevan
Brent Taylor . . . . .Michael McManus
Ann . . . . .Nicky Guadagni
Doug . . . . .Albert Schultz

■"The Squamish Five" represents a middle-class look at radical political activism. It crudely and sometimes laughably charts the sorry career of a small band of misguided Canadian revolutionaries in the early

scene in question might have trouble with this one, which begins with a drive-by killing and then picks up the useless life of ineffectual bandleader Lemmy. Barely able to keep his girlfriend and musicians on their feet, Lemmy deserves whatever he gets for hanging out at a scummy dive called the Bar Sinister and making a pact with its apparent owner, Tanas, who promises a vastly improved career for Lemmy in exchange for the dude's soul.

Few gigs are forthcoming, however, as most of the running time is given over to Lemmy and his g.f., Angel, boringly sinking into a drug-induced state of entropy, and Tanas' loathesome gang violently enforcing their narcotics contracts and indulging in bloodlust.

The relentless unpleasantness is utterly irredeemable and unrewarding for the viewer, and the pointedly unimaginative story possesses no dramatic momentum and makes little sense even on a simple narrative level. It's a trip to an asylum no one would want to visit even as a tourist.

Rock video director Richard Casey, making his feature debut here, manages to hide whatever he knows about the real music world in this dumb concoction.—*Cart.*

NORDIC FILM FEST

Karachi
(NORWEGIAN)

Torshavn (Faroe Islands)   A KF release of a Norsk Film production. Produced by Harold Ohrvik. Directed by Einar Oddvarson. Screenplay, Dan Taxbro, Finn Andreassen, adapted by Oddvarson; camera (Eastmancolor), Svein Krövel; editor, Terje Haglund; music, Eivind One Pedersen; production design, Harald Egede Nissen; sound, Ragnar Samuelsson; production management, Dan Taxbro, Inger Vatne; assistant directors, Inger Lise Langfeldt, Gamal al-Damaty. Reviewed at Nordic Film Festival, Torshavn, Faroe Islands, April 14, 1989. Running time: **95 MIN.**
Ted Hansen . . . . Jon Eikemo
Sara . . . . Amanda Ooms
Kramer . . . . Hans Ola Sörlie
   Also with: Stale Björnhaug, Oyvin Berven, Tonje Lunde, Ahmed Abubaia, Ahmed Kamis, Anne Krigsvoll, Robert Ryall, Nasrullah Qureshi, Lars Vik, Erik Hivju, Badi Uzzaman.

■With "Karachi," Norway's Einar Oddvarson has added to the cop thriller formula inventive production shine plus a subplot with strong erotic tension. The combination favors emotion and artistry over clean-cut thrills, making the item a dubious one in the international marketplace.

Why does the beautiful hippie girl let herself be talked into returning from Karachi to Oslo with heroin worth millions hidden in her suitcase? The answer along with the final shootout hangs in tatters as it is told in slick tv style.

It is in the film's middle part that things get really interesting. Here the girl is temporarily stashed away in a Norwegian cop's private hideout. The girl is both restless and reckless. Full of creative juices, she is left to such activities as burning patterns into the thigh of her pantyhose (while still wearing them) or to strip to put a coat of white on her body with a paint-roller.

The cop resists the sexual taunts of the girl by dulling himself with alcohol. A strange cat-and-mouse game develops with roles switching at odd moments.

There is clearly an influence here from Jean-Jacques Beineix' "Diva" and "Betty Blue" (Dutch-Swedish actress Amanda Ooms actually a Béatrice Dalle "Betty Blue" lookalike). Oddvarson does a juggling act of his own with interplay between actors, words and colors as applied by art designer Harald Egede Nissen and the beautiful cinematography of Svein Krövel.

The emotional charge of the best sequences marks Oddvarson as a writer-director of unusual insights and high technical skills. He does not get much help from Jon Eikemo, who is as dull as Maigret's old overcoat as the detective.

Amanda Ooms is another matter entirely. Whoever she may look like, she is no clone. Whether exuding sullenness, sauciness, wrath or joy, she is star material.

—*Kell.*

The Rainbow

Hollywood   A Vestron Pictures release and production. Executive producers, William J. Quigley, Dan Ireland. Line producer, Ronaldo Vasconcellos. Produced and directed by Ken Russell. Screenplay, Ken Russell, Vivian Russell, based on the novel by D.H. Lawrence; camera (Technicolor), Billy Williams; editor, Peter Davies; music, Carl Davis; production and costume design, Luciana Arrighi; art direction, Ian Whittaker; sound (Dolby), John Murphy; assistant director, Iain Patrick; casting, Doreen Jones. Reviewed at the Carolco screening room (American Film Market), L.A., Feb. 21, 1989. MPAA Rating: R. Running time: **112 MIN.**
Ursula Brangwen . . . . Sammi Davis
Anton Skrebensky . . . . Paul McGann
Winnifred . . . . Amanda Donohoe
Will Brangwen . . . . Christopher Gable
Uncle Henry . . . . David Hemmings
Anna Brangwen . . . . Glenda Jackson
MacAllister . . . . Dudley Sutton
Mr. Harby . . . . Jim Carter
Miss Harby . . . . Judith Paris
Mr. Brunt . . . . Ken Colley
Gudrun . . . . Glenda McKay
Molly . . . . Molly Russell
Rupert . . . . Rupert Russell

■Ken Russell achieved his breakthrough success as a director with "Women In Love" back in 1970, and he's now gone back to the well of D.H. Lawrence for "The Rainbow." Russell remains the ideal interpreter of the author's lusty, unconventional attitudes, as the picture brims with life.

Some stronger cast names would have helped give it more profile with the public, but b.o. should still be reasonable.

"The Rainbow" was Lawrence's fourth novel and concludes with the sexual awakening of Ursula Brangwen, whose story was continued in "Women In Love." The current film reps a prequel to the earlier one, in which Jennie Linden played Ursula and Glenda Jackson won an Oscar as her sister Gudrun.

Artistic considerations to the side, "Women In Love" struck a chord with audiences because its portrait of sexual adventurousness, questioning of standard morality and pre-feminist notions paralleled the similar explorations of young people at that time. "The Rainbow" doesn't enjoy that contemporary advantage, but deals with the same concerns in somewhat less electrifying but perhaps more mature and subtle ways.

Concentrating on the last section of the novel, Russell charts the spasmodic, often brutal maturation of Ursula (Sammi Davis), a country girl at the turn of the century whose parents can only conceive of her life in the most narrow, normal terms.

Ursula's very out-of-the-ordi-

nary sexual initiation comes at the persuasive hands of her swimming instructor, the strikingly beautiful Winnifred (Amanda Donohoe), one of Lawrence's patented free spirits who sports men's clothes on strenuous hiking expeditions, lectures her pupil on the pervasive unworthiness of the male animal and inspires her to break loose from society's chains.

Not incidentally, the two share an extensive scene of undraped swimming, massage and firelit hanky panky that represents the female equivalent of the Alan Bates-Oliver Reed nude wrestling match in "Women In Love."

Ursula develops a heightened awareness of nature's arbitrary injustices and cruelties, and impulsively begins lashing out at them. Rebelling against her parents, she moves to London to take a lowly position as a grade school teacher. The institution fits precise Dickensian specifications, from its sooty, impoverished students to its lecherous, impossibly stern headmaster, his birdlike spinster sister and the squashed but quietly sympathetic assistant, Mr. Brunt.

Inclined to be understanding of the children's problems, Ursula is eventually forced by extreme circumstances to become a disciplinarian, but is nonetheless disillusioned when Winnifred abandons her stated principles to marry Ursula's Uncle Henry, a mining magnate.

Before long, however, Ursula finds himself attracted to a man as well, the career soldier Anton (Paul McGann), who is mostly occupied fighting the Boer War. Despite the rough deflowering, Ursula's feelings grow into love, and she struggles with the temptations of a "normal" marriage and life as a military wife before coming to grips with her true nature and rushing off to the adventures that will be "Women In Love."

Compared to the ripe, often amusing indulgences of his previous pictures for Vestron, "Gothic," "Salome's Last Dance" and "Lair Of The White Worm," "The Rainbow" finds Russell working in a most restrained, classical style. The director, who wrote the script with his wife Vivian, plainly identifies and sympathizes with his heroine's fierce search for independence, identity and freedom for women, and can therefore approach this material with an entirely straight face.

Often reminding of a more

robust Mia Farrow, Sammi Davis, who came to the fore as the man-hungry teenager in "Hope And Glory," throws herself into Ursula with all the physical and emotional energy she can muster, and comes up a winner. Facing life without blinders, her Ursula takes it all in, the good and the bad, agonizes over much of it, but emerges vastly enriched by a raw experience.

Amanda Donohoe is absolutely on the money as the liberated Winnifred, who recognizes one of her own kind in Uncle Henry, very nicely embodied by David Hemmings (after the implausibly cast Elton John dropped out). Paul Mc-Gann makes Anton too languid and remote to get excited about.

Glenda Jackson and Christopher Gable, veterans of "Women In Love," reappear in different roles here, with Jackson effectively playing her own mother.

Also returning from the previous film is cinematographer Billy Williams, who helps bring the tale to life with his vibrant lensing but can't entirely disguise the somewhat reduced circumstances of the production. Carl Davis' score is lushly romantic in the grand tradition. —*Cart.*

Loverboy

Hollywood   A Tri-Star Pictures release. Produced by Gary Foster, Willie Hunt. Executive producers, Leslie Dixon, Tom Ropelewski. Directed by Joan Micklin Silver. Screenplay, Robin Schiff, Ropelewski, Leslie Dixon, from story by Schiff; camera (Technicolor), John Hora; editor, Rich Shaine; music, Michel Colombier; production design, Dan Leigh; art direction, Ann Champion; set decoration, Ethel Robins Richards; costume design, Rosanna Norton; sound (Dolby), Peter Hliddal; assistant director, Louis D'Esposito; casting, Meg Simon, Fran Kumin. Reviewed at Fairfax Odeon Cinemas, L.A., April 28, 1989. MPAA Rating: PG-13. Running time: 98 MIN.
Rancy Bodek . . . . Patrick Dempsey
Diane Bodek . . . . Kate Jackson
Joe Bodek . . . . Robert Ginty
Jenny . . . . Nancy Valen
Alex . . . . Barbara Carrera
Jory . . . . Charles Hunter Walsh
Joyce . . . . Kirstie Alley
Monica . . . . Carrie Fisher
Kyoko . . . . Kim Miyori

■ "Loverboy" is as cute as it is conventional. If not for the exuberant performance of Patrick Dempsey, pic might not even be tempting to its target audience of teenage girls. B.o. looks bland.

Dempsey is a frisky pizza delivery boy, representing to his handful of wealthy, aging women the opposite of what one imagines as the anonymous fantasy Adonis.

It seems pizza lovers Barbara Carrera, Kim Miyori, Kirstie Alley and Carrie Fisher appreciate Dempsey for his Woody Allenish clumsiness, adolescent enthusiasm in the sack and, amazingly, for his pale, 100-pound weakling-type body.

Dempsey appreciates them for their big tips.

It's probably no fault of director Joan Micklin Silver that "Loverboy" rarely rises above its pat conventions or clichéd predictability.

She's stuck with a script that allows little room for spontaneity or nuance — elements that were certainly characteristic of her previous pic, "Crossing Delancey."

Dempsey has to carry the whole show. His energy, in part, makes up for the endless scenes delivering pizza to sexily clad femmes living in snazzy, nameless Southern California neighborhoods.

The audience knows this debauchery can't go on all summer, so the scripters have thrown in a sweet g.f. (Nancy Valen) for Dempsey to win back before school starts and parents (Kate Jackson, Robert Ginty) who unwittingly get caught up in an infidelity game of their own just before their 20th anniversary.

Everything ends up a big misunderstanding, which is a lame excuse for passing off immoral acts these days in motion pictures. This is okay when things go so awry they are funny, something that doesn't happen here often enough. Tech credits are fine. —*Brit.*

K-9

Hollywood   A Universal Pictures release of a Gordon Co. production. Produced by Lawrence Gordon and Charles Gordon. Executive producer, Donna Smith. Coproducer, Steven Siegel. Directed by Rod Daniel. Screenplay, Siegel, Scott Myers; camera (Deluxe color), Dean Semler; editor, Lois Freeman-Fox; music, Miles Goodman; production design, George Costello; costume design, Eileen Kennedy; sound (Dolby), Richard L. Anderson; art direction, Jay Burkhardt; associate producer, Lloyd Levin; animal action by Karl Lewis Miller; casting, Judith Weiner. Reviewed at the Samuel Goldwyn theater, Beverly Hills, Calif., April 24, 1989. MPAA Rating: PG-13. Running time: 102 MIN.
Dooley . . . . James Belushi
Tracy . . . . Mel Harris
Lyman . . . . Kevin Tighe
Brannigan . . . . Ed O'Neill
K-9 . . . . Jerry Lee
Byers . . . . James Handy
Gilliam . . . . Cotter Smith

■ The mismatched-buddy cop picture has literally and perhaps inevitably gone to the dogs, and the only notable thing about "K-

9" is that it managed to dig up the idiotic premise first.

It's doubtful James Belushi alone has the star power to feed this mutt's boxoffice kitty more than a few initial scraps, followed by a quick trip to the video kennel.

Since the black-white pairing in "48 HRS.," there have been humerous cop film teamings. K-9 has all the trappings of its predecessors: a flimsy plot dealing with the cop (Belushi) trying to break a drug case, an unwanted partner (Jerry Lee, a gifted German shepherd) being foisted on him and a grudging respect that develops between the two during the course of a series of shootouts, brawls and sight gags.

There are a few amazing moments (the dog's rescue of Belushi in a bar). In between lingers lots of standard action-pic fare, plenty of toothless jokes and some downright mangy dialog.

A big problem stems from the almost total reliance on Belushi. His swaggering bravado routine is good for a chuckle or two but hardly enough to carry a film when leashed to a silent partner.

Mel Harris of tv's "thirtysomething" doesn't embarass herself in a predictable turn as Belushi's girlfriend and thus fares better than nearly everyone else involved, except for Jerry Lee. —*Bril.*

Out Of The Dark

Detroit   A New Line Cinema release of a Cinetel Films presentation of a Zel Films production. Produced by Zane W. Levitt. Coproduced by David C. Thomas. Directed by Michael Schroeder. Screenplay, J. Greg DeFelice, Levitt; camera (Foto-Kem color), Julio Macat; editor, Mark Manos; music, Paul F. Antonelli, David Wheatley; production design, Robert Schulenberg; casting, Abbie Joseph. Reviewed at AMC Americanna 8, Southfield, Mich., April 22, 1989. MPAA Rating: R. Running time: 90 MIN.
Kevin . . . . Cameron Dye
Ruth . . . . Karen Black
Stringer . . . . Bud Cort
Kristel . . . . Lynn Danielson
Camille . . . . Starr Andreeff
Det. Langella . . . . Divine
Clerk . . . . Paul Bartel
Dennis . . . . Geoffrey Lewia
Lt. Meyers . . . . Tracey Walter
Driver . . . . Tab Hunter

■ Too little suspense combined with a hackneyed plot turn "Out Of The Dark" into a routine trip through slasher material that's been better served many times before. Short theatrical life seems likely.

Film combines plot lines from last year's dreary "Party Line" and dozens of "Halloween" clones.

Robo the clown is a deranged client of Suite Nothings, a phone sex service that finds its staff being strangled and slashed to death.

The setting is ripe for a soft-porn treatment, and director Michael Schroeder never misses an opportunity to bare a breast and reveal a thigh.

As the tough-as-nails proprietor of Suite Nothings, Karen Black works on her grimace. She is also a single parent whose daughter, in a pointless plot turn, fears she is the cause of her parents' separation.

The police suspect Kevin (Cameron Dye), a freelance photographer and boyfriend of one of the phone sex girls. Kevin and his girlfriend suspect Stringer (played with wild-eyed fervor by Bud Cort), an accountant down the hall who lusts for the Suite Nothings staff.

Suspicion around Stringer heightens when one of the girls breaks into his office and finds pornographic magazines and S&M paraphernalia, but there are the requisite other potential suspects, including the boozing photographer who taught Kevin everything he knows.

Film is notable for cult buffs as the last vehicle for Divine, the "male actress" of several John Waters pics, who recently passed away. Divine's appearance as Det. Langella is so fleeting as to disappoint anyone but the most hardcore fans.

Also brief is Tab Hunter's appearance as a driver. (Performances by Paul Bartel and Geoffrey Lewis make this a mini reunion for the "Lust In The Dust" troupe.)

Unfortunately, the script is not up to the campy potential raised by a killer clown snuffing out women who are literally call girls.

Special effects and pacing never rise above made-for-tv fare.
—*Advo.*

New Year's Day

Hollywood   An International Rainbow Pictures presentation. Produced by Judith Wolinsky. Written and directed by Henry Jaglom. Camera (Technicolor), Joey Forsyte; additional camera, Hanania Baer, Nesya Blue; sound, Judy Karp; additional sound, Sunny Meyer, Catherine Calderon; associate producer, Phyllis Curott. Reviewed at the AFI/L.A. Fest, L.A., April 22, 1989. No MPAA Rating. Running time: 89 MIN.
Lucy . . . . Maggie Jakobson
Annie . . . . Gwen Welles
Winona . . . . Melaine Winter
Drew . . . . Henry Jaglom
Billy . . . . David Duchovny
Lazlo . . . . Milos Forman

Dr. Stadthagen	Michael Emil
Dr. Stadthagen's friend	Donna Germain
Marjorie	Tracy Reiner
Lucy's father	Harvey Miller
Lucy's mother	Irene Moore
Lucy's shrink	James DePreist

■An undifferentiated extension of the same themes, concerns and artistic strategies featured in Henry Jaglom's previous films, "New Year's Day" is nonetheless notable for introducing a luminous new actress, Maggie Jakobson.

Whenever she is onscreen, which fortunately is frequently, she proves herself to be a young lady whom the camera adores unreservedly, and convincingly displays a vast array of emotions. Commercial prospects are firmly in line with the director's earlier pics.

As with some of Jaglom's other outings, this effort takes place at a party and features a succession of artsy yuppie types who instantly fall into a psychosexual confessional mode upon meeting strangers.

Recalling, as he has done before, Woody Allen with his straight-to-camera opening monolog, Jaglom again stars as a depressed Me Generation obsessive who returns to New York from Los Angeles in the midst of a mid-life crisis.

Arriving on New Year's morning, Jaglom finds his apartment still occupied by three young ladies who thought they had until the end of the day to vacate the premises. Instead of booting them out, Jaglom immediately imposes himself upon their most personal concerns, especially those of Jakobson, whose boyfriend continues to fool around with other women throughout the open house the trio holds on their last day as roommates.

Lots of people show up for a drink or two in the course of the day, including Jakobson's parents and shrink, helmer's brother Michael Emil as a randy "psychosexologist," and director Milos Forman.

Despite the extensive mix of people, nearly every scene consists of a tête-à-tête encounter in which one character pours out his/her heart to another. Aside from her boyfriend problems, raven-haired Jakobson is intending to move to L.A., an idea almost all these New Yorkers find appalling. Resigned to never finding the right guy, blond roomie Melanie Winter is now searching for the appropriate genetic mate to father her child, and redhead Gwen Welles ultimately confesses to the passion she's hidden for years.

Jaglom, the morose stranger, encourages everyone to bare their souls, and some of the results prove quite spontaneous and amusing. On the other hand, this is such well-worn territory for the writer-director that one would hope that he'd know how to spot the pitfalls in his approach by now, to avoid the irrelevancies, redundancies and aggravating moments.

Pic is a mixed bag that lives and dies from moment to moment depending on who is onscreen. Jakobson is a luminous delight from whom more should soon be heard. Gwen Welles comes off as a pleasant ditz, but her shift to desperation seems very sudden, and Melanie Winter suffers from the most clichéd character conception. Jaglom is, well, Jaglom, and most of the other guests have at least a couple of nice moments to themselves.

Despite having been lensed under the most minimal conditions in one apartment, pic looks attractive and doesn't feel too claustrophobic. Buffs will note the appearance of Orson Welles (in a scene from Jaglom's "A Safe Place") in the Jaglom company logo, as well as the copy of Barbara Leaming's Welles biography by the hero's side at the end. —Cart.

Esh Tzoleveth
(Crossfire)
(ISRAELI)

Tel Aviv A Gelfand Films presentation of a Parlex production. Produced by Marek Rosenbaum. Directed by Gideon Ganani. Screenplay, Benny Barbash, based on original story by Ganani, Hanan Peled; camera (color), Danny Schneur; editor, Danny Schik; music, Eldad Lidor; art direction, Ariel Roshko; costumes, Rona Doron; production manager, Emanuel Amrami. Reviewed at Gordon Cinema, Tel Aviv, April 14, 1989. Running time: 92 MIN.

Miriam	Sharon Hacohen
George	Dan Turgeman

Also with: Miriam Gavrieli, Sinai Peter, Shlomo Tarshish, Don Friedman, Yoel Drori, Makhram Khouri Makhul, Gabi Shoshan, Adiv Geakhshan.

■Gideon Ganani's first shot at feature filmmaking, after many years in documentary, starts with a strong story, but he lacks both the experience and the budget to exploit its potential.

Based on a true story, the plot follows the doomed affair of a Jewish girl and a young Arab on the eve of the Independence War in Tel Aviv. Naturally there are pressures from both sides to put an end to the embarrassing relationship, but the lovers refuse to listen. As shooting erupts, they plan to escape abroad.

The extremist group Lehi Underground (Premier Itzhak Shamir was one of its leaders at the time) has an eye on the couple and just as they are about to leave, the girl is kidnaped and executed as a traitor. tor.

Given the present mood of the country, had the impact of the finale been stressed, the film would have zoomed into front page news. Ganani treats it, and the rest of the story, in a rather bland fashion. —Edna.

The Return Of Swamp Thing

Hollywood A Miramax Films release of a Lightyear Entertainment production. Produced by Ben Melniker, Michael Uslan. Executive producers Tom Kuhn, Charles Mitchell. Directed by Jim Wynorski. Screenplay, Derek Spencer, Grant Morris, based on D.C. Comics character; camera (Deluxe color, Zoran Hochstatter; editor, Leslie Rosenthal; music, Chuck Cirino; production designer, Robb Wilson King; set decorator, Frank Galline; sound, Blake Wilcox; special effects, Special Effects Intl.; Swamp Thing creators, Len Wein, Berni Wrightson; coproducer, Annette Cirillo; assistant director, Bruce Meade, Eric Moss; casting, Shay Griffin (Atlanta), Joey Alfieris (Georgia). Reviewed at Lorimar screening room, Culver City, Calif. April 20, 1989. MPAA Rating: PG-13. Running time: 88 MIN.

Dr. Anton Arcane	Louis Jourdan
Abby Arcane	Heather Locklear
Dr. Lana Zurrell	Sarah Douglas
Swamp Thing	Dick Durock
Dr. Rochelle	Ace Mask
Gunn	Joey Sagal

■"The Return Of Swamp Thing" is scientific hokum without the fun. Second attempt to film the D.C. Comics character will disappoint all but the youngest critters.

They may be entertained by watching crossbred creatures squirm helplessly or buy into the Swamp Thing's (Dick Durock) instant love for Heather Locklear. He's a plant; she's a vegetarian.

Director Jim Wynorski gets off the track of spoofing this swamp version of "Beauty And The Beast" by venturing into murky thematic territories that add noise but not liveliness to the adventure in the remote Florida slough.

Pic is set against a backdrop of evil where Dr. Arcane (Louis Jourdan) has turned the disco-looking basement of his ante-bellum mansion into a mutant lab inhabited by failed experiments as he tries to discover the genetic equivalent of the Fountain Of Youth.

The Swamp Thing escaped, but most of his more unfortunate distant cousins of the Petri dish have not, like the cockroach/man stuck in his back flailing his legs while Drs. Lana Zurrell and Rochelle (Sarah Douglas and Ace Mask, respectively) lament another misfire.

Locklear arrives at the scene — actually the fake-looking set facade — to confront Jourdan, her evil stepfather, who has never quite adequately explained her mother's mysterious death.

It doesn't take a genius to figure out Mom's fate, though it takes the dense Locklear character an hour and a half.

Durock and Locklear's too-sincere affection for one another weighs the production too much toward sentimentality.

All their scenes are shot through a gauze lens directed skyward with lush music playing in the background. In one, they engage in some sort of fantasy lovemaking (he's a plant) that can only occur after she eats one of his leaves. It couldn't be sexy, but it could have been funny if the lovers had acted as dumb as it looked.

With the exception of Jourdan, who never looks serious, the filmmakers seemed to have lost the feel for what makes a spoof. —Brit.

The Horror Show

New York An MGM/UA Distribution release from United Artists Pictures of a Sean S. Cunningham production. Produced by Cunningham. Directed by James Isaac. Screenplay, "Alan Smithee" (Allyn Warner), Leslie Bohem; camera (Metrocolor, Deluxe prints), Mac Ahlberg; editor, Edward Anton; music, Harry Manfredini; sound (Dolby), Hans Roland; stunt coordinator, Kane Hodder; special photographic effects, VCE/Peter Kuran; production manager, Debbie Hayn; casting, Melissa Skoff. Reviewed at 23d St. West 1 theater, N.Y., April 28, 1989. MPAA Rating: R. Running time: 95 MIN.

Lucas McCarthy	Lance Henriksen
Max Jenke	Brion James
Donna McCarthy	Rita Taggart
Bonnie McCarthy	Deedee Pfeiffer
Scott McCarthy	Aron Eisenberg

Also with: Thom Bray, Matt Clark, David Oliver, Terry Alexander, Lewis Arquette, Lawrence Tierney, Alvy Moore.

■Beneath the generic title "The Horror Show" lies "House III," least and silliest of the Sean Cunningham series, headed for poor b.o. as a low-end release from United Artists.

Unlike the two prior "House" pics released by New World, this edition features few special effects to distract diehard fans from the ridiculous storyline and howler dialog. Understandably one scripter, credited as Allyn Warner in ads for foreign release, uses the heretofore directors' pseudonym "Alan Smithee" to hide behind.

Lance Henriksen is miscast (he should have played the baddie) as a cop haunted by nightmares, daydreams and hallucinations stemming from the execution of a maniacal killer (hambone Brion James) he locked up. Killer's spirit apparently infests his house and wreaks havoc on Henriksen's family until a sappy, unbelievable happy ending is inserted to imply nothing we've watched *really* occured.

With James quoting stupid catchphrases from ther films, pic disintegrates early on, resulting in more unintentional laughs than its two NW predecessors yielded on purpose. Silliest scene has wifey Rita Taggart serving a vast turkey for lunch (!), which turns into a cheapjack monster with James' head on it. Bulk of listless footage consists of cast wandering into the basement of Henriksen's unatmospheric house.

Tech credits are acceptable, with the usual pro lighting job by Mac Ahlberg. —Lor.

Teen Witch

Hollywood   A Trans World Entertainment release. Produced by Alana Lambros, Rafael Eisenman. Executive producers, Moshe Diamant, Eduard Sarfui. Directed by Dorian Walker. Screenplay, Vernon Zimmerman, Robin Menken; camera (CFI color), Marc Reshovsky, editor, Natan Zahavi; music, Richard Elliot; songs, Larry Weir; production design, Stephen Rice; art direction, Dana Torrey; set decorator, Anna Rita Raineri; sound, Robert Janiger; casting, Alana H. Lambros. Reviewed at AMC Americana B. Southfield, Michigan, April 22, 1989. MPAA Rating: PG-13. Running time: 105 MIN.
Louise . . . . Robyn Lively
Brad . . . . Dan Gauthier
Richie . . . . Joshua Miller
Margaret . . . . Caren Kaye
Frank . . . . : . . . . Dick Sargent
Randa . . . . Lisa Fuller
Polly . . . . Mandy Ingber
Serena . . . . Zelda Rubinstein
Ahet . . . . Noah Blake
Shawn . . . . Tina-Marie Caspary
Kiki . . . . Megan Gallivan
Vincent . . . . Alsari Al-Shehali
Mr. Weaver . . . . Shelly Berman

■ Comedy potential of "Teen Witch" is limited in this well-intentioned, young teen vehicle burdened by a nice message and predictable outcome. Profit potential is limited to the 8-to 13-year-old set.

Whatever points "Teen Witch" gets for its upbeat message has to be penalized by the plebeian way it is handled on several fronts, not the least of which is its tepid script and expressionless acting.

Fifteen-year-old Louise has a crush on Brad, captain of the football team. Brad is going steady with Randa, the school's blonde bombshell cheerleader.

Louise considers her plight hopeless until a fortune teller/psychic reveals she is a descendant of witches from the days of Salem. When she reaches 16 next week, Louise will have the power to get anything she wants.

Her sweet 16th turns sour when Louise realizes that even with magical powers, being the most popular girl in school is too much to handle.

Film uses this tired plot device to drive home the message that you don't have to be something you're not to be liked.

Zelda Rubinstein ("Poltergeist") walks through her role as Louise's spiritual guide and fails to generate any magic of her own.

Shelly Berman as a stuffy English teachers grabs the few laughs there are in a scene in which Louise's voodoo doll causes him to disrobe in class. Later, when her mother tosses the doll into the washing machine, Berman succumbs to an uncontrollable urge to walk through a car wash.

Where "Teen Witch" does score is its bouncy score, provided by Larry and Tom Weir.
—Advo.

Depeche Mode 101
(DOCU)

Hollywood   A Westwood One Radio release of a Mute Film production. Produced by Frazer Pennebaker. Executive producers, Bruce Kirkland, Daniel Miller. Directed by David Dawkins, Chris Hegedus and D.A. Pennebaker. Camera (color), uncredited; editor, Dawkins, Hegedus, Pennebaker; re-recording, Dominick Tavella. Reviewed at AMC Century theaters, L.A., April 25, 1989. No MPAA Rating: Running time: 117 MIN.

■ London-based techno-rockers Depeche Mode quietly invade America in "Depeche Mode 101," but the group remains as aloof and enigmatic by the end of their 1988 World Tour as when this guitarless and drummerless band broke the scene in the early '80s.

Pic won't broaden their appeal, but plenty of teen word-of-mouth and skedded limited-run engagements could make for good biz on the cult circuit before encore on homevid.

From the start, it appears light will be thrown on this shadowy band, but instead, the four Englishmen escape exposure through the smoke screen of eight fans who've won the opportunity to tour with the band. These eight fans are the subject of segues in between concert footage. Unfortunately, more is learned about the fans' feelings on everything from art to fashion than about what is on the mind of the Depeche Mode ("fast fashion" in French).

Most performance footage — up to their big Rose Bowl closing gig — is flat, restrained and all too much alike. However the sound quality is exemplary.

There is reason to chronicle this aberrant band that has become big without the use of the traditional rock elements, and to D.A. Pennebaker's and co-directors Chris Hegedus and David Dawkins' credit, they have captured a unique band at its possible peak. Lack of insight into the brooding, unabashed band keeps the pic from emerging from the pack of rockumentaries. —Vors.

The Unbelievable Truth

Hollywood   An Action Features presentation. Produced by Bruce Weiss, Hal Hartley. Executive producer, Jerome Brownstein. Written and directed by Hartley. Camera (color), Michael Spiller; editor, Hartley; music, Jim Coleman; production design, Carla Gerona; set decoration, Sarah Stoleman; costume design, Kelly Reichardt; sound, Nick Gomez; assistant director, Ted Hope. Reviewed at Raleigh Studios (AFI/L.A. Fest), L.A., April 12 1989. No MPAA Rating. Running time: 98 MIN.
Audry Hugo . . . . Adrienne Shelly
Josh Hutton . . . . Robert Burke
Victor Hugo . . . . Christopher Cooke
Pearl . . . . Julia McNeal
Emmet . . . . Gary Sauer
Mike . . . . Mark Bailey
Liz . . . . Katherine Mayfield

■ "The Unbelievable Truth" is a promising, reasonably engaging first feature of the art school film variety. Very consciously designed and stylized in all departments, pic has a minorkey feel to it.

Narrative has Josh, a good-looking, taciturn guy who is still young enough to have his life in front of him, showing up in his small New York home town after a spell in the slammer. An ace mechanic, Josh manages to land a job in a garage owned by Vic, a loud, heavily opinionated man whose daughter, Audry is a 17-year-old sexpot due to enter Harvard at summer's end.

A most contrary girl, Audry drops her longtime boyfriend, moans about the impending end of the world, resists going to college, then shocks everyone by going materialistic and hitting it big as a model in Manhattan, where she shacks up with a photographer she detests. She also makes passes at Josh, and the eventual sexual suspicions and permutations nearly take on the dimensions of a French farce.

All of this is told by way of an acting style that could be described as heightened naturalism, the broadness of which constantly provokes a tickling humor while simultaneously emphasizes the banality of what is being said.

Framing the middle-class melodrama is director Hal Hartley's manipulative artistry, which uses such devices as orchestrated color schemes, highly unrealistic sound, Godardian intertitles, repeated motifs and careful scoring. A veneer of pretentiousness hangs over the proceedings, but the effect is more exhilirating than off-putting.

Adrienne Shelly's quicksilver Audry, Robert Burke's reserved Josh and Christopher Cooke's hotheaded Vic all come off well.

Technically, film is superb. Michael Spiller's lensing is exceedingly handsome, Carla Gerona's production design helps greatly in achieving the director's desired look, and Jim Coleman's score makes a strong impression.
—Cart.

Speed Zone
(U.S.-CANADIAN)

Hollywood   An Orion Pictures release of an Entcorp Communications production, presented by Raymond Chow. Produced by Murray Shostak. Executive producers, Albert S. Ruddy, Andre Morgan. Coproducer, Vivienne Leebosh. Line producer, Wendy Green. Directed by Jim Drake. Screenplay, Michael Short; camera (Film House color), François Protat, Robert Saad; editor, Mike Economou; music, David Wheatley; production design/art direction, Richard Hudolin; set decoration, Gillee Aird, Patti Hall; costume design, Paul Andre Guerin; sound, Don Cohen, Richard Lightstone; assistant directors, Michael Williams, Jack Cash; second unit director, Fred Waugh; 2d unit camera, Al Smith, David Nowel. Reviewed at Cineplex Odeon Fiarfax Cinemas, L.A., April 21, 1989. MPAA Rating: PG. Running time: 95 MIN.
Charlie . . . . John Candy
Tiffany . . . . Donna Dixon
Alec . . . . Matt Frewer
Vic . . . . Joe Flaherty
Jack . . . . Tim Matheson
Heather . . . . Mimi Kuzyk
Lee . . . . Melody Anderson
Margaret . . . . Shari Belafonte
Chief Edsel . . . . Peter Boyle
Also with: Dick Smothers, Tom Smothers, John Schneider, Jamie Farr, Lee Van Cleef, Eugene Levy, Michael Spinks, Brooke Shields, Carl Lewis.

■ The makers of "Cannonball Run II" may not have set out to

make "Speed Zone" a lesser film than its stupefying predecessor but they succeeded.

Director Jim Drake and scripter Michael Short spend the first 34 minutes of the 95-minute pic on talk scenes introducing a bunch of silly characters the night before the race. Throughout the race itself the director somehow manages to make it look as if most of the cars are cruising along at about 45 mph, except during a few crash set-pieces.

Since those scenes are clumsily staged and poorly timed, the photography is amateurish and the dialog is lame and unfunny, there are hardly any thrills or laughs of any kind whatsoever.

The filmmakers' most amazing achievement, however, has to be their mysterious success in persuading so many good comic actors to lend their names (if not their talents) to such an awful project. The money must have been good for John Candy, Joe Flaherty, Tim Matheson, Peter Boyle, the Smothers Brothers, Jamie Farr, Eugene Levy and Brooke Shields, among others.

Candy salvages a few winning moments as the driver with the most screen time, and his companion Donna Dixon is adorable as an aspiring actress who bears an uncanny resemblance to Marilyn Monroe.

Former heavyweight champ Michael Spinks has a hilarious reaction when he sees his car being trashed in a parking lot. That's about all, folks. —*Mac.*

The Experts

New York   A Paramount Pictures release of a James Keach production. Produced by Keach. Executive producers, Jonathan Krane, Jack Grossberg. Directed by Dave Thomas. Screenplay, Nick Thile, Steven Greene, Eric Alter, from story by Green, Alter; camera (Alpha Ciné color, Technicolor prints), Ronnie Taylor; editor, Bud Molin; music, Marvin Hamlisch; sound (Dolby), Rick Patton; production design, David Fischer; set decoration, Kim MacKenzie; assistant director, Dennis P. Maguire; production manager, George Grieve; additional editor, Eric Strand; special effects, George Erschbamer; casting, Marci Liroff, Michelle Allen (Canada); associate producers, Marilyn Black, Diana Greenwood. Reviewed on Paramount Home Video vidcassette, N.Y., April 19, 1989. MPAA Rating: PG-13. Running time: 83 MIN.
Travis . . . . John Travolta
Wendell . . . . Arye Gross
Bonnie . . . . Kelly Preston
Jill . . . . Deborah Foreman
Yuri . . . . James Keach
Cameron Smith . . . . . Charles Martin Smith
   Also with: Jan Rubes, Brian Doyle Murray, Mimi Maynard, Eve Brent, Rick Docommun, Steve Levitt, Tony Edwards.

■ "The Experts" is an innocuous, simpleminded comedy vehicle for John Travolta, briefly released Jan. 13 by Paramount and likely to prove an effective timekiller for undemanding pay-cable and video viewers.

Shot in Canada in 1987, pic is first of three completed "comeback" films for the star, whose most recent releases "Two Of A Kind" and "Perfect" flopped.

He's cast (a bit too dead-on) as a Gotham hipster who, with fellow aspiring nightclub owner Arye Gross, is drugged and shanghaied to Russia by KGB agent Charles Martin Smith.

One-joke story premise is a cousin to that old standby on Par's tv series "Mission: Impossible." Smith pretends the boys are in the Midwest when actually they're to serve as experts on up-to-date Americana in a KGB village, Indian Springs, whose denizens are studying to be all-American infiltrating spies.

Instead of the possible cultural clash, pic seques into a rather tired version of "Back To The Future." True to corny assumptions, the Russkies' image of U.S. culture is decades behind the times, so the unwitting heroes try to bring them up to date with modern music and dancing. When they talk Smith into obtaining gadgets and electronics, the townsfolks become fully Americanized. In fact they all jump at the chance to defect to the U.S. when our two dolts finally figure out they're in the USSR.

Overly cutesy direction by SCTV comedian Dave Thomas doesn't help sustain credibility. How Travolta and Gross fail to tumble to the ruse for weeks on end is hard to swallow, as is the hokey payoff in which traditional American values and smalltown lifestyles are reaffirmed.

Travolta has fun, verging on self-parody, reliving past glories as he teaches new dance steps to sexy spy Kelly Preston and the other townsfolk. Gross is an able, wisecracking sidekick. Trouble is it's all too predictable, lacking in genuine satire and ultimately degenerating into slapstick when producer James Keach pops up as a Soviet ne'er-do-well pilot to help everyone escape. —*Lor.*

Fast Food

Hollywood   A Fries Entertainment release of a Double Helix Films production. Produced by Stan Wakefield, Michael A. Simpson. Executive producer, Jerry Silva. Directed by Simpson. Screenplay, Clark Brandon, Lanny Horn, story by Scott B. Sowers, Jim Bastille; additional dialog, Randal Patrick; camera (color), Bill Mills; editor, John D. Allen; music, Iris Gillon; art direction, Shad Leach; set decoration, Julie Malm; sound, Mary Ellis; assistant director, Jerry Pece; associate producer, Phil Walden. Reviewed at Fries Entertainment, L.A., April 27, 1989. MPAA Rating: PG-13. Running time: 92 MIN.
Auggie . . . . Clark Brandon
Drew . . . . Randal Patrick
Samantha . . . . Tracy Griffith
Bud . . . . Michael J. Pollard
Calvin . . . . Lanny Horn
Wrangler Bob Bundy . . . . Jim Varney
E.G. McCormick . . . . Blake Clark
Dixie Love . . . . .Traci Lords
Mary Beth Bensen . . . . Pamela Springsteen
Alexandra Lowell . . . . Randi Layne
Judge Reinholt . . . . Kevin McCarthy

■ "Fast Food" may not be fine cuisine, but it's more nourishing than the wrapper would indicate. There's some genuine fun in this low-budgeter about young scam artists trying to beat burger tycoon Jim Varney at his own greasy game.

The Fries Entertainment release, lensed mostly in the Atlanta area, opens in regional markets, and should do okay with teen audiences.

Scripters may be copying such exploitation comedies as "Porky's," and "Hot Dog . . . The Movie," but they also make solid use of the more traditional David-and-Goliath formula. Despite the film's uneven tone and periodic indulgence in crude teenage humor, there's a winningly Capraesque feeling to the story and the characters which lifts it above its generic origins.

Clark Brandon and Randal Patrick are expelled from college after eight years of fleecing their fellow students, but they smell big bucks when "Wrangler Bob" Bundy (Varney, in good comic form) casts covetous eyes on a failing college-area gas station owned by spunky Tracy Griffith.

Defying Wrangler Bob, they transform it into their own burger stand and make a bundle peddling burgers laced with an aphrodisiac sauce whipped up by Horn in his college lab, before they're shuttered by the Food and Drug Administration.

Griffith (Melanie Griffith's half-sister) is dandy in the pic's most complex role. Besides Varney, other name actors in the cast include a greying Michael J. Pollard as a saner version of his "Bonnie & Clyde" mechanic; former porn star Traci Lords, as a sexpot sent by Varney to spy on the kids; and Kevin McCarthy, as a lubricious judge.

The film's pacing is sluggish at times, and the ending could have used more work, but there's enough meat on this burger to leave customers feeling pleased to have found a tasty bargain.

Tech credits are pro. —*Mac.*

NORDIC FEST REVIEWS

Kuutamosonaatti
(The Moonlight Sonata)
(FINNISH)

Torshavn (Faroe Islands)   A Finnkino release of a Filminor production with the Finnish Film Foundation. (Intl. sales, DB Media.) Produced by Heikki Takkinen. Written and directed by Olli Soinio. Camera (Eastmancolor), Kari Sohlberg; editor, Irma Taina; music, Antti Hytti; production design, Torsti Nyholm; sound (Dolby), Matti Kuortti, Paul Jyrälä. Reviewed at Nordic Film Festival, Torshavn, Faroe Islands, April 15, 1989. Running time: 85 MIN.
Anni Stark . . . . Tiina Björkman
Johannes, her brother . . . . Kim Gunell
Arvo Kyyrölä . . . . Kari Sorvali
Sulo, his brother . . . . Mikko Kivinen
   Also with: Soli Labbart, Ville-Veikko Salminen.

■ Olli Soinio's Finnish horror feature "The Moonlight Sonata" is told with wit, skill and speed. Item has been a hit at home and has deservedly earned an early pickup for world sales (by Italy's DB Media).

Tiina Björkman plays a dark-haired model who needs rest from too much media attention. But even out in the woods one should not carelessly undress in front of uncurtained windows. Soon the girl has a dimwit on a tractor trying to knock down her bastions. When she seeks refuge elsewhere, she runs right into the arms of the dimwit's even more brain-darkened hulk of a brother who is wielding a scythe.

The remote area's few other inhabitants soon turn out to be Charles Addams characters in league with the two super-loons.

Fortunately, the girl's kid brother turns up and proves adept at improvising electrically wired traps for the maniacs. The girl handles herself quite well with whatever she picks to bash the brute's heads with.

The genre cards are shuffled with virtuosity, while some new and funny trumps are added. Tiina Björkman acts as good as she looks, and the loons are allowed some redemption by way of a behavioral explanation. It seems their mother has beaten them since their early childhood and that she is still dishing out corporal punishment with lusty, loving care.

Kari Sohlberg's cinematography has shine and flash and the Dolby stereo-rendered music and sound effects enhance chills as well as laughs. —*Kell.*

Cha Cha Cha
(FINNISH)

Torshavn (Faroe Islands) A Finnkino release of Villealfa production with the Swedish Film Institute. Produced by Mika Kaurismäki. Executive producers, Klas Olofsson, Katinka Farago. Directed by Mika Kaurismäki. Screenplay, Kaurismäki, Richard Reitinger; camera (Eastmancolor), Timo Salminen; editor, Kaurismäki; music, Anssi Tikanmäki; sound, Jouko Lumme. Reviewed at Nordic Film Festival, Torshavn, Faroe Islands, April 14, 1989. Running time: **88 MIN.**
Matti . . . . Matti Pellonpää
Kari . . . . Kari Väänänen
Sanna . . . . Sanna Fransman
Also with: Siiri Nordin, Soli Labbart.

■ **"Cha Cha Cha" cannot make up its mind whether to believe in its characters as human comedy players or to push them over the line as farcical grotesques. So it moves in fits and jerks into some barren middle ground.**

For Finnish show business insiders, it may provoke a chuckle that helmer Mika Kaurismäki and coscripter Richard Reitinger have based their plot on real-life thesp and private life competition between actors Matti Pellonpää (the lead player in brother Aki Kaurismäki's "Shadows In Paradise" and "Ariel"), Kari Väänänen (the title lead in Mika's "Rossi") and Sanna Fransman (married to Väänänen as in "Cha Cha Cha").

The rest of the world is likely to find Väänänen's charm and good looks vanished as he now appears as a brash used-car salesman with shaven head. He leaves his wife and home so that his best friend can move in to be converted into a gentleman of culture from his present state as a vagrant boozehound sleeping under Helsinki's bridges. The goal behind all this moving around is for the bum to become eligible for a $1-million inheritance.

This old "Brewster's Millions" plot works, along with yet another role-switching character investigation (attempted and abandoned) with much overacting on Kari Väänänen's part. Matti Pellonpää does another humble clown turn but doesn't get a chance to really develop it.

As the wife, Sanna Fransman is left swaying to and fro between acting styles while the camera alternately makes her look beautiful and downright hideous (maybe there is another inside joke here).

There is usually a lot of energy in Mika Kaurismäki's filmmaking. This time around he just rambles along at high speed, cutting corners and banging any kind of logic out of shape. He knows all the mechanics of cinematic fun but in "Cha Cha Cha" their orchestration has danced out of his reach. — *Kell.*

Atlantic Rhapsody
(FAROE ISLANDS)

Torshavn (Faroe Islands) A Kaleidoskop release and production. Produced, written and directed by Katrin Ottarsdottir. Camera (Eastmancolor), Andreas Fischer-Hansen, Lars Johansson; editor, Jens Bidstrup; music, Hedin Meitil; sound, Peter Mogensen, Torben Christiansen, Steen K. Anderson; production management, Elis Poulsen, Ulla Boje Rasmussen, Elin Karbech Mouritzen; production consultant, Kirsten Bonnén Rask (the Danish Film Institute). Reviewed at Nordic Film Festival, Torshavn, Faroe Islands, April 13, 1989. Running time: **78 MIN.**
With: Erling Eysturoy, Katrin Ottarsdottir, Elin Karbech Mouritzen, Pall Danielsen Mikkjal Helmsdale, Birita Mohr, Hjördis Heindriksdottir, Asa Lützhöff, Sverri Egholm, Elis Pouslen, Egi Dam.

■ **"Atlantic Rhapsody" is a modest but still conspicuous feature film bow for writer-helmer Katrin Ottarsdottir. It also is the first such item from Denmark's self-governing Faroe Islands.**

Stringing together 52 quickie closeups of tiny slices of everyday life in the archipelago's minuscule capital city, Ottarsdottir displays wit, irony and a canny eye for the revealing detail. While offshore theatrical pickups may loom as few, tv sales are likely to pile up.

The Faroe Islands have their own language and a strong nationalistic pride, so continental Danes are in for pretty icy portraiture in "Atlantic Rhapsody." The Faroese themselves are seen engaging in such diverse pursuits as putting out a fire (was it arson?), childbirth (very close up, and the attending father faints), joining (clad in merry colors) a funeral procession, queuing up at the post office for liquor coupons (alcohol restrictions are severe and so over-drinking abounds), backseat love-making, etc.

Everything happening in Torshavn might just as well have happened in Brooklyn, Dubuque or Rome, and that is just Ottarsdot-

tir's point. She has, fortunately, added a few poetic visions of her own in the shape of child ghosts or Avenging (female) Angels popping up now and again to mock the busy mortals.

Where technique may here and there fail Ottarsdottir, she moves ahead undaunted and keeps one intelligently entertained all the way. With a few exceptions, all her players are amateurs (a total of 112 are seen on screen), and are caught as if unaware. Fortunately, only a few (the Danes again) are held up to ridicule. —*Kell.*

Kristnihald undir Jökli
(Christianity Under The Glacier)
(ICELANDIC)

Torshavn (Faroe Islands) An Icelandic Films release of an Umbifilm production (Reykjavik), with Magma/SDR/Maranfilm (West Germany). Produced by Halldor Thorgeisson, Ralp Christians. Directed by Gudny Halldorsdottir. Screenplay, Gerald Wilson, based on novel by Halldor Laxness; camera (Eastmancolor), W.P. Hassenstein; editor, Kristen Palsdottir; music, Gunnar Reinir Sveinsson; production design, Karl Juliusson; sound, Martien Coucke. Reviewed at Nordic Film Festival, Torshavn, Faroe Islands, April 16, 1989. Running time: **91 MIN.**
Embi . . . . Sigurdur Sigurjonsson
Ua . . . . Margrét Helga Johannsdottir
Mundi . . . . Helgi Skulason
Rev. Jon Primus . . . . . Baldvin Halldorsson
Fina . . . . Solveig Halldorsdottir
Jodinius Elverock . . Thorhallur Sigurdsson

■ **You have to be crazy to live in the shadow of a glacier, and to be a Christian on pagan Icelandic soil will get you nowhere. These seem to be among the morals, if any, to be deduced from "Christianity Under The Glacier," a comedy of the absurd.**

Based on Halldor Laxness' novel, directed by the Nobel Prize-winning author's daughter Gudny Halldorsdottir, item is for extremely specialized situations but holds some potential for eventual cult adulation.

Embi, a befuddled young divinity student, is sent by Reykjavik's bishop to conduct a discreet investigation of what goes on in the little-heard-from vicarage of Jon Primus up under the Snafells Glacier on Iceland's northern coast.

Embi, played with subdued charm by Sigurdur Sigurjonsson, soon finds his mind boggled by weirdo characters who blind him with wild visions and stuff his ears with dusty answers.

The vicar is tormented with guilt for not being able to embody his own Christian message. A resident foreign industrialist courts wan-

dering Oriental resurrectionists in the hope of escaping death. Once, it seems, the rich man was married to a witch. Currently, she is encased in ice, having taken the shape of a fish.

The visiting student hears and sees everything and understands nothing. Neither is he supposed to. Audiences may take it or leave it.

The fish is not the story's only red herring. At the end, the fish turns woman again and beds down with young Embi before sending him back to reality.

"Christianity Under The Glacier" is a handsomely mounted production, shot on stunningly dramatic natural locations and within fancifully designed sets. All actors perform with deadpan assuredness.

What it lacks is the mad logic without which comedy of the absurd does not really work. Too many dusty answers bury the fun and leave one with no real goods delivered. —*Kell.*

S/Y Glädjen
(S/Y Joy)
(SWEDISH)

Torshavn (Faroe Islands) Filmstallet production for Exat, the Swedish Film Institute and Hagafilm. Produced by Anders Birkeland, Börje Hansson. Directed by Göran du Rées. Screenplay, Göran du Rées, Inger Alfvén, based on Alfvén's novel; camera (Eastmancolor), Henrik Paersch; editor, Tomas Holéwa; music, Göran Lagerberg; production design, Anna Skagerfors; costumes, Görel Engstrand; sound, Wille Petterson-Berger, Jean-Frédéric Alexsson; production management, Johan Clason. Reviewed at Nordic Film Festival, Torshavn, Faroe Islands, April 14, 1989. Running time: **98 MIN.**
Annika . . . . Lena Olin
Klas . . . . Stellan Skarsgard
Maja-Lena . . . . Viveka Seldahl
Herbert . . . . Hans Mosesson
Liv . . . . Nina Lager
Johan . . . . Nicolaus Rubensson
The Physician . . . . Helge Jordal

■ **"S/Y Joy," based on a best-selling 1979 Swedish novel, is a bad case of warmed-over "Scenes From A Marriage"-type Ingmar Bergman melodrama. Action sequences save it from being phonily intellectualized soap fare.**

Annika and Klas (Lena Olin and Stellan Skarsgard, both lately in "The Unbearable Lightness Of Being") buy and shine up a recently ship-wrecked yacht bearing the film's moniker. They want to travel the oceans for a year to save their marriage, having taken to fighting each other after the loss of their young son.

When Annika by chance finds

out that the S/Y Joy at the time of her shipwreck had aboard another married couple with kids who suffered the tragic loss of husband and son, she sets out to investigate.

Klas is supposed to appear callous to their mutual loss, but director Göran de Rées actually makes him into a more sensitive person than Annika, who soon just seems to be wantonly prying (in the book, she has all the author's sympathy).

All through the film there is constant crosscutting between today's fights between Annika and Klas and past troubles, real or imagined by Annika. About halfway through the film, the crosscutting is action footage between the little sailing yacht's first and its present voyage.

Stellan Skarsgard is an actor in control of mute nuance. Lena Olin and Viveka Seldahl struggle in vain against the meanness in their roles. Du Rées even succeeds in making Lena Olin look ugly at the end, no mean feat but a destructive one. —*Kell.*

Getting It Right

Hollywood   An MCEG release. Produced by Jonathan D. Krane, Randal Kleiser. Executive producer, Rusty Lemorande. Directed by Kleiser. Screenplay, Elizabeth Jane Howard, based on her book; camera (Fuji color, Rank prints), Clive Tickner; editor, Chris Kelly; music, Colin Towns; production design, Caroline Amies; art direction, Frank Walsh; costume design, Hazel Pethig; sound (Ultra-Stereo), John Midgley; casting, Joyce Gallie. Reviewed at Raleigh Studios screening room, L.A., May 2, 1989. MPAA Rating: R. Running time: 102 MIN.
```
Gavin Lamb . . . . . . . . . . . . .Jesse Birdsall
Minerva Munday  . .Helena Bonham Carter
Mr. Adrian . . . . . . . . . . . . . . . .Peter Cook
Joan . . . . . . . . . . . . . . . . . .Lynn Redgrave
Jenny . . . . . . . . . . . . . . . . . .Jane Horrocks
Harry . . . . . . . . . . . . . . . . . .Richard Huw
```
   Also with: John Gielgud, Pat Heywood, Judy Parfitt, Bryan Pringle.

■ Sweet love triumphs over hollow class consciousness in "Getting It Right," a wonderful made-in-Britain sex comedy that celebrates romance in funny, quirky ways. Pic should notch healthy returns on both sides of the Atlantic.

Maggie Thatcher's England, specifically London, is satirized here. It is also the perfect setting in which self-taught hairdresser (Jesse Birdsall) can mix with pretentious nouveau upper crusties only to find that he is more sophisticated than they.

Birdsall plays a 31-year-old virgin still living at home but doing nothing about it. He suffers in silence, preferring instead to daydream about girls — how he might love them and what they would do together. If only he could make a move to ask one out, which he can't. He can't even bring himself to smile back at one on the London Transport bus.

To his clients, however, he's charming, the most sought-after coiffeur at Mr. Adrian, a tony West End salon that caters to the aging gentry and is run by a smarmy, Dickensian owner, the hysterically funny Peter Cook.

Birdsall gets yanked out one night by one of his chums to a trendy loft party along the Thames hosted by a trendy socialite who dresses like a man dressed in drag (Lynn Redgrave).

What ensues remines one of a bit of Griffin Dunne's predicament in "After Hours" except this is a much more complex adventure. It's filled with a cast of delightful English eccentrics.

Birdsall is rather nonplussed to find his best friend, Harry (Richard Huw) in the tub with another man, though he is taken aback to see the spurned g.f.

Lady Minerva Munday (Helena Bonham Carter) in bed nearby, miffed and stark naked. Redgrave, meanwhile, is determined to relieve the mystified Birdsall of his virginity.

In a short space of time, this once shy, sensitive guy becomes at least three women's savior and in ways that are consistently surprising if typically British.

His encounter with Bonham Carter's crass father, Sir Gordon Munday (John Gielgud), his title owed to making a fortune in seatbelts and who now presides over a tacky, ersatz country manor with his alcoholic wife (Judy Parfitt), is a cinematic morsel. Bonham Carter, the innocent maiden in "A Room With A View," is a terrific and surprisingly convincing bulimic tramp parading as an aristocrat.

Director Randal Kleiser is in touch with his subjects and treats them well. The actors clearly know what they are speaking about and seem to enjoy every word of Elizabeth Jane Howard's clever, textured script.

Particularly memorable is Pat Heywood as Birdsall's overbearing Mum. One would like to strangle her one minute and hug her the next.

Jane Horrocks as Jenny is well matched as the sweet, unsophisticated counterpart to Birdsall's winsome character. What endears her to him is that she knows who she is — a single mother trying to get on with life — while the others around him refuse. Theirs is not a lushly romantic story; it's real — and ultimately touching too.

Tech credits are fine and Dusty Springfield is a particularly good choice to sing the title track, nice and throaty. —*Brit.*

Two Wrongs Make A Right

New York   A Paradigm Films Intl. production and release. Produced by Ivan Rogers. Directed by Robert Brown. Screenplay, Rogers; camera (Southwest color), David Yosha; editor, Sheri J. Galloway; music, Tony Byrne; sound, William B. Jenkins Jr.; art direction, Yosha; assistant director, William P. Jackson; production manager, J.D. Wilson; additional camera, Chris Minnick; fight choreography, Ron E. White. Reviewed on Unicorn Video vidcassette, N.Y., April 21, 1989. No MPAA Rating. Running time: 83 MIN.
```
Fletcher Quinn . . . . . . . . . . . .Ivan Rogers
Jayna . . . . . . . . . . . . . . . . . . . . . .Eva Wu
Lake . . . . . . . . . . . . . . . .Rich Komenich
Lt. Zander . . . . . . . . . . . .R. Michael Pyle
Sgt. Vellosi . . . . . . . . . . .Michael G. Rizk
Jack Balantine . . . . . . . . . .Ron Blackstone
```

■ Lean, low-budget actioner with a catchy moniker shapes up okay for homevideo release.

Directed in Indianapolis by Robert Brown for topliner-filmmaker Ivan Rogers, "Two Wrongs..." resembles the blaxploitationers of nearly two decades ago, but has a cool, almost abstract tone resembling the policiers of late French master Jean-Pierre Melville (especially his Alain Delon classic "Le Samourai").

Rogers is the low-key hero Fletcher Quinn, whose nightclub is shot up by gangsters when he refuses to sell. They also beat up his Asian-American girlfriend (Eva Wu) and soon the local cops also are on Quinn's case due to his vigilante tactics.

Rather flat during its middle reels, pic is competently made but could have used a bigger budget to provide more oomph. Technical credits are modest. —*Lor.*

Listen To Me

Hollywood   A Columbia Pictures release of a Weintraub Entertainment Group presentation of a Martin Bregman production. Produced by Marykay Powell. Written and directed by Douglas Day Stewart. Camera (CFI, color), Fred Koenekamp; editor, Anne V. Coates; music, David Foster; sound (Dolby), Tom Causey; production design, Gregory Pickrell; set design, Joe Hubbard; set decoration, Kim Samson; costume design, Durinda Rice Wood; assistant director, Bill Scott; coproducer, Jerry A. Baerwitz; associate producer, Dolly Gordon; casting, Nina Axelrod. Reviewed at Samuel Goldwyn theater, L.A., May 3, 1989. MPAA Rating: PG-13. Running time: 107 MIN.
```
Tucker Muldowney . . . . . . . .Kirk Cameron
Monica Tomanski . . . . . . . . . . .Jami Gertz
Charlie Nichols . . . . . . . . . . .Roy Scheider
Donna Lumis . . . . . . . . . .Amanda Peterson
Garson McKellar . . . . . . . . . . . .Tim Quill
Dean Schwimmer . . . . . . . .George Wyner
Sen. McKellar . . . . . . . . . .Anthony Zerbe
Bruce Arlington . . . . . . .Christopher Atkins
Susan Hooper . . . . . . . . .Quinn Cummings
Hinkelstein . . . . . . . . . . . . . .Jason Gould
```

■ Luck couldn't get much worse for Weintraub Entertainment Group than to have a picture whose focus is a college debate on the red-hot abortion issue rolling down its release chute in 1989. Those who hang in through the film's awkward first half will find the trick pulled rather neatly out of the hat at the climax.

Feel-good ending will no doubt appease the masses, but luring them will depend on appeal of young stars Jami Gertz and Kirk Cameron. Beyond preliminary rounds, b.o. looks unpersuasive.

Writer-director Douglas Day Stewart does backflips trying to make an inherently soft subject — the pursuits of a college debate team — the stuff of big-screen drama. He constantly backs away from the essence of the sport — ideas and wits — and toward broad-appeal diversions like the lewd hijinks and uncute antics of supposedly charming main characters. In one segment, students blow up condoms during a sex education debate.

Students give their debate coach (Roy Scheider) the raucous welcome usually accorded sports chiefs, while Stewart creates false drama with portentous camera angles. Cliché is a mainstay of both the direction and writing here, while for the most of the film, the few debate scenes are so clumsy as to hold no interest at all, dampening any hopes "Listen" will stimulate on the intellectual level.

Instead, Stewart substitutes a barroom scene with team hero McKellar (Tim Quill) exciting freshmen Tucker (Kirk Cameron) and Tomanski (Jami Gertz) with tales of how much more their mental gymnastics will bring in the job market ("the National Rifle Assocation will hire you as a lobbyist").

Most disturbing aspect is that cautious script has brainy protagonists taking no real positions on anything, as if points of view were as disposable as Reeboks.

They're defined mainly by their styles — Cameron is an outgoing country boy with confidence to spare, Gertz is brainy and brittle, Quill is a rich kid with looks, smarmy charm and a bombastic, generalized debate style that's widely admired.

In a big switch, pic kicks into gear in last half, as McKellar's conflict between a pre-planned political future and his dream of being a writer begins to consume him. Events turn dramatic and even moving as team goes to New York to compete and simmering conflicts between the three leads explode.

The climactic abortion debate in Washington, which all along seems destined to hang the film for at least half the audience, is actually quite nimble and impressive.

Most viewers will leave the theater pleased, even if "Listen," just like the debaters it portrays, relies more on calculation and trickery than soul.

Gertz is a standout in the cast, the subtlest facial expression or cast of her eyes conveying the depth of character the script holds back 'til the end.

Among the supporting cast,

Amanda Peterson is particularly effective as a handicapped debater who's romanced by teammate Christopher Atkins, and Jason Gould adds subtle interest as a sketch artist who notices all.

—*Daws.*

Elef Neshotav shel Naftali Simantov
(A Thousand Wives)
(ISRAELI)

Tel Aviv A Shani Films presentation. Produced by Effi Atad. Directed by Michal Bat-Adam. Screenplay, Bat-Adam, based on Dan Benaya-Seri's story; camera (color), Yoav Kosh; editor, Yoseff Grinfeld; music, Alon Olearchik; art direction, Yoram Shayer; costumes, Rina Dorman; production manager, Amitan Mendelsohn. Reviewed at Lev Cinema, Tel Aviv, April 20, 1989. Running time: **90 MIN.**

Flora	Rita
Naftali	Yossi Polak
Rabbi	Nissim Azikri
Hamadian	Jonathan Cherchi
Matchmaker	Salim Daw

Also with: Levana Finkelstein, Geula Noni, Rivka Bachar, Etti Grottas, Nava Ziv, Ishai Meshulam, Ziporah Zabari, Tikva Aziz.

■ **Michal Bat-Adam's film is a record of life in Jerusalem between the World Wars that will appeal to audiences and festivals who prize this type of ethnic information. At home, the name of the country's No. 1 warbler Rita (in her film debut) will not hurt.**

Unfortunately, the script leaves many baffling details unexplained and often retreats into long and moody silences, good for atmosphere but not for the pace.

Naftali Simantov is an older merchant whose first two wives died in mysterious circumstances. A matchmaker persuades him to try once again with Flora, a simple and homely girl who is petrified by the prospect of leaving her mother's home.

Simantov, a kindly person who suffers from sexual malfunctions (as revealed in the wedding night scene) desperately wants an heir. Flora is too innocent to know what is to be done. Their barren marriage takes a bad turn when the husband sends his wife to buy cloth for a new dress and she falls prey to the lecherous salesman. Several months later, when her pregnancy is visible (and she still doesn't understand what happened), Simantov has to protect his honor. By the end of the film he is a widower once again.

Treated as a period piece and shot with admirable reserve, Bat-Adam's film is tightly controlled, the background finely sketched and some of the secondary charac-

ters, such as Nissim Azikri's earthly Rabbi, show a lot of promise. The problem rests with the central couple. Their plight does not justify the footage dedicated to it. Neither Rita, who shows definite potential, nor Yossi Polak, who fits the part physically, can keep up interest without more substantial support from the script, which in its present state leaves far too much to the audience's discretion.

More elaborate and incisive writing would have vastly benefited this handsome and carefully fashioned production, whose technical credits are of a high order.

—*Edna.*

The Distribution Of Lead

Hollywood A Zeno Films production. Produced, written, directed, edited by Charles Libin. Camera (Duart color, 16m), Paul A. Cameron; music, John Zorn; art direction, Donna Vega; sound, Mark Weingarten, Christopher O'Donnell; assistant director, Paul Holahan; associate producer, Mindel Goldstein. Reviewed at AFI/L.A. FilmFest, L.A., April 23, 1989. No MPAA Rating. Running time: **77 MIN.**

Maude	Katherine Rose
Fred	Ely Rowe
Gus	Ghasem Ebrahimian
Albert	Derek Lynch
Dylan	Corey Shaff
Paula	Pouran Esrafily
Girl with luggage	Ellen Berkenblit
Joanne Ford	Mindel Goldstein
Duke West	Paul Libin

■ **"The Distribution Of Lead" is a serious-minded but oppressive story of misguided revolt and violence, lensed almost entirely in a single New York apartment.**

First feature from Charles Libin offers two or three provocative scenes and an overall intensity, but also proves dull and sometimes ludicrous. Distribution prospects are leaden.

Arriving at a working class apartment, five nattily dressed, intense young Wall Street types announce to the occupant that they've botched an attempt to take over the firm they worked for and have killed a board member in the process.

The four men in the group display, in the circumstances, an inexplicable loyalty to their leader, Paula, a sleek, hardbitten, ruthless hellcat who has no problem shifting from the role of ambitious executive to urban terrorist.

Apartment dweller Maude is the sister of one of the guys, and is held captive in her own home while the gang of five works out its strategy for what to do next. After

a while, however, bullets come cracking through the windows at intervals, sometimes managing to pick off members of the group.

Latter development creates an eerie sense of big-city unease fostered by the unknowability of who is out there shooting in. Most original scene in the film has a mortally wounded man begging Paula to fulfill his last desire — that she make love to him on the spot — only to see her wriggle out of it.

Unfortunately, the majority of the claustrophobic picture is aggressively unsympathetic, largely because the "cause" for which the group attempted its corporate coup goes entirely unexplained, and because Paula comes off as such a cold, arrogant bitch that one feels the company was fortuante she didn't succeed in her takeover attempt.

Paula weirdly spends most of the picture running around the apartment acting threatening in a bra and shoulder holster, and her cronies are occasionally stuck with such ridiculous lines as, "You are really sexy when you're in a crisis."

As Maude, Katherine Rose, who appealingly resembles Greta Scacchi, suffers the fate of being handcuffed to a radiator most of the time. —*Cart.*

Have You Seen Drum Recently?
(SOUTH AFRICAN-BRITISH-DOCU-COLOR/B&W)

Hollywood A Bailey's African Photo Archive presentation. Produced by Claudia Schadeberg, Jurgen Schadeberg. Executive producer, JRA Bailey. Directed by Jurgen Schadeberg. Commentary by Richard Beynon; editor, Sharron Hawkes; in color, b&w. Reviewed at American Film Institute (AFI/L.A. Fest), L.A., March 29, 1989. Running time: **77 MIN.**

With: Miriam Makeba, Stan Motjuwadi, Can Themba, Thoko Thomo, Ntemi.

■ **"Have You Seen Drum Recently?" chronicles black South African life in the 1950s from the perspective of the late Drum magazine, a lively, very hip and politically progressive publication.**

Messy and unfocused, docu remains fascinating for its view of a vital black culture before the full weight of apartheid crushed it. Public tv outlets and educationally oriented venues couldn't go wrong with this.

Director Jurgen Schadeberg was photo editor of Drum and trained many of the young blacks who soon became outstanding photographers for the magazine. First and best section of the film draws heavily on the Drum archives to present a vivid portrait of life in Sophiatown.

As pictured here, Sophiatown was quite a happening place, full of hot music, sharp dressers, artists, writers, aspiring political leaders, athletes, gangsters and foxy ladies, a sort of transposed

Harlem of the 1920s and '30s. American influences, notably in music and clothing, were clearly at an all-time high, and the film strongly conveys the heady, cautiously hopeful atmosphere of the times.

Suddenly, after the beginning of the defiance campaign against apartheid laws, the picture lurches into history lessons and quickly unravels. There are fascinating glimpses of the very young Nelson Mandela and Oliver Tambo, of political meetings and confrontations. These are bewilderingly intercut with extensive coverage of black entertainers of the time as well as clips from two feature films, "Come Back Africa" and "The Magic Garden."

All of this material may be interesting unto itself, but thrown together it has no rhyme or reason. The thread provided by Drum is lost and, astonishingly, one never learns when and why the magazine ceased publication. Pic ends on a frustrating low note, but the opportunity to observe the excitement that was Sophiatown before it was razed proves more than worth tolerating these deficiencies. —*Cart.*

The Terror Within

New York   A Concorde Pictures release. Produced by Roger Corman. Coproducers, Rodman Flender, Reid Shane. Directed by Thierry Notz. Screenplay, Thomas M. Cleaver; camera (Foto-Kem color), Ronn Schmidt; editor, Brent Schoenfeld; music, Rick Conrad; sound, Bill Robbins; production design, Kathleen B. Cooper; creature design & makeup effects, Dean Jones; assistant director, Albert Dickerson; additional camera, Dick Buckley; 2d unit director, John Wentworth; 2d unit camera, David Gasperik; casting, Al Guarino. Reviewed at Criterion 2 theater, N.Y., May 6, 1989. MPAA Rating: R. Running time: **86 MIN.**

Hal	George Kennedy
David	Andrew Stevens
Sue	Starr Andreeff
Linda	Terri Treas
Andre	John LaFayette
Neil	Tommy Hinchley
Karen	Yvonne Saa
Gargoyle	Roren Sumner

■ "The Terror Within" is a low-budget, no frills monster pic from Roger Corman. It lacks freshness and is a routine entry in regional release, with only modest video prospects.

Corman is no stranger to the apocalyptic sci-fi genre, having helmed the similar "The Day The World Ended" in 1956. Here newcomer Thierry Notz helms a version of Ridley Scott's "Alien" on Earth: With their rations running out, the scientists — led by George Kennedy at the underground Mojave Lab for Disease Control in California — are fighting off mutants topside, as virtually the entire human race has been killed off by a plague.

They discover a pregnant girl (lovely Yvonne Saa), whose fetus has a vastly accelerated gestation rate. Group's doctor, Terri Treas, operates to remove the little monster, which pops out ("Alien" chestburster-style) to quickly grow and terrorize our heroes.

Pic benefits from a streamlined screenplay by Thomas Cleaver, who pares down the obviously derivative plot to bare essentials with no flab. Dean Jones' creature effects are interesting, but production is too chintzy to make the film required viewing for genre fans.

Kennedy punches the clock in a routine assignment; ditto hero Andrew Stevens. Femme cast fares better, with Starr Andreeff quite sympathetic in a dramatic role (she finds out she's carrying a mutant fetus as well) and Treas authoritative as the pic's take-charge character.—*Lor.*

Fallgropen
(The Trap)
(SWEDISH)

Malmö, Sweden   A Sandrews release of a Facta & Fiction production for SVT/Malmö, the Swedish Film Institute and Sandrews. Produced by Janne Wallin. Executive producer, Lena Hansson. Written and directed by Vilgot Sjöman. Camera (Eastmancolor), Ralph Evers; editor, Leif Kristiansson; music, Sven-Erik Bäck; production design, Jan Lynbech; sound, Ake Sjöberg, Lars Schön; costumes, Bo Skovborg; production management, Tommy Starck. Reviewed at Sandrews 1-3, Malmö, Sweden, April 26, 1989. Running time: **85 MIN.**

Larry Pedersen	Börje Ahlstedt
Pix	Maria Kulle
Maud	Ewa Fröling
Elisabeth	Kajsa Reingardt
Mattias	Duncan Green
Police lieutenant	Halvar Björck

Also with: Emy Storm, Kenneth Milldoff.

■ Maybe everybody in the cast of Vilgot Sjöman's "The Trap" must share the guilt in the sudden death of Elisabeth, a young theology student. If the philosophy spouted in this so-called "love thriller" is murky, so is its plot dénouement.

Still, there is some excitement in watching the old Sex-As-Redemption master ("I Am Curious, Yellow") play around with taboos and symbols once again.

Börje Ahlstedt, who bowed as an actor in "Curious" in 1967, now plays the recently divorced and still woozy professor who one morning has Elisabeth's corpse on his hands. One day earlier, she had

flunked her exam as his student. Later he had found her in the campus park, drunk and beaten up by her young boyfriend.

Whether Elisabeth took the pills that killed her or whether they were administered to her by somebody else never becomes quite clear. The professor has a brief but hectic encounter with his ex-wife (Ewa Fröling). He always returns to his slides, however, one of them coming alive in his imagination as a nude woman opening up her body from a position of crucifixion to a sexual embrace.

Symbols and expressions of guilt, angst and the gamut of other psychotic behavior patterns mix with the characters' moves and movements through the Ivy League environment of the ancient city of Lund University. Cinematographer Ralph Evers captures it all in beautifully lit, carefully composed frames.

Sjöman's message seems to be the Biblical one of the soul's union with God being epitomized also in the sexual union between man and woman. It takes considerable effort on the part of the actors to keep their lines from derailing into pomposity but they do pass this test with honors. —*Kell.*

Midnight Cop
(WEST GERMAN)

New York   A Vidmark presentation of a Lisa/KS/Roxy Film production. Executive producer, Dieter Nobbe. Directed by Peter Patzak. Screenplay, Paul Nicholas, Julia Kent, Patzak; camera (color), Toni Peschke; editor, Michou Hutter; music, Carl Carlton, Bertram Engel; sound (Dolby), Milan Bor; production design, Rainer Schaper; assistant director, Anna Georgiades. Reviewed on Vidmark videocassette, N.Y., April 21, 1989. MPAA Rating: R. Running time: **96 MIN.**

Inspector Alex Glas	Armin Mueller-Stahl
Lisa	Morgan Fairchild
Karstens	Michael York
Jack Miskowski	Frank Stallone
Shirley	Julia Kent

Also with: Monika Bleibtreu, Allegra Curtis, Harvie Friedman.

(English soundtrack)

■ Aimed at the international market, "Midnight Cop" is an okay tongue-in-cheek cop thriller, benefiting immensely from casting of top German character actor Armin Mueller-Stahl in title role.

Bookended, like Martin Scorsese's "New York Stories" segment, with "A Whiter Shade Of Pale" on the soundtrack, pic limns Berlin inspector Glas (Mueller-Stahl) hunting for a serial killer of pretty girls who's m.o. is to rub vaseline all over the corpses' faces. Julia Kent (who also co-scripted) is his pretty new sidekick. Bad guys include guest stars Michael York and Frank Stallone.

Morgan Fairchild dresses things up a bit as a callgirl who eventually serves as decoy to trap the killer. Tony Curtis' daughter Allegra, who looks a lot like mom Christine Kaufmann, makes a good impression as one of the victims.

Though plot meanders a bit, Mueller-Stahl holds it together

with his mock-impression of "Dirty Harry" tactics. Handling his English-language dialog with ease, he has subsequently landed a costarring role opposite Jessica Lange in Costa-Gavras' "The Music Box."

Tech credits are fine and pic overall marks a step up in the mid-Atlantic genre for Austrian helmer Peter Patzak. —*Lor.*

Lucky Stiff

New York   A New Line Cinema release of a Copeland & Power, Perlman & Proft presentation of a New Line Cinema production. Executive producers, Laurie Perlman, Pat Proft, Miles Copeland, Derek Power. Produced by Gerald T. Olson. Line producer, Deborah Moore. Directed by Anthony Perkins. Screenplay, Proft; camera (Deluxe color), Jacques Haitkin; editor, Michael N. Knue, Tom Walls; music, Tom Jenkins, Mike Tavera; sound, John Pritchett; production design, C.J. Strawn; art direction, Thomas O'Conor; assistant director, Robert Engelman; production manager-2d unit director, Olson; additional camera, Russell Carpenter; 2d unit camera, Don Burgess; additional music, Gary Falcone; casting, Annette Benson. Reviewed on RCA/Columbia Pictures Home Video vidcassette, N.Y., April 29, 1989. MPAA Rating: PG. Running time: **82 MIN.**

Cynthia Mitchell	Donna Dixon
Ron Douglas	Joe Alaskey
Ike	Jeff Kober
Frances	Barbara Howard
Ma	Fran Ryan
Pa	Morgan Sheppard
Eric West	Leigh McCloskey
Arlene	Elizabeth Arlen
Durel	Charles Frank

Also with: Bill Quinn, Joe Unger, Andy Wood, Jean-Paul Vignon.

■ "Lucky Stiff" is a genuinely amusing black comedy that got lost in the distribution shuffle when released late last year. Video prospects are much better.

Originally named ''Mr. Christmas Dinner,'' pic revolves around portly Joe Alaskey, jilted at the altar, who's spotted by siblings Donna Dixon and Jeff Kober as the ideal meal ticket for their family of inbred cannibals.

Some crazy slapstick ranges from the Lake Tahoe ski lodge where seductive Dixon picks Alaskey up, to the remote family homestead where everyone tries to fatten up the slow-witted Alaskey for their next meal.

Poor taste material (there's plenty of references to incest to complement the cannibalism plot) is made to work by some terrific 1-liners by scripter Pat Proft. As demonstrated by his previous ''Psycho III'' assignment as well as his choice of acting roles, helmer Anthony Perkins has a real affinity for dark humor.

Rotund comic Alaskey has a smooth delivery and does a great job executing the physical bits. Glamorously styled, Dixon is alluring and her arch readings suggest more sophisticated roles are in order.

Tech credits are solid. —*Lor.*

Garum
(SPANISH)

Madrid A Juan Vivó, TMT Prods., Mac Fusion production. Produced by Juan Vivó. Directed by Tomás Muñoz. Screenplay, Muñoz, Francesc Llovet, based on novel by Manuel Pedrolo; camera (color), Juan Gelpi, Antonio Piñero; editor, Emilio Ortiz; music, Juan G. Poveda; production design, Enrique Guevara; sets, Pere Daussa; visual effects, José Jorna, José Maria Aragonés; Juan Palleja, Tomás Muñoz. Reviewed at Madrid Film Festival, April 27, 1989. Running time: **110 MIN.**

Enric Germa	Tony Isbert
Lebia	Nuria Hosta
Jan	Enric Majo
Maia	Eulalia Ramón

Also with: Eva Cobo, Victoria Vivas, Enric Casamitjana, Felip Peña, Gal Soler, Sergi Tula.

■ **This amateurish pic about a painter who drives his car into a kind of fantasyland is so inept that the only enjoyment is laughing at the pretentious dialog which alternates with girls running about nude.**

Scripter-helmer Tomás Muñoz' mix of satanism, eternal love and sci-fi mumbo jumbo fails on every level. There is no action, no sex, no cohesion in the story, only a rambling succession of 1-liners

that seem to strive for epic banality.

The artist encounters a series of women in a small town in Spain (near Barcelona), all of them minions of the devil. He beds down with many of them, consults an expert on the occult and spends a lot of time hallucinating.

Poor camerawork, wooden thesping and disjointed pacing add up to a visual ordeal. —*Besa.*

Witchery
(ITALIAN)

New York A Filmirage production. Produced by Aristide Massacesi, Donatella Donati. Directed by ''Martin Newlin'' (Fabrizio Laurenti). Screenplay, Daniele Stroppa; camera (Telecolor), Lorenzo Battaglia; editor, Rosanna Landi; music, Carlo Maria Cordio; sound, Michael Barry; art direction, Alex Colby; special makeup effects, Maurizio Trani; casting, Paul Werner. Reviewed on Vidmark vidcassette, N.Y., April 26, 1989. No MPAA Rating. Running time: **95 MIN.**

Gary	David Hasselhoff
Jane Brooks	Linda Blair
Linda Sullivan	Catherine Hickland
Rose Brooks	Annie Ross
Lady in Black	Hildegard Knef
Leslie	Leslie Cumming
Freddie Brooks	Bob Champagne

Also with: Rick Farnsworth, Michael Manchester, Frank Cammarata.

(English soundtrack)

■ **''Witchery,'' previously titled ''Witchcraft,'' is a well-made Italian gore thriller lensed on location in Massachusetts. Film goes out direct-to-video in the U.S.**

Script makes an explicit reference to the classic ''Sunset Boulevard,'' but plot is strictly conventional. Hildegard Knef guests stars as a former German movie star, now sort of a ghost haunting the hotel location on a Mass. island where she used to live.

A storm strands the cast on this island and they're predictably killed one-by-one via Knef's demonic means. Various cast members represent individual deadly sins, playing into Knef's hands.

Pic's in-jokes make it fun for horror fans, though some grisly gore content marks it towards the hardcore fringe. Typical of this is a very sadistic routine whereby legendary jazz singer turned actress Annie Ross has her mouth sewn shut (!) so she can't yell for help when suspended in a fireplace to be burned alive.

Also of interest is casting of Linda Blair as a young pregnant woman who is possessed at film's climax, only this time the heavily made-up ''Exorcist'' star is dubbed by Knef rather than Mer-

cedes McCambridge.

Pic's Italian origins are well-hidden (vidcassette lists very few behind-the-camera credits), but one ringer is sexy young leading lady Leslie Cumming. Delivering a very stimulating sex scene when she's raped by a demon, Cumming is evidently a European bombshell (she looks like Italian thesp Lara Wendel) whose unemotional line readings and slurred diction are typical of the telltale phonetic approach to filmmaking.

Tech credits are fine, but the attempt at a spooky keyboards musical score is repetitive.—*Lor.*

Trois Pommes à côté du Sommeil
(Three Apples)
(CANADIAN)

Montreal A Malofilm Group release of a Malofilm Group and Canadian National Film Board production. Produced by Pierre Latour, Suzanne Dussault. Directed by Jacques Leduc. Screenplay, Leduc, Michael Langlois; camera (color), Pierre Letarte; editor, Pierre Bernier; sound, Claude Beaugrand. Reviewed at Cineplex Odeon Berri 5 cinema, Montreal, April 25, 1989. Running time: **92 MIN.**

Him	Normand Chouinard
Madeleine	Paule Baillargeon
Pascale	Paule Marier
Nicole	Josée Chabiollez
Hubert	Hubert Reeves
The editor	Guy Nadon
Eva	Elzbieta Koczorowski
The beautiful stranger	Mikaëlle Jean

■ **Three apples, three women and a freelance journalist are fruitfully unified in the profound reflections of an everyday man on his 40th birthday, in one of the most psychological films to come out of Quebec in a decade.**

Clearly aimed at a cinephile audience sprouting their first few silver hairs, ''Trois Pommes'' would be lost on any other age group or in any other format but the silver screen.

Short on action and long on philosophical pondering, Jacques Leduc has helmed a film which deftly captures the essence of a generation of babyboomers facing the proverbial midlife crisis.

There is neither an English version (yet) nor a sensible literal translation for the title. ''Trois Pommes à côté du sommeil'' means three apples besides sleep. The apples are in ''his'' night dreams. The women are in ''his'' daydreams.

''He'' is a vanilla fudge vacuum (played by Normand Chouinard), that ''you'' are obviously supposed to project your own life experiences onto. He has no name.

During his birthday he inevita-

bly bumps into all three of the women (Madeleine, Pascale and Nicole) which have each made a separate and indelible stamp on his future.

Although crafted to evoke compassion for this typically Quebec male, ''Trois Pommes'' carefully skirts male misogyny and the three women aren't bimbos.

Madeleine (played superbly by Paule Baillargeon) is an intelligent and direct woman who mirrors his fears and inability to make decisions.

Pascale is more absorbed in his identity than her own and serves as the key which unlocks the secrets of his youth.

Nicole is the young, passionate upstart whose self-concerns and possessiveness once drew him out of his apathetic shell.

Needless to say, none of the three relationships are kindling by his 40th. So after a day of Deep self-reflection, he winds up in a luxurious bathtub in an obscure hotel with yet another young beauty.

This fantasy-filled ending doesn't jibe with the overall tone of the film but provides an interesting twist which offers hope for the future. —*Suze.*

Der Fluch
(The Curse)
(W. GERMAN-AUSTRIAN)

Madrid An Extrafilm Produktion (Berlin), Bayricher Rundfunk (Munich), SDR (Stuttgart) and ORF (Vienna) coproduction. Produced and directed by Ralf Huettner. Screenplay, Huettner, Andy T. Hoetzel; camera (color), Diethard Prengel; editor, Ulla Möllinger; sets, Esther Walz; costumes, Evelyn Stosser; sound, Manfred Banach; music, Andreas Kobner. Reviewed at Cine Palafox, Madrid. April 24, 1989. Running time: **92 MIN.**

With: Dominic Raacke, Barbara May, Tomina Nowack, Ortrud Beginnen, Gerd Lohmeyer, Eva Ordóñez, Barbara Valentin, Vanessa Toth, Eva Schmidt-Klingerberg.

■ **The curse of this would-be thriller is its wobbly, meandering script which leaves all leads going nowhere and all ends untied. Slow pacing and ho-hum thesping contribute to the dullness.**

Story concerns a young married couple and their little girl, who decide to go climbing in the Bavarian Alps during a weekend excursion from Munich. There are oblique intimations that the little girl is in touch with occult powers. She is not averse to spotting an occasional ghost, whether on a city bicycle path or up among the mountains. The hills seem to cast some sort of spell on her, as does a mountainside chapel and three other children, real or imaginary.

The hocus-pocus is driving the kid's parents up the mountain. They discover, and then lose, frozen corpses in a glacier. They can't understand what's gotten into their little girl. Neither can the audience.

The finishing touch is ... of all things, an earthquake, which finishes off mom and dad (off-camera), leaving the little girl, or her ghost, perhaps, to wander the summits. —*Besa.*

Heaven Becomes Hell

New York   A Taurus Entertainment release of a Nivelli Intl. production. Produced by Lotte Nivelli. Written and directed by Mickey Nivelli. Camera (color), Larry Revene; editor, Richard Dama; music, Jonathan Hannah, Suzie Cioffi; lyrics, Mickey Nivelli; sound, Dale Whitman; production manager-casting, Arthur C. Lambert. Reviewed on (Taurus) vidcassette, N.Y., April 15, 1989. MPAA Rating: R. Running time: **99 MIN.**
Michael Walker . . . . Himself
Nick Cooney . . . . James Davies
Joanie Cooney . . . . Regan Vann
Gloria Johnson . . . . Myla Churchill
Rita . . . . Ruth Collins
David . . . . John Altamura

■ "Heaven Becomes Hell" is a low-budget melodrama dealing with the ongoing topic of fake evangelists. Treatment becomes campy in later reels, making pic a minor entry, currently in regional theatrical release.

Originally titled "Jealous," pic explores various aspects of that sin by focusing on a fake evangelist played by James Davies. Teamed with pal Michael Walker, he uses the faith healing religious scam in an effort to raise money to back a film to star the both of them, first seen as struggling Gotham actors.

A series of hokey marital problems and extracurricular love affairs build to several trick endings, all designed to point up inspirationally Davies' folly and instruct the viewer to proper behavior. It gets to be pretty funny, unintentionally.

Singer Michael Walker provides comic relief on purpose and also gets to sing a couple of okay songs. More earnest thesping is provided by leads Davies and his loyal wife Regan Vann.

Local actors pop up in different sorts of roles. Ubiquitous Ruth Collins is a brunet this time (instead of her usual blond bombshell) as the lonely housewife who seduces Davies, and John Al-

tamura, erstwhile New Jersey's beefy Toxic Avenger, is convincing in a dramatic assignment.

Credit filmmaker Mickey Nivelli (previously monikered Harbance Mickey Kumar) with pursuing the B-movie clichés with a straight face. —*Lor.*

Bloodstone

New York   An Omega Pictures presentation of a Nico Mastorakis production, in association with Metro Film Corp., Amritraj Prods. Executive producers, Murali Manohar, Ashok Amritraj. Produced by Mastorakis. Directed by Dwight Little. Screenplay, Curt Allen, Mastorakis, from story by Mastorakis; camera (Technicolor), Eric Anderson; editor, Mastorakis, Nancy Morris; music, Jerry J. Grant; sound (Ultra-Stereo), Andrew Achladis; art direction, Steve Russin, Manzoor; associate producer, Perry Husman. Reviewed on Forum Home Video vidcassette, N.Y., April 19, 1989. MPA Rating: PG-13. Running time: **91 MIN.**
Sandy McVey . . . . Brett Stimely
Shyam Sabu . . . . Rajni Kanth
Stephanie . . . . Anna Nicholas
Inspector Ramesh . . . . Charlie Brill
Paul Lorre . . . . Jack Kehler
Van Hoeven . . . . Christopher Neame
Kim Chi . . . . Laura Albert

■ Despite its exotic locale in India, "Bloodstone" is a pedestrian, uninvolving adventure pic that's understandably been released direct-to-video in the U.S.

Pic was filmed prior to director Dwight Little's successful "Halloween 4." Stilted screenplay by Curt Allen and producer Nico Mastorakis concerns a huge, cursed ruby that's stolen by Jack Kehler for baddie Christopher Neame.

Brett Stimely is an ex-cop on his honeymoon with Anna Nicholas, a textile heiress, who becomes involved in the chasing around action when Kehler secretes the stolen gem in Anna's tennis bag. Protagonists and their problems are dwarfed by scenic, remote locations including an impressive climax on a foot bridge across roaring rapids.

Hero Stimely is stymied by dubbing of his dialog while costar Nicholas looks nice but makes little impression in a stock role. Ditto transparent bad guy Neame, while decision to cast Charlie Brill as the stereotyped bumbling Indian police inspector is completely out-of-date and destroys credibility.

Tech credits are okay. —*Lor.*

Menja Zovut Arlekino
(My Name Is Harlequin)
(SOVIET)

Sydney   A Belarus Film Studio production. Directed by Valery Rybarev. Screenplay, Yuri Shchekochikhin, Rybarev, based on the

play "Catch 46, Size 2;" camera (Sovcolor), Felix Kuchar; music, Marat Kamilov; production design, E. Ignatiev. Reviewed at Mandolin, Sydney, April 20, 1989. Running time: **130 MIN.**
Andrei (Harlequin) . . . . Oleg Fomin
Lena . . . . Svetlana Kopylova
Andrei's mother . . . . L. Gavrilova
Neighbor . . . . V. Poshidayev
    Also with: I. Sorokin, V. Begunov, I. Domrachev.

■ Hard on the heels of "Little Vera" comes this new Soviet film about rebellious youth. This one's even more hard-hitting, though not as well handled as the earlier pic. Still, it could make its mark on the international scene.

The teenagers here live in a provincial town near the city of Minsk, and seem exceptionally influenced by fashions from the West. They go to discos and concerts where the songs are sung in English; they wear leather, chains and earrings, and one revealing scene has a group of youths watching a (presumably pirated) video of Walter Hill's "Streets Of Fire," sans dubbing or subtitles.

Andrei, who likes to be called Harlequin, is leader of a gang called The Commuters; gang members have names like Ghoul, Crutch and Crowbar. They're an aggressive bunch who pick fights on commuter trains and at discos.

Andrei's home is drab and unhappy. The one real hope in his life is Lena, the pretty girl with whom he's been involved but who's now a student going around with a group of college friends who despise Andrei and his gang.

These young people discuss a bleak future where, without "connections," they'll just "slave till we die" and where life means "queuing up for a little bit of happiness." Authority figures seem important.

"My Name Is Harlequin" is based on a play, though it bears no traces of its stage origins. It's rather long-winded, and tighter editing could make it more accessible. It paints a sometimes startling picture of life in the provinces of the Soviet Union, and the brutal gang-rape that climaxes the film is strong stuff by Soviet standards.

Oleg Fomin is impressive as the sullen, anti-social Andrei, while Svetlana Kopylova is a find as Lena. A stunning looker, she's become the latest Soviet actress to do a nude scene.

"Harlequin" should find its way to fests and Soviet film weeks, with arthouse chances in the West definitely indicated.
—*Strat.*

COMPETING AT CANNES FESTIVAL

Lost Angels

Hollywood   An Orion Pictures release. Produced by Howard Rosenman, Thomas Baer. Line producer, Andrew Z. Davis. Directed by Hugh Hudson. Screenplay, Michael Weller; camera (Duart color, Deluxe prints), Juan Ruiz-Anchia; editor, David Gladwell; music, Philippe Sarde; sound (Dolby), Edward Tise; production design. Assheton Gorton; art direction, Alex Tavoularis; set decoration, Robert Kensinger; costume design, Judianna Makovsky; costume design consultant, Milena Canonero; assistant director, Peter Kohn; casting, Nancy Foy. Reviewed at Orion Pictures screening room, L.A., May 2, 1989. (In Cannes Film Festival, competing.) MPAA Rating: R. Running time: **116 MIN.**
Dr. Chalres Loftis . . . . . Donald Sutherland
Tim Doolan . . . . Adam Horovitz
Cheryl Anderson . . . . Amy Locane
Andy Doolan . . . . Don Bloomfield
Felicia Marks . . . . Celia Weston
Richard Doolan . . . . Graham Beckel
Mrs. Anderson . . . . . . Patricia Richardson
Barton Marks . . . . Ron Frazier
Sweeney . . . . Joseph d'Angerio
Link . . . . William O'Leary
Paco . . . . Leonard Porter Salazar

■ "Lost Angels" suffers from some of the communication problems which bedevil its young, inarticulate hero. Hugh Hudson's wannabe "Rebel

Without A Cause" update tries to be a serious exploration of throwaway middle-class teens in the San Fernando Valley, but despite some gripping moments it's often cliched and incoherent.

Adam Horovitz of the Beastie Boys rap band has a sympathetic presence but not enough to do as the troubled lead of this so-so market entry for Orion.

(Handled by Vestron Intl. overseas, pic is in the main competition at the Cannes Film Festival. —*Ed.)*

The British director means to indict the hollowness and aridity of southern California, a theme which certainly has validity but has been done so often to require more originality than is on display here.

Michael Weller's screenplay is too often facile where it should be insightful, oblique when it should be emotional, and elliptical when it should be telling a story. Neither Weller nor Hudson seems to know how much to blame on his parents, his peers, society at large, and the crazy-making Santa Ana winds that blow symbolically through the pic.

It's another of those films about mental illness that tries to have it both ways, perhaps for fear of turning off the audience by presenting a lead who is truly disturbed.

The film powerfully conveys the latent violence just below the brooding surface of Horovitz' quiet demeanor. Whether it's the prelude to a freakout as he learns he's being locked up, or a fistfight with shrink Donald Sutherland, or a nightmarish violence-seeking trip to a Latino area, Horovitz has the ability to impersonate a stick of dynamite.

Character relationships, which should be paramount in a film dedicated to exploring problems between teens and parents, are underdeveloped. Sutherland brings subtlety to his occasional scenes as a scruffy shrink who has enough emotional problems to be empathetic, but he's in the film only intermittently, dissipating what could have been an intense focus of dramatic interest.

The parents and most adults are grotesque, 1-note caricatures. Mom is a ghastly type played by Celia Weston, Graham Beckel obviously needs more help than his son, and stepdad Ron Frazier is a cipher. With this gallery of losers, it's hard to understand the grin on Horovitz' face as he goes home in the contrived happy ending.

The young actors don't fare much better than the adults under Hudson's heavy hand. Horovitz' g.f. Amy Locane is a cute bubblehead who gets stoned watching a vidcassette of "Gigi."

Rather than mining its background for insights into materialism, drugtaking and heavy drinking, parental indifference, and the other ills blamed by Hudson and Weller, pic seems more interested in finding ways to pose its attractive young cast in stylized backgrounds that look like shots from "Vogue" or "Vanity Fair."

Lenser Juan Ruiz-Anchia, production designer Assheton Gorton, and others responsible for the film's fastidiously pallid look are all expert, but they help drain "Lost Angels" of the emotional impact it might have had. —Mac.

Torrents Of Spring
(ITALIAN-FRENCH)

Rome   An Erre Produzioni/Reteitalia/Les Films Ariane (Paris) coproduction, in association with Curzon Film Distributors (London). Produced by Angelo Rizzoli. Executive producer, Mario Cotone. Directed by Jerzy Skolimowski. Screenplay, Skolimowski, Arcangelo Bonaccorsi, based on a short story by Ivan Turgenev; camera (Technovision, Kodak color), Dante Spinotti, with Witold Sobocinski; editor, Cesare D'Amico; music, Stanley Myers; art direction, Francesco Bronzi. Reviewed at Fonoroma, Rome, April 12, 1989. (In Cannes Film Festival, competing.) Running time: 101 MIN.
Dmitri Sanin . . . . Timothy Hutton
Maria Nikolaevna . . . . Nastassja Kinski
Gemma Roselli . . . . Valeria Golino
Gemma's mother . . . . . Francesca De Sapio
Polizof . . . . William Forsythe
Baron . . . . Urbano Barberini
Old servant . . . . Jacques Herlin

■ "Torrents Of Spring" is a sensuous, beautifully lensed film rendition of an Ivan Turgenev short story. Shot by Polish emigré helmer Jerzy Skolimowski, pic is a fine period piece full of delicate underground emotion.

Its virtue and shortcoming is the same: a faithful transcription of 19th century literature to the 20th century screen. International cast headlining Timothy Hutton and Nastassja Kinski should earn this classic good audiences in Europe and an okay shot in the U.S.

No "Dangerous Liaisons," "Torrents Of Spring" has none of the malicious subcurrents that readily lend themselves to modern appreciation. Tale falls into the category of bittersweet sentimental education.

Dmitri Sanin, played by Hutton, is an idealistic young gentleman whose naiveté gets in the way of good intentions. Passing through a German town on his way back to Petersburg, he meets a comely, fun-loving Italian girl, Gemma (Valeria Golino), whose family owns a pastry shop. One word from her is enough to convince him to free his serfs; another day and he proposes.

At a country fair, capricious noblewoman Maria Nikolaevna (Kinski) has her admirer Urbano Barberini rob Gemma of a rose. This occasions one of the pic's more memorable scenes, a duel in the woods between Dmitri and Barberini. Maria Nikolaevna watches from a distance and sets her sights on Dmitri.

Her husband, Prince Polizof (William Forsythe), invites Dmitri round to their Versailles-like dwelling to sell his estate. It is Maria Nikolaevna, illegitimate offspring of a peasant woman and an estate owner, who is buying. Initially appearing as a calculating heart-breaker and vulgar nouveau-riche, Kinski skillfully turns her character into a woman of feeling and even principle. Dmitri succumbs to her taunting in a passionate tryst amid the ruins.

That night, unable to choose between Gemma and Maria Nikolaevna out of cowardice and indecision, Dmitri loses his youthful illusions and both women. He returns to Russia a hollow man.

As the pastry cook's daughter, Valeria Golino conveys just the right mixture of sensibility, bourgeois propriety and girlishness. She is a perfect counterpart to Kinski's sensual recklessness born of desperation (and the knowledge she is fatally ill). Hutton makes an attractive hero, but at times seems as arbitrary as a poorly translated novel. He inspires tenderness, but as the young man who knows himself too little fails to take off.

Production values are high throughout. Art direction by Francesco Bronzi is often striking, with Prague and surroundings doubling for old Germany. Final surrealist sequence during the Venice Carnival, where Dmitri goes in search of Maria Nikolaevna, is a fine set piece. Dante Spinotti's lensing and Stanley Myers' score underline pic's romantic side.

—Yung.

Sweetie
(AUSTRALIAN)

Sydney   A Filmpac (Australia) release of an Arenafilm production. (Intl. sales, UGC.) Produced by John Maynard. Directed by Jane Campion. Screenplay, Campion, Gerard Lee; camera (color), Sally Bongers; editor, Veronica Heussler; music, Martin Armiger; production design, Peter Harris; sound, Leo Sullivan; costumes, Amanda Lovejoy; production manager, Patricia L'Huede; assistant director, John Fretz; casting, Jane Campion. Reviewed at Hoyts screening room, Sydney, March 8, 1989. (In Cannes Film Festival, competing.) Running time: 97 MIN.
Dawn (Sweetie) . . . . Genevieve Lemon
Kay . . . . Karen Colston
Louis . . . . Tom Lycos
Gordon (Father) . . . . Jon Darling
Flo (Mother) . . . . Dorothy Barry
Bob . . . . Michael Lake
Clayton . . . . Andre Pataczek

■ "Sweetie" is an original, audacious tragicomedy about two sisters, one who's afraid of trees but believes in fortune tellers, the other who's plump and plain and eager to make her mark in showbiz.

Director Jane Campion, whose short films "A Girl's Own Story" and "Peel" and telefilm "Two Friends" were screened at Cannes a couple of years ago, is competing in the fest with this, her first cinema feature.

Though early scenes play a little flat, the picture quickly gets into its stride and manages to amuse and intrigue throughout. It's a genuinely different kind of pic, and shows a distinctively original vision on the part of Campion. If it garners the critical word of mouth it deserves, pic could do well in international arthouses.

At the beginning, focus is on Kay (Karen Colston) who works in an undefined factory in the inner city. She becomes convinced that a man described by a fortune teller as the man of her life is Louis (Tom Lycos), who just became engaged to a workmate. Kay sets about seducing him (in the factory parking lot) and before long they're living together in a rundown house in an unfashionable part of town. After a while, though, they stop having sex.

Enter Dawn (Genevieve Lemon), known as Sweetie, Kay's sister, who with her drugged-out boyfriend Bob (Michael Lake) simply breaks into the house and moves into the spare room. Always garbed in black, Sweetie is decidedly odd, and though Louis takes a liking to her, Kay refers to her as "a dark spirit."

The pic's other major characters are the girls' parents, Gordon (Jon Darling) and Flo (Dorothy Barry), who split up after several years of marriage. Flo heads north to cook for farmhands in the outback, while Gordon moves in with the sisters and Louis.

Campion and writer Gerard Lee have created some most unusual characters here, characters who are recognizable suburban types, yet slightly off-center. The out-of-kilter approach is a factor in Sally Bongers' outstanding camerawork, with its strikingly different compositions.

The characters are inarticulate for much of the time, yet given to speaking home truths on occasion. Campion keeps the viewer guessing throughout, shifting attention from one to another, including seemingly unimportant incidents that assume importance later. It climaxes with a tragicomic drama in which the hated trees play a major role.

Genevieve Lemon is so good as the overweight, slow-witted Sweetie that her part seems too small (she's introed late in the film, and even then disappears from the action for a while). Karen Colston is fine as the sensitive, constantly nervous Kay, with the supporting players all reacting well to Campion's direction. As Sweetie's tacky, somnolent boyfriend, Michael Lake steals his scenes.

Use of choral music is a plus and the film is tightly edited. In all, a refreshing, exciting debut from an obviously talented director.
—*Strat.*

SHOWING AT CANNES FILM FESTIVAL

Malpractice
(AUSTRALIAN)

Sydney A Film Australia production. Executive producers, Bruce Moir, Aviva Ziegler. Produced by Tristram Miall. Directed by Bill Bennett. Screenplay, Jenny Ainge and the cast; camera (color), Steve Arnold; editor, Denise Hunter; music, Michael Atkinson; sound, Max Hensser; production manager, John Russell; assistant director, Corrie Soeterboek; casting, Forcast. Reviewed at Film Australia screening room, Sydney, April 12, 1989. (In Cannes Film Festival, Un Certain Regard section.) Running time: **91 MIN.**

Coral Davis	Caz Lederman
Doug Davis	Bob Baines
Dr. Frank Harrison	Ian Gilmour
Sr. Margaret Beattie	Pat Thomson
Dr. Tom Cotterslow	Charles Little
Sr. Diane Shaw	Janet Stanley
Maureen Davis	Dorothy Alison

■ A gripping docudrama about a childbirth that goes wrong, "Malpractice" is, for most of its length, a powerful experience. Fest outings are indicated followed by tv sales, with theatrical possibilities slim.

Coral Davis, superbly played by Caz Lederman, is a workingclass woman married to an auto mechanic (Bob Baines) and mother of two girls. Her third pregnancy appears to be normal until she enters hospital (on a Saturday) for delivery and things start to go awry.

Her regular gynecologist (Charles Little) is out on his boat, and a junior doctor (Ian Gilmour), overworked and immature, has to cope. He makes a series of decisions, that obviously alarm the nursing sisters present, and tries a forceps delivery which doesn't work. The patient ends up in the operating theater undergoing a caesarian. Because he lost oxygen during birth, the newborn boy may be retarded or crippled.

After she recovers from the experience Coral is determined to find out what happened, against the wishes of her husband who just wants to accept the situation. At first, the doctors close ranks to protect Harrison, but when the nurses express their concerns publicly the matter can no longer be hushed up. Harrison is called before a medical tribunal.

Director Bill Bennett ("Backlash," "Jilted") handles this case history as though shooting an on-the-spot event on the run. He mixes professional actors with non-professionals (a couple of senior nurses and all the legal types play themselves) and has everyone improvise their dialog. Cameraman Steve Arnold, using hand-held 16m equipment, keeps up with the action as best he can.

This works brilliantly for most of the film. The long sequence in the hospital is extremely suspenseful.

The film's impetus does flag a bit in the final tribunal sequence, partly because the focus of attention is no longer on Coral, but also because the lawyers who play themselves lack the flair of the professional actors.

Fortunately, this drop in tension never diminishes the overall quality of the film. Apart from the stand-out performance of Lederman, also notable are Bob Baines as her husband, Ian Gilmour as the brash young medico and Pat Thomson and Janet Stanley as nursing sisters. It's sad to note that Stanley died shortly after shooting was completed. —*Strat.*

Speaking Parts
(CANADIAN)

Toronto A Cinephile release of an Ego Film Arts production. Directed by Atom Egoyan. Screenplay, Egoyan; camera (color), Paul Sarossy; editor, Bruce McDonald; music, Mychael Danna; art direction, Linda Del Rosario; sound, Steven Munro; executive producer (Europe), Don Ranvaud. Produced with the assistance of Telefilm Canada, Ontario Film Development Corp., Academy Pictures, Rome, Film Four Intl. Reviewed at Film House, Toronto, May 2, 1989. (In Cannes Film Festival, Directors Fortnight.) Running time: **92 MIN.**

Lance	Michael McManus
Lisa	Arsinée Khanjian
Clara	Gabrielle Rose
Producer	David Hemblen
Housekeeper	Patricia Collins
The Father	Gerard Parkes
The Bride	Jackie Samuda
The Groom	Peter Krantz

■ "Speaking Parts," the third feature from Toronto's Atom Egoyan, is a brooding, personal effort, adroitly blending film and video, but with mixed results overall.

Hero cleans hotel rooms, sexually services female clients off screen on orders from the housekeeper, but seeks a speaking part in films after playing extra roles.

He spurns advances from an equally brooding hotel laundry worker and persuades a scriptwriter guest to advance him for the role as her dead brother in a forthcoming pic.

That she does to a producer, who is seen almost throughout on a video screen communicating with his staff. She seems more absorbed replaying shots of her brother on a video screen mounted on a futuristic mausoleum.

Meanwhile, the laundry worker replays videos of the would-be-actor's bit part scenes at home and attaches herself to a vidstore owner who tapes a sexual orgy and a wedding. She is no better off after embarrassing the bride on camera about relationships that might go sour.

Almost everything in Egoyan's script is projection, external and internal. Egoyan's technical conception fascinates but his direction leaves most key performers speaking in pregnant pauses as if they were a bit dazed.

Maybe it's intended as a comic comment on commercial filmmaking when the scriptwriter treats script changes forced by the producer as life and death. She puts a gun to her head on a tv talk show, a sequence added to her film, but these scenes are played too seriously and go nowhere.

Michael McManus is a handsome male lead. Actress Arsinée Khanjian (Egoyan's wife), Gabrielle Rose and Patricia Collins do well. David Hemblen is a suitably domineering producer.

Technical credits are classy. Egoyan's talent impresses.

Pic should draw interest from specialized audiences. —*Adil.*

Communion

Hollywood A Vestron Pictures release (international) of a Pheasantry Films presentation, in association with Allied Vision Ltd. and The Picture Property Co. Produced by Philippe Mora, Whitley Strieber, Dan Allingham. Executive producers, Paul Redshaw, Gary Barber. Coproducer, Ed Simons. Directed by Mora. Screenplay, Strieber, based on his book; camera (Deluxe color), Louis Irvin; editor, Lee Smith; music theme, Eric Clapton; additional score, Allan Zavod; production design, Linda Pearl; art direction, Dena Roth; costume design, Melissa Daniel; sound (Dolby), Ed White; special visual effects, Michael McCracken, Michael McCracken Jr., Jim MacPherson, Steve Frakes; assistant director, Sharon Mann; associate producer, Richard Strieber; casting, Penny Perry, Donna Anderson. Reviewed at the Carolco screening room, L.A. (American Film Market), Feb. 23, 1989. (In Cannes Film Festival Market.) No MPAA Rating. Running time: **109 MIN.**

Whitley	Christopher Walken
Anne	Lindsay Crouse
Andrew	Joel Carlson
Dr. Janet Duffy	Frances Sternhagen
Alex	Andreas Katsulas
Sara	Terri Hanauer
Dr. Friedman	Basil Hoffman

■ "Communion" emerges as a rare science-fiction-oriented film that is actually dominated by its acting. Christopher Walken has never been stranger, more intense or compelling than he is here as, in effect, Whitley Strieber, author of the 1986 bestseller about his perceived contact with advanced nonhuman beings.

Made independently in partnership with the writer, absorbing film has yet to take on a domestic distributor, but should be promotable to strong openings in wide release due to notoriety of the book and interest in the subject matter among kids, New Agers and readers of sensational supermarket-rack publications.

As interpreted by Walken, Whitley is kind of a nutty guy, self-absorbed as novelist, moody and unpredictable as a husband, a fun father to his 7-year-old son, but utterly rational in his approach to life.

As a foretaste of things to come, Whitley and his family take to their mountain cabin for a vacation, but are greeted on their first night by a display of noises, bright lights, commotion and, to Whitley, apparent creatures, a combination so unsettling that their guests insist upon returning to New York the next day.

Unsure about what he really experienced, Whitley begins suffering from writer's block and a strange sadness, and his state of mind is hardly helped when the family returns to the cabin for Christmas, when unexplainable events continue to haunt him.

Initially inclined to suspect he is the victim of hallucinations, Whitley is finally convinced by a psychiatrist to undergo hypnosis, which ultimately leads him to a full recollection of his apparent encounter with the aliens.

Through it all, scenarist Strieber and director Philippe Mora have placed their greatest attention on the family crisis engendered by Whitley's visions and slow psychological transformation. Much more than a sci-fi thriller, "Communion" is a domestic drama in which a marriage is put to a ridiculously unfair test.

The give-and-take and small tensions of family life are nicely observed in the early-going, so as to make all the more palpable the tearing apart at the seams that comes with Whitley's approach to awareness.

Given the emphasis on character rather than extended pyrotechnics, it was essential to assemble a strong cast. Seemingly given his head here, Walken puts on a extensive display of minutely worked out mannerisms that some will undoubtedly say go too far over the top. Nevertheless, the performance rivets the attention at all times, deepens the film and provides a solid anchor for the questionable events paraded out.

Lindsay Crouse is more than up to the numerous confrontations she has with her frequently maddening husband, Joel Carlson is appealing as their son, and as the psychiatrist, Frances Sternhagen makes one take seriously the notion of legitimate inquiry into other-worldly contacts.

Although competently directed by Mora, the film falls short on the level of production values. Visual sheen of major studio projects is missing, and special effects come off as rather homemade and not enough to stun the audience and send it into the state of consciousness experienced by Whitley.

Actual aliens come in two varieties — hooded, wizened, blue-faced midgets and slender, tan-colored androgynes with black, almond-shaped eyes. While the former appear more lifelike than the latter, which seem entirely wooden, neither is convincing enough to withstand extended visibility afforded them.

Pic's intensity slackens in the final act, as Whitley struggles to clarify his visions, and film could profitably be cut by up to 10 minutes and not lose any of its import. —*Cart.*

Bad Blood

New York A Platinum Pictures production. Produced and directed by Chuck Vincent. Screenplay, Craig Horrall; camera (color), Larry Revene; editor, James Davalos; music, Joey Mennonna; sound, Larry Provost; art direction, Hilary Wright; production manager, Chip Lambert. Reviewed on Academy Entertainment vidcassette, N.Y., April 23, 1989. (In Cannes Film Festival Market.) MPAA Rating: R. Running time: **103 MIN.**
Arelene Billings . . . . Georgina Spelvin
Ted Barnes . . . . Gregory Patrick
Jack Barnes . . . . Troy Donahue
Wanda . . . . Carolyn Van Bellinghen
Evie Barnes . . . . Linda Blair
Jasper . . . . Harvey Siegel
Henry . . . . Scott Baker
Crystal . . . . Christina Veronica
Also with: Daniel Chapman, Jane Hamilton.

■ **"Bad Blood," originally titled "Son," is an engrossing gothic thriller that allows a tour de fource by Georgina Spelvin, her best performance since "Devil In Miss Jones."**

R-rated pic is being shopped at the Cannes fest market and is headed for video release Stateside in July.

Spelvin, billed here under a new pseudonym, "Ruth Raymond," plays Arlene Billings, a wealthy artist who's reunited with long-lost son Gregory Patrick after he spots her portrait of lookalike daddy in an art gallery.

Melodramatic plot is set into motion when Patrick and his wife, Linda Blair, visit Spelvin's Long Island mansion. Blair is poisoned and Spelvin starts to make an incestuous move on Patrick, whom she imagines is her late husband come back to life.

Pic plays well in the Robert Aldrich "What Ever Happened To Baby Jane?" mode, though director Chuck Vincent's pacing drags a bit, especially during a lengthy monolog by Patrick's foster mom, Carolyn Van Bellinghen.

Spelvin's performance is top-notch, mixing dramatic, camp and sexy elements in uninhibited fashion (while she and Vincent keep the pic within the bounds of an R rating). Name talent Troy Donahue and Linda Blair have little to do, but newcomer Christina Veronica makes a nice impression as a ditzy, sexy maid. —*Lor.*

Tree Of Hands
(BRITISH)

London A Greenpoint Film for Granada Film Prods. in association with British Screen. Produced by Ann Scott. Directed by Giles Foster. Screenplay, Gordon Williams, from novel by Ruth Rendell; camera (color), Kenneth MacMillan; editor, David Martin; music, Richard Hartley; production design, Adrian Smith; sound, David Stephenson; costumes, Barbara Kidd; associate producer, Ann Wingate. Reviewed at Cannon preview theater, London, March 7, 1989. (In Cannes Film Festival Market). Running time: **90 MIN.**
Benet Archdale . . . . Helen Shaver
Marsha Archdale . . . . Lauren Bacall
Dr. Ian Raeburn . . . . Malcolm Stoddard
Terence . . . . Peter Firth
Barry . . . . Paul McGann
Carol . . . . Kate Hardie

■ **"Tree Of Hands" tries hard to be a contempo psychological thriller but falls short of the mark. Topliners Helen Shaver and Lauren Bacall add, but the script isn't on a par with their performances. Pic is unlikely to travel well.**

A strong cast is poorly used as helmer Giles Foster strains to give the film a darker, more disturbing edge. The characters never properly tie together and the violence of the conclusion seems to come as an afterthought.

Pic is set in contempo London where bestselling author Shaver lives with her young son. Her mother (Bacall) with a history of mental illness — arrives from the U.S. determined to rebuild a relationship with daughter and grandson, but plans are cut short when the child is rushed to hospital and later dies.

Days later Bacall arrives home with a young boy stolen from the streets, and out of a misguided concern for the child, who has been beaten, Shaver provides shelter for the boy. Posing as a journalist, she visits the child's parents and decides to keep the boy for a while.

Shaver in turn is romanced by a kindly doctor and blackmailed by a sleazy chauffeur, while the boy's parents alternate between bickering and kinky sex. In pic's climax, parents and blackmailer are shot and killed, leaving Shaver to bring up the youngster.

Distinguished television helmer Giles Foster has yet to prove himself in the theatrical form — his previous effort was the dreadful "Consuming Passions" — and clearly needs to align himself with a worthier script than "Tree Of Hands."

Scripter Gordon Williams obviously had a tough time adapting Ruth Rendell's novel with its plethora of characters and subplots, but didn't bring it off. The Bacall character is only around for the film's first quarter; the boy's parents (Paul McGann and Kate Hardie) seem to be in a different film, while Peter Firth's campy blackmailer is an embarrassing caricature.

As a tv drama, "Tree Of Hands" would pass, but as a movie with a tighter format within which to explain itself it just doesn't work. —*Adam.*

Options

New York A Vestron Pictures release, in association with Silver Lion Films, of a Lance Hool production. Produced by Hool. Coproducers, Conrad Hool, Edgar Bold. Directed by Camilo Vila. Screenplay, Edward Decter, John J. Strauss, from story by Decter, Strauss, Stephen Doran, Paul Schneider; camera (color), Tony Imi, James Robb; Leo Napolitano (L.A.); editor, Christopher Greenbury; music, Roger Bellon; sound (Dolby), David Stone; production design, Hans Van Den Zanden; assistant director, Vito Linguini; production manager, Ian Ross; associate producers, Doran, Schneider, Michael Barclay; casting, Jane Warren. Reviewed on Vestron Video vidcassette, N.Y., April 29, 1989. (In Cannes Film Festival Market.) MPAA Rating: PG. Running time: **92 MIN.**
Donald Anderson . . . . Matt Salinger
Princess Nicole . . . . Joanna Pacula
Jonas . . . . John Kani
Philippe . . . . Danny Keogh
Rajid . . . . Tobie Cronje
Ed Sloan . . . . James Keach
Raff . . . . Alan Pierce
Priscilla . . . . Siobhan Taylor
Also with: Bobby Unser, Eric Roberts, Susan Anton.

■ **Hollywood's recent back to southern Africa movement continues with the meek comedy "Options," currently in regional theatrical release .**

Sort of a destitute man's "Romancing The Stone," pic limns the misadventures of nerdy Matt Salinger, a Stanford Business School grad working in Hollywood as a studio specialist in optioning real-life stories for the purpose of making telefilms.

He's sent to Zambia by greedy boss James Keach to track down Princess Nicole (Polish star Joanna Pacula), heir to the Belgian throne and descendent of Queen Victoria. She's been disinherited, is on the rebound from a failed marriage and is currently studying African elephants.

Slapstick footage goes nowhere in a hurry, with Pacula and later Salinger kidnaped, escaping several times with the aid of money-grubbing black sidekick John Kani. Salinger persists his stuffy talk and stuffier attitude until going native and eventually bedding the lovely Paula.

Helmer Camilo Vila, who previously made the Vestron horror release "The Unholy," displays little flair for comedy. Oddest gag has Salinger & Pacula in a dark cave singing "Do You Know The Way To San Jose?" which has thematic relevance and is reprised by Dionne Warwick over the end credits.

Very dumb touch has prominently credited guest stars Eric Roberts and Susan Anton only appearing for a few seconds following the end credits, portraying Salinger & Pacula in the telefilm version of their adventures.

Salinger struggles with an unflattering role. Pacula looks great as ever, but is still awaiting a worthy Hollywood assignment.

Tech credits are fine. —*Lor.*

Scenes From The Class Struggle In Beverly Hills

Hollywood A Cinecom Entertainment Group release of a North Street Films production. Production by J. C. Katz. Executive producers, Amir J. Malin, Ira Deutchman. Directed by Paul Bartel. Screenplay, Bruce Wagner, from story by Bartel, Wagner; camera (CFI color), Steven Fierberg; editor, Alan Toomayan; music, Stanley Myers; production design, Alex Tavoularis; art direction, Bob Kensinger; costume design, Dona Granata; sound (Ultra-Stereo), Trevor Black; assistant director, Dennis White; associate producer, Wagner; casting, Elisabeth Leustig. Reviewed at Filmland screening room, Culver City, Calif. March 28, 1989. (In Cannes Film Festival Markets.) MPAA Rating: R. Running time: **102 MIN.**

Clare Lipkin	Jacqueline Bisset
Frank	Ray Sharkey
Juan	Robert Beltran
Lisabeth Hepburn-Saravian	Mary Woronov
Peter	Ed Begley Jr.
Howard Saravian	Wallace Shawn
To-bel	Arnetia Walker
Zandra Lipkin	Rebecca Schaeffer
Willie Saravian	Barret Oliver
Rosa	Edith Diaz
Dr. Mo Van De Kamp	Paul Bartel
Sidney Lipkin	Paul Mazursky
June-bug	Jerry Tendo
Kelly	Susan Saiger
Michael Feinstein	Himself

■ "Scenes From The Class Struggle In Beverly Hills" is a **lewd delight. In top form here, director Paul Bartel brings a breezy, sophisticated touch to this utterly outrageous sex farce and thereby renders charming even the most scabrous moments in Bruce Wagner's very naughty screenplay.**

The highly adept cast could help this Cinecom release crossover from limited urban playoff to more general audiences.

Fans of Bartel's memorably perverse "Eating Raoul" should lap up this latest effort, which displays his jovial attitude toward sexual polymorphism in equally undiluted form. Some viewers will no doubt be shocked by much of what goes down here, but even middle-of-the-roaders may well end up more disarmed than offended by the film's knowing approach to lust among the uppercrust.

Wagner's script is structured in the manner of a classical French farce, and features more seductions and coitus interruptus than a season of soap operas. Hoity-toity divorcée Mary Woronov is having her house fumigated and so, with her sensitive son, checks in for the weekend next door at the home of former sitcom star Jacqueline Bisset, whose husband has just kicked the bucket.

Joining the menagerie of the filthy rich are Woronov's pretentious playwright brother Ed Begley Jr., his brand-new sassy black wife Arnetia Walker, Woronov's crazed ex-husband Wallace Shawn, Bisset's precocious daughter Rebecca Schaeffer, "thinologist" Bartel and, in a surprisingly real apparition, Bisset's late hubby, Paul Mazursky.

Up to their own brand of mischief are the housemen of the neighboring abodes, Robert Beltran and Ray Sharkey. Much of the mutty nonsense is set into motion when the two make a bet that they each can score with the other's boss over the weekend. It's a wager Beltran would prefer to win, since the alternative is a night of submission to the indiscriminately ambidextrous Sharkey.

No one misses out on the fun as they skulk from room to room between elaborate meals, a wake and shopping trips to Rodeo Drive.

Droll tone is set at the outset by the quaintly 1950s titles and Stanley Myers' witty score, and the comic champagne is kept bubbly with only the most momentary of missteps. A wonderful sequence in which some bedtime girl chat between Bisset and Woronov about the virtues of working class men is deftly intercut with a barroom heart-to-heart between Beltran and Sharkey concerning the preference of rich women is typical of the unchecked rawness of Wagner's clever script. It is the prime virtue of Bartel's direction that he makes it all so enjoyably palatable.

As he did in "Raoul," Bartel slyly sends up square sexual attitudes, racial stereotypes, social posturing and trendy lifestyles, and playfully posits the virtues of an enlightened hedonism. Film's title is a tip-off to the winking, satirical approach, which hardly introduces any notable social criticism but does feature the help taking advantage of the masters at least as much as they are exploited.

Cast enters into the spirit of the proceedings with evident glee. Never particularly associated with light comedy, Bisset excels at it here, spitting out the foul language with carefree dexterity and making light of her actress character's egotistical self-absorption. As he was in "Raoul," Beltran is both magnetic and very funny as a self-consciously macho Latino. Sharkey adroitly manages to endow his slim smooth operator with a great deal of charm.

Newcomer Arnetia Walker plays the resident sex bomb with raucous abandon, Shawn has hysterical moments in both senses of the word, and Begley and Mazursky are comically on target with their self-important impersonations. Ironically, only Bartel stalwart Woronov seems a bit uptight and starchy.

Bartel and lenser Steven Fierberg execute a great many subtle, just-right camera moves, Alex Tavoularis' production design and Dona Granata's costumes bestow the desired rich look on a limited indie budget and Alan Toomayan's editing is tight and keeps the frenzied action clear. —*Cart.*

Le Peuple singe
(The Ape People)
(FRENCH-INDONESIAN-DOCU)

Paris A UGC release of a Cinéma 7/Films A2/Revcom/GVFI/Sept/Blue Dahlia Films/-Indonesian Ministry of Information coproduction. Produced by Jacques Perrin. Directed and camera (Eastmancolor), by Gérard Vienne. Commentary, Jacques Lanzmann, Antoine Halff, Yves Coppens; editor, Jacqueline Lecompte; music, Jacques Loussier; sound, Philippe Barbeau, Pierre Ley, Antoine de Maximy, Bruno Tarrière, Martine Todisco, Jean-Paul Loublier; scientific adviser and assistant director, Jean-Yves Collet. Reviewed at the UGC screening room, Neuilly-sur-Seine, April 19, 1989. (In Cannes Film Festival, noncompeting.) Running time: **85 MIN.**
Narrator: Michel Piccoli.

■ There's plenty of engaging monkey business in "Le Peuple singe," wildlife documentarian Gérard Vienne's fascinating ode to the ape kingdom. Film was five years in the making (including a year of editing) and the care, keen interest and sympathy show in the finished film.

A Cannes selection (in a special noncompetitive slot), it's nonetheless a highly specialized item that seems limited for theatrical release. Vienne and his producer, Jacques Perrin, have prepared an entirely different miniseries version from the masses of footage recorded.

Vienne, codirector (with François Bel) of two previous feature docus on animal life, receives sole credit on this one, both for direction and camerawork, which is excellent and fluidly edited. Vienne clearly knows his subject and has organized the material to underscore common experience and response among varying families of primates.

Film (which was shot around the globe in Indonesia, Japan, Ethiopia, Brazil and Sri Lanka) introduces us to a wide-ranging variety of monkeys: macaques, baboons, gorillas, chimpanzees, orangutans, etc. Material is blocked out according to behavioral themes, such as maternal relationships, weaning, play, nourishment and social aggression. Film concludes on a trite cautionary note with montage effects of apes reacting with alarm to the infringements of man, symbolized by a buzzsaw felling trees.

Commentary, spoken by Michel Piccoli, keeps to the spare essentials. Jacques Loussier's music is effective.—*Len.*

Cleo/Leo

New York A Platinum Pictures presentation, in association with DB Films. Produced, written and directed by Chuck Vincent. Camera (color), Larry Revene; editor, "Martha Ubell" (Vincent); music, Joey Mennonna; sound, Dale Whitman; art direction, Todd Rutt; production manager, Chip Lambert; assistant director-casting, Edd Rockis; associate producers, Vita Di Bari, Riccardo Di Bari. Reviewed on New World Video vidcassette, N.Y., April 25, 1989. (In Cannes Film Festival Market.) MPAA Rating: R. Running time: **94 MIN.**

Cleo Clock	Jane Hamilton
Leo Blockman	Scott Baker
Marvin Blockman	Alan Naggar
Karen	Ginger Lynn Allen
Bob Miller	Kevin Thomsen
Sally	Ruth Collins

Also with: Frank Stewart, Jennifer Delora, Joe Giardina, Daniel Chapman.

■ The screen's current body-switching craze receives an effective variation in "Cleo/Leo," a direct-to-video feature satirizing male chauvinism.

Scott Baker spouts all the familiar clichés as a sexist businessman, who falls in the river after being chased by an irate redhead on the street who doesn't like his insulting comments.

Director Chuck Vincent glosses over the fantasy gimmick, as hero emerges from the drink a woman, Jane Hamilton. She's foulmouthed and unaware at first that a transformation has taken place.

Through this role reversal, Hamilton learns the error of her/his ways as guys make moves on her. The technique of a recent similar film, NW's George Burns vehicle "18 Again," is used as Baker's voice is voiced over from time to time as an alter ego to Hamilton's ongoing expanding consciousness.

Pic effectively capsules archaic sexual attitudes and stereotyping, though it fails to achieve the humor and nuttiness of a forebear like Thorne Smith's "Turnabout," the Hal Roach 1940 feature that's ripe for an update.

What makes the film work is an enthusiastic performance by Hamilton (a.k.a. Veronica Hart), getting a nice showcase here in her 20th feature assignment for Vincent. Baker is okay in a briefer role.

Former porn star Ginger Lynn Allen has her best crossover role to date, both sexy and sympathetic as Hamilton's roommate.—*Lor.*

Java Burn
(INDONESIAN)

Hollywood A Novacom Intl. presentation of a Parkit Films production (foreign sales, Manson Intl.). Produced by Dhamoo, Gobind and Raam Punjabi. Written and directed by Robert Chappell. Camera (color), John Foster; editor, Michael Spence; music, Lance Rubin; sound (Ultra-Stereo), Lee Orloff. Reviewed at Beverly Center Cineplex 2, L.A. (American Film Market), Feb. 26, 1989. (In Cannes Film Festival Market.) No MPAA Rating. Running time: **90 MIN.**

Nicky Hogan	William Penn Sullivan
Samantha	Ava Lazar
Lomax	David Thornton
Dustin	Peter Fox
Aileen	Ayu Azhari

(English soundtrack)

■A poor man's "The Year Of Living Dangerously," "Java Burn" exudes blood, sweat, sex, foul language and a passion for guns and fisticuffs, adding up to a generically correct action pic. This assures some playoff in overseas urban grindhouses before pic fulfills its homevideo destiny.

American bail-jumper Nicky Hogan (William Penn Sullivan) is a pimp living in an Indonesian city, but he's a nice pimp. The viewer knows this at the outset because the collegiate-looking dude declines an unsavory associate's invitation to partake in a drink of blood from a freshly killed snake.

He's in love with prostie Aileen (Ayu Azhari), but their relationship is tested when he sends her off to service a kinky State Dept. official. After his assassination, she escapes from the hotel with the victim's jacket which has the key to a fortune in diamonds. The hitmen drive Aileen into hiding.

Hogan's got to cherchez his femme as well as Samantha (Ava Lazar), a full-lipped American blond who got the relatively happy interracial couple in the fix in the first place. Turns out she and her b.f. (Peter Fox), also with the State Dept., are after the diamonds, too.

Making his directorial debut, Chappell was cameraman on Errol Morris' "The Thin Blue Line" and Charles Kaufman's "Jakarta," also produced by the busy Punjabi brothers production team. With his cinematographer John

Foster ("Wild Style"), "Java Burn" has a crisp, clean look. They are at their best in the pic's climactic scene in which a Mercedes crashes through the ceiling of a folk theater, raining the diamonds over the destitute crowd.

Still, the mix of commercial elements is all too ordinary. The actors deliver the artless dialog blandly, which doesn't matter since it probably will be seen more in dubbed form than in its original English lingo. —*Binn.*

Party Incorporated
(Party Girls)

New York A Platinum Pictures and Private Screenings presentation. Executive producers, Gary P. Conner, Ernest G. Sauer. Produced and directed by Chuck Vincent. Screenplay, Craig Horrall, Edd Rockis; camera (color), Larry Revene; editor, James Davalos; music, Joey Mennonna; sound, Dale Whitman; art direction, Todd Rutt; production manager, Chip Lambert; assistant director-casting, Rockis. Reviewed on New World Video vidcassette, N.Y., May 3, 1989. (In Cannes Film Festival Market.) MPAA Rating: R. Running time: **79 MIN.**

Marilyn	Marilyn Chambers
Peter	Kurt Woodruff
Christina	Christina Veronica
Felicia	Kimberly Taylor
Ronald Weston	Kurt Schwoebel
Griswald	Frank Stewart
Betty	Ruth Collins

Also with: Michelle Levine, Karen Nielsen, Maraya Chase, Debbie Rochon, Joey Mennonna, Ed Mallia, Derrick Roberts, John Altamura, Harvey Siegel, Robinette Lloyd, Chuck Vincent, Edd Rockis, Larry Revene, James Davalos, Jeffrey Wallach, Dale Whitman.

■Chuck Vincent's experiment in "interactive" cinema comes off as too much of an in-joke in "Party Girls" (retitled "Party Incorporated" after NW objected to moniker). Pic is merely okay pay-cable fodder.

Film was originally planned as a pay-tv stunt in which several alternate reels of footage would be prepared and a live phone-in would determine ending and plot twists by audience vote.

Ultimately simplified concept has resulted in a tongue-in-cheek film in which (fake) audience participation has been built in. Marilyn Chambers, in character, invites Vincent & his film crew into her mansion to shoot a tv docu about her. As the very minor plotline of her becoming a professional party arranger in order to raise $250,000 for back taxes unfolds, audience is represented on screen by three guys in a bar watching the tv docu and four girls at a pyjama party doing likewise.

Typical softcore sex comedy (of which Vincent is a prolific practi-

tioner) is satirized by the constant intrusion of not only the two audiences, but also Vincent and his crew, who end up on camera almost as much as the actors they're filming. Fantasy element is introed, "Purple Rose Of Cairo" style, by having the actors and audiences intermingle.

This ambitious format doesn't come off due to rather lame writing and Vincent's indulgent direction. When the helmer joins in the chorus as part of a threadbare production number behind Chambers, singing as she strolls through a Toronto shopping mall, it seems a bit desperate. Buffs may have some fun with the concept, which legitimately allows for frequent use of boom or camera reflection in the frame, on purpose.

Chambers has fun with a self-absorbed role that would have been tailormade for Mae West. Supporting cast is functional, highlighted by Christina Veronica's old-fashioned striptease. —*Lor.*

Spirits Of The Air, Gremlins Of The Clouds
(AUSTRALIAN)

Sydney A Meaningful Eye Contact production. Produced by Andrew McPhail, Alex Proyas. Directed by Proyas. Screenplay, Proyas; camera (color), David Knaus; editor, Craig Wood; music, Peter Miller; production design, Sean Callinan; sound, Miller, David White, Craig Wood; costumes, Angela Tonks, Mathu Anderson. Reviewed at Film Australia screening room, Sydney, Aug. 13, 1988. (In Cannes Film Festival Market.) Running time: **93 MIN.**

Felix Crabtree	Michael Lake
Betty Crabtree	Melissa Davis
Smith	Norman Boyd

■Still awaiting Australian release several months after its completion, "Spirits Of The Air…" is an offbeater looking for a cult audience. It's a film with a distinctive style and vision, but it adds up to a minimal screen experience.

Setting is the desert, some time in the future. Felix, a manic type, and his sister, Betty, live in a wood house in the middle of nowhere. The siblings have a religious fixation, so the place is filled with crucifixes, burning candles and other icons. For reasons inadequately explained, the couple are trapped in this desolate spot, but are trying to build a primitive aircraft which will fly them out.

Enter Smith, a stranger lost in the wilderness. They take him in, and he helps them build their flying machine, but all their early at-

tempts at getting liftoff end in crashes. Eventually they manage to construct a workable aircraft. By this time Betty has gone mad, Felix elects to stay on with her and Smith flies out alone.

It's a film forever dashing one's expectations. (Will Betty and Smith become lovers? Will the danger that appears to threaten the trio ever be fully explained?) Pic is striking to look at, with inventive production and camerawork.

The three actors can't sustain this kind of material and even Michael Lake (so effective in his brief role in "Sweetie") gives a monotonous portrayal. The music by Peter Miller also is uninspiring.

The vision of director Alex Proyas is ill-served by his screenplay and the actors. The final impression is of some clever ideas never properly realized. The credit titles, written in spidery handwriting, are virtually illegible. —*Strat.*

See No Evil, Hear No Evil

Hollywood A Tri-Star Pictures release. Produced by Marvin Worth. Executive producers, Burtt Harris, Earl Barret, Arne Sultan. Directed by Arthur Hiller. Screenplay, Barret, Sultan, Eliot Wald, Andrew Kurtzman, Gene Wilder from a story by Barret, Sultan, Worth; camera (Technicolor). Victor J. Kemper; editor, Robert C. Jones; music, Stewart Copeland; production design, Robert Gundlach; art direction, James T. Singelis; set decoration, George deTitta Jr.; costume design, Ruth Morley; sound, Dennis Maitland Sr.; assistant director, Mark McGann; casting, Lynn Stalmaster. Reviewed May 10, 1989, at the UA Coronet, L.A. MPAA Rating: R. Running time: **103 MIN.**

Wally	Richard Pryor
Dave	Gene Wilder
Eve	Joan Severance
Kirgo	Kevin Spacey
Adele	Kirsten Childs
Braddock	Alan North

■ With Richard Pryor and Gene Wilder in the lead roles, "See No Evil, Hear No Evil" could only be a broadly played, occasionally crass, funny physical comedy. As such, film is a surefire hit for Tri-Star.

How the blind Pryor ends up working for the deaf Wilder at a Manhattan lobby newsstand really is inconsequential, since neither their first encounter, nor anything that follows, is believable for a minute, including the thing that binds them in the first place — how each denies his limitations.

Wilder, who makes customers speak to him directly so he can read their lips, finds he can't turn down the equally vulnerable Pryor for a job.

The five writers, including Wilder, have worked up a fitting scenario for these nimble screen comedians to play off one another in a series of silly gags that are consistently amusing and — amazingly — rarely insulting to real people who suffer from these handicaps.

If anything, the duo, reteamed here under director Arthur Hiller ("Silver Streak"), are more in sync than ever. One doesn't step on the other's lines unless it's intended or get a bigger laugh unless the other gets a follow-up two seconds later.

They do a lot of actual stepping on toes, tripping over things and miscommunicating that bonds them into their bumbling relationship.

Their street-level repartee begins immediately, but really starts to move from the first morning they work together.

While Wilder's back is turned, a customer is shot in the back. Pryor is out on the curb listening for the New York Daily News to make its morning drop — so he misses hearing anything inside.

By the time Wilder turns around, he's only able to catch a glimpse of the assailant's (Joan Severance) sexy gams. Pryor has missed it all, though he does manage to catch a whiff of Severance's perfume before she slips by him onto the crowded street.

The cops arrive and, in predictable fashion, arrest the only suspects around, the two numbskulls who couldn't possibly coordinate anything, much less a murder.

What ensues is how Pryor and Wilder try to outwit the NYPD, the killers on their trail and, ultimately, the evil criminal mastermind. In essence, it's a chase scene that lasts 103 minutes.

The thin plot device is the whereabouts of a gold coin (which looks like foil-wrapped chocolate) that keeps getting stolen from the individuals involved in the caper.

For those who enjoy unrefined, sometimes clever, ribald humor, this is the ticket.

Besides the leads, everyone else does good turns in limited roles. Kirsten Childs is notable for being the only cast member who never acts stupid.

Tech credits are adequate to poor (continuity is a problem that probably won't be noticed much) and it's annoying to always have the music pounding in the background. There's plenty else going on.—*Brit.*

Fist Fighter

Hollywood A Taurus Entertainment Co. release of an Izaro Films, Eagle Film Corp. and Esme production. Produced by Carlos Vasallo. Directed by Frank Zuniga. Screenplay, Max Bloom, from story by Vasallo. Camera (Kodak color), Hans Burman; editor, Drake Silliman; music, Emiliano Redondo; set design, Francisco Magallon, Seth Santacruz; postproduction sound mixers, T.A. Moore Jr. and Jeff Gomillion; fight choreography, Jimmy Nickerson; second unit camera, Alberto Arellanos, Gerardo Manero; associate producer, Abraham Cherem; casting, Daniel Travis. Reviewed at Carolco screening room, Los Angeles, May 10, 1989. MPAA Rating: R. Running time: **100 MIN.**

C.J. Thunderbird	George Rivero
Harry "Punchy" Moses	Edward Albert
Billy Vance	Mike Connors
Ellen	Brenda Bakke
Rhino	Matthias Hues
Moreno	Simon Andreu

■ This exceedingly violent, ultra-low-budget actioner lensed in Mexico is redeemed somewhat by Edward Albert's memorable portrayal of a dissolute conman who helps a tough fistfighter avenge his buddy's death. Pic should yield satisfaction to intended fringe audience.

George Rivero plays C.J. Thunderbird, who arrives in a corrupt South American town to challenge a huge blond fighter, Rhino (Matthias Hues), who's controlled by a smooth, snake-eyed fight fixer, Vance (Mike Connors).

When C.J. begins to win, Vance has the local police interrupt the fight and make off with the money. But a peglegged former champ, Harry "Punchy" Moses (Albert), spots C.J.'s potential. Punchy, given a soulful, gravelly voiced portrayal by Albert, becomes C.J.'s trainer and the soul of the story as the two beat the local power structure.

When C.J. is thrown in prison after being provoked by the local police captain, Punchy makes a drunken, anguished attempt to fight Rhino and is beaten to a pulp.

Meanwhile, C.J. escapes from prison, is captured, but wins his freedom by defeating a hairy giant who's kept chained up for the purpose of tearing escapees apart.

By the time he reaches Punchy, his friend is on his deathbed, and C.J. vows to destroy his killers.

Pic's unrelenting violence and grinding cruelty is overwhelming, but director Frank Zuniga and scripter Max Bloom salvage some sweeter moments, particularly in the characters of Punchy and Brenda Bakke as a sympathetic g.f. who deserts Vance.

Rivero, with his chiseled physique and blow-dried silver hair, has limited emoting skills. But his portrayal of a fearless, stubborn hero is likely to click with intended viewers.

Grainy, often underlit fight footage is graphically choreographed by Jimmy Nickerson ("Raging Bull," "Rocky"). Mixed-up sound of fists thudding on flesh is practically the film's soundtrack.

Exotic atmospherics are aptly handled in scenes of shirtless fighters sparring in dark, crowded clubs, but editing often is jarringly abrupt, cutting without preamble into the thick of a fight scene, even at climax. Pic shows signs of hasty patching in the cutting room.

Connors gives a gritty, controlled perf as the icy power-broker, but best is Albert, whose contribution as the feisty fighter far exceeds the demands of the genre. —*Daws.*

Twister

Hollywood A Vestron release of a Wieland Schulz-Keil production. Produced by Schulz-Keil. Executive producers, William J. Quigley, Dan Ireland. Written and directed by Michael Almereyda, based on the novel "OH!" by Mary Robison. Camera (Duart color), Renato Berta; editor, Roberto Silvi; music, Hans Zimmer; production design, David Wasco; art direction, Don Bishop; set decoration, Dianna Freas; costume design, Carol Wood; sound (Dolby), Ed Novick; assistant director, Eric N. Heffron; second unit camera, Chris Squires. Reviewed at the Beverly Center Cineplex (American Film Market), L.A., Feb. 28, 1989. (In USA Film Festival.) MPAA Rating: PG-13. Running time: **94 MIN.**

Eugene Cleveland	Harry Dean Stanton
Maureen Cleveland	Suzy Amis
Howdy Cleveland	Crispin Glover
Chris	Dylan McDermott
Stephanie	Jenny Wright
Lola	Charlaine Woodard
Virginia	Lois Chiles
Man in barn	William Burroughs

■ "Twister" is an oddball family drama about some Kansas nuts who bounce off the walls of their mansion while a storm brews outside. Appealing for its ambition to achieve a unique tone and for its wildly disparate cast, pic never entirely comes together.

With an estate in the flattest part of the Midwest, Harry Dean Stanton is a retired soda pop tycoon who casually presides over a brood consisting of his layabout daughter Suzy Amis, the latter's 8-year-old daughter, his pretentious, would-be *artiste* son Crispin Glover, the latter's fiancee Jenny Wright, unconventional black maid Charlaine Woodard and his own fiancee, children's tv evangelist Lois Chiles.

Trying to work his way back under the same roof is Dylan McDermott, father of Amis' child, a ne'er-do-well who seems like too nice a guy for the fruitcakes populating Stanton's family. For no apparent reason other than basic disagreeability, Amis keeps adamantly rejecting McDermott's apologies and advances, although he just bounces right back every time.

Other than McDermott's attempts to ingratiate himself, tale offers neither a strong dramatic thread nor psychological insight, and thus must get by on its screwy mood and isolated moments of mostly deadpan humor. The former is achieved to a great extent through heavily emphasized background ambient noise and music, abetted by Hans Zimmer's imaginative score.

Latter stems largely from weird mix of performances, from Stanton's exaggeratedly flat, matter-of-fact patriarch and Glover's archly theatrical loser of a son to Amis' impressively more realistic and detailed mother-daughter.

Although it's impossible to see what first-time writer-director Michael Almereyda, working from a novel by Mary Robison, is trying to get at, he doesn't at this point display the powers to unify the set of performances or to consistently control the tone.

His plain visual approach and lax timing fails to punch up the latent but mostly unrealized comic possibilities, and the event referred to in the title is so unintegrated into the action that it remains strictly symbolic.

Renato Berta's shadowy lensing doesn't help the humor emerge, and other tech contributions are okay. Novelist William Burroughs puts in a brief appearance, the most exceptional aspect of which is the utter authenticity of his flat Midwestern accent. —*Cart.*

Midnight Warrior

New York   A P/M Entertainment Group production. Produced by Richard Pepin, Joseph Merhi. Directed by Merhi. Screenplay, Charles T. Kanganis; camera (color), Pepin; editor, Paul Volk; music, John Gonzalez; additional music, Jastereo Coviare; sound, Mike Hall; assistant director, Kanganis; 2d unit director, Red Horton; special makeup effects, Judy Yonemoto; stunt coordinator, Joe Murphy; associate producer, Charla Driver. Reviewed on Raedon Entertainment vidcassette, N.Y., April 19, 1989. No MPAA Rating. Running time: **86 MIN.**
Nick Branca . . . . Kevin Bernhardt
Angelina . . . . Lilly Melgar
Buddy . . . . Bernie Angel
Liz Brown . . . . Heidi Paine
Sam . . . . Marty Brinton
   Also with: Michelle Berger, Rita Rogers, David Parry, Jeanette Mateus, Marta Dargham, Addison Randall.

■ "Midnight Warrior" is a low-budget made-for-video feature that captures an authentic film noir mood in approximating the B pictures of yore.

Tv star Kevin Bernhardt portrays a principled tv news cameraman in L.A. who resists the blandishments of his boss Bernie Angel, who is more interested in a fast buck than integrity. Pic documents in episodic form a series of assignments leading to hero becoming cynical and replacing Angel as the exploiter.

Modestly lensed, pic is buoyed by a persuasive Bernhardt performance and capable supporting cast. Topic of tv news as exploitation remains a t..nely one and is treated convincingly here. —*Lor.*

Time Trackers

Hollywood   A Concorde Pictures release. Produced by Roger Corman. Written and directed by Howard R. Cohen. Camera (Foto-Kem), Ronn Schmidt; editor, Brent Schoenfeld; music, Parmer Fuller; art director, Peter Flynn; sound, Michael Clark; costume design, 21st Century; special effects makeup, Roy Knyrim; special effects, Gregory Landerer; second unit director, Andy Blumenthal; second unit camera, Richard Buckley; casting, Al Guarino. Reviewed on videotape, May 9, 1989. MPAA Rating: PG. Running time: **87 MIN.**
Harry . . . . Ned Beatty
Charles . . . . Wil Shriner
R.J. . . . . Kathleen Beller
Madeline . . . . Bridget Hoffman
Edgar . . . . Alex Hyde-White
Zandor . . . . Lee Bergere

■ **For preteen girls entranced with stories about knights in shining armor who slay villains for the maidens they love, "Time Trackers" is passably entertaining fare.**

Using the worn plot device of time travel, writer-director Howard R. Cohen puts a group of young scientists-intellectuals aboard a capsule that will journey backward from the year 2033 to stop the evil inventor Zandor (Lee Bergere) from changing the course of history.

Not showing too much of the braininess they purportedly have, pretty R.J. (Kathleen Beller, formerly of tv's "Dynasty"), prettier Madeline (Bridget Hoffman) and earnest escort Charles (Wil Shriner) stop at a West Hollywood park during a political rally circa 1991 (that appears to have been filmed in the middle of a swap meet) where they thwart Bergere's attempt to assassinate a Congressman.

It's never explained why this would be significant in history, although it sets up a silly enough scenario to introduce Ned Beatty as a cop who mistakes the heroes for the would-be killers. Beatty grabs the time capsule as the innocents escape from L.A. and finds himself, along with them, smack dab in the middle of England circa 1146.

Production is saddled with a weak stand-in for Abelard named Edgar (Alex Hyde-White), who cuts a dashing figure but otherwise acts a bit dim-witted to be the legendary swordsman Red Duke, deposed head of the realm. Bergere, his foe now on the throne, acts equally nonthreatening.

Thin material is spread even thinner as the entire middle of the pic has little to do with unseating Bergere and a lot to do with wandering down dank corridors or

among the revelers in the castle courtyard.

That there is a sci-fi element here (computers and laser guns) doesn't change the overall presentation to anything other than a reworking of a fairy tale. The lovers ultimately are united and the villain gets his just desserts.

Beller, Shriner and Hoffman are about as credible as the story, even if they do look to be enjoying themselves in their medieval garb. Production values are okay.
—*Brit.*

LATE CANNES REVIEWS

Dom Za Vesanje
(Time Of the Gypsies)
(YUGOSLAV)

Cannes   A Columbia Pictures presentation of a Forum Film, Sarajevo Television production. Produced by Mirza Pasic. Directed by Emir Kusturica. Screenplay, Kusturica, Gordan Mihic; camera (color), Vilko Filac; editor, Andrija Zafranovic; music, Goran Bregovic; sound, Ivan Zakic; art direction, Miljen Kljakovic; costumes, Mirjana Ostojic. Reviewed at Cannes Film Festival, competing, May 15, 1989. Running time: **136 MIN.**
Perhan . . . . Davor Dujmovic
Ahmed . . . . Bora Todorovic
Grandmother . . . . Ljubica Adzovic
Uncle . . . . Husnija Hasimovic
Azra . . . . Sinolicka Trpkova
   Also with: Zabit Memedov, Elvira Sali, Suada Karisik, Predrag Lakovic, Mirsad Zulic.

■ **Running over two hours, with a rambling story which takes a break every once in a while to indulge in fantasy and poetic license, the new Emir Kusturica picture is more demanding and less immediately appealing than his earlier Cannes winner, "When Father Was Away On Business."**

Dealing with the exploitation of gypsy children smuggled from Yugoslavia to Italy and put on the streets to steal and beg for their bosses, the film emerges as a relative latecomer, echoing numerous headlines in recent years and awardwinning picture, "Guardian Angel," by fellow Yugoslav Goran Paskaljevic.

Kusturica, obviously conscious of the delay (he even mentions Paskaljevic's film in his own), is far more ambitious than his predecessor. He is not content with a straightforward account of a specific case, but attempts to paint a much larger canvas of the gypsy experience, their fatalism, self-destructiveness and the misery of their existence, their colorful charm and inspiration, and their rejection of any type of organized society which would threaten to turn them into law-abiding citizens.

All of which is woven into the story of Perhan, a clumsy teenager who accompanies his younger sister to hospital in town. But instead of staying there to care for her, he is taken to Italy, forced to join the illicit labor force of a petty criminal, rises through the ranks to become his second in command and almost believes he has it made. Then he discovers he has been double crossed by his pretended benefactor.

Kusturica starts with the same elements that worked so well in his earlier picture, a blend of humor, poetry and a touch of surrealism. He has trouble, though, keeping the dosage right. Midway between folk opera, social protest and fantasy, the film has the potential to distinguish itself in each of these territories but does not invest sufficiently in either one of them.

On top of which it lacks a solid script to tighten up all the loose ends. This is particularly evident in the last half-hour, as the plot stumbles in search of a satisfactory denouement.

The film's best moments are its flights of fancy, in which Kusturica, delivered from the necessity of following a strict plotline, seems to be most comfortable. The cast, headed by Davor Dujmovic (one of the boys in "When Father Way Away") and consisting primarily of amateurs, offers some highly imaginative and deeply felt instinctive performances.

While some sequences stand out (the religious celebration on the river, the gypsy hut lifted up into the air), the film as a whole, with its overabundant soundtrack and nervous camera technique, is more difficult to accept. It will be interesting to see whether an international audience will duplicate the terrific response the film already has obtained at home, where it has broken most boxoffice records.
—*Edna.*

Brenda Starr

Cannes   A New World Intl. presentation of AM/PM production with Tribune Entertainment. Produced by Myron A. Hyman. Executive producer, John D. Backe. Directed by

Robert Ellis Miller. Screenplay by Noreen Stone, James David Buchanan, Jenny Wolkind, based on story by Stone and Buchanan and on the Brenda Starr comic strip by Dale Messick; camera (Eastmancolor), Freddie Francis; editor, Mark Melnick; music, Johnny Mandel; sound, Sharon Smith Holley; costumes for Brooke Shields, Bob Mackie; other costumes, Peggy Farrell; animation produced by Japhet Asher, Colossal Pictures/USFX; casting, Pat McCorakle. Reviewed at Cannes Film Festival (Market), May 15, 1989. MPAA Rating: PG. Running time: **87 MIN.**

Brenda Starr . . . . Brooke Shields
Basil St. John . . . . Timothy Dalton
Mike Randall . . . . Tony Peck
Libby (Lips) Lipscomb . . . . Diana Scarwid
Newspaper editor . . . . Charles Durning
Police chief . . . . Eddie Albert
President Truman . . . . Ed Nelson
   Also with: Nestor Serrano, Jeffrey Tambor, June Gable, Kathleen Wilhoite, John Short, Henry Gibson, Tom Aldredge, Matthew Cowles, Avner Eisenberg, Mary Lou Rosato.

■ **The comic strip girl reporter of Dale Messick's "Brenda Starr," the brash beauty with the celebrated gams, has been around since the 1940s. A much briefer lifespan is in the cards for this Robert Ellis Miller feature starring Brooke Shields.**

The picture loses every element of suspense as it staggers jerkily along in a style that opts more for farce than for comedy. Jerky movement and telescoped suspense sequences work well for a cartoon strip but take the narrative breath away from a film.

It does not help that Miller ("Reuben, Reuben") works from a story that insists on chopping up the action with animated or semi-animated inserts that show the cartoon artist at work with his strip and, reluctantly, falling in love with the live version of his creation.

While the plot takes the characters from New York to Puerto Rico and to high adventure among Russian spies and Amazon crocs, Shields looks lost most of the time. Miller is obviously not the director to help her release whatever energies she may possess as an actress. To tell the truth, baby fat still prevails in her pretty face (or at least it did in 1986, when pic was shot), and her body does not radiate much sexiness either.

Timothy Dalton lends his sardonic good looks (enhanced by a black eyepatch) to Basil St. John, the mysterious stranger who occasionally comes to the rescue of the heroine. Anthony Jay Peck as the cartoonist is as bland as he is blond, while Charles Durning and Eddie Albert turn up in small roles to give witty displays of what the fleshing out of a paper character is all about. *—Kell.*

Caracas
(AUSTRIAN)

Cannes   A Neue Studio Film Ges. production. Directed by Michael Schottenberg. Screenplay, Michael Horowitz, Schottenberg; camera (color), Walter Kindler; editor, Ingrid Koller; music, Erich Kleinschuster; sound, Walter Amann; art direction, Christopher Kanter. Reviewed at Cannes Film Festival (Directors Fortnight), May 14, 1989. Running time: **90 MIN.**
   With: Regula Bill, Gerhard Zemann.

■ **Director Michael Schottenberg introduces his first film as an evil picture for an evil audience. He couldn't be more accurate. Obviously no sympathy is lost between him and his characters, whom he mistreats royally and punishes with relish. However, it is highly improbable this is the right way to the heart of an audience.**

The story evolves around a middle-aged couple keeping a gas station and diner. She pretends to be a dancer; he dabbles in scientific research. The husband, humiliated and ignored by his wife who sleeps around with the customers, first is resigned to his situation. When he can't take it anymore he gets working on his revenge.

He intends to kill the wife, replace her with a hooker who is her double, and escape with that hooker and all the money to Caracas.

Schottenberg seems to enjoy debasing his characters, showing them in a mean and ugly light and denying the slightest chance of identification with either of them. The last part of the film turns into a thriller, as the husband goes about preparing the perfect murder, which turns out to be pretty messy as well. The final twist turns the table at the last moment, depriving once again the hardworking criminal of his spoils.

Regula Bill, playing both the wife and the hooker, looks the ultimate bitch and Gerhard Zemann is the personification of the born loser. Schottenberg moves the story heavily at a slow pace, making use of an insistent music track, justified by the woman's dancing hobby. The film quite efficiently builds up the audience's antagonism to the couple to the point viewers will be delighted to see them get their just desserts. The only problem is that the ones left behind don't look much nicer. *—Edna.*

COMPETING AT CANNES FESTIVAL

Jésus Of Montréal
(Jesus Of Montreal)
(CANADIAN-FRENCH)

Cannes   A Max Films Intl. (Canada)-Gerard Mital Prods. (France) coproduction, in association with the National Film Board of Canada. Produced by Roger Frappier, Pierre Gendron. Written and directed by Denys Arcand. Camera (color), Guy Dufaux; editor, Isabelle Dedieu; music, Yves Laferrière; production design, François Séguin; sound, Patrick Rousseau; Montreal cityscapes, Jacques Leduc; casting, Lucie Robitaille. Reviewed at Cannes Film Festival (competing), May 15, 1989. Running time: **120 MIN.**

Daniel . . . . Lothaire Bluteau
Mireille . . . . Catherine Wilkening
Constance . . . . . . Johanne-Marie Tremblay
Martin . . . . Rémy Girard
René . . . . Robert Lepage
Father Leclerc . . . . Gilles Pelletier
Richard Cardinal . . . . Yves Jacques
The Judge . . . . Denys Arcand

■ **Audaciously conceived and brilliantly executed, "Jesus Of Montreal" should be a surefire arthouse hit worldwide, and anticipated controversies surrounding the film will only garner it free publicity. It should be in the running for a major Cannes prize.**

Writer-director Denys Arcand tops his "Decline Of The American Empire" with this wickedly funny, searingly honest satire on the way the message of Jesus Christ has been distorted through history. Story involves a young actor, Daniel, hired by the priest of a Montreal church to direct an annual Passion Play on the mountain overlooking the city. Daniel, who's been away in India, is to play Jesus himself (he looks the part), and he gathers around him four other actors to play multiple roles in his rewritten version of the play.

Mireille, with whom has has an affair, is a pretty French girl whose former boyfriend thought her body was her only asset; she's only done commercials. Constance, secretly the mistress of the priest, had been in the previous year's production; a sensual single mother, she works in a soup kitchen. Martin dubs voices in porno films (he's hilariously introed as he voices two studs engaged in hectic, unseen, sexual activity). And Rene is an actor who longs to play Hamlet (and gets to insert the famous soliloquy into the Christ story).

The play's a success, but life starts imitating art. The church finds it offensive (Daniel has incorporated fresh information about Jesus) and wants it stopped. Daniel himself starts to act like Jesus offstage: At an audition in which Mireille's ex wants her to strip, Daniel destroys equipment and drives the commercial's sponsors from the theater. He's arrested, but released, and later resists the temptations of a devilish showbiz lawyer who offers him the world — if he sells out.

When the police try to stop the play mid-performance, there's an accident in which Daniel is critically injured, leading to other parallels with the Christ story coming to pass.

Arcand's consistently witty screenplay pokes fun at many aspects of contemporary life, including gushy critics and talkshow folk, tv commercials, church attitudes, overcrowded hospitals, the police — and much more. A marvelous irony is that the wounded Daniel can't get a bed in the crowded St. Marks hospital, but is well cared for in a Jewish hospital. Other religious jokes abound, such as the lawyer, superbly played by Yves Jacques, who orders Bloody Marys and a Lobster Magdalene for lunch.

Arcand always has been a fine director of ensemble casts, and this film is no exception. Lothaire Bluteau is properly esthetic and sensitive as Daniel, while Remy Girard steals all his scenes as the jokey Martin. A sequence in which members of the cast play out a scene from the play in different theatrical styles (Method, Comedie Française, Kabuki, etc.) is a showstopper.

There were walkouts (as well as beaucoup applause) at the Cannes unspooling, and no doubt the very religious will object to aspects of the film, especially the character of the self-serving Catholic priest (Gilles Pelletier) with his secret mistress and double standards. For the rest, everything that happens involves an actor *playing* Christ, and miracles — like a temporary return from the dead, or the way Daniel eventually lives on — are easily explained by modern science.

Pic should provoke argument, but it's sophisticated entertainment of the highest order. It's Arcand's best film, and one of the most original and successful pics ever produced in Canada.*—Strat.*

Trop Belle Pour Toi
(Too Beautiful For You)
(FRENCH)

Cannes An AMLF release of a Ciné Valse-D.D. production. (Intl. Sales: Roissy Films, Paris.) Written and directed by Bertrand Blier. Camera (Panavision, Eastmancolor), Philippe Rousselot; editor, Claudine Merlin; music, Franz Schubert; production design, Théobald Meurisse; sound, Louis Gimel; Paul Bertault; costumes, Michèle Mermande-Cerf; production manager, Bernard Marescot; assistant director, Luc Goldenberg; casting, Margot Capelier, Marie-Christine Lafosse. Reviewed at Cannes Film Festival, competing, May 11, 1989. Running time: **91 MIN.**
Bernard Barthélémy . . . .Gérard Depardieu
Colette Chevassu . . . . . . .Josiane Balasko
Florence Barthélémy . . . . . .Carole Bouquet
Marcello . . . . .Roland Blanche
Pascal Chevassu . . . . .François Cluzet
Also with: Didier Benureau (Leonce), Philippe Loffredo (Tanguy), Sylvie Orcier (Marie-Catherine), Myriam Boyer (Genevieve).

■ Bertrand Blier, whose films usually have made sardonic fun of such staple themes as friendship and sexual relationships, has come up with a new charmer in "Too Beautiful For You," this time bringing fresh insight to the old, old story of marital infidelity. This witty, cleverly structured film should have audiences chuckling wherever quality French films are screened.

In his last film, "Ménage" ("Tenue De Soirée"), Blier had husky Gérard Depardieu play a gay guy hopelessly in love with wimpy Michel Blanc. His new film stars Depardieu too, this time as a successful car dealer married to a sublimely beautiful woman (Carole Bouquet) and the envy of all his friends. Perversely, he falls passionately in love with a temporary secretary who comes to work for him — a plump, somewhat plain, middle-aged woman who would seem to be the least likely type to woo him away from his family. Josiane Balasko plays the sweet, sensual mistress with a warmth which makes Depardieu's passion acceptable.

The plot is simple enough, but Blier keeps his audience in a constant state of surprise, and delight, with the complex but frequently funny way he tells his essentially banal story. All the ingredients for a film about infidelity are here: the motel where the lovers meet; the apartment lent to them by one of Depardieu's employees; the increasingly agitated wife; the trip the lovers make to the countryside to get away from it all, the ending which leaves the philandering husband without either wife or mistress.

But Blier gleefully takes every cliché and turns it on its head, juggling time, allowing his characters to address the audience and including such genuinely charming scenes as one in which the blissful Balasko shares her happiness with a complete stranger at a railway station, telling him she's been making love for the last three hours.

Essential to the success of the film is the fact that there's a good deal of painful truth to be found in these situations. Two scenes in which the wife and the mistress meet, once in the office and again in the motel, are exquisitely written and acted emotional encounters. Another highlight is a complex flashback to the Depardieu/Bouquet wedding which is intercut with a dinner party they give for friends in the present; at both events, Balasko is a real, or imagined, interloper.

Depardieu, appearing in his fifth Blier film, brings the right comic touch to his impassioned, confused character. His constant railing against the mournful music of Shubert, heard throughout the film, is a running gag perfectly capped at fadeout. Carole Bouquet, a former James Bond girl, is properly elegant and cool as the betrayed wife, and also does a cameo as Balasko's distraught neighbor, a woman abandoned by her husband. Balasko herself is a joy as the mistress, while François Cluzet does a fine turn as her frustrated spouse.

A major asset to the film is Philippe Rousselot's constantly gliding Panavision camera, while Claudine Merlin's intricate editing also deserves a nod. The aforementioned music by Shubert adds to the success of the film which, like "Ménage," is about sex but sans nudity, although the dialog is raunchy at times. —*Strat.*

Reunion
(FRENCH-W. GERMAN-BRITISH)

Cannes A Les Films Ariane-FR3 Films (Paris) NEF Film Produktion und Vertriebs (Munich)-CLG Films (Twickenham) coproduction, in association with Tac Ltd. and Arbo-Film Maran GmbH. Executive producer, Vincent Malle. Produced by Anne François. Directed by Jerry Schatzberg. Screenplay, Harold Pinter, from the novel by Fred Uhlman; camera (Panavision, Eastmancolor and Fujicolor), Bruno de Keyzer; editor, Martine Barraqué; music, Philippe Sarde; production design, Alexandre Trauner; sound, Laurent Quaglio; production manager, Juergen Kussatz; assistant director, Eric Bartonio; casting (London), Debbie MacWilliams; casting (Germany), Henry Ohlmeier. Reviewed at Ariane Films screening room, Paris, May 8, 1989. (In Cannes Film Festival, competing). Running time: **110 MIN.**
Henry Strauss . . . . .Jason Robards
Hans Strauss . . . . .Christian Anholt
Konrad von Lohenburg . . . . . .Samuel West
Countess von Lohenburg .Françoise Fabian
Lisa . . . . .Maureen Kewin
Mme. Strauss . . . . .Barbara Jefford
Dr. Jakob Strauss . . . . .Bert Parnaby
Young Countess Gertrud . . .Shebah Ronay
Old Countess Gertrud .Dorothea Alexander
Also with: Tim Barker (Zimmerman), Struan Rodger (Pompetski), Roland Schaefer (Judge Freisler), Frederick Warder (gymnastics teacher), Alexandre Trauner (caretaker), Gerhard Fries (Brossner).
(In English)

■ Since 1989 marks the 50th anniversary of the start of World War II, interest in the subject is likely to increase, which will doubtless help launch "Reunion" in quality situations worldwide. This enormously impressive film ranks as one of the best of countless pics dealing with the rise of Nazism in Germany in the early '30s.

"Reunion" will be seen by many as a familiar subject, but it contains new insights into the genesis of a tragedy for Germany and the world. Intelligent and technically highly accomplished, the film should attract audiences seeking serious, thought-provoking fare.

Harold Pinter has fashioned an intelligent and well-constructed screenplay based on Fred Uhlman's autobiographical novel. Core of the drama is set in Stuttgart in 1933 and deals with the growing friendship between two schoolboys from different backgrounds: Hans (Christian Anholt), son of a Jewish doctor and World War I vet who, till now, was considered a pillar of the community; and the aristocratic Konrad (Samuel West), who's led a sheltered life, taught by private tutors, and who finds himself stimulated by the intelligent, sensitive Hans.

At the beginning of the year, portents of what's to come are few: small groups of Nazis march in the streets; a friend advises Hans' father to leave before Hitler takes over. Gradually, as the year progresses, the Facist movement takes hold. On a cycling trip to the Black Forest, the friends get in a fistfight with Nazis thugs, and Konrad is embarrassed when he takes Hans to meet his pretty cousin, Gertrud, who makes anti-Semitic remarks.

After the summer vacation, and the election that brought Hitler to power, the tide clearly has turned. A sympathetic teacher has been replaced by a diehard Nazi, and boys are expected to salute the Nazi flag. The home of Hans' Jewish neighbors is burned to the ground, and three children die in the blaze. Konrad reveals he's come to believe that Hitler sincerely wants to help Germany through this "stage of flux."

This long central part of the film is framed by a present-day narrative in which Hans, now Henry Strauss (Jason Robards), decides to return to Stuttgart to locate his parents' grave and to discover what happened to his old friend. Henry has lived in America since his parents sent him there at the end of 1933, and hasn't visited Germany since.

Needless to say, he finds Stuttgart radically changed (his old school was destroyed) but there still are traces of anti-Semitism. The final revelation as to the fate of his old friend comes as a genuine surprise.

Director Jerry Schatzberg has made what probably is his best film to date, a sober, thoughtful pic that recreates a seemingly authentic world of 56 years ago. He's aided immeasurably by the magnificent camerawork of Bruno de Keyzer, who uses desaturated color for the '30s sequences, giving an authentically drab look to the drama. The impeccable production design is by veteran Alexandre Trauner, who's done an amazing job throughout (one example: the conversion of the palatial home of the Von Lohenburgs in 1933 to a provicinal tax office in 1988).

In a memorable moment, Robards walks down a corridor, bathed in red light, before entering the cellars in which his parents' belongings still are kept.

Robards, with a small role, is fine as the adult Strauss, while newcomers Christian Anholt and Samuel West (son of actor Timothy West) are so good they seem to have stepped from an authentic movie of the '30s. Casting is excellent down the line. —*Strat.*

Mystery Train

Cannes A JVC presentation of an MTI Production (Intl. sales: Saredi Film, Zurich). Executive producers, Kunjiro Hirata, Hideaki Suda. Produced by Jim Stark. Written and directed by Jim Jarmusch. Camera (color), Robby Müller; editor, Melody London; music, John Lurie; sound, Mark Goodermote; production design, Dan Bishop; costumes, Carol Wood; line producer, Rudd Simmons; associate producer, Demetra MacBride; production manager, Kathie Hersch; assistant director, Eric (Elvis) Heffron; casting, Novella Smith, Noriko Murao. Reviewed at Cannes Film Festival (competing), May 13, 1989. No MPAA rating. Running time: 113 MIN.

Far From Yokohama

Jun	Masatoshi Nagase
Mitzuko	Youki Kudoh
Night clerk	Screamin' Jay Hawkins
Bellboy	Cinqué Lee
Man in station	Rufus Thomas

A Ghost

Luisa	Nicoletta Braschi
DeeDee	Elizabeth Bracco
News vendor	Sy Richardson
Man in diner	Tom Noonan
The Ghost	Stephen Jones

Lost In Space

Johnny	Joe Strummer
Will Robinson	Rick Aviles
Charlie	Steve Buscemi
Ed	Vondie Curtis-Hall
Voice of radio d.j.	Tom Waits

■ Wholly financed by Japanese electronics giant JVC, a first for an American production, "Mystery Train" is a 3-episode pic handled by indie writer-director Jim Jarmusch in his usual playful, minimalist style. Somewhat uneven, the film could stand some fine-tuning but still should find appreciative audiences the world over.

It could be almost dubbed "Memphis Stories," as this is Jarmusch's tribute to the city of Elvis and other musical greats. Characteristically, the director explores the crumbling, decaying edges of the city through the eyes of foreigners: Japanese teenagers, an Italian widow and a British punk.

All three stories take place during the same night mainly at the same hotel, the somewhat seedy Arcade; the three sets of characters never actually meet (until one brief encounter at fadeout).

Story one, "Far From Yokohama," intros teenagers Jun (Masatoshi Nagase) and Mitzuko (Youki Kudoh), who arrive by train, do a puzzling guided tour of Sun Studio (they can't understand a word the guide says), sit awed in front of a statue of Presley and check into the Arcade Hotel, where Jun photographs the fixtures and they argue about who was greater, Elvis or Carl Perkins (Jun thinks the latter). They make love, listen to the radio and hear a gunshot next morning as they're about to leave.

Story two, "A Ghost," features Nicoletta Braschi as Luisa, in Memphis to take her deceased husband's body back to Rome. After being conned by a news vendor and a sinister man (Tom Noonan) in a diner, she checks into the Arcade and meets talkative DeeDee (Elizabeth Bracco) in the lobby. They share a room, DeeDee talks about the English boyfriend she's just walked out on, Luisa thinks she sees the ghost of Elvis, and they, too, hear a gunshot next morning.

Final segment, "Lost In Space," picks up the story of the abandoned Brit Johnny (Joe Strummer), who goes on a drunken binge with DeeDee's brother (Steve Buscemi) and a black friend (Rick Aviles). Johnny shoots a liquor store clerk, and the trio hides out in the Arcade; next morning, trying to stop Johnny from shooting himself, Buscemi gets shot in the leg.

This third story is typical Jarmusch. As in "Down By Law," a trio of assorted males bicker away revealingly. But, oddly, it's the least interesting segment of "Mystery Train," adding nothing much to what's preceded it. The first story is by far the best, thanks to the wonderfully laid-back performances of the young leads and the genuinely amusing cultural differences they encounter. Central segment is rather touching in its depiction of two women from widely different backgrounds becoming friends.

Appearing in all three stories, and stealing the film, are Screamin' Jay Hawkins, as the scarlet-garbed night clerk, whose slow burns are a joy to behold, and Cinqué Lee as the wide-eyed bellhop. They make a great comedy team.

Working in color for the first time since his 1980 debut with "Permanent Vacation," Jarmusch makes the backstreets of Memphis, with its shuttered cinema and crummy stores, look marvelously rundown. Robby Müller's striking camerawork is a major asset, as is Dan Bishop's superior production design, which contrasts the three hotel rooms most amusingly. There's an expectedly superior music score by John Lurie.

Jarmusch is a minimalist, but his audience probably is growing and "Mystery Train" contains enough of the right ingredients to find the same market as "Stranger Than Paradise" and "Down By Law," though it isn't quite up to the standards set by them. Its international casting obviously will assist offshore marketing.—*Strat.*

El Niño de la Luna
(The Moon Child)

Cannes A Ganesh Producciones Cinematográficas Film. Executive producer, Julián Mateos. Written and directed by Agustín Villaronga. Camera (Eastmancolor), Jaume Peracaula; editor, Raul Román; music, Dead Can Dance; sets, Cesc Candini, Sadok Majri; costumes, Montse Amenós, Isidro Prunés; in Dolby. Reviewed at Cannes Film Festival, competing, May 12, 1989. Running time: 118 MIN.

Victoria	Maribel Martín
David	Enrique Saldaña
Georgina	Lisa Gerrard
Directress	Lucia Bosé

Also with: David Sust, Mary Carrillo, Günter Meissner, Hedi Ben Amar, Lydia Azzopardi, Jack Birket.

■ This beautifully shot, imaginatively directed, nigh-surrealistic Spanish pic works film magic for the first half-hour of its excessive running time, but then tries to substitute moonlight for steam. Its poetic imagery and striking visual effects are forceful in first part of pic, ultimately becoming onerous as script resorts to solutions that are far-fetched even within the context of the parapsychological premises.

Set before World War II, yarn concerns a village orphan who is told by his guardian that he, somehow, is the "child of the moon." The boy has occult powers, and can make physical objects move at a distance just by concentrating hard.

Presently, he becomes the prey of a kind of occult Center, resembling a hospital. He is adopted by one of its lady members, who takes him under her wing. The boy gives visual proof of his "powers" while continuing to be convinced that he is a moonchild.

The plot thickens as those running the Center decide to mate two of its members, so as to produce a "moonchild" who would possess extraordinary psychic powers. However, the chosen two, in league with the boy, rebel and escape.

Second part of pic takes a completely new tack, as the Center decides to pursue and try to kill the fugitives, who attempt to escape to Africa, supposedly the homeland of the boy's father.

Throughout, story is approached as a fantasy rather than a sci-fi or action pic. Interest is likely to be limited to select arthouse circuits. Good performances are turned in by Maribel Martin and Lisa Gerrard as the caretaker and the mother. Enrique Saldaña as the boy is effective for first part of film, but then becomes repetitive, and by end of pic his tiptoeing, furtive manner tends to exasperate. Good technical credits. Excellent direction points to Villaronga as one of the most imaginative directors on the Spanish scene today. —*Besa.*

DIRECTORS FORTNIGHT

Chine ma douleur
(China, My Sorrow)
(FRENCH-WEST GERMAN)

Paris An AMLF release of a Titane/Flach Film/La Sept/ZDF/Das Kleinfernsehspiel co-production. Produced by Jean-Luc Ormieres. Directed by Dai Sijie. Screenplay, Dai Sijie and Shan Yuan Zhu; camera (Eastmancolor and Agfacolor), Jean-Michel Humeau; editor, Chantal Delattre; music, Chen Qi Gang; art direction, Christian Marti; sound, Jean Pierre Fenie, Joel Rangon; costumes, Isabelle Filleul; casting, Marie France Michel, Eric Morille; assistant director, Patrice Martineau; technical adviser, Jean Rouch; production manager, Joey Fare; associate producers, Jean Luc Farguier, Isabelle Fauvel. Reviewed at Max Linder cinema, Paris, April 20, 1989. (In Cannes Film Festival, Directors Fortnight). Running time: 87 MIN.

With: Guo Liang Yi (Tian Ben, "Little Four-Eyes"), Tieu Quan Nghieu (the monk), Vuong Han Lai (the chief), Chi-Vy Sam (Beimo), Chang Cheung Siang (the cook), Truong Loi (the artist), Nguyen Van Thoi (the professor), Ngo Thuon, Souvannapadith Viradeth, Su Xio Ming, Miss Lius.

■ This is a Chinese film about political prisoners during the Cultural Revolution — Made In France.

Chinese-born Dai Sijie, 35, graduated from France's IDHEC film school in 1987 and chose to make his first theatrical feature about his homeland without getting farther than the Pyrénées, where most of this Chinese-speaking Franco-West German production was lensed with Chinese cast and Gallic tech crew. (The late exiled Turkish filmmaker Yilmaz Güney recreated the universe of his native land on local turf in his last film, "The Wall.") Apart from the production peculiarities, it stands out on its own right as a promising film debut.

Story, set in 1966, begins in a small Chinese provincial city, where a 13-year-old orphan, living hand-to-mouth, is arrested for owning and playing an outlawed (and apparently innocuous) recording. He is publicly humiliated as a public enemy and forced to wear a sort of paper dunce cap denouncing his "crime." Then he's shipped off to a reeducation (work) camp in the mountains, where he comes into contact with a group of adult outcasts, which include an apparently deaf and mute Taoist monk.

Film offers a cool, ironic group portrait of this small forsaken outpost, whose warden is himself a potential prisoner.

In one grotesquely poignant sequence, a lost group of acrobats, touring the area to provide entertainment to the poor peasants, mistakenly provides a tantalizing show for the prisoners and spins chicken-laden dishes in front of their famished audience.

Emotional center of the picture, however, remains the young boy and his tacit fascination with the monk, who keeps to himself and is surrounded by a court of wild pigeons. When the youth steps on a nail (gratuitously planted by a fellow prisoner) he falls dangerously ill and is nursed back to health by the monk.

Drama peaks when the warden orders the pigeons slaughtered. The despairing monk creates a sacrificial shadow theater, then slits his own throat. The boy thinks he's returning a favor when he saves the monk's life, only to learn that latter is deaf and mute by choice and reproachful of his young friend's intervention. In the moving final scene (reminiscent of "One Flew Over The Cuckoo's Nest") the youth smothers the monk to death, then flees.

The ingenious art direction, credited to Christian Marti, is made up of French buildings (apparently near Toulouse) resembling a provincial Chinese cityscape. He also erected a crumbling temple-cum-work camp atop a French mountain ridge. Other tech credits are fine. —*Len.*

Yaaba
(Grandmother)
(BURKINA FASO)

Cannes   An Arcadia Films (Paris)/Les Films de L'Avenir (Ouagadougou)/Thelma Film (Zurich) coproduction, in association with Burkina Faso, Télévision Suisse Romande, ZDF, La Sept, Centre National de la Cinémagraphie (Berne), Départment Fédéral des Affaires Etrangerès (Berne), COE (Milan). Produced by Freddy Denaës, Pierre-Alain Meier, Idrissa Ouedraogo. Written and directed by Ouedraogo. Camera (color), Matthias Kälin; editor, Loredana Cristelli; music, Francis Bebey. Reviewed at Cannes Film Festival (Directors Fortnight), May 12, 1989. Running time: **90 MIN.**
Yaaba . . . . Fatimata Sanga
Bila . . . . Noufou Ouedraogo
Nopoko . . . . Roukietou Barry
Kougri . . . . Adama Ouedraogo
Tibo . . . . Amade Toure

■ **The dry, brown plains of Burkina Faso offer a spare backdrop to Idrissa Ouedraogo's exquisitely simple tale "Grandmother." Ouedraogo's second feature (after the acclaimed "The Choice" and short "Issa The Weaver") establishes him as one of Africa's most sensitive directors, capable of communicating with international auds.**

Besides arthouse exposure. "Grandmother" has a pair of 12-year-old leads with built-in appeal for younger viewers.

Bila (Noufou Ouedraogo, an exceptional child performer) is a spunky boy who lives in a small village with his father and stepmother. He befriends Sana (Fatimata Sanga), an ancient old lady shunned by the villagers as a witch. Bila defends her from rock-hurling boys, brings her food, and calls her "grandmother."

When a little girl Bila plays with, Nopoko (Roukietou Barry), becomes fatally ill with tetanus, he enlists the aid of Sana. Against the villagers' wishes, Bila and his stepmother use Sana's herbal medicine to cure the girl. Though never reintegrated into the village, Sana remains the children's friend until she dies a peaceful death.

"Yaaba" turns these simple ingredients into a powerful film whose subject is essential human traits of goodness and generosity, evil, fear, superstition, intolerance. It is professionally lensed by Matthias Kälin and charmingly scored by Francis Bebey. Shot in helmer's own village, pic is full of very credible nonpro actors.
—*Yung.*

CANNES OFFICIAL SELECTIONS

Duende
(SWISS-FRENCH-
COLOR/B&W)

Cannes   Sophie Brandt presentation of a Strada Films (Geneva)-Les Films Du Phare (Paris)-Television Suisse Romande production. Produced by Ferrier, Brandt. Directed by Jean-Blaise Junod. Screenplay, Junod, Vincent Adatte; camera (Kodak color/b&w), Hugues Ryffel, editor, Christine Benoit; music, Michel Fano, traditional songs, Pilar del Castillo; sound, Luc Yersin. Reviewed at Cannes Film Festival Intl. Critics Week. May 12, 1989. Running time: **90 MIN.**

■ **Strictly for bullfight aficionados, this semi-documentary has 20-year-old matador Carmelo replay for the benefit of the camera the ceremony which marked his transition from novice to fully accredited bullfighter.**

Shot in Andalusia, pic makes the best use of the landscape and the scenery offered by local architecture. Film painstakingly follows in detail Carmelo's routines in the last few days before the decisive corrida. Slow and deliberate observation focuses on the emotional stress and on the necessity of concentration and mental preparation for the test ahead.

Black & white interviews with an experienced bullfighter and with the mother and sister of another, lend more depth to this ritual so very dear to Latin hearts. The final corrida is an appropriate climax to all the preparations.

This is a studious treatise on the bullfighting myth which Swiss director Jean-Blaise Junod obviously adores, rather than an exciting portrayal of it. Well shot and cut, using traditional music to enhance authenticity, the picture gives an interesting glimpse behind the glitter of a matador's glory. There is no exact English translation of the title, which means, according to the press-book, something between charm, power to bewitch and intuition.

Still, it's doubtful it will win any new hearts for this sport, or will calm animal rights advocates' protests against it. —*Edna.*

Tjoet Nja'Dhien
(INDONESIAN)

Cannes   A Cie Eka Praya Films production. Produced by Alwin Arifen, Alwin Abdullah, Eros Djarot. Written and directed by Djarot. Camera (color), George Kamarullah Penata; editor, Karsano Hadi; music, Idris Sardi; production design, Benny Benhardi; sound, Hartanto; costumes, Eddy Zaenuddin; production manager, Slamet Rahardjo Djarot; assistant director, Salmon Bouke Roring. Reviewed at Cannes Film Festival Intl. Critics Week, May 12, 1989. Running time: **118 MIN.**
Tjoet Nja'Dhien . . . . Christine Hakim
Teuku Um . . . . Slamet Rahardjo Djarot
Nja' Bantu . . . . Rita Zaharah
Pang Laot . . . . Pietradjaja Burnama
Penjair . . . . Ibrahima Kadir

■ **A sumptuously filmed epic about a turn-of-the-century rebellion against Dutch colonial rule, "Tjoet Nja'Dhien" has a fair number of good moments but overall pacing and mood make it unlikely to appeal widely to international audiences.**

Pic's title is the name of the legendary heroine who led the people of the Sultanate of Aceh (on the northern tip of the island of Sumatra) after her husband Teuku Uma was killed in a Dutch ambush. Indefatigable femme continued the resistance against increasingly powerful Dutch forces from 1896-1906, despite poor health (she suffered from failing eyesight and acute rheumatism).

Christine Hakim gives a sterling performance as the eponymous heroine.

Some of the battle scenes are well staged, especially early in the film, but so many sequences take place at night or in subdued lighting, that after a while a certain monotony of style becomes apparent (this subdued lighting, allied to the Scope format, will make the pic an iffy prospect for video and tv).

On the other hand, the inspiring saga, little known outside Indonesia, is passionately unfolded here. The film will have its champions and be a useful entry in Asian sections of forthcoming fests the world over. Commercial prospects outside home turf aren't good, except perhaps in the Netherlands.
—*Strat.*

Treffen In Travers
(Rendezvous In Travers)
(EAST GERMANY)

Cannes   A Defa producti on and presentation. Produced by Herbert Ehler. Written and directed by Michael Gwisdek, based on drama outline by Thomas Knauf and dialog by Christoph Prochnow. Camera (color), Claus Neuman; editor, Evelyn Carow; music, Reiner Bredemeier; production design, Hans Poppe; costumes, Katrine Cremer; sound, Hans-Joachim Kreinbrig; production management, Antje Wittfoth; Peter Vogel; assistant director, Hanna Seydel. Reviewed at Cannes Film Festival (Un Certain Regard), May 14, 1989. Running time: **97 MIN.**
Georg Forster . . . . Hermann Beyer
Therese Forster . . . . Corinna Harfouch
Ferdinand Huber . . . . Uwe Kockisch
Röschen Forster . . . . Susanne Bormann
Klärchen Forster . . . . Lucie Gebhardt
Liese . . . . Astrid Krenz
     Also with: Peter Dommisch, Heide Kipp, Wolf-Dietrich Köllner, Andreas Schneider, Hark Bohm, Michael Kind, Herbert Olschok, Horst Krause, Jochen Ziller.

■ **In "Rendezvous In Travers," a separated couple and the wife's lover spend a week in 1793 in a Swiss Alpine village inn to have their passions, erotic as well as political, tested in what often amounts to hand-to-hand combat.**

Veteran East German actor Michael Gwisdek has switched to writing and directing, and his bow is a conspicuous one, with Ingmar Bergman and John Cassavetes as his declared idols. Gwisdek has turned out an item that is steamy indeed for its country of origin, which may well see some rare offshore sales for it.

Two children and an innkeeper couple are used as stage props. Centerstage (and the film remains a drawing room/bedroom drama in spite of inventive camera work) is dominated by the woman and the two men in her life.

All three are historical characters. Georg Forster, a German author, scientist and world traveler, left his family and his country to become a Mainz province separatist and a member of France's National Convent. Therese Forster took Ferdinand Huber, a political journalist and Georg's best friend, as her lover.

The trio's little-accounted-for meeting on neutral Swiss ground had the purpose of instituting friendly divorce proceedings, but no sooner have the three been reunited before they start fighting, drinking, throwing hysterical fits, making up and breaking down again.

Georg is consumptive as well as impulsive. He spouts political philosophy and throws fits to gain his wife's sympathy. She feels tenderness for him while reserving her physical passion for Huber,

with whom she indulges in much inventive sex.

It is self-indulgency in general, however, rather than any expressions of passions in the screenplay that eventually makes the three protagonists stagger on to the border of the ludicrous.

At rare moments, the action is taken out of the dark inn interiors into the open Alpine spaces where the majestic mountains dwarf the cavorting humans in more ways than one.

A handsome production dress and fine acting, especially by Monica Vitti-lookalike Corinna Harfouch help "Rendezvous" hold the attention even where its spiritual contents turn shallow and its plot repetitive. Film has an inconclusive ending, since Forster died a year later in Paris, alone but undivorced. —*Kell.*

CANNES MARKET REVIEWS

The Return Of The Musketeers
(BRITISH-FRENCH-SPANISH)

Paris   A Universal Pictures release (Vision Intl. foreign; UGC in France) of a Michelle De Broca-Pierre Spengler presentation of a Timothy Burrill Prods. (London)-Filmdebroc-Cine 5 (Paris)-Iberoamericana Films (Madrid) co-production. Produced by Spengler. Directed by Richard Lester. Screenplay, George MacDonald Fraser, based on "Twenty Years After" by Alexander Dumas; camera (Rank color), Bernard Lutic; editor, John Victor Smith; music, Jean-Claude Petit; production design, Gil Arrondo; sound, Jean-Louis Ducarne; costumes, Yvonne Blake; production manager, Fernando Marquerie; assistant director, Clive Reed. Reviewed at UGC Normandie, Paris, May 6, 1989 (In Cannes Film Festival Market). Running time: **94 MIN.**
D'Artagnan . . . . Michael York
Athos . . . . Oliver Reed
Porthos . . . . Frank Finlay
Raoul . . . . C. Thomas Howell
Justine De Winter . . . . Kim Cattrall
Aramis . . . . Richard Chamberlain
Cardinal Mazarin . . . . Philippe Noiret
Planchet . . . . Roy Kinnear
The Queen . . . . Geraldine Chaplin
Rochefort . . . . Christopher Lee
Beaufort . . . . Eusebio Lazaro
Cyrano De Bergerac . . . . Jean-Pierre Cassel
King Louis . . . . David Birkin
Oliver Cromwell . . . . Alan Howard

■ **Fifteen years ago, Richard Lester boosted his then-flagging career with "The Three Musketeers" and its sequel "The Four Musketeers," lavish swashbucklers with a comic touch. His attempt at a comeback by returning to these past hits is, sadly, a stillborn event which looks as tired as its re-assembled cast.**

Boxoffice prospects are poor.

Pic has opened to quiet business in France, and that seems to be the likely pattern worldwide for this essentially second-hand material.

The charm of the original films was the deft way Lester combined an affection for the timeless Alexander Dumas story with his own distinctive style of throwaway comedy, a style he'd perfected in the Beatles films "A Hard Day's Night" and "Help," and in the Cannes Grand Prix winner "The Knack." He tries for the same blend of comedy and epic adventure here, but misses by a mile.

It's 20 years since the four musketeers ordered the execution of the evil Milady De Winter, and they've been separated ever since. But now King Charles is dead, and his son Louis, a 10-year-old, reigns with his mother (a reprise by Geraldine Chaplin). She's the secret mistress of Cardinal/Prime Minister Mazarin (Philippe Noiret), who is as much a plotter as was his predecessor, Richelieu.

D'Artagnan (Michael York) is assigned to bring together his three former comrades to fight for the Queen and Cardinal. He quickly recruits Porthos (Frank Finlay) and Athos (Oliver Reed), together with the latter's son, Raoul (C. Thomas Howell); however, Aramis (Richard Chamberlain), now a womanizing Abbé, is reluctant to

join the band (Chamberlain has only a marginal role in the film).

There follows a complicated and sometimes hard to follow plot involving a failed attempt to rescue King Charles I of England from execution. According to this, the executioner of the King was actually Justine (Kim Cattrall), evil daughter of Milady, who's intent on avenging herself on the four musketeers who she blames for the death of her mother.

Though Lester packs the film with action, it's rarely very exciting until the climactic assault on a moated castle to rescue the King, kidnaped by the Cardinal. Most of the time the director is so anxious that he merely confuses. He strains too hard to make fun of his material, and succeeds only in deadening it.

To be sure, there are lavish production values (most of the film was lensed in Spain), costumes and gadgets, plus a regular series of sword fights and derring-do. But a sense of genuine fun and adventure is absent.

Pic is dedicated to Roy Kinnear, whose accidental death during production must have cast a pall over the entire project. The credit sequence unfolds over a typical comedy routine involving Kinnear's Planchet attempting to steal food from diners at a busy eating-house, and from then on the portly comic is seen from time to time muttering and enacting typical bits of business. In two scenes, however, Lester is forced to make obvious use of a double whose face isn't seen, presumably in order to complete the film after the actor's death. —*Strat.*

The Rachel Papers
(BRITISH)

Cannes   A United Artists release (Virgin in U.K.) of an Initial production in association with Longfellow Pictures. Executive producers, James T. Roe 3d, Eric Fellner. Produced by Andrew S. Karsch. Coproduced by Paul Raphael. Written and directed by Damian Harris, based on the novel by Martin Amis. Camera (Agfacolor), Alex Thomson; editor, David Martin; music, Chaz Jankel; production design, Andrew McAlpine; sound, Ian Voigt; production manager, Mary Richards; assistant director, Michael Zimbrich; casting, Gail Stevens. Reviewed at Cannes Film Festival (Market), May 13, 1989. MPAA Rating: R. Running time: **95 MIN.**
Charles Highway . . . . Dexter Fletcher
Rachel Noyce . . . . Ione Skye
Norman . . . . Jonathan Pryce
DeForrest . . . . James Spader
Charles' father . . . . Bill Patterson
Jenny . . . . Lesley Sharp
Oxford Don . . . . Michael Gambon

■ **Written some 15 years ago,**

before home computers started to catch on, Martin (son of Kingsley) Amis' novel "The Rachel Papers" was a popular mirror of its times. Now Damian (son of Richard) Harris has adapted the novel and brought it to the screen in his directorial debut. Pic may play better for those who haven't read the book than for those who have.

Charles Highway is a 19-year-old with no money problems who maps out his sexual conquests via his desktop. He lives with his older sister Jenny and her bohemian spouse Norman, and is never short of female company.

He meets beautiful American Rachel Noyce, also 19, at a party she's given and where he's crashed. It's love at first sight, but she already has a boyfriend. After a bit of frustration, he sends her a funny love message on videotape, and she comes around. They have a steamy, passionate affair, of which he tires all too soon. They part. End of story.

The basic material is as old as the hills, but Amis explored it in fresh directions. Harris' isn't able to capture the book's special charms, and resorts to having his young hero address the camera to keep the viewer in the picture. Unfortunately, Dexter Fletcher, the young actor who was impressive in Derek Jarman's "Caravaggio," is rather too self-conscious here, and makes Charles a less than endearing hero. On the other hand, Ione Skye seizes her chances as Rachel and gives a glowingly sensual performance. Their lengthy love scenes together, often in a bathtub, are certainly steamy.

Though often amusing, the film isn't consistently funny and too often sinks into banality. Among the better scenes are a confrontation with Charles' father and his mistress at a screening of a nudie movie, and a family gathering at which the despised Norman (delightfully played by Jonathan Pryce) behaves with cheerful vulgarity.

In the end, it's a bit hard to understand from the film why Charles tires of the delectable Rachel so soon, even if she does hog the bathroom. Skye comes on so strongly as Rachel that she completely overshadows Fletcher, shifting audience sympathy away from the pic's supposed hero.

Sharply acted, beautifully lensed by Alex Thomson, and with a suitably trendy score, "The Rachel Papers" may catch on with the yuppie crowd, but the basic material should have made a more interesting film. —*Strat.*

Driving Force
(AUSTRALIAN)

Cannes   A European Film Management production (Intl. sales: J&M Entertainment). Executive producers, Antony I. Ginnane, Marilyn Ong. Produced by D. Howard Grigsby, S.M. Confesor. Directed by A.J. Prowse. Screenplay, Patrick Edgeworth; camera (color), Richard Michalak; editor, Prowse; music, Paul Schutze; production design, Toto Castillo; sound, Paul Wyhowski; stunts, Grant Page; 2d unit directors, Page, Grigsby; production manager, Ana Maria Dans; assistant director, Sol Jose; casting, Rosemary Welden. Reviewed at Cannes Film Festival (Market), May 12, 1989. Running time: **91 MIN.**
Steve . . . . Sam Jones
Harry . . . . Catherine Bach
Nelson . . . . Don Swayze
Becky . . . . Stefanie Mason
Surf . . . . Angel Cook

■ Lensed in the Philippines, this quickie is a Z-grade actioner for fast video payoff. Macho nonsense for undemanding viewers, the derivative plot is a cross between "The Cars That Ate Paris" and (inevitably) "Mad Max," falling many miles short of both.

Set in the near-future, pic deals with rival towtruck operators who cause pile-ups (often fatal) to drum up business. A series of unexciting car chases vies with an unexciting romance with numbing results.

Even the stunting is below par, with a dummy carelessly left in clear view during one smashup. Fact that the manic villain (Don Swayze) is dying of cancer adds nothing to the sum total.

Fans of the genre will be infuriated by this feeble offering, which has one of the weakest payoffs imaginable. Actors go strictly through the motions, while a subplot involving hero Sam Jones' daughter is for the birds.

Pic was prepared by the talented Rolf De Heer ("Incident At Raven's Gate") who wisely ankled from the resulting mess.—*Strat.*

Riverbend

Cannes   An Intercontinental Releasing presentation of a Vandale production. Executive producers, Regina Dale, Troy Dale. Produced by Sam Vance. Directed by Sam Firstenberg. Screenplay, Vance; camera (Allied color), Ken Lamkin; editor, Marcus Manton; music, Paul Loomis; sound (Ultra-Stereo), Michael Haines; art direction, Jack Marty; production manager-line producer, Norman Stevens; assistant director, David Womark; 2d unit director, Mike Shanks; coproducer, Valerie Vance. Reviewed at Cannes Film Festival (Market), May 12, 1989. No MPAA Rating. Running time: **100 MIN.**
Major Quinton . . . . Steve James
Bell . . . . Margaret Avery

Sheriff Jake . . . . Tony Frank
Tony . . . . Julius Tennon
Butch . . . . Alex Morris
Pauline . . . . Vanessa Tate
Capt. Monroe . . . . T.J. Kennedy
    Also with: Linwood Walker. Norm Colvin, Keith Kirk, John Norman, Al Evans.

■ On the heels of "Mississippi Burning" comes "Riverbend," an entertaining though outlandish fantasy about race relations set in Georgia in 1966. Pic has a chance of breaking through from its target black audience to wider acceptance.

Producer Sam Vance's quirky screenplay relies on a *deus ex machina* that is akin to time travel. Into the sleepy town of Riverbend, Ga., is injected a set of three black soldiers, headed by Steve James, who have escaped from military police while headed towards a court martial for failing to follow orders in Vietnam.

The black townsfolk are being persecuted (and murdered at will) by the evil white sherrif (Tony Frank). James hits upon the scheme of using his military expertise to train the locals ("Magnificent Seven" style) to take over the town, imprison the white folks and thereby focus statewide media attention on the hotspot in order to air his beef with the army.

Almost overwhelmed by too many twists and climaxes in the later reels, "Riverbend" works due to the inherently interesting switcheroo of its wish-fulfillment premise and James' solid central performance. Muscular thesp has appeared as sidekick in several Cannon features made by director Sam Firstenberg, but gets the opportunity here to dominate the proceedings. His low-key, authoritative delivery, very modern styling and martial arts abilities give the 1966 tale a 1989 perspective.

Almost stealing the show is arch-villain Tony Frank, whose rubbery face and ample girth launch a definitive portrayal of the hissable southern sheriff.

Margaret Avery provides the film's emotional center as a widow who befriends James. Julius Tennon scores as James' mutinous aide who almost diverts the good guys into a understandable revenge mode.

Texas-lensed production is modestly mounted but includes some effective imagery, notably the final confrontation when black and white throngs stream into the town square, separated at first by an invisible (but palpable) barrier before becoming reconciled.

—*Lor.*

Strapless
(BRITISH)

Cannes   A Granada Film production in association with Film Four (Intl. sales: Gavin Film, London). Produced by Rick McCallum. Written and directed by David Hare. Camera (Technicolor), Andrew Dunn; editor, Edward Marnier; music, Nick Bicat; production design, Roger Hall; sound, Clive Winter; production manager, Gillian Bates; assistant director, Christopher Hall; casting, Mary Selway. Reviewed at Cannes Film Festival (Market), May 14, 1989. Running time: **97 MIN.**
Dr. Lillian Hempel . . . . Blair Brown
Raymond Forbes . . . . Bruno Ganz
Amy Hempel . . . . Bridget Fonda
Mr. Cooper . . . . Alan Howard
Douglas Brodie . . . . Michael Gough
Colin . . . . Hugh Laurie
Romaine Salmon . . . . Suzanne Burden
    Also with: Camille Coduri (Mrs. Clark), Gary O'Brien (Mr. Clark), Julian Bunster (Carlos), Imogen Annesley (Imogen), Ann Firbank (Daphne Brodie), Rohan McCullough (Annie Rice), Joe Hare (Richard Forbes).

■ Writer-director David Hare's third feature is consistent with his other two in that it centers on the concerns of a middle-aged professional woman whose personal problems relate to wider political and social issues in Britain today. An unsentimental tale of love and betrayal, pic won't be easy to market, but will have its enthusiastic followers.

This time the central character is an American, Dr. Lillian Hempel (Blair Brown), who's lived in Britain for 12 years and feels she may care more for British values than the British do themselves. At the outset there's no man in her life, but while on vacation in Portugal she meets an apparently wealthy stranger, Raymond Forbes (Bruno Ganz), who woos her but fails to get her into his bed.

Back in London, Forbes continues his courtship, begging Lillian to marry him; initially, however, they live together and she soon discovers that this supposed millionaire actually doesn't have the money to pay his bills. They marry secretly, and soon after he simply disappears. Lillian discovers he already has a wife and son, also abandoned.

Lillian's serious, well-ordered life is contrasted with her flighty younger sister Amy (Bridget Fonda), who has a series of Latin lovers and gets pregnant by one of them. The pregnancy sobers the girl, and Lillian is impressed to see her sister get her life together.

Meanwhile, Lillian gradually is being drawn toward political activism as the British government's health service cutbacks begin to hurt.

Hare is a cerebral filmmaker, as he proved in both "Wetherby"

and "Paris By Night," and "Strapless" is a film for serious filmgoers. It raises important issues about contemporary life and lifestyles, while intelligently probing the lives of its characters. Although his work hasn't really caught on internationally, Hare is building up a body of work somewhat akin to that of Michelangelo Antonioni in the '50s and early '60s and it's only a matter of time before he comes up with a major success which will place his early films into perspective (and increase their value).

"Strapless" isn't that film, but it's an intelligent, ironic, multilayered drama that's consistently intriguing. Performances are impeccable, with Brown a standout as the protagonist: Her accent perfectly captures the tone of a Yank who's lived in London many years. Bridget Fonda, too, is fine as the irresponsible sister.

Technically, "Strapless" (so-named because both the sisters wind up with no visible means of support) is first-class. Opening credits play against a background of Nat King Cole's "When I Fall In Love," which is ironic given what follows.—*Strat.*

A Festa
(The Party)
(BRAZILIAN)

Cannes   An Embrafilme release of a Nello De'Rossi production. Written and directed by Ugo Giorgetti. Camera (color), Rodolfo Sanchez; editor, Marc De Rossi; music, Mauro Giorgetti, Decio Cascapera Filho; art direction, Isabel Giorgetti. Reviewed at Cannes Film Festival (Market), May 13, 1989. Running time: **82 MIN.**
    With: Antonio Abujamra, Adriano Stuart, Jorge Mautner, Iara Jamra, Otavio Augusto, Ney Latorraca, Patricia Pillar, Lala Deheinzelin, José Lewgoy.

■ Shot in just one location, "The Party" is nevertheless a fluent piece, well acted and potentially attractive to audiences searching for non spectacular amusement.

Third feature directed by Ugo Giorgetti, "The Party" reveals substantial progress from his previous credits, "Quebrando a Cara" (1981) and "Jogo Duro" (1984). Narrative structure is simple, personal and perfectly adapted to the low-budget production. Story, written by Giorgetti, takes place in the basement of a mansion in which a first-floor party is taking place. Two professional snooker players and a musician, hired to show their acts, are waiting to do same. But as the party goes on they realize they will never be called.

The endless waiting is shared by the frequent presence of waiters going downstairs to refill the glasses or by other artists — famous, unlike the three main characters — who are immediately cheered by the hosts.

Dialog makes good use of São Paulo's current slang in a coherent way. Fine interpreters Jose Lewgoy and Ney Latorraca have supporting roles. Supported by well-balanced photography and fine editing, Giorgetti dominates the action and achieves the difficult task of avoiding being boring.

Produced for $250,000, pic may delight audiences looking for an auteuristic work not especially committed to social issues but aiming to entertain and produce some laughs. —Hoin.

The Killer
(HONG KONG)

Cannes A Film Workshop production and release presented by Golden Princess/Magnum. Produced by Taui Hark. Written and directed by John Woo. Camera (color), Won Wing-Hang; music, Lowell Lowe. Reviewed at Cannes Film Festival (Market), May 12, 1989. Running time: **110 MIN.**
Jeffrey . . . . Chow Yun-Fat
Jenny . . . . Sally Yeh
Detective Lee . . . . Danny Lee
Detective Randy . . . . Kenneth Tsang
Sydney . . . . Chu Kong
Johnny Wang . . . . Shing Fui-on

■ **This extremely violent and superbly made actioner is another example of the polish and technical skill evident in current Hong Kong pics aimed at general audiences.**

More specifically, "The Killer" demonstrates the tight grasp that director John Woo has on the crime meller genre, and his ability to twist the form into surprisingly satisfying shapes. The picture creeps up on an audience. Melodramatic from the start, it finally goes over the top to deliver a solid emotional punch.

"The Killer" is a buddy-buddy outing with a vengeance. Male bonding between a maverick hitman (Chow Yun-Fat) and a dissaffected cop (Danny Lee) is pushed to almost homoerotic extremes. Sexual aspect is implicit, of course, as the bonding is presented largely as two tough guys living by the same rules.

The plot itself is all too familiar. The cold-blooded assassin is doublecrossed by underworld bosses after knocking off a drug kingpin. The determined cop, on the outs with his superiors, has to

catch his man or else. The setup works, pushing the characters into an airtight and fateful relationship.

Director Woo skillfully employs the standard tools of the genre. There are explosions and car chases aplenty. What distinguishes "The Killer" are its extraordinary ways of handling all the gunplay and physical action.

Chow Yun-Fat, a Hong Kong actor of considerable marquee value, is adept at combining pathos and chilling moral callousness. His soft underside is exposed when the plot has him falling for a cabaret singer (Sally Yeh) accidently blinded during a hit. Lee displays appealingly boyish determination and physical grace as the cop. Shing Fui-on is superb as the super-nasty villain.

Director Woo has worked for Golden Harvest, Cinema City and now indie Film Workshop. Pic has strong commercial potential. Cineastes should also give it a gander. "The Killer" proves that copgenre mallers shouldn't be dismissed out of hand — especially when they're made in Hong Kong.
— Sege.

That Summer Of White Roses
(BRITISH-YUGOSLAVIAN)

Cannes An Amy Intl./Jadran Film production. Executive producers, Susan George, Sulejman Kapic. Produced by Simon MacCorkindale, Mike Mihalic. Directed by Rajko Grlic. Screenplay, Grlic, MacCorkindale, Borislav Pekic, from Pekic's book "Defense And The Last Days;" camera (Eastman color), Tomislav Pinter; editor, Damir F. German; music, Brane Zivkovic, Junior Campbell, Mike O'Donnell; sound (Dolby), Louis Kramer; assistant director, Zvonimir Ilijic; coproducers, Paul Lichtman, Arnie Fishman; associate producer, Maestro Film. Reviewed at Cannes Film Festival (Market), May 14, 1989. Running time: **103 MIN.**
Andrija Gavrilovic . . . . Tom Conti
Ana . . . . Susan George
Martin . . . . Rod Steiger
Danny . . . . Nitzan Sharron
Zemba . . . . Alun Armstrong
Doctor . . . . John Gill
Mayor . . . . John Sharp
Clerk of council . . . . . Geoffrey Whitehead
Major von Richter . . . . Vanya Drach
Ostoja . . . . Miljenko Brlecic

■ **This warm and humanistic feature about the delayed impact of World War II in an idyllic beach community in Yugoslavia requires meticulous handling to attract a connoisseur audience for traditional cinema.**

Second production from the team of Simon MacCorkindale and Susan George taps a talented local director, Rajko Grlic, whose visual mastery and control of atmosphere are much in evidence. In looks and mood film resembles a

'60s classic of Eastern European cinema, Jiri Menzel's "Capricious Summer."

Heading a mixed British and Yugoslav cast, Tom Conti stars as a friendly but somewhat simpleminded lifeguard at a remote lake in Yugoslavia during the last summer of the war. Though the Germans are camped nearby and there is partisan activity in progress, the conflict has pretty much passed the residents by.

Conti provides refuge for a young widow (Susan George) and her son (Nitzan Sharron), both refugees from the Germans. At the suggestion of his friend Martin (Rod Steiger), he agrees to marry Ana to protect her, since she has no papers.

In danger of losing his job since he's never had the chance to save anyone from drowning in the placid lake, Conti ironically saves a man who turns out to be the new German commandant. Saluted for the act in a ceremony staged for German newsreel cameras, Conti unwittingly becomes a pariah, hated by the locals for "collaborating."

Screenplay by novelist Borislav Pekic (collaborating with MacCorkindale and the director) carefully develops the moral issues as well as a background of superstition that gives the film a fresh appeal and avoids the overly direct approach of so many war films. Helmer's suggestive use of odd details and symbols, such as a beautiful blond singer who sunbathes in the nude or a giant catfish (only its bubbles and wake are glimpsed) living in the lake add to the pic's rich texture.

Bringing the deliberately paced, episodic film to life is Conti's subtle central performance. Thesp tackles the challenging assignment of playing a simpleton by avoiding cliché or obvious effect, and result is moving without bathos.

Exec producer George is self-effacing and supportive in her platonic lover role, with solid portrayals by Steiger and Alun Armstrong as the local innkeeper. Slavic thesps are expertly dubbed with well-conformed British accents. Grlic scores high marks for his first English-language effort.

Ace cameraman Tomislav Pinter captures painterly compositions, with striking night photography and use of the lake's mirroring surface.—Lor.

Solidão
(Loneliness)
(BRAZILIAN)

Cannes An Embrafilme release of a Sambola Filmes production. Produced by Avelino Dias dos Santos, José Caruzzo Escafura. Directed by Victor di Mello. Camera (color), Antonio Goncalves; music, Wando; associate producer, Carlo Mossey. Reviewed at Cannes Film Festival (Market), May 12, 1989. Running time: **90 MIN.**
With: Pelém Marcella Praddo, José Wilker, Tarcisio Meira, Nuno Leal Maia, Rogerio Samora, Maite Proenca.

■ **This essentially kitsch story won't involve those not familiar with its subject, "Jogo do Bicho," an illegal form of gambling in Brazil.**

Jogo do Bicho is practiced throughout Brazil. Its "bankers" are rich people who have organized themselves in a structure similar to Mafia — "families," territories — although intimidation and murder are not necessarily part of their daily activity.

"Loneliness" is based on the real life of a "banker" from his own point of view, which includes nothing but his relationship with his beloved girlfriend. Newcomer producers Avelino Dias dos Santos and José Caruzzo Escafura spent lots on the production — reportedly over $2-million, much above Brazilian standards. The expensive cast includes soccer idol Pelé and first-rank tv stars such as José Wilker, Maite Proenca, Tarcisio Meira and Nuno Leal Maia.

The main characters, however, are portrayed by relatively unknown Rogerio Samora and Marcella Praddo. It makes little difference since the inconsistency of the roles could hardly be overcome by any actor.

Director Victor di Mello's most important previous credit is "Giselle," a softcore porn pic from the early '70s. "Loneliness" is not exactly a film intended to stimulate esthetic reflections. —Hoin.

Ängel
(SWEDISH)

Cannes A Swedish Film Institute release of a Golden Films production with Omega Film and the Swedish Film Institute. Produced by Peter Kropénin. Written and directed by Stig Larsson. Camera (color), Gunnar Källström. Lennart Peters, Lil Trulsson; editor, Bengt Johansen; music, Wlodek Gulgowsai; sound, Darek Hodor, Anders Larsson, Mats Lindskog, Lars Rechlin, Thomas Samuelsson; production manager, Maud Diamant, Micke Södersten. Reviewed at Cannes Film Festival (Market), May 13, 1989. Running time: **78 MIN.**
Kim . . . . Kim Kuusisto
Jon . . . . Leif Andrée
Stig . . . . Stig Larsson
The Mother . . . . Sissela Kyle

Eva ....Katarina Huldt
Also with: Nils Claesson, Helena Bergström, Peter Kneip, Simon Birnbaum.

■ Official publicity info for Stig Larsson's improvisational first feature film, "Ángel," fails to disclose the pertinent fact that the lead is played by a young drink & dope addict and convicted murderer given temporary parole due to Larsson's plea that his participating in a film about himself might serve as therapy.

It is to be hoped the therapy has worked where the film does not. Larsson has improvised almost everything. Slim, pale, golden-haired Kim Kuusisto is serviceable, no more, as the boy with the angelic looks who goads male and female friends and random strangers into committing vile acts. The narrative style relies, however, on dry, flat frames filled with little movement and much murky dialog.

Helmer Larsson also plays himself as Kim's writer-friend who is accused of being a passive bystander to life. Another friend is really being abused verbally and physically to the point where he, zombie-like, chokes a sleeping girl to death.

Why Kim grew up to become a devilish manipulator and eventually a murderer is indicated in flashbacks that yell of maternal neglect in his early boyhood. These do not explain very much, and it would seem Larsson and his nonpro actors are mostly content with keeping up serious miens during their extemporaneous input.

"Angel" tries very hard to be a "different" film but winds up being indifferent. —*Kell.*

Big Man On Campus

Hollywood   A Vestron Pictures release of an Arnon Milchan production. Executive producers, Mitchell Cannold, Steven Reuther. Produced by Milchan. Directed by Jeremy Paul Kagan. Coproducers, Scott Rosenfelt, Mark Levinson. Screenplay, Allan Katz; camera (Deluxe color), Bojan Bazelli; editor, Howard Smith; music, Joseph Vitarelli; costume design, Lisa Jensen; sound, David Brownlow; line producer, Susan Vogelfang; art direction, Michael Day; set decoration, Lauri Gaffin; makeup, Ronnie Specter; casting, Paul Ventura. Reviewed at Warner-Hollywood Studios, Hollywood, May 12, 1989. (In Cannes Film Festival Market.) MPAA Rating: PG-13. Running time: 105 MIN.
Bob ....Allan Katz
Alex ....Corey Parker
Diane Girard ....Cindy Williams
Cathy ....Melora Hardin
Dr. Webster.............Tom Skerritt
Dr. Fisk ....Jessica Harper
Stanley Hoyle ....Gerrit Graham
Judge Ferguson..........John Finnegan

■ This pic's original title, "The Hunchback Of UCLA," would have been the best thing about this woefully formulaic pabulum, which is far more misshapen structurally than its lead character.

Since the pic was shot crosstown at USC, UCLA balked, and it's no wonder. In football parlance, the end result would rank as subpar even for Northwestern. Unless Vestron has some marketing gimmick up its sleeve (or perhaps stuffed under its shirt), boxoffice prospects appear dismal.

Whatever homage or inspiration may have been drawn from "The Hunchback Of Notre Dame" dissipates within the first 10 minutes, as Bob (veteran tv writer Allan Katz, who wrote and stars) descends from the college belltower to defend Cathy, the blond girl (Melora Hardin) with whom he's become enamored from afar.

In a preposterous set of circumstances, the troll-like Bob is released into the custody of a psych professor (Tom Skerritt) who arranges for Cathy's boyfriend Alex (Corey Parker) to live with the hunchback and observe him. Some merry mix-ups — and three laughs, tops — ensue.

Parker gets fed all the wisecracks and ends up playing Alex as a cross between Matthew Broderick and Woody Allen circa "Bananas." The delivery's fine, but the material proves undernourished.

Katz' hunchback rendition swings all over the map, from a tiresome Yoda voice to makeup that has him resembling a '60s lovechild trying to sneak a keg into a party. Similarly, his rapid development from monosyllabic grunts to oracular wisdom in a matter of weeks is indicative of the slipshod quality of the entire film.

A number of firstrate actors inexplicably turn up in the margins, ranging from Skerritt to Jessica Harper. No one emerges with passing grades.

Any hope of redemption for the film is shattered in the finale, which takes place on the set of a talkshow clearly meant to recall "The Morton Downey Jr. Show."

Director Jeremy Paul Kagan mercifully brings very little sentiment to the story; unfortunately, there's very little comedy, and the film plods along so drunkenly its midsection seems interminable.

The only tech credit of note is Joseph Vitarelli's lighthearted

score. —*Bril.*

True Blood

Cannes   A Fries Entertainment presentation of a Maris Entertainment Corp. production. Produced by Peter Maris. Written and directed by Frank Kerr. Camera (CFI color), Mark H.L. Morris; editor, Mac Haight; music, Scott Roewe; associate producer, Sunny Vest; production manager, Michelle Brookman; assistant director, Katarina Witich; stunts, James Lovelett; casting, Valerie McGafferey. Reviewed at Cannes Film Festival (Market), May 13, 1989. MPAA Rating: R. Running time: 97 MIN.
Ray Trueblood...............Jeff Fahey
Donny Trueblood ....Chad Lowe
Jennifer ....Sherilyn Fenn
Lt. Joe Hanley ....James Tolkan
Spider Masters ....Billy Drago
Charlie....................Ken Foree

■ "True Blood" is a strictly ho-hum crime drama with the requisite number of beatings and car chases slotted around a tepid plot about brothers separated for 10 years. Theatrical prospects are zilch, but vid looks better.

Pic opens with a gang rumble in which Ray Trueblood (Jeff Fahey) scars rival Spider Masters (Billy Drago) across his eye. Soon thereafter Spider kills a cop and Ray is blamed; he's forced to go on the run, abandoning his 8-year-old kid brother.

Ten years later Ray, looking not a month older, returns to find brother Donny (Chad Lowe) is now running with Spider's gang and that bald, gum-chewing cop Hanley (James Tolkan) still is after the guy who killed his partner. Unfolding drama is strictly predictable. Sherilyn Fenn is given a thankless role in which she seemingly can't decide which brother she prefers.

Writer-director Frank Kerr shows no special aptitude for the genre, and technical credits are only average. A credit to the Wyoming Film Commission is odd, since though the characters talk a lot about going to Wyoming, they never actually get there. —*Strat.*

Paganini
(ITALIAN)

Cannes   A Medusa release of a Scéna Film Prods. Reteitalia-President Films coproduction. Produced by Augusto Caminito. Written and directed by Klaus Kinski. Camera (Eastmancolor, Telecolor prints), Pier Luigi Santi; music, Nicolo Paganini, performed by Salvatore Accardo; art direction, Massimo Lentini. Reviewed at Cannes Film Festival (market), May 12, 1989. Running time: 85 MIN.
Nicolò Paganini...........Klaus Kinski
Antonia Bianchi ....Debora Kinski
Achille Paganini ....Nikolai Kinski
Caffarelli ....Bernard Blier
Mime ....Marcel Marceau

Baroness ....Dalila Di Lazzaro
Also with: Donatella Rettore, Eva Grimaldi, Beba Balteano, Tosca D'Aguino, Carfora, André Thorent.

■ In his behind-the-camera debut, Klaus Kinski goes on the rampage in a delirious biopic of the great Italian violinist Nicolò Paganini. Alternate title "Kinski Paganini" is entirely appropriate, as helmer not only penned the script and performs without restraint in the title role, but has as costars young family members Debora and Nikolai Kinski playing Paganini's wife and son.

Pic is a willful orgy of excess which will end up either as a cult or curiosity item, as normal duds are unlikely to put up with plotless genius.

Pic opens on a fever pitch and rarely lets the temperature drop. Opening shows the unkempt violinist receiving the hysterical adulation of well-dressed 19th century ladies at the opera hall, as hysterical as girls at a Beatles' concert. Dalila Di Lazzaro is so overcome with emotion she can't resist masturbating, a scene she repeats in more explicit detail later in a carriage.

Paganini's story is told with the greatest liberty of expression. The violin, women and money woes hold centerstage. A virtually incomprehensible woman's voiceover sings the maestro's praises all through the beginning. Pic's saving grace is that, however simple-minded Paganini's after-hours pursuits may seem, the performance of violinist Salvatore Accardo on the soundtrack — continuously present — does convey the kind of passionate, goosebump-playing that makes a genius.

Nor is Kinski unconvincing in the main role. Physically rather more repellent than his Nosferatu incarnations, with tangled locks and long black sideburns, he nonetheless gets across a sense of haunted intensity. If anything, Kinski identifies with the role too closely, in the mistaken idea a film can be made from tons of unadultered emotion and no rhythm, no retakes, no story.

All thesps — including 10-year-old Nikolai Kinski, a standout as Paganini's beloved son — are dubbed horribly into American voices. There is a lot of diabolical fiddling, a lot of repetition, mini-cameos by mime Marcel Marceau and Bernard Blier as a nasty priest. A gruesome death scene, with

Paganini spitting blood all over his violin while his son looks on in horror, caps this pathological and occasionally riveting pic. —*Yung.*

Fortress Of Amerikkka

Cannes A Troma release of a Lloyd Kaufman/Michael Herz production, in association with Mesa Films. Prouduced by Kaufman, Herz. Executive producers, Laurel A. Koernig, Jeffrey W. Sass. Written and directed by Eric Louzil. Camera (TVC color), Ron Chapman; editor, Diane Robinson; music, David Ouimet; sound, Jim Magdaleno; art direction, Gary Randall; production manager, Sylvia Smith; assistant director, Danny Spear; special makeup effects, John (J. Frog) Garcia; stunt coordinator, William J. Kulzer; associate producers, Kulzer, Xavier Barquet, David Greenspan; casting, Jerry Bresler & Associates. Reviewed at Cannes Film Festival (Market), May 13, 1989. No MPAA Rating. Running time: **97 MIN.**

John Whitecloud	Gene LeBrok
Jennifer	Kellee Bradley
Sheriff	David Crane
Elizabeth	Kascha LePriol
Comdr. Karl Denton	William J. Kulzer
Leslie	Karen Michaels

Also with: Douglas C. Fox, Scot Perlstein, Wendy St. Claire, Shadow Eastwood, François Papillon.

■ "Fortress Of Amerikkka," a.k.a. "The Mercenaries," is an old-fashioned sexploitation film that will appeal to that fringe which enjoys truly bad acting, t&a and gore effects.

Second Troma release from filmmaker Eric Louzil, pic is a slight step from his "Lust For Freedom," but still suffers from awkward direction and the annoying Troma practice of adding hokey dialog and sound effects to fill up dead air.

Handsome, low-key Gene LeBrok (he looks like Christopher Reeve playing Superman) plays an Indian halfbreed fresh out of prison who has a score to settle with the Georgia County, Calif., sheriff (stolid David Crane) who killed his brother in cold blood.

Personal grudges soon take a backseat to the main problem: A band of mercenary soldiers calling themselves "Fortress Of Amerikkka," led by evil William J. Kulzer, is camped nearby. Instead of mere survivalist wargames, this coed bunch is killing folks right and left. Pic's anticlimax — coming after the sheriff is wiped out — is the townfolk and cops banding together to fight the mercenaries.

Until then, Louzil contrives to include as many scenes of women going topless as time will permit. Heroine Kellee Bradley abstains, but exotic porno star Kascha shows off her surgical implants memorably, given a run for the money by busty blond Karen Mi-chaels. Oddly enough, the statuesque blond featured on the film's poster doesn't show up in the film; she's the same model who was postergirl for another recent pic, "Shotgun," without appearing on screen in that one either.

While LeBrok glides through the picture without losing his cool, there is hysterically bad acting provided by Kulzer (a regular in Louzil films who also handles the stuntwork), Crane and especially Michaels, who smiles (unintentionally) in the face of danger. Pic's campiest scene occurs when Kascha and her boyfriend recite patriotic sentiments, echoed by the foolish narration.

Apart from some scenic views of forests and mountains, film's technical credits are weak. The background score is extremely poor. —*Lor.*

Divine enfant
(Divine Child)
(FRENCH)

Paris Forum Distribution release of an R. Films/Koala Films/La Sept coproduction. Produced by François Ravard. Directed and edited by Jean-Pierre Mocky. Screenplay, Mocky, André Ruellan; camera (Eastmancolor), Marcel Combes; music, Hubert Rostaing; sound, Bernard Rochut; art direction, Alain Cordonnier, Michel Modai; production manager, Josette Combes. Reviewed at Pathé Wepler theater, Paris, May 4, 1989. (In Cannes Film Festival Market.) Running time: **83 MIN.**

Sarah	Laura Martel
Aurelien Brada	Jean-Pierre Mocky
Yacinthe Jacob Fontaine	Sophie Moyse
Catherine Morhange	Louise Boisvert
Graton	Luc Deihumeau
Franquette	Jean-Pierre Clami
Carboni	Tolsty

■ Writer-director Jean-Pierre Mocky tries to subvert the kidpic genre in "Divine enfant," about a sweet little French orphan on the run from insensitive adults in the company of her dog and a vagabond, played by Mocky himself.

Mocky has lost none of his nerve and insolent bad taste, but the social satire is puerile and he directs in his familiar slipshod manner. Contrary to the local ad claims of "A Mocky For Everybody," this seems a mockery for few other than followers of the director.

The little heroine is a 6-year-old, freckle-faced redhead, Laura Martel, who runs away from her orphanage when the institution orders to have all pets impounded. She is immediately taken under the wing of Mocky a former race car driver who's hit the skids and finds new purpose by protecting the in-nocent moppet and her mutt.

Subsequent pursuits and farcical complications (due to an escaped woman lunatic and a frenetic *flic*) allow Mocky to exhibit his usual gallery of facile grotesques and social types, often portrayed by helmer's familiar stock company of supporting players.

Tech credits are passable. —*Len.*

Dealers
(BRITISH)

Cannes A Rank Organisation release of a Euston Films production. Executive producers, Andrew Brown, John Hambley. Produced by William P. Cartlidge. Directed by Colin Bucksey. Screenplay, Andrew MacLear; camera (Rank color), Peter Sinclair; editor, Jon Costelloe; music, Richard Hartley; production design, Peter J. Hampton; sound, Richard Dunford; production manager, Loretta Ordewer; assistant director, Roger Simons; casting, Joyce Gallie. Reviewed at Cannes Film Festival Market, May 11, 1989. Running time: **89 MIN.**

Daniel Pascoe	Paul McGann
Anna Schuman	Rebecca DeMornay
Robby Barrell	Derrick O'Connor
Frank Mallory	John Castle
Lee Peters	Paul Guilfoyle
Bonnie	Rosalind Bennett
Lennox Mayhew	Adrian Dunbar
Jamie Dunbar	Nicholas Hewetson
Elana	Sara Sugarman

■ A British "Wall Street" probably is not what the world is waiting for right now. "Dealers," though well produced, is a less than enthralling pic about a yuppie high-flyer and his glamorous mistress. B.o. prospects look slender.

Paul McGann (from "Withnail & I") is a dollar dealer in a London bank, set for promotion when his superior suicides after a botched deal. To his chagrin, McGann's boss brings in an outsider over his head, beautiful Rebecca DeMornay, the latest whiz-kid in the banking business (and the boss' mistress to boot). Before long, though, McGann is romancing his rival and taking her home for a nightcap in his seaplane, which he parks near Tower Bridge.

A drama that centers on the rise and fall of the dollar isn't likely to reach a very wide public unless it's remarkably well handled, and "Dealers" isn't. Nor is there much spark in the McGann-DeMornay twosome. Pic's most interesting character is Derrick O'Connor as a cockney dealer who's pinkslipped from the bank and sinks into a coke-snorting decline. While O'Connor makes the most of the character, it remains a sketchy role.

Judging by the lifestyles of these effete folk, there's still oodles of money in the banking business, but the bland goings-on depicted here aren't likely to enthrall the average moviegoer. Despite top-quality technical credits, and a feisty central performance from McGann, prospects for "Dealers" look bearish. —*Strat.*

My Mom's A Werewolf

Cannes A Crown Intl. Pictures release of a Hairy Production. Executive producer, Marilyn J. Tenser. Produced by Steven J. Wolfe. Directed by Michael Fischa. Screenplay, Mark Pirro; camera (color), Bryan England; editor, Claudia Finkle; music, Barry Fasman, Dana Walden; associate producer, Brian J. Smith. Reviewed at Cannes Film Festival (Market), May 13, 1989. MPAA Rating: PG. Running time: **84 MIN.**

With: Susan Blakely, John Saxon, Katrina Caspary, John Schuck, Ruth Buzzi, Marcia Wallace, Marilyn McCoo.

■ According to recent filmmaking, anyone from teenagers to grizzled seafarers can fall prey to the werewolf's curse, so why not your average suburban housewife? That's the comedy premise of "My Mom's A Werewolf," and it works quite well. Pic isn't strong enough for theatrical durability but has potential as a solid midline homevid offering.

Susan Blakely is the good-looking wife and mother who gets bitten on the toe by John Saxon, pet store owner-cum-lycanthrope, who eats mice for snacks, can't use cutlery and wants a werewife to continue the line.

She then undergoes a slow and often amusing transformation, which she tries to stop by shaving her legs, filing down teeth, and so on. Daughter Katrina Caspary slowly cottens to what's happening, just managing to vanquish Saxon (with a few silver forks tied to a pole).

Blakely pulls the pic through, playing the role in a suitably dizzy fashion. There are good makeup effects, and some not so good, and some good comedy ideas. Rest of the cast is okay, although they ham it up a bit. There are a few pacing problems and some intrusive overdubbing, but on the whole pic is effective enough to garner okay ancillary business. —*Doch.*

ISTANBUL FILM FESTIVAL

Gomlek
(The Shirt)
(TURKISH)

Istanbul A Pinar Film release produced by Altan Senol. Written and directed by Bilgé Olgac. Camera (color), Salih Dikisci; music, Serdar Yalcin. Reviewed at Istanbul Film Festival (competing), April 13, 1989. Running time: **100 MIN.**
With: Berhan Simsek, Erdal Ozyagcilar, Sehnaz Dilan, Savas Yurttas.

■ "Gomlek," a drama about feudal machinations and exploitation of workers, received an enthusiastic audience response at its emotional finish.

Semo is a greedy landowner in a poor village who breaks promises to his serfs when he divides the crops. The serfs are furious and rebellion simmers.

When a neighboring lord is shot during a workers' occupation of his land, Semo panics. He goes to live in his village and attempts to gain his subjects' favor by making Eno, leader of the dissension, his equal. He pulls a large symbolic gomlek (shirt) over the two of them, but events take a tragic turn before earnest Eno becomes aware of the ruse.

Helmer Bilgé Olgac again displays a flair for recreating the atmosphere of male-dominated village life evident in "The Spoon Haters" (1982).

Adept camerawork and an eclectic score add to film's appeal. It could get some exposure at ethnic fests. —Sam.

Ucurtmayi Vurmasinler
(Don't Let Them
Shoot The Kite)
(TURKISH)

Istanbul An Odak Film release of a Cengiz Ergun, Tunc Basaran, Odak Film/Magnum Film production. Directed by Basaran. Screenplay, Feride Cicekogly; camera (color), Erdal Kahraman. Reviewed at Istanbul Film Festival (competing), April 12, 1989. Running time: **100 MIN.**
Inci . . . . Nur Surer
Baris . . . . Ozan Bilen
Also with: Rozet Hubes, Sevgi Sakarya, Yasemin Alkaya.

■ In "Don't Let Them Shoot The Kite," a simple drama about the friendship between a lonely 5-year-old and a sensitive inmate in a woman's prison is both touching and true to life.

Pic, which won the Eczecibasi Foundation prize for best Turkish film at the Istanbul Film Festival, is a considerable improvement over veteran helmer Tunc Baseran's "One And The Others," winner of top prize in last year's fest.

Baris, the son of a woman arrested for drug-dealing, grows up in prison with little companionship or amusement. Inci, a political prisoner who befriends Baris, brightens his life by becoming both friend and teacher to him, roles his mother seems incapable or unwilling to adopt. Ozan Biler, remarkably unaffected as Baris, steals the show, and Nur Surer is memorable as Inci.

The title refers to a colorful kite Baris spies from the courtyard and mistakes for a bird. Inci explains what it is and promises she will take him to fly one when they are free. Inci is released first and in Baris' mind assumes the identity of the kite. The symbolic implications of the kite, which appears over the prison a.id is greeted with exuberant cheers by Baris and the women but ordered to be shot down by the warden, are only too obvious.

Focus is on the interaction between the prisoners, and the main hardships seem to be boredom and depression rather than physical abuse. Fixed longshots impart a cinema vérité feel to exterior scenes, a contrast to the close camerawork in festivities such as Baris' sunet (circumcision celebration).

Dramas set in women's prisons seem to be surefire draws in Turkey and in the video market in expatriate communities. Film could get some exposure at specialty fests as well. —Sam.

Ucuncu Goz
(The Third Eye)
(TURKISH)

Istanbul Produced by Tarik Akan, Orhan Oguz, Yol Film Ltd. Directed by Oguz. Screenplay, Nuray Oguz; camera (color), Orhan Oguz; editor, Ismail Kalkan; music, Onay Oguz, Onder Focan. Reviewed at Istanbul Film Festival (competing), April 13, 1989. Running time: **93 MIN.**
With: Tarik Akan, Selcuk Ozer, Merel Konrat, Aliye Rona, Ferdag Ferdag, Yaman Okay.

■ "The Third Eye," chronicling the creative crisis of a film director unable to complete a script, is technically adept and well rendered, but might prove too heavy-handed for general audiences.

Pic got a special mention from the Istanbul Film Festival for its "courageous approach to the problems of creativity." Powerful actor Tarik Akan is cast as the director who is grappling with an existential dilemma revolving around his humble origins, as well as a creative block.

He is in the middle of a melodramatic scenario about a married villager who has been raped and has a child during her husband's absence. Scenes from the work in progress are skillfully woven into contemporary events, whetting the viewer's appetite for more.

The director is biding his time during a visit to his neighbor, a faded beauty, when a comment she makes acts as a catalyst to shake him up. After going through agonizing physical reactions and imbibing vast amounts of red wine, he confronts his protagonist and has the final breakthrough, the opening of his "third eye," that allows him to complete his project.

Pic has excellent cinematography by the helmer and a catchy jazz piano and horn score. It succeeds in providing insight into both the angst of a modern intellectual and the intrigues of traditional society. —Sam.

Arabesk
(Arabesque)
(TURKISH)

Istanbul An Arzu Film-Erler Film production. Directed by Ertam Egilmaz. Screenplay, Gani Mujde; camera (color), Aytekin Cekmakci; music, Atilla Ozdemiroglu. Reviewed at Istanbul Film Festival (competing), April 12, 1989. Running time: **105 MIN.**
With: Mudge Ar, Sener Sen, Ugar Yucel, Ustun Asutay, Nacati Bilgic, Kadir Savun.

■ "Arabesque" is a delightful sendup of Turkish melodrama toplining Mudge Ar and Sener Sen, two of Turkey's most beloved stars.

It scored a huge success in domestic release, attracting the audience of the genre it mocks as well as those who grasped its satirical qualities.

"Arabesque" is a widely popular form of Turkish music considered lowbrow by purists. One of these haunting Middle Eastern refrains is the theme song that is heard throughout the saga.

It begins as two children, a landowner's daughter and a servant's son, plant a tree and vow eternal love. As they grow older, the boy (Sener Sen) asks for her hand, but her father cannot accept her marrying a peasant. The landowner tricks his daughter into rejecting her beloved.

When the daughter is forced to marry someone else, she runs away on her wedding night. The image of Mugde Ar, sprinting into Istanbul in her tattered lace wedding dress with a pack of sexcrazed thugs chasing her, is one of the movie's most hysterical.

The two lovers repeatedly have happiness snatched away from them each time they are about to be reunited. Clichés are played to the hilt.

The film is in danger of overstaying its welcome and nearly exhausts some of its gags by the last third. It's still great fun and could find some offshore action in ethnic or comedy fests. —Sam.

Zengin Mutfagi
(The Kitchen Of The Rich)
(TURKISH)

Istanbul An Arzu Film-Erler Film release produced by Er-Ar Film. Directed by Basar Sabuncu. Screenplay, Sabuncu, based on a play by Vasif Ongaren; camera (color), Erdal Kahraman. Reviewed at Istanbul Film Festival (out of competition) April 14, 1989. Running time: **85 MIN.**
With: Sener Sen, Nilufer Acikalin, Oktay Korunan, Gokhan Mete, Osman Gorgen.

■ "The Kitchen Of The Rich" is based on a play of the same name about Lutfu Usta, a cook in a wealthy household during the political turbulence of the early 1970s. Renowned comedian Sener Sen carries the film with his expressive personality. Otherwise the static camera and interior settings could become tedious.

The cook is a simple, kindly man whose life revolves around his work. The young maid who works in the house is like a daughter to him. Politically passive, the maid is disappointed by her boyfriend Selim's ideological extremes. As he switches from informing the police to becoming one himself, his loving attitude toward her changes to one of nonchalance, even disdain.

The denouement occurs when Usta poisons the huge guard dog of the household. The rash act causes speculation that it was politically motivated, and the maid is dismissed. Usta then has to acknowledge the decadence of the people around him.

Basar Sabuncu's films have been shown in many countries, and a tribute was organized at the National Theater in London, inspiring the description "works which shattered the prejudices about Turkish cinema." —Sam.

Kara Sevdeli Bulut
(Cloud In Love)
(TURKISH)

Istanbul An Ozkino Purtelas release produced by Kinomozaik. Directed and written by Muammar Ozer. Camera (color), Ozer; music, Ahmet Guvenc. Reviewed at Istanbul Film Festival (competing) April 12, 1989. Running time: **105 MIN.**

With: Zuhal Olcay, Haluk Bilginer, Sahika Tekand, Bulent Oran, Gokhan Mete, Sonat Bilgin.

■ In "Cloud In Love," a family's tranquility disintegrates after the mother is tortured during the 1980 military coup in Turkey. Pic focuses on the psychological effects of the brutality.

In a suspenseful scene, soldiers break into the home and take away the mother. She is tortured, although the scenes are not shown, and returned crushed and deranged. Versatile Zuhal Olcay gives a good performance in scenes reminiscent of "A Woman Under The Influence." She sets the radio on fire and paints her face and that of her daughter's. The girl relates to this irrational behavior, but the husband becomes increasingly disturbed. His sympathies are lessened even more when he becomes convinced that his wife has been raped.

The film won a censorship battle just a week before its fest bow. It holds interest for this reason, but may prove too 1-dimensional for some viewers. The soundtrack is both obtrusive and repetitious.
—*Sam.*

Gece Dansi Tutsaklari
(Captives Of A Night Dance)
(TURKISH)

Istanbul A Hakan Film Release produced by Hakan Balimir. Written and directed by Mahinur Ergun. Camera (color), Erdogan Engin; editor, Mevlut Kocak; music, Fuat Dominic. Reviewed at Istanbul Film Festival (competing) April 13, 1989. Running time: **98 MIN.**

Zeynap . . . . Hulya Kocyigit
Haluk . . . . Cihan Unal
Hayal . . . . Amanda J. Grant
Also with: Orcun Sonat, Suhan Baydar, Ali Surmeli, Meltem Savci.

■ "Captives Of A Night Dance" imparts the flavor of the lifestyle of modern middle-class Istanbulites. Although uneven and veering dangerously close to melodrama, it sustains interest through its lively, believable characterizations.

Hulya Kocyigit is Zeynap, an art director at a newspaper who writes short stories in her spare time. Her colleagues are buzzing about the arrival of Haluk, the new and reportedly unorthodox and difficult director of the paper. A close work collaboration between Zeynap and Haluk develops into a love affair.

A subplot deals with the changing relationship between Zeynap and Hayal, an uninhibited dance student who rents a room in Zeynap's house. Hayal is envious of Zeynap's writing, although she is better suited temperamentally to more active pursuits.

Director Mahinur Ergun shows promise in her first theatrical feature, especially in unpretentious segments such as the long dinner in the garden during which the women get tipsy.

The triangle that develops does not evolve naturally, and the plot's film-within-a-film resolution is somewhat contrived. Pic should be a big draw domestically, but hopes for offshore release are faint.
—*Sam.*

Indiana Jones And The Last Crusade

Hollywood A Paramount Pictures release of a Lucasfilm Ltd. production. Executive producers, George Lucas, Frank Marshall. Produced by Robert Watts. Production executive (U.S.), Kathleen Kennedy. Directed by Steven Spielberg. Screenplay, Jeffrey Boam, from a story by Lucas, Menno Meyjes, based on characters created by Lucas and Philip Kaufman; camera (Rank color), Douglas Slocombe; additional photography, Paul Beeson, Robert Stevens; editor, Michael Kahn; music, John Williams; sound (Dolby), Ben Burtt; production design, Elliot Scott; art direction, Stephen Scott, Richard Berger (U.S.), Benjamin Fernandez (Spain), Guido Salsilli (Italy); set designer, Alan Kaye (U.S.); set decorators, Peter Howitt, Ed McDonald (U.S.), Julian Mateos (Spain); visual effects supervisor, Michael J. McAlister, Industrial Light & Magic; mechanical effects supervisor, George Gibbs; costume design, Anthony Powell, Joanna Johnston; makeup supervisor, Peter Robb-King; stunt coordinator, Vic Armstrong; associate producer, Arthur Repola; assistant directors, David Tomblin (U.K.), Dennis Maguire (U.S.), Carlos Gil, Jose Luis Escolar (Spain), Gianni Cozzo (Italy); second-unit directors, Michael Moore, Frank Marshall; second-unit camera, Rex Metz (U.S.); second-unit assistant director, Gareth Tandy (U.K.); production supervisor, Patricia Carr (U.K.); unit production managers, Roy Button (U.K.), Joan Bradshaw, Ian Bryce (U.S.), Denise O'Dell (Spain); location managers, Bruce Rush (U.S.), Christopher Hamilton (Italy); casting, Maggie Cartier, Mike Fenton, Judy Taylor, Valerie Massalas. Reviewed at Mann National theater, L.A., May 16, 1989. MPAA Rating: PG-13. Running time: **127 MIN.**

Indiana Jones . . . . Harrison Ford
Professor Henry Jones . . . . . Sean Connery
Marcus Brody . . . . Denholm Elliott
Elsa . . . . Alison Doody
Sallah . . . . John Rhys-Davies
Walter Donovan . . . . Julian Glover
Young Indy . . . . River Phoenix
Vogel . . . . Michael Byrne
Kazim . . . . Kevork Malikyan
Grail Knight . . . . Robert Eddison
Fedora . . . . Richard Young
Sultan . . . . Alexei Sayle
Young Henry . . . . Alex Hyde-White
Panama Hat . . . . Paul Maxwell

■ To say that Paramount's "Indiana Jones And The Last Crusade" may be the best film ever made for 12-year-olds is not a backhanded compliment. What was conceived as a child's dream of a Saturday matinee serial has evolved into a moving excursion into religious myth.

More cerebral than the first two Indiana Jones films, and less schmaltzy than the second, this literate adventure should make big bucks by entertaining and enlightening kids and adults.

The Harrison Ford-Sean Connery father-and-son team gives "Last Crusade" unexpected emotional depth, reminding us that real film magic is not in special effects.

For Lucas and Spielberg, who are now entering middle age, the fact that this is more a character film than f/x extravaganza could signal a welcome new level of ambition.

Jeffrey Boam's witty and laconic screenplay, based on a story by Lucas and Menno Meyjes, takes Ford and Connery on a quest for a prize bigger than the Lost Ark of the Covenant — the Holy Grail.

Connery is a medieval lit prof with strong religious convictions who has spent his life assembling clues to the grail's whereabouts. Father and more intrepid archaeologist son piece them together in an around-the-world adventure, leading to a touching and mystical finale that echoes "Star Wars" and "Lost Horizon." The love between father and son transcends even the quest for the Grail, which is guarded by a spectral 700-year-old knight beautifully played by Robert Eddison.

This film minimizes the formulaic love interest, giving newcomer Alison Doody an effectively sinuous but decidedly secondary role. The principal love story is between father and son, making Ford's casually sadistic personality more sympathetic than in the previous pics.

The relationship between the men is full of tension, manifesting itself in Connery's amusing sexual one-upmanship and his string of patronizing putdowns.

There's also a warmth and growing respect between them that makes this one of the most pleasing screen pairings since Newman met Redford.

Connery confidently plays his aging character as slightly daft and fuzzy-minded, without blunting his forcefulness and without sacrificing his sexual charisma.

The cartoonlike Nazi villains of "Raiders" have been replaced by more genuinely frightening Nazis led by Julian Glover and Michael Byrne. Most of the film takes place in 1938, and Spielberg stages a chilling scene at a Nazi book-burning rally in Berlin, where Ford has a brief encounter with Adolf Hitler.

But exec producers Lucas and Frank Marshall, producer Robert Watts and Spielberg do not neglect the action set-pieces that give these films their commercial cachet.

There's the opening chase on top of a train in the Utah desert, involving a youthful Indy (River Phoenix) in 1912; a ferocious tank battle in the desert; a ghastly scene with hundreds of rats in a Venice catacomb; some aerial hijinks with a zeppelin and small planes, and many more outlandish scenes.

Perhaps the film's most impressive technical aspect is the soundtrack, designed by Ben Burtt. While the noise level sometimes becomes painful, the artistry is stunning.

Douglas Slocombe's lensing has a subtly burnished look, and Elliott Scott's production design is always spectacular.

The Industrial Light & Magic visual effects — supervised by Michael J. McAlister with Patricia Blau producing for the aerial unit — are artful and seamless.

John Williams' score again is a major factor in the appeal and pacing, and editor Michael Kahn makes the film move like a bullet. Other tech contributions are impeccable.

This is a film of which Lucas and Spielberg and their collaborators long will be proud. —*Mac.*

Season Of Fear

Hollywood   An MGM/UA release of a Filmstar Inc. production. Produced by Scott J. Mulvaney. Executive produced by Ryan J. Carroll, Charles F. Overton, Tod E. Gibbo, Roland Carroll. Directed by Doug Campbell. Screenplay, Campbell based on a story by Campbell and Mulvaney; camera (Monaco color), Chuy Elizondo; editor, Dan Selakovich; music, David Wolinski; production design, Phillip Michael Brandes; casting, Richard Pagano, Sharon Bialy. Reviewed at the AMC Americana 8, Southfield, Mich., May 16, 1989. MPAA Rating: R. Running time: 89 MIN.
Mick Drummond . . . . Michael Bowen
Fred Drummond . . . . Ray Wise
Ward . . . . Clancy Brown
Sarah Drummond . . . . Clara Wren
Bob . . . . Michael J. Pollard

■ "Season Of Fear" is a punchless spinoff of "Body Heat." Thanks to Clara Wren, it has the body, all right, but it never generates enough heat to sustain interest.

Riddled with unbelievable plot twists and preposturous finale, this likely will be a short "Season" theatrically with little expectation for much video interest.

Mick Drummond is the 24-year-old boozing son of a well-heeled entrepreneur who hopes to hit it big selling wind-driven energy devices.

His father, Fred Drummond, left his wife and Mick more than 20 years ago, and Mick has grown up bitter and resentful.

Nevertheless, when the father unexpectedly writes, Mick hops in his car and drives to see him the very next day. Improbable circumstance No. 1.

He arrives to find his father gone for the weekend but the house attended by a beautiful blond named Sarah.

Despite dialog that anywhere else would get you a cold shoulder, if not a slap in the face — "It must be pretty lonely out here." — Mick scores his very first night, only to learn the next day that he spent the night with his own stepmother. Improbable circumstance No. 2.

Michael J. Pollard turns in his stock performance as a sadistic mechanic who has spent too many hours under too many cars.

Ward, Sarah's cop brother, launches into a bizarre speech about the benefits of the electric chair if you're ever convicted of killing your sister. And Fred Drummond seems to have attended one too many board meetings, intermittently glowering, staring and flying off the handle.

When Pollard tries to kill Mick and Sarah, she stabs him to death, and Mick decides this was all a plot by his father.

"Season" creeps along for a good 45 minutes before any of this becomes clear. But this is about all that is clear.

The sluggish direction and anemic dialog fail to generate much interest. Unlike "Body Heat," there is little chemistry between Bowen and Wren.

Director Doug Campbell clearly enjoys the wind as a motif. Fred Drummond is trying to strike it rich selling energy-generating windmills. And the wind constantly is blowing here. If it's not ruffling Mick's hair, then it's blowing near gale force against the house or it's swirling seductively around Wren's legs.

But there is little to be fearful of in "Season Of Fear." And despite all this wind, most of what is exchanged on the screen is a lot of hot air. —*Advo.*

Road House

Hollywood   An MGM/UA Distribution release from United Artists Pictures of a Silver Pictures production. Executive producers, Steve Perry, Tim Moore. Produced by Joel Silver. Directed by Rowdy Herrington. Screenplay, David Lee Henry, Hilary Henkin; story by David Lee Henry. Camera (Deluxe color), Dean Cundey; editors, Frank Urioste, John Link; music, Michael Kamen; sound (Dolby), Bud Maffett; costume design, Marilyn Vance-Straker; set decorator, Phil M. Leonard; stunts, Charles Picerni; makeup, Scott H. Edde; casting, Ferne Cassel. Reviewed May 15, 1989, at the Directors Guild of America, Hollywood. MPAA Rating: R. Running time: 114 MIN.
Dalton . . . . Patrick Swayze
Doc . . . . Kelly Lynch
Wade Garrett . . . . Sam Elliott
Brad Wesley . . . . Ben Gazzara
Jimmy . . . . Marshall Teague
Denise . . . . Julie Michaels
Red Webster . . . . Red West
Emmet . . . . Sunshine Parker
Cody . . . . Jeff Healey
Tilghman . . . . Kevin Tighe

■ With "Road House," United Artists has hotwired Patrick Swayze a star vehicle shackled by a couple of flat tires in the script department. Ill-conceived and unevenly executed, pic should motor off with big early boxoffice among teens enamored of its well-oiled lead before stiffer competition (and undoubtedly better films) drives it from theaters.

Actually, the solution might have been to take Swayze's Mercedes away and give him a horse. The film essentially is a Western — a loner comes in to clean up a bar, of all things, and ends up washing and drying the whole town — but its vigilante justice, lawlessness and wanton violence feel ludicrous in a modern setting.

The film even has problems from a simple marketing perspective. Swayze established himself as an appealing romantic lead in "Dirty Dancing," yet this film's constant brawling and graphic violence likely will alienate the female audience that should have been its base, gratuitous nudity notwithstanding.

The choice leaves Swayze, as budding star, precariously straddling worlds: "Road House's" look and cast could have meant hit potential had it gone along the same lines "Cocktail" tapped for Tom Cruise; instead, Swayze postures like an under-inflated Stallone or Schwarzenegger ("Over The Top" and "Raw Deal" come to mind) and ends up in the center of a mediocre, reactionary bloodfest.

In fact, the many unintentional laughs won't entirely elude even savvy kid viewers, as the escalating fights ultimately make "Road House" start to look like an Anglicized kung fu flick.

Even with the hokey concept — which imparts a sort of mythic quality on the toughness of bouncers, loose women and smoke-filled bars — the film has some initial promise. A club owner (Kevin Tighe) recruits Dalton (Swayze) to clean up his bar, which is frequented by lowlifes and bikers.

At first, Dalton (apparently bouncers, like gunfighters, need only one name) has some intrigue about him. He avoids fighting when possible yet carries a big rep — including the label of having killed a man.

One becomes wistful for those early moments as "Road House" degenerates into a seemingly endless series of fistfights, egged on by bad guy Brad Wesley (Ben Gazzara), who runs the town.

The wispy subplot involves a flat romantic attachment for Dalton by a leggy and beautiful local doctor (Kelly Lynch) who turns up with thick glasses and her hair in a bun. Another unintended guffaw comes later when she appears outside the bar wearing a low-cut dress and come-hither look.

Director Rowdy Herrington, aptly named to oversee this mayhem, has a flair for lensing the fisticuffs — especially a particularly brutal encounter between Swayze and Wesley's top mugger (Marshall Teague). But there's just far too much of it.

Swayze has his moments during the first act as a monosyllabic stoneface but fades as the pic wears on (and on). Nearly everyone else is cartoonish at best, though Sam Elliott breathes some life into things as a grizzled bouncer — which, at least in the film, doesn't look like such a great career in terms of longevity.

Credit cinematographer Dean Cundey with giving the entire production a fabulous look, from the smoke-filled honkytonks to the parade of bodies beautiful, male and female, that inhabit them, That they resemble no bars a real person might wander into represents no insult to Cundey, though it is indicative of the sort of glossy tripe "Road House" serves up. —*Bril.*

How I Got Into College

Hollywood   A Twentieth Century Fox release of a Michael Shamberg production. Produced by Shamberg. Coproducer, Elizabeth Cantillon. Directed by Savage Steve Holland. Screenplay, Terrel Seltzer. Camera (Deluxe color), Robert Elswit; editors, Sonya Sones Tramer, Kaja Fehr; music, Joseph Vitarelli; production design, Ida Ransom; costume design, Taryn DeChellis; art direction, Richard Reynolds; set decoration, Kathe Klopp; sound (Dolby), Petur Hliddal; casting, Vickie Thomas Casting. Reviewed at the Avco Center Cinema, Westwood, May 18, 1989. MPAA Rating: PG-13. Running time: 89 MIN.
Kip . . . . Anthony Edwards
Marlon . . . . Corey Parker
Jessica . . . . Lara Flynn Boyle
Nina . . . . Finn Carter
Leo . . . . Charles Rocket
Oliver . . . . Christopher Rydell
Coach . . . . Brian-Doyle Murray
Vera Cook . . . . Tichina Arnold
Flutter . . . . Bill Raymond
Dean Patterson . . . . Philip Baker Hall

■ For the most part about as exciting as filling out a college entrance exam, "How I Got Into

College'' is a tepid but mercifully harmless little picture lacking the résumé to make the grade at the boxoffice but which cribs a few bits of comic inspiration and sweeter moments off its script.

Director Savage Steve Holland seemed destined for *wunderkind* status when he wrote and directed his first feature at 24, ''Better Off Dead'' — a reasonable alternative to seeing it. He then followed with ''One Crazy Summer,'' giving Savage Steve a decidedly tame rap sheet.

Now 29 and still mired in the high school experience, Holland again dabbles in interesting camera angles and lots of hit-or-miss humor, missing more often than not. Saying this film marks his best work thus represents damnation with faint praise, but it's a start.

There's at least a passing effort here to sketch a 3-dimensional character other than the protagonist — again a love-crazy high school senior (Corey Parker), in this case basing his college preference on the destination of Jessica (Lara Flynn Boyle), the all-everything girl with whom he's smitten.

The concurrent plot deals with politicking on the admissions board of their college of choice, where romantic Kip (Anthony Edwards) vies with pompous Leo (Charles Rocket) for the ear of the dean over what direction entrance standards will take.

Flat throughout, the film has some unexpected blips of humor (Jessica's nightmarish college interview comes to mind) and then compassion — the latter stemming from efforts to admit an underprivileged student (well-played by Tichina Arnold) who flips through books in between flipping french fries.

It's hardly enough to keep ''College'' off probation, but newcomer Terrel Seltzer's script takes the high road for the most part, respecting its young characters.

Never mind their self-absorbed preoccupation with SAT scores, which will likely seem remote and cartoonish to anyone who hasn't tried to solve a word problem during the last four years.

Parker's been spending plenty of time in school, also fronting Vestron's Cannes entry ''Big Man On Campus.'' He's learned to play a pretty fair cut-rate Matthew Broderick-type that's appealing but still hardly worth the price of tuition.

In addition to Rocket, pic squanders the talents of ''Saturday Night Live's'' Phil Hartman and Nora Dunn, who turn up as a pair of smarmy quick-buck artists.

Tech credits won't require anyone to stay after class, though the upbeat ending and sprightly pop score might keep those who last sitting through the credits. —*Bril.*

The Long Weekend (O'Despair) (B&W)

Hollywood   A Desperate Pictures presentation. Produced, written, directed and edited by Gregg Araki. Camera (b&w, 16m), Araki; music, Steven Fields, Iron Curtain, Fred's Crashshop, Steve Burr, Dirt Tribe, Harepeace. Reviewed at American Film Institute (AFI/L.A. Fest), L.A., March 17, 1989. No MPAA Rating. Running time: **87 MIN.**
Michael . . . . Bretton Vail
Rachel . . . . Maureen Bondanvile
Leah . . . . Andrea Beane
Sara . . . . Nicole Dillenberg
Greg . . . . Marcus D'Amico
Alex . . . . Lance Woods

■ Los Angeles' lowest-budget filmmaker, Gregg Araki, has scraped together his second feature, ''The Long Weekend (O'Despair),'' a sometimes whimsically depressive immersion in postpunk angst.

As was the case with the director's initial pic, ''Three Bewildered People In The Night,'' playoff for this iconoclastic effort will be limited to fests, midnight shows and highly specialized venues, but one has to hand it to Araki for putting together a legitimate theatrical feature for $5,000.

Pic was lensed in grainy 16m black & white in apartments and on the streets, and sound was entirely post-recorded. The disenfranchised characters are mostly gay or bisexual, have no direction, and are given to bemoaning how, ''It's tough being the new Lost Generation.''

Unfortunately, Araki is no cinematic Hemingway. The greatest amusement to be found here lies in observing how many ways the writer-director and his benumbed cast can invent to express stoned-out disillusionment, while enacting a severely alienated Los(t) Angeles weekend.

Michael is tired of his bisexual lover's irresponsibility, and Rachel doesn't quite know how to tell her outlandishly stupid bimbo g.f. to get lost. New horizons would be good for all of these victims of mental sunburn, but the ennui on view here could well be terminal.

Filmmaking technique is rudimentary, but Araki manages to convey a sporadically amusing world view on the most limited of means. In the process, he comes to embody the antithesis of the traditional well-made, slick industry ''product,'' which makes him a needed banner carrier for a certain fringe of the independent movement. —*Cart.*

Buying Time (CANADIAN)

Hollywood   An MGM/UA release of a Richard Gabourie production. Produced by Richard Gabourie. Directed by Mitchell Gabourie. Screenplay, the Gabouries; camera (Film House color), Manfred Guthe; editor, Michael Todd; music, David Krystal; sound, Steve Jones; art direction, Bill Flemming; casting, Laela Weinzweig. Reviewed at UA Caruth Plaza Theater, Dallas, May 16, 1989. MPAA Rating: R. Running time: **97 MIN.**
Jabber . . . . Jeff Schultz
Curtis King . . . . Page Fletcher
Jessie . . . . Laura Cruickshank
Reno . . . . Leslie Toth
Dez . . . . Martin Louis
Detective Novak . . . . Dean Stockwell

■ A sluggishly moving melodrama written by Mitchell and Richard Gabourie, produced by the latter and directed by the former, ''Buying Time'' relies on the tried-and-true for characters, their relationships and plot elements. It would have little appeal to an audience seeking anything but routine film fare.

The youthful hero is a clean-cut inner city carwash employee, Jabber (Jeff Schultz). Jabber's life would be relatively conflict-free if not for his sense of responsibility for friends Reno (Leslie Toth) and Dez (Martin Louis).

Reno, a small-time hustler always in the hole, gets Jabber in trouble after a sleazeball bookie welshes on a bet and they pull a robbery to square accounts. Jabber is blackmailed by a couple of cops into helping them get the goods on the killers of Dez, a small-time drug pusher.

Predictably, Jabber at first refuses to cooperate with the cops. Outraged when told of Dez' brutal murder (which, of course, is graphically enacted, complete with a psychopathic killer of cartoonish dimensions), he agrees to help.

The film profits enormously from the presence of Dean Stockwell as a cop. It is more than a cameo appearance, surprising considering the relatively unknown cast and low-budget appearance of the project.

Detective Novak (Stockwell) reappears whenever Jabber's resolve to help out seems to be weakening or when his passions take over, threatening to wreck the investigation.

Stockwell digs beneath the surface of an essentially superficial character and invests it with a depth largely missing elsewhere in the film. You begin to wonder if Novak is more — or, perhaps, something — other than he appears.

The youthful principals surrounding Stockwell throw themselves into their roles with energy and enthusiasm. Director Gabourie pretty much lets them have their heads, resulting in some heavy-handed emoting. Page Fletcher also lays it on as the limping mastermind behind the dope and horse-racing scheme. Laura Cruickshank makes for an appealing love interest for Jabber.

City and rural settings have a seedy, depressing look as captured by Manfred Guthe. Balance of the technical work, including the physical action sequences, is adequate. —*Bopo.*

CANNES OFFICIAL SELECTIONS

Old Gringo

Cannes A Columbia Pictures release of a Fonda Films production. Executive producer, David Wisnievitz. Produced by Lois Bonfiglio. Directed by Luis Puenzo. Screenplay, Aida Bortnik and Luis Puenzo, based on the novel "Gringo Viejo" by Carlos Fuentes; camera (Deluxe color), Félix Monti; editor, Juan Carlos Macias, William Anderson, Glenn Farr; music, Lee Holdrige; sound (Dolby), Simon Kaye; production design, Stuart Wurtzel, Bruno Rubeo; art direction, Scott Ritenour; set design, Steve Saklad, Tom Warren; set decoration, Tessa Davies; costume design, Enrico Sabbatini; production manager, Luis Bekris; assistant director, Raul Outeda; stunt coordinator, Mickey Gilbert; casting, Wallis Nicita; casting (Mexico), Claudia Becker. Reviewed at the Cannes Film Festival (official selection, non-competing), May 22, 1989. MPAA Rating: R. Running time: **119 MIN.**

Harriet Winslow	Jane Fonda
Ambrose Bierce	Gregory Peck
Arroyo	Jimmy Smits
Col. Frutos Garcia	Patricio Contreras
La Garduna	Jenny Gago
Ron	Jim Metzler
La Luna	Gabriela Roel
Mrs. Winslow	Anne Pitoniak
Pancho Villa	Pedro Armendariz Jr.
Zacarias	Sergio Calderon
Monsalvo	Guillermo Rios
Pedrito	Samuel Valadez (De La Torre)
Consul Saunders	Stanley Grover
Clementina	Josefina Echanove
Captain Ovando	Pedro Damian
Dolores	Maya Zapata
Trinidad	Jose Olivares

■ Luis Puenzo's "Old Gringo" has the star names needed for initial appeal Stateside and abroad, and huzzahs go to topcast Jane Fonda, Gregory Peck and a smoldering Jimmy Smits.

With $24-million on the line, Columbia handles this lush but somewhat limited pic with kid gloves to ensure the performances don't get lost in the opening weeks. Come Oscar-time, compelling performances will overcome the script's limitations to qualify for long, hard looks.

Based on Carlos Fuentes' novel "Gringo Viejo," the complex psychological tableau makes it easy to see why Fonda plopped herself in the plum role of 40-ish spinster on the run Harriet Winslow. She is swept up by accident in the Mexican Revolution and swept off her feet by a charismatic general in Pancho Villa's popular front. A rakish Jimmy Smits (from tv's "L.A. Law") as Gen. Arroyo is superbly cast. He conveys the cocksure yet sensitive machismo and motivations of his character's torment between the revolution he lives and the woman he loves.

As the embittered, sardonic journalist Ambrose Bierce, Gregory Peck has found a role that suits him to a T. He portrays the world-weary Bierce with relish and wit.

The paternalistic figure in a nebulous love triangle with Fonda and Smits, Peck exudes a sympathetic mien despite his crusty exterior. His best moments come long before the denouement, and the film's wittiest lines are his alone.

Although technically proficient and well directed, something got lost in the translation from novel to screen. There's a hollow ring to the proceedings, and the script by Aida Bortnik and Puenzo is the weak link. The narrative threads at times wave in the wind, and some compelling bits must have ended up on the cutting-room floor.

The look of early 1900s Mexico is captured quite well. Lee Holdridge's unintrusive score sets the mood particularly well in a scene in which Winslow shimmies and shakes while being seduced by Arroyo. It's one of the most tender, non-graphic (but still erotic) sequences to come down the pike in a long while.

If beautiful scenery and lensing are "Old Gringo's" skeleton, and the neat portrayals by the actors (even supporting cast here don't go unnoticed) its flesh, pic lacks the heart to bring it to life. Nevertheless, "Gringo" is a worthy view for audiences with more upmarket tastes and literary sensibilities.
—Silv.

Kvinnorna pa taket
(The Women On The Roof)
(SWEDISH)

Cannes A Swedish Film Institute presentation of Filmhuset production with the Swedish Film Institute, Svensk Filmindustri and SVT-1. Produced by Katanka Faragó. Executive producer, Waldemar Bergendahl. Directed by Carl-Gustaf Nykvist. Screenplay by Nykvist and Lasse Summanen; camera (color), Ulf Brantas, Jörgen Persson; editor, Summanen; music, Hakan Möller; sound, Owe Svensson, Lars Rechlin; production design, Brigitta Brensén; costumes, Inger Pehrsson; associate producer and assistant director, Henrik von Sydow; production management, Göran Lindberg. Reviewed at the Cannes Film Festival, competing, May 22, 1989. Running time: **96 MIN.**

Linnea	Amanda Ooms
Anna	Helena Bergström
Willy	Stellan Skarsgard
Officer Cadet Fischer	Ori Bäckström
Officer Cadet Oskar	Leif Andrée
Photo shop owner	Percy Brandt
Photographer Halling	Johan Bergenstrahle

Also with Katarina Olsson, Stig Ossian Ericsson, Ulla Sallert, Anna Söder, Marie Dahlgren.

■ Photography as fate is the theme of Carl-Gustaf Nykvist's "The Women On The Roof," helming debut by cinematographer Sven Nykvist's son. "Women" puts him in the ranks of Sweden's top filmmakers, past and present.

Nykvist wrote the story on which the pic was based with Lasse Summanen, the editor who has allowed nary a seam to show in the narrative fabric of the film.

Story takes place in Stockholm in 1914. Anna, a young photographer, has escaped from Austria to set up business in an attic studio. She takes Linnea, her neighbor who has just arrived in town from the country to seek a job, as her partner. Anna is blond, brash and sophisticated. Linnea is dark, shy and pretty.

Linnea maintains her innocence even when she is taught to steal and pose nude for what Anna calls fairy tale illustrations. It is summer, and the two women soon sleep in the same bed. That may or may not be innocent.

One day, Willy, a lean, charming gypsy from a circus, practically falls from the sky, or at least from a skylight, landing at Anna's feet. She takes him along to the bed, and Linnea does not find out until the next morning that she has been sleeping next to a stranger.

It seems that Willy helped Anna escape from Austria and from a particularly nasty man named Halling. Willy now introduces a new note of gaiety to the household. He and Anna are lovers, but it is obvious that a more romantic love is budding with Linnea.

By now, Linnea understands that Anna's real business is pornography, subdivision whips and chains. She also has learned that Anna's escape from Halling is not yet complete. Willy wants the three of them to find refuge in America, and even scares up the money for the journey.

But Anna does not really want to go. What follows is violent and ghastly: In a fight, Anna accidentally kills Willy and has Linnea help her dispose of the body. This is when the attic-dwellers climb to the roof for real.

If this is chiller stuff, other chills that give meaning to Anna's professional cool in all respects are to follow. A box of glass slides tells of Anna's having lived in bondage with Halling, also a photographer, since she was a child.

Nykvist's tale may be too strange for mass-audience stomachs and minds, and sometimes he seems preoccupied with forcing his characters into situations.

The film is full of references to photography, and the cinematography of Ulf Brantas and Jörgen Persson is just about as exquisite as any ever seen. Their lighting of night interiors and action in the dark calls to mind Rembrandt.

As Anna, Helena Bergström has a pert face that turns sullen and bright with convincing ease. Amanda Ooms' Linnea proves she has the spirit and intelligence of a good actress.

Stellan Skarsgard adds another great achievement to the gallery of characters he has created for the Swedish stage and screen. His graceful Willy is a larger-than-life gypsy who also is so lifelike that even his quotings of Shakespeare echo with new meaning.

The costumes by Inger Pehrsson are a delight of invention within period restrictions. Hakan Möller's score alternates between piano musings and gypsy strains, melting in unison with the action and its moods.—*Kell.*

Eat A Bowl Of Tea

Cannes A Columbia Pictures release of an American Playhouse Theatrical film. Executive producers, Lindsay Law, John K. Chan. Produced by Tom Sternberg. Directed by Wayne Wang. Screenplay, Judith Rascoe, based on novel by Louis Chu; camera (Deluxe color), Amir Mokri; editor, Richard Candib; music, Mark Adler; production design, Bob Ziembicki; associate producer, Patricia Chong; production manager, Diane V. Raike; assistant director, Mark Bashaar. Reviewed at Cannes Film Festival (Directors Fortnight), May 17, 1989. MPAA Rating: PG-13. Running time: **102 MIN.**

Mei Oi	Cora Miao
Ben Loy	Russell Wong
Wah Gay	Victor Wong
Bok Fat	Lee Sau Kee
Ah Song	Eric Tsiang Chi Wai

■ Wayne Wang returns to Chinatown with "Eat A Bowl Of Tea," and recaptures the relaxed humor and deep emotions of his earlier "Dim Sum" in the process. By its very nature, this will be a limited-release film, with fest outings indicated, but it should find enthusiastic responses in the right outlets.

Film starts with a voiceover reminder that, for 60 years, American policy was to bar entry of women from China into the U.S. As a result, men who came from China in the years prior to World War II were forced to leave behind mothers, wives and sisters. That changed after the war, in which China was a U.S. ally, and the pic starts off with Wah Gay (Victor Wong), who runs a New

York gambling club, deciding to send his soldier son Ben Loy (Russell Wong) to China to marry the daughter of his best friend. Fortunately, it's love at first sight between Ben and Mei Oi (Cora Miao), and they marry and return to the States, where Ben's delighted father presents him with a Chinese restaurant for a wedding present.

Unfortunately, Ben finds the pressures of running the business so severe that his lovelife suffers. A doctor advises a vacation, which is a successful remedy, but only in the short term. Basically, poor Ben is impotent, causing grief to his wife as well as to the couple's fathers, who eagerly want to become grandfathers.

Enter Ah Song (Eric Tsiang Chi Wai), a cheerful, rascally gambler who becomes Mei's secret lover, and who succeeds in getting her pregnant. But when word gets out that Ben isn't the father, it's Wah Gay who tries to restore family honor by attacking Ah Song with a meat ax.

Typically, the aforementioned scene is played for laughs, and indeed is the comic high point of a generally charming and amusing film. As in "Dim Sum," Wang takes his time to allow the audience to get to know characters he himself obviously has great feeling for, and the result is a most pleasant experience. He also creates the atmosphere of the late '40s via filmclips (the lovers first kiss at a screening of Frank Capra's "Lost Horizon" and later take in a screening of Orson Welles' "The Lady From Shanghai") and some evocative songs (the meat ax scene is backed by a vocalization of "How High The Moon").

Judith Rascoe has done a great adaptation of Louis Chu's 1961 novel (the title refers to the eventual cure for Ben's impotence) which has provided perfect material for Wang to demonstrate his skill with this kind of gentle comedy. Production values are on the highest level.—*Strat.*

Sfayah Min Dhahab
(The Golden Horseshoes)
(TUNISIAN)

Cannes   A Cinetelefilms production. Produced by Ahmed Eddine Attia, Hassen Daldoul. Written and directed by Nouri Bouzid. Camera (color), Youssef Ben Youssef; editor, Kalena Attia; music, Anouar Braham. Reviewed at Cannes Film Festival (Un Certain Regard), May 14, 1989. Running time: **104 MIN.**
Youssef . . . . Hicham Rostom

■ A Tunisian intellectual relives the political ideals and personal failure of his life during one long night in "The Golden Horseshoes." This sensitive think piece in nocturnal colors has a built-in local and fest audience from helmer Nouri Bouzid's controversial first film, "Man Of Ashes."

Not an easy or cheerful picture, "Horseshoes" is likely to have a more restricted aud than "Man Of Ashes," which was a resounding hit onshore once it got on screens.

Dissent is to be expected over "Horseshoes," too, for the way it shows political prisoners being brutally tortured in Tunisian jails in the 1970s, and its outspoken condemnation of an Islamic fundamentalist character.

Youssef (Hicham Rostom), a 45-year-old communist, is a hard hero to like. Torn between his progressive ideas and the psychological residue of a traditional upbringing, he alternately mopes, drinks, rants and raves, hurting the people he loves most — his aged mother, his son and daughters, the woman he lives with.

Though he preaches freedom, and has spent six years in prison for it, Youssef can't bear to think of his girlfriend or daughters in the arms of men. By divorcing his wife and moving in with beautiful, rich Zineb, he has climbed up the social ladder, without finding peace of mind.

This tormented man is haunted by the humiliation he has had to endure in prison. The torture scenes are few but horrifying, and show the systematic oppression of those who deviated from the line of the ruling regime.

Also unique in Arab films is the portrait of the hero's brother, a fundamentalist shown as an intolerant bigot who substitutes doctrine for thought and feeling.

Film's political references and time period are not perfectly clear to the uninitiated (actually, Youssef's Maoist magazine "Perspectives" came out 1963-68, and '68 was the year heavy prison sentences were being doled out to left-wing militants — two of whom are Tunisian ministers today). The reasons behind Youssef's suffering and explosion of violence also are murky at times, particularly in the sluggishly paced first part.

Yet, closing scenes are a dramatically moving payoff, when Youssef makes up his mind to do something and sets off with his rebellious son on a trip to see his daugh-

ter and brother. After a bitter confrontation in a blood-stained slaughterhouse, Youssef's angst melts away into a symbolic white horse running free.

Technically fine, with a well-directed cast. —*Yung.*

Fool's Mate
(WEST GERMAN)

Cannes   A Von Vietinghoff Filmproduktion, with ZDF. (Intl. sales: Jupiter Communications, Paris.) Produced by Joachim von Vietinghoff. Directed by Matthieu Carrière. Screenplay, Carrière; camera (Agfacolor), Rolf Liccini; editor, Galip Iyitanir; music, Klaus Buhlert; production design, Jennifer Bartlett; commissioning editor for ZDF, Gabriele Heuser; production manager, Udo Heiland; assistant director, Sabine Eckhardt. Reviewed at Cannes film fest (Un Certain Regard), May 20, 1989. Running time: **95 MIN.**
Alice Gordon . . . . Victoria Tennant
Lucas Tillman . . . . Michael Marwitz
Nikos Mitradis . . . . Stuart Wilson
Teresa . . . . Maria Barranco
Judy Miller . . . . Mareike Carrière
Alex . . . . Alexander Rasic
Clarence White . . . . Clayton George
Hausermann . . . . Peter Sattmann
The Chess Player . . . . Anatoli Karpov
(In English)

■ Actor Matthieu Carrière makes his move to the director's chair with this cosmopolitan melodrama set in Berlin. Tale of a former pianist heading for the skids is familiar and lacks tension. Theatrical chances aren't good, but the pic could make useful small-screen fodder.

Carrière found an actor not unlike himself in Michael Marwitz, who plays Lucas, a German former concert pianist who's given up touring to be with his English wife Alice (Victoria Tennant), and their small child; the wife is an architect engaged in work in Berlin. Bored, Lucas, who has a passion for chess, gets into gambling and coke-snorting, and falls in with a group that includes a sinister Greek gangster (Stuart Wilson), latter's sexy Mexican wife (Maria Barranco) and her lover, a Yugoslav (Alexander Rasic). There's also a black New Yorker (Clayton George) involved with the group.

Before long, Lucas is so deep in debt that he loses his wife and child, and winds up taking the rap for a murder he didn't commit. Michael Marwitz' rather monotonous performance prevents much audience identification with the troubled character. Film's best thesping comes from Maria Barranco (from "Women On The Verge Of A Nervous Breakdown") as the fiery Mexican.

Carrière himself does a brief, uncredited, guest spot, and he also rings in Russian chess master

Anatoli Karpov for a brief, but telling scene. The production is handsome enough, but like its protagonist, it lacks energy and charm. Main problem is the screenplay, for which Carrière was also responsible. —*Strat.*

Maria von den Sternen
(Mary Of The Stars)
(WEST GERMAN)

Cannes   A Metropolis Film presentation of Filmproduktion Thomas Mauch production with Hamburger Filmbüro and Film Fonds Hamburg. Produced and directed by Thomas Mauch. Screenplay, Mauch, Eva Hiller; camera (color), Mauch; editor, Bettina Böhler; music, Christoph Oliver; production design, Christian Bussman; costumes, Sabine Josst; production manager, Jan Weber; sound, Michael Saketzski. Reviewed at Cannes Film Festival (Directors Fortnight), May 16, 1989. Running time: **90 MIN.**
Maria . . . . Katja Junge
Johannes . . . . Robert Duessler
Manfred . . . . Heikko Deutschmann
    Also with: Michael Lott, Eric Schildkraut, Malte Jaeger.

■ "Mary Of The Stars" is about the perennial whore-goddess who confuses every man in her vicinity until her heart suddenly melts for one man only. The film is shot in muddy colors and badly lighted frames by Thomas Mauch, who also bows as producer-writer-helmer. He once manned a camera magnificently for Werner Herzog ("Aguirre") but clearly is in too deep here.

The low-budget item has the sound, look and feel of a youthful project that should have remained hidden in the filmmaker's bottom drawer. Bogged down by stilted reading of bookish dialog invoking poets and philosophers of the past, "Mary Of The Stars" is seen, and bedded down, by several men in and around the rundown suburban apartment house where she lives.

Actually, most of Mary's love encounters are spied upon by a young teacher who spends his summer vacation as an amateur astronomer in a small ramshackle hut of an observatory in the park across from Mary's house. He does not have to do much spying before Mary comes to spy, too, and to crawl into his bed.

The pretty young woman claims to want to give love to all men. When the teacher is picked to become the one and only, he submits, but without much conviction. We soon see that he actually much prefers to look at women from afar. About Mary, the film really does not reveal anything at all.

Electronic music rising to non-musical noise is used to provide psychological scare (and birds by the thousands fly away as if in anger). Katja Junge has okay looks but nothing in way of the femme fatale that her role requires. As the young teacher, Robert Duessler looks suitably bewildered throughout. —Kell.

Venus Peter
(BRITISH)

Cannes An Atlantic release (U.S.) of a British Film Institute production, in association with Channel 4, Scottish Film Production Fund, Orkney Islands Council and British Screen. (Intl. sales: Gavin Film). Executive producer, Colin McCabe. Produced by Christopher Young. Directed by Ian Sellar. Screenplay, Sellar, Christopher Rush; camera (Fujicolor), Gabriel Beristain; editor, David Spiers; music, Jonathan Dove; sound, David Stephenson; production design, Andy Harris; associate producer, Alan J. Wands; costumes, Sandy Powell; production manager, Jill Pack; assistant director, John Watson; casting, Priscilla John. Reviewed at Cannes Film Festival (Un Certain Regard), May 16, 1989. No MPAA Rating. Running time: **92 MIN.**
Peter . . . . Gordon R. Strachan
Grandfather . . . . Ray McAnally
Kinnear . . . . David Hayman
Miss Balsilbie . . . . Sinead Cusack
Peter's mother . . . . Caroline Paterson
Peter's father . . . . Peter Caffrey
Beadle . . . . Alex McAvoy
Jenny . . . . Emma Dingwall
Also with: Robin McCaffrey (Georgina), Louise Breslin (Leebie), Juliet Cadzow (Princess Paloma), Sheila Keith (Epp), George Anton (Billy), Alan Tall (McCreevie).

■ Ian Sellar's first feature, shot in the windswept Orkney Islands, north of Scotland, is a film about childhood which moves very slowly to a quite moving climax. Careful nurturing may help find an audience, but critical support will be essential if the film is to have a chance in the tough theatrical market.

Central character is young Peter who lives with his mother and fisherman grandfather; he's not certain where his father is, but imagines him to be a ship's captain. Much of the film is taken up with Peter's observations; family scenes, scenes in church and at school, the discovery of a stranded whale. Then the father returns, and it seems he'd simply tired of island life and gone to the mainland. His arrival triggers embarrassing family scenes, and brings Peter's story to its climax.

The evocative background of the Orkneys is a major asset to the film, as is the unaffected performance of young Gordon R. Strachan, an Orkney schoolboy, as Peter. Professional players, like Ray McAnally as the grandfather and David Hayman as the local priest, work generously alongside the youthful tyro.

If the film is, ultimately, less involving and exciting than it should be, it's because it shares with a few other British films an annoying habit of withholding information from the audience. We're never told exactly when it's taking place (obviously not the present), or what relationship some characters have to others, or why the local madwoman is unable to bathe herself (Peter spies on the priest swabbing her naked body). Indeed, the printed synopsis contains a good deal of information the film itself wilfully omits.

In Britain, where many of the allusions may be more easily understood, the film should have modest success, with offshore prospects more problematic. There'll be kudos for young Strachan, for Gabriel Beristain's moody camerawork, and for Jonathan Dove's rousing music.

Sellar shows great promise, but needs to unfold his story with more clarity. Among the supporting cast, Sinead Cusack makes her mark as a teacher who instills in the boy a love of poetry.—Strat.

Zanzibar
(FRENCH-SWISS)

Paris A Gaumont release of a French Production/SGGC/Film & Vidéo Production (Lausanne) coproduction. Executive producer, Emmanuel Schlumberger. Produced by Robert Boner. Directed by Christine Pascal. Screenplay, Pascal, Catherine Breillat, Robert Boner; camera (Eastmancolor), Pascal Marti; editor, Jacques Comets; music, Bruno Coulats; sound, Georges Prat, Georges Rousseau; art direction, Solange Zeitoun; production manager, Pierre Sayag. Reviewed at CNC, Paris, April 28, 1989. (In Cannes Film Festival, Perspectives on French Cinema.) Running time: **96 MIN.**
Vito Catene . . . . André Marcon
Marechal . . . . Francis Girod
Camille Dor . . . . Fabienne Babe

■ Movieland again contemplates its dirty navel in "Zanzibar," about a determined young indie producer trying to mount a production against all odds.

If the situations (sex, drugs, power) and relationships (producer beds actress, who in turn is "cannibalized" by the director) basically are familiar, actress Christine Pascal, in her third helming effort, succeeds in some acid personal-professional portraits. Pascal herself claims to have spent four years trying to get backing for this film, which preemed in Cannes sidebar Perspectives on French Cinema.

Script, by Pascal, Catherine Breillat (writer-director of "36 Fillette") and producer Robert

Boner, also is an interesting exposé of the way French auteur pictures are frequently made (or unmade). Story's idealistic producer André Marcon knows the film he wants to make (something about drugs), the director he wants to impose (a commercially washed-out tyrant played by filmmaker Francis Girod) and notably the star who is supposed to generate the financing (Fabienne Babe). But there's no script. This is the cart-before-the horse method of moviemaking that is the bane of the industry everywhere.

Marcon of course has a rough time, both with potential backers and his talent. Girod is excruciatingly obnoxious, and Babe is a junkie. Still he makes the mistake of falling in love with her, which proves his undoing. In the course of the best sequence, Girod — a superb portrait of the artist and vampire — puts Babe through some unorthodox screen tests, during which she ends up shooting dope for real. Crushed, Marcon sells his share in the film (to Girod) and withdraws to some godforsaken corner of Africa (Zanzibar). Irony of ironies, the film is made, proves a success, and wins Babe an award.

Pascal, who's first film was the abrasively autobiographical "Felicite" (followed by the unsuccessful "La Garce"), does her most accomplished directing, notably with her fine lead trio. Babe is vulnerable and touching, and Marcon, recruited from the theater, has strong introspective sensibility. Tech credits are good.—Len.

Devet kruhu pekla
(Nine Circles Of Hell)
(CZECHOSLOVAKIAN-CAMBODIAN)

Cannes A Ceskoslovenski Filmexpert (FEX) presentation of Barrandov Film Studios (Prague) coproduction with the Film Dept. of the Ministry of Culture of the Kampuchean People's Republic. Produced by Jan Syrovi. Directed by Milan Muchna. Screenplay by Muchna with Alexander Cukes; camera (color) Petr Hodja; editor, Dalibor Lipsky; music, Michael Kocab; production design, Milos Cervinka. Reviewed at the Cannes Film Festival (Un Certain Regard), May 20, 1989. Running time: **88 MIN.**
Tomas . . . . Milan Knazko
Khema . . . . Oum Savanny
Chivan . . . . Nov Chandary
Also with: Kveta Fialova, Jan Schmidt, Jiri Schmitzer, Milan Lasica, Jiri Samek, Jan Pohan, Bronislav Poloczek, Hang Chamrith, Som Dorin, Ban Thavi.

■ The uniqueness of the Czechoslovakian-Cambodian coproduction setup plus the sincerity of its theme of Love

Among The Ruins must have prompted the inclusion of Milan Muchna's "Nine Circles Of Hell" in the Cannes fest's prestigious Un Certain Regard section. Away from the Croisette, item's appeal is likely to begin and end with television.

It is a rare thing indeed to have a film team from a European East Bloc nation, and one of the more repressive ones at that, travel to Khmer Rouge-ravaged and still-Communist Kampuchea to join forces with the locals in shooting a picture that combines the elements of a tragic love story with an indictment of Khmer Rouge atrocities.

Eager to wash itself clean of the Khmer Rouge war of terror that killed millions of innocent Cambodians, the local authorities have helped provide backdrops of still-standing architectural wonders and other touristy sights for Milan Muchna's old-fashioned women's magazine story. It's about a visiting Czech doctor (stodgy Milan Knazko) who marries a Cambodian beauty (Oum Savanny has the right, bland Beauty Queen looks with an Oriental accent) despite her family's reluctance, only to be separated from her and their newborn infant by the advancing Khmer Rouge forces.

Before a few perfunctory scenes depicting the Kmher's atrocities (killing fields complete with skulls but obviously set up by the art director in a hurry), the doctor and his girlfriend have been seen swimming nude in the Pacific sunset. She has also had time to give birth to their child. The girl's brother and is now a Khmer commander.

Since there must be a limit to how happy an ending such a story may afford itself, the young mother dies and the doctor is sent back to Czechoslovakia. When peace of a kind prevails again, he is allowed to return and is united with his child. A few times, "Nine Circles Of Hell" moves with newsreel speed and a semblance of authenticity. Most of the time it looks liked a tied-together slide show with dialog emanating from a box hidden in the tropical flowers. —Kell.

Melancholia
(BRITISH-WEST GERMAN)

Cannes A British Film Institute (London)-Lichtblick Filmproduktion (Hamburg) coproduction, in association with Channel

4, NDR, Film Fonds Hamburg and Hamburger Filmbuero. Produced by Colin Mac-Cabe. Directed by Andi Engel. Screenplay, Engel, Lewis Rodia; camera (color), Denis Crossan; editor, Christopher Roth; music, Simon Fisher Turner; production design, Jock Scott; sound, Nigel Holland; executive in charge of production, Jill Pack; assistant director, Mary Soan; associate producer, Katy Radford; casting, Gilly Poole. Reviewed at the Cannes Film Festival (Director's Fortnight), May 20, 1989. Running time: **87 MIN.**

David Keller . . . . Jeroen Krabbé
Catherine . . . . Susannah York
Manfred . . . . Ulrich Wildgruber
Sarah Yelin . . . . Jane Gurnett
Rachel . . . . Kate Hardie
Dr. Vargas . . . . Saul Reichlin

■ Despite a dauntingly uninviting title, "Melancholia" proves to be a stimulating contemporary thriller about an idealist from the '60s who decides to take violent action in support of his long-submerged beliefs. It's a good bet for specialized theatrical outings worldwide.

Names of Jeroen Krabbé and Susannah York will be of help, though the latter has a relatively small role. Krabbé plays a German, Keller, long resident in London, who works as a critic but would like to return to novel writing. Keller lives alone, drinks too much, and is depressed with the way the world is heading. He is aroused from his inertia by a phone call from Hamburg which reminds him of his '60s activism.

The caller, Manfred, asks him to assassinate a Chilean torturer Vargas, currently visiting London. Keller is at first appalled by the idea, then agrees. But Manfred later visits London to tell Keller the assassination is off: the Chilean can now be of use to "our side."

Soon after, Keller is approached by Sarah Yelin (Jane Gurnett), a torture victim, whose husband was horribly murdered by Vargas. He makes up his mind, tracks down the Chilean, and kills him. He then goes to Hamburg and kills Manfred, betrayer of his former ideals.

The film raises questions about the use of violence to prevent further violence, and about the passivity of idealists. It doesn't play as a straight commercial thriller, but as a serious pic exploring provocative themes with intelligence. The pacing is unhurried, but the drama flows smoothly until its logical conclusion.

"Melancholia" is the first film directed by Andi Engel, German-born, London-based former critic who's best known as a distributor and exhibitor in Britain via his Ar-tificial Eye company. He's made an impressive directorial bow, though a less gloomy title would do wonders for the boxoffice.

Jeroen Krabbé is fine as the brooding protagonist, and Susannah York brings needed warmth as his ex-girlfriend with whom he's still on friendly terms.

Technically pro, the film will provoke and even enthrall audiences who lived through the radical period of 20 years ago. As a cry against today's complacency, it's more than just a thriller, though it works well on that level too. In all, a very promising debut.
—*Strat.*

Louss
(Rose Of The Desert)
(ALGERIAN)

Cannes A CAAI (Algiers) presentation of a CAAIC production. Produced by Med Tahar Harhoura. Written and directed by Mohamed Rachid Benhadj, based on an idea by Maria Cristina Paterlina and Benhadj. Camera (color), Ismaï Lakdhar Hamina, Mustapha Belmihoub; no editor's credit; music, Maria Cristina Paterlini; production design, Ahmed Kobi; costumes, Keltoum Mazif, Madani Meraabi. Reviewed at Cannes Film Festival (Intl. Critics Week), May 13, 1989. Running time: **90 MIN.**

Moussa . . . . Boubakeur Belaroussi
Zineb . . . . Dalila Helilou
Tahar . . . . Atmane Ariquet
Rachid . . . . Boumedienne Serat
Also with: Nawal Zaatar, Karima Hadjar.

■ "Rose Of The Desert" is a beautifully realized sensuously executed feature by Algerian writer-director Mohamed Rachid Benhadj. Pic tells of a few days in the life of a crippled man and other inhabitants of an oasis in the Algerian Sahara. Item, however, is insufficiently plotted and won't stand much of a chance with offshore audiences beyond the fest circuit.

Moussa (played with subdued strength, radiating from a strongly masculine face, by Boubakeur Belaroussi, who is crippled in real life) has no arms but uses his bent legs to get around pretty quickly. His feet substitute with grace and ease for his missing hands.

Living with his younger sister, Moussa knows that some day he'll have to give her away in marriage. He is told that he himself ought to find a wife.

While he finds it hard to make up his mind about much beyond filling his place in the small working community, life around him goes on in its languid desert rhythms. There are brief vignettes of men and women at work or at rare play, such as wedding preparation and women gathering to gossip.

The desert is the continuous backdrop — majestic, beautiful and rarely menacing — to the slow action that trails across its surfaces. A happy outcome is sensed towards the ending. The beauty in patience with the human condition is richly conveyed in the calm and ease of performance as well as the cinematography and editing.

Benhadj has avoided the twin traps of the maudlin and the morbid throughout. The symbolic meaning of film's original title takes on the shine of true awe of life. *Louss* is the Arab word not for a rose but for a crystalline formation of the desert's natural elements: wind, sand and nocturnal humidity. If some Third World survival symbolism is also implied, Banhadj is not hectoring about it. —*Kell.*

Il Decimo Clandestino
(To Save Nine)
(ITALIAN)

Cannes A Reteitalia production. Produced by Carlo and Enrico Vanzina. Written and directed by Lina Wertmüller. Camera (Eastmancolor; Luciano Vittori), Carlo Tafani; editor, Pierluigi Leonardi; art direction, Enrico Job; music, Dangio-Greco. Reviewed at Cannes Film Festival (Un Certain Regard), May 12, 1989. Running time: **86 MIN.**

Cesira . . . . Piera Degli Esposti
Landlady . . . . Dominque Sanda
Also with: Hartmut Becker, Susanna Marcomeni, Giorgio Trestini.

■ Originally made as a 1-hour tv drama for Italy's private web Reteitalia, "To Save Nine" found its way into Cannes in an extended feature-length version. Since it already aired on tv, pic's future as a theatrical looks limited — particularly in view of syrupy content and sluggish story.

Lina Wertmüller seems to have tossed this one off between major engagements. Fans of the director's caustic social commentary will find little to munch on here. Pic's appeal lies mainly as a heart-tugging fable about good children (there are nine in the cast) and picturesque poverty.

When her husband dies, farm woman Piera Deglia Esposti is forced to move her brood of nine bambini to the nearest metropolis — Bologna. She gets up a grocery shop selling country produce with no trouble, but can't find a landlord willing to rent her and kids an apartment. Finally, patrician Dominique Sanda rents her a scenic attic, and Piera insists she's alone.

An eternal grin on her face, Degli Esposti manages to hide her brood by getting them out of the building before dawn and home late at night. Eventually the kids are discovered. Glum landlady Sanda laments the trickery poor rich people are subjected to these days — only hint of the barbed social with that made Wertmüller famous. Yet here it lacks that crumb of paradoxical truth that would make it sting. Sanda remains "a bad woman," like the kids say, and a maudlin explanation about how she lost her own 7-year-old son makes things worse.

More than a story, "To Save Nine" is a situation. Characters are flatly drawn, though Degli Esposti manages to communicate warmth despite her inhumanity and unflagging good spirits. Sanda is dignified in a thankless role. Each of the nine kids is strikingly cute, and none bears the least resemblance to the parents. Score is dominated by cheery kids song.
—*Yung.*

Yun No Machi
(The Town Of Yun)
(JAPAN)

Cannes A Shigoto production. (Intl. sales, Hiroko Govaere, Roony-Soue-Boie, France.) Coproducers, Fumio Kannari, Jung Suk Kang, Ei Itoh. Directed by U Son Kim. Screenplay, Su Gil Kim, U Son Kim; camera (color), Dok Chol Kim; music, Kurodo Mori; art direction, Yuji Maruyama; sound, Katsuhisa Yano; lighting, Hideaki Yamakawa. Reviewed at Cannes Film Festival (Intl. Critics Week), May 17, 1989. Running time: **90 MIN.**

Yun . . . . Mi Bom Kang
Yuji . . . . Minoru Tanaka
Yun's grandmother . . . . Kotoe Hatsui
Yun's stepfather . . . . Hisashi Igawa
Yun's mother . . . . Rei Sen Lee
Yun's father . . . . Makoto Sato

■ Japan in its own way is as stratified racially as is Great Britain along economic-social lines. As "Yun No Machi" (The Town Of Yun) points out, Koreans — even those born and raised in Japan — are treated less favorably, sometimes wretchedly, because of who they are.

This is a first film by helmer U Son Kim, himself a Japanese of Korean descent. It's essentially a love story involving a Japanese youth and a girl of Korean heritage.

She lives in contemporary Osaka with her parents. When romantic sparks fly his parents become concerned. She is after all considered Korean although born in Japan — subject to annual fingerprinting and alien registration processes.

This pic has all the virtues of a maiden outing. It is buoyed by a force reflecting the director's personal concerns. It also has many of the flaws — ineptly staged action scenes (the boy fights for the girl's honor when threatened by Japanese toughs) and limp performances.

In all, an essentially parochial effort that promises more than it delivers. Technical credits are exceptionally strong, a not inconsiderable achievement for a pic debut.—*Sege.*

Sandra
(FRENCH)

Paris   A Les Films en Hiver production. Directed by Franck Landron. Screenplay, Landron, Pierre Sigwalt, Philippe Le Guay, Pierre Schoeller; camera (color), Florent Montcouquiol; sound, Philippe Donnebert, Mathiu Imbert, Jean-François Auger; editor, Nathalie Le Guay; art direction, Louis Soubrier; music, Jean-Claude Guignard; production manager, Frédéric Henault. Reviewed at CNC, Paris, April 27, 1989. (In Cannes Film Festival Perspectives on French Cinema). Running time: **76 MIN.**
  With: Christine Boisson (Sandra), Christophe Oden (Pierre), Jean-Michel Martial (Blaise), Bernard Ballet (father), Hélène Roussel (mother).

■ **Actress Christine Boisson comes out unscathed by this murky first feature by Franck Landon, a professional cameraman. Film, as described by one of its scripters, is a "love story plotted like a thriller, a thriller edited like a family movie, and a family movie with the immodesty of a film romance." Which is to say it's finally not much of anything.**

Boisson is a modern young woman with two lovers and something of a secret death wish. One of her boyfriends is a young diplomat involved in mysterious intrigues (about which we're never enlightened), while the other is a black photographer. The relationship with the latter hits the rocks, and Boisson soon breaks off with her diplomat. The latter's father tries to plead with her to take his son back but finally murders her in a fit of desperation.

Landon has technical savoir-faire but the story is ragged and unconvincing. Yet Boisson, who usually is not superior to a bad script, by moments makes her personage touchingly genuine. —*Len.*

Chorni Kvadrat
(The Black Square)
(SOVIET-DOCU-
COLOR/B&W)

Cannes   A Moscow Documentary Film Studios production. Directed by Iossif Pasternak. Screenplay, Olga Sviblova; camera (color/b&w), Vladimir Golovnia; music, Alfred Schnitke, M. Beresovsky, V. Tarassov. Reviewed at Cannes Film Festival (Intl. Critics Week), May 12, 1989. Running time: **60 MIN.**

■ **If perestroika seems slow to influence Soviet features, its effect on documentaries is clear in "The Black Square," an original and lively look at 20th century avant-garde painting in the USSR. Dedicated to Kasimir Malevich, it should receive wide screenings in art circles and tv culture slots.**

Director Iossif Pasternak, an orchestra conductor making his behind-the-camera debut, approaches his subject with a real feeling for the visual and the joys of filmmaking. The Soviet avant-garde is traced from Russian constructivism to a brief flowering in the Krushchev years, stagnation under Brezhnev, and the current revival of interest in this kind of art.

What most impresses about "Black Square," however, apart from its informative side, is the way it links artist production to the changing political climate. Revealing repertory footage shows Nikita Khrushchev skeptically viewing a modern, "non-official" canvas; another typical newsreel has the head of the Artists Union in the 1950s making fun of the same, while his audience laughs in agreement.

Numerous short interviews with contemporary painters point up the atmosphere of creative liberation that has followed perestroika.

Film certainly is more a sample of Soviet painting in this century than a comprehensive study. Watching fascinated Russians at a show of what used to be "unofficial art," one wonders how many avant-garde works have left the country, never to be seen again. More is the marvel that Pasternak succeeds so well in tracing the cultural politics after the evolution in so concise and engrossing a film.
  —*Yung.*

Barroco
(Baroque)
(SPANISH-CUBAN)

■ **Cannes**   A Televisión Española presentation of an Opalo Films/ICAIC (Cuba)/Quinto Centenario production. Executive producer, J.A. Pérez Giner. Directed by Paul Leduc. Screenplay, José Joaquin Blanco, Jesús Díaz, Leduc, based on "Concierto Barroco" by Alejo Carpentier; camera (Eastmancolor), Angel Goded; editor, Rafael Castanedo; sets, Julio Estéban; in Dolby. Reviewed at Cannes Film Festival (Un Certain Regard), May 14, 1989. Running time: **115 MIN.**
  With: Francisco Rabal, Angela Molina, Ernesto Gómez Cruz, Roberto Sosa, Alberto Pedro, Juan Peña, Elena Burke, José Antonio Méndez, Pablo Milanes, César Portillo de la Luz, Omara Portuondo.

■ **What this seemingly long, self-indulgent film is even about will elude most of those seeing it. Pic has no dialog and consists of a succession of scenes apparently set in Latin America during colonial times.**

Director Paul Leduc never identifies any of the personages. Instead, his rambling camera dwells on folkloric dances and music, and presents a cross-section of colonial life, Indians, blacks, slaves, masters and colonizers, the last-named cast as the oppressors.

There seems little rhyme or reason to the string of staged images, and audiences may interpret them as they wish. Presumably, they rep an allegory putting down the Spaniards. Near end of epic, Leduc jumps briefly ahead in time to the Spanish Civil War and winds up in a Madrid disco.

What any of it means is anyone's guess. The colonizers were facists? Evil pervades through the centuries? Spain has mellowed through the centuries?

Whatever the answer, it is hardly worth searching for. This turgid exercise in obscurity probably will never see the light of commercial screens. —*Besa.*

Wallers letzter Gang
(Waller's Last Trip)
(WEST GERMAN-
COLOR/B&W)

Cannes   A Metropolis presentation of Christian Wagner Film production in association with Bavarian Television. Produced, written and directed by Wagner, based on novel "Die Strecke" by Gerhard Köpf. Camera (color/b&w), Thomas Mauch; editor, Norbert Herzner; music, Florian Ernst Müller; production design, Myriande Heller; sound, Benedikt Röskau; production management, Jürgen Tröster, Thomas Wommer, Doris Salat. Reviewed at Cannes Film Festival (Intl. Critics Week), May 15, 1989. Running time: **100 MIN.**
Waller . . . . Rolf Illig
Rosina . . . . Sybille Canonica
Stumpf . . . . Franz Boehm
Young Waller . . . . Herbert Knaup
Also with: Crescentia Dunber, Rainer Egger, Dietlinde Elsasser.

■ **"Waller's Last Trip" is a slow one in more ways than one and is doomed to move even more slowly into any kind of marketplace. It is a sincere but dour exercise in minimalist cinema by debuting writer-helmer Christian Wagner.**

An old rails inspector trudges along the single-track railway line that has been his lifeline while looking back, in prolonged inserts in black & white, at the few events that have made up his only off-the-rails life.

Waller's old face is a closed one. As a young man, he looks more open, but obviously a stubborn streak in his character has always been there to help shape the man into the essential loner. He has a daughter who runs a village *bier-stube* (the setting is th Bavarian mountains), but he will never sit down with anybody there for a drink and a chat.

The flashbacks tell of Waller going away briefly to World War II, of which nothing is seen. He comes back unscarred, while a good friend does not. He has a love affair and eventually a child with the local factory-owner's pretty daughter, whose family rejects him. The woman dies and Waller's walks continue with a dullness meticulously recorded.

The acting in all roles also hews closely to the minimalist mode. Brief flashes of humor do occur but the melancholy mood prevails. It may not be meant that way by the filmmaker, but Waller appears to have always been a man of no drive and hence he winds up being pretty uninteresting, too.—*Kell.*

Dharmaga tongjoguro
kan kkadalgun?
(Why Did Bodhi-Djarma
Go East?)
(SOUTH KOREAN)

Cannes   A Bae Yong-Kyun presentation and production. Produced, directed, screenplay, camera (color) and edited by Yong-Kyun Bae. Music, Kyu-Young Chin. Reviewed at Cannes Film Festival (Un Certain Regard), May 16, 1989. Running time: **135 MIN.**
Hyegok . . . . Pan-Yong Yi
Kibong . . . . Won-Sop Sin
Haejin . . . . Hae-Jin Huang
The Superior . . . . Su-Myong Ko
The other disciple . . . . Hae-Yong Kim

■ **South Korea's Yong-Kyun Bae has spent several years making "Why Did Bodhi-Djarma Go East?," a film about the emptiness of earthly existence. Audiences that will not accept this as enough spiritual fodder after sitting through more than two hours of beautiful scenery and a few deep-think utterances from a trio of mostly stony-faced non-actors had better stay away.**

Those who do stick around will be put in the right minimalist frame of mind to appreciate the meditative cinematic moves of

Yong-Kyun Bae. There are scripture words; a rundown mountain monastery, and an old master teaching his two pupils the ways of Zen, which has nothing happening meaning that actually everything, including space beyond space, happens.

The tiniest inkling of a storyline is found in a small boy's wanton downing of a bird's nest with a stone throw. The boy is guilt-stricken but eventually absolved when the old master dies and fire consumes his corpse as the bird of the destroyed nest rises to spread its wings against the sunset.

Anyone for therapy classes?
—Kell.

Erreur de jeunesse
(Youthful Indiscretion)
(FRENCH-B&W)

Paris   An M 87 Prods./MC Films coproduction. Produced by Philippe Cosson. Written and directed by Radovan Tadic. Camera (Kodak b&w), Pierre Novion; editor, Dominique Gallieni; music, Jean-Louis Valero; sound, Bruno Tarriere, Dominique Hennequin; art direction, Thierry Francois; technical adviser, Gérard Zingg; assistant director, Pierre Soubestre. Reviewed at CNC, Paris, April 27, 1989. (In Cannes Film Festival, Perspectives in French Cinema.) Running time: 93 MIN.
    With: Francis Frappat (Antoine), Muni (Thérèse), Geraldine Danon (Françoise), Patrick Bauchau (Paul), Didier Flamand (Patrick), Irène Jacob, Gaspard Manesse, Eric Vieliard, Isabelle Weingarten, Yann Dedet.

■ A first feature by Yugoslav-born Radovan Tadic, "Erreur de jeunesse" seems like a throwback to the sort of French black & white auteur cinema that detractors described as being low-budget and set mostly in tiny maids' rooms.

Many clichés creep into Tadic's script about three lonely people living on the top floor of a Paris apartment house, but the assured direction gives this tale some melancholy appeal.

Central character is Antoine (Francis Frappat), an aspiring poet with a passion for T.S. Eliot. He works nights in a printing plant and befriends a cynical layabout (Patrick Bauchau) with an anecdotal knowledge of poetry. His neighbors include an old woman (Muni) who makes mysterious latenight phone calls from a public booth to a rich businessman, and a pretty young blond girl of good family (Geraldine Danon) who tries to draw Frappat into her sexually desperate void.

Tadic handles the crisscross poignancy adroitly, and the players are convincing. Nothing is re-solved, of course, and the film's coda is fuzzily symbolic. Pierre Novion's lensing is an atmospheric plus. —Len.

Montalvo et l'enfant
(Montalvo And The Child)
(FRENCH-B&W)

Paris   A CDN/La Sept/Groupe Emile Dubois/FR3/La Maison de la Culture of Grenoble/SGGC/TNDI Chateauvallon, Théatre de la Ville coproduction. Produced by Gilles Sandoz. Written and directed by Claude Mouriéras, based on choreography by Jean-Claude Gallota, ''Pandora.'' Camera (b&w), Walther Van Den Ende; editor, Monique Dortonne; sound, Francis Wargnier, Dominique Gaborieau; music, Arvot Part, art direction and costumes, Yves Cassagnes. Reviewed at Empire theater, Paris, April 24, 1989. (In Cannes Film Festival, Intl. Critics Week.) Running time: 76 MIN.
    With: Mathilde Attaraz (Pandora), Christophe Delachaux (Montalvo), Robbert Seyfried (Roberto), Jean-Claude Gallota (Gigi), Michel Ducret (Valerio), Marceline Bertelot (the grandmother).

■ "Montalvo et l'enfant" is based on a dance work by modern French choreographer Jean-Claude Gallota, but is not a conventional dance film. Director Claude Mouriéras, a videaste who's done several previous shorter productions from Gallotta's work, uses dance as an element of stylization in this sometimes compelling experimental feature about innocence and passion.

Lensed in hypnotic black & white by Walther Van Den Ende, story centers on a young boy and his uncle in and around an Italian immigrant housing block. Somewhat cinematically arty first part deals with their relationship, the man's escapist passion for bullfighting and act of killing a sheep that deeply hurts the child.

When the action shifts to local femme fatale named Pandora, Gallotta's choreography, mediated by Van Den Ende's camera, makes a vivid and exciting entry, as the uncle and romantic rival fight for her favors in a tangle that doesn't exclude homosexual overtones.

With words (in Italian) reduced to accessory (sociological) presence and music used sparely, film achieves some unusual cinematic force. It could gain, though, by some trimming. The excellent actor-dancers, which include Gallotta, are from choreographer's dance theater, the Emile Dubois groupe, which coproduced feature with national Drama Center (CDN) of Gennevilliers. —Len.

COMPETING AT CANNES FESTIVAL

Do The Right Thing

Cannes   A Universal Pictures release of a 40 Acres And A Mule Filmworks production. Produced and directed by Spike Lee. Coproducer, Monty Ross; line producer, Jon Kilik. Screenplay, Lee; camera (Duart color, Deluxe prints), Ernest Dickerson; editor, Barry Alexander Brown; music, Bill Lee; sound (Dolby), Skip Lievsay; production design, Wynn Thomas; set decoration, Steve Rosse; assistant director, Randy Fletcher; costumes, Ruth Carter; casting, Robi Reed. Reviewed at Cannes Film Festival, competing, May 19, 1989. MPAA Rating: R. Running time: 120 MIN.
Sal . . . . Danny Aiello
Da Mayor . . . . Ossie Davis
Mother Sister . . . . Ruby Dee
Vito . . . . Richard Edson
Buggin' Out . . . . Giancarlo Esposito
Mookie . . . . Spike Lee
Radio Raheem . . . . Bill Nunn
Pino . . . . John Turturro
Tina . . . . Rosie Perez
ML . . . . Paul Benjamin
Coconut Sid . . . . Frankie Faison
Sweet Dick Willie . . . . Robin Harris
Jade . . . . Joie Lee
Mr. Senor Love Daddy . . . . . . Sam Jackson
Smiley . . . . Roger Guenveur Smith
Clifton . . . . John Savage

■ Spike Lee combines a forceful statement on race relations with solid entertainment values in "Do The Right Thing." Militant approach presents distrib Universal with a marketing challenge to tap a potentially wide audience for a thought-provoking pic amongst this summer's fluff.

Lee adopts the durable theatrical format of "Street Scene" as his launching point, painstakingly etching an ensemble of neighborhood characters on a Bedford Stuyvesant block in Brooklyn. Centerpiece is Danny Aiello's pizza parlor, which he runs with his sons John Turturro and Richard Edson, with Lee delivering take-out orders.

Setting his day in a community's life on the hottest day of the summer, filmmaker sets up a running dialectic: A myriad of contemporary issues covering personal, social and economic matters are laid on the table in often shrill but sometimes funny confrontations. Ossie Davis is perfect casting as a sort of conciliator, a hobo nicknamed the Mayor who injects folk wisdom into the discussion.

Tempers in this melting pot flare throughout the day, but it is at quitting time when violence erupts. One of the more militant blacks, Giancarlo Esposito, marches into Aiello's shop backed up by muscular Bill Nunn (called Radio Raheem because of his ever-present ghetto blaster), demanding that some photos of prominent blacks be put on the wall next to Aiello's proud array of Italian-American idols.

Aiello destroys Nunn's radio with a baseball bat and when the ensuing fistfight spills out into the street, Nunn is killed by an over-zealous white cop. The neighborhood standoff after the police leave is broken when Lee himself, previously on the sidelines, steps forward and throws a garbage can through Aiello's window, cueing an all-out riot; fire destroys the store.

Vividly enacted, this violent and cathartic scene proves to be insightful rather than inciteful. End credits match a Martin Luther King Jr. quote on the impractical and immoral nature of violence with a Malcolm X statement reserving the "right to do what is necessary," calling violence as self-defense "intelligence." Pic's omnipresent deejay Sam Jackson ends the film with a voiceover reminder to register to vote — an election's coming up. In yet another case of synthesis, balancing Davis' nonviolent message of "Do The Right Thing," which he tells Lee in the opening reel, is pic's oft-played hypnotic theme song "Fight The Power," performed by Public Enemy.

Standing out in a uniformly solid cast are Ruby Dee, the Earth Mother of the microcosmic community; Aiello, Turturro and Edson as three quite different variations on an ethnic theme; Paul Benjamin, Frankie Faison and Robin Harris as the funny trio of kibitzers on the block, and Roger Guenveur Smith as he creates an unusual, poetic figure of a stammering simpleton (who sells photos of black leaders) in the midst of such confident figures.

Lee continues his comfortable screen role from prior films as a lovable nebbish with a backbone lurking in his makeup, ably supported by his real-life sister Joie Lee, cast as his sibling. In telephoto shots of the filmmaker in his Mookie role ambling down the block, glad-handing his neighbors, one is aware of his thorough knowledge and control of his material, literally shot on his home turf.

Dynamite opening credits sequence intros super-sexy dancer-choreographer Rosie Perez, cavorting to "Fight The Power;" she also plays Lee's Puerto Rican girlfriend in the film.

Topnotch technical credits include atmospheric amber lighting and startling camera moves by Lee's regular cinematographer Ernest Dickerson.

The director's father, Bill Lee, provides a varied and evocative background score, highlighted by sinuous saxophone solos by Branford Marsalis. One of the film's most stirring moments comes when deejay Jackson simply recites a meticulously compiled rollcall of great black musicians past and present. —Lor.

Kuroi Ame
(Black Rain)
(JAPAN)

Cannes A Toei Co. release of a Imamura Production Ltd., Hayashibara Group, Tohokushinsha Film Co. production. Produced by Hisa Iino. Directed by Shohei Imamura. Screenplay, Toshiro Ishido, Imamura, based on the novel by Masuji Ibuse; camera (black & white), Takashi Kawamata; editor, Hajime Okayusu; music, Toru Takemitsu; art direction, Hisso Inagaki; sound, Ken'ichi Benitani; lighting, Yasuo Iwaki. Reviewed at Cannes Film Festival (competing), May 17, 1989. Running time: **123 MIN.**

Yasuko . . . . Yoshiko Tanaka
Shigematsu . . . . Kazuo Kitamura
Shigako . . . . Etsuko Ichihara
Shokichi . . . . Shoichi Ozawa
Kotaro . . . . Norihei Miki
Yuichi . . . . Kaisuka Ishide

■ **This is a rigorous, highly disciplined film that like the superb novel on which it is based treats a terrible, albeit familiar, subject — the atomic bombing of Hiroshima on Aug. 6, 1945 — with an admirable absence of special pleading.**

Because "Kuroi Ame" (Black Rain) builds its considerable emotional punch by meticulous observation of detail rather than melodramatic flagwaving, it emerges as an exceptionally strong film and a probable Cannes prizewinner of some sort.

More importantly, it marks the return of director Shohei Imamura to an earlier, more fruitful phase of his career. He provided an obvious misfire at Cannes four years ago with "Zagan" after triumphing in 1983 with "Narayama Bushiko" (The Ballad Of Narayama), which copped the Golden Palm.

"Black Rain" is more reminiscent of the director's previous pics such as "Nippon Konchuchi" (Insect Woman). "Rain" uses the bombing and devastation as a point of departure for a tragic sequence of events afflicting ordinary peo-

ple: a young woman and her immediate family.

Because they were traveling just outside the city of Hiroshima, they survived the immediate devastation only to pay an even more insidious price — lingering death by nuclear radiation. Imamura vividly symbolizes the initial contamination when the woman (Yoshiko Tanaka) is splattered by inky drops of rain during a ferry ride to her uncle's home.

The ruthless aftermath of the bombing is effectively handled early in the film. As the girl and her uncle (Kazuo Kitamura) examine the debris, they witness: a woman succoring a charred infant, a blinded man falling out of a window, a wrenching encounter of a boy deformed beyond recognition and his brother who can't recognize him; tough stuff made poignant by Imamura's restrained treatment.

The film concentrates on the ensuing five years as the family unsuccessfully tries to marry off the young girl — tainted as a virtual social pariah because of the radiation exposure. Imamura here plays to his strength. He presents a telling array of physical detail of rural Japanese life that blends with his characterizations — giving them extraordinary appeal. Although shot in black & white, "Rain" is unusually handsome. (Budgeted at about $3.5-million, it was lensed from June to the end of last year in a small mountain village in Okayama Prefecture, facing the Sea of Setonaikai off the southern Japanese island of Shikoku.)

The minor characters are convincingly drawn, although the director appears less sure how to handle a crazed soldier with whom the girl finds warm romantic rapport. Nonetheless, the overall effect facilitates an inevitable ending conveyed with enormous grace and even a touch of surprise.

There are some flaws. The film tends at times to be paced monotonously, a situation that isn't helped by Tanaka's passive portrayal of the young woman. The plot is moved along by the all-too-familiar device of off-screen narration, a reading of the uncle's diary compiled to medically certify the young woman as cured. And, the special effects are wanting in some respects. The charred corpses occasionally resemble rejects from a low-budget special effects department.

These are minor glitches.

Takashi Kawamata's photography is excellent. Toru Takemitsu's score is fittingly spaced but very moving. Kitamura as the uncle is a standout.

In all, an uncompromisingly strong film. —Sege.

M. Hire
(FRENCH)

Paris A UGC release of a Cinéa/Hachette Première et Cie/FR3 Films coproduction. Produced by Philippe Carcassonne, René Cleitman. Directed by Patrice Leconte. Screenplay, Leconte, Patrick Dewolf, based on Georges Simenon's novel "Les Fiancailles de M. Hire;" camera (color), Denis Lenoir; editor, Joelle Hache; music, Michael Nyman; art direction, Yvan Maussion; sound, Pierre Lenoir, Dominique Hennequin; production manager, Frédéric Sauvagnac. Reviewed at UGC screening room, Neuilly, April 25, 1989. (In Cannes Film Festival, competing.) Running time: **79 MIN.**

M. Hire . . . . Michel Blanc
Alice . . . . Sandrine Bonnaire
Emile . . . . Luc Thuillier
Inspector . . . . André Wilms

■ **Michel Blanc, the bald, diminutive funnyman who won Cannes honors in 1986 in Bertrand Blier's previous pic "Tenue de soirée," plays it utterly straight in "M. Hire," an unconvincing adaptation of a 1933 novel by Georges Simenon, first filmed as "Panique" by Julien Duvivier in 1946.**

Competing at Cannes, pic also is first non-comic effort by director Patrice Leconte, who helmed a number of Blanc's early screen comedies before showing more personal abilities in the 1986 "Tandem," a piquant male-bonding comedy-drama.

Simenon's novel, about a lonely misanthropic man framed for a murder by a ruthless pair of lovers and hounded to death by a mob of neighbors, has been watered down. Script by Leconte and Patrick Dewolf (who coauthored "Tandem"), virtually does away with the social background and the frightening depiction of mob violence, which figured prominently in Duvivier's film.

Worse, M. Hire, the protagonist, a sleazy minor felon chez Simenon (and memorably portrayed by Michel Simon under Duvivier), has been morally sanitized. Unlike Simon, Blanc is aptly dour but unable to suggest the deep antipathy that is essential to the drama — it's hard to believe Blanc could be so disliked, as the script predicates but never forcefully dramatizes. Furthermore, the character is, if not a model citizen, a basically conventional outsider

who's always impeccably dressed, keeps a cage of pet white mice, and regularly visits a brothel.

He also has another pastime, which is the seed of his personal tragedy. He's transfixed by the attractive young woman (Sandrine Bonnaire) who lives across the courtyard and who doesn't believe in curtains. Night after night, the lonely Blanc stands at the window of his darkened apartment and spies on her, to the obsessive accompaniment of Michel Nyman's theme music on his record player.

Blanc knows her secret. Bonnaire's good-for-nothing boyfriend (Luc Thuillier) is guilty of a young woman's murder, for which the police suspect the unloved tailor, who has a police record for unspecified immoral acts. When Bonnaire realizes she is being watched, she begins coming on to the lovesick voyeur who offers to take her abroad away from her sordid life.

Bonnaire not only stands Blanc up at the train station but profits from his absence to plant an incriminating piece of evidence in his apartment. Running from the police, Blanc falls to his death from the rooftop, but has left a letter to the police that exposes Bonnaire's boyfriend.

Given the compromises and weaknesses of the script, Blanc does a creditable if not credible job as M. Hire in a dour, no-nonsense performance. Bonnaire gives some ambiguities and touching shadings to the twofaced girl. Luc Thuillier, however, has nothing much to do as Bonnaire's ne'er-do-well lover, and André Wilms does what he can with the conventional part of the snide police inspector who harasses Blanc.

Leconte's direction is competent but atmospherically less sure than in "Tandem," depending too much on Blanc, on whom too many ineffectual closeups are lavished. Tech credits are slick.

Film apparently is the 50th motion picture adapted from Simenon. —Len.

Rosalie Goes Shopping
(WEST GERMAN)

Cannes A Weltvertrieb des Autoren presentation of a Pelemele production. Produced by Percy and Eleonore Adlon. Directed by Percy Adlon. Screenplay, Percy and Eleonore Adlon, Christopher Doherty; camera (color), Bernd Heinl; editor, Heiko Hindkers; music, Bob Telson; art direction, Stephen Lineweaver; costumes, Elizabeth Warner Nonkin; makeup, N. Christine Chadwick. Reviewed at Cannes Film Festival, competing, May 18, 1989. Running time: **94 MIN.**

Rosalie . . . . .Marianne Sägebrecht
Liebling Ray . . . . .Brad Davis
Priest . . . . .Judge Reinhold
Rosalie's father . . . . .Willy Harlander
Rosalie's mother . . . . . . .Erika Blumberger
Barbara . . . . .Patricia Zehentmayr
Schnuki . . . . .John Hawkes
Schatzi . . . . .Alex Winter
April . . . . .Courtney Kraus
Also with: David Denney, Lisa and Lori Fitzhugh, Dina Chandel, Bill Butler, Ed Geldhart, John William Galt.

■ **Percy Adlon apparently believes nothing succeeds like success and that he can't miss in giving his audiences more of the "Cafe Bagdad" medicine which worked so well. However, this time he has tried too hard and delivered too little.**

The formula is evident. Adlon again picked an American location with an outlandish name, in this case Stuttgart, Ark. He put his favorite diva, the voluminous Marianne Sägebrecht, in it, let her loose on the American system and hoped for the best. With no real plot to hang on to, he attempts a madcap satire of consumerist society — broad gimmickry and driven at a hectic pace, to dissimulate its obvious inconsistency.

Sägebrecht plays a "peacetime war bride" who married an American pilot stationed in Bavaria and came back with him to the Midwest. Devoted to him and to her seven children, she provides princely standards of living for all of them by juggling around 37 different credit cards, issuing checks which bounce all over town, and rushing daily to church like a good Catholic to confess her sins and have the slate wiped clean.

As she is about to run out of tricks, she discovers the wonders of computers and electronic mail. Breaking codes and inventing phantom companies, she jumps at them with a vengeance and by the end of the picture the system itself contemplates the possibility of jumping off the roof in sheer despair.

Adlon, whose forte until now has been gentle, understated comedy, keen observation of human nature and great sympathy for his characters, is way out of his depth, trying to compensate for lack of quality with quantity. He goes for a frenetic pace, but his characters are never better than sketchy caricatures. His grasp of the system he parodies here is simplistic at best, and he denies Sägebrecht the leisurely pace she needs to build her on-screen charm. She

comes off as little better than a petty crook and the audience never gets to share the secret of her manipulations.

Brad Davis is miscast as her dimwitted husband who can't think of anything but flying old planes. Judge Reinhold is wasted as her confessor in a part which never develops. The rest of the actors are rushed on and off screen before they can display any real gifts.

There's plenty of music, camera tricks, filters and weird angles and neat art direction — all supposed to offer a cockeyed view o American life, but Adlon seems either too close or too removed to comment succinctly. While immediate reaction might be au dience identification with anyone who can beat the banks, in the long run the pic's prospects look less promising. *—Edna.*

Das Spinnennetz
(The Spider's Web)
(WEST GERMAN)

Cannes A Beta/Kirch Group presentation of Provobis production with ZDF, Beta/Kirch, ORF, Rai-Due, TVE and Filmexport Bratislava. Produced by Jürgen Haase. Executive producer, Peter Hahne. Directed by Bernhard Wicki. Screenplay, Wolfgang Kirschner, Wicki, based on Joseph Roth's novel; camera (Eastmancolor), Gerard Vandenberg; editor, Tanja Schmidbauer; music, Günther Fischer; sound, Detlev Fichtner; production design, Georg von Kieseritzki; sets, Götz Heymann, Karel Vacek; costumes, Marion Jacobs; production coordinator, Jan Kadlec. Reviewed at Cannes Film Festival, competing, May 17, 1989. Running time: **198 MIN.**
Lenz . . . . .Klaus Maria Brandauer
Theodor Lohse . . . . .Ulrich Mühe
Baron von
  Rastschuk . . . . .Armin Mueller-Stahl
Rachel Efrussi . . . . .Andrea Jonasson
Anna . . . . .Elisabeth Endriss
Baron von Köckwitz . . . . . . .Ullrich Haupt
Also with: Agnes Fink, Ernst Stötzner, Andras Frisay Kali Son, Peter Roggisch, Rolf Henninger, Hans Korte, Kyra Mladeck, Hark Bohm, Kalus Abrahamowsky, Yvonne Remé.

■ **"The Spider's Web" is great miniseries fodder and was conceived that way from the outset, but veteran German helmer Bernhard Wicki's giant picture of the rise to eventual power of a weak man also is traditionalist cinema of sufficient narrative drive to make theatrical distribution likely in at least some territories outside Germany.**

Basing his film on Austrian novelist Joseph Roth's book, written in installments from 1923-33, Wicki has East Berlin actor Ulrich Mühe as the antihero Lohse, who is wounded and patriotically indignant when a navy mutiny puts an end to World War I. Very little reason beyond this event is given

for Lohse's subsequent and consistent betrayal of friends, including killing them, whether male or female.

It probably is the two major weaknesses of an otherwise thoroughly professional job of cinematic storytelling that Ulrich Mühe has the looks and lack of expression of a mannequin rather than the look of evil, and that he is depicted throughout as anything but a man of power. On the contrary, he lucks onto every career step in his move to power, and whenever he encounters actual danger, he cringes and whines. He wets his pants too.

Mühe's facial expressions do not change much either during his many sexual trysts with gorgeous women, who may help him to achieve more power (one of them the Jewish wife of his early benefactor), and he is just as bland when he opens fire and thus instigates a bloodbath on striking Polish peasants.

Fortunately, Klaus Maria Brandauer supplies nuance (his role is much better written, too) as

Lohse's major adversary, the Jewish anarchist double agent, who is a much more intelligent schemer than Lohse. For a while the two men work the same side of the fence, but their final meeting steams with mutual hate. Explicit brutality is depicted in several scenes, especially in the first anti-Jewish pogrom and in the suppression of the Polish strike, but the gushing and spouting blood never is exploitative.

All through the film, the narrative moves at a brisk clip. Every scene and every event tie together neatly. Women, mostly powerless, and men, all ruthless, sometimes verge on stock characterization, but a long list of fine actors overcome the cliché excesses.

"The Spider's Web" lacks the swell of a great tragic epic, but Wicki (who created the classic antiwar film "Die Brücke" in 1959) is still a superior craftsman. He has been expertly helped by a production design and execution of impressive authenticity. *—Kell.*

CANNES MARKET REVIEWS

Breaking In

Cannes A Samuel Goldwyn Co. release of an Act III Prods. presentation of a Harry Gittes production. Executive producers, Andrew Meyer, Sarah Ryan Black. Produced by Gittes. Directed by Bill Forsyth. Screenplay, John Sayles; camera (color), Michael Coulter; editor, Michael Ellis; music, Michael Gibbs; production design, Adrienne Atkinson, John Willett; associate producer-production manager, Jack Cummins; assistant director, Richard Feury. Reviewed at Cannes Film Festival (Market), May 17, 1989. Running time: **91 MIN.**
Ernie Mullins . . . . .Burt Reynolds
Mike Lefebb . . . . .Casey Siemaszko
Carrie . . . . .Sheila Kelley
Delphine . . . . .Lorraine Toussant
Johnny Scat . . . . .Albert Salmi
Shoes . . . . .Harry Carey

■ **The challenge posed by "Breaking In" is to find the right audience for this charming buddy-caper comedy, which marks a change of style for Burt Reynolds. Customers expecting a familiar star vehicle will be sorely disappointed, but there should be an appreciative audience out there for another off-center film from Scottish director Bill Forsyth, whose last was the beautiful but drastically mishandled "Housekeeping."**

Forsyth teams up with screenwriter John Sayles for the comedy lensed in Portland, Ore. Reynolds plays Ernie Mullins, a 61-year-

old, graying, professional burglar with a gammy leg and the beginning of a pot belly.

He teams up with young Mike Lefebb (Casey Siemaszko), a garage hand who likes to break into houses to raid the fridge and read the mail, when they both hit the same place one night. They become partners, with the oldtimer teaching the youngster the tricks of the trade.

What follows is a gentle comedy, filled with incisive observation, which builds to a wry conclusion which won't set well with action fans. So it's essential to pitch the film's campaign to customers who'll be delighted by the Forsyth/Sayles approach to the material.

Forsyth's very special sense of humor already was apparent in his Scottish films, especially "Gregory's Girl" and "Local Hero." Here, he and cameraman Michael Coulter are constantly on the lookout for the amusing setup, whether it be Mullins' house, which is right in the flight path of Portland airport, or a supermarket with a roof adorned with huge, garish fake fruit.

The supermarket is one of the targets for the robbers, and sparks an amusing confrontation with a couple of friendly guard dogs. There's a nod to the Jules Dassin classic "Rififi" in the way Mullins uses an umbrella as part of his burglary equipment.

After a while, the partners fall out, and Lefebb ignores the older man's advice about not flashing his ill-gotten gains around. Trying to impress a kooky prostie (Sheila Kelley), the young thief acquires a flashy apartment and an expensive car, paying in cash. As a result, the law is soon on to him, and he cheerfully admits not only to his own crimes, but to those of his partner, basking in the glow of his notoriety. Given a stiff prison sentence, he finds life behind bars surprisingly pleasant, and the pic ends with a visit from Mullins in which each man pities the other, not realising that each has found a kind of happiness.

The two players carry the film with style. In a sharp change of character, Reynolds plays the old-timer with a relaxed charm that's wholly delightful; after a string of disappointing performances in dud pictures, this one should find favor with critics and select audiences. Siemaszko is fine, too, as the initially nervous and ultimately relaxed and confident young criminal. Kelley is fun as the prostie who favors colored condoms and likes to be known as an actress, though, as she says, "I'm not at performance level yet; I'm developing my instrument." Lines like that from Sayles are seized upon with relish by Forsyth.

Pic is technically fine in all departments, with production design by Adrienne Atkinson and John Willett making an especially fine contribution. Under Forsyth's sympathetic direction, performances down to the smallest bit part are most enjoyable.—*Strat.*

Crazy Horse
(She Drives Me Crazy)
(CANADIAN)

Cannes A Fries Distribution release of SC Entertainment production. Executive producers, Syd Capp, George Flak. Produced by Nicolas Stiliadis; line producer, Brian Dennis. Directed by Stephen Withrow. Screenplay, Michael Taav; camera (color), Douglas Koch; editor, Michael McMahon; production design, Alan Fellows. Reviewed at Cannes Film Festival (Market), May 17, 1989. Running time: **90 MIN.**
Matt .Daniel Stern
Kathy . . . . .Sheila McCarthy
Harry . . . . .Damir Andrei
Davey . . . . .Elias Koteas
Buddy . . . . .Page Fletcher
Annie. . . . . .Deborah Foreman

■ Described by its producers as

a romantic adventure in the genre of "Something Wild," this turns out to be something awful.

It would seem at first that it might be something different from the SC mill. A couple has split up, she to go off with another man, he to suffer and eventually follow them to their country retreat. Trying desperately to be funny, there is a faint hope that it might indeed be a romantic and witty affair.

But all hopes fade when a couple of thugs enter the scene and hold them hostage. Thug No. 1 is incensed over the loss of his motorcycle, and the non-events which then transpire are loud, tiresome and ugly. It seems every other utterance is one of today's favorite four-letter words.

What is unfortunate about this misplaced production is that two excellent Canadian actors, Sheila McCarthy ("I've Heard The Mermaids Singing") and Elias Koteas ("Malarek") are totally wasted. Only McCarthy rises above the vulgarity — she has nothing to do and little to say! —*Prat.*

Cold Feet

Hollywood An Avenue Pictures release. Produced by Cassian Elwes. Executive producer, Cary Brokaw. Coproducer, Mary McLaglen. Directed by Robert Dornhelm. Screenplay, Tom McGuane, Jim Harrison; camera (Deluxe color), Bryan Duggan; editors, David Rawlins, Debra McDermott; music, Tom Bahler; sound, Robert J. Anderson; production design, Bernt Capra; art direction, Cory Kaplan; costumes, Carol Wood. Reviewed at Wadsworth Theater, L.A., May 17, 1989. (In Cannes Film Festival Market.) MPAA Rating: R. Running time: **91 MIN.**
Monte . . . . .Keith Carradine
Maureen . . . . .Sally Kirkland
Kenny . . . . .Tom Waits
Buck . . . . .Bill Pullman
Sheriff . . . . .Rip Torn
Laura . . . . .Kathleen York
Store owner . . . . .Macon McCalman
Airline passenger . . . . . . .Bob Mendelsohn
Vet. . . . . .Vincent Schiavelli
Rosemary . . . . .Amber Bauer
Cowboy in bar . . . . .Tom McGuane
Bartender . . . . .Jeff Bridges

■ Tom McGuane and Jim Harrison collaborated on the script of "Cold Feet" in 1976 by correspondence, so maybe the Postal Service should be blamed for losing some of their mail. The offbeat, offputting result seems to have some pages missing. It is rife with incongruities and uncertainties of tone.

This misfired Avenue Pictures release is a marginal b.o. entry.

Filmed in McGuane's Montana hometown of Paradise Valley, with McGuane playing a cowboy barfly and pal Jeff Bridges making an unbilled appearance tending

bar, "Cold Feet" is set in the same turf the writer used in his script for the underrated 1975 film "Rancho Deluxe."

This film about the odd relationships among a trio of petty criminals aims to be a darker comedy than "Rancho," but the dark elements overwhelm the comedy.

When a film starts with a quack veterinarian in Mexico sewing a box of stolen emeralds into a live stallion, and then being shot by a hit man in the operating room, you know it's going to have some problems sustaining a coherent tone.

The hit man, played by Tom Waits, is so unnerving that his menace kills the chances for the whimsical character comedy in which McGuane thrives. Keith Carradine and Sally Kirkland, as Waits' reluctant partners in crime, are hopelessly overwhelmed by his maniacal presence.

The three characters are so silly it's hard to get interested in their romantic tangles, or to believe Carradine when he talks vaguely about still having a few ideals. The only evidence is that he wants to settle down to a quiet life on the ranch, coveting his brother's wife and being sort of nice to his daughter.

At least the film is unpredictable. Under Robert Dornhelm's direction, however, the characters (Waits excepted) never develop fully, and the script isn't inventive or funny enough to overcome the story's hybrid nature.

Lensing by Bryan Duggan is attractive, and Tom Bahler's music is evocative. Other tech credits are pro.—*Mac.*

Blood And Sand
(SPANISH)

Cannes An Overseas Filmgroup presentation of José Frade production. Produced by José Frade. Directed by Javier Elorrieta. Screenplay by Rafael Azcona, Ricardo Franco, Thomas Fucci, based on novel by Vicente Blasco Ibanez; camera (Eastmancolor) Antonio Rios; editor, Juan Antonio Pio; music, Jesus Gluck; production design; Luis Arguelo. Reviewed at Cannes Film Festival (Market), May 17, 1989. Running time: **117 MIN.**
Juan Gallardo . . . . .Christopher Rydell
Dona Sol . . . . .Sharon Stone
Carmen . . . . .Ana Torrent
Chiripa . . . . .Antonio Flores
Juan's uncle . . . . .Simon Andreu
Juan's manager . . . .José Luis de Villalonga
Juan's trainer/bandillero . . . .Tony Fuentes
(English soundtrack)

■ Producer José Frade has claimed his "Blood And Sand" is the first truly Spanish film version of Vicente Blasco Iba-

nez' famous novel. Frade's claim turns out to be empty. His picture is about as Spanish as Coke spiked with Fundador brandy.

The new version of "Blood And Sand" was shot with English (American) dialog and an American-Spanish cast in and around the bullrings of Madrid, Jerez and Sevilla. The bullfighting shown is cleansed of all blood except that shed by a couple of hu-

1922 Version
(B&W)

"Jesse L. Lasky presents Rudolph Valentino," the billing reads, "In a Fred Niblo production." Lila Lee and Nita Naldi head the supporting company. The picture is adapted by June Mathis from the novel by Blasco Ibanez and the play by Tom Cuching. At the New York Rivoli Aug. 6, 1922.
Juan Gallardo . . . . .Rudolph Valentino
Carmen .Lila Lee
Dona Sol . . . . .Nita Naldi
El Nacional . . . . .George Field
Plumitas . . . . .Walter Long
Senora Agustas . . . . .Rose Rosanova
Antonio . . . . .Leo White
Don Joselito . . . . .Charles Belcher
Potaje .Jack Winn
El Carnacione . . . . .Marie Martsini
Garabata . . . . .Gilbert Clayton
El Pontelliro . . . . .Harry Lamont
Marquise de Guevera . . . . .George Periolat
Dr. Ruiz . . . . .Sidney De Gray
Don Jose . . . . .Fred Becker

mans. The mortal *espada* entry in the bull's neck at the Moment Of Truth is never seen. The actual excitement of the *corrida* is

1941 Version

20th-Fox release of Darryl F. Zanuck production; associate producer, Robert T. Kane. Stars Tyrone Power; features Linda Darnell, Rita Hayworth. Directed by Rouben Mamoulian. Screenplay, Jo Swerling; based on novel by Vicente Blasco Ibanez; camera (Technicolor), Ernest Palmer and Ray Rennahan; editor, Robert Bischoff; Technicolor director, Natalie Kalmus. Previewed at Four Star, L.A., May 19, 1941. Running time: **123 MIN.**
Carmen Espinosa . . . . .Linda Darnell
Dona Sol . . . . .Rita Hayworth
Senora Augustas . . . . .Nazimova
Manolo de Palma . . . . .Anthony Quinn
Garabato . . . . .J. Carrol Naish
Nacional . . . . .John Carradine
Encarnacion . . . . .Lynn Bari
Natalio Curro . . . . .Laird Cregar
Guitarist . . . . .Vicente Gomez
Antonio Lopez . . . . .William Montague
Captain Pierre Lauren . . . . .George Reeves
Don Jose Alvarez . . . . . .Pedro de Cordoba
Pedro Espinosa . . . . . . .Fortunio Bonanova
Priest . . . . .Victor Killian
La Pulga . . . . .Michael Morris
Pablo Gomez . . . . .Charles Stevens
Carmen (as child) . . . . ,. . . .Ann Todd

reproduced only in a series of beautifully executed *veronicas* with the cape drawing magnificent bulls in ever smaller circles around a stand-in for Christopher Rydell's Juan.

What is left to tell of Blasco Ibanez' novel is told with plodding care and brief sex scenes between Rydell (who is better when clad in his Suit Of Light and looking haughty) and Sharon Stone. Stone appears to be not much more than a pudgy-faced teenager with a body that one might say strips well.

The beauty, symmetry and finely tuned dance of death of a bullfight at its best is sensed only via an introductory black & white newsreel clip. The rest of this ''Blood And Sand'' is, sad to say, pure bull, even if Tony Fuentes and José Luis de Villalonga put in brave performances and Jesus Gluck has built a strong score around excerpts from the works of Spain's best old and newer composers. —*Kell.*

Night Visitor
(Never Cry Devil)

Chicago   An MGM/UA release from United Artists of a Premiere Pictures Corp. production. Produced by Alain Silver. Executive producers, Tom Broadbridge, Shelley E. Reid. Directed by Rupert Hitzig. Screenplay, Randal Visovich; camera (color), Peter Jansen; editor, Glenn Erickson; music, Parmer Fuller; production design, Jon Rothschild; sound, Bill Oliver. Reviewed at the Randhurst Theater, Chicago, May 13, 1989. MPAA Rating: R. (In Cannes Film Festival Market.) Running time: **93 MIN.**
Ron Devereaux . . . . Elliott Gould
Captain Crane . . . . Richard Roundtree
Zachary Willard . . . . Allen Garfield
Stanley Willard . . . . Michael J. Pollard
Billy Colton . . . . Derek Rydall
Kelly Fremont . . . . Teresa Van Der Woude
Lisa Grace . . . . Shannon Tweed
Mrs. Coulton . . . . Brooke Bundy
Det. Dolan . . . . Kathleen Bailey
Dr. Lawrence . . . . Henry Gibson

■ **Despite a plot that involves devil worship, hookers, ritual murder and voyeurism, ''Night Visitor'' is remarkably dull. Picture is likely to sleepwalk through theatrical release and head straight to the video store.**

Tale of a high school boy (Derek Rydall) who witnesses his obnoxious, nasal-spray sniffing history teacher slaughtering the beautiful call girl who lives next door in a satanic rite and then can't get the police to believe his story has plenty of exploitable elements, but they are never used to advantage.

Instead, the outrageous material is treated in a fairly realistic manner, resulting in lengthy exposition and several tedious subplots. Even the occasional outbreaks of sex and violence are handled in a surprisingly restrained manner.

Only real exploitation going on here is the casting of a handful of well-known actors, including Henry Gibson in a cameo as a police expert, Richard Roundtree as the investigating detective and Elliott Gould as an old family friend who returns to help the troubled teen. Gould is the nominal topliner though his screen time is minimal.

Allen Garfield and Michael J. Pollard provide the only entertaining moments, camping it up as the bargain basement satanist and his half-witted brother/evil assistant. —*Brin.*

Warlock

London   A New World Pictures production. Executive producer, Arnold Kopelson. Produced and directed by Steve Miner. Screenplay, David Twohy; camera (color), David Eggby; editor, David Finfer; production design, Roy Forge Smith; art direction, Gary Steele; costume design, Louise Frogley; sound, Lee Strosnider, James M. Tanenbaum; assistant director, Matt Earl Beesley. Reviewed at Century Preview Theater, London, May 9, 1989. (In Cannes Film Festival Market.) Running time: **102 MIN.**
Giles Redferne . . . . Richard E. Grant
The warlock . . . . Julian Sands
Kassandra . . . . Lori Singer
Chas . . . . Kevin O'Brien
Mennonite . . . . Richard Kuse
Daughter-in-law . . . . Juli Burkhart
Farmer . . . . Chip Johnson
Pastor . . . . David Carpenter
Fastor's wife . . . . Anna Levine

■ **''Warlock'' is an attempt to concoct a pic from a pinch of occult chiller, a dash of fantasy thriller and a splash of ''stalk 'n' slash.'' But what could have been a heady brew falls short, despite some gusto thesping from Richard E. Grant and Lori Singer.**

The slightly confused nature of the film, combined with a lack of big-pull names indicates little box-office promise, though good marketing could create a buzz.

The brave casting of two English actors in lead roles — both regarded as up-and-coming talent in the U.K. — pays off, and helmer-producer Steve Miner shows admirable restraint, focusing more on the esoteric and arcane than the plain gore.

Pics opens in the Masschusetts Bay colony in 1691 where a contemptuous warlock (Julian Sands) is being readied for execution. But with a bit of nifty hocus-pocus, both he and witch-hunter Richard E. Grant are sent to 1988 L.A.

Sands soon gets back to his nasty habits — including chopping off a finger, gouging out eyes and skinning a child — as he pursues the magical book the ''Grand Grimoire.'' Naturally enough, the world would be destroyed should he find the book.

Waitress Lori Singer meets Sands when he crashes through a window into her house. After he puts an aging spell on her, she teams up with Grant to try to kill the warlock.

Their chase takes them to a showdown in a Boston cemetery, where Singer cleverly kills Sands by injecting him with salt water. Warlocks, we are told, hate salt.

Nicholas Meyer's ''Time After Time'' (1980), in which Jack The Ripper is chased through modern San Francisco, was a better example of a baddy being chased through time, but suffered from the same problem as ''Warlock.'' They're both uncomfortable mixtures of thriller and gore.

The English actors give their roles a fine ''out of place'' quality, which is needed. Sands virtually walks through his part, though Grant is excellent as the softspoken witch-hunter. Singer merely has to wear short skirts and act spunky in the first half of the film, but proves to be made of stronger stuff as the pic wears on.

Miner directs ably but didn't pull away from some of the horror clichés. Other technical credits are fine, though some special effects don't quite work.

Pic is worth seeing for an excellent final scene. Singer buries the evil ''Grand Grimoire'' in the middle of the massive Bonneville Salt Flats, then drives away across the brilliant white salt desert. —*Adam.*

Welcome Home

Cannes   A Columbia Picures and Rank Organisation presentation of Martin Ransohoff production. Produced by Martin Ransohoff. Executive producer, Don Carmody. Directed by Franklin J. Schaffner. Screenplay, Maggie Kleinman; camera (Eastmancolor), Fred J. Koenekamp; editor, Bob Swink; music, no credit given; title song sung by Willie Nelson; production design, Dan Yarhi, Dennis Davenport; assistant director, Don Granberry; casting, Lynn Stalmaster (Canada, Stuart Aikins). Reviewed at Cannes Film Festival (Market), May 17, 1989. Running time: **87 MIN.**
Jake . . . . Kris Kristofferson
Sarah . . . . JoBeth Williams
Jake's father . . . . Brian Keith
Woody . . . . Sam Waterston
Colonel Barnes . . . . Trey Wilson
Dwayne . . . . . J.J. (John Marshall Jones Jr.)
Tyler . . . . Thomas Wilson Brown
Leang . . . . Kieu Chinh (Nguyen)
   Also with: Lela Ivey, Jamie Jones, Jeremy Ratchford, Norah Grant, Bill Lynn.

■ **A fine opportunity to explore the emotional conflict and military-political hush-hush regarding the unexpected reappearance of U.S. soldiers record-** ed as dead in Vietnam or Cambodia is missed almost totally in Franklin J. Schaffner's ''Welcome Home.'' The picture comes out as mostly soap, headed for the homevid drain.

Kris Kristofferson looks suitably haggard and tired as Lt. Jake Robbins, who returns to Vermont after 17 years in Cambodia. He was shot down there and put in a POW camp. He had been reported dead even as he escaped to a more pleasant isolation. Although surrounded by the Khmer Rouge, Jake settled down to married village life with Cambodian Leang who bore him two children.

It is not until he wakes up in a New York State Air Force hospital that Jake remembers that he had just married his American sweetheart Sarah (mournfully played by JoBeth Williams) before he set out on his Far East tour of duty. He is told that she is now remarried and lives happily in Vermont with her second husband and 17-year-old son, who is actually Jake's.

The military fights to keep Jake from ''coming back to life.'' This would jeopardize their secret negotiations with the Vietnamese for the release of other U.S. servicemen listed as dead although still held as POWS. Jake, however, feels he must at least see his son, so he bungles on to the Vermont scene where he upsets everybody and nearly destroys the happiness of his now widowed father (Brian Keith) and Sarah's new family (Sam Waterston and Thomas Wilson Brown).

Having accomplished enough misery (don't worry, it eventually is repaired), Jake again defeats the military, this time by going back to the Far East. Leang has died, but their two kids are doing just fine and are happy as larks when Jake returns with them to Vermont to settle down with Granddad and with Sarah's family as their next-door neighbors.

An uninspired screenplay does not help Schaffner in making the film forward more than sluggishly. The plot and subplot (a U.S. senator is brought in to help defeat the military) flounder in shallow waters. Willie Nelson sings the title tune on a soundtrack that is otherwise soapily sentimental or gushily dramatic. —*Kell.*

Nobody's Perfect

Cannes   An August Entertainment presentation of Panorama Film Intl./Just Betzer production in association with SAP. Produced by Benni Korzen. Executive producers, Steven Ader, Dennis Spiegelman. Directed by Robert Kaylor. Screenplay, Annie Korzen, Joel Block, based on story by Steven Ader; camera (Eastmancolor), Claus Loof; editor, Robert Gordon; music, Robert Randles; music supervision, David Chackler; production design-art direction, Gilbert Wong; Don Maskovich; costumes, Lennie Barin. Reviewed at Cannes Film Festival (Market), May 17, 1989. No MPAA Rating. Running time: **91 MIN.**

Stephen/Stephanie	Chad Lowe
Shelly	Gail O'Grady
Andy	Patrick Breen
Jackie	Kim Flowers
Tennis coach	Vitas Gerulaitis
Doctor	Robert Vaughn
Professor Lucci	Annie Korzen

Also with: Eric Bruskotter, Todd Schaefer, Mariann Aalda, Marcia Karr, Nikky Lusty, Devon Kaylor.

■ "Nobody's Perfect" takes its title from Joe E. Brown's exit line in Billy Wilder's "Some Like It Hot." The theme of Robert Kaylor's little Californian youth comedy also has somebody in drag in explosive contact with an unsuspecting member of the truly feminine gender. The fun may not be of classic proportions, but it should work the picture into cinemas catering to the teenage trade, with neat results.

Chad Lowe, Rob's kid brother, puts on a wig and make-up when shyness keeps him from getting as close as he would like to Gail O'Grady, his prep school classmate who now accepts him as her roommate. She does so mostly to get rid of a dumb-ox suitor. As alternately Stephen and Stephanie, Lowe digs into his parts with wit and charm and never overdoes any of his acts.

He would seem so far to have less in the way of romantic good looks than brother Rob, but obviously is out to prove himself the better actor. He may well be.

As Shelly, the object of his affection, O'Grady is more of a bland blond, but she does have a fresh face. A smoothly developing screenplay and no-nonsense direction give everybody in the cast a chance to shine, if ever so briefly, as do Robert Vaughn and tennis veteran Vitas Gerulaitis in cameos.

The good, clean fun is spiced with a few saucy witticisms to please such adults who may wander in. —*Kell.*

No Holds Barred

Cannes   A New Line Cinema release of a Shane production. (Intl. sales, Filmstar.) Executive producers, Vince McMahon, Hulk Hogan. Co-executive producer, Richard Glover. Produced by Michael Rachmil. Directed by Thomas J. Wright. Screenplay, Dennis Hackin; camera (Metrocolor), Frank Beascoechea; editor, Tom Pryor; music, Jim Johnston; sound (Dolby), Scott Smith; produc-

tion design, James Shanahan; set decoration, Lynn Wolverton; production manager, Robert Anderson; assistant director, John Hockridge; stunt coordinator, Buck McDancer; additional editor, William Essary; additional music, Richard Stone; associate producer, Michael M. Donnell; casting, Karen Rea. Reviewed at Cannes Film Festival (Market), May 17, 1989. MPAA Rating: PG-13. Running time: **91 MIN.**

Rip	Hulk Hogan
Brell	Kurt Fuller
Samantha Moore	Joan Severance
Zeus	Tom (Tiny) Lister
Randy	Mark Pellegrino
Charlie	Bill Henderson
Ordway	Charles Levin
Unger	David Palmer
Neanderthal	Stan (The Lariat) Hansen
Sadie	Armelia McQueen

Also with: Jesse (The Body) Ventura, Gene Okerlund, Howard Finkel.

■ A disappointing big-screen vehicle for wrestling champ Hulk Hogan, "No Holds Barred" should nonetheless bring out the Hulkster's legions of fans to generate good openings but wobbly legs this summer for New Line.

Despite pro wrestling's renewed popularity in recent years, the films about grapplers have all flopped, even with casts including Sylvester Stallone, Roddy Piper and Sgt. Slaughter.

Here Hogan plays himself, still the World Wrestling Federation champ (pic's executive producer is WWF's head honcho Vince McMahon). He's named Rip for story's sake. He strikes the same poses, makes the same grimaces and uses the same holds the fans are accustomed to, and is even accompanied by the same announcers (in cameos): Mean Gene Okerlund, Jesse (The Body) Ventura and Howard Finkel.

Extremely lame plotline has tyrannical tv network boss Kurt Fuller unable to coax Rip away from a rival web. Fuller's countermove is to telecast live tough-guy contests, with muscular and mean black wrestler Tiny Lister emerging the winner. In clichéd fashion, Rip must meet Lister (as Zeus) in the octagonal ring while a race against the clock goes on to find his kidnapped girlfriend (Joan Severance) or Rip will have to "throw" the match to save her pretty neck.

Fans are bound to be disappointed by the uninteresting wrestling action on display here, poorly photographed to boot. Toilet humor abounds and far too much footage is devoted to Fuller's wimpy, bumbling henchmen Charles Levin and David Palmer.

Best scenes, sure to please smallfry, are when Hogan as Rip takes his rassling into the street and

applies it comicbook-style to smash up limos and anything else in his way.

Unfortunately, Hogan's acting is poor, his line readings lacking any conviction. His talented and beautiful leading lady Severance has to carry all their scenes together, including a misjudged homage to Frank Capra's famous Walls Of Jericho bedroom scene in "It Happened One Night."

As archvillain, Fuller closely resembles Bill Murray in "Scrooged," but overacts unbearably. Lister, with frightening crossed eyes, is physically right but stuck with unfortunate stereotyping, as is the rest of the film's black cast. An engaging and funny supporting role is essayed by another pro wrestling champ, Stan (The Lariat) Hansen. —*Lor.*

La cintura
(The Belt)
(ITALIAN)

Cannes   A Medusa Distribuzione release of a San Francisco Film/Metrofilm coproduction in association with Reteitalia. Produced by Giovanni Bertolucci, Galliano Juso. Directed by Giuliana Gamba. Screenplay, Gloria Malatesta, Francesca Archibugi, Claudio Sbarigia, based on Alberto Moravia's novel; camera (color), Luigi Verga; editor, Carlo Bartolucci; music, Ron; art direction, Claudio Cinini. Reviewed at the Cannes Film Festival (Market), May 17, 1989. Running time: **93 MIN.**

Bianca	Eleonora Brigliadori
Vittorio	James Russo

■ Marketed as a sexy s&m picture, but based on an Alberto Moravia novel with some pretense to seriously examine human behavior, Giuliana Gamba's "The Belt" is neither fish nor fowl. It's too tame for voyeurs and too insipid for connoisseurs.

It is finished off by casting two nearly unwatchable actors as the loving couple. Pic failed to score at the Italo boxoffice this season.

Tv personality Eleonora Brigliadori gave the film some notoriety when she sued a men's magazine that published risqué photos, thereby getting her in trouble with the network. The suit was dismissed in court and seems to have had little effect commercially.

Brigliadori plays Bianca, a neurotic young lady from a nice middle-class family. She passes from an affair with a married college prof to one with his American student Vittorio (James Russo), who marries her. Something is wrong with their relationship: Bianca discovers she gets turned on by being beaten up.

Both partners are horrified when they realize their attraction to sadomasochism. This doesn't stop Bianca from giving Vittorio the fatal belt for his birthday, a scene audience has been waiting for. Like most of pic's eros, it is handled with more reserve than most viewers are led to expect. This is the kind of film where everyone seems to make love with underwear on.

Story is framed by a ridiculous court trial, where Bianca is suing her husband for beating her. The female judge, initially ill-disposed to the brutal wife-beater, hears the story and advises the couple to reconcile, which they do.

James Russo gets so few closeups he is practically invisible as a character, his female costar is all too visible with her sudden bouts of hysteria, which seems to originate less in her neurosis than a bad script. Both are grating.

Technically pic is on the coy and arty side. —*Yung.*

Diamond Skulls
(BRITISH)

Cannes   A Film Four Intl. and British Screen presentation of a Working Title production. Produced by Tim Bevan. Directed by Nick Broomfield. Screenplay, Tim Rose Price; camera (Technicolor), Michael Coulter; editor, Rodney Holland; music, Hans Zimmer; sound, John Midgley; production design, Jocelyn James; associate producer, Jane Frazer; production manager, Lorraine Goodman; assistant director, Waldo Roeg; casting, Lucy Boulting. Reviewed at Cannes Film Festival (Market), May 16, 1989. Running time: **87 MIN.**

Sir Hugo Buckton	Gabriel Byrne
Lady Virginia Buckton	Amanda Donohoe
Hugo's father	Michael Hordern
Hugo's mother	Judy Parfitt
Jamie	Douglas Hodge
Rebecca	Sadie Frost
Peter	Struan Rodger
Exeter	Ian Carmichael

■ A stylish melodrama about sex and violence among the British aristocracy, "Diamond Skulls" never quite delivers the punches it promises. However, it has enough solid elements to intrigue audiences willing to enter this world of titled luxury and minimal morals.

Gabriel Byrne, looking more than ever like Prince Charles, is Sir Hugo, an ex-guards officer, now in business. He has a lovely wife (the delectable Amanda Donohoe) of whom he's extremely jealous, suspecting her of having an affair with an Argentine business colleague (for the British, with the Falklands War a recent memory, such a liaison is definitely a no-no).

One night, after a drunken dinner with his friends, Hugo is driving someone else's car when he hits a young woman, fatally injuring her. He and his friends leave her to die, though one of them, Jamie, the car owner, wants to report the accident.

Hugo is unburdened by guilt, and just wants everyone to keep quiet. But Jamie, who's having an affair with Hugo's sister Rebecca, threatens to spill the beans, and the friends are forced to silence him.

The plot itself is on the thin side, and Tim Rose Price's screenplay could certainly have used more punch. Nevertheless, former docu director Nick Broomfield makes a fine cross to feature films, showing style and confidence. He packs plenty of sex and intrigue into the pic, though he does tend to whip up unfulfilled suspense.

Donohoe gives another hot performance as the elegant Virginia whose name belies her actions. Struan Rodger also is effective as Hugo's somewhat sinister friend Peter, while Sadie Frost makes her mark as Hugo's sexually active sister. Veteran Michael Hordern is amusing as Hugo's titled father, though comedy actor Ian Carmichael is totally wasted as the family butler.

Michael Coulter's camerawork is tops, and the helicopter shots that bookend the picture are classy. If more time had been spent on beefing up the screenplay, this might have been a knockout drama; it isn't that, but it's certainly never dull, though the amoral ending will strike many as being exceptionally cynical. The title is meaningless. —*Strat.*

Zilch
(NEW ZEALAND)

Cannes A Park Avenue Prods. and Vardex Group production, in association with the New Zealand Film Commission. (Intl. sales, NZFC.) Produced by Amanda Hocquard, Richard Riddiford. Directed by Riddiford. Screenplay, Riddiford, Jonathan Dowling; camera (color), Murray Milne; editor, Chris Todd; music, Chris Knox. Reviewed at Cannes Film Festival (Market), May 16, 1989. Running time: **95 MIN.**

Sam ....Michael Mizrahi
Anna...................Lucy Sheehan

■ **This modest offering from New Zealand — only new pic for N.Z. at Cannes following a downturn over the past year — is an offbeat semi-comedy that works well enough but hasn't the strength for theatrical success.**

Pic follows the rather haphazard exploits of Michael Mizrahi, skinheaded telephone tolls operator-cum-double bass player, who enjoys listening in on and taping phone conversations (although the purpose of keeping all the tapes is never made clear).

He happens upon a plot to blackmail a minister by a construction company keen to win a tender for building a harbor crossing. Blackmail is by way of videoing the minister getting his kicks by standing naked in a shower while Lucy Sheehan, Mizrahi's friend and occasional lover, pelts him with tomatoes.

That's complicated by the presence of another video detailing flaws in the company's plans. Much of the film thus follows the pursuit of both videos while Mizrahi tries to piece together the plot. Audience is doing much the same thing for the confusing first half-hour.

There's some good comedy while all this untangles but not much else that stands out in this low-key offering. Acting is okay, with Mizrahi's oddball character leading the cast competently. Tech credits are average. Relevance of the film's title is elusive.

Mark this one down as a good learning experience for first-time feature director Richard Riddiford, and a passable small-screen entry. —*Doch.*

Identity Crisis

Cannes A Block & Chip production. (Intl. sales, Manley Prods.) Produced and directed by Melvin Van Peebles. Screenplay, Mario Van Peebles; camera (Precision color), Jim Hinton; editor, Victor Kanefsky, Melvin Van Peebles; music, E. Pearson; costumes, Bernard Johnson. Reviewed at Cannes Film Festival (Market), May 16, 1989. No MPAA Rating. Running time: **90 MIN.**

Chilly D. ....Mario Van Peebles
Sebastian ....Ilan Mitchell-Smith
Roxy ....Shelly Burch
Yves Malmaison ....Richard Fancy
Also with: Nicholas Kepros, Richard Clarke, Rick Aviles, Tab Thacker.

■ **"Identity Crisis" is a fast-lane action comedy of the absurd, written, produced, directed by and starring father and son team Melvin and Mario Van Peebles.**

This nonstop parade of impossible characters and assorted NYC outrages makes for enjoyable, unpretentious dementia. The Van Peebles should win new fans if "Crisis" gets the right handling.

Story spins around the sudden death by poisoning of French fashion designer Yves Malmaison (Richard Fancy) and his subsequent reincarnation in the youthful body of black rapper Chilly D. (Mario Van Peebles), who happens to fall off a ledge at the same moment.

Waking up in his new body, Yves finds his son Sebastian (Ilan Mitchell-Smith), a yuppie with a heart of gold who is slightly embarrassed by Dad's clear proclivities for his own sex. Once convinced it's really Pop, Sebastian embarks on a wild search for the murderers, a gang of evil Indians in turbans who are in cahoots with Uncle Max to take over the house of Malmaison. Only trouble is, every time Yves gets hit in the head (frequently), he reverts to Chilly D.'s personality — and vice versa.

Pic has a good time romping through gay bars, way-out clubs for women mudwrestlers, rap concerts, jails, etc. The Van Peebles keep the gags coming (especially from talented comedian Mario), fearlessly spoofing gays, blacks, women and about anyone else who runs through the film with no light hand. Only the finale, a chase-and-fight scene, falls into the routine and leaves a predictable taste pic doesn't deserve.

Music track is spunky, thesps well cast, and lensing lively and colorful. —*Yung.*

Relentless

Cannes A New Line Cinema release of a Cinetel Films presentation of a Hertzberg, Hansen, Smith production. Executive producers, Paul Hertzberg, Lisa M. Hansen. Produced by Howard Smith. Directed by William Lustig. Screenplay, "Jack T.D. Robinson" (Phil Alden Robinson); camera (Foto-Kem color), James Lemmo; editor, David Kern; music, Jay Chattaway; sound (Dolby), Craig Felburg; production design, Gene Abel; set decoration, Ann Job; assistant director, Whitney Hunter; stunt coordinator-2d unit director, Spiros Razatos; 2d unit camera, Chuck Colwell; casting, Annelise Collins, Susan Vash. Reviewed at Cannes Film Festival (Market), May 18, 1989. No MPAA Rating. Running time: **92 MIN.**

Buck Taylor ....Judd Nelson
Bill Malloy ....Robert Loggia
Sam Dietz ....Leo Rossi
Carol Dietz ....Meg Foster
Todd Arthur ....Patrick O'Bryan
Francine ....Mindy Seger
Capt. Blakely ....Ron Taylor
Ike Taylor ....Beau Starr
Carmen ....Angel Tompkins
Angela Taylor ....Harriet Hall
Also with: Ken Lerner, Frank Pesce, George (Buck) Flower, Armand Mastroianni.

■ **"Relentless" is a riveting, splendidly acted suspense thriller. New Line can look forward to good returns and super word-of-mouth this fall for the Cinetel picture.**

Phil Alden Robinson's fresh and invigorating script strikes a careful balance in focusing not just on maniacal killer Judd Nelson's murderous escapades but also putting at film's center the story of dedicated cop Leo Rossi and his supportive wife Meg Foster.

Format follows a pure Hitchcock suspense pattern: The audience immediately knows that Nelson is the socalled "Sunset Killer" murdering L.A. denizens seemingly at random and leaving snotty messages for the police on telephone book pages.

With brief flashbacks and other clues, the reason for his psychotic behavior gradually becomes clear to both the viewer and Rossi, who is a recently promoted police detective anxious to go all out to find the killer while his experienced partner (Robert Loggia in a solid turn) moves slowly. Climax set at Rossi's home is spellbinding, with excellent visual imagery to round off the story in satisfying fashion.

Director William Lustig keeps the screws tightened for an exciting, sometimes scary ride, while allowing for considerable warmth to be generated in the idiosyncratic family scenes involving Rossi, Foster and their young son.

Nelson provides shading and control to keep the maniac role from going over the top, succeeding in winning the viewer's understanding, if not sympathy. Rossi, in his best screen assignment since costarring in "Heart Like A Wheel," is a breath of fresh air to the recently overexposed police detective genre and should be getting bigger and better parts on the basis of this performance and a telling one in "The Accused."

Tech credits are fine and pic benefits from a full-bodied score by Jay Chattaway.—*Lor.*

Happy Together

Cannes A Vidmark Intl. presentation of an Apollo Film production. Produced by Jere Henshaw. Directed by Mel Damski. Screenplay, Craig J. Nevius; camera (Eastmancolor), Joe Pennella; editor, O. Nicholas Brown; music, Robert Folk; production design, Marcia Hinds; costumes, Dona Granata; choreography, Jeff Calhoun; associate producer, Jeffrey Fleisig; production manager, Russell H. Chesley; casting, Caro Jones. Reviewed at Cannes Film Festival (Market), May 15, 1989. MPAA Rating: PG-13. Running time: **96 MIN.**

Christopher Wooden ....Patrick Dempsey
Alexandra Page ....Helen Slater
Gooseflesh ....Dan Schneider
Slash ....Kevin Hardesty
Denny Dollenbacher ....Maris Weyers
Ruth Carpenter ....Barbara Babcock
Luisa Dellacova ....Gloria Hayes
Also with: Brad Pitt, Aaron Harnick, Ron Sterling, Eric Lumbard, Michael D. Clarke, Wendy Lee Marconi, Yvette Rambo.

■ **Patrick Dempsey and Helen Slater pour their considerable energy and talent into "Happy**

Together" and may win some theatrical audiences for Mel Damski's youth comedy about the duo's enforced (through a computer error) cohabitation of one dorm room in a California college.

Damski, unfortunately, too often wallows in farce rather than in exploration of his story's romantic comedy potential. This leaves Dempsey and Slater no chance of ever emerging as truly convincing let alone engaging characters.

Dempsey is the rather shy boy who has come to learn the craft of fiction writing but lacks sources of true inspiration via personal experience of suffering or joy. Slater is the extrovert drama class student who supplies him with both but has a hard time facing life beyond exuberant play-acting.

Slater is a jumping bean of sexuality, too, but also in this respect she is all show and no substance. This brings pain to Dempsey who is beginning to seek solace from a dorm neighbor, fat and (seemingly) jolly Gooseflesh (played sweetly by Dan Schneider) who has learned to live alone and like it.

After avalanches of musical cavorting (takeoffs of famous film dance numbers) and frenzied acting out of various common college occurrences, a happy ending is achieved for Dempsey and Slater. They are taken, in a written postscript, to more artistic struggle in New York, but by this time everything about them has been reduced to theatrical noises off.—*Kell.*

Erik
(CANADIAN)

Cannes   SC/Creswin release of SC Entertainment Corp. production. Executive producers, Syd Cappe, George Flak. Produced by Nicolas Stiliadis; associate producer, Angel Gonzalez; coproducer, Paco Alvarez. Written and directed by Michael Kennedy. Camera (color), Ludek Bogner; editor, Nick Rotundo; music, Mychael Danna; production design, John Dondertman; casting, Adriana Michel. Reviewed at Cannes Film Festival (Market), May 18, 1989. Running time: **90 MIN.**
Erik . . . . .Stephen McHattie
Liliana . . . . . . .Deborah Van Valkenburgh
The General . . . . .Aharon Ipale
   Also with: Ismael Carlo, Michael Champion, Dennis A. Pratt.

■ **This film opens with noble sentiments about political oppression, torture and assassination. What follows never lives up to the promise.**

Erik, a Vietnam veteran suffering from nightmares, finds himself in an unnamed South American country working as a mercenary for whichever side pays the most.

Oppression is everywhere, people whisper about "the dictatorship," and "the General" appears to be running everything, including the drug-smuggling business.

What follows is hopelessly confusing, highly predictable and never convincing. An enormous amount of shooting goes on and the body count is high. Erik (Stephen McHattie) is barely able to cope with it all and hardly seems to know what to do next. Even if he did, his performance would be no better. Deborah Van Valkenburgh appears from time to time as the inevitable photojournalist seeking out the truth who provides our hero with some relief.

Filmed in Mexico, the scenery looks good. The score is all rumble and crash. "Erik" is soon destined for pay-tv and video. —*Prat.*

Kokoda Crescent
(AUSTRALIAN)

Cannes   A Phillip Emanuel production. Produced by Emanuel. Directed by Ted Robinson. Screenplay, Patrick Cook; line producer, production manager, John Hipwell; camera (Eastmancolor), Dan Burstall; editor, Rob Gibson; music, Peter Best; sound, Sid Butterworth; production design, Les Binns; art direction, Stuart Menzies; casting, Liz Mullinar. Reviewed at Cannes Film Festival (Market), May 16, 1989. Running time: **83 MIN.**
Stan . . . . .Warren Mitchell
Russ . . . . .Bill Kerr
Alice . . . . .Ruth Cracknell
Margaret . . . . .Madge Ryan
Eric. . . . . .Martin Vaughan
Brett . . . . .Patrick Thompson
Policeman. . . . . .Steve Jacobs

■ **The talents of some of Australia's most estimable actors are squandered in "Kokoda Crescent," an anemic comedy-drama that ranks as one of the last and worst legacies of the Oz tax shelter era.**

Aussie distrib Village Roadshow will be hardpressed to extract any juice from this lemon. Outlook for the rest of the world is similarly bleak.

The blame can be apportioned equally among the participants. Patrick Cook, a clever cartoonist and satirist, wrote the screenplay, an absurd tale about three World War II vets who set out to avenge the death of one's grandson.

The kid — played by Patrick Thompson, son of thesp Jack Thompson — dies of a heroin overdose without exhibiting any of the symptoms of a junkie.

They suspect a crooked cop is the supplier. Their pleas for help to the media and a politician are spurned, so, after a minimal

amount of soul searching, the old-timers decide to mount a commando raid on the cop's heavily guarded mansion with the intention of killing him. A sense of morality is not this pic's strong suit, and it's sprinkled with gratuitous, puerile and offensive jokes and references to the Japanese, blacks and even the disabled.

The climax is bloody, ineptly handled, and as wildly implausible as what precedes it.

The less said about the overwrought performances, the better. If Ted Robinson's direction attempted to exert any control or method to the proceedings, it isn't evident. —*Dogo.*

Dead Poets Society

Hollywood   A Buena Vista release from Touchstone Pictures, in association with Silver Screen Partners IV. Produced by Steven Haft, Paul Junger Witt, Tony Thomas. Directed by Peter Weir. Screenplay, Tom Schulman; camera, (Duart color), John Seale; music, Maurice Jarre; sound (Dolby), Charles Wilborn; production design, Wendy Stites; art direction, Sandy Veneziano; set decoration, John Anderson; costume supervision, Marilyn Matthews; assistant director, Alan B. Curtiss; associate producer, Duncan Henderson; casting, Howard Feuer. Reviewed at Avco Cinema Center, Westwood, Calif., May 25, 1989. MPAA Rating: PG. Running time: **128 MIN.**
John Keating . . . . .Robin Williams
Neil Perry. . . . . .Robert Sean Leonard
Todd Anderson . . . . .Ethan Hawke
Knox Overstreet . . . . .Josh Charles
Charlie Dalton . . . . .Gale Hansen
Richard Cameron . . . . . . .Dylan Kussman
Steven Meeks . . . . .Allelon Ruggiero
Gerard Pitts . . . . .James Waterson
Mr. Nolan . . . . .Norman Lloyd
Mr. Perry. . . . . .Kurtwood Smith
Mrs. Perry . . . . .Carla Belver
McAllister . . . . .Leon Pownall

■ **A lyrical, gorgeous and tough evocation of the unsteady fires of youth, "Dead Poets Society" invites viewers to confront some central questions of their being at the same time competing distributors are releasing an avalanche of escapist fare.**

Summer release slot stacks the boxoffice odds against it, but quality and classic theme and treatment should make it a sturdy, if modest, performer for Disney's Touchstone label.

Pic is not so much about Robin Williams as an unconventional English teacher at a hardline New England prep school as it is about the youths he teaches and how the creative flames within them are kindled and then stamped out.

Williams' frequent absence from the screen and the sketchy, barely serviceable development of his character, Jack Keating, are likely to be the chief complaint of those who aren't swept up in pic's overall themes.

Director Peter Weir fills the screen with a fresh gang of compelling teenagers, led by Robert Sean Leonard as outgoing Neil Perry and balanced by Ethan Hawke as deeply withdrawn Todd Anderson.

Keating enters their rigidly traditional world (much as airman Adrian Cronauer entered the absurdly regimented Saigon Army base in "Good Morning, Vietnam", and has them literally rip out the pages of their hidebound textbooks in favor of his inventive didactics on the spirit of poetry.

Captivated by Keating's spirit, the influential Neil provokes his mates into reviving a secret club, the Dead Poets Society, that Keating led in his prep school days. Minus their teacher, the lads sneak off nights to a cave deep in the woods, where they begin with an invocation by Thoreau and then take turns reading favorite poets aloud.

Meanwhile the gifted, medical-school-bound Neil begins to pursue acting, his true aspiration, against the strenuous objections of his domineering father (Kurtwood Smith). Hope flares briefly, when Neil shines in the lead of "A Midsummer Night's Dream" at a neighboring campus, but is destroyed when his father yanks him permanently out of school.

Anytime anyone in "Dead Poets Society" dares to diverge from the rutted road, the consequences are swift and severe. That is the film's greatest strength — it's as brutally realistic as it is romantic — but it also may be its boxoffice downfall, as word of mouth about the very grim, tearstained segments surrounding Neil's eventual fate may deter summertime viewers.

Pic ends on a gritty, uncompromising high note, with a marvelous final image that will likely be indelibly imprinted in viewers' minds.

Message of Tom Schulman's resonant screenplay is that the subversive spirit ignited by Keating will continue to burn steadfastly, if quietly, among boys who will forever be members of the society of at least one dead poet.

Weir, who got bogged down in the climate of "Mosquito Coast," returns to form here among elements similar to his stirring "Gallipoli."

Camera (lenser is longtime collaborator John Seale) revels in the visual evocation of tradition, from the dark wood and dark suits of school corridors to the glorious images of autumn Vermont landscapes.

Story sings whenever Williams is onscreen. Most often his contribution is in zesty delivery of poetry and snappy rejoinders, and his imaginative approach to the boys.

Screen belongs just as often to Leonard, who as Neil has a quality of darting confidence mixed with hesitancy. Hawke, as the painfully shy Todd, gives a haunting performance.

Weir's direction can be heavy-handed. There is no missing the symbolism in the scene where a despondent Neil — naked in his room before an open window on a forbidding, wintry-cold world —

dons the crown of brambles from his Shakespeare play. It's the kind of thing that the younger audience, likely to be the most fervent respondents to this film, will drink up. —Daws.

Pink Cadillac

Hollywood A Warner Bros. Pictures release of a Malpaso production. Produced by David Valdes. Executive producer, Michael Gruskoff. Directed by Buddy Van Horn. Screenplay, John Eskow; camera (Technicolor), Jack N. Green; editor, Joel Cox; music, Steve Dorff; production design, Edward C. Carfagno; set decoration, Thomas L. Roysden; sound (Dolby), Willie D. Burton; assistant director, Matt Earl Beesley; casting, Phyllis Huffman. Reviewed at Raleigh Studios, L.A., May 22, 1989. MPAA Rating: PG-13. Running time: **122 MIN.**

Tommy Nowak . . . . Clint Eastwood
Lou Ann McGuinn . . . . . Bernadette Peters
Roy McGuinn . . . . Timothy Carhart
Waycross . . . . John Dennis Johnston
Alex . . . . Michael Des Barres
Ricky Z . . . . Geoffrey Lewis

Also with: William Hickey, Bill McKinney, Paul Benjamin, Frances Fisher, Jim Carrey, Mara Corday.

■ "Pink Cadillac" is mediocre duo-in-pursuit material only marginally brightened when Clint Eastwood parodies other personalities. Warner Bros. entry may be the weakest Eastwood release ever.

Here, to odd results, Eastwood tries to be both that laconic, stalwart persona and, strangely, kind of a pushover for an energetic damsel-in-distress (Bernadette Peters) with whom he develops little visible rapport and zero sexual chemistry.

The actor, still toned but by now considerably grey, doesn't seem to have his heart into playing it totally straight as a hard-edged bail bondsman's skip tracer who tracks down felons on the lam — Peters being one of the lucrative catches. Nor does he seem even slightly romantically inclined, though clearly that's what's intended in his pairing with Peters.

Peters plays a young mother living in a Sacramento trailer park who's fed up with her dull-witted husband's get-rich schemes — an Amway franchise and chinchilla farm among them — and is determined to escape. She does, in his precious convertible pink caddy which, unbeknownst to her, also happens to be where he and his drugged-out ex-con friends have stashed a quarter-million bucks in counterfeit bills.

Eastwood's adversaries are a bunch of survivalist types lead by

a stereotypical goon (Michael Des Barres) whose idea of toughening up his equally mentally impaired followers is to stand them against a backboard and shoot all around them with an automatic rifle to see if they'll wimp out.

In order to get their booty back, Peters' hubby (Timothy Carhart, in a thankless role) swipes the baby and brings her back to camp.

Eastwood, who reluctantly accepted the assignment to capture Peters and now finds he has to worry about a baby too, goes through the exploitative steps it takes to get her back with the enthusiasm of a government worker.

Peters is peppy and acts hysterical at the appropriate moments, though it's curious how she developed such a rapier wit considering her background and the circumstances.

Film's redeeming moments come from a number of funny Eastwood turns — striking silly poses as a disk jockey, clown and casino huckster and, rather amusingly, a lisping former Folsom prison inmate, all in an effort to foil his bait.

The only secondary character of note is Ricky Z (Geoffrey Lewis), known to Eastwood and others as a competent fake i.d. maker and hippie burnout from the '60s who is given some hilarious lines appropriate to anyone who has taken too much mescaline.

First-time scripter John Eskow has an ear for dialog and longtime Eastwood collaborator, director Buddy Van Horn, a good sense of actioner pacing, though these two elements don't mix well enough in this outing.

Whatever energy is sustained throughout the pic's 122 minutes comes about almost entirely from quick scene changes, an occasional laugh and a steady score of singable country western tunes.

Tech credits are fine. —Brit.

Igla
(The Needle)
(SOVIET)

Minneapolis A Kazakhfilm Studios release. Produced and directed by Rashid Nugmanov. Screenplay, Alexander Baranov and Bakhyt Kilibayev; camera (color), Murat Nugmanov; design, Murat Musin; music, Viktor Tsoi. Reviewed at Rivertown Intl. Film Festival, Minneapolis, May 5, 1989. Running time: **81 MIN.**

With: Viktor Tsoi, Marina Smirnova, Pyotr Mamonov, Aleksandr Baschirov.

■ The drug scene in the Soviet Union is as pernicious as it is in

other countries, and Soviet dealers are as venal and dangerous as their counterparts elsewhere. That's the conclusion one draws from "The Needle" by Rashid Nugmanov. While the low-budget film gives a fresh slant on Soviet society, it has slim prospects for U. S. distribution other than an occasional arthouse booking.

Main drawback is torpid pacing, which makes its 81 minutes seem much longer. This hasn't crimped its style in the USSR where 1,000 prints have spread Nugmanov's message throughout the land.

Heading the unschooled cast is Viktor Tsoi as Moro, a young vagrant who renews friendship with a former girlfriend, played by Marina Smirnova. The girl has become addicted to heroin. The youth's attempts to help her break her habit and his run-ins with dealers come acropper when he's knifed by a hit man.

Tsoi, a rock musician in his first film role, and Smirnova are believable as the principals. Technical credits are okay in view of Nugmanov's limited bankroll. Murat Nugmanov's camerawork is particularly impressive.

"The Needle" drew favorable responses from Rivertown Intl. Film Festival audiences, enhanced by the director's presence. —Rees.

Rembrandt Laughing

Minneapolis A Jon Jost release. Producers, Jost and Henry Rosenthal. Directed by Jost. Screenplay by Jost and den Darstellern; camera (color), Jost; sound, Alenka Pavlin, Rosenthal, Jon A. English, Jost; music, English. Reviewed at Walker Art Center, Minneapolis, May 8, 1989. Running time: **100 MIN.**

With: Jon A. English, Barbara Hammes, Jennifer Johanson, Ed Green, Nathaniel Dorsky, Jerry Barrish.

■ If there's a cult for independent filmmaker Jon Jost's work, it's the only conceivable market for his latest effort. "Rembrandt Laughing" is a mishmash of snips of conversation, much of it apparently improvised, and arty, desultory photography.

Focus is on a pair of ex-lovers five years after their breakup. In cinéma vérité fashion, the film follows their daily encounters with friends and associates. None of these dalliances is of more than passing interest to onlookers. In essence, nothing happens.

Given the material at hand, Jon A. English and Barbara Hammes are okay in the roles of the couple whose passion has cooled. The rest of the cast is adequate. The filmmaker's direction is superficial, and editing isn't evident. Jost is intrigued with endless lensing of soup cooking and sands shifting. When a seated character gets up and moves away, Jost keeps his camera grinding away at the empty chair. It may be art, but it isn't filmworthy. Film was shot on 16m and transferred to 35m.

Pic, preemed at the '89 Berlin Film Festival, was screened at the Walker Art Center as a sidebar to the '89 Rivertown Intl. Film Festival. —*Rees.*

Hotaru
(Firefly)
(JAPANESE)

Tokyo   A Toei release. Produced by Takeshi Motomura, Harumichi Otani. Directed by Koichi Kajima. Screenplay, Goro Hanawa, Kajima; camera (color), Masahiko Iimura; editor, Kioaki Saitoh; music, Masahide Sakuma; art direction, Tadayuki Kuwana; lighting, Shigeru Umeya; sound, Koichi Hayashi; assistant producers, Kazuyuki Satoh, Hikaru Kawase, Takashiro Mitome, Aimi Yoshikawa. Reviewed at Marunouchi Toei, Tokyo, April 27, 1989. Running time: **103 MIN.**

Kenji	Toshiro Yanagiba
Asako	Kaho Minami
Hideo Kiuchi	Hiroshi Fuse
Yoko	Kyoko Tsujisawa
Ninomiya	Tetsu Masoaka
Yokoyama	Takeshi Naito

■ **Japan is justly proud of its low crime rate and academic achievements, but "Hotaru" shows the country to be populated by dumbbells just waiting to be fleeced by bigger dumbbells.**

Take, for instance, the cunning scheme devised by the film's lowlife hero, Kenji. It consists of having his girlfriend, Asako, cajole men in the street into coming to his hole-in-the-wall bar where he charges an arm and a leg for drinks. Kenji has named his bar Kuro Neko, or Black Cat, anticipating that this symbol of bad luck will have a reverse psychological effect on his dopey customers, lulling them into a false sense of security and keeping them from running to the nearest policeman.

Kenji and his ilk must resort to increasingly elaborate stratagems to snooker each other. To avenge the killing of his boss, Kenji and an associate wait for the murderer in a toilet on board a train, rightly intuiting that their unsuspecting victim will come straight to them.

On the run from the police, Kenji hides out with Yoko, an old flame who convinces him that his current flame, Asako, no longer

wants to see him. Kenji fails to consider that a woman he dumped might be the teensiest bit self-serving. Makes you wonder how someone so naive could have lasted as a gangster.

Though set in the criminal underworld, it would not be incorrect to call "Hotaru" a "boy meets girl" film, even though the boy in question is a hardened criminal and the girl an employee of a place called Virgin Club.

The heroine retains the countenance and disposition of an angel even after she is sold by her boyfriend into prostitution and develops a drug habit.

The title of this feature, which is accompanied by the helpful French subtitle, "Ver Luisant," means "Firefly," and is a reference to the brief but luminous lives of the hero and heroine. It also gives an indication of how large their brains are. —*Bail.*

Zui Hou De Feng Kuang
(Desperation: The Last Frenzy)
(CHINESE)

Minneapolis   An Xi'an Film Studio release. Produced and directed by Zhou Xiaowen. Screenplay, Si Chengfeng; camera (color), Fen Wei; editor, Li Bing; music, Gue Feng; sound, Hui Dongzhi; set design, Lui Yichuan; costumes, Su Jianjun. Reviewed at Rivertown Intl. Film Festival, Minneapolis, May 13, 1989. Running time: **102 MIN.**

With: Zhang Jianming, Liu Xiaoning, Jing Lili, Zheng Jianhua, others.

■ **"Desperation: The Last Frenzy" is an eye-opener, a bang-bang Chinese action film that explodes many stereotypes of urban life in China today. Neither fish nor fowl — foreign art film nor Hollywood adventure pic, its potential outlets in the U.S. are limited, but as a solid attention-grabber, it's a sleeper that could pay dividends.**

Plot involves an intense manhunt for an escaped killer who has bumped off three people, including a police officer. Heading the chase is an Asian Clint Eastwood, a deadpan, no-nonsense copper whose tactics sometimes defy official sanction. There's no Charlie Chan posturing at work here.

Chinese crime detection systems — as up to date as those in the U.S. — employ computers, videotapes, helicopters and other sophisticated gear. As in the West, Chinese cops resent the paperwork and the public animosity.

Chase scenes are as hairy as any in American films, particularly one in which the quarry afoot is

pursued through city streets by the cop on a motorcycle. There's a bit too much coincidence in the police's frequent encounters with the desperado, bu the action is stark and believable for the most part. The ending is an absolute shocker.

Zhou Xiaowen's helming is top-notch, building suspense to a crescendo and holding the audience's interest throughout. Dynamic pacing makes the film's 102-minute running time pass quickly. Liu Xiaoning as the determined cop and Zhang Jianming as the killer are first-rate, and there are many fine performances in lesser roles.

Camerawork, sound and other technical efforts are of high quality. Subtitles are comprehensive, causing the viewer to miss part of the action. —*Rees.*

Hell High

New York   A JGM Enterprises release of a DGS presentation of a Grossman/Steinman production. (Intl. sales, ADN Associates.) Produced by David Steinman, Douglas Grossman. Directed by Grossman. Screenplay, Leo Evans, Grossman; camera (Precision color), Steven Fierberg; editor, Claire Simpson-Crozier, Greg Sheldon; music, Rich Macar, Christopher Hyans-Hart; sound (Dolby), Judy Karp, Phoebe Bindiger, Felipe Borrero; art direction, William Bilowit. Joan Brockschmidt; assistant director, Sandra Tait; production manager, Brooke Kennedy; casting, Louis Di Giaimo, Sarah L. Grossman. Reviewed on vidcassette (JGM), N.Y., May 27, 1989. MPAA Rating. R. Running time: **79 MIN.**

Dickens	Christopher Stryker
Brooke Storm	Maureen Mooney
Jon Jon	Christopher Cousins
Queenie	Millie Prezioso
Smiler	Jason Brill

Also with: Kathy Rossetter, J.R. Horne, Daniel Beer, Karen Russell, Webster Whinery.

■ **"Hell High," a.k.a. "Raging Fury," is an above-average teen horror flick destined for modest returns in current regional theatrical release.**

Subject is a pretty high school biology teacher (Maureen Mooney), shown in prolog being traumatized 18 years earlier when she witneessed a double murder of two teens in nearby swampland.

Incident started a local legend and her uppity students (led by mean Christopher Stryker) terrorize her one night wearing masks as monsters from the swamp. When they try to rape her (including a brief lesbian interlude with student Millie Prezioso), Mooney goes hurtling through a window and is left for dead.

In familiar genre fashion, Mooney comes back to wreak her revenge in grisly fashion. Pic's

hero Christopher Cousins gets involved in the mayhem (which is blamed on innocent football player Daniel Beer) and in a neat open-ended finale is nearly driven nuts with guilt.

Film benefits from good acting by its unknown cast, most of whom fit the age bracket for a change. Steven Fierberg's night photography of Westchester, N.Y., locations is solid. Only drawback is apparent use of body doubles for the femme leads' nude scenes. —*Lor.*

Fakebook

Hollywood   A Vested Interests/Fakebook production. Produced and directed by Ralph Toporoff. Screenplay, Gilbert Girion, from story by Toporoff. Girion; camera (Technicolor), Joey Forsyte; editor, Jack Haigis; music, Larry Schanker; sound, Dale Whitman; production design, Charles Lagola; art direction, Katharine Fredericks; costume design, Nina Canter; assistant director, Mike Listo; associate producers, Girion, Bill Hart; casting, Stanley Sobel. Reviewed at American Film Institute (AFI/L.A. Fest), L.A., March 17, 1989. No MPAA Rating. Running time: **96 MIN.**

Jack Solow	Peter MacNicol
Jerry	Carl Capotorto
Bobby	Tim Guinee
Lee	Bill Christopher-Myers
Tommy	Jonathan Walker
Benita	Charlotte d'Amboise
Abe Katz	Louis Guss
Louise	Zohra Lampert
Sharon	Margaret Devine
Lorraine	Trini Alvarado

■ **The overworked charm and innocence of the early 1960s are back once again in "Fakebook," a decent but innocuous little picture about a jazz group going nowhere fast.**

Good-natured Peter MacNicol thinks he can launch a successful jazz band, and his four cohorts give him a year to prove it. Instead of landing on 52d Street, however, the proficient but hardly inspiring group must drive miles for the only gigs they can land, at weddings and ridiculous rural dives.

Gilbert Girion's screenplay takes the boys from one amusingly depressing job to the next, until they finally pack it in after playing Tchaikovsky at a children's dance recital. Interspersed is MacNicol's sort-of romance with dancer Charlotte d'Amboise. Latter is so appealing that it is impossible to believe that she would be so patient with the impossibly slow fellow, who seems as though he is terminally constipated.

MacNicol's character is just too simple and bland to hold center-screen for more than 90 minutes, and none of the others ever emerge as more than 1-dimensional.

Although their allotted time is brief, several of the other women besides d'Amboise — Zohra Lampert as MacNicol's mother, Trini Alvarado as one of the guy's girlfriends and Margaret Devine as a well-meaning waitress — come off more favorably than the men.

Technically, film is just fine, but the entire enterprise suffers from a fatal lack of ambition. —*Cart.*

Ubit Drakona
(Kill The Dragon)
(SOVIET-WEST GERMAN)

Madrid A Goskino (USSR) and ZDF (Germany) coproduction. Directed by Mark Zakharov. Screenplay, Zakharov, Grigori Gorin, based on a work by Evgueni Shvarts; camera (color), Vladimir Nakhabtsev; music. Guennadi Gladkov; sets, Oleg Sheintsis, Said Menailschikov, Rolf Zehetbauer; sound, E. Fiodorov. Reviewed at Cine Palafox, Madrid, April 22, 1989. Running time: **132 MIN.**

With: Alexander Abdulov, Oleg Yankovski, Evgeni Leonov, Viacheslav Tijonov, Alexandra Zakharova, Victor Rakov, Alexandr Zbruev, Frant Mut.

■There is some spectacular photography and many imaginative sets in this parable about a dragon in a medieval Russian town. However the stirring sequences are diluted by overlong, wordy scenes, so end result is soporific.

Yarn concerns a "dragon," who manifests himself first as a kind of combative flying saucer, with dazzling light. It capriciously shoots bolts of explosives at unsuspecting passers-by, but also appears in the guise of a human ruler, a kind of big-brother dictator.

Hero of the often tongue-in-cheek story is a certain Lancelot who is captured by three fisherman and brought in a net to the village/metropolis. After escaping he meets the pretty daughter of the village keeper-of-the-files, who offers to sacrifice herself to appease the dragon. Lancelot vows to kill the dragon with his sword instead.

Throughout the script, played with unbridled theatricality, there are references to power, freedom, libertinism and honor, with many clear references to the modern-day Soviet situation. At the end the dragon is destroyed, but it is not clear whether another dragon will come to take his place. —*Besa.*

CANNES OFFICIAL SELECTIONS

Kuarup
(BRAZILIAN)

Cannes An Art Films/Columbia Pictures release of a Grapho Pictures and Guerra Films production. Executive producers, Mair Tavares, Ary Pini, Rachel Arruda. Produced by Roberto Fonseca, Paulo Brito, Ruy Guerra. Directed by Guerra. Screenplay, Guerra, Rudy Lagemann based on a novel by Antonio Callado; camera (color), Edgar Moura; editor, Mair Tavares; music, Egberto Giamonti. Reviewed at Cannes Film Festival (competing), May 21, 1989. Running time: **115 MIN.**
Nando .... Taumaturgo Ferreira
Francisca .... Fernanda Torres
Ramiro .... Claudio Mamberti
Fontoura .... Umberto Magnani
Lauro .... Ewerton de Castro
Olavo .... Roberto Bonfim
Sonia .... Claudia Raia
Also with: Andre Ceccato, Rui Rezende, Vinicius Salvatori, Dionisio Azevedo, Claudia Ohana, Maite Proenca, Lucelia Santos, Adilson de Barros, Mauro Mendonca, Stenio Garcia, Mauricio Mattar, Rui Polanan, Mac Suara Radivel, Claudio Ferrario, Aiupu, Jose Fernandes, Betty Goffman, Paulo Moska, Diana Burle, Rudy Lagemann, Celso Tadei, Solange Coutinho, Francisco Carlos, Roger de Renor, Macuama, Paulo Falcao.

■Inspired by the Amazon jungle-set novel "Kuarup" by Antonio Callado, film shows a deep commitment to the ideas of the author. It features, as expected, impressive landscapes. But it is questionable if the great amount of information on Brazil's political history can be absorbed within this fragmented narrative.

Callado's book relates the facts that led to the creation of Xingu National Park (originally aimed as an independent state for the Indians): the desegregation of the political system in Brazil, from the crisis of the second Getulio Vargas government (which led to the president's suicide in 1954) to the 1964 military coup and the repressive regime installed since then.

In the center of the action is Nando, a young Jesuit priest tormented by his own sexual desire and by the political action undertaken by his closest friends against the growing military influence. Nando believes in an ideal society organized by the Indians, where there would be no corruption, no injustice, no sin.

Even before going to the Xingu area in the Amazon jungle, Nando is faced with the corruption and the lack of conscience of the government officials designated to "protect" the Indians. At the Xingu, Nando meets Fontoura, a forest ranger who is opposed to any attempt to "educate" the Indians.

Eventually his dream of the ideal society in the jungle tends to fade, and discovers he no longer fits in the civilized world.

After joining a senseless and disastrous expedition to find the geographical center of Brazil, Nando realizes his destiny is not to serve as a missionary, but to fight for his political beliefs.

Ruy Guerra, a film director with a political commitment as strong as Callado's, aims not only to be faithful to the book but to place the saga of Nando amongst the events that changed Brazilian political history over the 10 years in which the action takes place.

Guerra pulverizes his narrative in several flashes back and forward, making it difficult to follow the action. Nando's character turns out to be inconsistent, and fragile acting by Taumaturgo Ferreira is no help.

Casting otherwise is good, especially with Umberto Magnani as Fontoura, the forest ranger, and alcoholic, Claudio Mamberti as Ramiro, a corrupt official of Brazil's Office for the Protection of Indians. Claudia Raia is also good as Sonia, the secretary of the corrupt minister of African culture and a compulsive lover of several men.

For viewers who can dismiss the lack of involvement with the central character and pic's lack of feeling, "Kuarup" is a strong and quite appealing work. —*Hoin.*

Piccoli equivoci
(Little Misunderstandings)
(ITALIAN)

Cannes A Massfilm production. Produced by Franco Committeri. Directed by Ricky Tognazzi. Screenplay, Claudio Bigagli, Ruggero Maccari, Simona Izzo, based on Bigagli's play; camera (color), Alessio Gelsini; editor. Carla Simoncelli; music, Enzo and Paolo Jannacci; art direction, Mariangela Capuano. Reviewed at Cannes Film Festival (Directors Fortnight), May 19, 1989. Running time: **90 MIN.**
Paolo .... Sergio Castellito
Francesca .... Lina Sastri
Sophie .... Nancy Brilli
Enrico .... Nicola Pistola
Giuliano .... Roberto Citran
Piero .... Pino Quartullo

■Young thesp Ricky Tognazzi (son of Ugo) makes his feature directing debut in the small but delightful "Little Misunderstandings." It is an enjoyable comedy whose talkiness makes it mainly suitable onshore.

Based on Claudio Bigagli's play, pic is entirely shot in a Roman apartment and relies on a sextet of young actors — who play actors — to carry it through.

Paolo (played by up-and-coming thesp Sergio Castellito) is waiting for girlfriend Francesca (Lina Sastri) to come home from touring with a play. They broke up before she left and Paolo is supposed to move out of her apartment before she returns.

He delays, talking with his pals Enrico (Nicola Pistola), an out-of-work actor he suspects has been to bed with Francesca, and Giuliano (Roberto Citran), madly jealous of his fetching fiancée Sophie (Nancy Brilli).

To save face in front of Francesca (returning with her new lover, Pino Quartullo), Paolo invites Sophie over for dinner. The characters come together and couples get happily reshuffled into their original arrangements during the night.

Making no attempt to disguise script's theatrical origins, Tognazzi concentrates on his thesps. Dialog is witty, cynical, bitchy, anxious. Characters come across as human beings of the Roman variety, subgenre actors.

Good comic pacing keeps things lively and moving. Whole cast deserves applause, especially Castellito and Nancy Brilli. —*Yung.*

Ganashatru
(Enemy Of The People)
(INDIAN)

Cannes A National Film Development Corp. production. Directed by Satyajit Ray. Screenplay, Ray, based on the play by Henryk Ibsen; camera (Eastmancolor) Barun Raha; editor, Dulal Dutt; music, Ray, art direction, Ashoke Bose. Reviewed at Cannes Film Festival (official selection, noncompeting), May 20, 1989. Running time: **100 MIN.**
Dr. Ashoke Gupta ..... Soumitra Chatterji
Nishith Gupta .... Dhritiman Chatterji
Maya Gupta .... Ruma Gubathakurta
Indrani Gupta .... Mamata Shankar
With: Dipankarde (Haridas), Subhendu Chatterji (Biresh Guha), Manoj Mitra (Adhir), Vishwa Guhathakurta (Ranen), Satya Banerji (Mammatha), Rajaram Yagnik (Bhargava).
(In Bengali)

■Satyajit Ray returns to the set after a four year absence due to illness with "Ganashatru," closely adapted from Henryk Ibsen's play "An Enemy Of The People." The idea of setting tale about a courageous doctor's unpopular stand against polluted water in an imaginary West Bengal town is a fascinating one, but results are static and a bit dull.

This is the first time Ray has made a film from a play, necessary because of his doctor's orders that he shoot only in the studio. The audience for Ray's films has always been mainly offshore, but "Enemy" could have trouble attracting more than his faithful fans.

Ray's favorite actor, Soumitra Chatterji, plays the good Dr. Ashoke Gupta as a man who hasn't lost his ideals through years of adversity. Gupta and his family are in debt to his brother Nishith (Dhritiman Chatterji), mayor of the town, who has got him a job as chief medical officer at the local hospital. When he discovers that the water from the local temple, town's main tourist attraction, is polluted and is causing cases of hepatitis and typhoid, Gupta insists on making the news public before it reaches epidemic proportions.

Nishith is linked to building interests, and cold-bloodedly sets about sabotaging his brother's information campaign, first discrediting him at the leftist newspaper where he has submitted an article, then at a public meeting Gupta calls. Turning the doctor's not being a practicing Hindu against him, Nishith manages to rile up the populance.

Offscreen, we hear shattering glass as the crowd throws rocks at the house. Just when the Guptas are on the verge of giving up and leaving town, however, the offscreen noise changes to "Long Live Gupta!" shouted by a group of supporters organized by daughter Mamata Shankar's fiancé.

At the same time, an honest newspaperman (Subhendu Chatterji) offers to send a protest to the big Calcutta papers about the affair. Gupta immediately takes heart and in an uplifting ending agrees to struggle on to inform people about the danger.

Entire story, which has been very credibly transplanted to Bengal, unfolds in the Guptas' living room, the newspaper office, and a courtyard where the meeting is held. Only one brief scene of people drinking water at the temple takes us out of this closed stage world.

The public meeting is film's best scene, becoming suspenseful and dramatic as tension is skillfully built up. In the main role, Chatterji is a very human figure who instantly claims sympathy. —*Yung.*

Chimère
(FRENCH)

Cannes A UGC release (France) of a Cinea production. (Intl. sales, President Films, Paris.) Produced by Philippe Carcassonne, François Cuel. Directed by Claire Devers. Screenplay, Arlette Langmann, Devers; camera (Fujicolor), Renato Berta; editor, Hélène Viard; music, John Surman; production design, Jacques Bufnoir; sound, Antoine Ouvrier, Jacques Thomas-Gérard, Philippe Lemenuel; production manager, Jean Achache; assistant director, Didier Creste; casting, Frederique Moidon. Reviewed at Cannes Film Festival (competing), May 19, 1989. Running time: **94 MIN.**
Alice . . . . Béatrice Dalle
Leo . . . . Wadeck Stanczak
Fred . . . . Francis Frappat
Mimi . . . . Julie Bataille
Alice's mother . . . . Adriana Asti

■A major disappointment after her intriguing first feature, "Black And White," Claire Devers' "Chimère" is a listless drama about a relationship that breaks up over a pregnancy that delights the woman but appalls the man. B.o. prospects are poor for this self-absorbed item.

Béatrice Dalle, who set the screen on fire in "Betty Blue," is wasted here as Alice, a young meteorologist working at a weather station on the coast near Bordeaux. She's been dating Leo (Wadeck Stanczak), a selfish young architect for a year when she announces she's pregnant. Since he's planning work in Senegal and feels he might be tied down, he reacts badly, and the relationship starts deteriorating.

On the sidelines is Fred (Francis Frappat), friend of both and maybe a bit in love with both; he's their father-confessor. Alice's young sister, Mimi (Julie Bataille), is strongly affected when her sister's affair ends. After she sees Leo with another girl, she drowns herself and her pet cat. Leo departs for Africa and Alice has a miscarriage. Leo returns, but they drift their separate ways.

This is perilously thin material, and Devers never manages to give it the charge of her first film. These are simply rather dull characters given to arguing, fighting and slapping each other. Maybe the director is trying to make a statement about the shallowness of French men in the late '80s, but whatever her theme she doesn't connect strongly enough with her audience.

Dalle proves once again that she's an accomplished actress, but the men in the film are merely types and irritating ones at that. Production dress is fine, with lush images from Renato Berta and an interesting music score from John Surman. In the end, the film is as elusive as its title. —*Strat.*

Santa Sangre
(Holy Blood)
(ITALIAN)

Cannes An Intersound production. Produced by Claudio Argento. Directed by Alexandro Jodorowsky. Screenplay, Jodorowsky, Roberto Leoni, Argento; camera (color), Daniele Nannuzzi; editor, Mauro Bonanni; art direction, Alejandro Luna; music, Simon Boswell. Reviewed at the Cannes Film Festival (Un Certain Regard), May 19, 1989. Running time: **118 MIN.**
Fenix . . . . Axel Jodorowsky
Concha . . . . Blanca Guerra
Orgo . . . . Guy Stockwell
Alma . . . . Sabrina Dennison
With: Thelma Tixou.

■Wild man director Alexandro Jodorowsky, who delighted and disgusted audiences with shock-value artfilms like "El Topo," is back in full form in "Santa Sangre." This ultimate Oedipus complex tale about a madman who becomes the arms of his mutilated mother is a sensational piece of filmmaking likely to end up a cult classic.

Its violence, though more psychological than evident on the screen, could keep it out of many venues and even get it into trouble with censors.

Fenix is a little boy whose American father, Orgo (Guy Stockwell, huge and wearing long blond tresses) runs the Gringo Circus in Mexico. His beautiful mother, Concha (Blanca Guerra, only thesp who turns in a serious performance), is a trapeze artist and religious fanatic. Her patron saint is a girl who was raped and had both arms cut off. The Church of Holy Blood, with its pool of "blood" where devotees bathe, is bulldozed away in pic's first hysterical scene.

Two newcomers appear at the circus: the screen's most lascivious tattooed lady and her angelic deaf daughter. Little Fenix and Alma have an instant rapport, as do Orgo and the tattooed lady. In a fit of jealousy, Concha throws a bottle of acid on her husband's delicate parts. He cuts off her arms and slits his throat — all before the innocent eyes of Fenix.

Many years later we find Fenix, now a handsome young man (Axel Jodorowsky), perched naked in a tree in a mental asylum. He sees his armless mother calling to him from the street and escapes to join her. Together they put together a bizarre variety act in which Concha signs and mimes with Fenix' arms.

At home Concha plays the Hollywood movie star, all feathered dressing gowns and temper tantrums, while Fenix butters her toast from behind with painted fingernails. But mama still is as jealous as ever, and every time Fenix becomes interested in a girl she orders "her hands" to kill. The first victim, is the tattooed lady, now a blowsy hooker trying to prostitute her daughter. When Alma finds her mother lying in a pool of blood, she quickly guesses who's responsible.

Meanwhile, Fenix and mama's hands have knifed or strangled various other victims, including an opulent stripper and "the world's strongest woman."

A cross between "Psycho," "The Hands Of Orlac" and the schlockiest B horror films ever made, "Santa Sangre" is an unadulterated romp. Jodorowsky goes over the top in every scene, but his undeniable sense of cinema grips throughout.

Film screened in Cannes' Directors Fortnight was dreadfully dubbed into English, and acting, except the case of Guerra, was poor. Daniele Nannuzzi's lensing, Alejandro Luna's sets, and Simon Boswell's score contribute to the atmosphere of freakish excess. —*Yung.*

Smertch
(The Tornado)
(SOVIET)

Cannes A Tadjikfilm Studios production. Directed by Bako Sadykov. Screenplay, Sadykov, Chingiz Aitmatov; camera (color), Rifkat Ibraguimov; editor, Sadykov; music, Sofia Gubaidulina; art direction, Chavkat Abdusalamov. Reviewed at Cannes Film Festival (Un Certain Regard), May 21, 1989. Running time: **100 MIN.**
With: Vladimir Msrian, Dimitru Fusu, Mukhamadali Makhmadov, Isfandior Gulamov.

■Tadjikistan helmer Bako Sadykov is known in the West as a documaker and for shorts like "Adonis XIV." "The Tornado," his first feature film, started as a short and was expanded to full-length, which may explain the feeling it has been padded.

The illusory quest of a tribe of people for the Land of Happiness makes a more interesting political metaphor than a watchable picture, and takers for this work look scarce.

Nor are Sadykov's documentary

interests put aside. Pic opens with breathtaking aerial shots of a glacier, mountains, plains. The stunning vastness of the natural landscape — apparently shot in several Central Asian republics — is the backdrop for all the action.

Leader of the tribe is woolly haired Mavrut, who has his followers fanatically convinced they must roam the most barren corners of the earth under the direst conditions to reach the land of their dreams.

Barbaric music, written by top composer Sofia Gubaidulina, blends voices and drums in a hypnotic rhythm, as the exhausted men and women force themselves to cross one more steppe, one more mountain.

When a young woman tells Mavrut she wants to have a baby, he reminds her she is wearing a chastity belt and has vowed never to have ties that would detract from the great quest. She gets pregnant anyway, chastity belt or no, and she and her lover are brutally punished.

She dies in childbirth and the baby is proclaimed a kind of savior for the tribe, but is lost when they try to cross some rapids. A little child is present on the far shore, however, singing a haunting tune.

Apart from the landscapes and some good shots of Samarkand without tourists, pic has a few nice touches, like a dauntless poet constantly being tortured by the others "because I'm a poet." He also says things like, "For you, thought is the enemy of the people." The metaphor is plain enough, and in the end the authoritarian leaders seem ready to topple, and a New Age to begin.

Bad Russian dubbing with sporadic lip synch doesn't help bridge the imagination gap needed to get into "Tornado." Real problem is its lack of rhythm, which perhaps film had more of as a short. —*Yung.*

Gorod Zero
(Zero City)
(SOVIET)

Cannes A Mosfilm Studios production. Directed by Karen Shaknazarov. Screenplay, Alexandre Borodianski, Shaknazarov; camera (color), Nikolai Nemoliaev; music, Edouard Artemiev; art direction, Ludmila Koussakova. Reviewed at Cannes Film Festival (Directors Fortnight), May 20, 1989. Running time: **102 MIN.**
Varadin . . . . Leonid Filatov
Also with: Oleg Bassilachvili, Vladimir

Menchov, Armen Djigarkhanian, Evgeni Evstigneev, Elena Arjanik.

■**Karen Shaknazarov's "Zero City" is one of Russia's first certifiable post-perestroika films.**

This comedy of the absurd about a Moscow engineer who gets trapped — seemingly forever — in a remote town that still has a Stalin exhibit in its local museum is a straightforward metaphor that part of today's Soviety society holding out against leader Mikhail Gorbachev's reforms.

Shot without pretentions by a solid commercial director, film should find its way to Western audiences in specialized playoffs and be enjoyed by all.

Alexei Varadin (Leonid Filatov) arrives in Zero City to ask local suppliers to alter some air-conditioner parts they produce for his Moscow machine shop. He knows it's a funny town when he finds the boss' secretary working in the nude, though he is the only one who seems to notice.

The boss puts Varadin on indefinite hold — his chief engineer died eight months ago. Varadin returns to his hotel, resigned to leave for Moscow. That night in a restaurant, the cook shoots himself because Varadin won't eat a cake decorated to look like his head.

Varadin finds no trains at the station and takes a cab, which drops him off in the middle of a forest. Waiting for a lift to town, he is forced to visit the town's museum and takes a hilarious guided tour full of absurd misinformation. He gets a lift from a beautiful woman, but police stop them and take Varadin in for questioning about the "murder" in the restaurant.

Ordered to stay in town, Varadin begins to feel that a child's prediction he will die in Zero City is going to come true. The town fathers treat him as a celebrity and insist he's the son of the dead cook, who was the town's first rock 'n' roller. Varadin's nightmare goes on and on through ever more absurd situations, until he finally escapes in a rowboat without oars on a still, moonlit lake.

In the main role, Filatov makes a good, nondescript everyman caught in a web of Kafkaesque nonsense. Parts of pic are very funny, and its portrait of suffocating Russian provincials all too true to life. —*Yung.*

Der 7. Kontinent
(The 7th Continent)
(AUSTRIAN)

Cannes A WEGA-Filmproduktion. Written and directed by Michael Haneke. Camera (color), Toni Peschke; art direction, Rudi Czettel; editor, Marie Homolkova. Reviewed at the Cannes Film Festival (Directors Fortnight), May 20, 1989. Running time: **111 MIN.**
Anna . . . . Birgit Doll
Georg . . . . Dieter Berner
Eva . . . . Leni Tanzer
Alexander . . . . Udo Samel

■**Austrian helmer Michael Haneke explores the deadening impact of everyday life on a couple who carried their alienation to its extreme consequences.**

Though the subject of group suicide is piquant, Haneke rejects any kind of scandalistic or voyeuristic approach.

Instead, he has made a beautifully lensed, stylistically austere work whose very sensitivity and slow pacing will scare off big audiences.

Film opens with a catalog of banal details — an alarm clock going off at six, feet entering slippers, hands making breakfast, brushing teeth, starting a car. Thanks to Toni Peschke's precision lensing, these familiar shots become a poem to the minutiae of modern life.

Gradually we meet the family: mother Anna (Birgit Doll), who works for an optician; husband Georg (Dieter Berner), a well-groomed young manager on the rise; little daughter Eva (Leni Tanzer), with her big, sad eyes. All is not s well, however, as Anna reports in perfunctory letters to her mother-in-law. The problem surfaces when Eva pretends to be blind to gain affection.

Punctuated by black frames and divided into three parts, "The 7th Continent" ends the second part with a wordless trip through an automatic carwash, very much like death. Anna begins to cry and the family joins hands.

Third part shows the family preparing for suicide. Georg and Anna quit their jobs and take their money out of the bank, explaining they are emigrating to Australia. Georg buys power tools, Anna orders a huge amount of food from the delicatessen, and they systematically set about destroying every single record, lamp, and piece of furniture in the house. They poison themselves in a drawn-out finale.

Haneke conveys the bleakness of the family's life within its apparent normality. He offers no explanation as to how Georg and Anna reach their decision, undercutting the inherent drama of the situation to concentrate on the family's alienation and distance from the world around them.

Technical credits are top-notch. The trio of main actors perfectly convey emotional incapacity and helplessness of adults and child alike. —*Yung.*

Sis
(Mist)
(TURKISH/SWEDISH/SWISS)

Cannes An Ulker Livanelli Interfilm production. Written and directed by Omer Zülfü Livanelli. Camera (color), Jürgen Jürges; editor, Hilmi Guver; music, Livanelli, Mikis Theodorakis, art direction, Gurel Yontan. Reviewed at Cannes Film Festival (Directors Fortnight), May 16, 1989. Running time: **108 MIN.**
Ali . . . . Rutkay Aziz
Idil . . . . Sevtap Parman
Also with: Asli Altan, Ugur Polat, Elia Kazan (captain of fishing boat).

■**Turkish musician Ömer Zülfü Livanelli, composer of several scores for Yilmaz Güney, makes his second venture into directing (first was "Iron Earth, Copper Sky") with "Mist." Story is politically grounded in recent Turkish history, but lacks the clarity needed for foreign auds to appreciate its setting. Prospects look mainly local.**

As film opens, Ali (Rutkay Aziz), a successful lawyer, is pleased by the country's new military rulers, whom he and his father see as imposing order. He has two small sons.

The sons grow into young men belonging to different political factions. Offscreen, one of the sons is shot to death. His brother Eral finds the body.

Even before the police start looking for Eral, Ali suspects his son of fratricide. They never discuss the matter, but Ali does everything in his power to hide Eral from the police and to try to pin the blame on a crazed young killer. Idil, feminist girlfriend of the dead son, has a brief relationship with Eral.

In the end, it turns out the father's suspicions are groundless. Police know it, too, but the newspapers have decided to pin the murder on Eral. An attempt to get him on the fishing boat bound for Rumania fails (briefly cameoing as the captain is none other than Elia Kazan). Father and son are left driving aimlessly around Istanbul, waiting to be caught.

Pic is lensed in dark, lugubrious colors. Thesps are understated and morosely laconic. Rhythm is slow.

Musical score was cowritten by the director and Greek composer Mikis Theodorakis, with whom Livanelli has often staged concerts.

—Yung.

CANNES MARKET REVIEWS

Ten Little Indians

Cannes A Cannon Entertainment presentation of a Breton Film Prods. Ltd. production. Executive producer, Avi Lerner. Produced by Harry Alan Towers. Directed by Alan Birkinshaw. Screenplay, Jackson Hunsicker, Gerry O'Hara, based on Agatha Christie's play; camera (Rank color), Arthur Lavia; editor, Penelope Shaw; music, George C. Clinton; sound (Ultra-Stereo), Alan Gerhardt; art direction, George Cains; production design, Roger Orpen; assistant director, Gregory Dark; costumes, Dianna Villiers; casting, Gianna Pisanello. Reviewed at Cannes Film Festival (Market), May 17, 1989. No MPAA Rating. Running time: **98 MIN.**

Justice Wargrave	Donald Pleasence
Capt. Lombard	Frank Stallone
Vera Claythorne	Sarah Maur Thorp
Gen. Romensky	Herbert Lom
Marion Marshall	Brenda Vaccaro
Blore	Warren Berlinger
Dr. Hans Werner	Yehuda Efroni
Elmo Rodgers	Paul L. Smith
Ethel Rodgers	Moira Lister
Anthony Marsden	Neil McCarthy

■Cannon's new version of Agatha Christie mainstay "Ten Little Indians" is a dud, and ranks near the bottom of all Christie adaptations. Low-grade effort won't even be able to match the sorry performance of Cannon's previous Christie, "Appointment With Death."

This version is based, per the credits, on the play by Christie and the curious credit seems more like a legal expedient than anything else. Center of the action is an African safari party — try and stage that — as 10 disparate people have been summoned by invitation by someone none of them knows to attend his get-together. After they listen to a record that accuses each of them of murder, they begin getting killed off according to the nursery rhyme "Ten Little Indians."

Plotline doesn't vary much from the source material, except of course in adapting the dialog to suit the African setting. The film is set in the '30s and it's a bit of a jolt when one of the guests (Brenda Vaccaro, playing an actress) remarks casually about a past lesbian affair. Definitely not Christie.

The filmmakers convey little sense of danger, with characters often seen in exaggeratedly long reaction shots (though it's hard to figure what they're reacting to). The cost efficiency of the produc-

ORIGINAL FILM
And Then There Were None
(B&W)

20th-Fox release of a Harry M. Popkin production. Stars Barry Fitzgerald, Walter Huston, Louis Hayward; features Roland Young, June Duprez, C. Aubrey Smith, Judith Anderson, Mischa Auer, Richard Haydn, Queenie Leonard, Harry Thursston. Directed by Rene Clair. Screenplay, Dudley Nichols from the Satevepost story and play, "10 Little Indians," by Agatha Christie; camera, Lucien Andriot; editor, Harvey Manger. Reviewed at Tradown L.A. July 6, 1945. Running time: **97 MINS.**

Judge Quincannon	Barry Fitzgerald
Dr. Armstrong	Walter Huston
Philip Lombard	Louis Hayward
Blore	Roland Young
Vera Claythorne	June Duprez
General Mandrake	Sir C. Aubrey Smith
Emily Brent	Judith Anderson
Prince Starloff	Mischa Auer
Rogers	Richard Haydn
Mrs. Rogers	Queenie Leonard
Fisherman	Harry Thurston

not on her 1939 novel. Christie did write a stage version in 1943, but

1965 Version
(B&W)

Seven Arts Pictures release of a Tenlit Films production. Produced by Oliver A. Unger in association with Harry M. Popkin. Directed by George Pollock. Screenplay, Peter Yeldham, based on a Dudley Nichols script, adapted by Peter Welbeck; camera (b&w), Ernie Steward; editor, Peter Boita; music, composed and conducted by Malcolm Lockyer. Reviewed Dec. 10, 1965, at Seven Arts Pictures homeoffice, N.Y. Running time: **92 MIN.**

Hugh Lombard	Hugh O'Brian
Ann Clyde	Shirley Eaton
Mike Raven	Fabian
General Mandrake	Leo Genn
William Blore	Stanley Holloway
Frau Grohmann	Marianne Hoppe
Judge Cannon	Wilfrid Hyde-White
Ilona Bergen	Daliah Lavi
Dr. Armstrong	Dennis Price
Herr Grohmann	Mario Adorf

tion shows to a woeful degree. And there's nothing of the humor or sheer style of such past grade-A Christies as "Evil Under The Sun."

Donald Pleasence as the tired judge gets most of the banal dialog, and the putative romantic lead, Frank Stallone, doesn't cut it (he smirks his way through the picture). Herbert Lom, Yehuda Efroni and Warren Berlinger try to bring something to their underwritten parts but with little effect.

The lovely Sarah Maur Thorp alone brings passion to her part of an English governess whose crime was that she accidentally caused a boy's death; the film doesn't deserve her. It's a tough job to screw up such a spiffy story as Christie's, but together Jackson Hunsicker

1975 Version

A Talia Films (Madrid)-Coralta Cinematografica (Rome)-Corona Production (Munich) and Comeci, S.A. (Paris) coproduction. Directed by Peter Collinson. Features entire cast. Screenplay, Enrique Llovet, Erich Krohnke, based on story by Agatha Christie; camera (Eastmancolor), Fernando Arribas; music, Bruno Nicolai; sets, Jose Maria Tapiador. Reviewed at Cine Vergara (Madrid), Feb. 1, 1975. Running time: **105 MIN.**

Cast: Oliver Reed, Elke Sommer, Richard Attenborough, Gert Frobe, Teresa Gimpera, Alberto de Mendoza, Stephane Audran, Adolfo Celi, Herbert Lom, Maria Rohm, Charles Aznavour.

and Gerry O'Hara have done it. One line of dialog serves to sum up the film: "Maybe that's the way they do things in Hollywood," Berlinger tells Vaccaro, "but we're nowhere near there."

Where exactly are they? Africa, with its topless natives, is the obvious setting, but there's none of the usual end credits thanking any particular state or nation. *—Gerz.*

Street Of No Return
(FRENCH-PORTUGUESE)

Cannes A Thunder Films Intl./FR 3 Films Prod./Animatografo coproduction, with Soficas Investimage. Investimage 2, Slav 2. Instituto Portugues de Cinema. Produced by Jacques Bral. Executive producers, Jacques-Eric Strauss, Patrick Delauneax, Antonio da Cunha Telles. Directed by Samuel Fuller. Screenplay, Jacques Bral, Fuller, based on David Goodis' novel "Sans Espoir de Retour;" camera (Fuji color), Pierre-William Glenn; music, Karl-Heinz Schafer; art direction, Geoffroy Larcher. Reviewed at Cannes Film Festival (Market), May 17, 1989. Running time: **90 MIN.**

Michael	Keith Carradine
Celia	Valentina Vargas
Borel	Bill Duke
Rhoda	Andréa Ferréol
Morin	Bernard Fresson

Also with: Marc de Jonge (Eddie), Rebecca Potok (Bertha), Jacques Marital.

(English soundtrack)

■Samuel Fuller directs his 23d feature with "Street Of No Return," adapted from a David Goodis thriller. Starring Keith Carradine as a singing star who gets his throat cut over a girl, pic is disappointing as a chiller and especially as a Fuller, though its large doses of action could in-terest B markets.

Those looking for auteur elements will find them, mainly in Michael, Carradine's idealistic revenger. Michael was a wildly popular singer made rather arrogant by success. He treats manager and ex-lover Andréa Ferréol brusquely, demanding she find him the address of a sexy dancer, Celia (Valentina Vargas, the girl from "The Name Of The Rose"). Celia agrees on bed but resists romance, being already attached to a crooked real estate operator. The man reclaims Celia and slashes Michael across the throat.

Years later, reduced to the state of a Klaus Kinki lookalike, Michael is a rasping, alcoholic bum. He stumbles across Celia's bunch again, but gets arrested, quite absurdly, as a cop-killer and is taken to the police station. Black police chief Borel (Bill Duke) is busy beating up black and white riot suspects. Realizing he's in for the same treatment, Michael makes an improbable escape thanks to a handy firehose — also allowing the rioters to get away.

Taken before the cruel boss of a black gang, he narrowly avoids death aboard a cargo ship, but makes another breathtaking and unbelievable escape down the anchor rope. Clinging to the underside of a jeep, he reaches the house where Celia is living. Surprise — her criminal lover is in cahoots with the black tough to create riots and lower property values.

Michael runs to the police chief and gets the whole force involved in a bloody shootout with the baddies. The cargo ship explodes, too. In a happy ending, beauty Celia leads beast Michael out of the gutter toward a new and better life.

Lensing is uneven, acting even more so. The cartoonish aspect of script and characters isn't consistent as a style, and leaves the viewer perplexed about whether the whole thing is a joke.

Though clearly lensed in Europe, pic has no signs of a definite locale of any sort, giving it an odd nowhere look. Re-edited version shown at Cannes opens with a rousing, all-out street brawl, apparently to foreground it as an actioner.

Carradine sings three songs before he loses his voice. Fuller wrote the lyrics to the title song. *—Yung.*

Ladder Of Swords
(BRITISH)

Cannes   A Film Four Intl./British Screen presentation of an Arden Films production. Produced by Jennifer Howarth. Directed by Norman Hull. Screenplay, Neil Clarke, based on story by Clarke, Hull; camera (Eastmancolor), Thaddeus O'Sullivan; editor, Scott Thomas; music, Stanley Myers; production design, Caroline Hananis; sound, Colin Nicholson; production manager, Olivia Stewart; casting, Priscilla John. Reviewed at Cannes Film Festival (Market), May 14, 1989. Running time: **98 MIN.**
Don Demarco . . . . .Martin Shaw
Denise Demarco . . . . .Eleanor David
Det. Inspector Atherton . . . . .Bob Peck
Alice Howard . . . . .Juliet Stevenson
Sergeant Bilby . . . . .Simon Molloy
Constable Lowe . . . . .Pearce Quigley
Grumpy Gun . . . . .Anthony Benson

■ Title refers to a set of lethally upturned Samurai swords which a minor circus performer ascends very, very carefully. Could be a metaphor for life's risktakers, or for any distrib willing to take a change on this offbeat, quirky British picture.

With a few exceptions, this species of film has lost its footing lately, either fading out at the b.o. or failing to get picked up at all.

This offering from first-time helmer Norman Hull and scripter Neil Clarke, commissioned by indie web Channel 4, won't be an easy sell either. Cast of well-known British thesps probably will help deliver modest returns on home turf for distrib Hobo Film Enterprises. Elsewhere pic likely will be confined to specialized situations.

But for audiences who don't have to go further than their loungeroom or vidstore, it offers some engrossing moments after a languid start, and a dramatic punch at the finale.

The Three Dees are a down-and-out circus act comprising Don Demarco (Martin Shaw), his booze-sodden wife Denise (Eleanor David) and Daley, their none-too-agile dancing bear.

Holed up in a trailer on a remote moor, they attract the attention of a suspicious cop, Atherton (Bob Peck). After a domestic set-to, Denise takes off. The bear dies, which seems to upset Demarco more, and he's consoled by pretty widow Alice (Juliet Stevenson).

They join a circus, where Demarco perfects the balancing-on-swords trick, but their happiness is shortlived, as Atherton accuses them of murdering Denise. They beat that rap, then Denise reappears and precipitates a crisis.

Acting by the principal players is uniformly excellent, and tech credits, especially Thaddeus O'Sullivan's luminous photography, are highly polished. —*Dogo.*

Ihmiselon ihanuus ja kurjuus
(The Glory And Misery Of Human Life)
(FINNISH)

Cannes   A Neofilmi presentation and production. Produced by Päivi Hartzell. Written and directed by Matti Kassila, based on the novel by F.E. Sillanpää. Camera (Eastmancolor), Kari Sohlberg; editor, Irma Taina; music, Jukka Linkola; production design, Ensio Suominen; sound, Johan Hake; line producer, Matti Ollila. Reviewed at Cannes Film Festival (Market), May 21, 1989. Running time: **95 MIN.**
Martti Hongisto . . . . .Lasse Pöysti
Anna Lepaa . . . . . .Liisamaija Laaksonenen
Laimi Hongisto . . . . .Tuula Nyman
Jalmari Roimela . . . . .Antti Litja

■ Based on Finnish Nobel Prize winner F.E. Sillanpää's autobiographical novel, veteran helmer Matti Kassila's "The Glory And Misery Of Human Life" tells of lovers, separated in their youth, who meet again when approaching old age.

If this sounds like "On Golden Pond," Kassila's film actually does it one better. It avoids any trace of the sentimental or the syrupy. But it lacks the star names to bring broader audiences into offshore theaters.

Kassila is, however, a superior craftsman, as are his cinematographer Kari Sohlberg and the crew. Add to this Lasse Pöysti's disciplined but highly expressive acting in the dominating lead as the writer who retraces his steps, and you have a film that will do well for itself on the minor fest circuit.

Pöysti as novelist Martti Hongisto, Sillanpää's fiction name for himself, lives in a fine country house with a nagging wife. He has five grown children, the youngest of whom gives him typical teen trouble. So, now and then, Hongisto just ups and leaves for days or weeks.

Although no longer going on the alcoholic binges of the youth, Hongisto must suffer the indignity of having his wife order his brother to keep watch on him. That the brother is really a more incurable alcoholic himself is the stuff of a strongly narrated subplot.

Leaving home once again, Hongisto calls on Anna, widowed during Finland's civil war 20 years earlier (story is set in 1939) and now celebrating the wedding of one of her sons. Hongisto is asked to join in festivities. Afterwards, he stays and spends the night with Anna in consummation of the love they once shared.

Back then, it seems, Anna had weighed Hongisto's potential as a husband and found it wanting. On the rebound, he had married a pretty country girl who soon grew fat and suspicious of his artistic visions and work.

The reunion between Hongisto and Anna is briefly but poignantly and poetically told. Since it is more than Anna's heart can take, she becomes melancholy while Hongisto actually is revitalized.

Pöysti has a bullet-shaped head and the withered face of a turtle. It

It is a marvel to see Poysti change from the weary man who leaves home to the confident personality you can believe in both as a great writer and as a romantic lover.

Anna is acted well but in a more traditional way by Liisamaija Laaksonen. All in the cast perform convincingly but the only true match for the great Pöysti is Antti Litja as the heavy drinker. Finnish films abound in heavy drinkers but this one plumbs the depths of the misery. —*Kell.*

Medium Straight

Cannes   An Overseas Filmgroup presentation. Produced by I.M. Ecks. Executive producers, Hisa Ota, Marie Torro Tark. Directed by Adam Friedman. Screenplay, Robert Litz; camera (color), Douglas E. Carnevale; editor, Michael Blocher, Susan Brookman; music, Rick Borgia, Lisa G. Bond. Reviewed at Cannes Film Festival (Market), May 18, 1989. No MPAA Rating. Running time: **85 MIN.**
Nick Harding . . . . .Jerome Lepage
Pat Harding . . . . .Richard Schiff
Grandee .Anne Lilly
Joey Mannucci . . . . .Ron Sanborn
Mel Burns . . . . .Brian Straub
Hilton . . . . .Patrick Minietta

■ The opening sequence of "Medium Straight" leads one to expect a routine crime adventure with a suitably gory finale. Instead, the violence is almost nonexistent and some surprisingly sensitive touches are incorporated into the script.

A volatile smalltime thug, Nick Harding (Jerome Lepage), sets up a drug deal with Joey Mannucci, the CPA son of New Jersey outfit kingpin Mo Mannucci. While struggling over a gun during the bungled transaction, it goes off and Nick believes he has offed Joey.

Nick hides out at his absent uncle's South Jersey farm with this tough-talking girlfriend Grandee. Nick's level-headed older cousin

Pat, who has bailed him out of trouble before, joins them. When Pat discovers Mannucci is not dead, he arranges a meeting between Nick and Mannucci to exchange money and Mo's gun that Nick has taken. Mannucci arrives with his bodyguard but the transfer is complicated by Nick and Grandee's conniving.

The female characters are mainly 1-dimensional. The bodyguard's playmate is a horny bimbo, ditto Grandee whose lust is matched by her greed. The males are childish lowlifers but more individualized. Pat (Richard Schiff) is sympathetic and becomes almost poetic in his philosophical voiceovers, through which we learn Nick's amorality may be attributed to losing his mother at an early age.

Pic won an award at the Fort Lauderdale Film Festival and word-of-mouth publicity gives it an edge in theatrical release.

The tech credits are above average, impressive for a low-budget flick shot in 2½ weeks. The camerawork, from intricate handheld shots to long takes, is especially good and the atmospheric score has some nice blues slide guitar riffs.

Director Friedman shows talent in his first feature and is a name to watch. —*Sam.*

Trapper County War

Cannes   A Noble Entertainment Group and Alpine Releasing Group presentation of a Noble production. Produced by Michael W. Leighton. Directed by Worth Keeter. Screenplay, Russel V. Manzatt; camera (Foto-Kem color), Irl Dixon; editor, Miriam L. Preisel; music, Shuki Levy; sound (Ultra-Stereo), Dave Henson; production design, R. Clifford Searcy; art direction, Everett D. Wilson; line producer, John O'Connor; associate producer, George Cook; assistant director, Fred Dresch; makeup, Starr Jones; costumes, Michael Nations; casting, Pat Orseth. Reviewed at Cannes Film Festival (Market), May 14, 1989. MPAA Rating: R. Running time: **95 MIN.**
Ryan Cassidy . . . . .Robert Estes
Lacey Luddigger . . . . .Betsy Russell
Sheriff Sam Frost . . . . .Bo Hopkins
Walt Luddigger . . . . .Don Swayze
Bobby Keal . . . . .Noah Black
Mom Luddigger . . . . .Sarah Hunley
Pop Luddigger . . . . .R.G. Armstrong
Jefferson Carter . . . . .Ernie Hudson
    Also with: Terrence Evans, Sage Parker, Royce G. Clark, Todd Maxwell, Wallace Merk, Mark J. Miller.

■ "Trapper County War" is a straightforward rednecks-vs.-city-boys yarn that's involving for most of the way. Lensed in the remote hills of North Carolina, viewers will believe the lawless goings on seen here could really happen unchecked by the authorities. **Pic does well on a low budget, but more business will be done via ancillary sales than from theatrical performance.**

Two young musicians from New Jersey, Ryan and Bobby, lose their way on a cross-country drive to California where they hope for record-making success. Barely have they driven into a small rural town when they're roughed up and told to leave by a seedy deputy (Don Swayze). Unfazed, they lunch in a diner in town where they hook up with bored waitress Lacey (Betsy Russell), who also hankers to be a singer but hasn't the gumption to pick up and leave. An orphan, she had been taken in, along with her timid older brother Elmore, by the town of Luddigger's first family.

After more scuffles between her new friends and her despised stepbrother Swayze, Lacey takes off with the clearheaded Ryan and Bobby. A chase across Trapper County ensues, the boys are jailed and released, and Bobby is killed by the Luddiggers after matriarch (Sarah Hunley) accidentally kills her adopted son. Ryan escapes into the thick forest. Bo Hopkins plays the laidback town sheriff who tries to keep the demented Luddiggers and their posse from going too far outside the law to bring back Ryan, who they say killed Elmore.

Hopkins adds some needed sanity to the proceedings, as does Ernie Hudson as an embittered Vietnam vet who provides the fugitive Jerseyite with food and sanctuary.

Performances are geneally solid. Robert Estes as Ryan is an attractive hero, and Betsy Russell as the lonely waitress brings unexpected conviction to the role (plus a solid Southern accent). Hudson adds life to a part that's been done to death. Local actors are authentic looking and sounding, and Sarah Hunley as Crazy Mama is scary in a "Deliverance" mode.

Director Worth Keeter keeps the story going at a good clip, and the dank mountainsides add greatly to the mood.

Pic takes a troubling turn at its violent climax, with the number of rifles in unreasonable hands making a good argument for gun control. —*Gerz.*

Sons

Cannes A Pacific Pictures production. (Intl. sales, Manley Prods.) Produced by Mark Toberoff. Directed by Alexandre Rockwell. Screenplay, Rockwell, Brandon Cole; camera (Duart color), Stefan Czapsky; editor, Jay

Freund; art direction, Virginia Fields; music, Mader. Reviewed at Cannes Film Festival (Market), May 14, 1989. Running time: **88 MIN.**
Mikey . . . . .William Forsythe
Ritchie . . . . .D. B. Sweeney
Fred . . . . .Robert Miranda
Father . . . . .Samuel Fuller
Florence . . . . .Stéphane Audran
Also with: Judith Godreche (Florence Jr.), William Hickey (Roger), Bernard Fresson (baker), Jennifer Beals (transvestite), Shirley Stoler (German housewife).

■ **"Sons" is a lively, funny and well-acted indie lensed between New Jersey and France. Three sons take their incapacitated father (played by the redoubtable Samuel Fuller) on a trip to Normandy to find his long-lost love. Helmer Alexandre Rockwell communicates his affection for the characters, giving their loudmouthed clowning a deeper dimension. Right handling should put this one over.**

Opening introduces Fred (Robert Miranda), a hot-headed small-time businessman, Mikey (William Forsythe), a sentimental, out-of-work eccentric, and Ritchie (D. B. Sweeney), the youngest brother and go-between. Pop (Fuller) is in a V.A. hospital, paralyzed from a stroke. His roommate William Hickey knows he wants to go back to Normandy, where he met a French girl during the war, and Mikey decides to take him there.

Action switches to France, where all three sons go along on Fred's cash. Bearing no physical or temperamental resemblance to one another (they have different mothers), the fraternal trio has constant clashes, yet conveys an underlying sense of affection, especially toward the father. All is done in spicy vernacular dialog with fine comic thesping from all hands.

Pic indulges in an exotic picture of Paris, all Arab dives and transvestite bars (most attractive transvestite is played by none other than Jennifer Beals in a cameo). Normandy, when they get there, is equally scenic, though the obvious fabrications are partially excused as New Jersey's idea of Europe.

Not all of it works, and Fuller's final meeting with his old flame, played by a severe Stéphane Audran, is emotionally barren. Yet pic's good humor gets it over credibility humps — like Fuller's convenient demise in Normandy, and brother Mikey's decision to stay and work for baker Bernard Fresson and his fetching daughter Judith Godreche.

Technically, pic is quite good

overall, notably Stefan Czapsky's lensing and Virginia Fields' sets. Music by Mader keeps up a pleasantly ironic beat. —*Yung.*

Personal Choice

Cannes A Moviestore Entertainment release of a Five Star Entertainment production. (Intl. sales, The Movie Group.) Executive producer, Mike Plotkin. Produced by Joseph Perez. Written and directed by David Saperstein. Camera (TVC color), John Bartley; editor, Pat McMahon; music, Geoff Levin, Chris Smart; sound (Ultra-Stereo), Eric Batut; production design, Jay Moore; art direction, Douglas Higgins; production manager, Colleen Nystedt; assistant director, Jacques Hubert; special visual effects, Lumeni Prods. Reviewed at Cannes Film Festival (Market), May 14, 1989. MPAA Rating: PG. Running time: **88 MIN.**
Paul Andrews . . . . .Martin Sheen
Eric . . . . .Christian Slater
Richard Michaels . . . . . . .Robert Foxworth
Laurie McCall . . . . .Sharon Stone
Mara Simon . . . . .Olivia d'Abo
Harry . . . . .F. Murray Abraham
Phil . . . . .Don Davis

■ **Martin Sheen's ever-ready support for liberal causes isn't enough to put over "Personal Choice," a sappy, heavy-handed message picture aimed at theaters but too weak to qualify as even a made-for-tv feature.**

"Cocoon" author David Saperstein offers a lifeless tale of an astronaut (Sheen) stricken with eventually fatal radiation poisoning during his moonwalk on a mid-'70s Apollo mission.

His bitter memories and disillusionment are rekindled when a gung-ho teen (Christian Slater) who idolizes him befriends the hermit-like Sheen while visiting his divorced father, who lives nearby. Script contrivance has dad (Robert Foxworth), a NASA scientist who has been laid off, cuing a late-in film confrontation with Sheen over who really did the work, the space scientists or the flyboys.

Despite the presence of beautiful leading ladies Olivia d'Abo and Sharon Stone (as Slater's and Foxworth's girlfriends), pic is all talk with almost no physical action. Characters remain remote and Saperstein muffs an emotional climax scene by framing a sentimental photo of a character with an in-joke presence of a "Cocoon" paperback in the foreground.

With cryptic flashbacks of Sheen's moonwalk ladled out every so often, film finally delivers its message direct to the camera long after viewers have lost interest: From out in space one can obtain the perspective to see what

we're doing to Earth, and want to fix it right now.

Icing on the cake is a laughable cameo by no less than F. Murray Abraham as a wheelchair-bound scientist (injured in an incident with a nasty Japanese whaling ship!) who exhorts us to stop killing the whales. Saperstein's message is, of course, correct and timely, but delivered in a form suitable for showing only at fundraisers attended by the committed.

Sheen is relentlessly earnest and boring, while Slater still displays those annoying Jack Nicholson inflections and mannerisms (apparently internalized) that have plagued his recent roles. If Nicholson had been cast as the astronaut (à la "Terms Of Endearment") Slater's idolizing might have come off.

Lensed largely in Vancouver (with a touristy stopoff in Huntsville, Ala., to visit NASA artifacts), pic is visually bland. A brief special-effects finale looks tacked on and silly. —*Lor.*

The Lemon Sisters

Cannes A Miramax release of a J&M Entertainment presentation of a Lightyear Entertainment production. Executive producers, Tom Kuhn, Charles Mitchell, Arne Holland. Produced by Diane Keaton, Joe Kelly. Directed by Joyce Chopra. Screenplay, Jeremy Pikser; camera (Technicolor), Bobby Byrne; editor, Michael R. Miller; music, Howard Shore; production design, Patrizia von Brandenstein; production manager, Carl Clifford; assistant director, Tony Lucibello; choreography, Anita Mann; casting, Mary Coloquhon. Reviewed at Cannes Film Festival (Market), May 15, 1989. MPAA Rating: PG-13. Running time: **89 MIN.**
Eloise Hamer . . . . .Diane Keaton
Franki DeAngelo . . . . .Carol Kane
Nola Frank . . . . .Kathryn Grody
Fred . . . . .Elliott Gould
Frankie . . . . .Aidan Quinn
C.W. . . . . .Ruben Blades
Nicholas Panas . . . . .Richard Libertini

■ **Set in Atlantic City, "The Lemon Sisters" is a romantic comedy about three women whose friendship overcomes all obstacles. Underwritten and awkwardly structured, the pic fails to deliver the promise of its strong cast. B.o. prospects aren't good.**

The film opens well with the three, Eloise (Diane Keaton), Franki (Carol Kane) and Nola (Kathryn Grody), performing a musical routine for the last time in a nightclub that's shuttering. Despite heckling, they sock over such standards as "Under The Boardwalk" and "Friends."

Eloise is an asthmatic who won't

give up her beloved cats (which cause the asthma) and who reveres her late father's collection of tv memorabilia (including Jack Benny's violin). She has a desultory relationship with cab driver Ruben Blades.

Franki is a scatty type taken in hand by Frankie (Aidan Quinn) who tries to groom her for a solo act; she succeeds, however, only when she inadvertently turns her number into a comedy routine.

Nola has a husband (Elliott Gould) and children, but loses her cash in a failed attempt to set up an elaborate taffy shop on the Boardwalk. Her friends rally round to help her save her home at fadeout.

The main problem with the film is an under-developed screenplay by Jeremy Pikser which is light on plot and lighter on genuine humor. Given such thin material, a huge load falls on director Joyce Chopra, and she fails to provide the light touch required. On the contrary, she tends to allow her actors to shout a lot, which becomes wearisome. Coproducer Diane Keaton comes off worst: Always an actress in need of a strong director, Keaton here allows her mannerisms to take over, and as a result her Eloise is the least endearing of the trio.

Best performance comes from Richard Libertini as a rich businessman who winds up buying Daddy's memorabilia.

Patricia von Brandenstein's production design is a major asset to the look of the film, and there's a well assembled music score. Keaton warbles a couple of songs charmingly.

Commercial prospects look poor for this one once the word gets around, though there might be first-weekend interest in the Keaton-Kane combo with the right ad campaign. —*Strat.*

Mes nuits sont plus belles que vos jours
(My Nights Are More Beautiful Than Your Days)
(FRENCH)

Paris   An AAA release of a Saris production. Produced by Alain Sarde. Written and directed by Andrzej Zulawski, based on the novel by Raphaële Billetdoux. Camera (Eastmancolor), Patrick Blossier; art direction, Jean-Baptiste Poirot; sound, Jean-Pierre Duret, Jean-François Auger; editor, Marie-Sophie Dubus; music, Andrzej Korzynski; production manager, Christine Gozlan; assistant director, Leslie Fargue. Reviewed at UGC Champs-Elysées theater, Paris, May 11, 1989. (In Cannes Film Festival Market.) Running time: **110 MIN.**
Blanche . . . . Sophie Marceau
Lucas . . . . Jacques Dutronc

Mother . . . . Valérie Lagrange
Hedwige . . . . Myriam Mezières
Inès . . . . Laure Killing
Concierge . . . . François Chaumette

■ **Paris-based Polish director Andrzej Zulawski continues to confuse hysteria with style in this adaptation of a bestselling romantic novel by Raphaele Billetdoux, who understandably had her name removed from the credits.**

It's not as indigestible as "L'Amour braque," Zulawski's unmentionable variation on Dostoyevsky's "The Idiot" — still "Mes nuits" is about as engaging as bouncing one's head against the wall, which is what the hero winds up doing to the heroine.

Sophie Marceau, who did unsavory things in "L'Amour braque," is the heroine, a talented young medium with a particularly frenzied entourage. Jacques Dutronc, the gifted pop singer-actor, plays a catatonic computer genius with a brain tumor who's speech faculties begin to break down, though the film beats him to it. Both characters have had traumatic childhood experiences.

Zulawski swings his camera around their passionate collision, first in a Paris cafe, then in a posh Biarritz hotel, where Marceau is being exploited to the hilt as a showbiz phenomenon. In addition to Marceau's nympho mom and jealous husband, there's a verse-speaking hotel concierge, plus torrents of verbal alliteration and word associations as Dutronc struggles to keep his brain and his tongue in touch with one another.

Dutronc, who's film appearances are frustratingly scarce, gives a performance of impressive technical control that perfectly captures the disconnected protagonist. Marceau adapts fairly well to Zulawski's directives, but she would do better in another director's cinematic fantasy.

Technically, film is first-rate, which contributes to the general feeling of artistic futility. —*Len.*

Othello

Cannes   An Uptown Films release of a Rockbottom production. (Intl. sales, Intercontinental Releasing.) Executive producer, Ted Lange. Produced by Katherine A. Kaspar. Supervising producer, James M. Swain. Directed by Lange. Screenplay adaptation, Lange, based on William Shakespeare's play; camera (CFI color), Swain; editor, Tim Tobin; music, Domenick Allen, Tom Borten; sound, John V. Speak, Mark Overton; production design, Christine Remsen; assistant director, Linda Manson Rockstroh; associate producers, Speak, Craig Lietzke, Myra Morris. Reviewed at Cannes Film Festival (Market), May

19, 1989. No MPAA Rating. Running time: **123 MIN.**
Othello . . . . Ted Lange
Iago . . . . Hawthorne James
Desdemona . . . . Mary Otis
Cassio . . . . Domenick Allen
Emilia . . . . Dawn Comer
Bianca . . . . Marina Palmier
Roderigo . . . . Stuart Rogers
Also with: David Kozubel, Ben Schick, John Serembe, Nelson Handel, Darryl Wright, Christa Marcione.

■ **Latest film version of the Shakespeare play offers some novelty elements that could generate theatrical and video interest.**

Ted Lange, after experience helming tv shows such as "The Love Boat," makes his feature debut directing himself alongside the cast of an "Othello" stage production.

Chief gimmick is not merely having a black actor in the Moor's role, but also casting black thesps as Iago and Iago's spouse, Emilia, in an otherwise all-white group of principal players.

This switch works primarily because of a forceful, dominating performance by Hawthorne James as Iago. With Lange eschewing the flamboyant effects associated with Olivier and Welles' screen versions of the role in favor of simplicity and underplaying, the contrast with Iago succeeds. Adding to the effective combination is James being nearly a head taller than Lange, making his evil counseling in the Moor's ear visually stimulating.

Low-budget production is straightforward, with extensive use of exteriors to avoid a stagey feel. Supporting cast is okay with the exception of Stuart Rogers' inappropriately high-pitched voice as Roderigo. —*Lor.*

The Dead Pit

Cannes   A Cornerstone Production Co. film. (Intl. sales, Skouras Pictures.) Executive producer, Jack A. Sunseri. Produced by Gimel Everett. Directed by Brett Leonard. Screenplay and editor, Leonard, Everett; camera (Monaco color), Marty Collins; music, Dan Wyman; sound, Stephen Powell; art direction, Ransom Rideout, assistant director, Brian Rogers. Reviewed at Cannes Film Festival (Market), May 14, 1989. Running time: **92 MIN.**
Dr. Gerald Swan . . . . Jeremy Slate
Dr. Colin Ramzi . . . . . . Danny Gochnauer
Jane Doe . . . . Cheryl Lawson
Christian Myers . . . Steffen Gregory Foster

■ **"The Dead Pit" is a low-budget horror flick about a chamber in the sub-basement of a mental institute which is the tomb of a deranged scientist and his lobotomized victims. The**

special effects are only moderately scary, and pic seems destined to go straight to video.

Twenty years ago, Dr. Gerald Swan, head administrator for the State Institute for the Mentally Ill, discovers his brilliant researcher has gone bonkers himself and is performing fiendish experiments on lobotomized patients. Swan is forced to kill Ramzi and seal him in a chamber (the "dead pit") in order to avoid a scandal that would ruin his career.

Back in the present "Jane Doe," a lovely young amnesiac, is found wandering around the streets and brought to the institute. She goes into hypnotherapy with Dr. Swan. Her presence somehow reactivates the evil Dr. Ramzi, who breaks the seal and begins stalking the lower regions of the wards. Eventually he unleashes his ghoulish former patients to terrorize the patients, but their deformed heads are more humorous than scary.

Some tongue-in-cheek jokes and puns liven up a fairly mindless script. The views of the victims lying with needles stuck in their exposed mangled grey matter is fairly sickening but other attempts to chill through blood-and-gore are not as successful. The more appealing nubile flesh of promising newcomer Cheryl Lawson as Jane Doe is given lots of exposure as she pads about the institution in t-shirt and panties. —*Sam.*

Estacion Central
(Central Station)
(SPANISH)

Cannes   A Septimania Films production. Produced by Manuel Valls and Albert Sagalés. Written and directed by J.A. Salgot; camera (Eastmancolor), Josep Maria Civit; editor, Ernest Blasi; sets, Vicenç Viaplana, Balter Gallart; music, Jordi Nogueras. Reviewed at the Cannes Film Festival (Market), May 21, 1989. Running time: **105 MIN.**
Alex . . . . Feodor Atkine
Elena . . . . Katarzyna Figura
Clara . . . . Paola Dominguin
Juan . . . . Gunter Meisner
Lucas . . . . Sergi Mateu

■ **This film about a photographer who accidentally takes a picture of a woman murdered in a train in Barcelona's Central Station has enough action and soft sex in it to generate modest sales in offshore markets, though these probably will be limited mostly to homevid and tv packages.**

Despite weak scripting and dialog, pic holds attention during most of its running time. The photog gets involved in a plot involving his pretty prostitute neighbor, her pimp, a police inspector (the least convincing of the characters) and members of the Barcelona underworld.

Alex, well thesped by Feodor Atkine, is on the verge of divorcing his unattractive wife. Before he can say "alimony," though, she's murdered, and he is accused of committing the crime. To aggravate matters, the police find photos of the girl murdered in the train in his studio after he inexplicably has lied to the cops about it.

Meanwhile, his pimp-pal and hooker neighbor have woven a complicated web of intrigue incriminating him. Perhaps a bit more violence, sex and special effects would have made it more saleable. —*Besa.*

Cavka
(Blackbird)
(YUGOSLAV-BRITISH)

Cannes A TRZ Film I Ton (Belgrade)-Smart Egg Pictures (London)-Croatia Film (Zagreb) production. (Intl. sales, Smart Egg Pictures). Executive producers, Jovan Markovic, Dorde Zecevic. Directed by Misa Radivojevic. Screenplay, Svetozar Vlajkovic, Radivojevic; camera (color), Radoslav Vladic; editor, Petar Jakonic; music, Kornelije Kovac; production design, Nemanja Petrovic; production manager, Momcilo Pesic. Reviewed at Cannes Film Festival (Market), May 15, 1989. Running time: 93 MIN.
Blackbird . . . . Marko Ratic
Prof . . . . Slobodan Negic
Prof's father . . . . Aleksander Bercek
Teacher . . . . Milena Dravic
Headmaster . . . . Bogdan Diklic
Psychiatrist . . . . Sonja Savic

■ **Simple, straightforward comedy-drama about the friendship between two schoolboys from very different backgrounds, "Blackbird" isn't strong enough to play the fest route, but will appeal to expatriate Yugo audiences and fans of kidfare.**

Prof is the nickname of a brainy, bespectacled kid with well-to-do parents he doesn't much like. Blackbird is the name given to a street kid, abandoned years earlier by his mother and left alone since his father was sent to prison. He lives in an old tramcar in the woods, and makes a living after school by washing car windshields.

Problem is that Prof's father disapproves of the friendship between his son and Blackbird, even after the latter saves Prof from drowning during a school outing.

Pic is standard fare, adequately made and technically fine, with

relaxed performances from the children. The supporting cast includes the ever-popular Milena Dravic in a marginal role as a teacher. —*Strat.*

Blowing Hot And Cold
(AUSTRALIAN)

Cannes A Chancom Ltd. presentation of a Rosa Colosimo production. Executive producers, Kevin Moore, Reg McLean. Produced by Colosimo. Directed by Marc Gracie. Screenplay, Colosimo, McLean, Luciano Vincenzoni, Sergio Donati; camera (color), James Grant; editor, Nicolas Lee; music, Joe Dolce; sound, Joe Wilkinson. Reviewed at Cannes Film Festival (Market), May 14, 1989. Running time: 85 MIN.
Jack Phillips . . . . Peter Adams
Nino . . . . Joe Dolce
Sally Phillips . . . . Kate Gorman
Shelagh McBean . . . . . . Elspeth Ballantyne
Jeff Lynch . . . . Bruce Kane

■ **A vehicle for Italo-Australian Joe Dolce, whose comedy disk "Shaddap You Face" became the most successful ever Aussie-produced single a while back, "Blowing Hot And Cold" is a minor entry better suited to the small screen than for theatrical release.**

Four writers labored to produce a tired screenplay in which Dolce appears as a rascally Italian salesman (of porno magazines and sex aids) who befriends a lazy small-town garage-owner (Peter Adams) after first trying to cheat him.

Adams' teenage daughter (Kate Gorman) has run off with her drug-running boyfriend, a piece of plotting which allows for the usual male buddy/road movie format, with some modest criminal action thrown in.

Dolce's fractured English is mildly amusing for a while, but becomes tiresome. Adams is more effective as the typical beer-swilling Aussie who finds unexpected friendship from this always optimistic "new Australian."

Elspeth Ballantyne is sympathetic as Adams' middle-aged, married mistress, and pic's only really funny scene is when her husband almost catches them in the act, but they're saved thanks to Dolce's quick thinking. As the young runaways, Kate Gorman and Bruce Kane fail to spark.

Modestly budgeted film is technically oke, with Dolce's music generally better than his performance. Director Marc Gracie can do little with the perfunctory, predictable screenplay.—*Strat.*

Mery Per Sempre
(Forever Mary)
(ITALIAN)

Cannes A Sacis-Intra Films release of a Numero Uno Intl. production. Produced by Claudio Bonivento. Directed by Marco Risi. Screenplay, Sandro Petraglia, Stefano Rulli; camera (color), Mauro Marchetti; editor, Claudio Di Mauro; art direction, Massimo Spano; music, Giancarlo Bigazzi. Reviewed at Cannes Film Festival (Market), May 12, 1989. Running time: 100 MIN.
Marco Terzi . . . . Michele Placido
Pietro . . . . Claudio Amendola
Also with: Alessandro Di Sanzo, Francesco Benigno, Roberto Mariano, Alfredo Li Bassi, Salvatore Termini, Matteo Mondello.

■ **Young helmer Marco Risi takes a look at a tough reform school in Palermo in "Forever Mary."**

Star Michele Placido, who plays the new teacher, is one of the only pro actors in the pic. Its appeal and conviction lie in its cast of boys really incarcerated for reasons similar to those they portray in the film. Two of the leads were unable to be flown in for the Cannes Market screening since they still are serving time. Pic has been picked up for the Montreal fest.

A predictable script by Sandro Petraglia and Stafano Rulli follows the rules of the genre, and it is the boys themselves who put some life into the film. Pietro (Claudio Amendola, an actor who does a good petty thief and hood) is caught after a mugging. Mary is a young transvestite whose father hates him. Claudio is an innocent, wide-eyed 14-year-old on his first conviction.

Marco Terzi (Placido) takes a job in the reform school while he waits for something better to turn up. Despised by the brutal guards as a bleeding-heart liberal, because he doesn't treat the boys like animals, as they do, Marco is equally scorned by his pupils for his lack of toughness.

He lets their leader Natale throw chalk in his face and write on him with pens. In the end Marco's peaceful determination wins the boys over. Even Natale, son of a Mafioso who killed his father's murderer, is impressed by Marco's lesson on why there is no water in Palermo's slums thanks to the Mafia.

Just when he's making progress, Natale turns 18 and is transferred to prison, Pietro runs away and is killed in a holdup, and gentle Claudio knocks a boy's eye out to keep from being raped. Despite all, Marco decides to stay in the reformatory.

Though it has plenty potential for violence, pic wisely avoids sensationalism. Language — some in Sicilian dialect — is frank and 4-letter. Placido makes a predictable liberal teacher in a cliched role, but has some clever dialog in his war to win the boys' trust. Technically well shot, pic boasts fine performances from its nonpro cast.

—*Yung.*

River Of Death

Cannes A Cannon Intl. release of a Breton Film Prods. Ltd. production. Produced by Harry Alan Towers, Avi Lerner. Directed by Steve Carver. Screenplay, Andrew Deutsch, Edward Simpson, based on Alistair MacLean's novel; camera (Rank color), Avi Karpick; editor, Ken Bornstein; music, Sasha Matson; sound, in Ultra-Stereo; art direction, John Rosewarne; associate producers, Michael Hartman, Erwin Hillier; casting, Caroline Zelder. Reviewed at Cannes Film Festival (Market), May 15, 1989. MPAA Rating: R. Running time: 100 MIN.
John Hamilton . . . . Michael Dudikoff
Dr. Manteuffel . . . . Robert Vaughn
Heinrich Spaatz . . . . Donald Pleasence
Col. Diaz . . . . Herbert Lom
Hiller . . . . L.Q. Jones
Maria . . . . Cynthia Erland
Anna . . . . Sarah Maur Thorp
Dahlia . . . . Foziah Davidson
Long John . . . . Ian Yule

■ **Generally ill-served on screen during his lifetime, novelist Alistair MacLean gets a posthumous slap in the face with Cannon's "River Of Death," an impoverished quota quickie.**

Tipped off immediately by his languid voiceover narration, erstwhile action star Michael Dudikoff gives a sleepy performance as John Hamilton, a guide whose pretty client (Sarah Maur Thorp) is captured in the Amazon jungle by cannibals. He mounts a motley expedition to go back after her, including mercenary L.Q. Jones, a couple of Israeli Nazi-hunters plus a shady rich guy (Donald Pleasence) and his young girlfriend (Cynthia Erland).

Everyone wants to get to a lost city, and final confrontation between a couple of feuding Nazis ends with a whimper, not a bang as the daughter of yet another Nazi they both wronged comes back to haunt them.

Director Steve Carver fails to disguise the pic's woeful absence of action. Similarly, the pic's South African locations do not convincingly double for its South American setting, reaching ludicrous extremes when black Africans are outfitted with stringy wigs to simulate indians.

Pleasence and Robert Vaughn barely try in their umpteenth assignment as Nazis; pic is set in 1965 so they don't have to look too old. Herbert Lom is laughingly cast as a Brazilian police chief, while blond newcomer Erland bears an uncanny resemblance to the slain Playboy model Dorothy R. Stratten, except for her oversize front teeth.—*Lor.*

Après le pluie
(After The Rain)
(FRENCH)

Paris A Forum Distribution release of an IMA Films production. Produced by Georges Benayoun, Paul Rozenberg. Written and directed by Camille de Casabianca. Script consultant, Yves Dangerfied; camera (color), Patrick Blossier; editor, Denise de Casabianca; sound, Philippe Senechal, Gérard Rousseau; music, Mamoud Ahmed; assistant director, Jacques Royer; production manager, Marcel Godot. Reviewed at Gaumont Ambassade theater, Paris, April 20, 1989. (In Cannes Film Festival, Market.) Running time: **90 MIN.**

Bertrand Cohen	Etienne Chicot
Marc Lafaye	Jacques Penot
Christine Faget	Camille de Casabianca
Salomon	Hassan Moussa Hassan

■ In 1987 Marco Ferreri made a feeble satire on humanitarian aid to the Third World, "Y'a Bon les blancs." Now actress, screenwriter and director Camille de Casabianca (who cowrote "Thérèse" with her father Alain Cavalier) covers the same theme in "After The Rain," her second feature.

Though made with more spirit and curiosity than Ferreri's fiasco, this modest-budgeted pic, shot on location in Djibouti, doesn't deliver the goods either.

Casabianca plays one of the leads, a naive, romantically disappointed young woman who enrolls with a relief organization in an African trouble zone. Her two principal colleagues are Etienne Chicot, a group leader with an incongruous nostalgia for Gaullist colonialism, and Jacques Penot, a barefoot, easygoing young medic.

Plot revolves around an illfated convoy into the desert during which they are taken prisoner by guerrillas and held hostage in a tiny village. Unlike Ferreri, who tried to push black comedy to its extremes, Casabianca's relatively realistic comedy is more concerned with characters, but fails to develop them sufficiently. The film plods once they are in captivity.

Chicot, a fine straight actor, has some delightful moments in a rare comic role, and Casabianca provides a good foil. Penot is appealing as the only well-balanced member of the crew. —*Len.*

High Stakes

Cannes A Vidmark Entertainment presentation. Executive producer, Michael Steinhardt. Written, produced and directed by Amos Kollek. Camera (color), Marc Hirschfeld; editor, Robert Reitano; music, Mira J. Spektor; associate producer, Julia Robinson. Reviewed at Cannes Film Festival (Market), May 14, 1989. MPAA Rating: R. Running time: **97 MIN.**

With: Sally Kirkland, Robert LuPone, Richard Lynch.

■ Sally Kirkland should have been more careful picking up parts after her nomination for an Oscar last year. Here she plays a hooker with a heart of gold caught between her procurer and a Wall Street broker who's been mugged on her street. There isn't much she can do to relieve the drudgery of this picture.

Kirkland, who kicks off with a strip act and tries for the rest of the film to look cheap and soulful at the same time, became a prostitute after her husband was killed in a car accident. Now she's had enough of it and wants out.

Robert LuPone is the stockbroker shocked by his partner's suicide.

The unlikely meeting between these two is followed by an even unlikelier relationship, burdened by pretentious philosophical reflections about nobody caring anymore, souls on sale, the differences between blue- and white-collar crime and more. One-liners such as "another day, another million," uttered by the broker's associates, are hard to beat.

Amos Kollek should at least have written a bit more plot to go with these dialogs, and pepped it up with more action than just another Russian roulette sequence. Kirkland is out of her depth, LuPone is remarkably unmemorable and Richard Lynch tried to soften his heavy image with a touch of sentimentality.

Technical credits won't carry this one much farther than the next-door video shop. —*Edna.*

Posed For Murder

Cannes A Fox/Fury Ventures presentation. (Intl. sales, Double Helix Films.) Produced by Carl Fury, Jack Fox. Directed by Brian Thomas Jones. Screenplay, John A. Gallagher, Chuck Dickenson, from Fox' story; camera (Technicolor), Bob Paone; editor, Brian O'Hara; music, Tom Marolda; sound, Rolf Pardula; production design, Claudia Mohr; assistant director, Colin Herrman; special makeup effects, James Chai; line producer, Steven Wren; casting, Dennis M. Lee, Nancy Winter-Cook. Reviewed at Cannes Film Festival (Market), May 15, 1989.

MPAA Rating: R. Running time: **85 MIN.**

Laura Shea	Charlotte J. Helmkamp
Rick Thompson	Carl Fury
Det. Steve Barnes	Rick Gianasi
Danny	Michael Merrings
Clifford Devereux	William Beckwith
Serge LaRue	Roy MacArthur
Terri	Terri Brennan
Sid	Jack Fox

■ Competently executed but unexciting, "Posed For Murder" is a slasher thriller that might generate decent video sales on the basis of its attractive leading lady and exploitable genre content.

Charlotte Helmkamp, who posed for Playboy magazine using the moniker Charlotte Kemp, doesn't stray too far in her role here as a buxom model for Thrill magazine, trying to get a lead role in a horror picture called "Meat Cleavers From Mars."

A nut is stalking her, killing her friends and acquaintances one by one.

Prime suspects include ex-boyfriend Michael Merrings, just out of jail, and new boyfriend Carl Fury. Cop on the case is another hunk, Rick Gianasi.

Director Brian T. Jones enjoys the many in-jokes and knowing references here. Unfortunately, little suspense is generated, cast gives extremely bland (and boring) line readings and final-reel payoff is unconvincing. Casting of coproducer Carl Fury in the male lead smacks of a vanity production.

Helmkamp is definitely an eyeful, but needs to work long and hard on her acting. Bob Paone's lensing is pro.—*Lor.*

Compo
(AUSTRALIAN)

Cannes A Sunrise Pictures production (Intl. sales, Kim Lewis Marketing). Produced by Nigel Buesst, Joanne Bell, Matthew Lovering. Directed by Buesst. Screenplay, Abe Pogos, based on his play "Claim NO: Z84;" camera (Eastmancolor), Vladimir Oscherov; editor, Nubar Ghazarian; music, Iain Mott; sound, Ray Boseley. Reviewed at Cannes Film Festival (Market), May 15, 1989. Running time: **82 MIN.**

Paul Harper	Jeremy Stanford
David Bartlett	Bruce Kerr
Carlo Garbanzo	Christopher Barry
Gina	Elizabeth Crockett
Dale Bradley	Cliff Neate
Tom Little	Rowan Woods
Vince Caruana	Peter Hosking
Eddie	Leo Regan

■ "Compo" — Australian slang for workers' compensation — is a likable enough but slight comedy that seems more appropriate as a telepic than a theatrical offering.

It follows the arrival of eager young graduate Jeremy Stanford at the claims department of a state compensation office. Far from his concept of a speedy and reasonable sympathetic outfit, he encounters a morass of civil service apathy and a bunch of appropriate no-hopers.

Subplot follows two bumbling investigators (Peter Hosking, Leo Regan) trying to assess a claim by tough detective Cliff Neate, who's trying to rejoin the force. Stanford's diligence, meanwhile, soon is seen as a liability by jaded boss Bruce Kerr and wisecracking, womanizing offsider Christopher Barry. But he manages to transfer to a better position anyway, while having an office romance with receptionist Elizabeth Crockett.

Pic is very low-key for a comedy. Much of that comedy derives from Aussie culture, so it may not mean as much to other audiences.

Performances generally are good, although Stanford's understated approach is a big contributor to the pic's mildness. Kerr, Barry and Rowan Woods (as a dim coworker) make a good showing. Tech credits are competent.

—*Doch.*

Society

Cannes A Wild Street Pictures presentation of a Keith Walley, Paul White production. Executive producers, White, Keizo Kabata, Terry Ogisu. Produced by Walley. Directed by Brian Yuzna. Screenplay, Woody Keith, Rick Fry; camera (Foto-Kem color), Rick Fichter; editor, Peter Teschner; music, Mark Ryder, Phil Davies; sound (Ultra-Stereo), William Fiege; production design, Mathew C. Jacobs; special makeup effects, Screaming Mad George; stunt coordinator, Dan Bradley. Reviewed at Cannes Film Festival (Market), May 13, 1989. No MPAA Rating. Running time: **99 MIN.**

Bill Whitney	Billy Warlock
Clarissa	Devin Devasquez

Also with: Evan Richards, Ben Meyerson, Charles Lucia, Connie Danese, Patrice Jennings, Ben Slack, David Wiley, Heidi Holm.

■ "Society" is an extremely pretentious, obnoxious horror film that unsuccessfully attempts to introduce kinky sexual elements into the extravagant makeup effects format of recent genre hits.

Rick Fry and Woody Keith's heavy-handed, shaggy dog script is a freaked-out variation on "The Stepford Wives." Teen Billy Warlock is thought to be paranoid by everyone, including his shrink, when he starts suspecting not only that he must have been adopted but also that his parents are having incestuous orgies with his sister.

Following many strange occurrences, red herrings and repetitive nudges about the class sytem and "fitting into society," it's finally revealed that rich and powerful folk really are some sort of undead monsters preying on Billy and all us other have-nots.

Sickening climax, notable for its poor continuity, is a sexual orgy called shunting, in which makeup expert Screaming Mad George indulges in what's credited as "surrealistic makeup effects." They turn out to be elaborations of the gooey stuff in "The Thing" remake and "From Beyond," latter produced by Brian Yuzna who makes his rather awkward directing debut here.

Though it's a fictional hint, the frequently emphasized incest plot element is unnecessary. The orgy itself is designed to blur the sexes and is pretty hard to watch, amounting to a fantasy film adaptation of what might be shown graphically in a rough trade porno film. The dubious points Yuzna and company are trying to make are smothered by the nastiness of the visuals.

Warlock is 1-note and surprisingly unsympathetic as the hero we're supposed to identify with, and his supporting cast is weak. Sole bright spot is a very sexy turn by former Playboy magazine model Devin Devasquez, yet she is stuck with one particularly tasteless line of dialog and an inconsistent characterization.

Of the technical credits, only the makeup counts, certain to gross out the fringe group that cares only about the goop content of a film. —*Lor.*

Summer Job

Cannes An SVS Films release of a Kenneth Dalton/Kuyes Entertainment picture, a Movie Job Inc. production, in association with Gomillion Studios. Produced by Josi W. Konski. Executive producers, John O'Donnell, Jeffrey Ringler, Ron Gell, David Walker, Ralph Wilson, Kenneth A. Dalton. Directed by Paul Madden. Screenplay, Wilson; camera (Agfa-Gevaert color), Orson Ochoa; editor, Christopher Cibelli; music, Ike Stubblefield; sound, Phil Pearle; assistant director, Bob Presner; 2d unit camera, Henry Lynk; coproducer, Dalton; casting, Brad Davis. Reviewed at Cannes Film Festival (Market), May 15, 1989. MPAA Rating: R. Running time: **90 MIN.**

Susan	Amy Baxter
Kathy	Sherrie Rose
Donna	Cari Mayor
Herman	George O.
Karen	Renee Shugart

Also with: James Summer, Chantal, Dave Clouse, Fred Bourdin, Kirt Earhardt, Hilly Gordon, Sherry Reichart, Orkestra.

■ Unbelievably in theatrical release Stateside, "Summer Job" represents the nadir of the teen sex-comedy genre, an amateur-

night film deficient on all levels.

Plotless wonder, with seven producers credited, including underachieving scripter Ralph Wilson, runs through tired sight gags and stupid dialog that is so badly acted and mechanically executed one can only marvel at the cynicism of its makers.

Sherrie Rose is the young supervisor of college kids working at a Florida resort for the summer. There's some practical joking, fraternizing with grotesque guests and boring partying. None of it works or is the least bit diverting.

Paul Madden's minimalist direction repeats camera setups in the manner of early D.W. Griffith, avoids camera movement and omits any hint of action footage. Apparently some pretty girls dropping their tops for a second or two is supposed to justify the rest.

Flat line readings are par for the course, while the token nerd is overplayed embarrassingly by thesp billed as simply George O. Cannes Market audience laughed only once, when a foppish waiter ineptly took a stab at reciting French dialog. —*Lor.*

A Chorus Of Disapproval

Seattle A South Gate Entertainment release. (Intl. Sales, J&M Entertainment). Executive producers, Andre Blay and Elliott Kastner. Produced and directed by Michael Winner. Screenplay, Winner, Alan Ayckbourn, based on Ayckbourn's play; camera (Rank color), Alan Jones; editor, Chris Barnes; music, John DuPrez; art direction, Peter Young; sound, Bob Taylor; assistant director, Marcia Gay. Reviewed at Harvard Exit, Seattle Intl. Film Festival, May 12, 1989. No MPAA Rating. (In Cannes Film Festival Market.) Running time: **100 MIN.**

Guy Jones	Jeremy Irons
Dafydd Llewellyn	Anthony Hopkins
Hannah Llewellyn	Prunella Scales
Fay	Jenny Seagrove
Rebecca	Sylvia Syms
Ian	Gareth Hunt
Jarvis	Lionel Jeffries
Bridget	Alexandra Pigg
Linda	Patsy Kensit
Ted	Richard Briers
Enid	Barbara Ferris
Crispin	Pete Lee-Wilson

■ It's tricky trying to convert stage to screen, and this is one play that suffers in translation. As a movie, "A Chorus Of Disapproval," chugs along when Alan Ayckbourn's play raced. His eccentric characters also fared better when viewed from the distance theater requires, their bizarre personalities appearing more believable and even human.

The movie is certain to please fans of Jeremy Irons, who delivers

a sympathetic performance as the hapless Guy Jones, although b.o. looks unpersuasive.

Irons shines as Jones, a shy, rather nervous widower who comes to work in the small English seaside town of Scarborough. He is lonely and, to meet people, he joins the local amateur group, which is practicing "A Beggar's Opera."

The production is directed by Dafydd Llewellyn (Anthony Hopkins), a scruffy solicitor whose only passion is the theater and who only really comes alive when he is directing a new play. Hopkins presents a credible Llewellyn, managing a smooth transition from a stand-up comic stick figure to one deserving true sympathy and understanding.

Jones, without really trying, soon becomes a small Lothario, his actions having hilarious effects on the various members of the drama group. Jones becomes involved with Llewellyn's lonely wife, Hannah (Prunella Scales), but she finds she is not alone in his affections.

In the stage version, a large part of the play's appeal lies in its clever juxtaposition of reality and make-believe, the subtle contrasts of what really is happening to the love trio to what is happening in the group's rehearsals. This similarity of events is all but obscured in the movie version. The result is funny, but a rather uningenious storyline.

Tech credits are fine. Pic is a fine, if uninspired, first screen adaptation of one of Great Britain's favorite playwrights. —*Magg.*

Les Matins Infideles (Unfaithful Mornings) (CANADIAN)

Cannes An Aska Film Distribution release of Les Productions du Lundi Matin film, with the financial participation of Telefilm Canada, Sogic, Radio-Canada and Commandigaires de la Societe en Commandite Duluth. Produced, written and directed by François Bouvier. Associate producers, Claude Cartier, Marc Daigle; camera (color), Alain Dupras; editor, Jean Beaudry; music, Michel Rivard; sound, Claude Beaugrand, Esther Auger; set decoration, Karine Lepp. Reviewed at Cannes Film Festival (Market), May 18, 1989. Running time: **90 MIN.**

Marc	Jean Beaudry
Jean-Pierre	Denis Bouchard
Laurent	Laurent Faubert-Bouvier
Julie	Violaine Forest
Pauline	Louise Richer
Young Woman on Corner	Nathalie Coupal

(French soundtrack)

■ Jean Beaudry and François

Bouvier, who made the notable "Jacques And November" in 1984, have come a cropper this time in presenting themselves as two of this year's more boring screen characters in a banal tale of everyday existence.

Jean-Pierre takes a picture every morning at 8:00 of the shop across the street. He takes these to Marc to inspire him in the writing of his novel. When nothing works he masturbates at the typewriter or stands on his head, imagining himself as a tree, whose roots are growing into the pavement.

Both men have trouble with the various women in their lives. Everything goes wrong, everyone is awash with misery and self-pity; both lack any sense of direction, purpose or responsibility in their lives. Finally, Jean-Pierre cuts down the tree outside the shop and hangs himself. Marc, it seems, might find a future with a "mysterious lady" whom Jean-Pierre had met at the bus stop, taken to bed, and made pregnant.

These dismal events are portrayed at a snail's pace, interspersed with daily scenes of snow shoveling in winter and jogging in summer, and other ordinary goings on. A serious, introspective study of all this might have some relevance with a powerful screenplay, performances and direction. But these are lacking here, and audiences who attempt to cope with it are in for a punishing time. —*Prat.*

The Kill-Off

Cannes A Filmworld Intl. production. (Intl. sales, Films Around The World.) Executive producers, Alexander W. Kogan Jr., Barry Tucker. Produced by Lydia Dean Pilcher. Directed by Maggie Greenwald. Screenplay, Greenwald, from Jim Thompson's novel; camera (Technicolor), Declan Quinn; editor, James Y. Kwei; music, Evan Lurie; sound, Mark Deren; production design, Pamela Woodbridge; production manager, Pat De Rousie. Reviewed at Cannes Film Festival (Market), May 17, 1989. No MPAA Rating. Running time: **95 MIN.**

Luane DeVore	Loretta Gross
Bobby	Andrew Lee Barrett
Pete	Jackson Sims
Ralph	Steve Monroe
Danny Lee	Cathy Haase
Rags	William Russell
Myra	Jorjan Fox

■ "The Kill-Off" is a rigorous, well-acted adaptation of a hard-boiled novel by Jim Thompson. Unrelentingly grim view of human nature plus a claustrophobic approach mark this for specialized audiences only.

Loretta Gross gives a strong performance (notable for excellent diction and projection) as Luane DeVore, an acid-tongued gossip-monger hated by almost everyone in her little community. She feigns a bedridden, feeble condition so that her husband (Steve Monroe), 20 years her junior, will take care of her hand and foot.

Things come to a head when folks decide to get rid of her, including Monroe, a slow-witted fellow whose new girlfriend (Cathy Haase) plots against his wife. Gross' death is followed by some bitter confrontations and a nihilistic finish.

Ensemble acting brings out the bitterness and hopelessness of a ragtag group of trapped characters. It's not a pretty picture, but helmer Maggie Greenwald keeps tight control of mood and tone.

Film's defects stem primarily from a low budget: More exteriors and action footage would give it the feel of a feature film rather than a stage piece, and Declan Quinn's underlit interiors overstay their welcome. Model-turned-actress Jorjan Fox gives a tentative performance as a young junkie that's not up to the level of her costars.

Tech credits are very modest. Evan Lurie's unusual score combines such instruments as saxophone and bandoneon (South American version of an accordion), but becomes repetitious and grating. —Lor.

O Grande Mentecapto
(The Blissful Misfit)
(BRAZILIAN)

Cannes   An Embrafilme release of an Oswaldo Caldeira production. Produced by Caldeira, Filmes Gerass and Embrafilme. Directed by Caldeira. Screenplay, Oswaldo Oroz, based on novel by Fernando Sabino; camera (color), Nonato Estrela; editor, Amauri Alves; music, Wagner Tiso; in Dolby stereo; art direction, Anisio Medeiros. Reviewed at Cannes Film Festival (Market), May 15, 1989. Running time: 105 MIN.
With: Diogo Vilela, Deborah Bloch, Osmar Prado, Regina Case, Luis Fernando Guimaraes, Imara Reis.

■ A light comedy on the Quixotesque adventures of a globetrotter from Minas Gerais, "The Blissful Misfit" displays attractive images of an inland Brazilian state and may appeal to young audiences.

Fernando Sabino is a writer with the typically "mineiro" humor, one of the reasons he has been among the widest-selling authors in Brazil for several decades. He was present at different stages of the production of this well-known

romance, whose main character is a blend of Don Quixote, Candide and the traditional mad dreamer of the tales of Minas Gerais.

Unlike Oswaldo Caldeira's previous credits — especially "Ajuricaba" (1976) and "O Bom Burgues" (1982) — helmer here strives for a very light and commercial adaptation of the work, filling the hero's tale with fine recreations of colonial Brazil and language suitable for children.

Geraldo Viramundo (Diogo Vilela), the globetrotter, becomes a priest, a soldier and a beggar in his search for assimilation into the society, but is always thrown out, until he becomes a leader of idiots and prostitutes attempting to take over the government palace.

The metaphor may not be appreciated by all, but the acting is efficient as are most technical credits — including the Dolby stereo — which will help make the film attractive to its target audience abroad. —Hoin.

Laura Laur
(CANADIAN)

Cannes   A Cinema Plus Distribution release of a Lux Films production. With the financial participation of Telefilm Canada, Societe Generale (SOGIC), the National Film Board, Super Ecran (Premier Choix), Bellevue Pathé Quebec, Societe Radio-Canada. Produced by Nicole Robert. Written and directed by Brigitte Sauriol, based on Suzanne Jacob's novel. Camera (color), Louis de Ernsted; editor, Andre Corriveau; art direction, Jean-Baptiste Tard; costumes, Nicoletta Massone; sound, Marcel Fraser, Jean-Pierre Joutel; music, Jean Corriveau. Reviewed at Cannes Film Festival (Market), May 17, 1989. Running time: 92 MIN.
With: Paula de Vasconcelos. Dominique Briand, Andre Lacoste, Andree Lachapelle, Eric Cabana, Johanne Fontaine.

(French soundtrack)

■ Based on the novel by Suzanne Jacob, this film attempts the difficult task of unravelling the impenetrable character of a young woman from a strange family background. Audiences may be left as much in the dark about Laura as when she first appears on the scene.

Brigitte Sauriol is a sensitive and talented filmmaker whose "Just A Game" (1983), dealing with incest, was a notable achievement. In "Laura Laur," however, she finds it almost impossible to explain why Laura behaves the way she does.

The center of her activities is her meeting (she is 20) with a well-to-do 50-year-old man who is tired of married life and has little zest for living. In a brief encounter every

man in his condition probably fantasizes over, she picks him up at a car-race, is cheeky and provocative, and before long is giving him a sexual experience the like of which he has never imagined.

Then she disappears, to return once a week to torment him. From then on, the story with its many psychological implications goes dark. It is almost impossible to figure out from flashbacks and conversations, the father, mother, brother, other lover implications. Worse, everyone is so glum and unhappy. Not a humorous word from anyone. The pace is slow, the camerawork unimaginative, the acting uneven. Paula de Vasconcelos does her best, but as Laura she is not likely to find much sympathy or understanding.—Prat.

Kotia päin
(Homebound)
(FINNISH)

Cannes   A Filminor presentation of Filminor (Heikki Takkinen) with Filmzolfo production. Directed by Ilkka Järvilaturi. Screenplay, Järvilaturi, Annina Enckell, Outi Nyytäja; camera (Eastmancolor), Kjell Lagerroos; editor, Tuula Mehtonen; music, Atso Almina; production design, Janusz Sasnowski; costumes, Merja Väisänen. Reviewed at Cannes Film Festival (Market), May 20, 1989. Running time: 90 MIN.
Mika . . . . Ilkka Koivula
Elli . . . . Leena Suomu
Kurkela . . . . Risto Tuorila
Ulla . . . . Jonna Järnefelt

■ "Homebound" is a bleak look at misfits in a Finnish provincial town. A misfit in itself, Ilkka Järvilaturi's drama about a young man's feeble attempts to tear himself away from the losers and scum surrounding him is unlikely to get much foreign exposure.

Basing his story on the records of a murder case, Järvilaturi pastes a double suicide ending onto a story that actually had a fairly happy outcome. The suicides of the film (real-life survivors in relatively good circumstances in Oulu) are a blowsy blond owner of a dockside vodka-mill and her bright math student son.

When young Mika's father died, the son wanted to break away to pursue a scholar's career in Helsinki. He is, however, drawn back to Oulu by his mother Elli's pleas for protection.

Elli, protected or not, is obviously a glutton for punishment. She submits with bovine patience to the sadistic treatment exerted by her new husband Kurkula, who one day forces her to "join" her dead spouse in latter's grave. On

other occasions, he locks her out to roam the streets naked or to crawl on all fours behind him.

In Helsinki, young Mika is disturbed by what is happening. To soothe his conscience, he starts beating up his pretty young girlfriend or having violent sex with her. He does occasionally go home, however. The last time he is too late: Elli's brother has hired a brutish, drunkard killer to do away with Kurkula.

More violence follows. Mika finds himself blackmailed by the hired killer and decides to do some killing of his own.

All of this is told jerkily and with the narration often obscured by over-inventive camera angles, fantasy flashbacks, or other devices meant to display artistic dash.

The mother is played with the proper dumb desperation by Leena Suomi. Most of the other characters are out of a rogues' gallery of illiterate public menaces. The really serious miscasting, however, is that of Ilkka Koivula as Mika, who is seen throughout as an unsmiling and self-absorbed young man of dull eyes and a bad complexion. Uncommunicative as he is as a character, his persona as an actor communicates even less. —Kell.

Easy Wheels

Cannes   A Fries Distribution release of a New Star Entertainment production. Executive producers, Sam Raimi, Robert Tapert, Bruce Campbell. Produced by Dmitri Villard, Robby Wald. Coproducer, Jake Jacobson. Directed by David O'Malley. Screenplay, O'Malley, Celia Abrams, Ivan Raimi; camera (Technicolor), James Lemmo; editor, John Currin; music, John Ross; sound, Dennis Carr; production design, Helen Dersjam; production manager, Julie Francis; assistant director, Robert Leveen; 2d unit director, Villard; 2d unit camera, Eugene Shlugleit; associate producer, Sara Altshul. Reviewed at Cannes Film Festival (Market), May 15, 1989. No MPAA Rating. Running time: 90 MIN.
Bruce . . . . Paul Le Mat
She-Wolf . . . . Eileen Davidson
Wendy . . . . Marjorie Bransfield
Prof . . . . Jon Menick
Animal . . . . Mark Holton
Candy . . . . Karen Russell
Merilee . . . . Jami Richards
Tondaleyo . . . . Roberta Vasquez
Allie . . . . Theresa Randal
Also with: Barry Livingston, Stevie Sterling, Mike Leinert, Robert Miano, Ted Raimi, George Plimpton.

■ "Easy Wheels" is a very cute, knowing throwback to drive-in movies of the early '70s, with genuine cult potential.

Bearing the trademark slapstick/comic book violence approach of the "Evil Dead" team of Sam Raimi, Bruce Campbell and Robert Tapert, pic limns the adventures on the road of a femme motorcycle gang, Women of the Wolf. Its leader is She-Wolf (Eileen Davidson), a tough cookie raised in the woods by wolves.

Her man-hating goal is to create a new world order run by women. To this end, she and her ladies in leather are on a kidnaping spree across the Midwest, absconding with baby girls to be raised in the forest by wolves.

Opposing force is a scruffy band of male bikers led by mystic Paul Le Mat. The sexes clash in several hilarious battles, featuring crazy, violent gags and inspired double entendres.

Direction by David O'Malley is functional but uneven, with too many talky, static stretches to satisfy hard action fans. However, whenever the script is really cooking, which is frequently, the combo of highbrow dialog and lowlife physical shtick is terrific.

With his "Melvin And Howard" background, Le Mat is perfect casting as the hippy-dippy biker, and Eileen Davidson, with her Joanna Pacula-like visage and cool manner, is more than his match. Almost everyone in the deep supporting cast gets a chance to shine as well.

Tech credits are modest. Running in-joke satirizes elements of "Raising Arizona," whose creators Joel & Ethan Coen previously were writers ("Crimewave") for Raimi & Co. —*Lor.*

Slow Burn
(CANADIAN)

Cannes A North American Releasing and EGM Film Intl. release of EGM Film Intl. production. Produced by Geoff Griffiths. Directed by John E. Eyres. Screenplay, Steven Lister; camera (color), Nathaniel Massey; music, Alan Grey. Reviewed at Cannes Film Festival (Market), May 16, 1989. Running time: **100 MIN.**
With: Anthony James, William Smith, Ivan Rogers, Scott Anderson, Mellisa Conroy.

■ **Filmed under the title "Brothers In Arms" but changed to "Slow Burn" when the producers found another film being shown with that name, this is not likely to find its way anywhere under any title.**

Filmed in Vancouver, which is passed off unconvincingly as New York City, this is a dark and dismal piece of gangster double-cross between the mafia and a Chinese gang. A prelude shows the murder of a family by a mafia hood. He

spares the young son. A great mistake. The audience must endure his determination to take revenge.

Watching the picture, this seems to take an eternity. Confusion abounds, the noise level is high, and everything looks as though it were copied from all previous low-budget pics on the same subject. A video release seems to be the only hope for this empty exercise in violence. —*Prat.*

Valentino Returns

Cannes A Skouras Pictures release of an Owl production. (Intl. sales, Vidmark Entertainment.) Produced by Peter Hoffman, David Wisnievitz. Directed by Hoffman. Screenplay, Leonard Gardner, based on his story "Christ Has Returned To Earth And Preaches Here Nightly;" camera (Alpha Cine color), Jerzy Zielinski; editor, Denine Rowan; music, source songs only; sound, Lee Strosnider; art direction, Woody Romine; assistant director, Ben Dossett; additional camera, Jeff Jur; associate producers, Nathaniel Dunn, Rowan; casting, Susan Shaw. Reviewed at Cannes Film Festival (Market), May 12, 1989. MPAA Rating: R. Running time: **88 MIN.**
Wayne Gibbs . . . . Barry Tubb
Sonny Gibbs . . . . Frederic Forrest
Patricia Gibbs . . . . Veronica Cartwright
Sylvia . . . . Jenny Wright
Also with: David Parker, Seth Isler, Miguel Ferrer, Kit McDonough, Macon McCalman, Jenny Gago, Leonard Gardner, William Frankfather, Jerry Hardin.

■ **Quite well-acted, "Valentino Returns" is an okay bit of Americana that has only modest theatrical prospects.**

Lanky young thesp Barry Tubb is featured as a small-town teen in the '50s whose rites of passage (presented rather episodically by helmer Peter Hoffman) include scrapes with the law, romancing neighborhood chicken farmer's daughter Jenny Wright and getting his even more adolescent dad, Frederic Forrest, out of trouble.

Adapted by Leonard Gardner from his own short story, pic is picaresque in tone, but given to dramatic outbursts, especially when concerned with Forrest's womanizing, confrontations with his long-suffering wife (Veronica Cartwright, excellent in an interesting interpretation) and various outlandish behavior.

Tubb, an appealing performer, is overburdened with a plot that places too much nostalgic weight on his treasured steed, a new pink Cadillac. Soundtrack echoes the overemphasis on atmosphere with a long list of song hits but no background score to cover the draggy sketches.

Jerzy Zielinski's lensing is evocative and film climaxes on an entertaining note: Tubb's family

finally is drawn together as a unit in protecting Wright from her mean father's wrath (and belt). Though pic was filmed in both California and Florida, with an extended production history, finished product bears little evidence of behind-the-scenes headaches.

Thank you credits on print go out to Sundance Institute, Fred Roos and Michael Hausman, among others. —*Lor.*

Kopytem sem, kopytem tam
(Tainted Horseplay)
(CZECH)

Cannes A Barrandov Film Studios production. Directed by Věra Chytilová; screenplay, Pavel Skapik, Chytilová; camera (color), Jaroslav Brabec; art direction, Zbynek Hloch; music, Jiri Chlumecky, Jiri Vesely. Reviewed at Cannes Film Festival (Market), May 19, 1989. Running time: **150 MIN.**
Pepe . . . . Tomás Hanák
Dedek . . . . M.. Steindler
Frantisek . . . . ʾav.. Vávra
Jirina . . . . Tereza Kucerová
Jana . . . . Bára Dlouhá
Hana . . . . Renáta Becerová
Actress . . . . Chantal Poullain-Polivková

■ **One of the first Czech films on on AIDS, Věra Chytilová's "Tainted Horseplay" (previously "Snowball Reaction") is a long, meandering tale about bored singles who use casual sex as an escape and end up in the nightmare of AIDS. Plentiful nudity (male and female) should assure wide local viewing, but pic lacks tightness to work as a film as well as a moral tale.**

First hour introduces three pals in their 30s: good-looking Pepe (Tomás Hanák), an incorrigible playboy; wiry, would-be playwright Frantisek (David Vávra), and Dedek (Milan Steindler), a paunchy vet. The trio clowns around at parties, in the office, on the ski slopes. Though Pepe has a firebrand girlfriend (Tereza Kucerová), that doesn't stop him from sleeping with every girl he meets. There's also a good deal of bed-switching among the pals and their girlfriends.

Pepe is the first to fall sick. It takes forever for the nature of his illness to come out. When the friends discover they too may be infected, they turn into ferocious animals, shunning each other. They're scared out of their wits.

Many gags don't make it over the subtitles. Sex scenes are kept mild and playful, but soon become tiresome.

Chytilová's penchant for dizzying moving camerawork and

crooked framing gets limited play. The three main thesps turn in good work, but script keeps audience from identifying with any of them. Dede's illness and group's dissolution make no great emotional impact.

Lesson of film is clear, however, and it ought to serve a didactic purpose. —*Yung.*

L.A. Bounty

Cannes A Noble Entertainment Group and Alpine Releasing Group presentation of an Adventuress Prods., Leighton & Hilpert production. Produced by Sybil Danning, Michael W. Leighton. Directed by Worth Keeter. Screenplay, Leighton, from story by Danning; camera (Foto-Kem color), Gary Graver; editor, Stewart Schill; music, Howard Leese, Sterling; sound, David Waelder, George Alch; art direction, Phil Brandes; production manager-assistant director, Tony Brewster; stunt coordinator, Bob Bralver; line producer, Leighton; coproducer, Robert P. Palazzo; associate producer, George Cook; casting, Pat Orseth. Reviewed at Cannes Film Festival (Market), May 13, 1989. No MPAA Rating. Running time: **81 MIN.**
Ruger . . . . Sybil Danning
Cavanaugh . . . . Wings Hauser
Lt. Chandler . . . . Henry Darrow
Kelly Rhodes . . . . Lenore Kasdorf
Also with: Robert Hanley, Van Quattro, Bob Minor, Frank Doubleday, Maxine Wasa, Robert Quarry, Blackie Dammett, J. Christopher Sullivan.

■ **Sybil Danning executes something of a self-parody in the lame action vehicle "L.A. Bounty," a minor title for video usage.**

Also coproducing and providing the weak storyline, Danning portrays a macha bounty hunter patterned after Clint Eastwood's Man With No Name, including his trademark mannerisms and cheroots. There the resemblance ends.

She's after nemesis Wings Hauser, a wigged-out artist and drug kingpin with a price on his head. Hauser has mayoral candidate Robert Hanley kidnaped and Danning is one step ahead of the police in trying to free him and put away Hauser for good.

Director Worth Keeter includes lots of filler in this uninvolving opus. Hauser is allowed to ham it up preposterously while Danning, unflatteringly photographed, merely looks sullen.

Best technical credit is the often rousing musical score by Howard Leese and Sterling, which fails to disguise how listless the action scenes are. —*Lor.*

Pasion de Hombre
(A Man Of Passion)
(SPANISH)

Cannes A Golden Sun production. Executive producer, J.A. de la Loma Jr. Written and directed by José Antonio de la Loma. Camera (Eastmancolor), Tote Trenas; editor, J.A. de la Loma Jr.; sets, Juan Ferrer; art consultant, Modest Cuixart; sound, Jaime Puig; English dialog, Robert Miller; production manager, Joaquin Densalat; Spanish casting, Marta Flores; U.S. casting, Claire Newell. Reviewed at Cannes Film Festival (Market), May 20, 1989. Running time: **97 MIN.**

Mauricio	Anthony Quinn
George (child)	R.J. Williams
Susana	Maud Adams
Basillo	Ray Walston
Nuria	Victoria Vera
Jose Pedro	Pepe Martin
Gloria	Elizabeth Ashley

Also with: Ramon Sheen, José Maria Caffarel, Shari Shattuck, Robert Miller, Josep Minguell.

(English soundtrack)

■ **Anthony Quinn puts in a fine, though overfamiliar, performance in this pic about an aged womanizing painter living on the Costa Brava. Though some of the dialog is stilted and the situations are often clichés, pic could garner some commercial interest, especially with Quinn as a draw.**

Yarn is partly told through the eyes of an 11-year-old boy whose actress mother takes him to Spain to spend a summer with his grandfather, an artist.

The artist, Mauricio, is a freewheeling, bohemian eccentric, who's big on talent but short on money. The boy is a budding concert pianist who at first remains skeptically aloof from the painter, but whose heart is soon won by Mauricio.

The painter manages to get a baby grand for the boy, shows him the countryside and preaches to him the joy of life. Mauricio's pleasures alternate between impassioned bouts with his canvas, conquests of pretty women living in the neighborhood and good-natured drinking. It is all a bit too pat, and the director-writer provides no twists to his main character.

Pic concludes 12 years after main action of film, when the boy, now a seemingly successful pianist, is called back for a final meeting with the painter.

Technical credits are good, lensing in picturesque sites are a plus and most of the thesping adequate.

—*Besa.*

Out Of Time
(BRITISH-EGYPTIAN)

Cannes A Motion Picture Intl. presentation of an ATP and Tamido Films production. Executive producers, Wagih Khairy, Joseph Nassar. Produced and directed by Anwar Kawadri. Screenplay, Jesse Graham; camera (color), Fred Tammes; editor, John Shirley; music, Alan Parker. Reviewed at Cannes Film

Festival (Market), May 14, 1989. Running time: **94 MIN.**

Jake	Jeff Fahey
Rene	Camilla More
Stavros Eliomotis	Spiros Focas
Haros	Michael Gothard
Nikos	Michael Russo
Donald	Tuck Milligan
Omar	Gamil Rateb

■ **"Out Of Time" weaves a pleasant but innocuous modern romantic adventure against an ancient historical background. It merits a wide screen to show off its stunning lensing, but video appeal should be strong as well.**

Archeologist Jake and his assistants retrieve a marble bust of Alexander the Great from the sea near a Greek island, and discover a clay serpent with hieroglyphics concealed within. The news travels fast and Jake soon has rivals for possession of the serpent, including the suavely persuasive Greek tycoon Stavros Eliomotis.

During a lecture he is giving later, Jake is distracted by Rene, a mysterious beauty who asks a question, revealing she has only a foggy notion exactly who Alexander the Great was. He spies her later across a crowded taverna and runs off with her after dumping a truckload of watermelons on her companion Nicos, the son of the Greek tycoon. When the serpent is stolen, Jake is thrown out of Greece. He heads for Egypt accompanied by Rene in a race to find Alexander's treasures before the others do and clear his name.

The rest of the movie proceeds in a "Romancing The Stone" mode with Jake characterized as an obsessed scientist eager to get to the site while Rene seems more at home having a bellydance lesson with college chums she's run across in an Alexandria nightclub. She proves she's made of sterner stuff, as the search for the treasures, when she has blood smeared over her in a purification ritual, is chased up treacherous rocks by an adversary, and treks for miles without water across the desert.

The plot, except for the unique way of bumping off those who prove troublesome, is predictable and the dialog less than profound. Viewers looking for visually appealing escapist entertainment should find it enjoyable. Archeological experts were consulted during the shoot and mini history lessons are painlessly interjected. Tech credits are fine and scenery in the remote Siwa desert of Egypt is especially striking. —*Sam.*

Tale Of Two Sisters
(COLOR-B&W)

Cannes A Vista Street Entertainment presentation of an L.A. Dreams production. Executive producers, Jerry Feifer, Tony Miller. Produced by Lawrence Bender, Randoll Turrow. Supervising producer, James R. Hanson. Directed and created by Adam Rifkin. Screenplay, improvised by cast; camera (color), John F.K. Parenteau; editor, King Wilder; music, Marc David Decker; sound, Steve Evans, Bob Murawski; additional camera, Mark Parry; special makeup effects, Tony Gardner. Reviewed at Cannes Film Festival (Market), May 18, 1989. No MPAA Rating. Running time: **89 MIN.**

Phil	Valerie Breiman
Liz	Claudia Christian
Dad	Sydney Lassick
Mom	Dee Coppola
Butler/Auntie Sparkle	Tom Hodges
Taxi driver	Jeff Conaway
Gardener	Pete Berg
Adult bug girl	Danielle Von Zerneck
Bug girl	Samantha Hallie Culp
Gravedigger	Brian Belknap

Narration and poetry by Charlie Sheen.

■ **"Tale Of Two Sisters" is an experimental feature combining improvised conversations with surreal imagery. Commercial prospects are nil, but a small cult following could be developed.**

Filmmaker uses a basic storyline of two adult siblings, Valerie Breiman and Claudia Christian, having a reunion after five years and mulling over their childhood and unresolved mutual resentments.

Upon this he overlays, in the shredded footage manner not used often in American films since Henry Jaglom's 1971 "A Safe Place," memories and nightmarish or surreal images to illustrate the women's feelings. Unfortunately, some of Adam Rifkin's imagery smacks of the usual film student's fondness for Fellini, particularly "8½."

More damaging to the film's overall impact is the frequent appearance of Dee Coppola as the girls' mom. Her huge breasts and grotesque makeup create a silly figure at odds with what the women say about their family life as kids.

Christian does best at improvising anecdotes and her true feelings, while pretty younger sister Breiman comes off as mannered and phony without a script to rely on.

Rifkin delivers some interesting photographic effects, particularly in brief black & white sequences, while voiced-over poetry by Charlie Sheen adds another dimension to the footage and should spur curiosity to see this offbeat film.

—*Lor.*

Summer Of The Colt
(CANADIAN)

Cannes A Cinema Plus release of Les Productions la Fête film. Produced by Rock Demers, Lita Stantic. Directed by Andre Melançon. Screenplay, Genevieve Lefebvre, Rodolfo Otero, based on Otero's story; camera (color), Thomas Vamos; editor, Andre Corriveau; music, Osvaldo Montes; sound, Yvon Benoit; art direction, Esmeralda Almonacid; production manager, Dolly Pussi; costumes, Lucrecia Matilde de Ricart. Reviewed at Cannes Film Festival (Market), May 19, 1989. Running time: **100 MIN.**

Federico	Hector Alterio
Ana	China Zorrilla
Laura	Alexandra London-Thompson
Daniel	Juan de Benedictis
Martin	Santiago Gonzalez
Felipe	Mariano Bertolini
Manuela	Gabriela Felperin
Luis	Manuel Callau
Damasia	Emilia Farah

■ **This is No. 8 in Rock Demers' successful series "Tales For All," family films which have won large audiences in Quebec and Europe. This one is more than likely to join them; horses and children seldom miss at the b.o.**

Filmed entirely in Argentina, this coproduction between Les Productions la Fête (Canada) and GEA Cinematografica is a simple, sensitive story by Rodolfo Otero, set against the beautiful pampas scenery surrounding a family ranch. Here 12-year-old Martin, his friend Daniel, his brother Felipe and sister Laura come to visit their grandfather and his sister, Ana, from Buenos Aires. There are hundreds of beautiful horses to be ridden and enjoyed, a family tradition; a long, pleasant, lazy summer in peace and quiet, in which the children become aware of the land and learn to love nature.

This year however, Laura has turned 13 and her grandfather, usually kind and loving, turns against her because, it transpires, she brings back his long buried pain of the memory of having been deserted by his young wife (who looked like Laura) after the birth of their only child. Before the summer is over, these emotional disturbances are laid to rest and the children leave happily, looking forward to returning the following year.

All credits are exceptionally good: the fine photography of Thomas Vamos; the lovely, restrained score by Osvaldo Montes; the understanding direction by Andre Melançon of the delicate screenplay by Genevieve Lefabvre from Otero's story. Well-known Argentine actor Hector Alterio is perfect as the grandfather and the children are natural and likable.

China Zorrilla, distinguished actress from Uruguay, doesn't have much to do or say as the sister, but her presence is effective. Film was shot in Spanish, and then dubbed into French and English versions. This English version is carefully done. The French title is ''Fierro ou l'ete des Secrets.'' —*Prat.*

Aprés la guerre
(After The War)
(FRENCH)

Paris An AMLF release of a Caméra Noire/TF1 Films/GPFI coproduction. Produced by Jean-Claude Fleury. Written and directed by Jean-Loup Hubert. Camera (color), Claude Lecomte; editor, Benedicte Brunet; music, Jurgen Knieper; art direction, Thierry Flamand; sound, Bernard Aubouy, Dominique Dalmasso; assistant director, Patrick Poubel; production manager, Alain Depardieu. Reviewed at Pathé Clichy, Paris, May 5, 1989. (In Cannes Film Festival, Market.) Running time: **108 MIN.**

Antoine . . . . Antoine Hubert
Julien . . . . Julien Hubert
German soldier . . . . Richard Bohringer
Victor Toulis . . . . Martin Toulis
La Crochue . . . . Isabelle Sadoyan
Gaby . . . . Olivier Nembi
The mayor . . . . Raoul Billerey

■ Two French kids and a German provide the sentimental movieland formula in this wartime drama by Jean-Loup Hubert, whose ''Grand Highway'' enjoyed a merited critical and commercial success.

''After The War'' commendably avoids the winsome pitfalls of the subject, but it's predictable fare that fails to dredge up much emotion. Basic ingredients and slick packaging, however, could give it some offshore selling strength.

Hubert's original script, set in August 1944, tells of how two smalltown kids, on the run after committing a tragic gaffe, fall in with an invalid German soldier who's deserted as advancing Allied forces rout the occupying armies. After an inevitably difficult acquaintanceship, the boys and the soldier take a liking to each other and share their flight. But the German is caught by American soldiers and executed for looting.

Director has cast his own sons, Julien, 8, and Antoine, 12, (he was the boy in ''Grand Highway''), and they are perfect. But Richard Bohringer as the German is a major mistake. Though his fluent, unaccented French is attributed to his Alsatian origins, one is too aware of a French star playing a German who's a hardened veteran of two world wars (his climactic horror and outrage at a massacred French village strikes a particularly false note). Foreign auds

with no perception of French speech or familiarity with Bohringer may accept the imposture with less difficulty. —*Len.*

The Last Warrior
(BRITISH)

Cannes An SVS Films release of an ITC Entertainment Group presentation of a Label Prods/Martin Wragge production. Executive producer, Wragge. Produced by Keith Watkins. Written and directed by Wragge. Camera (Technicolor), Fred Tammes; editor, Jacqueline Le Cordeur; music, Adrian Strijdom; sound (Dolby), Henry Prentice; associate producer, Roger Orpen. Reviewed at Cannes Film Festival (Market), May 15, 1989. No MPAA Rating. Running time: **94 MIN.**

Jim Kemp . . . . Gary Graham
Katherine . . . . Maria Holvöe
Imperial marine . . . Cary-Hiroyuki Tagawa
Priest . . . . John Carson

■ ''The Last Warrior,'' alternately called ''Coastwatcher,'' is a subpar World War II drama whose penchant for closeups, even during action scenes, betrays its video targeting.

Filmmaker Martin Wragge misses the boat right at the outset by choosing and styling a loner hero (Gary Graham) who is strictly modern '80s though cast as a U.S. soldier at a surveillance post in the South Pacific in April 1945.

A Japanese warship arrives and kidnaps all the natives and missionaries on the island, except for Graham and a beautiful blond nun-in-training, Maria Holvöe.

It's a very poor man's ''Heaven Knows, Mr. Allison,'' as the two bicker but survive together, with Graham excessively lucky that the Nipponese soldiers always choose to attack him singly. Relentlessly padded film climaxes halfway through when skilled warrior Cary-Hiroyuki Tagawa decides to spare Graham's life so he can (quite improbably) train him to fight as an equal.

Mumbo-jumbo about ''honor'' and learning how to die properly won't fool an audience that will easily sniff out the artificial prolonging of a skimpy story.

Some attractive forest and mountain locations perk up the action, with the highlight scenes taking place on a rusted old ship that looks suspiciously like the set used for Wragge's previous South African-lensed sci-fier ''Survivor.'' Director's overuse of slow motion during shootouts and swordfights is a drag.

While Graham obviously is miscast, Holvöe as the novice nun is a ringer, ready for entry in a wet t-shirt contest. Tagawa gives a stalwart performance that works to-

ward overcoming the idiotic nature of his character, a killing machine without the killer instinct. —*Lor.*

Rabid Grannies

Cannes A Troma release of a Stardust Pictures production. Executive producer, James Desert. Produced by Desert, Jonathan Rambert. Written and directed by Emmanuel Kervyn. Camera (Eastmancolor), Hugh Labye; editor, Philippe Ravoet; music, Peter Castelain, J.B. Castelain; production design Luke Bertrand; special effects, Steven Fernandez; sound, Frederic Ullman. Reviewed at Cannes Film Festival (Market), May 18, 1989. Running time: **83 MIN.**

With: Catherine Aymerie, Caroline Braekman, Danielle Daven, Raymond Lescot, Elliot Lison, Michel Lombet, Anne Marie Fox, Paule Herreman, Bobette Jouret, Françoise Lamoureux, Jack Mayar, Françoise Moens, Sebastien Radovitch, Richard Cotica.

■ Apart from having one of the best titles of the year, ''Rabid Grannies'' is a real treat for gore aficionados. Troma's Lloyd Kaufman and Michael Herz should have a solid genre home-vid item here, perhaps theatrical too, although pic's graphic content will mean narrow release.

Typically offbeat story sees various family members congregate for the birthday of their sweet, kindly grannies, Danielle Daven and Anne Marie Fox. Elderly duo also are loaded, and each of the family is looking to get a big share of an inheritance, as soon as possible.

Amidst the proceedings a present arrives from the black sheep of the family, spurned because of his satanic activities. When opened the duo are transformed into hideous cannibalistic monsters (that scene and their first act of retribution are quite striking). From there it's the usual cat and mouse plot, yielding some of the most gruesome scenes imaginable.

Like it or loathe it, effects creator Steven Fernandez has created some truly eye-averting, gut-wrenching scenes. Pic as such isn't scary — an audience has to divorce itself from such goings on — but horrible in the true sense. Director Emmanuel Kervyn tries to weave in some black humor, but most of it's probably lost to all but the most hardened of audiences by pic's end.

Quality of acting in this effects-driven pic is irrelevant; suffice to say there's a market there for something as nasty but well done as ''Rabid Grannies.'' — *Doch.*

Rising Storm

Cannes A Gibraltar Releasing and Crawford/Lane Prods. presentation. (Intl. sales, Im-

age Organization). Executive producer, Joel Levine. Produced by Jay Davidson, James Buchfuehrer. Directed by Francis Schaeffer. Screenplay, Gary Rosen, William Fay; camera (color), Robb D. Hinds; editor, Alan Baumgarten; music, Julian Laxton; sound (Dolby), Henry Prentice; art direction, Jon Jon Lambon; assistant director, Buchfuehrer; associate producers, Karl Johnson, Barrie Saint Clair; casting, Barbara Remsen & Associates. Reviewed at Cannes Film Festival (Market), May 12, 1989. No MPAA Rating. Running time: **96 MIN.**

Artie Gage . . . . Zach Galligan
Joe Gage . . . . Wayne Crawford
Mila Hart . . . . June Chadwick
Don Waldo . . . . John Rhys-Davies
Blaise Hart . . . . Elizabeth Keifer
Lt. Ulmer . . . . Graham Clark
Also with: William Katt, Gordon Mulholland, Patrick Mynhart, Deep Roy.

■ Alternating at will between futuristic satire and hard action sequences, ''Rising Storm'' a.k.a. ''Rebel Waves,'' is an entertaining hybrid in the ''Mad Max'' genre, likely to scare up a video following.

Lensed in South Africa (spotlighting the scenic views of the now over-familiar Namib desert), pic is set in the U.S. in the year 2099, when what's left of the country is ruled by a totalitarian theocracy headed by oily televangelist Jimmy Joe 2d.

Spoof elements get underway with a bang as Richard Strauss' ''Thus Sprach Zarathustra'' plays during the opening credits sequence, in which a huge Big Boy hamburger statue is excavated like some rare artifact.

On-the-run plot has brothers Wayne Crawford and Zach Galligan (former just sprung from stir) thrown in with blond sisters June Chadwick and Elizabeth Keifer, the gals being chased by various heavies headed by John Rhys-Davies (whose penchant for sadistic torture is film's roughest element).

Femmes turn out to be freedom fighters, who with the heroes' unwitting assistance uncover the ancient radio station of a militant deejay. They use cassettes he left behind to broadcast the truth to a brainwashed populace and bring about a revolution.

Helmer Francis (a.k.a. Franky) Schaeffer overlays the usual post-apocalypse shenanigans with high style, including some smooth Steadicam work and solid action scenes. Exaggerated tongue-in-cheek nature of the script skews the film's potential audience toward cultists, however.

Crawford, better known as producer (though he previously starred in his own pic, ''Jake Speed''), does very well as the mercenary hero. Newcomer Keifer complements spunky Chadwick as heroines willing to muss up their hair a bit. William Katt, who previously starred for Crawford and his producing partner Andrew Lane in "White Ghost," is effective in an unbilled cameo as the d.j. —Lor.

Lover Boy
(AUSTRALIAN)

Cannes A Seon Films production, with assistance from the Australian Film Commission and Independent Film Makers' Fund of Victoria. (Intl. sales, Kim Lewis Marketing, Melbourne.) Produced by Daniel Scharf. Directed by Geoffrey Wright. Screenplay, Wright; camera (color), Michael Williams; editor, Grant Fenn; music, John Clifford White; production design, Judy Borland; sound, Mark Tarpey; associate producer, Ian Pringle; production manager, Elisa Argenzio. Reviewed at Cannes Film Festival (Market), May 19, 1989. Running time: **60 MIN.**
Mick	Noah Taylor
Sally	Gillian Jones
Gaz	Ben Mendelsohn
Duck	Daniel Pollock
Rhonda	Alice Garner
Lex	Peter Hosking
Mick's mother	Beverley Gardiner

■A promising debut for writer-director Geoffrey Wright, "Lover Boy" unfortunately doesn't provide enough material to play as a solo feature and will be too strong for tv in many countries. Double-billing would be the answer.

Clocking in at just an hour, pic toplines Noah Taylor, from "The Year My Voice Broke," as Mick, a suburban 16-year-old who prefers the company of a lonely 43-year-old woman Sally (Gillian Jones), to that of friends his own age. He meets Sally when she employs him to cut her grass, and all too soon they're involved in a passionate affair. She rejects him when a former lover returns, but when Mick discovers that Sally has been beaten by the lover, he attacks him and is fatally stabbed as a result.

All of this is fine as far as it goes. Performances are excellent, especially Jones as the world-weary woman attracted to the scrawny teenager. Lovemaking scenes between them are fairly forthright, and quite emotional. Scenes involving Mick's layabout friends are more conventional, and inadequate sound recording has rendered much of the dialog muffled. Nevertheless, "Lover Boy" certainly introes a new director to watch for in Geoffrey Wright.

It's a pity that more money couldn't have been found to expand the film to more conventional feature length: There was certainly the material for a longer movie here, and one that might have had real theatrical possibilities.

Technically, "Lover Boy" just scrapes by, its minuscule budget always apparent. It makes up for its lack of resources with the evident talent at work here. —Strat.

Phantom Of The Mall

Cannes A Fries Entertainment release and production. Produced by Tom Fries. Directed by Richard Friedman. Screenplay, Scott Schneider, Richard King, Tom Schneidman, from story by Fred Ulrich, Schneider; camera (CFI color), Harry Mathias; editor, Amy Tompkins, Gregg Plotz; music, Stacy Widelitz; sound, David Kelson; production manager, Michael Johnson; assistant director, Steve Ray; director of additional photography, Fries; additional camera, Tony Cutrono; special makeup effects, Matthew Mungle; stunt coordinator, David Zellitti; casting, Rosemary Welden. Reviewed at Cannes Film Festival (Market), May 17, 1989. No MPAA Rating. Running time: **88 MIN.**
Melody	Kari Whitman
Mayor Karen Wilton	Morgan Fairchild

Also with: Derek Rydall, Jonathan Goldsmith, Rob Estes, Pauly Shore, Kimber Sissons, Tom Fridley, Gregory Scott Cummins, Ken Foree.

■Horror movie clichés get a ho-hum airing in "Phantom Of The Mall," a sleep-inducing effort which generates camp humor only in its ridiculous final reel, probably too late for most fans.

Mayor of Midwood, Calif., Morgan Fairchild inaugurates a new shopping mall, but a masked figure stalking the airshafts starts killing people. His main target is pretty young waitress Kari Whitman, who in her nightmares is convinced the killer is her dead boyfriend Eric.

Rather strained script contrives an additional killer plus a couple of nefarious villains, but presentation is strictly routine. Visual references to the "Phantom Of The Opera" don't come off, and the phantom's makeup job is poor and unscary.

Final reel features some effective stuntwork and breathless pacing, with the deaths and twists suddenly coming so fast that it's funny. If only helmer Richard Friedman had turned up the throttle earlier. (Producer Tom Fries is credited with directing additional footage.)

Kari Whitman makes an empathetic heroine, but her flashback sex scenes are poorly shot and use of a nude body double is obvious. Fairchild has little to do until the slambang finale, while rest of the cast is adequate. —Lor.

Time Of The Beast

Cannes A Liberty Films presentation of an A Cut Above production. Executive producer, John R. Bowey. Produced by Russell Markowitz. Directed by Bowey; screenplay, Lynn Rose Higgins; special effects, Robert Burman (Burman Studios); music, Rene Veldsman. Reviewed at Cannes Film Festival (Market), May 15, 1989. Running time: **89 MIN.**

With: Brion James, Carolyn Ann Clark, Milton Raphael Murrill, Neil McCarthy, Brian O'Shaughnessy.

■"Time Of The Beast" is a technically competent but forgettable horror offering, no doubt headed straight for the undiscerning end of the homevid market.

There are so many salivating big-fanged creatures on offer these days it's hard to imagine any of them have any shock factor anymore. "Time Of The Beast's" contribution — a genetic mutation apparently derived from a cat — has hardly any impact, and barely shows, anyway.

Beastie is the result of an experiment gone wrong in a genetic laboratory. Routine scenario sees the protagonists trying to escape its clutches as they find themselves trapped in the locked complex. Amidst this is apparently a basic concern over animal experimentation, relentlessly referred to by a group of activists (one of them is the daughter of the lab's owner) who have broken in to free the animals.

Director John Bowey has tried to build a suspenseful atmosphere but doesn't pull it off. That's not helped by a silly ending, some gaps in the plot and no real concentration on the beast in question. There are many shots of hairy talons and a manlike body, but it's never seen in whole (the prosthetic mask is seen only as a head shot once or twice). Scary it ain't.

Acting is mediocre. Brion James makes the most of his lead role as genetic scientist (formerly working at the lab) who is trying to expose the operation by working undercover as a security guard (which takes quite a while to work out). Carolyn Ann Clark looks lovely but does little else. Tech credits are good. —Doch.

Hellgate

Cannes A Ghost Town Film Management, Distant Horizon, Ananh Singh presentation. (Intl. sales, New World Intl.) Executive producer, Sudhir Pragjee. Produced by Anant Singh, Shan Moodley. Directed by William A. Levey. Screenplay, Michael O'Rourke; camera (Technicolor), Peter Palmer; editor, Mark Baard, Max Lemmon, Chris

Barnes; art direction, David Howard; assistant director, Gavin Sweeney. Reviewed at Cannes Film Festival (Market), May 18, 1989. No MPAA Rating. Running time: **88 MIN.**
Matt	Ron Palillo
Josie	Abigail Wolcott
Lucas	Carel Trichardt
Pam	Petrea Curran
Chuck	Evan J. Klisser
Bobby	Joanne Ward
Buzz	Frank Notard
Zonk	Lance Vaughan
Jonas	Victor Mellaney

■A puerile script, hamfisted acting and large slabs of incoherence take "Hellgate" to new depths in the already much abused horror genre. Mark this one down as homevideo fodder.

Standard group of college youths is this time terrorized by the deranged owner of a tourist ghost town, "Hellgate." It's populated by real ghouls, although that's never really explained, and doesn't seem to have any great impact on overall plot.

Presumably it's linked to a crystal the owner has that brings things back to life, or changes living things. (Goldfish are turned into snarling nasties that then explode, although the model is carelessly left on the grass in the foreground of a much later shot.) Dead daughter Abigail Wolcott is brought back to life, luring unfortunates into the lair so revenge for her death (by "strangers") can be wreaked.

Hero Ron Palillio is almost a goner but Wolcott takes a liking to him before dad starts chopping, so he escapes, only to return to find "who the hell did this."

Some truly stupid dialog and inappropriate acting totally eradicates any vestige of hope or suspense in this pic as the four ever-joking bimbos wander around the town. Palillo and girlfriend eventually escape (there's a shot of them taking an almost leisurely stroll through the ghoul-laden town). Actual climax is unsatisfying — hardly surprising given the events leading up to it — and mainly incomprehensible.

Special effects are average and offer nothing new to today's audiences. The okay camera work is not good enough though to save this offering.—Doch.

Night Life

Cannes A Creative Movie Marketing presentation of a Wild Night production. (Intl. sales, Image Organization.) Produced by Charles LIppincott. Directed by David Acomba. Screenplay, Keith Critchlow; camera (Foto-Kem color), Roger Tonry; editor, Michael Bateman; music, Roger Bouland; sound (Ultra-Stereo), Craig Felburg; production design, Philip Thomas; assistant director, John Jakes; makeup, Craig Reardon; associate producer, Susan Nicoletti; casting, Susan Young. Reviewed at Cannes Film Festival (Market), May 16, 1989. MPAA Rating: R. Running time: **89 MIN.**

Archie Melville	Scott Grimes
Charly	Cheryl Pollak
Verlin Flanders	John Astin

Also with: Anthony Geary, Alan Blumenfeld, Kenneth Ian Davis, Darcy DeMoss, Lisa Fuller, Mark Pellegrino, Phil Proctor.

■ **"Night Life"** is an uneven comic horror film owing much to George Romero's "Night Of The Living Dead" and subsequent pics. Unnecessarily gruesome footage of cadavers come to life to chase down the living isn't as funny as apparently was intended, and isn't sufficiently scary or outrageous to make it as straight horror fare.

Opening credits sequence in which teenager Archie Melville disposes of various human limbs and organs promises (?) a gorefest about a demented youth. Instead, it turns out the kid is working in his uncle's (John Astin) mortuary to pay for college. The boyish-looking Archie is continually taunted by two high school jocks and their cheerleader girlfriends, and when the four die in a car accident, their bodies wind up in Astin's lab.

During a lightning storm, the corpses are brought to life "Frankenstein"-style and begin to chase Archie around the house and, later, throughout the countryside. He has a tomboy buddy (Cheryl Pollak) and together they manage after much trying to eliminate the undead four.

Performances are a mixed lot, with Pollack's and Scott Grimes' Archie attractive and energetic leads. Astin plays it more for laughs, as does Anthony Geary in a small role as a dippy racecar driver who temporarily takes Pollack away from it all. Canadian helmer David Acomba sets the action in some attractive California countryside. Most tech credits, particularly the music by such metal groups as Fastway, are snazzy. A plot twist at fadeout is really the only jolting moment in the film. —*Gerz.*

Heaven Can Help

Cannes A United Entertainment production. (Intl. sales, Overseas Filmgroup.) Executive producers, Gordon H. Alexander, Sorgie Gwen. Produced and directed by Tony Zarindast. Screenplay, Zarindast; additional dialog, Bud Fleisher; camera (Foto-Kem color), Robert Hayes; editor, Ronald Goldstein; music, Allen Dermardrosian; sound (Dolby), T.C. Williams; production design, Don Scott;

assistant director, William Pressman; special effects, Ken Balles. Reviewed at Cannes Film Festival (Market), May 13, 1989. No MPAA Rating. Running time: **111 MIN.**

Val	Tony Bova
Vyra	Jinx Dawson
Angel Crystal	Dianne Copeland
Mrs. Ferrari	Diane Hayden
Matthew	Joe Balogh
Angel Billy	Ted Prior
Devil	Myron Natwick

Also with: Collette Rounsavall, Lenny Rose, Kimberly Dawn.

■ **Angels interfere with humans' problems one more time in the inept comedy "Heaven Can Help,"** a laughably amateurish attempt at whimsy by action specialist Tony Zarindast.

Tony Bova earns a couple of honest laughs as a real estate honcho who styles himself like Frankie Valli or James Darren in the '60s. For no good reason (a subplot involving an angel hooking up with his son Joe Balogh's computer makes no sense), he becomes the battleground between the devil (impersonated inadequately by Myron Natwick) via his witch henchwoman Jinx Dawson and a couple of angels.

Pic's quota of slapstick is mechanically rendered and Zarindast's script lacks the necessary wit to pull this fantasy premise off. Special effects, including flying scenes (with thick wires plainly visible) and pointless animated rays are very poor.

Silliest gimmick has both femme adversaries styled to look like British singer Samantha Fox: Dawson reps Fox' musical persona when the witch is granted youth and made a rock singer, while the angel is personified by short, muscular, ultra-stacked Dianne Copeland. Unintentional camp humor overwhelms the pic's few legit gags.

Cast, especially Ted Prior as a very California type of angel, tries hard but can't bring this extremely overlong film to life.—*Lor.*

Destiny To Order
(CANADIAN)

Cannes A Cineplex Odeon Films release (Canada) of an Atlantis Films Ltd. production. Executive producers, Michael MacMillan, Peter Sussman. Produced by Seaton McLean, Jonathan Goodwill, John Kramer. Written and directed by Jim Purdy. Camera (color) Ludek Bogner; editor, Ian Webster; music, Dave Gray; costumes, Laurie Drew; production design, Richard Harrison; sound, Jack Heeron, Chris Cook. Reviewed at Cannes Film Festival (Market), May 15, 1989. Running time: **97 MIN**

J.D. Baird	Stephen Ouimette
Thalia	Alberta Watson
Kenrick	Michael Ironside
Anne	Victoria Snow

■ **The visit to the twilight zone to**

meet an assortment of characters from the world of an author's non-singing detective has some effective moments, but on the whole fails to live up to an intriguing premise.

This Atlantis production, written and directed by Jim Purdy, starts with a trick beginning which leads audiences to believe they are in for another thick-ear chapter about biker bullies, sex and drugs. Only a purple prose off-screen commentary gives pause to an early exit. When the reason for this becomes apparent, the film takes on a different look and proceeds in another direction.

The off-screen voice belongs to a young author working at his word processor. He is reading aloud as he writes. He stops, he is out of imagination, he is lost; he wonders about his life and work (sigh). A violent thunderstorm puts a jolt into his computer. He finds himself in contact with his characters who have become real people, with himself taking on different disguises and determined to save his heroine (a rock singer) from the biker brigade whose leader is equally determined to finish off the author.

While much of this is pointed and funny, it is not always consistent within the idea of reality suspended; scenes go on too long, and the screenplay doesn't take full advantage of the twists and turns which a more imaginative treatment could provide. Fortunately it has a marvelous portrayal by Alberta Watson as the lively performer who keeps changing her identity, and a brisk yet sympathetic supporting part by Victoria Snow as the author's girlfriend trying to bring him back to himself.

Michael Ironside is, as always, thoroughly effective as the villain, while Stephen Ouimette does well as the author who, one suspects, will never amount to much.

The language is vile and the proceedings are loud and violent. However, it's a cut above the usual and should find a place with audiences who want rock and shock — the main background to its twilight zone. Pic identifies and makes good use of Toronto locations. —*Prat.*

Freakshow
(CANADIAN)

Cannes A Brightstar Films presentation. (Intl. sales, Shapiro Glickenhaus Entertainment.) Executive producer, Don Haig.

Produced by Anthony Kramreither. Directed by Constantino Magnatta. Screenplay, Bob Farmer; camera (Film House color), Gilles Corbeil; editor-2d unit director, Claudio De Grano; music, Steve Shelski, Dan LeBlanc; sound, Gord Thompson; production design, Andrew Deskin; assistant director, Fergus Barnes; special makeup effects, Gordon Smith; casting, Sue Magee. Reviewed at Cannes Film Festival (Market), May 18, 1989. Running time: **92 MIN.**

Shannon Nichols	Audrey Landers
Dr. Borges	Peter Read
Fidge	Dean Richards

Also with: Micheline Scattolon, Will Korbut.

■ **"Freakshow"** is a rock-bottom horror film that only a tax loss specialist could love. Prospects are rotten in all media.

Amateurishly directed and acted opus consists of four horror stories, linked by the flimsy premise of loathsome tv newscaster Audrey Landers trapped in a curiosity collection exhibit by its goofball curator Peter Read.

Tales, wholly lacking in awe or ingenuity, go from bad to worse: an endlessly padded episode of a drug addict lured to his death by a poodle with a bag of heroin in its mouth; a pizza delivery boy who survives a night at an evil mansion located at 1313 Bram Stoker Blvd.; a ripoff of a classic "Alfred Hitchcock Presents" tv episode in which a paralyzed girl (from drugs again) is subjected to an autopsy while still alive and conscious; and a stupid story of ghouls rising from their graves to punish two gravediggers who are stealing the dirt from the cemetery to sell it to a golf course (!).

Level of tastelessness here is evidenced in the final segment when a goon finds out the dead can come back, and exults: "That's great! That means there'll be a Beatles reunion."

Director Constantino Magnatta embarrassingly tries to simulate musicvideos, with terrible rock songs frequently thrown in and girls sashaying in their underwear (one couldn't call it dancing). Heavy-handed use of spiral patterns to try and hypnotize the audience plus bookended setting of the pic in a movie theater doesn't work. —*Lor.*

Lethal Woman
(The Most Dangerous Woman Alive)

New York An Independent Network-Film Ventures Intl. presentation of a Pure Gold Film Enterprises production. Produced by John Karie, S.D. Nethersole, Josh Spencer. Executive producers, Joseph Goldenberg, Irv Holender, Michael R. Ricci, Robert B. Steuer.

Directed by Christian Marnham. Screenplay, Michael Olson, Gabriel Elias; camera (color), Vincent G. Cox; supervising editor, Ettie Feldman; editor, Wayne Lines; music, Meir Eshel; sound, Mark Phillips; art direction, Graeme Orwin; production manager, Carol Hickson; assistant director, Rory Sales; second unit camera, Spencer; casting Kevin Albers. Reviewed on Vidamerica vidcassette, N.Y., May 4, 1989. (In Cannes Film Festival Market.) No MPAA Rating. Running time: **95 MIN.**

Christine/Diana	Merete Van Kamp
Major Derek Johnson	Robert Lipton
Tory	Shannon Tweed
Col. Maxim	James Luisi
Grizabella	Deep Roy
Major Burlington	Graeme Clarke

Also with: Prudence Solomon, Nita, Linda Warren, Phillipa Vernon, Adrienne Pearce, Deon Stewardson, Larry Taylor.

■ **"Lethal Woman" is an unconvincing revenge pic, suitable as a direct-to-video exploitation genre title.**

Pic originally was called "The Most Dangerous Woman Alive" and in fact is a sex-switch on the classic "Most Dangerous Game" horror format of humans as prey.

Merete Van Kamp, Dutch thesp who closely resembles Michelle Pfeiffer this time out, plays an army brat who's raped by her commanding officer Col. Maxim (James Luisi, playing heavy in the old twirling-mustache mode). Fellow soldiers and even Van Kamp's fiancé (Deon Stewardson) cover up for the colonel.

Embittered, Van Kamp has rounded up other rape victims, including statuesque Shannon Tweed, and set up shop on an all-women island. There she lures all the men involved in the original rape incident and court-martial one by one, hunts them down and kills them in bloodthirsty fashion. Robert Lipton is the retired special forces expert who's assigned by the army to put a stop to Van Kamp's antisocial behavior.

Lensed in South Africa, site of several Film Ventures '70s hits (e.g., "Kill Or Be Killed" with James Ryan), pic is competently made but phony. Supporting cast has trouble simulating the all-American accents and no suspense is generated in final reels when the obviously competent Lipton fights various starlets for survival.

Vam Kamp is hamstrung in a nasty role, with Tweed stealing the spotlight, especially when latter delivers the exploitation goods in a topless tryst in the surf with Lipton, simulating the "From Here To Eternity" pose. Pic could have used more lighter moments. It's played dead-serious by helmer Christian Marnham and is ultimately boring.—*Lor.*

Quarantine
(CANADIAN)

Cannes An Atlantis Release of an Apple Pie Pictures production. Executive producer, Stephen Cheikes/Beacon Group. Written, produced and directed by Charles Wilkinson. Camera (color), Tobias Schliessler; editor, Allan Lee; art direction, Robert Logevall; production manager, David Hauka; casting, Lindsay Walker. Reviewed at Cannes Film Festival (Market), May 14, 1989. Running time: **97 MIN.**

Ivan Joad	Beatrice Boepple
Spencer Crown	Garwin Sanford
Sen. Edgar Ford	Jerry Wasserman
Lt. Beck	Tom McBeath
Berlin Ford	Michele Goodger
The Kid	Kaj-Erik Eriksen
Councilwoman Campbell	Susan Chappelle
Dr. Jim	Lee Taylor
Ford's doctor	Don Mackie
Dr. Currie	Amy Newman

Also with: Mark Atcheson, Kim Kondrashoss, Steve Dotto, Roman Podhora, Frank Ferrucci, Susan Astley, Sheila Paterson, Jeremy Mathews, Curt Bonn.

■ **After a promising first film, "My Kind Of Town" in 1984, Charles Wilkinson has written, produced and directed "Quarantine," a film providing no good reasons why he thought it necessary to do so.**

This is a minor film in every respect, with little to recommend it. A city is under siege from an unnamed disease. People everywhere (although we never see them) are dying from it. Worse, all those who were associated with the dead and contaminated by their sickness — or they might just be unwanted politically — are given a quick trial and unceremoniously carted off to camps. All this is the work of a crazed, dictatorial senator who wants "a healthier world".

Late in the developments a Dr. Jim emerges as some kind of hero trying to save his patients, and a woman who breaks into the camp turns out to be his daughter hoping to save him. In this confused mission she wins over a scientist working on a super-computer which, one gathers, will eradicate the disease. But in the general confusion and lack of any point or purpose to this thin and superficial plot, it is hard to know what anything is all about, to say nothing of the ending.

Is this a veiled reference to AIDS? The characters are sketchily drawn and unconvincing; it is neither good science-fiction nor horror; it is not commercial, and it is not a personal statement with relevant social comment.

Filmed in Vancouver, the only Canadian reference to be gleaned from the goings-on is a mention of the "Provincial Ministry Of Health." The cast does its best with its ill-defined material and cardboard characters. Other credits are good enough. —*Prat.*

Renegades

Hollywood A Universal Pictures release of a Morgan Creek Prods. presentation of a Interscope Communications production. Produced by David Madden. Executive producers, James. G. Robinson, Joe Roth, Ted Field, Robert Cort. Coproducer, Paul Schiff. Directed by Jack Sholder. Screenplay, David Rich; camera (Deluxe color), Phil Meheux; editor, Caroline Biggerstaff; music, Michael Kamen; production design, Carol Spier; art direction, James McAteer; sound (Dolby), Bryan Day; costume design, Gina Kiellerman; line producer, Gabriella Martinelli; casting, Junie Lowry. Reviewed at Avco Cinemas, Westwood, Calif., May 31, 1989. MPAA Rating: R. Running time: **106 MIN.**

Buster	Kiefer Sutherland
Hank	Lou Diamond Phillips
Barbara	Jami Gertz
Marino	Rob Knepper
Finch	Bill Smitrovich
Red Crow	Floyd Westerman

■ **Positioned in its atrocious ad campaign as a sort of bratpacker's "48 HRS.," "Renegades" offers some rollercoaster thrills thanks to Jack Sholder's full-throttle direction but ultimately exhausts itself with unrelenting bedlam. Released amid a wave of summer blockbusters, b.o. may fire off a fair round or two before the chambers come up empty, despite the teen lure of its two young guns.**

Story resembles an earlier quest film, "Red Sun," which cast Charles Bronson as a gunslinger shackled with a stone-faced samurai (played by Toshiro Mifune) jointly pursuing the bad guy who swiped Mifune's ceremonial sword.

Better there than Philadelphia, where "Renegades" essentially reenacts that plot — all the while liberally employing such clichéd elements as crooked cops, GQ-outfitted villains and a touch of incongruous Indian magic that feeds on old stereotypes.

Kiefer Sutherland plays an undercover cop chasing a baddie who's stolen $2-million in diamonds. In the process, Marino (Rob Knepper) kills the brother of Hank (Lou Diamond Phillips) and makes off with an ancient spear, an artifact sacred to their Lakota Indian tribe.

Phillips must recover it to satisfy his father, throwing him together with Sutherland, who's intent on exposing the "dirty cop" working with the gang because *his* father was ousted from the force with a blemished record.

Unfortunately, the sins of the fathers are visited not on the sons, but the screenplay. There's some terrific action, to be sure, which should come as no surprise to anyone who saw Sholder's impressive sleeper "The Hidden."

The frenetic pace, however, provides scant opportunity to flesh out the two leads, let alone any of the supporting cast, who all remain cardboard cutouts bordering on ethnic slurs.

Even the action yields diminishing returns under the weight of repetition, so that the final showdown elicits few whoops and hollers despite its obvious desire to do so.

Phillips fares best among the performers, though he's yet to find any role even remotely tapping the promise he exhibited in "La Bamba." He probabaly hasn't hurt his star appeal much with films like "Young Guns" and "Disorganized Crime," but it's hard to maintain a career by cornering the market on knife-wielding young Indian/Hispanic types.

Sutherland seems miscast as a grown-up tough guy, while Jami Gertz looks smashing but has precious little to do in a walk-through part as the mobster's gal.

In addition to Sholder's undeniable flare for breakneck action, pic benefits immeasurably from Michael Kamen's evocative score, setting the mood with everything from tom-tomming Indian themes to more urgent chords during the mutliplex melees.

Credit Phil Meheux' camera and an army of sound technicians with capturing the remarkable first chase scene, though the final night-time shootout looks a trifle murky. —Bril.

Code Name Vengeance

New York   An Action Intl. Pictures presentation of a Killmasters Co. Ltd. production. Executive producer, Hope Holiday. Produced and directed by David Winters. Screenplay, Anthony Palmer; camera (Irene color), Keith Dunkley; editor, Brian G. Frost; music, Tim James, Steve McClintock, Mark Mancina; sound, Bob Hay; assistant director, Barry Van Bilion; associate producer, Barrie Saint Clair. Reviewed on Forum vidcassette, N.Y., May 26, 1989. MPAA Rating: R. Running time: 96 MIN.
Monroe Bieler . . . . .Robert Ginty
Sam . . . . .Shannon Tweed
Dutch. . . . . .Cameron Mitchell
Harry Applegate . . . . .Don Gordon
Chuck . . . . .Kevin Brophy
Tabrak . . . . .James Ryan

■ "Code Name Vengeance" is a perfunctory action pic for the homevideo market boasting some name value but very weak execution.

Story involves the kidnaping of a Middle Eastern magnate's wife and son, with the U.S. government sending in ex-CIA man Robert

Ginty to get them back alive.

Endless trekking by Ginty and his helpers is boring, leading to the predictable cynical finale indicting corrupt U.S. policies. Heavy-handed climax has U.S. government baddie Don Gordon accidentally wrapped up in the American flag as he gets his just desserts from Ginty's revolver.

Though set in Northern Africa, pic is one of the first of the current spate of U.S. productions lensed in South Africa (shot there at the end of 1986), technically adept but low on inspiration. Filmmaker David Winters is credited properly on screen, but given the odd pseudonymn "Maria Dante" in written materials.

Ginty gives a tired performance, which makes Gordon's baddie look overacted by comparison. Shannon Tweed provides the requisite undraped pulchritude and Cameron Mitchell strives to inject a bit of comic relief. Surprise is a quite convincing turn by South African star James Ryan as a hawk-nosed, Anthony Quinn-esque Arab rebel.—Lor.

Food Of The Gods II
(CANADIAN)

Detroit   A Concorde Pictures/Centauri Films release of a Canadian Entertainment Investors No. 1 and Company Limited Partnership presentation of a Rose & Ruby production. Executive producers, Andras Hamori, Robert Misiorowski. Produced by David Mitchell, Damian Lee. Directed by Lee. Screenplay, Richard Bennett, E. Kim Brewster, story by Richard Bennett; camera (color), Curtis Petersen; editor, Mitchell; music, Parsons/Haines; visual effects, Ted Rae. Reviewed at Americanna 8, Southfield, Mich., May 31, 1989. MPAA Rating: R. Running time: 91 MIN.
Neil Hamilton . . . . .Paul Coufos
Alex Reed . . . . .Lisa Schrage
Edmund Delhurst . . . . .Colin Fox
Jacques . . . . .Frank Moore
Mark . . . . .Real Andrews
Dr. Treger . . . . .Jackie Burroughs
Al . . . . .Stuart Hughes

■ "Food Of The Gods II" is a silly sequel to two previous efforts at scaring up an audience with overgrown rats. Failing once again, perhaps this is the last we'll see of Lassie-sized rodents.

"Food's" theatrical life will be short, and even though its makers hope to rush it into videocassette, it should get lost on the shelves there, too.

Alternately titled "Gnaw," "Food Of The Gods II" is only loosely connected to "Food Of The Gods," a tepid 1976 remake of the wretched "Village Of The Giants" (1965), both films by Bert

I. Gordon.

In those earlier efforts, a menagerie of wasps, worms, chickens and rats feast on a strange substance that causes them to grow into giants, terrorizing the countryside.

This hackneyed theme did little terrorizing of audiences, however. So it's unclear why director Damian Lee felt this tale worth trotting out once again.

This time it's only rats that do the expanding. The film tries to assume a modicum of social commentary by opening on a university campus in which students are protesting the use of animals for laboratory experimentation.

The filmmakers never explore that theme, opting instead for a tired thriller without much thrills.

Prof. Neil Hamilton is working on a botanical growth serum. Miles away, however, a former teacher of his has experimented with a growth hormone of her own. When she tried it out on an undersized youth, he grew to such heights that he could kick sand in Michael Jordan's face with impunity.

Hamilton agrees to work on an antidote to the growth drug. But due to a series of unlikely circumstances, a pack of rats has taken the drug and is now terrorizing the campus.

With such a trite premise, "Food's" only hope of keeping interest is through interesting special effects.

Instead, audiences must sit through a series of murders all played out essentially the same way: A stuffed rat head darts out from a side of the screen, squirting coeds with fake blood as the students scream unconvincingly and otherwise let the rodents have their way.

A jiggling hand-held camera substitutes for suspense. The few scenes in which rats terrorize the cast are mostly accomplished by juxtaposing shots of people running and screaming with shots of real rats running around miniature sets.

The film opens with a band of students protesting the animal research, chanting "Animals have rights, too." Animals come off pretty well in "Food Of The Gods II." It's the audience that doesn't seem to have any rights. —Advo.

Thrilled To Death

New York   A Platinum Pictures presentation. Executive producer, Anant Singh. Pro-

duced and directed by Chuck Vincent. Screenplay, Craig Horrall; camera (color), Larry Revene; editor, James Davalos, "Marc Ubell" (Vincent); music, Joey Mennonna; sound, Gary Rich, Dale Whitman; art direction, Mark Hammond; production manager, Jeremiah Hawkins; casting, Chip Lambert. Reviewed on Republic Pictures vidcassette, N.Y., May 26, 1989. MPAA Rating: R. Running time: 92 MIN.
Cliff Jackson . . . . .Blake Bahner
Elaine Jackson . . . . .Rebecca Lynn
Darryl Christie . . . . .Richard Maris
Nan Christie . . . . .Christine Moore
Val . . . . .Harvey Siegel
Bill . . . . .Scott Baker
Trudy . . . . .Karen Nielsen
    Also with: Al Goldstein, Gloria Leonard, Wanda Logan, Miriam Zucker, Christina Veronica, Daniel Chapman, Jacqueline Lorians, Tasha Voux.

■ Direct-to-video feature "Thrilled To Death" is a suspenser presenting an interesting situation of everyday peril, but faltering in a limp final reel.

Initial surprise is the solid performance of two porn stars, Krista Lane (here credited as Rebecca Lynn) and Rick Savage (credited as Rick Maris).

Central premise is an innocent young couple, Blake Bahner and Lane, who unwittingly fall in with a sinister couple (Savage and lovely Canadian thesp Christine Moore) while Bahner is researching a novel at a club for swingers.

They get involved in drugs, sex and murder and become amateur investigators. Final reel bogs down in endless exposition, including a dull airport phone conversation when action footage would have sufficed.

Except for this glaring lapse, director Chuck Vincent develops the melodramatic situations well, capturing and sustaining one's interest.

In the supporting cast, Christina Veronica impresses in her portrayal of an adult film actress, giving Bahner inside stuff in an interview. Inside joke is she's a straight thesp, while porn vet Lane as Bahner's wife is cast as the innocent type, quite convincing and sympathetic in a change-of-pace assignment. Guest stars Al Goldstein and Gloria Leonard play themselves, given a scene each to state their points of view.

Tech credits are okay. —Lor.

Deathstalker And The Warriors From Hell

New York   A Concorde Pictures presentation from New Classics of a Triana Films production. Executive producer, Robert North. Produced by Alfonso Corona, Antonio De Noriega. Directed by Corona. Screenplay, Howard R. Cohen; camera (color), Xavier Cruz; editor, uncredited; music, Israel Torres,

Alejandro Rulfo; sound, Miguel Sandoval; art direction, Francisco Magallon; assistant director, Alejandro Todd; production manager, Abel Marin. Reviewed on Vestron vidcassette, N.Y., May 27, 1989. MPAA Rating: R. Running time: **86 MIN.**

Deathstalker	John Allen Nelson
Carissa/Elezena	Carla Herd
Camisarde	Terri Treas
Troxartas	Thom Christopher
Nicias	Aaron Hernan
Inares	Roger Cudney
Makut	Agustin Salvat
Marinda	Claudia Inchaurregui

■Third edition in Concorde's "Deathstalker" series is a bland, made-in-Mexico affair constituting little more than a title and pretty package for undiscriminating video retailers.

Soap opera thesp John Allen Nelson is miscast in title role, smirking his way through a nonadventure in a mythical medieval land searching for the secret treasure city of Erendor. He accompanies Princess Carissa (Carla Herd) and her big diamond in quest for a matching stone. She's killed and he finds her twin Princess Elezena (also Herd) and eventually two matching gems, for chintzy visual effects when the powerful diamonds are joined.

Herd is upstaged by a pretty Amazonian warrior played by Claudia Inchaurregui, as well as Concorde regular Terri Treas as a villainess with arch dialog readings. Nelson's all-American approach is way out of place and supporting cast is weak. Previous pics in this series had some campy material, but this one's a stiff.—*Lor.*

Chasing Dreams

New York   A Nascent production. Executive producer, Marcus Robertson. Produced by David G. Brown. Directed by Sean Roche (1st unit), Conte (2d unit). Screenplay, Brown; camera (CFI color), Connie Holt; editor, Jerry Weldon, Robert Sinise; music, Gregory Conte; sound, Ken Wiatrak; production design, Bobbi Peterson Himber; production manager, Tim Silver; stunt coordinator, Scott Cook; coproducer, Marc Schwartz. Reviewed on Prism Entertainment vidcassette, N.Y., May 27, 1989. MPAA Rating: PG. Running time: **94 MIN.**

Gavin	David G. Brown
Parks	John Fife
Father	Jim Shane
Ben	Matthew Clark
Sue	Lisa Kingston
Mother	Claudia Carroll

Also with: Cecilia Bennett, Kelly McCarthy, Don Margolin, Marc Brandes, Dan Waldman, Kevin Costner.

■"Chasing Dreams" is a lackluster attempt at an inspirational film, notable only for a brief cameo appearance in yet another baseball-themed movie by the reigning genre king, Kevin Costner.

Lensed in 1981, pic gets a belated homevideo release primarily because of Costner's fleeting presence on screen.

Young David G. Brown toplines and penned this lame tale of a junior college freshman who had taken a year off after high school "to find himself" and now is attracted to baseball, favorite sport of his wheelchair-ridden, ailing younger brother Ben (Matthew Clark).

Though college coach John Fife quickly befriends Brown, artificial plot device has his dad forcing the "unmotivated" youth to devote all his free time to farm chores. Getting little sleep, he devotes himself to baseball practice on the sly as well and predictably becomes the team hero. Final reel creaks with ridiculous melodramatic gimmicks (sudden death of cute little Ben while Brown is away on a pro scout visit; Brown's sudden catatonia when beaned in a championship game) and hokey sentimental finish.

Production and most of cast is at best semi-pro. Costner's easygoing manner and delivery is as confident and developed here as in "Field Of Dreams."

With others yet to be released (including NW's 1983 Canadian pic "The Gunrunner") Costner has more movie marginalia in his past then virtually any other contemporary star. In this one his role is limited to giving the hero (his younger brother) a peptalk in opening scene on his way to medical school. Cast talks a lot about him but unfortunately for the filmmakers Costner never shows up again.—*Lor.*

Med döden inde pa livet (Dying — A Part Of Living) (DANISH-DOCU)

Copenhagen   A Danish Government Film Office and Hanne Höyberg Film release of Hanne Höyberg Film production. Produced by Hanne Höyberg. Directed by Dola Bonfils. Camera (Eastmancolor), Björn Blixt, Claus Baadsgaard; editor, Niels Pagh Andersen; music, Keith Jarrett performing J. S. Bach's "Das Wohltemperierte Klavier;" sound, Morten Degnböl, Henrik Garnov; research, Peter Elsass; production management, Henning Jensen, Per Neumann. Reviewed at the Delta Bio, Copenhagen, May 30, 1989. (In Montreal Documentary festival.) Running time: **95 MIN.**

■"Dying — A Part Of Living" is a calm and controlled documentary look at patients, nurses and doctors at work and in conversation with each other in the Infectious Diseases ward of the Copenhagen Hvidovre hospital where about five patients draw their last breath every day.

The ward is also one of Europe's leading treatment centers for AIDS patients in particular, but Dola Bonfils' film is a discovery of the fact that the terminally ill are actually less concerned with the causes than with the effects of their disease whatever its origin.

In discreet listening and viewing closeups, a few patients are followed as they approach death's door. None of them acknowledge their death as imminent. When they express despair, it is mostly because they feel defeated by sheer mental and physical fatigue. Otherwise, they insist on clinging to the belief, whether justified or not, that the doctors may help them live quite a few years more.

The doctors and nurses all admit (nobody talks to the camera) that the are actually unable, maybe even unsuited, to really do anything much about the latest epidemiological disease. Often, they find themselves frustrated by the impersonal intramural policies of a big hospital. At other times, they feel their own shortcomings in the psychological aspects of their work.

Dola Bonfils spent the months of January and February 1988 with her small film crew in "a fly on the wall" position at Hvidovre. She has come back with a both keen and compassionate documentary of obvious international attraction to highly specialized situations, while some tv sales are likely, too.—*Kell.*

Deadly Reactor

New York   An Action Intl. Pictures production. Executive producers, David Winters, Mark Winters, Bruce Lewin. Produced by Fritz Matthews. Directed by David Heavener. Screenplay, Heavener, from story by Thomas Baldwin; camera (Image Transform color), David Hue; editor, Brian Evans; music, Brian Bennett; songs, Heavener; sound, James Hassel; art direction, Mark Holmes; assistant director, Randy Maiers; production manager, Kimberly Casey; stunt coordinator, Bob Ivy; associate producer, Manoj Parekh; casting, John Mickland. Reviewed on AIP vidcassette, N.Y., May 27, 1989. No MPAA Rating. Running time: **88 MIN.**

Duke	Stuart Whitman
Cody	David Heavener
Hog	Darwyn Swalve
Shawna	Allyson Davis

Also with: Barbara Kerek, Arvid Holmberg, Ingrid Vold, Kimberly Casey.

■"Deadly Reactor," formerly titled "The Reactor," is an offbeat Western in sci-fi clothing that could attract a modest following among homevid aficionados.

Filmmaker-singer David Heavener demonstrates, as he did in previous pic "Outlaw Force," a fondness for the Clint Eastwood/Sergio Leone Westerns. Here he plays a preacher-styled gunslinger in a post-nuclear war West, appointed town sheriff and charged with defending the righteous citizens from a marauding gang (styled like contemporary bikers) led by fatso Hog (Darwyn Swalve).

Relying overmuch on Heavener's voiceover exposition, pic opens with him recuperating from wounds inflicted by Hog's gang. Hog raped his sister and killed his family, so Heavener has lots of avenging to do. He's known as "the Reactor," a tag acquired from learning gunfighting from wise old mountain man Stuart Whitman, who taught him to observe the other guy, prompt the adversary to make the first move and then react.

Heavener, who resembles Tommy Lee Jones with beard, is quite effective doing Eastwood's Western shtick, abetted here by a catchy, folksy musical score by Brian Bennett that is inspired by Ennio Morricone's "For A Few Dollars More" theme. —*Lor.*

Deadly Breed

New York   A P/M Entertainment Group presentation. Produced by Richard Pepin, Joseph Merhi. Written and directed by Charles T. Kanganis. Camera (color), Rick Lamb; editor, Paul Volk; music, John Gonzalez; sound, Mike Hall, Marty Kasparian; art direction, Alisa Williams; assistant director, John Weidner; stunt coordinator, Mike John Sarna; associate producer, Charla Driver. Reviewed on Raedon Entertainment vidcassette, N.Y., May 24, 1989. No MPAA Rating. Running time: **83 MIN.**

Captain	William Smith
Kilpatrick	Addison Randall
Jake	Blake Bahner
Vincent	Joe Vance
Lana	Michelle Berger
Alex	Rhonda Grey
Mr. Lewis	John Grantham

■"Deadly Breed" is an interesting B picture taking the Skinheads phenomenon as launching point for a cop thriller. It's a direct-to-video release.

Handsome Blake Bahner plays a parole officer whose charges suddenly are getting killed. It turns out the local police captain (William Smith) actually is behind the murders (as well as in charge of their investigation), executed by his cop henchman Addison Randall, who leads a gang of right-wing Skinheads.

Randall frames Bahner for the

murders and rapes and kills Bahner's lovely wife, Michelle Berger. Bahner teams up with femme cop Rhonda Grey to track down the murderers.

Efficient thriller benefits from solid performances, especially Randall's no-nonsense effort, whether spouting racist slogans or posing as a cool cop. Berger's a beautiful blond who adds eye-appeal to the proceedings.

Tech contributions are adequate for a video-aimed feature. —*Lor.*

Gator Bait II: Cajun Justice

New York A Paramount Video presentation of a Sebastian Intl. Pictures production. Produced and written by Ferd and Beverly Sebastian. Camera (color), Ferd Sebastian; music, George H. Hamilton, Angelique theme, Ferd Sebastian; Cajun music, Julius Adams, Vernon Rodrique; sound, Walt Martin; production design, Beverly Sebastian; costumes, Martha Marcantel; special effects, Beverly Sebastian; associate producer, Joan McCormick. Reviewed on Request TV, April 26, 1989. MPAA Rating: R. Running time: **94 MIN.**
Angelique . . . . Jan MacKenzie
Big T . . . . Tray Loren
Leroy . . . . Paul Muzzcat
Luke . . . . Brad Kepnick
Joe Boy . . . . Jerry Armstrong
Elick . . . . Ben Sebastian
Geke . . . . Reyn Hubbard

■ "Gator Bait" was an adept 1973 B-film starring the late Claudia Jennings that later found some success in the homevid market. This direct-to-video sequel made by the original directors, Ferd and Beverly Sebastian, is a more routine exploitationer unlikely to penetrate many VCR slots.

Film opens with the wedding of Big T (Tray Loren), the now grown up brother of Desiree (Jennings' character in the original). His bride Angelique (Jan MacKenzie) is a city girl unused to the ways of the swamp Big T inhabits. Big T delivers lectures to her on surviving in the wild, in itself an amazing feat of nature since his original character had no tongue.

Central idea is that after being brutalized by the baddies the demure bride will explode into action like the heroine of the first flick. Unfortunately, MacKenzie's character never develops sufficiently to counter the loss of Jennings' star power and atavistic vigor.

The villains also are a comedown from the earlier enterprise. Where the antagonists in "Gator Bait 1" consisted of two fathers and their sons with a revenge mission of their own, the heavies here are simply a group of beer-slurping redneck louts intent on ter-

rorizing their Cajun neighbors. Attempts to individualize them and include a surviving miscreant from the original film register weakly. Even more problematic are the drawn out sequences of their rape and brutalization of MacKenzie that consume far more screen time than the running amok in the first film.

This leaves relatively little time for MacKenzie's action antics to win the day. This film does competently but with little conviction. For viewers of the earlier movie the respective means of disposing of the last two villains will seem embarrassingly familiar.

As in the first "Gator Bait," tech credits are solid for a movie of this ilk, with the Sebastians wearing numerous production hats.
—*Lomb.*

Teen Vamp

New York A New World Pictures presentation of a Jim McCullough production. Produced by McCullough. Written and directed by Samuel Bradford. Camera (color), Richard Mann; editor, uncredited; music, Robert Sprayberry; sound, Rob Smith; production manager, Jill Duvall; stunt coordinator, Gary Paul; makeup, Cathy Glover. Reviewed on New World vidcassette, N.Y., May 25, 1989. No MPAA Rating. Running time: **89 MIN.**
Reverend . . . . Clu Gulager
Mom . . . . Karen Carlson
Connie . . . . Angie Brown
Murphy . . . . Beau Bishop
    Also with: Mike Lane, Evans Dietz, Edd Anderson, Jude Gerard.

■ Only related by title to New World's "Vamp," "Teen Vamp" from NW Video is an amateurish, Southern-fried horror comedy with little to offer homevid fans.

Shot in Shreveport, La., on an evidently threadbare budget, pic wallows in '50s nostalgia for a nonstory of nerd Beau Bishop transformed (very unconvincingly) into a leather-jacketed hip dude after a whore at a road house bites him.

His vampire status is taken very matter-of-factly by all concerned, except his pretty girl friend Angie Brown, who demands he bite her too!

Cornpone approach to the vampire genre doesn't work, and isn't helped by amateur sound recording, poor makeup effects and a far too talky script. Guest stars Karen Carlson as Bishop's mom and Clu Gulager as a hammy minister have little to do. Bishop's charmless performance is a drag.—*Lor.*

SEATTLE FEST REVIEWS

Bloodhounds Of Broadway

Seattle A Vestron Pictures release of an American Playhouse production. Executive producer, Lindsay Law. Produced and directed by Howard Brookner. Screenplay, Brookner, Colman DeKay, adapted from short stories by Damon Runyon ("The Bloodhounds Of Broadway," "A Very Honorable Guy," "Social Error" and "The Brain Goes Home"); camera (color), Elliot Davis; music, Jonathan Sheffner; casting, Richard Pagana. Sharon Bialy. Reviewed at Seattle Intl. Film Festival, May 29, 1989. No MPAA Rating. Running time: **101 MIN.**
Harriet Mackyle . . . . Julie Hagerty
Feet Samuels . . . . Randy Quaid
Hortense Hathaway . . . . Madonna
Handsome Jack Maddigan . . . Esai Morales
Basil Valentine . . . . Ethan Phillips
Regret . . . . Matt Dillon
Lovey Lou . . . . Jennifer Grey
Waldo Winchester . . . . Josef Sommer
Missouri Martin . . . . Anita Morris
The Brain . . . . Rutger Hauer

■ Howard Brookner (who died recently after completing this first feature) and Colman DeKay interweave four of Damon Runyon's famous "Broadway" short stories about New Year's Eve on Broadway in 1928 to produce a gangster's farce that falls somewhat short of true comic inspiration, but moves quickly enough to provide some light-hearted entertainment.

Strong character acting by an all-star cast enlivens this fluffy little piece about romance and gangsters during Prohibition. Boxoffice prospects appear dim.

"Bloodhounds Of Broadway" first introduces its host of characters at one of Broadway's watering holes as they prepare to celebrate the coming New Year in grand style with raucous parties, bootleg hooch, clandestine crap games and chorus girls ready to sing and shimmy at the stroke of midnight.

Narrated by newspaper scribe Waldo Winchester (Josef Sommer), who helps sort out the host of characters, "Bloodhounds" blends the stories of some of the colorful creatures of that time.

There's Harriet Mackyle, played by Julie Hagerty, who delivers a fine performance as a rich society babe who's throwing the party and invites some local mobsters for added color.

Randy Quaid as Feet Samuels does a satisfying job as an honorable dimwit who's madly in love with a beautiful, diamond-hungry showgirl, Hortense Hathaway,

very adeptly played by Madonna.

Matt Dillon gives a rather tepid performance as Regret, Broadway's lousiest horse player, especially in comparison with Jennifer Grey, who does a good job as Lovey Lou, an angel-faced showgirl in love with Regret.

Rutger Hauer provides an appropriately restrained performance as a powerful gangster who spends the entire night being driven around with a knife in his stomach in seach of some refuge.

Inspired costuming, particularly during the showgirl sequences, lends strong support to the production. The pic does suffer from a flawed sound system that delivers too many 1-liners garbled and otherwise incomprehensible, which inadvertently slows down an otherwise quickly moving plot.
—*Magg.*

Amanda

Seattle A film written, produced, directed and edited by Jeff Meyer and Gail Kappler Rosella. Camera (color), Mark Shapiro; sound, Eric L. Thomas, Philip Royal, Pat Plyley; casting, Gail Kappler Rosella. Reviewed at Seattle Intl. Film Festival, May 26, 1989. No MPAA Rating. Running time: **120 MIN.**
Jason . . . . Jeff Meyer
Amanda . . . . Gail Kappler Rosella
Bill Bettman . . . . William Mitchell
Trudy . . . . Ann Bowden
Patricia . . . . Claire Janell
Nelson . . . . Drew Forsythe
Elliot Tanner . . . . Vern Taylor

■ Filled with lots of dreamy and picturesque shots of Seattle, "Amanda" is visually pleasing. But pretty scenery can't make up for an insufficient storyline, which begins to drag early in the film and fails to gather much steam later on. Chances for a regular run are doubtful.

"Amanda" is the second film in six years for local filmmaker Jeff Meyer, who, along with partner Gail Kappler Rosella, wrote, directed, produced and starred in the film, as well as financed the project.

It's billed as a romantic fantasy and follows the story of Jason (Jeff Meyer), a down and out photographer who lives on a dilapidated houseboat. Jason, it becomes clear, is down and out not because he is untalented, but because he no longer wants to work "commercial." He is dedicated to photography as art. Jason hopes to receive a grant to pay off mounting debts and continue work on a book of his photographs.

By chance he meets a beautiful young woman, Amanda (Gail Kappler Rosella), takes her picture and falls in love with her. Just as Jason learns he did not get his grant and is being evicted from his boat, Amanda turns up and says she's rich, single and wants him to come live with her. Jason's life changes overnight as he's swept into Amanda's world and she uses her contacts in the art scene to get his book published.

The rest of the plot centers on the notion that all is not as it seems in Amanda's world, but it gives only vague hints at what that might be. In fact, the storyline becomes somewhat confused. It unsuccessfully attempts to deal with the issue of whether wealth corrupts creativity. Several references also are made to Amanda as a poor little rich girl, yet fail to ever explain what this has to do with the plot. In addition, there are too many scenes which fail to advance the plot at all (such as a camping trip which includes some nice shots of scenery), and instead seem to make the action drag even more.

The climax comes as a surprise mostly because the audience was given little clue that the plot might take this twist. The ending itself — when Jason wakes up and realizes it was all a dream only then to meet Amanda not only lacks originality, but it reinforces the notion that the picture has failed to pass along the kind of information needed to draw some conclusions when the film fails to do so itself.—*Magg.*

Romero

Seattle A Four Seasons Entertainment release of a Paulist Pictures production. Produced by Ellwood E. Kieser. Directed by John Duigan. Screenplay, John Sacret Young; camera (color), Geoff Burton; music, Gabriel Yared; sound, Edward Beyer. Reviewed at Seattle Intl. Film Festival, June 1, 1989. No MPAA Rating. Running time: 94 MIN.
Archbishop Oscar Romero . . . . .Raul Julia
Father Rutilio Grande . . . . .Richard Jordan
Arista Zalads. . . . . .Ana Alicia
Father Morantes. . . . . .Tony Plana
Francisco Galedo . . . . .Harold Gould

■ "Romero" is a compelling and deeply moving story about Father Oscar Romero, archbishop of El Salvador, and his transformation from an apolitical, complacent priest to a committed leader of the Salvadoran people before his assassination in 1980.

Scheduled for platform release later this year, the film holds promise for strong b.o. return as it has the potential to become one of the most politically influential films of the 1980s.

"Romero's" strength and appeal lies in its ability to present a complex political situation in a very personal, dramatic manner which emphasizes one person's belief that he can make a difference. Instead of relying on a third party view of Central American politics, usually by using American reporters, film actively and unabashedly engages the emotions and feelings of the audience.

Raul Julia, in the central role of Romero, delivers a flawless and impassioned performance of the mousy, shy man who gradually emerges from passive anonymity to the reluctant leader in the struggle to bring social justice and political reform to the El Salvadoran nation until his martyrdom at the hands of the military junta in March 1980.

Australian writer-director John Duigan, making his American directorial debut with "Romero," deserves credit for maintaining an even keel on a story that could easily become too depressing or violent for public consumption. Likewise, he manages to keep Romero's personal struggle the focus of the film, and to avoid polemic arguments about U.S. involvement in El Salvador or church-vs.-state rights.

The film is supported by a fine cast, including a particularly satisfying performance by Richard Jordan as Father Grande, a close friend of the archbishop and whose assassination helped to galvanize Romero into action.

Several years in the planning, the pic represents the first foray into feature filmmaking by Paulist Pictures, owned by the Paulist Fathers, an order of Catholic priests dedicated to service of those outside the church. Father Ellwood Kieser, president of Paulist Pics and "Romero" producer, along with screenwriter John Sacret Young, traveled to El Salvador to conduct research for the screenplay, and to ensure "Salvadoran input." —*Magg.*

First Date
(TAIWANESE)

Seattle A Peter Wang Films production. Executive producers, Lin Deng Fei, Xu Xing Zhi, Wang. Planning producer, Zhao Qi Bing; producer, Xu Guo Liang; line producer, Nie Yang Xian; associate producers, Jennifer Fong, He Ying Li. Written and directed by Wang. Camera (color), Larry Banks; editor, Li Shin Yu; music, Zhang Hong Yi; production design, Ren Shi Zheng. Reviewed at Seattle Intl. Film Festival, May 31, 1989. Running time: 90 MIN.
Yang Jia Luo . . . . .Chang Shi
Yo Fu Sheng . . . . .Li Xing Wen
Teacher Liu . . . . .Shi Jun
Jade Cloud Lin . . . . .Huang Jin Qing
Mousie Guo . . . . .Zhang Zhi Hua
Birdie Gu . . . . .Xie Zu Wu
Yang Huai Xun . . . . .Peter Wang

■In this era of heightened awareness of the economic and political power of Pacific Rim countries, "First Date" offers an interesting glimpse of Taiwan in the 1950s through the story of a young boy whose growth into manhood parallels that of Taiwan emerging from uncertainty to find a place in the world.

Shot entirely in Taiwan, "First Date" follows Yang Jia Luo (Chang Shi) as a mischievous adolescent who attends a strict disciplinary high school. Bored and unchallenged, he nearly fails out of school until befriended and inspired by one of his teachers, Teacher Liu (Shi Jun).

Life at home is dominated by the comic babbling of his drunken, dissolute father (adeptly played by Peter Wang). Confronted with both an unhappy home life and his own sexual awakening, Jia Luo frequently fantasizes about love, both erotic and "true."

As the son of a civil servant, Jia Luo is fascinated with the braggart Yo Fu Sheng (Li Xing Wen), son of a high official who seems to embody all that the new Taiwan can offer: wealth and power to those who work within the system.

The friendship between Jia Luo and Yo reaches a crisis after Yo sets off an explosion in the chemistry lab and Liu strikes him for his carelessness. (Hitting students, it appears, is a normal practice.) Yo is humiliated and after the incident, Liu disappears, and Jia Luo suspects Yo's father used his influence. Jia Luo embarks on revenge, and along the way learns some lessons in responsibility and friendship.

Written and directed by Peter Wang, "First Date" adeptly employs a gentle humor to provide a satisfying portrait of both the complex emotions of youth and the simple pleasures of growing up.

The film successfully recaptures a time where the discovery of holding hands and a casual kiss shook the world.—*Magg.*

Star Trek V: The Final Frontier

Hollywood   A Paramount Pictures release of a Harve Bennett production. Executive producer, Ralph Winter. Produced by Bennett. Directed by William Shatner. Screenplay, David Loughery, from story by Shatner, Bennett, and Loughery, based on "Star Trek" tv series created by Gene Roddenberry; executive consultant, Roddenberry; camera (Panavision, Technicolor), Andrew Laszlo; editor, Peter Berger; music, Jerry Goldsmith; sound (Dolby), David Ronne; sound effects, Mark Mangini; production design, Herman Zimmerman; art direction and costume design, Nilo Rodis-Jamero; set design, Ronald R. Wilkinson, Richard Frank McKenzie, Andrew Neskoromny, Antoinette Gordon; set decoration, John M. Dwyer; visual effects, Bran Ferren; special visual effects, Associates & Ferren; visual effects coordinator, Eric Angelson; optical unit supervisor, Dick Swanek; effects animation supervisor, Dick Rauh; matte paintings, Illusion Arts Inc., Syd Dutton; makeup artists, Wes Dawn, Jeff Dawn; special makeup design, Kenny Myers; associate producer, Brooke Breton; assistant director, Douglas E. Wise; production manager-coproducer, Mel Efros; Yosemite climbing sequence, Denali Prods., directed by Robert Carmichael, produced by Stephen J. Ross; casting, Bill Shepard. Reviewed at Village Theater, Westwood, Calif., June 6, 1989. MPAA Rating: PG. Running time: **106 MIN.**

Kirk . . . . William Shatner
Spock . . . . Leonard Nimoy
McCoy . . . . DeForest Kelley
Scotty . . . . James Doohan
Chekov . . . . Walter Koenig
Uhura . . . . Nichelle Nichols
Sulu . . . . George Takei
St. John Talbot . . . . David Warner
Sybok . . . . Laurence Luckinbill
Korrd . . . . Charles Cooper
Caithlin Dar . . . . Cynthia Gouw
Captain Klaa . . . . Todd Bryant
Vixis . . . . Spice Williams
J'onn . . . . Rex Holman
"God" . . . . George Murdock
Amanda . . . . Cynthia Blaise
McCoy's father . . . . Bill Quinn

■ **Even diehard Trekkies may be disappointed by "Star Trek V: The Final Frontier." Coming after Leonard Nimoy's delightful directorial outing on "Star Trek IV: The Voyage Home," William Shatner's inauspicious feature directing debut is a double letdown.**

The sluggish, murkily plotted and visually uneven Paramount release probably won't light any fires at the b.o. after the opening weekend.

What can you say about a "Star Trek" pic that takes 30 minutes to get the crew of the Enterprise into outer space, or a "Star Trek" whose best scenes are those early ones on Earth? The trouble began with the story, which Shatner cowrote with producer Harve Bennett and scripter David Loughery. Exec consultant Gene Roddenberry should have been pressed back into service for a major overhaul.

Shatner, whose prior directing experience was mostly on his vid series "T.J. Hooker," doesn't bring much energy to the film. Nor does he keep the focus on the human elements, as Nimoy did in the last installment. Aside from some broad but welcome comic scenes with the crew, Shatner fritters away most of the 106-minute running time (which seems longer) on so-so action and special effects which often verge on the tacky.

A major flaw in the story is that it centers on an obsessive quest by a character who isn't a member of the Enterprise crew, a renegade Vulcan played by Laurence Luckinbill in Kabuki-like makeup. The crazed Luckinbill kidnaps the crew and makes them fly to a never-before-visited planet at the center of the galaxy in quest of the Meaning of Life.

Better they should have stayed home and watched reruns of the tv series, which had a lot more to say about the meaning of life. It's a shame that in doing his own translation of the series to the big screen, Captain Kirk doesn't trust the virtues of character interaction and contemplative dialog which made the series so extraordinary.

Shatner also sabotages himself by not riding herd over the tech shop. Despite its big budget, the film often has a shoddy low-budget look.

What genuine entertainment there is in the film is supplied by the patented exchanges among the crew. Shatner, Nimoy and DeForest Kelley have some good moments around a campfire as they take "shore leave" in spectacular surroundings at Yosemite National Park.

Shatner also rises to the occasion in directing a dramatic sequence of the mystical Luckinbill teaching Nimoy and Kelley to re-experience their long-buried traumas. The recreations of Spock's rejection by his father after his birth, and Kelley's euthanasia of his own father are moving highlights.

Overall, the tired, offhand feeling of this pic seems to underscore the advancing years of the crew in a negative way. Some of the stuff Shatner has them do is embarrassing, including an incredible mountain-climbing exploit he performs with the obvious aid of a double, and a raunchy dance scene that undercuts the mature dignity of Nichelle Nichols' Uhura. —*Mac.*

Manika: The Girl Who Lived Twice
(FRENCH-SWISS)

Paris   A Labrador Films/Carlton Film Export/Almira Films (Lausanne) coproduction. Executive producer, Raoul Katz. Directed by Francois Villiers. Screenplay, Villiers and Brian Phelan. Camera (color), Alain Levent; art direction, Ram Yadekar; editor, Hélène Piemiannikov; sound, Paul Lainé; music, Naresh Sohal; production manager, Patrice Millet. Reviewed at the CNC, Paris, April 27, 1989. (In Cannes Film Festival, Perspectives on French Cinema.) Running time: **106 MIN.**

Manika . . . . Ayesha Dharker
Father Daniel . . . . Julian Sands
Ranit Sharma . . . . Suresh Uberoi
Sister Ananda . . . . Stéphane Audran
Father René . . . . Jean-Philippe Ecoffey
(English soundtrack)

■ **"Manika" is a mild-mannered and mildly interesting tale of reincarnation. Director Francois Villiers' original script, written with Brian Phelan, fails to burrow to any psychological depth but relates an unusual story with sympathy.**

Shot in English on location in Sri Lanka and Nepal, this Franco-Swiss picture should have okay commercial value for theatrical and tv.

Manika is a 10-year-old girl in a poor southern Indian fishing village who believes with growing insistance that she had an earlier life some decades before as the adolescent wife of a rich Brahman in Nepal and died in childbirth. Her teacher at the local Catholic mission school, a young Jesuit priest (Julian Sands), befriends Manika and is ordered by his superiors to bring her around to orthodox reason, since reincarnation doesn't accord with Catholic doctrine (the story is set in the early '60s).

When Manika runs away, headed north towards her previous Life, Sands is sent after her. Instead of bringing her home, priest agrees to accompany her and satisfy his own curiosity and doubts.

In Nepal they indeed find everything as Manika's troubled dreams had indicated, especially the husband, Suresh Uberoi, a prominent businessman who has remarried, despite his deathbed promise to Manika.

Uberoi, unperturbed by this unexpected homecoming (he innately believes in reincarnation like most Brahmans), invites her into his home. His new wife, understandably less happy, takes their baby and leaves. Realizing the upheavals she is causing, Manika decides to return to her fishing village though now at peace with herself.

Sands, in whom Manika has caused a crisis of faith, decides to pursue his mission in a more secular manner, after meditating at a mountain-top retreat run by an ecumenical nun (Stéphane Audran, in an 11th hour cameo).

Villiers, making his comeback to theatrical features after a long career in tv, has given the story a brisk colorful production though the latter sections of the plot (Manika in her husband's house; Sands in hot theological debate with an old seminary pal Jean-Philippe Ecoffey) are treated too superficially to be convincing.

Sands has the right quiet inquisitive sensibility as the young Irish Jesuit, and Ayesha Dharker, a nonprofessional recruit in an Indian dance school, is good as the girl with two lives. Supporting cast is solid. —*Len.*

Curfew

New York   A New World Pictures presentation of a York Image production. Executive producers, David Feder, Rick Hilton, Jonathan A. Weisgal. Produced by Julie Philips. Directed by Gary Winick. Screenplay, Kevin Kennedy; camera (CFI color), Makoto Watanabe; editor, Carole Kravetz; music, Cengiz Yaltkaya; sound, Debbie Spinelli; assistant director, Melitta Fitzer; stunt coordinator, Chuck Borden; coproducers, Gregory Choa, Gregory Cundiff. Reviewed on NW vidcassette, N.Y., June 3, 1989. MPAA Rating: R. Running time: **84 MIN.**

Stephanie Davenport . . . . Kyle Richards
Ray Perkins . . . . Wendell Wellman
Bob Perkins . . . . John Putch
Megan . . . . Jean Brooks
Walter . . . . Frank Miller
    Also with: Peter Nelson, Nori Morgan, Bert Remsen, Christopher Knight, Niels Mueller, Bob Romanus.

■ **"Curfew" is an uninvolving update of the format of "The Desperate Hours," substituting sadism for dramatics. It's a very minor direct-to-video title.**

Wendell Wellman and John Putch portray two brothers who break out of jail to terrorize the judge, d.a., etc., and their families responsible for sending them up for raping and killing a young girl.

They take the d.a.'s family hostage and pic dwells predictably on the psychological and physical torture inflicted as well as the victims' attempts to turn the brothers against each other.

Title refers to sexy heroine Kyle Richards (the d.a.'s daughter) having to be home by 10 p.m. according to her parents' strict rules. This is contrasted heavy-handedly with the severe treatment meted out by the brothers.

A subplot of pranks by Kyle's high school classmates has little force except to set up a "boy who cried wolf" gimmick.

Acting is acceptable, though Wellman is overly theatrical as the domineering older brother. Richards is styled intriguingly as an innocent sort of bombshell, but her performance is unimpressive.

—*Lor.*

Femme de Papier
(Front Woman)
(FRENCH)

New York   A Pierre Grise Prods. and La Sept production. (Intl. sales, Metropolis Film, Zurich.) Produced by Martine Marignac. Directed by Suzanne Schiffman. Screenplay, Schiffman, Pierre Zucca; camera (color), Ramon Suarez; editor, Marie-Aimée Debril, music, Jean-Pierre Mas; sound, Alix Compte, Paul Bertolt; assistant director, Patrick Delabrierre. Reviewed at French Institute (AFI European Community Film Festival), N.Y., June 7, 1989. Running time: **91 MIN.**

Marc	Jean-Pierre Léaud
Paule	Hélène Lapiower
Julie	Caroline Loeb
Berthier	Rufus
Etienne	Thierry Fortineau
Bernard	Laszlo Szabo

■ "Femme de Papier" is a delightful French comedy offering a few twists on a traditional imposture theme of having a photogenic front for the anonymous author of popular novels ("Front Women" is pic's English-language moniker).

Playing in the U.S. at the traveling AFI European Community Film Festival, pic stands a good chance at the b.o. back on its home turf, and has decent export prospects.

For her second feature following the period drama "Sorceress," Suzanne Schiffman changes pace to a light and peppy style associated with early New Wave pics by Jean-Luc Godard and François Truffaut (on which she apprenticed as script girl). Casting of Jean-Pierre Léaud in an emblematic role continues the link with that tradition.

Léaud portrays a Parisian publisher of romance novels who hits on the gimmick of having his live-in girlfriend (carrot-top cutie Hélène Lapiower) pose as author Rosine de Beaumont for bookjacket and autograph signings. She's an immediate hit but rebels against being exploited, and throws Léaud out of their apartment.

Complications occur when she meets a nerd (Rufus) claiming to be the book's author, leading to discovery of the real author (Thierry Fortineau), a bookseller who's so happy to be in print at last that he's not too miffed at the deception. Climax shot at Charles de Gaulle Airport neatly weaves plot threads together for a blissfully happy ending.

Schiffman's light touch makes this typical French fluff soar, abetted by a very peppy cast. Léaud's fussy mannerisms are a nostalgic throwback to his '60s persona, while newcomer Lapiower scores as a personable, energetic gamin in the Malène Jobert mold. Particularly fun are several impromptu song numbers belted (directsound) by Lapiower and her best pal Caroline Loeb. Rufus is properly eccentric (with a M. Hulot-esque gait) as the introverted "writer."

Sprightly score by Jean-Pierre Mas is in sync with the director's self-conscious approach. Hidden-camera type photography of street scenes (with apparent use of real-life extras) adds to pics' verve.

—*Lor.*

L'Insoumis
(Fight For Us)
(FRENCH-FILIPINO)

Paris   A Pathé release of a Giancarlo Parretti Production presentation of a Bernadette Intl. production. Executive producer, Salvatore Picciotto. Produced by Leonardo de la Fuente. Directed by Lino Brocka. Screenplay, Jose F. Lacaba; camera (color), Rody Lacap; editor, George Jarlego, Sabine Mamou, Bob Wade; sound, Alfredo Sabile; art direction, Benjie de Guzman, Buboy Tagayon; special effects makeup, Cecille Baun; assistant director, Bey Vito; production managers, Boy C. de Guia; Bernard P. Guiremand; casting, Zenny Basco. Reviewed at Cannon France, Paris, May 12, 1989. Running time: **94 MIN.**

Jimmy Cordero	Phillip Salvador
Trixie	Dina Bonnevie
Esper	Gina Alajar
Major Kontra	Bembol Roco
Sister Marie	Ginnie Sobrino
Django	Abbo de la Cruz

■ A harrowing fictionalized report on political terror and lawlessness in post-Marcos Philippines, "Fight For Us" is Lino Brocka's red-hot exposé of the reality behind his country's apparent democratization.

Financed entirely from France by new Cannon and Pathé honcho Giancarlo Parretti, but lensed entirely on home turf with local cast and technicians, film is certain to be a hot topic of discussion and controversy, which should have beneficial effects on its commercial chances. The Cannes fest saved it for one of its last but not least attractions.

Brocka, the best known and most prolific of Filipino filmmakers, has used melodrama before to convey social realities of his homeland, and the approach here is the same, perhaps even more violent and angrier than the films he made under the Marcos dictatorship. Though the thriller format limits its intrinsic cinematic value and emotional depth, the director's outrage makes this a rivetting political pamphlet.

Script by journalist Jose Lacaba paints an unrelentingly bloody picture of the Philippines since the rise to power of Corazon Aquino in 1985. Behind the facade of a country rediscovering its democratic instincts, Lacaba and Brocka show us a cowered people, prey to the fanatical terror and violence and untouchable paramilitary vigilante groups (here called the Orapronobis), whose extralegal executions, tortures, summary massacres and brazen kidnappings continue to reach with impunity from remote peasant villages to the very heart of metropolitan Manila.

The dramatization of what the filmmakers claim to be factual events harshly indicts the army and police, who are shown here as turning a complicitous blind eye and deaf ear to the guerrilla activities. The Orapronobis claim to be engaged in a holy war against communism, which aligns them ideologically with the new (capitalist) order just as it had with the Marcos regime.

Lacaba stresses the continuity of terror with a prolog illustrating a gratuitous vigilante murder (of a priest) under the former dictatorship, before the action leaps ahead to late 1988, when the same bands continue to infest city and country.

Lacaba and Brocka, however, stop short of implicating Corazon Aquino in the violation of civil liberties and human rights that they denounce. Their film seems rather a celluloid inquiry directed to the nation's ostensibly sympathetic leader, cautiously asking if she is aware of the corruption that continues to rot the Philippines.

Like any melodrama, film has its hero, Phillip Salvador, a one-time priest who gave up the cassock to join the rebels against the Marcos regime. Imprisoned, he is released by the new "democracy" and devotes his energies to a human rights group investigating reports of torture and murder. He also is now a family man with an attractive wife (and fellow activist), Dina Bonnevie, who is expecting their first child.

Movement of the story will be obvious to any casual filmgoer. Salvador, the former rebel who has turned over a new leaf and vowed himself to lawful humanitarian activities, finds himself gradually sucked back into the universe of violence he believes a thing of the past. After witnessing numerous examples of sanguinary human rights violations, Salvador loses his brother-in-law and is himself seriously wounded in one urban guerrilla ambush.

The coup de grace comes when a former lover of his (Gina Alajar), and the son he gave her, are kidnapped (in broad daylight on a busy Manila thoroughfare), tortured and subsequently murdered by the Orapronobis. In an emotional scene, Salvador clutches the bloodied corpse of his son to his chest, staring blankly ahead. Film ends as he returns home and brings out the pistol a former resistance colleague left with him when trying (unsuccessfully) to recruit him back to clandestine service.

(Lacaba and Brocka never define the political coloring — communist? — of what is referred to vaguely throughout the film as the "resistance.")

Some viewers undoubtedly will blanch at the film's emphatic violence, which occasionally belongs more to the realm of Movieland than of real life (such as in the climactic bloodbath in the Orapronobis den, ironically staged against a backdrop of an American flag, and neighboring portraits of Marcos and Stallone/Rambo!). Yet other dramatic large-scale scenes have a wrenching documentary immediacy, enforced by the unflamboyant, committed acting.

Brocka, however, seems to go overboard in the depiction of the Orapronobis vigilantes, with their sadistic fanaticism, rabid anti-communist cant and cannibalistic religious rituals. All true, Brocka apparently claims, but outrageous documented reality sometimes needs to be toned down or stylized in a coventionally contrived fiction if audiences are to accept it.

Though reportedly shot in relatively clandestine conditions in the Philippines, film benefits from good lensing by Rody Lacap and fluid editing by George Jarlego, Sabine Mamou and Bob Wade.

—*Len.*

Kunst & Vliegwerk
(At Stalling Speed)
(DUTCH)

Amsterdam A Cannon Film Distribution Nederland release of a Castor Films production. Directed by Karst van der Meulen. Screenplay, Van der Meulen, Piet Geelhoed; camera (color), Fred Tammes; editor, Hans Walther; music, Tonny Eyk; sound, Victor Dekker; art direction, Hendrik Jan Visser. Reviewed at City theater, Amsterdam, March 31, 1989. Running time: 110 MIN.
With: Toon Agterberg, Herman van Veen, Saskia van Basten Batenburg, André van den Heuvel, Kitty Janssen.

■ A winsome entertainment for the whole family, "Kunst & Vliegwerk" is the latest by Karst van der Meulen, a kidpic specialist who's turned out eight features in the past 16 years.

The story is simple and linear with well-spaced attention-grabbers for smaller children, and a gimmick — a homemade mini-rocket. There's also a hungry escaped tiger, a stuntman with amnesia, a gun, a lot of loot, a wimpish artist father, a sensitive mother, Dutch soldiers, policemen and a happy ending which is some time in coming.

Child players, all amateurs, have fun, which can be fun to watch. The grown-ups, all professional, occasionally have difficulty balancing the tomfoolery and acting. Tech credits are okay, without frills. It looks like the sort of pic that could branch out into a miniseries. —Wall.

Lady Terminator
(INDONESIAN-U.S.)

New York A Studio Entertainment release of a Soraya Intercine Film presentation, in association with 108 Sound Studio. Produced by Ram Soraya. Directed by Jalil Jackson. Screenplay, Karr Kruinowz; camera (color), Chuchu Suteja; editor, uncredited; music, Ricky Brothers; production design, Yansen J.; assistant director, Kenn Thimoty; makeup, Tetty, Barbara Anne Constable. Reviewed at Criterion 3 theater, N.Y., June 3, 1989. No MPAA Rating. Running time: 82 MIN.
With: Barbara Anne Constable, Christopher J. Hart, Claudia Angelique Rademaker, Joseph P. McGlynn, Adam Stardust, Ikang Fawzi.

(English soundtrack)

■ An unusual domestic release of a sex/action pic made in Indonesia, "Lady Terminator" provides mainly camp and novelty value in its mixture of grotesque situations and laughable dialog.

Distributed by Gotham-based Studio Entertainment, pic is a bit rougher than current R-rated fare, and goes out sans MPAA rating, with a self-imposed equivalent to an R advertised.

Farfetched story is credited as based on the legend of the South Sea Queen, shown in prolog losing her life force, après sex, to her 100th husband Elias, who transforms the snake she keeps inside her into a magical dagger. The Queen curses him, vowing vengeance in 100 years' time on Elias' great-granddaughter, and walks into the sea.

A pretty American anthropology student, Tanya, is elected as the reincarnation of the Queen, transformed in a goofy special effects scene into the title zombie avenger. Dressed in black leather, like Pam Grier as "Foxy Brown," she goes on the rampage, wiping out hundreds of Indonesians with a machine gun in quest for singer Erika, the descendant of Elias.

Much of pic's humor comes from a Yank cop in Indonesia, Max, whose flippant attitude (he likes to joke in morgues and hospitals) and poor acting enrich the film's lousy post-synched dialog. He ultimately saves Erika from the indestructible Tanya, with the running gag being his improbable ability to escape death while Tanya merely uses supernatural means.

Gamiest element here is Tanya's bloody murdering of her sexual partners. She provides some appealing nude scenes until being turned into a monster (via makeup) for the finale. Credits do not identify individual cast members with their roles.

Action scenes are okay, but visual effects are subpar. —Lor.

The Jitters

New York A Gaga Communications presentation of a Fascination production. (Intl. sales, Skouras Pictures.) Executive producer, Tetsu Fujimura. Produced and directed by John M. Fasano. Screenplay, Jeff McKay, Sonoko Kondo; additional dialog, Fasano; camera (Medallion color), Paul Mitchnick; editor, Ray Van Doorn, Fasano; music, Dann Linck, Tom Borton; sound, Jin Hong; production manager, Cindy Sorrell; assistant director, Bob Urquhart; special creature, Steven Wang; special makeup effects, Richard Alonzo; stunt coordinator, Rick Forsayeth; coproducer, Sonoko Sakai. Reviewed on Prism Entertainment vidcassette, N.Y., June 3, 1989. MPAA Rating: R. Running time: 79 MIN.
Michael . . . . Sal Viviano
Alice Lee . . . . Marilyn Yokuda
Tony Yang Sr. . . . . James Hong
Rat . . . . Frank Dietz
Frank Lee . . . . Handy Atmadja
Tony Yang Sr. . . . . James Hong
Also with: Jonathan Goldstein, Jesse D'Angelo, Raymond Wong, Lana Davies, Clara Rater, Andrea Roth.

■ This mixed-up attempt at a live-action comic strip heads to videostores with no warning on how fans are to react to an overly goofy fantasy effort.

With Japanese funding, American production and Toronto Chinatown setting, John Fasano's film is a mishmash to start with. He doesn't help things out by overlaying a noisy musical score and sound effects track that either drowns out or distracts from the dialog exchanges.

Wacky premise concerns the Chinese undead, known as Gyonsii, a group of vampire-like beings trapped in limbo on Earth (between heaven and hell). Heroine Marilyn Yokuida's toystore-owner dad (Handy Atmadja) joins the zombie ranks when he's mudered by sneak thieves, their leader wearing a Batman t-shirt (in timely fashion).

Yokuda and her Caucasian boyfriend Sal Viviano team up with a pair of young magicians to sort out the undead and avenge daddy's death. Gimmick of the vampires hopping along lets the viewer know quickly it's all tongue in cheek. A silly scene of a zombie suddenly turning into a reptilian monster is inserted as an excuse for the makeup effects crew to trot out pulsating bladders and dribbling goo.

Performances are hard to judge thanks to the soundtrack overlay. Best thing in the pic is a fancy cartoon opening-credits sequence; end credits are unreeled slowly to pad the abbreviated running time. —Lor.

Alexa

New York A Platinum Pictures and B/Tru Prods. presentation of a Hydra Film Partners production. Produced by Peggy Bruen. Directed by Sean Delgado. Screenplay, Bruen, Delgado; camera (color), Joey Forsyte; editor, James Davalos; music, Gregory Alper; sound, Tim Harvey; art direction, Liz Deutsch; production manager, Richie Vetter; assistant director, Barry Shapiro. Reviewed on Academy Entertainment vidcassette, N.Y., May 28, 1989. MPAA Rating: R. Running time: 80 MIN.
Alexa Avery . . . . Christine Moore
Tony . . . . Kirk Baily
Marshall Newhouse . . . . Ruth Collins
Jan . . . . Joseph P. Giardina
Tommy . . . . Tom Voth
March . . . . Adam Michenner
Also with: Thomas Walker, Sarah Halley, Trula Hoosier, Leslie Lowe, Mary Round, Joseph Haddock, Sharon Kane, Sheri St. Claire.

■ "Alexa" is an ambitious but unsatisfying character study of a Gotham prostitute; it's scheduled as a summer homevideo release.

Unlike the courtroom/psychoanalytic approach of the play and subsequent film "Nuts," filmmakers Sean Delgado and Peggy Bruen take a behavioral approach that creates initial interest in the plight of high-priced callgirl Alexa (Canadian thesp Christine Moore), but is nullified by a misjudged melodramatic final feel.

After eight years hooking, Alexa is pondering whether to retire and take up best buddy Ruth Collins' offer to open a restaurant together. Key plot catalyst is young playwright Kirk Baily interviewing her for a show he's writing about prostitution. Alexa falls in love with him but her nasty pimp (Joseph P. Giardina) intervenes with fatal results.

Moore, a Jacqueline Bisset-type beauty who's been impressive in a series of east coast thrillers, plays it mean here, creating a central figure that's nearly as unsympathetic as the male cast. With no one to root for the film is hurting, and cemetery finale leads to bathos. Emphasis on Baily's play proves an empty device since it's never enacted on screen.

Baily remains a cipher in his lead role, seen only from Alexa's perspective. Collins does her reliable sidekick part, and Frank Zappa-esque Giardina is briefly scary as the violent hustler. Tech credits are inconsistent (several key scenes, including a prolog, are shot silent with poor post-synch while others use direct sound), but Gregory Alper's moody jazz score is a plus. —Lor.

Outback
(AUSTRALIAN)

Sydney A Samuel Goldwyn Intl. release of an Intl. Film Management-Burrowes Film Group-John Sexton Prods. production. Executive producers, Antony I. Ginnane, Kent Lovell. Produced by John Sexton. Directed by Ian Barry. Screenplay, Sexton; camera (Eastmancolor), Ross Berryman; editor, Henry Dangar; music, Mario Millo; sound, Ben Osmo; production design, Owen Paterson; line producer, Su Armstrong; costumes, Terry Ryan; production manager, Grant Hill; assistant director, John Wild; casting, Forcast. Reviewed at Colorfilm screening room, Sydney, Aug. 26, 1988. Running time: 91 MINS.
Creed . . . . Jeff Fahey
Alice Richards . . . . Tushka Bergen
Jack Donaghue . . . . Steve Vidler
Thompson . . . . Richard Moir
Allenby . . . . Shane Briant
Henry Iverson . . . . Drew Forsythe
Aunt Maude . . . . Sandy Gore
Richards . . . . Fred Parslow
Caroline Richards . . . . Cornelia Frances

■ A turn-of-the-century Australian Western, which is visually sumptuous and filled with intriguing characters, "Outback" nevertheless looks a bit too much like a rerun of the "Snowy River" sagas, complete with spectacular scenes of galloping horses and a feisty heroine who's as tough as any man about the place.

This familiarity may mitigate against the film's critical and box-office chances, though family audiences could respond to its beauty and sense of old-style adventure.

The teen heroine is Alice (Tushka Bergen) whose father runs a lavish property, with magnificent old homestead, but whose poor business management is driving him to the brink of bankruptcy. His neighbor, a slimy villain (Shane Briant), covets the land and will stop at nothing to get it.

The willful Alice is involved with two men. First, a working-class drover, Donaghue (well played by Steve Vidler), and then a somewhat mysterious Yank businessman (Jeff Fahey) who secretly pays off her father's debts until his own business is sabotaged by Briant and he, too, faces bankruptcy.

Climax consists of a breakneck gallop across country with a mob of 100 horses that, if sold to the British army (in need of the nags for war against the Boers in South Africa) might save the day.

There are plenty of other characters here, including Donaghue's devious business partner (Richard Moir) and Creed's loyal accountant (Drew Forsythe) as well as, amusingly, Alice's free-thinking aunt (the splendid Sandy Gore) at whose Melbourne salon she spends some time.

Drama boils down, essentially, to which of the two men Alice will choose. For a turn-of-the-century gal, she seems to be quite free with her sexual favors.

Director Ian Barry handles the material at a brisk pace, indeed too brisk at times. The quite complex plotting is covered in all-too-brief scenes, cut to the bone by editor Henry Dangar, with the result that some details of the behind-the-scenes dealing over the Richards property remain hazy.

Director of photography Ross Berryman deserves a special nod for the film's superb look, and production designer Owen Paterson has likewise done sterling work, aided by location shooting in a couple of magnificent old country homes.

Despite the basic familiarity of the material, "Outback" could click in the Aussie market but needs the change of title to "Min-

namura" it has been given in some markets. The "outback" is considered to be far more remote country than the locations used in the film, and in any event "Outback" was the international title given by UA to the 1971 Ted Kotcheff pic known in Australia as "Wake In Fright." Current pic's overseas chances will depend on handling and favorable critical attention. —*Strat.*

To Die For

Detroit   A Skouras Pictures release of a Greg H. Sims presentation of an Arrowhead Entertainment/Lee Caplin production. Executive producers, Greg H. Sims, Lee Caplin. Produced by Barin Kumar. Directed by Deran Sarafian. Screenplay, Leslie King; camera (Foto-Kem color), David Boyd; music, Cliff Eidelman; art direction, Greg Oehler; special effects supervisor, Eddie Surkin; special makeup effects, Mike Deak, John Foster, Greg Johnson, Wayne Toth; assistant director, Mike Johnson. Reviewed at AMC America-na 8, Southfield, Mich., June 7, 1989. MPAA Rating: R. Running time: 90 MIN.
Vlad Tepish	Brendan Hughes
Kate Wooten	Sydney Walsh
Celia Kett	Amanda Wyss
Martin Planting	Scott Jacoby
Mike Dunn	Micah Grant
Simon Little	Duane Jones
Tom	Steve Bond
Jane	Remy O'Neill
Lt. Williams	Al Fann
Det. Bocco	Philip Granger
Paula Higgins	Julie Maddalena

■ "To Die For" is a well-intentioned but poorly executed vampire film that tries to mix horror, eroticism and universal concepts of love and friendship. Because it ultimately fails in each of these goals, "To Die For" won't spend much time in the theater.

Due to the popularity of the genre alone, it may generate some video buzz before getting lost on the shelves.

To their credit, director Deran Sarafian and writer Leslie King have tried to incorporate some of the original lore from the Dracula tale, including the demon's sexual attraction to women. One bite from the original Dracula may have meant death or worse, an eternity as one of the walking dead. The bite also represented a pleasure/pain experience that some victims found worth the consequences.

Trouble is, the acting, direction and writing in "To Die For" are so weak, they sabotage the movie's good intentions. What's left is a horror film buoyed by few horrors and weighed down by overacting, ludicrous plot twists and weak special effects.

The story centers on Vlad Tep-

ish, a handsome vampire who has fallen for Kate Wooten, a young real estate agent dismayed at the thought that she may never find someone who can give her passionate, uncontrollable, blind love.

She breaks off the comfortable but unexciting relationship she has with her boyfriend Martin and instead finds herself irresistibly drawn to Vlad.

Vlad has a dark history. His friend Tom, also a vampire, is seeking revenge because in the past Vlad killed Tom's true love. Now Tom wants to kill Kate.

Kate's search for forbidden love, and finding it in Vlad (get it, Vlad the Impaler) is an interesting concept. Rather than developing it, "To Die For" quickly degenerates into a silly vampire spat between Vlad and Tom.

First Tom snuffs out Kate's friends, starting with her roommate Celia, who also has taken a shine to Vlad.

Celia, played by Amanda Wyss, provides a campy transformation from goody-goody to sex-starved vamp. Had the whole movie taken on a campy air, "To Die For" might have succeeded.

Instead the picture quickly falls into the familiar monster motif. Tom kills the small band of characters we've been introduced to. The local cops don't know what to make of it.

Ultimately there is a final confrontation between Tom and Vlad. Even here, however, "To Die For" is disappointing. The scene is too brief. The confrontation is unexceptional and the special effects look cheesy. —*Advo.*

Underground Terror

New York   An SVS Films presentation of a Triangle production. Produced by Steven Mackler. Line producer, Robert Zimmerman. Directed by James McCalmont. Screenplay, Zimmerman, Brian O'Hara, from O'Hara's story; additional material, Tennyson Bardwell; camera (Technicolor), Anghel Deca; editor, Keith Reamer; music, Taj; sound, Pawel Wdowczak; production design, Mikhail Fishgoyt; art direction, Claudia Mohr; production manager, Philip Dolin; 2d unit director, Zimmerman; associate producer, Bernard E. Goldberg; casting, Dennis M. Lee, Nancy Winter Cook. Reviewed on Sony vidcassette, N.Y., June 3, 1989. MPAA Rating: R. Running time: 90 MIN.
John Willis	Doc Dougherty
Boris	Lennie Loftin
Kim Knowles	B.J. Geordan
Weasel	Ric Siler

Also with: Joe Bachana, James Davies, Allen L. Rickman, Christopher Koron, Herb Farnham, Charles J. Roby, Andrea Black, Regan Vann.

ish, a handsome vampire who has

■Gotham-lensed video feature, previously called just "Underground" is an okay thriller about a ruthless gang living in the subway and preying on hapless travelers.

Pic avoids the horrific approach of such predecessors as "Raw Meat" (which dealt with cannibals in the British underground) but is still grisly in limning sadistic nutcase Lennie Loftin's antics beneath Gotham's streets.

Doc Dougherty, convincingly uptight in his verbal explosions, is the gung-ho cop who's suspended from the force for excessive violence. He teams up with femme reporter B.J. Geordan to track down the killers.

Pic benefits from atmospheric location lensing. Other tech credits are ordinary. —*Lor.*

LATE FILM REVIEWS

Batman

Hollywood   A Warner Bros. release of a Guber-Peters production. Produced by Jon Peters, Peter Guber. Executive producer, Benjamin Melniker, Michael Uslan. Coproduced by Chris Kenney. Directed by Tim Burton. Screenplay, Sam Hamm, Warren Skaaren, from a story by Hamm based on characters created by Bob Kane appearing in magazines published by DC Comics; camera (Eastmancolor, Technicolor prints), Roger Pratt; editor, Ray Lovejoy; music, Danny Elfman; songs, Prince; production design, Anton Furst; supervising art direction, Les Tomkins; art direction, Terry Ackland-Snow, Nigel Phelps; set decoration, Peter Young; costume design, Bob Ringwood, Linda Henrikson; special visual effects, Derek Meddings; supervising sound editor, Don Sharpe; rerecording mixer, Bill Rowe; makeup, Paul Engelen; stunt coordinator, Eddie Stacey; assistant director, Derek Cracknell; second unit director, Peter MacDonald; associate producer, Barbara Kalish; casting, Marion Dougherty. Reviewed at Cary Grant Theater, Culver City, June 9, 1989. MPAA Rating: PG-13. Running time: 126 MIN.
Batman/Bruce Wayne	Michael Keaton
Joker/Jack Napier	Jack Nicholson
Vicki Vale	Kim Basinger
Alexander Knox	Robert Wuhl
Commissioner Gordon	Pat Hingle
Harvey Dent	Billy Dee Williams
Alfred	Michael Gough
Grissom	Jack Palance
Alicia	Jerry Hall
Mayor	Lee Wallace
Bob The Goon	Tracey Walter

■Anyone expecting a replay of the campy tv series "Batman" will get quite a shock from this dark and brooding saga of the Caped Crusader. Director Tim Burton effectively echoes the visual style of the original Bob Kane comics while conjuring up a nightmarish world of his own.

But the uneven Warner Bros. release treats its thin plot too reverentially, and Jack Nicholson's incandescent Joker overwhelms Michael Keaton's subdued title character. Definitely not for small children, this "Batman" will find admirers and detractors in equal numbers.

Going back to the source elements of the cartoon figure, who made his debut in 1939 for Detective (now DC) Comics, the Jon Peters-Peter Guber production will appeal to purists who prefer their heroes as straight as Clint Eastwood. Others may be bothered or mystified by the grim and gruesome goings-on which eschew warmth and humor.

The filmmakers have gone out of their way to avoid anything which would evoke the 1960s biff-bam-pow humor of the vidseries. Even Robin is missing, perhaps also a reflection of a nervous contemporary attitude toward the homosexual overtones many found in his relationship with Batman.

But Robin wasn't there at the beginning, when Kane (a consultant on this film) introduced Batman as a solitary nocturnal man whose strange behavior stemmed from his trauma at witnessing the murder of his parents. In a striking departure from his usual amiable comic-style, Keaton captures the haunted intensity of the character, and seems particularly lonely and obsessive without Robin around to share his exploits.

The gorgeous Kim Basinger takes the sidekick's place, in a determined bow to heterosexuality which nonetheless leaves Batman something less than enthusiastic. This Batman is an aloof '80s guy who has a problem getting emotionally involved, and the film never hits the right tone in dealing with the often banal romantic chatter.

It comes as no surprise that Jack Nicholson steals every scene in a sizable role as the hideously disfigured Joker. By this stage, in his career, calling Nicholson "over the top" is beside the point because he makes a glorious style of playing the most extravagantly psychotic characters.

Nicholson embellishes fascinat-

Original Film

A 20th Century Fox release of William Dozier production. Directed by Leslie H. Martinson. Screenplay, Lorenzo Semple Jr., based on characters created by Bob Kane; camera (Deluxe color), Howard Schwartz; editor, Harry Gerstad; music, Nelson Riddle; assistant director, William Derwin. Reviewed at 20th-Fox Studio, Hollywood, July 14, 1966. Running time: **105 MIN.**

Batman	Adam West
Robin	Burt Ward
The Catwoman	Lee Meriwether
The Joker	Cesar Romero
The Penguin	Burgess Meredith
The Riddler	Frank Gorshin
Alfred	Alan Napier
Commissioner Gordon	Neil Hamilton
Chief O'Hara	Stafford Repp
Aunt Harriet Cooper	Madge Blake
Commodore Schmidlapp	Reginald Denny
Fangschliester	Milton Frome
Bluebeard	Gil Perkins
Morgan	Dick Crockett
Quetch	George Sawaya

ingly baroque designs with his twisted features, lavish verbal pirouettes and inspired excursions into the outer limits of psychosis. It's a masterpiece of sinister comic acting.

But his Joker is disturbing enough to cause small kids to run up the aisles screaming.

The character works in a black-humor vein, although the accumulated brutalities become wearying long before the finale. Another off-putting element is a sequence of the Joker defacing some of our culture's most beloved art works, which not only is the opposite of funny but also could inspire vicious copycat behavior.

What keeps the film arresting is the visual stylization. Bearing in mind that comic books were a major influence on the film noir style that flourished after World War II, it was a shrewd choice for Burton to emulate the jarring angles and creepy lighting of film noir. He daringly combines it with suggestions of art deco architecture and "Blade Runner"-like future shock into a seamless whole.

But Burton and his superlative tech staff are undercut by the common failing of so many contemporary pics — the story. Scripters Sam Hamm and Warren Skaaren, working from Hamm's adaptation of the comic, fail to bring the richness and complexity to Batman that would complement the visuals.

Kudos go to the craftsmen on the British-made pic for their powerful support. Lenser Roger Pratt, production designer Anton Furst and visual effects creator Derek Meddings have done yeomanly work. Also making first-rate contributions are Joker makeup designer Nick Dudman and costume designers Bob Ringwood and Linda Henrikson.

Danny Elfman's eerie score is a big plus, although the songs by Prince are excrescence on the soundtrack.

Maybe next time around, if the boxoffice warrants a "Batman II," they'll come up with a story to match the visual pyrotechnics.
—*Mac.*

Licence To Kill
(BRITISH)

London An MGM/UA Distribution release from United Artists of an Eon production. Produced by Albert R. Broccoli, Michael G. Wilson. Directed by John Glen. Screenplay, Richard Maibaum, Wilson; camera, (Panavision, Technicolor) Alec Mills; editor, John Grover; music, Michael Kamen; sound (Dolby), Edward Tise; production design, Peter Lamont; art direction, Dennis Boshner; special effects supervisor, John Richardson; production supervisor, Anthony Wayne; stunt supervisor, Paul Weston; set decoration, Michael Ford; second unit director-cameraman, Arthur Wooster; costumes, Jodie Tillen; associate producers, Tom Pevsner, Barbara Broccoli; title sequence, Maurice Binder; casting, Jane Jenkins, Janet Hirschenson. Reviewed at Odeon Leicester Square, London, June 12, 1989. MPAA Rating: PG-13. Running time: **133 MIN.**

James Bond	Timothy Dalton
Pam Bouvier	Carey Lowell
Franz Sanchez	Robert Davi
Lupe Lamora	Talisa Soto
Milton Krest	Anthony Zerbe
Sharkey	Frank McRae
Killifer	Everett McGill
Joe Butcher	Wayne Newton
Dario	Benicio Del Toro
Q	Desmond Llewelyn
Felix Leiter	David Hedison
Della Churchill	Priscilla Barnes
M	Robert Brown
Miss Moneypenny	Caroline Bliss

■The James Bond production team has found its second wind with "Licence To Kill," a cocktail of high-octane action, spectacle and drama. It's a sure-fire click worldwide for the 16th in the United Artists 007 series and one that will rate among the best.

Presence for the second time of Timothy Dalton as the suave British agent clearly has juiced up scripters Richard Maibaum and Michael Wilson (who also coproduces) and director John Glen, who helms a Bond pic for the fifth consecutive time.

Out go the self-parodying witticisms and over-elaborate high-tech gizmos that slowed pre-Dalton pics to a walking pace. Exotic settings now serve the narrative rather than provide a glossy travelog.

Dalton plays 007 with a vigor and physicality that harks back to the earliest Bond pics, letting full-bloodied actions speak louder than words.

The thrills-and-spills chases are superbly orchestrated as pic spins at breakneck speed through its South Florida and Central American locations. Bond survives a series of underwater and mid-air stunt sequences that are above par for the series.

He's also pitted against a crew of sinister baddies (led by Robert Davi and Frank McRae) who give the British agent the chance to use all his wit and wiles. Femme elements in the guise of Carey Lowell and Talisa Soto add gloss but play second fiddle to the action.

Plot revolves around Bond's mission of vengeance for his Yank friend Felix Leiter (David Hedison), formerly of the CIA and now with the Drug Enforcement Agency in South Florida. Leiter's wife (Priscilla Barnes) has been murdered by drug baron Franz Sanchez (Davi) and Leiter himself is badly mauled in the attempt to arrest him.

Bond, temporarily relieved of his special license-to-kill status, tracks Sanchez to his Central American hideout, nerve center of a worldwide multibillion-dollar drug operation. A thrilling chase sequence with three Kenworth trucks careening down a mountain road brings the pic to a stunning climax.

The usual secret service team of Q, M and Miss Moneypenny is fleetingly present, with Q's imaginative gadgetry playing an essential but low-key role in Bond's brushes with death.

Two gripes in the otherwise outstanding tech credits department are the sometimes poor clarity of the dialog and the occasional lapses in lipsync. Otherwise the repeat crew on "Licence" has served up a scorcher. —*Coop.*

Ghostbusters II

Hollywood   A Columbia Pictures release. Executive producers, Bernie Brillstein, Joe Medjuck, Michael C. Gross. Produced and directed by Ivan Reitman. Screenplay, Harold Ramis, Dan Aykroyd, based on their characters; camera (Panavision, Deluxe color), Michael Chapman; editor, Sheldon Kahn, Donn Cambern; music, Randy Edelman; sound (Dolby), Gene Cantamessa; production design, Bo Welch; art direction, Tom Duffield; set decoration, Cheryl Carasik; set design, Nick Navarro, Gregory Papalia, Rich Heinrichs; costume design, Gloria Gresham; visual effects supervisor, Dennis Muren; visual effects, Industrial Light & Magic; effects photography, Mark Vargo; visual effect producer, Janet Mohler; visual effects art director, Harley Jessup; creature makeup design, Tim Lawrence; optical photography supervisor, Thomas J. Rosseter; key effects camera, Kim Marks; animation supervisor, Tom Bertino; matte painting supervisor, Mark Sullivan; additional visual effects, Apogee VCE Inc.; assistant director, Peter Giuliano; associate producers, Kahn, Gordon Webb; casting, Michael Chinich. Reviewed at the Cineplex Odeon Century City Cinema, L.A., June 12, 1989. MPAA Rating: PG. Running time: **102 MIN.**

Dr. Peter Venkman . . . . Bill Murray
Dr. Raymond Stantz . . . . Dan Aykroyd
Dana Barrett . . . . Sigourney Weaver
Dr. Egon Spengler . . . . Harold Ramis
Louis Tully . . . . Rick Moranis
Winston Zeddemore . . . . Ernie Hudson
Janosz Poha . . . . Peter MacNicol
Mayor . . . . David Margulies
Vigo . . . . Wilhelm Von Homburg
Also with: Harris Yulin, Kurt Fuller, Janet Margolin, Christopher Neame, Cheech Marin, Brian Doyle Murray, Judy Ovitz, Ben Stein.

■ "Ghostbusters II" is baby-boomer silliness as opposed to the juvenile silliness of the original. Kids will find the oozing slime and ghastly, ghostly apparitions to their liking and adults will enjoy the preposterously clever dialog.

In "II," the foe is slime, a pinkish, oozing substance that has odd, selective powers — all of them (humorously) evil. Its origins have something to do with a bad imitation Rembrandt painting, the lecherous art historian with an indecipherable foreign accent who's restoring it (Peter MacNicol), and all the bad vibes generated by millions of cranky, stressed-out New Yorkers. The worse their attitude, the worse the slime problem, which is very bad indeed.

The Ghostbusters, naturally, are the only guys for the job.

Bill Murray gets the plum central role (or he forced it by seemingly adlibbing dozens of wisecracks) at the same time his character also manages to skip out on a lot of the dirty ghostbusting work, leaving it to his pals Dan Aykroyd, Harold Ramis and Ernie Hudson.

While they are zapping Slimer, the main nasty creature from "Ghostbusters," his swirling friends or venturing into Manhattan's underground version of the river Styx (a churning fast-flowing stream of red goo), Murray's time is spent wooing back Sigourney Weaver, now a single mother.

For the umpteenth time, another human is to be sacrificed by a demon with aspirations to rule the world, in this case Weaver's kidnaped baby to Vigo (Wilhelm Von Homburg), the Nordic-looking figure in the painting.

It may be a first time, but Weaver gets to play a softie, a nice break for the actress and her admirers (even if shots with her cute imperiled baby are scene-stealers).

Scripters Ramis and Aykroyd filled the film with dumb/funny dialog, none better than when the Ghostbusters are together in the lab talking sweet talk to the bowl of slime in an effort to neutralize its evilness. Once that's accomplished, Ramis pronounces the stuff effectively neutralized into "mood slime."

From the frenetic pacing and cacophonous tone, director Ivan Reitman is clearly in his element.

The special effects go a long way in camouflaging the thin, overwrought story. Industrial Light & Magic is up to its usual technical brilliance, especially in the last scene where the memory of Staypuff, the gargantuan meanie from "Ghostbusters," is upstaged forever by a much greater and even more imposing American symbol.

Rick Moranis is a riot. Hudson, who can make terrific comic faces, is underused. Good for sly smiles are cameos by Judy Ovitz, Cheech Marin, Janet Margolin and Ben Stein.

Other tech credits (too numerous to mention) look like they cost a mint. —*Brit.*

Beeld van een kind
(Image Of A Child)
(DUTCH-DOCU)

Amsterdam   A NFI release of a Yuca Film production. Produced by Suzanne van Voorst. Written and directed by Albert van der Wildt. Camera, (color, 16m), Peter Brugman, Bernd Wouthuysen; editor, Menno Boerema; sound, Bert van den Dungen, Floor Kooij, Eric Langhout. Reviewed at Desmet theater, Amsterdam, April 25, 1989. Running time: **60 MIN.**

■ Albert van der Wildt, cameraman of many features and director of a few docus, made this film on "cot death" — officially, SIDS (Sudden Infant Death Syndrome) — as a way of coping with the loss of his own first child.

Van der Wildt deals with parents' problems and attitudes of the medical profession with an integrity and honesty that is gripping.

Cot death strikes babies without warning. There are no symptoms, no known causes, even autopsies shed no light. Although the experts and reason tell them they are not to blame, parents harbor a sense of guilt; rebellion, despair and numbness alternate.

Van der Wildt shows all this mainly through his own experience, his broken marriage, a fetishistic attachment to boys, clothes, the grave.

There also is another couple with a young son. When their first child died of cot death, their relationship became fragile. The second child, now about six, has added permanent stress and an abiding terror about cot death striking again.

The film's frankness may leave some viewers with an uneasy feeling of intruding, but it's a docu that will travel. —*Wall.*

Ice House

New York   An Upfront Films release of a Cactus Films production. Executive producer, Rick McCartney. Produced by Bo Brinkman. Coproducer, Kenneth Schwenker. Directed by Eagle Pennell. Screenplay, Brinkman, based on his play "Ice House Heat Waves;" camera (Duart color), Brown Cooper; editor, John Murray; music, Carmen Yates, Tony Fortuna; sound editor, John W. Donaldson; production design, Lynn Ruth Appel; casting, Nancy Frigand. Reviewed at Quad 3 theater, N.Y., June 12, 1989. No MPAA Rating. Running time: **77 MIN.**

Kay/Mother . . . . Melissa Gilbert
Pake . . . . Bo Brinkman
Vassil . . . . Andreas Manolikakis
Also with: Lynn Miller, Buddy Quaid, Nikki Letts.

■ Play-to-film adaptation "Ice House" boasts impressive performances by husband and wife team of Bo Brinkman and Melissa Gilbert, but is too claustrophobic a piece to attract much interest.

Ironically, film works best when bearing down on the two principals in closeup monologs or angry bickering. Texan helmer Eagle Pennell unwisely injects illustrated flashbacks (shot in Texas) which are banal and silly and fail miserably at opening out Brinkman's play, which Brinkman adapted for the screen and produced as well.

He toplines as Pake, a ne'er-do-well from Texas, who's escaped the oil fields to become a bum rather than the recording star he dreamed to be. Pic concerns a long night in an L.A. hotel room (actually lensed at Gotham's Chelsea Hotel) during which Pake cajoles his former girlfriend from back home, Kay (Gilbert), to go off with him to Texas to get married and start a new life. Odd man out is Andreas Manolikakis as Kay's current pal, anxious to marry her to get his U.S. citizenship.

Pic's highpoint is Brinkman's lengthy monolog, filmed in continuous take, recalling a symbolic nightmare he had. Gilbert, child star on tv's "Little House On The Prairie," excels in an adult role played mainly hard as nails. Manolikakis is saddled with a stereotyped assignment, all gestures and outbursts.

Tech credits are modest, with purposefully unflattering photography of the leads. —*Lor.*

Zwerfsters
(Wayfarers)
(DUTCH)

Amsterdam   A Cinemien release of a Vereniging Videodrama production. Produced by Hoel van Eekhout. Written and directed by Marja Kok. Camera (color, 16m), Onno van der Wal; editors, Kok, Van der Wal, Pascale, Bunink. No other credits available. Reviewed at Desmet theater, Amsterdam, April 10, 1989. Running time: **70 MIN.**

Louise . . . . Loudhi Nijhoff
Catherine . . . . . . Catherine ten Bruggencate
Bag lady . . . . Catherine Holland

■ "Wayfarers," a drama about aging, doesn't invite speculation or deep thought, but provides Loudhi Nijhoff the opportunity of a memorable performance.

Nijhoff, 88, star of Dutch film, theater and tv, makes the most of what she claims is her last role. One sincerely hopes not.

Nijhoff is Louise, an octogenarian who lives comfortably in a good neighborhood with her two cats. She has a grown daughter and friends. Her faculties are fading but there are no complaints.

One Sunday she goes out, elegantly dressed as usual, and on several occasions runs into a good-natured bag lady. Nijhoff follows her, watches how she goes to sleep on a bench, then herself dozes off on another bench. When she returns home she realizes she has died, that no one sees or hears her, that the bag lady will henceforth be her guide.

Marja Kok, an experienced actress and legit and vid director, wrote and helmed this first theatrical feature. The script is flimsy and without point. Except for Nij-

hoff, there are only two other roles worthy of note, the bag lady and the daughter, well handled respectively by Catherine Holland and Catherine ten Bruggencate. Direction and technique are adequate.
—*Wall.*

Street Justice

New York A Lorimar and Sandy Howard presentation. Executive producers, Howard, Harold Rick, Anita Rick. Produced by David Witz, Michael Masciarelli. Directed by Richard C. Sarafian. Screenplay, James J. Docherty; camera (Medallion color), Roland (Ozzie) Smith; editor, Mark Goldberg; music, Jamii Szmadzinski, Paul Hertzog; sound, David Cochrane; art direction, Joanne Chorney; assistant director, Tony Thatcher; production manager, Dennis Chapman; additional camera, Roger Olkowski; associate producer, Risa Gertner; casting, Paul Bengston, David Cohn, Anne Tait. Reviewed on Warner Home Video vidcassette, N.Y., June 10, 1989. MPAA Rating: R. Running time: **94 MIN.**

Curt Flynn	Michael Ontkean
Katharine Watson	Joanna Kerns
Tamarra	Catherine Bach
Arthur Dante	J.D. Cannon
Edith Chandler	Jeanette Nolan
Sam Chandler	Richard Cox
Father Burke	William Windom
Mandy	Sandra Currie
Taxi driver	Richard C. Sarafian

■ **"Street Justice" is a minor action drama going direct to video by WB as part of the Lorimar acquisition. Good cast is mired in routine scripting.**

Michael Ontkean toplines as a U.S. government agent who's now an embarrassment to Uncle Sam: his mission to pick up a Soviet defector in Leningrad was terminated out of expediency. Escaping after 12 years in a Russian prison, he finds the CIA has ordered a hit on him.

Ontkean returns home to Hoboken where his wife (Joanna Kerns) has remarried. City (including corrupt police force) is run by the Chandler family led by matriarch Jeanette Nolan. When the Chandlers seriously injure his daughter, Ontkean goes on the warpath to clean house.

Pic lacks novelty in limning a tv-type tale en route to a bittersweet romantic finish. Helmer Richard C. Sarafian pilots efficiently but there's nothing here to grab one's attention. Tech credits for the mainly-in-Canada shoot are solid.
—*Lor.*

Natalia
(FRENCH-SWISS)

Paris Imperia release of a Fakhoury Productions/Slotint coproduction Executive producer, Jean-Pierre Dupuy. Produced by Michèle Dimitri. Directed by Bernard Cohn. Screenplay, Cohn, Claude Heymann; camera (color), Denys Clerval; editor, Cécile Decugis; music, Michel Portal; sound, Pierre Lorrain, Joel Faure; costumes, Regina Gothe; art direction, Nicole Rachline; assistant director, Serge Dupuy-Malbray. Reviewed at the 3 Luxembourg cinema, Paris, May 3, 1989. Running time: **116 MIN.**

Natalia Gronska	Philippine Leroy-Beaulieu
Paul Langlade	Pierre Arditi
Catherine Valence	Ludmilla Mikael
Tomasz	Michel Voita
Jacqueline Leroux	Dominique Blanc
Mr. Gronska	Lionel Rocheman
Madam Gronska	Elisabeth Kaza

■ **First-timer Bernard Cohn tackles a potentially rich dramatic subject in "Natalia," but lacks the means to give it the requisite scope and texture.**

"Natalia" is an ambitious young Jewish actress who forsakes friends, family and religion to carve a niche for herself in the French film industry under the German Occupation, but finally is denounced and packed off to a concentration camp. She survives but returns a broken woman.

A fascinating theme is treated in the most superficial, unconvincing manner in a parsimonious production. Despite the writing collaboration of a seasoned filmmaker, Claude Heymann (who did not work during the war), Cohn, for lack of budget (but also for lack of directing skill), never brings the period and its contradictions to dramatic life.

The *coup de grace* is the casting and acting of Philippine Leroy-Beaulieu as the young actress and Pierre Arditi as the gentile director who becomes her lover and instrument of her rise to brief stardom on wartime screens. The charming Leroy-Beaulieu strikes one as too nice a girl to abandon her orthodox Polish parents to their grim fate as Natalia does hers with insensitive determination. Arditi is even less convincing as a successful purveyor of innocuous escapist movies for an occupied French audience.

It's a particularly sorry waste of a good subject. Jewish theme already has helped give it exposure in festivals, but its commercial chances are poor. Film first unspooled at Cannes in 1988, but bowed theatrically only recently.

Cohn served his apprenticeship as assistant to such name directors at Luis Buñuel, François Truffaut, Robert Bresson, Otto Preminger and Woody Allen. —*Len.*

Rituelen
(Rituals)
(DUTCH)

Amsterdam A Cannon Nederland release of a Sigma Filmproductions production. Produced by Matthijs van Heijningen. Written and directed by Herbert Curiel, based on the novel by Cees Nooteboom. Camera (color), Marc Felperlaan; editor, August Verschueren; music, Eric van Tijn, Joches Fluitsma; sound, Victor Dekker; production manager, Kees Groenewegen; casting, Margarete van Dam. Reviewed at Bellevue theater, Amsterdam, April 17, 1989. Running time: **95 MIN.**

Inni Wintrop	Derek de Lint
Philip Taads	Thom Hoffman
Arnold Taads	Ton Lensink
Roozenboom	Jerome Reehuis
Riezenkamp	Johan Ooms
Zita	Sheryn Hylton Parker
Petra/Sanne	Camilla Braaksma
Girl with dove	Roswitha Bergmann
Monseigneur	Bert Andre

■ **An often gripping adaptation of Cees Nooteboom's much-translated novel, "Rituals" is a meticulously filmed drama about an antihero who coasts through life, bouncing with every current. Sprinkled with humorous dialog and dosed with sex, it stands good offshore chances.**

Derek de Lint gives probably his most accomplished film performance to date as the good-looking nonentity, a man orphaned at an early age, well off, a dabbler in art, journalism and the stock market, but a weak man without passion or compassion.

De Lint loses his money when the market crashes in 1987, but dabbles on, not without success. He meets the son of a man who had treated him generously but had been monstrous with his own offspring.

Stunningly portrayed by Thom Hoffman, son is a specialist in antique Japanese pottery and a devotee of Zen. His fanatical ambitions are to acquire a certain type of Japanese bowl and to rid himself of all earthly and bodily attachments.

Herbert Curiel scripted and directed, but he is stronger in the latter department. Viewers unfamiliar with the novel will find some character relationships unclear. Certain scenes are dramatically overloaded. Lengthy stretches of voiceover narration and long monologs are overly literary and lend themselves more to being read than heard. In fact, a subtitled export version will work better for foreign audiences than the original.

Supporting roles, art direction and music are particularly fine.
—*Wall.*

Journey To The Center Of The Earth

New York A Cannon Films presentation. Executive producers, Adam Fields, Tom Udell, Avi Lerner. Directed by Rusty Lemorande. Screenplay, Debra Ricci, Regina Davis, Kitty Chalmers, Lemorande, based (uncredited) on Jules Verne's novel; camera (TVC color), David Watkin, Tom Fraser; editor, Roxanne Zingale, Victor Livingston; music, uncredited; sound, Alan Gerhardt, Edward L. Moskowitz; production design, Geoffrey Kirkland; production manager, Ron Grow; visual effects, Fantasy II; visual effects supervisor, John Scheele; line producer, Karen Koch; casting, Nicola van der Walt, Perry Bullington. Reviewed on Warner & Cannon vidcassette, N.Y., June 7, 1989. MPAA Rating: PG. Running time: **79 MIN.**

Chrystina	Nicola Cowper
Bryan	Ilan Mitchell-Smith
Richard	Paul Carafotes
Gen. Rykov/Shank	Janie du Plessis
Tola	Jeff Weston
Sara	Jaclyn Bernstein
Wanda	Kathy Ireland
Professor	Lochner de Kock

Also with: Simon Poland, Jeremy Crutchley, Emo Philips.

■ **Cannon's much-touted remake emerges as an unfinished film, pasted together crudely for direct to video release via Warner's video distribution.**

Pic rolled in L.A. in June 1986 but Cannon pulled the plug mid-

Original Film

A 20th Century Fox release of a Charles Brackett production. Stars Pat Boone, James Mason, Arlene Dahl and Diane Baker. Features Thayer David and Peter Ronson. Directed by Henry Levin. Screenplay, Brackett and Walter Reisch, based on the novel by Jules Verne; camera (Cinemascope, color), Leo Tover; editor, Stuart Gilmore and Jack W. Holmes; music, Bernard Herrmann; special songs by James Van Heusen and Sammy Cahn. Previewed at Paramount theater, N.Y., Dec. 4, 1959. Running time: **132 MIN.**

Alec McEwen	Pat Boone
Prof. Oliver Lindenbrook	James Mason
Carla	Arlene Dahl
Jenny	Diane Baker
County Saknussemin	Thayer David
Hans	Peter Ronson
Groom	Robert Adler
Dean	Alan Napier
Prof. Bayle	Alex I'inlayson
Paisley	Ben Wright
Kirsty	Mary Brady
Chancellor	Frederick Halliday
Rector	Alan Caillou

way through production leaving debuting helmer Rusty Lemorande stranded. What emerges on video is an incomprehensible mishmash which makes the film almost a sequel to Albert Pyun's Kathy Ireland-starrer "Alien From L.A.," lensed in Zimbabwe a year later with overlapping characters. Ad-

1977 Version
(SPANISH)

An Almena Films production. Directed by Juan Piquer Simon. Screenplay, Juan Piquer Simon and Carlos Puerto based on novel by Jules Verne; camera (Eastmancolor), Andres Berenguer; editor, Maruja Soriano; music, Juan Jose Garcia Caffi; sets, Emilio Ruiz; special effects, Francisco Prosper and E. Ruiz; costumes, Gumersindo Andres. Reviewed at Cine Rhearmond, Madrid, Sept. 5, 1977. Running time: **90 MIN.** *(Soundtrack in English available.)*

Professor Lindenbrook	Kenneth More
Axel	Pep Munne
Glauben	Ivonne Sentis

Hans	Frank Brana
Olsen	Jack Taylor
Molly	Lone Fleming
Prof. Fridleson	José Mará Caffarel
Prof. Kristoff	Emiliano Redondo

ditional lensing is uncredited, presumably helmed by Pyun.

With few Jules Verne elements present, tale has four kids in a cave in Hawaii falling into a world below. Amidst sudden dream sequences (one of which briefly features comic Emo Philips, otherwise cut out of the picture) and virtually no continuity, two of the kids (including pic's original lead Paul Carafotes) get left behind. That leaves young British nanny Nicola Cowper and Carafotes' brother Ilan Mitchell-Smith to reach Atlantis, i.e., Zimbabwe.

Denizens of Atlantis include numerous characters from "Alien From L.A.," notably an eye-patched Gen. Rykov (Janie du Plessis) and a professor (Lochner de Kock) planning a trip to the surface world to conquer humanity. Object of worship is an alien girl named Wanda, played briefly by Kathy Ireland in her role from the Pyun film.

Pic ends abruptly followed by highlights and outtakes as padding. Names of the producers (then-Cannon toppers Menahem Golan and Yoram Globus) are missing from the credits, as is the music listing.

Tech contributions and acting are impossible to evaluate under the circumstances, though Geoffrey Kirkland's outsized sets for the L.A. shoot (lensed by David Watkin) are impressive. Zimbabwe footage (photographed by Tom Fraser) matches "Alien From L.A." —*Lor.*

Ongedaan gedaan
(Deed Undone)
(DUTCH)

Amsterdam A Nederlands Film Museum release of a Frans van de Staak production. Produced and directed by Van de Staak. Screenplay, Van de Staak, Gerrit Kouwenaar, Stan Lapinski; camera (color, 16m), Bernd Wouthuysen; editor, Jan Dop; music, Bernhard Hunnekink; sound, Piotr van Dijk; production manager, Ab Praamstra. Reviewed at Nederlands Film Museum, Amsterdam, May 16, 1989. Running time: **73 MIN.**

Anton	Thom Hoffman
	Martien van den Ouwelant
Brigitte	Olga Zuiderhoek
	Catherine ten Bruggencate
Clemens	Titus Muizelaar
	Hans Hausdörfer
Diane	Chris Jolles
	Lineke Rijxman

■Two couples, four characters portrayed by eight actors, plus some poems by Gerrit Kouwe-

naar — these are the elements of this gripping and imaginative film from Holland's most prominent avant-garde director, Frans van de Staak.

Helmer's objective was a film "about people who want to get something done. I leave out the why as well as the results. What's left is the moment of endeavor."

There's no story, just a number of sequences in which each character is acted by one of two players. They walk a lot and quickly, heels clicking rhythmically through an impersonal quarter of Amsterdam. One never knows where they're going. They have difficulties in communicating. Writing is sometimes easier than talking: It's easier to leave a note on a table saying "you're it" than to say "I love you" face-to-face.

Script is full of humor and irony — people bursting with purpose being distracted by a badly tied shoelace, or a couple exasperated beyond reason by each other's mannerisms. —*Wall.*

Force majeure
(Uncontrollable Circumstances)
(FRENCH)

Paris An AAA release of a CAPAC/-Fildebroc coproduction. Produced by Paul Claudon, Michèlle de Broca. Directed by Pierre Jolivet. Screenplay, Jolivet, Olivier Schatzky; camera (color), Bertrand Chatry; editor, Jean-Francois Naudon; music, Serge Perathoner, Jannick Top; sound, Yves Osmu, Dominique Daimasso; art direction, Eric Simon; assistant director, Jean-Claude Marchant; production manager, Georges Pellegrin. Reviewed at Georges V theater, Paris, May 13, 1989. Running time: **85 MIN.**

Philippe	Patrick Bruel
Daniel	François Cluzet
Katia	Kristin Scott-Thomas
Malcolm	Alan Bates
Jeanne	Sabine Haudepin
Hans	Thom Hoffman
Philippe's mother	Lucienne Hamon
Journalist	Marc Jolivet
Hans' father	Wim Meeuwisse
Gloria	Béatrice Assenza

■Pierre Jolivet and his co-scripter, Olivier Schatzky, have hit on a solid original story idea in "Force majeure," which dramatizes the predicament of two young Frenchmen who are asked to save the life of a casual acquaintance by accepting to share his fate in a Southeast Asian prison.

Feature is Jolivet's third and his first commercial (and critical) success. It has low-key but effective psychological force, which could take it into foreign specialized outlets.

Patrick Bruel and François Cluzet are two dissimilar young Gauls who meet during an Asian

backpack holiday and fall in with a footloose Dutchman. Bruel and Cluzet leave their share of a hash purchase with their Dutch mate, who plans to stay on.

Nearly two years later, Bruel and Cluzet, who have not kept in touch, each receive a visit from an Amnesty Intl. lawyer (Alan Bates) who informs them that the Dutch traveler is in an Asian prison and has been sentenced to death as a drug trafficker. That's unless the two return within five days and confess to owning part of the hash, for which all three apparently would serve a 2-year prison term for possession of drugs.

Story, which is not without its strains on credibility, is nonetheless skillfully structured and developed. Cluzet, an unemployed layabout in Lille with a girlfriend and a baby to support, says yes to going, while Bruel, a career-minded Paris university student, hesitates to sacrifice his degree exams for a casual acquaintance.

There are complications that modify the attitudes of the two youths. Cluzet, who has sold exclusive rights to his story to a local newspaper, begins to realize the devastation and emptiness of his life, while Bruel slowly comes around to saying yes, but gets romantically involved with the Dutchman's ex-girlfriend (Kristin Scott-Thomas), who has been recruited by Bates as an emotional lever. Outcome is downbeat for all involved.

Cluzet is fine as the increasingly confused ne'er-do-well and is movingly balanced by Sabine Haudepin as his fed-up girlfriend. Bruel, an up-and-coming young lead with a limited dramatic palette, is credible but less moving as the intellectual who discovers untapped romantic capacity at the wrong moment, and Scott-Thomas plays off him with touching ambivalence.

Only Bates strikes a false note as the British lawyer, a thankless role that is not redeemed by the unconvincing scene Jolivet and Schatzky devise to give the character some depth.

Tech credits are good. Imaginative scoring by Serge Perathoner and Jannick Top reinforces the script's thematic tensions. —*Len.*

Danger Zone II:
Reaper's Revenge

New York A Skouras Pictures presentation of a Jason Williams and Tom Friedman

production. Produced by Williams, Friedman. Directed by Geoffrey G. Bowers. Screenplay, Dulany Ross Clements, from story by Williams, Friedman; camera (Foto-Kem color), Daniel Yarussi; editor, Susan Medaglia; music, Robert Etoll; sound, Kenneth Segal; art direction, Richard Wirsich; production manager, Todd King; assistant director, Michael Grossman; 2d unit director, Williams; stunt coordinator, Mike Tino. Reviewed on Forum Home Video vidcassette, N.Y., June 10, 1989. MPAA Rating: R. Running time: **95 MIN.**

Wade Olson	Jason Williams
Reaper	Robert Random
Donna	Jane Higginson
Francine	Alisha Das
Doug	Walter Cox
Rainmaker	Barne Wms. Subkoski

■"Danger Zone II: Reaper's Revenge" is a worthy successor to the 1987 release, a model of crisp, well-scripted B-picture entertainment.

Filmmaker Jason Williams returns as the taciturn hero Wade Olson, whose biker nemesis Reaper (Robert Random) is released from prison on a legal technicality. Reaper kidnaps Olson's girlfriend Jane Higginson and our hero is on his trail.

Structured as a trek in the desert en route to a violent showdown, pic is interesting not only for colorful details of its biker milieu but a cleverly interwoven script by Dulany Ross Clements that links (almost mystically) the history and fates of disparate characters.

Olson keeps meeting people on the road who've also been wronged by Reaper. They tag along with him to settle their own scores: Rainmaker (Barne Wms. Subkoski) who's been cursed and can't start rain anymore; Doug (Walter Cox) who needs the Reaper's signature to sell a Vegas building and save his wife and adopted daughter, and Francine (Alisha Das), introed to prostitution by Reaper, who also sold her baby daughter. It all ties together.

Acting, especially by the low-key Random (who probably would kick Charles Manson out of the neighborhood for being too nice a guy) and the attractive female leads, is a plus. Daniel Yarussi's lensing on location is effective as is a hard rock soundtrack. —*Lor.*

Mijn vader woont in Rio
(My Father Lives In Rio)
(DUTCH)

Amsterdam A Hungry Eye Pictures release of an Added Films Holland production. Produced by Dirk Schreiner, Paul Voorthuysen. Directed by Ben Sombogaart. Screenplay, Burny Bos, Sombogaart, based on novel by Bos; camera (color), Jules van den Steenhoven; editor, Gys Zevenbergen, Rimko Haanstra; sound, Erik Langhout; art direction, Marjolein Stokkink; production manager, Marc van der Bijl. Reviewed at Netherlands

Film Museum, Amsterdam, April 24, 1989.
Running time: **97 MIN.**

Liesje . . . . Wenneke
Mama . . . . Geert de Jong
Frits . . . . Thall Boermans
Granddad . . . . Hans Veerman
Papa . . . . Peter Faber

■ **A children's jury chose this ingratiating Dutch entry as winner of the kidpic section of the last Berlin Film Festival. Ironically, "My Father Lives In Rio" was refused support from Dutch funding committees when submitted as a project by first-time feature director Ben Sombogaart, who had a track record of several fine shorts, docus and tv programs, all children-themed.**

It's entertaining in any country and any language for anybody after his or her eighth birthday.

Pic's greatest virtue is that it's not a standard kiddie item — no secret treasures, no gang of baddies. There are no baddies at all, in fact, nor any goody-goodies, or the slightest glimmer of saintliness anywhere. Most amazing of all, the only child is the little girl whose father of the title supposedly lives in Rio.

Little Liesje's parents met, married and lived in Rio until mama got homesick and took her daughter back to Holland to live with grandfather. Papa was to follow after having made more money. Granddad is super but dies early on, when Liesje is nine. She resents Frits, who moves into granddad's room and begins an affair with mama.

The girl has a correspondence with dad, then secretly sells some stamps grandfather left her to pay for a plane ticket to Rio. As it turns out, father was not in Rio, nor hunting crocodiles with a big gun and bushy beard. He was in Holland all along, serving a prison term for smuggling.

Acting of the principals is perfect, and supporting roles are meticulously cast. Wenneke's performance as the daughter is a joy to behold — maybe American acting coach Nancy Gould must share credit with helmer Sombogaart.

Tech credits are high order, though everyone helped to cut costs. This feature and a 5-part tv spinoff cost a mere $500,000, yet never looks skimped. A clever screenplay, enthusiastic collaborators, discipline and imagination replaced a hefty budget. — *Wall.*

The Guests Of Hotel Astoria
(DUTCH-U.S.)

Amsterdam   A Melior Films release of a Take 7 production. Produced by Rafigh Pouya. Executive producer, Bijan Shamoradi. Written and directed by Reza Alamehzadeh. Camera, (color), Charles Burnett; music, Esfandiar Monfaredzadeh; sound, Yousef Shahab; production manager, Barbara Bryan. Reviewed at Cinecenter, Amsterdam, May 25, 1989. Running time: **115 MIN.**

With: Shohreh Aghadashloo, Mohsen Marzban, Hooshang Touzi, Naser Rahmany Nejad, Kamran Nozad.

■ **This film by an émigré director, Reza Alamehzadeh (born 1943), about émigrés, especially those from Iran, forcefully captures the feeling and frustration of exile, giving renewed vital meaning to the word "refugee."**

Helmer, sentenced to life imprisonment under the Shah, was freed after six years by the Islamic Revolution. He made five documentaries, several of which were banned. The new masters of Iran couldn't very well accuse him of aiding and abetting the old regime, but his films displeased — he was forced to flee, on foot, across the mountains to Turkey. He eventually wound up in the Netherlands, where a short film he made with backing from Iranians in the U.S., "The Guests," won acclaim and prizes.

The Hotel Astoria of the title isn't really a hotel, but a small guest house in Istanbul where a dozen or so Iranian refugees huddle, nurse coffees in the tiny bar, hoard secrets, spread rumors and get rid of their money, jewels and other belongings. Everything can be bought in the Turkish capital: passports, visas, police protection. The thing is to get out before the money runs out.

A young couple tries to be smart. They buy tickets to Cuba and declare themselves political refugees during a stopover in the Netherlands. The Dutch authorities diagnose them as a Turkish problem and ship them back to Istanbul, where their money goes, most of it into police pockets.

There's just enough left for a 1-way ticket (for the woman, pregnant) to the U.S., where the American-born child can bring the mother a permit to stay and the father legal entry later. So it is said, but the lawyer says otherwise.

When the mother dies in childbirth, there remains the possibility of the child staying and the father being allowed to come and raise it. There's a modern end to the modern fairy tale.

Acting is generally fine. Charles Burnett's camerawork is a standout among okay credits. — *Wall.*

Honey, I Shrunk The Kids

Hollywood   A Buena Vista release of a Walt Disney Co. production. Produced by Penney Finkelman Cox. Executive producer, Thomas G. Smith. Directed by Joe Johnston. Screenplay, Ed Naha, Tom Schulman, based on a story by Stuart Gordon, Brian Yuzna, Naha; camera (Metrocolor), Hiro Narita; editor, Michael A. Stevenson; music, James Horner; production design, Gregg Fonseca; art direction, John Iacovelli, Dorree Cooper; costume design, Carol Brolaski; sound design, Wylie Statemen; sound (Dolby), John Reitz, David Campbell, Gregg Rudloff; stunt coordinator, Mike Cassidy; special vocal effects, Frank Welker; assistant director, Betsy Magruder; casting, Mike Fenton, Judy Taylor, Lynda Gordon (U.S.), Jory Weitz (N.Y.). Reviewed at Avco Center theater, L.A., June 13, 1989. MPAA Rating: PG. Running time: **86 MIN.**

Wayne Szalinski . . . . Rick Moranis
Big Russ Thompson . . . . Matt Frewer
Diane Szalinski . . . . Marcia Strassman
Mae Thompson . . . . Kristine Sutherland
Little Russ Thompson . . . . . Thomas Brown
Ron Thompson . . . . Jared Rushton
Amy Szalinski . . . . Amy O'Neill
Nick Szalinski . . . . Robert Oliveri

■ **When this summer's blockbusters have come and gone, "Honey, I Shrunk The Kids" might well be remembered as the most endearing and entertaining release of all. Disney's family-oriented feature should grow big over time — perhaps even to loom larger than some of its b.o. competition.**

Borrowing to good end elements from two '50s sci-fi pics, "The Incredible Shrinking Man" and "Them," scripters Ed Naha and Tom Schulman pit two sets of unfriendly neighbor kids, mistakenly shrunk to only ¼-inch high, against what ordinarily would be benign backyard fixtures, both alive and inanimate.

Their misfortune was to get caught in the beam of ne'er-do-well inventor Wayne Szalinski's (Rick Moranis) molecule-reducing contraption while he's out giving a lecture to a group of skeptical scientists.

Moranis (only slightly less nerdy than in his previous roles) returns frustrated and angry to pound on the enlarged laser-looking zapper as bits fall to the floor, where the kids are found screaming for him to recognize them.

He doesn't, and instead sweeps them into the dustpan along with the other flotsam that goes out with the trash.

Now, they must make it back to the house among towering vegetation, humongous bugs and fierce water showers on a quest that would be nightmarish except that it seems mostly like a lot of fun.

Pic is in the best tradition of Disney and even better than that because it is not so juvenile that adults won't be thoroughly entertained.

For one thing, none of the youngsters is unlikable, and each has a distinct personality.

The most colorful of the group is Moranis' lookalike son Nick (Robert Oliveri), a know-it-all at age 10 who is humbled very humorously by a hair-raising E-ticket aerial ride on the back of a bee searching for pollen.

He and his sweetly self-conscious teenage sister (Amy O'Neill) are supposed to hate the boys next door — little Russ Thompson, who is O'Neill's age, and his younger brother Ron (Jared Rushton from ''Big'') — because they hated them first.

That's because big Russ Thompson (Matt Frewer, tv's Max Headroom) thinks Moranis is a nut case and in Frewer's intimidating way (bullyish, really) has influenced his sons to have the same narrow thoughts.

Bound together in adversity with the Szalinski girl and boy, Brown and Rushton are free to believe what they will — whether that means communicating with their former ''enemies'' or insects, who they also find can make great friends.

Everything is treated in such a light, imaginative tone that the kids' conversations breaking down those silly misconceptions are as delightful to listen to as the creepy, sometimes harrowing obstacles they deftly deal with are to watch.

The adults are no less entertaining, even in their wildest farcical moments. Moranis and Frewer are well cast to play opposites, though it's not until the end that they even appear on screen together. Marcia Strassman and Kristine Sutherland also are good as their respective wives.

Special effects make up a good part of the pic and most are executed well. Visual effects coordinator Michael Muscal and creatures and miniatures supervisor David Sosalla deserve special mention.

Film was lensed entirely at the Churubusco Studios in Mexico City. —Brit.

Silence Like Glass
(WEST GERMAN)

Munich   A Bavaria/Lisa/Roxy release. (Intl. sales, Majestic Films Intl.) Executive producer, Michael Röhrig. Produced by Gunter Rohrbach, Carl Spiehs, Luggi Waldleit-ner. Directed by Carl Schenkel. Screenplay, Bea Hellmann, Schenkel; camera (color), Dietrich Lohmann; editor, Norbert Herzner; music, Anne Dudley; production manager, Dieter Minx, Peter Sterr. Reviewed at Munich Film Festival, June 24, 1989. Running time: **105 MIN.**

Eva . . . . .Jami Gertz
Claudia . . . . .Martha Plimpton
Eva's father . . . . .George Peppard
Dr. Burton . . . . .Bruce Payne
Dr. Markowitz. . . . . .Rip Torn
Eva's mother . . . . .Gayle Hunnicutt

■ **''Silence Like Glass'' is a melodramatic story of a friendship between two young girls from opposite backgrounds, whose common bond is that they are victims of cancer. Despite brilliant acting and tight direction, the morbid, clinical atmosphere makes b.o. prospects doubtful. Film seems a natural for tv, however, providing some of the explicit language is removed.**

Film is a true story, based on 1,-200 pages of diary kept by Bea Hellmann, who collaborated on the script with Schenkel. It begins with 19-year-old ballerina Eva Martin's collapse on stage during a New York ballet premiere. She is taken to a clinic specializing in cancer cases where her illness is diagnosed as a usually terminal form of lymphatic cancer.

Eva (Jami Gertz) shares a room with Claudia (Martha Plimpton), whose working class background sharply contrasts with the refined and sensitive dancer from a well-to-do family. They probably would never have met under normal circumstances, let alone become friends.

Since the medics have been unable to give either woman a favorable prognosis, they feel doomed and are under great stress. Claudia, who is bald as a result of chemotherapy, is loud, obscene and aggressive; Eva is depressed and wonders whether she will ever dance again. After a series of operations and chemotherapy, Eva also loses her hair and nearly all hope, till tests show the cancer has taken a surprise turn for the better. On the down side, all hope for Claudia vanishes.

Gertz and Plimpton turn out fine performances, ditto the rest of the cast. Technical credits are excellent apart from a few unclear passages in the soundtrack. The film ends on an upbeat note, since Eva, unlike the moribund Claudia, recovers and begins a career teaching ballet to children.

''Silence Like Glass'' opened the Munich Film Festival, but, as a downer, didn't provide the inspi-ration of last year's opener, ''Stand And Deliver.'' —Kind.

Tummy Trouble

■ **Playing in an exclusive arrangement with ''Honey, I Shrunk The Kids'' is a new Walt Disney-Amblin Entertainment cartoon, ''Tummy Trouble,'' which reunites klutzy Roger Rabbit — star of Buena Vista blockbuster ''Who Framed Roger Rabbit'' — with his nemesis Baby Herman.**

The 7½-minute short, directed by veteran Disney animator Rob Minkoff, finds the hysterical Roger Rabbit (voice by Charles Fleischer) rushing Baby Herman (voices by April Winchell and Lou Hirsch) to the hospital after the infant swallows a rattle.

The characters' entanglements in hospital corridors, on gurneys and in the o.r. are about on a par with the frenetically paced misadventures they shared in the opening sequence of ''Who Framed Roger Rabbit,'' but with more visual jokes for adults.

Billed as a Maroon Cartoon, the first animated short produced by Disney since ''Goofy's Freeway Trouble'' in 1965, ''Tummy Trouble'' was produced by Don Hahn (associate producer on ''Who Framed Roger Rabbit'') with music by James Horner. Kathleen Turner gets a screen credit as sultry songstress Jessica Rabbit where she didn't in the previous feature.

Frank Marshall, exec producer along with Steven Spielberg and Kathleen Kennedy, directed the live-action/animation ending.

Disney is planning a series of of these shorts. The next one, ''Roller Coaster Rabbit,'' is in production at the Walt Disney/MGM Studios in Florida. —Brit.

Puss In Boots

New York   A Cannon Films release of a Golan-Globus production. Executive producer, Itzik Kol. Produced by Menahem Golan, Yoram Globus. Directed by Eugene Marner. Screenplay, Carole Lucia Satrina, from fairy tale by Charles Perrault; camera (Rank color), Avi Karpick; editor, Satrina, Marner; music, Rafi Kadishson; songs, Michael Abbott, Anne Croswell; sound (Dolby), Eli Yarkoni; production design, Marek Dobrowolski; costume design, Ora Strikovsky; production manager, Ron Isak; assistant director, Tamir Paul; 2d unit director, Satrina; casting, Daliah Hovers. Reviewed on Warner Video/Cannon Video vidcassette, N.Y., June 13, 1989. MPAA Rating: G. Running time: **96 MIN.**

Puss . . . . .Christopher Walken
Corin. . . . . .Jason Connery
Vera . . . . .Carmela Marner
King . . . . .Yossi Graber
Lady Clara . . . . .Elki Jacobs
Ogre. . . . . .Amnon Meskin

■ **One of the better examples of Cannon's ''Movie Tales'' feature series of a couple of years back, ''Puss In Boots'' offers a fine change of pace for Christopher Walken as a song & dance cat.**

Jason Connery plays a young man out on the road with his inheritance, a tabby cat that turns into human form (Walken) at will. Cat promises him wealth and success, which Walken proceeds to earn by fooling a king (Yossi Graber) in awarding his daughter's hand to Connery, while appropriating the vast castle and wealth of an ogre (Amnon Meskin).

Briefly released last year theatrically and now a homevid title, ''Puss'' features several fun songs, belted with verve by Walken; Connery is dubbed for his vocals. Sets and other tech credits are okay for this lensed-in-Israel pic. —Lor.

Far From Home

New York   A Vestron Pictures release of a Lightning Pictures presentation. Produced by Donald P. Borchers. Executive producers, Lawrence Kasanoff, Ellen Steloff. Directed by Meiert Avis. Screenplay, Tommy Lee Wallace, from story by Ted Gershuny; camera (CFI color), Paul Elliott; editor, Marc Grossman; music, Jonathan Elias; sound, William Fiege; production design, Victoria Paul; costume design, Donna Linson; production manager, Fred Culbertson; casting, Linda Francis. Reviewed at Westside Cinema 2 theater, N.Y., June 23, 1989. MPAA Rating: R. Running time: **86 MIN.**

Charlie Cross . . . . .Matt Frewer
Joleen Cross . . . . .Drew Barrymore
Duckett . . . . .Richard Masur
Louise . . . . .Karen Austin
Agnes Reed . . . . .Susan Tyrrell
Pinky Sears . . . . .Anthony Rapp
Amy .Jennifer Tilly
Jimmy Reed . . . . .Andras Jones
Sheriff . . . . .Dick Miller
    Also with: Connie Sawyer, Stephanie Walski, Teri Weigel.

■ **The poorly scripted would-be thriller ''Far From Home'' is of note only as a transition film to adult roles for child actress Drew Barrymore. Vestron release heads to video end of August.**

Film is set in remote Banco, Nev., where Joleen (Barrymore), just turned 14, is stranded with no gas at a trailer park with her dad (Matt Frewer) on a vacation tour of national parks. A mad killer is offing people in the vicinity.

Chief suspect is sinister youngster Jimmy Reed (Andras Jones), who tries to rape Barrymore by the local swimming hole. Audience will spot blatant clues as early as the second reel as to the real killer's identity, however.

Loaded with atmosphere, pic suffers from first-film-itis for director Meiert Avis — a surplus of odd camera angles and poor pacing. It's not as campy as producer Donald Borchers' previous heavy-breather, "Two Moon Junction," but often as silly with a roster of caricatures.

With a baby face, dreamy eyes and a Playboy model's body, Barrymore is sexy but ill-used by a tawdry screenplay that has her volunteering to "go for a swim" no matter how many dead bodies pile up around her. Interestingly, pic was shot less than six months after her child's role in "See You In The Morning."

Frewer is styled to look like Bruce Dern but embarrassingly lapses into his "Max Headroom" tv voice in one scene.

Standout in supporting cast is Richard Masur. —*Lor.*

Weekend At Bernie's

Hollywood   A 20th Century Fox release of a Gladden Entertainment production. Produced by Victor Drai. Executive producers, Robert Klane, Malcolm R. Harding. Directed by Ted Kotcheff. Screenplay, Klane; camera (Deluxe color), François Protat; editor, Joan E. Chapman; music, Andy Summers; sound (Dolby), Walter S. Hoylman, W.A. Grieve-Smith (N.Y.); production design, Peter Jamison; art direction, Michael Novotny, Dean Taucher (N.Y.); set design, Keith Burns, Dawn Serody; set decoration, Jerie Kelter, R.W. Carpenter (N.Y.); costume consultant, Joe Tompkins; costume supervisor, Richard Butz; stunt coordinator, Conrad Palmisano; assistant director, Henry Bronchtein; second-unit director, Palmisano; second-unit camera, Frank Holgate; casting, Lynn Stalmaster. Reviewed at UA Coronet, Westwood, Calif., June 22, 1989. MPAA Rating: PG-13. Running time: **97 MIN.**
Larry Wilson . . . . Andrew McCarthy
Richard Parker . . . . Jonathan Silverman
Gwen Saunders . . . . . . Catherine Mary Stewart
Bernie Lomax . . . . Terry Kiser
Paulie . . . . Don Calfa
Tina . . . . Catherine Parks
Tawny . . . . Eloise Broady
Marty . . . . Gregory Salata
Vito . . . . Louis Giambalvo
Jack Parker . . . . Ted Kotcheff

■ As shlepping-the-stiff pics go, "Weekend At Bernie's" ranks below the classic black comedy of "The Trouble With Harry" and "S.O.B.," but there's

enough farcical fun in the Fox release to make it an okay summer program filler.

Terry Kiser steals the show as the corpse hauled around by frantic Andrew McCarthy and Jonathan Silverman, but the film is more mechanical than imaginative.

Scripter Robert Klane's premise probably sounded better on paper and at story conferences than it plays on screen. When Gotham insurance company go-getters McCarthy and Silverman show up for a weekend in the Hamptons with slimy boss Kiser, only to find him bumped off by the mob, it's a scream for a few minutes before the gags become repetitive.

Gross caricatures abound as Kiser's decadent party guests fail to notice their host is much more laid-back than usual. For reasons which are not made totally credible, the boys feel they have to keep Bernie's demise a secret from everyone, and only their hilarious attempts to get the stiff off the island put the film back on track.

Director Ted Kotcheff draws amiable perfs from the two leads, but his lackadaisical style too often fails to sustain and build the physical comedy. The film also suffers from ugly lensing by François Protat that can't be excused as a satiric comment on Bernie's crudely materialistic lifestyle, as expressed in Peter Jamison's garish production design.

But when things get draggy, there's always Kiser, with his wonderfully droll manipulation of his rubbery limbs, expertly aided and abetted by McCarthy and Silverman, and his sly changes of expression as rigor mortis progresses.

Klane comes up with the occasional outrageous invention, such as a scene in which Kiser's sex-crazed mistress engages him in strenuous lovemaking, causing McCarthy to lament that Bernie does better dead than he's been doing alive.

But the film is too much a one-joke effort, lacking the cleverness and brio to be a first-rate farce, or the consistent wildness to be a truly memorable black comedy.
—*Mac.*

Bunker Palace Hotel
(FRENCH)

Paris   A Bac Films release of an AFC/-Téléma/La Sept/FR3 coproduction. Produced by Maurice Bernart. Directed by Enki Bilal.

Screenplay, Bilal, Pierre Christin; camera (Fujicolor), Philippe Welt; music, Philippe Eidel, Arnaud Devos; art direction, Michele Abbe-Vannier; sound, Pierre Gamet; production manager, Alain Centonze. Reviewed at Marignan-Concorde theater, Paris, June 20, 1989. Running time: **95 MIN.**
Holm . . . . Jean-Louis Trintignant
Clara . . . . Carole Bouquet
Nikolai . . . . Benoit Regent
Muriel . . . . Maria Schneider
Orsini . . . . Yann Collette
Destoop . . . . Philippe Morier-Genoud
Solal . . . . Jean-Pierre Léaud
Zarka . . . . Roger Dumas
The President . . . . Hans Meyer
Matron . . . . Jezabelle Amato

■ Comic strip artist Enki Bilal has transferred his striking pictorial style but little else to the screen in this dramatically still-born sci-fi feature about a subterranean refuge for politicos in a totalitarian government besieged by revolution.

Sole interest here is the visual designs, transposed from Bilal's fantasy strips with the effective aid of matte-shot special effects and the unsettling Eastern European cityscapes provided by Bilal's home town, Belgrade, where exteriors and studio work were shot. Bilal's previous film work includes set and costume designs for Michael Mann's "The Keep" and storyboard elements for "The Name Of The Rose."

Bunker Palace Hotel is a concrete and marble haven deep in the earth's core where honchos of a mythical state are shuttled by locomotive and elevator. Here the regime's cream of the crop huddle, waited on by androids that keep breaking down.

Late arrivals are Jean-Louis Trintignant, the mysterious industrialist who designed the place, Carole Bouquet, an undercover revolutionary, and Benoit Regent, a disgraced official who has murdered a fleeing minister to take his place (plastic surgery aiding). Everybody is awaiting the arrival of the President, though the cracks in the walls and the black goo oozing from the water faucets provide ominous signs of a fate unexpected by them. What happens will come as a surprise only to moviegoers who have just debarked from the planet Mars.

Bilal and Pierre Christin, the scenarist of his comic strips, have piled a vast number of genre clichés into their feebly programmed script, without taking the trouble to create any psychological tensions or develop plot ideas (absolutely nothing is made of the fact that Bouquet and Regent had once been lovers).

Trintignant shaved his pate to

resemble a typical Bilal humanoid and plays the cold-blooded manufacturer with some relish. Bouquet, her own hair cropped short, is wasted in a totally passive role; ditto for the long absent Maria Schneider (originally planned for Bouquet's part). Among other supporting parts is the distressingly weird Jean-Pierre Léaud, whose appearances are now virtually interchangeable. Actors playing the androids in fact come out ahead of the main cast.—*Len.*

Vent de galerne
(They Were Giants)
(FRENCH-CANADIAN)

Paris   A 20th Century Fox (France) release of a Prod 27/BLM Productions/Cleo 24 (Montreal) coproduction. Executive producer, Claude Nedjar. Coproducer, Francine Forest. Produced by Gérard Martin. Directed by Bernard Favre. Screenplay, Favre, Marcel Jullian, Claude Nedjar, with collaboration of Marie Paule Caire and Jérome Bimbenet, based on novel "Sous le vent de galerne" by André Guilloteau; camera (color), Jean Francis Gondre, editor, Emmaneulle Thibault; music, François Dompierre; art direction, Patrice Mercier; costumes, Etienne Couleon; sound, Dominique Chartrand, Marcel Pothier. Reviewed at 15 Juillet Parnasse theater, May 16, 1989. Running time: **102 MIN.**
With: Jean-François Casabonne, Charlotte Laurier, Roger Jendly, Jean-François Blanchard, Monique Melinand, Francis Reddy, Pierre Charras, Daniel Martin, Jean Claude Leguay, Laurent Relandeau, Elizabeth Tamaris, Thierry Fortineau, Bruno Wolkowith, Patrick Bonneli, Alain Lenglet, Valerie Lefort.

■ First-time director Bernard Favre evokes the genocide of 1793 in this grim evocation of the Vendée uprising against the young Republic. A counterweight to the satiating French Revolution Bicentennial celebrations, "Vent de galerne" unfortunately fails to fulfill its epic design.

Favre and his producer Claude Nedjar wrote the script (loosely based on a historical novel) and have kneaded in a good deal of fascinating historical material, much of it little known. Yet the drama and grandeur of the group protagonist — film's suggested English title is "They Were Giants" — gets little beyond the level of intentions.

Ironically, Favre subtly suggested the epic in his first fiction feature "La Trace" (1983), which followed the lonely peregrinations of a 19th century Alpine peddler. "Vent de galerne" is adequately peopled on a larger scale but somehow remains crimped.

Film attempts to epitomize the Vendée revolt in the fate of one small township. The Republican government in Paris is making unjust demands on the local population with its heavy quotas of military conscriptions. The inhabitants mobilize to raise an army, appoint the village blacksmith as their chief and ask a local nobleman to lead them into battle with the revolutionary government. Before they can move out, Republican forces ambush and massacre the entire population.

Not much of a valentine to the Revolution, but the generally undistinguished acting (by a Franco-Canadian cast) and Favre's loose grip deprive "Vent de galerne" of its cinematic impact. Tech credits are okay. —*Len.*

The Gunrunner
(CANADIAN)

New York A New World Pictures and Video Voice presentation. Executive producers, Ernest J. Schmizzi, Gregory F. Schmizzi. Produced by Richard Sadler, Robert J. Langevin. Directed by Nardo Castillo. Screenplay, Arnie Gelbart; camera (Foto-Kem color), Alain Dostie; editor, Diane Fingado, Andre Corriveau; music, Rex Taylor Smith; sound, Serge Beauchemin; production design, Wendell Dennis; assistant director, Jacques Méthé; production manager, Ann Burke; casting, Flo Gallant. Reviewed on NW vidcassette, N.Y., June 10, 1989. No MPAA Rating. Running time: **84 MIN.**

Ted Beaubien	Kevin Costner
Maude	Sara Botsford
Lochman	Paul Soles
Wilson	Gerard Parkes
George	Ron Lea
Rosalyn	Mitch Martin
Robert	Larry Lewis
Max	Daniel Nalbach

■**Before playing Eliot Ness in "The Untouchables" Kevin Costner starred in this unreleased Canadian pic as a Montreal good-guy gangster. Video debut six years after has weak prospects since it's a very dull show.**

In an otherwise Canadian cast, Costner toplines as Ted Beaubien, returning home to Montreal from China in 1926 to become embroiled in local politics, class struggles and family infighting. Boring plotline has him ultimately launching a 1-man vendetta against corruption, with anticlimax that his gunrunning is actually on the side of the angels, to back a revolution in China.

For Costner fans, pic would have been more interesting if he had played a baddie to contrast with his recent all-American hero stardom. Instead, he's laidback, self-assured and stuck in an almost actionless vehicle that plays like a subpar telefilm. Sara Botsford brightens things up as a villainous gambling club operator, but her sex scene with Costner is extremely tame.

Tech credits are chintzy, with variable sound recording. —*Lor.*

Saturday The 14th Strikes Back

New York A Concorde Pictures release. Produced by Julie Corman. Directed by Howard R. Cohen. Screenplay, Cohen; camera (Foto-Kem color), Levie Isaacks; editor, Bernard Caputo; music, Parmer Fuller; sound, Michael Clark; production design, Stephen Greenberg; assistant director, Murray Miller; production manager, Reid Shane; 2d unit director, Jeffrey Delman; 2d unit camera, Stephen R. Sharp; associate producer, Lynn Whitney; casting, Al Guarino. Reviewed on MGM/UA Home Video vidcassette, N.Y., June 17, 1989. MPAA Rating: PG. Running time: **78 MIN.**

Eddie Baxter	Jason Presson
Gramps	Ray Walston
Frank	Avery Schreiber
Kate	Patty McCormack
Linda	Julianne McNamara
Alice	Rhonda Aldrich
Bert	Daniel Will-Harris
Charlene	Pamela Stonebrook

Also with: Joseph Ruskin, Riad, Leo V. Gordon, Michael Berryman, Phil Leeds, Tommy Hall.

■**This unnecessary, unfunny sequel to the 1981 parody received some theatrical play last year ahead of current homevideo availability.**

Filmmaker Howard R. Cohen again maximizes the references to familiar horror icons, but dialog is lame and level of spoofing obvious rather than inspired.

First pic had the team of Richard Benjamin and Paula Prentiss fronting the action. This time teen Jason Presson is slated by an assortment of baddies — ranging from Michael Berryman's mummy to Leo V. Gordon's Evil One ringleader — to take over the world on his birthday, the title date.

While monsters, including pretty vampire Pamela Stonebrook and werewolf Tommy Hall, come up out of the basement, the dingbats in Presson's family never notice anything's wrong. Armed with a bell and amulet presented by his fake grandpa Ray Walston, Presson does battle with evil, culminating in an embarrassing montage of stock footage including shots from numerous Roger Corman films, even including "Avalanche" and gangster pics.

Poverty budget is apparent in chintzy special effects, as well as stillborn ideas like Stonebrook suddenly belting a song with a 3-girl chorus appearing to dance around the room amateurishly.

Though "Bad Seed" Patty McCormack is cast as Presson's mom, Cohen fails to make any reference to her film background. —*Lor.*

Offerings

New York An Arista Films presentation. Produced and directed by Christopher Reynolds. Screenplay, Reynolds; camera (Allied & WBS color), R.E. Braddock; editor, Reynolds; music, Russell D. Allen; sound, John Menier, Jonathon Bensley; assistant director, Bill Edumund; production manager, Paul P. Murphy; casting, Becky Grantham. Reviewed on South Gate Entertainment vidcassette, N.Y., June 14, 1989. MPAA Rating: R. Running time: **92 MIN.**

Gretchen	Loretta Leigh Bowman
Kacy	Elizabeth Greene
Sheriff Chism	G. Michael Smith
Jim Paxton	Jerry Brewer
John Radley	Richard A. Buswell

■**"Offerings" is a pale imitation of the "Halloween" series of films, right down to derivative musical theme.**

Oklahoma-lensed opus refreshingly features thick regional accents, but story is tired. A mute boy ends up in a mental hospital 10 years after killing and eating his mean mom. Cannibalism theme continues as he goes on the rampage, offering body parts to young heroine Gretchen (Lorette Leigh Bowman) in ritualistic fashion.

Film is unpleasant rather than scary, with an unwholesome emphasis on a scene where Gretchen and her teen pals dine on a pizza left on their doorstep (no one knows why the delivery boy skedaddled) that contains a "sausage" topping nobody ordered.

Film lacks the usual genre sex and makeup effects values. —*Lor.*

On The Make

New York A Taurus Entertainment release of a Rayfield Co. presentation. Produced by Fred Carpenter. Directed by Samuel Hurwitz. Screenplay, Carpenter, James McTernan, from story by Carpenter; camera (Duart color), Gerard Hughes; editor, Ross Gelosi; music, Phil Cardonna, Don Kehr, Michael Stein, Kirk Fisher; sound (Dolby), Cathy Calderon; assistant director, Bart Herbstman; 2d unit director, Alan Jacobson; associate producers, John P. Melfi, Michael Nolan. Reviewed on vidcassette (Taurus), N.Y., June 11, 1989. MPAA Rating: R. Running time: **74 MIN.**

Bobby	Steve Irlen
Kurt	Mark McKelvey
Lori	Teresina
Richard	Kirk Baltz
Jane	Tara Leigh
Vivian	Jennifer Dempster
Tina	Laura Grady
Danny	Michael Ross
Paul	Don Alexander

■**"On The Make" is an unusual picture, not the teen sex comedy its title implies but rather a cautionary tale about AIDS in the** heterosexual community. A bit preachy, it's nevertheless a nicely executed drama, currently in regional theatrical release.

Structured as a flashback from a young man's funeral (we later learn he had AIDS), pic mainly takes place at a disco where leads Bobby (Steve Irlen) and Kurt (Mark McKelvey) go through the usual dating rituals. There's some sharp writing by producer Fred Carpenter and coscripter James McTernan on the range of lines (both clever and hoary) used to break the ice with members of the opposite sex.

Generally light tone becomes serious when Irlen's problems in finding a permanent relationship come up, and melodrama intrudes when he barely saves his young sister (Teresina) from being raped by an old high school nemesis (Kirk Baltz).

Payoff is Kurt's announcement of his 100th female conquest (he's even compiled a complete list of names). That contrasts with news that he's got AIDS. Pic's message is to assume responsibility; Kurt also is painted as a bad guy due to his callous treatment of Tina (Laura Grady). He's made her pregnant and then insists she have an abortion.

Safe sex message here is still timely, though pic's skirting of the AIDS transmission issue dates it a bit. Another drawback is that the characters don't do anything but dance and date; material focusing on their jobs and schooling would have helped flesh out the 1-note story.

Acting by a cast of fresh talent is generally good, with McKelvey and villain Baltz particularly distinctive. Lensing on locations in Nassau County, N.Y., is crisp. —*Lor.*

Thank You Satan
(CANADIAN-FRENCH)

Paris Cout de Coeur release of a Ciné-flor/SGGC/Prods. Karim (Montreal) coproduction. Produced and directed by André Farwagi. Screenplay, Christian Carini, Farwagi, Nelly Alard, Jean Cosmos; camera (Fuji-color), Daniel Jobin; editor, Elisabeth Fernandez; music, Martial-Kool Louis, Léo Ferré; art direction, Clorinde Mery. Reviewed at Georges V cinema, Paris, June 12, 1989. Running time: **83 MIN.**

Alain Monnier	Patrick Chesnais
France Monnier	Carole Laure
Nathalie Monnier	Marie Fugain
Sylvie Monnier	Muriel Brener

■**This is a trifle of a family comedy about a 14-year-old girl who makes a pact with the devil** in order to save her parents from breaking up and to prevent their apartment from going on the block. Patrick Chesnais is the dad, a gynecologist with a young actress-mistress, and Carole Laure is the resigned mom.

André Farwagi directed this routine item that, despite a domestic black cat and a satanic representative at a local church, never really incorporates the feeble supernatural premise into the action. In fact it could easily be cut without altering the storyline.

Eric Blanc, a local standup comic and impersonator, is featured as a black street-musician who shares a winning lottery with the conspiring daughter (newcomer Marie Fugain), who uses her share of the money to buy the family flat when mom and dad finally are reconciled.—*Len.*

Loos
(No Potatoes)
(DUTCH)

Amsterdam   A Hungry Eye Pictures release of a Shooting Star Filmcompany production. Produced by Dave Schram, Hans Pos, Maria Peters, José Steen. Executive producers, Otger Merckelbach, Robert Swaab. Directed by Theo van Gogh. Screenplay, Guus Luijters, Van Gogh; camera (color), Tom Erisman; editor, Willem Hoogenboom; music, Rainer Hensel; sound, Jan van Sandwijk; art direction, Jan Roelfs, Ben van Os; production manager, Erwin Godschalk. Reviewed at Kriterion theater, Amsterdam, May 2, 1989. Running time: **97 MIN.**
Loos . . . . .Tom Jansen
Anna . . . . .Renée Fokker
Maria . . . . .Marie Kooyman
Dorrius . . . . .Leen Jongewaard
Wery . . . . .Max Pam
De Vries . . . . .Cas Enklaar

■Theo van Gogh's direction is superb, the lensing is inventive and eloquent, the editing is smooth, art direction striking and acting is good to excellent, but "Loos" is a bore.

The fault lies in the script — futile complications and wanton complexity larded with puerile humor. Large portions of kinky sex (from bondage and blind prostitutes to sado-killers, snuff movies and masochistic nymphos) can't compensate for the lack of real dramatic interest.

Loos is a lawyer who specializes in defending rapists and sex murderers, provided they can pay. He's blackmailed into defending a particularly repulsive underworld czar, falls for tricky and troubled females, smokes, drinks and beds to excess and ends up snared and disillusioned.

This story may have been meant not only as a thriller but also as an account of a man's moral and physical downfall, but this is one of many things in the film which remain obscure.

What is clear is that director, cast and crew could have made a memorable picture had there been a clear, professional script, not to mention a producer capable of keeping Van Gogh from playing private cinema games. —*Wall.*

Consuelo
(SWEDISH-CHILEAN)

Santiago   Produced by Swedish Filminstitute, Arauco Films, Film Stallet, Andrés Martorell y Cia, Latinofilms, Swedish TV 2. Executive producers, Anders Birkeland, Abdullah Ommidvar. Directed by Luis R. Vera. Screenplay, Vera, Edgardo Mardones, Hugo Amore; camera (color), Andrés Martorell H.; editor, Thomas Holéwa; music, Jan Tolf, Claes Wang; sound, Eugenio Gutierrez, Thomas Holéwa; art direction, Myriam Pilowsky, Patricio Carvajal. Reviewed at Teatro Cervantes, Santiago, Chile, May 28, 1989. Running time: **105 MIN.**
Manuel . . . . .Sebastian Dahm
Lena . . . . .Gunnel Fred
Consuelo . . . . .Loreto Valenzuela
Francisco . . . . .Luis A. Vera
Also with: Mats Bergman, Alex Zissis, Charlotta Larsson, Rodolfo Bravo, Jorge Gajardo, Myriam Palacios, Cora Dīaz, Monica Carrasco and special appearances by Tennyson Ferrada, Schlomit Baytelman and Carlos Caszely.

■Although "Consuelo" aims at the right targets, it misses most of them. It is the story of Manuel, exiled from Chile after the 1973 military coup, and his painful adaptation to life in Sweden plus, years later, the return to his native Valparaiso where he finds that things aren't what they used to be.

The subject of exile, living in another country, feeling oneself into its way of life and then facing the choice of staying or returning (often with adolescent children, to whom "home" is the country where they grew up) has affected many Latin Americans in recent years and surely deserves less superficial treatment.

Film was partly shot in Sweden and partly in Chile, and the European segments' quality is better. Maybe that's because director Luis R. Vera, a Chilean who became a Swedish citizen, lived this part of the story himself while his return visits to Chile tended to be on the brief side.

Although an improvement on his earlier "Hechos Consumados," "Consuelo" is unlikely to leave much of a mark, either in Chile or abroad. At best, fair b.o. can be expected.

Sebastian Dahm and Gunnel

Fred, as the exile and his Swedish girlfriend, provide pleasantly natural performances, but most of the Chilean cast is inadequate.

The film's idea is that Manuel, on his return, finds a different and worse society, in which his former friends have sold out and Consuelo, his girlfriend of yore, now dances at a rundown nightclub. The protagonist's dilemma between the Swedish Lena and the Chilean Consuelo is uninvolving.

Technical credits are better than average for Chilean films, but Andrés Martorell's cinematography has too much of a pretty postcard style. —*Amig.*

Judgement Day

New York   A Rockport/Ferde Grofé Films presentation. Executive producer, Guy F. Coomes. Produced by Ferde Grofé Jr., Keith Lawrence. Written and directed by Grofé. Camera (color), Pete Warrilow; editor, Joe Zucchero, William Schleuter; music, Lucas Richman; associate producers, Jack Weaver, Sidney Djanogly, Zucchero. Reviewed on Magnum Entertainment vidcassette, N.Y., June 4, 1989. MPAA Rating: PG-13. Running time: **93 MIN.**
Pete Johnson . . . . .Kenneth McLeod
Charlie Manners . . . .David Anthony Smith
Priest . . . . .Monte Markham
Octavio . . . . .Cesar Romero
Maria . . . . .Gloria Hayes
Sam . . . . .Peter Mark Richman

■Taking advantage of current media fascination with Satan worship, the exploitation vehicle "Judgement Day" panders to obvious titillation without treading any new ground. Actioner has gone directly to homevid.

Fairly predictable plot concerns two backpacking youths (McLeod and Smith) who stumble into an isolated village in an unnamed Latin American country. They soon discover that, besides being quaint and picturesque, said pueblo also has an odd custom: Once a year residents pack their bags and leave for 24 hours.

As local lore puts it, on that day the devil takes up residence, the result of an escape clause in a diabolic pact drawn up by the Prince of Darkness and a 17th century Spanish conquistador (Cesar Romero). Unfortunates caught within the city limits become permanent citizens of Hades. Needless to say, our two heroes end up in town after midnight and spend the rest of the tape trying to get out.

While pic is not without some fun moments, Dante might look gravely on these devilish doings that contain very little traditional fire and brimstone. At times the

stygian darkness seems more like a euphemism for bad lighting.

Acting is passable, and Satan and his damned crew sport some rather unconvincing rubber masks. Other tech credits are okay —*Lent.*

Sleepaway Camp 3:
Teenage Wasteland

New York   A Double Helix Films production. Executive producer, Stan Wakefield. Produced by Jerry Silva, Michael A. Simpson. Directed by Simpson. Screenplay, Fritz Gordon, from story idea by Robert Hiltzik; camera (Cinefilm color), Bill Mills; editor, Amy Carey, John David Allen; music, James Oliverio; sound, Mary Ellis; assistant director, Jerry Pece; production manager-associate producer, Bob Phillips; special makeup effects, Bill Johnson; stunt coordinator, Lonnie Smith; casting, Shay Griffin. Reviewed on Orion/Nelson Entertainment vidcassette, N.Y., June 11, 1989. MPAA Rating: R. Running time: **79 MIN.**
Angela . . . . .Pamela Springsteen
Marcia . . . . .Tracy Griffith
Herman . . . . .Michael J. Pollard
Tony . . . . .Mark Oliver
Cindy .Kim Wall
Also with: Kyle Holman, Daryl Wilcher, Haynes Brooke, Stacie Lambert, Kashina Kessler, Cliff Brand, Randi Layne, Jill Terashita.

■Third edition in the horror series continues the deep black humor of Part 2, as Pamela Springsteen is back murdering campers and counselors with gay abandon. Direct-to-video release is nasty but fun.

Filmed back-to-back with Part 2, pic has Springsteen impersonating a camper to return to the scene of the crime, Camp Rolling Hills, where she offed 19 folks the year before. Renamed Camp New Horizons, place is now run by Michael J. Pollard (that's real scary!) as an experiment in sharing — it's 50% underprivileged kids and 50% rich brats.

At the slightest excuse, usually evidence of sexual promiscuity or drugtaking, Springsteen kills the offender in grisly fashion while cracking jokes at the victim's expense. It's fun because it's not realistic or taken seriously. Imaginative makeup effects by Bill Mills deliver the goods.

Springsteen (yes, Bruce's sister) again manages the tricky feat of being appealing yet vicious, while Pollard is his usual wacky self, seeming to enjoy himself in a softcore sex scene with voluptuous Stacie Lambert. Second-billed Tracy Griffith (Melanie's sister) has little to do but try and survive the bloodletting. —*Lor.*

Violent Zone

New York   An Arista Films presentation. Executive producer, Louis George. Produced and directed by John Garwood. Screenplay, John Bushelman, Daved Pritchard; camera (United color), Roger Estrada; editor, Steve Bushelman; music, Mark Josephson, Malcolm Cecil; sound, Alejandro Cabrales; art direction, Pete Manansala; assistant director, Joe Dagumboy. Reviewed on South Gate Entertainment vidcassette, N.Y., June 15, 1989. MPAA Rating: R. Running time: 90 MIN.

Steve Ryker . . . . .John Jay Douglas
Charles Townsend. . . . .Christopher Weeks
Norman McCloskeY . . . . . .Chard Hayward
Linda Blomberg . . . . .Cynthia Killion
Rick O'Brien . . . . .Daved Pritchard
Doris . . . . .Michael Myracle
Ronald . . . . .Willie Olmstead
Clarence Hartwell . . . . . . .Alphonse Walter
Old Mishima . . . . .Ken Watanabe

■ "Violent Zone" is an above-average war picture; focusing on some clever twists and turns in a 40-years-later plotline. It's a direct-to-video U.S. release for new South Gate banner.

John Jay Douglas, who resembles Alan Hale Jr., plays a vet summoned by rich guy Christopher Weeks for a special mission 43 years after he fought the Japanese on Kao Teng Island. Pic follows the routine caper format of rounding up the team and training them to go in to rescue Weeks' son from a commie prison camp he's been imprisoned in since 1974.

Twist is that group never leaves their base island, caught in a battle for survival against an unseen enemy. Is it the Japs or the CIA? Several climactic revelations come as surprises in John Bushelman and Daved Pritchard's script.

John Garwood directs efficiently on Philippine locations.
—Lor.

Lethal Weapon 2

Hollywood   A Warner Bros. release of a Silver Pictures production. Produced by Richard Donner and Joel Silver. Directed by Donner. Screenplay, Jeffrey Boam from story by Shane Black, Warren Murphy; camera (Technicolor), Stephen Goldblatt; editor, Stuart Baird; coproducers, Steve Perry, Jennie Lew Tugend; music, Michael Kamen, Eric Clapton, David Sanborn; production design, J. Michael Riva; art direction, Virginia Randolph, Richard Berger; set decorator, Marvin March; sound (Dolby), Robert Henderson, Alan Robert Murray; assistant directors, Terry Miller Jr., Michael Alan Kahn, Albert Cho; associate producer, Peter Frankfurt; casting, Marion Dougherty, Gail Levin. Reviewed at the Samuel Goldwyn Theater, Beverly Hills, June 28, 1989. MPAA Rating: R. Running time: 113 MIN.

Martin Riggs . . . . .Mel Gibson
Roger Murtaugh . . . . .Danny Glover
Leo Getz . . . . .Joe Pesci
Arjen Rudd . . . . .Joss Ackland
Pieter Vorstedt . . . . . . .Derrick O'Connor
Rika van den Haas . . . . .Patsy Kensit
Trish Murtaugh . . . . .Darlene Love
Rianne Murtaugh . . . . .Traci Wolfe
Capt. Murphy. . . . . .Steve Kahan

■ An immensely crowd-pleasing sequel, "Lethal Weapon 2" proves better than its predecessor in most respects and should have a fair chance of outgunning it at the boxoffice.

Loaded with the usual elements, "Weapon 2" benefits from a consistency of tone that was lacking in the first film, which started with an extremely intriguing premise — a psychopathic cop made dangerously effective because of his suicidal bent — then abandoned it to pursue the route of a conventional shoot-'em-up.

This time, screenwriter Jeffrey Boam (who also penned the third Indiana Jones pic) and director Richard Donner have wisely trained their sights on humor and the considerable charm of Mel Gibson and Danny Glover's onscreen rapport.

They've also dreamed up particularly nasty villains and incorporated enough chases and shootouts to hold the attention of a hyperactive 9-year-old. So even if the last reel seems too familiar, it doesn't really matter.

Plot sets the duo after South African diplomats using their shield of immunity to smuggle drugs. Tagging along for the ride in a hilarious comic turn is Joe Pesci ("Raging Bull") as an unctuous accountant who laundered the baddies' money and now needs witness protection to stay out of the washing machine himself.

There's also a fleeting entanglement between Riggs (Mel Gibson) and the lead villain's secretary (the sparkling Patsy Kensit) that adds some welcome sex appeal.

Some may take exception to the use of South Africans as heavies. Although pic delivers some jabs at the evil of apartheid, the villains are really more about convenience than politics: Their racism makes them instantly despicable, while the diplomatic immunity compels (or perhaps excuses) the good guys to step outside the confines of the law to foil them.

It's a clever plot device that doesn't entirely compensate for its political shallowness, since both the villains and the filmmakers are so clearly motivated by commerce.

Mel Gibson's Martin Riggs has overcome much of the torment from his wife's death by the time this film starts and has meshed into the life of partner Roger Murtaugh (Danny Glover) and the other precinct cops.

Gibson nonetheless maintains a sense of residual madness, an over-the-edge quality that prompts him to plummet out a seventh-story window or quote the Three Stooges while holding numerous armed thugs at gunpoint.

Unusual as it is for most sequels, Gibson takes Riggs beyond where he was the first time out, making the character more accessible while maintaining a quirkiness that charges the film at every turn. It's an impressive bit of acting and the kind that rarely gets enough recognition.

Glover plays off that eccentricity beautifully, while Pesci brings to mind Gilbert Gottfried's scene-stealing antics in "Beverly Hills Cop II." Joss Ackland and Derrick O'Connor merit the appropriate hisses as the Gestapo-like villains.

Tech credits are superb, most notably the crackling sound from each gunshot's recoil. Stuntwork and Stuart Baird's editing are equally impressive, and Michael Kamen, Eric Clapton and David Sanborn provide a properly understated (if suprisingly undistinguished) score.

Blink and you'll miss a quick plug for one of Donner's other ventures, "Tales From The Crypt." Based on this latest outing, odds are also good he'll be exhuming another "Weapon."
—Bril.

The Karate Kid Part III

Hollywood   A Columbia Pictures release of a Jerry Weintraub production. Produced by Weintraub. Executive producer, Sheldon Schrager. Coproducer, Karen Trudy Rosen-felt. Directed by John G. Avildsen. Screenplay, Robert Mark Kamen; camera (Deluxe color), Stephen Yaconelli; editors, John Carter, Avildsen; music, Bill Conti; sound (Dolby), Barry Thomas; production design, William F. Matthews; art direction, Christopher Burian-Mohr; set decoration, Catherine Mann; associate producer, Douglas Seelig; casting, Caro Jones. Reviewed at Samuel Goldwyn theater, Los Angeles, June 26, 1989. MPAA Rating: PG. Running time: 111 MIN.

Daniel . . . . .Ralph Macchio
Miyagi . . . . .Noriyuki (Pat) Morita
Jessica . . . . .Robyn Lively
Terry . . . . .Thomas Ian Griffith
Kreese . . . . .Martin L. Kove
Mike Barnes . . . . .Sean Kanan

■ The makers of "The Karate Kid Part III" — also responsible for its successful predecessors — have either delivered or taken a few too many kicks to the head along the way, resulting in a particularly dimwitted film that will likely spell the death of the series.

Even if it enjoys a review-proof opening weekend, it will require some real heroics in homevid to rescue this one and allow "Kid" to make another comeback — by which point "Martial Arts Man" may have become a more fitting title.

The only remarkable things about it are that Ralph Macchio still looks young enough to play a 17-year-old, and that Noriyuki (Pat) Morita can still milk some charm from his character by mumbling sage Miyagi-isms about things like life and tree roots, despite their utter inanity this time around.

If the second film was silly it at least benefited by moving out of the L.A. suburbs to Okinawa, and even the previous film's most glaring shortcomings seem forgivable compared to the third installment's horrid script, with villains as cartoonish as World Wrestling Federation regulars.

Director John G. Avildsen and writer Robert Mark Kamen appear to have succumbed to the "Rocky" syndrome — where the epic nature of the hero demands bigger and more despicable bad guys to justify his attention, resulting in the creation of some smoke-spewing menace lacking only horns and a tail.

Martin L. Kove reprises his role from the first pic as Kreese, the nasty karate master previously humbled by Miyagi (Morita) and still bitter from the experience.

This time, however, he has a patron — former Vietnam buddy Terry (Thomas Ian Griffith), who apparently has made millions dumping toxic chemicals yet has nothing better to do than devote his time to seeking vengeance against Miyagi and protégé Daniel (Macchio) on Kreese's behalf.

Terry enlists the services of a sneering young foot for hire (Sean Kanan) who spends the next two-thirds of the film trying to lure Daniel into a grudge match to defend his karate title.

In his first screen role, Griffith is left to twist appallingly as the villain, emerging as a sort of wild-eyed Gordon Gekko with a pony-tail and a penchant for shattering blocks of wood. His speech before the final match is laughable, indicating he didn't make his fortune (working for an outfit called "Dynotox") thanks to his brains.

Kove's role is equally absurd, and even Macchio — whose kid-next-door manner fueled the earlier films — suffers from material that lets him do little but whine. Morita is likable but his sage-of-the-Orient lines have lost their punch.

Even the veteran production team comes up lame. Bill Conti's score is frequently sappy, Kamen's dialog fails to generate a single laugh to lighten the mood, and Avildsen's pace is plodding before jumping to an abrupt and unsuspenseful conclusion. —*Bril.*

Great Balls Of Fire!

Hollywood   An Orion Pictures release. Produced by Adam Fields. Executive producers, Michael Grais, Mark Victor. Directed by Jim McBride. Screenplay, Jack Baran, McBride, based on book by Myra Lewis with Murray Silver; camera (Deluxe color), Affonso Beato; editors, Lisa Day, Pembroke Herring, Bert Lovitt; source music, Baran, McBride; sound (Dolby), Petur Hliddal; production design, David Nichols; art direction, Jon Spirson; set design, Kathleen McKernin, Lauren Polizzi; set decoration, Lisa Fischer; costume design, Tracy Tynan; choreography, Bill and Jacqui Landrum; co-executive producer-unit production manager, Art Levinson; associate producers, Baran, Karen Penhale; first assistant director, Baran; casting, Judith Holstra. Reviewed at Directors Guild of America Theater, Los Angeles, June 27, 1989. MPAA Rating: PG-13. Running time: **108 MIN.**
Jerry Lee Lewis . . . . Dennis Quaid
Myra Gale Lewis . . . . Winona Ryder
J.W. Brown . . . . John Doe
John Phillips . . . . Stephen Tobolowsky
Sam Phillips . . . . Trey Wilson
Jimmy Swaggart . . . . Alec Baldwin
Steve Allen . . . . Himself
Lois Brown . . . . Lisa Blount
Dewey Phillips . . . . Joe Bob Briggs
Rusty Brown . . . . Joshua Sheffield
James Van Eaton . . . . Mojo Nixon
Roland James . . . . Jimmie Vaughn
    Also with: David Ferguson, Robert Lesser, Lisa Jane Persky, Paula Person, Valerie Wellington, Booker T. Laury, Michael St. Gerard.

■ Rock 'n' roll and its legendary characters have always been a tempting subject for filmmakers, but rare is the non-

documentary that adds anything to the music. "Great Balls Of Fire!" is no exception. It's a thin, cartoonish treatment of the hellbent, musically energetic young Jerry Lee Lewis.

Pic will disappoint ardent fans of the Killer with its lack of depth and off-kilter campiness, though it hits the mark with some sizzling musical numbers. Boxoffice is likely to ignite briefly then smolder out.

Full-bore performance by Dennis Quaid as the kinetic piano-pumper stops at surface level, and 108 minutes of his gum-cracking smirks and cock-a-doodle-doo dandyism are hard to take.

Pic focuses on the years 1956-59, when Lewis' career took off with the provocative hit "Whole Lotta Shakin' Goin' On" and was nearly destroyed by his marriage to 13-year-old cousin, Myra Gayle Brown (Winona Ryder), which shocked British fans and cut short his first overseas tour.

Mixed up in the Memphis milieu are the presence of Elvis Presley, who preceded Lewis at Sun Studios; Jimmy Swaggart, Lewis' Bible-thumping cousin; and the heady, devilish allure of the jumpin' black juke joints from which Lewis lifts his best music.

Filmmakers haven't created a story with the imagination and depth of "Hellfire," Nick Tosches' vivid book on Lewis' life, from which several incidents are duplicated. But script by Jack Baran and director-cowriter Jim McBride is based on a book by Myra Lewis and is by-the-numbers, suffering from a lack of grace or metaphor, stating and restating the obvious in dialog, and relying on cash and flash as character motivations.

McBride's direction leans toward comedy, camp and music-vid-style diversions. At one point, Elvis (Michael St. Gerard) is shown curling his lip as he watches his rival on tv. Local high-schoolers break into dance numbers whenever Lewis drives by in a convertible. A dim joint called the Rebel Room has a sign proclaiming "World's Toughest Nightclub" above its entrance, and its slack-jawed clientele are literally bashing each other with bottles before the Killer gets their attention with "Whole Lotta Shakin'."

Lewis' storied torment over the conflicting forces of light and dark, of church and "devil music," are shown here as confronta-

tions with Swaggart (Alec Baldwin) in which Quaid always seems to have his mind firmly made up (thus, no drama).

Other characters also get short shrift. Sun recording studios owner Sam Phillips (the late Trey Wilson) comes across as a manipulative snake-oil salesman, and his goony brother Judd (Stephen Tobolowsky rounds out the cliché.

Pic does come across with some smoking musical moments. Quaid is just fine pumping the keyboard and grinning, and can really kick back a piano stool. Best are the barroom "Whole Lotta Shakin'," "Real Wild Child (Wild One)" and a concert hall "Great Balls Of Fire," in which Lewis lights his piano afire and invites headliner Chuck Berry to "top that."

Much time is spent on the mutual attraction between the twice-married Lewis and virginal Myra. Ryder brings a mix of comic vulnerability and precocious enthusiasm to the role.

Rock musician John Doe is fine as Myra's easygoing father (also Lewis' bass player) in a perf that's mercifully understated next to Quaid's.

It seems the filmmakers have backed away from the true fascination of their subject and gone the safe and silly route. Production design is often appealing; cinematography is just okay.—*Daws.*

Action U.S.A.

New York   A Stewart & Berger Inc. presentation. Executive producers, Wolfram Berger, Gunter Simon, John Stewart. Produced by Alan Stewart, Susan Stewart. Directed by John Stewart. Screenplay, David Reskin, from story by Reskin, John Stewart; additional material, James J. Desmarais; camera (Allied & WBS color), Thomas L. Callaway; editor, Gabrielle Gilbert; music, Del Casher; sound, Kirk Cameron; art direction, John Perdichi; assistant director, Jeff Schiffman; associate producer, Ross Hagen. Reviewed on Imperial Entertainment vidcassette, N.Y., June 17, 1989. No MPAA Rating. Running time: **89 MIN.**
Carmen . . . . Barri Murphy
Osborn . . . . Gregory Scott Cummins
McKinnon . . . . . . William Hubbard Knight
Hitch . . . . Hoke Howell
Conover . . . . William Smith
Frankie Navarro . . . . Cameron Mitchell
Drago . . . . Ross Hagen
    Also with: David Sanders, Rod Shaft, Claire Hagen.

■ "Action U.S.A.," originally called "A Handful Of Trouble," is an above-average chase picture headed direct to video in American stores this month.

This is an excellent example of the type of escapist fun that packed drive-in theaters as recently as a decade ago but is now without a

natural home. Title change to a generic moniker reflects the pic's aim toward foreign audiences.

Unusual heroine Barri Murphy (not afraid to get her hair mussed up in the action) stars as Carmen, on the run from gangsters when her boyfriend (Rod Shaft, a good handle for a car-pic thesp) is rubbed out for stealing diamonds and she's a witness.

Chase format involves topnotch stunts, with cars frequently flying through the air and luxury cars demolished. Solid teaming of Gregory Scott Cummins and William Hubbard Knight as a pair of FBI men protecting Murphy adds flesh to the streamlined Texas-lensed opus. —*Lor.*

Order Of The Eagle

New York   An Action Intl. Pictures production. Executive producers, David Winters, Bruce Lewin. Produced by William Zipp. Directed by Thomas Baldwin. Screenplay, Zipp; camera (United color), Stephen Ashley Blake; editor, Rick Brown, Steve Nielson; music, William Stromberg; sound, David Eddy; production design, Thom Atcheson; assistant director, Brian DeMellier; production manager-associate producer, Karen Pilcher; special effects, Chuck Whitton, stunt coordinator, Ken Ganim. Reviewed on AIP videocassette, N.Y., June 3, 1989. No MPAA Rating. Running time: **82 MIN.**
Quill . . . . Frank Stallone
Billings . . . . William Zipp
Monica . . . . Jil Foor
Freddie . . . . Perry Hill
Greg . . . . Casey Hirsch
Leo . . . . David Roger Harris
Jack LaRouse . . . . David Marriott
    Also with: Brian O'Connor, John Cianetti, David Campell, Steve Horton, Sonny King.

■ "Order Of The Eagle" is a better-than-average pic from the Action Intl. stable, headed directly to U.S. videostores.

Actor William Zipp also wrote and produced this story of Eagle Scout Casey Hirsch who gets a real-life test in earning his title survival badge when he finds secret computer disks inside a plane wreck.

They contain the codes for a prototype Star Wars defense design, which corrupt businessman Frank Stallone wants back at all costs to protect his government contracts. David Roger Harris and David Marriott are the ruthless henchman who go after Hirsch. The boy is protected by Zipp and other good Samaritans.

Clean-cut pic pays more attention to story values than others of its ilk, with interesting final scenes to round off the tale (rather than mindless action footage and the non-endings of so many recent videos). Acting is fun, buttressed by unusual casting of tall, pretty tomboy leading lady Jil Foor as Zipp's girlfriend.

William Stromberg's musical score, with its echoes of Bernard Herrmann's work, is a decided plus. —Lor.

Skull: A Night Of Terror
(CANADIAN)

New York   A Geonib Properties presentation of a Lightshow production. (Intl. sales, Tom Parker Motion Pictures.) Executive producers, George Niblett, Donald J. McMillan. Produced and directed by Robert Bergman. Screenplay, Bergman, Gerard Ciccoritti, from Ciccoritti's story; camera (Film House color), Bergman; editor, Bergman; music, Philip Strong; sound, Mark Tolleeson; art direction, Nicholas White; production manager-assistant director-associate producer, Allan Levine. Reviewed on Academy Entertainment vidcassette, N.Y., June 20, 1989. MPAA Rating: R. Running time: **77 MIN.**
David King . . . . Robert Bideman
Jennifer King . . . . Nadia Capone
Skull . . . . Robbie Rox
Lisa King . . . . Erica Lancaster
Gideon King . . . . Nial Lancaster
Kiel Adams . . . . Paul Saunders
Sarah Adams . . . . Bonnie Beck
Ash . . . . Isabelle Merchant
    Also with: Banito Brown, Paul Babiak, Debbie Cooper.

■ "Skull: A Night Of Terror" is an uninvolving hostage pic from Canada. Direct-to-video title originally was called "Don't Turn Out The Light."

Robert Bideman is a cop haunted by nightmares of the time he killed an innocent girl while she was being used as a human shield by thugs. Now he's living in the country with wife Nadia Capone and two cute kids, when the nightmare literally comes back to haunt him: Cons use a woman as shield and this time he backs down, allowing them to escape.

They coincidentally take over his farmhouse, torment Capone and kill Bonnie Beck, Bideman's secret mistress who also is the wife of Bideman's partner, Paul Saunders. Final siege, sort of "Straw Dogs" in reverse, is not very exciting.

Title heavy Robbie Rox is not as menacing as one would expect, and his scenes with Capone's little daughter are almost fatherly rather than exploitation-oriented. Both monikers for the film are misnomers, as very little action takes place at night. —Lor.

Hardcase And Fist

New York   A United Entertainment production. Executive producer, Gordon Alexander. Produced and directed by Tony Zarindast. Screenplay, Bud Fleischer, Zarindast, from story by Zarindast; camera (Foto-Kem color), Robert Hayes; editor, Bill Cunningham; music, Tom and Matthew Tucciarone;

sound (Dolby), Steve Evans; production design, Alan Scott; assistant director, Robert Heusser; production manager, James Driscoll; additional camera, Jack Anderson; associate producer, Joyce Johnson. Reviewed on Forum vidcassette, N.Y., June 18, 1989. MPAA Rating: R. Running time: **92 MIN.**
Bud McCall . . . . Ted Prior
Eddy Lee . . . . Carter Wong
Sharon . . . . Christina Lunde
Nora . . . . Maureen Lavette
Tony Marino . . . . Tony Zarindast
Vincent . . . . Vincent Barbi
    Also with: Tony Bova, Beano, Stacey Nemour, Bill Summers, Debra Lamb, Angelyne.

■ Routine action pic has its moments, making for a decent video title pitting mafia against two cons (the title combo).

Ted Prior is an L.A. cop framed by the mob but ordered rubbed out in prison so as not to spill the beans to the FBI about a mafia chieftain. His old Vietnam vet buddy Tony (played by the filmmaker Tony Zarindast) is ordered to carry out the hit, but decides to help Prior and his martial arts expert cellmate Carter Wong escape instead.

Film loses credibility as Zarindast and his girlfriend Maureen Lavette tag along with the cons as good Samaritans until getting conveniently wiped out in a siege by the gangsters.

In addition to good stuntwork, best thing about the film is Zarindast's canny casting of beautiful women, especially Christina Lunde as Prior's girlfriend. Plotting is too loose to be riveting, notably the cavalier treatment of Wong's wife, Debra Lamb, who is talked about a lot, finally shown doing a striptease in a nightclub and cryptically dropped from the story.

Tech credits are up to par except for variable sound. —Lor.

Eye Of The Eagle II: Inside The Enemy

New York   A Concorde Pictures presentation of a New Classics production. Executive producer, Cirio H. Santiago. Produced by Catherine Santiago. Directed by Carl Franklin. Screenplay, Franklin, Dan Gagliasso; camera (color), Christopher Jones Lobo; editor, Edgar Viner; music, Justin Lord; additional music, Jody C. Robinson; sound, Do Bulatano; production design, Joe Mari Avellana; art direction, Jo Jo Magno; production manager, Aurelio Navarro; assistant director, Leo Martinez; special effects, Juan Marbella Jr.; stunt coordinator, Fred Esplana; associate producer, Christopher Santiago. Reviewed on MGM/UA Home Video vidcassette, N.Y., June 17, 1989. MPAA Rating: R. Running time: **79 MIN.**
Anthony Glenn . . . . William Field
Scratch . . . . Ken Jacobson
Dino Reynaldo . . Ronald William Lawrence
Mai . . . . Shirley Tesoro
Major Sorenson . . . . Andy Wood
    Also with: Archie Adamos, Paul Holme, Carl Franklin, Mike Monty, Leo Martinez.

■ This followup, alternately titled "Killed In Action (K.I.A.)," has little relationship to its direct-to-video ancestor save both are Filipino-lensed Vietnam War movies.

Several crew members and one G.I. (Mike Monty) encore in a minor tale of a private (William Field, cast for his resemblance to Charlie Sheen) who befriends a lovely Vietnamese girl (Shirley Tesoro) with dire consequences.

She's turned into a drug addict and forced into prostitution by Field's commanding officer, evil Major Sorenson (Andy Wood in a bland portrayal). When Field tries to spill the beans, instead of the promised court martial all he gets is a coverup by Sorenson. Pic ends up with lots of chasing around and a thoroughly unsatisfying finale.

Actor-turned-director Carl Franklin displays the requisite technical skill but had better find better scripts. Cast is okay but unchallenged by this material. —Lor.

Whiteforce
(AUSTRALIAN-FILIPINO)

New York   An Eastern Film Management and FGH presentation. Executive producer, Antony I. Ginnane. Produced by Lope V. Juban, Marilyn G. Ong. Directed by Eddie Romero. Screenplay, Henry Tefay; camera (Eastman color), Jose Batac; editor, Gervacio Santos; music, Ryan Cayabyab; art direction, Roy Lachica; production manager, Jessie Cunenta; assistant director, Ricardo B. DeGuzman; stunt coordinator, Renato Morado. Reviewed on New Star vidcassette, N.Y., June 3, 1989. No MPAA Rating. Running time: **85 MIN.**
Johnny Quinn . . . . Sam Jones
Nicki . . . . Kimberley Pistone
Alex Korda . . . . Timothy Hughes
Briggs . . . . Raoul Aragonn
Wizard . . . . Jimmy Fabregas
    Also with: Vic Diaz, Rubin Rustia, Ken Metcalfe, Mike Monty.

■ Sam Jones makes a convincing he-man hero in the otherwise hohum "Whiteforce," one of three actioners with "Force" in the title he's made recently.

Headed direct to video, Far East opus marks an underwhelming return of Eddie Romero, whose '70s exploitation films for AIP and Dimension Pictures were a lot more fun for drive-in fans.

Jones is accused of murdering his partner Ken Metcalfe, when in fact Timothy Hughes, a megalomaniacal drug lord, is responsible. The former "Flash Gordon" (billed as Sam J. Jones a decade back) is stuck with Metcalfe's spunky daughter Kimberley Pistone dodging bullets as both sides

search for a laserdisk which has the incriminating information about the drug cartel on it.

Jimmy Fabregas provides a modicum of comic relief as Jones' sidekick. Henry Tefay's script is merely functional; in-joke that the villain is named "Alex Korda" is hardly yock-inducing for film buffs. Action scenes are perfunctory and Romero omits the t&a footage that once was his forte. —Lor.

Assault Of The Party Nerds

New York   A Check Entertainment production. Executive producer, David DeCoteau. Produced by Richard Gabai, M. Alex Becker. Written and directed by Gabai. Camera (color), Howard Wexler; editor, Richard Deckard; music, Larry Berliner, Mike Morrell; songs, Gabai; sound, Peter Michaels 2d, Freddy Rottensy; production design, Royce Mathew; assistant director, Michael A. Becker; associate producer, David L. Gabai. Reviewed on Prism Entertainment vidcassette, N.Y., June 1, 1989. MPAA Rating: R. Running time: **79 MIN.**
Muffin . . . . Michelle Bauer
Bambi . . . . Linnea Quigley
Sid Witherspoon . . . . Troy Donahue
Ritchie . . . . Richard Gabai
Diane . . . . Deborah Roush
T.K. Joe Whyte
Scott . . . . Marc Silverberg
Bud . . . . C. Paul Dempsey
Chip . . . . Robert Mann
Cliff . . . . Kevin Glover
    Also with: Tantala Ray, Casey Fleming, Richard Rifkin, Amy Burr.

■ This low-budget, direct-to-video feature in the vein of "Revenge Of The Nerds" is an okay timekiller, more silly than funny.

All-purpose filmmaker Richard Gabai also toplines as Ritchie, prexy of Lambda Alpha Eta fraternity which is down to just four members (all seniors) at its State U. chapter. With the blessing and funding of national frat honcho Troy Donahue, he decides to throw a fabulous rush party to get new members.

Film's shenanigans involve the frat nerds' natural adversaries, the football jocks of rival Zeta house. Key plot twist (tastefully handled) is the revelation that the jocks are gay, causing them to lose face and girlfriends by the final reel.

Though using the pseudonym "Michelle McClellan," film's lead role is played by B-star Michelle Bauer, who provides the requisite nudity for vidfans as well as a campy performance as an overage, gushy college coed. Costar Linnea Quigley also is getting a bit old for this type of role and defers to Bauer for most of the dialog scenes.

Gabai and male cast are earnest but not very amusing. Porn actress Tantala Ray shows up at a party for a tasteless routine that is counterproductive. —*Lor.*

When Harry Met Sally

Hollywood A Columbia Pictures release of a Castle Rock Entertainment production in association with Nelson Entertainment. Produced by Rob Reiner, Andrew Scheinman. Coproducers, Jeffrey Stott, Steve Nicolaides. Directed by Reiner. Screenplay, Nora Ephron; camera (Duart and CFI color), Barry Sonnenfeld; editor, Robert Leighton; music adapted and arranged by Marc Shaiman; special musical performances and arrangements, Harry Connick Jr.; sound, Robert Eber; production design, Jane Musky; set decoration, George R. Nelson, Sabrina Wright-Basile; costume design, Gloria Gresham; assistant director, Aaron Barsky; associate producer, Ephron; casting, Jane Jenkins, Janet Hirshenson. Reviewed at Pathé screening room, L.A., June 29, 1989. MPAA Rating: R. Running time: 95 MIN.

Harry Burns . . . . Billy Crystal
Sally Albright . . . . Meg Ryan
Marie . . . . Carrie Fisher
Jess . . . . Bruno Kirby
Joe . . . . Steven Ford
Alice . . . . Lisa Jane Persky
Amanda . . . . Michelle Nicastro
Documentary couples . . . . . Kuno Sponholz
Also with: Charles Dugan, Connie Sawyer, Katherine Squire, Al Christy, Bernie Hern, Frances Chaney, Donna Hardy, Jane Chung.

■ Despite its glibness and superficiality, Columbia's "When Harry Met Sally" is likely to do well with audiences starved for a good romantic comedy.

Can a man be friends with a woman he finds attractive? Can usually acerbic scripter Nora Ephron sustain 95 minutes of unrelenting cuteness? Can the audience sit through 11 years of emotional foreplay between adorable Billy Crystal and Meg Ryan?

Abandoning the sour, nasty tone of some of her previous writing about contemporary sexual relationships, Ephron cuddles up to the audience in this number about the joys and woes of (mostly) platonic friendship. With its safe and formulaic approach set against modern sexual anxiety and cynicism, the film suggests an uneasy marriage between "Pillow Talk" and "Manhattan."

Rob Reiner directs with deftness and sincerity, making the material seem more engaging than it is, at least until the plot mechanics begin to unwind and the film starts to seem shapeless. The only thing that's unpredictable about the story is how long it takes Harry and Sally to realize they're perfect for each other. By the time they figure that out, though, it may be too late for many viewers to care.

Two characters who seem to have nothing on their minds but each other (even though they won't admit it), Harry and Sally are supposed to be a political consultant and a journalist, but it's hard to tell from the evidence presented.

Crystal is seen shuffling papers on his kitchen table, but he never talks about politics. Given the actor's comic talents, it might have been interesting to portray him as a hardball prankster, but it's never clear what Harry believes.

Ryan once in a while pecks at a word processor in her comfy apartment, but displays no interest in public personalities, events or issues.

Not only are the characters and social context fuzzily presented, there isn't much sense of life going on around them. The only other characters in the story with any definition are their respective best friends, Bruno Kirby and Carrie Fisher, two loser types who ironically find happiness before the more attractive but even more neurotic leads.

In a film whose main story never manages to warm the heart, a fatal flaw for a romantic comedy, the only genuine emotion comes from pseudo-documentary interludes of elderly couples reminiscing about the haphazard ways in which they found happiness together. The vignettes are endearing, but they seem like a crutch for an uncertain screenplay.

It's a tribute not only to Reiner but also to Crystal and Ryan that they manage to find such charm in the early stages of the relationship. Ephron's witticisms sometimes crackle, and the actors manage to shade them with occasional suggestions of depth that the second half of the film dissipates.

With attractive lensing by Barry Sonnenfeld and a delightful soundtrack of romantic oldies as well as new musical performances and arrangements by Harry Connick Jr., the film conjures up an image of Manhattan that recalls Woody Allen's cinematic love affair with the island.

But lacking the sharp edges and lifelike unpredictability of the Allen films it so obviously emulates, "When Harry Met Sally" suffers most by raising those comparisons. —*Mac.*

Hajen som visste för mycket
(The Shark That Knew Too Much)
(SWEDISH)

Malmö A Svensk Filmindustri release of an SF production with Kulturtuben and Filmhuset. Produced by Waldemar Bergendahl. Written and directed by Claes Eriksson. Camera (Eastmancolor), Dan Myhrman, free fall cinematography, Blue Sky Film; editor, Jan Persson; music, Eriksson; musical arrangements, Charles Falk; sound, Christjan Persson, Anders Larsson; choreography, Sandy Mansson; production design, Rolf Allan Hakanson; stunt coordination, special effects, Johan Toren/Svenska Stuntgruppen; production management, Anne Otto, Thomas Allercrantz; assistant director, Michael Sevholdt. Reviewed at the Royal Malmö, Sweden, July 6, 1989. Running time: 84 MIN.

Joachim, Alexander and
Luther Plottner . . . . Anders Eriksson
Samuel Plottner . . . . Claes Eriksson
Benny Hörnsteen . . . . Per Fritzell
Dixie Hopper . . . . Kerstin Granlund
Helge Lock . . . . Jan Rippe
Cilly Cumberland-
Brons . . . . Charlotte Strandberg
Lennart Cumberland-
Brons . . . . Peter Rangmar

■ Writer-director-composer-lyricist-actor Claes Eriksson bowed successfully as a filmmaker two years ago with "Leif," a satire on the Swedish arms industry. With "The Shark That Knew Too Much," he takes on Stockholm's Wall Street with joyous overkill and satirical firepower way out of control.

Eriksson has again used himself and his fellow singer-actors from the popular Galenskaparna stage ensemble and the Aftershave vocal group in all leading roles, assuring a sympathetic reaction from local audiences. But although consisting of many individually funny parts, "Shark" has no cumulative narrative bite.

Killed in the general blast is a storyline that has several stock exchange sharks outbidding (and biting) each other in preposterous maneuverings, illustrated by avalanches of sightgags. Super-shark Samuel Plottner (played too frenetically by Eriksson himself) has the final bite put on himself by his son who poses as a triplet to obtain a majority of the shares in dad's company.

Anders Eriksson displays innocuous charm as the trio of brothers (only one is seen at a time), and Per Fritzell has the right touch of suave menace as daddy's chief rival. Charlotte Strandberg, Kerstin Granlund and veteran musical star Gaby Stenberg do distaff duty with mature wit.

Loans and inspirations from Harold Lloyd, Buster Keaton and Monty Python appear without noticeable disguise. The film and the performing ensemble are at their collective best in a couple of grand-style song-&-dance numbers, both of them employing male dancers only. Technical credits rate tops throughout. —*Kell.*

GRAMADO FESTIVAL REVIEWS

Jardim de Allah
(The Garden Of Allah)
(BRAZILIAN)

Gramado, Brazil An Embrafilme release of a Jupiter Filmes production. Executive producers, Walter Ribeiro, Armando Santone. Directed by David Neves. Screenplay, Onezio Paiva; camera (color), Jaime Schwartz; editors, Marta Luz, Marie Dominique Maciel; music, Claudio Daulsberg, Mario Telles, Tito Madi; set design, Paulo Dubois; costumes, Izabel Paranhos. Reviewed at Gramado Film Festival, June 11, 1989. Running time: **91 MIN.**

With: Françoise Forton, Joel Barcelos, Paulo Barbosa, Grande Otelo, Raul Cortez, Imara Reis, Isabel Garcia, Betina Viany, Valeria Frascino.

■ A good interpreter of the "carioca" soul, helmer David Neves comes out with another personal work, the end of a trilogy initiated with "Muito Prazer" and "Fulaninha," featuring an authentic look at current moral values in Rio de Janeiro.

Pics like "Muito Prazer" (1979), "Luz de Fuego" (1982) and especially "Fulaninha" (1986) have in common low budgets but also a very personal approach to Rio, a city Neves treats as a character in most of his films.

Low budget and Rio also are present in "Jardim de Allah." Title refers to a public garden that defines the boundary between the Ipanema and Leblon districts. The garden also is close to the Cruzada São Sebastiao, a tenement built long ago by the Catholic Church to accommodate thousands of homeless families and rehouse slum dwellers.

Film is intended to be a chronicle of ambiguity. Characters are beggars, drug dealers and middleclass families who are supposed to live harmoniously in the same environment. Neves' approach is centered on one particular beggar (well portrayed by Grande Otelo) who tells the story of "Jardim de Allah" in a rather didactic way.

This is less important, however, than parallel stories involving the cocaine habit of a daughter of a bourgeois family, her involvement with the drug dealer and the efforts of her father to succeed at business, which eventually includes the murder of his partner. Father and mother, Raul Cortez and Imara Reis, achieve fine performances, as does Paulo Barbosa as an amateur robber who invades a wealthy home and gets drunk on their scotch.

Neves directs as if spreading some inside jokes, not caring much about minor syntax errors but caring enough to be sincere. Technical and artistic crew are somehow part of this dialog, which includes a subtle homage to veteran film critic Alex Viany.

The result is sometimes amateurish, but that is Neves' style. Though not as technically well finished as "Fulaninha," this is work of integrity and a reliable chronicle of a city that has long been Neves' main subject. —*Hoin.*

Faca de Dois Gumes
(Two-Edged Knife)
(BRAZILIAN)

Gramado, Brazil An Embrafilme release of a DWD production. Executive producer, Patrick Moine. Directed by Murilo Salles. Screenplay, Leopoldo Serran, Alcione Araujo, Salles, based on original story by Fernando Sabino; camera (color), José Tadeu Ribeiro; editor, Isabelle Rathery; music, Victor Biglione; sound, Valeria Mauro; set design, Maria Helena Salles; costumes, Barbosa Mendonca; associate producers, Videofilmes, MSC. Reviewed at Gramado Film Festival, June 16, 1989. Running time: **95 MIN.**

With: Paulo José, Marieta Severo, José de Abreu, Flavio Galvao, Paulo Goulart, Fernando Peixoto, Jose Lewgoy, Ursula Canto.

■ Carefully produced with funds raised partially from French tv, "Faca de Dois Gumes" is a well-told thriller with elements of adultery, scandal and violence. Despite some problems with the Portuguese dialog, product can raise interest abroad, especially for the universality of the genre and for technical achievement.

This is the second feature directed by Murilo Salles, one of the top Brazilian cinematographers of the '70s and early '80s. Previous work, "Nunca Fomos Tao Felizes" (1984), dealt with a former political activist and his son. "Faca de Dois Gumes" can also be seen as a political statement, for the torture, the violence, the arbitrariness of the state are always present.

Fundamentally, pic is a thriller in which a wealthy businessman discovers his wife is having an affair with his partner. He kills both of them, resulting in deep involvement not only with police but with an unknown — and extremely cruel — gang seeking the $5-million the betrayed husband and his partner supposedly raised in an illegitimate deal.

Salles directs clearly keeping tv in mind, with medium shots and most of the action over-explained. Actors, especially Paulo José and Marieta Severo, never really get involved with their characters, maybe derived from the necessity to shoot a comprehensible story.

Music by Victor Biglione — generally a sax solo — is overused, and screenplay is generally consistent but very weak as far as the Portuguese dialog is concerned. Pic should gain from French dubbing. Torture scenes and the relation between the father and the kidnaped son are otherwise strong and resistant to such deficiency.

Other technical credits, especially cinematography by José Tadeu Ribeiro, are very good. —*Hoin.*

UHF

New York An Orion Pictures release of a Cinecorp production, in association with Imaginary Entertainment. Executive producer-production manager, Gray Frederickson. Produced by Gene Kirkwood, John Hyde. Coproducers, Kevin Breslin, Deren Getz. Directed by Jay Levey. Screenplay, Al Yankovic, Levey; camera (Alpha Cine color, Deluxe prints), David Lewis; editor, Dennis O'Connor; music, John Du Prez; songs, Yankovic, others; sound (Dolby), Bo Harwood; production design, Ward Preston; costume design, Tom McKinley; assistant director, John R. Woodward; stunt coordinator, George Fisher; Introvision fantasy sequence — additional camera, John Hora; associate producers, Becki Cross, Joe Aguilar; casting, Cathy Henderson, Barbara Hanley, Michael Cutler. Reviewed at Criterion 3 theater, N.Y., July 14, 1989. MPAA Rating: PG-13. Running time: **96 MIN.**

George Newman	Weird Al Yankovic
Teri	Victoria Jackson
R.J. Fletcher	Kevin McCarthy
Stanley Spadowski	Michael Richards
Bob	David Bowe

Also with: Stanley Brock, Anthony Geary, Trinidad Silva, Gedde Watanabe, Billy Barty, John Paragon, Fran Drescher, Sue Ane Langdon, David Proval, Grant James, Emo Philips, Jay Levey.

■ On-target film and music parodies by Weird Al Yankovic highlight his feature bow "UHF," but pic's tedious and conventional narrative make it unlikely to compete effectively for big summer b.o. Subsequent tv use probably will attract Yankovic fans.

As scripted by Yankovic and his regular collaborator (making his feature helming debut) Jay Levey, "UHF" pales by comparison with hit-forebears "The Groove Tube" and "Tunnelvision" in alloting too much footage to the boring framework story.

Yankovic is named station manager of dinky Channel 62 when his uncle wins it in a poker game. Satire of its cut-rate operation provides a few laughs, with station suddenly vaulting into local ratings supremacy when Yankovic promotes janitor Michael Richards to host a kiddie show, with wacky results. Evil manager of a network affiliate (Kevin McCarthy) plots Channel 62's demise leading to a Richards-hosted telethon to save the UHFer.

Pic soars when Yankovic daydreams a fantasy sequence, including excellent parodies of Steven Spielberg films, as well as during brief tv commercials or program promos, including a clever spoof of violence starring Levey in "Gandhi II."

Most inspired, off-the-wall segment is a musicvideo featuring claymation effects by the Chiodo Bros. in which Yankovic merges

Dire Straits' hit "Money For Nothing" with Paul Henning's "Ballad Of Jed Clampett" theme for tv's "The Beverly Hillbillies." It's a showstopper, but immediately we're thrown back to cornball plot developments.

Other highlights include Richards' manic turn as the hilariously dimwitted janitor/superstar (Yankovic kindly lets him keep his old job even as he hits it big), frequently upstaging Yankovic's rather mild (in character) screen persona. The late Trinidad Silva (to whom film is dedicated) is very funny as host of "Raul's Wild Kingdom," a nature show in extremely poor taste.

McCarthy is delightfully hammy as the villain while comedienne Victoria Jackson plays it straight as Yankovic's girlfriend.

Tech credits are modest but support the various types of footage (including musicvideos) on display.—*Lor.*

The Prisoner Of St. Petersburg
(AUSTRALIAN-W. GERMAN-B&W)

Sydney A Seon Films (Melbourne)-Panorama Film (W. Berlin) coproduction. Intl. sales, Kim Lewis; Marketing, Melbourne). Produced by Daniel Scharf, Klaus Sungen. Directed by Ian Pringle. Screenplay, Michael Wren; camera (b&w), Ray Argall; editor, Ursula West; music, Paul Schutze; production design, Peta Lawson; sound, Eckhard Kuchenbecker; production manager/casting, Jolanda Darbyshire. Reviewed at Australian Film Commission screening room, Sydney, July 7, 1989. Running time: **80 MIN.**
Jack . . . . Noah Taylor
Elena . . . . Solveig Dommartin
Johanna . . . . Katja Teichmann
Also with: René Schönenberger (businessman), Dennis Staunton (Irishman), Johanna Karl-Lovy (old woman), Olivier Picto (Stefan), Christian Zertz (Lorenzo), Hans-Martin Stier (truckdriver), Manfred Salzgeber (Russian man with coat).

■ **Already seen at the Rotterdam, Melbourne and Cannes (Un Certain Regard) fests so far this year, "The Prisoner Of St. Petersburg" is obviously going to be a fest fave, but finding a paying audience, even in art houses, might prove to be a trickier proposition.**

Filmed entirely in West Berlin, pic involves the experiences of a strange young man, presumably Australian, who arrives in the city by train. At first Jack (played by Noah Taylor, the young thesp from "The Year My Voice Broke") speaks only Russian (subtitled in English), quoting from the works of Gogol and Dostoyevsky who apparently hold him in thrall. Berliners are, not surprisingly, baffled by the stranger who insists on speaking a foreign language nobody understands.

Jack has various encounters. He attacks an old woman, recreating a scene from one of the Russian books that obsess him. He is nearly picked up by a gay businessman. Then he meets two older women, Elena (Solveig Dommartin from Wim Wenders' "Wings Of Desire") and Johanna (newcomer Katja Teichmann). To Jack, Elena resembles Sonya, his Russian ideal woman, and he falls in love with her. The three speak English together, and wander the cold city streets, stopping at bars, a railway station and a truck-stop.

There's not much more to it than that. Jack has dream images of himself with Sonya/Elena in pre-revolutionary St. Petersburg, but whether he's mad, or simply, as one character suggests, a "prisoner of St. Petersburg" is never made very clear. He remains an unexplained cypher, and Taylor only gives a surface reading of the character. Similarly, the two women appear motiveless, with one, Elena, fearing love while the other, Johanna, falls for the young stranger at first sight.

Writer Michael Wren and director Ian Pringle weren't after realities here: This is a dank mood piece which relies heavily on Ray Argall's superlative, razor-sharp black and white photography to create its strange mood. Pringle's earlier features ("The Plains Of Heaven" and "Wrong World") were also about displaced, disoriented characters in a desolate environment. Both were moderately well received by buffs (Jo Kennedy won best actress award at Berlin for "Wrong World") but had limited release. Commercially, "Prisoner" looks to be equally dubious.

However, there's no doubting that the atmosphere Pringle and Argall create is effective, and the film emerges as an intriguing exercise in style which, despite self-conscious artiness, exerts a certain spell over the viewer. Pic has already sold to Scandi and Japan, with U.K. and Italy pending; a direct to exhib release in Oz is likely. —*Strat.*

Que Bom Te Ver Viva
(Good To See You Alive)
(BRAZILIAN)

Gramado, Brazil An Embrafilme release of a Taiga Producoes Visuais/Fundacao do Cinema Brasileiro production. Executive producers, Katia Cop, Maria Helena Nascimento. Written and directed by Lucia Murat. Camera (color), Walter Carvalho; editor, Vera Freire; music, Fernando Moura; sound, Heron Alencar; art direction, Adolfo Orico Rosenthal; set design, costumes, Beatriz Selgado. Reviewed at Gramado Film Festival, June 16, 1989. Running time: **100 MIN.**
With: Irene Ravache.

■ **Basically a documentary on women tortured under Brazil's military dictatorship, "Que Bom Te Ver Viva" introduces a single character as the imaginary counterpoint to the actual revelations of the victims. Pic will be of interest to those searching for political docudramas.**

About 10 women tortured 20 years ago are interviewed today, mostly at their homes. They talk about their new lives, their work, their families. All were involved in political activities in the years of the dictatorship, and many took part in terrorist actions.

Director Lucia Murat is a tv journalist and approaches the subject much like a newscast. Her goal is to find out if torture has driven the women to madness and how they manage to survive. Since the stories do not provide much new information on torture techniques, the answer to the first question is usually no.

Project would have failed but for the introduction of one fictional character, a woman who wraps up the stories, assembling madness, coherence and a deep knowledge of the world. Irene Ravache gives a great performance as the woman, constantly making the interviewed women, who have nothing to say except to praise their babies, interesting.

Some interviews, on the other hand, raise good questions about the shame of the torture victims — and how in most cases they are condemned by society to silence forever. —*Hoin.*

Missing Link

New York A Universal Pictures release of a Kane Intl. production, in association with Guber-Peters-Barris Prods. Produced by Dennis D. Kane. Executive producers, Peter Guber, Jon Peters. Written, directed and camera (color) by David and Carol Hughes. Editor, David Dickie; music, Mike Trim, Sammy Hurden; sound (Dolby), David Hughes; special makeup effects, Rick Baker; narrator, Michael Gambon. Reviewed on MCA Home Video vidcassette, N.Y., July 10, 1989. MPAA Rating: PG. Running time: **91 MIN.**
Ape-man . . . . Peter Elliott

■ **An interesting companion piece to "Gorillas In The Mist," Universal's no-dialog feature "Missing Link" had a brief theatrical run last November and currently is in videostores.**

Pic limns the travails a million years ago of the last apeman (genus Australopithecus Robustus), doomed to extinction by the more violent race of man. Coming from the "Gorillas" executive producers (and featuring effective makeup effects by Rick Baker, also from that film), pic carries its similar ecological message and warning with agreeable understatement.

The handsome visuals of the Namib desert and various national parks in Namibia shot by filmmakers David and Carol Hughes deserve a big-screen treatment, but absence of a strong narrative makes it more appropriate for the lower involvement of a video audience.

Peter Elliott is expressive and quite sympathetic underneath Baker's variation on an apesuit makeup. After finding his mate and compatriots dead, killed by man's invention of the ax, he wanders to the sea in vain search for other survivors of his kind.

Mood and some setups are similar to Stanley Kubrick's classic "Dawn Of Man" sequence in "2001: A Space Odyssey," but with a further inversion as here the viewer is inevitably rooting for the gentle guys our ancestors knocked off. By extension, all other animals on the planet are in danger until we come to our senses, film implies.

Fascinating views of wildlife ranging from bullfrogs to lions and elephants make this picture of interest to fans of nature shows. Besides "Gorillas In The Mist," it also fits in thematically with producer Dennis B. Kane's previous National Geographic Society docu feature "People Of The Forest." —*Lor.*

Proichi Schpana Zamoksvaret Skaia
(Farewell, Street Urchins)
(SOVIET-B&W)

Barcelona A Mosfilm Studios/Goskino production. Directed by Alexander Pankratov. Screenplay, Eduard Volodarsky; camera (b&w), Boris Novoselov; music, Nikolai Karetnikov; production design, Vasily Scherbak. Reviewed at Barcelona Film Festival, July 8, 1989. Running time: **87 MIN.**
With: Larisa Borodina, Sergei Makarov, Nikolai Dobrynin, Mikhail Puzyrev, Oleg Golubitskys.

■Set in 1956 in working class neighborhood in Moscow, this well-acted and directed pic is a neo-realistic indictment of Soviet life in the penurious postwar era.

Main interest for a Westerner is in the portrayal of the drab daily life of the period, rather than in the story of a tragic puppy love between a 15-year-old boy and a slightly older waitress.

Writer Eduard Volodarsky has woven various revealing elements into the story. The boy is the son of a dissident who is serving a jail term as an "enemy of the people." As a poor student he is a disappointment to his bedraggled, hardworking mother and spends much of his time with a group of street urchins.

The girl, besides slinging borscht in a soup kitchen, hangs out with a gang of toughs and delinquents. One of these has become her lover. He has a nasty temper and a ready blade.

Despite the disparity in their ages, the young couple falls in love. Their romance flowers against the sordid background of poverty, crime, crowded apartments and hopeless drudgery.

We are given occasional glimpses into the lives of those residing in the nabe, and their shabby, worn existences. Story comes to a head when the knife-toting thug pockets a wad of bills in a momentarily unattended till. The cashier faces a long jail term for her negligence, but the culprit is apprehended when the girl squeals to the police, hoping therewith to rid herself of the obstacle that stands between herself and her young lover.

Though in b&w, pic has a sepia tint that adds to the dreary ambience. The downbeat ending is softened by the arrival of the boy's dissident father, who has been released from prison. The boy's fate is to spend the rest of his days in a futureless job as an underpaid linotype operator.

Item could cull some interest in select art circuits, more for its depiction of Soviet society than for the familiar love story. —Besa.

She's Back

New York   A Vestron Pictures release of a Tycin Entertainment production. Produced by Cynthia DePaula. Executive producers, Lawrence Kasanoff, Richard Keatinge. Directed by Tim Kincaid. Screenplay, Buddy Giovinazzo; camera (Precision color), Arthur D. Marks; editor, Mary Hickey; music, Jimmie Haskell; sound (Dolby), Micah Solomon; art direction, Kim Meinelt; set design, John Paino; assistant director, Joe Derrig; production manager, Geraldine Caulfield; casting, Judy Henderson, Alycia Aumuller. Reviewed on Vestron vidcassette, N.Y., July 13, 1989. MPAA Rating: R. Running time: 90 MIN.

Beatrice . . . . Carrie Fisher
Paul . . . . Robert Joy
Sherman Bloom . . . . Matthew Cowles
Razorface . . . . Joel Swetow
Det. Brophy . . . . Sam Coppola
Sally . . . . Donna Drake
Bob . . . . Bobby DiCicco
    Also with: Anthony Mannino, Gary Yudman, Erick Avari, Sam Cagnina, Robert Bottone.

■This black comedy farce in the "Topper" vein offers a few laughs, but despite a July 7 release in Miami it's more likely to attract a following, based on presence of topliner Carrie Fisher, in subsequent video release via Vestron.

Low-budgeter originally was titled "Dead & Married," limning the hapless fate of Robert Joy, who moves to Queens with wife Fisher. The house is robbed by a neighborhood gang the first night. The thugs, led by evil-looking Joel Swetow, kill Fisher, but she's soon back as a ghost only Joy can see.

Script by Buddy Giovinazzo starts promisingly with Fisher's endless nagging (both while alive and dead) driving Joy crazy. Now she wants him to go out every night and kill another gang member responsible for her death.

Poor Joy acquiesces and fortunately is aided in his task by gung-ho neighbor (a Korean War vet) Matthew Cowles. Bodies pile up, makeup effects become more elaborate and, unfortunately, Fisher's funny role gets diminished by the final reels.

En route, it's a fun turn for her as a first-class kvetch, well-matched to comic foil Joy. Helmer Tim Kincaid keeps things hopping, though the fantasy premise and ghost's in-and-out presence seem arbitrary in what amounts to a sendup of the spate of revenge and vigilante justice pics.

Tech credits and supporting cast are okay, but this is strictly Fisher and Joy's show.—Lor.

Nam Angels

Boca Raton, Fla.   A Concorde Pictures release of a New Classics presentation. Produced by Christopher R. Santiago. Directed by Cirio H. Santiago. Screenplay, Dan Gagliasso; camera (color), Rick Remias, Chris Squires; editor, Edgar Viner; music, Jaime Fabregas; associate producer, Anna Roth; casting, Al Guarino. Reviewed on Cinemax, Boca Raton, Fla., June 27, 1989. (Also available on Media Home Entertainment vidcassette.) MPAA Rating: R. Running time: 93 MIN.

With: Brad Johnson (Calhoun), Vernon Wells, Kevin Duffis, Rick Dean, Mark Venturini, Jeff Griffith, Romy Diaz, Ken Metcalfe.

■This oddball picture introduces Hell's Angels on their bikes into the Vietnam War with entertaining (though unconvincing) cross-genre results. Released in Miami in January, it's now simultaneously available on paycable and vidcassette.

Filipino helmer Cirio H. Santiago has made several conventional films about the Vietnam conflict (including two "Eye Of The Eagle" pics), but here goes wild with a crazy gimmick. A group of Hell's Angels happens to be hanging out in a Saigon bar. They're recruited by young Lt. Calhoun (Brand Johnson) to help him rescue two comrades captured behind enemy lines.

Gimmick is that he needs specialists to take dirt bikes into the rugged terrain before a massive offensive is launched. He offers the rowdy quartet a chance to earn $10-million in gold hoarded by local warlord Vernon Wells.

Though that key plot twist is hard to swallow, Santiago stages action scenes well and it's fun to see the free-spirit bikers in gung ho war action. Predictably, they don't take kindly to following orders.

Cast is serviceable and tech credits fine. —Lor.

L'Air de Rien
(Easy In Mind)
(FRENCH-BELGIAN-CANADIAN-B&W/COLOR)

Barcelona   A Lamy Films presentation of a Les Films de la Phalène (Belgium). Neuf de Coeur (France) and Bleu Blanc Rouge (Canada) coproduction. Produced by Benoit Lamy. Written and directed by Mary Jiménez. Camera (b&w, Fuji color), Raymond Fromont; editor, Philippe Bourgueil; music, Thierry De Mey; sets, Marc Philippe Guerig; sound, Miguel Rejas. Reviewed at Barcelona Film Festival, July 5, 1989. Running time: 89 MIN.

Jessie . . . . Carole Courtoy
Théo . . . . Gabriel Arcand
Marcel . . . . Josse De Pauw
Francis . . . . Lucas Belvaux
Constance . . . . Bernadette Lafont
Mathilde . . . . Eugenie De Mey
Cécile . . . . Maria de Medeiros

■Mood of this inconclusive, rambling pic is conditioned by a young woman's uncertainty about whether she is terminally ill.

Rather than wait to learn the results of her clinical analysis, she decides to take a train to a neighboring city where she tries to experience life anew.

Audience never finds out if the girl is really ill. She wanders the streets aimlessly, meets up with a man in a cafe who spouts philosophical verities, has an affair with a timid bartender in the hotel where she lodges and dwells on the objects and people that she encounters.

Problem is that there is virtually no plot or dramatic development, so that the rambling nonstory makes the film seem twice its real length. Much of the dialog is self conscious and heavyhanded as the pic strives for profundity.

Carole Courtoy as the wayward girl (who appears in almost every scene) is plain and charmless. Most of pic conveys an "air of nothingness" which probably will relegate it to terminal commercial limbo. —Besa.

MOSCOW FILM FESTIVAL REVIEWS

Huguan
(The Shining Arc)
(CHINESE)

Moscow   A Guangxi Studio production. Directed by Zhang Jun Zhao. Screenplay, Zhang Jun Zhao, Xu Xiao Bin; camera (widescreen, color), Xiao Feng. Reviewed at Moscow Film Festival (competing), July 12, 1989. Running time: **100 MIN.**

With: Bai Ling, Zhang Guang Bei, Xiao Xiung.

■ "The Shining Arc" is an ambitious psychological study of a gifted girl called mentally ill by others, a witch by herself.

Directed by Zhang Jun Zhao ("One And Eight"), pic has moments of great poetry and intensity, a degree of mysticism, and insights into the lives of the Chinese middle class that may be a matter of historical record now. Though not an easy film, it could attract an art house following with special handling.

In a superbly eerie opener, a young man and woman gaze at a frozen lake while she (heroine Jin-won) remembers skating a figure eight on it in her dream, and seeing a line of fire appear. An able mix of closeups, widescreen lensing drained of color, and music set the tone for what is to come.

As it turns out, scene is a flash-forward to pic's end. Jin-won is actually living in a mental hospital, surrounded by concerned doctors. A young woman medic, Sun-ni, encourages her lover to make the girl fall in love with him and so bring her out of her shell. Sun-ni brings the girl home to live with her family, many of whom are musicians. In this refined setting, Jin-won blossoms.

Eventually, Sun-ni's plans succeed too well, and Jin-won and boyfriend fall in love. He gives the girl moral support when her father dies, but cannot bring himself to leave his pragmatic girlfriend for this dreaming girl with extrasensory gifts. Film closes enigmatically.

Film is darkly atmospheric, with its desaturated colors, shadowy lensings, and smoky images. It captures the imagination in all but a few scenes, notably those involving a bohemian artist who seems more comical than real.

Principals are sensitive thesps and believable whatever they do. Only trouble is keeping characters straight in the gloom of the lensing.

Pic's admiration for extreme individuality, as evidenced in its psychic heroine who is referred to as "far beyond us," makes a clearcut break with mass ideology. The family of intellectuals who love Western music is notable.

—Yung.

Aje Aje Bara Aje
(Come, Come, Come Upward)
(SOUTH KOREAN)

Moscow   A Motion Picture Promotion Corp. release of a Tae-hung Production Co. Ltd. production. Produced by Lee Tae-Won. Directed by Im Kwon-t'aek. Screenplay, Han Sung-Won; camera (color), Gu Jung-mo; music, Kim Jong-gil. Reviewed at Moscow Film Fetival (competing), July 9, 1989. Running time: **125 MIN.**
Sun-Nyo . . . . Kang Soo-yeon
Jin-Song . . . . Jin Yong-mi
Hyon-Jong . . . . Yu In-chon
Un-son . . . . Jun In-ja
Also with: Han Ji-il, Jon Mu-Song.

■ "Come, Come, Come Upward" by prolific helmer Im Kwon-t'aek ("Surrogate Mother") is the first South Korean film to compete at the Moscow Film Festival.

Tale of two girls who enter a Buddhist monastery but are drawn back into the world is an intriguing psychological study which gets a little lost in novel-like complexity and length.

Its shrewd exploitation of Korea's exotic beauty and canny tale-spinning should earn it attention in specialized foreign markets.

Sun-Nyo (played by young Kang Soo-yeon) decides to become a nun after she gets into an innocent scrape over a handsome teacher at school. At the monastery, she is judged too much of a know-it-all to achieve Zen. Yet she perseveres and, in a kinky scene, has her head shaved like the other nuns.

When Sun-Nyo saves a drunk who tries to kill himself, she is persecuted by the over-greatful man. Result is she gets thrown out of the convent and is forced to follow the brute. After he graphically rapes her, Sun-Nyo grows attached to him and is expecting a baby, when pic switches to the story of another young novice, Sister Chong-hwa.

The mother superior's pet, she is the rigid, orthodox type. She sets off to live in a cave for three years of hyper-ascetism, only a devilish old monk is already living there and demands her body in another graphic rape scene. Pic goes on to show the first girl, Sun-Nyo, working in a kind of General Hospital on an island, jinxing every man she loves (at least three die), and returning to the mother superior's deathbed to be recognized as the true nun.

Though story connects, pic loses much of its punch by too much meandering. Pro lensing underscores the beauty of interiors and exteriors. Thesping is okay.

—Yung.

Follow Me
(WEST GERMAN)

Moscow   A Europolis release. Intl. sales, Cine-Intl. An Alpha Film/Allianz Film-produktion coproduction, in association with Bayerischen Rundfunk, La Sept, FFA, LFA, FKT and Joself Radl Filmproduktion. Produced by Monika Aubele, Norbert Schneider. Directed by Maria Knilli. Screenplay, Knilli, Vera Has; camera (color), Klaus Eichhammer; editor, Fritz Baumann, Knilli; music, Tzveton Marangosoff; art direction, Winfried Hennig. Reviewed at Moscow Film Festival (competing), July 9, 1989. Running time: **104 MIN.**
Pavel Navratil . . . . Pavel Landovsky
Ljuba . . . . Marina Vlady
Judity . . . . Katharina Thalbach
Barber . . . . Rudolf Wossley
Milos . . . . Ulrich Reinthaller
Also with: Hans Jakob (violinist), Mark Zak (soldier), Sylva Langova, Hana-Maria Pravda, Renata Olarova.

■ West German helmer Maria Knilli has concocted an East-West comedy set between Prague and Germany. Originality it has, humor it largely lacks, and storyline is so frail, it leads to seat-squirming ennui. Offbeat effort is a curiosity item with a tough b.o. life before it.

Coyly lensed in a variety of languages, including German, Czech and Russian, pic does without dialog for long stretches, attempting to hang together with visual humor and German intertitles summing up the conversation. Device is okay, but would've been more successful if dialog was funny in the first place or, indeed, made more sense.

Opening is a typically overloaded scene that introduces hero Pavel Navratil (played by well-known Czech theater thesp Pavel Landovsky, not a newcomer to these roles). He is presented digging a grave in a cemetery while three old biddies watch and make catty comments, explaining how he is a college prof who has lost his job for entertaining "wrong ideas."

Next he gives away all his possessions to a group of young people (his students?) and takes off for Germany. The airport becomes a recurrent logo in the film; Pavel says airport and cemeteries are the two póles of his life that he'd like to escape.

In Germany, Pavel hangs out in the "Jetcut" barbershop, where he debates with the (Czech?) barber. Other friends are Ljuba (Marina Vlady), a homesick Russian emigré who runs a brothel, and a violinist who plays Smetana and makes Pavel dream of Prague. Another emigré, young Milos (Ulrich Reinthaller), weeps for his homeland.

Pic gets more abstract and artificial as it goes on. Pavel returns clandestinely to Prague with a shipment of nighthawks, which he releases on the airport runway. Then he spends a night in the cemetery conversing with a nice Russian soldier. The police find him next morning and obligingly toss him back on a Westbound plane.

Point of all this is vague. There are a lot of funny characters (led by Landovsky) but little fun. It's technically professional.

—Yung.

Stan Posiadania
(Inventory)
(POLISH-W. GERMAN)

Moscow   A Polish Film Unit TOR/Polish TV/Regina Ziegler Filmproduktion (Berlin) coproduction. Written and directed by Krzysztof Zanussi. Camera (color), Slowomir Idziak; editor, Marek Denys; music, Wojciech Kilar; art direction, Wieslawa Chojkowska; production manager, Michal Szdzerbic. Reviewed at Moscow Film Festival (competing), July 8, 1989. Running time: **101 MIN.**
Julia . . . . Krystyna Janda
Tomek . . . . Artur Zmijewski
Mother . . . . Maja Komorowska
Also with: Andrzej Lopicki, Artur Barcis, Tadeusz Bradecki, Adam Bauman.

■ Latest Krzysztof Zanussi film, "Inventory" (also called "State Of Possession") traces the difficulty of human relations in a 3-cornered tale — a neurotic woman, idealistic young man and his mother.

Director concentrates on ethical and human factors in a talky script with too little movement to hold one's attention. Art houses will have to reach for this one.

Tomek (Artur Zmijewski) is a clean-cut, high-minded geography student. He lives with mother Zofia (Maja Komorowska), a sensitive, practicing Catholic like her son. When Tomek meets Julia (Krystyna Janda), a depressed woman older than he, he first tries to comfort her, then selflessly invites her to stay with him and his mother.

As Julia, Janda is a convincing neurotic who calls out for sympathy even when she's most irritating. Komorowska fills the mother's role to a T, trying to be Christian to Julia while worrying about her affect on her son.

Young Zmijewski is a Tomek too good to be true. He goes to West Berlin where his separated father has made a good life for himself, refuses the money that would solve his problems, and looks for work as a humble house painter. His patience dealing with Julia's fits also far exceeds the audience's.

Film is open-ended, leaving Julia in a rest home for treatment while Tomek vows to keep trying to make their relationship work.

Whether one accepts Tomek's saintliness or not (what attracts him to Julia remains closer to pity than love), film poses its moral problem and works it out as a chamber piece for three strong thesps, much the way Krzysztof Kieslowski does in his Ten Commandments series. Difference is "Inventory makes little use of cinema and relies heavily on words to make its point. Result is a slow-moving film with a little grip on the imagination. —*Yung.*

Blind Fury

Sydney A Tri-Star Pictures release of a Tri-Star/Interscope Communications production. Executive producers, Robert W. Cort, David Madden. Produced by Daniel Grodnik, Tim Matheson. Directed by Phillip Noyce. Screenplay, Charles Robert Carner, based on a screenplay by Ryozo Kasahara; camera (Technicolor), Don Burgess; editor, David Simmons; music, J. Peter Robinson; production design, Peter Murton; stunt coordinator, Dick Ziker; sword fight choreographer, Steven Lambert; car stunts, Dennis (Danger) Madalone; assistant director, Tom Davies; associate producers Dennis Murphy, Charles Robert Carner; production manager, Murphy; casting, Junie Lowry. Reviewed at Fox-Columbia/Tri-Star screening room, Sydney, July 20, 1989. MPAA Rating: R. Running time: **85 MIN.**

Nick Parker . . . . Rutger Hauer
Billy Deveraux . . . . Brandon Call
Frank Deveraux . . . . Terrance O'Quinn
Annie Winchester . . . . Lisa Blount
MacCready . . . . Noble Willingham
Lynn Deveraux . . . . Meg Foster
Lyle Pike . . . . Nick Cassavetes
Tector Pike . . . . Rick Overton
Slag . . . . Randall (Tex) Cobb
Cobb . . . . Charles Cooper
Japanese Swordsman . . . . Sho Kosugi

■ "Blind Fury," which is currently enjoying a successful world preem engagement in Brisbane, Australia, is an action film with an amusing gimmick. Toplining Rutger Hauer, as an apparently invincible blind Vietnam vet who wields a samurai sword with consummate skill, pic is light on plot but simply aims to please the action fans. Prospects look promising.

Nick Parker, Hauer's character, is actually based on Zatoichi, the heroic blind samurai who starred in a couple of dozen popular actions films for Japanese company Daiei in the '60s and early '70s. Shintaru Katsu played Zatoichi with skill and humor in the series. Current pic's credits note it's based on a screenplay by Ryozo Kasahara.

First problem for writer Charles Robert Carner is to find a way to Americanize such a character. This is solved by having Parker blinded and lost in action in Vietnam and then trained by friendly Vietnamese to use his other senses to survive. (Why they'd teach him traditional samurai technique remains unanswered.)

Twenty years later, Parker is back in Miami to look up an old army buddy, Frank Deveraux (Terrance O'Quinn) who's in trouble with the mob in Reno. Parker's in time to prevent the kidnaping of Billy (Brandon Call), Frank's son, but not to stop the murder of Frank's ex-wife, Lynn (Meg Foster, in for only one scene) by the vicious Slag, played by Randall

(Tex) Cobb.

The rest of the film is simply a series of fights and chases as Parker heads for Reno to reunite Billy with his father. Parker's senses are so acute that he's more than a match for a seemingly endless stream of gun-toting villains. He can even slice an annoying insect in two with his lightning-fast sword. In the film's obligatory car chase scene, the blind man gets to drive.

Hauer manages to make his miraculous hero more convincing than might have seemed possible, though, of course, these adventures are hardly to be taken seriously, any more than were those of the Japanese prototype. The sword-fight scenes are well staged by Steven Lambert.

The numerous villains in the film are the comic-strip variety, including the maniac duo of Nick Cassavetes and Rick Overton, the very nasty Randall (Tex) Cobb, and Noble Willingham as the chief baddie. Young Brandon Call holds his own, though Lisa Blount's heroine is a perfunctory presence.

Aussie director Phillip Noyce hasn't extended himself with this one, which is a much less interesting film than his "Dead Calm," but which may well have a wider appeal among action aficionados. Noyce handles the material with brisk confidence, and he and editor David Simmons have come up with a commendably concise 85 minutes of almost nonstop action. Other technical credits are fine.

Writer Carner's screenplay contains a few funny lines, like the one in which one of the villains, confronted by a gun-toting old lady, remarks that it was to prevent this kind of situation that he voted for gun control. Who needs guns, anyway, when a blind man can defeat all these bad guys without one? —*Strat.*

The Understudy:
Graveyard Shift II

New York A Cinema Ventures production. Produced by Stephen R. Flaks, Arnold H. Bruck. Supervising producer, Michael Kravitz. Directed by Gerard Ciccoritti. Screenplay, Ciccoritti; camera (Film House color), Barry Stone; editor, Neil Grieve; music, Philip Stern; sound, Gordon Thompson; production design, Ciccoritti; art direction, Nicholas White; assistant director, Tom Willey, production manager, Allan Levine; special makeup effects, Arianne Scova; casting, Roger Mussendun; associate producer, Maurice Visser. Reviewed on Virgin Vision videcassette, N.Y., July 17, 1989. MPAA Rating: R. Running time: **88 MIN.**

Camilla/Patti . . . . Wendy Gazelle
Matthew . . . . Mark Soper
Baissez . . . . Silvio Oliviero
Ash . . . . Ilse Von Glatz
Duke/Larry . . . . Tim Kelleher
Also with: Leslie Kelly, Paul Amato, Carl Alacchi.

■ **This sequel to the 1987 vampire pic dwells on the behind-the-scenes aspects of horror filmmaking. Direct-to-video release should scare up some genre fan interest.**

Silvio Oliviero encores as the real-life vampire who appears on a movie set and replaces the missing leading man (who's actually been killed by one of Oliviero's bitten minions). He causes no end of trouble until the director (Mark Soper) finally figures out he's the real thing. Rather silly plot twist has Soper and Oliviero shooting a game of 9-ball to determine the heroine's fate.

Canadian helmer Gerard Ciccoritti generally eschews humor here, going for a fragmented structure as well as a dark and dour mood. Cast is effective, especially sexy heroine Wendy Gazelle.
—*Lor.*

Babar: The Movie
(CANADIAN-FRENCH-ANIMATED)

Hollywood A New Line Cinema release of a Nelvana-Ellipse production in association with the Clifford Ross Co. Produced by Patrick Loubert, Michael Hirsh, Clive A. Smith. Executive producers, Loubert, Hirsh, Smith, Stephanie Sperry, Pierre Bertrand-Jaume, Yannick Bernard. Directed by Alan Bunce. Screenplay, Peter Sauder, J.D. Smith, John De Klein, Raymond Jaffelice, Bunce, based on a story by Sauder, Loubert, Hirsch. Based on characters created by Jean and Laurent de Brunhoff. Director of animation, John Laurence Collins; picture editor, Evan Landis; voice director, Debra Toffan; music, Milan Kymlicka; production design, Ted Bastien; art direction, Clive Powsey, Carol Bradbury; associate producers, Lenora Hume, Stephan Hodgins; creative consultant, Clifford Ross; casting, Arlene Berman. Reviewed at Sunset Towers screening room, L.A., July 19, 1989. MPAA Rating: G. Running time: **70 MIN.**
Voices of:
King Babar (the elder) . . . . Gordon Pinsent
Boy Babar . . . . Gavin Magrath
Queen Celeste . . . . Elizabeth Hanna
Young Celeste . . . . Sarah Polley
Cornelius . . . . Chris Wiggins
Pompadour . . . . Stephen Ouimette
Zephir . . . . John Stocker
Rataxes . . . . Charles Kerr

■ **An agreeable and nicely animated tale for youngsters, "Babar: The Movie" should do good matinee business worldwide and even better vidcassette rentals based on the familiarity of the well-loved picture book pachyderms.**

Gentle spirit and minimalist drawing style of the original characters created by Parisians Jean and Laurent de Brunhoff is well-preserved, and an unusually good score extends pic's appeal.

Unfortunately, too-familiar storyline is almost as flat as the 1-dimensional elephant drawings, but that may not be a problem for pic's intended audience, who are too young to have seen it all before.

Pic unfolds in the form of a bedtime story told by wise King Babar to his children, describing the origin of the spirited Victory Parade that opens the film. Babar, on his first day as boy king of Elephantland, learns of a rhinocerous attack on a nearby village that is home to his sweetheart, Celeste.

Since none of his elders can fathom the danger, stalwart Babar sets out through the jungle with Celeste to help. Story then follows the tried and true kidpic line of separation from the mother (Celeste's) and a perilous journey toward reunion, with little added dimension.

The young elephants arrive to witness the decimation of Celeste's village and the enslavement of the pastoral pachyderms to the ruthless rhinos.

Celeste, unfortunately, plays the damsel-in-distress and admiring prop for Babar's heroics — not too interesting for young female watchers.

Jungle is full of characters — a wisecracking monkey, an Australian crocodile — who aid Babar's struggle after admiring his brave and generous ways — illustrating the story's basic lessons that one good turn deserves another. friendship is the best policy.

Voices are nicely done, if only mildly interesting. Though far from classic, Babar is no discredit to its storybook origins.

Animation style has a gentle, bouncy appeal, and vivid jungle backdrops and a smart production design make up for the (intentional) flatness of the elephants, who rely mainly on voice, costume and animated use of their trunks for expression. —Daws.

Tainted

New York   A Cardinal Pictures presentation. Produced by Orestes Matacena, Phyllis Redden. Written and directed by Matacena. Camera (TVC color), Ramon Suarez; editor, Stephen Sheppard; music, Hayden Wayne; sound, Phil Pearle; art direction-costume design, Randy Barcelo. Reviewed on South Gate Entertainment vidcassette, N.Y., July 19, 1989. No MPAA Rating. Running time: **93 MIN.**

Cathy Lowell . . . . .Shari Shattuck
Marian . . . . .Park Overall
Frank . . . . .Gene Tootle
Tom . . . . .Magilla Schaus
Rapist . . . . .Blaque Fowler
Principal . . . . .Ross Taylor
Guard . . . . .Ruben Rabasa

■ **An American film noir in the French tradition, "Tainted" is a well-shot and acted thriller that unfortunately relies on too many unbelievable plot pegs.**

Lensed in 1984 in Hendersonville, N.C., pic was planned for theatrical release by Film Concept Group under the title "Body Passion," but surfaces belatedly in vidstores instead.

Shari Shattuck toplines as a smalltown teacher married to mortician Gene Tootle and resented by her sister-in-law Park Overall. Her world falls apart one evening when a prowler (Blaque Fowler) breaks into her home and attacks her. Tootle arrives and kills the prowler in the nick of time, but suffers a fatal heart attack.

Instead of telling the police, Shattuck decides to cover up the incident, fearing smalltown disapproval of her involvement in such violent doings. She successfully stages a mock-death of her husband in his car and buries the rapist in the backyard.

She is forced to involve Overall in the body disposal coverup (in return for ownership of the family mortuary business she's inherited) when workmen start digging up the grounds. Pic climaxes at the crematorium with greedy violence breaking out via Overall and her workman lover, Magilla Schaus.

With echoes of such French classics as "Rider On The Rain" and "Diabolique," filmmaker Orestes Matacena creates some suspenseful sequences, but it's heard to swallow much of the characters' behavior, notably that imposed on Overall's role. Shattuck and Overall (latter now a tv regular on "Empty Nest") are arresting-looking and forceful heroines topping an interesting cast, all of whom bear odd stage names.

Ramon Suarez' cinematography is topnotch. —Lor.

Bille en tête
(Headstrong)
(FRENCH)

Paris   AMLF release of a Carthago Films/Renn Prods./Générale d'Images/FR3 Films coproduction. Produced by Tarak Ben Ammar. Directed by Carlo Cotti. Screenplay, Cotti, Alexandre Jardin, based on latter's novel; camera (color), Jean-Claude Larrieu; editor, Jennifer Auge; music, Jean-Claude Petit; sound, Henri Roux, Jean-Paul Loublier; art direction, Jean-Pierre Clech; assistant director, Jacques Cluzaud; production manager, Bernard Lorain. Reviewed at Marignan-Concorde theater, Paris, July 5, 1989. Running time: **94 MIN.**

Virgile . . . . .Thomas Langmann
Carla . . . . .Kristin Scott-Thomas
L'Arquebuse . . . . .Danièlle Darrieux
Raoul . . . . .Patrick Raynal
Jean . . . . .Michel Albertini

■ **"Bille en tête" is a misfired comedy-drama about a headstrong 16-year-old boy who's in a hurry to grow up, decides to seduce an older married woman and carries it off.**

This variation of "Devil In The Flesh" is based on a book by young novelist Alexandre Jardin, who wrote the script with helmer Carlo Cotti, an opera director and former assistant to Franco Zeffirelli.

Film would be utterly obnoxious without the gracious charm and humor of Kristin Scott-Thomas, who plays the classy young married woman, and Danielle Darrieux as the young upstart's wonderful grandmother.

As the impulsive youth, Thomas Langmann, who was the appealing Jewish orphan in last year's sentimental "The Sandwich Years," is all push and shove but never graduates beyond being a cute nuisance. Pic never recovers from the disbelief caused by Scott-Thomas' rather early surrender to his annoying advances. —Len.

Lawa
(Lava)
(POLISH)

Moscow   A Polish Film Producers' Corp., Perspektywa Unit production. Written and directed by Tadeusz Konwicki, based on a dramatic poem by Adam Mickewicz. Camera (color), Piotr Sobocinski; editor, Elzbieta Kurkowska; music, Zygmunt Konieczny; art direction, Allen Starski. Reviewed at Moscow Film Festival (competing), July 16, 1989. Running time: **125 MIN.**

Pilgrim/Wizard . . . . . . .Maja Komorowska
Poet . . . . .Gustav Holoubek
Gustw-Konrad . . . . .Artur Zmijewski
Senator . . . . .Henryk Bista
Priest . . . . .Tadeusz Lomnicki
Angel . . . . .Grazyna Szapolowska
    Also with: Jolanta Pietek-Gorecka, Teresa Budzisz-Kryzyzanowska, Janusz Michaelowski, Jan Nowicki, Arunas Smajlis, Andrzej Lapicki.

■ **Distinguished Polish writer and filmer Tadeusz Konwicki's has carried out a nobel assignment in "Lava:" filming a national monument of Romantic literature, Adam Mickewicz' dramatic poem "Dziady" (Forefather's Eve).**

Result is a remarkable picture painstakingly shot with an excellent cast skilled in dramatic recital. Unfortunately, it is virtually unwatchable for non-Polish speakers, forced to listen to a rapid-fire, 2-hour reading of the poem in translation (as was done at the Moscow fest). Subtitles seem unusable here. Audiences abroad will be confined to Polish literature students, to whom pic is recommended highly.

Konwicki doesn't limit himself to a slavish visual transcription of a famous work. All through the film, but especially at the end, defiant references are launched to the present. Considering story deals with the loss of Polish independence and the partitioning of the country in the early 19th century, the contemporary comparison is a bitter one indeed.

Mickewicz' poem is considered a masterpiece that embodies the Polish soul in all its religious and moral aims, its impetuous idealism and neuroses. Title "Forefather's Eve" refers to the custom in Lithuania (lost to Russia at the end of the 18th century) of worshiping the memory of dead ancestors who have been killed in battle or some other historical struggle.

On the Day of the Dead, Mickewicz' ghost (Gustaw Holoubek) appears in Vilnius (now in Soviet Lithuania). He remembers when he was a young poet (Artur Zmijewski), the girl he loved, and his imprisonment with a group of Vilnius students who conspired against the Russian Czar, who had partitioned Poland.

A large cast ably led by a magic Maja Komorowska, carries off scenes in the graveyard, in prison and in a glittering salon, where that part of Vilnius' population that has collaborated with the Russians is living the high life.

Here and there images of today's Poland appear in all its workaday hurry, with Grazyna Szapolowska walking through the crowds dressed as a lovely angel. Narrator's final comment wryly notes no Pole today can be surprised at how hard life was in the old days.

Sterling performances from all hands breathe life into the metered lines of Polish dialog. Sets are lavish, editing snappy and imaginative. Score by Zygmunt Konieczny underlines the haunting weight of history. —*Yung*.

Lady Makbet Mtsenskovo Uezda
(Lady Macbeth Of The Mtsensk District) (SOVIET)

Moscow   A Mosfilm Studio production, in association with Mediactuel (Switzerland), Sovinfilm and Sovexportfilm. Directed by Roman Balayan. Screenplay, Balayan, Pavel Finn, based on story by Nikolai Leskov; camera (color), Pavel Lebeshev; music, Yevsei Yevseyev; art direction, Said Menyalschikov, Alexander Samulekin. Reviewed at Moscow Film Festival (market), July 11, 1989. Running time: **81 MIN.**
Katerina Izmailova . . Natalia Andreichenko
Sergei . . . . Alexander Abdulov
   Also with: Nikolai Pastukhov.

■Impressively fresh in Roman Balayan's version of the Leskov story (made into a film, "Siberian Lady Macbeth," in 1962 by Andrzej Wajda) "Lady Macbeth Of The Mtsensk District" has a sophisticated simplicity that should appeal to arthouse audiences.

Set in the 19th century, tale has no apparent link to Shakespeare's Lady Macbeth other than its heroine's ruthless willingness to murder to get what she wants. Married to an old merchant, beautiful Katerina Izmailova (Natalia Andreichenko) leads a bored provincial life till she meets handsome over-

Original Film
Siberska Ledi Magbet
(Siberian Lady Macbeth) (YUGOSLAV-B&W)

Avala Films production and release. With Olivera Markovic, Ljuba Tadic, Bojan Stupica, Miodrag Lazovic. Directed by Andrzej Wajda. Screenplay, Sveta Likic, from novel by Nikolai Leskov; camera (b&w), Alexandre Sekulouic; music, Dmitri Shostakovitch. Reviewed at Cannes Film Festival, May 12, 1964. Running time: **90 MIN.**
Sergei . . . . Olivera Markovic
Wife . . . . Ljuba Tadic
Kulak . . . . Bojan Stupica
Husband . . . . Miodrag Lazovic

seer Sergei (Alexander Abdulov).
   Love so overwhelms Katerina she makes little attempt to hide the affair. When her husband learns of it, she hits him over the head and kills him.
   The lovers are free now to enjoy pastoral romps and rolls in the hay. Alas, Sergei's real interest is money, and when a cute little blond heir turns up, he forces Katerina to kill the child, too.
   Last part of this brief tale is the hardships en route to a penal colony where they are sent. There a humiliated, destroyed Katerina

kills herself and her rival in a splendidly concise finale.
   Natalia Andreichenko's on-target performance gives the heroine dignity in spite of all her vanity and vices. Pavel Lebeshev's cinematography is first-rate.
                            —*Yung*.

Primeriro de Abril, Brasil
(April 1, Brazil) (BRAZILIAN)

Gramado, Brazil   An Embrafilme release of an Estudio Pesquisa e Criacoes production. Produced and directed by Maria Leticia. Screenplay, Leticia, Emiliano Queiroz; camera (color), Edson Santos, Jose Tadeu Ribeiro; editor, Marilia Alvim; music, Sergio Dias, Joao Paulo Mendonca; sound, Hercilia Cardillo; set design, Mixel; costumes, Natalia Stepanenko. Reviewed at Gramado Film Festival, June 12, 1989. Running time: **90 MIN.**
   With: Rosamaria Murtinho, Ida Gomes, Tessy Callado, Maria Leticia, Ana de Fatima, Ticiana Studart, Aline Molinari, Melise Maia, Chico Diaz, Emiliano Qauerioz, Aldizio Abreu, Sergio Otero, Eduardo Lago, Ricardo Blat.

■A metaphor for the Brazilian military coup of 1964 about a women's boarding house, this first feature by Maria Leticia was almost five years in production. Result reflects these difficulties but also inspires laughs and can be helpful for an understanding of modern Brazilian history.

Script by actor and dramaturg Emiliano Queiroz establishes a parallel between the facts that led to the military coup of 1964 and the degrees of power inside the boarding house, where young women fight the severe authority of an old manager.
   Leticia uses tv and newsreel footage to insert the actual characters in the action, achieving good results.
   Final product is fluent and often funny, though by no means sophisticated. A predominantly female cast is efficient despite the fragmented shooting, which involved at least two cinematographers. Editing deals with material shot or collected over several periods of time, and is responsible for the main narrative gimmick, so it becomes almost a character. Editors won an award at Gramado, as did actress Rosamaria Murtinho in the difficult lead role. —*Hoin*.

Perigord noir
(Black Perigord) (FRENCH)

Paris   A UGC release of a Capricorne

Prod./Générale d'Images coproduction. Produced by Joelle Bellon. Directed by Nicolas Ribowski. Screenplay, Philippe Conil; camera (Eastmancolor), Yves Dahan; editor, Pierre Gillette; sound, Roger di Ponio; art direction, Jean-Claude Sevenet; production supervision, Septieme Production; production manager, Philippe Guez. Reviewed at UGC Normandie theater, Paris, July 16, 1989. Running time: **96 MIN.**
Antoine . . . . Roland Giraud
Jean-Tou . . . . Jean Carmet
Adiza . . . . Lydia Galin
Constance . . . . Odette Laure
Victoire . . . . Laurence Semonin
Charles . . . . Jacques Rosny
Amédée . . . . Pierre Vassiliu
Djibril . . . . Robert Liensol
Youssouff . . . . Maka Kotto
Felicien . . . . Jean-Paul Muel

■This mildly amusing racial comedy confronts French rubes and Black Africans who are out to exploit one another for their own ends.

Basic idea of Philippe Conil's original script — it's the Africans who debark intent on colonizing a small economically troubled village — is promising but the development is hesitant and the payoff something of a copout. There are inevitable echoes of recent French hit "Black mic-mac," which pitted African immigrant wits against Paris bureaucracy.

Still, director Nicolas Ribowski has rounded up a good cast and manages to maintain an ambience of unmalicious good humor. The material easily could have backfired into tastelessness.

Plot gets into gear when a college-educated young African beauty (played by newcomer Lydia Galin) hits on a plot to help her friends buy a banana plantation they have been expelled from. Galin hunts up one of her mother's ex-soldier lovers in France and presents herself as his daughter, then has her compatriots brought over. The locals welcome the group as a source of cheap labor while vying for Galin as a potential spouse. In typical comic tradition, all's well that ends well, with a triple mixed marriage as chief compensation.

· Roland Giraud, as Galin's targeted French (sugar) daddy, and Jean Carmet, as the conniving mayor, head the lively cast, which includes Robert Liensol, Odette Laure and songwriter Pierre Vassiliu, who wrote the clever score. Pic was shot entirely in the lovely Perigord region in southwestern France. —*Len*.

Cappuccino
(AUSTRALIAN)

Sydney   A Ronin Films (Australia) release of an Archer Films production. Produced by Anthony Bowman, Sue Wild. Directed by Bowman. Screenplay, Bowman; camera (color), Danny Batterham; editor, Richard Hindley; music, William Motzing; production design, Darrell Lass; sound, Ross Linton; production manager, Sue Wild; assistant director, Corrie Soeterboek. Reviewed at Valhella theater, Glebe, Sydney, July 18, 1989. Running time: **84 MIN.**
Max . . . . John Clayton
Anna French . . . . Rowena Wallace
Maggie Spencer . . . . Jeanie Drynan
Larry . . . . Barry Quin
Celia . . . . Cristina Parker
Bollinger . . . . Ritchie Singer
Nigel . . . . Simon Matthew
   Also with: Ernie Dingo (himself), Saturday Rosenberg (Lulu), Francois Bocquet (Sal).

■A low-budget light comedy about a group of middle-aged actors and their relationships, "Cappuccino" is a modest but appealing film which is getting a Christmas release Down Under and which should find its audience among older, more serious filmgoers at that time of the year.

Overseas theatrical prospects look slight, but it's a natural for the small screen.

The story is narrated by Max (John Clayton) who graduates from being a Sydney taxi driver to standup comic to playwright (after a spell in prison). His friends include ex-lovers Anna (Rowena Wallace) and Maggie (Jeanie Drynan), who stay on good terms even though they're often rivals for the same roles. Anna is the more secure of the two, whereas Maggie, recently divorced and denied custody of her dog, is less sure of herself.

They meet regularly at an inner-city cafe where the titular cappuccino is the favorite beverage. At the outset, Max is dating the much younger, and vulgar, Celia (Cristina Parker) and Anna is involved with Larry (Barry Quin), a star of tv soaps. Soon Larry is shacked up with Celia, and Maggie has found herself a lustful Brazilian who can't speak English.

What amounts to a plot involves a crooked cop (Ritchie Singer) and a videotape showing a VIP in a compromising situation.

Director Anthony Bowman's screenplay contains some bitter jokes about the plight of actors ("If it wasn't for actors there'd be no taxis out there") and other aspects of showbiz (the audition, the tv commercial, the member of the public who identifies an actor too closely with the role he's playing). Some of the jokes are a bit "in," but older audiences should relish this inside look at the private lives of rather ordinary, unglamorous, thesps.

The cast is good, with Rowena Wallace and Jeanie Drynan standouts as the friendly rivals. Bowman writes and directs with affection for his characters. Technical credits are passable.

Though it may not set the world afire, "Cappuccino" is a likeable film filled with chuckles. It will have to be well marketed to compete against bigger product out in the marketplace. —*Strat.*

La Barbare
(The Savage)
(FRENCH)

Paris Films Number One release of a CTV/TF1 Films/SGGC coproduction. Produced by Norbert Saada. Line producer for Tunisia, Carthago Films. Directed by Mireille Darc. Screenplay, Darc, Jean Curtelin, Catherine Cohen, based on novel by Katherine Pancol; camera (Fujicolor), Claude Agostini; editor, Jacques Witta; music, Jean Marie Senia; sound, Alain Curvelier, Jean Paul Loublier; art direction, Claude Bouvard; technical advisor, Marc Angelo; assistant director, Serge Dupuy-Malbray; production manager, Michel Bernède; associate producers, Norbert Chalon, Jacques Bokobsa; casting, Shula Siegfried. Reviewed at Georges V cinema, Paris, June 19, 1989. Running time: **88 MIN.**
Michael . . . . Murray Head
Alice . . . . Angela Molina
Sophie . . . . Aurélie Gibert

■ "La Barbare" is a drab variation on the husband-wife-mistress triangle. Actress Mireille Darc's filmmaking debut has some colorful Tunisian backgrounds but limited dramatic range as middle-aged hubbie and teen lover go through on-again/off-again rituals that leave him wasted and her cured of a childhood trauma.

British singer Murray Head and Angela Molina are the (dubbed) leads, a couple with a solid home relationship and a successful medical clinic in Tunisia. Their undoing is to welcome the 17-year-old daughter of a just-deceased friend and neighbor who had abandoned wife and child years earlier. Girl (newcomer Aurélie Gibert) returns their hospitality by seducing Head. He lets his marriage and practice go to seed as he invests himself deeper into the fling, which for Gibert is a way of getting even with her dead dad.

Script by Darc and Jean Curtelin, based on a local bestseller, limns the young girl's psychosexual range with clichés, though

Gibert's tart aggressiveness has convincing heat. Head and Molina are less lucky with thin characterizations that wear thinner with the repetitive situations.

Film was reportedly shot in double English-French tracks. English version, not seen here, apparently is for foreign markets. —*Len.*

Jadup und Boel
(Jadup And Boel)
(EAST GERMAN)

Moscow A DEFA Film, Babelsberg Group production. Directed by Rainer Simon. Screenplay, Paul Kanut Schafer, based on his novel; camera (Orwocolor), Roland Dressel; editor, Helga Gentz; music, Rainer Bredemeyer; art direction, Hans Poppe. Reviewed at Moscow Film Festival (competing), July 17, 1989. Running time: **102 MIN.**
Jadup . . . . Kurt Bowe
Boel . . . . Katrin Knappe
Barbara . . . . Gudrun Ritter
Mrs. Martin . . . . Kathe Reichel
Max . . . . Timo Jacob
Also with: Franciszek Pieczka, Michael Gwisdek, Horst Lebinsky, Rolf Martin-Kruckenberg, Christian Bowe, Inga Kaltenhauder, Uta Rachfuss, Susanne Wisniewski.

■ Shown at the Moscow Fest after being on the shelf between 1981 and 1987, "Jadup And Boel" is a subtle work of mainly local interest. There is little that is obviously controversial in the film, besides the irregular life the town mayor (a Party man) leads.

Jadup, the mayor (Kurt Bowe), is a little too outspoken for comfort and often is called on the carpet by the small town's Party leaders. Rumors are flying about his relationship to a strange girl named Boel (Katrin Knappe) he knew many years ago.

She was raped and her rapist never caught — was it Jadup or — uncomfortable but more plausible — a Russian soldier? Now Boel has disappeared, and some even speculate he killed her.

All this is told in enigmatic flashbacks integrated with Jadup's life today: his understanding wife (Gudrun Ritter), his impatient teenage son Max (Timo Jacob), preparations for celebrating the town's 800th anni. Jadup is forced to take a critical look at himself and those around him, and in doing so succeeds in growing closer to his son.

Pic is alternately intriguing and involuted, leaving a mixed taste. It will appeal more to highbrows than emotional viewers. Editing is swift and mixes the stories well. Lensing is fine. —*Yung.*

Lady Avenger

New York A Marco Colombo presentation. (Intl. sales, Filmtrust.) Executive producer, Colombo. Produced by John Schouweiler, David DeCoteau. Directed by DeCoteau. Screenplay, Will Schmitz, Keith Kaczorek; camera (Foto-Kem color), Thomas Callaway; editor, Miriam L. Preissel; co-editor, Mary Schmitz; music, Jay Levy; sound, D.J. Ritchie; production design, Royce Mathew; production manager, Ellen Cabot; assistant director, Nigel Parker; stunt coordinator-2d unit director, John Stewart; associate producers, Thomas Keith, Saranne Rothberg, Christian Halsey. Reviewed on South Gate Entertainment vidcassette, N.Y., July 11, 1989. MPAA Rating: R. Running time: **82 MIN.**
Maggie Blair . . . . Peggie Sanders
Jack . . . . Tony Josephs
Mary . . . . Jacolyn Leeman
Annaline . . . . Michelle Bauer
Ray . . . . Daniel Hirsch
Kevin . . . . Bill Butler
Also with: Rodger Hurt, Steve Artiaga, Billy Frank, Adam Englund, Mike Jacobs Jr.

■ "Lady Avenger" is a direct-to-video release of an off-beat woman vigilante pic from director David DeCoteau, who's usually involved in fantasy projects.

Peggie Sanders, distinctively styled with shades and tight t-shirt, is the marauding lady who has escaped from prison and is after the L.A. gang that murdered her brother. Pic holds out genre promise of a "Colors" at outset but soon downplays the gang aspect as Sanders gradually finds out that her corrupt stepdad (Tony Josephs) and her best friend (DeCoteau regular Michelle Bauer) have dirty hands.

Besides Sanders' adept action performance, Bauer (billed here with her alternate moniker Michelle McClellan) is impressive in a character role that still finds excuses for sexploitation footage. Director's usual black humor is eschewed in favor of melodrama played straight. —*Lor.*

Ijintachi Tono Natsu
(The Discarnates)
(JAPANESE)

Moscow A Shochiku Eizo Co. Ltd. production and release. Executive producer, Shigemi Sugisaki. Directed by Nobuhiko Obayashi. Screenplay, Shinichi Ichikawa, from Taichi Yamada's novel; camera (color), Yoshihisa Sakamoto; music, Masatsugu Shinozaki; art direction, Kazuo Satsuya. Reviewed at the Moscow Film Festival (competing), July 17, 1989. Running time: **109 MIN.**
Harada . . . . Morio Kazama
Mother . . . . Kumiko Akiyoshi
Father . . . . Tsurutaro Kataoka
Kei . . . . Yuko Natori
Mamiya . . . . Toshiyuki Nagashima

■ "The Discarnates" is a modern-day ghost story that doesn't quite make it. Essentially

a 1-idea film, it elaborates the fantasy of a 40-year-old man meeting his dead parents. Well-lensed, it might drum arthouse interest.

Film played in Los Angeles in January at the Little Tokyo Cinema.

Harada (Morio Kazama) is a tv writer who has moved into a lonely, isolated apartment after a divorce. When a beautiful neighbor appears in desperate need of company, he cruelly sluffs her off. The next day, however, Harada's nasty personality is transformed into that of reverent son, when he stumbles cross Mom and Dad — who were killed when he was a boy — living in their old house, and younger than he is.

The pair must qualify as the most clean-cut, wholesome ghosts on film. Soon Harada has gotten over his surprise and is playing catch with Pop and having his back rubbed by Mom. At the same time, he starts romancing his good-looking neighbor.

Rules of the Japanese ghost story seem to require Harada to pay for his ghostly affections by growing prematurely old, although it is only apparent when he looks in a mirror. Harada's friends beg him to get more rest, and his girlfriend finally forces him to bid Mom and Dad adieu. It does him little good, because she herself is a ghost, having committed gory suicide the night he rebuffed her.

A pal saves him in pic's best scene, an unexpected bit of bloody horror that offers a nice climax.

Helmer Nobuhiko Obayashi is a prolific pro who lenses well. Cinematography is first-rate, thesps attractive. Most interesting because she's the most consistent, is Harada's lover (Yuko Natori), a mysterious and tragic being in a film peopled mostly by cheerful 1950s characters. —*Yung.*

Revenge Of The Living Zombies

New York An H&G Films Ltd. production. (Intl. sales, Cinevest.) Executive producer, David Gordon. Supervising producer-production manager, Andrew Sands. Produced and directed by Bill Hinzman. Screenplay, Bill Randolph, Hinzman, from story by Hinzman; camera (color), Simon Manses; editor, Paul McCollough, Hinzman; music, Erica Portnoy; sound, Deborah Cottrill, Greg Kellerman; special makeup effects, Gerald Gergely; associate producer, Manses. Reviewed on Magnum Entertainment vidcassette, N.Y., July 12, 1989. MPAA Rating: R. Running time: **84 MIN.**
Flesh Eater . . . . Bill Hinzman
Bob . . . . John Mowood
Sally . . . . Leslie Ann Wick

Ralph . . . . Kevin Kindlin
Eddie . . . . James J. Rutan
Also with: Denise Morrone, Charles Kirkpatrick Acuff, Lisa Smith, Mark Strycula, Rik Billock, David A. Sodergren, Kathleen Marie Rupnik, Matthew C. Danilko, David Ashby, Susan Marie Spier.

■ "Revenge Of The Living Zombies" is a 20-years-after tribute to George A. Romero's "Night Of The Living Dead," made by one of the pic's zombie thesps, Bill Hinzman. Gory direct-to-video release is aimed at cult fans.

Shot in the Pittsburgh area (as was the original), pic has Hinzman literally rising from the ground to reprise his role as "Flesh Eater" (pic's alternate title). He attacks two sets of partying teens on Halloween, turning them into flesh-eating ghouls.

Several scenes, notably a siege at a farmhouse and the mistaken-identity finale, are direct re-dos of the Romero film. Hinzman also stresses that pic's invention that the sure way to destroy a zombie is to shoot it in the head.

Some of the thesping here is amateurish, but pic generally achieves its modest aims. —Lor.

Bye Bye Baby
(ITALIAN)

New York A Seymour Borde & Associates release of a Reteitalia presentation of an Intl. Dean Film production. Executive producer, Tony Renis. Produced by Pio Angeletti, Adriano De Michelli. Directed by Enrico Oldoini. Screenplay, Liliana Betti, Paolo Costella, Oldoini, from story by Oldoini; camera (Image Transform color), Giuseppe Ruzzolini; editor, Raimondo Crociani; music, Manuel De Sica; sound (Dolby), Robert E. Forrest; art direction-costume design, Luciano Sagoni; production manager, Mario D'Alessio; assistant director, Costella. Reviewed on Prism Entertainment vidcassette, N.Y., July 20, 1989. MPAA Rating: R. Running time: 85 MIN.
Sandra . . . . Carol Alt
Paolo . . . . Luca Barbareschi
Lisa . . . . Brigitte Nielsen
Marcello . . . . Jason Connery
Daria . . . . Alba Parietti
Also with: Paul A. Royd, Bruno Mori.
(English soundtrack)

■ Carol Alt makes a good impression toplining in "Bye Bye Baby," the first of her series of recent Italian films to be released theatrically in the U.S. Unfortunately, the romantic comedy is too corny to score a breakthrough.

Alt plays a Milanese doctor married to rich guy Luca Barbareschi, their marriage seemingly breaking up with a fight during the opening credits (as Marilyn Monroe sings "Bye Bye Baby" from "Gentlemen Prefer Blondes" on the tv).

After dallying romantically with friend of the family Alba Parietti, Barbareschi takes up with sexy billiards player Brigitte Nielsen, while Alt becomes involved with fellow doctor Jason Connery. Pic skips along at several-year intervals charting the couple's reconciliations and breakups, usually accompanied by rainstorms.

Chief gimmick involves Barbareschi's hokey attempts, during a vacation at Club Med in Mauritius, to fix up Connery with Nielsen so that he can ride off into the sunset with his estranged wife.

Excellent handling of English dialog by the entire principal cast makes this way above par for an Italian production aiming at mid-Atlantic audiences. Unfortunately, that dialog is frequently pretentious or old-fashioned, missing the wit of its Hollywood forebears.

Cast can't be faulted, with Alt a glamorous and feisty heroine, matched by Barbareschi's shaggy-dog appeal. Nielsen is far more natural in her acting and delivery than in her U.S. films, though she doesn't come across convincingly at the dramatic climax (when she finds out Barbareschi has been two-timing her). Connery, son of Diane Cilento and Sean Connery, adds to the idealized look aimed for by filmmaker Enrico Oldoini. Lensing by Giuseppe Ruzzolini is quite pretty, with okay songs warbled by Phyllis Rhodes and Nielsen on the soundtrack. —Lor.

Le Crime d'Antoine
(The Crime Of Antoine)
(FRENCH)

Paris A Capital-Cinéma release of a Cathala Prods./CTV/TF 1 Films coproduction. Produced by Norbert Saada. Directed by Marc Rivière. Screenplay, Rivière, Dominique Roulet, based on Roulet's novel; camera (Fujicolor), Claude Agostini; editor, Jacques Witta; music, Charlélie Courture, Tom Novembre; sound, Philippe Loioret, Jean-Paul Loublier; art direction, Alain Gaudry; production manager, Bernard P. Guirmand; assistant director, Philippe Besnier. Reviewed at Saint Lazare Pasquier theater, Paris, July 15, 1989. Running time: 84 MIN.
Antoine Bourjois . . . . Tom Novembre
Lea . . . . Catherine Wilkening
Julien . . . . Jacques Weber
Jean . . . . Patrick Timsit
Marc . . . . Stéphane Jobert
Pilou . . . . Yves Robert

■ This is a routine thriller that is better than most in the intelligent handling of situation, dialog and actors.

Scripter Dominique Roulet, who adapted his own novel, and first-time helmer Marc Rivière have concentrated their energies on providing credible personages who generate dramatic interest and

suspense, rather than dropping human marionnettes into a contrived plot. Still, the makers don't provide enough wrinkles on a formula mystery to give this far-reaching commercial prospects.

"Le Crime d'Antoine" is superficially indebted to "Vertigo." Tom Novembre is a young composer whose wedding day ends in tragedy when his beloved is fatally electrocuted. Two years later he has not recovered from the loss and is morbidly intrigued by an ad placed by a woman with the same first name as his lost love. He responds, goes to a rendezvous and meets a girl who is the spitting image of his bride (both are played by Catherine Wilkening).

Romance blossoms predictably but Novembre is disturbed by Wilkening's mysterious comings and goings, her frequent no-shows for dates, and chronic lying. Trailing her one day to an antique shop, he gets wind of her shady connection with shop owner Jacques Weber and his sidekick Stéphane Jobert. The lovestruck Novembre only comes to realize the implications of his relationship when he finally takes off with Wilkening and her supposed five-year-old daughter.

Novembre, a lanky pop singer-actor with Buster Keaton eyes and a seductive voice, is fine as the protagonist desperate not to lose the love of his life a second time. Wilkening's darkly passionate mystery lady is both disturbing and sympathetic.

Jacques Weber and Stéphane Jobert strike some sinister sparks off their mostly stock charactizations. Newcomer Patrick Timsit is winning as Novembre's pal.

Actors are aided by Roulet's sober, well-turned dialog and Rivière's attentive direction. Tech credits are good. —Len.

Sadoth Yerukim
(Green Fields)
(ISRAELI)

Jerusalem A Ruty production. Produced by David Torr. Written and directed by Itzhak Zeppel Yeshurun. Camera (color), Gadi Danzig; editor, Tova Asher; music, Adi Renert; sound, David Liss; art direction, Sophie and Skachav Bar-Adon. Reviewed at Jerusalem Film Festival, July 3, 1989. Running time: 90 MIN.
With: Shmuel Shilo, Lya Dulizkaya, Ruth Harlap, Shmuel Edelman, Amit Leor, Sharon H. Brandon.

■ Itzhak Zeppel Yeshurun tackles here the most sensitive and controversial subject in Israel, the uprising in the Occupied

Territories, the first one to do so in an Israeli fiction film.

Yeshurun places three generations of Israelis at the heart of the confrontation. They are on their way to a military base on the West Bank. Through a series of circumstances which do not always make much sense, they are stuck there and have to find their way back.

Yeshurun, who deals only with the Israeli side of the conflict, is horrified at the sight of the emotional change taking place in his compatriots as a result of the political situation. The Arab presence throughout the film is limited to the background, a constant threat that is spelled out only once, but is felt all the time.

The characters are neatly divided by their age. The old farmer and his wife are the idealists who came to Israel in order to build a different kind of society; their roots are deep in the land they work. Their son belongs to the consumerist era: He has left Israel to make money in America and is back for a visit with his American wife. The grandson, a soldier, and his girlfriend are of today's generation — confused, frustrated, neglected and unloved.

The film is a series of explosive clashes with no respite between them, directed, acted and shot in naturalistic fashion. The plot, however, is clearly intended as an allegory for the human and political condition of Israel today.

While the women are relatively more restrained, none of the male parts succeeds in eliciting sympathy. The most problematic of them is the prodigal son (Shmuel Edelman) who refuses to come home for good from America. Edelman plays it on a hysterical level.

The late cinematographer Gadi Danzig (killed in May while shooting a Cannon film in the Philippines) stressed the almost documentary authenticity of the scenes, which, taken separately, probably could work better than put together, one next to the other. No doubt this is a relevant film, but a hard one to take. —Edna.

Dasi
(A Bonded Woman)
(INDIAN)

Moscow A Little India production, sponsored by Doordarshan Tv. Produced by B. Ramachandra Rao. Written and directed by B. Narsing Rao. Camera (color), A.K. Bir; editor, D. Rajagopal; music, B. Narsing Rao; art direction, T. Vaikuntam. Reviewed at Moscow Film Festival (competing), July 15, 1989.

Running time: **94 MIN.**
Kamalakshi . . . . .Archana
(Soundtrack in Telegu)

■ **Judged best Telegu film of 1988 and awarded national prizes for lensing, art direction, and costumes, "Dasi" (A Bonded Woman) stands out in the crass commercial panorama of the Telegu film industry.**

Tale about a child sold as a slave to a family of landowners in the 1920s is a serious, well-lensed work. It is too monotone to take off as a film, but has plenty of color for exotica shoppers.

Misfortune after misfortune are piled onto the frail shoulders of dark-skinned beauty Kamalakshi (played by rising actress Archana). She weeps over her lot of being sold for a handful of rupees to become part of a rich lady's dowry.

The wife is so spoiled she expects Kamalakshi even to wash her face. The husband expects sexual availability day and night, and isn't put off by his wife stumbling onto them. In between pampering the lord and lady, Kamalakshi is given 1,000 endless chores.

When guests drop by, the lord hands the household's bonded woman over to them for the evening. Kamalakshi submits in silent anguish to it all. She gets pregnant and struggles to keep the baby, but they remind her she has no right to have a child of her own. Her voice is heard at last in a wrenching scream during an abortion.

If the heroine's exploitation is outrageous, her resigned submission makes it hard to identify with her closely. Archana plays the "dasi" as a miserable, voiceless victim, far too intimately caught up in the system to rebel against it.

Film is sprinkled with lots of exotica, from local ways of running the household to the lady's beauty treatments, folk dancing, local musicians and fighters. Story hardly exists; film just goes from one humiliation to another. Music is by the director. —*Yung.*

Mentiras Piadosas
(White Lies)
(MEXICAN)

Moscow A Filmicas Internacionales-Fondo de Apoyo production. Directed by Arturo Ripstein. Screenplay, Paz Alicio, Garcia Diego; camera (color), Carlos Fuente; music, Lucio Alvarez; art direction, Juan Jose Urbini. Reviewed at Moscow Film Festival (competing), July 11, 1989. Running time: **116 MIN.**
With: Delio Casanova, Alonso Echanove, Ernesto Yanes, Luiga Huertas.

■ **Arturo Ripstein paints a fresh and curious picture of love in the lower depths in "White Lies." The overwhelmingly sordid love affair between a health inspector and a grocer has a gritty true-to-life feel, but is still emotionally moving. It should be a good art-house pickup.**

Israel is a little man with a small store, always being fined. He has a nagging wife and three hungry kids, one of whom is blind. His passion is constructing a mechanical exhibit of store dummies wearing traditional Mexican costumes, which he is making with his buddy "Mathilde," a fat, gentle man with a taste for boys.

Clara meets Israel when she comes to his store to fine him. She returns to have her fortune told (Israel's sideline) and later ends up in bed with him. Unhappy with her husband, Clara finds passion and love with the grocer. They decide to leave spouses and kids in order to live together.

Their dream of love is crushed under daily problems, guilt feelings about leaving their families and Israel's pathological jealousy. Ending is bleak but not hopeless, as plans are laid for life to go on.

Ripstein fills the screen with rich detail and convincing clutter. The little motorized exhibit, which Israel and Mathilde dream of selling to some rich gringo for an ethnic museum, is the height of kitsch, in poignant contrast to its makers' very genuine enthusiasm. Clara and Israel's homes are masterpieces of overcrowding.

"Lies" boldly depicts love-making between two not very attractive people and manages to be moving rather than comic. Principals are finely cast. —*Yung.*

Evil Altar

New York A Ryan Rao presentation of an Om production. Executive producer, Rao. Produced by Robert A. Miller, George L. Briggs. Directed by Jim Winburn. Additional scenes directed by Rao. Screenplay, Brend Friedman, Scott Rose, Jon Geilfuss; camera (Foto-Kem color), Peter Wolf; editor, Rick Mitchell; music, Bruce Lowe, Briggs; sound (Ultra-Stereo), Paul Coogan; art direction, Gary Bentley; additional camera, Howard Anderson 3d; coproducer, Merlin Miller; associate producer, Chris Eguia. Reviewed on South Gate Entertainment vidcassette, N.Y., July 15, 1989. MPAA Rating: R. Running time: **87 MIN.**
Reed Weller . . . . .William Smith
Collector . . . . .Pepper Martin
Sheriff O'Connell . . . . .Robert Zdar
Teri Connors . . . . .Theresa Cooney
Daley Long . . . . .Tal Armstrong
Also with: David Campbell, Jack Vogel, Connie Lolan, Lee Nicht.

■ **Satanism rears its head once more in "Evil Altar," a direct-to-video release with few new wrinkles for the genre.**

William Smith portrays a guy who's sold his soul and become powerful enough to run the little town of Red Rock. He's sent his minion (Pepper Martin) to collect 103 young souls for sacrifice.

With burly local cop Robert Zadar under Smith's spell, the disappearance of various youngsters is covered up until a visiting lawyer (Tal Armstrong) teams up with locals to root out the evil.

Pic suffers from meager special effects, including a poorly done climax in which heroine Theresa Cooney is threatened in her bedroom by a floating ball reminiscent of "Phantasm." Bald-pated Smith makes a solid villain. —*Lor.*

Los Dias del Cometa
(The Days Of The Comet)
(SPANISH)

Barcelona A Tornasol Films, Aiete Films, Ariño P.C. production. Executive producer, Gerardo Herrero. Written and directed by Luis Ariño. Camera (Agfa color), José Luis López Linares; editor, Juan San Mateo; music, Alejandro Masso; sets, Gonzalo Polo; sound, Miguel Angel Polo. Reviewed at Barcelona Film Festival, July 9, 1989. Running time: **77 MIN.**
Aurora . . . . .Maribel Verdú
Samuel . . . . .Antonio Dechent
Paloma . . . . .Carmen Conesa
Montero . . . . .Nacho Martínez
Also with: Abel Folk, Pep Molina, Mario Gas, Mireya Ross, Terele Pávez.

■ **Most of this rambling pic seems to be a pretext for showing pretty young Spanish thesp Maribel Verdú disporting with various lovers in bedroom scenes.**

Her obsession with a comet which presages evil and other sidereal mumbo jumbo is loosely linked to a tale of the Madrid underworld, with the usual doses of prostitution, drugs and violence.

Aurora takes up with a shady macho man she meets in a cafe, who promptly becomes her pimp. She seems to string along more for the fun of it than out of necessity. Among her assignations is a wealthy weirdo who gets his kicks more from morphine than sex, and who also seems to nurture a death fixation.

The girl, under the influence of the stars, bops about from the pimp, to the weirdo, to a struggling painter who is more interested in her soul than her body, though he does not disdain sampling the latter.

Following a fatal mishap, the pimp has to blow town, leaving his young protégé free to cavort with the artist in search of true love. The girl's real nemesis is the guy with the morphone syringes, who finally invites her to the ultimate oblivion.

Clumsy dialog, halfhearted sex scenes and a diffuse story probably will limit pic's commercial future to a very brief run in Spanish houses. —*Besa.*

Montoyas y Tarantos
(SPANISH)

Madrid A Comunicacion Visual Creativa production. Produced by Teo Escamilla. Directed by Vicente Escrivá. Screenplay, Escrivá, Alfredo Mañas; camera (Agfa color), Escamilla; editor, José Antonio Rojo; music, Paco de Lucia; sets, Alfonso López; special effects, Carlos de Marchi; sound, Antonio Bloch. Reviewed at Tecnison screening room, Madrid, July 3, 1989. (In Montreal Film Festival, competing.) Running time: **103 MIN.**
Maria La Taranta . . . . .Cristina Hoyos
Antonio Montoya . . . . .Sancho Gracia
Manuel Taranto . . . . .Juan Paredes
Ana Montoya . . . . . .Esperanza Campuzano
Also with: Juan Antonio Jiménez, José Sancho, Mercedes Sampietro, Queta Claver, Antonio Canales, Daniel Martin, Carlos Torrescusa, Carmen Encalado, Jesús Bernabé.

■ **This handsome remake of "Los Tarantos" should please flamenco enthusiasts, thanks to some superb dance numbers, outstanding music by Paco de Lucia and an effective retelling of the Romeo and Juliet story set in a gypsy milieu.**

Veteran Spanish helmer Vicente Escrivá handles yarn as a poetic fable, getting off to a rousing start with a stylized street fight between the Montoyas and the Tarantos which turns into a memorable flamenco dancing duel between the rival families.

Story pretty well follows the classic lines, with son and daughter of each respective family falling in love with each other. Their love is thwarted by the boy's proud, intransigent father, well played by Sancho Gracia, while the girl's mother tries in vain to make peace between the feuding families.

Though the poetic ending of the two lovers on an isolated beach is followed by an unconvincing shootout (in which the girl's family members take revenge on those who have brought tragedy upon both families), most of pic is solidly made. Major attractions are the music and dancing.

Technical credits are excellent, with fine choreography by Cristina Hoyos and crisp cinematography by Teo Escamilla, who also produced the film. —*Besa.*

Dans la nuit
(In The Night)
(FRENCH-B&W)

La Rochelle A Cinémathèque Française restoration and presentation of a Fernand Weill production and release (1929-30). Written and directed by Charles Vanel. Camera (b&w), Georges Asselin, Marc Bujard, Gaston Brun, Henri Stuckert; sets, Armand Bonamy; assistant director, Jean Cassagne. First released in Paris May 31, 1930. Reviewed at the La Rochelle Film Festival, July 7, 1989. Length: 5,933 ft. Running time (at 20 frames per second): **79 MIN.**
The worker ....Charles Vanel
His wife.............Sandra Milowanoff

■One of those films you won't find in any of the standard film history books, "Dans la nuit" was the first and only feature film directed by actor Charles Vanel, who died recently.

Shot silent in 1929 as the talkies were taking over, it is a brilliant tour de force that heralded Vanel as a talent to reckon with. Unfortunately, nobody noticed this commercially antiquated picture when it opened in 1930. Vanel directed a short film two years later at the Pathé-Natan studios, where he was under contract, but clearly his heart was no longer in it.

"Dans la nuit" has little in the way of innovation, but Vanel brilliantly employs all the means of the silent art, which had reached its acme of expression. Vanel sets out to dazzle the filmgoer and keep him on tenterhooks, and largely succeeds.

The story might have been taken from the Grand Guignol repertory. A newly wed quarry worker, played by Vanel, has his face so hideously mutilated in a work accident that he must wear a mask so as not to repel his young wife (Sandra Milowanoff, a Russian émigré actress who was phased out of pictures by sound). She eventually gives in to the advances of another laborer who visits here when Vanel is at work.

Climactic scene pits husband and lover, who has donned another mask to escape recognition. The two fight, Vanel apparently is killed, and his body dumped in a quarry pit. But Milowanoff gets the fright of her life when she again is alone with her "lover."

Vanel breaks his film into two different sections, two different moods. The first part is set on the couple's wedding day and uses mobile camera and virtuoso editing to capture the sunlit holiday spirit and the accompanying popular fête in a mining village. With the accident, the picture darkens into terrifying chiaroscuro effects and moves inexorably towards its horrific conclusion.

Unfortunately the original distrib desperately tacked on a happy ending (it was just a dream!) but the film did screen at specialized houses with its original grim climax, which is how it should be seen today. Superb restoration by the Cinémathèque Française includes the trite coda, which should be removed from show prints out of respect for the film Vanel conceived.

Stunning location photography was the work of at least four ace silent film lensers Georges Asselin, Gaston Brun, Marc Bujard and Henri Stuckert.—*Len.*

Les Misérables
(FRENCH-B&W)

Paris A Pathé-Cinéma presentation of a Pathé-Natan production (1933). Produced by Emile Natan. Directed by Raymond Bernard. Screenplay, Bernard, André Lang, from novel by Victor Hugo; camera (b&w), Jules Kruger; editor, Charlotte Guilbert, music, Arthur Honegger, under Maurice Jaubert's direction; sets, Jean Perrier; costumes, Paul Colin; sound, Antoine Archimbaud; makeup, Vladimir Tourjansky; assistant director, Lucien Grunberg; production manager, André Gargour. First released by Pathé Consortium Cinéma in three parts, "Une Tempete sous un crane," "Les Thenardiers" and "Liberté, liberté, chérie," Feb. 9, 16, 23, 1934. Reviewed at Cinémathèque Française, Paris, June 1, 1989. Running time (restored version): **280 MIN.**
Jean Valjean ....Harry Baur
Inspector Javert ....Charles Vanel
Thenardier ....Charles Dullin
Mme. Thenardier .....Marguerite Moreno
Fantine......................Florelle
Cosette ....Josselyne Gael
Marius ....Jean Servais
Cosette (child) ....Gaby Triquet
Gillenormand ....Max Dearly
Enjolras ....Robert Vidalin
Eponine ....Orane Demazis

■**Rather than unearth its abominable 1957 Technicolor version starring Jean Gabin — as was done in Gotham just recently — French major Pathé-Cinéma would do better to revive its rare 1933 adaptation of "Les Misérables," which certainly is the finest of the many screen adaptations of the Victor Hugo classic.**

That it was made in glorious black & white should not keep it from selected overseas repertory arthouse exposure.

With his gift for blending the intimate and the large-scale, it was only natural that Raymond Bernard be assigned to direct this 5-hour super production of Hugo's novel, which Pathé had already filmed twice — and memorably — in silent form in 1912 and 1925.

Bernard made the perfect choices for collaborators. Critic-turned-scripter André Lang helped him reshape Hugo's unwieldy and frequently ludicrous plot into a smoothly articulated screenplay that preserved both the melodramatic armature and the historical timeframe. Bernard's long-time art director Jean Perrier rebuilt the Paris of 1832 on a stretch of land outside Antibes.

Jules Kruger, who shot "Wooden Crosses" for Bernard — not to mention Abel Gance's "Napoleon" — was brought back to provide the master lighting (Kruger here systematized the use of the tilt shot, which quickly became a cliché). Arthur Honegger was commissioned to compose the broodingly powerful music (arranged incidentally, by the no less brilliant Maurice Jaubert).

A magnificent cast incarnates Hugo's beloved gallery of larger-than-life fictional creations. Harry Baur is a Jean Valjean for all times. No actor before or since has conveyed the emotional and spiritual dimensions of the brutish convict who becomes a secular saint. His death scene remains an example of the finest film acting. Opposite him, Charles Vanel deploys equal subtlety in the more monolithic role of Javert, the implacable cop who has made Valjean's capture the goal of his career.

The famous stage actor-director Charles Dullin is a memorably grotesque Thenardier, as twisted in body and voice as he is in mind. Florelle, a music hall singer turned actress, is effectively heartbreaking in the seduced and abandoned Fantine. Jean Servais is a romantic, rich-voiced Marius, while the irrepressible Max Dearly plays his sprightly royalist grandfather Gillenormand with wonderful eccentric humor.

Henry Krauss, the great silent actor who in 1912 was the first Jean Valjean, here plays Monseigneur Myriel, the saintly ecclesiastic who catalyzes Valjean's spiritual redemption.

From the unforgettable opening image — the superhumanly mighty Valjean shouldering a grotesque caryatid into place on a building facade — Bernard captures the Hugolian spirit and bears it forward in a measured, hypnotic rhythm. Though the narrative falters on occasion in the first two sections, the action opens to its full breadth as the characters are embroiled in the 1832 Revolution.

Here Bernard's mastery of sweeping spectacle explodes in the romantic description of the tumultuous fighting at the barricades, and out-Hollywoods Hollywood.

"Les Misérables" was released in France in 1934 in three separately shown films, but was clumsily reduced to a 200-minute version (in two parts) in 1944. This latter cut, disowned by Bernard and André Lang, remained the only available one until the 1970s, when Pathé invited Bernard to reconstruct the original negative for French tv airings (one key scene, detailing Valjean's theft of the churchman's candlesticks, still is missing).

Unfortunately Pathé continues to peddle the shorter version commercially, so fests, tv stations and arthouses who want "Les Miz" should take care to insist on the original 3-film version and not the Readers Digest-style recut. —*Len.*

Parenthood

Hollywood A Universal Pictures release of an Imagine Entertainment production. Produced by Brian Grazer. Executive producer, Joseph M. Caracciolo. Directed by Ron Howard. Screenplay, Lowell Ganz, Babaloo Mandel, based on story by Ganz, Mandel, Howard; camera (Deluxe color), Donald McAlpine; editor, Michael Hill, Daniel Hanley; music, Randy Newman; production design, Todd Hallowell; art direction, Christopher Nowak; set decoration, Nina Ramsey; costume design, Ruth Morley; sound (Dolby), Richard C. Church; assistant director, Joe Napolitano; 2d unit director, Walter Von Huene. Reviewed at Samuel Goldwyn theater, L.A., July 24, 1989. MPAA Rating: PG-13. Running time: **124 MIN.**
Gil .Steve Martin
Karen . . . . .Mary Steenburgen
Helen . . . . .Dianne Wiest
Frank . . . . .Jason Robards
Nathan . . . . .Rick Moranis
Larry . . . . .Tom Hulce
Julie . . . . .Martha Plimpton
Tod . . . . .Keanu Reeves
Susan . . . . .Harley Kozak
David Brodsky . . . . .Dennis Dugan
Gerry . . . . .Leaf Phoenix
Marilyn . . . . .Eileen Ryan
Grandma . . . . .Helen Shaw
Kevin . . . . .Jason Fisher
George Bowman . . . . .Paul Linke

■An ambitious, keenly observed, and often very funny look at one of life's most daunting passages, "Parenthood" is likely to sweep the Baby Boom generation like nothing since "The Big Chill."

Though a syrupy ending and some saccharine twists nearly sink it, pic has enough impressively good moments to keep 'em lined up at the boxoffice well into the fall.

Film's masterstroke is that it covers the range of the family experience, offering not just the situation comedy of one child-fixated couple but the points of view of everyone in an extended and wildly diverse middle-class family.

At its center is over-anxious dad Steve Martin, who'll try anything to alleviate his 8-year-old's emotional problems, and Mary Steenburgen, his equally conscientious but better-adjusted wife.

Rick Moranis is the yuppie extreme, an excellence-fixated nerd who forces math, languages, Kafka and karate on his 3-year-old girl, to the distress of his milder wife (Harley Kozak).

Dianne Wiest is a divorcée and working mother whose rebellious teens (Martha Plimpton and Leaf Phoenix) dump their anger in her lap.

Jason Robards is the acidic patriarch of the family whose neglectful fathering made his eldest son (Martin) grow up with an obsession to do better. The old man is forced to take another shot at fatherhood late in life when his ne'er-do-well, 27-year-old son (Tom Hulce) moves back in.

Director Ron Howard, in his most mature work to date, brings his middle-Americana vision to the kind of family comic-drama previously done in New York accents by Woody Allen, even borrowing some cast members from Allen's stable. Moving among households, pic covers a lot of ground, from the mundane to the painful to the hilarious.

Lowell Ganz and Babaloo Mandel's deft and perceptive script zings with 1-liners, expertly delivered by this amazing cast.

Admirably, script doesn't shy from real life, on one hand poking fun at yuppie obsessiveness but on the other exploring the mass of emotions entailed in parenthood.

The irrepressible Martin plays it mostly straight in an impressive lead performance, but lets go in pic's marvelous comic centerpiece, when he plays balloon-twisting Cowboy Bob to save the day at his son's birthday party. In a baseball scene, his dance of delight when his son finally catches that all-important pop fly is a cinematic classic.

In a moodier but just as essential side of the story, Wiest and her troubled household nearly steal the show. Wiest is vastly compelling as the mom who's both rejected and needed by her spooky, surly kids. Plimpton is eerily on-target as her flippant, trouble-seeking daughter and Keanu Reeves is an inspired touch as Plimpton's crazed but ardent boyfriend Tod (annoyingly referred to by Wiest as "that Tod").

Howard stretches as a director and usually hits his mark, particularly in a darkly funny scene where Martin hallucinates a worst-case scenario in which his disturbed son turns into a campus sniper.

Pic sometimes dives into the sentimental, but Howard usually pulls its nose up with deft comedy. Not so in the last reel, when all loose ends get tied up in bright packages, and in a rather incredible development, middle-aged Wiest and the new man in her life have another baby.

Camera's lingering lovefest with cooing infants at the end also tends to reverse favorable sentiments. Also, in these heated times, pic's intimation that all pregnancies should be brought to term is bound to raise a few eyebrows.

Pic was the first feature filmed at Universal's new Orlando, Fla., studios. Settings and technical contributions are excellent.

Particularly fine is Donald McAlpine's rich cinematography. Randy Newman's score makes the perfect aural accompaniment.
— *Daws.*

Turner & Hooch

Hollywood A Buena Vista release of a Touchstone Pictures presentation, in association with Silver Screen Partners IV. Executive producer, Daniel Petrie Jr. Produced by Raymond Wagner. Coproducer, Michele Ader. Directed by Roger Spottiswoode. Screenplay, Dennis Shryack, Michael Blodgett, Petrie, Jim Cash, Jack Epps Jr., from story by Shryack, Blodgett, Petrie; camera (Metrocolor; Technicolor prints), Adam Greenberg; 2d unit camera, Michael A. Benson; editor, Garth Craven; music, Charles Gross; sound (Dolby), Jim Webb; production design, John DeCuir Jr.; art direction, Sig Tinglof; set decoration, Cloudia; "Hooch" owned and trained by Clint Rowe; animal trainer, Scott Rowe; stunt coordinator, Conrad E. Palmisano; assistant director, Albert M. Shapiro; 2d unit director, Craven; casting, Mike Fenton, Judy Taylor, Lynda Gordon, Karen Hendel. Reviewed at Avco Cinema, Westwood, Calif., July 25, 1989. MPAA Rating: PG. Running time: **100 MIN.**
Scott Turner . . . . .Tom Hanks
Emily Carson . . . . .Mare Winningham
Chief Hyde . . . . .Craig T. Nelson
David Sutton . . . . . . .Reginald VelJohnson
Zack Gregory . . . . .Scott Paulin
Walter Boyett . . . . .J.C. Quinn
Amos Reed . . . . .John McIntire
Hooch . . . . .Beasley

■Until its grossly miscalculated bummer of an ending, "Turner & Hooch" is a routine but amiable cop-and-dog comedy enlivened by the charm of Tom Hanks and his homely-as-sin canine partner.

The Buena Vista release nips too closely on the heels of "K-9," and after a strong opening on Hanks' name, audience interest probably will evaporate abruptly as word of mouth spreads about the disastrous finale.

The quality of a film usually can be calculated in inverse proportion to the number of writers laboring on it, and in this case five scribes have striven to bring forth a tired and derivative molehill.

Imagine another actor in the role of the fussy smalltown California police investigator played by Hanks, and the film would seem like a telepic ripoff of Universal's "K-9," which did surprisingly well this spring with its comic variation on the mismatched-police-partners formula.

Hanks has an ease and precision to his comic underplaying which makes the character's anal-retentive personality amusing rather than offputting, and brings some winning results when his life is disrupted by a messy junkyard dog with a face only a furry mother could love.

In the numbingly unoriginal plot, the dog named Hooch (delightfully played by Beasley, who was trained by Clint Rowe) witnesses a double murder and is Hanks' only means of catching the drug smugglers responsible for the slayings. The rather mechanical style of director Roger Spottiswoode (who took over the film after original director Henry Winkler departed) fails to enliven the stereotypical criminal proceedings.

As long as the plot takes a back seat, the interplay between Hanks and the dog keeps the film watchable. Hanks bravely flies in the face of the old adage against working with animals or small children, and has a fine time freaking out over the chaos Hooch wreaks on his fastidiously arranged home.

The drab romantic scenes with veterinarian Mare Winningham are mostly a snooze, since the true love story here is that between Hanks and the 4-legged creature. Hanks' fellow cop (Reginald VelJohnson) has better luck than Winningham, because his scenes also revolve around the dog's antics.

Given the fact that the film is nothing more until this point than a light comedy, it is astonishing no one in the Disney hierarchy blew the whistle on the screenwriters' nutty idea for climaxing the story with a gut-wrenching act of violence that flipflops the film from comedy to melodrama. "Turner & Hooch" is no "Old Yeller," and the sudden tugging at the heartstrings only causes bafflement and resentment.

A feeble attempt to lighten the mood again seems crassly dismissive of the audience's feelings, and an advertisement for a sequel that will never be made.—*Mac.*

Lenny Live And Unleashed (BRITISH)

London A Miramax Films release of a Palace/Sleeping Partners production, in association with Telso Intl. and British Satellite Broadcasting. Executive producers, Stephen Woolley, Nik Powell. Produced by Martyn Auty, Andy Harries. Directed by Harries. Screenplay, Lenny Henry, Kim Fuller; camera (color), Peter Sinclair; editor, Gerry Hambling; sound, Clive Barrett; production design, Christopher Hobbs; costumes, Sharon Lewis. Reviewed at Odeon Haymarket, London (also in Blacklight Festival, Chicago), July 24, 1989. Running time: **94 MIN.**
With: Lenny Henry, Robbie Coltrane, Jeff Beck.

■"Lenny Live And Unleashed"

ably displays Lenny Henry as a fine British alternative to Yank standup comedians, though his pic may be too parochial for many offshore markets.

Henry is well known to British audiences, who have followed him from teenage mimic to a mature, politically savvy comic who is established as an actor as well. He has performed in the U.S., but apart from a role in James Bruce's "The Suicide Club," he's relatively unknown outside the U.K.

Comic-in-concert films tend to be rather similar, so in an attempt to be original, this one opens with Henry being driven to the theater by an obnoxious London cabbie (Robbie Coltrane) followed by scenes of Henry giving himself advice while accurately impersonating (and costumed as) Steve Martin, Richard Pryor and (especially good) Eddie Murphy.

Rest of the film is devoted to Henry's stage show, filmed over a week at the Hackney Empire Theater in London, with Henry doing standup material as well as trotting out his tv characters, including reggae artist Fred Dread, Brixton DJ Delbert Wilkins, oldtimer Deakus and (in a duo with guitarist Jeff Beck) blues singer Smith.

Climax is an impression of sex-machine singer Theophilus P. Wildebeeste, who selects a hapless girl from the audience and serenades her as she sits on a red silken bed. The characters are all well known to U.K. audiences and some overtly parochial, reflecting the situation of blacks in Britain.

Unobtrusive direction by Andy Harries — who resists the temptation of repeated reaction shots of the audience — and excellent editing by Gerry Hambling keep the pic bubbling at an enjoyable pace. Henry's material is not cruel or offensive, and even though the big-screen format gives him a chance to use the F-word, he never goes over the top.

Fun as it is, "Lenny Live And Unleashed" is bound to have a limited theatrical life — probably quite a good one in the U.K. — before finding its rightful home on the video shelves —*Adam.*

Cher frangin
(Dear Brother)
(FRENCH-CANADIAN-BELGIAN)

Paris   A Capital Cinéma release of a Stephan Films/Productions Bleu Blanc Rouge (Montreal)/Lamy Films (Brussels) coproduction. Produced by Vera Belmont. Directed by Gérard Mordillat. Screenplay, Jean Marie Es-

tève, Richard Morgis, Philippe Triboit, David Milhaud. Yvan Leduc, Mordillat; camera (Fujicolor), Michel Baudour; editor, Nicole Saunier; art direction, François Koltes; music, Jean Louis Negro; sound, William Flageollet; assistant director, François Koltes; production manager, Linda Gutemberg. Reviewed at Saint-André-des-Arts theater, Paris, May 16, 1989. Running time: **95 MIN.**

Alain . . . . Luc Thuillier
Marius . . . . Marius Colucci
Lou . . . . Julie Jezequel
Maurer . . . . Philippe Caroit
Vacher . . . . Eric Denize
Coudrier . . . . Charles Mayer
Jarlot . . . . Riton Liebman
Ahmed . . . . Najim Laouriga

■ A low-budget treatment of an all-but-taboo subject in French films — the Algerian War — "Cher frangin" deals with the fate of a young deserter in 1959 who is caught and pressed into service in a disciplinary battalion.

Director Gérard Mordillat, inheriting a screenplay concocted by others — but which he rewrote — doesn't transcend the conventions of the war movie, but he manages a grimly realistic re-creation of small-scale desert combat. Pic was an immediate b.o. casualty, boding ill for more films on a traumatic moment in contemporary French history.

Script is a double-layered affair that attempts descriptions of conditions at the front and how it's viewed from back home. Linking device is the young protoganist's correspondence to his kid brother and his young pregnant wife. These Paris scenes are sketchy and uninvolving.

Though straitened by the budget, Mordillat does better with the war scenes (shot in Tunisia), which follow a French unit's raid on a tiny Arab village harboring guerrilla fighters, and a subsequent series of brief but violent skirmishes. There's a "Lost Patrol" familiarity to the plot, which finally has everybody but our hero exterminated in an ambush. Survivor manages to escape across the border into Tunisia where he plans to spill the truth about the Algerian conflict in a pirate pamphlet.

. Luc Thuillier is adequate as the 2-time deserter and a well-picked cast gives some credible substance to the various typed members of the platoon. Julie Jezequel is Thuillier's gentle spouse and Marius Colucci (son of the late comic Coluche) is the 10-year-old kid brother. —*Len.*

Marquis
(BELGIAN-FRENCH)

Paris   A Bac Films release of an YC Alligator Films/Constallation Production/Tchin Tchin Prod. coproduction. Executive producer, Eric Van Beuren. Directed by Henri Xhonneux. Screenplay, Roland Topor, Xhonneux; camera (Fujicolor), Etienne Fauduet; editor, Chantal Hymans; music, Reinhardt Wagner; creature designs and artistic direction, Topor; creatures created by Jacques and Fréderérique Gastineau; art direction, Pierre-François Limbosch; costumes, Maryvonne Herzog; gestural direction, Philippe Bizot; sound, Joel Rangon, Dominique Hennequin; assistant director, Joseph Claes, production manager, Eric Plateau; associate producers, Claudie Ossard, Roger Cornu. Reviewed at Accatone cinema, Paris, July 20, 1989. Running time: **83 MIN.**
With: Philippe Bizot, Bien de Moor, Gabrielle van Damme, Olivier Dechaveau, Bernard Cognaux, Pierre Decuypere; and the voices of : Francois Marthouret, Valérie Kling, Michel Robin, Isabelle Canet-Wolfe, Vicky Messica, Nathalie Juvet, René Lebrun, Bob Morel, Roger Crouzet, Willem Holltrop, Eric de Saria, Henri Rubinstein.

■ Roland Topor, the abrasive, bawdy satirist-caricaturist, has imagined the most subversively offbeat feature in the current crop of costume films set during the era of the French Revolution. It's a randy fable of decadent French society gone to the dogs — and other beasties — on the eve of the storming of the Bastille.

The cast of characters are animals à la Fontaine, but played by human performers — themselves dubbed by other actors — who wear masks designed by Topor. This is an elegantly raunchy, slyly amusing intellectual romp cleverly spiced with socio-sexual-political musings and farcical bestiality. Not for the prudish, "Marquis" could be an arthouse and cult favorite.

The protagonist, an aristocratic canine (or top dog), is a thinly disguised representation of the Marquis de Sade, whose own writings (as well as those of Mirabeau) are used textually. The politically outspoken de Sade's imprisonment at the Bastille in 1789 on trumped up charges of sexual perversity is the prime inspiration of Topor's story and setting (the Bastille prison, from which de Sade was transferred before the Revolution).

When he isn't writing, Marquis does a lot of talking — denouncing dogma in favor of art and freedom (political and sexual). His principal interlocutor is his own phallus, an imposingly erect fellow named Colin who has human features, and impulsive below-the-belt opinions. Marquis and his member don't see eye to eye and finally decide to part ways in the end, on July 15, 1989.

Marquis is the quietly thoughtful center of a storm of turpitude and conspiracy at the Bastille, patrolled by chicken guards. There's the prison governor, a masochist rooster who gets serviced by a whip-wielding revolutionary filly named Juliette; a libertine Jesuit camel; a promiscuous rat-faced turnkey; and fetchingly bovine Justine, seduced and abandoned by the king and imprisoned at the Bastille, where a plot is hatched to have Marquis framed as her seducer and father of the soon-to-be-born child — who comes into the world wearing an Iron Mask.

Topor's collaborator is coscripter and director Henri Xhonneux, with whom he made the popular children's tv series "Tele-cat." The wittily articulated masks and animation effects are the work of Jacques and Frédérique Gastineau.

The actor-mimes match physical fluency to their bestial comportment and the voices are well chosen. Etienne Fauduet's lighting and Pierre-François Limbach's studio sets heighten the film's seductively fantastical ambience.
—*Len.*

Nunca Estuve en Viena
(I've Never Been To Vienna)
(ARGENTINE)

Moscow   An Incine production. Written and directed by Antonio Larreta. Camera (color), Ricardo Aronovich; music, Pepe Nieto. Reviewed at Moscow Film Festival (competing), July 14, 1989. Running time: **100 MIN.**
With: China Zorrilla, Sergi Mateu, Alberto Segado, M. Teresa Constantini.

■ "I've Never Been To Vienna" tells of the breakup of a rich aristocratic family in Argentina in the early years of the century. Pic has the look of Luchino Visconti doing a telenovela.

Watchable and very pretty to look at, with a sort of feminist heroine, it could find some arthouse takers offshore.

A tough granny fixated on her own noble blood runs the sprawling country house where her grown grandchildren live. The three girls are all lovely. One marries a suitably wealthy man, one is commandeered by granny as a secretary-slave, and the third, Adela, falls for the handsome young gardner, who wants to become a theater designer.

There is also a tubercular brother who plays piano and is in and out of sanatoriums.

The gardener falls hard for Adela, but is tempted to the city by her uncle Marcelo, who has been his lover for 15 years. Adela only learns of their relationship after she has gotten pregnant.

Granny receives such a shock over the double revelation of Adela having a baby out of wedlock and her son Marcelo being gay she drops dead.

Helmer Antonio Larreta treats his characters with intimate affection, making them come alive. His picture of genteel life is a pleasant fantasy. Costumes and decor are embellished with an aura of nostalgia. The drama that takes center stage, however, isn't very moving, and the family's final destruction is as much a relief to the viewer as it is to the characters.

Cast is fine. —*Yung.*

Le Café des Jules
(The Guys In The Cafe)
(FRENCH)

Paris A Films de l'Atalante release of a Diagonale/La Sept coproduction. Produced, directed and edited by Paul Vecchiali. Screenplay, Jacques Nolot; camera (color), Georges Strouvé; music, Roland Vincent; sound, Antoine Bonfanti; assistant director, Pierre Sénélas. Reviewed at Studio 43, Paris, June 20, 1989. Running time: **65 MIN.**
With: Jacques Nolot, Brigitte Rouan, Lionel Goldstein, Patrick Raynal, Raymond Aquilon, Georges Téran, Raphaeline Goupilleau.

■ **A hackneyed piece of naturalistic film writing, "Le Café des Jules" is partially redeemed by fine ensemble playing. Set entirely in a glum suburban cafe on a Saturday night, it could easily be put on a legit stage without textual alteration.**

Producer-director Paul Vecchiali has helmed with unobtrusive skill.

Script by actor Jacques Nolot (who plays one of the leads) is a plotless slice-of-life look at the simmering discontents and frustrations among a disparate group of male cafe regulars and a woman (Brigitte Rouan) who has been involved with some of them. The alternating banter, soulful thinking out loud, and booze-whetted tensions climax in Nolot's rape of Rouan in the back of the cafe.

Nolot and Rouan are standouts among a well-picked and skillfully directed cast. The script is just another wrinkle on a familiar theatrical situation which doesn't gain much extra depth from the cinema. Tech credits are modest.
—*Len.*

Friday The 13th Part VIII
— Jason Takes Manhattan

Hollywood A Paramount Pictures release of a Horror Inc. production. Produced by Randolph Cheveldave. Written and directed by Rob Hedden. Camera (Technicolor prints), Bryan England; editor, Steve Mirkovich; music, Fred Mollin; sound, (Ultra-Stereo), Lars Ekstrom; production design, David Fischer; set decoration, Linda Vipond; costume design, Carla Hetland; special makeup effects, Jamie Brown; stunt coordinator, Ken Kirzinger; assistant director, Jeffrey Authors; production manager, Mary Guilfoyle; special effects coordinator, Martin Becker; special effects camera, Brenton Spencer. Reviewed at Paramount Studio theater, L.A., July 28, 1989. MPAA Rating: R. Running time: **100 MIN.**
Rennie Wickham . . . . .Jensen Daggett
Sean Robertson . . . . .Scott Reeves
Charles McCulloch . .Peter Mark Richman
Colleen Van Deusen . . . .Barbara Bingham
Julius Gaw . . . . .V.C. Dupree
Jason . . . . .Kane Hodder
Tamara Mason . . . . .Sharlene Martin
Wayne Webber . . . . .Martin Cummins
Young Jason . . . . .Timothy Burr Mirkovich
Young Rennie . . . . .Amber Pawlick

■ **Paramount's latest cynical excursion into sadistic violence is lifted slightly above its generic mire by the stylish efforts of debuting director Rob Hedden and his lenser, Bryan England.**

"Friday The 13th Part VIII — Jason Takes Manhattan" is basically the same musty slice-and-dice formula jazzed up by being moved from Crystal Lake to Gotham's mean streets. The cash should pour in as usual from teens wanting a sick kick on date night.

There's little attempt at subtlety in these films, and that's how the fans like it — raw and bloody, with giggles periodically thrown in to break the tension.

The minimal variation this time in Hedden's script is to have most of the action take place on a cruise ship taking the Crystal Lake high school grads to Manhattan, where some humor naturally arises from the locals' indifference to the madman in their midst.

This low-budgeter devotes less time to the Big Apple scenes than the ad campaign would indicate, and it's too bad, because Hedden and England conjure up a nightmarish vision of garbage-strewn, rat-infested, skinhead-ridden streets that rivals the verbal diatribes of Robert De Niro in "Taxi Driver" and out-Scorseses Martin Scorsese for operatic grottiness.

Maybe these scenes are also more riveting in light of that when Jason pursues the young leads through Manhattan, most of the killing is over, because most of the kids didn't survive the boat trip.

Before that, the film devotes its energies to recycling all the tried-

and-true methods of dispatching teens by stabbing, strangling, electrocuting, burning, head-smashing, slashing and spearing. For slasher pic aficionados, there are no nifty new murder methods on view, and for the more civilized segment of humanity, it's strictly lose-your-lunch time.

Given the meager opportunities for character development in these films, it's a wonder that some of these performers show such promise. Jensen Daggett is a standout as the troubled young girl on whom Jason is fixated. V.C. Dupree has vibrant energy in his boxing scenes, Sharlene Martin has a fine time with the bitch role, and Martin Cummins is funny as a video freak who compulsively films the proceedings.

Then there's Jason, the all-but-unkillable human tower of slime who perpetually rises from the bottom of the lake to wreak revenge for his drowning long ago. The imposing Kane Hodder, ghoulishly made up by Jamie Brown, plays the role with unholy relish and even stirs up a bit of sympathy at the end.

The director and lenser surely will rise to better things, while quickly dumping this title from their resumés. —*Spel.*

Doida Demais
(She Can Drive A Person Crazy)
(BRAZILIAN)

Gramado An Embrafilme release of a Morena Filmes/Cininvest/Embrafilme production. Executive producers, Mariza Leao, Paulo Cesar Ferreira. Directed by Sergio Rezende. Screenplay, Sergio Duran; camera (color), Antonio Luis Mendes, Cesar Charlone; editor, Mauro Alice; music, David Tygel; song "A Fina Poeira do Ar" by Paulo Ricardo, sung by Paulo Ricardo and Rita Lee; sound (Dolby), Juarez Dagoberto, Valeria Mauro, Jose Louzeiro; art direction, Clovis Bueno; sets, Tony Vanzolini; costumes, Isabel Paranhos; production director, Paulo Fernando Pijnappel. Reviewed at Embaixador theater, Gramado Film Festival, June 17, 1989. Running time: **102 MIN.**
Leticia . . . . .Vera Fischer
Gabriel . . . . .Paulo Betti
Noé . . . . .José Wilker
Also with: Italo Rossi, Carlos Gregorio, Alvaro Freire, Chico Expedito, Gilson Moura, Luca de Castro, Manfredo Bahia.

■ **"Doida Demais" is a carefully produced and professionally directed drama. Excessive stress apparent in actress Vera Fischer, however, is unbalancing and dilutes some potentially good situations.**

Story concerns a classic triangle: Leticia (Fischer), an ambitious businesswoman involved in a forged painting; her former lover

(José Wilker), an extremely possessive man, also involved in the fake; and her new lover (Paulo Betti), a pilot working for gold miners deep in the Amazon jungle.

What is potentially an involving screenplay, however, centers too often on Fischer. A beautiful woman, she is nevertheless far less gifted as an actress.

Helmer Sergio Rezende probably realized the mistake while still shooting the film, as some characters are obviously inflated while others just shrink.

Leticia is supposed to drive men crazy, but her actions never explain why. The male characters are far more consistent, especially Italo Rossi as a wealthy art collector and Wilker as his obsessed assistant.

Action takes place in appropriate locations as efficient art direction by Clovis Bueno achieves the miracle of bringing the film to the Amazon without taking an exotic approach to the area. Original music by David Tygel is his best; it furnished the speed the narrative demands.

All other technical credits, including the Dolby stereo sound, match any international standard.
—*Hoin.*

And The Violins
Stopped Playing
(U.S.-POLISH)

Moscow A David Films production, in association with Film Polski, Tor Unit. Executive producer, Krzysztof Zanussi. Produced, written and directed by Alexander Ramati, based on his novel. Camera (color), Edward Klosinski; editor, Mirowslawa Garlicka; music, Leopold Kozlowski, Zozislaw Szostak; art direction, Teresa Smus-Barska; costumes, Elzbieta Radtke; production manager, Michal Szczerbic; associate producer, Judy Hecht. Reviewed at Moscow Film Festival, July 16, 1989. Running time: **119 MIN.**
Dymitr . . . . .Horst Buchholz
Zoya . . . . .Maya Ramati
Roman Mirga . . . . .Piotr Polk
Wala Mirga . . . . .Didi Ramati
Shero Rom . . . . .Zitto Kazann
Dr. Josef Mengele . . . . . . .Marcin Tronski
Koro . . . . .Wojciech Pastuszko
Pawel . . . . .Jacek Sas-Uchrynowsky

■ **"And The Violins Stopped Playing" is Alexander Ramati's dramatization of the Nazi persecution of European gypsies during World War II, based on his own novel. Lensed on location in Poland (Kryzstof Zanussi exec produced), film has an authenticity of locale that contrasts with its highly invented story.**

Between gypsy fiddlers, dances, camps and caravans, blossoming young love and death in Auschwitz, "Violins" abounds with color and human interest that should get audiences through the tragic final scenes. Tv programmers will likely be the most interested.

Dymitr (Horst Buchholz) is a sensitive violinist who learns that the Warsaw ghetto has been cleared of Jews and the Germans plans to move the gypsies in soon. He takes his wife (Didi Ramati) and teen-age son Roman (Piotr Polk) to a gypsy camp outside town and convinces the camp council they are in imminent danger. He is appointed camp head to lead them to safety, ousting the old leader who pooh-poohs the danger.

Dymitr's son Roman falls for wild gypsy beauty Zoya (Maya Ramati) when he sees her dancing around the fire. Zoya already has been spoken for, and it takes a knife fight to win Roman her hand in marriage. The wedding takes place on the road, as the gypsies flee the omnipresent Nazis. Some Polish partisans warn them to break up the caravan and pretend to be Ukrainian peasants. Though they follow this advice, many are caught and killed.

Reaching Hungary, they are welcomed warmly and momentarily lulled into thinking they're safe. It is then that a German patrol chances upon them and ships them to Auschwitz, a name Dymitr has heard before. The gypsies are treated better than the Jews, and Roman is privileged as interpreter for the sinister Dr. Josef Mengele. In the end, Zoya falls ill and dies, and Dymitr plays his violin in the camp's gypsy orchestra while his wife goes to the gas chamber. Then the violins stop playing.

Story is tragic, but a varied pace and lots of gypsy gaiety keep it from becoming maudlin. Firmly on the gypsies' side, Ramati shines them up quite a bit, with consequent strain on their believability. Nonetheless, "Violins" is a watchable, highly dramatized film dealing with a little-known part of history.

Top-notch technical work includes cinematography by Edward Klosinski. —*Yung.*

Posetitel Muzeia
(Visitor To A Museum)
(SOVIET)

Moscow   A Lenfilm Studio production, Creative Unit 3. Written and directed by Konstantin Lopushanski. Camera (color), Nikolai Pokoptzev; art direction, Vaseli Yurkevich; music, Arthur Schnitke, Viktor Kusin. Reviewed at Moscow Film Festival (competing),

July 16, 1989. Running time: **135 MIN.** With: Viktor Mikhailov, Irina Rakshina, Vera Maiorova.

■ **"Visitor To A Museum" is a highbrow Soviet horror film set in a world destroyed by an ecological disaster. It is directed by young Lenfilm helmer Konstantin Lopushanski, whose "Letters From A Dead Man" about life after a nuclear holocaust was screened abroad and earned him a critical reputation.**

In many ways very similar to "Letters," "Visitor" lacks the first film's gripping power. Running a very long 135 minutes, its offshore life looks limited.

A man comes to what remains of a city — now just an isolated house here and there. He wants to spend his holidays visiting a famous museum which is now in the middle of the sea, result of the ice caps melting. It can only be reached at low tide after days of perilous marching, and few who have set out to see it have returned.

In addition, the few scared residents left keep fires burning in their windows at night against the retarded mutants who roam the land. Most of these freakish creatures are kept locked in concentration camps, but the house where the man stays has two of them as servants (later it turns out they're the couple's own kids).

The groundwork is laid for a fine adventure to the mythical museum (could it be the Hermitage?). Instead, film takes off on a different tack along religious lines. The visitor — a nondescript being who looks half-demented from the beginning — is both drawn to and repulsed by the mental defectives, whom Lopushanski depicts very touchingly as truncated human beings struggling to be whole. He attends one of their religious ceremonies, where priests chant nonsensical prayers and the congregation follows in a trance.

Somehow the visitor is picked out as their awaited savior. At first he refuses the role and tries to escape. Then, repeating "everything is foretold," he lets himself be inducted into their number and is turned into an inspired zombie himself. He sets off at last across the sea in the midst of a tempest, but somehow reaches land on the other side and, screaming hysterically, begins to cross it.

The interesting, apocalyptic set design fills every frame with the rubbish and rubble of a decayed civilization. The smoky, dark lensing, with figures lit by red neon

light, imparts a sense of gloomy prophecy.

This trip through hell in search of a God is not made more light-hearted by Lopushanski's fondness for prolonged scenes of hysterical screaming. There are numerous bows to the late Andrei Tarkovsky, from the existential angst to religious metaphor, yet little of the master's spirituality comes through. —*Yung.*

Never On Tuesday

New York   An Elliott Kastner and Andre Blay presentation, in association with Palisades Entertainment of an Elwes/Wyman production. Executive producer, Cassian Elwes. Produced by Brad Wyman, Lionel Wigram. Written and directed by Adam Rifkin. Camera (Foto-Kem color), Alan Jones; editor, Ed Rothkowitz; music, Richard Stone; sound, Tom Cunliffe; production design, Bobby Bernhardt; art direction, Tiffanie Winton; assistant director, Paul Kimatian; production manager, Michael D. Carlin; special makeup effects, David Anderson; casting, Tony Markes; associate producers, Frances Fleming, Kimatian. Reviewed on Paramount vidcassette, N.Y., July 22, 1989. MPAA Rating: R. Running time: **90 MIN.**
Tuesday . . . . .Claudia Christian
Matt . . . . .Andrew Lauer
Eddie . . . . .Pete Berg
Larry Lupin . . . . .Gilbert Gottfried
Thief . . . . .Charlie Sheen
Motorcycle cop . . . . .Judd Nelson
Tow-truck man . . . . .Emilio Estevez

■ **The talent and beauty of Claudia Christian is showcased in "Never On Tuesday," an unreleased 1987 vanity production that should give Paramount Home Video sleeper possibilities due to the presence of several big-name gueststars.**

As in his more recent pic "Tale Of Two Sisters," also toplining Christian, filmmaker Adam Rifkin shows great potential in his handling of varied film techniques. Unfortunately, his experimental approach has no extant audience; he might have done better to start with conventional features before plunging into uncharted waters.

Here he sets himself the insurmountable goal of making a static road movie. Andrew Lauer and Pete Berg are two Ohio youths driving to California to meet those fabled west coast beauties. Pic is barely underway when they recklessly crash into Christian's Volkswagen, stranding the three of them in the middle of nowhere.

Passersby refuse to give the hapless trio a lift and Christian announces in the second reel, "I'm a lesbian," thwarting the lecherous intent of our heroes. Rifkin manages to create some variety (and wish-fulfillment sexiness) with frequent fantasy sequences, but it

is the periodic visits of quirky, uncredited cameo performers that keep the film going.

Standup comic Gilbert Gottfried pops up with his usual shouting routine to sell the folks a brush, but won't give them a ride. Charlie Sheen has the best guest spot as a violent ex-con who robs the trio at knifepoint — he plays it for real. Brother Emilio Estevez makes a brief appearance and his "Breakfast Club" costar Judd Nelson is too hammy as a mustachioed cop to get any laughs.

Golden oldies on the soundtrack make the film easy to take, but Rifkin's bittersweet ending is unsatisfying.—*Lor.*

Up Your Alley

New York   A Seymour Borde & Associates release of an Unknown Film Co. and Loganworks Ltd. production. Produced by Murray Langston. Directed by Bob Logan. Screenplay, Langston, Logan; camera (Foto-Kem color), Mark Melville; editor, Tom Siiter; music, Paul Ventimiglia; sound, Monti S. Rainbolt; assistant director, Stephanie Hunt; coproducers, Gerald Cutter, Michael Borkin; associate producer, Chris Trimarche. Reviewed on IVE vidcassette, N.Y., July 22, 1989. MPAA Rating: R. Running time: **88 MIN.**
Vickie Adderly . . . . .Linda Blair
David . . . . .Murray Langston
Sonny .Bob Zany
Marilyn . . . . .Ruth Buzzi
Nick . . . . .Johnny Dark
Joe . . . . .Jack Hanrahan
Lance . . . . .Glen Vincent
Pauline . . . . .Melissa Shear
   Also with: Kevin Benton, Yakov Smirnoff, Kent Perkins, Vic Dunlop, Tom Dreesen, Myles Thoroughgood.

■ **"Up Your Alley" is an engaging shoestring production in which numerous comedians play it straight in limning the plight of homeless street people. Pic had a brief theatrical run in Miami in April ahead of video release.**

The brainchild of erstwhile bag-over-head "Unknown Comic" Murray Langston, pic is a sweet tale of marginals, investigated by undercover reporter Linda Blair, who fakes being one of them. The largely unsung Czech director in Hollywood, Hugo Haas, made similar pics, "Paradise Alley" and "Edge Of Hell," 30 years earlier.

Some extraneous suspense is introduced in a subplot of a mad killer preying on L.A. bums, and pic works in its character study of oddball types. Langston scores as the taciturn, sometimes drunken beggar whose demeanor is softened by the friendship of a big, slow-witted guy fresh to the streets (Bob Zany) as well as a platonic romance with Blair.

Blair has a nice change of pace

from her horror assignments. Various standup comics, including Langston, inject needed comic relief with their crazy routines, which fit the characters. —*Lor.*

Les Deux Fragonard
(The Two Fragonards)
(FRENCH)

Paris   A Capital Cinéma release of a CFC/Capital Cinéma/FR3 Films/La Sept co-production. Produced by Christian Charett. Directed by Philippe Le Guay. Screenplay, Le Guay, Jérome Tonnerre; camera (Eastman-color), Bernard Zitzermann; editor, Denise de Casablanca; music, Jorge Arriagada; art direction, Bénédicte Beaugé; costumes, Christian Gasc; sound, Pierre Lenoir, Gérard Rousseau; special effects, Reiko Kruk; assistant director, Yvon Rouvre; casting, Simone Amouyal; production manager, Alain Darbon. Reviewed at Pathé Hautefeuille theater, Paris, May 23, 1989. Running time: **110 MIN.**
Jean-Honoré
  Fragonard . . . . Joachim de Almeida
Cyprien Fragonard . . . . Robin Renucci
Marianne . . . . . . Philippine Leroy-Beaulieu
Salmon d'Anglas . . . . Sami Frey
Saint-Julien . . . . Jean-Louis Richard
La Guimard . . . . Christine Fersen
Rudolphi . . . . Philippe Clevenot
Mme. Dantes . . . . Nada Strancar

■ "Les Deux Fragonard," a first-time feature by former critic Philippe Le Guay, is an overlong, uneasy marriage of biopic and costume melodrama. Real-life protagonists are the 18th century painter Fragonard and his more obscure cousin, an anatomist.

Le Guay and his co-scripter Jérome Tonnerre present both as artists in their own right. Predictably, they are in love with the same woman.

Jean-Honoré Fragonard, as played by Joachim de Almeida, is your typical romantic artist, an inspired hedonist who falls for a fetching young laundress, Philippine Leroy-Beaulieu, and uses her as the model for his celebrated commission "The Swing." Cousin Cyprien (Robin Renucci) is more introverted, involved in his artful dissections and embalmings of corpses, and also falls for Leroy-Beaulieu.

Story's biographical elements, awkwardly conventional, make way for more interesting fictional intrigues involving a decadent art-loving aristocrat, played with stylish cold-bloodedness by Sami Frey. Frey, bested in his bid to be the painter's patron, adopts the vengeful option of sponsoring the anatomist: He plots to have Leroy-Beaulieu murdered and delivered to Renucci for a brilliant feat of embalming.

Le Guay, who perhaps has aimed too high for a first film, lacks assurance with dramatic pacing and his lead actors, but has a feeling for the period setpieces and mood, and the macabre tensions are effectively handled. Bernard Zitzermann's smart lensing is an elegant atmospheric plus. —*Len.*

Slash Dance

New York   A Glencoe Entertainment Group presentation. (Intl. sales, Double Helix Films.) Produced by Andrew Maisner. Directed by James Shyman. Screenplay, Shyman; camera (Foto-Kem color), Geza Sinkovics; editor, Lawrence Rosen; music, Emilio Kauderer; sound, Kip Gynn; art direction, Wayne Lehrer; choreography, Shari Blum; associate producer, Tom Koranda. Reviewed on Glencoe vidcassette, N.Y., July 13, 1989. No MPAA Rating. Running time: **83 MIN.**
Tori Raines . . . . Cindy Maranne
Logan . . . . James Carrol Jordan
Edison . . . . Jay Richardson
Amos . . . . Joel von Ornsteiner
Rupert . . . . John Bluto
Jeff . . . . Jackson Daniel
  Also with: William Kerr, Deanna Booher, Shari Blum, Susan Kay Deemer, Kelle Favar, Cynthia Cheston, Joleen Troop, Lanell Henson, Vinece Lee, Janice Patterson.

■ Catchy title notwithstanding, "Slash Dance" is a meek horror thriller headed for home-video shelves.

Filmmaker James Shyman's tame approach is more slasher-film-meets-"A Chorus Line" than the Jennifer Beals pic punned upon. A maniac is killing the young women auditioning for a role in a musical show at the Van Slake theater. Lovely cop Cindy Maranne goes undercover as a dancer to root out the baddie.

Minor plot pits Van Slake heirs Joel von Ornsteiner and William Kerr as prime, too-obvious suspects.

Pic suffers from too much attempted comic relief (Von Ornsteiner's geek-style overacting is a pain) and surprising prudishness. Dancing, endlessly shown in rehearsal form, is boring and staged without style. Tech credits, especially Geza Sinkovics' colorful lensing, are above average. —*Lor.*

Deadly Weapon

New York   An Empire Pictures production. Executive producer, Charles Band. Produced by Peter Manoogian. Directed by Michael Miner. Screenplay, Miner, from story by George Lafia, Miner; camera (Foto-Kem color), James L. Carter, editor, Peter Teschner; music, Guy Moon; sound (Ultra-Stereo), Ed Parente; art direction, John Myhre; assistant director, Betsy Pollock; production manager, Hope Perello; casting, Anthony Barnao; associate producers, Perello, Debra Dion. Reviewed on TWE vidcassette, N.Y., July 22, 1989. MPAA Rating: PG-13. Running time: **90 MIN.**
Zeke . . . . Rodney Eastman
Traci . . . . Kim Walker
Dalton . . . . Gary Frank
Indian Joe . . . . Michael Horse
  Also with: Gary Kroeger, Barney Martin, Sam Melville, Joe Regalbuto, William Sanderson, Ed Nelson, Michael Hennessey, Susan Blu, Richard S. Horvitz, John Stuart Wildman, John Lafayette, Sasha Jenson.

■ "Deadly Weapon" is a failed attempt at a high-concept picture from Charles Band's late fantasy factory, Empire Pictures. Story of a bullied youngster who goes high-tech for revenge went unreleased, inherited, as a video, by TWE.

Debuting helmer Michael Miner exhibits technical skill but does not establish a consistent tone for this mishmash. Rodney Eastman is Zeke, a 15-year-old in the small town of King Bee, Ariz., who thinks he's a visitor from Outer Space, waiting for the Mother Ship to come for him. He finds an anti-matter pistol belonging to the army, lost in a train wreck nearby.

Zeke proceeds to blast his enemies (including his mean daddy) with the formidable revolver and comically rounds up the town preacher, sheriff and mayor, locking them up in the car trunk as he goes joyriding in thrillseeking Kim Walker's pink Cadillac convertible.

While the army mobilizes to carefully put Zeke out of commission (the gun's power source can explode like a 200-kiloton bomb), pic turns maudlin en route to a tragic finish.

Eastman displays convincing angst in the central role, with Walker, a beautiful blond who was one of the "Heathers" in the recent New World release, making a solid impression in an underwritten part. Special effects and other tech credits are fine. —*Lor.*

The Evil Below

New York   A Gibraltar Releasing presentation of a Legend Film production. Produced by Barrie Saint Clair. Executive producer, Sol Pienaar. Directed by Jean-Claude Dubois. Screenplay, Art Payne; camera (color), Keith Dunkley; supervising editor, Ettie Feldman; editor, Micki Stroucken; music, Julian Laxton; sound, Bob Hay; art direction, Adrianne Grabman; production manager, Coenie Dipinaar; assistant director, David Jooste; stunt coordinator, Paul Siebert. Reviewed on Raedon vidcassette, N.Y., July 19, 1989. No MPAA Rating. Running time: **92 MIN.**
Max Cash . . . . Wayne Crawford
Sarah Livingstone . . . . June Chadwick
Tracy . . . . Sheri Able
Adrian Barlow . . . . Ted Le Platt
  Also with: Gordon Mulholland, Brian O'-Shaughnessy, Paul Siebert, Art Payne.

■ This routine South African-lensed thriller about legendary evil scares up little interest in its video release.

Comfortable team of Wayne Crawford and June Chadwick go diving for a treasure ship that sank in 1683. They encounter rivals for the booty, as well as shark attacks and lots of local talk about "the devil walks on this island." Incoherent nightmares pad out the running time.

It's ho-hum low adventure. Crawford is okay in his typical ne'er-do-well action role. —*Lor.*

The Abyss

Hollywood   A 20th Century Fox release. Produced by Gale Anne Hurd. Written and directed by James Cameron. Camera (Duart color; Deluxe prints), Mikael Salomon; editor, Joel Goodman; music, Alan Silvestri; sound (Dolby), Leo Orloff; sound design, Blake Leyh; production design, Leslie Dilley; conceptual design, Ron Cobb; supervising art direction, Peter Childs; art direction, Russell Christian, Joseph Nemec 3d; set design, Andrew Precht, Tom Wilkins, Gershon Ginsburg; set decoration, Anne Kuljian; costume design, Deborah Everton; underwater unit supervisor and camera, Al Giddings; underwater unit production supervisor, Terry Thompson; visual effects supervisors, John Burno, Hoyt Yeatman, Dennis Muren, Robert Skotak; Gene Warren Jr.; special visual effects, Dream Quest Images, Industrial Light & Magic, Fantasy II Film Effects; production manager, Charles Skouras, 3d; assistant director, Robin Oliver, Stephen J. Fisher, Newt Arnold; stunt coordinator, Dick Warlock; casting, Howard Feuer. Reviewed at Avco Cinema Center, Westwood, Calif., Aug. 2, 1989. MPAA Rating: PG-13. Running time: 140 MIN.

Bud Brigman . . . . Ed Harris
Lindsey . . . . . Mary Elizabeth Mastrantonio
Lt. Coffey . . . . Michael Biehn
Catfish . . . . Leo Burmester
Hippy . . . . Todd Graff
Jammer . . . . John Bedford Lloyd
Sonny . . . . J.C. Quinn
One Night . . . . Kimberly Scott
Lew Finler . . . . Capt. Kidd Brewer Jr.
Wilhite . . . . George Robert Klek
Schoenick . . . . Christopher Murphy
Ensign Monk . . . . Adam Nelson
Dwight Perry . . . . Richard Warlock
Leland McBride . . . . . Jimmie Ray Weeks
DeMarco . . . . J. Kenneth Campbell
Gerard . . . . Ken Jenkins
Bendix . . . . Chris Elliot

■A firstrate underwater suspenser with an otherworldly twist, "The Abyss" suffers from a payoff unworthy of its buildup. Same sensibilities that enable writer-director James Cameron to deliver riveting, supercharged action segments get soggy when the "aliens" turn out to be friendly.

This $50-million-plus pic is likely to start taking on water well before it breaks even.

Action is launched when a Navy nuclear sub suffers a mysterious power failure and crashes into a rock wall. Bud Brigman (Ed Harris) and his gamy crew of undersea oil-rig workers are hired to dive for survivors.

At the last minute Brigman's flinty estranged wife, Lindsey (Mary Elizabeth Mastrantonio), who designed their submersible oil rig, insists on coming aboard to lend an uninvited hand.

Crew finds nothing but a lot of corpses floating eerily in the water-filled sub, but meanwhile, Lindsey has a close encounter with a kind of swift-moving neon-lit jellyfish she's convinced is a friendly alien.

When turbulence from a hurri-cane rocking the surface outs off the crew's ties to their command ship, their underwater stay is perilously extended.

Another creature comes aboard to look them over in the form of a shimmering water tentacle that changes shape to mimic the looks on their faces. The beginnings of a beautiful friendship are aborted by the ticking time-bomb on board, a stressed-out Navy Seal commando, Lt. Coffey (Michael Biehn) who's convinced the creature is a Soviet war tool.

Coffey sets out to nuke the aliens with a warhead from the stricken sub. The plot becomes a dangerous game of chase between the crew and the psycho Coffey, with a time-detonated nuclear bomb dangling between them. The future of the oceans and of extraterrestrial relations hang in the balance.

Almost all of the action is exceedingly well-rendered by Cameron and crew, with layers of tension woven into the plot until the experience becomes engulfing and nearly exhausting.

Yet when pic arrives at its major metaphorical question — what lies at the bottom of the abyss — it founders. Cameron hasn't got the answer, only a vague, optimistic suggestion.

The special effects teams are also in the dark, providing so many versions of the extraterrestrials that we're clueless what they're all about.

What are they doing on the ocean floor? Do they know what a nuclear bomb is? Why don't they crack the code in the typed messages they intercept from Bud and actually say something to him? Do they eat fish? (There's not a single fish in this ocean.)

Pic's rush-to-the-surface ending (which brings pic in at an unfinished-feeling 140 minutes) leaves audience high and dry on these questions, and Cameron dodges back into the love story for a big kiss finalé. It's not distracting enough.

Although it ultimately underwhelms, "The Abyss" has plenty of elements in its favor, not least the performances by Harris as the compassionate crewleader and Mastrantonio as his steel-willed counterpart. Not even the pic's elaborate technical achievements can overshadow these two.

Mastrantonio displays unexpected capacities and Harris should jump ahead in boxoffice rankings

after this exposure.

Biehn is powerfully convincing as the crumbling commando, and other casting is diverse enough to add some engaging dimensions.

Script is mostly topnotch, loaded with lively, humanizing dialog, but it's awkward when it comes to describing the aliens.

Production design, lighting and camerawork make this a very watchable underwater epic, with diving masks that don't hide faces, a slew of well-designed watercraft and an action-packed underwater dogfight between two submersibles.

Technical obstacles surmounted by "The Abyss" crew during an arduous eight weeks of underwater filming are remarkable.

Score by Alan Silvestri is lean and taut. Amusingly, it seems to echo the "Star Trek" theme whenever the alien is sighted.

—*Daws.*

Wired

New York   A Taurus Entertainment release of an F/M Entertainment, Lion Screen Entertainment production. Executive producers, P. Michael Smith, Paul Carran. Produced by Edward S. Feldman, Charles P. Meeker. Directed by Larry Peerce. Screenplay, Earl Mac Rauch; camera (Agfa XT color), Tony Imi; editor, Eric Sears; music, Basil Poledouris; sound (Dolby), Robert Wald; production design, Brian Eatwell; assistant director, Jerram Swartz; production manager-associate producer, Austen Jewell; casting, Kathleen Letterie. Reviewed at Technicolor screening room, N.Y., Aug. 3, 1989. (In Montreal Film Festival, noncompeting). MPAA Rating: R. Running time: 108 MIN.

John Belushi . . . . Michael Chiklis
Angel Valesquez . . . . Ray Sharkey
Bob Woodward . . . . J.T. Walsh
Cathy Smith . . . . Patti D'Arbanville
Judy Belushi . . . . Lucinda Jenney
Arnie Fromson . . . . Alex Rocco
Dan Aykroyd . . . . Gary Groomes
Lou . . . . Jere Burns
Coroner . . . . Clyde Kusatsu
Also with: Tom Bower, Earl Billings, Dakin Matthews, J.C. Quinn, Steve Vinovich, Matthew Faison, Jon Snyder, Finis Henderson 3d, Amy Michelson, Blake Clark, Scott Plank, Brooke McCarter, Paul Ben-Victor, Richard Feldman, Ned Bellamy, John Apicella, Joe Urla, Billy Preston.

■In a brief but outstanding career on tv and in pics, John Belushi was an engaging personality. His drug overdose death further enthralled the public. "Wired," however, is relentlessly offputting, and that spells boxoffice trouble.

. Fondness for the comedian/actor/singer and curiosity about his downfall might mean strong opening business, but word-of-mouth will be negative, if not nil.

Screenwriter Earl Mac Rauch

and director Larry Peerce may have been trying to revolutionize the biopic genre (were they thinking of "Citizen Kane?"), but their screenplay counts as one of the most peculiar ever realized. Structured far afield of Bob Woodward's straightforward investigative biography of the same name (a bestseller), "Wired" is told in episodes, flashbacks and dream sequences.

In a fanciful, less-than-successful effort to string together the events in Belushi's tragicomic life, "Wired" begins after Belushi (Michael Chiklis) has died. He rises, dressed in an autopsy gown, to join another "spirit," Angel Valesquez (Ray Sharkey), in a cab ride down memory lane, a sort of hip, but sordid, "This Is/Was Your Life."

The professional benchmarks in Belushi's life are there: the Blues Bros., the comic performances on "Saturday Night Live" (which seem to be invented just for this pic), his Hollywood films. One episode is interrupted by others, including graphic glimpses of Belushi's cocaine habit and the devastating effect it has on his confidantes and colleagues.

Several sequences make no sense at all, such as Gary Groomes as Dan Aykroyd as Richard Nixon as Beldar Conehead and Chiklis/-Belushi as a prim Bob Woodward.

In yet another script quirk, Woodward (J.T. Walsh) joins Belushi and Angel in their observations of Belushi's life. Part the inquiring reporter played by William Alland in "Citizen Kane" and part Jack Webb in "Dragnet," deadpan Woodward ends up interviewing Belushi on his deathbed at the Chateau Marmont.

That's after he watches Belushi take the final injection from Cathy Smith (Patti D'Arbanville), who looks up and says "How 'bout you, Woody? Want a hit?"

"Wired?" Weird.

Somehow, Chiklis ekes out an estimable performance as the doomed comic actor, sweating flashes of Belushi's intensity and vulnerability.

In their brief scenes as trampy drug supplier Smith and beleaguered wife Judy, D'Arbanville and Lucinda Jenney are as effective as the script allows. So is Sharkey. Tech credits are satisfactory.

But, ultimately, the performances are diluted by the uncontrolled crosscutting. Just as Belushi could have run his life a lot smarter — the unmistakable cautionary message of "Wired" — the filmmakers could have made a smarter picture. —*Binn.*

Lock Up

Hollywood A Tri-Star Pictures release of a White Eagle/Carolco Pictures production. Produced by Lawrence Gordon, Charles Gordon. Executive producer, Michael S. Glick. Directed by John Flynn. Screenplay, Richard Smith, Jeb Stuart, Henry Rosenbaum; camera (Technicolor), Donald E. Thorin; editors, Michael N. Knue, Donald Brochu; music, Bill Conti; production design, Bill Kenney; art direction, William Ladd Skinner (L.A.), Bill Groom (N.Y.); set decoration, Jerry Adams (L.A.), George DeTitta Sr. (N.Y.); sound (Dolby), Charlie Wilborn; assistant directors, Newt Arnold, David Sosna; 2nd unit director, David Lux; stunt coordinator, Frank Orsatti; coproducer, Lloyd Levin; casting, Joy Todd. Reviewed at Cineplex Odeon Century City, L.A., July 31, 1989. MPAA Rating: R. Running time: 105 MIN.

Frank	Sylvester Stallone
Warden Drumgoole	Donald Sutherland
Meissner	John Amos
Chink	Sonny Landham
Dallas	Tom Sizemore
Eclipse	Frank McRae
Melissa	Darlanne Fluegel
Braden	William Allen Young
First Base	Larry Romano

■ **Sylvester Stallone seems content to be the current cinema's leading gladiator. For those who don't care if their warrior is ever more charmless, violent and glum, "Lock Up" meets most expectations.**

It's doubtful, however, that most filmgoers will find the hardcore prison setting a top choice to escape to this summer.

"Lock Up" is made in the same, simplistic vein as most other Stallone pics — putting him, the blue-collar protagonist, against the odds over which he ultimately prevails.

Emotional guy that he is, Stallone couldn't wait for his 6-month prison term to be up because in the meantime, his foster father may die so he escapes to see him one last time. It seems his cold-hearted warden (Donald Sutherland) wouldn't allow him a supervised furlough to make the trip.

This is all told in dialog at the opening of "Lock Up" to explain Stallone's wrenching midnight transfer from a low security prison to "hell," a maximum security one run now by Sutherland.

As revealed through his monosyllabic posturing, Sutherland is the vengeful, sadistic type. He whines to Stallone about the media and the public and how they "made you (Stallone) into a hero and a warden into a criminal."

So much for the institutional rationale. The rest of the film is Stallone trying to survive "hell" that

Sutherland, as the Devil, has diabolically allowed to run amok.

Short of ordering, "kill, kill," Sutherland allows certain of his uniformed henchmen backed up by lifer prisoner/ringleader Chink (Sonny Landham) to bring Stallone down.

What better place to launch the defense than during a prison yard football game in which Stallone, in good, muscular form, plays better than Joe Montana.

This is the muddiest confrontation, but there are others that are as dirty or bloody or both — a real modern-day version of fighting, Roman-coliseum style, only held in usual prison settings like the cafeteria, the rec room, the isolation cell.

Under John Flynn's well-paced direction, the film seems to move faster than its plot suggests. Donald E. Thorin's good, gritty cinematic eye and editors Michael N. Knue and Donald Brochu's rapid p.o.v. cutting help.

Also to heighten tension — or more likely, mask the script's weaknesses — Bill Conti's uninspired score pounds on in the background.

A weak attempt to film a Rocky-esque car-fixing scene in the prison shop where Stallone has become the resident motor whiz to the tune of the upbeat song "Vehicle" elicits unintentional laughter instead.

This is macho posturing at its nadir, though Stallone has legions of fans who think otherwise.

Darlanne Fluegel, as his faithful girlfriend, shows up occasionally to present the soft side of things (when Conti's score turns to Mantovani) but her character's only interesting attribute is that she's not a man.

To use the term loosely, Stallone is likable given that the screenwriters (Richard Smith, Jeb Stuart, Henry Rosenbaum) have given him less (if that's possible) to do or say than he's had in earlier performances. He just wants out — it's that simple.

The best lines (another loose use of the term) are given over to fellow inmate Dallas (Tom Sizemore), a hyper "30-year man" and a schemer — whose energies are spent working up crazy ideas like escaping via climbing the steam pipes or racing cockroaches for money.

Others are given little to no shading, notably Sutherland in a very forgettable and lamentable role, and decent, if underused,

secondary parts played by Frank McRae, the gentle giant of a shop steward, and John Amos, the prison's No. 2 man.

Pic has a surprisingly well-executed ending that delivers on two counts; Stallone walks free and audiences get to walk out.

—*Brit.*

One Man Force

New York A Shapiro Glickenhaus release of a Shapiro Glickenhaus Entertainment and Academy Entertainment presentation. Executive producers, Martin F. Gold, Alan M. Solomon. Produced and directed by Dale Trevillion. Screenplay, Trevillion; camera (Alpha Ciné color), Constantine Makris; editor, Lori Kornspun; music, David Michael Frank; sound (Ultra-Stereo), Bill Robbins; production design, Stephen Rice; assistant director, Ted Mather; production manager, John S. Engel; stunt coordinator-2d unit director, Spiro Razatos; additional camera, Levie Isaacs, Zoran Hochstatter; coproducer, Jef Richard; casting, Cathy Henderson, Barbara Hanley. Reviewed on Academy vidcassette, N.Y., July 26, 1989. MPAA Rating: R. Running time: 89 MIN.

Jake Swan	John Matuszak
Lt. McCoy	Ronny Cox
Dante	Charles Napier
Shirley	Sharon Farrell
Pete	Sam Jones
Ronnie	Chance Boyer
Adams	Richard Lynch
Lea Jennings	Stacey Q

Also with: Robert Tessier, Shirley Jo Finney, George (Buck) Flower, Daniel Rojo.

■ **An okay action pic, "One Man Force" is notable as a rare starring role for the late John Matuszak, who does well as a sensitive, tough guy detective.**

Film was briefly test-released theatrically in June but more logically will find its niche in videostores.

Matuszak plays an L.A. cop who goes on the rampage when his partner (Sam Jones) is killed by drug dealers. His boss is a police lieutenant essayed by Ronny Cox, identical to his "Beverly Hills Cop" film roles but with a twist at pic's end.

Main plot has him hired (after being suspended from the force) to solve the kidnaping of a rock star (played by Stacey Q), which Matuszak ultimately links to a money-laundering ring.

Pic is buoyed by an excellent supporting cast of familiar talent including Sharon Farrell as a diner owner and Charles Napier as a villain. Matuszak handles the physical action with aplomb and also is effective in several dramatic scenes.

Tech credits are above average, including an energetic musical score by David Michael Frank.

—*Lor.*

Cemetery High

New York A Titan Prods. presentation of a Generic Film production. Produced by Gorman Bechard, Kristine Covello. Directed by Bechard. Screenplay, Bechard, Carmine Capobianco; camera (Foto-Kem color), Patrick J. Donoghue; editor, Timothy Snell; sound, Shaun Cashman, Frank Christopher; production manager, Cashman; assistant director, Covello; costume design, Debi Thibeault. Reviewed on Unicorn Video vidcassette, N.Y., July 25, 1989. No MPAA Rating. Running time: 80 MIN.

Kate	Debi Thibeault
Kathy	Karen Nielsen
Michelle	Lisa Schmidt
Dianne	Simone
Lisa	Ruth Collins

Also with: Tony Kruk, David Coughlin, Frank Stewart, Kristine Waterman, Carmine Capobianco, Donna Davidge, Kathy Milani, Elizabeth Rose.

■ **"Cemetery High" is a threadbare horror comedy being released direct to video.**

Made-in-Connecticut pic originally was titled "Assault Of The Killer Bimbos" when lensed for Charles Band's Empire Pictures in June 1987, but that catchy moniker was reassigned several months later by Empire to a west coast-lensed feature instead.

With backyard movie production values, talky tale concerns a quartet of angry women who following highschool graduation become vigilantes to wipe out "male slimeballs," after having been assaulted. Led by Debi Thibeault, they later recruit voluptuous Ruth Collins to join their army and help in the seduction of unwitting males.

Flat line readings by much of the cast and too many unfunny in-jokes and self-references to the film in progress sink this exercise. Old-fashioned gimmick of inserting shots of a Gore Gong and Hooter Honk to announce impending explicit violence or nudity merely breaks up the action in tiresome fashion. Gore content turns out to be relatively tame. —*Lor.*

The Arrogant

New York A Cannon Intl. release. Produced by Philippe Blot. Line producer, Rick Nathanson. Written and directed by Blot. Camera (TVC color), Claude Agostini; editor, Ken Bornstein; music supervision, Paula Erickson; sound, Bernard Rochut; assistant director, Robert Schwartz; second unit camera, Gideon Porath; casting, Jodie Sloate, Eddie Foy. Reviewed on Playboy Channel (via vidcassette), N.Y., July 20, 1989. MPAA Rating: R. Running time: 87 MIN.

Julie	Sylvia Kristel
Giovanni	Gary Graham
Leticia	Leigh Wood
Senator	Joe Condon

Also with: Brian Strom, Michael Justin, J. R. Zdvorak, Dale Segal, Kimberly Baucum, Teresa Gilmore, Sean Faro, Bill Mullikin.

■An obscure disaster from Cannon, "The Arrogant" is a pretentious road movie shot in Nevada in 1986 that received only a test booking in Miami in March 1987 but recently surfaced on the Playboy Channel.

Alternately titled (pointlessly) "Sylvia Kristel's Desires," pic pairs the erstwhile "Emmanuelle" thesp with director Philippe Blot, who also helmed her in the conventional European pic "Hot Blood" (a.k.a. "Flamenco Blue"), a Cannon pickup.

Here Blot mounts an abstract nonstory about title figure Giovanni (Gary Graham), on his motorcycle headed for nowhere after killing his father-in-law at film's outset. On his tail are his two brothers-in-law, doubly angry because they caught Giovanni dallying with their other sister.

Giovanni picks up sexy hitchhiker Julie (Kristel), supposedly a waitress en route to her job. She never arrives, but they stop off for encounters with bikers, pick up a couple for some impromptu swapping, etc. Giovanni, who thinks of himself as God in numerous stilted speeches, seems to be wiped out in a highway accident but pops up in priest's garb at the finale.

Blot's script is a shambles, throwing in pointless fantasy sequences and tons of unutterable dialog at will. Kristel and Graham do their best to avoid embarrassment, but it's an uphill battle.

Supporting cast makes little headway, though Teresa Gilmore has a sexy scene. —Lor.

Me And Him
(WEST GERMAN)

Copenhagen   An Egmont Film release in Scandinavia (Columbia Pictures in U.S.) of a Neue Constantin Film (Munich) production. Produced by Bernd Eichinger. Line producer, G. Mac Brown. Directed by Doris Dörrie. Screenplay, Warren L. Leight, Michael Juncker, Dörrie, based on novel "Io e lui" by Alberto Moravia; camera (Eastmancolor), Helge Weindler; editor, Raimund Barthelmes; title song, Jonathan Kelp; other music: classical and popular recordings in arrangement by Nora York and Doug Purviance; casting, Ellen Lewis; sound, Bonnie Finnegan; production design, Suzanne Cavedon; assistant director, Howard McMaster; production management, Diana Pokorny; production supervisor, Dieter Meyer. Reviewed at MBR, Copenhagen, Aug. 3, 1989. MPAA Rating: R. Running time: 90 MIN.
Bert Uttanzi . . . . .Griffin Dunne
Annette, his wife . . . . .Ellen Greene
Me (voice) . . . . .Steven Marcus
Peter Karamis . . . . .Craig T. Nelson
Mrs. Karamis . . . . .Kelly Bishop
Janet Landerson . . . . .Carey Lowell
Juliette . . . . .Kara Glover
Corazon . . . . .Kim Flowers

Also with: Robert LaSardo, Nancy Giles, Rocco Sisto, David Alan Grier, Bill Raymond, Jodie Markell, Jarrod Scott Gormick.
(English soundtrack)

■West Germany's Doris Dörrie and producer Bernd Eichinger have crossed the Atlantic to do a New York story, "Me And Him," with a U.S. cast. A hit last year at home, pic might have fared better by staying in Munich.

Using a cinematically shopworn formula of having half the dialog spoken by somebody unseen and heard only by one on-screen person, helmer Dörrie and two co-writers have adapted an Alberto Moravia spoof novel. It's the story of Bert, a career-bent young architect who is detoured badly from the twin paths of professional and marital virtue when his lower abdominal promontory starts developing a will and a voice of its own.

Good, clean and funny vulgarity inspired by similar concepts used to make great screwball comedies spring from the novels of America's Thorne Smith. In Dörrie's hands, everything turns limp and repetitive as the title's Him (Griffin Dunne looking suitably embarrassed throughout) struggles valiantly and in vain to resist the temptations he is alerted to by the hidden Me (given voice by Steven Marcus) through a plot of minuscule twists and turns.

Bert creates the design for a building that will revolutionize New York. Bert's boss (Craig T. Nelson, as suave as ever) has designs on Janet (pert Carey Lowell) who competes with Bert as company's project manager. Bert, urged on by Me and protesting only meekly, falls for both Janet and sundry other women, including the boss' wife, while his life with a wife comes apart.

While the plot moves ploddingly and predictably through a series of sitcom tableaux, the conflict between Me and Him is evidenced mostly via a milking of every conceivable pun on the subjects of *raising, rising, standing up, pushing ahead* plus *stand and deliver* and *mouth-to-mouth resuscitation.* Acting in most distaff roles is either shrill or bland and none of the women around Bert is made to look particularly attractive by Helge Weindler's rather blunt lensing.

In describing life among well-to-do Manhattanites at work, "Me And Him" holds not even the flicker of a candle to Mike Nichols' "Working Girl." Dörrie's

sympathy seems to lie more with Me than with Him, while women, not to mention their liberation, must feel badly let down by her. At the end, Bert has seemingly lost all but he still grins sheepishly as a chorus of dancing women do a clumsy "Everything Is Going To Be All Right" on a midtown sidewalk. —Kell.

A Nightmare On Elm Street 5: The Dream Child

New York   A New Line Cinema release of a New Line, Heron Communications, Smart Egg Pictures presentation of a Robert Shaye production. Produced by Shaye, Rupert Harvey. Executive producers, Sara Risher, Jon Turtle. Directed by Stephen Hopkins. Screenplay, Leslie Bohem, from story by Bohem, John Skip, Craig Spector, based on characters created by Wes Craven; camera (Metrocolor), Peter Levy; editor, Chuck Weiss, Brent Schoenfeld; music, Jay Ferguson; sound (Dolby), Joseph Singer; production design, C.J. Strawn; art direction, Tim Gray; set decoration, John Jockinsen; assistant director, Kristine Peterson; special makeup effects, Chris Biggs, Todd Masters, Greg Nicotero; Freddy Krueger makeup/Baby Freddy creator, David Miller; special visual effects, Peter Kuran, Phillip Downey; visual effects supervisor, Alan Munro; optical special effects, Ted Rae, Doug Beswick; 2d unit camera, Russ Carpenter; 3d unit camera, Chris Nibley; stunt coordinator, Mike Cassidy. Reviewed at Loews N.Y. Twin 2 theater, N.Y., Aug. 2, 1989. MPAA Rating: R. Running time: 89 MIN.
Freddy Krueger . . . . .Robert Englund
Alice . . . . .Lisa Wilcox
Dan. . . . . .Danny Hassel
Yvonne . . . . .Kelly Jo Minter
Greta . . . . .Erika Anderson
Jacob . . . . .Whitby Hertford
Alice's father. . . . . .Nick Mele
Amanda Krueger . . . . .Beatrice Boepple
Mark . . . . .Joe Seely
Dan's mother . . . . .Valorie Armstrong
Dan's father . . . . .Burr DeBenning
Greta's mother . . . . .Pat Surges
Mark's father . . . . .Clarence Felder

■Fifth edition of the hit "Nightmare" series is a poorly constructed special effects showcase, destined for solid b.o. based on series' brand name.

Whether fans will be disappointed with this flashy but unsuspenseful concoction is a moot point — the ongoing horrific adventures of undying slasher Freddy Krueger have the momentum to likely yield 1989's top indie release. However, New Line honchos should reexamine the formula after this less-than-riveting effort.

Pic's storyline dovetails closely with Parts 3 and 4: Alice (Lisa Wilcox, surviving from last pic) learns that the vengeful monster Freddy (steady Robert Englund) is now preying on her friends, materializing through the dreams of the fetus she's carrying. New title character is Jacob (Whitby Hert-

ford), 10-year-old dream child who reps what Alice's child will become and is the focus of her war with Freddy. Key to battling the monster is contacting the spirit of Freddy's mom (Beatrice Boepple), a nun who committed suicide following his birth.

Unfortunately, Aussie helmer Stephen Hopkins adopts a music-video approach, delaying the boring exposition for several reels and usually cutting away from climaxes to destroy much of the film's impact. Acting is highly variable, with an early high school graduation scene strictly dullsville and a mini-abortion debate (loaded way in favor of pro-lifers) embarrassingly simplistic in Leslie Bohem's script.

Saving grace is the series of spectacular special effects set pieces featuring fanciful makeup, mattes, stopmotion animation and opticals. Noteworthy is a sequence (makeup by Todd Masters) of Alice's beautiful model friend (Erika Anderson) grotesquely distorted as Freddy forces her to eat at a nightmarish dinner. Hardcore fans definitely get their money's worth from such visuals, but better narrative values are needed if the series is to continue.

Englund scores again as the scary yet sympathetic monster, though his sexist 1-liners are disturbingly repetitive this time out. Wilcox is strong reprising her lead role and young Hertford is eerie as the dream child. Aussie lenser Peter Levy's edgy camerawork is a plus. —Lor.

Un Tour de manège
(Roundabout)
(FRENCH)

Paris   A Gaumont release of an A.B. Films/Au Progrès du Singe/Chapeau Rouge Films/Les Prods. du 3ème Etage/Orly Films coproduction. Produced by Albert Prevost. Directed by Pierre Pradinas. Screenplay, Pierre and Simon Pradinas, with the collaboration of Alain Gautré; Camera (Fujicolor), Jean-Pierre Sauvaire; editor, Chantal Delattre; music, Albert Maroeur; sound, Antoine Ouvrier, William Flageollet; art direction, Michel Vandestien, Jacques Rouxel; assistant director, Gabriel Julien Laferrière. Reviewed at Denfert cinema, Paris, June 13, 1989. Running time: 75 MIN.
Elsa . . . . .Juliette Binoche
Al . . . . .François Cluzet
Duc . . . . .Thierry Jimenez
Sylvain . . . . .Daniel Jégou
Rateau . . . . . .Jean-Chretien Sibertin-Blanc
Berville . . . . .Denis Lavant
Jo . . . . .Thierry Fortineau
Montaigne . . . . .Albert Prevost
Bank manager . . . . .Michel Aumont
Filmmaker . . . . .Riccardo Freda

■Pierre Pradinas, a young theater director, reveals an eager cinematic sensibility in his first feature, "Un tour de manège." As a fully realized film it leaves something to be desired, but it's an often imaginative test run that in its best moments recalls the experimental exuberance of the French New Wave.

Pradinas deliberately reminds viewers that he's of the same generation as Léos Carax: Juliette Binoche is one of his two stars, and Denis Lavant, Carax' plug-ugly male actor, has a supporting role as an obnoxious social parasite.

Story, which Pradinas wrote with his brother Simon (and improvised upon during shooting), deals with the banal situation of a young couple trying to stick together but finally lost to each other. François Cluzet is a ne'er-do-well young man desperately dependent on the love of Binoche, so ethereally dissatisfied that she does a literal vanishing act in the film's ultimate sequence.

Cluzet sees an end to their material hassles when he is offered a movie role by a casting agent who lets the couple occupy his tastelessly fashionable Paris apartment.

Pradinas' exploration of the medium is saved from annoying self-indulgence by his sympathy for his leads, who give the fragile tale a melancholy emotional base. Supporting cast of assorted odd characters provides levity to the proceedings. Pradinas recalls a New Wave trait by casting veteran Italo action helmer Riccardo Freda in a cameo as the movie director Cluzet may work for.

Tech credits are fine.—*Len.*

Criminal Act

New York   An Independent Networks Inc./Film Ventures Intl. presentation. Executive producers, Robert B. Steuer, Irv Holender. Produced by Daniel Yost. Line producer, Richard Hench. Directed by Mark Byers. Screenplay, Yost; camera (Image Transform color), Roxanne di Santo; editor, M. Kathryn Campbell; music, Wayne Coster; sound, James Bennett; production design, Cole Lewis; art direction, Eric M. Townsend; assistant director, James C. Gordon; production manager, Gerard DiNardi; stunt coordinator, Jeff Smolek; coproducers, Myron Meisel, Bill Stern; associate producers, Stephen Kay, DiNardi. Reviewed on Prism Entertainment vidcassette, N.Y., July 22, 1989. No MPAA Rating. Running time: 93 MIN.

Pam Weiss . . . . .Catherine Bach
Sharon Fields . . . . .Charlene Dallas
Ron Bellard . . . . .Nicholas Guest
Herb . . . . .John Saxon
Also with: Cork Hubbert, Victor Brandt, Luis Avalos, Ray Tillotson, Rick Zumwalt, Syd Beard, Barbara Lusch, Vic Tayback, Jeanie Moore.

■ **Previously titled, more appropriately, "Tunnels," "Criminal Act" is a shaggy-dog, made-for-video feature that promises fantasy and horror but delivers a cornball story of greedy real estate developers.**

When a rat appears in their bathroom at work, newspaper reporter Catherine Bach and photographer Charlene Dallas are escorted to basement tunnels by the exterminator (Vic Tayback). They imagine the sight down there of monsters (humanoid rats). But after many a weary reel it turns out no monsters exist, only nasty guys kidnaping and killing street bums to pave the way for a multimillion-dollar real estate development scheme.

Though the two heroines make for a pleasant sparring team, poorly scripted pic fails to deliver an interesting or credible adventure for them. Bach shows off martial arts skills kicking some bad guys and there's one plot twist involving a double cross. If not for the video boom, this pic wouldn't have been made.

Overlong, padded feature has a pointless scene tacked on after the end credits. —*Lor.*

The Phantom Empire

New York   An American Independent production. Produced and directed by Fred Olen Ray. Screenplay, T.L. Lankford, Ray; camera (United color), Gary Graver; supervising editor, Robert A. Ferretti; editor, William Shaffer; music, Robert Garrett; sound, Dennis Fuller; production design, Cory Kaplan; costume design, Jill Conner; special visual effects, Mark D. Wolf, Wizard Works, Kaplan; special makeup effects, Paul M. Rinehard; special effects animation, Bret Mixon; assistant director-production manager, Tony Brewster; coproducer, Brewster; associate producers, Nick Marino, Salvatore Richici. Reviewed on Prism Entertainment vidcassette, N.Y., July 23, 1989. MPAA Rating: R. Running time: 83 MIN.

Cort Eastman . . . . .Ross Hagen
Andrew Paris . . . . .Jeffrey Combs
Eddy Colchilde . . . . .Dawn Wildsmith
Prof. Artemis Strock . . . . . .Robert Quarry
Denea Chambers . . . . .Susan Stokey
Cave bunny . . . . .Michelle Bauer
Bill .Russ Tamblyn
Alien queen . . . . .Sybil Danning
Picnic guy . . . . .Michael D. Sonye
Picnic girl . . . . .Victoria Alexander
Robby the Robot . . . . .Himself

■ **Named after a famous Gene Autry serial, "The Phantom Empire" is an affectionate nod to old-time lost world sci-fi pics, which should amuse homevideo fans.**

Helmer Fred Olen Ray shot this 1986 picture on a shoestring budget, ingeniously making up for lack of resources by stressing snap-py dialog and in-jokes (even Robby the Robot pops up as a bad guy).

Plot is simple: After a mutant creature emerges from a cave and kills two picnickers, Susan Stokey hires salvage experts Ross Hagen and Dawn Wildsmith to mount an expedition into the caves to search for the lost city of Rilah.

Robert Quarry and Jeffrey Combs tag along as mineral experts. Crew finds a race of mutants, plus beautiful girls in bikinis led by Michelle Bauer. Sybil Danning pops up as a queen from Outer Space mining for diamonds to fuel her crashed space ship on the return trip home.

There's some fun animated footage of dinosaurs plus endless chasing around, but pic mainly works via the tongue-in-cheek dialog exchanges of its cast, most of whom are cult favorites from fantasy and horror pics.

Wildsmith is in particularly good humor, cracking sarcastic jokes in a tough-girl role. Bauer is funny in exaggerated mime as, with no knowledge of English, she's pressed into service as the expedition's guide. Danning has one of her better, campier latter-day roles in a flashy black leather outfit. —*Lor.*

Witchtrap

New York   A Cinema Plus and GCO Pictures presentation of a Mentone Pictures production. Executive producers, Jackson Harvey, David A. Bowen. Produced by Kevin S. Tenney, Dan Duncan. Line producer, Joan C. Morisaki. Written and directed by Tenney. Camera (Monaco color), Thomas Jewett; editor, William O. Sullivan; music, Dennis Michael Tenney; sound, Rod Ellis; art direction, Ken Aichele; assistant director, Kelly Schroeder; special makeup effects, Judy Yonemoto; stunt coordinator, Richard Fraga; associate producer, Heino G. Moeller. Reviewed on Magnum Entertainment vidcassette, N.Y., July 29, 1989. MPAA Rating: R. Running time: 90 MIN.

Tony Vicente . . . . .James W. Quinn
Whitney . . . . .Kathleen Bailey
Agnes .Judy Tatum
Felix .Rob Zapple
Frank Murphy . . . . .Jack W. Thompson
Levi Jackson . . . . .Clyde Talley 2d
Ginger . . . . .Linnea Quigley
Also with: Hal Havins, Kevin S. Tenney, J.P. Luebsen.

■ **A followup to the successful 1986 release "Witchboard," "Witchtrap" is an occasionally interesting haunted house thriller that would have benefited from better casting and a more ample budget.**

Filmmaker Kevin S. Tenney, who also acts in this one, provides some hip dialog but gets disturbingly flat line readings from much of the cast. Pic, originally titled "The Presence," bypassed theatrical to go directly to videostores.

Devin Lauter (Tenney) calls in paranormal experts to exorcise the haunted house he's inherited from his uncle and renovated at considerable cost. Crew, led by siblings Judy Tatum and Rob Zapple, finds ample evidence that Uncle Avery (J.P. Luebsen) is stalking the premises. The only way to put his soul to rest is to merge his missing heart with the rest of his remains.

While the ghost kills off much of the cast, including guest star Linnea Quigley, James W. Quinn and Kathleen Bailey team up to outwit it. Unfortunately, pic's ending is cryptic.

Makeup effects by Judy Yonemoto are okay. —*Lor.*

Murder Story
(DUTCH-BRITISH)

New York   A Contracts Intl. and Elsevier-Vendex Film presentation of a Tom Reeve production. Produced by Murder Story B.V. Holland for Reeve & Partners Film Co. Ltd. Produced by Reeve. Executive producers, Jim Reeve, Ronnie Gerschtanowitz. Written and directed by Eddie Arno, Markus Innocenti. Camera (Cineco color), Marc Felperlaan; editor, Rodney Holland; music, Wayne Bickerton; sound, Victor Dekker; production design, Morley Smith; assistant director, Will Koopmans; production manager, Simon Jansen; stunt coordinator, Henk Wams. Reviewed on Academy Entertainment vidcassette, N.Y., July 26, 1989. Running time: 90 MIN.

Willard Hope . . . . .Christopher Lee
Corrigan . . . . .Bruce Boa
Tony Zonis . . . . .Alexis Desinof
Marty . . . . .Stacia Burton
Also with: Kieron Jecchinis, Jeff Harding, Kate Harper, Garrick Hagon, Marie Stillin, Bill Bailey.

■ **Dutch-made thriller "Murder Story" is a passable light entertainment where youngsters become involved in real-life murder and espionage (à la Universal's "Gotcha" and "Cloak & Dagger").**

With British backing and casting, pic shapes as an okay video.

Interesting screenplay by tandem directors Eddie Arno and Markus Innocenti focuses on aspiring young novelist Alexis Desinof, living in Amsterdam, who's copying the technique of his author hero Willard Hope (Christopher Lee), whereby seemingly random newspaper clippings are merged as genesis for a mystery.

When Desinof meets his hero at a book-signing session and finds out he also lives in Amsterdam, he inveigles for assistance from Lee. Duo, plus Desinof's pretty girlfriend Stacia Burton, start putting disparate clues together and soon become targets for extinction by real-life killers involved in stolen scientific research.

Film unfolds suspensefully but is hampered by an open ending which (on purpose to prove a point) does not resolve the mystery.

Lee is authoritative as the cultivated armchair hero pressed into action, in a depature from his sinister roles. Young leads Desinof and Burton are engaging.

Pic is relatively tame compared to other films in its genre. Big-name casting for the youngsters plus a more topical central mystery could have elevated this acceptable picture to must-see status. —*Lor.*

The Adventures Of Milo And Otis
(JAPANESE)

The Japanese outdoor adventure film "The Adventures Of Chatran" is being released domestically by Columbia Pictures Aug. 25 as "The Adventures Of Milo And Otis," with narration by Dudley Moore added and running time cut from 90 to 76 minutes.

Original pic, directed by Masanori Hata (with associate director Kon Ichikawa) was reviewed by *Sege.* from the Cannes Film Festival market as "Koneko Monogatari" in the May 21, '86, issue of VARIETY. Mark Saltzman wrote the U.S. version's screenplay based on Hata's story, and Michael Boddicker composed the score for the Col release.

Sege. called the picture "a stunning achievement ... The film is about a male cat and the animals and reptiles he encounters during extended and risky forays into the Hokkaido countryside. There is not a single human being in the picture.

"(Hata) treats the animals anthropomorphically — that is, he puts them in situations and shows them acting much like humans. This, however, is done while maintaining a sense of dignity, even reverence, for his charges."

Casualties Of War

Hollywood A Columbia Pictures release of an Art Linson production. Produced by Linson. Coproducer, Fred Caruso. Directed by Brian DePalma. Screenplay, David Rabe, from an article by Daniel Lang; camera (Deluxe color; Technicolor prints), Stephen H. Burum; editor, Bill Pankow; music, Ennio Morricone; sound (Dolby), Gary Wilkins; production design, Wolf Kroeger; art direction, Bernard Hydes; set decoration, Hugh Scaife, Peter Hancock; costume design, Richard Bruno; special effects supervisor, Kit West; stunt coordinator, Jeff Jensen; assistant director, Brian W. Cook, Sompol Sungkawess, Aldric Porter; casting, Lynn Stalmaster. Reviewed at The Burbank Studios, Calif., Aug. 9, 1989. MPAA Rating: R. Running time: **113 MIN.**

Eriksson	Michael J. Fox
Meserve	Sean Penn
Clark	Don Harvey
Hatcher	John C. Reilly
Diaz	John Leguizamo
Oahn	Thuy Thu Le
Brown	Erik King
Rowan	Jack Gwaltney
Lt. Reilly	Ving Rhames
Hawthorne	Dan Martin
Capt. Hill	Dale Dye
Chaplain Kirk	Sam Robards
Cherry	Darren E. Burrows
Oahn's Mother	Ba Thuan T Le

■ **A powerful metaphor of the national shame that was America's orgy of destruction in Vietnam, Brian DePalma's film is flawed by some punch-pulling but is sure to rouse strong audience interest, even if the Columbia release will be a bitter pill for many.**

Turning one of America's most distinctive directors of horror films loose on the Vietnam War is perfect casting, at least for the part of "Casualties Of War" dealing directly with the harrowing rape and murder of a Vietnamese woman by four GIs.

Journalist Daniel Lang's account of the actual 1966 atrocity first appeared in 1969 as a New Yorker article and was later reprinted in book form. Methodically examining the spiral of violence unleashed in young Americans by the absence of moral standards in Vietnam, Lang uses the incident to raise unspoken questions about the insanity of the U.S. mission there.

The effortlessly authentic script by David Rabe is eloquent in its simplicity and sticks to Lang's account in all but a few of its awful particulars. Unfortunately, Rabe and DePalma have also flinched from the most truly horrific aspect of the crime, and have skimmed through the aftermath en route to a simplistic happy ending.

Screen newcomer Thuy Thu Le is the Vietnamese woman kidnapped by a reconnaissance patrol as what the deranged sergeant (Sean Penn) calls "a little portable R&R to break up the boredom, keep up morale." When the men are through using her sexually, they stab and shoot her to death, over the futile objections of the lone holdout, a "cherry" private played by Michael J. Fox.

Casting Fox was a brilliant coup on DePalma's part, since he brings with him an image of all-American boyishness and eager-beaver conservatism that makes him an ideal audience surrogate figure for this story. Fox' beautifully acted cowardly passivity in the face of the unthinkable challenges and implicates the viewer to examine his own conscience on the subject of Vietnam.

This seems a film DePalma was born to make, given his early antiwar subject matter in the 1960s and his fascination with the most extreme forms of cinematic violence. Here he abandons his usual sly humor in the face of a genuinely appalling subject.

DePalma's greatest gift is the visceral power he is able to bring to violence, sucking the viewer into the giddy madness of the murderous impulse. It is a dangerous gift, one that can spill over into irresponsibility, but here DePalma subordinates his p.o.v. shots and sinuous camera movements to shock the viewer out of any lingering complacency about what we were doing in Vietnam.

Always riveting to watch even if he often crosses into overacting, Penn is able to shade his rampaging maleness with overtones of sexual uncertainty that weren't present in Lang's account. While he taunts Fox for supposed sexual inadequacy in not participating in the gang rape, it is Fox' moral impotence that is the most subtly disturbing character trait on display here.

Far from an admirable figure, the Fox character is able to indulge the luxury of contempt for the other men in the squad while registering only a few muted protests and never turning his weapon on them or taking the woman to safety. Fox movingly conveys the character's growing self-disgust over this failure to act, even as he assumes a heroic posture in bucking the system by turning the others over to flawed military justice.

Where the film falters most seriously is by dropping the element of premeditation that existed in the actual murder. Lang chillingly relates that the sergeant told the men in advance that "they would avail themselves of her body, finally disposing of it, to keep the girl from ever accusing them of abduction and rape."

Perhaps figuring that watching such a cold-blooded procedure would be too hard for the audience to take, Rabe and DePalma have diluted some of the impact of the woman's death at the same time as they have subtly reduced Fox' moral responsibility by making the murder more of an ad hoc occurrence.

They also have skimmed much too quickly over Fox' struggle to bring the crime to light and the court-martial that followed.

Rather than leaving the Fox character with anxious feelings of his real-life counterpart — fearful of retribution from the men he turned in, still unable to sort out his past and his future — Rabe and DePalma have concocted a pat Stateside ending that too easily pretends that he has put the nightmare behind him.

As usual for a DePalma film, the tech contributions are firstrate. Stephen H. Burum's lensing is suitably dark, airless and claustrophobic, making striking use of the Steadicam. Wolf Kroeger's production design turns the Thailand locations into a convincing evocation of Vietnam's Central Highlands in 1966.

The profound emotions stirred by this flawed but often majestic film are served best of all by the somber and heartfelt score by Ennio Morricone, who brings home in a stabbing rush all of the tragedy of Vietnam. —*Mac.*

Bal poussière
(Dusty Ball)
(IVORY COAST)

Paris An Imperia release of a Focale 13 production. Written, produced and directed by Henri Duparc. Camera (color), Bernard Dechet; editor, Christine Aya; music, Boncana Naiga; sound, Pierre André Gauthier. Reviewed at Gaumont Ambassade theater, Paris, Aug. 1, 1989. Running time: **88 MIN.**

"Half-God"	Bakary Bamba
Binta	Tchelly Hanny
Nya	Naky Sy Savane
Fanta	Thérèse Taba

■ **This slight comedy about polygamy in the Ivory Coast won the Grand Prize (and critics award) at this year's Humor Film Festival in Chamrousse. It has an engaging premise but Henri Duparc's screenplay and direction don't do it comic justice.**

Pic has been doing pleasantly

enough at local wickets but isn't likely to be another "The Gods Must Be Crazy."

Story is set in a village whose leading citizen, a rich peasant called "Half-God" — because he's second to God only — decides to take a sixth wife to round out his week. He beds one a night, on the seventh day he rests, or awards a conjugal bonus to "best-behaved" member of his harem.

Unfortunately for him, the new light of his loins is a modern-minded young beauty who is pressed into the union by her self-serving traditional parents. She sets out to turn the household upside down with her iconoclastic behavior, and comes into a rivalry with her fellow spouses. When a musician boyfriend turns up for the local ball of the title, she runs away with him, however.

There is some mild satire here in Bakary Bamba's benignly self-infatuated machismo and his household conferences with his womenfolk. The complications introduced by the street-smart Tchelly lack the mounting tensions and humor of good situation comedy. Whatever charm the film has is created by its actors more than script or helming.

Tech credits are mediocre.

—*Len.*

Uncle Buck

New York   A Universal Pictures release. Produced by John Hughes, Tom Jacobson. Written and directed by Hughes. Camera (Deluxe color), Ralf D. Bode; editor, Lou Lombardo, Tony Lombardo, Peck Prior; music, Ira Newborn; additional music, Matt Dike, Michael Ross; sound (Dolby), James Alexander; production design, John W. Corso; visual consultant, Douglas Arthur Kraner; set decoration, Dan May; costume design, Marilyn Vance-Straker; assistant director, Thomas Mack; 2d unit director, Bill Brown; 2d unit camera, Gregory Lundsgaard; associate producers, Brown, Ramey E. Ward; casting, Risa Bramon, Billy Hopkins. Reviewed at National 1 Theater, N.Y., Aug. 9, 1989. MPAA Rating: PG. Running time: **100 MIN.**
Buck Russell . . . . John Candy
Chanice Kobolowski . . . . Amy Madigan
Tia Russell . . . . Jean Louisa Kelly
Maizy Russell . . . . Gaby Hoffman
Miles Russell . . . . Macaulay Culkin
Cindy Russell . . . . Elaine Bromka
Bob Russell . . . . Garrett M. Brown
Marcie . . . . Laurie Metcalf
Bug . . . . Jay Underwood

■ **John Hughes unsuccessfully tries to mix a serious generation gap message between the belly laughs in "Uncle Buck," a warm-weather John Candy vehicle unlikely to hold its theaters for a long run.**

The talented comic had better choose his assignments more carefully, given he's already had two flops released this year: "Who's Harry Crumb?" and ensemble comedy "Speed Zone."

On paper the rotund Second City veteran seems ideal for the title role: a ne'er-do-well, coarse black sheep of the family suddenly pressed into service when his relatives (Elaine Bromka, Garrett M. Brown), a suburban Chicago family, have to rush off to visit Bromka's dad, stricken with a heart attack.

Enter Uncle Buck, put in charge of the three youngsters for an indefinite period. Audience knows immediately that the clash will lead to sitcom humor as well as sentimentality as the kids wear down Buck's rough edges and he teaches them some seat-of-the-pants lessons about life.

Unfortunately, Candy is too likable to give the role any edge. When called upon to be tough or mean he's unconvincing, as in the slapstick dealings with the precociously oversexed boyfriend Bug (Jay Underwood) of eldest daughter Jean Louisa Kelly. This crude version of a Mr. Belvedere role calls for an actor who can be cuddly and threatening simultaneously, e.g., Mr. T.

Candy does deliver the gags well, e.g., microwaving the laundry after abusing the recalcitrant washer-dryer; or funny bits involving his grotesque junker of a car with its thunderous backfiring.

Hughes' decision to emphasize the nastiness of teen Kelly (who calls Bromka "the mother figure" and is bleakly sarcastic at all times) as a way of showing youngsters' estrangement from their parents is a fatal blow to the film. Kelly's performance is technically okay, but the character is so unsympathetic and Hughes' dialog so cruel that the picture stops dead for each of her big scenes, forcing Candy to recover the light tone rather than build gag upon gag. Cornball final-reel clinch as she's reconciled with her parents following Candy's going to bat for her is a transparent attempt at audience manipulation.

Beyond principals Candy and Kelly, there's a thankless role for Amy Madigan, miscast as Candy's long-suffering g.f.; no way could one believe the feisty thesp would sit still for a minute let alone eight years of the lowlife gambler's antics. Young kids Gaby Hoffman and Macaulay Culkin are supportive, particularly Culkin in a "Dragnet"-voices routine with the star. Rest of the cast is caricatured.

Tech credits for the Chicago-locationed pic are excellent, with an eclectic selection of mainly '50s songs brightening up the soundtrack. —*Lor.*

Puppet Master

New York   A Full Moon production. Executive producer, Charles Band. Produced by Hope Perello. Directed by David Schmoeller. Screenplay, Joseph G. Collodi, from story by Band, Kenneth J. Hall; camera (color), Sergio Salvati; editor, Tom Meshelski; music, Richard Band; sound (Ultra-Stereo), William Fiege; production design, John Myhre; assistant director, David Turchi; production manager, Gary Schmoeller; puppet effects, David Allen Prods. — supervisor, Allen; special makeup effects, Patrick Simmons; 2d unit director, Perello; additional camera, Russ Carpenter; casting, Vivian Levy. Reviewed on Paramount vidcassette, N.Y., Aug. 5, 1989. MPAA Rating: R. Running time: **90 MIN.**
Alex . . . . Paul Le Mat
Dana Hadley . . . . Irene Miracle
Frank . . . . Matt Roe
Clarissa . . . . Kathryn O'Reilly
Megan Gallagher . . . . Robin Frates
Theresa . . . . Merrya Small
Neil . . . . Jimmie F. Scaggs
Andre Toulan . . . . William Hickey
Also with: Barbara Crampton, David Boyd.

■ **"Puppet Master" is a well-crafted horror feature from Charles Band's reborn production outifit. Paramount direct-to-video release should scare up solid interest from fans of last year's "Child's Play."**

Stars of this effort are various cute/scary little puppets, brought to life by Dave Allen Prods., which terrorize a group of psychics summoned to the Bodega Bay Hotel when a man they worked with (Jimmie F. Scaggs) commits suicide.

The puppets were crafted by the title character (William Hickey), who committed suicide in 1939 at the same site.

Pic's human characters, led by a miscast Paul Le Mat (as a Yale anthropology prof), are stock figures out of an Agatha Christie tale, but the puppets are lively and a treat. For example, the Pin Head has burly arms but a tiny dome (working by a combo of stopmotion animation and little person Cindy Sorensen handling the arm movements). Goofiest creation is a femme puppet that emits live leeches from its mouth.

Script gimmick of almost the entire cast being psychic (with varying powers) is not exploited well, and director David Schmoeller's pacing is off-kilter, notably in a laborious 10-minute prolog starring Hickey. Gory finale fulfills genre cliches, including most of the victims' corpses gathered together at a party.

It is the realistically fluid movements of the tiny beasties that audiences will remember, aided by the dramatic lighting and low-angle camerawork of imported Italian cinematographer Sergio Salvati.

Kathryn O'Reilly provides some sexy scenes before the puppets get her, while guest star Barbara Crampton (of "The Re-Animator") has little to do in her brief spot. Tech credits are way above average for video-oriented features. —*Lor.*

The Gods Must Be Crazy 2
(BOTSWANA)

Paris   A Weintraub Entertainment Group (U.S.) release, 20th Century Fox in France, of a Boet Troskie production. Written and directed by Jamie Uys. Camera (color), second unit direction and stunt coordinator, Buster Reynolds; editor, Renée Engelbrecht, Ivan Hall; music, Charles Fox; sound, Eward Pearse; narrator, Paddy O'Byrne; production manager, Gerda van den Broek. Reviewed at Marignan-Concorde cinema, Paris, Aug. 6, 1989. MPAA Rating: PG. Running time: **99 MIN.**
With: N!xau, Lena Farugia, Hans Strydom, Eiros, Nadies, Erick Bowen, Treasure Tshabalala, Pierre Van Pletzen, Lourens Swanepoel.

■ **Jamie Uys has concocted a genial sequel to his 1983 international sleeper hit "The Gods Must Be Crazy" that is better than its progenitor in most respects. If initial response in France — where it is preeming — is an accurate gauge, "Gods 2" could receive favor from the boxoffice deities in other territories.**

20th Century Fox is releasing in eight European markets, include France, West Germany and the U.K., while Weintraub Entertainment Group has domestic rights.

Uys, who wrote, "conceived" and directed, is lucky and clever: lucky to have hit upon a formula — call it ethnological burlesque — that is sympathetically exotic and fertile in story possibilities; and clever in the comic, but unpatronizing, exploitation of his characters and environment.

His tongue-clicking Kalahari Bushman hero, again played by a real McCoy named N!xau, is once more unwittingly embroiled in the lunacies of civilization. Uys has orchestrated a desert farce of criss-crossing destinies with more assured skill and charming sight-gags, marred only by facile penchant for speeded-up slapstick motion.

Pic also harks back charmingly to silent movie comedy in its thorough and often imaginative use of props and accessories. Uys manages to find in his desert setting an extraordinary range of objects and animals that take active part in the funmaking.

Filmmaker too is aware of what's been in commercial fashion these past seasons. Kids and animals? — "Gods 2" has both.

First plotline has N!xau's two adorable offspring getting innocently borne away on the trailer truck of a pair of unsuspecting ivory poachers. N!xau follows the tracks and comes across two other odd couples from the nutty outside world.

There is a New York femme lawyer (Lena Farugia), a guest lecturer at a local convention, who is stranded in the middle of the Kalahari with a handsome, phlegmatic game warden (Hans Strydom) when their ultra-light plane is downed in a sudden storm. In their attempts to get airborne again they are plagued by the desert fauna, which include elephants, rhinos, ostriches, snakes, giraffes, monkeys, leopards, tigers and hyenas.

Then there are two hapless mercenaries, an African and a Cuban, who keep taking one another prisoner in a series of table-turning pursuits through the brush.

These four tandems (kids, poachers, stranded whites and mercenaries) meet up under the desert-smart aegis of the guileless N!xau, who teaches everybody a lesson in survival tactics and human decency before returning home with his children.

Cast is straight-faced and engaging. Adequate tech credits suggest Uys had the time and money to give this one more professional polish. —*Len.*

Eddie And The Cruisers II: Eddie Lives (CANADIAN)

New York   A Scotti Bros. Pictures release, in association with Aurora Film Partners, presented by Tony Scotti, of a Les Prods. Alliance production. Executive producers, Victor Loewy, Denis Héroux, William Stuart, James L. Stuart. Produced by Stéphanie Reichel. Line producer, Wendy Grean. Directed by Jean-Claude Lord. Screenplay, Charles Zev Cohen, Rick Doehring, based on characters created by P.F. Kluge; camera (Sonolab color), René Verzier; editor, Jean-Guy Montpetite; music, Marty Simon, Leon Aronson; music supervision, Kenny Vance; songs, John Cafferty, performed by Cafferty & the Beaver Brown Band; sound (Dolby),

Don Cohen; art direction, Dominic Ricard; set decoration, Gilles Aird; costume design, Ginnette Magny; assistant director, Pedro Gandol; dance staged by Claude Thompson. Reviewed at Magno Review 2 screening room, N.Y., Aug. 9, 1989. MPAA Rating: PG-13. Running time: 103 MIN.
Eddie Wilson/Joe West . . . . . Michael Paré
Diane . . . . Marina Orsini
Rick . . . . Bernie Coulson
Sal . . . . Matthew Laurance
Dave Pagent . . . . Michael Rhoades
Hilton . . . . Anthony Sherwood
Quinn . . . . Mark Holmes
Stewart . . . . David Matheson
Charlie . . . . Paul Markle
    Also with: Kate Lynch, Harvey Atkin, Vlasta Vrana, Larry King, Bo Diddley, Martha Quinn, Merrill Shindler, Sunny Joe White, Michael (Tunes) Antunes.

■ This sequel shapes up as one of the most commercial indie pics since "Dirty Dancing." Scotti Bros. could have an all-media hit on its hands if audiences deign to sample a small feature amid the blockbusters.

Martin Davidson's 1983 original, based on P.F. Kluge's novel and boasting a stars-of-the-future cast headed by Tom Berenger and Ellen Barkin, was a flop release from Embassy Pictures. Subsequent brisk sales of the soundtrack album spurred by HBO showings of the pic made a sequel viable.

In key ways, "Eddie Lives" corrects the dramatic deficiencies of the original, while retaining such potent elements as John Cafferty's songs (solid new ones) and central character of Michael Paré as fictional rock totem Eddie Wilson.

This time, Paré is center stage throughout, not some flashbacks-only remote figure from 1960s New Jersey. Celebrating numerous tried-and-true showbiz clichés, plotline has Paré in 1989 as a Montreal construction worker named Joe West, his moustache and character-lined face differentiating him from the singing superstar everyone thinks died in a car crash in 1964 (but whose body was never found).

He's brought back to performing when his record label issues his previously unreleased final album as well as singles from a "mystery tapes" session that may or may not be the real McCoy. A young guitarist (Bernie Coulson in a fun performance) coaxes Paré to join his band, which the purist musical taskmaster soon revamps into a super group selected to play at a Montreal Arts Festival. Paré finally comes out of the closet and reveals himself as Eddie Wilson at the climax of that concert, lavishly staged (at a real Bon Jovi gig) in Las Vegas.

Pic very well could be the career boost for Paré that "Wiseguy" on

tv was for Ken Wahl, as the ruggedly handsome thesp delivers forcefully in a near-mythic role. His lip-synced emotional readings of songs sung by Cafferty on the soundtrack are convincing.

Supporting cast, largely Canadian, is overshadowed, but besides Coulson there are effective spots for Geena Davis-lookalike Marina Orsini as Paré's girlfriend; Anthony Sherwood as the new group's charismatic tenor sax player, and on recall from the first film, Matthew Laurance as the folksy "guy from Jersey" left high and dry by Eddie's disappearance. Extended cameos by the likes of Larry King, Martha Quinn and Bo Diddley are fun and fit the film's mythic approach.

Cafferty's songs include at least two possible hits, a rousing (and frequently reprised here) "Running Through The Fire" and a hard-driving number, "Pride And Passion."

Helmer Jean-Claude Lord, known for horror pics starring Pam Grier and William Shatner, pilots efficiently with especially dynamic results during the musical sequences. Noteworthy among these is an energetic nightclub dance routine staged by Claude Thompson. Unusual among recent Canadian productions aimed at general U.S. audiences, pic refreshingly doesn't hide its north-of-the-border content, with frequent emphasis on the Montreal locale (including snowy scenes and hockey games). —*Lor.*

Rude Awakening

New York   An Orion Pictures release of an Aaron Russo Entertainment presentation. Produced by Aaron Russo. Directed by Russo and David Greenwalt. Screenplay, Neil Levy, Richard LaGravenese, from a story by Levy; camera (Film House color), Tom Sigel; editor, Paul Fried; music supervised by Paul Rothchild; music, Jonathan Elias; sound, Greg Sheldon; production design, Mel Bourne; set decoration, Carol Nast; costumes, Peggy Farrell; production manager, Mitch Gamson; assistant director, Joel Segal; associate producer, Bill Carraro; casting, Joy Todd. Reviewed at Magno Review 1 Screening Room, N.Y., Aug. 11, 1989. MPAA Rating R. Running time: 100 MIN.
Hesus . . . . Cheech Marin
Fred Wouk . . . . Eric Roberts
Petra . . . . Julie Hagerty
Sammy . . . . Robert Carradine
Lloyd Stoole . . . . Buck Henry
Ronnie . . . . Louise Lasser
June . . . . Cindy Williams
April Stoole . . . . Andrea Martin
Brubaker . . . . Cliff DeYoung
Voice of fish . . . . Aaron Russo
    Also with: Timothy Leary, Jerry Rubin, Bobby Seale, David Peel, Greg Rex, Dion Anderson, Peter Boyden, Nicholas Wyman, Michael Luciano, Ed Fry, Timothy L. Halpern, Davidson Thomson, Kevin Dornan, Deena Levy.

■ A good-natured comedy, "Rude Awakening" offers an entertaining cast of characters whose antics aim for the conscience as well as the funny bone, but since belly laughs are sparse, producer Aaron Russo's directorial debut gives off only modest boxoffice prospect vibes.

Nostalgia for the 1960s and the harsh realities of the 1980s clash seriocomically as two career hippies (Eric Roberts and Cheech Marin) return to New York after 20 years of commune life in a Central American (actually Florida) forest.

Hoping to maintain peace, they bring with them classified plans for a war in Central America given to them by a dying CIA man. Other U.S. agents (headed by Cliff DeYoung's broadly comic psychotic G-man) tail Roberts and Marin from one old friend's New York pad to another. But a chase yarn this isn't.

Filmmakers instead choose to concentrate on what happens when Marin and Roberts' hippie outlook on life, intact for two decades, mixes with the newfound materialism of their old friends — starting with Louise Lasser, a loopy eatery owner whose Nouveau Woodstock has a big yuppie clientele "that I can't get rid of."

Then there are Julie Hagerty, a successful but neurotic designer, and Robert Carradine, owner of a chain of tanning salons who brags, "People will pay for a suntan." "How do you get the sun to fall on just the guys who pay" asks Marin, the stoned-out innocent.

In the ensemble cast's dominant role, Roberts is great as the free spirit who can walk into a room and immediately cure anyone of his or her uptightness. Second City Television's Andrea Martin steals the pic's funniest scene as the prim and proper co-op owner who visits prospective buyers Carradine and wife (Cindy Williams). Martin, too, loosens up (hilariously) as the hippies descend on their orderly life.

Soon things turn grave as Roberts finds out the way of the world: Everyone is more interested in money than peace or pollution. In fact, he breaks down crying until a few young idealogues-come-lately ask for help in organizing a movement to clean up the environment.

In the first pic from his recently formed production company (buttressed by a $100-million budget for seven pics over three years and

Orion for domestic distribution), Russo took over helming chores following departure of David Greenwalt ("Secret Admirer") midway through production. Thus the codirector credit.

Unevenness of the comedy is probably more a function of the screenplay than the directorial upheaval. Overall, "Rude Awakening" has hints of a sleeper hit, but it'll take a lot of luck and marketing savvy to wake that potential. *—Binn.*

Angels Of The City

New York A Raedon Home Video release of a PM Entertainment Group production. Produced by Richard Pepin, Joseph Merhi. Directed by Lawrence-Hilton Jacobs. Screenplay, Raymond Martino, Merhi, Jacobs; camera (color), Pepin; editor, Paul Volk; music, Jastereo Coviare, John Gonzalez, Jacobs; assistant director, Addison Randall; special makeup effects, Judy Yonemoto; associate producers, Charla Driver, R.W. Munchkin. Reviewed on Raedon videcassette, N.Y., Aug. 2, 1989. No MPAA Rating. Running time: **89. MIN.**

Catherine	Kelly Galindo
Wendy	Cynthia Cheston
Gold	Michael Ferrare
Lee	Renny Stroud
Tavares	Jastereo Coviare
Det. Jon Chance	Lawrence-Hilton Jacobs
Mick	Brian Ochse

Also with: Rusty Schmidt, Lisa Axelrod, Richard Allen, Kari French, Meryl Swartz, Danny Acevdeo, Kym Elizabeth Whitely, Ron Preston.

■ **Former "Welcome Back, Kotter" costar Lawrence-Hilton Jacobs makes an impressive feature helming debut with "Angels Of The City," an action pic released direct to video.**

Coeds Kelly Galindo and Cynthia Cheston pose as L.A. hookers as part of their sorority initiation. They're kidnaped as part of a turf war between rival pimps and are subsequently on the run for much of the film after witnessing a bloody shootout between the mack men.

Jacobs reprises his acting role as tough detective Jon Chance (previously featured in "L.A. Heat"). His direction here is tight, balancing action and exploitation elements of the seamy underworld setting with an interesting subplot of Galindo using her traumatic experience (which leaves Cheston a vegetable at pic's end) as part of a sociology class project for getting in touch with real-life people. Unusual construction has a seemingly minor character, a runaway girl, turning out to be the catalyst for Galindo's new awareness.

Cast (including several impressively evil-looking villains) and tech credits are okay for this low-budgeter. *—Lor.*

Lykken er en underlig fisk (Happiness Is a Curious Catch) (DANISH)

Copenhagen A Warner and Metronome release of a Metronome Film production in association with DR/TV and the Danish Film Institute. Produced by Mads Egmont Christensen. Written and directed by Linda Wendel. Camera (Eastmancolor), Björn Blixt; 2d unit camera, Dan Lausten; editor, Janus Billeskov Jansen; music, Thomas Koppel/Savage Rose, vocals, Anisette; sound, Morten Degnbol, Henrik Langkilde; production design, Claus Bjerre; screenplay consultants, Sören Ulrik Thomsen, Kristen Thorup; production management, Marianne Christensen; DFI consultant producer, Kirsten Bonnén Rask. Reviewed at Dagmar, Copenhagen, Aug. 10, 1989. Running time: **90 MIN.**

Mia	Stine Bierlich
Lotta, her mother	Helle Ryslinge
Mia's kid brother	Sebastian di Lucci
Christian	Lars Knutzon
Sandvik	Ole Ernst
Manfred	Pelle Koppel

Also with: Tom Jacobsen, Lise Schröder, Jen Jörn Spottag, Carsten Bang, Mogens Brix-Pedersen, Beatrice Palner.

■ **Linda Wendel's "Happiness Is A Curious Catch" is a group portrait of abject people in a small fishing community on Jutland's North Sea Coast.**

Sketchily told film never gets off the ground as dramatic narrative, but neat little human insights and keen social observations should help usher "Happiness" into some offshore tv sales.

Sadness reigns throughout this muted film about Lotta (Helle Ryslinge), a former beauty queen who 17 years ago found refuge (she thought) for herself and for Mia, her newborn, fatherless daughter. Her marriage to a steady fisherman, however, long ago turned sour.

Mia (Stine Bierlich) is left to take charge of a lately arrived kid brother, while Lotta, now withered and haggard, works days in a fish cannery and at night runs a casino of sorts from her home for her husband and his cronies, including the small-town big shot (Ole Ernst), everybody's employer.

The employer has designs on both mother and daughter. The mother dreams of running away with this uncaring Mr. Big, while his nice son defeats humiliations to marry the daughter.

Since everybody has been seen as thoroughly miserable in spite of their unsuccessful attempts to be nice to each other, the humorous surprise ending, with the wedding party posing outside the church, seems to radiate nothing beyond bitter irony.

Bierlich, left to look chubbily morose too much of the time, has some fine interplay with Sebastian di Lucci as her kid borther, a true and stubborn survivor of the shabby warfare between adults and near-adults endowed with scant intelligence.

"Happiness" has fine cinematography that rarely gets a chance to work itself naturally into the film's dramatic context. The near-absence of supporting music is a conscious conceit. *—Kell.*

En verden til forskel (A World Of Difference) (DANISH)

Copenhagen A Pathé-Nordisk Film release of an L&M production, in association with Nordisk Film and the Danish Film Institute. Produced by Kristian Levring. Written and directed by Leif Magnusson. Camera (Eastmancolor), Steen Veileborg; editor, Janus Billeskov Jansen; music, Torbjörn Tuvom, Yevgeni Doga; sound, Henrik Langkilde; production design, Claus Bjerre; production management, Thomas Lydholm, Maja Dich. Reviewed at Lille Björn screening room, Copenhagen, Aug. 11, 1989. Running time: **96 MIN.**

Jens	Adam Kozlowski
His father	Boguslaw Linda
Vicky	Hilda Jensen
Hassec	Miroslaw Dymitrow
Bente	Kirsten Lehfeldt

Also with: Poul Hagen, Morten Lorentzen, Rasmus Haxen, Svank Djukic, Lars von Trier, Peter Schröder, Jens Jörgen Spotag.

■ **"A World Of Difference" by tv graduate Leif Magnusson is yet another attempt at seeing the confusion of immigrants/refugees in the post-World War II Europe through the eyes of a child.**

Due to confused storytelling and mixing of cinematic styles, only pic's charmingly subdued and natural 12-year-old Adam Kozlowski may help it get some foreign exposure.

The boy, bearing the Danish name of Jens, is first seen as an unhappy Polish immigrant pupil in a tough Yugoslav boarding school from which he flees. He gets to Denmark as a stowaway on a train and finds his Polish father, who lives a tawdry existence as a gambler/dreamer/schemer. He welcomes his long-lost son, but he gets nowhere with his plans even when the boy helps him retrieve some money he has been robbed of by fellow immigrants.

The Danes around the father and the boy are a cold lot. Feeling let down by his dad, the boy sets out to return to Yugoslavia where, inexplicably, an old granddad welcomes him into some never-never land rural idyll. Has the boy actually inherited his father's aptitude for hiding behind dreams? This point remains undeveloped.

Magnusson's film seems to have the child as victom of a careless-to-callous world as its theme. Mercifully, however," "A World Of Difference" never turns maudlin, and opposite Kozlowski, Boguslaw Linda as the father and Hilda Jensen as a sub-teen slum vamp perform with admirable restraint. *—Kell.*

LOCARNO FESTIVAL REVIEWS

Piravi (Birth) (INDIAN)

Locarno A NFDC, Discovery of India presentation of a film Folk Trivandrum production. Directed by Shaji N. Karun. Screenplay, S. Jayachandran Nair, Ragunath Paleri, Shaji; camera (color), Sunny Joseph; editor, Venugopal; music, G. Aravindan. Reviewed at Locarno Festival (competing), Aug. 6, 1989. Running time: **110 MIN.**
With: Premji, Archana, C.V. Sreeraman, Mullene, Krishna Moorty.

■ **This is a slow-moving, touching and tender first film by a director of photography who is evidently in love with the landscape of Trivandrum in the south of India, and gets the best out of it.**

It's inspired by a real incident that took place in the late '70s when a student who dared to sing a protest song and was never heard of again. This is the student's imaginary story told from the point of view of his family, living in a faraway village.

Raghu studies in the big city to become an important person. As holidays are approaching, the father goes every day to wait for him at the bus station. Days go by and Raghu is not there. Strange rumors make their way to the isolated village.

The old man finally decides to go into the city and find out the truth, but all he gets is polite and meaningless information. Only when the daughter goes to Raghu's student friends does the terrible truth of his disappearance come out.

The story is affecting because of its simple, unadorned approach, and thanks to the remarkable expressiveness of each face, particularly the father, Premji, and the daughter, Archana.

It takes some time getting used to the slow, meticulous pace of the film, but it becomes a painfully compelling elegy dealing with the generation gap and the destruction of the family unit. It's also a sad political comment on a country that has still not quite managed its transition to democracy. —*Edna*.

Khaneh-je Doost Kojast
(Where Is My Friend's House)
(IRANIAN)

Locarno A Farabi Cinema Foundation presentation of an Institute for Intellectual Development of Children and Young Adults (Teheran) production. Written, directed and edited by Abbas Kiaros-tami. Camera (color), Farhad Saba. Reviewed at Locarno Film Festival (competing), Aug. 6, 1989. Running time: **83 MIN.**
With: Babak Ahmadpoor, Ahmad Ahmadpoor, Khodabakhsh Defai, Iran Otari, Ayat Ansari, Sedigheh Tohidi, Peiman Moafi, Tayebeh Soleimani, Mohammad Reza Parvaneh, Farhang Akhavan.

■ **This agonizingly slow film is recommended to patient film-goers who are not bothered by endless repetition designed to help drive home the picture's theme.**

Basically, it's a children's film about 8-year-old Ahmad, who has taken his friend's copybook by mistake, and wastes an entire afternoon trying to find him in a neighboring village. Not knowing his friend's address, he wanders back and forth on the narrow streets, asking in vain everybody he meets until night falls and he has to return home.

There is something admirable in the boy's insistence on delivering the copybook to save his colleague another scolding. The persistence of director Abbas Kiarostami to document all of Ahmad's fruitless attempts to do his duty (always thwarted by the insensitivity of the adults around him) allows the audience to see the story through the boy's eyes and to understand his state of mind.

Shot in a sensitive, straightforward manner in a real village, using unknown but expressive children, this film is a throwback to the quality Iranian cinema of 15 years ago.—*Edna*.

Arusi-ye Khuban
(Marriage Of The Chosen)
(IRANIAN-COLOR/B&W)

Locarno A Farabi Cinema Foundation presentation of an Institute for the Cinematographic Affairs of the Mostazafan Foundation production. Written, directed and edited by Mohsen Makhmalbaf; camera (color, b&w),

Ali Reza Zarrindast; music, Babak Bayat. Reviewed at Locarno Film Festival (special screenings), Aug. 8, 1989. Running time: **75 MIN.**
With: Mahmoud Bigham, Roya Nonahali, Ebrahim Abadi, Mohsen Zehtab; Hossein Hosseinkhani, Ameneh Kholdabarin, Mohammed Reza Bahmanpoor.

■ **Over-emotional, repetitive, and even ideologically suspect at times, this is nevertheless the type of Iranian film many people will want to see due to its subject: the trauma of a shell-shocked soldier trying to reintegrate to normal life.**

A photographer wounded on the Iran-Iraq front is released into the hands of his wealthy fiancée's family, with instructions to take it easy. Memories from the front and also of the revolution, the Lebanon war and the famine in Africa, constantly haunt him. He feels the new order in his country has little to claim to its crdit, poverty is as terrible as it ever was, and injustice still rules.

He goes back to work as a press photographer, together with his girl, who is preparing an exhibition of her own photos. They toil in the sleaziest corners of the city and unveil a dark, desolate image of Teheran, which nobody wants to see or publish. Without going into any kind of political discussion, the film is nevertheless clearly disenchanted with the face of Iran today. It ends inconclusively as the hero is stranded, with no place to go.

Shot in color and black & white with considerable visual imagination plus a cast of dedicated actors, the film often resorts to surrealism for the hero's nightmares. Trying to tackle too many themes at the same time, director Mohsen Makhmalbaf spreads himself thin.

It's most interesting aspect is the film's attempt to use shell shock as the national symptom. It's detached from its basic medical context and looked at not only as the result of the war, but of everything that led to it and is still unsolved, e.g., crime, poverty and women's condition in Iran. It takes guts to say something like this, even if it is not sufficiently substantiated. —*Edna*.

Amori in Corso
(Loves In Progress)
(ITALIAN)

Locarno A Rai Due, Academy Films presentation of a Rai Due, Mita Films production. Directed by Giuseppe Bertolucci. Screenplay, Linda Revera, Domenico Raffaele, Bertolucci; camera (color), Fabio Cian-

chetti; editor, Fiorella Giovanelli; music, Beethoven. Reviewed at Locarno Piazza Grande, Aug. 7, 1989. Running time: **82 MIN.**
Anna . . . . .Francesca Prandi
Bianca . . . . .Stella Vordemann
Daniela . . . . .Amanda Sandrelli

■ **This intimate tv production, a first-prize winner at the Salsamaggiore Festival, is dramatically too thin to sustain audience interest for long.**

Two adolescent girls (Anna and Bianca) face their first serious sexuality crisis as they spend a few days together in Bianca's country house, supposedly to study for their exams. Since a man is due to come over, his eventual presence is the topic that simultaneously pulls the friends apart and unites them.

Entire film is dedicated to the emotional duel between Anna and Bianca, with a short intermezzo when the third girl (Daniela) joins the party.

The story is told from Anna's point of view, adding a first-person narration to already copious dialog. The homosexual undercurrent is evident very early on, as director Giuseppe Bertolucci insists on having the svelte Anna always in trousers with almost no make-up, while the doll-like Bianca is carefully groomed. When this is finally brought into the open at the end, the audience has long outguessed the girls' secret yearnings.

Bertolucci, a talented women's director ("Secrets, Secrets"), moves in predictable circles around Francesca Prandi (Anna) and Stella Vordemann (Bianca), working hard to keep a degree of irony and distance. Film comes alive briefly with the intentionally vulgar performance of Amanda Sandrelli (Daniela).

On the small screen some of these shortcomings might be less visible, but not so on Locarno's spectacular Piazza Grande, one of Europe's largest venues. Photography is no more than adequate, a pity considering the lovely locations, and editing is slack even at 82 minutes. General effect is of an unsuccessful attempt to make a warmed-over Italian equivalent of the French New Wave. —*Edna*.

Riding The Rails

Locarno An Adventure Film production. Written and directed by Neil Hollander. Camera (color), John Cressey; editor, Valerie Schwartz; music, Galt McDermot; sound, Paul Zehrer; art direction, Reine Michelet. Reviewed at Locarno Film Festival (competing), Aug. 9, 1989. Running time: **90 MIN.**

Sam .Jim Babchak
Enrique . . . . .Jose Zuniga

■ **This type of film used to be made during the Depression, when unemployment was responsible for a class of homeless people always on the road and looking for work. Nowadays, it looks largely gratuitous, a road movie exercise of no real consequence.**

Jim Babchak plays a washed-out stockbroker who has to tramp his way from New York to California, where he has been promised another job. He starts riding the freight trains, quickly learning the ropes from Jose Zuniga, who travels with a dog.

On the way, the stockbroker is taught a couple of lessons in tramp ethics as well. He also reviews his life and tries to reach some conclusions concerning his future.

Told in the first person as a long monolog, this is supposed to be an analysis of the hobo mentality, a survey of these marginals forgotten by society.

Shot in documentary style, the social comments it has to make are familiar and the action is repetitious. Director Neil Hollander evades any issue that he finds uncomfortable. In the '30s people wanted work but couldn't get any. No such thing is mentioned in this film's context. Even the hero's Mexican pal, who sneaked across the border to make some money, doesn't seem to have any purpose in his wanderings, and neither do the other unfortunates they meet on their way.

As a coast-to-coast survey of unfamiliar landscapes, this film may make some sense. As a social statement, it definitely lacks substance. —*Edna*.

The Top Of His Head
(CANADIAN)

Locarno A Films Transit presentation of a Rhombus Media, Grimthorpe Film production. Produced by Niv Fischman. Written and directed by Peter Mettler. Camera (color), Tobias Schliesser, Mettler; editor, Mettler, Margaret van Eerdewijk; music, Fred Frith, additional music, Jane Siberry; sound, John Martin, Egidio Coccimiglio; art direction, Valanne Ridgeway, Angela Murphy; costumes, Beth Pasternak. Reviewed at Locarno Film Festival (competing) Aug. 8, 1989. Running time: **110 MIN.**
Gus . . . . .Stephen Ouimette
Policeman . . . . .Gary Reineke
Lucy Ripley . . . . .Christie MacFadyen
Also with: David Fox, Julie Wildman, David Main, Alexander Maidan, Diana Barrington, John Paul Young, Julian Richings, Joey Hardin.

■ **This is another protest film**

about alienation, using all the tricks of the trade to confuse the issue and leave the audience wondering what it is all about.

There is little Swiss-Canadian director Peter Mettler doesn't throw into the pot. The communication explosion, the age of computers, the materialism of a society judging its members on their salesmanship, social paranoia and impending ecological disaster are only some of the evils of Western society taken into consideration here.

They serve as background for the story of a crack salesman of satellite dishes who falls in love with a performance artist who's also a dedicated conservationist. All the salesman's ideals collapse as he progresses through the film, desperately trying to find her.

On his journey, he discovers new ways of seeing man and nature. At the same time, by identifying with his beloved and her ideas, he is suspected by the law. He's followed every step he takes, since anything unconventional is considered subversive as well.

The trouble with the film is that Mettler mixes up his ideas. Instead of developing them, he simply throws in more, achieving a kind of experimental mishmash.

To his credit, the film is technically highly polished. Stephen Ouimette as the salesman has an adequately befuddled look and Christie MacFadyen is every bit the determined artist with a cause. Yet following them around is the kind of bumpy ride only a few film buffs will be ready to try. —*Edna*.

Lüzzas Walkman
(SWISS)

Locarno   A Look Now Films presentation. Produced by Christian Schocher, ZDF, SRF. Written and directed by Schocher. Camera (color, 16m), Jürg Hassler; editor, Franz Rickenbach; music, Fredy Studer, Christy Doran, Baby Jail; sound, Felix Singer. Reviewed at Locarno Film Festival (Swiss section), Aug. 5, 1989. Running time: **102 MIN.**
   With: Thomas Pfister (Lüzze), Bice, Fredi Meier, Le Lupa, Hannes R. Bossert.

■ **Switzerland may well be one of the most prosperous countries in the world, but certainly not one of the happiest, judging by films like this one, which persistently show only the dark and gloomy side of it.**

Lüzze is an 18-year-old who lives in the mountains with his father. He helps with the farm work, distributes the milk, fills in on odd jobs during the winter sports season and is totally alienated. He

lives by himself with his walkman and his admiration of Kiss.

One night, after being teased by a couple of city girls on a ski vacation, he steals their car and drives to Zurich. Most of the film takes place there, as he wanders by himself around town and meets solitary social outscasts and freaks.

This is the opposite of the pretty postcard picture of Switzerland. It's a cold and uncommunicative place, where loneliness is a general affliction for which there is no real remedy. One explicit scene of a junkie shooting up without even getting a kick out of it anymore is the most extreme example of the despair which takes hold of these marginals, living in one of the richest and most opulent cities in the world.

Shot in 16m, mostly with handheld camera, the film is a gritty, authentic (albeit unflattering) portrait of Zurich by night, which has its poetic moments, particularly when using music performed on screen. Unfortunately, there is absolutely no sense of pace: each scene is self-indulgently allowed to run too long and therefore overstay its welcome.

Most of the acting is of the spontaneous but unprofessional kind, an advantage since the film has the look of an improvised picture of life in the raw. —*Edna*.

Piano Panier
(SWISS)

Locarno   A Light Night (Geneva) presentation. Produced by Light Night, Patricia Plattner, Gemini Films, Paulo Branco, TSF, Portuguese Radiotelevision. Written and directed by Plattner. Camera (color, 16m), Matthias Kaelin; editor, Loredana Cristelli; music, Jacques Robcllaz; sound, Paulo de Jesus. Reviewed at Locarno Film Festival (competing), Aug. 5, 1989. Running time: **95 MIN.**
Marie . . . . Anne-Laure Luisoni
Filipa . . . . Rita Blanco
   Also with: Maria Filomena, Daniel Wolf, Paulo Branco, Antoine Basler, Diego Doria, Stefan Gubser.

■ **Made on a shoestring budget and shot in 16m, Patricia Plattner's first feature is a story of female friendship, put to the test of contrasting backgrounds.**

Marie is an aspiring musician from Geneva with a knack for unhappy love affairs. Her best friend, Filipa, catches her on the rebound after one such disappointment and suggests Marie should join her on a trip to her native Portugal.

The reason for the trip, which Marie ignores, is Filipa's impending marriage in the old country.

Once they get to Portugal, they spend most of the time in a house by the beach, discussing their options and preferences.

Their friendship is never really endangered. It is obvious that dreamy, indolent Marie, who has no pressing financial worries, can afford to speculate longer about her future and take more detours before making a decision, while practical, down-to-earth Filipa, for whom the material future is of immediate concern, looks at life from an entirely different perspective.

There is a world of difference in the sexual traditions each one of the girls represents, as well as in the romantic concepts guiding them. Plattner, who wrote her own script, loses her grip on the story once she makes her premises clear, which is at a pretty early stage. She relies on the sympathetic personality of her two actresses and some of the guests (including co-producer Paulo Branco in a featured role), to carry the story through, but the burden turns out to be too heavy.

By the end of it, it looks like another buddy-buddy picture moving around in pleasant but not very compelling circles. Every little mood is verbalized at length, falling back on many clichés (Swiss solitude against Latin family warmth). —*Edna*.

The Package

Hollywood   An Orion Pictures release. Executive producer, Arne L. Schmidt. Produced by Beverly J. Camhe. Coproducers, Andrew Davis, Dennis Haggerty. Directed by Davis. Screenplay, John Bishop; camera (Astro color; Deluxe prints), Frank Tidy; editor, Don Zimmerman, Billy Weber; music, James Newton Howard; sound (Dolby), Scott D. Smith; production design, Michael Levesque; costume design, Marilyn Vance-Straker; art direction, Colleen Kennedy, Wynn Thomas; set decoration, Rick T. Gentz; production manager, Charles J. Newirth; assistant director, Craig Huston; stunt coordinator, Terry Leonard; 2d unit director, Leonard, James A. Dennett; associate producers, Newirth, Dennett; casting, Louis Digiamo, Richard S. Kordos, Nan Charbonneau. Reviewed at Directors Guild theater, L.A.. Aug. 17, 1989. MPAA Rating: R. Running time: **108 MIN.**
Johnny Gallagher . . . . Gene Hackman
Eileen Gallagher . . . . Joanna Cassidy
Thomas Boyette . . . . Tommy Lee Jones
Col. Glen Whitacre . . . . John Heard
Milan Delich . . . . Dennis Franz
Ruth Butler . . . . Pam Grier
Walter Henke . . . . Kevin Crowley
Police Lt. . . . . Reni Santoni
Karl Richards . . . . Ron Dean
Secret Service . . . . Thalmus Rasulala
   Also with: Nathan Davis, Chelcie Ross, Joe Greco, Ike Pappas, Marco St. John.

■ **Smartly written, sharply played and directed at a crackling pace that never sacrifices clarity for speed, "The Package" is an enormously satisfying political thriller.**

If properly placed and exploited, it has the potential to shape up as a word-of-mouth hit with moviegoers longing for a well-mounted, no-frills, "meat and potatoes" nail biter. Unfortunately this doesn't look likely to happen, as the Orion release is coming to theaters late in the season with none of the fanfare attendant on other, lesser summer items.

The plot confected by screenwriter John Bishop isn't exactly fresh, mixing elements out of John Le Carré and Richard Condon thrillers. Director Andrew Davis keeps things moving so skillfully that one is easily drawn into following the story's every twist and turn. Aiding this process immeasurably is the film's star, Gene Hackman — who is quite simply the finest journeyman actor in American cinema today.

Poised and professional as ever, Hackman is perfectly cast as a career Army officer assigned to a special detail guarding a top-level diplomatic conference in East Berlin — where American and Soviet authorities are on the verge of signing a treaty bringing the threat of nuclear warfare to an end.

After a violent encounter with submachine-gun-toting backpackers, Hackman is off on another assignment — escorting a troublesome soldier (Tommy Lee Jones) stateside to stand trial. This cynical, snarling character amuses the seasoned Army man at first. That evaporates when this ''package'' (the military term for the person being delivered) takes a powder via an obviously staged fight in an airport men's room.

Trying to track the man, Hackman visits his estranged wife — and soon realizes the package is posing as someone he's not. When the woman turns up murdered — and Hackman's under house arrest for the killing — the action really heats up.

Our hero knows he's a marked man, but he doesn't know who has marked him or why. Moreover, he senses it's part of some larger plot — its meaning and purpose veiled. Looking for help, he turns to his ex-wife (Joanna Cassidy), also an Army officer. Soon she finds herself behind the eight ball along with her ex.

Now on the run from nameless forces whose purpose they can't comprehend, the couple head for Chicago — and a grand showdown with the mysterious ''package,'' who, we learn, is part of a plot to assassinate one or both of the heads of the U.S. and Soviet governments.

As wild and woolly as this may seem on paper, Davis and his collaborators make this seemingly improbable story unfold with ruthless logic. The fact that this sort of ultimate detente may indeed be a near-future reality gives a special zest to the film's notion of how the cold war might be continued — for the betterment of high-level, cloak-&-dagger parties on both sides. Thanks to top-notch location scouting, editing and cinematography, the film's grand finale — in which various forces are seen converging on a Chicago hotel to either kill or prevent a killing — is very effective. You know exactly where each character is in relation to the other in this very complex piece of staging.

In the brief but pivotal title role, Tommy Lee Jones shows it's possible to play an out-of-control psychopath without turning into a gargoyle. Joanna Cassidy is as smooth as ever, particularly in a key moment when she realizes that the men who've stopped her and claim to be police are really assassins. Dennis Franz is effective as a Chicago cop who helps the couple.

As usual, top honors go to Hackman. It's a simple, straight-forward part, but there are precious few performers who could make as much of it as he does. Of special note is a pivotal early scene where he tangles with a sinister military man (John Heard) who faults him for failing to get the backpacking killers. Nine actors out of 10 would have played the scene through clenched teeth or blustered their way through. Hackman plays it simply, full out yet calm, allowing one to read the emotions on the character's face. If this moment had been bungled, it would have been impossible to care about what the character does afterward or to read his moves as he tries to decode the clues to the puzzle. Hackman makes it look easy. *This* is acting. —*Rens.*

Cheetah

Hollywood A Buena Vista release of a Walt Disney Pictures presentation, in association with Silver Screen Partners III, of a Robert Halmi production. Executive producer, Roy Edward Disney. Produced by Robert Halmi Sr. Directed by Jeff Blyth. Screenplay, Erik Tarloff, John Cotter, Griff Du Rhone, from story by Cotter, based on the book ''The Cheetahs'' by Alan Caillou; camera (TVC color, Metrocolor prints), Tom Burstyn; editor, Eric Albertson; music, Bruce Rowland; sound (Dolby), Bill Daly; production design, Jane Cavedon; costume design, Elizabeth Ryrie; animals trained by Animal Actors of Hollywood; animal trainers, Wally Ross, Julian Sylvester, Kun Istvan, Cristie Miele, Doree Sitterly; assistant director, Lester Berman, John Houston; associate producer, Cotter; casting, Lynn Kressel. Reviewed at National theater, Westwood, Calif., Aug. 12, 1989. MPAA Rating: G. Running time: **84 MIN.**

Ted	Keith Coogan
Susan	Lucy Deakins
Morogo	Collin Mothupi
Earl Johnson	Timothy Landfield
Jean Johnson	Breon Gorman
Kipoin	Ka Vundla
Lani	Lydia Kigada
Patel	Kuldeep Bhakoo
Abdullah	Paul Onsongo
Nigel	Anthony Baird

■ **Although the title suggests a true-life adventure docu, Walt Disney Pictures' ''Cheetah'' is a bland and formulaic story film about two American teens in Kenya and their pet cheetah. While the animal footage and the African landscapes are well shot, those more appealing elements unfortunately take back seat to the plot.**

The G-rated Buena Vista release is serviceable family fare, but ''Cheetah'' will finish far behind the four other pics BV has put out with such remarkable success this summer.

Likable Keith Coogan (Jackie Coogan's grandson) and flintier Lucy Deakins are the white-bread Pasadena siblings who accompany their scientist father Timothy Landfield and medical worker mother Breon Gorman to Kenya. Warned by their sniffy mom to stay clear of natives and wild animals, the kids rebel by befriending adorable Masai urchin Collin Mothupi and by adopting an orphaned baby cheetah, who is later kidnaped by poachers.

Director Jeff Blyth, whose background is in travel pics, has a good eye and lets Tom Burstyn's camera linger unhurriedly on the serene and spacious Kenyan vistas. The filmmaker's treatment of Africa and the natives is respectful and free from condescension. Yet ''Cheetah'' rushes over what should be a key element in building its emotion, the initial 6-month period of domesticating the cheetah, which is tossed off in a quick montage.

Before the film has hardly begun, the clunky screenplay announces the family's imminent departure and starts grinding its expository gears for the sentimental necessity of returning the animal to the wilderness.

It's hard to care deeply about an animal whose relationship with the kids has been so perfunctorily presented. The cheetah and the other animals on view are so much more compelling to watch than most of the humans that it's continually frustrating when Blyth and editor Eric Albertson cut away from the beasts too quickly.

Although the villains in ''Cheetah'' are pure cardboard — money-grubbing Indian merchant Kuldeep Bhakoo, phlegmatic African Paul Onsongo, and seedy Britisher Anthony Baird — the sluggishly undramatic mood gradually perks up as Coogan, Deakins, and Mothupi journey to Nairobi to recapture the cheetah and set it free.

While the ending is predictable, it is also genuinely touching, and redeems some of the film's earlier blandness.

''Cheetah'' mostly leaves one yearning for the good old days of the True-Life Adventure films, or the likes of ''Bambi,'' ''The Yearling,'' ''Old Yeller,'' and ''Hatari!'' when Hollywood really knew how to make a story about animals spring to life on screen.
—*Mac.*

Millennium

London A 20th Century Fox release of a Gladden Entertainment production. Executive producers, John Foreman, Freddie Fields, Louis M. Silverstein, P. Gael Mourant. Produced by Douglas Leiterman. Coproducer, Robert Vince. Supervising producer, John M. Eckert. Directed by Michael Anderson. Screenplay, John Varley, based on his short story ''Air Raid;'' camera (color), Rene Ohashi; editor, Ron Wisman; music, Eric N. Robertson; sound (Dolby), Jim Hopkins; production design, Gene Rudolf; art direction, Charles Dunlop; costumes, Olga Dimitrov; special visual effects, Light and Motion. Reviewed at Rank preview theater, London, Aug. 11, 1989. MPAA Rating: PG-13. Running time: **108 MIN.**

Bill Smith	Kris Kristofferson
Louise Baltimore	Cheryl Ladd
Arnold Mayer	Daniel J. Travanti
Sherman	Robert Joy
Walters	Lloyd Bochner

■ **''Millennium'' tries hard to combine sci-fi special effects and a love story, but unfortunately neither are convincing and the pic ends up looking like a failed pilot for a tv series. Boxoffice prospects look slender.**

Veteran science-fiction director Michael Anderson does the best he can with a mediocre script, which spends more time analyzing the paradoxes of time travel and not enough developing characters or giving the pic drama or suspense.

There is a degree of sophistication about the special effects, and there are some quality actors involved — but for an audience used to the likes of ''Batman'' and the ''Ghostbusters'' and Indiana Jones pics, the film is likely to be passed over.

Pic opens with an investigation of a mid-air collision between a 747 and a DC-10, with Kris Kristofferson leading the experts' probe of the crash.

During his investigation, he meets Cheryl Ladd, leader of a commando unit of women from 1,000 years in the future. The complicated remainder of the pic involves movement through time, the search for the powerful ''stunner'' and the future civilization's efforts to continue. Seems that world is peopled by a race that can't procreate.

Kristofferson gives the film his best shot and breathes some life into the tired lines, while Ladd sports many outfits and wacky hairstyles but lacks real passion. Daniel J. Travanti just has to look studious for a few scenes. The rest of the cast is fine.

Special effects are adequate, with mechanical effects looking better than the opticals.

The big problem with time travel films is that it is so easy to pick holes in the storyline. In the case of ''Millennium,'' the story is so slight and poorly developed that it only really gets off the ground thanks to a few nice pieces of direction and game-playing by the leads. —*Adam.*

Let It Ride

Hollywood   A Paramount Pictures release. Executive producer, Richard Stenta. Produced by David Giler. Coproducers, Ned Dowd, Randy Ostrow. Directed by Joe Pytka. Screenplay, "Ernest Morton" (Nancy Dowd), based on Jay Cronley's novel "Good Vibes;" camera (Technicolor), Curtis J. Wehr; editor, Dede Allen, Jim Miller; music, Giorgio Moroder; sound (Dolby), Cecelia Hall; production design, Wolf Kroeger; set decoration, William D. McLane; assistant director, Austin McCann, Linda Montanti; casting, Wallis Nicita. Reviewed at Paramount Studios, L.A., Aug. 18, 1989. MPAA Rating: PG-13. Running time: **86 MIN.**

Trotter ....Richard Dreyfuss
Looney ....David Johansen
Pam ....Teri Garr
Vicki ....Jennifer Tilly
Greenberg ....Allen Garfield
Marty ....Ed Walsh
    Also with: Michelle Phillips, Mary Woronov, Robbie Coltrane, Richard Edson, Cynthia Nixon, Richard Dimitri, Tony Longo.

■**Richard Dreyfuss finds himself gamely struggling to keep a lame mount on track in this plodding comedy about a compulsive gambler on a hot streak.**

Directed by Joe Pytka, an award-winning director of commercials making his feature film debut, the pic never really gets out of the starting gate largely due to an exceptionally weak script that fails to take the premise far enough.

The setting is also something of a put-off, since it makes fun of its various beer-swilling, chain-smoking horseracing bettors without paying any real attention to the downside of what is obviously for many a dangerous and destructive compulsion.

Dreyfuss plays the aptly named Jay Trotter, a cab driver who picks up a sure-thing tip on a horserace through the vulgar dealings of simple minded buddy Looney (David Johansen).

Starting with $50, Trotter parlays a single win into a streak amounting to thousands of dollars, allowing him to rub elbows with the upper crust in the Jockey Club and a cast of colorful stereotypes to counter the lowlifes in his local bar.

All the while, however, his betting orgy is keeping him away from home and endangering his reconciliation with his wife (Teri Garr), left waiting in a rather fetching negligee.

That subplot actually makes "Let It Ride" a failure on several levels rather than just as a muddled comedy, since we never see how

Trotter's excesses broke up the marriage or what's pulling it back together. Despite the fairy-tale ending, it's hard to force a glass slipper onto such an ugly stepsister of a film.

Showing signs of his creative origins, Pytka handles 10-second gags well enough but doesn't flesh out his characters at all. There's also little in the way of innovation in terms of shooting the horseracing, which employs too much slow-motion and has all the suspense of professional wrestling.

Garr is essentially wasted as the exasperated wife and Johansen may be carving out the world's most unusual niche for typecasting, having played a grungy cab driver previously in "Scrooged."

The real scene stealer is Jennifer Tilly, packed into an impossibly low-cut dress with a bombshell body and pipsqueak voice. Riotous almost every time she opens her mouth, she even brings a bit of pathos to her character as, shucks, a gal who had to get her money somewhere.

Unfortunately, that sort of wide-open humor proves sorely lacking. The idea of a day where everything's clicking on all cylinders and, as Dreyfuss proclaims, "God likes me," has real potential, yet the filmmakers can't tap it for as many good laughs as a light beer commercial.

An overbearing score doesn't help, and Curtis J. Wehr's cinematography — especially in the bar — is at times too murky to navigate. —*Bril.*

Tennessee Nights
(U.S.-SWISS)

Locarno   A Nelson Entertainment presentation. A Condor Films production with Allianz Films. Intermonda, WDR. Produced by Bernard Lang, Peter-Christian Fueter. Executive producers, Jürg Staubli, Roger Weil. Directed by Nicolas Gessner. Screenplay, Gessner, Laird Koenig, based on "Minnie" by Hans Werner Kettenbach; camera (color), Pio Corradi; editor, Marie-Therese Boiché; music, Gabriel Yared; costume design, Hilary Wright; associate producers, Hartwig Schmidt, Bill Hartman. Reviewed at Locarno Piazza Grande, Aug. 6, 1989. Running time: **95 MIN.**

Leighton ....Julian Sands
Minnie ....Stacey Dash
    Also with: Ed Lauter, Ned Beatty, Denise Crosby, Brian McNamara, Rod Steiger.

■**This psychological thriller about the nightmarish trip of a young, uptight British lawyer into the deep South is one of the costliest Swiss productions of the year.**

Spoken in English and boasting

a strong supporting cast, it is intended as an entry into mainstream American commercial cinema, but neither plot nor performances are strong enough to get it there.

Specialized in the music business, Wolfgang Leighton (British thesp Julian Sands) visits Nashville to finalize European distribution contracts for a new Johnny Cash album. He takes a weekend off to go fishing but instead finds himself involved in a Kafkaesque plot.

He lands in a ramshackle motel and has a white girl make a play for him. He then hears strange noises from her room as if she were being beaten up, leaves in a rush before his presence is noticed, only to discover that a car is following him and trying to run him off the road.

He picks up a teenaged black girl (Stacey Dash), who asks to be taken to Memphis but doesn't mind driving around wherever he goes, sharing with him some good old Southern wisdom and even finding a shelter for the night. The weekend ends in jail, before he is brought before a freakish, Bach-loving judge (Rod Steiger) in a preposterously pretentious courtroom scene.

The details of the story don't really add up, diversions and red herrings being pulled out constantly for lack of a solid plot. The identity of the mysterious car chasing Leighton is given a lame explanation, as are most other motivations in this film. As a symbolic encounter between a prissy, paranoiac foreigner and the South, the film is far too condescending, resorting to old-fashioned cliches like the bigot cop, pervert jail inmates, or pretty sunsets.

The cast itself seems to have trouble believing the story. Julian Sands, on screen for most of the time, displays minimal dramatic range and elicits no sympathy whatsoever for Leighton. The rest of the cast is more relaxed but not much better, except possibly for Rod Steiger playing the judge, who seems to have strayed here from another movie. Character actors like Ned Beatty and Ed Lauter have very little to sink their teeth in.

Technical credits are all of a high order, veteran director Nicholas Gessner making sure the film has the polished look of a first-class production. It may finally do better on smaller screens than in theatrical distribution. —*Edna.*

Un Eté d'orages
(Stormy Summer)
(FRENCH)

Paris   An AAA release of a Slav Prods./Films A2/SGGC/AFC coproduction. Produced by Xavier Larère. Directed by Charlotte Brandstrom. Screenplay, Brandstrom, Nicolas Bernheim, based on novel "Le Dernier été" by Pierre-Jean Rémy; camera (color), Willy Kurant; editor, Michèle Boehm; music, Murray Head; sound, Michel Brethez; production manager, Franz Dammame; assistant director, Alain Wermus; Françoise Combadière. Reviewed at Marignan Concorde theater, Paris, July 5, 1989. Running time: **95 MIN.**

Laurence ....Judith Godrèche
Louis ....Stanislas Carré de Malberg
Jack ....Murray Head
Anne ....Marie-Christine Barrault
Hélène ....Eva Darlan
Yves ....Roger Van Hool
Robert ....Jean Bouise
Grandmother ....Gisèle Casadesus

■**Newcomer Charlotte Brandstrom shows directorial promise in this mostly familiar tale of teen growing pains set against the greater agony of German-occupied France.**

Action is set in the Auvergne country home of a far-flung bourgeois family whose members gather there each summer. This summer happens to be in 1944 — the Normandy invasion has begun, but the clan seems immersed in its down domestic epicureanism.

Two 16-year-old cousins, Judith Godrèche and Stanislas Carré de Malberg, experience first love, though not precisely with one another. Malberg is mad about Godrèche. She seems keen on him until an outsider turns her head: a handsome, talented British officer — played with quiet seductive presence by Murray Head — who has been parachuted in to organize underground forces for the liberation. He is brought incognito into the household by Godrèche's militant father.

Malberg's jealousy peaks when he learns his cousin and Head have made love. He rushes to town to deliver an anonymous denunciation to the collaborationist militia. Immediately torn by remorse, he tries to avert the tragedy but arrives to see Head shot dead by the militia. He subsequently learns that he is not responsible for the Brit's death because another cousin has intercepted the letter.

Aided by a fine ensemble cast, Brandstrom does well with her descriptions of the family — dominated by a dilettante patriarch wonderfully played by the late Jean Bouise — and the more intimate byplay of amorous youngsters and philandering (or resistance-minded) parents.

Director is particularly subtle in suggesting the presence of encroaching war on this seemingly cossetted brood without succumbing to the goosestepping clichés of most wartime dramas.

Tech credits are fine. Willy Kurant's lensing is a standout.

—*Len.*

Estacio Central
(Central Station)
(SPANISH)

Locarno A Septimania Films presentation of a Septimania Films, Spanish Television (TVE) production. Produced by Manuel Valls, Albert Sagales. Written and directed by Josep Anton Salgot. Camera (Eastmancolor), Josep Maria Civit; editor, Ernest Blasi; music, Jordi Nogueras; art direction, Vincenc Viaplana, Balter Gallart; associate producers, Josep Estany, Tomas Garrofe. Reviewed at Locarno Film Festival (competing), Aug. 7, 1989. Running time: **105 MIN.**

Alex . . . . Feodore Atkine
Elena . . . . Katarzyna Figura
Policeman . . . , ... Sergi Mateu
Also with: Paola Dominguin (Alex' wife), Günther Meisner (Alex' friend).

■ **Sex, crime, police brutality and chic photography rub elbows in this uncertain attempt at a Hitchcockian thriller, whose slick, fashionable looks belie its contents.**

French actor Feodore Atkine plays a photographer who is out at night to catch life in the raw, in Barcelona's Central Railway Station. Bored with his wife and considering divorce, he nevertheless ignores her illicit affair with his best friend, who turns out later to be a pimp and a pusher.

One night at the station, he photographs a woman who is later killed on the train. This is the first step into a vortex of furious passions and unexplained crimes. He falls madly in love with his friend's girl. At the same time his own wife is murdered on the train in mysterious fashion. The police consider him the prime suspect.

The film pretends to place the passionate love story of the photographer and his neighbor in the context of a mystery thriller, but the plot is clumsily manipulated. Wooden performances by all actors look even worse because of mediocre dubbing, quite visible in this film since three of the leads obviously do not speak Spanish.

—*Edna.*

Denj Angela
(The Name-Day)
(SOVIET-B&W)

Locarno A Sovexportfilm presentation of a Lenfilm Studios production. Directed by Serghei Selianov, Nikolai Makarov. Screenplay, Mikhail Konvaltchuk, from his unpublished novel; camera (b&w), Serghei Astakhov; music, Arkadi Gagulashvili; art direction, Larissa Shilova. Reviewed at Locarno Film Festival (competing), Aug. 8, 1989. Running time: **77 MIN.**

With: Leonid Konovalov, Alexander Belov, Yekaterina Kuklina, Larissa Shumilkina, Ludmilla Yampolskaya.

■ **Shot in 1980 in bits and pieces of borrowed film stock from a novel still unpublished to this day, this item is one of the latest glasnost discoveries to be cleared off the shelf.**

An allegory of Soviet history, it uses an isolated family living in a rambling old house as a metaphor. The story is told through the eyes of a simpleton, whose interpretation of events is sufficiently distorted to give them all an ironic, surrealist slant. This allows the film to deliver some biting remarks on ignorance and corruption, favoritism and stagnation. Telling is an incident of a policeman who goes up a tree in an early scene to keep an eye on the family's conduct, and is still there, years later, when the tree catches fire at the end of the film.

Pic has loose and shaky construction, allusions that are not always quite clear, impressionist camerawork reminiscent of Andrei Tarkovsky's work but lacking the same degree of control, and a grand finale in which the great issues of humanity are discussed around the dinner table. These indicate ambitions that didn't quite materialize, possibly because of the conditions under which the film was made.

As uneven as it is, this simpleton's version of the recent past has its promising moments and produces some sharp barbs. —*Edna.*

Curse II: The Bite
(U.S.-ITALIAN-JAPANESE)

New York An Ovidio Assonitis presentation, in association with Viva Entertainment and Towa Prod. Executive producers, Assonitis, Kenichi Timinaga, Federico Prosperi. Directed by Fred Goodwin. Screenplay, Susan Zelouf, Prosperi; camera (Fujicolor; Technicolor prints), Roberto D'Ettore Piazzoli; editor-2d unit director, Claudio Cutry; music, Carlo Maria Cordio; sound (Dolby), Jim Pilcher; production design, William Jett; assistant director, Matthew Clark; production manager, David Dodson; special effects, Screaming Mad George; associate producer, Stefano Priori; casting, Ted Hann. Reviewed on TWE vidcassette, N.Y., Aug. 4, 1989.

Running time: **98 MIN.**
Lisa . . . . Jill Schoelen
Clark . . . . J. Eddie Peck
Harry . . . . Jamie Farr
Iris . . . . Savina Gersak
Sheriff . . . . Bo Svenson
Big Flo . . . . Marianne Muellerleile
Gas jockey . . . . Al Fann
George . . . . Sydney Lassick
Also with: Sandra Sexton, Terrence Evans, Shiri Appleby, Bruce Barchiano, David Coe.

■ **This gory horror film brings back snakes as a screen menace, but is defeated by an uninteresting storyline and listless action.**

Originally titled "The Bite," it's been renamed "Curse II" by video distributor TWE to follow up producer Ovidio Assonitis' 1987 release "The Curse" (a.k.a. "The Farm"). That unrelated pic was directed by David Keith from an H.P. Lovecraft tale.

New one, filmed in New Mexico, plays as a road movie. Jill Schoelen and boyfriend J. Eddie Peck are driving to Albuquerque but take a dangerous shortcut through Yellow Sands. Peck gets bitten by a snake and, quite improbably, is given the wrong antidote by Jamie Farr, a traveling salesman posing as a doctor (for no good reason).

Nuclear testing and waste dumping have upset the balance of nature in the region, which (along with Farr's wrong antidote) causes Peck's arm to mutate into a giant snake's head that attacks people. Courtesy of outrageous makeup effects by Screaming Mad George, this yields some fun for gore fans but makes no sense. When Peck cuts the snake's head off with a meat cleaver, it simply grows back again.

There's an exciting climax set in a mudpit. Acting is acceptable in a pic aimed squarely at monster snake fans, a rather small group among general film enthusiasts.

—*Lor.*

Mind Games

New York An MGM/UA Distribution release from MGM of an MTA/Persik production. Executive producers, Mary Apick, William J. Immerman, Bob Yari. Produced by Apick. Directed by Yari. Screenplay, Kenneth Dorward; camera (Foto-Kem color), Arnie Sirlin; editor, Robert Gordon; music, David Richard Campbell; sound (Ultra-Stereo), Tom Cunliffe; art direction, Richard Way; costume design, Del Adey-Jones; assistant director, Liam O'Brien; second unit camera, Ernesto Melara; line producers, Louis Lawless, Randy Turrow; associate producer, Dorward; casting, Yasmine Golchan. Reviewed on CBS/Fox vidcassette, N.Y., Aug. 15, 1989. MPAA Rating: R. Running time: **93 MIN.**

Eric Garrison . . . . Maxwell Caulfield
Dana Lund . . . . Edward Albert
Rita Lund . . . . Shawn Weatherly
Kevin Lund . . . . Matt Norero

■ **Though briefly receiving film fest exposure and west coast bookings in March, MGM/UA's "Mind Games" is a small-scale psychological thriller that will play better on tv.**

A piece for four actors (there is no supporting cast), Bob Yari's pic follows the traditional format of an appealing but dangerous stranger disrupting a family. Maxwell Caulfield (previously effective as a heavy in "The Boys Next Door") is Eric, a psych student who attaches himself to Edward Albert and Shawn Weatherly, who are traveling in the Southwest in their rec vehicle with 10-year-old Matt Norero.

Caulfield, as part of a self-assigned psych project, manipulates the threesome, working on the son first (with discreet overtones of homosexuality), then the adults. Tension among the characters is dissipated when the film turns to unconvincing melodrama.

Caulfield is a commanding presence here, even when the script has him reveal too much of his ulterior motives. Weatherly is dramatic and provides needed sex appeal, while Albert is saddled with an underwritten part as the weak husband. Newcomer Norero gives a subtle reading of the kid's part.

With good technical contributions, Yari keeps the pot boiling up to a point. Ambitious finale tries for an open-ended effect, but lacks credibility. —*Lor.*

The Stay Awake
(SOUTH AFRICAN)

New York A Nelson Entertainment presentation of a Stay Awake Investment & Management production. Executive producer, Avi Lerner. Produced by Thys Reyns, Paul Raleigh. Directed by John Bernard. Screenplay, Bernard; camera (color), Alwyn Kumst; editor, Bernie Buys; music, Dan Hill, Kevin Kruger; sound, Darryl Martin; assistant director, David Howard; production manager, Gavin Sweeney; prosthetics, Robbie Guess; associate producer, Barry Wood; casting, Nicola van der Walt. Reviewed on Orion/Nelson vidcassette, N.Y., Aug. 12, 1989. MPAA Rating: R. Running time: **88 MIN.**

With: Shirley Jane Harris, Tanya Gordon, Jayne Hutton, Heath Potter, Ken Marshall, Lindsey Reardon, Michelle Carey, Christobel D'Orthez, Maxine John.

■ **"The Stay Awake" doesn't live up to its title. South African-made horror pic imported to U.S. vidstores is a snoozer.**

Moniker refers to a Britishism for a slumber party. The young heroines at St. Mary's School for Girls stay up all night in the gym as a stunt to help raise money for the institution. They're terrorized by a demon, calling itself Angel of Darkness, summoned up by a vengeful guy executed in the gas chamber in 1969.

Cast is good-looking but weak in the acting department. (An actor named Ken Marshall is credited, but he's not the U.S. thesp from "Krull" and tv's "Marco Polo.") Picture is so tame that when the requisite shower room scene is presented, one girl is even shown showering with clothing still on.

Monster shows up looking like a green reptile man, mostly limited to closeups emphasizing its orange eyes. Minor special effects are used in the final reel, but disposal of the beastie is unimaginative.

—*Lor.*

HEADED FOR MONTREAL FESTIVAL

Shirley Valentine

Hollywood A Paramount Pictures release. Executive producer, John Dark. Produced and directed by Lewis Gilbert. Screenplay, Willy Russell, based on his play; camera (Technicolor), Alan Hume; editor, Lesley Walker; music, George Hadjinassios, Russell; production design, John Stoll; costume design, Candice Paterson; sound (Dolby), Jonathan Bates; casting, Allan Foenander. Reviewed at Paramount Studios, L.A., Aug. 14, 1989. (In Montreal Film Festival, noncompeting.) MPAA Rating: R. Running time: **108 MIN.**
Shirley Valentine-
  Bradshaw . . . . .Pauline Collins
Costas Caldes . . . . .Tom Conti
Jane . . . . .Alison Steadman
Gillian . . . . .Julia McKenzie
Marjorie . . . . .Joanna Lumley
Joe Bradshaw . . . . .Bernard Hill
Headmistress . . . . .Sylvia Syms
Young Shirley . . . . .Gillian Kearney
Young Marjorie . . . . . . .Catherine Duncan
Milandra Bradshaw . . . . . . .Tracie Bennett
Brian Bradshaw . . . . .Gareth Jefferson

■ **Paramount offers adult filmgoers a funny valentine with "Shirley Valentine," an uneven but generally delightful romantic comedy that has as its lead the irresistible Pauline Collins.**

Pic reteams "Educating Rita" director Lewis Gilbert and writer Willy Russell, so surely "Valentine," which has a broader appeal, could be an even bigger hit for this British filmmaking duo.

Collins *is* Shirley Valentine, the perfect match of actress and character. She starred in the 1-

Original Play

A Bob Swash presentation of a solo play in two acts by Willy Russell. Staged by Simon Callow. Sets, Bruno Santini; lighting, Nick Chelton. Stars Pauline Collins. Opened Jan. 21, 1988 at the Vaudeville theater, London; £13.50.
Shirley Valentine . . . . .Pauline Collins

woman show for more than a year on stage, first in a London West End production, then on Broadway, a run that earned her hearts, plaudits and a plethora of awards, including the Tony.

The legit work was a monolog in which Collins, a middle-aged Liverpool housewife who yearns to drink "a glass of wine in a coun-

try where the grape is grown," described other characters and gave them life through her fanciful imagery.

As the vulnerable, ever-so-slightly rebellious type who is lonely in her marriage, she keeps her spirits afloat by entertaining herself talking aloud about other people's foibles, notably those foisted on her by dullard husband Joe (Bernard Hill) and snoopy neighbor Gillian (Julia McKenzie).

In Russell's film adaptation, "Shirley Valentine" becomes a full-blown location shoot with those and other characters now cast as separate speaking parts, mostly by other terrific British actors. Tom Conti, who performed with her in the recent stage production "Romantic Comedy," is barely recognizable here playing a very convincing swarthy Greek tavern keeper whose specialty is the romantic sail to a secluded cove.

The filmmakers wisely have Collins continue her role as the stage Shirley by going with the correct instinct that "The Wit and Wisdom of Shirley Valentine," as Russell's work is billed, is best spoken directly into the camera as Collins did to theater crowds.

Under Gilbert's jovial direction, this p.o.v. becomes one of the film's more charming features — as if the audience just dropped in to take tea and sympathy with the working-class mum, perhaps to jot down one or more of her original homilies or just have a good laugh.

Half the film — the first and better half — follows Collins along her humdrum, domestic chores in and out of her row house. Her chatter is lively, occasionally indecipherable (it's the thick Liverpool accent) and always amusing. For all her candidness about marriage, family and friends (language and split-second nudity earned pic an R rating), it is never spoken

with an ounce of vulgarity or malice. A chance encounter with former school rival Marjorie (Joanna Lumley) is a delicious treat.

Collins' best, most true friend is "Wall," as in the kitchen wall, against which she bounces off ideas — like going to Greece with a g.f. (Alison Steadman) without telling her mate.

In Greece she talks to the camera less and so too does she keep company with less interesting types than could be found back in rain-soaked, dreary England. Her hotel is occupied by Ugly Brits (as opposed to Ugly Americans) with Conti (attractive though he is) stuck playing the stereotypical rogue.

The white-washed island of Mykonos, its emerald waters and breathtaking sunsets (shot stunningly by cinematographer Alan Hume) — not to mention the little tryst — do much to make Shirley feel alive again. Director Gilbert has some fun himself, even going so far as to shoot some silly slo-mo footage of a crashing shoreline that in other pics might be the fireworks. Why not? This isn't serious stuff.

Shirley's journey of self-realization ends on a sweet, sentimental note — one relevant to couples everywhere.

Shirley Valentine-Bradshaw, the mildly sour Liverpool housewife, was more entertaining than Shirley Valentine, the contented reborn woman. Even so, it would be impossible not to smile along with this very happy person as the curtain/sunset falls. —*Brit.*

Cookie

Hollywood A Warner Bros. release of a Lorimar Film Entertainment presentation of a Laurence Mark production. Produced by Mark. Executive producers, Susan Seidelman, Nora Ephron, Alice Arlen. Coproducer, Jennifer Ogden. Directed by Seidelman. Screenplay, Ephron, Arlen; camera (Duart color; Metrocolor prints), Oliver Stapleton; editor, Andrew Mondshein; music, Thomas Newman; production design, Michael Haller; art direction, Bill Groom; set decoration, Les Bloom; costume design, Albert Wolsky; sound (Dolby), Tod Maitland; assistant director, David Dreyfuss, Chris Stoia; casting, Ellen Chenoweth. Reviewed at The Raleigh Studios, Hollywood, Aug. 11, 1989. (In Montreal Film Festival, noncompeting.) MPAA Rating: R. Running time: **93 MIN.**
Dino . . . . .Peter Falk
Lenore . . . . .Dianne Wiest
Cookie . . . . .Emily Lloyd
Carmine . . . . .Michael V. Gazzo
Bunny . . . . .Brenda Vaccaro
Vito . . . . .Adrian Pasdar
Enzo Della Testa . . . . .Lionel Stander
Arnold Ross . . . . .Jerry Lewis
Segretto . . . . .Bob Gunton

Henry Solomon . . . . .Ben Rayson
Pia . . . . .Ricki Lake
Dominick . . . . .Joe Mantello

■ **Half-baked, bland and flat as a vanilla wafer, "Cookie" rolls out the tired marriage of comedy and organized crime to produce a disorganized mess with little nutritional or comedic value. Fortune appears grim and should probably read, "Don't make any longrange plans. You'll soon be moving to homevideo."**

With deserved plaudits coming her way for writing "When Harry Met Sally," this is a pic Nora Ephron (who cowrote with Alice Arlen) may want to omit from her summer of '89 resume; similarly, director Susan Seidelman shows she still knows how to dress a female lead up — à la "Desperately Seeking Susan" — but then leaves star Emily Lloyd with no place to go.

Indeed, "Cookie's" greatest offense is how it squanders its intriguing cast with such lifeless material. Only Dianne Wiest emerges in top form with her brassy portrayal of a weepy red-haired gun moll in the Lucille Ball mode.

Aside from that everyone gets wasted — unfortunately not in the mob use of the term, based on the film's interminable lapses with nothing going on. At 93 minutes, it feels longer than the chronologically assembled "Godfather" saga, with profuse apologies to Francis Ford Coppola. It's enough to make one yearn for a shooting or car chase.

That wouldn't be necessary if the film worked as a comedy, which it fails to do in a puzzling way: Seidelman and the writers (who all doubled as exec producers) don't go for big laughs or black comedy, as was done with "Married To The Mob" or "Prizzi's Honor."

The result proves completely shapeless — so much so it would have been difficult to walk out and label it a comedy had Warner Bros. not so identified it — as a "high-spirited comedy," at that — in press materials.

The story gets set in motion, such as it is, when mobster Dino Capisco (Peter Falk) is released from prison after 13 years, rejoining his wife (Brenda Vaccaro), mistress (Wiest) and the headstrong daughter he had with the latter played by Lloyd, who burst onto the scene in the 1987 British pic "Wish You Were Here."

Sadly, about the only thing

Lloyd gets to do here is prove she can affect a New York accent and chew gum at the same time. Thrown together with Falk as his driver, the two fail to build any of the warmth or even grudging admiration they display in the final reel.

The film ultimately turns into an elaborate scheme by which Falk can get even with his treacherous former partner (played by Michael V. Gazzo from "The Godfather, Part II"), and the payoff is hardly worth the protracted build-up. Lionel Stander and Jerry Lewis poke their heads in along the way, the latter served much better by his recent work in a similar setting on tv's "Wiseguy."

Seidelman still possesses a nice visual flair. Working from a second-rate script, however, she can create no excitement or pathos around these thinly drawn characters.

Thomas Newman's bouncy score provides one of the few bright spots, while Albert Wolsky's costumes for Lloyd look aptly picked from the Madonna wanna-be section at K mart. When it's time to call roll on "Cookie," most of those involved will want to be someplace else. —Bril.

Nocturne indien
(Indian Nocturnal)
(FRENCH)

Paris A UGC release of an A.F.C./Sara Films/Ciné-5/Christian Bourgois Production coproduction. Produced by Maurice Bernart. Directed by Alain Corneau. Screenplay, Corneau, Louis Gardel, from novel "Notturno Indiano" by Antonio Tabucchi; camera (Fujicolor), Yves Angelo; editor, Thierry Derocles; music, Franz Schubert; sound, Pierre Gamet, Gérard Lamps; art direction, Partho Sengupta; assistant director, Frédéric Blum; production manager, Patrick Lancelot. Reviewed at UGC, Neuilly, Aug. 8, 1989. Running time: **110 MIN.**
The man . . . . Jean-Hugues Anglade
Christine . . . . Clementine Célarié
Peter Schlemihl . . . . Otto Tausig
Doctor . . . . T.P. Jain
Theosophy professor . . . . Iftekhar
Vimla Sar . . . . Dipti Dave

■ **A strangely beautiful adaptation of a beautifully strange short novel by Antonio Tabucchi, "Nocturne indien" follows a young man's vain search for a friend who has vanished in India.**

Despite the thematic déjà vu, the acting, photography and direction lift this far above the mystical tourism of previous Gallic films lensed in the East (i.e., "The Bengali Night" and "Manika"). Shot mostly in English, film will be a tough sell because of its anti-dramatic, enigmatic style. It is competing at the Montreal fest.

Director Alain Corneau's thriller experience has helped him create the unforgettable ambience of "Nocturne indien," which might be described as a film noir without guns, physical action, or climactic unraveling of the mystery.

Corneau adapted Tabucchi's book with Louis Gardel, the author of his previous pic, "Fort Saganne." It is unusually faithful in structure — even retaining the precise identification of locations, here placed in intertitles — and makes generous use of Tabucchi's terse dialog. Yet they have managed to turn something fundamentally literary into a fascinating cinematic experience.

The unnamed protagonist is Jean-Hugues Anglade, who debarks in Bombay in search of a Portuguese friend who had been living there with a prostitute. Latter had written to him in the hope of saving her lover from a mysterious psychological malaise.

Anglade's quest begins in a sordid hotel where he interviews the lovely melancholy hooker. He then takes the train to Madras to meet the director of a Theosophical Society, the friend with whom he had been in correspondence. Finally he makes his way to Goa, which is his last hope. He finds nobody, but meets a young French photographer whom he invites to dinner. The film ends as they part for the night.

The metaphysical development may seem familiar: Anglade begins to take himself for the person he is seeking, though he seems to be acting at the transformation more than living it. The film exerts a fascination that's skillfully sustained by Corneau's austerely measured direction.

Much credit is due to the superb acting. At first neutral in character, Anglade (seen notably in "Betty Blue") is an actor whose mere presence is magnetic and who knows how to listen. As his (real or adopted) personality begins to emerge, he infuses the scenes with warm ambiguity.

Anglade's episodic interlocutors are no less vivid: Each performance is a beautifully modulated miniature. Among them are Dipti Dave as the romantic prostitute; and T.P. Jain as the resigned doctor at a lurid Bombay hospital where Anglade looks for his friend.

Otto Tausig is a Jewish Holocaust survivor who purportedly has come to India to visit a statue that has haunted him since seeing a facsimile in the bureau of a Nazi concentration camp doctor, and Iftekhar is the theosophical professor who engages Anglade in some literary chat. Finally the excellent Clementine Célarié portrays the depressed French photographer. Non-professionals also contribute striking cameos.

Yves Angelo's photography is wondrous: no glossy tourist snapshots, but a series of richly composed and framed images that record the garishness, luxury and distress of hotel rooms and lobbies, overcrowded hospital wards and bureaus, a Bombay train station and its vast improvised waiting room, the grandeur of a Portuguese monastery, etc.

Other tech credits are first-class.
—Len.

My Left Foot
(BRITISH)

London A Miramax Films release of a Granada Film production. Executive producers, Paul Heller, Steve Morrison. Produced by Noel Pearson. Directed by Jim Sheridan. Screenplay, Shane Connaughton, Sheridan; camera (color), Jack Conroy; editor, J. Patrick Duffner; music, Elmer Bernstein; art direction, Austen Spriggs; costumes, Joan Bergin; casting, Nuala Moiselle. Reviewed at Bijou Preview theater, London, Aug. 14, 1989. (In Montreal Film Festival, competing.) Running time: **98 MIN.**
Christy Brown . . . . Daniel Day Lewis
Mr. Brown . . . . Ray McAnally
Mrs. Brown . . . . Brenda Fricker
Mary . . . . Ruth McCabe
Dr. Eileen Cole . . . . Fiona Shaw
Older Benny . . . . Eanna McLiam
Older Sheila . . . . Alison Whelan
Older Tom . . . . Declan Croghan
Younger Christy . . . . Hugh O'Conor
Lord Castlewelland . . . . Cyril Cusack

■ **First and foremost, "My Left Foot" is the warm, romantic and moving true story of a remarkable man: the Irish writer and painter Christy Brown born with cerebral palsy into an impoverished family. That it features a brilliant performance by Daniel Day Lewis and a fine supporting cast lifts it from mildly sentimental to excellent.**

With careful handling and positive reviews, pic could click moderately at the boxoffice. Its audience obviously is limited, but the success of "Rain Man" proves there is a market out there for films about special people.

Film is virtually always uplifting, with its low moments short and sharp, and uncomfortable though some may find the scenes of Christy's anger and frustration, it is a film that leaves the viewer with a warm feeling.

Pic opens with Day Lewis being taken to a charity event and being looked after by a nurse (Ruth McCabe). She starts to read his autobiography, "My Left Foot," and his life then is shown in flashbacks.

At his birth, his parents are told their child would be little more than a vegetable, but through his mother's insistence that he fit in with family life, he shows intelligence and strength inside his paralyzed body.

His brothers and sisters push him around in a homemade "chariot," and in one splendid scene he keeps goal for a street soccer game, stopping the ball with his head. The young Christy is wonderfully played by 13-year-old Hugh O'Conor.

The older Christy amazes his family by writing the word "mother" on the floor with a piece of chalk gripped in his left foot. He goes on to become an artist — still using that left foot — and is helped by therapist Fiona Shaw, with whom he falls in love.

She announces her marriage to an art gallery owner during a dinner, and in one scene, Day Lewis expresses his drunken rage.

He learns to type with his reliable left foot, and becomes a local celebrity. Pic ends as he and the nurse fall in love. In real life, they married and lived together until his death in 1981.

All performances are on the mark in this perfect little film. Brenda Fricker, as his loving and resilient mother, is excellent, as is the late Ray McAnally as his bricklayer father.

"My Left Foot" is not a sad film. In fact, there is a great deal of humor in Day Lewis' Brown. First-class and unobtrusive direction by first-time helmer Jim Sheridan and a fine script by Sheridan and Shane Connaughton shape the pic perfectly, but they are blessed with an actor who can pull off this difficult role.

And if there is any justice, Day Lewis should win an Oscar for "My Left Foot." —Adam.

High Fidelity —
The Guarneri
String Quartet
(DOCU)

New York A Four Oaks Foundation release. Executive producer, Walter Scheuer. Produced and directed by Allan Miller. Camera (Duart color), Dyanna Taylor; editor, Tom Haneke; sound editor, Donald Klocek; additional camera, Don Lenzer, Joachim Prim, Boyd Estus, William Megalos, Nicholas Kuskin. Reviewed at Magno Review 1 screening room, N.Y., Aug. 8, 1989. (In Montreal Film Festival, Cinema of Today and Tomorrow.) No MPAA Rating. Running time: **85 MIN.**

With: Arnold Steinhardt, John Dalley, Michael Tree, David Soyer.

■ **"High Fidelity" is a painless, entertaining intro to classical music and its practitioners, focusing on the longest-running act in the string quartet business. Specialized theatrical chances loom for this well-made documentary.**

Filmmakers eschew a canned performance approach to spotlight what makes these guys tick: a trio of chums who met at the Curtis Institute of Music in Philadelphia and teamed up with an eminent cellist with classical and tv pit orchestra experience to form Guarneri Quartet in 1964.

What makes this film interesting is how, in a natural, undramatic way, it brings out the dynamics of the group — how they frequently argue, yet manage to produce precise and challenging music. There are plenty of excerpts from performances and rehearsals to satisfy the classical music fan, but Miller's personal approach makes the pic just as accessible as if he were spotlighting the Modern Jazz Quartet or the Beatles instead.

From the group's charismatic violinist, Arnold Steinhardt, to its droll cellist, David Soyer, these fellows emerge as ordinary people with simple lifestyles but extraordinary talent. It's refreshing to get to know superstars in a given showbiz niche who have no time for airs but in perfectionist fashion want to give their best to an audience, then go home to their families.

Dyanna Taylor's flexible camera tracks them on tour around the world (their manager Harry Beall complains that they don't expand their schedule enough to meet demand, however) as well as in quiet moments at home. The arguments during rehearsals are revealing — individuals always express their unvarnished opinion, but with civility. Notable is a scene of Steinhardt pumping for the inclusion of a Kreisler quartet in their next season's repertoire, but getting thumbs down from the other three for the umpteenth time. *—Lor.*

A Whisper To A Scream
(CANADIAN)

New York A Distant Horizon and Lighthouse Communications presentation. Executive producer, Anant Singh. Written and produced by Gerard Ciccoritti, Robert Bergman. Directed by Bergman. Camera (Film House color), Paul Witte; editor, Richard Bond; music, Barry Fasman, Dana Walden; additional music, Philip Strong; sound, Eric Fitz; production design, Ciccoritti; art direction, Nicholas White; assistant director, Tom Willie; production manager-associate producer, Allan Levine; choreography, Maxine Heppner. Reviewed on Virgin Vision vidcassette, N.Y., July 22, 1989. (In Montreal Film Festival, Panorama Canada section.) MPAA Rating: R. Running time: **96 MIN.**

Gabrielle	Nadia Capone
Frank	Silvio Oliviero
Det. Taillard	Yaphet Kotto
Ohwyn Peters	Lawrence Bayne
Tullio	Michael Lebovic
Mia	Denise Ryan
Mimi	Soo Garay

Also with: Danny Wengle, Klea Scott, Susan Hamann, Denise Daigle, Leslie Kelly, Audrey Rose, Annette Schaffer, Leanne Burton, Tessa.

■ **This Canadian horror film is more pretentious than most, but suspensefully tells the tale of an obsessed soundman who kills strippers.**

Nadia Capone, also toplining for director Robert Bergman in the current vid release "Skull: A Night Of Terror," plays a dancer having trouble with her boyfriend (Silvio Oliviero), an artist who can't find work. She takes a job as a phone-sex girl, working at Michael Lebovic's nightclub.

Early on, Bergman reveals the identity of the killer who's preying on the dancers at the club, but story gimmick has Capone increasingly suspecting (with good reason) that her nutty boyfriend is the monster. This leads to an ironic climax in which she rushes to the real killer for help against innocent Oliviero.

Bergman emphasizes topless footage of the dancers in providing exploitation content, but they are cast as performance artists rather than strippers (Gotham starlet in this field, Phoebe Legere, originally was announced as pic's costar but does not appear). *—Lor.*

FESTIVAL LATINO REVIEWS

El Secreto de Romelia
(Romelia's Secret)
(MEXICAN)

New York A Fondo de Fomento a la Calidad Cinematográfica-U. Autonoma de Guadalajara-STIC-Centro de Capacitación Cinematográfica-Imcine production. Directed by Busi Cortés. Screenplay, Cortés, based on novel "El Viudo Román" by Rosario Castellanos; camera (color), Francisco Bojórquez; editor, Federico Landeros; music, José Amozurrutia; sound, Miguel Sandoval; art direction, Leticia Venzor. Reviewed at Festival Latino (competing), Biograph theater, N.Y., Aug. 6, 1989. Running time: **100 MIN.**

Dolores	Diana Bracho
Dr. Carlos Román	Pedro Armendáriz Jr.
Doña Romelia Orantes	Dolores Beristáin
Young Romelia	Arcelia Ramírez
Romi	Nuria Montiel
Aurelia	Alina Amozurrutia
Cástula	Josefina Echánove

Also with: María Carmen Cárdenas, José Angel García, Lumi Cavazos, Lisa Owen, Alenjandro Parodi, Pilar Medina, Román Echánove.

■ **Based on Rosario Castellanos' short novel "Román, The Widower," "Romelia's Secret" is a complex first feature by Mexican director Busi Cortés. With special handling, pic could do okay on the arthouse circuit.**

Complicated story contrasts Latino notions of honor, revenge and changing attitudes toward women through the juxtaposition of several generations. Memories and dramatized diary accounts toggle pic's action between the 1930s and present day.

Theme hinges on the character of Romelia Orantes (Dolores Beristáin), a widow who returns to her native Tlaxcala after a near half-century absence. Reason is to claim an inheritance left to her by her husband, Dr. Román.

She is accompanied by recently divorced daughter and three granddaughters, who discover that instead of being a longtime widow, granny's ex died only recently. They also discover that Romelia has a secret.

Film is deliberately laden with ambiguous symbols working to disorient the viewer. At times, clarity would be a welcome relief. The viewer is left with disturbing questions: What is the contrast between the three Orantes sisters and the three granddaughters? Why so many instances of voyeurism? What inference can be drawn between the political changes in the 1930s and Mexico's 1968 student movement?

While thesping is good, the makeup department should have been called in to show effects of time on the character of the maid Cástula, who doesn't change a bit in 50 years.

Despite occasional glitches, dense tale is compellingly told. Francisco Bojórquez' lush photography and scenic setting work to create a rich environment that makes the sad tale all the more palpable. *—Lent.*

Aventurera
(VENEZUELAN)

New York A P.B.R. Producciones-Foncine production. Directed by Pablo de la Barra. Screenplay, José Ignacio Cabrujas, De la Barra; camera (color), Julio Sosa Pietri; editor, Armando Silva; music, Rodrigo Troconis; sound, Edgar Torres; art direction, Tania Manelo. Reviewed at Festival Latino (competing), Biograph theater, N.Y., Aug. 8, 1989. Running time: **108 MIN.**

Braulio Fernández	Flavio Caballero
Rosario	Verónica Cortés
Buffalo	Toco Gómez
Ronco	Jorge Canelón
Montanita	Luis Rivas
Pres. Rómulo Betancourt	Gustavo Rodríguez

Also with: Alejo Felipe, Cayito Aponte.

■ **Venezuelan feature "Aventurera" touts a smorgasbord storyline, unsuccessfully mixing elements of a sitcom, love story and political adventure into an unsavory mishmash.**

Actioner takes place in 1960, soon after the Cuban Revolution and Venezuela's return to a democratic government. Though only given lip service, both incidents are meant to present pic's political backdrop. To aid the romantic angle, helmer Pablo de la Barra uses Mexican songwriter Agustín Lara's theme "Aventurera," which replays ad infinitum.

Story centers on striving actor Braulio Fernández (Flavio Caballero), who gets mixed up with a professional wrestler, the wrestler's g.f. and a group of revolutionaries. Said political malcontents plot to assassinate President Rómulo Betancourt, played by Gustavo Rodríguez in a role that basically demands that he smoke cigars disinterestedly.

The revolutionaries, never numbering more than half a dozen, espouse ties with both the Dominican Republic and Cuba. Yet it seems improbable this small group could ever take over a government, much less carry out a successful assassination. Even when their plot is put into action, they don't act on it.

Fernández plays the innocent, getting in over his head on all fronts. The wrestler wants to kill him and the revolutionaries try to hire him. For some reason never explained, they need him to steal a car which they could easily get elsewhere.

Forced script, cowritten by playwright José Ignacio Cabrujas, somehow manages unconvincingly to bring everything together by the end.

Acting is okay, especially Toco Gómez as wrestler Buffalo (Gómez picked up best supporting actor nod at Bogota's Intl. Film Festival). Other tech credits are also up to par. —*Lent.*

Little Monsters

Hollywood   An MGM/UA Distribution release from United Artists, in association with Vestron Pictures, of a Davis Entertainment Co., Licht/Mueller Film Corp. production. Produced by Jeffrey Mueller, Andrew Licht, John A. Davis. Executive producers, Mitchell Cannold, Dori B. Wasserman. Directed by Richard Alan Greenberg. Screenplay, Terry Rossio, Ted Elliott; camera (Technicolor), Dick Bush; editor, Patrick McMahon; music, David Newman; sound (Dolby), Kim Harris Ornitz; production design, Paul Peters; costume design, Marilyn Vance; special makeup effects, Robert Short; production manager, Jack Grossberg; assistant director, Randall Badger; casting, Bonnie Finnegan, Steven Jacobs. Reviewed at Mann Westwood theater, L.A., Aug. 23, 1989. MPAA Rating: PG. Running time: **100 MIN.**

Brian	Fred Savage
Maurice	Howie Mandel
Glen	Daniel Stern
Holly	Margaret Whitton
Snik	Rick Ducommun
Boy	Frank Whaley
Eric	Ben Savage
Todd	William Murray Weiss
Ronnie	Deven Ratray
Kiersten	Amber Barretto

■ **Under the bed is where this pic takes place, and under the bed is where it appears to have come from. UA's homely little pickup from Vestron about mischief-making monsters who get kids in trouble deserves permanent shelter from the light of day. Boxoffice will evaporate quickly.**

If anything, pic resembles "Beetlejuice" in a parallel universe plagued by bad scripting, bad directing and bad lighting.

Brian (Fred Savage), his brother and their bickering parents move into an old house where things are always turning up in the wrong places, bringing blame down on the kids. Culprit proves to be Howie Mandel as a raucous, hyperactive monster with a bad complexion who pops out from under the bed at night to wreak havoc.

After Brian traps him, the monster, named Maurice, lures Brian through the floorboards and into his underworld, kind of a surreal Halloween party where the ogres get to break things they've filched from above and eat all the junk food they want.

Brian becomes kind of a regular at this underground goon club, even going along with Maurice on his rounds of wrongdoing, including a tasteless prank played at the home of the school bully.

Eventually, though, the monsters kidnap Brian's brother, Eric (Ben Savage), and he recruits his school chums to help rescue his bro and wipe out the brutes.

Even the divorce-bound parents (Daniel Stern and Margaret Whit-ton) are brought back together out of worry.

Although the concept has a certain amount of charm, it's clumsily rendered in a pedestrian script credited to Terry Rossio and Ted Elliott.

Director Richard Alan Greenberg tries a patchwork of borrowed styles and angles to jazz it up, but camera usually seems to be in the wrong place. Ditto Greenberg's instincts with the actors.

Fact that the monsters can't tolerate daylight poses a lighting challenge cinematographer Dick Bush never surmounts. Pic looks murky most of the time, and one has a hard time knowing when it's supposedly dark and when it supposedly isn't.

Editing is choppy and sound mix abrupt — particularly at the finale, when Talking Heads' "Road To Nowhere" enters the mix at an absurdly loud volume. Costumes and effects are sometimes intriguing, but uneven overall.

As the star, Fred Savage (of tv's "The Wonder Years") is amiable enough but hardly exciting. Mandel is buried as the monster, and Stern and Whitton seem out of place and constrained.

Pic won't be around long enough for many people to notice. —*Daws.*

Out On Bail

New York   A Trans World Entertainment release of a Shuster/BSB Entertainment production. Produced by Alan Amiel. Executive producers, Harry Shuster, Brian Shuster. Coproducers, Stanley Shuster, Ron Isaacs, Kevin Krog. Directed by Gordon Hessler. Screenplay, Michael D. Sonye, Jason Booth, Tom Badal; camera (color), Johan van der Vyfer; editor, Brian Varaday; music, John David Hiler, Briani; sound (Ultra-Stereo), Allan Gerhardt, Andy van Eeden, Marcus Post; production design, Gavin Bitter; art direction, Leon Schutte; assistant director, Mark Gilbert; production manager, Barrie Kriel; 2d unit director, Neal Sundstrom; stunt coordinator, Scott Ateah. Reviewed on TWE vidcassette, N.Y., Aug. 3, 1989. MPAA Rating: R. Running time: **102 MIN.**

John Dee	Robert Ginty
Sally Anne Lewis	Kathy Shower
Sheriff Taggert	Tom Badal
Smiley	Sydney Lassick
Mayor Farley	Leo Sparrowhawk

■ **"Out On Bail" tells a standard tale of corrupt Southern rednecks, made unbelievable by lensing this Tennessee-set picture in South Africa with fake local supporting roles. Direct-to-vid release faces bleak prospects.**

Robert Ginty is comfortably cast as the stranger in town, thrown in a Fairfield, Tenn., jail for brawling with thugs involved in a drug deal. Corrupt sheriff (Tom Badal, who also coscripted) and lawyer (Sydney Lassick) offer him a deal to escape while out on bail if he does a dirty job for them: assassinate the reform candidate for mayor.

Ginty predictably outwits the baddies, cueing some fun chasing around in a stolen hearse with girlfriend Kathy Shower in tow. Gordon Hessler-helmed project, which reportedly went through many changes including a U.S.-lensed false start called "Johnny Blade" sporting a different cast and filmmakers, plays all right except for the poor attempts at Southern accents by South African supporting players. They all look like ringers and destroy credibility.

For his part, Ginty is solid in a role familiar from his "The Exterminator" pics. Costar Kathy Shower is far too beautiful to be convincing as a lonely, smalltown hotel operator. The sentimental "Shane" subplot involving her little son (Dewaal Stemmit) is ultra-cornball. Topnotch stunts highlight the tech credits. —*Lor.*

Lone Wolf

New York   A Flash Features production, in association with Prism Entertainment. Executive producer, A.B. Goldberg. Produced by Sarah Liles, Doug Olson. Directed by John Callas. Screenplay, Michael Krueger; additional material, Callas, Nancy M. Gallanis; camera (color), David Lewis; editor, Kurt Tiegs; music, Jon Kull; songs, Greg Leslie, performed by Tyxe; sound, Bob Abbott; art direction, Lad de Glopper; special effects coordinator, Ted A. Bohus; special effects, Vincent J. Guastini; additional special effects, Patrick Denver; werewolf prosthetic makeup, Paul C. Reilly Jr.; production manager, Bruce Granger; coproducer, Krueger. Reviewed on Prism vidcassette, N.Y., Aug. 16, 1989. No MPAA Rating. Running time: **96 MIN.**

Julie Martin	Dyann Brown
Joel	Kevin Hart
Eddie	Jamie Newcomb
Deirdre	Ann Douglas
Colleen	Siren
Joseph Simmons	Jeff Harris
The wolf	Tom Henry

■ **This made-for-video werewolf feature is moderately interesting but unfortunately adds nothing to the lore of the lycanthrope.**

Shot in Denver, pic unfolds as a whodunit with mostly students as suspects when a rash of killings breaks out in a small town. Police are slow to pick up on the clues, such as sightings of wild dogs near the murder scene. Young computer hackers decide to investigate on their own, leading to a surprise revelation of the werewolf's identity.

Gore content increases as film goes on (first few attacks are presented tamely) and a fair amount of suspense is built up. However, the cast members are a bit too old for their roles, though heroine Dyann Brown is a beauty. Gimmick of building evidence to make each principal potentially the killer is fun.

Tech credits are okay, including unspectacular werewolf effects.
—*Lor.*

Kickboxer

London A Pathé Entertainment release of a Kings Road Entertainment production. Produced by Mark DiSalle. Directed by DiSalle, David Worth. Fight scenes directed, choreographed by Jean-Claude Van Damme. Screenplay, Glenn Bruce; story by DiSalle, Van Damme; camera (Technicolor), Jon Kranhouse; editor, Wayne Wahram; music, Paul Hertzog; production design, Shay Austin; sound, (Ultra-Stereo), Grant Roberts; casting, Madalena Chan, Teddy Chen, Wong Siu Lung. Reviewed at Cannon Panton St., London, Aug. 18, 1989. MPAA Rating: R. Running time: **105 MIN.**
Kurt Sloane . . . . . Jean-Claude Van Damme
Eric Sloane . . . . Denis Alexio
Xian Chow . . . . Dennis Chan
Tong Po . . . . Himself
Winston Taylor . . . . Haskell Anderson
Mylee . . . . Rochelle Ashana

■ Combine "Karate Kid" and "Rocky" with a bit more blood and gore, dull direction and a smattering of inept actors and you have "Kickboxer." On the plus side there are a few amusing jokes and there's no denying hero Jean-Claude Van Damme moves well, but pic seems destined for the video shelves.

Van Damme is a shorter, chunky version of Arnold Schwarzenegger, but without Arnie's developing sense of humor and willingness to poke fun at himself. They are also similar in that any film either is in has to use up valuable moments explaining why he speaks with a thick foreign accent. Van Damme is struggling to rid himself of his Belgian twang.

Thankfully "Kickboxer" has a simple storyline which barely extends the actors and allows codirectors Mark DiSalle and David Worth to shoot travelog-style footage of Thailand and have the muscular Americans eventually show their superiority over wily Orientals.

Pic opens with Dennis Alexio (Eric Sloane) being crowned World Kickboxing champion, watched by his younger brother Jean-Claude Van Damme. The duo head off to Thailand to take on the originators of kickboxing after being asked some inane questions by a journalist.

Alexio fights, and is crippled by top Thai fighter Tong Po, leaving Van Damme to swear revenge. He finds out the only way he can defeat Po is by learning Muay-Thai fighting and sets off to convince eccentric Dennis Chan (Xian Chow) to teach him.

Much of the pic is taken up with the training process — Van Damme kicking trees, Van Damme practicing fighting underwater, Van Damme having his legs stretched — until he is ready for the showdown with Tong Po.

The two face-up with hands wrapped with hemp and resin and dipped in broken glass, and after the blood flies for a few minutes Van Damme (unsurprisingly) emerges as champion, being hailed Bak Shung (White Warrior) by the fickle crowd.

Much of "Kickboxer" is macho nonsense full of cliché characters and risible dialog. There is no denying, though, that the fight scenes — choreographed by Van Damme — are well handled. Van Damme may not yet be in the Jackie Chan league, but he is eventually carving out a niche for himself with this style of simplistic actioners. Direction and tech credits are okay.

Highpoint of the film is the performance by Dennis Chan as Van Damme's oddball Oriental mentor. His role owes much to Joel Grey's similar part in Guy Hamilton's 1985 pic "Remo Williams" (which cohelmer David Worth worked on), but he instills the role with enjoyable wry humor and elegance. —*Adam.*

Kill Slade
(SOUTH AFRICAN)

New York A Nelson Entertainment presentation of a Kill Slade Investment & Management production. Executive producer, Avi Lerner. Produced by Thys Heyns, Paul Raleigh. Directed by D. Bruce McFarlane. Screenplay, Terry Asbury; camera (color), Chris Schutte; editor, Robert Simpson; music, Johnny Boshoff; sound, Shaun Murdoch; art direction, Jan Horn; assistant director, Gavin Sweeney; production manager, Cameron Nolan-Sondegaard; associate producer, Barry Wood. Reviewed on Orion/Nelson vidcassette, N.Y., Aug. 16, 1989. MPAA Rating: PG-13. Running time: **88 MIN.**
Slade . . . . Patrick Dollaghan
J.J. . . . . Lisa Brady
Flanigan . . . . Danny Keogh
Kostas . . . . Anthony Fridjhon
Major Bayela . . . . Vusi Dibakwane
President Dere . . . . Alfred Nokwe

■ This South African thriller, released direct-to-video in the U.S., apes the format of "Romancing The Stone" with very minor results.

Slade is played in easygoing fashion by Patrick Dollaghan: a soldier-of-fortune hired by bad guys in the African nation of Kungola to kidnap U.S. reporter Lisa Brady. She's getting too close to exposing corruption involving U.N. food shipments to the country, and all sorts of folks, good guys and heavies, want to keep the problem under wraps.

Trekking across the veldt, Dollaghan and Brady develop the usual romantic sparring routine. Odd touch of Brady supposedly blinded during the kidnaping is awkwardly handled. Having a group of albino blacks called "the Hunting Dogs" pursuing the duo a tasteless script element.

Film suffers from a shortage of large-scale action until an exciting stunt climax staged across a vast gorge. Cast is nondescript with toothy beauty Brady not very convincing in her line readings.
—*Lor.*

Nightmare Sisters

New York A Dave DeCoteau presentation of a Cinema Home Video production. (Intl. sales, Filmtrust.) Executive producer, Johnny Schouweiler. Produced and directed by DeCoteau. Screenplay, Kenneth J. Hall; camera (color), Voya Mikulic; editor, Tony Malanowski; music, Del Casher; songs, Haunted Garage; sound, D.J. Ritchie; production design, Royce Mathew; special effects animation, Bret Mixon; assistant director, Will Clark; production manager, Ellen Cabot; associate producer, Hall. Reviewed on TWE vidcassette, N.Y., Aug. 14, 1989. No MPAA Rating. Running time: **81 MIN.**
Melody . . . . Linnea Quigley
Marci . . . . Brinke Stevens
Mickey . . . . Michelle Bauer
Kevin . . . . Richard Gabai
Freddy . . . . Marcus Vaughter
Phil . . . . Timothy Kauffman
Amanda . . . . Sandy Brooke
Omar . . . . Michael D. Sonye

■ "Nightmare Sisters," a.k.a. "Sorority Sisters," is a low-budget fantasy comedy that demonstrates one can make an entertaining if minimal genre pic in four days. It was released last year on video.

Film shares cast, filmmakers and fantasy material with same team's earlier pic, "Sorority Babes In The Slimeball Bowl-O-Rama." Director Dave DeCoteau's gimmick this time is take his stock company of beauties (Linnea Quigley, Michelle Bauer and Brinke Stevens) and present them as ugly or plain Jane sorority girls who, with the aid of a magic crystal ball, become sexy knockouts.

This provides their nerd dates with a pleasant surprise, until the gals' fanged teeth start showing.

Pic uses many static, talky scenes to read the story rather than dramatize it, a necessity on such a limited shooting schedule but making the result a tough slog. Though the special effects are minor, the cast is enthusiastic.—*Lor.*

Living The Blues

New York A Gwyn & Alan Görg production. Produced and written by Gwyn & Alan Görg. Directed by Alan Görg. Camera (color), Philip Holahan; editor, Clay Mitchell; music, Sam Taylor, Andrew Albright, Louie Stone, Mitchell, the Görgs; sound, John Hays; production manager, Alan Görg; costumes, Gwyn Görg; associate producer, Dan McLoughlin. Reviewed on Raedon Home Video vidcassette, N.Y., Aug. 12, 1989. No MPAA Rating. Running time: **78 MIN.**
Mana Brown . . . . Galyn Görg
Sam Brown . . . . Sam Taylor
Abel Wilson . . . . Michael Kerr
Zanzibar Brown . . . . Martin Raymond
Effie Brown . . . . Gwyn Görg
Mary Wilson . . . . Karlene Bradley
George Wilson . . . . Fred Nelson

■ "Living The Blues" is a pleasant though slight family production about breaking into the music biz, made in 1986 and now arriving via vidcassette.

Spotlight is on attractive dancer Galyn Görg, who later was featured to good effect in the film "Body Beat." Vaguely in the tradition of Irene Cara and Jennifer Beals, she plays an aspiring dancer in love with Michael Kerr, who wants to become a blues guitarist. It's not exactly "Romeo And Juliet," but both families object to the relationship.

Pic benefits from some nice musical performances led by Sam Taylor, as Görg's uncle, with filmmaker Gwyn Görg limning the heroine's mother. Director Alan Görg falls back on various genre clichés but generally whips up interest in the characters. Low-budget is reflected in the absence of the finalé scene, when everyone sets off for a gig in Denmark.

Galyn Görg is an appealing screen presence, and cryptic but interesting scenes of her dancing on the sidewalk are interspersed with the main narrative. Kerr is bland as the male lead but supporting cast is okay. —*Lor.*

MONTREAL FESTIVAL REVIEWS

Lo Zio Indegno
(The Sleazy Uncle)
(ITALIAN)

Montreal An Ellepi Film production. Produced by Leo Pescarolo, Guido de Laurentiis. Directed by Franco Brusati. Screenplay, Leo Benvenuti, Piero De Bernardi, Brusati; camera (color), Romano Albani; editor, Gianfranco Amicucci; music, Stefano Marcucci; production design, Dante Ferretti. Reviewed at Montreal World Film Festival (competing), Aug. 26, 1989. Running time: **105 MIN.**
Luca . . . . Vittorio Gassman
Riccardo . . . . Giancarlo Giannini
Teresa . . . . Andréa Ferréol
Andrea . . . . Kim Rossi Stuart
la chanteuse . . . . Beatrice Palme
Marina . . . . Simona Cavallari
Isabella . . . . Stefania Sandrelli

■ **An artful and affecting comedy about a successful businessman's life-altering reunion with a roguish uncle, Franco Brusati's new film is highly exportable and likely to appeal to arthouse audiences in North America and elsewhere.**

Uncle Lucca (Vittorio Gassman) is no model citizen. He lies, cheats and steals with the brazen belief that all will be forgiven tomorrow. Worse yet, he's unrepentantly lecherous for schoolgirls and blatantly indiscreet about approaching them. Chased from a cinema one day he suffers a seizure, collapses in the street and lands in a posh private clinic.

In need of 3-million lire for an operation, Gassman summons his nephew Riccardo (Giancarlo Giannini), who hasn't seen the salty old dog since childhood and doesn't remember him. A sharp-dressed, self-made man with a flourishing industrial cleaning business and a compassionate nature, Giannini forks over the money.

The next day, at a ritzy restaurant rendezvous with a woman not his wife, nephew discovers uncle tossing a bacchanal for a bevy of young ladies. It's a hilarious surprise but only one of a succession of comic twists that Brusati deftly sustains throughout.

Gassman and Giannini unfold their deepening relationship with an exquisitely balanced chemistry that infuses the story with irresistible charm. An artist of life with the proverbial twinkle in his eye, grey-beard Gassman can smooth-talk his way out of anything without surrendering a drop of pride. So, he blows the medical money on a party and adds insult to injury by seducing his nephew's restaurant date. Giannini is furious but also fascinated with this untamed bohemian who's unlike anyone he knows in a life neatly ordered between business in Milan and an ostentatious home in the countryside.

Gassman lives in a messy atelier, which he proceeds to set afire after his nephew remodels it as a surprise. Visiting Giannini's home, uncle scandalizes female party guests by proffering blood-test papers certifying his freedom from sexually transmittable diseases.

Gassman is uncomfortable in his nephew's bourgeois world, and Giannini's fussy wife is not sorry to see him leave. After a separation, uncle returns uninvited to nephew's home, fails to find him there and steals a valuable painting on his way out.

Giannini has been at uncle's city flat, where he discovers that the old man is a poet of narrow but respected international reputation. During Gassman's trial for theft — a wonderful sequence of dialog between the old man and an unseen inquisitor — he attempts to explain his existential code of living. "I write in the morning. The rest of the day I'm free to do as I please."

Gassman's dazzling performance builds convincingly to this summing up, and his brief imprisonment seems as amoral as the acts he is punished for.

Giannini's perfectly executed work as Gassman's foil is resonant with understated poignance. He never discovers the secret of his uncle's liaison with his mother, but Giannini, in the film's emotional final moments, apparently has gained some valuable insights about living and himself.—*Rich.*

La Vie est rien d'autre
(Life And Nothing But)
(FRENCH)

Paris A UGC release of a Hachette Première/AB Films/Little Bear/Films A2 coproduction. Executive producer, René Cleitman. Produced by Frédéric Bourbouion, Albert Prevost. Directed by Bertrand Tavernier. Screenplay, Tavernier, Jean Cosmos; camera (Eastmancolor), Bruno de Keyzer; editor, Armand Psenny; music, Oswald d'Andrea; art direction, Guy-Claude François; costumes, Jacqueline Moreau; sound, Michel Desrois, Gérard Lamps, William Flageollet; makeup, Eric Muller; production manager, Claude Albouze; assistant director, Tristan Ganne; associate producer, Clea Prods. Reviewed at UGC, Neuilly, Aug. 10, 1989. (In Montreal Film Festival, noncompeting.) Running time: **135 MIN.**
Maj. Dellaplane . . . . Philippe Noiret
Irène de Courtil . . . . Sabine Azéma
Alice . . . . Pascale Vignal
Mercadot . . . . Maurice Barrier
Perrin . . . . François Perrot
André . . . . Jean-Pol Dubois
Lt. Trevise . . . . Daniel Russo
Gen. Villerieux . . . . . . Michel Duchaussoy

■ **Bertrand Tavernier scores vibrantly with his 12th feature, "Life And Nothing But," which is excellent and nothing but. It's a moving drama of women looking for their missing menfolk on the ex-battlefields of World War I while the French army seeks a candidate for the Unknown Soldier.**

Film is unspooling at Montreal (it was pulled by Tavernier from Venice at the last minute) and is likely to earn helmer among his finest kudos internationally.

First laurels go to a densely textured, finely constructed screenplay, the fruit of Tavernier's collaboration with Jean Cosmos, a veteran legit and tv scripter, here tackling his first cinema script. Enriched by their thorough research into a little-known historical topic, story offers several probing character studies of men and women hesitating on the frontier between morbid obsession with the past and anxious hope in the future. The dialog, credited solely to Cosmos, is abundant but always pertinent in its psychological richness.

Set in a war-scarred region of eastern France in 1920, story centers essentially on three people: Sabine Azéma, a well-heeled Parisian seeking an industrialist husband who had enlisted late in the war to escape domestic boredom; Pascale Vignal, a schoolteacher looking for a fiancée she knew little but loves still, and Philippe Noiret, the French officer in charge of army's daunting task of finding and identifying the estimated 350,000 soldiers reported missing in action.

Noiret has his hands full with his grim routine functions when he is given another job: exhume unidentified cadavers for an upcoming lottery at the citadel of Verdun in a few days' time. The winning remains are to be dubbed the Unknown Soldier and paraded to a final resting place under the Arch of Triumph. The ceremony at Verdun provides one of the film's final setpieces.

Script uses this actual historical quest as a general background, an abstract, ironic and somewhat absurd contrast to the more mundane but desperate human concerns embodied by the principals.

Tavernier and Cosmos concentrate dramatic interest in the character conflict between the supercilious Azéma and the uncouth Noiret, who harbors a black hatred for her industrialist-politician father-in-law (a war profiteer, he charges).

Their antagonism, begun in a coastal military hospital, is played out in a former battle zone where Noiret is preoccupied with the excavation of a tunnel in which a troop and hospital train was buried by German mines in the last months of the war. Here families of missing soldiers are escorted in hope of identifying the remains being extricated from the tragic wreck.

Noiret, a deeply lonely man performing an heroic but ungrateful mission, begins to fall secretly in love with Azéma, whose inner strength and tenacity revive his feelings. She too undergoes a transformation as Noiret's passionate integrity and outrage ultimately move her to taking the first step in declaring her love — a gesture that terrifies the lovesick soldier into evasive silence.

The acting is deeply felt and first-class. This is Noiret's 100th film and his rendering of a hardened career officer caught between bitter resignation and the chance of emotional rebirth is a new milestone in an admirable career. Azéma channels her passionate manner into a vibrant portrait of a woman bent on providing retrospective meaning for a loveless marriage by a false sense of devotion. Pascale Vignal is a newcomer of vital sensibility as the schoolmistress of modest origins who blindly pursues a romantic quest and is brutally yanked to reality by Noiret.

Every supporting player — and they are many — is perfect. Deserving mention are Maurice Barrier, as a hack sculptor swimming in commissions for war monuments, François Perrot, as a hapless sub-officer assigned to dig up bodies with a crew of Asians (whose religion forbids contact with corpses), Jean-Pol Dubois, as Azéma's smug chauffeur and Michel Duchaussoy as a contemptuous general.

Tavernier directs with a masterful balance of the large-scale and the intimate, as well as a passionate sympathy for his personages. Despite the grimness of the setting and action, there is no cheap recourse to sensationalism, no special effects gruesomeness. The sense of loss, horror and absurdity is omnipresent from the opening scenes. Story's coda is a lyrical swell of hope and love that confirms film's title.

Though there is much talk, the plastic qualities are outstanding. Bruno de Keyzer superbly captures the austere winter light of the Meuse region where film was shot. In an era when production design in France has become a euphemism for mere set dressing, the contributions of Guy-Claude François and his team of art directors — and let's not forget the propmen — cannot be underestimated. Jacqueline Moreau's costumes are a subtle component of the visual impact.

Armand Psenny's editing keeps this long film flowing harmoniously. Oswald d'Andrea, who has adapted Kurt Weill and "Cabaret" for the French stage, contributes a fine score. —*Len.*

Drugstore Cowboy

Hollywood   An Avenue Pictures release. Produced by Nick Wechsler, Karen Murphy. Executive producer, Cary Brokaw. Directed by Gus Van Sant Jr. Screenplay, Van Sant, Daniel Yost, based on novel by James Fogle; camera (Alpha Ciné & Deluxe color; Color-film prints), Robert Yeoman; editor, Curtiss Clayton; music, Elliot Goldenthal; sound, Ron Judkins; production design, David Brisbin; art direction, Eve Cauley; costume design, Beatrix Aruna Pasztor; assistant director, David B. Householter; casting, Richard Pagano, Shirley Bialy. Reviewed at Raleigh Studios, L.A., Aug. 24, 1989. (In Montreal Film Festival, Cinema of Today and Tomorrow.) MPAA Rating: R. Running time: **100 MIN.**
Bob . . . . Matt Dillon
Dianne . . . . Kelly Lynch
Rick . . . . James Le Gros
Nadine . . . . Heather Graham
Gentry . . . . James Remar
Also with: William Burroughs.

■ No previous drug-themed film has the honesty or originality of Gus Van Sant's drama "Drugstore Cowboy." Carefully handled, this provocative and extremely topical work could make an enormous impression on serious-minded moviegoers. Even the unserious should sober up quickly at the sight of a film this daring.

"Drugstore Cowboy" addresses the fact that people take drugs because they *enjoy them.*

Set in Portland, Ore., in the early '70s, "Drugstore Cowboy" tells of one self-confessed and completely unrepentant "drug fiend" (his own description), Bob Hughes (Matt Dillon). Without ex-

cuses or apologies, Hughes frankly admits he "loves the stuff — the whole drug lifestyle." The way he manages to keep his "lifestyle" going is simple: He robs drug-stores, not for money — for drugs.

Backed up by a "crew" consisting of his willowy but tough wife Dianne (Kelly Lynch), his dimwitted but true-blue pal Rick (James Le Gros) and Le Gros' weepy, bumbling girlfriend, Nadine (Heather Graham), Dillon revels in his self-described life of crime. Lording over his tiny band as its self-appointed father, he lectures on junkie dos and don'ts (particularly regarding superstitions like leaving a hat on the bed), and plans his petty crimes with care. He takes especial pleasure in outsmarting the police adversary, Officer Gentry (James Remar).

Dillon's world begins to sour when Graham dies of an overdose while the "crew" is staying at a motel whose other guests are conventioneering policemen. He manages to spirit the body away, but the incident so frightens him, he vows to give up drugs entirely. Unfortunately, Lynch refuses to go along with him.

It's a novel conflict. Dillon is kicking the habit for personal reasons — he still likes drugs. He and Lynch still love each other, but for junkies, drugs make every romance a triangle.

Author William Burroughs, cleverly and delightfully cast as a junkie elder statesman, counsels Dillon "that in the future, the right wing in this country will demonize drugs as the first step in establishing a police state." The film couldn't state its position more clearly.

"Drugstore Cowboy" is heartening proof that Van Sant's first low-budget feature, "Mala Noche," wasn't a 1-shot wonder. He has a real feel for the underside of American life. He also has a sure visual sense. With the help of cinematographer Robert Yeoman he's made a film without one cliché shot.

Van Sant draws fine performances from his cast, particularly Kelly Lynch, who up to now has appeared as the obligatory Sexy Girl. This is her *acting* debut.

In addition Van Sant gets one truly great performance from Matt Dillon. —*Rens.*

VENICE FESTIVAL

Island
(AUSTRALIAN)

Sydney   An Atlantis Releasing presentation of an Illumination Films production. Executive producers; William Marshall, Jeannine Seawell. Produced by Paul Cox, Samantha K. Naidu. Directed by Cox. Screenplay, Cox; camera (color), Mike Edols; editor, John Scott; music consultant, Anil Acharya; production design, Neil Angwin; sound, Jim Currie; production manager, Paul Ammitzboll; assistant director, Alexandra Christou; associate producer, Takis Emmanuel. Reviewed at Cannes Film Festival (Market), May 17, 1989. (In Venice Film Festival, competing.) Running time: **93 MIN.**
Eva . . . . Eva Sitta
Marquise . . . . Irene Papas
Sahana . . . . Anoja Weerasinghe
Janis . . . . Chris Haywood
Henry . . . . Norman Kaye
Frenchman . . . . François Bernard

■ "Island" is the first dramatic feature that Paul Cox has made outside Australia, but it confirms his reputation as a personal and idosyncratic film-maker profoundly interested in humanity and human emotions.

Exceptional performances from Irene Papas and Chris Haywood should help the film find international art house audiences.

The island in question is Astypalea, in the Dodecanese chain of Greek islands in the Aegean. The tiny place has been lovingly photographed by Mike Edols, with the narrow, hilly streets, stark white buildings and intense blue of the sea all strikingly evoked.

The drama centers on three women, all refugees of one kind or another. Irene Papas plays Marquise, who comes from the Greek mainland and lives alone with tragic memories. Eve Sittes is Eva, a Czech-born, Australian drug-addict, trying to sort out her life and personal problems. Third character is Sahana (Anoja Weerasinghe), a Sri Lankan woman whose husband, a political refugee, abandoned her on the island and told her to wait for him.

The lives of these three intertwine as they reach out to one another in time of crisis. Eva is threatened by a vicious French drug dealer and Sahana comes to the realization that her husband will never return.

Film's principal assets are the vivid images and some (not all) of the performances. Papas is extraordinary as Marquise, and gives an attention-grabbing performance. In contrast, Sittes is rather thin as Eva; a stronger actress

could have made the character more convincing. Anoja Weerasinghe is moving as Sahana.

Chris Haywood, stalwart of many Australian films, is entirely convincing as Janis, a deaf-mute Greek fisherman. Able only to communicate in grunts and gestures, Haywood creates a genuinely touching and kindly character — it's a virtuoso piece of acting, and he has justly been nominated in the acting category of the 1989 Aussie film awards. So has Papas, and the pic is nominated for best film, director, original screenplay, editing and production design but not, oddly enough, cinematography.

On the debit side, Cox' pacing is ultra-slow, and he lingers too much on minor details, especially in the early scenes. Also, the director seems more detached from this film than he was with some of his earlier work (especially "Man Of Flowers," "My First Wife" and "Cactus") and, as a result, "Island" seems at times contrived and too deliberately packaged for the international art house audience. Cox regular Norman Kaye flew to the Aegean for a nothing role as a tourist — good actor as he is, Kaye's presence in this film is clearly redundant.

The use of Greek songs and Sri Lankan music adds to the mood of the picture, and a sequence in which the principals spontaneously start to dance in a cafe is a delight. Audiences seeking a picture with more plot and brisk pacing won't be impressed, but Cox' affection for his women characters, and for the island location, will please his many followers around the world.

Character of the French drug peddler is presented with a lack of subtlety, emphasizing the character's violence and sickness: this, allied to a few other anti-French remarks in the film, will ensure pic's lack of popularity in that territory (where, to date, "Cactus" remains unreleased, despite presence of Isabelle Huppert in the cast).

Pic should be well received in Venice, and may be in the running for a prize, especially in the acting stakes. —*Strat.*

BOSTON FESTIVAL REVIEWS

Strawman
(TAIWANESE)

Boston A Central Motion Picture Corp. release. Produced by Hsu Kuo-liang. Directed by Wang T'ung. Screenplay, Wang Hsiao-di, Sung Hung; camera (color), Li P'ing-pin; editor, Ch'en Sheng-ch'ang; music, Chang Hung-yi. Reviewed at Loews screening room, Boston, Aug. 9, 1989. (In the Boston Film Festival.) Running time: **97 MIN.**

With: Chang Pao-chou, Cho Sheng-li, K'o Chung-hsiung.

■ This 1987 Taiwanese film was a prizewinner in its homeland for best pic and best script. Stateside commercial prospects are dim, but it may attract some friendly attention on the festival circuit.

Story plays like a Chinese version of "Hope And Glory," with World War II serving as a backdrop for an affectionate look at life in a small rural village under Japanese occupation in 1944. Film is episodic, mixing comedy with occasional pathos, latter mostly derived from poverty of the villagers.

Best comic bit involves Japanese overseer of the village warning the women that "our enemies are the terrible Americans" who are known for their promiscuity. The same official shows his dark side when he coldy confiscates the town's cattle for the war effort.

Final and most sustained portion of the film involves the two main characters finding an unexploded American bomb and taking it to the big town for their supposed reward.

Tech credits are mixed, but Li P'ing-pin's cinematography is a definite plus, while English subtitles obviously were done by someone unfamiliar with the language. Line that one character's husband was killed in battle is translated as "He was died by American plane bomb." One is almost grateful for those lines that are left untranslated. —*Kimm*.

The Dybbuk
(POLISH-B&W)

Boston A Rutenberg and Everett Yiddish Film Library of the National Center for Jewish Film presentation. Production company (1937), Feniks. Released in 1938. Directed by Michal Waszynski. Screenplay, Alter Kacyzne, Andrzej Marek, based on the play by S. Ansky; subtitles, David G. Roskies, Sylvia Fuks Fried; camera (b&w), A. Wywerka; music, H. Kon; cantorial music, Gershon Sirota; choreography, Judith Berg; artistic director, Andrzej Marek. Reviewed at the Coolidge Corner Moviehouse, Boston, March 8, 1989. (In the Venice and Boston Film Festivals.) Running time: **123 MIN.**

Tsaddik of Miropole . . Abraham Morewski
The Messenger . . . . Issac Samberg
Sender . . . . Moshe Lipman
Leah . . . . Lili Liliana
Khonnon . . . . Leon Liebgold
Note . . . . M. Bozyk
Also with: Dina Halpern, Judith Berg, G. Lemberger, Samuel Landau, S. Bronecki, M. Messinger, Z. Katz, Abraham Kurtz, David Lederman.

■ After more than two years of work, the National Center for Jewish Film's restoration of the 1938 Yiddish film "The Dybbuk" turns out to have been worth the wait. Film should be of serious interest not just to Jewish audiences curious about their cultural heritage, but cineastes of all stripes.

Tale is based on the play by S. Ansky, telling how two old friends vow that their soon-to-be-born children should marry, but one friend dies before the promise can be conveyed to his family. Several years later the now grown daughter Leah (Lili Liliana) meets Khonnon (Leon Liebgold), the son of the dead friend, when her father invites the scholar to take a meal in his home.

Neither is aware of the vow, but Khonnon becomes obsessed with Leah, and begins to dabble in the mystical form of Judaism known as kabbala. He dies during a forbidden ceremony where he summons evil spirits, but his own spirit comes back to possess Leah on her wedding day. The stricken family takes her to the Tzaddik of Miropole (Abraham Morewski), a saintly rabbi, to exorcise the spirit from Leah.

Film has the courage of its convictions in taking the story to its logical conclusion, a dark ending that may not satisfy contemporary viewers used to movie climaxes that have been test-marketed for high approval ratings. Original audience presumably found the film tragic but not downbeat.

Besides the fascination with getting a somewhat stylized glimpse of life in the Polish Jewish community before the war, film boasts a moody, almost surreal tone. In one scene the bride shares her happiness by dancing with the townspeople only to suddenly find herself in the arms of Death (played by choreographer Judith Berg).

In the lead roles husband and wife team of Leon Liebgold and Lili Liliana — already stars of the Yiddish stage when the film was made — show a depth of characterization sometimes absent from broader melodramas of the era. Other notables in the cast include Abraham Morewski as the bewildered rabbi who must perform the exorcism and Isaac Samberg as the eerie messenger who literally appears and disappears throughout the film, warning the characters of their fates. (The late M. Bozyk, who plays the comic servant Note, was the husband of Reizl Bozyk of "Crossing Delancey" fame.)

Tech credits are solid, given the time and place the film was made, with some of the special effects still impressive. Mixture of studio and location work jells except for exterior sets which seem artificial by today's standards.

Reconstruction was funded in part by Kenneth and Justin Freed, the latter the current proprietor of the Coolidge Corner Moviehouse in Brookline, Mass.—*Kimm*.

Religion, Inc.

Boston A Chronicle Films presentation of a Michael Mailer production. Produced by Mailer. Executive producers, Laury Pense, Emanuel Goldberg, Daniel Adams. Line producer, Hank Blumenthal. Directed by Adams. Screenplay, Adams, Mailer, from story by Adams; camera (color), John Drake; editor, Thomas R. Rondinella; music, Kip Martin; sound, Jeff Pullman; production design, Paola Ridolfi; assistant director, Simon Brook; 2d unit camera, Denise Brassard; casting, Robin Monroe. Reviewed at Loews screening room, Aug. 14, 1989. (In the Boston Film Festival.) No MPAA Rating. Running time: **87 MIN.**

Morris Codman . . . . Jonathan Penner
Dr. Ian Clarity . . . . Gerald Orange
Debby . . . . Sandra Bullock
God . . . . George Plimpton
Peggy . . . . Wendy Adams
Brendan Collins . . . . Chuch Pfiefer
Also with: Jerzy Kosinski, Tama Janowitz, Jose Torres, Earl Hagan Jr., Michael Mandell, Jaffe Cohen.

■ "Religion, Inc." plays like a satiric short story that has been padded to feature length. In-jokey nature of the enterprise combined with indifferent thesping by principals suggests a rocky road ahead.

Film marks feature debut of director Daniel Adams, who co-wrote the script with producer Michael Mailer, son of author and sometime filmmaker Norman Mailer. Premise is strong, with ad exec Morris Codman (Jonathan Penner) at a low point in his life when a decidedly preppy God (writer George Plimpton) appears on his tv screen and suggests that he start a new religion.

Codman forms the title corporation, hiring janitor Ian Clarity (Gerald Orange) to front the religion, which preaches selfishness and greed as positive virtues. The idea of a religion formed and run on the basis of what marketing surveys say "religious consumers" want has promise, but the script hasn't really been thought through. Why cruelty and adultery would be publicly acknowledged precepts of a religion inspired by corporate robber barons is never made clear.

Story also has unsatisfying ending when Codman and Clarity's consciences suddenly begin bothering them and they experience a change of heart. Press notes indicate that Hemdale may be acquiring the film and recutting the ending, making the Boston festival appearance a final viewing of the director's cut.

Script's problems are worsened by actors apparently unfamiliar with film acting and sound recording that highlights their playing to back rows. Writer Jerzy Kosinski, who has acted before (in Warren Beatty's "Reds") fares best in a cameo as a panhandler.

Strongest plus in the film is its look, with credit going to director of photography John Drake and production designer Paola Ridolfi, whose contributions suggest film might play better with the sound off.

Most likely prospects for film are quick theatrical playoff followed by sale to cable. Pic will probably work a lot better on the small screen. —*Kimm*.

Route One/USA
(FRENCH-DOCU)

Boston A Les Films D'Ici and La Sept presentation in association with Channel 4 and RAI-3, of a Richard Copans production. Directed by Robert Kramer. Camera (color), Kramer; editor, Guy LeCorne, Kramer, Pierre Choukroun, Claire Laville, Keja Kramer; music, Barre Phillips; sound, Olivier Schwob, Jean-Pierre Laforce. Reviewed at Loews screening room, Boston, Aug. 23, 1989. (In the Boston Film Festival.) Running time: **253 MIN.**

With: Paul McIsaac.

■ "Route One/USA" wants to be a study of the dark underside of late '80s America, but instead it's like being locked in a closet with CBS newsman Charles Kuralt and his "On The Road" crew for four hours plus.

There's some wonderful material here, but commercial possibilities seem almost nil in its present form.

Premise is that American filmmaker Robert Kramer, who lives in Europe, is returning to the

States with a friend known as "Doc" who has been practicing medicine in Africa for the past 10 years. (Paul McIsaac, who plays Doc, is listed in the credits as actor.)

Together the two of them decide to rediscover their native land by traveling Route One, an old highway that runs more than 2,000 miles from Fort Kent, Maine, to Key West, Fla. Journey took place from fall of 1987 until March 1988.

Along the way we see the real people and places they visit, from a bingo tourney run by the Penobscot Indians to a Pat Robertson for President meeting in New Hampshire. Among the celebrities who pass through the film are candidates Robertson and Jesse Jackson and performers Ossie Davis and Helen Hayes. We see little if anything of Kramer; instead pic focuses on Doc, who is trying to figure out what he wants to do with himself now that he's back.

What's curious is that Kramer seems not to understand that the film he has made is not the film he intended. His statement in the press notes refers to being "surrounded by big trouble and hard times," but in fact many of the stories we come to see are downright inspirational, from a Hispanic community activist in Bridgeport, Conn., to the people working at an inner city public school in Manhattan.

After a stay in North Carolina, Doc drops out of the movie, saying he's decided what he's going to do, and the remaining hour of the film is quite pointless. Doc reappears, without explanation, in Florida and we leave him seemingly about to be evicted from his home.

Using this fictional character to get into the real lives of the people in the film was a clever idea, but filmmaker Kramer seems disappointed that both the fictional and real people in the film are largely upbeat about their lives in late '80s America.

Given the nature of the film, tech credits are about as solid as can be expected under the circumstances, with several sequences movingly rendered. —*Kimm.*

LOCARNO FESTIVAL

Kornblumenblau
(POLISH)

Locarno   A Film Polski presentation. Produced by K. Irzykowski Film Studios. Executive producer, Jerzy Fidler. Directed by Leszek Wosiewicz. Screenplay, Wosiewicz, Jaroslaw Sander, based on Kazimierz Tyminski's memoirs "To Silence The Dream;" camera (color), Krzysztof Ptak; editor, Wanda Zeman, Jaroslaw Wolejko; music, Zdzislaw Szostak; sound, Leszek Wronko; art direction, Zenon Rozewicz, Krzysztof Baumiller; artistic manager, Janusz Morgenstern. Reviewed at Locarno Film Festival (competing), Aug. 11, 1989. Running time: **89 MIN.**
Tadzik . . . . Adam Kamien
Moskva . . . . Marcin Tronski
Wlodek . . . . Piotr Skiba
   Also with: Krzysztof Kolberger, Wieslaw Wojcik.

■ **Dramatizing the Holocaust is risky business, because nothing can match the intensity of the real horror. That's the problem with "Kornblumenblau," as admirable as intentions may have been.**

Based on the true story of a Polish musician who survived the extermination camp only because he could play on the accordion the title melody, the picture pulls no punches. A brief pre-credits sequence summarizes the hero's life until his arrest by the Nazis for resistance activities. Film proper is dedicated to the dehumanization he goes through from the moment he is put in a camp. The relentless terror allows for one instinct only, that of survival.

Any act is justified to get one more piece of bread, to resist one more beating. Watching heinous crimes perpetrated is routine.

Director Leszek Wosiewicz drives the picture at a fearful pace, pitilessly brutalizing the audience with terrifying images and breathless rhythm. Gray is the predominant color, while the acting strives to capture despair.

It's all very impressive, but still a movie. It is painfully obvious the actors look too healthy and well fed and the images are too clean, with the presence of a director pulling the strings behind the camera quite evident.

In his hands, the sickening monstrosity of the Holocaust is raw material for artistic purposes. Particularly unsettling is the final sequence, when the Nazis are celebrating a grotesque masquerade of Beethoven's Ninth Symphony while Jews are decorously dispatched to the gas chambers and exterminated by a bored execu-

tioner who's munching his sandwich. —*Edna.*

Dreissig Jahre
(30 Years)
(SWISS)

Locarno   A Look Now presentation. Produced by Dschoint Ventschr, Videoladen. Produced and directed by Christoph Schaub. Screenplay, Martin Witz, Schaub; camera (color), Patrick Lindenmaier; editor, Fee Lichti; sound, Felix Singer; music, Thomas Baechli, Andrea Caprez; art direction, Maya Weymuller. Reviewed at Locarno Film Festival, Aug. 11, 1989. Running time: **89 MIN.**
   With: Joey Zimmerman, Stefan Gubser, Laszlo I. Kish.

■ **This portrait of men in their 30s suffering from growing pains is just one more Swiss film about how sad it is to conform. Neither characters nor story suggest any better alternative.**

Once upon a time, when they were only 18, Franz, Thomas and Nick were about to change the world. They lived together and shared ideals. Now 13 years later, only one of them sticks to his dreams of an unconventional, freewheeling style of life. He comes back from a long trip abroad and tries to persuade his friends to break away again, but with only limited success.

Filmmaker Christoph Schaub doesn't make any tough choices. It is clear that he thinks compromises deprive his heroes of their chance for happiness, but he also concedes it is damn hard being an original when everybody else has given it up.

Schaub ultimately offers little impact. His protagonists are nice and presentable, but the less than fascinating camerawork is reminiscent of early New Wave. Andrea Caprez' songs are pleasant but unmemorable. —*Edna.*

Ad, Bad, Khak
(Water, Wind, Dust)
(IRANIAN)

Locarno   An Islamic Republic of Iran Broadcasting (Channel One) production. Written, directed, edited and makeup by Amir Naderi. Camera (color), Reza Pakzad; sound, Nezam Kiai; executive director, Freydun Azma. Reviewed at Locarno Film Festival, Aug. 11, 1989. (Also in Toronto Film Festival.) Running time: **94 MIN.**

■ **Shot by director Amir Naderi in 1985, shelved when he defected to America and still unreleased, this companion piece to his fest favorite "The Runner" probably will make the fest circuit as well.**

Shot in one of the most desolate places imaginable, a dried-up lake on the border of Iran and Afghanistan, the film is an almost abstract confrontation of man and nature at its worst. A boy (Majid Nirumand, who also was in "The Runner") comes back to his village, which has been ravaged by a terrible drought. He wanders through what used to be the shores of a lake — now a dry, forbidding desert. Animal carcasses are lying everywhere.

Small groups of refugees depart, leaving all their belongings — sometimes even their children — behind. The hot wind blows unrelentingly, sweeping away the last signs of human life. Only the boy won't go away with the others; he will stay and fight the dust and the wind.

All through the film the camera follows this boy as he runs aimlessly in circles. No one ever will accuse Naderi of trying to entertain his audience, but he certainly manages to shock it. The images of men crushed by the desert are shattering. So is the overwhelming, unrelenting sound of the sand storm.

The film may be taken as an allegory of the Iranian people, or maybe of the entire Third World, struggling against its fate. With its repetitive images and uncompromising insistence on gruesome details (hungry dogs tearing apart the carcass of a cow), it is a tough film to watch.—*Edna.*

Affetuose Lontananze
(Affectionate Distances)
(ITALIAN)

Locarno   A Maestranza & Tecnici Cinema production. Produced by Beppe Scavuzzo. Directed by Sergio Rossi. Screenplay, Rossi, Age, with Caterina de Martiis, Maria Giovanna Pintus, based on story by Rossi; camera (color), Franco Lecca; editor, Massimo Palumbo Cardella; songs, Maurizio Areni, Anna Karin Klockar; sound, Roberto Petrozzi, Bruno Pupparo; art direction, Maria Silvia Farci. Reviewed at Locarno Film Festival (competing), Aug. 12, 1989. Running time: **100 MIN.**
   With: Lina Sastri, Angela Finocchiaro, Fiorenza Marchegianni, Gianpiero Bianchi.

■ **Once upon a time, this would have been considered a woman's picture. In the perspective of the late '80s, however, this condescending portrait of three modern single women, supposedly independent and liberated, but obsessed by the men in their lives, is annoying rather than gratifying for female audiences.**

Mostly, this is the story of Luisa, a mature art teacher who has just broken up a longstanding affair and is pining for another. Her friends, one an obstetrician, the other a librarian, are about the same age and face the same kind of problems. Both are professionally successful but unfulfilled in their personal lives. The first changes partners all the time, while the second is faithful to one man, until he tells her he wants to divorce his wife and marry her instead, which makes her unhappy because she is too fond of her freedom.

Nothing much happens in the first half of the picture, until Luisa meets a cartoonist who seems to be a promising prospect. Unfortunately, his diffidence prevents his committing himself further than a night in the sack or a day on the town. This is frustrating for a woman who needs affection, and she finds it difficult to function without it.

Excessively talky, explaining the obvious at length and in detail, the script doesn't skip any of the clichés. Luisa is a sort of Mr. Chips, always siding with her students, who adore her. There is simply no flaw in her character. All she wants is a man who can appreciate her qualities, but as the film ends, she still is looking for him.—*Edna.*

Noch Ein Wunsch
(One More Wish)
(SWISS-WEST GERMAN)

Locarno A Westdeutsche Rundfunk, Koln (WDR), Swiss German tv, Zurich (DRS) production. Produced by Hartwig Schmidt, Claudio Ricci. Directed by Thomas Koerfer. Screenplay, Koerfer, Dieter Feldhausen, based on story by Adolg Muschg; camera (color), Ueli Steiger, Michael Fueter; editor, Marie-Ann Naumann, Marina Nickel, Brita Soerensen; music, Louis Crelier; sound, Klaus Esefeld, Josef Baum; art direction, Heinz Melchior, Torsten Hindersin; costumes, Detlef Papendorf, Caludia Schmelter, Georg Widmann; makeup, Klaus Mack. Reviewed at Locarno Film Festival (Swiss section), Aug. 11, 1989. Running time: **103 MIN.**
Martin . . . . Matthias Habich
Brigitte . . . . Hannelore Eisner
Anne . . . . Johanna Lier
Anne's mother . . . . Marianne Nentwich
Also with: Thomas Nock, Joachim Spiess, Stefan Gubser, Michael Gempart, Babett Arens, Jurgen Cziesla, Salahedinne Ben Sad, Claudia Burckhardt, Hildegard Ziegler, Thomas Koerfer, Daniel Schmid, Bruno Ganz.

■ **Bearing all the signs of a commissioned film done without any real personal involvement, this is a routine family melodrama.**

It depicts the midlife crisis of a successful lawyer who drops out of his birthday party and goes to Paris. There he meets a young girl, has a 1-night affair and is shocked later to discover that she

goes on with her life without his constant presence. It's sprinkled with clichés throughout. The philandering husband, the understanding wife and the emancipated lover fit into well-known patterns, with a couple of pretty ridiculous tearjerking gimmicks (the girl hospitalized after participating in an anti-establishment demonstration) for a bonus.

Thomas Koerfer, once a direc-

tor seeking a personal language, evidently has decided to take it easy for a while. He tells the story without any frills or thrills, making the best of the Swiss locations. The handsome actors too often are allowed to slip into histrionics, especially Matthias Habich.

Produced for tv, it looks like the small screen is its natural home.
—*Edna.*

NORWEGIAN FESTIVAL REVIEWS

Landstrykere
(Wanderers)
(NORWEGIAN)

Haugesund, Norway A KF release of a Norsk Film production for Landstrykere Ans. Produced by Gunnar Svensrud. Directed by Ola Solum. Screenplay, Hans Lindgren, Lars Saabye Christensen, Solum, from Knut Hamsun's novel; camera (Eastmancolor). Harald Paalgard; editor, Yugve Refseth; music, Henning Sommero; production design, Anne Siri Bryhni; costumes, Kari Elfstedt; sound, Conrad Weyns; production management, Peter Boe; assistant director, Eva Isaksen. Reviewed at Norwegian Film Festival, Haugesund, Norway, Aug. 19, 1989. Running time: **135 MIN.**
Edevart . . . . . . Trond Peter Stamsö Munch
Lovise Margrete . . . . . . Marika Lagercrantz
August . . . . Helge Jordal
Ragna . . . . Liv Helöe
Ane Maria . . . . Liv Steen
Knoff . . . . Espen Skjönberg
Also with: John Sigurd Kristensen, Lasse Lindtner, Hildegunn Riise, Frank Krog, Karl Sundby, Kristian Figenschow, Stale Björnhaug, Hans Peter Korff, Karl Boman-Larsen, Siri Enger Karlsen, Grete Nordra, Paul Ottar Haga, Egil Lorch, Per Christensen, Bernhard Ramstad.

■ **"Wanderers" takes Norse Nobel Prize-winning Knut Hamsun's 1927 novel about common folks in the North Atlantic coastal areas of Norway in the 1870s to the big screen as a series of handsome postcards.**

Although obviously stamped for foreign destinations (and presold to West Germany's ARD as a 3-hour tv miniseries) film has an uncertain offshore future theatrically. At 135 minutes, it is tediously overlong and obscure and inconclusive in most of its choppy episodes.

Helmer Ola Solum took over the production of "Wanderers" when others had left it during the early stages of its costly shooting. (At $4.5-million, it's reportedly the costliest pic in local history.) He has done a workmanlike job without adding any personal insight or original viewpoint to the subject matter. The film has no narrative sweep or emotional gut-punch two areas in which novelist Hamsun excelled.

Edevart, a young country lad, is so impressed by roguish August, a charmingly aggressive trader, that he follows him on his travels up and down the coast.

Eventually, Edevart sees through August's trickery and cuts loose to pursue his own goals, one of them being a young mother left behind with two kids and some sheep in a rustic cabin. Since the husband has not been reported dead, Edevart gets nowhere with this all-too-good Lovise, at least not until after years of waiting for the return, and renewed departure, of her vicious spouse.

August, seen as both tramp and hero, disappears from the action for greater parts of the film and is sorely missed. Played by Helge Jordal, he may come on as a monotonous, self-obsessed clown, but he also remains convincing as a man of his age with the wits to survive.

As Edevart and Lovise, Trond Peter Stamsö Munch and Sweden's Marika Lagercrantz are all surface youthful good looks. Hamsun's rich gallery of sharply observed characters surrounding the lead trio is left dangling as a set of sketchbook outlines.

All production credits are professional, and Henning Sommero's score suggests the somber longings of the people and place better than the rough-sledding picture itself.

"Wanderers" falls way short of its ambition to match the epic storytelling achievements of Sweden's Jan Troell ("The Emigrants") and Denmark's Bille August ("Pelle The Conqueror").
—*Kell.*

Bryllupsfesten
(The Wedding Party)
(NORWEGIAN)

Haugesund, Norway A UIP release of a Mefistofilm production. Produced, written and

directed by Svend Wam, Petter Venneröd. Camera (Eastmancolor), Svein Krövel; editor, Inge-Lise Langfeldt, Randi Weum; music, Svein Gundersen; production design, Viggo Jönsberg, Tone Skjeldfjord; sound, Ragnar Samuelsson; choreography, Morten Ruda; costumes, Kari Baade, Kathrine Tolo; special effects, Jan Valland; production management, Halvor Bodin. Reviewed at Norwegian Film Festival, Haugesund, Norway, Aug. 22, 1989. Running time: **115 MIN.**
Totto Holm . . . . Knut Huseby
Dyveke Holm . . . . Eli Anne Linnestad
Uncle Eugene . . . . Ernst-Hugo Järegard
Lise Holm . . . . Julie Wiggen
Henry Balstad . . . . Jon Eikemo
Gerd . . . . Mari Björgan
Roger Balstad . . . . Philip Tellman
Mutter . . . . Aud Schönemann
Fatter . . . . Leif Juster
Rakel . . . . Fröydis Armand
Tony . . . . Calvin Ray Stiggers
Also with: Lasse Lintner, Tord Nygard, Are Sjaastad, Anne Marie Ottersen.

■ **Firebrand filmmakers with leftish leanings through 12 diverse fatures, the do-it-all duo of Petter Venneröd and Svend Wam just relax and have fun with "The Wedding Party," an outright farce.**

Watching top talent of stage and screen tumbling headlong into slapstick and pratfalls seems sure to lure plenty of locals to the wickets.

This time around, Venneröd and Wam have served up too much of a good thing in a poorly edited series of star turns for "Party," making it unlikely to reach foreign shores.

The mechanics of rhythmic editing are lacking most of the way through an otherwise solid enough plot framework. A bride's rich father uses the wedding party to conceal an insurance swindle via the rigged theft of some Edvard Munch fakes on his walls. The real paintings are hidden in the basement.

Wedding party guests, burglars, servant staff and police constantly bump into or chase each other, with the most predictable results. Dialog is spoken too loudly by all but Sweden's Ernst-Hugo Järegard and Oslo comedian Leif Juster.

Virtually all roles are cameos and the actors are encouraged to overact furiously.

Throwing the final vestiges of caution to the wind, the ending has everybody diving into the bushes to crouch and emit loud noises after having eaten over-spiced soup. At this point, a raspberry response from audiences would seem merited. —*Kell.*

The Rose Garden
(WEST GERMAN-U.S.)

Haugesund, Norway   Pathé Intl. presentation of CCC Filmkunst (Berlin) in association with Cannon Film, ZDF (Mainz), ORF (Vienna). Produced by Artur Brauner. Directed by Fons Rademakers. Screenplay, Paul Hengge; camera (Eastmancolor), Gernot Roll; editor, Kees Lindhorst; music, Egisto Macchi; production design, Jan Schlubach; costumes, Monika Jacobs; sound, Karl Laabs; production manager, Ingrid Windisch; special effects, Adolf Woytinek; Liv Ullmann's wardrobe, Jil Sander; casting, Horst Scheel. Reviewed at Norwegian Film Festival, Haugesund, Norway, Aug. 21, 1989. Running time: **112 MIN.**
Gabriele Freund . . . . .Liv Ullmann
Aaron Reichenbacher . . .Maximilian Schell
Herbert Schlüter . . . . .Peter Fonda
Pässler . . . . .Jan Niklas
Tina . . . . .Katarina Lena Müller
Arnold Krenn . . . . .Kurt Hübner
Prof. Eckert . . . . .Hanns Zischler
Ruth Levi . . . . .Gila Almagor
    Also with: Marcike Carrière, Georg Marischka, Nicolaus Sombart, Ozay Fecht, Achim Ruppel, Friedhelm Lehmann, Lutz Weidlich, Peter Kortenbach.

■ "The Rose Garden," made for both cinema and tv , looms to fare best via the home screen. Its title refers to a plot of flowered land next to a Hamburg street where 20 Jewish children were hanged April 20, 1945, as the British army appoached the city.

The children had been used for medical experiments, and their execution was ordered by an SS officer who lives in West Germany. He has avoided prosecution on legal technicalities.

Holland's Fons Rademakers, who gained a best foreign language film Academy Award for "The Assault" (which also had a World War II theme), fictionalizes the incident by having the SS officer brought to court in today's Frankfurt as a witness in a related case. The old man has been assaulted in the city's airport by Aaron Reichenbacher (Maximilian Schell), who is assigned defense attorney Gabriele Freund (Liv Ullmann).

Reichenbacher will not talk, and Freund has to do extensive detective work to find out her client was the only one to escape the group hanging. He has returned from Montevideo exile to find his sister, and had chanced to see the SS officer in the airport.

As it develops into a courtroom melodrama-detective story, the heavily talky pic is relieved only by a few scenes of Freund's daughter being terrorized by neo-Nazi hoodlums. A running fight between Ullmann and the girl's father (Peter Fonda) over custody is mixed up in a flimsy subplot.

Just as the SS officer appears to be brought to justice, he escapes it once more. Rademakers makes the German judicial system look hollow and its administrators callous.

A reconstruction of the 1945 hangings is delivered in grayish tones and subdued style to look like a documentary.

With its near-total dependence on expository dialog, the main part of "The Rose Garden" has only its theme to keep it from being flat-out dull. Schell avoids his usual mannerisms and delivers a touching portrait of a tortured, anguished man.

Ullmann is brisk and convincing as a matter-of-fact intellectual awakened emotionally by the case. Fonda's part is mostly a cliché, but he walks through it with a conviction mellowed by self-irony. —Kell.

En handfull tid
(A Handful Of Time)
(NORWEGIAN)

Haugesund, Norway   A KF release of a Norsk Film production, in association with the Swedish Film Institute. Produced by Harald Ohrvik. Directed by Martin Asphaug. Screenplay, Erik Borge; camera (Eastmancolor), Philip Oegard; editor, Einar Egeland; music, Randall Meyers; sound, Magne Mikkelsen; production design, Edith Stylo; production management, Erik Disch; assistant director, Egeland. Reviewed at the Norwegian Film Festival (competing), Haugesund, Norway, Aug. 20, 1989. Running time: **95 MIN.**
Older Martin . . . . .Espen Skjönberg
Younger Martin . . .Nicolay Lange-Nielsen
Anna . . . . .Camilla Ström Henriksen
Anker . . . . .Per Jansen
Else . . . . .Minken Fosheim
Daniel . . . . .Björn Sundquist
Kari . . . . .Brit Elisabeth Haagensli
Ada . . . . .Lotte Tarp
Hannibal . . . . .Arve Opsahl
Henrik . . . . .Hans Krövel
Susan Walker . . . . .Susannah York
Ted Walker . . . . .Nigel Hawthorne
    Also with: Carl Bomann Larsen, Jan Harstad, Henrik Scheele, Erik Hivju, Liv Thorsen, Jack Fjeldstad, Gunnar Enekjär, Frode Rasmussen.

■ "A Handful Of Time" is a sit-up-and-gasp feature film bow for the unlikely team of young helmer Martin Asphaug and writer Erik Borge, latter being actually a top Norse film business exec in retirement.

Technically impressive, dramatically dazzling and emotionally uncompromising, this gothic thriller about love, guilt and redemption is clearly marked for the major festival circuit.

It should obtain theatrical sales in just about any territory as well.

It's a minor miracle that the director avoids getting bogged down in flashbacks in a film that constantly jumps between today and yesterday. Borge's story recounts an old man's struggle to come to terms with a certain sin of omission of his youth.

Old Martin heeds the voice of Anna, who calls him back to the mountain cabin where he left her to die while she gave birth to their surviving son.

Anna actually had been forced upon the young man by an uncle, who gave him the money to seek his fortune as a horse trader in Norway's rugged west. She was raped by her father, who was killed by Martin. The two youngsters find love as well as social bonding with another couple in the wilderness.

Throughout the travels and travails of young and old, past and present, both story and camera move naturally to create a seamless drama in which violent action (always seen with awesome nature as a direct participant) interchanges with compassionate and often witty observations of wilderness people.

Every character in "A Handful Of Time" is fully fleshed and nuanced. Old Martin is given an especially fine honing of both sorrow and survivor's wit by Espen Skjönberg, while Nicolay Lange-Nielsen and Camilla Ström Henriksen as young Martin and Anna find emotions to add exciting shadings to their otherwise still unmarked faces. Lange-Nielsen is great in physical action, too.

Plot contrivances jar at times, and too much blood is allowed to gush. The brief appearance of Susannah York and Nigel Hawthorne as a couple of very British angels constitutes a comedy routine of no real relevance.

But they do not detract seriously from the joy and almost physical pleasure of watching this strong and beautiful film move forward. Editor Einar Egeland has worked in perfect musical empathy with Asphaug, while producer Harald Ohrvik deserves special credit for having made the clearly ebullient helmer toe the (story) line in moments of temptation, avoiding empty technical fireworks.
—Kell.

Hamlet Goes Business
(FINNISH-B&W)

Haugesund, Norway   A Finnkino presentation of a Villealfa Film production. Produced, written and directed by Aki Kaurismäki. Camera (b&w), Timo Salminen; editor, Raija Talvio; sound, Jouku Lumme; production design, Pertti Hilkamo; production management, Jaakko Talaskivi; assistant director, Pauli Pentti; costumes, Tuula Hilkamo. Reviewed at Norwegian Film Festival (special screening), Haugesund, Norway, Aug. 24, 1989. Running time: **86 MIN.**
Hamlet . . . . .Pirkka-Pekka Petelius
Klaus . . . . .Esko Salminen
Ophelia . . . . .Kati Outinen
Gertrud .Elina Salo
Polonius . . . . .Kari Väänänen
Simo . . . . .Hannu Valtonen
Helena . . . . .Mari Rantasila
Rosencrantz . . . . .Turo Pajala
Guildenstern . . . . .Aake Kalliala
Father/ghost . . . . .Pentti Auer
The Guard . . . . .Matti Pellenpää
    Also with: Vesa Mäkelä, Maija Leino, Pertti Sveholm, Vesa Vierikko, Miitta Sorvali, Erkki Astala.

■ "Hamlet Goes Business" actually was shot in 1987, between filmmaker Aki Kaurismäki's internationally acclaimed comedies "Shadows In Paradise" and "Ariel." In "Hamlet" the joke element prevails at the expense of the warmly human involvement of the other films, but there is little doubt that an original director has delivered another item for offshore circulation

Shot in black & white on a tiny budget, "Hamlet" ambles leisurely and tongue-in-cheek through present-day events that neatly parallel those that befell Shakespeare's Danish prince. Moods of classic film noir and old Warner Bros. thrillers also are evoked as Hamlet (played with bemused mien by Pirkka-Pekka Petelius) roams the corridors of his murdered father's business empire, now in the hands of an uncle with designs on roping in a world monopoly in the manufacture of rubber ducks.

All characters bear the original Shakespearean names. Ophelia weeps bitterly in her chambers as Rosencrantz and Guildenstern are dispatched to Norway (!), where they expect to be bored to death. At film's midnight screenings at the 17th Norwegian Film Festival, audiences were kept wide awake, guffawing.—Kell.

Miraklet i Valby
(Miracle In Valby)
(DANISH)

Haugesund, Norway   A Syncron Film release (Norway) of a Nordisk Film (Denmark) production, in association with the Danish Film Institute, the Swedish Film Institute and Esselte Entertainment (Sweden). Produced by Bo Christensen. Directed by Ake Sandgren. Screenplay, Sandgren, Stig Larsson; camera (Eastmancolor), Dan Lausten; editor, Darek Hodor; music, Vladek Gulgowski, Roxette; production design, Henning Bahs; sound, Michael Dela; Danish Film Institute consultant producer, Ida Zeruneith. Reviewed at Norwegian Film Festival (Children's section), Haugesund, Norway, Aug. 23, 1989. Running time: **85 MIN.**
Sven .Jakob Katz
Bo . . . . .Troels Asmussen
Petra . . . . .Lina Englund

Hanna . . . . Amalie Alstrup
Also with: Ingvar Hirdvall, Mona Seilitz, Karen Lise Mynster, Nis Bank Mikkelsen, Peter Hesse Overgaard, Jens Okking.

■ **Time travel and devious special effects are involved in Swedish Ake Sandgren's Danish kiddie feature "Miracle In Valby." Jerky, insecure storytelling and editing, plus generally stiff acting, sink it.**

The ambition of the story itself has defeated the filmmakers. Sven, an 11-year-old radio amateur, receives signals from the past in Latin. He one day finds Petra, his Swedish neighbor's daughter, abducted by medieval warriors. With his friend Bo he sets out on a time travel in the wreck of a small mobile home where he keeps his radio gear. His kid sister is a stowaway in the radio shack.

The Middle Age warriors capture a new batch of kids from the future, and their monks make an altar of the mobile home while they listen in awe as the kid sister reads aloud to them from a Horror Comix book. Their fun soon comes to an end when Bo has everybody tricked by a chicken popping out of a mechanical egg he has brought along.

Hints of young love emerging among the kids and unnuanced ridicule of all adults are woven into the proceedings. They remain as underdeveloped as everything else in a bottom-heavy fantasy film that never gets off the ground. — *Kell.*

For harde livet
(For Dear Life)
(NORWEGIAN-DOCU)

Haugesund, Norway A Europa Film release of a Motlys production. Produced by Svein Toreg. Written and directed by Sigve Endresen. Camera (Eastmancolor), Halgrim Oedegaard; editor, Hans Otto Nicolaysen; music, Knut Reiersrud; sound, Peik Borud. Reviewed at Norwegian Film Festival, Haugesund, Norway, Aug. 19, 1989. Running time: **98 MIN.**

■ **"For Dear Life," a documentary about teenage dope addicts given an institutional second chance in a ski resort area, earned a theatrical release with subsequent neat boxoffice business.**

It also went on to win Norway's most prestigious film award, the Amanda, in three categories (best docu, best director and best editor) at the Norwegian Film Festival. Offshore exposure, however, is not likely to go beyond the educational circuit.

For 18 months, helmer Sigve

Endresen and his expert crew recorded what they saw and heard at Tyrili, where a group of youngsters, rescued from the streets of Oslo, went through a physical and mental survival school. This encompasses discussion sessions with Tyrili teachers; rock climbing; grouse hunting; riding in rubber rafts over rapids, and soul searching and talks.

The kids were given the freedom to "run away" (all came back), and a few are seen back on the city streets. The film, however, nearly too-studiously avoids all melodramatics. No needle or self-abasement is seen, no whining or anger is heard.

What "For Dear Life" tells us is mostly that hope lies in the good will of educators and victims alike. Refraining from depicting the sordid aspects of the young drug scene, Endresen may be praised for soberness, but not necessarily for any in-depth realism in his approach to his subject. — *Kell.*

Dykket
(The Dive)
(BRITISH-NORWEGIAN)

Haugesund, Norway A Filmeffekt (Norway), Millennium and British Screen presentation; a KF release (Norway), Gavin Film (intl. sales) of a Filmeffekt production. Produced by Dag Alveberg. Coproducer, Patrick Casavetti. Directed by Tristan De Vere Cole. Screenplay, Leidulv Risan, Carlos Wiggen; camera (Eastmancolor), Harald Paalgard; editor, Russel Lloyd; music, Geir Böhren, Bent. Aserud; title tune, Stein Berge Svendsen, Stein Osvoll; production design, Jarle Blesvik; special effects, Petter Borgli; sound, Kari Nyströ, Peter A. Stoop; costumes, Anne Hamre; production management, Arve Figenschow; casting (U.K.), Mary Selway; casting (Norway), Eva Isakson. Reviewed at Norwegian Film Festival, Haugesund, Norway, Aug. 24, 1989. Running time: **95 MIN.**
Bricks . . . . Michael Kitchen
Dobs . . . . Frank Crimes
Gunnar . . . . Bjjörn Sundquist
Ann . . . . Marika Lagercrantz
The captain . . . . Sverre Anker Ousdal
Akselsen . . . . Nils Ole Oftebro
(English soundtrack)

■ **In full command of technical credits and not overdoing its special effects, Tristan De Vere Cole's "The Dive" is a gutwrenching thriller about two divers stuck in a bell on the ocean floor.**

Item is sure to become a nice sales commodity for Gavin Film.

This British-Norwegian film has an English-only version and one in which the Norwegian characters speak their own language when alone together. The dialog is spare and to the point anyway, and the play on emotion beyond outright suspense is neatly low-key. Au-

diences will be involved in a drama that is for real.

An atmosphere of playful camaraderie is struck as two divers, Bricks (Michael Kitchen) and Gunnar (Björn Sundquist), prepare for their helicopter lift back home after an overlong tour of duty. Gunnar lets himself be talked into doing the 3-minute job of going down in the diving bell an extra time to repair a trawler-damaged valve. Rolf goes with him, and soon the two of them find themselves trapped 100 yards below the surface.

Wire netting latches on to the bell, and the three minutes develop into hours. The men run out of oxygen. The bell gets unhooked from its line to the vessel above. Only a tv monitor and the radio work.

The measures taken by the rescue crew seem to be absolutely authentic. Most faces are tough and bitten by sea and wind, but all actors go well beyond cliché in their performances. As Gunnar, Sundquist comes on as a man of action and tempered emotion.

Deadly irony follows the drama: The dive was forced by a greedy company owner. Fortunately, this theme is not overworked in a film that rings sober and true. — *Kell.*

LATINO FESTIVAL REVIEWS

El Escándalo
(The Scandal)
(VENEZUELAN)

New York A Yekuana Films-Foncine production. Directed by Carlos Oteyza. Screenplay, José Ignacio Cabrujas, Oteyza; camera (color), Hernán Toro; editor, Freddy Veliz; music, Pablo Manavello; sound, Edgar Torres; art direction, Sandy Jelambi. Reviewed at Festival Latino (competing), Biograph theater, N.Y., Aug. 6, 1989. Running time: **104 MIN.**
Antonio Campos . . . . Flavio Caballero
Aroldo Benavides . . . . Daniel López
Julia Campos . . . . Corina Azopardo
Nicolás "El Príncipe" . . . . . . Juan Manuel Montesinos
Harry Dixon . . . . Giles Bickford
Oscar Mateos . . . . Iván González
Doble Feo . . . . Alejo Felipe
    Also with: Carlota Sosa, Cecilia Martínez, Lucia Rikos, Mariano Alvarez, Carlos Moreán, Cayito Aponte, Vlctor Cuica, Félix Landeta, Ernesto Balzi.

■ **Dealing with such timely topics as insider trading and corruption, Venezuelan feature "El Escándalo" (The Scandal) is a well-made, surface-deep journalistic exposé about how power and money ultimately corrupt the innocent. While tech credits are high, cliché-laden script inhibits potential impact.**

Pic delves into the *haute* lifestyles of the rich and famous within the national petroleum industry, Venezuela's single most important dollar-earner. Action takes place before the drastic fall in world oil prices circa 1981.

Storyline is simple: Amiable production chief Antonio Campos (Flavio Caballero) is hoisted to national attention when he makes a commercial touting the oil industry. He is promoted and suddenly courted by oily info-dealer Aroldo Benavides (Daniel López). Aroldo has a flair for life: When a Caracas

restaurant runs out of lobster, he merely borrows a helicopter and flies to the Caribbean for a fresh barbecue lunch.

The fastlane takes its toll on Campos' family life as he becomes more deeply involved. He learns that once compromised, there's no where to go but down.

Cowritten by playwright José Ignacio Cabrujas, story offers few surprises. Fast-paced editing keeps the action moving while the brash music adds drive to this moral tale.

Acting is fine, especially by López and Corina Azopardo, who plays Campos' wife, Julia. — *Lent.*

El Jinete de la Divina Providencia
(The Horseman Of The Divine Providence)
(MEXICAN)

New York An Imcine-Conacite 2-Cooperativa Séptimo Arte-U. Autonoma de Sinaloa production. Directed by Oscar Blancarte. Screenplay, Blancarte, Sergio Molina, Xavier Robles, based on the play by Molina; camera (color), Antonio Ruiz; editor, Juan Manuel Vargas; music, Oscar Reinoso; sound, Robert Camacho; art direction, Zeth Santacruz. Reviewed at Festival Latino (competing), Biograph theater, N.Y, Aug. 14, 1989. Running time: **100 MIN.**
    With: Bruno Rey, Martha Navarro, Claudio Obregón Germán Robles, Carlos East, Alonso Echanove, Abril Campillo, Héctor Monge, Ernesto Schwartz, Antonio Subiaga, Rodolfo Arriaga, Ernesto Yáñez.

■ **Mexican helmer Oscar Blancarte's second feature "The Horseman Of The Divine Providence" is an interesting yet marred work about a real-life 19th-century horseman who took local crooked politicos to task.**

Storyline centers on Jesús Malverde, a mysterious figure from the Sinaloan town of Culiacán, a type of Mexican Robin Hood à la Joaquín Morietta, who steals from the rich to give to the poor.

Pic's genesis is a legit work of the same name by Sergio Molina, with the bandit-hero as the play's central character. In scripting an adaptation, helmer Blancarte made a wise decision to keep Malverde off-screen, inferring that he is really a metaphor for the greater will of the town.

Film begins in present day: Malverde is proposed for canonization. Several members of the clergy unconvincingly try to gather information and are met with contradictory ''Rashomon''-style tales. The main question arises: Did the horseman exist at all? Although Blancarte concedes his existence, the legendary hero emerges rather as a symbol of justice against gross corruption and cruelty.

Story is not without humor, especially as the town spontaneously collaborates to protect Malverde against the evil state governor, an opera buffo character.

Director shows a weakness in his portrayal of women, who come off as vapid clichés or mere victims of violence lacking characterization. Three separate rape scenes are excessive and serve little purpose.

Overall production values are inconsistent. While the past is lovingly painted, contemporary scenes suffer from directorial indifference. Photography by Antonio Ruiz is lush and admirable while Oscar Reinoso's synthesized music seems out of place and grating. —*Lent.*

El Camino Largo A Tijuana (The Long Road To Tijuana) (MEXICAN)

New York   Produced by Luis Estrada, Emmanuel Lubezki. Directed by Estrada. Screenplay, Brian Stern, Aaron Sorice; camera (color), Carlos Marcovich; editor, Tony Salgado; music, Santiago Ojeda, Diego Herrera; sound, Salvador de la Fuente, Akie Ozono; art direction, Vito Ilardi, Natalie Weiss. Reviewed at Festival Latino (noncompeting), Public theater, N.Y., Aug. 5, 1989. Running time: **92 MIN.**
Juan . . . . Pedro Armendáriz Jr.
Rita . . . . Ofelia Medina
Lila . . . . Patricia Pereyra
Tubo . . . . Daniel Jiménez Cacho
Gas . . . . Jaime Keller
Chino . . . . Alfonso Arau
Nana . . . . Carmen Salinas
Fogonero . . . . José Carlos Rodríguez
Dealer . . . . Julián Pastor

■ **First feature by Luis Estrada, son of w.k. Mexican helmer José**

Estrada, "The Long Road" tries to lead viewers into uncharted territory, yet an obvious low budget presents several insurmountable roadblocks.

Story deals with a heroin-addicted runaway (Patricia Pereyra), who stumbles into an automobile graveyard while fleeing from two lowlifes. Yard proves to be home for itinerant junk dealer Juan (Pedro Armendáriz Jr.), who happens to have a daughter about the same age living somewhere in Tijuana.

The bad guys — who feel compelled by the turgid script to rough up anyone in their way — are out to collect a substantial reward offered by the teen's parents. Both characters are completely without color.

Armendáriz plays a variation on Stacy Keach's Mike Hammer role, while the impressive cast includes some of Mexico's hottest talent — Armendáriz, Ofelia Medina, Alfonso Arau and Carmen Salinas — mostly in bit parts.

Camerawork tends to be flat and badly lit, especially within the stark surroundings of deserted buildings, abandoned industrial plants, empty streets and junkyards that pose as oblique metaphors for spiritual and moral decay. Sound levels also need work.

While film is not without interest, the poor technical quality will repel all but the most diehard viewers. —*Lent.*

Todo Por Nada (All For Nothing) (CHILEAN)

Santiago   A LAK production. Executive producer, Hernán Swart. Directed by Alfredo Lamadrid. Screenplay, Patricio Campos; camera (color), Miguel Montenegro, Marcelo González; editor, Ismael Morales; music, Miguel Zabaleta; costumes, Alexis Paredero; associate producer, René Kreutzberger. Reviewed at Cine Rex I, Aug. 14, 1989. Running time: **99 MIN.**
Alejandra . . . . Ana Maria Gazmuri
Juan José . . . . Fernando Kliche
Joaquín del Río . . . . Mauricio Pesutic
Andrés del Campo . . . . Osvaldo Silva
Claudio García . . . . Patricio Achurra
Also with: Marcel Edwards, Ernesto Rompeltien, Rodrigo Bastidas, Patricia Larraguibel, Verónica González, Luis Wigdorsky, Grimanesa Jiménez, Gladys del Río.

■ **The unconscious parody of telenovela backstage shenanigans may be "Todo Por Nada's" only point of interest.**

The main difference is that on tv the commercials come separate from the story, which is certainly not the case in the film. Lead

character Alejandra promotes a brand of instant coffee (lovingly identified) at a supermarket (lingering long shots of its marquee) and dreams of becoming a tv star.

The road to fame is paved by an advertising executive who uses her as a model, a fashion photographer, a tv director, a variety show host and the owner of a production company. Bed-hopping from one to the other, Alejandra finally makes it, although her one true love gets lost on the way.

With the honorable exceptions of Mauricio Pesutic and Patricio Achurra, acting ranges from bad to deplorable. Transfer from videotape to 35m film (done in the U.S.) was serviceable, which can not be said for the other technical credits. A cast of well-known telenovela performers could help initial b.o., but is unlikely to sustain the film. —*Amig.*

Erik The Viking (BRITISH)

London   An Orion Pictures release (U.S.) of a John Goldstone/Prominent Features production, in association with Svensk Filmindustri. Executive producer, Terry Glinwood. Produced by John Goldstone. Written and directed by Terry Jones; camera (Fujicolor), Ian Wilson; editor, George Akers; music, Neil Innes; sound, Alan Bell; production design, John Beard; art direction, Gavin Bocquet, Roger Cain; costumes, Pam Tait; special effects, Richard Conway; associate producer, Neville C. Thompson; casting, Irene Lamb. Reviewed at Prominent Studios preview theater, London, Aug. 30, 1989. MPAA Rating: PG-13. Running time: **103 MIN.**
Erik . . . . Tim Robbins
Keitel . . . . Gary Cady
Erik's grandfather . . . . Mickey Rooney
Freya . . . . Eartha Kitt
King Arnulf . . . . Terry Jones
Princess Aud . . . . Imogen Stubbs
Halfdan the Black . . . . John Cleese
Loki . . . . Antony Sher
Ivor the Boneless . . . . John Gordon Sinclair
Helga . . . . Samantha Bond
Sven the Berserk . . . . Tim McInnerny
Thorfinn Skullsplitter . . . . . Richard Ridings
Harald the Missionary . . . . . . Freddie Jones
Also with: Charles McKeown, Danny Schiller, Tsutomu Sekine.

■ **The idea of telling the story of a Viking warrior who thought there must be more to life than rape and pillage is an amusing one, and for the most part "Erik The Viking" is an enjoyable film, only slipping when it comes to the special effects toward the end of the pic.**

Danger is film could get classed as a kid-pic (especially when writer-director-actor Terry Jones' book "The Saga Of Eric The Viking" is for kiddies, though not a basis for this pic) when in fact its humor is adult fare. But on the whole it could do well at the wickets — especially with its Monty Python links and strong international cast.

Pic opens with Erik (Tim Robbins) falling in love with a girl just as he kills her, piercing her heart with his sword while at a raiding/pillaging party. Spurred by her death he decides to try and bring the Age of Ragnarok — where men fight and kill — to an end, and seeks advice from Freya (Eartha Kitt) who tells him he must travel over the edge of the world.

He sets off with an unruly band of followers — including the local blacksmith who wants Ragnarok to continue as it helps his swordmaking business and who plots to scupper the mission — and is pursued by Halfdan the Black (John Cleese), the local warlord who quite enjoys Ragnarok and wants it to continue.

After overcoming the fearsome Dragon of the North Sea with judicious use of a pillow, they arrive at

Hy-Brasil (Celtic for Atlantis), ruled by the overly friendly King Arnulf (Terry Jones). The inept Vikings cause Hy-Brasil to sink, but not before Princess Aud (Imogen Stubbs) falls for Robbins and the band makes off with the Horn Resounding, which helps them travel over the edge of the world, and across space to the gates of Asgard.

They find that the gods actually are a bunch of children, don't want to help, and banish the Vikings to the Pit of Hell. Ironically they are saved by Harald the Missionary (Freddie Jones) — 16 years and not a single conversion — who is unable to see Asgard because he doesn't believe in their gods. Happy ending sees the Vikings home again, the Age of Ragnarok over, and Robbins in love with Stubbs.

American Tim Robbins is fine as the softly spoken and sensitive Erik, and especially seems to enjoy himself in the battle scenes. The film's great strength, though, is the Viking crew, which is full of wonderful characters, such as Tim McInnerny's manic Sven the Berserk, heavily disguised Antony Sher's scheming Loki and best of all Freddie Jones' put-upon missionary.

John Cleese nicely plays evil Halfdan the Black as a calm company director, but has few scenes, while Mickey Rooney and Eartha Kitt really only have small cameo roles, with Rooney hamming madly.

As he showed with the Monty Python films "The Holy Grail" and "Life Of Brian," Terry Jones is most adept at historical-based movies, and with "Erik The Viking" he has wonderfully recreated the time of Norse sagas and written a funny script packed with typically weird and wonderful characters. The locations in Norway and Malta serve him well and notably good are the specially built Viking longship and Pam Tait's costumes.

Where the film falters is when the Vikings head towards Asgard over the Rainbow Bridge. Poor matte drawings and only okay special effects detract from what up till then is a stylish and slick film. The fantasy element seems to force "Erik The Viking" into a hurried climax where the humor seems to dry up. —Adam.

When The Whales Came
(BRITISH)

London   A 20th Century Fox release (in U.S.) of a Golden Swan presentation, produced in association with Central Independent TV and American Continental Corp. Executive producer, Geoffrey Wansell. Produced by Simon Channing Williams. Directed by Clive Rees. Screenplay, Michael Morpurgo, based on his novel "Why The Whales Came;" camera (color), Robert Paynter; editor, Andrew Boulton; music, Christopher Gunning; sound, Peter Glossop; production design, Bruce Grimes; costume design, Lindy Hemming; associate producer, Alexander Myers. Reviewed at Edinburgh Film Festival, Aug. 22, 1989. MPAA Rating: PG. Running time: **99 MIN.**

The Birdman	Paul Scofield
Jack Jenkins	David Threlfall
Clemmie Jenkins	Helen Mirren
Will	David Suchet
Gracie Jenkins	Helen Pearce
Daniel Pender	Max Rennie
Mr. Wellbeloved	Jeremy Kemp

Also with: John Hallam, Barbara Ewing, Dexter Fletcher, Nicholas Jones, Joanna Bartholomew.

■ "When The Whales Came" is a slight story beautifully dressed to give the appearance of more substance. Performances, direction and design are all first-rate, but there is the overwhelming sensation that there is a lot less there than meets the eye. Prospects should be limited, via 20th Century Fox release domestically.

Pic is obviously a labor of love for all concerned and it is to producer Simon Channing Williams' credit that he managed to get the project off the ground. The film has a gentle, lyrical quality that is slightly spoiled by the so-so whale animatronics at the close of the pic.

Film opens on the island of Samson in the Scilly Isles in 1844 where locals leave the island they believe cursed. Then in 1914 on the neighboring island of Bryher youngsters Max Rennie (Daniel) and Helen Pearce (Gracie) play on the beach, watched by the mysterious Paul Scofield (Birdman).

Though warned against Scofield (Birdman) by other villagers they make friends with him and he warns them about never going to Samson. When World War I starts David Threlfall (Jack) joins the navy leaving Helen Mirren (Clemmie) and daughter Pearce alone. She and Rennie take the boat out fishing, against orders, and find themselves temporarily stranded on Samson.

On their return Scofield tells them of the curse of Samson — the locals killed a whale washed up on the beach and after that their wells dried up — and when a tusked whale (a narwhal) is beached on the shore it seems the curse will strike Bryher. Scofield explains the story of Samson and convinces the islanders to carry the whale back to the seas and help drive off a herd of narwhals heading for the island.

Cinematographer Robert Paynter and helmer Clive Rees give the pic a grainy, realistic quality, though that does not detract from the glorious beauty of the Scilly Isles. Direction is first rate and excellent tech credits give the pic a classy distinction.

It is always a pleasure to see Paul Scofield, and his portrayal of the deaf Birdman has the quality of sadness and pride that only he can give a role. Strong cast also includes top notch performances by Helen Mirren, David Suchet and David Threlfall.

Most endearing performance is by radiant young Helen Pearce as Gracie. A nonactor, she is a resident of Bryher (where pic is set) and was only found when she turned up for work as an extra. Most disappointing, though, are the animatronic narwhals which are either indistinct or obviously artificial and in some ways detract from the gritty realism of the preceding storyline.

Pic is based on the book "Why The Whales Came" by Michael Morpurgo, which was used as the shooting title during production. Why film has had the title changed from "Why..." to "When..." is unclear, and certainly does nothing to enhance the production. —Adam.

The Favorite
(La Nuit du Serail)
(SWISS)

Paris   A 20th Century Fox release of an Ascona Films production. Executive producers, Guy Collins, Klaus Hellwig. Produced by Georges-Alain Vuille. Directed by Jack Smight. Screenplay, Larry Yust, based on the novel "Sultana" by Prince Michael of Greece; camera (color), Howard Wexler, Giorgio Tonti; editor, Dennis Virkier; music, William Goldstein; sound, Hal Whitby; art direction, Bryan Ryman, Allan H. Jones; costumes, Tami Morr; casting, Don Pemrick. Reviewed at Georges V cinema, Paris, Aug. 15, 1989. Running time: **101 MIN.**

Aimée Dubucq de Rivery	Amber O'Shea
Abdul Hamid	F. Murray Abraham
Sineperver	Maud Adams
Selim	James Michael Gregary
Tulip	Ron Dortch
Sebastiani	Laurent Le Doyen

(English soundtrack)

■ "The Favorite" is a moldy wad of Turkish taffy about a French girl who is kidnaped by pirates and sold into the harem of none less than the Sultan of the Ottoman Empire.

Somewhat similar in plot to the expensive 1985 French-produced fiasco "Harem," it is based on a true story novelized by Prince Michael of Greece in a bestseller, from which the screenplay has been extracted in the worst movieland manner. This Swiss-produced English-lingo 19th century costumer seems headed for the homevid seraglio.

Topbilled F. Murray Abraham may have been intended as a main selling point, but his is a glorified supporting character who dies not long after his screen entry. His dignified ineffectual Sultan Abdul Hamid recalls Ben Kingsley's equally passive Arabian prince in "Harem." Both seem helpless before life and bad scripts.

Story is fancifully based on the life of Aimée Dubucq de Rivery, a convent-bred daughter of French aristocrats whose enforced departure for the West Indies took a permanent detour by Constantinople. Presumably her willfulness and beauty turned the trick against her harem equals — she became the Sultan's favorite, and when he died, wiggled her way into his successor's heart.

In Larry Yust's nonsensical screenplay, cast in the form of a flashback from the moment of the protagonist's death years later in the presence of a Catholic priest, we find her taking sides with the nice spineless Sultans against a palace revolt fomented by jealous Maud Adams, a harem harridan bent on enthroning her own son.

Yank newcomer Amber O'Shea is cast as the young innocent aristocrat who becomes a sultana, but she is less Dubucq de Rivery than Dubuque, Iowa. (France's Sophie Marceau, originally sought by the producers, would have gotten by more credibly.)

James Michael Gregary has agreeable presence but a rotten part as Selim, Abraham's son and embattled successor. Ron Dortch is the kindhearted head eunuch with the film's funniest outburst — after stabbing a rebellious janissary he moans: "You're bleeding on the carpet!"

Speaking of carpets, the film was partly shot in the Topkapi Palace in Istanbul and as such has some exotic color and costumes. Otherwise production is stingy, notably in the deployment of extras for the "big" scenes (the rebellion, the departure for the war against Russia). Lensing and other credits are passable.

Jack Smight directed without apparent Turkish delight. —Len.

Los Hermanos Cartagena
(The Cartagena Brothers)
(BOLIVIAN)

New York   A Productora Cinematográfica Ukamau production. Written and directed by Paolo Agazzi, based on the book "El Hijo Opa." Camera (color), César Pérez; editor, Ursula West; music, Cergio Prudencio; sound, Antonio Gonzáles. Reviewed at Festival Latino (noncompeting), N.Y., Aug. 12, 1989. Running time: **92 MIN.**
With: Juan José Taboada, Edwin Morales, Eduardo Vargas, Eddy Bravo.

■ "The Cartagena Brothers," by Bolivian helmer Paolo Agazzi, is an empty political tract that bears none of the charm of char-acterization that distinguished director's 1982 pic "Mi Socio."

Obvious dialectical work attacks racism while fostering the class struggle between the oppressed and oppressors. Pic relates the parallel tale of two half brothers, one the heir apparent of a rich landowner, the other an illegitimate son of a deranged Indian servant woman.

Needless to say, they end up on opposite sides of a bloody class war rife with political demonstrations and strikes countered by harsh repressive measures including disappearances, torture and murder.

Characters are never more than black hat/white hat caricatures ·
—Lent.

MONTREAL WORLD FEST REVIEWS

Ser
(Freedom Is Paradise)
(SOVIET)

Montreal   A Mosfilm Studios production. Written and directed by Sergei Bodrov. Camera (color), Youri Skirtladze; production design, Valery Kostrin; music, Alexander Raskatov. Reviewed at Montreal World Film Festival (competing), Sept. 2, 1989. Running time: **75 MIN.**
With: Sasha Grigoriev (Volodya Koryzer), Alexander Bureyev, Svetlana Gaitau, Vitautus Tomkus.

■ From "The 400 Blows" to "My Life As A Dog," the theme of a child adrift in a stormy world has produced indelibly poignant cinema. Now glasnost has enabled Sergei Bodrov to offer a searing new variation on the theme in his powerful "Freedom Is Paradise," a riveting journey through the underside of Soviet working-class and institutional life as seen through the eyes of an untamed 13 year-old drifter.

Sasha, whose mother is dead and father is in prison camp, lives at a boarding school for "difficult" youths. The institution enforces tough paramilitary discipline and operates on the assumption that its wards are condemned to a life on society's scrap heap. "They're all the offspring of drunken parents," says one sardonic administrator. The young inmate-students tattoo themselves with the letters "Ser," an acronym for "freedom is paradise."

Director Bodrov opens his tightly compressed narrative with Sasha busing through the country-side after escaping from the school. A rail-thin skinhead in a black leather jacket, Sasha projects a sullen, laconic demeanor that masks a wounded vulnerability.

He scrounges for shelter, food and money as best he can, an improbably grave child-man moving among world-weary, cynical adults. Arriving at the door of a childless unmarried woman who knew his parents, Sasha gets a bed for the night, only to be handed over to the police and returned to the institution the next day. Resourcefully true to form, he soon escapes again, determined to find the remote prison camp holding the father he's never known.

Bodrov's skillful use of documentary realism lends a sharp, unsentimental edge to Sasha's on-the-road experiences as he tramps through the sprawling Soviet landscape. Taken in for the night by a sympathetic prostitute, he asks for money and receives some U.S. dollars ("you can trade them one for six") from one of her officer clients. Sasha jumps a train, is caught stealing and uses the greenbacks to bribe his way out of certain arrest and return to the dreaded school.

The drab and circumscribed lives of ordinary Soviet citizens, the existence of a very real Soviet class system and the persistence of a rigid police state infrastructure into the age of glasnost are presented without apology in "Freedom Is Paradise." Nevertheless, Sasha finds small kindnesses along the way and finally reaches the Arkhangelsk region of the USSR and the grim, gulag-like prison where his father resides. The military commander, a soldierly but avuncular man, takes a measure of pity on the boy and feeds him in a "visitors' room" discreetly graced with a photo of Mikhail Gorbachev.

In a sequence of understated emotional intensity, Sasha is permitted to visit for a few days with his father, the emaciated, beaten-down image of what the boy almost certainly will become if his life continues on its present course. Sasha offers the alienated convict barely articulate expressions of love, manly protestations of self-reliance and pathetic optimism about a better future together. His father remorselessly recounts for the boy the story of his own life as a prison camp orphan born from the union of a guard and a woman sentenced to 36 years for stealing six cucumbers. In a bitter, uncompromising resolution, the filmmaker suggests that Sasha's own prospect for a better life will depend entirely on the indomitability of his spirit.

Volodya Koryzev's performance as the child antihero is sensitively directed and builds up with accumulating force to the film's confrontational climax. Quality cinematography and editing help the filmmaker open up a revealing window on contemporary Soviet life within the picture's admirably taut timespan. —Rich.

Comedie d'été
(Summer Interlude)
(FRENCH)

Montreal   An Ariel Zeitoun partners production. Directed by Daniel Vigne. Screenplay, Colo Tavernier O'Hagan, Vigne, based on Eduard von Keyserling's novel "Versant sud;" camera (color), Andre Neau; editor, Vigne; music, Jean-Claude Vannier; production design, Françoise Deleu. Reviewed at Montreal World Film Festival (competing), Aug. 28, 1989. Running time: **104 MIN.**
Vicky . . . . Maruschka Detmers
Adrien . . . . Remi Martin
Also with: Jean-Claude Brialy, Nelly Borgeaud, Jessica Forde, Jean-François Perrier, Mila Parely, Sophie Tribout, Thierry Fortineau, Jeanne Marine.

■ A stylishly produced, nicely performed period ensemble about a wealthy French family resisting the onset of change in the years before World War I, "Comedie d'été" is too confined by its genre and frame of reference to travel successfully beyond France, French-speaking territories and sophisticated European markets.

In the summer of 1912 Adrien (Remi Martin), an expelled military cadet, returns to the family's country estate in a borrowed lieutenant's uniform, for fear of enraging his father. The old man, a retired Colonel, is a bigot, militarist and believer in a rigid 19th century class system soon to be forever torn asunder by the Great War. Adrien's father cannot tolerate "impropriety," which is why his wife keeps secret the divorce of her friend and house guest, the ravishing Vicky (Maruschka Detmers).

Also on hand are Adrien's older sister and foppish brother-in-law, a younger brother, nieces, a predictably old-fashioned grandmother, a lusty servant couple and a tutor whose working-class origins and social idealism mark him as a radical in this company. The family insulates itself from the injustices suffered by the poverty-wracked peasants living in the surrounding countryside. According to local custom, when a man can no longer afford to feed his wife he is free to sell her into virtual slavery for whatever the market will bear.

Adrien is quickly smitten by the beautiful, irreverent, free-spirited Detmers. The tutor already is obsessed with her. Fully aware of her sexual magnetism and reveling in her newfound freedom, Detmers toys with the young scion and the teacher. The two young men form a friendship based upon their shared attraction for the intriguing older woman and their disdain for the Colonel's unyielding social code.

Martin plays Adrien as a buoyant, self-confident youth blessed with the natural arrogance of the rich. Detmers — who contrary to past form remains (disappointingly) buttoned-up in costume throughout — is ideal as the unconventional beauty. Director Daniel Vigne choreographs Martin's courtship of Detmers as a tense emotional chess game between two proud, wily opponents. Sebastien the tutor, on the other hand, is lovestruck unto death by the unattainable siren.

Vigne and his collaborators stage the obligatory generational confrontations and reconciliations common to this genre, and lacerate the stultifying mores of the era in familiar "Masterpiece Theater" fashion. Also derivative, but effectively handled, is a code in which

Adrien, who survived a duel with his father's help, returns from the war front to a transformed world, crippled in body but not in spirit.—*Rich.*

Troudno Perviya Sto Let
(Patience Is A Virtue)
(SOVIET)

Montreal A Sovexportfilm release of a Lenfilm production. Directed by Viktor Aristov. Screenplay, Georgy Markov, Eduard Shim; camera (Sovcolor), Yuri Vorontsov; production design, Vladimir Bannykh; music, Aracy Gagulashvili; sound, L. Shumyacher. Reviewed at Montreal World Film Fest (Cinema of Today & Tomorrow section), Aug 25, 1989. Running time: **138 MIN.**
Varya . . . . Lubov Krasavina
Ivan . . . . Nikolai Shatokhin
Alyona . . . . Olga Nikolayeva
Liza . . . . Natalia Lvova

■ **The grim life of the Russian peasant in today's Soviet Union is the background of this ambitious, lengthy drama that incorporates Federico Fellini-inspired dream and nightmare sequences. It adds up to intriguing drama, but it needs pruning to sharpen the rambling narrative.**

Varya, well played by Lubov Krasavina, is a young wife who lives in a cramped cottage with her simple-minded husband, feisty mother-in-law and her husband's little brother. She's pregnant, and yearns to escape her dull, miserable daily grind.

Sometimes she escapes via dreams: She soars over the village, or witnesses what seems to be a '60s-style love-in (naked couples frolicking in verdant countryside), or visits a plush seaside resort. But there are nightmares too: she and her baby in a postnuclear war world, trying to escape a strangely deserted city.

Real life is another matter. Varya, whose child may not be that of her husband, longs to escape, tries (unsuccessfully) for an abortion and even contemplates suicide. There are violent arguments involving her husband and mother-in-law.

Viktor Aristov's pic paints a grim picture of country life, where corruption (stealing bricks and cement to build a private house) and drunkenness are still a factor and where people talk cynically about the new Mikhail Gorbachev "Line," noting that the party line has regularly zigzagged over the years.

Like many other contemporary Soviet films, this one's inordinately long. But performances are strong, and the camerawork is inventive. Offshore theatrical chances aren't optimistic, however.

Pic's alternative English title is "It Is Hard for The First Hundred Years." —*Strat.*

Queen Of Hearts
(BRITISH)

London A Cinecom Pictures release (in U.S.) of an Enterprise Pictures presentation, in association with Nelson Entertainment, of an Enterprise/TVS Films production. Executive producer, Graham Benson. Produced by John Hardy. Directed by Jon Amiel. Screenplay, Tony Grisoni; camera (Rank color), Mike Southon; editor, Peter Boyle; music, Michael Convertino; sound (Dolby), Peter Glossop; production design, Jim Clay; art direction, Philip Elton; costume design, Lindy Hemming; associate producer, Caroline Hewitt. Reviewed at Edinburgh Film Festival Aug. 21, 1989. (Also in Montreal Film Festival.) Running time: **112 MIN.**
Nonno . . . . Vittorio Duse
Danilo . . . . Joseph Long
Rosa . . . . Anita Zagaria
Mama Sibilla . . . . Eileen Way
Barbariccia . . . . Vittorio Amandola
Eddie . . . . Ian Hawkes
Beetle . . . . Tat Whalley
Also with: Ray Marioni, Sarah Hadaway, Anna Pernicci, Jimmy Lambert, Frank Rozelaar-Green, Frank Coda, Roberto Scateni.

■ **"Queen Of Hearts" has a unique, magical charm that sets it apart from other British releases, not least because it features the attractive feature film directing debut of Jon Amiel and includes a fine cast of unknowns.**

The film is seen entirely through the eyes of a young boy whose world is an Italian community in central London where time seems to have stood still. Pic will need careful handling, but could be worthwhile.

If anything, though, the gentle strangeness and eventual sadness that the film comprises may stand against it — pushing the pic into the film festival bracket and limited arthouse release.

Pic opens in Italy, filmed in a misty, dreamy style, where would-be lovers Joseph Long (Danilo) and Anita Zagaria (Rosa) flee the violent Vittorio Amandola (Barbariccia) who is promised to Zagaria. With a charming twist they escape their pursuers and travel to England where, with some luck at the cards, Long gets enough money to buy a cafe.

Within no time they have four children and live the quiet life in their cocooned Italian quarter where they live with Zagaria's shrewish aged mother Eileen Way (Mama Sibilla). That life is altered when Long's father Vittorio Duse (Nonno) arrives from Italy and when the now wealthy Amandola starts to plan his revenge on the family.

Young Ian Hawkes (Eddie, son of Danilo) and his friend Tat Whalley (Beetle) relish the mischievous Duse, but when he dies and Amandola schemes the cafe away from the family the friends fall out and the once tight family seems in ruins. Family and friends are finally reconciled when the whole community joins to perform a "sting" on Amandola.

"Queen Of Hearts" is a very simple story, but decked with such charm that its gentle humor and off-the-wall references don't seem out of place. The Italian quarter is decked in '50s style with old cars parked in the street — during a wedding scene a brand new Volkswagen appears on the street, emphasizing the unworldly quality of the community as seen through the child's eyes.

Joseph Long and Anita Zagaria are excellent as the loving couple to whom family is everything, but they are eclipsed by Eileen Way and Vittorio Duse as the bickering old folks, who give a fine display of their veteran acting skills. Ironically one scene shows the family watching the 1958 film "The Vikings," in which Way had the role of Kitala the soothsayer.

The small shoulders of 11-year-old Ian Hawkes ably support the film, easily handling the charming narrative of Tony Grisoni's script. The combination of helmer Jon Amiel (who directed BBC's "The Singing Detective") and cameraman Mike Southon manages to create a rich, warm atmosphere of a small community of winding streets and marking Amiel as a director to watch.

"Queen Of Hearts" is a hard film to categorize. The unknown cast and simple setting may stand against it, but the underlying charm and affectionate skill that has gone into its production sets it apart from the rest of the field.
—*Adam.*

Der Bruch
(The Break)
(EAST GERMAN)

Montreal A DEFA-Studio fur Spielfilme production. Directed by Frank Beyer. Screenplay, Wolfgang Kohlhasse; camera (Orwocolor), Peter Ziesche; editor, Rita Hiller; music, Gunther Fischer. Reviewed at Montreal World Film Festival (noncompeting), Aug. 28, 1989. Running time: **118 MIN.**
Graf . . . . Götz George
Markward . . . . Rolf Hoppe
Lobowitz . . . . Otto Sander
Kollmorgen . . . . Hermann Beyer
Biegel . . . . Jens-Uwe Bogadtke
Lotz . . . . Gerhard Hahndel
Tina . . . . Ulrike Krumbiegel
Anita . . . . Angelika Waller

■ **Opening and closing party line promo reels touting postwar East Berliners' "will to survive" serve as comic bookends for the bumbling thievery of this film's characters, Graf, Lobowitz, Bruno and company.**

A huge cast of crotchety characters, including Hitchcockian inept cops, are established quickly as the stage is set for the ultimate heist, to rob the weekly train payroll from the vault on Christmas Eve.

Although lacking American-style fast-paced action, the pic's steady pace relies on intricately developed characters, their foibles, faults and virtues. Their persistence and ineptitude supply a hefty dose of humor. Poignant yet sympathetic attacks on the pitfalls of the political system justify their sordid ways. And several overlapping love triangles add the necessary dash of romance. Long running time flies by quickly.

Subtitling is tight, although lack of dubbing may reduce pic's obvious tv chances. —*Suze.*

Ultimas Imagenes
Del Naufragio
(Last Images Of The Shipwreck)
(ARGENTINE-SPANISH)

Montreal An Enrique Marti, Films Cinequanon SRL, Virrey Olaguer y Feliu production. Written and directed by Eliseo Subiela. Camera (color), Alberto Basail; editor, Marcela Saenz; music, Pedro Aznar; production design, Abel Facello. Reviewed at Montreal World Film Festival (competing), Aug. 30, 1989. Running itme: **127 MIN.**
Roberto . . . . Lorenzo Quinteros
Estela . . . . Noemi Frenkel
Also with: Hugo Soto, Pablo Brichta, Sara Benitez, Andres Tiengo and Alicia Aller.

■ **Like Eliseo Subiela's 1986 metaphysical parable "Man Facing Southeast," the Argentine director's new film, "Last Images Of The Shipwreck," serves up deadpan meditations on the spiritual barrenness of modern existence.**

Subiela has not advanced significantly as a stylist, however, and the filmmaker has scuttled the marketability of "Shipwreck" by failing to navigate the shoals of tedium.

The film's narrative unfolds through the flashback recollections of Roberto (Lorenzo Quinteros), a novelist manqué weary of the emotional deadness and numbing routine of his life as a Buenos Aires insurance agent. As he rides the metro back and forth from his unhappy home to his dead-end job, the middle-aged intellectual is lost in an interior world of pessimistic ruminations. His fellow passengers appear to him as plastic-wrapped zombies, and Subiela's deft set-up of such images begins the film on a promisingly surrealistic note.

On the metro one day, Roberto races to prevent a beautiful young girl from jumping in front of a train, then discovers she's a hooker who uses this technique to pick up tricks. The seductive and enigmatic Estela (Noemi Frenkel) intrigues the somber Roberto, who is interested only using her as source material for his stalled novel. Roberto accompanies her on the bus to her family home on the outskirts of Buenos Aires. At a bus stop near a cemetery, the spirits of the dead come aboard, but Estela ignores her late aunt and uncle because she does not want to talk about her father.

This father, who heartlessly abandoned the family long ago, hovers over the movie as an unseen presence and a metaphor for modern humanity's loss of faith. One look at Estela's family also might explain his absence. One brother, traumatized by the death-squad reign of terror in the '70s, lives a life of monkish reflection, grows pumpkins and tries to keep his mind empty for new thoughts.

Another brother supports the home with a day job and devotes the rest of his time to building an airplane in which he plans to escape his prison-like existence through a "tunnel in the sky." A third brother is a common criminal fond of guns and girls. Mother is an around-the-bend eccentric whose bitterness over life may represent mother Argentina's crushed expectations of greatness.

Initially suspicious of Roberto, Estela's family soon accepts him and slowly comes to depend on his visits. Roberto becomes "dangerously melancholic" and obsessed with transmuting their lives into fiction. He's sacked from his job, leaves a marriage bed that "smells like a cadaver," moves into a hotel and is soon writing "scripts" for the criminal brother's stick-up jobs.

Estela is a mystic fond of taking salami sandwiches to church and sharing them with Jesus, who's always available, thorned crown and all, to give her spiritual pep talks. She asks Jesus for advice on how

to get through to Roberto, whom she ultimately seduces. The emotionally cut-off intellectual eventually realizes that her love is his salvation. Roberto's recollections, in fact, are being narrated to his uncomprehending baby son, who does not heed the writer's warnings in the film's final scene that one day he will be pushed out of his infant's paradise.

These transparent reflections on human corruption and original sin are at the heart of a film that could stand some rigorous editing. Subiela does evince flashes of an original filmmaking sensibility and skill in directing a good group of actors. In the future, he'd be advised to get out from under the weight of the philosophical self-importance that sinks "Shipwreck" in its own metaphysical murkiness. —*Rich.*

Stalin S Nami?
(Stalin With Us?)
(SOVIET-DOCU)

Montreal   A Sovexportfilm release of a Chance Studio production. Directed by Tofik Shahverdiyev; screenplay, Shahverdiyev, A. Streliani; camera (color), E. Karavayev; editor, Igor Robertus; music, V. Baboushkin. Reviewed at Montreal World Film Festival (Cinema of Today & Tomorrow section), Aug. 25, 1989. Running time: **74 MIN.**

■Not everyone in the Soviet Union approves of glasnost and perestroika, as evidenced by this documentary featuring a clutch of ardent and unrepentant Stalinists.

Subjects, mostly elderly, include a woman schoolteacher, a taxidriver, a farmer and a retired military man. They look back fondly on an era of harsh discipline, and comment that, were Stalin alive today, the country would be in a better shape and those guilty for Chernobyl and other disasters would be shot.

Most interesting of these extreme right-wingers, Soviet-style, is a youthful fanatic who's eventually revealed to be a policeman who works at a top security prison.

Filmmaker Tofik Shahverdiyev adds his own visual comments by intercutting an image of a flock of sheep, during comments on why Stalin was so popular in his day, or juxtaposing newsreel images of mass crowds fêting the dictator with similar crowds praising Hitler and Mao.

Pic ends with a group of the Stalinists toasting their "beloved" hero, and predicting the film will be suppressed.

Commendably brief, "Stalin With Us?" is a fascinating look at some of the opposition to Gorbachev, and will be of interest to fests and tv programmers looking for unusual docu material. —*Strat.*

Kingsgate
(CANADIAN)

Montreal   A Thomas Howe Releasing Ltd. (Canada) release of a One Prods. Ltd. production. Produced, written and directed by Jack Darcus. Camera (color), Doug McKay; editor, Doris Dyck; music, Michael Conway Baker; sound, Rob Young; production design, Michael Nemirsky; associate producer, Paul Mears. Reviewed at Montreal World Film Festival (Panorama Canada), Aug. 25, 1989. Running time: **110 MIN.**
Fee . . . . Elizabeth Dancoes
Ellis . . . . Duncan Fraser
Brenda Kingsgate . . . . Barbara March
Marlene . . . . Roberta Maxwell
Daniel Kingsgate . . . . Alan Scarfe
Tom . . . . Christopher Plummer

■Three couples spend 110 minutes of screentime boozing and yelling at each other in "Kingsgate," a sub-sub-Edward Albee-style exercise. Writer-director Jack Darcus doesn't provide the screenplay, nor his actors the performances, to make this material begin to work.

Fee (Elizabeth Dancoes) is a literature student having an affair with Ellis (Duncan Fraser), her older teacher. After a weekend together she unwisely asks him home to meet Mum and Dad; unwise because Mum (Roberta Maxwell) hates Dad (Christopher Plummer), an airline pilot, for his infidelities and neglect, and because both are drunk most of the time.

Having survived half an hour of that encounter, we proceed to the next. Famous writer Daniel Kingsgate (Alan Scarfe) has invited Ellis and Fee to stay on his country property. We know we're in for a bad time when Kingsgate's wife Brenda (Barbara March) starts weeping the moment she sees them. It doesn't take too much to guess that Kingsgate will make a pass at Fee, or that Ellis will try to console Brenda, or that everyone, audience included, will have a simply terrible time.

The actors suffer most in the film, though, since Darcus encourages most of them to overact embarrassingly; only Christopher Plummer manages to salvage something out of his role. The actors shouldn't be blamed, though, since they are saddled with clichéd dialog and absurdly contrived situations.

It's hard to see theaters willing to give "Kingsgate" a run, and equally hard to see it being a fave on vidcassette or cable. Plummer's name is about the only plus the pic has going for it. —*Strat.*

The Imported Bridegroom

Boston   A Lara Classics presentation. Executive producer, Frank Moreno. Produced and directed by Pamela Berger. Associate producer, Chris Schmidt. Screenplay, Berger, from a story by Abraham Cahan; camera (color), Brian Heffron; editor, Amy Summer; music, Bevan Manson, Rosalie Gerut; sound, Ted Evans; production design, Martha Seely; first assistant director, Frank Kosa. Reviewed at Loews Copley Place, Aug. 28, 1989. (Also in Montreal and Boston film festivals.) No MPAA Rating. Running time: **90 MIN.**
Asriel Stroon . . . . Gene Troobnick
Shaya . . . . Avi Hoffman
Flora . . . . Greta Cowan
Mrs. Birnbaum . . . . Annette Miller
    Also with: Miriam Varon, Andreas Teuber, Ted Jacobs, Ira Solet, Ira Goldenberg, Barry Karas, Helene Lantry, Moshe Waldocks, Seth Yorra.

■Pamela Berger, writer-producer of "Sorceress," makes her directorial bow with a comedy-drama set in the Jewish community in turn-of-the-century Boston. Low-budget film will require special nurturing to reach audiences on the arthouse circuit before finding its eventual home on the small screen.

As Joan Micklin Silver did with "Hester Street," Berger has turned to the writings of the great Yiddish journalist Abraham Cahan. "The Imported Bridegroom" centers on three characters, all of whom find that their lives haven't turned out quite as expected. Film is a charmer, if one is willing to overlook its shortcomings.

Asriel Stroon (Gene Troobnick) is a Polish Jew who has become a successful landlord in the New World. Now he wonders if he has abandoned his spiritual side, and decides to visit the old country to renew his roots. There he meets Shaya (Avi Hoffman), a young scholar set to marry the daughter of the richest man in town. As much to spite an old rival as to do good, Asriel arranges for Shaya to come to America and marry his daughter instead.

Asriel's daughter Flora (Greta Cowan), born in America, plans to marry a doctor and become part of the better society in town. She wants nothing to do with the scholar who is the opposite of everything she thinks she wants in a husband.

Berger's strength is in her script, where she retains Cahan's bemused attention to detail to the various ways the Jewish immigrants adapted to life in America. The twist is that as Shaya becomes more attractive to Flora, he becomes a less desirable son-in-law to her father.

Berger makes good use of Boston locations to re-create turn-of-the-century locations, including some suburban locales which stand in for Asriel's hometown in Poland. Principal performers are able, with Hoffman the standout as the shy student who becomes Americanized.

Production is hampered by the limited budget, with tech values varying throughout. Director of photography Brian Heffron achieves some beautiful effects with interior lighting, especially a synagogue study group seemingly lit only by candlelight, but many exterior shots are too bright, seeming more suitable for a contemporary sitcom than a period piece. Berger also exhibits the strengths and weaknesses of a first-time director, with film's highs and lows attributable to someone learning by doing.

Film was shot on 16m, and it is being presented in that format at festival screenings. Berger hopes to have it blown up to 35m for general release. —*Kimm.*

Uneasy Silence

Montreal   A Full Circle Films production. Executive producers, Maria and Joy Silverman. Produced by Wanda Rohm, Robert Rothman. Directed by John Strysik. Screenplay, Rothman, Strysik; camera (color), Michael Goi; editor, Strysik, Goi; music, Elliott Delman; sound, Diego Trejo; production design, Thomas B. Mitchell; casting, Payne Leavitt Group; production manager, Colleen McNichols; assistant director, Neil Kinsella. Reviewed at Montreal World Film Festival (Cinema of Today & Tomorrow), Aug. 27, 1989. Running time: **90 MIN.**
Sam . . . . .Robert Rothman
Sarah . . . . .Kathleen Sykora
Astro . . . . .Michael Bacarella
Terry Quinn . . . . .Carolyn Kodes
T.J. . . . . .Charles Gerace
Also with: Irv Alberts, Tom Taverna, Marcel Lussier, Mark Sugar.

■An earnest downbeater about homeless people trying to eke out an existence in a big American city (Chicago), "Uneasy Silence" deserves full marks for the sincerity of its creative talent.

Sincerity alone won't sell tickets, though, and the film doesn't shape up as a boxoffice attraction, even in limited arthouse release.

Problem is that lead actor Robert Rothman, who coproduced and coscripted, simply doesn't look convincing in his role as Sam, an ex-Screaming Eagle, now reduced to scavenging the city's gutters. Rothman looks simply too fit, speaks too well, thinks too fast to be convincing as a vagrant; there may be vagrants like him, but he doesn't persuade us he is authentic in the way Jack Nicholson did in "Ironweed." Kathleen Sykora is no Meryl Streep either, but she is several notches more effective than her costar.

They meet when he gets savagely beaten while trying to come to her aid, and the film's most telling scene has him kept waiting at an emergency hospital though he's been brought there by the police, in an ambulance, badly hurt. Still, he recovers, they become friends, and he's taken in tow by a friendly tv journalist (Carolyn Kodes) out to do a story on the homeless. The film's attacks on the superficiality of tv journalism are rather obvious shafts.

Commercially, the film faces an uphill battle, not helped by a gratuitously downbeat ending which, again, may be authentic but just adds one more nail in the coffin. Kudos go to cameraman Michael Goi whose location work is fine, and to production designer Thomas B. Mitchell who makes Sarah's hideaway look convincingly lived-in. Other credits are fine, though the presence of a production astrologer in the final crawl (as well as a rat wrangler) is worthy of note.—*Strat.*

An Unremarkable Life

Montreal   An SVS Films release of a Continental Filmgroup Ltd. production. Executive producers, Navin Desai, Gay Mayer, Watson Warriner. Produced and directed by Amin Q. Chaudhri. Screenplay, Marcia Dineen; camera (color), Alan Hall; editor, Sandi Gerling; music, Avery Sharpe; production design. Norman B. Dodge Jr.; associate producer, Brian Smedley-Aston; production manager, Stan Bickman; assistant director, Steven Pomerey; casting, Pennie DuPont. Reviewed at Montreal World Film Festival (Cinema of Today & Tomorrow section), Aug. 26, 1989. MPAA Rating: PG. Running time: **98 MIN.**
Frances McEllany . . . . .Patricia Neal
Evelyn McEllany . . . . .Shelley Winters
Max Chin . . . . .Mako
With: Rochelle Oliver, Charles Dutton, Lily Knight, Jenny Chrisinger, Michael O'Neill, Madeleine Sherwood.

■Two distinguished veteran femme movie stars play sisters living together in a claustrophobic old house: it's almost the formula for some gothic horror pic, but the results are more akin to "The Whales Of August."

Pic is aimed at the older set, so probably will play better on the small screen than in theatrical outings.

Shelley Winters is Evelyn, a bitter widow unable to relate to her daughter or granddaughter. She's bossy and crotchety and basically racist. Her sister, Frances (Patricia Neal), who never married, still has happy memories of the war years, when she was a pilot; she's basically good-natured and rather sweet.

The harmony of the sisters' closed world is shattered when Frances meets Max Chin (Mako), an elderly garage mechanic, who comes courting. Evelyn is appalled, not only at this disruption to routine but also because of Max' Asian background. The sisters quarrel, Frances is persuaded for a while to end her friendship with Max, but ultimately decides he's more important to her. They marry, and go off to Greece for a honeymoon, while Evelyn moves out of the house in which she's lived all her life.

The film relies heavily on its leads, and they don't fail, both giving solid performances. If, ultimately, Patricia Neal dominates it's because she has more screen time (though Shelley Winters makes the very most of her bitter, rather sad, character). Mako plays the Chinese suitor on a single, rather monotonous, note of cheerful amiability.

Producer-director Amin Q. Chaudhri handles the talky script adequately, but without much involvement. The last-minute trip to Greece seems extraneous. Technically, the film is fine, except for some rather jarring cuts (indicating dropped footage). Production design is good, as its camerawork, though the music tends to underscore the drama too insistently.

"An Unremarkable Life" (not the best title) might spark some limited interest in theatrical runs, but seems more suited to cable and vidcassette since the senior citizens, at which it's aimed, will lose little by seeing it at home. —*Strat.*

Staying Together

Montreal   A Hemdale release of a Joseph Feury production. Produced by Feury. Executive producers, John Daly, Derek Gibson. Directed by Lee Grant. Screenplay, Monte Merrick; camera (CFI color), Dick Bush; editor, Katherine Wenning; sound (Dolby), Jan Erik Brodin; art direction, W. Steven Graham; costume design, Carol Oditz; assistant director, John T. Kretchmer, Carole Keligian; casting, Marsha Keiman & Associates. Reviewed at Montreal World Film Festival (noncompeting), Aug. 27, 1989. MPAA Rating: R. Running time: **91 MIN.**
Duncan McDermott . . . . Sean Astin
Nancy Trainer . . . . .Stockard Channing
Eileen McDermott . . . . . . .Melinda Dillon
Jake McDermott . . . . .Jim Haynie
Denny Stockton . . . . .Levon Helm
Lois Cook . . . . .Dinah Manoff
Kit McDermott . . . . .Dermot Mulroney
Brian McDermott . . . . .Tim Quill
Kevin Burley . . . . .Keith Szarabajka
Beverly Young   . . . . .Daphne Zuniga

■Like a cross between a warmed-over "Mystic Pizza" and an "American Playhouse" formula film, "Staying Together" serves up familiar homilies about family values in changing small-town America and the indomitable power of love.

Regional release would be best for testing its limited theatrical prospects, but this sincerely made coming-of-age tale is better suited for paycable playoff.

In a bucolic town somewhere in South Carolina, Mr. and Mrs. McDermott and their three strapping sons run a self-named home-cooked-chicken restaurant. Mom is a tower of strength and a paragon of understanding; dad is gruff but caring, and the brothers confine their red-blooded oats-sowing, boozing and pot-smoking to their off hours. Everyone is brimming with pep and familial fellowship and content with a Main Street existence far removed from the chaotic realities of urban USA.

The yuppies have landed in this woodsy town to build condos near the lake, and pop McDermott takes an offer he can't refuse for the restaurant and its choice land site. Big brother Kit, middle sibling Brian and little bro Duncan can't believe dad has sold out their birthright without consulting them. He explains that he's been slinging chickens all his life to provide for his family, but that he doesn't intend to die on the spit.

Brian (essayed by Tom Cruise-John Travolta hybrid Tim Quill) has been having an affair with an older woman who's championing the developers' cause and running for mayor to make her point. When his dad decides to cash in, the hot-tempered kid denounces pop, leaves home and talks his way into a job on the condo construction site.

The yup developer doesn't like the McDermott brothers and would like them less if he ever found out (he doesn't) about his roadrunning fiancée's prenuptial fling with big brother Kit, the good-mannered marathoner. Feisty baby brother Duncan, meanwhile, is mostly obsessed with losing his virginity (he finally does) and is always willing and able to outdrink the older guys.

Shortly after mom and dad return from a vacation to Yosemite, pop's set-up premonitions of mortality are payed off when he drops dead gardening. Lee Grant and screenwriter Monte Merrick push all the preprogrammed melodrama buttons, including prodigal son Brian's too-late-to-say-goodbye dash to the hospital.

Can the McDermotts weather the emotional crisis that threatens to tear their love asunder? The outcome is never in doubt and the ending — which includes mom's hookup with high school sweetheart and storekeeper/bar band drummer Levon Helm — is resolutely upbeat if not particularly uplifting. —*Rich.*

Les Baisers de secours
(Emergency Kisses)
(FRENCH-B&W)

Paris   A Films de l'Atalante release of a Films de l'Atalante/La Sept/Planète et Compagnie coproduction. Produced by Gérard Vaugeois. Directed by Philippe Garrel. Screenplay, Garrel, Marc Cholodenko; camera (b&w), Jacques Loiseleux; editor, Sophie Coussein; music, Barney Wilen; sound, Claudine Nougaret, Alain Garnier, Daniel Fromaget. Reviewed at Club 13, Paris, Aug. 23, 1989. (In the Montreal Film Festival and Venice Film Festival-non-competing.) Running time: **83 MIN.**
With: Philippe Garrel (Mathieu), Brigitte Sy (Jeanne), Louis Garrel (LO), Anémone (the actress), Maurice Garrel (Mathieu's father), Yvette Etievant (Mathieu's mother), Jacques Kabadian, Valérie Dreville.

■Philippe Garrel makes auteur navel-contemplation a family affair in his latest black & white opus, "Baisers de secours," an emotionally ineffectual series of scenes from a couple's domestic crisis.

Garrel has cast himself as the man, a filmmaker (what else?), as well as his own real-life companion, child and father (professional actor Maurice Garrel). Hard not to avoid the feeling that the director is hanging his own dirty laundry across the screen. Pic is getting excess of honors with double exposure at the Montreal and Venice festivals.

The slender storyline deals with Garrel's plans to make a film about his marriage to Brigitte Cy. Only problem is that, though he will play himself, his mate is to be portrayed by a well-known professional actress (Anémone). Cy, a struggling legit thesp, is wounded deeply by Garrel's unwillingness

to cast her. Rest of the film dramatizes the couple's breakup, their cautious rendezvous and shared soul-searchings. The two finally get back together again and there is no more mention about the film.

Garrel, grungy and shaggy-haired, is as inarticulate an actor as he is a helmer, but his companion gives her sincere best as a woman offended both privately and professionally by her self-involved lover. Their kid, Louis Garrel, provides a facile (but desperately needed) source of endearment since it's hard to warm up to his embattled parents.

Anémone, who appeared in Garrel's first film (in 1966), has two major scenes with Garrel and Cy (who tries to persuade her to give up the role to her), then disappears until the final sequence, which is meant to be poetically vague but is merely emptily distended.

Garrel the elder dispenses paternal philosophy. Ironically, the nicest performance is a cameo by Yvette Etievant as Garrel's mom — maybe because she in fact is *not* his off-screen mother.

Jacques Loiseleux' b&w lensing is clean and unaffected. Barney Wilen's jazz underscoring has some effective moments. Marc Cholodenko, a novelist, makes his filmwriting debut with some axiomatic dialog on love and loving and being a couple —*Len.*

Cold Comfort
(CANADIAN)

Montreal   A Norstar Entertainment production. Executive producers, Peter R. Simpson, Dan Johnson. Produced by Ilana Frank, Ray Sager. Directed by Vic Sarin. Screenplay, Richard Beattie, L. Elliott Simms; camera (color), Sarin; editor, Nick Rotundo; music, Jeff Danna, Mychael Danna; art direction, Jo-Ann Chorney; associate producer, Nick Rotundo. Reviewed at Montreal World Film Festival (Panorama Canada), Aug. 28, 1989. Running time: **90 MIN.**
Floyd . . . . .Maury Chaykin
Dolores . . . . .Margaret Langrick
Stephan . . . . .Paul Gross

■Cinematographer Vic Sarin's directorial film debut is a well-shot psychological thriller but lacks thrills and suffers from a story which is all over the place.

On the cold and comfortless praries in Manitoba, a mentally deranged father (Maury Chaykin), essentially kidnaps a traveling salesman (Paul Gross) to present to his pubescent daughter (Margaret Langrick) as a birthday present. It's a twisted tale of jealousy verging on incest. Semi-nude scenes of the daughter in well-

choreographed erotic dances limit the film's tv potential, which otherwise would be its obvious venue.

The first half-hour drags as the improbable storyline is developed. Floyd, the father, heads out from his desolate gas station to a neighboring town for doughnuts. By the time he gets back from the 15-mile drive, it's nightfall and a raging blizzard sets the stage for him to "rescue" Stephen, the salesman, from a car accident.

In what clearly is supposed to be the establishing of Floyd and his daughter Dolores' eccentric characters, pic builds at a snail's pace until Stephen is clearly a prisoner since he's chained to a pipe in the kitchen.

Violence between the father and Stephen is kept to a minimum visually. The script lacks the necessary tension to make the conflict credible, and the father's vulgarity when describing his daughter's body parts to the prisoner is regrettably what begins to reveal the depth of Floyd's insanity and latent incestuous desires.

However, all that's implied is never dealt with. It is unclear whether the daughter desires Stephen even when presenting herself to him naked. There is no passion anywhere, and the father's lust becomes the vehicle to justify the whole misdirected tale.

Acting is weak on all fronts. Dreary music lacks the necessary fear-inducing edge. Pic's saving grace is Sarin's picture postcard cinematography. —*Suze.*

Matinee
(CANADIAN)

Montreal   A Thomas Howe Releasing release of a Summit Entertainment presentation of a D. Slayer Prods. film. Executive producer, Richard Davis. Produced by Kim Steer, Cal Shumiatcher. Written and directed by Richard Martin. Camera (color), Cyrus Block; editors, Bruce Lange, Debra Rurak; music, Graeme Coleman; sound, Lars Ekstrom. Reviewed at Montreal World Film Festival (Panorama Canada), Aug. 28, 1989. Running time: **90 MIN.**
Marilyn . . . . .Gillian Barber
Al Jason . . . . .Ron White
Oslam . . . . .Tim Webber
Lawrence . . . . .Jeff Schultz
Sherri . . . . .Beatrice Boepple
Warren . . . . .R. Nelson Brown

■A horror film buffet of comedy and schlock, this tongue-in-cheek suspense thriller makes up for its lack of shock value with a solid cast, liquid imagery and innovative editing. A treat for buffs hot on horror film trivia, pic should fare well in specialty outlets and on vidcassette.

Set in a small town where "burying the past has been elevated to the level of a virtue," burying film buffs at the local horror festival becomes the pic's central theme.

From the opening shot of a young couple kissing in the back row of a cinema while watching "Murder Camp," and the boy is knifed through the neck at the same time as "Murder Camp's" victim, jump-cut editing sets the rapid-pace juxtaposition between film and "reality." The ensuing string of campy murders at the local matinee, many witnessed by the local cinephiles, elevates voyeurism and the lust for visual gore to a level that Godard might snicker at.

Al Jason (adeptly played by Ron White) is the detective who tries to solve the murder mystery, despite the fact he moved to the country to escape big-city corruption. He encounters a bevy of eccentrics dead set on keeping the horror fest alive

Warren is the weirdo who executes the theater lighting amid his "ship of fools where Vivien Leigh is the divorcée." Marilyn (Gillian Barber) is the puritan mother protecting her daughter Sherri (Beatrice Boepple) from the pending bright lights of Hollywood via her ex-husband and horror director, who also gets the ax at the premiere of his "Bad Blood II."

A tight and intentionally corny script, a claustrophobic camera and upbeat eerie music make this a must-see for all fans of Trivial Pursuit's Silver Screen Edition. —*Suze.*

Jena Kerosinshika
(The Kerosene Seller's Wife)
(SOVIET)

Montreal   A Sovexportfilm release of a Mosfilm production. Directed by Alexander Kaidanovsky. Screenplay, Kaidanovsky; camera (Sovcolor), Alexei Rodionov; music, Alexander Goldstein; sound, E. Fedorov; production design, Teodor Tezhek, Viktor Zenkov. Reviewed at Montreal World Film Festival (Cinema of Today & Tomorrow), Aug. 28, 1989. Running time: **99 MIN.**
With: Anna Myasoyedova, Alexander Balouyev, Vitautas Paukste, Sergei Veksler.

■This intriguing, offbeat item is filled with bizarre, surreal moments which catch the eye, but has, at one viewing at least, a storyline that's perversely difficult to unravel.

Despite that, it's one of the more intriguing films to emerge from the Soviet Union this year, and will doubtless get fest exposure.

Setting is a small town in 1953.

Petravicius, an investigator, arrives in town to follow-up bribery charges. Meanwhile, three years earlier, Pavel Uldatsov, a surgeon with a beautiful wife, was betrayed by his evil twin brother Sergei, who lusted after the wife. Sergei had deliberately caused one of Pavel's patients to die; Pavel had been blamed and imprisoned. Now he's out and ekeing out a living as a door-to-door seller of kerosene, while his evil brother is chairman of the local Soviet.

Writer-director Alexander Kaidanovsky doesn't tell this yarn in straightforward manner, preferring to indulge in any number of visually striking scenes of surreal beauty which nevertheless blur the narrative. They include images of angels, a flutist burned to death during a concert without anyone noticing, and a visit to an insane asylum where the mad seem saner than the sane.

There's a political message to be found here, about the evils of corruption, said to be at the core of the Soviet Union's problems. But while trying to sort out the plot and characters, let alone the message, most Western viewers will simply enjoy the rich visuals which are invariably witty and often startling.
—*Strat.*

Spasi I Sokhrani
(Save And Protect)
(SOVIET)

Montreal   A Lenfilm Kirovsky production. Directed by Aleksandr Sokurov. Screenplay, Yuri Arabov, based on Gustave Flaubert's novel "Madame Bovary;" camera (color), Sergei Yurisditski; music, Yuri Khanine; design, Elena Amachinskaia. Reviewed at Montreal World Film Festival (competing), Aug. 29, 1989. Running time: **165 MIN.**
With: Cecile Zervoudaki, Robert Vaab, Aleksandr Tcherednik, Viatcheslav Rogovoi, Daria Chpalikova.

■An excruciatingly self-indulgent film, "Save And Protect" is most interesting for demonstrating the freedom of wretched excess permitted by glasnost to contemporary Soviet filmmakers.

Extensive walkouts during a Montreal festival screening did not bode well for its prospects abroad, though generous helpings of nudity and sexual frankness make this unbearably long effort a good bet to rake in the rubles in Russia.

Allegedly modeled on Flaubert's "Madame Bovary," the story is set in some godforsaken corner of Russia in a period that time-shifts in deliberately ana-chronistic fashion between the 19th and 20th centuries. The heroine, nameless like all the characters, is a high-strung, no longer young housewife given to babbling in French and dreaming of faraway places. Justifiably bored with her loutish country doctor husband, she channels her creativity into sexual adventurism.

With hubby none the wiser this charismatic village eccentric keeps liaisons with various lovers (stablehand, student, shopkeeper) anywhere convenient, including the backseat of a horse-drawn jitney. Actress Cecile Zervoudkai disrobes so often and is mounted so frequently that the film's emotionless eroticism peters out quickly into self-caricature.

In this filthy fly-ridden town maladies are commonplace and treated by bleeding or primitive surgery. Director Aleksandr Sokurov contrasts disease as a metaphor for existence in this village of fools with the heroine's life-affirming sexual drive as a quest for freedom from convention. "I want to live," she proclaims to a lover, standing naked to the sky during an interlude in a weed field. But as her passion slowly and steadily degenerates into raving madness, the filmmaker does his utmost to make it impossible to care about her grim, prefigured fate.

Sokurov evinces little sense of style and less regard for narrative as he veers between heightened naturalism and hallucinatory surrealism with scant redeeming artistic purpose. Most maddening is his penchant for real-time sequences, a technique that induces mounting queasiness over the course of a seemingly infinite 165 minutes. Sensitive cinematography does little to compensate for dreadfully overwrought performances and the portentous, muddled philosophy that permeates the rambling dialog.—*Rich.*

226
(Four Days Of Snow And Blood)
(JAPANESE)

Montreal   A Shochiku release of a Shochiku-Fuji Co. Ltd. production. Executive producer, Kazuyoshi Okuyama. Produced by Yoshinobu Nishioka. Directed by Hideo Gosha. Screenplay, Kazuo Kasahara; camera (Fujicolor), Fujio Morita; editor, Tsukasa Kono; music, Akira Senju; production design, Yoshinobu Nishioka. Reviewed at Montreal World Film Festival (noncompeting), Aug. 27, 1989. Running time: **114 MIN.**
Capt. Nonaka . . . . Kenichi Hagiwara
Capt. Ando . . . . Tomokazu Miura

Capt. Kono . . . . Masahiro Motoki
Asaichi Isobe . . . . Naoto Takenaka
Takaji Muranaka . . . . Daisuko Ryu
Mihoko . . . . Yuko Natori
Ando's wife . . . . Kaho Minami
Admiral Suzuki . . . . Shinsuke Ashida

■Top production values and some suspenseful drama are the ingredients of this dramatization of the events of Feb. 26, 1936, when junior officers staged a coup against government ministers, assassinating several of them in the name of the Emperor.

For non-Japanese audiences, though, the film will pose some problems, partly because of a lack of knowledge about the real-life event, and partly because of the way the film is structured, with rugged violent action at the start followed by long scenes of debate and discussion.

In the mid-'30s Japan quit the League of Nations and invaded Manchuria; meanwhile, there was widespread unemployment and starvation. The junior officers blamed corrupt politicians, and felt the Emperor was ignorant of the true state of affairs; they decided to kill the Prime Minister and senior cabinet members.

The plan worked up to a point, though the PM escaped, as did some others. But the rebellious officers weren't backed up by their superiors, and, after four tense days, backed down and ordered their troops back to barracks. The officers were executed by firing squad (three of them suicided).

Hideo Gosha's film begins with the plotters deciding to proceed, and then shows the events of the night of Feb. 26 (the date is the film's original Japanese title) in graphic detail as soldiers smash their way into the homes of the politicos and gun them down before their horrified families. The agonizing debates that follow will be more interesting to domestic audiences, no matter how hard Gosha tries to make them dramatically involving.

There's a strong emphasis on the effect of the events on the wives of the rebels, and these scenes tend to become cloying.

The film is technically firstclass, with top credits in every department. Performances are strong down the line, with Tomokazu Miura standing out as the most fanatical of the rebels. The film may have some theatrical possibilities outside Japan, but video looms as a better bet. —*Strat.*

Asthikal Pookkunnu
(And Bones Do Blossom)
(INDIAN)

Montreal   A Peebles Movie Makers production. Directed by P. Sreekumar. Screenplay, R. Narendra Prasad, Sreekumar; camera (Widescreen, color), Gopi Nath; editor, Venu Gopal; music, Raveendran. Reviewed at Montreal World Film Festival (Indian Cinema section), Aug. 27, 1989. Running time: **125 MIN.**
With: Murali, Chithra Nair, Chandran Nair, A.R. Antony, Shantha Devi.

■An overlong drama from southern India, "And Bones Do Blossom" deals with the murder of a union leader during a period of labor unrest.

The familiar theme is treated lethargically by director P. Sreekumar, whose sometimes confusing flashback structure also diminishes audience involvement.

Story involves the arrival of a stranger who comes to stay with the dead man's widow and parents, but the stranger is hiding a secret that's all too predictable and is revealed at fadeout.

Main assets here are the widescreen photography of Gopi Nath and the interesting score by Raveendran. Offshore chances are minimal. — *Strat.*

Der Geschichtenerzähler
(The Story Teller)
(WEST GERMAN)

Montreal   A Common Film production, in association with Ula Stöckl Filmproduktion, PDK Pictures (L.A.) and SFB. Executive producer, Wilbur Stark. Produced by Helmut Wietz. Directed by Rainer Boldt. Screenplay, Bolt, Dorothea Neukirchen, Wolf Christian Schröder and Hans Kwiet, from the novel by Patricia Highsmith; camera (Agfacolor), Rolf Liccini; editor, Petra Heymann; music, Serge Weber; sound, Wolf-Dietrich Peters; production design, Rainer Schaper; production manager, Udo Heiland; assistant director, Barbara von Wrangell. Reviewed at Montreal World Film Festival (competing), Aug. 26, 1989. Running time: 93 MIN.
Nico Thomkins . . . . Udo Schenk
Helen Thomkins . . . . Anke Sevenich
Clara Lilienthal . . . . . . Christine Kaufmann
Eduard Hanstock . . . . Peter Sattemann
Alex Hanson . . . . Rüdiger Wandel
Ivy . . . . Jalo Arikan
Herr Jensen . . . . Hans Michael Rehberg
Frau Jensen . . . . Christina Horn
Inspector . . . . Gunnar Möller

■The sinister world of Patricia Highsmith is well served by writer-director Rainer Boldt in this intriguing thriller about some rather unpleasant people involved in ultimately lethal game-playing.

The handsomely produced film, though tops of its kind, probably is not the sort of fare international arthouse audiences are looking for, but this one deserves to be an exception to that rule.

European directors have, in recent years, proved especially adept at adapting Highsmith's pessimistic thrillers to the screen: Claude Miller and Claude Chabrol in France and Hans Werner Geissendörfer in Germany have come up with classy Highsmith pics. Add to them "The Story Teller," a typical Highsmith tale of a marriage breaking up thanks to the writer-husband's mordant gameplaying; Nico even jokes about killing his wife, and unashamedly cheats on her.

Finally, she's had enough and leaves without a forwarding address. Nico is suspected of murdering her, and goes along with the game, even planting false evidence: but in fact Helen is holed up in a beachside house on the island of Sylt, where she's having an affair with Eduard, lover of Clara, a crippled artist neighbor from back home. When Nico decides finally to track down his wife, tragedy results.

Rainer Boldt convincingly captures a mood of dark cynicism, and creates a set of principal characters who are convincingly decadent. Udo Schenk is particularly fine as the faithless husband, while Christine Kaufmann makes the crippled artist a genuinely devious character.

Pacing is brisk, Rolf Liccini's camerawork is superior, and there's an apt music score from Serge Weber. "The Story Teller" is in every respect exemplary, but probably will have trouble finding cinema audiences outside Germany partly because the dark world of Highsmith has proved in the past rather too cynical for audiences (with the notable exception of Hitchcock's "Strangers On A Train") and partly because arthouse audiences tend to seek nongenre fare. Pic was a worthy addition to the Montreal fest. —*Strat.*

Les Bois noirs
(Dark Woods)
(FRENCH)

Paris A Bac Films release of a Paradis Film/Mondex Film/FR3 Films coproduction. Executive producer, Eric Heumann. Produced by Jean Labadie, Stéphane Sorlat. Directed by Jacques Deray. Screenplay, Deray, Pascal Bonitzer, based on novel "Le Chateau des bois noirs" by Robert Margerit; camera (color), Carlo Varini; editor, Hugues Darmois; music, Romano Musumarra; art direction, François de Lamothe; sound, Alain Sempe, François Groult; costumes, Martine Rapin; production manager, Dominique Toussaint; assistant director, Robert Kechichian; associate producer, Guy Amon. Reviewed at the Club Gaumont, Paris, Aug. 17, 1989. (In Montreal Film Festival, competing.) Running time: **113 MIN.**

Violete	Béatrice Dalle
Gustave Dupin	Philippe Volter
Bastien Dupin	Stéphane Freiss
Nathalie Dupin	Geneviève Page
Antoine	Hervé Laudiere
Anna Bourderias	Jenny Cleve
Dr. Charles	Pierre Vial

■Jacques Deray dusts the cobwebs off a hoary Gothic romance plot in "Les Bois noirs," about a young Parisian woman who marries a handsome but disquieting provincial squiare with odd family and somber castle. If story seems dated to contemporary eyes, it nonetheless has the merits of sound scripting, fine acting and direction. Pic is competing at Montreal.

Film begins conventionally enough as a flashback testimony by recently widowed Béatrice Dalle, charged with the fatal poisoning of her husband (Philippe Volter), a local landowner whom she married after an unusual courtship in Paris. Typically, the flashback device proves faulty since the audience is privy to scenes that do not involve Dalle.

Volter brings Dalle home to his chateau in southwestern France where his mother (Geneviève Page) indoctrinates her into the household. Apart from the governess and her son, there is Volter's brother (Stéphane Freiss) who prefers to spend his time away from home.

Not surprisingly, there is a sibling rivalry between Volter and Freiss that is aggravated by the presence of Dalle. She and Freiss strike up a platonic friendship strengthened by her deepening alarm and dissatisfaction with her husband, whose surface charm begins peeling away almost immediately to reveal a violent morbid sensibility. The family falls apart in Cain and Abel bloodshed, conjugal disgust and suicide made to look like murder.

Story is drawn from a '50s French provincial novel and has been intelligently adapted by Deray and Pascal Bonitzer, a Cahiers du Cinéma critic and auteur film scripter. This odd-couple screenwriting pair succeeds in enriching stock characters and inflecting genre clichés, such as bats and dangerous dogs. Here the bats are harmless victims of human brutality, and the dogs are symbols of fidelity.

Script does run into trouble when it's time to get Dalle off the hook with the revelation of Volter's murder of Freiss. It takes nothing less than a providential bolt of lightning to provide the macabre denouement. This may be in the manner of the Gothic novel, but it's counter to the style Deray and Bonitzer have chosen.

Dalle is fine as the young Parisian who romantically marries into a nightmare and Freiss is appealing as the brother-in-law. Geneviève Page's mother-in-law is a well-limned portrait in moral resignation. Jenny Cleve and Hervé Laudière are vivid as the chateau governess and her son.

The performance that carries the picture is by Volter, recently seen in Belgium's boxoffice smash "The Music Teacher." He deepens and shades the conventional portrait of the ominous squire with unusual dramatic power and screen presence. Volter is someone to watch.

Deray's direction is his most assured in quite a long while. Tech credits are classy. —*Len.*

Terezin Diary
(DOCU)

Montreal A Terezin Foundation Inc. presentation in association with Visible Pictures Ltd. Executive producer, Zuzana Justman. Produced and directed by Dan Weissman. Screenplay, Justman; camera (Duart color), Ervin Sanders; editor, Mark Simon; sound, Jaroslav Detak, Nikolaus Ochs; production manager, Jiri Jezek; narrator, Eli Wallach. Reviewed at Montreal World Film Festival (Cinema Of Today & Tomorrow section), Aug. 25, 1989. Running time: **88 MIN.**

■This addition to the distinguished number of documentary films centering on aspects of the Holocaust is a little different from the others and as a result will play well on tv, with specialized theatrical bookings also indicated.

Terezin was a small fortress town near Prague which, in 1939, was established as a Jewish ghetto by the Germans. Some 140,000 people passed through Terezin, many of them artists and intellectuals; 15,000 were children, and for many Terezin merely was a stopover on the way to Auschwitz.

Dan Weissman and Zuzana Justman, the latter a Terezin survivor herself, focus their film on a 1986 reunion of survivors. Stories are told about life in what at first was a relatively benign community, referred to by one commentator as "the most bizarre" of the camps.

Footage is included from the 1944 film "Hitler Gives The Jews A Town," made by the Germans as a propaganda exercise. Indeed, during the war an investigating international commission was rooted into thinking Terezin was a genuinely productive community.

There are many moving stories told here, all lovingly brought together by the filmmakers. All who see the film are likely to be touched by the simply presented but forceful material. —*Strat.*

Tian Yin
(Thrown Together By Fate)
(CHINESE)

Montreal A China Film Export release of a Beijing Film Studio production. Directed by Zhang Huaxun. Screenplay, Zhang Huaxun, Li Guangliang, Yang Congjié, Geng Yucuan; cmaera (color), Zhang Li, Zhao Peng; music, Lei Lei; production design, Ma Jesheng. Reviewed at Montreal World Film Festival (competing), Aug. 27, 1989. Running time: **106 MIN.**

Hainiu	Xu Shouli
Fusako	Zhao Xiaorui

■After the recent events in China, it comes as no real surprise that the country's competing entry in the Montreal fest is a bland programmer like "Thrown Together By Fate," a well made but old-fashioned melodrama in the "Hell In The Pacific" tradition.

It's 1942, and a brave Chinaman, Hainiu, finds himself on a desert island with a Japanese woman, Fusako, who had been brought from her home to China to be an unwilling prostitute. Hainiu's first instinct is to kill this "enemy," but he spares her and, inevitably, they become lovers and have a child (though nothing approaching a lovemaking scene is shown).

The couple survive rather well, though their pet dog is killed while defending their infant from a poisonous snake. However, when a Japanese unit lands on the island, tragedy results, and the child is left an orphan at fadeout.

All this is handsomely photographed, but not very compelling. The love story is handled in a remote way, and the habit of having the heroine's Japanese dialog translated by voiceover is extremely irritating.

As a plea for international understanding, the film is naive indeed. It would be a pity if this were to be the standard of Chinese films of the future. —*Strat.*

Mandoukhai Tsetsen Khatan
(Mandoukhai The Wise)
(MONGOLIAN)

Montreal A Mongolkino presentation. Produced by L. Zenemeder. Directed by B. Baljinnyam. Screenplay, Sh. Natsagdorj,

based on the novel by Natsagdorj; camera (color), L. Sharavdorj; editor, Maam; music, N. Jantsannorov; set design, B. Purevsukh. Reviewed at Montreal World Film Festival (Cinema of Today & Tomorrow), Aug. 29, 1989. Running time: 180 MIN.
Mandoukhai (empress) .... Nansrayn Suvd

■ Set in the 15th century after the collapse of Genghis Khan's empire, this pic follows Mandoukhai from her youth when she's forced to marry the new ruler to her violent death after unifying the vast Mongolian empire.

Pic easily could be cut from a 3-hour saga to a 2-hour tv movie by trimming excessive battle scenes and gory closeups.

Like "The Last Emperor," film is a rich historical document, revealing ancient customs, traditions and power struggles that are the roots of today's republic.

Regrettably, Mandoukhai's forceful vision gets buried in endless shots of the cavalry, which she rules with an iron fist. Her personal tragedy and loss of three children testify to the will of a remarkable woman who was known as the empress of wisdom. —Suze.

Mona et Moi
(Mona And I)
(FRENCH)

Montreal   A Chrysalide, RGP Prods. and Skyline production. Produced by Olivier Owen, Christopher Giercke. Directed by Patrick Grandperret. Screenplay, Grandperret, Dominique Gallieni; camera (color), Louis Bihi; editor, Yann Dedet; sound, Julien Cloquet. Reviewed at Montreal World Film Festival (Cinema of Today & Tomorrow), Aug. 29, 1989. Running time: 90 MIN.
Pierre (I) .... Denis Lavant
Mona .... Sophie Simon
Ricky .... Antoine Chappey
Johnny Valentine ...... Johnny Thunders
The father .... Jean-François Stevenin
Olivier .... Olivier Owen
The Manager .... Christopher Giercke

■ "Mona And I" is a sex, drugs and rock 'n' roll pic that has little to do with Mona and him (Pierre).

Most of the sex is slyly captured in the first 10-minutes in a string of images that resemble photo album snap shots. Offbeat opening has potential, but after Mona and Pierre's sketchy relationship is established, film plummets to the dodgy drugs and rock 'n' roll scenario bemoaning the financial woes of Pierre and the guys in band. Opening style is abandoned and scenes drag through back alleys, rehearsal sessions and drugs.

Sophie Simon (Mona) has a refreshing screen presence and does as much as she can with a role in

which she's reduced to a prop, backdrop or sidekick to the guys. After being ignored by Pierre, it's no surprise when she takes off with lead singer Johnny Valentine, emulated by the rest of the losers. Even as the "winner," Johnny's

philosphy is that "there are junkies that have junky mentalities, and there are people who take drugs."

Pic's mediocre rock 'n' roll doesn't even give it much chance as a rock film. —Suze.

TORONTO FEST REVIEWS

Bye Bye Blues
(CANADIAN)

Toronto   A Festival Films release in Canada of an Allarcom-True Blue Films production. Executive producer, Tony Allard. Produced by Anne Wheeler, Arvi Liimatainen. Written and directed by Wheeler. Camera (color), Vic Sarin; editor, Christopher Tate; production design, John Blackie; art direction, Scott Dobbie; music, George Blondheim; sound, Garrell Clark; costumes, Maureen Hiscox. Reviewed at Famous Players screening room, Toronto, Aug. 30, 1989. (In Toronto Festival of Festivals.) Running time: 118 MIN.
Daisy Cooper .... Rebecca Jenkins
Teddy Cooper .... Michael Ontkean
Max Gramley .... Luke Reilly
Slim Godfrey .... Stuart Margolin
Frances Cooper .... Robyn Stevan
Mary Wright .... Kate Reid
Arthur Wright .... Leslie Yeo
Pete .... Wayne Robson
Doreen Cooper .... Sheila Moore
Lady Wilson .... Susan Wooldridge
Bernie Blitzer .... Leon Pownall
Richard Cooper (9 years) .... Kirk Duffee
Emma Cooper .... Aline Levasseur

■ Baked in vivid nostalgic 1940s colors and mood, "Bye Bye Blues" is one of the best English-Canadian pics in many years. It should find happiness in commercial houses and later on tv and video.

The most accessible feature yet from Canadian scripter-director Anne Wheeler, pic begins in wartime India, where opening scenes were shot. They focus on a loving young couple. He's in the army and she's pregnant with their second child.

He is abruptly posted but isn't told where; she returns with two children to her parents' home in the snow-covered Alberta farmland back in Canada. Her letters to him are returned undelivered.

She receives no news about him and no money. She teaches herself to play piano, joins a local dance band and becomes its singer, despite her father, who is against working mothers. She moves to a house in town.

The band travels to nearby dates and she leaves the children with her love-starved sister-in-law, who's involved sexually with Australian soldiers at the town's base.

The band's clarinetist, a lonely drifter, befriends the young moth-

er. Despite her loneliness, she politely resists his advances, preferring to remain faithful.

Over the years, the band's popularity grows and it lands a national radio contract. Just then, the doctor husband returns from a prisoner-of-war camp in Singapore. She wistfully lets the bandmembers go to their big break without her, to resume the role of wife.

Delineated from a quiet feminist sensibility of women coping alone in various ways, from forbearance to challenging small-town values, the pic glows with an engrossing story well told.

It owes as much to Vic Sarin's lush, properly stylized camerawork as it does to Wheeler's careful work with script, characterizations and sympathetic direction.

Singer-actress Rebecca Jenkins, a new find, is standout and perky as the young mother-pianist. Michael Ontkean shines in brief scenes as the loving husband. Stuart Margolin is smooth as an alcoholic bandleader who gets booted out for defrauding his players. Robyn Stevan scores as the hedonistic sister-in-law who decides not to have an abortion and reconciles with her own mother.

Lanky Luke Reilly comes across strongly as the drifter, whose past remains mysterious.

And there are topnotch character performances by bandmember Wayne Robson; Kate Reid and Leslie Yeo, who play Jenkins' parents; mother-in-law Sheila Moore; Leon Pownall, the band's booker; Susan Wooldridge, in a cameo in the India scenes, and Jenkins' children at various ages, most notably Kirk Duffee and Aline Levasseur.

John Blackie's production design, Scott Dobbie's art direction and other technical values are excellent.

Pacing at times is slower than necessary; further tightening would help. Ontkean's long-awaited return is anticlimactic but, as the quietly unfolding pic itself, that has the touch of reality.
—Adil.

Leningrad Cowboys Go America
(FINNISH)

Toronto   A Villealfa Filmproduction/-Swedish Film Institute production. Executive producer, Klaus Heydemann. Producer, Klas Oloffson, Katinka Farago. Written and directed by Aki Kaurismäki. Camera (color), Timo Salminen; editor, Raija Talvio; art direction, Heikki Ukkonen, Karl Laine; music, Mauri Sumen; sound, Jouko Lumme. Reviewed at Bloor Cinema, Toronto, Aug. 28, 1989. (In Toronto Festival of Festivals.) Running time: 78 MIN.
With: Matti Pellonpaa, Kari Vaananen, Sakke Jarvenpaa, Heikki Keskinen, Pimme Korhonen, Sakari Kuosmanen.

■ Prolific Finnish director Aki Kaurismäki takes his quirky cues in "Leningrad Cowboys Go America" from Jim Jarmusch and Mack Sennett in this wacky tale of a Finnish musical octet trying to make it as a hip rock 'n' roll band in America.

Curiosity-seekers of Kaurismäki's growing body of work will consider this a must-see on the fest circuit, but it'll be an iffy leap into the mainstream.

Pic starts "somewhere in the tundra," where an 8-man band, which plays painfully bad accordion riffs a la "SCTV's" Schmenge brothers, is advised by a local record producer to go to more tolerant America.

The group and its self-aggrandizing manager sport ludicrously exaggerated ducktail hairdos, black wraparound sunglasses, cumbersome fur coats and pointed flipper footwear. One of the bandmembers freezes to death while practicing before the departure, but the group takes the stiff with them and carts him around in a coffin tied to the top of their car.

In New York City, a scuzzball producer tells them to go to Mexico and play at his cousin's wedding, and to consider learning rock 'n' roll. What follows is a fish-out-of-water road pic. The band, after buying a used Cadillac from Jim Jarmusch (in a cameo as a used-car salesman), stops off in every sleazy bar from New Orleans to San Antonio to Galveston to Del Rio, and polishes its pathetic repertoire to include hard rock, Springsteen, country and Latin.

These guys are almost as at home in America as Percy Adlon's German hausfrau in "Bagdad Cafe," but Kaurismäki doesn't tap the situation for rich cultural observations. The main characters, including the village idiot, who stows away in a Finnair jet to follow his idols, are all caricatures, and the manager is played strictly on one note.

Kaurismäki uses black & white title cards to announce the tongue-in-cheek flat action that follows. When the band agrees on a "revolution" to gang up on their manager, it's a Keystone Kops binding-and-gagging routine. When the boys are starving, their leader throws them a bag of onions, while his personal supply of endless

Budweisers is stashed away in the ice preserving the dead body in the peripatetic coffin.

The smart black humor of Kaurismäki's "Hamlet Goes Business" is forsaken for a giddy little ditty whose 1-joke plot would fare much better as a comedy club sketch.—*Devo.*

BLACKLIGHT FEST REVIEWS

Making 'Do The Right Thing' (DOCU)

Chicago A Chamba Organization/40 Acres and a Mule Filmworks production. Produced and directed by St. Clair Bourne. Associate producer, Dolores Elliott. Camera (Duart color), Juan Cobo, Joseph Friedman; editor, Susan Fanshel; music, Steve Coleman; sound, Donald Klocek; additional camera; Crystal Griffith, Neil Shapiro, Rosemary Tomosky-Franco, James Fealy, Joan Siegler. Reviewed at Blacklight Film Festival, Chicago, Aug. 25, 1989. No MPAA Rating. Running time: **60 MIN.**

With: Spike Lee, Danny Aiello, Ossie Davis, Ruby Dee, Giancarlo Esposito, Bill Nunn, Richard Edson, John Turturro.

■St. Clair Bourne's behind-the-scenes look at Spike Lee's "Do The Right Thing" offers a suitably penetrating companion piece to Lee's latest feature.

Given the amount of interest, both critical and popular, generated by Lee's tale of black/white relations in Bedford-Stuyvesant, demand for the making-of docu should be high and this effort undoubtedly will satisfy.

Bourne incorporates the customary motifs for this type of film, including scenes of the actors at work, the director instructing same and nitty-gritty actualities as the cameras roll. However, Bourne goes one step further by incorporating into the matrix the actual residents of the neighborhood Lee chose as a setting for his film.

Therein lie the weaknesses and the strengths of "Making 'Do The Right Thing.' "

By including more than backstage activities in his film, Bourne both expands and dilutes its effectiveness as a document. His attempt to detail the effect "Do The Right Thing" had on the Bed-Stuy block on which it was shot is necessarily compromised by his duty to chronicle the making of Lee's film.

Even so, the scenes that record the sense of importance imparted

to the neighborhood residents by their participation in the film, and their abandonment after the shoot was completed, serve to heighten the direness of their situation — and to lift "The Making Of 'Do The Right Thing' " above other films of its type. —*Brin.*

The Game

New York A Visual Perspectives release of a Curtis Films Ltd. production. Executive producer, Julia Wilson. Produced and directed by Curtis Brown. Screenplay, Wilson, Brown, from Brown's story; camera (Duart color), Paul Gibson; supervising editor, Gloria Whittemore; editor, Daniel Barrientos; music, Wilson; sound, Michael Lazar; production design, Walter Jorgenson; production manager, Wilson; 2d unit camera, Steve McNutt; casting, Lee Winters. Reviewed at TVC screening room, N.Y., Aug. 17, 1989. (In the Blacklight Film Festival, Chicago.) No MPAA Rating.:Running time: **116 MIN.**

Leon Hunter	Curtis Brown
Jason McNair	Richard Lee Ross
Silvia Yearwood	Vanessa Shaw
Vail Yearwood	Billy Williams
Ben Egan	Charles Timm
George Paturzo	Michael P. Murphy
Carl Rydell	Dick Biel
Gloria	Carolina Beaumont
Norman	Bruce Grossberg
Arrington	Damon Clark

Also with: Erick Shawn, Erick Coleman, Joanna Wahl, Rick Siler, Claire Waters, Jerome King.

■A timely pic about a N.Y. mayoral election, "The Game" is a diamond in the rough — low-budget, no-name filmmaking with a punch. It augurs the arrival of another talented black indie filmmaker, Curtis Brown.

Like Spike Lee, Brown is a Brooklynite who studied at New York U. and bootstrapped his way into film. For his debut feature, he takes a Lee-esque strategy of a militant screenplay in which he plays the role of the heavy himself.

Script by Julia Wilson and Brown is an ingenious and insightful look at politics and power. Brown portrays Leon Hunter, a chess expert working at a top p.r. firm who's assigned (for expedient reasons) by his boss to run the

mayoral campaign of a white candidate (Dick Biel). Like the current real-life Gotham mayoral race, there are two leading white candidates and one black in the film, but characters bear no resemblance to Edward Koch, Rudolph Giuliani or David Dinkins (Giuliani's name is mentioned in the film only in his prior U.S. Attorney status).

Fancying himself a kingmaker, Brown maneuvers to have Biel win at any cost. Key plot twist, worthy of classic B movies of yore, has Brown exploiting a hospital identification mixup following the unwarranted police shooting of a messenger (Billy Williams). Switching bodies, he instigates a situation wherein candidate Biel can simultaneously attack the administration and take a hard-line stand on corruption/police brutality while the black candidate waffles.

A clever subplot manages to develop sympathy for several contrasting positons: the bigoted cop (Charles Timm) who shot the messenger; the cop's deeply religious partner (Richard Lee Ross) has a crisis of conscience over whether to tell the truth or be blindly loyal to Timm, and the messenger's wife (Silvia Yearwood), a former Black Panther whose subsequent assimilation is put to the test by the violent act. Thesping is solid, especially by Ross and Timm, though Brown's lowkey performance fails to maximize the character's potential in a role tailor-made (if pic had a bigger budget) for Clarence Williams 3d or Billy Dee Williams. Bruce Grossberg provides terrific comic relief as the roly-poly hospital morgue attendant.

Despite budget limitations, film is consistently interesting and offers many novel touches. For example, Brown's constant chess-playing by phone with a mysterious adversary adds suspense and is neatly resolved. A blackmail setup scene (shades of Gore Vidal's "The Best Man") in which Brown entraps his own candidate for future post-election control is staged off-camera while we watch a sexy dancer (Claire Baker) instead, a stylish and tasteful form of representation. Ending is delicious, capped with a memorably cynical tag line of dialog.

Tech credits are acceptable, with an okay score by Wilson. Pic reportedly has been trimmed from its original length by a reel to 103 minutes for release.—*Lor.*

Rising Tones Cross (DOCU)

Chicago An Ebba Jean/DFFB production. Executive producers, Udo Rabek, Hans Muller. Directed by Ebba Jahn. Camera (color), Jahn; editor, Jeannette Menzel; sound, Karola Michalic Ritter, Renate Saml, Jose Gebers; 2d camera, Brian Denitz; lighting, Roy Wilson; production manager, Peter Kowald. Reviewed at Blacklight Film Festival, Chicago, Aug. 25, 1989. No MPAA Rating. Running time: **119 MIN.**

■This feature-length docu chronicling the hard life and times of a group of avant-garde jazz musicians in New York could be a delight for hardcore jazzbos, but nonbuffs are likely to find it slow moving. Picture doubtless will fare better in Europe than in the States.

Most interesting aspect of "Rising Tones Cross" in the insider's view it offers of the jazz community.

Pic effectively deromanticizes the jazz myth by illustrating just how difficult it is to survive as a dedicated jazz musician in the U.S. Artists are shown at home in meager, sometimes blighted apartments, rehearsing endlessly and playing in tiny basement clubs and on streetcorners — wherever they can attract an audience.

Story of Charles Gayle, a black tenor saxophonist who lives in abandoned buildings and eats out of garbage cans when necessary so he can be free to play his music, is particularly moving. Also effective is Peter Kowald, a German bass player who comments wryly on the irony that allows American jazz artists to be revered in Europe and ignored in the country where the form was created.

"Rising Tones Cross" also features a healthy does — maybe an overdose — of N.Y.-style new wave jazz, which ranges from the incomprensible to the sublime.
—*Brin.*

Sea Of Love

New York   A Univeral Pictures release of a Martin Bregman production. Produced by Bregman, Louis A. Stroller. Directed by Harold Becker. Screenplay, Richard Price; camera (Deluxe color), Ronnie Taylor; editor, David Bretherton; music, Trevor Jones; sound (Dolby), Keith Wester; production design, John Jay Moore; costume design, Betsy Cox; production manager, Barbara Kelly; assistant director, Michael Steele, N.Y. — Herb Gaines; additional camera, Adam Holender; associate producer, Michael Scott Bregman; casting, Mary Colquhoun, Canada — Stuart Aikins. Reviewed at Universal Screening room, N.Y., Aug. 29, 1989. MPAA Rating: R. Running time: 112 MIN.

Frank Keller . . . . Al Pacino
Helen . . . . Ellen Barkin
Sherman . . . . John Goodman
Terry . . . . Michael Rooker
Frank Keller Sr. . . . . William Hickey
Gruber . . . . Richard Jenkins
Gina Gallagher . . . . Christine Estabrook
Miss Allen . . . . Barbara Baxley
Older woman . . . . Patricia Barry
Helen's mother . . . . Jacqueline Brookes
Raymond Brown . . . . Michael O'Neill
Also with: Paul Calderon, Gene Canfield, Larry Joshua, John Spencer, Mark Phelan.

■ Hot summer b.o. should continue into autumn with Universal's "Sea Of Love," a suspenseful film noir boasting a superlative performance by Al Pacino as a burned-out Gotham cop.

Handsomely mounted Martin Bregman production benefits from a witty screenplay by Richard Price ("The Color Of Money" scripter), limning the bittersweet tale of a 20-year veteran NYC cop (Pacino) assigned to a case tracking down the serial killer of men who've made dates through the personal columns.

He teams up with fellow cop John Goodman to set a trap for the murderer by matching fingerprints with those found at the crime scenes. Clues point to a woman being the killer, placing rhyming romantically inclined ads in the personals and leaving a 45 rpm disk of '50s hit "Sea Of Love" on the record player. Using a romantic poem of his mother's, Pacino places an ad and with Goodman take turns interviewing femme suspects at dinner trysts to get their fingerprints on the wine glass for matching.

Early on, Ellen Barkin appears as one of the suspects, but after an initial rebuff Pacino is smitten with her and crucially decides not to get her fingerprints for analysis. Pic builds some hair-raising twists and turns as the evidence mounts pointing to her guilt, climaxing in a very surprising revelation

Thankfully closer in character to "Serpico," his previous Bregman-produced hit policier by Sidney Lumet, than his morbid Jerry Weintraub flop, William Friedkin's "Cruising," Pacino here brings great depth to the central role. A loner with retirement after 20 years facing him, this cop is a sympathetic, self-divided individual and Pacino makes his clutching at a second chance with femme fatale Barkin believable. It's a significant screen comeback after four years' absence following Pacino's disastrous miscasting (in period dress) in the Irwin Winkler pic, Hugh Hudson's "Revolution."

Chemistry between the two stars is palpable in the modern "Body Heat" vein and Barkin's unconventional (in a movie star sense) good looks add to the credibility of her key role. Goodman provides solid comedy relief, while Patricia Barry stands out in a well-chosen supporting cast as an older woman who heartbreakingly picks up the wrong vibes at dinner after answering Pacino's phony personals ad.

Director Harold Becker, known for his series of thrillers starring James Woods, puts his own stamp on the picture with tight control of several explosive scenes. Price's script is both edgy and funny, balancing solid entertainment values with the dark, obsessive strains of the genre.

Tech contributions are excellent, especially British lenser Ronnie Taylor's atmospheric photography of familiar Manhattan locales (interiors were shot in Toronto). Besides a punchy score by Trevor Jones, title song by George Khoury and Phillip Baptiste is repeated endlessly on the soundtrack in its 1959 hit version of Phil Phillips & the Twilights with a hypnotic effect; Tom Waits warbles a new version over the end credits. —Lor.

A deux minutes près
(A Question Of Minutes)
(FRENCH)

Paris   A Production du Daunou production and release. Produced by Denise Petitdidier. Directed by Eric Le Hung. Screenplay, Françoise Dorin; camera (Eastmancolor), Philippe Théaudière; editor, Anne-Marie Cotret; music, Marc Hillman; assistant director, Xavier de Cassan. Reviewed at Georges V cinema, Paris, Aug. 28, 1989. Running time: 100 MIN.

Tristan . . . . Jacques Weber
Virginie . . . . Charlotte de Turckheim
Paul . . . . François-Eric Gendron
Christine . . . . Dominique Regnier

■ Françoise Dorin, the French stage's own female Neil Simon, makes a disappointing screen writing debut with this romantic comedy of errors about mismatched would-be lovers trying to get a passionate affair going. Charmless direction by Eric Le Hung and mediocre tech credits add up to a bum date between Dorin and the movies.

Jacques Weber and Charlotte de Turckheim star as hapless glumly married souls who dream of a passionate "brief encounter" promised by astrological readings. When they met, they believe this is "it," but their successive dates are plagued by petty accidents and mishaps that dampen their laboriously stoked romantic fires.

Turckheim is okay as a schlumpy suburban, but Weber, who often plays romantic heroic parts in the theater, is an egregious miscast — and his slightly bored manner betrays the character. A number of secondary parts and cameos are recruited from the legit stable of the producer, Denise Petitdidier, who runs a leading Paris commercial playhouse (and nicely portrays an astrologer in the film). —Len.

Le Mariage de Figaro
(The Marriage Of Figaro)
(FRENCH)

Paris   A Lydie Media production and release. Produced by Fanny Cottencon. Directed by Roger Coggio. Screenplay, Coggio, Bernard G. Landry, based on the play by Beaumarchais; camera (color), André Diot; editor, Raymonde Guyot; art direction, Thierry Leproust; music, Pierre Jansen; costumes, Yvonne Sassinot de Nesle; sound, Jean-Marcel Milan; production manager, Thierry Pyrolley; assistant director, Regis des Plas. Reviewed at Club Gaumont, Paris, Sept. 5, 1989. Running time: 171 MIN.

Suzanne . . . . Fanny Cottencon
Figaro . . . . Roger Coggio
Countess Rosine . . . . Marie Laforet
Count Almaviva . . . . Claude Giraud
Marceline . . . . Line Renaud
Cherubin . . . . Yannick Debain
Bartholo . . . . Michel Galabru
Bazile . . . . Jean Lefebvre
Antonio . . . . Paul Proboist
Brid Olson . . . . Roger Carel

■ Beaumarchais' splendid 18th century comedy "The Marriage Of Figaro" has been made into a overwrought, enervating film by Roger Coggio.

This is the latest in the "classics illustrated" series Coggio began well enough in 1980 with Molières "Les Fourberies de Scapin." But with one exception — Marivaux' "Les Fausses confidences," handsomely canned by Daniel Mossman — the program has degenerated into overproduced screen travesties of great literature, starring the ubiquitous Coggio.

"Figaro" cost some $6-million — financed in good part, like the previous films, by advance ticket sales to the public — and runs nearly three hours. But for all its gratuitous physicality and cinematic fussing it's a pictorially graceless bore which gives a falsely bombastic impression of one of the great theatrical comedies.

First staged in 1784, play enjoyed an immediate success which was in part fueled by attempts — by none less than Louis XVI himself — to ban it as seditious (which it was). Coggio is not one to let didactic opportunity go by so we periodically watch lackeys lugging a huge portrait of the unfortunate King Louis throughout the film, even though the action is set in Spain. True, Spain was a thin mask for Louis XVI's France, but this geographic convention, acceptable in the artificial world of the stage, is jarring in a film where veristic detail is piled on thickly and pointlessly.

Coggio throws a portentous pall over Beaumarchais' subtly observed characters, marvelously contrived comic complications and scintillating wit, destroying the delicate balance between the comic gaiety and the beguiling melancholy. Pierre Jansen's music and André Diot's lighting tip us off from the first shot that Coggio is out to teach us that Beaumarchais is Serious Stuff.

Coggio heads the casting casualty list. As Figaro, the wily valet to a proud Spanish lord, who is preparing to wed chaste chambermaid Suzanne when he learns his master is planning to seduce her, the actor-director indulges in the barely modulated scenery-chewing that weakened his "Scapin" film (otherwise buoyed by fine comic support) and reduced Gogol's "Diary Of A Madman" to a sinister one-man psychodrama.

Suzanne is Fanny Cottencon, whose habitual vivacity fails to dispel the ponderous airs of her partner (she also produced with Coggio). Claude Giraud plays Count Almaviva, not as a corrupt yet dignified nobleman, but as a neurotic wolf, a high-born lowlife on the make. Marie Laforet entirely misses the offended virtuousness of the countess Rosine. Yannick Debain's Cherubin, the poetic lovesick page, displays a shocking physical familiarity with the countess that makes nonsense of this exquisite role.

Veteran comedians Michel

Galabru, Paul Preboist, Roger Carel and Jean Lefebvre fall back on their familiar tics in more stock characterizations.

The one pleasant surprise comes from French music hall star Line Renaud, who has the reserve and embattled dignity of Marceline, the aging housekeeper who pursues Figaro with marital intentions until she discovers him to be her long-lost son. Renaud has what the other principals and the film in general lack: style and substance.

Film was shot in and around a chateau near Paris which (at least as photographed) doesn't reflect the grandeur and importance of its occupants.

Film, like the play, includes Beaumarchais' alternate title "La Folle journée" (The Mad Day), referring to the action's morning-to-night development.—*Len.*

Cage

Hollywood   A New Century/Vista release of a Lang Elliott Entertainment presentation. Produced and directed by Elliott. Coproducer, Jack Roe. Executive producer, Larry J. Lebow. Screenplay, Hugh Kelley; camera (Deluxe color), Jacques Haitkin; editor, Mark S. Westmore; music, Michael Wetherwax; production design, Joseph M. Altadonna; costume design, Sandra Culotta; sound (Dolby), Jon Earl Stein, John G. Geisinger; technical adviser, Kelley; martial arts coordinator, Ketrick (Kit) Kelley; stunt coordinator, Phil Culotta; assistant director, Peter Berquist; associate producer, A. Edward Ezor. Reviewed at AMC Century 14, L.A., Sept. 1, 1989. MPAA Rating: R. Running time: **101 MIN.**

Billy Thomas	Lou Ferrigno
Scott Monroe	Reb Brown
Tony Baccola	Michael Dante
Mario	Mike Moroff
Morgan Garrett	Marilyn Tokuda
Tiger Joe	Al Leong
Tin Lum Yin	James Shigeta
Diablo	Branscombe Richmond
Chang	Tiger Chung Lee
Costello	Al Ruscio
Mono	Daniel Martine

■ "Cage" is an efficient but depressingly brutal exploitation pic about "cage fighting," a gladiatorial sport in which men fight to the death while locked in a steel cage.

New Century/Vista release starring Lou Ferrigno should do okay with undiscriminating action audiences.

Highly offensive ethnic stereotypes abound in this low-rent, lowbrow film produced and directed by Lang Elliott, who depicts Orientals, Mexicans, Italians, blacks and others as equally vile and mercenary types.

The two white heroes are a lovable simpleton who breaks necks when he gets mad (Ferrigno) and a square-jawed blond Aryan type (Reb Brown) who sets a bad guy

on fire and coolly stands back to admire his handiwork.

Hugh Kelley's simpleminded script contends that "human cockfights" are big business in underground establishments in L.A.'s Chinatown, where most of the film is set, and "in Chinese communities all over the world," according to the film's Tong boss, James Shigeta.

In the hands of better filmmakers, this tale could have had elements of genuine tragedy, as did "The Harder They Fall," the powerful 1956 boxing pic about a dimwitted giant brutalized by crooked fight promoters. "Cage" seldom takes Ferrigno's point of view, watching the action instead from the crassly voyeuristic vantage point of the depraved spectators.

Elliott's direction keeps things moving but often strains credibility in presenting the action, failing to rouse truly visceral involvement and relying heavily on crunch-bang-bam soundtrack noises. Jacques Haitkin's lensing is too much on the murky side, perhaps to disguise the poverty-level sets, and Michael Wetherwax' score leans toward the crude   —*Mac.*

Edgar Allan Poe's Masque Of The Red Death

Hollywood   A Concorde Pictures release. Produced by Roger Corman. Directed by Larry Brand. Screenplay, Daryl Haney, Brand from an Edgar Allan Poe story; camera (Foto-Kem color), Edward Pei; editor, Stephen Mark; music, Mark Governor; art direction, Troy Meyers; costume design, Sania M. Hays; sound, Michael Clark; assistant director, Jonathan Allen Winfre; associate producers, Sally Mattison, Adam Moos; casting, Al Guarino. Reviewed at the Hollywood screening room, L.A., Aug. 23, 1989. MPAA Rating: R. Running time: **85 MIN.**

Machiavel	Patrick Macnee
Prospero	Adrian Paul
Julieta	Clare Hoak
Claudio	Jeff Osterhage
Lucrecia	Tracy Reiner

■ If you're attempting a venture as ambitious as this, you'd better have the production wherewithal to back it up. The new "Masque Of The Red Death" doesn't, making it a dubious theatrical release, and an only marginal video item.

The 1964 "Masque" was the seventh of Roger Corman's eight Edgar Allan Poe films. Less adaptations of the stories than gothic melodramas "inspired" by Poe themes, these AIP releases are among the most enjoyable pro-

Original Film

An American Intl. Pictures release of a Roger Corman production. Stars Vincent Price. Features Hazel Court, Jane Asher. Directed by Corman. Screenplay, Charles Beaumont, R. Wright Campbell, from story by Edgar Allan Poe; camera (Panavision, Pathecolor), Nicolas Roeg; editor, Ann Chegwidden; music, David Lee; assistant director, Peter Price. Reviewed at Lytton Center, Hollywood, June 15, 1964. Running time: **86 MIN.**

Prince Prospero	Vincent Price
Juliana	Hazel Court
Francesca	Jane Asher
Gino	David Weston
Alfredo	Patrick Magee
Ludovico	Nigel Green

grammers of the '60s. "Masque Of The Red Death" was Corman's shoot-the-works exercise in style. Its high point was an inspired sequence in which Hazel Court found herself lost in a maze of lushly multicolored rooms.

The rooms in the new "Masque" (shot locally and *very* cheaply), are considerably smaller. In fact, the primary danger on view would appear to come less from the plague dealt with in the plot than the danger of cast members trampling one another.

In the '64 version Vincent Price played Prince Prospero, the film's antihero, as a despot in the grand tradition. Astonished that anyone would object to his taking of his sadistic pleasures, he appeared more annoyed by than fearful of the plague raging just beyond his castle walls. In the new version, director Larry Brand (who also co-scripted with Daryl Haney) Prospero as an oversensitive, sulky, periodically hot-tempered youth. This would be perfectly acceptable, save for the fact that the actor cast — Adrian Paul — seems capable of portraying only the sulky part.

Top-billed Patrick Macnee, cast in the dual role of the prince's tutor and the Red Death himself, shows considerably more acting energy in his brief part.

As the innocent village maiden whose beauty sets Prospero's blood boiling, Clare Hoak is comely, but won't eclipse pleasant memories of Jane Asher in the original. Tracy Reiner, as the prince's sister (and incestuous sex interest) manages better in the Hazel Court role.

For the record, there's another "Masque Of The Red Death" on the way from Menahem Golan's 21st Century Pictures, to be followed by a "(Fall Of) The House Of Usher" from the same company. —*Rens.*

Chud II: Bud The Chud

New York   A Vestron Pictures, Lightning Pictures presentation from MCEG Prods. of a Jonathan D. Krane production. Produced by Krane. Executive producers, Lawrence Kasanoff, Richard Keatinge. Directed by David Irving. Screenplay, "M. Kane Jeeves" (Ed Naha); camera (color), Arnie Sirlin; editor, Barbara Pokras; music, Nicholas Pike; sound (Ultra-Stereo), Richard Waddell; production design, Randy Moore; art direction, Don Day; assistant director, Darcy Brown; production manager-line producer, Anthony Santa Croce; special makeup effects, Makeup & Effects Labs; stunt coordinator, Hubie Kerns; coproducer, Simon R. Lewis; casting, Marla Tate. Reviewed on Vestron vidcassette, N.Y., Aug. 5, 1989. MPAA Rating: R. Running time: **84 MIN.**

Steve	Brian Robbins
Kevin	Bill Calvert
Katie	Tricia Leigh Fisher
Bud the Chud	Gerrit Graham
Masters	Robert Vaughn
Graves	Larry Cedar

Also with: Bianca Jagger, Larry Linville, Judd Omen, Jack Riley, Sandra Kerns, Norman Fell, June Lockhart, Clive Revill, Priscilla Pointer, Rich Hall.

■ One of the least necessary of recent sequels, "Chud II" turns out worse than expected — an unfunny farce dotted with pointless cameos. Ailing Vestron is sending this one direct to video, where, reportedly, the 1984 predecessor developed a following.

Storyline by Ed Naha (hiding behind a pseudonym borrowed from W.C. Fields) has the cannibalistic ghouls of the title slated for extinction when the government cancels a research project. Gerrit Graham is the last one, nicknamed Bud, who escapes when high school students Brian Robbins and Bill Calvert steal his corpse as a replacement for their biology class experiment and accidentally reanimate him with electricity.

Everytime Bud bites somebody (human or animal) it joins him in zombie state. Soon an army of the beasts is prowling the streets of a small town. With evil military commander Robert Vaughn and his men in pursuit, the zombies naturally invade a Halloween party for film's climax.

Stupid gags are executed with poor timing by helmer David Irving, whose mom Priscilla Pointer is part of the endless cameo role roster. Despite her high-up billing, Bianca Jagger pops in for just a few seconds at the end of the picture.

Graham's mugging as the monster is the only fun thing on view. Principal cast is bland. —*Lor.*

Killing Dad
(BRITISH)

London A Scottish Television Film Enterprises in association with British Screen presentation of an Applecross production. Produced by Iain Smith. Written and directed by Michael Austin, based on the novel ''Berg'' by Ann Quinn. Camera (color), Gabriel Beristain; editor, Edward Marnier; production design, Adrienne Atkinson; sound, Ian Voigt; costumes, Sandy Powell. Reviewed at Cannon Shaftsbury Avenue, London, Aug. 10, 1989. (In Edinburgh Film Festival.) Running time: **93 MIN.**
Nathy ....Denholm Elliott
Judith ....Julie Walters
Alistair Berg ....Richard E. Grant
Edith ....Anna Massey
Luisa ....Laura del Sol
Also with: Ann Way, Jonathan Phillips, Kevin Williams.

■ **It would be nice to report that Scottish Television's first foray into feature filmmaking had been successful, but even a first-rate cast giving their all are unable to make ''Killing Dad'' funny. Prospects look dim.**

Following a background of writing scripts for pics like ''Greystoke: The Legend Of Tarzan, Lord Of The Apes,'' first-time writer-director Michael Austin here proves he can direct; unfortunately his script is not up to par. The black humor he is trying for does not come off and he has to resort to slapstick to get the odd laugh.

Pic opens when Edith Berg (Anna Massey) receives a letter from her long-lost husband Nathy (Denholm Elliott) who left home 23 years ago claiming he was going to buy some cigarets. He wants to come home, but the news doesn't please his son Alistair Berg (Richard E. Grant) who enjoys a peaceful existence with his mother.

He travels to Southend, on the coast, checks into the same faded hotel as his father with the plan to kill Elliott. What he finds is an unreformed character who gets drunk, lies and ''borrows'' money and lives with Judith (Julie Walters).

Grant makes friends with Elliott, whose behavior convinces Grant he must kill him. What follows of one of those farcical cases of mistaken identity, with Grant strangling Elliott's ventriloquist's dummy instead of his intended victim and Walters convinced Grant's love for her forced him to kill Elliott.

With Walters in tow he returns to his mother, only to find her in bed with Elliott. Finally disillusioned, he escapes out the back door to try and find Laura del Sol

(Luisa), the exotic dancer who took a shine to him at the hotel in Southport.

The acting is all first-rate; Denholm Elliott has his drunk act down to a fine art, and gives his character an added sly and charming edge. Julie Walters as the faded Judith is excellent, but for her the role is not particularly testing. Richard E. Grant sports a wacky pudding bowl haircut in an attempt to get laughs, but his performance is gently menacing and proves he doesn't always play a role as manic (as in ''Withnail & I'' and ''How To Get Ahead In Advertising''). Grant is fast shaping up as one of Britain's brightest new hopes.

The big problem is Austin's script, which isn't as funny as it thinks it is. The supposed black humor is not on the mark often enough, and even Gabriel Beristain's slick photography, Adrienne Atkinson's fine production design and the excellent actors cannot make up for that fact. —*Adam.*

Cipayos
— La tercera invasión
(Sepoys
— The Third Invasion)
(ARGENTINE)

Buenos Aires An Argentina Sono Film release of a Magma Producciones presentation. Produced by Victor Gabriel Chiesa. Directed by Jorge Coscia. Screenplay, Julio Ferrández Earaibar, Coscia; camera (color), Miguel Miño; editor, Carlo Tedesco, Liliana Nadal; music, José Luis Castiñeira de Dios; sound, Daniel Mosquers; choreography, Irene Castro; sets, Gustavo Fidler; costumes, Angélica Fuentes. Reviewed at Concorde theater, Buenos Aires, Aug. 10, 1989. Running time: **115 MIN.**
With: Guillermo Gramuglia, Virginia Innocenti, Inés Estévez, Carlos March, Claudio Rissi, Eric Morris.

■ **An interesting premise appears to have suffered from sidetracking during execution. A political parable in musical format, this bilingual (Spanish and English) production may attract attention in venues where there is lingering interest in the Falklands/Malvinas war of 1982.**

Another selling point is the flashy — but sometimes derivative — dancing. Film's drawbacks appear mainly attributable to its being designed by a committee, rather than sticking to director-screenwriter Jorge Coscia's original conception.

International audiences may require an introductory explanation to fully understand the film, the characters' motivations, and par-

ticularly the subtitle, ''The Third Invasion.'' Britain militarily invaded Buenos Aires twice, in 1806 and 1807. Defeated by local forces in the capital on both occasions, it instead overran the lightly garrisoned Malvinas/Falkland islands in 1833, where it remained.

The word ''sepoy'' designates the native soldiers who fought on the British side in India, and by extension, anyone who works for an invader. The film imagines a situation in which — presumably as a result of a rekindling of the war in the South Atlantic — Britain has invaded Buenos Aires for the third time, this time successfully, and is in occupation.

The tango has been proscribed, and the only remaining resistance to the occupiers is offered by a group of dancers who keep up that dance form.

The surfeit of dance clutters up and clouds the film's apparent message that military solutions, from either side, are really no solution.

Proficient performances are extracted from a no-name cast — which, as in most Argentine films requiring plentiful English speaking parts, draws heavily from the ranks of the local English-community amateur theater groups. —*Olas.*

Priceless Beauty
(ITALIAN)

Paris A Films Jacques Leitienne release of a Gruppo Bema/Reteitalia coproduction. Executive producers, Ciro Dammicco, Danny B. Besquet. Produced by Nicole Seguin. Written and directed by Charles Finch. Camera (color), Luciano Tovoli; editors, Mirko Garrone, Ruggero Mastroianni; music, Danny B. Besquet; sound, Cario Caputo; music, Danny B. Besquet; production manager, Gianni Stellitano. Reviewed at Triomphe theater, Paris, Aug. 6, 1989. Running time: **90 MIN.**
With: Christophe Lambert (Menroe), Diane Lane (China), Francesco Quinn, Claudia Ohana, Joaquim de Almeida.
(French dialog track)

■ **''Priceless Beauty'' trots out the old genie-in-the-bottle-and-three-wishes routine for this dumb romantic tale starring Christophe Lambert.**

Italo-produced feature, ostensibly shot in English (but reviewed here in French-track version), has premiered in France with minimal publicity and little apparent interest from Lambert-watchers. One can predict a quick home-video reincarnation.

Newcomer Charles Finch (son of the late star Peter Finch) wrote and directed without story sense or new ideas. Lambert plays a pop

star who quits the public spotlight after the death of his brother, killed in a bike accident for which Lambert feels responsible. He withdraws to a Mediterranean isle to nurse his guilt feelings but his agent tracks him down.

In the meantime Lambert fishes a mysteriously luminescent antique vase out of the sea and unleashes its occupant: a nubile young (apprentice) genie who offers him the fulfillment of his dreams. Lambert is skeptical but slips into a grudging romance with the otherworldly messenger.

Although she has promised him anything, she unfortunately can't bring the dead brother back to life, but does arrange for a brief posthumous reunion, which allows Lambert to shed his remorse. Genie has to be sent back to the sea, but the next day Lambert meets on the beach a lovely young girl who's the spitting image of his supernatural amour.

For Lambert this is hardly a congenial vehicle, especially after the pretentious posturing of Michael Cimino's ''The Sicilian.'' The bottle lady is played gauchely by Diane Lane. Francesco Quinn and Claudia Ohana have luckless supporting roles. Luciano Tovoli lensed without great effort, and Ruggero Mastroianni is credited as having supervised the editing. —*Len.*

The Emissary
(SOUTH AFRICAN)

New York A Lars Intl. Pictures presentation of a Scholtz Films production. Executive producers, Johann Schoeman, Les Arlow. Produced, written and directed by Jan Scholtz. Camera (Irene color), Johann Scheepers; editor, Johan Lategan; music, Robyn Smith; sound, Mike Berridge; art direction, François du Plessis; assistant director, Bob Riley; production manager, Desirée Markgraaff. Reviewed on Virgin Vision vidcassette, N.Y., Aug. 16, 1989. MPAA Rating: R. Running time: **94 MIN.**
Jack Cavanaugh ....Ted LePlat
Caroline Cavanaugh ....Terry Norton
Hesse...................Andre Jacobs
Brochard ....Patrick Mynhardt
Ambassador MacKay .....Robert Vaughn
Also with: Jonathan Taylor, Colin Sutcliffe, Hans Strydom, Ken Gampu, Brian O'Shaughnessy.

■ **''The Emissary'' is an okay political nail-biter, unusual among the scores of recent South African-made features aimed at an international audience by not hiding its locale. Pic is a direct-to-video release Stateside.**

Espionage tale concerns the U.S. assistant secretary of state for Africa (Ted LePlat), whom the KGB tries to get under control through his wife Caroline (Terry Norton). Filmmaker Jan Scholtz' screenplay cleverly employs several interesting gambits by which the baddies blackmail her, including drugging her and staging incriminating sex photos as well as exploiting her old flame.

The marital discord between LePlat and Norton adds some dramatic meat to standard spy stuff, though pic never develops the kind of memorable moral ambiguity present in Hitchcock's "Notorious," for example. LePlat is effective in a John Glover-type role, while Norton triumphs over a shaky U.S. accent to make a forceful impression. Robert Vaughn, who's made numerous pics in South Africa in recent years, pops up briefly as the U.S. ambassador.
—*Lor.*

Uma Avenida Chamada Brasil
(An Avenue Called Brazil)
(BRAZILIAN-DOCU)

Rio de Janeiro A Skylight release of an Octavio Bezerra/Uberto Molo production. Executive producer, Jonas Breitman. Written and directed by Octavio Bezerra. Camera (Eastmancolor and video), Miguel Rio Branco; editor, Severino Dada; music, Bruno Nunes, Edson Maciel, Gil Benjamim; sound, Carlos Dela Riva, Antonio Cesar, Walter Goulart; assistant director, Claudia Dutra. Reviewed at Star Ipanema theater, Rio de Janeiro, Aug. 11, 1989. Running time: **85 MIN.**

■ A documentary on Rio's outskirts, "Uma Avenida Chamada Brasil" is a piece of superlative perversity, for it shows nothing but reality. Not a light entertainment, it's highly recommended for people willing to think about the extent to which a society can be cruel.

Thirty-mile-long Brazil Avenue is the gateway to Rio de Janeiro, on which 1-million people circulate every day, coming from suburbs to work in downtown Rio. It also is the link between downtown Rio and virtually every highway leaving for other Brazilian cities, not to count the international airport.

Framed by outdoors, Avenida Brasil in fact camouflages some of the worst living conditions in the world.

Pic goes beyond the outdoors to reveal not an avenue but a country. In doing so, director Octavio Bezerra (who won a special award at Festrio in 1987 for "Memoria Viva," a documentary on artist Aloisio Magalhaes) does not fabricate some of the saddest images a man can see. He just documents — a work that took him two years —

the current cruelty, violence and disregard for human beings. Helmer makes extensive use of video footage. Part of the material in this film was shown at the Intl. Film & TV Festival of New York in 1988 and won the Silver Medal in the national affairs category.

Most sequences are shocking — but also cool. A few shots are staged, but aid comprehension of the situations described. It's hard to discern what is a real cold-blooded shooting or what is staged; what is a rape, a robbery, a drug deal and what is not.
—*Hoin.*

Baptême
(Baptism)
(FRENCH-BELGIAN)

Paris An AAA release of a Films Alyne/SGGC/Man's Films coproduction. Produced, written and directed by René Féret. Camera (Fujicolor), Pierre Lhomme; music, Evelyne Stroh, Chopin; sound, Michel Vionnet, Jacques Thomas-Gérard; art direction, Renaud Sanson; costumes, Barbara Kidd; makeup, Marie-Hélèn Duguet; line producer, Louis Wipf; production manager, Laurent Rigaut; assistant director, Philippe Roussel. Reviewed at Pathé Clichy theater, Paris, Sept. 4, 1989. Running time: **125 MIN.**
Aline . . . . Valérie Stroh
Pierre . . . . Jean-Yves Berteloot
André . . . . Jacques Bonnafé
Maurice . . . . Pierre-Alain Chapuis
Also with: Edith Scob, René Ozo, Clarisse Weber, Dominique Reymond, Valérie Lacombe, Jean Pierre Bonnot, Quentin Ogier.

■ Writer-director René Féret lovingly retraces his own family history in "Baptême," which follows the life of his parents from the time of their marriage in 1935 to the moment of his father's death in 1962.

Made from the heart, it benefits from lucid sincerity and unmannered performances by Valérie Stroh and Jean-Yves Berteloot. It's the kind of unostentatious intimate filmmaking that has appeal in overseas arthouse markets.

Féret keeps his screenplay largely free of dramatic contrivance and thus strengthens the quiet poignancy of its domestic observation. Direction is straightforward, without flourishes or studied effects — as a result picture has a homey, almost artless, simplicity.

Film is set in a mining region of northern France and it's a tribute to Féret and his fine lenser Pierre Lhomme that it isn't bathed in the usual gloom French directors associate with the working-class north.

We are introduced to the principals in the cafe of Stroh's parents where she meets Berteloot, who sells butter at the local market with

his brother, Jacques Bonnafé. Stroh knows what she wants and she wants him — so she does the proposing. She invents a phony pregnancy to override her parents' objections.

After a romantic honeymoon in Corsica, the couple are abruptly yanked back to reality with the sudden death of Stroh's mother. They sell the cafe and take in Stroh's now alcoholically inert father, who soon disappears from the film without comment. We are left to assume he has died. Féret also leaves us largely in the dark as to how the couple fare during the dark war years.

Féret picks up the thread in 1945, when they have a third son, who is given the name of a first child killed in a fire at age three. This last son — Féret presumably — suffers from the feeling that his mother loves him less for himself than as a reincarnation of the dead baby.

The postwar scenes follow the couple's personal and professional difficulties: Stroh's near-affair with a local schoolteacher, Berteloot's discouragement at his poor business acumen and a series of grindingly mediocre jobs. At one point they are reduced to personally collecting debts among local mining families.

The family finally attains a hard-won domestic harmony when a final blow falls: Berteloot is doomed by cancer. Yet it is decided that the sons will go off as planned to pursue their careers and leave the parents alone to see out the remaining months with courage. In the poignant final scene, Stroh, aware that Berteloot has but minutes to live, brings out glasses and a symbolic bottle of champagne to relive a sublime moment of their honeymoon.

Stroh and Berteloot suggest that passing of years without recourse to heavy makeup, but with subtle attention to gestural and psychological verisimilitude of their characters. Among supporting cast, Bonnafé is fine as Berteloot's more materially successful brother, obsessed with having a son (after five daughters) and finally getting one.

Production is modest but professional. —*Len.*

L'Invité surprise
(The Surprise Guest)
(FRENCH)

Paris A Gaumont release of a Gaumont/-

Gaumont Intl./TF-1 Films coproduction. Produced by Alain Poiré. Directed by Georges Lautner. Screenplay, Didier van Cauwelaert, Lautner; camera (Eastmancolor), Yves Rodallec; editor, Michelle David; music, Philippe Sarde; sound, Alain Lachassagne; art direction, Jacques Dugied; assistant director, Dominique Brunner; production manager, Marc Goldstaub, Guy Azzi; casting, Mamade. Reviewed at Gaumont Ambassade theater, Paris, Aug. 28, 1989. Running time: **86 MIN.**
With: Eric Blanc, Victor Lanoux, Jean Carmet, Michel Galabru, Jacques François, Renée Saint-Cyr, Françoise Dorner, Gérard Hernandez, Florence Geanty, Jean Rougerie, Agnes Blanchot.

■ This awful suspense farce casts funnyman Eric Blanc as the witness of a car bombing that transforms him overnight into a reluctant media celebrity and the bugbear of a French secret service department, which apparently is behind the incident and eager to shut him up.

Director Georges Lautner and price-winning novelist Didier van Cauwelaert (who dialogued Lautner's previous film, "The Murdered House") pile pointless incident and stock characters into a plot that splutters and starts without genuine wit or comic tension. Direction is flabby from the start with a faked assassination during a tv quiz show.

The glib looselimbed Blanc joshes fearlessly through the action. No wonder, since he is the stepson of ace crimebuster Victor Lanoux, who's been ousted for excess of zeal and now feigns a physical handicap. The ex-cop comes out of his wheelchair to help keep Blanc out of the clutches of commissioner Michel Galabru (funny in his usual facile manner) and secret service honcho Jean Carmet.

But this is one of those films that should have remained in the files.
—*Len.*

Täcknamn Coq Rouge
(Cover Name Coq Rouge)
(SWEDISH)

Stockholm A Sandrews release of a Spice Film production in association with the Swedish Film Institute, Sandrews, STV-2, Sonet Media. Produced by Peter Hald, Hans Iveberg. Written and directed by Pelle Berglund, based on the novel by Jan Guillou. Camera (Eastmancolor), Göran Nilsson; editor, Björn Gunnarsson; music, Ulf Dageby; sound, Lars Liljeholm, Patrik Strömdahl; production design, Anders Barréus; costumes, Lenamari Wallström; special effects, Horst Stadlinger, Soft Effects, Lars Höglund; production management, Sweden, Jutta Ekman; Morocco, Mohammed Abbazi. Reviewed at Sandrews-1, Stockholm, Aug. 29, 1989. Running time: **90 MIN.**
Hamilton . . . . Stellan Skarsgard
Näslund . . . . Lennart Hjulström
Fristedt . . . . Krister Henriksen
Appeltoft . . . . Philip Zandén
The Old One . . . . Bengt Eklund

Also with: Saim Ursay, Tuncel Kurtiz. Anette Kischinowsky, Lars Green, Roland Hedlund, Harald Hamrell, Lena T. Hansson, Gustaf Skarsgard, Janos Hersko, Ulrikka Hansson, Gerhard Hoberstorfer, Lars Engström, Lars (Tjadden) Hällström.

■ Sweden, forever boastful of her neutrality, tends to get involved with offshore, big-time politics every so often, and "Cover Name Coq Rouge," a secret agent thriller, has the Nordic Kingdom knee-deep in Middle East plotting and terrorist killings.

Writer-director Pelle Berglund and novelist Jan Guillou, on whose book the film is based, more than indicate that all this is for real. Maybe so, but seen from the outside, this item has that homevideo look.

Stellan Skarsgard, the brilliant Royal Dramaten Theater actor who also appeared in Philip Kaufman's "The Unbearable Lightness Of Being," seems to be mostly sleepwalking through his lead role. He's an aristocratic former leftist intellectual, now naval officer Carl Gustav Gilbert Hamilton, who is recruited by Sweden's Säpo (secret service) to look into the allegedly Palestinian killing of a foreign office Mideast expert. When the killer turns out to be an Israeli, a tight lid is slammed on the case.

Hamilton, however, travels to Israel to follow certain clues. At home, he has been surrounded by police and establishment clowns or, at best, dour skeptics. In Israel and Lebanon (apart from stock shots of Jerusalem, Morocco is the location used), Mossad agents are fooled while Al Fatah chieftains are convinced the Swede merits their help. Hamilton finds his clues and returns home in time for Christmas except that his Yuletide idyll with a small nephew entrusted to his care nearly gets spoiled because he first has to kill off four Israeli ultrarightist terrorists.

Pic cites the real case of a decade ago in Lillehammer, Norway, where Mossad agents defied Norse sovereignty to kill what they took to be a Palestinian terrorist (the man turned out to be an innocent Moroccan worker). "Cover Name Coq Rouge" really goes to town in describing wholesale carnage instigated by the Israelis (supplied with Lebanese passports) before Hamilton gets to them.

The film actually is at its best when describing agent Hamilton as the classic lone wolf sleuth walking the corridors of stupid officialdom. When the blood and gore occur, they do not tie together too clearly with the general narrative.

Cinematographer Göran Nilsson has supplied fluent work throughout to accentuate both action and atmosphere. —*Kell.*

TORONTO FESTIVAL OF FESTIVALS REVIEWS

In Country

Toronto A Warner Bros. release of a Richard Roth production. Produced by Norman Jewison, Roth. Executive producer, Charles Mulvehill. Directed by Jewison. Screenplay, Frank Pierson, Cynthia Cidre, based on novel by Bobbie Ann Mason; camera (Technicolor), Russell Boyd; editor, Anthony Gibbs, Lou Lombardo; music, James Horner; sound (Dolby), Scott Smith; production design, Jackson DeGovia; art direction, John Jensen; costumes, Aggie Guerard Rodgers; assistant director, H. Gordon Boos; associate producer, Michael Jewison; casting, Howard Feuer. Reviewed at Toronto Festival of Festivals, Sept. 7, 1989. MPAA Rating: R. Running time: 120 MIN.
Emmett Smith . . . . Bruce Willis
Samantha Hughes . . . . Emily Lloyd
Irene . . . . Joan Allen
Lonnie . . . . Kevin Anderson
Tom . . . . John Terry
Mamaw . . . . Peggy Rea
Anita . . . . Judith Ivey
Dwayne . . . . Dan Jenkins
Earl . . . . Jim Beaver
Grampaw . . . . Richard Hamilton
  Also with: Heidi Swedberg, Ken Jenkins, Jonathan Hogan, Patricia Richardson, Kimberly Faith Jones.

■ Norman Jewison usually is a commanding storyteller, but "In Country" is a film with two stories that fail to add up to something greater: a country girl's coming of age, and a troubled Vietnam veteran's coming to terms with his haunting memories of war.

While it aims at the noblest sentimental impulses, "In Country" never transcends its own sincerity. It's possible, but not very likely, that the film will tempt large audiences to participate with it in a collective catharsis of unresolved Vietnam-era grief.

Emily Lloyd, in a sparky performance that seizes control of the movie, plays Samantha Hughes, a spirited, just-minted high school graduate from the small town of Hopewell, Ky. She lives in a ramshackle house with Bruce Willis, who turns in a likable but unremarkable interpretation of her moody uncle Emmett, a veteran who has suffered lasting emotional damage from his nightmarish tour of duty in 'Nam. He's a stolid, brooding man who suffers from punishing headaches, rashes and a general disinterest in life. Some townfolk think he's crazy, but the character most certainly is not.

Lloyd's father, who also served "in country," was killed in combat before she was born. She likes the freedom of living with Willis, who permits Lloyd unsupervised liaisons with her callow basketball star boyfriend (Kevin Anderson). She's not especially close to her mother, Willis' sister, played deftly by Joan Allen. Mom has had the bad taste to move from hick Hopeful to Lexington, marry a yuppie, enroll in college, have a baby and otherwise get on with her upwardly mobile life. Lloyd does have an affinity for her cliché hillbilly grandparents, "Mamaw" (Peggy Rea) and "Grampaw" (Richard Hamilton), wise old folks who have endured.

An obsessive jogger, Lloyd presumably is running toward an undefined future filled with the freedom she craves. Her peripatetic workouts to the Walkman accompaniment of Bruce Springsteen's "I'm On Fire" provide a convenient device for touring Hopewell. It's a changing hill town, where people are better off and better educated than they were 20 years ago.

The only ones living in the past are Emmett and his small circle of Vietnam veteran buddies. The rambling screenplay, based on the novel by Bobbie Ann Mason, hangs on to the point that the kids who lost their youth and lives in Vietnam were mostly country boys. Having been to hell and back, the vets have seen the unspeakable, and consequently they relate better to one another than to their wives and girlfriends. Their collective pain intensifies when a Vietnam veterans dance is virtually ignored by neighbors, who've dismissed the war as just another bad, long-forgotten tv show.

Lloyd seizes the bittersweet social occasion to seduce a good-looking mechanic (John Terry) who also has been physically scarred by his wartime experience. Like Willis, he keeps Lloyd at bay when her interest in Vietnam and the circumstances of her father's death begin to intensify. She makes an icon of her father's military photo, which she discovered in a cache of his love letters from the field that was abandoned by her mother. Poring through the missives — read by the soldier in a maudlin voiceover-from-the-grave — Lloyd becomes so upset that she leaves a scalding message on mom's answering machine condemning her disloyalty to his memory.

In one of the film's best scenes, Allen confronts the pain of recollection to explain to her daughter the way things were 20 long years before: She was married for a month to a boy she hardly knew then and can hardly remember now. "Go on with life," is her advice to Lloyd. Their reconciliation is one of several that fill the film up with its own big-heartedness.

Lloyd's quest for the truth of Vietnam and her father's death is uncertainly achieved through elegiac flashbacks that combine Willis' terrible memories of combat with the last patrol of Lloyd's father. Jewison evokes an otherworldly Vietnam jungle nightscape lit with ghostly flares and fraught with terror. Yet the warzone flashbacks seem gratuitously staged and manipulative in a film that never ceases to call attention to its concern with the big theme of memory and reconciliation.

When Lloyd comes to realize her father may have participated in atrocities, Willis upbraids her for her loss of faith in his memory. He argues that the slaughter of innocents could not be avoided under the war's dirty circumstances, and that the perpetrators have paid the price through a lifetime of suffering.

In dutiful formula fashion, "In Country" arrives at an affirmative resolution with a visit by Lloyd, Willis and Mamaw to the Vietnam Memorial in Washington, D.C. It's a scene that's sensitively handled and moving, but also manipulative and self-serving. It's a resolution that's too pat a tidying up of all the inarticulated grief and yearnings that have led up to it.

Willis generates sympathy for his tormented character, but the 1-dimensional script and his still limited range (not compensated for by a Fu Manchu beard and diz) conspire to make Emmett a stolid caricature of the spiritually wounded veteran. Lloyd is permitted to dominate the movie and does so with an appealing but uncontrolled energy that makes "In Country" essentially Samantha's story.

Supporting performances, particularly Rea's Mamaw, are solid, and the film has good-to-look-at cinematography and design. Yet "In Country," unlike the superior "Jacknife," is so earnest that it never breaks through to the buried commonality of hurt that it self-righteously strikes to evoke.

—*Rich.*

Itanong Mo Sa Buwan (The Moonchild)

Toronto   A Double M Films Intl. production. Executive producer, Roberto Genova. Produced by Edgardo Instrella. Directed by Chito Rono. Screenplay, Armando Lao; camera (color), Charlie Peralta; editor, Chito Rono; music, Toto Fentica; sound, Ramon Reyes; art direction, Leo Ataya. Reviewed at Toronto Festival of Festivals, Sept. 8, 1989. Running time: **115 MIN.**
Josie . . . . Jaclyn Jose
Angel . . . . Mark Gil

■ **Seductive and disturbing images emerge from helmer Chito Rono's portrait of a fictionalized hostage-taking "love affair" in the Philippines.**

After Angel robs a bank and takes the bank teller (Josie) hostage, their conflicting accounts of the incident to family and police smear lies and reality into an indecipherable melting pot.

In flashback, Josie (played provocatively by Jaclyn Jose), spins a tale where she used both wit and sexual prowess to escape her captor's beatings and abuse. Her husband doubts the story and her stuffy mother-in-law's outright accusations foretell Angel's version.

In real time, Angel swears on his death bed that they were lovers and had contrived the holdup together as a means of escaping their spouses.

Rono decidedly avoids revealing which is the "true" story, yet hints strongly that Josie is a she-devil who manipulates both the lover and husband. Audience is left to judge.

Erotic scenes indicate pic will fare well in appropriate outlets. Soap opera-type storyline implying infidelity, stale marriage and uncontrollable lust is ideal for pay-tv and vidcassette venues. —*Suze.*

A Dry White Season

Toronto   An MGM/UA Distribution release of an MGM Pictures presentation. Produced by Paula Weinstein. Executive producer, Tim Hampton. Directed by Euzhan Palcy. Screenplay, Colin Welland, Palcy, based on the novel by Andre Brink; camera (Deluxe color), Kelvin Pike, Pierre-William Glenn; editor, Sam O'Steen, Glenn Cunningham; music, Dave Grusin; art direction, Alan Tomkins, Mike Phillips; production design, John Fenner; associate producer, Mary Selway; production supervisor, Vincent Winter; sound (Dolby), Roy Charman; assistant director, Michael Cheyko; casting, Selway, Wallace Nicita. Reviewed at Toronto Festival of Festivals, Sept. 6, 1989. Running time: **97 MIN.**
Ben du Toit . . . . Donald Sutherland
Gordon Ngubene . . . . Winston Ntshona
Stanley . . . . Zakes Mokae
Captain Stolz . . . . Jurgen Prochnow
Melanie Bruwer . . . . Susan Sarandon
Ian McKenzie . . . . Marlon Brando
Susan du Toit . . . . Janet Suzman
Emily Ngubene . . . . Thoko Ntshinga
Suzette du Toit . . . . Susannah Harker
Mr. Bruwer . . . . Leonard Maguire
Johan du Toit . . . . Rowen Elmes
 Also with: Gerard Thoolen, Stella Dickin, David de Keyser, Andrew Whaley, John Kani, Sophie Mgcina, Bekhithemba Mpofu, Tinashe Makoni, Precious Thiri, Richard Wilson, Derek Hanekom, Michael Gambon, Paul Brooke.

■ **If audiences are prepared for a wrenching picture about South Africa that makes no expedient compromises with feel-good entertainment values, the riveting performance and visceral style on display in "A Dry White Season" could help it to succeed where "Cry Freedom" failed.**

Comparisons between the two films are inevitable, and some critics are bound to protest that Hollywood once again has been unable to make a film about apartheid state terror without spotlighting a white hero. "Cry Freedom" left itself open to such charges by carelessly shifting its focus from the cruel reality of South Africa's black townships to the melodramatic escape of a liberal white editor.

Filmmaker Euzhan Palcy — who is black — never tempers her outrage, but "A Dry White Season" drives home the point that the story of South Africa is a story of two races that's unlikely to be resolved by either one alone.

Set in 1976, the film moves quickly to a searing sequence in which a demonstration by black schoolchildren of Soweto is broken up with gratuitous lethal force. Police and troops teargas, then open fire on the fleeing children, killing many. Others are brutally beaten and arrested, including the son of Winston Ntshona, a gardener who works at the comfortable home of naive prep school teacher Donald Sutherland.

Sutherland is a basically decent man who cares enough to pay for the missing boy's schooling but not enough to question society's blatantly unjust status quo. In the film's opening scene, when Ntshona's son is arrested and beaten for the crime of not running fast enough, Sutherland tells the father upon his release that the authorities "must have had a reason."

When Ntshona's boy does not return from his second trip to prison, Sutherland promises the distraught father he'll use his influence to investigate. He learns the boy has been killed and buried in an unmarked grave. When Ntshona presses his own investigation into his son's fate, he is arrested and tortured unto death by Jurgen Prochnow, a sadistic captain of the feared Special Branch police. The filmmaker's graphic depiction of this bloody business manipulates the viewer's sympathies, but is believable in light of South Africa's recent history.

When Sutherland learns of the gardener's fate he undergoes a crisis of conscience. With mounting astonishment this community pillar — a respected family man, ex-rugby star and old-line Afrikaner — comes to discover what he's always closed his eyes to: South African "justice and law could be described as distant cousins — not on speaking terms."

Those words are spoken by Marlon Brando, rising with a world-weary magnificence to the role of a prominent human rights attorney whose idealism has been battered into resignation. Reluctantly, he's persuaded by Sutherland to haul Prochnow into court on a murder charge. Brando's phlegmatic attorney is beyond outrage at playing his courtroom hand against a stacked deck. Sarcasm is his only tactic, the moral high ground his only refuge as Brando proves Prochnow a murderer, but loses his case before a judge who makes no effort to hide his disgraceful bias.

The jurist is the defender of all that the film's smug white characters hold sacred: separation of the races, the equation of human rights with "communism" and the concept that their civilization can be saved from the "savages" only by savagery.

Brando disappears after these transfixing moments on screen, but the Catch-22 trial radicalizes Sutherland. His family, friends and coworkers are astonished and scandalized by the burning metamorphosis of the mild-mannered teacher. Soon he is visiting Soweto and working with dedicated activist Zakes Mokae to build a new case against Prochnow.

Also unsympathetic, but from a different perspective, is cynical liberal journalist Susan Sarandon.

A hardened veteran of the white anti-apartheid minority, she scoffs at Sutherland's late awakening but agrees to help him by publishing whatever evidence can be dug up against the Special Branch. Sarandon is English, not Afrikaner, and the screenplay hints at wanting to further explore the historical antipathies between South Africa's two white groups. Sarandon's character, however, is used only as a device to further the plot, and the actress is given no opportunity to do anything but demonstrate a competent Anglo accent.

The story of South Africa has not had a happy ending, and neither does "A Dry White Season." Palcy offers the viewer the bittersweet satisfaction of vengeance and an opaque ray of hope, but hope, as Mokae tells Sutherland, "is a white man's word." Nevertheless, the film's dual perspective crystalizes its heroes' resistance to systemized evil as a moral imperative.

Sutherland gives one of his best recent performances as the reluctantly galvanized Ben du Toit, and his evolving relationship with the charismatic Mokae serves to personalize the film's concern with big issues.

In her first film since the charmingly crafted "Sugar Cane Alley," Palcy demonstrates a firm grip on bigger-budget logistics, and moves the story inexorably toward its grim conclusion. Zimbabwe locations are thoroughly authentic, as are the song track by Hugh Masekela, Ladysmith Black Mambazo and the cast of "Sarafina."

—*Rich.*

The Traveller (CANADIAN)

Toronto   A BLP/Lighthouse Films production. Produced by Bruno Lazaro Pacheco, Raymond Massey. Directed by Pacheco. Screenplay, Pacheco, Jean Pierre Lefebvre, based on an original story and French screenplay by Guy P. Buchholtzer; camera (color), Thomas H. Turnbull; editor, Pacheco, Patricia Lambkin; music, Daniel Ross; sound, Michael Williamson, Jeff Butterworth. Reviewed at Bloor Cinema, Toronto, Aug. 31, 1989. (In Toronto Festival of Festivals.) Running time: **96 MIN.**
 With: R. Lewis Morrison, Ginette St. Denis, Denise Brillon, Phillip Stewart, James Stevens, Arlen Jones.

■ **A plodding, melancholy journey of self, "The Traveller" will find very few takers for its trip tics. Sluggish direction and script by Bruno Lazaro Pacheco make it a difficult outing, saved only by lovely photography of**

British Columbia's mountain and lake vistas.

Story focuses on Robert Braun (R. Lewis Morrison), who arrives in Vancouver on a buying trip for his thriving business in Pacific Northwest Indian masks. He's deeply troubled, and through a series of flashbacks, we learn that he was raised as a white among native Indians, was married to a Haida woman, and was a strong native rights activist during his university days.

Now his midlife turning point is manifested in coming to terms with the financial benefits of his craft business vs. the emotional and psychological break he does not seem to have made with his roots.

He has an adulterous encounter with a woman he meets at his hotel, Ginette (Ginette St. Denis), who enlists his ex-anthropology professor status to narrate a series of videotapes about Indian lore for her academic needs.

He then feels compelled to drive up north to search out his land, initially in Ginette's car and then solo when she says she's not into it. He visits the majestic mountains where he raced hand-carved canoes with his Indian buddies. After being rescued in the boat he buys to paddle up to his old home, he winds up at a local dance hall at which he meets up with his ex-wife.

Morrison is as wooden as the carved masks he sells. The romantic relationship between him and St. Denis is completely unconvincing, and Morrison's angst is more annoying than existential.

In his feature directorial debut, Pacheco is not successful at unfolding a midlife crisis of culture. Even the pastoral beauty of the Canadian west cannon carry the pic further than the limited actors can take it. —Devo.

The Reincarnation Of Golden Lotus
(HONG KONG)

Toronto   A Golden Harvest Group production. Executive producer, Raymond Chow. Produced by Teddy Robins. Directed by Clara Law. Screenplay, Lee Pik Wah; camera (color), Ma Chor Shing; editor, Hamilton Yu; music, Teddy Robins, Richard Lo; art direction, Lee King Man, Yuen Ching Yeung, Tang Wei Ling, Chan Yiu Wing. Reviewed at Toronto Festival of Festivals, Sept. 8, 1989. Running time: 99 MIN.
Lotus . . . . Joi Wong
Wu Dai, husband . . . . Eric Tsang
Brother-in-law . . . . Lam Chun Yen
Designer/lover . . . . Sin Lap Man

■The ancient myth of China's most reputed fallen woman is married seamlessly to a contemporary tragic love story in a festival gem that should fare well with film buffs.

After the necessary leap of logic where "the number one slut in ancient Chinese history" is reincarnated as Lotus, pic begins in Shanghai, 1966, amid political upheaval. Young Lotus is quickly labeled as counter-revolutionary without reason, and her hopeless tale begins to unfold again.

Subtly denouncing Maoist partyline propaganda, film focuses on the tragedies which accompany impersonal, hard-line politics, not on politics itself.

Like the ancient Golden Lotus, the young Lotus is doomed from the start by her innocent desires. After being raped, she falls in love with a young man (who later becomes her brother-in-law), but political pressures on the man result in her being labeled a "slut." She marries a rich man from Hong Kong to escape her vile existence.

Comical sex scenes with her husband justify her buried desire, which, after once again being rejected by the brother-in-law, is focused on a trendy fashion designer, who will cause her nothing but grief.

Flashback sequences serve as the temptress' surrealist visions, where the same actors play similar characters in ancient China. When contemporary Lotus finally reads the old myth — now outlawed as pornography — the two stories meet for a romantic and tragic finale.

Editing and camerawork enhance the story. Music is over-dramatized, but otherwise film is a fine effort. —Suze.

Where The Spirit Lives
(CANADIAN)

Toronto   An Amazing Spirit production, in association with the Canadian Broadcasting Corp., Mid-Canada TV and TV Ontario. (Intl. sales, Atlantis Releasing, Toronto.) Executive producer, Paul Stephens. Produced by Heather Goldin, Eric Jordan, Mary Young Leckie. Directed by Bruce Pittman. Screenplay, Keith Ross Leckie; camera (color), Rene Ohashi; editor, Michael Todd; music, Buffy Sainte Marie; art direction, Valanne Ridgeway. Reviewed at Toronto Festival of Festivals, Sept. 9, 1989. Running time: 97 MIN.
Komi/Amelia . . . . Michelle St. John
Pita/Abraham . . . . Clayton Julian
Rachel . . . . Heather Hess
Kathleen . . . . Ann-Marie Macdonald
Taggert . . . . Ron White
Miss Appleby . . . . Chapelle Jaffe
Reverend Buckley . . . . David Hemblen
Mrs. Barrington . . . . Patricia Collins

■If all low-budget Canadian pics were as original, well made and superbly acted as "Where The Spirit Lives," the millions of dollars pumped into production every year by public agencies would be wisely spent.

Reaching back to a horrifying chapter of Canadian history, the family pic fictionalizes the routine kidnaping by the federal government of native Indian children from their reserves and their incarceration in religious schools where all traces of their background and language were beaten out of them.

Keith Ross Leckie's always riveting and unsentimental tale centers on a rebellious teenage girl (Michelle St. John) airlifted from home with her younger brother (Clayton Julian) and locked in the school.

She is taught by a compassionate white schoolteacher (Ann-Marie Macdonald), a newcomer who's also an outsider and appalled (but most times shyly silenced) by the treatment the children receive. The federal goverment Indian agent (Ron White) openly loathes his work and finally quits.

Doing "God's work," school officials brutalize the children. One female teacher (Chapelle Jaffe) even commits lesbian acts off-camera with a native Indian student too terrified to protest to authorities.

The young heroine, who finally succumbs, is about to let herself be "adopted" by the school's rich white patroness when she discovered that the school's clergyman has lied about her parents being dead. In a final defiance, she escapes with her brother and her teacher's blessing.

Bruce Pittman's direction bursts with talent. Lecke's first produced screenplay demonstrates storytelling without polemic.

Screen newcomer St. John is outstanding in the lead role. Pic boasts excellent performances in all roles, from professionals including Jaffe, White, David Hemblen and Patricia Collins to nonpro native children including Clayton Julian and Franklin Doss in film debuts.

Rene Ohashi's camerawork is superb. Technical credits are first-class. So is music composed and sung by Buffy Sainte Marie. Credit, too, to Norman Jewison for personally providing extra funds for completion of postproduction.

This pic deserves theatrical life, more than many made in Canada, but because the Canadan Broadcasting Corp. is a key investor it is to go directly to tv, airing on CBC-TV Oct. 29. Too bad. Outside the country, it should be treated better. —Adil.

Penn & Teller Get Killed

Boston   A Warner Bros. release of a Lorimar Film Entertainment presentation. Produced and directed by Arthur Penn. Coproduced by Timothy Marx. Screenplay, Penn Jillette and Teller; camera (Panavision, color), Jan Weincke; editor, Jeffrey Wolf; music, Paul Chihara; sound (Dolby), John Sutton 3d; production design, John Arnone; costumes, Rita Ryack; assistant director, Lewis Gould; casting, Meg Simon, Fran Kumin. Reviewed at Loews screening room, Boston, Aug. 31, 1989. (In Boston and Toronto film festivals.) MPAA Rating: R. Running time: 89 MIN.
Penn . . . . Penn Jillette
Teller . . . . Teller
Carlotta . . . . Caitlin Clarke
Fan . . . . David Patrick Kelly
Ernesto . . . . Leonardo Cimino
Jesus freak . . . . Christopher Durang
Old cop . . . . Alan North
Also with: Jon Cryer.

■ "Penn & Teller Get Killed" is a funny, albeit sick movie which should attract notice among the comedy team's fans in first run, and then begin a long life as a cult hit on the midnight circuit.

Humor is on the order of a cult film of the past, "Harold And Maude," with jokes turning on suicide and attempted murder.

Penn & Teller, self-styled "bad boys of magic," play themselves, opening with one of their bizarre acts on a national tv program. During the interview segment, Penn makes a joke about how much fun it would be if a killer actually was stalking him. What follows is a series of practical jokes between Penn and Teller that suddenly turns serious as it appears there is a real-life killer out to get them.

The trick of the film is that each of the practical jokes gets more and more bizarre, but the real joke is on the audience who have to wonder whether any given sequence is "real" or another one of their stunts. Final payoff fully lives up to all that came before it. Moral of the story, according to Penn, is that "one should never go on national tv and beg psychopaths to kill one."

Besides their various outlaw magic acts, Penn and the usually speechless Teller are required to act, and they are able to carry off the job of playing a variation of their stage personalities. Teller speaks only briefly late in the film.

Among the supporting cast, standout is Caitlin Clarke who has several roles to play in the various pranks, and carries them off flawlessly. Other familiar faces popping up in bits are actors Alan North and Jon Cryer and playwright Christopher Durang.

Visually, film seems to be a bit on the flat side, with director Arthur Penn leaving the flamboyance to his stars. There also is an unusual number of plugs for Trump Tower (where part of the film was shot) and Diet Coke.

Result is a pic that people will either love or hate, but those who love it are likely to want to go back and see it again. Get those midnight slots ready. —*Kimm*.

Roger And Me
(DOCU)

Toronto A Dog Eat Dog Films production. Produced and directed by Michael Moore. Camera (color, 16m), Chris Beaver, John Prusak, Kevin Rafferty, Bruce Schermer; editors, Wendey Stanzler, Jennifer Berman; sound, Judy Irving, Charley Arnot. Reviewed at Toronto Festival of Festivals, Sept. 9, 1989. (Also in New York Film Festival). Running time: 90 MIN.

■ "Roger And Me" is a cheeky and smart indictment against General Motors for closing its truck plant in Flint, Mich., throwing 30,000 employees out of work and, as a result, leaving many neighborhoods abandoned.

Michael Moore, a Flint native who recalls the prosperous "Great American Dream" days of his 1950s childhood, launches a 1-man documentary crusade to bring GM chairman Roger Smith back to town. He wants Smith to see the human tragedy caused by the plant closing.

With cameras turning, Moore tries several times but never gets past the ground floor of GM headquarters. He is refused an interview because he "doesn't represent anyone" and later has the microphone cut off while attempting to confront Smith at a GM stockholders meeting he has infiltrated.

He interviews fired workers, shows decaying houses across the city and two grandiose schemes to reactivate the town: the opening of a Hyatt Regency hotel and a huge shopping mall. Both fail quickly for lack of business. Tourists don' come to Flint.

The local sheriff is shown evicting ex-autoworkers, some even on Christmas Eve, a job he does not enjoy. Moore interviews Flint native Bob Eubanks, of tv's "The Newlywed Game," on a return visit and Eubanks openly make offensive jokes about women and gays.

Pat Boone and Anita Bryant entertain local audiences at a GM funded theater and in interview just advise workers to look to better days. Evangelist Robert Schuller delivers virtually the same empty message.

Intercut are scenes of the town' rich, who seem oblivious to the plight of their fellow citizens and wonder what the fuss is about.

The crime rate rises and civic officials spearhead the public burning of an issue of Money magazine that names Flint "the worst place to live in the U.S."

GM's only response is to build a theme park, Autoworld, which ironically features a puppet autoworker singing a love song to a robot.

Moore, who describes his tracking of Smith across the U.S. at his own expense, finally catches his quarry only long enough for Smith to refuse to come to Flint.

Moore's father worked at the GM spark plug plant for 33 years and the son has carved out a dandy personal docu that makes hash of the American Dream, which was fostered, as he shows, by 1950s GM-sponsored tv variety series with Dinah Shore and Boone.

Pic is 1-sided, for sure, but Moore makes no pretense otherwise. The irony of the title pervades the piece. The effect is absorbing. Its prospects: festivals and public tv and possible limited theatrical life. —*Adil*.

American Boyfriends
(CANADIAN)

Toronto An Alliance Entertainment release (in Canada) of an Alliance Entertainment in association with First Choice production. Executive producer, Robert Lantos. Produced by Steve De Nure. Written, directed and coproduced by Sandy Wilson. Camera (color), Brenton Spencer; editor, Lara Mazur; music, Terry Frewer; production design, Philip Schmidt; costumes, Sheila Bingham; associate producer, Ralph Zimmerman. Reviewed at Cineplex Odeon screening room, Toronto, Aug. 31, 1989. (In Toronto Festival of Festivals.) Running time: 100 MIN.

Sandy Wilcox	Margaret Langrick
Butch	John Wildman
Marty	Jason Blicker
Julie	Liisa Ropo Martell
Thelma	Michele Bardeaux
Lizzie	Dela Brett
Daryl	Scott Anderson
Spider	Troy Mallory

■ With "My American Cousin" director Sandy Wilson cornered the market on charm with her joyful coming-of-age story, but she seems to have lost her touch in the sequel, "American Boyfriends."

Audiences will naturally be curious about heroine Sandy's social development and her relationship with her blond hunk of an American cousin, Butch, but film's focus is too scattered and what was once fetching now plays flat.

Although pic kicks off with another of Sandy's (Margaret Langrick's) diary entries, "Love changes everything," Sandy is no longer the real center of gravity of the film, and her plucky point of view is missing.

It's the mid-'60s in British Columbia, and Sandy's off to Vancouver's Simon Fraser U. Her girlfriends are getting married and everyone's talking about "doing it" as they set their hair in curlers, watch "The Jetsons" and eat Metrecal wafers.

When Sandy gets an invitation to Butch's (John Wildman) wedding, she convinces her soon-to-be married friend Thelma, her now roommate Julie, and her best buddy Lizzie to take a ride in Julie's VW bug to Portland and crash the affair.

The buzzword at the wedding is Vietnam, and American boys are being drafted. Butch gives Sandy his fire-engine red Cadillac as a wedding present, so she and Julie decide to cruise down the coast to California and find some American dream surfer boys of their own.

The only guys they meet on the beach at Santa Cruz are from Canada, until they rescue a black UCLA student, Spider, and his Bronx-born, Jewish Dylanesque sidekick, Marty, from a bar brawl and hang out with them.

Sandy wakes up to social concerns, to Spider and Marty's freedom fighter speeches, and to U.S.'s involvement in an undeclared war. When she calls Lizzie (who's lost her virginity to a marine she met at Butch's wedding) she finds out that Butch was killed in a car crash, so she rushes back to the funeral.

Butch's role is reduced to a cameo, and his relationship with Sandy is almost incidental here. Too bad it wasn't fleshed out more fully in this film, as it was the crucial dynamic in the first one.

Wilson still crystalizes the burning issues of giggling teenage girls' lives — neverending discussions about losing your virginity, birth control, makeup, boys, and parental gripes.

Art direction, costumes, hairstyles and musical score are on the mark, establishing a clear sense of time and place.

Wilson is undermined by her own weak script filled with unexceptional teen life events. She needed a clearer point of view to focus the agenda of her story here. Sandy the heroine doesn't get a chance to be as feisty as she was — she can mature but it doesn't have to be at the expense of her endearing personality. —*Devo*.

The Vacant Lot
(CANADIAN)

Toronto A Picture Plant Ltd. production. (Intl. sales Film Transit). Produced by Terry Greenlaw. Written and directed by William D. MacGillivray. Camera (color), Lionel Simmons; editor, Angela Baker, MacGillivray; art direction, Angela Murphy; sound, Jim Rillie. Reviewed at Bloor Cinema, Toronto, Sept. 6, 1989 (in Toronto Festival of Festivals). Running time: 100 MIN.

With: Trudi Petersen, Grant Fullerton, Barbara Nicholson, Rick Mercer, Caitlyn Colquhoun, Cheryl Reid, Tara Wilde.

■ "The Vacant Lot" is the moniker of the all-girl, postpunk feminist rock band that is the anchor in Novia Scotia director Bill MacGillivray's latest feature. It could also describe the soul of the film as well as its characters.

This one will play much better on the small screen than theatrically.

Two alienated people living in Halifax hook up through their love of music in this odd couple tale. Trudi (Trudi Petersen) is a pretty blond teenager living in a mobile home with her embittered mother and sister after the family was abandoned by her father, a peripatetic musician. David (Grant Fullerton) is an older ex-great guitarist from the '60s who never made it, but gets gigs where he can. He generally sits around, strumming chords and feeling sorry for himself.

David meets Trudi at the library, where she works on Saturdays, and they hang out together. When Trudi breaks her arm in a car accident, she enlists David to replace her as the rhythm guitarist of the Vacant Lot. Lead singer Patti scrutinizes David's ability and physique, and she provides the only deadpan character that director MacGillivray usually supplies in numbers.

The band gets a mini road trip going, which turns out to be nightmarish and funny. There's an ambiguous sexual relationship budding in Trudi and David's friendship that doesn't get resolved till the last frame.

The need for professional and personal success for these depressing lives in flat, gray Nova Scotia doesn't seem to be able to click unless the two leads escape to L.A.

The script is emotionally bleak, and MacGillivray doesn't use enough humor to break up the desolation. Fullerton's guitar riffs are engaging, but can't sustain an uninteresting storyline. —Devo.

Dr. Caligari

Toronto A Steiner Films presentation of a Joseph F. Robertson production. Executive producer, Gerald M. Steiner. Produced by Robertson. Directed by Stephen Sayadian. Screenplay, Jerry Stahl, Sayadian; camera (color), Ladi von Jansky; editor, G. Martin Steiner; music, Mitchell Froom; production design, Sayadian. Reviewed at Bloor Cinema, Toronto, Aug. 30, 1989. (In Toronto Festival of Festivals.) Running time: **80 MIN.**

With: Madeleine Reynal, Fox Harris, Laura Albert, Jennifer Balgobin, John Durbin, Gene Zerna.

■ It's a twisted, skewed, day-glo world that Stephen Sayadian has conjured up in his version of "Dr. Caligari." The pic's weak attempts at campy dialog and bizarre plot twists don't make it an easy sell, and even discriminating cult movie mavens may sit this one out.

This Dr. Caligari is a sadomasochistic, metal breast-plated woman with a morbid fascination with pain and suffering who runs the CIA (Caligari Insane Asylum). She's the granddaughter of the 1919 Dr. Caligari of "cabinet" fame and is carrying on in the same tradition as her namesake. She doesn't kill people, though, but organizes hormonal interfacing experiments.

Her patient, sex fiend Mrs. Van Heusen, is readmitted to the CIA by her husband in hopes to modify her outrageous libido. Dr. Caligari transplants the hypothalamus liquid of another patient, Gus Platt, a guy who loves electroshock therapy ("it's like a thousand points of light"), into Mrs. Van Heusen's brain.

She also turns the CIA's chief male administrator, Dr. Awol, into Mamie Van Doren, so he can better service her, and Mrs. Van Heusen is given enough drug therapy to inspire her to mesquite-grill her husband to death.

Sayadian (who also directed the porno film "Café Flesh" under the name Rinse Dream) uses his camera to attack his subjects from every angle. The highly stylized sets, neon costumes and stark lighting make it a visual explosion reflecting a mad world. Too many oozing sores and exposed internal organs dilute the shock effect.

All the actors, notably Madeleine Reynal's Dr. Caligari and the late Fox Harris' Dr. Awol, deliver their lines in purposely affectless rhythms, and when they're trying to be cute it doesn't often work. Mitchell Froom's score captures the eerie moments. Tongue-in-cheek subtleties are missing, but giant slurping tongues abound. —Devo.

The Plot Against Harry
(B&W)

Toronto A King Screen production. Produced by Robert Young, Michael Roemer. Written and directed by Roemer. Camera (b&w), Young; editor, Terry Lewis, Georges Klotz; music, Frank Lewin; art direction, Howard Mandel; sound, Peter Vollstadt, Paul Jaeger; costumes, Lily Partridge. Reviewed at Bloor Cinema, Toronto, Aug. 31, 1989. (In Toronto Festival of Festivals.) Running time: **80 MIN.**

With: Martin Priest, Ben Lang, Henry Nemo.

■ "The Plot Against Harry" is hilarious and often poignant — with proper handling it could be an arthouse fave.

It was shot in 1969 by Michael Roemer ("Nothing But A Man"), but was held up because of a lack of completion funding. Watching this b&w pic is like unearthing a sociological fossil of manners, mores and life in the 1960s.

Harry Plotnick (Martin Priest), a smalltime Jewish numbers racketeer, gets released from prison and expects to pick up the gambling circuit he ran in his old neighborhood. His loyal schlemiel assistant/chauffeur Max, in cruising through his old turf in Manhattan, makes him realize the world has changed, and blacks and Hispanics now have dibs on his area.

In a farcical accident, Harry hits the rear end of a car carrying his ex-wife Kay and his ex-brother-in-law Leo and wife. Without missing a beat, Kay introduces Harry to the daughter he never saw, Margie (now pregnant), and her husband Mel, in an almost touching encounter.

Later, Harry calls on his overprotective sister Mae, gets back into the swing of things by hiring a prostitute for the night and then proceeds to have a heart attack.

With Harry's gambling empire becoming more precarious, he decides to take up Leo's offer to buy into the legitimate synagog catering business with him. In the meantime he decides to appear before a comically filmed government commission on organized crime to turn in evidence on an Italian buddy who hasn't protected his interest.

As the story unfolds, Harry is faced with a new world and the gnawing lures of the solid middle-class family life that he's always eschewed.

The Plotnick family is boisterous, upfront, multilayered and Jewish in a way that Philip Roth would savor parodying. Among the many gems of quick scenes are the candlelighting ceremony at one of Leo's catered bar mitzvahs, ex-wife Kay's afternoon at a dog obedience school, nubile daughter Millie (another offspring Harry didn't know he had) modeling brassieres for a local department store, and Harry's voodoo-like initiation into a Shriner-type fraternal organization.

The cast is uniformly solid, delivering their sparklingly crisp dialog straight. Roemer's screenplay is funny, honest and moving.

Priest brings a rich interpretation to Harry, focusing on his naivete, his conflicts, his addictive passion for gambling and his primal need for familial approval. The sets, costumes and locations shots are pure late '60s, something that could never be reproduced on a contempo soundstage.

Harry's comic transformation from gambler to benefactor (at a heart fund telethon sponsored by the nouveau riche future in-laws of Millie) to middle-aged man surrounded by family love is acted and directed in a refreshingly direct way that is a joy to watch unfold. — Devo.

VENICE FILM FEST REVIEWS

The Mahabharata
(BRITISH-FRENCH-U.S.)

Venice A Reiner Moritz presentation of a Les Prods. du 3ème Etage production. Produced by Michel Propper. Co-producers, Ed Myerson, Rachel Tabori, Micheline Rozan, William Wilkinson, Channel 4, Brooklyn Academy of Music, Mahabharata Ltd. Executive producers, Michael Birkett, Michael Kustow, Harvey Lichtenstein. Directed by Peter Brook. Screenplay, Jean-Claude Carrière; camera (color), William Lubtchansky; editor, Nicholas Gaster; music, Toshi Tsuchitori, Djamchid Chemirani, Kudsi Erguner, Kim Menzer, Mahmoud Tabrizi-Zadeh; sound, Daniel Brisseau; production design, Chloe Obolensky; executive art director, Emmanuel de Chauvigny, Raul Gomez; costumes, Pippa Cleator; makeup, Josee de Luca. Reviewed at Venice Film Festival, Sept. 3, 1989. Running time: **171 MIN.**

Vyasa	Robert Langton-Lloyd
Boy	Antonin Stahly-Vishwanadan
Ganesha/Krishna	Bruce Myers
Arjuna	Vittorio Mezzogiorno
Yudhishthira	Andrzej Seweryn
Bhima	Mamadou Dioume
Nakula	Jean-Paul Denizon
Sahadeva	Mahmoud Tabrizi-Zadeh
Droupadi	Mallika Sarabhai
Kunti	Miriam Goldschmidt
Madri & Hidimbi	Erica Alexander
Abhimanyu	Nolan Hemmings
Dhritharashtra	Ryszard Cieslak
Gandhari	Helen Patarot
Dushassana	Urs Bihler
Karna	Jeffrey Kissoon
Drona	Yoshi Oida
Bishma & Parashurama	Sotigui Kouyate
Shakuni	Tuncel Kurtiz

Also with: Georges Corraface, Tapa Sudana, Bakary Sangare, Corrine Jaber, Clement Masdongar, Ken Higelin, Joseph Kurian, Myriam Tadesse, Hapsarif Hardjito.

■ The Venice kickoff this year was no more and no less than the entire history of the world in three hours: the sensational Peter Brook production based on the most voluminous literary work in existence, the Indian Mahabharata.

Based on his stage production, Brook has directed tv and theatrical film versions, running respectively 321 and 171 minutes. On stage, the show went on for nine hours and spread over three separate evenings.

First unveiled at the Avignon Festival, this mammoth production was a cultural shock, unveiling a vastly unknown monumental legend next to which even the Iliad and the Odyssey look modest in scope and content.

Jean-Claude Carrière worked 11 years on the stage adaptation, reducing the enormous Indian manuscript (15 times longer than the Bible) to a manageable length, which had to be shrunk here once more. It's still built around Vyasa, the storyteller who unfolds for the benefit of a young boy an allegory of the entire history of the human race from creation through destruction to eventual redemption.

The Brook-Carrière adaptation finds in the Indian classic all the universal motivations of human conduct, such as greed, sex and power, to which they adroitly add some pure Judeo-Christian symbols, such as the myth of Moses' birth.

Using actors of every race and origin takes this legend out of its strict Asian source and lends it a majestic, universal sense. Vyasa's interpretation even has its humble side, as his several incursions into the action, discussing the proceedings with his characters, hint that other interpretations may be equally valid to explain our existence.

The poem, which narrates the war between two groups of five cousins for the rule of the world, is divided into three main sections. The first, "The Game Of Dice," introduces the two sides and their origins up to the point where one family loses all its properties to the other in a game of dice.

The second part, "Exile In The Forest," follows the diaspora of the losers on the one hand, and the anguish of the victors who fear eventual vengeance, on the other.

The third part, "The War," shows the bloody clash between them, leading to the brink of Apocalypse.

This is an intellectual feast providing lots of food for thought, and Brook packs the film with meaningful insight. Film buffs, however, will be less happy with the results. There is no reason, of course, to expect the film to be realistic (after all, it is a legend). Brook, whose suggestive powers on stage are tremendous, fails to inspire in his choice of visual style, which is neither spare enough to be symbolic nor elaborate enough to produce the fantasy itself on the screen.

Looking at the result, one could quite easily imagine how impressive the setups might have been in a theatrical performance, and how stagy they look here. With the camera never more than a few feet from the action, the sets look unimaginative. The acting is declamatory, the staging unnatural and the production values, seen at close range, leave much to be desired. Image always is subservient to the text, and the exotic soundtrack music contributes more to the atmosphere than does the eye of the camera.

As a followup event to the show itself, the film version may find its way into arthouses, but the better bet is on the tv series, the smaller screen being less sensitive to visual limitations and less fussy about masses of dialog. Cultural tv programmers will have a field day with this one. Don't be surprised if this finally will turn out to be the best possible advertisement for the live show, of which the film evidently is only a shadow. —*Edna.*

Berlin Jerusalem
(FRENCH-ISRAELI)

Venice   A Simon Mizrahi presentation of an AGAV Films production. Coproduced with Channel 4, La Sept, Nova Films, RAI-2, Orthel Films, NOS, Transfax, La Maison de Culture du Havre, the Hubert Bals Fund, CNC. Directed by Amos Gitai. Screenplay, Gitai, Gudie Lawaetz; camera (color), Henri Alekan, Nurith Aviv; editor, Luc Barnier; music, Markus Stockhausen; sound, Antoine Bonfanti; art direction, Marc Petitjean, Emannuel Amrami; costumes, Gisela Storch. Reviewed at Venice Film Festival (competing). Running time: **84 MIN.**
    With: Lisa Kreuzer (Elsa), Rivka Neuman (Mania), Markus Stockhausen, Benjamin Levy, Vernon Dobtcheff, Bernard Eisenschitz, Juliano Merr, Ohad Shachar, Keren Mor, Bilha Rosenfeld, Daniel Roth, Ori Levy, Yossi Graber.

■**Give Amos Gitai credit for making different movies, the kind that intellectuals will love analyzing to death but normal audiences will take in only with great difficulty.**

The idea of tracing the parallel histories of two women, German expressionist poet Elsa Lasker-Schuller and Russian revolutionary Mania Schochat, is certainly interesting. Both women, not really related to each other in real life, looked forward to the Zionist ideal of establishment of a Jewish national identity as a chance for a new start in a new country, and a new kind of society.

Gitai, who rejects traditional film narrative as superfluous and finds realism boring, makes it hard on himself and on his public. Moving constantly along parallel lines with Schuller in decadent Berlin of the '20s about to be taken over by the Nazis, and Schochat in Palestine, laying down the ground rules for an egalitarian, collective society abolishing private property, he tries to evoke moods in a poetic, metaphorical fashion, rather than supply facts. Both lines lead finally to a similar conclusion, disenchantment with the outcome of their Zionist dream.

For Schochat, taking up arms against the Arabs before all peace attempts have been explored and exhausted is a tragic mistake she is unable to prevent. For Schuller the new Jewish identity she finds there does not satisfy the ideals she believes in.

To convey this, Gitai favors very long traveling shots, stages living tableaux whose inspiration derives from painters like Georg Grosz and uses declamatory dialog to clarify his positions.

Until 10 minutes before the end, it is a historical piece, half German expressionism, half social realism in its visual design. The last 10 minutes take place today, a long traveling through ravaged scenery which suggests recent events on the West Bank, accompanied by a complex soundtrack which mixes effects with excerpts of authentic broadcasts reporting on the violence. This epilog points, of course, to the defeat of the ideas promoted by both women in the first part of the film.

None of the performers ever gets the chance to develop a character properly. On the other hand, camerawork and sound are both remarkable, the strongest features of this film.

The film will doubtless ride the festival circuit successfully. Commercially, however, it will be probably restricted to specialized positions, catering to audiences preferring innovative to emotive cinema. —*Edna.*

Sieben Frauen
(Seven Women)
(WEST GERMAN)

Venice   A Moana Film GmbH production. (Intl. sales, Pyramide Intl., Paris.) Produced, written and directed by Rudolf Thomé. Camera (color), Martin Gressmann; editor, Dörte Völz; music, Wolfgang Böhmer; sound, Gunther Kortwich; production design, Eve Schaenen; production manager, Joan Spiekermann. Reviewed at Venice Film Festival (Venice Horizontal), Sept. 6, 1989. Running time: **90 MIN.**
Hans Hummel . . . . . Johannes Herrschmann
Ati Hollmann . . . . Adriana Altaras
Johanna Hollmann . . . . . Elizabeth Zuendel
Sylvie Hollmann . . . . Alexandra Schnaubelt
Catharina Hollmann . . . . Margarethe Raspe
Grandmother . . . . Johanna Danubius

■**"Seven Women" — no connection with John Ford's last film — is the final film in a trilogy, "Forms Of Love," of which "The Philosopher," seen this year in Berlin, was the second. The same two lead actors appear again, but in different roles, and the new film generally is less amusing and attractive.**

Johannes Herrschmann plays Hans, who seems to have been abroad for some years. He returns on the death of his rich banker father and, after a brief visit to his mother in the country, arrives in Berlin and moves into his father's house.

He quickly discovers (a) that his father had some pretty nasty, threatening enemies and (b) that the old man, a lover of games, is playing a last game with his son from beyond the grave; the clues are in computer messages he left behind.

Next door is a house with seven women: grandmother, mother and five daughters. The eldest, Johanna, is away, but Ati and Sylvie, both karate experts, move in with Hans to "protect" him. They manage to subdue three assailants one night. Ati's attracted to Hans, but they do no more than share a shower (unseen) before the absent Johanna returns and, for Hans, it's love at first sight.

All of this could have been a lot more amusing than it is. Little is made of the computer game the dead father plays with his son. The sparring between Hans and the women lacks excitement (Herrschmann is very bland here, after his sex-object role in the last film). Several scenes are elaborately set up but ultimately seem to have little point (a trip to Hamburg to see a Japanese businessman; the employment of a Dutch assistant).

Film is technically smart and adequately acted, but the screenplay is too thin to carry a feature, and audiences are liable to be left feeling frustrated.—*Strat.*

I Want To Go Home
(FRENCH)

Paris   An MK2 production and release. Coproducers, Films A2/La Sept. Produced by Marin Karmitz. Directed by Alain Resnais. Screenplay, Jules Feiffer; camera (color), Charlie Van Damme; editor, Albert Jurgenson; music, John Kander; art direction, Jacques Saulnier; sound, Jean-Claude Laureux, Jean-Paul Loublier; costumes, Catherine Leterrier; production manager, Yvon Crenn; assistant director, Yann Gilbert. Reviewed at Club 13, Paris, Aug. 31, 1989. (In Venice Film Festival, competing.) Running time: **105 MIN.**
Joey Wellman . . . . Adolph Green
Christian Gauthier . . . . . . Gérard Depardieu
Lena Apthrop . . . . Linda Lavin
Elise Wellman . . . . Laura Benson
Isabelle Gauthier . . . . Micheline Presle
Terry Armstrong . . . . . . Geraldine Chaplin
Harry Dempsey . . . . John Ashton
Dora Dempsey . . . . Caroline Sihol
Cohn-Martin . . . . . . François-Eric Gendron
(English Soundtrack)

■**Jules Feiffer and Alain Resnais make strange bedfellows — the product of their union is a stillborn satiric comedy called "I Want To Go Home," about an American cartoonist in Paris.**

Though occasionally pleasant in a bland way, it leaves an aftertaste of perplexed dissatisfaction and faint embarrassment. The head-scratching is likely to be general at the Venice festival, where this English-language production by leading French indie Marin Karmitz is competing.

Resnais' involvement will surprise only those who don't know about his lifelong passion for comic books and pulp literature (images of which can be glimpsed in his famous early short films). Resnais' profoundly European artistic sensibility is alien to Feiffer's loose caricatural style. Worse, the prestigious helmer hasn't the slightest inkling about comedy, its rhythms and tones.

Nor is Feiffer's screenplay anything to write home about. A soft sendup of culture shock and parent-child relations, it lines up stick figures and half-baked sentimental or farcical situations. The initial fun at the expense of Americans abroad is facile, often secondhand, and sometimes odd (the hero, pondering the oddities of French currency, puzzles over why the 5-franc coin is bigger than a 10-franc coin — hasn't he ever seen a nickel and dime?).

Alongside his cartoonish characters, Feiffer also injects conventional film animation with cartoon creatures who pop up periodically in balloons to upbraid or advise the principals, Adolph Green and Laura Benson. This touch isn't enough to create a style.

Central character is a cantankerous American cartoonist, played as a likable kvetch by songwriter and musical comedy veteran Green (who in a climactic scene literally launches into a medley of golden oldies). One of Noel Coward's wrong people who travel, Green is making his first trip abroad, accompanied by Linda Lavin, to attend an exhibition of comic strip art in which his work figures.

Green's real reason in braving Gallic rudeness, snobbery and indifference is to see his neurotic daughter, Laura Benson, who's fled uncivilized Cleveland, self-centered Green and incompatible Lavin to enroll in a literature student at the Sorbonne. Mad about Flaubert, on whom she's written her thesis, she has become starry-eyed before her evasive professor Gérard Depardieu, who happens to be a comic book fan and one of Green's most ardent admirers.

When Depardieu meets Green at the exhibition, it's the beginning of a whirlwind intro to French hero-worship and cultural shallowness. Depardieu drags the flattered Green and Lavin to the posh country manor of his mother, Micheline Presle, who indulges her son's obsessive Yank-collecting. During a masquerade party thrown in the cartoonist's honor, Green is reconciled with his daughter, finds a kindred spirit in Presle, and manages to make a basic contact with grassroots French through his cartoon talents. Green stays on in France, while Lavin and Benson, who have made up as well, return to the States.

The performances are broad Broadway. Resnais is at a loss to extract nuance and coordinate his cast as an ensemble, especially when the story moves clumsily toward farcical complications in the party scene.

Depardieu, in his first English-speaking part, knows how to charm with blithe timing perfected in Francis Veber's comedies, and raises some smiles with such accented slanguage as "Ain't that the berries?" (the trademark utterance of Green's cartoon creation, Hepp Cat). The role is a dead end, never growing beyond the cultural stereotype of the philandering Paris intellectual who courts Yank pop culture personalities.

Lavin and Benson are notable only as foils for the crotchety but basically sweet Green. Presle is wasted in yet another role beneath her rich possibilities. Geraldine Chaplin, John Ashton and Caroline Sihol do ineffectual part-time service as other Depardieu house-guests.

John Kander is along for this Franco-American hayride with a brisk score. Tech credits are fully professional, but it ain't the berries. —Len.

El Mono Loco
(The Mad Monkey)
(SPANISH-FRENCH)

Venice   An Iberoamericana Films-French Production coproduction. (Intl. Sales, Majestic Films Intl., London.) Produced by Andres Vicente Gomez. Directed by Fernando Trueba. Screenplay, Trueba, Manolo Matij, based on "The Dream Of The Mad Monkey" by Christopher Frank; camera (color), Jose Luis Alcaine; editor, Carmen Frias; music, Antoine Duhamel; sound, Georges Prat; production design, Pierre-Louis Thevenet; associate producer, Emmanuel Schlumberger; production supervisor, Jose Lopez Rodero; assistant director, Radu Milhaileanu. Reviewed at Venice Film Festival (competing), Sept. 5, 1989. Running time: **107 MIN.**
Dan Gillis . . . . Jeff Goldblum
Marilyn . . . . Miranda Richardson
Marianne Gillis . . . . Anemone
Malcolm Green . . . . Dexter Fletcher
Legrand . . . . Daniel Ceccaldi
Jenny Green . . . . Liza Walker
Danny Gillis . . . . Jerome Natali
Marion Derain . . . . Arielle Dombasle
Ariane . . . . Micky Sebastian
Juana . . . . Asuncion Balaguer
(English soundtrack)

■ "The Mad Monkey" is, for much of its length, an intriguing psychological drama, laced with sex, about an American screenwriter in Paris and his involvement with a young English director and the latter's child-like, sensual sister.

Thanks to a typically strong performance by Jeff Goldblum, the English-language Spanish-French coproduction could stir up some international interest, though it's marred by a frustratingly unresolved conclusion.

Goldblum plays Dan Gillis, who's based in Paris and whose marriage to a Frenchwoman (Anemone) is ending, leaving their small son unhappy and disturbed. Legrand (Daniel Ceccaldi), an urbane producer, offers Gillis a job working with a tyro British director, Malcolm Green (Dexter Fletcher). At first, Gillis is hesitant. He hates British directors, he says, and his British agent, Marilyn (Miranda Richardson), who's confined to a wheelchair, also is doubtful, suggesting Gillis work on an Alain Delon project instead.

But the clincher comes when Gillis meets Jenny (Liza Walker), Malcolm's child-woman sister and star of his disturbing, awardwinning short film. As the work progresses, Gillis finds himself becoming obsessed with the beautiful, enigmatic girl who comes on with sexual favors whenever her brother needs help.

"The Mad Monkey" is based on a book by Christopher Frank, whose earlier book, "La Nuit Americaine," was filmed in 1974 as "The Important Thing Is To Love," which became a longrunning cult item in France. "The Mad Monkey" may well make its mark in certain European territories, though in the end it's frustratingly ambivalent about its character's motives and obscure in its resolution.

Spanish director Fernando Trueba, who has never quite matched the success of his first film, "Opera Prima" (1980), does a fine job in creating a mood of suspense and eroticism, and handles some individual scenes with great skill. But overall he's trapped by a screenplay (which he cowrote) that doesn't deliver.

The players, however, are excellent. Goldblum is totally convincing as the writer whose fondness for women has, we gather, always been his undoing and who becomes haunted by the mysterious Jenny. In this role, Liza Walker is a find, combining childlike innocence with a disturbing sexuality. Miranda Richardson is scorching as the crippled but very sexy agent.

Technical credits are all highly professional, but it's a pity the film builds up such a mysterious mood and then refuses to reveal, in a coherent way, what's really been going on. Incidentally, pic has an old-fashioned air about it in that every character smokes constantly throughout; seldom, in recent years, have so many cigarets been smoked in a pic.

In the end, "The Mad Monkey" looms as a better bet in Europe than Stateside, but it could become a cult item with proper handling.
—Strat.

Koma
(Coma)
(SOVIET)

Venice   A Lenfilm production. Produced by Juri Pavlov. Directed by Nijole Adomentajte, Boris Gorlov. Screenplay, Adomentaje, Gorlov, Michail Konovalchuk; camera (b&w, color), Juri Voroncov; editor, Irina Vigdrochik; music, Algirdas Paulavicus; sound, Leonid Shumjacher; art direction, Michail Gavrilov. Reviewed at Venice Film Festival (Critics Week), Sept. 5, 1989. Running time: **62 MIN.**
With: Natalyia Nikulenko (Maria), Aleksander Balurov (Nikifor), Oleg Krutikov, A. Zavjalov, O. Torban, L. Ulianova.

■ Glasnost films keep pouring out of the Soviet Union and it seems there is no end to the number of dark corners of the past that need to be explored. This film is based on thousands of stories collected by the two writer-directors, about re-education camps for women, as these gulags were referred to in Stalin's time.

The film takes place in 1950, three years before Stalin's death, but an unsettling epilog clearly states the past is still very much alive.

The story, not always very clearly told, follows a young inmate who out of both affection and interest has an affair with one of the head guards. To save her son, who was born in the camp, she is forced to denounce her lover and bear false witness against him. The plot is of lesser importance, the point of the picture being to paint the gruesome conditions under which the prisoners had to survive. It's hard labor, malnutrition, a constant process of dehumanization and degradation imposed by brutal, corrupt guards in everyday iniquities intended to break every bit of self-respect in these women's spirit. The grim, desolate landscape and the freezing northern climate only stress the bleakness of their existence.

With mood much stronger than story, this is the kind of film that festivals and cultural centers will welcome.—*Edna.*

Christian
(FRENCH-DANISH)

Venice A Leo Pescarolo, Luciano Martino, Victoria Film presentation of a Victoria Film, Chrysalide Film, Ellepi Film, Dania Film, DMV Distribution production. Produced by Soren Staermose, Ole Sondberg. Written and directed by Gabriel Axel. Camera (Eastmancolor), Morten Bruus; editor, Nils Pagh Andersen; sound, Morten Dengbol, Lars Lund, Niels Arnt Torp; music, Beethoven, Nikolaj Christensen; costumes, Françoise Nicolet, Maria Seddiki. Reviewed at Venice Film Festival (competing), Sept. 5, 1989. Running time: **105 MIN.**
Christian . . . . .Nikolaj Christensen
Aicha . . . . .Nathalie Brusse
Grandfather . . . . .Preben Lendorff Rye
Johnny . . . . .Jens Arentzen
Francoise . . . . .Nadine Alari
Vagabond . . . . . .Bernard Perre Donnadieu
Waitress . . . . .Carole Aymond
Ambassador . . . . .Aser Bonfils

■ Borne on the wings of his awardwinning "Babette's Feast" Danish helmer Gabriel Axel comes back with a youth-oriented picture, too bland and too naive for its own good.

The story of a young man, Christian, searching for love and finding no peace of mind until he finds it, the film rambles undecidedly from cold Denmark to the scorching heat of a Moroccan village, as the hero is jilted by his girlfriend, drifts away from his family, almost embarks on a career of crime, and is rescued from perdition by the dark eyes of an Arab girl.

There is very little that is likable or even explicit about Christian, and much less about the cardboard characters he meets on his travels, all of them superficially sympathetic. These people invariably and amazingly welcome Christian on his long trip across Europe, even if there is no evident reason for such a reception, except a vague air of innocence he has about him. This innocence does not prevent his helping himself to other people's property whenever in need. Manipulative script arbitrarily arranges events to keep him moving constantly on a journey in the classic tradition of Scandinavian obsession with the mirage of the South.

However, not only is there a basic lack of urgency in all these proceedings, but the film also suffers from the inexpressive per-

formance of Nikolaj Christensen as Christian. Christensen, who performs several of his own songs in the film, may be a talented musician but he is no great shakes as an actor, and being required to carry the film on his shoulders is simply too great a burden. As a matter of fact, he is often upstaged by the secondary roles, as thin and incomplete as they may be.

At one point the film almost suggests the possibility of a travelog, but this obviously is not Axel's intention, as he dwells more on people's faces than on the landscapes that Christian crosses. Technical credits are of a high order, but the soundtrack, which easily accommodates Christensen's type of folk-rock, also features Beethoven's Emperor Piano Concerto, a classic warhorse a bit too familiar to use as background music.

Finally, the only trace of *Babette* and her feast you may encounter here is the advice of a Moroccan grandmother to her niece about the influence of food on the disposition of men. It's one of the film's rare highlights.—*Edna.*

Sedim na konari a je mi dobre
(I'm Sitting On A Branch And I Feel Fine)
(CZECH-WEST GERMAN)

Venice A Slovensky Film/Taurus Film (KirchGruppe) production with participation by Television de Espana/Sacis/RAI-TV 1. Directed by Juraj Jakubisko. Screenplay, Jakubisko, Jozef Pastéka; camera (color), Laco Kraus; editor, Patrik Pass; music, Jiri Bulis; art direction, Stanislav Mozny. Reviewed at Venice Film Festival (competing), Sept. 4, 1989. Running time: **105 MIN.**
Pepe . . . . .Boleslav Polivka
Prengel . . . . .Ondrej Pavelka
Ester . . . . .Marketa Hrubesova
Zelmira . . . . .Deana Horváthová
Kornet . . . . .Stefan Kvietik

■ Slovakia's best-known filmer, Juraj Jakubisko, confirms his talent for telling local history as a fairytale in "I'm Sitting On A Branch And I Feel Fine."

Tale of a soldier and circus performer who sets up house with a mysterious mute girl has been picked up by several arthouse distribs in Europe and is Czechoslovakia's nominee for the European Oscars.

The war is over and survivors are straggling home amidst confusion, soup lines and American airdrops of food, clothes and bubble gum. Pepe (fine comic Boleslav Polivka), a circus hand released from a concentration camp, steals a bicycle and sells it to returning

soldier Prengel (boyishly appealing Ondrej Pavelka). The bike turns out to be stuffed with gold, and sets off a dangerous treasure hunt that cements Pepe and Prengel's friendship.

Together they open a bakery in an abandoned villa that once belonged to a Jewish baker — possibly the treasure's owner. One day a Titian-haired girl (the sensuous Marketa Hrubesová) appears. The boys think she is Ester, the baker's daughter, but the poor girl's resemblance to Ester's picture is coincidence; she has been traumatized into silence by the war and is pregnant. Both men fall instantly in love.

Jakubisko and scriptwriter Jozef Pastéka skillfully show Slovakia's postwar rebirth turning somber as notes of Stalinism rise.

Ester is killed by bandits after bearing a daughter, and the two clowning bakers are sent to prison by a greedy postman, envious of their gold, and a vengeful lady Party boss spurned by Pepe (villainously played by Deana Horváthová, Jakubisko's wife). Many years will pass before good and innocence can be reunited — ending takes place in a mythical future time.

Film's openness about Stalinism is new in Czech cinema, even if there still is some reading between the lines to do. The heroes' anarchic individualism celebrates the lightness of being so long repressed.

Polivka and Pavelka are a perfectly balanced duo. Technical credits fill the bill. —*Yung.*

The Cook, The Thief, His Wife & Her Lover
(DUTCH-FRENCH)

Venice An Allarts Cook (The Hague), Erato Films and Films Inc. (Paris) coproduction. (Intl. sales, Recorded Releasing, London.) Produced by Kees Kasander. Coproduced by Denis Wigman, Pascal Dauman, Daniel Toscan du Plantier. Directed by Peter Greenaway. Screenplay, Greenaway; camera (Widescreen, color), Sacha Vierny; editor, John Wilson; music, Michael Nyman; production design, Ben Van Os, Jan Roelfs; sound, Garth Marshall; casting, Sharon Howard Field; assistant director, Gerrit Martijn. Reviewed at Venice Film Festival (Venice Night section), Sept. 4, 1989. Running time: **126 MIN.**
Richard, The Cook . . . . .Richard Bohringer
Albert Spica, The Thief . .Michael Gambon
Georgina Spica, His Wife . . .Helen Mirren
Michael, The Lover . . . . .Alan Howard
Mitchell .Tim Roth
Cory . . . . .Ciaran Hinds
Spangler . . . . .Gary Olsen
Harris . . . . .Ewan Stewart
Turpin . . . . .Roger Ashton Griffiths
Mews .Ron Cook
Grace .Liz Smith

Patricia . . . . .Emer Gillespie
(English soundtrack)

■ Supporters of the work of British writer-director Peter Greenaway will welcome this new outing from the iconoclastic filmmaker. This is a confronting film which will appeal to a specific arthouse audience willing to go along with Greenaway's grim sense of humor and cheerful assault on all our sacred cows.

Setting is a smart restaurant, La Hollandaise, where Richard, the chef (Richard Bohringer) prepares a lavish menu every night. Among his regular customers are Albert Spica (Michael Gambon), a loudmouthed, vulgar, violent gangster ("thief" is too nice a word for him), who dines with his entourage of seedy yes-men, and his bored, beautiful wife, Georgina (Helen Mirren).

At another table each night sits Michael, a quiet, diffident man who's always reading books. He and Georgina make eye contact, and soon they're having a series of secret rendezvous, first in the ladies' toilet, later (with the connivance of Richard) in a pantry where they make passionate love. Eventually Albert discovers his wife's infidelity, and takes a typically violent revenge, triggering a more unusual retaliation from her.

Albert Spica is one of the ugliest characters ever brought to the screen. Ignorant, over-bearing and violent, he's first seen covering a victim with filth before abusing his long-suffering wife about her toilet habits and his minions over their appearance and manners. He also brutally tortures a kitchen boy (who has frequently entertained with a beautiful soprano voice) and, indeed, has no redeeming features: it's a gloriously rich performance by Gambon.

In contrast, Helen Mirren (in a role which was originally to have been played by Vanessa Redgrave) is all calm politeness and mute acceptance until her passion is aroused by the (far from handsome) Michael. The actress is simply superb, as Georgina sheds her clothes and her inhibitions for a series of scorching lovemaking scenes.

As the Cook, top-billed French star Richard Bohringer is kept on the sidelines until near the end, when his culinary skills are brought to bear as part of the wife's ingenious revenge on her husband.

Past Greenaway films have played games with letters of the alphabet ("A Zed And Two Noughts") and numbers ("Drowning By Numbers"). Here the game is with colors: each section of the restaurant, plus the parking lot, is given one of the colors of the rainbow: and the colors of the clothes the principal characters wear change as they pass from place to place.

Greenaway's fascination for paintings and architecture, as well as his witty literary references, have always been an intriguing element in his films. Here, painterly effects abound and, using a widescreen process for the first time, the director has his brilliant cameraman Sacha Vierny use only lateral tracking shots, as the camera follows characters from room to room. The film looks magnificent.

There are religious references too (the Garden of Eden being only one), but the main inspiration seems to be Jacobean tragedy with its violence and vulgarity and unabashed treatment of primal urges. Greenaway isn't afraid to assault his audience with aural and visual excesses (of which the torture of the boy is only one example); but his vision is extraordinary, and the film will repay repeated viewings. Certainly it seems destined to become a talking-point.

Another important plus factor is the music by the director's regular collaborator, Michael Nyman: the style is familiar from the earlier films, but it's extremely effective.

At 126 minutes, the film is on the long side, but it provides such a rich, intelligent, dynamic, mordantly funny experience that few audiences will have time to be bored. There will certainly be those who will find aspects of the film repulsive, but there should be enough people out there willing to experience this challenging experience to give the film the international art house success it deserves. It confirms Greenaway as being in the forefront of European film directors.—*Strat.*

In una notte di chiaro di luna
(On A Moonlit Night)
(ITALIAN-FRENCH)

Venice An Italian Intl. Film/Istituto Luce-Italnoleggio/Carthago Films coproduction, in association with RAI-TV 2. Produced by Fulvio Lucisano, Tarak Ben Ammar. Executive producer, Vittorio Galiano. Written and directed by Lina Wertmüller. Camera (color), Carlo Tafani; editor, Pierluigi Leonardi; art direction, Enrico Job; costumes, Gianni Versace, Gino Persico; music, Greco, Dangiò, Avion Travel, Tom Waits; associate producer, Federica Lucisano. Reviewed at Venice Film Festival (competing), Sept. 4, 1989. Running time: **107 MIN.**

John Knot	Rutger Hauer
Joelle	Nastassja Kinski
Prof. McShoul	Peter O'Toole
Mrs. Colber	Faye Dunaway
Carola	Dominique Sanda
Sheila	Lorraine Bracco
Massimo	Massimo Wertmüller
Zaccaris	Luigi Montefiori

■ **Lina Wertmüller gives up comedy but not the grotesque caricature that is her stylistic signature in "On A Moonlit Night."**

Pic attacks the delicate subject of AIDS head-on, perhaps a bit too fearlessly. Though nixed by most critics at its Venice premiere, pic has a great hold on auds through its first half, but they lose sympathy for hero Rutger Hauer after a bizarre script turn. It is likely to drum up some initial boxoffice on the strength of the subject and strong performances by Hauer and Nastassja Kinski.

Pic opens in high gear with a sickening reenactment of a real event: the double suicide of two newlyweds who mistakenly believe they have AIDS. The dead woman's distraught father blames the media for creating a climate of hysteria around the illness.

Film's message is that irresponsible journalists have built a general psychosis around AIDS, in which fear takes the greatest toll. During the film, scientist/AIDS expert Peter O'Toole delivers the optimistic message that humanity will overcome the illness.

Insofar as all infected characters remain HIV positive without developing the disease, and there is not a homosexual or intravenous drug user in the film, "On A Moonlit Night" can be faulted for simplifying both problem and solution. The main thing is it boldly tackles a subject of great interest in Wertmüller's usual lively and controversial way, forcing auds to face painful reality and examine their own attitude.

John Knot (Hauer) is a jaunty, devil-may-care American reporter who poses as an AIDS carrier to record people's reaction for an AIDS series in a Paris paper. In highly colored scenes, Hauer is thrown out of fancy restaurants, bars and the house of lustful artiste Dominique Sanda. His photographer buddy Max (Massimo Wertmüller) hangs around to snap a picture.

Crossing paths again with a pretty, gutsy photographer he had an affair with in Beirut (played with conviction and charm by Kinski), John finds the old flame still burning and — surprise — that he is the father of a small child. But another old acquaintance, an amoral Venetian aristocrat (Luigi Montefiori), puts him onto the chilling truth: John really *is* HIV positive.

Wandering aimlessly around London, accompanied by a lonely and ironic Tom Waits tune, he faces the truth in a moving and — for a change — realistic scene of despair.

Grasping at straws, John goes to see AIDS authority O'Toole in a finely acted and directed scene of pretense and discovery. O'Toole advises John to accept the necessary compromises and open himself to the comprehension and affection of family and friends. And here the intense concern for Hauer's dilemma peaks — and ends.

For some reason, John now decides to play the hero and disappear from Joelle and the baby, without so much as telling her their wedding is off. He flies to New York, where he hits on the unlikely plan of blackmailing millionaire widow Faye Dunaway to manufacture condoms and finance AIDS research (she is a secret carrier, too). At this point all credibility has flown out the window, and pic climaxes with a violent confrontation between John and his Venetian pal (who has gone to bed with Joelle without telling her about his health) and a final showdown between John and Joelle.

Yet the feeling remains that, despite pic's deliberate excesses (and its sins include laughably over-the-top luxury sets by art director Enrico Job and overdressed chic by costume designer Gianni Versace), there was an intriguing film that got lost.

Hauer gives John debonair intelligence and sensibility that render his plight more anguishing, while Kinski is surprisingly believable as the kooky, sensual, never-let-go photographer. Dunaway has too abstract a role to do much with and some of pic's worst dialog. Supporting cast is professional.

—*Yung.*

Corsa di Primavera
(Spring Race)
(ITALIAN)

Venice An Artisti Associati presentation of a Clemi Cinematografica production. Produced by Giovanni di Clemente. Directed by Giacomo Campiotti. Screenplay, Campiotti, Lucia Maria Zei; camera (color), Carlo Tafani; editor, Roberto Missiroli; music, Stefano Caprioli; sound, Alessandro Zanon; set design, Antonia Rubeo; costumes, Alexandra Toesca. Reviewed at Venice Film Festival (Critics Week), Sept. 5, 1989. Running time: **100 MIN.**

With: Alessandro Borrelli (Issaco), Giusi Cataldo (Issaco's mother), Roberto Citran (Issaco's father), Massimo Filimberti (Fiorello), Federico Campiotti (Gabriele), Chiara Campiotti (Gabriele's mother), Ernesto Giorgetti, Sergio Tramonti, Alessio Beninca, Maria Teresa Spertini.

■ **Sweet, unpretentious and straightforward, a film like this would seem more suited to a children's film festival rather than the ambitious Venice Critics Week. That it did manage to worm its way through, should be a credit to its natural, unspoiled charm.**

A series of episodes evolving around three 8-year-old boys, the film takes place in a small Italian village, with one brief sequence in Venice. The movie begins with one of the boys, Issaco, moving into the town with his mother, a hairdresser, who has just separated from her husband. There, among his new classmates, Issaco befriends two other boys his own age, Gabriele, the son of the village doctor, and Fiorello, the son of a simple farmer. The entire film relies on close and sensitive observation of these children's routines.

Episodes like the visit of a circus, the strange disappearance of soap cakes from the school's lavatory, or the attempt to run away from home, are some of the pegs on which first-time helmer Giacomo Campiotti hangs his story, not always exploiting all the potential there is in each of them, but never allowing his picture to sink into sentimental excesses.

Sequences like Issaco's Christmas visit with his father who still lives in Venice, or Fiorello accompanying his father silently on an early morning wild duck hunt, are remarkably well handled, both by the actors and the director.

Campiotti, 32, who shot the film in the village where he was born and based his script on many of his childhood memories, obviously feels very comfortable with this material. He has only two professional actors, Issaco's parents, in the entire cast. It isn't difficult to identify the freshness, but also awkward stances, which are inevitable in such cases.

Well shot and briskly edited, there is no reason why such a film couldn't find its own profitable slot, if carefully handled for the right kind of audience. —Edna.

Johnny Handsome

Venice   A Tri-Star release (in U.S.) of a Carolco presentation of a Guber-Peters Co. production. Executive producers, Mario Kassar, Andrew Vajna. Produced by Charles Roven. Directed by Walter Hill. Screenplay, Ken Friedman, based on the book "The Three Worlds Of Johnny Handsome" by John Godey; camera (Technicolor), Matthew F. Leonetti; editor, Freeman Davies; music, Ry Cooder; sound, Richard Goodman; production design, Gene Rudolf; stunts, Allan Graf; associate producers, Mae Woods, Ted Kurdyla; special makeup, Michael Westmore; production manager, Kurdyla; assistant director, James R. Dyer; casting, Bonnie Timmermann. Reviewed at Venice Film Festival (Venice Night), Sept. 6, 1989. Running time: 95 MIN.
John Sedley . . . . Mickey Rourke
Sunny Boyd . . . . Ellen Barkin
Donna McCarty . . . . . Elizabeth McGovern
Drones . . . . Morgan Freeman
Dr. Resher . . . . Forest Whitaker
Rafe Garrett . . . . Lance Henriksen
Mikey Chalmette . . . . Scott Wilson

■ A promising idea is gunned down by sickening violence and a downbeat ending in "Johnny Handsome," a Mickey Rourke vehicle that faces an uphill battle for the boxoffice dollar.

At the outset, John Sedley is anything but handsome. Born with a cleft palate and badly disfigured face, he's struggled through life and wound up a petty criminal. In the opening sequence, old buddy Mikey (Scott Wilson), persuades Johnny to join him in the robbery of an antique coin store; Johnny goes along, but both men are double-crossed by Rafe (Lance Henriksen) and Sunny (Ellen Barkin), the other gang members. Rafe kills Wilson, and Johnny is sent to the pen where Rafe's hoods make a stabbing attack on him.

That's when he comes to the attention of kindly Dr. Resher (Forest Whitaker), a plastic surgeon who, after a series of painful ops, has Johnny looking like Mickey Rourke. Johnny is allowed out of prison each day to work on the docks, where he meets pretty accountant Elizabeth McGovern and a relationship blossoms.

But Johnny isn't content with his new circumstances: He wants revenge. He plots with Rafe and Sunny (who don't recognize him) to rob the dockyard payroll, meaning to double-cross them. It all leads to a grim, violent downer of an ending.

Rourke works hard at his character but fails to make Johnny the least bit sympathetic. Barkin creates one of the ugliest femme characters seen in recent films, while Henriksen is typecast as yet another seedy hood.

Walter Hill, who's capable of far better genre pics than this, hardly tries. He makes nothing of the New Orleans location, and revels in the over-the-top violence of the opening and closing sequences.

With much more subtle treatment, the film could have been quite moving, and certainly the special makeup by Michael Westmore is effective enough to make Rourke's transformation a third of the way into the film an affecting moment. But sympathy for the character is thrown to the wind once he abandons McGovern.

A brief theatrical run is indicated, followed by a much more durable life on video. But it could have been so much more. —Strat.

Australia
(BELGIAN-FRENCH-SWISS)

Paris   A UGC release of a Films de la Dreve/AO Prods./CAB Prods./Christian Bourgois Prods./RTBF/Ciné 5 coproduction. Produced by Marie Pascale Osterreith. Directed by Jean-Jacques Andrien. Screenplay, Andrien, Jean Gruault, Jacques Audiard; camera (color), Yorgos Arvanitis; editor, Ludo Troch; supervising editor, Henri Colpi; art direction, Herbert Westbrook; costumes, Yvonne Sassinot de Nesle; music, Nicola Piovani; sound, Henri Morelle, Gérard Lamps; production manager, Jef Van de Water. Reviewed at UGC, Neuilly, Aug. 30, 1989. (In Venice Film Festival, competing.) Running time: 118 MIN.
Edouard Pierson . . . . Jeremy Irons
Jeanne Gauthier . . . . Fanny Ardant
Julien Pierson . . . . Tcheky Karyo
Agnès Decker . . . . Agnès Soral
Madam Pierson . . . . Hélène Surgère
Francois Gauthier . . . . Maxime Laloux
André Gauthier . . . . Patrick Bauchau
Saturday Pierson . . . . . . Danielle Lyttleton

■ "Australia" is a quietly affecting drama of expatriation and homecoming by Jean-Jacques Andrien, one of Belgium's finest film talents. Film's very subtlety and discretion however may work against its commercial possibilities beyond arthouse and fest circles.

Tripartite in coproduction (Belgium, France, Switzerland) and bilingual (French-English), it remains a successful example of multinational European filmmaking dictated by subject matter.

Andrien, who grew up in the heart of the Belgian wool industry in Verviers, chose his hometown as one of the main settings of his screenplay, written in collaboration with French scripters Jean Gruault and Jacques Audiard. The other chief location is southern Australia, where we first meet the story's Belgian-born hero, an Aussie wool merchant.

Played with introspective strength by Jeremy Irons, protagonist is a laconic Belgian-born war veteran who decided to remain in Australia — for whom he served as a fighter pilot — to raise a daughter he had from a woman who had died (his many years away from birthplace and language tacitly explain Irons' accent). His reticence about his past creates one of the film's currents of psychological "mystery" since even his daughter, now 12, has been deliberately kept in the dark about her mother's identity and her father's own family back in Belgium.

It is the child's quest for her own roots that Andrien interweaves with Irons' return to Belgium, summoned by his brother and mother to help save their failing wool-carbonizing plant. Irons quickly sums up the industrial situation as hopeless, though his tradition-minded brother (played with fierce commitment by Tcheky Karyo) is too blinded by his artisan's pride to admit that the factory is doomed in the general economic crisis.

But Irons' resolve to return quickly to Australia and his daughter wavers when he meets Fanny Ardant, a young woman of peasant stock who moved into the urban middle-class through a marriage with a lawyer (Patrick Bauchau). As (geographically, spiritually and emotionally) rootless as Irons is, she arouses a dormant passion in him. His invitation to join her on a business trip to England at first shocks her, but she shows up unannounced at his London hotel, then the next day takes fright and runs back to Belgium, resolved not to continue the affair.

Film ends on a note of hope in the future — and reconciliation with the past. Irons, who has succeeded in arranging a business deal that could save the family enterprise, reveals to Ardant the circumstances of his life he has repressed. At the same moment, on the other side of the globe, his daughter (who in a phone conversation has spoken with her Belgian grandmother), discovers the mother she never knew in an old reel of film Irons has kept hidden in his room.

Andrien's direction has an elegiac finesse that is lyrically enhanced by the lensing of Greece's Yorgos Avanitis (associated notably with compatriot Theo Angelopoulos). Avanitis' magical images of the vast Australian landscapes and claustrophobic Belgian industrial zones transcend facile geographic contrasts to suggest the spiritual moods of Andrien's characters — their loneliness as well as their possibilities.

A sequence that owes its essential power and ethereal beauty to the lighting is the tense climax when Karyo, in apparent despair over impending bankruptcy, takes a dangerous nocturnal glider plane as the other principals anxiously gather at the air terrain, fearing tragedy.

The cast is faultless. Ardant is especially poignant in her self-revelatory monolog in London (which Irons reciprocates later). Agnès Soral is just right as the extroverted friend who encourages Ardant's leap into the love affair. The classy Hélène Surgère is the grandmother who makes secret phone contact with a grandchild whose existence she never suspected. Young Aussie newcomer Danielle Lyttleton has thoughtful melancholic warmth as Irons' daughter.

Nods as well to Herbert Westbrook's art direction, Yvonne Sassinot de Nesle's costumes and Nicola Piovani's score. —Len.

MONTREAL WORLD FILM FEST REVIEWS

Angry Earth
(BRITISH)

Montreal A Bloom Street production. Produced by Ruth Kenley. Written and directed by Karl Francis. Camera (color), Roger Pugh Evans; editor, Christopher Lawrence; music, Ken Howard; production design, Francis Pugh. Reviewed at Montreal World Film Festival (Cinema Of Today & Tomorrow), Sept. 3, 1989. Running time: **106 MIN.**
  With: Sue Roderick, Mark Lewis Jones, Maria Pride, Dafydd Hywell, Jack Shephard, Phyllis Logan, Robert Pugh.

■ In this bitter period piece Welsh filmmaker Karl Francis attempts to link the oppression of coal miners in late 19th- and early 20th-century Wales to conditions in the present-day U.K. "Angry Earth" is a competent but unevenly styled exercise in political advocacy through historical filmmaking.

Its lack of commercial polish makes it more suitable for the festival circuit than theatrical distribution.

The director has a good idea for framing his film: the recollections on her 110th birthday of Gwen from Wales, "the oldest woman in Great Britain." Nurses fuss over her, the queen sends a telegram and reporters from the BBC and the tabloids descend. Silent and detached, but bemused, the ancient lady drifts into memories.

Wales in the 19th century is under the boot of England, and its coal miners' lives are worth far less than horses. Life in the pit is the Hobbesian paragon of nastiness, brutishness and shortness. Young Gwen can only persevere when her husband and son are killed in a coal gas explosion. The evil mine owners do not fork over one halfpence.

Francis' depiction of cruel laissez-faire capitalism could make the most callow yuppie stand up and sing "The International." The miners lead lives of virtual slavery in thrall to their unspeakably greedy masters. The filmmaker effectively recreates their life of misery in the splendid Welsh countryside, using stretches of Welsh language dialog (subtitled in French at the Montreal fest) for authenticity.

To survive, Gwen takes on the job of washing miners' corpses, disemboweling them (so the stiffs won't go putrid) and laying them out for burial. The young woman writes ringing pleas for justice in letters to the editor of a London paper, which are read in voiceover throughout the film.

Francis follows the travails of her life and times, through bloody strikes, a rape by British soldiers (wickedly avenged by her son), a nervous breakdown, recovery with the help of a kind doctor and liberal rich lady, remarriage and new tragedy.

Somewhat puzzlingly, the film ends on the eve of World War I (Gwen implores the young men not to fight), with a good 75 years left to the indomitable woman's story. Given his "oldest woman" device, Francis might have devised a brief coda addressing his heroine's life from 1914-1989.

Sue Roderick is sturdy as the young Gwen and the supporting cast are convincing enough as the downtrodden miners. "Angry Earth" might have benefited, however, from more focus on its undeveloped contention that things have not changed all that much in Margaret Thatcher's England.
  —Rich.

El Costo De La Vida
(The Cost Of Living)
(MEXICAN)

Montreal A Rafael Montero, Producciones Volcan, Martin Mendalde production. Directed by Rafael Montero. Screenplay, Jose Luis Benlliure, Rafael Montero, Oscar Montero; camera (color), Mario Luna; editor, Manuel Rodriguez; production design, Darsel Salinas; music, Alfonso Munoz. Reviewed at Montreal World Film Festival (Latin American Cinema), Sept. 1, 1989. Running time: **95 MIN.**
Miguel . . . . Rafael Sanchez Navarro
Patty . . . . Alma Delfina
  Also with: Alonso Echanove, Lucia Guilmain, Patricio Castillo, Hector Ortega.

■ A downbeat morality tale about an unemployed Mexican yuppie who desperately turns to crime, "The Cost Of Living" offers caustic commentary on Mexico's current economic crisis. It's best suited for festival sidebars on contemporary Latin cinema.

Miguel is a staff architect in a large Mexico City firm. Well-dressed, well-mannered and diligent, his greatest desire is to save enough money to buy a boxed set of the complete works of the Rolling Stones. His wife Patty punches a computer in a department store, and dreams of a camping vacation at the seashore. Their love gets them through the ups and downs of life, such as no shower water in the morning. Everyone they know is talking about "the crisis" — Mexico's collapsing economy and the impossibly spiraling cost of living.

One day the government pulls some contracts from Miguel's firm and suddenly he's fired because he lacks a college degree. A round of humiliating job interviews goes nowhere, and then Miguel is swindled out of bribe money he's been advanced for a taxi license.

A disciple of the Mexican code of machismo, Miguel is terrified at the prospect of being supported by his caring and compassionate wife. This notion is reenforced by Miguel's drinking buddies. Soon a surly and disheveled Miguel takes to holding up grocery stores, reluctantly accompanied by his spouse. Inevitably, and all too predictably, he comes to a bad end.

Director and co-writer Rafael Montero makes no secret of his feelings toward the Mexican political establishment, and the film's up-to-date look at life in Mexico City does not offer an optimistic view of the country's future. The slangy dialog and lead performances are spirited, though the melodramatic flourish of a heavy metal guitar riff each time the plot takes a new negative turn is more amusing than probably intended.
  —Rich.

Sabirini Centar
(Meeting Place)
(YUGOSLAVIAN)

Montreal An Avala Film-Belgrade Art Film-Centar Film-TV Belgrade-Terra-Novi Sad production. Produced by Aleksandar Stojanovic. Directed by Goran Markovic. Screenplay, Dusan Kovacevic; camera (color), Tomislav Pinter; editor, Snezana Ivanovic; music, Zoran Simjanovic; production design, Veljko Despotovic. Reviewed at Montreal World Film Festival (competing), Aug. 30, 1989. Running time: **98 MIN.**
  With: Rade Markovic, Bogdan Diklic, Bata Stojkovic, Olivera Markovic, Rada Zivkovic, Mirjana Karnovic and Anica Dobra.

■ Goran Markovic's fable about life after death has its amusing moments and is a respectable enough film festival entry, but "Meeting Place" is too parochial in its humor and a touch too heavy-handed in its execution to successfully compete in the American specialty film market.

In an appealing setup graced with a (low-budget) Spielbergian flourish, an aging archeologist and his bumbling team excavate by accident a mysterious slab from the time of the Roman empire. The old professor realizes what his inebriated workers do not: After a lifetime of questing he finally has found the passageway to the realm of the dead. Unfortunately, the excitement proves too much for the old man who suffers a heart attack and (apparently) dies. His timing is unfortunate, because the townfolk are in the midst of a wild wedding party and not inclined to break off and mourn him.

The professor finds himself in a purgatorial limbo that doesn't look much different from the dig site. Scattered among the ruins in a surreal tableau are the dead souls of his neighbors, looking just the way they did when alive. They while away the eons carping at one another and reminiscing about life among the living. This particular vision of the afterlife does not present death as a very enlightening experience. In a mordant comment by the filmmaker on the limitations of human nature, the dead carry bitter grudges and recriminations with them to the other side.

Back in the village the professor's son has arrived from Belgrade and goes berserk when he learns that the old man has bequeathed his house — packed with the excavated treasures of a career — so that the silly village might have a museum. The son proceeds to discard or destroy the old man's work of a lifetime, so upsetting the professor's principal aide that he commits suicide in order to rejoin his master.

That's another case of bad timing, because the professor soon emerges from his coma, not yet dead after all. This frightens the villagers somewhat, but most are so drunk and so dense that they quickly accept his resurrection. An agile cast helps director Markovic lampoon the village characters, but much of what may be pertinent to the Yugoslavian audience is likely to be lost on foreigners.

Inspired by the professor's visit, a group of the dead makes for the crypt-like passageway, the titular "meeting place," in order to return and settle old scores with the living. They journey through time, encountering the crucifixion, the crusades, the assassination of archduke Ferdinand, Hitler and Stalin, before finally emerging in the village. It's 1969 and astronauts are walking on the moon. The dead souls arrive just in time to join the wedding party, but soon discover you can't go home again.
  —Rich.

Lun Hui
(Samsara)
(CHINESE)

Montreal A China Film Export Corp. release of a Xi'An Film Studio production. Directed by Huang Jianxin. Screenplay, Wang Shuo, based on his novel "Floating On The Sea;" camera (color), Zhao Fei; music, Qu Xiaosong; production design, Yang Gang. Reviewed at Montreal World Film Festival (Cinema of Today & Tomorrow), Aug. 30, 1989. Running time: **117 MIN.**
With: Lei Han, Tan Xiaoyan, Liu Lijun, Kan Lijun.

■ **Completed well before the upheavals that took place in China earlier this year, "Samsara" is an angst-ridden study of a young man trying to cope with life in the new China. Fests and limited arthouse theatrical engagements are indicated.**

Shi-Ba's parents are dead, and he lives in a large apartment, maintaining his lifestyle by means of some shady deals. He falls in love with a young dancer, who comes to live with him, but is threatened by hoodlums (he owes them money) and permanently crippled when they use an electric drill on his knee.

This is a world where young people visit discos, drink Cokes and Sprites, and are constantly thinking up new ways to make money. One young woman has married a foreigner simply to get alimony after a divorce. The resolution is extremely pessimistic.

Director Huang Jianxin, who previously made "The Black Cannon Incident," shows himself capable of handling suspense well, as for example in a tense scene in an art gallery where the young hero nervously goes to meet the extortionist without knowing who he's looking for. Love scenes between the dancer and Shi-Ba are quite touching.

This is a long way from the kind of Chinese film we've come to expect, many of which have rural settings. The young people here could be living in almost any big city, and the film has something of the feel of the kind of urban dramas Edward Yang has been making in Taiwan.

This may be one of the last gasps of the trailblazing Xi'An Film Studio, and will be want-to-see fare for the growing worldwide audience for Chinese cinema.—*Strat.*

Justice Denied
(CANADIAN)

Montreal A National Film Board of Canada-CBC production. Executive producer, Colin Neale. Produced by Adam Symansky. Line producer, Mike Mahoney. Written and directed by Paul Cowan. Camera (color), David de Volpi; editor, Rita Roy, Cowan; music, Jean Corriveau; sound, Hans Oomes; production design, Emmanuel Jannasch; production manager, Wayne Cormier; assistant director, John Houston; casting, John Comerford. Reviewed at Montreal World Film Festival (Panorama Canada), Aug. 31, 1989. Running time: **98 MIN.**
Donald Marshall Jr. . . . . Billy Merasty
John MacIntyre . . . . Thomas Peacocke
Roy Ebsary . . . . Wayne Robson
Harry Wheaton . . . . Peter MacNeill
Jim Carroll . . . . J. Winston Carroll
Jimmy MacNeill . . . . Daniel McIver
Maynard Chant . . . . Steve Marshall
John Pratico . . . . Vincent Murray

■ **Documentary director Paul Cowan dramatizes a celebrated real-life miscarriage of justice in "Justice Denied," a sober tale of an Indian youth who served 11 years in prison for a murder he didn't commit.**

In Canada, where the case is well known, there'll be an audience (especially on tv) for the pic, but offshore chances are less likely because writer-director Cowan has made an academic, uninvolving case history.

The facts seem indisputable: One night in 1971 in Sydney, Nova Scotia, Donald Marshall Jr., a Micmac Indian, and his black friend Sandy Seale, went to a park intending to mug someone. Instead they were confronted by Roy Ebsary, a profoundly disturbed man, who stabbed Seale to death.

The investigating officer, MacIntyre, however, pinned the blame on Marshall, who was found guilty when some unreliable witnesses testified they saw him do the killing. Protesting his innocence, Marshall, in the succeeding years, managed to escape from custody briefly and was involved in a prison riot. Finally, the Canadian Mounties pinned the murder on Ebsary, who served a brief sentence.

Cowan has treated all this rather gingerly, and it might even have been better to have made a wholly fictionalized account of the drama. There's a lack of emotion and drama in what should have been a very emotional and dramatic film; a bit of excess would have been welcome amid all the restraint.

Billy Merasty is totally convincing as the unjustly convicted man, and his parents in the film are played by Marshall's real-life parents. Thomas Peacocke makes MacIntyre a very enigmatic character, while Wayne Robson's Ebsary is a weirdo who could have been presented as even weirder (for seven years, he left his home only to have sex with a neighbor's dog).

Pic was shot in Halifax, Nova Scotia, and at the prison where Marshall served time. It makes for an undoubtedly authentic but dramatically disappointing drama. Technical credits are good, though Jean Corriveau's score drowns out the dialog at one key moment in the drama.—*Strat.*

Nijusseiki Shonen Dokuhon
(Circus Boys)
(JAPANESE-B&W)

Montreal A CBS/Sony Group production. (Intl. sales, Shibata Organization, Tokyo). Executive producers, Hisamitsu Hida, Yoichi Sakurai. Produced by Ryuzo Shirakawa, Kaizo Hayashi. Written and directed by Hayashi. Camera (black & white), Yuichi Nagata; editor, Osamu Tanaka; music, Hidehiko Urayama, Yoko Kumagai; sound, Ichiro Kawashima; production design, Takeo Kimura, Hidemitsu Yamazaki; assistant director, Tempei Masuda. Reviewed at Montreal World Film Festival (Cinema of Today & Tomorrow), Sept. 1, 1989. Running time: **106 MIN.**
Jinta . . . . Hiroshi Mikami
Wataru . . . . Shu Ken
Omocha . . . . Moe Kamura
Maria . . . . Michiru Akiyoshi
Sayoko . . . . Yuki Asayama
Yoshimoto . . . . Yoshio Harada
Samejima . . . . Sanshi Katsura

■ **Evidently, writer-director Kaizo Hayashi's first film, the silent "To Sleep So As To Dream," was no fluke. The director's followup is an equally beautiful film, and also an advance; this deft blend of tragic drama and fantasy is hauntingly well done. Fests, and then the international arthouse circuit, are definitely indicated.**

It's a pity, though, that the English title given the film is so prosaic and uninviting. The original Japanese translates as "The Boys' Own Book Of The 20th Century," which captures the feel of this very special film much better. The story begins early this century, establishing two children, Jinta and Wataru, in training to become stars of the circus one day, though the older Jinta is much more cynical about his efforts than his kid brother.

A few years pass and the brothers are, in fact, circus stars, but before long Jinta ankles to try his skills at sleight of hand in the outside world. He becomes a conman, and eventually is forced to join the gang of Yoshimoto, a rural gangster.

Meanwhile, back at the circus, things aren't going well, especially when an aged elephant runs amok one night and is shot dead by police. Still, Wataru and his girlfriend Maria persevere and start to work up a new act, while always hoping Jinta will return.

In the film's stunning final section, Jinta falls passionately in love with Omocha, the mistress of Samejima, one of the gangster's clients. They kill Samejima and go on the run with the gangsters in pursuit. It ends in a sequence of sheer poetry, in which the magic of the circus reasserts itself.

Yuichi Nagata's sublime black & white photography is a major asset to the film. The circus scenes are handled with raffish élan, and, amusingly enough, the "elephant," who figures prominently, is "played" by a fake elephant (which sheds a tear as it expires). It sounds like a precious idea, but it works and adds to the magic of these delightful scenes.

The final part of the film, involving the gangsters who still seem to be living in the samurai past, is quite strong. A chase at night through a forest, with the pursuers carrying blazing torches to light their way, is a sequence of genuine beauty. The climax is wholly satisfactory.

Hayashi obviously is a special talent whose affection for old cinema remains undiminished and is incorporated into this new film without pretension. Word of mouth should be strong on the film, and with proper handling and positive reviews it could become a cult item on the arthouse circuit. Technically, it's tops in every department.—*Strat.*

Termini Station
(CANADIAN)

Montreal An Astral Bellevue Pathé release (in Canada) of a Saturday Plays Ltd. production. (Intl. Sales, Transit Film). Executive producers, Douglas Leiterman, Donald Haig. Produced and directed by Allan King. Screenplay, Colleen Murphy; camera (color), Brian Hebb; editor, Gordon McClellan; music, Mychall Dama; sound, Peter Shewchuk; production design, Lillian Sarafinchan; associate producers, Nicholas Gray, John Board; production manager, Nicholas Gray; assistant director, John Board; casting, Dorothy Gardner. Reviewed at Montreal World Film Festival (Market), Aug. 30, 1989. (Officially preeming at Toronto Festival of Festivals). Running time: **108 MIN.**
Molly Dushane . . . . Colleen Dewhurst
Micheline . . . . Megan Follows
Harvey Dushane . . . . Gordon Clapp
Val . . . . Norma Dell'Agnese
Also with: Debra McGrath, Leon Pownall.

■**Director Allan King makes a return to the big screen after quite a long absence with "Termini Station," a wintry drama about a smalltown family in crisis. Well-made but overwritten film could perform decently domestically, with homevid indicated as the best bet for international distribution.**

Colleen Dewhurst gives a full-throttle performance as Molly Dushane, an alcoholic widow who lives with her businessman son Harvey and his wife. Molly spends her time boozing, listening to opera or watching tv soaps.

Her young daughter Micheline works as a hooker in the little Ontario mining town, and yearns to get out and start a new life in the big city. It's gradually revealed that the family troubles sprang from Molly's longstanding love affair with a local businessman, Stein, who actually was Micheline's real father. When Molly's husband discovered the truth, he nearly killed the girl, but shot himself instead. Now Stein is dead, though Harvey hasn't told his mother.

The guilty secret comes out into the open in a series of dramatic but slightly overwrought scenes that culminate in Michelene deciding to take her mother along with her on the crucial trip to Montreal.

Screenwriter Colleen Murphy writes dialog in the form of speeches, to the extent that the film has the feel of a stage play (which it wasn't). Despite this, most of the film works thanks to some strong performances and the control producer-director King keeps over the material. After an uncertain start, the drama exercises its spell over the viewer.

This won't be an easy film to market, but if reviews are good the pic could find an appreciative audience, especially on home turf. It's preeming at the Festival of Festivals in Toronto, and was sneaked at a market screening during the Montreal fest. —*Strat.*

Konec Starych Casu
(The End Of The Good Old Days)
(CZECH)

Montreal Barrandov Film Studios, Czechoslovak Film, production. Directed by Jiri Menzel. Screenplay, Menzel, Jiri Blazek, based on a novel by Ladislav Vancura; camera (color), Jaromir Sofr; editor, Jiri Brozek; music, Jiri Sust; sound, Karel Jaros; production design, Zbynek Hloch; assistant director, Jan Prokop. Reviewed at Montreal World Film Festival (competing), Sept. 1, 1989. Running time: **97 MIN.**

Duke Alexei . . . . Josef Abrham
Stoklasa . . . . Marian Labuda
Spera . . . . Jaromir Hanzlik
Jakub Lhota . . . . Rudolf Hrusinsky
Michaela . . . . Barbara Leichnerova
Suzanne . . . . . . Chantal Poullain-Polivkova
Pustina . . . . Jan Hartl
Jan Lhota . . . . Jan Hrusinsky
Kotera . . . . Jiri Adamira
Ellen . . . . Alice Dvorakova

■**Jiri Menzel is back in typically winning form with this lightweight but quite disarming comedy of class, sex and capitalism in post-World War I Czechoslovakia.**

Handsome production design and a gentle, typically Czech sense of humor should help this charmer find audiences in many parts of the world.

The setting is a country estate currently being rented by a plump nouveau riche businessman, Stoklasa (another fine performance from Marian Labuda, remembered as the fat guy in Menzel's last film, "My Sweet Little Village"). Stoklasa wants to keep the chateau permanently, but some of his neighbors are after it as well.

Enter Duke Alexei, a cheerful, bearded nobleman who arrives unexpectedly, moves in for a long stay, and proceeds to delight the children and seduce the women. Josef Abrham, in this role, bears an uncanny resemblance to David Puttnam.

What follows is told from the perspective of Spera (Jaromir Hanzlik), a typical Menzel hero who is always yearning for something (usually a pretty girl) but is quite unable to get it. He has his eye on a couple of women in the household, including French tutor Suzanne and housekeeper Cornelia, but in both cases the ebullient Duke pips him to the post.

Meanwhile, Stoklasa's pretty daughter Michaela is being courted by Jan, son of a neighbor; but all their efforts to find somewhere private to consummate their passion are frustrated.

The film is structured around a series of running gags, pratfalls, embarrassments, misunderstandings and goucheries. It's low-key humor, the kind at which you chuckle rather than laugh outright, but then so was "My Sweet Little Village," and that got an Oscar nomination.

Among the joys here are the throwaway moments: the pompous butler constantly correcting his un-aristocratic boss; the mysterious nocturnal wanderings of Ellen, a woman described as of "uncertain age and uncertain sex;" the arrival into this peaceful world of a large motorcar, and so on.

Menzel's timing for comedy always has been on the button, and so it is here, though his basic material is, as is often the case, very slight. Fans of the work of this amiable filmmaker will be as enchanted as ever, and also will be looking forward to the imminent release of his long-banned, 20-year-old "Larks On A String."
—*Strat.*

The Midday Sun
(CANADIAN)

Montreal A Missing Piece production. (Intl. Sales, Films Transit, Montreal.) Executive producer, Don Haig. Produced by Christopher Zimmer. Coproduced by John Hunter. Written and directed by Lulu Keating. Camera (color), Manfred Guthe; eidtor, Miume Jan; music, Sandy Moore; sound, Daniel Pellerin; production design, Mary Steckle; production manager, Peter Reid; assistant director, David Robertson; casting, Susan Hains. Reviewed at Montreal World Film Festival (Panorama Canada), Aug. 30, 1989. Running time: **95 MIN.**

Maggie Cameron . . . . Isabelle Mejias
Julian . . . . George Seremba
Bruno . . . . Robert Bockstael
Lillian . . . . Jackie Burroughs
Watson . . . . Roland Hewgill
Anthony . . . . Dominic Kanaventi
Elizabeth . . . . Kathy Kuleya

■**The misadventures of a naive young Canadian woman working at a mission in an unnamed African country are the subject of this sometimes intriguing first feature about culture clash.**

Reminiscent in some ways of the French arthouse success "Chocolat," the film could spark audience interest if carefully handled.

At the onset, a voiceover states, "When you travel, the strangest creature you encounter is yourself." That's certainly true of Maggie Cameron (Isabelle Mejias), a pretty, 20-year-old redhead who comes to Africa to work on a mission with Julian, a hardworking priest. Though eager to learn, Maggie is chronically naive, imposing all her Western values on everything she sees, and making mistake after mistake. One of her worst moves is to have an affair with Bruno, a superficially charming but intrinsically racist German.

When her home is robbed, her houseboy Anthony immediately is blamed and sentenced quickly to prison for 10 years. Though outraged at what she sees as an injustice, Maggie can do nothing but befriend Anthony's wife Elizabeth — and, for the first time, gets some insight into the real lifestyle of the African people.

There are numerous subplots, including one involving Jackie Burroughs and Roland Hewgill as leftovers from the colonial days. But the black actors overshadow the white actors in this film, and Robert Bockstael, as the minister, and Kathy Kuleya, as Elizabeth, are standouts.

Mejias tries her best, but can't prevent Maggie from being an almost unbearably irritating character.

The film was shot in Zimbabwe, and an authentic feel for the provincial city (Bulawayo) is one of its main assets. Technical credits are fine and first-time director Lulu Keating, who also scripted, has made a promising debut.
—*Strat.*

Tutajosok
(Memories Of A River)
(HUNGARIAN-FRENCH)

Montreal A Budapest Studio, Mokep, Kerszi-Feeling production, in association with the Ministry of Culture and Communications, Paris. Produced by Gabor Hanak, Hubert Niogret. Directed by Judit Elek. Screenplay, Elek; camera (Eastmancolor), Gabor Halasz; editor, Katalin Kabedo; music, Peter Eotvos; sound, Gyorgy Kovacs; art direction, Tamas Banovich; costumes, Erzsebet Mialkovszky. Reviewed at Montreal World Film Festival (competing), Sept. 2, 1989. Running time: **147 MIN.**

David Hersko . . . . Sandor Gaspar
Csepkanics . . . . Pal Hetenyi
Amsel Vogel . . . . Franciszek Pieczka
Matej . . . . Andras Stohl

■**This is a landmark film for Hungary which indicates a relaxing of politics as helmer Judit Elek succeeds in fictionalizing a historical event and denouncing anti-Semitism for the first time.**

Set in the confines of the Austro-Hungarian empire in the 1880s, the peaceful life of Jewish loggers is turned upside down by the ritualistic murder of a young Jewish girl, Eszter Solymosi. The 3-part television version is a more suitable format than the 147-minute film, which feels like a long three hours.

The deeply religious Jewish community has its tranquil, hard-working existence involuntarily overcome by violence when the loggers, taking a load of logs to the next town, find the body of the girl floating in the river. Unjustly accused of murder and subsequently whipped and beaten, several of the group members are corrupted by the jail system. They begin accusing one another to escape further torture.

Most of the pic bogs down in a long and drawn-out court scene, but all are finally acquitted. The drama has taken its toll on each of them even after they return to their majestic mountain in the wilderness.

Pic's theatrical potential is limited to its own territory, but historical and folklorish aspects should give it a fair chance in tv outlets.
—*Suze.*

Guerriers et Captives
(Warriors And Prisoners)
(ARGENTINE-SWISS-FRENCH)

Montreal An MGI presentation. A Films du Phare, Jorge Estrada Mora Prods., Television Suisse Romande, La Sept production. Produced by Jorge Estrada Mora, Jean Marc Henchoz, Sylvette Frydman. Executive producer, Sabina Siegler. Written and directed by Edgardo Cozarinsky. Camera (color), Javier Miquelez, Hector Collodoro, Carlos Ferro, Ignacio Musich, Florent Bazin, Michel Amathieu; editor, Alberto Borrelo; music, Jose Luis Castineira de Dios; sound, Dante Amoroso, Antonio Gonzales, François Musym, Pierre Alain Besse, art direction, Miguel Angel Lumaldo, Rolando Blanco, Rodolfo Navarro, Osvaldo Maldonado; costumes, Nene Murua, Marisa Centanin, Julieta Hanono, Caroline de Vivaise. Reviewed at Montreal World Film Festival (Cinema of Today & Tomorrow), Aug. 29, 1989. Running time: **97 MIN.**
Marguerite . . . . Dominique Sanda
Garay . . . . Federico Luppi
Yvonne . . . . Leslie Caron
 Also with: China Zorilla (the sergeant), Gabriela Toscano (the prisoner), Selva Aleman (the teacher), Duilio Marzio, Carlos Merola, Juan Palomino, Alexandro Cutzarida, Gabriela Otero.

■ **Interesting both for its trinational backing and its exploration of Argentina's 19th-century war against its indigenous natives, Edgardo Cozarinsky's "Warriors And Prisoners" mixes history and myth in an unusual take on the cavalry vs. Indians genre.**

Although watchable and competently performed, it doesn't have an obvious marketing hook for North American distribution.

It's 1880 and the Argentine army is on the brink of subjugating the country's Indian population. The natives still are resisting as the cavalry pushes deeper into the vast plains of Patagonia, far from the European sophistication of Buenos Aires.

Cozarinsky sets his film in a dusty outpost town near a frontier fort. Soldiers and civilians have been drawn to this remote place in search of the common dream of all colonists — the fortune and social stature unattainable at home.

The commanding colonel has returned from an assignment to Paris with a younger but by no means girlish French wife (Dominique Sanda). She's a woman of limited means but aristocratic aspirations who hopes to fulfill her ambitions in Patagonia. Her sophisticated Spanish- and French-speaking officer husband promises that her dreams of family and gentry living will be realized just as soon as the nasty business of the last stubborn tribes is taken care of. "Your children will be Argentine," he assures her.

The townspeople deceive themselves with signs of progress, such as a new school mistress to educate the barefoot natives in European ways, and a railway connection with the distant capital. Stunning cinematography enables Cozarinsky to evoke the Patagonian vastness and the notion of man's puniness.

The colonialists have imported the barbarisms of their old world into the new one. Soldiers are summarily executed for desertion and the cruel economics of the age compel them to re-enlist or be imprisoned for vagrancy. When the survivors of the Indian wars are finally granted the land promised to them, they are easily persuaded to sell it back to powerful opportunists for a fraction of its worth.

The colonel's wife, meanwhile, has busied herself with the notion of re-educating a French girl recently rescued by the troops after a decade as an Indian captive. Ultimately, the colonel's wife fails to wean the girl from her Indian ways, and her dashing soldier literally loses his head as a consequence.

Cozarinsky's sympathies are obviously with the downtrodden, represented here by the "noble savage" natives and the peasant troopers. The colonel's heroism and essential decency while pressing the Indians' extermination are meant to reflect the contradictory impulses of the "civilizing" colonizers. Argentina, the expatriate filmmaker is saying, can only come to terms with its present by understanding its past. —*Rich.*

Black Lights, White Shadows
(B&W)

Montreal A Novamerica Films production. Produced by Gabe von Dettre, Adam Goldfine. Executive producer, Ron Rodriguez. Written and directed by Von Dettre. Camera (b&w, 16m), Goldfine; music, Yo-Yo Ma, Joan Clement. Reviewed at Montreal World Film Festival (Cinema of Today & Tomorrow), Aug. 25, 1989. Running time: **96 MIN.**
Judith . . . . Rita Mate
Boyfriend . . . . Arch Stanton
Narrator . . . . Kathi Gati

■ **If there is such a thing as cinematic torture, this abysmally pretentious exercise in pseudo-surrealism is it. A dutiful reviewer could only envy the Montreal festival filmgoers who headed in droves for the exits long before this dreary dirge about existential disaffection dragged to its pointless conclusion.**

Judith and her boyfriend are Hungarian expatriates living in New York. She works a routine office job, while he spends his days "scribbling" fiction at the kitchen table. Through Judith's tortuous stream-of-consciousness reflections, it's apparent that they don't want to live together but cannot live apart.

Interminable real-time sequences, bargain-basement dream psychology, bad poetry, boring sex and jumbled impressionism are offered up here in a miserably recorded, poorly photographed and irredeemably pompous narrative. She's a jabbering drag, he's a loathsome slob, and why anyone, should care about their lives is a question the filmmaker obviously never asked himself. —*Rich.*

Rikyu
(JAPANESE)

Montreal A Shochiku release of a Teshigahara Prods.-Shochiku Eizo Co.-Itoh & Co.-Hakuhodo Inc. production. Executive producers, Shizuo Yamanouchi, Hisao Minemura, Kazuo Watanabe. Produced by Yoshisuke Mae, Hiroshi Morie. Directed by Hiroshi Teshigahara. Screenplay, Genpei Akasegawa, Teshigahara, based on the book by Yaeko Nogami; camera (color), Fujio Morita; editor, Toshio Taniguchu; music, Toru Takemitsu; production design, Yoshinobu Nishioka, Shigemori Shigeta; costumes, Emi Wada; production manager, Toru Okuyama. Reviewed at Montreal World Film Festival (competing), Sept. 2, 1989. Running time: **134 MIN.**
Sen-no Rikyu . . . . Rentaro Mikuni
Hideyoshi Toyotomi . . . . Tsutomu Yamazaki
Soji Yamonoue . . . . Hisashi Igawa
Riki . . . . Yoshiko Mita
Nobunaga Oda . . . . Koshiro Matsumoto
Ieyasu Tokugawa . . . Kichiemon Nakamura
Hidenaga Toyotomi . . . . Ryo Tamura
Casper . . . . Donald Richie

■ **Lovers of Japanese art and culture will go for "Rikyu" in a big way. Hiroshi Teshigahara has returned to feature films, after a 17-year absence, with a** supremely beautiful, stately biopic of the 16th century artist credited with perfecting the tea ceremony.

Prestige, big-city arthouse exposure is indicated, though the steady pace and length of the film will limit audience appeal.

Rikyu was teamaster for the man who became Japan's most powerful warlord of the period, Hideyoshi Toyotomi. Under Rikyu's guidance, the tea ceremony became a crucial centerpiece for social and political life, but the man also was adept at flower arrangement, painting and design of all kinds. His advice also was sought after by his master, until Hideyoshi decided Rikyu was "insolent" for disagreeing about the wisdom of a proposed invasion of China. In 1591, Rikyu was forced to commit ritual suicide.

Teshigahara will be remembered above all else for his 1964 Cannes prizewinner "Woman Of The Dunes," which he followed up with a couple of powerful dramas, "The Face Of Another" and "Man Without A Map." But since "Summer Soldiers" (1972), his only film has been a short documentary on the Spanish architect Antonio Gaudi. Much of the director's time has been spent running a famous school of flower arrangement established by his late father.

The director's screen comeback has all the visual power of his earlier work but lacks the narrative impetus. Teshigahara has deliberately left the "big" events of the drama — the battles and beheadings and even the final suicide — off-screen. Instead, he's opted for a stately film that is perfect in every visual respect; costumes, sets, camerawork are all impeccable. Some viewers may wish for more obvious drama, though there's plenty of intrigue going on.

As Rikyu, Rentaro Mikuni gives a performance of calm strength that seems exactly right for the role. Supporting players are all well cast and effective. Toru Takemitsu's music is haunting.

This is a film in the best tradition of Japanese cinema, and harks back to the great days of Mizoguchi and others who portrayed court intrigues of the past. With careful handling and positive word of mouth, the film could cash in on worldwide interest in Japanese art and do solid arthouse business. It was a worthy contender in the Montreal fest competition.
—*Strat.*

Kolahal
(The Turmoil)
(INDIAN)

Montreal   A Saikia production. Produced and directed by Bhabendra Nath Saikia. Screenplay, Nath Saikia; camera (color), Kamal Nayak; editor, Nikunja Bhattacharjee, Atish Nandi; music, Mukul Barua. Reviewed at Montreal World Film Festival (Indian cinema section), Aug. 29, 1989. Running time: **118 MIN.**

    With: Runu Devi Thakur, Bibhu Ranjan Choudhury, Chetona Das.

■This drama from Assam centers on the plight of a woman left alone to care for her small son when her husband leaves to find work. It's a gloomy, tragic story, very slowly paced, and of interest only to Indian cinema buffs.

The woman gets a job in a nearby rice warehouse, but tragedy strikes when her son is crushed to death by the rice. In a macabre touch, she's presented with a sack of rice that is stained with her son's blood. To add to her woes, she discovers that her husband is a bigamist, and she's lusted after by local men who know of her desperate situation.

The film, based on a 1969 book called ''Rats,'' takes its time to tell this sad little story, which is really no more than an anecdote. Color processing is poor and editing is ragged, but the writer-producer-director gets a strong performance from Runu Devi Thakur as the woman. Commercial chances are negligible.—Strat.

Off Off Off ou Sur le toit de Pablo Neruda
(Off Off Off Or On The Roof Of Pablo Neruda)
(CANADIAN)

Montreal   A Les Films de l'Insomniaque production. Directed by Jorge Fajardo. Screenplay, Fajardo, based on ''Off Off Off'' by Alberto Kurapel; camera (color), Philippe Amiguet; editor, Claire Boyer; music, Alberto Kurapel; set design, Marinea Mendez. Reviewed at Montreal World Film Festival (Panorama Canada), Aug. 31, 1989. Running time: **80 MIN.**

■''Off Off Off'' is a seriously artsy pic in which a Spanish-speaking neon chicken plays a supporting role in the revolution. Those who like experimental cinema that dabbles in South American politics will love it.

Entire film is shot in a darkly lit studio with several obscure exteriors of a jogger who's part of the gang. All actors wear white make-up and mime the sorrows of torture victims. Bring ear plugs for the piano solos.—Suze.

Portion d'éternité
(Looking For Eternity)
(CANADIAN)

Montreal   Prima Film presents a Les Productions du Regard in association with the National Film Board of Canada production. Executive producer, Jean-Roch Marcotte. Produced by Marie-Andrée Vinet. Written and directed by Robert Favreau. Camera (color), Guy Dufaux; editor, Hélène Girard; sound, Serge Beauchemin; scientific consultant, Jacques Testart; art direction, Vianney Gautheir. Reviewed at Montreal World Film Festival (competing), Sept. 2, 1989. Runnning time: **96 MIN.**

Marie	Danielle Proulx
Pierre	Marc Messier
Hélène	Patricia Nolin
Antoine	Paul Savoie
M. Lemieux (father)	Gilles Pelletier
Michelle	Maryse Gangé
Luc	Raymond Cloutier
Julie	Johanne-Marie Tremblay
François	Daniel Gadouas

■This drama of middle-age baby-craving has a witty script with enough emotional impact to make it a sure winner on quality tv outlets.

A car crash that kills the parents-to-be, Marie and Pierre, instantly launches the pic into a problematic flashback formula pitted against the followup investigation scenes by a government minister, Hélène, of the mad scientist-type genetics biologist, Antoine.

As evidenced by a recent Life magazine issue called Baby Craving, Marie and Pierre's problem is a common scenario. Despite all attempts, the wife cannot get pregnant; the clock is ticking; mid-30s sets the woman into a state of panic. Desperation sets in and the couple is willing to resort to any scientific hope of fertility, including the often-futile and expensive process of in vitro fertilization, more commonly known as test-tube babies. Pic addresses a slew of current issues including legal rights of embryos.

To spice up the docu-type story, pic's biologist is a slightly crazed Canadian version of Dr. Frankenstein who dabbles in cloning experiments and envisions a world where babies can be brought to term in a test tube. The would-be guardian of morality, Hélène, is the voice of popular ethics who questions the role of science in reproduction.

Yet despite the heavy subject matter, Favreau exploits realistic, comic situations in the flashback scenes between the couple. ''I'm ovulating,'' says Marie waking up Pierre. ''Congratulations,'' he snores in one of numerous scenes that make light of their crisis.

Melodrama takes a serious turn when the in vitro process finally works, Marie is pregnant with quadruplets her body can't handle, and the couple's preoccupation with further scientific interruption lead to the car crash.

Pic makes no pretense of answering the big questions it poses. Lack of action and problematic structure nullify any hope of successful theatrical release. But high-quality technical aspects, especially Guy Dufaux' gorgeous camera-work make it a topnotch pic for tv and vidcassette. —Suze.

Black Rain

Hollywood   A Paramount Pictures release of a Jaffe/Lansing production in association with Michael Douglas. Produced by Stanley R. Jaffe, Sherry Lansing. Executive producers, Craig Bolotin, Julie Kirkham. Directed by Ridley Scott. Screenplay, Warren Lewis; camera (Super 35, Technicolor), Jan DeBont; editor, Tom Rolf; music, Hans Zimmer; sound (Dolby), Keith A. Wester, James J. Sabat; production design, Norris Spencer; art direction, John J. Moore, Herman F. Zimmerman, Kazuo Takenaka (Japan); set design, Alan S. Kaye, Robert Maddy, James R. Bayliss; set decoration, John Alan Hicks, Leslie Bloom, Richard C. Goddard, John M. Dwyer, Kyoji Sasaki (Japan); costume design, Ellen Mirojnick; special effects supervisor, Stan Parks; second unit director, Bobby Bass; additional photography, Howard Atherton; aerial photography, David Nowell; additional editing, William Gordean, Jacqueline Cambas; line producer (Japan), Yosuke Mizuno; associate producer, Alan Poul; assistant directors, Aldric La'auli Porter, Benjamin Rosenberg, Masayuki Taniguchi (Japan), Dennis Maguire (second unit); casting, Dianne Crittenden, Nobuaki Murooka (Japan); additional casting, Melissa Skoff. Reviewed at Mann National Thater, Westwood, Calif., Sept. 12, 1989. MPAA Rating: R. Running time: **126 MIN.**

Nick	Michael Douglas
Charlie	Andy Gracia
Masahiro	Ken Takakura
Joyce	Kate Capshaw
Sato	Yusaku Matsuda
Ohashi	Shigeru Koyama
Oliver	John Spencer
Katayama	Guts Ishimatsu
Nashida	Yuya Uchida
Sugai	Tomisaburo Wakayama
Miyuki	Miyuki Ono

■Since this is a Ridley Scott film, ''Black Rain'' is about 90% atmosphere and 10% story. But what atmosphere! This gripping crime thriller about hardboiled N.Y. cop Michael Douglas tracking a yakuza hood in Osaka, Japan, boasts magnificent lensing by Jan DeBont and powerfully baroque production design by Norris Spencer. Though it may be too dark for some viewers, and cops out a bit in the overlong finale, the Paramount release looks like a b.o. winner.

Smoothly and intelligently blending the conventions of American film noir with those of Japanese yakuza (gangster) films, ''Black Rain'' is much more effective than its forerunner, Sydney Pollack's 1975 ''The Yakuza,'' which also had Japanese icon Ken Takakura in a sidekick role to the American protagonist.

Until a misguided last-minute attempt to show that he's really a nice guy underneath, Douglas is utterly believable as a reckless and scummy homicide detective who takes kickbacks from drug dealers and resorts to the most brutal methods to capture escaped counterfeiter Yusaku Matsuda.

First collaring Matsuda after a shocking outbreak of violence in a N.Y. restaurant, Douglas is sent with him to Osaka, where he promptly loses him to the yakuza and watches helplessly as his partner Andy Garcia is murdered. Coming into conflict with the Japanese police, Douglas turns to the criminal underground to help bring in his prey.

Scripters Craig Bolotin (who also exec produced with Julie Kirkham) and Warren Lewis fascinatingly depict the growing influence of Takakura's higher concepts of honor and loyalty on Douglas, who in turn causes some of his expedient lack of morality to rub off on the Japanese police inspector.

It isn't long before the entire world begins to seem like "one big grey area," as the cynical Douglas describes New York City.

Lavishly backed up by producers Stanley R. Jaffe and Sherry Lansing — who overcame the hazards of a reportedly difficult location to help create a seamlessly exotic Osaka — Scott brings a "Blade Runner"-like density to his smoggy, hellish visual stylization. DeBont's Oscar-caliber lensing gives an electric intensity to a film which is never less than riveting to watch.

The mood of omnipresent menace and descent into an amoral quagmire is evocatively summed up in the film's title, a metaphor for the postwar corruption that spawned the yakuza. Crime boss Tomisaburo Wakayama, recalling the waves of American B-29s that firebombed Japanese cities in World War II, tells Douglas that Americans "made the black rain" and created an enduring climate for crime.

Though generally depicting the nearly psychotic Douglas character from a critical distance, Scott sometimes lapses into the too-frequent failing of contemporary pics and encourages the audience to cheer when Douglas gives the villain a gratuitous punch in the face or acts like Rambo in assaulting a gangster stronghold.

The clumsily sentimental ending seems to reflect an inability to come to terms with this complex s.o.b. of a cop. By attempting to sugarcoat him to let the audience go out feeling good, "Black Rain" may succeed in doing just the opposite, squandering some of its earlier impressiveness.

Takakura's quiet sense of stature and Garcia's resigned acceptance of death are among the finest things in the film. The rest of the Japanese supporting cast is first-rate, particularly Wakayama's godfather. Although Kate Capshaw's film noir B-girl role is corny, she plays it with a suitably Claire Trevor-like heart of gold.

Tech credits are uniformly stunning. —*Mac.*

Heart Of Dixie

New York   An Orion Pictures release of a Steve Tisch production. Produced by Tisch. Executive producer, Martin Davidson. Directed by Davidson. Screenplay and associate producer, Tom McCown, based on Anne Rivers Siddons' novel "Heartbreak Hotel;" camera (Deluxe color), Robert Elswit, editor, Bonnie Koehler; music, Kenny Vance; additional music, Vance, Phillip Namanworth; sound (Dolby), Glenn Berkovitz; production design, Glenda Ganis; art direction, Sharon Seymour; costume design, Sandy Davidson; assistant director, Deborah Love; production manager-coproducer-2d unit director, Paul Kurta; stunt coordinator, Danny Aiello 3d; additional camera, Tom Sigel; 2d unit camera, Kim Marks; casting, Marci Liroff, N.Y.-Julie Hughes, Barry Moss. Reviewed at Quad 1 Theater, N.Y. Sept. 16, 1989. MPAA Rating: PG. Running time: 95 MIN.

Maggie	Ally Sheedy
Delia	Virginia Madsen
Aiken	Phoebe Cates
Hoyt	Treat Williams
Boots	Don Michael Paul
Tuck	Kyle Secor
Keefi	Francesca Roberts
Jenks	Peter Berg
Sister	Jenny Robertson
M.A.	Lisa Zane
Jean	Ashley Gardner

Also with: Kurtwood Smith, Richard Bradford, Barbara Babcock.

■ "Heart Of Dixie" is a silly, relentlessly high camp drama reducing the civil rights movement of the '50s to a Whitman's sampler nostalgic exercise. Orion understandably has given this stinker a low-profile release.

Following the widespread criticism of Orion's "Mississippi Burning" for failing to accurately portray '60s civil rights activism (and the blacks' p.o.v.), it is doubly problematic that "Dixie" not only commits the same mistake (there is only one major black character) but also has a disastrously light-hearted tone that unintentionally comes off far closer to John Waters' satirical "Hairspray" (also a pic about race relations) than to "Burning."

Deficient script by Tom McCown is based on Anne Rivers Siddons' novel "Heartbreak Hotel." That title was lost to a Buena Vista 1988 Tuesday Weld-David Keith comedy release that, like "Dixie," contains an Elvis Presley impersonation as the original title tie-in period hook.

It's 1957 and Ally Sheedy is a sorority senior at Alabama's Randolph U., working at the school paper. First 50 minutes of the pic laboriously document the silly concerns of the sorority sisters, e.g., getting pinned (for which pretty blond Jenny Robertson will even submit to date-rape) or being named Honeysuckle Queen (stunning Virginia Madsen competes immediately following the death of her boyfriend).

The pastel visuals by Robert Elswit, loaded down with endlessy cute period costumes and vintage cars, continue to be pretty even after the film suddenly turns "serious." At a Presley concert in Tupelo, Miss., Sheedy witnesses a black kid being beaten viciously by police for daring to listen to Elvis in the "white" section of the stadium rather than the balcony reserved for "colored."

She's instantly radicalized and with the goading of Associated Press photographer Treat Williams becomes a mini-crusader, writing a blistering plea for tolerance and equality for the campus newspaper, which gets her expelled. Extremely hokey, tearjerker finish has her visiting Randolph as the first black student enrolls (filmed on location at U. of Mississippi, no less).

This nonsense could have played acceptably, perhaps in the manner of a Deanna Durbin film, if the audience were made to care about Sheedy's character and share her concerns. Instead she's a drip, overacting in mannered fashion as does the rest of the giddy cast. Her transformation is phony as is virtually everything else on screen. Not helping matters is the principals looking too old for their college roles (Sheedy and Madsen were both 26 at time of lensing), though guest star Phoebe Cates (24 then) carries across the same credible pixie look as in "Shag," filmed a year earlier.

Madsen, who did a good job for director Davidson in the HBO baseball pic "Long Gone," is tiresome here. Jenny Robertson stands out in the supporting cast while the director is unkind to fellow sorority gal Ashley Gardner, who gets numerous unintentional laughs as she consistently overdoes simple reaction shots or functional line readings.

In the only black role of consequence, the sorority housekeeper, Francesca Roberts brings nobility and bearing to a cornball assignment.

Behind-the-camera credits including a nonstop parade of golden oldies on the soundtrack are technically excellent, but sabotage what should have been a serious, gritty story; besides the civil rights theme, examples of honest film depiction of sorority life exist, e.g., the classic docu "Rush." —*Lor.*

Je n'aurai jamais du croiser son regard (FRENCH)

Paris   An AMLF release of a Productions Pacific/Générales d'Images/Miniato Productions coproduction. Produced by Patricia and Pierre Novat. Written and directed by Jean Marc Longval. Camera (Eastmancolor), Jean-Claude Larrieu; editor, Yves Deschamps; music, Jacques Davidovici; sound, Philippe Senechal, Gérard Rousseau; assistant director, Jean-Luc Olivier; technical adviser, Elie Chouraqui; production manager, Georges Marshcalk. Reviewed at Marignan-Concorde theater, Paris, Sept. 4, 1989. Running time: 94 MIN.

With: Nathalie Cardone (Zoe), Smain (Bambi), Luc Thuillier (Lucky), Marie Caries, Philippe Chambon, Hélène de Saint Pére, Béatrice Lord, Gérard Sergue, Marius Colucci.

■ Young girl with a troubled past closing in on her meets sympathetic lovestruck delinquent who's ready to do anything to protect her in this tedious, nonsensical romantic thriller.

Newcomer Jean-Marc Longval contrived the poorly plotted script and inane dialog and directed with as much gimmickry as he could muster (which includes a lot of self-indulgent Steadicam shots).

Sole interests here are the young leads: Nathalie Cardone, as the attractive footloose teen, stood out in intense supporting roles in last season's "Drole d'endroit pour une rencontre" and "The Little Thief," and Smain is a likable Algerian comedian who's equally active on the stage. There's also Luc Thuillier, who plays Smain's buddy. All three deserve better than this hand-me-down story which leaks its feeble mysteries in cryptic flashback dream fragments. —*Len.*

Midnight

New York   An SVS Films release of an SVS and Midnight Inc. presentation, produced in association with Kuys Entertainment Group and Gomillion Studios. Executive producers, Michael Holzman, Ron Gell, John O'Donnell, Jeff Ringler, Gloria J. Morrison. Produced by Norman Thaddeus Vane, Morrison. Written and directed by Vane. Camera (United & Filmservice color), David Golia; editor, Sam Adelman; music, Michael Wetherwax; sound (Ultra-Stereo), Marty Kasparian; art direction, Mark Simon; assistant director, Patrick

Wright; casting, Barbara Remsen & Associates. Reviewed at Westside Cinema 1, N.Y., Sept. 2, 1989. MPAA Rating: R. Running time: **84 MIN.**

Midnight (Vera)	Lynn Redgrave
Mr. B	Tony Curtis
Mickey Modine	Steve Parrish
Heidi	Rita Gam
Siegfried	Gustav Vintas
Missy	Karen Witter
Ron	Frank Gorshin
Arnold	Robert Miano

Also with: Wolfman Jack, Barry Diamond, Gloria Morrison, Robert Axelrod, Tom (Tiny) Lister Jr.

■ **"Midnight" is an amateurish Hollywood satire typified by atrocious overacting, consistently unfunny gag lines and pathetic in-jokes. Pic didn't draw flies during its Gotham midnight bookings and video prospects are poor.**

Lynn Redgrave toplines (pulling faces and screeching her lines as if intent on dominating 1989's worst acting sweepstakes) as a tv horror hostess copied after Elvira but with a crude Tallulah accent. She's warring with her greedy network boss Tony Curtis while romancing young gigolo Steve Parrish, an aspiring actor who moves into her mansion.

When killings of her adversaries occur, beginning with her double-crossing agent Frank Gorshin, no suspense is generated since writer-director Norman Vane slavishly imitates the classic "Sunset Boulevard" — right down to a doting Stroheim-like butler played by Gustav Vintas.

Thesps are poorly directed right down to the gawking extras. Lighting and editing are poor. Karen Witter provides alluring pulchritude as Parrish's new love interest while Redgrave is fitted out with ugly makeup and unflattering costumes and hairpieces.

Though Curtis and Gorshin have scenes together, Vane foolishly misses the chance for some genuine humor by not pairing Gorshin's classic Burt Lancaster carbon to Curtis à la "Sweet Smell Of Success."

Pic's oddest element, undoubtedly unintentional, is recurring imagery out of pro wrestling: Redgrave's pet boa (wrapped around Parrish's neck après sex) that looks like Jake (The Snake) Roberts' pet Damien; Parrish playing his big scene more like the antics of the Honky Tonk Man than his characters' models James Dean and Elvis, and a bit part as a security guard played by no less than current rassling heel Zeus (Tiny Lister, Eddie Murphy's former bodyguard who costarred in "No

Holds Barred").

Lots of on-screen plugola includes Redgrave holding up a Hollywood trade paper to the camera (which duly earns a thank-you in the slow end crawl that pads pic's running time), a new low in product placement. —*Lor.*

Night Game

Hollywood A Trans World Entertainment release of an Epic Pictures production. Produced by George Litto. Executive producers, Moshe Diamant, Eduard Sarlui. Directed by Peter Masterson. Screenplay, Spencer Eastman, Anthony Palmer, from story by Eastman; camera (Technicolor), Fred Murphy; editor, Robert Barrere; music, Pino Donaggio; sound (Ultra-Stereo), Scott Smith; assistant director, David Womark; associate producer, Joe Regan; casting, Ed Mitchell, Ed Johnston. Reviewed in L.A., Sept. 14, 1989. MPAA Rating: R. Running time: **95 MIN.**

Seaver	Roy Scheider
Roxy	Karen Young
Nelson	Richard Bradford
Broussard	Paul Gleason
Alma	Carlin Glynn

■ A solid cast, professional production and attractive locations help, but can't hide, the threadbare script of this limp detective thriller.

Despite the slasher-programmer air of its ads (which cutely parody "Major League," whose ads in turn play off the ones for "Airplane"), "Night Game" isn't all that far from an average tv mystery series episode. Theatrical prospects are dim.

Set in Galveston, Texas, plot follows efforts of a veteran police detective (Roy Scheider) in tracking down a serial killer who has been slashing the throats of young women along the city's beachfront. Discovering there's a relationship between the killings and the strikeout victories of a star pitcher for the Houston Astros, our hero gets his man in fairly short order.

A halfhearted attempt is made to pad things out via the hero's sometimes rocky relationship with his feisty fiancée (Karen Young). It really doesn't amount to much, save helping to get her into position for the grand finale, which in standard-issue thriller tradition finds her trapped in the killer's clutches as our hero rushes to her aid.

There's a striking disparity between the relative sophistication of the methods used to discover the killer's identity, and the lack of same used to contrive the last reel. Why did he bother going to all that trouble when all he had to do was wait around his girlfriend for the

killer to strike? That's what girlfriends in programmers are for, aren't they? —*Rens.*

Henry V
(BRITISH)

London A Renaissance Films production, in association with the BBC and Curzon Film Distributors. Executive producer, Stephen Evans. Produced by Bruce Sharman. Adapted and directed by Kenneth Branagh, based on play by Shakespeare; camera (color), Kenneth MacMillan; editor, Michael Bradsell; music, Patrick Boyle; production design, Tim Harvey; costumes, Phyllis Dalton; associate producer, David Parfitt. Reviewed at Mr. Young's preview theater, London, Aug. 15, 1989. (At Cinema '89, Brighton.) Running time: **137 MIN.**

Henry V	Kenneth Branagh
Chorus	Derek Jacobi
Exeter	Brian Blessed
Fluellen	Ian Holm
French king	Paul Scofield
Dauphin	Michael Maloney
Ely	Alec McCowen
Katherine	Emma Thompson
Alice	Geraldine McEwan

Also with: Simon Shepherd, James Larkin, John Sessions, Christian Bale, Michael Williams, Richard Briers, Geoffrey Hutchings, Robert Stephens, Robbie Coltrane, Judi Dench, Harold Innocent.

■ There is a limited market for film adaptations of Shakespeare plays, but "Henry V" is an exceptionally watchable and accessible pic.

It offers a plethora of fine performances from some of the U.K.'s brightest acting talents and

Original Film
(BRITISH)

A United Artists release of a Two Cities (Laurence Olivier-Dallas Bower) production. Directed by and starring Olivier. Features Robert Newtee, Esmond Knight, Leslie Banks, Felix Aylmer, Renee Asherson, Leo Genn. Screen adaptation by Olivier, Alan Dent and Reginald Beck from the play by William Shakespeare; camera (Technicolor), Robert Krasker and Jack Hildyard; score, William Walton, conducted by Muir Mathieson and played by London Symphony Orchestra; text editor, Dent; film editor, Beck; art, Paul Sheriff; costumes, Roger Furse. Previewed at N.Y., April 17, 1946. Running time: **127 MIN.**

King Henry V	Laurence Olivier
Ancient Pistol	Robert Newton
Chorus	Leslie Banks
Princess Katherine	Renee Asherson
Fluellen	Esmond Knight
Constable of France	Leo Genn
Archbishop of Canterbury	Felix Aylmer
Mountjoy	Ralph Truman
King Charles VI	Harcourt Williams
Alice	Ivy St. Holier
French ambassador	Ernest Thesiger
The dauphin	Max Adrian
Duke of Orleans	Frances Lister
Duke of Burgundy	Valentine Dyall
Duke of Bourbon	Russell Thorndike
Capt. Gower	Michael Shepley
Sir Thomas Erpingham	Morland Graham
Court Soldier	Brian Nissen
Earl of Westmoreland	Gerald Case
Queen Isabel of France	Janet Barnell
Duke of Exeter	Nicholas Bannen
Bishop of Ely	Robert Helpmann

Mistress Quickly	Freda Jackson
Williams	Jimmy Hanley
Capt. Jamie	John Laurie
Capt. MacMorris	Niall MacGinnis
Sir John Falstaff	George Robey
Lieut. Bardolph	Roy Emerton
Earl of Salisbury	Griffith Jones
Bates	Arthur Hambling
Corporal Nym	Frederick Cooper

an attractive debut by tyro helmer Kenneth Branagh.

Pic should fare well in its own distrib arena.

Branagh is being hailed as the new Laurence Olivier in the U.K., and with "Henry V" — like Olivier's 1944 version — he takes on adaptation, direction and starring responsibilities. While Branagh does not yet possess the acting abilities of the young Olivier, he has fashioned a stirring, gritty and enjoyable film.

Olivier's "Henry V" was filmed toward the end of World War II and designed to rally the English with its glorious battle scenes and patriotic verse. Branagh's version is more realistic and tighter in scale — mainly because of the smaller budget — and while his film is equally rousing, it is a contempo version of Shakespeare: high on acting, low on glamour.

Branagh has taken the sensible step of gathering the cream of British acting talent around him and making his directorial debut with unfussy use of the camera. He favors many close-ups and slow tracking shots, and appears to be enjoying the performances rather than trying to do too much.

Pic opens with Derek Jacobi as the chorus wandering around a film studio setting the scene. Branagh (Henry V, King of England) prepares for an invasion of France to secure his legal claim to the French throne.

Despite dissent among some nobles, Branagh and his followers arrive in France and battle to capture various towns. Paul Scofield (the French king) sadly ponders his country's situation and is urged to enter in bloody battle by Michael Maloney (the dauphin).

After many battles, Branagh's tired and bedraggled army prepares for the final conflict with the massive French forces. After wandering among his troops in disguise, Branagh makes an impassioned speech and his forces win.

One subplot has Emma Thompson (the French king's daughter Katherine) and her maid (Geraldine McEwan) playing at learning English. Branagh declares his love for Thompson after he has won the

French throne. Another subplot has Branagh's old buddies Richard Briers, Robert Stephens and Geoffrey Hutchings, remembering the good old days when they and Robbie Coltrane (Falstaff) would all go drinking together.

For such a large and varied cast, all of the performances are fine, with Brian Blessed as the loyal Exeter and Scofield as the sad French king especially good. Branagh's Henry V appears gentle, but displays his inner strength and maturity as the battles wear on. The likes of Ian Holm, Michael Williams, Robert Stephens and Maloney always brings class to a production.

The female roles, as with the play, are slight but still effectively played.

There are bound to be many comparisons between the two versions of "Henry V," though the bottom line is that any intelligent and caring adaptation of Shakespeare for the cinema should be cherished. —*Adam*.

VENICE FILM FEST REVIEWS

Beiqing Chengshi
(A City Of Sadness)
(TAIWANESE)

Venice   A 3-H Films Ltd.-Era Intl. Ltd. production. (Intl. sales, Era Intl., Taipei, and Jane Balfour Films, London.) Executive producers, Yan Xiongzhi, H.T. Yan, Yang Dengqui, Michael Yang. Produced by Qui Fusheng. Directed by Hou Hsiao-hsien. Screenplay, Wu Nianzhen, Zhu Tianwen; camera (color), Chen Huaien; editor, Liao Qingsong; music, Chang Hongyi, Naoki Tachikawa; production design, Liu Zhihua, Chang Zaimin; sound, Du Dujie, Yang Jingen; assistant director, George Chang. Reviewed at Venice Film Festival (competing), Sept. 9, 1989. Running time: **158 MIN.**
Lin Wen-ching . . . . Tony Leung
Hinomi . . . . Hsin Shu-fen
Lin Wen-heung . . . . Chen Sown-yung
Lin Wen-leung . . . . Kao Jai
Lin Ah-lu . . . . Li Tien-lu
Hinoe . . . . Wu Yi-fang
Shisuku . . . . Ikuyo Nakamura
Ah-ga . . . . Kenny Cheung
Mio . . . . Chen Shu-fang
Red Monkey . . . . Ai Tsu-tu

■ Hou Hsiao-hsien's "A City Of Sadness" is a majestic family saga, rich in detail and character, and impeccably made. It's undoubtedly a demanding film, but also a film of considerable stature and richness.

The tale centers on a Taiwanese family, the Lins, during the crucial years 1945-49. In 1945, the 51-year Japanese occupation of Taiwan came to an end: Japanese contacts were severed, and local Taiwanese looked forward to asserting their own lifestyle on the island. All too soon, however, mainland Chinese started to arrive, bringing with them crime and corruption. When the Communists won the struggle on the mainland, Taiwan became the unwilling h.q. of the ousted Nationalist government.

Against this political background, Hou unfolds a dense family saga. Old man Lin had four sons: No. 1, Wen-heung, a businessman who gets involved in the rackets and meets a violent end; No. 2, Wen-sun, a doctor who was sent by the Japanese to fight in the Philippines and has never returned, though his wife waits in vain for him; No. 3, Wen-leung, who spent the war in Shanghai and has returned a madman, and No. 4, Wen-ching, a photographer who's been deaf since a childhood accident.

Wen-ching is the focus of the film, both through his friendship with Hinoe, a young radical opposed to the Chinese takeover of Taiwan, and especially because of his love for Hinoe's sister, Hinomi, who communicates with him through endless notes, and who winds up his wife.

Hou fills the film with details about the life of these people. We learn how, after the Japanese left, Japanese flags were used for clothing and that many people weren't quite sure which way up to fly the Taiwanese flag. A variety of languages is spoken in the film (Japanese, Taiwanese, Mandarin, Cantonese); in one scene, a group of businessmen discuss a problem in three different languages.

There's an exquisite moment of parting as Hinomi's Japanese girlfriend gives her friend a kimono as a farewell gift. There's another memorable moment when, during a heated political discussion, Wen-ching puts on a record (which of course he can't hear) of a German folk song for Hinomi.

Not all the details of the film are easily understood at one viewing: The relationships of the gangster to the oldest brother aren't always clear, nor are the reasons for the sudden outbursts of violence. These are relatively minor problems in a film of great scope and individuality, which combines family drama, humor and tragedy in equal proportions. Gradually, the emphasis is placed more and more on Hinomi.

"A City Of Sadness" is a fine technical achievement: production credits are superior, with the glowing camerawork and intricate soundtrack especially fine. The print caught, which had English subtitles, was marred only by a lengthy opening explanatory crawl that was too fast for comprehension.

The pic certainly deserved its major prize in Venice, which may help it reach the world's arthouse audiences, where Hou's previous films have become known. This is certainly a major achievement for Taiwanese cinema.
—*Strat*.

Jaded

Venice   An Olpal production. Executive producer, Andres Holzer. Produced by Gary Graver, Oja Kodar. Directed by Kodar. Screenplay, Kodar; camera (Eastmancolor), Graver; editor, Maria Foss; music, Alexander Welles; production design, Julia Riva; sound, Sasha Devici; production manager, Gaylynn Baker. Reviewed at Venice Film Festival (Critics Week), Sept. 8, 1989. Running time: **93 MIN.**
Joe . . . . Randall Brady
Rita . . . . Elizabeth Brooks
Angel . . . . Scott Kaske
Sara . . . . Jillian Kesner
Rossanda . . . . Oja Kodar
Jennifer . . . . Kelli Maroney
George . . . . Todd Starks

■ "Jaded" harks back to the Andy Warhol/Paul Morrissey school of filmmaking. This drama about a bunch of lowlife characters living at Venice Beach, Calif., is skillfully structured but repetitive and ugly, and makes a disappointing debut for writer-director Oja Kodar.

The pic begins abruptly with a sickening scene of violence in which Angel (Scott Kaske), a transvestite, is brutally beaten by Joe (Randall Brady), sadistic husband of Rita (Elizabeth Brooks). Rita already has been bashed by her husband, and flees, seeking help from her cousin Sara (Jillian Kesner), despite the fact that Sara and Joe had an affair. Angel also arrives at Sara's apartment.

Meanwhile, the bixsexual Sara's current male lover, George (Todd Starks), a masseur, is making it with his latest client, Italian opera singer Rossanda (Kodar), who later also makes it with her chauffeur, Joe.

The series of interlocking love affairs seems inspired by "La Ronde," and the circular structure of this film is its biggest asset. Unfortunately, Kodar elects to present her characters in the tackiest of milieus and situations. They're a uniformly unappealing bunch (with Angel eliciting the most sympathy) and audiences may quickly cease to care who's having sex with whom.

The numerous sex scenes are presented without much inhibition, and the scene in which a nude Kesner is thrown between Todd Starks and Randall Brady as if they were playing ball with her is so over the top as to achieve a grim humor.

Mostly, though, these scrungy characters are too miserable to create much interest or sympathy.

"Jaded" may achieve some kind of cult status, but for the most part looks like a tough sell.
—*Strat*.

O Sangue
(The Blood)
(PORTUGUESE-B&W)

Venice   A Uniportugal presentation. A Tropico Filmes production. Produced by Victor Goncalves. Written and directed by Pedro Costa. Camera (b&w), Martin Schäfer; editor, Ana Luisa Guiamares; music, Igor Stravinsky; sound, Pedro Caldas. Reviewed at Venice Film Festival (Critics Week), Sept. 6, 1989. Running time: **95 MIN.**
Vicente . . . . Pedro Hestnes Ferreira
Clara . . . . Ines Medeiros
Nino . . . . Nuno Ferreira
Also with: Luis Miguel Cintra, Isabel de Castro, Henrique Canto e Castro.

■ No one can accuse Pedro Costa of commercial compromises in his film "O Sangue." Strange and hermetic, it is perfect for intellectual acrobatic exercises, intended for a highly restricted and exclusive audience.

Two brothers, whose father keeps going away for reasons that aren't quite clear, share a secret bond between them. When the father disappears completely, they almost manage (with the help of a girl) to establish a happy household of their own.

Strange incidents keep occuring. The boys' uncle comes from the big city and demands explanations, goons obviously associated with the departed father try to force information out of the boys, they are separated and the brittle, tentative bond is broken forever.

Costa shoots in a highly personal, poetic style, allowing for numerous interpretations, from conflict between generations to corruption in labor organizations. Evidently, he is more interested in conveying moods than information.

There are numerous references for film buffs, from Jean Cocteau to Manoel de Oliveira. However, for those not familiar with such names, Costa's film will probably remain an unsolved riddle.

—*Edna.*

Blauäugig
(Blue Eyes)
(WEST GERMAN)

Venice A Bioskop Film production. Produced by Eberhard Junkersdorf. Directed by Reinhard Hauff. Screenplay, Dorothee Schön; camera (Eastmancolor), Hector Morini, Jaroslav Kucera; editor, Heidi Handorf; music, Marcel Wengler; sound, Hubert Henle; assistant director, Peter Carpentier. Reviewed at Venice Film Festival (competing), Sept. 8, 1989. Running time: **87 MIN.**
Johann Neudorff . . . . Götz George
Daniel . . . . Miguel Angel Sola
General von Elz . . . . Julio de Grazia
Alfredo Neudorf . . . . Alex Benn
Laura Neudorf . . . . Emilia Mazer
Gomez . . . . Alberto Segado
Ana . . . . Noemi Morelli
Elena . . . . Monica Galan
(In Spanish)

■ **The problems of Latin America have fascinated German filmmakers in the past, and now Reinhard Hauff looks at the tragedy of Argentina in the '70s in "Blue Eyes," a suspenseful, but rather contrived, political thriller along "Missing" lines.**

Götz George plays Johann Neudorff, a successful and influential Argentine businessman with a Czech-German background. It's 1978, and Neudorff, who doesn't oppose the military dictatorship, is shocked to discover his daughter (Laura) is living with Daniel, a political activist, and is on a military hit list. When Laura is kidnaped, he sets out to use his powerful government contacts to help her, and in doing so discovers for himself the full horror and violence of the military regime.

Although he tries to help Daniel, he's betrayed by his own son, Alfredo. Daniel is killed and Neudorff himself winds up in a grim military prison. The discovery that his daughter also is dead leads to his decision to seek revenge.

Alongside the main story are ironic flashbacks showing that, as a small boy in Czechoslovakia, the blond, blue-eyed Johann was "adopted" by Nazi parents. Now the same thing is happening to his grandson.

Though there are elements of "The Official Story" as well as "Missing" here, "Blue Eyes" isn't up to the standard of either. It works best as a suspense thriller, and Hauff whips up considerable tension in the central part of the film. The final scene smacks of overkill.

Götz George gives a powerful performance as the conservative father radicalized by his experiences. He's supported by a strong cast. Apart from the wartime flashbacks, all the dialog is in Spanish, and the film gains a good deal of strength from its authentic Buenos Aires locations.

Production values are high, and the film could do solid business in Germany and Spanish territories, with arthouse possibilities in the rest of the world. Video sales also look promising. Despite its flaws, pic emerged as one of the stronger entries in the Venice competition.

—*Strat.*

She's Been Away
(BRITISH)

Venice A BBC Films production. (Intl. sales, The Sales Co.) Produced by Kenith Trodd. Directed by Peter Hall. Screenplay, Stephen Poliakoff; camera (color), Philip Bonham-Carter; editor, Ardan Fisher; music, Richard Hartley; production design, Gary Wilkinson; sound, Clive Derbyshire; production associate, Carolyn Montagu; assistant director, Dermot Boyd; casting, Joyce Nettles. Reviewed at Venice Film Festival (competing), Sept. 10, 1989. Running time: **106 MIN.**
Lillian Huckle . . . . Peggy Ashcroft
Harriet Ambrose . . . . Geraldine James
Hugh Ambrose . . . . James Fox
Dominic Ambrose . . . . Jackson Kyle
Young Lillian . . . . Rebecca Pidgeon
Gladys . . . . Rosalie Crutchley
Matilda . . . . Rachel Kempson
George . . . . Hugh Lloyd

■ **A luminous performance from Peggy Ashcroft is the centerpiece of the BBC's second 35m theatrical feature (following John Hurt-starrer "Little Sweetheart"), which is notable also for being the first film Peter Hall has directed since "Akenfield" in 1974. This story of an old woman who emerges from a mental home after 60 years seems likely to connect with serious filmgoers worldwide.**

Stephen Poliakoff's screenplay links two women: Lillian Huckle (Ashcroft), who, in the late '20s, was seen by her family as mad, though flashbacks (with Rebecca Pidgeon as the young Lillian) show her more as a slightly manic nonconformist; and Harriet Ambrose (Geraldine James), wife of Lillian's great-nephew Hugh (James Fox).

Lillian comes to stay with Hugh and Harriet (and their worldly wise son, Dominic) when the mental home in which she's lived all these years is demolished (apparently the result of government cutbacks). The Ambroses live in the same house Lillian lived in as a girl, cueing memories of her frustrated youth.

The point Poliakoff and Hall are making (a shade laboriously) is that Harriet today is no worse than Lillian was in the '20s. She's pregnant, not sure she wants the baby and getting more and more hysterical about it. Two-thirds into the film, the two women set out together without telling Hugh, and provoke a police search (a kidnaping is suspected).

Ashcroft is splendid as the puzzled old lady who would really rather be back in the hospital. She can't cope with the modern world of traffic and supermarkets, and the return to her old home triggers painful memories.

James is almost as successful as the hard-bitten Harriet, who keeps smoking though she's pregnant, can't park her husband's car and has a fierce temper and sarcastic wit. James Fox is also very good as the finicky, fastidious husband driven to the brink of despair by his wife's strange behavior.

Peter Hall, best known in recent years for his work at Britain's National Theater, doesn't attempt any cinematic flourishes, but handles Poliakoff's screenplay adroitly.

In Britain, the film is to have a short theatrical release prior to a scheduled airing on BBC-TV next month, but a Venice prize might modify those plans. International release is indicated for this quality British production.

Above all, pic is likely to bring well-deserved kudos to Ashcroft, who, in countless films and plays over the years (including most notably David Lean's "A Passage To India"), has made her considerable mark.—*Strat.*

Der Aten
(The Spirit)
(WEST GERMAN-SWISS)

Venice A Visual Filmproduktion-Xanadu Film coproduction. (Intl. sales, Metropolis Film, Zurich). Executive producer, Elke Haltaufderheide. Directed by Niklaus Schilling. Screenplay, Schilling, Gad Klein, from the novel by Herbert W. Franke; camera (Eastmancolor), Bernd Neubauer, Thomas Meyer; editor, Schilling; music, Georges Delerue, Francis Lai, Vladimir Cosma; production design, Maria Buchner, Harald Rüdiger; sound, Martin Müller, Markus Urchs; video/com-

puter techniques, Wolfgang Hirsch; production manager, Pierrot Egger; assistant director, Gundula Ohngemach. Reviewed at Venice Film Festival (Venice Night section), Sept. 11, 1989. Running time: **120 MIN.**
Brock . . . . Charles Brauer
Jens . . . . Ian Moorse
Evelyn . . . . Karina Fallenstein
Li Sun . . . . Ankie Beilke
Police Chief . . . . Katharina Welser
Iris Wege . . . . Liane Hielscher
Devenisch . . . . Franz Boehm
Under Secretary of State . . Dorothea Moritz

■ **An ingenious idea for an ultramodern thriller is given lethargic treatment in "The Spirit," an overlong and seldom thrilling suspense film.**

Set in 1995, pic centers on Jens Lohkamp (Ian Moorse), a computer whiz still troubled by the incident 20 years earlier when his young sister was kidnaped and murdered by a stranger: Jens had seen the kidnaper, who was never caught.

He's encouraged by Evelyn (Karina Fallenstein), who works at a tv station, to use his computer to "predict" what her long-lost father will look like today, and provides a 20-year-old photograph. Jens soon realizes that Brock (Charles Brauer), the father, is the kidnaper who's obsessed him all these years. Brock becomes aware that his identity has been rumbled . . .

Given this intriguing basic idea, Niklaus Schilling has made a disappointing movie. Far too much footage is spent with Jens at the computer, and the director seems so fascinated with the images on the computer screen that he loses track of the plot.

It's a pity, because once we're away from the computer Schilling is able to whip up a certain amount of suspense, especially toward the end of the film when Brock comes out into the open and finds that his credit cards are worthless and that his fate is sealed. There are solid performances from the three leads, and from Ankie Beilke as Jens' Asian wife, but as the film's editor as well as director Schilling should have been more ruthless in shaping his material. As it is, "The Spirit" is mainly for computer buffs.

—*Strat.*

Che ora è
(What Time Is It?)
(ITALIAN-FRENCH)

Venice A Warner Bros. Italia release of a Cecchi Gori Group-Tiger Cinematografica/ Studio El/Gaumont coproduction. Produced by Mario and Vittorio Cecchi Gori. Directed by Ettore Scola. Screenplay, Scola, Beatrice Ravaglioli, Silvia Scola; camera (color), Luciano Tovoli; art direction, Luciano Ricceri; editor, Raimondo Crociani; music, Armando

Trovajoli; production manager, Franco Cremonini. Reviewed at Venice Film Festival (competing), Sept. 12, 1989. Running time: **97 MIN.**

Marcello . . . . Marcello Mastroianni
Michele . . . . Massimo Troisi
Loredana . . . . Anne Parillaud
Sor Pietro . . . . Renato Moretti
Fisherman . . . . Lou Castel

■ **Ettore Scola pairs two electric thesps, Marcello Mastroianni and Massimo Troisi (who also toplined in his previous "Splendor"), in a slight but charming picture that should have a dignified run ahead of it, at home and offshore.**

Premise is as willfully banal as the title, "What Time Is It?" A father spends a day with his son, who is doing his military service. It works thanks to on-key performances by the two leads, who could well be in line for laurels in Venice.

Mastroianni, the 60-year-old father, is a successful Roman lawyer who has risen from poor origins. He wants to shower all the trappings of middle-class life on son Troisi — fancy car, fancy apartment, trip to America. Michele, his son, is his opposite, a modest literature grad who prefers the company of fishermen and books. He takes after his Neapolitan mother (ergo Troisi's strong accent, at complete variance with Pop's Roman tongue).

The two spend a Sunday together in the port of Civitavecchia, where Michele is stationed. Script hits the expected notes of awkward conversation (Dad is glib and expansive, son reticent and embarrassed), affectionate gestures (Dad gives son Grandpa's railway watch), tension, misunderstanding, a final clash. Story concludes with forgiveness and comprehension between a father and son who live in different worlds, but who have managed to really communicate for the first time.

Film dutifully illustrates the gap in values between the materialistic middle class, always rushing after money and success, and the simple, unpretentious life Michele wants. His girlfriend (Anne Parillaud), pretty and disorderly, cusses like a sailor but is completely natural, like the crusty fishermen in Sor Pietro's bar, where Michele likes to hang out. Though Michele doesn't despise his father's choices, he rejects them for himself. Film is clearly on his side, but Mastroianni injects so much good humor and love for life into the father, the two are pretty well balanced in the end.

Troisi, often self-indulgent when he directs himself, toes the line under Scola's direction without losing any of his amiable spontaneity. He turns what could have been a schematic outsider into a believable character with his head on straight. Armando Trovajoli's sophisticated score and top technical work give pic quality backup.

—*Yung.*

Sen No Rikyu
(The Death Of A Tea Master)
(JAPANESE)

Venice   A Metropolis Film presentation of a Seiyu production. Produced by Kazunobu Yamaguchi. Executive producer, Sueaki Takaoke. Directed by Kei Kumai. Screenplay, Yoshimata Yoda, based on the novel "Honkakubo ibun" by Yasushe Inoue; music, Teizo Matsumura; sound, Yukio Kubota; art direction, Takeo Kimura; assistant director, Kazuo Hara. Reviewed at Venice Film Festival (competing), Sept. 8, 1989. Running time: **108 MIN.**

Rikyu . . . . Toshiro Mifune
Uraku . . . . Kinnosuke Yorozuya
Oribo . . . . Go Kato
Honkakubo . . . . Eiji Okada
Hideyoshi . . . . Shinsuke Ashida
  Also with: Eijiro Tono, Taketoshi Naito, Tsunehiko Manijuo, Taro Kawano, Teizo Muta.

■ **This is the second recent film about the Grand Master of the Tea Ceremony, Rikyu, whose fourth centenary is soon to be celebrated in Japan. Kei Kumai chooses to evoke the Master's last years in this heavy-handed, academic version, leading to his ritual suicide, in the general context of the historical events of the time.**

Kumai does this in retrospect, placing his story 27 years after Rikyu's death occurred. Digging into the past, his characters try to clarify the reasons which led the Master and two of his illustrious colleagues to take their own lives within a short period of time.

Honkakubo, Rikyu's closest disciple, is used as the one source of information which can supply answers once he focuses his memory in the right direction. In a series of encounters with real people, imaginary meetings with his late master and extensive flashbacks, it turns out the reason for the extreme act lay in the conflict between the masters of the tea ceremony and the Princes they served.

This conflict is to be taken as the traditional clash between the spiritual and the material. It is in order to preserve the absolute freedom of the spirit that Rikyu is finally compelled to commit hara-

kiri, this being the only way he could prove true to the principles of his art. Somewhere, along the road, the film also tries to raise the issue of artists barging into political territory, an action that can only end with their defeat.

The film moves ponderously along at a snail's pace, preferring to take Rikyu and his life on a metaphorical level rather than a realistic one. There is much more concern for confrontation between him and his prince than in the fine art he has laid down in the rules for the tea ceremony. While it is repeatedly performed during the film, precious little is said about its significance or meaning.

Kumai relies heavily on the presence of Toshiro Mifune as Rikyu, but fails to explore the potential of the actor. Eiji Okada gives the most balanced performance as Honkakubo, the disconsolate disciple who still lives in the shadow of his departed master.

Soundtrack is grandly melodramatic, while photography is glossy and eye-catching. —*Edna.*

Scugnizzi
(Street Kids)
(ITALIAN)

Venice   A Titanus Distribuzione release of a Clemi Cinematografica production, in association with Titanus Produzione. Produced by Giovanni Di Clemente. Directed by Nanni Loy. Screenplay, Loy, Elvio Porta; camera (color), Claudio Cirillo; editor, Franco Fraticelli; music, Claudio Mattone; art direction, Bruno Garofalo. Reviewed at Venice Film Festival (competing), Sept. 7, 1989. Running time: **122 MIN.**

Fortunato Assante . . . . Leo Gullotta
Don Nicola . . . . Aldo Giuffre
Judge . . . . Pino Caruso
  Also with: Claudia Muzil, Piero Pepe, Nicola Di Pinto (Cotenella), Stefano De Sando, Gerardo Scala, Lina Polito, Imma Piro, Italo Celoro, Giuseppe De Rosa, Marco Leonardi.

■ **The tragedy of street kids in Naples becomes musical entertainment in Nanni Loy's highly original "Scugnizzi." Without trying to sweeten the bitter life of the orphans and abandoned youngsters who live and work on the streets, Loy and cowriter Elvio Porta bypass the usual straight drama to alternate film and theater.**

Result is a more distanced look at the problem than last season's acclaimed drama about Sicilian waifs, "Forever Mary." An emotional score by Claudio Mattone and several good dance numbers might give this unusual pic a shot at the boxoffice.

A 2-bit actor, Fortunato (played

by a fine, low-key Leo Gullotta) is roped into organizing a musical in a boy's reformatory. Though he takes the job strictly for the money (he has to repay a loan — or else), Fortunato gradually is won over by the hardy, intelligent kids with so much talent and so little chance to use it.

Their stories are told as flashbacks while the show is going on in Naples' rich San Carlo theater for an audience of the city's elite. Quality of music, choreography, singing and performances are so high the scugnizzi could go on a world tour tomorrow, but their impossible professionalism and bravura may be one of pic's techniques to remind us it's only a film world. It balances the horrors of the other half, showing the misery and suffering of street life.

Episodes are skillfully interwoven into Fortunato's preparations for the show. One tyke who works for a bar is recruited by a boss to murder another scugnizzo with a gasoline-filled lightbulb. A teenager sees his apartment burn down with his grandmother in it because the fire engines can't get past all the illegally parked cars.

Another hears there's a job open making fireworks, because the owner's son — a boy of five or six — has blown both hands off and can't work anymore.

"Scugnizzi's" merit is that it gets the sense of horror and social waste across in a genuinely entertaining format, keeping the tone light and ironic. The shifting between stage numbers — some of which are excellent — the rehearsals and the boys' lives outside keeps things lively.

Inevitably story's drama suffers somewhat, and a backstage murder of one of the boys doesn't have the punch for a grand finale. Yet film makes its point when the somber cast returns to the reformatory with the audience enthusiastic, their companion dead and the city lost in frenzied joy over the victory of its soccer team.

The boys, all nonpros, turn in surprising performances and stay fresh from the beginning to end.

—*Yung.*

TORONTO FESTIVAL OF FESTIVALS REVIEWS

The Big Bang
(DOCU)

Toronto A Kanter-Toback production. Produced by Joseph H. Kanter. Directed by James Toback. Camera (color), Barry Markowitz; supervising editor, Stephanie Kempf; editor, Keith Robinson. Reviewed at Toronto Festival Of Festivals, Sept. 8, 1989. Running time: **81 MIN.**

With: James Toback, Don Simpson, Jose Torres, Eugene Fodor, Darryl Dawkins, Charles Lassiter, Elaine Kaufman, Emma Astner, Missy Boyd, Max Brockman, Polly Frost, Veronica Geng, Julius Hemphill, Fred Hess, Sheila Kennedy, Anne Marie Keyes. Marcia Oakley, Jack Richardson, Tony Sirico, Barbara Traub, Joseph H. Kanter.

■ **Just who are we and how did we get here? How did it all begin anyway? Does God exist and if so, in what form? James Toback raises all of these questions and answers none of them, but has fun doing so in this engaging exercise in documentary q&a.**

Specialty distributors willing to gamble on an oddball longshot might mull taking a pop at "The Big Bang."

An amusing preamble shows the filmmaker trying to persuade producer Joseph H. Kanter to invest in a film without a story, characters or script. Even the idea is a little vague. Toback, director of the semi-autobiographical "The Pick-Up Artist" has a pet theory that the universe is the fruit of God's orgasm. He wants to interview a disparate group of people about their views on the Big Questions in order to better understand his own. In return for Kanter's financing this whim, Toback promises him the dubious immortality of a full-screen credit.

Toback introduces his subjects: A Hollywood producer, an NBA basketball star, a former boxing champion, a reformed career criminal, a prominent Manhattan restaurateur, a concert violinist, a writer, a survivor of the Auschwitz death camp, a jazz musician, a painter, a fashion model, an astronomer, two children, a Columbia U. student from the inner city, and three women of diverse backgrounds.

Probing their life histories down to the most intimate details, Toback attempts to elicit the group's innermost thoughts on sex, life, death, the afterlife, God and the filmmaker's own version of the big bang theory.

The skip-jump editing with which Toback juxtaposes his interviews keeps the documentary moving along even as it minimizes its inability to grasp a transcendent "truth." Hollywood insiders may find the confessions of Don Simpson (coproducer of "Flash Dance," "Beverly Hills Cop" and "Top Gun") of passing interest. Raised in Alaska in a rigid Baptist fire-and-brimstone milieu, the moviemaker forthrightly describes the rest of his life as one long act of revenge against his upbringing.

Basketball star Darryl Dawkins is full of humorous sexual bravado, but ultimately evinces a deeper vulnerability and hints of religiosity. Boxing champ and author Jose Torres recounts his life as a series of startling progressions somehow foreordained.

The story of the Auschwitz survivor (Barbara Traub) is respectfully employed by Toback to illustrate humankind's infinite capacity for evil. The reflections of the ex-mobster (Tony Sirico) are brimful of irony and regret, but he insists under Toback's point-blank interrogation that he never knowingly killed anyone. People talk about their great romances, nervous breakdowns, sexual initiations, departed parents, triumphs, tragedies and dreams fulfilled and unrealized. Very few it seems have a cogently thought-out world view.

Ultimately, "The Big Bang" acts as a kind of litmus test for self-reflection and audience identification with its subjects. Even as it demonstrates the futility of arriving at a universal formulation of humankind's place in grand design, the loosely linked strands of speculation, rumination and recollection on display make it easy to go along with Toback's wry quest for the revelatory insight. —*Rich.*

Eversmile, New Jersey
(ARGENTINE-BRITISH)

Toronto A J&M Entertainment presentation of a Los Films de Camino production. Executive producers, Julia Palau, Michael Ryan. Produced by Oscar Kramer. Directed by Carlos Sorin. Screenplay, Jorge Goldenberg, Roberto Sheuer, Sorin; camera (color), Esteban Courtalon; editor, Bryan Oates; music, Steve Levine. Reviewed at Toronto Festival of Festivals, Sept. 10, 1989. Running time: **94 MINS.**

Fergus O'Connell . . . . . . Daniel Day Lewis
Estela . . . . Mirjana Jokovic
Also with: Gabriela Acher, Julio de Grazia, Ignacio Quiros, Miguel Ligero.

■ **"Eversmile, New Jersey" is a pretentious road pic that spends much of its running time doing nothing but showing off the lovely rugged landscape of Patagonia as photographed by Estéban Courtalón.**

Daniel Day Lewis is wasted as a silly, dogmatic American dentist motorbiking through Patagonia giving free treatment and urging the unconcerned population to take better care of their teeth.

He allows the about-to-be-married daughter of a tow-truck driver to travel along as his assistant. When she offers sex, he initially refuses by repeating, "I am a dentist." That is just one of the many non sequiturs in a non-realized script.

Title is a reference to name and location of sponsoring foundation, whom he no longer can reach by phone. He also cannot contact his wife back home.

Except for the camerawork, the pic also fails to make contact. Dim future is predicted. —*Adil.*

As Tears Go By
(HONG KONG)

Toronto An In-Gear Film production. Produced by Rover Tang. Executive producer, Alan Tang. Written and directed by Wong Kar-wai. Camera (color), Andrew Lau; editor, Peter Chang, Hai Kit-wai; music, Danny Chung; art direction, William Chang; sound, Roony Ching. Reviewed at Toronto Festival Of Festivals, Sept. 9, 1989. Running time: **102 MIN.**

With: Andy Lau, Maggie Cheung, Jacky Cheung, Alex Man, Wong Un, Lam Gao, Wong Bun.

■ **Tyro director Wong Kar-wai makes the subculture of petty Hong Kong street gangsters the stuff of flashy, entertaining moviemaking in "As Tears Go By." Joltingly violent, sentimental and profane, "As Tears Go By" is a must for festivals and programs on present-day Asian film, and has potential for international video distributors.**

The story is shaped by the hierarchical pecking-orders of the Hong Kong underworld's Triads and the fierce code of honor by which its denizens redress "loss of face." Andy Lau, an aspiring "big brother" in a local Triad, is awakened at his Kowloon slum apartment one morning by a surprise visitor. Maggie Cheung, a beautiful distant cousin from the country, needs a place to stay in Hong Kong while she seeks a cure for a lung virus.

The young hood makes her welcome, then rushes to the aid of his "little brother," Jacky Cheung, who's having a hard time collecting an overdue debt for the gang boss. A first-person p.o.v. tracking shot, used frequently here to set up showdowns, follows Lau into the welsher's gang den. He orders his little brother to stop talking, bashes the debtor bloody with a beer bottle, collects the money and ignites the first of many frenetic chase scenes.

Wong propels his narrative with a glitzy array of cinematic flourishes such as slo-mo, stop-printing, overhead shots and dizzying, off-kilter camera angles. Spatially distorting closeups, like a freshly lit cigaret in full-frame blowup, lend interludes of visual poetry and dreamy romanticism to the film's superheated realism.

The netherworldliness is further enhanced by portentously chorded rock soundtrack colorations modeled after Jan Hammer's "Miami Vice" scoring. The pic is also studded with song-over-action sequences obviously intended for the local musicvideo market.

The Hong Kong of "As Tears Go By" is a neon-lit night world of mean streets, smoky pool halls, macho posturing, unforgiving vendettas and overweening ambition. Loyalty, friendship and respect are precious, particularly to those whose only wealth is their honor, courage and raw toughness. The thought of a straight life is not a viable consideration to Lau and his little brother.

In trying to climb out of poverty and up the slippery rungs of the gangland power structure, the two outsiders from the countryside make bitter enemies. Wong directs with a keen instinct for rollercoaster cause-and-effect dynamics and populates his pic with a gallery of street-real intimidators. Tense confrontational scenes escalate with a kind of brutal lyricism from vicious insult to sudden explosions of primitive violence.

Ultimately the two blood brothers commit themselves to murdering an informant in police custody in order to win favor with the Triad's "godfather" and to erase a serious loss of face incurred in a sadistically brutal street fight. Predictably, Lau's relationship with his sweet country cousin has blossomed slowly into love. Before the hero can give up the life of crime, his ingrained code of honor sets him on a fateful course of action.—*Rich.*

Zazie
(JAPANESE)

Toronto   An Amuse Cinema City presentation. Executive producers, Yokichi Osato, Hisashi Yamamoto, Takaomi Deghuchi, Masami Aritake. Produced by Akira Morishige. Hideaki Tsushima, Tatsuo Hatanaka. Directed by Go Riju. Screenplay, Riju; camera (color), Jyoji Ide; editor, Kan Suzuki; sound, Kunio Ando; art direction, Masanori Yamada. Reviewed at Toronto Festival of Festivals, Sept. 13, 1989. Running time: **95 MIN.**
Zazie . . . . Yoshito Nakamura
Kyoko . . . . Masumi Miyazaki
Megumi . . . . Rikaco
Sunada . . . . Tetta Sugimoto
Bun . . . . Yuki Matsushita

■ "Zazie" is a stunning feature debut that could be titled "Rock Lies And Videotape In Downtown Tokyo." Helmer Go Riju, 27, has taken the navel-gazing out of Japanese experimental video, and like "Sex, Lies..." uses the techno pop format as vehicle of self-discovery in this scenario for former rock star Zazie. If handled properly, pic could be an arthouse hit.

Zazie (played by hot young actor Yoshito Nakamura) is alienated from modern-day Tokyo. He obsessively records his life and his thoughts on tape. He monitors himself on screen. His search for identity is as telling of youth's preoccupations in Japan as "Sex, Lies And Videotape" is of Americans.

Brilliant use of the screen space depicts Zazie's inner angst, a volcano which he can no longer suppress. It's a cauldron that must be explored, a void that must be filled.

Zazie finally begins to re-ignite lost ties with other band members who in turn become frustrated when he continues to indulge in his own preoccupations.

Lack of action and simplistic script work in a minimalist context. Technical qualities are super. Riju has emerged as a talented and potentially explosive new Japanese director whose work will appeal to film buffs and aficionados. —*Suze.*

In The Blood
(DOCU-COLOR/B&W)

Toronto   A White Mountain Films production. Executive producers, William E. Simon, R.L. Wilson. Produced, written and directed by George Butler. Coproducers, Deborah Boldt, Jacqueline Frank, John Leisenring; camera (color), Dyanna Taylor; editor, Janet Swanson; music, Michael Case Kissel; associate producers, Elizabeth Alexander, Elisabeth Bentley. Reviewed at Toronto Festival of Festivals, Sept. 9, 1989. Running time: **90 MIN.**
With: Robin Hurt, Tyssen Butler, Larry Wilson, Greg Martin, Theodore (Ted)

Roosevelt 4th, Theodore (Bear) Roosevelt 5th, Bartle Bull, Harry Muller, Webster Kalipswa, George Butler.

■ "In The Blood," a slick adventure documentary celebrating the primordial urge to hunt, constantly seeks to reconcile its paeans to bloodsport with the cause of conservation. Not nearly as controversial as it aspires to be, the film's best moments come during its literally red-blooded hunting action sequences.

It should prove satisfying to safari-buffs, armchair or otherwise, and could attract curious viewers seeking a vicarious exotic experience.

Filmmaker George Butler, creator of the then-refreshing 1977 docu "Pumping Iron" and its stagey sequel, "Pumping Iron II: The Women," hopes to draw a bead on audiences by tracking an alleged hunting renaissance symbolized by none other than President George Bush. Indeed, the docu is steeped in presidential lore, and on one level plays as a sophisticated home movie featuring a bunch of bluebloods in the brush.

Butler's original plan was to make a docu titled "African Game Trails," modeled on President Theodore Roosevelt's published account of his 1909 safari with his son Kermit. The clever enough concept called for a recreation of that expedition featuring Wall Street investment banker Theodore (Ted) Roosevelt 4th (T.R.'s great-grandson) and his 10-year-old son T.R. 5th (Bear). When the gentlemen's agreement between Butler and T.R. 4th went awry, the filmmaker restructured the docu as an account of the coming-of-age big game "blooding" of his appealing 13-year-old son Tyssen, who narrates the film.

Although T.R.'s descendants have been edited into bit players, the docu is redolent with the spirit of the larger-than-life President Teddy. T.R.'s original antique safari gun (a Holland & Holland in the possession of one of the party) is treated with iconographic reverence by the filmmaker and his colleagues. Butler makes good use of fascinating footage (courtesy of the Smithsonian Institution) shot during T.R.'s safari in the quick-speed, silent b&w style of the day. Some sound effects were added in post-production. Less effective are the first-person excerpts from T.R.'s book read by an actor in breathless voiceover.

The principal voiceover, however, is the narrative of the unprecocious Tyssen Butler, an all-American kid whose grandfather was a British officer in colonial Africa and an enthusiastic hunter. That passion for the hunt was passed down to the filmmaker. Under the wing of great white hunter Robin Hurt of Kenya, Tyssen has come to Tanzania to be initiated into the Butler family's hunting tradition. He's accompanied by his father, a film crew, a party of well-heeled Wasps and some native guides.

In Hemingwayesque fashion, "In The Blood" celebrates the communion alleged to exist between the stalker and the stalked. The hunters forever evoke the *noblesse oblige* concept of "respect" for their prey and obey an elaborate code of honor. Above all, a hunter must never kill an animal before its time (a few years short of natural death), and the killshot must be clean and relatively painless if it's to be judged a sporting one. The frisson of the kill is depicted as the climax of an intricate ceremony the requires skill, patience, cunning and courage. The hunter's reward is the adrenaline-rushing sensual exhilaration of reverting to the primitive state, of meeting the beast — in this case dangerous wild bulls — "on the ground."

Viewers must accept on faith the assertion by Hurt and the other hunting advocates that their bloodsport brings revenues to underdeveloped African nations and encourages conservation by driving away the vicious and unprincipled poachers who reportedly run wild in those countries that have banned hunting. In one tingling sequence the hunting party accompanies Tanzanian paramilitary game wardens in an armed raid on elephant poachers. More dangerous was the setting of a "backfire" enabling some hunters to escape a raging brushfire. Although an African hunter was killed during this sequence, the docu lamely avoids any reference to his fate.

A parallel hunt for a wily man-eating crocodile inspires a brief campfire debate about the morality of hunting that is abruptly terminated in favor of a fest of (allegedly delicious) barbecued bull. Because the documentary attempts to justify hunting on ecological grounds, more time should somehow have been given to critics of this position. "In The Blood" is better off when it is unabashedly paying homage to the visceral pursuit of the hunt. The exciting climax in which Tyssen bags his first bull and subsequently is smeared with its blood in the time-honored "blooding" ceremony crystalizes the film's true nature.

The documentary makes passing anthropological reference to the good-natured natives upon whose turf these holiday hunters are intruding. The tribal spirit is best evoked, however, in a wonderful, under-utilized soundtrack of songs by Toure Kunda, Olatunji and some lesser known but musically mesmerizing tribal groups. —*Rich.*

Kopffeuer
(Heads On Fire)
(WEST GERMAN)

Toronto   A Lerm-Film/NDR production. Executive producer, Julius Leufen, Thomas Wullenweber. Produced by Joachim Rusenberg. Directed by Erwin Michelberger. Screenplay, Michelberger; camera (color), Jorg Schalk; editor, Irmingard Buttler; music, CYAN; sound, Einar Marell; art direction, Maximilian Johannsmann. Reviewed at the Toronto Festival Of Festivals, Sept. 9, 1989. Running time: **87 MIN.**
With: Ameise, Nobuyuki Takayama, Seyran Ates, Klaus Pawlak, Peter Kern, Volker Spengler, Ernst Johan Reinhardt.

■ Angry urban punks living off the fringe of society paint a grim picture of Germany's rebellious youths.

Film focuses on four teens who "prefer a mental hospital than a family," as they take refuge from the world in an abandoned warehouse.

Pic lacks the action or intensity to warrant cult status. However, first-time helmer Erwin Michelberger has courageously and naively tackled a subject most would rather forget: directionless, raging youths whose screams go unheard.

Alev is a Turkish girl escaping a pre-arranged marriage. Yukio is a Japanese youth whose dream of being in a band will never materialize. David is the group's pinnacle who "decorates" the warehouse in a hopeless attempt to create a pseudo-family atmosphere. Gerold is a male prostitute constantly on the rampage. Their band continually strengthens until their home and dreams are once again shattered by vandals.

It's a commendable effort which adds another chapter to the rebel without a cause theme, despite the fact that pic doesn't quite live up to its fiery title. —*Suze.*

Tongdang Wansui
(Gang Of Three Forever)
(TAIWANESE)

Toronto   A Wanli Film production. Produced by Lee Ching-Fu, Chu Gee-Cheung. Directed by Yu Wei-Yen. Screenplay, Shau Sa; camera (color), Lee I-Shu; editor, Chen Buo-Wan; sound, Fu Kuo. Reviewed at Toronto Festival Of Festivals, Sept. 9, 1989. Running time: **97 MIN.**
    With: Shu Kwei-Yin, Lee Ming-I, Lee Jee-Shee, Chang See, Teng An-Ning, Tsang Che-Jen.

■ **The only thing this film is missing is the kitchen sink. Pic follows the gang of three from youth through old age with a mish-mash of supporting char-** acters whose ties with the three are never made clear and never resolved.
    Smatterings of politics, romance and culture are introduced extraneously.
    Pic slides from one segment of the gang's life to the next without warning or continuity. The evolution of American rock 'n' roll is the only accurate way to identify decade and time frame.
    Dreadful lighting casts an eerie yellow glow on the entire film, rendering it visually lifeless. Speed reading is required to follow the English subtitles. —*Suze.*

BOSTON FILM FEST REVIEWS

Gokiburi
(Twilight Of The Cockroaches)
(JAPANESE/ANIMATED/-
LIVE ACTION)

Boston   A Streamline Pictures release of a TYO production; a Gaga Communications presentation. Produced by Hiroaki Yoshida, Hidenori Taga. Written and directed by Yoshida. Camera (color), Kenji Misumi; animation design, Hiroshi Kurogane; music, Morgan Fisher; sound (Dolby), Susumu Aketagawa; art direction, Kiichi Ichida; lighting, Masaaki Uchiba. Reviewed at Loews screening room, Boston, Sept. 7, 1989. (In Boston Film Festival.) No MPAA Rating. Running time: **105 MIN.**
    With: Kaoru Kobayashi, Setsuko Karasumara.

■ **This 1987 subtitled fantasy entry mixes animation with live action, but any similarities to "Who Framed Roger Rabbit" end there. Rather than family audiences, pic is geared to grown-ups with predilection for serious fantasy, a genre with unproven appeal Stateside.**
    Story centers on an (animated) cockroach colony in an apartment belonging to a Mr. Saito. Bugs are depicted as humanoid except for antennae and an extra set of arms. (Arms are gloved to sidestep the creatures' lack of hands.) All seems idyllic for a young female roach and her fiance, until a warrior from "the other side of the field" — actually another apartment — arrives to tell how the roaches are engaged in a terrible battle with the woman there.
    Audiences may be hardpressed to side with roaches against the humans, but they are asked to suspend disbelief and sympathize with peaceful vermin who simply wish to feast on our leftovers and live in peace. Problems arise when the female human and Saito get to- gether, with the woman insisting he rid his apartment of infestation.
    Mixture of live-action humans and animated cockroaches is done well, with anthropomorphized bugs dying valiantly amid clouds of bug spray and the occasionally well-placed shoe. Sound is especially effective in playing up how the world is perceived by roaches. Bulk of film is fully animated, with most bizarre sequence featuring a femme roach getting directions from a talking pile of dog droppings.
    The story ends on a triumphant note with a survivor proving that roaches will indeed inherit the Earth. Pic, which is playing the Boston Film Festival as part of an all-night "Comics And Cartoons" sidebar, seems best suited to venues able to handle such esoteric animation/fantasy material.
    —*Kimm.*

American Blue Note

Boston   A Vested Interests production. Produced and directed by Ralph Toporoff. Associate producers, Gilbert Girion, Bill Hart. Screenplay, Girion, from a story by Toporoff and Girion; camera (Technicolor), Joey Forsyte; editor, Jack Haigis; music, Larry Schanker; sound, Dale Whitman; production design, Charles Lagola; costumes, Nina Canter; first assistant director, Mike Liston; casting, Stanley Soble. Reviewed at Loews screening room, Boston, Aug. 30, 1989. (In the Boston Film Festival.) No MPAA Rating. Running time: **97 MIN.**

Jack	Peter MacNicol
Jerry	Carl Capotorto
Bobby	Tim Guince
Lee	Bill Christopher-Myers
Tommy	Jonathan Walker
Benita	Charlotte d'Amboise
Lorraine	Trini Alvarado

Also with: Louis Guss, Zohra Lampert, Eddie Jones, Sam Behrens.

■ **With an ad campaign that** played down the jazz elements and focused on the idea of young adults starting out on their careers, "American Blue Note" has some sleeper potential.
    Following a few weeks in the life of a struggling jazz quintet circa 1961, film has several nicely etched episodes of the highs and lows of being young and uncertain about the future.
    Pic focuses on the band's leader Jack (Peter MacNicol) who takes the group on weekend gigs to weddings and backroad dives, trying to get a chance to make it at a 52d Street nitery in New York. Episodic nature of the film makes one think of session players telling stories about when they were still wet behind the ears. There are the endless auditions, the publicity photographs, the latenight dinners and the wedding that requires both Italian and Irish standards.
    Jack also begins a relationship with a ballet instructor (Charlotte d'Amboise), proving himself to be as tentative a romantic as he is a bandleader. Ultimately film shows how Jack has to grow up a bit and take a more realistic look at his future.
    First-time feature director Ralph Toporoff previously worked as a camera operator and assistant cameraman (as well as directing for tv), and his eye for visual composition is obvious. In one sequence, the band begins an impromptu roadside performance for a bride and groom whose car has a flat. Toporoff takes his time in easing a police car into frame and building the gag to its payoff. A few other scenes tend to drag, especially a scene between Jack and his uncle which is pointlessly ambiguous.
    Performances are professional, with several players in smaller roles standing out, particularly James Puig as a gas station attendant forced into the quintet when one of its members fails to arrive for a club date.
    Gentle, often wry style should please audiences provided they're tipped off that this is a "people's" story and not another jazz film that's incomprehensible to outsiders. —*Kimm.*

Champions Forever
(DOCU)

Hollywood   An Ion Pictures release, in association with Champions Forever Inc. Produced by Nabeel Zahid, Joseph Medawar. Executive producers, Tom Bellagio, Hollister Whitworth. Directed by Dimitri Logothetis. Written by Kenneth W. Griswold, from Story Consultant F. Daniel Somrack; no camera or color process credit; music, Bebu Silvetti; no sound credit; coproducer, Griswold. Reviewed at AMC Century 14 Cinemas, L.A., Sept. 19, 1989. No MPAA Rating. Running time: **90 MIN.**

■ **While theatrical prospects for this sports documentary are rather limited, it should have a long life as a cable tv and homevideo item. For this lovingly assembled tribute to the fighters of what can truthfully be called "the Muhammad Ali era," is a natural for hardcore boxing fans that should even attract the attention of those with only a passing interest in the sport.**
    Consisting of newly filmed interviews with Ali, George Foreman, Joe Frazier, Larry Holmes and Ken Norton, juxtaposed through judicious use of split screens with footage of their various fights, "Champions Forever" can lay claim to genuinely show boxing from the inside out.
    In the process, without consciously intending to do so, the film goes a long way toward answering critics of the sport who view it as nothing more than sheer physical brutality for its own sake. For as we see in these carefully chosen clips, and hear from these boxers, explaining things in their own words (the film is mercifully free of narration), the object of the game is strategically outwitting your opponent — a process at which Ali was past-master.
    It's fascinating to look and listen to boxers like Norton and Frazier, who were physically far more imposing than Ali, explain how his speed and agility conspired to exhaust and defeat them. Fascinating too are their related remarks.
    Foreman speaks with pride of his being a by-product of the Johnson administration's "Headstart" poverty program. "It was fashionable to be compassionate about people then," he says. "It hasn't been so fashionable lately."
    Norton, still recuperating from a calamitous auto accident that ended his career and nearly cost him his life, speaks with obvious respect and appreciation of his onetime opponent, Ali, who he says rushed to the hospital when he

heard of Norton's fate. "Before he came along the purses for boxing were small," Norton notes. "After Ali, they just went through the roof."

The object of all this respect (somewhat grudging on Frazier's part, it must be said) is not the man he once was physically — crippled as he is by Parkinson's disease. Though his speech is somewhat slurred, his mind is as alert as ever. It's a joy to hear Ali talk about his career, and for those too young to have seen it, something of a revelation to watch in retrospect.

It's amazing to see once again images of the brash, funny, and incredibly forceful figure then known as Cassius Clay speaking to sports reporters in a manner no fighter ever did before or since. Using newsreel clips, the film puts Ali's story in perspective, showing the relation of his conversion to Islam to the struggles of the civil rights movement.

Appropriately Ali has the last word in the film. Asked how he'd like to be remembered, he says the days of his calling himself "the greatest" are past. "All I have to say is when I retired from boxing the sport *died*."

After seeing "Champions Forever," few would be likely to disagree with him.—*Rens*.

Mutant On The Bounty

Hollywood A Skouras Pictures release of a Canyon Films presentation. Produced by Robert Torrance, Martin Lopez. Directed by Torrance. Screenplay. Lopez, from story by Lopez, Torrance; camera (Foto-Kem Color). Randolph Sellars; editor, Craig A. Colton; music. Tim Torrance; production design. Clark Hunter; art direction Hilja Keading; sound, Robert Janiger; mutant makeup design. Brian Penikas & Associates; assistant director. Michael N. Grossman; associate producer. Karen J. Lewis; casting. John Jackson. Reviewed at AMC Century 14, L.A., Sept. 22. 1989. MPAA Rating: PG-13. Running time: **94 MIN.**

Carlson . . . . John Roarke
Justine . . . . Deborah Benson
Dag . . . . John Furey
Babette . . . . Victoria Catlin
Lizardo . . . . John Fleck
Max . . . . Kyle T. Heffner
Rick O'Shay . . . . Scott Williamson
Manny the Weasel . . . . John Durbin
Captain Lloydes . . . . Pepper Martin

■ **Lame, sophomoric, dumb, crude — none of these words adequately conveys the experience of watching "Mutant On The Bounty," a prime candidate for the next Golden Turkey Awards.**

"From the people who saw 'Star Wars,'" as the trailer puts it, this cheapie sci-fi parody made by Robert Torrance and Martin Lopez would have earned an F if it had been a film school project. B.o. future is grim for the Skouras Pictures release, which had its first playdates last month.

The witless screenplay is a graphic demonstration of just how bad a script can be and still reach the screen in today's anything-goes marketplace. The sparse audience at a first-day showing in L.A. laughed only two or three times, perhaps more from embarrassment than anything else.

Kyle T. Heffner is the title character, a saxophone player who was beamed up to a gig 23 years ago and never made it there. When he's beamed back to life on the spaceship USS Bounty in 2048, his mutated face makes him resemble General Noriega with a severe case of eczema.

There's no menace or suspense emanating from this "alien," since he's a regular guy who soon becames pals with the laid-back crew and starts a nonchalant romance with sweet-natured magazine reporter-photographer Deborah Benson.

The crew also includes a flighty humanoid robot (John Fleck) who sometimes sounds like James Earl Jones and sometimes like Tammy Faye Bakker, a cynical doctor (Victoria Catlin) with an accent like Inspector Clouseau's, a pot-bellied captain (Pepper Martin) who drops dead on his first sight of the mutant, and two other guys (John Roarke and John Furey) who mostly hang around looking bored.

Heffner and Benson are enjoyable enough under the dismal circumstances, but the less said about the others the better, except for giggling villain Scott Williamson, who becomes an active irritant in the last half-hour of the pic when he's beamed aboard to make something happen.

Most of the film takes place in a single small set, with occasional cutaways to wobbly special effects shots of obvious model spaceships. Lenser Randolph Sellars brings some splash to the threadbare goings-on, and Tim Torrance's music works hard to feign some pacing.

One of the characters says that in the early years of space exploration, Earth would execute criminals by beaming them out into oblivion. That would be the kindest fate for "Mutant On The Bounty." —*Mac*.

Trust Me

New York A Cinecom Pictures release of a Bruce Feldman, Harry Clein and David Weisman presentation. Executive producer. Curt Beusman. Produced by George Edwards. Directed by Bobby Houston. Screenplay. Houston, Gary Rigdon; camera (United color). Thomas Jewett; editor, Barry Zetlin; music. Pray For Rain; music supervised by Peter Afterman. Diane Delouise Wessel; sound. David Waelder; set decoration. Richard Dearborn; production manager-assistant director. Tony Brewster; associate producer. Bert Swartz; casting. Barbara Remsen, Ann Remsen Manners. Reviewed at Review 1 screening room, N.Y., Aug. 1. 1989. MPAA Rating: R. Running time: **104 MIN.**

James Callendar . . . . Adam Ant
Sam Brown . . . . David Packer
Catherine Walker . . . . Talia Balsam
Billy Brawthwaite . . . . . . William DeAcutis
Nettie Brown . . . . Joyce Van Patten
Mary Casal . . . . Barbara Bain
Also with: Brooke Davida. Simon McQueen. Alma Beltran. Marilyn Tokuda. Barbara Perry. Virgil Frye. Morri Beers. Anna Cray Carduno.

■ **"Trust Me," Bobby Houston's hip satire on the art world, presents a clique of engagingly quirky characters played by a strong cast of fresh faces and reliable veterans. The nice-looking low-budget production starts out clever, but falls flat at the windup.**

Indie production's modest scale as well as soft ending make it a commercial challenge for Cinecom, which inked for distribution quite a while ago with publicists Bruce Feldman and Harry Clein and "Kiss Of The Spider Woman" producer David Weisman. Similarity with Wayne Wang's "Slam Dance" won't help.

Not that Wang and Houston's works are bad; they're just not extraordinary. Returning, post-"Slam Dance," as another cynical Brit facing off with naive Los Angelenos, Adam Ant plays James Callendar, a financially strapped art gallery owner who doesn't know much about art.

Callendar does know, however, that in terms of commercial success, "dead means bread." He sets out to drive innocent young artist Sam Brown (David Packer) over the brink to drive up the price of Brown's poignant paints of cherubs in flight. When Brown isn't self-destructing fast enough and the cost of hitmen proves prohibitive, Callendar personally attempts to off the artist.

That's pretty much the plot, except for what becomes a predictable romantic subplot between Brown and adorable art gallery employee Catherine Walker (Talia Balsam). "Trust Me's" aces are its well-drawn characters who have some genuinely funny lines.

Faring much better than in the misfired "You Can't Hurry Love," Packer turns in a winsome performance as the reluctant artist, although he often acts like Crispin Glover in "Back To The Future." Exuding confidence in her role, Balsam also gets to do a scene with her real-life mother, Joyce Van Patten, playing Packer's long-suffering mom to the comic hilt.

Also featured are William DeAcutis as the fey gallery assistant; Barbara Bain, as an icy, scheming art gallery owner, and the work of artists such as David Salle, Robert Longo, Keith Haring, Jiri Georg Dokoupil, Joel Peter Witkind, Linus Correggio, Jean-Michel Basquiat and Andy Warhol.

That ending, though, is a big problem, raising more questions than it answers. The filmmakers pretty much abandoned characters they made the audience care about.—*Binn*.

Time Burst — The Final Alliance

New York An Action Intl. Pictures production. Executive producers. David Winters, Bruce Lewin. Produced and directed by Peter Yuval. Screenplay. Yuval. Michael Bogert; camera (Image Transform color), Paul Maibaum; editor, Todd Felker; music, Todd Hayen; sound, Karen Perron; art direction, Eric Warren; production manager, Robert Katz; assistant director, Peter Flynn; coproducer, Bogert; associate producer, Sadie Winters. Reviewed on AIP vidcassette. N.Y., Aug. 18. 1989. No MPAA Rating. Running time: **93 MIN.**

Urbane . . . . Scott David King
Jane English . . . . Michiko
Master . . . . Gerald Okamura
Mueller . . . . Jay Richardson
Takeda/Akira . . . . Craig Ng
Also with: Chet Hood, Jack Vogel. Richard Rogers, Beano.

■ **A modest made-for-video sci-fi feature, "Time Burst" lacks the special effects and straightforward storytelling needed to attract a following.**

Filmmaker Peter Yuval's previous genre effort, "Dead End City," was a crisp B picture while "Time Burst" is awkwardly constructed. Nutty opening has hero Scott David King walking away from a Cessna plane crash after he's kidnaped an antiquity dealer (Richard Rogers) killed in the plane mishap. Vintage Japanese samurai are battling in the California forest nearby for no reason.

King has amnesia but is soon chasing hither and yon with pretty (and violent) teammate Michiko, a CIA operative. Snippets of exposition finally reveal that everyone's after a set of ancient Japanese tablets, held by Gerald Okamura, that offer the key to immortality. King turns out to be 350 years old and impervious to bullets and such, making for some cute though silly plot twists during shootouts.

King, a handsome young thesp vaguely resembling Stephen Collins, delivers a straightforward performance in a confusing role while Michiko adds a distinctive, offbeat beauty to the pic. —*Lor.*

Un Père et passe
(Fathers)
(FRENCH)

Paris A Films Number One release of a Ca Films/Films A2/SGGC coproduction. Produced by Anne Fleischi, Sophie Deloche. Directed by Sébastien Grall. Screenplay, Grall, Alex Varoux, Patrick Braoude; camera (color), Manuel Teran; editor, Jacques Comets; music, Pierre Papadiamandis; sound, Pierre Lorrain, Gérard Lamps; art direction, Valérie Grall; assistant director, Veronique Labrid; casting, Shula Siegfried. Reviewed at Marignan-Concorde theater, Paris, Aug. 15, 1989. Running time: **84 MIN.**

With: Véronique Genest (Marianne), Eddy Mitchell (Nikos), Guy Marchand (Jacques), Luc Thuillier (Pascal), François Berleand (Maxence), Penelope Schellenberg (Camille), Christian Charmetant, Ged Marlon.

■ **Too many papas spoil the child in this latest product of the paternalistic baby boom engendered by "Three Men And A Cradle." Amusing in some of its characterizations, comedy is less assured in its often broad unconvincing plot turns.**

Chances to travel are probably limited to fest exposure.

The youngster here is the 10-year-old girl who has been brought up by her mother but doesn't know who her dad is. One day, youngster (Penelope Schellenberg) finds three letters addressed to three men who were romantically involved with mom (Véronique Genest) shortly before Schellenberg was born. Genest, on a dangerous photojournalism assignment in Lebanon, intended to ask the men to look after Schellenberg in the event that she's killed, but she never posted them.

Curiosity (and the desire for a paternal presence) now prompts the girl to mail the letters during Genest's professional absence. The three men quickly answer, which creates confusion galore in the lives of everyone concerned, including mom's current boy-

friend (François Berleand) and her employer, another ex-beau (nicely played by rock star Eddy Mitchell).

Band of confused papas are uptight middle-class teacher Guy Marchand, charmingly sleazy antique dealer Christian Charmetant, and footloose young Luc Thuillier (only a teen when he knew the older Genest). Their communal adventures include "kidnaping" Schellenberg from an orphanage when Genest is reported a political prisoner in Africa.

Patrick Braoude, who coauthored recent comedy hits "Black Mic Mac" and "L'Oeuil au buerre noire" wrote the wobbly script with Alex Varoux. Direction by Sébastien Grall is adequate. —*Len.*

Cutting Class

New York A Republic Pictures release of a Gower Street Pictures presentation of an April Films production. Executive producers, Peter S. Davis, William N. Panzer. Produced by Rudy Cohen, Donald R. Beck. Directed by Rospo Pallenberg. Screenplay, Steve Slavkin; camera (Image Transform color), Avi Karpick; editor, Nathan Zahavi, Bill Butler; music, Jill Fraser; sound, Peter Bentley; production design, Richard Sherman; costume design, Kelly Troup; assistant director, Donald Newman; production manager, Cohen; second unit director, Beck; casting, Eric Boles. Reviewed on Republic Pictures videcassette, N.Y., Aug. 22, 1989. MPAA Rating: R. Running time: **90 MIN.**

Brian Woods	Donovan Leitch
Paula Carson	Jill Schoelen
Dwight Ingalls	Brad Pitt
Dr. Dante	Roddy McDowall
William Carson	Martin Mull
Colleen	Brenda Lynn Klemme

Also with: Mark Barnet, Robert Glaudini, Eric Boles, Dirk Blocker, Nancy Fish, Robert Machray, David Clarke, Norman Alden, Tom Ligon.

■ **Several notches above the typical slasher film, "Cutting Class" dares to satirize the genre while suspensefully engineering enough plot twists to be taken straight by genre fans.**

Donovan Leitch (son of the folksinger) heads a talented cast, portraying a loony who's the prime suspect in a rash of high school murders. Coed Jill Schoelen sympathizes with him and helps Leitch try to clear himself, while her boyfriend (Brad Pitt) has mixed motives; he still harbors guilt for having shown Leitch how to fiddle with daddy's car, resulting in the death years back of Leitch's papa.

Murders, via ax and other grisly modes, are matched with comic relief. Notable is a running gag of Shoelen's dad, Martin Mull, left in the woods for dead, but turning

up at the end of the picture in a clever gag. Nancy Fish also scores in a perfect caricature of a mean old biddy as principal Roddy McDowall's second in command.

Final reel is loaded with credible switches shifting the blame, made all the more interesting by scripter Steve Slavkin's careful detailing and clues. Director Rospo Pallenberg uses the school setting atmospherically in staging suspense scenes.

As in "The Stepfather," Jill Shoelen is quite convincing as the anything-but-helpless heroine, while Leitch and Pitt square off effectively as the alternate good guys/bad guys. Tech credits are fine. —*Lor.*

Nowhere To Run

New York A Concorde Pictures release. Produced by Julie Corman. Directed by Carl Franklin. Screenplay, Jack Canson, Nancy Barr, from Canson's story; camera (Foto-Kem color), Phedon Papamichael; editor, Carol Oblath; music, Barry Goldberg; sound, Gregory Choa; production design, Sherman Williams; costume design, Darcee Olson; production manager, Albert T. Dickerson 3d; assistant directors, Dickerson, Eddie Ziv; 2d unit director, Melitta Fitzer; 2d unit camera, Igor Meglic; associate producer, Lynn Whitney. Reviewed on MGM/UA Home Video vidcassette, N.Y., Sept. 16, 1989. MPAA Rating: R. Running time: **85 MIN.**

Harmon	David Carradine
Howard	Jason Priestley
Jerry Lee	Kieran Mulroney
Cynthia	Jillian McWhirter
Judge Culbert	Henry Jones
Saralynn	Kelly Ashmore
Joanie	Brenda Bakke
Sheriff Tooley	Andy Wood
J.W.	Sonny Carl Davis

Also with: Ed Call, Tony DeCarlo, Matt Adler, Sonia Curtis, Richard Partlow, Jocelyn Jones, Don Steele, Brigett Butler.

■ **"Nowhere To Run" is an unconvincing, poorly scripted nostalgia piece lamely trying to merge "American Graffiti" with "Phenix City Story." It's in regional theatrical release awaiting its date with video destiny next month.**

Title confusion here is rampant: Pic initially was released as "Temptation Blues" and had earlier shooting titles of "Caddo Lake" and "Heroes Stand Alone;" the "Heroes" moniker has since been reassigned to another Concorde picture made in South America starring Chad Everett. Besides a 1978 tv movie by that name, two new productions also are called (tentatively) "Nowhere To Run" — a Sandy Tung-helmed pic starring Rick Schroeder and a soon-to-roll Cannon/Pathé project.

This edition is set at a Texas high school in 1960 where, in between puppy love romances, all the students are planning what object to put in the time capsule for posterity. Caddo County (actually lensed in California) is filled with corruption. Local crime boss David Carradine has just been sprung from jail and is warring with rival politicians (notably the judge, played by Henry Jones) over control of local rackets.

Hero Kieran Mulroney becomes involved when he goes to work at Carradine's bait house and witnesses many things he shouldn't. Contrived script has Carradine going on the revenge warpath, with a whirlwind final reel of stupid plot twists handled quite cynically. Writers Jack Canson and Nancy Barr obviously didn't take this one seriously, as in a serious scene punctuated by anachronistic dialog such as "It's a done deal."

Overburdened by explanatory voiceover narration by Mulroney, pic is pleasantly directed by Carl Franklin except for a botched incest subplot: Pretty heroine Jillian McWhirter has been raped by her dad (Andy Wood), who's running for office. This fact is relied upon for several of the final plot twists and doesn't work at all.

Acting is okay, with a standout turn by sexy Brenda Bakke as Carradine's ex-wife and resident goodtime girl. —*Lor.*

Quicker Than The Eye
(SWISS)

New York A Condor production, coproduced by SRG, ZDF, ORF, Crocodile Prods., Paul-Boris Lobadowsky, William Hartman. Produced by Peter-Christian Fueter. Directed by Nicolas Gessner. Screenplay, Joseph Morhaim, Gessner, from Claude Cueni's novel; additional dialog, Brian Strasman; camera (Schwarz Filmtechnik color by Fuji), Wolfgang Treu; editor, Daniela Roderer; music, George Garvarentz; sound (Dolby), Jürg von Allmen; production design, Max Stubenrauch; assistant director, Urs Egger; dialog director, Robert Rietty; casting, Paul Bengston, David Cohn. Reviewed on Academy Entertainment vidcassette, N.Y., July 22, 1989. MPAA Rating: PG. Running time: **92 MIN.**

Ben Norell	Ben Gazzara
Mary Preston	Mary Crosby
Inspector Sutter	Jean Yanne
Catherine Lombard	Catherine Jarrett
Kurt	Wolfgang Berger
Gertrude	Dinah Hinz
Schneider	Ivan Desny
Silke	Sophie Carle
Pres. Makabutu	Robert Liensol
Christian	Eb Lottimer

(English soundtrack)

■ **"Quicker Than The Eye" is a modest Swiss-made programmer headed shortly for the U.S. video market. It plays like an** elongated tv episode.

Ben Gazzara is a bit uncomfortable in the lead role of a semi-successful magician touring Europe with his whiny ("Let's get married") assistant Mary Crosby. Nasties, led by Ivan Desny, plot to use him as the dupe to kill an African leader attending a summit conference in Lucerne, with the blame to fall on Gazzara.

The hitmen fail to complete their mission, with Gazzara escaping rather than being murdered. With the aid of Crosby and other beautiful women he adapts his long-in-the-works super magic trick to outwit and catch the baddies.

Pic is well lensed on lovely locations but fails to generate suspense. Gazzara's magic feats are perfunctory, and little interest is generated by the cornball romantic rivalry between Crosby and their employer (Catherine Jarrett) for Gazzara's boudoir attentions.

Tech credits are good, including English dubbing of support roles supervised by Robert Rietty.

—*Lor.*

Domino
(ITALIAN)

New York A Taurus Entertainment release of a Compagnia Distribuzione Intl. presentation of a Clemi Cinematografica production. Produced by Giovanni Di Clemente. Executive producer, Michal Janczarek Kapuscinski. Directed by Ivana Massetti. Screenplay, Massetti, Gérard Brach, from story by Massetti; camera (Cinecittà color), Tonino Nardi; editor, Anna Rosa Napoli; music, Alessandro Murzi, Massimo Terracini; sound, Mario Dallimonti; art direction, Giantito Burchiellaro; costume design, Silvana Fusacchia. Reviewed on IVE vidcassette, N.Y., Aug. 19, 1989. MPAA Rating: R. Runnng time: **91 MIN.**

Domino . . . . Brigitte Nielsen
Also with: Thomas Arana, Daniela Alzone, Lucien Bruchon, Pascal Druant, Cyrus Elias, Stephane Ferrara, Joy Garrison, Giancarlo Geretta, Yves Jouffroy, Kim Rossi Stuart, Antonella Tinazzo, David Warbeck.

(English soundtrack)

■Though pretty to look at, "Domino" is a Brigitte Nielsen vehicle that's hopelessly pretentious. Falling between art film and sex pic, Italo import has had a modest theatrical release but is likely to bewilder curious video fans.

With a murky script by Nielsen and frequent Roman Polanski collaborator Gérard Brach, filmmaker Ivana Massetti tries in vain for avant-garde effects and an almost sci-fi atmosphere: All the action is shot on abstracted sets at Cinecittà with even car-driving scenes reverting to process photography. Though the pithy, pretentious

English dialog is delivered well by an unidentified cast, none of it makes sense.

Nielsen is Domino, a platinum-blond beauty (given to wearing numerous dark wigs) who's working on a video docu about Billie Holiday. We're treated to "You Don't Know What Love Is" and other terrific recordings by Lady Day, plus vintage footage of her, but Massetti's endless homage has little to do with the plot.

There is little action, but a lot of languorous scenes of masturbation (R-rated in terms of explicitness), Nielsen operating her videocamera and soul-searching talk about sex. Lest this sound like the Italian version of "Sex, Lies And Videotape," note that Massetti has little interest in character interaction — she prefers monologs directed to human sounding boards.

Nielsen sees a silhouetted couple making love in the apartment across the street and a voyeur with telescope. And she's plagued by obscene phone calls. She wanders around, talks to several beautiful black women and consorts with a sexy sound man. Pic's silliest stretch for philosophical import is her monolog about the meaning of a growing spot on her skin (not shown), diagnosed as dermatitis.

Viewer does get to see plenty of Nielsen's unblemished skin, presumably the film's drawing card. However, unlike previous Italian effort "Bye Bye Baby," in which her acting was fine, Nielsen's bored line readings here are embarrassing. Rest of cast is functional, with British thesp David Warbeck popping up as a blind neighbor.

Massetti's visual expertise is evident, with fascinating lighting by Tonino Nardi and some amazing (if occasionally trashy) costumes for Nielsen by Silvana Fusacchia. —*Lor.*

VENICE FILM FEST REVIEWS

Dekalog
(The Ten Commandments)
(POLISH)

Venice A Polish TV presentation of a Polish TV production, with Sender Freies Berlin. Directed by Krzysztof Kieslowski. Screenplay, Krzysztof Piesiewicz, Kieslowski; camera (color, 16m), Wieslaw Zdort (1st episode), Edward Klosinski (2d episode), Piotr Sobocinski (3d & 9th episodes), Krzysztof Pakulski (4th episode), Slawomir Idziak (5th episode), Witold Adamek (6th episode), Dariusz Kuc (7th episode), Andrzej Jarosiewicz (8th episode), Jacek Blawut (10th episode); editor, Ewa Smal; music, Zbigniew Preisner; sound Malgorzata Jaworska (episodes 1, 2, 4, 5), Nikodem Wolk-Laniewski (episodes 3, 6, 7, 9), Wieslawa Dembinska (8th episode); art direction, Halina Dobrowolska. Reviewed at Venice Film Festival (Special Events section), Sept. 5-14, 1989. Running time: **584 MIN.** (1st episode: **55 MIN.**, 2d episode: **59 MIN.**, 3d episode: **58 MIN.**, 4th episode: **58 MIN.**, 5th episode: **60 MIN.**, 6th episode: **61 MIN.**, 7th episode: **57 MIN.**, 8th episode: **56 MIN.**, 9th episode: **60 MIN.**, 10th episode: **60 MIN.**)

First Commandment (I am the Lord thy God. Thou shalt have no other God but me):
Father . . . . Henryk Baranowski
Son . . . . Wojciech Klata
Aunt . . . . Maja Komorowska
Second Commandment (Thou shalt not take the name of the Lord thy God in vain):
Doctor . . . . Aleksander Bardini
Wife . . . . Krystyna Janda
Husband . . . . Olgierd Lukaszewicz
Third Commandment (Honor the Sabbath day):
Ewa . . . . Maria Pakulnis
Janusz . . . . Daniel Olbrychski
Janusz' wife . . . . Joanna Szczepkowska
Fourth Commandment (Honor they father and thy mother):
Anka . . . . Adrianna Biedrzynska
Michal . . . . Janusz Gajos
Anka's boyfriend . . . . Artur Barcis
Fifth Commandment (Thou shalt not kill):
Murderer . . . . Miroslaw Baka
Lawyer . . . . Krzysztof Globisz
Taxi driver . . . . Jan Tesarz
Sixth Commandment (Thou shalt not commit adultery):
Magda . . . . Grazyna Szapolowska
Tomek . . . . Olaf Lubaszenko
Tomek's landlady . . . . Stefania Iwinska
Seventh Commandment (Thou shalt not steal):
Ewa . . . . Ana Polony
Majka . . . . Maja Barelkowska
Stefan . . . . Wladyslaw Kowalski
Wojtec . . . . Boguslaw Linda
Eighth Commandment (Thou shalt not bear false witness):
Zofia . . . . Maria Koscialkowska
Elzbieta . . . . Teresa Marczewska
Tailor . . . . Tadeusz Lomnicki
Ninth Commandment (Thou shalt not covet thy neighbor's wife):
Hanka . . . . Ewa Blaszczyk
Roman . . . . Piotr Machalica
Tenth Commandment (Thou shalt not covet thy neighbor's goods):
Jerzy . . . . Jerzy Stuhr
Artur . . . . Zbigniew Zamachowski
Shop owner . . . . Henryk Bista

■For true film buffs, this series of ten 1-hour films is the cinema event of the year. Coveted by practically every festival in sight, it was displayed in full for the first time in Venice.

Two of the episodes (the fifth and the sixth) won awards in their feature film form, titled, respectively "Thou Shalt Not Kill" (a.k.a. "A Short Film About Killing") and "A Short Film About Love," while the First, Ninth and 10th have been traveling from one fest to another since first unveiled in Cannes this year. Seeing the full cycle only confirms the immense talent of Polish director Krzysztof Kieslowski and the originality of this project.

The 10 modern moral stories he spins are inspired by the Ten Commandments, but do not refer directly to the Biblical text, nor do they apply theological interpretation to it. This is why Kieslowski insists on using only the number of the commandment as the title for each film, and never mentions the commandment itself in the credits. The audience is invited to identify them and to figure out the connection between the moral aspect of the plot and the Letter of the Divine Law.

All 10 stories are placed in the same gray and depressing block of new concrete buildings in a Warsaw suburb, where university professors and taxi drivers live side by side. It's a drab and unattractive solution offered by the Socialist regime to growing housing problems. Leading characters in one episode will emerge again, as passersby or secondary characters, in another episode. One plot may be mentioned again in a later one and familiarity is bred with this little world, which accurately reflects a much bigger one.

On the most immediate level, this is a downbeat, perceptive and pitiless image of Polish reality. Kieslowski has no wish to make any political statement, but makes some very serious observations about the quality of life in his country and the effect it has on the people living there.

A profound sense of guilt accompanies all his characters. It varies in nature from episode to episode, but is always there, a determining factor in their conduct. This is probably the reason critics have found a strong Catholic influence in the cycle.

The mystical, unexplained presence of the same character in nine of the 10 episodes, a silent youth who looks sadly and even disapprovingly at the proceedings but takes no part in them, seems to confirm this interpretation. Such is denied by Kieslowski, who evidently feels it limits the scope of his project.

The conflicts he portrays are ethical rather than religious, with the possible exception of the first two installments, in which man tries, for a little while, to take on the authority of God. In both cases he fails piteously. The first episode is about the trust and affection between a father, his son and their personal computers. In the second one, an old doctor is coerced into predicting the chances of one of his patients to survive. His answer shows how unreliable science is.

In the third episode, a man is forced by a former mistress to drive all over town on New Year's Eve. The fourth explores the dark, incestuous passions of a daughter for her widowed father. In the fifth, best known until now in its feature-length film version, he points out the fallacy of justice, which demands an eye for an eye.

The sixth, the most romantic of all, deals with the loss of innocence that prevents an older woman from responding to the advances of a much younger man. In the seventh episode, a little girl is the object of a ruthless struggle between her mother and her grandmother.

The eighth, the one episode in which ethics are clearly stated as the object of the story, has a professor of ethics faced with her own past and decisions during the Holocaust. The ninth has an impotent husband struggling helplessly to believe in his wife's fidelity. The 10th, in which black humor abounds, has destitute brothers fall prey to temptation when they inherit their father's stamp collection. When they decide against selling it (as they originally intended), they find themselves wheeling and dealing to enlarge it to the best of their limited ability.

Being a pessimist at heart, Kieslowski, who cowrote all 10 scripts, unfolds a variety of human weaknesses, shows how difficult it is to conform to one commandment, let alone 10, and considers human frailty with sympathy but little hope. All his characters are defeated and disappointed in the end, conscious of the nagging doubt that will stay with them forever, even when it seems they have reached satisfactory solutions to their problems. Kieslowski seldom

allows that to happen.

All the stories are relatively simple, almost elementary in their construction. They involve two or three characters at the most and proceed in a straightforward, unadorned, linear fashion. The visual style is spare and precise, wasting no time or space. Dialog usually is kept to the absolute minimum, but acting is of such high standard that most of the time there is no real need for words.

It is difficult to single out performances in the uniformly excellent casts, which feature some of the top talent in Poland. Even Krystyna Janda and Daniel Olbrychski, probably best known because of their careers in the West, are toned down from their normal stentorial tones to the general level of subtle, understated and moving contributions of the rest.

Direction is so perfectly controlled, that in 10 hours of film, there rarely are any instances of voices being raised above normal. This only makes the emotional stress they hide more explosive. Kieslowski remains faithful to the intimate mood he establishes in the first few minutes, and the result is overwhelming.

One editor and one art director worked on all 10 films, resulting in a steady, unhurried but inexorable rhythm throughout the series. Set design shrewdly establishes a separate background for each story, yet they share something basic in common.

Kieslowski uses the same composer and the same opening theme throughout, a simple, heartbreaking tune that sets the mood even before the first image comes on the screen.

He changes cameramen from film to film, not only to accommodate their schedules, but to give a slightly different look to each film. The most obvious example is the discolored, filtered images of the fifth episode, the only instance in the entire cycle of graphic horror, featuring one of the most shocking murder scenes ever filmed.

After the Venice screenings, the general opinion was that in spite of its being produced for tv, the cycle should be given theatrical exposure first. With judicious handling it could fit perfectly in slots that accommodated earlier film events of the same scope, like "Berlin Alexanderplatz," "Heimat" and "Shoah."

One problem concerns the rights for the fifth and sixth episodes. The aforementioned feature films

have been on the market for over a year now (handled by Film Polski). The cycle as a whole, containing the same two films in shortened versions (at least as effective as the longer ones), is sold by the Polish TV sales bureau, Poltel.—*Edna.*

Storia Di Ragazzi E Di Ragazze
(A Story Of Boys And Girls)
(ITALIAN-B&W)

Venice A Warner Bros. release (in Italy) of a Duea Film-Unione Cinematografica production, in collaboration with RAI Uno. (Intl. sales, Sacis, Rome.) Produced by Antonio Avati. Written and directed by Pupi Avati. Camera (b&w), Pasquale Rachnini; editor, Amedeo Salfa; music, Riz Ortolani; production design, Daria Ganassini, Giovanni Zighetti; sound, Raffaele De Luca; costumes, Graziella Virgili; production managers, Francesco Guerrieri, Luca Bitterlin; assistant director, Massimo Tomagnini. Reviewed at Venice Film Festival (Venice Night section), Sept. 7, 1989. Running time: **92 MIN.**

With: Felice Andreasi (Domenico), Angiola Baggi (Maria), Davide Bechini (Angelo), Lina Bernardi (Olimpia), Anna Bonaiuto (Amelia), Massimo Bonetti (Baldo), Claudio Botosso (Taddeo), Valeria Bruni Tadeschi (Valeria), Claudia Casaglia (Donatella), Monica Cervini (Paola), Marcello Cesena (Lele), Consuelo Ferrara (Dolores), Stefania Orsola Garello (Antonia), Alessandro Haber (Giulio), Lucrezia Lante della Rovere (Silvia), Susanna Marcomeni (Renata), Claudoi Mazzanga (Marco), Enrica Maria Mondungo (Linda), Ferdinando Orlandi (Nando), Roberta Paladini (Loretta), Claudia Pozzi (Gina), Massimo Sarchielli (Don Luciano), Mattia Sbragia (Augusto), Ciro Scalera (Alberto).

■Pupi Avati specializes in comedies, often with large groups of people. His latest, "A Story Of Boys And Girls," is one of his best: a wholly delightful film that invites the audience to join in the engagement celebrations of a city boy and a country girl in the winter of 1936.

The traditional feast (a 30-course meal) has been prepared by the girl's extended family — and the local priest — in the large old farmhouse where she lives. Meanwhile, the upper-middleclass family of the young man, who live in Bologna, are not exactly looking forward to meeting their future inlaws.

Matters are complicated because the girl's father has just been caught in his latest infidelity, and is reduced to tears by the news that his mistress has been unfaithful to him. Also, a traveling salesman who has rented a room each year for his wife and family arrives unexpectedly with his young French mistress in tow, causing additional woes for the hostess.

Much of the film takes place during the long meal, where all

kinds of Tuscan delicacies are consumed. As the wine takes its hold, some tearful stories are told and a rifle is fired carelessly (nicking the arm of the bride-to-be's mother, but nobody seems very concerned about it).

The meal is followed by a siesta, and some amorous activity between the two families. In the end, the city folk leave and everyone heaves a collective sigh of relief.

The film is splendidly cast and acted: It would be invidious to pick out individual performances, since the ensemble cast is near flawless.

Avati's warm, generous vision encompasses amusing details (such as the groom-to-be's family maid, who, the night before the party, is caught between dinner courses by her lover and emerges flushed and disheveled to serve the meat). There are some genuinely lovely characters (like the working-class boy from Rome, friend of one of the country girls, who, when quizzed by the visitors, doesn't know any of the city's fashionable streets).

The black & white photography (slightly soft, because it was shot on color negative) is so beautiful that it gives the illusion of being filmed many years ago. Riz Ortolani's score is one of his best: attractive and not overused. Amedeo Salfa's editing is extremely good.

This could be Avati's international breakthrough film, if the black & white photography isn't seen as a negative point by distribs. Good to very good arthouse runs in major cities worldwide are indicated for this generous, charming movie, which is filled with sentiment but never crassly sentimental. —*Strat.*

Layla, ma raison/
Mágnún Layla
(Mágnún And Layla)
(TUNISIAN-ALGERIAN-FRENCH)

Venice A Tanit Prods. (Tunis)/Centre Algérien pour l'Art et l'Industrie Cinématographique (Algiers)/Ben Aknoun Entreprise Nationale pour l'Audiovisuel (Algiers)/ATRIA Films (Paris) coproduction. Executive producer, Lofti Layouni. Written and directed by Taieb Louhichi, based on the novel "Layla, ma raison" by André Miquel; additional dialog, Miquel; camera (color), Ramón Suárez; editor, Moufida Tlatli; music, Egisto Macchi. Reviewed at Venice Film Festival (competing), Sept. 14, 1989. Running time: **107 MIN.**

Qays/Mágnún . . . . Safy Boutella
Layla . . . . Anca Nicola
Qay's father . . . . Tarak Akan
Layla's father . . . . . Abderrahmane al Rachi
Mute girl . . . . Fatma Ben Saidane

Also with: Mouna Noureddine. Fatima Helilou. Hichem Rostom. Sid Ahmed Agoumi.

■ **A seventh century Arab legend about the tragic love between a poet and his beloved provides the frame for "Magnún And Layla."** This Tunisian-Algerian-French coprod starts slow but builds to an emotional climax that should be appreciated by audiences interested in Afro-Arab cinema. In other respects it looks thin for arthouse circulation.

Tunisian helmer Taieb Louhichi earned a sizable reputation with "Shadow On The Earth," film about a nomadic tribe destroyed by modernity. In "Layla," his third feature, he abandons ethnographic concerns for pure storytelling, with mixed results.

Based on a novel by Frenchman André Miquel, tale is the familiar one of starcrossed love, opposed by the young couple's elders for no good reason. Qays (Algerian thesp Safy Boutella) and Layla (Rumanian actress Anca Nicola) have their parents' blessings to marry. Unable to contain his joy and desire, Qays breaks with the custom of the time and sings verses exalting his love. Layla's harsh father (Syrian thesp Abderrahmane al Rachi) feels so dishonored over having his daughter's virtues enumerated in public, he calls off the marriage.

Qays' loving père (a moving performance by Turkish thesp Tarak Akan) does everything he can to change Rachi's mind, but after multiple refusals he marries the girl off to another man. Qays becomes known as Mágnún (the madman, in Arabic), and goes on singing wondrous verses about his love as a hermit in the desert. In the end the lovers die, unable to live without each other.

Multinational cast includes Tunisian actress Fatma Ben Saidane in the curious role of a mute girl who observes the tragedy unfold like a Greek chorus. Film's epic ambitions stumble on indifferent performances by leads, who lack the stuff legends are made of. One senses the grandeur of the story rather than sees it on the screen.

Louhichi turns the sunburned desert sands into an eternal backdrop; wisely, decor and costumes are kept spartan and have a biblical feel. —*Yung.*

Palombella Rossa
(Red Lob)
(ITALIAN)

Venice A Titanus release of a Sacher Film production in association with Nella Banfi-Palmyre Film/RAI-TV Channel 1/So.Fin.A. (Intl. sales, Sacis, Rome.) Produced by Angelo Barbagallo, Nanni Moretti. Written and directed by Moretti. Camera (color), Giuseppe Lanci; editor, Mirco Garrone; music, Nicola Piovani; art direction, Giancarlo Basili, Leonardo Scarpa. Reviewed at Venice Film Festival (Special Event), Sept. 9, 1989. Running time: **87 MIN.**
Michele . . . . Nanni Moretti
Reporter . . . . Mariella Valentini
Also with: Silvio Orlando, Alfonso Santagata, Claudio Morganti, Asia Argento, Eugenio Masciari, Mario Patane, Antonio Petroce''i, Remo Remotti, Fabio Traversa, Giovanni : - tafava, Imre Budavari, Raul Ruiz.

■ **Maverick helmer Nanni Moretti provides more evidence he's the most intelligent spokesman for his generation of 35-year-olds in "Red Lob."** Title refers to a technique for scoring a goal in water polo, and virtually the whole film takes place in a swimming pool during a wild and woolly water polo match. The game is great fun in itself, but Moretti uses it to reflect on the Italian Communist Party and its present impasse.

As brilliantly as he turns water polo into politics and back again, the sophisticated in-jokes are not likely to be understood much beyond the borders, both geographical and cultural. In Italy, pic has the makings of a season smash — or maybe a cult item.

Moretti plays Michele Apicella, the character who has appeared in many of his films, here an important young politician who repped the CP on tv in a pre-election "Meet The Press"-type show. After a car accident, he loses his memory, and his first great discovery as he tries to reconstruct his life — and pic's first big laugh — is, "I'm a communist!"

Swept along with his team to a water polo meet, Michele finds himself besieged by a reporter (Mariella Valentini), whose trite questions drive him into a diatribe against journalism and the imprecise used of words. Michele takes frequent breaks in the match to watch the key scenes of "Doctor Zhivago" on tv, clash with his teenage daughter and reflect on (or try to remember) why he is a communist.

In between insidious moves by the opposing team and failed strategy on his side (the referee even throws Michele's coach out of the match), Michele is hounded

by a pair of dissatisfied militants and a Catholic fundamentalist who keeps repeating, "I'm glad you exist. Are you glad I exist?" He's especially dogged by his and other people's memories of what the Party used to be like, when he went selling militant papers door to door (a funny insert of a younger Moretti in his own Super-8m footage from the '70s). "Do you remember. . ." becomes an unbearable refrain.

In "Red Lob," politics, sports and the neurotic hero's existential crisis are interwoven in a clever, often hilarious film with a strongly autobiographical ring to it. Interesting as the attempt is, it probably can be fully appreciated only with a good knowledge of Italian politics of the last two decades. Other audiences are likely to feel lost in the web of jokes and references and leave the pic wondering what side the actor-director is on after all. (Actually, Moretti declares he's a non-card-carrying communist.)

Pic's strong points are fine comic timing, on-target observations transformed into gags and original thinking. Less compelling is its overall structure, and film struggles to find a way to end. Cast includes many nonpros, but little does it matter: Faces and 1-liners are the thing. Moretti, who is a water polo player offscreen, opens himself up in one of his most personal and enjoyable performances.
—*Yung.*

Tempo di Uccidere
(The Short Cut)
(ITALIAN-FRENCH)

Venice A Titanus release of an Ellepi Film/Dania Film/SURF Film/D.M.V. Distribuzione/Italfrance coproduction, in association with Reteitalia. Produced by Leo Pescarolo, Guido De Laurentiis. Directed by Giuliano Montaldo. Screenplay, Furio Scarpelli, Giacomo Scarpelli, Paolo Virzi, Montaldo, based on Ennio Flaiano's novel "A Killing Time;" camera (color), Blasco Giurato; editor, Alfredo Muschietti; music, Ennio Morricone; art direction, Davide Bassan; associate producer, Giancarlo Bertelli. Reviewed at Venice Film Festival (Venice Night), Sept. 10, 1989. Running time: **110 MIN.**
Enrico Silvestri . . . . Nicolas Cage
Mario . . . . Ricky Tognazzi
Mariam . . . . Patrice Flora Praxo
Major . . . . Giancarlo Giannini
Also with: Gianluca Favilla, Georges Claisse, Robert Liensol, Vittorio Amandola.

■ **The interior drama of a soldier who believes he's been infected with leprosy is soberly lensed with no bow to touristic exoticism, yet "The Short Cut" has an inner tension that grabs**

hold. Careful handling should land it offshore business.

Many directors have wanted to shoot Ennio Flaiano's 1949 war novel "A Killing Time," among them Jules Dassin, Valerio Zurlini and Francesco Rosi. Darryl F. Zanuck held onto an option for almost 20 years, and only last year producers Leo Pescarolo and Luciano Martino acquired rights from 20th Century Fox. At last brought to the screen by Giuliano Montaldo (director of tv's "Marco Polo" as well as the classic "Sacco And Vanzetti"), "The Short Cut" proves worth the wait.

Nicolas Cage plays Enrico, an Italo lieutenant in Ethiopia disappointed in his expectations that Africa was an earthly paradise. One day, separated from his regiment, he takes an ominous short cut that leads him to a lake where an enticing native girl (French thesp Patrice Flora Praxo) is bathing nude.

Enrico rapes her, but afterward the girl is so gentle and attentive he spends the night with her in a cave. During the night he fires at a strange animal; the bullet ricochets and gravely wounds the girl, as Enrico tells his buddy Ricky Tognazzi in a flashback. What he only reveals much later — this time to the girl's father — is that he panics and finishes the dying girl off with his gun. Then he hides the body and all traces of their presence.

Though Enrico escapes detection, he can't avoid punishment. Second part of the film centers around his growing conviction the girl's blood has infected him with leprosy through a scratch on his hand. At this point, most audiences are bound to read leprosy as a metaphor for AIDS, even though in the original novel it had no such connotation. This accidental echo gives his drama a contemporary edge.

Enrico nervously visits a medic, gets hold of a gruesomely illustrated book on the disease, and turns into a desperate runaway, terrified of going back to Italy and infecting his wife and child. In his anxiety he also becomes a thief, stealing money from a corrupt major, Giancarlo Giannini (hammy in an out-of-place comic role).

Eventually it is Africa that takes pity on him in the person of the dead girl's father, who nurses him back to health and dispels his groundless fears. A healthy Enrico heads homeward at war's end, while the lesson of tolerance he's learned so painfully is lost both on him and on Italy with its cruel postwar colonial decrees.

Cage gives the lieutenant a dull irritability and thoughtless presumption that keeps the viewer at a distance from the character — in this case, the right distance. Pic is told partly from Enrico's p.o.v., partly from his pal's, partly as a simple story, and again this apparent defect works out well in the end, creating multiple entry points into the mysterious tragedy.

Blasco Giurato's curiously cool, desaturated camerawork works out unexpected tonalities in the African landscape (pic was lensed in Kenya, Zimbabwe and Spain). Tognazzi and Flora Praxo are good in supporting roles. —*Yung.*

Donator
(The Donator)
(YUGOSLAV)

Venice A Jadran Film production, in collaboration with Meteor Film. Directed by Veljko Bulajic. Screenplay, Ivan Bresnan, Bulajic; camera (Eastmancolor), Boris Turkovic; editor, Sandra Botica; music, Arsen Dedic; production design, Vladimir Tadej; costumes, Jasna Novak; production manager, Ante Deronja. Reviewed at Venice Film Festival (Venice Night section), Sept. 8, 1989. Running time: **108 MIN.**
Eric Slomovic . . . . . . .Ljubimir Todorovic
Siegfried Handke . . . . .Peter Carsten
Juana. .Urska Hlebec
François Yvette . . . . .Charles Millot
Rosa Slomovic . . . . .Ana Karic
Ambroise Vollard . . . . .Tonko Lonza

■ "The Donator" is an unenthralling wartime drama about a German officer's search for a priceless French art collection. Unconvincing backgrounds and characters limit this to local exposure.

The story, told in flashback, is structured around the search by German officer Handke (Peter Carsten) for a Yugoslav Jew, Eric Slomovic (Ljubimir Todorovic) who, before the war, befriended a famous French collector of impressionist paintings and, on his death inherited the collection.

Unfortunately, the characters (as written and performed) fail to come to life, and the familiar tale lacks tension and drama. Another major problem is that, try as he might, production designer Vladimir Tadej is unable to make Zagreb streets look remotely like Paris.

Director Veljko Bulajic, best known for large-scale pics like "The Battle Of Neretva" (1969), just goes through the motions with this stolid tale. The actors fail to register, though Urska Hlebec is fetching as the Spanish model who

becomes Eric's lover.

Apart from production design, technical credits are adequate.
—*Strat.*

Et la Lumière Fut
(Let There Be Light)
(FRENCH-W. GERMAN-ITALIAN)

Venice A Films du Triangle production with La Sept (Paris), Direkt Film (Munich), RAI-1 (Rome). Produced by Alain Queffelean. Written and directed by Otar Iosselliani; camera (color), Robert Alazraki; editor, Iosselliani, Ursula West, Marie-Agnes Blum; music, Nicolas Zourabichvili; sound, Alix Comte; set decoration, Yves Brover; costumes, Charlotte David; production director, François Xavier Decaene. Reviewed at Venice Film Festival (competing), Sept. 13, 1989. Running time: **106 MIN.**
With: Sigalon Sagna (old healer), Saly Badji (wife leaving husband), Binta Cisse (girl riding crocodile), Marie-Christine Dieme (young mother), Fatou Seydi (potter), Alpha Sane (Yere the traveller), Abdou Sane, Souleimane Sagna, Marie-Solange Badiane, Moussa Sagna, Ousmane Vieux Sagna, Salif Kambo Sagna, Fatou Mounko Sagna, Oswaldo Oliveira Bouba Sagna.

■ For a festival insisting on defining films by their national origins, this is a tough nut to crack. It's by a Georgian director who lives in the West, uses French, West German and Italian coin to shoot a film in Africa.

Whatever the official designation, this is an Otar Iosselliani movie, true to his reputation as a poet of the screen who refuses to tell stories and prefers to catch moments of life, who turns down professional actors in favor of amateurs less polished but more authentic, who reaches for gentle allegories and sometimes delivers unexpectedly sardonic conclusions.

His intentions in this film are perfectly clear. Mankind systematically and consciously destroys the world it has inherited, and spoils its chance for bliss and happiness through greedy, unthinking, foolish actions. The human race needs no vengeful God to banish it from paradise — it writes its own sentence without any difficulty.

Paradise for Iosselliani is an African village, living in perfect harmony under a matriarchal sort of social system. Women hunt for food, men do the washing, nature is bountiful in every respect, contentment is general and life goes on peacefully and uneventfully from one day to another. People don't need any clothes, for the climate is mild, they don't need entertainment as long as they can watch the sunset every evening, and they don't need property as long as

there is enough around for all. Heavy trucks carry lumber through the village once in a while, but nobody pays attention to them. They belong to an alien world which doesn't concern the inhabitants of this village.

The camera adopts the position of the unobtrusive observer and registers village routines, inserting incidents such as a woman leaving her lazy husband for another man with the approval of the entire village, or the old healer bringing down rain to fill up a freshly dug well. Speaking their own language, the protagonists are naturally unintelligible outside their own home, but Iosselliani does not feel the need to supply any translation. Only once in a long while is there a title indicating what is being said, but the actions are eloquent enough to make everything clear.

The village idyll is disrupted once the men in the trucks stop there and start cutting down the trees. The paradise is lost, the villagers are sent packing into exile, forced to adapt to a modern world of military camps, shanty towns, passports, borders and misery.

If Iosselliani's message is not that original, his way of conveying it certainly is. He has an uncanny talent to fix on screen human behavior in its natural state. His sensitive eye lovingly catches the beauty and ridicule of human conduct.

Africa is obviously an allegory, the film referring to the state of mankind. Well served by Robert Alazraki's camera, he creates a lyrical image of what human society could be and then, ironically but also sadly, follows its destruction. The villagers must have taken the presence of Iosselliani's crew and the necessities of filming in their stride, for they look as unaffected and spontaneous as if this were a documentary, not a fiction film.

Not everyone will take to this type of filmmaking, which is entertaining only for those prepared to accept Iosselliani's uncompromising approach. Film fests and cultural events will surely cheer, while commercial distribution needs careful handling and judicious choice of exhibition outlets. —*Edna.*

Ek Din Achanak
(Suddenly One Day)
(INDIAN)

Venice A National Film Development Corp.-Doordarshan production. Executive producers, Ravi Malik, Debashis Mujumdar. Directed by Mrinal Sen. Screenplay, Sen, based on a story by Ramapada Chaudhuri; camera (Eastmancolor), K.K. Mahajan; editor, Mrinmoy Chakraborty; music, Jyotishka Dasgupta; production design, Gautam Bose; sound, B.K. Chaturvedi, Anup Mukherji. Reviewed at Venice Film Festival (competing), Sept. 12, 1989. Running time: **105 MIN.**
Neeta . . . . .Shabana Azmi
Aparna . . . . .Aparna Sen
Sudha (mother) . . . . .Uttra Baokar
Shasanka (father) . . . . .Sreeram Lagoo
Seema . . . . .Roopa Ganguly
Anu . . . . .Arjun Chakraborty
Samar (uncle) . . . . .Manohar Singh

■ Bengali director Mrinal Sen's latest is an intriguing story about the sudden disappearance of a retired academic; but the director's unemotional handling of an emotional subject will restrict the film's b.o. possibilities.

The opening scenes set up an interesting situation: during a heavy rainstorm, Shasanka tells his wife, two daughters and son that he's going out for a walk — but he never returns. What happened? We might expect a police investigation, but the police never come into the picture.

Instead, members of the family recall (in flashback) moments spent with the missing man to search for clues as to his disappearance. One such clue involves an envelope on which he'd written, over and over, the name of one of his students, Aparna; and flashbacks show the visits the lovely Aparna (Aparna Sen) made to the apartment. But when she's located, she denies any relationship with the missing man.

The mystery remains unresolved at fadeout, and we haven't been given much insight into the characters. Since most of the film is set in the family apartment, it has the feeling of a play rather than a film.

Shabana Azmi is fine as the older daughter, but Sen's approach gives the actors little chance to bring depth to their roles. The film winds up as dusty as the books that line the apartment shelves. —*Strat.*

Un Monde Sans Pitié
(A World Without Pity)
(FRENCH)

Venice A Les Productions Lazennec production. (Intl. sales, UGC.) Executive producer, Alain Rocca. Directed by Eric Rochant. Screenplay, Rochant; camera (color), Pierre Novion; editor, Michèle Darmon; production design, Thierry François; music, Gerard Torikian; sound, Jean-Jacques Ferran; production manager, Adeline Lecallier. Reviewed at Venice Film Festival (Critics Week), Sept. 10, 1989. Running time: **87 MIN.**

Hippo	Hippolyte Girardot
Nathalie	Mireille Perrier
Halpern	Yvan Attal
Xavier	Jean-Marie Rollin
Francine	Cécile Mazan

■ **Eric Rochant emerges as an impressive new director with "A World Without Pity," a raffish tragicomedy which seems to accurately capture a particular way of life for the youth of Europe's big cities right now. The pic's freshness and wit will guarantee it a life on the fest circuit, with possible arthouse runs indicated.**

The film's central character, Hippo (disarmingly played by Hippolyte Girardot) is not exactly cynical about life: He's just resigned to a dull existence. He hasn't a job, he doesn't seem to go to the movies or concerts or restaurants; he hangs out with a few friends, drives a battered car (the front doors won't open) and half-heartedly dreams of a love affair he knows in advance will end badly.

He sets his sights on the pretty Nathalie (Mireille Perrier) and eventually gets invited over to her place to tea(!) which leads to a night together, but — wouldn't you know? — she's leaving next day on a trip. When she returns, things (including the police, who are always harassing Hippo) conspire to keep the lovers apart.

Rochant, who previously made some interesting short films, seems to be on the verge of an exciting career. He and his wonderful cast have created an authentic, sad-funny world, peopled with characters who manage to be both touching and maddening. The seemingly casual style of direction exactly fits the milieu of the drifting characters, who find it hard to communicate directly, and yet dream impossibly romantic dreams.

The performances and the skillful direction more than make up for the wafer-thin plot. It may be a hardsell, but responses should be good to this modestly impressive debut.—*Strat.*

Chameleon Street

Toronto A Prismatic One-Filmworld Intl. production. (Intl. sales, Films Around the World.) Produced by Dan Lawton. Executive producers, Helen B. Harris, Hobart W. Harris. Written and directed by Wendell B. Harris Jr. Camera (color), Daniel S. Noga; edi-

tor, Matthew Mallinson; music, Peter S. Moore; art direction, Tim Alvaro; sound, Bernard Hajdenberg. Reviewed at Toronto Festival Of Festivals, Sept. 14, 1989. (Also in Venice Film Festival, Critics Week.) Running time: **98 MIN.**

With: Wendell Harris, Angela Leslie, Aminaa Fakir, Paula McGee, Anthony Ennis, David Kiley.

■ **Using the real life story of an Afro-American "great imposter" for inspiration, auteur-actor Wendell B. Harris Jr. has fashioned an erratic low-budget comedy that veers wildly from stretches of bizarre originality to misdirected overreaching.**

Like its hapless protagonist, "Chameleon Street" tends to undermine itself just when its wacko momentum seems to be going places.

Harris will come up short in the inevitable comparisons to Spike Lee and Robert Townsend. Yet there's enough twisted wit and contempo black attitude on display in "Chameleon Street" to draw the core audience of black college students and "buppies" apparently targeted by the filmmaker. Its appeal to the hip crossover crowd is questionable, and will depend on word-of-mouth.

Told in flashback through an interview with a prison psychiatrist, the mostly true story of William Douglas Street (Harris) starts off in Detroit, circa 1978. The overbearingly well-spoken hero is going berserk from the boredom of working in his father's burglar alarm business and frittering away his diffuse intelligence in banal rap sessions with coworkers and drinking buddies.

Divorced, restless and living with his parents, Street's greatest asset is his unbridled imagination. Soon he begins to exteriorize his fantasies: "I think, therefore I scam."

A scam plan to blackmail Detroit Tigers star Willie Horton is absurdly botched when one of Street's nutty cohorts sends the extortion letter to a local newspaper over the hero's signature. Making the best of a bad situation, Street exploits his new-found status as a "media darling," giving inane interviews to junk journalists voracious to devour the hot topic of the moment.

Remarriage to a sexy and materialistic woman galvanizes Street to pursue a rewarding and prestigious career in medicine. Why bother with a trifle like medical school? Street breezily convinces a hospital that he's a Harvard-trained resident transfer, and the

filmmaker scores some tart sociological points about appearance and reality as the imposter mesmerizes his white medical colleagues. Using his faux-Harvard resume like a talisman, he bluffs his way through a surgery scene in which the gross-out humor unfortunately overwhelms the satire.

Harris sets "Chameleon Street" on a jittery episodic course, steering the film with an illogical, freewheeling loopiness. Too frequently the situations concocted by Harris the director are not exploited fully by Harris the comic actor. He bug-eyes and deadpans his way through a sequence in which Street interviews an Amazon-like female basketball star by posing as a reporter for Time magazine.

The film's black man's point-of-view on black women owes a clear stylistic debt to Spike Lee, but Harris can't push his sexual humor over the top. After he's apprehended and sentenced for his doctor act, Street talks his way out of a jailhouse rape in another underdeveloped situation.

Harris is capable of cutting loose with short bursts of comic verbal inventiveness. A highlight is his rapid-fire explanation of the "f-word's" etymology to an obnoxious redneck. In spite of the film's narrative ambitions, however, its funniest moments have the disconnectedness of a series of skits.

The narrative of "Chameleon Street" breaks down seriously during an overlong interlude at Yale University, where Street flees after escaping prison. Easily crashing the campus, he poses (shades of Eddie Murphy) as an African exchange student speaking hopelessly fractured French. A visually surreal costume ball sequence during which the hero is literally unmasked could have been a nice metaphor for the character's life, but is permitted to meander where it should have kicked butt.

Street's "intricate web of lies" entangles him just as his self-created persona has taken a promising new turn in the Detroit government bureaucracy. The enigma and the joy of the character ultimately flow from his refusal to concede to rehabilitation. Harris is smart to treat the imposter as a provocative anti-hero but only partially successful in evoking Street's complexity and the comic pathos of his story.—*Rich.*

Venezia Rosso Sangue
(Venice Blood Red)
(ITALIAN-FRENCH)

Venice A Sena Intl.-Reteitalia-Clea Prods.-President Films coproduction. (Intl. sales, President Films, Paris.) Produced by Augusto Caminito, Adolphe Viezzi, Jacques-Eric Strauss, Henri Lassa. Directed by Etienne Périer. Screenplay, Périer, Matthew Pollack, from story by Georges Garone; camera (Eastman color), Marcello Gatti; editor, Noelle Balenci; music, René Michel Dazey, Antonio Vivaldi; sound, Daniel Couteau; production design, Luciano Spadoni; costumes, Jost Jakob, Stefania D'Amario; production manager, Angelo Zemella; assistant director, Vivalda Vigorelli. Reviewed at Venice Film Festival (noncompeting), Sept. 14, 1989. Running time: **110 MIN.**

Carlo Goldoni	Vincent Spano
Vivaldi	Wojtek Pszoniak
Nicoletta	Isabel Russinova
Tiepolo	Massimo Dapporto
Princess Ortensia	Andréa Ferréol
Grand Inquisitor	Victor Lanoux
Torelli	Yorgo Voyagis
Celia	Valérie Mairesse
Silvio Conio	Galeazzo Benti

■ **"Venice Blood Red" must have been chosen for the closing night attraction at this year's Venice festival solely because of its setting: Venice in 1735. The city at carnival time is marvelously photogenic, but nothing else about this clammy coproduction is memorable.**

The basic idea is serviceable. Carlo Goldoni, a would-be playwright, finds a backer for his latest effort in the wealthy Spinoza; his benefactor is murdered by a masked man who leaves a red silk handkerchief beside the corpse. Subsequent backers, including Princess Ortensia, are similarly rubbed out, and the Grand Inquisitor suspects the hapless author, who eventually becomes a potential victim himself.

Unfortunately, director Etienne Périer handles his material without flair. Mixing very labored comedy with swashbuckle and mystery, the director seems to be aiming for the kind of off-beat humor Richard Lester brought to the best of his period films; he falls wide of the mark, however.

Vincent Spano doesn't register much as Goldoni, but might fare better in the English-track version currently being prepped (there's also a French version, titled "Venise Rouge"). Polski actor Wojtek Pszoniak seems to be having more fun than anyone else in the cast; he plays the composer Antonio Vivaldi as a Harpo Marx type, with long hair, extravagant gestures and a nagging wife. Victor Lanoux is very dour as the Grand Inquisitor, though Isabel Russinova does bring some charm to a routine role as the hero's love interest (who has a wealthy and influential papa). As in all too many whodunits, the murderer is all too easy to spot.

Star of the film is undoubtedly Venice itself, the world's greatest movie set. Nods, too, for Marcello Gatti's camerawork and the costumes of Jost Jakob and Stefania D'Amario.

The film is technically slick, but overlong at 110 minutes. International prospects aren't promising, but a video career is possible, even though the film satisfies neither as a murder mystery nor as a romantic comedy. —*Strat.*

Es ist nicht leicht ein Gott zu sein
(Hard To Be A God)
(WEST GERMAN-SOVIET)

Venice A Jugendfilm-Verleih (in West Germany)/Titanus (in Italy) release of a Hallelujah Film (Munich)/Sovinfilm (Moscow)/Dovzhenko Studio (Kiev) coproduction, in association with Garance (Paris)/Mediactuel (Switzerland). Executive producer, Angelika Stute. Produced and directed by Peter Fleischmann. Screenplay, Fleischmann, Jean-Claude Carrière, based on novel by Arkady and Boris Strugatsky; camera (color), Pavel Lebeshev, Klaus Müller-Laue, Jerzy Goscik; editor, Marie Jo Audiard; music, Jurgen Fritz; art direction, Oksana Medwid, Sergei Chotimski; special effects, Yuri Lemeshev. Reviewed at Venice Film Festival (Venice Night), Sept. 12, 1989. Running time: **133 MIN.**
Rumata . . . . Edward Zentara
Kyra . . . . Anne Gautier
Suren . . . . Hugues Quester
Reba . . . . Aleksandr Filipenko
Okana . . . . Christine Kaufmann
Anka . . . . Birgit Doll
Baron . . . . El Gudsha Burduli
Also with: Werner Herzog (Mita), Regimantes Adomaitis, Pierre Clementi (king), Thomas Schücke, Aleksandr Boltnev.

■ **Eight years in the making, Peter Fleischmann's tribulations on the pioneering West German-Soviet coproduction "Hard To Be A God" will act as a warning to other producers eager to launch blockbusters with the Russians.**

Happily film has been completed at last, though pic screened in Venice was a work print with special effects and color-correction missing. In addition, both producers and Fleischmann are eager to recut, though whether in the interest of making a faster adventure film or a fuller philosophical parable remains to be seen. Pic is reviewed here as a work print bound to undergo modifications before release in February.

Film is based on a sci-fi tale by the Russian Strugatsky brothers, who've provided material for Andrei Tarkovsky and others. Earth

scientists of the future send men to a distant planet to study its civilization, which still is in the Middle Ages. What the explorers don't know is that the real purpose of their mission is to see whether they'll lose their nonviolent instincts and revert to violence and barbarism.

In the form unspooled in Venice, "Hard To Be A God" works fairly well as a straight adventure yarn, and presumably will improve when special effects are added. Playing Rumata of Estoria, Polish thesp Edward Zentara is gruff scientist sent to rescue colleague Werner Herzog (in a short but sweet acting role), something he fails to do. Herzog has gone mad and — horrors — lost his scientific objectivity. Rumata, sent to replace him, loses his, too, after much dilly-dallying. He finally comes in on the side of the oppressed peasants, using his futuristic powers, a helicopter and a zap gun that wipes out bunches of meanies at one blow.

Back in the space station, a white-coated team of historians led by Birgit Doll watch the proceedings on a surround screen very much like viewers in a movie theater. Two hours of screen time later, medieval cruelty and barbarism begin to get to them, too, and Doll finally weeps — something they don't do in the future. In a rousing climax, the space station enters the fray, puts everyone to sleep, and takes the injured Rumata back to calmer times.

A great deal of violence is, necessarily, written into the film, though much of it takes place off-screen, like the sex scenes. Enough is suggested — particularly in the torture scenes — to keep weak stomachs anxious.

Invincible heroes, evil councilors, and imperiled women are the stuff computer games are made of, and "Hard To Be A God" has a hard time looking new. There are hints Fleischmann is aiming beyond simple sci-fi adventure, which ought to be further developed in the final cut. It remains an enjoyable yarn that needs some trimming, but it's a long way from "Indiana Jones."

As Rumata, Zentara lacks the roguish charm normally associated with adventure heroes. Aleksandr Filipenko is an evil but 1-dimensional villain, and the two or three femmes hardly emerge at all. Only vital player is El Gudsha Burduli as a fearless fighting baron with a sense of outlandish hu-

mor. Pierre Clementi has a small role as an amusingly camp king.

Camera crew headed by Russian lenser Pavel Lebeshev casts a grey powder over the awesome landscapes, while composer Jurgen Fritz gives tale an austere, serious score. —*Yung.*

Il prete bello
(The Handsome Priest)
(ITALIAN-FRENCH)

Venice A BIM Distribuzione release of a Nickelodeon (Rome)/Partner's Production (Paris) coproduction in association with RAI-TV 3. Produced by Valerio De Paolis. RAI-TV producer, Cecilia Valmarana. Directed by Carlo Mazzacurati. Screenplay, Franco Bernini, Carlo Mazzacurati, Enzo Monteleone, based on a novel by Goffredo Parise; camera (color), Giuseppe Lanci; editor, Mirco Garrone; music, Fiorenzo Carpi; art direction, Leonardo Scarpa. Reviewed at Venice Film Festival (Critics Week), Sept. 13, 1989. Running time: **94 MIN.**
Sergio . . . . Massimo Santelia
Cena . . . . Davide Torsello
Don Gastone . . . . Roberto Citran
Fedora . . . . Jessica Forde
Immacolata . . . . Adriana Asti
The Accountant . . . . Marco Messeri
Also with: Antonio Petrocelli, Silvana De Santis, Luisa De Santis, Leonardo Sartori, Raffaele Foscarini, Andrea Calgaro, Jacopo Simini, Bianca Osborne, Vasco Mirandola, Amy Werba.

■ **Young helmer Carlo Mazzacurati made a splash with his debut feature, "The Italian Night." "The Handsome Priest," a hymn to friendship and the golden age of childhood, is a slicker, less risky picture, which trusts on emotion in the place of realism.**

Based on a Goffredo Parise novel, this well-heeled film should raise initial b.o. interest, with offshore arthouse audiences a possibility.

Helmer returns to his native Northern Italy, nostalgically described by Giuseppe Lanci's moody, fog-ridden lensing and Fiorenzo Carpi's dreamy score. Pic's elegiac opening gradually turns into the story of a gang of poor kids living in Vicenza in the 1930s.

Hero is 11-year-old Sergio (played with great aplomb by newcomer Massimo Santelia), whose best friend is Cena (Davide Torsello, two years older). Cena is the leader of the band; Sergio the more introspective follower.

One day a new priest is assigned to the parish, Don Gastone (the gentle, eternally naive Roberto Citran). He ropes Sergio into a poetry recital with a bunch of nasty rich kids. Spinster Adriana Asti, hopelessly infatuated with the

priest, pays for Sergio's new clothes and Don Gastone's silly book on the Spanish Civil War.

Another new face in town is Fedora (Jessica Forde), a pretty young hooker from Venice. In the same spirit of innocent opportunism as the priest, Fedora sets up shop upstairs from Asti's respectable household. When jealous Asti finds her in bed with Don Gastone, she gets the girl deported and the priest defrocked.

Meanwhile, Sergio's boyish adventures with his crew continue, the bad events sandwiched between too many lyrical interludes. Grandpa dies and Mom (Amy Werba) gets engaged to a smug merchant. Best scenes are those with Marco Messeri as the accountant, an innocent-at-heart burglar who gets the boys involved in his last robbery, and dies. Cena is caught and sent to prison, and Sergio forced to make the transition from boyhood to adult life.

Though determinedly unsentimental, "The Handsome Priest" may be too soft for some palates. It shines mainly in Mazzacurati's creation of atmosphere (a simpler 1930s, with little mention of Fascists or premonitions of war) and direction of his young cast of non-pros, particularly the excellent hero. Technically very fine, pic reveals a director completely at home with professionality.
—*Yung.*

Muzh i doch Tamari Aleksandrovni
(Tamara Alexandrovna's Husband And Daughter)
(SOVIET)

Venice A Mosfilm Studio production. Directed by Olga Narutskaya. Screenplay, Nadejda Kozhushanaya; camera (color), Valeri Martinov; music, Oleg Karavaichuk; art direction, Mikhail Kartashov. Reviewed at Venice Film Festival (competing), Sept. 11, 1989. Running time: **108 MIN.**
Valeri Sergeievich . . . . . Aleksandr Galibin
Katia . . . . Anna Bazhenova
Also with: Valentina Maliavina, Antonina Dmitrieva.

■ **Moscow as an irrational, loveless hell of tauntingly empty relationships and nauseating street violence provides the background for "Tamara Alexandrovna's Husband And Daughter." First feature by Olga Narutskaya offers a peek into a harsh urban world deprived of its old, rigid roles and duties, plunging into violence as it inches towards freedom.**

Lensed in an expressionistic key, which the director doesn't always have under control, "Tamara Alexandrovna" is a curiosity item likely to attract limited audiences abroad, as it has at home.

The lady of the title is glimpsed only fleetingly in the opening credit sequence. Story centers on her 13-year-old offspring Katia (played appealingly, if wildly, by non-pro Anna Bazhenova, who looks and acts like a French pre-teen discovery) and divorced husband Valeri, a boy who never grew up. When the mother has to go to the hospital for an operation, Katia moves into Daddy's place, a single room in a big Moscow apartment, cohabited by a batty fat lady.

At first impish Pop seems like the ideal companion to lonely Katia. They shriek and scream together; he helps her escape from a sadistic gym teacher and lets her throw a big party in the flat. His prankishness never ends and soon he tires of the girl, asking her to move back in with her mother. Searching desperately for love, Katia almost gets gang raped by a nice boy and his two not-nice pals. She ends up running away from her indifferent parents.

Miffed at being stood up by Katia, the three boys take out their frustration on her father. In the middle of town, they hunt him down and beat him within an inch of his life in pic's most memorable sequence, rivaling the West for sickening violence. Pic leaves him in the hospital, his handsome face toothless and disfigured, flirting with a nurse.

"Tamara Alexandrovna" is a noisy film (both in its confused, dark images and cacophonic soundtrack) whose scenes and actors often spin out of control, drowned out in an attempted stylishness pic never achieves. Yet, beyond the squeaking actors trying hard to act unconventional, film manages to suggest a terrifying sense of desperation plaguing the Soviet post-ideology era, now empty of morals, ethics and a basic sense of responsibility.

Film was produced by Rolan Bykov's group for young people's films "Junost," an indie spinoff of Mosfilm Studios. —*Yung.*

TORONTO FESTIVAL OF FESTIVALS REVIEWS

Chattahoochee

Toronto A Hemdale production and release. Produced by Faye Schwab. Executive producer, Aaron Schwab. Directed by Mick Jackson. Screenplay, James Hicks; camera (color), Andrew Dunn; editor, Don Fairservice; music, John Keane; art direction, Patrick Tagliaferro; coproducer, Sue Baden Powell. Reviewed at Toronto Festival of Festivals, Sept. 16, 1989. No MPAA Rating. Running time: **103 MIN.**
Emmett Foley . . . . Gary Oldman
Walker . . . . Dennis Hopper
Also with: Frances McDormand, Pamela Reed, Ned Beatty, M. Emmet Walsh.

■ **At last year's Toronto Festival of Festivals, Hemdale might have learned that the considerable acting skills of Gary Oldman could not help a British tv director salvage a misconceived picture like "Criminal Law." Yet Hemdale unwisely returned to the Toronto fest this year with "Chattahoochee," a similarly botched Oldman vehicle helmed by another British tv director, Mick Jackson.**

Oldman's bravura performance as a victimized patient in a Deep South prison hospital for the criminally insane, circa 1950s, fails to cure the film of its manifold structural and stylistic ills. Theatrical and video prospects for "Chattahoochee" are as dim as its gloomy, squalid mise-en-scene.

The tale of Oldman's Emmett Foley allegedly is based on a true story of one Chris Calhoun, who could not handle the "expectations" of others when he returned from the Korean War to the Deep South as a "certified hero." In an opening setup that's frenetically bizarre, Oldman goes beserk one morning. He shoots up his small tropical town with a handgun, but wounds his only victim just slightly. Oldman really wants to to shot dead by the police.

The hick lawmen — whose ignorance and incompetence serve as the butt of the entire film's dudgeon — try to oblige him, but can't hit the broad side of a barn. He then tries to shoot himself through the heart, but aims the pistol at the right side of his chest.

Upon recovering and after a cursory psychiatric evaluation by the first of several no-nothing medicos, Oldman is promptly packed off to Chattahoochee, a maximum security hospital for the criminally insane. Cocky, and apparently not all that disturbed an individual, Oldman soon learns he's been thrown into an institution whose attitude towards mental illness is downright medieval.

The "hospital" is modeled as sort of a cross between the Turkish prison barracks of "Midnight Express," the hard-time joint reformed by Robert Redford in "Brubaker" and the good ole' prison farm of "Cool Hand Luke." Similarities to those three excellent movies end there.

Inmates wallow in filth and the food is excremental. Beatings and various forms of water torture are employed by the redneck cavemen who run the place. Thoughtless prison medical bureaucrat Ned Beatty turns aside all complaints of maltreatment. Oldman's bunkmates are maniacs, blithering idiots and worldly wise weirdos like Dennis Hopper and M. Emmet Walsh. In short, it's a madhouse.

When the tough, inherently decent Oldman tries to challenge the system he is beaten back. He tries again, is beaten back harder, and so forth. Meanwhile, his superbly sexy, self-centered wife (Frances McDormand is threatening to him. He receives increasingly brutal punishments that eventually include electro-shock and chemical sedation.

In one absurdly staged scene, totally devoid of narrative logic, Oldman and a small group inexplicably escape from the prison in an unsuccessful attempt to rob a bank in order to pay their legal fees for an appeal. More inexplicably, they return to Chattahoochee, apparently because they have nowhere else to go.

He becomes a jailhouse lawyer, discovers the rule of habeas corpus, and with the help of his steadfast sister (Pamela Reed), eventually gets the governor to investigate. Oldman shaves, and is released around 1960 to get on with whatever will become of his life. A lame, genre-standard crawl tells of the lasting reforms supposedly enacted after the investigation.

Oldman's accent, demeanor and presence as the Kafkaesque victim Emmett are up to his general standards of immersion in character. Hopper is sympathetic as his worn-down compatriot, and McDormand effective as the spouse. In spite of a few good interludes (Oldman and Hopper face-lit in the dark, reminiscing about sex), the film is largely a chaotic mess of repetitive, badly written sequences of institutional brutality piled on to numbing effect.

"Chattahoochee" is a most unpleasant film to look at, even if its murky design is meant to serve its message. It's a little too late for Jackson to wax indigant over the abysmal backwardness of '50s Dixie with so many urgent contemporary problems to address in this country and his own. —*Rich.*

Les matins infidèles
(Unfaithful Mornings)
(CANADIAN)

Toronto A Les Productions du Lundi Mahn production. Produced by François Bouvier. Directed by Bouvier, Jean Beaudry. Screenplay, Bouvier, Beaudry; camera (color), Alain Dupras; editor, Beaudry; sound, Claude Beaugrand, Esther Auger. Reviewed at Toronto Festival of Festivals, Sept. 16, 1989. Running time: 90 MIN.
Marc . . . . Jean Beaudry
Jean-Pierre . . . . Denis Bouchard

■ **This film has an interesting premise, but unfortunately few comic moments and it's difficult to muster any compassion for either of its protagonists.**

Marc and Jean-Pierre have trouble with women, children and life in general. Marc is a writer and idealist. Jean-Pierre is an irresponsible photographer. In a project doomed from the start, Jean-Pierre is supposed to take a photo at 8 a.m. on the same street corner every day for one year. Marc writes a novel based on the photos.

It's no surprise when their women leave them or when Jean-Pierre systematically loses his apartment, car and job. Jean-Pierre's untimely suicide in the last scene doesn't work in a pic which lacks the intensity for such a finale.

Outside pic's native Quebec, commercial potential is as dismal as its protagonists' misdirected lives. —*Suze.*

White Lake
(CANADIAN-DOCU)

Toronto Produced and directed by Colin Browne. Camera (color, 16m), Tom Westman, Karl Spreitz, Rolf Cutts, Paul Guenette, Randy Rotheisier, Tom Turnbull; editor, Browne; music, Jean Piche; sound, Peg Campbell, Jill Haras. Reviewed at Toronto Festival Of Festivals, Sept. 14, 1989. Running time: **80 MIN.**

■ **First-time director Colin Browne has directed a glorified home movie that daringly defies docu traditions in content and style. Although pic has zero commercial potential, it is ideal for a university with a film** studies department, or for similar specialized venues.

Punctuated with shots of buildings being demolished, pic largely is talking-head shots of the late Herbert Guernsey's descendants. Guernsey was a British-born patriarch who settled in Canada's White Lake region. Separate interviews with his children, and their descendants, reveal extremely contradictory versions of the man's life.

Pic's strength is that it doesn't attempt to provide a definitive portrait and uses contradictions to challenge the "truthfulness" attributed to the docu format.

Cinephile-oriented tv outlets should offer a second life for this clever pic. —Suze.

Life Is Cheap

Toronto A Far East Stars production. Produced by Winnie Fredriksz. Executive producers, John Koon-chung Chan, Wayne Wang. Directed by Wayne Wang. Codirected and written by Spencer Nakasako; camera (color), Amir M. Mokri; editor, Chris Sanderson, Sandy Nervig; music, Mark Alder; art direction, Collete Koo; production manager, Jessinta Liu; assistant director, Johnny Lee; sound, Curtis Choy. Reviewed at Toronto Festival of Festivals, Sept. 15, 1989. Running time: **90 MIN.**

Man With No Name	Spencer Nakasako
Money	Cora Miao
Blind Man	Victor Wong
The Anthropologist	John K. Chan
The Duck Killer	Chan Kim Wan
Uncle Cheng	Cheng Kwan Min
Taxi Driver	Allen Fong
Kitty	Cinda Hui
The Red Guard	Lam Chung
The Big Boss	Lo Wai

Also with: Gary Kong, Rocky Ho, Lo Lieh, Bonnie Ngai, Wu Kin Man, Yu Chien, Mr. and Mrs. Kai-Bong Chau.

■ Audaciously stylish and visually mesmerizing, "Life Is Cheap" aims to evoke the uncertain mood of present-day Hong Kong as viewed from the perspective of an Asian-American naif. Director Wayne Wang's tart take on the conundrum of Chinese identity has all the narrative logic of a tilted pinball machine, but its outrageous élan could appeal to the hip arthouse crowd.

Screenwriter-star Spencer Nakasako is the retro-Eastwoodian "man with no name," a half-Chinese, half-Japanese, all-American stablehand from San Francisco who has agreed to act as a courier for a San Francisco Triad, the Chinese mafia, in return for an all-expenses-paid sojourn in Hong Kong. The black-Stetsoned, cowboy-booted hero wants to see the legendary port before its takeover by China. In the wake of Tiananmen Square, it's a city of "5½-million sitting ducks."

Handcuffed to an attaché case destined for the "Big Boss" in Hong Kong, the hero seeks to unlock the enigma of "5,000 years of Chinese culture." Wang skewers the lofty notion of Chinese self-superiority by populating his film with a widely variegated gallery of funny and flawed characters.

There's a sardonic slaughterer of ducks; a profane taxi driver; a slick-tailored mobster tormented by his youth as a Maoist Red Guard; an uncle with a passion for Western song & dance routines; a squeamish prostitute; a dominating young beauty who's the mistress of the Triad boss and the lesbian lover of his daughter; filthy rich socialites; an arcane anthropologist; hack movie soundtrack dubbers, and a 1-armed concert pianist.

Character and plot in "Life Is Cheap" serve mostly as catalysts for a careening impressionistic excursion into the realm of — dare say it — Oriental inscrutability. Wang blips and zaps his narrative with Godardian bursts of subliminal imagery, much of it bloody (the hero recurringly fantasizes his arm cleaved from its handcuffed package). Wild juxtapositions of disconnected sequences are linked by the slow-to-comprehend American kid's deadpan ruminations on the inverted rules of Eastern conduct. There also are ceaseless japes at traditional Confucian wisdom: Life in Hong Kong is cheap, allows the grinning blood-splattered duck killer in a typical monolog — "but toilet paper is expensive."

The director is enamored of composition and relies on it to energize his film whenever the prop-like plot fails to do so. The American kid must deliver the briefcase to the Big Boss only. The gangster knows he's in town but declines delivery for reasons unstated and opaque. The contents eventually are revealed to be paradoxical: Italian salamis, cigarets, masks, a wig, a porn mag featuring pregnant women, etc.

The hero's frustration at his inability to consummate his mission soon evaporates into irrelevancy as he wends his way through Hong Kong's byways and folkways, senses bombarded with culture shock. He feeds on experience, digests it during vertiginously framed interludes alone in his cheap hotel room, then reemerges for another helping. Hero is initially respectful and well-intentioned; his Western qualities of impatience and chivalry cause him to grope and stumble into a situation in which he causes the mob boss grievous loss of face.

Wang tips his hat to the chop-socky genre by staging what must be among the very longest foot chase sequences in the history of film. It's a breathless hand-held camera gambit that may exhaust the patience of intolerant viewers but pays off with a giddily tangible sense of being inside the film.

Wang is by no means the first to collapse and expand film time with accordion-like playfulness, but his compositional inventiveness keeps things fresh.

An interior shot in a subway car has an elegiac dreaminess sublimely reflecting the hero's state of mind after the chase ends in crushing defeat. The interplay of a roiling punk-rock song and a Buddhist prayer ceremony artfully reflect the protagonist's jolted state-of-mind after weeks in the East. In "Life Is Cheap," interior contemplation carries the burden of the real action.

Wang attends to his linear plot with a climactic scene of confrontation and redemption sure to revolt some, but daringly transfixing in its setup and execution.

The filmmaker's proverbial reach surely has exceeded his grasp here, but the experimental and experiential energy of "Life Is Cheap" transcends flip, hip cartoonishness to arrive at something unique. —Rich.

Marocain
(WEST GERMAN)

Toronto A Hyane I/II Filmproduction. Directed by Elfi Mikesch. Screenplay, Mikesch; camera (color), Mikesch; editor, Brita Pohland; sound, Frieder Schlaich, Irene V. Alberti; art direction, Uta Reichardt. Reviewed at Toronto Festival of Festivals, Sept. 15, 1989. Running time: **86 MIN.**
With: Eva Lehmann, Traute Hoess, Abdelhadi El Aidi.

■ This is a touching story of an old woman and her daughter trying to reconcile their differences and misunderstandings at the mother's bedside. Their recollections of adventures in North Africa slice the psychological drama with stunning location shots of Morocco.

The daughter is a filmmaker. The crotchety old mother has seen her daughter's films "five times and understands nothing." She wants to live for another year just to clean up her daughter's "pigsty." Daughter listens in quiet shock to her mother's adventures with a man 35 years her junior after father died.

Elfi Mikesch's work as a cinematographer on pics for Monika Treut and Werner Shroeter plus codirection of "Seduction: The Cruel Women" (1983) explain why pic doesn't look like a first feature. However, subject matter and slow pace limits film's potential to festival venues and tv outlets. —Suze.

Surname Viet Given Name Nam
(DOCU-COLOR/B&W)

Toronto A Woman Makes Movies release of an Idera Films production. Produced, written, directed and edited by Trinh T. Minh-ha; camera (color, 16m), Kathleen Beeler; art direction, Jean-Paul Bourdier; sound, Linda Peckham. Reviewed at Toronto Festival Of Festivals, Sept. 8, 1989. Running time: **108 MIN.**

■ Rising above the stridency of feminist polemics, "Surname Viet Given Name Nam" is a sorrowful, lyrical and skillfully constructed filmed essay on the repression of women in Vietnamese society. It has a particular beauty and power best appreciated on screen, but public tv and specialty cable outlets should take notice.

Filmmaker Trinh T. Minh-ha elicits confessional interviews from five Vietnamese women as the cornerstone of her film. Her subjects include a doctor, an embassy maid, a former refugee, a student who has grown up in America, and a woman whose husband was imprisoned after the Communist takeover of South Vietnam. All of them have in common an indoctrination in the "four virtues" and "three submissions" which rigidly codify the lives of Vietnamese women in a society wholly dominated by men.

According to the documentary, the Communist triumph in the Vietnam war brought no change to the time-honored status of women as chattels. The popular concept of a woman's life divides it into three stages: a "Lady," before marriage, a "maid" during marriage and a "monkey" after marriage.

The women's testimonials unfold as painful confessional monologs, told in halting but eloquent

English, about their quotidian struggle for survival in a police state society where injustice is commonplace. In a country that has known unceasing turmoil and bitterly hard times, women apparently have been victimized with the worst burdens of hunger and poverty.

As one participant says, she has had "to bear witness to the unbearable." Another recounts the "law of the jungle" in the inhuman refugee camps of Guam. Yet they feel an abiding love for their country, indeed, consider themselves eternally married to it, hence the film's title.

Brightly lit against a background of deep shadows, the interviews build over long takes that heighten their accumulated impact. Intercut with the interviews are a latticework of beautifully photographed scenes of folk dances and village life, archival footage from the days of French Indochina and of course, footage from the long American war in Vietnam.

Further layers of meaning are provided by the juxtaposition of folk songs and a famous epic poem about a female warrior. These lyrics and verse, translated in overtitles, suggest that the subjects' experiences are timeless and representative of their society's as a whole.

The filmmaker also makes a parallel foray into the meaning of her own work and the elusive nature of documentary truth. "Surname Viet Given Name Nam," by illuminating the sequestered world of its subjects, sheds disturbing new light on their hard-to-fathom homeland. It has the haunting resonance of the best documentaries. —*Rich.*

Onde Bate o Sol
(Where The Sun Beats Down)
(PORTUGUESE)

Toronto   A GER production. Produced by Joao Pedro Benard. Directed by Joaquim Pinto. Screenplay, Pinto; camera (color) Pinto; editor, Claudio Martinez; music, Miso Ensemble; sound, Francisco Veloso, Vasco Pimentel. Reviewed at Toronto Festival of Festivals, Sept. 13, 1989. Running time: **88 MIN.**
     With Laura Morante, Antonio Pedro Figueiredo, Marcello Urehgue, Manuel Lobao.

■**Nothing ever happens where the sun beats down. Audiences are so far ahead of the young men discovering their homosexuality that nothing remains but the scenery.**

Ever-popular repressed sexuality theme is not new to North American cinema buffs, who otherwise would be the film's target market. What is perhaps radical to a Portuguese audience proves no revelations in content or treatment of material here. Audience is left to contemplate the burning sun, an image that induces what a real burning sunset induces: sleep. —*Suze.*

Brown Bread Sandwiches
(CANADIAN)

Toronto   A Brown Bread Sandwiches Inc.-Eagle Pictures production. Produced by Nellie Zucker, Carlo Liconti. Executive producers, Ciro Dammicco, Stefano Dammicco. Written and directed by Liconti; camera (color), Paul van der Linden; editor, Ron Wisman; music, Lawrence Shragge, Raymond Pennal; art direction, David Moe; sound, Paul Barr. Ian Hendry. Reviewed at Toronto Festival of Festivals, Sept. 10, 1989. Running time: **92 MIN.**
Michelangelo . . . . Daniel DeSanto
Giulia . . . . Lina Sastri
Aunt Eva . . . . Kim Cattrall
Alberto . . . . Giancarlo Giannini
     Also with: Kim Coates, Tony Nardi, Peter Boretski.

■**The beleagured Canadian cinema is poorly served by "Brown Bread Sandwiches," a painfully contrived ensemble about Italian emigrés in Toronto circa 1957.**

"Brown Bread" is likely to go stale the very week it opens in Canada, and with the possible exception of Italian and Canadian tv, its prospects are deservedly moldy.

Allegedly about displacement, culture shock, assimilation and familial disintegration in an alien land, Carlo Liconti's apparently semi-autobiographical film is badly written, woodenly directed, stiffly performed and embarrasingly executed. Liconti uses the hackneyed device of an alter-ego narrator split between a child protagonist and the same character's grown-up self reminiscing in voiceover about the onscreen goings on. These center on the travails of a fractious extended Italian family packed together with scant privacy in a Toronto boarding house.

In an unbearably precocious performance, Daniel DeSanto, as young Michelangelo, aspires to an assimilated life as an Anglicized Canadian, eating brown bread (not crunchy Italian white) and winning the love of his blue-eyed blond teacher.

Clunky dialog, meandering scene structure and flat jokes

abound in this kitchen table melodrama. Most of the gags are about sex, pregnancy, child-bearing, Italian machismo and bodily functions. Saccharine, strings-to-go musical arrangements smother virtually every traditional moment.

Lina Sastri, as the remote mother whose love and attention Michaelangelo craves, manages little more than a surly caricature of the abrasive tower-of-strength matriarch all too familiar in immigrant melodramas.

The rest of the cast fares no better, with one notable exception. Giancarlo Giannini, portraying a bitter laborer who eventually marries the cousin made pregnant by his younger brother, is so far over the heads of his compatriots that he seems to be acting in another movie.

In fact, another, far superior film similarly set in the Italian emigré milieu exists. It's called "Queen Of Hearts" and should be studied closely by the makers of "Brown Bread Sandwiches".
—*Rich.*

Space Avenger

Toronto   A Manley Prods. production. Produced by Ray Sundlin, Robert A. Harris, Richard W. Haines. Executive producers, Timothy McGinn, David Smith. Directed by Richard W. Haines; screenplay, Haines, Lynwood Sawyer; camera (Technicolor), Mustupha Barat; editor, Haines; music, Richard Fiocca. Reviewed at the Toronto Festival of Festivals, Sept. 10, 1989. No MPAA Rating. Running time: **88 MIN.**
     With: Robert Prichard, Mike McCleric, Charity Staley, Gina Mastrogiacomo, Kirk Fairbanks Fogg, Angela Nicholas.

■**An amiably dopey takeoff on the possession-by-lizardly-aliens genre common to such as "Alien," "Aliens" and "The Hidden," Richard W. Haines' "Space Avenger" is best suited for midnight movie playoff (its Toronto festival venue), European cinematheques that cater to fringe buffs and B-video addicts.**

Four alien convicts escape from an outer galaxy prison and land in the woods, somewhere in the U.S.A. circa 1930. Hoping to hide out from pursuing "agents" on "off-limits biosphere" Earth, the slimy lizard beings quickly possess the bodies of two airheaded young couples driving through the woods.

Seeking plutonium for their damaged spacecraft they go into town, seize some guns and shoot up the local pub in the first of countless sequences of off-the-wall

violence. Then they return to their ship to wait out the evolution of primitive Earthly technology.

Fifty years later their saucer is dug up by a construction crew and the possessed beings come out shooting. Seeking a more inconspicuous environment they head for Greenwich Village. The invaders wind up not far from the pad of an obsessed comic book artist who's a lot more interested in his job than in his sexy girlfriend.

The aliens go off to the Tunnel club in Manhattan, still looking for plutonium. There they are spotted by the comic maven, who soon ties them together with a series of strange, unexplained incidents of violence.

When the artist saves his job by creating a "Space Avenger" series about these weirdos in 1930s clothes, the creatures come after him. Things begin to get complicated when the artist's girlfriend also is possessed. In the end, all is resolved happily, except ...

Filmmaker Haines undoubtedly is hoping to spawn a cult following that will demand a sequel, but that's not necessarily apparent from the sophomoric tone of these goings-on.

The script, quite possibly by design, overflows with authentic 1-line groaners. ("Are you the agent? No, I don't have an agent — I freelance.")

Although the producers are touting the film's use of the dye transfer Technicolor printing process now owned by China, the candy-colored print is unremarkable. Herky-jerky editing is in keeping with the pic's skit-like episodic "structure." Special effects are okay and humorously employed but have all been seen before.
—*Rich.*

Foreign Nights
(CANADIAN)

Toronto   A Norstar release of a Mahaba Films production. Executive producers, David Semple, Shawky Joe Fahel. Produced by Justine Estee, Alan Doluboff, Izidore K. Musallam. Directed by Musallam. Screenplay, Alan Zweig. Musallam; camera (color), Paul Mitchnick; editor, Robert Benson; sound, Max Sartor. Reviewed at Toronto Festival of Festivals, Sept. 16, 1989. Running time: **91 MIN.**
Leila . . . . Terri Hawkes
Youssef (her father) . Youssef Abed-Alnour
Basma (her mother) . . . . . Bushra Karaman
Morad . . . . Mohammad Bacri
Karim . . . . Paul Morasutti
Jamie . . . . Gillian Doria
Paul . . . . Stephen Foster

■**This teen pic about a Canadian-born Palestinian girl**

whose desire to dance is thwarted by her extremely strict and traditional father, is a slice-of-life example of cross-cultural tensions in metropolitan Toronto. Simple storyline is ideal for family-time tv in Canada or on multicultural tv venues abroad.

Leila is a "good girl" who wants to learn modern dance in high school. Afraid of Western influence, her father gives her a 5 p.m. curfew, forbidding her to dance, date or party with her friends. However, only when father plans an arranged marriage for Leila "back in the home land" does she rebel and run away. Not surprisingly, she takes up dance and gets a successful role in a play.

The father's total inability to accept her choices is the ultimate point of the pic: Try to understand today's kids, especially your own. It's ideal viewing for families with teens in similar situations. —*Suze.*

MONTREAL WORLD FILM FEST REVIEWS

Boda Secreta
(Secret Wedding)
(ARGENTINE-DUTCH-CANADIAN)

Montreal   A Cinephile release of an Allarts Enterprises, Cinephile Ltd., Movie Center production. Executive producers, Juan Collini, Kees Dasander, Denis Wigman, Andre Bennett, Brigette. Directed by Alejandro Agresti; screenplay, Agresti; camera (Fujicolor), Ricardo Rodriguez; editor, Rene Weigmans; music, Paul M. Van Brugge; set design, Juan Carlos Alvarez. Reviewed at Montreal World Film Festival (competing), Aug. 31, 1989. Running time: **95 MIN.**
Fermin . . . . Tito Haas
Tota . . . . Mirtha Busnelli
Pipi . . . . Sergio Poves Campos
Priest . . . . Nathan Pinzon

■ "Boda Secreta" is a fantasy love story with softcore politics where Fermin is resurrected 13 years after disappearing as an activist in Argentina.

He relocates Tota, the woman he promised to marry, and despite the fact that she doesn't recognize him, their romance reignites in a politically repressed small town miles from Buenos Aires.

Pic carefully skirts current South American politics, indulging in long-lost couple sentimental meanderings, with commercial potential if handled carefully.

Reminiscent of "The Official Story" in its denunciation of the previous military regime, pic has more diverse characters including the town fool, Pipi, a rebel whose cause is gone with the wind. Pipi has learned to keep his mouth shut, and should appeal to bureaucratic ex-hippies.

Pic's pro-democracy, freedom-of-speech stance makes it a winner for PBS-type outlets. —*Suze.*

Hungry Heart
(AUSTRALIAN)

Montreal   A Chancom Ltd.-Lions Den Prods. production. Executive producers, Kevin Moore, Reg McLean, Rosa Colosimo. Produced by Colosimo. Directed by Luigi Acquisto. Screenplay, Acquisto; camera (color), Jaems Grant; editor, Courtney Page; music, Separate Tables, David Bride, John Phillips; production design, Michael Kourri; sound, Mark Tarpey; production manager, Colosimo; assistant director, Kathryn Hughes. Reviewed at Montreal World Film Festival (noncompeting), Aug. 28, 1989. Running time: **95 MIN.**
Sal Bono . . . . Nick Carrafa
Katie Maloney . . . . . Kimberley Davenport
Jane . . . . Lisa Schouw
Mr. O'Ryan . . . . Norman Kaye
Mrs. Bono . . . . Dasha Blahova
Vito . . . . Osvaldo Maione
Charlie . . . . Mark Rogers
Tony . . . . Gaetano Scollo
Mr. Maloney . . . . John Flaus
Connie Bono . . . . . Carmelina di Gugliemo
Anna Bono . . . . Amanda Colosimo

■ A love affair that starts passionately but quickly descends into a painful parting is the main theme of "Hungry Heart," but there are so many subplots and minor characters juggling for attention that the main story gets lost all too often.

The 1987 production, unreleased to date in Australia, has many qualities but is unlikely to get the opportunity to find audiences, except on video.

Sal (Nick Carrafa) is an Italo-Australian who, though he's completed medical school, seems mysteriously listless about starting work. He drifts around with his mates, getting involved in marginally criminal activities, which lead to nothing. When he meets the attractive Katie (Kimberley Davenport) there's an instant attraction. Before long a passionate love affair is in progress, though the attraction fades as quickly as it started when she tires of his criticisms of her. When he thinks she's gone off with an ex-boyfriend, he spends a night with her flat-mate, a singer (Lisa Schouw).

Alongside the central duo are a number of interesting characters struggling for screen time. There's Sal's mother (played by Czech actress Dasha Blahova, who's hard-ly ideal casting as an Italian momma, but gives a creditable performance nonetheless). Her friendship with a former Catholic priest (Norman Kaye, looking as if he'd strayed in from a Paul Cox film) is a subplot that gets nowhere.

There's also an excellent cameo from John Flaus as Katie's father, a country farmer who finds his daughter's city lifestyle perplexing. More might have been made of the clash between the Irish-Australians, repped by Katie's family, and the Italians.

Ultimately, the film gets Serious, when Katie confronts Sal over his infidelity with Jane (who ankles the morning after, apparently for good). It's never clear why Jane would agree to go to bed with Sal, or whether Katie's upset at her betrayal or Sal's or both.

Luigi Acquisto directs his own screenplay better than he writes, and there's enough talent on display here to make the film's ultimate failings all the more frustrating. It adds up to a pleasant, occasionally appealing, ultimately disappointing pic. —*Strat.*

Fontan
(Fountain)
(SOVIET)

Montreal   A Sovexportfilm release of a Lenfilm production. Directed by Yuri Mamin. Screenplay, Vladimir Vardounas; camera (Sovcolor), Anatoli Lapshov; music, Alexei Zalivalov; production design, Yuri Pougach; sound, Leonid Gavrichenko. Reviewed at Montreal World Film Festival (noncompeting), Aug. 29, 1989. Running time: **101 MIN.**
Kerbabayev . . . . . . Assankul Kouttoubayev
Peter . . . . Sergei Dreiden
Maya . . . . Janna Kerimtayeva
Mitrofanov . . . . Viktor Mikhailov
Slavik . . . . Anatoli Kalmikov
Katya . . . . Liudmila Samokhvalova
Shestopalov . . . . Alexei Zalivalov
Ivan . . . . Nicolai Trankov
Popov . . . . Ivan Krivorouchko

■ A feature with a very biting wit, "Fountain" is a perestroika comedy that could spark international interest. Its savage attack on living conditions in a large Russian city and its escalating, off-the-wall humor make it one of the more accessible films to come out of the Soviet Union this year.

Pic opens up in an Asian republic where Kerbabayev, an old man, is in charge of the local spring. He can only stand by aghast when a couple of Russian-speaking truck drivers blast the spring to get a faster flow of water.

Later the old man, who speaks no Russian, arrives in a large city in the west of the country (Lenin-grad?) to stay with his daughter and son-in-law (Peter) who live in a crumbling, crowded apartment building. Peter is in charge of the maintenance of the building, but fights a losing battle against cracks in the walls, a collapsing roof and blocked drains.

The old man inadvertently sets in motion a series of events that result in hot water and power being cut off from the building — the apartment dwellers are praised for their efforts to conserve much-needed energy. A tv crew descends on the building, whose inhabitants also include a man illegally growing tulips in his apartment and a spaced-out composer who likes to attach large wings to his body and attempt to fly from the top of the roof.

While much of this is funny, there's a bitterness to the humor that suggests that the plight of these apartment dwellers is all-too-familiar to Russian audiences. Fadeout has the old man rocketed up into space in the building's faulty elevator.

Director Yuri Mamin has a deft way of building gag upon gag, and the large cast of performers is directed with droll precision. Some of the night scenes seemed overly dark in the print caught.

"Fountain" is a film that pokes fun at efforts to reform the chronically troubled Soviet society at the most basic grassroots level. In laughing at the very real problems exposed here, Mamin and his team have come up with one of the most enjoyable of recent Soviet films. —*Strat.*

Az, grafinyata or
Hoi, La Comtesse
(I, The Countess)
(BULGARIAN-B&W/COLOR)

Montreal   A Bulgariafilm presentation. Directed by Peter Popzlatev. Screenplay, Raymond Wagenstein, Popzlatev; editor, Madlene Raditcheva; camera (b&w, color), Emil Cristov; music, Georgi Genkov; art direction, Georgi Todorov. Reviewed at Montreal World Film Festival (noncompeting), Sept. 1, 1989. Running time: **119 MIN.**
Sissi (the countess) . . . . Svetlana Yancheva

■ This is a simple enough tale which proves that drugs, sex, illegal abortion and disillusioned youth did not bypass Bulgaria in the late 1960s.

The self-named countess begins her slow downward spiral with her first shot of heroin at a music fest in Sophia, in a film whose excessive length limits its appeal.

Her sad story is reminiscent of the anti-drug pic "Christiane F.," yet lacks the latter's provocative shock value. The countess' formative years are lived out in juvenile delinquent centers, asylums and dimly lit institutions where the doctors seem to need as much psychological treatment as their patients.

Heavy scenes of Sissi's encounters with other patients paint a grim picture of rehabilitation, yet paradoxically warn of the dangers of drug abuse.

Sissi's few moments of happiness are filmed in color and contrast sharply with the film noir-type camerawork which rivets her grim world to a dark future.

Pic would serve well as an educational exercise for teens who over-glorify the '60s heyday. Trimming of occasional violent or sexually graphic scenes might be required for the small screen, an otherwise good venue for a film with limited theatrical potential.

—*Suze.*

Welcome To Canada
(CANADIAN)

Montreal A National Film Board of Canada production. Executive producer, Colin Nealle. Directed by John N. Smith. Screenplay, Sam Grana, Smith; camera (color), David de Volpi, Roger Martin; editor, Smith, Grana, Martial Ethier; sound, Jacques Drouin; associate producer, Paul Pope. Reviewed at Montreal World Film Festival (Panorama Canada), Aug. 29, 1989. Running time: **88 MIN.**

With: Noreen Power, Brendan Foley, Madonna Hawkins, Kasivisanathan Kathrigasoo, Kumaraselvy Karthigasoo, Pathanjali Prasad.

■ In 1987, Tamil refugees from Sri Lanka were dropped off the coast of Newfoundland where they were detained by Immigration Dept. officers. The latest docudrama from John N. Smith explores a fictional encounter between Tamils and Newfoundland villagers, and does so with insight and humanity.

Using nonprofessional actors, Smith ("Sitting In Limbo," "Train Of Dreams") explores what might have happened had the Newfies been able to make personal contact with the refugees. Members of the little fishing community of Brigus South treat the freezing Tamils (who arrive in the middle of a snowstorm) with great kindness and sympathy. The daughter of one of them already has died after being immersed in the freezing sea.

A priest tries to bring comfort to the bereaved father, and explain that he's unable to fulfill Tamil religious tradition of cremating the body within 12 hours of death. Meanwhile, a Tamil boy plays with local children, and villagers, who aren't even sure where Sri Lanka is, try to get to know their unexpected visitors. Eventually, Immigration officials arrive to take the refugees away.

All of this is intercut (a bit unnecessarily) with footage shot in Sri Lanka which gives some indication of why the refugees fled in the first place.

It's a pity Smith chooses to be frustratingly uninformative about the background to his film. He gives the impression of filming actual events, but it seems no such encounters between villagers and refugees actually took place. Smith is, instead, speculating what might have happened had Canadians had a chance to welcome the Tamils on a person-to-person basis without official interference. But this information is withheld from the viewer and, indeed, for some time into the film we're not even told where we are, or when.

Where the director succeeds, and succeeds admirably, is in the scenes where he just allows his amateur actors to react to each other, as these ordinary people from totally different backgrounds try to find common ground. The performances are natural, unforced and totally artless.

The film is technically very fine, with crisp camerawork and fine use of traditional Newfoundland and Sri Lankan music. A lengthy church service towards the end could be pruned a little, but otherwise the film is appealing enough to play the fest circuit, with tv exposure also indicated. —*Strat.*

A Hecc
(Just For Kicks)
(HUNGARIAN-W. GERMAN)

Montreal A Hunnia Film Studio (Budapest)-Infafilm (Munich) coproduction. Directed by Péter Gárdos. Screenplay, Gárdos, Andras Osvat; camera (color), Tibor Mate; editor, Maria Rigo; music, Janos Novak; production design, Jonsef Romvari. Reviewed at Montreal World Film Festival (competing), Aug. 31, 1989. Running time: **93 MIN.**
Tamas Holl . . . . .Gabor Reviczy
Marno . . . . .Armin Müller-Stahl
Juli . . . . .Dorottya Udvaros
Bela Stocker . . . . .Dozso Garas
Judit . . . . .Eniko Eszenyi
Brocher . . . . .Peter Andorai
Wife . . . . .Juli Basti
Zeiss-Ikon Woman . . . . .Mari Torocsik

■ "Just For Kicks" is an aptly titled comedy of no great consequence, but it's enjoyable and unpredictable, and those are useful assets. It may be deemed a bit insubstantial for theatrical release outside Hungary, but it deserves attention.

It looks like a holiday film for Péter Gárdos after his weightier comedy "Whooping Cough." The new film centers on Tamas Holl, a selfish, devil-may-care auctioneer who thinks he has everything. He's left his wife for the delectable Juli (Dorottya Udvaros, in good form); he has tickets for the opera; he's having a fling on the side with the ardent wife of a gymnastics teacher; and he's making a fair bit of extra money by cheating his clients.

Suddenly, things start to go wrong. Three tough guys start to harass him, day and night, and he doesn't know why. They ring his doorbell, smash his car windshield, invade his office and beat him up, even shave his head — all of which reduces him to a wreck. Who's responsible? The gym teacher? His ex-wife? His best friend (Armin Müller-Stahl), a bath-house attendant who's having a secret affair with Juli? His brother (Peter Andorai) whose wife Tamas once got pregnant? Or perhaps the woman (Mari Torocsik) he cheated when she wanted to sell a valuable old camera? The final resolution is satisfactorily unexpected.

Tamas is indeed a rogue and deserves everything he gets, but Gárdos obviously wants us to like him too, and Gabor Reviczy plays the character with plenty of charm. The film's something of a charmer too, though not to be taken at all seriously. The action moves briskly along, there are plenty of amusing characters and situations, and a fair amount of nudity (mostly in the bath-house scenes). The exceptionally strong cast provides a series of strong performances.

"Just For Kicks" isn't a memorable film, but it's an enjoyable diversion. —*Strat.*

The Long Road Home
(CANADIAN)

Montreal A Lauron Pictures presentation. Executive producer, Ronald Lillie. Produced by Ronald Lillie, William Johnston. Directed by William Johnston. Screenplay, Dan Datree; camera (color), Vic Sarin; editor, Judy Krupanszky, William Johnston; sound, Steven Cole; set design, Megan Less. Reviewed at Montreal World Film Festival (Panorama Canada), Aug. 31, 1989. Running time: **95 MIN.**
Michael Posen . . . . .Denis Forest
Cynthia . . . . .Kelly Rowan
Ronald Schubert . . . . .Gareth Bennett

■ Squeaky clean story of a 1969 American draft dodger who spends his summer at a kid's camp would qualify as an Ontario travelog promo reel save for a few quirks.

Pic so typical of good-guy Canadian morality, and story so sweet that it requires sugarless gum, it is perfect fare for family-time tv.

Wishy-washy Vietnam premise is lost in glorious Canadian sunsets due to a feeble script and dominant camera. Some scenes drag endlessly because producers seem determined to get their money's worth out of 1960s song rights.

The lack of passion, action or adventure, and editing ideal for commercial breaks, destine this pic to tv outlets with conservative family audiences. —*Suze.*

Henry . . .
Portrait Of A Serial Killer

Boston A Maljack Prods. presentation. Executive producers, Waleed B. Ali, Malik B. Ali. Produced by John McNaughton, Lisa Dedmond, Steven A. Jones. Directed by McNaughton. Screenplay, Richard Fire, McNaughton; camera (color), Charlie Lieberman; editor, Elena Maganini; music, McNaughton, Ken Hale, Jones; art direction, Rick Paul. Reviewed at Loews screening room, Boston, Sept. 14, 1989. (In the Boston Film Festival.) No MPAA Rating. Running time: **83 MIN.**
Henry . . . . .Michael Rooker
Otis. . . . . .Tom Towles
Becky . . . . .Tracy Arnold

■**Hard-driving, riveting film will be tough for many to take, but "Henry . . . Portrait Of A Serial Killer" marks the arrival of a major film talent in the person of director, coproducer and cowriter John McNaughton. Pic is an unsentimental look at a sociopath as his bloody trail passes through Chicago.**

Finished some two years ago, the film has gone begging until achieving cult status on the midnight circuit in the Windy City. Movie will require creative selling as it is too serious for the gorehounds but too grisly for the arthouse crowd. (Producers rejected an X rating from the MPAA.)

From the opening shot of a woman's nude body lying in a ditch to the closing shot of a bloody suitcase, there isn't a wasted moment in the film. Story follows Henry (Michael Rooker) while he rooms with his old prison buddy Otis (Tom Towles) and Otis' sister Becky (Tracy Arnold).

Henry has a philosophy about murder, which he shares with Otis. Simply put, Henry always keeps on the move and constantly changes his methods so as not to leave a pattern for the police to follow. Somewhat nervous at first, Otis quickly joins in.

Film uses two strategies to keep audiences off balance. First is the use of violence, which starts off subtly but finally moves to a gory extreme that mainstream audiences are likely to find unnerving. Early killings are shown in flashback, where we only see bodies as grotesque still lifes.

By the time we're shown Henry in action, we've come to realize that he doesn't seem like anything out of the ordinary, thus denying audiences the distancing that typical movie mass murders like Jason or Freddy Krueger permit. Fact that Henry is not killed or brought to justice in the end but instead simply moves on is even more disturbing.

The second tactic is the use of Becky to humanize Henry. A young woman down on her luck, her affection for the similarly troubled Henry seems to promise some hope of redemption. Film keeps tantalizing us with that possibility until the very end.

Low-budget pic looks surprisingly good, capturing the gritty feel of the characters' lives. Thesping is solid, with Rooker — currently onscreen as the repairman in "Sea Of Love" — a standout as Henry. His casualness about the brutal killings makes him all the more frightening.

Result is that this is a movie that will anger and frighten audiences, with walkouts reported when film unspooled at the Telluride fest. Many will also find this one of the most impressive film debuts of the '80s. —*Kimm.*

No Safe Haven

New York An Overseas Filmgroup presentation of a Vanguard Prods./Soltar production. Executive producers, G. Don Olsen, John G. Ciesar. Produced by Gary Paul. Coproducer, Carlos Vasallo. Directed by Ronnie Rondell. Screenplay, Wings Hauser, Nancy Locke; camera (color), Steven McWilliams; editor, Drake Sullivan; music, Joel Goldsmith; sound (Ultra-Stereo), Michael Haines; assistant director, Charles Nul; stunt coordinator, Shane Dixon; 2d unit camera, Michael Delahoussaye. Reviewed on MCEG/-Virgin vidcassette, N.Y., Sept. 24, 1989. MPAA Rating: R. Running time: **91 MIN.**
Clete Harris . . . . .Wings Hauser
Randy . . . . .Robert Tessier
Carlos . . . . .Robert Ahola
Carol . . . . .Marina Rice
Manuel . . . . .Branscombe Richmond
Buddy Harris . . . . .Tom Campitelli
Harvey Latham . . . . .Harvey Martin
Mrs. Harris . . . . .Evelyn Moore
J.J. Harris . . . . .Chris Douridas
Roberta . . . . .Nancy Locke

■**"No Safe Haven" is an okay action pic that curiously has sat on the shelf nearly three years before heading for videostores.**

Written by husband-wife team Wings Hauser and Nancy Locke, pic toplines Hauser as a U.S. spy in Honduras who heads home for revenge when mobsters kill his mom and young brother. Teamed with sidekick Robert Tessier (bald thesp cast as a good guy for a change), he then heads back south of the border to clean up the drug lords.

Under Ronnie Rondell's direction, pic moves at a fast clip and has solid stunt scenes. Subplot involving pro football is not very interesting or germane to the story.

Hauser is fine as the toughguy hero, while there is some odd injoke banter between him and **Locke, who plays a Peace Corps worker in Honduras.** —*Lor.*

J'ai Ete Au Bal
(I Went To The Dance)
(DOCU)

Montreal A Brazos Films-Flower Films production. Produced and directed by Les Blank, Chris Strachwitz, based on Ann Allen Savoy's book "Cajun Music — The Story Of A People;" camera (color, 16m), Blank; editor, Maureen Gosling; music, Michael Doucet. Reviewed at Montreal World Film Festival (Cinema of Today & Tomorrow), Aug. 27, 1989. Running time: **84 MIN.**
With: Michael Doucet, Marc and Ann Savoy, D.L. Menard, Clifton Chenier, Dewey and Rodney Balfa, Wayne Toups and Barry Ancelet.

■**The intertwined histories of Louisiana's French Cajun music and its Afro-American cousin Zydeco are lovingly traced by Les Blank and Chris Strachwitz in a documentary that should delight audiences at the various festivals and specialty houses into which it's already been booked.**

Festival directors, cinematheque programmers and tv buyers who haven't seen it should make a point of checking out "J'ai Ete Au Bal."

"Cajun" is a corruption of "Aracadians," the French Canadian settlers who were driven from Quebec by the British and journeyed across the continent to Louisiana and East Texas early in the 19th century. As the title implies, Cajun was the music of the dance halls in which the tight-knit French community gathered each week.

A partytime gumbo of old world melodies and new world counterpoints, Cajun's singers, fiddlers and accordionists made up the genre's rules as they went along. Rendered in a plaintive French patois the Cajun laments about lost or unrequited love invariably channeled sadness into exuberance. As one observer explains, it was a music of "hard times" for people who wanted to escape their troubled lives.

Interviews with musicians and folklorists, archival footage and old photographs are used by the filmmakers to fill out a story they realize is best told by the music itself. They track the permutations of Cajun music through successive eras of American history, during which it evolved by adapting itself chameleon-like to various instruments and new cultural influences such as Afro-American voodoo and blues and country & western music from neighboring Texas.

When Huey Long opened Louisiana to the outside world in the 1930s, the French Cajun community came under pressure to assimilate as "Americans" but the music, though eclipsed for a while, never entirely disappeared.

When Louisiana boys returned home after WWII ready for home cooking and good times they sparked a Cajun renaissance. Although it was once again obscured by rock and roll in the 1950s, Cajun was revived by folkies in the 1960s and in recent years has caught on nationally with music aficionados eager to discover a "new" sound.

The resilience of Cajun as documented here is a tribute to the music's timelessness and the rich cross-cultural contributions that made it so. —*Rich.*

Il Maestro
(The Conductor)
(FRENCH-BELGIAN)

San Sebastian A Man's Films (Brussels), Flach Film (Paris), RTBF.BRT Belgian TV coproduction. Written and directed by Marion Hänsel, based on story by Mario Soldati. Camera (Fujicolor), Acacio de Almeida; editor, Susana Rossberg; music, Frédéric Devresse; art direction, Emita Frigato; costumes, Anne Verhoeven; sound, Henri Moreile. Reviewed at San Sebastian Film Festival, Sept. 19, 1989. Running time: **90 MIN.**
Goldberg . . . . .Malcolm McDowell
Romualdi . . . . .Charles Aznavour
Dolores . . . . .Andréa Ferréol
Administrator . . . . .Francis Lemaire
(English soundtrack)

■**This elegant and sensitively made pic is a delight to watch and should appeal to discriminating highbrow audiences around the world, despite problems in casting and flaws in linguistic logic.**

Set in Italy, story begins intriguingly with the arrival of a famous conductor who is to conduct four concerts. However, as he is rehearsing "Madame Butterfly" with the orchestra and a soloist, he suddenly cannot go on, evidently under a crippling traumatic strain.

The impresario, who also is an old friend, gradually gets the story out of the conductor. It is told to the viewer in various long flashbacks to 1943 when the conductor, Goldberg (Malcolm McDowell), was escaping from the Nazis.

In one of his convent hideouts he met a man (Charles Aznavour) who was passing himself off as a great maestro while Goldberg, a Jew, was feigning being a bank clerk. The relationship between the two, one a great conductor and the other a poseur, develops touchingly as a kindly widow hides them for a while.

Near end of the pic, the maestro's secret finally is revealed, a secret less dramatic than might be expected, but touching nonetheless.

Both McDowell and Aznavour put in fine, often moving performances; however, they don't come across convincingly as two supposed Italians. Also, since they are speaking in English (Aznavour, of course, with a strong French accent), the linguistics of the film are haywire.

Excellent production values, crisp lensing and fine direction mark this distinguished European production. —Besa.

Urotsukidoji
(Legend Of The Over-Fiend)
(JAPANESE-ANIMATED)

Toronto   A Japan Audio Visual Network production. Executive producer, Yoshinobu Nishizaki. Produced by Yasuhito Yamaki. Directed by Hideki Takayama. Screenplay, Noboru Aikawa, based on a comic written by Toshio Maeda; camera (color), Nobuyuki Sugaya; editor, Shigeru Nishiyama; sound, Yasunori Honda. Reviewed at Toronto Festival of Festivals, Sept. 16, 1989. Running time: **108 MIN.**

■ **This is a violent sci-fi-horror schlock extravaganza verging on porno. Films like this are why the word misogynist was invented.**

A young girl is raped several times by a monster from Outer Space that takes refuge in the body of schoolteachers and other teens. A young boy who will "save" her is a Peeping Tom in his spare time.

Midnight Madness section at fests is a perfect type of venue for this animated pic. Techinical aspects and animation quality are excellent. It should do well in vidcassette format for adult viewers. —Suze.

Ume No Matsuri
(A Festival Of Dreams)
(JAPANESE)

Montreal   A Herald Ace release of a Nippon Herald-Herald Ace production. Produced by Masato Hara, Koichi Murakami. Directed by Hideo Osabe. Screenplay, Osabe; camera (Fujicolor), Masaki Tamura; editor, Akira Suzuki; music, Toshiaki Yokota; production design, Osamu Yamaguchi; sound, Koshiro Jinbo. Reviewed at Montreal World Film Festival (Cinema of Today and Tomorrow section), Aug. 29, 1989. Running time: **114 MIN.**
With: Kyohei Shibita, Shiro Sano, Mariko Kaga, Kei Sato, Narimi Arimori.

■ **This is a simple tale of a young farmboy who longs to make a success of playing the** *shamisen,* **a banjo-type instrument.**

Set in the extreme north of Honshu island, the film involves the rivalry between Kenkichi, a farmer's son, and Yuzo, whose family is rich. Both are in love with Chiyo, who prefers Kenkichi and agrees to wait when, defeated in an early music contest by Yuzo, he sets out accompanied by a blind *shamisen* maestro to learn his craft.

The film is beautifully made, but predictable and slowly paced. Offshore chances are slim. —Strat.

Notater om Körlighedon
(Notes On Love)
(DANISH-B&W/COLOR)

Copenhagen   A Columbus Film release of a Jörgen Leth production, with Columbus Film in association with the Danish Film Institute. Produced by Vibeke Windelöv. Written and directed by Leth. Camera (b&w, Eastmancolor), Henning Camre, Dan Holmberg; editor, Camilla Skousen; sound, Per Meinertsen, Per Streit; production design, Per Kirkeby; creative adviser, Marlyn Czajkowski; Danish Film Institute consultant producer, Claeas Kastholm Hansen; assistant director, Susanne Bier; screenplay consultants, Jonas Cornell, Ann Bierlich; production management, Marianne Mouritzen. Reviewed at Delta Bio, Copenhagen, Sept. 18, 1989. Running time: **88 MIN.**
With: Claus Nissen, Stina Ekblad, Jan Nowicki, Baard Owe, Edith Guillaume, Charlotte Sieling, Jörgen Leth, Mette Ida Kirk, Anders Hove, Peter Eszterhas, Linda Hindberg, Pia Tröst Nissen, Lars Daingard, Arne Willumsen.

■ **"Notes On Love" is another installment in poet-filmmaker Jörgen Leth's series of mock docus, actually fictionalized essays (mainly on sports and ballet) that over the years have garnered a following via specialized situations. "Love" will be, at best, restricted to that same route.**

Inherent in Leth's style have always been large quantities of outrageous self-indulgence. This time he may have crossed the line irretrievably into self-parody with an endless series of tableaux of minimal movement depicting the before's (shaving, putting on makeup, meditative fingertip-caressing of faces) and after's (the lighting of cigarets, the putting on and tearing off again of clothes).

It is Leth's conceit that he follows in the footsteps of anthropologist Bronislaw Malinowski who 70 years ago visited the New Guinean Trobriand Islands and came back to write "The Sexual Life Of The Savages." While staying home in sparse Danish interiors most of the time, Leth does go the Trobrian Islands, too, but brings home mostly some incredi-

bly blurry color shots and a few in black & white with neat enough portraiture of natives engaged in ritual face-painting and skull-shaving.

The ritualistic love preludes aside, there is precious little amorous feel, let alone passion, in "Notes On Love." Claus Nissen, a Danish actor and master of noncommittal expression, is seen as a writer in trouble with love even at the wishful thinking print stage.

Although restricted to displays of melancholy, only actors Jan Nowicki from Poland and Stina Ekblad from Sweden plus Denmark's Nissen and mezzo-soprano Edith Guillaume (for comic relief and fine singing, respectively) succeed in lifting credible performances out of the pretentious mumbo-jumbo. The monotone of Leth's own commentary serves as this filmmaker's traditional but by now absolutely unnecessary additional signature. —Kell.

Fear, Anxiety And Depression

Las Vegas   A Samuel Goldwyn Co. release of a Propaganda Films production. Produced by Stanley Wlodowski, Steve Golin, Joni Sighvatsson. Executive producers, Michael Kahn, Nigel Sinclair. Written and directed by Todd Solondz. Screenplay, Solondz; camera (Foto-Kem color), Stefan Czapsky; editor, Peter Austin, Emily Paine, Barry Rubinow; music, Karyn Rachtman, Joe Romano, Moogy Klingman; sound, Al Martinez; production design, Marek Dobrowolski; art direction, Susan Block; costume design, Susan Lyall; assistant director, Lisa Zimble, Howard McMaster. Reviewed at Cinetex, Bally's Casino Resort, Las Vegas, Sept. 25, 1989. MPAA Rating: R. Running time: **85 MIN.**
Ira . . . . .Todd Solondz
Jack . . . . .Max Cantor
Janice . . . . .Alexandra Gersten
Junk . . . . .Jane Hamper
Donny . . . . .Stanley Tucci

■ **Writer-director-performer Todd Solondz first caught Hollywood's attention with a comic short. The major problem with this, his first feature, is that he essentially hasn't left that mode.**

Running out of gags, and a viewer's patience, long before it runs out of running time, the commercial prospects for this sketchlike satire of creativity-obsessed New Yorkers are dim.

Though the playwright hero of this cartoonish comedy is an admirer of Samuel Beckett, it's clear from the start who Solondz truly idolizes — Woody Allen.

As film follows the adventures of his would-be intellectual hero looking for love and artistic success, scene after scene remorse-

lessly retreads characters and situations out of "Annie Hall," "Manhattan" and "Play It Again, Sam."

Still, Solondz can't be accused of plagiarism, for no one would ever mistake him for Allen — or anyone else for that matter.

He's a thin, spindly figure with thick-lensed, black-rimmed glasses, a high whiny voice, huge splayed lips and pale shrimp-pink features topped with a mass of stringy-curly black hair. Solondz resembles nothing so much as a cross between Arnold Stang and a Giacometti sculpture.

Ordinarily it wouldn't be seemly to dwell on a performer's physical characteristics, but Solondz leaves no choice. He does everything possible to accentuate and celebrate his presentational oddities.

Most of the time he uses his inert figure (only his arms show any sense of animation) for Buster Keaton-like gags of nonplussed reaction to disastrous situations. Solondz' approach can best be seen in relation to his costar, Alexandra Gersten.

Solondz' distaff nerd equivalent (sweating, whining and traipsing about in the ugliest lime green parka known to man), Gersten plays a grasping, demanding shrew whose constant pursuit of the hero is a major source of annoyance to him. The trouble is, she's just as annoying to the viewer.

It's easy to see what Solondz is after — a Diane Arbus-like sense of unease. Just because you strike poses that suggest you're an escapee from one of Arbus' portraits doesn't mean you've reached her artistic level.

Jane Hamper does fairly well as a punk performance artist the hero pursues. Unfortunately, as her character is obsessed with gay men, her performance becomes the occasion for one of the most tasteless and insensitive AIDS jokes to reach the screen.

Max Cantor is good in the Tony Roberts/Michael Murphy part of the hero's lovable but insincere best friend. Stanley Tucci does a nice turn as a charming but shallow record producer friend of the hero's.

Like all the other performers, they're hampered by Solondz' insistence on framing the action in blocklike compositions centering their figures in Arbus style. Other tech credits are acceptable. —Rens.

Noiembrie, Ultimul Bal
(November, The Last Ball)
(RUMANIAN)

Montreal A Romaniafilm release of a Film Co. No. 4, production. Produced by Villy Auerbach. Directed by Dan Pita. Screenplay, Pita, Serban Velescu, from the novella "The Place Where Nothing Ever Happens," by Mihail Sadoveanu; camera (color), Calin Ghibu; editor, Cristina Ionescu; music, Aurelian Popa; sound, Sotir Caragata; production design, Constantin Simionescu; costumes, Catalina Ghibu; production manager, Gheorghe Piriu. Reviewed at Montreal World Film Fest (noncompeting) Aug. 25, 1989. Runnng time: 105 MIN.
With: Stefan Iordache, Soimita Lupj, Gioni Popovici, Serglu Tudose, Florian Potra, Gabriela Baclu, Gabriel Costea, Corneliu Revent, Catalina Mugea, Vasile Nitulescu.

■This desultory costume drama, set on a country estate in 1890, centers around a nobleman in love with a much younger girl who marries someone else. Prospects for this one are small outside Rumanian communities.

The story is based on a novella, "The Place Where Nothing Ever Happens," and this is, indeed, minimalist drama. But Dan Pita, one of Rumania's best known directors (and a prizewinner at Berlin in 1985), goes for the ultrasomber approach and has cast actors who lack much charisma.

The result makes for plodding, uneventful drama, and the monotonous music and slow pacing don't help. Tale of unrequited love builds up to a last reel tragedy that lacks impact.

Poor color processing, giving the film a muddy look, is another drawback. —Strat.

Los amores de Kafka
(The Loves Of Kafka)
(ARGENTINE)

Buenos Aires A Jorge Estrada Mora Prods. presentation. Produced by Jorge Estrada Mora. Executive producer, Karel Skop. Directed by Beda Docampo Feijóo. Screenplay, Docampo Feijóo, based on a pilot developed by Docampo Feijóo, Juan Bautista Stagnaro; camera (color), Frantisek Uldrich; editor, César D'Angiolillo; music, Mozart, Donizetti, Gershwin, Schubert; sound, José Luis Díaz; sets, Boris Moravec; costumes, Dagmar Brizinova. Reviewed at Ambassador theater, Buenos Aires, Aug. 4, 1989. Rating in Argentina: Suitable for ages 13 and up. Running time: 103 MIN.
Franz Kafka . . . . Jorge Marrale
Milena Jesenska . . . . Susú Pecoraro
Kafka's father . . . . Villanueva Cosse
Kafka's sister . . . . Cecilia Roth
Max Brod . . . . Salo Pasik
Kafka's mother . . . . Ljuba Skorepova
Julie . . . . Sofia Viruboff
Sigmund Freud . . . . Karel Chromik
Interpreter . . . . Jana Krausova-Pehrova
Also with: Karel Habl, Jan Schanilec, Jiri Nemecek, Oldrich Vlach, Dana Moravkova, Jiri Havel.

■An Argentine film successfully tackles an international subject in "The Loves Of Kafka" — a subject pertaining not just to Czechoslovakia, but to the history of world literature. With proper handling, this is one prestige presentation that could make a mark in the mainstream.

Within a visually attractive package, and without seeming to crowd the subject matter, the plot goes considerably beyond the Czech writer's love life (a fiancée, Julie, whom Kafka doesn't love and whom he might have treated with greater delicacy, and a married woman, Milena, with whom he strikes up overpowering physical and intellectual bonds).

What the viewer gets is a full-length portrait of the quintessential 20th-century writer who created troubling parables of the powerless individual in a world he cannot fathom, let alone control.

Included are Kafka's family relations, particularly with his supportive sister and his contemptuous father, whose disapproval determines the shape of Kafka's life. The latter's passion for literature; his position in society as a Jew; his tuberculosis, and even a number of his story plots are outlined. Sigmund Freud also pops up in the story.

The whole package, featuring a splendid period atmosphere, is wrapped into a contemporary tale — that of an Argentine director who goes to Prague to make a film also called "The Loves Of Kafka," but finds the Barrandov studios too busy filming Milos Forman's "Amadeus." The hoary film-within-a-film format is trotted out for an effective whirl, and several of the actors in the contemporary story double up for roles in the film within.

"Loves" is a major enterprise by an Argentine production company that contracted Barrandov's services for the Prague location filming. The same production company and director previously made another film in Czechoslovakia with services contracted there, "Under The World," codirected by Juan Bautista Stagnaro, who co-plotted "Loves."

The two lead actors, Jorge Marrale and Susú (Camila) Pecoraro, are able to deliver dialog about the importance of literature with conviction, keeping it from sounding pretentious and pedantic.

An important subject has reached the screen with class and it's a notable achievement for the Argentine cinema. There are plot elements for a range of interests: a romance one can sympathize with; faithfulness toward a key literary goal of the century and a tortured psychological case history. All of it is served up with doses of humor. Also, the Prague location is lovely.

One plot element — a fleeting flashforward to Milena, decades later, in a Nazi concentration camp — is made to seem gratuitous by the filmmakers' ambivalence. Through dialog, the film manages to cue it in while pretending not to want to include it. Better to have put it in straight, without any disclaimer. —Olas.

Sidewalk Stories
(B&W)

Toronto An Island Pictures release of a Rhinoceros production. Executive producers, Howard M. Brickner, Vicki Lebenbaum. Produced, written, and directed by Charles Lane. Camera (b&w), Bill Dill; editor, Anne Stein, Charles Lane; music, Marc Marder; art direction, Ina Mayhew. Reviewed at Toronto Festival of Festivals, Sept. 15, 1989. MPAA Rating: R. Running time: 97 MIN.
With: Charles Lane, Nicole Alysia, Sandye Wilson, Darnell Williams, Trula Hoosier.

■Director-writer-actor Charles Lane takes a plucky gamble and mostly wins in his feature film debut, "Sidewalk Stories," a silent b&w comedy about the homeless. The challenge will be met mostly by fest and arthouse audiences who could succumb to the vulnerability and charm of the lead thesps.

Filmmaker owes a great debt to Charlie Chaplin in evoking the compassion of the little man and his impotence in living in a sociologically defeatist environment. Lane plays a street artist who draws charcoal caricatures in Greenwich Village. He witnesses the murder of man who once had his baby daughter sit for a portrait, and Lane saves the abandoned child.

Lane adopts the adorable tyke and provides her with shelter in the abandoned building which serves as his "home" — mattress, light bulb, table, and chair. One almost expects to see him dining on Chaplin's boiled shoelaces, but he musters up a few cornflakes for the kid.

Lane tries to find the baby's mother, and is befriended by a classy children's clothing store owner, who also once sat for a portrait.

Lane ultimately reunites baby and mom, but not without the requisite car chase. In this instance, he runs off with a horse-drawn carriage to pursue the murderers.

Bill Dill's black & white cinematography is crisp and evocative, panning street scenes, generally eliciting the chilly feel of New York City's Village scene in winter, and allowing the baby and Lane to mug for he camera. Marc Marder's musical score has the pathos of Chaplin's piano riffs.

Some of the comedy is sledgehammer subtle (an irrepressibly demanding librarian), but more restrained bits shine through in effective sight gags, such as Lane capitalizing on the baby's scribblings on his easel, which he sells as art, and the baby pointing to a picture of herself as a missing child on a milk carton.

The only sounds in the film are voiced just before the closing credits when individual street people in a downtown park warming their hands over a communal fire ask for spare change and plead, "Won't you do anything about the homeless?"

Lane, although entertaining and agile, is not a slick mime, and the story has some heavy social-conscience finger-wagging. But the idea works and Lane is to be commended for pulling off an alternative way of looking at a pressing social issue. —Devo.

300 mil til himlen/
300 mil do nieba
(300 Miles To Heaven)
(DANISH-POLISH)

Copenhagen A Warner & Metronome Film release of an LLM Film (Denmark) and Film Unit TOR (Poland) production, in association with the Danish Film Institute and Trans Europe Film (Paris). Produced by Lise Lense-Möller. Directed by Maciej Dejczer. Screenplay, Dejczer, Cezary Harasmowicz; camera (Eastmancolor/Orwocolor), Krzysztof Ptak; editor, Jaroslaw Wolejko; music, Michal Lorenc, production design, Wojciech Jaworski; sound, Piotr Domaradski; costumes, Dorota Roquelpo, Lotte Dandanell; assistant director, Maria Kuzemko, Zdzislawa Hausner, Morten Henriksen; production management, Iwona Ziulkowska, Didier Brunner; Danish Film Institute consultant producer, Hans Hansen. Reviewed at Warner & Metronome Film screening room, Copenhagen, Sept. 15, 1989. Running time: 88 MIN.
Grzes . . . . Wojciech Klata
Jedrek . . . . Rafal Zimowski
Their mother . . Jadwika Jankowska-Cieslak
Their father . . . . Andrezej Mellin
Elka . . . . Kama Kowalewska
Elka's father . . . . Krzysztof Stroinski
Refugee photographer . . . . Adrianna Biedrzynska
Also with: Peter Steen, Holger Vistisen, Alexander Bednarz, Hans Christian Aegidius.

■Partly financed by Danish Film Institute coin earmarked for kiddie and youth productions, "300 Miles To Heaven" by Maciej Dejczer of Poland's Film Unit TOR deals in uncompromisingly adult terms with the plight of two Polish kids escaping to the West as well as that of their left-behind parents. Film is cleancut and eloquent melodrama that never resorts to the maudlin or the sensational.

It is already assured French distribution (but as yet none in Poland) and should appeal to young and adult audiences everywhere.

Two brothers, bird-watcher Jedrek, 13, and accordion-playing Grzes, 10, decide to run off to whatever imagined never-never land a foreign truck passing their remote village will take them; they hide between its wheels as stowaways. They have seen their parents try to set up a small brick kiln only to be hounded by corrupt local officialdom.

Elka, a bright young girl with a daydreaming, ineffectual father, tries to make a getaway and taunts her dad to help. This only lands him in jail and herself in a reform school, while the boys, starving and dirty, actually make it. They cross the Baltic Sea with the truck and wind up amidst the seeming benevolence of a Danish camp for refugees.

In Denmark, the boys are given food, clothes, money and partial freedom to investigate Yuletide life in the opulent streets of affluent Copenhagen. While officials back home keep pestering their parents, the boys run into stern Danish bureaucracy.

Even if a fellow refugee, a woman photographer, seems ready to help the kids, film's final frame leaves them as street loners on Christmas Eve. They have succeeded in having a phone conversation with their parents, who defy the police and their own hearts by encouraging them to stay in Denmark.

"300 Miles To Heaven" is stark in its portraiture of the rundown qualities of life in a Communist dictatorship. It is a credit to the emerging new powers in Poland that the film was shot there at all and with such fine actors as Krzysztof Stroinski (shining in particular in a Peter Lorre-ish role as Elka's father), Adrianna Biedrzynska (the photographer) and Jadwika Jankowska-Cieslak (the boys' mother).

Wojciech Klata is a scene-stealer as the younger brother who believes in a future in a Louisiana street parade band, but Rafal Zim-

owski as Jedrek and Kama Kowalewska as Elka move with natural ease and honesty, too.

Cinematography and editing are to the point and writer-director Maciej Dejczer is a born film storyteller who knows when a pulled punch is stronger than a jab to the heart. The majority of dialog is in Polish. —Kell.

Peaux De Vaches
(Thick Skinned)
(FRENCH)

Montreal   A Titane production. (Intl. sales, Cinexport, Paris.) Produced by Jean-Luc Ormières. Directed by Patricia Mazuy. Screenplay, Mazuy; camera (color), Raoul Coutard; editor, Sophie Schmit; music, Théo Hakola, Passion Fodder; production design, Yves Brover; sound, Jean-Pierre Duret; production manager, Baudouin Capet. Reviewed at Montreal World Film Festival (noncompeting), Aug. 29, 1989. Running time: 88 MIN.
Annie . . . . Sandrine Bonnaire
Roland . . . . Jean-François Stevenin
Gérard . . . . Jacques Spiesser
Also with: Laure Duthilleul, Salomée Stevenin, Yann Dedet, Jean-François Gallotte.

■ Screened in the Un Certain Regard section at Cannes, and winner of the 1989 Prix Georges Sadoul, "Peaux De Vaches" is a tense, atmosphereic drama set on a farm.

Sandrine Bonnaire gives another strong performance as Annie, wife of Gérard (Jacques Spiesser), whose peaceful life is interrupted by the arrival of her husband's older brother, Roland (Jean-François Stevenin), who's spent 10 years in prison.

Seems that a decade earlier, the brothers had drunkenly set fire to a barn. A man sleeping in the barn died in the blaze. Roland took the rap for his younger brother, but now that he's out he wants some recompense for the years behind bars.

Writer-director Patricia Mazuy sets up an intriguing situation here. During the 10 years his brother has been in the pen, Gérard has modernized the farm, and seems to have deliberately put his brother's plight out of his mind; he's never told his wife about Roland. Now, he finds himself affected by conflicting emotions — guilt, love, fear — without knowing how to cope with Roland's demands.

Bonnaire is ably supported by Stevenin and Spiesser, two excellent actors in good form here. Unfortunately, the promising idea never really develops, and the interesting themes are set aside in the rather obvious plotting in the second half of the film.

Nevertheless, this is a quality,

small-scale French item which could score a modest success in selected venues. —Strat.

What's Up, Hideous Sun Demon
(B&W/COLOR)

New York   A Wade Williams Prods. presentation from Greystone Picture Corp. of a 24 Horses production. Produced by Greg Brown, Jeff Montgomery, Hadi Salem. New version directed by Craig Mitchell. Written by Mitchell. Camera (Technicolor, b&w; Foto-Kem prints), John Lambert, Steve Dubin; additional camera, William Pope; supervising editor, Glenn Morgan; music, Fred Myrow; associate producer, Kevin Kelly Brown; in Dolby stereo. Additional cast: Cameron Clarke, Googy Gress, Alan Stock, Mark Holton. Voices of: Jay Leno, Susan Tyrrell, Barbara Goodson, Bernard Behrens. Reviewed at Film Forum 2, N.Y., Sept. 1, 1989. No MPAA Rating. Running time: 71 MIN.
Original film: A Pacific-Intl. release (1959) of a Clarke-King Enterprises production. Produced by Robert Clarke. Directed by Clarke, Thomas Cassarino. Screenplay, E. S. Seeley Jr., Doane Hoag, from story "Strange Pursuit" by Clarke, Phil Hiner; camera (b&w), John Morrill, Vilis Lapenieks, Stan Follis; editor, Cassarino; music, John Seely; sound, Doug McGuire. Running time: 74 MIN.
Gil/Pitnik . . . . Robert Clarke
Polly . . . . Patricia Manning
Trudy/Bunny . . . . Nan Peterson
Major . . . . Patrick Whyte
Also with: Del Courtney, Fred La Porta, Bill Hampton.

■ This revamped version (with silly voice dubbing) of Robert Clarke's 1959 monster pic packs enough belly laughs to merit midnight bookings, as well as serving to renew interest in the campy original.

Already parodied in the '60s by amateur filmmaker Don Glut, Clarke's "The Hideous Sun Demon" was redubbed in a "Special Edition" prepared between 1983 and 1986 but never released. This 1989 second re-do is in the vein of Woody Allen's famous dub job "What's Up, Tiger Lily?"

In his film, Clarke toplined as a research scientist exposed to radioactive isotopes that cause him to regress into a humanoid reptilian monster when exposed to direct sunlight. Melodramatic plot has him falling in love with statuesque torch singer Nan Peterson, but ultimately destroyed in a cheapie climax reminiscent of Raoul Walsh's classic "White Heat" set atop a vast gasoline storage tower.

Satirist Craig Mitchell makes fun of the cornball story and shoestring-budget footage emphasizing lots of stiff reaction shots (original was lensed during 12 weekends on a budget under $50,000). New dialog brings out front the sexually risqué material of the original (Peterson is an im-

pressive '50s bombshell) while hilariously adding drug references. One side-splitting sequence takes innocent footage of a cute little girl and her mom, turning it into a hip, Cheech & Chong-style drugged-out rap routine.

Jay Leno (uncredited) is hilarious dubbing Clarke's role and providing off-the-wall narration, while Susan Tyrrell is a perfect choice for re-doing Peterson's role and her "Strange Pursuit" ballad number. Several new b&w insert shots matched to the original are funny, but a color prolog of college kids (including Googy Gress and Mark Holton) watching Clarke's film on the late show is a pointless framing device.

Fans are advised to also check out the original (also distributed by Wade Williams) which features excellent exterior photography (including work by Vilis Lapenieks) and actually is funnier in its integral nightclub scenes (where Peterson's fake keyboard moves are a hoot) than the new version. —Lor.

The First Season
(CANADIAN)

Toronto   An Orange production film. Produced by Robert Frederick. Directed by Ralph L. Thomas (uncredited). Screenplay, Brian Ross, Victor Nicolle, from story by Nicolle; camera (color), Richard Leiterman; editor, Frank Irvine; music, Graeme Coleman; production design, David Fisher. Reviewed at Carlton Cinemas, Toronto, Sept. 14, 1989. (In Toronto Festival Of Festivals.) Running time: 92 MIN.
Eric . . . . R.H. Thomson
Alex Cauldwell . . . . Kate Trotter
Jodie Cauldwell . . . . Christianne Hirt
Frank Cauldwell . . . . Dwight Ross

■ Ringing performances by three of its leads and Richard Leiterman's fine camerawork do not save "The First Season" from being a slight, mediocre story tossed adrift on British Columbia's big Pacific coast.

Ralph L. Thomas, who directed, had his name removed from the credits to protest newcomer producer Robert Frederick's final edit.

Pic deals with financially precarious fishermen, one of whom commits suicide, leaving his feisty wife and teenage daughter to carry on. The pair is helped by a troubled Vietnam War vet recruited against his will to help the pair keep their boat and business afloat.

R.H. Thomson delivers resoundingly as the vet given to alcoholic rages and repressed loneliness who finally finds peace and love. Kate Trotter, given little time to mourn the death of her husband, is class casting and fine throughout. Comely Christianne Hirt is a talented screen presence.

With many awkward, unexplained scenes, predictable unraveling and overall flatness, pic is best suited to quick tv playoff. —*Adil.*

Sous les draps, les étoiles
(Under The Sheets, The Stars)
(CANADIAN)

Toronto An Aska Film Intl. release of a Vision 4/National Film Board of Canada production. Produced by Suzanne Hénaut, Doris Girard. Directed by Jean-Pierre Gariépy. Screenplay, Gariépy; camera (color), Pierre Letarte; editor, Yves Chaput; music, Jean Vanasse; sound, Richard Besse. Reviewed at Toronto Festival of Festivals, Sept. 13, 1989. Running time: **90 MIN.**
With: Guy Thauvette, Marie-Josée Gauthier, Marcel Sabourin, Joseph Cazalet, Gilles Rénaud.

■ This is a stylish debut feature about two unlikely lovers whose secrets remain bottled up despite their heated encounters. Like Pandora's box, a flood of revelations surface when opened, mounting the intensity that leads to an inevitable downfall.

It's a very personal story which is unlikely to rack up much theatrically outside Quebec, but content and taut camerawork make it a high-quality pic for tv venues.

Thomas (Guy Thauvette) is an astronomer returned from South America with memories he would rather forget once back in Montreal. He meets a travel agent, Sylvie (Marie-Josée Gauthier), in a strange cafe, but her existentialism forces her to seek escape from the alienating urban center.

She just wants to leave with no particular destination in mind. He just wants to stay put. The verbal distance between the two restricts their bond and sparks their lust. They spend hours under the sheets discussing the stars.

A strange intruder who threatens to kill Thomas serves as a catalyst to the past, yet finally provokes Thomas' confession via Sylvie. His involvement with the CIA in South America comes back to haunt him.

Good technical production is exhibited on all fronts. It's a natural for French-language tv outlets.
—*Suze.*

B.O.R.N.

New York The Movie Outfit production. Executive producer, Skip Holm. Produced by Claire Hagen. Directed by Ross Hagen.

Screenplay, Hoke Howell, Ross Hagen; camera (Foto-Kem color; Getty prints), Gary Graver; editor-coproducer, Diana Friedberg; music, William Belote; art direction, Shirley Thompson; assistant director, Steven Pomeroy; production manager-line producer, Herb Linsey; stunt coordinator, Louie Elias; 2d unit director, John Stewart; 2d unit camera, Thomas Callaway; associate producers, Howell, P.J. Soles. Reviewed on Prism Entertainment vidcassette, N.Y., Aug. 8, 1989. MPAA Rating: R. Running time: **92 MIN.**
Buck Cassidy . . . . Ross Hagen
Liz . . . . P.J. Soles
Charlie . . . . Hoke Howell
Dr. Farley . . . . William Smith
Hugh . . . . Russ Tamblyn
Rosie . . . . Amanda Blake
Also with: Rance Howard, Clint Howard, Claire Hagen, Wendy Cooke, Debra Lamb, Kelly Mullis, Corine Cook, Louie Elias, Aspa Nakapoulou, Greg Cummins, Debra Burger, Dawn Wildsmith.

■ A thriller in the genre of Michael Crichton's "Coma," "B.O.R.N." is a direct-to-video feature notable for its veteran cast and pleasantly old-fashioned approach.

Title is an acronym for Body Organ Replacement Network.

Actor-director Ross Hagen has made this a family affair, with numerous relatives and pals doubling both in front of and behind the camera. He portrays an ordinary guy caught in a deadly situation in which evil doctors (led by ever-villainous William Smith) kidnap his pretty daughters to kill them and obtain organs for lucrative black-market transplants.

With the aid of chums Charlie (Hoke Howell) and Rosie (the late Amanda Blake), he goes after the baddies himself, since the police, notably corrupt detective Morrison (Rance Howard), offer little help.

Pic combines its exploitation elements with a solidly moralistic tone, just like its low-budget counterparts from the '50s. Pace is swift and acting effective, especially Russ Tamblyn as a vicious heavy. Poster girl Kelly Mullis (who's graced the artwork for such pics as "Shotgun" and "Fortress Of Amerikkka") gets an acting role here as Hagen's blond daughter, and has a good screen presence.—*Lor.*

Si Te Dicen Que Cai
(If They Tell You I Fell)
(SPANISH)

San Sebastian An Ideas y Producciones Cinematográficas production. Executive producer, Enrique Viciano. Written and directed by Vicente Aranda, based on Juan Marsé's novel. Camera (Agfacolor), Juan Amorós; editor, Teresa Font; music, José Nieto; sound, Licio Marcus de Oliveira; production design, Jaime Fernandez Cid; sets, Josep Rosell. Reviewed at San Sebastian Film Festival, Sept. 17, 1989. Running time: **120 MIN.**
Menchu-Ramona-

Aurora Nin . . . . Victoria Abril
Java . . . . Jorge Sanz
Marcos . . . . Antonio Banderas
Conrado-Sr. Galán . . . . . Javier Curruchaga
Also with: Guillermo Montesinos, Ferrán Rané, Lluis Homar, Joan Miralles, Carlos Tristancho, Juan Diego Botto.

■ Those with the patience to see this film two or three times, or read the novel by Juan Marsé upon which it is based ahead of time, may understand its convoluted plot. Ordinary filmgoers will be hard-pressed to make any sense out of what they see on the screen.

The complex story is told in four time frames, 1936, 1940, 1970 and 1988. These are mixed and jumbled about, with one actress, Victoria Abril, playing three parts, a fact which may be lost on most audiences.

The story concerns a prostitute, fascist types, revolutionaries left over from the Spanish Civil War, an ambitious boy, a voyeur and various others whose lives are intertwined. It is virtually impossible to make out the plot, or why things are happening or what the motivations are.

Pic has a lot of rather nasty sex scenes in it. These include voyeurism, flagellation, urinating upon one's mate, sadomasochism and similar divertissements not for the squeamish. None of them contribute to clarifying the plot.

Thesping, production values and direction are good. The period scenes belie the relatively modest budget with which the film was made. —*Besa.*

La Luna Negra
(The Black Moon)
(SPANISH)

San Sebastian An Origen production for Spanish TV. Executive producer, Antonio Cardenal. Written and directed by Imanol Uribe. Camera (color), Javier Aguirresarobe; editor, Teresa Font; music, Jose Nieto; sets, Luis Valles. Reviewed at San Sebastian Film Festival, Sept. 21, 1989. Running time: **82 MIN.**
Eva . . . . Lydia Bosch
Manuel . . . . Fernando Guillén
Adrian . . . . José Coronado
Also with: Patricia Figón, Emma Suárez, Yolanda Rios, Amparo Muñoz, Fernando Sancho.

■ Second segment of a Spanish TV series on witchcraft, this pic has little to justify its presence at the Basque fest other than the coincidence that its director is Basque.

Poor direction, thesping, lighting, effects and dialog probably will limit its exposure to European tv.

Yarn supposedly is based on the

Biblical story of Lilith, transposed to modern Spain. Within 48 hours, Eve conceives a daughter, loses her husband and runs down an "enigmatic" woman on the road. Nine years pass, during which the child grows and attains occult powers.

The mumbo-jumbo is mixed with puerile dialog, bad special effects and wooden thesping as the personages trip about a fancy house with a swimming pool. All of it is as flat as a pancake, but far less appetizing. —*Besa.*

Homer And Eddie

San Sebastian A Kings Road Entertainment presentation of a Borman/Cady production. Produced by Moritz Borman, James Cady. Directed by Andrei Konchalovsky. Screenplay, Patrick Cirillo; camera (Eastmancolor), Lajos Koltai; editor, Henry Richardson; music, Eduard Artemyev; production design, Michel Levesque; art direction, P. Michael Johnson; costume design, Katherine Kady Dover; casting, Robert McDonald. Reviewed at San Sebastian Film Festival, Sept. 16, 1989. No MPAA Rating. Running time: **99 MIN.**
Homer Lanza . . . . James Belushi
Eddie Cervi . . . . Whoopi Goldberg
Also with: Karen Black, John Waters, Robert Glaudini, Jim Mapp, James Thiel, Jeffrey Thiel, Andy Jarrel, Anne Ramsey, Wayne Grace, Beah Richards.

■ This road film about a mentally deficient dishwasher and a homicidal escaped cancer patient is a downer from beginning to end. Unfavorable comparisons with "Rain Man" are bound to be made.

The problem is not James Belushi's or Whoopi Goldberg's thesping, but a script that gets bogged down in religious arguments and dubious symbolism.

Homer, a mentally retarded dishwasher in Arizona, decides to hitchhike up to Oregon to see his father, who is dying of cancer. Almost immediately two crooks in a car roll him and steal the little money he has. Before long, he meets up with wacky vagabond Eddie in an old jalopy, and soon they become pals.

On the road Eddie tries to enlighten Homer to the ways of the world. She takes him to a brothel and gets the money to pay for it by holding up a store. Her criminal activities increase, and she winds up shooting people while robbing their stores. The twosome argue about the existence of God, and at the end the atheistic Eddie sees Christ dragging a cross in the streets of a small town in Oregon.

Meanwhile, Eddie tells Homer that the doctors have only given her a month to live. Pic has some touching scenes in it, as when Eddie tries to cheer up Homer by dancing with him, or Homer huddling with Eddie in a bathroom when she becomes terrified at the sound of some planes overhead.

Yet it is hard to feel much sympathy for these two mental patients, especially when Eddie goes about shooting down innocent shopkeepers and spews little but foul language throughout the film. The image of two underprivileged people in a cruel world is rather too pat to be convincing, and pic ends in a predictable way with Eddie getting her due.

Item might garner some interest on the basis of Belushi and Goldberg, but thus far seems to have failed to find a distrib in the States, following initial distrib Cineplex Odeon Films' decision to cease its domestic theatrical release program. —*Besa.*

Forced March

Boston A Shapiro Glickenhaus Entertainment release of an A-Pix production. Executive producers, Richard Karo, George Selma. Produced by Dick Atkins. Supervising producer, Gerrit van der Meer. Directed by Rick King. Screenplay, Atkins, Charles K. Bardosh; camera (color), Ivan Mark; editor, Evan Lottman; production design, Laszlo Rajk. Reviewed at Loews screening room, Boston, Sept. 15, 1989. (In Boston Film Festival.) No MPAA Rating. Running time: **104 MIN.**

Kline/Miklos Radnoti	Chris Sarandon
Myra	Renée Soutendijk
Hardy	John Seitz
Father	Josef Sommer

■ "Forced March" is a curiously uninvolving story about the Holocaust that tries to approach the situation through the eyes of an actor making a movie on the subject. Resulting pic is really two movies at war with each other, with neither one succeeding in making its point.

Movie opens on tv star Benjamin Kline (Chris Sarandon) who dies in the final episode of his hit detective series so he can escape from it. He has signed on to travel to Hungary to appear in a film about Miklos Radnoti, a Hungarian poet who was killed during a forced march from a Nazi labor camp.

Much of the film is the movie-within-a-movie, with long sequences suddenly interrupted by the onscreen director (John Seitz). The director argues that no Holocaust film can capture what it was really like, but they have to make it as truthful as they can. As a result, Kline starts sleeping in the work camp and tries to get inside the mind of the dead poet. Problem is that this serves to distance us from the horror of the Radnoti story, since we are constantly reminded this is only a re-creation.

On the other hand, the problems of actor Kline — a non-observant Jew whose Hungarian-born father (Josef Sommer) refuses to talk about his own wartime experiences — seem somewhat trivial by comparison. This is exacerbated by the selection of Chris Sarandon for the role, a competent actor who lacks the dramatic weight of someone like Meryl Streep or Jeremy Irons in the similarly structured "The French Lieutenant's Woman."

Film might have worked better if it simply told Radnoti's story, or focused more on the making of such a film. Combined, it's unlikely to satisfy anyone. —*Kimm.*

Hanna Monster, Liebling
(Hanna Monster, Darling)
(AUSTRIAN-B&W)

Venice A TTV Films presentation of a TTV Films, Cult Films production. Written and directed by Christian Berger. Camera (b&w), Berger; editor, Eliska Stibrova; music, Carmel; sound, Reinhold Kaiser; sets, Lois Weinberger, Uta Rechhardt; production manager, Danny Krausz. Reviewed at Venice Film Festival, Sept. 12, 1989. Running time: **100 MIN.**

Hanna	Marika Green
Leo	Hagnot Elishka
Arthur	Peter Turrini

Also with: Hannes Nicolussi, Claudia Holldack, Elert Bode, Ignaz Kirchner, Paulus Manker, Rosemarie Wohlbauer, Zbigniew Kasztan.

■ More interesting for the theme than its treatment, Christian Berger's film follows a married woman from a state of bliss to dejection and from dejection to independence. The trip is emotional and physical as the woman leaves her Austrian home to cross the continent.

Early sequences are misleading in a sense, as they create suspense and the impression the pic is developing into a horror movie. Hanna, a former dancer, radiantly pregnant, is rushed to the hospital, but something goes wrong in labor. She and her husband are denied access to the baby, who turns out to be a monster. The trauma is too much for her. She leaves the hospital without warning, improvises a hold-up in a supermarket, rents a car and begins a trip that will take her to the North Sea.

Berger, who shot the film himself, chose a grainy black & white texture. Actress Marika Green is on the screen almost constantly, most of the time by herself. Both script and performance are too vacuous to hold one's attention for long, but once Berger's intentions become clear, this solitary voyage begins to make sense.

Hanna, who realizes she never has been more than a darling possession for the men in her life, takes fate into her own hands. Even if she still hasn't decided which way she wants to go, she knows by film's end that she is at least completely free in her choice.

The film certainly will be appreciated, mostly by feminists, for its uncompromising approach. That won't endear it much to the conventional distribution channels. —*Edna.*

Courage Mountain

Toronto A Trans World Entertainment release of an Epic Prods. presentation of a Stone Group Ltd.-France production. Executive producer, Joel A. Douglas. Produced by Stephen Ujlaki. Directed by Christopher Leitch. Screenplay, Weaver Webb, from story by Fred and Mark Brogger; camera (color), Jacques Steyn; editor, Martin Walsh; music, Sylvester Levay; production design, Rob King; sound, Bernard Bats. Reviewed at Toronto Festival of Festivals, Sept. 16, 1989. No MPAA Rating. Running time: **96 MIN.**

Heidi	Juliette Caton
Grandfather	Jan Rubes
Peter	Charlie Sheen
Jane Hillary	Leslie Caron
Signor Bonelli	Yorgo Voyagis
Signora Bonelli	Laura Betti

■ Despite a beloved heroine, a strong international cast, and the lush Swiss Alps as a backdrop, "Courage Mountain" turns out to be a disappointing followup to the classic Heidi story. While the pic will probably find family audiences curious to see their memory of Shirley Temple's Heidi grown up as a teenager, it will play much better on video and tv.

On the eve of World War I in 1914, Heidi (Juliette Caton) is accepted at a posh boarding school in Italy. She's encouraged to further her education by grandfather Jan Rubes, but she's upset that she must say goodbye to her perky love interest, Peter (Charlie Sheen), who himself is off to be a soldier in the Swiss army.

At the school run by headmistress Leslie Caron, Heidi is scoffed at for her country bumpkin ways by her snotty classmates. The idyllic life soon crumbles when the Italian army takes over the school building, and the girls are sent to live and work as slave laborers in Signor Bonelli's (Yorgo Voyagis) Dickensian rat-infested orphanage.

Heidi and four friends make a daring escape through the drain pipe, and must forge their way on foot across the glacial Swiss Alps to safety in Switzerland, all the while followed by the evil, mustachioed Bonelli. Peter gets word that Heidi needs saving, and pulls some daredevil ski slaloms to rescue the group.

Jacques Steyn's camera caresses the beautiful snow-capped mountains and cozy thatched huts that dot the countryside. That's not enough to compensate for the weakness of Weaver Webb's script, which includes an unconvincing adolescent love interest (due mainly to the incongruent casting of Sheen as an 18-year-old Swiss boy with a blatant American accent), and a frustratingly brief interaction between Heidi and her cherished grandfather, played perfectly by Jan Rubes.

Caton looks right as the spunky heroine, but Caron and Voyagis are given less to do with their 1-dimensional characters. Director Christopher Leitch tries to combine heart-racing chase scenes with heartfelt displays of affection and friendship, but the result does not encapsulate the grand sweep of classic storytelling. —*Devo.*

Crimes And Misdemeanors

New York   An Orion Pictures release of a Jack Rollins and Charles H. Joffe production. Executive producers, Rollins, Joffe. Produced by Robert Greenhut. Written and directed by Woody Allen. Camera (Duart color; Deluxe prints), Sven Nykvist; editor, Susan E. Morse; music, various; sound, Frank Graziadei; production design, Santo Loquasto; art direction, Speed Hoplins; set decoration, Susan Bode; costume design, Jeffrey Kurland; production manager, Joseph Hartwick; assistant director, Thomas Reilly; associate producers, Reilly, Helen Robin; casting, Juliet Taylor. Reviewed at Loews Tower East, Oct. 5, 1989. (In Denver Intl. Film Festival.) MPAA Rating: PG-13. Running time: **104 MIN.**

Judah Rosenthal	Martin Landau
Cliff Stern	Woody Allen
Halley Reed	Mia Farrow
Lester	Alan Alda
Dolores Paley	Anjelica Huston
Ben	Sam Waterston
Wendy Stern	Joanna Gleason
Barbara	Caroline Aaron
Jack Rosenthal	Jerry Orbach
Miriam Rosenthal	Claire Bloom
Sharon Rosenthal	Stephanie Roth
Jenny	Jenny Nichols
Sol Rosenthal	David S. Howard
Aunt May	Anna Berger
Detective	Victor Argo
Prof. Louis Levy	Martin Bergmann
Lisa	Daryl Hannah

■ **Woody Allen ambitiously mixes his two favored strains of cinema, melodrama and comedy, with mixed results in "Crimes And Misdemeanors." Laudable effort is unlikely to break his or Orion's losing streak at the box-office.**

Two loosely linked stories here concern eye doctor Martin Landau and documentary director Allen, each facing moral dilemmas. The structural and stylistic conceit is that when Landau is onscreen, the film is dead serious, even solemn (harking back to Allen's controversial series of Ingmar Bergmanesque pictures starting with "Interiors"), while Allen's own appearance onscreen signals hilarious satire and priceless 1-liners.

What makes this odd mix interesting is that both halves of the piece, presented in alternating scenes, deal with an ethical Big Theme borrowed from Bergman, namely, correct human behavior in a modern, godless world. Unfortunately, the characters' specific problem is banal and unnatural dialog (a failing of Allen's recent flops "September" and "Another Woman"), making Landau's story needlessly remote.

Landau's problem is simple: His mistress (Anjelica Huston, shrill in an underwritten role) threatens to go to his wife (Claire Bloom) and reveal all, including Landau's previous embezzlement activities. At wit's end, he seeks the assistance of his ne'er-do-well brother (Jerry Orbach), who orders up a hitman from out of town to waste Huston.

Meanwhile, Allen, unhappily married to Joanna Gleason, has fallen in love with tv documentary producer Mia Farrow, whom he meets while directing a tv docu profiling his enemy and brother-in-law, Alan Alda. Alda is perfect casting as a successful tv comedy producer, whose pompous attitude and easy romantic victories with women (including Farrow) exasperate Allen. Though portrayed as filled with sour grapes and envy, Allen's plight is basically sympathetic.

Picture uses several subplots effectively, notably the plight of Sam Waterston (excellent in an unusual characterization) as the Landau family rabbi who's tragically going blind; and Allen's frequent visits to the Bleecker St. Cinema to watch old movies with his cute adolescent niece (Jenny Nichols). Also helping to knit themes together is the subject of Allen's serious, longrange docu project, a philosophy professor (played by Martin Bergmann) whose pronoucements give both the characters and audience food for thought, especially when this life-affirming guy commits suicide.

Landau's thesping is another career milestone, following his Oscar-nomination performance last year in Francis Coppola's "Tucker." He creates and holds one's interest in a selfish character who, defying all dramatic conventions, becomes increasingly corrupt and even learns to live with his evil and guilt rather than overcoming them. Huston is less fortunate, unable to make much of a merely functional character, while Allen fails to provide any interesting scenes for Bloom to play in the role of his wife.

An homage to Bergman's "Wild Strawberries," when Landau improbably visits his ancestral home and walks into a seder ceremony from 40 years ago, is well-acted but far too blunt in laying the film's themes on the table. In this scene, as elsewhere, yellow-tinted visuals by Bergman's great collaborator Sven Nykvist (who did not lens "Strawberries," a Gunnar Fischer assignment) superbly stylize the action. A background score of standards ranging from Irving Berlin and Cole Porter to classical pieces is effective, though several Landau segments are overly austere sans underscoring.

Allen fans will enjoy, following his screen return in "New York Stories," another taste of the comedian's vintage nebbish character. Farrow, in her 10th straight Allen feature, provides a warm center. Besides Waterston's standout role, there is topnotch support by Gleason and Anna Berger as Landau's Aunt May (in the seder flashback). Daryl Hannah pops up (uncredited) as one of Alda's aspiring tv actresses in a party scene. —*Lor.*

The Salute Of The Jugger

Sydney   A Filmpac (Australia) release of Kings Road Entertainment production. Executive producer, Brian Rosen. Produced by Charles Roven. Written and directed by David Webb Peoples. Camera (Technicolor), David Eggby; editor, Richard Francis-Bruce; music, Todd Boekelheide; production design, John Stoddart; sound, Jay Boekelheide, Lloyd Carrick; special makeup, Michael Westmore, Bob McCarron; 2d unit director/stunts, Guy Norris; production manager, Carol Hughes; assistant director, Keith Heygate; U.S. casting, Bonnie Timmermann; Australian casting, Alison Barrett. Reviewed at Fox-Columbia screening room, Sydney, Australia, Oct. 4, 1989. MPAA Rating: R. Running time: **102 MIN.**

Sallow	Rutger Hauer
Kidda	Joan Chen
Young Gar	Vincent Phillip D'Onofrio
Mbulu	Delroy Lindo
Big Cimber	Anna Katarina
Gandhi	Gandhi Macintyre
Dog Boy	Justin Monju
Gonzo	Max Fairchild
Lord Vile	Hugh Keays-Byrne
Maria	Lia Francisa
Samohin Boy	Aaron Martin

■ **This is an action film that seems to be trying to lift itself above the rut of post-apocalyptic desert pics (the increasingly tired "Road Warrior" genre), but it gets bogged down in endless sequences of a rugged "game" of the future. The forceful ad campaign may result in strong openings, but word of mouth isn't likely to work in the film's favor.**

It's the first feature directed by screenwriter David Webb Peoples ("Blade Runner," "Leviathan") and he's provided himself with a murky, familiar screenplay about a band of wandering "juggers." They're futuristic gladiators, led by the deeply scarred Sallow (Rutger Hauer), who was once a member of the League, the ruling elite, but who was banished over a misdemeanor. Now Sallow is determined to challenge the League's juggers and regain his position.

His own team (which includes Vincent Phillip D'Onofrio, Delroy Lindo and Anna Katarina) is augmented by a feisty peasant girl, Kidda (Joan Chen), who proves invaluable in the climactic confrontation with the League's team, which is headed by the giant Gonzo (Max Fairchild).

Dialog is at a premium here: Most of the soundtrack consists of grunts and groans. Plot development is slim also. Much of running time is given over to the game itself, which seems to have no rules except that the winning team places the skull of a dog atop a pointed stick. Since participants mostly wear masks during play, it's often difficult to sort out who's doing what to whom.

Final scenes at the League's underground h.q. seem to aim at some kind of spiritual triumph for Sallow, but action fans may view the denouement as an anticlimax.

Pic was principally financed in Australia and shot on desert locations near the mining town of Coober Pedy, South Australia, as well as in studios in Sydney. An Aussie crew was utilized, plus a few actors including Fairchild and the formidable Hugh Keays-Byrne (who plays the sinister Lord Vile and whose last name is, unfortunately, misspelled as "Bryne" in the opening credits).

Peoples goes for action first and foremost, and the concentration on a violent, no-holds-barred sport of the future is likely to endear the pic more to sports fans than to those who like their action more linear and less confusing. David Eggby's camerawork is up to his usual high standards. Editor Richard Francis-Bruce has done a good job considering the complexities involved, and John Stoddart's production design, especially in the underground scenes, is tops, adding to the film's scrungy look and tone.

Hauer, whose character loses an eye halfway through the pic, seems to relish roles that require physical deformity: He gives Sallow a certain presence, but he certainly doesn't extend himself in this role. Chen comes off best with a graceful performance as Kidda; Her moves in the game sequences are often quite beautiful in the midst of all the ugliness.

On the basis of "The Salute Of The Jugger," writer-director Peoples isn't up there with the most creative action directors (James Cameron, John McTiernan, George Miller, the Coen brothers) and boxoffice prospects for his first outing look to be only fair. Pic opens in Australia Oct. 19, with sneak previews starting immediately. —*Strat.*

Abba Ganuv 2
(The Skipper 2)
(ISRAELI)

Tel Aviv   A Roi presentation. Produced by Yehuda Barkan. Executive producer, Udi Soffer. Directed by Avi Cohen. Screenplay, Pini Idan, Shlomo Mashiach; camera (color), Amnon Salomon; editor, Shlomo Hazan; music, Nancy Brandeis. Reviewed at Pe'er Cinema, Tel Aviv, Sept. 20, 1989. Running time: **95 MIN.**

Chico . . . . Yehuda Barkan
Galia . . . . Alona Kimchi
Ben . . . . Ben Zion

■ **A sequel to Yehuda Barkan's Mediterranean meller, which scored nicely out of town last year, this is bound to appeal to the same kind of audience and generate similar b.o.**

Barkan again plays the happy-go-lucky sailor from Tiberias who has only one real commitment in life, his son Ben. In the last film, he had fallen for a blond Tel Aviv lawyer. This time around, he moves to Tel Aviv, to be closer to her.

The perfect idyll is disturbed when there is another legal attempt by his former wife to remove his son from him and subsequently by his suspicion that the pretty lawyer is having an affair with a customer. Some tears and some laughs later, everything is settled for the satisfaction of all concerned.

Correctly directed by Avi Cohen, who gets mileage out of every bit of pathos and elaborates every comic invention (not many of them around), the film banks mostly on Barkan's popular appeal.

Tech credits are okay. —*Edna.*

Beverly Hills Brats

Hollywood   A Taurus Entertainment release of a Rupert A.L. Perrin presentation of a Moore/Rivers production. Produced by Terry Moore, Jerry Rivers. Executive producer, Perrin. Directed by Dimitri Sotirakis. Screenplay, Linda Silverthorn, from original story by Moore, Rivers; camera (Technicolor), Harry Mathias; editor, Jerry Frizell; music, Barry Goldberg; production design, George Costello; set decoration, Maria Caso; art direction, Jay Burkhart; assistant directors, Richard Abramitis, Scott Cameron; associate producers, Grant Cramer, Janet Sheen. Reviewed at the Cineplex Odeon theaters, Century City, Calif., Oct. 6, 1989. MPAA Rating: PG-13. Running time: **91 MIN.**

Clive . . . . Burt Young
Jeffrey Miller . . . . Martin Sheen
Veronica Miller . . . . Terry Moore
Scooter . . . . Peter Billingsley
Sterling . . . . Ramon Sheen
Tiffany . . . . Cathy Podewell

■ **Even allowing that they're intentionally playing down to the audience, the filmmakers have crafted a completely laughless comedy. Atrocious almost to epic proportions, "Beverly Hills Brats"** would seem a must for those who compile books about bad cinema and a threat to the mental health of most anyone else.

If there's a bright spot here, it may be that this film might bring about a moratorium on the use of Beverly Hills as a tool to fill theater seats. The depressing part is that a number of people who've been in decent films before sacrificed themselves in the process.

Indeed, seeing Martin Sheen and Burt Young waltzing through this monument to industry excess and nepotism (count the Sheens in the credits) makes what otherwise would be written off as another lousy exploitation pic downright annoying. The opulent Beverly Hills locations add to the feeling of waste that surrounds the project.

Sheen plays a Beverly Hills plastic surgeon whose wife (Terry Moore, who coproduced with Jerry Rivers) and three kids live in utter stereotypical luxury: driving sports cars to school, having a Latin houseboy at Moore's beck and call, using computer systems that put NASA to shame.

Still, 15-year-old Scooter (Peter Billingsley) feels unloved and has a would-be robber (Young) pretend to kidnap him to get some attention. The ordeal brings the family together while Scooter shows his pseudo-captor life in the fast lane.

The film's clichés and racial slurs would be troublesome if one didn't stop to consider the source.

It's interesting to see director Dimitri Sotirakis insert outtakes prior to the closing credits, since they're all but indistinguishable from the shots that preceded them. If you've ever wondered why there are so many aspiring filmmakers in Los Angeles, one need only look at "Beverly Hills Brats" — the kind of film that makes viewers say, "Heck, I could do better than *that*." And they'd be right.—*Bril.*

Near Death
(DOCU-B&W)

New York   A Zipporah Films release of an Exit Films production. Major funding by National Endowment for the Humanities, in association with Channel 4, La Sept. Produced and directed by Frederick Wiseman. Camera (b&w, 16m), John Davey; editor and sound, Wiseman. Reviewed at New York Film Festival, Oct. 7, 1989. No MPAA Rating. Running time: **348 MIN.**

■ **"Near Death" is a tedious,** repetitious documentary made at a Boston hospital critical care unit that sheds little light on the issues affecting terminally ill patients, their families and health-care workers.

Frederick Wiseman, whose 1970 docu "Hospital" was an insightful, wider-ranging work in the same genre, has fallen in love with his footage this time. The nearly 6-hour opus debuted at the New York Film Festival will hold some interest via public tv for devotées of Wiseman's cinéma vérité approach.

Four case studies form the core of pic's content, plus endless, repetitive discussions by doctors and nurses about these cases and the ethical issues involved, mainly when to "pull the plug" on these terminal patients. Because of the medical jargon and unfortunately inarticulate physicians focused on at Beth Israel Hospital in Boston, pic is boring and unable to educate the viewer the way a researched docu with experts' interviews might do.

Instead, Wiseman with his no narration, no music, no facts/titles approach bears down in almost real-time sequences with the hope that lightning will strike and something moving or novel will be recorded. Only in the final segment, nearly two hours devoted to the hopeless case of Charlie Sperazza, does anything of that sort happen, as Sperazza's wife is very real and very empathetic. Sperazza makes an unexpected comeback and it is genuinely inspiring when he wiggles his toes after being all but given up on.

Pic's logical finish is the scene of Charlie being successfully taken out of intensive care, but Wiseman chooses to then end the film with footage of a corpse being removed from the hospital morgue to a waiting hearse, before bookending pic with a shot of the Charles River.

Sperazza's doctor, with a boring monotone and endlessly reiterated (almost verbatim) clichés, unfortunately resembles most of the doctors and nurses shown before.

Main protagonist is a Dr. Weiss who seemingly presides over the the unit and disconcertingly talks about heavy issues more like a basketball coach than philosopher. He confesses to being a nihilist, comparing the health care for terminal cases to the Greek myth of Sysiphus, i.e., endlessly rolling a rock up a hill only to have it roll back again. Near the end of the pic he recites virtually the only fact or datum imparted during its duration: that on average two-thirds of a person's lifetime healthcare costs are incurred in the final 21 days of one's life.

Most of the film's thrust deals with the issue of the team decision of physicians/nurses/patient/family as to what measures should be taken to prolong life during the end game of this medical chess match with Death. Once the parameters of this painful process are laid on the table, Wiseman unwisely pours over the topic dozens of times more, presumably for the benefit of slow-witted viewers.

The other key deficiency of his approach is that while patients (mostly unconscious, however) and families pour their hearts out, the health-care workers are obviously (and inevitably) aware of the camera's presence and therefore are on their best behavior. Intramural criticism is kept to a minimum and all concerned are portrayed as saintly, if hardly all that brainy, technicians.

A hardnosed film editor could usefully cut this pic down to feature length by retaining only one or two of the case studies, while further removal of repetitious discussions during individual segments could reduce it to a tight, half-hour tv special.

As it stands, "Near Death" is surprisingly bland. Even exploitational elements such as an autopsy review segment (with organs displayed on camera) and two scenes of corpses being removed come off as remote and clinical. End credits reveal that all but one patient died soon after the events depicted. —*Lor.*

Raakh
(Ashes)
(INDIAN)

Montreal   An Emotion Picture Co./Second Image Enterprise production. Produced by Aditya Bhattacharya, Asif Noor. Directed by Bhattacharya. Screenplay, Bhattacharya, Nuzhat Khan; camera (color), Santosh Sivan; editor, A. Sreekar Prasad; music, Ranjit Barot. Reviewed at Montreal World Film Festival (Indian Cinema), Sept. 1, 1989. Running time: **153 MIN.**

With: Pankaj Kapoor, Aamir Khan, Spuriya Pathak, Homi Wadia, Chandu Parkhi.

■ **This debut of a young (26-year-old) director takes an interesting subject but makes heavy weather of it. International chances are slight.**

Set in the near future in a dictatorship that apparently has followed police riots, the film centers on Aamir, a young man from a wealthy family, whose woman friend Neeta is raped by Karmali, a gangster, and some of his minions. Aamir vows vengeance, and teams up with a vet police officer, Kapoor, to bring the gangsters to justice.

The drama takes a painfully long time to unfold, even by the generally lethargic standards of Indian films. And, when Aamir finally takes a gun and sets about righting wrongs, the scenes of gunfights and violence are presented without any conviction whatsoever.

Despite this, Pankaj Kapoor gives a creditable performance as the tortured hero. —*Strat.*

Otto — Der Ausserfriesische (WEST GERMAN)

Hamburg A Rialto/Rüssel Video & Audio production. Directed by Otto Waalkes, Marijan Vajda. Screenplay, Bernd Eilert, Robert Gernhardt, Peter Knorr, Waalkes; camera (color), Egon Werdin; music, Thomas Kukuck, Christoph Leis-Bendorff. Reviewed at Ufa Palast, Hamburg, Sept. 20, 1989. Running time: **92 MIN.**

With: Otto Waalkes, Barbara May, Volker Kleinert, Hans-Peter Hattwachs, Wolfgang Zerlett.

■ **This film is the third vehicle for West Germany's most popular standup comic, straw-haired beanpole Otto Waalkes. There's no good material in this pic, which attempts to be a spoof of well-known films and tv series.**

The title, itself, is a pun on the German version of "E.T. The Extra-Terrestrial," and translates very loosely as "Otto — The Far Out Frisian."

B.o. prospects outside Germany are nil, due to the film's reliance on in-jokes stemming from regional German stereotypes. (Germans tell Frisian jokes the way the English tell Irish jokes or Americans Polish ones.)

The threadbare plot involves a bumbling attempt by a yokel (Waalkes) to save his pastoral homeland from environmental destruction at the hands of the military industrial complex. His fumble-footed crusade takes him to Florida for an encounter on the set of "Miami Vice." He winds up on a tennis court with Wimbledon champ Steffi Graf.

It is painfully obvious that Waalkes and his team of writers assumed that the star's mere presence would ensure laughs. They've skimped on the material, which is dated and often just dumb. Too bad, since Waalkes is a gifted comic who is capable of much

more than what he delivers this time out.

Technical credits are adequate for what clearly was intended as a star vehicle and nothing more. —*Gill*

Sati (Suttee) (INDIAN)

Montreal A National Film Development Corp. production. Directed by Aparna Sen. Screenplay, Sen, Arun Banerjee; camera (color), Ashok Mehta; editor, Shaktipada Roy; music, Chidananda Das Gupta; production design, Kartick Basu. Reviewed at Montreal World Film Festival (competing), Aug. 31, 1989. Running time: **124 MIN.**

With: Shabana Azmi, Kali Banerjee, Pradip Mukherjee, Arindam Ganguly, Ketaki Dutta, Shakuntala Barua, Arun Banerjee, Ajit Banerjee, Bimal Dev, Manu Mukherjee, Dipankar Raha, Ratna Ghosal.

■ **"Suttee" must have one of the most bizarre plots in screen history: It's about a woman who marries a tree. Sadly, the offbeat storyline doesn't compensate for the ponderous treatment by one of India's few women directors, Aparna Sen.**

The drama is set in 1828 when the Brahmin branch of Hinduism seems to have been exceptionally conservative. Suttee, soon to be outlawed by the British, was still common. This meant that a widow was expected to join her dead husband on the funeral pyre.

In a small village, Umi (Shabana Azmi), a young Brahmin woman, is saddled with two dire disadvantages: She's mute, and her horoscope foretells she'll be a young widow. As a result it's not surprising she can't get a husband.

The extraordinary solution is to marry her to a magnificent old banyan tree by which she spends a lot of her time. The wedding ceremony is carried out with all seriousness, but the film ends in tragedy with poor Umi seduced and abandoned and finally experiencing a kind of suttee with her husband/tree.

This might have been the basis for a powerful, if strange, film, but Sen handles the story with so little sense of pacing or narrative that even the most patient viewer is likely to become restless. Azmi, a talented actress, does the best she can with her role, but some of the supporting actors are less successful. The film looks handsome, but is unlikely to appeal to audiences other than the most ardent followers of Indian cinema. —*Strat.*

Flying Fox In A Freedom Tree (NEW ZEALAND)

Wellington A Grahame McLean Associates production, in association with the New Zealand Film Commission. (Intl. sales, NZFC). Produced by Grahame McLean. Directed by Martyn Sanderson. Screenplay, Sanderson; camera (color), Allen Guilford; editor, Ken Zemke; music, Michelle Scullion. Reviewed at National Film Unit, Wellington, N.Z., (In Tokyo Intl. Film Festival competing.) Sept. 29, 1989. Running time: **92 MIN.**
Pepe . . . . .Faifua Amiga Jr.
Tagata . . . . .Richard von Sturmer

■ **The often uneasy cultural coexistence of Polynesia and Europe is a dominant theme of New Zealand feature films made within and outside the country. "Flying Fox In A Freedom Tree" is one of the most affecting to date.**

While it is a tricky theatrical prospect outside N.Z. and the Pacific Islands, it should have strong telefeature potential and film fest appeal following its competing booth at the Tokyo fest.

Set and filmed on location in Western Samoa, pic is adapted from Albert Wendt's novel by first-time helmer Martyn Sanderson. The strengths of the script are apparent in the clear focus given the protagonist, Pepe (Faifua Amiga Jr.), which ensures character is not subservient to overemphatic cultural and political posturing. Sanderson also understands visual and verbal irony.

Pepe is a young Samoan initially torn between two cultures. He is able to work out his particular destiny by force of individual spirit and the example of his best friend. This friend, Tagata (Richard von Sturmer), is the mythical "flying fox" of the title — a dwarf, and street-smart Europolynesian, who never could fit into conventional society.

The "example" Tagata ultimately provides Pepe might appear excessively grim. Yet it is a measure of Wendt and Sanderson's achievement that it emerges as an affirmation of life and death. In so doing, pic champions individuality over slavish allegiance to any so-called cultural identity.

There are some awkward and unduly slow-moving moments in the early part of the film as Pepe, from a hospital bed, begins to spin his tale. As the story deepens, initial misgivings dissolve before the gathering power of the piece that dictates its own momentum.

Faifua Amiga Jr. has the energy and intelligence, if not always the

technique, to bring veracity to the central role. He is at his best in the big scenes with his father, to whom he is opposed, and with the old high chief, Toasa, from whom he learns his ancestry. He also conveys wry humor, which is most important in Pepe.

As Tangata, Richard von Sturmer is an unmistakable find. Even allowing for his somewhat unusual stature, he has a presence in the camera eye that instantly compels.

Sanderson is a well-known actor in New Zealand and Australia and has made several short films. "Flying Fox" is an auspicious foray into the realm of features.
—*Nic.*

Tarzan Mama-Mia (DANISH)

Copenhagen A Pathé-Nordisk release of a Nordisk Film production, in association with DR/TV and the Danish Film Institute. Produced by Henrik Möller-Sörensen. Written and directed by Erik Clausen. Screenplay supervision, Dorthe Birkedal Andersen, Pernille Clausen, Morten Bruus; camera (Eastmancolor), Bruus; editor, Leif Axel Kjeldsen; music, Kim Larsen, Bellami; sound, Mike Nielsen; costumes, Merete Engbäk; production design, Sven Wichman; production management, Thomas Lydholm; Danish Film Institute consultant producer, Ida Zeruneith; casting, Jette Termann; Reviewed at the Palads, Copenhagen, Sept. 20, 1989. Running time: **84 MIN.**
Rikke . . . . .Christina Haagensen
Her father . . . . .Michael Falch
Charlotte . . . . .Tammy Öst
Ludvig . . . . .Leif Sylvester Petersen
The watchmaker . . . . .Erik Clausen
Bettina . . . . .Anne Sofie Fensmark
Anna . . . . .Anne Marie Norge
Also with: Ole Meyer, Bjarne Jensen, Elsebeth Nielsen, Susanne Höjsting, Suzanne Bjerrehus, Bo Leth Larsen, Arne Vang Jörgensen, Peder Jorde, Louise Clausen, Michela Thor Jensen.

■ **Writer-helmer Erik Clausen moves with his usual ease and empathy among society's lower strata in his new kiddie comedy "Tarzan Mama-Mia." It has appeal with fine acting and asides of grotesque humor to the parent generation as well.**

Pic tells of an 11-year-old motherless slum kid who lives alone with her father until a horse moves in with them in their tiny second floor rear apartment. Item should move at an easy trot into offshore children's film distribution.

Rikke (played like a serious-miened Pippi Longstocking by Christina Haagensen) lives a lonely life with her soccer-on-tv-obsessed father (Michael Falch). Fun enters her life, and that of the dreary neighborhood as well, when the girl wins a pony in a cornflakes promotion contest.

A local bum (Clausen's off-film comedy act partner Leif Sylvester Petersen) turns out to be a former stable boy, and soon one and all, including helmer Clausen himself as a quite morbidly amusing wheelchair cripple, are horsing around and contributing to a finer life for girl and pony.

Clausen is unabashedly sentimental about his little world of social have-nots but never cloyingly so. The curious title he came up with refers to the fact that the horse, when owned by another girl who tearfully had to sell hers to the cornflakes company, was named Mama-Mia, while Rikke's bum friend has for some reason insisted on Tarzan as the mount's moniker. The film is full of non sequiturs and sticks to no strong storyline. It is, however, lively within each of its strings of episodes and with a cumulative effect of goodwill and smiles all around.

Actress Tammy Ost turns in a finely honed performance as Rikke's school teacher who winds up in the dad's bed but not necessarily in the girl's heart. It is a Clausen specialty to keep audiences slightly off balance with offbeat shadings of otherwise stock characters and situations.

The richly imaginative and technically controlled cinematography of Morten Bruus is an added pleasure throughout. —*Kell.*

The Taste Of Hemlock
(BRITISH)

Boston   An Intl. Artists Film release of a Sean S. Cunningham presentation of a Tynan Young production. Produced by Eric Tynan Young. Coproduced by Jonathan G. Chambers. Directed by Geoffrey Darwin. Screenplay, Young, based on play "The Astrakhan Coat" by Pauline Macaulay; camera (color), Roger Tonry; editor, Henry Te; music, Young; sound, Tony Smyles; assistant director, Chambers. Reviewed at Loews screening room, Sept. 12, 1989. (In Boston Film Festival.) No MPAA Rating. Running time: **90 MIN.**

Claud Thatch . . . . Randy Harrington
James Hattan . . . . Eric Tynan Young
Barbara . . . . Anne Elizabeth Ramsey
Barry . . . . Reed Armstrong
Lt. Jordan . . . . David McKnight
Mrs. Dobrowski . . . . Barbara Pilavin
Sgt. Narducci . . . . Shea Young

■ **Shorn of about half an hour, "The Taste Of Hemlock" might have made an interesting segment on the old British teleseries "Roald Dahl's Tales Of The Unexpected." As is, it is a mixture of interesting weirdness and a bit too much padding.**

Film, carrying a 1987 copyright, focuses on hapless young Claud Thatch (Randy Harrington) who answers an ad at a laundromat announcing that the owner of a barely worn leather jacket must sell it for quick cash. Claud responds, and is summoned to meet James Hattan (played by the film's producer/writer/composer Eric Tynan Young).

James appears to be a well-heeled young Englishman with affected mannerisms and a tendency to manipulate those around him. This becomes clear upon the arrival of Barry (Reed Armstrong) and Barbara (Anne Elizabeth Ramsey) who are introduced as "twins" and dress in identical clothes. Claud is tricked into purchasing the expensive coat even though he cannot afford it.

Indeed, the entire film plays like an elaborate practical joke with Claud as the patsy, and since the audience knows only a little more than he does it is sometimes difficult to know what exactly is going on. The problem is that by the time everything is made clear, the "twist" ending has become all too easy to anticipate.

Chief problem here seems to be the pacing, as too much time is spent establishing how strange James and his friends are and how out of place Claud is among them.

Harrington is fine as Claud but Young gets to be a bit much as James, even given that the character is flamboyant and eccentric. Ramsey scores in the difficult role of the plotter who has second thoughts. —*Kimm.*

Echad Mi'Shelanu
(One Of Us)
(ISRAELI)

Tel Aviv   A Nachshon Films presentation of an Israfilm production. Produced by Zvi Spielman, Shlomo Mograbi. Directed by Uri Barbash. Screenplay, Benny Barbash, based on his play; camera (color), Amnon Salomon; editor, Tova Asher; music, Ilan Virtzberg; art direction, Eitan Levy; production manager, Gadi Levy. Reviewed at Lev cinema, Tel Aviv, Sept. 22, 1989. Running time: **110 MIN.**

Rafa . . . . Sharon Alexander
Yotam . . . . Alon Aboutboul
Amir . . . . Dan Toren
Tamar . . . . Dahlia Shimko
  Also with: Shaul Mizrahi, Alon Neuman, Ofer Shikartzi, Ruby Porat-Shuval, Eli Yatzpan, Arnon Tzadok (the Colonel).

■ **Uri Barbash's tense topical drama takes place at an Israeli army base, dealing with moral dilemmas facing officers of a crack commando unit. Compelling in spite of its flaws, this looks like a winner on the local market, picking up the army's ethical conflicts where an earlier** hit, "Ricochets," left off.

Based on a play by the director's brother, Benny, who adapted and expanded it for the screen, the script has a military police investigator dispatched to a West Bank camp to look into the death of an Arab suspect. The official report, considered unsatisfactory at headquarters, said death occurred when suspect attempted to escape interrogation for the murder of an Israeli officer.

For openers, the investigator finds out the dead officer was a close friend from training days, but so is the interrogator whose actions he has to review. It doesn't take long to discover the report was doctored. Barely concealed facts are soon unveiled, and the MP now has to make up his mind whether to incriminate fellow avenging officers or turn a blind eye.

He is expected by everybody around him to let it slide, because the whole issue is about "us" against "them," and normal justice does not apply in such cases.

Barbash offers some relevant and very critical insights into the mentality of the Israeli fighter, a combination of tough determination, male comradeship and adolescent innocence. The soldier is profoundly disturbed by the complex human and political situation he finds himself in, which he often prefers to ignore since he knows no other way of handling it.

Film bears down on what is one of the most controversial topics in Israel, but does it from a liberal perspective that will be familiar to a large segment of its potential audience.

To convey his positions in the clearest possible manner, Barbash compromises on both structure and characterization. He has a long flashback in the first half of the picture that almost becomes a film on its own, dedicated to the officers' training course and to the macho friendship between the three leading characters.

He also has a tendency to oversimplify the secondary parts and skip over relevant issues that might detract attention from the main ideological thrust of the script (the eventual guilt of the dead suspect is never even brought into question).

Sharon Alexander is remarkably subtle as the investigator who has trouble separating conscience, emotions and grudges. Alon Aboutboul, as his close friend and chief suspect, makes the best of his boyish, irresponsible charm, even if he can't fully cope with the subconscious guilt implied in his role.

Strong support is lent by Dan Toren, coming through in the flashback as the ideal image of the sabra, and by Arnon Tzadok in a brief but authoritative appearance as the colonel in command.

Well shot and briskly edited, this may be the item to pump some life into the abysmal b.o. performance of Israeli films this year, both at home and abroad. —*Edna.*

Roadkill
(CANADIAN-B&W)

Toronto   A Cinephile release (in Canada) of a Mr. Shack Motion Pictures production. Produced by Bruce McDonald, Colin Brunton. Executive producer, Mr. Shack. Directed by McDonald. Screenplay, Don McKellar; camera (b&w), Miroslaw Baszak; art direction, Geoff Murrin; editor, Mike Munn; music, Nash The Slash; sound, Steve Munro; associate producer, Keith Michael Bates. Reviewed at Toronto Festival of Festivals, Sept. 15, 1989. Running time: **80 MIN.**

Ramona . . . . Valerie Buhagiar
Roy Seth . . . . Gerry Quigley
Buddie . . . . Larry Hudson
Bruce Shack . . . . Bruce McDonald
Matthew . . . . Shaun Bowring
Russel . . . . Don McKellar
Luke . . . . Mark Tarantino
  Also with: Peter Morfea, Patricia Sims, Earl Pastko, Dean Richards, Jim Millan, Nash The Slash, Joey Ramone.

■ **A black & white rock 'n' roll road movie with a casual attitude and retro-psychedelic style, "Roadkill" scrambles a jigsaw of thematic pretensions that don't fit together but do fit its hallucinatory mood. "Roadkill" is not clever enough to travel theatrically outside of Canada, but deserves video exposure and would fit nicely into the movie programming slots of cable music services.**

The influence of Wim Wenders and Jim Jarmusch on filmmaker Bruce McDonald is apparent, but "Roadkill" lacks the coherence and sophistication these paradigms of "outlaw" cinema bring to their work. The skewed, cartoonish narrative revolves around Ramona (Valerie Buhagiar) a compliant young woman who works for a hyper rock promoter. He frantically dispatches her from Toronto to northern Ontario to track down and return a wayward band that disappeared while touring the boondocks. They're called Children of Paradise, in keeping with the film's inchoate groping at the theme of spiritual quest and realization.

Ramona can't drive, so she

takes a cab into the tundra-like countryside. Stranded by the garrulous, joint-toking cabbie, she's swept up in a dizzying series of road adventures. These include a film-within-a-film encounter with an itinerant documentary maker (McDonald), and meetings with an aspiring serial killer, a 15-year-old country kid who seduces her and a mute hotdog vendor who turns out to be the missing lead singer of the band but is meant to represent the godhead. The singer and the hapless would-be serial killer have a date with destiny, and its metaphysical symbolism is all too transparent.

The farther Ramona ventures from the ordered reality of her life in Toronto, the more self-reliant she grows. When she spontaneously learns to drive, her transformation is more or less complete, but the film keeps rolling aimlessly along to its absurd denouement.

Buhagiar has interesting screen presence and exotic, strongly chiseled features, which she uses to animate Ramona's character when the script fails to do so. The supporting performers are less compelling but adequate to the purpose.

Crisp black & white cinematography and a propulsive postpunk soundtrack (featuring the Ramones, Cowboy Junkies and Nash The Slash, among others) enhance the underground ambience "Roadkill" aims for. —*Rich.*

Den röde traad
(The Red Thread)
(DANISH)

Copenhagen   A Grasten Film release of Regner Grasten production. Produced by Regner Grasten. Executive producer, Sven Methling. Directed by Piv Bernth. Screenplay, Michael Bundesen, Michael Hardinger, Jörgen Thorup, based on story by same plus Regner Grasten; camera (Agfacolor), Peter Roos; editor, Mette Schramm, Sven Methling; music, Shu-bi-dua; sound, Stig Sparre Ulrich; production design, Pelle Arestrup; choreography, Mikela Lage; production management, John Hilbard. Reviewed at Palads, Copenhagen, Sept. 27, 1989. Running time: 85 MIN.
Heinz Heinicken Sr./Jr. . . . . . .Thomas Eje
Johnny Jazz Sr./Jr. . . . . .Michael Bundesen
Peter Pop Sr./Jr. . . . . . .Michael Hardinger
Balletskowitz Sr./Jr. . . . . . . .Kim Daugaard
Wehrmacht Pvt.
  Kettenraucher . . . . .Claus Asmussen
Patric . . . . .Jorgen Thorup
Mrs. Jensen . . . . .Birgit Sadolin
Cinderella . . . . .Mette Riis
  Also with: Uffe Pilgaard, Claus Ryskjär, Peter Andersen, Karina Von.

■The first feature film to be produced under a new Danish state subsidy system, "The Red Thread" will have to survive on home market returns only and may just about do so.

Producer Regner Grasten has entrusted the members of Shu-bi-dua, a rock group with a devoted national family-following, to write and perform in most of the skits and songs, many of which were hits, that pad out the film's farcical plot.

Lead singer Michael Bundesen plays a Yank soldier sharing a jeep in 1945 with a Russian and a Britisher as they come to the rescue of the lady owner of a small seaside resort hotel in Jutland. A German officer has forced his way into the house to use it as a (mock) hiding place for nothing less than the German Reich's gold reserve. Many years later, a second generation returns to retrieve the treasure.

The gold actually lies buried in a church vault, where ghosts dance as the combatants enter. Another busy ghost is Wehrmacht Pvt. Kettenraucher (the film's funniest performance, by Shu-bi-dua member Claus Asmussen, son of famed jazz violinist Svend Asmussen). Thomas Eje as the brute German officer delivers his lines with a glint of absurdist evil in his eyes. Eje is pretty funny, too.

A flimsy love story goes with the sometimes blurry fun. Short shots of animation (a rising and setting sun in particular) enliven the proceedings when they otherwise bog down in badly timed Mack Sennett imitation or flounder in non sequitur mugging. Piv Bernth in her directorial bow has been given neither time nor coin to more than stitch together loosely whatever material screenplay and performers offered her.

The final frame indicates a sequel for "The Red Thread." The current one's fate would seem to be hanging by one. —*Kell.*

Ts'e Ma Ju Lin
(Run Away)
(TAIWANESE)

Boston   A Central Motion Picture Corp. release. Executive producer, Hsu Kuo-liang. Produced by Hsu Hsin-chih. Directed by Wang T'ung. Screenplay, Hsiao Yeh, Ts'ai Ming-liang, from short story by Ch'en Yu-hang; camera (color), T'ang Wei-han, Li P'ing-pin; sound, Tu Tu-chih; editor, Wang Chin-ch'en, Ch'en Sheng-ch'ang; music, Chang Hung-yi; production supervisor, Lin Teng-fei; art direction, Ku Chin-t'ien, Lin Ch'ung-wen, Wang T'ung; costumes, Ku Chao-shih, Wang T'ung; assistant directors, Lin Chun-ch'eng, Ch'en Sheng-ch'ang, Chiang Pien. Reviewed at Loews Copley Place, Boston, Sept. 21, 1989. (In the Boston Film Festival.) Running time: 114 MIN.
Dan Ju, the girl . . . . .Chang Ying-chen
Ho Nan, the man . . . . .Ma Ju-feng
"Crow Face" . . . . .Teng Ping-ch'en
The Old Man . . . . .Kuan Kuan
  Also with: Ku Chun, Sha Li-wen, Ch'en Hui-lo, Wang Jui, Li Wen-t'ai, Tan Yang, Ho Wei-hsiung, Chieng Lung, Lu Yun-pao.

■"Runaway," 1985 pic appearing as part of Taiwanese series within the Boston Film Festival, shows regional cinema on the verge of making big waves in the international film community. Action-oriented drama is a few minutes too long for American tastes, but all aspects represent solid filmmaking.

Story is set in mainland China in the 13th century, as the government is cracking down on roving packs of bandits. One gang, a sort of medieval Chinese version of "The Wild Bunch," has fallen on hard times. Kidnaping a young woman (Chang Ying-chen) to coerce her small town to pay tribute they instead find themselves in retreat, their leader killed and the heir apparent (Ma Ju-feng) starting to fall in love with the girl.

Action sequences are rousing, from bloody swordfights to a comic 3-way fistfight over the unending appetite of one of the bandits. As the older generation dies off, the remaining bandits elect to pull off one last robbery — against the imperial tax collectors — and then go their separate ways.

Film's commercial value Stateside is severely hindered by the fact that the chief motivation for the young woman is that she has grown protective of the man who has kidnaped and raped her. Even arthouse crowds respectful of cultural diversity are likely to find that a bit too much.

Tech credits are solid, with director Wang T'ung showing equal facility with non-action scenes, including the grumblings of the older generation and a fascinating (and bawdy) shadow puppet show put on during the bandits' drunken revels. —*Kimm.*

Periodes met zon
(Sunny Spells)
(DUTCH-DOCU)

Amsterdam   A Cor Koppies Filmverhuur distribution of a Stichting Jura production. (Intl. sales, Seventh Heaven Films, Amsterdam.) Produced by Jan Ketelaar. Directed by, camera (color, 16m), editor, Ruud Monster; sound, Karel Evers, Mark Glynne, Jac Vleeshouwers, Geert de Bruin. Reviewed at Kriterion theater, Amsterdam, Sept. 17, 1989. Running time: 75 MIN.

■"Sunny Spells" is fascinating, but when it's all over one still doesn't know if it's fiction or documentary.

Director Ruud Monster wanted to film things, sites, happenings, events and non-events in the Netherlands during one year — that's documentary. He also wanted to mix in fantasy: what came into his head in connection with his filmed "reality." He succeeds so well that the viewer never quite manages to distinguish the two.

There are children, funerals, wolves, frogs, chickens, cows, road-building machinery, harvesters, meadows, factory sites, Dutch people on bikes doing cowboy work, bride and groom in full regalia on an old motorbike, and skylines. In his tightly edited flow of images, without beginning, middle or end, without commentary (but with music and natural sound), all these elements contribute to the spell of this picture.

Monster, active in tv and well repped in festivals, traveled some 25,000 miles for his images, acting as his own cameraman and editor. Film has enough going for it to reach beyond local fest circuits. —*Wall.*

La Femme de Rose Hill
(The Woman Of The Rose Hill)
(SWISS-FRENCH)

Venice   A Filmograph (Geneva) presentation of a Filmograph, Gemini Films, GPFI (Paris) production. Coproduced with West German Television (WDR), Television Suisse Romande (SRR), Film Four Intl., Airone Cinematografica. Executive producers, Jean-Louis Porchet, Gerard Ruey. Written, produced and directed by Alain Tanner. Camera (Cinemascope, Eastmancolor), Hugues Ryffel; editor, Laurent Uhler; music, Michel Wintsch; sound, Jean-Paul Mugel; art direction, Stephane Levy associate producer, Paulo Branco. Reviewed at Venice Film Festival (competing), Sept. 11, 1989. Running time: 95 MIN.
Julie . . . . .Marie Gaydu
Jean . . . . .Jean-Philippe Ecoffey
Jeanne . . . . .Denise Peron
Marcel . . . . .Roger Jendly
  Also with: Louba Guertchikoff, Andre Steiger, Jacques Michel, Marie-Christine Epiney.

■For the plot of his new movie, Alain Tanner goes back 15 years to one of his best films, "Middle Of The World." This love story also is a confrontation between cultures and mentalities, and it once again is triggered by the presence of a foreign woman in a Swiss ambience.

Here the crisis involves Julie, a black woman brought by a farmer from an island in the Indian Ocean. They had established contact through the mail, and within a week of landing in snow-covered Switzerland Julie marries Marcel. The rough manners of the middle-aged husband are to much for his young bride, who denies him access to her bedroom and finally leaves him.

She then embarks on a torrid romance with Jean, who works with his father in the family's brick factory. In spite of parental warnings, the young man installs Julie in the home of his eccentric aunt, and visits her regularly until he discovers she is pregnant.

When his pleas that Julie end the pregnancy are ignored, Jean leaves the country for several months but, on returning almost goes berserk when he is not allowed to see the baby. Worried about the condition of his son, he arranges to have Julie and the baby sent back to her island, which results in tragedy for all.

Marie Gaydu's strong screen presence, in her first film role, is a definite asset. So is the sympathetic performance of Denise Peron as the unconventional aunt who doesn't mind swimming against the current. Jean-Philippe Ecoffey, as the lover who is afraid

to commit himself at the right time, has some trouble making sense of his role.

Tanner overuses clichés, like the "mail-order bride" plot, images of black and white bodies intertwined and the notion of parents spoiling their children's love life "for their own good." Also, female audiences will protest the old-fashioned position willingly adopted by the film's heroine. She's only too happy to sweep floors, cook exotic food and jump into bed whenever her lover deigns to come by.

Technically, the film is highly polished. Hugues Ryffel gets full value from the Swiss landscape and the changing natural light of every season, carefully chosen to fit the mood of the story. The film's success, however, will depend mostly on audience reaction to the chemistry between Ecoffey and Gaydu. —*Edna.*

SAN SEBASTIAN FEST REVIEWS

Hab Ich Nur Deine Liebe
(If I Only Have Your Love)
(WEST GERMAN)

San Sebastian An Elizabeth Müller production. Written and directed by Peter Kern. Camera (Fujicolor), Eberhard Geick; editor, Müller; production manager, Patti Unwin; sound, Slavco Hitrov; costumes, Zwinki Jeannée. Reviewed at San Sebastian Film Festival, Sept. 20, 1989. Running time: **98 MIN.**
Grete . . . . .Christa Bernd
Michael Seebisch . . . . .Tilo Prückner
Hio Main . . . . .Ankie Beilke-Lau
   Also with: Marcelo Uriona, Wolf-Dietrich Sprenger, Brigitte Janner, Christiane Lemm, Hans-Peter Korff.

■**This zany and occasionally droll German comedy drew laughs and applause at its screening here to a young audience. Pic has enough outrageous and offbeat elements to generate some interest for specialized markets and tv.**

The story involves a bachelor computer executive who, too shy to approach women, resorts to porn shop fare for his kicks. His life totally changes on New Year's Eve and the following day as he gets embroiled with an elderly woman whom he accidentally hits with his car.

The victim seems to be mute, but then, on the most unexpected occasions, breaks into operatic song. The exec can't get rid of her. She follows him to a New Year's Eve party, then to his office, caus-

ing embarrassment and throwing the exec's life into confusion. The situation is complicated further when the timid exec shelters a Thai hooker who is being mistreated by her pimp.

Kern mixes the story with surrealistic touches to good comic effect, but the yarn goes awry with a weak finale. Even so, item manages to hold audience interest throughout.

Gay undercurrents are palpable, and the conservative exec has a rather improbable tattoo on his arm.

Production values are rather on the modest side. Both femme leads are too homely.—*Besa.*

Konsul
(The Consul)
(POLISH)

San Sebastian A Film Polski presentation. Written and directed by Miroslaw Bork. Camera (color), Julian Szczerkowski, editor, Krzysztof Oslecki; music, Zbigniew Karnecki; sound, Ryszard Patkowski; art direction, Tadeusz Kosarewicz; production manager, Andrzej Janowski. Reviewed at San Sebastian Film Festival, Sept. 17, 1989. Running time: **104 MIN.**
   With: Piotr Fronczewski, Maria Pakuinis, Krzysztof Zaleski, Jerzy Bonczak, Gustaw Lutkiewicz, Grazyna Kruk, Henryk Bista, Maciej Goraj, Ryszard Kotys.

■**This delightful, amusing film is about a Polish confidence man whose trickery starts with mod-**

est swindling of a vendor in a market and leads to the conning of Polish authorities.

The con man, who just has been released from jail for similar offenses, seeks out a former girlfriend, now married, and takes up his wily and ingenious conning game again. Thesp Piotr Fronczewski plays the part of the swindler to perfection, mostly with a straight face, but, when needed, with the proper soupçon of expression and irony.

The intricate ploys he invents are fascinating to watch, as he pretends to be an engineer, tricks a family in the sticks into giving him $3,000, and finally succeeds in passing himself off as a consul, hoodwinking everyone from local politicos to top government ministers.

There is plenty of ribbing of the Polish regime. Though criticism of the communist system certainly is a strong motif in the film, it is the clever twists in the con man's activities that make the film a winner.

Item could be of interest for release in arthouse circuits and for tv.—*Besa.*

Papeles Secundarios
(Supporting Roles)
(CUBAN-SPANISH)

San Sebastian A Cuban Film Institute (ICAIC) and Spanish TV (RTVE) coproduction. Directed by Orlando Rojas; Screenplay, Rojas, Jorge Alvarez, Osvaldo Sánchez; camera (color), Raúl Pérez Ureta; editor, Nelson Rodriguez; music, Mario Daly. Reviewed at San Sebastian Film Festival, Sept. 19, 1989. Running time: **117 MIN.**
   With: Rosa Fornes, Juan Luis Galiardo, Luisa Pérez Nieto, Ernesto Tapia, Mario Balmasedo.

■**This is a rambling, talky pic with minimal plot development about a group of legit thesps in Havana rehearsing a play.**

Intermingled in the nonstory are the lives and loves of the troupe, mixed with rather pretentious posing and prose.

A tedious script, awful music and clumsy editing are certain to restrict this muddle to Spanish and Cuban tv screens. —*Besa.*

El Mar y el Tiempo
(The Sea And Time)
(SPANISH)

San Sebastian An Ion Producciones film, with the collaboration of Spanish TV. Executive producer, José Luis García Sánchez. Written and directed by Fernando Fernán Gómez. Camera (color), José Luis Alcaine; editor, Pablo G. del Amo; music, Mariano Diaz; sets, Julio Esteban; production manager, Andrés

Santana; sound, Gilles Ortión. Reviewed at San Sebastian Film Festival, Sept. 22, 1989. Running time: **100 MIN.**
Eusebio . . . . .Fernando Fernán Gómez
Jesús .José Soriano
Doña Eusebia . . . . .Rafaela Aparicio
Mer . . . . .Aitana Sánchez-Gijón
Chus . . . . .Cristina Marsillach
   Also with: Iñaki Miramón, Ramón Madaula, Eulalia Ramón, Emma Cohen.

■**This tender glance into the life of a politically "progressive" Madrid family in 1968 has its touching moments, but is unlikely to stir up much interest except for those who want to cast a nostalgic look into their past.**

Much of the pic, which seems more like a play than a vehicle for film, is overfamiliar to Spanish audiences: the return of the Spanish exile for a look-see at modern Spain, the goings-on of a liberal family of the time and the struggles of the then-young generation against the establishment.

Buoying the pic are an amusing performance by Rafaela Aparicio as the cantankerous grandmother who is confined to her huge bed (an almost identical part to that in Carlos Saura's "Mom Turns 100") and fine thesping by Fernando Fernán Gómez as the lonely father and José Soriano as the returned exile from Argentina.

High points of the story concern the exile's rediscovery of Madrid and of his estranged family, and his inability to adapt himself to the "new" Spain. The tight family structure is breaking down, and the returned exile can see it more plainly than the others.

A few of the dramatic scenes are well done, such as when the exile visits his brother's ex-wife and she drinks herself into a stupor, or when he joins a game of cards in a local tavern and marvels at all the curse words used.

What "progressive Madrid" was like in 1968 is not apt to be of great interest to modern audiences who have doubtless been hearing of it from their parents for a decade or more. Item essentially is a nostalgia piece with lotsa talk but little action or plot.—*Besa.*

La Nación Clandestina
(The Secret Nation)
(BOLIVIAN)

San Sebastian A Channel 4, Spanish TV, AZF (Stuttgart) and Japan TV coproduction, made by the Grupo Ukamau. Produced by Beatriz Palacios. Written and directed by Jorge Sanjinés. Camera (color), César Pérez; music, Cergio Prudencio; sound, Juan Guarani. Reviewed at San Sebastian Film Festival, Sept. 23, 1989. Running time: **125 MIN.**
   With: Reynaldo Yujra, Delfina Mamani, Orlando Huanca, Roque Salgado.

■ Though Bolivian helmer Sanjinés has made seven earlier features, this pic has a totally amateur look about it, as though it were shot on a Bolivian shoestring budget.

Most of soundtrack is the local Indian lingo; pic has such a grainy look to it that it presumably is a blowup. Sound is often hard to understand and most scenes are shot with a hand-held camera. There isn't a single frame that isn't shaky.

Aside from these technical points, item comes across as a sincere effort and is of some ethnic and political interest. Using nonprofessional actors, most of them Indians living in the hills outside La Paz, pic tells story by means of long, sometimes confusing flashbacks of the life of a man who has wronged his village, his wife, his mother and virtually all those who have been in contact with him.

Repentant of his errors, and wishing to seek redemption, he decides to tramp back to his village carrying on his back an ancient dance-ritual costume and headgear. He knows that when he performs the ritual dance with it, it will cost him his life.

On the trek he meets up with various persons, such as a communist being hunted down by the police. He recalls how he met his wife, the death of his father, his estrangement from his brother after joining the army, and his betrayal of the villagers when he sells out to the gringos. He prevents the villagers from joining their mining comrades in a fight against the military and steals money from the village.

Pic may be of some interest on the fest circuit or for educational tv. Even so, it could be cut by at least a half hour without losing its point. —Besa.

Ke Arteko Egunak
(Days Of Smoke)
(SPANISH)

San Sebastian   A Bertran Filmeak and Trenbideko production, in association with Spanish TV. Produced by Luis Goya. Directed by Antxon Ezeiza. Screenplay, Ezeiza, Koldo Izagirre; camera (Agfa color), Alfredo Mayo; editor, José Salcedo; music, Michel Portal. Reviewed at San Sebastian Film Festival, Sept. 20, 1989. Running time: **95 MIN.**
With: Pedro Armendariz Jr., Elene Lizarralde, Iro Landaluze, Lankidetza Berezia, Xabier Elorriaga, Patxi Bisquert, Ikerine Letamendi.

(Basque soundtrack)

■ This bland, talky film about an exile returning to San Sebastian never makes a clear political statement, though sympathy for ETA terrorists clearly shines through.

Pic, with a Basque-language soundtrack, is made by a Basque helmer who himself lived for many years in exile in Cuba for having been involved with the ETA. However, Antxon Ezeiza provides no insight into the organization's operations or ideology. "Days Of Smoke," in fact, is strikingly similar to other pics made in Spain about the subject, but is less dramatic and more discursive.

Slim yarn concerns an exile who has been away for 20 years and returns to "find his roots," although in fact it is because of marital disagreements in Mexico where he had been living. In San Sebastian, he looks up his ex-wife, learns his daughter is in jail, yaks with some of his old pro-ETA cronies and watches street disturbances.

Naturally, there are the usual sneering digs at the police and the glorification of those "resisting" them. It has all been done before, and better. —Besa.

DUTCH FILM DAYS REVIEWS

Opstand in Sobibor
(Revolt In Sobibor)
(DUTCH-SOVIET-DOCU)

Utrecht   An Open Studio Productie/Leningrad Documentary Studio coproduction. Produced by Lily van den Bergh. Directed by Pavel Kogan, Van den Bergh. Screenplay, Patra Lataster, based on an idea by Peter Dep, Van den Bergh; camera (color), Sergei Skortsov; editor, Jan Dop; music, Gene Carl, Patricio Wang; sound, Sergei Litvakov; research, Jules Schelvis. Reviewed at Dutch Film Days, Utrecht, Sept. 22, 1989. Running time: **140 MIN.**
With: Alexander Pecherski, Stanislaw Szmajzner, Samuel Lerer, Regina Zielinski, Jules Schelvis.

■ Sobibor, the first Nazi extermination camp, is subject of this first Dutch-Soviet coproduction. The film cost $400,000 and talks to the leaders of the Sobibor camp uprising and with survivors in Australia, the Soviet Union, N.Y. and Brazil. It is a film one won't forget.

Some 250,000 died in Sobibor before the Nazis decided to raze it after the revolt. Some 30 Jews, brought in to do the dismantling, were executed immediately afterward. A total of 34,313 Dutch Jews were shipped there. We meet four of the few survivors in this film.

Producer-codirector Lily van den Bergh says the film's goal is to show what the survivors went through, but no footage of active violence is used. Instead, there are songs, music, humor, memories and tears. A hope for justice, albeit delayed, prevails.

Film manages to convey the sense of people in their own right, not just figures who got in the way of history. This is the film's main asset, and also its chief liability, because the intentions leave the whole with a disjointed feeling.

But the pic shows humanity as consisting of separate entities, even if they share the most traumatic experiences.

Harrowing memories are recorded: the boy who sees his father in line for the gas chamber, the girl put to work in the clothes repair shop and finds her mother's wedding ring hidden in the seam of her jacket, and who then gets her sister's shoes as a handout from an SS man.

Van den Bergh worked four years on the picture. Cooperation from the Soviets was generally good, though organization became difficult when Leningrad cohelmer Pavel Kogan fell ill during postproduction of this intensely moving film. —Wall.

Alles moet anders
(Everything Must Change)
(DUTCH-DOCU)

Utrecht   A Lowlands Pictures production. Written, produced and directed by René Seegers. Camera (color), Maarten Kramer; editor, Mario Steenbergen; music, Jan Willem van Mook; sound, Flip van den Dungen, Joris van Ballegoijen. Reviewed at Dutch Film Days, Sept. 21, 1989. Running time: **180 MIN.**

■ An overlong docu on postwar reconstruction in the Netherlands in 1944-50, pic employs historical documents as well as staged re-creations and scenes from novels of the time.

It was a tremendous feat for producer-director René Seegers to assemble the diverse materials, but the general impression is one of academic dryness. It could have been a lot shorter, more to the point and, as a result, more poignant.

Born in 1952, Seegers has a deep concern for the changes in his homeland in the years after the war, from which it suffered profoundly. The Netherlands recovered fast, gripping the shirttails of a former enemy, Germany. Holland, once an agricultural and colonial power, became an industrial and trading nation.

People were ready for new things, new faces, new centers of power, but nothing spectacular happened. Gradually, the familiar faces and centers of power returned. What people really wanted was for things to go on as they always had. Changes mainly were cosmetic.

The film's last line is "It is questionable if it would have been better if everything had changed." Seegers seems to suggest that it would have been better, but, on reflection, thinks that it would have been impossible. —Wall.

Max & Laura & Henk & Willie
(DUTCH)

Utrecht   A Netherlands Film Museum/IAAF release of a Fly by Night/Pieter Goedings production. Produced by Hermann Pohle, Frank Lucas. Directed by Paul Ruven, Sabine van den Eynden, Pim de la Parra. Screenplay, De la Parra, Van de Eynden. Camera (color, 16m), Frans Bromet; editor, Jessica de Koning; music, Hans Dulfer, Walther de Graaf; sound, Pander Roskam, Ludo Keeris, Kees Linthorst; art direction, Bartel Meyburg. Reviewed at Dutch Film Days, Utrecht, Sept. 20, 1989. Running time: **80 MIN.**
Willie . . . . Marina de Graaf
Max . . . . Pim De la Parra
Laura . . . . Manouk van der Meulen
Henk . . . . Jake Kruyer
Also with: Wim Verstappen, Jenny Arean.

■ This entertaining and artfully exuberant item is very much a Pim De la Parra film, although he declares it was a collective effort down the line with everybody working without salary and instead taking a piece of the picture.

Made in six days for $30,000, it has no scenario to speak of but lots of enthusiasm, pluck and nerve. It's a nicely pixilated story of "how it started, how it went on, how it went wrong and how it ended," as cowriter, codirector and star De La Parra describes plot.

De la Parra is a druggist and pigeon fancier with a longstanding attachment to stock exchange punster and former masseuse Marina de Graaf and a medium-term platonic relation to lovely Manouk van der Meulen. He fears longstanding attachments because they could become permanent. Van der Muelen falls for artist Jake

Kruyer.

There are other willing females in the cast ready for a roll in the hay, not to mention a beautiful pigeon named Bonita, who may be in fact Bonito. Everybody changes pads at the drop of a (pigeon) feather, but things all dovetail nicely in the end.

Pic, imaginatively lensed by Frans Bromet, doesn't shrink from using old devices such as direct discourse to the camera, which saves time and keeps up the pace. There is a fair amount of slapstick and some deadpan acting, notably from De la Parra's former partner Wim Verstappen. —*Wall.*

Immediate Family

Mill Valley, Calif. A Columbia Pictures release of a Lawrence Kasdan production in association with Sanford/Pillsbury Prods. Produced by Sarah Pillsbury, Midge Sanford. Executive producer, Kasdan. Directed by Jonathan Kaplan. Screenplay, Barbara Benedek. Camera (Deluxe color), John W. Lindley; editor, Jane Kurson; music, Brad Fiedel; sound (Dolby), Larry Sutton, Bruce Carwardine; production design, Mark Freeborn; art direction, David Willson; set design, Byron Lance King; set decoration, Kimberley Richardson; costume design, April Ferry; associate producer, John H. Starke; assistant directors, David Rose, Michael Steele; casting, Julie Selzer, Sally Dennison, Michelle Allen. Reviewed at Mill Valley (Calif.) Film Festival, Oct. 11, 1989. MPAA Rating: PG-13. Running time: **95 MIN.**

Linda Spector	Glenn Close
Michael Spector	James Woods
Lucy Moore	Mary Stuart Masterson
Sam	Kevin Dillon
Susan Drew	Linda Darlow
Michael's mother	Jane Greer
Bessie	Jessica James
Eli's mom	Mimi Kennedy
Eli's dad	Charles Levin
Eli	Harrison Mohr
Jason	Matthew Moore
Kristin ("Picasso")	Kristin Sanderson
Kristin's mom	Merrilyn Gann

■ Definitely no comedy, "Immediate Family" nonetheless explodes with bursts of laughter that lighten the heartbreak of a lot of nice people tormented by their own best intentions. If the public takes to this one, it's likely to take to it in big numbers, with awards for the performers falling in behind.

For Solomon and generations of juvenile judges since, there's no tougher case to call than competing claims for a baby. But Solomon's solution wouldn't work for "Family," in which Glenn Close and Mary Stuart Masterson are each so deserving.

Obviously reading the newspapers, writer Barbara Benedek and director Jonathan Kaplan have taken a familiar front-page conflict and fleshed it out into an involving drama, though the cynical may be temped to dismiss it as an overly obvious telesoap.

Granted, the plot requires no elaborate examination: After 11 years of marriage, James Woods and Glenn Close are still achingly childless. After no years of marriage, young Mary Stuart Masterson and boyfriend Kevin Dillon face impending parenthood under circumstances that could wreck their chances for a happier life later.

The solution, so obviously simple in a lawyer's office, is that Woods and Close will adopt Masterson's baby. But first — and some may rightfully quibble over this plot device — the lawyer thinks everybody should get better acquainted.

Since each individual in the quartet is genuinely decent, it's no surprise they get along well. But caught in their own increasingly beaming expectations, Woods and Close keep missing that shade passing over Masterson's face as the birth approaches.

Sympathetic, efficient lawyer Linda Darlow has arranged things very neatly. Upon arrival, the baby will immediately be placed in the possession of the adoptive parents and Masterson will be quickly moved off of the maternity ward to recuperate among the gall bladder and kidney patients less likely to remind her of the sacrifice of her firstborn.

Within their legal rights, there's always a chance at the last moment that Woods and Close will conclude they really don't want to be parents after all. Or maybe, Masterson could decide . . .

In its lighter moments, "Family" gives Woods a chance to apply his considerable talents to a different kind of character than those which occupy most of his résumé. He's a caring, loving husband willing to go to any lengths to be an equally dandy dad. (Early on, as Kaplan quickly covers the couple's futile efforts to conceive, Woods sums it all up with one expression as he retires to privacy with a copy of Penthouse to collect a sperm sample.)

Dillon also is appealing as the loyal, loving boyfriend, equally eager to do the right thing, whatever that may be. By necessity, however, the masculine contribution to the film stands in direct proportion to any man's contribution to motherhood. "Family" unavoidably belongs to Close and Masterson — and they make the most of it.

Clever as she is, Close keeps her potentially cloying part understated; there's no need to hang a sign on her suffering. Young Masterson is simply superb, managing to first earn the audience's sympathy and then keep hold when some might be tempted to turn away.

To their credit, Kaplan and Benedek have created a film a lot of people may want to see. But it's not a film many would want to live. —*Har.*

The Fabulous Baker Boys

Hollywood A 20th Century Fox Film Corp. release of a Gladden Entertainment presentation of a Mirage production. Executive producer, Sydney Pollack. Produced by Paula Weinstein, Mark Rosenberg. Written and directed by Steve Kloves. Camera (Deluxe color), Michael Ballhaus; editor, William Steinkamp; music, Dave Grusin, sound (Dolby), Stephan Von Hase; production design, Jeffrey Townsend; assistant director, Myers; coproducer, Bill Finnegan. Reviewed at 20th Century Fox, L.A., Oct. 5, 1989. MPAA Rating: R. Running time: **113 MIN.**

Jack Baker	Jeff Bridges
Susie Diamond	Michelle Pfeiffer
Frank Baker	Beau Bridges
Nina	Elie Raab
Monica Moran	Jennifer Tilly

■ Happily harkening back to the days when Hollywood put more stock in performer appeal than it did in special effects, this smoothly made little romantic comedy set on the fringes of show business could do very well if properly positioned in the marketplace, so that word of mouth is given a decent chance to build.

European prospects are likewise excellent as light, sophisticated entertainments are in very short supply these days.

There's nothing startlingly original about this tale of two piano-playing brothers who find an attractive young singer to give some much needed CPR to their dying lounge act. In fact, this is one of those rare cases where the material's very familiarity works as a plus.

The first look at cynical, seen-it-all Jack Baker (Jeff Bridges) and his bubbling, ever-optimistic brother Frank (Beau Bridges) tells all that's necessary to know about them.

When they're joined by sexy-surly singer Susie Diamond (Michelle Pfeiffer), it's obvious exactly where the film is headed. Jack and Susie are on a romantic collision course, with Frank bound to be hurt by the explosion.

The fun part is seeing it all play out. Thanks to a standout cast, and first-time director Steve Kloves' skill in handling them, there are any number of surprises along the way.

The key scene is a beautifully staged *pas de trois* on a hotel balcony, where the principals are celebrating a successful debut at a swank hotel.

Frank, very drunk, is mooning about the past and missing his absent wife. Jack is brooding on the sidelines, becoming increasingly aware of his attraction to Susie. She's onto herself too, but unwilling to make the first move. The tension can be cut with a knife. More important, it's easy to read everything on the characters' minds.

This same performing subtlety provides an enormous boost to the expected third-act revelations — Jack's bitterness stems from his failed serious-jazz career, Frank's not the solid professional showman he claims to be, and Susie is as vulnerable as all get-out beneath her flinty exterior.

Kloves, his performers and cinematographer Michael Ballhaus conspire to set these predictable "twists" off in high style.

Being one of the best underplayers around, Jeff Bridges has no trouble with the role of one of the most brooding musicians since James Mason in "The Seventh Veil." He's given a great assist by Beau Bridges — their real-life sibling status working neatly into their on-screen interaction. The focus of all eyes, however, is on Pfeiffer.

It's a very tricky part, as the actress, who does all her own singing, is required to play a character whose vocal abilities are good, but not so good as to make a viewer wonder why she hasn't been signed to a major label. Pfeiffer hits the nail right on the head.

She also hits the spot in the film's certain-to-be-remembered highlight — a version of "Makin' Whoopee" that she sings while crawling all over a piano in a blazing red dress. She's dynamite. — *Rens.*

Donna d'ombra
(Woman Of Shadows)
(ITALIAN)

Rome A Marina Piperno production, in assocation with RAI-TV Channel 2 and the Ministry of Tourism and Entertainment. Written and directed by Luigi Faccini. Camera (Telecolor), Franco Lecca; editor, Maddalena Colombo; music, Luis Bacalov; art direction, Michele De Luca; costumes, Lia Morandini; choreography, Elsa Piperno. Reviewed at Politecnico Cinema, Rome, Oct. 1, 1989. Running time: **90 MIN.**

Carla . . . . Anna Bonaiuto
Gianni . . . . Francesco Capitano
Father . . . . Luciano Bartoli
Vera . . . . Daniela Morelli
Also with: Carla Cassola (mother), Francesco Carnelutti (director), Roberto Posse (Pino), Antonio Cantafora, Elsa Piperno (dancer).

■ **Unspooling at the Jewish museum in New York in a series on the life and culture of Italian Jews, Luigi Faccini's "Woman Of Shadows" is the only new film being shown. Hardly a Jew-** ish picture, "Woman" is the affectionate portrait of an independent woman who happens to be Jewish.

A top-drawer performance by Anna Bonaiuto as a choreographer in search of herself carries pic through a talky, sometimes stagey script to win over the attentive viewer. Pic could find its way to specialized audiences. Italian theatrical release is being negotiated for February.

The death of her father comes as a great shock to Carla (Bonaiuto), and sets her on a trip to revisit her sentimental past — her old lovers. Following her doggedly is Gianni (Francesco Capitano), the faithful journalist who loves her and is determined not to let her walk out of his life.

The trip is a strange mix of realistic and unrealistic events. In the latter category is Carla's accidental meeting with her ex-husband, a pretentious film director, while Gianni overhears everything from behind a tree. Surviving this episode, viewer is increasingly drawn into Carla's restless wandering and memories of herself as Daddy's little girl.

Controlled, disciplined performances by stage thesps Bonaiuto and Capitano give "Woman Of Shadows" the sophistication it needs. Carla is presented unapologetically as a hard-driven, at times rapacious female, who has achieved success and recognition in a creative field without losing her femininity. Gianni is smart enough to swallow his false masculine pride and pursue her as she pursues old flames. Pic's originality lies in making both characters sympathetic without diluting them.

As the father, Luciano Bartoli looks and sounds disturbingly youthful even as a gray-haired old-timer, apparently to suggest that's how grown-up Carla remembers him. More successful are the handful of references to Jewish traditions, especially a striking scene in the hospital when Gianni prepares the father's corpse.

Lensing is serviceable; Luis Bacalov's score has its best moments in some lyrical passages. — *Yung.*

Look Who's Talking

Hollywood A Tri-Star Pictures release of a Jonathan D. Krane/MCEG production. Produced by Krane. Written and directed by Amy Heckerling. Camera (Alpha Ciné color, prints by Technicolor), Thomas Del Ruth; editor, Debra Chiate; music, David Kitay; art direction, Graeme Murray; costume design, Molly MacGinnis; set decoration, Barry W. Brolly; sound (Dolby), Ralph Parker; line producer, Bob Gray; assistant director, Bill Mizel. Reviewed at Cineplex Odeon Century Plaza Cinema, L.A., Oct. 6, 1989. MPAA Rating: PG-13. Running time: **90 MIN.**

James . . . . John Travolta
Molly . . . . Kirstie Alley
Rosie . . . . Olympia Dukakis
Albert . . . . George Segal
Grandpa . . . . Abe Vigoda
Voice of Mikey . . . . Bruce Willis
Mikey . . . . Jason Schaller,
Jaryd Waterhouse,
Jacob Haines,
Christopher Aydon

■ **Like a standup comic pouring "flopsweat," this ill-conceived comedy about an infant whose thought are given voice by actor Bruce Willis palpitates with desperation. Yuppie-targeted programmer is destined for a short life in theaters, and its video future seems likewise limited.**

One need look no further for underscoring the film's ineptitude than its title. "Look Who's Voice-Overing" would be a far more appropriate moniker, as Willis isn't heard by the film's other characters.

The camera simply homes in on one of the four strikingly dissimilar babies who play the leading role — or the three puppets assigned to the character in the film's prebirth sequence — and Willis lets fly with asides to match their "cute" expressions.

Kirstie Alley does the best she can as the child's mother — an accountant whose married boyfriend (George Segal) gets her pregnant. Convinced he'll leave his wife for her and the child, she spurns the attentions of the sweet, earnest young cab driver (John Travolta) who helped her at the hospital when she was going into labor.

There's no way to generate suspense from a plot whose outcome can be guessed simply by reading the casting credits.

John Travolta continues to exude the casual charm that once gave his name boxoffice potency, but it's wasted in a vehicle unworthy of him — or anyone else connected to it, for that matter.

All tech credits are acceptable. — *Rens.*

The Occultist

New York An Urban Classics presentation of a Tycin Entertainment production. Produced by Cynthia DePaula. Written and directed by Tim Kincaid. Additional material, George Lafia; camera (Precision & Foto-Kem color), Arthur D. Marks; editor, Joe Keiser, Bari Wheaten; music, Guy Moon, Carl Dante, from films "Creepozoids," "Cellar Dweller" and "Slave Girls From Beyond Infinity;" sound, Micah Solomon; production design, Kim Meinelt, John Paino; assistant director, Steve Shoup; production manager, Geraldine Caulfield; special makeup effects, Ed French; pyrotechnic special effects, Matt Vogel. Reviewed on Unicorn vidcassette, N.Y., Oct. 12, 1989. MPAA Rating: R. Running time: **80 MIN.**

Waldo Warren . . . . Rick Gianasi
Barney Sanford . . . . Joe Derrig
Anjanette Davalos . . . . Jennifer Kanter
Marianna Davalos . . . . Mizan Nunes
Harold . . . . Richard Mooney
Col. Esteve . . . . Matt Mitler
Mama Dora . . . . Betty Vaughn
Pres. Davalos . . . . Anibal Lleras
June . . . . Kate Goldsborough
Ciprian Lane . . . . Doug Delauder

■ **Originally titled "Maximum Thrust," this minor voodoo pic is another leftover title from Empire Pictures' 1987 production slate. It's being released direct to video.**

Rick Gianasi plays Waldo Warren, a private eye hired by reps of the island of San Caribe to protect their president (Anibal Lleras) during a New York visit. The prexy's lovely daughter (Jennifer Kanter) supports revolutionaries out to assassinate her dad.

Filmmaker Tim Kincaid mixes two extremes of campy acting here for a novel though somewhat cryptic effect. Most of the cast performs in monotone, robotic fashion (fitting the subject matter that involves macumba trances and even cyborgs) while other thesps overact outrageously.

There's one good plot twist involving two assassination attempts, but pic's resolution is unconvincing. Tech credits are pro but quite modest. — *Lor.*

Fat Man And Little Boy

Hollywood A Paramount Pictures release of a Lightmotive production. Produced by Tony Garnett. Executive producer, John Calley. Directed by Roland Joffé. Screenplay, Bruce Robinson, Joffé, from a story by Robinson; camera (Panavision, Technicolor), Vilmos Zsigmond; editor, Françoise Bonnot; music, Ennio Morricone; sound (Dolby), William J. Randall; production design, Gregg Fonseca; art direction, Peter Lansdown Smith, Larry E. Fulton; set decoration, Dorree Cooper; associate producer, Kimberly Cooper; assistant director, Bill Westley; casting, Nancy Foy. Reviewed at Paramount Studios, L.A., Oct. 10, 1989. MPAA Rating: PG-13. Running time: **126 MIN.**

Gen. Leslie R. Groves . . . . . Paul Newman
J. Robert Oppenheimer . . . . Dwight Schultz
Kitty Oppenheimer . . . . Bonnie Bedelia
Michael Merriman . . . . John Cusack
Kathleen Robinson . . . . Laura Dern
Peer de Silva . . . . Ron Frazier
Richard Schoenfield . . . . John C. McGinley
Jean Tatlock . . . . Nathasha Richardson
Jamie Latrobe . . . . Ron Vawter

■ **The first major studio "prestige" picture of the season, this historical drama about the creation of the atom bomb is bound** to garner initial attention. When the smoke clears, this well-intentioned, handsomely mounted Paramount release will have to be numbered among the major disappointments of the year. It may do acceptably in limited release, but wider audience appeal is unlikely.

Bruce Robinson and Roland Joffé are the writer-director team who (with producer David Puttnam) made "The Killing Fields." The balance between central story and wider sociopolitical context that made that production noteworthy isn't achieved here.

The film's problems are crystalized in its title. "Fat Man" and "Little Boy" were the nicknames given to the bombs dropped over Hiroshima and Nagasaki. These names aren't mentioned by any of the characters in the film, nor do the bombings figure in the action, which comes to an end prior to their taking place. This sense of misplaced emphasis dominates the entire production.

As the action begins, prior to the actual Manhattan Project's inception, it's important to underscore that the entire affair came about after a group of noted European refugee scientists petitioned the U.S. government to make an all-out effort at building a device to stop Hitler. When the "project" came into being this emphasis changed, and as it continued it shifted once again.

"Fat Man And Little Boy" gives the once-over-lightly to all of this, concentrating instead on Gen. Groves (Paul Newman), the man assigned to oversee the project, and J. Robert Oppenheimer (Dwight Schultz), the brilliant scientist with far-left-to-all-out-communist connections picked to lead it. This is all well and good, except that few dramatic sparks fly.

Newman has no trouble bringing the tough-talking "can do" general to life. The trouble is that life is limited, as the scriptwriters have no interest in exploring the man behind the mission.

This strategy tends to tilt the dramatic balance toward Oppenheimer. The film falls short here, too, partially because of Schultz' lackluster performance, but primarily because Robinson and Joffé fail to give a clue to what made this man tick.

"My politics are an open book," Oppenheimer declares at one point, but this book is by no means open to viewers. Oppen-

heimer never discusses his political views, and his communist connections are limited to an unhappy extramarital affair with a party member (nicely played by Natasha Richardson). The real Oppenheimer's politics were much more complex; while he denied having any views, his wife, brother and sister-in-law all were party members.

The film's Oppenheimer is largely a stuffed shirt with a snootily crooked cigaret whose most grievous error is his refusal to play baseball.

As if sensing their hero's lack of warmth, the filmmakers have concocted a subplot in which a young ballplaying scientist (John Cusack) has a romance with a nurse (Laura Dern) that's cut short when a uranium experiment results in his slow, painful death.

This is all very touching, but leaves the larger issues relating to the creation of the weapon in the lurch. Joffé and Robinson even leave out the true story's most important line. At the sight of the first atomic explosion, Oppenheimer recalled the words of the Bhaghavad-Gita: "I have become death, the destroyer of worlds." This Oppenheimer says nothing.

While the hero is silent, Joffé works at creating a considerable amount of visual "noise" with portentous camera angles.

All technical credits are outstanding. —Rens.

Mack The Knife

Chicago   A 21st Century Film Corp. release. Executive producers, Menahem Golan, Yoram Globus. Produced by Stanley Chase. Written and directed by Golan, based on legit musical "The Threepenny Opera" by Bertolt Brecht and Kurt Weill. Camera (Magyar color; Rank prints), Elemer Ragalyi; editor, Alain Jakubowicz; musical director, Dov Seltzer; choreography, David Toguri; production design, Tivadar Bertalan; costumes, John Bloomfield; sound (Dolby), Cyril Collick; assistant directors, Avner Orshalimy, Gabor Varadi; casting, Kate Kagan. Reviewed at Cinecenter screening room, Chicago, Oct. 9, 1989. (In Chicago Intl. Film Festival.) MPAA Rating: PG-13. Running time: **120 MIN.**
MacHeath . . . . Raul Julia
Mr. Peachum . . . . Richard Harris
Jenny . . . . Julia Migenes
Street Singer . . . . Roger Daltrey
Mrs. Peachum . . . . Julie Walters
Polly Peachum . . . . Rachel Robertson
Money Matthew . . . . Clive Revill
Tiger Brown . . . . Bill Nighy
Lucy . . . . Erin Donovan
Coaxer . . . . Julie T. Wallace

■It's strange to see material that was once radical — beggars, murderers and thieves railing at God and society — turn into a snoozer, but that's how it goes in

"Mack The Knife," Menahem Golan's earnest but intensely dull film version of "The Threepenny Opera."

Appeal will be limited to diehard theater buffs and fans of Raul Julia, though the latter probably would get more excitement out of an 8x10 glossy.

Fault is not entirely Golan's, be-

1976 Production

Threepenny Opera

N.Y. Shakespeare Festival presentation of a Joseph Papp revival of a musical in three acts, with book and lyrics by Bertolt Brecht and music and Kurt Weill, translated by Ralph Manheim and John Willett, based on "The Beggar's Opera," by John Gay. Staged by Richard Foreman; music direction by Stanley Silverman; scenery Douglas W. Schmidt; costumes, Theoni V. Aldredge; lighting, Pat Collins. Features C.K. Alexander, Blair Brown, Ellen Greene, Raul Julia, Caroline Kava, David Sabin, Elizabeth Wilson. General manager, Robert Kamlot; publicity, Merle Debusky, Faith Greer; stage managers, D.W. Koehler, Michael Chambers, Frank Di Filia; advertising, Case & McGrath. Opened May 1, '76, at the Vivian Beaumont Theater, N.Y.; $9 top weeknights, $10 weekend nights.
Ballad Singer . . . . Roy Brocksmith
Mack the Knife . . . . Raul Julia
Jenny Towler . . . . Ellen Greene
Jonathan Peachum . . . . C.K. Alexander
His assistant . . . . Tony Azito
Charles Filch . . . . Ed Zang
Mrs. Peachum . . . . Elizabeth Wilson
Matt . . . . Ralph Drischell
Polly Peachum . . . . Caroline Kava
Jake . . . . William Deull
Bob . . . . K.C. Wilson
Ned . . . . Rik Colitti
Jimmy . . . . Robert Schlee
Walt . . . . Max Gulack
Tiger Brown . . . . David Sabin
Smith . . . . Glenn Kezer
Lucy Brown . . . . Blair Brown

cause the social satire that drives "The Threepenny Opera" is almost completely out of date now, rendering the story and its shady characters little more than quaint, color relics. Even so, Golan's relentlessly artsy approach, exemplified by the use of vaselined lenses in a few of the more romantic scenes, aggravates the artificiality and tediousness of the proceedings.

Lead actors, for the most part, mug shamelessly. Worst offenders are Richard Harris, who hams it up as Mr. Peachum, the leader of the beggars, and Roger Daltrey, who cutes it up as Street Singer, the oversized urchin/narrator, leadfooting the whimsy and taking every opportunity to expose his blackened teeth to the camera.

Julia, by contrast, offers an almost lethargically underplayed interpretation of MacHeath, the role for which he won a Tony Award in

1976, and seems throughout to be wishing he were elsewhere.

Only outstanding performance comes from Julia Migenes, who more than holds her own as Low-Dive Jenny, the only woman who wises up to MacHeath. Migenes, a seasoned opera singer, also fares best with the complex Kurt Weill tunes.

Weill's songs are the foremost asset of this production, but they are too dark, cynical and dissonant to find favor with a broad cross-section of moviegoers. They also are strangely undercut by throngs of motley cockney extras who sing and dance in production numbers, making the film look at times like a roadshow version of "Oliver!"
—Brin.

Tropical Snow

New York   A PSM Entertainment release of a Howard W. Koch presentation. Produced by J.D. Leif. Executive producer, Kevin Brodie. Written and directed by Ciro Durán. Camera (color), Eduardo Serra; editor, Duncan Burns; music, Alan DerMarderosian; art direction, Oscar Alzate; casting, Mike Fenton, Jane Feinberg. Reviewed on Paramount/CIC videocassette, Oct. 11, 1989. MPAA Rating: R. Running time: **88 MIN.**
Gustavo (Tavo) . . . . Nick Corri
Marina . . . . Madeleine Stowe
Oskar . . . . David Carradine
Also with: Argermiro Catiblanco, Alfonso Ortiz, Merena Dimont, Libia Tenorio, Roger Melo, Celmira Yepes, William Mesa, Sonia Ceballos, Antonio Corral.

■In view of Colombia's war on local druglords, tropical becomes topical in this sluggish "exposé" on cocaine smuggling, helmed by Colombian filmmaker Ciro Duran. Lensed in Bogota and Barranquilla in 1986, pic had a limited release this April in Miami.

Movie begins with a declaimer noting that although this is not a true tale, it happens every day in Colombia.

Storyline concerns Colombian couple Gustavo and Marina (Nick Corri and Madeleine Stowe) hankering to go to Gotham to find a better life. Although Marina works evenings as a cocktail waitress, daytime hours are spent with Gustavo pick-pocketing recent arrivals at the airport.

Oskar (David Carradine) offers them a chance to travel all expenses paid — that is, if they each carry a bellyful of cocaine packets. Knowing the danger involved, they resist until circumstances force them to accept and the full tragedy is unraveled in more-or-less predictable fashion.

Tech credits are okay with attention paid to sleazy barroom atmosphere and hazy Bogota streets. Acting is also all right.

Abundant nudity may hinder tv sales, which seems like the most obvious market, especially with curent media focus on Colombia's cocaine connection. —*Lent.*

An Innocent Man

Hollywood A Buena Vista release of a Touchstone Pictures presentation, in association with Silver Screen Partners IV of an Interscope Communications production. Produced by Ted Field, Robert W. Cort. Executive producer, Scott Kroopf. Coproducer, Neil Machlis. Directed by Peter Yates. Screenplay, Larry Brothers; camera (Panavision, Technicolor), William A. Fraker; editor, Stephen A. Rotter, William S. Scharf; music. Howard Shore; production design, Stuart Wurtzel; costume design, Rita Ryack; art direction, Frank Richwood; set decoration, Chris A. Butler; assistant directors, Paul Deason, Kelly Wimberly; sound (Dolby), Dan Sable; associate producer, Brothers; casting, Howard Feuer. Reviewed at AMC Theaters, Century City, Calif., Oct. 5, 1989. MPAA Rating: R. Running time: 113 MIN.
Jimmie Rainwood . . . . Tom Selleck
Virgil Cane . . . . F. Murray Abraham
Kate Rainwood . . . . Laila Robins
Mike Parnell . . . . David Rasche
Danny Scalise . . . . Richard Young
John Fitzgerald . . . . Badja Djola
Robby . . . . Todd Graff

■ **Even Tom Selleck's residual appeal from his babysitting days will be hard-pressed to overcome this collection of cliches, which accomplishes the almost unthinkable by bringing the prison genre to a new low. Theatrical sentence should quickly be commuted to life in homevideo.**

If the idea was to put Selleck in a gritty setting that would cast him as a "serious" actor, then someone forgot to check Larry Brothers' screenplay for intentional guffaws and downright stupidity. One more clunker like this could make a fella awful wistful for the Hawaiian islands and "Magnum P.I."

Nightmarishly structured, the film takes half-hour before Selleck's everyman, Jimmie Rainwood, gets wrongfully framed by two corrupt vice cops (David Rasche and Richard Young). Then he spends more than an hour in stir before he gets released to seek vengeance on the duo in one of the more absurd finales in memory.

In between, Jimmie gets a lesson in prison survival from the cellwise Virgil (F. Murray Abraham), learning to do the previously unthinkable to survive the hellish conditions.

Brothers and director Peter Yates must realize that they're working from an unbelievably hackneyed premise. Why else would they hilariously skip huge chunks of exposition? One minute Jimmie's nervously defending himself against a massive thug (menacingly played by Bruce A. Young), and the next he's a real prison hard case, complete with shades and Fu Manchu mustache.

The prison scenes have some initial bite but soon squander any sense of reality or tension through sheer excess, paling next to memorable productions such as tv's "The Glass House." Similarly, the two bad cops are such maleficient cartoons they ought to be brandishing tridents instead of handguns.

From the first frame the film exhibits screaming flaws, as the credit sequence has Jimmie working at the airport to dripping background music that makes it seem as if the audience stumbled into a 70m airline commercial.

Selleck exhibits sensitivity that should only impress those who haven't gotten used to the "it's okay for men to cry" mentality. Abraham is more compelling in a smaller role but has consistently been underused since his virtuoso performance in "Amadeus."

Much like "Road House," "An Innocent Man" is simply a star vehicle that degenerates into violence to solve the emotional and moral dilemmas its script sets up and then either can't or doesn't care to intelligently resolve. (Based on the leaden dialog, the former seems the more plausible explanation.)

The closing is meant to be crowd-pleasing but should only surprise those so dense as to be entertained by what's gone before it. Ironically, if the film has any message about the dehumanizing aspects of prison, it tosses it away by trying to inspire the viewer to hoot at gore and carnage, thus diminishing one's own humanity.

There's some nifty stuntwork in the final reel and Yates and cinematographer William Fraker, who previously collaborated on "Bullitt," give the film a nice look — though one for which it's hardly worth enduring its cruel and unusual 113-minute term. —*Bril.*

Mortal Passions

Mill Valley, Calif. A Gibraltar Releasing Organization production. Produced by Gwen Field. Executive producers, Andrew Lane, Wayne Crawford, Joel Levine. Directed by Andrew Lane. Screenplay, Alan Moskowitz; camera (Foto-Kem color), Christian Sebaldt; editor, Kimberly Ray; music, Parmer Fuller; sound, Bill Robbins; assistant director, Darcy Brown; art direction, Tucker Johnston; casting, Maira Suro-Castles. Reviewed at the Mill Valley Film Festival, Calif., Oct. 6, 1989. No MPAA Rating. Running time: **98 MIN.**
Todd . . . . Zach Galligan
Berke . . . . Michael Bowen
Emily . . . . Krista Errickson
Adele . . . . Sheila Kelly
Dr. Powers . . . . David Warner
Darcy . . . . Luca Bercovici
Cinda . . . . Cassandra Gava

■ **Convincingly consummate along the way toward one of the best curtain lines in recent memory, "Mortal Passions" has enough sex and more than enough lies to be another indie hit in theaters, leaving the videotape for later.**

First, though, "Passions" must fight its way out of film-fest obscurity.

Boxoffice names would make the film easier to sell, but not necessarily better; the performers are more than able already. As for director Andrew Lane, writer Alan Moskowitz and producer Gwen Field, studio backing and a bigger budget might have smoothed some rough edges but couldn't have improved much on the dandy job they've done.

Delightfully silly beneath its earnestness, "Passions" revels in the amoral, murderous frustrations of a beautiful young wife (Krista Errickson) doing her best to bed and bounty any and all of the men in her life.

First, there's the likable rich husband (Zach Galligan), long on suicidal impulses and short on immediate career goals. Unaware of a hoard of hundred-dollar bills hubby has stashed away, Errickson thinks she has to support the couple working as a cocktail waitress while Galligan endlessly putters around the mansion left by his late father.

His own devotion unrewarded, Galligan suspects Errickson is having an affair. Indeed, being so innocent, he would be shocked to know what a tryst it is, with Errickson enthusiastically bound to the bedposts by her lounge-lizard boyfriend (Luca Bercovici) as the two of them plot murder.

The scene is undone by the appearance of Galligan's older brother (Michael Bowen) who used to break bones on his sibling's behalf when they were little and is even more psychotically over-protective now. Errickson has had an affair with him, too, before her uneven vows to Galligan.

Given the explosive circumstances, murder is inevitable but hardly conclusive. In fact, a corpse alongside the bed only drives Errickson to greater fits of amoré and enhanced ambitions for the now-discovered stash of cash.

There are clues aloose in the hands of outsiders. One is a befuddled psychologist (David Warner) whose insights fall far short of his pompously redundant shingle, "Dr. Terence Power Ph.D." The other is an airhead starlet (Sheila Kelly) whose sympathy for Galligan is offset by her own larceny. "I finally meet some guy I care about and I try to blackmail him," she later regrets.

There is absolutely nothing predictable about this wonderful group of loonies and Lane never lets slip where he and the tightly wrapped script are taking them. Given the low budget, there unfortunately are places where seams show in the production, but these never get in the way.

"No matter how bad things are, you don't expect to get killed for it," one potential victim notes about the homicidal developments taking place. Hopefully, these filmmakers won't be saying the same thing in the months ahead about the deadly difficult marketplace where able efforts like "Passions" often expire unfairly.
— *Har.*

Dancing For Mr. B: Six Balanchine Ballerinas
(DOCU-COLOR/B&W)

New York A Seahorse Films production, in association with WNET N.Y. Produced and directed by Anne Belle. Codirector, Deborah Dickson. Camera (color, 16m), Don Lenzer; editor, Deborah Dickson; sound, Peter Miller; associate producer, Martha Parker. Reviewed at New York Film Festival, Oct. 7, 1989. (Also in Chicago Film Festival.) Running time: **86 MIN.**
With: Maria Tallchief, Mary Ellen Moylan, Melissa Hayden, Allegra Kent, Merrill Ashley, Darci Kistler.

■ **In this devotional documentary, George Balanchine, who virtually invented ballet in America, is remembered as an inspirational genius by six dancers whom he molded in body and soul. "Dancing For Mr. B: Six Balanchine Ballerinas" is indispensable viewing for balletomanes, and also should interest more detached viewers.**

Theatrical prospects are limited outside of festivals and locked runs, but "Mr. B," a WNET N.Y. coproduction, will reach its intended audience on public television. It should be an attractive buy for European tv programmers.

The articulate recollections of the Balanchine disciples, including his ex-wife Maria Tallchief, paint a consensus portrait of the choreographer as a driven perfectionist whose students would "do anything for him." The dancers who developed through the ranks of Balanchine's School of American Ballet to win coveted spots in his New York City Ballet viewed him as a demigod.

If Balanchine was a martinet in his methodical approach to the smallest details of the dance (including the ballerinas' perfume), he was also a "master psychologist" who did not need to rule by fear. When the dancers entered the privileged circle of Balanchine's master classes they inevitably felt as if they were learning how to dance all over again. Balanchine's rigorous, physically arduous method was paradoxically ineffable. His notion of the ballet, says one dancer, was "revealed, but never explained." The Balanchine spirit hovers over classes taught by the retired ballerinas as they inculcate a new generation with the notion that "a body could sing."

Tracing Balanchine's rise from a Russian emigré to the architect of American ballet, filmmakers Anne Belle and Deborah Dickson intercut the dancers' talking head interviews with fascinating archival footage of memorable performance sequences. Balanchine's guidance of the School of American Ballet and New York City Ballet from the pioneering days of Ballet Society in the 1940s to instituional preeminence in the postwar era is recalled with unqualified reverence. If Balanchine had detractors, they have no voice in "Dancing For Mr. B."

Balanchine is evoked as the pure spiritual embodiment of dance. His love of cooking, his friendships with other exalted geniuses such as Igor Stravinsky and W.H. Auden, and his marriages are the only mentions of a life outside ballet. Tallchief, who eventually had her marriage to Balanchine annulled, recalls without bitterness that she was a "mute," compliant 20-year-old wife to a man 20 years her senior. The dilemma of reconciling a career in ballet with the irrepressible desire for a more "normal" life is candidly addressed by Tallchief and Allegra Kent, both of whom drifted from the powerful pull of Balanchine's orbit.

Balanchine was drawn to youth, Tallchief recalls. Although understated, a poignant unifying theme of the documentary is the transience of youthful beauty and energy and the supernova-like imper-

manence of the prima ballerina's stage life. —*Rich.*

Halloween 5

Hollywood   A Galaxy Intl. release of a Magnum Pictures production. Produced by Ramsey Thomas. Executive producer, Moustapha Akkad. Line producer, Rick Nathanson. Directed by Dominique Othenin-Girard. Screenplay, Michael Jacobs, Othenin-Girard, Shem Bitterman; camera (CFI color), Robert Draper; editor, Jerry Brady; costume design, Simon Tuke; set decoration, Steven Lee, Chava Danielson; music, Alan Howarth; Halloween theme by John Carpenter; sound (Ultra-Stereo), David Lewis Yewdall, Pat Bietz; assistant directors, Kelly Schroeder, L.A. McConnell, Troy Rohovit; casting, Dawn Steinberg. Reviewed at Hollywood Pacific Theaters, Oct. 13, 1989. MPAA Rating: R. Running time: **96 MIN.**
Dr. Loomis . . . . .Donald Pleasence
Jamie . . . . .Danielle Harris
Tina. . . . . .Wendy Kaplan
Rachel . . . . .Ellie Cornell
Michael Myers . . . . . . .Donald L. Shanks
Billy . . . . .Jeffrey Landman
Meeker . . . . .Beau Starr
Nurse Patsey . . . . .Betty Carvalho
Samantha . . . . .Tamara Glynn

■ In its only novel twist, "Halloween 5" takes the liberty of setting up its sequel (albeit clumsily) at the film's end rather than "killing" that pesky Michael Myers and then figuring out how to revive him after counting b.o. receipts. Otherwise, this is pretty stupid and boring fare.

Still, it's hard to accuse the filmmakers of being cocky or overly ambitious by assuming the fourth sequel will beget a fifth. Even an awkward, mindless outing like the latest installment has enough fatal walks down murky hallways to all but ensure a tidy take via the combination of boxoffice and homevideo.

The near-certainty of that potential exists despite the fact that the series is now practically indistinguishable from the "Friday The 13th" pics, except perhaps that the latter may be more appealing to hockey fans. John Carpenter's influence over the first "Halloween" has given way to the basest instincts, the most insidious aspects of the genre.

Indeed, rarely has the connection between sex and violence been as clear as in "Halloween 5," in which carnal instincts result in gory retribution, and in which much of the violence is voyeuristically directed at young women in various modes of undress.

The thread of a plot has the killer empathetically linked to his 9-year-old niece Jamie (Danielle Harris), who goes into a sort of epileptic seizure when she senses

he's about to kill again.

Meanwhile, the determined Dr. Loomis (Donald Pleasence, getting a bit long in the tooth for this sort of duty) also seems to sense that Michael Myers is still alive and keeps badgering the little girl — to the point of unintentional hilarity — to help him end this scourge.

Director Dominique Othenin-Girard doesn't bring much style to the action, with the exception of a protracted scene in which one of the dimwits in distress (Wendy Kaplan) harangues the killer in a car, thinking it's her boyfriend in Halloween garb.

For the most part, though, the film follows a dreary formula, milking scenes for far more suspense than they're worth, reveling in gore and ignoring logic — or will it strike anyone else as odd that the killer can walk around in his ashen mask in broad daylight, obscured by patches of shrubbery.

Rick Draper's photography is moody enough, and Alan Howarth's score, if a bit overbearing, at least sets the requisite tone.

Among the performers, Kaplan proves vivacious and fetching as the perky Tina even if the character is flaky. Harris is bright-eyed as the disturbingly beset Jamie, while Pleasence appears tired and a trifle bored, wheezing his way through the proceedings until the inane finish.

One footnote to the film involves a rare safe-sex message, as a teenage girl says no to sex because she lacks protection, then proceeds with gusto once her companion produces a condom. If it represents an effort to promote social responsibility, however, it seems out of place in such a crass and commercially exploitative context. —*Bril.*

George's Island
(CANADIAN)

Toronto   An Astral Films release in Canada of a Salter Street Films production. Produced by Maura O'Connell. Directed by Paul Donovan. Screenplay, Donovan, O'Connell; camera (color), Les Kriszan; editor, Stephan Fanfara; music, Marty Simon; art direction, Bill Fleming; production manager, Suzanne Colvin; coproducer, Stefan Wodoslawsky. Reviewed at Toronto Festival of Festivals, Sept. 16, 1989. Running time: **89 MIN.**
Capt. Waters . . . . .Ian Bannen
Miss Birdwood . . . . .Sheila McCarthy
Mr. Droonfield . . . . .Maury Chaykin
George Waters . . . . .Nathaniel Moreau
Bonie . . . . .Vicki Ridler
Mr. Beane . . . . .Brian Downey
Mrs. Beane . . . . .Irene Hogan
Capt. Kidd . . . . .Gary Reineke

Blinky . . . . .Chas Lawther
Buntwhip . . . . .Avery Baltzman

■ Orphans, pirates, buried treasure, evil foster parents, and a happy ending: "George's Island" has it all. Paul Donovan's adventure tale is great fun, with a bright script, a sparkling Canadian cast, and a story that will be most palatable to kids and their parents.

Orphan George Waters (Nathaniel Moreau) lives with his feisty wheelchair-bound grandfather (Ian Bannen) in a cluttered shack near Halifax, Nova Scotia, harbor. The old geezer amuses him with tales of buried treasure on George's Island, just across the water, where 250 years ago Capt. Kidd put away a trunkful of jewels and gold, much to the protestations of his band of drunken pirates who wanted a cut for themselves.

After a surprise assessment visit to the grog-guzzling grandfather's home by George's priggish, Lysol-spraying officious schoolteacher, Cloata Birdwood (Sheila McCarthy), and her fussy, Walter Mittyish social worker cohort Mr. Droonfield (Maury Chaykin), the 10-year-old boy is deemed to be living in an unfit environment. They send young George off to live in a colorless subdivision with the Beanes, wicked foster parents who make bizarre wine concoctions in their cellar and keep their charges locked up in windowless rooms behind bars.

On Halloween night, George and his fellow foster child tenant go trick or treating and are rescued by Capt. Waters, dressed as a motorized eye. They all sail to George's Island, followed in tow by Miss Birdwood and Mr. Droonfield, to witness the re-enactment of Capt. Kidd and company cavorting, dancing, and unveiling the treasure.

When George is told, at one point, that his grandfather wants to put him up for adoption, all the childhood fears of abandonment come to the fore, and when he is housed in the Beanes' domain, where Mrs. Beane (Irene Hogan) saves the remaining breakfast Cream of Wheat lumps each morning to recycle the next day, it's a kid's worst nightmare come true.

Donovan and Maura O'Connell's screenplay is full of twists and turns and good yuks. All the adults here are loony, and the director allows them carte blanche madness with their roles. Mc-

Carthy sniffs it up as the prissy schoolmarm; Chaykin dribbles and scribbles as the pathetically downtrodden, adolescent-arrested social worker; Hogan gives her foster parent the perfect Ruth Gordon touch, and Bannen shoots blanks at teachers and downs the booze with gusto as the grandpa.

The only sanity comes from Moreau and Vicky Ridler, as foster children No. 1 & 2, who play it straight. Tech credits are good, and although kids are used to slicker special effects in sci-fi pics, the story keeps rolling along in its whimsical way to keep the young ones interested. —*Devo.*

Savage Beach

New York   A Malibu Bay Films release. Produced by Arlene Sidaris. Written and directed by Andy Sidaris. Camera (Filmservice color), Howard Wexler; editor, Michael Haight; music, Gary Stockdale; sound (Ultra-Stereo), Craig Stewart; production design, Jimmy Hadder; costume design, Fionn, with Garrick; assistant director, M.M. Freedman; special effects, Steve Lombardi, Gary Bentley. Reviewed at Magno Preview 9 screening room, N.Y., Oct. 11, 1989. MPAA Rating: R. Running time: **95 MIN.**
Donna .Dona Speir
Taryn . . . . .Hope Marie Carlton
Capt. Andreas . . . . .John Aprea
Bruce Christian . . . . .Bruce Penhall
Martinez. . . . . .Rodrigo Obregon
Japanese warrior . . . . . . .Michael Mikasa
Shane Abilene. . . . . .Michael Shane
Anjelica . . . . .Teri Weigel
Also with: Dann Seki, Al Leong, Eric Chen, Paul Cody, Lisa London, Patty Duffek.

■ "Savage Beach" is an entertaining action pic, the third followup film to Andy Sidaris' "Malibu Express." Newest effort should do modestly well in regional theatrical release commencing Oct. 13 in Gotham, ahead of its guaranteed video/cable market.

Lovely blond thesps Dona Speir and Hope Marie Carlton return for the third time (following "Hard Ticket To Hawaii" and "Picasso Trigger") in their lead roles as government drug inforcement agents who moonlight as air cargo haulers. Returning home from an emergency serum delivery to ailing kiddies on a remote island, they crash land on Knox Island, 600 miles from their Molokai homebase.

Coincidentally, numerous apposing forces are converging on the island in search of a horde of gold stolen by the Japanese from the Philippines and originally lost in 1943 when its transport ship sunk. Among these are U.S. army & navy types, led by John Aprea, a secret CIA infiltrator (Bruce Penhall), a pair of Japanese mercenaries plus two communist insurgents from the Philippines (Rodrigo Obregon and Teri Weigel).

There is a surprisingly serious subplot, involving a Japanese warrior (Michael Mikasa) still left on the island 46 years later guarding the gold but guiltridden for having killed defenseless U.S. navy men who washed up on the island. He takes a liking to Carlton and protects her in the ensuing action.

Filmmaker Andy Sidaris ensures that most of the action is campy fun with his oddball dialog and predilection for having the female cast strip in the least likely situations. For equal time to appease women in the audience there is a new, handsome leading man Michael Shane as Shane Abilene, nominal leader of the good guys.

Speir is an impressively tough heroine, while Carlton is allowed to show her soft side via the platonic romance with warrior Mikasa. Unfortunately, the wrinkly makeup converting young Mikasa into an ancient WW II vet is unconvincing.

Odd touch has all of the sex scenes devoted to the heavies, as Obregon and smouldering brunet Weigel hilariously discuss "the revolution" while bedding down.

Howard Wexler's lensing makes for a colorful package and producer Arlene Sidaris gets a lot of production value on screen within a modest budget. Action fans who favor a tongue-in-cheek approach will enjoy this one. —*Lor.*

L.A. Vice

New York   A Raedon Entertainment Group presentation of a P/M Entertainment Group production. Produced by Richard Pepin, Joseph Merhi. Directed by Merhi. Screenplay, Charles T. Kanganis; camera (color), F. Smith Martin; editor, Steve Waller; music John Gonzalez; sound, Paul Coogan; art direction, Matt Manis; assistant director, Steve Rockmael; 2d unit director, Red Horton; special makeup effects, Judy Yonemoto; associate producers, Charla Driver, Richard W. Munchkin. Reviewed on Raedon vidcassette, N.Y., Oct. 9, 1989. No MPAA Rating. Running time: **83 MIN.**
Jon Chance . . . . . .Lawrence-Hilton Jacobs
Capt. Joe Wilks . . . . .William Smith
Evelyn . . . . .Jean Levine
Bear . . . . .Jastereo Coviare
Victoria . . . . .Bonnie Paine
Also with: R.J. Walker, Josh Sailor, Sue Nelson, Berni Angel, R.W. Munchkin, Joe Palese, Greg Allan Martin, Nick Testa, Donn Nardini, Charla Driver, Linda Holdahll.

■ This okay sequel to "L.A. Heat" brings back police detective Jon Chance in a vengeance saga for the homevideo audience.

Lawrence-Hilton Jacobs plays Chance (for the third time on screen), assigned to a big kidnaping case for which he recruits his retired captain (William Smith) as backup. Smith is killed and Chance quits the police force.

He's brought back into the case by the kidnaped girl's father, however, and brings in a willing though neophyte pal (Jastereo Coviare) to help.

Action is predictable but well-staged and Jacobs' smooth performance is film's chief asset. Coviare, who also composes musical scores for action pics, is appealing as Jacobs' American Indian sidekick.—*Lor.*

Bloodfist

New York   A Concorde Pictures release of a Concorde/New Horizons production. Produced by Roger Corman. Directed by Terence H. Winkless. Screenplay, Robert King; camera (color), Ricardo Jacques Gale; editor, Karen Horn; music, Sasha Matson; assistant director, Jose Torres; associate producer, Sally Mattison. Reviewed at Criterion 2 theater, N.Y., Oct. 9, 1989. MPAA Rating: R. Running time: **85 MIN.**
Jake . . . . .Don (The Dragon) Wilson
Kwong. . . . . .Joe Marie Avellana
Baby . . . . .Michael Shaner
Nancy . . . . .Riley Bowman
Raton . . . . .Rob Kaman
Black Rose . . . . .Billy Blanks
Chin Woo . . . . .Kris Aguilar
Detective . . . . .Vic Diaz

■ Several notches below the level of Chuck Norris and Jean-Claude Van Damme pics is "Bloodfist," a cheapo martial arts actioner for undiscriminating fans of the genre.

Pic gets underway with a novel opening credits sequence, in which each leading actor (i.e., kicker) is listed with his karate and/or kickboxing titles. Film quickly heads downhill with formula script, utilizing virtually the same premise as recent Van Damme vehicle "Kickboxer."

Don (The Dragon) Wilson plays Jake (yes, the knowing screenplay by Robert King makes an in-joke about Robert Towne's "Chinatown"), who heads from L.A. to Manila when his brother is murdered following a kickboxing match. Under the tutelage of Kwong (Joe Marie Avellana), Wilson trains for a Ta Chang fighting competition, seeking vengeance on one of the combatants who he suspects killed his brother.

Pic has a couple of plot twists plus a statuesque blond leading lady (Riley Bowman) to distinguish it from others in the genre. Unfortunately, the editing is ragged and photography hit-and-miss, while the fighters-turned thesps show little acting ability.

Lead Wilson, who's vaguely in the Mike Stone school of martial arts heroes, has a bland screen personality. Fans undoubtedly will be attracted by the high kicks and bloodletting. Roger Corman followers will be glad to see Vic Diaz again, stalwart of so many Filipino-lensed actioners of the early '70s. —*Lor.*

Dad

Hollywood   A Universal Pictures release of an Amblin Entertainment presentation. Produced by Joseph Stern, Gary David Goldberg. Executive producers, Steven Spielberg, Frank Marshall, Kathleen Kennedy. Written and directed by Goldberg, based on the novel by William Wharton. Camera (Deluxe color), Jan Kiesser; editor, Eric Sears; music, James Horner; production design, Jack DeGovia; costume design, Molly Maginnis; art direction, John R. Jensen; sound (Dolby), Stephen H. Flick, Ron Bartlett; special makeup, Dick Smith; coproducers, Sam Weisman, Ric Kidney; casting, Judith Weiner. Reviewed at Academy of Motion Picture Arts & Sciences, Beverly Hills, Calif., Oct. 19, 1989. MPAA Rating: PG. Running time: 117 MIN.

Jake Tremont	Jack Lemmon
John Tremont	Ted Danson
Bette Tremont	Olympia Dukakis
Annie	Kathy Baker
Mario	Kevin Spacey
Billy	Ethan Hawke
Dr. Chad	Zakes Mokae
Dr. Santana	J.T. Walsh

■ The syrupy quality that's become endemic to Spielberg/Amblin Entertainment productions stifles several memorable performances in "Dad," an otherwise engaging mix of comedy and drama.

It's precisely that cloying sweetness and annoying excess which may serve up a major slice of the fall boxoffice pie to this highly calculated tearjerker, destined to reinforce Ted Danson's status as a major bigscreen star.

It also represents a promising feature directorial debut for tv producer Gary David Goldberg. There's certainly much that's funny, warm and endearing about "Dad," which, based on William Wharton's novel, deals with the familiar theme of a grown child resolving his sense of duty toward an aging parent.

Unfortunately, prolonged tilling of that emotional terrain and seemingly endless verbalization of feelings — all set to James Horner's overbearingly sentimental score — diminish most of what's good about the film.

As for makeup magician Dick Smith's labors to turn Jack Lemmon and Olympia Dukakis into the film's 78-year-old Jake Tremont and his wife Bette, it amounts to little more than a gimmick, a novelty that would soon wear thin were it not for the lusty portraits turned in by the two actors.

The real breakthrough comes from Danson in the pivotal role of Lemmon's somewhat estranged son, who returns from his sheltered world of Wall Street opulence to find his parents failing and infirm.

Bound by what he describes as a pact between parents and their children — essentially "I'll raise you, you take care of me when the time comes" — John (Danson) moves in with his parents to ease their final days, in the process finding new meaning in his relationship with his own college-age son ("Dead Poets Society's" Ethan Hawke, also splendid here).

The theme hardly breaks new ground, but Goldberg's script frequently makes it work — especially in comic moments, with quick repartee nicely delivered by the principals, including Kathy Baker and Kevin Spacey as Danson's sister and brother-in-law.

Known for his charm on "Cheers" and in lesser film roles, Danson brings tremendous depth to this big-league assignment, pulling off the film's one truly great moment in the scene where, his voice breaking, he yanks his shock-ridden father from the hospital care of an unfeeling doctor.

Structurally, however, the film rides a bizarre rollercoaster over emotional peaks and valleys as the parents face death and recovery almost in repertory. There's also a jarringly incongruous (if occasionally funny) section where the revivified Lemmon takes to wearing garish outfits reminiscent of Jack Nicholson's Joker in "Batman" — perhaps cute, but hardly believable.

The film also fails to convey the passage of time, in a way that begins to gnaw at the mind when it isn't flooded with mush. How long has Danson been away from his job? When does his son's next school term start, or has he missed it already?

"Dad" banks on the fact that such plot points will get washed away, becoming superfluous in its wave of emotion. That will doubtless be true for many, even with its slow stretches and excessive length.

Technical aspects augment Goldberg's efforts to make "Dad" more a visceral experience than an intellecutal one, another Amblin trademark. Credit goes to cinematographer Jan Kiesser for the beautifully shot flashbacks of Jack in his youth, with the unnervingly similar Chris Lemmon standing in for his father.

There's a powerful wallop to be found in the labyrinth of emotions raised by aging, death and generational responsibility, as was the case in "On Golden Pond."

The elder Lemmon adds an amiable old coot to his résumé that, the makeup ordeal notwithstanding, doesn't really rank with his great roles. —Bril.

Gross Anatomy

Hollywood   A Buena Vista release of a Touchstone Pictures presentation, in association with Silver Screen Partners IV, of a Hill/Rosenman production, produced in association with Sandollar Prods. Produced by Howard Rosenman, Debra Hill. Executive producers, Sandy Gallin, Carol Baum. Directed by Thom Eberhardt. Screenplay, Ron Nyswaner, Mark Spragg, from story by Spragg, Rosenman, Alan Jay Glueckman, Stanley Isaacs; camera (Technicolor), Steve Yaconelli; editor, Bud Smith, Scott Smith; music, David Newman; production design, William F. Matthews; art direction, P. Michael Johnston; set design, Lauren Polizzi; set decoration, Catherine Mann; costume design, Gale Parker; sound (Dolby), Jim Tanenbaum; casting, Judith Weiner. Reviewed at Avco Cinema, Westwood, Calif., Oct. 16, 1989. MPAA Rating: PG-13. Running time: 107 MIN.

Joe Slovak	Matthew Modine
Laurie Rorbach	Daphne Zuniga
Rachel Woodruff	Christine Lahti
David Schreiner	Todd Field
Miles Reed	John Scott Clough
Kim McCauley	Alice Carter
Dr. Banks	Robert Desiderio
Dr. Banumbra	Zakes Mokae
Papa Slovak	J.C. Quinn
Mama Slovak	Rutanya Alda

■ "Gross Anatomy," a serio-comic look at the first year of medical school, should be required viewing for anyone with aspirations in that direction, but for all others, film is about as exciting as a pop quiz. Boxoffice prognosis is not hopeful.

Matthew Modine stars as the 26-year-old son of a fisherman; he's just beginning his medical studies. The film, trying to be another "Paper Chase," follows him and other students through their courses, with particular focus on the anatomy lab, in which he's teamed with four classmates to work on a cadaver throughout the school year.

Dissecting group includes his too-serious, driven roommate Todd Field; married young mother Alice Carter; Modine's nemesis, the judgmental, ultrapreppy John Scott Clough, and hardworking Daphne Zuniga, who reluctantly provides love interest for Modine.

"Gross" offers some nice, unexpected details: The anatomy profs, and key figures of authority, just happen to be a woman and a black man, played by Christine Lahti and Zakes Mokae.

Another plus is the film's convincing portrayal of med-school life, with its demanding regimen of reading, memorization of names and facts, and the infectious smell of formaldehyde. (Oddly, financial problems are all but ignored.)

A series of hardships is meaningless without interesting characters, however. The writers — Ron Nyswaner and Mark Spragg, working from a story by Spragg, Howard Rosenman, Alan Jay Glueckman and Stanley Isaacs — could come up with nothing more than stick figures and repetitive, 1-note problems.

Director Thom Eberhardt does well under the circumstances, generating as much energy and sympathy as possible for the characters, but he's let down by the writing.

Biggest problem is Modine's character; though there's little on-screen evidence of his intelligence, he frequently is described as being so smart he can get by with minimum study.

He's content to just coast, continually coming to class late, being flip with his teachers and seeming not to care about the whole process.

Since opening scene establishes that he wants to become a doctor strictly for financial considerations, there's nothing at stake here. The thought persists that if he gets thrown out for his insubordination, he could open up a Pizza Hut franchise and be just as happy.

In the film's last half-hour, several melodramatic developments unconvincingly change Modine into a caring, committed student, but the transformation is too sudden and too late to generate interest. Character, supposedly out of touch with himself, simply comes off as a smarty-pants goof-off, and the filmmakers are lucky that the talented Modine brings such charm and likability to a role that would have been disastrous in other hands.

In the John Houseman-style role, Lahti hasn't much to do but look stern, but she's good in her Big Scene near the end.

Carter and Clough add fine support. Though Zuniga is quite bland, pic is generally well cast by Judith Weiner. Particularly nice are bits by Robert Desiderio as a doctor and J.C. Quinn as Modine's dad.

Technically, film is above par, with especially notable contributions by cinematographer Steve Yaconelli, editors Bud Smith and Scott Smith, production designer William F. Matthews and scorer David Newman. —Gray.

Next Of Kin

New York A Warner Bros. release of a Lorimar Film Entertainment presentation of a Barry & Enright production. Executive producer, Larry Dee Waay. Produced by Les Alexander, Don Enright. Directed by John Irvin. Screenplay, Michael Jenning (based, uncredited, on screenplay by Jenning, Jeb Stuart); camera (Metrocolor prints), Steven Poster; editor, Peter Honess; music, Jack Nitzsche; music supervision, Jackie Krost, David Kershenbaum; additional music, Gary Chang, Todd Hayen; sound (Dolby), Glenn Williams; production design, Jack T. Collis; set decoration, Jim Duffy; costume design, Donfeld; assistant director, Bruce Moriarty; production manager, Scott Maitland; associate producer, Jeb Stuart; casting, Jane Alderman, Shelley Andreas, Mindy Marin. Reviewed at Chelsea 4 theater, N.Y., Oct. 21, 1989. MPAA Rating: R. Running time: **108 MINS.**
Truman Gates . . . . Patrick Swayze
Briar Gates . . . . Liam Neeson
Joey Rosselini . . . . Adam Baldwin
Jessie Gates . . . . Helen Hunt
John Isabella . . . . Andreas Katsulas
Gerald Gates . . . . Bill Paxton
Lawrence Isabella . . . . Ben Stiller
Harold . . . . Michael J. Pollard
Also with: Ted Levine, Del Close, Valentino Cimo, Paul Greco, Vincent Guastaferro, Paul Herman.

■ **John Irvin's atmospheric direction lifts the Patrick Swayze cop vehicle "Next Of Kin" from routine programmer level to sleeper status. Unfortunately, Warners' no-press-screenings policy is indicative of this intriguing B+ picture getting the heave-ho in the marketplace.**

Pic is of historical interest as the final film to go into production (August 1988) at Lorimar, while the indie was being swallowed by Warner Communications.

Interesting wrinkle in Michael Jenning's screenplay (based on a script by Jenning and pic's associate producer, Jeb Stuart) is a mixing and matching of two ethnic strains of the vendetta: backwoods Appalachian version and revenge Sicilian-style.

These plot threads are set in motion when Bill Paxton, a Kentucky boy from the hills now working in Chicago, is ruthlessly murdered by mafia enforcer Adam Baldwin as part of a strong-arm move in the vending machines racket. Paxton's older brother, Patrick Swayze, is a Chicago cop determined to find the killer.

Interfering with Swayze's efforts is the old-fashioned "eye for an eye" vengeance demanded by eldest brother Liam Neeson. Picture climaxes with an elaborate war in a Chicago cemetery between Baldwin's mafioso and Neeson's Kentucky kin, matching automatic weaponry with primitive (but reliable) crossbows, hatchets, snakes and knives. Treachery on the Cosa Nostra side bring out a parallel "next of kin" subplot that concludes the film effectively.

Director Irvin's technical skill and Steven Poster's muted-color photography bring out the flavor of both Kentucky and Chicago locations, with consistent tongue-in-cheek elements (and outright comic relief by the delightful Michael J. Pollard) balancing the film noir mood.

Swayze is sold as the mixed-motives hero, and inspired casting teams him with Irish thesp Neeson, most convincing as a throwback whose fish-out-of-water misadventures in Chicago are a treat. Cast against type, Baldwin, the hulking youngster familiar from "My Bodyguard," builds a fascinating portrait of evil lurking behind the innocent face. Supporting cast is convincing and physically perfect. — *Lor.*

Present Memory
(DOCU-B&W/COLOR)

Boston A Cine Research presentation of a Full Moon production. Produced by Richard Adelman. Directed by Richard Broadman. Camera (color), John Bishop; editor, Broadman; music, Bruno Destrez, Jimmy Giuffre; sound, Stephen Olech; assistant director, Susan Steiner; associate producer, Steiner. Reviewed at the Brattle theater, Oct. 12, 1989. No MPAA Rating. Running time: **88 MIN.**

■ **This tight documentary is sure to provoke discussions in Jewish populations as it boils down the 20th-century Jewish experience to 88 minutes. In touching on issues from the Holocaust to Israel to assimilation in America, filmmakers Richard Broadman, Susan Steiner and Richard Adelman manage to get beneath the surface rather than settling for a once-over-lightly approach.**

Film uses interviews and archival footage, avoiding overused material in favor of such clips as scenes of the Warsaw Jewish community in the 1930s and early settlements in the Holy Land. Mixed with "average" folks are people like Israeli politician Rabbi Meir Kahane — sounding surprisingly moderate — and Harvard law professor Alan Dershowitz.

Some of the film's best moments come from Dershowitz' mother, an observant Orthodox Jew, talking not only about her son but also about how her old New York neighborhood has become increasingly Hasidic.

Ultimate point of the film is to raise — but not answer — the question of what it means to be a Jew in America. —*Kimm.*

It Had To Be You

Hollywood A Limelite Studios release of a Frank B. Tolin, Harve S. Tolin and Ronald B. Fenster presentation of a Tom Yanez and Richard Abramson production. Produced by Abramson, Yanez. Executive producers, Tolin, Fenster. Written and directed by Renée Taylor, Joseph Bologna. Camera (Metro color), Bart Lau; editor, Tom Finan; music, Charles Fox; lyrics, Hal David, production design, Stephen Wolf; costume design, Leslie Herman; set decoration, Regina McLarney; sound, Henry Lopez; assistant director, Robert P. Cohen; casting, Marcia Shulman. Reviewed at AMC Century 14 Cinemas, L.A., Oct. 17, 1989. No MPAA Rating. Running time: **105 MIN.**
Theda Blau . . . . Renée Taylor
Vito Pignoli . . . . Joseph Bologna
Schornberg . . . . William Hickey
Judith . . . . Eileen Brennan
Dede . . . . Donna Dixon
Milton . . . . Tony Randall
Alfred . . . . Gabriel Bologna

■ **Limited release of this stage-to-screen transfer of Renée Taylor and Joseph Bologna's comedy is appropriate, for there's limited appeal for this writer-director-performer-husband-and-wife team's brand of fey schmaltz. Video prospects appear limited as well.**

Back in 1971 in "Made For Each Other," Taylor and Bologna managed to pull off the final twist on "kooky" couplings — a favorite theme of stage and screen comedies of the '60s (e.g., "The Owl And The Pussycat"). Their obvious maturity gave that project a patina of poignance, too. It wasn't just another performance, but the climax of a decade of toiling in the fields of "offbeat" comedy.

That was 18 years ago. Any attempt to repeat it is understandably doomed from the start. Codirecting as well as co-scripting, Taylor and Bologna come up with the most cramped, squalid parade of medium 2-shots this side of a "poverty row" programmer. Disbelieving stares, far more than laughter, quickly become the primary spectator response.

The subject of "It Had To Be You" is a broken-down bit player who is convinced she is glamorous, sexy and talented as a playwright. Taylor gives every indication that the line between herself and the character she's playing is an exceedingly thin one.

Luring a middle-aged "creative director" of tv commercials back to her apartment, our heroine schemes to keep him there via the most time-honored of porno-flick traditions — she gets his clothes wet. As he waits for them to dry, she makes only a half-hearted attempt at a straight seduction, however.

She wants to read him her play. He may hate it (and her), but that doesn't matter. For underneath it all she suspects he's really a frustrated artist who has wasted his life trying to make a business success. After confessing some selected sorrows of her own (a child and a husband who are now both — sob! — dead), she even gets him to call up the son (Gabriel Bologna) he hasn't spoken to in two years.

Joseph Bologna can just barely get by with a scene or two of this sort of thing. Renée Taylor is a non-starrer from scene one. It's a distinctly odd experience watching an actress trying to pass for 40 and failing — especially when the 40-year-old she's playing is trying to pass for 30.

Technical credits are poor, with frequent focus problems (not projection-related) in the print viewed. —*Rens.*

Catch Me If You Can

Minneapolis An MCEG release of a Jonathan D. Krane production. Produced by Krane, Don Schain. Written and directed by Stephen Sommers. Camera (color), Ronn Schmidt; editor, Bob Ducsay; music, Tangerine Dream; sound (Dolby), Leslie Shatz; art direction, Stuart Blatt; production manager, Cristen M. Carr; stunt coordinator, George Fisher; assistant directors, Randy Pope, Betsy Bangs; additional camera, Alan Oltman; associate producers, Rachel Langsam, Alan Lasoff; casting, Riki Woulle Co., Minnesota. Reviewed at Willow Creen Cinema, Minneapolis, Oct. 14, 1989. MPAA Rating: PG. Running time: **105 MIN.**
Dylan . . . . Matt Lattanzi
Melissa . . . . Loryn Locklin
Nevil . . . . Grant Heslov
Monkey . . . . Billy Morrissette
Mr. Johnson . . . . Geoffrey Lewis
Johnny Phantmun . . . . . . M. Emmet Walsh
Manney . . . . Dan Bell

■ **A plot involving high school kids trying to save the old alma mater by betting on drag races is too much to swallow even for "Catch Me If You Can's" targeted teenage audience. Too few young 'uns will catch this action pic, which appears headed for cable and tape.**

Helmer Stephen Sommers' first effort isn't a total disaster. Despite an implausible script and a predictable ending, Sommers maintains an element of suspense and maneuvers his no-name cast reasonably well. He rates low marks, however, for the story he penned.

It's a nonsensical premise to begin with: Senior class president Melissa, played by Loryn Locklin, has promised to raise a couple hundred grand to dissuade a rapacious school board from closing Cathedral High. Button and bake sales can't do the trick, so the coed, as a last resort, teams up with Dylan (Matt Lattanzi), the school's black sheep who is majoring in drag racing.

The pitch is to bet fatter and fatter purses on Lattanzi's winning a series of races. Given the growing number of government-sponsored lotteries these days, maybe that isn't so farfetched at that.

One hopes impressionable young filmgoers won't be taken in by the pic's winking at breaking traffic laws, flimflamming the cops and other illegalities.

Locklin and Lattanzi are attractive and do the best they can with the material. Grant Heslov is appropriately square as the class nerd. Geoffrey Lewis as the school principal and M. Emmet Walsh as a bigtime gambler (the only adults in the cast) add little believability to the goings-on, but the roles hardly call for Oscar-level thesping.

Technical credits are generally okay; the stunt driving is fairly exciting but palls in its repetitiousness. —Rees.

Silent Night, Deadly Night III: Better Watch Out!

New York A Quiet Films presentation of an Arthur H. Gorson production. Produced by Gorson. Executive producers, Ronna Wallace, Richard N. Gladstein. Directed by Monte Hellman. Screenplay, Carlos Laszlo, from story by Laszlo, Hellman, Gladstein; camera (Foto-Kem color), Josep M. Civit; editor, Ed Rothkowitz; music, Steven Soles; sound, Dennis Carr; production design, Philip Thomas; art direction, Laurie Post; costume design, Pia Dominguez; assistant director, Tom Herod Jr.; special makeup effects, Nina Kraft; stunt coordinator, Rawn Hutchinson; coproducer, Patricia Foulkrod; associate producer, Rothkowitz; casting, Kimba Hills. Reviewed on IVE vidcassette, N.Y., Sept. 23, 1989. MPAA Rating: R. Running time: 91 MIN.
Dr. Newbury . . . . Richard Beymer
Ricky . . . . Bill Moseley
Laura . . . . Samantha Scully
Chris . . . . Eric Da Re
Jerri . . . . Laura Herring
Granny . . . . , Elizabeth Hoffman
Lt. Connely . . . . Robert Culp
Receptionist . . . . Isabel Cooley
Psychiatrist . . . . Leonard Mann
Truck driver . . . . Carlos Palomino

■Direct-to-video sequel to the notorious "Santa Claus" horror series is a competently made but strictly standard fright pic bound to disappoint fans of helmer Monte Hellman.

Widely respected by cineastes, especially in Europe, Hellman has been out of the limelight of late, not getting top-drawer assignments as he did back when "Two-Lane Blacktop" became a cult

classic. He began his career three decades ago working on horror pics for Roger Corman (a film clip from Corman's "The Terror" is excerpted here as an homage) and now returns full circle.

Film tastefully avoids the objectionable material of its predecessors; there is just a brief setup clip from Part One. Heroine Samantha Scully is a blind girl linked up with the youngster (now grown-up Bill Moseley) responsible for the Santa Claus killings by scientist Richard Beymer. He experimenting on Mosely, who's been in a coma for six years since being apprehended and nearly killed; sci-fi element here is mixed with psychic connection phenomena.

Despite this adventurous premise, pic quickly becomes a standard suspenser, as Moseley escapes and goes on the rampage, threatening Scully, her brother (Eric Da Re) and bro's pretty girlfriend (Laura Herring). Climax is out of "Wait Until Dark," with Scully evening up the odds in a darkened basement.

Interesting casting has Scully and Herring the same physical type (both earthy brunets), and they team up in the final reels to combat the monster. Unfortunately, pic offers little novelty or thematic interest, analogous in underachievement within Hellman's output to Alan J. Pakula's similarly woebegone "Dream Lover."

Tech credits are good, with an eerie, droning score by Steven Soles. Carlos Laszlo's script is filled with red-herring suspense sequences and dumb dialog.—Lor.

Recordçoês da Casa Amarela
(Recollections Of The Yellow House)
(PORTUGUESE)

Venice An Invicta Filmes/GER coproduction. Produced by Joaquim Pinto, João Pedro Bénard. Executive producer, Bénard. Written and directed by João César Monteiro. Camera (color), José António Loureiro; editor, Helena Alves, Claudio Martinez; music, Franz Schubert, Antonio Vivaldi; art direction, Luis Monteiro. Reviewed at Venice Film Festival (competing), Sept. 13, 1989. Running time: 120 MIN.
João de Deus . . . . João César Monteiro
Violeta . . . . Manuela de Freitas
Mimi . . . . Sabina Sacchi
Armando . . . . Ruy Furtado
Julieta . . . . Teresa Calado
Also with: Henrique Viana (police captain), Duarte de Almeida (Ferdinando), Luis Miguel Cintra (Livio).

■Utterly irreverent, hilariously deadpan, Portuguese helmer João César Monteiro ("Silves-

tre") is destined to win a place in the hearts of sophisticated filmgoers with "Recollections Of The Yellow House."

A work of pure anarchy, pic traces the inconsequential ramblings of a mangy old goat (played to a T by Monteiro himself) who goes from boarding house to madhouse and comes back to infect the world with his nonconformism. Pic wowed Venice (winning a Silver Lion) and should catch on elsewhere with the right launch.

João de Deus (Monteiro) is a scrawny but erudite eccentric inhabiting a room in Manuela de Freitas' boarding house, which may or may not have bedbugs. He's a connoisseur of the bathwater left by the landlady's daughter (Teresa Calado), a trumpet player. Mimi (Sabina Sacchi), a sweet, not-too-bright girl of easy virtue, becomes his confidante and 1-shot lover before she dies of a botched abortion. There also are cafe buddies, a doctor who prescribes difficult remedies for sensitive body parts and João's 70-year-old mother, a charwoman whom he still takes money from.

More than black humor, "Yellow House" is infested with a fatalistic view of life that's both outrageous and exhilarating. When João discovers the tender Mimi has just been taken to the morgue, his first thought is to search for her savings — which he then leaves behind when the landlady surprises him attempting to seduce her daughter.

Penniless and homeless, but as elegant in his manners as ever, he dons an old army uniform and fools a number of people before being locked up in the city asylum. Even there it's clear no walls can hold him back for long.

Vulgar, theatrical, much too talky, "Yellow House" captures its audience anyway. Whole cast deserves kudos, but Monteiro (born 1939) outshines all as the old boy. Camerawork by José António Loureiro is a limpid joy; Schubert and Vivaldi have never been funnier.—Yung.

In Krakende welwtand
(Squatters' Delight)
(DUTCH-B&W)

Amsterdam A Studio Nieuwe Gronden production. Produced by René Scholten. Directed by Mijke de Jong. Screenplay, De Jong, Jan Eilande. Camera (b&w, 16m), Peter Mariouw Smit, Jan Wich; editor, Menno Boerema; sound, Ben Zijlstra. Reviewed at Film Museum, Amsterdam, Sept. 11, 1989. Running time: 65 MIN.
With: Sophie Hoebrechts, Ottolien

Boeschoten, Matthias Maat, Angela van de Zon.

■A well-acted, nicely shot first feature, "Squatters' Delight" is a lively, intelligent tale of squatters (Krakers) in Holland.

The subject was played up by the media early in the 1980s, when housing shortages and squatters were a prominent issue. Today it's different: Most "inhabitants" no longer are motivated by political slogans or community ideals, but by low rent, the absence of prying landlords, the "democratic" voting and the few regulations.

The very Dutch tale is set in one building, which the authorities offer to buy, renovate and re-rent to the present tenants. If the tenants accept, they must move out for about a year, before returning to the premises for a rent that's still low.

This provokes some hard thinking and forces clear points of view. Most of the tenants will move out and wait for the work to be completed. But the old-timers won't play. If they move out, it's for good.

Then some members of the old guard think again. With the help of enthusiastic newcomers, they squat their own squatted house. Everything will be hunky-dory in their domain — a squatter's life in squatters' delight. Communal happiness is the goal.

Mijke de Jong, who coscripted and directed, brings the squatters' lives into fine relief. —Wall.

Unni

Boston A Malabar production. Executive producers, Kitty Morgan, Bill Rothman, Paul Varghese. Produced by Morgan, Rothman. Coproducer, National Film Development Corporation (India). Directed by G. Aravindan. Screenplay, Rothman, Morgan; camera (color), Sunny Joseph, Shaji; editor, Beena Venugopal; music, Aravindan; sound, Krishnan Unni; art direction, Aravindan. Reviewed at Loews Copley Place, Boston, Sept. 13, 1989. (In Boston Film Festival.) No MPAA Rating: Running time: 113 MIN.
Tara . . . . Tara Johannessen
Unni . . . . Gijie Abraham
Sethu . . . . Sethu
Mary . . . . Elizabeth Anthony
Maggie . . . . Vivian Colodro
Bill . . . . Bill Swotes

■American writer/producers and an Indian director combining to tell the story of American students in India sounds like an interesting idea. Some of that idea is still visible in "Unni," a film with limited commercial appeal at best.

Story focuses on Tara (Tara Johannessen) and other American

college students spending an un-specified amount of time in Kera-la, a section of southern India. Tara, a moody, introspective girl, becomes involved with Unni (Gijie Abraham), a young Indian boy who was discovered by a student in the program the previous year.

Story is perhaps too strong a word for a meandering film in which most of the interesting things seem to be taking place off-screen. There is little motivation for most of the characters' actions in the film and, indeed, Unni — the title character — gets very lit-tle screentime.

Problems are exacerbated by cast members (many of whom were former students of writers/-producers Kitty Morgan and Wil-liam Rothman) who are well-meaning but unconvincing. Situa-tion is not helped by director G. Aravindan, apparently well known in India, but making his Stateside bow. Aravindan seems to have his own agenda, which he won't share with the audience, so that scenes of interest are cut short while a seem-ingly endless amount of time is de-voted to such trivialities as the stu-dents' bus passing other buses on the road.

Tech credits are a drawback as well, especially the sound, which changes level from scene to scene and often in the same scene. Grat-ing narration by Johannessen's character becomes means by which most of the story gets told.

"Unni" seems to be the victim of its good intentions, and addi-tional and extensive postproduc-tion may be able to salvage the travelog aspect of the pic. As is, it's got some rough sledding ahead. —*Kimm*.

VANCOUVER FEST REVIEWS

Cold Front
(CANADIAN)

Vancouver A Shapiro Glickenhaus re-lease of a Beacon Group production. Produced by Ed Richardson, Sean Allan. Executive producers, Grant Allan, Gins Doolittle, Stephen Cheikes, Kenneth Tolmie. Directed by "Paul Bnarbic" (Allan S. Goldstein). Screenplay, Sean Allan, Stefan Arngrim; cam-era (color), Thomas Burstyn; editor, Martin Hunter; music, Braun Farnon, Craig Zurba; production design, Sarina Rotstein-Cheikes; art direction, Bob Bottieri; set decoration, Bryn Finer; associate producer, Don McLean; casting, Lynn Stalmaster & Associates. Reviewed at Vancouver Film Festival, Sept. 19, 1989. Running time: **96 MIN.**

John Hyde	Martin Sheen
Derek MacKenzie	Michael Ontkean
Mantha	Kim Coates
Amanda	Beverly D'Angelo
Inspector Duchesne	Yvan Ponton
Jeannie	Shelagh McLeod
Matthew	Joshua Murray
Katie	Katie Murray
Jackie Clearly	Doug McGrath

■ **Commercial potential for this spy vs. spy tale in the "cold front" of Vancouver is tough to predict. Star attraction Martin Sheen has been pretty cold him-self lately, but pic has some nice moments that could generate strong word of mouth through a platform release.**

Sheen plays a U.S. Drug En-forcement Agency operative who teams up with a Royal Canadian Mounted Police Criminal Intelli-gence agent (Michael Ontkean) to track down a terrorist killing the female partners of men he has tar-geted for assassination.

As Sheen and Ontkean get closer to their quarry, he gets closer to Sheen's ex-wife, lounge singer Beverly D'Angelo, who sees herself as a free agent. The killer becomes a regular at the lounge, eventually making his move on the singer. Aware that she is the closest thing to a partner that his adversary has, he is deter-mined to kill her before he murd-ers the agent.

Both Sheen and Ontkean under-play their roles here, giving sets that portray an unusually dark vi-sion of Vancouver an opportunity to take the spotlight. The Stefan Arngrim/Sean Allan screenplay has some nice moments.

Problems include a paint-by-numbers approach to the plot. In the hands of an experienced direc-tor ("Bnarbic" doesn't exist; director Allan S. Goldstein with-drew his name after an undivulged "disagreement" with producer Beacon Group), the screenplay could have put moviegoers on the edge of their seats.

A mediocre ending doesn't help the film, but tech credits are more than adequate. Pic could have used stronger music for D'Angelo's lounge scenes. The final chase, though shot with care, is old news. — *Cadd*.

The Feud

Vancouver A Feud Co. production. Ex-ecutive producer, Frank Scaraggi. Produced by Bill D'Elia, Carole Kivett. Directed by D'-Elia. Screenplay, D'Elia, Robert Uricola, based on novel by Thomas Berger; camera (color), John Beymer; editor, Bill Johnson; music, Brian Eddolis; production design, Charles Lagola; casting, Stuart Howard, Amy Schecter; associate producers, Gary Nolin, Mike Listo. Reviewed at Vancouver Film Festival, Oct. 11, 1989. Running time: **96 MIN.**

Reverton	René Auberjonois
Dolf Beeler	Ron McLarty
Bud Bullard	Joe Grifasi
Tony Beeler	Scott Allegrucci
Bernice Beeler	Gayle Mayron
The Stranger	David Strathairn
Harvey Yelton	Stanley Tucci
Eva Bullard	Lynne Killmeyer
Freida Bullard	Kathleen Doyle
Bobby Beeler	Libby George

■ **"The Feud" is an accom-plished debut by New York hel-mer Bill D'Elia, offering an off-beat and darkly funny view of middle America in the 1950s. Despite a lack of big names, pic could fare well on the indie cir-cuit with careful handling.**

The film's unhurried pace, and sometimes subtle humor, may have been a problem if not for D'Elia's polished and professional helming. Considering pic is a first-time ef-fort, it is smooth and confidently structured with high production values.

Pic focuses on the Beeler fami-ly of Hornbeck and the Bullards of Millville and the feud that takes over their lives and encompasses death and ruin, love and hate, but all in an affectionate and amusing way.

In the Millville hardware store Ron McLarty as Dolf Beeler tries to buy some paint remover but gets into an argument with Joe Grifasi as Bud Bullard over his refusal to get rid of his unlighted stogie be-cause no smoking is allowed on the premises. Grifasi's cousin René Auberjonois intervenes, pulling a gun and saying he's a cop, and handcuffs McLarty. It later turns out Auberjonois just works for the railway.

That night the hardware store burns to the ground, and the fol-lowing day McLarty's car is bad-ly damaged by a bomb. Each man blames the other, and the feud be-gins.

Complications arise when Scott Allegrucci (Beeler's son Tony) falls in love with Lynne Killmeyer (Bullard's teenage daughter Eva). Not a good move considering their parents' battle, and when more family members and townspeople intentionally — and unintentional-ly — get involved in the feud things go from bad to worse.

The dark ending sees McLarty dying of a heart attack, Grifasi in a mental home and the nearest per-son to a villain — Auberjonois — hailed a hero for shooting a bank robber.

What makes "The Feud" are its well-drawn characters with their odd smalltown obsessions, envies and gripes. They seem to have leapt out of a Norman Rockwell painting and landed in an oddball America.

D'Elia is well served by his cast, with Auberjonois playing the freaky Reverton just right — he is manic and weird, but just about avoids overacting. Standouts, though, are the young lovers Scott Allegrucci and Lynne Killmeyer, who have an appealing naive charm amid the outlandish animos-ity.

Helmer D'Elia shows a confi-dent ability (he is certainly a talent to watch) and is aided by lush camerawork by John Beymer and excellent production design by Charles Lagola. D'Elia's exten-sive background in commercials pays off in the crisp and clear way he tells his story and also in the stylish bits of camera movement he slips in.

In all "The Feud" is a nice small film and certainly worth a look. —*Adam*.

Mob Story
(CANADIAN)

Vancouver An O'Meara production. Ex-ecutive producers, Anthony Kramreither, Don Haig. Produced by Kramreither. Directed by Jancarlo Markiw, Gabriel Markiw. Screen-play, Markiw, Markiw and Dave Flaherty; camera (color), Gilles Corbeil; editor, Michael Todd; sound, Leon Johnson; art direction, Kim Forrest; associate producers, Vonnie Von Helmolt, Orval Fruitman. Reviewed at Van-couver Film Festival, Oct. 8, 1989. Running time: **103 MIN.**

Luce	John Vernon
Mindy	Kate Vernon
Sam	Al Waxman
Dolores	Margot Kidder
Maria	Diana Barrington
Gianni	Robert Morelli
Tom	Angelo Pedari
Heinrich	Brian Paul
Lance	Eric Zivot

■ **In-jokes about the subzero temperatures of the Canadian city Winnipeg abound in "Mob Story," unfortunately giving the pic a parochial feel that it could well have resisted, judging by its strong cast. Local prospects may be good, but it seems unlikely to make the grade elsewhere.**

Helmers Jancarlo and Gabriel Markiw (they're brothers) make good use of their locations. The sometimes slapstick humor works best toward the end of the pic as gangsters romp in the snow. In most ways the characters are bet-ter than the script, which is essen-tially simplistic and unadven-turous.

Pic opens with Mafia don John Vernon informing the treacherous Al Waxman that he is off to Palm Springs to avoid Senate hearings. Instead he jets to freezing Winnipeg to track down his ex-lover and long-lost son.

His son, Angelo Pedari, and the boy's mother, Diana Barrington, run an Italian restaurant. She is tough and sly, even conning the local hood out of protection money.

Waxman blows up Vernon's Palm Springs condo, but finds out he must travel to Winnipeg to finish the job. Helping Waxman in Canada are local second-rate hood Robert Morelli and his ambitious moll, Margot Kidder.

Plot gets complicated as various factions try to get hold of Vernon, but true to tradition, everyone lives happily ever after.

Kidder seems to relish the opportunity to play a real tart, but the poorly written script has her killed off just after halfway through. Vernon looks suitably bemused at the antics of everyone around him.

Best of all is Barrington, the strong widow who is seemingly superior to the rest of the characters. Also fine is Eric Zivot as vain tv anchorman.

Some may say it is admirable that the Markiws have not tried to hide the film's Canadian origin, but the in-jokes detract from the overall pleasure of an occasionally amusing piece. Pic is a shade too long and tries to be too clever, though highlights include a well-constructed car chase and Winnipeg's own truly awful weather.
—*Adam.*

THESSALONIKI FEST REVIEWS

Gamos Sto Perithorio
(A Wedding On The Fringe)
(GREEK)

Thessaloniki   A Greek Film Center/Compass Film Production. Written and directed by Vassilis Kessissoglou. Camera (color), Stavros Chasapis; editor, Andreas Andreadakis; music, Panaqiotis Calatzopoulos; sound, Marinos Athanasopoulos; sets-costumes, Maria Coularmani; production manager, Giorgos Diamantis. Reviewed at Thessaloniki Film Festival (competing), Oct. 6, 1989. Running time: **97 MIN.**
Photini . . . . Aleka Paizi
Elias . . . . Stavros Xenidis
Son . . . . Vangelis Kazan
Daughter . . . . Olga Tournaki
    Also with: Yoto Fessta, Dinos Avgoustides, Nikos Garofallou, Eleni Mavromati, Dimitris Poulikakos, Vassilis Vassilopoulos, Lilian Palantza, Zano Danias, Elena Akrita.

■**This is a charming romantic comedy laced with gentle parody about a couple who separated during World War I and reunited decades later. With proper marketing, pic should do well at home, and its timeless, universal theme will facilitate travel.**

Elias (Stavros Xenidis), a vigorous, widowed octogenarian, decides to go to his northern Greek village to vote. While there he spies Photini (Aleka Paizi), his fiancée years ago, also now widowed.

Elias' awkward overtures eventually break down Photini's reserve. In a touchingly intimate tryst in the cemetery, they renew their old passion and begin a surreptitious courtship.

When Photini tells her incredulous daughter about her plans to marry Elias, the daughter insists she break off the relationship before they become the laughing-stock of the community. Implicit in this statement is a basic part of Greek life, even today: "philotimo," or maintaining one's honor, a deeply embedded concept that molds the lives of most villagers and many city dwellers.

Photini is intimidated by her daughter but swept away by Elias on a giddy visit to Athens. The timing and expressions of the leads are perfect, giving warmth and sensuality to their interaction.

Paizi as Photini won the best actress award at the Salonika fest and Xenidis won a special award for his role as Elias and for his career contribution. Olga Tournaki is convincingly nagging as the daughter, a role that helped her win best supporting actress.

The camerawork is adept, although purposely conventional. Bits of Greek history are revealed in flashbacks, and satirical commentary on current affairs such as the June general elections is incorporated into fast-paced episodes.

Some of the in-jokes, such as the raunchy bump-and-grind "tsifteteli" (belly dance), done by two miniskirted teenagers at a wedding celebration, had Greek viewers howling with laughter while the foreigners at the fest preem also were highly amused. —*Sam.*

Xenia
(GREEK)

Thessaloniki   A Greek Film Center/ET-1/Patrice Vivancos/Lezard Vert Prods. production. Directed by Vivancos. Screenplay, Malvina Karali, Vivancos, Giorgos Bramos; camera (color), Giorgos Arvanitis, Yannis Daskalthanassis; editor, Yannis Tsitsopoulos; music, Dimitris Papadimitriou; sound, Thanassis Arvanitis; sets-costumes, Giorgos Patsas. Reviewed at Thessaloniki Festival (competing), Oct. 5, 1989. Running time: **92 MIN.**
Xenia . . . . Themis Bazaka
Matthieu . . . . Denis Podalides
    Also with: Frantzesco Algora, Kostas Foudoukis, Giorgos Sabanis, Brizio Montinaro.

■**Patrice Vivanco's sometimes ponderous road movie "Xenia," which won him the best first feature film prize at the Thessaloniki fest, shows he has promise. However, its high-level production values cannot overcome the plot's weakness and its uneven handling.**

Xenia is a pregnant woman (Themis Bazaka) who is compelled to have her child in Andalusia. She meets another motorist, the young actor Matthieu (Denis Podalides), on his way to an audition. When his car breaks down, they form an uneasy alliance.

Some interesting observations are revealed through their conversations, but are tossed out and blown to the wind rather than developed. For example, Xenia mocks Matthieu's platitudes about the beauty of Greece and its light, saying she finds the light depressing. The conversation ends abruptly before a real point can be made.

Bazaka, one of Greece's most expressive actresses, comes across as a tough-talking individualist, a bohemian who has defied conventional society. Unfortunately, she resorts to overacting when experiencing prenatal pains, yet seems perversely aloof in other scenes. Podalides' performance is understated, but he is more believable as the shy young actor.

Some exchanges and plot developments — sinister pursuers, a visit to a mysterious man — are incomprehensible. The last scenes, in which Matthieu is taught to care for the newborn, would have had more emotional power if sufficient audience rapport had been established with the protagonists.

The lensing by often-laureled cameraman Giorgos Arvanitis and Yannis Daskalthanassis is outstanding and does justice to the rugged beauty of the Mediterranean, especially Spain. The piano-string score with some flamenco

guitar segments, although sometimes resorting to overbearing string arrangements, is on the whole appealing. —*Sam.*

Kleisto Kykloma
(Television Closed Circuit)
(GREEK)

Thessaloniki   An ET-1 production. Directed by Nikos Yannopoulos. Screenplay, Soula Pierakou, Nikos Yannopoulos; camera (color), Andreas Bellis; editor, Andreas Andreadakis; music, Giorgos Christianakis; sound, Argiris Lazaridis; sets-costumes, Eleni Blassopoulou. Reviewed at Thessaloniki Film Festival (competing), Oct. 7, 1989. Running time: **72 MIN.**
Stephania . . . . Pemi Zouni
Dimitris . . . . Peris Michailidis
    Also with: Joanna Pridezi, Athina Pappa, Gounar Kernich, Marilena Thoma.

■**"Television Closed Circuit" is one of the few current Greek films to focus on quotidian activities in contemporary Athens. The entertaining comic drama brings up timely concerns that should draw local audiences, but the low quality of the production from pubcaster ET-1 will make it difficult to export to anything but tv.**

A married couple, Stephania (talented actress Pemi Zouni) and Dimitris (Peris Michailidis) separate, apparently because of his irresponsible work patterns and philandering. They decide to keep a closed-circuit tv in their flats in the same neighborhood so that Dimitris can share in the nurturing of their 7-year-old girl, who lives with Stephania.

The presence of the camera both facilitates and hinders communication in a way that is symbolic of how the mass media have programmed our expectations in personal relationships. The agony of trying to end a love affair in a dignified manner while overcoming jealousy is highlighted when both Stephania and Dimitris "tune in" while the other is entertaining a new love interest.

The young girl steals the scenes in which she discusses her concerns with each parent, and the affection shown is natural and heartwarming.

Pic should be particularly relevant at home, since Greece has the highest divorce rate in the European Community, but the poor quality of pic's color and problems with sound limit its theatrical appeal.—*Sam.*

Rom
(GREEK-DOCU)

Thessaloniki An ET 1 production. Written and directed by Menelaos Karamaggiolis. Camera (color), Andreas Sinanos, Elias Konstantakopoulos; editor, Takis Yannopoulos; music, Nikos Kipourgos; sound, Dimitris Athanasopoulos, Mimis Kasimatis; research, Miranda Terzopoulou, Katerina Loutsou, Vaggelis Marsellos; singing, Kostas Pavlidis, Dora Masklivanou; narration, Electra Alexandropoulou, Marika Giralidou, Giorgos Konstas, Menelaos Karamaggiolis. Reviewed at Thessaloniki Film Festival (competing), Oct. 3, 1989. Running time: 74 MIN.

■ "Rom" is a colorful, thoroughly researched portrait of gypsy life, giving insight into this much-maligned subculture's origins and customs. The narrative is at times overwhelming, distracting from the visual flow.

One of the more successful of recent productions of pubcaster ET 1, "Rom" expresses four different perspectives on gypsy culture: that of a teacher, photographer, older gypsy woman and a young girl, revealed through the voiceovers.

The title comes from the word "Romeos," a term for a member of the East Roman culture and their language as well. In 1979, the UN recognized the people with gypsy origins under the name Rom.

The docu conveys myriad bits of information about the gypsy myths, including the belief that gypsies made the nails for the crucifixion of Christ, placing a taint upon their race and the reason the gypsies are destined to roam forever.

The photography is adept, particularly in hand-held closeups that capture the striking features of typical gypsies. "Rom" is chock full of info on the background of various gypsy crafts such as circus acrobatics and horse training but only skims the surface of contemporary issues such as housing and education.

An actual interview with a "king" of a large gypsy group in one of the Athenian suburbs, such as Ano Liosion, might have added to the pic's appeal for docu festivals. Even so, it can easily fit into such a slot based on its educational value. Its lively street scenes and musical interludes will be a draw for educational tv.

Pic won an award at the Thessaloniki fest for best docu, somewhat gratuitous since it was the only docu in competition. —*Sam.*

Athoos H Enochos
(Guilty Or Not Guilty)
(GREEK)

Thessaloniki A Dimitris Arvanitis/ET-1 production. Directed by Dimitris Arvanitis. Screenplay, Yannis Giotis; camera (color), Lakis Kirlidis; editor, Andreas Andreadakis; music, John Alex, Yannis Drolapas; sound, Mimis Kasimatis; sets-costumes, Agni Doutsi. Reviewed at Thessaloniki Film Festival (competing), Oct. 5, 1989. Running time: 121 MIN.

With: Spyros Drosos, Yannis Bezos, Despo Diamandidou, Tikita Blaxopoulou, Olga Tournaki, Dinos Karidis, Giorgos Moutsios.

■ "Guilty Or Not Guilty," a psychological drama about the trial and execution of a suspected rapist in northern Greece, is an overwrought, crudely made tv production that will have difficulty sustaining audience interest for two hours, even at home.

The movie is based on the actual case of Aristides Pangratides, who was charged with attempted rape in a Thessaloniki orphanage. Despite the uncertainty of witnesses and the circumstantial nature of the evidence, Pangratides was sentenced to death and executed by a firing squad.

"Guilty Or Not Guilty" uses the same technique as Theo Angelopoulos' memorable first feature, "Reconstruction," in which the crime and alleged criminals are known, so attention is focused on the reconstruction of the events.

In this case, the technique merely deprives Dimitris Arvanitis' film of suspense, as there is little development of the proper psychological tension. Melodramatic overacting replaces the finely honed performances of Angelopoulos' thesps.

The remarks of the prosecutor, who recommends a life sentence rather than the death penalty because of the accused's traumatic youth — he was forced to prostitute himself — make him seem pathetic but not sympathetic. Camerawork and film quality are poor and the distorted electric guitar-synthesizer score is grating.

Olga Tournaki was honored at the Salonika fest for her role as the distraught mother. Another standout performance is by Despo Diamandidou, who may be recognized by foreign audiences from her role as the mother in Woody Allen's "Love And Death." Here she's cast as "The Lady Of The Villas." —*Sam.*

A Un
(Buddies)
(JAPANESE)

Tokyo A Toho Pictures and Film Face production. Directed by Yasuo Furuhata. Screenplay, Tutoma Nakamura; camera (color), Daisaku Kimura; art direction, Shinobu Muraki; costumes, Reiko Yamada; sound, Yasuo Hashimoto. Reviewed at Tokyo Film Festival, Sept. 29, 1989. Running time: 114 MIN.
With: Shuzo Kadokura, Ken Takadura Kimiko, Nobuko Miyamoto, Senichi Mizuta, Eiji Bando Tami, Samuko Tuji Satoko, Yasuko Tomita.

■ This pic, which opened the Tokyo Film Festival, is a local drama modestly shot on indoor sets. Despite some fine thesping, item has a static quality and stylized lensing that will make it of little interest to Western audiences. Excessive running time takes its toll.

Yarn, set in 1936, concerns two "buddies" who have been in the army together. Both are married, but one, Shuzo Kadokura, continues to have a crush on his friend's wife, though by now she has a grown-up daughter. He never makes a pass at her, however, and becomes a well-liked friend of the family, lends money to his buddy when latter is involved in embezzling and plays godfather to the friend's nubile daughter.

There is little movement or plot development, as director Yasuo Furuhata's camera remains positioned in front of ritual conversations over tea, while the dialog is mostly dull. The painted backgrounds are embarrassingly bad, and there is minimal effort to convey the idea that we are in 1937.

After a confrontation between the buddies, all ends inconclusively well after Kadokura convinces his buddy to let his friend allow his daughter to go spend the night with her boyfriend, who has been drafted and is about to go off to to war. —*Besa.*

The Enchantment
(JAPANESE)

Tokyo A Fuji Television production. Produced by Toshiro Kamata, Kei Sasaki. Directed by Shunichi Nagasaki. Screenplay, Goro Nakajima; camera (color), Makato Watanabe; music, Satosi Kadokura. Reviewed at Tokyo Film Festival, Oct. 3, 1989. Running time: 109 MIN.
Miyako . . . . .Kumiko Akiyoshi
Sotomura . . . . .Masao Kusakari
Harumi . . . . .Kiwako Harada

■ Storyline of a psychiatrist dealing with a split-personality case having homicidal tendencies whom he falls in love with is familiar enough. Yet, even retold here in a modern Tokyo setting and using a shoestring budget, yarn holds interest.

Pic involves a triangle comprising the shrink, his pretty patient and his secretary. Doc has been carrying on an affair with the secretary, so when the new patient arrives she turns jealous and establishes her own contact with the new patient.

While one of the personalities of the patient makes up amorously to the shrink, the other is consumed with jealousy and on two occasions knifes the doc. Meanwhile, the secretary and the patient establish a lesbian relationship.

Pic concludes rather confusingly with a double murder, but this seems to be a dream sequence, since at the end the shrink is inconclusively seen driving away leaving the two women watching his car receding in the distance.

Production values are pretty basic and pic will be limited to the local market, since pacing is slow, and there is a lack of dramatic build-up. It has good thesping and some interesting insights into modern Tokyo. —*Besa.*

Interdevotchka
(Intergirl)
(SOVIET-SWEDISH)

Tokyo A Goskino and Filmstalet (Sweden) coproduction. Directed by Pyotr Todorovski. Screenplay, Vladimir Kunin; camera (color), Valery Shuvalov; music, Pyotr Todorovsky; production design, Valentin Konovalov. Reviewed at Tokyo Film Festival, Oct. 4, 1989. Running time: 155 MIN.
Tatyana . . . . .Elena Yakovleva
Edvard . . . . .Tomas Laustiola
Alla Sergeevna . . . . . .Larisa Malevannaya
Lyalka . . . . .Anastasiya Nemolaeva

■ This is a solid, well-made, albeit overlong film about the adventures of a Leningrad call girl who marries a client from Sweden and goes straight.

What might have been a tawdry, routine film on an overfamiliar subject is handled here with captivating freshness and makes a fascinating study of a milieu not heretofore reflected with such frankness in Soviet cinema.

Buoying up the film is a fine performance by Elena Yakovleva as the pretty hooker who must overcome Soviet bureaucracy in order to pull off a marriage of convenience which will enable her to move to Sweden to enjoy the offerings of Western consumerism.

Most of the pic is set in Leningrad where Tatyana works as a nurse in a hospital, but supplements her income as a call girl who gets paid in hard currency by businessmen bedding down with her. One of these, a Swede, offers to marry her. He is a retiring, punctilious bookkeeper-type man, who has sincerely fallen in love with the girl.

She sees him as her passport to a better life. After being blackmailed by her father, whom she hasn't seen for 20 years, and raising the coin by selling herself for a long night to a Japanese client, she finally gets to "the promised land." Soon she feels nostalgia for Russia, despite her abundance of luxury items. She alternately befriends a Soviet truckdriver who hails from the same nabe as herself in Leningrad, and a Soviet hooker from Moscow, now trying to work in Sweden. She pines to see her mother back in Leningrad.

Pic ends with tragic poignancy, as Tatyana is no longer able to endure her lonely exile and pointless existence. Despite the criticism of Soviet life, pic underlines the difficulties of adaptation to foreign climes.

Item could be of interest for arthouse release around the world, but perhaps could do with a half-hour less running time and a more expressive title. It has good production values, credible thesping and a nice insight into a profession that does not legally exist in the USSR. —*Besa.*

Music For Old Animals
(ITALIAN)

Tokyo A Unione Cinematografica production. Executive producers, Piccioli and Leopardi. Written and directed by Stefano Benni, Umberto Angelucci. Camera (color), Pasqualino de Santis; editor, Ugo di Rossi; music, Arturo Annecchino; sets, Lorenzo Barraldi. Reviewed at Tokyo Film Festival, Oct. 4, 1989. Running time: **109 MIN.**
Lucio . . . . .Dario Fo
Lee . . . . .Paolo Rossi
Lupetta . . . . .Viola Simoncioni
Museum guard . . . . .Francesco Guccini
Libellula . . . . .Maddalena de Panfilis
Also with: Betty Prado, Carlo Monni.

■This is a quirky, alternately ebullient, zany, but occasionally tiresome adventure comedy that occasionally lurches off to the serious side. Item revolves about an odd threesome wandering through a city during an undetermined State "emergency."

This is a kind of "road" movie without a road, as the writer/directors follow their whims and fancies, sometimes opting for surrealism, at other times for broad street humor. Often they hit their mark, but sometimes their results go awry.

Main characters are an old professor, a car mechanic with a passion for Zen and a young girl who prefers to live in her own dreamworld rather than go off to the first day of school.

As the three walk and drive about the city they occasionally meet up with the owner of the fancy convertible they have "borrowed," or run into a military road block, or philosophize about life and purpose, or fall upon an odd gathering of outcasts, where they witness a strange symbolic dance and so on.

What it all adds up to is never told. Their final destination is a hospital, where the professor is put into an intensive care unit. The episodes of the day's journey are related to his former life, but the point is left vague.

There's fine thesping by all players. Pic is rather too oddball to generate much commercial interest, but could find its way on the fest circuit.—*Besa.*

Rezerva La Start
(The Benchwarmer)
(RUMANIAN)

Tokyo A Romania Film presentation. Produced by Dan Vasinov. Directed by Anghel Mora. Screenplay, Mora, Serban Marinescu; camera (color), Marian Stanciu; editor, Melania Obriou; music, Adrian Enascu; production manager, Titi Pobescu. Reviewed at Tokyo Film Festival, Oct. 1, 1989. Running time: **85 MIN.**
With: Mihai Stan, George Alexandru, Ion Roxin, Florentin Duse, Boris Pertroff.

■This sad excuse for a film certainly will warm benches while other films play. A dull story, inept dialog, clumsy lensing and strident music combine for a filmic cacophony.

Story concerns a trainer with a heart problem trying to get a national team into shape for a pentathlon. Pic bounces between yakking and clips of team members exercising.

Naturally the surly trainer has a stroke just as the team is competing, but all is told in episodic, disjointed and undramatic fashion.
—*Besa.*

Kharej Az Mahdoudeh
(Off The Limits)
(IRANIAN)

Tokyo A Cooperative Group of Filmmakers, Institute for the Cinematographic Affairs of the Mostazafan Foundation production. Directed by Rakhshan Bani'etemad. Screenplay, Farid Mostafavi; camera (color), Ali Reza Zarrindast; editor, Ruhollah Emami; music, Mohammad Reza Aligholi; production manager, Habib Esmaili; sets, Amir Estabi; sound, Rubik Mansouri. Reviewed at the Tokyo Film Festival, Oct. 2, 1989. Running time: **100 MIN.**
With: Mehdi Hashemi, Parvaneh Masoumi, Mahmud Jafari, Jamshid Layegh, Mahmud Bahrami, Hassan Raziani, Mohammad Varshochi, Farhad Khanmohammadi, Soroush Khalili, Esmail Mohammadi, Mehri Mahrnia.

■"Off The Limits" is an occasionally droll, very low-budget pic about a civil servant who moves into a new house he has just bought with his wife and the bureaucratic snafus he runs into after a burglary.

Indeed, the otherwise timid, law-abiding and penny-saving Halimi catches the culprit and takes him to the police, only to discover that his new house, due to a zoning mistake, is not under the jurisdiction of any of the authorities.

Pic pokes fun at the Iranian bureaucracy, but is cautiously set in 1972, under the Shah's government. Pic concludes humorously with Halimi and his neighbors taking justice into their own hands.

Technical level is rudimentary; print shown was grainy, washed out and scratched. English subtitles flicker and are full of pidgin English and spelling mistakes.
—*Besa.*

Salim Langde Pe Mat Ro
(Don't Cry For Salim,
The Lame)
(INDIAN)

Tokyo A National Film Development Corp. production. Written and directed by Saeed Akhtar Mirza. Camera (color), Virendra Saini; music, Sharang Dev. Reviewed at Tokyo Film Festival, Oct. 6, 1989. Running time: **120 MIN.**
With: Pavan Melhetra, Makarand Deshpande, Ashutesh Gowarikar, Rajendra Neelima Azim, Vikram Gokhale, Surekha Sikri.

(Hindi soundtrack)

■An overtly political plea for unity between Muslims and Hindus, this pic could arouse some interest on the fest circuit and perhaps even in limited art locations despite its poor technical quality and excessive length.

Story concerns a group of young hoods in Bombay, one of whom, a Muslim, awakens to the broader issues of life and starts to turn away from his life of petty crime.

Salim, who has a slight limp, struggles to survive in the squalid Bombay underworld, while his parents and sister vainly struggle to make ends meet. Influenced by a scholarly but poor suitor who wants to marry his sister, Salim is made aware of the futility of the struggle between the religious factions in his country.

Little by little he starts to question his own life. As he does so, he turns away from his former associates in crime, but before he can start an honest life as a car mechanic, his past catches up with him.

Helmer/writer Saeed Mirza uses Salim as a mouthpiece for his own political views, which lay all the blame on "those who partitioned the country." Much of pic is overdeveloped, and English subtitles are full of mistakes in grammar and spelling. —*Besa.*

Worth Winning

Hollywood   A 20th Century Fox release of an A&M Films production. Produced by Gil Friesen, Dale Pollock. Executive producer, Tom Joyner. Directed by Will Mackenzie. Screenplay, Josanne McGibbon, Sara Parriott, based on Dan Lewandowski's novel; camera (Deluxe color), Adam Greenberg; editor, Sidney Wolinsky; music, Patrick Williams; music supervision, David Anderle; production design, Lilly Kilvert; art direction, Jon Hutman; set design, David Klassen; set decoration, Linda Spheeris; costume design, Robert Blackman; sound (Dolby), Dave McMillan; assistant director, Randy Cordray; associate producers, Neil Koenigsberg, Wendy Dozoretz; casting, Wallis Nicita. Reviewed at 20th Century Fox, L.A., Oct. 25, 1989. MPAA Rating: PG-13. Running time: **102 MIN.**

Taylor	Mark Harmon
Veronica	Madeleine Stowe
Eleanor	Lesley Ann Warren
Erin	Maria Holvöe
Ned	Mark Blum
Claire	Andrea Martin
Terry	Tony Longo
Howard	Alan Blumenfeld
Howard Jr.	Devin Ratray
Auctioneer	David Brenner

■ "Sex, Lies And Videotape" would have been an apt title for this soufflé about a man who cons three women into accepting marriage proposals that he videotapes to win a bet. But the comparison, to be sure, ends there. Pic may at first engage some viewers, but ultimately Fox will be stood up at the boxoffice altar.

Mark Harmon plays the glib and callow bachelor whose 6-figure salary and "glamorous job" (a tv weatherman) make him irresistible to scores of vapid, leggy babes whom he reels in and then tosses back.

Either to take him down a notch or fix him up, his surreally immature yuppie friend Ned (Mark Blum) makes him a high-stakes bet that he can't get three women of Ned's choice to agree to marry him, with the proof in the taping.

Ill-motivated premise for what follows, a series of hollow deceptions in the name of the male ego, strains both credibility and Harmon's likability.

Pic is at least half over before it strikes a single honest note, when Harmon falls for the flintiest of the women (Madeleine Stowe) and issues her a sincere and desperate marriage proposal.

The three women he has preyed upon find out about each other — via videotape — and plot his humiliation. Second half of the film is considerably better paced and motivated than the first, but no more worthwhile. Do we really care of this 30-ish cad ever learns his lesson, to be followed, of course, by a happy ending?

Also, in a smarmy device, Harmon talks directly to the camera, letting us in on a personality not worth investigating.

Director Will Mackenzie (tv's "Family Ties," "Moonlighting") apparently set out to make a '40s-style screwball comedy, but pic lacks the wit or style by a longshot, substituting titillation and crass humor.

Script, chock-full of bimbos and pushovers, was penned by women (Josanne McGibbon and Sara Parriott) from a novel by Dan Lewandowski. Apparently picture set out to be something quite different but missed.

Lesley Ann Warren, in an unfortunate turn, plays a slithering nymphomaniac in Frederick's of Hollywood attire.

Stowe has moments of radiance but at other times is just as confounded by the pic as other cast members. Lensing and tech credits are, in general, straightforward and tv-like. —Daws.

Maddalena Z

Mill Valley, Calif.   A Teacup Films production. Produced and directed by Mark Schwartz. Executive producer, George Ow Jr. Screenplay, Geoffrey Francis Dunn; camera (color), Gene Evans; editor, Mona Lynch; music, Randy Masters; sound, Bayard Carey; production design, George Arthur, Edith Hutton; assistant director, Jeff Buchanan; associate producer-casting, Bonita Anne Mugnani. Reviewed at Mill Valley Film Festival, Mill Valley, Calif., Oct. 8, 1989. No MPAA Rating. Running time: **88 MIN.**

Dominic	Bill Ackridge
Zandy	Dunja Djordjevic
Tony	Geoffrey Dunn
Stella	Liz Rolfe
Mario	Gene Matisoff
Dirk	Ken Hill
Julia	Lorna Ho
Sally	Deborah Gray

Also with: Darian Ratcliff, Jeremy Slate, Richard Conti, Bette Laws, Lenny Calandrino, Frank Diamanti, John R. Patterson, Simon Kelly, Valentina Belenky Belova.

■Limited by obvious indie production difficulties, "Maddalena Z" nonetheless is an engaging little romance, unusual for its background and subject matter.

Film is a good showcase for its leads, Bill Ackridge and Dunja Djordjevic, drawn into a May-December romance that might have turned out much worse than it does, with wedding bells ringing in his mind but not hers.

The aging Ackridge is a dying breed of fisherman on the California coast whose traditional skills and small tub are no match for the big boats and regulatory bureaucracy. Djordjevic is a college girl writing about the fishing biz, taken aboard by the older man for first-hand experience.

The clash of class and generations makes for predictable material, but writer Geoffrey Francis Dunn wrings the most out of it and producer-director Mark Schwartz sets it well against nice ocean vistas and colorful Italian locals.

A lifelong bachelor who has retained a senior-citizen version of good looks, Ackridge knows his women and recognizes the girl's infatuation but foolishly entertains an old fool's notion that there could be permanency here. She, too, acknowledges her attraction but isn't deceived by any illusions that the relatively simple old fisherman is a hot prospect.

Can she disengage without causing permanent damage? Fortunately, the seaman's own sense of humor puts the situation into perspective, leaving only a bit of elderly melancholy as the sun sinks in the west, with Randy Masters' lovely Italian score in the background. —Har.

Shocker

Hollywood   A Universal Pictures release of an Alive Films presentation. Executive producers, Shep Gordon, Wes Craven. Produced by Marianne Maddalena, Barin Kumar. Coproducer, Peter Foster, Bob Engelman. Written and directed by Craven. Camera (Foto-Kem color), Jacques Haitkin; editor, Andy Blumenthal; music, William Goldstein; production design, Cynthia Kay Charette; costume design, Isis Mussenden; art direction, Randy Moore; set decoration, Naomi Shohan; sound (Ultra-Stereo), Robert Janiger; associate producer, Warren Chadwick; casting, Gary M. Zuckerbrod. Reviewed at Writers Guild theater, Beverly Hills, Calif., Oct. 24, 1989. MPAA Rating: R. Running time: **110 MIN.**

Lt. Don Parker	Michael Murphy
Jonathan Parker	Peter Berg
Horace Pinker	Mitch Pileggi
Alison	Cami Cooper
Rhino	Richard Brooks
Pac Man	Theodore Raimi
Tv newscaster	John Tesh
Tv evangelist	Dr. Timothy Leary
Victim	Heather Langenkamp
Bartender	Bingham Ray

■Universal arrives years late and thousands of brain cells short with this apparent effort to get in on the slasher-film genre at a time when Freddy Krueger, Jason and Michael Myers all appear to be running out of steam, if not victims.

Even with Wes Craven ("A Nightmare On Elm Street") at the helm, pic should set off few sparks at the boxoffice except for perhaps an initial jolt from the morbidly curious.

At first glance (or at least for the first 40 minutes) "Shocker" seems a potential winner, an almost unbearably suspenseful, stylish and blood-drenched ride courtesy of writer-director Craven's flair for action and sick humor.

As it continues, however, the camp aspects simply give way to the ridiculous while failing to establish any rules to govern the mayhem. The result is plenty of unintentional laughs that undermine the few legitimate chuckles and most of the remaining action.

Craven never bothers to adequately explain the why and how of latest matinee idol of mass murder Horace Pinker (Mitch Pileggi), who in this case resembles Mr. Clean with a big knife.

Instead, the overlong story simply leapfrogs among ludicrous clichés of the genre, with deceased girlfriends coming to the rescue, the wraith of a killer floating around and possessing people and the sturdy young protagonist (Peter Berg) moronically linked to the murderer via his dreams.

The emphasis on dreams isn't the only thing that brings "Nightmare's" Freddy to mind, since ol' Horace — unlike his silent, masked, lurching brethren in "Friday The 13th" and "Halloween" — has a penchant for spewing infrequently funny vulgarities at his victims and intended target Jonathan (Berg).

The obtuse story has Pinker, already a mass killer of several families, slaying the foster family of Jonathan and his police captain father (Michael Murphy). Jonathan "sees" the events in a prescient dream that indicates he's linked to the murderer.

That leads the police to Pinker's door, and after a series of misadventures he's caught and executed. Something goes wrong, which for all the audience knows could be due to black magic or bizarre static cling, and Horace lives on after the execution as a disembodied malevolent spirit who strikes out by possessing others.

The only original twist involves an emphasis on television that pervades the film; Horace is a tv repairman, somehow uses tv to affect his resurrection and eventually becomes an inhabitant of the airwaves in the film's best section, albeit one that's horribly overplayed.

Still, what may have been the original idea — a "tv killer" who gains access to homes when viewers numbly turn the tube on — was lost in transition among unimpressive pyrotechnics, unneeded side trips and an insipid post-death romance between Jonathan and his girlfriend (Cami Cooper). It may have been a romantic invention when a female warrior returned from beyond to pull her lover's fat out of the fire in ''Conan The Barbarian,'' but this woman hangs around long enough to cook breakfast.

Craven produces a few memorable moments along the way (the killer's possession of a cherubic little girl is an absolute scream) but not enough to sustain the weight of ''Shocker's'' shortcomings in terms of plot and dialog.

Tech credits are generally fine, the special effects are many but unspectacular. The music also plays an important part, most notably the use of the song ''No More Mr. Nice Guy,'' which provides the basis of the pic's clever marketing campaign.—*Bril.*

Kill Me Again

Hollywood   An MGM/UA Distribution release of a Polygram Pictures and MGM presentation of a Propaganda Films production. Produced by David W. Warfield, Sigurjon Sighvatsson, Steve Golin. Executive producers, Michael Kuhn, Nigel Sinclair. Line producer, George J. Roewe 3d. Directed by John Dahl. Screenplay, Dahl, Warfield; camera (Deluxe color), Jacques Steyn; editor, Frank Jimenez, Jonathan Shaw, Steyn; music, William Olvis; production design, Michelle Minch; sound (Ultra-Stereo), Craig Felburg, Bill V. Robbins; assistant director, Jeff Morrell; associate producers, Carol Lewis, Scott Cameron; casting, Carol Lewis. Reviewed at Filmland theater, L.A., Oct. 25, 1989. MPAA Rating: R. Running time: **94 MIN.**

Fay Forrester . . . . . Joanne Whalley-Kilmer
Jack Andrews . . . . Val Kilmer
Vince Miller . . . . Michael Madsen
Sammy . . . . Pat Mulligan
Marty . . . . Nick Dimitri
Jack's Secretary . . . . Bibi Besch
Alan Swayzie . . . . Jonathan Gries
Tim, Motel Clerk . . . . Michael Sharrett

■The regional release MGM/-UA is giving this low-key crime melodrama is understandable in terms of today's market demands. However, this tale of a down-and-out detective and a seamy femme fatale is a thoroughly professional little entertainment.

It should find a welcome home in foreign and ancillary markets.

Set in contemporary Nevada, ''Kill Me Again'' gets off to a fast start with a small-time con couple (Michael Madsen and Joanne Whalley-Kilmer) scoring big when they cop a suitcase full of cash from a pair of Mafia bagmen.

Deciding she wants the ill-gotten gains for herself, the antiheroine

beans her beau with a rock and takes off for a round of fast living in Reno. To make sure she kicks over all the traces, she asks a seedy detective (Val Kilmer) to fake her murder.

As he's in hock to a group of ruthless loan sharks, Kilmer is only too happy to oblige. His employer's physical charms are an added incentive. Reckless as he may be to get involved in this sort of thing, he's still smart enough not to trust her. Consequently he's well prepared for the round of murders, double crosses and escapes that make up the film's last half.

Fresh from playing a carnal innocent in ''Scandal,'' Whalley-Kilmer takes to the role of a *really* bad girl with glee. Always seeming to be just barely wearing whatever outfit she's shimmied into, she's perfectly suited to playing the sort of woman who'd change her name from ''Fay'' to ''Vera'' in order to escape detection.

Val Kilmer is somewhat less successful with his part, largely because, as written, it's difficult to tell how smart or stupid his detective is supposed to be.

Both Kilmers plainly had a wonderful time with the love scenes (one of which is scored to a purposely off-key rendition of ''Smoke Gets In Your Eyes''). They get fine support from Michael Madsen as a fully functioning psychotic.

All technical credits are superior.—*Rens.*

Meet Market
(CANADIAN)

Montreal   A Malofilm Group release of a Les Prods. Vidéofilms Limitée film, in association with the National Film Board of Canada. Executive producer, Robert Ménard. Produced by Claude Bonin. Directed by Robert Ménard. Screenplay, Ménard, Claire Wojas, Michel Côté; camera (color), Pierre Mignot; editor, Michel Arcand; music, Richard Grégoire; sound, Michel Charron; makeup, Jacques Lafleur, Pierre Saindon. Reviewed at Cineplex Odeon Cinema Berri, Montreal, Oct. 15, 1989. Running time: **96 MIN.**

Jean-Jacques (the Peacock), Gérard (the
   Bull), Patrice (the Lion), Serge
   (the Worm) . . . . Michel Côté
The Divine . . . . Louise Marleau
Sonia . . . . Géneviève Rioux

■This sizzling comedy can attribute its imminent success to actor and cowriter Michel Côté, who audaciously plays all four leading roles with the wit and cunning of four radically different actors.

Film was released in Quebec with the title ''Cruising Bar.''

Côté struts his stuff in designer silk suits as Jean-Jacques, the Peacock. He adopts the air of an overweight middle-aged womanizer as married suburbanite Gérard, the Bull. As Patrice, the Lion, he dons long blond hair, buck teeth and a hockey shirt to personify an aging rocker. As the Worm (Serge), Côté becomes a zit-popping nerd.

Makeup masters Jacques Lafleur and Pierre Saindon help Côté carry off the character switches.

Jean-Jacques, Gérard, Patrice and Serge — who frequent drastically different Montreal night clubs — are doomed to failure in their shallow pursuit of women. While somewhat predictable, their strategies are humorously scripted and executed with bumbling perfection.

The Peacock gets lucky with ''the Divine'' at a chic hotspot but fails to perform between his designer sheets. The Bull proves he can still do the locomotion but gets nabbed by his disguised wife.

When Patrice's luck runs out at the disco, he figures he'll take up with his old girlfriend . . . until his pals slip him three hits of acid. And Serge, by far the most pathetic, winds up cruising transvestites by accident.

Helmer Robert Ménard has tapped a nerve with a pic that drives home the point that cruisers are losers in the decade of ''safe sex.'' Pic should do well in territories where simplistic humor, clever acting and an original concept are a plus. Vidcassette venue is a natural second life.—*Suze.*

Jungle Assault

New York   An Action Intl. Pictures production. Executive producer, David Winters. Produced by Fritz Matthews. Written and directed by David A. Prior. Camera (Image Transform color), Stephen Ashley Blake; editor, Paul O'Bryan; music, Brian Bennett; sound, Lisa Kempton; art direction, Ted Prior; production manager, Michael Bogert; assistant director, Kimberley Casey; student coordinator, Bob Ivy; casting, William Zipp. Reviewed on AIP vidcassette, N.Y., Sept. 23, 1989. No MPAA Rating. Running time: **85 MIN.**

Gen. Mitchell . . . . William Smith
Kelly . . . . William Zipp
Becker . . . . Ted Prior
Rosa . . . . Maria Rosado
McClusky . . . . David Marriott
Crusher . . . . Darwin Swalve
Elaine Mitchell . . . . Jeannie Moore
   Also with: John Cianetti, Chris Gable, Deke Anderson, Chet Hood, Angela Porcell, Shaun Summers.

■Nicely made actioner ''Jungle Assault'' has prolific made-for-

vid helmer David Prior switching his sights from war in the Far East to skirmishes in Latin America.

William Smith toplines as a retired U.S. Army general who organizes a small force to go south of the border for his daughter (Jeannie Moore), who has been duped and is helping the anti-American forces down there.

There are effective battle scenes here, but best element is a feisty rebel leader, played to the hilt by Maria Rosado, who's both sexy and sinister. —*Lor.*

Animal Behavior

Hollywood   A Millimeter Films release. Produced by Kjehl Rasmussen. Executive producer, Randolph Clendenen. Co-executive producers, Bob Weinstein, Harvey Weinstein. Coproducers, Dale Aj Rose, Edward Glass. Directed by ''H. Anne Riley'' (Jenny Bowen, Rasmussen). Screenplay, Susan Rice; camera (Filmhouse color), David Spellvin; editor, Joseph Weintraub; music, Cliff Eidelman; sound (Ultra-Stereo), John Pritchett; production design, Jeannine Oppenwall; art direction, David Brisbin; set decoration, Lisa Fischer. Reviewed at Lorimar Studios, Los Angeles, Oct. 23, 1989. MPAA Rating: PG. Running time: **90 MIN.**

Alex Bristow . . . . Karen Allen
Mark Mathias . . . . Armand Assante
Coral Grable . . . . Holly Hunter
Mel Gorsky . . . . Josh Mostel
Dr. Parrish . . . . Richard Libertini
Sheila Sandusky . . . . Alexa Kenin
Tyler Forbes . . . . Jon Mathews
Mrs. Norton . . . . Nan Martin
Cleo Grable . . . . Crystal Buda

■This long-on-the-shelf release from Miramax' Millimeter Films subsidiary is a romantic comedy pitched to young adults. This tale of the coming together of a self-obsessed animal behavior researcher and a lonely composer-turned-music-teacher is going to need all the help it can get. Boxoffice prospects are poor.

The core of Susan Rice's script is a perfectly straightforward Sleeping Beauty story about a woman hiding her emotional needs in her work: She finds those needs unwittingly answered by a patient but persistent male. There's nothing straightforward about this curiously constructed saga, which moves in fits and starts, mirroring all too well the distracted state of its heroine.

Narrative uncertainty springs from the fact that the project was started by one director (Jenny Bowen) and completed by another (the film's producer, Kjehl Rasmussen). Add to that what appears to be a considerable amount of postproduction tinkering and you've got a film in which scenes end before they start, characters make formal entrances only to be whisked away at a moment's notice, and the finale appears to be a flashback from actions that took place at the halfway point.

Even if the filmmakers had come up with something narratively smoother, they wouldn't have been able to smooth out the rough edges of star Karen Allen's performance.

As a researcher committed to proving that chimpanzees can communicate with humans through sign language, Allen's character has a hard time convincing other professionals (and the viewer) of the validity of her ideas.

The chimp she works with is very cute, but so what? And why is Armand Assante, wildly miscast as a tweedy-shy composer, so taken with her snippy, superior ways?

Allen's isn't the only chalk-on-a-blackboard performance on view here. Holly Hunter weighs in with an equally charmless turn as a neighbor of Assante's whose daughter refuses to speak. With Hunter braying and strutting about as she does, one can scarcely blame the child. —Rens.

Astérix et le coup du menhir
(Asterix And The Stone's Blow)
(FRENCH-WEST GERMAN-ANIMATED)

Paris   A Gaumont release of a Gaumont Prod./Extrafilm Prod. (Berlin) coproduction. Produced by Yannick Piel. Directed by Philippe Grimond. Screenplay, Yannick Voigt, Adolph Kabatek, based on the cartoon albums "Le Devin" and "Le Combat des chefs" by René Goscinny and Albert Uderzo; animation director, Keith Ingham; camera (Eastmancolor), Craig Simpson; editor & sound effects, Jean Goudier; music, Michel Colombier, art direction, Michel Guérin. Reviewed at Gaumont Ambassade theater, Paris, Oct. 9, 1989. Running time: **77 MIN.**
Voices: Roger Carel, Pierre Tornade, Henri Labussière, Marie-Anne Chazel, Julien Guiomar, Henri Poirier, Roger Lumont, Patrick Préjean.

■ "Astérix et le coup du menhir" is Gaumont's third effort, and sixth in the total line of animated Asterix pics. Like the predecessors it's a graphically unadventurous but agreeable kidpic that no doubt will please fans (which are particularly legion in West Germany, coproducer of this feature).

New adventures, drawn from two published albums, once again pit Astérix, his brawny dimwitted companion Obelix, and their mutt Idéfix against the Roman legions who have conquered all of Gaul, with the exception of Asterix' village, which is protected by a strength-endowing potion concocted by the community's Druid priest.

Trouble brews when the Druid gets konked into dotty amnesia and no longer can remember the formula for the potion. This leaves the Gauls vulnerable not only to Roman invasion but to the greed of an itinerant charlatan soothsayer, who is quickly recruited by the Latins for their empire-building ends.

Feature was helmed by Philippe Grimond, who was production manager on the previous Asterix cartoon, and produced in Gaumont's specially established animation studio in Paris. —Len.

Aufzeichnungen zu Kleidern und Städten
(A Notebook On Clothes And Cities)
(WEST GERMAN-DOCU)

Montreal   A Road Movies (Berlin) production. Produced by Ulrich Felsberg. Written and directed by Wim Wenders. Camera (color, 16m), Robby Müller, Muriel Edelstein, Uli Kudicke, Wenders, M. Nakajima, M. Chikamori; editor, Dominique Auvrey, Lenie Savietto, Anne Schnee; music, Laurent Petitgand; sound, Jean-Paul Mugel, Axel Arft, Reiner Lorenz. Reviewed at Festival intl. du nouveau cinéma et de la video Montréal, Oct. 25, 1989. Running time: **80 MIN.**

■Vanguard filmmaker Wim Wenders is back on the edge with his latest film, an intellectual exposé of fashion designer Yohji Yamamoto.

Forget Paris, Texas. The principal setting is Paris — complete with a long shot of the famous tower — but that's as close as it gets. Wenders' "notebook" on clothes and cities essentially is an experimental docu that would be classified as educational art if helmed by anyone other than the latest Cannes fest jury prexy.

Wenders innovatively displays his penchant for video images (minus the sex and lies) with a mini hand-held monitor layered on numerous shots of everything from superhighways to film editing machines. The mini Sony displays Yamamoto's talking head intoning theories on fabrics, forms and fashion. Large screen — often used as a backdrop — is filled with desktops, car dashboards, studios and yes, cities.

Unfortunately, this intriguing technique often overpowers the dull subject matter and pretentious script. Droning music further slackens the pace.

Pic is a festival film for diehard Wenders fans. Its potential outside educational or video art outlets is abysmal. — Suze.

Tango War
(ARGENTINE)

Washington   A Magma Prods. presentation of a Eustace production. Executive producer, Víctor Gabirel Chiesa. Directed by Jorge Coscia. Screenplay, Coscia, Julio Fernández Baraibar; camera (color), Miguel Mino; editor, Dario Tedesco; music, José Luis Castiñeira de Dios; sound, Daniel Mosquera; art direction, Gustavo Fidler; choreography, Irene Castro; special effects, Emilio Kauderer; casting, Jorge Tejada. Reviewed at Americas Festival, AFI, Washington, D.C., Oct. 14, 1989. Running time: **98 MIN.**
Angel . . . . William Gramuglia
María . . . . Virginia Innocenti
Ivonne . . . . Inés Estévez
Dick . . . . Charles March
Zakir . . . . Claudio Rissi
Colonel Beresford . . . . Eric Morris
Raguzzi . . . . Alexander Urdapilleta
Also with: Paul Verón, Irene Castro, William James, Julio Fernández Baraibar, James Murray, Ernest Ceretti, Mario Suárez, Willy Lemos, Cecilia Allassia, Robert Murphy, Miguel Fernández Alonso, Sergio Lupardo.

■ "Tango War," first feature by Argentine helmer Jorge Coscia, is a commercial fantasy musical that combines humor and politics into an interesting hybrid. Despite its somewhat obscure theme — British-Argentine relations — it may find international acceptance.

Action takes place sometime after the Falklands war. Buenos Aires has been occupied by the British Army, a multinational lot made up of Scots, Gurkhas, Irishmen, Hindus and Africans. The tango has been outlawed and Argentina turned into a British colony.

A group of tango territorists, led by chief hoofer Angel (William Gramuglia), plots to save national sovereignty by sabotaging British events and dancing in the streets. They are opposed by the Poplins, a rock-inspired street gang topped by Dick (Charles March), whose members counterdance in support of the Brits.

Pic uses broad humor and blatant satire in its depiction of events. Some may find the humor is a bit too broad, in the British slapstick tradition.

Hoofing is excellent, and the stylized streetfighting scenes smolder with aggressive passion. Lensing is imaginative, and occupied B.A. resembles sections of Belfast.

Production viewed is bilingual — the Brits speak English and the Argentines speak Spanish; English-only version also was shot.
                                                    — Lent.

Los espiritus patrióticos
(The Patriotic Spirits)
(ARGENTINE)

Buenos Aires   A Faro Films release of an H M Producciones Cinematográficas presentation. Produced by Mario Levit. Directed by María Victoria Menis, Pablo Nisenson. Screenplay, Menis, Nisenson; camera (color), Salvador Melita; editor, Norberto Rapado; music, Leo Sujatovich, Daniel García; sound, Ernesto Viales; sets Alfredo Iglesias; costumes, María Angélica Iglesias. Reviewed at Trocadero theater, Buenos Aires, April 20, 1989. Rating in Argentina: suitable for ages 16 and up. Running time: **95 MIN.**
Ana . . . . Alicia Zanca
Gigliotti . . . . Héctor Malamud
Carlos . . . . Mauricio Dayub
Mariela . . . . Ana María Caso
Milcer . . . . Juan Manuel Barrau
Belén . . . . Ricardo Fasán
Evaristo . . . . Alfredo Iglesias
Conquistador . . . . Pacheco Fernández
Felicitas . . . . Diana Ingro
Manucho . . . . Jorge D'Elía
Also with: Max Berliner, Ricardo Sendra, Hernán Vargas, Ricardo Belén, Guillermo Marín, Derli Prada, Leo Murray, Carlos March.

■A pleasant, if lightweight, political satire, this is an imaginative and amusing first feature for the codirectors. If it is to travel, it probably will require an explanation for foreign audiences of the archetypes that crop up in its cast.

In this topical ghost story, a crew of Argentine journalists sets out to investigate a plot against the country's democracy. Latter is threatened — literally — by many ghosts from the past.

These specters gather in the dark basement archives of the National Library, forming what they call the Patriotic Spirits' Club. Its pasty-faced ranks include everything from a Spanish conquistador to veterans, wearing camouflage blackface, of the most recent military uprisings against the government.

Prominent members of the club also include a couple of hoity-toity farm owners who always lug their own milk cow around, a friar, a John Bull-like character and an army general from last century's "desert wars." They are organizing a coup with the help of a political cutthroat who hopes to become immortal like them.

This clever plot idea is, unfortunately, cartoonishly developed. Everything is baldly schematic. In this universe all it takes to form one's own government is to blow up the incumbent president.

The satire, however, not only takes aim at anti-democratic forces active in Argentine society, but also at such targets as excessive psychoanalysis (a policeman who spouts nonsensical psychological interpretations of events), cliché-ridden journalistic prose and the country's lousy telephone service (one public telephone, seen in passing, has a sign reading, "It's working").

Costumes, sets and visuals in general are firstrate. A highlight is a spectral party sequence in which the conspirators dance a splendid twist with lyrics by the writer-directors. —Olas.

Face Of The Enemy

Hollywood A Tri-Culture Pictures production. Produced by Behrouz Gueramian, Elizabeth Lynch Brown, Catherine Rocca. Executive producers, David Sahakian, Michael King. Directed by Hassan Ildari. Screenplay, Philip Anderson, based on story by Ildari; camera (CFI color), Peter Indergand; editor, Toby Brown; music, Esfandiar Monfaredzadeh; production design, Marina Kieser, Pierluca DeCarlo; costume design, Sylvia Vasquez; line producer, Bob Jones; art direction, John Allen; sound (Ultra-Stereo), Giovanni Di Simone. Reviewed at Raleigh Studios, L.A., Oct. 13, 1989. (In Women In Film Festival.) No MPAA Rating. Running time: **92 MIN.**

Neiloufar . . . . Rosana DeSoto
James Wald . . . . George DiCenzo
Darya . . . . Cindy Cryer

■ **As a topical melodrama, this low-budget effort wins points for novelty. Despite good performances, its exploration of lives left in the backwash of the Iran hostage crisis strains credibility, undermining audience interest. Theatrical and video prospects would appear to be limited.**

Set in the U.S. in the present, story centers on a former U.S. embassy hostage (George DiCenzo) now working as a security guard at a chemical factory. Haunted by memories of his ordeal (shown in frequent brief flashback montages), this ex-government operative has become so mentally unhinged that he's driven his wife and child away.

Convinced that a woman he sees visiting the plant one day (Rosana DeSoto) was part of a team that tortured him in Iran, he kidnaps her, holding her prisoner in his basement.

For a while, director Hassan Ildari creates some dramatic tension, as we're not entirely sure if the former captive is right about his prisoner or not. When we learn that he is, interest increases; there's great dramatic potential in seeing tables turned.

With this potential comes a new set of questions. Who is this woman? What is she doing living and working Stateside? Is she still an Iranian agent, or has she given up politics in search of the quiet life she's apparently sharing with her school-age daughter? Did captivity drive him batty, or was he always that way?

As none of these questions is answered, the film leaves us with the decidedly ugly spectacle of a woman being held against her will.

Both DiCenzo and DeSoto do yeoman's work, but there's only so much even the best actors can do with material that suggests a low-budget remake of "The Collector."

Technical credits are good. Score by Esfandiar Monfaredzadeh is overinsistent.—Rens.

Goodnight, Sweet Marilyn

New York A Studio Entertainment release of a Chaparral Intl. production. Produced and directed by Larry Buchanan. Screenplay, Buchanan; camera (color), Miles Anderson; editor, Jeff D. Buchanan, Larry Buchanan; music, uncredited; sound, Peter Wolff; associate producer, Marlene O'Connell. Reviewed on Off Hollywood vidcassette, N.Y., Oct. 13, 1989. MPAA Rating: R. Running time: **94 MIN.**
Norma Jean Baker . . . . Misty Rowe
Marilyn Monroe . . . . Paula Lane
Mesquite . . . . Jeremy Slate
Ralph Johnson . . . . Terrance Locke
Ruth Latimer . . . . Patch Mackenzie
Hal James . . . . Preston Hanson
Irving . . . . Marty Zagon
Psychiatrist . . . . Joyce Lower
Gladys Baker . . . . Phyllis Coates
Doctor . . . . Kenneth Hicks
Announcer . . . . Gerry Hopkins
Masseur . . . . George Niles Berry
Also with: Andre Phillipe, Adele Claire, Sal Ponti, Paula Mitchell, Jean Frost, Lillian McBride, Stuart Lancaster, Ivy Bethune, Robert Gribbon, Garth Pillsbury.

■ **"Goodnight, Sweet Marilyn" is an interesting elaboration by conspiracy film specialist Larry Buchanan on his 1975 feature "Goodbye, Norma Jean." Pastiche feature is scheduled for theatrical release before its homevideo usage.**

Though known primarily for his numerous '60s sci-fi pics, Buchanan has made many topical biopics covering everyone from Lee Harvey Oswald and Bonnie & Clyde to Jean Harlow, Howard Hughes, Janis Joplin, Jimi Hendrix and Jim Morrison. Common thread is a healthy interest in exploiting conspiracy theories.

Here he focuses on Marilyn Monroe's final day in August 1962, as fictional pal Mesquite (Jeremy Slate) confesses how he "took her life, to save it." Flashbacks from her deathbed (as two evident spooks from the CIA hover, removing photos of RFK and JFK from the mantelpiece) reveal her life history. A murder attempt by a fake masseur (presumably a deranged fan) also is depicted, but over an hour of the film is made up of footage from the 1975 picture, with a topnotch, moving performance by Misty Rowe as the young Norma Jean Baker in the '40s.

New scenes topline Paula Lane as Marilyn, whose physical and vocal carbon of the Hollywood icon is most effective. For fans unfamiliar with Buchanan's 1975 picture, package should satisfy, though it relies too heavily on old material that will be instantly recognizable to anyone who watched the Misty Rowe picture when it came out or on tv.

Phyllis Coates, erstwhile Lois Lane on tv, has a small role as the ghost of Norma Jean/Marilyn's mother. — Lor.

Real Men Don't Eat Gummy Bears
(WEST GERMAN)

Munich A K.S. Film Karl Spiehs/Lisa Film production. Produced by Karl Spiehs. Directed by Walter Bannert. Screenplay, Florian Burg; camera (color), Hanus Polak; assistant director, Regina Gmeiner; set design, Claus Kottman. Reviewed on vidcassette, Munich, Oct. 7, 1989. Running time: **89 MIN.**
Elephant Joe/Father
  Johannes . . . . Christopher Mitchum
Peter . . . . Robby Rosa
Padre . . . . John Hillerman
Susi . . . . Angela Alvarado
Tony . . . . Bentley C. Mitchum
Bishop . . . . Ernest Borgnine
Col. Menninger . . . . Arthur Brauss
Gundula . . . . Käte Jaenicke
Agent KX 3 . . . . Julia Kent
Agent K 712 . . . . Art Metrano
(English soundtrack)

■ **The laughs are few and far between in "Real Men Don't Eat Gummy Bears." This comedy fails with wornout slapstick, predictable gags and banal plot. It may have some appeal to adolescent males, but few others. Theatrical prospects are nil. Video and tv prospects aren't much better.**

Story is a hodgepodge of confused identities. Tony, played by Bentley C. Mitchum, is a teenage boy in search of his father, whom he has never met. The boy, his friend Peter (Robby Rosa) and their traveling companion Susi (Angela Alvarado) drive to a Spanish village where they believe the father works as a priest.

They show up in the village about the same time as African adventurer Elephant Joe (Christopher Mitchum), the twin brother of Father Johannes (also Mitchum), a village priest. The adventurer is in the village in search of his son, whom he has never seen. He does not know his brother is alive.

Predictable confusion reigns as everyone confuses the celibate, peaceable priest with his macho brother. John Hillerman, as a village priest, becomes irked at his fellow priest's apparent misbehavior. Ernest Borgnine, as the outraged bishop, enters the scene to restore propriety.

Nonsensical subplot barely holds together. It involves bungling spies, chiefly Art Metrano as Agent K 712. Meanwhile, jealousy between the two boys over their female companion threatens their friendship.

Film is loaded with comedy clichés that weren't very funny to begin with. The dialog has no wit or originality. The story often loses its flimsy thread of logic.

Mitchum is stiff and unconvincing in his dual roles. Just about everyone else merely goes through the motions. The exceptions are Borgnine, playing an implausible role with vigor, and Käte Jaenicke, who plays Gundula, the village priest's housekeeper, with charm. Director Walter Bannert could do little with this dismal screenplay. —Dem.

Wilde Harten
(Wild Hearts)
(DUTCH)

Amsterdam A Concorde Film release of an Added Films production. Produced by Dirk Schreiner, Paul Voorthuysen. Written and directed by Jindra Markus. Camera (color), Peter de Bont; editor, Henk van Eeghen; music, Erik Brusse, Michiel Jansen; sound, Marcel de Hoogd; casting, Frank Krom. Reviewed at Cinema theater, Amsterdam, Sept. 1, 1989. Running time: **94 MIN.**
  With: Alexandra van Marken, Hans Oldigs, Herbert Flack, Wim van Rooij, Frank Schaafsma, Joop Doderer, Andrea Domburg.

■ **Jindra Markus, who wrote and directed three successful and original shorts, has made a feature that strings together several episodes that do not automatically add up to a full-length film. Pic creates little sympathy for characters who are sometimes staggeringly stupid full-fledged members of the Me Generation.**

"Wild Hearts" tells of a small-time singer trying to build a career and a small-time crook trying to make his reputation. They meet, fall in love and couple in artistically arranged poses.

Then we get a conman who can swim and run fast, forgeries, extortions, hold-ups, murder, mayhem, drug abuse, plus an operation gone wrong. It's never quite clear who does what to whom, when and why, and why nobody thinks of calling the cops.

Lack of budget shows here (pic was brought in for about $700,000) but so, too, does absence of a producer with discerning control. It's a shame because there are some nice sequences, but Markus' directorial left too often doesn't know what the right is doing.

Veteran actors Andrea Domburg and Joop Doderer rely (successfully) on their routine to stay on course. The new discoveries, Alexandra van Marken and Hans Oldigs, flounder a bit, groping for material that doesn't exist. Van Marken, who is soon to star in a local legit staging of "Cabaret," sings nicely, and Oldigs benefits from some astonishing makeup.
—*Wall.*

Norman's Awesome Experience
(CANADIAN)

New York . A Norstar Entertainment production, in association with Salter Street Films. Produced by Paul Donovan, Peter Simpson. Supervising producer, Ray Sager. Written and directed by Donovan. Camera (Medallion color), Vic Sarin; editor, Stephan Fanfara; music, Paul Zaza; production design, Emanuel Jannasch, Bruce McKenna; additional direction, Ron Oliver; 2d unit director, Cordell Wynne; associate producer, Michael McTegue. Reviewed on South Gate Entertainment vidcassette, N.Y., Oct. 8, 1989. MPAA Rating: PG-13. Running time:

90 MIN.
Norman	Tom McCamus
Erika	Laurie Paton
Umberto	Jacques Lussier
Titanus	Lee Broker
Fabius	David Hemblen
Serpicus	Marcos Woinsky
Felix	Gabriela Salas
Blacksmith	Armando Capo
Dr. Nobbelmeyer	Brian Downey

■This entertaining time-travel feature, released direct to video, was made in 1987 as "A Switch In Time" but retitled to take advantage of the hit Orion release "Bill & Ted's Excellent Adventure."

Oddball premise has hip young lab assistant Norman (Tom McCamus) transported back to the days of ancient Rome due to a power surge at the Geneva high-energy physics installation where he works. Accompanying him are a pretty model (Laurie Paton) and her Italian photographer (Jacques Lussier), who've secretly entered the facility to shoot a glamour layout for Omni magazine.

Unlike "Bill & Ted," pic doesn't hop around but takes the cast on a single adventure, fighting barbarians in remote European colonies controlled by ancient Rome. It's nicely filmed on Argentine locations. Lack of variety is a drawback in a genre in which time paradoxes and sci-fi gimmickry usually makes for most of the fun.

Cast does a fine job, particularly Paton as the feisty heroine. Golden oldies on the soundtrack aim for the target youth audience. Special effects are modest. —*Lor.*

DENVER FEST REVIEWS

Yours To Keep
(DOCU)

Denver A Forum production. Produced and directed by Merce and Laurie Taylor-Williams. In color. Reviewed at Denver Intl. Film Festival, Oct. 15, 1989. Running time: 75 MIN.

■In John Taylor, 19-year-old brother of filmmaker Laurie Taylor-Williams, "Yours To Keep" has the ideal subject for a probing of the life of a man held back from normal pursuits by Down's syndrome. Engrossing, affecting film makes clear he is not retarded but does need more time to think things through (an effect of imbalanced body chemistry).

Raised in circumstances as close to normal as feasible, John Taylor connects to the "real" world through his passion for '70s rock music, about which he is extraordinarily knowledgeable.

The Taylor-Williams docu moves close to its subject, watching him prepare for a high school graduation dance, receive his diploma and go job hunting as he explores his potential for independent living. With his family he expresses himself freely, but the intensity of his thinking and memory collide with his efforts to express himself to strangers.

First job is at an animal-care center; he takes his work so literally that he spends his time petting the dogs rather than carrying out his assigned responsibilities. He interviews with a radio station where he feels his familiarity with '70s rock will be of use but is told his hiring would not be economically justifiable.

Out of the blue, he lands a supporting role in the feature film "The Seventh Sign," starring Demi Moore. Nurtured in this democratic environment by cast members and crew, Taylor acquires a resilience that tames his hesitancy in speech and pulls him further into the "real" world. At film's end, he gets a job with the Sam Goody music chain that draws on his intelligence and strengthened ability to communicate.

The world for Taylor is difficult, but in this study, which exudes considerable optimism for handicapped individuals, the promise of independent living seems quite possible.

Lensing is good, but soundtrack in blackout sequences where Taylor converses with his toy friend Kermit is affected by extraneous noise. There may be more rock music than all but aficionados will like.—*Alyo.*

Forevermore: Biography Of A Leach Lord

Denver An Eric Saks production. Produced and directed by Saks. In color. Reviewed at Denver Intl. Film Festival, Oct. 15, 1989. Running time: 83 MIN.

■Blend of avant-garde filmmaking and environmental concerns results in a messy film, short on coherence and long on ways of disorienting viewers.

Skittish in coming to grips with a personal story as well as the problem of pollution in America, this film puts viewers off by playing around with time, simultaneously moving forward and backward, without bringing pertinent insights to bear.

The pseudonymous figure of Isaac Hudak is the son of a brilliant physicist who uses the son in bizarre experiments that succeed in turning the son against the father, as well as against toxic producers whom he identifies with his father.

Figure of Hudak is played by three actors who do not age well. Hudak as young man does not emerge intact though the elderly, ailing figure who haunts racetracks comes across as believable if not particularly interesting. Events in these lives are obscure and the en-

vironmental aspects of the film are slighted by poorly lit photography.
—*Alyo.*

In A Pig's Eye

Denver An Elsinore production. Produced by David Brownstein, John Saffron. Written and directed by Saffron. Camera (color), Jim Hayman; editor, Peter Friedman; art direction, Bonnie Saltzman; costumes, Alison Lances. Reviewed at Denver Intl. Film Festival, Oct. 14, 1989. Running time: 86 MIN.
With: Marian Seldes, David Canary, Tudor Sherrard, Alexa Lambert, Bobbi Jo Lathan, David Bailey.

■Zany without going over the brink, this spoof of "Grand Hotel" intrigues is comically diverting with its absurd incidents, batty characters and bizarre setting.

Action focuses on the arrival at the Hotel Copacabana of Isabel Purvis (Marian Seldes), paranoid tobacco industry p.r. lady, for that group's convention. The hotel's run-down exterior masks its day-glo interiors and the jungle of its conservatory. Everyone is confused as to who is who.

Purvis is convinced that villains are out to subvert her gathering, but certain a good eight hours' sleep will enable her to halt the enemy attack. But it is clear no such respite is in store. Her hotelowner husband, a quack scientist, is working on proof that smoking is not injurious to the health.

The guest list of the hotel is not long, but the staff is weird enough to extend the foolishness. Besides the owner, there is a blond, sleepwalking bimbo seeking an acting career; the bellboy Woodrow, the not-so-devoted son of the owner, and the chambermaid, none other than the daughter of the tobacco p.r. woman.

Writer-director John Saffron sustains his whimsy amiably. Sparkle is brought to the film by leading lady Seldes, who kindles something of the gravity and hauteur of Margaret Dumont. Seldes is an eccentric blend of elegance and idiocy, truly a polished performer.

David Canary, from the tv soap "All My Children," fails to get an edge on his hotelier role to make him sufficiently extravagant. Tudor Sherrard is a capable young talent. Alexa Lambert could have brought more sparkle to her slight role.

David Brownstein's score bounces the film along with its musical jokes and upbeat tropicana. Camerawork by Jim Hayman captures Bonnie Saltzman's dazzling interiors smartly.

The film's satirical jabs against smoking will be appreciated by nonsmokers. —Alyo.

Because Of That War
(ISRAELI-DOCU)

Denver   An Israel Film production. Directed by Orna Ben Dor Niv. Camera (color), Oren Schmukler. Reviewed at Denver Intl. Film Festival, Oct. 15, 1989. Running time: 93 MIN.
With: Yehuda Poliker, Jaco Poliker, Ya' acove Gilad, Halina Birnbaum.

■This painful documentary places its cameras in front of two survivors with particularly ghastly histories of the Holocaust to relate and lets them talk and reminisce about that period of cataclysmic violence.

Were the materials of this documentary dramatized it would be difficult if not impossible to accept its horrors. In the crudely captioned, shakily translated, poorly shot film, understatement is perhaps the only way the survivors could tell of their loss and near slaughter.

Distanced though the film may make the Holocaust, the reality of the brutality is expressed by Halina Birnbaum and Jaco Poliker, who barely escaped horrifying deaths. Each has a son in music, Yehuda Poliker and Ya' acove Gilad, two well-known Israeli musicians whose material comes out of that time of terror.

Their melancholy and wild songs are welcome diversions in a film that concentrates on the Holocaust to the exclusion of forward-looking aspects of Israeli life. —Alyo.

The Little Mermaid
(ANIMATED)

Hollywood   A Buena Vista release of a Walt Disney Pictures presentation; in association with Silver Screen Partners IV. Produced by Howard Ashman, John Musker. Written and directed by Musker, Ron Clements; based on the fairy tale by Hans Christian Andersen. Directing animators, Mark Henn, Glen Keane, Duncan Marjoribanks, Ruben Aquino, Andreas Deja, Matthew O'Callaghan; music, Alan Menken; songs, Ashman, Menken; art direction, Michael A. Peraza Jr., Donald A. Towns; supervising editor, John Carnochan; visual effects supervisor, Mark Dindal; layout supervisor, David A. Dunnet; backgrounds supervisor, Towns; computer animation, Tina Price, Andrew Schmidt; supervising sound Edemann; animation camera (color), supervi-Edemann; animation camera (color), supervisor, John Cunningham; assistant director, Michael Serrian; associate producer, Maureen Donley; casting, Mary V. Buck, Susan Edelman. Reviewed at Walt Disney Studios, Burbank, Calif., Nov. 1, 1989. MPAA Rating: G. Running time: 82 MIN.

Voices of:
Ariel . . . . .Jodi Benson
Ursula .Pat Carroll
Sebastian . . . . .Samuel E. Wright
Triton . . . . .Kenneth Mars
Scuttle . . . . .Buddy Hackett
Flounder . . . . .Jason Marin
Eric . . . . .Christopher Daniel Barnes
Louis . . . . .René Auberjonois
Grimsby . . . . .Ben Wright

■ Look for Disney to be awash in a sea of green thanks to this gloriously animated blend of classic fairy tale elements with broad humor.

Borrowing liberally from the studio's classics, "The Little Mermaid" may represent its best animated feature since the underrated "Sleeping Beauty" in 1959 and, based on recent returns on lesser films, seems destined to swim into the sunset leaving boxoffice records for the genre in its wake.

That should come as no surprise to admirers of "The Great Mouse Detective," writer-director collaborators John Musker and Ron Clements' exceptionally appealing 1986 animated feature that helped salvage the art form at the studio after it had nearly sank into "The Black Cauldron."

Once again, Clements and Musker have anchored the film with a wonderfully camp villain, Ursula the seawitch, who provides menace and a marvelously droll flair — à la "Mouse Detective's" Ratigan — here thanks to the vocal wizardry of Pat Carroll.

The other key is equally consistent with the genre but marvelously realized, stemming from the clear positioning of the film as an animated musical us-

Original Version
Rousalochka
(The Little Mermaid)
(SOVIET)

A Sovexport release of Gorki Studios production. Features entire cast. Directed by V. Bychkov. Screenplay, V. Vitkovitch from the story by Hans Christian Andersen; camera (Sovcolor), Emil Vageschain; music, Evgueni Krylatov. Reviewed at Karlovy Vary Film Fest, July 17, 1976. Running time, 80 MIN.
Mermaid . . . . .Vika Novikova
Troubador . . . . .Valentin Nikulin
Princess . . . . .Galina Artemova
Prince . . . . .Y. Senkevitch
Witch . . . . .G. Volchek

ing songs (hummable, lilting, and in one instance piercingly beautiful on the order of "Les Misérables") to carry and advance the story.

The source material is a Hans Christian Andersen tale that's been tailored to the conventions of the animated feature, which may rob the original story of some of its emotional wallop but nonetheless provides a fertile seabed for the wild imaginations of the animators.

The mermaid princess Ariel lives in her sea-lord father Triton's undersea kingdom but yearns for a life above, made all the more haunting to her when she rescues a handsome young prince from the sea. Disobeying her father, she makes a pact with the seawitch enabling her to go ashore and get the prince to fall in love with her — her soul hanging in the balance, her beautiful voice as collateral.

Adults and children who've devoured the Disney classics will recognize various inspirations for the characters: "Fantasia's" mythology sequence for Triton, "Pinocchio" for Ariel's crustacean conscience Sebastian and the underwater sequences, a pair of eels reminiscent of "Lady And The Tramp's" evil Siamese cats and "Sleeping Beauty's" diabolical Maleficent.

Still those parts, as assembled, produce an utterly satisfying whole — one that's romantic, suspenseful and at times extremely funny.

The character design helps immensely, as animals of the cartoonishly cute variety counterbalance the classical approach to the human (and humanlike) leads. Ursula alone proves a visual feast, a thick-jawed nightmare who swishes about on eight octopus legs in one of the film's more inspired inventions.

The animation proves lush and fluid, augmented by the use of shadow and light as elements like fire, sun and water illuminate the characters. An early action sequence featuring a shark may not be one of the more innovative designs but provides enough thrills that it would likely have served as the finale of one of the studio's other recent features.

Key contributions are made by lyricist Howard Ashman (who coproduced with Musker) and composer Alan Menken, whose songs frequently begin slowly but build in cleverness and intensity.

Menken's score is outstanding, and the film's sprightly "Under The Sea" number (voiced by the Jamaican-accented Samuel E. Wright in another bravura turn) emerges as an instant classic. Newcomer Jodi Benson (Ariel) also exhibits a show-stopping set of pipes on the ballad "Part Of Your World," a "Les Miz" ringer.

Most technical aspects are superb, though the filmmakers succumb to the annoying MTV-influenced convention of some too-quick cuts (why not let us look at some of these scenes?) and jarringly awkward edits, as if overly concerned with rushing the story along.

No need to hurry, except perhaps to the bank as "The Little Mermaid" shows off its legs. —Bril.

Last Exit To Brooklyn
(WEST GERMAN)

Paris   AMLF release (Cinecom in the U.S.) of a Neue Constantin Film production, in collaboration with Bavaria Film and Allied Filmmakers. Executive producer, Bernd Eichinger. Coproducer, Herman Weigel. Directed by Uli Edel. Screenplay, Desmond Nakano, based on novel by Hubert Rechy; camera (color), Stefan Czapsky; editor, Peter Przygodda; music, Mark Knopfler; art direction, David Chapman; costumes, Carol Oditz; sound, Danny Michael, Milan Bor; makeup, Kathryn Bihr; assistant directors, Don French, Carla Corwin; production manager, Dieter Meyer; associate producers, Anna Gross, Jake Eberts. Reviewed at the Marignan-Concorde theater, Paris, Oct. 30, 1989. Running time: 102 MIN.
Harry Black . . . . .Stephen Lang
Tralala . . . . .Jennifer Jason Leigh
Big Joe . . . . .Burt Young
Vinnie . . . . .Peter Dobson
Boyce . . . . .Jerry Orbach
Sal . . . . .Stephen Baldwin
Georgette . . . . .Alexis Arquette
Spook . . . . .Cameron Johann
(English soundtrack version)

■West Germany's latest slumming expedition into the hinterlands of American society, "Last

Exit To Brooklyn" is a bleak tour of urban hell that will have a tough audience sell ahead of it.

Bernd Eichinger's $16-million Stateside-lensed production of Hubert Rechy's controversial 1964 novel seemed an unlikely choice for screen translation by Europeans, though the story's dark, oppressive social vision must have struck a quasi-expressionist chord.

Eichinger, screenwriter Desmond Nakano and director Uli Edel have succeeded in presenting a conscientious illustration that is well acted and technically impeccable, but it doesn't hold a scalpel to the lacerating torrential prose that made the book so cringingly urgent. The film's brute dramatics, sordid naturalism and candid treatment of violence and sexuality now seem blandly conventional by current movie standards.

For the spectator, film's abiding obstacle is an unsavory gallery of largely contemptible characters who are at best pitiable and at worst have not developed beyond Neanderthal awareness. Edel, whose international reputation was made on the 1980 teen drug drama "Christiane F.," proves himself an accomplished professional ripe for Hollywood assignments. What he lacks here is that fundamental gift of empathy that would make these damned souls more than just figures under a cinematic microscope.

Optioned by a number of filmmakers since its publication (notably Stanley Kubrick and Brian DePalma), novel long was thought unfilmable, in part because of its short-story structure and large cast of characters. This obstacle largely has been surmounted in Nakano's well-structured screenplay, which sets time and place, introduces the players and interweaves their destinies with economical story logic. Peter Przygodda's editing brings it all together for a taut 102-minute run.

Action is set in a working-class section of Brooklyn in 1952, close by the Navy yards where young Americans are embarking for the Korean War. Residents, however, couldn't care less about happenings beyond their own back yards — many engaged in a bitter 6-month strike against a local factory. A sense of stagnation intensifies personal and group discontents and passions. Film's spectacular centerpiece is a well-staged riot pitting strikers against police when factory management uses scab labor to break the picket lines.

One of the protagonists is Stephen Lang, a venal married shop steward and secretary of the strike office who has been dipping into the union till to subsidize his first homosexual affair. When union boss Jerry Orbach boots him out for failing to show at the factory clash, the penniless Lang is in turn dropped by his mercenary lover. His despair drives him to make a pass at a young boy. Ironically, a subhuman band of local goons rescues the boy and thrashes Lang to within an inch of his life (and "crucifies" him on a wooden crossbeam).

These roughnecks (used by Orbach to attack the scab workers) are linked with film's other major character, a tawdry, hard-drinking teen hooker named Tralala (Jennifer Jason Leigh), who lures unsuspecting bar-hopping servicemen to a back lot where they are mugged and robbed by the band.

Leigh abandons the guys when she is picked up by a gentle, sentimental soldier who wants to treat her like a real girlfriend during his last days before shipping out. Leigh plays along, expecting a handsome payoff for her company; instead she gets only a tender farewell letter any normal-hearted woman probably would cherish. Returning to the neighborhood bar she gets drunk and defiantly declares herself open for sexual services to joint's entire clientele.

The resulting gangbang, one of the most horrific passages in Rechy's book, is here sanitized and given a hopeful finish. While Rechy's tart is literally raped to death, the film's heartless hooker not only survives but shows her first signs of feeling when she tries (in a Pietà-like pose) to console the local teen admirer (the boy Lang has tried to pick up) who comes across her battered naked body.

Other Rechy characters who wind through the film include notably the young, doped-out tranvestite (Alexis Arquette) who first arouses Lang and later is fatally struck by a car (driven by cameo player Rechy himself). In a more caricatured subplot, a worker arranges a hypocritical marriage between his fat stupid daughter and the lowlife who seduced and impregnated her.

Apart from the trite Christian symbolism, some heavy social satire and occasional portentous touches (such as smoking manholes à la Martin Scorsese), Edel's direction is relatively restrained (much of the graphic violence was edited out of the picture after a private screening for west coast film execs). Stefan Czapsky's lensing makes evocative nocturnal use of the notorious Red Hook section of Brooklyn, where most of the exteriors were filmed at night in conditions just as dangerous as those described in the book.

Edel is adept with his native American cast, notably Lang, Leigh and Arquette (whose screen time is unfortunately curtailed). Orbach is fine as the unscrupulous union leader. Peter Dobson, Steve Baldwin and Cameron Johann are okay in supporting roles. Tech credits are all firstrate. —Len.

The Bounty Hunter

New York   An Action Intl. Pictures production. Executive producers, David Winters, Bruce Lewin. Produced by Fritz Matthews. Directed by Robert Ginty. Screenplay, Thomas Baldwin; camera (Image Transform color), Robert Baldwin; editor, David Campling, Jonathan Shaw; music, Tim James, Steve McClintock, Tim Heintz; sound, Todd Felker; art direction, Laurey Lummus; assistant director, Scott Clark; stunt coordinator, Bob Ivy. Reviewed on AIP vidcassette, N.Y., Oct. 24, 1989. No MPAA Rating. Running time: 90 MIN.
Duke Evans . . . . Robert Ginty
Sheriff Bennett . . . . Bo Hopkins
Marion Foot . . . . Loeta Waterdown
Kevin Foot . . . . Melvin Holt
Barnes . . . . John White
Jimmy Gibbons . . . . Robert Knott

■Robert Ginty makes an underwhelming directorial debut in "The Bounty Hunter," a routine vengeance feature, released direct-to-video.

Reportedly doubling as a pilot for a hoped-for tv series, pic fails to set up the requisite characters for such a venture. Instead, topliner Ginty is his usual taciturn self, heading to a small Oklahoma town to avenge the death of an Indian with whom he served in Vietnam. His skills as a bounty hunter are displayed briefly in a prolog but irrelevant to the main action.

Villain is Bo Hopkins, playing his familiar smalltown sheriff role. This time he's corrupt, involved in a land deal with oilmen. Other key character is the Indian's pretty sister (Loeta Waterdown), who gives Ginty a tour of local Indian culture that provides pic's upbeat message and avoids stereotyping.

Redneck bad buys in league with Hopkins are stereotypes, however, and pic offers no suspense. Contrived finish doesn't hold water.
—Lor.

Meet The Hollowheads

Hollywood   A Moviestore Entertainment release of a Linden production. Produced by Joseph Grace, John Chavez. Executive producer, Pippa Scott. Directed by Tom Burman. Screenplay, Burman, Lisa Morton; additional dialog, Stanley Mieses; camera (Foto-Kem color), Marvin Rush; editor, Carl Kress; music, Glenn Jordan; production design, Ed Eyth; visual consultant, Ron Cobb; costume design, Eduardo Castro; sound (Dolby), Bo Harwood; assistant director, Matt Hinkley. Reviewed at Raleigh Studios, L.A., Nov. 1, 1989. MPAA Rating: PG-13. Running time: 86 MIN.
Henry Hollowhead . . . . John Glover
Miriam Hollowhead . . . . Nancy Mette
Mr. Crabneck . . . . Richard Portnow
Billy Hollowhead . . . . Matt Shakman
Cindy Hollowhead . . . . Juliette Lewis
Bud Hollowhead . . . . Lightfield Lewis
Joey . . . . Joshua Miller
Babbleaxe . . . . Anne Ramsey
Top Drone . . . . Logan Ramsey
Oliver . . . . Chaz Conner
Grandpa . . . . Shotgun Britton

■ "Meet The Hollowheads" is a dismally unfunny attempt at futuristic comedy by noted special effects makeup creator Tom Burman.

The debuting director and coscripter manages some visual inventiveness on a low budget, but the witless attempt to blend sitcom characters and gross-out humor falls completely flat.

The Moviestore Entertainment release, which has had some fest exposure, is a marginal b.o. entry.

Lensed under the title of "Life On The Edge," "Hollowheads" has been described by coscripter Lisa Morton as a blend of "Father Knows Best" and "Eraserhead," which should make both Robert Young and David Lynch feel insulted. The scripters' conception of a post-nuclear age in which people live in tunnels, receiving sustenance through a network of tubes, is repetitiously developed, and the story seems pointless.

The Hollowhead family — played in broad sitcom style by John Glover, Nancy Mette, Matt Shakman, Juliette Lewis and Lightfield Lewis — are supposed to be typically vapid members of a society that is preoccupied with preparing and eating weird-looking food. Mette's dithering mother character spends most of her time in the kitchen working with bizarre instruments and creatures to produce disgusting concoctions.

The scripters' sophomoric idea of wit is to spin off endless feeble and vulgar puns around such words as tubes, orifices, reaming, suction, purging, viscosity, leaking, discharge and going with the flow.

Although the film could have some limited appeal to subteens who like sick humor of the "Garbage Pail Kids" variety, for most viewers "Hollowheads" simply will seem unpleasant, with its fixation on crude and cruel humor.

Taking as its centerpiece the familiar sitcom situation of bringing the boss home for dinner, Burman indulges in graphic violence that lays any idea of comedy to rest.

Among the hapless cast stuck in this much, Juliette Lewis manages some bright moments as the pubescent teenage daughter, and the late Anne Ramsey brings a touch of genuine weirdness to her role as an angry tube worker called Babbleaxe. Ramsey, who had a severe speech defect, has her dialog displayed in subtitles as she colorfully rants.

The industrious production design by Ed Eyth, with Ron Cobb as visual consultant, makes the most of the inexpensive sets. Marvin Rush's lensing is suitably gaudy, although the overuse of a wide-angle lens to make characters look geekish gets tiresome, as does Glenn Jordan's intentionally discordant music.

Exec producer Pippa Scott, who worked with producers Joseph Grace and John Chavez, could have looked a lot harder for material in launching her Linden Prods. indie banner.—*Mac.*

Best Of The Best

New York   A Taurus Entertainment release, in association with Kuys Entertainment Group, of an SVS and The Movie Group presentation. Executive producers, Michael Holzman, Frank Giustra. Produced by Phillip Rhee, Peter E. Strauss. Line producer, Marlon Staggs. Directed by Bob Radler. Screenplay, Paul Levine, from story by Rhee, Levine; additional dialog, Max Strom; camera (CFI color), Doug Ryan; editor, William Hoy; music, Paul Gilman; sound (Dolby), Bill Daly; production design, Kim Rees; art direction, Maxine Shepard; costume design, Cynthia Bergstrom; assistant director, Chuck Conner; production manager, Joel Deloach; stunt coordinator, Simon Rhee; 2d unit camera, Jerry Watson; associate producer, Deborah Scott; casting, Jack Tarzia. Reviewed at Magno Review I screening room, N.Y., Oct. 30, 1989. MPAA Rating: PG-13. Running time: 95 MIN.
Alex . . . . Eric Roberts
Coach Couzo . . . . James Earl Jones
Catherine Wade . . . . Sally Kirkland
Tommy . . . . Phillip Rhee
Travis . . . . Christopher Penn
Virgil . . . . John Dye
Sonny . . . . David Agresta
Also with: Tom Everett, Louise Fletcher, John P. Ryan, Edan Gross, Simon Rhee, Ahmad Rashad, Master Hee Il Cho, James Lew, Ken Nagayama, Ho Sik Pak, Dae Kyu Chang, Samantha Scully, Adrianne Sachs, Kane Hodder.

■A lot of talent is wasted in "Best Of The Best," a corny, uninvolving sports competition pic about martial artists. B.o. should be tame.

Feature is a showcase for Phillip Rhee, Korean-American martial arts teacher who coproduced the film, worked on the story and toplines as a member of the U.S. national team headed for South Korea to compete. He also wants to settle the score with the Korean champ who killed his brother in a match.

Also on the team, despite a shoulder injury, is Eric Roberts; an overweight Christopher Penn, looking more like a wrestler than karate expert, as well as contrasting types John Dye and David Agresta. Thankless roles go to James Earl Jones as the martinet of a coach; Sally Kirkland, overly restrained as the mystical assistant trainer who's deeply into oriental philosophy, and Louise Fletcher as Robert's sobby mom.

Under debuting helmer Bob Radler's by-the-numbers direction, "Best" is dull and remote throughout. Considerable unintentional humor is developed by imitation: slavish aping of John Avildsen's "Rocky" and "Karate Kid" formats, plus a slow-motion training jog through the surf right out of "Chariots Of Fire."

If it weren't sunk by its derivative nature, "Best" would flounder through sickly, unbelievable plot devices that have the cast displaying pained expressions. Worst gimmick in Paul Levine's script is placing Roberts' 5-year-old son in the hospital in serious condition so that Roberts must nearly miss out on the competition to visit him; suddenly, the kid and Fletcher are in the stands in Korea (!) watching Roberts win through improbable (undoubtedly an afterthought) intercutting.

Finale tries to be different in stressing brotherhood rather than the genre's surefire elements of vengeance and black hat bloodlust. However, the "uplift" switcheroo proves counterproductive when the hero (Phillip Rhee) backs off wimpily just when revenge is nigh, and then the heinous villain (Simon Rhee) turns into mister nice guy after kicking Phillip in the groin repeatedly.

Phillip Rhee shows promise here, while the big-name cast is stifled by poor material. Fights are unexciting, including a stupid barroom brawl during the boys' "last night out" before training, and won't satisfy an action audience weaned on the visceral predecessors of Bruce Lee and Jean-Claude Van Damme.

Tech credits are modest, with one song even echoing "Eye Of The Tiger" from the "Rocky" films. —*Lor.*

No Justice

New York   A Richfield's Releasing release of a Richfield's Prods. Ltd. production. Executive producer, Theresa Marie Martin. Produced, written and directed by Richard Wayne Martin. Codirector, Fred Dresch. Camera (CFL and Cinefilm color), Karen Edmunsen Bean; editor, Barbara J. Boguski; music, Mike Headrick; sound, David Rodgers; art direction, Gretchen Oehler; associate producer, Michael McVerry. Reviewed on vidcassette (Richfield's), N.Y., Oct. 21, 1989. MPAA Rating: R. Running time: 91 MIN.
Virgel Johnson . . . . Bob Orwig
Mayor Johnson . . . . Cameron Mitchell
Sheriff Smith . . . . Steve Murphy
Bo Johnson . . . . Phillip Newman
Susie Willis . . . . Susan Ashley Pohlman
Sissy Taylor . . . . Liza Case
Preacher Smith . . . . Richard Wayne Martin
Preacher's wife . . . . Camille Keaton
Also with: Mike McVerry, Bobby Storm, Tise Tansil, Randall K. Pierce, Donald Farmer.

■"No Justice," a pleasant throwback to drive-in movies, is an action tale of corruption and vengeance in a small Tennessee town. Picture has been in local theatrical release since August.

Debuting director Richard Wayne Martin gets things off to a fast start in a lengthy opening that crosscuts among several spheres of action, ending in a fiery car crash by speeders trying to escape police pursuit.

Main plotline involves the mayor (Cameron Mitchell) pursuing an oldtime vendetta to displace a rival clan so he can use the property for a marijuana and moonshine business. Mitchell installs his dim-witted nephew Virgel (Bob Orwig) as the new sheriff after Sheriff Smith (Steve Murphy) leaves town abruptly with pretty Susie (Susan Ashley Pohlman).

All hell breaks loose when Virgel turns out to be a sadistic ogre, raping his girlfriend (Liza Case) and then imprisoning and torturing her brother (Mike McVerry). When state officials refuse to intervene in the local mayhem, the feud escalates and isn't resolved until Sheriff Smith returns and the feds finally arrive.

Though cast is uneven, pic builds up convincing good ole boy atmosphere and has enough interesting subplots to keep the viewer alert. Violence and sexual scenes are handled tastefully.
—*Lor.*

Rakevet Ha'Emek
(The Valley Train)
(ISRAELI)

Tel Aviv   A Rakevet Ha'Emek production. Produced and directed by Jonathan Paz. Screenplay, Nissim Zohar, Yaakov Lazar, Hanan Zess, Paz; camera (16m, color), Ofer Inov; editor, Tamar Yaron; music, Kobi Hess; art direction, Ariel Glazer; production manager, Israel Arieli. Reviewed at Tel Aviv Cinematheque, Oct. 14, 1989. Running time: 85 MIN.
Gadi . . . . Dan Turgeman
Yoav . . . . Ami Ushpitz
Ruthie . . . . Netta Moran

■With all due sympathy and appreciation for the efforts invested here, Jonathan Paz' first feature is a pretty amateurish affair, whose aims are much higher than its means.

The confrontation between Yoav, an unimaginative but charming macho bully who is the hero of all the kids in the kibbutz, and Gadi, who starts by adoring him and ends by pitying him, is supposed to reflect the change of mentality in a kibbutz from the '50s to the '60s. The idea itself is a legitimate one, even if some of the conflicts have been better exploited in films like "Noa At 17" and "Stalin's Disciples."

The problem lies with the direction, clumsy and insecure most of the way, and with a cast that is more than willing to do anything required, if not necessarily capable of doing it. Except for Dan Turgeman (Gadi), none has any real acting experience, and they perform accordingly.

Ami Ushpitz (Yoav) is the most embarrassing case. He is on camera almost constantly, but is so obviously conscious of it, that he can't relax one single minute in a role which demands spontaneity most of all.

Given the strict budget, the film is technically acceptable. —*Edna.*

Stepfather II

New York   A Millimeter Films release of an ITC Entertainment Group production. Executive producer, Carol Lampman. Produced by William Burr, Darin Scott. Directed by Jeff Burr. Screenplay, John Auerbach, based on characters created by Carolyn Lefcourt, Brian Garfield, Donald E. Westlake; camera (Foto-Kem color), Jacek Laskus; editor, Pasquale A. Buba; music, Jim Manzie, in association with Pat Regan; sound (Dolby), David Brownlow; production design, Bernadette Disanto; art direction, Aram Allen; set decoration, Johnna Butler; costume design, Julie Carnahan; assistant director, Jan Ervin; production manager, Llewellyn Wells; special makeup effects, Michelle Burke; casting, Rosemary Welden. Reviewed at Loews Astor Plaza, N.Y., Nov. 4, 1989. MPAA Rating: R.

Running time: **86 MIN.**
Dr. Gene Clifford . . . . Terry O'Quinn
Carol Grayland . . . . Meg Foster
Matty Crimmins . . . . Caroline Williams
Todd Grayland . . . . Jonathan Brandis
Dr. Joseph Danvers . . . . Henry Brown
Phil Grayland . . . . Mitchell Laurance
Also with: Leon Martell, Renata Scott, John O'Leary, Eric Brown.

■ **This dull sequel reduces the intriguing premise of Joseph Ruben's original "Stepfather" to the level of an inconsequential, tongue-in-cheek slasher film. Theatrical prospects are poor, but there's name recognition in ancillary markets.**

Terry O'Quinn as the murderous, average guy vainly trying to mimic the American Family ideal was killed off at the end of the Ruben pic. Sequel opens with recap of previous finalé (including brief footage of previous costars Shelley Hack and Jill Schoelen), followed by O'Quinn waking up in a Washington State asylum with several chest scars indicating his not-quite-fatal wounds. Some 80 minutes later he's repeatedly stabbed in the chest again for a phony open ending.

John Auerbach's deficient screenplay has characters badly state all the interesting themes that were developed dramatically in the Carolyn Lefcourt-Brian Garfield-Donald Westlake original. Another drawback is the use of silly taglines ("Make room for daddy" is used to anchor the pic's ad campaign as well) assigned O'Quinn during his periodic bouts of mania. They're silly, not funny, and reduce the film to camp.

Another damaging change is shift in emphasis, despite the title, away from the stepchild to new mama. Daughter Jill Schoelen was the central character previously, with much of that pic's danger and suspense due to her realization her new daddy wasn't the ideal husband mom Shelley Hack took him to be. This time, O'Quinn bamboozles the shrink at the asylum (Henry Brown) and escapes, lifts the identity of a deceased family therapist from the newspaper obituary, and moves into an L.A. suburb. He romances the pretty real estate divorcée who's his neighbor (Meg Foster).

Pic builds towards their impending marriage, but 13-year-old son Todd (Jonathan Brandis) is only a minor character who does not figure in the dramatics, leaving a hole in the story structure. Instead, it is another neighbor (Caroline Williams), the postal delivery woman, who is suspicious of O'Quinn. She, like Foster, is being coun-

seled by O'Quinn in his group-therapy-style family sessions. Her suspicion grows when she starts reading his mail illegally. Although Williams' tumbling to his fake identity makes for a funny scene, final clues (humming a tune, stealing an incriminating wine bottle) leading to Foster's unraveling the mystery are stupidly injected into the narrative and crudely resolved.

Auerbach's script also is unconvincing on simple matters such as escaped looney O'Quinn's never-mentioned source of income which enables him to rent a new home while on the run. Even David Janssen on tv's "The Fugitive" had to work at menial jobs to keep afloat.

Jeff Burr, who also has horror pics "The Offspring" and "Leatherface: The Texas Chainsaw Massacre III" under his belt, directs the piece claustrophobically and fails to whip up any atmosphere. In fact, there's very little to look at during the tedious stretches between O'Quinn's violent outbursts, thanks to a cheapjack production typical of video-driven sequels (original pic was a b.o. failure which evidently made its bucks via homevid).

Acting is merely okay, with O'Quinn still on-target casting as bland Mr. Normal, but becoming quite hammy when riled. Foster is extremely sympathetic, but duo's sex life is played for laughs. Absence of original's mother/daughter sexual tension re: the new man in the house has no counterpart in the sequel. —*Lor.*

Ghost Writer

New York   A Rumar Films presentation of a Ruth Landers production. Executive producers, Landers, Mark Polan. Produced by David DeCoteau, John Schouweiler. Written and directed by Kenneth J. Hall. Camera (Image Transform and Foto-Kem color), Nicholas von Sternberg; editor, Tony Malanowski; music, Reg Powell, Sam Winans; sound (Ultra-Stereo), D.J. Ritchie; production design, Royce Mathew; assistant director, Michael Becker; special makeup effects, John Vulich; casting, Clair Sinnet. Reviewed on Prism Entertainment vidcassette, N.Y., Oct. 9, 1989. MPAA Rating: PG. Running time: **94 MIN.**
Angela Reid . . . . Audrey Landers
Billie Blaine . . . . Judy Landers
Tom Farrell . . . . Jeff Conaway
Vincent Carbone . . . . . . Anthony Franciosa
Also with: David Doyle, Joey Travolta, John Matuszak, Peter Paul, David Paul, Dick Miller, Ken Tobey, Nels van Patten, Richard Gabai, Pedro Gonzalez-Gonzalez, George (Buck) Flower.

■ **"Ghost Writer" is an overly timid romantic comedy, made as a feature for homevideo fans but emerging closer to the tone of a**

network tv movie.

Casting of sisters Audrey and Judy Landers works well (their mom, Ruth Landers, is pic's executive producer). Audrey is a magazine writer seeking peace and quiet at a beach house in Malibu that turns out to be haunted by her aunt's half-sister, Billie Blaine. Ghost role is a pastiche on Marilyn Monroe, well played by Judy in her familiar ditzy blond persona.

Audrey writes interview stories with Blaine, attributing them to a journal she found. Instead of being a suicide, it turns out Blaine was murdered by a mobster (Anthony Franciosa) who now is eager to get his hands on the nonexistent journal. At first only Audrey can see the ghost, but later havoc begins when it becomes visible to others.

Comedy here is light; ditto the scares in a silly climax shot at the Movieland Wax Museum. Both Landers sisters get to sing on the soundtrack and their performances are perfectly in character.

Unfortunately, vid fans are likely to get restless at filmmaker Kenneth J. Hall's overly chaste handling of risqué scenes involving Judy Landers, undoubtedly a function of having mama in charge.

Tech credits are fine, but large supporting cast, ranging from the late John Matuszak to the Barbarian Bros. (Peter and David Paul) has little to do. —*Lor.*

The Toxic Avenger Part III: The Last Temptation Of Toxie

Hollywood   A Troma release of a Lloyd Kaufman/Michael Herz production. Produced and directed by Kaufman, Herz. Screenplay, Gay Partington Terry, Kaufman, from story by Kaufman; camera (TVC color), James London; editor, Joseph McGirr; music, Christopher DeMarco (based on music by Antonin Dvorak); sound, Abe Nejad; art direction, Alexis Grey; costume design, Susan Douglas; stunt coordinator, Scott Leva; assistant directors, William Jennings, Ander Wolk; associate producer, Jeffrey W. Sass; casting, Phil Rivo. Reviewed at Denny Harris of California, W.L.A., Nov. 2, 1989. No MPAA Rating. Running time: **89 MIN.**
The Toxic Avenger . . . . Ron Fazio,
                                John Altamura
Claire . . . . Phoebe Legere
Chairman/The Devil . . . . Rick Collins
Malfaire . . . . Lisa Gaye
Mrs. Junko . . . . Jessica Dublin

■ **Laboring under the theory that if silly is good then stupid is better, the Troma team remains consistent to ludicrous extremes with this too-rarely funny second sequel to its oozing 1984 film. Sporting a nice production design that's almost epic by Troma**

standards, pic should do limited boxoffice before mopping up enough in homevideo to guarantee future toxic shocks.

Only the Troma guys would joke within the film about its low budget after opening with a melee in a videostore where "Toxie" (alternately Ron Fazio and John Altamura) disembowels "the Warner brothers" — terrorists who want to limit the denizens of Tromaville's rental options.

That, alas, is about the funniest thing in the film, except perhaps for its title and the way femme lead Phoebe Legere is always shot at a 45-degree angle from the crotch up.

Like most anything else, however, it gets stale pretty fast, and Troma's Lloyd Kaufman and Michael Herz haven't bothered to freshen the toxic stew that, in no particular order, mixes lots of entrails, half-naked women and sound effects plucked from the Three Stooges.

As for special effects, who else would think of shooting a bus falling off a hill and then running it *backwards* to depict it being "magically" elevated from the bottom?

The story unfortunately offers no such magic, as Toxie finds himself out of work as a superhero after ridding Tromaville of all evil. Needing $357,000 for an operation to cure his sightless girlfriend (Legere), he takes work for mega-corporation Apocalypse Inc., a front company for a corporation from way down under, namely Hell.

Putting the film's grotesque protagonist in jogging shorts and turning him into an over-sized yuppie serves as inspiration for a seemingly endless parade of rather lame jokes.

Working on a tight budget, special effects coordinator Pericles Lewnes manages to come up with some reasonably hellish visuals, and the foreboding Apocalypse building — with spiral stairway and trident logo — actually has a rather impressive design.

The rest is strictly grade-school stuff with lots of screaming and noise, noise, noise. In terms of performances the peripheral players are bad but not quite bad enough to be funny, while Rick Collins' booming voice and solid line readings as the devil seem almost too good for the film. Legere makes a firstrate floozy and has most of the best laughs.

Overlong climax ranks as a real yawn, though they do mention the need to save the day to ensure a "Toxic Avenger Part IV." Based on the third's mere existence that obviously won't require any excessive heroics.—*Bril.*

The Phantom Of The Opera

Hollywood A 21st Century Film release of a Menahem Golan production. Produced by Harry Alan Towers. Directed by Dwight H. Little. Screenplay, Duke Sandefur, based on a screenplay by Gerry O'Hara, from Gaston Leroux' novel; camera (Rank color), Elemer Ragalyi; editor, Charles Bornstein; music, Misha Segal; art direction, Tivada Bertalan; costume design, John Bloomfield; special makeup effects, Kevin Yagher; sound (Ultra Stereo), Cyril Collick; assistant director, Avener Oshalimy; associate producer, Eliezer Ben-Chorin. Reviewed at Mann's Chinese theater, L.A., Nov. 3, 1989. MPAA Rating: R. Running time: **90 MIN.**

The Phantom	Robert Englund
Christine	Jill Schoelen
Richard	Alex Hyde-White
Barton	Bill Nighy
Carlotta	Stephanie Lawrence
Hawking	Terence Harvey
Davies	Nathan Lewis
Meg (New York)	Molly Shannon
Meg (London)	Emma Rawson

■ Casting "Nightmare On Elm Street's" Robert Englund in "The Phantom Of The Opera" is about as "high concept" as it's possible for an exploitation horror film to get these days. Laboriously dull, this "Phantom" may attract enough of the Englund faithful to make for a halfway decent opening weekend, but after that boxoffice prospects are poor.

"This motion picture is not associated with any current or prior stage production or motion picture of the same title," runs a disclaimer at the end of the film. It's all too true. Not only are audiences unlikely to confuse this competent but flatly directed in Budapest production with Andrew Lloyd Webber's stage musical, or the classic Lon Chaney silent, it has precious little to do with Gaston Leroux' novel.

Opening in contemporary New York, this "Phantom," much like the film-within-a-film "The Duel-

Original 1925 film
(B&W/COLOR)

Universal production featuring Lon Chaney, Mary Philbin and Norman Kerry. Directed by Rupert Julian. Adapted from the novel of the same name by Gaston Leroux. At the Astor, New York, for run starting Sept. 6, '25. Running time: **101 MIN.**

The Phantom	Lon Chaney
Christine Dane	Mary Philbin
Raoul de Chagny	Norman Kerry
Ledoux	Arthur Edmund Carewe
Simon Buquet	Gibson Gowland
Philip de Chagny	John Sainpolis
Florine Papillon	Snitz Edwards

ing Cavalier" in "Singing' In The Rain," starts with its heroine being hit on the head by a sandbag and mentally transported back to the mid-19th century for the bulk of the plot. Set in London, rather than the Paris of "Phantom" tradition, this rendition seems faithful in broad outline to the original, save for the fact that its tragic anti-

1943 version

Universal release of a George Waggner production. Directed by Arthur Lubin. Stars Nelson Eddy, Susanne Foster, Claude Rains. Screenplay, Eric Taylor, Samuel Hoffenstein; adaptation, John Jacoby; based on composition 'Phantom Of The Opera' by Gaston Leroux; stage director, opera sequences, William Wymetal; musical director, Edward War; camera, Hal Mohr; Technicolor camera, Duke Green; operatic score and libretto by Edward Ward and George Waggner; 'Lullaby of the Bells' music by Edward Ward, lyrics by Waggner. Tradeshown in N.Y. Aug. 12, '43. Running time: **92 MIN.**

Anatole Carron	Nelson Eddy
Christine Dubois	Susanna Foster
Enrique Claudin	Claude Rains
Raoul de Chagny	Edgar Barrier
Biancarolli	Jane Farrar
The Aunt	Barbara Everest
Vercheres	Steve Geray
Villeneuve	Frank Puglia
Marcel	Hans Herbert
Lacours	Fritz Feld
Amolt	J. Edward Bromberg
Gerard	Hume Cronyn
Jennie	Gladys Blake
Maid	Elvira Curel
Franz Liszt	Fritz Lelbez

hero is a Jack the Ripper style maniac who apparently would rather kill the young soprano to whom he's devoted than kiss her.

Running about encased in makeup that makes him appear a kind of Jack Palance gone to seed, Englund is his usual broad self. Yet gorehounds expecting a "Freddy

1962 version
(BRITISH)

Rank and Universal release of a Hammer production. Stars Herbert Lom, Heather Sears. Produced by Anthony Hinds. Directed by Terence Fisher. Screenplay, John Elder; camera (color), Arthur Grant; editors, James Needs, Alfred Cox; music, Edwin Astley. Previewed, Leicester Square Theatre, London, June 6, '62. Running time: **84 MIN.**

The Phantom	Herbert Lom
Christine	Heather Sears
Lattimer	Thorley Walters
Lord D'Arcy	Michael Gough
Harry	Edward De Souza
Rossi	Martin Miller
Cabby	Miles Malleson
Charwoman	Miriam Karlin
Vickers	John Harvey
Bill	Harold Godwin
Dwarf	Ian Wilson
Xavier	Marne Maitland
Yvonne	Sonia Cordeau
Mrs. Tucker	Renee Houston

Of The Opera" are bound to be disappointed, for the stabbings,

stranglings and decapitations he executes lack suspense, surprise or innovation.

As the object of his decidedly mixed emotions, Jill Schoelen is pretty but vapid. The other performers go through their paces admirably, but there's little they can do with a screenplay that has difficulty making the simplest plot points and finds the problem of moving from one scene to another nearly insurmountable.

The film's contemporary framing device is apparently in place to allow for a sequel, an announcement of which already has been made. —*Rens.*

Beverly Hills Vamp

New York An American-Independent Prods. presentation of an Austin Enterprises production. Produced by Grant Austin Waldman. Coproduced and directed by Fred Olen Ray. Screenplay, Ernest D. Farino; camera (color), Stephen Ashley Blake; editor, Chris Roth; music, Chuck Cirino; sound, Ken Fuller; assistant director, Waldman; production manager, Michelle Morgan; 2d unit directors, Dan Golden, Grant Waldman; 2d unit camera, Gary Graver; special effects animation, Bret Mixon; creative consultant, T.L. Lankford; associate producers, Carlyle Waldman, Henry Waldman. Reviewed on Vidmark vidcassette, N.Y., Oct. 25, 1989. MPAA Rating: R. Running time: **89 MIN.**

Kyle Carpenter	Eddie Deezen
Madam Cassandra	Britt Ekland
Brock	Tim Conway Jr.
Aaron Pendleton	Jay Richardson
Kristina	Michelle Bauer
Russel	Tom Shell
Jessica	Debra Lamb
Claudia	Jillian Kesner
Balthazar	Ralph Lucas
Molly	Brigitte Burdine
Sherry Santa Monica	Dawn Wildsmith

Also with: Robert Quarry, Carlyle Waldman, Pat McCormick, Tony Lorea, Susan Olar, Greta Gibson, Jeffrey Hogue.

■ A pleasant addition to the overworked vampire comedy genre, "Beverly Hills Vamp" is of special interest to industryites by virtue of its nonstop stream of in-jokes parodying the world of low-budget filmmaking.

Helmer Fred Olen Ray, who has bootstrapped his way to prominence in the field of quickie production, pokes fun at himself as well in a film free of the bitterness usually associated with backstage efforts.

Eddie Deezen toplines in his familiar nerd role as a guy who survives an evening with vampire callgirls that, however, takes the lives of his two chums, Tim Conway Jr. and Tom Shell. Viewer is taken on a Cook's tour of Hollywood, notably the milieu of producer Aaron Pendleton, who specializes in 5-day wonders like

"Motorcycle Sluts In Heat." Deezen's girlfriend, Brigitte Burdine, shows up to help him combat Britt Ekland, the vampire madam of a BevHills brothel.

With Michelle Bauer, Debra Lamb and Jillian Kesner providing the pulchritude, easy-to-take pic has some clever moments for the fans, including Robert Quarry making fun of his revered "Count Yorga" character. Vampire lore is handled inconsistently, but there are good special effects by Bret Mixon when the creatures disintegrate. —*Lor.*

Valmont
(FRENCH-BRITISH)

New York An Orion Pictures release of a Claude Berri and Renn Prods. presentation of a Renn Prods. (Paris)-Timothy Burrill Prods. Ltd. (London) coproduction. Produced by Paul Rassam, Michael Hausman. Directed by Milos Forman. Screenplay, Jean-Claude Carrière, from the novel "Les Liaisons Dangereuses" by Choderlos de Laclos; camera (Panavision, Eastman color; Deluxe prints), Miroslav Ondricek; editor, Alan Heim, Nena Danevic; music, Christopher Palmer; additional music, John Strauss; sound (Dolby), Chris Newman; production design, Pierre Guffroy; art direction, Albert Rajau, Loula Morin, Martina Skala; costume design, Theodor Pistek; production managers, Xavier Castano, Patric Bordier; assistant director, Olivier Horlait; choreography, Ann Jacoby; casting, Ellen Chenoweth, Maggie Cartier — France: Margot Capelier, Gérard Moulevrier. Reviewed at Cinema 1, N.Y., Nov. 6, 1989. MPAA Rating: R. Running time: 137 MIN.

Valmont	Colin Firth
Merteuil	Annette Bening
Tourvel	Meg Tilly
Cécile	Fairuza Balk
Madame de Volanges	Siân Phillips
Gercourt	Jeffrey Jones
Danceny	Henry Thomas
Madame de Rosemonde	Fabia Drake

Also with: T.P. McKenna, Isla Blair, Ian McNeice, Aleta Mitchell, Ronald Lacey, Vincent Schiavelli, Sandrine Dumas.

■ Milos Forman's meticulously produced "Valmont" is an extremely well-acted period piece that suffers from stately pacing and lack of dramatic high points. Expensive French-British production shapes as a special event for European audiences, who flocked to Forman's "Amadeus," but is less likely to attract sizable U.S. patronage.

Plot of Choderlos de Laclos' 1782 novel is quite familiar due to Stephen Frears' 1988 hit film, "Dangerous Liaisons," from Christopher Hampton's 1987 play, as well as recent revival of Roger Vadim's modernized 1959 feature version that starred Gérard Philipe.

Forman has met the challenge of breathing new life into the material, but key plot twists and revelations are robbed of their surprise and novelty by the widely seen 1988 WB release.

Basic story revolves around a bet by two 18th Century French aristocrats, Valmont (Colin Firth) and his old flame Marquise de Merteuil (Annette Bening). She wants Valmont to seduce 15-year-old Cécile (Fairuza Balk) to cuckold Cécile's fiancé, Gercourt (Jeffrey Jones), who is Merteuil's unfaithful lover. Valmont counters with the bet that he can bed timid married lady Madame de Tourvel (Meg Tilly). If he wins Merteuil must submit to his lust as well.

With action alternating between Paris (particularly well realized in attractive sets and brief street scenes) and the country estate of Valmont's aunt (Fabia Drake), duel between the two protagonists unfolds in measured, spoonfed dramaturgy. Jean-Claude Carri-

Original film
Les Liaisons Dangereuses
(The Dangerous Meetings)
(FRENCH)

Marceau release of Marceau-Cocinor production. Stars Gerard Philipe, Jeanne Moreau; features Annette Vadim, Jeanne Valerie, Simone Renant, Jean-Louis Trintignant. Directed by Roger Vadim. Screenplay, Roger Vailland, Claude Brule, Vadim from the novel by Chaderlos De Laclos; camera, Marcel Grignon; editor, Victoria Mercanton. At Colisee, Paris, Sept. 22, 1959. Running time, 108 MIN.

Valmont	Gerard Philipe
Juliette	Jeanne Moreau
Cecile	Jeanne Valerie
Marianne	Annette Vadim
Volange	Simone Renant
Danceny	Jean-Louis Trintignant

ère's dialog is in simplified English that makes matters easy to follow yet lacks the poetry usually employed in period pieces.

What keeps the film interesting, if not riveting, is the generally on target casting and resulting topnotch interpretations. Forman's approach generally emphasizes younger thesps than previously associated with the roles, and scores a coup in stage actress Bening as the schemer Merteuil. It's a star-making turn (Bening ironically subsequently has earned a starring role in Frears' new film, "The Grifters"), with Bening's constant, slightly evil smile and very subtle villainy the film's steadiest aspects.

In dramatic terms, however, Carrière denies her the mad scene and extremely bitter outbursts that helped earn Glenn Close an Oscar nomination in the Frears-Hampton version.

Casting of U.K. thesps Colin Firth as Valmont and Siân Phillips as Cécile's no-nonsense mother is adroit, overcoming the Americanized miscasting in the Frears edition. Firth's rake is very convincing. Meg Tilly is a bit flat as the object of his desire, especially disappointing following her unexpurgated sensuality in "The Girl In A Swing."

Film shifts emphasis away from her to Cécile, a role that wide-eyed child star Balk attacks with relish. Grownup "E.T." topliner Henry Thomas is a blank as Balk's young paramour; his ultimate swordfight with Firth is sloughed off by For-

man in a too-tasteful, undramatic finale.

Stealing all her scenes is Fabia Drake as the knowing but somno-

---

1988 version
Dangerous Liaisons

Hollywood A Warner Bros. release of an NFH Limited production from Lorimar Film Entertainment. Produced by Norma Heyman, Hank Moonjean. Coproducer, Christopher Hampton. Directed by Stephen Frears. Screenplay, Hampton, based on his play and the novel "Les Liaisons Dangereuses" by Choderlos de Laclos; camera (color), Philippe Rousselot; editor, Mick Audsley; music, George Fenton; production design, Stuart Craig; art direction, Gerard Viard, Gavin Bocquet; set decoration, Gerard James; costume design, James Acheson; sound (Dolby), Peter Handford; assistant director, Bernard Seitz; casting, Juliet Taylor, Howard Feuer. Reviewed at Glen Glenn sound, L.A., Dec. 6, 1988. MPAA Rating: R. Running time: 120 MIN.

Marquise de Merteuil	Glenn Close
Vicomte de Valmont	John Malkovich
Madame de Tourvel	Michelle Pfeiffer
Madame de Volanges	Swoosie Kurtz
Chevalier Danceny	Keanu Reeves
Madame de Rosemonde	Mildred Natwick
Cecile de Volanges	Uma Thurman

lent matriarch a bit bemused by all the youngsters' foolish games of love. Incidental roles are well-filled, particularly Aleta Mitchell as Bening's slightly mysterious black maid, spying on the young lovers in an elaborately staged tryst scene.

Pierre Guffroy's lavish design work and Theodor Pistek's nonpareil costumes certainly will be noted come awards time, as carefully captured in muted color tones by Miroslav Ondricek's Panavision camera. Varied musical score also adds to the period atmosphere in a production whose casting and language tend to leaven and universalize the material rather than fix it in France at the time of revolution. —*Lor.*

Steel Magnolias

Hollywood A Tri-Star Pictures release of a Rastar production. Produced by Ray Stark. Executive producer, Victoria White. Directed by Herbert Ross. Screenplay, Robert Harling, based on his play; camera (Technicolor), John A. Alonzo; editor, Paul Hirsch; music, Georges Delerue; costumes, Julie Weiss; production design, Gene Callahan, Edward Pisoni; art direction, Hub Braden, Michael Okowita; set design, Steven Wolff; set decoration, Lee Poll, Garrett Lewis; sound (Dolby), Al Overton; associate producer, Andrew Stone; casting, Hank McCann; assistant director, Bob Engelman. Reviewed at Cineplex Odeon Century Plaza theater, L.A., Nov. 10, 1989. MPAA Rating: PG. Running time: 118 MIN.

M'Lynn Eatenton	Sally Field
Truvy Jones	Dolly Parton
Ouiser Boudreaux	Shirley MacLaine
Annelle Dupuy Desoto	Daryl Hannah
Clairee Belcher	Olympia Dukakis
Shelby Eatenton Latcherie	Julia Roberts
Drum Eatenton	Tom Skerritt
Spud Jones	Sam Shepard
Jackson Latcherie	Dylan McDermott
Sammy Desoto	Kevin J. O'Connor
Owen Jenkins	Bill McCutcheon

■ Shrewdly cast, handsomely mounted and professional as all get-out, "Steel Magnolias" delivers the good laugh and the good cry that today's moviegoers just can't seem to resist. It should be an enormous hit.

Robert Harling's (still running) play was set solely in the beauty parlor where his heroines — a group of the liveliest, warmest Southern women imaginable — gather to dish dirt, crack jokes, do hair and give one another some solid, post-feminist emotional support. In opening up his own play for the screen, Harling has made actual characters of the menfolk only talked about in the play. This is still the women's show, so these males (Tom Skerritt, Sam Shepard, Dylan McDermott and Kevin J. O'Connor) don't get much to do other than contribute to background atmosphere. As producer Ray Stark has wisely spared no ex-

Original play

WPA Theater presentation of a play in two acts by Robert Harling. Staged by Pamela Berlin. Setting, Edward T. Gianfrancesco; costumes, Don Newcomb; lighting, Craig Evans; sound, Otts Munderloh; hair, Bobby Grayson; Casting, Darlene Kaplan; production stage manager, Paul Mills Holmes. Opened March 21, '87 at the WPA Theater, N.Y. $16 top.

Cast: Margo Martindale, Constance Shulman, Kate Wilkinson, Blanche Baker, Rosemary Prinz, Mary Fogarty.

pense in filling that background in, it's an attractive place for them to spend their time.

This is a straight-ahead piece of stagecraft, with every "surprise" carefully prepared (and cushioned), and every scene making its one point before moving on. Harling's 1-liners are often funny, but just as often they strain after cleverness (as in "She worships the quicksand I walk on"). Still they *work*, and under Herbert Ross' direction, this cast gives them a memorable going-over.

As Sally Field's troubled yet ever-hopeful seriously diabetic daughter, Julia Roberts has real freshness and charm of the sort that can't be faked. This film is going to make her a star.

As the beauty shop owner around whom all the action swirls, Dolly Parton is thoroughly in her element. Wisely she doesn't press her luck through overemphasis, remaining instead in character as a particular good ole gal — with the Dolly her fans love peeking out from underneath.

From the unbridled caricature of "Madame Sousatzka," Shirley MacLaine has rebounded with a nicely bridled caricature this time out. As the town curmudgeon she looks a wreck, talks trash and obviously loves every minute of it.

As her partner in hamming-as-an-art-form, Olympia Dukakis just about walks away with the picture, even though she's never the center of attention in any of the film's scenes.

Daryl Hannah, not unexpectedly, has her hands full keeping up with this company. She's a trouper and almost makes a viewer believe she's a gawky, nerdish beautician's assistant.

This leaves Sally Field in the most important and problematic role. She does some spectacular underplaying through the bulk of the action, revealing layer after layer of the feelings of this kindly tempered, deeply worried mother. In the last act she's saddled with a graveside solo that — even in a film like this — is miles over the top.

This lapse aside, plus a few rocky transitions and a series of finales that seems to go on forever (a problem this film shares with "Parenthood"), "Steel Magnolias" is a solid success.

Audiences are no more likely to quibble over these lapses than they are to question a story in which women from widely different social classes band together through thick and thin. This is a fairy tale, and it's one millions of Americans (not without reason) desperately want to believe. —*Rens.*

All Dogs Go To Heaven

New York   An MGM/UA Distribution release from United Artists, in association with Goldcrest Films, of a Sullivan Bluth Studios Ireland Ltd. production. Executive producers, Morris F. Sullivan, George A. Walker. Produced by Don Bluth, Gary Goldman, John Pomeroy. Directed by Bluth. Codirected by Goldman, Dan Kuenster. Screenplay, David N. Weiss, from story by Bluth, Ken Cromar, Goldman, Larry Leker, Linda Miller, Monica Parker, Pomeroy, Guy Schulman, David Steinberg; animation camera supervisors (Technicolor), Ciaran Morris, Jim Mann; editor, John K. Carr; music, Ralph Burns; songs, Charles Strouse, T.J. Kuenster; in Dolby stereo production design, Bluth, Leker; production managers, Gerry Shirren, Thad Weinlein; directing animators, Pomeroy, Miller, Ralph Zondag, Dick Zondag, Lorna Pomeroy-Cook, Jeff Etter, Ken Duncan. Reviewed at Guild 50th St. theater, N.Y., Nov. 10, 1989. MPAA Rating: G. Running time: 85 MIN.
Voices of:
Charlie . . . . Burt Reynolds
Anne-Marie . . . . Judith Barsi
Itchy . . . . Dom DeLuise
Carface . . . . Vic Tayback
Killer . . . . Charles Nelson Reilly
Whippet Angel . . . . Melba Moore

Vera . . . . Candy Devine
King Gator . . . . Ken Page
Flo . . . . Loni Anderson

■**Family audiences are ill-served by Don Bluth's "All Dogs Go To Heaven," an animated musical that's confusing, pointless and miscast (in voices). Pic doesn't stand a chance in competition with Disney's superior "The Little Mermaid."**

Though nominally set in Louisiana in 1939, this animated-in-Ireland concoction is woefully in need of a workable story and continuity. First reel lacks any interest, as a junkyard dog just out of prison, Charlie (Burt Reynolds), and his Dachshund pal Itchy (Dom DeLuise) return to watch rat races (rats instead of dogs, for wagering) and go back to work at the night club co-owned by Carface (Vic Tayback).

Carface greedily has partner Charlie killed, whereupon the doggie goes up to heaven to sing with Melba Moore as a cute greyhound-type angel. Supposedly, all dogs go to heaven because they're naturally good and kind, yet pic's unredeeming heavies like Carface also are dogs.

Pointless fantasy premise has Charlie obtaining the pocket watch that controls his life, getting it started again and returning to Earth to live on. He and Itchy befriend an overly cute little human girl, Anne-Marie (Judith Barsi), who talks to animals and proves useful in predicting the outcome of horse races. Pic turns into a minor-league "Little Miss Marker."

Whether adults or smallfry will be able to sit through the remainder of the picture depends on their tolerance for filler and confusing construction, with nightmare sequences and off-the-track material causing considerable head-scratching.

A promising setpiece of Mardi Gras lasts only a few seconds and similarly brief is pic's most atmospheric scene, a setting of vintage New Orleans streets where neighborhood dogs remark on the protagonists' predicament. Setpiece of a huge alligator (nicely voiced by Ken Page) singing with and infatuated by Charlie is clumsily inserted into the action.

Though there is comic relief, Bluth gets no laughs here and is ill-served by wretched songs, several by "Annie's" Charles Strouse. Reynolds' vocals on four numbers are embarrassing; he is a curious choice as lead singer after one assumed his musical comedy screen

career was over following "At Long Last Love." Several of his cronies, including wife Loni Anderson in a small role as a collie, add little to the action.

Quality of animation is highly variable, even during any given scene. —*Lor.*

Crack House

Hollywood   A Cannon release of a Silverman Entertainment production. Produced by Jim Silverman. Executive producer, Jack Silverman. Coproducer, Joan Weidman. Directed by Michael Fischa. Screenplay, Blake Schaefer, from story by Jack Silverman; camera (Foto-Kem color), Arledge Armenaki; editor, Claudia Finkle; music, Michael Piccirillo; sound (Ultra-Stereo), Bill Robbins; production design, Keith Barrett; assistant directors, J. Daniel Dusek, Robert Leveen; associate producer, John Quinn; casting, Anthony Barnao, Lisa London. Reviewed at Hollywood Pacific theater, L.A., Nov. 10, 1989. MPAA Rating R. Running time: 90 MIN.
Steadman . . . . Jim Brown
Dockett . . . . Anthony Geary
Lt. Johnson . . . . Richard Roundtree
Melissa . . . . Cheryl Kay
Rick . . . . Gregg Gomez Thomsen
Mother . . . . Angel Tompkins
B.T. . . . . Clyde R. Jones
Chico . . . . Albert Michel Jr.
Annie . . . . Heidi Thomas
Tripper . . . . Kenneth Edwards
Buzz . . . . Joey Green

■**Cheaply made, routinely executed, and obviously destined for a short theatrical life, "Crack House" offers exploitation-minded viewers little that they can't see for free on tv "tabloid" shows. Video prospects likewise appear to be limited.**

While the drug scene has changed, exploitation movie versions of it haven't altered all that much, if "Crack House" is anything to go by.

As per usual we have our young lovebirds, albeit from less than middle-class circumstances. She (Cheryl Kay) is a budding art student, determined not to make the mistakes her alcoholic mother (Angel Tompkins) made in her life. He (Gregg Gomez Thomsen) is an ex-gang member, determined to tread the straight and narrow.

When a former gang buddy is gunned down in a drive-by shooting, our hero lends the remaining gang members in a bloody vendetta against their enemies. The police capture him, and in his absence our heroine drifts into drugs, thanks to a slimy pusher (Clyde R. Jones). Jones loses her to an evil drug kingpin (Jim Brown), who takes her in trade over a drug deal gone sour.

When our hero learns of her fate he makes a deal with the police, goes undercover, and helps to rout

the evil drug lord. The End — and not a moment too soon.

Sluggishly paced, indifferently lit, and semi-professionally acted, save for an alarmingly vigorous performance by Brown as the woman-beating drug lord, "Crack House" is a downer in every way. —*Rens.*

Ministry Of Vengeance

Hollywood   A Concorde Pictures release of a Motion Picture Corp. of America presentation. Produced by Brad Krevoy, Steven Stabler. Directed by Peter Maris. Screenplay, Brian D. Jeffries, Mervyn Emryys, Ann Narus, story of Randal Patrick; camera (color), Mark Harris; editor, Michael Haight; music, Scott Roewe; sound, Glen Marullo; production design, Stephen Greenberg; set decoration, Troy Myers; costume design, Terry Dresbach; associate producers, Bjorn Friberg, Peter Fornstam; assistant director, Randy Pope. Reviewed at Highland theater, L.A., Nov. 5, 1989. MPAA Rating: R. Running time: 93 MIN.
David Miller . . . . John Schneider
Reverend Bloor . . . . Ned Beatty
Colonel Freeman . . . . James Tolkan
Mr. Whiteside . . . . Yaphet Kotto
Reverend Hughes . . . . George Kennedy
Zarah . . . . Apollonia Kotero
Ali Aboud . . . . Robert Miano
Al-Hassan . . . . Daniel Radell
Fatima . . . . Maria Richwine
Gail Miller . . . . Meg Register
Kim Miller . . . . Joey Peters

■**"Ministry Of Vengeance" is the kind of film that makes the viewer come out feeling as if he had been covered with sludge. When minister John Schneider takes off his clerical collar and heads to Lebanon to gun down the terrorist who killed his wife and daughter, a dramatic situation that could have been compelling quickly descends into stupid and ugly mayhem.**

Schneider's wooden performance never adequately conveys the torment his character is supposed to feel after his family is massacred at the Rome airport, or the conflict between his religious ideals and his human desire for vengeance. Scripters Brian D. Jeffries, Mervyn Emryys and Ann Narus (working from Randal Patrick's story) sidestep the moral issues implicit in a man of the cloth turning to the gun rather than turning the other cheek, as he is urged to do by pastor George Kennedy.

Not interested in exploring the toll revenge exacts on the human soul, the scripters and director Peter Maris are more eager to turn the hero loose on a gang of grossly caricatured Arab terrorists. Schneider actually receives a standing ovation from his congregation when he returns home with his bloody mission completed.

The film introduces Schneider with the by-now obligatory shorthand for complexity in action heroes, a prolog showing him receiving his Vietnam War trauma. His abrupt transformation into a minister is not adequately explained by his guilt over having killed a female Vietcong.

The film perks up briefly when the embittered Schneider turns for help to his rugged old Vietnam colonel (James Tolkan), who is running a paramilitary training camp. Effortlessly believable down to the white strip left by his cap band on the back of his sunburned bald head, Tolkan throughout the film conveys a sense of complexity in his relationship with Schneider that the story otherwise lacks.

The Lebanon section, which occupies more than half of the running time, is dismal to watch and even more dismal to think about. Not only does Schneider locate the supposedly elusive master terrorist (Robert Miano) by looking up his whereabouts in a magazine, he gets himself posted to Ned Beatty's mission right down the road from the terrorist's compound, and then sneaks into the heavily guarded compound with the help of a female missionary (the incongruously sexy Apollonia Kotero).

Not only the terrorist but also Tolkan and Beatty turn out to be on the CIA's payroll, under the supervision of Yaphet Kotto, a situation the audience understands long before Schneider does.

The fact that the terrorist is working for the CIA evidently is supposed to mitigate the film's blatant anti-Arab slant, but a racial stereotype is a racial stereotype no matter how you slice it.

Tech credits are mostly routine, although Mark Harris' photography is so dark that it's often hard to see what is happening. That's probably less the fault of the lenser and more a result of the dim projection on the dirty screen at the L.A. nabe where this film was caught.—*Mac.*

Survival Quest

Toronto An MGM/UA Distribution release from MGM of a Starway Intl. production. Executive producer, Dac Coscarelli. Produced by Roberto Quezada. Written and directed by Coscarelli. Camera (color), Daryn Okada; editor, Coscarelli; music, Fred Myrow, Christopher L. Stone; production design, Andrew Siegel; costume design, Carla Gibson; associate producer, Aaron A. Goffman; casting, Casting Co., Denise Chamian.

MPAA Rating: R. Reviewed at Cumberland Four, Toronto, Nov. 11, 1989. Running time: **96 MIN.**
Hank . . . . .Lance Henriksen
Jake . . . . .Mark Rolston
Raider . . . . .Steve Antin
Harper . . . . .Michael Allen Ryder
Joey . . . . .Paul Provenza
Hal . . . . .Ben Hammer
Jeff . . . . .Dominic Hoffman
Olivia . . . . .Traci Lin
Gray . . . . .Dermot Mulroney
Cheryl . . . . .Catherine Keener
Checker . . . . .Ken Daly
Pilot . . . . .Reggie Bannister

■ **"Survival Quest," a 1986 production, deserves the quick and dirty playoff it's getting from MGM/UA: a 1-week theatrical run, but matinees only, at a small midtown Toronto house before homevid release.**

Plot concerns two separate survival courses run over the same rugged northern Rockies terrain. One is shepherded by a firm but kindly guy, the other, by a firm but nasty guy. Former group includes two women, an older man and a jail prisoner. The other group is out for blood of humans and animals.

Friction between the two groups is telegraphed at the outset, as is all ensuing action.

Blood is spilled, but justice and heroism prevail. As the kindly leader says, art, not hardware, is what survival courses are all about.

Daryn Okada's camerawork is smooth. Acting is pedestrian. Script, direction and music score belong to the bygone days of Western Union. —*Adil.*

Otokowa Tsuraiyoo Toraijiro Kokoro no Tabiji
(Tora-san Goes To Vienna)
(JAPANESE)

New York A Kino Intl. release of a Shochiku Co. production. Executive producer, Makoto Naito. Produced by Kiyoshi Shimazu, Kiyo Kurosu. Directed by Yoji Yamada. Screenplay, Yamada, Yoshitaka Asama; camera (Panavision, color), Tetsuo Takaba; editor, Iwao Ishii; music, Naozumi Yamamoto; sound, Isao Suzuki; art direction, Mitsuo Degawa. Reviewed at Magno Preview 9 screening room, N.Y., Nov. 2, 1989. Running time: **111 MIN.**
Torajiro Kuruma
  (Tora-san) . . . . .Kiyoshi Atsumi
Sakura Suwa . . . . .Chieko Baisho
Hiroshi Suwa . . . . .Gin Meada
Ryozo Kuruma . . . . .Masami Shimojo
Tsune Kurma . . . . .Chieko Misaki
President of printing co. . . . . .Hisao Dazai
Gozen-Sama, priest . . . . .Chishu Ryu
Mitsuo . . . . .Hayato Nakamura
Kumiko . . . . .Keiko Takeshita
The madam . . . . .Keiko Awaji
Hermann . . . . .Martin Loschberger
Therese . . . . .Vivien Dybal

■**It is questionable whether former President Ronald Rea-** gan had any hard evidence for his assertion that Japanese inroads into Hollywood would bring back decency to American films, but Japan's Tora-san movies, the world's longest-running film series, could serve him if he is ever pressed for specifics.

The series boasts comedic formats devoid of sex and violence. "Tora-san Goes To Vienna," the latest and 41st in the series, is the first getting a New York premiere and a regular commercial American opening outside of ethnic conclaves. Despite its charms, its gentle and unsophisticated comic tone and languid pacing will require very special handling to attract audiences.

Tora-san, an itinerant peddler before returning home to visit his sister and her family, encounters a troubled executive who tries to throw himself in front of a train the protagonist is riding. Tora-san befriends the would-be suicide and agrees to accompany him to his dream vacation spot, Vienna, which the iconoclastic Tora-san for some time believes is in Japan.

When Tora-san arrives in Vienna suffering from homesickness and culture shock he restricts himself to his hotel room until he meets Kumiko, a young Japanese woman who has been living in the Austrian capital for eight years. At film's climax she is set to go back to Japan with Tora-san, but as in the other 40 films of this series he loses the object of his affection, in this case to her Austrian boyfriend. Tora-san returns to his family to provide a bewilderingly uneventful and nondescriptive account of his Viennese stay.

Part of the challenge of U.S. distribution will be selling a foreign film of little arthouse appeal though it shares some affinities with the family sagas of Yasujiro Ozu and even includes Ozu veteran Chishu Ryu in a small part. Tora-san's Chaplinesque character is another quality selling point, but while endearingly played by stocky Kiyoshi Atsumi he remains far more passive than most American comic actors.

This is not to say Tora-san's ethereal denseness does not have its moments. (It seems to take his family almost five minutes to explain to him that Japanese is not spoken in Vienna.) In this Tora-san entry at least, comic moments are far outnumbered by the wistful spells of its middle-aged but boyish protagonist who sees the whole world in terms of his hometown province.

It is this sense of wistful longing that Tora-san manages to trigger in his encounters with other characters and their mundane problems. The charm of Tora-san and this *reductio ad sentimentum* could see viewers through the plot's lengthy configurations and banalities.

Foreigners used to the image of high-tech sophisticated Japanese may be taken aback by the film's provincial characters and their stunned reaction to the news of Tora-san's going abroad. The extent to which American audiences share this Japanese fondness for small-town feelings and nostalgia for a time when the world seemed larger will be a major factor in determining Stateside success.

Supporting players, including both Tora-san regulars such as Chieko Baisho and guest stars like Keiko Takeshita as Kumiko, acquit themselves well. Tech credits, including Panavision lensing, are fine. —*Lomb.*

Second Sight

Hollywood A Warner Bros. release of a Lorimar Film Entertainment presentation of an Ursus Film production. Produced by Mark Tarlov. Executive producer, Joe Caracciolo Jr. Directed by Joel Zwick. Screenplay, Tom Schulman, Patricia Resnick; camera (Technicolor), Dana Christiaansen; editor, David Ray; music, John Morris; production design, James L. Schoppe; art direction, Paul W. Gorfine; set decoration, Bryan Thetford; costume design, Cynthia Bales; sound (Dolby), Chris Newman; special visual effects, Bran Ferren; assistant director, Robert Warren; associate producer, Margaret Hilliard; casting, Pat McCorkle. Reviewed at Mann's Chinese theater, Hollywood, Nov. 3, 1989. MPAA Rating: PG. Running time: **84 MIN.**
Wills . . . . .John Larroquette
Bobby McGee . . . . .Bronson Pinchot
Sister Elizabeth . . . . .Bess Armstrong
Preston . . . . .Stuart Pankin
Manoogian . . . . .John Schuck
Coolidge . . . . .James Tolkan
Cardinal O'Hara . . . . .William Prince
Bishop O'Linn . . . . .Michael Lombard
Priscilla . . . . .Christine Estabrook
Maria . . . . .Marisol Massey

■**How "Second Sight" ever got a first look from backers is beyond even paranormal powers to figure out. Exhibs aren't likely to give it a second weekend.**

Slapped-together story about a struggling detective agency that uses a psychic (Bronson Pinchot) for a secret weapon plays like a rejected tv series idea that perversely mutated into a feature film. That Tom Schulman ("Dead Poets Society") and Patricia Resnick ("9 To 5") scripted it is an embarrassment.

From the first unattractive image — the three detectives rising from a manhole to make inane comments — it's plain this picture is going to be all over the place and way off track. It's as if director Joel Zwick wanted to make "The Three Stooges" with the wrong cast, or "Ghostbusters" with the wrong budget.

John Larroquette and Stuart Pankin play detectives depending on Pinchot's "channeling" abilities to put their agency on the map. Inexplicably, they take a 2-bit case that involves finding the hit-and-run thugs that smashed a nun's car. They wreck lots more cars in the process. Then the thugs kidnap the cardinal, so they're onto a really big case.

Pic's coup de grace is when the sleuths board a plane headed for Philly, then get a telepathic message their friend is in trouble in a dark alley. So they take over the plane and drive it through the Boston Tunnel to the rescue. "Don't worry, you can have your plane back as soon as we rescue our friend Wills," the nun (Bess Armstrong) tells the airline pilot.

Though Zwick's direction is as out of control as the berserk spirit guide that puts Pinchot through his foolish paces, pic does have a few moments of wit thanks to Larroquette, whose dry, adept delivery creates cohesiveness now and then.

Low production values make this one of the most unattractive films in memory, and musical tracks are cheesy and stale. Coming out just after Halloween, this one takes the costume prize for worst concept, worst execution in a project masquerading as entertainment.—*Daws.*

La Revolution française: Les Années lumière/Les Années terribles
(The French Revolution: The Light Years/The Terrible Years)
(FRENCH-WEST GERMAN-ITALIAN-CANADIAN)

Paris   An Ariane Films production and release. Coproduced by Films A2, Laura Films, Antea, Les Prods. Alliance, Alcor Films. Executive producer, Antoine de Clermont-Tonnerre. Produced by Alexandre Mnouchkine. Directed by Robert Enrico, Richard Heffron. Screenplay, David Ambrose, Daniel Boulanger, Enrico, Heffron; historical adviser, Jean Tulard; camera (Eastmancolor), François Catonné; editor, Bernard Zitzermann; editor, Patricia Neny, Annie Baronnet; music, Georges Delerue; art direction, Jean-Claude Gallouin, Gérard Daoudal; special effects, Georges Demetreau, Emilio Ruiz; costumes, Catherine Leterrier; makeup, Thi Loan N'Guyen, Eric Muller; sound, Guillaume Sciama, Jacques Thomas-Gerard, Jean Charles Rualt, Claude Villand, Bernard Le Roux; assistant directors, Clément Delage, Marc Jeny; production supervisors, Jean-Claude Bourlat, Janine Ruault, Xavier Quignon-Fleuret; production managers, Edith Colnel, Henri Jaquillard; casting, Margo Capelier, Laurence Lustyk, Michelle Guillermin, Claire Maubert. Running time: 174 MIN. (Les Années lumière) and 163 MIN. (Les Années terribles). Total running time: 337 MIN.

Louis XVI . . . . .Jean-François Balmer
Maria Antoinette . . . . .Jane Seymour
Danton . . . . .Klaus Maria Brandauer
Robespierre . . . . .Andrzej Seweryn
Desmoulins . . . . .François Cluzet
Mirabeau . . . . .Peter Ustinov
Lafayette . . . . .Sam Neill
Marat . . . . .Vittorio Mezzogiorno
Bailly . . . . .Michel Duchaussoy
Luci Desmoulins . . . . .Marie Bunel
Gabrielle Danton . . . . . . .Marianne Basler
Duchess of Polignac . . . .Claudia Cardinale
Princess de Lamballe . . . .Gabrielle Lazure
Saint-Just . . . . .Christopher Thompson
Sanson . . . . .Christopher Lee
(French-track version)

■In terms of scope, investment and logistics, "The French Revolution" is the biggest motion picture ever undertaken in Europe. Ariane Film's $50-million international coproduction is technically polished and spectacular, with enough plausible performances, sophisticated production design and colorful historical interest to keep the general filmgoer happily involved.

However, it never rises to any genuine heights of artistry or epic emotion, reflects no personal vision of history.

In France, where French Revolution bicentennial celebrations peaked months ago, filmgoers are coming slowly, but early statistics suggest a possible longrange following. For foreign viewers, the subject may have just that blend of the exotic and the familiar (everybody has some partial knowledge of the events) to recruit. Real obstacle for the theatrical release is its length and twin-feature format, which most likely will limit offshore exposure to the tv miniseries spinoff. To cut the film would be to kill it.

If this is no revolution in film style, it does have pretentions to being a prototype of the new trend in international ventures. Coproduced by Italy, Canada and West Germany (cofinanced in part by new pan-European film aid funds), codirected (as two separate features) by France's Robert Enrico and Yank Richard Heffron, scripted by Briton David Ambrose, film is especially cosmopolitan in its casting.

Opposite a purely Gallic King Louis XVI (Jean-François Balmer) and Camille Desmoulins (François Cluzet) filmmakers have cast an Austrian Danton (Klaus Maria Brandauer), a British Marie Antoinette (Jane Seymour), a Polish Robespierre (Andrej Seweryn), an Italian Marat (Vittorio Mezzogiorno), a Kiwi Lafayette (Sam Neill) and a Mirabeau of Franco-Russian descent (Peter Ustinov).

Cast performed in both French and English to provide separate negatives for French-speaking and Anglo-Saxon territories.

Post-synching of the cast for French version reviewed here is on the whole satisfactory, though doesn't entirely erase the discomfort many filmgoers feel in watching dubbed popular actors.

It covers the major events of the French Revolution, from the covening by a reluctant Louis XVI of the Estates General in Versailles and the storming of the Bastille in 1789; it moves right on through to the execution of Robespierre and his henchmen in 1794, marking the end of the Terror and more generally the revolution.

Enrico directed the first part, "Les Années lumière," which concludes with the siege of the Tuileries palace in 1792 and the refuge of the king in the National Assembly. Heffron picks up the thread in "Les Années terrible," which essentially dramatizes the battle of the Republican titans (Danton, Robespierre, Marat and company) for the control of the revolution.

Faced with a daunting screenwriting task, David Ambrose (counseled by prominent historian Jean Tulard) does a pretty decent job of cut-and-paste composition. History and psychology are both simplified and on occasion twisted for the sake of clarity, rhythm and showmanship. There's a fair balance of dramatized public events and imagined private scenes inspired by known facts. There are also moments of movieland hokum (such as prolog with teen schoolmates Robespierre and Desmoulins already raging against Louis).

Overall, Heffron fares better than Enrico in animating this vast picture book of the Revolution. Enrico stirs up only moderate excitement in such spectacular sequences as the storming of the Bastille prison (with the series of tragic misunderstandings that led up to it) and the march to Versailles by the women in Paris. Enrico seems hindered by the expository passages of his assignment, which flipflop between the large-scale public scenes and the intimate ones.

Heffron's direction has more sustained rhythm and nerve. He also has the part of the story with greater dramatic intensity and pathos, dealing essentially with the trial and execution of Louis XVI and Marie Antoinette, then with the political infighting and personal rivalries of the revolutionary factions.

As Louis XVI, Balmer dominates the cast. His interpretation of the unhappy monarch, whose clumsiness and arrogance often sabotaged his good intentions, is a credible, subtle and finally moving portrait of spineless royalty. Seymour is less lucky as the queen, in part because the role is dully written, but also because she is oddly post-synched by a French actress, whereas Marie Antoinette was an Austrian, whose foreignness and accent added xenophobic oil to the revolutionary fires.

Brandauer's Danton is only occasionally effective. Temperamentally he's wrong for the part of the volcanic demagog whose oratory power dazzled friends and foes (the dubbing doesn't suggest this incendiary force). The part too is psychologically underwritten, glossing over the personage's ambiguities and complexities.

Seweryn, however, is a surprisingly effective — and strangely touching — Robespierre, moving the role from the monolithic stereotype of the stone-faced revolutionary heavy. Though playing on the ideological and moral intransigence, Seweryn captures the more tortured human qualities of a man forced to sacrifice values and friends for a (finally perverted) sense of social morality and government. Seweryn is extremely well post-synched (by legit actor Gérard Desarthe, who dubbed the other Polish Robespierre — Wojciech Pzoniak — in Andrzej Wajda's "Danton").

Mezzogiorno is a conventionally rabid Marat, not complex enough to explain his vast popularity during the revolution. Sam Neill is an elegant, moody Lafayette, torn between his revolutionary ideals and his aristocratic sympathies.

Ustinov plays Mirabeau as a dirty old man rather than the 40-year-old firebrand with a stormy reputation for adultery and sexual athletics, and trivializes one of the period's most colorful demagogs.

Supporting cast is huge and ranges from blandly caricatural to colorfully cogent. Latter include well-cut silhouettes such as Jan-François Stévenin's Legendre, Michel Duchaussoy's Bailly (who became Paris' first mayor), Raymond Gérome's Necker and Christopher Lee — who else? — bringing lugubrious mute dignity to Sanson, the Revolution's chief executioner.

Adequate supporting womenfolk include Marianne Basler, as Madame Danton and Marie Bunel as Lucie Desmoulins. Roles for Claudia Cardinale and Gabrielle Lazure are ornamental.

Production expertly blends real historical locations (notably the Palace of Versailles), with well-reconstituted sets (by art directors Jean-Claude Gallouin and Gérard Daoudal), and special effects work. A castle in Tarascon in the south of France convincingly stands in for the Bastille prison, complemented by some large-scale street sets.

Model set specialist Emilio Ruiz deserves special mention for the completely convincing miniatures that help recreate the Place de la Revolution (today Place de la Concorde), where the guillotine stood, the Hotel du Ville (City Hall), among other historical evocations.

The French government lent the army for some of the big crowd and battle scenes. One of the first set pieces to be filmed, the Battle of Valmy (which symbolized the Revolution's triumph over foreign intervention), anticlimactically lacks mass and sweep. (John Guillermin began this shooting before being replaced by Heffron a few days into production, which may explain the crimped feeling of the sequence.)

Music of Georges Delerue has color and pomp and never degenerates into a facile hit-parade of revolutionary tunes. Jessye Norman gives a forceful rendition of the end-credit "Hymn to Liberty."

François Catonné lensed the Enrico chapter and Bernard Zitzermann the Heffron film, both with a fine sense of atmosphere. Catherine Leterrier's costumes are well-appointed and the editing by Patricia Neny (for Enrico) and Martine Barraqué and Peter Hollywood (for Heffron) is fluid. Other tech credits are professional.
—*Len.*

Prancer

Hollywood An Orion Pictures release of a Nelson Entertainment presentation in association with Cineplex Odeon Films. Produced by Raffaella De Laurentiis. Coproducers, Greg Taylor, Mike Petzold. Directed by John Hancock. Screenplay, Taylor; camera (Film House color), Misha Suslov; editor, Dennis O'Connor; additional editing, Jack Hofstra; music, Maurice Jarre; sound (Dolby), James Thornton; production design, Chester Kaczenski; art direction, Marc Nabe; set design, Thomas Wilkins; set decoration, Judi Sandin; costume design, Denny Hurt; head animal trainer, David Meeks; associate producer, Hester Hargett; assistant director, Donald P.H. Eaton; reindeer unit camera, Buzz Feitshans; casting, Susan Willett, Craig Campobasso. Reviewed at National Theater, Los Angeles, Nov. 11, 1989. MPAA Rating: G. Running time: **103 MIN.**

John Riggs	Sam Elliott
Jessica Riggs	Rebecca Harrell
Mrs. McFarland	Cloris Leachman
Aunt Sarah	Rutanya Alda
Steve Riggs	John Joseph Duda
Orel Benton	Abe Vigoda
Mr. Stewart/Santa	Michael Constantine
Carol Wetherby	Ariana Richards
Prancer	Boo
Prancer's Voice	Frank Welker

■**Though it's the kind of story that could have used the Spielberg touch, "Prancer" is an earnest, slick, mildly engaging children's fantasy for the holidays. Greg Taylor's tale of a little girl nursing a reindeer back to health in the belief it is Santa's Prancer benefits from snowy Midwestern locations, but suffers from the overly prosaic nature of John Hancock's direction.**

The film never seems truly magical, never soars. Orion's release of the Nelson Entertainment/Cineplex Odeon presentation should do some family trade, but will have a hard time making a serious dent in the b.o. done by Disney's "The Little Mermaid" and other splashier seasonal entries.

Taylor admits in the publicity notes for "Prancer" that his screenplay deliberately follows the "E.T." formula of a child from a troubled household encountering an alien creature lost in the woods, hiding it at home, seeing it taken away by crass adults, and ultimately setting it free in a bittersweet finale. But the comparisons all are unfavorable to "Prancer," which is plodding where Spielberg's film is deft, workmanlike rather than inspired, and heart-tuggingly formulaic rather than deeply moving.

Still, Rebecca Harrell is fine in her pro acting debut as the child who retreats from the unpleasant reality of life at the failing family farm with her strung-out widower dad, Sam Elliott, into a stubborn conviction that the wounded reindeer actually is a strayed member of Santa's sleigh-pulling team. Harrell never stoops to cuteness or mawkishness, playing the role with an intelligence, determination and humor that keep the audience involved with the character even when the script and direction become sluggish.

The brooding Elliott also lends credibility to the tale, with his rugged good looks shadowed by the unrelenting pressure of financial anxiety. When he and his daughter first see the reindeer, he automatically tries to shoot it before she frantically stops him, and later his itchy trigger finger almost leads him to fire a wild shot at the animal in the midst of a group of kids. He provides some, but not enough, of the sense of danger a film like this needs to provide weight to the fantasy.

For too long, "Prancer" rambles without much tension or suspense as Harrell brings in a grumpy but kindly old vet (Abe Vigoda) to treat its leg, and struggles comically to raise money to feed the animal behind her father's back. Although her father is supposed to be preoccupied, it strains credibility that Prancer goes undiscovered for so long, and in place of "E.T.'s" sinister government agents, "Prancer" merely substitutes a local merchant who exhibits the animal to sell Christmas trees.

"Prancer" unsuccessfully reaches for the kind of evergreen emotion aroused by George Seaton's classic 1947 film "Miracle On 34th Street" or by Francis Pharcellus Church's "Yes, Virginia, there is a Santa Claus" editorial in the New York Sun in 1897. The scripter has Elliott quote from Church's editorial as he finally becomes more empathetic with his daughter's vision; it's a touching scene, but its derivative nature is part of what's wrong with the film.

There's a simplicity and charm to "Prancer" at its best, with Harrell brightening the life of an emotionally disturbed recluse sweetly played by Cloris Leachman, trying to persuade Michael Constantine's weary department store Santa to pass along her message to the genuine article, or being surprised by her neighbors' excited reaction when her secret is exposed in the local newspaper.

But the narrative and visual style are far too earthbound. The reindeer is photographed matter-of-factly, as if he were just another reindeer. Misha Suslov's lensing of landscapes and Chester Kaczenski's production design have their moments, but their work mostly is merely serviceable, as is Maurice Jarre's score. And the special-effects mechanics of the fantasy ending call attention to themselves, as they never would in a truly magical film. —*Mac.*

Back To The Future, Part II

Hollywood A Universal Pictures release of a Steven Spielberg/Amblin Entertainment presentation. Produced by Bob Gale, Neil Canton. Executive producers, Spielberg, Frank Marshall, Kathleen Kennedy. Directed by Robert Zemeckis. Screenplay, Gale, from story by Zemeckis and Gale based on characters they created in "Back To The Future;" camera (Deluxe color), Dean Cundey; additional camera, Jack Priestley; editor, Arthur Schmidt, Harry Keramidas; music, Alan Silvestri; production design, Rick Carter; art direction, Margie Stone McShirley; set design, Martha Johnston, Stephen Homsy, Paul Sonski, Beverli Eagan, Steve Wolff, Nancy Nickelberry, Larry Hubbs, Joseph G. Pacelli; set decoration, Linda De Scenna; costume design, Joanna Johnston; sound (Dolby), William B. Kaplan; special visual effects, Industrial Light & Magic, supervisor, Ken Ralston; makeup created by Ken Chase; Michael J. Fox' makeup, Bron Roylance; assistant director, David McGiffert; 2d unit director, Max Kleven; 2d unit camera, Don Burgess; associate producer, Steve Starkey; casting, Mike Fenton, Judy Taylor, Valorie Massalas. Reviewed at Cineplex Odeon Universal City Cinemas, L.A., Nov. 18, 1989. MPAA Rating: PG. Running time: **107 MIN.**

Marty McFly/Marty McFly Jr./	
Marlene McFly	Michael J. Fox
Dr. Emmett Brown	Christopher Lloyd
Lorraine	Lea Thompson
Biff Tannen/Griff	Thomas F. Wilson
Marvin Berry	Harry Waters Jr.
Terry	Charles Fleischer
Western Union Man	Joe Flaherty
Needles	Flea
Jennifer	Elizabeth Shue
Strickland	James Tolkan
George McFly	Jeffrey Weissman/
	Crispin Glover
3-D	Casey Siemaszko
Match	Billy Zane
Skinhead	J.J. Cohen

■**The "Back To The Future" franchise basically is a license to print money, so Universal and Amblin Entertainment will have no trouble recouping their hefty (reportedly about $35-million) investment on this sequel. But "Future II" probably won't reach the $104-million domestic-rentals hilltop scaled by the first one in 1985.**

Too clever and intricate for its own good, the sequel lacks the warmth and seemingly effortless brio of the original, but it still is an impressive technical achievement, and director Robert Zemeckis keeps things entertaining with his unrelenting kinetic drive. The Steven Spielberg presentation should have a huge opening.

The energy and heart which Zemeckis and strong-writing partner Bob Gale (who takes solo screenplay credit this time) poured into the ingenious story of part one is diverted into narrative mechanics and camera wizardry in "Future II." Zemeckis and Gale have chosen to keep themselves amused by making an intensely self-referential film that restages scenes from the original with a different p.o.v., while Michael J. Fox struggles to rectify the damage done to the space-time continuum by a thoughtless blunder he commits on a visit to the year 2015.

The story starts exactly where the original left off, with Fox' Marty McFly and Christopher Lloyd's visionary inventor Dr. Emmett Brown taking off in their flying DeLorean time machine for 2015 on an urgent mission to save Fox' children from a terrible fate. "Future II" finds the McFly family living in shabby lower-middle class digs in a world that isn't so much Orwellian as a gaudier and tackier projection of the present day.

Though the explanation for what happened to the family is tossed off unsatisfactorily in a few lines of dialog, what matters to Fox is that his son has become a wimp, just like his father was in the 1955 segment of the original film. He himself has become a weary loser in the corporate ratrace, kowtowing unsuccessfully to a Japanese boss, while his daughter (also played by Fox in a pointless stunt) resembles Tracy Ullman's caricature of a teenager.

Then, in a curious narrative lapse, the film veers off on a tangent that occupies the rest of the running time and ultimately leaves the future problem unresolved, which helps account for "Future II's" somewhat bleak emotional impact. Fox picks up a sports almanac which, if taken back to the past, will enable him to get rich by gambling on future events. But villainous Biff (Thomas F. Wilson) absconds with it in the time machine to give it to his 1955 self, and the chase begins.

Zemeckis has a wonderful new toy of his own to play with, a computerized camera called the Vistaglide, improved from its prototype use on his "Who Framed Roger Rabbit," which enables the director to have actors interact with themselves in two or more roles simultaneously with much more freedom than has been possible in the past. However, the results are an equivocal success. The interaction of the characters is amazing to watch, but the quality of the photography suffers. Dean Cundey's lensing of the original was crisp and sunny, but here is grainy and murky, and not just in sections that are supposed to be garish and ugly, such as the altered 1985. It seems that to accommodate the harsher lighting requirements and layered images of

the Vistaglide system, and the elaborate, Industrial Light & Magic visual effects of the 2015 section, Cundey had to dull out the overall look of the rest of the film as well, which produces a generally unattractive set of images.

Zemeckis' fascination with having characters interact at different ages of their lives also hurts the film visually, and strains credibility past the breaking point, by forcing him to rely on some very cheesy makeup designs.

The mass audience, so quick to disparage whatever they think looks "fake," will not be amused by these transformations. Nor are the character turns by the resourceful Fox and the others an adequate substitute for the touchingly comic story of the original, in which Fox went back in time to make sure his nerdy father (Crispin Glover) became a man and married his mother. Glover, who reportedly bowed out of "Future II" because of the financial terms he was offered, is glimpsed in old footage and doubled by Jeffrey Weissman but is otherwise sorely missed.

In what must be one of the wettest prints to ever hit the screen, footage from next summer's "Future III" — which is still being filmed, although a few scenes were shot simultaneously with "Future II" — is displayed in an effective trailer attached to this film. "Future III" is revealed to be a Western, with Fox pursuing Lloyd back to what the inventor calls "my favorite historical era" (1885), and Wilson providing the villainy as Biff's ancestor Buford (Mad Dog) Tannen.

Perhaps the daring novelty of doing a large-scale Western might just provide the jump-start that hallowed genre needs to revive itself, and could also revive the creative energies necessary to keep the "Back To The Future" franchise a going concern. —Mac.

Harlem Nights

Hollywood   A Paramount Pictures release in association with Eddie Murphy Prods. Produced by Robert D. Wachs, Mark Lipsky. Executive producer, Eddie Murphy. Written and directed by Murphy. Camera (Technicolor), Woody Omens; editor, George Bowers; music. Herbie Hancock; sound (Dolby), Gene S. Cantamessa; production design, Lawrence G. Paull; costume design, Joe I. Tompkins; co-producer-production manager, Ralph S. Singleton; art direction, Martin G. Hubbard, Russell B. Crone; set decoration, George R. Nelson; assistant director, Alan B. Curtiss; associate producer, Ray Murphy Jr.; casting, Robi Reed. Reviewed at the Mann's Village theater, Westwood, Calif., Nov. 14, 1989.

MPAA Rating: R. Running time: 118 MIN.
Quick . . . . .Eddie Murphy
Sugar Ray . . . . .Richard Pryor
Bennie Wilson . . . . .Redd Foxx
Phil Cantone . . . . .Danny Aiello
Bugsby Calhoune . . . . .Michael Lerner
Vera .Della Reese
Annie . . . . .Berlinda Tolbert
Jack Jenkins . . . . .Stan Shaw
Dominique La Rue . . . . .Jasmine Guy
Crying Man . . . . .Arsenio Hall

■ **This blatantly excessive directorial debut for Eddie Murphy should initially light up Paramount's boxoffice with its marquee appeal but fade to borderline hit status as it turns off fringe fans. Overdone, too rarely funny and, worst of all, boring, the film won't hurt Murphy's stardom but may inhibit future behind-the-camera aspirations.**

Essentially a reworking of "The Sting" with elements of "The Cotton Club," the film features Richard Pryor as the sage Sugar Ray to Murphy's hot-tempered Quick, who risk losing their 1930s Harlem nightclub when a corpulent crime boss (Michael Lerner) sets his sights on it.

The pair hatches up a predictable scheme to turn the tables on the mobster, whose henchmen include a cold-hearted mistress ("A Different World's" Jasmine Guy) and a crooked cop (Danny Aiello, becoming a familiar white face in films with largely black casts).

Still, any similarity between "Harlem Nights" and "Do The Right Thing" ends there — largely because Murphy has done the write thing, and done it poorly. Even the comic talents of such gifted peripheral players as Redd Foxx and Della Reese have to work overtime to generate laughs.

Dialog plays like a black tv sitcom except for the constant use of profanity. Four-letter words are fine in the context of a larger story, but relying on them as the basis of comedic material and as a substitute for invention, as is done here, is numbing.

There's an obnoxious cameo by Murphy's chum Arsenio Hall that proves pointless and unnecessary, as well as a mean-spirited recurring gag involving the stuttering heavyweight champ (Stan Shaw).

The film does have its moments, such as when Murphy dukes it out with Reese's growling club madam or beds the carnivorous Dominque (Guy).

There's also a subtle message to the inner-city youths who flock to

Murphy's films. Sugar Ray lectures Quick on the merits of avoiding conflict rather than fighting and dying, noting that it does little good to have a tombstone that reads, "He died, but he ain't no punk."

The film hasn't enough of those moments to sustain its tired storyline, however, and has too many trite lines and awkward scenes in between, most of them supporting the merits of being a punk.

Murphy's direction is competent if unevenly paced, though his own performance only sporadically shows the flash of earlier films. Similarly, Pryor mumbles his lines and is often left to smile insipidly.

Another annoyance lies in the film's look: It appears to be the studio backlot it is, with vintage cars and rain-slicked streets set against obvious matte shots of New York's skyline. Only the exquisite costumes, hairstyles and interior designs give the film any sort of period feel.

Tech credits are otherwise okay, especially Herbie Hancock's bluesy score. Those with keen eye also will notice boxer Roberto Duran as, ironically, a bouncer at "Club Sugar Ray," plus the motion picture debut of Charles Q. Murphy, a dead ringer for his writer-director-star brother.
—Bril.

Beyond The Doors

New York   An Omni-Leisure Intl. production. Executive producer, Murray M. Kaplan. Written and directed by Larry Buchanan. Camera (color), Nicholas Joseph von Sternberg; editor, uncredited; music supervision, Jeffrey Dann, David Shorey; songs, Shorey, Richard Bowen, Janet Stover; sound, Al Ramirez; art direction, Shay Austin; production manager-assistant director, John Curran. Reviewed on Unicorn vidcassette, N.Y., Nov. 11, 1989. MPAA Rating: R. Running time: 116 MIN.
Jimi Hendrix . . . . .Gregory Allen Chatman
Janis Joplin . . . . .Riba Meryl
Jim Morrison . . . . .Bryan Wolf
Alex Stanley . . . . .Sandy Kenyon
She (Morrison's g.f.) . . . . .Susanne Barnes
Frank Stanley . . . . .Steven Tice
Mrs. Stanley . . . . .Toni Sawyer
Ellen . . . . .Jennifer Wilde
J. Edgar Hoover . . . . .Richard Kennedy
    Also with: Karen Mayo-Chandler, Stuart Lancaster, Joseph A. Tornatore, Logan Carter, Harold Wayne Jones.

■ **Perhaps the screwiest of Larry Buchanan's series of conspiracy-theory films, "Beyond The Doors" is a direct-to-video release postulating that the government put a hit out on Janis Joplin, Jimi Hendrix and Jim Morrison.**

Filmed in 1983 with the Joplinesque title "Down On Us," it's fun but extremely silly entertainment, opening with a George Bernard Shaw quote: "Assassination is the extreme form of censorship."

Unlike his other films about Marilyn Monroe and Lee Harvey Oswald, Buchanan is on pretty shaky ground here, trying to create links and conspiracies involving three of the shooting stars from the '60s.

Episodic pic unfolds awkwardly in flashbacks dating from 1968-71, as Steven Tice reads a file left him by his just assassinated dad (Sandy Kenyon), a government mole who was assigned to kill the three singers, supposedly because of their political stands and influence on young people.

Namedropping script mentions Richard Nixon (especially in somewhat cryptic quotes from a 1977 interview) and others in vaguely pointing a finger, and depicts another deceased figure, J. Edgar Hoover, onscreen. Links between the three stars and their personal interrelationships remain quite unconvincing, however. Buchanan is far more circumspect than the recent "Wired" film in depicting surviving folks; no one will recognize, for example, sidemen Mitch Mitchell or Ray Manzarek from the characters shown on screen.

Main content, filled with sexploitation material involving groupies going topless, is a rather campy re-creation of concerts and backstage/out-on-the-town incidents. It's all rendered goofy by the decision to save big bucks and rely on a dozen soundalike songs by David Shorey, Richard Bowen and Janet Strover that give the feel but do not replicate the impact of the singers' actual hits.

Three thesps in the lead roles don't look like their targets, but Riba Meryl as Joplin and Gregory Allen Chatman as Hendrix do pretty well in mimicking their voices and manner. Bryan Wolf does a poor job recalling Morrison, while his unidentified girlfriend (called simply "She" in the credits) is well played by Susanne Barnes.

Pic's only revelation is the claim that Morrison faked his own death in order to regain his privacy. According to Buchanan, Morrison went to live in a monastery in Spain, dying there quietly in January 1974. If you believe that one, Buchanan has the real story of Howard Hughes and Jean Harlow in the can for perusal as well. —*Lor.*

Race For Glory

Hollywood A New Century/Vista release of a BPS production. Produced by Jon Gordon, Daniel A. Sherkow. Executive producer, David G. Stern. Directed by Rocky Lang. Screenplay, Scott Swanton, from story by Lang; camera (Technicolor), Jack N. Green; editor, Maryann Brandon; music, Jay Ferguson; production design, Cynthia Charette; art direction, Kurt Gauger (U.S.), J.M. Hugon (France); set decoration, Donna Casey (U.S.), Annie Seneghal (France); sound (Dolby), Collin Charles; stunt coordinator, Bill Anagnos (U.S.), Remy Julienne (France); associate producer, Tricia Levine; assistant director, Curtis Lee Collins (U.S.), J.M. Carbonnaux (France). Reviewed at Hollywood Pacific theater, Hollywood, Nov. 3, 1989. MPAA Rating: R. Running time: **96 MIN.**

Cody	Alex McArthur
Chris	Peter Berg
Jenny	Pamela Ludwig
Jack	Ray Wise
Klaus	Oliver Stritzel
Yoshiro Tanaka	Burt Kwouk
Ray Crowley	Jerome Dempsey
Joe Gifford	Lane Smith

■ A by-the-numbers sports drama about friendship tested under the pressures of international motorcycle racing, "Race For Glory" is nonetheless solid in direction, acting and script. Though it lacks imagination, it has heart.

With its attractive actors and skillful race footage, pic could find a following among young filmgoers here and add mileage overseas and in video.

Alex McArthur plays daredevil bike racer Cody and Peter Berg his best friend and mechanic, Chris. They leave smalltown America together to pursue their dream of glory on the international circuit, but tension develops when the bike blows up in a race and it looks like hotheaded Chris can't cut it as Cody's "tuner."

Meanwhile Cody's star is rising — he gets an offer from a Japanese company to join their team and accepts, abandoning both Chris and his hometown girlfriend, Jenny (Pamela Ludwig), for the big time. Too late, he learns the team owners have sold him out (they put him on an inferior bike) to prevent him from threatening their star, world champion racer Klaus (Oliver Stritzel).

After a dirty track tactic by Klaus sends Cody crashing into another racer, who's nearly paralyzed, Cody returns home with his dreams and friendships destroyed, and finds his father died while he was gone. His hurt but loyal friends attend the funeral, pic begins its upswing again, and anyone can guess the rest.

This familiar formula works here. Second-time helmer Rocky

Lang ("All's Fair") obviously has strong feelings for the material and gets impassioned performances from his three lead actors.

Berg is especially affecting as the bullheaded young mechanic who battles to keep things on a true course.

McArthur, with his teen-idol looks and moves, gives an assured peformance as the bound-for-glory racer, and Ludwig is very adept as his tuned-in girlfriend. Rainy night fistfight between the two best friends is among the best scenes — the acting shows, but not to disadvantage.

Lang's tone works in this simplistic, teen-oriented tale — it plays like solid low-budget entertainment with some sizzling race footage for icing. Even the soft-focus romantic montage of the young lovers frolicking at the seaport can be swallowed in the right spirit. The director fares best with teens and sports; scenes involving the corporate puppeteers laying out their evil plans are laughably wooden.

While script gets a bit too misty-eyed about "dreams" and "our shot" now and then, at least it's a lucky break and not an unrealistic screenwriter that lets Cody win the final race.

Shooting and editing of the race-track footage, from Grand Prix races in Belgium, France and Yugoslavia, is first-rate. Costuming is apt, and music is on-target — it sounds like the kind of stuff these characters would listen to. —*Daws.*

Magnus
(ICELANDIC)

Reykjavik A Nytt lif release of a Nytt lif/New Life production. Written, produced and directed by Thrainn Bertelsson. Camera (Eastmancolor), Ari Kristinsson; editor, Skafti Gudmundsson; music, Sigurdur Runar Jonsson; production design, Geir Ottarr; sound, Martien Coucke, Caroline Hooper; costumes, Sigrun Gudmundsdottir; production management, Vilhjalmur Ragnarsson. Reviewed at private screening, Reykjavik, Oct. 12, 1989. Running time: **88 MIN.**

Magnus	Egill Olafsson
Helena, his wife	Gudrun Gisladottir
Edda, their daughter	Maria Ellingsen
Theodir Olafsson	Laddi
Laufey, his wife	Magret Akadottir
Olafur Theodorsson	Jon Sigbjörnsson

Also with: Ingimar Oddsson, Erlingur Gislason, Thröstur Leo Gunnarsson, Arni Petur Gudjonsson, Randver Thorlaksson, Orn Arnasson, Lilja Thorisdottir.

■Thrainn Bertelsson's "Magnus" is a sweetly witty black comedy about a man in his prime being informed that he has cancer. Although melancholy at heart, the film is a fine

balancing act between comedy and farce.

Its way to offshore exposure should be eased by its fine use of local color to set off characters and action.

Magnus has a painter-wife with a secret lover. It is just a fling really, but the lover insists on telling Magnus all. Magnus also has a father whose property he signs away by mistake: he is a lawyer and public servant. Then there is Magnus' daydreaming cabbie brother-in-law, who has wife trouble.

Magnus furthermore has a home made noisy by a daughter's young friends, but the knowledge that he may be going to die somehow relaxes him toward what would otherwise be serious problems. He flirts briefly with taking his own life, then plunges into its mainstream instead, head first and pursuing an old dream of one day riding into Reykjavik on a white stallion.

Egill Olafsson, who has a handsome if balding head framed by closely cropped black hair, gives the role of Magnus a suitably deadpan reading. Everybody around him is never shy of giving vent to his feelings. Magnus' father (Olafur Theodorsson), a slyly crazy gun-toter and owner of an illegal whisky still, is a new sprout on the old Donald Pleasence tradition, and popular local comedy actor Laddi is all mildly befuddled charm as the brother-in-law.

Every single thesp has quite obviously had a high old time performing under Thrainn Bertelsson's direction that never for a moment allows excess. His screenplay is similarly strong on logic even when introducing the oddest twists of action. Editing using cross-cutting serves to keep things moving at the same lively clip as the Icelandic horses on which the human protagonists move about as expertly (or more so) as in their cars. —*Kell.*

After Midnight

Chicago An MGM/UA release from United Artists of a High Bar Pictures production. Produced by Ken and Jim Wheat, Richard Arlook, Peter Greene. Executive producers, Barry J. Hirsch, Allen Dennis. Written and directed by the Wheat Bros. Camera (Foto-Kem color), Phedon Papamichael; editor, Phillip Linson, Quinnie Martin Jr.; music, Marc Donahue; art direction, Chris Henry; sound (Ultra-Stereo), Steven Williams; assistant director, Josh King; line producer, Michael Bennett; casting, David Cohn. Reviewed at the Northtown theater, Chicago, Nov. 4, 1989. MPAA Rating: R. Running time: **90 MIN.**

Allison	Jillian McWhirter

Cheryl	Pamela Segall
Professor Derek	Ramy Zeda
Joan	Nadine van der Velde
Kevin	Marc McClure
Alex	Marg Helgenberger
Ray	Billy Ray Sharkey

■ **Tedium runs rampant in this weak anthology of ersatz scare tales, which blends excessive violence with worn storylines to deadly dull effect. Picture may scare up a few dollars from undiscerning filmgoers in regional release, but it seems destined to haunt videostore shelves.**

"After Midnight" uses higher education as a framing device, as new college students come to grips with a psychology of fear course taught by a nutty professor whose teaching methods include pressing a loaded gun into the class loudmouth's forehead and causing him to wet his pants. Teacher subsequently blows out his own brains in front of the class, but unfortunately it's just a gag and the movie goes on.

The anthology kicks in as a group of foolhardy coeds meets at the professor's house at night for some extracurricular fear. Each is told to recount a scary story because "when we fear, we approach our essence."

Essentially, the tales are the sort that have been told 10-million times around campfires: A couple is lured into a dark old house when the car mysteriously blows a tire; four girls meet the bogeyman when Mom and Dad's car runs out of gas on the wrong side of town; a girl working in an empty office building is terrorized by a random psycho. Meanwhile, a freshman p.o.'d from the first day of class is lurking outside the house with an ax, seeking revenge.

Such goings-on might raise a little gooseflesh on a 13-year-old, but the violence in "After Midnight" makes the film too rough for the only audience that would find its stories surprising or scary. Among other grace notes, a husband hacks off his wife's head with a sword, a pack of Dobermans attacks a panicky woman and a distraught office worker skewers a security guard with a broken desk chair.

By the time the climactic carnage rolls around, even self-immolation, ax-murder and a rampaging skeleton fail to arouse the sensibilities. —*Brin.*

Laser Mission
(WEST GERMAN)

Munich A Zimuth-Interfilm, IMV Vertrieb Intl. Medien & Karat Film Intl. production. Produced by Claus Czaika. Executive producer, Hans Kühle Sr. Directed by Beau Davis. Screenplay, Phillip Guteridge, based on story by David A. Frank; camera (color), Hans Kühle Jr.; editor, E. Selave; music, David Knopfler; sound, Alex Berner. Reviewed on vidcassette, Munich, Nov. 6, 1989. Running time: **95 MIN.**

Gold	Brandon Lee
Professor Braun	Ernest Borgnine
Alissa	Debi Monahan
Eckhardt	Werner Pochath
Kalishnakov	Graham Clarke
Manuel	Pierre Knoessen
Roberta	Maureen Lahoud

(English soundtrack)

■ **A lively, well-made actioner with humor, "Laser Mission" toplines Brandon Lee, who lives up to the chopsocky skills of his father, the legendary kung fu star Bruce Lee. Prospects for cable and homevideo are good, with theatrical limited to offshore areas especially in Asia where the Lee name is still an attraction.**

The implausible plot begins with the theft of the world's largest diamond at a Sotheby's auction and the subsequent abduction of the world's leading laser-weapons expert, Professor Braun, in a distant, fictitious African country known as Kavanga, but clearly recognizable as Angola via the presence of Cuban and Russian soldiers.

U.S. special agent Michael Gold goes to Kavanga on an assignment to persuade Braun to defect to the West. Braun is kidnaped; Gold is captured by the KGB and sentenced to death on espionage charges. After his escape, shooting his way out amid much carnage, the CIA sends him on a special mission to rescue the professor, who holds the secret of making a deadly laser weapon using the stolen diamond.

Gold links up with Braun's daughter, Alissa, who he thinks can help him find her father. Action, much of it taking place in the desert or at a remote diamond mine, doesn't spare the usual car chase sequences. Gold, employing fists and martial arts in hand-to-hand situations, pulls out of one tight spot after another, leaving scores of machine-gunned bodies in his wake.

Comic relief scenes of the two Cuban soldiers, Manuel and Roberta, played by Pierre Knoessen and Maureen Lahoud, fail to amuse. Graham Clarke is convincing as the steely-eyed KGB officer, Kalishnakov, ditto Werner Pochath as the stereotyped ruthless German arms dealer and sadist, Eckhardt. Ernest Borgnine pleases as the kindly, somewhat bewildered professor, while Lee and Debi Monahan struggle with a mediocre script.

David Knopfler's rock music is a solid plus.—*Kind.*

Wilt
(BRITISH)

London A Rank Film Distributors and London Weekend TV presentation of a Picture Partnership production, in association with Talkback. Produced by Brian Eastman. Directed by Michael Tuchner. Screenplay, Andrew Marshall, David Renwick, based on novel by Tom Sharpe; camera (color), Norman Langley, editor, Chris Blunden; music, Anne Dudley; production design, Leo Austin; art direction, Richard Elton, Diane Dancklefsen; costumes, Liz Waller; casting, Rebecca Howard. Reviewed at Rank preview theater. Sept. 14, 1989. Running time: **91 MIN.**

Wilt	Griff Rhys Jones
Flint	Mel Smith
Eva	Alison Steadman
Sally	Diana Quick
Hugh	Jeremy Clyde
Dave	Roger Allam
The Rev. Froude	David Ryall
Dr. Pittman	Roger Lloyd-Pack

■ **Popular British comedy actors Griff Rhys Jones and Mel Smith are still looking to make the breakthrough into movies. Though "Wilt" is amusing in places and features some attractive performances, this won't be the pic. It will do well in the U.K., but stands little chance of succeeding elsewhere.**

Producer Brian Eastman was involved in transferring two other Tom Sharpe novels — "Blott On The Landscape" and "Porterhouse Blue" — to tv, but "Wilt" does not make a comfortable big-screen transition, looking as if it would be more than happy as a small-screen feature.

There is still, though, a good deal of enjoyment to be derived from "Wilt," mainly thanks to a uniformly excellent cast and unpretentious, straightforward direction by Michael Tuchner, as well as the charmingly honest urban provincial settings.

Rhys Jones is the title character, a disillusioned college lecturer, who spends his spare time walking his dog and dreaming about murdering his domineering wife, Alison Steadman.

She has made friends with upwardly mobile couple Diana Quick and Jeremy Clyde. When Steadman and Rhys Jones attend a party at their posh country home Rhys Jones gets dead-drunk, and due to Quick's machinations finds himself locked in a naked passionate embrace with a life-size inflatable doll named Angelique.

He drunkenly roams the town trying to get rid of the doll, eventually dumping it in a building site hole at his college. The next day, Steadman goes missing and Rhys Jones' nocturnal activities are noted — especially by the ambitious inspector, Mel Smith.

The most amusing scenes are those with Rhys Jones and Smith indulging in the banter they are known for from their tv appearances. They make a fine double act, with Smith — who recently made his debut as a helmer with "The Tall Guy" — especially funny as the blundering Inspector Flint.

Alison Steadman is fast becoming a mainstay in British comedy films — she recently also appeared in "Shirley Valentine" and "The Adventures Of Baron Munchausen" — and is a consistently excellent supporting actress.

Helmer Michael Tuchner gives "Wilt" a gritty, realistic feel and seems rightly unashamed that pic is a domestic comedy through and through. Many of the scenes work well, and the blow-up doll certainly gives a good performance, only to be killed off early on.

The laughs do not come often enough given the cast and storyline. Credit should go to Leo Austin for constructing the life-size inflatable doll. Other tech credits are fine. —*Adam.*

Forbidden Sun
(Bulldance)
(BRITISH)

New York A Filmscreen production, in association with Marlborough Prods. Produced by Peter Watson-Wood. Executive producers, Robin Hardy, Timothy Woolford. Co-executive producer, James Reeve. Line producer, David A. Barber. Directed by Zelda Barron. Screenplay, Hardy, from his story; screenplay collaboration, Jesse Lasky Jr., Pat Silver; camera (Technicolor), Richard Greatrex; editor, George Akers, Dennis Mc-Taggart; music, Hard Rain; music producer, John Du Prez; sound, David Stephenson; production design, Miljan Kljakovic; costume design, Siobhan Barron; assistant director, Zoran Andric; production manager, Peter Cotton; stunt arranger, Bill Weston; 2d unit director, David Brockhurst; 2d unit camera, Chris Cox; casting, Mike Fenton, Jane Feinberg, Valorie Massalas. Reviewed on Academy Entertainment vidcassette, N.Y., Nov. 18, 1989. MPAA Rating: R. Running time: **83 MIN.**

Francine Lake	Lauren Hutton
Charles Lake	Cliff DeYoung
Jack	Robert Beltran
Jane	Viveka Davis
Elaine	Renée Estevez
Steph	Christine Harnos
Paula	Samantha Mathis
Betsey	Renee Props
Ulysses	Svetislav Goncic
Lt. Ionnides	Enver Petrovci

■ A belated followup to the cult classic "The Wicker Man," "Forbidden Sun" (better known by its shooting title, "Bulldance") is a lamentably silly exploitation film devling into ancient myths; it's headed directly for U.S. videostores.

A brief cause célèbre due to having gone overbudget (putting its production company behind the eight ball), film awkwardly combines the talents of director Zelda Barron, a helmer of pics about school girls such as "Shag" and "Secret Places," and "Wicker Man" helmer Robin Hardy, this time the scripter. It's not the production but the concept that went awry.

The school girls this time are American beauties training as Olympic gymnasts at Lauren Hutton and Cliff DeYoung's school on the island of Crete (actually filmed on rugged Yugoslavian locations, with Slavic thesps in the supporting cast portraying Greeks). Samantha Mathis is the new arrival from whose perspective the story starts being told, though picture structurally goes askew midway when she is raped and written out of the film.

Leading role actually goes to lovely blond Viveka Davis, a headstrong student who's a former juvenile delinquent. She's in love with handsome instructor Robert Beltran, and goes nuts when she spots him in a sexual tryst with Hutton. Davis goads the girls to exercise vigilante justice against the rape suspect (Svetislav Goncic) and then proceeds to persecute Beltran for a different type of revenge.

The classical myth of the Minotaur, half-man/half-bull, is the basis for the film's most ludicrous motif, as Davis becomes obsessed with the ancient ritual of the bulldance — a gymnast vaulting over a live bull's horns, landing on its back and flipping over via dismount. At first practicing this with men wearing bull-masks, by film's end she's trying the real thing. Under Barron's "Shag"-gy direction, such antics emphasize plenty of jiggle rather than Olga Korbut-style beauty of movement.

Add a British rock group, Hard Rain, which appears on camera and provides the music score, and film becomes more a package of incompatible ingredients than mythic fantasy. Tech credits are fine but acting leans to the gee whiz end of the spectrum. —*Lor.*

Blind Fear
(CANADIAN)

Montreal A Malofilm Group release of a Lance Entertainment production, in association with Allegro Films. Executive producer, René Malo. Produced by Pierre David, Franco Battista. Directed by Tom Berry. Screenplay Sergio Altieri; camera (color), Rodney Gibbons; editor, Franco Battista, Yves Langlois; music, Michael Malvoin; production design,

Richard Tasse. Reviewed at Cineplex Odeon cinema Université 2021, Nov. 20, 1989. Running time: **90 MIN.**

Erika Breen	Shelley Hack
Bo	Jack Langedijk
Ed	Kim Coates
Marla	Heidi Von Palleske
Cal	Ron Lea
Lasky	Jan Rubes
Heinemann	Geza Kovacs

■ What begins as the ultimate exploitation pic of the "frail blond young thing" slowly turns into a twisted tale of wits and murder boasting moderate suspense and a snappy ending.

It plods through opening scenes and character establishment, but gets rolling when the blind victim is trapped in an abandoned country lodge and hunted by three psycho robbers, including the trigger-happy killer, Ed.

Supporting actors don't measure up, but Shelley Hack is convincing as the blind Erika, whose only weapon is her knowledge of the old lodge where she worked.

Erika cunningly lures Ed into the attic and rigs a floor hole so he plummets to the second level, a trick that only enrages him. Ever resourceful, she leads Bo into a bear trap in the basement and finishes off Marla with lantern fuel and an explosive gas stove in the kitchen.

The friendly neighborhood cop, Cal, arrives in the nick of time to shoot Ed and it appears to be a wrap.

However, Erika orchestrated the robbery with "Uncle Harry" (alias Heinemann) who loomed outside the lodge during her unplanned ordeal. Realizing she's been betrayed when they head back to the lodge to pick up the loot, she kills him too. With $1.5-million in her knapsack, she hitches a ride ... with the friendly neighborhood policeman.

However silly, the last few twists in the story are its strength. Mediocre editing lacks the speed and punch for theatrical venues. Homevid and pay tv are pic's obvious outlets where viewers can be riveted to the edge of their sofa. —*Suze.*

To Teleftaio Stoixima
(The Last Bet)
(GREEK-COLOR/B&W)

Thessaloniki A Kostas Zirinis/Greek Film Center production. Written and directed by Kostas Zirinis. Camera (color, b&w), Tossos Alexekis; editor, Aristidis Karidis-Fuchs; music, Stavros Papastavrou; sound, Marinos Athanassopoulos; sets-costumes, Tassos Zografos. Reviewed at Thessaloniki Film Festival, Oct. 6, 1989. Running time: **99 MIN.**
With Daniel Olbrychski (Orestes), Katerina Razelou (the wife), Mary Igglesi, Christos Tsangas, Eva Kotamanidou, Nikos Papakonstantinou, Stratos Pachis, Giorgos Nezos, Michalis Orphanos, Antonis Vlissidis, Richard Svere.

■ "The Last Bet" is a talky, slow-moving police thriller about Orestes, a journalist with former militant leanings who becomes a prime suspect in a murder case.

Orestes (Polish actor Daniel Olbrychski) is at the center of a group of disillusioned leftists. He supposedly suffers from a more intense existential crisis because of his higher sensitivity. His self-imposed isolation takes its toll on his wife (comely Katerina Razelou) and child, and she eventually turns to another.

Imposed on this dreary psychological study is the story of a series of executions by an unknown assailant, which leads to Orestes' imprisonment. The confinement seems easier to bear than his own mental entrapment.

The cinematography is adept, with nicely integrated black & white sequences from student demonstrations. Yet little empathy is aroused by Orestes or the rest of the cast whose talents are largely wasted, so it is difficult for an audience to have much concern over the outcome. —*Sam.*

L'Orchestre rouge
(The Red Orchestra)
(FRENCH-ITALIAN)

Paris AAA release of a Mod Films/Antenne 2/Clesi Cinematografica coproduction, in association with the RTBF. Produced by Jacques Kirsner. Directed by Jacques Rouffio. Screenplay, Gilles Perrault, from his book; camera (color), Pierre-William Glenn; editor, Anna Ruiz; music, Carlo Savina; sound, Michel Desrois, Claude Villand, Bernard Leroux; art direction, Laurent Peduzzi; costumes, Olga Pelletier; production manager, Hubert Merial; casting, Lisa Pillu. Reviewed at Marignan-Concorde theater, Paris, Nov. 15, 1989. Running time: **127 MIN.**

Trepper	Claude Brasseur
Giering	Daniel Olbrychski
Lydia	Dominique Labourier
Grossvogel	Etienne Chicot
Katz	Serge Avedikian
Kent	Martin Lamotte
Berzine	Roger Hanin
Georgie	Barbara de Rossi
Piepe	David Warrilow

■ An extraordinary true story becomes just another spy movie in "The Red Orchestra," an overlong cloak and dagger tale cast with some familiar faces when less familiar ones might have better enforced the theme of anonymous heroism.

Jacques Rouffio directed without flare from a screenplay by **Gilles Perrault, who brought the exploits of the Red Orchestra spy ring to light in his 1967 bestseller** (just reissued in Paris in an enlarged and revised edition).

The Red Orchestra was the legendary Soviet espionage network that operated with incredible efficiency in occupied western Europe during World War II, until the Gestapo ruthlessly dismantled it and executed most of its agents.

The one that got away was its charismatic chief, Leopold Trepper, played with tight-jawed determination but no charisma by Claude Brasseur. Like his lieutenants, Trepper was a Polish Jew and a lifelong communist with a history of political activism (notably in Palestine). He was appointed by Soviet military intelligence to set up an espionage network in the West in 1937 (the height of the Stalinist purges) in anticipation of a war with Germany.

Trepper's heterogeneous organization was tentacular and potent, with informants as high up as Hitler's headquarters in Rastenburg. Stalin more often than not failed to act on momentous leaks, such as Germany's treacherous invasion of Russia in 1941, which Trepper had details on months in advance. Network did play a decisive role in preparing the Soviets for the Battle of Stalingrad.

When Brasseur is nabbed by a specially appointed German police ace (played with cynical relish by Polish thesp Daniel Olbrychski), action centers somewhat theatrically on a duel of personalities as the Nazis attempt to use the Red Orchestra to remove the Soviet Union from the Allied coalition. Brasseur holds out and manages to escape, but is rewarded by Stalin with a cell at Moscow's Lubyanka prison, where he remains for 10 years.

Film's attempts at realism are denatured by casting and language conventions. Brasseur and his cohorts, Dominique Labourier, Etienne Chicot and Serge Avedikian, are supposed to be Poles, but of course they all speak fluent French, as do the Germans and the Soviets (though toward the end somebody suddenly begins declaiming in Russian). This sort of linguistic statelessness is one of the major maladies in the new pan-European production push.

Still, Roger Hanin's opening cameo as Soviet secret service boss Berzine and David War-

rilow's German officer are fairly effective silhouettes. Barbara de Rossi brings some indifferent romantic interest as Brasseur's companion.

Producer Jacques Kirsner was one of those who originally hounded French and Polish authorities to get the real Treppler an exit visa for Israel. It's a shame that so much obvious longterm dedication to a subject should result in so ordinary a movie. —*Len.*

Warlords

New York An American-Independent production. Executive producers, Ronnie Hadar, Michael Plotkin. Produced by Harel Goldstein. Coproduced and directed by Fred Olen Ray. Screenplay, Scott Ressler; camera (Foto-Kem color), Laslo Regos; editor, William Shaffer; music, William Belote; sound, David Waedler; art direction, Corey Kaplan; costume design, Jill Conner; assistant director, Grant Waldman; production manager-associate producer, Herb Linsey; special makeup effects, John Nolan; stunt coordinator, John Stewart; 2d unit director, Sid Haig; 2d unit camera, Dan Golden; additional camera, Stephen Ashley Blake. Reviewed on Vidmark vidcassette, N.Y., Oct. 25, 1989. MPAA Rating: R. Running time: **85 MIN.**

Dow	David Carradine
Danny	Dawn Wildsmith
Warlord	Sid Haig
Beaumont	Ross Hagen
Col. Cox	Fox Harris
Dr. Mathers	Robert Quarry
Dow's wife	Brinke Stevens
Desert girl	Victoria Sellers

Also with: Sam Hiona, Cleve Hall, Debra Lamb, Michelle Bauer.

■ **Yet another "Mad Max"-styled entry, "Warlords" benefits from a tongue-in-cheek approach but is still of only limited interest to sci-fi completists.**

Pic is set after a nuclear war during an uprising by mutants. David Carradine portrays a cloned version of a famous hero, searching for his wife (Brinke Stevens) who's in the clutches of a powerful warlord (Sid Haig).

Taking the familiar sparring twosome trek of films ranging from "Soldier Blue" to "Spacehunter," Carradine reluctantly teams up with tough babe Danny (Dawn Wildsmith, in one of her best, earliest screen roles to date). Later they're joined by nutty Col. Cox (the late Fox Harris). In pic's silliest routine, Carradine converses with Ammo, his little talking mascot, played by a childish puppet.

Dim plotline concerning cloning experiments and warlord Haig's true identity fails to rouse much interest. Main fun is watching Wildsmith's antics as she makes the most of Scott Ressler's putdown dialog. Victoria Sellers, daughter of Peter Sellers and Britt Ekland,

makes an unimpressive film debut as a girl Wildsmith abandons in the desert.

Tech credits are extremely modest. —*Lor.*

Wait Until Spring, Bandini (BELGIAN-FRENCH-ITALIAN-U.S.)

Ghent An Orion Classics release of a Dusk-CFC-Zoetrope Studios production, in collaboration with Intermedias (France) and Basic Cinematografica (Italy). Produced by Erwin Provoost, Tom Luddy, Fred Roos. Directed by Dominique Deruddere. Screenplay, Deruddere, based on novel by John Fante; camera (Eastmancolor), Jean-François Robin; editor, Ludo Troch; music, Angelo Badalmenti, Paolo Conte; sound, Frank Struys; production design, Robert Ziembicki; costume design, Shaye Cunliffe. Reviewed at Ghent Film Festival, Oct. 14, 1989. Running time: **100 MIN.**

Svevo Bandini	Joe Mantegna
Maria Bandini	Ornella Muti
Mrs. Effi Hildegarde	Faye Dunaway
Arturo Bandini	Michael Bacall
Rocco Saccone	Burt Young
Sister Celia	Tanya Lopert
Mr. Helmer	François Beukelaers
Mr. Craik	Josse De Pauw

■ **Likable, if leisurely, this bittersweet family drama of Italians in wintry Colorado could melt boxoffice resistance with its topnotch casting.**

For his second feature, Belgium's Dominique Deruddere, the *enfant terrible* who burst onto the fest circuit adapting Charles Bukowski for "Crazy Love," a.k.a. "Love Is A Dog From Hell," again takes on an American book.

Pic is adapted from John Fante's semiautobiographical chronicle of the Bandini family of Italian immigrants battling financial and emotional hazards in 1925.

Svevo (a nicely downtrodden turn from Joe Mantegna), an out-of-work bricklayer, wastes his few bucks in the pool hall before becoming an oddjobber for a wealthy widow (Faye Dunaway, effortlessly vampish in sumptuous period costumes).

Maria (the beautiful Ornella Muti, credibly acting in her own voice in English) bravely keeps the family together while Svevo moves in with his new "employer." Only the machinations of little Arturo (impressive first-timer Michael Bacall, natural and never cute) bring his parents back together.

Rich in period detail, the story accurately depicts the plight of Europeans struggling to make ends meet in the New World. Plenty of gentle humor offsets the Catholic angst (playing of Tanya Lopert as teacher-nun is expertly pitched) as

12-year-old Arturo's confessions punctuate the narrative, offering wry commentary on the daily duplicities.

Astute direction of young and seasoned players should make the melodrama (in the original sense, a story with lotsa music) of interest to a more general audience. —*Phil.*

Tolérance (FRENCH)

Paris An AMLF release of a Top Films Productions/GPFI/Films A2/La Sept coproduction. Produced by Raymond Blumenthal. Written and directed by Pierre-Henry Salfati. Camera (color), Michael Abramowicz; music, Bernard Cavanna; art direction, Bernard Vezat; costumes, Dominique Borg; sound, Jean-Paul Mugel, Gérard Rousseau; production manager, Farid Chaouche; associate producer, Jean-Claude Fleury; casting, Shula Siegfried. Reviewed at Elysées Lincoln theater, Paris, Oct. 1, 1989. Running time: **104 MIN.**

Marmant	Ugo Tognazzi
Assuerus the hermit	Rupert Everett
Tolerance	Anne Brochet
Cabanes	Marc de Jonge
Marie-Thé	Catherine Samie

■ **An ambitious but turgid period satire, "Tolérance" sets up an intriguing premise about an aristocratic family and a household hermit they receive as an inheritance from England.**

Pierre-Henry Salfati's original script has bizarre historical motifs and echoes of Molière's "Tartuffe," Marco Ferreri and Peter Greenaway, but the seriocomic manner curdles into unappetizing metaphysical sludge.

Story was inspired by a late 18th century English aristocratic eccentricity of owning an ornamental hermit for home and salon. Salfati's idea was to transpose the situation to France during the decadent years of the Directory (1795-1799) and describe what happens when an English hermit is set loose in the chateau of an emigré Italian nobleman (Ugo Tognazzi) and his mystical young wife (Anne Brochet) who have escaped the ravages of the French Revolution.

The hirsute unwashed hermit (Rupert Everett), after spending an ascetic period up a tree, at last comes down to begin a surprise transformation: under Tognazzi's guidance, he becomes a libertine dandy who leads many of the principals to death (Tognazzi's head falls under a travelling guillotine).

Despite a number of offbeat scenes (occasioned by Tognazzi's gastronomical passions), weird characterizations (including an aristocrat whose hobby is collecting the heads of guillotine victims), superb photography and costuming that capture the often grotesque luxuriance of the time, film labors under mirthless direction that's as heavy as the actors' makeup.

Acting too tends towards the ponderous, with a starchy Tognazzi and a bland Everett. However, the ethereal Anne Brochet confirms herself as one of the most graceful and gifted of young French actresses. —Len.

Heroes Stand Alone

New York A Concorde Pictures release of a Concorde-New Horizons production. Executive producer, Roger Corman. Produced by Luis Llosa. Directed by Mark Griffiths. Screenplay, Thomas McKelvey Cleaver; camera (Foto-Kem color), Cusi Barrio; editor, Michael Thibault; music, Eddie Arkin; sound, Edgar Lostanau; art direction, Esteban Mejia; assistant director, Augusto Tamayo; stunt coordinator, Jose Luy. Reviewed at Criterion 3 theater, N.Y., Nov. 25, 1989. MPAA Rating: R. Running time: **83 MIN.**

Zack Duncan	Chad Everett
Walt Simmons	Bradford Dillman
Major Grigori	Wayne Grace
Willie	Rick Dean
Killer	Michel Chieffo
Johnson	Timothy Wead
Rosa	Elsa Olivero

■ **"Heroes Stand Alone" is a subpar war film notable only for its attractive Peruvian locations.**

Chad Everett, who toplined in a more thoughtful WWII war pic for WB back in 1966 ("First To Fight"), stars as CIA mercenary Zack Duncan, serving in Central America in the guerrilla war of fictional country San Pedro. Film's shooting title was "Duncan's Dodgers," but it's a far cry from such action forebears as "Merrill's Marauders" and "Dayton's Devils."

Ridiculous screenplay concerns an abortive U.S.-backed flyover mission that violates a San Pedro ceasefire. When the plane is shot down, Everett and his men are sent in to recover survivors and the incriminating flight recorder black box before Cuban and Russian troops find them and create an international incident.

Bradford Dillman is the bad guy, an ex-CIA operative who's now a dirty, doublecrossing arms dealer. As a sign of the times, pic makes the Russian adviser a good guy and even humanizes the set of stereotyped Cubans; "the company" (CIA) and its alumni are naturally the easy targets for scorn. A pretty Indian girl (Elsa Olivero) is artificially put on the Cuban team as a tracker, mainly to set up a topless bath at a Peruvian waterfall.

Mark Griffiths directs limply, with poorly staged battle scenes. Hokey finalé of Everett and the Russkie throwing away their weapons (more a case of detente than glasnost) is laughably bad.
—Lor.

Olga Robards (GREEK)

Thessaloniki A Greek Film Center/Christos Vakalopoulos/ET 1 production. Directed by Christos Vakalopoulos. Screenplay, Vakalopoulos, Antonis Kioukas; camera (color), Andreas Sinanos; editor, Costas Iordanis; music, Nikos Xidakis; sound, Dimitris Athanassopoulos; sets-costumes, Alexis Kritsopoulos; production manager, Stavros Tsiolis. Reviewed at Thessaloniki Film Festival (competing), Oct. 7, 1989. Running time: **89 MIN.**

With: Olia Lazaridou (Olga Robards), Antonis Kafetzopoulos, Costas Tsakonas, Stavros Tsiolis, I. Simeonidis, E. Sofroniadou, N. Liaskos.

■ **The problem with "Olga Robards," a stylized thriller with top-notch technical credits, is the viewer knows less at the end than at the beginning about who Olga Robards is and what her relationship is with the other characters.**

The action starts out promisingly enough in a carnival as Olga (Olia Lazaridou) adeptly picks off targets at a shooting range and wins a kewpie doll from a sinister attendant. Some suspense is created as an unknown assailant shoots a victim with a camera-lens weapon.

In an unrelated incident, a sexy pickpocket (Costas Tsakonas), hides in a coatroom after a theft and happens to see Olga picking up a cello case. The intrigued thief trails her and discovers her use of the instrument in the case would win her more kudos from the Mafia than music critics.

Most of Olga's day is spent either bumping off well-dressed Arab businessmen from the rooftops of Athens or lounging seductively on her penthouse terrace, waiting for gentlemen callers. Her slightly sullen expression varies so little it is difficult to determine if either of these pastimes brings her any pleasure.

The pickpocket is lured to her bed while the reclusive neighbor seems content to observe her actions. A subplot about a gas station operator who is the ringleader of a band of petty thieves adds some welcome humor. The jazzy score, with a lively theme song and catchy accordion playing by local celeb Vanias, adds interest.

The film's visual style, for which Andreas Sinanos shared the best cinematography award at the Salonika fest, is highly derivative of French films with a hint of German expressionism.

The visual appeal cannot compensate for an incomprehensible plot, which is bound to induce as much ennui in an audience as that expressed by Olga Robards.
—Sam.

Raiders Of The Living Dead

New York An Independent-Intl. Pictures presentation of a Cineronde-Canada production. Executive producer, Charles Baldwin. Produced by Dan Q. Kennis. Directed by Samuel M. Sherman. "Inceptive effects and direction," Brett Piper. Screenplay, Sherman, Piper; camera (Duart color), Douglas Meltzer; editor, John Donaldson; music coordinator, Tim Ferrante; production design, Ruth Seidman; assistant director-associate producer, David Weisman; production manager, Timothy Speidel; makeup effects, Scott Suger. Reviewed on USA Network, N.Y., Nov. 3, 1989. MPAA Rating: PG-13. Running time: **83 MIN.**

Morgan Randall	Robert Deveau
Shelly	Donna Asali
Jonathan	Scott Schwartz
Dr. Carstairs	Bob Allen
Man in black	Bob Sacchetti
Librarian	Zita Johann
Michelle	Corri Burt

Also with: Leonard Corman, Christine Farish, Nino Rigali, Barbara Patterson.

■ **"Raiders Of The Living Dead" is a very minor zombie picture, reviewed here for the record after being cablecast on USA Network's "Up All Night" series.**

Picture was begun in 1983 by Brett Piper (credited for "inceptive effects and direction") under the title "Graveyard" and completed two years later by Independent-Intl. topper Samuel M. Sherman.

Hodgepodge relies heavily on library music and weakly inserted verbal exposition to spin a tale of newspaper reporter Robert Deveau, who's stumbled on the mystery of zombies. Befriended by Donna Asali, he tracks the undead down to an island prison, abandoned for 40 years, where a mad scientist is still up to no good in reanimating corpses. Two kids, Scott Schwartz and Corri Burt, come to their rescue with laser guns Schwartz designed, as well as grandpa Bob Allen, sporting a trusty bow and arrow.

Timekiller doesn't make much sense but has a couple of spooky scenes in a cemetery and the prison. Zita Johann, who costarred with Karloff in Universal's 1932 classic "The Mummy," pops up as a librarian telling Deveau about the prison's history. —Lor.

Future Force

New York An Action Intl. Pictures production. Produced by Kimberley Casey. Executive producers, David Winters, Bruce Lewin. Directed by David A. Prior. Screenplay, Prior; created by Thomas Baldwin; camera (Image Transform color), Andrew Parke; editor, Paul O'Bryan; music, Tim James, Steve McClintock, Mark Mancina; sound, Bob Grant; production manager, Karen King; assistant director, Lorene Duran; stunt coordinator, Bob Ivy; associate producers, Gail Jensen, David Carradine; casting, Bill Zipp. Reviewed on AIP vidcassette, N.Y., Nov. 12, 1989. No MPAA Rating. Running time: **84 MIN.**

John Tucker	David Carradine
Becker	Robert Tessier
Marion	Anna Rapagna
Adams	William Zipp
Grimes	Patrick Culliton
Billy	D.C. Douglas
Roxanne	Dawn Wildsmith
Alicia	Kimberley Casey

Also with: August Winters, John Cianetti, Brian O'Connor, Judy Styres.

■ **This straight-to-video feature offers some offbeat social commentary in its sci-fi approach to the future of law enforcement.**

David Carradine toplines as an elite bounty hunter in 1991, working for the Civilian Operated Police Systems (COPS), a result of turning law enforcement over to the private sector. Film gets underway with a bang as Carradine reads a parody of Miranda rights to a suspect & blows him away.

Soon the shoe is on the other foot as COPS' head honcho William Zipp puts a $100,000 bounty out on Carradine's head when our hero sides with Anna Rapagna, a tv news reporter who's got the goods on the out-of-control civilian police.

Pic climaxes in an interesting mixture of cynicism and hope for reform following Carradine's showdown with Zipp's chief henchman (Robert Tessier), as well as Zipp's ironic comeuppance.

With a nod to "Robocop," Carradine wields a high-tech "arm" that fits over his real one (or works via remote control) and operates like a cannon. Otherwise, "Future Force" is low-tech but scores high in imagination.

The taciturn Carradine is appealing as the good-bad guy and already has filmed a sequel. Supporting cast is effective, notably Dawn Wildsmith who essayed a similar tough gal role opposite Carradine in "Warlords." —Lor.

En afgrund af frihed
(An Abyss Of Freedom)
(DANISH)

Copenhagen   A Regner Grasten Film release and production. Produced by Regner Grasten. Directed by Peter Eszterhas. Screenplay, Eszterhas, based on novel by Bo Green Jensen; camera (Agfacolor), Tom Elling; editor, Tomas Gislason; music, Moonjam, title tune by Dodo & the Dodos; assistant director, John Hilbard. Reviewed at Palads, Copenhagen, Nov. 7, 1989. Running time: **88 MIN.**

Maria	Anne Herdorf
Dan	Jörn Lendorph
Tine	Christine Skou
Henrik	Jeppe Kaas
Tine's father	Waage Sandö
Tine's mother	Karen Margrethe Bjerre
Dan's father	Dick Kaysöe
Dan's grandmother	Elin Reimer

Also with: Finn Storgård, Michael Lindvad, Merete Voldstedlund, Jens Arntzen.

■ Facing life beyond graduation seems far more difficult for the four 18-year-olds in "An Abyss Of Freedom" than the imminent final exam itself. "Freedom" writer-director Peter Eszterhas, basing his film on a straight and stringent novel by Bo Green Jensen, mixes too many music videostyle non sequiturs into what could otherwise have become a fine youth meller.

The dialog sounds authentic and there is fine acting in all youth roles. Young audiences offshore, steeped in the tradition of casual zooming, slow motion juggling and other cinematic junk food, may well take to it all.

The foursome spends its final days in school by roaming the city of Copenhagen, videotaping each other at play (as an amateur rock group with no serious intention of becoming a professional one) or just generally cavorting around the city of Copenhagen). They are the seemingly self-assured but really pretty bewildered children of parents who have gradually defected from their 1968 stands and attitudes and who have had nothing but cliché values to pass on to their offspring.

Two of the kids, Tine and Henrik, are essentially straight arrows, not really too wary of the establishment future that their parents once rebelled against. The other two, Maria and Dan, are just as essentially loners and ready for rebellions of their own. Maria flirts dangerously with drugs and Dan just as dangerously with Maria.

All four fight each other and make up again. They speak the language of their day, age and environment. We come to see the parents of the straight arrows as truly hell-bent (murder is attempted in an out-and-out sex and social status war), but Tine and Henrik remain the obvious survivors, while Maria and Dan will not conform and wind up in pools of blood, Dan knifed by a pusher, Maria having cut her own wrist.

None of the four leads are given much of a chance to develop their characters, but as recruited from a tv series in which they bowed last year, Anne Herdorf (Maria), Christine Skou (Tine), Jörn Lendorph (Dan) and Jeppe Kaas (Henrik) radiate true talent. The older professional thesps fare less well, abandoned almost totally by Eszterhas both as writer and director.

Film's music might serve better on a concert stage. Dramatically, it makes no sense at all. When not mired in tried-and-untrue stylistics, Tom Elling's cinematography is smooth and to the point. —*Kell.*

Vals de la Habana Vieja
(Waltz In Old Havana)
(CUBAN)

San Juan   An Icaic (Instituto Cubano de Artes e Indústrias Cinematográficas) production. Produced by Ricardo Avila. Directed by Luis Felipe Bernaza. Screenplay, Bernaza, Reynaldo Montero, based on an idea by Ana Viña; camera (color), Jorge Haydú; editor, Glayds Cambre; music, Aneire and Tony Taño; art direction, Pedro G. Esperanza. Reviewed at San Juan Cinemafest, Teatro Tapia, San Juan, P.R., Nov. 12, 1989. Running time: **78 MIN.**

Solidad Reina	Ana Viña
Epifanio Glorioso	
Rey	Reynaldo Miravilles

Also with: Takini Alvariño, Jorge Luis Garcia.

■ Cuban director Luis Felipe Bernaza's "Waltz In Old Havana" is an amusing commercial comedy with a surprisingly audacious political subtext, which alone may spark international b.o. interest.

Storyline concerns a coming-out party, planned by Solidad Reina (Ana Viña) to celebrate her daughter's 15th birthday. Husband Epifanio (Reynaldo Miravilles) wants none of it. He considers such conventions old-fashioned and bourgeois. Besides, he wants to spend the money on a color tv. Daughter Odry (named after Audrey Hepburn) doesn't seem to care one way or the other.

Solidad and her friends work on the sly, making secret preparations and decorating the old Vienna Palace, located in the historic part of Old Havana. These arrangements reach levels of absurdity and humor. Meanwhile, Odry's spats with her boyfriend show that Cuban machismo still is very much present within revolutionary society.

Film also is a tribute to cinema. Epifanio works as a projectionist at a cinema that seems to endlessly unspool "Casablanca" and a docu on the debutante tradition. Gaudy period movie posters and memorabilia that line the projection booth and Epifanio's home spill over into lenser Jorge Haydú's cinematography, infusing the film with color.

With "Waltz," helmer Bernaza has created a socially critical comedy that entertains while metaphorically pointing to particularly Cuban idiosyncrasies. Unlike most Icaic productions, the filmmaker shows the decaying façades of Old Havana and the inherent shabbiness of the city.

Neither can pic's political subtext be ignored. The hysteria depicted with its cry-in-the-dark ending makes one wonder how Cuba ever released this film internationally. —*Lent.*

Sweet Lies

New York   An Island Pictures presentation of a Goldeneye production. Executive producer, Chris Blackwell. Produced by Serge Touboul. Directed by Nathalie Delon. Screenplay, R. Dunn, from Delon's story; camera (LTC-Franay and Metrocolor), Dominique Chapuis; editor, Marié-Sophie Dubus; music, Trevor Jones; title song, Robert Palmer; sound, Pierre Gamet, Gérard Lamps; art direction, Bruno Held; set decoration, Laurent Barbat; assistant director, Bernard Seitz, (L.A.): Matia Karrell; 2d unit camera, Arthur Cloquet; casting, Elisabeth Leustig. Reviewed on CBS/Fox vidcassette, N.Y., Nov. 7, 1989. MPAA Rating: R. Running time: **96 MIN.**

Peter Nicholl	Treat Williams
Joëlle	Joanna Pacula
Dixie	Julianne Phillips
Lisa	Laura Manszky
Bill	Norbert Weisser
Maggie	Marilyn Dodds Frank
Isabelle	Aina Walle
Nemo	Gisèle Casadesus
Mr. Leguard	Bernard Fresson
Bradshaw	Lucy Morgan

■ After three years on the shelf, "Sweet Lies" emerges in vidstores as a pleasant but dated romantic comedy of the sort popular 20 years ago.

Treat Williams toplines rather self-consciously as an insurance company snoop who pursues his quarry, a guy faking an injury who's in an unnecessary wheelchair, to Paris. There three gorgeous young women are immediately spellbound by Williams. The elder two (Joanna Pacula, Julianne Phillips) make a bet over which one can bed him, all to impress the youngest (Laura Manszky).

That's the entire plotline, a slim hook for actress-turned-director Nathalie Delon to hang a feature film on. Along the way there's some minor slapstick, the usual romantic complications and pretty location scenery. Williams' indulgent impressions of James Cagney and Robert De Niro are less appetizing, however.

Femme castmembers do little more than look pretty. Film's key drawing card probably is Robert Palmer's sinuous title song, endlessly repeated. —*Lor.*

Leedvermaak
(Polonaise)
(DUTCH)

Utrecht   A Cannon release of a Riverside/Toneelgroep Amsterdam production. Produced by Gys Veraluys. Executive producer, Remmelt Remmelts. Directed by Frans Weisz. Screenplay, Judith Herzberg, Weisz, based on play "Leedvermaak" by Herzberg; camera (color), Goert Giltay; editor, Tom Ruys; sound, Marcel de Hoogd; art direction, Ben van Os; production manager, Fabienne Hulsebos; costumes, Inger Kolff; casting, Hans Kemna. Reviewed at Netherlands Film Days, Rembrandt theater, Utrecht, Sept. 24, 1989. Running time: **90 MIN.**

Lea	Catherine ten Bruggencate
Nico	Pierre Bokma
Simon	Peter Oosthoek
Ada	Kitty Courbois
Zwart	Rijk de Gooyer
Duifje	Sigrid Koetse
Alexander	Hugo Haenen
Dory	Marjon Brandsma
Riet	Annet Nieuwenhuijzen
Hans	Edwin de Vrice

■ "Leedvermaak" is a superbly acted film adapation of a legit work by Judith Herzberg. Pic won awards for director, actor and actress at the recent Dutch Film Days, and is nominated for the European Film Award.

Director Frans Weisz filmed the basically 2-set drama on 20-night sked and a $500,000 budget. Though tech credits are above average, the tight budget and the filmmaker's admiration for the play seems to have hindered Weisz' cinematic handling of Herzberg's moving work, for a feeling of filmed theater prevails.

Pic is set during a big party thrown by a Jewish couple, Kitty Courbois and Peter Oosthoek, for their only child (Catherine ten Bruggencate) who is to marry a successful doctor (Pierre Bokma). The action moves between the family's large country house and the voluminous tent erected for the occasion.

It is a fête rocked, if not wrecked, by memories of the Holocaust. Courbois and Oosthoek are survivors of Auschwitz. Bokma's mother did not survive the death camps. One of the guests, Annet Nieuwenhuijzen is a gentile woman who took in ten Bruggencate during the war — and Courbois still is jealous of her.

Weisz' lyrical manner makes the best of the early scenes as he sets time, place and brings on players with fluid rhythm.

Characters emerge and develop: the bride, egocentric, spoiled frustrated; the groom, kindly, hardworking and philandering; the bride's father, decent and unimaginative, and the groom's ex-wife, a war orphan and professional violinist.

Despite the abundance of stage dialog and occasional theatrical symbolism, Weisz does transcend theater restrictions.

Bokma and Nieuwenhuijzen won the Dutch Film Days Golden Calf prizes, but such is the high quality of the performances that any of the other members of the cast could have staked a claim to the honors. —*Wall.*

Dexiotera Tis Dexias
(Further Right Than The Right)
(GREEK)

Thessaloniki A Greek Film Center/Public Movement Ltd. production. Written and directed by Nikos Antanakos. Camera (color), Lefteris Pavlopoulos; editor, Giorgos Triantafyllou; music, Christos Leontis; sound, Mimis Kassimatis; art direction, Mikes Karapiperis; costumes, Rene Georgiadou; makeup, Stella Votsou; production manager, Babis Apostolopoulos. Reviewed at Thessaloniki Film Festival (competing), Oct. 7, 1989. Running time: **121 MIN.**
With: Vassos Andronidis, Antonis Antoniou, Antonis Vlissidis, Vassilis Kolovos, Takis Moschos, Giorgos Ninios, Timos Perlengas, Gerrasimos Skiadaressis, Nikitas Tsakiroglou, Yota Festa, Petros Fissoun, Minas Hadjisavvas.

■ "Further Right Than The Right" is an uneven blend of psychological drama and political thriller, about a group of people who have been physically and psychologically wounded during the period of the Greek junta (1967-74).

Each of the individuals represents a particular political ideology, which some express defiantly, others timidly. The enormous cast, including some of Greece's finest actors (Yota Festa and Takis Moschos), is given little chance to flesh out its roles. The emphasis is on the characters as symbols of a viewpoint that fits into an historical perspective.

Gerrasimos Skiadaressis stands out in his performance as a soldier; role gave him the nod for best actor at the Salonika fest, and Giorgos Ninios won the award for best supporting actor. Stella Votsou got the prize for best makeup.

The cinematography by Lefteris Pavlopoulos captures the claustrophobic atmosphere of the mostly dark interiors with a few hazy, surrealistic outdoor shots and the cello, guitar and accordian music is appropriately gloomy. —*Sam.*

Lo Que Le Pasó a Santiago
(What Happened To Santiago)
(PUERTO RICAN)

San Juan A Dios los Cria Producciones-Pedro Muñiz production. Written and directed by Jacobo Morales. Camera (color), Agustin Cubano; editor, Alfonso Borrel; music, Pedro Rivera Toledo; sound, Antonio Betancourt; art direction, Bonita Huffman. Reviewed at Cine Plaza II, San Juan, P.R., Nov. 5, 1989. Running time: **105 MIN.**
Santiago Rodríguez . . . . Tommy Muñiz
Angelina . . . . Glady Rodríguez
Aristides Esquilin . . . . Jacobo Morales
Daughter . . . . Johanna Rosaly
Geraldo . . . . Roberto Vigoreaux
Also with: Claribel Medina, Pedro Javier Muñiz, René Monclova.

■ "Lo Que Le Pasó a Santiago," third feature by Puerto Rican filmmaker Jacobo Morales, is a charming and intriguing story about love after 60. Story, coupled with competent tech credits, points to strong crossover b.o. appeal.

Popular tv actor Tommy Muñiz plays Santiago Rodríguez, a cantankerous, recently retired widower who tries to establish some routine in his now-empty life. His family is in turmoil: One daughter lives abroad, another is separated from her husband and his son receives mental care at a local hospital.

A former accountant, Santiago is a stickler for precision, leaving him unprepared for a chance meeting with a mysterious woman, Angelina (Glady Rodríguez), who shares his quiet joys as he strolls around the plazas and parks of Old San Juan. She is elusive and reluctant to share her past with him. She schedules meetings at odd hours, refusing to give a phone number or even her last name.

While the relationship gives his life new meaning, the enigma brings him to hire a private investigator to discover the truth about Angelina.

Although Muñiz and Rodríguez basically reprise their roles from the longrunning national tv series "Los García," Muñiz distinguishes himself, especially in the relationships with his children and grandchild, which are complex and well developed.

Narrative is straightforward and rife with detail and humor. Dialog

is fresh and believable, avoiding cloying sentimentality. Competent lensing by Agustin Cubano and San Juan locations give the pic a sense of Old World charm within a modern context.

With "Santiago," Morales has achieved a mature film that should find offshore acceptance. —*Lent.*

Puta Miseria!
(Damned Misery!)
(SPANISH)

San Juan, Puerto Rico A ELS Films de la Rambla-A. Llorens Olivé-Mare Nostrum Productions-TVE production. Produced and directed by Ventura Pons. Screenplay, Pons, based on novel by Rafael Arnal. Trinitat Satorre; camera (color), Macari Golferichs; editor Amat Carreras; music, Xavier Capellas; art direction, Josep Ma. Espada. Reviewed at San Juan Cinemafest, Nov. 9, 1989. Running time: **90 MIN.**
Ximo . . . . Antonio Ferrandis
Coloma . . . . Amparo Moreno
Mellat . . . . Angel Burgos
Felo . . . . Paco Morell
Plasencia . . . . Joan Monleón
Amparito . . . . Carme Molina
Cura . . . . Manolo Melia
Pataca . . . . Enric Majó

■ Third film in what Spanish filmmaker Ventura Pons calls his "lumpen trilogy," "Puta Miseria!" is an irreverent commercial farce that takes potshots at the capitalist system. Despite some genuine laughs, uneven treatment may limit international appeal.

Filmed in Catalan, story concerns two poor layabouts and pretty thieves, who plot the kidnaping of a prominent citizen for a rich ransom. They team up with a fat masseuse (Amparo Moreno), who leads them to the former town butcher. Little do they know that she wants to punish him for leading her into a life of depravity.

The two bunglers manage to accomplish their task, only to learn that the butcher has no money. In reality, he has plenty of money — embezzled money — along with a plane ticket to Rio. His disappearance sparks a police investigation, complicating his return.

While situations prove to be humorous, rhythm is uneven and the ending is unraveled much too easily. —*Lent.*

Try This On For Size
(FRENCH)

Paris A Film Number One release of a Candice production. Produced by Sergio Gobbi. Executive producer, Yannoula Wakefield. Directed by Guy Hamilton. Screenplay, Alec Medieff, Gobbi, Hamilton, from James Hadley Chase's novel; camera (color), Jean-Yves Le Mener; editor, Georges Klotz; music,

Claude Bolling; costumes, Jacqueline Gamard; sound, Jean-Pierre Ruh; makeup, Charly Koubesserian; assistant director, Marc Barbault; associate producers, Jean-Bernard Fetoux, Bernard Cherry. Reviewed at Georges V Cinema, Paris. Oct. 17, 1989. Running time: **105 MIN.**
Lepski . . . . Michael Brandon
Bradley . . . . David Carradine
Maggie . . . . Arielle Dombasle
Ottavioni . . . . Guy Marchand
Radnitz . . . . Mario Adorf
Igor . . . . Peter Bowles
(English soundtrack)

■ Despite having all the ingredients of a James Bond thriller, including a parody Bond opening logo, veteran Bond helmer Guy Hamilton, dazzling women, breathtaking chases, international crime and humor, "Try This On For Size" just doesn't make it.

In fact this clunker is so off-target, it's hard to believe the same Hamilton directed "Goldfinger." The only bright note is that, as the first in a 12-part series, part tv, part theatrical, it can only be uphill from here.

Michael Brandon, portraying James Hadley Chase's insurance investigator hero Tom Lepski, overacts with good-natured buffoonery. David Carradine is wooden as the bad guy, while awardwinning French actor Guy Marchand puts in one of his least memorable performances as a bumbling stereotyped Gallic cop. Marchand mumbles his forgettable lines in an incomprehensible English that makes one wish there were subtitles.

The film's main problem, however, is that it doesn't clearly fit the crime-thriller or the crime-thriller spoof mold, being too serious for the latter and not serious enough for the former.

Plot revolves around the heist of a 16th-century Russian icon by master thief Lew Bradley, played by Carradine. Lepski's insurance company holds the policy for the icon. The pic does have one outstanding scene, a car-van chase that ends in a spectacularly long tumble from a high cliff.

This film has very little theatrical potential overseas. Domestically it belly-flopped in a brief theatrical run in Paris. —*Bald.*

Dansen med Regitze
(Waltzing Regitze)
(DANISH)

Copenhagen A Pathé-Nordisk release of a Nordisk Film & TV production, with the Danish Film Institute. Produced by Lars Kolvig. Directed by Kaspar Rostrup. Screenplay, Rostrup, based on novel by Martha Christensen; camera (Eastmancolor), Claus Loof; editor, Grete Möldrup; music, Fuzzy; production design, Henning Bahs; sound, Bjarne Risbjerg; costumes, Annelise Hauberg, Ole Gläsner; choreography, Britt Bendixen; assistant director, Tom Hedegaard; Danish Film Institute consultant producer, Kirsten Bonné Rask. Reviewed at the Palads, Copenhagen, Nov. 13, 1989. Running time: **85 MIN.**

Karl Age	Frits Helmuth
Karl Age as a young man	Mikael Helmuth
Regitze	Ghita Nörby
Regitze as a young woman	Rikke Bendsen
Börge	Henning Moritzen
Börge as a young man	Michael Moritzen
Ilse	Anne Werner Thomsen
Ilse as a young woman	Dorthe Simone Lang
Regitze's mother	Kirsten Rolffes
Gloria	Birgit Zinn

Also with: Henning Ditlev, Kim Römer, Birgit Sadolin, Nanna Möller, Torben Jensen, Hans Henrik Clemmensen, Peter Zhelder, Sylvester Zimsen, Troels Thers.

■ Respectable blue-collar sentiment and working-class nostalgia constitute the heart of writer-director Kaspar Rostrup's "Waltzing Regitze." It's an unabashedly old-fashioned film about 60-ish Karl Age's taking stock after a life with tough, strong-willed and warm-hearted Regitze.

Local heartstrings will respond to Rostrup's shrewd tugging, especially with exquisite performances from Danish vets Frits Helmuth and Ghita Nörby. "Regitze" has more sincerity than art; its slow pacing and absence of escalated drama make export prospects dim.

Karl Age's reminiscences take place in his moments of absent-mindedness during a summer reunion of friends and relations staged by Regitze in and around the couple's minuscule garden-colony house.

Toward the very end of the film, tragedy is introduced when Regitze's exuberant party mood and Karl Age's absent-mindedness are revealed as being caused by the news that Regitze has terminal cancer. It seems rather too much of a *deus ex machina* gimmick pulled out of Rostrup's hat.

Helmuth has finely tuned expressions of inner depth, and Nörby's Regitze radiates wit as well as lusty emotion. The players performing in the "as young" roles all function well, and so do several older character actors in cameos, especially Henning Moritzen as the family friend who has "defected" into a career in business and Torben Jensen as a remorseful wife-beater.

Grete Möldrup's editing surmounts the odds of constant flashback with rhythmic neatness. —*Kell.*

ARCHIVE REVIEW

Uncle Moses
(B&W)

Boston A Rutenberg and Everett Yiddish Film Library of the National Center for Jewish Film presentation. Production company, Yiddish Talking Pictures. Released in 1932. Directed by Aubrey Scotto, Sidney Goldin. Story, Sholem Asch; dialog, Maurice Schwartz; subtitles, Sylvia Fuks Fried; camera (b&w), Frank Zucker, Buddy Harris; editor, Bob Snody; music, Samuel Polonsky; sound, March Asch, Gerre Barton, Armond Schettini; artistic director, Anthony Continer. Reviewed at Museum of Fine Arts, Boston, Oct. 26, 1989. (In the Boston Jewish Film Festival.) Running time: **83 MIN.**

Uncle Moses	Maurice Schwartz
Alter Melnick	Rubin Goldberg
Masha	Judith Abarbanell
Charlie	Zvee Scooler
Aaron	Mark Schweid
Rosie	Sally Schor
Grendel	Rebecca Weintraub
Berel	Jacob Mestrel
Sam	Sam Gertler
Mannes	Leon Seidenberg
Nachman	Wolf Goldfaden

■ Maurice Schwartz was celebrated as the "Olivier of the Yiddish stage," and this reconstruction of his first sound film gives ample evidence to back the claim. While primarily of interest to Jewish audiences, film scholars should welcome the opportunity to again see one of only four performances Schwartz committed to celluloid.

Schwartz plays Uncle Moses, a mere butcher in the old country, but a wealthy garment manufacturer in the new world of New York. Here he gives to charity, hires "landsmen" from his old village to work in his sweatshop, and fights the garment workers union since he considers his workers to be "family" rather than employees. In return he expects hard work and undying loyalty.

The focus of the film is Moses' union troubles, and the desire of this widower to put his various love affairs behind him and settle down with Masha (Judith Abarbanell), the feisty daughter of one of his employees and one of the few who refuse to kowtow to him. In fact she is involved with a young radical (Zvee Scooler), but her parents are pushing for the match with Moses. The drama plays out as Moses reaches the heights of his powers and then begins the long descent down.

Production is quite lavish for a Yiddish film of the era, with the look of the Warner Bros. social dramas from around the same time. Unfortunately the National Center for Jewish Film had to work from existing prints which were in 16m, with an occasionally fuzzy soundtrack. All-new subtitles were added.

Schwartz' larger-than-life performance dominates the film, while the supporting cast seems largely stagebound, with Scooler's radical an exception. Schwartz creates a complex figure who can be egotistical one moment and generous the next, successfully turning him into someone with whom audiences will sympathize when he receives his eventual comeuppance.

"Uncle Moses" is the 16th restoration of the Center, which previously did "Tevye" (1939), Schwartz' only other sound film. Two other films, "Yizkor" (1922) and "Unfortunate Bride" (1926), are in the Center's collection but have not yet received funding for repair. —*Kimm.*

She-Devil

Hollywood An Orion Pictures release. Produced by Jonathan Brett, Susan Seidelman. Directed by Seidelman. Screenplay, Barry Strugatz, Mark R. Burns, based on the novel "The Life And Loves Of A She-Devil" by Fay Weldon; camera (Duart color), Oliver Stapleton; editor, Craig McKay; music, Howard Shore; production design, Santo Loquasto; art direction, Tom Warren; set decoration, George DeTitta Jr.; costume design, Albert Wolsky; sound (Dolby), Tod A. Maitland; assistant director, Glen Trotiner; 2d unit director, Andrew Mondshein, casting, Ellen Chenoweth. Reviewed at UA Coronet theater, Westwood, Calif. Nov. 28, 1989. MPAA Rating: PG-13. Running time: **99 MIN.**

Mary Fisher	Meryl Streep
Ruth	Roseanne Barr
Bob	Ed Begley Jr.
Hooper	Linda Hunt
Mrs. Fisher	Sylvia Miles
Nicolette	Elisebeth Peters
Andy	Bryan Larkin
Garcia	A Martinez

■ A dark and gleeful revenge saga set in a world of unfaithful husbands and unfair standards of beauty, "She-Devil" is likely to massage a sore spot for female viewers and draw an enthusiastic all-around following.

Curious combo of Meryl Streep and Roseanne Barr guarantees boxoffice lineups, particularly as word-of-mouth grows on Streep's amazing comic turn.

Pic offers a unique heroine in Ruth Patchett (Barr), a dumpy but dedicated housewife afflicted with a conspicuous facial mole and an uninterested husband (Ed Begley Jr.).

When Begley, an accountant, strays into the arms of a fabulously wealthy and affected romance novelist (Streep), Barr puts up with it — to a point.

However, when Begley, bags more or less packed, sets her blood boiling with crude put-downs, Barr clicks into an inspired attack mode.

Making a list of everything her absentee hubby holds near and dear, Barr sets out to rock his world — first by blowing up the house, then by dumping off the children at his love nest·on her way to Whereabouts Unknown, then by ingeniously dismantling his career.

Along the way she finds her self-esteem and does some good in the world, partly by establishing an employment agency for unloved, unskilled women.

In the hands of director Susan Seidelman, this revenge fantasy is both unabashedly feminist and a great deal of fun, even if it amounts to not much more than a good, savory joke.

Framed and photographed as a high-camp spoof, pic romps

through the wreckage of Streep's once-perfect dream house — a pink palace by the sea — while tossing subversive social observations over its shoulder.

The casting is a real coup, with Barr going her everywoman tv persona one better by breaking the big screen heroine mold, and Streep blowing away any notion that she can't be funny.

Inhabiting the archly ridiculous role of uppity authoress Mary Fisher as deftly as she has any other, Streep punctuates her lines with adroit, inventive physical comedy.

Barr ambles less spectacularly through her role, delivering her lines in her flat, matter-of-fact voice, but her restraint puts an edge on the proceedings, and she exudes a steady fix on her character.

Barr's transition from tolerant wife to diabolical she-devil is a bit shaky, but gets help from special effects, splashy lighting and Howard Shore's Sturm und Drang score.

Begley, by turns frenetic, gallant and absurd, makes an appropriate centerpiece, while Sylvia Miles is a scene-stealer as Streep's blunt and cackling mother. A Martinez draws the short straw as the stereotypical Latin-lover houseboy, a role he plays with high-camp poutiness.

Fay Weldon's novel, basis of "She-Devil," took the ending much further, having Barr's character transform herself through plastic surgery to another Mary Fisher.

Seidelman dispensed with that to maintain a tone more affirming of who Ruth Patchett is. It's less funny and a bit soft and open-ended, but does give audiences more to go home with.

Production design by Santo Loquasto is marvelous and witty, particularly Streep's palace, pool and hot tub. Costumes by Albert Wolsky add amusing layers to the Streep and Barr characters while still being coolly appropriate. Handsome and sometimes skewed cinematography by Oliver Stapleton and savvy editing by Craig McKay are also assets. —Daws.

The War Of The Roses

Hollywood   A 20th Century Fox release of a Gracie Films production. Produced by James L. Brooks, Arnon Milchan. Coproducer, Michael Leeson. Executive producers, Polly Platt, Doug Claybourne. Directed by Danny DeVito. Screenplay, Leeson, based on the novel by Warren Adler; camera (Deluxe color), Stephen H. Burum; editor, Lynzee Klingman; additional editing, Nicholas C. Smith; music, David Newman; sound (Dolby), Jeff Wexler; rerecording mixers, Michael J. Kohout, Leslie Schatz, Matthew Iadarola, Bill W. Benton; production design, Ida Random; art direction, Mark Mansbridge; set design, Stan Tropp, Mark Fabus, Perry Gray; set decoration, Anne McCulley; costume design, Gloria Gresham; associate producer, J. Marina Muhlfriedel; assistant director, Thomas Lofaro; Philadelphia 2d unit camera, Robert Dalva; Philadelphia 2d unit assistant director, Robert Rooy; casting, David Rubin. Reviewed at Century City Cineplex, L.A., Nov. 30, 1989. MPAA Rating: R. Running time: 116 MIN.
Oliver Rose . . . . Michael Douglas
Barbara Rose . . . . Kathleen Turner
Gavin D'Amato . . . . Danny DeVito
Susan . . . . Marianne Sägebrecht
Josh at 17 . . . . Sean Astin
Carolyn at 17 . . . . Heather Fairfield
Harry Thurmont . . . . G.D. Spradlin
Larrabee . . . . Peter Donat
Josh at 10 . . . . Trenton Teigen
Carolyn at 10 . . . . Bethany McKinney

■ What Michael Douglas does to the fish at Kathleen Turner's dinner party in "The War Of The Roses," director Danny DeVito does to the audience. Piddling notions of humor are the least of this misanthropic comedy's offenses, however. Trying to wring yocks from a deranged couple locked in mortal combat over possession of their house — a situation more suited to film noir than to black comedy — the misfired Fox release will bring in audiences for a week or two, but then it's straight down the tubes.

W.C. Fields once offered a simple prescription for comedy involving destruction: If a beat-up old jalopy is pushed off a cliff, the audience will laugh. If a glistening new Rolls-Royce is pushed off a cliff, the audience will be appalled at the waste and excess. That, in a nutshell, is what goes haywire with "The War Of The Roses."

Everything beautiful on screen in this glossily photographed film, from the house to Douglas' antique sportscar to the couple's china figurines to the ravishingly leonine Turner herself, is thoroughly trashed by DeVito, whose sicko humor will wind up alienating virtually everyone in the audience.

The most dismaying thing about the Gracie Films production is that it starts out winningly as a sharp, cynical and sexy modern romantic comedy, but soon deteriorates into sordid and tedious nonsense.

The aptly intense Douglas is a workaholic Washington, D.C., lawyer on the rise in the early years of his marriage to Turner, a saucy former college gymnast who channels her fierce energies into raising two children and remodeling their stately old house.

Once her work is completed, she realizes the marriage is a shell, but Douglas refuses to change his ways and causes her to seek a divorce.

In outline, up to this point, the adaptation of a Warren Adler novel follows predictable lines, with Douglas' rampant sexism challenged by Turner's burgeoning feminism. What keeps it fresh are the sexually charged performances of the two attractive leads — who previously teamed with such success in "Romancing The Stone" and "The Jewel Of The Nile" — and the sarcastic twists DeVito and scripter Michael Leeson pull from the material.

Part of the fun comes from DeVito's own performance, stealing the show every time he appears as Douglas' sleazy and utterly jaundiced divorce lawyer, who narrates the story as a cautionary tale to another client. DeVito's gnomish persona, which also manifests itself in his directorial penchant for sudden cuts to bizarre low-angle shots, imparts an engagingly bent tone to the proceedings.

But once the battle lines are drawn, with both parties insisting on keeping the house and living together in mutual hate after Turner refuses Douglas' $490,000 buyout offer, the cruelty underlying DeVito's gags comes to the forefront in an increasingly ugly fashion. The director's attempt to make jokes about Douglas running over Turner's cat with his sportscar are merely a foretaste of Gothic ruination to come.

The film reaches its nadir of loathsomeness when Turner decides to retaliate against her maniacal husband by serving him liver pâté and telling him he's eating his beloved dog. A quick cut to the living dog outside the house doesn't mitigate the offensiveness of the gag, nor does a disclaimer in the end credits stating that "no harm to any animal" was caused by the filmmakers. What about the harm caused to the audience's sensibilies?

Despite it all, Turner has seldom been more stunning than she is in this film, which was lensed by Stephen H. Burum. Though DeVito, with his violently misogynistic approach, tries to defile her beauty in the horrific final sequences, she remains a great camera subject, this generation's Lauren Bacall.

The only question about Turner is why she sometimes shows such questionable taste in scripts, and acquiesces in such offputting finales as this one or the similarly nihilistic end which marred John Huston's otherwise splendid "Prizzi's Honor."

The audience watches the last part of "The War Of The Roses" with a mounting sense of dread, which is not the best approach for a comedy, even a black one. An aghast spectator overheard at a Hollywood preview perhaps summed up "Roses" best: "It's about how love turns to hate, and that's exactly my reaction to the film." —Mac.

National Lampoon's Christmas Vacation

Hollywood   A Warner Bros. release of a Hughes Entertainment production. Produced by John Hughes, Tom Jacobson. Executive producer, Matty Simmons. Directed by Jeremiah S. Chechik. Screenplay, Hughes; camera (Panavision, Technicolor), Thomas Ackerman; editor, Jerry Greenberg; music, Angelo Badalamenti; production design, Stephen Marsh; art direction, Beala B. Neel; set decoration, Lisa Fischer; costume design, Michael Kaplan; sound (Dolby), James Alexander; associate producers, William S. Beasley, Mauri Syd Gaton, Ramey E. Ward; assistant director, Matt Earl Beesley; 2d unit director, Charles Picerni Sr.; 2d unit camera, Eric Engler; casting, Risa Bramon, Billy Hopkins, Heidi Levitt. Reviewed at Samuel Goldwyn theater, Beverly Hills, Calif., Nov. 29, 1989. MPAA Rating: PG-13. Running time: 97 MIN.
Clark Griswold . . . . Chevy Chase
Ellen Griswold . . . . Beverly D'Angelo
Eddie . . . . Randy Quaid
Nora . . . . Diane Ladd
Clark Sr. . . . . John Randolph
Art . . . . E.G. Marshall
Francis . . . . Doris Roberts
Margo Chester . . . . Julia Louis-Dreyfus
Aunt Bethany . . . . Mae Questel
Uncle Lewis . . . . William Hickey
Frank Shirley . . . . Brian Doyle-Murray
Audrey . . . . Juliette Lewis
Rusty . . . . Johnny Galecki
Todd Chester . . . . Nicholas Guest
Catherine . . . . Miriam Flynn
Ruby Sue . . . . Ellen Hamilton Latzen

■ Solid family fare with plenty of yocks, "National Lampoon's Christmas Vacation" is Chevy Chase and brood doing what they do best. With the laugh level boosted by the rambunctious return of Randy Quaid, pic is a partridge in a pear tree for Warner Bros.

Despite the title, which links it to previous pics in the rambling "Vacation" series, this third entry is firmly rooted at the Griswold family homestead, where Clark Griswold (Chase) is engaged in a typical over reaching attempt to give his family a perfect, old-fashioned Christmas.

As usual for the genre, script relies on simple situational humor. In a major sequence, Chase staples 25,000 Christmas bulbs to the outside of the house and then can't get them to light.

Another gag has to do with his insistence on stuffing a gargantuan Christmas tree into the living room.

Acidic contrast to his fanatical focus on family comes from next-door neighbors Todd and Margot (Nicholas Guest and Julia Louis-Dreyfus) as a pair of suave young urbanites repelled by Chase's behavior. Script gets off some zingers at their lifestyle, too.

A group piece in which the ensemble keeps growing as relatives arrive, pic really gains momentum when Randy Quaid shows up as redneck ne'er-do-well cousin Eddie, driving an RV that looks like a septic tank on wheels.

Until then, script drags a bit, with some dusty sketches, like one in which Chase gets goggle-eyed over the cleavage of a department store clerk, going on too long.

For the most part, helmer Jeremiah S. Chechik makes an adept debut, injecting plenty of energy and spirit, and getting great performances from such minor characters as Mae Questel in an adorable turn as a daffy 80-year-old aunt.

Chase is in peak form, his mugging and slapstick offset by his droll persona and perfect timing. Background of his obsession with family is revealed in scenes showing how he's ignored, despite best efforts, in a job at a huge, anonymous firm.

Beverly D'Angelo provides excellent support in her third turn as his tolerant wife.

Production design is both handsome and cheeky, special effects are amusing and music tracks are cleverly timed to the actions (such as the playing of Gene Autry's "Here Comes Santa Claus" while a SWAT team surrounds the house). —*Daws.*

Tank Malling
(BRITISH)

London A Pointlane Films production. Executive producer, Terence Murphy. Produced by Glen Murphy, Jamie Foreman. Directed by James Marcus. Screenplay, Marcus & Mick Southworth; camera (color), Jason Lehel; editor, Brian Peachey; music, Rick Fenn, Nick Mason; production design, Geoffrey Sharpe; costumes, Liz Da Costa. Reviewed at Cannon Oxford Street, London, Nov. 28, 1989. Running time: **108 MIN.**

Tank Malling	Ray Winstone
Helen Searle	Amanda Donohoe
Robert Knights	Peter Wyngarde
Cashman	Glen Murphy
Dunboyne	Jason Connery
Salena	Marsha Hunt
Danny	Jamie Foreman

Campbell Sinclaire | John Bett

Also with: John Conteh, Terry Marsh, Nick Berry, Maria Whittaker, Don Henderson.

■ **"Tank Malling" is a home movie masquerading as a low-budget British movie. While it is admirable that a group of London actors managed to raise the budget for this crime thriller, they let themselves down with a clichéd and caricature-ridden pic that ends up being just plain nasty.**

Pic is destined for a limited vid life.

Film is packed with models, boxers and barmen who would be familiar to readers of British tabloids. This aspect would be more tolerable if the film didn't take itself so seriously, but the cast's celebrity ends up detracting from the good aspects — fluid direction, nice production values and excellent editing.

Investigative reporter Tank Malling (played by an aggressive Ray Winstone) is just out of prison — he was framed for perjury — and covering equestrian events (cue simplistic attack at so-called upper classes). He is approached by highclass prostitute Amanda Donohoe, who has information on powerful national figure Peter Wyngarde.

Winstone sets about uncovering the story of vice and corruption with the help of his East End buddies, while killer Glen Murphy pursues him and Donohoe, leaving bodies in his wake. But the only publisher willing to take the story is John Bett, who runs an underground magazine (cue cheap gay caricatures).

What follows is Winstone's fight to clear his good name and see Wyngarde behind bars, while his friends regularly fall to Murphy's switchblade.

The acting tends to fall into the tough-guy category. Winstone spends his time ranting; Jason Connery's thesping technique as lawyer Dunboyne amounts to wearing glasses and having his hair slicked back. Murphy at least looks the part of psychokiller Cashman. Donohoe (probably the U.K.'s busiest actress) saves the day with a classy performance — even though she has to spend most of the time crying or getting drunk.

What is missing from the script by James Marcus and Mick Southworth is a sense of humor. As "The Long Good Friday" showed, British gangland movies can work if the acting is topnotch

and if there is some humor. Instead, "Tank Malling" relies on clichés and lets any friend of the producers get a walk-on. —*Adam.*

Triumph Of The Spirit

Hollywood Nova Intl. Films and Shimon Arama presentation of an Arnold Kopelson production. Produced by Kopelson, Arama. Directed by Robert M. Young. Screenplay, Andrzej Krakowski, Laurence Heath, based on story by Arama, Zion Haen; camera (Rank color), Curtis Clark; editor, Arthur Coburn; music, Cliff Eidelman; production design, Jerzy Maslowska; art direction, Krystyna Maslowska; set decoration, Izabela Paprocka; costume design, Hilary Rosenfeld; sound (Dolby), Eli Yarkoni; production manager, Tadeusz Baljen; boxing choreographer & trainer, Teddy Atlas; assistant director, Miguel Gil; associate producers, Evan Kopelson, Sonja Karon; casting, Mike Fenton, Judy Taylor, Valorie Massalas. Reviewed at Samuel Goldwyn theater, L.A., Nov. 2, 1989. MPAA Rating: R. Running time: **120 MIN.**

Salamo	Willem Dafoe
Gypsy	Edward James Olmos
Poppa	Robert Loggia
Allegra	Wendy Gazelle
Elena	Kelly Wolf
Avram	Costas Mandylor
Jacko	Kario Salem
Janush	Edward Zentara
Maj. Rauscher	Hartmut Becker

■ **An event as oft-dramatized as the Holocaust becomes difficult to portray anew, a circumstance that blunts the impact of "Triumph Of The Spirit."**

Film's raison d'être — its true story of a Greek boxing champ who survived life-or-death bouts in the ring at Auschwitz — is murkily underplayed within the harrowing chronicle of death-camp suffering, leaving producer Arnold Kopelson's pic with little to add to what has been done better. Boxoffice looks subdued.

Though this is the first feature filmed almost entirely inside the Auschwitz/Birkenau camps, project was likely a more deeply affecting experience for its makers than it is for viewers.

Kopelson ("Platoon"), bucking indifference from the studios, spent seven years bringing the story to the screen. The story was brought to him by Shimon Arama, who eventually financed the film with Kopelson, via Nova Intl. Films.

In conveying the experience of the Greek middleweight boxer Salamo Arouch (Willem Dafoe), writers Andrzej Krakowski and Laurence Heath were hamstrung by history, as Arouch did not take part in the film's climactic event — an uprising that leads to the blowing up of the crematorium (and the death of most of the conspirators).

Focus is therefore spread among

Arouch's family and friends, including his love interest, Allegra (Wendy Gazelle), but none of the characters is compelling enough to make the pic pass quickly.

Arouch's bouts in the ring for the entertainment of Nazi officers — dramatically lensed by Curtis Clark and choreographed by Teddy Atlas in gritty, realistic style — fall short of being great material, as he is set against other prisoners, who usually were sent to the gas chambers when they lost, making these life-or-death struggles more degrading than inspiring.

The moral anguish that might have beset the boxer goes unarticulated, though at least Arouch shares the hunk of bread he gets for winning with his family, including ailing Poppa (deftly played by Robert Loggia).

The boxing story might still have been a powerful metaphor in the right hands, but it seems incidental in "Triumph," as Arouch's fights don't commence until 45 minutes into a very slow film, after he prevails in a scuffle with a sadistic guard, or kapo, and is recruited for the ring.

For the most part, screen time is devoted to retelling the Holocaust story in a version that, lacking distinctive characters, relies heavily on images chosen by director Robert M. Young.

An empathetic, humanistic stylist, Young refrains from graphic depictions of the camp's horrors, letting them be reflected in the faces of the prisoners. For a scene in which Arouch's brother (Costas Mandylor) is sent into the crematorium to work and backs away in rebellion, Young keeps the camera on the actor the whole time.

Film is notably short on dialog, and what little it has — expanded somewhat by Dafoe's subdued voiceover narration — almost works against it. "All I cared about was fighting and winning," is not a line an actor of Dafoe's subtlety was born to deliver.

Aside from coveying quiet suffering and pained resignation, Dafoe finds little to do. Like the others, he just tries to exude sorrowful stamina.

Edward James Olmos at least brings a mordant sense of humor to his role as a gypsy kapo who mockingly entertains the SS by night, but his is a character one never quite gets a fix on. A scene in which he and Dafoe share a stolen cigaret and bottle of liquor is frustratingly wordless, as if even the writers didn't have a handle on the characters.

"Triumph" has some fine cinematic moments, like a striking shot of the train loaded with Greek prisoners as it steams into Birkenau's yawning "gates of·hell" on a snowy night, and camera work overall is artful, particularly in the boxing scenes, where deep black background contrasts with ghastly white of the gaunt fighters.

In the ring, with the Oscar in one corner and the century's most momentous human event in the other, "Triumph" isn't likely to induce a clinch. —*Daws.*

Alien Seed

New York   An Action Intl. Pictures presentation of a Fitzgerald Films production. Produced by Mark Paglia. Executive producers, Dale Mitchell, Jerry Graham, John Fitzgerald. Directed by Bob James. Screenplay, Douglas K. Grimm, James; camera (color), Ken Carmack; editor, Grimm, Tom Matthies; music, John Standish; sound, Camille Freer; production design, Kari Stewart; assistant director, Ted Ferrari; production manager, Scott Jessup; special makeup effects and creatures design, Patrick Denver; associate producers, Erik Estrada, Robert Hyatt; casting, Gerald I Wolff & Associates. Reviewed on AIP vidcassette, N.Y., Nov. 11, 1989. No MPAA Rating. Running time: **88 MIN.**

Lisa Jordan . . . . Heidi Paine
Mark Timmons . . . . Steven Blade
Dr. Stone . . . . Erik Estrada
Mary Jordan . . . . Shellie Block
Rev. Bolam . . . . David Hayes
Gen. Dole . . . . Terry Phillips
Col. Hobbs . . . . Michael Ford

■**This interesting sci-fi film went direct to video, but is an entertaining entry for fans of suspenseful storylines rather than special effects bombast.**

Steven Blade portrays a writer who's been obsessed with UFO incidents since childhood, when his family was involved in one. He's summoned by Shellie Block, a young blond who reports she's been kidnaped by aliens on a spaceship.

By the time he arrives in Colorado to meet her, Block has been murdered by sinister Erik Estrada (effectively cast against type as the ruthless baddie here). He finally gets Block's pretty sister (Heidi Paine) to cooperate with him after she, too, is abducted by aliens and, like her deceased sister, is impregnated by them.

Director Bob James keeps the action tight and suspenseful for first half of the pic, as details gradually are revealed showing the government's coverup activities regarding UFOs, as well as the existence of a renegade force of operatives, including former CIA

man Estrada, also at large. Pic loses some steam in later reels as it degenerates into standard chase segments. An open ending of Paine and her new baby signals a possible new age.

Cast is lackluster, though Paine cuts a mean figure in tight t-shirt when she turns into a Rambette wielding a machine gun late in the film. Tech credits are okay. —*Lor.*

Boris Godunov (FRENCH-YUGOSLAV-SPANISH)

Paris   A UGC release of an Erato Films production, coproduced by La Sept/SGGC/-Blue Dahlia Prods./Iberoamericana de TV/-Avala Films. Executive producer, Daniel Toscan du Plantier. Produced by Toscan du Plantier, Claude Abeille. Directed by Andrzej Zulawski. Screenplay, Zulawski, based on opera libretto by Modeste Mussorgsky; camera (Fujicolor), Andrzej J. Jaroszewicz, Pierre Laurent Chenieux; editor, Marie-Sophie Dubus; music, Mussorgsky; musical direction, Mstislav Rostropovich; art direction, Nicolas Dvigoubsky, Vlastimir Gavrik; costumes, Magda Biernawska-Teslawska; makeup, Michel Deruelle; sound, Michel Lepage, Guy Level, Dominique Hennequin; assistant director, Patrick Poubel; production manager, Farid Chaouche. Reviewed at UGC screening room, Neuilly-sur-Seine, France, Nov. 27, 1989. Running time: **117 MIN.**

Boris Godunov . . . . Ruggero Raimondi
Prince Chouisky . . . . Kenneth Riegel
Grigory/Dimitri . . . . Pavel Slaby
(voice: Vyaceslav Polosov)
Pimene . . . . Bernard Lefort
(voice: Paul Plischka)
Marina Mnichek . . . . Delphine Forest
(voice: Galina Vichnievskaya)
The Innocent . . . . Pavel Slaby
(Nicolai Gedda)

■**After a stagey unadventurous "La Bohème" by Luigi Comencini, producer and opera film specialist Daniel Toscan du Plantier now delivers a deliriously unstately "Boris Godunov," directed in Yugoslavia by Andrzej Zulawski in his typically epileptic manner.**

Zulawski, who inherited the assignment when fellow Pole Andrzej Wajda backed off, sets out to deflate the turgid grand manner of opera and succeeds only too well. As tumultous as Mussorgsky's great opera is, Zulawski's galloping camera and manic actors more often compete with rather than support or illustrate the music and epic drama. Opera purists will howl at the wholesale cuts (some 105 minutes worth) and Zulawski's often outlandish scenic interpolations. Mussorgsky's magnificent music, even in truncated form, still KO's Zulawski's lunatic-asylum histrionics. Possible controversy may fuel b.o. chances, which are limited anyway to specialty theaters.

Zulawski even injects some political anachronisms, such as a crowd of extras suddenly framed through concentration camp barbed wire, and Soviet soldiers on patrol with watchdogs.

Director's trademark tracking shots and wild-eyed marionette-like performances divert attention from the tragedy of Boris Godunov, the 16th-century Czar, feverishly acted and sung without any pathetic majesty by Ruggero Raimondi. Zulawski goes in for acrobatic fornications by the novice monk-turned-false Czarevitch Dimitri (personified by Pavel Slaby mostly in his birthday suit). Delphine Forest provides equally pointless female nudity as Marina Mnichek, who's introduced already in bed with Slaby and later takes her bath with an inflated toy duck. Slaby also plays the Innocent, a village idiot.

Only three of the leads — Raimondi, Kenneth Riegel as Prince Chouisky and Romuald Tesarowicz as the hermit Varlaam — sing their own parts; other roles are portrayed by actors post-synched by professional singers, which allows Zulawski more leeway in bending thesps to his own style. Among other players are Bernard Lefort, former administrator of the Paris Opera, cast as the old monk Pimene.

Toscan du Plantier pulled this one off for a $7-million pricetag and got spectacular production values for his money from the Belgrade studios. Sizable part of budget was sunk into the recording of the full opera version, which will be released by Erato records. —*Len.*

Otokowa Tsuraiyo Torajiro Sarada Kinenbi (Tora-San's Salad-Day Memorial) (JAPANESE)

San Juan   A Kiyoshi Shimazu, Shochiku Co. production. Directed by Yoji Yamada. Screenplay, Yamada, Yoshitaka Asama, based on a collection of poems by Machi Tawara; camera (Widescreen, color), Tetsuo Takaba; editor, Iwao Ishii; music, Naozumi Yamamoto; art direction, Mitsuo Dekawa. Reviewed at San Juan Cinemafest, Teatro Tapia, San Juan, P.R., Nov. 6, 1989. Running time: **101 MIN.**

Torajiro (Tora-san) . . . . . . Kiyoshi Atsumi
Machiko . . . . Yoshiko Mita
Also with: Iliroko Mita, Chieko Balsho, Gin Maeda, Masami Shimojo, Chieko Misaki, Hisao Dazai, Hidetaka Yoshioka, Chishu Ryu.

■**The 40th installment in Japan's popular Tora-san series, "Tora-san's Salad-Day Memori-**

al," is a strange blend of comedy and poetry combined with a troubled love story. Off-shore marketing chances seem slim outside ethnic venues.

(No. 41, "Tora-san Goes To Vienna," reviewed in VARIETY Nov. 15.)

Pic again teams writer-helmer Yoji Yamada and his itinerant creation Tora-san, the lovable bumbling peddler, perennially played by Kiyoshi Atsumi. Title refers to a tome of Tanka poems written by a young woman poet in honor of the day she tossed Tora-san a salad. Character of the poet is based on Machi Tawara, whose tome of Tanka verse was a national bestseller.

Story finds Tora-san hooking up with an ailing old woman during his travels. Through her, he meets and falls for her doctor, a young widow named Machiko (Yoshiko Mita). Although he is attracted, Tora-san is afraid to commit himself.

The rest of the film revolves around Tora-san's relations with his family in Tokyo, while he tries to come up with excuses to see the doctor. When it looks like they will finally get together, he bolts and returns to his adventurous life.

Throughout, pic is peppered with Tanka verses that highlight poetic scenes.

While tech credits are up to par, main marketing problem is cultural. Although Tora-san is charming and a bit of a rogue, his context is defined within Japanese society. Foreigners lacking reference undoubtedly will be puzzled by much of the humor and situations depicted.—*Lent.*

Alienator

New York   An Amazing Movies presentation of an American-Independent Prods./-Majestic Intl. production. Produced by Jeffrey C. Hogue. Executive producers, Tom Howard, Daniel Q. Kennis. Directed by Fred Oien Ray. Screenplay, Paul Garson; camera (color), Gary Graver; editor, Chris Roth; music, Chuck Cirino; sound, Christopher Endicott; art direction, Lindah Lauderbaugh; costume design, Jill Conner; assistant directors, Joseph Zimmerman, Grant Austin Waldman; production manager-associate producer, Jeffrey B. Mallian; stunt coordinator, Bobby Bragg. Reviewed on Prism Entertainment vidcassette, N.Y., Nov. 18, 1989. MPAA Rating: R. Running time: **92 MIN.**

Commander . . . . Jan-Michael Vincent
Ward . . . . John Phillip Law
Kol . . . . Ross Hagen
Orrie . . . . Dyana Ortelli
Benny . . . . Jesse Dabson
Caroline . . . . Dawn Wildsmith
Tara . . . . P.J. Soles
Alienator . . . . Teagan Clive

Also with: Robert Clarke, Richard Wiley, Leo V. Gordon, Robert Quarry, Fox Harris, Hoke Howell, Jay Richardson, Dan Golden, Jeffrey C. Hogue.

■ "Alienator" is a tongue-in-cheek sci-fi thriller geared toward homevideo fans with a soft spot for the old stars and old-fashioned serials.

Film dovetails closely with previous pics by Fred Olen Ray, particularly "Star Slammer," in a tale of rebel leader Ross Hagen, who escapes execution on a remote prison planet and travels to Earth. Muscle lady Teagan Clive (as title "Alienator") is sent to destroy his Earthling youngsters, led by Jesse Dabson and Dawn Wildsmith, befriend Hagen.

The appearance of genre vets like Robert Clarke and Robert Quarry is a plus, but "Alienator" suffers from a weak script. Leads Jan-Michael Vincent and John Phillip Law have little to do; Wildsmith is cast against type in an uncharacteristically wimpy role, and P.J. Soles is stuck in a rather goofy costume as an outer space technician.

Not enough is made of Teagan Clive as the title character; she's strange and awesome looking in a revealing heavy metal outfit but had a much better role in the Italian horror film "Obsession: A Taste For Fear."

Tech credits are adequate.
—Lor.

Dial: Help
(ITALIAN)

New York A Metro Film and San Francisco Film production, presented by Giovanni Bertolucci, Galliano Juso, in association with Reteitalia. Directed by Ruggero Deodato. Screenplay, Joseph and Mary Carava, Deodato, from Franco Ferrini's story; camera (Telecolor), Renato Tafuri; editor, Sergio Montanari; music, Claudio Simonetti; sound, Massimo Loffredi; art direction, Antonello Geleng; costumes, Giovanna Deodato; production manager, Tullio Gentili; special effects, Germano Natali; U.S. casting, Jeff Gerrard. Reviewed on Prism Entertainment videcassette, N.Y., Oct. 26, 1989. MPAA Rating: R. Running time: **96 MIN.**
Jennie Cooper . . . . Charlotte Lewis
Prof. Klein . . . . William Berger
    Also with: Marcello Modugno, Mattia Sbragia, Carola Stagnaro, Victor Cavallo, Carlo Monni, Giorgio Tirabassi, Jole Silvani, Cesare Di Vito, Antonietta Di Vizia, Emanuela Fuin, Cyrus Elias, Fausto Lombardi, Monica Dorigatti.

(English soundtrack)

■ Despite its absurd premise, "Dial: Help" emerges as an above-average Italian horror thriller, imported direct to U.S. vidstores.

Charlotte Lewis, the mega-voluptuous costar of "Pirates" and "The Golden Child," is cast against type as a vulnerable British heroine whose innocent dialing of a wrong number sets off a series of supernatural murders.

It seems (rather preposterously) that she's made contact with a long-gone phone romance service whose pent-up energy ("of love and hate," per psychic expert William Berger) finds a mystical outlet through the phone lines. She's plagued by weird voices; the phone kills her tropical fish and her friends are murdered by an invisible presence. Pic climaxes with Lewis retracing her steps and finding the secret room that unlocks the mystery.

Helmer Ruggero Deodato again demonstrates he's near the head of the class in making America-style films in Rome, with an excellent direct English soundtrack. Pic is something of a challenge for fidgety video fans, in that star Lewis doesn't really get down and boogie until the final reel; her prudish performance up until that point is definitely misleading.

Finale, however, is worth waiting for, as Deodato combines voyeurism and bondage motifs memorably in a kinky payoff for which Lewis takes on the idealized look of a John Willie adult cartoon character. Pic definitely is a showcase for the exotic star, whose physical attributes could well win her an extended Italian career parallel to current reigning local star Serena Grandi.

Unidentified supporting cast is good and all tech credits are solid.
—Lor.

LONDON FILM FESTIVAL

Children Of Chaos
(FRENCH)

London A Les Films de l'Equinoxe production. Executive producer, Patrick Delauneux. Produced and directed by Yannick Bellon. Screenplay, Bellon, Loleh Bellon, Gerard Segue, Remi Waterhouse; camera (color), Pierre-William Glenn; editor, Kenout Peltier; music, Michel Portal; sound, Bruno Charrier, Elvire Lerner; art direction, Jacques Voizot; costumes, Zorica Lozic, Françoise Tournafond. Reviewed at London Film Festival, Nov. 20, 1989. Running time: **98 MIN.**
Marie . . . . Emmanuelle Béart
Robert . . . . Robert Hossein
Patrick . . . . Patrick Catalifo
Lena . . . . Mona Bausson
Pierre . . . . Pierre Bergez
Xavier . . . . Thierry Miroux
Richard . . . . Adel Bellali
Hassina . . . . Yamina Meraihi

■ "Children Of Chaos" is a thoughtful study of drug abuse among French youth. While its setting — a therapeutic theater group — and characters are vaguely romantic, helmer Yannick Bellon shows an impressive hard edge.

The theatrical environment may be romantic, but at lest the drug-taking never is portrayed as such. And the pic offers a message of hope.

Story opens in a women's prison, where Emmanuelle Béart is watching a play. She later speaks to one of the castmembers, who inexplicably arranges her parole as long as she joins the Theatre de Fil troupe.

Béart finds herself in a kind of worthy reform school, where criminals are supposed to rehabilitate themselves through acting. Naturally she finds it all a bit stupid, but gradually she joins in, eventually turning to tutor Robert Hossein for help.

Subplot is the fact that Béart is the mother of a small child, and through her work with the troupe grows closer to the child. Béart has a few days away from the theater when she slips back into prostitution and drugs, but finally returns, and the picture ends with a sense of optimism.

Béart's low-key acting is appropriate for the washed-out, confused Marie. The rest of the young cast is enthusiastic, while Hossein as the teacher Robert is suitably sage-like.

The direction is sharp and sometimes crude, but Bellon has made a caring and humanistic film that offers no simple answers. Pic may be overly liberal in its outlook, but it still amounts to a quality feminist film. Tech credits are fine.
—Adam.

Quest For Love
(SOUTH AFRICAN)

London A Distant Horizon production. Executive producer, Anant Singh. Produced by Shan Moodley. Written and directed by Helena Nogueira, from the novel "Q.E.D." by Gertrude Stein and the writings of Antonio A. Goncalves. Camera (Technicolor), Roy Macgregor; editor, Noguiera; editor, Noguiera; music, Tony Rudner; production design, Beverly Lanyon; art direction, Adrianne Grabman; sound, Owen Keyser; costumes, Leigh van de Merwe. Reviewed at London Film Festival, Nov. 18, 1989. Running time: **93 MIN.**
Alex . . . . Jana Cilliers
Dorothy . . . . Sandra Prinsloo
Michael . . . . Andrew Buckland
Mabel . . . . Joanna Weinberg
Zaccharia . . . . Wayne Bowman
Isabella . . . . Lynn Gaines
Cokwana . . . . S. Prince Mokhini
Mapule . . . . Frances Ndlazilwana

■ "Quest For Love" is an intelligent and compassionate film tracing the political and sexual confusion of a woman recently released from prison in South Africa. It is well directed by Helena Nogueira.

The pic benefits from an excellent performance by Jana Cilliers as the tormented Alex, in whom she instills an innate intelligence and commitment. Pic is complex, with a lot of emphasis on flashbacks, but always manages to maintain interest.

"Quest For Love" opens with Cilliers spends her time getting to prison and returning to her home country of Manzania to stay with Sandra Prinsloo in her cottage in the bush.

Prinsloo is not at the cottage, so Ciliers spends her time getting to know the locals and reminiscing on the period just before she was arrested. Through flashbacks she is seen boarding Prinsloo's yacht (the "Q.E.D."), where she has to confront her sexual and political confusion.

On board she is met by her boyfriend, Andrew Buckland (later murdered in prison), who gives her photographs of atrocities committed by the South African Defence Force. Also on board she makes love with Prinsloo, but cannot commit herself to that relationship.

Back in Manzania she sets about rebuilding a school destroyed by the South Africans and has a fling with a muscular painter. Ultimately, though, she is waiting for Prinsloo's return so she can admit that she is able to fully commit herself.

Cilliers seems easily able to handle the intellectual and sexual complexities of her character. Prinsloo is fine, though she makes Dorothy a little blander than the characters around her seem to think she is. The male characters really are little more than caricatures — the boyfriend Buckland is set up just to get shot, while Wayne Bowman is asked to do little more than be lusty and sweaty.

"Quest For Love" is an impressive film from relative newcomer Helena Noguiera, who ably handles the directing, screenplay and editing chores. Other tech credits are fine.—*Adam*.

Sophisticated Lady
(BRITISH-DOCU)

A Davids Film Co. production for Channel 4. Produced and directed by David Mingay, David Robinson. Camera (Eastman color), Jack Hazan; editor, Mingay; music, Duke Ellington, Harold Arlen; sound, Manor Mobile; art direction, Michael D. Howells. Reviewed at London Film Festival, Nov. 14, 1989. Running time: **78 MIN.**
With: Adelaide Hall, Benny Waters, the Mike Pyne Trio.

■ **This enjoyable portrait of American singer Adelaide Hall presents a picture of an irresistibly happy and even joyful woman, and one of showbiz' great survivors. Pic is a captivating documentary with real appeal to music fans.**

"Sophisticated Lady" is a smooth and knowledgeable production, which takes in an interview with Hall, film from an April concert in London and archival footage and recordings. On stage with her at the concert is Benny Waters, and together they give a performance of vitality and skill.

Hall wears a warm smile and shares nothing but fond memories of her early years with black revues, recalling her Broadway debut in 1921, her years at the Cotton Club, and working in Paris and London. She is encouraged to recall the people and the tunes, and tends to gloss over the racism aspect.

The inclusion of old footage — Fats Waller accompanies her on a Hammond organ on "That Old Feeling" — makes a nice contrast to the concert footage. Codirectors David Robinson (critic and director of the Edinburgh Film Festival) and David Mingay include rendi-

tions of classics like "Ill Wind," "Diga Diga Do," "Drop Me Off In Harlem" and "When A Man Loves A Woman." Hall's sense of enjoyment makes the scenes truly pleasurable.—*Adam*.

A Private Life
(BRITISH)

London A Totem producton for BBC TV. Executive producer, Innes Lloyd. Produced by Francis Gerard, Roland Robinson. Directed by Gerard. Screenplay, Andrew Davies; camera (Eastman color), Nat Crosby; editor, Robin Sales; music, Trevor Jones; production design, Mark Wilby; sound, Robin Harris; costumes, Diane Cilliers; associate producer, Moira Tuck. Reviewed at London Film Festival, Nov. 14, 1989. Running time: **95 MIN.**

Jack	Bill Flynn
Stella	Jana Cilliers
Older Paul	Kevin Smith
Older Karen	Embeth Davidtz
Older Gary	Lance Maron
Young Paul	Justin John
Young Karen	Talia Leibman
Young Gary	Warren Hetz
Sgt. Smith	Ian Roberts
Dickie	Jamie Bartlett
Abe Kotlowitz	Anthony Fridjhon

■ **"A Private Life" is a moving and compassionate film about the effects of apartheid on a couple, one of whom happens to be white, the other "colored." Despite the drama, it's not a totally downbeat story, and the pic features attractive performances and direction.**

Helmer/producer Francis Gerard had been planning the film since 1977 when he met the couple the story is based on in Cape Town. Pic is a BBC TV production that rightly has received a theatrical release in the U.K., and it would be an important addition to any film festival.

Bill Flynn is a policeman in 1950s Cape Town purely because he needs a job (he gets lectures from superiors because he never arrests anyone). He meets Jana Cilliers in a local cafe, and slowly they fall in love.

Cilliers discovers her application for a "white" identity card has been turned down. Because she can't fully trace her family she is classified as colored — meaning her marriage to Flynn would be illegal.

She finds herself pregnant and Flynn buys himself out of the force. They begin a life of lies across the color bar. While they have no problems fitting into the community, where it is assumed she is "white," attempts to get her reclassified fail.

As the years go by, the strain of trying to protect their three children from the consequences of col-

or bias grow heavier, and their eldest son, Kevin Smith, begins to blame his mother for his problems. He falls in love with a "white" girl, but cannot marry her, and chooses to kill himself after an argument with Cilliers.

Performances by Flynn and Cilliers are excellent, and they ably show how apartheid can harm even the most harmless couple. Smith is fine in his early scenes, though his part becomes a melodramatic device.

"A Private Life" is obviously a labor of love for filmmaker Gerard, and he treats it with intelligence and understanding. He is greatly aided by a fine script by Andrew Davies and outstanding camerawork by Nat Crosby.

—*Adam*.

Driving Miss Daisy

Hollywood A Warner Bros. release of a Zanuck Co. production. Produced by Richard D. Zanuck, Lili Fini Zanuck. Executive producer, David Brown. Coexecutive producer, Jake Eberts. Directed by Bruce Beresford. Screenplay, Alfred Uhry, based on his play; camera (Technicolor), Peter James; editor, Mark Warner; music, Hans Zimmer; production design, Bruno Rubeo; art direction, Victor Kempster; set decoration, Crispian Sallis; costume design, Elizabeth McBride; sound (Dolby), Hank Garfield; makeup supervisor, Manlio Rocchetti; assistant director, Kaherli Frauenfelder; associate producers, Robert Doudell, Uhry; casting (Atlanta), Elyn S. Wright. Reviewed at The Burbank Studios, Calif., Nov. 29, 1989. MPAA Rating: PG. Running time: **99 MIN.**

Hoke Colburn	Morgan Freeman
Daisy Werthan	Jessica Tandy
Boolie Werthan	Dan Aykroyd
Florina Werthan	Patti LuPone
Idella	Esther Rolle

■ **With guaranteed Oscar nominations for career-crowning performances by Morgan Freeman and Jessica Tandy, Warner Bros.' "Driving Miss Daisy" is a touching exploration of 25 years of change in Southern race relations (1948-73) as seen through the relationship of an elderly Jewish widow and her stalwart black chauffeur.**

Bruce Beresford's sensitive direction complements Alfred Uhry's skillful adapation of his Pulitzer Prize-winning play. The gemlike Zanuck Co. film should be a good b.o. performer.

The rare kind of story whose small observations suggest large social truths without pretension, "Driving Miss Daisy" manages to make its two central characters memorably individualized even as it uses them to illustrate profound social developments.

Freeman, re-creating his Obie-winning role of Hoke Colburn, and the veteran Tandy as Daisy Werthan triumphantly and indelibly bring these characters to life.

Set in the relatively tolerant city of Atlanta, where white matrons in the pre-Civil Rights era could pride themselves on their lack of prejudice while still acting as

Original play

Playwrights Horizons presentation of a comedy-drama in one act by Alfred Uhry. Staged by Ron Lagomarsino. Settings, Thomas Lynch; costumes, Michael Krass; lighting, Ken Tabachnick; music, Robert Waldman; production manager, Carl Mulert; stage manager, Anne Marie Kuehling; publicity, Bob Ullman; artistic director, Andre Bishop; executive director, Paul Daniels. Opened April 16, '87, at Playwrights Horizons, N.Y. $17.50 top.
Cast: Morgan Freeman, Ray Gill, Dana Ivey.

bossy as all get out to their black help, "Daisy" effortlessly evokes the changing periods on a limited budget.

This is one play that not only shows no strain in being opened up for the screen, but actually improves in the process. Since forward motion is partly what it's about, and the settings through which Hoke and Daisy pass are so germane, Uhry's expansion of his intimate three-character play enhances his themes and broadens the audience's social perspective on the characters.

Tandy is a powerful stroke of casting, for she is not only the right age for Daisy but also has the flinty, stubborn, somewhat chilly personality that keeps the film from falling into easy sentimental traps.

Her Daisy is a captious and lonely old stick, living a bleakly isolated widow's life in her empty old house, and her inability to keep from tyrannizing Freeman, housekeeper Esther Rolle, and other black helpers gives the film a current of bitter truth, making her gradual friendship with Freeman a hard-won achievement.

Freeman's Hoke is the essence of tact, a man whose lifelong habituation to a white person's slights has given him a quiet, philosophical acceptance of his role in life and a secret sense of amusement toward whites' behavior.

A lesser actor might have been tempted to view Hoke from the outside, to graft a contemporary sensibility onto him, to wink at the audience or indulge in implausible outbursts.

Freeman has the wisdom and compassion to absorb himself into situations which can only be painful for a black actor to recall, remaining true to history and paying tribute to the people who lived it.

It's a satisfying road from Daisy rebuffing Hoke's attempts to ingratiate himself in 1948, to his refusal to keep driving when he wants to relieve himself on a 1955 journey, to the infirm old woman finally taking his hand in 1973 and murmuring, "Hoke, you're my best friend." His habitual and laconic "Yassum," repeated in different keys, becomes the moving emblem for the character.

Dan Aykroyd, shedding his smart-ass comic persona, is fine as Daisy's longsuffering son Boolie, who forces Hoke onto his mother and runs diplomatic interference between them throughout.

Pulling off the difficult task of growing from young manhood to late middle age, Aykroyd is a sympathetic audience surrogate figure, yet a man whose liberal instincts can't quite transcend the limitations of his time and place.

Uhry is less successful fleshing out the script with characters who didn't appear in the play. Patti LuPone is never allowed to develop Boolie's social-climbing wife Florina beyond a vulgar caricature.

Rolle has some choice moments in a sort of Hattie McDaniel part as Idella, but her funeral scene doesn't become the emotional epiphany it should be despite soloist Indra A. Thomas' superb rendition of "What A Friend We Have In Jesus." —Mac.

Blaze

Hollywood   A Buena Vista release of a Touchstone Pictures presentation, in association with Silver Screen Partners IV, of an A&M Films production. Produced by Gil Friesen. Dale Pollock. Executive producers, David Lester, Don Miller. Written and directed by Ron Shelton, based on book "Blaze Starr: My Life As Told To Huey Perry," by Blaze Starr, Huey Perry; camera (Duart color), Haskell Wexler; editor, Robert Leighton; music, Bennie Wallace; sound (Dolby), Kirk Francis; production design, Armin Ganz; art direction, Edward Richardson; set design, Harold Fuhrman; set decoration, Michael J. Taylor, Rosemary Brandenburg; costume design, Ruth Myers; assistant director, Yudi Bennett; 2d unit director, David Lester, 2d unit camera, John Toll; associate producer, Wendy Dozoretz; casting, Victoria Thomas. Reviewed at Mann's Bruin theater, Westwood. Calif., Dec. 7, 1989. MPAA Rating: R. Running time: 108 MIN.

Earl Long	Paul Newman
Blaze Starr	Lolita Davidovich
Thibodeaux	Jerry Hardin
LaGrange	Gailard Sartain
Tuck	Jeffrey DeMunn
Doc Ferriday	Garland Bunting
Picayune	Richard Jenkins
Red Snyder	Robert Wuhl

■ A bawdy and audacious tale of politics and scandal, "Blaze" delivers one of the best love stories of the year and a brave and marvelous character turn by Paul Newman. Audiences may at first be indifferent to period piece drawn from dusty New Orleans headlines, but word-of-mouth should lead to solid box-office.

Writer-director Ron Shelton is emerging as one of the most refreshing entertainers around. Like his "Bull Durham," "Blaze" fields a quirky and original chunk of Americana, and loads the bases with rich dialog and comedy.

Pic, like most based on real life, doesn't tie up into a satisfying whole. The rhythms are inconvenienced by actual events, and some issues must be tiptoed around. What extraordinary material there is, Shelton makes the most of, taking generous liberties here and there.

Newman plays Louisiana governor Earl K. Long, brother of the equally notorious former guv'nor Huey P. Long, in 1959-60 during his May-December romance with famed New Orleans stripper Blaze Starr (Lolita Davidovich).

"Ol' Earl," a self-decribed "pro-gressive thinker," was a stump speaker extraordinaire, an advocate of black voting rights and a friend of the poor man. He was also, many believed, a tax evader, a drunk and a madman. Starr was a queen of tawdry New Orleans showbiz who'd come up from poverty in the Tennessee hills.

In Shelton's hands, their relationship, which churned up newspaper headlines and plagued Long's teetering career, is a great and comic love story. From the beginning we know these two individualists are a fine match, and so do they.

Blaze, deftly played by newcomer Davidovich, knows what a man needs and what she needs, and with Earl makes a solid match of the two. Davidovich is impressive, taking the character from a clunky, overripe hillbilly teenager to a woman with her powers fully focused. Despite the showbiz savvy, Davidovich plays Blaze unhardened — she loves Earl, and the audience never doubts it. Drawback is that she comes across so upright and good it seems like a whitewash.

Newman is less careful with his character — anybody would question Earl's fitness for public office while admiring his unhinged passion. Newman transforms into Earl — mussed hair, gravelly voice, wild blue eyes and arched brow, with an old man's faraway fix on a vision that's behind him now.

A role this ribald and colorful would have been cartoonish in other hands; Newman tamps it down with his natural gravity. At the same time, he's funny and touching in the love scenes. Role is packed with marvelous moments for him; it was a challenge well met.

Shelton wisely emphasizes the love story. Earl's support of the politically deadly voting rights bill for blacks wins him our interest and sympathy, but lands him in a mental hospital after he storms the floor of the Legislature to make a crazily impassioned argument for it. It's an amazing true incident, but after that the issue is dropped.

"Blaze" is packed with entertainment, a reminder of an era when politics reflected the passions of its practitioners, and presents a couple of memorable characters who remain true to themselves.

Armin Ganz' production design is richly authentic, and Haskell Wexler's photography makes pic a treat to behold. Well-selected score of regional standards adds much to the pic's appeal. —Daws.

Family Business

Hollywood   A Tri-Star Pictures release in association with Regency Intl. Pictures of a Gordon Co. production. Produced by Lawrence Gordon. Executive producers, Jennifer Ogden, Burtt Harris. Directed by Sidney Lumet. Screenplay, Vincent Patrick, based on his novel; camera (Technicolor), Andrzej Bartkowiak; editor, Andrew Mondshein; music, Cy Coleman; sound (Dolby), Maurice Shell; production design, Philip Rosenberg; art direction, Robert Guerra; set decoration, Gary Brink; costume design, Ann Roth; assistant director, Michael Haley; casting, Meg Simon, Fran Kumin. Reviewed at the Burbank Studios, Burbank, Calif., Nov. 29, 1989. MPAA Rating: R. Running time: 115 MIN.

Jessie	Sean Connery
Vito	Dustin Hoffman
Adam	Matthew Broderick
Elaine	Rosana DeSoto
Margie	Janet Carroll
Christine	Victoria Jackson

Also with: Bill McCutcheon, Deborah Rush, Marilyn Cooper, Salem Ludwig, Rex Everhart, James S. Tolkan, Marilyn Sokol, B. D. Wong.

■ Sean Connery steals scenes as well as merchandise in an immensely charismatic turn to make "Family Business" one of the year's better films — a darkly comic tale about three generations brought together and torn apart by their common attraction to thievery.

"Business" should heist its share of seasonal boxoffice, its astral cast appealing to both young and old.

Director Sidney Lumet has crafted a film with real pathos mercifully bereft of the shameless sentimentality that's run rampant this season, while writer Vincent Patrick (adapting his own novel) injects enough bawdy humor to create a delightful mixed bag spiced with almost a European sensibility.

The key, however, is Connery, who dives head-first into his part as amoral family patriarch Jessie, surfacing with a character to rival his Oscar-winning role in "The Untouchables."

Despite fine performances by Dustin Hoffman and to a lesser degree Matthew Broderick, without Connery the house of cards on which the film is built might easily tumble down.

He's an unabashed rogue well into his 60s who, when we meet him, must be bailed out of jail after savaging an off-duty cop in a bar fight. Connery cuts an irresistible figure to his sheltered Ivy League grandson (Broderick), who enlists the old man's aid to carry out a high-tech robbery.

Caught in the middle, literally and figuratively, is the boy's father, Hoffman, who once had the same relationship with his father and ended up doing hard time for it.

Hoffman is now a semirespectable businessman who dabbles only in white-collar crime, though there's clearly a darker side to him that misses his wayward past despite his resentment toward Connery. Broderick, meanwhile, hopes to prove himself to the elder members of the McMullen clan by demonstrating his courage — even if he has to wear preppy-looking glasses over his ski mask.

Lumet brings out the nuances of these family relationships in a breezy fashion that's rarely heavy-handed, including Rosana DeSoto's refreshingly tough presence as Vito's wife to break up all the male bonding.

Still, the heart of the film involves the men learning to deal with one another, as each father must resolve feelings toward his son, and vice versa.

The richness of Connery's character allows Lumet to deal with the comic overtones of crime without having to preach about it. While it's subtly made clear there is a right and wrong here, Connery never bows to such conventions, nor would it be believable for him to do so.

Hoffman has worked his own quiet magic following his Oscar for "Rain Man" with another deft performance that's less flashy but calls for great inner strength.

(As for those who might question Connery playing father to an actor only eight years his junior, the casting proves far more believable than the Cruise-Hoffman brother pairing in "Rain Man." It's also notable that the film jokes about the disparity between them since Connery towers over Hoffman.)

Lumet nimbly straddles the line between comedy and drama without resorting to the camp elements of something like "Prizzi's Hon-

or." The tone more closely resembles Lumet's "Dog Day Afternoon," a mix of big laughs with strong drama.

Like that film's "Attica" sequence, "Family Business" also has one scene destined to become a much-repeated classic, as Connery demonstrates prison ground rules to a van full of prospective inmates.

Tech credits are firstrate, with Cy Coleman's jazzy score perfectly setting the mood.—*Bril.*

Glory

Hollywood A Tri-Star Pictures release of a Freddie Fields production. Produced by Fields. Coproducer, Pieter Jan Brugge. Directed by Edward Zwick. Screenplay, Kevin Jarre, based on books "Lay This Laurel" by Lincoln Kirstein and "One Gallant Rush: Robert Gould Shaw And His Brave Black Regiment" by Peter Burchard, and letters of Col. Robert Gould Shaw; camera (Technicolor), Freddie Francis; editor, Steven Rosenblum; additional editing, T. Battle Davis; music, James Horner, The Boys Choir of Harlem; production design, Norman Garwood; supervising art director, Keith Pain; art direction, Dan Webster; set decoration, Garrett Lewis; costume design, Francine Jamison-Tanchuck; sound (Dolby), Russell Williams; stunt coordinator, Bob Minor; battle consultant, B.H. Barry; special effects coordinator, Phil Cory; special visual effects, Syd Dutton, Bill Taylor, Illusion Arts Inc.; makeup effects, Kevin Yagher; assistant director, Skip Cosper; 2d unit director, Dan Lerner; 2d unit camera, David Wagreich; associate producers, Ray Herbeck, Jr., Sarah Caplan, P.K. Fields Zimmerman; casting, Mary Colquhoun, Shay Griffin (Atlanta). Reviewed at AMC Century 14, Hollywood, Nov. 28, 1989. MPAA Rating: R. Running time: **122 MIN.**
Col. Robert Gould
  Shaw . . . . Matthew Broderick
Ptv. Trip . . . . Denzel Washington
Maj. Cabot Forbes . . . . Cary Elwes
Sgt. Maj. Rawlins . . . . Morgan Freeman
Pvt. Jupiter Sharts . . . . Jihmi Kennedy
Pvt. Thomas Searles . . . . . Andre Braugher
Sgt. Maj. Mulcahy . . . . John Finn
Gov. John A. Andrew . . . . Alan North
Gen. Harker . . . . Bob Gunton
Col. James Montgomery . . . Cliff DeYoung
Edward Pierce . . . . Christian Baskous
Mute Drummer Boy . . . . RonReaco Lee
Maj. Gen. George C.
  Strong . . . . Jay O. Sanders
Quartermaster . . . . Richard Riehle
Bigoted Soldier . . . . Mark A. Levy
Sarah Shaw . . . . Jane Alexander
Frederick Douglass . . Raymond St. Jacques

■ **A stirring and long overdue tribute to the black soldiers who fought for the Union cause in the Civil War, "Glory" has the sweep and magnificence of a Tolstoy battle tale or a John Ford saga of American history.**

The Tri-Star release is a courageous achievement for producer Freddie Fields, director Edward Zwick and screenwriter Kevin Jarre to have brought forth in today's marketplace.

"Glory" tells the story of the 54th Regiment of Massachusetts

Volunteer Infantry, the first black fighting unit raised in the North during the Civil War.

As the war went on, 186,107 blacks fought for the Union, and 37,300 of them died.

"Glory" provides a fitting memorial to that chapter of the nation's history previously celebrated by Robert Lowell in his poem "For The Union Dead" but not on the screen, where the treatment of the Civil War for the most part has been conspicuously skewed toward romanticizing the Confederacy in such landmark films as "The Birth Of A Nation" and "Gone With The Wind."

Matthew Broderick's starring role as Col. Shaw, the callow youth from an abolitionist family who proved his mettle in training and leading his black soldiers, is not only beautifully acted but perfectly judged in terms of dramatic proportion, never overwhelming the importance of the supporting parts played by black actors.

Broderick's boyishness initially seems incongruous in a role of command, but that becomes a key element of the drama, as the film shows him confiding his inadequacies in letters home to his mother (the unbilled Jane Alexander) and struggling to assert leadership of his often recalcitrant men.

Although the film indulges in some romanticism of its own by portraying blacks as unambiguously eager to enlist in the Union Army in 1862 — when in fact the initial refusal of the North to let them fight caused some to resist later recruitment — it does not neglect to show the inequities that existed in the Union Army and in Northern society for the men who were willing to give their lives to help save it.

The rage caused by ill treatment is searingly incarnated in a great performance by Denzel Washington, as an unbroken runaway slave whose combative relationship with Broderick provides the dramatic heart of the film.

An unjust whipping ordered by Broderick when Washington goes AWOL to find shoes, and their silent mutual acknowledgement of the wrong, is the beginning of an understanding which culminates in Washington's battlefield heroism as the bearer of the regimental colors.

Both Washington and regiment's first black officer (Morgan Freeman, whose sagacity and strength go beyond acting) should be remembered for these roles at

Oscar time (Freeman may well be nominated twice, for supporting actor here and for best actor in "Driving Miss Daisy").

Jihmi Kennedy is winningly believable as a stuttering country boy with a deadly aim, Andre Braugher is delightful in his film debut as an educated Boston social friend of Broderick's, and Raymond St. Jacques is magisterial in his unbilled cameo as the abolitionist Frederick Douglass.

Of the white characters, Cary Elwes is suitably muddled and warmhearted as Broderick's second-in-command, John Finn has an unsettling presence as an Irish racist drill sergeant, Jay O. Sanders has the stature for Maj. Gen. George C. Strong, and Bob Gunton, Cliff DeYoung, and Richard Riehle effectively play officers whose contempt for black soldiers is surpassed only by their own venality and corruption.

From the carnage of Antietam through the hand-to-hand struggle of James Island to the climactic decimation of the regiment at Fort Wagner in Charleston harbor, "Glory" portrays Civil War combat in all its horror, with a ferocity matched in previous cinematic recreations only by Ford's Shiloh sequence in "How The West Was Won."

"Glory" simplifies history by presenting the decision to have the 54th lead the suicidal assault on Fort Wagner as Shaw's alone, for reasons of regimental honor, despite the debate that persists over whether superior officers used the blacks as cannon fodder.

Freddie Francis' masterful photography, eschewing the sepia haze that too often makes period films seem comfortably distant, plunges the audience into the battles with a vividness that is both spectacular and chilling. —*Mac.*

Enemies, A Love Story

Hollywood A 20th Century Fox release of a Morgan Creek production. Executive producers, James G. Robinson, Joe Roth. Produced by Paul Mazursky. Coproducers, Pato Guzman, Irby Smith. Directed by Mazursky. Screenplay, Roger L. Simon, Mazursky, based on novel by Isaac Bashevis Singer; camera (Deluxe color), Fred Murphy; editor, Stuart Pappé; music, Maurice Jarre; clarinet soloist, Giora Feidman; production design, Guzman; art direction, Steven J. Jordan; set decoration (N.Y.), Ted Glass; costume design, Albert Wolsky; sound (Dolby), Don Cohen; assistant director, Henry Bronchtein; casting, Ellen Chenoweth. Reviewed at 20th Century Fox, L.A., Dec. 7, 1989. MPAA Rating: R. Running time: **119 MIN.**
Herman Broder . . . . Ron Silver

Tamara . . . . Anjelica Huston
Masha . . . . Lena Olin
Yadwiga . . . . Margaret Sophie Stein
Rabbi Lembeck . . . . Alan King
Masha's Mother . . . . Judith Malina
Mrs. Schreier . . . . Rita Karin
Pesheles . . . . Phil Leeds
Yasha Kotik . . . . Elya Baskin
Leon Tortshiner . . . . Paul Mazursky
Baby Masha . . . . Marie-Adele Lemieux

■Haunting, mordantly amusing, deliciously sexy — it's a special film that can manage to be all three at once. "Enemies, A Love Story," Paul Mazursky's triumphant adapation of the Isaac Bashevis Singer novel about a Holocaust survivor who finds himself married to three women in 1949 New York, is perhaps the best film the adventurous producer-director has ever made.

Sophisticated filmgoers will respond with delight to the Fox release of Morgan Creek's production.

Ron Silver is fascinatingly enigmatic in the lead role of Herman Broder. He's a quietly charming, somewhat withdrawn man whose cushy job as a ghostwriter for a very reformed rabbi (Alan King) gives him plenty of time to attend to his deliriously complicated love life.

Glorifying in the perversities of the human heart, Singer has slyly concocted a situation in which the character simultaneously is married to a devoted but cloddish woman (Margaret Sophie Stein), is carrying on a passionate affair with a sultry married woman (Lena Olin), and also finds himself back in the arms of his long-vanished wife (Anjelica Huston), who was thought to be lost in the war.

With the exception of Stein's character, a Polish Gentile peasant who saved Silver's life by hiding him from the Nazis, all of these people are human wreckage of the Holocaust. European immigrant Jews, their devastating experiences have led them to reject the consolations of their former religious faith and to doubt the existence of a God who could allow such an event to occur.

Silver finds himself of necessity reinventing morality day-by-day in a world in which traditional rules seem pointless and absurd. Mazursky and his writing collaborator Roger L. Simon carry off the difficult feat of making this strange man an empathetic figure for the audience even as he strews further ruin in his circuitous path through the boudoirs of Brooklyn, the Bronx and Manhattan.

Like Silver, the audience will find it difficult to prefer one of his three women over the others, since Stein, Olin, and Huston are equally captivating, equally endearing in their entirely different ways.

A Swedish actress best known for her erotically charged performance in "The Unbearable Lightness Of Being," Olin is sensational here as the doomed Masha, for whom lovemaking is the best assertion of life over the inevitability of self-destruction. Although her fate resembles that of Meryl Streep's Holocaust survivor in "Sophie's Choice," this vibrant woman is not so much a victim as a controller of destiny.

All three women, in fact, prove stronger and more capable of dealing with life than Silver is. The film turns from a comedy of adultery into a celebration of the female life force.

Huston is delightfully cynical and courageous as a wry "angel" whose miraculous return seems to give her quasi-mystical powers of healing. Stein, with her broad peasant smile, is adorable as the earth-mother figure who risked her life for Silver and now fiercely defends her marriage and her child against his compulsive philandering.

Maurice Jarre contributed a bewitching, bittersweet score, incorporating klezmer music with clarinet solos by Giora Feidman. Traditional Jewish liturgical music and 1940s pop tunes add to a most captivating soundtrack. —*Mac.*

Resan till Melonia
(The Voyage To Melonia)
(SWEDISH-ANIMATED)

Malmö, Sweden   A Sandrews release of Penn Film production with Sandrews/Filmhuset/SVT2/Skrivstugan/Läskonsten/Film Teknik (Sweden) and Norsk Film(Norway). Produced by Klas Olofsson and Katinka Farago. Directed by Per Ahlin; screenplay, Ahlin, based on "The Tempest" by Shakespeare; editor, Ahlin; camera (color), Pelle Svensson, Piotr Jaworski; music, Björn Isfält, Mats Nörklit; sound (Dolby) Christer Furubrand; production design, Ahlin; directing animators, Kjeld Simonsen, Ahlin, Flemming Jensen, Ulf Ebeling, Lasse Persson, Lise Jörgensen, Guttorm Larsen, Alicja Uchymiak, Thomas Holm, Peter Jando, Hakan Westford. Reviewed at Sandrews 1-3, Malmö, Sweden, Dec. 5, 1989. Running time: 104 MIN.
Prospero. . . . . .Allan Edwall
Miranda. . . . . .Robin Carlsson
Ferdinand. . . . . .Olle Sari
Ariel. . . . . .Tomas von Brömssen
Caliban. . . . . .Ernst Günther
William. . . . . .Jan-Olof Strandberg
Slagg. . . . . .Hans Alfredson
  Also with: Eva Rydberg, Ingvar Kjellson, Jan Blomberg, Nils Eklund.

■"The Voyage To Melonia" by

Per Ahlin, Sweden's past master of animated films, probably has aimed above everybody's head with this go at "The Tempest." Seven years in the making at a locally extraordinary cost of $3.5-million, pic looks big but soon sags dangerously, and eventually ruptures.

The debris includes a claimed Shakespearean inspiration devoid of poetry and drama; plot additions from "Machine Island," a Jules Verne sci-fi novel, and "Robinson Crusoe;" grotesque characters; highfalutin' literary dialog, and a witless score.

Retained from Shakespeare are Prospero as an exiled king-cum-magician on the enchanted island of Melonia, his daughter Miranda, and Ariel and Caliban. But Prospero, with a chin competing for length with his nose, is seen as hapless, Miranda as a doll with nobody to romance her, Ariel as a clumsy yellow albatross and Caliban as giant composite of garden vegetables and fruit.

From the crater of a volcano on the island, Caliban has filled a glass tube with Power Soup. Two evil weapons manufacturers from neighboring Plutonia island arrive, via a tempest-caused shipwreck, to steal the Power Soup. They need it to make the rest of the world just as grim and dirty as Plutonia.

The wrecked ship's master and its boatswain and Prospero's lady cook fill in with some song and dance. William, an Ahlin-invented dog, is given a lot of poetry to recite. Pic slows to near-standstill as everybody from Melonia travels to Plutonia to destroy the munitions plant, free the child slaves and return with the film's ecological moral spelled out in caps.During the Plutonia sequences, some backgrounds and action animation have touches of the grimness of Ralph Bakshi's work.

Otherwise, the backgrounds are mostly pretty, but the characters move about jerkily. Toward the of the pic, "The Tempest" is reintroduced as William has everybody take part in a performance (a tribute to the original Stratford performances of the Bard's works?) of the play in an abandoned theater.

Some of Sweden's best actors and comedy talents have supplied film's voices, but dialog director Per-Arne Ehlin has them all sounding as if they were reciting from books.—*Kell.*

Glass
(AUSTRALIAN)

Sydney   An Oilrag production. Produced by Patrick Fitzgerald, Chris Kennedy. Written and directed by Kennedy; camera (color), Pieter de Vries; editor, James Bradley; music, Mario Gregory; sound, David Glasser; production design, Kerry Ainsworth; production manager, Dathy Flannery; assistant director, Corrie Soeterboek; casting, Chris Kennedy. Reviewed at Mosman screening room, Sydney, Nov. 20, 1989. Running time: 93 MIN.
Julie Vickery. . . . . .Lisa Peers
Richard Vickery. . . . . .Allan Lovell
Peter Breen. . . . . .Adam Stone
Alison Baumer. . . . . . . .Natalie McCurry
Inspector Ambrosoll. . . . . .Bernard Clisby
Charlie. . . . . .Rowan Jackson
Dianne. . . . . .Lucinda Walker-Powell
Brenda. . . . . .Julie Herbert
Veronica. . . . . .Felicity Copeland

■A small-scale thriller, set in Australia's business world of glass skyscrapers and double-dealing, "Glass" emerges as a routine debut for Chris Kennedy. Theatrical chances are slim, though, with electronic media outlets the best bet.

Pic opens with striking images of Sydney's skyline and repeated shots of broken glass. Plot involves Richard Vickery (Alan Lovell), a yuppie business exec who's being fleeced by his lawyer, Breen (Adam Stone). Breen is having an affair with Vickery's wife, Julie (Lisa Peers), and they're trying to con Vickery into approving the development of a casino and hotel complex.

In an early scene, Vickery's secretary (Felicity Copeland) is murdered by an unseen assailant using a shard of glass; she'd tried to tell Vickery something just before her death. Was the killer Breen, or was she victim of a serial killer?

What follows is at times confusing, at times predictable. Once we discover Vickery's new g.f. (Natalie McCurry) is a makeup artist, there are no prizes for guessing an apparent death later in the drama will have been faked.

Peers gives the best performance as the scheming wife, with both Lovell and Stone looking too young for their roles.

For a first effort, Kennedy keeps within a modest but conventional range. The film contains few surprises, and lacks genuine tension. Technical credits are fine.

Item is too slim to qualify for a cinema outing, but could perform modestly on video and other ancillary markets. —*Strat.*

Jydekompagniet III
(The Jut-Nuts III)
(DANISH)

Copenhagen A Pathé-Nordisk Film release of Nordisk Film production in association with the Danish Film Institute. Produced by Michael Obel. Written and directed by Finn Henriksen, based on ideas by Henriksen, Finn Norbygaard, Jacob Haugaard, Michael Obel; camera (Eastmancolor), Lasse Spang Olsen; editor, Jorgen Kastrup, Finn Henriksen; music, Soren Dahl; sound, Preben Mortensen; production design, Soren Skjaer; costumes, Bente Ranning; production management, Pernille Utzon Ravn, Lene Nielsen; assistant director Sanni Sylvester Petersen. Reviewed at the Palads, Copenhagen, Dec. 6, 1989. Running time: **85 MIN.**

Finn.	Finn Norbygaard
Jacob.	Jacob Haugaard
Kordtzack.	Benny Poulsen
Emmy.	Berrit Kvorning
Swiss surgeon.	Jean-Claude Flamant
Arab prince.	Hussein Shehaded

Also with: Poul Huttel, John Martinus, Bjarne Buur, Lillian Tillegreen, Poul Clemmesen, Sune Otterström, others.

■"The Jut-Nuts III" actually is only the second Jut-Nuts pic, but it may be the better one.

As in the first "Jut-Nuts," Finn Norbygaard and Jacob Haugaard are seen as a couple of would-be Bogart-like private eyes in the remote Jutland sticks. They can't make ends meet without hiring out for extracurricular chores like posing as Stone Age cannibals for Japanese tourists or participating in organ transplant experiments (Norbygaard scores big by selling his buddy's heart).

A corrupt hospital manager, a French surgeon, a nurse with a nose fixation and an Arab prince are involved in a series of amicable, rather ploddingly delivered farcial turns.

"The Jut-Nuts III" boasts firstrate technical credits. —*Kell.*

Oiji
(Mr. Canton And Lady Rose)
(HONG KONG)

Honolulu A Golden Harvest presentation of a Golden Way Films Ltd. production. Produced by Wong Jo-yi. Directed by Jackie Chan. Screenplay, Tang King-sang; camera (Scope color), Wong Ngok-tai; editor, Cheung Yui-jung. Reviewed at Hawaii Intl. Film Fest, Nov. 29, 1989. Running time: **125 MIN.**

Kuo Cheng-wah (Mr. Canton).	Jackie Chan
Luming.	Anita Mui
Chief Detective Ho.	Richard Ng

■Hong Kong superstar Jackie Chan, whose films combine breathtaking action, amazing stunts and self-effacing humor, tries a change of pace with "Mr. Canton And Lady Rose."

He adds a Damon Runyon story about rival gangsters, dumb cops and a poor flowerseller whose pretty daughter wants to break into high society. The result is an entertainment package that could find Chan fans worldwide.

Set in the '30s, pic opens with Chan as a naive newcomer to Hong Kong, fresh off the boat from Canton. Swindled out of his meager savings, his luck changes when he's persuaded to spend his last coins on a lucky rose. Almost immediately, he inherits a raffish gang of gamblers from their expiring boss, and finds himself in the money. He's also in the middle of a gang war, and facing the hamfisted investigations of detective Ho and his men.

Much of the plot is freely borrowed from the Runyon story that formed the basis for two Frank Capra classics ("Lady For A Day," and "Pocketful Of Miracles.") The flower-seller's beauteous daughter wants to marry the son of a fabulously wealthy Shanghai merchant, and Chan and his men have to pose as members of Hong Kong's upper-crust to impress the woman's future in-laws. All this is handled with flair and a fine feeling for comedy.

Chan and his formidable stunt team have devised a number of show-stopping action sequences. A sequence in a rope-factory is a classic of its kind, and Chan obviously does all his own work.

The combination of action and comedy, plus the snappy, surefire direction, should enable this pic to play to appreciative audiences the world over; pic already unspooled at the Vancouver film fest.

Production design is a major asset, with much of the action taking place on a vast, beautifully designed outdoor set. All technical credits are great. Pic's original title translates as "Miracles." —*Strat.*

Fengkuang De Daijia
(Obsession)
(CHINESE)

Honolulu A Xi'an Film Studio production. Produced by Wu Tianming. Directed by Zhou Xiaowen. Screenplay, Zhou Xiaowen, Lu Wei; camera (color), Wang Xinsheng. Reviewed at Hawaii Intl. Film Fest., Nov. 28, 1989. Running time: **100 MIN.**

Qingqing.	Bai Yujuan
Lanlan.	Li Xing
Li Changwei.	Xie Yuan
Sun Dach.	Chang Rong

■The renowned Xi'an Film Studio has produced an action piece complete with revenge theme, car chase and soft-core nudity. "Obsession" rates little more than passing interest, even amazement.

Pic opens and closes with a David Hamilton-like sequence, shot in misty light, in which sisters Qingqing and Lanlan bathe each other in a communal shower. Soon after, young Lanlan is raped by a muscular layabout driving a stolen car. Qingqing becomes obsessed with tracking down the rapist and extracting revenge.

Drama unfolds with minimal suspense, a Western-style car chase (in which vehicles drive right through a supermarket) and some soul-searching about the effect of porno literature on disturbed minds.

Pic also comments on the status of young people who live apart from their families (against Chinese tradition): The sisters live alone, and the rapist lives with his brother in a tower apartment from which he spies on people with binoculars.

An important film could have been made from these themes, but "Obsession" comes across as superficial and derivative. Technical credits are passable, and there are good performances from Bai Yujuan (as the older sister) and Li Xing (as the rape victim). The rape itself takes place offscreen, but most of the subsequent drama is unsubtly realized, especially the "Death Wish" style finale at which, one gets the impression, audiences are supposed to barrack for the avenger.

Pics original title translates as "The Cost Of Frenzy." —*Strat.*

Yuanyang lou
(Young Couples)
(CHINESE)

London A Peking Film Academy Youth Film Studio production. Directed by Zheng Dongtian. Screenplay, Wang Peigong. Camera (color), Gu Wenkai, Qu Jianwei; editor, Zhang Langfang; music, Zhang Ruishen; production design, Liu Ying. Reviewed at London Film Festival, Nov. 14, 1989. Running time: **126 MIN.**

Matchmaking wife.	Ji Ling
Husband.	Tian Shaojun
Factory Director's wife.	Fang Hui
Husband.	He Wei
Painter's wife.	Song Chunli
Husband.	Guo Kaimin
Sexually ignorant wife.	Zhao Yue
Husband.	Liu Jian
Hard-working wife.	Song Xiaoying
Husband.	Zhao Fuyu
Studious wife.	Xiao Xiong
Husband.	Liu Xinyi

■This refreshing series of amusing vignettes is a useful reminder that Chinese cinema is not purely about peasants, rice-crops or the Cultural Revolution.

"Young Couples" focuses on a day in the lives six young married couples living in the same high-rise, all trying to cope with assorted domestic problems. The vignettes vary from amusing to insightful, but present the couples simply and without propaganda or political grandstanding.

While Zheng Dongtian's direction may be straightforward, he inspires attractive performances from his band of young actors. Pic, actually shot in 1987, gives fascinating insight into ordinary life in contempo China.—*Adam.*

Ori
(BRAZILIAN-DOCU)

London An Angra Filmes, Fundacao do Cinema Brasileiro production. Produced by Ignacio Gerber. Directed by Raquel Gerber. Screenplay, Beatriz Nascimento; camera (Eastmancolor), Hermano Penna; editor, Renato Neiva Moreira; music, Nana Vasconcelos; sound, Francisco Carneiro, Lia Camargo, Walter Rogerio. Reviewed at London Film Festival, Nov. 13, 1989. Running time: **91 MIN.**

■"Ori" means "head" in the language of the Yoruba people of West Africa. In terms of this worthy documentary (originally shot as a 2-part series), it refers to black consciousness in relation to history and time. Pic is ideal for certain film festivals with its strong mixture of political and racial awareness.

It uses the research of black historian Beatriz Nascimento to probe the history of the "Quilombos" and their hero Zumbi, who wanted to build a new Brazilian nation in the 17th century, integrating black people and Indians.

That concept is at the core of "Ori," which follows the black movement in Brazil and the Americas, and traces the black culture brought to the Americas from West Africa. Docu draws on historical footage and film of black movement meetings to show how black cultures are linked and are becoming strengthened.

At times fascinating and thought-provoking, "Ori"occasionally lapses into the pompous and indulgently intellectual and sometimes the pic's 90 minutes drag. —*Adam.*

The 13th Floor
(AUSTRALIAN)

Sydney A Premiere Film Marketing presentation in association with Medusa Communications. Produced by David Hannay, Charles Hannah. Executive producer, Tom Broadbridge. Directed by Chris Roache; camera (Eastmancolor), Stephen Prime; editor, Peter McBain; music, Mick Coleman; sound, David Glasser; production design, Darrell Lass; production manager, Julia Ritchie; assistant director, Ian Astridge; casting, Shauna Crowley. Reviewed at Mosman screening room, Sydney, Nov. 15, 1989. Running time: **94 MIN.**

Heather Thompson	Lisa Hensley
John Burke	Tim McKenzie
Rebecca	Miranda Otto
Bert	Jeff Truman
Brenner	Vic Rooney
Dr. Fletcher	Michael Caton
Thompson	Tony Blackett
Nick	Paul Hunt
Alistair	Adam Cook
Boy	Matthew Nicholls

■ **"The 13th Floor" is a creaky ghost story gone direct to video in Oz. It's the weakest in a quartet of pics assembled by Premiere Film Marketing and Medusa Communications.**

Pic starts with 8-year-old Heather Thompson witnessing her politician father order the torture of a man on the 13th floor of an uncompleted building. The man's son is electrocuted accidentally.

Heather, now age 20 and played by Lisa Hensley, is estranged from her father. With druggie friend Rebecca (Miranda Otto), she camps on the 13th floor of the office building, a floor that remains vacant because it's rumored to be haunted.

It is, indeed, haunted — by the ghost of the electrocuted lad. But he's a friendly spook, and comes to Heather's aid against assorted baddies, including a private eye (Vic Rooney) sent by her father to kill her because she has incriminating info on him.

Pic is light on thrills, since the ghost obviously is on the heroine's side. The villains, including the building's macho caretaker and another hitman, aren't very threatening.

A rather nasty sequence has Heather captured and drugged by her father's underlings.

Hensley has little to do except look nervous. Technically, the film is fine except for the great banks of light in the supposedly deserted office. Newcomer Chris Roache, who wrote and directed, misses an opportunity here. —*Strat.*

Wan-ch'un ch'ing-shih
(Spring Swallow)
(TAIWANESE-HONG KONG)

London A Central Motion Picture Corp./KCI Prods. (Taiwan)/Golden Harvest (Hong Kong) production. Executive producers, Hsu Hsin-chih, Raymond Chow, Sun Ta-ch'iang. Produced by Lin Teng-fei, Ho Kuan-ch'ang, Sun Ta-wei. Directed by Richard Chen. Screenplay, Hsi Sung, Ko Pi; camera (Agfacolor), Lin Wen-chin; editor, Ch'en Po-wen; music, Chang Fan Chi-yu; production design, William Cheung, Li Pao-lin; sound, Hsin Chiang-sheng; costumes, Fan Chi-yu. Reviewed at London Film Festival, Nov. 24, 1989. Running time: **99 MIN.**

Yin Ch'un-yen (Spring Swallow)	Lu Hsiao-fen
Chang	Chang Fu-chien
Ping-chung	Ma Ching-t'ao
Chang's mother	Chuang Yuan-yung
Lin	Chiang Hou-jen
Mrs Yang	Wen Ying
Ch'un-yen's mother	Ting Yeh-t'ien
Ch'un-yen's father	Ch'ang Feng

■ **"Spring Swallow" is a finely crafted period drama about a woman trapped in a marriage she doesn't want and the repercussions she endures when she takes a lover. Veteran helmer Richard Chen has fashioned a classic (and classy) pic, with a fine lead performance by Lu Hsiao-fen.**

Set in the Fujian province of southern mainland China in 1916, pic follows a very traditional structure, even using chapter introductions to separate sections. Excellent production design, costumes, and camerawork give it a lush, elegant quality.

After her husband dies, Lu Hsiao-fen, an intelligent peasant, is traded into an arranged marriage with wealthy businessman Chang Fu-chien. She tries to make the best of the relationship, but finds him uninterested and uncommunicative.

While he is away on business she succumbs to the temptation of local merchant Ma Ching-t'ao. But she runs into the unexpected interference of Chang's mother Chuang Yuan-yung.

"Spring Swallow" is a simple tale, but per production info, helmer Chen struggled 20 years to make the pic. He directs with assured skill, and is aided by Lu Hsiao-fen's topflight performance. —*Adam.*

Hider In The House

London A Vestron Pictures production. Produced by Edward Teets, Michael Taylor. Coproduced by Stuart Cornfield, Lem Dobbs. Directed by Matthew Patrick. Screenplay, Lem Dobbs; camera (color), Jeff Jur; editor, Debra Smith; production design, Vicki Paul. Reviewed at Cannon Oxford Street Theater, London, Dec. 4, 1989. MPAA Rating: R. Running time: **105 MIN.**

Tom Sykes	Gary Busey
Julie Dryer	Mimi Rogers
Phil Dryer	Michael McKean
Neil Dryer	Kurt Christopher Kinder
Holly Dryer	Candy Hutson
Rita Hutchinson	Elizabeth Ruscio
Gary Hufford	Bruce Glover
George	Leonard Termo

■ **Despite the stalk-and-slash trappings, "Hider In The House" is an intelligent, gripping and sometimes compelling psychological thriller featuring attractive performances by Mimi Rogers and Gary Busey. Pic needs delicate handling to click.**

What makes this pic stand apart is that helmer Matthew Patrick and writer Lem Dobbs have bothered to explore the background of its disturbed central character Tom Sykes (Busey), providing an underlying sympathy for him.

Over the opening credits is an explanation that Busey's character was mistreated as a child by his father, from whom he often chose to hide. He eventually killed his parents by setting fire to the house.

As a man, Busey is released from a state institution. In his search to find a real home, he breaks into a recently renovated house and builds himself a secret space behind a false wall in the attic.

Unfortunately, his dreamhouse also is that of the well-to-do Dryer family (Rogers, Michael McKean and children Kurt Christopher Kinder and Candy Hutson). While they settle into their new home, Busey taps into the intercom system and starts drawing on their relationships, making the family his own.

Busey at first sees Rogers as a mother figure, but he becomes increasingly obsessed with her. When he discovers her husband is having an affair he arranges for Rogers to catch the pair together.

Despite trying to control himself, Busey still kills a couple of people — an exterminator and Rogers' friend Elizabeth Ruscio — but also shows a degree of affection toward the children. When McKean and Rogers finally get back together Busey is pushed over the edge.

Busey gives a fine performance as the obsessed murderer and Rogers is excellent as the unknowing object of Busey's attentions. The rest of the cast is strong.

Patrick directs "Hider In The House" with a good deal of thought and intelligence and does not rely on violence or shock value. He has constructed an admirable psychological thriller, greatly helped by Jeff Jur's elegant camerawork. Other tech credits are fine. —*Adam.*

LATE FILM REVIEW

We're No Angels

New York A Paramount Pictures release. Produced by Art Linson. Executive producer, Robert De Niro. Coproducer, Fred Caruso. Directed by Neil Jordan. Screenplay, David Mamet, suggested by 1955 screenplay by Ronald MacDougall, adapted from the play "My Three Angels" by Sam and Bella Spewak, based on the play "La Cuisine de anges" by Albert Husson. (Panavision, Alpha Cine color, Technicolor prints), Philippe Rousselot; editor, Mick Audsley, Joke Van Wuk; music, George Fenton; sound (Dolby), Kant Pan; production design, Wolf Kroeger; costume design, Theoni V. Aldredge; production manager, Warren Carr; assistant director, Patrick Clayton; art direction, Richard Harrison; set decoration, David Birdsall, Peter Lando; 2d unit director, Jim Devis; casting, Wallis Nicita. Reviewed at Loews Tower East, N.Y., Dec. 11, 1989. MPAA Rating: PG-13. Running time: **108 MIN.**

Ned	Robert De Niro
Jim	Sean Penn
Molly	Demi Moore
Father Levesque	Hoyt Axton
Deputy	Bruno Kirby
Warden	Ray McAnally
Bobby	James Russo
Translator	Wallace Shawn

Also with: John C. Reilly, Jay Brazeau, Ken Buhay, Elizabeth Lawrence, Bill Murdoch, Jessica Jickels.

■ **Teaming the combustible on-screen personalities of Robert De Niro and Sean Penn is a stirring idea, but what might have been a volatile mix of acting pyrotechnics fails to ignite in the disappointingly bland morality comedy "We're No Angels." The indifferent boxoffice histories of both stars are unlikely to be reversed with this release.**

Described by its producer as "very loosely based on some of the ideas" in the eponymous 1955 movie about convicts on the lam, "We're No Angels" is precisely about a pair of jailbirds on the run. The year is 1935 and De Niro and Penn are hard-timers in a hellish north country penitentiary that may be a metaphor for Depression-era America.

The late, great Ray McAnally, reduced here to a caricature of cruelty as the Big House warden, forces the heroes to witness the electrocution of a remorseless murderer. But in a sequence whose rollercoaster cartoonishness sets the tone for what follows, the condemned con and two heroes pull an improbable breakout and head for the Canadian border.

Separated from their accomplice, De Niro and Penn reach a remote border town renowned for a shrine of "the weeping Madonna" and a monastery. The town is swarming with police on their trail, but the cons are happily mistaken for visiting ecclesiastical scholars. Director Neil Jordan and screenwriter David Mamet thus set the stage for a parable about virtue, wisdom, faith and redemption.

The thick-skulled cons improvise in their newfound roles as priests and their misadventures multiply as they bumble their way toward freedom in Canada. Their flight suggests a kind of Pilgrim's Progress by way of "Black Friday," the Three Stooges, Norton & Kramden, "The Bells Of St. Mary's," the Coen Brothers and objets d'homage ad infinitum.

But the film never gets into satirical orbit. Instead of the remorselessly reductive Mamet of "Glengarry Glen Ross" or the cunning Mamet of "House Of Games," this Mamet is joltingly sentimental, sparing juicy targets like the Church while lavishing good intentions on these sprouted-up angels with dirty faces.

Pugfaced, slack-jawed and marble-mouthed, De Niro and Penn mug their semiarticulate proles with relish, but as religioso fish out of water their con game

Original Film

Paramount release of Pat Duggan production. Stars Humphrey Bogart, Aldo Ray, Peter Ustinov, Joan Bennett and Basil Rathbone; features Leo G. Carroll, John Baer, Gloria Talbott, Lea Penman and John Smith. Directed by Michael Curtiz. Screenplay, Ranald MacDougall, based on the Albert Husson play; camera (Technicolor), Loyal Griggs; editor, Arthur Schmidt; music, Frederick Hollander; songs, "Sentimental Moments" by Hollander (music) and Ralph Freed (lyric) and "Ma France Bien-Aimee, G. Martini (music) and Roger Wagner (lyric). Previewed in Hollywood, June 13, '55. Running time, **103 MIN.**

Joseph	Humphrey Bogart
Albert	Aldo Ray
Jules	Peter Ustinov
Amelie Ducotel	Joan Bennett
Andre Trochard	Basil Rathbone
Felix Ducotel	Leo G. Carroll
Paul Trochard	John Baer
Isabelle Ducotel	Gloria Talbott
Madame Parole	Lea Penman
Arnaud	John Smith

becomes a tiresome joke. The edgy, fabulist style employed skillfully by Jordan in "The Company Of Wolves" and "Mona Lisa" emerges intermittently in this film but is subsumed by the predictable plot conventions of the big-studio holiday movie.

In "We're No Angels," Jordan sacrifices the no-net highwire spirit of his independent films but doesn't get broad, boxoffice hilarity in return. De Niro and Penn are left to make their great imposters an engaging vaudeville act on the road to a pumped-up climactic en-

lightenment. The bracing redemptiveness of it all is embarrassingly clarioned by George Fenton's pompous scoring.

Demi Moore is solid as a fiery townie who complicates De Niro's life. Hoyt Axton is well cast as the monastery rector. Wallace Shawn is typically absurd as a punctilious and unctuous little monk.

Most outstanding is the multi-textured camera work of Philippe Rousselot and the synergystic period design of Wolf Kroeger.

—*Rich.*

Born On The Fourth Of July

Hollywood A Universal Pictures release of an A. Kitman Ho and Ixtlan production. Produced by Ho, Oliver Stone. Directed by Stone. Screenplay, Stone, Ron Kovic, based on the book by Kovic; camera (Deluxe color), Robert Richardson; editor, David Brenner; co-editor, Joe Hutshing; music, John Williams; sound (Dolby), Todd A. Maitland; production design, Bruno Rubeo; art direction, Victor Kempster, Richard L. Johnson; set decoration, Derek R. Hill; costume design, Judy Ruskin; assistant directors, Joseph Reidy, Stephen J. Lim, David Sardi, Donald J. Lee Jr.; associate producers, Clayton Townsend, Reidy; casting, Risa Bramon, Billy Hopkins. Reviewed at Alfred Hitchcock Theater, Universal Studios, Hollywood, Dec. 14, 1989. MPAA Rating: R. Running time: **144 MIN.**

Ron Kovic	Tom Cruise
Mr. Kovic	Raymond J. Barry
Mrs. Kovic	Caroline Kava
Donna	Kyra Sedgwick
Charlie	Willem Dafoe
Young Ron	Bryan Larkin
Steve Boyer	Jerry Levine
Tommy Kovic	Josh Evans
Jimmy Kovic	Jamie Talisman
Susanne Kovic	Anne Bobby
Timmy	Frank Whaley
Marine major	John Getz
Lieutenant	David Warshofsky
Marvin	Corkey Ford
Willie	Rocky Carroll
Maria Elena	Cordelia Gonzalez
Mr. Wilson	Tony Frank
Mrs. Wilson	Jayne Haynes

■ **Oliver Stone again has shown America to itself in a way it won't forget. His collaboration with Vietnam veteran Ron Kovic to depict Kovic's odyssey from teenage true believer to wheel-chair-bound soldier in a very different war results in the most gripping, devastating, telling and understanding film about the Vietnam era ever.**

Pic will be a mighty contender for the best picture Oscar, as well as best actor (Tom Cruise as Kovic), best director and a platoon of others. Boxoffices both here and abroad will be hosting a very long parade.

Stone, who coproduced, directed and wrote the script with Kovic, creates a portrait of a fiercely pure-hearted boy who loved his country and believed that to serve it and to be a man was to fight a war. It turned out to be Vietnam, and that's where the belief was shattered.

Shooting from very much inside this intense young man's perceptions, Stone creates an often surreal vision of an all-American smalltown Catholic upbringing in which the forces shaping Kovic's values and goals are about as gentle as a blast furnace forging steel.

Way before his hero sees action, Stone shoots this like a war film, with nearly every early scene infused with desperate intensity.

From boys playing war in the woods to a Fourth of July parade to a wrestling match, the camera races or slows or sweeps around in circles, until the picture becomes a rollercoaster of feeling.

Even with little dialog, Stone piles up images and sound to make the audience aware of what drives a young man who is packing for the Marines the night his classmates are dancing at the prom.

In 'Nam, things go terribly wrong — young Sgt. Kovic accidentally kills a fellow Marine in battle. His attempted confession is harshly denied him by a c.o. Later, he's shot in the foot, gets up for a gritty round of Sgt. Rock grandstanding, and is hit again and paralyzed.

Typically, Stone drenches the picture in visceral reality, from the agonizing chaos of a field hospital to the dead stalemate of a Bronx veteran's hospital infested with rats, drugs and the humiliation of lying helplessly in one's own excrement.

The U.S. Kovic left behind is unrecognizable, yet as he struggles uselessly to regain control of his body he remains steadfast in his ideas, shouting "Love it or leave it!" at his peacenik brother (Josh Evans).

Sprawling picture unveils one incredible scene after another, from a night when a drunk and unbearably pained Kovic wakes the entire neighborhood shouting about the lies he fell for, to the film's horrifying and comedic emotional nadir, a scene in which two drunken, crazed, wheelchair-bound vets (Cruise and Willem Dafoe), stranded on the roadside in the midst of a desert in Mexico, vent their rage on each other.

Until his turnaround, Kovic's life becomes one long surrealistic nightmare from which there is no escape, not even in Mexico. Film's enormous achievement is that it finds a coherent, dramatically beautiful way to tell this story, so that Kovic does become a soldier and does find his war.

Pic's latter scenes at the political conventions where Kovic's activism takes hold also are stunning in that they bring the story powerfully into the present. Watching the protesters forcibly evicted from the gatherings of establishment and vested interests, with John Williams' moving score rising behind the action, it becomes clear Stone is not telling this story to evoke nostalgia.

Cruise, who takes Kovic from clean-cut eager teen to impassioned long-haired activist, is stunning.

Pic comes from a place so deep inside the character's wounded heart that it is almost unbearable.

Dafoe, as a disabled vet hiding out in a Mexican beach town in a haze of mescal, whores and poker, gives a startling, razor-sharp performance.

Also notable are Caroline Kava as Kovic's religious mother and Frank Whaley as a fellow hometown vet.

Tech credits are all superb, particularly the sound-related work; film gains significant energy and dimension from its complex audio tracks.

Cinematographer Robert Richardson and production designer Bruno Rubeo, both longtime Stone collaborators ("Platoon," "Salvador," "Talk Radio"), make firstrate contributions. That Rubeo's 1950 Massapequa, N.Y., was created near Dallas, where "Talk Radio" was shot, is a circumstance few filmgoers will notice. All design and costume elements re-create the '60s in fascinating authenticity.

"What happened?" cries a veteran in this picture, raising the central question of the Vietnam era. Stone's "Born On The Fourth Of July" is perhaps the most relevant answer yet. —*Daws.*

Bearskin:
An Urban Fairytale
(BRITISH-PORTUGUESE)

London   A Film Four Intl./British Screen/Cinema Action IPC (Portugal)/RPT (Portugal) production. Produced by Leontine Ruette and Eduardo Guedes. Written and directed by Ann and Eduardo Guedes. Camera (Metrocolor), Michael Coulter; editor, Edward Marnier; music, Michael McEvoy; sound, Joaquim Pinto; art direction, Jock Scott, Luis Monteiro; costumes, Michael Jeffrey. Reviewed at London Film Festival, Nov. 5, 1989. Running time: **95 MIN.**

Silva . . . . Tom Waits
Johnny Fortune . . . . Damon Lowry
Kate . . . . Charlotte Coleman
Laura . . . . Julia Britton
Jordan . . . . Bill Paterson
Mrs. J . . . . Isabel Ruth
Barman . . . . Ian Dury
Broker . . . . David Gant
Harold . . . . Alex Norton
George . . . . Mark Arden

■ **Co-helmers-writers Ann and Eduardo Guedes are keen to fashion a film full of fanciful ideas, visual analogies and philosophical comment, but the ponderously titled "Bearskin: An Urban Fairytale" remains less than entertaining. Strong**

presence of American singer-actor Tom Waits could help b.o. appeal.

A fine performance by the endearingly gruff Waits helps give the pic a good deal of cosmopolitan charm. He is a charismatic talent, and well suited to the role of an enigmatic traveling entertainer with a dark past. Some of the other actors around him, though, are less able to cope with the often pretentious lines.

The meandering script by the Guedes becomes an uncomfortable blend of chase-thriller and philosophical diatribe, and perhaps a stronger producer could have taken them in hand and curbed the self-indulgence. The direction itself is stylish and proficient, but the awkward contempo "fairytale" format works against the pic being an easy commercial success.

Pic opens with wayward young hero Damon Lowry on the run from a pair of casino heavies after he has ripped off a large sum of money. After leaving his snooker-playing girlfriend (Charlotte Coleman) in the lurch, he gets a job counting theatrical costumes in a bleak warehouse run by the strangely somber Isabel Ruth. From there he joins a Punch and Judy show run by the enigmatic Waits and his silent assistant (Julia Britton). Lowry's job is to prowl around the show dressed in a bearskin. Not only does he find the job satisfying, but it also provides and ideal disguise.

As the casino hoods continue to seach for Lowry, so a mysterious American arrives looking for Waits, culminating in a car trying to run down Lowry and Waits being shot in the back. Later Lowry, in his bearskin, gets captured by the hoods, who beat him up. But before they can finish him off he is rescued by Britton. She tends his wounds, but like an idiot he wanders off and is chased by the gun-wielding hoods. But guess who comes to the rescue? Yes, Waits isn't really dead, and in an unexciting bluff fools the bad guys.

Throughout the film, Bill Paterson, as a philosophical guardian angel, pops up to offer Lowry advice and help — hence the "fairytale" of the title.

Waits seems to be getting better and better as an actor and certainly gives pic a much needed boost of class. Lowry is pretty hamfisted as the supposed rough diamond Johnny Fortune, while Paterson — unusual for him — is just hammy

as the guardian angel. Britton is fine in what is virtually a mime role, and, besides Waits, is the only sympathetic character.

Art direction by Jock Scott and Luis Monteiro is excellent, making good use of the mostly Portuguese locations to double as a strange, dark London. Nicest location is a disused airport, but it seems to have been put into the pic purely because it is a nice location rather than integral to the plot.

Ann and Eduardo Guedes wrote and produced the pretentiously dull "Rocinante" in 1986, and say "Bearskin" is the second pic in a trilogy. It certainly is more accessible than "Rocinante," though as a thriller it is uninvolving and slow.—*Adam.*

Comédie d'amour
(Love Comedy)
(FRENCH)

Paris   A Pan Européene release of a Show-Off/Ciné-5/Clara Films/Zoom 24 coproduction. Executive producer, Robert Kuperberg, Jean-Pierre Rawson. Produced by Victor Beniard and Antonio da Cunha Telles. Directed by Rawson. Screenplay, Hélène Doering, Kuperberg, Rawson; literary adviser, Edith Silve; camera (Fujicolor), Dominique Chapuis; art direction (adviser), Alexandre Trauner; editor, Jacquelin Thiédot; sound, Jean-Claude Laureux; music, Karl Heinz Schafer; assistant director, Vincent Canaple. Reviewed at UGC Biarritz cinema, Paris, Nov. 15, 1989. Running time: **89 MIN.**

Paul Léautaud . . . . Michel Serrault
Le Fléau . . . . Annie Girardot
Marie D . . . . Aurore Clément
    Also with: Patrick Bauchau, Roger Carel, Christine Delaroche, Jean-Paul Roussillon.

■ **"Comedie d'amour" is an unilluminating biopic of Paul Léautaud, a misanthropic French writer and drama critic whose personal diaries are considered by many to be his major achievement.**

No surprise then that producer-director Jean-Pierre Rawson and his co-adaptors have been largely content to dip generously into Léautaud's bilious, often obscene, sarcastically funny jottings and epigrams. Film won a prize from a French booksellers association for best literary adaptation but seems an unlikely export item.

As film, it is inert. Rawson's direction is limited to arranging the scenery (with "adviser" Alexandre Trauner) and camera setups for a star turn by Michel Serrault at his most waspish. As an essentially oneman stage show, this might have had more bite and perhaps some emotion, but Serrault's familiar acting idiosyncracies leave no room for pathetic observation into a vile, grungy, dirty-minded but deeply wounded man.

Screenplay evokes a moment in Léautaud's life in 1933, when he was occasionally rolling under the table with his mistress of 20 years (a shrewish Annie Girardot) and beginning to drool after an admiring younger librarian (a wooden Aurore Clément). She resists long enough for Serrault to reel off a sufficient arsenal of 1-liners that would chill Woody Allen to the funnybone. —*Len.*

Goitia — Un Dios Para Si
Mismo
(Goitia — A God For Himself)
(MEXICAN)

San Juan   A Latina release of an Imaginaria-Instituto Mexicano Cinematografía (Imcine)-Fondo de Fomento a la Calidad Cinematográfica Gobierno del Estado de Zacatecas production. Executive producer, Julio Derbez del Pino. Directed by Diego López. Screenplay, López, Jorge González de León, Javier Sicilia, José Carlos Ruiz, Enrique Vargas T., Raúl Zermeño; camera (color), Arturo de la Rosa, Jorge Suárez; editor, Sigfrido García; music, Amparo Rubín; art direction, Teresa Pecanins. Reviewed at San Juan Cinemafest, Teatro Tapia, San Juan, P.R., Nov. 10, 1989. Running time: **112 MIN.**

    With: José Carlos Ruiz, Patricia Reyes Spíndola, Alejandro Parodi, Ana Ofelia Murguía, Angélica Aragón, Alfonso Echánove, Fernando Balzaretti.

■ **Although conceived earlier, imagistic biopic "Goitia", on Mexican artist Francisco Goitia, suffers through obvious comparisons to Paul Leduc's 1985 pic "Frida," about Mexican painter Frida Kahlo. Second feature by Diego López, "Goitia" probably will have a difficult time at international wickets.**

Pic revolves around Goitia's struggle with art and faith, beginning at the end of his life when he asks God's permission to complete one more painting. Story then plunges back to the days of the Mexican Revolution.

Overlong pic's principal problem lies in its lack of dramatic tension, even though the action is an interior one. Rather, we get a parade of anguish and spiritual angst with little change in tone as the nonlinear script follows the painter's tortured life.

Admirable lensing by Arturo de la Rosa and Jorge Suárez is lush in capturing both the majestic beauty of the Mexican countryside — the scenic deserts and dense jungles — and documenting the painter's troubled works. It is underscored by Amparo Rubín's fine score.

José Carlos Ruiz puts in a believable turn as Goitia, reflecting the passing of time and the changes in his perception of self and the world he lives in. —*Lent.*

Always

Hollywood   A Universal Pictures release of a Universal/United Artists presentation from Amblin Entertainment. Produced by Steven Spielberg, Frank Marshall, Kathleen Kennedy. Coproducer, Richard Vane. Directed by Spielberg. Screenplay, Jerry Belson, based on film "A Guy Named Joe," with screenplay by Dalton Trumbo, adaptation by Frederick Hazlitt Brennan, story by Chandler Sprague, David Boehm; camera (Deluxe color), Mikael Salomon; editor, Michael Kahn; music, John Williams; sound (Dolby), Willie Burton; production design, James Bissell; art direction, Chris Burian-Mohr, Richard Reynolds (Montana), Richard Fernandez (Washington); set design, Carl Stensel; set decoration, Jackie Carr; costume design, Ellen Mirojnick; sound design, Ben Burtt; visual effects, Industrial Light & Magic; visual effects supervisor, Bruce Nicholson; visual effects producer, Jim Morris; visual effects camera, Hiro Narita; special effects supervisor, Mike Wood; aerial sequence design, Joe Johnston; forest fire plates director, Bissell; additional aerial sequences director, James Gavin; aerial unit camera, Frank Holgate, Alexander Witt; underwater camera, Pete Romano; assistant director, Pat Kehoe; 2d unit director, Marshall; 2d unit additional camera, John Toll, Gary Graver; casting, Lora Kennedy. Reviewed at Universal Studios, Hollywood, Dec. 8, 1989. MPAA Rating: PG. Running time: 121 MIN.

Pete Sandich . . . . Richard Dreyfuss
Dorinda Durston . . . . Holly Hunter
Ted Baker . . . . Brad Johnson
Al Yackey . . . . John Goodman
Hap . . . . Audrey Hepburn
Dave . . . . Roberts Blossom
Powerhouse . . . . Keith David
Nails . . . . Ed Van Nuys
Rachel . . . . Marg Helgenberger
Bus driver . . . . Doug McGrath
The singer . . . . J.D. Souther

■Not every Steven Spielberg film can or should be a grandiose cinematic event. The kind of film he would have made if he had been a studio contract director during Hollywood's golden era, "Always" is a relatively small-scale, engagingly casual, somewhat silly, but always entertaining fantasy.

Richard Dreyfuss charmingly inherits the lead role of a pilot returned from the dead in this remake of the 1943 Spencer Tracy pic "A Guy Named Joe" set among firefighters in national parks. The Universal release may not reach the b.o. stratosphere, but should be a high flier, nevertheless.

The fondly remembered original film, scripted by Dalton Trumbo and directed by Victor Fleming, used the omnipresence of death in World War II to give emotional weight to Tracy's self-sacrificing beyond-the-grave encouragement of the romance between bereaved flame Irene Dunne and tyro flier Van Johnson, who also benefits from his tutelage in the air.

Spielberg's transposition of the story to the spectacularly burning Montana forests — incorporating footage shot during the devastating 1988 fires at Yellowstone National Park — is a valid equivalent, for the most part, especially since his action sequences using old World War II-era planes are far more thrilling than those of "A Guy Named Joe," whose strengths are more in its character relationships.

The supernatural elements of "Always" may cause some tittering. In place of the fliers' heaven in "Joe," with starchy commanding officer Lionel Barrymore giving Tracy a moving pep talk on his role in the war effort, Spielberg has nothing more to offer than a fey sylvan afterlife supervised by bromide-spouting Audrey Hepburn. She's alluring as always, but corny as a live-action fairy godmother.

Holly Hunter's dispatcher and semi-skilled aspiring pilot, lacking the womanly grace Dunne brought to the part, comes off as gawky and ditzy in the early parts of "Always." Bereavement seems to visibly mature the actress, whose emotional struggle between the memory of Dreyfuss and new love Brad Johnson becomes spirited and gripping.

Not quite the transcendent adult love story one might have hoped to

Original film

A Guy Named Joe

Metro release of Everett Riskin production. Stars Spencer Tracy and Irene Dunne; features Lionel Barrymore, Van Johnson, James Gleason, Ward Bond, Barry Nelson. Directed by Victor Fleming. Screenplay, Dalton Trumbo, adaptation by Frederick Hazlitt Brennan from original story by Major Chandler Sprague and David Boehm; editor, Frederick Brennan; camera (b&w), George Folsey, Karl Freund. Reviewed at Capitol theatre, New York, Dec. 23, '43. Running time: 120 MIN.

Pete Sandidge . . . . Spencer Tracy
Dorinda Durston . . . . Irene Dunne
Ted Randall . . . . Van Johnson
Al Yackey . . . . Ward Bond
Nails Kilpatrick . . . . James Gleason
The General . . . . Lionel Barrymore
Dick Rumney . . . . Barry Nelson
Ellen Bright . . . . Esther Williams
Colonel Sykes . . . . Henry O'Neill
James J. Rourke . . . . Don DeFore
Sanderson . . . . Charles Smith

find Spielberg capable of at this point in his career, "Always" has a predominantly goofy, adolescent tone. Dreyfuss' debonair approach and the delightful antics of his sidekick pilot John Goodman (in the old Ward Bond part) help keep the film from getting maudlin.

Stepping into Tracy's shoes without strain, Dreyfuss has a similar kind of amiability and kindliness, a gentlemanly ease with women that is unusual in to-

day's films. His ghostly dance with Hunter is one of the film's most touching scenes.

Spielberg is not so successful with Johnson, who has the square-jawed good looks of a comic-book character. But with his terrible John Wayne impressions, oafish courting behavior and dimwitted expressions, he comes off as the male equivalent of a dumb blond with a great figure.

Among the superlative tech credits are Mikael Salomon's lensing, Michael Kahn's editing, James Bissell's production design, Bruce Nicholson's supervision of the Industrial Light & Magic visual effects, and Mike Wood's supervision of the forest fire special effects.

John Williams' music is rousing, and Spielberg wittily substitutes "Smoke Gets In Your Eyes" for "I'll Get By" as the couple's theme music. It's a shame that the haunting melody from Irving Berlin's "Always," which would have been so appropriate here, reportedly was denied to Spielberg.—Mac.

Ansouy-e Atash
(Beyond The Flames)
(IRANIAN)

Nantes   A Utopia release (Paris) of an Islamic Iranian Republic Broadcasting (Channel One) production. Written, directed and edited by Kianoush Ayyari. Camera (color), Dariush Ayyari. No other credits available. Reviewed at Festival of Three Continents, Nantes, France, Dec. 3, 1989. Running time: 97 MIN.

With: Khosro Shojazadeh, Siamak Atlasi, Mehrdad Vafadar, Atefeh Razavi, Nematollah Larian, Parvin Soleimani.

■Strident, overlong but forceful, this 35m feature production of Iranian tv won the grand prize at the recent FIPA tv festival in Cannes. Released theatrically at home and set for a limited arthouse release in France, pic is a natural for festival exposure and specialized theatrical and tv circuits.

Writer-helmer Kianoush Ayyari's tale of greed that divides a peasant family is blunt and abrasive. Set in rural Iran in the 1970s, he describes the stubborn clash of two brothers over an indemnity for the family house razed to make way for an oil rig. In selling the house they have also turned out their own mother, who now lives like an animal in the carcass of a bus and spends her time cursing her fate and her heartless offspring.

One brother has cheated the other out of his share and has sent him to prison after getting slashed with a knife. The prisoner gets out and makes his way straight back to the destroyed village, where his brother lives in a tiny shack as a pipeline gatekeeper and wastes his money incongruously on clothing and cosmetics.

Director keeps the tone high-pitched and somewhat repetitive as the family conflict widens to include a mute milkmaid and her young brother. When the ex-con brother falls in love with her, he realizes he can marry her only if his now-estranged mother makes the request as tradition requires.

Performances are adequate, though the behavior may strike foreign audiences as caricatural. Stark color lensing and camerawork by Dariush Ayyari (helmer's brother) captures the glaring oppressiveness of desert and oil rigs, which provide the backdrop to these naked human passions.

—Len.

Walter & Carlo I Amerika
(Walter & Carlo In America)
(DANISH)

Copenhagen   An Egmont Film release of Egmont Film production with MSM A/S and the Danish Film Institute. Produced by Steen Leise-Hansen. Executive producer, Kim Magnusson. Written and directed by Jarl Friis-Mikkelson and Ole Stephensen; camera (Eastmancolor), Claus Loof; editor, Maj Soya; music, Jan Glaesel; sound, John Nielsen, Leif Jensen, Niels Arnt Torp; production design, Linda Del Rosario; costumes, François Nicolet; assistant director, Peter Flint; associate producer (Toronto locations), Barbara Kelly. Reviewed at Imperial, Copenhagen, Nov. 22, 1989. Running time: 86 MIN.

Carlo . . . . Jarl Friis-Mikkelsen
Walter . . . . Ole Stephensen
Wally La Rouge . . . . Tony Curtis
Annatolij Chekov . . . . Jan Malmsjö
KGB Agent . . . . Jan Teigen
Danish police chief . . . . Björn Watt Boolsen
His wife . . . . Ghita Nörby
Natasja . . . . Belinda Metz
Anastasia . . . . Claire Celluci
    Also with: Ulrik Cold, Jesper Klein, Rummy Bishop, Charles Seixas, Bob Zidel, Bill Lake, Arnie Achtman, Sören Ostergaard, Kirsten Lehfeldt, Sös Egelind, Jack Newman, Ho Chow, Frank Nakashima.

■Having scored maximum Danish boxoffice and ditto negative reviews with their first two "Walter & Carlo" items, "Up At Dad's Hat" and "It's Dad's, Too," writer-helmer-thesps and tv-comedy graduates Ole Stephensen and Jarl Friis-Mikkelsen opt for offshore attention with "Walter & Carlo In America."

Filmed primarily in Toronto (standing in for N.Y.) and featuring foreign talent ranging from Tony Curtis to Norway's Jan

Teigen, Sweden's Jan Malmsjö and Canada's Belinda Metz and Claire Celluci, "Walter & Carlo In America" is designed as a spoof to end all secret agent spoofs. It pours an abundance of 007 clichés and just as many strictly Danish tv comedy turns into a cauldron that helmers proceed to overturn by adding speeded-up musicvideo stylistics.

The friends Walter (Stephensen as a dumb-handsome airline pilot) and Carlo (Friis-Mikkelsen as a shrill, vicious and lecherous know-it-all) somehow get involved in a race by the FBI, Danish police and the KGB for a life-size Little Mermaid statue. In the statue's mouth are hidden four CDs containing a secret weapon formula.

Curtis' FBI boss is given no motivation, but he speaks his lines with an amused authority that eludes most of the rest of the cast. Metz and Celluci do run-of-the-mill pin-up duty as a couple of Russian spies, and Malmsjö as another Russian has nothing to do but beg for food while looking chubbily well fed. —*Kell.*

Las Cosas Del Querer
(The Things Of Love)
(SPANISH)

Madrid A Lince Films production for Iberoamericana Films with the participation of Spanish Television (RTVE) and the Productora Andaluza de Programas. Executive producers, Luis Sanz, Francisco Belinchón. Directed by Jaime Chávarri. Screenplay, L. Irazábal, Fernando Colomo, Chávarri, based on story by A. Laretta and Irazábal; camera (color), Hans Burmann; editor, Pedro del Rey; music, Gregorio García Segura; choreography, Eduardo Montero; sets, Gloria, Marti; sound, Carlos Faruolo. Reviewed at Cine Capitol, Madrid, Nov. 5, 1989. Running time: **100 MIN.**
Dora . . . . Angela Molina
Mario . . . . Angel de Andrés López
Juan . . . . Manuel Bandera
Also with: Maria Barranco, Amparo Baró, Mari Carmen Ramirez, Juan Geo, Eva León, Diana Penalver, Santiago Ramos, Miguel Molina.

■ **This is an entertaining pic set in the Spain of the 1940s with lotsa musical numbers that have strong nostalgia appeal for those who lived the era in Spain. Though local in scope, pic could score with Hispano and Latino audiences, but the Andalusian dialect will prove a handicap.**

Handsomely produced and well lensed, directed and acted, item involves a trio of vaudeville thesps, two men and a woman, slightly reminiscent of old Yank dance films. Much of plot revolves around gay singer Mario and his homosexual liaisons.

Juan and Dora first meet during an air raid during the Spanish Civil War. She is a singer in a cheap theater, and is not averse to having a fling with any attractive male; if he pays, so much the better.

After the war, the two meet again by chance at an audition for Mario, the pretty gay singer. A friendship springs up among the three. Juan, who plays the piano, loves Dora, who in turn plays it fast and loose, while Mario runs through a string of male lovers, among them a nobleman.

Situation takes a nasty turn when, after an affair, Mario rejects the nobleman, upon which the latter's mother vows that Mario will rue the day.

Major attraction of pic is the numerous musical numbers. All are well executed, with both Angela Molina and Angel de Andrés López putting in excellent performances. Technical credits are fine, with a good evocation of the period. —*Besa.*

The Wizard

Hollywood A Universal Pictures release of a Finnegan-Pinchuk production. Executive producer, Lindsley Parsons Jr. Produced by David Chisholm, Ken Topolsky. Directed by Todd Holland. Screenplay, Chisholm; camera (Panavision, Deluxe color), Robert Yeoman; editor, Tom Finan; music, J. Peter Robinson; sound (Dolby), J. Paul Huntsman; production design, Michael Mayer; art direction, Rob Sissman; set decoration, Claire J. Bowin; costume design, Scilla Andreen-Hernandez; assistant directors, Jerry Ketchum, David O'Vidio; casting, Mali Finn. Reviewed at Cineplex Odeon Theaters, Universal City, Calif., Dec. 9, 1989. MPAA Rating: PG. Running time: **99 MIN.**
Corey Woods . . . . Fred Savage
Sam Woods . . . . Beau Bridges
Nick Woods . . . . Christian Slater
Haley . . . . Jenny Lewis
Jimmy Woods . . . . Luke Edwards
Putnam . . . . Will Seltzer
Bateman . . . . Sam McMurray
Christine . . . . Wendy Phillips

■ **It didn't take any magic to conjure up this plot, which ought to have been subtitled "Rain Boy." Fred Savage, 13, kidnaps his near-catatonic brother — a wiz, it turns out, at videogames — and takes him on a cross-country trek to Los Angeles.**

Boxoffice score should be pint-sized too, though an undeniably crowdpleasing finale and Savage's allure may rack up some bonus points with the Nintendo generation.

Tyro director Todd Holland serves up a few morsels far tastier than the sum of the film's parts, but the basic story proves so inane as to make the whole meal unpalatable. It's hard enough to figure out what the kids eat or do in terms of hygiene on the road.

They immediately pick up a 13-year-old babe (Jenny Lewis) and head off to $30,000 grand prize "videogame championships" in L.A.

In hot pursuit, meanwhile, are the boys' dad and brother, played by Beau Bridges and Christian Slater, as well as a cartoonish bounty hunter (Will Seltzer), hired by Bridges' ex-wife and her unctuous husband.

Unfortunately, the only thing more idiotic than the convenient timing (or even existence) of a big-buck videogame tourney and the "Rocky"-like manipulation that goes with it is the actual execution of the event itself — an overblown, high-tech setpiece complete with shrieking emcee and adoring fans.

That the whole sequence serves as a blatant promotion for Universal Studios' tour in this Universal release only increases the feeling of queasiness. This isn't film, it's a 90-minute product-placement opportunity.

The extended videogame playing presents a fundamental problem that seems lost on the filmmakers: playing such games may be fun, but watching someone else do it, even on a big screen, isn't.

The predictable finish works, as the old underdog-comes-from-behind ploy overcomes the limp editing and direction and was cheered raucously by a moppet-laden preview audience.

Even kids may be bored silly, however, by much of what leads up to it. Except for the broadest gags — the best being Bridges' growing infatuation with videogames himself — most of the events that punctuate writer-producer David Chisholm's script are bland.

Savage remains consistently wonderful in his tv role of "The Wonder Years," but has yet to find a film part of that caliber. He plays much the same character here, minus the quality writing in support or an adult voiceover to point out the stupidity of these situations.

Lewis is a find as the female lead and actually gets much of the film's good material, which is in short supply. With the animated film alternatives out for kids, pickings for "The Wizard" should be equally slim.—*Bril.*

Mutants In Paradise

New York A Caridi Entertainment presentation of a Blue Ridge Cinema Associates production. Produced by William Moses Jr. Line producers, Renee Harris, Beth Pfeifer. Written and directed by Scott Apostolou. Camera (Commonwealth Films color; Duart prints), G. Neal Means; editor, Apostolou, Thomas Lucas; music, Jep Epstein; sound, James Shore; production design, Frank Harris; art direction, Tomasina Keremes; assistant director, Scott Sullivan; associate producers, Brian Cartier, William Megalos, Peter M. Hargrove; casting, Bob Ewing. Reviewed on TWE vidcassette, N.Y., Nov. 23, 1989. No MPAA Rating. Running time: **77 MIN.**
Steve Awesome . . . . Brad Greenquist
Alice Durchfall . . . . Anna Nicholas
Oscar Tinman . . . . Robert Ingham
Boris/Bob . . . . Skipp Suddeth
Dr. Durchfall . . . . Edith Massey
Trainer . . . . Ray (Boom Boom) Mancini

■ **"Mutants In Paradise" is a cute sci-fi spoof, made on a student film level (at U. of Virginia), but with enough gags to keep homevideo fans amused. Plans for midnight movie bookings for the pic (shot about five years ago) fell through.**

Brad Greenquist, who later did a good job in "The Bedroom Window," toplines as a nerd who plays guinea pig in venal scientist Robert Ingham's genetic experiments, trying to come up with a nuclear-proof man to survive impending war. It all turns out to be a ruse to get grant money, but along the way Greenquist has funny misadventures caused by several bumbling Soviet spies and attempted romances with lovely Anna Nicholas.

The late Edith Massey (a regular in John Waters' films), plays the heroine's mom, supposedly a genetic scientist. Boxing champ Ray (Boom Boom) Mancini makes what would have been his screen debut (if film had been released in a timely way) as the hero's trainer.

Writer-director Scott Apostolou shows some promise as a satirist, though too many sketches are thrown in that don't belong.

Cast performs well in this 16m effort shot in Charlottesville, Va. —*Lor.*

A Sting In The Tale
(AUSTRALIAN)

Sydney A Rosa Colosimo Films release and production. Produced by Rosa Colosimo, Reg McLean. Directed by Eugene Schlusser. Screenplay, Patrick Edgeworth; camera (Eastmancolor), Nicholas Sherman; editor, Zbigniew Friedrich; music, Allan Zavod; production design, Lisa (Blitz) Brennan; sound, Michael Piper; production manager, Alison Sadler; assistant director, Arthur D'Aprano. Reviewed at Mosman screening room, Sydney, Oct. 26, 1989. Running time: **96 MIN.**

Diane Lane	Diane Craig
Barry Robbins	Gary Day
Louise Parker	Lynne Williams
Roger Monroe	Edwin Hodgeman
Prime Minister Falcon	Don Barker
P.M.'s minder	Jon Noble
Michael Meadows	Tony Mack
Peter (editor of Daily Echo)	Patrick Edgeworth
Permanent Secretary	Bob Newman
Wilson Sinclair	Gordon Goulding
Leader of Opposition	Gary Bishop
Barmaid	Joanne Cooper

■ A whimsical fable about the woman who becomes Australia's first female prime minister and brings down a powerful media baron, "A Sting In The Tale" (titled "Scorpio" during production) suffers from awkward dialog and an obviously restricted budget. Theatrical success, at home and abroad, is unlikely, with local tv and video chances more favorable.

Diane Craig plays Diane Lane, an ambitious politician who wins a hotly contested seat for the ruling government party. She is having a secret affair with Barry Robbins, the (married)-minister for health. Her best friend is Louise Parker, a once-radical journalist who works for the Echo, a paper owned by a ruthless Australian media tycoon with interests in the U.S. and U.K. Edwin Hodgeman's Roger Monroe bears a striking resemblance to a well-known media magnate with the same initials.

Robbins is plotting to oust the increasingly unpopular prime minister, and Diane also has her eye on the top spot. She wants revenge on Monroe, whom she blames for the death of her coalminer father.

Though there are a few twists in the tale, the situations are familiar from many a tv soap. Patrick Edgeworth's script has too much corny dialog, and some of the supporting actors are barely serviceable, though Craig is modestly effective and Hodgeman convincingly devious. End titles reveal that he winds up selling newspapers on a Melbourne street corner, a clear case of wishful thinking.

For Australian audiences, the oddest thing about the film is its location. These federal government high jinks occur not in Canberra, Australia's capital, but in Adelaide; it's akin to setting an American political subject in Boston.

A limited budget is obvious in the underuse of extras, especially in some of the scenes in which Parliament is sitting. Russian-born cinematographer Nicholas Sherman tries to jazz things up visually with tracking shots, but adds little to the proceedings. —*Strat.*

Talvisota (The Winter War) (FINNISH)

Helsinki A Finnkino release of National Filmi production, in association with the Finnish Film Foundation. Produced by Marko Röhr. Executive producer Jukka Mäkelä. Directed by Pekka Parikka. Screenplay, Parikka, Antti Tuuri, based on Tuuri's novel; camera (Eastmancolor), Kari Sohlberg; 2d unit camera, Antti Hellstedt; editor, Keijo Virtanen; music, Juha Tikka; "Lt. Haavisto's Theme," Jukka Haavisto; sound, Paul Jyrälä, David Lewis Yewdall; production design, Aarre Kiovisto, Raimo Mikkela; costumes, Tuula Hilkamo, Ilpo Nurmi; special effects, Esa Parkatti; production management, Juhani Jotuni, Terhi Tammila. Reviewed at the Rex, Helsinki, Nov. 30, 1989. Running time: **198 MIN.**

Martti Hakala	Taneli Mäkelä
Jussi Kantola	Vesa Vierikko
Pentti Saari	Timo Torikka
Vilho Errkilä	Heikki Paavilainen
Erkki Somppi	Antti Raivio
Juho Pernaa	Esko Kovero
Arvi Huhtala	Martti Suosali
Matti Ylinen	Tomi Salmela
Maari Haapasalo	Samuli Edelman
Yrjö Haavisto	Vesa Mäkelä
Battallion Commander	Aarno Sulkanen
Marjatta Hakala	Pirkko Hämäläinen

Also with: Kari Kihlström, Esko Salminen, Kari Sorvali, Ari-Kyösti Seppo, Esko Nikkari, Ville Virtanen, Eero Melasnieme, Pertti Sveholm, Helena Havisto, Kalevi Kahra, Tarja Heinula, Leena Suomo.

■ "The Winter War" celebrates the 50th anni of the outbreak of the first Russo-Finnish war in epic fashion.

Already picked for a competion run in the Berlin fest and released Dec. 8 in Los Angeles to qualify for Academy Award consideration, the foreign legs of 'The Winter War' would seem assured. Such legs, however, will be wobbly unless severe editing is performed from an excessive running time of 198 minutes with no intermission.

Pic recounts the 105 days of violent hostilities along a border of 2,000 miles where 275,000 ill-equipped but psychologically well-prepared Finns fought 500,000 Russians in full fighting trim to a stand-off truce that saved Finland's sovereignty at a time when its three Baltic sister nations were swallowed up by the Stalinist empire.

Pekka Parikka wrote the script with Antti Tuuri, author of the 1984 novel telling what he saw and felt as an enlisted man. A single platoon of Finnish soldiers is followed from prewar call-up back home in their village to their diminished numbers' lying in an open dugout during an apocalyptic yet hopeful ending.

Russian air and infantry attacks are seen only from the Finnish soldier's point of view. The foe is seen beaten back bloodily either in hand-to-hand fighting or by Molotov cocktails utilized by the Finns in mid-battle when they ran out of other ammo.

Much of this is old-style war film storytelling. Parikka avoids melodramatics and phoniness from his cast. The film is completely realistic, but its editing and music give it the look, sound and feel of a symphonic work.

When a halt was called to the fighting, 23,000 Finns had died. The Russian death toll was 200,000.

"The Winter War" has no lead roles on which to focus attention or sympathies. Still, several faces are given memorable expressions by fine actors such as Taneli Mäkelä and Antti Raivio.

Of special merit is Kari Sohlberg's cinematography, which retains a calm eye for strange beauty amid the horrors it records. —*Kell.*

Noce blanche (White Wedding) (FRENCH)

Paris A Film du Losange production and release. Coproducers, La Sept, La Sorcière rouge. Produced by Margaret Menegoz. Written and directed by Jean-Claude Brisseau. Camera (color), Romain Winding; sound, Georges Prat, Dominique Hennequin; music, Jean Musy; editor, Maria Luisa Garcia. Reviewed at the Marignan-Concorde theater, Paris, Dec. 10, 1989. Running time: **92 MIN.**

Francois Hainaut	Bruno Cremer
Mathilde Tessier	Vanessa Paradis
Catherine Hainaut	Ludmila Mikael
Carpentier	Francois Negret
Academic adviser	Véronique Silver
Concierge	Jean Dasté

■ "Noce blanche" recycles a hackneyed plot with some poignant variations and an impressive film acting debut by French pop singer Vanessa Paradis.

Jean-Claude Brisseau, a onetime literature prof, has directed with intensity, though his script might have benefited from an extra hand to iron out the peripheral platitudes. Paradis' popularity domestically has pulled film out of the arthouse ghetto. Pic has okay chances on fest and arthouse circuits abroad.

Film is about a married man falling for a much younger woman. Bruno Cremer is a high school philosophy teacher who takes an interest in the troubles of a problem student (Paradis) who's up for expulsion for absenteeism and antisocial attitudes.

He discovers in her a lonely, potentially brilliant student who, he considers, only needs some special attention. He begins to give her private tutoring, and the inevitable happens.

Their liaison last for some time and Paradis makes a remarkable academic comeback. Cremer tries to back off from the relationship, which has all but wrecked his marriage and composure. The affair comes to light in an embarrassing climax at school, and Paradis is expelled and Cremer transferred.

Brisseau has imagined a heartbreaking denouement for his romance, which is lifted out of the ordinary by 17-year-old Paradis. Her adolescent stage offered no hint of the subtlety and disturbing passion she brings to the role of the self-destructive teen. Cremer is adequate as the bemused and bewitched prof.

Film slumps in Cremer's home scenes with his wife, a stereotype of the intelligent wronged spouse that the lovely Ludmila Mikael fails to redeem. Other supporting roles also lack substance and interest.

Romain Winding's lighting gives the action a rarefied quality. Other tech credits are fine. —*Len.*

Agni Feu (Fire) (FRENCH-INDIAN-DOCU)

Florence Produced and distributed by Camelus/Viswanadhan. Directed by Viswanadhan. Camera (color, 16m) Adoor Gopolakrishann, Mankada Ravi Varma; editor, Nicole Oudinot; sound, Jacques Guillot. Reviewed at the Festival dei Popoli, Florence, Nov. 30, 1989. Running time: **120 MIN.**

■ Artist-filmmaker Viswanadhan's overly long and slow-moving documentary on the uses and manifestations of fire in his native India fails to ignite much interest.

Although it has some well-lensed footage, lack of dialog and narration leaves the viewer confused and bored.

Film, shown in competition at the Festival dei Popoli, may end up being slotted at other fests but commercial prospects are nil.

Viswanadhan, who won the Festival dei Popoli's top prize in 1986 for a docu on the Ganges River, stresses the importance of fire as a tool for survival and as a religious symbol. Indians are shown warming themselves over the fire, cooking with it, using it to forge tools and employing it in religious rituals.

There also are many scenes that appear to have nothing to do with the pic's subject. In on seemingly endless segment, people haul bags of cement over a bleak landscape to what could be a power plant. Whether the director is trying to illustrate the "fire" of work or equate electricity with fire is impossible to determine.

Film, which was lensed in dozens of locales around India, could have provided an enlightening look at the country and its people. Instead, its many pretty images end up being so many sparks in the wind. —*Thom.*

La ciudad oculta (Hidden City) (ARGENTINE)

Buenos Aires A Transeuropa Films release of an Orsai Cine production. Produced by Isabel Eugenia Lettner. Directed by Osvalso Andéchaga. Screenplay, Andéchaga, with collaboration of Miguel Briante, Chino Collado, Nacho Wisky; camera (color), Miguel Rodríguez; editor, Diego García Gutiérrez; music, Antonio Tarragó Ros; sound, Mario Antognini; art direction, Pablo Olivo, Jorge Marchegiani; sets, Walter Lettner; costumes, Gloria Linigier. Reviewed at Vigo screening room, Buenos Aires, Sept. 27, 1989. Running time: **82 MIN.**

Roberto . . . . Leandro Regúnaga
Teresa . . . . Isabel Quinteros
Maidana . . . . Edguardo Suárez
Ruiz . . . . Vito Catalano
Also with María Vaner, Alberto Benegas, Rubén Maravini, Raúl Lavié, Paulino Andrada, María Fiorentino, Gustavo Garzón, Marta Roldán, Fausto Collado.

■ **Good intentions are in evidence in this socially committed work, but the result is a collection of hits and misses. Abroad, pic is likely to function best at venues where the main consideration is the standpoint it adopts in favor of the oppressed.**

The title "Hidden City" refers to a Buenos Aires shantytown. The film, inspired by actual events, is a heartfelt first feature by director Osvaldo Andéchaga. Centering on the fictionalized story of one of its inhabitants, Roberto, it describes a drive by the former military government to eliminate the slum. The chosen methods for the squatter eviction program are subterfuge, lies, humiliations, violence and even murder. The shantytown dwellers make inchoate attempts to resist.

For exhibition in foreign countries, pic would benefit greatly if some notes or titles were added clarifying points which may leave even Argentine audiences in the dark.

At the end of the film Roberto is seized in the street adn thrust into the trunk of a car by government bullies, and the lid slammed shut. Argentine audiences, but not necessarily all foreign viewers, know that in the military years, being kidnap-

ped and stuffed into the trunk of a car meant death after torture, with no traces left.

Main failing of this drama is its haphazard plotting and editing, awash in loose ends.

One of its best scenes takes place at the beginning, when, in a country with virtually no Indian consciousness, a teacher is seen lecturing her class about the high moral virtues of the military campaigns of extermination of the natives at the turn of the century.

The camera pans around the classroom, and the children being given this indoctrination are seen to be Indian descendants themselves. Typically, however, this effective scene is not integrated into the rest of the film.

Some false-sounding dialog and uneven acting skills are further minuses. Miguel Rodríguez' color photography is one of the pluses. — *Olas.*

Dance Of Hope (DOCU)

New York A First Run Features release of a Copihue production. Produced by LaVonne Poteet, Deborah Shaffer. Directed by Deborah Shaffer. Camera (color), Jaime Reyes; editor, Marcelo Navarro; music, Wendy Blackstone; sound, Mario Diaz, Patricio Valenzuela; assistant camera, Rodrigo Rivas; production consultant, Gustavo Becerra. Reviewed at Public Theater, N.Y., Dec. 6, 1989. No MPAA Rating. Running time: **75 MIN.**

■ **"Dance Of Hope," docu about the victims (living and dead) of Chile's dictatorship, rejects a voiceover device and uses instead affecting on-camera interviews and somber images of Chilean women fighting for justice and peace of mind. This approach and a cameo by Sting give the Deborah Shaffer pic a shot at developing a sizable following.**

Released coincident with Chile's first elections (Dec. 14) since the 1973 coup which ousted Salvador Allende and installed August Pinochet, pic features eight Chilean women. They're but a handful of the many whose fathers and sons, husbands and brothers are still unaccounted for since the right-wing military seized power with the Nixon administration's help.

The women symbolize their plight by dancing the Chilean national dance without partners. Thus, the title of Oscar-winning director Shaffer's heartfelt docu as well as "They Dance Alone," the song

Sting is seen performing (with Peter Gabriel) in an Amnesty Intl. concert in 1988.

That concert took place just across the border in Argentina, presumably for safety reasons. As members of the Assn. of Relatives of the Detained and Disappeared, Violeta, Gala, et al. are outspoken in their criticism of the Pinochet government. One has to wonder for their well-being.

Docu is 1-sided, but not detrimentally so. For 16 years, the survivors got the official run-around ("psychological torture," in their words). How far, then, could the filmmakers have gotten in seeking government comment?

The women's on-camera testimony is informative, but is periodically delivered in monotone but that could be because they've become anesthetized to their grief and hardened to their campaign.

The true story is told best by images such as Pinochet's clownishly ornate uniform, the freedomfighting rallies and subsequent police clampdowns and, most of all, the women hunched over a desert poking stick in the dried soil in the vain search for the remains of their loved ones. —*Binn.*

D.N.I. (I.D.) (ARGENTINE)

Buenos Aires A Transeuropa Films release of a Grupo Cine Argention production. Produced by Clara Segesdi. Directed by Luis Brunati. Screenplay, Julio Fernández Baraibar, Brunati; camera (color), Aníbal Di Salvo; editor, Remo Chiarborello; music, Diego Boris, Carlos Viola; sound, Pepe Gramático; art direction, Carlos Galetttini, Juan Schoder. Reviewed at Vigo screening room, Buenos Aires, Nov. 21, 1989. Running time: **92 MIN.**

With: Carlos Carella, Tina Serrano, Lorenzo Quinteros, Paulino Andrada, Paco Fernández de Rosa, Rubén Stella, María Fiorentino, Irma Roy, Juan Brunati, Miguel Requejo.

■ **Mixing documentary footage, reconstructed historical events, still photos and sundry other ingredients, "D.N.I." is an angry political tract giving the leftwing Peronist view of history. It is unlikely to travel well.**

"D.N.I." is of the opinion that the government of General Juan Perón became repressive only when "Perón fell into the trap set by provocateurs."

"D.N.I." lacks any sense of film style and is depressingly amateurish in execution. The director is a Peronist politician. The film's title is the initials of the identity papers

issued by the Argentine government.

As a Peronist pamphlet, pic became outdated by the time of its release. Current Peronist government of President Carlos Menem, which was in opposition at the time the film was made, has since adopted policies sharply different from Brunati's stridently anti-free-enterprise, anti-foreign posture.

Main interest of "D.N.I.," from a cinematic point of view, are two narrative devices it employs, with different degrees of success.

The first is designed to overcome the lack of resources. Lacking the wherewithal to put armies on screen in its reconstruction of diverse events in Argentine history, pic symbolizes them with the members of a murga — a rough-and-tumble Carnival (Mardi Gras) dancing band — wearing appropriate uniforms, or elements thereof.

It's an intriguing idea. Unfortunately, the execution is less prepossessing than the concept and the murga's prancing and facial mugging turn out to be more distracting than suggestive.

The second interesting narrative device is to include numerous shots of street signs and other place names bearing the names of Argentine historical characters. The device is employed for people whom the filmmakers hate (for not being nationalistic or anti-popular, etc.). It has a rhetorical purpose: irony. Its unspoken message: Despite these villains' heinous crimes, see how many streets and public squares have been given their names!

On the other hand, the device is not employed to depict the blanketing of the country with the names of Juan and Eva Perón in their heyday. Being fully deserved, in the filmmaker's view, there is no irony in this.

There is little else in their film deserving praise. —*Olas.*

Houseboat Horror (AUSTRALIAN)

Sydney A PM Terror Prods. presentation. Intl. sales, All Media Enterprises. Executive producer, Greg Petherick. Produced by Ollie Martin. Directed by Kendal Flanagan, Martin. Screenplay, Martin; camera (color), Bill Parnell; editor, Clayton Jacobson; music, Brian Mannix, Steve Harrison, Ross McLennan; production design, Brian Gunst; sound, Scott Findlay; production managers, Warren Amster, Bosley Spry; assistant director, Collin Morris; associate producer, Rick Lappas; casting, Deborra-Lee Furness. Reviewed at Mosman screening room, Sydney, Dec. 8, 1989. Running time: **85 MIN.**

Grant Evans. . . . . .Alan Dale
Tracy. . . . . .Christine Jeston
Sam. . . . . .Craig Alexander
Ziggie. . . . . . . .Des (Animal) McKenna
Costello. . . . . .Gavin Wood
"J". . . . . .John Michael Howson
Zelia. . . . . .Louise Silversen
Teresa. . . . . .Peppie D'Or
Bernie. . . . . .Steve Whittacker
Jennie. . . . . .Julie Thompson
Dagger. . . . . .Mark Muggeridge
Harold. . . . . .Wilkie Collins
Bill. . . . . .David Blackman
Con. . . . . .Greg Latts

———

■ A straight-to-video slasher pic made two years ago and slavishly modeled on the "Friday The 13th" formula, "Houseboat Horror" has nothing new to offer, but could please undemanding horror freaks.

This time the killings are taking place at remote Lake Infinity, where a film crew is shooting a musicvid. The killer, unseen for much of the pic, but revealed near the end as a scarred, bald psycho, is seeking revenge on the film people because he was badly burned on a film set. This doesn't stop him slaughtering a hitchhiker, her boyfriend and a forest ranger, in the first reel.

Codirectors Ollie Martin (who produced and scripted) and Kendal Flanagan provide the requisite number and variety of killings, but little else.

Apart from the butchery, there's a touch of nudity in the standard swimming and shower scenes. Humor is confined to a lame "Psycho" joke.

The cast, mostly drawn from tv soaps, barely registers and there's a pointless cameo from John Michael Howson, known on Aussie tv as a gushy commentator on movies.

Only other point of (mild) interest is the credit for casting given to actress Deborra-Lee Furness, star of "Shame" a couple of years ago. Presence of Alan Dale, from the popular soap "Neighbors," also may help the pic's exposure in the U.K., where "Neighbors" plays twice a day to a huge audience. —*Strat.*

———

Kuma Hula: Keepers Of A Culture (DOCU)

———

Florence A Mug-Shot production for Cover Enterprises Inc. Executive producer, Neil Abercrombie. Produced by Robert Mugge, Vicky Holt Takamine. Directed by Mugge. Camera (color 16m), Lawrence McConkey; editor, Mugge; sound, William Barth; 2nd unit camera, Erich Roland; associate producer, Ricardo Trimillos; project administrator, Toy Tokujo. Reviewed at Festival dei Popoli (noncompeting), Florence, Italy, Nov. 27, 1989. Running time: **85 MIN.**

■ "Kuma Hula" is a colorful, expertly lensed and edited documentary that takes a serious but refreshing look at the history and ancient traditions represented in the dance of the Hawaiian people.

Those expecting lots of shapely young women in flimsy grass skirts will be disappointed, but anyone with more than a passing interest in the hula and the islands should find the film rewarding. Commercial prospects appear limited to public tv and homevideo.

Director Robert Mugge, known for film portraits of such musicians as Al Green, Sonny Rollins and Sun Ra, relates the dance's long history through interviews with kuma hulas, the dedicated master teachers responsible for passing the secrets of the hula down from generation to generation.

Interviews cover how the hula was brought to the islands nearly 1,500 years ago, its repression by missionaries in the 19th century, and the many years dancers must spend to master its difficult techniques. In the interviews, as well as the 14 hula performances shown, Mugge wisely concentrates on the dancing itself rather than what each dance means.

The hulas feature various troupes of dancers attired in vibrantly colored costumes performing against the backdrop of some of Hawaii's most scenic panoramas. The dances, most of which are examples of traditional hula (rather than the modern Western version most visitors to the islands see), are well lensed.

A couple of segments feature the notorious grass skirts. In one, a brief b&w film clip taken from 1937's "Waikki Wedding," numerous beauties are so attired as Shirley Ross and Bing Crosby croon a tune. In the other, three very overweight Hawaiian women, who also are obviously very skilled dancers, swirl their skirts in a rousing rendition of the "Aerobics Hula." —*Thom.*

———

Suivez cet avion (Follow That Plane) (FRENCH)

———

Paris An AAA release of a Slav Prods./SGGC/Madeleine Films coproduction. Produced by Xavier Larère, Gilbert de Goldschmidt. Directed by Patrice Ambard. Screenplay, Ambard, Alain Estève; camera (color), Bertrand Chatry; editor, Nicole Saunier; music, Didier Vasseur; art direction, Jimmy Vansteenkiste; sound, Eric Devulder; costumes, Rosine Lan; casting, Nicole Agnès Cottet. Reviewed at Marignan-Concorde theater, Paris, Nov. 5, 1989. Running time: **87 MIN.**
Remi Cerneaux. . . . . .Lambert Wilson
Elisabeth Martini. . . . .Isabelle Gélinas
Ascar. . . . . .Claude Pieplu
Associate. . . . . .Clovis Cornillac
Combette. . . . . .Maria Meriko

———

■ "Follow That Plane" taxis along the runway of ersatz screwball comedy, but crashes on takeoff. Newcomer Patrice Ambard has contrived some occasionally amusing gags, but masters neither plot, rhythm nor engaging characterization.

Story is more comic book than comic, despite its open salutes to Hollywood masters such as Capra, Wilder and Lubitsch.

Lambert Wilson looks lost as a timid, mother-dominated computer specialist (with specs à la Cary Grant) who becomes a prime suspect in a bank heist masterminded by his supposedly devoted landlady. Isabelle Gélinas provides bubbly romantic interest as the fellow office worker out to get her man —Wilson.

Claude Pieplu is dropped ineffectually into the pointlessly convoluted shenanigans as a pretentious but slow-witted detective. Clovis Cornillac is the deceptively bright assistant. —*Len.*

———

Ten For Two (DOCU)

———

Florence A Joko Film production. Produced by John Lennon, Yoko Ono. Directed by Stephen Gebhardt. Camera (color, 16m) Gebhardt, Robert Fries, Joseph Pipher, George Manupelli; editor, Laura Lesser; sound, Carl Sjodahl. Reviewed at Festival dei Popoli (noncompeting), Florence, Italy, Nov. 26, 1989. Running time: **78 MIN.**

———

■ This unreleased film of a 1971 rock concert/rally for imprisoned radical leader John Sinclair is entertaining musically but mainly of interest as a look at the turbulent political mood of the early '70s.

Film's title alludes to the 10-year prison term given Sinclair, head of the Rainbow People's Party, for possession of two marijuana cigarettes.

The pic features performances by its producers, John Lennon and Yoko Ono, plus Stevie Wonder and popular groups of the era, as well as brief speeches by Bobby Seale, Rennie Davis and Jerry Rubin. Likely destination for distribution would be the college circuit and homevid specialty shops.

Although not up to the technical standards of today's concert features, lensing and sound quality of the film's 18 songs are solid enough to be satisfying. Filmed in Ann Arbor, Mich., the concert opens with The Up belting out "Free John Sinclair" and Allen Ginsberg, accompanied on guitar by Gary Williamson, singing "Dear John Sinclair."

Best musical performances come from Bob Seger and Tee Garden and Van Winkle on the standard "Oh! Carol," and Wonder with "For Once In My Life."

Wonder also performs "Heaven Help The Child" and "Someone Is Watching You," the latter dedicated to "any undercover agents who might be in the audience."

Seale, flanked by several Black Panther guards, gives the longest and most free-wheeling speech, telling the 14,000-plus crowd that the "only solution to pollution is a humane revolution."

Lennon and Ono close the concert with four political tunes -- "Attica State," "The Luck Of The Irish," "Sisters O Sisters" and "John Sinclair." Their participation in the campaign to free Sinclair led to the government's attempt to deport Lennon, which in turn kept "Ten For Two" from being released as planned.

Film wraps with footage of Sinclair being released from prison and reunited with his family and friends three days after the concert. —*Thom.*

———

Vanille fraise (Vanilla-Strawberry) (FRENCH-ITALIAN)

———

Paris An Ariane Films production and release, coproduced by G. Films, Films A2 and Cristaldifilms. Executive producers, Alexandre Mnouchkine, Antoine de Clermont-Tonnerre. Produced by Christian Ferry, Michel Cheyko. Directed by Gérard Oury. Screenplay, Oury, Danièle Thompson; camera (color), Luciano Tovoli; art direction, Aurelio Crugnola; sound, Alain Sempé, Jean-Paul Loublier; editor, Albert Jurgenson; music, Jean Musy; songs, Gipsy Kings and Mia Martini; assistant directors, Michel Cheyko, Victor Tourjansky. Reviewed at Gaumont Ambassabe theater, Paris, Nov.·29, 1989. Running time: **103 MIN.**
Antoine Boulanger. . . . . .Pierre Arditi
Clarisse Boulanger. . . . .Sabine Azéma
Hippolyte. . . . . .Isaach de Bankolé
Guillaume. . . . . .Jacques Perrin
Andreani. . . . . . . .Riccardo Cucciolla
Muso. . . . . .Giuseppe Cedrena

———

■ A blend of marital farce and espionage comedy set in Capri, "Vanille fraise" is a routine but agreeable Gallic laugh machine that owes most of its easy charm to a perfectly tuned star trio.

Latest from veteran comedy director Gérard Oury and co-writer (and daughter) Danièle Thompson should be okay for team's usual markets, but has poor overseas potential.

Premise is inspired by the 1985 incident in which French agents posing as a married couple plotted the sinking of the Greenpeace ship Rainbow Warrior in New Zealand.

In "Vanilla-Strawberry" (code names for the agents), Isaach de Bankolé and Sabine Azéma are brought together for a similar assignment in the Mediterranean. They've been ordered to sink a luxury yacht operating under the cover of a Third World charity organization, but which in fact is preparing to smuggle French warheads to terrorist groups.

Part of the fun is generated by the ill-matched "couple" attempting to act the loving newlyweds without succumbing to genuine romance. Bankolé, a blithe, polygamous black intelligence officer, and Azéma, a former diver for the French secret service who goes back into active service to escape an intolerable marital crisis, can't avoid the inevitable.

Unexpected headaches come when Azéma's hypocritical, philandering husband, Pierre Arditi, gets wind of her presence in Capri with another man and rushes down to catch her in the act.

Verbal humor and farcical misunderstandings are mostly predictable, but script thankfully is free of the pontificating and pseudo-serious asides. Directorial invention is of a fairly low order, but at least provides a swift, bouncing rhythm.

This is one of Oury's best-cast efforts, with Bankolé and Azéma playing off one another with breezy skill.—*Len.*

Tell Me Sam
(FRENCH-DOCU)

Florence Produced by M.W. Prods. Directed by Emil Weiss. Camera (16m color), Pierre Bofferty; editors, Francoise London, Michele Darmon; sound, Jean Pierre Duret. Reviewed at the Festival dei Popoli (competing) Nov. 25, 1989. Running time: **76 MIN.**

■ The "Sam" of the title is veteran helmer Sam Fuller, who tells all about his career in this uneven by moderately entertaining English-language documentary.

Primarily of interest to hardcore Fuller fans, film should get some additional fest invites and has a chance at some tv pickups.

Pic is composed of interviews with Fuller intercut with scenes and stills from his work, including "The Big Red One" and such cult classics as "Pickup On South Street," "White Dog" and "Run Of The Arrow."

Interviews take place as Fuller takes a boat up the Seine, a train across Germany, walks around Prague and watches himself being interviewed in a monitor wile smoking one of his ever-present cigars.

He waxes philosophical about everything from his early days as a newspaperman and his controversial film career to his experiences as part of the U.S. Army's 1st Infantry Division during World War Two and its liberation of the Falkenau concentration camp. —*Thom.*

Music Box

Hollywood A Tri-Star Pictures release of a Carolco Pictures presentation of an Irwin Winkler production. Produced by Winkler. Executive producers, Joe Eszterhas, Hal W. Polaire. Directed by Constantin Costa-Gavras. Screenplay, Eszterhas; camera (Panavision, color), Patrick Blossier; editor, Joele Van Effenterre; music, Philippe Sarde; sound (Dolby), Pierre Gamet, Gerard Lamps, William Flageollet; production design, Jeannine Claudia Oppewall; costume design, Rita Salazar; art direction, Bill Arnold; set decoration, Erica Rogalla; assistant directors, Rob Cowan, Jeanne Caliendo; associate producer, Nelson McCormick; casting, Mary Goldberg, Pam Dixon. Reviewed at Carolco Pictures screening room, W. Hollywood, Nov. 28, 1989. MPAA Rating: R. Running time: **123 MIN.**

Ann Talbot	Jessica Lange
Mike Laszlo	Armin Mueller-Stahl
Jack Burke	Frederic Forrest
Harry Talbot	Donald Moffat
Mikey Talbot	Lukas Haas
Georgine Wheeler	Cheryl Lynn Bruce

■ **Ponderous and predictable with only the presence of Jessica Lange as a popular draw, "Music Box" strikes a dissonant chord and should play a sad tune for Tri-Star at the boxoffice.**

"Music Box" marks the second straight mound of overbearing glop generated by the trio of writer Joe Eszterhas, producer Irwin Winkler and director Constantin Costa-Gavras, who last collaborated on the dismal "Betrayed." All have seen their time and energy put to much better use and hopefully will again.

Lange plays an accomplished Chicago defense attorney, Ann Talbot, who must defend her own father (Germany's Armin Mueller-Stahl, veteran of several Rainer Werner Fassbinder pics) in extradition proceedings when he's accused of having committed war crimes in Hungary during World War II.

Slowly losing her conviction as to her father's innocence, Lange's character pulls out all the stops, including the political connections of her former father-in-law, to try to exonerate her dad.

Even the film's accounts of Holocaust atrocities — which should have the impact of a blow to the stomach — prove for the most part strangely unaffecting under Eszterhas' limp dialog and Costa-Gavras' stodgy direction, which relies on a concussive score to try to create tension where there is none.

The director's use of blatant symbolism proves equally jarring and bothersome. Lange repeatedly sees herself in mirrors during the course of the film, once for a ridiculously long stretch, before her opposing counsel (Frederic Forrest) urges her to look at herself.

That might provide some insight if the audience had any idea what she was opposed to see. Viewers aren't privy to Ann's relationship with her father prior to the start of the film, and aside from the fact he raised his kids as a widower there's scant explanation of her feelings.

The film feels longer than it is, and offers a payoff that's not only too late but woefully incomplete. After sitting there that long some sort of emotional resolution would seem forthcoming, though it's a tepid one at best.

Lange does a fair job but fails to flesh out a terribly 1-dimensional character — a fatal flaw, since she's the film's focal point. Peripheral players are largely wasted, including Lukas Haas of "Witness" as Ann's son. Donald Moffat distinguishes himself in his brief time as the power-broker father-in-law.

Tech credits are unspectacular, though Patrick Blossier's camera may do some good for Hungarian tourism while making the Windy City look utterly bleak, two words that apply to the film in general.
—*Bril.*

Cat Chaser

London A Vestron Pictures presentation of a Whiskers production. Executive producer, Guy Collins. Produced by Peter Davis, William Panzer. Directed by Abel Ferrara. Screenplay, Elmore Leonard, Jim Borrelli, Alan Sharp, based on novel by Leonard; camera (Technicolor), Anthony Richmond; editor, Kim Kennedy; music, Chick Corea; production design, Dan Leigh; sound, Henry Lopez; costumes, Michael Kaplan; casting, Brad Davis. Reviewed at London Film Festival, Nov. 20, 1989. No MPAA Rating. Running time: **90 MIN.**

George Moran	Peter Weller
Mary de Boya	Kelly McGillis
Jiggs Scully	Charles Durning
Nolan Tyner	Frederic Forrest
Andres de Boya	Tomas Milian
Rafi	Juan Fernandez

Also with: Phil Leeds, Tony Bolana, Adrianne Sachs, Robert Escobar, Vivian Addison.

■ "Cat Chaser" is another example of how difficult it is to transform a sharp and racy novel into a classy movie. Despite a fine cast and atmospheric direction by Abel Ferrara, the pic doesn't quite make the grade, though it certainly is worth a look.

Pic looks destined for a limited theatrical life, but may click on video.

There is a decided *film noir* quality about the film, with nice use of the steamy Miami locations and intelligent lead actors, in a similar vein to "Body Heat." Unfortunately, pic gets bogged down with its own cleverness. The script is overly wordy, occasionally preposterous and eventually too complex.

Peter Weller plays Miami hotel owner George Moran who fought during the American intervention of Santo Domingo. Years later he is drawn back to try and find the woman who taunted him with the name "Cat Chaser," but also let him live when he was captured by rebels.

He doesn't find the woman, but instead is joined by Kelly McGillis. Ensuing affair convinces Mary (McGillis) that she must end her marriage. Unfortunately she is married to Tomas Milian, former head of the Santo Domingo secret police, who has other thoughts on the matter.

Milian sends Charles Durning to lean on Weller, while drunk ex-Army man Frederic Forrest also arrives at Weller's Miami hotel. It turns out Forrest also works for Milian, but neither man makes much of an impression, and McGillis is determined to leave her husband.

Climax of the pic involves Durning plotting to steal $2-million in cash that Milian keeps about the house. Unfortunately when Milian beats up McGillis she decides the $2-million should be her divorce settlement, and takes the cash before Durning can get it.

Weller is fine as the intelligent, self-contained hero, but best of all is Kelly McGillis, seemingly relishing the part of a sexually charged femme fatale. The role is quite different from the more repressed characters she has played recently. Charles Durning, as always, gives the pic a dose of class, and manages to make his manipulative killer vaguely charming. Frederic Forrest, however, blusters badly and thankfully comes to a sticky end halfway through.

Helmer Abel Ferrara displays a stylish, confident hand — it is obvious from some of the locations and camerawork that he had directed episodes of "Miami Vice" — and is aided by excellent photography by Anthony Richmond. Experienced costume designer Michael Kaplan lets himself down, though, with some quite repulsive outfits that McGillis is forced to wear. Other tech credits are fine. —*Adam.*

Tango & Cash

Hollywood A Warner Bros. release of a Guber-Peters Co. production. Produced by Jon Peters, Peter Guber. Executive producer, Peter Macdonald. Coproduced by Larry Franco. Directed by Andrei Konchalovsky. Screenplay, Randy Feldman; camera (Panavision, Technicolor), Donald E. Thorin; supervising editor, Stuart Baird; editor, Huber De La Bouillerie, Robert Ferretti; music, Harold Faltermeyer; production design, J. Michael Riva; art direction, David Klassen, Richard Berger; set decoration, Marvin March; costume design, Bernie Pollack; sound (Dolby), Robert R. Rutledge, Mark Stoeckinger; assistant directors, Marty Ewing, Artist Robinson, Dan Suhart; casting, Glenn Daniels. Reviewed at the Mann Village theater, Westwood, Calif., Dec. 20, 1989. MPAA Rating: R. Running time: **98 MIN.**
Tango . . . . Sylvester Stallone
Cash . . . . Kurt Russell
Kiki . . . . Teri Hatcher
Yves Perret . . . . Jack Palance
Courier/Requin . . . . Brion James
Quan . . . . James Hong
Lopez . . . . Marc Alaimo
Gunman/Chinese guy . . . . Phillip Tan
Owen . . . . Michael J. Pollard

■ **Peter Guber and Jon Peters flew off to Columbia leaving Warner Bros. to serve up this holiday turkey — a mindless buddy cop pic, loaded with non-stop action that's played mostly for laughs and delivers too few of them. Based on the frigid yule season thus far, it doesn't promise to be a very lethal boxoffice weapon.**

Inane and formulaic, the film relies heavily on whatever chemistry it can generate between Sylvester Stallone and Kurt Russell, who repeatedly trade wisecracks while facing life-or-death situations.

For Stallone it's a chance to put on glasses and lighten up a bit while Russell repeats his swaggering pec-flexing from "Big Trouble In Little China." Trying to top what's gone before, the action snowballs so absurdly that, rather than the sought-after "Lethal Weapon" feel, the film most closely resembles by its end other Warner Bros. properties with Bugs Bunny in them.

The film starts with two pre-credit action sequences that establish just how ludicrous what follows will be. They also contain the film's one memorable line, when an observer suggests that Stallone's maverick cop "thinks he's Rambo."

Jack Palance re-creates down to each gasp his role from "Batman" as a snarling crime boss who decides to bring down the two cops who have separately plagued his drug-dealing schemes — their exploits recapped via blaring headlines in the Los Angeles Chronicle.

Framed and sent to prison, the two rival cops (named, as opposed to nicknamed, Tango and Cash) become a reluctant team in an effort to exonerate themselves. Along the way, they hitch up with Tango's bombshell sister (Teri Hatcher), who happens to be an exotic dancer at some "Star Wars"-esque nightspot.

The thinking seems to be if you're going to be ridiculous you might as well go at it full throttle, and director Andrei Konchalovsky does just that — staging fiery action sequences set to a pulsing, synthesized Harold Faltermeyer score much like the composer's yeoman work for "Beverly Hills Cop."

(Albert Magnoli, helmer of WB's hit "Purple Rain," directed the final two weeks of lensing after Konchalovsky quit in a dispute over pic's ending. —*Ed.*)

The pace, in fact, recalls the title if not the tone of Konchalovsky's 1985 pic "Runaway Train," but the headlong chase to keep attention spans from flagging unfortunately has yielded to a film lacking any redemptive core to its characters.

Indeed, they're all style, no substance — simply too busy having a good time kicking butt, taking names and playing with logarithmically bigger guns and cars to bother with character development, even when in prison being threatened and tortured by goons resembling the cast from "The Road Warrior."

Russell gets dealt all the best lines, while Stallone at least shows he doesn't have to take himself so seriously all the time, though it's hard to describe this brawling shoot-'em-up — glasses or no — as much of a reach.

Hatcher is stunning to look at but has little else to do, while Brion James makes a menacing heavy. As for Palance, he would have been better off had Jack Nicholson repeated recent cinematic history and burst in to shoot him early in the storyline.

The camerawork and editing are superb and the production design noteworthy, especially as it relates to the prison sequences. —*Bril.*

Sexbomb

Hollywood A Phillips & Mora Entertainment/Film Barn Prods. production. Produced by Rick Eye. Executive producers, Jim Phillips, Anthony Mora, Fred Olen Ray, Jeff Goldsten. Directed by Jeff Broadstreet. Screenplay, Robert Benson; camera (color), Dale Larson; editor, Todd Felker; music, Leonard Marcel; sound, Reinhardt Stergar; art direction, Liz Simakis; costumes, Patty Breen; special effects, Scott Colter; assistant director, Lisa Campbell. Reviewed at Film Services Laboratories, Hollywood, Nov. 20, 1989. No MPAA Rating. Running time: **89 MIN.**
King Faraday . . . . Robert Quarry
Phoebe Love . . . . Linnea Quigley
Lou Lurrod . . . . Stuart Benton
Candy . . . . Delia Sheppard
Gersch/Steve . . . . Stephen Liska
Lola . . . . Kathryn Stanleigh
Rake . . . . Spice Williams

■ **"Sexbomb" is an ultra-low-budget spoof of ultra-low-budget filmmaking with enough clever lines and cheeky characterizations to keep it amusing. Pic had a world preem 1-day engagement Nov. 29 but it's way too thin for theatrical release.**

Shot in nine days on a $160,000 budget, pic demonstrates handy, if self-referential, resourcefulness on the part of producer-director Jeff Broadstreet and writer Robert Benson, who've created a darkly comic parody of the cheesy netherworld of quickie filmmaking that should be most amusing to graduates of same.

At fictional Faraday Intl. Prods., production on "I Rip Your Flesh (With Pliers)" consists of having a thug in a rubber·mask chase a topless blond (B-movie queen Linnea Quigley) around the couch with intent to maul her.

"Sexbomb's" dramatic tension, as it were, comes from Robert Quarry's intervention as King Faraday, a raging gasbag of a rich, penny-pinching producer whose blistering takedowns of everyone within range make for a bracing, if depressing scenario.

His bored bombshell wife (Delia Sheppard) seizes on a footloose would-be screenwriter, Lou Lurrod (Stuart Benton), as the stooge she can get to murder him.

Broadstreet, who appears in a cameo as "the cheapest writer in Hollywood," finds the right insouciant, self-mocking tone to keep the pic appealing in line with its own low aspirations, and writer Benson supplies wit.

Drawing card for some viewers will be Quigley (billed simply as Linnea), who plays the supportive girl-next-door (albeit barebreasted and in black garters), in contrast to Sheppard's scheming seductress. Both femme leads are frequently topless.

Also of interest is "the music video," a searingly energetic version of "Rhythm" by bizarro rock band Food For Feet.—*Daws.*

Black Rainbow
(BRITISH)

London A Goldcrest Films and Tv production. Executive producer, George A. Walker. Produced by John Quested, Geoffrey Helman. Written and directed by Mike Hodges. Camera (color), Gerry Fisher;· editor, Malcolm Cooke; music, John Scott; sound, Blake Wilcox; production design, Voytek; art direction, Patty Klawonn; costumes, Clifford Capone; associate producer, Don Anderson. Reviewed at London Film Festival, Nov. 26, 1989. Running time: **113 MIN.**

Martha Travis	Rosanna Arquette
Walter Travis	Jason Robards
Gary Wallace	Tom Hulce
Lloyd Harley	Mark Joy
Lt. Weinberg	Ron Rosenthal
Ted Silas	John Bennes

Also with: Linda Pierce, Olek Krupa, Marty Terry, Ed. L. Gray, John Thompson, Helen Baldwin, Darla N. Warner.

■ Helmer Mike Hodges displays a fine return to form with "Black Rainbow," an enjoyable supernatural thriller making fine use of its North Carolina locations, and even better use of the excellent Rosanna Arquette who gives a chilling performance. Pic could work at the boxoffice if handled properly.

Film is set in the fundamentalist society of crumbling industrial towns where folks have a deep-rooted faith in the spiritualist movement. In many ways its chills and thrills are played so low-key — and well — that a shootout climax doesn't seem to match the tone of the rest of the film.

Pic opens with journalist Tom Hulce tracking down spiritualist Arquette to fill in the background to a story he himself was involved in some years before. The flashback shows Arquette and her alcoholic father (Jason Robards) presenting a traveling clairvoyant act at various small-town venues throughout North Carolina.

During one act Arquette receives a message from a murdered man to pass on to his wife in the audience. Unfortunately he is not dead and his wife gets rather upset. Later that night the man is killed in his home.

Small-town reporter Hulce sets about uncovering the scoop, and follows Arquette and Robards to their next town. There he gets drunk with Robards and sleeps with Arquette, but still doesn't believe her "gift." That night she predicts even more deaths, and again her vision comes true.

While all this is going on, a factory owner who ordered the murder of the first man has put a hit out on Arquette because he has discovered she can identify his assassin. While on stage the next night, Arquette "sees" the killing of her father by the assassin. The killer is trapped and shot by the police after he follows a "vision" of her about their hotel.

Enigmatic ending sees the photographs Hulce took of Arquette at her hideaway cottage showing only a tumbledown shack — no sign of her.

Arquette is excellent as the strange but seductive Martha. She has an ethereal quality combined with innate sexuality, though she looks vaguely uncomfortable in the actual scenes of clairvoyance on stage. Robards is in his element as the drunkard father, and lends effortless class and humor to the pic. Hulce is intelligently restrained, and gives a fine performance as the stumbling reporter in way over his head.

Hodges the writer has fashioned an enjoyable and compelling pic, with references to religion, conspiracies and the environment as well as providing the requisite thrills. As a director he is confident and fluid, and extracts good performances as well as finding excellent locations. Fine contributions are made by cinematographer Gerry Fisher and editor Malcolm Cooke.

Pic is uncompromisingly strange and does not let itself get drawn into the concession of a happy ending or simple explanation. "Black Rainbow," the first live-action pic from the new-look Goldcrest, offers its leads meaty roles that they take on with relish. —*Adam.*

Moontrap

New York A Shapiro Glickenhaus Entertainment presentation of a Magic Films production. Executive producers, James A. Courtney, Brian C. Manoogian, Alan M. Solomon. Produced by Robert Dyke. Coproduced by John Cameron. Directed by Dyke. Screenplay, Tex Ragsdale; camera (Deluxe color), Peter Klein; editor, Steven C. Craig, Kevin Tent; music, Joseph LoDuca; sound, Frank Biondo; production design, B.K. Taylor; assistant director, Todd Jeffries; production manager, Victor Malone; special visual effects, Acme Special Effects Co. — supervisor, Gary Jones; miniature supervisor, David Wough; associate producer, Stephen Roberts. Reviewed on SGE vidcassette, N.Y., Nov. 22, 1989. MPAA Rating: R. Running time: **90 MIN.**

Col. Jason Grant	Walter Koenig
Ray Tanner	Bruce Campbell
Mera	Leigh Lombardi
Koreman	Robert Kurcz
Barnes	John J. Saunders
Haskell	Reavis Graham

■ "Moontrap" is a very entertaining though highly derivative sci-fi adventure, currently available in homevid stores.

Shapiro Glickenhaus probably missed an opportunity by deciding against releasing the film to U.S. theaters, as there haven't been any Outer Space pics out lately, and this one's a goodie.

Canny casting has "Star Trek's" resident Russian, Walter Koenig, moving up to a William Shatner-type role here as an astronaut who jumps at the opportunity to head up the first manned U.S. moon mission in decades. He's sent to find the base there from which a derelict spaceship emanated. Bruce Campbell, star of the "Evil Dead" pics, is his trusty copilot and both thesps rise to the occasion.

Tex Ragsdale's script has some similarities to that of Tobe Hooper's "Lifeforce," except that most of the action here takes place in space or on the moon. Pods are found which create robots using scrap or even corpses as spare parts, and heroes' encounters with these mechanical monsters are excitingly staged by helmer Robert Dyke.

Good special effects follow the look of "2001" for inspiration, which along with "Alien" adds to the film's derivative aspect (throw in "Saturn 3" for the robot design). The beautiful alien they find and befriend is well-played by Leigh Lombardi, a looker in the Mathilda May ("Lifeforce") school.

Despite all the references to previous films, "Moontrap" is exciting and suspenseful. Made in Detroit, its technical qualities are up to international standards. Hopefully it will receive some theatrical exposure for buffs despite having landed on homevideo first. —*Lor.*

La Grieta
(The Rift)
(SPANISH)

Madrid A Dister Group film. Executive producer, José Escrivá. Produced by Escrivá, Francesca de Laurentiis and Juan Piquer Simón. Written and directed by Piquer Simón. Camera (Eastmancolor), Juan Marine; editor, Antonio Gimeno; music, Joel Goldsmith; art direction, Gonzalo Gonzalo; underwater design and special technical effects, Carlo de Marchis; special makeup effects & creatures, Colin Arthur; other special effects, Basilio Cortijo; costumes, María Escrivá; sound, Jim Willis. Reviewed at Cine Palafox, Madrid, Nov. 25, 1989. Running time: **86 MIN.**

Wick Hayes	Jack Scalia
Captain Phillips	R. Lee Ermey
Robbins	Ray Wise
Nina	Deborah Adair

Also with: Emilio Linder, John Toles Bey, Tony Isbert, Ely Pouget, Alvaro Labra, Luis Lorenzo, Frank Braña, J. Martinez Bordiu, Edmund Purdom, Garick Hagon.

■ "The Rift" comes just a little too late, since comparisons with "The Abyss" will be inevitable. Ingredients are similar: a nuclear sub sunk in an underground rift, a rescue operation, two former lovers on the crew, etc.

Though shot on a low budget (cost was that of *four minutes* of "The Abyss," quipped the producer), pic has enough ingredients to make it suitable for homevid and tv release. RCA/Col reportedly has picked up world tv rights.

The all-important effects are on the whole well-handled, especially the sea monsters, though corpse dummies are not very convincing and the sub seems rather too small. The horror effects are graphically grisly.

Story is a kind of mix of the old "Star Trek," "The Abyss" and "Alien," but on a very modest level. Mission is to find a nuclear sub that has sunk into an underground rift off the coast of Norway.

The crew includes a pretty marine biologist and a handsome nuclear sub designer who has been falsely blamed for the Navy Department's mistakes that led to the sinking of the first sub. They and others are under the command of a martinet captain.

Eventually, the first sub is located, stuck in a deep abyss. The crew members of the rescue mission descend and discover that, in fact, an underwater lab had been set up by the first mission, in which genetic mutation experiments were carried out. These had been hushed up by the government.

The experiments gave rise to the appropriate sea monsters, who now kill and contaminate the crew members. Most succumb to a slimy death, but the hero and heroine make it to the happy end. —*Besa.*

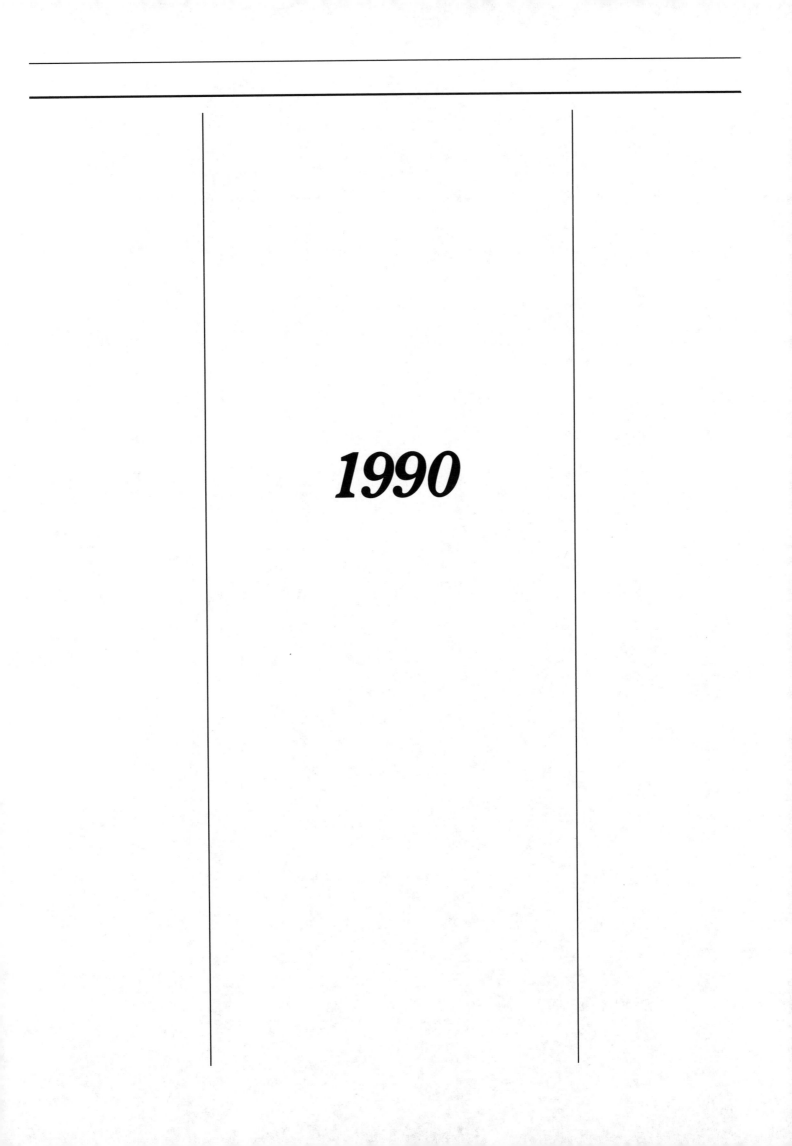

1990

The Delinquents
(AUSTRALIAN)

Sydney   A Greater Union Distributors release (Warner Bros. in U.S.) of a Village-Roadshow presentation of a Cutler-Wilcox (The Delinquents) production, in association with Silver Lining Entertainment. Executive producers, Graham Burke, Greg Coote, John Tarnoff. Produced by Alex Cutler, Michael Wilcox. Directed by Chris Thomson. Screenplay, Clayton Frohman, Mac Gudgeon, from novel by Criena Rohan; camera (color), Andrew Lesnie; editor, John Scott; music, Miles Goodman; production design, Laurence Eastwood; sound, Paul Brincat; line producer, Irene Dobson; production manager, Rosslyn Abernethy; assistant director, Colin Fletcher; casting, Michael Lynch, Rae Davidson; costumes, Bruce Finlayson. Reviewed at Village Cinema City, Sydney, Dec. 20, 1989. Running time: **101 MIN.**

Lola Lovell . . . . .Kylie Minogue
Brownie Hansen . . . . .Charlie Schlatter
Mrs. Lovell . . . . .Angela Punch-McGregor
Bosun . . . . .Bruno Lawrence
Mavis . . . . .Desirée Smith
Lyle . . . . .Todd Boyce
Aunt Westbury . . . . .Melissa Jaffer
Mrs. Hansen . . . . .Lynette Curran

■ The success of "The Delinquents" in Australia and Britain (pic opens simultaneously in both territories) will depend on reaction to teen fave Kylie Minogue, star of soaps and the song charts, seen here in her first feature. Pic should open to very big business, but probably fade, whereas domestically it faces an uphill battle which the crucial miscasting of Charlie Schlatter won't alleviate.

This story, set in the late '50s, about the passionate love affair of a couple of teens, is trite stuff. Lola (Minogue) and Brownie (Schlatter) live in the small town of Bundaberg in Queensland. She's still at school when they become lovers and she gets pregnant. The youngsters plan to elope, but are parted by Lola's alcoholic mother (Angela Punch-McGregor), who forces her daughter to have a back-street abortion (offscreen).

Brownie spends about a reel searching for his lost love in the city of Brisbane, then goes to sea in despair. However, via a piece of contrived plotting of monumental proportions, he happens to walk into a Melbourne bar one night and sees Lola, her hair bleached, sadder but wiser.

Love blossoms again, but, once more, the lovers are parted by the authorities; Lola is sent to a Dickensian welfare home for a year. When she emerges Brownie is waiting for her, but the couple's problems aren't over.

The screenplay is repetitive and tame. Despite the numerous bedroom scenes, and some fleeting nudity, there's no hint of genuine passion between the young lovers. Far more interesting characters are Mavis (Desirée Smith) and Lyle (Todd Boyce), who befriend Lola and Brownie. Their scenes have a warmth that's lacking in the central relationship, and their tragedy toward the end of the film carries far more impact than the problems of Minogue and Schlatter.

Authority figures are caricatured in the film: the police are all violent, welfare officers are chillingly heartless and parents are brutal and/or unfeeling. Teens may repond to this approach, but adults won't get much joy from the 1-dimensional treatment.

Technically, pic is good, with great care taken by production designer Laurence Eastwood to make the late '50s setting as authentic as possible. Unfortunately, this visual precision is betrayed by the casting of Schlatter, whose broad American accent and style make nonsense of the character of a small-town Australian boy (the inevitable, laborious line explaining that he spent time in Seattle doesn't help at all). Nor is Schlatter a strong enough actor to justify the casting.

As for Minogue, the verdict still is out regarding a future acting career. She pulls off a couple of scenes well, including one where she rebels against an unctuous do-gooder (Melissa Jaffer) in whose care she's been placed by a court, but it's unfair to judge her on this material.

Supporting players are tops, with Punch-McGregor making the most of her role as Lola's mother, and Bruno Lawrence most sympathetic as Brownie's sailor mentor.

During production, it was announced that David Bowie would compose the film's score; he dropped out, but Miles Goodman's score is perfectly pleasant. Some standard rock numbers from the era are well used. —*Strat.*

Skulduggery
(BRITISH)

London   A BBC TV production. Produced by Ann Scott. Directed by Philip Davis. Screenplay, Davis from his play; camera (Eastmancolor), Barry McCann; editor, Peter Harris; music, Carl Davis; sound, Roger Long; production design, Gerry Scott; costumes, Pat Godfrey. Reviewed at London Film Festival, Nov. 18, 1989. Running time: **90 MIN.**

Tony . . . . .David Thewlis
Sweeney . . . . .Steve Sweeney
Terry . . . . .Paul McKenzie
Gombo . . . . .Chris Pitt
Kak . . . . .Robin Weaver
Tony's mum . . . . .Gillian Raine

■ At first glance, this impressive BBC feature is an amusing study of contempo life in a typical British public housing project, but toward the climax it subtly changes from mild-mannered to dark and mildly weird.

Writer-director Philip Davis has acted in three Mike Leigh productions — most recently "High Hopes" — and uses a similar realistic, improvisational style. There is the same dark humor and underlying social comment along with unpretentious direction of the actors.

Though "Skulduggery" is very much a 4-hander, it is the impressive performance of David Thewlis that catches the eye. He is an oddball British talent who was the best thing in the recent "Vroom" and "Resurrected."

Pic opens with three kids and a slightly older friend (Thewlis) meeting in a local woods, ready to break into a shop. Their inept plan gets canceled when Thewlis tells about a new alarm system, but one of them — Chris Pitt — decides to go ahead, but is caught by the police.

The other two — Steve Sweeney and Paul McKenzie — idly spend their time about the estate planning crimes, chatting-up girls, generally acting the aggressive no-hopers. When Pitt is released from reform school, allegiances are swapped and McKenzie changes his clothes and style when he takes up with a rich girl who lives nearby.

Thewlis is the strange character who takes to observing his friends, especially McKenzie. When the three younger kids break into a large house, pic takes a strange turn when Sweeney and Pitt are beaten up by Thewlis, who then declares his love for McKenzie.

Pic nixes a rough charm with an honest sense of the ridiculous, and while it is limited in its scope, Davis' direction is proficient — he even allows himself a brief walk-on part. "Skulduggery" has a correctly bleak quality and is an attractive debut by Davis. —*Adam.*

1939
(SWEDISH)

Stockholm   A Svensk Filmindustri release of an SF production, in association with the Swedish Film Institute and SVT-1. Produced by Waldemar Bergendahl. Executive producer, Lennart Wiklund. Directed by Göran Carmback. Screenplay, Brasse Brännström, adapted by Catti Edfeldt, Kjell Sundstedt; camera (Eastmancolor), Jens Fischer; editor, Susanne Linnman; music, Anders Berglund; production design, Lasse Westfeldt, Jimmy McGann; costumes, Inger Pehrsson; makeup, Kjell Gustavsson, Britt-Marie (Ludde) Kling; sound, Willie Peterson-Berger, Jean-Frederic Axelsson; production management, Thomas Allercrans, Lars Blomgren; assistant director, Eva Bagge; casting, Daniel Alfredson. Reviewed at the Globe, Stockholm, Dec. 18, 1989. Running time: **192 MIN.**

Annika . . . . .Helene Egelund
Berit . . . . .Helena Bergström
Bengt Hall . . . . .Per Morberg
Annika's father . . . . .Ingvar Hirdwall
Her mother . . . . .Anita Ekström
Her granddad . . . . .Per Oscarsson
Her brother . . . . .Per Grytt
Harald . . . . .Johan Ulveson
Hans . . . . .Stefan Larsson
Alfred Hall . . . . .Keve Hjelm
Cecelia Hall . . . . .Anita Wall
Also with: Willie Andreasson, Krister Henriksson, Gunilla Larsson, Gino Samil, Heinz Hopf, Runo Sundberg, Björn Aronsson, Thomas von Brömssen, Stefan Graebe, Balthazar Silvera, Anders Lönnbro, Michael Druker, Louise Hoffsten, Meta Roos.

■ "1939" is the catchy title of an epic melodrama that deals with Swedish people during World War II. Serving also as a 3-part tv miniseries, "1939" is too long-winded and too superficial as national soul-searching and overall drama to stand much of a chance as a theatrical export item.

Director Göran Carmback delivers a bright-looking series of mostly amiable characters performing in sequences that only rarely touch upon tragedy.

Death appears only in thrown-in flashes like one of wounded German soldiers glimpsed through the windows of a train permitted transit from fighting Norway to occupied Denmark. Watered down from an actual event is a young girl's witnessing of a Swedish officer saluting his Nazi counterpart who has shot down a Norse trooper just as latter had crossed the border.

Other grim glimpses are of wartime black marketeering on a small scale and profiteering on a larger international business scale, particularly with Germany. An underdeveloped subplot discloses that the Swedish government was warier of local left-wingers (they were interned) than of Nazi sympathizers (they were left alone).

Otherwise, audiences will be stuck with a common enough poor-rural-girl-meets-rich-city-boy story that drags on for 112 minutes of the film's 192-min. running time. The sweet friendship between the country girl Annika (blandly performed by soft-contoured Helene Egelund) and quick-witted city survivor Berit (a cute-as-a-button Helena Bergström) does have its tragic undertones, but these soon turn maudlin.

As charming boy turned male chauvinist pig, Per Morberg displays strength. Also notable are such older thesps as Keve Hjelm, Ingvar Hirdvall, Per Oscarsson and Anders Lönnbro. The rest of a huge cast also contribute with well-modulated performances.

The ending develops mild irony in an old black & white shot of local crowds celebrating V-Day in Europe just as wildly as it was done on Piccadilly and the Champs-Elysées.

Expert production dress brings the era back to life imaginatively. —*Kell.*

Deadly Spygames

New York   A Sell Entertainment and Double Helix Films presentation of a Sell Pictures production. Executive producer, M. George Henry. Produced by Jack M. Sell, Adrianne Richmond. Directed by Sell. Screenplay, Sell, Richmond; camera (Video Masters color), Wayne Kohlar; editor, Maurits Guépin; music, Hutch Deloach; sound, Irving Nafshun; art direction, Jim Bandsuh; costume design, Wendi Joan; assistant director, Richmond; production manager, Val Christman; stunt coordinator, Mike Stymaks; associate producer, Bruce Richmond; casting, Shirley Hamilton, Darlene Davis (Bahamas). Reviewed on Sell Pictures vidcassette, N.Y., Nov. 1, 1989. No MPAA Rating. Running time: **86 MIN.**

Python	Troy Donahue
Stephen Banner	Jack M. Sell
Chastity	Tippi Hedren
Jacqueline	Adrianne Richmond
Ling Choy	Joni Le Goddessa
Russian general	Bob McDonald
Karlov	Kathlyn Miles
Mr. E.	Peter Abbott
Cuban general	Les Golden
Det. Brody	Curt Colbert

Also with: Natasha Pinder, Jim Fay, Joleen Lutz, Bobbi Wexler, John Martinez.

■ **"Deadly Spygames" is an entertaining spoof of the James Bond pics, with good video prospects domestically and some foreign potential as a theatrical title.**

Beginning with the Maurice Binder-esque credits sequence, filmmakers Jack M. Sell and Adrianne Richmond have fun with the familiar format of the Ian Fleming films, but the twist is having the twosome also toplining as ordinary folks in the superspy roles. Sell plays Banner, government spy assigned by CIA agent Troy Donahue to knock out a Cuban radar installation, while Richmond is his assistant and onetime romantic partner.

Plot escalates toward a possible World War III as a Soviet general (Bob McDonald) sends agent Karlov (Kathlyn Miles) to steal a secret film incriminating his grandson as a mass murderer. She succeeds and Banner has to steal it back from the Soviet computer room at the UN.

Pic is fun due to its extreme tongue-in-cheek approach, especially noticeable in the frequent, functional use of stock footage whenever largescale military operations occur. Only drawback is extensive reliance on a sequence from Sell's previous film, "Outtakes," in which that pic's satire on Santa Claus slasher films is recycled unconvincingly into a supposed documentary film about the general's son being a killer.

Guest star Tippi Hedren makes wisecracks as she screens the film for the CIA, but its inappropriateness sticks out.

Acting and tech credits are okay. —*Lor.*

Jakarta
(INDONESIAN-U.S.)

New York   A Novacom Intl., Parkit Films and Troma presentation. Executive producers, Lloyd Kaufman, Michael Herz. Produced by Dhamoo Punjabi, Gobind Punjabi, Raam Punjabi. Directed by Charles Kaufman. Codirector, E.G. Bakker. Screenplay, Charles Kaufman; additional writing, Ralph Soll; camera (PPFN, TVC color), Robert Chappell; additional camera, Kasiyo Hadiwijoyo; editor, Michael Spence; music, Jay Chattaway; sound (Ultra-Stereo), David Pastecchi; production design, Susan Kaufman; casting, Judy Henderson & Associates. Reviewed on MCEG/Virgin vidcassette, N.Y., Dec. 19, 1989. MPAA Rating: R. Running time: **95 MIN.**

Falco	Christopher Noth
Esha	Sue Francis Pai
Dolph	Ronald Hunter
Jack	Franz Tumbuan
Lola	Zoraya Perucha
Bernie	David Sharp

■ **"Jakarta" is a well-crafted film noir made in Indonesia and New York. The 1986 production is a belated direct-to-video release Stateside.**

Christopher Noth is the down-on-his-luck hero who used to be a government agent. He's sent against his will back to Jakarta, where three years earlier he botched a bodyguard assignment to protect witnesses planning to testify against druglords. He becomes reinvolved with femme fatale Sue Francis Pai en route to an ironic finish.

Helmer Charles Kaufman, best known for his 1980 horror film "Mother's Day," dots the action with excellent chase scenes. Of special interest is the pic's ample local color, including authentic Javanese puppet shadow plays.

Noth is okay as the brooding hero, but Pai steals the show as the extremely alluring beauty whose evil nature is a satisfying throwback to the dark '40s pictures "Jakarta" recalls.

Tech credits are fine. —*Lor.*

La Otra Ilusión
(The Other Illusion)
(VENEZUELAN)

Havana   An R.Z. Cine y Video-Departamento de Cine de la Universidad de los Andes (ULA) production. Written and directed by Roque Zambrano. Camera (color), Césare Javorsky; music, Juan Carlos Nuñez, Grupo Sentimento Muerto. No other credits available. Reviewed at Havana Intl. Film Festival, Dec. 13, 1989. Running time: **112 MIN.**

With Julie Restifo, Javier Vidal, Luz Urdaneta.

■ **"The Other Illusion" by Venezuelan director Roque Zambrano is an overlong, beautifully photographed and orchestrated exercise in self-indulgence that boasts no discernible storyline nor real characters. Potential outside the local territory seems slim.**

Theme concerns a musician and his painter wife, both victims of some sort of existential angst. They mope about their luxurious country home and mutter pretentious, philosophically tinted lines of text, counterpointed by endless boring flashbacks revealing mutually misunderstood childhoods.

Actors Julie Restifo and Javier Vidal are not allowed enough dimension in the script to provide any sort of texture, which leaves a sameness of tone throughout. Although admirable, the excellent tech credits are wasted. —*Lent.*

The Banker

New York   A Westwind production. Executive producer, Robert W. Mann. Produced and directed by William Webb. Screenplay, Dana Augustine, from story by Webb, Richard Brandes, Augustine; camera (color), John Huneck; editor, Patrick Dodd; music, Sam Winans, Reg Powell; sound, Ken Segal; production design, James R. Shumaker; assistant director, Bruce Franklin; production manager, Jeff Spielman; coproducer, Kurt Anderson; casting, Al Onorato, Jerry Franks. Reviewed on MCEG/Virgin vidcassette, N.Y., Dec. 19, 1989. MPAA Rating: R. Running time: **95 MIN.**

Sgt. Dan Jefferson	Robert Forster
Spalding Osbourne	Duncan Regehr
Sharon Maxwell	Shanna Reed
Cowboy	Jeff Conaway
Fowler	Leif Garrett
Lt. Lloyd Hughes	Richard Roundtree

Also with: Juan Garcia, Michael Fairman, Deborah Richter, Teri Weigel, Karen Russell, Julie Hayek, Leigh Wood, E. J. Peaker.

■ **A bank chairman as heartless monster? What sounds like a job description is the basis for an effective horror tale in the slasher genre.**

William Webb, whose films have invariably gone direct to video, makes no pretense at making a whodunit here. We're immediately informed that banker Duncan Regehr is killing call girls, then ritualistically mutilating their bodies. It seems he's following some ancient South American Indian practice, even painting his face and using a crossbow.

Robert Forster is the plodding cop tracking him down. Giving the film an interesting wrinkle is Forster's old flame, Shanna Reed, who becomes a successful newscaster and wins popular support when her uncensored outrage at the killer is allowed to be broadcast. Regehr becomes one of her biggest fans and then turns against her in love-hate fashion.

Though low on suspense, pic benefits from casting of such luscious actresses as Teri Weigel and Deborah Richter as the targets of Regehr's bloodlust. There are overt overtones of "The Most Dangerous Game" as he often prefers to hunt down his human prey.—*Lor.*

Mestizo
(VENEZUELAN)

Havana   A Mario Handler Producciones-Instituto Cubano del Arte e Indústria Cinematográficos (Icaic) production. Produced and directed by Mario Handler. Screenplay, Handler, Antonio Larreta, based on novel "El Mestizo José Vargas," by Guillermo Meneses; camera (color), Julio Valdés; editor, Handler; art direction, Ramón Aguirre; sound, Ricardo Istueta. Reviewed at Havana Intl. Film Festival, Dec. 7, 1989. Running time: **82 MIN.**

José Ramón Vargas	Marcos Moreno
Cruz Guaregua	Zezé Motla
Aquiles Vargas	Aldo Tulián
Pacha	Víctor Cuica

Also with: Nancy González, Omar Gonzalo, Eduardo Gil, Hilda Vera.

■ **Mario Handler's period pic "Mestizo" leaves most viewers wondering what exactly is the point. While the film supposedly is an indictment against racism in Venezuelan history, the confused, slapdash handling of the storyline muddles any sense of cohesion.**

Based on the novel "El Mestizo José Vargas," pic relates the episodic erotic ventures of a young mulatto, José Vargas (Marcos Moreno), in his dealings with white society. We are shown something about his relationship with his black mother and his rich, white racist father. We also see him at work and in his drunken sexual exploits. Yet there are not enough elements to jell into any semblance of a plot.

While tech credits are okay, international interest seems nil.
—*Lent.*

In Fading Light
(BRITISH)

London An Amber Films/Channel 4/British Screen production. Produced and directed by the Amber Production Team: Viv Dawson, Kitty Fitzgerald, Rich Grassick, Ellie Hare, Sirkka-Liisa Konttinen, Pat McCarthy, Murray Martin, Jane Neatrour, Lorna Powell, Pete Roberts, Annie Robson, Ray Stubbs, Judy Tomlinson. Screenplay, Tom Hadaway; camera (color), Amber Production Team; music, Alasdair Robertson. Ray Stubbs; sound, Dave Eadington. Reviewed at London Film Festival, Nov. 25, 1989. Running time: **102 MIN.**
Yopper . . . . Joe Caffrey
Irene . . . . Maureen Harold
Alfie Olsen . . . . Dave Hill
Micky Molloy . . . . Brian Hogg
Dandy Mac . . . . Sammy Johnson
Karen Olsen . . . . Joanna Ripley
Betty . . . . Amber Styles

■Amber Films is a collective based in the north of England dedicated to making films about the lives of working-class people. "In Fading Light" is group's ambitious lowbudget pic told with almost documentary realism and compassion for the realistic characters involved.

It's also an important reminder that there is a British film industry outside London, and that there still is room for pics about real people and real problems. Unfortunately, the Amber team is so uncompromising in striving for realism that much of the dialog — in thick northern accents — will be incomprehensible even to most U.K. audiences.

The arrival of a young woman at the dockside where the crew of a fishing boat are working stirs interest. It turns to upheaval when it turns out Joanna Ripley is the daughter of skipper Dave Hill and wants to stay with him. Neither the crew nor his common-law wife (Maureen Harold) are thrilled at the prospect.

The crew is even less thrilled when they find Hill has decided to take Ripley on their next fishing trip. She proves to be an excellent fisherman and even wins the grudging respect of Sammy Johnson who refused to talk to her for the entire trip. They return with a paltry catch and the boat is taken away.

Pic ends, however, with a vague sense of optimism as Ripley and Joe Caffrey head off to find a new fishing fleet to work with. An overwhelming sense of honesty makes the film most enjoyable, with an emphasis on the small, important things in life. When Caffrey loses a finger in an accident it is treated with matter-of-factness by everyone.

Best direction by the Amber team is on board the boat, and they are well served by a cast lacking in pretensions, willing to give their all. A worthy and fascinating pic, "In Fading Light" is important in showing a way of life unknown to many in England. —*Adam.*

Venir al Mundo
(To Come Into The World)
(CUBAN)

Havana An Instituto Cubano del Arte e Indústria Cinematográficos (Icaic) production. Produced by Ricardo Avila. Written and directed by Miguel Torres. Camera (color), Raúl Rodríguez; editor, Gladys Cambre; music, Frank Fernández; art direction, Heriberto Echevarría. Reviewed at Cine Chaplin, Havana Intl. Film Festival, Dec. 12, 1989. Running time: **79 MIN.**
Luis . . . . Mario Balmaseda
Mariana . . . . Susana Pérez
Carlos . . . . Alberto Pujols
Enrique . . . . Miguel Navarro
Claudia . . . . Tahimi Alvariño
    Also with: Luisa María Jiménez, Tito Junco, Mireya Chapman, Ramoncito Veloz, Oneida Hernández, Elvira Vladés.

■"Venir al Mundo" is a feature-length soap opera whose short running time nevertheless will prove too long for most filmgoers. Although popular at domestic screens, offshore sales are chancy at best.

Employing a bevy of national tv actors, writer-director Miguel Torres narrates the tired tale of a doctor, played by well-known legit and screen actor Mario Balmaseda, and his bedside manner.

Specializing in fertility problems, several case histories supplement the meager storyline about the doc's adulterous behavior. Title refers to his success in the maternity ward.

Tech credits are okay, while dialog abounds with shopworn cliches better suited for the small screen. —*Lent.*

Mamá Querida
(Mama Dear)
(ARGENTINE)

Havana A Vanguardia Cinematográfico-Instituto Nacional de Cinematografía production. Directed by Silvio Fischbein. Screenplay, Fischbein, Diana Fischbein, Adrián Desiderato; camera (color), Andrés Silvart; editor, Jorge Valencia, Armando Blanco; music, Jorge Rapp; sound, Jorge Grammatico. Reviewed at Havana Intl. Film Festival, Dec. 5, 1989. Running time: **75 MIN.**
Berta . . . . Chela Ruiz
Mario . . . . Victor Laplace
Marta . . . . Selva Alemán
Natario . . . . Omar Fanucchi
Rosa . . . . Laura Marino
Susan . . . . Beatriz Irusta
    Also with: Héctor Tealdi, Noemi Kazán, Elita Aizenberg, Carolina Fischbein, Beatriz Raiter, Fernando di Leo, Susana Sisto, Omar Tiberti, Fernando de la Torre, Silvana Silveri.

■Argentine director Silvio Fischbein's "Mamá Querida" is a well-intentioned study of a family in conflict over an aging parent. Although well acted and argued, pic's strident tone is a drawback.

Story begins with the death of the patriarch of a Buenos Aires Jewish family. Returning for the funeral is artist son Natario (Omar Fanucchi), who lives abroad. Daughter Marta (Selva Alemán) is preparing for her marriage to Mario, played by w.k. actor Victor Laplace.

At the beginning of the film, the mother (Chela Ruiz) is able to care for herself, but her health deteriorates until she is completely debilitated. She eventually moves into Marta's home, sparking strife between her and Mario.

Worse than ill health, the mother's bleats for attention and her constant complaints wear at daughter and viewer alike, and the issue of the mother's care engulfs everyone. —*Lent.*

Rosa de Dos Aromas
(Rose With Two Scents)
(MEXICAN)

Havana A Gazcón Films production. Directed by Gilberto Gazcón. Screenplay,, Gazcón, Emilio Carballido, based on play by Carballido; camera (color), Agustín Lara; music, Eduardo and Karen Roel. Reviewed at Havana Intl. Film Festival, Dec. 16, 1989. Running time: **90 MIN.**
    With: Olivia Collins, Patricia Rivera, Tere Velázquez, Wolf Ruvinskis, Ana Colchero, Hilda Aguirre, Humberto Elizondo, Sonia Piña, Gina Leal, Diana Herrera.

■Based on Emilio Carballido's popular legit comedy, "Rosa de Dos Aromas" fits into Mexico's sex comedy genre, with the exception that it has a well thoughout script.

Directed by Gilberto Gazcón, storyline concerns two women, one a professional translator and the other a hairdresser, who suddenly find out they are married to the same man. The man in question has been jailed for a traffic accident.

Although at first the two women hate each other, they unite to raise bail money. In the end, they come to realize friendship is stronger than their love for the cad and the bail is spent on a holiday cruise.

Film has some funny moments, because of the combination of the script and strong thesping by Olivia Collins and Patricia Rivera as the wronged wives. —*Lent.*

El Ausente
(The Absent)
(ARGENTINE)

Havana A Cinematográfica de Santa Fe release of a Rafael Filippelli-Unión de Cineastas Argentinos Cooperativa de Trabajo production. Executive producer, Antonio Ottone. Directed by Rafael Filippelli. Screenplay, Filippelli, Carlos Dámaso Martínez, based on a story by Antonio Marimón; camera (color), Andrés Silvart; editor, Diego García Gutiérrez; music, Jorge Candia; sound, Mario Antognini; art direction, Hugo Guzzo. Reviewed at Havana Intl. Film Festival, Dec. 10, 1989. Running time: **85 MIN.**
Raúl Salas . . . . Omar Rezk
Muñiz . . . . Roberto Suter
Elena . . . . Ana María Mazza
Rios . . . . Omar Viale
Lencinas . . . . Daniel Grecco
    Also with: Ricardo Bertone, Nicolás Jair, Coco Santillán, Beatriz Sarlo, Miguel Quiroga, Darío Fernández, Alejandro Cuevas, Miguel Iraiarte, Pepe Nov.

■"The Absent," a low-budget Argentine reconstruction of the turbulent Peronist years preceding the 1976 military coup, suffers from a simplified pamphlet approach to a historically complicated theme, one that may be obscure to most non-Argentines.

Fictional biopic centers on the work of union leader Raúl Salas (Omar Rezk) in the town of Córdova, and his struggle with local and national authorities.

Director Rafael Filippelli unwisely has chosen to reveal the film's mechanics by showing camera and crew crosscut with the fictional narrative. Rather than adding to the pic's texture, the device distances the viewer by emphasizing tale's inherent artifice.

Pic seems part of Argentina's post-junta glasnost, in which past political sins are paraded out for contemporary contemplation and condemnation — an "at last it can all be told" tabloid approach to history. While possibly important domestically, offshore interest is questionable. —*Lent.*

La Vida en Rosa
(La Vie en Rose)
(CUBAN)

Havana An Instituto Cubano del Arte e Indústria Cinematográficos (Icaic) production. Produced by Humberto Fernández. Written and directed by Rolando Díaz. Camera (color), Roberto Fernández; editor, Jorge Abello; music, Edesio Alejandro, Manuel Eugenio; sound, Ricardo Istueta; art direction, Raúl de la Nuez. Reviewed at Havana Intl. Film Festival, Dec. 12, 1989. Running time: **86 MIN.**
Old Ramón . . . . Manuel Porto
Young Ramón . . . . Tony Cortés
Old Elena . . . María de los Angeles Santana
Young Elena . . . . Lavinia Castro
Old Alberto . . . . Orlando Casín
Young Alberto . . . . Roli Pena
    Also with: Elena Huerta, Odalys García, Lazaro Nuñez, Luis F. Flores, Jorge Prieto, Berardo Forbes, Pedro Alvarez, Tony Salup,

Joel Nuñez, Katia Caso.

■ The misfired Cuban teenage fantasy "La Vie En Rose" presents the confrontation of a group of teens with their future selves in a tossed-salad script that goes nowhere.

Written and directed by Rolando Díaz, pic presents two realities — present and future — side by side. Díaz is best known outside Cuba for the 1984 "Los Pájaros Tirándole a la Escopeta."

Fantasy theme seems inspired from Steven Spielberg's "Amazing Stories" tv lineup, and although "La Vie" may have made for an interesting short, film suffers from a meandering search for structure and form.

Story concerns a typical teen (Tony Cortés), who one day meets himself as an old man (Manuel Porto). His friends also meet their older selves and find former bonds have shifted and romances traded.

When the youngsters are dissatisfied by their future, they are told they cannot change them. The future selves blame the youngsters for events that have yet to happen, etc.

Tech credits are high and acting competent. Directorial quirks, such as a party shown in fast motion and a plethora of quick cuts, are annoying and better suited to tv. —Lent.

Internal Affairs

Hollywood   A Paramount Pictures release, of a Frank Mancuso Jr. production, in association with Pierre David. Executive producers, David, René Malo. Coexecutive producer, David Streit. Produced by Mancuso. Directed by Mike Figgis. Screenplay, Henry Bean; camera (Technicolor), John A. Alonzo; editor, Robert Estrin; music, Figgis, Anthony Marinelli, Brian Banks; sound (Dolby), Gary Gerlich; production design, Waldemar Kalinowski; art direction, Nicholas T. Preovolos; set decoration, Florence Fellman; costume design, Rudy Dillon; assistant director, J. Stephen Buck; additional camera, Curtis Clark; associate producers, Mara Trafficante, Pam O'Har; casting, Carrie Frazier, Shani Ginsberg. Reviewed at Paramount Pictures screening room, Hollywood, Jan. 5, 1990. MPAA Rating: R. Running time: 117 MIN.
Dennis Peck . . . . .Richard Gere
Raymond Avila . . . . .Andy Garcia
Kathleen Avila . . . . .Nancy Travis
Amy Wallace . . . . .Laurie Metcalf
Grief . . . . .Richard Bradford
Van Stretch . . . . .William Baldwin
Dorian Fletcher . . . . .Michael Beach
Penny . . . . .Faye Grant
Tova . . . . .Katherine Borowitz
Heather . . . . .Annabella Sciorra

■ Stylish and slick, this tightly constructed cop yarn should reward Paramount with arresting boxoffice receipts and lift Andy Garcia another rung up the star ladder. Even its unsatisfying finale and the overused convention of police corruption can't undermine the film's grit.

The title proves a clever double entendre, as Garcia plays LAPD internal affairs division investigator Raymond Avila, pulled into a psychological game of chicken with quarry Dennis Peck (Richard Gere), a much-honored street cop who manipulates his position as easily as he does the people around him.

Played by Gere with a constant sense of menace, Peck preys on Raymond's insecurities by insinuating that he's bedded his wife (Nancy Travis) — increasingly neglected, ironically, as Raymond thrusts his all into the case.

While hardly new territory, director Mike Figgis wrings every ounce of tension from tyro writer Henry Bean's screenplay and, most impressively, elicits firstrate performances from top to bottom, including the film's smaller roles.

The look, too, immeasurably helps in creating a foreboding atmosphere, along the lines of Michael Mann's feature work or William Friedkin's "To Live And Die In L.A.," where it was shot.

Credit should especially go to cinematographer John A. Alonzo, who captures the same alluring essence of corruption he did in "Scarface." His achievement peaks with a pastel, blue-tinged

glimpse into Raymond's tequila-addled mind as he envisions his wife hotly entangled with Peck.

Granted, the film is all mood draped over a by-the-numbers plot, but its style wins out. Figgis never lets the pace slow long enough to expose the story's thinness despite, in retrospect, a moderate amount of action.

What violence there is proves brutally realistic, and Gere's pummeling of Garcia in an elevator is one of the film's best moments.

Reaching back in time, Gere revives his psycho, over-the-edge persona from "Looking For Mr. Goodbar;" he's a smoothly believable defiler of married women and one very scary dude.

With a role in the third "Godfather" film on the way and "The Untouchables" and "Black Rain" behind him, Garcia is becoming one of Paramount's most visible stars and promises to become a more and more bankable one. His quiet seething brings needed complexity and depth to a thinly drawn character.

The leggy Travis is fine as Garcia's wife, while Laurie Metcalf — a costar of tv's "Roseanne" — turns in the film's most memorable supporting role, terrific as Garcia's tough femme partner.

All tech credits are excellent, including heart-thumping music by a trio that includes director Figgis, who also scored his previous film "Stormy Monday." —Bril.

Lola
(MEXICAN)

Havana   A Concite Dos-Cooperativa José Revueltas-Televisión Española (TVE)-Macondo Cine Video production. Executive producer, Dulce Kuri. Produced by Jorge Sánchez. Directed by María Novaro. Screenplay, Novaro, Beatriz Novaro; camera (color), Rodrigo García; editor, Sigfrido Barjau; music, Gabriel Romo; sound, Carlos Aguilar; art direction, Marisa Pecanins. Reviewed at Havana Intl. Film Festival, Dec. 9, 1989. Running time: 92 MIN.
Lola . . . . .Leticia Huijara
Daughter . . . . .Alejandra Vargas
Chelo . . . . .Martha Navarro
    Also with: Roberto Sosa, Mauricio Rivera, Javier Zaragoza, Chell Godínez, Gerardo Martínez, Laura Ruiz.

■ First feature by María Novaro, "Lola" is a small but impressive film about the relationship between a mother and daughter. If handled carefully, pic stands a fair chance on the arthouse circuit.

"Lola" explores new territory in depicting the fragile world of an

imperfect modern woman, one who must fend for herself and daughter in the absence of the traditional family unit. As a backdrop, post-earthquake Mexico City appears as fragile and wounded as its inhabitants.

The storyline is slim. Lola (Leticia Huijara), a single mother abandoned by her rock musician lover, lives her marginal life as best she can selling irregular-sized clothing on the streets of Mexico City. She and others stay only one step ahead of the police, whose frequent raids attempt to clean the sidewalks of unlicensed vendors.

Lush lensing by Rodrigo García and Sigfrido Barjau's abrupt editing jar the viewer through irregular rhythm and pacing.

Although pic could stand trimming by about 15 minutes, "Lola" remains a significant first film. —Lent.

Tremors

Hollywood   A Universal Pictures release of a No Frills/Wilson-Maddock production. Executive producer, Gale Anne Hurd. Produced by S.S. Wilson, Brent Maddock. Line producer, Ginny Nugent. Directed by Ron Underwood. Screenplay, Wilson, Maddock, from story by Wilson, Maddock, Underwood; camera (Deluxe color), Alexander Gruszynski; editor, O. Nicholas Brown; music, Ernest Troost; production design, Ivo Cristante; art direction, Don Maskovich; set decoration, Paul Ford; sound (Dolby), Steve Flick, Richard Anderson; creature effects, Tom Woodruff Jr., Alec Gillis; assistant director, Mike Topoozian. Reviewed at Universal screening room, Universal City, Calif., Jan. 12, 1990. MPAA Rating: PG-13. Running time: 96 MIN.
Valentine McKee . . . . .Kevin Bacon
Earl Basset . . . . .Fred Ward
Rhonda LeBeck . . . . .Finn Carter
Burt Gummer . . . . .Michael Gross
Heather Gummer . . . . .Reba McEntire

■ An affectionate send-up of schlocky 1950s monster pics, but with better special effects, "Tremors" has a few clever twists but ultimately can't decide what it wants to be — flat-out funny, which it's not, or a scare-fest. Confusingly marketed, pic has "Aliens" producer Gale Anne Hurd's stamp on it but should unearth only limited boxoffice before crawling off to homevid.

The film draws its inspiration from latenight-tv horror flicks — à la "The Night Of The Living Dead" or the more obscure "The Killer Shrews" — with a bunch of bumpkins trapped in a house trying to fend off a mutated menace.

In this case, the threat — and a pretty downright repulsive one at that — comes in the form of four house trailer-sized worm-creatures, with multiple serpent like tongues, that tunnel underground before bursting up to devour human prey.

More than anything else the four "things" (why there are four is anybody's guess) resemble a smaller version of the giant worms in "Dune," which also found b.o. somewhat lonely in the desert. Director Ron Underwood shoots them in "Jaws"-type fashion set to similarly urgent music, providing a sort of worm's-eye view.

All the conventions of the genre are here: a small town in the middle of nowhere isolated from outside help, with a scientist on hand to study strange seismic phenomena.

After that, however, Underwood, S.S. Wilson and Brent Maddock begin to play with those clichés, going after knowing laughs from the audience, with mixed results.

The scientist, for example, is a pretty young woman (Finn Carter) who doesn't know where the monsters come from or understand why everyone keeps asking her to explain, while the heroes — handymen types Kevin Bacon and Fred Ward — carry on like Curly and Larry in search of Moe.

The opening also is thoroughly dreadful — a painful combination of low-brow gags bottoming out with a leaky cesspool hose, all set to twangy country music and interspliced with gory doings-in of local townfolk.

The pacing and action improve considerably as the film goes on, maintaining a tongue-in-cheek approach while the situation becomes more dire. The most inspired moments remain comic, such as when an unfortunate worm invades the rec room of gun enthusiasts Michael Gross and Reba McEntire.

Performance are fine if bland, with Bacon and Ward making an appealing pair, though only because they're so relentlessly dim. They resort to the paper-rock-scissors game to make any decision.

Gross is amusing as the crazed survivalist, while country singer McEntire found a strange vehicle in which to make her screen acting debut, belting out the closing song and proving she can handle a shotgun all in one.

Tech credits are firstrate, particularly the sound, creature effects and Ernest Troost's John Williams-inspired score — enough to evoke images of a fin knifing through the desert sand. —*Bril.*

Downtown

New York   A 20th Century Fox release of a Gale Anne Hurd production. Executive producer, Hurd. Produced by Charles H. Maguire. Directed by Richard Benjamin. Screenplay, Nat Mauldin; camera (Deluxe color), Richard H. Kline; editor, Jacqueline Cambas, Brian Chambers; music, Alan Silvestri; sound (Dolby), Jerry Jost; production design, Charles Rosen; art direction, Gregory Pickrell; set decoration, Don Remacle; costume design, Daniel Paredes; assistant director, Stephen J. Fisher; production manager-associate producer, Jack Roe; stunt coordinator-2d unit director, Terry Leonard; 2d unit camera, Robert Thomas; associate producer, Mauldin; casting, Reuben Cannon. Reviewed at 23d St. West 3 theater, N.Y., Jan. 13, 1990. MPAA Rating: R. Running time: **96 MIN.**

Alex Kearney	Anthony Edwards
Dennis Curren	Forest Whitaker
Lori Mitchell	Penelope Ann Miller
White	Joe Pantoliano
Jerome Sweet	David Clennon
Henry Coleman	Art Evans
Christine Curren	Kimberly Scott
Mickey Witlin	Rick Aiello
Lt. Sam Parral	Roger Aaron Brown
Lowell Harris	Ron Canada
Luisa Diaz	Wanda De Jesus
Inspector Ben Glass	Frank McCarthy

■ **"Downtown" is a routine buddy cops film, with no chance to give 20th Century Fox a hit in that genre to parallel its loner cop annuity, "Die Hard."**

Scripter Nat Mauldin's by-the-numbers premise has white bread young cop Anthony Edwards become the fish out of water transferred from the comfy suburbs to Philadelphia's inner-city Diamond Street district. He's had a run-in trying to arrest powerful businessman David Clennon for speeding. It's telegraphed that Clennon will be back as the main plot cog.

Emphasizing his flair for slapstick (with oodles of blood and bruises that the Three Stooges never incurred), Edwards displays myriad forms of incompetence, instantly incurring the wrath of his new boss (Art Evans). He attaches himself, unwanted, to young but seasoned black detective Forest Whitaker and tries to solve the murder of his former partner from the 'burbs, perpetrated near the Diamond Street police station. A scam involving stolen Mercedes autos and corrupt police provides some interest along the way.

Chemistry between the two leads occasionally works, but helmer Richard Benjamin fails to maintain a consistent tone. Atop the slapstick and black humor there is some unnecessary ultra-violence and both mawkish and dramatic scenes that clash with the intended good-timey feel. Best attempt at injecting depth beyond the surface gags is Whitaker's lengthy monolog recalling the death of his

first partner, delivered movingly by the "Bird" star.

Supporting turns by Penelope Ann Miller and Kimberly Scott as the leads' wives are well-played, and pic's most memorable role is Evans' showy effort as the foul-mouthed, explosive top cop downtown. Villains Clennon and Joe Pantoliano seem miscast and the thesps play it tongue-in-cheek and way too light.

Pic's biggest boner comes when Whitaker is written out of the film before the last reel. It's designed as a plot twist, but comes off as pointless — one infers while watching that the thesp had to run off and fulfill another film assignment. He pops back in for a coda scene but it's too late since he's missing at the de rigeur shootout with the heavies.

Tech credits are impressive, notably Terry Leonard's frequent and scary car chases and stunts. War zone atmosphere of the Philly setting is well conveyed, though film was shot primarily in L.A.

— *Lor.*

Ski Patrol

Hollywood   A Triumph release of an Epic Prods. and Sarlui/Diamant presentation of a Paul Maslansky production. Produced by Phillip B. Goldfine, Donald L. West. Executive producer, Maslansky. Directed by Richard Correll. Screenplay, Steven Long Mitchell, Craig W. Van Sickle, based on story by Mitchell, Van Sickle, Wink Roberts; camera (Deluxe color), John Stephens; editor, Scott Wallace; music, Bruce Miller; production design, Fred Weiler; art direction, Seven L. Nielsen; set decoration, Steven A. Lee; costume design, Angee Beckett; sound (Ultra-Stereo), John Earl Stein; choreography, Jeff J. Adkins; stunt coordinators, Lane Parrish, Tony Jefferson; assistant director, Denis Stewart; 2d unit director, Parrish. 2d unit camera, Edgar Boyles, David Nowell; casting, Fern Champion, Pamela Basker, Sue Swan. Reviewed at Epic Prods. screening room, L.A., Jan. 9, 1990. MPAA Rating: PG. Running time: **91 MIN.**

Jerry	Roger Rose
Lance	Corby Timbrook
Iceman	T.K. Carter
Murray	Leslie Jordan
Eddie	George Lopez
Maris	Martin Mull
Pops	Ray Walston
Stanley	Paul Fieg
Tiana	Tess
Suicide	Sean Gregory Sullivan

■ **Daredevil comic ski stunts, punchy party scenes and a few bright spots in the cast make watching this lightweight, formulaic pic at least more fun than a snowball down your back. Unless marketing is able to give it a big lift, boxoffice conditions look slushy.**

Exec producer Paul Maslansky, who created the "Police Academy" mold takes the format to the

slopes in this outing, which pits scheming developer Martin Mull against the fun-loving guys and gals of the Snowy Peaks Ski Patrol.

Mull wants to close down their employer, ol' Pops Sandrich (Ray Walston), so he can win the license to operate on the mountain for himself. He and his ski-bum henchmen, led by corrupt golden boy Lance (Corby Timbrook), sabotage the ski patroller's efforts to pass their certification tests.

It's boilerplate entertainment, but more watchable than the "Police Academy" series because the characters are not complete pinheads.

Best things going here are tiny Leslie Jordan as the ranting, drawling Southern drill sergeant of the ski patrol and T.K. Carter as the life-of-the-party team member who sings, dances and does impressions. George Lopez' small part suggests he's ready for a bigger one; he exudes a rollicking comic presence.

A schizophrenic character named "Suicide" (Sean Gregory Sullivan) brings unfunny tedium to the screen whenever he appears, which is often.

First-time director Richard Correll has a flair for bringing party and stunt scenes alive, and those, along with a high-energy soundtrack of rock chestnuts, keeps the pic diverting.

Production values suggest a tight budget and hasty schedule. Editing is sometimes abrupt and opening segment seems tacked on and is a dismal start to an otherwise okay pic.

Despite the thin writing, wild ski scenes keep film lively. —*Daws.*

Ni Con Dios Ni Con el Diablo
(With Neither God Nor The Devil)
(PERUVIAN-FRENCH-BRITISH)

Havana   A URPI Producciones Cinematográficas (Peru)-JBA Prod. (France)-Channel 4 (U.K.) production. Executive producer, Monica Brown. Written and directed by Nilo Pereira del Mar. Camera (color, 16m), Pereira del Mar; editor, Hitler Mego; music, Raúl Pereira; sound, Eduardo Cayo; art direction, Lidia Denegri. Reviewed at Havana Intl. Film Festival, Dec. 5, 1989. Running time: **90 MIN.**

Jeremias	Marino León

Also with: Patricia Cabrera, Diana Escobar, Reinaldo Arenas, Ivone Frayssinet, Eduardo Cesti.

■ **A decidedly low-budget 16m venture, "With Neither God**

Nor The Devil'' relates the tale of a Peruvian youth who is dealt a bad hand by destiny.

Story concerns a sheepherder in the Andean highlands caught between the Shining Path guerrillas and the Army. In defense, he flees to Lima where he becomes a further victim of the urban jungle.

Film is most effective in its depiction of the youth in his element, among the mountain people and their customs. The appearance of the Shining Path in the village and the subsequent harsh justice for the villagers are well handled. Scenes with the local witch doctor are also of interest.

The film loses its charm and momentum when Jeremias arrives in the city and encounters the expected fresh batch of horrors. The theme has been dealt with better in other films.

Director Nilo Pereira del Mar inserts some humor, such as the boy's first experience with a telephone, but the abrupt ending seems forced and far too coincidental.

Young actor Marino León carries the role of the affable, sincere youth and maintains interest throughout. Lensing tends to be grainy and editing is sometimes jerky. —*Lent.*

Leatherface: Texas Chainsaw Massacre III

New York A New Line Cinema release. Produced by Robert Engelman. Directed by Jeff Burr. Screenplay, David J. Schow, based on characters created by Kim Henkel, Tobe Hooper; camera (Deluxe color), James L. Carter; editor, Brent A. Schoenfeld; music, Jim Manzie, with Pat Regan; sound (Dolby), Robert Janiger; production design, Mick Strawn; costume design, Joan Hunter; stunt coordinator, Kane Hodder; mechanical effects, Bellissimo Belardinelli Effects; special makeup effects, Kurtzman, Nicotero & Berger Efx Group; associate producer, Michael DeLuca; casting, Annette Benson. Reviewed at Loews 19th St. East Sixplex, N.Y., Jan. 11, 1990. MPAA Rating: R. Running time: **81 MIN.**
Michelle . . . . Kate Hodge
Tex . . . . Viggo Mortensen
Ryan . . . . William Butler
Benny . . . . Ken Foree
Tinker . . . . Joe Unger
Alfredo . . . . Tom Everett
Sara . . . . Toni Hudson
Mama . . . . Miriam Byrd-Nethery
Leatherface . . . . R.A. Mihailoff
   Also with: David Cloud, Beth Depatie, Dwayne Whitaker, Jennifer Banko.

■ ''Leatherface'' is a toothless sadistic horror film that ranks at the bottom of the barrel among recent, pointless sequels. New Line can kiss this series goodbye.

Tobe Hooper's 1974 original film, released by Bryanston and reissued by New Line, was a horror breakthrough in unrelieved tension. Same helmer's outré 1986 sequel for Cannon toplining Dennis Hopper was a fast flop.

Third time isn't lucky, as David Schow's thin screenplay has about enough material for a 1-reeler, padded out to feature length. Kate Hodge and William Butler play a boring yuppie couple driving from L.A. to Florida who are lured down a remote Texas road by a family of cannibals. Pic consists of their survival efforts, assisted by two other innocent bystanders, Toni Hudson and Ken Foree.

Jeff Burr's lethargic direction turns completely inept during the film's incoherent (and infrequent) action scenes where one can't tell what's happening or who's getting killed. Worst example is that reliable Foree, a familiar face from George Romero and Peter Maris pics, seems to be killed in several scenes but keeps popping up when needed.

Providing zero fun for gore fans is the fact that the killings take place off-screen, presumably due to cuts needed to get the film its R rating in place of the original X that delayed its release from last November. Much of the action consists of dimlit night scenes, which make the picture unwatchable at its natural venue, drive-ins.

Acting is shrill, and the attempt to create some sympathy for the disgusting cannibals (especially Joe Unger) is ridiculous. Unlike the original film, where Gunnar Hansen as Leatherface ran frighteningly at top speed after his victims, new Leatherface (played by R. A. Mihailoff) shambles along with a gamy leg in a brace and is thereby a cornball, oldfashioned monster.

Valencia, Calif., locations do not adequately convey the rural Texas atmosphere. —*Lor.*

Wild Orchid

Rome An Artisti Associati release (Triumph in U.S.) of a Vision Intl. presentation of a Damon/Saunders production. Produced by Mark Damon, Tony Anthony. Coproduced by Howard North. Executive producers, David Saunders, James Dyer. Directed by Zalman King. Screenplay, King, Patricia Louisianna Knop; camera (color), Gale Tattersall; music, Geoff MacCormack, Simon Goldenberg; costumes, Luciano Soprani. Reviewed at Quirinale Cinema, Rome, Jan. 4, 1990. Running time: **100 MIN.**
Wheeler . . . . Mickey Rourke
Claudia . . . . Jacqueline Bisset
Emily . . . . Carré Otis
   Also with: Assumpta Serna.
   (Italian-dubbed soundtrack)

■ If ''Wild Orchid'' aims to grab audiences with a hot-house atmosphere of erotica, it mainly teases until a pay-off in the last sequence. Italian opener obviously hoped to generate talk in the footsteps of ''Nine ½ Weeks,'' a local hit, which also toplined Mickey Rourke and was co-scripted by ''Wild Orchid'' director Zalman King.

Over the holidays ''Orchid'' filled houses with a limited release strategy. Off-shore, pic's chances are somewhat less than its predecessor's. Film bowed in Rome in a dubbed-in-Italian version; original English soundtrack version will play in the U.S. via Triumph release.

Claudia (Jacqueline Bisset) is a wired jet-set businesswoman who hires tyro lawyer Emily (Carré Otis) to help her close a deal. Prim Emily, a Midwest farm girl still wet under the collar — but highly attractive — is dazed to find herself on a plane to Rio. There she meets Claudia's old flame Wheeler (Rourke), a self-made millionaire with perverse sexual tastes.

Hypnotizing Emily with his original personality (?), he forces her to forget her good-girl upbringing and do liberating things. At first, it upsets her to watch a rich German couple making love in the back seat of a limo all four are riding in. Later, Wheeler's mere gaze is enough to make reluctant Emily go to bed with the first guy who picks her up in a bar.

The guy turns out to be the lawyer for Claudia's antagonist and in film's best scene — the only one that could be called psychologically intriguing — Claudia uses Emily's ''shame'' to turn the tables on the two smirking men, beating them on their own sexual territory.

What doesn't work is the hold Rourke is supposed to have over Otis. Looking pudgy and puffyfaced, with a little gold earring, he is anything but an appetizing sex object. Why first Claudia, then Emily, should fall under his spell requires considerable suspension of disbelief.

''Wild Orchid'' scarcely tries to be believeable, preferring to load film with over-the-top characters, places, and situations. Locations alternate between outdoor tropical paradise and indoor 5-star hotel, with the lambada being danced a lot.

As Emily, Otis really is hypnotically attractive, but she plays the still-waters-run-deep country beauty with expressionless immobility. Bisset, always a class act, here bubbles over with caricatured joie de vivre — throwing herself into people's arms, dancing up a storm at weddings, hitting the ceiling when she finds something going on between Emily and Wheeler. Rourke has his truest moments tooling down jungle roads on his motorcycle, ''Easy Rider''-style.

As for eros, King tries hard to build atmosphere via voyeurism in three or four scenes which show little flesh. Only when Emily breaks through Wheeler's reserve/impotence in the last sequence does pic deliver what its ad campaign promises, in a torrid, highly choreographed but equally explicit bedroom session between the two. Nudity is complete for both actors and so are the Kama Sutra positions, at least in the Italo version, worth a sure-fire X-rating Stateside.

Costumes by Luciano Soprani are fashionably gorgeous, fitting in with the rest. Pic is technically fine. —*Yung.*

The Wolves Of Willoughby Chase
(BRITISH)

London A Zenith production. Produced by Mark Forstater. Directed by Stuart Orme. Screenplay, William M. Akers, based on novel by Joan Aiken; camera (color), Paul Beeson; editor, Martin Walsh; music, Colin Towns; production design, Christopher Hobbs; sound, Peter Glossop; associate producer, Raymond Day. Reviewed at Institute of Contemporary Arts, London, Dec. 21, 1989. Running time: **93 MIN.**
Slighcarp . . . . Stephanie Beacham
Grimshaw . . . . Mel Smith
Bonnie . . . . Emily Hudson
Sylvia . . . . Aleks Darowska
Mrs. Brisket . . . . Geraldine James
Simon . . . . Lynton Dearden
James . . . . Richard O'Brien
Pattern . . . . Jane Horrocks
   Also with: Eleanor David, Jonathan Coy.

■ ''The Wolves Of Willoughby Chase,'' despite a long wait — pic was shot in early 1988 — is a thoroughly enjoyable children's fantasy-adventure and deserves a better theatrical life than it will unfortunately get. Pic may have a better life in the kid-vid market.

Film was backed by Atlantic Entertainment in the States, but was never released in America due to company's financial problems.

Pic has a suitable Dickensian feel, set during the imaginary reign of King James III some time in the last century in a snowbound part of North Yorkshire where wolves seem to rule the countryside. Based on Joan Aiken's children's novel, it has an attractively sinister quality and centers on the fight by two young girls to foil a dastardly plot by their evil governess.

Lord and Lady Willoughby have to travel overseas for reasons of health and daughter Bonnie (Emily Hudson) and her timid cousin Sylvia (Aleks Darowska) are left to the not so tender mercies of new governess, the hissable Slighcarp (Stephanie Beacham).

It transpires that Beacham and her ever-hungry companion Grimshaw (Mel Smith), apparently have arranged the Willoughbys' death so they can take over the family estate, and when the girls defy Beacham they are packed off to the orphanage of Blast burn.

There they are forced to work in the massive laundry night and day, watched over by the vindictive Mrs. Brisket (Geraldine James). With the help of forest boy Lynton Dearden, the girls escape and are chased through the snow by Beacham and James until they reach Willoughby Chase. There they find the Willoughbys have returned safely and Beacham's plans eventually are thwarted.

Tyro theatrical helmer Stuart Orme handles his chores well; they must have been doubly hard since pic was shot at the Barrrandov Studios in Prague and on location around snowy Czechoslovakia.

Especially good are the studio-built sets of the castle interiors and the laundry, designed by the talented Christopher Hobbs (he designed Derek Jarman's "Caravaggio"). He also designed the costumes and engineered a wonderful steam-driven sled contraption used in the final chase scenes across the snowy wastes.

Hudson and Darowska are excellent as the plucky youngsters, but best of all is Beacham who outdoes herself as the wicked Slighcarp, making her "Colbys" character of Sable look like a sweetheart.

The excellent cast is boosted by attractive tongue-in-cheek performances by Mel Smith and Geraldine James, though the irritating playing by Jane Horrocks as maid Pattern is a slight detraction.

The wolves themselves obviously are Alsatians with shaggy jackets, but it all adds to an atmosphere of gothic-style children's stories fondly remembered by many — mildly frightening but essentially good fun. —*Adam.*

Love Or Money

Boston A Hemdale Films release of a Salah M. Hassanein production. Executive producer, Hassanein. Produced by Elyse England. Directed by Todd Hallowell. Screenplay, England, Michael Zausner, Bart Davis; camera (color), Igor Sunara; editor, Ray Hubley; music, Jim Lang; sound, Paul Cote; art direction, Robert P. Kracik; costume design, Ileane Meltzer; assistant director, Kyle McCarthy; associate producers, Zausner, Davis; line producer, Kathie Hersch; casting, Deborah Aquila. Reviewed at Allston Cinema, Boston, Jan. 5, 1989. MPAA Rating: PG-13. Running time: **89 MIN.**

Chris Murdoch	Timothy Daly
Jeff Simon	Michael Garin
Jennifer Reed	Haviland Morris
William Reed	Kevin McCarthy
Lu Ann Reed	Shelley Fabares
Arthur Reed	David Doyle
Baskin	Katherine Cortez
Bradley	James Patrick Gillis

Also with: Alan Havey, Tisha Roth, Robert Stanton, Geoffrey Nauffts, Tom Signorelli, Rex Robbins.

■ **Presumably Hemdale is airing out this 2-year-old film prior to video release, as it seems exactly the wrong time of year for this summer-themed piece of fluff. Lightweight fare is amiable enough for the undemanding.**

Chris Murdoch (Timothy Daly) and Jeff Simon (Michael Garin) are two yuppies involved in real estate who have left a big firm to strike out on their own. Their last chance to save their fledgling firm is landing the business of William Reed (Kevin McCarthy). However, their former employers (Katherine Cortez, James Patrick Gillis) have been sucking up to Reed's partner and brother, Arthur (David Doyle).

On top of this double rivalry is a romance between William's daughter Jennifer (Haviland Morris) and Chris. The film tries to present them as a latter-day Tracy and Hepburn, with Chris the pragmatic businessman and Jennifer — she's a marine biologist — the intellectual. The situations are resolved predictably.

The film does serve to showcase the talent of its young cast. Daly and Garin are not without comic charm as the yuppies on the make, while Morris proves that having an actress who can be the love interest as well as believably intelligent always will be a plus.

Vet performers McCarthy and Shelley Fabares, as his wife with a roving eye, add what passes for star quality here. Only Doyle embarrasses himself with a ridiculously over-the-top performance as the obnoxious brother.

Tech qualities are no more than adequate, with much of the film (shot largely on Long Island) looking as if it's anticipating its transition to the small screen. Someone apparently was asleep at the switch as far as continuity, with an exit sign in one scene moving noticeably from one position to another. Presumably on tv no one will be able to tell the difference. —*Kimm.*

FLORENCE FILM FESTIVAL

Hearing Voices

Florence A Sharon Greytak production, with the sponsorship of the New York Foundation for the Arts. Written and directed by Greytak. Camera (color), Doron Schlair; art direction, Chere Ledwith; sound, Micah Solomon; music, Wes York; line producer, Robby Henson. Reviewed at Florence Film Festival, Dec. 8, 1989. Running time: **87 MIN.**

Erika	Erika Nagy
Lee	Stephen Gatta
Michael Krieger	Tim Ahearn
Carl	Michael Davenport

■ **"Hearing Voices" is an unabashed, often intriguing indie that fearlessly tackles not one but two taboo topics at the same time. Not only does the heroine, a New York model, have to live with ileostomy surgery, in which her digestive tract is deviated, she also struggles with a probably doomed love affair with a gay man.**

Documaker ("Weirded Out" and "Blown Away") Sharon Greytak makes a brave if offbeat feature film debut in a pic that will have to struggle for audiences and foreign sales.

Dignity and courage are the defining characteristics of Erika (Erika Nagy), a top hand model who believes the life-long scars on her back (from a childhood operation) have made her excel in her work. She has a violent, priming boyfriend, also a model, who cruelly bullies her. Erika puts up with him stoically.

Early in the film, in a simple but shocking scene, she delicately changes the bag she must wear at her waist, following recent surgery. She generously allows her doctor (Tim Ahearn) to use her infirmities to instruct medical students.

This is how she meets Ahearn's sensitive male lover. Long-haired Lee (Stephen Gatta) falls for Erika and leaves the doctor, with all the difficulties that may be imagined in converting to a heterosexual relationship.

Pic's other shock scene shows Erika making love to Lee, both in their underwear. Despite good intentions, pic here often slips into the ridiculous. It's unaided by the wooden Nagy, who has one wild, out-of-character shouting scene, and the over-emoting Gatta, allowed to reach points of near hysteria. One wishes Greytak's delicacy and matter-of-factness in dealing with physical handicaps would have extended to interpersonal relations, which seem seen from a distance.

Pic is most stimulating in bringing up graphic questions of a woman's relation to her own body, narcissistic and otherwise, and here Greytak is inspired in her coupling of model with physical abnormalities.

Doron Schlair provides top-flight cinematography, while Wes York's piano score is effective in downplaying the highly charged themes. Backstage scenes of the gritty world of modeling are witty and refreshingly debunking.

—*Yung.*

Everybody Wins
(BRITISH-U.S.)

New York An Orion Pictures release of a Jeremy Thomas production, made by Recorded Picture Co. Executive producers, Terry Glinwood, Linda Yellen. Produced by Thomas. Coproducer, Ezra Swerdlow. Directed by Karel Reisz. Screenplay, Arthur Miller; camera (Duart color; Deluxe prints), Ian Baker; editor, John Bloom; music, Mark Isham; additional music, Leon Redbone; sound (Dolby), Ivan Sharrock; production design, Peter Larkin; art direction, Charley Beal; set decoration, Hilton Rosemarin; costume design, Ann Roth; assistant director, Timothy M. Bourne; production managers, Mike Haley, Robert Girolami; stunt coordinator, David Ellis; casting, Ellen Chenoweth. Reviewed at Embassy 1 theater, N.Y., Jan. 19, 1990. MPAA Rating: R. Running time: **97 MIN.**

Angela Crispini	Debra Winger
Tom O'Toole	Nick Nolte
Jerry	Will Patton
Connie	Judith Ivey
Amy	Kathleen Wilhoite
Judge Murdoch	Jack Warden
Charlie Haggerty	Frank Converse
Felix	Frank Military
Father Mancini	Steve Skybell
Jean	Mary Louise Wilson

■ "Everybody Wins" is a very disappointing picture. Repping Arthur Miller's first feature film screenplay since "The Misfits" in 1961, the Karel Reisz-helmed film noir is nearly unreleasable and has virtually no chance of attracting an audience.

Eyebrows in the trade were raised when Orion opened the film cold with no press screenings, despite its Miller and Reisz pedigrees plus presence of stars Debra Winger and Nick Nolte. Reason is obvious: This big-budget prestige picture is obscure and artificial, with appeal only for handful of film buffs.

As such, it casts doubt on the commercial acumen of producer Jeremy Thomas, repping the first film under this much-trumpeted internationally funded production program (the second, currently in production for Warner Bros. release, also stars Winger — Bernardo Bertolucci's "The Sheltering Sky"). Pic has the oddball, easily resistible cryptic qualities of such Thomas productions as "Eureka" and "The Shout" rather than the appeal of his Oscar-winner "The Last Emperor."

Overladen with pompous and frequently dated dialog, Miller's script (developed from his 1982 pair of 1-act plays, "Two-Way Mirror") is essentially a routine whodunit. Nolte plays an investigator called in by seeming good Samaritan Winger to get young Frank Military out of jail for a murder she claims he did not commit. Nolte doggedly pursues various leads, interviews odd people and discovers a web of corruption engulfing a small Connecticut town.

Unfortunately, film founders immediately due to the miscasting of Winger as a schizo femme fatale who is, Nolte finds out in later reels, a notorious local prostitute. She copes uneasily with Miller's overblown dialog, which has her alternately putting on airs to a bewildered Nolte or handing him non sequiturs.

Not helping matters is the lack of chemistry between Nolte and Winger in their sex scenes here.

Supporting cast has rather brief assignments, with self-destructive baddie Will Patton overplaying his hand. Jack Warden as a smoothie judge is transparent, while Judith Ivey is wasted in an undeveloped part as Nolte's sister. A subplot involving what might be a Manson-like religious cult run by Patton is introduced but never properly followed up.

The production captures the gloomy look of a decaying rust-belt town in Connecticut well; its shot in Norwich with studio work in Wilmington, N.C. Funky songs by Leon Redbone are inserted to try and pep up the downbeat pic, but come off as artificial.

Miller's cynical ending fits the piece, but is overly glib in painting a society beyond hope of reform. Warden enunciates his corny tagline, "You can't save the goddamn world," and the viewer is likely to yawn in response. —Lor.

Heart Condition

Palm Springs A New Line Cinema release. Produced by Steve Tisch. Executive producer, Robert Shaye. Coproducers, Marie Cantin, Bernie Goldman. Written and directed by James D. Parriott. Camera (Deluxe color), Arthur Albert; editor, David Finter, music, Patrick Leonard; production design. John Muto; costume design, Louise Frogley; casting, Karen Rea. Reviewed at Palm Springs Film Festival, Jan. 12, 1990. MPAA Rating: R. Running time: **95 MIN.**

Jack Moony	Bob Hoskins
Napoleon Stone	Denzel Washington
Crystal Gerrity	Chloe Webb
Capt. Wendt	Roger E. Mosley
Mrs. Stone	Janet DuBois
Dr. Posner	Alan Rachins
Harry Zara	Ray Baker
Graham	Jeffrey Meek
Dilnick	Kieran Mulroney

■ From what seems like a far-fetched premise — a cop who gets a heart transplant ends up depending on his worst enemy's ticker — writer-director James L. Parriott spins a most engrossing and rewarding tale in this auspicious feature debut.

Pic may not set sirens wailing at the boxoffice, but with ancillary returns and prestige payoffs, should be an A-positive type investment for New Line.

Bob Hoskins plays vice detective Moony, an intense, crazy, racist slob who briefly has a girl in his life — a hooker, Crystal (Chloe Webb). She disappears and gets involved with her black lawyer, Stone (Denzel Washington), a handsome self-possessed smooth operator who becomes the object of Moony's obsessive rage.

Moony, who lives on greaseburgers and booze, has a heart attack the same night Stone is killed in a car crash. Thanks to the expedient transplant surgery and to the amusement of his colleagues at the precinct, he ends up a "blood brother" to his enemy.

To Moony's horror, the sarcastic, clever Stone appears in ghost-like form visible only to him, and becomes his constant, unwanted companion, dispensing advice on what to eat, how to dress, and women.

Stone wants Moony to solve the mystery of who murdered him that night in an automobile ambush; Moony wants to get back to Crystal, who's now living with a dangerous, jetset drug supplier (Jeffrey Meek). Crystal wants Moony to leave her alone so she doesn't get killed.

From a fantasy premise, Parriott develops a clever, action-laden comedy about racism bred from insecurity and male competition in a script well worthy of this top-notch cast.

Washington creates a most compelling character in Stone, finding the rhythm of the role with an assurance that never flags; Hoskins is gutsy and amusing, exhibiting bug-eyed discomfort when he's manicured and barbered in a Stone-style transformation; Webb makes Crystal unique and reachable, establishing her corner of the triangle with far less screen time.

Among the supporting cast, Roger E. Mosley adds plenty of attitude as the police captain who can't wait for the volatile Moony to hang himself.

L.A. locations in Hollywood, Westwood, Beverly Hills and the beach are artfully used, and production design is excellent, from Moony's cluttered dive to the ruined beach house used at the finale.

Sharp music tracks add a contempo bracket for the action and some amusing touches. —Daws.

Fellow Traveller
(BRITISH-U.S.)

London A British Film Institute/BBC Tv/HBO Showcase production. Executive producers, Colin McCabe, Jill Pack. Produced by Michael Wearing. Directed by Philip Saville. Screenplay, Wearing; camera (Technicolor), John Kenway; editor, Greg Miller; music, Colin Towns; production design, Gavin Davies; sound, Roger Slater, (U.S.) Mark Weber, Bruce Gerstein; costumes, Al Barnett; associate producer, Ian Brindle. Reviewed at Metro Cinema, London, Jan. 8, 1990. Running time: **97 MIN.**

Asa Kaufman	Ron Silver
Clifford Byrne	Hart Bochner
Sarah Aitchison	Imogen Stubbs
Jerry Leavy	Daniel J. Travanti
Joan Kaufman	Katherine Borowitz
Sir Hugo Armstrong	Richard Wilson
Sheriff of Nottingham	Jonathan Hyde
Robin Hood	Alexander Hanson
Little John	John Labanowski

Also with: Peter Corey, Briony McRoberts, Julian Fellowes, Doreen Mantle, David O'Hara. Allan Mitchell, Roger Hammond.

■ "Fellow Traveller" has the rare distinction of being a British film that actually looks international. It has an impressive cast, intelligent story and glossy U.S. and U.K. locations give it an edge over many British productions. Pic will be screened on HBO in the U.S.

Helmer Philip Saville shows a big-screen feel with this story of a blacklisted Hollywood screenwriter during the McCarthy era who is forced to Britain to find work. Writer Michael Eaton's script gets too complex and tries to pack in too many flashbacks and psychological ramblings, to the extent that pic feels long but watered down.

Pic goes some way in covering the commie-bashing McCarthy Era '50s, but eventually becomes rather simplistic when trying to debate the actual politics of the time rather than concentrating on the emotional impact, which is when it is strongest.

Glossy opening is set beside a luxury swimming pool in Hollywood where film star Clifford Byrne (Hart Bochner) shoots himself. At the same time in London, his friend Asa Kaufman (Ron Silver) is escaping the McCarthyist witch-hunt and — illegally — looking for work.

A series of flashbacks shows that Bochner and Silver were best friends — Bochner the dashing Errol Flynn-type star and Silver the writer. Silver starts seeing psychoanalyst Jerry Leavy (Daniel J. Travanti), and shortly afterwards flees the country when he hears he is named by the House Un-American Activities Committee.

In England he takes a false name, starts writing a tv series, "The Adventures Of Robin Hood," and searches for Bochner's English girlfriend (Imogen Stubbs), whom he has a brief affair with; he also mulls over politics with her leftie friends.

It is only when Travanti makes an appearance in London to lecture that it clicks with Silver that he was set up by the psychoanalyst and he sets about exposing Travanti during his speech. Happy ending has Silver's wife and kid settling in Blighty.

What spoils "Fellow Traveller" is some of the soap opera plotting that insists Silver have an affair with Stubbs. A series of dream sequences of Silver's mother being ravished by a G-man also serves little purpose and only complicates matters.

Daniel J. Travanti lends little to the film. Silver is convincing as the cynical writer thrown into a strange English environment, and Hart Bochner looks the handsome leading man, replete with Errol Flynn mustache.

Pic is excellent at re-creating the early heady days of independent tv in the U.K. Best point in the film is the series of imaginary scenes from the "Robin Hood" series Silver is writing. The sepia-tinted scenes suitably catch the mood of the era, and as the film wears on reflect Silver's heightened paranoia and mounting anger.

Philip Saville displays a confident directorial hand and gives the film a good deal more gloss and glamor than its tv origins imply. Excellent production design by Gavin Davies and costumes by Al Barnett add to the quality. Unfortunately, Michael Eaton's script is a letdown — it offers plenty of fascinating insight, but pads out the film with too many unnecessary distractions. —Adam.

Paint It Black

Palm Springs A Vestron production. Produced by Anne Kimmel, Mark Forstater. Directed by Tim Hunter. Screenplay, A.H. Zacharias, Michael Drexier (see below); camera (CFI color), Mark Irwin; editor, Michael J. Sheridan; music, Jurgen Knieper; production design, Steve Legler; art direction, Jeff Ozimek; costume design, Leonard Pollack; sound (Dolby). Charlie Wilborn. Reviewed at Palm Springs Film Festival, Jan. 14, 1990. MPAA Rating: R. Running time: **101 MIN.**
Jonathan Dunbar . . . . Rick Rossovich
Marion Easton . . . . Sally Kirkland
Gina . . . . Julie Carmen
Lambert . . . . Martin Landau
Eric . . . . Doug Savant
Lt. Wilder . . . . Jason Bernard

■**Director Tim Hunter ("River's Edge"), who took the reins on short notice from exiting director Roger Holzberg, lacks a compelling story or point of view with "Paint It Black."**

This uneven, amateurish thriller will probably move directly from its Palm Springs Film Festival unveiling to video shelves.

Hunky Rick Rossovich plays Jonathan, a Santa Barbara artist whose metal sculptures are not paying the rent, primarily because his lover/patroness, gallery owner Marion Easton (Sally Kirkland), is stealing the money she gets for them.

After Jonathan saves the life of a kid he finds stabbed in an alley, the kid, a rich brat with a loose brainpan, decides to do him a favor by murdering Marion in her office.

Moments before, Jonathan has broken into the gallery to go through the files and find out once and for all if he's being cheated. He drops a card on the floor with his girlfriend's number on it and ends up a murder suspect.

Then the new girlfriend (Julie Carmen) reveals that her father (Martin Landau) is a major gallery owner, and Jonathan is on his way up. But the card, which has fallen into the hands of the killer (Doug Savant), keeps threatening him.

Pic ends up focusing more and more on the psycho killer and his creepy ways, all the way to the clifftop finale.

Hunter is working with a lightweight, illogical script and brings no redeeming style or attitude to it.

"Paint It Black" spends half the time fawning embarrassingly over the idea of Jonathan as an artist who won't be compromised, and the rest trying to titillate with sex scenes and nasty murders.

Worse is the way the hero is so worried about his own hide that he lets the killer keep walking around loose even after he knows who he is.

Performances are just okay and tech credits are unremarkable or sub-par.

Script credit, which is a pseudonym for original writers Tim Harris and Herschel Weingrod, whose shooting script was rewritten by both directors, is currently in dispute. —Daws.

Simple Justice

Florence A Panorama Entertainment release of a Street Law Associates production. Produced by Gigi Pritzker. Directed by Deborah Del Prete. Screenplay, T. Jay O'Brien, Michael Sergio; camera (color), Rob Draper; art direction, Nancy Deren; editor, Richard Del Prete; music, Eric Turkel, John Pati. Reviewed at Florence Film Festival, Dec. 10, 1989. Running time: **97 MIN.**
Vincenzo DiLorenzo . . . . . . .Cesar Romero
Anna DiLorenzo . . . . Doris Roberts
Janet DiLorenzo . . . . .Cady McClain
Frankie DiLorenzo . . . . .Matthew Galle
Also with: John Spencer (Inspector Sullivan), Kevin Geer (Inspector Warren), Michael Genet (Mitchell Jackson), Priscilla Lopez (Dr. Gail Gitterman).

■**An indie pic without moral complexes or artistic pretensions, "Simple Justice" champions a nice family from the Bronx forced by an over-lenient court to take injustice into its own hands. Mixing "Death Wish" with a lot of tv-type corn, "Simple Justice" is a no-surprise pic salvaged by astute storytelling.**

It should appeal to the drive-in crowd and to audiences who like their law and order minus legality.

Cesar Romero has the undemanding armchair role of grandpa Vincenzo DiLorenzo, a tranquil oldster who lost his policeman son in an unsolved crime 20 years back. Now he gardens while granny Doris Roberts makes spaghetti dinners for grandson Frankie (Matthew Galle) and his sweet, pregnant wife, Janet (Cady McClain).

Life at the cheerful DiLorenzos' is all church, kitchen and babies — until Janet and Frankie get beaten up during a brutal bank robbery. Janet loses the baby and spends the rest of the film in a coma.

An over-the-top gang of belching, red-eyed blacks and Hells' Angels so mean, dangerous and guilty they'd make the Joker in "Batman" blush are set free by the black woman judge for lack of evidence. The time is ripe for homemade justice.

Frankie embarks on "Rocky"-style home training sessions to build up his bankteller's muscles. Blood starts spurting out of park sprinklers, and meat hooks sink into flesh, as a mysterious hand strikes. Suspicion falls on Frankie, natch.

Could the crusading avenger really be Inspector Sullivan (John Spencer, best performance in the film), belatedly revenging his old partner, Frankie's father? Of course, it's neither, and the murderer isn't hard to guess.

Tv helmer Deborah Del Prete shows an equal penchant for gooey sentiment and violent bloodshed. From the chirping grandmother and simpering wife down to the drug-crazed hoodlums, characters are more cartoonish than real specimens. Apart from Spencer, thesping follows the stereotypes.

On the plus side is pic's pacing, which holds the attention even if story is predictable. Final twist has audiences cheering at this sitcom family's last murderous act of "justice."

Lensing is pro. —Yung.

Chambre à part
(Separate Bedrooms)
(FRENCH)

Paris A Flach Films production and release, coproduced by Solus Prod, TF1 Films Prods. Produced by Jean-François Lepetit. Directed by Jacky Cukier. Screenplay, Serge Frydman, Cukier. Camera (color), Yves Angelo; editor, Anne Lafarge; music, Philippe Sarde; sound, Bernard Aubouy, Dominique Hennequin; art direction, Jean-Louis Poveda; assistant director, Valérie Othnin-Girard; production manager, Yvon Crenn. Reviewed at the Triomphe theater, Paris, Jan. 5, 1990. Running time: **93 MIN.**
Martin . . . . .Michel Blanc
Gert . . . . .Frances Barber
Francis . . . . .Jacques Dutronc
Marie . . . . .Lio
Also with: Catherine Frot, Engelbert Humperdinck, Christine Murilo, Nicolas Asken, Roger Ashton-Griffiths, Peter Moffat, Lollie May, Sheila Gish.

■**"Chambre à part" is a cross-channel odyssey that brings Michel Blanc, Jacques Dutronc and Lio (a pop singer and sometime actress) to London.**

Newcomer Jacky Cukier, a former assistant director, co-wrote and directed this bitter comedy-drama in a manner that often recalls the abrasive carnal romances of Bertrand Blier. Despite a first half with bite and humor, the film loses itself in the dour aimlessness of a script that plays its trump cards too quickly.

Blanc is a Frenchman living in London. His wife is a doctor (Frances Barber) who has a son from a previous marriage. Their relationship seems blandly satisfying until they run into a maverick French couple, Dutronc and Lio, who are professional parasites, living off their victims' need for companionship and love.

Before anybody can figure out what's hit them, Blanc and Lio begin having an affair, and Dutron's sleazy charm takes its effect on the strait-laced Barber. The dizzy game of musical beds breaks up when Blanc and Lio, taking their liaison seriously, flee back to Paris, where their relationship founders.

Film works best in its description of the expatriate blues and the romantic longings that motivate the oddly matched quartet. When the picture returns to familiar ground, though, it begins to resemble just another French movie about romantic misfits.

Blanc, Dutronc and Lio are fine as the Gallic players, but the most genuine performance comes from Barber as the British spouse jarred out of her middle-class complacency by emotional turmoil.

Supporting cast and tech credits are solid. Engelbert Humperdinck plays himself in the opening New Years' Eve night club scene, in which the principals meet. —*Len*.

Russicum
(The Third Solution)
(ITALIAN)

London A Tri-Star Pictures release. A Cecchi Gori Group/Tiger Cinematografica production, in collaboration with RAI. Produced by Mario and Vittorio Cecchi Gori. Directed by Pasquale Squitieri. Screenplay, Valerio Riva, Robert Balchus, Squitieri, from the novel "Il Martedi del Diavolo" by Enzo Russo; camera (color), Mario Cimini; editor, Mauro Bonnani; music, Renato Serio; sound, Benito Alchimede; set design, Emilio Baldelli; costumes, Blanche Cardinale. MPAA Rating: R. Reviewed at Odeon Kensington, London, Dec. 12, 1989. MPAA Rating: R. Running time: **111 MIN.**
Mark Hendrix . . . . .Treat Williams
Father Carafa . . . . . . .F. Murray Abraham
George Sherman . . . . .Danny Aiello
Alexandra . . . . .Rita Rusic
Michael Wessling . . . . .Robert Balchus
Marini . . . . .Rossano Brazzi
Father Hanema . . . . .Nigel Court
Father Isidoro . . . . . . .Leopoldo Mastelloni

■ "Russicum," shot in Rome and produced by Mario and Vittorio Cecchi Gori, is a rambling pre-glasnost spy thriller full of over-elaborate camera angles, over-complex plotting and over-elaborate thesping from its Italian — and sometimes American — actors. Prospects are nil.

Some dastardly villains are trying to sabotage a proposed visit to the USSR by the Pope, and it takes the blundering intrusion of young American attaché Treat Williams to save the day.

Representing the Americans are Williams and Danny Aiello, who plays the U.S. Secret Service head in Rome. The Italians are repped by Rossano Brazzi as a counter-espionage expert nicknamed "The Cook," while F. Murray Abraham heads the Russicum, a Catholic institute involved in preparing the pastoral mission by the Pope.

Pic begins with the assassination of an American nun, who it later turns out was a CIA agent. Williams sets about finding out who

the murderer is, and discovers the killing was part of the plot to stop the papal visit. After a few more killings it turns out Aiello is the bad guy, under the misguided impression the U.S. doesn't want to Pope to visit the USSR.

Williams appears to sleepwalk his way through the film, though he is given no help by the preposterous script. Abraham is going through a phase of appearing in many Italo dramas, but at least gives his part some much needed intensity and commitment. Aiello tries his best, but can do nothing to pull the film up into the "ordinary" category.

The charismatic Brazzi pops up in a few scenes, but his part is virtually a cameo. Sole femme role is handled by Rita Rusic, who blandly sets about double-crossing everyone.

Helmer Pasquale Squitieri tries hard to give the pic some appeal, but unfortunately resorts to a barrage of high crane shots or very low-level angles which add nothing to the film. Music is overpowering and other tech credits aren't worth recording. —*Adam*.

Suffering Bastards

Florence A Cinelux production. Produced by Tom Mangan, Neil Hodges, George F. Andrews. Directed by Bernard McWilliams. Screenplay, McWilliams, John C. McGinley; camera (color, 16m), Neil Hodges; editor, Steve Wang; music, Dan Di Paola. Reviewed at Florence Film Festival, Dec. 9, 1989. Running time: **89 MIN.**
Buddy Johnson . . . . .John C. McGinley
Al Johnson . . . . .David Warshofsky
Mrs. Johnson . . . . .Pam LaTesta
Bernard . . . . .Rene Rivera
Mr. Leech . . . . .Eric Bogosian
Chazz . . . . .Michael Wincott
Sheena . . . . .Eloise Marion
Sharnetta . . . . .Gina Gershon

■**Bernard McWilliams' demented comedy "Suffering Bastards" was one of the hits of the Florence film fest, and has all the credentials to become a cult item if it finds the right venues. Shot on a shoestring in 16m, it soars with sheer zaniness and outrageous invention, heralding a talented director and actors ready to go places.**

Pic is framed by a scene in an unlikely Honolulu bar in which womanizing Buddy Johnson (John C. McGinley) is trying desperately to seduce a girl plumber with his hard-luck story. This takes us back to Atlantic City, many years ago. Buddy and his brother Al (David Warshofsky) sing and swing in their mother's tawdry nightclub. The irrepressible brothers, who

bear as much resemblance to each other as Laurel did to Hardy, find the club taken over by a smooth-talking swindler.

Out of a job, but vowing to Mommy (a delectable Pam LaTesta) they'll buy the club back someday, they find employment in a sinister warehouse. Buddy's irresponsible flirting with the secretary makes a permanent enemy out of her violent boyfriend, Bernard (fine Rene Rivera), a Hispanic hitman who becomes their undefeatable, hilarious nemesis. When a little innocent burglary nets the a big drug payoff, Buddy and Al joyfully buy the old club, only to have disaster strike, via Rene, on opening night.

They take to the woods and end up in Hawaii, running an appropriately kitsch bar, while diabolical Rene survives a plane crash to stalk them again.

Scripters McWilliams and McGinley take goliardic humor one notch up the sophistication ladder, mixing sight gags (Mommy suffocating on a sandwich at the beach is a classic) with a deadpan offscreen narrator.

Both McGinley, a regular in Oliver Stone's films, and Warshofsky carry of their inane brother roles with unrepentant relish. Imagination helps make up for the sub-Hollywood sets, whose tackiness fits the plot.—*Yung*.

Pentimento
(FRENCH)

Paris An AMLF release of a Téléma production, coproduced by FR3 Films Prod. Produced by Charles Gassot. Directed by Tonie Marshall. Screenplay, Marshall, Sylvie Granotier; camera (Eastmancolor), Pascal Lebèque; editor, Luc Barnier; art direction Jean-Pierre Fouillet, Jacques Wieber; costumes, Eve-Marie Arnault; sound, Henri-Morelle, Dominique Hennequin; music, Steve Beresford; assistant director, Alain Peyrollaz; production manager, Mamade, Cannelle et Chloé. Reviewed at Publicis theater, Paris, Jan. 8, 1990. Running time: **84 MIN.**
Lucie . . . . .Patricia Dinev
Charles . . . . .Antoine de Caunes
Madeleine . . . . .Magali Noël
Aline . . . . .Laurence César
Lambert . . . . .Etienne Berry
Claude . . . . .Jean-Pierre Jorris
Christiane . . . . .Micheline Dax

■**This is the second Gallic screwball comedy of the season and largely superior in execution to "Follow That Plane," a misbegotten salute of sorts to the romantic farces of '30s Hollywood. In "Pentimento," actress Tonie Marshall makes a pleasantly promising directing debut without succumbing to self-indulgent**

movieland tributes.

Marshall's strengths are a sense of pacing and precision in handling actors, two requisites for good screen farce. Script, which she concocted with Sylvie Granotier, is a soap bubble of a plot about a giddy young woman who rushes to the funeral of a father she never knew and gets involved in the wrong party. The resulting mixups land her in the middle of art smugglers and a romantic sprint with a young man she mistakenly thinks is her brother.

The blithely eccentric cast is dominated by pretty newcomer Patricia Dinev, who bursts onto the screen in irresistible high gear and stays there. If there is any homage at all in the picture, it could be to Marshall's own actress mother, Micheline Prèsle, whom Dinev recalls at certain moments. Antoine de Caunes, a popular young tv personality, plays the romantic straight man with elegance and charm, and Magali Noël provides a seasoned comic mien as Dinev's spaced-out mother.

Luc Barnier deserves a special nod for his fast-forward editing. Other tech credits are bright.

— *Len*

China Lake

Florence A Cairo Cinemafilms production. Produced by Dieter Wiehl, Ruth Johnson. Written and directed by Wiehl. Camera (color), Jasper Marquandt; editor, Christoph Schmid-Maybach. Reviewed at Florence Film Festival, Dec. 7, 1989. Running time: **94 MIN.**
Edmont Wodzinski . . . . .L.A. Davis
Scooter Wodzinski . . . . .Joe Toppe
Laura Wodzinski . . . . .Amielia Richer-Hart
Aunt Edna . . . . .Sandi Stutz
   Also with: Richard Edson (Connie Veesk), Veltha E. Race (Angie), Bob Bumgarner (Clyde), Red Cahoon (bus driver).

■**Winner of the Grand Prize at the Mannheim Film Week, "China Lake" is a hip, stop-motion road movie set in the American desert. Its deadbeat humor and sarcastic attitude toward the monotonous American lifestyle, raised to the point of surrealism, ought to appeal to younger fans.**

If the shoestring indie look is an undisturbing hallmark, neo-helmer Dieter Wiehl has a hard time getting controlled performances out of pic's quartet of actors. In the end, "China Lake" remains in the amateur category, though its originality and fine lensing herald a talent to watch out for.

Story revolves around the family reunion of four sublimely obtuse characters who can hardly communicate with each other. Fat, beer-swigging Edmont (L.A. Davis) has chosen a spectacular but totally isolated desert to park his mobile home, where he lives with his 18-year-old son Scooter (Joe Toppe, a zombified James Dean lookalike). Dad spends his days glued to the tv set.

The arrival of Aunt Edna (Sandi Stutz, playing with a comic German accent) and Scooter's punkette sister Laura (Amielia Richer-Hart), whom he hasn't seen since his mother's death, bring a breath of life to the arid trailer.

Soon a mutual, shy attraction blooms between the two teens. In pic's most exhilarating moment, Scooter beheads the old station wagon and abducts bored Laura in his new "convertible" for a liberating joyride to Las Vegas. The threat of casual incest, handled with humor and sensitivity, recedes in a happy farewell and a note of hope.

Jasper Marquandt's lensing of majestic desert locations (shot in Deep Springs Valley, Calif.) opens up the cramped wide angles of the interior scenes. Wiehl demonstrates a good sense of place and minimalist modern wit in the Jim Jarmusch school. Thesps look right, though a bit self-conscious. Dialog runs all over the place.
—*Yung.*

Stanley & Iris

Park City, Utah An MGM/ UA Distribution release from MGM of a Lantana production. Executive producer, Patrick Palmer. Produced by Arlene Sellers, Alex Winitsky. Directed by Martin Ritt. Screenplay, Harriet Frank Jr., Irving Ravetch, based on Pat Barker's novel "Union Street;" camera (Duart color), Donald McAlpine; editor, Sidney Levin; music, John Williams; sound (Dolby), Richard Lightstone; production design, Joel Schiller; art direction, Alicia Keywan; costume design, Theoni Aldredge; associate producer, Jim Van Wyck. Reviewed at U.S. Film Festival, Park City, Utah, Jan. 19, 1990. MPAA Rating: PG-13. Running time: **102 MIN.**

Iris. . . . . .Jane Fonda
Stanley. . . . . .Robert De Niro
Sharon. . . . . .Swoosie Kurtz
Kelly. . . . . .Martha Plimpton
Richard. . . . . .Harley Cross
Joe. . . . . .Jamey Sheridan
Leonides. . . . . .Feodor Chaliapin

■**The elements are in place but they don't add up to great drama in this well-meant effort to personalize the plight of illiterate people via a love story between a man who can't read and his teacher. Boxoffice payoff for MGM/UA looks modest.**

Project reunites director Martin Ritt with screenwriting team of Harriet Frank Jr. and Irving Ravetch, same talents that produced the Oscar-winning "Norma Rae," which also had a working-class setting and underdog social concern.

"Stanley & Iris" lacks the communal backdrop that propelled "Norma Rae." The millworker protagonist in that pic struggled on behalf of a whole caste of workers in a hometown factory, but Robert De Niro's plight as an illiterate cook proves too small for a feature film framework. What's more, pic's natural dramatic climaxes are undercut or bypassed in scenes that don't live up to expectations.

Jane Fonda plays Iris, a recent widow still struggling with grief while trying to support a whole household, including her unemployed sister and brother-in-law, on her wages as an assembly-line worker in a cake factory.

She catches the eye of Stanley Cox, a cafeteria cook who mostly shuns intimacy to avoid having anyone discover his embarrassing deficiency — that at middle age, he has never learned to read or write.

Fired by his boss for being potentially dangerous, Stanley no longer can afford to care properly for the aging father who lives with him. The old man dies soon after being placed in a nursing home, and the bereft Stanley finally confronts his fears and asks Iris to teach him to read.

Sitting in her kitchen each night, they begin an old-fashioned courtship hampered by Iris' continued attachment to her dead husband. Though he's clever and inventive, building contraptions in his garage at night, Stanley has plenty of trouble with reading. He finally gives up and disappears after one humiliating incident.

What would seem the high point of the reading story — his epiphany when he finally grasps the system by which marks on paper turn into meaning — takes place offscreen, as Stanley does some homework of his own.

There is, however, a nice comical scene in a library where Stanley excitedly reads aloud for Iris everything he picks up. Likewise, the love story reaches fruition in three unsatisfying episodes.

Fonda has some trouble evoking a woman whose life would have dropped her off at such a humble station — her voice and carriage belong to a person of far more ability. De Niro, as a quiet, prideful man who feels foolish and like "a big dummy" trying to learn, does in fact come across as self-consciously awkward and a tad silly, though his performance includes some muted, winning comedy in its details.

Where "Stanley & Iris"does succeed admirably is in its compassionate portrayal of the insecure, prison-like existence of illiterate people. Script offers some fine, revealing moments, but it's also somewhat untidy and ham-handed. Characters speak in simple sentences with big meanings in order to sound like low-born folk; it doesn't ring true.

Pic is attractively shot in straight-forward fashion, but the John Williams score is mediocre.

As its title suggests, this is a 2-character show, though there are brief supporting performances by Martha Plimpton, Jamey Sheridan and Swoosie Kurtz as Iris' family, down-on- their-luck examplars of blue-collar woes. -- *Daws.*

Men Don't Leave

Hollywood A Warner Bros. release of a Paul Brickman/Jon Avnet production, presented by the Geffen Co. Produced by Avnet. Executive producer, Brickman. Directed by Brickman. Screenplay, Barbara Benedek, Brickman, from a story by Benedek, suggested by Moshe Mizrahi's film "La Vie Continué;" camera (CFI color), Bruce Surtees; editor, Richard Chew; music, Thomas Newman; sound (Dolby), Curt Frisk; production design, Barbara Ling; art direction, John Mark Harrington; set design, William Arnold; set decoration, Karen O'Hara (Chicago), Cricket Rowland (Baltimore); costumes, J. Allen Highfill; Jessica Lange's costumes, Susan Becker; assistant director, Dan Kolsrud; 2d unit director, Jon Avnet; helicopter camera, Rexford Metz; casting, David Rubin. Reviewed at the Burbank Studios, Burbank, Calif., Jan. 17, 1990. MPAA Rating: PG-13. Running time: **113 MIN.**

Beth Macauley. . . . . .Jessica Lange
Chris Macauley. . . . . .Chris O'Donnell
Matt Macauley. . . . . .Charlie Korsmo
Charles Simon. . . . . . .Arliss Howard
John Macauley. . . . . . . .Tom Mason
Jody. . . . . .Joan Cusack
Lisa Coleman. . . . . .Kathy Bates
Winston Buckley. . . . . . .Core Carrier
Mr. Buckley. . . . . .Jim Haynie
Mrs. Buckley. . . . . . . .Belita Moreno
Dale Buckley. . . . . . .Shannon Moffett
Nina Simon. . . . . .Lora Zane
Polka dancer. . . . . . .Theresa Wozniak

■**Though stuck with a preachy title and weighed down by a dismal beginning, Warner Bros.' "Men Don't Leave" recovers its equilibrium to become a quietly moving tale of a widow (Jessica Lange) and her struggle to support her two sons in shabby Baltimore surroundings.**

Director-coscripter Paul Brickman's flair for comedy enlivens what could have been an overly sudsy story, and Lange's performance is finely shaded. The uneven Geffen Co. film lacks a strong b.o. hook, however, and needs favorable critical response to survive in the marketplace.

Suggested by Moshe Mizrahi's 1981 French film "La Vie Continué" (Life Goes On) with Annie Girardot, "Men Don't Leave" is Brickman's first film as a director since the sparkling 1983 comedy "Risky Business," which was coproduced by "Men's" producer, Jon Avnet. Lacking the sureness of touch that film had, "Men Don't Leave" nevertheless shows that Brickman and his coscripter, Barbara Benedek (who also gets screen story credit), are skillful, empathetic observers of the problems of everyday life.

Since the title can't refer to the death early in the film of Lange's debt-ridden husband (Tom Mason) in an unsatisfactorily explained accident (or can it?), it must refer (somewhat obscurely) to the constancy of her new b.f., Arliss Howard in contrast to the desertion of Girardot in the original by Jean-Pierre Cassel.

But the title misleadingly suggests a feminist tract, not the warmhearted comedy-drama this pic becomes after getting past the disjointed kitchen-sink melodrama of Mason's death and Lange's selling of the family's suburban home. The move to Baltimore revives what seemed a terminally ill film and brings its compellingly to life.

Playing the role af first with an unmodulated emotional glaze, surrounded by that hushed reverential aura that too often seems to accompany her work, the taciturn Lange is pulled back to life by the spirited behavior of her boys, superbly played by newcomers Chris O'Donnell and Charlie Korsmo; by O'Donnell's sweet but loopy g.f. Joan Cusack, and by the engagingly offbeat Howard. Barely getting through the day in a humiliating job delivering food for a trendy restaurant run by rough-edged Kathy Bates, Lange can't handle O'Donnell's precocious sexual involvement with Cusack or her own conflicted emotions over the insistent attentions of Howard, an avant-garde cellist.

She starts to blossom, though, in a lovely scene in a working-class polka hall, when she's asked to dance by the portly but grace-

Original Film

La Vie Continué
(Life Goes On)
(FRENCH)

Paris A GEF/CCFC release of a Cineproduction/SFPC coproduction. Produced by Lise Fayolle, Giorgio Silvagni. Written and directed by Moshe Mizrahi. Dialog collaborator, Rachel Fabien; camera (color), Yves Lafaye; editor, Martine Barraque; music, Georges Delerue; sound, Serge Deraison; art direction, Dominique Andre; production manager, Charlotte Fraisse. Reviewed at the UGC Marbeuf theater, Paris, Oct. 12, 1981. Running time: 93 MIN.
Jeanne. . . . . .Annie Girardot
Pierre. . . . . .Jean-Pierre Cassel
Max. . . . . .Pierre Dux
Henri. . . . . .Michel Aumont
Catherine. . . . . .Giulia Salvatori
Elizabeth. . . . . .Paulette Dubost

ful Theresa Wozniak as Howard plays the accordion with spirited good humor.

The film's dramatic heart is a sequence showing Lange, after losing her job in a blowup against Bates, descending into a catatonic state and refusing to leave her bed

for days as the apartment turns into a quiet vision of hell. It's a scary piece of acting by Lange, beautifully directed by Brickman, and it turns a somewhat meandering film into a memorable emotional experience.

Despite his earlier insolence toward his mother, O'Donnell goes to see the disaffected Howard, and in a powerful monolog, begs him to come back. Meanwhile, the younger Korsmo, who has been drifting into petty thievery, runs away to the family's old home, and the boys' distress helps shock Lange to her senses, along with some psychic first aid from both Howard and Cusack, who are both endearing in their roles.

"Men Don't Leave's" inability to be pinned down into convenient niches may keep it from having wide appeal, but that quality also gives it the unusual feeling of life being lived, messily, upsettingly but affectingly.

The film is dedicated to the memory of the late Geffen Co. president David Bombyk, who oversaw and helped develop the film before he died of AIDS, which also claimed the life of the film's costume designer, J. Allen Highfill.—*Mac.*

Brain Dead

Hollywood A Concorde Pictures release of a Julie Corman production. Produced by Corman. Directed by Adam Simon. Screenplay, Charles Beaumont, Simon, based on Beaumont's story; camera (Foto-Kem color), Ronn Schmidt; editor, Carol Oblath; music, Peter Francis Rotter; sound, Michael Clark, Geraint Bell, Joe Earle; production design, Catherine Hardwicke; art direction, Gilbert Mercier; set decoration, Gene Serdena; costume design, Catherine Taieb; associate producer, Lynn Whitney; casting, Barbara Cohen, Leslie Litt. Reviewed at Raleigh Studios, Hollywood, Jan. 25, 1990. MPAA Rating: R. Running time: 85 MIN.
Rex Martin. . . . . .Bill Pullman
Jim Reston. . . . . .Bill Paxton
Jack Halsey. . . . . .Bud Cort
Conklin/Ramsen. . . . . .Nicholas Pryor
Dana Martin. . . . .Patricia Charbonneau
Vance. . . . . .George Kennedy

■A confusing case of dreams within nightmares within more dreams, the only wave "Brain Dead" makes is in the shape of an indecipherable headache. Dribbling out in regional release, the film may generate some curiosity in homevideo among sci-fi buffs, if only due to its unusual credits.

Unfortunately, the story behind the story is more interesting than the film itself. Adam Simon, making his feature directing debut, discov-

ered an unused 1963 script (titled "Paranoia") by Charles Beaumont, who along with Rod Serling and Richard Matheson wrote the lion's share of original "Twilight Zone" tv episodes.

Simon updated and expanded upon the story. Film emerges as a morass of fantasy sequences that eventually implodes. Twisting and turning like a paler version of the final sequence in Terry Gilliam's "Brazil," film seeks to sustain that sense of lunacy for at least 45 minutes. It suffers badly from stretching.

Bill Pullman plays a neurologist studying brains and paranoia who is asked by his sleazy chum Jim (Bill Paxton), corporate drone for a faceless conglomerate, to study a cracked-up mathematician with a secret formula locked in his addled mind.

The film's one revelation comes in the form of Bud Cort as the crazed scientist Halsey — gaunt and pale, babbling in a Bowery-boy accent.

Pullman performs an operation on Halsey but ultimately gets yanked into the delusions and madness himself, until it's hard to recall or even care where the entrance to the maze began.

The film's confusing nature yields mostly indifference and undercuts its visual flair. The actors also seem a bit lost with the exception of Cort.

Tech credits are okay, with stark production design of sterile white rooms by Catherine Hardwicke and an urgent score by Peter Francis Rotter that's, alas, more compelling than the source material. —*Bril.*

Strike It Rich
(BRITISH-U.S.-COLOR/
B&W)

New York A Millimeter Films release, in association with Ideal Communications Films, British Screen and BBC, of a Flamingo Pictures production. Executive producers, Bob Weinstein, Harvey Weinstein. Produced by Christine Oestreicher, Graham Easton. Directed by James Scott. Screenplay, Scott, based on Graham Greene's novella "Loser Takes All;" additional dialog, Richard Rayner; script contributions, Julian Mitchell, Dick Vosburgh; camera (Technicolor, b&w), Robert Paynter; editor, Thomas Schwalm; music, Shirley Walker, with musical themes by Cliff Eidelman; sound (Dolby), David Wynne Jones; production design, Christopher Hobbs; costume design, Tom Rand; assistant director, Guy Travers; associate producer, Susan Slonaker; casting, Joyce Gallie. Reviewed at Bay theater, N.Y., Jan. 27, 1990. MPAA Rating: PG. Running time: 84 MIN.
Ian Bertram. . . . . . . .Robert Lindsay
Cary Porter. . . . . . . .Molly Ringwald
Herbert Dreuther. . . . . . .John Gielgud
Bowles. . . . . .Max Wall
Philippe. . . . . . . .Simon de la Brosse

Blixon. . . . . .Marius Goring
Bowles' nurse. . . . . . . .Margi Clarke
Kinski. . . . . .Vladek Sheybal
Hotel manager. . . . . . . .Michel Blanc
Mrs. De Vere. . . . .Frances De La Tour

■"Strike It Rich" is a poorly directed piece of light (i.e., low calorie) entertainment. Miramax didn't press screen this pic and even removed its name afer trumpeting its production two years ago, releasing it via Millimeter Films, its B-level film subsidiary.

Film is the second mid-Atlantic venture by the Gotham indie and has in common with previous film "Scandal" a nostalgic bent towards England (here the '50s) plus the original casting of Emily Lloyd in both pics. British thesp elected to play Americans in two U.S. films instead, "Cookie" and "In Country," while her British roles were ironically filled for Miramax by Yank actresses, Bridget Fonda and here, Molly Ringwald.

Helmer James Scott closely follows the letter of Graham Greene's 1955 novella "Loser Takes All." He adds an opening reel (shot partly in black & white) that fleshes out the romance of accountant Robert Lindsay and half-his-age Ringwald, portraying a British lass raised in America after being evacuated during the Blitz (accounting for her all-American accent).

Unfortunately, the Greene material is merely a trifle that would have needed the talents and charm of say, Stanley Donen, Kenneth More and Audrey Hepburn in the '50s to constitute a viable theatrical feature. As executed here, it's hopelessly old-fashioned, remote and even fusty.

Plotline has the lovers spending their honeymoon in Monte Carlo on the whim of Lindsay's boss (John Gielgud). Predictably, Lindsay contracts gambling fever and uses his mathematical abilities to perfect a winning system for roulette. Angry at being stranded there by the forgetful Gielgud, he plots to use his casino winnings to buy the swing shares in Gielgud's business and drive the grand old man out, but relents cornily in final reel to spend time with the neglected Ringwald.

Greene's themes are laid on with a trowel here and a promising subplot of superstition (heralded by cute, old-fashioned credits featuring a black cat in split-screen) is poorly developed. Scott, who has been making shorts, docus and feature-length material for over 25 years, doesn't seem suited to handling mainstream films. He never shows Lindsay winning at roulette, denying the viewer the genre's vicarious pleasure (Lindsay might as well be robbing banks and just pretending to have a winning system for Ringwald's benefit). Final reels are filled with clumsy crosscutting that kills off any residual attachment to the characters.

There's no chemistry between the stars. Ringwald's frequently flat line readings are a drag. With her recent string of flop vehicles, she's failed to get an adult role of substance following her breakthrough five years ago as a teen fave. With this dull outing and megaflop "Bert Rigby, You're A Fool," Lindsay's screen career remains stillborn. Gielgud's role is just a brief walkthrough.

Coming off best here are two leading French thesps making their English-language debuts. Simon de la Brosse as Ringwald's younger love interest is appealing; he costarred in Miramax' French import "The Little Thief" and is a Gallic dead ringer for former Ringwald costar Judd Nelson. Michel Blanc is very effective in his underplaying as the very understanding hotel manager. — *Lor.*

Flashback

Hollywood A Paramount Pictures release of a Marvin Worth production. Produced by Worth. Coproducer, David Loughery. Executive producer, Richard Stenta. Directed by Franco Amurri. Screenplay, Loughery; camera (Technicolor), Stefan Czapsky; editor, C. Timothy O'Meara; music, Barry Goldberg; sound (Dolby), John Pritchett; production design, Vincent Cresciman; art direction, James Terry Welden; set decoration, Cecilia Rodarte; costume design, Eileen Kennedy; assistant director, Frank Bueno; 2d unit camera, Frank Beascoechea; casting, Nancy Foy. Reviewed at Mann Bruin theater, West L.A., Calif., Jan. 25, 1990. MPAA Rating: R. Running time: 108 MIN.
Huey Walker. . . . . .Dennis Hopper
John Buckner. . . . . .Kiefer Sutherland
Maggie. . . . . .Carol Kane
Stark. . . . . .Paul Dooley
Sheriff Hightower. . . . . .Cliff DeYoung
Barry. . . . . .Richard Masur
Hal. . . . . .Michael McKean
Sparkle. . . . . .Kathleen York
Phil Prager. . . . . .Tom O'Brien

■Dennis Hopper does a delightful self-parody in Paramount's "Flashback" as an Abbie Hoffman-like fugitive "radical jester" brought to farcical justice in 1989 by uptight FBI agent Kiefer Sutherland. Unfortunately, the film's promising premise is dissipated by character clichés, mechanical plot twists and an uncertain grasp on political satire.

"Flashback's" debatable assumption that today's audience feels nostalgic for the hippie era of the late 1960s won't make the Marvin Worth production another b.o. "Woodstock."

The fun part of "Flashback" is the Rip Van Winkle story of the gray-bearded Hopper, looking like he's been sleeping off a 20-year o.d., expounding on the political and sexual mores of the 1960s and the 1980s to Sutherland while en route to jail between San Francisco and the Pacific Northwest.

Hopper — Huey Walker, who originally was busted in 1969 on the charge of playing a malicious prank on Vice President Spiro T. Agnew — has a field day with his character's ranting monologs and weird, manic gestures. The lines he's given by scripter David Loughery about "your government's madness" usually hit their satiric targets.

When he tells Sutherland that in the Reagan era all the poor people were homeless and all the rich people were in the Betty Ford Clinic, he displays a winning, wily humor.

There's also a riotous vein of laughter in such off-kilter reactions as his addressing a bewildered black train porter as "soul brother" and declaring, "You're a prisoner of the system, like I am."

One trouble with "Flashback" is that there isn't enough of that kind of material. Too much screen time is wasted on predictably contrived situations in which Hopper repeatedly escapes from Sutherland and is recaptured, and in a tedious chase of the pair by implausibly vengeful smalltown sheriff Cliff DeYoung.

A deeper problem is that both Loughery and director Franco Amurri seem to be suffering from a serious case of cultural amnesia when it comes to remembering what was going on in the late 1960s. Amurri, making his American feature debut, was in Italy at the time, but Loughery should have known better.

Perhaps it's a sign of how depressing the 1980s were that the events of 1967-69, one of the worst periods in American history, can be portrayed as nostalgia fodder by comparison.

Hopper does get to point out that the U.S. then was dropping more bombs on Vietnam than it dropped on Germany and Japan combined during World War II, but the line is a throwaway underneath some slapstick visual antics.

Sutherland, who was ashamed of his hippie upbringing and invented a middle-class past to become an FBI agent, is turned back into a flower child under Hopper's benign influence, but it happens with such incredible abruptness that even Hopper has to remark, "Man, when you change, you really change."

When the pair find themselves back on the rundown commune in Oregon where Sutherland lived as a child, encountering dilapidated hippie Carol Kane dwelling among the portraits of martyred 1960s figures, the film taps briefly into the sadness of the time.

Yet, as Sutherland tearfully watches inane home movies of himself gamboling with his parents and their fellow hippies, "Flashback" labors under the delusion that the summer of 1967 was a halcyon era and has the FBI agent blithely discard his gun and career, buy a motorcycle and hit the road.

The film's tricky finale, contriving to include both 1960s apocalyptic imagery and a yuppieish happy ending for Hopper, seems symptomatic of its fuzziness toward a subject that could have been turned into a first- rate comedy.

Though Amurri is good with actors, his direction is visually flat and his pacing sluggish. The lensing by Stefan Czapsky too often is murky and colorless, and the loud rock score by Barry Goldberg is uninspired, as is the formulaic use of period music.—*Mac.*

Atame
(Tie Me Up! Tie Me Down!)
(SPANISH)

Madrid A Miramax Films release (U.S.) of an El Deseo production. Executive producer, Agustin Almodóvar. Written and directed by Pedro Almodóvar. Camera (Eastmancolor), José Luis Alcaine; editor, José Salcedo; music, Ennio Morricone; sound (Dolby), Goldstein & Steinberg; sets, Ferrán Sánchez; costumes, José Maria Cossio; production manager, Esther Garcia; assistant director, José Luis Escolar; makeup, Juan Pedro Hernández. Reviewed at Cine Fuencarral, Madrid, Jan. 22, 1990. (In Berlin Film Festival, competing.) Running time: 101 MIN.
Marina. . . . . .Victoria Abril
Ricki. . . . . .Antonio Banderas
Lola. . . . . .Loles León
Máximo Espejo. . . . . .Francisco Rabal
    Also with: Julieta Serrano, Maria Barranco, Rossy de Palma, Lola Cardona, Montse G. Romeu, Emiliano Redondo, Oswaldo Delgado, Concha Rabal, Alberto Fernández, José Maria Tasso, Angelina Llongueras, Manuel Bandera, Virginia Diez.

■Pedro Almodóvar's newest pic combines all of the winsome ingredients that have made his recent films b.o. attractions.

Though not matching "Women On The Verge Of A Nervous Breakdown" for sheer madcap zaniness, its controlled humor and occasional touches of the outlandish should draw large audiences worldwide.

In contrast to "Women," this film harks back to Almodóvar's earlier features where sexuality was a central theme. Though milder than "Law Of Desire," "Atame" does contain numerous sex scenes, frontal nudity and a bathtub episode that could become a classic.

The film was given an "over 18" classification in Spain. However, virtually all the sex scenes are spiced with touches of humor, making them more like off-color jokes than a scatalogical assault.

Almodóvar's control increases with each film. He has moved away from sight gags, shock tactics and glamorized kitsch. These elements still lurk in the background, as in the clever opening titles, but they have been molded into a subtler narrative.

Yarn concerns Ricki (Antonio Banderas), a 23-year-old man who is released from a mental institution. From the time he was a child he has been in and out of institutions. Now he decides it is time to marry, have kids and maybe even get a job.

He sees the picture of Marina (Victoria Abril) in a film buff magazine. She is a hooker and porno actress he once paid to spend a night with, and Banderas decides to marry her.

After unsuccessfully trying to pick her up at a film set on the last day of shooting, Banderas forces his way into her apartment and declares his intentions. After a scuffle, he decides to tie her to the bed, certain that she will learn to love him.

The relationship between the protagonists gradually shifts from that of captor and captured to lovers. Meanwhile, the elderly porno film director, who is confined to a wheelchair, teams up with Abril's sister to try and find the missing thesp.

Just as the film threatens to flag and the Abril's fate becomes claustrophobically tiresome, Almodóvar changes pace. He switches to a focus on the porn director, throws in a short tv skit and adds various amusing antics.

By the time her sister finally finds Abril, who is still tied to the bed, the captive girl tells her she's fallen in love with Banderas. Pic ends in a delightful scene with the sisters and Banderas singing as they drive back to Madrid. Almodóvar's inventive direction, superb lensing by José Luis Alcaine, a fine score by Ennio Morricone and top technical credits make "Atame" a pleasure to watch. The film has the same Spanish framework as its predecessors, reflecting the modern, amoral, sex & drug culture of modern Madrid, intertwined with long-entrenched religious and social values. (Abril typically wears a necklace with a cross.)

Abril and Banderas are compelling to watch as the central couple. Good supporting performances by Paco Rabal as the porno helmer (whose antics include "dancing" a flamenco in his wheelchair), Loles León as the effusive sister and Rossy de Palma as a drug pusher further buoy up the film. —*Besa.*

Mountains Of The Moon

New York   A Tri-Star Pictures release of a Mario Kassar and Andrew Vajna presentation of a Daniel Melnick/Indieprod production. (Intl. sales, Carolco.) Executive producers, Kassar, Vajna. Produced by Daniel Melnick. Directed by Bob Rafelson. Screenplay, William Harrison, Rafelson, from Harrison's book "Burton And Speke" and the journals of Richard Burton and John Hanning Speke; camera (Rank color; Technicolor prints), Roger Deakins; editor, Thom Noble; music, Michael Small; sound (Dolby), Simon Kaye; production design, Norman Reynolds; costume design, Jenny Beavan, John Bright; assistant director, Patrick Clayton; stunt coordinator, Alf Joint; choreography, Eleanor Fazan; additional camera, Dick Pope; associate producer, Chris Curling; casting, Celestia Fox. Reviewed at Todd-AO screening room, N.Y., Jan. 25, 1990. MPAA Rating: R. Running time: **135 MIN.**

Richard Burton. . . . . . . .Patrick Bergin
John Hanning Speke. . . . . . . .Iain Glen
Isabel Arundell. . . . . .Fiona Shaw
Laurence Oliphant. . . . .Richard E. Grant
Lord Houghton. . . . . . . .Peter Vaughan
Edgar Papworth. . . . . . . .Roger Rees
David Livingstone. . . . . . . .Bernard Hill
Mrs. Arundell. . . . . .Anna Massey
Mr. Arundell. . . . . .Leslie Phillips
Mabruki. . . . . .Delroy Lindo
Sidi Bombay. . . . . .Paul Onsongo
Also with: Peter Eyre, James Villiers, Omar Sharif, Roshan Seth, Doreen Mantle, Pip Torrens, Frances Cuka

■**Bob Rafelson's "Mountains Of The Moon" is an outstanding adventure film. Its balance of the cerebral and emotional should prove an audience pleaser worldwide if marketing difficulties presented by arcane subject matter and unknown cast can be overcome.**

Daniel Melnick production for Carolco gives Tri-Star two challenges in a row, as distrib currently is making b.o. headway with another against-the-grain production, the Civil War epic "Glory."

Adapted by "Rollerball" writer William Harrison and Rafelson from Harrison's book and the journals of 19th century explorers Richard Burton and John Hanning Speke, "Mountains" covers the same territory as the Emmy-winning 1971 tv docudrama "The Search For The Nile," which toplined Kenneth Haigh and John Quentin. Without sacrificing the historical context, new pic provides deeply felt performances and refreshing, offbeat humor to bring the tale back to life.

Starting in 1854, pic documents duo's ill-fated first two expeditions to Africa, climaxing with Speke's discovery of what became named Lake Victoria, the true source of the Nile (though Speke could not prove same). Roger Deakins' gritty, realistic photography of rugged Kenyan locations contrasts with segments of cheery beauty back home in England between treks.

In only his seventh feature film in a distinguished career that spans 22 years, Rafelson brings expert detailing to the saga. The male bonding theme of the two explorers is forcefully and tastefully told (with a key scene of intimacy as Speke cradles and kisses a feverish Burton midway through the pic). Besides its vivid presentation of the dangers posed by brutal, hostile African tribes (whose turf the white geographers are violating), pic strongly develops its major themes of self-realization and self-aggrandizement.

Chief drawback is film's inability to make pressing to modern audiences the Holy Grail-like quest to find the Nile's tributaries, a hot topic in the 19th century but of little import now.

Rafelson's casting is a key to film's success. Irish thesps Patrick Bergin and Fiona Shaw are earthy choices for Burton and his wife, Isabel. Bergin is an arresting cross between musical comedy's Jim Dale and a lumberjack, noticeably growing in stature as the film progresses.

As Speke, Scots actor Iain Glen creates sympathy for a wayward character. He resembles David Bowie on screen, a reminder that project originally was planned as a vehicle for British rock stars including Bowie until wiser heads prevailed; pic benefits immensely from lack of distraction thanks to having unfamiliar faces in the lead roles.

Technically, "Mountains" never strays from its dramatic thrust to become merely picturesque. —*Lor.*

U.S. FILM FESTIVAL REVIEWS

Metropolitan

Park City, Utah   A Westerly Film-Video production. Produced, written and directed by Whit Stillman. Coproducer, Peter Wentworth. Line producer-production manager, Brian Greenbaum. Camera (color), John Thomas; editor, Chris Tellefsen; music, Mark Suozzo, with original music by Tom Judson; costume design, Mary Jane Fort; sound, Antonio Arroyo. Reviewed at U.S. Film Festival, Park City, Utah, Jan. 23, 1990. No MPAA Rating. Running time: **98 MIN.**

Audrey Rouget. . . . . . .Carolyn Farina
Tom Townsend. . . . .Edward Clements
Nick Smith. . . . . . .Christopher Eigeman
Charlie Black. . . . . . . .Taylor Nichols
Jane Clarke. . . . . .Allison Parisi
Sally Fowler. . . . . . . .Dylan Hundley
Cynthia McClean. . . . . . .Isabel Gillies
Fred Neff. . . . . .Bryan Leder
Rick Von Sloneker. . . . . . .Will Kempe
Serena Slocum. . . . .Elizabeth Thompson

■**Filmmaker Whit Stillman makes a strikingly original debut with "Metropolitan," a glib, ironic portrait of the vulnerable young heirs to Manhattan's disappearing debutante scene. With its sophisticated, gently mocking wit and the introduction of an intriguing ensemble cast, pic is a strong candidate for specialized theatrical release.**

Story centers on a set of East Side friends who dub themselves the SFRP (or "Sally Fowler Rat Pack," after the girl whose sprawling Park Avenue apartment they gather in) and, more amusingly, UHBs, for Urban Haute Bourgeoisie.

They drag into their number a newcomer, Tom (Edward Clements), who openly disapproves of them but nonetheless shows up every night for a private gatherings after black-tie parties and dances.

A self-serious but insensitive young man, Tom inspires the first-time love of Audrey, a quiet, good-humored literature lover who feels a bit outside the group. Tom repeatedly humiliates her as he continues to pursue an old flame, Serena (Elizabeth Thompson).

For Tom, the comforting sense of permanence the group offers proves an illusion — just as he comes to rely on them, they scatter as Christmas holidays end. In an amusing errand of rescue with his romantic rival, Charlie (Taylor Nichols), Tom tries to resurrect what he's lost.

Apparently seeking to portray in comic detail the surviving remnants of the world described in F. Scott Fitzgerald's "This Side Of Paradise," "Metropolitan" succeeds on several levels, offering rich, sparkling dialog, distinct characters and an intriguing peek into a seldom-seen milieu.

Among the fine cast, Christopher Eigeman stands out as Nick, the funny, arrogant group leader who's as jovially self-aware and self-mocking as his new friend, Tom, is stilted and blind to himself. Carolyn Farina gives a sensitive, perceptive performance as Audrey.

Pic is a true independent production, financed by 37-year-old Stillman (who sold his Manhattan apartment) and several friends. Stillman's previous film experience was his involvement in making a 1984 indie production, "Skyline," about the comic adventures of Spaniards in New York.—*Daws.*

Preston Sturges: The Rise And Fall Of An American Dreamer

Park City, Utah   Barking Dog Prods. and American Masters production. Produced and directed by Kenneth Bowser. Executive producers, Susan Lacy, Marilyn Haft. Coproducer, Caroline Baron. Written by Todd McCarthy. Narrated by Fritz Weaver. Camera, Dennis Maloney; editor, Ken Werner; composer, Michael Bacon; sound mixers, Mark Bovos, Russel Fager, Thomas Payne, Roger Pietschsmann, John Vincent; coordinating producer for American Masters, Herlene Freezer; associate producer for American Masters, Diane Dufault. Reviewed at the U.S. Film Festival, Park City, Utah, Jan. 21, 1990. Running time: **75 MIN.**

With: Eddie Bracken, Thomas Quinn Curtiss, Edwin Gillette, Betty Hutton, A.C. Lyles, Joel McCrea, Frances Ramsden, Cesar Romero, Andrew Sarris, Paul Schrader, Sandy Sturges, Rudy Vallee, Priscilla Woolfan.

■**The life of the great 1940s writer-director Preston Sturges proves as vivid as his work in this lively documentary created for PBS' "American Masters" series. Extensive clips from Sturges' highly entertaining and distinctive films and revealing interviews with ex-wives, friends and colleagues give docu both general interest and value to scholars.**

Beginning with the Chicago-born Sturges' turbulent upbringing in the lap of European culture by his mother, a constant companion of the dancer Isadora Duncan, pic follows him into adutlhood as the reigning genius of 1940s Hollywood and the first screenwriter to be entrusted with a slate of films to direct.

For Sturges, real life was as full of irony as his screen stories. It was his mother who gave Isadora Duncan the long scarf by which she strangled when it caught in a car wheel. In another incident, Sturges, despondent after the breakup of his first marriage, was poised to jump from a tall building when a workman fell from it to his death at the same moment, changing Sturges' mind.

Interviews reveal how Sturges' private life influenced the remarkable characters he placed before the public; his free-thinking mother apparently was the spark for the character played by Barbara Stanwyck in "The Lady Eve."

Docu dwells for some time on the making of Sturges' dazzling comedies, such as "The Great McGinty," "The Lady Eve," "Sullivan's Travels," "The Palm Beach Story" and "The Miracle Of Morgan's Creek," before exploring the disastrous partnership he formed with Howard Hughes after leaving Paramount.

Clips are skillfully edited and docu is fastpaced and insightful throughout. Fritz Weaver's narration and Todd McCarthy's clever, fluidly informative script offer smooth transitions between clips and interviews.

Piece is scheduled for airing on PBS this summer or fall and may find specialized theatrical play.
— *Daws.*

The Horseplayer

Park City, Utah A Relentless Entertainment production. Produced by Larry Rattner. Executive producers, Daryl Jamison, Robert Nau. Directed by Kurt Voss. Screenplay, Voss, Rattner; camera (Duart color), Dean Lent; editor, John Rosenberg; music, Gary Shuyman; sound, William Weir; art direction, Steve Karman; costume design, Elisabeth Scott; associate producer, Lee Ann Kaplan. Reviewed at U.S. Film Festival, Park City, Utah, Jan. 20, 1990. No MPAA Rating. Running time: **92 MIN.**

Bud. . . . . .Brad Dourif
Randi. . . . . .Sammi Davis
Matthew. . . . . .M.K. Harris
George. . . . . .Vic Tayback
Kid. . . . . .Max Perlich

■Second indie feature from director Kurt Voss is an uninspired followup to "Border Radio,"lacking that pic's spare syle and striking visuals.

Brooding study of a disturbed loner who is preyed upon by a cynical artist and his idle female companion has few prospects beyond foreign or video exposure.

Brad Dourif plays Bud, an emotionally fragile type who divides his life between stocking the icebox in a liquor store and betting the horses, until his routine is disrupted by Randi (Sammi Davis), a flirtatious blond, and Matthew (M.K. Harris), the callous painter she lives with.

As the couple imposes heavy-handed companionship on Bud, it develops that Matthew depends on his girlfriend's outside affairs as subjects for his work.

Unsuspecting Bud is portrayed in a series of paintings Matthew is preparing for a show. Meanwhile, his affair with Randi rattles him so that he takes up drinking and loses his job before she leaves him. It also develops that weirdo Bud is a killer on parole, whose father was an abusive artist.

Shot in L.A. on a minimal budget, "The Horseplayer" attempts a half-hearted psychological study of the players in this confused, unpleasant triangle, but comes up with no convincing insights.

Voss, who cowrote the script with producer Larry Rattner, finds a few compelling images, such as Bud bundled up in a ski mask in the icebox, looking both sinister and absurd.

Unfortunately, pic's themes are not fully realized and Voss' style generally stays on the surface of a story that seems thrown together for convenience.

Dourif, playing yet another psycho on the edge, and Harris as a nasty, thieving manipulator, are so unsympathetic as to deter interest.

Lensing by Dean Lent, who also collaborated on "Border Radio,"is often quite effective, though pic's few locations become claustrophobic. — *Daws.*

To Sleep With Anger

Park City, Utah An SVS Films release of an Edward R. Pressman production. Produced by Caldecot Chubb, Thomas S. Byrnes, Darin Scott. Executive producers, Pressman, Danny Glover, Harris E. Tulchin. Written and directed by Charles Burnett. Camera (color), Walt Lloyd; editor, Nancy Richardson; music, Stephen James Taylor; music supervision, Budd Carr; production design, Penny Barrett; art direction, Troy Myers; costume design, Gaye Shannon-Burnett; sound, Veda Campbell; assistant director, Johnathan Meizler; associate producers, Michael Flynn, Linda Koulisis. Reviewed at U.S. Film Festival, Park City, Utah, Jan. 24, 1990. No MPAA Rating. Running time: **95 MIN.**

Harry Mention. . . . . . . .Danny Glover
Babe Brother. . . . . . . .Richard Brooks
Gideon. . . . . .Paul Butler
Suzie. . . . . .Mary Alice
Junior. . . . . .Carl Lumbly
Linda. . . . . .Sheryl Lee Ralph
Pat. . . . . .Vonetta McGee
Preacher. . . . . .Wonderful Smith
Hattie. . . . . .Ethel Ayler

■**Writer-producer Charles Burnett's first major feature, about a visitor from the Deep South who brings superstition and evil into a divided L.A. household, simmers for a long time before it begins to percolate a pungent, stimulating brew. With special handling, pic could appeal to a sizable audience.** The visitor, Harry Mention (Danny Glover), seems all vibrant charm and quaint back-home ways until family members begin to notice an unsettling aura about him; he has a talent for scattering seeds of doubt in people and stirring up conflicts.

"You got to work at evil," Glover says, and he works at it. His superstitious tokens and rituals soon fill the middle-class household and family members begin to take sick or go crazy. Glover sucks the weakest one, Babe Brother (Richard Brooks), toward a dangerous crossroads, turning him sullen and abusive.

Like playwright August Wilson, Burnett draws on the potency of symbols and traditions in black folkloric history — in this case the trickster who stirs up ill winds — but sets them against the conflicting currents of contemporary black life.

The one person who's impervious to Glover is an old consort of his, Hattie (Ethel Ayler), a former brothel singer who's born again. Yet it isn't religon that ultimately trips him.

Once its theme takes hold, "To Sleep With Anger" is a fascinating piece that proves Burnett a filmmaker of rich imagination and talent.

Glover, aged for the role, is a powerfully unsettling presence as Harry. Brooks is strikingly effective as the complex, troubled brother who draws family criticism for his materialistic goals. Mary Alice is excellent as the quietly centered midwife and matriarch who must confront Harry.

Handsomely designed and shot in South Central Los Angeles, production features fine original music by Stephen James Taylor and a rich compilation of gospel and blues tunes.—*Daws.*

Stella

Hollywood A Buena Vista release of a Touchstone Pictures/Samuel Goldwyn Co. presentation. Produced by Samuel Goldwyn Jr. Directed by John Erman. Executive producer, David V. Picker. Coproducer, Bonnie Bruckheimer-Martell. Screenplay, Robert Getchell. Camera (Medallion Color, Technicolor prints), Billy Williams; production design, James Hulsey; editor, Jerrold L. Ludwig; art direction, Jeffrey Ginn; set decoration, Steve Shewchuk; music, John Morris; sound (Dolby), Bill Phillips; costume design, Theadora Van Runkle; assistant directors, Brian Cook, Michael Steele, Carl Goldstein; casting, Howard Feuer, Stuart Aikins. Reviewed at the Crest Theater, Westwood, Jan. 30, 1990. MPAA Rating: PG-13. Running time: **114 MIN.**
Stella Claire. . . . . .Bette Midler
Ed Munn. . . . . .John Goodman
Jenny Claire. . . . . .Trini Alvarado
Stephen Dallas. . . . . . .Stephen Collins
Janice Morrison. . . . . . .Marsha Mason
Mrs. Wilkerson. . . . . . .Eileen Brennan
Debbie Whitman. . . . . . . .Linda Hart

■The semitragic "Stella Dallas" shows her years in this hopelessly dated and ill-advised remake, which suffers from both slavish faith to the pattern of the 1937 version and the few alterations it dares make. Some amusing moments, Bette Midler's astral presence and the Disney marketing machine should sew up a big weekend or two at the boxoffice before wanton simpering causes "Stella" to unravel.

One can understand what attracted Midler to the part, which earned Barbara Stanwyck an Oscar nomination. Few stories have more melodrama about them than this one.

Still, the idea of a lower-class mother who selflessly sends her daughter off to her upper-crust dad and his new wife — all so daughter can land the right beau — must sound like nails on a blackboard to Equal Rights Amendment proponents, and Midler's ballsy wit completely misses the redeeming lower-class yearning Stanwyck gave the role originally.

In addition, even in a year of

1925 Version

Stella Dallas

Hollywood Samuel Goldwyn production directed by Henry King. Adapted from Olive H. Prouty's novel of the same name by Francis Marion. Cameraed by Arthur Edeson. At the Apollo, New York, for special run beginning Nov. 16. Running time: **106 mins.**
Stella Dallas. . . . . .Bella Bennett
Stephen Dallas. . . . . . .Ronald Colman
Helen Morrison. . . . . . . .Alice Joyce
Ed Munn. . . . . .Jean Hersholt
Laurel Dallas. . . . . .Lola Moran
Richard Grovesnor. .Douglas Fairbanks, Jr.
Miss Philiburn. . . . . .Vera Lewis
Mrs. Grovesnor. . . . . . . .Beatrix Prior

tearjerkers many will have a hard time suppressing a gag reflex wading through all this hokum, which at times resembles a "disease of the week" telefilm under the heavy hand of telepic director John Erman.

All of the significant changes in the story come early, as Stella (Midler) meets a young doctor (Stephen Collins) while tending bar and quickly gets pregnant by him.

She refuses his half-hearted offer of marriage as well as any financial help, letting him run off to New York while she raises their daughter on her own.

Contrast that with the original, where Stella clearly sets out to woo Stephen Dallas as a means of escaping her lower-class existence, fascinated by the elite and trappings of wealth.

It's a small point but one that provided motivation and pathos in the original for what ultimately occurs; those plot points hinged on Depression-era values and class conflict that could have proven equally

1937 Version

Stella Dallas

United Artists release of a Samuel Goldwyn production. Associate producer, Merritt Hulburd. Features Barbara Stanwyck, John Boles, Anne Shirley; Barbara O'Neil, Alan Hale. Directed by King Vidor. Based on novel by Olive Higgins Prouty; screenplay, Harry Wagstaff Gribble, Gertrude Purcell; camera, Rudolph Mate; musical director, Alfred Newman; film editor, Sherman Todd; asst. director, Walter Mayo. Reviewed in Projection Room, N.Y., July 28, '37. Running time: **104 mins.**
Stella Martin Dallas. . . . .Barbara Stanwyck
Stephen Dallas. . . . . .John Boles
Laurel Dallas. . . . . .Anne Shirley
Helen. . . . . .Barbara O'Neil
Ed Munn. . . . . .Alan Hale
Mrs. Martin. . . . . .Marjorie Main
Mr. Martin. . . . . .Edmund Elton
Charlie Martin. . . . . . .George Walcott
Carrie Jenkins. . . . . . . .Gertrude Short
Richard. . . . . .Tim Holt
Mrs. Grosvenor. . . . . . .Nella Walker
Con.. . . . . .Bruce Satterlee
Con. (grown up). . . . . . .Jimmy Butler
Lee. . . . . .Jack Egger
John. . . . . .Dickie Jones
Miss Phillibrown. . . . . .Anne Shoemaker

valid today (see "Roger & Me") but that are eschewed by the filmmakers in favor of the story's more insipid emotional foundation.

Erman and writer Robert Getchell instead try to inject some levity into the maudlin proceedings, perhaps to make the film less an unre-

lenting sob story. On that front, at least, they largely succeed, thanks primarily to the winning performance by John Goodman as Stella's long-suffering admirer Ed as well as Midler's natural comic flair.

That smart streak, however, undercuts the don't-know-any-better brashness Stanwyck brought to the role and makes Stella less sympathetic. It's hard to believe, for example, that Midler would be unaware that her embarrassing display at a snooty Boca Raton club wouldn't filter back to her daughter.

The relationship between mother and daughter doesn't prove compelling enough to make the film fly on that alone. Midler and Trini Alvarado have their moments, but they have their problems as well — among them an inexplicable Canadian-sounding accent both affect.

Despite her protests to the contrary, Midler's Stella simply seems too smart and tough to engender much sympathy. Her decision to have a child out of wedlock and go it alone (Stella was married in the 1937 pic) also seems relatively tame in light of social mores circa 1990.

Goodman is more effective and, throwing in his role in "Always," has the distinction in recent months of carving out memorable performances in two otherwise-lame remakes. Collins is forgivably bland as the father, while Marsha Mason provides a warm presence in a small role as his new flame.

Based on tv's affection for film remakes, "Stella" might very well have gone that route without Midler's participation, and Erman certainly makes it feel that way. His use of long, lingering fade-outs between scenes makes one half expect to see the words "Insert commercial here."

Tech credits are unspectacular, and the sound in particular comes out garbled in some of the early scenes. John Morris' overbearing, ever-present score is in keeping with the film's overall tone. — Bril.

La Voce della Luna
(The Voice Of The Moon)
(ITALIAN-FRENCH)

Rome A Penta Distribuizione release of a C.G. Group Tiger Cinematografica/Cinemax coproduction, in association w/RAI-TV. Produced by Mario and Vittorio Cecchi Gori. Executive producers, Bruno Altissimi, Claudio Saraceni. Directed by Federico Fellini. Screenplay, Fellini, with Tullio Pinelli, Ermanno Cavazzoni, freely adapted from Cavazzoni's novel "The Poem Of Lunatics;"

camera (Technicolor), Tonino Delli Colli; editor, Nino Baragli; music, Nicola Piovani; art direction, Dante Ferretti; costumes, Maurizio Millenotti. Reviewed at CDS, Rome, Jan. 26, 1990. Running time: **120 MIN.**
Salvini. . . . . .Roberto Benigni
Prefect Gonnella. . . . . .Paolo Villaggio
Aldina. . . . . .Nadia Ottaviani
The Steamer. . . . . . . .Marisa Tomasi
Oboe player. . . . . .Sim
Aldina's sister. . . . . .Syusy Blady
Nestore. . . . . .Angelo Orlando
Also with: Dario Ghirardi (journalist), Dominique Chevalier, Nigel Harris, Vito, Eraldo Turra, Giordano Falzoni, Ferruccio Brambilla, Franco Javarone, Lorose Keller (Duchess), Uta Schmidt (grandmother).

■"The Voice Of The Moon" will be cherished in a special way by Federico Fellini fans, being almost a summation of the themes, characters and obsessions that have haunted his films since "8 1/2." Other viewers may find the film a little perplexing, so much does it build on the maestro's past work.

Story is gossamer and not all audiences will follow its meanderings raptly. Pic opened Feb. 2 at 200 sites in Italy, where its stars -- popular comics Roberto Benigni and Paolo Villaggio — are as much a drawing card as the director. Abroad it will attract the usual Fellini audiences.

Film has the twilight mood of a career drawing to a close (the director recently turned 70). For the first time, Fellini bases his film on a novel (coscripter Ermanno Cavazzoni's "The Poem Of Lunatics"), but actors and crew worked more from a skeleton outline than a shooting script, inventing scenes day by day at Rome's Pontini Studios. The loosely structured adventures of demented dreamers in a small Emilian town soon turn into a circus parade of favorite Fellini leitmotifs.

Film opens with Salvini (Benigni), poet, dreamer and visionary, communing with nature in the country. He joins a group of locals spying on a house, where a fat, middle-aged woman is performing a comical striptease for their benefit. This causes Salvini to flashback to his grandmother (Uta Schmidt), a big country woman who laughed at his funny face. He ends up in a cemetery where an oboe player (Sim) who's sleeping in a marble tomb tells the story of the ghosts who used to haunt him.

One by one, other village characters come to the fore. There is the prefect Gonnella (Villaggio), a hopeless paranoiac whose brand of lunacy is alienating and pathetic. A rough sewage worker with a handkerchief on his head fascinates Salvini with his hole drilling; Salvini is always trying to peer down wells to see what's on the other side.

He is also, obviously, hypnotized by the moon. He makes a midnight call on puffy Syusy Blady (a fine new comedienne known for her tv skits) to ogle her beautiful sister Aldina (Nadia Ottaviani) asleep. For Salvini, Aldina is the moon incarnate — and cinematographer Tonino Delli Colli's superb lighting makes us almost believe her round, glowing silver face is that of a moon-woman.

Rebuffed by Aldina, Salvini steals her sparkling slipper, which he will later try on several females and discover to his delight it fits them all. For the moment he is heartbroken, however, and takes comfort sitting on the rooftops listening to the bittersweet tale of gentle little Nestore's (Angelo Orlando) fling with a steamy manicurist (Marisa Tomasi). He marries her but can't keep up with her sexual demands, as overpowering as a runaway train. Though she leaves him for a butcher, he bears her no rancor.

Salvini, another saintly innocent, takes delight in the whole world, untouched by its evil and corruption. Pic's main set is a bitter joke by production designer Dante Ferretti — a typical Italian piazza where medieval, Renaissance and Umbertine buildings coexist with a depressing piece of Fascist architecture, a hideous modern church, choking traffic and a forest of tv antennas.

In a rousing sequence, the square comes alive in a chaotic beauty pageant, where Aldina is elected Miss Flour and Salvini is trapped under the platform. Released at last, he takes revenge on Aldina's sleazy dance partner, sparking a general chase scene. Typically, it ends with a dreamlike abruptness when Salvini is transported back to his old family home by a loving sister. Left to himself, he fearfully opens the door to an empty room and finds Nestore, urging him to come outside and see the event of the century: the sewage worker and his brothers have captured the moon and tied it down. Before it is assembled an awed crowd, a panel of authorities and tv anchormen. Finally someone shoots the glowing silver ball and as it deflates cardinals and politicians scurry away in their limousines.

Like Salvini, Gonnella is the director's alter ego, ranting against the "infection of old age," knowing

"there's not much time left." In a triumphal fantasy scene, he overcomes his fears and dances a waltz with his long-suffering consort, the Duchess d'Alba (Lorose Keller). Salvini is rewarded, too — the moon is back in the sky and at last he hears its voice, the voice of Aldina (which interrupts itself for a "commercial break").

Film is really one long dream, in which thought and poetry continually dissolve into modern chaos. Fellini's horror is evident concerning this brave new world, seen as mindless teens bopping to deafening disco music and an invasion of Japanese tourists. Then the day's noisy chaos becomes the strange, empty sensuality of the night.

The message is silence — listen to the voices and try to understand something.

Headlining a cast of weirdos, Benigni is unrecognizable — a wan elf in Dickensian spectacles. He's a cross between poet and puppet, Giacom Loepardi and Pinocchio. Tightly reined in by the dialog, so unlike the off-the-cuff ravings of his 1-man shows, Benigni still manages to inject a whimsical rush of energy into pic. Villaggio, too, puts aside most of his mannerisms to play the paranoid prefect with bitter relish.

The haunting little melodies of the background score are the work of Nicola Piovani, the perfect successor to the late Nino Rota in the Fellini oeuvre. —Yung.

Adrenaline
(FRENCH-COLOR/B&W)

Paris A Sinfonia release of a Manitou Prods. production. Produced by Yann Piquer. Directed by Yann Piquer, Jean-Marie Maddeddu, Anita Assal, John Hudson, Barthelemy Bompard, Alain Robak, Philippe Dorison. Camera (b&w, color), Bernard Cavalie; editor, Pierre Didier; music, Scoop!; art direction, Jean-Pierre Camus. Reviewed at Cannon screening room, Paris, Jan. 25, 1990. Running time: 73 MIN.

With: Jean-Marie Maddeddu, Clementine Célarié, Bernardette Coqueret, Ged Marlon, Alain Aithnard, Jean-François Gallotte, Franck Baruk.

■ "Adrenaline" is a baker's dozen of sketches with a fantasy or horror premise, made by seven directors and packaged to vie as a feature theatrical attraction. It's a motley series of mostly mediocre quality, redeemed on occasion by flashes of macabre humor and parody. Ironically, it will probably

end up quickly enough where other short efforts do — as filler on tv. Film premiered at the recent Avoriaz fantasy fest.

Many of the shorts exploit the theme of inanimate objects which acquire a deadly will of their own: a nearly empty subway train runs out of control; a ceiling descends inexorably on a bedroom occupant; an empty wine bottle attacks a human; aged automobiles solemnly roll towards a car cemetery with their helpless drivers locked inside to accompany them into the compressing machines.

Among the better entries, played for sinister laughs, are Anita Assal and John Hudson's "T.V. Buster" in which a boob tube couple, personally harangued by the images on their tv screen, call in a specialist to exorcize their set. "Corridor" by Alain Robak (whose gore feature "Baby Blood" got a special mention at Avoriaz) is a lampoon of the Indiana Jones-style booby-trap gauntlet setpiece, reset in an house being visited by a potential buyer.

Yann Piquer and Jean-Marie Maddeddu crown the collection with "Physical Culture,"a good 1-joke item about a man who literally has his head punched into a shapeless pulp in order to exhibit it in an abstract art gallery. Short separately has won numerous prizes, notably in the shorts competition at the 1988 Cannes film festival. —Len.

Ein Wolk van Groen
(A Cloud Of Green)
(DUTCH)
(DOCU)

Rotterdam An IAF release of a Rolf Orthel production. Executive producers, Sandra van Beek, Anet van Barneveld, Toni Garcia. Directed by Kees Hin. Camera (color, b&w, 16m), Jules van den Steenhoven, Frans Bromet, Rob Brouwer; editor, Kees Linthorst, Frans van de Staak; sound, Piotr van Dijk, Noah van der Lely, Jan Wouter van Reijen. Reviewed at Rotterdam Film Festival, Jan. 26, 1990. Running time: 87 MIN.

With: Aus Greidanus, Carol Linssen, Johan Leysen.

■ "Ein Wolk van Groen" is a Dutch docu about very Dutch subject, made for the 111th anniversary of Dutch weekly magazine, "Green Amsterdammer." Pity that Holland is such a small country and that so few people will see this witty, sophisticated film about a Dutch institution.

When asked to direct this anni picture, Kees Hin decided to focus

on the publication's (too few) readers. They are intellectuals, liberals not committed to any one dogma, critical thinkers, worriers. Hin found in his subjects an affinity with Hamlet, who thought so much and did so little — so Hamlet becomes a character in the film.

Film works through an amazing interplay of the most diverse images, a few interviews, a mosaic of still lives, some old movie clips, and of course Hamlet, the individualist. Hin skillfully, and very gently, pulls everybody's leg, so that would could easily have been a boring compilation of old material, journalistic coups and gossip for the initiated becomes classy entertainment.
—Wall.

Streets

Hollywood A Concorde production and release. Produced by Andy Ruben. Executive producer, Roger Corman. Directed by Katt Shea Ruben. Screenplay, Katt Shea Ruben, Andy Ruben; camera (Foto-Kem color), Phedon Papamichael; editor, Stephen Mark; music, Aaron Davis; sound, Bill Robbins; production design, Virginia Lee; art direction, Johan Le Tenoux; set design, Abigail Scheuer; set decoration, Michelle Munoz; costume design, Fionn; associate producer, Rodman Flender; assistant director, Terry Edwards; 2d unit directors, John Wentworth, Jon Winfrey; 2d unit camera, Janusz Kaminski. Reviewed at Van der Veer Photo Effects screening room, Burbank, Calif., Jan. 23, 1990. MPAA Rating: R. Running time: 83 MIN.

Dawn	Christina Applegate
Sy	David Mendenhall
Lumley	Eb Lottimer
Policewoman on horse	Starr Andreeff
Bob	Patrick Richwood
Dawn's blond roommate	Kady Tran
Dawn's tattooed roommate	Julie Jay
Elf	Mel Castelo
Allen	Alan Stock
Paramedic	Rhetta Green
Lieutenant	Kay Lenz

■ Despite its B-film framework involving a maniacal killer stalking street kids, "Streets" transcends its genre with a gritty and affecting portrait of a teenage throwaway (Christina Applegate of tv's "Married... With Children") struggling to exist in L.A.'s demimonde.

Director Katt Shea Ruben's previous work has shown promise that this film builds on, and she should move on to major pics shortly. The Concorde release opened to mild boxoffice on Jan. 19 in the Atlanta area.

Ruben, who scripted with her producer-husband Andy Ruben, clearly had more ambitious things in mind than just another Concorde thriller in which nubile girls are stalked and murdered.

Applegate's solid performance in her first starring feature as the jaded but still sensitive Dawn, who sells sex to survive and shoots up heroin to get through the day, speaks volumes about the scuzzy side of L.A. life, and the director's deft touch with actors gives the film a strong feeling of credibility.

Working with a minimal budget and a 19-day shooting sked, Ruben conjures up an impressive, subtly fantastic atmosphere with the stylish assistance of lenser Phedon Papamichael.

Giving an ironic golden sheen to the daytime scenes and a sinister blue cast to the night scenes, "Streets" is always compelling to watch and wordlessly creates a spooky vision of urban alienation.

The Rubens' script is admirably short on exposition and character monologs, building the particulars of Applegate's horrifying life through low-key, incremental observation and dialog.

When she remarks that she survives by eating dead animals found by the side of the road, or tries to explain the difference between prostitution and her casual "whoring," the filmmakers convey the character in a moving yet unsentimental fashion.

Yet since this is a Roger Corman film, neorealism isn't enough, and there has to be a psycho killer (vampirish policeman Eb Lottimer), who preys on street kids and becomes obsessed with eliminating Applegate.

Although the situation is clichéd and somewhat farfetched, the female director avoids any feeling of exploitiveness, making the murders and attempted rapes powerfully ugly and chilling.

With something of the feel of a low-budget "Klute," although without much insight into the character of the killer, "Streets" has a compelling pattern of visual suspense, greatly aided by Papamichael's resourceful photography of tawdry Santa Monica and Venice locations and by Lottimer's creepy, Rutger Hauer-like presence.

Though the film would have been better if it had managed to explore the complex social causes of a street kid's plight rather than focusing so much on one aberrant cop, there are a certain languor and artiness that creep into Ruben's direction at times, and the suspense plot provides a counterbalance.

Among the solid supporting cast members are David Mendenhall,

appealing without being wimpy as a straight kid from Santa Barbara who becomes drawn into Applegate's life and tries to help her escape it; Patrick Richwood, as a street character whose sweetness meets a sadistic response from Lottimer; Mel Castelo, Kady Tran and Julie Jay as girls menaced by the killer, and Alan Stock, as Applegate's gentle, stuttering john.

Tech credits are fine considering the budget, including the inventive production design by Virginia Lee and the eerie music by Aaron Davis.

Besides its sheer dramatic value, the film also should serve as a warning to kids across the country about the unglamorous realities of L.A. street life and as an effective diploma for its director and producer as they graduate from Corman's stable. — *Mac.*

Love At Large

Park City An Orion Pictures release. Produced by David Blocker. Written and directed by Alan Rudolph. Camera (color), Elliot Davis; editor, Lisa Churgin; music, Mark Isham; sound (Dolby), Susumu Tokunow; production design, Steven Legler; costume design, Ingrid Ferrin; associate producer, Stuart Besser; casting, Pam Dixon. Reviewed at U.S. Film Festival, Park City, Utah, Jan. 27, 1990. MPAA Rating: R. Running time: **97 MIN.**

Harry Dobbs	Tom Berenger
Stella	Elizabeth Perkins
Miss Dolan	Anne Archer
King/MacGraw	Ted Levine
Mrs. King	Annette O'Toole
Mrs. MacGraw	Kate Capshaw
Doris	Ann Magnuson
Marty	Barry Miller
Art	Kevin J. O'Connor
Rick	Neil Young

■**Latest Alan Rudolph film is a tongue-in-cheek take on the gumshoe genre that mostly seeks to explore the perplexing possibilities of love. A hard pic to get across in a marketing campaign, it nonetheless offers many moments of delight and should do steady if discreet business with specialized audiences.**

Recruiting Mark Isham to create the sophisticated, sexy score that sets the tone for a moody fantasy lensed in rainy Portland, Ore., Rudolph sets up a bunch of half-cocked, lovelorn characters and lets them bumble around entertainingly.

Wealthy and idle Miss Dolan (Anne Archer) hires rumpled cheap detective Harry Dobbs (Tom Berenger) to trail a lover she underdescribes. Berenger picks the wrong guy and ends up pursuing a quarry far more interesting than the intend-

ed — this one's not only married, he's got two separate families.

Meanwhile, he's being followed by novice detective Stella (Elizabeth Perkins), who's been hired by his unreasonably jealous, crockery-throwing girlfriend, Doris (Ann Magnuson).

Berenger and Perkins fall in love, but not easily. When she slaps him, he observes, "That's the first time we've touched."

As pic progresses, its story convolutions become rather hard to make sense of, but the plot never seems to be the point.

It's the endless round of illogical but irresistible liaisons and the characters' own unfathomable peculiarities that form the basis of this dizzy sendup of romance.

Berenger, with his squashed hat and growling delivery, is slyly amusing as Dobbs, while Perkins exudes a flinty, provocative chemistry that ignites in scenes with Berenger and Ted Levine, who's most intriguing in a dual role as an urban businessman and rough-hewn rancher who can scarcely figure himself out.

Archer is certainly arch as the absurdly pampered and melodramatic Miss Dolan, but musician Neil Young hits a flat note in a cameo as Dolan's lover that takes him way out on a ledge.

Production designer Steven Legler and cinematographer Elliot Davis make first-rate contributions to pic's beguiling mystery and atmosphere. —*Daws.*

House Party

Park City A New Line Cinema release. Executive producer, Gerald Olson. Produced by Warrington Hudlin. Written and directed by Reginald Hudlin. Camera (Metrocolor), Peter Deming; editor, Earl Watson; music, Marcus Miller; sound (Dolby), Oliver Moss; production design, Bryan Jones; art direction, Susan Richardson; set decoration, Molly Flanegin; costume design, Harold Evans; assistant director, Kelly St. Rode. Reviewed at U.S. Film Festival, Park City, Utah, Jan. 20, 1990. MPAA Rating: R. Running time: **100 MIN.**

Kid	Christopher Reid
Pop	Robin Harris
Play	Christopher Martin
Bilal	Martin Lawrence
Sidney	Tisha Campbell
Sharane	A.J. Johnson
Stab	Paul Anthony
Pee-Wee	Bowlegged Lou
Zilla	B. Fine

■**"House Party" captures contemporary black teen culture in a way that's fresh, commercial and very catchy. New Line should have a hit.**

Filmmaking team of Reggie and Warrington Hudlin make a strikingly assured debut feature blending comedy, hip-hop music and dancing in a pic that moves to a kinetic, nonstop rhythm.

Rap duo Kid 'N' Play (Christopher Reid and Christopher Martin) play colleagues in rhyme, trying to get away with throwing a booming house party the night Play's parents are away and Kid is grounded by his Pop (Robin Harris) for getting in a fight at school.

En route to the party, Kid is pursued by the school thugs (rap trio Full Force), and all of them are pursued by the neighborhood cops. Then unwitting Kid becomes an object of desire for both of the young ladies Play is trying to impress (Tisha Campbell and A.J. Johnson).

Writer-director Reggie Hudlin, who expanded "House Party" from a short he made while a student at Harvard, injects pic with the cartoonish style and captivating rhythm of today's rap scene in a way that will be a major draw for teens, who'll manage to see it despite its R rating (for colloquial language and sexual references).

Hudlin demonstrates a rare degree of talent on all fronts, from the fresh, funny script loaded with black slang and gleeful cultural references to a flair for visual comedy that presents itself at every turn.

Camerawork is astonishingly fluid, smooth and expressive, with the vantage point always seeming to be in the right place, particularly in the tight, riotous party scenes.

From a production standpoint, pic easily outshines its $2.5-million budget and appears to lack nothing in casting or locations. Shot in L.A., with most outdoor lensing done at night in suburbs, it succeeds in achieving a nonspecific look.

Christopher Reid as Kid (also his musical persona) makes a winning lead with his tree-stump haircut and gentle mugging; the comedy starts as soon as you see him. Harris delivers a fresh performance as the slouchy, widowed dad who doles out discipline.

Pic takes an admirable stand on drugs, drinking and sexual responsibility, delivering the message without stifling the beat. Production design and costumes are sharp. Editing by Earl Watson is first-rate. Soundtrack sales on Motown label should be brisk. — *Daws.*

Return Home
(AUSTRALIAN)

Sydney A Musical Films production, produced with the assistance of the Australian Film Commission and Film Victoria. (Intl. sales, Kim Lewis Marketing.) Produced by Cristina Pozzan. Directed by Ray Argall. Screenplay, Argall; camera (color), Mandy Walker; editor, Ken Sallows; music, Joe Camilleri; sound, Bronwyn Murphy; production design, Kerith Homes; production manager, Elisa Argenzio; assistant director, Euan Keddie; casting, Gregg Apps. Reviewed at Mosman screening room, Sydney, Jan 23, 1990. (Also at Berlin Film Festival, Panorama section.) Running time: 87 MIN.

Noel McKenzie . . . . Dennis Coard
Steve McKenzie . . . . . Frankie J. Holden
Gary Wilson . . . . Ben Mendelsohn
Judy McKenzie . . . . . . Micki Camilleri
Wendy . . . . Rachel Rains
Barry Marshall . . . . Alan Fletcher
Brian . . . . Paul Nestor
Gail . . . . Michelle Stanley

■Cinematographer Ray Argall, who has won plaudits for his camerawork of "Wrong World" and "The Prisoner Of St. Petersburg" among others, makes an assured crossover to the director's chair with "Return Home," a modest but extremely impressive new film which rings true in every minute detail. Critical support should help this little gem find an appreciative audience on the arthouse circuit.

Newcomer Dennis Coard plays Noel, a successful big city insurance broker, whose personal life appears to be in tatters after a recent divorce. He decides to go home, back to the beachside suburb in Adelaide where he grew up at his father's gas station with older brother, Steve.

Steve (Frankie J. Holden) still runs the gas station, in partnership with his hard-working wife, Judy (Micki Camilleri), but things aren't going well since the place isn't on a main road and a new shopping mall has taken trade away; the couple are struggling to pay their bills, yet live a contented life with their two small children.

The other principal character in the film is Gary (Ben Mendelsohn), Steve's teenage mechanic, a well-meaning, awkward youth who's had a falling out with Wendy (Rachel Rains), his girlfriend. These teenagers are light years away from the teens that usually inhabit films these days: they're painfully shy and gauche with each other.

But, then, all the characters in "Return Home" ring true. Argall, who wrote as well as directed, has created a group of instantly recognizable, and very Australian, types, whose speech patterns and actions are totally naturalistic. There's no melodrama in the story, and no false note. Noel hangs out with Steve, Gary and Judy; he observes their lives, and evidently sees in them what he's lost in his own world of the rat race. He goes back to the city for a while, but, at fadeout, returns home again.

For some audiences, the story Argall is telling with such understatement may seem too slight and too ordinary. As a result, pic will need most careful treatment, and critical support is essential. Its first public outing will be at the Berlin fest (Panorama section) where it deserves to make its mark.

The low-key performances perfectly fit the mood Argall is aiming for.

Dennis Coard, who worked for Australia's telephone company for 15 years before he decided to take up acting, is a natural as Noel; through his eyes, we observe this little backwater and its people. Frankie J. Holden and Micki Camillari are perfectly cast as the working-class couple battling to pay their bills, and Ben Mendelsohn (remembered as the young tearaway in "The Year My Voice Broke") is touching as the vulnerable Gary.

Mandy Walker's camerawork captures the details of the suburb with loving affection; Ken Sallows' editing is on the button, and Kerith Holmes' production design is in keeping with the overall mood. Music is a combination of rock (played by Gary in his hot-rod car) and classical (preferred by Noel).

Clearly, Ray Argall is a talent to watch out for in future. — Strat.

Tiden har inget namn
(Time Has No Name)
(SWEDISH-DOCU)

Lübeck, West Germany A Stefan Jarl presentation of Stefan Jarl Film production with the Swedish Film Institute, others. Produced, written and directed by Jarl. Camera, Per Källberg; editor, Annette Lykke- Lundberg; music, Ulf Dageby; sound (Dolby), Bengt Andersson. Reviewed at 31st Nordic Film Days, Lübeck (West Germany), Nov. 3, 1989. Running time: 61 MIN.

■Like other Stefan Jarl documentaries ("The Soul Is Stronger Than The World," "The Threat," etc.), "Time Has No Name" is an indictment, in the guise of a documentary, of man's violence against nature.

Jarl admits to juggling facts to suit his cause: "I am 100% subjective. Commonly accepted truth as such is of no interest to me," he says. Jarl has trouble finding a distributor, even at home in Sweden.

Offshore fests, however, usually welcome him and bestow prizes on his films. "Time Has No Name" may well appeal to the limited environmental activist audience, but it will need a bent for enigmatic poetry at the same time. (Jarl quotes Pier Paolo Pasolini thus in the main titles: "There is no other poetry than action.")

"Time" shows us, more or less, a day in the life of an elderly farm couple in the province of Skane. Teodor and Asta Svensson wake up to the radio's droning of disasters (all environmental and clearly rigged) before tending to kitchen, feeding their pigs and cows, milking and doing field chores. They hardly open their mouths except when Teodor gives vent to misanthropy of a kind not unusual to old men.

Shots of landscapes and animals and closeups of working hands interchange endlessly, but not hurriedly. Jarl continues to run counter to cinematic wisdom: Not a single shot lasts fewer than seven seconds.

The poetic qualities of Jarl's cinematic art are such that his message of doom is likely to impress far less than his obvious yen for Zen. Jarl is a terrible preacher, but he is a firstrate artist. That combination is a dangerous one, but Jarl is as unafraid as he is stubborn. — Kell.

Blue Steel

Park City An MGM/UA Distribution release from United Artists, in association with Vestron Pictures, of a Lightning Pictures presentation of an Edward R. Pressman production. Executive producer, Lawrence Kasanoff. Produced by Pressman, Oliver Stone. Coproduced by Michael Rausch. Directed by Kathryn Bigelow. Screenplay, Bigelow, Eric Red; camera (color), Amir Mokri; editor, Lee Percy; music, Brad Feidel; sound, Tom Frandau; production design, Toby Corbett; costume design, Richard Schissler; associate producers, Michael Flynn, Diane Schneier; casting, Risa Bramon, Billy Hopkins. Reviewed at U.S. Film Festival, Park City, Utah, Jan. 26, 1990. (Also in Berlin Film Festival, Panorama section.) MPAA Rating: R. Running time: 102 MIN.

Megan Turner . . . . Jamie Lee Curtis
Eugene Hunt . . . . Ron Silver
Nick Mann . . . . Clancy Brown
Tracy . . . . Elizabeth Peña
Mrs. Turner . . . . Louise Fletcher
Mr. Turner . . . . Philip Bosco

■A taut, relentless thriller that hums with an electric current of outrage, "Blue Steel" should shoot down a sizable chunk of boxoffice for MGM/UA.

Director and cowriter Kathryn Bigelow makes the most of her hook — the use of a female star (Jamie Lee Curtis) in a tough action pic — by stressing the character's vulnerability in remarkable early scenes that galvanize audience sympathy.

Most interesting is the way the character's range seems to explode against all the abusive, victimizing men in the picture and a system in which attitudes are stacked against her.

As rookie cop Megan Turner, Curtis is hit with doubts and resistance from all corners, then suspended after she kills an armed robber (Tom Sizemore) her first night out and no gun is found at the scene.

The psycho bystander who picked the gun up (Ron Silver) starts commiting serial murders with bullets he's carved her name onto, and Curtis, under deep suspicion, gets dragged back onto the force to help find him.

The day she loses her badge, the lonely Curtis is easy prey for a charming suitor, a commodities trader named Eugene (Silver) who also happens to be the serial killer.

Curtis gives an eerily effective performance as Turner, getting across in palpable waves her shaky determination and an inner steeliness born of anger against her abusive father (Philip Bosco).

Script is at its weakest where the villain (Silver) is concerned — the way he picks up Turner's name and her trail defies credibility, and his characterization as a schizophrenic nutso with violent religious hallucinations is a writeoff.

Even so, pic lacks nothing for menace and suspense, and should score big audience points with its frightening, explosively violent second half.

Director seems fascinated with violence, as blood has not been splattered this sensuously and abundantly since Sam Peckinpah.

Brad Feidel's score is heartstoppingly effective and production values are high. — Daws.

A Matter Of Degrees

Park City, Utah A Backbeat production in association with New Front Films, Linus Associates, George Gund and Fujisankei Communications Intl. Produced by Roy Kissin, Randall Poster. Coproducer, Lynn Goldner. Directed by W. T. Morgan. Screenplay, Poster, Jack Mason, Morgan; camera (color), Paul Ryan; editor, Curtiss Clayton, Charlie Mullin; music, Jim Dunbar; sound, Fred Burham; production design, Mark Friedberg; art direction, Ginger Tougas; set decoration, Bonita Flanders; assistant director, Raoul Madera; associate producers, Paul Moen, John H. Stout, Barbara Katz. Reviewed at U.S. Film Festival, Park City, Utah, Jan 22, 1990. No MPAA Rating. Running time: **100 MIN.**

Max. . . . . .Arye Gross
Zeno. . . . . .Tom Sizemore
Kate. . . . . .Judity Hoag
Wells. . . . . .Wendell Pierce
Isabelle. . . . . .Christina Haag
Peter Downs. . . . . .John Doe

■An indie project developed through the Sundance Institute, "A Matter Of Degrees" enters uncharted territory — the dilemmas of disaffected college students in the '80s — and bumbles around in it, coming up with a few bright passages in a mostly uneven film. Commercial prospects appear to be slight.

On the plus side are the film's soundtrack — chockful of the alternative music of contempo bands like Firehose, the Minutemen and Fetchin' Bones — and a chrismatic supporting turn by Tom Sizemore as a student and part-time mechanic with a passion for steel.

But the story's protagonist, reluctant graduating senior Maxwell Glass (Arye Gross) doesn't know what he wants to be and neither does the film.

"Degrees" is at its best when it relaxes into being a rambling coming-of-age story about friends approaching graduation into a world they're not ready for.

But it spends much of its time trying to be funny and reaching to be hip, posturing its nebulous characters as holdouts against Reagan-era values but not finding anything compelling for them to represent.

Max' rants against the "apathy" of the times are neither fresh nor eloquent, and one sometimes wonders if he is supposed to be a parody of a nonconformist.

Shot on location at the Brown U. campus in Providence, R.I., pic follows a group of students whose on-and-off activism centers around preserving the campus radio station, domain of renegade deejay Peter Downs (rock musician-actor John Doe).

Pic begins with an attempt at striking a satiric tone — a series of MBA-bound students sit in the same "inverview" chair and describe their goals, in contrast to Max, who has none — that's soon abandoned for various other styles of storytelling.

Whatever poignancy the characters evoke is undercut by an improbable, commercial-style big finish.

Overall, pic has the insular feel of a project made for a small circle of friends, many of whom where in on it.

Director W. T. Morgan, who made the undergroud rock docu "The Unheard Music," contributes some amusing touches.

Lensing is attractive, and production design by Mark Friedberg is apt and amusing. Soundtrack also includes selections by Doe, Miracle Legion, Throwing Muses, the Lemonheads and Yo La Tengo. — *Daws.*

Bedroom Eyes II

New York A Vidmark release of a Distant Horizon and Anant Singh presentaton. Executive producer, Singh. Produced and directed by Chuck Vincent. Screenplay, Gerard Ciccoritti; camera (Agfa Gevaert color; Technicolor prints), Larry Revene; editor, James Davalos; music supervision, Budd Carr; sound, Larry Provost, Dale Whitman; art direction, Todd Rutt; costumes, Jeffrey Wallach; assistant director, Kathleen Phelan; production manager, Chip Lambert; associate producer, Mickey Nivelli; casting, Edd Rockis. Reviewed on Vidmark vidcassette, N.Y., Jan. 12, 1990. MPAA Rating: R. Running time: **87 MIN.**

Harry Ross. . . . . .Wings Hauser
Carolyn Ross. . . . . . . .Kathy Shower
Sophie. . . . . .Linda Blair
JoBeth. . . . . .Jane Hamilton
Vinnie. . . . . .Joe Giardina
Matthew. . . . . .Kevin Thomsen
Gwendolyn. . . . . .Jennifer Delora
Det. Briar. . . . . .Harvey Siegel
Karen. . . . . .Maraya Chase
Michelle. . . . . .Kimberly Taylor

■This sequel to a 1986 Canadian- made thriller is notable for snappy pacing and a rather complicated plotline. Helmer Chuck Vincent downplays his usual skin quotient, however.

Wings Hauser plays a fairly sympathetic role for a change, an unscrupulous stockbroker married to art dealer Kathy Shower who decides to have a romance with Linda Blair after he spies on Shower in a sexual tryst with an artist.

All hell breaks loose when Blair is murdered and both Hauser and Shower are prime suspects. Key to unravelling the mystery is a wall portrait of Hauser's late first wife,

which closely resembles one of the other characters.

En route to a bittersweet finale cast does a good job in alternately creating sympathy and suspicion. Vincent's favorite actress, Jane Hamilton, pops up in a key supporting role. It's all played on the surface, but plot is intriguing enough to hold one's interest. — *Lor.*

What The Moon Saw
(AUSTRALIAN)

Sydney A Boulevard Films production. Executive producer, Peter Boyle. Produced by Frank Howson. Directed by Pino Amenta. Screenplay, Howson; camera (color), David Connell; editor, Marc Van Buren; music, John Capek; sound, Andrew Ramage; production design, Otello Stolfo; costumes, Rose Chong; line producer, Barbi Taylor; coproducer, James Michael Vernon; casting, Greg Apps; assistant director, John Wild; production manager, Deborah Samuels. Reviewed at Mosman Screening Room, Sydney, Jan 24, 1990. (Also in Berlin Film Festival, Kinderfest section.) Running time: **96 MIN.**

Steven Wilson. . . . . . .Andrew Shephard
Pearl Wilson (Gran). . . . . . .Pat Evison
Mr. Zachary. . . . . .Max Phipps
Emma Pearce. . . . . . . .Danielle Spencer
Jim Shilling. . . . . .Kim Gyngell
Tony. . . . . .Mark Hennessy
Mrs. Melrose. . . . . .Jan Friedl
Also with: Kurt Ludesher (George), Adrian Wright (Kurt), Murray Fahey (Ali), Ross Thompson (Hardy), Gary Sweet (Wilson), Nicki Paull (Night).

■"What The Moon Saw" is predominantly a film for children, but it aims for adult appeal as well, especially at adults fond of old-style theater. Unfortunately, the uncertain direction makes it an iffy commercial prospect though it could have a life on video.

Basic idea is a good one. Young Steven, attractively played by Andrew Shepherd, is sent from the country to Melbourne by his mother and his crippled father. His colorful Grandma (Pat Evison), a former showgirl ("Best legs on the Tivoli Circuit") now sells tickets at a city theater currently staging a pantomime production of "Sinbad."

Though the production is amateurish and tatty, the boy's eyes are opened to a wonderful world. He befriends the young lead actors, and also the theater's cleaner and candy-seller, but falls foul of the theater's owner, a cranky character called Mr. Zachary. Latter is given over-the-top treatment by Max Phipps.

There was a promising film in this notion, but what emerges is disappointingly unfocused. The relationship between the child and his delightful old Gran is a promising

start, but little is made of this as the film progresses. Instead, we get lengthy scenes of the stage production and of a dream in which the child imagines himself as Sinbad experiencing various adventures.

A few questions remain unanswered, too. The ominous opening scene, in which the boy is put aboard a country bus, suggests he's being sent away from home for a long time, perhaps forever; but it turns out to be only for the school holidays. Nor is the father's disability referred to again, or the reason he's apparently estranged from his seemingly benign old Mum.

Kim Gyngell does an OK turn as the show's author, accused at one point of including Communist propaganda and a satire of Ronald Reagan, but his impersonation of Groucho Marx for the dream sequence is indulgent.

Danielle Spencer is charming as the femme lead, and warbles "I Only Have Eyes For You" appealingly.

The film is technically fine though John Capek's music tends to underline every point made in script and direction.

This is the second production of Boulevard Films (after last year's "Boulevard Of Broken Dreams") and, like its predecessor, it indicates a fascination for show business in all its forms. This one avoids the sentimentality that marred the first film, but the narrative thread proves too tenuous to carry the story, and children may well become fidgety. They may respond, though, to the scene in which the courageous moppet dares to call the theater owner "a tyrant" to his face. — *Strat.*

Why Me?

New York A Triumph release from Epic Pictures of a Sarlui/Diamant presentation of a Carolina production. Produced by Marjorie Israel. Executive producer, Irwin Yablans, Directed by Gene Quintano. Screenplay, Donald E. Westlake, Leonard Mass Jr., from Westlake's novel; camera (Consolidated color), Peter Deming; editor, Alan Belsam; music, Basil Poledouris; sound (Dolby), Rob Janiger; production design, Woody Grocker; assistant director, Yudi Bennett; production manager, Robert P. Schneider; 2d unit director, David Lipman; 2d unit camera, Walt Lloyd, Reviewed at Magno Preview 4 screening room, N.Y., July 27, 1989. MPAA Rating: R. Running time: **88 MIN.**

Gus Cardinal. . . . .Christophe Lambert
Bruno. . . . . .Christopher Lloyd
June. . . . . .Kim Greist
Inspector Mahoney. . . . . .J.T. Walsh
Ralph. . . . . .Michael J. Pollard
Benjy. . . . . .Tony Plana
Tiny. . . . . .John Hancock
Also with: Wendel Meldrum, Rene Assam, Gregory Millar, Lawrence Tierney, Jill Terashita, Thomas Callaway.

■Caper comedy "Why Me?" is a frantic but only intermittently funny U.S. vehicle for French star Christophe Lambert. Gallic reaction should be brisk but pic shapes as a weak entry for American audiences.

Film just opened in Paris and is due out May 4 in the U.S.

Pic is a throwback to '60s-style films — not surprising since it's based on a followup novel to Donald Westlake's "The Hot Rock," which spawned the 1972 Fox film and was followed up in '74 by "Bank Shot."

With aid of rewrite, Lambert follows in the footsteps of previous pics' Robert Redford and George C. Scott as the charming con man who's an expert safecracker. Teamed with sidekick Bruno (Christopher Lloyd in a variety of wacky costumes) and g.f. June (Kim Greist), he steals the cursed ruby, the Byzantine Fire. This sets up a film-long chase around Los Angeles for the stone, wanted by the police, other criminals, the Turkish government and a nutty group of Armenian terrorists.

Helmer Gene Quintano has fun with the knockabout chases and slapstick (often using distorting camera angles) but this material is old hat. "A Fish Called Wanda" proved the traditional caper film isn't dead, but "Why Me?" lacks its inspired casting and hilarious bits.

Lambert isn't funny in the lead role, though his scary stuntwork dangling from a skyscraper in the finale is impressive (and, again, well-suited to French audiences, being in a Jean-Paul Belmondo mold). Rest of cast plays it overly cutesy, except for J.T. Walsh who's effective as the mean police chief.

Tech credits are first-rate, with a bouncy score by Basil Poledouris.

—Lor.

Sundown: The Vampire In Retreat

Palm Springs, Calif. A Vestron production. Produced by Jef Richard. Executive producer, Dan Ireland. Director, Anthony Hickox. Screenplay, Hickox, John Burgess; camera (color), Levie Isaacs; editor, Chris Cibelli; music, Richard Stone; sound (Dolby), Jon Earl Stein; production design, David Brian Miller; art director, Fernando Altschul; assistant director, Jonathan Tzachor. Reviewed at the Palm Springs Film Festival, Jan. 13, 1990. MPAA Rating: R. Running time: **104 MIN.**

Count Mardulak. . . . . . .David Carradine

David Harrison. . . . . .Jim Metzler
Sarah. . . . . .Morgan Brittany
Shane. . . . . .Maxwell Caulfield
Milt. . . . . .M. Emmet Walsh
Sandy. . . . . .Deborah Foreman
Van Helsing. . . . . . . .Bruce Campbell
Jack. . . . . .Dana Ashbrook
Jefferson. . . . . .John Ireland
Alice. . . . . .Elizabeth Gracen

■"Sundown" is a vampire-comedy-Western-daytime soap without a moment of wit or logic in it. U.S. theatrical release is most unlikely.

Shot in Moab, Utah, "Sundown" is about bloodsuckers who try to get straight by forming a desert community around an artificial plasma plant that churns out a yellow protein for them to drink instead of human blood.

We are treated to the unpleasant sight of a town full of sallow-skinned uglies cringing from the desert sun in sunglasses, hats and too many clothes.

Into town to fix the malfunctioning plasma plant comes a bland yuppie engineer (Jim Metzler) and his big-eyed wife (Morgan Brittany), who behaves as if she's escaped from a romance novel. She secretly lusts after her husband's college buddy, Shane (Maxwell Caulfield), who's secretly the father of one of her children and is now a vampire working at the plasma plant.

These suburban annoyances get caught in the middle of a showdown between David Carradine, the creator of the vampire Betty Ford Clinic, and Shane and Jefferson (John Ireland), who want to go back to preying on human beings and have armed their band of gunslingers with wooden bullets so they can go up against the other vampires.

That could have been fun, but it takes director Anthony Hickox a full hour of dreadful dialog and inane situations to get to the action, and then it's badly shot. The few moments of gruesome special effects are like fireworks that turn out to be quick-fizzling duds.

There are some interesting scenes with rabid little bats created by Tony Gardner, and when filming is done from the bat's red-filtered point of view as they zero in on prey, it's quite effective.

The cast seems to be in a conspiracy against acting. Most of the bit players apparently were rounded up in Moab. The mishmash of period costumes, cars and furnishings that passes for production design is offensive to the eye and the senses, and if there is a bad choice to make in framing, shot sequence or guid-

ance to an actor, Hickox goes for it with unerring instinct. — Daws.

A Better Tomorrow III (Love And Death In Saigon) (HONG KONG)

Chicago A Golden Princess presentation of a Film Workshop production. Produced and directed by Tsui Hark. Screenplay, Tai Fu-Ho, Leung Yiu-Ming; camera (color), Wong Wing-Hang; music, Lowell Lo; art direction, Luk Tse-Fung; production managers, Andy Ma, Shirley Lau; stunt coordinators, Lau Fong-Sei, Lau Chi-Ho; associate producer, Rudolf Chiu. Reviewed at Film Center of the School of the Art Institute, Chicago, Jan. 13, 1990. No MPAA Rating. Running time: **100 MIN.**

Cheung Chi-Keung (Mark). .Chow Yun-Fat
Chow Ying-Kit (Kitty Chow). . .Anita Mui
Cheung Chi-Mun (Mun). . . . .Tony Leung
Ho Cheung-Ching. . . . . .Saburo Tokito
Pat. . . . . .Cheng Wai Lan
Uncle. . . . . .Shek Kin
Ling. . . . . .Maggie Cheung

■Admirers of John Woo's Hong Kong gangster blockbusters "A Better Tomorrow I & II" undoubtedly will be satisfied by this exotic prequel, though Tsui Hark has taken the series in a somewhat surprising direction with this entry, scaling down the action and tossing in a romantic subplot.

By rights, this highly entertaining film, which blends shameless melodrama, low comedy, hyperbolic action sequences and bigger-than-life performances, should find a viable audience in the West. Unfortunately, despite the fact that all three pics have been major hits in Asia, market here for these and other Hong Kong actioners currently is limited to Chinatown theaters and nonprofit film societies, where they are all the rage among cineastes.

As the alternate title, "Love And Death In Saigon," suggests, pic takes place in Vietnam (for the most part) during the chaotic withdrawal of U.S. troops in 1974. This ambitious setting gives Hark the opportunity to enlarge his canvas significantly and move away from the claustrophobic milieu of warring gangster clans defined in the first two films.

Pic's basic plot follows the efforts of amiable yet deadly Hong Kong hustler Mark (Chow Yun-Fat), who travels to Saigon to secure exit visas for his uncle and cousin. Needless to say, he doesn't accomplish this by standing in long lines at the customs office.

Requiring large sums of cash for bribery, he becomes involved in

smuggling U.S. currency with his cousin Mun (Tony Leung) and black market temptress Kitty Chow (Anita Mui).

This scheme leads to the film's most spectacular action sequence when the trio is doublecrossed by a sleazy North Vietnamese Army sergeant and required to outgun what seems to be a full regiment of soldiers. Only cognoscenti of Hong Kong-style screen carnage can accurately imagine the outlandish scope of the violence that ensues.

During this orgy of destruction (peculiarly scored with low-key, ominous music — as is the rest of the film), Mui surprisingly takes the lead, protecting Mark and Mun while putting on an impressive show of force. In many ways, Mui emerges as the most memorable performer in the film. Even in her love scenes, she seems almost invulnerable.

Topliner Chow Yun-Fat is unusually subdued in this outing, though he does have a few moments in classic form during a climactic gun battle near the end of the film, striding in slow motion through a burning house in his trademark unbuttoned trenchcoat, calmly looking for someone to shoot.

The action scenes that serve as denouement to "Love And Death In Saigon" are almost overwhelming by Western standards, but they are subtle in comparison to the kill-fest that capped "A Better Tomorrow II." — Brin.

Scherzo Furioso (DUTCH)

Amsterdam A Classics Film release of a Grace Films production. Produced by Ank Muller. Written and directed by Marianna Dikker. Camera (color, 16m), Wouter Suyderhoud; editor, Maurits Guépin; sound, Lukas Boeke. Reviewed at the Movies theater, Amsterdam, Jan. 9, 1990. Running time: **62 MIN.**

Laurens. . . . . .Hans Dagelet
Stephanie. . . . . .Will van Kralingen

■"Scherzo Furioso" is an elegant, witty, ironic medium-length feature whose awkward length may help for tv exposure but impede any theatrical chances.

Pic has the casual mastery of detail in acting and direction that is the hallmark of good cinema.

Hans Dagelet and Will Van Kralingen turn in beautiful performances as an artist couple. They are in handsome middle age, charming, sexy, financially well off. For their eighth wedding anniversary they decide to throw a party.

Though they seem the ideal couple, there is strain. Dagelet takes the expression "modern marriage" as license to bed all females. His mate doesn't seem to mind, but then she surprises everybody at the party by announcing in an ironically charming speech that she is leaving Dagelet for a new, unknown, lover that very night, after she helps clean up.

Dagelet, uncomprehending, is hurt, cueing a quarrel. Film comes to a surprising, very funny and quite open conclusion. The way in which his seduction tricks become futile when he tries them out on his wife are delightful, as is the manner in which she dominates her drooping Don Juan.

Writing and direction by Marianna Dikker and Wouter Suderhoud's lensing perfectly support the performance. — *Wall.*

Beverly Hills Bodysnatchers

New York A Shapiro Glickenhaus Entertainment release of a Hess-Kallberg Associates and McGuffin Prods. presentation of a Busybody production. Executive producers, Oliver G. Hess, Kevin M. Kallberg. Produced by Jon Mostow, P.K. Simonds Jr. Directed by Mostow. Screenplay, Simonds, from story by Mostow, Simonds; camera (Foto- Kem color), Zoran Hochstätter; editor, Barry Zetlin; music, Arthur Barron; sound (Ultra-Stereo), Don Sanders; production design, Lea Anna McConnell; art direction, Debra Hatch; set decoration, Greg Benge; assistant director, Kristine Peterson; production manager- coproducer, Susan Stremple; additional camera, Stephen Ashley Blake; associate producers, Kurt Eggert, Margaret Breitenstein; casting, Sharon Nederlander. Reviewed on Shapiro Glickenhaus vidcassette, N.Y., Jan. 10, 1990. MPAA Rating: R. Running time: **85 MIN.**

Lou	Vic Tayback
Doc	Frank Gorshin
Vic	Art Metrano
Freddie	Rodney Eastman
Vincent	Warren Selko
Don Ho	Keone Young
Mona	Brooke Bundy
Don Carlo	Seth Jaffe
Nunz	Steven Field
Stu	Christian Hoff
Julie	Allison Barron
Heather	Linda Carol

■A meager attempt at black humor, "Beverly Hills Bodysnatchers" makes little use of its title locale in spoofing "Burke & Hare" genre antics. Pic briefly played in Phoenix last September ahead of h.v.

Jon Mostow's pic actually is more a mafia spoof than fantasy film, giving it an archaic early '70s feel. Vic Tayback plays a funeral home owner assisted by mad scientist Frank Gorshin who has young kids imposed on him as workers by mobster Art Metrano. They're Rodney Eastman and Warren Selko, Metrano's nephews, who use the grim workplace to throw ghoulish parties for their friends.

Plot sickens when the current mafia don, Seth Jaffe, is killed on a golf course and Gorshin foolishly re- animates the corpse in one of his experiments. It escapes and unfunny mayhem ensues.

Lack of solid laughs is a big defect (e.g., an oriental mobster played by Keone Young is named "Don Ho") and pic does nothing interesting with the zombies subplot. Cast becomes increasingly agitated to ill effect. Even Gorshin, who one would expect to do an impression (Colin Clive maybe?), simply walks through this one.

— *Lor.*

Monsieur
(FRENCH-BELGIAN- B&W)

Paris A Bac Films release of a Films des Tournelles/ Films de l'Etang/La Sept coproduction. Produced by Anne-Dominique Toussaint. Written and directed by Jean-Philippe Toussaint, based on his novel; script collaboration, Anne-Dominique Toussaint, Patrick Deville, Madeleine Santandrea; camera (b&w), Jean-François Robin; editor, Sylvie Pontoizeau; music, Olivier Lartigue; art direction, Wim Vermeylen; sound, Dominique Warnier, François Groult. Reviewed at Cannnon France screening room, Paris, Jan. 9, 1990. Running time: **89 MIN.**

Monsieur	Dominique Gould
Kaltz	Wojtek Pszoniak
Mme. Pons- Romanov	Eva Ionesco
Mme. Dubois-Lacour	Alexandra Stewart
Anna Bruckardt	Aziliz Juhel
The friend	Tom Novembre

■"Monsieur" is an encouraging debut by Jean- Philippe Toussaint. Results are mixed but there's little doubt that Toussaint has a cinematic eye and a style.

Toussaint is the eccentric young Belgian novelist who collaborated on the screen adaptation of his offbeat tale "The Bathroom," which newcomer John Lvoff filmed in 1987. With no other experience Toussaint has personally tackled a film of his other published novel, "Monsieur."

Like "The Bathroom" (about a man who decides to relocate his domestic activities in his bathroom), "Monsieur' is a black & white existential comedy of alienation with a deadpan hero drifting through an indifferent and sometimes hypocritically hostile world.

The eponymous hero is a passive young man who works in an insurance company and lives with the family of his girlfriend — until she brings another man home to dinner one evening. This seems to disturb no one, least of all the girl's oddly hospitable parents.

Monsieur finally gets the message and takes an apartment of his own. No sooner is he settled than he is set upon by his overbearing Polish landlord- neighbor (Wojtek Pszoniak) who exhorts him into working as his personal typist on weekends. This involves the protagonist in encounters with other rather weird individuals, before a climactic romance that finally seems to go right for the hapless Monsieur.

Toussaint's script is a string of slightly off-kilter social sketches that don't always click or hang together, but when they do, the film is absurdly inspired. Among the best sequences are a couple of hilarious sporting scenes involving a gym football scrimmage (with a wheelchair referee furiously trying to keep up with the players) and a water polo match (which inevitably recalls Nanni Moretti's current "Red Lob").

The blandly persevering hero is played with amusing impassivity by Dominique Gould, a promising young American actor who's been working in France since 1986. Pszoniak's typical hamminess (unbearable in many French films) provides a perfect complement to Gould, and Tom Novembre, the Buster Keaton-like protagonist of "The Bathroom," does a brief turn as Monsieur's friend. Rest of the cast is at home in Toussaint's poker-faced universe.

Tech credits, notably Jean-François Robin's b&w lensing and Olivier Lartigue's score, are excellent. Film may be limited commercially. Hopefully Toussaint will persist with another film; one not hampered by its literary premise. — *Len.*

3615 Code Père Noël
(Dial Code Santa Claus)
(FRENCH)

Paris A Deal/UGC release of an LM Prods./ Deal/Garance coproduction. Executive producer, Francis Lalanne. Produced by Jungle Prods. Written and directed by René Manzor. Camera (color), Michel Gaffier; editor, Christine Pansu; music, Jean-Felix Lalanne; sound, Jean-Charles Ruault, Jean-Paul Loublier; art direction, Eric Moulard; assisant director, Thierry Lasheras. Reviewed at UGC Normandie theater, Paris, Jan. 23, 1990. Running time: **87 MIN.**

Thomas	Alain Musy
Julie	Brigitte Fossey
Grandpa	Louis Ducreux
Santa Claus	Patrick Floersheim
Roland	François-Eric Gendron

■This dumb chiller, made in France, exploits a psycho killer-on-the-loose plot, minus the gore — or anything else that adds up to a boxoffice attraction for the cheap thrills and ketchup crowd. There's little bloodletting and only two victims (not counting the audience): a dog and a policeman.

Ineptly derivative script and vidclip-style direction is the work of a young director, René Manzor, whose better known pop singer brother, Francis Lalanne, produced. Manzor made a negative impression with his first feature, "Le Passage" (1986), an awful fantasy melodrama whose turgid pop metaphysics somehow appealed to Alain Delon, who produced and starred in it.

Manzor has no such boxoffice glory to boost "3615 Code Père Noël," which pits a poor little rich boy (Alain Musy, who appeared in "Le Passage") against a bearded lunatic (Patrick Floersheim) in a Santa Claus outfit on Christmas Eve. Arena of this confrontation is the vast, labyrinthine country mansion in which the boy lives with his preoccupied tycoon mother (Brigitte Fossey) and his lovable, ill-sighted grandad (Louis Ducreux).

Musy, decked out as a pint-sized cross between Rambo and a Toshiro Mifune samurai, manages to keep the killer at bay much of the time through his daunting arsenal of war toys, electronic surveillance systems, secret passages and booby-trapped rooms. By the time the deadly game of hide-and-seek is over, the kid, understandably, no longer believes in Santa Claus. Nor is film one to hope for as a vidcassette in your next yuletide stocking.

Title refers to the Minitel, the French phone-based teletext information system, which precipitates the drama when the nutcase intercepts Musy's request for Santa to come and visit. —*Len.*

Angels
(SPANISH-SWISS)

Madrid A CAB Prods. (Lausanne), Marea Films (Madrid, Cadrage (Paris), K2 (Brussels) production, in association with Cannon Group Iberoamerica, Television Suisse Romande (SSR), Television Espanola (TVE). A Gerard Ruey, Jean-Louis Porchet, Adrian Lipp presentation, in collaboration with Daniel Vaissaire and Dominique Janne. Executive producer, Adrian Lipp. Written and directed by Jacob Berge. Camera (Eastmancolor), Emmanuel Machuel; editor, Joella Hache; art director, Felipe de Paco; sound, Laurent Barbey; music, Michel Portal; production manager, Teresa Enrich; associate producer, Alain Tanner. Reviewed at Cine Dore, Madrid, Feb. 7, 1990. (In Berlin Film Festival, competing.) Running time: **95 MIN.**

Rickie.	.Steven Weber
Sara.	.Belinda Becker
Thomas.	.Justin Williams
Tonio.	.Jose Esteban Jr.
Molina.	.Cristina Hoyos
Natacha.	.Angela Molina
Hugo.	.Feodor Atkins

■Before the opening credits, there are a few moments of magic in this film, as we see a black dancer performing a hypnotic dance in a dive in postwar Barcelona. But the promise is never fulfilled in this European hybrid which gets bogged down in excessive talk, a rambling story and European auteurism.

Though set in modern Barcelona, it is a Barcelona few Catalans today would recognize, for it is one seen through the eyes of non-Spaniards. In this mishmash underworld setting, the lingos are Spanish with an Andalusian accent and American English. Spanish thesps try to pronounce English as best they can. Most of track is in English, but quite a bit also is in Spanish.

The pre-title dance sequence is seen by a young American boy when he was in Spain. As a grown man, he returns from Brooklyn to Barcelona upon learning of his mother's death. She was a poetess and viewers are treated to some of her verses.

So, being in Barcelona, Rickie (whose background is never revealed; all we know is that he plays a trumpet) tries to seek out the black dancer of his memory. He finds her easily enough in a brothel, and strikes up a strange sort of masochistic romance with the girl. She is more than a hooker, it would seem. She says she is an ex-African princess. Rather, she is the idol of a mob of street urchins called the Angels.

Good thesping by Belinda Becker as the black girl, and by Justin Williams as the brother who breathes some life into the film. But protagonist Steven Weber is a dud. Cristina Hoyos, Spain's top flamenco dancer, is cast as a madame and never gets to dance; Angela Molina appears only a few seconds on screen as a hooker. Feodor Atkins is at his menacing best as a pimp, but is part is irrelevant.

Financed by European tv and government film groups, item is basically a quota-filler for tv.
—*Besa.*

Hjälten
(The Hero)
(SWEDISH)

Malmö, Sweden An SF release of AB Filmhuset production with the Swedish Film Institute, Svensk Filmindustri and SVT-2. Produced by Katinka Farago. Executive producer, Waldemar Bergendahl. Written and directed by Agneta Fagerström-Olsson; camera (Eastmancolor), John Olsson; editor, Christin Lohman; music, Björn Schüldt; production design, Sören Krag-Sörensen; sound, Adel Kjellström, Stephan Apelgren. Reviewed at the Downtown, Malmö, Feb. 1, 1990. (In Berlin Film Festival, Forum of Young Cinema.) Running time: **118 MIN.**

Rita.	.Lena Carlsson
Her father.	.Helge Jordal
Jimmi.	.Ulf Friberg
Edit.	.Marianne Mörk

Also with: Birgitta Ahlgren, Carl Sjöström, Magnus Skogsberg, Lotta Hansson, Yvonne Schaloske, Pär Ericson, Magnus (Mankan) Nilsson, Mona Seilitz, Joakim Pietras, Karin Emard, Jerk Rysjö, Nils Moritz, Lars Väringer.

■Although full to the brim of beautifully observed behavioral detail, absence of narrative build and suspense gives "The Hero" dim prospects even at back-home wickets.

In the pic, penned and helmed by Agneta Fagerström-Olsson, Rita turns 17 during a 1965 summer holiday on Sweden's west coast with her upper (business) class parents. She also goes through the rites of coming-of-age and falls in and out of love with 1) her father and 2) Jimmy, the young driver of a laundry van.

With "Seppan," a meller about sub-teenage working class kids, Fagerström-Olsson delighted the international fest circuit three years ago. In her new and more ambitious picture, she is defeated by her own screenplay which is cliché-ridden in all adult character delineations. There also is some heavy-handed symbolism to contend with plus several serious plot development non sequiturs. Too many comings and goings are downright aborted in mid-telling.

Fagerström-Olsson does work hand-in-glove with cinematographer John Olsson to create fine frames in which she also has all actors perform with a maximum of expressive facial and body language within their written limitations. Especially fine are Norway's Helge Jordal as Rita's bewildered and bedeviled father and, in the dominating lead, Lena Carlsson as the still kiddie-chubby budding beauty who wants to probe and test her own strength.

The hero of the title is probably meant to be whoever Rita chooses to attach her affections to. The temptations of an incestuous daughter-father relationship is indicated, then left dangling. Psychological clashes are followed by social ones when Rita turns left of her tennis-playing swain to run off instead with the laundry van driver. Latter's gypsy inclinations soon scare her off, however, but when she returns home, home is a suicide away from being what it used to be.

The stuff of true drama is there all right, but the director seems to feel herself above exploiting it to even the basic degree of moving things along in a natural way. She goes off on tangents (Rita and her clumsy girlfriend explore a traveling carnival or they get themselves dangerously tipsy on a boat-ride to a big city), and she keeps wagging a nemesis finger at audiences with symbolic close-ups of dead birds, shot down by Rita's elders.

The males of those elders are all boozers and they all walk the edge of bankruptcy and suicide, while their wives are Fellini grotesques seen mostly in the company of their ditto dogs. Generally, the kids are sketched in more convincingly, and Marianne Mörk shines especially in her comic-relief role as Rita's morose girlfriend. Local and international pop music idols are seen and heard throughout as unwitting heralders of the impending 1968 end of the Age of Innocence.—*Kell.*

Milou en mai
(Milou In May)
(FRENCH-ITALIAN)

Paris A Pyramid release of a Nouvelles Editions de Films/TF1 Films/Ellepi Films production. Produced and directed by Louis Malle. Screenplay, Malle, Jean-Claude Carrière; camera (color), Renato Berta; editor, Emmanuelle Castro; music, Stéphane Grappelli; sound, Jean-Claude Laureux, Dominique Hennequin; art direction, Willy Holt; production manager, Gérard Molto; assistant director, Michel Ferry. Reviewed at the Gaumont Ambassade theater, Paris, Feb. 2, 1989. Running time: **108 MIN.**

Milou.	.Michel Piccoli
Camille.	.Miou-Miou
Georges.	.Michel Duchaussoy
Claire.	.Dominique Blanc
Lily.	.Harriet Walter
Grimaldi.	.Bruno Carette
Daniel.	.François Berieand
Adele.	.Martine Gautier
Mme. Vieuzac.	.Paulette Dubost

■Louis Malle's latest is a family chronicle mixed with social satire that pokes fun at the French middle class of 1968. Though bourgeois-baiting is an old Malle specialty, "Milou en mai," despite its attractive name cast and a reasonably pleasant first half, is a bland disappointment.

Pic should ride on the international wave of popularity created for Malle by the prize-winning "Au revoir, les enfants." Locally, it is the first domestic success of the new year.

A momentous occasion in French history, the events of May 1968 are not illuminated by Malle. Working with an oblique, far-end-of-the-telescope idea, Malle and his co-scripter Jean-Claude Carrière have fabricated an artificial, seriocomic situation in which a solemn family reunion far from Paris degenerates as news of the uprisings and strikes are alarmingly blown out of proportion by fragmented news reports and paranoid rumors.

The far-flung members of a provincial bourgeois clan gather at the homestead (in the Bordeaux region, where Malle has a house) for the funeral of the matriarch, who has died suddenly.

The business of the funeral arrangements, the reading of the testament and the division of property is disturbed by the social shock waves emanating from Paris. Burial itself becomes impossible when local gravediggers join the nationwide strikes that have paralyzed industry and commerce.

The breakdown of communications and order has at first a liberating effect on the gathered family, temporarily united in a festive mood (they even dance around the corpse of the grandmother still lying in the salon). The sense of freedom turns to terror with rumors that the revolution is on their doorstep and that the bourgeoisie are to get their due. Everybody literally heads for the hills.

Up till here Malle and Carrière have some facile fun. This is not '60s Gallic Chekhov, nor Buñuel (hard to forget Carrière's old ties with the Spanish master, especially when the dead grandmother is suddenly brough back for a couple of mysterious live appearances). The portraits are largely stock. When the script sends its characters scurrying, the story and direction become dull and never recover.

At least there are the actors. Michel Piccoli gives the film's most sincere, heartfelt performance as Milou, the elder son who never left home, a bucolic gentle dreamer who quotes Virgil for an audience of bees and who cannot face the thought of losing the ancestral property. (He's too obviously patterned on the weak-willed Gayev in Chekhov's "The Cherry Orchard," a role played by Piccoli in Peter Brook's Paris stage production in the early '80s).

Miou-Miou is Piccoli's grasping middle-class daughter, brazenly cuckolding hubby with her old flame, the family notary (François Berieand); Dominique Blanc is his niece, a tense, embittered lesbian actress who arrives with latest lover in tow; Michel Duchaussoy is the young brother, a vaguely left-leaning journalist with a British hippie wife (Harriet Walter).

Bruno Carette, a young tv comedian who died shortly after making his film debut here, does a bright stereotypical turn as a sympathetically macho truck driver who joins the party. Paulette Dubost, best remembered as the coquettish catalyst of trouble and tragedy in Jean Renoir's "Rules Of The Game," silhouettes the thankless role of the departed (but supernaturally present) grandmother and spends most of her screentime playing dead. Unfortunately, the film eventually lies down with her.

With Renato Berta at the camera, Malle renders the vibrant pastoral sensuousness of the southwestern France dear to him. It's a shame that the freshness of the setting is wasted on the shallow staleness of much of the material.

The breezy score is by another old Malle collaborator, jazz master Stéphane Grappelli. Other tech credits are firstrate. — *Len.*

Loose Cannons

Hollywood A Tri-Star Pictures release of an Aaron Spelling/Alan Greisman production. Executive producer, René Dupont. Produced by Spelling, Greisman. Directed by Bob Clark. Screenplay, Richard Christian Matheson, Richard Matheson, Clark; camera (Panavision, Technicolor), Reginald H. Morris; editor, Stan Cole; music, Paul Zaza; sound (Dolby), Ken Heeley-Ray; production design, Harry Pottle; art direction, William J. Durrell Jr.; set decoration, Denise Exshaw; assistant director, Ken Goch; casting, Mike Fenton, Judy Taylor, Valorie Massalas. Reviewed at AMC Theaters, Century City, Feb. 7, 1990. MPAA Rating: R. Running time: **93 MIN.**

Mac.	.Gene Hackman
Ellis.	.Dan Aykroyd
Gutterman.	.Dom DeLuise
Smiley.	.Ronny Cox
Riva.	.Nancy Travis
Von Metz.	.Robert Prosky
Grimmer.	.Paul Koslo
Captain.	.Dick O'Neill

■This pic's title begs for puns about firing blanks, being a dud, going off half-cocked. Those dispensed with, it can be said that Dan Aykroyd's dexterous multipersonality schtick is the only redeeming feature of this chase-heavy comedy, destined for a quick pileup on the homevid heap.

Director Bob Clark manages to make his low-brow comedy "Porky's" look like "Amadeus" with this latest salvo into the police-buddy genre, while Gene Hackman continues his befuddling penchant for sprinkling his overflowing résumé with shameful losers.

"Loose Cannons" may be best remembered for its unbelievably convoluted screenplay — a concoction of elements from "Lethal Weapon 2," "Midnight Run" and "Beverly Hills Cop," all played at the speed of a Warner Bros. cartoon.

Foremost, it provides a rare cinematic chance for Aykroyd to display the rapid-fire mimickry that proved his signature on "Saturday Night Live," rifling through impersonations of everyone from the crew of "Star Trek" to the Roadrunner, the latter a rare highlight.

Plot involves gruesome murders, a secret 45-year-old porno film, a candidate for the chancellorship of West Germany and a horde of uzi-brandishing neo-Nazis.

All of that is irrelevant to the main plot, which pairs the gruff Mac (Hackman) with the Sybil-like Ellis (Aykroyd) — recently (and apparently prematurely) reactivated by his police-captain uncle after suffering a nervous breakdown that causes him to lapse into multiple personalities.

Such talented actors as Ronny Cox and Robert Prosky walk through in brief, stereotypical roles.

The film does little to capitalize on the D.C. setting, while a climactic encounter in the New York subway at least incorporates one rather nifty stunt. Tech credits are unspectacular, with the frequent chases shot in by-the-numbers fashion.
— *Bril.*

The White Girl

New York A Tony Brown Prods. release and production. Executive producer, Sheryl Cannady. Produced by James Cannady. Line producer, Dwight Williams. Written and directed by Tony Brown. Camera (Precision color), Joseph M. Wilcots; editorial supervision, Wilcots; editor, Tony Vigna; music, George Porter Martin, Jimmy Lee Brown; sound (Ultra-Stereo), Gary Cunningham; set design, Bill Webb; costume design, Paul Simmons; assistant director, Randy Fletcher; production manager, Brent Owens; associate producers, Joseph Ray Martin. Reviewed at Metro 2 theater, N.Y., Feb. 10, 1990. MPAA Rating: PG-13. Running time: **88 MIN.**

Kim Barnes.	.Troy Beyer
Bob.	.Taimak
Vanessa.	.Teresa Yvon Farley
Nick.	.O.L. Duke
Debbie.	.DiAnne B. Shaw
Dr. McCullough.	.Petronia Paley
Karl.	.Don Hannah
Mr. W.	.Donald Craig
Mrs. Barnes.	.Sherry Williams
Charles.	.Mike Deurloo
Tracy.	.Twila Wolfe
Roger.	.Kevin Campbell

■A public service announcement masquerading as a feature film, "The White Girl" is antidrug propaganda aimed in condescending fashion at educating black audiences. It has zero crossover potential.

Shot in 1987, pic was shown last year at fundraisers and it waves its "good cause" flag wildly; an opening credit card declares it the "first buy-freedom motion picture." Why black people should be shamed into attending a lecture is not clear or fair.

Debuting filmmaker Tony Brown, who hosts the tv interview show "Tony Brown's Journal," tries here to fight drugs and raise black consciousness: His oft-repeated message for his constituency is, "Don't try to be white."

While trying to avoid the clichés of early '70s blaxploitation pics (except for directing O.L. Duke's overplayed stereotype of a pimp/pusher), Brown unwittingly reaches back to '30s exploitation film modes. Structurally and in terms of content, film often resembles Dwain Esper's "Maniac" or the more famous "Reefer Madness."

Lovely Troy Beyer toplines as a college student hooked on cocaine (her parents told her it was okay "for recreational use") who seems headed for recovery when fellow black students (at an integrated Southern college) DiAnne B. Shaw and heartthrob Taimak befriend her. Unfortunately, gorgeous roommate Teresa Yvon Farley keeps offering her "the white girl" (punning slang for the dreaded powder).

Worse still, Farley is sleeping her way to the top in hopes of a news anchor position at the local tv station, and even has promised to deliver Beyer's body for sexual favors to the evil white tv producer (Mike Deurloo).

Brown interrupts this barnstorming dramaturgy with even more overt devices, such as assemblies at the black student union where enlightened German student Don Hannah (Daryl's brother in an okay performance) tells us that Ludwig von Beethoven was "of African origin." He even throws in a segment on tv of "Tony Brown's Journal" wherein comedian George Kirby recites his poem "King Heroin" to warn how drugs affected his life.

Cast is well-chosen though sabotaged by the strident script. Beyer and Taimak are beautiful to look at in an endless stream of costume changes while Farley steals the show in pic's most dramatic role. Decent support is offered by Petronia Paley as a friendly psychologist, and Kevin Campbell might have an Elisha Cook Jr. career ahead of him on the basis of his bug-eyed, drug-crazed white lecher assignment here. — *Lor.*

Hard To Kill

New York A Warner Bros. release of a Lee Rich production, in association with Adelson/Todman/Simon Prods. Executive producers, Rich, Michael Rachmil. Produced by Gary Adelson, Joel Simon, Bill Todman Jr. Directed by Bruce Malmuth. Screenplay, Steven McKay; camera (Technicolor), Matthew F. Leonetti; editor, John F. Link; music, David Michael Frank; sound (Dolby), Glenn Anderson; production design, Robb Wilson King; art direction, Louis Mann; assistant director, Douglas Wise; stunt coordinator, Buddy Joe Hooker; martial arts choreography, Steven Seagal; coproducer, Jon Sheinberg; associate producer, McKay; casting, Glenn Daniels. Reviewed at Chelsea 6 theater, N.Y., Feb. 9, 1990. MPAA Rating: R. Running time: **95 MIN.**

Mason Storm.	.Steven Seagal
Andrea Stewart.	.Kelly Le Brock
Vernon Trent.	.Bill Sadler
O'Malley.	.Frederick Coffin
Mrs. Storm.	.Bonnie Burroughs
Sonny Storm.	.Zachary Rosencrantz
Quintero.	.Branscombe Richmond

■Steven Seagal's smooth moves give the lackluster vehicle "Hard To Kill" a good shot at b.o. among action fans. Chance to groom the star for a step up to heavyweight class in the genre is missed, however.

Seagal won fan approval with his debut "Above The Law" two years back while having the unusual distinction of above-the-title billing on a major release first time out. "Kill" is more of a B picture for the popcorn trade that WB elected not to press screen.

Steven McKay's threadbare screenplay, which went into production as "Seven Year Storm," uses a Rip van Winkle gimmick. As Mason Storm, cop Seagal is nearly killed in the first reel after shooting surveillance film of corrupt politico Bill Sadler. His wife (Bonnie Burroughs) is murdered by Sadler's minions, his son disappears in the massacre and Seagal is pronounced dead.

Cop buddy Frederick Coffin recognizes the danger and hides evidence of Seagal's last-minute recovery. Seven years later, under the tutelage of impossibly beautiful nurse Kelly Le Brock, Seagal comes out of his coma (sporting a laughable phony beard), uses Oriental methods of recovery and plots his revenge.

Sluggish direction by Bruce Malmuth doesn't help, but whenever Seagal is allowed to whip into action the film is a crowdpleaser. Unlike other loner prototypes ranging from John Wayne and Clint Eastwood through to James Bond, he goes beyond merely ruthless into the realm of sadistic, breaking opponents' limbs just for starters (as in a memorable fight here with latino heavy Branscombe Richmond). It ain't pretty, but it gets the action fans off.

Though Coffin is effective in the nice guy role and Sadler (soon to be in "Die Hard 2") earns his hisses as the sleazy senator, film could have used a boost with some names in the supporting cast. Seagal's real-life wife Le Brock is a pleasant matchup opposite him (especially when handling in-joke double entendres), but is far too glamorous for the role and not up to the dramatic moments.

Tech credits are low-budget looking, with cameraman Matthew Leonetti again, as in "Red Heat," emphasizing tv-style 2-shot closeups too often.

— Lor.

Longtime Companion

Hollywood A Samuel Goldwyn Co. release of an American Playhouse production. Produced by Stan Wlodkowski. Executive producer, Lindsay Law. Directed by Norman Rene. Screenplay, Craig Lucas; camera (color), Tony Jennelli; editor, Katherine Wenning; music supervision, Liz Vollack; sound, Paul Cots; production design, Andrew Javknoss; art direction, Ruth Ammon; set decoration, Kate Conklin; costume design, Walker Hicklin; coproducer, Lydia Dawn Pilcher; assistant director, Howard McMaster. Reviewed at U.S. Film Festival, Park City, Utah, Jan. 24, 1990. No MPAA Rating. Running time: **96 MIN.**

David. . . . . .Bruce Davison
Willy. . . . . .Campbell Scott
Fuzzy. . . . . .Stephen Caffrey
Sean. . . . . .Mark Lamos
Howard. . . . . .Patrick Cassidy
Liza. . . . . .Mary-Louise Parker
Paul. . . . . .John Dossett
Bob. . . . . .Brian Cousins
John. . . . . .Dermot Mulroney
Alec. . . . . .Brad O'Hara
Michael. . . . . . . .Michael Schoeffline

■A project like American Playhouse's "Longtime Companion," the first feature film to tell the story of how AIDS devastated and transformed the gay community throughout the 1980s, would need to be outstanding to draw an across-the-board audience in theaters, and this picture most certainly is.

Word-of-mouth should benefit pic's distribution by Samuel Goldwyn Co., firmed a week before its world premiere at the U.S. Film Festival.

In the hands of writer Craig Lucas (plays "Blue Window," "Prelude To A Kiss") and his frequent stage collaborator, director Norman Rene, "Longtime Companion" is simply an excellent film, with a graceful, often humorous script and affecting performances.

Story begins during the carefree pre-AIDS party days on Fire Island, where Willy (Campbell Scott) and Fuzzy (Stephen Caffrey) meet and begin a relationship that brings together an extended circle of friends. It's the same day a New York Times article announces a rare disease spreading among gay men.

A year later, Willy's best friend John (Dermot Mulroney) becomes violently ill and dies. It's only the beginning. One by one, this community of actors, writers and lawyers is affected.

Among the most piercing events is the deterioration of a tv scripter, Sean (Mark Lamos), who is cared for by his lover, David (Bruce Davison), who owns the beach house where the friends always have gathered.

Davison gives a tremendously sensitive, compassionate performance as the caretaker who sees his friend through to the end.

Strength of Lucas' script is the way it weaves emotional and informational material together. The many ways in which the AIDS crisis rubs against an uneasy society — in insurance, hiring and housing matters — are conveyed.

Main characters are crisply drawn, and the grimness is alleviated with buoyant, ribald little jokes that prop up even in the darkest moments.

The accumulated losses depicted in "Longtime Companion" and the bravery and endurance of those who confront the disease constructively make the pic extremely moving.

Though it is bound by its subject to cover certain ground, the film never seems like a disease-of-the-week telepics, as the writing and performances are so compelling.

Mary-Louise Parker shines as Fuzzy's supportive sister. Production values seem well above pic's $1.5-million budget. — Chas.

La Messe en si mineur (Mass In C Minor) (FRENCH)

Paris An FCF release of a Films de la Concorde/Eurisma coproduction. Executive producer, Philippe Gandrille. Produced by Emmanuel Serenot. Written and directed by Jean-Louis Guillermou. Camera (Panavision, color), Jean Badal; sound, Philippe Lioret; editor, Jean Kargayan; music, Johann Sebastian Bach. Reviewed at Georges V theater, Paris, Feb. 5, 1990. Running time: **85 MIN.**
Sophie. . . . . . . .Margaux Hemingway
Philippe. . . . . .Denis Charvet
Laurent. . . . . .Pierre Amoyal
Laura. . . . . .Annabella Mouloudji
Mme. Villegrain. . . . .Stéphane Audran
M. Villegrain. . . . . .Yves Barsacq

■This inane melodrama about two French musician buddies romancing an Franco-American woman should have been called "Mess in C Minor." Screenplay, or what was actually filmed of it, manages to accommodate Johann Sebastian Bach with Margaux Hemingway, church weddings, French chateaux, shady aristocrats, drugs, murder and mental hospitals — a cinematic cacophony of ineptness.

Jean-Louis Guillermou, who wrote and directed, comes from sports journalism and commercials, but one is at a loss to say what he's peddling here. According to the press materials, film was conceived as a homage to Bach. All that remains, as a pointless motif, is a rehearsal of the title piece that climaxes in a final full-scale performance.

To add to the absurdities, Guillermou imported Hemingway as film's star, and cast her alongside two Gallic screen amateurs in their movie debuts: an acclaimed violinist, Pierre Amoyal, who plays a violinist, and a rugby football jock, Denis Charvet, who plays Amoyal's bassist buddy. They form a trio of wooden acting instruments under the Guillermou's tone-deaf direction.

The musicians meet Hemingway while performing at the upper class chapel wedding of her sister. A nascent romance between Amoyal and Hemingway is sabotaged by former's dire financial problems and the girl's disdainful snobbish stepmother, Stphane Audran, who in fact is plotting to use the musician to smuggle dope into Italy. When Amoyal catches on he is killed in a car "accident." Hemingway, who has begun seeing Charvet, is abducted, drugged and locked up in a mental hospital. Just as suddenly as she's kidnaped, she's released for a happy reunion with Hemingway, under the auspices of Johann Sebastian.

An obtrusive and often ridiculous voiceover narrative (by Charvet) seems tacked on to hide the holes in the plot and the important shots and sequences that apparently never were made. The production ran into unspecified problems. In addition, Amoyal understandably disassociated himself with the finished picture in a pre-credit disclaimer that is not on the screen long often to be read by the audience.

There was some early mention of an English-track version. That would save nothing — excepting the French language, which Hemingway grinds flat with her graceless inexpressive accent. — Len.

Daredreamer

Seattle A Lensman Co. release. Produced by Pat Royce. Executive producers, Meier Mitchell & Co. Directed by Barry Caillier. Screenplay, Royce, Caillier, based on story by Tim Noah, Royce, Caillier; camera (Eastman color), Christopher G. Tufty; editor, Karen Thorndike; music, Paul Speer, David Lanz; songs written and performed by Tim Nosh; in Dolby stereo; choreography, Wade Madsen; costume design, Lahly Poore, Dan Gregory; production manager, Carolyn Johnson; associate producers, Johnson, Josh Conescu, Tom Hechim. Reviewed at Oak Tree Cinemas, Seattle, Feb. 1, 1990. MPAA Rating: PG-13. Running time: **108 MIN.**

Winston	Tim Noah
Jennie	Alyce LaTourelle
Max	Adam Eastwood
Zach	Michael A. Jackson

Also with: Jim Hechim, Billy Burke, Thomas Arthur, Whitey Shapiro, Renee Parent, Kirk Woller.

■**Cowriters Pat Royce and Barry Caillier's first full-length film about an ordinary high school senior who constantly escapes into daydreams is a fast-paced musical romp. An ingenious storyline and sterling performances by a cast of newcomers make for an engaging pic, which could appeal to a sizable audience with proper handling.**

"Daredreamer" tells the story of Winston (Tim Noah) who "zones out" at the slightest provocation, escaping into the fantasy world of his daydreams in which he is always powerful and in control. In real life, however, he's a wimp.

The pic deals with Winston's immediate problem: Having been "kept back" a number of years, his high school graduation depends upon the completion of a speech assignment due within the next 24 hours. As usual, Winston panics, escaping into daydreams even though he knows he must "learn to face reality."

To further complicate matters, Winston is tormented by tough-guy classmates, the Three D's (Jim Hechim, Billy Burke and Thomas Arthur), taunted by the "popular girl" Cindy (Renee Parent) and berated by his teachers, particularly the speech teacher Mr. Bigley (Whitey Shapiro).

The plot picks up considerably, however, when Winston discovers himself mysteriously entangled in the daydreams of classmate Jenny (Alyce LaTourelle), who finds Winston's secret life — and Winston — exciting. In fact, the pic's strongest scene comes when Winston and Jenny initially confront each other in their daydreams and attempt to decide who is in whose daydream.

From then on, the pic begins to operate on a much more subtle and interesting level.

Winston daydreams one time too many and is expelled. Lacking a belief in himself, he has nowhere to turn. Enter Zach (Michael A. Jackson, former Seattle Seahawks linebacker), the soft-spoken, sax-playing custodian of the school, who is a sort of mystical guardian to Winston.

Zach taps into Winston's inherent magic and shows the daydreamer how to be a "daredreamer," leading Winston to a very upbeat ending. If anything, the ending is a bit too optimistic, and threatens to turn off a potential segment of its teen audience.

The film's high points, of course, are in the daydreams. Featuring brisk choreography, the fantasy sequences are filled with plenty of action, romance, comedy, as well as topnotch performance art and entertaining rock 'n' roll sequences. Noah, a well-known children's entertainer, gives a solid performance in his first feature film, deftly handling the personality changes between fumbling, inept nerd to suave, confident hero. Although well past the age of high school, Noah delivers a very convincing performance as the failing student.

Among the pic's remarkably fine performances are newcomers Alyce LaTourelle as Jennie and Jim Hechim as Dicky of the Three D's. It also marks a strong debut for director Barry Caillier, who elicits sympathetic and respectable performances form a cast of frosh.

Handsomely designed and lensed in Seattle, the film features original music written and performed by Noah, and solid production values despite a shoestring budget of less than $1 million. — *Magg.*

Hiver 54, l'Abbé Pierre
(Winter Of '54: Father Pierre)

Paris AMLF release of a Les Productions Belles Rives/Miships Associs coproduction. Produced by Christian Ardan. Directed by Denis Amar. Screenplay, Marie Devort, Amar; camera (color), Girard de Battista; editor, Jacques Witta; sound, Philippe Lioret, William Flageollet; art direction, Jean-Jacques Caziot; assistant director, Jean-Francois Chaintron; production manager, Alain Depardieu; casting, Shula Siegfriend. Reviewed at Gaumont Ambassade theater, Paris, Nov. 27, 1989. Running time: **102 MIN.**

Father Pierre	Lambert Wilson
Hélène Vartnier	Claudia Cardinale
Raoul	Robert Hirsch
Castaing	Bernie Bonvoisin

Also with: Laurent Terzieff, Philippe Leroy-Beaulieu, Vladimir Vordanov, Bernard Lefort, Isabelle Petit-Jacques, Eric Metayer.

■**"Hiver 54, l'Abbe Pierre" is a conventional, less than inspirational biopic about the crusading French priest who founded the Ragpickers of Emmaus, a charity organization that has performed social miracles in providing shelter and food for the homeless and dispossessed in three decades of activity.**

Still active at 78, Father Pierre — known as the Abbé (Abbot) Pierre — remains a beloved public figure today, which has been an dominant factor in film's local success. Offshore prospects seem limited, though the existence of affiliates of the Emmaus communities abroad may be useful for attracting more ecumenical audiences.

Film limits its scope to the events of the brutally cold winter of 1953-54 when Father Pierre, as yet a little-known cleric who had been a resistance fighter and parliamentary deputy, pulled off an extraordinary media coup to stir up government and popular support for the thousands of poor who were literally freezing to death on the streets, in back lots and under bridges.

His conscience-raising began with an open letter to the housing minister on the front page of a leading French newspaper and was topped off with a moving appeal on a national radio station. Donations and contributions poured in from around the country in a tidal wave of support and concern that made Father Pierre an international celebrity overnight (and ripe for cinematic sanctification as early as 1955 in a now-forgotten feature, "Le Chiffoniers d'emmaus").

Screenplay by Marie Devort and director Denis Amar may be based on fact, but it rings with hokey artifice, replete with snappy dialog effects, 2-dimensional characterizations and calculated dramatic reversals. (Father Pierre's confidential plans to political figures, press moguls and the like invariably meet with the same initial rejection, and later with the same sudden surprise change of heart.)

Amar, an unlikely choice as helmer — his specialty has been action melodramas — plays for plot and suspense, which keeps film from getting overly mawkish. Ironically, "Winter Of '54: Father Pierre," for a film about humanitarian concerns lacks real depth of emotion.

Lambert Wilson's Father Pierre is unaffected and direct, but doesn't fully suggest the persuasive force that vanquished the barriers of official and public selfishness (but it has nabbed him a César nomination as best actor).

In a foolishly overblown role, Claudia Cardinale wears an indestructible smile as a big-hearted hotel owner who accepts heavy financial loss by transforming her Champs-Elsyées establishment into a nerve center for the charity drive. Legit star Robert Hirsch (a César nominee as best supporting actor) plays to the galleries as one of the priest's tramp lieutenants.

Some interesting silhouettes are etched by Laurent Terzieff, as a press boss, and former Paris Opera adminstrator Bernard Lefort, as the Paris Prefect of Police. — *Len.*

Le Party
(CANADIAN)

Montreal A Cinepix release of a ACPAV production. Produced by Bernadette Payeru. Written and directed by Pierre Falardeau; director's consultant, Francis Smiardi. Camera (color), Alain Dostie; editor, Michel Arcand; music, Richard Desjardins; sound (Dolby), Serge Beauchemin; art direction, Jean-Baptiste Tard; associate producer, Marc Daigle. Reviewed at Famous Players Imperial Cinema, Montreal, Feb. 1, 1990. Running time: **100 MIN.**

Sylvie Nantel	Lou Babin
Pierre Boyer	Julien Poulin
Alexandra	Charlotte Laurier
Julien	Luc Proulx
Romeo Mongrain	Michel Forget
Pinceau	Pierre Powers
Journalist	Louise Laprade
Francis	Roger Léger
Mimi	Angele Coutu
Becique	Benoit Dagonais
Ginette	André Doucet
Jacques	Guildor Roy
Lili	Andréa Parro
Pierrot	Alexis Martin

■**A potent rock 'n' roll film about liberty and lust, "Le Party" undulates between gut-wrenching authenticity and genuine eroticism. Subtitled English version will need critical acclaim and a carefully handled release to have any success in English-speaking North America.**

A variety show in a scuzzy prison is the premise for this pic sure to be heralded by critics for its compassion with convicts. Comedy and striptease sequences make pic seem more like a college flick at times, but also make palatable a pic which would otherwise be too heavy.

Quebec and Euro markets are more the speed for this pic where panties are worth their weight in gold; where booze is concocted from fire extinguisher fluid; where cigarettes are currency; and where prisoners prepare for "the party" as if the Statue of Liberty were arriving with Lady Godiva on horseback.

"The Party" is a fiction film based entirely on "facts" recounted to helmer Pierre Falardeau by his colleague Francis Simard who spent 11 years in prison himself. Simard took the liberty to organize such parties — regarded as rehabilitation by the authorities — to prevent himself and the other men from going mad. That's understandable, per the film.

The onstage party hosts a gamut of Quebec musicians — from heavy rock'n'rollers to country and blues singers — who belt out their version of what it means to be free. Magicians, comedians, and two strip tease artists also take center stage.

Backstage and offstage, numerous scenarios unfold as the party rages on: stories intricately woven together delineate the whole picture of life in a cage.

There's a touching drama. Stripper, Alexandra — a role which will put Charlotte Laurier ("Les Bon Debarras") back on the map — spends the better part of the film backstage listening to inmate Julien's story. Thesp Luc Proulx brings years of theater experience to the role of a man who hasn't touched a woman in 11 years. Theirs is a tender encounter.

The other stripper, Lili, isn't quite so lucky. Turning a few tricks on the side, she winds up getting beaten and raped, a scene which leads another prisoner, Bécique (Benoit Dagenais) to reprimand the beast for forgetting the code of prison ethics.

Meanwhile, there's a suspense story building as inmate Francis (Roger Léger) prepares for his escape by transforming himself into a woman. Teamwork with other prisoners provides him with the dress, wig, shoes and "visitor's pass," stolen from a woman in the balcony.

The balcony is a sea of hypocrisy where the administration and their spouses have perched for the show.

A tragedy builds in an isolation cell where an inmate (Julien Poulin)

prepares for a grizzly suicide because he is detained from the party where his lover (Lou Babin) sings her country and western ballad for other ears.

Tying all the stories together is the straight-laced female journalist, the character guaranteed to quell feminist criticism. Asking Alexandra if it bothers her to be regarded as a sexual object, the dancer retorts, "I find it better than showing my face on tv beside a can of dog food."

After eight years of silence, Falardeau's "Party" marks a directorial comeback. Relentless in his adoration and criticism of Quebec ("Elvis Gratton," "Speak White," "Pea Soup"), this pic is perhaps the first which will travel beyond provincial boundaries.

Pic is everything "Weeds" tried to be and more. Technical elements are excellent. Soundtrack is very strong. "Le Party" has a natural second life in paytv and homevid.
— *Suze.*

Dog Tags

New York A Cinevest Entertainment Group release of an Arthur Schweitzer and Krishna Shah presentation of a Daars production Executive producer, Romano Scavolini. Produced by Alain Adam, Dalu Jones. Line producer, Charles Wang. Written and directed by Scavolini. Camera (Panavision, Technicolor; Kay Metrocolor prints), John McCallum; editor, Nicholas Pollock; music, John Scott; sound (Dolby), Ron Green; production design, Art Nicdao; art direction, Mor Nicdao; special effects makeup, Medy Alpa; casting, Mik Gribben. Reviewed at Quad 1 theater, N.Y., Feb. 3, 1990. MPAA Rating: R. Running time: 93 MIN.
Cecil. . . . . .Clive Wood
Capt. Newport. . . . . .Mike Monty
Also with: Baird Stafford, Robert Haufrecht, Peter Erlich, Chris Hilton, Gigi Doenas.

■"Dog Tags" is a standard issue patrol film, set during the Vietnam War. Pretentious direction and laudable technical skill fail to lift this from action pic status to art house entry.

Filmmaker Romano Scavolini, known Stateside for his 1981 horror pic "Nightmare" after numerous Italian film credits as director and cameraman, proves himself here a talented helmer of individual setpieces but unable to put them together into a cohesive whole.

British thesp Clive Wood (also in "Buster") ably portrays a commando codenamed Cecil who saves some GIs from their imprisonment in Tiger

Cages. Instead of heading for rescue pickup, Wood and his ragtag band of soldiers are ordered by the captain (Mike Monty, a regular in Philippines-lensed pics) on a secret mission across the border into Cambodia.

Instead of finding secret information in a downed helicopter, Wood discovers four boxes of gold and the men predictably turn greedy en route to a cynical finish.

Film's strong points include John McCallum's sharp widescreen lensing, a vigorous musical score by John Scott and sustained tension within several harrowing sequences.

Pic is sabotaged by extremely crude editing (which makes the appearance of a pretty Vietnamese girl and her family tagging along with the heroes needlessly cryptic) and an unnecessary device of dividing the story into separate "acts," plus prolog and epilog. Tale is unconvincingly told in flashback by author Chris Hilton.

Tech credits, particularly vivid Dolby sound recording and some spectacular explosions, are on a par with big-budget films in this genre.
—*Lor.*

Mortgage
(AUSTRALIAN)

Sydney A Film Australia production. Produced by Bruce Moir. Directed by Bill Bennett. Screenplay, Bennett; camera (color), Steve Arnold; editor, Sara Bennett; music, Michael Atkinson; sound, Max Hensser; production manager, Hilary May; assistant director, Nikki Long; casting, Rae Davidson. Reviewed at Film Australia screening room, Sydney, Dec. 7, 1989. Running time: 90 MIN.
Dave Dodd. . . . . .Brian Vriends
Tina Dodd. . . . . .Doris Younane
George Shooks. . . . . . .Bruce Venables
Kevin Grant. . . . . . . .Andrew Gilbert
Jack Napper. . . . . .Paul Coolahan
Philosophical drunk. . . . . . .Bob Ellis

■"Mortgage" is the second docudrama Bill Bennett has made for Film Australia; the first, "Malpractice," unspooled at several fests, including the Un Certain Regard section of Cannes this year, and the new offering should go the same route with lively tv sales indicated, especially in Europe.

Pic comes across as an ultrarealistic "Mr. Blandings Builds His Dream House," sans much in the way of comedy. Dave and Tina Dodd are average working-class types who want a home of their own. They purchase land in the western

suburbs of Sydney, and sign a contract with a display home company run by shifty Jack Napper. Napper recommends a builder, George Shooks, whose business already is in a shaky state, thanks mainly to the ineptitude of his assistant, Kevin.

The ensuing sorry saga will be familiar to most home builders. The work is slow, mistakes are made (a toilet in the laundry instead of the bathroom, window frames of the wrong color, etc.) and the Dodds are hit by rising interest rates and escalating rental for their temporary apartment. When Tina gets pregnant it's almost the last straw, and lawyers give conflicting advice about how to proceed.

Ultimately, "Mortgage" is as much a film about a marriage as about the problems of home building. As forcefully played by newcomers Brian Vriends and Doris Younane, Dave and Tina come across as painfully real, unglamorized characters. Their arguments, improvised as is almost all the dialog in the film, are often bitter, bordering on violent. A sequence in which Dave returns home after a drunken night out is an extremely powerful one.

The improvisation works well throughout, though the unseen interviewer whose voice (that of the director) is heard from time to time seems an unnecessary device. Nonetheless, "Mortgage" works as a powerful exposé of the pitfalls into which young couples, with limited resources can fall when they seek a home of their own.

Performances down the line are on the button, and Bennett's direction is up to his usual high standard.

There's an amusing cameo from writer-director Bob Ellis as a drunken taxi passenger who waxes philosophically about the financial situation and helpfully suggests that Tina, who's out of work, might find an opening in a suburban Deep Massage Parlor. —*Strat.*

Il bambino e il poliziotto
(The Boy And The Policeman)
(ITALIAN)

Rome A Penta release of a Mario and Vittorio Cecchi Gori Tiger Cinematografica production, in association with Reteitalia. Produced by Mario and Vittoriio Cecchi Gori. Directed by Carlo Verdone. Screenplay, Verdone, Leo Benvenuti, Piero DeBernardi; camera Cinecitta (color), Danilo Desideri; editor, Antonio Siciliano; music, Fabio Liberatori; art direction, Giovanni Natalucci. Reviewed at Rivoli Cinema, Rome, Jan. 6, 1990. Running time: 110 MIN.

Carlo Vinciguerra. . . . . . .Carlo Verdone
Giulio. . . . . .Federico Rizzo
Mother. . . . . .Adriana Franceschi
Also with: Barbara Cupisti, Isabella Di Bernardi, Francesco Gabriele, Tony Brennero.

■Latest from comedian-helmer Carlo Verdone is an amusing family comedy that has climbed Christmas b.o. charts at home. Given pic's pro craftsmanship and the universal appearl of adopted waif fables. "The Boy And The Policeman" could leap across national boundaries to related markets.

Verdone's evolution from a pungent satirist of mealy Italo characters to a well-heeled professional willing to tone down his own role in the interest of film as a whole (and its commercial entertainment value) is mighty apparent here. This middle-of-the-road Christmas carol to those big-hearted men in blue is an easy watch. While "The Boy" lacks originality, it makes contact with mainstream audiences, adults as well as kiddies.

Commissioner Carlo Vinciguerra (Vardone), masquerading as a late hippie. slips into a party to crash a drug ring. In the course of the police action, the attractive hostess (Adriiana Franceschi is arrested, though her crime is mainly protecting others. Carlo is surprised to find she has a 6-year-old son, a smart-taking, adorable gap-toothed redhead (Federico Rizzo, a true child acting discovery). After a little hemming and hawing, he agrees with the judge to watch out for little Giulio until Mom gets out of jail.

Body of film shows bachelor Carlo's masked delight in entertaining his little guest, even when he breaks windows, ruins spaghetti dinners and leaves skates on the floor to be stepped on. Material is extra-familiar, but in the hands of Vardone the gags grab laughs without exception. Finale has Carlo rescue Giulio, who has been kidnaped by the drug dealers to keep his mother silent.

Giulio is even responsible for breaking up Carlo's tepid romance with a married coworder (Barbara Cupisti), but that leaves the door open for a 3-way happy ending, with policement, boy and beautiful mom walking into the sunset together.

Pic plays up the thrill of speeding, crime-busting police cars in action, even as it gently spoofs the clumsiness (but not inefficiency) of Commissioner Carlo. Verdone's sure sense of timing brings off the laughs, while technical work is professional and unobtrusive. —Yung.

Rodrigo D. — No Futuro (Rodrigo D. — No Future) (COLOMBIAN)

New York A Compania de Fomento Cinematografico (Focine)-Tiempos Modernos-Foto Club 76 production. Directed by Victor Gaviria. Screenplay, Gaviria, Luis Fernando Calderon, Angela Perez, Juan Guillermo Arredondo; camera (color), Rodrigo Landine; editor, Luis Alberto Restrepo; music, German Arrieta: sound. Gustavo de la Hoz; art direction, Ricardo Dugue. Reviewed at Duart screening room, N.Y. Oct. 10, 1989. Running time: 90 MIN.
With: Ramiro Meneses, Carlos Mario Restrepo, Jackson Idrian Gallego, Vilma Dias.

■First feature by documentary and short helmer Victor Gavira, "Rodrigo D. (No Future)" is a powerful exploration of the bleak and precarious lives of working-class street kids in Medellin. So dangerous is this world, that three of the non-pro actors have been killed violently since production wrapped in 1988.

(Pic is part of the series "Colombian Cinema: From Magic To Realism" organized by MoMA, and received a Jan. 20 U.S. preem at the U.S. Film Fest in Park City, Utah.)

The naturalistic script, written in near-impenetrable Medellin street slang, won second prize in Colombia's 1986 annual screenplay competition. It was based on an article that appeared in the local newspaper "El Mundo" about a teeenager, Rodrigo Alonso, who leaped from the top floor of a downtown building.

Rather than pursue a linear plot, pic presents a slice of life as we follow Rodrigo and his teenage friends over a several-day period, exploring their world as they live it as best they can.

Rodrigo (Ramiro Meneses) can't sleep at night. He has headaches and thinks about his mother, who died sometime previous to the story. He is also looking for a drum kit so he can start a punch band with his chums, who sell cocaine to school kids, steal cars, listen to raucous punk music or just hang around.

The story is unsettling, more often for things unsaid. Rodrigo's suicide becomes an existential decision in the face of a hopeless future.

Gavaria manages to capture the essence of his nether world through able camerawork and judicious selection of locations, the shanty towns that line the valley walls overlooking modern Medellin. Non-pro actors are always believable. —Lent.

A Man Called Sarge

San Francisco A Cannon Pictures release, produced by Gene Corman. Executive producers, Yoram Globus, Christopher Pearce. Written and directed by Stuart Gillard. Camera (color), David Gurfinkel; no editor credited; music, Chuck Cirino; sound, Dani Natovitch; assistant director, Dev Maoz; casting, Jeremy Zimmerman. Reviewed at the Alexandria theater, San Francisco, Feb. 6, 1990. MPAA Rating: PG-13. Running time: 88 MIN.
Sarge. . . . . .Gary Kroeger
Von Kraut. . . . . .Marc Singer
Fifi LaRue. . . . . .Jennifer Runyon
Sadie. . . . . .Gretchen German
Chevalier. . . . . .Michael Mears
Browning. . . . . .Andy Greenhalgh
Anazalone. . . . . .Bobby Di Cicco
Billy Bob. . . . . .Travis McKenna
Bearpaw. . . . . .Andrew Bumatai

■Skipping critics' screenings, Cannon Pictures doubtlessly thought "A Man Called Sarge" was one of those comedies that benefits from a group experience. You can't get much of a group together at an afternoon screening when there's only one other paying customer — and he's not laughing.

Right at the start, an off-screen narrator promises, "This is not an important story, but it's a darn good way to kill 90 minutes." He lied. What can an off-screen narrator know; he was probably paid to say that without ever seeing the picture. His 90 minutes weren't killed slowly and excruciatingly, each precious moment of a lifetime dying an agonizing death at the hands of writer-director Stuart Gillard.

In memorium of the tortured time, however, let it be recorded that the "Sarge" in question takes place during the North Africa campaign of what the script calls "World War Eye Eye," pitting a company of Americans led by Gary Kroeger against legions of Germans commanded by Marc Singer. There is lots of shooting and many explosions but the favorite weapon of choice is bad jokes.

Inspired by the likes of much more successful silliness, Gillard obviously believes it's hilarious for an officer to say, "All right, gentlemen, take your seats" and film the gentlemen picking up their seats. There is a lot of that, all of equal quality. The cast is not to blame, but the work must have been embarrassing to carry out in front of each other. Imagine the difficulty of playing a French officer who mispronounces English words and those trying to decipher what he's saying while pretending nobody ever saw Peter Sellers do it all so much better so long ago.

Gillard gets a kick out of trick photography, too, discovering that if you slow down the camera and project the film at regular speed, characters will scurry around the desert like they're running real fast.

Equally hilarious, Gillard can run the film backwards and the characters will move backwards. There's a pioneer mind at work here, no doubt about it.

Unfortunately, the director has yet to master the notion that when characters are seen on a train in one scene, they should not be shown walking on the tracks in the next scene unless there's some hint of how or why they got off the train. An editor would have helped, but there's no editor credited. A writer would have helped but, as noted, the director was the writer.

It's possible "Sarge" will do better in the international market, provided everything gets lost in translation. With any luck the Netherlands will get a print dubbed in Sengalese and the 90 minutes will pass away more gently.—Har.

Wildest Dreams

New York A Platinum Pictures production. Exeuctive producer, Richard Keatinge. Produced and directed by Chuck Vincent, Screenplay, Craig Horrall, from Vincent's story; camera (color), Larry Revene; editor, James Davalos; music, Joe Mennonna; sound, Dale Whitman; art direction, Mark Hammond; custumes, Jeff Wallach; line producer, Bill Tasagal; assistant director, Bill Slobodian; casting, Chip Lambert, Reviewed on Vestron vidcassette, N.Y., Jan 3, 1990. MPAA Rating: R. Running time: 80 MIN.
Bobby Dalancy. . . . . . . .James Davies
Dancee. . . . . .Heidi Paine
Joan Peabody. . . . . .Deborah Blaisdell
Stella. . . . . .Ruth Collins
Rachel Richards. . . . . . .Jill Johnson
Isabelle. . . . . .Jeanne Marie
Claudia. . . . . .Angela Nicholas
Dexter. . . . . .Scott Baker
Louie. . . . . .Daniel Chapman
Also with: Murray Pilch, Jane Hamilton, Harvey Siegel.

■Made in 1987 with alternate title "Bikini Genie," "Wildest Dreams" is a below-par sex comedy belatedly being released direct-to-video.

It was shot in Gotham for the since defunct Lightning Pictures wing of also defund Vestron Pictures, whose video arm is distributing.

Pic's natural outlet, however, is paycable, where director Chuck Vincent's formula of bare bosoms and slapstick has proved to be a programming staple.

James Davies, who did a good job playing an evangelist in the recent theatrical release "Heaven Becomes Hell," is a bit old for the lead role here. He's a nerd left to run his parents' Greenwich Village antique shop in their absence. A bottle arrives from ancient Egypt and out pops lively Heidi Paine as a genie, who soon switches from the Barbara Eden look to wear a bikini.

Cornball complications arise when she grants his third wish for "true love." A succession of women, including Jeanne Marie as a hausfrau addicted to cleaning and buxom delivery girl Ruth Collins, become infatuated with Davies but none of them are "true." Predictably, the plain Jane who's his assistant at the shop, Deborah Blaisdell, becomes his soulmate in the end. In-joke is that she's actually porn star Tracey Adams, demure this time out.

Cast tries hard, but film isn't funny. It lacks the special effects associated with this fantasy genre.
—Lor.

Who Shot Patakango?

Florence A Patakango Ltd. production. Produced by Halle Brooks. Directed by Robert Brooks. Screenplay and editing, Robert and Halle Brooks; camera (color), Robert Brooks; art direction. Lionel Driskill. Reviewed at Florence Film Festival, Dec. 9, 1989. Running time: **104 MIN.**
Bic Bickham. . . . . .David Knight
Devlin Moran. . . . . . . .Sandra Bullock
Mark Bickham. . . . . . . .Kevin Otto
Cougar. . . . . .Aaron Ingram
Patakango. . . . . .Brad Randall
Freddie. . . . . .Chris Cardona
Goldie. . . . . .Michael Puzzo

■"Who Shot Patakango?" is a rollicking evocation of the 1950s as lived by teen pals growing up in Brooklyn's Bedford-Stuyvesant district. Seen through a nostalgic lens, helmer Robert Brooks' film is a tale well told, distinguished by a lack of self-consciousness rare in such efforts. This one indie is engrossing enough to capture larger mainstream audiences with the right handling.

The Patakango of the title is a minor character, a slow-witted clod who turns up at vocational high school with a bloody arm from a gunshot he doesn't remember getting. Who shot him remains an unanswered question, as pic zeroes in on good-looking Bic Bickham (played by engaging newcomer David Knight).

Bic is a natural leader, fun-loving and not afraid of a fight. When the gang visits a beat hangout in Greenwich Village, he makes a play for a sophisticated college girl, Devlin Moran (Sandra Bullock). Devlin responds to his attentions, despite her girlfriends' teasing and a college boyfriend she eventually opts for. Pic takes a light view of the poor boy/rich girl romance.

In this golden age before racial tension and drugs turned slum schools into hell, blacks and whites are separate but friendly. The personal grudge of a black girl against a new Hispanic student gets artificially blown out of proportion. The police arrest Bic and a black student as the warring ringleaders, take them to the station and beat them up until they invent nonexistent gangs to satisfy their elders. The incident ends unsentimentally, when Bic's blind father comes down to the station and belts the cop who beat up his son.

"Patakango" is lively throughout and almost always believable, thanks to its sense of humor and creditable performances from dozens of young thesp. Period tunes pepper scenes with the rhythm of the times. Professional lensing is a plus. —Yung.

La Vengeance d'une femme (A Woman's Revenge) (FRENCH)

Paris An AMLF release of a Sara Film production. Produced by Alain Sarde. Directed by Jacques Doillon. Screenplay, Doillon, Jean-Francois Goyet, inspired by Fyodor Dostoyevsky's novel "The Eternal Husband;" camera (color), Patrick Blossier; editor, Catherine Quesemand; sound, Jean-Pierre Duret, Dominique Hennequin; art direction, Raul Edoardo Giminez; assistant director, Etienne Albrecht; production manager, Christine Gozlan. Reviewed at AMLF screening room, Paris, Jan. 8, 1990. (In Berlin Film Festival, competing.) Running time: **133 MIN.**
Cecile. . . . . .Isabelle Huppert
Suzy. . . . . .Béatrice Dalle
Stephan. . . . . .Jean-Louis Murat
Laurence. . . . . .Laurence Cote

■Jacques Doillon is in a restrained mood in "A Woman's Revenge," a drama of jealousy and vengeance, vaguely inspired by a Dostoyevsky tale. Though he's usually stronger when quieter, filmmaker only turns out a lukewarm drama here that's overlong and visually seems better suited to the tv screen.

Pic is being shown in a competitive slot in the Berlin Film Festival.

Script by Doillon and his usual coauthor, a variation on "The Eternal Husband" with the roles sexually reversed, will interest less for its character insights than for the acting duet by Isabelle Hppert and Béatrice Dalle. Confrontation of the cool, distant Huppert and the more sensually spontaneous Dalle lacks heat until a final half hour when both let off steam and mutual recriminations.

Huppert is a widow with convoluted designs of revenge on Dalle, who had been a friend of the couple before becoming Huppert's husband's lover. Huppert tries to warm her up as girlfriend and confidante, then deliberately pushes her new lover into her arms. Though aware of the setup, Dalle plays along, but still falls into the trap set by the other woman and finally is backed into suicide.

Clocking in at over two hours, this apparently is Doillon's longest feature to date, though the material doesn't justify it. Long static dialog scenes, delivered in hushed voices, tend to pursue obvious psychological points before the expected climax finally arrives. — Len.

City Life (DUTCH)

Rotterdam A Nederlands Film Museum/ Intl. Art Film release of a Rotterdam Films production. Executive producer, City Life Foundation. Produced by Dick Rijneke, Mildred van Leeuwaarden, Jan Heijs. General editor, Mario Steenbergen. **Part One: "Thou Shalt Not Speak Evil"** (Tbilissi) Produced by Gruzia-Film and Gosteleradio. Directed by Tato Kotetishvili. Camera (color), Dato Meparishvili. **"Disorder In Progress"** (São Paolô). Produced by Juliq Calasso Jr., Casa de Imagens Cinema e Video. Directed and camera (color) by Carlos Reichenbach. **"Unheavenly City"** (Houston). Produced by Eagle Pennell, Southwestern Alternate Media Project. Directed by Pennell. Camera (color), Levie Isaacks. **"Seven Days A Week"** (Warsaw). Produced and camera (color) by Jacek Petrycki. Directed by Krzysztof Kieslowski. **"A Short Film About Nothing"** (Buenos Aires). Produced by Movimiento Falso. Directed by Alejandro Agresti. Camera (color), Nestor Sanz. **"Urban Jungles"** (Randstad). Produced by Rotterdam Films. Directed by Dick Rijneke and Mildred van Leeuwaarden. Camera (color), Rijneke. **Part Two: "The Last Boat"** (Budapest). Produced by Joszef Marx. Directed by Bela Tarr. Camera (color), Gabor Medvigy. **"Poleshift"** (Hamburg). Directed by Gabor Altorjay. Camera (color), Jorgö Jeshel. **"Eulalia — Marta April 1988"** (Barcelona). Produced by Manuel Alminana. Directed by José Luis Guerin. Camera (color), Gerardo Gormezano. **"Dakar — Clando"** (Dakar). Produced by Mame Yande Films. Directed by Ousmane William M'Baye. Camera (color), Bara Dionkhane. **"Stones, Storm And Water"** (Bevagna). Produced and camera (color) by Clemens Klopfenstein. **"Calcutta, My Eldorado"** (Calcutta). Produced and directed by Mrinal Sen. Camera (color), Shashi Anand. Reviewed at Rotterdam Film Festival, Jan. 25, 1990. (In Berlin Film Festival, Forum.) Running time, Part One: **110 MIN.**; Part Two: **141 MIN.**

■ Too uneven for general release, "City Life" — with its four solid hours of film — is a rich banquet for buffs. Dutch filmmaking couple, Dick Rijneke and Mildred van Leeuwaarden invited young indie helmers from all over the globe to make a short about their city. (Gotham, London and Paris, too large and well-known, were eliminated).

"City Life" opened the Rotterdam Film Festival and will close the Forum at the Berlin fest.

A few conditions were imposed on the directors: all had to use the same negative film stock and the same Dutch lab and do the editing in Rotterdam (where a number of the participants had been habitués of the festival). No episode was to exceed 20 minutes. Every film had to include a reference to the sinking of the Titanic, a floating city of sorts which sank like Atlantis.

All but one of the directors complied. Only Hungary's Bela Tarr broke a rule by submitting a 32-minute picture and threatened to make a stink if it was shortened. Producers gave in to avoid bitterness and undesirable publicity.

Inevitably there are differences in quality and mood. They reflect not only the differences in quality of living in each city, but also the character of the filmmakers.

Krzysztof Kieslowski's contribution on Warsaw and Alejandro Agresti's on Buenos Aires were the best appreciated for their originality by festgoers at Rotterdam. Georgia's Tato Kotetishvili's piece on Tbilisi appealed with its honest indignation and craftmanship.

The disputed Hungarian entry was completed before the recent revolutionary changes there. Gloom and fear permeate the atmosphere. Why it took Tarr 32 minutes instead of 20 to make this point is not clear.

The liveliest contribution came from the senior director, India's Mrinal Sen. His Calcutta is big, noisy, smelly and full of people scrambling for light and air. The rhythm of the film is beautifully controlled, its impending stampede of images always held in check.

There was no indifference at Rotterdam to the other contributions in "City Life." One either loved them or hated them. There is no corner for fuddy-duddies in the lives of these cities.

"City Life" is dedicated to the memory of Hubert Bals, who created and ran the Rotterdam festival until his untimely death.—*Wall.*

BERLIN FILM FESTIVAL REVIEWS

The Handmaid's Tale

New York A Cinecom Entertainment Group release of a Danny Wilson production, in coproduction with Bioskop Film, and in association with Cinetudes Film Prods. and Odyssey/Cinecom Intl. Produced by Wilson. Executive producer & production manager, Wolfgang Glattes. Directed by Volker Schlöndorff. Screenplay, Harold Pinter, based on Margaret Atwood's novel; camera (Technicolor), Igor Luther; editor, David Ray; music, Ryuichi Sakamoto; sound (Dolby), Danny Michael; production design, Tom Walsh; art direction, Gregory Melton; set decoration, Jan Pascale; costume design, Coleen Atwood; conceptual advisor, Jennifer Bartlett; assistant director, Anthony Gittelson; associate producers, Gale Goldberg, Alex Gartner; casting, Pat Golden. Reviewed at Magno Review 1 screening room, N.Y., Feb. 8, 1990. MPAA Rating: R. Running time: **109 MIN.**

Kate	Natasha Richardson
Commander	Robert Duvall
Serena Joy	Faye Dunaway
Nick	Aidan Quinn
Moira	Elizabeth McGovern
Aunt Lydia	Victoria Tennant
Ofglen	Blanche Baker
Ofwarren/Janine	Traci Lind
Doctor	David Dukes
Aunt Helena	Zoey Wilson
Aunt Elizabeth	Kathryn Doby
Rita	Lucile McIntyre

■"The Handmaid's Tale" is a provocative portrait of a future totalitarian theocracy where women have lost all human rights. Pic's theme and near-perfect cast will attract an audience, but its lack of fire will prevent it from being a breakthrough film.

Preeming in competition at the Berlin Film Festival, this adaptation of Margaret Atwood's best seller belongs to that rare category of science fiction film dealing with dystopias, cautionary views of our future. It's among a handful of pics such as "Metropolis," "Things To Come," "1984" in two incarnations, "Soylent Green" and "THX-1138" (which starred Rober* Duvall 20 years before his assignment as the heavy here), and the boldest to date, "A Clockwork Orange."

Even rarer, "Handmaid's Tale" is sci-fi from a woman's point-of-view. Following a military coup, this future society called Gilead operates under martial law in a perpetual state of warfare (a la "1984"), with Old Testament religion the rule. The socalled sins of late 20th Century society, ranging from pollution to such activities birth control & abortion are blamed by the authorities as causing God's plague of infertility in most women, requiring drastic measures to preserve the race.

Though fictional country is not identified as America, its insignia is the familiar All Seeing Eye and pyramid symbol for the Great Seal of the U.S., as displayed on the backside of the dollar bill.

Natasha Richardson portrays a young mother whose husband is killed and daughter kidnaped when she's rounded up by the authorities to serve as a breeder, or handmaid, assigned to the barren family of state security chief Robert Duvall and his wife Faye Dunaway.

Her travails unfold in Harold Pinter's uncharacteristically straightforward screenplay rather mechanically, beginning with the roundup with other young women including sympathetic lesbian Elizabeth McGovern. Pic's subtlest touch is glimpses of trucks carting away ethnic minorities, who we soon find out have no role in this future state. After horrific training under martinet Victoria Tennant, she segues to Duvall's idyllic, almost ante bellum mansion to service him in an odd sexual ritual that also involves infertile wife Dunaway (tastefully presented).

Uncredited thesp David Dukes plays a doctor who suggests at her monthly checkup that he can surreptitiously father her child -- in this male-dominated society no testing is done on daddy (Duvall) so the possibly fatal burden of procreating falls on the handmaid alone. Richardson's problem is solved (rather unconvincingly) by Dunaway's scheme of fixing her up with chauffeur Aidan Quinn. Pic resolves too neatly and unbelievably with pregnant Richardson escaping to a new life "in the mountains," after she has assassinated Duvall.

Though helmer Schlöndorff succeeds in painting the bleakness of this extrapolated future, he fails to create a strong and persistent connection with the heroine's plight. The cold, clinical sex act of the handmaid is convincing enough, but the expected cathasis of her romantic liaison with her lover is dully presented and sabotaged by cross-cutting. Despite some comic relief, film's heartless, remote mood works against its overall effectiveness.

Thematically, pic is most similar to Ira Levin's "The Stepford Wives," especially in rather grim party scenes when the white bread, aristocratic ladies of the future display all too well the false, country-club values of our culture, only magnified.

Cast can't be faulted, as Richardson's everywoman hits the right note of plainess with strength. Duvall and Dunaway underplay admirably, relying on the viewer's identification of their similar personas of lawyer Tom Hagen from "The Godfather" and Joan Crawford in "Mommie Dearest" to fill in the blanks. Unfortunately, Aidan Quinn overplays his stock role.

Tennant is effectively cast against type as an evil taskmaster while McGovern adds life to the proceedings in a quirky part — she'd rather be an honest prostitute than play the handmaid game. Traci Lind, who's changed her billing after several films as Traci Lin, is a standout as a persecuted young mother who, unlike strongwilled Richardson, is ultimately brainwashed by the system.

Ryuichi Sakamoto's electronic music score is insidious, most vital in its unusual presaging of the Duvall assassination. That familiar screen standby spiritual "Shall We Gather At The River" is used ironically, in its most perceptive appearance since Sam Peckinpah's Westerns.

Film's technical contributions, notably Igor Luther's sharp, colorful photography and Coleen Atwood's precise costuming, support pic's concept, but lacking is the original, stylistic vision of Lang in "Metropolis," Kubrick in "A Clockwork Orange" or George Lucas in the memorably white-on-white "THX-1138." Opting for plainness backfires in stunting pic's impact.

—*Lor.*

Überleben In New York (Surviving In New York) (WEST GERMAN)

Hamburg A Rosa von Praunheim and WDR tv production, distributed by Filmwelt. Directed by von Praunheim. Camera (color, 16m), Jeff Preiss; editor, von Praunheim, Mike Shepard; music, Roy Campbell; sound, Philip Roth. Reviewed at Abaton theater, Munich, Feb. 4, 1990. (In the Berlin Film Festival, Forum section.) Running time: **90 MINS.**

■Rosa von Praunheim has departed from his usual fare of gay-rights topics for this endearing docu-style look at German expatriates living in Manhattan.

Von Praunheim has lived in New York on and off for 20 years, picking up the public tv mode of documentary filmmaking. The result is a highly watchable and often moving portrait of three young German women struggling to pay the rent and get that all-important green card in the Big Apple.

Pic is a natural for the specialty theater and fest circuit.

Key to the film's success is judicious editing and the often amazing openness of the three women. One, for example, works as a Catholic school psychiatrist and does the shimmy at a midtown go-go bar by night.

All three women have tales to tell which range from the inspiring to the harrowing. Von Praunheim's sense of absurd campiness and Jeff Preiss' roving camera never lets things get too heavy.

Tech credits are adequate on this low-budget 16m job shot in just four weeks. — *Gill.*

La Baule-Les Pins (FRENCH)

Paris A UGC release of an Alexandre Films/SGGC/Films A2 coproduction. Produced by Robert Benmussa. Directed by Diane Kurys. Screenplay, Kurys, Alain Le Henry; camera (color), Giuseppe Lanci; editor, Raymonde Guyot; music, Philippe Sarde; sound, Bernard Bats, François Groult; assistant director, Michel Thibault; second unit director, Marc Angelo; production manager, Philippe Lievre; casting, Pierre Amzallag. Reviewed at UGC, Neuilly-sur-Seine, France, Feb. 5, 1990. Running time: **97 MIN.**

Lena Korski	Nathalie Baye
Michel Korski	Richard Berry
Leon Mandel	Jean-Pierre Bacri
Bella Mandel	Zabou
Odette	Valeria Bruni-Tedeschi
Ruffier	Didier Benureau
Frederique	Julie Bataille
Sophie	Candice Lefranc
Daniel	Alexis Derlon
Suzanne	Emmanuelle Boidron
Rene	Maxime Boidron
Titi	Benjamin Sacks

■Diane Kurys covers familiar ground in a routine manner in "La Baule-Les Pins." Family comedy-drama is a followup to Kurys' fine 1983 film "Coup de Foudre" (Entre Nous), which movingly dramatized the story of the director's parents. Despite its affiliation to an earlier critical and commercial success, prospects for "La Baule" probably will be more modest.

"La Baule" begins where "Coup de Foudre" ends: with the separation and impending divorce of Kurys' parents, called Lena and Michel Korski in both films, a provincial petit bourgeois Jewish couple who had met during the war in an internment camp, married, had kids and continued to struggled together through the difficult postwar years in Lyon.

The cramped middle-class family life weighed heavily on the mother, especially when she befriended another frustrated young married woman, who was a catalyst for the couple's breakup.

In the new script Kurys wrote with her usual collaborator, Alain Le Henry, the breakup, situated during the summer of 1958, is just beginning.

But the girlfriend (played in "Coup de Foudre" by Miou-Miou) has disappeared without a trace. Kurys' parents, originally portrayed by Isabelle Huppert and Guy Marchand, now are embodied by Nathalie Baye and Richard Berry.

Except for the opening scenes, film is set in a coastal resort, the "La Baule" of the title, where the family traditionally vacations in a rented house. This time, however, mom sends the kids ahead with their governess, promising to come later.

In fact Baye uses the time to look for work and an apartment in Paris, where she hopes to bring the children after she leaves Berry.

Kurys recounts this fateful summer in her family's history from the point of view of the two daughters, aged 13 and eight, who are only vaguely aware of parental strife and tend to go about their holiday in the usual carefree manner.

This narrative angle is not consistently respected, since the film dramatizes intimate scenes among the adults that the kids are not witness to.

Film's major faults, however, are the banality of the script and the relative staleness of Kurys' direc-

tion. The personal commitment that informed "Coup de foudre" is strangely absent here.

The autobiographical elements are evoked without insight, the beachside escapades of the children are familiar comic stuff of countless films about kids, and the violent quarrels of the parents were shown with more effective pathos in "Coup de foudre."

Baye, more emotionally direct than the hermetic Huppert, is good as the wife and mother fighting to assert her freedom from a mediocre life and husband. But Berry has little of the uncomprehending fragility that made Guy Marchand's performance in the early film so memorable.

Jean-Pierre Bacri and Zabou provide light-hearted support as the uncle and aunt also vacationing with their brood (Bacri was featured in "Coup de foudre," but played Miou-Miou's husband). Vincent Lindon is engaging as Baye's summertime lover, but he disappears rather suddenly.

Newcomer Valerie Bruni-Tedeschi is perfect as the children's long-suffering governess and Didier Benureau is the eccentric landlord who rents his house to the family and moves into the basement. The kids, led by pretty Julie Bataille as the older daughter, are perfectly natural and entertaining. Tech credits are fine. —Len.

Full Moon In New York
(HONG KONG)

Berlin   A Shiobu Film Co. production. (Intl. sales, Kwan's Creation Co.) Produced by Henry Fong. Directed by Stanley Kwan. Screenplay, Zhong Acheng, Yan Tai On Ping; camera (color), Bill Wong; editor, Steve Wong, Chow Cheung Kan; music, Chang-Hung Yi; sound, Yeung Woi Keung; production design, Pan Lai; line producer, Nancy Tong; assistant director, Season Ma. Reviewed at Berlin Film Festival (Panorama section), Feb. 10, 1990. Running time: **88 MINS.**
Wang Hsiung Ping . . . . . . .Sylvia Chang
Li Feng Jiao. . . . . Maggie Cheung
Chao Hong. . . . . .Sichingowa

■"Full Moon In New York," which centers on three Chinese women from different backgrounds who become friends in New York, is strong on atmosphere and character but thin on plot. It will play the fests, with arthouse exposure more problematical.

For the internationally growing audience of China film buffs, pic has been eagerly awaited as it's the latest from director Stanley Kwan,

whose "Rouge" was widely admired two years ago.

Sichingowa plays a woman from Mainland China who has come to the U.S. to marry a Chinese American; she misses her mother and is finding it hard to come to terms with life in the Big Apple.

Sylvia Chang plays a Taiwanese actress who's lived in New York for several years. She breaks up with her American boyfriend, and seems uncertain of her future. The most assured of the three is Hong Kong-born Maggie Cheung, who owns a restaurant (where her father is chef) and property in the U.S. and Hong Kong. A successful businesswoman, she has no time for men.

Kwan does surprising little with the women after establishing them. There are long scenes in which they get to know each other and find a bond despite the differences of background, status and language (Cheung speaks Cantonese, the other two Mandarin). They get drunk together, sing songs and help each other.

All of this is finely observed, and beautifully photographed by Bill Wong, adding up to a moody, atmospheric film. It demands patience from audiences, but they will be rewarded with these portraits of strong, attractive women. Pic lacks the impact of "Rouge," but compensates with a gentle, understated beauty all its own. New York seldom has looked more attractive that it does here. — Strat.

The Exiles
(DOCU)

Berlin   An Exiles Project presentation and production. Produced by Richard Kaplan, Catharine Taylor. Directed by Kaplan. Screenplay by Kaplan and Lou Potter; camera (Image Transform, newsreel excerpts b&w), Dick Blofson, Kit Davidson, Rob Issen, Axel Reinhardt, Dyanne Taylor; editors, Anne Borin, Walter Hess, Richard Kaplan; music, Arthur Cunningham; sound, Laurent Lafran, Larry Loewinger, Peter Miller, Scott Nielsson, Horst Stroemer, Gerd Willert. Reviewed at Berlin Film Festival (Panorama section), Feb. 10, 1990. Running time: **116 MINS.**

■For "The Exiles," noted documentarist Richard Kaplan combines newsreel shots of Nazi or Nazi-inspired atrocities with filmed comments gathered in interviews with 70 European intellectuals, artists or scientists who escaped the Holocaust to the U.S.

A sure tv attention-getter, "The Exiles" has on its roster such names as Alfred Eisenstadt, Bruno Bettel-

heim, Fritz Lang, Rod Steiger, Billy Wilder, Sabine Thomson, Nuria Nono, Hanna Gray, Dolly Haas, Edward Teller, Felicia Deyrup, Herbert Marcuse, Mary Jane Gold, Golo Mann and Erich Leinsdorf.

Not a single boastful claim is made, but Kaplan somehow makes it appear that Western culture has been built on survivors alone. This conceit is an innocent one, since the contributions of these exiles — whether to painting, music, nuclear physics or advertising — have been obvious.

What is interesting is to discover how their troubles were not quite over once they left the Nazi realm. They faced xenophobia and anti-Semitism, and there was a struggle, often in vain, to maintain their language and way of life.

They haven't forgotten and they don't want anybody else to forget. That guilt should remain common for all is this docu's message.

—Kell.

Samlaren
(The Collector)
(DOCU)

Berlin   A Swedish Film Institute release of an Erik Stroemdahl Film with the Swedish Institute. Produced, written, directed, filmed (Eastmancolor) and edited by Erik Stroemdahl; music, Bo Anders Persson; sound, Anders Hammar, Patrik Stroemdal. Reviewed at Berlin Film Festival (Market), Feb. 10, 1990. Running time: **82 MINS.**

■Documentarist Erik Stroemdahl profiles an old bag man, "The Collector," who, despite his appearance, is an environmental activist.

Sympathetic to the man's philosophy of never letting anything or anybody go to waste, Stroemdal never questions his inefficient ways.

The old man, Kurre Hellstroem, used to run a school for pastry chefs, he says, but always was in trouble with the authorities, and even spent time in jail for driving without a license.

Hellstroem, now in a good house and neighborhood, annoys his neighbors and the police by scrounging things that can be recycled, and his yard looks and smells like a junkyard. The amiable Hellstroem will support prostitutes or drunks who come to his door for help.

When he is arrested for various offenses, the authorities tend to be gentle with him, considering him feeble-minded or illiterate.

Actually, Hellstroem seems to have the last laugh on everybody, including Stroemdahl.

The film may be too long for easy tv slotting. But in times when environmentalist sentiment runs high, Hellstroem may come across to many as a kind of latter-day folk hero. —*Kell.*

The Natural History Of Parking Lots

Park City, Utah A Little Deer production. Produced by Aziz Ghazal. Written and directed by Everett Lewis. Camera, Hisham Abed; lighting, Roy Unger; editor, Lewis; music, John Hammer; sound, Mark Decew, Sreescanda; production manager, Chester Wong; second unit camera, David Dechant. Reviewed at the U.S. Film Festival, Park City, Utah, Jan. 25, 1990. (In Berlin Film Festival, Panorama). No MPAA Rating. Running time: **92 MIN.**

Chris. . . . . .Charlie Bean
Lance. . . . . .B. Wyatt
Sam. . . . . .Charles Taylor
P.O.. . . . . .Mark Williams
Kelly. . . . . .Sara
Neo-Nazi. . . . . .Roy Heidicker
Mrs. Porter. . . . . .Eli Guralnick

■**This black & white film is as much about the sheer joy of image-making as about its subject, but it still manages to tell a sharp, simple story, all the more affecting for the depth of its visual expression.**

With a style that recalls the French New Wave films of Robert Bresson and Jean-Luc Godard, pic should find strong interest on the festival circuit and in arthouses.

The desolation of Los Angeles' anonymous urban jungle is personified in Chris (Charlie Bean), a teenager more or less abandoned by his splintered, preoccupied family. He finds consolation in stealing '50s cars, apparently as a link to a more innocent time.

On probation and rarely in school, Chris lives alone with a maid in the house left behind by his divorced parents, and occasionally sees his stockbroker father, who says things like, "The real question is what my investment procedure is going to be between now and 1990."

When his older brother Lance (B.

Wyatt) shows up to stay with him, the alienated siblings begin to form a bond that gives Chris what he most needs — a sense of security and family ties.

But Chris discovers that his father is paying Lance a hefty sum to "babysit" him at about the same time his older brother's drug-dealing business catches up with him.

"Parking Lots," created by Everett Lewis, a Los Angeles art school film professor, and lensed on a low budget with several nonactors in the cast, burns with visual poetry and intensity, from the energy of a wobbly handheld camera veering in reckless circles around its subjects to such startling effects as an empty white screen followed by a slow pan to a shot of a man speaking at the camera.

Actors are often backlit, with faces in shadow, and the pristine natural-lit interiors are artsy indeed.

Lewis also gets across some lovely scenes between his actors, particularly the ones at a swimming hole where they frolic, and later, mend a fight.

Scenes of the brothers in their similar haircuts and leather jackets wrestling and engaging in roadside urinating rituals are funny and memorable.

Story has some structural flaws and one gets the sense that some of the things it intended to say, particularly about parking lots as a metaphor for abandonment and impermanence, didn't show up on the screen.

The aggressive camerawork can be overbearing at times, and when a road trip to Tijuana provides absolutely no change in lighting or atmosphere, it gets in the way of the story.

John Hammer's austere, synthetic score complements the European feel of the visuals. —*Daws.*

L'Homme Imaginé (The Man Of Her Imagination) (FRENCH)

Berlin A CDN production, with Oculus 57/Le Largo. (Intl. sales, Motion Media, Paris.) Directed by Patricia Bardon. Screenplay, Bardon; camera (Eastmancolor), Pascal Caubere; editor, Catherine Maurice; music, Bernard Sandoval; production design, Stephane Levy Kuentz; sound, Laurent Langlois; production manager, Olivier Girard; assistant director, Alain Monne. Reviewed at Berlin Film Fest

(Panorama section), Feb. 10, 1990. Running time: **83 MINS.**

Marie. . . . . .Marie Carré
The man. . . . . .Jacques Spiesser
Also with: Helene Bascoul, Yann Dedet, Paul Balin, Betrice Houplain, Pierre Gerard, Benoit Thivel.

■**A charming but insubstantial first feature, "The Man Of Her Imagination" is likely to be sympathetically received on its home turf, but is too familiar and gentle to travel well. Still, critical notice might help Patricia Bardon find an audience.**

Her story revolves around an shy, elfin heroine who's painfully thin, lives alone, works in a suburban town hall, has two kittens, a nagging mother and no man. Also, she can't sleep at night.

Into her life comes a stranger, much older than she and already looking a little worse for wear. But he's charming, she's attracted, and they become passionate lovers. Then days go by and he doesn't call. And the very night he does call, she's in bed with someone else.

It's as simple as that, but Marie Carré is an appealingly vulnerable heroine and grabs audience attention. Slim on narrative as it is, the film is filled with interesting settings, including the local swimming pool or various bars, cafes and restaurants.

It's a promising debut, filled with tenderness and humor, but it may be too lightweight to make the grade. Still, Bardon's second feature can be awaited with anticipation.
—*Strat.*

INDIA FILM FESTIVAL REVIEWS

Mathilukal (The Walls) (INDIAN)

Calcutta Produced, written and directed by Adoor Gopalakrishnan for Adoor Gopalakrishnan Prods. Sponsored by Doordarshan (Indian tv). Based on a story by Vaikom Muhammad Basheer. Camera (Eastmancolor), Ravi Varma; editor, M. Mani; art direction, Sivan; music, Vijaya Bhaskar. Reviewed at the India Film Festival, Calcutta (Indian Panorama), Jan. 18, 1990. Running time: **120 MIN.**

Basheer. . . . . .Mammootty
Head warden. . . . . .Thilakan
Classmate. . . . . .Murali
Razak. . . . . .Ravi Vallathol
With: Karamana, Sreenath, Babu Namboodiri, Jagannatha Varma, Vempayam, Azees.

■**In "The Walls," leading Kerala director Adoor Gopalakrishnan films a tale based on the prison writings of local Malayalan scribe Vaikom Muhammad Basheer. Film has the masterful simplicity of a fable and the refinement of experienced filmmaking. One of the strongest new Indian pics of the season, it should find release in specialized venues after a fest run.**

Setting is the early 1940s. Basheer is serving a jail sentence for his support of India's freedom struggle. A good-tempered, even-keeled philosopher, Basheer has a contagious love of life that makes him popular with convicts and jailers

alike — to say nothing of his fame as a writer. Though sentenced to two years for his books, Basheer doesn't take it too hard.

And no wonder — daily life in the Trivandrum Central jail looks like a tropical picnic in paradise. The first guard he meets lets him keep his matches, cigarets and a razor blade; the second supplies him with tea and special food; a third with admiring companionship. Basheer spends his time chatting with other political prisoners and puttering around his rose garden. When the other politicos are abruptly pardoned, however, Basheer inexplicably gets left behind. He grows moody with no one to talk to, and even plans escape. Then a voice from the other side of the garden wall, a young girl serving a life sentence in the women's prison next door, arrives to brighten his day. He falls in love with the unseen stranger, but before they can meet in the infirmary, as they plan, Basheer is pardoned. He leaves jail with a heavy heart.

Despite some long moments, "The Walls" is an engrossing film. It finds its sincerity in the unhurried, linear unfolding of events, where Ravi Varma's honest, upright lensing mirrors the hero's character. Gopalakrishnan agains demonstrates his command of camera, actors (all convincing), and almost nude sets. As Basheer, Mammootty communicates the writer's fascinating intelligence and humanity. — *Yung.*

Alicinte Anweshanam
(Alice's Search)
(INDIAN)

Calcutta A Neo Vision production, in association with the National Film Development Corp. Produced, written and directed by T.V. Chandran. Camera (color), Sunny Joseph; editor, Venugoplal; music, Ousephachan; art direction, C. N. Karunakaran. Reviewed at India Film Festival (Indian Panorama), Calcutta, Jan. 12, 1990. Running time: **120 MIN.**
Alice . . . . .Jalaja
Also with: Raveendranath, Nedumudi Venu, Sreeraman, Nilambur Balan, P.T.K. Mohamed.
(In Malayalam)

■ "Alice's Search," like another fine Malayalam film from last season, Shaji's "The Birth," centers on a missing person. Pic's uniqueness lies in its feminist slant, and the surprisingly liberated conclusions reached by the heroine. It looks headed for more fests and film weeks.

Here it is the man's young wife Alice (actress Jalaja) who follows his tracks, and learns more about him than she knew when he was around. A lecturer in a local college is to a!! appearances a respectable fellow. He, wife Alice and the two kids are a middle-class Catholic family without problems. One day he disappears.

Roaming up and down Kerala in search of him, Alice shows not only a lot of bravery and determination, but sensitive intelligence in putting together the jigsaw pieces of a man whose real nature she scarcely knew. He now appears as a whoring, boozing wastrel.

Alice is transformed from a self-effacing wife whose existence revolves around her man to an independent person. Film ends not in an emotional climax, but in Alice's simple realization she's better off without the cad.

"Alice's Search" trails through the exotic pageantry of tropical Kerala in a fluid tale without punches. The mystery is gentle, politics and religion softly touched on, characters quietly introduced.

Lensing and thesping are quality work. —*Yung.*

Bagh Bahadur
(The Tiger Dancer)
(INDIAN)

Calcutta A Doordashan production. Produced by Buddhadeb Dasgupta. Executive producer, Dulal Roy. Written and directed by Dasgupta. Camera (color), Venu; editor, Ujjal Nandi; music, Shantanu Mahapatra; art direction, Nikhal Sengupta; production manager, Somnath Das. Reviewed at the India Film Festival (Indian Panorama), Calcutta, Jan. 19, 1990. Running time: **90 MIN.**
Ghuram . . . . .Pavan Malhotra
Radha. . . . . .Archana
Sibal. . . . . .Vasudev Rao
Also with: Biplab Chattopadhyay, Rajeswari Roychowdhury, Masood Akhtar.
(In Hindi)

■Veteran director Buddhadeb Dasgupta mines the rich lode of Indian folk tales in "The Tiger Dancer." Short and sweet, pic tells the tragic story of a man the West would call a street artist who undergoes a human and artistic crisis. Given the director's reputation and pic's refined simplicity, the film is bound to make fest rounds and be in line for special releases.

Ghunuram (played by versatile Hindi actor Pavan Malhotra) takes a month off work at a rock quarry to wander back to the village of Nonpura for its annual folk festival. He dons the elaborate body makeup of a tiger and prepares to enchant audiences with his Tiger Dance, as he has in other years. He also hopes to marry Archana, young daughter of his aged host and drummer, Vasudev Rao.

To his and Rao's shock, the villagers ignore the Tiger Dance to gape at a leopard some circus people have caught. Upstaged by the leopard show, Ghunuram feels like a has-been. Far worse than losing his public's economic support is the loss of their respect. Archana changes her mind about him, too, enamored of a circus performer. In desperation, and with old Rao drumming fiercely to give him courage, Ghunuram enters the leopard's cage. He succeeds in rousing the tame creature into a fight and loses his life.

To quibble with an undeniably moving finale, last scene could have been improved by a more realistic-looking confrontation between man and beast. It's obvious the leopard is a fun-loving fellow, and a sense of real menace fails to come across — camera simply cuts away to show Ghunuram dead in the cage. However, the two main thesps, Malhotra and Rao, are a dynamic combo as the spirited and feeling folk artists, too proud to be bested by a fake. Film is well lensed, and the tiger makeup is tops. — *Yung.*

Banani
(The Forest)
(INDIAN)

Calcutta A Purbanchal Film Cooperative Society production. Directed by Jahnu Barua. Screenplay, Sushil Goswami; camera (color), Anoop Jotwani; editor, Heu-En Barua; music, Satya Baruah, Prashanta Bordoloi; art direction, Phatik Baruah. Reviewed at India Film Festival (Indian Panorama), Calcutta, Jan. 13, 1990. Running time: **108 MIN.**
With: Mridula Baruah, Sushil Goswami, Bishnu Kharghoria, Golap Duttta, Lakshmi Sinha, Munin Sharma, Jyoti Bhattacharya, Shasanka Debo Phukan.
(In Assamese)

■ "The Forest" is an honest, if sometimes overly explicit, protest about how India's forests are being illegally cut down with the complicity of political powers. Pic should find limited play abroad in fests and Indian film weeks.

The ecology angle is well played up in the lush countryside of Assam by director Jahnu Barua (whose "The Catastrophe" was another memorable social critique).

An evil logger is merrily chopping down trees when Tapan Barua, idealistic forest ranger, gets transferred to the area. He immediately starts blocking the logs, stationing guards on forest roads, and warring with his corrupt superiors. The villagers love him; his wife detests him because he keeps getting transferred.

Film is laced with a number of didactic speeches, apparently aimed at informing local auds about the devastating ecological effects of deforestation. Story is predictable enough, but the characters help flesh it out. Most of film's emotional charge resides in its undisguised contempt for the officialdom that protects the timber smugglers, summed up in the line: "No one can stop corruption in this country" Hopefully the message will reach honest ears. —*Yung.*

Chhandaneer
(The Nest Of Rhythm)
(INDIAN)

Calcutta An Abhishek Prods. film. Written and directed by Utpalendu Chakraborty. Camera (color), Girish Padhiar; art direction, Prasad Mitra; editor, Bulu Ghosh; music, Chakraborty; playback, Balmurali Krishna, Ajay Chakraborty, Maya Sen. Reviewed at the India Film Festival (Indian Panorama), Calcutta, Jan. 16, 1990. Running time: **130 MIN.**
Seema. . . . . .Anjana Banergi
Also with: Dipak Sarkar, Madhabi Chakraborty, Satya Banerjee, Anup Kumar, Sreela Majumdar, Jnanesh Mukherjee, Ratna Ghosal, Kanika Majumdar.
(In Bengali)

■ "The Nest Of Rhythm" is unusually successful in overlaying a convincing story with an exposition on Indian classical dance. Though it looks something like a hybrid, Utpalendu Chakraborty's tale of a classical dancer becomes more entertaining as it goes on, thanks to a rigorous performance by Anjana Banerji as actress and dancer. It would be a good choice for an Indian cultural program.

Seema (Banerji) is a rich girl who has trained in the Bharat Natyam tradition since she was little. Like any great ballerina, she's all iron will, determination, and practice. Her middle-class parents are proud of her international success, but worry about marrying her off to someone able to pay for her expensive costumes.

Scorning her parents' choice, Seema chooses a blind musician, Ayan, as mate. She marries not for love of him, but for love of his great talent. They begin doing shows together, with Seema dancing to Ayan's classically innovative music.

A true purist, Seema gives dance lessons to make ends meet, but refuses to compromise with her art. When Ayan gets them a gig with a vulgar pop singer, Seema walks out. Their final break comes when Ayan agrees to write music for a commercial film — and is exploited by the producers for his trouble. Seema continues on the true path, and earns ever greater fame. After a leg injury, she makes up with a repentant Ayan.

Despite Seema's single-mindedness, or because of it, she is an unusual and appealing character, an independent woman.

Story comes decked with a number of fine dance numbers, which illustrate the graceful beauty and expressiveness of Bharat Natyam. Viewer also is given some sense of the different classical traditions in Bengal and the South, when Seema attempts to blend Eastern dance with Southern music.

— *Yung.*

Percy
(INDIAN)

Calcutta A National Film Development Corp. production in association with Channel 4 Television. Directed by Pervez Merwanji. Screenplay, Cyrus Mistry, Jill Misquitta; camera (Eastmancolor), Navroze Contractor; editor, Priya Krishnaswamy; art direction, Roshan Kalapesi; music, Vanraj Bhatia; produc-

tion manager, Sorab Irani. Reviewed at the India Film Festival (Indian Panorama), Calcutta, Jan. 18, 1990. Running time: **128 MIN.**
Percy. . . . . .Kurush Deboo
With: Ruby Patel, Hosi Vasunia, Sharad Smait, Rajan Bane, Zenobia Shroff.
(In Parsi-Gujarati)

■A first feature film by Pervey Merwanji, "Percy" is hardly what one expects an Indian film to be. This light, ironic comedy about a meek loser has an almost Western edge of ethnic humor. Pic's appeal is sorely tried, however, by a drawn-out running time that needs radical trimming. Coproduced by Channel 43, it could make it at specialized venues in a 90-minute format.

Pic's inherent fascination is its setting in Bombay's Parsi community, a small but influential Zoroastrianism sect originating in Persia. Unlike last season's "Pestonjee," also about the Parsis, "Percy" is played out in contemporary times and in local dialect.

Hero, incarnated to a T by the lanky Kurush Deboo, is a 28-year-old mama's boy, an overgrown daydreamer with no friends. Life revolves around trudging off to work in an office and coming home to Mother's (Ruby Patel) cooking.

One day he joins the Bombay Music Society, an oddball group who get together to listen to recordings of Western music. Percy is struggling out of his shell when he gets beaten up by a delivery boy whom he got sacked for stealing. The office is bombed, too, and Percy becomes even more shiftless without a job. Final blow is the death of his domineering mother, but the traumatic event carries a promise that Percy will become self-sufficient at last.

With no story to sink its teeth into, "Percy" founders in meandering scenes casually linked together. Yet Merwanji excels at sharply observed details and affectionately critical portraits of the Parsis — like Percy's big-hearted, coarse father. Pic's offbeat sense of humor combines with personal tragedy in a telling melange. — *Yung.*

Revenge

Hollywood   A Columbia Pictures presentation in association with New World Entertainment of a Rastar production. Produced by Hunt Lowry, Stanley Rubin. Executive producer, Kevin Costner. Directed by Tony Scott. Screenplay, Jim Harrison, Jeffrey Fiskin, based on the novella by Harrison; camera (Deluxe color), Jeffrey Kimball; editor, Chris Lebenzon; music, Jack Nitzsche; production design, Michael Seymour, Benjamin Fernandez; art direction, Tom Sanders, Jorge Sainz; costume design, Aude Bronson-Howard; set decoration, Crispian Sallis, Fernando Solorio; production/sound mixer, David MacMillan; assistant director, Lowry. Reviewed at Mann Bruin theater, Los Angeles, Feb. 14, 1990. MPAA Rating: R. Running time: **124 MIN.**
Cochran. . . . . .Kevin Costner
Tibey. . . . . .Anthony Quinn
Miryea. . . . . .Madeleine Stowe
Cesar. . . . . .Tomas Milian
Mauro. . . . . .Joaquin Martinez
Texan. . . . . .James Gammon
Madero. . . . . .Jesse Corti
Rock star. . . . . .Sally Kirkland
Amador. . . . . .Miguel Ferrer
With: Luis De Icaza, Gerardo Zepeda, John Leguizamo, Joe Santos, Christofer De Oni.

■This far-from-perfect rendering of Jim Harrison's shimmering novella has a romantic sweep and elemental power that ultimately transcend its flaws. Contempo tale of a doomed love triangle in lawless Mexico should rack up hot numbers for Columbia for several weeks, despite a marketing campaign that emphasizes its least distinctive aspects.

Audiences will see Kevin Costner in a different light here as a man whose passions lead him afoul of the boundaries of right and wrong. As J. Cochran, a hotshot Navy pilot who retires after 12 years, he heads down to Puerto Vallarta for recreation at the home of a wealthy sportsman friend, Tibey (Anthony Quinn) and is right away smitten with his host's gorgeous and unhappy wife Miryea (Madeleine Stowe).

Despite his friend's graciousness and reputation as a cold-blooded killer, Cochran takes the suicide plunge into passion, running off with Miryea for a sexual idyll that is soon enough blasted into oblivion by Tibey and his henchmen. They pound Cochran to a pulp and leave him in the desert to die, then pack Miryea off to a whorehouse to be drugged and abused.

Cochran recovers and sets off on a perilous quest to search out his lover, ultimately confronting Tibey in a scene that crackles with conflict and remorse.

It is a measure of the quality of Harrison's book that it was so hotly pursued. The late John Huston once intended to film it, and contributed to the script (uncredited). Costner sought it separately from Rastar, thus his exec producer credit.

Originally shot to follow more closely the tone of the pristine narrative, the much-fiddled-with footage was eventually pasted into its current form, and though much is lost, the tale's simplicity, grace and subtlety shine through.

All three elements of the love triangle are compelling, and as a crucial fourth character Mexico performs radiantly.

Stowe is emerging as a great screen beauty, her teasing eyes and mocking smile recalling Meryl Streep, and she is certainly a match for Costner's charisma, which flags out but is ultimately winning in this roughly molded role.

Director Tony Scott ("Top Gun," "Beverly Hills Cop II") is all thumbs for a few reels, with too-tight framing setting an oppressive tone. Also, the pic is forced roughly through its emotional paces. Not until the first screen appearance of the magnificent Quinn do things improve. His perf as a political puppeteer is so rich and sympathetic that he threatens to steal away the audience despite his brutality.

While Scott has trouble setting a tone in pic's reworked beginning (the opening dialogue and "Top Gun" jet-fighter footage is a groaner), he finds his footing in Mexico, where landscapes and Jack Nitzsche's music establish a mesmerizing atmosphere, and adventure is set loose in the wild-frontier environs.

Pic's vitality is enhanced by several castings, including Sally Kirkland in an obnoxious/infectious turn as a loose-living rock star, Mel Ferrer as the hepcat tough who teams with Cochran to find the femme, and, best of all, gravelly voiced James Gammon as a Texas horse dealer raging along with the last breath left in his body.

There are some other lovely touches, such as the perf of Alfredo Cienfuegos as Antonio, the young transvestite who watches over Miryea in the brothel, and the use of 98-year-old non-pro Trini Rodriguez, found on location, as the healer who aids Cochran.

A crucial weakness of the pic is that Cochran recovers so quickly, whereas in the book, the severity of his brush with death was at the core of the tale's power.

Though "Revenge" is far from a masterpiece, it has many attractions to blot out its faltering steps, including the chemistry that catches fire among its lead characters; Mexico included. — *Daws.*

Hollywood Mavericks
(DOCU)

Park City, Utah   An American Film Institute and NHK Enterprises production. Coordinating producer, Florence Dauman. Written by Todd McCarthy, Michael Henry Wilson; camera (color), John Bailey, Steve Baum, Frederick Elmes, Marc Gerard, Mead Hunt, Todd McClelland, Peter S. Rosen, Steve Wacks; editor, Stacey Foiles; creative consultants, Foiles, McCarthy, Wilson; production manager, Dale Ann Stieber; Reviewed at U.S. Film Festival, Park City, Utah, Jan. 22, 1990. Running time: **90 MIN.**
Participants: Martin Scorsese, Paul Schrader, Peter Bogdanovich, D.W. Griffith, Erich Von Stroheim, Josef Von Sternberg, King Vidor, John Ford, Orson Welles, Samuel Fuller, John Cassavetes, Dennis Hopper, Francis Coppola, Sam Peckinpah, Robert Altman, Alan Rudolph, David Lynch, Robert De Niro.

■"Hollywood Mavericks," financed by Japanese media company NHK and produced under the auspices of the American Film Institute, takes a stimulating look at American directors who have adhered to their own visions regardless of the pressures of the system.

With Martin Scorsese, Peter Bogdanovich and Paul Schrader as commentators and critics on clips of the groundbreaking works they've admired, "Mavericks" offcers an insightful and enriching probe of who the innovators were and why they mattered.

D.W. Griffith is described as a playwright who came to the cinema by default and "had such little regard for the movies that he broke every rule there was."

Francis Coppola, describing his long and troubling journey to make "Apocalypse Now," says he came to the decision that "since I'm already washed up, I'll just be washed up and at least make the movie I believe in."

Schrader describes his backing for the admittedly uncommercial "Mishima" — "I think a lot of the money I received was a form of patronage" — and John Cassavetes describes the genesis of his innovative independent films "Shadows" and "Faces."

Alan Rudolph observes how the studios stifle creativity: "Hollywood approaches its most talented offspring and says, 'We'll pay you a lot of money to behave like an artist — just don't produce any art.'"

Feature-length docu relates how Orson Welles persisted in shooting pieces of "Othello" over three years despite a collapse of producer backing and how Samuel Fuller turned low-budget pics into dynamic personal statements.

Scorsese opines that "The Last Temptation Of Christ" was "the most maverick" of all his films; David Lynch declares he likes a film to be entertaining and tell a strong story, but also to be "full of mystery and abstraction and things that are happening beneath the surface."

Told minus narration through thoughtfully structured commen-

Hollywood Mavericks

Continued from page 306

tary, abundant film clips and some rare interview footage, pic begins with subjects like Fuller and Welles attempting to define "maverick" and cuts to brief snatches of milestone films as diverse as "Raging Bull" and "Eraserhead."

Excerpts from 68 pics are included, from Griffith's "The Musketeers Of Pig Alley" (1912) to Spike Lee's "Do The Right Thing" (1989).

The makers of "Mavericks" have limited their field to iconoclastic Americans who operated at least somewhat within the system; all sorts of omissions could be argued for.

But, by starting back in the silent era, docu packs into its 90 minutes a more enriching view of how the struggle for independence has been waged than if it had loitered in the present. Absence of such figures as Woody Allen, John Sayles, Lee, Stanley Kubrick and Jim Jarmusch is somewhat mitigated by their inclusion in a montage of film clips at docu's conclusion.

Created for worldwide tv and possible theatrical release, docu is the first coproduction of Japanese pubcaster NHK-Japan Broadcasting Corp. with the AFI. — *Daws.*

Mr. Leedii — Yoake No Shinderera (Mr. Lady — Cinderella At Daybreak) (JAPANESE)

Tokyo A Toho release of a Nichiei production. Produced by Hiroaki Kato. Directed by Shoji Segawa. Screenplay, Segawa, Kikuma Shimoizaka, Masato Hayashi; camera (color), Makoto Hayashi; lighting, Hideaki Yamakawa; editor, Keiichi Uraoka;music, Ryudo Uzaki; sound, Shoji Tanimura; art direction, Hiro Kitagawa, Kiotaka Sawada; assistant director, Jin Kato; associate producer, Michiko Kato. Reviewed at Shinjuku Village 1, Jan. 31, 1990. Running time: **110 MIN.**
Daisuke Yamazaki. . . .Tsurutaro Kataoka
Tetsuro Tsujimoto. . . . . .Akira Onodera
Sakurako Hayase. . . . . . .Mari Yagisawa
Tetsuya Nakahara. . . . . .Kenichi Kaneda
Yoko Yamazaki. . . . .Hideko Nagashima
Yumi Hagiawara. . . . . . .Yumi Morio

■"**Mr. Lady — Cinderella At Daybreak" happily confounds fears of predictability, despite allowing its actors to dress up in women's clothing and despite starring Tsurutaro Kataoka.**

In fact, one of the more pleasant surprises is Kataoka. The ubiquitous and none-too-funny tv comedian managed to give a beautifully understated performance in "Ijintachi no Natsu," an accomplishment many attributed to the direction of Nobuhiko Obayashi. Here Kataoka again distances himself from his small-screen inanities to project a winning gentleness.

Fired from his job at a usurious loan company, Kataoka runs into a long-lost male friend, Akira Onodera, the bewigged proprietor of a gay club. Hired by Onodera to handle the club's finances, Kataoka is soon dressing in drag to earn more money for his son's operation and trying to sort out his feelings for a beautiful club employee who may be a man.

Much of the detailed plot suggests that the scenarists familiarized themselves with the subject by watching gay-themed Western films. Kataoka's initial discomfort in drag, his efforts to avoid being recognized by a certain customer and his disastrous participation in a floor show all seem inspired by similar moments in "The Ritz."

Moreover, his uneasiness over being attracted to a person of (possibly) the same sex is a lift from "Victor/Victoria." And the titular reference to "La Cage aux Folles" (released here as "Mr. Lady-Mr. Madame") acknowledges indebtedness to that European comedy as does Onodera's love for his son from a brief marriage, reminiscent of Ugo Tognazzi's affection for his own son.

The derivative nature should not obscure the fact that the film is radical for Japan, treating gays

with a surprising lack of condescension. Interestingly, the film was made with what the credits term the "support" of a leading cosmetics firm (Max Factor) and a hairpiece manufacturer (Art Nature). — *Bail.*

Pink Ulysses (DUTCH-COLOR/B&W)

Rotterdam An NFM-IAP release of a Yuca Film production. Produced by Suzanne van Voorst. Written and directed by Eric de Kuyper. Camera (16m, color and b&w), Stej Tijdink; editor, Ton de Graff; sound, Jan van Sandwijk. Reviewed at Rotterdam Film Festival, Jan. 28, 1990. Running time: **98 MIN.**
With: Jose Teunissen, Jos Ijland, Dolf Wilkens, Erik de Bruyn.

■**This could easily become a cult film. Question is: the cult of what? Of lovers of music, of dance, of bodies and eroticism,** sensuality, gay movies, of astonishing shots? In any case, "Pink Ulysses," by Eric de Kuyper, is an attention-grabber.

There's no plot, only the theme of Ulysses' return from Troy as a thread to hold the whole together. Film is a sensuous flow of music (from Wagner to Zarah Leander) and images (including clips of old pics), filled with bodies and colors, and a very explicit sequence of male masturbation.

Pic was made with little money but lots of humor. It searches continuously. For beauty? Perhaps. For things and feelings to be grateful for? Probably. Direction is technically and artistically of a high order. "Pink Ulysses" made a positive impression on auds at the Rotterdam Film Festival and also played the Berlinale. — *Wall.*

AMERICAN FILM MARKET REVIEW

King Of New York (ITALIAN-U.S.)

New York A Reteitalia and Scena Film Intl. presentation of an Augusto Caminito film. Executive producers, Jay Julien, Vittorio Squillante. Produced by Mary Kane. Directed by Abel Ferrara. Screenplay, Nicholas St. John; camera (Duart color), Bojan Bazelli; editor, Anthony Redman; music, Joe Delia; sound (Dolby), Drew Kunin; production design, Alex Tavoularis; art direction, Stephanie Ziemer; set decoration, Sonja Roth; costume design, Carol Ramsey; assistant director, David Sardi; production manager, Kane; 2d unit director-stunt coordinator, Phil Neilson; special effects coordinator, Matt Vogel; associate producer and casting, Randy Sabusawa. Reviewed at Loews Astor Plaza, N.Y., Dec. 28, 1989. (In American Film Market.) No MPAA Rating. Running time: **103 MIN.**
Frank White. . . . . .Christopher Walken
Dennis Gilley. . . . . . . .David Caruso
Jimmy Jump. . . . . . . .Larry Fishburne
Ruth Bishop. . . . . .Victor Argo
Thomas Flannigan. . . . .Wesley Snipes
Jennifer. . . . . .Janet Julian
Larry Wong. . . . . .Joey Chin
Lance. . . . . .Giancarlo Esposito
Joey Dalesio. . . . . .Paul Calderon
Also with: Steve Buscemi, Theresa Randle, Leonard Lee Thomas, Roger Guenver Smith, Carrie Nygren, Freddie Jackson, Sari Chang, Ariane Koizumi, Vanessa Angel, Phoebe Legere, Pete Hamill.

■**A violence-drenched fable of Gotham druglords, "King Of New York" is a potent film for international audiences. Its unsympathetic, nihilistic thrust makes it a tough sell to domestic audiences, though Christopher Walken's unin-** hibited title performance could be a draw.

Pic is unusual in being an all-American production fully financed by European sources (Italy in this case), after being developed at New World and Universal. Unlike such projects as the recent West German-backed "Last Exit To Brooklyn," there are no imported cast or crew members involved here.

Nicholas St. John's screenplay presents no point of audience identification, coolly depicting Walken as a fresh-out-of-prison gangster who vows to take over Gotham's $1-billion-plus drug industry. With his mainly black henchmen he blows away leading Colombian, Italian and Chinese kingpins and soon sets up shop at the Plaza Hotel (protected by two beautiful femme bodyguards) as the King of New York.

Film is sketchy as to Walken's true motives, though we see his humanitarian efforts in backing a hospital. This antihero apparently is seizing power in an attempt to subsequently reform the city's ills, but his erratic behavior and ruthless ultraviolence prevent audience empathy with the character. His ongoing war with vicious police, headed by hothead David Caruso, gives one a chance, nevertheless, to root for Walken en route to a tragic finale.

Director Abel Ferrara has visualized an ominous view of New York where deadly violence can erupt instantaneously. It is the suddenness of Walken's fatal outbursts that gives the film its greatest impact. Also impressive are large-scale setpieces, including a climax shot in Times Square, as well as a balletic orgy of bloodletting (in which Walken's bodyguards are killed) stylized by cinematographer Bojan Bazelli's pastel lighting effects.

Complementing Walken's bra-vura turn are equally flamboyant performances by Caruso as the young Irish cop out to destroy Walken, and Larry Fishburne as Walken's slightly crazy aide-de-camp. Victor Argo underplays and is a steadying influence as Caruso's partner. Almost every principal character gets to emote during a dramatic death scene. Among several cameos, Freddie Jackson pops in to sing during a party dedicating the hospital Walken has backed.

Tech credits are above average for this modestly budgeted picture. — *Lor.*

HUNGARIAN FILM WEEK REVIEWS

Cellovolde
(Shooting Range)
(HUNGARIAN-B&W)

Budapest An MTV Films-Hunnia Films-Bela Balazs Studio production (Intl. sales: Cine Magyar, Budapest). Directed by Arpad Sopsits. Screenplay, Sopsits, Gyula Elian; camera (b&w), Tibor Klopfler; editor, Maria Magdolna Kovacs; music, Laszlo Melis; production design, Csaba Stork; sound, Tamas Markus; assistant director, Zoltan Salgo. Reviewed at Hungarian Film Week, Budapest, Feb. 7, 1990. Running time: **88 MIN.**

Feri.	Zoltan Lengyel
Jutka.	Judit Danyi
Father.	Lajos Kovacs
Mother.	Lili Monori
Interrogator.	Fero Nagy

■"Shooting Range" is a grim case history based on a 1982 incident: a youth shot and killed his father for no apparent reason. Director Arpad Sopsits has used this crime as the basis for a bleak study of youthful hopelessness and lack of direction. Fests could be interested but commercial opportunities are slim.

Pic, winner of the Hungarian Film Week's Gene Moskowitz prize and a special prize, is shot in two shades of black & white; sepia for the flashbacks, traditional monochrome for the scenes in which the youth is interrogated by a police officer. Sober and well-made, the film nevertheless fatally lacks any kind of emotion which might have gained audience attention. Even when the aggressive father humiliates his son (trying to have sex with a prostitute when the father arrives and simply takes over), there's little impact.

The story could and should have been really chilling: the boy eventually shoots his father, and his mother helps him bury the corpse; but it all goes for very little.

On the plus side, the cool images are beautiful and the leading performances solid. — *Strat.*

Meteo
(HUNGARIAN)

Budapest A Hunnia Filmstudio production (Intl. sales: Cine Magyar, Budapest). Directed by Andras M. Monory. Screenplay, Monory, Geza Beremenyi; camera (Eastmancolor), Gabor Szabo; editor, Agnes Incze; music, Janos Masik, Tibor Szemzo; production design, Laszlo Zsoter; sound, Istvan Sipos; assistant director, Elemer Kaldor. Reviewed at Hungarian Film Week, Budapest, Feb. 4, 1990. Running time: **102 MIN.**

Berlios.	Karoly Eperjes
Eckermann.	Laszlo Kistamas
Vero.	Zoltan Varga
Marilyn.	Cecilia Esztergalyos
Czech girl.	Denissa Der
Henrik.	Vilmos Vajdai

■This is a visually striking film burdened with a slight and sometimes confusing narrative. A favorable reception at the Berlin film fest (where it unspooled in the Panorama section) might mean some international attention and sales, but prospects are doubtful.

Director Andras M. Monory, seemingly under the influence of Ridley Scott, presents images of a decaying, sinister city, at times evoking Scott's "Black Rain." He obviously isn't short of visual ideas, but lacks a strong narrative to accompany his striking images. (Lenser Gabor Szabo garnered the Hungarian Film Week's best cinematographer award for this and "Condemned To Die.")

His central characters are outsiders — lawbreakers out to crack the system by means of a computer scam. The computer whiz is Eckermann (Laszlo Kistamas) who spends most of his time in a bathtub where he inhabits a strange dream world peopled by toy animals, including a Miss Piggy clone.

However, he rouses himself from the tub long enough to help his dissolute pals (Karoly Eperjes, Zoltan Varga) devise a computer key to a gambling joint in the city. Later, Eckermann meets his fate at the lovely hands of a femme fatale, apparently a Czech refugee, who tantalizingly shares his bath and then leaves a hair dryer behind her before she departs, causing the inevitable fatal accident.

The plot is none too clear and none too interesting. Monory is trying for an ultrahip, modern picture, complete with rock music. But clever as much of this is, it doesn't connect because the narrative is too fuzzy. The fact that the characters are generally unsympathetic doesn't help either.

Camerawork and production design are the main features here, and they're impressive. The actors do their best with the rather drab characters they have to play. "Meteo" may click with the young, in-crowd, both on its home turf and, perhaps, in Berlin. Beyond that, prospects look murky.

— *Strat.*

Vattatyuk
(Cotton Chicken)
(HUNGARIAN)

Budapest A Hunnia Filmstudio production. Directed by Andras Szoke, Maria Dobos, Gabor Ferenczi. Screenplay, Szoke, Dobos, Ferenczi; camera (color), Dobos; editor, Szoke; sound, Bela Prohaszka, Antal Szabo, Elek Korosfalvy. Reviewed at Hungarian Film Week, Budapest, Feb. 4, 1990. Running time: **71 MIN.**

Wife/waitress.	Gabriella Juhasz
Kovacs.	Agnes Kovacs
Nagy.	Ilona Nagy
Sgt. Badar.	Sandor Badar
Gazdag.	Tibor Gazdag
Lance-Sgt. Vizi.	Janos Horvath
Marinka.	Csaba Marinka
Economic director Szoke.	Andras Szoke
Little girl.	Rahel Ada Hudi

■It's possible that Hungarian filmmakers of the future were involved in this modest student production, which has been blown up from Super 8m after being shot in only six days. Offshore prospects aren't good, however, since this is strictly a local item.

Seemingly haphazard screenplay pokes fun at politicians and official-dom in general as it tells a fractured tale of an investigation into a missing golden egg (Hungary's economy?).

On one level, the film is extremely amateurish, though its youthful anarchy and sense of the ridiculous are definite assets. The jokes are too local for "Cotton Chicken" to find a roost in other countries, except in student fests and the like.

Still, the production team, led by Andras Szoke, may well come up with something more accessible next time around. — *Strat.*

Konnu Ver
(Fast And Loose)
(HUNGARIAN)

Budapest A Hunnia Filmstudio production, in association with ZDF (Intl. sales: Cinemagyar, Budapest). Directed by Gyorgy Szomjas. Screenplay, Ibolya Fekete, Ferenc Grunwalsy, Szomjas; camera (Eastmancolor), Grunwalsky, Zsolt Haraszti; editor, Anna Kornis; music, Janos Karacsony; sound, Gyorgy Kovacs. Reviewed at Hungarian Film Week, Budapest, Feb. 3, 1990. Running time: **86 MIN.**

Margo.	Margo Kiwan
Ildi.	Ildiko Deim
Attila.	Janos Derzsi
Dragan.	Zsolt Kortvelyesi
German tourist.	Peter Andorai
Attila's friend.	Karoly Eperjes

■Over the last decade, Gyorgy Szomjas has chronicled the underside of contemporary Hungary in a series of raffish, gritty pics ("Bald Dog Rock," "Light Physical Injuries," "The Wall Driller"). His latest is equally unsparing in its depiction of a society in moral decline, and may, indeed, prove too probing and relentless for many tastes. It's bound to spark controversy in its study of two Budapest women who are, essentially, prostitutes.

Szomjas, who won the Hungarian Film Week's best director prize for this pic, found his actresses, Margo Kiwan and Ildiko Deim, when he was making "The Wall Driller" in 1985. Since then, he kept in touch with the women and interviewed them regularly.

The interviews form the basis for the new screenplay, but the pic has a prominent end title declaring that it is a work of the imagination. Imagination it may be, but the grotesquely furnished apartment seen in the film actually belongs to Kiwan, and both women wear their own clothes throughout as they enact a story close to their own experiences.

Pic begins with Attila (Janos Derzsi) in prison sharpening a knife in preparation for his release that day. On the outside, he tracks down his girlfriend, Ildi, who lives with her working-class parents. Ildi and her friend, Margo, work as nude models at an art college, but they earn most of their money picking up foreign tourists and having sex with them. They don't consider themselves prostitutes; they're "adventuresses." They have to give Attila the slip when a German tourist becomes a likely target and, indeed, pays $200 for sex with both women, though his pleasure is interrupted by the arrival of an angry Attila at Margo's apartment.

Pic continues through the day as the two uninhibited femmes go about their normal activities, but it ends in tragedy as Attila takes his revenge on the faithless Ildi during a rock concert.

Szomjas sees Margo and Ildi as representing a deep malaise in Magyar society at a time when an impoverished, eager country is opening up to Western capital and reaping the benefits as well as suffering in the downside of the situation. He certainly seems to be fond of Margo and Ildi, cheerful hedonists who know exactly what they want and how to get it.

Some may find the film uncomfortably voyeuristic as the camera frequently caresses the bodies of the women, but the lack of inhibition seems the right way to portray women who presumably went along with the way the filmmakers depicted them, warts and all.

There's a disturbing moment when Margo allows Attila to make love to her, and he cuts her with his knife during the act. Scenes like this may incur the wrath of film censors in some countries, and some women may be offended, yet "Fast And Loose" clearly is based on reality.

There's humor, too, as one young woman recalls how she advised a tourist that Budapest's imposing parliament building actually was the railway station.

Szomjas uses various devices to distance audiences, such as images that are repeated and shots that switch from color to black & white and back. He introduces some fascinating characters against a background of society that, like his own two heroines' society, is

trying to overcome years of economic stagnation. Pic, whose original title literally means "Easy Blood" (as in "easy virtue") deserves to be taken seriously.
— *Strat.*

Felrevert Harangok
(Tolling Church Bells)
(HUNGARIAN-DOCU)

Budapest A Movi Forum Filmstudio production. Directed by Alajos Paulus. Camera (color), Laszlo Harrach, Tibor Ormos; editor, Emoke Venczel; sound, Peter Szucs. Reviewed at Hungarian Film Week, Budapest, Feb. 3, 1990. Running time: **90 MIN.**

■This up-to-the-minute documentary about refugees from the Transylvanian part of Rumania, despite its topicality, is not made with sufficient skill to merit more than tv exposure.

The three couples spotlighted, all ethnic Hungarians, tell of their suffering under the recently deposed Ceaucescu regime. One, a former aide to the Rumanian leader, escaped with his family to Budapest; another went to America, while a third found work in the Budapest Opera House.

The refugees have sad stories to tell, which are illustrated by photos and old newsreels. Pic ends with footage of last December's demonstrations that led to the fall and execution of the Rumanian dictator.

Strictly for politically inclined docu fests or specialized tv programming. — *Strat.*

Potyautasok
(Stowaways)
(HUNGARIAN)

Budapest A Journal Film, MTV FMS, Hunnia Filmstudios production. Directed by Sándor Söth. Screenplay, Géza Bereményi, Söth; camera (Eastmancolor), Piotr Sobocinki; editor, Mária Rigó; music, Zygmund Konieczny; sound, György Kovács; sets, Wojcech Saloni-Marczewskip; costumes, Malgorzata Moskwa-Braszka. Reviewed at Hungarian Film Week, Budapest, Feb. 4, 1990. Running time: **94 MIN.**
Móni. . . . . .Laura Favalli
Arpi. . . . . .Karl Tessler
Tamás. . . . . .Luke Mullaney
Prison Boss. . . . . .Jan Nowicki
Piotr. . . . . .Boguslaw Linda
Szimanski. . . . . .Jan Tesarz

■The novelty of this film by 25-year-old Sándor Söth exists in the astonishing animosity of its story, based on real facts, which presents one socialist

country as seen through the eyes of another in the blackest, most unflattering colors.

Two boys and a girl, bored with their easy life in Budapest, decide to take a trip to Poland and go all the way to Gdansk, for their first glimpse of the sea. The year is 1982, Poland is under martial law, and Gdansk is, of course, a boiling cauldron of political confrontations.

For the three insouciant dropouts, coming from the relatively well-off and relaxed Hungarian atmosphere, Poland is something of a grim shock, but they won't discontinue their voyage until they get to the sea. And once there, they cannot resist the temptation of taking one little step further, stealing a boat and trying to reach the nearest Swedish island.

Caught by the police, the boys are thrown into jail until the investigation is completed which, under the circumstances could take as long as six months, while the girl, who had not accompanied them on the last leg of their adventure, hits blank walls when she tries to apply for support from official authorities.

While there is no effort to spruce of the image of the two Hungarians or reduce their share of the guilt, they soon turn out to become victims, as the second part of the film develops into a socialist version of "Midnight Express," complete with all the sadistic trimmings of the original.

The script also goes on to elaborate the corruption of the Polish system and throws in, for good measure, sexual bribery as well. Political prisoners are delivered into the hands of hardened criminals who delight in torturing and humiliating them. Even the religion factor is not forgotten. The criminals are devout Catholics who never forget their prayers before they set out to beat up somebody.

A one-sided, angry and relentless picture, it starts out as a social satire and grows into a sordid prison melodrama before it delivers it final message, common to many Hungarian pics this year: Youth in this part of the world is possessed by a desperate urge to run away, at any cost, to any place.

The initial stages show Söth to have a rich visual style, and with the help of top Polish cameraman Piotr Sobocinski, he maps for himself devilishly complicated and intricate shots, displaying originality and daring.

Pity this impetuous flow of images is not maintained throughout the film, which falls into established routines, but maybe this is too much to expect of a director of Söth's years. Romantic and political problems alike are resolved in an arbitrary manner, and there isn't much to do in a prison film that hasn't been worn thin already by previous pics of the same genre.

Acting is adequate, but the three protagonists are often upstaged by such seasoned veterans as Jan Nowicki or Boguslaw Linda, capable of fleshing out roles from one or two lines.

Promising but far from satisfactory, the film is, however, one of the best reflections of anger and hostility exploding recently in the socialist countries and directed mostly at themselves. — *Edna.*

Hagyjatok Robinsoni!
(Leave Robinson Alone!)
(HUNGARIAN-CUBAN)

Budapest A Dialog Filmstudio (Budapest)-ICAIC (Havana) coproduction. Produced by Gabor Sarudi. Written and directed by Peter Timar. Camera (color), Sandor Kardos; choreography, Alfredo Gonzales Planes; sound, Tamas Markus; assistant director, Csilla Szigeti. Reviewed at Hungarian Film Week, Budapest, Feb. 3, 1990. Running time: **83 MIN.**
Robinson. . . . . .Istvan Miko
Daniel Defoe. . . . . .Dezso 'Garas
Also with: Miguel Navarro, Raul Pomarez, Jose M. Rodriguez, Enrique Arredondo, Anna Nagy, Gabor Hegyi.

■An abysmal attempt to breathe fresh life into the Robinson Crusoe legend, "Leave Robinson Alone!" is an all-round embarrassment.

Structured around labored sequences in which Robinson tells his story to writer Defoe in London in the early 18th century, pic is set mostly on a beautiful desert island.

Director Peter Timar's ideas of comedy, however, are juvenile when they're not racist and sexist. He has black natives, all of them near-naked, dancing some kind of fertility dance as the porcine hero ogles the women. Istvan Miko as the castaway gives a dismally unfunny performance matched only by the ugly camerawork and silly, flashy editing. Having Robinson mistake a monkey and a rabbit for naked women is just one of many insulting jokes crammed into this nasty effort.

Before the end, Defoe is seen

sleeping through Robinson's story, and potential viewers of "Leave Robinson Alone!" may do just the same. — *Strat.*

Eszterkönyv
(The Book Of Esther)
(HUNGARIAN)

Budapest A Cine Magyar presentation of an Objecktiv Filmstudio production. Written and directed by Krisztina Deák; camera (Eastmancolor), Iván Márk; editor, Ferenc Szécsényi; music, Ferenc Darvas; lyrics, Zoltán Solyó, Szabolcs Várady; sound, György Fék; sets, József Romvári; costumes, György Szakács. Reviewed at Hungarian Film Week, Budapest, Feb. 4, 1990. Running time: **87 MIN.**
Esther. . . . . .Eszter Nagy-Kálózy
Zsolt. . . . . .András Bálint
Herman. . . . . .Károly Eperjes
Nick Kovacs. . . . . .Can Togay
Jusztinia. . . . . .Mari Töröcsik
Aranka. . . . . .Enikö Eszenyi
Rózsi. . . . . .Erzsi Pártos

■No relation to the Biblical text, this film is inspired by the diary of a 13-year-old girl, Anna Herman, an Auschwitz gas chamber victim. Polished camera work and a solid supporting cast help this debut effort (and best first film prizewinner at the Hungarian Film Week) to a certain extent, but the theme promised more than the young director was able to deliver.

Discovered in Hungary after the war, and published, the diary was compared with the young Anne Frank's testimony of the Holocaust. However, later rumors, substantiated by some remarks in the memoirs of the girl's stepfather, insist Anna's mother, Esther, wrote most of the material after the war to atone for abandoning her child to follow her second husband into exile.

The script explores the possibility and focuses on the mother's obsessive search for Anna when she comes back after the war, the gradual realization that she is dead and the self-destructive process that settles in. Esther tries to punish everybody around her, including herself, for what she did.

Using historical facts and background (the stepfather was a w.k. writer involved in abortive postwar attempts to establish a free press in the country), Krisztina Deák's script evolves around Esther, who walks a thin line between insanity and despair.

While Eszter Nagy-Kálózy offers a remarkably affecting performance in the lead, her thin, pale, devastated face constantly haunted by her personal demons, she has to struggle against a script that allows some fuzziness in the story, and relies too often only on her facial expressions to carry the plot forward without any help.

No doubt this is a moving picture, but dramatically, after a certain point, it just marks time before delivering the inevitably gruesome climax. — *Edna*

Aki Nekiszaladt
A Demokracianak
(He Ran Against Democracy)
(HUNGARIAN-DOCU)

Budapest A Movi Forum Filmstudio production. Directed by Bela Szobolits. Camera (color), Gyorgy I. Kiss; editor, Judit Kollanyi; sound, Janos Gonda; production manager, Norbert Solymosi. Reviewed at Hungarian Film Week, Budapest, Feb. 7, 1990. Running time: **95 MIN.**

■With the political changes taking place in Eastern Europe, more and more documentaries are being produced criticizing the now discredited old-style Communism. "He Ran Against Democracy" is one such film, which is of considerable local interest, but is unlikely to travel except to docu fests or specialist tv networks.

The filmmakers probe the suicide of a small-town mayor who had been the subject of critical newspaper articles written by a young woman journalist. In an interview, she claims to have been threatened over her story, which suggested the mayor gave valuable favors to members of his family and others. Also interviewed is the widow who appears to be appalled at the democratic events sweeping the country. It adds up to a fascinating document, but is not in any way cinematically interesting. — *Strat.*

Iskolakerülök
(Truants)
(HUNGARIAN)

Budapest A Cine Magyar presentation of a Budapest Film Studios production. Produced by Gábor Hanák. Directed by Ferenc Kardos. Screenplay, István Kardos; camera (Eastmancolor), András Szalai; editor, Margit Galamb; music, György Selmeczi; sound, János Réti; art director, Eva Martin; costumes, Klára Gulyás; production manager, Lajos Gulyás. Reviewed at Hungarian Film Week, Budapest, Feb. 3, 1990. Running time: **93 MIN.**

With: Károly Eperjes (teacher), Dorottya Udvaros (mother), Ildiko Bansagi, Eszter Csakanyi, Maria Gladkowska, Akos Madarász, Miklós Szekely B., Eszter Nagy-Kálozy, Dzoko Rosic, Erszi Pasztor, Renata Szalter, Edit Soós, László Czikéli, István O. Szabó, Zsuzsa Szilágyi.

■Ferenc Kardos' new picture emerges from the Hungarian tradition of films about misguided youth rejected by an unfeeling society. Unlike remarkable precedents such as "Sunday Children" and "Stand-Up," however, Kardos can't make up his mind about what issues he wants to address.

The script mostly turns around an energetic and dedicated geography teacher and his relations with a compulsive runaway kid who keeps looking for his mother as she changes addresses and lovers. It's also about the teacher's problems at home, the comic infatuation of a female colleague with him, a young boy's attempt to commit suicide, the dilapidated state of the boarding school in which the entire action of the film takes place, the symbolic search for gold in the Danube, and lots more.

Any one ingredient could have blossomed into a full-scale feature, given the right treatment. Here, however, they are all thrown in one atop another, arbitrarily introduced and then dropped without further ado. Characters, including the principal ones, are superficial, which prevents any real identification with them or their problems.

While technical credits are of a high order typical in Hungarian pics, separate scenes often click. Acting, by a cast including some of the top names in Hungary, is more than adequate. The result looks like a collection of ideas, none of which has been fully exploited here. — *Edna.*

Szürkület
(Twilight)
(HUNGARIAN-B&W)

Budapest A Cine Magyar Presentation of a Budapest Studios, Hungarian Television, Paesens Films (Zurich) production. Written and directed by György Fehér; camera (black and white), Miklós Gurbán; editor, Mária Czeilik; sound, János Réti; sets, Tamás Vayer; costumes, Gyula Pauer. Reviewed at Hungarian Film Week, Budapest, Feb. 6, 1990. Running time: **105 MIN.**

With: Péter Haumann, János Derzsi, Gyula Pauer, László Németh, Miklós B. Székely, Erszike Nagy, Mónika Varga, Káti Lázár, István Lénárt, Pál Hetényi, Judit Pogany.

■"Sürkület" is an agonizingly slow but beautifully photographed thriller in which every shot seems to take forever and the story has the peculiar quality of never advancing.

Strangely reminiscent of a Friedrich Dürenmatt novel, "The Pledge," adapted to the screen as "It Happened In Broad Daylight," pic follows the investigation of a murder. A strange man roams over the countryside, attracts little girls by offering them chocolates and then kills them once they accompany him into the woods.

The policeman in charge becomes obsessed with the case and pursues it after he is taken off it, coming back again and again to the same spots and trying to reconstruct the crime in his mind, hoping this will lead him to the killer.

Scripter-director Fehér insists on denying the audience any satisfaction whatsoever, focusing exclusively on the obsession and refusing to introduce any kind of evidence that would lead the case forward.

On the other hand, he is lavish with dark moods. The magnificent images of wintry Hungarian landscapes in the mist, of rain beating down relentlessly, the desolation of the barren trees and the hardened faces of the peasants easily could make a perfect album of artistic black & white still photos of the highest order.

In this static, mostly immobile film, it is difficult to discuss either the acting, which consists mainly of fitting into a certain type of portrait, or editing, which is hardly in evidence. Practically impossible to handle as a normal release, there may be a spot on the art circuit and in festivals for this type of outlandish production. — *Edna.*

Szedules
(Don't Disturb)
(HUNGARIAN)

Budapest An Objectiv Filmstudio production. Written and directed by Janos Szasz. Camera (Eastmancolor), Tibor Mathe; editor, Anna Korniss; music, Peter Ogi; production design, Laszlo Rajk; sound, Istvan Sipos; production manager, Lajos Ovari; assistant director, Kalman Balogh. Reviewed at Hungarian Film Week, Budapest, Feb. 5, 1990. Running time: **80 MIN.**
The girl. . . . . .Andrea Kiss
The father. . . . . .Tamas Jordan
Gyuri. . . . . .Zoltan Hegyi

The younger brother	Aron Oze
The stranger	Lajos Kovacs

■This first feature from a young film school grad shows Janos Szasz has ideas and he's willing to take some risks, both useful attributes for a directing career. "Don't Disturb" takes a long time to establish its mood, and will try the patience of some viewers, but, by midpoint, it develops into a tense drama of sexual relationships.

The setting is a rundown city apartment occupied by a father and his two sons. They rarely talk to each other, occupy separate rooms, and seem to exist on a diet of canned sardines.

The older son, Gyuri, has a girl, which upsets the equilibrium of the apartment. They spend time together behind a locked door with a "Don't Disturb" sign on the door handle. The young brother and the father are affected by the girl's presence; when not with Gyuri, she wanders around wearing only a nightshirt, or stares from the window onto the street below.

Eventually, Gyuri makes way for the other two. His young brother, head shaven, is seduced by the girl in a lengthy and quite erotic sequence. Later, when she's left alone with the father, a more basic and desperate kind of sexual passion is aroused.

Different meanings can doubtless be read into what is evidently an allegorical story. Festivals, especially those interested in discovering new directors, should consider "Don't Disturb" for their programs. But audiences should be prepared for the lengthy (and almost dialog-less) preliminaries before the film's strange mood takes over.

Technical credits are all very good, and Janos Szasz bears watching in the future. Andrea Kiss, who is impressive as the young woman, also should have a career ahead of her. — *Strat.*

Mulatság
(Days Of Peace And Music)
(HUNGARIAN-DOCU-VIDEO)

Budapest A Cine Magyar presentation of a Közmüvelödési Információs Vállalat production. Directed by György Szomjas; camera (video), Gábor Balogh, Tibor Varjasi; editor, Ferenc Acs; musical director, Béla Hálmos;

sound, György Kovács. Reviewed at Hungarian Film Week, Budapest, Feb. 4, 1990. Running time: **90 MIN.**

■Omitting dialog and offering a simple, predictable structure alternating between song and dance and leisurely occupations such as wood carving, the interest of György Szomjas' picture about the Teka Folk Festival, shot entirely in video, is mostly ethnographic.

This initiative would like to be taken as a Hungarian version of Woodstock, 20 years later; an opening title indicates as much. Image quality is far from impressive and any comparisons with Woodstock, the event or the film, are largely exaggerated. It is difficult to accept this sympathetic but modest affair at more than its face value, a few days of peace and music for a few people.

Several hundred young men and women, some of them accompanied by their children, attended the folk fest, which took place in a summer camp. They lived together for 10 days, dancing to traditional tunes and singing along with a strictly nonelectric band.

In any case, if there is a market for this type of production, it will mostly be in educational tv.
— *Edna.*

A Halal Villamosa
(The Tram Of Death)
(HUNGARIAN-DOCU)

Budapest A Movi Forum Filmstudio production. Directed by Janos Veszi. Camera (color), Peter Vekas; editor, Agnes Kulics; sound, Gyula Traub; production manager, Norbert Solymosi. Reviewed at Hungarian Film Week, Budapest, Feb. 7, 1990. Running time: **84 MIN.**

■A good murder trial movie is always worth watching, and this real-life trial, filmed as it happened in a Budapest courtroom, is fascinating. It is the most accessible of the many docus unspooled at the 1990 Magyar Film Week.

On trial are several teens, one of whom is accused of the murder of an off-duty policeman. Seems that the youths were on a tram on a Friday night in November, 1988, and caused a disturbance. The cop, who was later discovered to have been drunk, fired a warning shot and one of the teens was hit in the leg. Apparently, the policeman

was overpowered, thrown off the tram and shot with his own gun.

Court procedures are markedly different from the U.S. system. The presiding judge, a very amusing character as it turns out, questions the witnesses himself and puts on quite an act. Testimony is conflicting, and though one of the teens is found guilty and sentenced to prison, the facts of the matter are still murky at fadeout.

The pic fascinates because it is well constructed and shot, and the case is genuinely interesting. Another plus is the knowledge that viewers witness the genuine trial, not a studio recreation, a fact that should give "The Tram Of Death" the overseas exposure it richly merits. — *Strat.*

Te Meg Elsz?
(Are You Still Alive?)
(HUNGARIAN-DOCU-B&W)

Budapest An Objektiv Filmstudio production. Directed by Sandor Sara. Production team, Sandor Csoori, Imre Gulyas, Gabor Hanak, Ferenc Jeli, Laszlo Szabo, others. Reviewed at Hungarian Film Week, Budapest, Feb. 3, 1990. Running time: **87 MIN.**

■"Are You Still Alive?" isn't a talking-heads documentary; it's a talking head. Pic contains interesting subject matter, but the treatment is more suited to radio than to cinema or even tv.

Bela Kemenfyi is an elderly Hungarian with an amazing survival story to tell. In 1944, at age 15, he was accused of being a traitor, and was shot by Russian soldiers and left to die. Still critically wounded, he was transported to a gulag, where he stayed for nine years. After his return home in 1953, crippled, he was unable to find work.

Vet feature and documentary director Sandor Sara lets Kemenfyi tell his grim story in medium closeup and black & white for nearly an hour and a half. Apart from a brief opening sequence, showing the old man leaving his home, the camera just shows us his face. The treatment is so rigorous it's self-defeating; the saga could have reached a wider audience if Sara had made it more of a film. As it is, offshore sales look to be nearly impossible. — *Strat.*

BERLIN FILM FESTIVAL REVIEWS

Georg Elser
(Seven Minutes)
(WEST GERMAN-U.S.)

Berlin A Deutscher Verleih/Senator Film Verleigh Gmbh release of a Saturn Movie and Mutoskop-Film coproduction. (Intl. sales: Walter Manley Prods., New York.) Produced by Moritz Borman, Rainer Soehnlein. Directed by Klaus Maria Brandauer. Screenplay, Stephen Sheppard from his novel "The Artisan," camera (color), Lajos Koltai; editor, Dagmar Hirtz; music, Georges Delerue; production design, Wolfgang Hundhammer; costumes, Barbara Baum. Reviewed at Berlin Film Festival (New German Films), Feb. 10, 1990. Running time: **97 MIN.**

Georg Elser	Klaus Maria Brandauer
Wagner	Brian Dennehy
Anneliese	Rebecca Miller
Frau Gruber	Elisabeth Orth

With: Nigel le Vaillant, Vadim Glowna, Peter Andorai, Marthe Keller, Maggie O'Neill, Roger Ashton-Griffiths, Hans Michael Rehberg, Dietrich Hollinderbaeumer, Hans Stetter, Robert Easton, Janos Acs, Ralph Richter, Werner Fritz, Dave Hill.

■Klaus Maria Brandauer gets thumbs up for this directorial debut, with himself in the lead, as the insignificant watchmaker who tried to assassinate Adolf Hitler in a beer hall bombing in 1939. Pic has good

offshore possibilities, especially now that Germany is back in the headlines.

Brandauer turns in a remarkably subdued performance in an almost mute role as the would-be assassin whose bomb goes off just seven minutes after Hitler leaves the beer hall. Despite the fact that everyone in the audience knows the outcome from the start, the pic gains momentum with mounting suspense right up to the final frames as bomber Eiser is nabbed at the Swiss border while his pregnant fiancée escapes to safety.

Lenser Lajos Koltai keeps in tight, accentuating the dark sense of forboding and claustrophobia of the film's primarily nighttime action. Lightness and air are reserved for the scenes with Rebecca Miller, as the waitress who falls in love with Elser and whose life is put at risk by his secret plan to bomb the beer hall during a speech by Hitler.

Brian Dennehy is well cast as the police official who has no sympathy for the Nazis, but whose sense of duty compels him to track down Elser. He provides the mirror image to the bomber, whose sense of responsibility drives him to plant the bomb. When the two men finally meet, they face each other without malice, but with a recognition that each has done what he had to do.

Supporting cast is strong, but this is clearly Brandauer's film all the way. Alone on screen much of the time, it is up to his facial expressions and body language to convey his mute revulsion as Jewish neighbors are hauled away and fascist acquaintances become ever more brazen. It is a challenging role, handled with skill.

This is the third "Nazi film" for Brandauer. His acting breakthrough came with Istvan Szabo's "Mephisto" in 1980-81, playing the role based on the true life story of legendary German "Faust" actor Gustaf Gründgens, who was never able to shake off accusations that he had collaborated with the Nazis. The second pic was Szabo's "Hanussen," about a true life stage showman who tried and failed to outwit the Nazis.

Top-drawer technical credits give this pic the look and feel of a big-budget production. — *Gill.*

Ono
(It)
(SOVIET)

Berlin   A Sovexportfilm presentation of Lenfilm Studio production. Directed by Serghei Ovtcharov. Screenplay, Ovtcharov, based on "Tale Of A City" by Mikhail Saltykov-Schtchedrin; camera (color), Valeri Fedossov; editor, Olga Amosova; music, Serghei Kuryochin, also incidental music by Tchaikovski, Glazunov, Zfassman, Soloviov-Sedoi, Lecuona; sound, Konstantin Sarin; art director, Natalya Vasilieva; costumes, Anshela Sapunova; special effects, W. Bianki, O. Nikolaiev, O. Kalyagina. Reviewed at the Berlin Forum, Feb. 11, 1990. Running time: **120 MIN.**
Klemantinka. . . . . . .Natalya Gundareva
Amalia. . . . . .Svetlana Kryutschova
Iraida. . . . . .Elena Sanayeva
Anelka. . . . . . . .Margarita Terechowa
Ferdystchenko. . . . . . .Rolan Bykov
   Also with: Leonid Kuravliov, Oleg Tabakov, Rodion Nachapetov, Vera Glagoleva, Irina Mazurkevitch, Alexander Polovzev, Anatoli Romaschin.

■A complex satire of Russia's entire history, Serghei Ovtcharov's film is more ambitious in form than "Zelig" and covers more ground than "Repentance." If there may be some doubts about the lightweight tone "Ono" uses to discuss past tragedies, there is no doubt about its originality.

The script is a faithful adaptation of an 1870 novel by Mikhail Saltykov, writing under the pseudonym of N. Schtchedrin. Entitled "Tale Of A City," it was supposed to be the history of the Russian people disguised as the saga of one town. Ovtcharov updated it without changing the original plot, thereby hinting that nothing has really changed in this country, and that what was true before the revolution remains so 70 years after.

Conceived as a collection of pseudodocumentary footage found in some forgotten archive, the film was kept for many months in the laboratory to destroy image and sound quality. The result is an authentically antiquated look. Ovtcharov not only satirizes historical events, he also apes the cinematic styles of the different periods in which the events took place.

Quick sequences display the various, despotic monarchs who ruled over the city, famous for its liquor and boiled eggs, with particular attention to three voracious ladies, one of whom speaks German to her subjects and is easily identified as Catherine the Great.

Ovtcharov uses one mayor Piotr Ferdystchenko to stand for Lenin, then Stalin and later Khrushchev (Rolan Bykov looks like he's enjoying himself immensely in the triple part). As the pic approaches the present, narration grows blacker by the minute, making abundant use of surrealist fantasy scenes deriding the mental and physical state of health of the various leaders, and the tempest gradually building up under them.

Ovtcharov, who comes back again and again to the haggard faces of the crowd which has long submitted meekly to ill treatment, doesn't try to imply that past suffering will be rewarded by a better future. The future is at best a chaotic uncertainty. The film's last image, identical to the first, shows the portrait of writer Saltykov, grimly staring at the audience, an ominous look in his eyes.

With all its levity and sarcasm, this isn't an easy film to watch. Ovtcharov's style is rewarding, but following all his allusions is pretty exhausting. Many of the barbs will be lost on those without a solid knowledge of Russian history and Soviet cinema.

Technically, the film is a tour-de-force, which may go unnoticed because it both works purposeful-

ly against the quality of the image, instead of contributing to it. The credits indicating the film is in color shouldn't be taken literally, for whatever color there is, is doctored beyond recognition.

A collector's item for the erudite, "Ono" is likely to surface in many festivals, but can't hope for much more than that away from the home turf. — *Edna.*

Visioni privati
(Private Screenings)
(ITALIAN)

Berlin   A Nutrimenti Terrestri, RAI 3, production. Written and directed by Ninni Bruschetta, Francesco Calogero, Donald Ranvaud; camera (16m, color), Angelo Strano; editor, Davide Azzigana; music, Giovanni Renzo; sound, Gigi Spedale. Reviewed at the Berlin Forum of the Young Cinema, Feb. 14, 1990. Running time: **100 MIN.**
Virginia. . . . . .Jessica Forde
Boris. . . . . .Patrick Bauchau
Ettore. . . . . .Antonio Caldarella
Gianfranco. . . . . .Antonio Alveario
Pino. . . . . .Maurizio Puglisi
Petronius. . . . . .Peter Berling
Donald. . . . . .Donald Ranvaud
Nathalie. . . . . .Nathalie Roche
   Also with: Cyd Charisse, Chris Severnich, Bob Swaim, Tatti Sanguinetti, Lelia Costa, Giovanni Moschella, Francesca Tardella, Maurizio Marchetti, Roberto de Francesco, Sandro Anastasi, Mario Veuti, Francesco Calogero.

■A light spoof of the film festival scene made by specialists on the subject, "Visioni privati" was shot mostly in Taormina during the 1988 fest. It's all done in good spirits, nobody is really insulted or hurt, which means it can be expected to materialize next year at festivals all over.

Originally, pic was intended as a short with a brief excuse of a narrative to tie in the various incidents registered by the camera together. Then, once the media got wind of it, the project blossomed into a full-fledged feature, with some of the actors returning later to fill up the parts they had sketched in their guest performances during the Taormina festival.

Entertaining for the initiates, who will immediately identify most of the barbs sneaked by the filmmakers in a supposedly innocent manner, the film will evidently register less well with general audiences. If any illusions have been left that film festivals are respectable cultural events, this film may well dispel them once and for all.

Fumbled schedules, misplaced

prints, improvised translations and unprofessional staff are only some of the incidents reviewed here. An energetic factotum (Donald Ranvaud, who has indeed filled this function more than once for various festivals) simultaneously sets up press conferences, consoles frustrated actresses and tries to solve a mysterious death on the premises, all at the same time.

Very much a spur-of-the-moment, tongue-in-cheek enterprise, this is bound to amuse the cognoscenti who will love seeing Ranvaud rushing off in all directions at the same time, observing producer Sievernich who fends off script offers and cups of coffee, or watching film critics rambling on meaninglessly about films they hate to see anyway. — *Edna.*

Denk Bloss Nicht, Ich Heule
(Don't Think
That I'm Crying)
(EAST GERMAN-B&W)

Berlin   A Defa Studios presentation. Directed by Frank Vogel. Screenplay, Manfred Freitag, Joachim Nestler; camera (b&w, Cinemascope), Günter Ost; editor, Helga Krause; music, Hans-Dieter Hosella; sound, Konrad Walle; art director, Harald Horn. Reviewed at the Berlin Forum of the Young Cinema, Feb. 13, 1990. Running time: **91 MIN.**
   With Peter Reusse, Anne Kathrein Kretzschmar, Helga Görin, Jutta Hoffman, Herbert Köffer, Hanns Hardt-Hardtloff, Harry Hindemith.

■Neat, dogmatic and irritatingly flat, this is another of East Germany's shelf films (made in 1965), courageous and ridiculous at the same time.

The opening statement that the film's hero is expelled from his school because he is too honest, was obviously enough to prick the ears of the censors. Once this is followed by his father's deathbed advice to fight bosses and functionaries, the censors couldn't possibly have had any alternative except to deny the film circulation.

Later on, it associates the hero with a gang of "halbstarke" (hooligans, all disgusted with the regime), elaborates on the boredom and pointless life of this gang, and frequently alludes to the Nazi past and the insecure moral position of the older generation, all of which couldn't have helped the film either.

All this is true and director Vogel, as well as his scriptwriters, should definitely be commended for it. The trouble starts with the script which is quite incapable of fusing these elements. Characters are sketchy, human relations are schematic, acting is crude, and the ostentatious use of Cinemascope camera delivers some nice pictures but too many pretentious poses.

It's natural to show such films in Berlin these days, and they may have some life left in the immediate future, especially in various retrospectives dedicated to forbidden films. It's doubtful, however, that once the novelty wears off, they can expect to be more than respected, but seldom seen, museum pieces. — *Edna.*

Das Kaninchen Bin Ich
(I Am The Rabbit)
(EAST GERMAN-B&W)

Berlin A Defa Film presentation of a Roter Kreis production. Directed by Kurt Maetzig. Screenplay, Manfred Bieler, based on his novel "Maria Morzeck or I Am The Rabbit"); camera (b&w), Erich Gusko; editor, Helga Krause; music, Gerhard Rosenfeld, Reiner Bredemeyer; sound, Konrad Walle; art director, Alfred Tomalla; costumes, Rita Bieler; production manager, Martin Sonnabend. Reviewed at the Berlin Forum of the Young Cinema, Feb. 12, 1990. Running time: **110 MIN.**
Maria. . . . . .Angelika Waller
Paul Deister. . . . . .Alfred Muller
Gabriele. . . . . .Irma Munch
Aunt. . . . . .Ilse Voigt
Dieter. . . . . .Wolfgang Winkler
With: Willi Narloch, Willi Schrade, Rudolf Ulrich, Anemarie Esper, Helmut Schellhardt, Werner Wieland.

■Had it not been forbidden for 24 years, it is difficult to imagine anyone would trouble to show this film. With all due respect to its courage, there is little to recommend in this woodenly acted and unimaginatively directed picture.

No doubt director Maetzig stepped on a lot of toes when he made this film. He features a power-hungry judge who not only manipulates justice to his own advantage, but also has an illicit affair with a girl who could be his daughter.

Justice is shown to be totally dependent on party politics, the harshness of the sentences defining the extent of the court's commitment to the party line. There is also total nudity in one scene, promiscuity and transparent, unflattering references to the changes which took place in East Germany around the time the Berlin Wall was put up.

Maria, a 16-year-old waitress who has been refused access to the university because her brother was jailed on a trumped-up charge of distributing reactionary propaganda, has an affair with the judge who sentenced him. This is supposed to be true romance until she discovers the man is too much in love with himself and his career to care for anybody else. At which point she leaves him and starts a life of her own.

The acting is amateurish and stiff, the script is transparently manipulative and the romance is ridiculous and incredible. Shot in a dogmatic, film-school manner, the plot is practically over half an hour before Maetzig wraps it up with a whimper.

Technically, pic is neat, correct, but uninspiring. The only reason to look at it now is to prove there were people who dared to criticize the regime 25 years ago. — *Edna.*

Kalmenhofkinder
The Children of Kalmenhof
(WEST GERMAN-DOCU)

Berlin A Nikolaus Tscheschner production. Director, Nikolaus Tscheschner. Camera (16m, color), Gerhard Braun, Anton Klima, Alberto Montani; editor, Johannes Beringer; sound, Beringer, Marlies Emmerich. Reviewed at Berlin Film Festival (New German Films), Feb. 11, 1990. Running time: **139 MIN.**

■This is a valuable piece of journalism by fledgling director Nikolaus Tscheschner, who has lived in both halves of divided Germany, but at two hours and 20 minutes, it is far too long.

Victims of the Nazi Holocaust included not only Jews, gypsies, Poles, homosexuals and political oppositionists, but also unknown numbers of handicapped persons, many of them children, who're the subjects of this documentary.

Kalmenhof was a home for disabled children who were the targets of Nazi racial-purity insanity, which resulted in the forced sterilization and even "mercy killings" of many of them. Moving interviews with some of the few who survived tell the story of Holocaust victims who have had to cope with their disabilities and the trauma of their experiences.

Pic requires major editing, which would only make the film's message more powerful. Tech credits are nothing special on 16m. — *Gill.*

Der VW-Komplex
(The VW Complex)
(WEST GERMAN)

Berlin A Coffin release of a Big Sky Film, FAS-Film, WDR tv production. Produced by Albert Schwinges. Directed by Hartmut Bitomsky. Camera (color), Axel Block; sound, Gerhard Metz. Reviewed at Berlin Film Festival (New German Films), Feb. 14, 1990. Running time: **93 MIN.**

■West German documentary filmmaker Hartmut Bitomsky has a topnotch ability to combine archive material and imaginative lensing, but this closeup look at the Volkswagon never gets out of first gear.

This is one German car-related product that won't export well.

"The VW Complex" draws parallels to Bitomsky's 1986 docu "Reichsautobahn," an overlong history of the building of German autobahns under the Nazis. Excellent newsreels clips were supplemented by tedious camera pans along power lines and bridge abutments. Same problems this time around.

No problem with the tech credits, though, that judicious editing would not solve. — *Gill.*

Mein Krieg
(My War)
(WEST GERMAN)

Berlin A Känguruh-Film and WDR tv coproduction. Directed by Harriet Eder, Thomas Kufus. Camera (color, 16m), Johann Feindt; editor, sound, Arpad Bondy. Reviewed at Berlin Film Festival (New German Films), Feb. 12, 1990. Running time: **90 MIN.**

■Young West German directors Harriet Eder and Thomas Kufus show remarkable promise in their first documentary film. The pic, a compilation of amateur films shot by frontline German soldiers in World War II, may have little offshore appeal, but German tv producers should sit up and take notice of this talented directorial pair.

Accompanying the film clips are interviews with the men who shot them. Their bittersweet recollections are in some cases cathartic, as the now-elderly men recall a young manhood marked by war.

Technical credits adequate for this 16m film. — *Gill.*

Verfolgte Wege
(Paths Of Survival)
(WEST GERMAN)

Berlin A Vulcano M. Film production. (Intl. sales: Metropolis Film, Zurich.) Produced by Christian Faust. Directed by Uwe Janson. Screenplay, Janson; camera (color), Egon Werdin; editor, Patricia Rommel; music, Michaela Dietl; production design, Susanne Dieringer; sound, Manuel Laval. Reviewed at Berlin Film Festival (New German Films), Feb. 11, 1990. Running time: **106 MIN.**
Hermann. . . . . .Peter Cieslinski
Marie. . . . . .Barbara Auer
Karl. . . . . .Michael Dick
Heindl. . . . . .Tilo Pruckner
Friedrich. . . . . .Adolf Laimbock

■Uwe Janson's first feature is a sober drama set in Germany in 1946. The theme is rehabilitation and readjustment to normal life after the horrors of the war, and pic is good enough to play the fest circuit and make a modest mark.

Central character is Hermann (Peter Cieslinski) who, towards the end of the war, was traumatized when a woman he tried to help was gunned down because of him. He's presented as being the archetypical good German, sensitive and withdrawn and horrified by the violence.

After his experiences, he spends time in a hospital, and is then assigned to work at a small country railway station, a setting very similar to that of Jiri Menzel's Oscar-winning "Closely Watched Trains."

In this peaceful environment, he starts to become human again, and falls in love with a local woman (Barbara Auer). But he also becomes involved, with a fellow worker, in stealing U.S. aid parcels from the trains that pass by.

The resulting film is modest in scale, but sufficiently well acted, written and directed to make its mark. The postwar mood is successfully captured and gives the film its impact. Not a world-beater, but a satisfying experience. — *Strat.*

A Halalraitelt
(Condemned To Death)
(HUNGARIAN)

Budapest A Reflex Film production. (Intl. sales, Cinemagyar, Budapest.) Produced and directed by Janos Szombolyai. Screenplay, Szombolyai, Ference Jeli, Akos Kertesz; camera (Eastmancolor), Gabor Szabo; editor, Marianna Miklos, Zsuzsa Posan; sound, Tamas Markus; production design, Eva Martin; production managers, Janos Herendi, Jozsef Bujtar; assistant director, Jeli. Reviewed at Hungarian Film Week, Budapest, Feb. 5, 1990. (In Berlin Film Festival, competing.) Running time: **91 MIN.**

Ferenc Gergo	Peter Malcsiner
Zsuzsa	Barbara Hegyi
Sandor Wagner	Gabor Mate
Bela Nagy	Istvan Bubik
Security officer	Peter Doczy
Mother	Teri Foldi

■Technically, "Condemned To Death" is first-class save for rather banal use of classical music. It could have an arthouse career around the world, especially in cities where there are significant Hungarian communities. Thesping is in the best tradition of Magyar cinema.

Over the years, several important Hungarian films have dealt with the traumatic events of November, 1956, when Soviet tanks crushed a popular uprising against Communist rule. With the new freedom sweeping through Central Europe, director Janos Szombolyai is able to go further in depicting those dramatic events.

The drama is set in 1958 and centers on a condemned man, Ferenc Gergo, awaiting execution for crimes allegedly committed during the uprising. In flashback, Gergo's story is told. An engineer in a military factory, he'd been having a secret affair with Zsuzsa, wife of his friend and colleague, Sandor.

Both men are accused of spying by the factory's security chief, Nagy. Sandor is imprisoned and apparently commits suicide, while his friend is freed and able to marry the widow. Not long afterward, they're caught up in the events of 1956, though Gergo is responsible for saving the hated Nagy from retribution at the hands of his fellow workers when the revolution first breaks out. Once the Russians restore the Communist regime, Gergo is falsely accused of being a coup leader.

Though traditional in form, "Condemned To Death" is a powerful picture, filled with ironies, such as in the opening sequence, set in 1953, in which Nagy has Gergo "stand in" for Stalin at a local memorial service for the dead Soviet leader.

The uprising itself is presented in far more detail than before, with the tensions and shifting loyalties lucidly evoked. As a fresh and angry depiction of troubled times, pic is significant and a forthright example of how very outspoken films can be now in the Eastern Bloc. — *Strat.*

Through The Wire
(DOCU)

Berlin A Daedalius production. (Intl. sales: Fox Lorber Associates, New York.) Produced by Alexandra White. Screenplay, Rosenblum; camera (color), Nancy Schreiber, Haskell Wexler; editor, Angelo Corrao; music, Nona Hendryx; narrator, Susan Sarandon. Reviewed at Berlin Film Festival (Panorama section), Feb. 10, 1990. Running time: **85 MIN.**

■Although few would imagine that the United States is holding political prisoners and torturing them, that's the contention of this angry documentary, and reports by Amnesty Intl. support the thesis.

The prisoners are women, specifically three political activists who spent October 1986-July 1988 in the Female High Security Unit at Lexington, Ky. The unit was entirely underground, and originally was painted a blinding white. The women were kept awake 24 hours a day, constantly observed and subjected to humiliating body searches by male officials.

The prisoners interviewed in the film were jailed for long terms (up to 58 years) for possession of illegal weapons and participating in violent attacks. The filmmakers interview the three, and also prison officials who maintain that the unit is not especially punitive. But the facts seem incontestible, and experts claim systematic pressure is being brought to bear on the women to destroy their will.

The elderly parents of one prisoner, Susan Rosenberg, are active in a campaign to give their daughter more humane treatment; scenes from her childhood are included to flesh out a portrait of a young woman politicized by the Vietnam War and racism.

Soberly narrated by Susan Sarandon, "Through The Wire" offers a disturbing insight into aspects of the prison system in the U.S. It's not a comfortable film, but should get attention. Some reenacted scenes, involving prison officials watching the prisoners showering on tv monitors, are problematical and really unnecessary additions to an already strong indictment. — *Strat.*

How To Be Louise
(B&W)

Berlin A Venus de Mylar production. Executive producer, Mark M. Green. Produced, written and directed by Anne Flournoy. Camera (b&w), Vladimir Tukan; editor, Kathleen Earle Killeen; music, Phillip Johnston; production design, Bradley Wester, Ceticia Stella; sound, Jeffrey Stern; production manager, Deirdre Fishel; assistant director, Marguerite Greiner. Reviewed at Berlin Film Festival (Panorama section), Feb. 11, 1990. Running time: **77 MIN.**

Louise/Lola	Lea Floden
Stanley Fastwalker	Bruce McCarty
Pinky	Maggie Burke
Dad	Mark Green
Lola	Lisa Emery
Nancy	Mary Carol Johnson
Rita	Mayda Sharrow

■"How To Be Louise," first feature from Anne Flournoy, tries hard but fails by a mile to make the grade. Commercial prospects look slim for this black and whiter.

Louise (Lea Floden) is an awkward young woman who wants to be an actress. She works in a store and shares a New York apartment with two confident girlfriends. She's haunted by the memory of her mother's accidental death 24 years earlier, and a visit from her beloved father becomes a disaster when she spills food over him.

Her clumsiness pays off when she walks into a taxi driven by Stanley Fastwalker (Bruce McCarty), with whom she finds romance (with some help from quotes from James Joyce) in the final reel. Meanwhile, conflict enters her life in the irritating form of Pinky (Maggie Burke), her snobbish, grasping stepmother who tries to trick her out of her father's will.

Flournoy's pic is as maladroit as her heroine. The screenplay is ragged, music horribly overused, supporting actors amateurish and the soundtrack is one of those in which rustling papers sound like cannon fire.

About an hour into the film, an intertitle brazenly bridges several pages of presumably unfilmed script. Camerawork is very grainy.

On the plus side, Floden makes Louise a sympathetic, if at times annoyingly inept, character, while McCarty has presence as the love interest. There's no doubt that Flournoy has some ideas for an offbeat, whimsical comedy, but plot contrivances (the grasping stepmother) aren't well integrated into the central story of the lovable, put-upon Louise. — *Strat.*

ARCHIVE REVIEW

Hell Bent
(B&W-SILENT)

New York A Universal release in 1918. Directed by John Ford. Screenplay, Ford, Harry Carey; camera (b&w), Ben Reynolds. Reviewed at the American Museum of the Moving Image, Queens, N.Y., Jan. 26, 1990. Length: 5,700 ft. (5 reels). Running time (at 20 frames per second): **77 MIN.**

Cheyenne Harry	Harry Carey
Bess Thurston	Neva Gerber
Cimarron Bill	Duke Lee
Bean Ross	Joseph Harris

■"Hell Bent" is a 1918 John Ford film rediscovered at the Czech Film Archives. Current print available in German titles is presently the only one of two complete films surviving from the director's 1917-1919 beginning years at Universal Studios. The other, "Straight Shooting" was Ford's first feature and also a Czech Archive rediscovery.

Less engaging than "Straight Shooting," "Hell Bent" still operates with the efficiency of a minor programmer boosted by some Ford touches. "Hell Bent" was Ford's 14th film and his ninth feature. Its leading player, Harry Carey was Ford's most frequent early star and collaborator. Here, Carey is again playing his laconic Cheyenne Harry protgagonist. At the outset of the film a Western author is asked to provide a more ordinary kind of hero. He walks over to a painting of Frederic Remington's "The Misdeal" which comes to life, a scene of a barroom racked by violence after a cheating cardplayer has been discovered. It is Carey's Cheyenne Harry who has fled the scene.

Harry rides into the town of Rawhide where in a long winded comic turn he strikes up a friendship with Cimmaron Bill (Duke Lee) and is then smitten by love for Bess (Neva Gerber), a "good girl" forced by circumstances to work in a dance hall. B-plot mechanics take over as Harry tries to rid town of outlaws but is stymied when he learns Bess' weak-willed brother is member of gang led by Bean Ross (Harris). Bess considers Harry a coward for his inaction but when Bess is kidnaped by the gang Harry rides to the rescue.

Film is enlivened by some of Ford's special moments. As his relationship with Bess develops Harry awkwardly carries her home in the rain while in the next shot his abandoned pal wanders through the darkened saloon. Exterior shooting demonstrates Ford's striking landscape compositions in his pre-Monument Valley days.

Unusual denouement has hero and villain, both wounded, agree to let heroine take the one surviving horse while they accept macho challenge to cross desert on foot. An oncoming sandstorm helps determine the fitter to survive. Ford fans may be reminded of the desert climax to his 1949 "Three Godfathers" (a remake of his still lost "Marked Men") a film he dedicated to Carey. — Lomb.

The Hunt For Red October

Hollywood A Paramount Pictures release of a Mace Neufeld/Jerry Sherlock production. Executive producers, Larry De Waay, Sherlock. Produced by Neufeld. Directed by John McTiernan. Screenplay, Larry Ferguson, Donald Stewart, based on Tom Clancy's novel; camera (Panavision, Technicolor), Jan De Bont; editor, Dennis Virkler, John Wright; music, Basil Poledouris; sound (Dolby), Richard Bryce Goodman; production design, Terence Marsh; art direction, Dianne Wager, Donald Woodruff, William Cruise; set decoration, Mickey S. Michaels; undersea submarines, Boss Film Corp.; special visual effects, Industrial Light & Magic, supervisor - Scott Squires; production manager-2d unit director, Beau Marks; assistant director, Jerry L. Balew; stunt coordinator, Charles Picerni Jr.; casting, Amanda Mackey. Reviewed at Mann National theater, L.A., Feb. 22, 1990. MPAA Rating: PG. Running time: **137 MIN.**

Capt. Marko Ramius	Sean Connery
Jack Ryan	Alec Baldwin
Capt. Bart Mancuso	Scott Glenn
Capt. Borodin	Sam Neill
Admiral Greer	James Earl Jones
Andrei Lysenko	Joss Ackland
Jeffrey Pelt	Richard Jordan
Ivan Putin	Peter Firth
Dr. Petrov	Tim Curry
Seaman Jones	Courtney B. Vance
Capt. Tupolev	Stellan Skarsgård
Skip Tyler	Jeffrey Jones
Admiral Painter	Fred Dalton Thompson
Capt. Davenport	Daniel Davis
Loginov	Tomas Arana

■"The Hunt For Red October" is a terrific adventure yarn, excitingly filmed by director John McTiernan. The Paramount release, produced by Mace Neufeld, looks like a b.o. smash.

Tom Clancy's 1984 Cold War thriller, well-thumbed at the White House in the days when the USSR was viewed as "The Evil Empire," has been thoughtfully adapted by Larry Ferguson and Donald Stewart to reflect the recent mellowing in the U.S.-Soviet relationship. Sean Connery is splendid as the renegade Soviet nuclear sub captain pursued by CIA analyst Alec Baldwin and the fleets of both superpowers as he heads for the coast of Maine.

With a Cold War plot that could have suffered from the changes in the Western filmgoing public's perception of the USSR, the filmmakers have wisely opted to keep the story set in 1984 — "shortly before Gorbachev came to power," as the opening title puts it —rather than to force it into a contemporary time frame. Though Clancy's conservative slant on the Soviet threat remains strong, the essentially hopeful nature of the story has been supported by recent events and makes the film accessible to more

liberal viewers as well.

Looking magnificent in his captain's uniform and white beard, Connery scores another career highlight as the Lithuanian Marko Ramius, an enigmatic seaman whose actions cause intense debate in the inner circles of Moscow and Washington as the action proceeds inexorably to a fail-safe point. Is he a madman planning to launch his own preemptive nuclear strike on the U.S.? Or is he a conscientious would-be defector trying to turn over his advanced new sub in order to prevent Soviet hardliners from being able to start World War III?

At first "Red October" leads the audience to believe that Connery, with his secretive and sometimes ruthless behavior, is the Soviet equivalent of Sterling Hayden's deranged Gen. Jack D. Ripper in "Dr. Strangelove." The film gradually shifts the viewer's perspective to consider the other alternative, urged on by Baldwin, who knows more than any other American about the character of Ramius.

Giving his role the complex stature of a man who has gone from a limited role in an underwater war with "no battles, no monuments, only casualties" to become a hidden but powerful player in a political "game of chess," Connery effortlessly conveys the dual nature of a coldblooded killer and a meditator on the Hindu scripture famously quoted by American nuclear physicist Robert Oppenheimer: "I am become death, the destroyer of worlds" (Connery dryly notes that Oppenheimer was "accused of being a Communist").

True to Clancy's example in its relentless quest for authenticity in military detail, and highly impressive in its display of the latest in U.S. government-supplied naval hardware, "Red October" nevertheless requires a willing suspension of disbelief in asking the audience to accept the notion that Baldwin's low-level CIA analyst would be thrust into such a James Bondian operational role, and that he would prove to be an idealistic seeker of detente and world peace.

Baldwin's intelligent and likable performance makes his Walter Mittyish character come alive as an audience surrogate with a fierce desire to push the course of events in a positive direction. He's combating not only the bulk of the Soviet fleet as it pursues the errant

sub, but also the reflexive anti-Communist mentality of most pursuing on the U.S. side — not including his wise and avuncular CIA superior James Earl Jones, equally improbable but masterful as the film's deus ex machina (a role far removed from his jittery bomber crew member in "Strangelove").

Director McTiernan, lenser Jan De Bont, production designer Terence Marsh, editors Dennis Virkler and John Wright, and the tech support staff, including the Industrial Light & Magic special visual effects unit have done yeoman work in staging the action with credibility and cliffhanger intensity. — Mac.

Where The Heart Is

New York A Buena Vista release of a Touchstone Pictures presentation, in association with Silver Screen Partners IV. Executive producer, Edgar F. Gross. Produced and directed by John Boorman. Screenplay, Boorman, Telsche Boorman; camera (Film House color; Technicolor prints), Peter Suschitzky; editor, Ian Crafford; music, Peter Martin; sound (Dolby), Bryan Day, Ron Yoshida (N.Y.); production design, Carol Spier; costume design, Linda Matheson; Chloe's paintings & body makeup, Timna Woollard; production manager, Sean Ryerson, Ira Halberstadt (N.Y.); assistant director, Tony Lucibello; associate producer, Ryerson; casting, Bonnie Finnegan, Stuart Aikins (Toronto). Reviewed at 57th St. Playhouse, N.Y., Feb. 20, 1990. MPAA Rating: R. Running time: **94 MIN.**

Stewart McBain	Dabney Coleman
Daphne	Uma Thurman
Jean	Joanna Cassidy
Lionel	Crispin Glover
Chloe	Suzy Amis
The !#&@	Christopher Plummer
Jimmy	David Hewlett
Harry	Maury Chaykin
Tom	Dylan Walsh
Hamilton	Ken Pogue
Sheryl	Sheila Kelley

■John Boorman's "Where The Heart Is" would be more at home released in the '60s than now. Visually arresting allegorical comedy suffers from gauche dialog, grotesque acting and a stupid ending.

Film is a companion piece to a picture Boorman made 20 years ago for Robert Chartoff and Irwin Winkler, the little-seen "Leo The Last," in which Marcello Mastroianni was an aristocrat who learns about life from ghetto denizens in London. This time it's tycoon Dabney Coleman who gets the message when he and his family end up in a Brooklyn tenement.

Topic harks back to the now-dated screwball comedies made during the Depression. Boorman also relies heavily on a '90s stock market crash, and his approach to the plight of street people and other current social problems is flippant.

Predictable plotting has tyrannical buildings demolitions expert Coleman, well-cast in an Archie Bunker role, getting fed up with his spoiled, grown-up kids. He throws them out of the mansion and (unconvincingly) orders them to live in a Brooklyn tenement that local protesters have succeeded in preserving against his wrecking ball, holding up a big redevelopment project.

Kids, led by Uma Thurman, are determined to make it on their own. Her sister (Suzy Amis) gets a gig doing a calendar for an insurance company, with Thurman the chief nude model for her body-painting and photography artwork.

Of course, stock market manipulation brings down Coleman's empire and soon he's reunited with his brood on the streets. There's some fun as the good guys succeed (Amis' calendar is a hit with her backers), but that good will is frittered away in an idiotic finish in which Boorman stubs his toe.

Cast reunites at a party and suffers through giddy dialog as they dance around, attempting to tie up loose plot threads. Glover is revealed to be a "closet heterosexual," merely posing as gay to make it in the fashion world.

Film's most successful element is the series of spectacular *trompe d'oeil* artworks by Timna Woollard, inspired by paintings by Ingres, Henri Rousseau, Picasso, etc., and personified by Thurman. Combined with the all-nighter atmosphere of the delapidated Brooklyn house, pic succeeds in capturing a '60s ambience.

Unfortunately, what audience will care about the question posed by Boorman and his daughter, coscripter Telsche Boorman: "How would '60s people react to today's world?"

Besides Thurman, who is perfectly cast as a sexy kook, Amis makes a very good impression as her artistic, romantic sister. Canadian thesp David Hewlett, who replaced Anthony Michael Hall in the son's role at the beginning of shooting, does not match his siblings (his accent is a problem). Coleman and especially wife Joanna Cassidy overact and pour on the unfunny slapstick. Christopher Plummer is tiresome as a street

bum/magician in heavy makeup, using a voice that sounds like Eddie (Rochester) Anderson.
— *Lor.*

Nightbreed

New York A 20th Century Fox release of a James G. Robinson and Joe Roth presentation of a Morgan Creek production. Executive producers, Robinson, Roth. Produced by Gabriella Martinelli. Directed by Clive Barker. Screenplay, Barker, based on his novel "Cabal;" camera (Deluxe color), Robin Vidgeon; editor, Richard Marden, Mark Goldblatt; music, Danny Elfman; sound (Dolby), Bruce Nyznik; production design, Steve Hardie; art direction, Ricky Eyres; costume design, Ann Hollowood, Marie France (L.A.); special makeup & visual effects, Image Animation; special makeup design, Bob Keen, Geoff Portass; special makeup (L.A.), Tony Gardner; creature supervision, Simon Sayce; model unit director, Julian Parry; model camera, Harry Oakes; camera (L.A.), Steven Fierberg; special effects supervisor, Chris Corboulo; animated optical effects, VCE/Peter Kuran; action unit director, Andy Armstrong; assistant director, Kieron Phipps, Mike Topoozian (L.A.); associate producer, David Barron; casting, Doreen Jones (U.K.), Todd Thayler (U.S.). Reviewed at 23d St. West 3 theater, N.Y., Feb. 17, 1990. MPAA Rating: R. Running time: **99 MIN.**

Aaron Boone	Craig Sheffer
Lori	Anne Bobby
Dr. Philip Decker	David Cronenberg
Capt. Eigerman	Charles Haid
Det. Joyce	Hugh Quarshie
Narcisse	Hugh Ross
Lylesberg	Doug Bradley
Rachel	Catherine Chevalier
Ashberry	Malcolm Smith
Pettine	Bob Sessions
Poloquin	Oliver Parker
Sheryl Ann	Debora Weston

■**Writer-director Clive Barker's "Nightbreed" is a mess. Self-indulgent horror pic could be the "Heaven's Gate" of its genre, of obvious interest to diehard monster fans but a turnoff for mainstream audiences.**

In a bit of poetic justice, Joe Roth, the Fox studio chieftain, inherited this turkey from Joe Roth, the Morgan Creek cotopper (with James Robinson). There were no press screenings, even for folks interviewing Barker about the pic.

It's the first big-budget horror film release since Fox' own "The Fly II" exactly one year ago. "Nightbreed" had a rocky production history that saw Morgan Creek replacing film's producer, Christopher Figg (who usually works with Barker), midway through shooting.

Rock singer Suzi Quatro also was prominent in the cast but doesn't appear in release version.

What emerges is an incoherent

mishmash in which lots of misguided effort (well over 300 crew members are credited) went into monster makeups and lavish effects that often last only fleeting seconds on screen.

Other than Fox' hit "Alien" series, not strictly a horror property, it would seem foolhardy to stage these costly gore production numbers only to have them cut to avoid an X rating. (Morgan Creek has William Peter Blatty's "The Exorcist: 1990" in the can for Fox release, however). For his second try at feature direction (after NW's successful cheapie "Hellraiser"), Barker unwisely imitates Ken Russell's "Altered States" (whose costar Charles Haid pops up here in the final reels) in structure: plot exposition is doled out in static dialog scenes alternating with hectic, almost psychedelic bursts of action.

His inverted story premise is not explained until halfway through the picture: the last survivors of shapeshifters (legendary monsters including vampires and werewolves) are huddled below ground in a tiny Canadian cemetery near Calgary called Midian, trying to avoid final extinction.

Hero Craig Sheffer is plagued by nightmares and heads there in hopes of becoming a monster, while his nutty shrink (David Cronenberg, in the Peter Cushing role) is on a messianic mission to destroy the undead critters. Sheffer's normal girlfriend tags along and ends up siding with the sympathetic (though disgusting looking) monsters, but unlike Sheffer doesn't want to become one.

What with Danny Elfman maintaining a dark, portentous mood with his post-"Batman" orchestral score, pic presents unrelated sequences of gore and slashing until the ridiculously overproduced finale taken from a disaster epic. As their subterranean world literally blows up under fire from Haid's armed-to-the-teeth group of survivalists, the monsters let loose their cousins, the Berserkers, who look like gooey versions of the Michelin Man. Sheffer is appointed Cabal, entrusted with the future of the surviving creatures of the night. Tacked-on coda is lifted from "Carrie."

Countering the oppressive mood are Barker's inept attempts at comic relief by giving the monsters catch-phrase throwaway lines that imitate Freddy Krueger's routine

in the "Nightmare On Elm Street" pics but aren't funny.

Sheffer is an unappealing protagonist, presumably cast since his angular facial features respond well to monster makeup disfigurement. Romantic costar Bobby manages to keep a straight face in the most ludicrous scenes.

Chief casting gimmick is giving the lead baddie role to revered Canadian director David Cronenberg. While he presented a pleasant screen presence in his fleeting role in John Landis' "Into The Night," Cronenberg overstays his welcome here. Horror cultists might enjoy his soft-spoken, monotone performances and in-jokes (his character is as screwy and fetishistic as the evil Jeremy Irons in Cronenberg's "Dead Ringers"), but others will merely wonder why a professional actor was cheated out of a salary.

Individual technical credits are often impressive but don't support each other. Most notably, Robin Vidgeon's stylized photography (he also shot Barker's "Hellraiser," its sequel and "The Fly II") is undercut by lack of matching between disparate studio shots, exteriors and fancy matte shots. Orson Welles (at a tender age) and crew put together all manner of complex effects shots to come up with "Citizen Kane," but all Barker has to show is lots of footage.
— *Lor.*

Dimenticare Palermo
(To Forget Palermo)
(ITALIAN-FRENCH)

Rome A Penta Distribuzione release of a Mario and Vittorio Cecchi Gori and Silvio Berlusconi Communications presentation. Produced by Mario, Vittorio Cecchi Gori for Reteitalia/C. G. Silver Group Leopard/Gaumont Prods. Directed by Francesco Rosi. Screenplay, Rosi, Gore Vidal, Tonino Guerra, based on a novel by Edmond Charles Roux; camera (Technicolor, Eastman Kodak negative), Pasqualino De Santis; art direction, Andrea Crisanti, Stephen Graham (U.S.); costumes, Enrico Sabatinti; editor, Ruggero Mastroianni; music, Ennio Morricone; production manager, Alessandro Von Normann. Reviewed at Barberini Cinema, Rome, Feb. 16, 1990. Running time: **110 MIN.**

Carmine Bonavia	James Belushi
Carrie	Mimi Rogers
Man of Power	Joss Ackland
Gianna Magnardi	Carolina Rosi
Hotel manager	Philippe Noiret
Prince	Vittorio Gassman
Also with: Harry Davies, Marco Leonardi.
(Italian soundtrack)

■**"To Forget Palermo" is Francesco Rosi's latest foray into the political thriller, though hardly his best work. Lensed** in New York and Sicily, it illustrates the long arm of the international Mafia. The U.S. connection is evident in setting, a main character who is a liberal Italoamerican politician, and Gore Vidal as coscriptwriter. Add in Yank topliners James Belushi and Mimi Rogers, and pic's bid for the international market could succeed with careful handling.

Loosely based on Edmond Charles Roux' Prix Goncourt 1966 novel, pic has been updated to encompass Sicily's present-day ills, while lensed in a style recalling classic Yank political thrillers. Unlike most Mafia operas, it avoids gory bloodshed and fancy murders in preference for psychological torture. This cerebral approach often makes pic a tepid watch.

Carmine Bonavia (Belushi) is just a few points behind the incumbent in the New York City mayoral race. A chance meeting with bright, attractive Italian tv reporter Carolina Rosi gives him two vote-culling ideas: to campaign for the legalization of drugs and to spend his honeymoon in dad's native Palermo.

After a lengthy and not very new look at behind-the-scenes politicking, it is a relief when pic switches to Italy. Carmine and new bride Carrie (Rogers), a poised photoreporter, check into a luxury hotel in Palermo. As seen through Pasqualino De Santis' camerawork, the city is a wrenching mixture of magnificence and ruin, and appears to decay while one watches.

The honeymooners dutifully hit the tourist spots, where Carrie snaps her shutter nonstop. Neither can hear the sinister notes that creep into Ennio Morricone's romantic score, sure tipoffs malice is afoot. They also ignore ultimate Man of Power Joss Ackland's bald pate, reappearing too often for comfort at the next table.

Soon over-innocent Carmine gets himself involved in an ambiguous knifing in the market. Ackland, in name of the Mafia, gives him a choice: to go to prison for murder, or drop legalizing drugs from his campaign platform. Carmine, the consummate politician, compromises unconvincingly, but a predictable surprise ending redeems him.

Onshore, "To Forget Palermo" will be read heavily in light of local politics. Pic's strong stand in favor of legalizing drugs, in fact, is strongly opposed by Rosi's own

political party. In a way, film seems custom-built around the argument, with the result the story has much less force than its thesis. A secondary theme is the way the media hype candidates and how easy it is to manipulate opinion polls.

Dubbed into Italian, the version here reviewed, Belushi offers a restrained performance as the candidate, hovering between cynical and likable, but ultimately tipping the scales in his favor with his all-too-human ("real Sicilian") weakness: jealousy. Strange he doesn't pay more attention to his father's good advice about staying clear of Sicily altogether.

As wife Carrie, Rogers, who bears a disturbing resemblance to a young Barbara Stanwyck, has enough of a hard edge to keep the character from fading into the background, and comes across as believable but not very sympathetic. Of the three, mafioso Ackland is the only one likely to sell a used car.

In cameos, Vittorio Gassman pops up as a latter-day Prince of Saline, condemned never to leave his hotel after slighting the Mafia 30 years ago. Philippe Noiret makes a guest appearance as the hotel manager.

Splendid lensing includes a number of breathtaking aerial shots. Technical work gives film a high quality veneer throughout. — *Yung*.

Madhouse

Hollywood An Orion Pictures release of A Boy Of The Year production. Produced by Leslie Dixon. Written and directed by Tom Ropelewski. Coproducer, Donald C. Klune. Camera (Fotokem color), Denis Lewiston; editor, Michael Jablow; production design, Dan Leigh; music, David Newman; art direction, C.J. Simpson; set decoration, Leslie Rollins; costume design, Jim Lapidus; sound, Peter Bentley; assistant directors, Jerram A. Swartz, Bob Nellans, Alan R. Green; casting, Sally Dennison, Julie Selzer, Justine Jacoby. Reviewed at the AMC Theaters, L.A., Feb. 16, 1990. MPAA Rating: PG-13. Running time: **90 MIN.**
Mark. . . . . .John Larroquette
Jessie. . . . . .Kirstie Alley
Claudia. . . . . .Alison LaPlaca
Fred. . . . . .John Diehl
Bernice. . . . . .Jessica Lundy
Jonathan. . . . . .Bradley Gregg
Wes. . . . . .Dennis Miller
Dale. . . . . .Robert Ginty

■The lunatics were surely running the asylum when Orion opted to unloose this pathetic comedy, though sanity returned when it was decided to cancel press screenings. Still,

someone had to see it eventually, even if few paying customers will be apt to unless they're a little wacko themselves.

That's unlikely, since the film primarily relies on the marquee value of three sitcom stars who can all be found being much funnier on tv. Kirstie Alley, for one, should thank her stars that this came out after "Look Who's Talking."

Alley, John Larroquette and Alison LaPlaca find themselves trapped in a seemingly endless maze of bad jokes based on cheap innuendo, long takes, shrieking fits and bodily excretions. Someone should have sensed they were in trouble when the best scene in the first half-hour involved a projectile-vomiting cat.

Minus the scatalogical humor (such as it is) first-time writer-director Tom Ropelewski basically structures the whole film as a dragged-out sitcom, with apologies to most sitcoms.

Larroquette and Alley play a yuppie couple whose prized, recently purchased home is invaded by a horde of repulsive houseguests, including Alley's golddigging sister (LaPlaca), Larroquette's cousin and his shrill wife (John Diehl, Jessica Lundy), as well as the next-door neighbor and his kids.

They all won't leave for various reasons, and the increasingly exasperated couple can't make them go. Audiences will be more fortunate and can wander out anytime they choose.

The concept is so hackneyed it might have worked as a screwball farce had the execution not been so dreadful, but the material and characters are played so broadly it's hard to endure.

Add to that the film's sheer volume, as Ropelewski seems to anticipate the audience's deafening silence by drowning nearly every scene in screams or thudding music. In a similar vein the leads emerge as blithering idiots, though Alley has one pulse-quickening striptease that should be bottled and saved for a better pic, while LaPlaca gets to model plenty of garish clothes. — *Bril*.

BERLIN FILM FESTIVAL REVIEWS

Conte de Printemps (A Tale Of Springtime) (FRENCH)

Berlin An Orion Classics release of a Roissy Films presentation of a Films du Losange production. Produced by Margaret Menegoz. Written and directed by Eric Rohmer. Camera (color), Luc Pages; editor, Lisa Garcia; sound, Pascal Ribier; music, Beethoven, Schumann; production manager, Françoise Etchegaray. Reviewed at the Berlin Film Festival (non-competing). Feb. 20, 1990. Running time: **110 MIN.**
Jeanne. . . . . .Anne Teyssedre
Igor. . . . . .Hugues Quester
Natacha. . . . . .Florence Durrell
Eve. . . . . .Eloise Bennett
Gaelle. . . . . .Sophie Robin

■Veteran French helmer Eric Rohmer inaugurates a new cycle of morality parables, entitled "Tales Of Four Seasons," with another one of his bright, urban, sophisticated conversation pieces, for which he is famous.

This is a subtly suggestive story of the relations among a small group of people, wittily scripted and directed. The theme is the tendency of certain persons to impose their will on others, and the various emotional types of black-mail employed to achieve this purpose.

Jeanne, a pretty philosophy teacher whose boyfriend is away on business, stays for a week with Natacha, an 18-year-old conservatory student she meets by chance. Natacha's parents are separated, she hates her mother, dotes on her father, can't stand his latest girlfriend, and would very much like to replace her with Jeanne.

To this end, she manipulates her new friend into her parents' graces, leading everybody involved into intriguing situations. All of them are resolved in long conversations, some of them highly literate, reflecting moral uncertainties and doubts on the part of all the leading characters.

Unlike his recent work, in which he seemed to thrive on a simpler and more immediate dialog, Rohmer is going back here to the philosophical mood of his earlier films ("Ma Nuit Chez Maud"). Jeanne, by her profession, is a natural for highbrow quotes. Eve, the g.f. of Natacha's father, is just preparing her own thesis in the same domain, and the rest are only too happy to go along and explore the possibilities of abstract thought. Characters, however, are finely limned and the verbal outpour sounds natural enough, coming from them.

The only big difference here is that Rohmer seems to have less patience with the whims and shortcomings of his characters and doesn't mind showing it clearly in casting the film. Anne Teyssedre is most sympathetic, offering a sensitive and nicely balanced performance as Jeanne, while Florence Durrell fits the teenage moods and caprices of Natacha.

It's hard to believe, however, Rohmer did not perceive the weakness of Hugues Quester, as Natacha's father, the irritating arrogance of Eloise Bennett as the lover and the false tone of Sophie Robin as Jeanne's cousin, Gaelle. The only explanation for their choice is that he doesn't like them very much (and the script leaves little doubt on this subject). There is no reason why the audience should try to like them better.

Rohmer fans, who have discovered new depths in each of his films, will certainly enjoy the latest one as well, but will find themselves walking through familiar territory. Tightly controlled camera work (back to 35m after several 16m forays), Beethoven's "Spring Sonata" as the opening and closing theme and Schumann's piano music integrated into the plot, lend the film that specific intellectual aura which is by now Rohmer's trademark. — *Edna.*

Dias Melhores Virao
(Better Days Ahead)
(BRAZILIAN)

Rio de Janeiro An Embrafilme release of a Cininvest/Multiplic production. Produced by Paulo Cesar Ferreira. Executive producers, Angelo Gastal, Renata Almeida Magalhaes. Directed by Carlos Diegues. Screenplay, Diegues, Antonio Calmon, Vicente Pereira, Vinicius Vianna, based on story by Calmon; camera (Eastmancolor), Lauro Escorel; editing, Gilberto Santeiro; art direction, Lia Renha; costumes, Emilia Duncan; music, Rita Lee, Roberto de Carvalho; sound (Dolby), Jorge Saldanha; musical production, RAC Som e Imagem; associate producers, CDK Producoes, Embrafilme. Reviewed at UIP screening room, Rio de Janeiro, Jan. 18, 1990. (In Berlin Film Festival, competing.) Running time: **92 MIN.**
Marialva/Mary Mattos. . . . . .Marilia Pera
Mary Shadow. . . . . .Rita Lee
Pompeu. . . . . .Paulo José
Dalila. . . . . .Zezé Motta
Wallace. . . . . .José Wilker

Also with: Marilu Bueno, Paulo Cesar Pereio, Antonio Pedro, Betina Viany, Benjamin Cattan, Patricio Bisso, Michel Royster, Sandra Pera, Jofre Soares, Leticia Monte, Lilia Cabral, Aurora Miranda.

■**A light comedy on the fantasy of a femme dubber who aims to be a star on the series she is dubbing for Brazilian tv, this 11th feature by Carlos Diegues shows the helmer at his best. Pic has a good chance to be enjoyed both by local and foreign audiences.**

Story may have been told before in different ways: A group of dubbers live their fantasies in the films they dub for tv. Most have a strictly professional approach to their scenes, but they're bored by the work and couldn't care less about the plot.

Not Marialva, who is dubbing the main star of the "Mary Shadow Show," something between Lucille Ball and Mary Tyler Moore shows. Marialva dreams of being a part of the show. She is played by Marilia Pera, a top Brazilian actress who was cited by New York Film Critics Circle for her role in "Pixote."

Marialva is fascinated by Mary Shadow, very adequately portrayed by rock singer Rita Lee, and even changes her name to Mary Mattos. She will not hesitate to use everybody around her — colleagues, lovers, best friend — to go Hollywood.

Best friend is played by Zezé Motta, who had the main role in Diegues' costly production "Xica da Silva." She heads a precious supporting cast including top stars like Paulo José ("Faca de Dois Gumes") and José Wilker ("O Homem da Capa Preta").

Narrated with simplicity and a fine sense of humor (where some inspiration in the Pedro Almodóvar style can be detected), "Dias Melhores Virao" results in the best recent work by Diegues, far more homogeneous than "Quilombo" or "A Train To The Stars," both already seen in New York. Spontaneity seldom seen in helmer's previous works is the key to this accomplishment. Diegues himself appears twice in the film, first lecturing on tv on the problems of Brazilian cinema, then directing a musical sequence with Rita Lee.

Besides Pera, Motta and José, pic is well supported by the technical credits, including the good stereo sound and especially editing by Gilberto Santeiro. It allows a fluency far above the expected standards of a Latin American production. "Dias Melhores Virao" is much more centered on a universal appeal than on the compromise of a strictly Brazilian narrative style. — *Hoin.*

Asteniceksij Sindrom
(The Weakness Syndrome)
(SOVIET-COLOR/B&W)

Berlin An Odessa Filmstudio production. (Intl. sales: Primodessa.) Directed by Kira Muratova. Screenplay, Muratova, Sergei Popov, Alexander Tschernych; camera (Fujicolor/b&w), Vladimir Pankov; editor, Valentina Olejnik; production design, E. Golubenko; sound, Elena Demidova; production manager, Nadja Popova; assistant director, T. Borodina. Reviewed at Berlin Film Fest (Competing), Feb. 19, 1990. Running time: **153 MIN.**
Nikolai. . . . . .Sergei Popov
Natasha. . . . . .Olga Antonova
Mascha (brunette). . . . . .Natalia Busko
Mascha (blonde). . . .Galina Sachurdaewa
Teacher. . . . . . . .Alexandra Ovenskaya
Iunikov. . . . . .Pavel Polischnuk
Mother. . . . . .Natalia Rallewa
Nikolai's wife. . . . .Galina Kasperovich
School director. . . . . . . .Viktor Aristov
Head doctor. . . . . . .Nikolai Semjonov
Woman on the train. . . . .Nadja Popova

■**With its full frontal nudity and explicit dialog, "The Weakness Syndrome" makes "Little Vera" look like a vicarage tea party. It's a challenging film that's too long and sometimes indulgent, but it could well attract arthouse audiences the world over with its kaleidoscopic vision of a society in decay.**

Femme director Kira Muratova, 55, whose work has often been shelved in the past, has come up with a caustic, unrelenting attack on every aspect of the Soviet system today. Pic is technically fine, with thesping so naturalistic that it's sometimes hard to discern between actors and people taken off the streets.

The film was entered in the Berlin festival not by the Moscow Committee for Cinematography (as is usual) but by the Odessa Film Studio, which produced it. Sovexportfilm apparently isn't involved in marketing the pic (it's Primodessa Film instead).

The film opens with a 40-minute black & white segment centering on a woman doctor, Natasha (Olga Antonova) who's been driven almost mad by the death of her husband. She attends his funeral, then rails against mankind in general, refuses to help a sick man, and picks up a drunk on the street to have sex with.

Abruptly "The End" appears on screen; it was a b & w film. In color, a moderator appears before the screen with the leading actress and inviting the unimpressed audience to discuss it.

For the next 110 minutes, Muratova shows a series of barely connected vignettes wih no linking plotline. It's an almost unrelievedly grim world where the subways are overcrowded and the shops are empty. People are violent or listless, angry and antisocial. Pupils pay no attention to the teacher, but speak in slogans they've learned in the past.

Near pic's end, a woman on a train (Nadja Popova) gives an obscene monolog addressed to the camera, using words worthy of James Joyce or D.H. Lawrence. Sequence apparently was responsible for the film's lack of distribution in the USSR, but the entire film would probably have been seen as exceptionally negative.

Moments of strange beauty mix with the gloom. A plump woman plays "Strangers In The Night" on a trumpet, and a young girl dances to music on a record player. But the woman is ignored by her lazy son, and the girl is beaten by her father. Even the isolated moments of pleasure have their downside.

Pic could be trimmed since some scenes go on long after the point has been well made. Western audiences are likely to be devastated and disturbed by Muratova's vision of her homeland. There are two references to Soviet leader Mikhail Gorbachev in the film: a man wearing a Gorby badge asks "Why do we fight?" during a typical scene of argument and dissension. Later, a man in a mental home starts: "Mikhail says..." and then lapses into silence.

For Muratova, "The Weakness Syndrome" is a considerable achievement unlike any previous Soviet film. It's a bitter, bleak film with little hope indicated, but the overall impression is of a dauntingly original and exciting pic which should cause a stir wherever it's shown. — *Strat.*

Die Tanzerin
(The Dancer)
(W. GERMAN-JAPANESE)

Berlin A Manfred Durniok-Herald Ace coproduction. Produced by Manfred Durniok, Masato Hara. Directed by Masahiro Shinoda. Screenplay, Hans Borgelt, Tsutomu Tamura, Shinoda, from a story by Ogai Mori; camera (color), Jurgen Jurges, Kazuo Miyagawa; editor, Barbara Hiltmann; music, Cong Su; production design, Harry Leupold, Setsuo Asakura. Reviewed at Berlin Film Fest (New German Films), Feb. 19, 1990. Running time: **123 MIN.**

Oota Toyotaro.	Hiromi Go
Elis Weigelt.	Lisa Wolf
Anna Weigelt.	Brigitte Grothum
Toyotaro's mother.	Haruko Kato
Baroness von Bulow.	Mareike Carriere
Von Meilheim.	Christoph Eichhorn
Soejima.	Takuzo Kadono
Aizawa.	Toru Mazuoka
Tanimura.	Shiro Sano
Robert Koch.	Rolf Hoppe

■One of Japan's top directors, Masahiro Shinoda, helmed this West German-Japanese coprod on locations in West and East Berlin. On the basis of his reputation and the romantic depiction of another era, pic might have some international arthouse chances, but the German obsession with dubbing will have to be modified.

In the print caught, Japanese dialog was overlaid with an unnecessary German narration, whereas it would have been more logical simply to subtitle the Japanese text. This could be fixed easily, however.

Plot concerns a Japanese medical student who, in 1885, is sent to Berlin to study. He meets and falls in love with a young dancer, who becomes pregnant. He neglects his studies and when news of this gets back to his mother, she attempts suicide. He returns sadly to Japan, leaving his German love behind.

The story's a simple and familiar one, and hardly justifies the leisurely treatment that results in a running time of over two hours. The film explores to some degree the attitudes of Germans towards Japanese, and vice versa, at this period in history, but the main thing is the romance, which is somewhat tentatively handled.

Visually, the film is most impressive with glorious images of old Berlin forming the background to this story of star-crossed lovers. Thesping is in keeping with the mood. — *Strat.*

Coupe De Ville

New York A Universal Pictures release of a Morgan Creek Prods. presentation of a Rollins, Morra, Brezner production. Executive producer, James G. Robinson. Produced by Larry Brezner, Paul Schiff. Coproducer, Mike Binder. Directed by Joe Roth. Screenplay, Binder; camera (Deluxe color), Reynaldo Villalobos; editor, Paul Hirsch; music, James Newton Howard; executive music producer, Joel Sill; sound (Dolby), Carey Lindley; production design, Angelo Graham; art direction, Jim Murakami; costumes, Deborah Scott; production manager-associate producer, Jerry Baerwitz; assistant director, Dennis Maguire; casting, Marci Liroff. Reviewed at Universal screening room, N.Y., Feb. 20, 1990. MPAA Rating: PG-13. Running time: **99 MIN.**

Bobby.	Patrick Dempsey
Buddy.	Arye Gross
Marvin.	Daniel Stern
Tammy.	Annabeth Gish
Betty Libner.	Rita Taggart
Uncle Phil.	Joseph Bologna
Fred Libner.	Alan Arkin

Also with: James Gammon, Ray Lykins, Chris Lombardi, Josh Segal, John Considine, Steve Boles, Don Tilley, Edan Gross, Michael Weiner, Dean Jacobson.

■ The best aspect of this ordinary coming-of-age/buddy bonding/road movie hybrid are the powder-blue '54 Caddy from which it takes its name and a nicely remixed soundtrack of vintage early '60s radio hits.

"Coupe De Ville's" facile appeal to nostalgia and inoffensive breeziness should ease the pic's flow into the video-cable pipeline following a perfunctory theatrical release.

The rivalrous Lipner siblings, big brother Marvin (Daniel Stern), middle brother Buddy (Arye Gross) and little brother Bobby (Patrick Dempsey) are maneuvered by their crusty but caring dad (Alan Arkin) into a reluctant reunion after a long separation. The time is 1963. Their mission: drive the titular convertible from their hometown of Detroit to their parents' retirement home in Florida.

The Coupe de Ville is a sentimental birthday present from Arkin to his wife (Rita Taggart). He's a failed inventor, still tinkering in search of the big one (a polyurethane stop sign). She's a cliché of loving steadfastness who's stuck by her man because "you take the card you're dealt."

Their three sons are burdened with a lifetime of emotional baggage to sort out as they uneasily hit the road. Bullying big brother Marvin, though matured by a hitch in the Air Force, remains imperious and remote. Rebellious little brother Bobby remains untamed by his tony reform school and has no use for "tight-ass" Marvin. Middle brother Buddy, a sexually awakened clever college grad, still mediates between them. All three are joined in fear of what Arkin will do to them if any harm comes to the car.

While the brothers negotiate the rocky road to reconciliation, their blue beauty suffers all too predictable mishaps. Director Joe Roth (now head of 20th Fox) does nothing to alleviate the monotony once the brothers are established in their blustery confrontational triangle. The flat narrative of "Coupe De Ville" is pushed along by routine cross-cutting between the parents in Florida and the feuding frères, who meet no one on their travels more interesting than a couple of Georiga traffic cops and a philosophical auto-chopper.

Things change with the maudlin revelation that Arkin is suffering from a terminal disease. United by this epiphany the brothers begin to reach out to one another and, with the help of a ne'er-do-well uncle (Joseph Bologna) raise some badly needed cash at the dog track.

Perhaps the best moment in Mike Binder's homiletic screenplay is an amusing quarrel in which the contentious brothers deconstruct the murky meaning of the Kingsmen's "Louie, Louie," according to their respective worldviews. Binder probably thought so as well, since he returns to this sequence for the punchline that brings this sentimental journey to its faux-poignant conclusion.

Dempsey, who was seen to much better advantage in the underregarded "Some Girls," brazenly seizes every opportunity to steal the screen from Gross and Stern, but his brother is the least likeable of the three. It's hard to tell if Arkin's irascibility stems from his character's malady or the actor's feelings about the script. — *Rich.*

Basket Case 2

New York A Shapiro Glickenhaus Entertainment release of an Ievins/Henenlotter production. Executive producer, James Glickenhaus. Produced by Edgar Ievins. Written and directed by Frank Henenlotter. Camera (TVC color), Robert M. Baldwin; editor, Kevin Tent; music, Joe Renzetti; sound (Dolby), Paul Bang; production design, Michael Moran; special makeup effects, Gabe Bartalos; original Belial design, Kevin Haney; animatronics supervisor, Kenneth Walker; assistant director, Ted Hope; production manager, Declan Baldwin; casting, Caroline Sinclair. Reviewed at Broadway screening room, N.Y., Feb. 26, 1990. MPAA Rating: R. Running time: **89 MIN.**

Duane Bradley.	Kevin Van Hentenryck
Granny Ruth.	Annie Ross
Marcie Elliott.	Kathryn Meisle
Susan.	Heather Rattray
Editor Lou.	Jason Evers
Phil.	Ted Sorel
Artie.	Matt Mitler

■ Belated sequel to the 1982 cult horror film, "Basket Case 2" is a hilarious genre spoof. With its imaginative makeup effects and cockeyed point of view, pic stands a chance of attracting a wider audience than just diehard monster fans.

With only four films under his belt (including "Frankenhooker," shot before "Basket Case 2" but yet to be released), Frank Henenlotter shows considerable knowledge and affection for the horror genre. Here he's paying homage to Tod Browning's 1932 classic "Freaks," updated and modernized.

Effective and funny exposition (opening reel is a riot satirizing clichés such as the evening newscast) fills in the viewer on what happened in the first film: Siamese twins Kevin Van Hentenryck and Belial are nabbed on a murder rampage in Manhattan. Separated at the hip, Van Hentenryck is normal-looking except for a hideous scar and Belial is little more than a head with some gruesome flesh attached — carried around in a wicker basket by his brother.

Annie Ross as Granny Ruth is a crusader for the rights of "unique individuals" (i.e., freaks) and welcomes the brothers into her home in Staten Island. Weird menagerie of youngsters, mostly crazy variations on the Elephant Man by makeup whiz Gabe Bartalos, are treated very sympathetically at first, but as in Browning's film (which primarily utilized real sideshow freaks as well as actors Wallace Ford and Roscoe Ates), their potential for scaring the audience also is exploited.

Pic climaxes with Belial's ultraviolent attacks on foes of the freaks, namely tabloid reporter Kathryn Meisle, her shutterbug assistant Matt Mitler and cop Ted Sorel. En route is one of the oddest scenes in recent horror pics, Belial making love to Eve, a similarly grotesque Siamese twin whose better half, Heather Rattray, is not coincidentally Van Hentenryck's girlfriend. The Siamese twins sex gambit was handled in extremely poor taste in the recent porno video "Joined," but Henenlotter overcomes that inherent problem with a wild sense of humor.

Van Hentenryck, who's styled to resemble Dwayne Hickman's Dobie Gillis on screen, is effective as the self-divided hero and Rattray offers a strange beauty that builds suspense re: *her* hidden deformity. Wide-eyed Meisle is fun to hate as the exploitative journalist and Jason Evers (of "The Brain That Wouldn't Die") is a fun, nostalgic choice to play her editor.

Casting coup is Annie Ross, the legendary jazz singer of Lambert, Hendricks and Ross, who is a lot of fun as the demented granny who goads her freakish charges to fight back.

Tech credits are impressive down the line, demonstrating what an underground filmmaker can do with an ample budget. — *Lor.*

Due Occhi Diabolici
(Two Evil Eyes)
(ITALIAN)

Rome An Artisti Associati Release of a Gruppo Bema/ADC production. Produced by Achille Manzotti, Dario Argento. Directed by George Romero, Dario Argento. Screenplay, Romero (first episode); Argento, Franco Ferrini (second episode) from a story by Edgar Allen Poe; camera, Peter Reniers; art direction, Cletus Anderson; costumes, Barbara Anderson; editor, Pat Buba; music, Pino Donaggio; makeup, Tom Savini. Reviewed at Quirinale Cinema, Rome, Feb. 18, 1990. Running time: **105 MIN.**
Jessica Valdemar. . . . . .Adrienne Barbeau
Steven Pike. . . . . .E.G. Marshall
Rod Usher. . . . . .Harvey Keitel
Annabel. . . . . .Madeleine Potter
Dr. Robert Hoffman. . . . . .Ramy Zada
Ernest Valdemar. . . . . . .Bingo O'Malley
Mr. Bee. . . . . .Martin Balsam
Mrs. Pee. . . . . .Kim Hunter
Eleonora. . . . . .Sally Kirkland
(Italian soundtrack)

■ **George Romero and Dario Argento team up on a double-episode thriller, "Two Evil Eyes." The shot-in-English Italo release has done respectably onshore. Prospects offshore are average, given the reputation of directors and the presence of Yank Harvey Keitel in one part.**

Romero's "The Truth About The Valdemar Case," pic's first half, is highest on genuine chills. Recycling the zombie theme, tale has a rich old man, on his death-bed, hypnotized by his wife's lover. While the guilty pair are making runs to the bank to empty his coffers, the fellow dies. They store him in the basement freezer but discover that dying under hypnosis leaves open a door for the restless dead to squeeze back into the world of the living. A legion of ghoulish zombies soon comes through and makes short work of wife and lover in a gory finale.

Episode is effectively chilling, with a lot of seat-hopping surprises. Thesps are borderline credible, and the American sets are soap-opera rich.

In second half, Argento shoots an update of Poe's "The Black Cat" with curious results. Keitel gives his all as a sleazy photographer specializing in gory murder and mayhem shots. His ethereal violinist girlfriend (Madeleine Potter) is his opposite.

Potter's affection for black felines, and Keitel's flashbacks to a previous lifetime (when he was impaled by an identical witch) start his paranoia going. When he uses her pet for a sadistic photo shoot, she decides to leave. Keitel kills her almost by chance, walls her up in the study, and covers his tracks perfectly — until a stomach-churning ending.

Keitel brings a sense of humor to the role that gets it over some routine work. As usual, Argento delights in gore more than psychology, making "Cat" the weaker of the two episodes. Technically, the whole pic is well-handled.
— *Yung.*

Collision Course

London De Laurentis Entertainment Group presents an Interscope Communications production. Executive producer, Rene Dupont. Produced by Robert Cort, Ted Field. Directed by Lewis Teague. Screenplay, Frank Darius Namei, Robert Resnikoff; camera (Technicolor), Donald E. Thorin; editor, Jerry Greenberg; music, Ira Newborn; production design, Harry Pottle; costumes, Ron Talsky. Reviewed on President Home Entertainment/CBS-Fox vidcassette, London, Feb. 20, 1990. MPAA Rating: PG. Running time: **96 MIN.**
Investigator Fujitsuka Natsuo. . .Pat Morita
Detective Tony Costas. . . . . .Jay Leno
Philip Madras. . . . . . .Chris Sarandon
Shortcut. . . . . .Ernie Hudson
Lt. Ryerson. . . . . . . .John Hancock
Dingman. . . . . .Al Waxman
Kitao. . . . . .Soon-Teck Oh
Scully. . . . . .Tom Noonan
Kosnic. . . . . . . .Randal (Tex) Cobb

■ **"Collision Course," one of the package of De Laurentis pics that never received a U.S. theatrical outing, gets a video release in the U.K. from President Home Entertainment/CBS-Fox. Pic is a standard jokey cop-buddy pic blessed with an amusing standout performance by Pat Morita who effortlessly reprises his "Karate Kid" role.**

A strong supporting cast gives the pic some weight, though comedian Jay Leno, topcast alongside the experienced Morita, doesn't show enough confidence to give "Collision Course" the humor it sometimes strives for.

Traditional chases and shootouts occur but eventually pic falls into the "also-ran" category.

Set in Detroit, a stolen secret Japanese prototype turbocharger has been sold to a dastardly local manufacturer. Japanese investigator Morita is dispatched to find the device, and after the obligatory misunderstanding (where he gets arrested by the local cops) he teams up with blundering Leno to solve the mystery.

Morita gets the chance to show off a few martial arts skills, Leno rattles off a few jokes, while villain Chris Sarandon seems to enjoy himself generally acting nasty. Script also allows for a few cheap shots about Japan being to blame for the Detroit motor recession, but thankfully doesn't dwell on the subject too long.

The mismatched couple eventually track down the bad guys after a chase which forces them onto the Grand Prix track, and naturally enough the tough-but-nice Leno is at the airport to wave Morita off.

Experienced helmer Lewis Teague, who was the third director on the project, does a workmanlike job with the script which offers little out of the ordinary, but at least amounts to agreeable, unpretentious entertainment best suited to the video shelf. Best point is Morita's usual charming performance which sets pic apart from the plethora of actioners in the local video store.● — *Adam.*

La Bella de la Alhambra
(The Belle Of The Alhambra)
(CUBAN)

Havana An Instituto Cubano del Arte e Industria Cinematograficos (Icaic) production. Produced by Humberto Hernandez. Directed by Enrique Pineda Bernet. Screenplay, Pineda Bernet, Miguel Barnet; camera (color), Raul Rodriguez Cabrera; editor, Jorge Abello; sound (Dolby), Raul Garcia; art direction, Derubin Jacome; music, Mario Romeu; choreography, Gustavo Herrara. Reviewed at Havana Intl. Film Festival, Dec. 12, 1989. Running time: **108 MIN.**
Rachel. . . . . .Beatriz Valdez
Federico. . . . . .Omar Valdez
Pedro Carreno. . . . . . . .Cesar Evora
Adolfito. . . . . .Carlos Cruz
Amargen. . . . . .Veronica Lynn
Rolen. . . . . .Ramon Veloz
La Mejicana. . . . . .Isabel Moreno
Eusebio. . . . . .Jorge Martinez
Lopez. . . . . .Miguel Navarro
Bazan. . . . . .Miguel Gutierrez
    Also with: Omar Padilla, Hector Echemendia, Argelio Jiminez, Gasper Gonzale, Carlos Mas, Adolfo Robal, Ulises Regueiro, Andres Pinero, Hector Eduardo Suarez, Yara Iglesias, Maria Elena Molinet.

■ **A marvel in period reconstruction of Cuba's former cabaret tradition, "The Belle Of The Alhambra" suffers sadly from lack of storyline. Lush lensing, able art direction, strong acting efforts and abundant musical numbers (this is Cuba's first Dolby venture) may spark some international interest.**

Directed by Enrique Pineda Barnet, pic recounts the story of Rachel, a beautiful young woman whose ambitions bring her to the top of the cabaret circuit in the 1920s and '30s, the Alhambra Theater. To achieve this, she must use and be used by a host of influential men, again and again.

Actress Beatriz Valdez gives an admirable turn as Rachel and is well able to carry off musical and hoofing demands. Music, both period favorites and original tunes by Mario Romeu is expectedly good, as is the stunning art direction by Derubin Jacome.

Film ends with a nostalgic nod to what has passed into memory, never to return. In his quest for nostalgia and beautiful glossy visuals, Pineda Barnet has overlooked the story in this go-nowhere script, based on Miguel Barnet's novel "Rachel's Song."

For a Cuban film, there is a surprising amount of nudity.
— *Lent.*

Lad isbjörnene danse
(Dance Of The Polar Bears)
(DANISH)

Copenhagen A Warner & Metronome release of a Metronome Film production with the Danish Film Institute and the Danish Film

Studio. Produced by Mads Egmont Christensen. DFI consultant producer, Hans Hansen. Directed by Birger Larsen. Screenplay, Larsen, Jonas Cornell, based on novel by Ulf Stark; camera (Eastmancolor), Björn Blixt; editor, Birger Möller-Jensen; music, Frans Bach; sound, Henrik Langkilde; production design, Peter de Neergaard; costumes, Manon Rasmussen; casting, Jette Termann; production management, Thomas Lydholm, Ditte Christiansen. Reviewed at Metronome screening room, Copenhagen, Dec. 20, 1989. Running time: **87 MIN.**

Lasse. . . . . .Anders Schoubye
His father. . . . . .Tommy Kentner
His mother. . . . . .Birthe Neumann
Hilding. . . . . .Paul Hüttel
Hilding's daughter. . . . . .Laura Drasbäk
Gubbi. . . .Hakim Frank Bellman Jacobsen
Tina. . . . . .Kristine Horn
The teacher. . . . . .Stig Hoffmeyer
   Also with: Henrik Larsen, Astrid Villaume, Gerda Gilboe, others.

■ **Birger Larsen bows convincingly with his own film, "Dance Of The Polar Bears," a kiddie feature that should please young as well as adult audiences at home and abroad with its witty and offbeat look at a child's adaptabilty and eventual independence.**

Helmer served his apprenticeship as a runner/handyman with directors Bille August ("Pelle The Conqueror") and Sören Kragh-Jacobsen "Emma's Shadow").

On Christmas Eve, 12-year-old Lasse's socially ambitious mother runs away from her "very good butcher" husband, an easygoing collector of Elvis Presley records and player of the harmonica. Although Lasse has closer ties to his dad than to his mom, he has to follow latter into her new life with a rich dentist, a widower with a precocious teenage daughter.

While Lasse used to be a lazy dreamer at school, he turns around completely, slicking down his hair, putting on a tie, getting his teeth fixed and developing into a paragon of virtue and scholarly effort.

Although small of stature, his girl classmates start giving him the eye, and the dentist's daughter taunts him sexually, too.

When Lasse's transition into the dentist's ideal of a Perfect Boy seems assured, Lasse revolts and returns to easy camaraderie and harmonica-playing in his father's modest appartment. There is, fortunately, no hint of the maudlin in this reunion.

Lasse is played by Anders Schoubye, who switches easily from ragamuffin charm to studious hauteur. Tommy Kentner as the butcher and Paul Hüttel as the dentist come through as real-life adults. All the female characters, children

as well as adult, are seen as sweet little she-devils.

It is, however, the constant unbalancing of conventional child meller material that makes "Polar Bears" so delightfully different. Nothing in the film is quite what it appears to be. And when Lasse, on loan one day to his father, visits the zoo to watch the polar bears, the grotto is empty. Their keeper just shrugs as he explains that they "are away for the day, probably out dancing."—*Kell.*

Hans de Wit
(DUTCH)

Amsterdam A Concorde release of a Zig-Zag Film production. Executive producer, Jane Waltman. Produced by Waltman, Joost Ranzijn. Directed by Ranzijn. Screenplay and editor, Ranzijn, Waltman, from the novel by Heere Heeresma. Camera (color), Lex Wertwijn; sound, Peter Flamman, Ad Roest; music, Kees van der Vooren, Wilfrid Snellens; art direction, Gert Brinkers. Reviewed at the Cinema theater, Amsterdam, Jan. 11, 1990. Running time: **92 MIN.**

Hans de Wit. . . . . .Koen de Bouw
Mother. . . . . .Nelly Frijda
Father. . . . . .Jim van der Woude
Nellie. . . . . .Jaloe Maat
Sailor. . . . . .Huub van der Lubbe
Bookkeeper. . . . . .Hans Beijer

■ **Joost Ranzijn strikes out in his first feature film, "Hans de Wit," which tries for a tragicomic style but comes out more like unsuccessful farce. Helmer was more successful with his earlier slightly surreal shorts, which won numerous prizes. Here his camera and editing are heavy and unimaginative.**

Title character is the son of a short-tempered but good-hearted blue collar worker who loses his job when his company goes bust and must move the family into a slum. He insists that Hans must start making money and should give up his lofty notions of education. So both become dustmen. Son then lands an office job where he works out a time-and-money-saving scheme for all the dustmen, but the idea fails and only gets him fired.

In the meantime dad has a work accident, and his legs are paralyzed. The doctors won't operate because it's too costly and risky. So Hans finds a job in the hospital, steals surgical equipment, practices surgery on birds and dogs and then operates on dad with mom as nurse. The operation is the central scene of the film, but instead of being funny, is merely bloody and

messy.

Hans is played by a young unknown who is not one of the discoveries of the year. On the other hand, the parents are adequately played by veterans Jim van der Woude and Nelly Frijda.
— *Wall.*

Willy Signori e Vengo da lontano
(Willy Signori And I Come From Afar)
(ITALIAN)

Rome A Warner Bros. release of a Mario and Vittorio Cecchi Gori Tiger Cinematographica/Unione P.N. Cinematografica coproduction. Produced by Gianfranco Piccioli, Giorgio Leopardi. Directed by Francenso Nuti. Screenplay, Giovanni Veronesi, Ugo Chiti, Nuti; camera (color), Gian Lorenzo Battaglia; editor, Sergio Montanari; music, Giovanni Nuti; art direction, Virginia Vianello, Chiti. Reviewed at Embassy Cinema, Rome, Dec. 22, 1989. Running time: **105 MIN.**

Willy Signori. . . . . . . .Francesco Nuti
Lucia. . . . . .Isabella Ferrari
Alessandra. . . . . .Anna Galiena
Ugo. . . . . .Allesandro Haber
Ilona. . . . . .Cristina Gaioni
   Also with: Antonio Petrucelli, Giovani Veronesi, Novello Novelli.

■ **"Willy Signore And I Come From Afar" rolls along pleasurably enough thanks to the hammy appeal of comedian-helmer Francesco Nuti. Pic performed solidly during holidy b.o. Offshore, audiences will be limited to Nuti fans.**

Once again Nuti is cast as a nice guy accidentally embroiled in a pretty stranger's troubles. In the end, the two get together.

Willy is a newspaperman on a big Milan paper, assigned to cover local disasters. One night his jalopy crashes into a speeding roadster, killing its drunk driver. Willy feels guilty, but it wasn't his fault. That's not what Lucia (Isabella Ferri), the dead man's pregnant girlfriend, thinks. She makes one accusing visit to Willy's office, and he's hooked.

Rest of pic is devoted to Willy taking responsibility for mother and unborn child, carrying her up six flights of stairs, leaving parties to go grocery shopping, etc.

Lest the viewer get the impression lovable, mugging Willy is a victim, he periodically vents his feelings by slugging everybody in the film, from disobedient Lucia, to his whining wheelchair-ridden brother (Alessandro Haber), to his nasty yuppie girlfriend (Anna Galiena). He also throws more than

one pesky cat out of a window.

These abrupt displays of manhood get a few laughs, but leave an uncomfortable feeling that behind Nuti's overflowing charm lies the heart of a killer.

When Willy's girlfriend interferes, Lucia nobly disappears for Willy's good. Last reel moves cast to a picture postcard Morocco, where poor brother Haber can play baseball in his wheelchair. Willy, too, finds true happiness with Lucia, who turns up, strangely, still pregnant.

Technically impeccable, "Willy Signori" has an excellently lensed rescue scene on a roof. Nuti is very good at sight gags, which he seems to have studied from Chaplin. Best of the rest is the irrepressible Haber, who throws himself into his role. — *Yung.*

Paperitähti
(Paper Star)
(FINNISH)

Helsinki A Finnkino release of Villealfa (Finland) and Swedish Film Institute production in association with Finnkino (Finland) and Esselte Video (Sweden). Produced by Klaus Heydemann. Directed by Mika Kaurismäki. Screenplay, Kaurismäki, Antti Lindquist; camera (Eastmancolor), Timo Salminen; editor, Veikko Aaltonen; music, Anssi Tikanmäki; sound, Jouko Lumme; production design, Risto Karhula; assistant director, Pauli Pentti; associate producers, Klas Olofsson, Katinka Farago. Reviewed at Nordia 3, Helsinki, Nov. 30, 1989. Running time: **86 MIN.**

Anna. . . . . .Pirkko Hämäläinen
Ilja. . . . . .Kari Väänänen
Ulf. . . . . .Hannu Lauri
Tauka. . . . . .Matti Rassila
Assi. . . . . .Minna Soisalo

■ **"Paper Star" is nothing more than the formulaic story of a fashion model's fall from grace caused by evil men.**

Femme lead is never explained as anyone but a dumb glutton for punishment, and nothing relieves the monotony of the series of ugly bumps.

Only the otherwise fine record of brother filmmakers Mika and Aki Kaurismäki will help this nostalgia-for-the-dirt item travel anywhere.

Hapless Anna finds herself in jail after killing, in self-defense, Ilja (Kari Väänänen), an alchoholic lover. She has had two other lovers: a nice but befuddled motorcycle racer (Matti Rassila) and a drug-dealing businessman (Hannu Lauri).

Beaten up by her photographer lover, Anna cannot get jobs as a model. She consoles herself with bubble-baths and remembering, in brief black and white flashes, herself as an innocent teen. Pirkko Hämäläinen sleepwalks sullenly through it all.

As the photographer, Väänänen comes on all slavering leer or screaming madness. As Anna's other men, Rasila and Lauri put in more subdued, convincing performances.

"Paper Star" looks professional in the way of later Rainer Werner Fassbinder pics, but it shares the German's naive ideas of the horrors of the lifestyle of the rich. When he approaches the lower classes (like a bag lady who befriends Anna), Kaurismäki turns maudlin.—*Kell.*

Ho vinto la lotteria di capodanno
(I Won The New Year's Lottery)
(ITALIAN)

Rome A Penta release of a Mario and Vittorio Cecchi Gori Tiger Cinematografica production, in association with Reteitalia. Associate producers, Bruno Altissimi, Claudio Saraceni for Maura Intl. Film. Directed by Neri Parenti. Screenplay, Parenti, Leo Bencivenni, Domenico Salerni; camera (color), Alessandro d'Eva; editor, Sergio Montanari; music, Bruno Zambrini; art direction, Maria Stilde Ambruzzi. Reviewed at Rouge et Noir Cinema, Rome, Jan. 8, 1990. Running time 90 MIN.
Paolo Ciottoli. . . . . . .Paolo Villaggio
  Also with: Antonio Allocca, Margit Newton.

■ "I Won The New Year's Lottery" is a local holiday comedy featuring Paolo Villaggio as the lucky bloke who can't find his winning ticket. Helmed by Neri Parenti, pic lays on a very thin plotline but is enlivened by a string of successful gags. It has done quite well at local wickets.

Playing on every Italian's fantasy of copping a cool $4 million without effort, "Lottery" starts with the traditional tv show where the winners are announced to an anxious nation glued to the set. Only Paolo Ciottoli (Villagio) shows no interest in hearing the results of the draw. He's too busy trying to commit suicide.

He realizes he's won as he's downing a glass of poison, which, like his other clumsy attempts, doesn't put a dent in him. When he comes back from having his stomach pumped, full of uncontainable joy, he finds his possessions have been confiscated to pay old debts. Included is the typewriter in which he hid the lottery ticket.

Rest of pic shows Paolo tracking down six identical typewriters sold at public auction. His misadventures include a visit to a home for the blind, masquerading as a fireman to rescue another machine and disrupting a variety show.

Villaggio's surrealist comic style, familiar from the Fantozzi series, hasn't changed much. Apartments explode cartoon-fashion; people fall out of windows and suffer nary a scratch. Running through "Lottery" are the misfortunes of Paolo's neighbors, who suffer injuries every time they're near him.

Based on a silent comedy, the gags are excellently timed and usually work. They would work better if Villaggio would blabber and shout less.

Some are in questionable taste, such as the string of blind man jokes, but pic's heart is basically in the right place, as shown by the ending, in which Paolo unwittingly donates his windfall to the home for the blind.

Pic is notable for its many costume and scenery changes. —*Yung.*

Love & Murder
(CANADIAN)

Toronto A Norstar Entertainment release in Canada of a Sharmhill Prods. presentation. Executive producer, Howard Deverett. Produced, written and directed by Steven Hilliard Stern. Camera (color), David Herrington; editor, Ron Wiseman; music, Matthew MacCauley; production design, Tony Hall. Reviewed at Famous Players screening room, Toronto, Jan. 16, 1990. Running time: 97 MIN.
Hal Caine. . . . . .Todd Waring
Brenda. . . . . .Kathleen Laskey
Officer Fred. . . . . .Ron White
Janitor. . . . . .Wayne Robson

■ This ever-so-seriously played pic has a handsome but dumb photographer selling dates for women, photographing a young girl's fall to her death from a room across the street and knowing he's next on the list of a killer of prostitutes.

There are several suspects, including a cop and a crazed, seedy janitor; the killer, however, is disclosed with no build-up.

Pic, filmed under the title "Ladykiller," has a much-borrowed, mainly anti-femme plot, lame direction and an indifferent look. There is little to recommend it, except for loved-by-the-camera Kathleen Laskey (a former Toronto Second City performer) as the photographer's girlfriend who deserves better.

Pic is as untended as the rundown apartment building in which the photog lives. Even the theme song, Frank Sinatra's rendition of "Love And Marriage," is wasted.

Quick road to homevid is certain. — *Adil.*

Buon Natale, Buon Anno Joyeux/
Noël, Bonne Année
(Merry Christmas, Happy New Year)
(ITALIAN-FRENCH)

Paris An AFMD release of a Cité Film/TF1 Films Prod./Titanus Prod. coproduction. Produced by Fabio Cricuolo, Luigi Patrizi for Videoschermo. Directed by Luigi Comencini. Screenplay, Cristina Comencini, Raffaele Festa Campanile, Luigi Comencini, André Brunelin (French version), freely adapted from the novel "Buon Natale Buon Anno"by Pasquale Festa Campanile; camera (Eastmancolor), Armando Nannuzzi; editor, Sergio Buzi; music, Fiorenzo Carpi; art direction and costumes, Paola Comencini; assistant director, Maurizio Sciarra; production manager, Gerardo Verrone. Reviewed at Marignan-Concorde theater, Paris, Jan. 20, 1990. Running time: 102 MIN.
Gino. . . . . .Michel Serrault
Elvira. . . . . .Virna Lisi
Patrizia. . . . . .Consuelo Ferrara
Pietro. . . . . .Paolo Graziosi
Giannina. . . . . .Tiziana Pini
Giorgio. . . . . .Mattia Sbragia
Abraham. . . . . .Nar Senne
(French soundtrack version)

■ "Merry Christmas, Happy New Year"is a geriatric romance from Luigi Comencini about the revival of passion in a retired Italian couple. Italo-French coproduction has its moments of warmth and humor but finally is not particularly convincing.

Comencini, who has made some of the finest movies about children, has not lost his touch in dealing with the problems of the elderly, but his intelligent grasp of characterization and emotion is below par.

Billing of France's Michel Serrault and Virna Lisi plus the Comencini name also may push film in specialized markets, though dramatically both thesps are somewhat too young — and thus less pathetic — as the aging principals who realize their intense need for one another only when they are physically separated.

They have been married for 40 years and have two daughters, both married with families, and domestic headaches galore. The elders no longer can pay the rent on their apartment and accept to live separately in the respective households of their children.

The separation weighs on them, becoming intolerable the day their dormant sexual need for each other awakens. Ashamed to admit their problems with their preoccupied children, they meet on the sly like young guilty lovers in a hotel room.

When summer comes, the old people are separated again as Lisi must accompany one daughter's family on holiday in Sicily, while Serrault remains in Rome, lonely and penniless. Determined to join his beloved, he resorts in desperation to arranging a phony burglary of the apartment to finance his trip.

Once reunited, Serrault and Lisi "elope" and end up living happily ever after — as lighthouse keepers off the coast of Sicily!

Script by Comencini, daughter Cristina and Raffaele Festa Campanile is loosely drawn from a novel by the late Pasquale Festa Campanile and is best in early sections describing the couple's disorientation in their domestic uprooting and new romantic awareness that takes both by surprise. Both script and direction hobble once Serrault begins to look for work with a group of clandestine African immigrants.

Serrault, in his first Franco-Italian coproduction, is a curious, not quite satisfying choice for the part. French actor is best in moments of sarcasm and ill humor and seems less at ease with pathos and expressions of straightforward sentiment. Yet Comencini is so in awe of his star that he personally supervised the French-track version of the film, which is the one he wants shown outside Italy.

If the integrity of Serrault's performance is respected, the other players suffer from the usual drawbacks of dubbing, which is technically competent but still obtrusive.

Tech credits are otherwise okay.
— *Len.*

Dagens Donna
(Donna Of The Day)
(DANISH)

Copenhagen A Dansk Filmindustri release of Dansk Filmindustri production. Produced by Torben Villesen. Associate producer, Johnny Johansen. Directed and edited by Stefan Henszleman. Screenplay by Hanne-Vibeke Holst, based on an idea by Torben Villesen; camera (Eastmancolor), Dirk Brüel; music, Randall Meyers; title song, words and lyrics Anne Linnet; sound, Jan Juhler; production design, Sören Skjär; costumes, Bente Ranning; production management, Henrik Möllerörensen; Danish Film Institute consultant producers, Peter Poulsen, Kirsten Bonnén Rask. Reviewed at the Palladium, Copenhagen, Jan. 22, 1990. Running time: **91 MIN.**

Donna . . . . .Birgitte Simonsen
Lasse . . . . .Ole Lemmeke
Britt . . . . .Hanne Windfeld Lund
Michael . . . . .Jesper Christensen
Per Kjär . . . . .Dick Kaysöe
Thomas . . . . .Jens Arentzen
Marie Tvede . . . . .Lizzi Lykke
Also with: Nanna Lüders, Eva Krogh, Birgit Conradi, Anders Hove, Jens Erik Roepsdorff, Anders Hove, Claus Flygare.

■ Stefan Henszleman's "Donna Of The Day" offers a sensitive look at homosexuality. Working from Hanne-Vibeke Holst's very heterosexual seriocomic screenplay, Henszleman is performing with some cinematic flash but with much less artistic assurance.

Photographer Donna and schoolteacher Britt have a hard time with men and careers in the big city. Donna suffers discrimination in the male-dominated world of fashion photography, but enjoys uncommitted flings with men. Britt, a timid romantic, clings to a one-and- only affair with a man who turns out to be married and a rover. Donna, pert, brash and raven-haired, tries to avoid falling in love with Lasse, a young man of strong romantic inclinations but far from settled into the establishment.

They make love, split up, make up, split up and make up again on the way to an open ending that still has the trimmings of conventional happy one. Donna never succeeds in pushing her girlfriend into real independence, so wedding bells with the rover are soon heard as a sarcastic echo.

No point other than one of female defeatism is really made, which was hardly the original idea and screenplay.

Henszleman's players are a mixed lot. Some are newcomers of promise like Birgitte Simonsen, who displays strength and wit in the title lead, while others speak their lines like amateurs in a dramatic void. Professional thesps like Ole Lemmeke as Donna's paramour, Jesper Christensen and Dick Kaysöe are allowed to dig into their roles, and Lemmeke especially exudes talent and screen presence.

While cinematographer Dirk Brüel, a superior craftsman of artistic independence, and Henszleman sometimes work at cross-purposes to kill pictorial beauty with dramatic dullness or vice versa, "Donna Of The Day" generally winds its way through the workplaces and watering holes of contemporary Copenhagen with speed and fluency.

One phenomenon regularly derailing "Donna" is the director's insistence on having his cinematographer dwell with loving detail on male nudity, while the naked females are invariably seen as next to ugly.—*Kell.*

The Last Winter
(CANADIAN)

Palm Springs A Rode Pictures, John Aaron Prods. and National Film Board of Canada production. Produced by Jack Clements, Ken Rodeck. Coproducers, Joe MacDonald, Ches Yetman. Written and directed by Aaron Kim Johnston. Camera (color), Ian Elkin; editor, Lara Mazur; music, Victor Davies; production design, Perri Gorrare; art direction, Nancy Panikiw; set design, Ken Hart-Swain; set decoration, Ane Christanson; costume design, Martha Snetsinger; sound, Clive Perry; assistant director, David McAree; casting, Anne Tait. Reviewed at Palm Springs Film Festival, Jan. 12, 1990. Running time: **103 MIN.**

Grampa Jack . . . . .Gerard Parkes
Will . . . . .Joshua Murray
Ross . . . . .David Ferry
Audrey . . . . .Wanda Cannon
John . . . . .Nathaniel Moreau
Winnie . . . . .Katie Murray
Kate . . . . .Marsha Moreau

■ This vivid, imaginative tale of a Manitoba farmboy's coming of age bears the hallmarks of classic family entertainment. Unlikely to see U.S. theatrical distribution, it nonetheless captures a uniquely Canadian heartland experience.

Writer-director Aaron Kim Johnston has crafted a tribute to his childhood in a tale seen through the eyes of a 10-year-old Will (Joshua Murray) as he resists his family's move to the city.

Beset with growing pains and upset by the prospect of being uprooted, Will creates a fantasy shield between himself and reality, hallucinating a white horse named Winter who charges across the farmland bearing some mysterious message.

His closest ties are to his Grampa Jack (Gerard Parkes) and his cousin Kate, whom he's in love with (it causes him no end of distress when he's informed by a schoolmate that "it's against the

law to marry your cousin").

Though the dialog sometimes rings a bit false and the pace at times resembles "The Waltons," Johnston is talented enough to keep things engaging with clever, simple episodes and funny lines and characters (clumsy Will falls down the stairs more often than he walks down).

The overwhelming presence of the land and weather are captured in Ian Elkin's clean, crisp photography, and the winter storms and snowdrifts painstakingly evoked by the art department.

Johnston draws lovely performances from the children, especially Murray. Parkes forges a convincing link with the young actor as his elderly confidante.

Working toward a climax at which Will is forced to accept the inevitabilty of change, Johnston finds a lyrical way to tie up the hallucination of the horse and the end of Will's childhood connection to Grampa, who won't leave the farm.

Audiences, especially kids, are bound to love the result. — *Daws.*

Theo & Thea
(DUTCH)

Amsterdam A Meteor Film release of a Van den Beginne production. Produced by Kees Kasander. Directed by Pieter Kramer. Screenplay, Arjan Ederveen, Tosca Niterink; camera (color), Erik Zuyderhoff; editor, Marina Bodbijl; music, Patty Trossel; sound, Roel Bazen; art direction, Ruud van Empel, Wilbert van Dorp. Reviewed at the Alfa theater, Amsterdam, Dec. 28, 1989. Running time: **92 MIN.**

Theo . . . . .Arjan Ederveen
Thea . . . . .Tosca Niterink
Marco Bakker . . . . .Himself
Brigitta Berber . . . . .Adele Boemendaal

■ This is a fun family picture, if jokes about the digestive tract, ballroom scenes with world leaders, drooping trousers and other belly-laugh material are favored.

Stars are Theo and Thea (T&T), who for four years hosted a tv show for kids that became even more popular with grownups. Their trademark — rabbits' teeth hanging from their upper lips — is known throughout Holland. This is basically local product not likely to travel.

They decided to make this film before splitting (on good terms) to pursue separate careers, so the team's debut feature also is its swansong. Script is a series of haphazardly linked sketches, and

the common denominator is that none has an ounce of logic to them.

T&T have their heads dunked in a toilet bowl, are immersed in medicinal mud and take tea with a (not very) lookalike of the Dutch queen. Finally, everybody takes a trip to Austria.

Also on board is legit and tv star Marco Bakker, who does everything asked of him (quite a lot), wears flowing fantastical costumes and, mysteriously, evening dress during the day. The sophisticated Adele Boemendaal plays a horrid witch who repents and becomes a nice witch, always bewitching.
— *Wall.*

Zaman-e az Dast Rafteh
(Lost Time)
(IRANIAN)

Teheran Produced by Puran Darakhshandeh, Mohammad Ali Farajollahi. Written and directed by Darakshandeh. Camera (color), Hossein Jafarian; editor, Ruhollah Emami; music, Kambiz Roshanravan; art direction, Keyhan Mortazavi; production manager, Khosro Taslimi. Reviewed at Fajr Film Festival, Teheran, Feb. 10, 1990. Running time: **115 MIN.**

Shakibey . . . . .Sanaz Sehati
Bahram . . . . .Framarz Sedighi
Mrs. Solori . . . . .Tania Johari
Lalie . . . . .Solmaz Asgharnezhad
With: Afsar Asadi, Zhaleh Olov, Shahla Riahi, Ali Asghar Garmsiri, Dariush Asadzadeh, Jahangir Foruhar, Behzad Rahimkhani, Parvin Soleimani, Mehri Mehrani, Purandokht Moheiman.

■ In "Lost Time," a startlingly feminist film by one of Iran's first woman directors, Puran Darakshandeh weaves a magical atmosphere around an old house, an orphan girl and a childless doctor who knows her own mind.

Fine lensing, believable acting and a lyrical flashback structure put pic among the top achievements in this season's Iranian cinema.

Pic's theme will draw most offshore attention. Shakibey (played with solemn firmness by Sanaz Sehati, a college prof in her first acting job) is a gynecologist who can't cure herself: she is sterile. Her architect husband Bahram (the realistically ambivalent Framarz Sedighi) feels doubly frustrated when Shakibey meets little Lalie (Solmaz Asgharnezhad) and wants to adopt her.

Fearing she'll stop trying to have a child of their own, he forces her to give the girl up. Wife responds by freeing him to divorce her and find another wife.

If film reaches a happy ending, it does so through an intense examination of what it means to be a woman in Iran today. Also unusual is the film's middle-class setting. Shakibey's status as a professional and her financial independence are emphasized as the source of her strength and her rebellion against social precepts.

"Lost Time" is a psychologically complex film that mostly sidesteps easy characters for emotional depth. As outrageous as the husband may seem to Western eyes for wanting to divorce his childless wife, he visibly struggles to come to terms with having no offspring.

Blending the perceptions of many women about themselves, Darakhshandeh adds an imaginary dimension. Dream images abound. All hands turn in sympathetic, down-to-earth performances. Hossein Jafarian's lyrical images find their counterpoint in Kambiz Roshanravan's poignant score.
— *Yung.*

Nama-ye Nazdik
(Close-Up)
(IRANIAN)

Teheran An Institute for the Intellectual Development of Children and Young Adults production. Written and directed by Abbas Kiarostami. Camera (color), Alireza Zarrindast; editor, Kiarostami; production manager, Hassan Aghakarimi. Reviewed at Fajr Film Festival, Teheran, Feb. 5, 1990. Running time: **100 MIN.**
Ali Sabzian . . . . .Himself
Reporter . . . . .Hassan Frazmand
Father . . . . .Abolfazi Ahankhah
Son . . . . .Mehrdad Ahankhah
Taxi driver . . . . .Hushang Shahai
Mohsen Makhmalbaf . . . . .Himself

■ In "Close-Up," a pic likely to be one of Iran's most successful fest exports this season, Abbas Kiarostami mixes cinema verité with reconstructed facts (and even some deliberate manipulation) to tell a funny-sad story about a man who masquerades as a famous director.

Though some criticized pic as pretentious, it has a lot going for it: an intriguing premise, structural experimentation and moving social critique.

Kiarostami, one of Iran's premier helmers whose last fiction film ("Where Is My Friend's House") found European theatrical release, supplies absolutely real story and characters. Ali Sabzian, an unemployed and divorced young man, casually tells a well-to-do lady on the bus he's Mohsen Makhmalbaf, a well-known filmmaker (who later appears).

One thing leads to another, and before long he has involved the lady's family in his next "film project" to be shot in their comfortable home, with their engineer-son in a main role. Within a week Sabzian is exposed and arrested. At this point, Kiarostami and his crew come in and film the trial.

Sabzian explains he's not a con artist, but couldn't resist feeling respected for once in his life. Audience sympathy is all for him, and a wise judge persuades the duped family to forgive him.

Instead of ending pic on this emotionally satisfying note, however, Kiarostami next reconstructs events leading up to Sabzian's arrest with characters playing themselves. Ending is less rosy and more critical this time round, showing the hero betrayed by his new friends and led away in despair.

Kiarostami's sharp, offbeat sense of humor keeps peeking out midst continual depictions of the financial straits endured by most characters, who long to have something more than life has doled out.

In one candid-camera sequence, Kiarostami deliberately doctors a tape recording to make it more apparent that Sabzian didn't know he was being taped. For the audience, the camera crew is a strongly felt presence throughout, even as it influences the events it's recording.

Film's main problem for foreign viewers will be its nonstop dialog, which will be hard to compress in subtitles. — *Yung.*

Stille Betrueger
(Sleepy Betrayers)
(SWISS-GERMAN)

Solothurn, Switzerland An Image Film of Zurich and Berlin Film School production. Produced by Joerg Helbling. Directed by Beat Lottaz. Screenplay, Lottaz; camera (color), Rainer Meissle; editor, Susanne Peuscher; music, Mariaus Odagiu; sound, Sabina Belcher; art direction, Ulrike Denk. Reviewed at Solothurn Festival, Jan. 19, 1990. Running time: **84 MIN.**
Paul . . . . .Norbert Muzzulini
Sandra . . . . .Annemarie Kneck
Georg . . . . .Andreas Schmnidt
Marion . . . . .Elke Reichardt
Miriam . . . . .Jale Arikan
Maike . . . . .May Buchgraber

■ This morality play about a modern couple by Swiss student Beat Lottaz is a thoroughly creditable debut effort from a talent to watch. The tiny budget and bleak subject matter mean it is unlikely to find release outside home territory, however.

Plot covers familiar emotional territory but is intentionally black and white in its depiction of the gender clash. "One imperfect man and a perfect woman" reads the blurb.

Paul is a moderately gifted but egotistical young writer who shares his flat with girlfriend Sandra, a mild-mannered and selfless sculptor. He is constantly unfaithful and prone to pompous intellectualizing about love, lust and meaningful relationships, while she watches in despair.

Following the advice of Paul's best friend George, a secret admirer, Sandra finally enlists in the battle of the sexes and starts pretending she has a lover too, to try and bring Paul to heel. Calling her bluff, he victoriously moves out to temporarily shack up with new conquest Marion. At this point the inevitable happens as Paul's cocksure world falls apart and he is deserted by all concerned.

One of the film's coscripters has been attending script seminars under Polish director Krzysztof Kieslowski and it shows. Dialog is economical and revealing throughout. Technical credits are okay.
— *Jaq.*

Rendez-vous au tas de sable
(FRENCH)

Paris A UGC release of a Girard Mital production, coproduced by Films A2. Produced by Philippe Guez for Septembre Prods. Directed by Didier Grousset. Screenplay, Richard Gotainer, Jean-Pierre Domboy; camera (color), Yves Dahan; editor, Herv Schneid; sound, Pierre Excoffier, Dominique Dalmasso; art direction, Ivan Maussion; production manager, Chantal Malrat. Reviewed at UGC Biarritz theater, Paris, Feb. 12, 1990. Running time: **90 MIN.**
Nickel . . . . .Richard Gotainer
Ganesh . . . . .Thierry Fortineau
Gerard . . . . .Jean-Claude Leguay
Grolu . . . . .Vincent Ferniot
Bazouk . . . . .Ged Marlon
Bali . . . . .Muriel Combeau
Starkey . . . . .Jean-Paul Muel
"Attila" singer . . . . . .Jango Edwards

■ Richard Gotainer is the latest in the line of local pop stars trying to make it into films —and the latest to fail. This self-made vehicle (he cowrote the script) is a feeble satire of the French pop music milieu, climaxing in a lampoon of the easy-to-kid Eurovision song contest.

A quick local flop, it won't carry a tune elsewhere either. Film's title, which literally translates as "rendezvous at the sand hill," is a slang expression among musicians and refers to a sort of performance cue.

Gotainer, a composer and performer of slangy humorous lyrics, casts himself as a sympathetic weirdo/mechanic who finds himself the reluctant manager of a woefully untalented pop group. In a predictable turn of events, Gotainer stands in for his singer during a crucial playdate, scores a personal success and is kidnaped by a crooked impresario to head another pop outfit. He hoodwinks his new master and successfully maneuvers his own group into the media spotlight.

There are flashes of Gotainer's kooky (and unexportable) stage charm in the musical numbers, but otherwise his film personality doesn't click.

The good players in other main roles include Ged Marlon and Jango Edwards, a Yank clown who's popular on the European 1-man-show circuit. He does a parodic turn as a macho rock singer who faces down Gotainer in a competitive concert bout.

Didier Grousset, former assistant to Luc Besson, helmed this unamusing nonsense. — *Len.*

Mashgh-e Shab
(Homework)
(IRANIAN-DOCU)

Tehran Produced by the Institute for the Intellectual Development of Children and Adults. Written and directed by Abbas Kiarostami. Camera (16m, color), Iraj Safavi; editor, Kiarostami; music, Mohammad Reza Aligholi; production manager, Mohammad Tolu Behbud. Reviewed at the Fajr Film Festival, Tehran, Feb. 7, 1990. Running time: **89 MIN.**

■ "Homework," one of two new Abbas Kiarostami films finished this season, uses simple documentary technique to highlight the problems of Iran's educational system. Pic's success in so doing has prompted the education ministry, which financed it via the Institute for the Intellectual Development of Children and Young Adults, to hold up release.

Most foreign audiences will have a hard time understanding in what way this gentle pic is controversial, although they should be charmed by the heartfelt complaints of dozens of little boys who feel overworked with homework. The underlying issue is how much discipline and rigor ought to be expected of tykes, and how unfeelingly adults treat them. Pic also points to the economical gap separating rich kids from poor.

Film is loaded with face-on monologues with the boys explaining why they haven't done their homework. One familiar excuse is that mom and dad are illiterate and can't correct their work.

Most moving child is a crybaby, afraid to stand in front of the camera without his friend, who explains that ever since the teacher beat his pal with a ruler, he's been nervous and fearful. In pic's lyrical ending, the first boy recites an Islamic poem, demonstrating his perfect memory, while his friend solemnly looks on.

Less interesting are the long harangues of a few fathers who concur with their kids.

Kiarostami constantly foregrounds his camera and crew. In a memorable scene in the schoolyard, he uses a telephoto lens to catch the boys being boys during group prayer. Sequence was criticized by the authorities as disrespectful, but is the pic's clearest demonstration that everything has it proper place, and children must be treated like children first of all. — Yung.

Joe Versus The Volcano

New York A Warner Bros. release of an Amblin Entertainment production. Produced by Teri Schwartz. Executive producers, Steven Spielberg, Kathleen Kennedy, Frank Marshall. Written and directed by John Patrick Shanley. Camera (Panavision, Technicolor), Stephen Goldblatt; editor, Richard Halsey; music, Georges Delerue; sound (Dolby), Keith A. Wester; production design, Bo Welch; art direction, Tom Duffield; set decoration, Cheryl Carasik; costume design, Colleen Atwood; assistant director, William M. Elvin; production manager, Ian Bryce; special visual effects, Industrial Light & Magic, supervisor - David L. Carson; associate producer, Roxanne Rogers; casting, Marion Dougherty. Reviewed at Coronet theater, N.Y., March 5, 1990. MPAA Rating: PG. Running time: 102 MIN.
Joe. . . . . .Tom Hanks
DeDe/Angelica/Patricia. . . . . .Meg Ryan
Graynamore. . . . . .Lloyd Bridges
Dr. Ellison. . . . . .Robert Stack
Waponi chief. . . . . .Abe Vigoda
Waturi. . . . . .Dan Hedaya
Marshall. . . . . .Ossie Davis
Luggage salesman. . . . Barry McGovern
Dagmar. . . . . .Amanda Plummer
Hairdresser. . . . . .Carol Kane

■ "Joe Versus The Volcano" is an overproduced, disappointing shaggy dog comedy. Its superstar frontline cast ensures a decent opening, but pic's sparse quota of put-on laughs and empty center should generate negative word-of-mouth.

It's easy to see what attracted executive producer Steven Spielberg to this material, another '40s-throwback tale of an average guy who winds up in fantastic circumstances, à la Spielberg's recent remake of "A Guy Named Joe" as "Always."

Debuting helmer John Patrick Shanley (Oscar-winner for writing "Moonstruck") has unwisely staged his story in a series of static tableaux: the picture doesn't move, either within the frame or via editing. Thanks to a creative technical team and a very big budget there are interesting things to consume, but not the full meal to which film audiences are accustomed.

Story in outline resembles a wacked-out version of Frank Capra's flawed classic "Meet John Doe"(like "Volcano," a Warner Bros. release): a nebbish is bamboozled by unscrupulous types to trade his meaningless existence for a grand adventure that's linked to a suicide pact.

Pic starts promisingly with Tom Hanks going to work in the ad department of the grungy American Panascope surgical supplies factory. Bo Welch's lavish production design gives the dreary place the oppressive scale of a set from Fritz Lang's "Metropolis."

Dan Hedaya is letter-perfect as his mean supervisor while Meg Ryan as DeDe (in the first of her three gimmicky roles) sports dark hair in an amusingly ditzy Carol Kane impression as his mousey coworker. As an in-joke, the real Carol Kane pops up also in black wig later in the film, uncredited.

Hanks is a hypochondriac and his doctor, guest star Robert Stack, diagnoses a "brain cloud," giving the hapless guy only six months to live. That cues a cornball wormturns scene as Hanks tells Hedaya what to do with his job.

Coincidentally, eccentric superconductors tycoon Lloyd Bridges pops in to offer Hanks a new life: unlimited expense money to "live like a king" for 20 days before heading for a remote Polynesian island to "die like a man," i.e., jump into an active volcano to

appease the fire god.

After an entertaining shopping spree in New York (with solid turns by down-to-earth Ossie Davis as his chauffeur and Barry McGovern as a luggage hondler), Hanks ends up in L.A. to meet Ryan Number Two, Angelica: Meg with red hair doing a high-strung Lesley Ann Warren routine.

On the yacht to the island, in comes Angelica's half-sister, Ryan Number Three as Patricia —thesp's usual, glamorous blond self. Pic falls apart completely at this point, with neither the dumb musical gags nor the golden oldies on the soundtrack able to punch up Shanley's lazy script.

A typhoon and islanders in rafts imitating "Mutiny On The Bounty" kill time en route to a nonclimax at the volcano as deadpan local chief Abe Vigoda marries the duo and Ryan decides to jump

in with her beau. That cues the unconvincing happy ending.

Hanks indulges himself in some rather unfunny solo bits here, notably a silly little dance out at sea, but nothing career-threatening. Most annoying are his soapbox soliloquies, to which Shanley provides the running gag of Ryan having no comeback — her Angelica repeatedly says, "I have no response to that." Ryan has fun in her three personas, but they're simply revue sketches.

Tech crew including Industrial Light & Magic's effects persons ably provide the film's Spielbergian component at sea as well as creating the volcano. Studio shots mix uncomfortably with location work during the latter adventure reels. — Lor.

BERLIN FILM FESTIVAL REVIEWS

Das Schreckliche Mädchen
(The Nasty Girl)
(WEST GERMAN)

Berlin A Filmverlag der Autoren release of a Sentana Film production. Written and directed by Michael Verhoeven. Camera (color), Axel de Roche; editor, Barbara Hennings; music, Mike Hertung, Elmar Schlöter, Billy Gorlt, Lydie Auvray; sound, Haymo H. Heyder; art direction, Hubert Popp; costumes, Ute Truthmann. Reviewed at Berlin Film Festival (competing), Feb. 14, 1990. Running time: 92 MIN.
Sonja. . . . . .Lena Stolze
Maria (mother). . . . .Monika Baumgartner
Paul Rosenberger (father). . .Michael Gahr
Uncle. . . . . .Fred Stillkrauth
Grandmother. . . . . . .Elisabeth Bertram
Martin. . . . . .Robert Giggenbach
Robert. . . . . .Michael Guillaume
Nina. . . . . .Karin Thaler
Dr. Juckenack. . . . .Hans-Reinhard Müller
Frälein Juckenack. . . .Barbara Gallauner
Father Brummel. . . . . . .Willi Schultes
Burgomaster. . . . . . .Richard Süsmeier
Schulz. . . . . .Udo Thomer
Merganthaler. . . . . .Ludwig Wühr
Dr. Fasching. . . . . . .Herbert Lehnert
Frau Stangl.Irmgard Henning-Bayrhammer
Abtretter. . . . . .Ossi Eckmüller
Roeder. . . . . .Hermann Hummel

■ Just in time for all the German reunification hoopla, along comes nasty old Michael Verhoeven with a viciously funny film accusing his fellow West Germans of being a bunch of incorrigible hypocrites who find no difficulty in being Nazi stooges yesterday, liberal-minded democrats

today and God only knows what tomorrow.

This well-crafted picture promises to be a crowd-pleaser on its home turf. Export possibilities are brightened by the timeliness of Verhoeven's scathing examination of the Teutonic psyche. The world is asking whether the Germans have learned from two world wars. Verhoeven's answer: Don't count on it.

His plot is based on the true story of a teenage girl in Bavaria a few years back who wanted to write an essay on the Nazis' impact on her town. She quickly became the object of scorn from townspeople who had a surprising lot to conceal.

Lena Stolze as pic's "nasty girl" deftly handles her character's development from winsome girlhood to maturity. A strong supporting cast convinces the audience that loving friends can become bitter foes when cornered.

The audience laughs from start to finish, primarily because every word of Verhoeven's biting screenplay rings true. The girl's questions about the past are met with the polite evasion and bristling condescension every enquiring young German knows well.

Verhoeven is an old hand at making his fellow Germans

squirm. His 1970 anti-Vietnam film "O.K." was rejected by the Berlin Film Fest jury as anti-American — blowing the festival wide open. His 1982 pic about Nazi resistance fighters, "Die Weisse Rose" (The White Rose), spawned a national debate over some wartime "treason" convictions that were never revoked.

Verhoeven makes it clear he wants his film to apply to any German town. To do that, he has departed from his usual straightforward storytelling approach to create a surreal setting where living room divans career through a town market square, and the mayor's office doubles as a nursing home deathbed.

The visual aspects work in large part because of lenser Axel de Roche, who shot nearly the whole film at wide-angle. Tech credits give the film a high-budget look.
—*Gill.*

Bail Jumper

Berlin An Angelika Films release of a Big Buildings production. Executive producer, Jessica Saleh Hunt. Produced by Josephine Wallace, Christian Faber. Directed by Faber. Screenplay, Faber, Wallace; camera (color), Tomasz Magierski; editor, James Bruce; music, Eddie Reyes; production design, Lynn Ruth Appel; costumes, Arianna Phillips. Reviewed at Berlin Film Festival, Feb. 17, 1990. No MPAA Rating. Running time: **96 MIN.**
Elaine. . . . . .Eszter Balint
Joe. . . . . .B.J. Spalding
Dan. . . . . .Tony Askin
Steve. . . . . .Bo Brinkman
Bambi. . . . . .Alexandra Audr
Athena. . . . . .Joie Lee
Reed. . . . . . . .Ishmael Houston-Jones

■ **The only pic that's ever managed to integrate several tornados, a flood, an earthquake, a meteorite, a grasshopper invasion, a tidal wave and a total solar eclipse, this story about a bail jumper and her derelict boyfriend is unlikely to find much of an audience beyond fringe cinephiles in any territory.**

In this far-reaching, meandering fantasy whose existential elements don't quite gel, bail jumper Elaine meets appliance-thief Joe at a beach party. A string of natural disasters keeps them one step ahead of the law as they drive to New York where they hole up in a friend's deserted house.

Pic dives into the totally implausible when a tidal wave submerges everything on Staten Island except their house, transforming it into a private island. However, Joe isn't happy with their new-found paradise: He doubts Elaine's love at which point a solar eclipse turns their world black.

Welcome finale arrives when Joe nearly shoots himself in the head (by accident) and a wailing Elaine hurls herself to the floor in despair. The sun comes out and disaster ceases.

Pic has its comic moments, but a thin script and weak thesping kill the pace of what could have been a very original idea.

Technical elements are fine except for grainy disaster stock shots which don't match the new film stock whatsoever.

"Bail Jumper" is best suited to late night tv where such a wacky tale would be an eye-opener.
— *Suze.*

Waiting For The Light

Berlin A Triumph release of Epic Prods. and Sarlui/Diamant presentation of an Edward R. Pressman production. Executive producer, Pressman. Produced by Ron Bozman, Caldecott Chubb; associate producers, Michael Flynn, Linda Koulisis. Written and directed by Christopher Monger. Camera (color), Gabriel Beristain; editor, Eva Gardos; music, Michael Storey. Reviewed at Berlin Film Festival (Panorama), Feb. 19, 1990. MPAA Rating: PG. Running time: **90 MIN.**
Tante Zena. . . . . .Shirley MacLaine
Kay. . . . . .Teri Garr
Emily. . . . . .Hillary Wolf
Eddie. . . . . .Colin Baumgartner
Joe. . . . . .Clancy Brown
Mullins. . . . . .Vincent Schiavelli

■ **"Waiting For The Light" is a warm tale of an eccentric former vaudeville magician (Shirley MacLaine), her strait-laced niece (Teri Garr as Kay), and Kay's two mischievous children who shake up a small town with their illusionary antics. Comic, simple and endearing, pic should have a good theatrical run with family audiences.**

MacLaine fans will appreciate her zany thesping, which equals her performance in "Steel Magnolias." In "Waiting For The Light," MacLaine shines as a wacky woman capable of shedding light on an otherwise ordinary neighborhood.

Pic gets rolling when the children are expelled from school (while imitating Aunt Zena) and Kay decides to move the family from Chicago to start anew in a smaller town. Trouble awaits when the kids are caught stealing veggies from a garden and Aunt Zena (an appropriate name) seeks revenge on the stuffy old neighbor, Mullins. When Zena and the children dress up as ghosts to teach Mullins a lesson, the town goes crazy and attracts tourists. Zena must produce a "miracle" for all those waiting for the light, or a ghost-like angel, as the rumor goes. Zena doesn't let them down.

With good technical elements on all fronts, pic is enriched by colorful costumes which match the characters. Homevid and tv are a natural afterlife. — *Suze.*

Cantate Pour Deux Généraux
(Cantate For Two Generals)
(FRENCH-DOCU)

Berlin A Mission du Bicentenaire Sodaperaga production in association with the Comite du film ethnographique and the Misee de l'homme in Paris. Directed by Jean Rouch. Camera (color), Rouch. Reviewed at Berlin Film Festival, Feb. 19, 1990. Running time: **60 MIN.**

■ **A visually disturbing docu in which a small group of Haitians and Africans conduct graphic voodoo rites on Napoleon's grave to free the spirit of a black general, Toussaint-Louverture, during the French bicentennial is not for the weak-stomached.**

Some rituals include closeups of chickens having their beaks bitten off, their wings and legs broken and finally bled to death. The only audience for this pic would be found in museums and territories where such customs are not considered barbaric.

Creole chanting accompanies all scenes, including some more appealing ceremonies where white sheets are slowly put into large ceramic jars. Unfortunately, the French-lingo voiceover only translates the lyrics and does not explain the significance of the objects or their movements.

While pic is classified as a docu, it is questionable as to whether the rituals were staged for the camera, since it's unlikely that a filmmaker would be allowed to film such voodoo scenes without pre-planning.

Pic is an interesting cultural experience which exposes the huge gap between what is socially acceptable to western civilizations versus those which still practice ancient rituals.

"Cantate" has no credits whatsoever, indicating pic is not intended for release. — *Suze.*

Krokodillen In Amsterdam
(Crocodiles In Amsterdam)
(DUTCH)

Berlin An Orthel Filmproductie production. Produced by Rolf Orthel. Directed by Annette Apon. Screenplay, Apon, Yolande Entius, Henriette Remmers; camera (color), Bernd Wouthuysen; editor, Danniel Daniel; music, Wonk van der Moulon; production design, Ruben Schwartz, Serge van Opzeeland; sound, Piotr van Dijk. Reviewed at Berlin Film Fest (Panorama section), Feb. 13, 1990. Running time: **90 MIN.**
Gino. . . . . .Joan Nederlof
Nina. . . . . .Yolanda Entius

■ **A modestly charming and amusing female buddy movie, "Crocodiles In Amsterdam" is lightweight fare from Dutch director Annette Apon, best known for "The Waves" (1981).**

In her new film, Apon teams two utterly dissimilar femmes. Ditzy Gino, a dreamy beauty just thrown over by her boyfriend, aims to travel to Sri Lanka to see elephants, but it looks like she'll never get there. Joan Nederlof plays the role with style.

In contrast, Nina (played by coscripter Yolanda Entius) is an anti-social type lacking the looks and style of Gino. She's apparently been involved with a terrorist group plotting to blow up a military target, but wanders off and meets Gino when a plot to rob her rich uncle backfires.

Most of the film involves the unlikely teaming and growing friendship of the two women, and their various adventures around the streets of Amsterdam. Along the way, Apon has a few serious points to make, such as the lack of communication between the generations (in a scene in which Nina visits her mother, but has nothing to say to her).

Entertaining pic is likely to have modest appeal both at home and in special situations abroad. "Desperately Seeking Susan" it's not, but it has endearing qualities, including the two actresses' splendid performances. — *Strat.*

Reise Nach Ostende
(Journey To Ostend)
(WEST GERMAN-DOCU)

Berlin A Stiftung Deutsche Kinemathek release of an NDR and WDR tv production. Directed by Klaus Wildenhahn. Camera (16m, color), Wolfgang Jost; sound, Wildenhahn; editor, Annemarie Lang-Johannsen. Reviewed at the Berlin Film Festival (New German Films), Feb. 10, 1990. Running time: **118 MIN.**

■ This made-for-tv film by veteran North German Broadcasting documentary director Klaus Wildenhahn confronts German viewers with a country most of them know next to nothing about, Belgium. Hence, little interest outside those two countries for this somewhat long pic.

As any American knows who visits Germany, the Germans complain that Americans know far too little about them. The best rejoinder is to point out how little they know of their own smaller neighbors, which is just what Wildenhahn does. He uses archive material and oldtimers' reminiscences to trace Germany's clashes with the hapless Belgians in two world wars, and tours the modern country, travelogue-style.

Technical credits are adequate for 16m format. — *Gill.*

Tobu yume o shibaraku minai
(A Paucity of Flying Dreams)
(JAPANESE)

Berlin An Araki presentation and production. Produced by Seiya Araki. Directed by Eizo Sugawa. Screenplay, Sugawa from a novel by Taichi Yamada; camera (Eastmancolor), Shinsaku Himeda; editor, Yoshitami Kuroiwa; music, Toshiaki Tsushima; production design, Kazuo Takenaka; sound, Koshiro Jimbo; production manager, Yoshiaki Hori, Koko Kajiyama. Reviewed at Berlin Film Festival (Panorama section), Feb. 11, 1990. Running time: **108 MIN.**
Shuji Taura. . . . . . .Toshiyuki Hosokawo
Mutsuko Miyabashi (young). . . .Eri Ishida
Mutsuko Miyabashi (old). . .Meiran Maeda
Yasuko Taura. . . . . .Meriko Kaga
Shinichi Taura. . .Shinnosuke Furomoto
Takeo Miyabashi. . . . . . .Katsuhiro Oida
Also with: Takashi Sasano, Hiromitsu Suzuki, Rei Okamoto, Toshie Kobayashi.

■ "A Paucity Of Flying Dreams" is an elegant, witty, erotic fairy tale by veteran helmer Eizo Sugawa, who proves that stylish entertainment values haven't entirely left mainstream Japanese cinema. This one is likely to spread its wings to reach offshore theatrical exhibition.

Shuji Taura, played by suavely handsome Toshiyuki Hokosawa. is a businessman who winds up in a hospital so overcrowded after a railroad accident that he has to share his room with Mutsuko Miyabashi, a female victim. The woman is hidden by a screen, but during the night a polite conversation between them develops into a steamy erotic dialogue.

The next morning, Taura catches a glimpse of his nocturnal "partner" and finds out that she is a badly scarred old woman. He returns to work in Tokyo where his bosses are beginning to find fault with his work and his wife is about to leave him in favor of a professional career of her own.

Out of a blue sky, Matsuko reappears, now beautiful and in her late 30s. Verbal love is soon exchanged with the real thing (choreographed and filmed with finesse), but the next morning Taura wakes up to yet another shock: The woman has disappeared without a trace.

Mutsuko, however, will reappear from time to time, each time seven years younger than before. Taura is obsessed with her. He feels that he is flying, but since he only has dreams to support his aerial flight, he is doomed to fall. His career and marriage in tatters, he one day spots a small girl of five staring at him.

At times, Sugawa tends towards overachieving by piling on effects that could have been dispensed with, but his film has an overall feel of ruthless logic and erotic warmth to compensate for subplot excesses.

The production dress of "Flying Dreams" is of the highest order and so are all technical credits. The acting is modern in a way more akin to everyday western than Japanese. Film may be a fairy tale, but it's a thoroughly contemporary one. — *Kell.*

Sprizneni volbou
(Selective Affinities)
(CZECHOSLOVAKIAN-DOCU-B&W)

Berlin A Ceskoslovensky Filmexport presentation of Kratky Film production. Written and directed by Karel Vacek. Camera (b&w), Josef Ort-Snep; editor, Jirina Skalska; sound, Sbynek Mader. Reviewed at Berlin Film Festival (Panorama) Feb. 13, 1990. Running time: **85 MIN.**

■ The title "Selective Affinities" describes what brought a number of Czechoslavakian Communist Party toppers together to create — with optimism, possibly opportunism and a modicum of open minds — the short-lived 1968 Prague Spring. As a tongue-in-cheek political docu it stands to become a small classic.

Karel Vacek's documentary has expert cameraman Josef Ort-Snep take a close, often intimate but never prying, look at the faces and body movements of Antonin Novotny, who resigned as president, and of Alexander Dubcek, Oldrich Cernik, Goldstruecker, Ota Sik, Josef Smerkovski and others as they juggle themselves into the positions they hope to keep in their vaunted "socialist state with a human face."

As the cinematography is intimate, so is Sbynek Mader's sound recording, which catches the tiniest nuances of tonal inflections that disclose alternately excessive self-assurance and creeping doubt. The documentarist obviously had the confidence of his subjects even if some of them jokingly claim that "we reserve our real thoughts for when you have gone."

Gustav Husak comes on with great confidence, too, although hardly expressing true belief in liberation of the system, and Army General Ludvik Svoboda keeps lips and eyelids half-closed during the sessions that would eventually end by having him elected president in a puppet position as the spring was squelched by the invading Russians.

Hacek made the entire film during 15 days in March. "Selective Affinities" has been around in a sharply abbreviated version. It was restored to its original form by the Czeckoslavakian Citizens Forum cinema section only a month before its Berlin Film Fest showing. — *Kell.*

Mixwix
(WEST GERMAN)

Berlin A Filmwelt release of a Herbert Achternbusch Filmproduktion. Written and directed by Achternbusch. Camera (color), Adam Olech, Hermann Fehr; sound, Heike Pillemann. Reviewed at Berlin Film Festival (New German Films), Feb. 13, 1990. Running time: **85 MIN.**
With: Monika Lemberger, Waggie Brömse, Alfred Edel, Josef Bierbichler, Annamirl Birbichler, Dietmar Schneider, Gabi Geist, Judit Achternbusch, Franz Baumgartner, Marion Moutell, Herbert Achternbusch.

■ West German poet-cum-filmmaker Herbert Achternbusch's latest foray into the absurdity of everyday life will appeal to his small clutch of groupies, but will get nothing but a shrug from anyone else. No offshore prospects for this poem set to pictures but still deeply imbedded in the German language.

Achternbusch is the dean of German anti-intellectual intellectuals; people who take swipes at snooty intellectuals by going over the top with intellectualism. For Achternbusch, this means turning the German language itself into a daunting weapon to wield against the intellectual establishment.

Ostensibly, this film concerns a department store owner named Mixwix (a word play on "masturbator") who spends his life squatting on the roof of his store while his minions attend to him and fawn over him. In reality, of course, the nonstop voiceover narration by Achternbusch allows the filmmaker to display his own intellectual prowess, weaving intricate genitive and dative clauses and shifting to and fro between the language's two subjunctive cases.

No amount of subtitling can help the foreign viewer, who remains baffled throughout. Even most Germans find this kind of thing heavy going, if not outrageous.

His fans in elite circles find Achternbusch's humor outrageously hilarious, but few hardtops can afford such a narrow-scope pic.
— *Gill.*

O Processo Do Rei
(The King's Trial)
(PORTUGUESE-FRENCH)

Berlin A Madragoa Filmes (Lisbon)/Gemini Films (Paris) coproduction, in association with Pandora Films (Frankfurt), AB Cinema (Rome). Directed by Joao Mario Grilo. Screenplay, Jean-Pierre Theilladde, Daniel Arasse, Grilo; camera (color), Eduardo Serra; editor, Rodolfo Wedeless; music, Jorge Arriagada; sound, Nicolas Lefebvre; assistant director, Manuel Joao Aguies. Reviewed at Berlin Film Festival (Panorama section), Feb. 16, 1990. Running time: **91 MIN.**
King Alfonso I. . . . . .Carlos Daniel
Dona Maria. . . . . . . .Aurelle Doazan
Pedro II. . . . . .Antonino Solmer
Count Castelo-Melhor. .Carlos de Medeiros
Preyssac. . . . . .Gerard Hardy
Ninon. . . . . .Muriel Brenner
Father Vieira. . . . . .Filipe Ferrer
Father Ville. . . . . . .Jean Lafront
Saint-Romain. . . . . .Jean Rupert

■ The serene and immaculate look of this slice of 17th century Portuguese history is deliberately at odds with the uncomfortable subject matter of this disturbing, beautiful pic. Though Portuguese films have seldom set arthouse boxoffices alight, buyers might take a look at this one.

It opens in 1640 when Alfonso I was the first king of a newly independent Portugal, married to a French princess (cousin of Louis

XIV). The crippled, simpleminded king became the focus of a plot to dethrone him. His wife took part in the scheme when she claimed publicly that he had never consummated their marriage. The Pope annulled the liaison, then the king was imprisoned.

This story of intrigue is shot on real locations. The images are tableau-like, beautifully composed, but always cinematic. So it comes as a shock when, in this stately setting, women witnesses at the trial describe in great detail the king's sexual problems. The explicit dialog coming from these elegant, graceful women, is unexpected to say the least.

"The King's Trial" isn't a swashbuckler, though there's a duel scene and the kind of intrigue and romance that, in another era, might have been made into a Hollywood romance. Director Joao Mario Grilo is aiming for a more aesthetic experience, and should have critics going along with his refined vision. This could be translated into modest b.o. returns, given proper handling.

English subtitles on the print caught were extremely poor, with "1667" at one point being translated as "1967." — *Strat.*

Leo Sonnyboy
(SWISS)

Berlin An Edi Hubschmid production. Produced by Hubschmid. Directed by Rolf Lyssy. Screenplay, Lyssy; camera (Eastmancolor), Hans Liechti, editor, Lilo Gerber; music, Rüdi Hausermann; production design, Edith Peier; sound, Remo Belli; assistant director, Ursula Bischof. Reviewed at Berlin Film Festival (Market), Feb. 17, 1990. Running time: **95 MIN.**
Leo Mangold. . . . . . .Mathias Gnadinger
Apia. . . . . .Ankie Beilke-Lau
Adrian Hauser. . . . . . .Christian Kohlund
Also with: Dieter Meier, Hilde Ziegler, Heinz Buhlmann, Peach Weber, Esther Christinat, Stephanie Glaser.

■ Rolf Lyssy's new comedy is a moderately amusing item about a marriage of convenience between a Swiss engine-driver and an Asian woman. Though it has bright moments, it's not in the same class as his earlier "The Swissmakers," which was immensely popular on its home turf and at fests abroad.

The new film is strikingly similar to the Canadian pic "A Paper Wedding" competing in the Berlin fest this year. In this case, Hauser, who is married but having a secret affair with Apia, a go-go girl from Thailand, asks his best friend, Leo Mangold, to marry

Apia so that she can stay in Switzerland.

Leo, an overweight, lonely train driver, agrees. Inevitably, he falls in love with the sympathetic and charming Apia and, just as inevitably, his friend is none too happy about it. Meanwhile, there are suspicious visits from the immigration department.

This is treated as comedy, but the laughs (at least for non-Swiss audiences) are few and far between. What does succeed, however, is the touching relationship between the decidedly odd couple at the film's center.

The film is technically excellent, but international possibilities, outside tv, look slight.
— *Strat.*

Nezna revoluce
(The Gentle Revolution)
(CZECHOSLOVAKIAN-DOCU)

Berlin A Ceskoslovensky Filmexport presentation of Kratky Film production. Written and directed by Petr Slavik, Jiri Strecha. Camera (color) and sound by a collective; editor, Vera Kutilova. No other credits available. Reviewed at Berlin Film Festival (Panorama) Feb. 14, 1990. Running time: **70 MIN.**

■ Thrown together in too much of a hurry, "The Gentle Revolution" is a haphazard documentation of events in the streets of Prague from August to early December, 1989. The very immediacy of the subject matter will, however, help pic's international sales until a better film comes along.

As helmed by Petr Slavik and Jiri Strecha, FAMU docu film school graduates, and their team of volunteer camera and sound people, "The Gentle Revolution" lacks style and personality and looks like bad television footage.

It's interesting and at times moving, however, to witness the gentle moods winning out over the temptation to respond to the violence of the regime with more violence. Whole avenues are seen overflowing with sitting youths, lighting candles as their only defense against police moving in with clubs.

Vaclav Havel is caught by the camera as he quietly and efficiently organizes protestors and sits down to a bargaining table across from a Communist chieftain who said earlier that Havel was a political zero. The bargaining leads to the Nov. 19 creation of the Citizen's Forum.

There are expressions of jubilation galore in "The Gentle Revolution," but the editing fails to sustain either mood or natural suspense. — *Kell.*

Tulitikkutehtaan tytto
(The Match Factory Girl)
(FINNISH)

Berlin A Villealfa presentation of Villealfa coproduction with the Swedish Film Institute and in association with Finnkino and Esselte Video. Produced by Aki Kaurismäki. Executive producers, Klas Olofsson, Katinka Farago. Written and directed by Aki Kaurismäki. Camera (Eastmancolor), Timo Salminen; editor, Kaurismäki; music, Reijo Taipale, the Strangers, Piotr Tchaikovski, Mauri Sumen, Badding Rockers, Nardis, Klaus Treuheit, Olavi Virta, Melrose; sound, Jouko Lumme; production design, Risto Karhula; production management, Klaus Heydemann, Jaakko Talaskivi; assistant director, Pauli Pennti. Reviewed at Berlin Film Festival (Forum of Young Film), Feb. 15, 1990. Running time: **70 MIN.**
Iris. . . . . .Kati Outinen
Her mother. . . . . .Elina Salo
Her stepfather. . . . . . . .Esko Nikkari
Man in dancehall. . . . . . .Vesa Vierikko
Also with: Reijo Taipale, Silu Seppälä, Outi Maenpaa, Marja Packalen, Klaus Heydemann.

■ Finnish cinema's wunderkind Aki Kaurismäki is back with "The Match Factory Girl," in which he has polished his deadpan realistic comedy style to a high gloss. His story about a tormented loser who takes a silent but gruesome revenge is sure to raise happy chuckles in specialized theaters.

Title's assembly line worker is a mousy Iris, abused by everybody including the parasitic mother and stepfather she lives with in a slum apartment. They hog her salary and even the meat chunks from her soup. She takes solace in reading romantic pulp and in sitting around in dancehalls, unapproached and listening to more romantic slush while sipping soda.

One day a man asks Iris to dance and afterwards to his plush apartment. They bed down, but next morning Iris gets the bounce. Her parents bounce her, too, when they find out that she is pregnant. But nobody figured on the hidden strength of this timid girl, who now sets out to calmly plan and execute her revenge.

Using minimum dialogue and composing sparse frames neverthless filled with telling detail, Kaurismäki accomplishes more than just a clever takeoff on Robert Bresson's quiet-violent style. He infuses every shot with real emo-

tion although his actors' facial expressions are kept at a minimum. If his story is obviously corny, it also rings painfully true.

In the lead, Kati Outinen is everything Hans Christian Andersen must have had in mind with his own version of a daydreaming girl selling matches on street corners. Outinen is Kaurismäki's favorite actress and he has her radiate a quiet glow even when expressing maximum sadness.

As in his earlier films ("Shadows In Paradise," "Ariel"), Kaurismäki uses romantic music sung by pop singers as a Greek chorus commenting on the value of dreams to sustain dreary lives. There is, however, never a condescending note. — *Kell.*

Stan Strachu
(State Of Fear)
(POLISH)

Berlin A Film Polski presentation of a OKO Group production. Directed by Janusz Kijowski. Screenplay, Cezary Harsimowicz, Kijowski; camera (Agfacolor), Przemyslaw Skwirczynski; sound, Jerzy Szawlowskiiart; production manager, Arkadiusz Piechal. Reviewed at Berlin Forum of the Young Cinema, Feb. 18, 1990. Running time: **126 MIN.**
Janek. . . . . .Wojciech Malajkat
Ewa. . . . . .Anna Majcher
Henryk. . . . . .Henryk Talar
Wanda. . . . . .Monika Niemczyk
Iwona. . . . . . . .Joanna Trzepiecinska
Also with: Jan Machulski, Piotr Machalica, Marcin Tronski, Mieczyslaw Voit, Jerzy Dominik, Cezary Harsimowicz, Ryszard Kotys, Jan Prochyra.

■ A tremendous amount of energy, pent-up frustration and anger, emerges in this almost, but not entirely, realistic account of the 1981 events in Poland, when the lid was temporarily clamped on Solidarity and a military government took over.

The plot takes place in a theater company and revolves around a mysterious briefcase whose contents are never revealed. The set painter hands it over to the actor, the police want to get their hands on it, the actor is submitted to the third degree, but he insists he knows nothing about it. He escapes from the police station, hides in a flat occupied by a young girl with whom he falls in love, is once again apprehended and thrown into jail, to be released years later. He never told anybody about the briefcase.

That, however, would be far too simple a story for director Janusz Kijowski to handle. So he starts piling up symbols at an amazing rate. The actor, Janek, refuses to play Hamlet in the company's next production, but he also has had a troubled relationship with his father, a party dignitary kicked out in the 1968 purges. Also, there is a kind of Cain and Abel situation, his brother being a major in the secret police who constantly meddles in the investigation.

While everybody around him chooses political allegiancies, Janek himself refuses to take a position; he only knows that he wants out, to leave Poland and go to Sweden. The trigger for every action is fear, exploited by the authorities to turn the entire population into a nation of informers, for it is only by informing on one person that there is any chance of saving another.

With lots of hand-held camera sequences, oversaturated photography for the flashbacks, authentic video newsreels of the Jaruzelski takeover in 1981, and characters tortured by doubts, anguish and guilt, Kijowski's film is a clash between generations, but also between brothers. It's a terrifying portrait of moral corruption as the only means of survival and of the profound mistrust destroying even the most intimate relations.

Trying to tackle so many themes at the same time, the narration becomes at times erratic, and more editing might have added to the film's impact. In any case, it is still a powerful, multilayered drama, distinguished by strong acting and tense direction. — *Edna.*

Franta
(WEST GERMAN)

Berlin An Allary Film production, in association with CWP. Produced by Dietrich Mack. Directed by Mathias Allary. Screenplay, Jan Christoph Jager, from the book "Franta Zlin" by Ernst Weiss; camera (Eastmancolor), Immo Rentz; editor, Monika Kretschmann; music, Peter Ludwig; sound, Reinhard Bihler; production design, Anette Ganders; production manager, Jurgen Venske; assistant director, Heidi Spies. Reviewed at Berlin Film Festival (New German section), Feb. 15, 1990. Running time: **96 MIN.**
Franta. . . . . .Jan Kurbjuweit
Mascha. . . . . .Micole Ansari
Vassili. . . . . .Ben Hecker
Vicky. . . . . .Daniela Lunkewitz
Woman in wood. . . . . .Sabine Gutberlet
Doctor. . . . . .Michael Richter

■ **This ambitious first film is adapted from a novel written in 1919 by Ernst Weiss, a colleague of both Franz Kafka and Stefan Zweig. The author's work hasn't been filmed till**

now, but Mathias Allary, though he obviously cares about the project, fails to make it acceptable to any but a limited audience.

Main protagonist Franta is a soldier during World War I and sympathy for him is quickly eroded when he brutally rapes a peasant woman whose cow he has killed for food. In the trenches he's emasculated during an explosion, and returns to his long-suffering wife bitter and twisted.

The war scenes are intercut with footage showing Franta furiously painting a series of large canvases, with the vivid colors of the oils commenting on the colors of the war scenes (red for blood and so on).

This might have worked on paper, but it's a bit obvious on film and the amaturish acting in this low-budgeter doesn't help.

"Franta" will be limited to university and fringe screenings, with commerical prospects very doubtful. — *Strat.*

Das Blinde Ohr Der Oper
(The Blind Ear Of Opera)
(WEST GERMAN)

Berlin A Giscia Films release of a ZDF and ORF tv coproduction. Directed and written by Hans Neuenfels. Camera (color, 16m), Benedict Neuenfels; editor, Inge Schneider; music and sound collage, Klaus Wagner, Stefan Schiske, Peter Kaizar; costumes, Dirk von Bodisco. Reviewed at Berlin Film Festival (Intl. Forum), Feb. 14, 1990. Running time: **86 MIN.**
With: Karan Armstrong, Roland Hermann, Elizabeth Laurence, James Johnson, Andreas Jäggi, Werner Hollweg, Jean-Marie Laujrens, Claudia Hollweg, Hans Neuenfels, Christiane Bruhn, York Höller, Johanna Karl-Lory, Marcus Bluhm, Stefan Wieland and others.

■ **This bizarre ode to opera buffs everywhere could prove a sleeper that earns a niche in festival programs.**

Plot, such as there is of it, involves a librettist's search through Paris, Moscow and Berlin for the perfect melody for his libretto, which is, of course, perfection itself. Helmer Hans Neuenfels as the wandering writer achieves a zany spoof of the opera world in a picture that works most of the time.

Benedict Neuenfels' camera gives this low-budgeter a sumptuous texture.

Other tech credits are adequate for its 16m format. — *Gill.*

Bumerang — Bumerang
(Boomerang Boomerang)
(WEST GERMAN)

Berlin A Geissendorfer Film production, in association with WDR, Pro-Ject Film. (Intl. sales, Filmveralg der Autoren, Munich.) Produced and directed by Hans W. Geissendörfer. Screenplay, Irene Fischer, Dorothee Schon; camera (color), Hans-Gunther Budking; editor, Helga Borshe; music, Dennis Hart; sound, Chris Price; production design, Michael Pilz; assistant director, Mika Kallwass. Reviewed at Berlin Film Fest (New German section), Feb. 13, 1990. Running time: **102 MIN.**
Evi. . . . . .Katja Studt
Pit. . . . . .Jurgen Vogel
Bond. . . . . .Jan Plewka
Reindl. . . . . .Lambert Hamel
Also with: Bernd Tauber, Michael Lerchenberg, Johanna Baumann, Erich Hallhuber.

■ **Hans W. Geissendörfer's first cinema feature since "Edith's Diary" (1983) is a pic squarely aimed at Germany's teen market. It's a mild thriller about a trio of environmentally conscious youngsters who kidnap a right-wing politician on the eve of an election. It looks to have strictly local possibilities.**

Evi, 16, is out on her bicycle when she's struck by the car driven by Reindl, a portly politico who favors the presence of nuclear weapons on German soil, something the teen abhors. She isn't hurt and, on the spur of the moment, uses Reindl's own gun to kidnap him. Since her mother is away, she takes him to her house, chains him in the bathtub, and elicits help from her two friends, fiery Pit and intellectual Bond (so called because he loves spy thrillers).

The promising theme is superficially handled. The director and writers never manage to develop it beyond its simplistic and wish-fulfilling premise. Pic is very well made, and young Katja Studt is a promising find as the young heroine. Lambert Hamel is convincing as the politico who gradually realizes he can use his plight to advantage in the upcoming elections.

African Timber
(WEST GERMAN-
FRENCH)

Berlin A Neue Deutsche Film (Munich)/ Project Film (Munich)/Torii Production (Paris) coproduction. (Intl. sales, Filmverlag der Autoren, Munich.) Produced by Chrostoph Mattner. Directed by Peter F. Bringmann. Screenplay, Mattner; camera (color), Frank Brühne; editor, Annette Dorn; music, Paul Vincent Gunia; sound, Rainer Wiehr; production design, Michael Pilz; production manager, Christine Stoltz; coproducer, Sylvia Montalti. Reviewed at Berlin Film Festival (New

German section), Feb. 15, 1990. Running time: **99 MIN.**
Peter Bechtle. . . . . . .Heiner Lauterbach
Girolles. . . . . .Julien Guiomar
Victoria St. Georges. . . .Deborah Lacey
Brasser. . . . . .Dietmar Schonherr
Samuel Moriba. . . . .Kofi Baba Bucknor
Philippe Djerdan. . . . . . .Said Amadis
Dr. Akoto. . . . . .Kofi Yirenkyi
Erhardt. . . . . .Claus Fuchs
Kweku. . . . . .Fred Amugi
Washington. . . . . . .Ernest Youngmann
(English soundtrack)

■ **Interesting locations in Ghana don't help this rather dim thriller get off the ground. Peter F. Bringmann is trying to make an English-lingo pic of international appeal, but prospects are distinctly iffy.**

The drama centers on a timber company in the hinterlands of Ghana, a small African country. Bechtle is brought from Germany to run a timber mill when the former manager is murdered. He finds to his surprise that the mill owner is a beautiful black woman, and soon they're in the sack together.

There's dirty work afoot, and it transpires that the femme's evil partner is trying to smuggle valuable mahogany out of the country illegally. It all winds up in a series of blandly handled chases and shoot-outs, with no surprises in store.

The hero, in which Heiner Lauterbach is as wooden as the trees that surround him, survives bullet wounds with amazing ease, and looks as if he, at least, understands what's going on. Audiences are likely to be less convinced.

Blacks in the film are presented as being servile, lazy or on the take, or all three. Only the aristocratic heroine escapes this labelling, and she's just too good to be true.

Pic's main asset is the fascinating backgrounds, especially the small town where many scenes take place. Those who care for the environment will be heartbroken at the numerous scenes in which magnificent old trees are felled to make timber. — *Strat.*

Exitus
(BULGARIAN-B&W)

Berlin A Bojana Film Studio production. Directed by Krassimir Krumow. Screenplay, Krumow, from a novel by Zlatomir Zlatanow; camera (b&w), Christo Bakalow; editor, Jordanka Batschwarowa; music, Stela Decheva; production design, Eugeni Apostolow; sound, Borislav Bojadjiev. Reviewed at Berlin Film Festival (Panorama section), Feb. 14, 1990. Running time: **97 MIN.**

With: Rumen Trajkov, Petar Popjordanov, Barbara Prkopjak, Ivan Grigorov, Prodan Noncher, Penka Tsitselkova, Rumjana Bocheva, Maja Tomova, Stojan Guder.

■ "Exitus" is an exceedingly bleak and somber film in which grim people live out desolate lives with little hope of escape. Black and whiter is a downer lacking the invention and poetry to make it a moving experience.

The central character is a failed academic working as caretaker of a cinema about to preem a Norwegian film. A grand opening is set with a beautiful Norwegian actress present. The caretaker is obsessed by his brother's death, apparently in a fire, and the death of a cinema employee in a similar fashion.

He tries to attach himself to the visiting actress, but to no avail. Empty sex with a woman in an office is the closest this loser comes to happiness.

Perhaps "Exitus" makes more sense in a Bulgarian context, but its depiction of agonized guilt and almost perpetual drunkenness makes it a chillingly unenjoyable cinema experience. It's technically fine, and the performances are solid, if predictable. — Mars.

Schweigen = Tod
(Silence = Death)
(WEST GERMAN-DOCU)

Berlin A Rosa von Praunheim Filmproduktion, with SR. Directed by Rosa von Praunheim. Screenplay, von Praunheim; camera (color), Mike Kuchar, Evan Estern; editor, Mike Shepherd, von Praunheim; music, Diamanda Galas; sound, Mark Milano. Reviewed at Berlin Film Festival (Panorama section), Feb. 16, 1990. Running time: 63 MIN.
(English soundtrack)

■The second of Rosa von Praunheim's AIDS trilogy (the third, "Asses On Fire," is now in postproduction), "Silence = Death" is a forceful followup to "Positive."

Like its predecessor, it evokes understandable anger at lack of government support for AIDS victims. The message the film carries is that those who are HIV positive don't want to be pitied, or to stop living, but want to continue to function in society.

Main focus is on a painter, David Wojnarowicz, who has the virus and whose lover died of it. Like other AIDS activists, he points an accusing finger at a complacent and ignorant general public.

"Silence = Death," along with von Praunheim's other docus, will be widely seen in the gay community, with public tv exposure also indicated. — Strat.

The Terra-Cotta Warrior
(HONG KONG)

Berlin An Art & Talent Group production. Produced by Hon Pou Chu. Coproduced by Kam Kwok Leung, Zhang Yimou, Ng Tin Ming. Directed by Ching Tung Yee. Screenplay, Lee Bik Wah; camera (Panavision, Eastmancolor), Peter Pau; editor, Mak Chi Shin; music, Joseph Koo; sound, James Wong; production design, Yee Chung Man;; costumes, Yu Ka On; production manager, Sze Sum Lam; special effects, Tsui Hark. Reviewed at Berlin Film Festival (noncompeting), Feb. 18, 1990. Running time: 111 MIN.
Mong. . . . . .Zhang Yimou
Twon. . . . . .Gong Li
Bai Yun Fei. . . . . .Yu Yung Kang

■ One of the most lavish films ever produced out of Hong Kong, "The Terra-Cotta Warrior" is a lively comedy adventure clearly inspired by "Indiana Jones" films as well as by Japanese samurai epics. Asian business should be busy, and the film should also find an audience in the west, if only a cult following.

Director Ching Tung Yee (best known for "A Chinese Ghost Story") is unperturbed by the loony screenplay of Lee Bik Wah which tells a love story that spans 3,000 years as well as packing in as many action and stunt scenes as the slight plotline will bear. The director goes for broke, and the result is enormously entertaining.

The pic opens in the distant past during the reign of a powerful emperor, Quin, whose capital is Xi'an (now the base of China's most famous film studio). Mong is the emperor's most loyal soldier, who thwarts an assassination attempt against his master. Mong is played with great authority by Zhang Yimou, who's better known as the director of the prize-winning Chinese pic "Red Sorghum."

Mong falls in love with a court handmaiden called Twon ("Winter") and they have an affair. Both are doomed to die when the emperor discovers their sin. Twon walks off into a wall of flame, while Mong is encased in clay to become one of thousands of terra-cotta warriors guarding the emperor's tomb.

At this point there's an abrupt shift forward in time to the early 1930s. Twon has been reincarnated as Lily, a ditzy actress in love with Bai, a suave film director working on China's first talkie. He takes her for a joyride in his 2-seater plane which crashes (thanks to her) into the mausoleum where the emperor lies buried guarded by the ghostly clay warriors. At this point Mong returns actively to life and Bai is revealed as being the villainous leader of a gang of grave robbers.

What follows is action and comedy all the way as the bemused Mong tries to cope with life in the 20th century and do battle with Bai Yun Fei's gun-toting gangsters, though he's armed only with his trusty sword.

It's all fun, and builds up to a splendidly crazy climax topped by a coda which has Twon in the present day assume the form of a Japanese tourist in China.

This is robust fare, handled in over-the-top style. The spectacular locations were lensed in Mainland China, and the picture looks expensive. Production design is splendid and stuntwork good (except for a shakily staged escape on horseback from a moving train).

The film was shown out of competition in Berlin's official section where the running time was incorrectly listed as 145 minutes. It could provide needed light relief at other noncompeting fests before seeking a wider audience through specialized screenings worldwide. — Strat.

Lord Of The Flies

Hollywood A Columbia Pictures release of a Jack's Camp/Signal Hill Ltd. production presented by Castle Rock Entertainment in association with Nelson Entertainment. Executive producers, Lewis Allen, Peter Newman. Produced by Ross Milloy. Coproducer, David V. Lester. Directed by Harry Hook. Screenplay, Sara Schiff, based on William Golding's novel; camera (Continental color; Deluxe prints), Martin Fuhrer; supervising editor, Tom Priestley; music, Philippe Sarde; sound (Dolby), Douglas B. Arnold; production design, Jamie Leonard; costumer design, Doreen Watkinson; first assistant director, Matt Hinkley; unit production manager, Matthew Binns; stunt coordinator, Jerry Gatlin; associate producer, Walker Stuart; casting, Janet Hirshenson, Jane Jenkins, Michael Hirshenson. Reviewed at Pathe Entertainment screening room, L.A., Feb. 21, 1990. MPAA Rating: R. Running time: 90 MIN.
Ralph. . . . . .Balthazar Getty
Jack. . . . . .Chris Furrh
Piggy. . . . . .Danuel Pipoly
Simon. . . . . .Badgett Dale
The twins. . . . .Edward Taft, Andrew Taft
Marine officer. . . . . .Bob Peck
Marine petty officer. . . . .Bill Schoppert
Pilot. . . . . .Michael Greene
Also with: Gary Rule, Terry Wells, Braden MacDonald, Angus Burgin, Martin Zentz, Brian Jacobs, Vincent Amabile, David Weinstein, Chuck Bell, Everado Elizondo, James Hamm, Charles Newmark, Brian Matthews, Shawn Skie, Judson McCune, Zane Rockenbaugh, Robert Shea, Gordon Elder.

■ The notion that the story of civilized boys reverting to savagery on a desert isle would be improved by shooting in color and substituting American actors for British child thesps is an odd one indeed. Look for a quick departure to video for this Columbia release.

Peter Brook's black and white version of William Golding's

Original film
(BRITISH-B&W)

Cannes A Continental release of a Lewis Allen-Dana Hodgion-Two Arts production. Written and directed by Peter Brook, from the book by William Golding. Camera (b&w), Tom Hollyman; editor, Brook, J.C. Griel, M. Lubtchansky. Reviewed at Cannes Film Festival, May 14, 1963. Running time: 90 MIN.
Ralph. . . . . .James Aubrey
Jack. . . . . .Tom Chapin
Piggy. . . . . .Hugh Edwards
Roger. . . . . .Roger Elwin
Simon. . . . . .Tom Gaman

"Lord Of The Flies" is no classic, but it stands miles above this thoroughly undistinguished and unnecessary remake. Lewis Allen, one of the producers of the earlier version and exec producer of the remake with Peter Newman, made this film "to protect the first film and to prevent television movie-of-the-week imitations after Golding received the Nobel Prize for literature," according to the press notes.

That's about as poor an excuse

for a remake as has been heard in recent years, especially since it's hard to imagine a telepic version much worse than this one.

In Brook's offbeat film, which for its time had some genuine shock value, the experiences of the castways were rendered in an eerie and nightmarish style. Here, director Harry Hook's literal, unimaginative visual approach makes the tale seem mundane and tedious. It's a textbook case of how color can be a backward step artistically, particularly since green foliage (as any lenser knows) as quickly becomes monotonous to the eye.

Time, perhaps, has also taken a toll on the novelty of Golding's allegory. Since its publication in 1954, the world has been through so many social upheavals and so much large-scale brutality from all quarters that it's no longer news that schoolboys have within them the seeds of savagery. Setting the story in the contemporary world makes it seem doubly superfluous.

Sara Schiff's flat screenplay makes all the boys seem like dullards and does little to help differentiate the cast members, most of whom seem cut from the same mold of bland cuteness. Nor do these boys seem to be living through the kind of gritty physical experience that would make the allegory spring to life. Indeed, one of the product plugs in the end credits is for a sunscreen lotion, which must have been liberally applied on the Jamaican location, since the cast all seem to have remained carefully shielded from the elements.

Hooks misguidedly cast the film not with skilled child actors, but with unknowns, beginners and neophytes. Since, in film acting terms, technique expresses civilization, a lack of technique robs the cast members of the veneer of culture they need for the story to work, and makes their transition to savages seem undramtic.

Nor does it make sense to change Golding's boys to Americans. Removing the rigid social context of the British class system robs the story of much of its irony and impact. The boys in the remake are from a military school, which is intended to stand in for British school discipline but remains an underexplored device. No one in this film has any stature or authority whatsover.

Individual performances mostly never rise above the semiamateur level. The inadequacy of the cast may be an indictment of the director's bad judgment, but by comparison with the professionalism of Brook's cast, it can also be seen as a glaring contract between the level of training received by young American and British thesps. — *Mac.*

Nuns On The Run (BRITISH)

Hollywood A 20th Century Fox release of a Handmade Films presentation. Executive producers, George Harrison, Denis O'Brien. Produced by Michael White. Written and directed by Jonathan Lynn. Camera (Agfa-Gevaert color; Technicolor prints), Michael Garfath; editor, David Martin; music, Yello, Hidden Faces; sound (Dolby), Tony Jackson, Robin O'Donoghue; production design, Simon Holland; art direction, Clinton Cavers; set decoration, Michael Scirton; costume design, Susan Yelland; makeup, Pat Hay; assistant director, David Brown; coproducer, Simon Bosanquet; casting Mary Selway. Reviewed at 20th Century Fox, L.A., March 8, 1990. MPAA Rating: PG-13. Running time: **90 MIN.**
Brian Hope/Sister Euphemia. . . .Eric Idle
Charlie/Sister Inviolata. . .Robbie Coltrane
Faith. . . . . .Camille Coduri
Sister Superior. . . . . . .Janet Suzman
Sister Mary of the Sacret Heart. .Doris Hare
Sister Mary of the Annuciation. .Lila Kaye
"Case" Casey. . . . . .Robert Patterson
Abbott. . . . . .Robert Morgan
Morley. . . . . .Winston Dennis
Father Seamus. . . . . . . .Tom Hickey

■ **If everyone who has ever had his ear yanked by a nun goes to see "Nuns On The Run," Fox will have a winner. This uproarious British import, with the irreverent antics of Eric Idle and Robbie Coltrane as two petty gangsters scared into convent drag, should have a blessed b.o. future. (Fox has it for the U.S. and Canada only.)**

Like Jack Lemmon and Tony Curtis in the Billy Wilder classic "Some Like It Hot," which this film more than casually resembles, Idle and Coltane are motivated by fear for their lives to dress in women's garb. In the old pic, the Chicago mob was in pursuit; new one has rival British and Chinese gangs trying to recover two suitcases full of illicit cash.

Idle, the skinny long-faced Monty Python alumnus, and the portly, ribald Coltrane (Falstaff in Kenneth Branagh's "Henry V") make a wonderful pair of dumbbells, both in and out of their habits. Both are oddly believable as nuns, even while writer/director Jonathan Lynn mines all the expected comic benefits of drag humor, more inherently funnier than crooks dressed as priests, as in the recent unsuccessful "We're No Angels."

Though "Nuns On The Run" has a PG-13 rating, it's raunchy enough to include a shower room scene of the phony nuns ogling their teenaged charges as well as some salty language. But the tone of the humor is essentially benevolent, and the film could even be enjoyed by some of the more enlightened members of the cloth. It's unlikely to arouse the kind of indignation that was vented on "Life Of Brian," Handmade Films' 1979 religious satire, in which Idle costarred.

Idle and Coltrane here are a lookout and a getaway driver for believably nasty London crime lord Robert Patterson. Their desire to escape their surroundings and the lure of easy cash backfire ominously, and after a relatively straight setup in the opening 22 minutes (including the sight of a well-ventilated corpse), they take refuge in a convent school run by Janet Suzman.

A crusty, no-nonsense type who prefers to be addressed as "Sister Liz," Suzman is having a little problem with a shortage in the books caused by tipling, horseplaying nun Lila Kaye. Suzman tolerates the strange appearance and behavior of Idle and Coltrane with an eye to sharing their cash.

The pragmatism of the genuine nuns goes refreshingly against pious stereotype, and the farcical mechanisms engineered by Lynn to keep the plot moving to its satisfying resolution never falter. Lynn and editor David Martin keep up a zippy pace throughout, aided by the energetic score by Yello and Hidden Faces, with co-exec producer George Harrison also tossing in one of his songs.

What makes the film so delightful is the relationship between Idle and Coltrane. Idle's Sister Euphemia of the Five Wounds is frantically ignorant of Catholic theology, and Coltrane's intricate attempts to explain it are hysterically funny and right on target. "It's a bit of a bugger," Coltrane's Sister Inviolata of the Immaculate Conception admits of the doctrine of the Holy Trinity.

Coltrane takes after Lemmon's character in the Wilder pic by getting a sly kick out of wearing women's clothing, and finds that pretending to be a nun also makes him think like a nun, recalling more and more and of his Catholic indoctrination. But he's not transformed enough to lose his lecherous eye toward the nubile students or to take double-edged umbrage when randy old Father Seamus (Tom Hickey), this film's equivalent of Joe E. Brown, can't keep his hand off Idle's prissy nun.

The constant double entendres are done with wit rather than crudity, and the slapstick is mostly agreeable and efficiently directed, although the sight gags about Camille Coduri's extreme myopia are pushed a little far on occasion. Coduri otherwise is sweet and endearing in the Marilyn Monroe part. As Idle's plucky inamorata, she does her best to help them escape without being unduly bothered that they are dressed like nuns. — *Mac.*

Bad Influence

Hollywood A Triumph release of an Epic Prods. and Sarlui/Diamant presentation of a Steve Tisch/Producer Representatives Organization production. Executive producers, Richard Becker, Morrie Eisenman. Produced by Tisch. Line producer, Iya Labunka; coproducer, Bernie Goldmann. Directed by Curtis Hanson. Screenplay, David Koepp; camera (color), Robert Elswit; editor, Bonnie Koehler; music, Trevor Jones; sound (Dolby), Dane A. Davis; production design, Ron Foreman; art direction, William S. Combs; set decoration, Leslie Morales; associate producer, Koehler; casting, Lisa Beach. Reviewed at Mann Regent theater, Westwood, Calif., March 6, 1990. MPAA Rating: R. Running time: **99 MIN.**
Alex. . . . . .Rob Lowe
Michael Boll. . . . . . . .James Spader
Claire. . . . . .Lisa Zane
Pismo Boll. . . . . .Christian Clemenson
Leslie. . . . . .Kathleen Wilhoite
Patterson. . . . . .Tony Maggio
Ruth Fielding. . . . . . . .Marcia Cross

■ **While it would be hard-pressed to achieve the notoriety of the last time Rob Lowe was seen before a camera, "Bad Influence" proves a reasonably taut, suspenseful thriller that provides its share of twists before straying into silliness during its final third.**

Boxoffice should carry some weight, no doubt augmented by curiosity-seekers who will savor its parallels to Lowe's recent off-screen antics.

Pic's most significant flaw may be that Lowe doesn't really project enough menace or charisma to pull off his role as Alex, a babyfaced psycho who slowly leads James Spader through a liberating fantasy that ultimately turns into a yuppie nightmare.

Spader might have been more compelling in the role of Alex, though that would hardly compensate for some of the film's lapses in logic.

Director Curtis Hanson ("The Bedroom Window") and writer David Koepp ("Apartment Zero") seem to draw their inspiration most closely from Alfred Hitchcock's "Strangers On A Train" — a chance meeting between a regular guy and an outwardly normal stranger whose hidden darkness ultimately leads to fatal complications.

Spader plays Michael, a buttoned-down yuppie heading toward a passionless marriage and vying with a coworker for a coveted promotion.

Along comes Lowe, rescuing him from a barroom beating, then gradually manipulating matters so that they fall Michael's way, including his promotion, bedding a provocative woman and extricating him from his marriage plans.

The last feat will provide the film's historical footnote, as Alex videotapes Michael having sex and then uses the tape to devastating effect — voyeurism being one of the film's recurrent themes as well as its most amusing parallel to Lowe's much-publicized career as a homevideo auteur.

Foremost, however, the film is about Michael's seduction by Alex' free-wheeling attitude, only to find that the rewards don't come cheap and that Alex isn't an easy friend to lose.

Spader delivers a terrific performance, and some of the scenes have tremendous impact, especially when — again via video — he discovers the depth of Alex' depravity, as fantasy turns into fatal distraction.

Unfortunately, Michael's initial transformation occurs too rapidly, and the pair's wild latenight spree through L.A. rings false.

Audiences may similarly be inclined to snicker at Michael's inept efforts to hide incriminating evidence, as well as some of the dialog as earnestly read by Lowe.

Hanson and writer Koepp create a continued sense of tension and invest many scenes with much-needed humor. Trevor Jones' score helps immeasurably, and L.A. night scenes are shot gorgeously by Robert Elswit, who seems to find a hundred different angles from which to shoot Michael's avant-garde apartment.

Other tech credits are fine. Christian Clemenson is well-cast as Spader's brother, given the two thesps' close physical resemblance. — *Bril.*

Body Chemistry

Hollywood A Concorde Pictures release. Produced by Alida Camp. Executive producer, Rodman Flender. Directed by Kristine Peterson. Screenplay, Jackson Barr; camera (Foto-em color), Phedon Papamichael; editor, Nina Gilberti; music, Terry Plumeri; production design, Gary Randall; art direction, Ella St. John Blakey; set design, Cee Parker; set decoration, Michele Munoz; costume design, Sandra Araya Jensen; sound, Cameron Hamza; assistant director, James B. Rogers; 2nd unit director, Melitta Fitzer; associate producer, Kevin Reidy. Reviewed at Raleigh Studios, L.A., March 7, 1990. MPAA Rating: R. Running time: **87 MIN.**

Tom	Marc Singer
Claire	Lisa Pescia
Marlee	Mary Crosby
Freddie	David Kagen
Jason	H. Bradley Barneson
Kim	Doreen Alderman
Wendy	Lauren Tuerk
Dr. Pritchard	Joseph Campanella

■ **A trashier, campier knock-off of "Fatal Attraction," "Body Chemistry" is an above-average effort from Concorde with enough provocative elements to do well in video and in its 60-print regional release. (A larger national send-out is being contemplated by distrib.)**

Down to the kitchen knife scene, "Chemistry," retitled from "Afterimage," borrows unabashedly from the aforementioned Adrian Lyne blockbuster, but offers some kinky twists of its own.

Setting in a sexual behavior research lab allows for screening of the erotic videos used to stimulate subjects. Married lab director Marc Singer is easily seduced when aggressive outside researcher Lisa Pescia, who controls a lucrative contract needed by his lab, shows one of these porn cassettes after hours and comes on to him.

There's plenty of steam as these two go at it everywhere but in bed, but Singer is soon caught in a squeeze as his insatiable, out-of-control colleague pulls such reckless stunts as parking a van outside his house and dragging him into it for bondage games, which she videotapes and uses to threaten him.

As in the prototype pic, the more Singer tries to shut her out, the more desperate and threatening she gets.

Mary Crosby plays the Anne Archer role as the supportive wife who suspects plenty and finally confronts the Jezebel interloper in a stony staredown scene at a party.

Despite its femme director (Kristine Peterson), ending of "Chemistry" is more mordant than the one in "Fatal Attraction," and is likely to fuel the misogynist sentiments the pic incites all along.

Despite the campy sex scenes, director Peterson mostly plays it straight, with some stylish touches and an aptitude for suspense and violence, particularly in a taut kitchen scene involving a struggle for a knife.

Among the cast, Crosby gives the strongest performance, while Singer as the beefcake philanderer displays his guilt a bit too broadly. Pescia is effective as the seductress and David Kagen an affable presence as the get-around single guy who's Singer's colleague.

Production values are solid.

— *Daws.*

The Last Of The Finest

New York An Orion Pictures release of a Davis Entertainment production. Executive producer, Jere Cunningham. Produced by John A. Davis. Directed by John Mackenzie. Screenplay, Cunningham, Thomas Lee Wright, George Armitage, from Cunningham's story; camera (Foto-Kem color; Deluxe prints), Juan Ruiz-Anchia; editor, Graham Walker; music, Jack Nitzsche, Michael Hoenig, featuring Mick Taylor; sound (Dolby), Kirk H. Francis; production design, Laurence G. Paull; set decoration, John Thomas Walker; costume design, Marilyn Vance-Straker; production manager-coproducer, assistant director, William P. Scott; stunt coordinator, David Ellis; associate producer, Darlene K. Chan; casting, Janet Hirshenson, Jane Jenkins. Reviewed at Art Greenwich 1 theater, N.Y., March 9, 1990. MPAA Rating: R. Running time: **106 MIN.**

Frank Daly	Brian Dennehy
Wayne Gross	Joe Pantoliano
Ricky Rodriguez	Jeff Fahey
Howard (Hojo) Jones	Bill Paxton
Linda Daly	Deborra-Lee Furness
R.J. Norringer	Guy Boyd
Capt. Joe Torres	Henry Darrow
Harriet Gross	Lisa Jane Persky
Anthony Reece	Michael C. Gwynne
Stant	Henry Stolow
Tommy Grogan	John Finnegan
Calvert	J. Kenneth Campbell
Rose	Patricia Clipper
Anita	Michelle Little
Fast Eddie	Xander Berkeley
Haley	Pam Gidley

■ **The Iran-contra affair becomes the plot device for a farfetched and preachy cop film offering Brian Dennehy an interesting star turn. Commercial prospects are bleak for this oddball Orion message picture.**

Originally titled "Street Legal," "The Last Of The Finest" belongs to a rarely attempted brand of pastiche film, last seen in the Watergate comedy "Nasty Habits," in which nuns led by Glenda Jackson and Geraldine Page portrayed thinly disguised members of the Nixon administration.

"Finest" is less interesting because it's one step removed. The central characters are Dennehy and his band of dedicated cops who tumble upon a bunch of corrupt characters (who parallel the Iran-contra protagonists) while working on a drug bust.

Like characters from a Don Siegel action pic (especially "Charley Varrick"), Dennehy and his loyal men Joe Pantoliano, Jeff Fahey and Bill Paxton bristle at L.A.P.D. rules and are suspended when their task force becomes overly zealous in its fight against drug trafficking. Audience immediately tumbles to the fact that higher-ups are blocking their noble cause: it's a combination of police brass and feds, working on an elaborate scheme to trade drugs for arms to supply Central American freedom fighters.

In pic's silliest plot twist, Dennehy and company too easily rip off minor drug dealers to finance their own purchase of heavy weapons to stage a 3-man war against the baddies (one of Dennehy's merry men is murdered early on, as a corny motivational device). Their victory against tall odds is phony and film's symbolism goes over the top in a climax of the drug money exploding in its cesspool hideaway, covering the baddies in excrement.

Despite the deficiencies of a script that unwisely mixes tongue-in-cheek elements with soapbox messages, Scottish director John Mackenzie keeps the pic moving and enjoyable on a strictly thriller level. Its unsubtle references to Iran-contra are more fun for film historians than action fans, leading to an ending on tv identical in purpose to the rabble-rousing conclusion of Alex Cox' similarly preachy "Walker."

Dennehy is excellent in delivering a liberal message in the form of a free-thinking independent who's tired of the expediency and greed of a system riddled with phony patriots. Guy Boyd ably leads the group of Machiavellian villains and Aussie thesp Deborra-Lee Furness makes a good impression as Dennehy's wife.

Former Rolling Stone Mick Taylor adds punch with his guitar solos. —*Lor.*

Skrivanci Na Nitich
(Larks On A String)
(CZECHOSLAKIAN)

Berlin A Barrandov Filmstudio production. Produced by Karel Kochman. Directed by Jiri Menzel. Screenplay, Bohumil Hrabal, Menzel, from a story by Hrabal; camera (color), Jaromir Sofr; music, Jiri Sust; assistant director, Josef Sandr. Reviewed at Berlin Film Festival (competing), Feb. 16, 1990. Running time: **94 MIN.**

With: Rudolf Hrusinsky, Vaclav Neckar, Vladimir Brodsky, Leos Sucharipa, Jitka Zelenohorska, Nada Urbankova, Jaroslav Satoransky.

■ **A full 21 years after it was made, Jiri Menzel's "Larks On A String" is finally off the shelf. Through perhaps not the banned masterpiece of legend, it is a courageous, bittersweet comedy of considerable charm and invention. Cowinner of the Berlin Fest's Golden Bear (with "Music Box") should spark interest worldwide.**

The film was made at the end of the Golden Age of Czech cinema. In 1987, Menzel won an Academy Award for his first feature, "Closely Watched Trains." In 1968, at the height of Alexander Dubcek's Prague Spring, his next film, "Capricious Summer," won the Grand Prix at the Karlovy Vary Film Fest. "Larks On A String" went into production just as the Warsaw Pact invaded the country (August 1968) and, as soon as it was finished, was banned.

Menzel's heresy, and that of his writer, Bohumil Hrabal, was to satirize the "reeducation" of "bourgeois elements" in the early '50s, immediately after the Communist takeover of the country. Much of the film is set on a scrapheap close to heavily polluting factories.

There, a small group of "bourgeois" types are forced to do manual labor. They include a former philosophy professor, a former state prosecutor, a musician, a milkman, a hairdresser and a Jewish hotelier. They're overseen by a functionary (Rudolph Hrusinsky) with a working-class background (who, naturally, does very little actual work).

Nearby, a group of young women, who had all tried unsuccessfully to escape the country, live in a makeshift prison. There's regular contact between the two groups, and a young bourgeois falls in love with a pretty prisoner. Eventually they marry, but by proxy. He's been arrested for daring to ask a party bigwig the

whereabouts of his missing friends.

A running joke through the film has a sinister black car and two men arriving periodically to take away anyone who asks awkward questions. The young hero winds up a victim in the same way as the others, and the film's extraordinary last image shows the political prisoners descending into a seemingly bottomless coal shaft. It's a chillingly prophetic fadeout, yet with a glimmer of hope as the former professor remarks: "I'm happy, I've found myself."

No doubt that "Larks On A String" was a daring and provocative film to have been made in Czechoslovakia at that point in history. Menzel mocks the slogans of the '50s (banners with 1984-style messages like "We Will Surpass The Norm") and the destructiveness of the era (hundreds of typewriters and crucifixes wind up on this symbolic scrapheap). A funny scene has a film director staging a scene of apparently happy workers, and another shows that Hrusinsky, a rigorous enforcer of the Hygiene Act, uses the law to bathe pretty young girls.

Unfortunately, "Larks On A String" is not as successful as the famous films that preceded it. A couple of scenes (the women fighting among themselves, their chief guard's strange honeymoon with his gypsy bride, where they simply run around their apartment turning the lights on and off) go on too long and have little point. The film is at its best when it's at its blackest; "This man will not die a natural death," says Hrusinsky, chillingly, of the rebellious Jew.

Despite its flaws, the film is sufficiently amusing, provocative, and in the end, uncannily prophetic, to make its mark in the art houses around the world. Thesping is great, and the cast contains several familiar faces from this period of Czech cinema. Technically, the film is excellent.

"One day we'll see where the truth lies," says one of the characters. It took a long time for the truths in Menzel's film to be revealed to the outside world, but his anger at the destructive system imposed on his country is as valid as ever.

Expectations are that other banned classics of the late '60s will be unveiled at fests this year, including Karel Kachyna's legendary "The Ear." Meanwhile, Men-

zel's film, despite its flaws, can be enjoyed at last. — *Strat.*

Leben BRD
(Life—Federal Republic of Germany)
(WEST GERMAN-DOCU)

Berlin A Harun Farocki presentation of a Farocki, ZDF, La Sept production. Written and directed by Farocki. Camera (16m, color), Ingo Kratisch; editor, Roza Merzedres, Irina Hoppe; sound, Klaus Klingler; research, Michael Trabtzsch. Reviewed at Berlin Film Festival (Forum of the Young Film), Feb. 10, 1990. Running time: **83 MIN.**

■ **Setting out to confirm some of the intrinsic fears expressed lately by Socialist countries looking westward, Harun Farocki lingers too long on one topic. It is likely that a 1-hour format would better catch the fancy of tv programmers, pic's main customers.**

His image of West Germany, as a place where nothing happens without careful rehearsal and preparation, is sarcastically well-documented, amusing and at the same time threateningly accurate. Life has no mystery and surprises when everything from sex to driving a car is dissected, analyzed and reprocessed in a clinical fashion and served back to the customers in an orderly, didactic manner.

Farocki devotes long sequences to subjects such as obstetrics, psychosocial conduct, police academies and hospitals. He concludes that the transformation of humans into programmed machines not only affects the private lives of the people here, but the political climate as well.

The effect of these sequences is sometimes hilarious because of the way instructors and students relate to each other, and ominous, because of their implied message. — *Edna.*

Uberall Ist Est Besser Wo Wir Nich Sind
(It's So Much Nicer Wherever We Are Not)
(WEST GERMAN-B&W)

Berlin A Daniel Zuta Film production, in association with ZDF. Produced by Daniel Zuta. Directed by Michael Klier. Screenplay, Klier, Gustav Barwicki; camera (b&w), Sophie Maintigneux; editor, Bettina Bohler; sound, Klaus Klingler; production design,

Jerome Burckhard-Latour. Reviewed at Berlin Film Festival (New German Films), Feb. 17, 1990. Running time: **74 MIN.**
Jerzy. . . . . .Miroslav Baka
Ewa. . . . . .Marta Klubowicz
Alex Gebel. . . . . .Michael Krause
Bronek. . . . . .Josef Zebrowski
Anna. . . . . .Anna Pastewka
Susi. . . . . .Anja Klein

■ **This is a modest, black and white pic about the problems of Eastern European refugees in the West.**

Item is of a scale that's better suited to tv than theatrical screens, but fests could be interested.

It opens in Warsaw, where Jerzy has decided to leave the country, intending to end up in the U.S. On his last day, he does some illegal money changing and meets Ewa, a waitress, in a bar. Next day he's in West Berlin.

Here he finds no paradise. He has to stay in shabby lodgings and take dubious work, either washing dishes or running errands for a loan shark. He quickly learns that money talks. Meanwhile, he meets Ewa again; she has left Poland too, and started work as a cleaner, soon drifting into prostitution. They have a brief affair, but she wants more than he can provide.

Despite the theme, Michael Klier's first feature isn't all gloom and doom. As played by Miroslav Baka, Jerzy is an optimistic character who will probably succeed in the end. Czech-born Klier doesn't stint in his depiction of West Berlin as a place where newcomers from the socialist East have a pretty hard time of it.

Production values here are modest but adequate. Lack of music is no drawback. Thesping is fine, with Marta Klubowicz as Ewa particularly good. — *Strat.*

Butterbrot
(Bread And Butter)
(WEST GERMAN)

Berlin A Senator Film Verleih release of a Bavaria and Iduna Film production. Produced by Michael Röhrig. Written and directed by Gabriel Barylli. Camera (color), Thomas Mauch; editor, Hannes Nikel; music, Harald Kloser; art direction, Egon Strasser. Reviewed at Berlin Film Festival (New German Films), Feb. 14, 1990. Running time: **93 MIN.**
Martin. . . . . .Gabriel Barylli
Peter. . . . . .Heinz Hoenig
Stefan. . . . . .Uwe Ochsenknecht
Maria. . . . . .Timna Brauer
Lilli. . . . . .Natascha Aghfurian

■ **Austrian-born playwright**

Gabriel Barylli has made a name for himself in West Germany with a trilogy of stage pieces about coming of age, and this screen adaptation of one of them should do well on home turf. Export prospects are dimmed by the lingo barrier thrown up by pic's wordy screenplay.

Plot involves three guys holed up in a secluded house who fret over problems with the opposite sex. They come to the realization that their own low self-regard is to blame.

Barylli, who plays one of the three, transferred this play to the screen without opening it up beyond the four walls of the house.

Kudos to Uwe Ochsenknecht, whom non-Germans will recognize as the jaded hippie from Doris Dörrie's 1985 comedy ''Men.''

Tech credits are adequate.
— *Gill.*

Je T'ai Dans La Peau
(I'm Hopelessly Yours)
(FRENCH)

Berlin A Les Films d'Ici, Video 13, Road Movies and La Sept production. Directed by Jean-Pierre Thorn. Screenplay by Thorn, Lorette Cordrie, Dominique Lancelot; camera (color), Denis Gheerbrant; editor, Thorn, Alain Debarnot; music, Jacky Moreau; sound, Pierre Exoffier, Dominique Hennequin; set designer, Florence Bes; costumes, Montserrat Casanova. Reviewed at Berlin Film Festival (Forum), Feb. 21, 1990. Running time: **120 MIN.**
Jeanne. . . . . .Solveig Dommartin
Lucien. . . . . .Philippe Clevenot
Henri. . . . . .Henri Serre
Renee. . . . . .Aurore Prieto
Superiorin. . . . . .Helene Surgere
Biquette. . . . . .Anna Acerbis
Odette. . . . . . . .Emmanuelle Chaulet

■ A woman's futile struggle to find justice in the extremes of both Christian and Communist creeds is filmed as if her life story absolutely must be told. Pic, a bit too long but eloquently recounted, should be especially well-received in eastern bloc countries where numerous tales of such personal and political quests are bound to surface.

Jeanne begins her conscientious search in the '60s as a nun. Thesp Solveig Dommartin's sensuality and defiance befits the inevitable failure of that short celibate chapter.

On the rebound, heroine gets a monotonous job operating a machine in a nonunion factory run by condescending businessmen. When one of Jeanne's coworkers is fatally injured by a faulty machine, her conscience drives her to lobby the other women to fight for improved working conditions. Her colleagues are justifiably afraid of losing their jobs, and the undiplomatic Jeanne has her thankless work cut out for her.

Jeanne's love life isn't much more successful. Her affair with Lucien screeches to a disastrous halt when he dies unexpectedly. This scene is terribly overdramatized and ridiculously edited (Jeanne runs repeatedly down the hospital corridor), an effect which flaws pic's steady flow. Reaction also is very out-of-character for Jeanne, who is more of a bulldozer than an emotional sop.

Nonetheless, Jeanne becomes even more committed to organizing rallies and demonstrations, but falls short of success once again. Twenty years later, she's managed to alienate everyone including her closest women comrades and suicide seems the only possible solution.

In the current times of crumbling frontiers and merging political theories, this pic is very dated. However, its 1960-80s span is also its strength: text ''documents'' a fading era.

Very grainy images suit the conquer-the-oppressor theme. Dommartin's strong acting carries the film through all its ideological twists and turns, a few of which could be tightened to make pic shorter. Length is a problem for tv but not for homevid where pic should find a second life in Europe. — *Suze.*

Tom et Lola
(Tom And Lola)
(FRENCH)

Paris An AFMD release of a Cinemanuel/ Cerito Films/Caroline Prods./EFVE Films/ Orly Films/Zoom 24 coproduction. Produced by Alain Belmondo, Gerardé Crosnier. Directed by Bertrand Arthuys. Screenplay, Arthuys, Christian de Chalonge, Muriel Teodori, Luc Goldenberg. Camera (Eastmancolor), François Catonné; art direction, Michèle Abbé-Vannier; sound, Guillaume Sciama, François Groult; editor, Jeanne Kef; music, Christophe Arthuys; casting, Francine Cathelain. Reviewed at Gaumont Ambassade theater, Paris, Feb. 1, 1990. Running time: **94 MIN.**
Tom. . . . . .Neil Stubbs
Lola. . . . . .Melodie Collin
Helen. . . . . .Cecile Magnet
Dr. Vaneau. . . . . .Marc Berman
Catherine. . . . . .Catherine Frot
Robert. . . . . .Celian Varini

■ This fable is about two 9-year-olds living in plastic bubbles because they've been diagnosed as lacking natural immunity to disease. Ex-assistant director Bertrand Arthuys' first feature has an interesting premise that is worked out without sustained charm or mystery. Pic failed locally and has no ostensible prospects abroad.

Script follows the nocturnal escapades of the androgynous Tom and Lola, naked and hairless, as they find out how to leave their bubbles and explore the aseptic, strangely empty clinic. Ostensibly, their vulnerability is a medical sham because their health and high spirits remain unimpaired. They finally escape the clinic with dreams of reaching Alaska, which symbolizes the purity and natural ambience they've missed.

François Catonné's lensing and Michèle Abbé-Vannier's art direction create the appropriate aquarium-like climate of emotional sterility and seclusion. Neil Stubbs and Melodie Collin are okay as the bubble children but never engage the audience on an empathetic level. Adult cast is less fortunate in caricatured roles.

This is recently founded Cinemanuel's second production. Firm is headed by former production managers Alain Belmondo (brother of Jean-Paul Belmondo, who put coprod money into the film) and Gerard Crosnier, who clicked with 1988 debut feature ''Chocolat.'' —*Len.*

Kuduz
(YUGOSLAVIAN)

Berlin An FRZ Bosna Film (Sarajevo)-Avala Film (Belgrade) coproduction. Directed by Ademir Kenovic. Screenplay, Abdulah Sidran, Kenovic; camera (Eastmancolor), Mustafa Mustafic; editor, Christel Tanovic; music, Goran Bregavic; production design, Milenko Simic; production manager, Bakir Tanovic. Reviewed at Berlin Film Festival (Panorama section), Feb. 20, 1990. Running time: **100 MIN.**
Becir Kuduz. . . . . . . .Slobodan Custic
Badema. . . . . . . .Snezana Bogdanovic
Brzahler. . . . . .Abdulah Sidran
Amela. . . . . .Ivana Legin
Alija Goro. . . . . .Branko Diric
Salem Pilav. . . . . .Bozo Bunjevac
Semso. . . . . .Mustafa Nadarevic
Safet. . . . . .Sasa Petrovic
Anja. . . . . .Radmila Zivkovic

■ Yugoslavia has a large Muslim minority, mostly living around Sarajevo, but few films, apart from those by Emir Kusturica, have explored these communities. Ademir Kenovic, in his first film, tells a straightforward tale about a Muslim living in a small village. Pic could interest fests.

Kuduz was imprisoned for seven years for wounding Semso, a policeman (who was demoted, suggesting he was also at fault). Released, Kuduz has to start his life again, and marries Badema, a waitress, even though she's an unmarried mother and doesn't know the name of the child's father. Their wedding is interrupted by a drunken Semso, who has to be overcome.

Married life is blissful at first, though Kuduz gets increasingly jealous of the easygoing Badema's men friends. Meanwhile, he tries to set up his own building company.

Kenovic depicts these people with sympathy and insight, though more orthodox Muslims would be outraged at some of the scenes: Badema never wears a veil, smokes a lot and flirts with other men, and is seen naked on her wedding night.

Lead actors are convincing in their roles, and the picture is well made though lacking any real surprises. Ademir Kenovic obviously has a feel for the subject and characters, and could come up with a stronger vehicle next time around.

Technically, the film is marred by faulty lab work resulting in an unhealthy yellow tone that dominates throughout. — *Strat.*

The Fourth War

New York A New Age Releasing (Cannon/ Pathé) release of a Kodiak Films presentation. Produced by Wolf Schmidt. Executive producers, William Stuart, Sam Perlmutter. Directed by John Frankenheimer. Screenplay, Stephen Peters, Kenneth Ross, based on Peters' novel; camera (Alpha Ciné color; Deluxe prints), Gerry Fisher; editor, Robert F. Shugrue; music, Bill Conti; sound (Dolby), Ganton/Trudel; production design, Alan Manzer; costume design, Ray Summers; production manager, Les Kimber; assistant director, Don French; 2d unit director-line producer, Robert L. Rosen; associate producer, Harry Bloom, Frank Spolar; casting, Bette Chadwick. Reviewed at Broadway screening room, N.Y., Feb. 26, 1990. MPAA Rating: R. Running time: **91 MIN.**
Col. Jack Knowles. . . . . .Roy Scheider
Col. Valachev. . . . . .Jürgen Prochnow
Lt. Col. Clark. . . . . .Tim Reid
Elena. . . . . .Lara Harris
Gen. Hackworth. . . .Harry Dean Stanton
Sgt. Major. . . . . .Dale Dye
M.P. Corporal. . . . . . .Bill MacDonald

■ Events in Eastern Europe

have overtaken "The Fourth War," a well-made Cold War thriller about private battling that might escalate out of control. Foreign prospects are better than U.S. for this John Frankenheimer effort.

Opening title sets the tale in November 1988 on the border of Czechoslovakia and East Germany. Roy Scheider is well-cast as a hardline colonel who's caused nothing but trouble in his career and is now stationed at a post near the border by his general, Harry Dean Stanton.

Soon after taking his new post, Scheider witnesses the murder of a fleeing defector through no man's land. He rightly blames the Soviet colonel (Jürgen Prochnow) for this dastardly deed and even throws a snowball at him in anger.

From this minor act of outrage ensues a man-to-man feud of Laurel & Hardy proportions, involving blowing up Scheider's jeep, and singlehanded invasions of each other's country by the worked-up colonels. Scheider's second in command, Tim Reid, brings a note of sanity to the proceedings, but even his reports to Stanton and Stanton reading the riot act to Scheider fail to halt the hostilities.

Things finally come to a head when Lara Harris, as a Czech working in West Germany who needs help to return home to her child, comes between the two Cold Warriors.

Tightly directed by Frankenheimer with an eye for comic relief as well as tension maintenance, "The Fourth War" holds the fascination of eyeball-to-eyeball conflict. It's not exactly "Hell In The Pacific," but with the shading provided by Scheider and Prochnow on their surface-unsympathetic characters, the film holds its grip.

Problem, as with another Cold War tale "The Hunt For Red October," is simply that an audience can no longer readily feel the imminent danger of WW III in a period of thaw. The chills of a Frankenheimer classic like "Seven Days In May" can't be generated by such an outlandish fable. Instead, one can vicariously enjoy a battle of dinosaurs, hardliners (and there are plenty of them still with us in both the East and West) who still view the world in simplistic us vs. them terms.

Besides the two stars, Reid is very effective as the man on the spot (his commanding officer is

out of control), and Harris is convincing as a duplicitous femme fatale. Gerry Fisher's lensing (on Calgary-area locations adequately subbing for Europe) is fluid and especially striking in night scenes, while Bill Conti's rousing score keeps one's pulse running.

Title refers to an Albert Einstein quote: The third world war may involve nuclear weapons, but the fourth will be fought with stones. — *Lor.*

Dancin' Thru The Dark
(BRITISH)

London A Palace Pictures and British Screen presentation of a BBC Films and Formost Films production. Executive producers, Richard Broke, Chris Brown, Charles Negus-Fancey, Nik Powell, Steve Woolley. Produced by Andree Molyneux, Annie Russell. Directed by Mike Ockrent. Screenplay, Willy Russell; camera (color), Philip Bonham-Carter; editor, John Stothart; music, Willy Russell; production design, Paul Joel; sound, Peter Edwards; costumes, Laura Ergis; casting, Ann Fielden. Reviewed at 20th Century Fox Preview Theater, London, Feb. 27, 1990. Running time: **95 MIN.**

Linda	Claire Hackett
Peter	Con O'Neill
Maureen	Angela Clarke
Eddie	Mark Womack
Bernadette	Julia Deakin
Kav	Simon O'Brien
Frances	Louise Duprey
Billy	Andrew Naylor
Carol	Sandy Hendrickse
Robbie	Peter Watts

Also with: Colin Welland, Peter Beckett, Conrad Nelson, Julian Littman, Ben Murphy.

■ Hard on the heels of his success with "Shirley Valentine," writer Willy Russell has again returned to his native Liverpool with a gritty low-budget comedy, which offers a fine cast of young British talent and an attractive debut by helmer Mike Ockrent.

Pic is unashamedly parochial, but Russell's growing rep could help, even though realistic overseas returns may be limited.

Pic started life as the play "Stags And Hens" in 1978 and though expanded to accommodate the big screen format, retains many stage-bound aspects, especially the male and female toilets where much of the action takes place.

Russell stamps his presence throughout the film, writing the script, composing the music and lyrics and even taking on a cameo role. Most of the Liverpudlian cast have been in Russell plays before, while tyro film helmer Ockrent directed the original West End and

U.S. stage versions of Russell's "Educating Rita."

Pic's great strength, as with "Rita" as well as "Shirley," is the biting dialogue, and the recurring theme of a strong female character debating the prospect of escape to a better life.

The strong femme role in "Dancin' Thru The Dark" is Linda (Claire Hackett), who is out on the town with friends on the night before her wedding. Unfortunately her hubbie-to-be and his friends also end up at the same nightspot.

Arriving back in Liverpool for a gig is now successful popster Peter (Con O'Neill), Claire's ex-boyfriend. His friends in the band can't believe the seedy side of Liverpool ("Like Beirut without the sun," comments one) and the bad news is they're signed to perform at that same nightspot.

Pic traces the two groups as they set about getting drunk and preparing for an evening of dancing and debauchery. In one amusing scene the girls — bar Claire — are all issued condoms, with the ever optimistic older girl Bernadette (Julia Deakin) keeping three.

First half of the film is out and out comedy, but when Linda starts talking to Peter, seeds of doubt are sown about whether she should get married and more importantly whether she should stay in Liverpool. All her friends battle to convince her to stay and get married, but she eventually makes a run to escape them and the prospect of a dreary life.

"Dancin' Thru The Dark" is a true ensemble piece. On a certain level, the varied characters are perfectly drawn by Russell, but because the cast is large, only Linda and Peter are given any depth. That leaves just tantalizing glimpses of what the others have to offer.

All of the young actors are excellent and instill their roles with a good deal of character. Topcast leads Hackett and O'Neill are fine and are certainly names to watch, while Russell makes an attractive cameo appearance as "pub drunk" in one of the opening scenes.

Ockrent makes a confident feature debut and is especially good at handling the large crowd scenes inside the nightclub Branskys, where much of the pic is set. He gets the best out of the young cast, and even the set-piece music scenes don't look awkward as they often do in many pics.

Pic is an amusingly accurate look at Liverpool lifestyles amongst the young and aimless, and while the transition from humor to drama is a bit uncomfortable — maybe due to some rough editing — and the premise that escape to London is a better bet than Liverpool is a bit naive, "Dancin' Thru The Dark" is ultimately a satisfying and enjoyable work. It would be interesting, though, to next see Russell examine the eventual reality of his female characters' "escapes." — *Adam.*

Harbour Beat
(AUSTRALIAN-BRITISH)

Sydney A Zenith presentation of a Palm Beach Picture in association with Australian Film Finance Corp. (Intl. sales: The Sales Co., London.) Produced by David Elfick, Irene Dobson. Directed by Elfick. Screenplay, Morris Gleitzman; camera (Eastmancolor), Ellery Ryan; editor, Stuart Armstrong; music, John Stuart; sound, Paul Brincat; production design, Michael Bridges; production managers, Catherine Knapman, Charles Salmon (Glasgow); assistant director, Colin Fletcher; casting, Christine King. Reviewed at Colorfilm screening room, Sydney, Feb. 23, 1990. Running time: **99 MIN.**

Neal McBride	John Hannah
Lance Cooper	Steven Vidler
Gavin Walker	Gary Day
Constable Mason	Emily Simpson
Det-Sgt. Cimino	Bill Young
Andrew De Santos	Tony Poli
Mrs. De Santos	Peta Toppano
Simone	Angie Milliken
Allie Muir	Jeannette Cronin
Bazza	Christopher Gummins
Beaumont	Ken Radley
Carol Walker	Rhondda Findleton
Secretary	Mercia Deane-Jones
Cabbie	Allan Penney

■ "Harbour Beat" is a formula cop/buddie pic, but it's far more rooted in reality than the cartoon fantasies of Yank actioners like the "Lethal Weapon" pics or "Tango & Cash." Commercially, this will prove to be both a blessing and a curse.

David Elfick, the established Aussie producer ("Newsfront," "Starstruck," "Around The World In 80 Ways"), turns his hand to direction with positive results. He's made a well-paced, entertaining yarn significantly more intelligent and witty than the norm. Morris Gleitzman's screenplay is good though the basic idea of two cops from different backgrounds forming an unlikely partnership is familiar.

The pic is unusually enjoyable because the characters are well-written and well-played. John

Hannah is a find as a zealous cop from Glasgow, Scotland, who's transferred to sunny Sydney and partnered with a surf-loving, laid-back local. In this role, Steven Vidler also makes his mark.

Vidler was previously partnered with a retired cop (Gary Day), who quit the force to go into real estate. Before long it becomes evident that Day was up to his ears in a scam involving a shady real estate man (Tony Poli), who plants drugs on properties ripe for development and then blackmails the owners into selling.

Elfick includes all the required ingredients of the genre, mixing suspense with romance and humor, and building up to a tense climax high up in a derelict warehouse. Stuntwork is good, but the emphasis is on character and suspense rather than violent action.

This will endear the film to audiences seeking something more than the average shoot-'em-up, but the first half of the film might play slowly for fans seeking more traditional action fare. These scenes establish Hannah's background in Glasgow (filmed on location there), his arrival in Sydney, his teaming with Vidler, and his acquisition of a beachside apartment, fancy car and masseuse girlfriend (Angie Milliken).

In addition to the leads, Gary Day is impressive as the crooked ex-cop. Bill Young, an immensely tall actor, is amusing as the detective sergeant distracted because of his unmarried daughter's unwanted pregnancy. Emily Simpson is a smash as an attractive but acid-tongued woman cop with ambitions for career and private life.

Other well-etched characters include Vidler's chatty cousin (Christopher Gummins), a gourmet plumber, and Peta Toppano (star of Elfick's "Fields Of Fire" vidseries), who does what amounts to a cameo as Poli's drug-addicted wife.

Technically, "Harbour Beat" is seamless. Ellery Ryan's great camerawork makes Sydney look sumptuous, Stuart Armstrong's editing is sharp, and Michael Bridges' production design spot-on.

Yank audiences may be put off by the relative lack of action, but the film should be appreciated in other territories, especially Britain and Australia. A miniseries spinoff is also indicated since audiences are likely to warm to the characters.

Elfick makes his move to the director's chair with confidence and style. He delivers an entertaining package that pumps new life into a tired formula. — *Strat.*

Corps perdus
(Lost Bodies)
(FRENCH-ARGENTINE)

Paris A Films de l'Atalante release of a Films de l'Atalante/DB Films/La Sept/SGGC/ Jorge Estrada Mora Producciones (Buenos Aires) coproduction. Executive producer, Gérard Vaugeois. Produced by Ricardo Freixa. Directed by Eduardo de Gregorio. Screenplay, De Gregorio, Suzanne Schiffman, Charles Tesson, with the collaboration of José Pablo Feinman, Roberto Scheuer; camera (Eastmancolor); Maurice Giraud, José Maria Hermo; editor, Nicole Lubtchansky; music, Gustavo Beytelman; sound, Bernard Aubouy, Dante Amoroso, Bernard Leroux; art direction, Emilio Basaldua; costumes, Mariana Polski; makeup, Mirta Blanco, Oscar Mulet; assistant director, Charles Tible. Reviewed at the Cinema Latina, Paris, Feb. 19, 1990. Running time: **92 MIN.**
Laura Canetti/Letizia Fiume.Laura Morante
Eric Desange/Juan Bax. . . .Tcheky Karyo
Carlos Mateoli. . . . . . .Gerardo Romano
Rafael Braun. . . . . . . .Georges Claisse
Mother. . . . . .Lucrecia Capello
Librarian. . . . . .Osvaldo Bonet

■ **A bilingual coprod between France and Argentina, this slick little melodrama was co-written and directed with a sure sense of atmosphere by Eduardo de Gregorio, an Argentine-born, Paris-based filmmaker best known for the scripts he wrote for Jacques Rivette.**

It's a good supernatural yarn that will no doubt appeal to specialized venues and genre fests.

Pic makes baroque use of literary motifs and conventions borrowed from Oscar Wilde, Borges, Robert Louis Stevenson and the classic gothic horror tale. It has a mysterious mansion, ghosts, hidden doors and secret corridors, a painting with supernatural influences and a drama of doubles.

Story begins in contemporary Buenos Aires where a French art historian and restorer (Tcheky Karyo) has been summoned to identify a painting, an unknown work of a once obscure but brilliant artist Karyo has championed. Painting's owner is a beautiful young architect (Laura Morante) who hopes to sell the canvas to finance a real estate deal on the site of the mansion she has inherited from her recently deceased mother.

But as Karyo, alone in the attic of the mansion, begins to remove the layers of the paint that have hidden the original work (a portrait of Morante's diva grandmother), he begins to suffer hallucinations that revive a morbid, violent past that encroaches on Karyo and Morante.

Karyo begins to see himself as the painter Bax, a hideously scarred artist of brutish temperament. Bax was desperately in love the beautiful singer, who resembles Morante and rejects his advances. Present mirrors past and eventually is displaced by it when the troubled art historian begins an affair with Morante, who later finds herself reenacting her grandmother's drama and the tragedy that takes the life both of painter and art historian.

Gregorio and his (Gallic) cowriters, Suzanne Schiffman and Charles Tesson, contrive a sophisticated game of mirrors and labyrinths which is given a flamboyantly decadent mounting. José Maria Hermo's lensing, Emilio Basaldua's art direction, Nicole Lubtchansky's editing and Gustavo Beytelmann's tango strains contribute to the hypnotic ambiance.

The lovely Morante and the feral Karyo, in a Jekyll/Hyde composition, are good in difficult, somewhat artificial double roles. Use of alternating French and Spanish dialogue between the principals subtly underlines the schizophrenic sense of foreboding. — *Len.*

Skyddsängeln
(The Guardian Angel)
(SWEDISH-B&W)

Malmö, Sweden A Sandrew Film release of Mekano Pictures production with Sandrew Film, the Swedish Film Institute, Filmhuset, SVT-2. Produced by Anders Birkeland. Directed by Suzanne Osten. Screenplay, Osten, Madeleine Gustafsson, Etienne Glaser, based on Ricarda Huch's novel "Der Letzte Sommer;" camera (b&w), Göran Nilsson; editor, Michal Leszczylowski; music, Frans Schubert, Richard Wagner, Boboul Ferkousad, Sten Kjellman; sound (Dolby), Ulf Darin, Klas Engström; production design/costumes, Mona Theresia Forsén; production management, Kaska Petras (Sweden). Gotfried Talboom (France). Reviewed at the Metropol, Malmö, Sweden, Feb. 28, 1990. Running time: **94 MIN.**
Jacob. . . . . .Philip Zandén
Joel Birkman. . . . . . . .Etienne Glaser
Livia Birkman. . . . . .Malin Ek
Welja. . . . . .Björn Kjellman
Katja. . . . . .Gunilla Röör
Jessica. . . . .Lena Nylén
Hanna. . . . . .Hanna Hartleb
Ivar. . . . . .Tuncel Kurtiz
Maria Demodov. . . . . .Pia Baeckström

Also with: Reuben Sallmander, Sven Lindqvist, Lars Wiik.

■ **"The Guardian Angel," a political thriller successfully merged with social comedy, depicts the conflicts of conscience arising when an idealistic assassin hires on as secretary/bodyguard to his designated victim, a government minister. A fine future on the international fest and arthouse circuit can safely be predicted for this one.**

With Göran Nilsson's expertly lit and adroitly moving cinematography imbuing the story with visual delights, film also portrays early 20th century upper-class family life in careful, often absurdist, nuance. Any initial satiric intent mellows into congenial sympathy as the action proceeds.

Were it not for some bombastic, symbolic interpolations of newsreel shots of violent demonstrations, "The Guardian Angel" might easily take its place alongside the comic work of Ingmar Bergman. Maybe Michal Leszczylowski's editing, so perfect in its enhancing of narrative rhythms, could have scissored these propaganda inserts.

Based on a 1910 novel by Germany's Ricarda Huch, who used prerevolutionary Russia as her locale, film is made to take place "anywhere and at any time," but clearly takes place at the turn of the century in some rural Swedish idyll (shades of "Smiles Of A Summer Night"). Joel Birkman (Etienne Glaser) has taken temporary refuge with his family after having beaten down a student revolt and jailed its leader, who is sentenced to death.

Once installed in the Brinkmans' elegant mansion, black-clad Jacob (Philip Zandén) gradually unbends to the sensual delights of a home where father may be a tyrant, but a benevolent one. Although an archsupporter of the political establishment, he lends an understanding ear to revolutionary ideas.

Birkman remains unruffled in office, in bedroom and most everywhere else, even if he does seem wary of his secretary's real identity. The politician knows that he is powerless against evolution, but that it is his duty to stem revolution. He argues his points well in conversations at elegant dinners while his wife lives her nights and days in more or less controlled terror.

The family's three grown children often join with their father in the playing of chamber music. Every family member is seen as a fullfledged individual, far beyond caricature. There is a lot of erotic byplay in their pursuits of pleasure during this enforced summer holiday, and Jacob is literally given more than a tumble. For awhile it even looks as if both the minister and the phony secretary may steer their own fates in other directions than those designed for them.

Director Suzanne Osten ("The Mozart Brothers") has her own regular troupe of film and stage actors. In the center as the minister, Glaser, who cowrote the screenplay with Osten and Madeleine Gustavsson, is fragile physically but exudes the unrelenting will of a professional politician along with a fine sense of the ludicrous in matters public and private.

Malin Ek generates poetic *angst* in her role as Birkman's tightly wound-up wife. As stern but temporarily malleable Jacob, Zandén has a zealot's tension fighting with temptation to play along with his social uppers, adding shades of light and charm to his dark, brooding mask.

This trio, a sextet including Björn Kjellman, Gunilla Röör and Lena Nylén as the young adult children, emulates a kind of Mozartian musicianship in witty movement and speech. Alone or in interplay, they create a near-operatic sense of cinematic acting.

The empathy between director, thesps and cinematographer resounds in every carefully composed frame. — *Kell.*

The Haunting Of Morella

Detroit A Concorde release. Produced by Roger Corman. Directed by Jim Wynorski. Screenplay, R.J. Robertson; camera, Zoran Hochstatter; editor, Diane Fingado; music, Fredric Nesign Teetsel, Chuck Cirino; production designer, Gary Randall; associate producers, Alida Camp, Rodman Flender. Reviewed at AMC Americana Theater, Southfield, Mich., Feb. 22, 1990. MPAA Rating: R. Running time: **87 MIN.**

Gideon	David McCallum
Morella/Lenora	Nicole Eggert
Guy	Christopher Halsted
Coed	Lana Clarkson
Diane	Maria Ford
Dr. Gault	Jonathan Farwell
Miles Archer	Brewster Gould
Ilsa	Gail Harris
Judge	Clement Von Franckenstein
Rev. Ward	R.J. Robertson
Serving girl	Debbie Dutch

■ Nudity, lesbianism, softcore sex, beer barrel-breasted babes: "The Haunting Of Morella" has it all. But that's still not enough to give this predictable, dull rendering of an Edgar Allan Poe tale much life at the boxoffice. Its chances on the crowded homevideo shelf are about the same.

Perhaps it was very warm in Poe's time. That might explain why so many people in "The Haunting Of Morella" keep taking their clothes off.

And maybe Fredericks of Hollywood got its start back in the days when witches were burned at the stake. That would explain some of the outfits in this horror film that lacks horror, pacing or compelling story.

"Haunting" begins with Morella (Nicole Eggert) pinned, crucifixion-style, to a stake as a crowd of witch-haters cheers on her death. Morella vows to return, and sure enough, 17 years later, she starts to come back with the help of the governess of her daughter Leonora (also Eggert).

The governess is one of several buxom beauties with whom Gideon (David McCallum), Morella's husband, has surrounded himself. She is also one of those people in this film who finds frequent excuses to take her clothes off; taking a bath, having a swim, getting ready to retire for the night, etc.

The governess' job is to bring victims to Morella's tomb, so they can be killed and their spirits used to revitalize Morella's decaying skeleton.

Meanwhile, Morella's spirit decides to invade her daughter's body and check things out. One of the things she checks out is attorney Guy Chapman (Christopher Halsted), who has taken a liking to Leonora.

This possession gives Eggert a chance to switch back and forth between the evil Morella and the innocent Leonora. It's clear when Morella is taking over because Eggert drops her head, then looks up with a sneer on her face. These scenes may be method acting, and they are clearly cheapo special effects.

That's right in keeping with the rest of the frugal makeup and special effects in this pic.

The best thing that can be said about David McCallum's performance is that it makes the audience want to, well, cry U.N.C.L.E.
— *Advo.*

Tong Tana — En Resa Till Borneos Inre
(Tong Tana — A Journey To The Heart Of Borneo)
(SWEDISH-DOCU)

Berlin A Swedish Film Institute presentation of Roed Krusenstjerna Film production with SVT-2, the Swedish Institute, TV2 Danmark, the BBC, Bayrische Rundfunk. Written and directed by Jan Roed, Frederik von Krusenstjerna, Bjoern Cederberg, Kristiian Petri; camera (Eastmancolor), Roed; lighting, Bjoern Ryd; editor, Michal Leszezylowski with Carina Hellberg; music, Harold Budd, Brian Eno; sound (Dolby), Ragnar Samuelsson; narration, interviews, Bjoern Cederberg. Reviewed at Berlin Film Festival (market), Feb. 19, 1990. Running time: **88 MIN.**

■ "Tong Tana" has a strong environmentalist message, plus visual and technical credits of a high artistic order.

Item's quick pickup by many Berlin marketeers (Seymour Wishman's First Run Features for the U.S.) may well be rewarded with some initial first-window distribution.

Pic's Swedish production collective is not the first to trace and meet Switzerland's Bruno Manser, who has lived for the past six years as a more or less natural member of the Bornean rainforest's Penan nomadic tribe. Nobody, however, has done either Manser, a clean-shaven, softspoken 34-year-old, or the poisoned-arrow hunters' justice in so balanced a way.

In film's first two thirds, Manser and the Penans and their life in the rainforest are seen as unhurried and happy, humans in nearly absolute harmony with nature. The beauty of the people under their tall trees is caught in rain and shine by stunning cinematography, sound that captures even the breathing of monkeys and rustle of leaves, and editing paced to perfection.

At its present rate, the logging of Borneo is expected to kill the rainforest of the world's third largest island by the mid-'90s. Thus, it was necessary for the filmmakers to also watch the bulldozers at work and to listen, in film's final third, to both sides in confrontations between the Malaysian government and Friends of the Earth.

Fortunately, "Tong Tana" avoids the stridency of propaganda in favor of letting everybody speak their piece. That includes the government spokesman, environment minister/logging concession owner James Wong, who is sticking his own head in a noose by mouthing platitudes, though the editing may have given that impression. — *Kell.*

Superstar
(DOCU)

Los Angeles A Marilyn Lewis Entertainment Ltd. presentation. Produced, written and directed by Chuck Workman. Executive producer, Marilyn Lewis. Coexecutive producer, Peter English Nelson. Production executive, Stephen Kern. Camera (CFI color), Burleigh Wartes; editor, Workman; line producer, James Cady; production coordinator, Jennifer McGonical; sound, Samantha Heilweil; associate producer, Larry Green; research director, Jessica Berman Bogdan; postproduction supervisor/assistant editor, Carol Streit. Reviewed at the Writers Guild theater, L.A., Feb. 24, 1990. No MPAA rating. Running time: **85 MIN.**

■ "Superstar" is an uneven documentary portrait of Andy Warhol which suffers most from what the late art celebrity himself points out early on: "Just look at the surface. . .and there I am. There's nothing behind it."

Still, public's persistent fascination with the Warhol enigma should bring these reels their 15 minutes of fame on the specialized circuit.

Pic, which world-preemed to soldout houses at the Berlin Film Fest, begins at a very engaging clip, with veteran documaker Chuck Workman applying his clever compilation skills to a barrage of ironic vidclips from the tv news that illustrate the pull of the pop culture from which Warhol spun his ideas, while sliding in biographical info via tv obits of the artist.

Ahead of that, there's an art-making sequence that shows printmakers turning out silkscreens of Warhol to the seductive pulse of Blondie's hit "Heart Of Glass."

But when pic gets down to biographical business, it turns a bit mundane, with nothing much to enliven relatives' fond remembrances of their Andy except Workman's irreverent editing.

Further on, there is much redundancy, and film dwells overlong on the unremarkable circumstances of Warhol's death in 1987 after routine surgery.

A sequence built around Warhol's famous soup can paintings, with interviews with execs and workers at the Campbell's soup factory, is amusing at first but overplayed.

A few moments of drama are

provided midway, with footage mostly from tv news of Warhol's near-fatal shooting in 1968 by the radical founder (and sole member) of the Society for Cutting Up Men (SCUM).

More interesting to the majority of viewers will be interviews with the wits, wags and exotic creatures Warhol knew, though none seemed to know him very well.

"I was just passing through —I was never close to any of these people," says rocker Lou Reed, whose music underscores much of the footage culled from the Factory, Warhol's creative center in New York City.

Interviewees also include Factory-ites Viva and Ultra Violet, actor Dennis Hopper, writer Fran Lebowitz and eccentric Taylor Mead, who recalls how hard it was for Warhol's creative collaborators to shake any coin out of him. It's virtually the only criticism of him in the docu.

Various people speculate on Warhol's elusive sexuality, all concluding they don't really know. "I think his turn-on was his connection to the sexual charisma of the stars," says Shelley Winters.

Of Warhol's obsession with celebrity, one wag quips, "Andy was everywhere. He would go to the opening of a drawer."

Pic traces the evolution of Warhol's enterprises from fashion drawings to fine arts to the founding of Interview magazine. Gallery owners contribute self-serving raves about the importance of his work and their early recognition of it.

Warhol's strikingly unusual films are given a light going-over, with a split screen used to unspool two at once.

The artist himself is present mostly in clips from disarming but maddening interviews in which he amiably gave 1-word answers to elaborate questions.

"I'm a commercial person," he says in footage explaining the directions his work took. "I've got a lot of mouths to feed. Gotta bring home the bacon."

Undecided whether to enshrine the artist or refuse to be taken in by his games, "Superstar" lacks edge. Its approach most resembles description Tom Wolfe gives of Warhol's influence: "He showed artists that you can have your cake and eat it too — you can wallow in (America's) excess and still be superior to it because you're mocking it." Ditto this film. — *Daws*.

Kurt Olsson — filmen om mit liv som mejsjälv (Kurt Olsson — The Film About My Life As Myself) (SWEDISH)

Malmö, Sweden A Svensk Filmindustri release and production. Produced by Waldemar Bergendahl. Directed by Hakan Wennberg. Screenplay by Wennberg and Lasse Brandeby; camera (Eastmancolor); editor, Thomas Täng; music, Elisabeth Engdahl; production design, Folke Strömbäck; sound, Christian Gyllensten; costumes, Gunilla Henkler, Britt-Marie Larsson; production management, Christer Nilsson, Magnus Stenberg. Reviewed at the Palladium, Malmö, Sweden, Feb. 28 1990. Running time: **95 MIN.**

Kurt Olsson, age 7	Joel Cederholm
Kurt as teen	Lasse Brandeby
Kurt as adult	Lasse Brandeby
Olle Olsson	Lasse Brandeby
Asta Olsson	Anki Rahlskog
Gun	Ulla Skoog
Arne Nyström, age 7	Tobias Olofsson
Arne as teen	Hans Wiktorsson
Arne as adult	Hans Wiktorsson
Arne's father	Hans Wiktorsson
Shipyard manager	Per Oscarsson

Also with: Ellenor Svensson, Elsie Rahlskog, Kent Andersson, Inger Hayman, Unni Brandeby, Thomas Nystedt, Gerd Hegnell, Harald Lönnbro, Ulf Dageby.

■ Having padded the wildly popular crazy tv antics of Swedish "brothers" Kurt and Lasse with plenty of production values, writer-actor Lasse Brandeby and helmer Hakan Wennberg deliver a plotless farce with tragic undertones that is unlikely to raise a chuckle with anybody but domestic couch potatoes.

Big, hulking and grim Kurt Olsson (played with deadpan conviction by Brandeby who also doubles as Olsson senior, while little Joel Cederholm as junior's son is all playful charm) is followed from literal birth, seen from inside his mother's womb, and up through grade school, army service, wedding to his ugly-duckling admirer and on to fatherhood and a self-destructive career as a phony shipbuilder.

What is funny about Kurt is that he never takes himself anything but dead seriously whether combing his hair in a futile effort to look like Bill Haley, his rock era hero, or coming on as a military zealot wreaking havoc while on guard duty. He is deaf to criticism and efforts to save him from the predicaments his outright stupidity plunges him into. This makes him the total survivor.

Such fun soon wears thin, however, when it has no plot; only a series of skits and an eventual void in which to function. It does not help that tv comedy partner Arne (Hans Wiktorsson) is allowed to pop up only occasionally and in a less than supportive role. Veteran dramatic actor Per Oscarsson plays his cameo with punch and precision, and as Kurt's paramour, Ulla Skoog is the hilarious epitome of powerless but persistent passion.

The tragedy of Kurt's one-track-mindedness comes through best in the sequences where Brandeby plays his own father, a fascist in streetcar conductor's clothing.

While Kurt himself is seen partly as a hapless victim, the father is a thoroughbred s.o.b. of no mitigating traits whatsoever. It is a truly evil pleasure to be in his company, which momentarily puts Brandeby in a class with Peter Sellers' Inspector Clouseau and the combined characters of John Cleese.

In Sweden, as anywhere else, the transition of a series and its characters from tv to the big screen is fraught with danger.
— *Kell*.

Positiv (Positive) (WEST GERMAN-DOCU)

Berlin A Rosa von Praunheim Filmproduktion, with WDR. Directed by Rosa von Praunheim. Screenplay, von Praunheim; camera (color), Mike Kuchar, Evan Estern, Elfi Mikesch; editor, Mike Shepard, von Praunheim; sound, Mark Milano, Klaus Klingler. Reviewed at Berlin Film Festival (Panorama section), Feb. 16, 1990. Running time: **90 MIN.**

(English soundtrack)

■ "Positive" is the first of three feature-length docus about the AIDS epidemic made in the U.S. by German director Rosa von Praunheim. As such it will be widely seen and used by everyone interested in the subject, but probably by few others.

Von Praunheim features a number of key AIDS activists, including writer Larry Kramer, founder of a self-help group, who makes extraordinary accusations against former New York mayor Ed Koch), and docu film director Phil Zwickler ("Rights and Reactions"). Also featured is singer Michael Callen, one of the longest survivors of AIDS.

Von Praunheim provides sobering statistics and interviews men who blame former President Ronald Reagan and Koch for the way the virus has spread, asserting they failed to act because the disease seemed at first to affect only the homosexual community.

At one point Zwickler half-jokingly tells the audience, "He (von Praunheim) wants me to die on camera," but this isn't a voyeuristic film, rather an angry and informative one.

Some hardcore gay footage would have to be trimmed before the film is aired on most tv stations around the world. — *Strat*.

Pretty Woman

New York A Buena Vista release of a Touchstone Pictures presentation, in association with Silver Screen Partners IV, of an Arnon Milchan production. Produced by Milchan, Steven Reuther. Executive producer, Laura Ziskin. Directed by Garry Marshall. Screenplay, J.F. Lawton; camera (Technicolor), Charles Minsky; editor, Priscilla Nedd; music, James Newton Howard; sound (Dolby), Jim Webb; production design, Albert Brenner; art direction, David Haber; set decoration, Garrett Lewis; costume design, Marilyn Vance-Straker; production manager, Roger Joseph Pugliese; assistant director, Ellen H. Schwartz; 2d unit director-associate producer, Walter Von Huene; coproducer, Gary W. Goldstein; casting, Dianne Crittenden. Reviewed at National 2 theater, N.Y., March 15, 1990. MPAA Rating: R. Running time: **117 MIN.**

Edward Lewis	Richard Gere
Vivian Ward	Julia Roberts
James Morse	Ralph Bellamy
Philip Stuckey	Jason Alexander
Kit De Luca	Laura San Giacomo
Hotel manager	Hector Elizondo
David Morse	Alex Hyde-White
Elizabeth Stuckey	Amy Yasbeck
Elevator operator	Patrick Richwood
Mr. Hollister	Larry Miller
Bridget	Elinor Donahue

Also with: William Gallo, Hank Azaria, Larry Hankin, R. Darrell Hunter, Dey Young, Stacy Keach Sr., Lucinda Sue Crosby, Nancy Locke, Amzie Strickland.

■ **Julia Roberts delivers a star-making performance in Disney's crowd-pleasing romantic comedy "Pretty Woman." Despite its obvious flaws, Garry Marshall's sentimental pic hits the right emotional targets to shape up as a monster hit.**

J.F. Lawton's formula screenplay owes plenty to "Pygmalion," "Cinderella" and "The Owl And The Pussycat" in limning a fairy tale of a prostitute with a heart of gold who mellows a stuffy businessman.

Pic's first two reels are weak, as corporate raider Richard Gere is unconvincingly thrown together with streetwalker Julia Roberts when he seeks directions to Beverly Hills while driving a sports car borrowed from his lawyer, Jason Alexander.

Roberts shows him how to drive the Cobra and soon inveigles her way into his penthouse hotel suite. Seducing this reluctant john, she's improbably hired by Gere to spend the week with him as escort since he's split up with his girlfriend and has big dinners on tap with shipbuilder Ralph Bellamy, his takeover target. Her price tag is $3,000; film's cryptic shooting title was "3000."

Fortunately for Marshall and the viewer, film blossoms along with Roberts at around the 30-minute mark, when she doffs her unflattering Carol Channing blond wig to get natural and embark on a massively entertaining (and class conscious) shopping adventure on Rodeo Drive.

Roberts handles the transition from coarse and gawky to glamorous with aplomb, aided by Marilyn Vance-Straker's appropriate costuming. Pic climaxes somewhat unconvincingly with previously unscrupulous Gere suddenly turning into Mr. Nice Guy and deciding to team up with Bellamy "to build boats together" instead of stealing his company. Industryites will note the cute parallel to Disney's own salvation and expansion following a Texan white knight's intervention six years ago. Act III is a bit corny as the inevitable parting leads to a predictable fairy tale ending for Roberts.

Pic's casting is astute, with Gere underplaying like a sturdy ballet star who hoists the ballerina Roberts on his shoulders. Underlying tastelessness of the material is diffused by placing the sex scenes mainly off screen, keeping nudity to a bare minimum and contriving that Gere is the sex object on screen, notably in a bathtub scene together.

Sexiest routine is almost identical with a "Fabulous Baker Boys" vignette: Gere playing solo jazz piano late at night in the hotel ballroom and joined for a tryst by Roberts.

Supporting cast is outstanding. Hector Elizondo, a regular in all of Marshall's features, takes the Alan Mowbray-style hotel manager role to understatedly set up (and steal) a dozen scenes with precise comic timing. Laura San Giacomo is perfect as Roberts' roommate and voice of prostie experience. Larry Miller is hilarious improvising comebacks when Gere takes Roberts shopping in his store, and Patrick Richwood does terrific takes as the elevator operator who sees all.

Lavish production is glossy and properly unrealistic. Roy Orbison title hit song is played twice to good effect. — *Lor.*

A Shock To The System

New York A Corsair Pictures release. Produced by Patrick McCormick. Executive producer, Leslie Morgan. Directed by Jan Egleson. Screenplay, Andrew Klavan, based on Simon Brett's novel; camera (Duart color), Paul Goldsraith; editor, Peter C. Frank, William A. Anderson; music, Gary Chang; sound (Dolby), Danny Michael; production design, Howard Cummings; art direction, Robert K. Shaw Jr.; set decoration, Robert J. Franco; costume design, John Dunn; production manager, Carl Clifford; assistant director, Amy Sayres; additional camera, Ken Ferris; associate producer, Alice Arlen; casting, Mary Colquhoun. Reviewed at Corsair screening room, N.Y., March 12, 1990. MPAA Rating: R. Running time: **87 MIN.**

Graham Marshall	Michael Caine
Stella	Elizabeth McGovern
Robert Benham	Peter Riegert
Leslie Marshall	Swoosie Kurtz
Lt. Laker	Will Patton
Melanie	Jenny Wright
George Brewster	John McMartin
Lillian	Barbara Baxley
Tara	Haviland Morris
Henry Park	Philip Moon

■ **"A Shock To The System" is a very dark comedy about escaping the current rat race via murder. Unsympathetic, poorly motivated central character and flat direction nullify Michael Caine's reliable thesping, spelling tepid b.o. for fledgling distrib Corsair's first release since "Miss Firecracker" a year ago.**

Caine is cast as a Britisher working for a N.Y. firm who's passed over for the post of marketing department head when John McMartin (in an affecting performance) is forced to take early retirement. Upstart Peter Riegert (way too sympathetic for the role) gets the job instead and starts throwing his weight around.

Caine is also fed up with his wife Swoosie Kurtz' habits, but Andrew Klavan's script (based on Simon Brett's novel) fails to motivate Caine's sudden turn to cold-blooded murder.

After doing away with Kurtz by rigging faulty electric wiring in the basement, he blows up Riegert (and obnoxious assistant Philip Moon) on his sailboat. Plodding Connecticut cop Will Patton discovers plenty of clues (a cigaret lighter lost by Caine is given inordinate screen time in a vain attempt to drum up suspense), but inexplicably is unable to nail the obviously guilty antihero.

Film's easy targets allow an undemanding audience to vicariously enjoy killing one's boss or nagging spouse, but events are unbelievable and thereby uninvolving. A key early scene of a beggar seemingly killed in the subway by Caine is clumsily staged and confusingly resolved. Jan Egleson's direction slows to a snail's pace during the middle reels and lacks the style of the classics in this genre: "Monsieur Verdoux" by Charles Chaplin and "Kind Hearts And Coronets" by Robert Hamer.

Despite script deficiencies, Caine almost pulls it off with a nasty turn (replete with James Cagney-isms) reminiscent of his early '70s "Get Carter" persona. His third-person voiceover narration further distances the already cold action, acting in an opposite matter to his "Alfie" intimate asides. Elizabeth McGovern is effective as his romantic interest, with Jenny Wright appealing in an underwritten role as her roommate.

Paul Goldsmith's lensing of N.Y. locations is functional and pic is punched up considerably by the catchy use of amplified acoustic bass in Gary Chang's score.
— *Lor.*

Driving Force
(AUSTRALIAN)

New York A J&M Entertainment presentation of an Eastern Film Management production. Executive producers, Antony I. Ginnane, Marilyn Ong. Produced by Howard Grigsby, Rod Confesor. Directed by A.J. Prowse. Screenplay, Patrick Edgeworth; camera (Philippine Information Agency and Cinevex Color), Kevan Lind, Richard Michalak; editor, Tony Paterson; music, Paul Schutze; sound, Paul Wyhowski; production design, Toto Castillo; assistant director, Soc Jose; production manager, Anna Maria Dans; second unit directors, Grigsby, Grant Page; associate producer, Mike Fuller; casting, Rosemary Welden. Reviewed on Academy Entertainment vidcassette. N.Y., Feb. 19, 1990. MPAA Rating: R. Running time: **90 MIN.**

Steve O'Neil	Sam J. Jones
Harry	Catherine Bach
Nelson	Don Swayze
Pete	Ancel Cook
Becky	Stephanie Mason
Pool	Billy Blanks
John	Gerald Gordon
Leslie	Renata Scott

■ **"Driving Force" is a contrived action pic that fails to whip up the populist sentiment of '70s trucker pics.**

Direct-to-video pic was shot in the Philippines by Aussie filmmakers, with several supporting players dubbed with American accents. Its foreign origins are betrayed when an all-American girl calls the bad guys "bikeys," Australian slang instead of the U.S. term bikers for motorcycle types.

Sam J. Jones gets a job driving a tow truck to earn a living and keep custody of his daughter. Unscrupulous fellow tow-truckers led by evil Don Swayze are causing accidents and strong-arming innocent folks to drum up business. When Jones interferes, a boring vendetta begins.

Film founders due to a series of idiotic, almost impossible coincidences in the final reels, all designed to pile *tsouris* on Jones until he gets mad and gets even.

Jones is okay in this standard issue role, with Catherine Bach adding some glamor as his girlfriend (she's also convincing in the action scenes). Swayze, Patrick's near lookalike brother, goes through the motions as the cardboard villain. — *Lor.*

Ripoux Contre Ripoux
(My New Partner 2)
(FRENCH)

Paris An AMLF release of a Films 7/Orly Films/Sedif/TF 1 Films coproduction. Produced and directed by Claude Zidi. Screenplay, Zidi, Simon Michael, Didier Kaminka; camera (color), Jean-Jacques Tarbes; sound, Jean-Louis Ughetto, William Flagollet; editor, Nicole Saunier; music, Francis Lai; art direction, Françoise Deleu; assistant director, Denis Seurat; production manager, Pierre Gauchet. Reviewed at the UGC Normandie Theater, Paris, Feb. 6, 1990. Running time: **107 min.**

Rene.	.Philippe Noiret
François.	.Thierry Lhermitte
Brisson.	.Guy Marchand
Simone.	.Line Renaud
Natasha.	.'Grace de Capitani
Commissioner Bloret.	.Michel Aumont
Portal.	.Jean-Pierre Castaldi
Banker.	.Jean-Claude Brialy
Cesarini.	.Jean Benguigui

■ The new adventures of Claude Zidi's cheeky Paris cops, the "ripoux" (slang for dishonest policemen), took off like a shot at local wickets and has fine prospects in markets wherever the first pic scored.

Pic's progenitor ("My New Partner") cleaned up in theaters in the 1984-85 season, grabbed César awards for best picture and director, and exported well. In the new pic, it's more of the same with inevitably less novelty and more convention but the same blithe (and slightly grating) cynicism about corruption as a social norm. Audiences won't feel they've been taken for a ride, though, in this slick cop versus cop comedy-cum-farce, whose title translates literally as "Ripoux Versus Ripoux."

Producer-director Zidi has rounded up most of the cast and crew of the original. His coauthors are again Didier Kaminka, whose dialog is cocky yet believably mundane when it has to be, and Simon Michael.

The latter, a retired cop turned screenwriter, was undoubtedly responsible for the wealth of detail that gave the first "Ripoux" an uncharacteristically convincing texture for a comedy and an edge on more seriously intended but less credible crime fights. There's less of that realism here.

Nonetheless, Michael's contribution may have largely to do with the importance of urban geography in the screenplay. Once again the action is set largely in the police territory of Paris 18th *arrondissement.*

However, center of activity has shifted from the sordid immigrant melting pot of the Goutte d'Or to the more middle-class heights of Montmartre. Two of the funniest scenes (one involving the zigzagging flight and arrest of a panicky robber) are based on a street-smart knowledge of the area's serpentine high and low topography.

Philippe Noiret and Thierry Lhermitte are back in fine form. They're still padding out their meager salaries with bribe-taking, petty racketeering and shakedowns of small-time felons and corrupt "honest" citizens.

Both still share their beds with gold-hearted hookers. Lhermitte has the blond, gracious Grace de Capitani; Noiret an over-the-hill pro, played by music hall star Line Renaud (succeeding nightclub luminary Regine in the original).

Only snag is that Lhermitte, the once-idealistic rookie corrupted by the veteran Noiret, is suffering a relapse of honesty. He even announces his intention to try for a promotion to commissioner. This change of heart naturally horrifies the cynical Noiret, whose passion for horses and the racetrack remains ruinously unabated.

Ironically, it's Lhermitte's first (and only) good deed that undoes them both. Exposed by a zealous anticorruption police crusader and denounced by their "clientele," the tandem find themselves relieved of their duty.

Their replacements, Guy Marchand and Jean-Pierre Castaldi, prove even more corrupt than their predecessors, and the treacherous clientele, now contrite, beg their former "protectors" to take back their turf.

This sequel lacks the freshness of the first film. The characters, pretty much fixed by the end of "Les Ripoux," don't grow or change significantly, and the plotting is somewhat mechanical.

But there are enough brisk comic highlights to keep the story moving and a climactic double-cross gag in a bank vault is a classic. Zidi handles it all with technical skill.

As in "Ripoux 1," it's really Noiret who creates much of the film's pleasure with his irresistible characterization of a lovable rogue that will always be the mainstay of any future "Ripoux" spinoffs. There are sure to be more if all the principals are willing.

Delightful supporting cast includes Jean-Claude Brialy as a guilt-ridden banker, Michel Aumont as the police chief and Jean Benguigui as the owner of a Montmartre strip joint.

Zidi has also retained his fine technical unit, including lenser Jean-Jacques Tarbes, editor Nicole Saumier (who also took a César for the first "Ripoux"), art director Françoise de Leu and composer Francis Lai. — *Len.*

The Witches

London A Warner Bros. release of a Lorimar Film Entertainment presentation of a Jim Henson Prods. film. Executive producer, Jim Henson. Directed by Nicolas Roeg. Screenplay, Allan Scott, based on the book by Roald Dahl; camera (color), Harvey Harrison; editor, Tony Lawson; music, Stanley Myers; production design, Andrew Sanders. Reviewed at 20th Century Fox preview theater, London, U.K., March 13, 1990. MPAA Rating: PG. Running time: **92 MIN.**

Miss Ernst/	
Grand High Witch.	.Anjelica Huston
Helga.	.Mai Zetterling
Luke.	.Jasen Fisher
Mr. Stringer.	.Rowan Atkinson
Mr. Jenkins.	.Bill Paterson
Mrs. Jenkins.	.Brenda Blethyn
Miss Ernst's assistant.	.Jane Horrocks

■ The combination of the wizardry of Jim Henson's creature shop and and a superbly over-the-top performance by Anjelica Huston gives Nicolas Roeg's "The Witches" a good deal of charm and enjoyment. Problem is, it's a toughie for distribs.

Pic is too sophisticated for the children's market but also not quite right for older audiences. Pic was shot in Norway and the U.K. in summer 1988 and had a limited release in the U.S. earlier this year.

Roeg shows a more restrained touch — during shooting he admitted he wanted to make the pic mainly because he had just become a father and wanted to try his hand at a children's film — due to the formal nature of the movie's structure. But he shows the old Roeg' touches with some clever camera angles as well as working easily with the special effects.

"The Witches" opens in Norway where grandmother Helga (Mai Zetterling) is telling her 9-year old grandson Luke (Jasen Fisher) about witches and their wicked ways. Witches, it seems, have purple eyes, are bald (so they wear wigs) and have square feet! His parents die in a car crash, and Luke and grandmother travel to England for a holiday.

They go to a stark Cornish hotel. Also checking in is the annual ladies meeting of the Royal Society for the Prevention of Cruelty to Children; in actual fact a meeting of the British witches, due to be addressed by the Grand High Witch, Huston. Young Luke accidentally overhears the meeting where Huston announces her grand plan to feed poisoned chocolate to all British children, which will turn them into mice. Luke gets captured and is forced to drink the magic potion. As a mouse he manages to escape their clutches and begins the tortuous journey up to his grandmother's room.

She and Luke cook up a plot to spoil the witches' plan. He steals a bottle of the potion, scampers into the kitchen and pours the poison into the soup being served to the witches. They turn into mice and are set upon by waiters and the angry hotel manager Rowan Atkinson (doing a fine impression of John Cleese's Basil Fawlty).

Back at their English home, Luke has just got used to the idea of spending the rest of his days as a mouse when a good witch, Jane Horrocks, who was originally Huston's assistant but quit, casts a spell to make Luke into a boy again. True to tradition, everybody lives happily ever after.

In a tight black dress and vampish haircut, Huston seems to enjoy herself as the evil chief witch, and in fact the pic seems to be merely plodding along until she arrives on the scene.

Swedish actress/director Zetterling, in her first time in front of the camera for more than 15 years, adds a nice counterbalance as the slightly doddery grandmother and old adversary of the witches. American Jasen Fisher shows the right amount of boyish enthusiasm, while the supporting cast of British character actors are fine.

As always Jim Henson's animatronics and makeup are excellent. Huston in her full witch makeup is a frightening sight, while rightly Henson's team have avoided making the animatronic mice look sickly sweet. The Luke/mouse is endearingly brave, though there is a note of sadness when he gets part of his tail chopped off.

Tech credits are top notch. "The Witches" is the work of a sensible Roeg; no convoluted flashbacks or sultry sexuality, but a controlled and suitably dark piece of filmmaking that marks an interesting change of direction for the usually controversial Englishman. — *Adam.*

Nikita
(FRENCH-ITALIAN)

Paris A Gaumont release of a Gaumont production/Cecchi Gori Group Tiger Cinematografica coproduction. Written and directed by Luc Besson. Camera (Eastmancolor), Thierry Arbogast; editor, Olivier Mauffroy; music, Eric Serral; sound (Dolby), Pierre Befvre, Gérard Lamps; art direction, Dan Weil; production manager, Jérome Chalou. Reviewed at the Gaumont Ambassade theater, Paris, Feb. 22, 1990. Running time: **115 MIN.**
Nikita. . . . . .Anne Parillaud
Marco. . . . . . . .Jean-Hugues Anglade
Bob. . . . . .Tcheky Karyo
Amanda. . . . . .Jeanne Moreau
Victor. . . . . .Jean Reno
Also with: Philippe du Janerand, Roland Blanche, Philippe Leroy-Beaulieu, Marc Duret, Jacques Boudet.

■ After the waterlogged mysticism of "The Big Blue," Gaumont's wonderboy director Luc Besson is back on terra firma in "Nikita," already nicknamed "The Big Black." It's an absurd, shrill, ultraviolent but soft-centered urban thriller about a pretty, young, cop-killing junkie who's re-educated as a crack secret service agent, with license to kill.

The local cult success of "The Big Blue" will probably keep "Nikita" out of the big red, but fans will not find the qualities that had them coming back for repeated viewings of the former. Foreign prospects are not rosy.

Nikita is Anne Parillaud, a punk drug fiend who survives a police assault when her mad-dog band burgles a neighborhood pharmacy. Sentenced to life imprisonment for having cold-bloodly executed one of the cops, Parillaud is drugged and wakes up in a cell where she is offered a second chance by Tcheky Karyo, an intelligence officer in charge of her training.

After some more violent antisocial behavior, Parillaud buckles under and agrees to play by the rules. She becomes an elite sharpshooter, specializing in public assassinations of undesirable foreign elements.

Parillaud seems resigned to her fate until she meets Jean-Hugues Anglade, an easygoing, affectionate supermarket cashier whom she picks up, romances and shacks up with. The idyll is complicated by the facade she must maintain — he thinks she's a nurse — and the dangerous periodic assignments. One such mission takes both Parillaud and Anglade to Venice for an apparent vacation, which is a cover for another cold-blooded execution.

Besson gets sole credit for the screenplay so he alone is to blame for the genre platitudes, the inconsistent characterizations and the unbelievable action highlights. Though the basic premise already makes suspension of disbelief difficult (why should a government intelligence service recruit a spaced-out delinquent, even if she does show unlikely and unexplained ability with firearms?), the film falls apart, along with the totally unnerved heroine, during a botched espionage mission in a foreign embassy.

Besson's bloated direction, relieved only occasionally by humor (and not always in the best taste), emphasizes the poverty of the confection. The pitched gun battles and pursuits, heavily underscored by Eric Serra's thumping rock track, are graphically violent to a gratuitous and sometimes sadistic degree.

Parillaud (a.k.a. Madam Besson) does her frenetic best to make Nikita something resembling a human being. But she remains a totally uninteresting figment of Besson's blinkered movieland imagination, especially when she's in the company of Karyo and Anglade, who provide balance to her overacting.

Jeanne Moreau provides a touch of class in a small role as over-the-hill agent who tutors Parillaud in feminine graces. Jean Reno, a Besson faithful, plays a killer with stone-faced parodic panache. Tech credits are glossy in the usual Besson manner. — *Len.*

The Krays
(BRITISH)

Hollywood A Rank release (foreign; no U.S. distrib) of a Parkfield Entertainment presentation of a Fugitive Features production. Produced by Dominic Anciano, Ray Burdis. Executive producers, Jim Beach, Michele Kimche. Directed by Peter Medak. Screenplay, Philip Ridley; camera (color), Alex Thomson; editor, Martin Walsh; music, Michael Kamen; sound, Godfrey Kirby; production design, Michael Pickwoad; costume design, Lindy Hemming; makeup, Jenny Boost; stunt arranger, Stuart St. Paul; assistant director, Michael Zimbrich; associate producer, Paul Cowan; casting, Noel Davis. Reviewed at American Film Market, L.A., Feb. 27, 1990. Running time: **119 MIN.**
Violet Kray. . . . . . . .Billie Whitelaw
Ronald Kray. . . . . .Gary Kemp
Reginald Kray. . . . . . . .Martin Kemp
Rose. . . . . .Susan Fleetwood
May. . . . . .Charlotte Cornwell
Cannonball Lee. . . . . . . .Jimmy Jewel
Helen. . . . . .Avis Bunnage
Frances. . . . . .Kate Hardie
Charlie Kray Sr.. . . . . . .Alfred Lynch
Jack (The Hat) McVitie. . . . . .Tom Bell
George Cornell. . . . . . .Steven Berkoff
Steve. . . . . .Gary Love
Mr. Lawson. . . . . .Victor Spinetti
Mrs. Lawson. . . . . . . .Barbara Ferris
Judy. . . . . .Julia Migenes

■ A chilling, if somewhat monotonous, biopic charting the rise and fall of two prominent hoods in 1950s-60s London, cockney lads whose psychosexual warping leads them into ultraviolence, "The Krays" is an unusual film that should shoot up strong b.o. in the U.K. this fall (via Rank). Stateside, it could do some biz as well (no U.S. distrib as yet).

Screenwriter Philip Ridley deftly explores the cynical amorality of the us-vs.-them lower-class milieu, and the destructive effect of smothering mom Billie Whitelaw (in a superb performance) on her sociopathic twins, while virtually ignoring the standard cops-and-robbers dramaturgy of gangster films.

As the Krays, the brothers Kemp, who both had considerable acting experience before beginning their rock careers in Spandau Ballet, are just right in their deadeyed portrayal of what a rival thug calls "a pair of movie gangsters." Indeed, they are among the most repellent gangsters to come along since Richard Widmark pushed an old lady in a wheelchair down the stairs in "Kiss Of Death."

Like a 2-headed fetus seen by the lads in a jar at a freak show, the Krays share a quasi-incestuous relationship that leads Ron into a displaced homosexual union and an intense envy of Reg's doomed attempt to reach beyond his lowlife milieu by marrying a middle-class girl (the touching Kate Hardie).

Director Peter Medak, who knew the Krays when he was an a.d. and they provided protection on the locations of Joan Littlewood's "Sparrows Can't Sing" in 1962, works skillfully with lenser Alex Thomson, production designer Michael Pickwoad and composer Michael Kamen to conjure up a cold and eerie atmosphere.

In the supporting cast, Susan Fleetwood is a standout as the boys' doting aunt, with an overwhelming monolog near the end of her life that reveals the despair she has so carefully concealed.

Also giving expert characterizations are man-hating granny Avis Bunnage, timid aunt Charlotte Cornwell, eccentric grandpa Jimmy Jewel, weakling dad Alfred Lynch, and reckless gangsters Tom Bell and Steven Berkoff. — *Mac.*

Strand Under The Dark Cloth
(CANADIAN-DOCU)

Montreal A John Walker Prods. film. Produced and directed by John Walker. Written by Walker, with Findlay and Tom Perlmutter; camera (color), Walker; editor, Cathy Gulkin, John Kramer, Geoff Bowie; sound, Aerlyn Weissman, Jean-Pierre Delorme, David Springbett, Bob Withey; music, Jean Drome assisted by Rene Lussier; associate producers, Tom Perlmutter and Anne Koyama; Reviewed at Intl. Festival of Films on Art, March 6, 1990. Running time: **81 MIN.**
Voice of Paul Strand. . . . . . .Paul Soles
Voice of Cesare Zavattini. . .Harvey Atkin

■ A beautifully crafted, thoroughly researched and intimately recounted docu on the life, art and avant-garde films of the late American photographer Paul Strand, pic is ideal fare for photography and film schools, clubs, festivals and special venues for art aficionados.

Via Walker's probing, but never intrusive, camera, oodles of details emerge about Strand's techniques, his habits, his inspirations based in "social reality," his three wives, and his one devotion: to take pictures of his immediate surroundings.

Per docu, Strand established himself in New York in the 1920s as a master of light and structure with his now famous photo of Wall Street, inspired by the forms and movement of Euro modernist painters such as Matisse and Picasso. Closeups of Strand's pics of poverty-stricken folk in Manhattan are equally profound.

Amusing stories told by his second and third wives pepper this serious portrait with comic relief, and offer insight into a photographer who believed that taking pictures isn't all that important: "It's what it is you have to say about the world that matters."

Walker uses interviews with Strand's collaborators such as Italian neorealist scriptwriter Cesare Zavattini ("Bicycle Thief") to explain the man's talent; not to hype the company he kept.

Dashes of humor lace other interviews, such as that of Fred Zinnemann who noted that when Strand was making docus, Hollywood defined a documentary as "a film without a woman in it."

Strand made "anti-fascist" docus in Mexico and Spain before tackling the issue of the Ku Klux Klan in the U.S.. A pic ("Native Land") which was released "the day after Pearl Harbor" and was consequently lost in the wind, signalling the end of Strand's short-lived cinematic career.

Walker made a concerted effort to ensure his own camerawork is as stunning as Strand's photos, and for the most part succeeds. Simple editing and personalized commentary give docu a distinctly unmanipulative, sometimes plodding, but ultimately genuine credibility.

Pic has no commercial potential but will undoubtedly win critical acclaim in photography and film circles for its content and methodology. Homevid also looks dismal, but there's some potential for educational tv outlets. — *Suze.*

The Great Wall of China: Lovers At The Brink (BRITISH-DOCU)

Montreal A Viz Ltd. production. Directed by Murray Grigor. Screenplay, Grigor, Marina Abramovic, Ulay; camera (color, 16m), Douglas Campbell; editor, Grigor. Reviewed at Intl. Festival of Films on Art, March 11, 1990. Running time: **65 MIN.**
With: Juna Chang (narration), Marina Abramovic, Ulay.

■ **Document of a novel concept where two lovers walk from opposite ends of the Great Wall of China to meet at a given point is more original than engaging. Pic could easily be trimmed to fit a 1-hour format for educational tv, its obvious venue.**

Packaged as a film inside a film, their meeting is used as an example of an ancient Chinese myth. An old woman holds an outdoor screening where the cur-

rent story unspools for a group of children.

Pic and the walk itself come off as a labor of love, an obsession, an unparallelled adventure. The landscape of China's remotest areas indirectly becomes the film's focus due to lack of action and human contact.

As a unique farewell to their 12-year relationship, Marina Abramovic begins her 2,000-kilometer walk at the "head of the dragon" (the Great Wall's nickname), and Ulay begins his 2,000-kilometer jaunt at the "tail." They trudge through desert (where parts of the wall are buried), up and down mountains (where the wall is disintegrating), past the restored segment, and on to Shenmu, the designated meeting place.

Their walk is intentionally filmed in real time. No sensationalism. No frills. Several imaginary sequences involving ancient Chinese dancers liven up the pace occasionally, but pic generally lacks zip.

Earnest narration gives a blow-by-blow description of their feelings every step of the way during their isolated trek, where for the most part, villagers and hermits blend in with the desolate landscape. When they finally meet, scene lacks the tension it could easily have had.

Pic slips into finale where the old Chinese woman takes down her makeshift movie screen and reminds the children it's only a myth. — *Suze.*

Ay Carmela! (SPANISH-ITALIAN)

Madrid An Iberoamericana Films (Madrid) and Ellepi (Rome) coproduction, in association with Television Espanola (RTVE). Executive producer, Andres Vicente Gomez. Directed by Carlos Saura. Screenplay, Saura, Rafael Azcona, based on book by Sanchis Sinisterra; camera (Eastmancolor), Jose Luis Alcaine; editor, Pablo G. del Amo; music, Alejandro Masso; sound, Guilles Ortion; production design, Rafael Palmero; production manager, Victor Albarran; makeup, Jose Antonio Sanchez. Reviewed at Cine Capitol, Madrid, March 15, 1990. Running time: **103 MIN.**
Carmela. . . . . .Carmen Maura
Paulino. . . . . .Andres Pajares
Gustavete. . . . . .Gabino Diego
Lieut. Ripamonte. . . . .Maurizio de Razza
Also with: Jose Sancho, Mario Candia, Miguel Angel Rellan, Edward Zentara, Antonio Fuentes.

■ **Carlos Saura returns to the subject of the Spanish Civil War, but this time with a touch of wry humor. Item boasts mem-**

orable performances by **Carmen Maura and Andres Pajares as two thesps caught on the front between the reds and the fascists. Pic should have wide popular appeal, despite some of the "in" references and situations.**

Pic zigzags from humor to pathos to buffoonery to tragedy, and the sardonic touch of coscripter Rafael Azcona is evident throughout. Evidently, it is the fascists who come in for all the ribbing (the Italian fascists are cast as operatic buffoons, in contrast to the fanatic Spanish nationalists), but pic is essentially nonpolitical.

Though Saura again discharges his spleen against Franco, the personal drama and ideals of the three itinerant thesps is the uppermost theme, as they try to wriggle out of threatening dilemmas and adapt to the fascist ideologies in order to survive.

Pic opens on the Aragon front in 1938, near the end of the war, when matters are already very bad in the republican camp. Carmela and Paulino put on a show to entertain the ragged troops, she doing a sexy dance, he a comic number, suitably vulgar for the rude soldiers. The musical accompaniment is provided by a young, mute bumpkin whom they have picked up in their wanderings.

Realizing that the war is drawing to a close, Carmela and Paulino decide to drive to Valencia. One foggy morning they suddenly find themselves in the midst of a nationalist column. Though they protest that they are merely traveling players, a Republican flag used in their show incriminates them, and they are hauled off to the small town where the nationalists have set up h.q.

After first being herded in with Polish prisoners from the international brigades and other "reds," some of whom are summarily executed, the two thesps manage to ingratiate themselves with an Italian officer who wants to put on a patriotic entertainment.

This give Azcona and Saura leave for some poignant humor, a few amusing musical numbers, and ultimately an unexpected finale as the two thesps grapple, Paulino following a basic instinct for survival, Carmela standing up for her beliefs.

Andres Pajares, a well-known stand-up comic heretofore working mostly in local comedies, makes an auspicious bow in his superb

performance as the adaptable survivor. Maura is outstanding as Carmela, and Babino Diego delightfully awkward as the mute.

Pic is punctuated with catchy songs from the period, from both bands, including the popular "Ay, Manuela" (from which title of pic was adapted.) Usual superb lensing by Alcaine, fine editing, good production values and skillful direction by Saura, who finally seems to be back on the right track.
— *Besa.*

The Forbidden Dance

Hollywood A Columbia Pictures release of a 21st Century Corp. and Menahem Golan presentation. Produced by Marc S. Fischer, Richard L. Albert. Directed by Greydon Clark. Executive producers, Golan, Ami Artzi. Screenplay, Roy Langsdon, John Platt, from a story by Joseph Goldman; camera (Panavision, Foto-Kem color), R. Michael Stringer; editor, Robert Edwards, Earl Watson; music, Vladimir Horunzhy; sound (Ultra-Stereo), Jan Eric Brodin; production design, Don Day; art direction, Frank Bertolino; set decoration, Shirley Starks; costume design, Susan Bertram; assistant directors, Paul Martin, Jeff Shiffman, Jessica Levin; choreography, Miranda Garrison, Felix Chavez; casting, Ted Warren, Gennett Tondino. Reviewed at Mann Westwood, L.A., March 16, 1990. MPAA Rating: PG-13. Running time: **97 min.**
Nisa. . . . . .Laura Herring
Jason. . . . . .Jeff James
Ashley. . . . . .Barbra Brighton
Mickey. . . . . .Miranda Garrison
Joa. . . . . .Sid Haig
Carmen. . . . . .Angela Moya
Benjamin Maxwell. . . . . .Richard Lynch

■ **Hot as the lambada dance may be or become, it's hard to imagine an audience exists for this pic, except for those who savor unintentional hilarity or yearn to hear the song "Lambada" until their ears bleed.**

The film does possess cult potential, since it's bad to the point of absolute giddiness. Any pic where a mother protests, "I do not want my son involved with an Indian princess from the jungle" almost demands to be seen to be believed.

The unfortunate twist on "Forbidden Dance" is that it seeks to disguise its effort to cash in on lambada by masquerading as a social-conscience film. Pic makes a pitch for saving the Amazon rainforests where a leggy princess (Laura Herring) and her dancin' tribe are being threatened by a multinational conglomerate.

So what does the princess do? She takes off to Los Angeles to try to stop the company, hooks up with a Beverly Hills rich kid (Jeff

James) and finds the solution to all her problems: television.

If Nisa and Jason (or as she calls him, Jace-own) can win a big dance contest and get on tv, then she can tell everyone about her tribe's plight and that will solve everything — if, that is, they can survive the scheming of Jason's petty ex-girlfriend (Barbra Brighton) and the company's leering "troubleshooter" (Richard Lynch).

That the performances are dreadful doesn't come as a big surprise, but even the dancing isn't particularly hot. Herring, a former Miss USA in her motion pic debut, is lovely and exotic, with a radiant smile and extremely pliable hips. Still, her hopelessly contrived pairing with James doesn't generate enough heat to melt an ice cube.

The focal point of the unintentional laughs, however, is Nisa's witch doctor escort Joa (Sid Haig), who specializes in strange noises and devilish looks. When he scopes out Jason's Beverly Hills home, the howls drown out most of the dialog, which isn't a big loss.

Like the wave of films that accompanied the emergence of rap and "Flashdance" imitators like "Footloose," "Forbidden Dance" won't amount to much domestically unless the lambada becomes the sensation here it's been elsewhere. Whatever the chances of that, this pic won't do anything to help the cause.

Tech credits are unspectacular, with ho-hum choreography and little innovation shooting the dance sequences. Costumers have a field day outfitting Herring's frame, though the script and direction ultimately leave her all dressed up with no place to go. — Bril.

Il male oscuro
(The Obscure Illness)
(ITALIAN)

Rome An Artisti Associati release of a Clemi Cinematografica production. Produced by Giovanni Di Clementi. Directed by Mario Monicelli. Screenplay, Suso Cecchi D'Amico, Tonino Guerra, based on Giuseppe Berto's novel; camera (color), Carlo Tafani; editor, Ruggero Mastroianni; music, Nicola Piovani; art direction, Franco Velchi; production manager, Domenico Lo Zito. Reviewed at Rivoli Cinema, Rome, March 8, 1990. Running time: **114 MIN.**
Giuseppe Marchi. . . . .Giancarlo Giannini
Wife. . . . . .Emmanuelle Seigner
Girlfriend. . . . . . . .Stefania Sandrelli
Psychiatrist. . . . . . . .Vittorio Caprioli

■ **Mario Monicelli's "The Obscure Illness" illustrates the pleasure of watching solid professionality and intelligence at work. Pic has done little business at local wickets, but should have a run in other European situations. It could be a fest candidate.**

Giuseppe Marchi (a frazzled, middle-aged Giancarlo Giannini) is a scriptwriter pressed for cash, struggling to finish an absurd screenplay on Judas Iscariot for a harried Roman producer. His father dies. Pic opens with a flashforward to Giuseppe on shrink Vittorio Caprioli's couch, denying his dreams about his father.

A sly comic tone gives otherwise familiar happenings an edge of sophistication. Giuseppe leaves girlfriend Stefania Sandrelli for a 17-year-old blond (Emmanuelle Seigner) he meets at a taxi stand. The girl, who is quite an armful, throws herself into his bed, gets pregnant, and drags him to the altar.

Meanwhile, Giuseppe has his first attack of a hysterical illness. Rushed to the hospital, he's operated on for a perforated ulcer, but after opening him the doctors can find nothing the matter. Another one diagnoses a floating kidney, sending the imaginary invalid into a spate of body braces.

Marriage to pretty Seigner calms him down for years. Then, while his family is on vacation, he has another "attack" and starts seeing a psychiatrist. More years pass. The day he finally announces he's cured, his wife informs him she's had a long-standing affair. Giuseppe abandons his home and opts for lonely isolation on a bare patch of land in Calabria.

Giannini puts a heavy note of weariness under the outward Roman frenzy of the neurotic intellectual, able neither to sell out nor to get past chapter one on his novel. Seigner is a surprise as the child-wife, who grows up as the years pass, selfish but in her own way also self-sacrificing.

Sandrelli makes a sympathetic ex. Her brief return at pic's end is a melancholy coda. Caprioli is one of the screen's most likeable shrinks, keeping to the spirit of understated humor that pervades "Obscure Illness," a tone that recalls Italo Svevo.

Monicelli walks sure-footed on a tight screenplay by Suso Cecchi D'Amico and Tonino Guerra, who adapted Giuseppe Berto's far-ranging novel without going out of cinematic bounds. Professional standards are more than upheld by Franco Velchi's sets, Carlo Tafani's cinematography, and Nicola Piovani's score. — Yung.

Lambada

Hollywood A Warner Bros. release of a Cannon Pictures production in association with Film and Television Co. Produced by Peter Shepherd. Directed by Joel Silberg. Screenplay, Silberg and Sheldon Renan, based on a story by Silberg; camera, Roberto D'Ettore Piazzoli; editor, Marcus Manton; sound (Dolby), Bill Robbins; music, Greg DeBelles; music supervisor, Seth Kaplan; soundtrack executive producer, Dick Griffey; choreography, Shabba-Doo; production design, Bill Cornford; art direction, Jack Cloud; assistant director, Sanford Hampton; second unit directors, R.M. Schroeder, Robert Bralver; casting, Ed Mitchell. Reviewed at Hollywood Pacific Theater, L. A., March 16, 1990. MPAA Rating: PG. Running time: **98 min.**
Kevin. . . . . .J. Eddie Peck
Sandy. . . . . .Melora Hardin
Ramone. . . . . .Shabba-Doo
Dean. . . . . .Ricky Paull Goldin
Supt. Leland. . . . . . . .Basil Hoffman
Uncle Big. . . . . . . .Dennis Burkley
Principal Singleton. . . . . .Keene Curtis

■ **Theatrical playoff for this one should be swift, as it doesn't take a calculator to figure out that "Lambada's" peripheral dance segs don't add up to $7 worth of lambada. Still, director/cowriter Joel Silberg keeps the story lively on a cartoonish-level, and pic should entertain patrons even if it doesn't quite deliver what the posters are selling.**

Warner Bros.' distrib investment in this exploitation quickie rides on how many tix can be sold before word gets out that it's about a "Stand And Deliver"-type math teacher who does his dirty dancing on the side. J. Eddie Peck plays the Beverly Hills teacher by day, East L.A. lambada dancer by night, his sculpted dancer's physique straining the credibility of this most unlikely of teen fantasy scenarios.

The blue-eyed protagonist has as many names as he has identities. He's called "Blade" at the lambada club, where he wears an earring and black leather; Kevin Laird at school, where he wears glasses and a tie; and he was Carlos Gutierrez in an earlier life as a poor, orphaned immigrant, before he was adopted by Anglo parents and found his gospel: that education is the road to success.

In the pic, Blade forgoes evenings at home with his wife and son to motorbike over to the lambada club where he teaches math in the back room to a gang of east side dropouts who want to pass their high school diploma equivalency tests.

First, though, he gains their admiration on the dance floor, where for some unexplained reason he's got the hottest moves around.

His lambada prowess intrigues one of his B.H. highschoolers, sexually precocious Sandy (Melora Hardin), who stumbles onto the scene and sets out to seduce or blackmail him, unaware of his real, noble reason for leading this double life.

The dancing occupies little screen time compared to the sudsy intrigue Sandy stirs up on the school front, and what lambadaing there is is photographed mostly in tight titillating shots that lack context and reflect minimal effort in choreography.

Blade's dance-club rival Ramone, played by Shabba-Doo, gets too much screen time as an actor and not enough as a dancer.

Filmmakers apparently wanted to avoid the dance-contest cliché and offer a message; either that, or they stuffed the lambada theme into a "Stand And Deliver" knock-off they already had going. It's hard to tell.

Either way, the "get an education" segs come off as patronizing in the extreme, and the dance sequences are unenlightening.
— Daws.

Vazeni pratele, ano
(It's All Right, Dear Comrades)
(CZECHOSLOVAKIAN)

Berlin A Cseskoslovensky Filmexport presentation of Film Studio Barrandov production. Directed by Dusan Klein. Screenplay, Klein, Ladislav Pechacek; camera (color), Joseph Vanis; editor, Jiri Brozek; music, Petr Hapka; sound, Karol Jaros. Reviewed at Berlin Film Festival (Panorama section) Feb. 15, 1990. Running time: **100 MINS.**
Bohous. . . . . .Milan Lasica
Bohous' wife. . . . . . . .Jana Hlavacova
Hanka. . . . . . . .Marcela Ovcackova
Kamila. . . . . . . .Michaela Ovcackova
Secretary. . . . . .Valerie Zawadska
Dlask. . . . . .Franticek Rehak
Also with: Pavel Zednicek, Zita Furkova, Rudolf Hrusinsky, Alene Kreuzmannova.

■ **Dusan Klein follows in the fine human comedy tradition of the early works of countrymen Milos Forman and Jiri Menzel with "It's All Right,**

Dear Comrades," which could work its way into international theatrical sales as solid family entertainment a good deal above Western sitcom levels.

The story of a honorably unambitious worker maneuvered to the top of the executive ladder at a big sanitation ceramics factory is genuinely funny. It contains many sly digs at management-labor relations and bureaucracy in a Socialist state. An especially fine "Life With Father" portrait comes with the bundle of fun, too.

At the factory, 50-year-old Bohous, a handsome bear of a man, one day finds himself promoted to finance manager. The promotion is given to him by a CEO who expects to be able to get away with various shenanigans by having Bohous in his pocket. Bohous would rather be back at tile-making, but he is a pragmatic man, and he strings along without compromising his honesty too much.

At home, Bohous plays an accordion to "get away from it all," meaning his less-than-satisfactory love life with his wife, who has acting ambitions, and their identical twin daughters who declare themselves "down" because they may fail their Russian exam. They would rather spend their free time in discos, anyway.

Moreover, Bohous' parents are prone to doing zany things at the old people's home. Bohous is expected to set things right wherever he goes, and he manages to make everybody happy. Just when he thinks he can go back to tile-making, he gets another promotion instead.

As Bohous, Milan Lasica is the embodiment of solid male charm with a fine worry-frown attached. As his wife, Jana Hlavacova displays mature warmth in a humorous way. As the twins, Marcela and Michaela Ovcackova are sweet and funny beyond cute. The characters are delineated in swift, precise strokes that avoid ridicule, and they are all played with discretion and wit. — *Kell.*

Volevo i pantaloni
(I Wanted Pants)
(ITALIAN)

Rome A Penta Distribuzione release of a Cecchi Gori Group Tiger Cinematografica/ Maura Intl. Film/Reteitalia production. Produced by Mario and Vittorio Cecchi Gori. Directed by Maurizio Ponzi. Screenplay, Leo Benvenuti, Piero De Bernardi, Bruno Garbu-

glia, Roberto Ivan Orano, Ponzi, based on Lara Cardella's novel; camera (Telecolor). Maurizio Calvesi; editor, Sergio Montanari; music, Giancarlo Bigazzi; art direction, Franco Velchi; associate producers, Bruno Altissimi, Claudio Saraceni. Reviewed at CDS screening room, Rome, March 2, 1990. Running time: **92 MIN.**

Annetta	Giulia Fossà
Grazia	Lucia Bosè
Aunt Vannina	Angela Molina
Angelina	Natasha Hovey

Also with: Pino Colizzi, Luciano Catenacci, Stefano Davanzati, Marcello Scuderi, Tony Palazzo, Ludovica Modugno, Antonella Famà.

■ **The notoriety of the source novel is bound to get "I Wanted Pants" off to a fast start in the Italo market, but rentals could drop off quickly if auds find Maurizio Ponzi's version too anguishing. Offshore pickups may be able to latch onto book's popularity in translation or the feminist theme.**

In spite of story's built-in fascination, "I Wanted Pants" tends to be ponderously obvious in its portrait of a Sicilian girl trapped between repressive parents and a hypocritical society. The novel by young Lara Cardella was a national bestseller that made headlines when righteous Sicilians contested the author's bleak view of small-town bigotry.

Annetta (Giulia Fossà) is a country girl attending high school in town. Too shy to don makeup and miniskirts in the bathroom before class like the other girls, she remains a wallflower until pretty rich girl Angelina (Natasha Hovey) takes her under her wing. A ruse gets Annetta away from her strict parents (Lucia Bosè and Luciano Catenacci personify heartless cruelty) to go to a swinging party at Angelina's house, where she meets Nicola.

When Annetta and Nicola are later discovered kissing on the beach, it's a public scandal. Beaten, humiliated, taken out of school, Annetta is finally sent to live with her aunt Vannina (Angela Molina) and uncle. Though Vannina is understanding and a free spirit (with a married lover), the uncle terrifies Annetta because of sexual advances he made to her as a child.

Sure enough, at the first opportunity he tries to rape her. Realizing he's already had his way with his two little girls, Annetta flees screaming through the streets. Courageously she presses charges against him while her parents and police look on disapprovingly.

Ponzi is a talented veteran good at communicating with audiences.

Though the characters aren't always believable, they are boldly drawn in terms easy to love and hate. Three generations of oppressed females are represented by mama Bosè, vituperatively sexophobic; the sensual Molina, rebelling against a brutish husband in an illusory affair, and heroine Fossà, abruptly transformed from a sensitive, shy adolescent into a rebellious woman.

Ponzi stresses the tale's overtly feminist side to the limit. Little Annetta is a tomboy who smokes cigarets and plays rough but gets punished when little boys get praised. She decides to become a nun because she thinks they wear pants under their habits. As a teenager, she finds society repressing her burgeoning sexuality while pushing marriage and kids.

Oddly, pic tacks on an unexpected upbeat ending in which Annetta finds happiness in marriage and maternity. The hopeful note is she's knitting pants for her infant daughter.

Technical work is top caliber.
— *Yung.*

Farewell To Autumn
(POLISH)

Warsaw A Ki Studio Filmowe production. Directed by Mariosz Trelinski. Screenplay by Wozcieski Nowak, Zanusz Wrsblewski based on the novel "Farewell To Autumn" by S.I. Witiewicz; camera (color), Zanek Zamojda; sound, M. Dobek. Reviewed at Polish Film Review, Feb. 24, 1990. Running time: **84 MIN.**

With: Mario Pauvlms, Jan Frycz, Grazyna Trela, Jan Peszeu.

■ **Decadence, homosexuality, excess wealth, infidelity, alcoholism and drugs all played a major role in the decline of aristocracy, per "Farewell To Autumn," a quasi-political pic that also condemns the terrorist tactics and genocide of the ensuing communist regime.**

Film ponders the transition of power from one dictatorship to another via a manipulative rogue, his wife, his evil mistress and his male lover. Plenty of nudity, some dicey sex scenes and a flashy visual style prevent pic from being just a political essay. Arthouse circuit and specialty venues are the only real theatrical possibility, although homevid, if properly packaged, should provide a second life.

Pic has a "wanna-be American" visual style typical of the

new wave of Polish films, but debutant helmer Mariosz Trelinski handles it more adeptly than most.

"Farewell To Autumn" moves swiftly from scene to scene as the protagonist swaggers from party to boardroom to bedroom without conscience. Such scenes of corruption are often crosscut with real black & white images of war.

Thesp Jan Frycz is believable as the male boor who personifies decay; he's a bully who hits his pregnant wife and unabashedly fornicates with other men and women, occasionally at orgies. Nonetheless, he emerges as an antihero and victim of the system, which is more than can be said for any of the women.

Rigidly 1-dimensional, ridiculously outdated female characters are pic's major flaw. The vamp/ mistress is evil incarnate. She's defined by symbols such as flames and snakes (yawn). Meanwhile, the only prop the angelic wife is missing is a halo (double yawn). Helmer scores zero for originality in that department and his portrayal of a Jewish man as greedy and narrow-minded could easily be labeled anti-Semitic.

Nonetheless, the pic, flaws and all, indicates Trelinski has potential as a filmmaker, but he desperately needs some fresh material. Technical elements are surprisingly good for pic's minuscule budget. — *Suze.*

Stan Wewnetrzny
(Inner State)
(POLISH)

Warsaw Produced by the Polish Film Producers Corp., Film Unit X. Directed by Krzysztof Tchorzewski. Screenplay, Tchorzewski, Jacek Janczarski. Camera (color), Jan Mogilnicki; editor, Lucja Osko; sound, Lech Branski; music, Branski, Zbigniew Holdys; production managers, Halina Kawecka, Antoni Sambor; art director, Barbara Nowak. Reviewed at Polish Film Review, Feb. 25, 1990. Running time: **87 MIN.**

With: Krystyna Janda, Jadwiga Kankowska-Cieslak, Junsz Gajos, Jan Englert, Marian Opania.

■ **Shot in 1982 and banned until 1989, "Inner State" is a fiction adventure depicting apolitical people's devastation by martial law in Poland. Treatment isn't nearly as hard-hitting as other Polish films dealing with the period, a flaw that limits pic's theatrical potential to an East bloc release.**

Yarn begins in October 1981.

Yachtswoman Eva (Krystyna Janda) is sailing merrily along, celebrating, with her ex-husband and her new business partner, her pending solo tour around the world. Their party is filmed by a tv journalist, whose coverage of the race becomes the inevitable symbol of state censorship after the clamp-down.

Pic pointlessly dwells on the "good life" prior to martial law before getting to the heart of the matter: whether or not a privileged woman will return to her homeland when it's in crisis. Not surprisingly, she does.

Fleeting scenes of unidentified people pursued by the military and rumors of others dissappearing without a trace are injected as a timeframe reference. The ex-hubbie loses his job when he refuses to sign a loyalty oath. The business partner's boat club goes down the drain.

When Eva arrives pregnant with the ex-husband's child, pic's potential as a political foray becomes muddled into a soap opera-like scenario.

In an honorable attempt to make harsh political reality palatable for foreign audiences, helmer Tchorzewski compromises on both content and style; in the process learning the hard way that it's impossible to copy the American action/adventure formula.

Tv may provide a second life for the pic, destined to be archive or festival material. — *Suze.*

La Fille des collines
(The Hill Girl)
(FRENCH)

Paris UGC release of a Partners production/Hachette Première/UGC/Cine 5/Nickleodeon coproduction. Produced by Ariel Zeitoun. Directed by Robin Davis. Screenplay, Davis, Patrick Laurent, Alain Le Henry, based on the novel "Hill Girl" by Charles Williams; camera (color), Michel Abramowicz; editor, Marie-Josephe Yoyotte; music, Philippe Sarde; sound, Harald Maury, Jean-Paul Loublier; art direction, Pierre Gompertz; production managers, Daniel Chevalier, Daniel Deschamps. Reviewed at the Marignan-Concorde theater, Paris, March 14, 1990. Running time: **98 MIN.**
Tom. . . . . .Florent Pagny
Vincent. . . . . .Tcheky Karyo
Angelina. . . . . .Nathalie Cardone
Augustin. . . . . . . .Jean-Pierre Sentier
Lisa. . . . . .Laura Killing

■ **"La Fille des collines" is a well-made but obvious melodrama about a hot-blooded rural nymphette who comes** between two brothers. **Robin Davis' film is a transposition of a novel by Yank thriller writer Charles Williams, whose books have been especially popular among Gallic helmers by René Clément, Marcel Ophüls and François Truffaut.**

Davis and coscripters Patrick Laurent and Alain Le Henry reset Williams' tale in southern France in 1958. Florent Pagny is a young hick back from three years of military service who wants to revive his grandfather's farm. His married older brother, Tcheky Karyo, in the meantime has inherited their father's factory and is leading a dissipated life.

Film opens with the brothers' rollicking reunion against breathtaking natural vistas in the Pyrenees. Davis so insists on their fraternal warmth that there's no question they'll end up deadly rivals before long. And sure enough the trouble comes in the luscious shape of a cloistered baby doll, Nathalie Cardone, whom Karyo has seduced. To save his brother from a father's wrath, the kid brother agrees to marry the dishonored girl.

Again, the dramatization of the initial mutual antagonism between Pagny and Cardone is so overdramatized that we know they'll be locked in a passionate embrace a few reels later. Just about everything in this tale is trite and predictable, right down to the cop-out happy end.

Karyo, however, is genuinely unsettling as the wild, violent brother and Cardone is a hot ball of suppressed sensuality. Beside them Pagny seems somewhat bland as the more level-headed and civilized of the three. Superb natural locations are well-lensed by Michel Abramowicz. — *Len.*

Bumashnyie Glasa Prischvina
(Prischvin's Paper Eyes)
(RUSSIAN)

Berlin A Sovexportfilm presentation of a Lenfilm production. Directed by Valeri Ogorodnikov. Screenplay, Ogorodnikov, based on scenario by Irakli Kvirikadze; camera (color), Valeri Mironov; editor, Tamara Denisova; music, Edison Denisov; sound, Gassan Sade; sets, Vladlen Ivanov; production manager, Valeri Yermolayev. Reviewed at the Berlin Forum of Young Cinema, Feb. 16, 1990. Running time: **150 MIN.**
Prischvin. . . . . . .Alexander Romazov
Chrustalyov. . . . . .Ole Kovalov
Eisenstein. . . . . . . .Serghei Lavrentiev
Schutov. . . . . .Piotr Rudakov
Also with: Yuri Zapkni, Piotr Barkov, Mikhail Vekshin, Jakov Stepanov, I. Zywina, A. Schelest, O. Lant.

■ **This film within a film moves back and forth in time and offers a wealth of interpretations for each premise it presents. It's the kind of pic no one can hope to unravel at one go, but most viewers won't really be tempted to go for a second helping.**

A tv reporter agrees to play the inquisitor in a picture being shot by a friend, but he's also supposed to prepare a report on the beginning of Soviet tv in 1949. He stumbles upon mysteries that have been thoroughly hushed up since then. A tv director was killed as the result of a romantic tragedy, but the motives are not all certain. The investigation influences the script of the fiction film. The tv reporter is victimized in one role and victimizing in another, but there are also the flights of imagination in which he explores other possible solutions to past riddles.

Since there is no clear way of telling one level of the script from the other and clarity seems to be director Ogorodnikov's least concern, the result is close to complete pandemonium, the kind of film cherished by puzzle fans and dreaded by others. Pic's replete with Christian symbols, surrealist scenes, implications of universal guilt, touches of anarchism, a satire of filmmaking and clips from Eisenstein films, and many other symbolic ingredients.

Two sequences, however, stand out. One equates Stalin, Hitler, Mao, Mussolini and Ivan the Terrible and considers them all capable of the Odessa Stairs massacre. Using manipulative intercuts, Ogorodnikov shows Stalin pointing his finger at victims to be shot in the famous "Battleship Potemkin" scene. The other sequence (toward the end of the film) shows Stalin's statue hanging by its neck as a helicopter carries it away into wasteland. Even by glasnost standards, this is a rare spectacle.

Few will hold still for it, however, because the film is so obscure, the photography so doctored the viewer often must guess what's being shown, the acting so extremely expressionistic and the moods so erratic. At 150 minutes, it's a test of endurance. — *Edna.*

Folley, Buschgeister Tanzen im Rauch
(Folley, Bush Spirits Dance In Smoke)
(WEST GERMAN-DOCU)

Berlin A Wilde Früchte production. Written and directed by Marlene Dittrich Lex. Camera (color, 16m), Eduard Hartmann; editor, Radkar Stanek, Dittrich-Lux; sound, Thomas Bock, music, Griot Karimama, Griot Monkassa. Reviewed at Berlin Film Festival (New German Films), Feb. 17, 1990. Running time: **88 MIN.**

■ **Powerful music highlights this documentary about African tribal medicine.**

Tribal chants are translated into German, but there's no narration to give this pic verbal structure. The result is interesting pictures and good music, but little real insight into what is going on.

Nevertheless, pic could find a place for itself in women's or New Age festival screenings. Tech credits limited by 16m format. — *Gill.*

De Avonden
(Evenings)
(DUTCH)

Amsterdam A Concorde Film release of a Praxino Pictures production. Produced by René Solleveld and Peeter Weijdeveld. Directed by Rudolf Van den Berg. Screenplay, Jean Ummels, Van den Berg, based on the novel by Gerard Reve; camera (color), Willy Stassen; editor, Mario Steenbergen; music, Bob Zimmerman; sound, René van den Berg; art director, Freek Bieslot. Reviewed at the Cineco, Amsterdam, Dec. 2, 1989. Running time: **120 MIN.**
Fritz van Egters. . . . . . .Thom Hoffman
Father. . . . . .Rijk de Gooijer
Mother. . . . . .Viviane de Muynck
Maurits. . . . . .Pierre Bokma
Bep. . . . . .Elja Pelgrom

■ **Rudolf van den Berg has made a good film of Gerard Reve's 1947 novel "De Avonden", whose impact in Holland is comparable to that to J. D. Salinger's "Catcher in the Rye" in the U.S. Reve's prose was long thought untranslatable to the screen, but an adroit screenplay leaps the adaptation hurdle, backed by an effective musical score.**

Like most of Reve's writings, "Evenings" is partly autobiographical. Frits van Egters (Thom Hoffman) is a young college flunkie holding down a dull office job during the day. In the evenings he dines with his tedious parents, who are long-time communists, then goes out to visit his no more exciting friends.

Book and film are about those evenings of (theoretical) freedom, from Christmas to New Year's of 1946; about sex less as a problem than as basis for clumsy experimentation; about despised maddening home life with an increasingly deaf and slovenly father and a fastidious talkative mother; and about appeals to God as one purveyor of imagination to another.

Van den Berg weaves his sequences into a pattern that recreates Reve's void on the screen, a nervous void. All the players are at their best and the technical credits are first class. — *Wall.*

Hemligheten
(The Secret)
(SWEDISH)

Malmö, Sweden A Sandrew Film release of Drakfilm production with Sandrew Film and the LO (Congress Of Trade Unions). Produced and directed by Ralf Karlsson. Screenplay, Karlsson, Ulla-Carin Nyquist; camera (Eastmancolor), Peter Kruse; editor, Christin Loman; music, Ulla-Carin Nyquist, Claes Wang; sound, Stefan Ljungberg; production design, Stig Limer, costumes, Ellinor Ejve; production management, Göran Lindberg. Marianne Persson; assistant director, Cilla Norborg. Reviewed at Sandrews 1-3, Malmö, Sweden, Feb. 28, 1990. Running time: **95 MIN.**
Valdemar. . . . . . .Carl-Gustaf Lindstedt
Greta. . . . . .Sif Ruud
Amanda. . . . . . . .Suzanna Björklund
Sam. . . . . .Peter Oberg
Amanda's father. . . . . .Jan Waldekranz
Amanda's mother. . . .Susanne Barklund
Sam's mother. . . . . . .Susanne Reuter
Sam's father. . . . . . . .Rolf Skoglund
Sofia. . . . . .Malin Berghagen
   Also with: Jonas Uddenmyr, Leif Löf, Britta Pettersson, Mimi Pollak, Per Eggers, Anna Godenius, Björn Lövgren, Per Myrberg.

■ "The Secret" is mild-mannered family entertainment which, away from Swedish home ground, will be destined mostly for subteen programs on public television. First-time producer-director-writer Ralf Karlsson makes far too many off-tangent runs to sustain real suspense in what is meant to be a thriller.

Plot deals with two kids who find a fun haven in an old bagman's run-down mansion. They are sworn to secrecy about the place and its treasures of junk converted into fine antiques or combined into curios of utility value.

No excitement is generated either in the kids' attempts to keep their schoolmates off the track or in a subplot involving the abduc-tion of the bagman's unhappy sister from the hospital.

Environmental damage and the iciness of the welfare state in dealing with the elderly come in for some broad satirical jabs, but the film is at its best when the kids (Suzanna Björklund and Peter Oberg) and the two old people (veteran thesps Carl-Gustaf Lindstedt and Sif Ruud) are seen in leisurely interplay. When nothing else moves, this quartet supplies moving moments. — *Kell.*

De Kassiere — Lily Was Here
(Lily Was Here)
(DUTCH)

Berlin A Movies Film (Amsterdam) presentation and production. Produced by Chris Brouwer, Haig Balian. Executive producer, Anna Brouwe. Directed by Ben Verbong. Screenplay, Verbong, Sytze van der Laan; camera (Fujicolor), Lex Wertwijn; editor, Ton de Graaf; music, David A. Stewart; production design, Willem de Leeuw; costumes, Yan Tax; special effects, Harry Wiessenhaan; production management, Patricia McMahon, Gelder de Haas. Reviewed at Berlin Film Festival (Panorama), Feb. 20, 1990. Running time: **115 MIN.**
Lily. . . . . .Marion van Thijn
Arend. . . . . .Thom Hoffman
Ted. . . . .Coen van Vrijberghe de Coningh
The doctor. . . . . . .Monique van de Ven
Alan. . . . . .Dennis Rudge
Lily's mother. . . . . . . .Truus de Selle
   Also with: Con Meyer, Adrian Brine, Yvonne Ristie, Jeroen Planting, Gunar Gritters-Doublet, Richard Messina, Hans Kesting.

■ **Writer-director Ben Verbong, who helmed "The Girl With The Red Hair," takes a close look at another young woman in "Lily Was Here." This girl is seen alternately with black and bleach-blond hair in a meller that practically o.d.'s on cinematic pop art.**

Verbong's "Lily" also suffers from maudlin sentiment in the midst of its story about the supermarket cash register girl whose black G.I. lover dies just as the couple are to embark for the U.S. and marriage. Lily is pregnant. Finding no understanding with her parents, she throws herself into a runaway's life, letting herself be picked up by shady characters and then turning to robbery herself.

One not-quite-shady man (Thom Hoffman) tries to help Lily (and himself) go straight. She also receives aid and friendly advice from a woman doctor (Monique van de Ven). Nevertheless, she seems as hellbent on committing more robberies as she is on having and keeping her child. As played in the sultry-demure style of Béatrice Dalle ("Betty Blue") by Marion van Thijn, Lily never comes across as anything but just plain dumb.

Closeups of the actual birth of Lily's child in a subway tunnel constitute phony drama, serving to enlist audience pity with Lily that her role, as otherwise written, does not really merit. Right away, Lily is on the run again, while the police has the baby in hospital custody and meant to serve as bait for Lily to turn up herself.

Then, bang, an utterly unbelievable happy ending is contrived. By this time, moody jazz saxophone playing and wanton splashings of Fujicolor have drowned "Lily Was Here" in sheer bathos anyway. — *Kell.*

NEW DIRECTORS/NEW FILMS

A Wopbopaloobop A Lopbamboom
(LUXEMBOURG-W. GERMAN-B&W)

New York A Frankfurter Filmproduktion for ZDF and Visuals presentation. Executive producer, Mike Smeaton. Produced by Norbert Walter. Directed by Andy Bausch. Screenplay, Bausch, Armand Strainchamps, from story by Bausch, Strainchamps, Michel Treinen; camera (b&w), Klaus-Peter Weber; editor, Wolfgang Raabe; music, Gast Waltzing, Maggie Parke; sound, Horst Zinsmeister; art direction, Strainchamps; costumes, Evelyne Wanderscheid; production manager, Jürgen Tröster; assistant director, Barbara Etz. Reviewed at Museum of Modern Art (New Directors/New Films series), N.Y., March 14, 1990. Running time: **85 MIN.**
Rocco. . . . . .Birol Uenel
Veronique. . . . . .Désirée Nosbusch
Petz. . . . . .Thierry Vanwerveke
Anke. . . . . .Sabine Berg
Daniel. . . . . .Serge Wofl
Erwin. . . . . .Nicolas Lansky
Ginette. . . . . .Geraldine Karier
   Also with: Konrad Scheel, Jochen Senf, Jaoued Deggouj, Georges Petro.

■ **Recently making the fest circuit, this Luxembourg feature about young people clashing in a provincial town in the early '60s is amateurish and incoherent with no chance of U.S. distribution.**

Fledgling helmer Andy Bausch bites off too much material, presenting a vast cast and confusingly edited subplots in limning the "Breaking Away" genre conflicts of French-speaking and German-speaking folks in the town of Dudelange.

It's New Year's Eve 1963 and Birol Uenel (as Rocco) is back in town with gangsters on his tail. He and most other cast members have a crush on Désirée Nosbusch, a striking Marthe Keller type. Tempers flare throughout the film due to regional differences, culminating in poorly staged violence and a nonending.

As a portrait of provincial atti-tudes, film would have worked better with a linear script focusing on fewer characters. Decision to stress intentionally bad music (culminating in an a capella performance of "Quando, Quando" at the party) gives the pic little to fall back on. There are no hit songs of the period used, even the Little Richard "Tutti Frutti" from which pic's title is lifted does not appear. A jazz background score is anachronistic, representing a synthe-sized sound not in vogue until a decade after the film's time frame.

Cast members are attractive, especially Nosbusch, Serge Wolf and Sabine Berg, but fail to develop interesting characters. The extremely grainy blowup from 16m of Klaus-Peter Weber's harshly lit, black & white photography gives the film an amateur aspect and doesn't work in the interior scenes, particularly the party.
                                        — *Lor.*

Untama Giru
(JAPANESE)

New York A Parco Film production. Executive producer, Tsuji Masuda. Produced by Junichi Ito, Natsuki Hariu. Written and directed by Go Takamine. Camera (color), Masaki Tamura; editor, Hiroshi Yoshida; music, Kouji Ueno; production design, Keiko Hoshino; costumes, Atsuto Yokoi; assistant director, Henriku Morisaki. Reviewed at Museum of Modern Art (New Directors/New Films series), N.Y., March 16, 1990. Running time: **120 MIN.**
Giru. . . . . .Kaoru Kobayashi
Chiru. . . . . .Jun Togawa
High commissioner. . . . . .John Sayles
Mare. . . . . .Chikako Aoyama
Andakue. . . . . .Edie
Nishibaru. . . . . .Susumu Taira
Utubasan. . . . . .Yoshiko Hazama
Terurin. . . . . .Rinsuke Teruya
Kijimuna. . . . . .Eikou Miyasato

■ **Okinawan director Go Takamine unsuccessfully tackles the very difficult cinematic genre** of allegorical fantasy in "Untama Giru," a painfully tedious and amateurish effort. Recently shown in the Berlin fest's Forum, pic has meager commercial potential.

As best represented by Jean Cocteau's classic "Orphée" and two great Latin American films of 20 years back, "Antonio Das Mortes" and "El Topo," this folkloric film requires both technical skill and unfettered imagination. Takamine's ponderous, obscure and minimalist approach produces poor results.

Though story is set in the late '60s, it attempts to cover aspects of Okinawan history dating back to the Japanese invasion in 1609, U.S. occupation after W.W. II and return of the territory to Japan in 1972. There's more factual and emotional content on the subject in Hollywood's "The Teahouse Of The August Moon," however.

Kaoru Kobayashi stolidly portrays Giru, a manual worker who becomes the legendary hero Untama Giru when he goes to haunted Untama Forest, has a magical object implanted in his forehead and leads battles against the U.S. military authorities.

Stupid subplots involve Giru's waif-like sister Jun Togawa, who is improbably a prostitute at the local brothel, coveted by evil U.S. high commissioner John Sayles (bland in a guest role). Emphasis is on fleeting but stimulating nude footage of a woman (credits are garbled, but actress is probably Chikako Aoyama) who turns out to be a werepig that transforms (off-camera) from pig to woman.

Special effects are used for levitating Giru and other fantasy characters, but film never takes flight. Technical credits are pro but undermined by lax editing and poor pacing. Besides Sayles' on-screen participation, the actor-filmmaker's producer Maggie Renzi gets an untranslated thank-you credit at the end. — Lor.

SANTA BARBARA FILM FESTIVAL REVIEWS

Stardumb

Santa Barbara, Calif. Produced by Christopher Keith and Lynda Lemon. Directed by Harrison Ellenshaw. Screenplay, Clete Keith; camera, Bryan Duggan; editor, Victor Livingston; music, Peter Francis Rotter; production design, Clark Hunter; art direction, Richard Hale; costume design, Riki Sabusawa; set decoration, Sarah Seager; sound, Samuel Lehmer and Jeffrey Kliment; assistant director, Pete E. Hirsh. Reviewed at the Santa Barbara Intl. Film Festival, March 9, 1990. No MPAA Rating. Running time: **103 MIN.**
Cliff . . . . .Clete Keith
Sherry . . . . .Doris Anne Soyka
Tony. . . . . .Craig Fleming
Howard. . . . . .Joseph Scott
Lazlo. . . . . .James Austin
Didi. . . . . .Leslie Charles
Arthur. . . . . .Bruce R. Barrett
Vicki. . . . . .Diane Adair
Papa Rotella. . . . . . . .Edmund Biagio

■ **"Stardumb" is a loosely crafted, low-budget spoof of independent filmmaking that has slim commercial prospects but enough verve and entertainment value to bode well for some of its creators.**

Clete Keith, who also scripted, plays Cliff Monroe, a first-time filmmaker who gets lucky when he finds a financier who's willing to give him $3.5-million for his film noir debut, "Dead Silence."

Then the bad news: The old man wants his nonactor son, a forklift operator named Tony (Craig Fleming) to play the lead.

This slack-jawed individual, accurately described by Cliff as "a pinheaded dork," has the capacity to send other actors storming off the set within seconds of opening his mouth.

Then, as if the harried young director hadn't enough trouble, he learns the money he's using was embezzled from the Mob. A trio of well-dressed goons puts the finger on him, giving him five weeks to hand over the completed negative so they can try to recover their dough.

In the end, it is only some snappy improvising and the benevolence of the absurd that saves Cliff from disaster.

Likewise, this project has a short reach and a conceived-on-the-fly feel, but there's enough cleverness and brio here to give it an appealing shine.

Keith is merely adequate as an actor, but his script is often hilarious, and the direction and editing maintain a good pace and tongue-in-cheek tone.

Fleming is a real hoot as the obtuse Tony, and there are some amusing sketches of other showbiz flakes. Spliced-in "interviews" with showbiz folk describing their weird encounter with Tony on the set are an inspired touch. — Daws.

Vietnam, Texas

Santa Barbara, Calif. An Epic Prods. film. Coproducers, Robert Ginty and Ron Joy, Executive producer, Mark Damon. Directed by Ginty. Written by Tom Badal and C. Courtney Joyner. Camera (Deluxe color), Robert M. Baldwin Jr.; editor, Jonathan P. Shaw; music, Richard Stone; production design, Phillip J.C. Duffin; art direction, Kate J. Sullivan; set decoration, Alison Cornyn; costume supervisor, Diane Crooke; sound, Russell O. Fager. Reviewed at the Santa Barbara Intl. Film Festival, March 9, 1990. No MPAA rating. Running time: **85 MIN.**
Thomas McCain. . . . . . . .Robert Ginty
Wong. . . . . .Haing S. Ngor
Max. . . . . .Tim Thomerson
Mailan. . . . . .Kieu Chinh
Lan. . . . . .Tomlyn Tomita
Harold. . . . . .John Pleshette
Minh. . . . . .David Chow
Msgr. Sheehan. . . . . . . .Burt Remsen
Sammy. . . . . .Chi-Muoi Lo
Tini. . . . . .Michelle Chan

■ **Good intentions are roughly served in this uneven actioner that, like Louis Malle's "Alamo Bay," displays some compassion for the stateside Vietnam community while exploiting its violent elements. Best prospects lie in the foreign market for this low-budgeter tentatively set for a fall release.**

Robert Ginty, who also directed, stars as Father Thomas McCain, a Vietnam vet turned priest who still suffers guilt about the Vietnamese woman he abandoned — pregnant with his child — when he returned to the States.

Fifteen years later, he tracks them down in Houston's Little Saigon and forces himself into their lives, despite the fact that his former flame Mailan (Kieu Chinh) is now comfortably established as the wife of a vicious drug runner, Wong (Haing S. Ngor), who terrorizes the fishing community.

Ginty hooks up with his old soldier buddy Max (Tim Thomerson), now a dissolute bar owner, and they set out to reach Mailan and her teenage daughter Lan (Tamlin Tomita), setting off beatings and murders as they run up against Wong's henchmen.

Mailan, who struggled through four years in Thai refugee camps with a half-breed child after McCain left her, has no interest in the danger he brings to her, and that, coupled with the fact that the Vietnamese who try to help him end up dead, makes McCain difficult to sympathize with.

Ginty travels a rough road trying to make this pic work, attempting to have it all ways at once as the tough-guy priest who happens to be an amateur boxer, fistfighting his way toward a futile goal.

In one scene, he stages some masochistic absolution for his hero, having goons "crucify" the priest in a fish freezer by stabbing ice picks through his hands.

Ending, in which McCain gets what he wants and everybody else pays the highest price, is completely unworkable, and will no doubt be the biggest obstacle to distribution for a film that otherwise has some scattered merits.

Among its plusses, pic features numerous Asian roles, with Tamlin Tomita a standout as the spirited teenage daughter. Ngor ("The Killing Fields") is suitably chilling as Wong; Chinh is well-cast as the graceful survivor of much hardship and Chi-Muoi Lo is promising as a young would-be entertainer who leads the priest through Little Saigon's nightclubs.

Thomerson does much to keep the action bright in an amusing turn as the shambling, hyperactive Max, who plays the jumpy joe sidekick to Ginty's cool, centered but selfish protagonist.

John Pleshette also aids the cause as Wong's irrepressible, wisecracking lawyer.

Lensed on short time and scant funds, pic is technically uneven, but scores high on action and pace, with editing and shooting often quite effective. — Daws.

Goin' To Chicago

Santa Barbara, Calif. A Poor Robert Prods. production. Produced, directed, written and edited by Paul Leder. Camera (Fotokem color), Francis Grumman; music, Bob Summers; sound, Scott Smith; art direction, Elpidio Vasquez; costumes, Ewa Zbroniec; associate producer, Summers; casting, Geraldine Leder. Reviewed at the Santa Barbara Intl. Film Festival, March 10, 1990. No MPAA rating. Running time: **105 MIN.**
Edward Sr.. . . . . .Cleavon Little
Helen. . . . . .Viveca Lindfors
Aaron. . . . . .Gary Kroeger
Elinor. . . . . .Eileen Seely
Edward Jr.. . . . . .Guy Killum
Darlene. . . . . .Penny Johnson
Aline. . . . . .Lydie Donier

■ "Goin' To Chicago" is an attempt to honor the spirit of political activism in the '60s that suffers from an ill-focused story and a budget so low that all historical action takes place off-screen. Commercial prospects are scant.

Aaron and Ellie (Gary Kroeger and Eileen Seely), a young couple campaigning for presidential candidate Eugene McCarthy, split apart when Aaron decides the struggle is useless and heads off for a hedonistic summer in Europe. He leaves behind his grandmother (Viveca Lindfors), who soon takes ill, while Ellie and a young black friend Eddie (Guy Killum) toil for McCarthy in the New Hampshire primaries.

Eddie's father (Cleavon Little) and Lindfors begin a friendship that's charming enough but adds little to the storyline, which rambles around too long without a center.

Indie filmmaker Paul Leder, who put up his own money and that of a few investors, avoids the cost of period filming by shooting all in-teriors, with almost no extras or establishing shots. Pic lacks even stock footage of European sights.

Result is a talky, static film that in most unsatisfactory fashion delivers all pivotal events via radio reports or television footage.

Though pic gains some emotional momentum in the final act, partly via the devastating video clips of Robert Kennedy's murder, its cause has already been lost, and the fine sentiments it delivers at the end are not likely to reach many ears.

Among the cast, the magnificent Lindfors brightens the screen considerably with her abundant humanity, and she and the talented Little make their scenes together palatable, if irrelevant.

Seeley gives a spirited perf and Killum is promising as young Eddie. Kroger, though, adds little interest to the unsympathetic role of Aaron.

The unfamiliar music tracks, usually a potent element in films about the '60s, are minus any impact. Sound mix and cinematography are poor, and production values minimal. — *Daws.*

ARCHIVE FILM REVIEWS

Karla
(EAST GERMAN-B&W)

Berlin A DEFA Films presentation of a Berlin Group production. Directed by Hermann Zschoche. Screenplay, Ulrich Plenzdorf, Zschoche; camera (Cinemascope, b&w), Gunther Ost; editor, Birgitte Krex; music, Karl-Ernest Sasse; sound, Wolf-Joachim Preugschat; art director, Dieter Adam. Reviewed at the Berlin Forum of Young Cinema, Feb. 17, 1990. Running time: **128 MIN.**
Karla. . . . . .Jutta Hoffman
Kaspar. . . . . .Jürgen Hentsch
Mrs. Janson. . . . . .Inge Keller
Principal. . . . . . .Hans Hardt-Hardtloff
Rudi. . . . . .Jörg Knoche
    Also with: Dieter Wien, Rolf Hoppe, Herwath Grosse, Harald Moszdorf, Gisela Morgen, Fred Delmare, Peter Sturm, Peter Plessow.

■ The best of the forbidden 1965 crop of East German films unveiled this year in Berlin, "Karla" is an enjoyable but far too long and elaborate melodrama of a young teacher trying to beat the system for its own good.

Karla, a naive and energetic young woman fresh out of the university, yearns to go out and share her knowledge with her future pupils. Dispatched to a re-mote little town, she is allowed more than the usual margin of freedom by her principal, a former anarchist.

She is eyed with suspicion by a supervisor, however, who doesn't like to have anybody rock the boat. She also enters an affair with a former journalist who tried once to write about Stalin's crimes and, as a result, works in a sawmill. She also meets a professional challenge in some of the bright students who refuse to be fed party formulas.

Believing in absolute honesty, Karla's positions are tested when she ignores warnings and insists on telling her students about the German author for whom the high school is named. It's the first step in her unintentional campaign of harassment against conformism, but ultimately she's forced to resign.

Putting much of the weight on the romance, to sweeten the pill of social criticism, the script nevertheless manages to deliver some pertinent remarks on the antiquated, unorganized school system, and the evils of conformism. It clearly sympathizes with individu-alists like Karla and her lover. There is even an allusion to the possible Nazi past of one character, but it is quickly swept under the carpet: This was a taboo subject in East German films at the time.

Trimmed to a normal length, the film can still be appreciated for Jutta Hoffman's lively performance, the crisp, widescreen black and white photography and a nicely balanced cast, which includes the young Rolf Hoppe, an East German actor best known in the West. — *Edna.*

Le Roman de Renard
(The Tale Of The Fox)
(FRENCH-B&W)

Paris An Acacias/Cineaudience release (1990) of a Ladislas Starevitch production (1929-1941). Produced by Louis Nalpas (1929-31) and Roger Richebé (1939-41). Originally released in Paris on April 10, 1941. Restored by Renov-Film laboratories with the participation of La Sept. Directed, designed, animated and photographed by Ladislas Starevitch, with the collaboration of Irene Starevitch. Screenplay, Ladislas, Irene Starevitch, based on "Le Roman de Renard," with dialog by Jean Nohain, Antoinette Nordmann; editor, Laura Sejourné; music, Vincent Scotto. Reviewed at the Cannon France screening room, Paris, Feb. 7, 1990. Running time: **65 MIN.'**
    Voices: Claude Dauphin, Romain Bouquet, Sylvain Itkine, Leon Larive, Robert Seller, Edy Debray, Nicolas Amato, Jaime Plana, Suzy Dornac.

■ Sixty years after it was made and half-a-century after its belated release in France, Ladislas Starevitch's legendary feature animation epic at last is visible again. If the delighted reaction of modern preview audiences here is any criteria, this time it's here to stay.

As a kidpic attraction, it's a surefire joy, but it will obviously be limited to French-speaking territories (unless a good imaginative dubbing job can be done). Sophisticated adult filmgoers here and abroad, however, will appreciate its undiminished technical virtuosity and wide-ranging humor.

Ladislas Starevitch (1892-1965) is one of the famous unknowns of European film history. A Moscow-born Pole (original spelling of his name is Wladyslaw Starewicz), he pioneered the early Russian cinema, making his name with innovative puppet animation shorts and live-action fantasy features.

After the revolution he took refuge in France, where he continued to write, direct, design, ani-mate and lense highly popular puppet shorts with the sole collaboration of his family (notably his daughter Irene, who still lives in the house outside Paris where Starevitch operated his tiny studio).

"Tale Of The Fox," his only animation feature, was completed as a silent feature in 1929-30. His producer, Louis Nalpas, intended to release it with music and sound effects recorded on synchronized phonograph records, a system that quickly became obsolete.

Starevitch retrieved all film rights and pacted with UFA for a German-track version, released in 1937. Then, on the eve of World War II, producer Roger Richebé agreed to make a domestic version with popular actors such as Claude Dauphin and Sylvie Bataille dubbing the puppet creations, and Vincent Scotto composing a popular parodic score.

Finished "talkie" was finally released during the Occupation. It subsequently disappeared until the French state archives restored a mediocre copy of the film in the early '80s and lent it to a few local fests and specialized film events.

Current reissue print is superior in picture and sound quality. It was made from the original nitrate negative his family found only last year in Starevitch's studio-home. Starevitch had made a specialty of reinterpreting classic fables and fairy tales, so an adaptation of "Le Roman de Renard," a medieval literary classic, was right up his alley.

Book's episodic nature, relating how Renard the fox dupes his fellow beasts in a feudal kingdom ruled by Noble the lion, perfectly suited the rollicking social satire and anachronistic lampooning that Starevitch had delighted in such silent shorts as "The Town Rat and the Country Rat" and "The Frogs Want a King"

Starevitch alternates scenes of the fox's resourceful escapades with hilarious tableaux of court life, where wronged animals come to file complaints against the fox's antisocial abuses. When Renard doublecrosses the king himself, the outraged monarch lays siege to the outlaw's castle, which has a complex defense system worthy of Rube Goldberg. The attack fails, so the king decides to make the fox his prime minister. The stinging irony of this subversive climax certainly was not lost on pic's first audiences of Vichy France.

The cast of animal characters is large and memorable. The puppets are animated in painstaking stop-animation technique with extraordinary virtuosity and sense of anthropomorphic detail. It's incredible to believe it was done in a mere 18 months.

The stentorian king and his coquettish queen lioness preside over a kingdom of troubador cats, double-talking barrister badgers, greedily gullible wolves, squealing orphan chicks, a chorus of frogs, topless dancer black rats à la Josephine Baker, diapered fox cubs and an inept army of donkeys and bears.

The silent images and the boisterous soundtrack are so perfectly matched one wouldn't guess that a full decade separated their respective productions. The delightful word play and verbal gags are the work of songwriter and radio producer Jean Nohain, brother of actor Claude Dauphin, who dubbed the pedantic monkey narrator. Vincent Scotto's music mocks his own popular ballads, notably in a classic scene where the cat serenades the sentimental queen under her window in a meowing parody of the '30s crooner.

French culture web La Sept financed film's restoration and is backing attempts by the Starevitch family to locate and restore other rare titles (many of which have been saved by archives). A major retrospective is announced for the Annecy Animation Festival in 1991. — *Len.*

Pikovaya dama
(The Queen Of Spades)
(RUSSIAN-B&W)

Paris A Joseph Ermolieff production (Moscow, 1915-16) First released in Moscow, April 19, 1916. Preserved by Gosfilmofond. Directed by Yakov Protazanov. Screenplay, Protazanov, Fedor Ozep, from the story by Alexander Pushkin, camera (b&w), Evgeny Slavinsky; sets, Vladimir Balyuzhek, Sergey Lillienberg, W. Przytinevski; assistant director, George Azagarov. Reviewed at the Orsay Museum of the 19th Century, Paris, Dec. 10, 1989. Length: 3,768 ft. Running time (at 16 frames per second): **63 MIN.**
Hermann. . . . . .Ivan Mozhukhin
Lisa. . . . . .Vera Orlova
Countess. . . . . .E. Shebuyeva
Countess (young). . . . . .Tamara Duvan
Count. . . . . .P. Pavlov
Count of St. Germain. . . .Nikolai Panov
Narumov. . . . . . . .Vladimir Strijewsky

■ **Of the six screen versions (including an opera film) of Alexandre Pushkin's famous tale of the supernatural, "The Queen of Spades," this second Russian production, made in 1915, is likely to remain the best, most haunting of the lot.**

Yakov Protazanov's film is literary adaptation at its innovative best and 75 years of aesthetic and technical developments have not diminished its dramatic force.

"Queen of Spades" consolidated Ivan Mozhukhin as the premier tragedian of Russia's prerevolutionary cinema. He brings mesmerizing intensity to the role of Hermann, the dour, ambitious Czarist career officer who will stop at nothing to learn the sure-fire gambling secret of an aged countess. Pretending to court the dowager's poor, lonely ward, he gains access to the mansion and surprises the fragile aristocrat in her rooms. When he threatens her with a pistol, she dies of heart failure.

Some nights later, the brooding Mozhukhin receives an otherwordly visit from the dead countess, who reveals the secret hand that will earn him untold fortune. But the obsessed officer finds himself the butt of a supernatural joke when he turns up the wrong card at the gambling table. Haunted by the mocking vision of the countess, he goes mad and is locked up, forever to repeat the gestures of the losing deal.

The film's portentous atmosphere remains extraordinarily potent. Among the many striking cinematic elements Protazanov and his co-adaptor (the future emigré Fedor Ozep) used to give the story greater visual impact are a series of complex, innovative flashbacks. The intricate web of past and present provides one of the story's most powerful jolts. Stark lighting and some sinister baroque set design heighten the film's eerie spell.

This was perhaps the first masterpiece by the extraordinarily eclectic Protazanov, most of whose films before the revolution have not survived. The film's negative was lost and remaining print materials are somewhat splicey. Bits and pieces of action are missing.

Gosfilmofond, the Soviet archive, has done all that is technically possible to preserve the hypnotic picture quality. Defective as the print is — and pending the discovery of other copies — "The Queen of Spades" remains a classic moment of screen fantasy and horror. — *Len.*

Opportunity Knocks

New York A Universal release of an Imagine Entertainment presentation of a Brad Grey/Meledandri-Gordon Co. production. Produced by Mark R. Gordon, Christopher Meledandri. Executive producer, Brad Grey. Directed by Donald Petrie. Screenplay, Mitchel Katlin, Nat Bernstein; camera (Deluxe color), Steven Poster; editor, Marion Rothman; music, Miles Goodman; sound (Dolby), Glenn Williams; production design, David Chapman; art direction, Leslie A. Pope; set decoration, Derek Hill; costume design, Nan Cibula; unit production manager-coproducer, Raymond Hartwick; assistant director, Don Hauer; casting, Ilene Starger. Reviewed at Cineplex Odeon Chelsea Cinemas 5, N.Y., March 23, 1990. MPAA Rating: PG-13. Running time: **105 MIN.**
Eddie. . . . . .Dana Carvey
Milt. . . . . .Robert Loggia
Lou. . . . . .Todd Graff
Annie. . . . . .Julia Campbell
Max. . . . . .Milo O'Shea
Sal. . . . . .James Tolkan
Mona. . . . . Doris Belack
Connie . . . . .Sally Gracie
Pinkie . . . . .Mike Bacarella
Harold Monroe. . . . .John M. Watson Sr.
Bubbie . . . . .Beatrice Fredman
    Also with: Thomas McElroy, Jack McLaughlin-Gray, Gene Honda, Del Close, Michael Oppenheimer, Paul Greatbatch, Sarajane Avidon, Mindy Suzanne Bell, Richard Steven Mann, Michelle Johnston.

■ **Television and standup comic Dana Carvey's deft mimicry and physical comedy are used to the max in "Opportunity Knocks," but pic's routine venture into action and romance genres subtracts from the laughs. Since overall product could have been consistently funnier, b.o. returns probably won't be that special.**

Since the late 1970s "Saturday Night Live," of course, has been a breeding ground for big-screen comedy stars. Of the current ensemble, Carvey has emerged as the front-running talent, largely due to his "Church Lady." Use of that click character in pic's advance trailer should help draw an audience, as long as it doesn't backfire since "she" is absent from this pic.

Youthful, fresh-faced Carvey is mainstream American good-looking as a straight man, but fiendishly hilarious when his malleable face and multifarious voice disappear into other characters. As Chicago con artist with a conscience Eddie Farrell he gets to mimic an East Indian, a Chinese, a Japanese and one President Bush.

In a change of pace from the low-paying street cons they commit, Carvey and accomplice Todd Graff break, enter and take up residence in a luxurious suburban house. Carvey is mistaken for a housesitting friend by the mother of the house's owner (Doris Belack). So begins a familiarly improbable plot.

Intending at the outset to milk the situation for all it's worth, Carvey heeds the advice of semiretired con artists Milo O'Shea and Sally Gracie, and starts a "love con" with Julia Campbell, the earthy doctor daughter of Belack and Robert Loggia. Naturally, they fall in love and Carvey ends up regretting the charade.

In a parallel story line, Carvey and Graff are pursued by baddies led by James Tolkan for stealing, and then losing, a cash-laden car. Naturally, Carvey and company orchestrate a sting that eliminates the Tolkan threat.

Everyone in the legitimate world falls for Carvey, including Loggia, who essentially reprises his character in "Big" as the successful businessman looking for a "fresh perspective." He finds it, all too willingly, in a guy who isn't entirely what he seems, and, again, Loggia fails to see that.

Fortunately, the conventional screenplay and direction is frequently interrupted by Carvey's winsome shticking. A bit in which he performs "Born To Be Wild" in a club's amateur spot works better than might be expected. Choreographer Jeffrey Hornaday gets a credit for the sequence and the detail put into it pays off.

Later, however, Carvey is expected to be a romantic lead, and the audience is expected to believe it. Filmmakers err on both counts. (This is director Donald Petrie's second effort after "Mystic Pizza.")

Virtually irresistible with the right material, Carvey finds himself carrying a pic with formulas that are proven or wornout, depending on POV and marketplace luck. Help from the supporting cast is minimal. Tv actress Campbell, a Trini Alvarado lookalike, makes her feature debut.

Chicago locations, including Wrigley Field, look nice. Pic also has a chart-tailored soundtrack, including yet again the work of Euro-synth duo Yello. — *Binn.*

Teenage Mutant Ninja Turtles

Los Angeles A New Line Cinema release of a Golden Harvest presentation of a Limelight production, in association with Gary Propper. Produced by Kim Dawson, Simon Fields, David Chan. Coproducer, Graham Cottle. Executive producer, Raymond Chow. Directed by Steve Barron. Screenplay, Todd

W. Langen, Bobby Herbeck, from story by Herbeck, based on cartoon characters created by Kevin Eastman and Peter Laird; camera (Technicolor, prints by Deluxe), John Fenner; editor, uncredited; music, John Du Prez; sound (Dolby), Lee Orloff, Steve Maslow, Michael Herbick, Gregg Landaker; production design, Roy Forge Smith; art direction, Gary Wissner; set design, Jerry Hall; set decoration, Brendan Smith, Barbara Kahn; costume design, John M. Hay; stunt coordinator & martial arts choreographer, Pat Johnson; special effects, Special Effects Unlimited; special effects supervisor, Joey Di Gaetano; creatures designed by Jim Henson's Creature Shop; Henson creative supervisor, John Stephenson; Henson visual supervisor, Ray Scott; Henson designers, Peter Brooke, Nigel Booth, John Blakeley; animaltronic puppeteers, David Greenaway, Mark Wilson, David Rudman, Martin P. Robinson, Kevin Clash, Ricky Boyd, Robert Tygner; assistant director, Michael Grossman; 2d unit camera, Tony Cutrono; voice casting, Barbara Harris. Reviewed at Cineplex Odeon Universal City Cinemas, L.A. March 24, 1990. MPAA Rating: PG. Running time: **93 MIN.**

April O'Neil . . . . Judith Hoag
Casey Jones . . . . Elias Koteas
Raphael . . . . Joch Pais
Michelangelo . . . . .Michelan Sisti
Donatello . . . . .Leif Tilden
Leonardo . . . . .David Forman
Danny Pennington . . . . .Michael Turney
Charles Pennington . . . . . .Jay Patterson
Chief Sterns . . . . .Raymond Gerra
The Shredder . . . . .James Saito
Tatsu . . . . .Toshishiro Obata

Also with the voices of: Robbie Rist, Kevin Clash, Brian Tochi, David McCharen, Michael McConnohie, Corey Feldman.

■ **Wacky, though uneven, live-action screen version of the "Teenage Mutant Ninja Turtles" cartoon characters should go over big with subteens. Jim Henson's Creature Shop has devised marvelous renditions of the title characters, four superhero turtles who speak a hilarious mishmash of teenage slang as they fight off a horde of baddies.**

While visually rough around the edges, sometimes sluggish in its plotting and marred by overtones of racism in its use of Oriental villains, the Golden Harvest presentation released by New Line scores with its generally engaging tongue-in-cheek humor as long as it focuses on the antics of the title characters. Adults should find it easy enough to take.

The Henson versions of the Keven Eastman-Peter Laird turtles — Raphael, Michelangelo, Donatello and Leonardo — are charmingly anthropomorphic, with their large, fully expressive eyes and faces and their goofy, supple teenage mannerisms.

Supposedly mutated by radioactive goop, the turtles live in the sewers, eat pizza, dance to rock music, play Trivial Pursuit and casually toss around such words

as "awesome," "bodacious" and "gnarly." A variety of human actors inhabiting the costumes and doing voice characterizations bring them amusingly to life.

The screenplay by Todd W. Langen and Bobby Herbeck, from a screen story by Herbeck, abandons some of the character distinctions the turtles have in the comics and makes all four of the green guys seem like clones, differentiated mostly by their variegated colored headbands. But they're such a likeable bunch that this defect doesn't sink the film.

The scripters and director Steve Barron wisely never bother to take the plot seriously, since it's nothing more than some nonsense about the turtles and a handful of human sidekicks trying to stop a gang called the Foot Clan from terrorizing N.Y. streets.

The Foot Clan, a bunch of teenage throwaways trained in martial arts by evil Japanese James Saito and Toshishiro Obata, kidnap the turtles' mentor and father-figure, Splinter, a large animatronic rat whose gentleness and wisdom put the viewer in mind (no doubt intentionally) of George Lucas' Yoda.

Though Splinter's abduction provides the film with whatever poignancy it can muster, that development also retards the action for a long stretch, with the turtles moping around far too passively for superheroes.

A bit too much time is devoted to the peculiar romance of unbelievably funky tv newswoman Judith Hoag and her off-the-wall vigilante b.f. Elias Koteas, who join forces with the creatures and misunderstood j.d. Michael Turney to rid N.Y. of the slimy villains.

It would have been much funnier if Hoag had been a typically bubbleheaded blonde anchorwoman reduced to grunginess by her "heroes in a half-shell," and, given the turtles' crush on her, it seems odd that they never become jealous of her attachment to Koteas.

A tawdry use of Japanese as grunting bad guys seems to be fashionable again, as it was in World War II propaganda films, now that many in the U.S. feel resentful over the Japanese dominance of the world economy. "Am I behind in my Sony payments again?" asks Hoag in a lamentable aside when accosted by the Foot Clan in a dark alley.

The unfortunate effect of such

stereotyping on kids' minds is mitigated somewhat by the fact that Splinter speaks with an Oriental voice and trained the turtles in martial arts learned from a Japanese master.

The martial-arts setpieces, deftly choreographed by stunt coordinator Pat Johnson, are amusingly outlandish, with the screen populated by hordes of attackers whom the nonchalant, graceful turtles have little trouble vanquishing as they toss off streams of surfer-lingo wisecracks.

Production designer Roy Forge Smith has done an effective job of conjuring up a nightmarish N.Y. setting (well suited to the frenetic music-video style of the director), but the lensing by John Fenner is very uneven. Sometimes appropriately strange and creepy, elsewhere the look is overly garish, particularly in the grainy flashbacks explaining the origins of the turtles and Splinter. — *Mac.*

Uchu No Hosoku
(Universal Laws)
(JAPANESE)

Tokyo A Daiei production. Produced by Katsunori Arai, Takashi Matsuki. Executive producer, Toshihiro Kojima. Directed by Kazuyuki Izutsu. Screenplay, Izutsu, Akira Asai; camera (color), Noboru Shinoda; editor, Satoshi Yoshioka; production design, Yuji Hayashida; music, Stardust Review; sound, Kazuo Numata. Reviewed at Yurakucho Subaruza, March 16, 1990. Running time: **119 MIN.**

Yoshiaki . . . . .Masato Furuoya
Reiko . . . . .Mari Torigoe
Miki . . . . .Megumi Yokoyama
Kazuya . . . . .Kyozo Nagatsuka
Mikiko . . . . .Haruko Mabuchi
Emiko . . . . Yoshimi Ashikawa

■ **This is by far Kazuyuki Izutsu's most accomplished film, but it illustrates why he still remains a hopeful contender. He cannot go the distance, cannot maintain a consistency of tone from beginning to end.**

Although Izutsu has been hailed by some as one of Japan's "best new-generation directors," he indeed strikes other observers as the Japanese cinema's Terry Malloy, someone who could have been a contender. Still, Izutsu cannot yet be written off, although he must now be beginning to try the patience of even his most ardent supporters.

For these supporters, hope is undoubtedly being kept alive by memory of Izutsu's official 1981

debut, "Gaki Teikoku," made two years before his 30th birthday. Prior to the release of this Art Theater Guild production, Izutsu coproduced his first 16m feature at the age of 18, directed his first 35m film four years after that and made several soft-core porn features, an apprenticeship omitted in English-language bio information supplied by the distributor of his latest film.

"Gaki Teikoku" focused on three lowlifes involved in an effort to break the stranglehold of a gang on the nightlife of the Kita section of late 1960s Osaka. Dialog was a head-swirling admixture of Osaka dialect, gangland slang and Korean. The screenplay, with its forging and breaking of alliance and its warring factions, recalled the murkier plot developments in some Shakespearean historical tragedies.

"Uchu No Hosoku" (Universal Laws) is far removed from the rumbles and rubouts of Izutsu's first film, which means that, 15 minutes into the film, the hero has thrown punches at his elder brother only twice. Other annoying displays of fisticuffs follow, but, for the most part, Izutsu manages to tell his story calmly.

Yoshiaki is a successful designer for a Tokyo fashion concern who returns to his hometown of Ichinomiya to take over his late father's small fabric factory. Much to his surprise and chagrin, he learns that his mother, believing Yoshiaki fully intended to remain in Tokyo, sold off his father's looms.

Determined to make a go of the business anyway, Yoshiaki consults a local wise man, who gives him predictable advice about being guided by his "heart" rather than his technique, and seeks financial backing from a disco owner, who steals Yoshiaki's designs and presents them as his own, a bit of baldfaced deception that unfortunately precipitates one of those interminable knock-down, drag-out fights Izutsu so loves.

Besides those troubles associated with business, Yoshiaki has to cope with his brother's rapidly disintegrating marriage as well as his own estranged relationship with a model.

Some moments almost justify comparisons to Ozu; others threaten to rend the fabric (no pun intended) of the pic as conflicting acting styles engage in a Godzilla vs. King Kong battle for primacy.

Masato Furoya is reliably good as Yoshiaki; Mari Torigoe, former model and campaign girl, is decorative as his lover; and Megumi Yokoyama, previously confined to tv and commercials, is winning as Yoshiaki's younger sister.

— *Bail.*

The Sleeping Car

New York A Triax Entertainment release of a Vidmark Entertainment presentation. Executive producer, Mark Amin. Produced and directed by Douglas Curtis. Screenplay, Greg O'Neill; camera (CFI color), David Lewis; editor, Allan Holzman, Betty Cohen; music, Ray Colcord; sound, Blake R. Wilcox; production design, Robert Benedict; assistant director, Bill Berry; production manager, Vicki B. Rocco; special visual effects & 2d unit director, Max W. Anderson; special makeup effects design, John Carl Buechler; special mechanical effects supervisor, Marty Bresin; coproducer, Bob Manning; associate producer, O'Neill. Reviewed on Vidmark vidcassette, N.Y., March 20, 1990. MPAA Rating: R. Running time: **87 MIN.**

Jason	David Naughton
Kim	Judie Aronson
Vincent Tuttle	Kevin McCarthy
Bud Sorenson	Jeff Conaway
Joanne	Dani Minnick
Mr. Erickson	John Carl Buechler
Mrs. Erickson	Ernestine Mercer
Dwight	Steve Lundquist
Kerry	Bill Stevenson
Harris	David Coburn
Clarice	Nicole Hanson
19-year-old girl	Sandra Margot

■ "The Sleeping Car" is an above-average horror flick released theatrically Feb. 2 in regional markets such as Pittsburgh and Nashville ahead of its video debut in mid-May.

Effort by Vidmark aimed at theatrical audiences would probably have gotten a better shot several years ago before horror pics glutted the market.

It has a stronger plot and cast than usual in limning the familiar tale of haunting, in this case a railroad car that was the scene of sex and murder 10 years earlier.

David Naughton is a little long in the tooth, but effective anyway, as the hero on the rebound from a failed marriage (with Dani Minnick) who goes back to school to study journalism with hip prof Jeff Conaway (a fun performance).

He rents the sleeping car as a cheap abode from goofy landlady Ernestine Mercer and has '60s hippie leftover Kevin McCarthy as an even goofier neighbor. Thanks to interesting gore and makeup effects by John Carl Buech-

ler (also doubling as actor in the 10-years-earlier segments), pic's depiction of poltergeist appearances has some novelty and drive.

It turns out that Naughton unwittingly is the catalyst for the unhappy ghost going on a killing spree in the RR car once more before a big showdown.

Douglas Curtis pilots the picture with self-assurance, stumbling only in a series of false wakeup endings that are a direct lift from John Landis' "An American Werewolf In London," which also starred Naughton.

Greg O'Neill's flippant and unpretentious script is refreshing, giving Naughton plenty of tongue-in-cheek rejoinders to lighten up the film and establish a tone early on that's amplified by Conaway's "everything is everything" approach.

Judie Aronson, who made a nice impression in a small role in "Cool Blue," is an unusual looking beauty who is arresting as the sexually liberated romantic lead. Effects by Buechler and others are solid. — *Lor.*

Prom Night III: The Last Kiss
(CANADIAN)

Toronto A Norstar Entertainment release (in Canada) of a Peter Simpson production, in association with Comweb Prods. Executive producers, Dan Johnson, Ilana Frank. Produced by Ray Sager, Peter Simpson. Directed by Ron Oliver, Simpson. Screenplay, Oliver; camera (color), Rhett Morita; editor, Nick Rotundo; music, Paul Zaza; production design, Reuben Freed; special effects, Light and Motion Corp.; makeup, Stephen Lynch. Reviewed at Famous Players screening room, Toronto, March 21, 1990. MPAA Rating: R. Running time: **95 MIN.**

Alex Gray	Tim Conlon
Sarah Munroe	Cyndy Preston
Shane	David Stratton
Mary Lou Mahoney	Courtney Taylor

■ Gore-filled and intended as a comedy, "Prom Night III: The Last Kiss," may find some reward in homevid (IVE in U.S.), not in theatrical.

Sequel brings a dead and failed beauty queen back to her high school 30 years later, still looking for love and retribution. She kisses and makes love to average student (Tim Conlon), kills the caretaker, two teachers, his football rival and his best pal, most of them by flying, whirring machines.

Only then he realizes he's in big trouble. Almost everyone else in

the busy school seems to have had surgical lobotomy, not noticing the absence of those killed. His blond girlfriend (Cyndy Preston) wants to know why he's acting strange and distant. He won't tell, having buried three of the dead in the school's football yard.

Mary Lou (Courtney Taylor), looking much older than his dead guidance counsellor, finally zaps him back to the late 1950s, again triumphant over the forces of good.

Acting, direction and script are flat. Two directors don't make a good one, in this case. Special effects are humdrum. — *Adil.*

La Fête des pères
(Fathers' Day)
(FRENCH)

Paris An AMLF release of a GPFI/TF 1 Films Prod./Ice Film/SGGC/Futures Prods. coproduction. Produced by Jean-Claude Fleury. Directed by Joy Fleury. Screenplay, Pierre Grillet, Joy Fleury; camera (color), Manuel Teran; editor, Jacques Comets; music, Bob Telson; sound, Paul Laine; production manager, Alain Depardieu. Reviewed at UGC Biarritz theater, Paris, March 15, 1990. Running time: **83 MIN.**

Thomas	Thierry Lhermitte
Stephane	Alain Souchon
Carole	Gunilla Karlzen
Mireille	Micheline Presle
Jerome	Rémi Martin

■ This dull romantic comedy could easily be called "Two Men And A Baby." The two men, Thierry Lhermitte and Alain Souchon, are a handsome, gay yuppie couple in Bordeaux and want to have a kid.

Their first attempt to clandestinely adopt a black baby in Martinique ends in a fiasco. Then they meet a beautiful young blonde (Gunilla Karlzen) who's fleeing a brutal boyfriend. They ask her to bear a kid for them, take her back home and install her in their apartment. She refuses artificial insemination, so the two guys, overcoming their sexual bias, tumble in the sack with her. Presto: twins.

Joy Fleury, who's first feature was a vain Gallicized adaptation of Japanese novel "Sadness and Beauty," directs unremarkably from a blandly predictable script she wrote with Pierre Grillet.

Lhermitte and Souchon have a laid-back charm that gives the film an occasionally mild lift. Karlzen is a Scandinavian eyeful introduced in a 1988 French ab-

surdist comedy, "The Bathroom." It's no fault of hers if the role here has no substance or poignance.

— *Len.*

Yksinteoin
(Going It Alone)
(FINNISH)

Tampere, Finland A Finnkino release of Kinofinlandia production. Produced and directed by Pekka Lehto. Screenplay, Jussi Parviainen; camera (Eastmancolor), Kari Sohlberg; editor, Olli Soinio; music, Matti & Pirjo Bergström; sound, Hannu Koski. Reviewed at Tampere Intl. Film Festival, March 9, 1990. Running time: **81 MIN.**

With: Jussi Parviainen (himself) and voices of Sanna-Kaisa Palo and Vesa Mäkinen.

■ A fiction-docu hybrid about a man, playwright-actor Jussi Parviainen, caught in the agonies of being left by his wife, "Going It Alone" should strike common denominator chords with adult audiences everywhere via specialized art houses.

Parviainen went through the ordeal of separation last fall, and captured it on film. In the presence of the topnotch filmmaking team of helmer Pekka Lehto ("Flame Top"), cinematographer Kari Sohlberg and sound recorder Hannu Koski, Parviainen spoke to himself but mostly to his ex on the (cordless) phone for the better part of five days and nights.

There is a curiously controlled intensity about Parviainen's voice and expressions throughout this catharsis — filmed with the camera rolling in front of him in his car, in his home and on the street — even when he is at his loudest and most abusive.

Large Finnish audiences have taken to the film because he is as well known to them as is his ex, stage actress Sanna-Kaisa Palo, whose voice is heard in the film. Also heard is Palo's new lover, 27-year-old pianist Vesa Mäkinen, who calls to tell Parviainen to lay off. Before pic's release there were also threats of lawsuits, later abandoned, on the part of Palo and Mäkinen for the unauthorized use of their voices.

This is titillation for home audiences, but "Going It Alone" does, as indicated, achieve artistic cinéma vérité value as well. A lightly bearded and handsome man in his 40s, Parviainen never whines to the point of being a bore, and when he uses foul language about the woman who left him, he is also quick to admit to having been quite a rover, and a male chauvinist pig, himself. Audiences used to the language of most films these days should not shrink at Parviainen's excessive use of sexual 4-letter words.

Even when he bawls about missing his small children, Parviainen escapes the maudlin and remains a body and soul in honorable torment. He never rolls around on the floor nor screams at the top of his voice. Being a chain-smoker does not keep him from being a good actor, too: he can create suspense merely by not immediately lighting the cigarette he has one-handedly fished out of its pack.

He may be a sad and sorry case, but he certainly comes out as a survivor as well. That was supported by his own announcement at film's Tampere fest showing that he has currently gained custody of his children. — *Kell.*

De Falschen Hond
(The Traitor)
(LUXEMBOURG)

Luxembourg City A Utopia release of an RTL-Hei Elei production. Produced by Jean Octave. Executive producer, Michel Welter. Directed by Menn Bodson, Gast Rollinger, Marc Olinger. Screenplay, Henri Losch, from the novel ''Der Verrater'' by Nikolaus Hein; camera (color), Bodson, Rollinger; editor, Roger Meulenbergs; music, Jacques Neuen; sound, Gast Casel, Bruno Ferrari, John Koenig, Gust Nussbaum; art direction, Luc Aulner, Jacques Dedye; costumes, Jeanny Kratochwil. Reviewed at Utopia 1, Luxembourg City, Dec. 11, 1989. Running time: **113 MIN.**
Matt. . . . . .Ander Jung
Benn. . . . . .Raoul Biltgen
Anna. . . . . .Denise Grégoire
Grandmother. . .Marie-Paule von Roesgen
Grandfather. . . . . .Paul Greisch
Mayor. . . . . .Marc Olinger
Mayor's wife. . . .Marie-Christine Faber
Priest. . . . . .Josy Braun
Teacher. . . . . .Henri Losch

■ Shot in 16m for a mere $400,000 and blown up to 35m, ''The Traitor'' is a remarkable if overlong pic. Strong historical/patriotic theme makes it a natural for home turf but problematic for foreign. It will certainly pop up at fests of neighboring countries.

Originally planned as a miniseries celebrating the 150th anniversary of Luxembourg's independence from its neighbors, this lavish production was quickly picked up theatrically by a local exhibitor. Melodramatic yarn is loosely based on a patriotric novel and manages to avoid much the book's

jingoism, but doesn't quite eliminate the bathetic excess.

Set in 1830-31, story centers on Matt Breckert (Ander Jung) who flees to Germany when he refuses to join countrymen in their struggle to throw off Dutch oppression and become citizens of Belgium. Jung wants only to be a Luxembourgish. He drowns during an attempt to return home after a long exile and becomes a national hero.

Despite the budget, Menn Bodson and Gast Rollinger, who cohelmed and colensed, have given material a striking if not quite convincing mounting. Jung and Marc Olinger (who shared in direction) are impressive, though the large supporting cast sometimes betray their stage origins. Synthesizer score by Jacques Neuen sometimes drowns out several well-staged sequences. Jeanny Kratochwil's costumes are lovely.
— *Jemp.*

Eden Miseria
(FRENCH)

Paris A Colifilm release of a Paolo Branco/Films Plain Chant production. Produced by Paolo Branco, Philippe Diaz. Directed by Christine Laurent. Screenplay, Laurent, Philippe Arnaud, based on ''Les Journaliers'' of Isabelle Eberhardt; camera (Eastmancolor), Thierry Arbogast; editor, Francine Sandberg; music, Az Dyne, Christine Gaudry; sound, Nicolas Lefevre, Antoine Rodet; art direction/costumes, Isabel Branco, Camilo Joao. Reviewed at the Utopia cinema, Paris, Feb. 15, 1990. Running time: **102 MIN.**
Si Mahmoud-Isabelle. . . . .Danuta Zarazik
Paul Herbst. . . . . . .Philippe Clevenot
Slimene Ehni. . . . . . . .Abdallah Badis
Lalla Gazhel-Stella. . . .Ines de Almeida
Henri Jagorn. . . . . . . .Stephané Jobert

■ ''Eden Miseria'' is a static, low-budget account about Isabelle Eberhardt, adventuress and writer active in late 19th century. Director Christine Laurent, working with lenser Thierry Arbogast, has an eye for striking compositions, but her direction lacks clarity and dynamics.

Eberhardt's fascination with the deserts of North Africa and her early death at age 27 earned her a monicker as the female Rimbaud. The subject of numerous books, her brief solitary life and mystical writings have become a hot international film property. Currently Mathilda May is portraying the heroine under Ian Pringle's direction in a Franco-Australian coprod.

Laurent's film in fact was begun several years ago and interrupted

when its producer, the Paris- and Lisbon-based Paolo Branco, went bankrupt. Film was finally bailed out by another indie producer (whose company has also gone under since), and completed only last year.

Most of the film was shot in the Cape Verde islands off the coast of Portugal, where the barren landscapes stood in adequately for the Algerian desert. The lack of financial means obviously has straitened director Laurent's intentions, even though she claims to have been uninterested in period reconstitution.

A greater weakness is Laurent and Philippe Arnaud's screenplay, which functions on the assumption that the viewer knows something about Eberhardt. Material is boiled down from her published diaries to her contacts with a stranded French painter and her inconstant relationship with an Arab lover. But the elliptical treatment of such moments as the heroine's death and the rather abstract talkiness make for meager film fare.

Danuta Zarazik, a young newcomer of Polish origins, plays Isabelle as a closed book that can't even be skimmed. Philippe Clevenot, a legit actor of commanding presence, steals the film from her as the exiled painter who's losing his eysight. Abdallah Badis is adequately forlorn as the handsome lover. — *Len.*

Stan The Flasher
(FRENCH)

Paris A Pyramide release of an R. Films/Canal Plus coproduction. Produced by François Ravard. Written and directed by Serge Gainsbourg. Camera (color), Olivier Gueneau; editor, Babeth Si Ramdane; music, Gainsbourg; sound, Michel Brethez, Gérard Rousseau; art direction, Raoul Albert; production manager, Jean Lara; assistant director, Richard Debuisne. Reviewed at Gaumont screening room, Neuilly, March 1, 1990. Running time: **67 MIN.**
Stan. . . . . .Claude Berri
Aurore. . . . . .Aurore Clément
David. . . . . .Richard Bohringer
Natasha. . . . . .Elodie
Rosalie. . . . . .Lucie Cabanis
Father. . . . . .Daniel Duval
Cell mate. . . . . .Michel Robin

■ Serge Gainsbourg, the gifted iconoclastic songwriter and sometime filmmaker, checks in with his fourth and most compact feature, ''Stan the Flasher,'' which relates the terminal despair of an aging impotent exhibitionist. Commercial potential is limited.

Film is typical of Gainsbourg's sexual preoccupations and interest in young nymphets, but is less repellent than his previous pic, ''Charlotte Forever'' and its incest-minded navel-watching. Though running only 67 minutes, this static though slickly made tale may seem hours long to many.

Title role is that of a sexually burned out intellectual played by Claude Berri, the megabuck producer (''The Bear,'' ''Valmont'') and filmmaker (''Jean de Florette''), here making a return to his first profession. Berri is a private tutor in English literature, and lives with a younger woman (Aurore Clément) whom he can no longer satisfy in bed and whom he suspects of infidelity.

His desire thus fixes on another object: one of his pupils, a budding moist-lipped beauty (played by a nubile newcomer identified only as Elodie). After he tries to get under her skirts during a bit of close quarters tutoring, he gets his head cracked by an indignant father and does a jail term, where his cell mate is a versifying murderer (Michel Robin). When he returns home to find that Clément has flown the coop, he blows his brains out.

Protagonist's ''flashing'' is not presented as chronic exhibitionism, only an occasional lapse, and it's not until the final minutes that he's seen in action, flapping his raincoat up a park staircase for an indifferent audience of schoolgirls, who include Elodie.

Gainsbourg's script is essentially a series of intimate encounters and monologues which reach for, and sometimes attain, a kind of seedy melancholy lyricism. Berri, revealing an underused acting temperament (along with pot belly and genitals), is the perfect embodiment of Gainsbourg's Shakespeare-quoting lowlife. But it's tough working up any sympathy for this Hamlet of the fleshpots, who's obviously a projection of the filmmaker. — *Len.*

Baby Blood
(FRENCH)

Paris A Neuf de Coeur release of a Partner's Prods./Exo 7 Prods. coproduction. Produced by Ariel Zeitoun, Joelle Malberg, Irène Sohm. Directed by Alain Robak. Screenplay, Robak, Serge Cukier; camera (Fujicolor),

Bernard Dechet; editor, Elisabeth Moulinier; music, Carlos Acciari; sound, Yves Laisné, Serge Richard, Frédéric Giovanelli, Pierre Lemenuel, Joel Rangon, Thierry Sabatier; assistant director, Dominique Truillou; production manager, Daniel Deschamps; special makeup and special effects, Benoit Lestang, Jean-Marc Toussaint. Reviewed at Georges V cinema, Paris, Jan. 28, 1990. Running time: **85 MIN.**

Yanka. . . . . . . .Emmanuelle Escourrou
Richard. . . . . . . .Jean-François Gallotte
Also with: Christian Sinniger, Roselyn Geslot, François Frapier.

———

■ **This unusual French-made chiller has all the crude earmarks of the knee-jerk gore genre, but it made a singular impression on the jury of the last Avoriaz Film Festival, which pushed through a special mention for the noncompetitive selection.**

Film has ample gruesomeness but the bloodletting and horror are tempered by a macabre, ironic sense of humor. It could be something of a sleeper in the glutted international horror market.

"Baby Blood" is an unspeakably slimy thing from the beginnings of time that snakes its way up between the legs and into the womb of a footloose young girl, and demands that she bring it into the world the human way. But milk and baby bottles won't do. This literal *enfant terrible* needs male human blood to grow and

exhorts its carrier to serial murders.

Though derivative of shock tactics from "Alien" and other fiend-on-the-loose pictures, cowriter-director Alain Robak effectively mixes gore and black humor (the conversations between the girl and her "baby," an electronically transmogrified voice, are often absurdly amusing).

Script and direction are occasionally sloppy and unlikely. The pregnant girl sometimes kills and walks away spotless, while on other occasions gets good and bloody. In latter instances, her potential victims conveniently seem not to notice.

Film wallows in sexual repulsion typical of horror movies. The heroine (fleshy newcomer Emmanuelle Escourrou) lures third-rate mashers and machos as prey. There's hardly an appealing man in sight. In a conclusion worthy of a feminist nightmare, she is threatened by a bus full of football jocks, but her now-born "baby" settles everybody's hash by bring-

ing about the climactic disaster.

Special effects by Benoit Lestang and Jean-Marc Toussaint are usually adequate and Elisabeth Moulinier's editing is good at hiding them when they're less so. In one of the script's best ideas the creature, first represented as phallic and serpentine, is born in a normal human baby body, then makes a sudden debut in its primeval form in the climactic bus sequence. — *Len.*

———

Stuff Stephanie In The Incinerator

———

Sydney A Troma release of an Allied Film Group production. Produced and directed by Don Nardo. Screenplay, Nardo, Peter Jones; camera (color), Herb Fuller; editor, James Napoli; sound, John Terry; associate producer, Jones. MPAA Rating: PG-13. Reviewed on Roadshow Home Video cassette, Sydney, Feb. 4, 1990. Running time: **98 MIN.**
Stephanie/Casey. . . . . . .Catherine Dee
Paul/Jared. . . . . .William Dane
Roberta/Robert. . . . . . . .M.R. Murphy
Nick/Rory. . . . . .Dennis Cunningham
Also with: Paul Nielsen, Andy Milk, Phil Vincent.

———

■ **This so-called psychological thriller comedy is so tedious and forgettable Troma has probably decided to resort to the typically Troma-esque title and artwork as about the only way of mustering any interest in it. Pic has been launched onto the unsuspecting Aussie homevid market.**

Even discerning Troma fans will be disappointed at this one: if it ever got released theatrically by mistake censors would find very little that remotely approaches the usual Troma explicitness. It doesn't work as a thriller relying on suspense instead of shock, and it's certainly not a comedy.

Wealthy decadents William Dane and Catherine Dee (Stephanie), along with associates M.R. Murphy and Dennis Cunningham, act out scenarios involving kidnaping, plot to murder one another, seduction, and so forth to make their lives more interesting.

Whole film is one of these scenarios, with various different parts and unenthralling twists until pic's finish when the quartet split up until their next game, which seems to be an annual occurrence.

Hamfisted acting — perhaps the actors are acting that way as part of the game, but the effect is the same — banal dialog and a com-

plete absence of mystery and suspense eradicate any chance of salvaging what may have been an okay idea. There is an incinerator (in a shot for about two seconds) but Stephanie isn't in any danger of being stuffed in it.

Tech credits are adequate, although pic obviously was shot on a minuscule budget. Barring unforeseen and unlikely cult exposure, theatrical opportunity would have to be nil.

— *Doch.*

———

Os Sermoes
(The Sermons)
(BRAZILIAN)

———

Rio de Janeiro An Embrafilme release of Embrafilme production. Produced by Marica Leite, Maria Helena Nascimento. Directed by Julio Bressane. Screenplay, Bressane; camera (Eastmancolor), Jose Tadeu Ribeiro; editor, Dominique Paris; music, Livio Tragtemberg; sound, Ricardo Giestas, Roberto Carvalho; sets, Roberto Granja, Rosa Dias; costumes, Bia Salgado. Nei Salgado. Reviewed at Sala 2, Estacao Botafogo Theatre, Rio de Janeiro, Feb 5. 1990. Running time: **75 MIN.**
Padre Antonio Vieira. . . . .Othon Bastos
Also with: Eduardo Tornaghi, Paschoal Villaboim, Bia Nunes, Breno Moroni, Karen Acioly, Guará, Caetano Veloso, Haroldo de Campos, Neville D'Almeida.

———

■ **New film by Julio Bressane is inspired by the work of Father Antonio Vieira, one of the most important preachers of the Portuguese language in the 17th century. Film will appeal to slim audience, but those few into Bressane's universe will like this new example of it.**

Bressane, an avant-garde filmmaker who has been contributing some of the most polemical works of the Brazilian cinema over the last 20 years, has been keeping his style and the faith in his aesthetic beliefs.

Vieira, a priest born in Lisbon in 1608, was killed in Salvador in 1697. Pic is about his famous sermons, but very little of the sermons themselves can be detected. A highly auteuristic work, "The Sermons" brings to screen the universe of Bressane much more than that of Antonio Vieira. It reveals, as in most of his films, a coherent discussion about the vehicle and its questions of narrative.

That discussion, for Bressane, started in the early '60s with "Cara a Cara" and developed in some of the most important moments of Brazilian avant-garde cinema: "Matou a Familia e Foi ao Cine-

ma," "A Familia do Barulho," "O Rei do Baralho" and several films made in England in the late '60s/early '70s.

Part of a broad statement about the cinema as a form of expression, "The Sermons" is, like any Bressane film, a work to be enjoyed — and highly enjoyed —by those interested in the cinema turned on itself.

Lack of specific sites for distribution of avant-garde films in Brazil drives "The Sermons" to a regular release in commercial screens. Obviously not a product for mass audiences, "The Sermons" is nevertheless an important part — in universal terms — of a conception of cinema usually intended for cinematheques, film archives and special sites. — *Hoin.*

———

Atoski vrtovi
(God's Witness)
(YUGOSLAVIAN)

———

Berlin An Otvoreni Ateljo Beograda/ Belgrade Open Studio presentation of Otvoreni Atelje Beograda production in association with Avala Film. Executive producer, Snejana Stoytchitch. Directed by Stojan Stojcic. Screenplay, Stojcic, Slaven Radovanovic; camera (Eastmancolor), Aleksandar Petkovic; editors, Vuksan Lukovac, Peter Jakonic; music, Ksenija Zecevic; sound, Marco Rodic; production design, Stojcic, Misa Miric. Reviewed at Berlin Film Festival (Panorama section), Feb. 18, 1990. Running time: **98 MIN.**
Igor Vasiljev. . . . .Tanasije Uzunovitch
Also with: Neda Arneric, Petar Bozcvic, Nedad Nedimic, Elizabeta Djorevska, Danica Maksimovic, Dusan Janicijevic, Mima Karadzic.

———

■ **Following in the Yugoslavian cinematic tradition of surrealism/magic realism (Dusan Makavejev, Emir Kusturica), Serbian first-time director Stojan Stojcic's "God's Witness" tells a story of spiritual resistance to physical political persecution. It does so on a large canvas filled to bursting-point with a regular circus of action and images.**

In the Balkans after the Russian Revolution, the new Communist zealots hunt down everyone who will not forswear their Orthodox Catholic ways and symbols. Chief targets in this hunt are Igor Vasiljev, an icon painter, and Randjel, an architect, who decide to rebuild their wrecked church.

Persecution and resistance are then put on display with vigor and imagination in a production in perfect technical control of its overall design. Its indulgence in off-tangent detail, however, will eventually doom "God's Witness" as an international boxoffice commodity beyond a specialized circuit.

Stojcic can't help throwing in quotes or inspirations from fellow filmmakers Tarkovski and Jodorowski or paying tribute to a series of painters such as Hieronymus Bosch, Marc Chagall and even Salvador Dali. In the midst of this, sundry characters of saints and grotesques act as if in passion plays or Brechtian cabaret.

"God's Witness" boasts plenty of violence and lustily vulgar sex. Its catchy music score makes easy transformations from liturgical strains to mainstream jazz. With plenty of magic in plot and scenery, the numerous anachronisms are calculated but weaken the film's essential message and clutter up its narrative stream. — *Kell.*

No Daireikai II
(Big Spirit World II)
(JAPAN)

Tokyo A Shochiku-Fuji release of a Tamba Kikaku production. Executive producer, Tetsuro Tamba. Chief producer, Kuniko Higashijima. Produced by Misako Saka, Tokuko Shishikura. Directed by Mitsunori Kube. Screenplay, Kanna Urata; camera (color), Jun Seikawa; music, Goro Awami; conceptual designer, Kiko Mozuna; technical adviser, Kozo Okazaki; adviser, Tsuneyuki Morishima. Reviewed at Tokyo Rex, Jan. 22, 1990. Running time: **105 MIN.**
Tsuyoshi Okamoto . . . . . Tetsuro Tamba
Yashiro . . . . Koji Takahashi
Mayumi Okamoto . . . . . Hitomi Nakahara
Goddess . . . . Judy Ongg
Mami Yamasi . . . . Maki Watase

■ This is the second feature-length investigation by Tetsuro Tamba — actor, director and very serious spiritualist — of the afterlife. It is subtitled "Shindara Odoroitall," or "Death Came as a Surprise."

What, after all, could be more surprising than to learn that the good spirit world is brightly lit, has lots of flowers, buildings of gold and spirits dressed in loose-fitting garments of white? Equally surprising is the revelation that the bad spirit world is dimly lit, has fiery topography and spirits wielding whips.

Okamoto (Tamba) is executed for a murder he didn't commit. The judges who sentence him are portrayed by comedians Tamori and Sanma Akashiya. Seems that Okamoto deserves capital punish-

ment because, 130 years previous, in a different incarnation, he did murder someone.

"There's no running away from your karma," he's told during a visit to the good spirit world by a magic wand-wielding Judy Ongg, who seems to have discovered the secret of eternal youth. It is obvious Ongg is photographed from no closer than 50 ft. and through a muslin-covered lens.

Prior to being instructed about cosmic inevitability, Okamoto wanders the streets of this world with other spirits, including those of Imperial Army soldiers. Remarkably sanguine at having walked away from his death by hanging, Okamoto amuses himself by inhabiting the bodies of others and by visiting grieving friends and relatives.

As was the case with American-made epics of a spiritual nature, this one features anonymous extras by the gross and stars by the dozen. Yoko Nogiwa, Tamba's costar on the fondly remembered tv series "Key Hunter," appears in the bad spirit world briefly enough to prevent damage to her reputation, if not her judgment.
— *Bail.*

Erdenschwer
(Earthbound)
(WEST GERMAN)

Berlin An Oliver Herbrich and WDR tv coproduction with Calypso Film of Cologne. Directed by Oliver Herbrich. Screenplay, Herbrich, Andreas Hamburger; dialog author, Friedemann Schulz; camera (color), Ludolph Weyer; editor, Romy Schumann; music, Hannes Thanheiser; sound, Gerd Metz; art direction, Tobias Siemsen, Gerald Damowsky. Reviewed at Berlin Film Festival, (New German Films), Feb. 16, 1990. Running time: **94 MIN.**
Franz Seeliger . . . . Hannes Thanheiser
Hanna Frey . . . . Vera Tschechowa
Dr. Frank . . . . Rüdiger Vogler
Head doctor . . . . Hark Böhm
Brittle man . . . . Peter Radtke
Circus director . . . . Alfred Edel
Young Seeliger . . . . Martin Abram
Midgit . . . . Alida Pisu

■ This gem of a first feature by 28-year-old Oliver Herbrich bodes well for the future. Pic has wit, charm and substance. German tv execs in search of directing talent will be looking his way.

The plot itself — a pinch of "One Flew Over The Cuckoo's Nest" and a dash of "King of Hearts" — is hardly new, but Herbrich seems in firm control of his

strong cast.

Vera Tschechowa is tops as the mental institution director who is going crazy being stuck with crazy people all the time. Hannes Thanheiser is a delight as the octogenarian who is convinced he can fly, and who helps the frau doctor loosen the fetters which keep her "earthbound."

Tech credits above average for this low-budgeter. — *Gill.*

Living Doll
(BRITISH)

Porto An MGM Video release in the U.K. A Spectacular Trading production. Produced by Dick Randall. Directed by Peter Litten, George Dugdale. Screenplay, Dugdale, Mark Ezra; camera (Agfacolor), Colin Munn; editor, Jim Connock; music, DeWolf Ltd.; special effects, Paul Catling. Reviewed at Porto (Spain) Film Festival, Feb. 2, 1990. Running time: **92 MIN.**
With: Mark Jax, Katie Orgill, Gary Martin, Freddie Earlle, Eartha Kitt.

■ This cheapo horror pic touches all the bases (sex, violence, gore) but arrives at home D.O.A. Suitable for the homevid market, but that's it.

Set in New York (a few exteriors are thrown in), pic concerns an antisocial medical student making some extra bucks working in a morgue. He has been ogling a pretty flower salesgirl, who, following a car accident, turns up on a slab.

Predictably, the student decides to abduct the corpse and set up a menage à deux in his tumbledown digs. Though the girl starts decomposing, the student still sees her in her pristine lifelike beauty. Neither rigor mortis nor the expected stench materialize, though an occasional rat does nibble away in the apartment.

The living doll then urges the 'lent to wreak revenge on her ex-boyfriend, who had been driving the car and is romping with her successor. That allows pic to enter into a bit of mayhem.

The tale is too slim and drags along as the makers fill out the requisite 90 minutes with twaddle. Special effects are decidedly unspectacular, pacing is mostly slow and the story unconvincing. Eartha Kitt has a cameo as the landlady. — *Besa.*

User Friendly
(NEW ZEALAND)

Auckland A Film Konstruktion production in association with the New Zealand commission. (Intl. sales, NZFC). Produced by Trevor Haysom, Frank Stark. Directed by Gregor Nicholas. Screenplay, Stark, Nicholas, Norelle Scott; camera (color), Donald Duncan; editor, David Coulson; music, Mark Nicholas. Reviewed at Cinema 2, Auckland, N.Z., March 18, 1990. Running time: **90 MIN.**
Billy . . . . William Brandt
Augusta . . . . Alison Bruce
Miranda . . . . Judith Gibson
Wayne . . . . David Letch
Monty . . . . Lewis Martin
Marjorie . . . . Joan Reid

■ Gregory Nicholas' first feature, "User Friendly," has many sly and stylish black delights and other, often flamboyant inventions, but is hardpressed to coherently unfold its tale of raunch and greed. This uncertain story structure may make pic a difficult proposition for broad theatrical release, although it should have a healthy life at certain fests and on homevid.

An exuberant romp turning the caper genre into Gothic gavotte, "User Friendly" begins when an ancient dog-goddess effigy possessing vast regenerative and erotic powers is stolen from the island of Tokabaru. It surfaces in Auckland, as the property of manic cosmetics tycoon, Miranda Matlock (Judith Gibson). Miranda uses it as a marketing symbol and a form of aphrodisiac to enhance her love life with companion Wayne (David Letch).

Footloose hippie Augusta (Alison Bruce) covets the wooden canine as a means of winning back ex-boyfriend and anthropologist Billy (William Brandt). On the other side of town, Monty (Lewis Martin) and Marjorie (Joan Reid) want it to carry through their experiments on eternal life with the goldie-oldie community of the Balmoral Bowling Center.

A battle for possession takes place with the dog-goddess ultimately fulfilling the desires of all.

Nicholas' particular strengths, and his success as a maker of short films, show in the pace and detail of individual scenes. One such sequence involves mad Marjorie running amok with a syringe filled with the dog-goddess's magic juices. But too often the drive of the main plot is slowed by scenes that are peripheral, and incipient involvement is marooned on a sandbank of whys and wherefores.

Of the players, Joan Reid's stone-eyed grimacing old bitch is a stand-out, and Gibson's frontal, all-stops-out Miranda, shines. The young leads, Brandt and Bruce, the characters mainly responsible for pushing the narrative along, have some difficulty convincingly establishing a presence. — *Nic.*

Wizards Of The Lost Kingdom II

New York A Concorde Pictures release of a New Classics presentation. Produced by Reid Shane. Directed by Charles B. Griffith. Screenplay, Lance Smith; camera (Foto-Kem color), Geza Sinkovics; editor, Jonas Thaler; music, David M. Rubin; sound, Kip Gynn; production design, Kathleen Cooper; costume design, Kimberly Guenther; production manager, Shane; assistant director, Albert T. Dickerson 3d; 2d unit director, Barbara Kallir; associate producer, Sally Mattison. Reviewed on Media Home Entertainment vidcassette, N.Y., Feb. 10, 1990. MPAA Rating: PG. Running time: **79 MIN.**
Dark One. . . . . .David Carradine
Tyor. . . . . .Bobby Jacoby
Anathea. . . . . .Lana Clarkson
Caedmon. . . . . .Mel Welles
Idon. . . . . .Susan Lee Hoffman
Erman. . . . . .Blake Bahner
Donar. . . . . .Sid Haig
Zerz. . . . . .Henry Brandon
Vanir. . . . . .Wayne Grace
Loki. . . . . .Edward Blackoff
Freyja. . . . . .Diana Barton

■ **Lost in the shuffle of recent sequels, this low-budget fantasy pic had a modest release theatrically last year in theaters and vidstores and is reviewed here for the record.**

A sequel to an equally minor 1985 release, film is piloted with little sense of involvement by Charles B. Griffith, legendary scripter of such pics as "A Bucket Of Blood" and "Little Shop Of Horrors. Wizard Mel Welles (shop owner Mushnick in "Little Shop") has the task of reuniting three kingdoms against evil in a far future era. He's aided by a youngster (Bobby Jacoby) and legendary warrior (David Carradine). During their boring trek, the heroes encounter many well-endowed women, including Lana Clarkson, but nothing happens to threaten the film's PG rating. It probably would have worked better targeted for the hard R tag most of Roger Corman's films generate. Chief area of interest is the chance to see old Corman regulars like Welles and Sid Haig again, plus one of the final roles for recently deceased Henry Brandon. — *Lor.*

Beautiful Dreamers
(CANADIAN)

Toronto A Cinexus/Famous Players and C/FP Distribution Inc. release (in Canada) in association with the National Film Board. Produced by Michael Maclear, Martin Walters. Executive producer, Stephen Roth. Executive producer for the National Film Board, Colin Neale. Written and directed by John Kent Harrison. Camera (color), François Protat; editor, Ron Wisman; music, Lawrence Shragge; production designer, Seamus Flannery; costume design, Ruth Secord. Reviewed at Famous Players screening room, Toronto, March 20, 1990. Running time: **105 MIN.**
Dr. Bucke. . . . . .Colm Feore
Walt Whitman. . . . . Rip Torn
Jessie Bucke. . . . . . . Wendel Meldrum
Mollie Jessop. . . . . . . Sheila McCarthy
Rev. Haines. . . . . Colin Fox
Dr. Lett. . . . . .David Gardner
Agatha Haines. . . . . . . Barbara Gordon
Birdie Bucke. . . . . . . .Marsha Moreau
Dr. John Burgess. . . . . .Albert Schultz

■ **A first pic directed by John Kent Harrison, "Beautiful Dreamers" is full of good intentions, but only some of them are realized.**

Pic centers on free-thinker Walt Whitman's actual visit to London, Ontario, in 1880, bringing fresh winds to the city's mental asylum and churning up most of the church and civic elite.

Much is made of the friendship between the older, white-bearded Whitman and the asylum's young superintendent, forcefully played by Canadian actor Colm Feore, who resists then traditionally harsh methods of treating the mentally ill. Maybe he resists because he, too, is injured and has a gimpy leg, about which he says too little.

Taking Whitman's advice, he appeals to the inmates' feelings and lets them out of the building. They play soccer against a team fielded by the town's mocking elite who wind up clapping.

Rip Torn plays Whitman large as a legend rather than on a human scale, but his grand actorly characterization bores quickly. Standout is Wendel Meldrum, a radiant beauty with classy acting skills to boot, who as the superintendent's wife is jealous of the time her husband spends with Whitman. But then, having read Whitman's "racy" poems, she becomes his ally. Meldrum abruptly announces her friendship by joining the two men stripped nude, as they are, at a swimming hole. It's a high point.

Sheila McCarthy makes a powerful wordless cameo appearance as a married patient driven to the point of mad despair by overwork. Rescued from ovary removal by the superintendent, she is among

his first successes while responding to music played in the women's section.

Harrison's script packs too much in yet leaves many key resolutions to over-quick explanation. His direction is uneven, as is François Protat's camerawork. Rest of the cast, particularly Colin Fox, Albert Schultz and David Gardner, does well. — *Adil.*

Hollywood Hot Tubs 2: Educating Crystal

New York An Alimar production. Executive producer, Carol Thompson. Produced by Mark Borde, Ken Raich. Directed by Raich. Screenplay, Brent V. Friedman; camera (Foto-Kem color), Areni Milo; editor, Michael Hoggan; music, John Lombardo, Bill Bodine; sound, William Dager; production design, Thomas Cost; art direction, Jack Licursi; assistant director, Steve Fitzgerald; production manager-associate producer, Shayne Sawyer; stunt coordinator, Eddie Braun; 2d unit director, Borde; 2d unit camera, Arledge Armenaki, casting. Michael Harrah. Reviewed on IVE vidcassette, N.Y., March 15, 1990. MPAA Rating: R. Running time: **100 MIN.**
Crystal. . . . . .Jewel Shepard
Jason. . . . . .Patrick Day
Gary. . . . . .David Tiefen
Pam. . . . . .Remy O'Neill
Billy. . . . . .Rob Garrison
Prince Ahmet. . . . . . . .Bart Braverman
Mr. Darby. . . . . .J.P. Bumstead
Jane. . . . . .Spice Williams
Sandy. . . . . .Dayna Danika
Prof. Drewton. . . . . . . .Michael Pataki
Nahbib. . . . . .Phil Diskin
Hardie. . . . . .Martina Castle
Mindy. . . . . .Tally Chanel
Rita. . . . . .Debra Lee Giometti

■ **Beneath its come-on title, this sequel to Chuck Vincent's 1984 feature moves out of the exploitation film arena to a well-scripted comic look at west coast life styles. Clearly aimed at the video market, pic could have modest theatrical potential as well.**

The Crystal of the title, Jewel Shepard, encores as the bubbly, jiggly valley girl who heads for business school to learn how to run her mom Remy O'Neill's hot tubs/health spa establishment. Evil Bart Braverman (convincing with beard as a prince) is conspiring to take over the business, even planning to marry O'Neill to achieve his ends.

Film is told from the point of view of handsome hero David Tiefen, who's working as a chauffeur to Braverman while writing a book about Shepard. Patrick Day is also appealing as a student who

teams up with her to work on a class project.

Under newcomer Ken Raich's direction, film works due to the quirky touches of Brent Friedman's screenplay. Notable is a strange but amusing subplot of a dinosaur rock guitarist (J.P. Bumstead) working as a hot tub installation man, who comes out of retirement to rock on.

Previously wasted in purely decorative assignments, Shepard comes into her own here in a funny and sympathetic role. It's not quite "Educating Rita," but the formula of gawky ingenue blossoming is a sure-fire one.

Tech credits are fine. — *Lor.*

A Matter of Degrees

Park City, Utah A Backbeat production in association with New Front Films, Linus Associates, George Gund and Fujisankel Communications Intl. Produced by Roy Kissin, Randall Poster. Directed by W.T. Morgan. Screenplay, Poster, Jack Mason, Morgan; camera (color), Paul Ryan; editor, Curtiss Clayton, Charlie Mullin; music, Jim Dunbar; sound, Fred Burnham; production design, Mark Friedberg; art direction, Ginger Tougas; set decoration, Bonita Flanders; assistant director, Raoul Madera; coproducer, Lynn Goldner; associate producers, Paul Moen, John H. Stout, Barbara Katz. Reviewed at the U.S. Film Festival, Park City, Utah, Jan. 22, 1990. No MPAA Rating. Running time: **100 MIN.**
Max. . . . . .Arye Gross
Zeno. . . . . .Tom Sizemore
Kate. . . . . .Judith Hoag
Wells. . . . . .Wendell Pierce
Isabelle. . . . . .Christina Haag
Peter Downs. . . . . .John Doe

■ **An indie project developed via Sundance Institute, "A Matter Of Degrees" enters uncharted territory — the dilemmas of disaffected college students in the '80s — and bumbles around in it, coming up with a few bright passages in a mostly uneven film. Commercial prospects appear slight.**

On the plus side are the film's soundtrack (chockful of the alternative music of contempo bands like Firehose, the Minutemen and Fetchin' Bones) and a charismatic supporting turn by Tom Sizemore as a student and part-time mechanic with a passion for steel.

The story's protagonist, however, reluctant graduating senior Maxwell Glass (Arye Gross), doesn't know what he wants to be and neither does the film.

"Degrees" is at its best when it relaxes into being a rambling coming-of-age story about friends approaching graduation into a world they're not ready for.

Pic spends much of its time trying to be funny and reaching to be hip, posturing its nebulous characters as holdouts against Reagan-era values but not finding anything compelling for them to represent.

Max' rants against the "apathy" of the times are neither fresh nor eloquent, and one sometimes wonders if he is supposed to be a parody of a nonconformist.

Shot on location at the Brown University campus in Providence, R.I., pic follows a group of students whose on-and-off activism centers on preserving the campus radio station, domain of renegade deejay Peter Down (rock musician/ actor John Doe).

Pic begins attempting to strike a satiric tone with a series of MBA-bound students, each sitting in the same "interview" chair and describing their goals, in contrast to Max, who has none. That's soon abandoned for various other styles of storytelling.

Whatever poignancy the characters evoke is undercut by an improbable, commercial-style big finish.

Overall, pic has the insular feel of a project made for a small circle of friends, many of whom were in on it. Director W.T. Morgan, who made the underground rock docu "The Unheard Music," contributes some amusing touches.

Lensing is attractive, and production design by Mark Friedberg is apt and amusing. Soundtrack also includes selections by Doe, Miracle Legion, Throwing Muses, the Lemonheads and Yo La Tengo. — *Daws.*

NEW DIRECTORS/NEW FILMS

Pekin Teki Suikaz
(Beijing Watermelon)
(JAPANESE)

New York A Shochiku (U.S.) release of a Maxdai Inc./Producers System Co. production. Produced by Michio Morioka. Executive producers, Kaneo Kawanabe, Kyoko Obayashi. Directed by Nobuhiko Obayashi. Screenplay, Yoshihiro Ishimatsu, from a story by Lin Xiao-Li and Toru Kugayama; camera (color), Shigekazu Nagano; editor, Nobuhiko Obayashi; music, Tetsuo Konda; art direction, Kazuo Satsuya. Reviewed at Museum Of Modern Art, N.Y. (in New Directors/New Films), March 24, 1990. (No MPAA Rating). Running time: **135 MIN.**

Shunzo . . . . .Bengal
Michi. . . . . .Masako Motai
Dr. Muraki. . . . . .Toru Minegishi
Yamada. . . . . .Takashi Sasano
Teramoto. . . . . .Akira Emoto
Ioka. . . . . .Haruhiko Saito
Li. . . . . .Wu Yue
Chen. . . . . .Fang Qing-Lin
Zhu. . . . . .Li Juan
Zhang. . . . . .Li Han
    Also with: Yang Xiao-Dan, Zhuang Pei-Yuan and Xu Hua.

■ **This meandering tale about a Tokyo greengrocer's obsession with a group of Chinese students may have some appeal in urban markets with sizable Asian-American audiences.**

Shochiku will find out when "Beijing Watermelon" is released in Los Angeles. But Nobuhiko Obayashi's ironic look at contemporary Sino-Japanese relations is best suited to festivals, such as the New Directors/New Films series where it had its U.S. debut.

When Shunzo, a greengrocer with a flourishi ng business, tries to chase a Chinese student for haggling over the price of vegetables, his wife Michi scolds him for being callous and makes him give the boy some odds and ends. Sounding a refrain that becomes a leitmotif of "Beijing Watermelon" she reminds Shunzo that the impoverished Chinese scholars are "strangers in a strange land." The students quickly gravitate to this reluctant benefactor, and gradually Shunzo's attitude softens.

Soon Shunzo is making regular visits to the students, who treat him as a surrogate father. Over the course of a leisurely narration that closely approximates the plot's 6-year time span, the grocer goes "China-mad," giving up ever bigger chunks of his life to the students. To the great distress of his wife, children and hired help, Shunzo's devotion to the students eventually costs him his grocer's license, his savings, his business, his family's harmony and his health. In return Shunzo achieves a type of Confucian fulfillment that, the film suggests, is all too rare in materialistic modern Japan.

An opening crawl states that the film will try to evoke the unrelenting noise that characterizes the" 'tepid peace" enjoyed by Japan. "Beijing Watermelon" works hard at cinematic anthropology, building an Ozu-like tatami-level's view of the crowded intimacy of workingclass Japanese home life. The film, which half-heartedly pretends to be a documentary about a real incident, is given over to dispassionate observation: the daily rituals of the nuclear Tokyo neighborhood, the camaradarie of greengrocers at the wholesale market, the pastimes of sunbathers at grimy harborside beaches and the bizarre agglomeration of the city's architecture.

On another level, "Beijing Watermelon" addresses Chinese-Japanese reconciliation — Shunzo's father was killed during Japan's brutal wartime occupation of China. The Asian neighbors might as well live on different sides of the world. The students are startled by skyscrapers and toll roads, and astounded by the dizzying pace of life in Tokyo. In China, one student observes, the Buddhas are always smiling, but in Japan they're forever meditating. For Shunzo and his family, their extended sacrifice for the students becomes a kind of meditation on the possiblility of a life unbound from the shackles of mercantile success.

"Beijing Watermelon" is technically assured. But Obayashi's late-in-the-game attempt to break through the "fourth wall" by confiding directly to the audience on the artifice of film is contrived and plays awkwardly.

Bengal as Shunzo and Masako Motai as his wife perform with understated grace that might have stayed fresher in a more compressed narrative. — *Rich.*

H-2 Worker

New York A Stephanie Black production, in association with Valley Filmworks. Produced and directed by Black. Camera (Duart color, 16m), Maryse Alberti; additional camera, Tom Sigel; editor, John Mullen; associate editors, Lise Engel, Nancy Salzer; title song, Mutabaruka; sound, Dan Walworth, Hannah Silverman, Scott Briendel, Neil Danziger, David Isay; archival research, Jo Applebaum; associate producer, Jean Casella. Reviewed at Museum of Modern Art (New Directors/New Films series), March 24, 1990. Running time: **66 MIN.**

■ **This to-the-point documentary exposes the problems of underpaid Jamaican workers who trek for six months to toil in the Florida sugar cane fields. It should arouse some action on a long-dormant issue.**

Tourists take for granted the dormitory-style barracks and company stores for field workers that dot the Florida roadside. There's virtually no interaction with the guest workers, who visit the U.S. for 6-month stretches under the H-2 visa program. It's hardly a topic for the nightly newscasts in West Palm Beach or Fort Lauderdale.

Debuting director Stephanie Black lays the issues on the table in clearcut fashion: Poverty in Jamaica makes the chance to earn U.S. bucks nearly irresistible, yet the heavily subsidized farm employers chisel the Jamaicans' wages.

Smug U.S. and Jamaican officials repeatedly assert there is no problem, though the Jamaican prime minister admits things could be improved and that poverty is the root cause here for supporting the program.

Pic's weakest segment presents a thorny issue, namely trade and international economics, in glib fashion. Black counterpoints (on the side of the angels) N.Y. and N.J. politicians arguing for cutting farm subsidies and quotas to help the sugar economies of other countries, with Floridians naturally supporting the status quo. Her crosscutting between the sad-eyed workers and shots of whites enjoying a sugar festival shifts the film into the realm of propaganda.

Black uses hidden-camera techniques to gather footage of the workers' cramped living conditions. There's nothing spectacular about what she shows, but the testimony of the workers points up injustice. Old black & white newsreels drive home the racism behind this phenomenon.

Pic would benefit from pruning, as the images of lonely workers become repetitive and a subplot involving a '40s field hand who now has to collect cans for subsistence is off the mark. Thick accents of the Jamaican interviewees should be subtitled for clarity. — *Lor.*

ARCHIVE FILM REVIEWS

Le Rendez-Vous des quais
(Rendezvous On The Docks)
(FRENCH-B&W)

Paris A Trinacra/Pan Europienné release of a Groupe des Réalisations Cinématographiques production (1953-55). Directed by Paul Carpita. Screenplay, Carpita, André Maufray; camera (b&w), Carpita, Maurette (uncredited); editor, Suzanne de Troye, Suzanne Sandberg; music, Jean Wiener; technical advisor, Marc Maurette. Reviewed at 14 Juillet Odeon theater, Paris, Feb. 19, 1990. Running time: **73 MIN.**

Jean	Roger Mannuta
Robert	André Maufray
Marcelle	Jeanine Moretti
The "yellow" worker	Albert Mannac
Jean's wife	Annie Valde
Toine	Georges Pasquini

Also with: Florent Munoz, Louisette Cavolini, Andrée Atarof, Rose Dominiquetti.

■ **Glasnost in France: This victim of French political censorship is an historical curiosity with modest but genuine qualities. Pic, shot entirely on locations (exteriors and interiors) with a cast of nonpro actors, will interest festivals as a rare example of French neorealism.**

"Le Rendez-Vous des quais" was made in Marseilles in 1953 and confiscated by police at its first local showing two years later. Paul Carpita, an activist schoolteacher who cowrote and directed, long believed prints and negative had been destroyed. Yet in 1988, the copies and the original negative, still under official lock and key, were located at the State Film Archives. With political censorship officially a thing of the past, film was rehabilitated and restored and has finally reached theaters, 35 years after an aborted premiere which nearly ended in bloodshed.

Carpita, the son of a dock worker, made this film about the 1950 Marseilles dockers' strike organized by the Communist labor unions to protest France's involvement in the Indochinese war. Marseilles was the embarkment point for the shipping of arms to Vietnam and the port of call for returning dead and wounded.

Carpita evokes the larger events through the personal difficulties of a young docker and his fiancée. When port authorities learn his brother is a union honcho, they try to set him up as strikebreaker in order to discredit the activist sibling. This strand of plot is not convincingly handled, but the love,

hopes and fears of the couple are affectingly dramatized.

Despite the subject, film contains none of the incendiary rhetoric that authorities claimed could "endanger public order" (official reason for film's ban). Dockers discuss the economic and social crises of the postwar years and the absurdity of the war quietly. A union leader's exhortation to fellow workers to strike is also staged without hyperbole.

This restraint can be taken for timidity, too. Carpita didn't have the means to recreate a dockers' strike or a police crackdown, and had to suggest a good deal to make auds believe that the great port of Marseilles has been paralyzed.

Carpita, however, deftly uses newsreels and clandestinely shot footage which give the film a social scope. Yet, the film works best in its more modest moments. As a portrait of life among the dockers and their families, it has believable warmth, understanding and faith that is alien to more heavy-breathing politically slanted pics.

Film also is a missing link in the history of regional French filmmaking. Author/filmmaker Marcel Pagnol lent Carpita his local studio and sound engineer for the post-synchronization work. The b&w lensing, not credited on film, is good. Only name contributor to the film is composer Jean Wiener, who had scored another commercially ill-fated workers drama, "Le Point du jour" (1949), Louis Daquin's superb neorealist chronicle of a mining community. — *Len.*

Dolgada scastivaja zhizn
(A Long and Happy Life)
(SOVIET-B&W)

Amsterdam An MFM/IAF release of a Lenfilm production (1967). Written and directed by Gennadi Schpalikov. Camera (b&w), D. Meshev; music, V. Ovtchinnikov. No other credits provided. Reviewed at the Rotterdam Film Festival, Feb. 2, 1990. Running time: **61 MIN.**

Victor	K. Lavrov
Lena	I. Gulaya

■ **A beautiful, fascinating Soviet film with an intriguing history, "A Long and Happy Life" will stir admiration for**

its writing and direction, straightforward yet cunning.

This was the only film directed by Gennadi Schpalikov, a popular screenwriter. It was released for a few days in 1967 in some out-of-the-way cinemas, then withdrawn suddenly, without explanation. Schpalikov continued to write scipts for successful films. Then, in 1974, he hanged himself.

It took Rotterdam fest director Marco Müller a good deal of negotiating to premiere the pic at this year's edition. It was certainly worth the effort. Pic shows how little money is needed to create a masterpiece.

Little happens in this film. Only two people matter. Schpalikov systematically "de-dramatizes" the action with what he called "little points of interruption" and "purely visual feelings."

A man and a woman meet on a bus carrying a group of young people to the theater. He (K. Lavrov) is an geologist, she (I. Gulaya) is a divorced factory worker. He impresses her with his talk of faraway places. She invites him to join the group of friends at the theater. He refuses, claiming he's too dirty and disheveled. But he rushes to a barber, changes his clothing and runs back to the theater only to learn the performance, Chekhov's "The Cherry Orchard," is sold out. Someone shows him how to crash the building.

Lavrov is not interested in the play, only in Gulaya. At the intermission, a long one with music and dancing, Lavrov kisses her and takes her out of the theater and walks her home. There they separate, because her mother and little daughter are upstairs.

The next day she appears with her child on a tourist boat where Lavrov has spent the night. He takes them to a restaurant where they sit like a family on a yearly outing. Suddenly Lavrov rushes off on a pretext of a phone call, but instead leaves and boards a bus. At the other end of the bus is Gulaya, dejected, but not desperate. She probably is going home to mother. He probably is going home, but to nowhere in particular.

Writer-director described the film as one "devoid of concreteness or heroes, which slipped through his fingers like the massive barge steaming off in the film's never-ending finale."

That's an unforgettable sequence — the barge gliding through the immense hostile river

delta. A young woman stands in the stern, playing an accordion and singing. An obstinate young man stands on the bridge, waving and whistling sharply. The barge glides on into the open sky, open water, open ending. — *Wall.*

Berlin Um Die Ecke
(Berlin Around The Corner)
(EAST GERMAN-B&W)

Berlin A DEFA Films presentation of a Berlin Group production. Directed by Gerhard Klein. Screenplay, Wolfgang Kohlhaase; camera (b&w), Peter Krause; editor, Evelyn Carow; music, Georg Katzer; sound, Hans-Joachim Kreinbrink; art director, Alfred Drosdek; costumes, Barbara Braumann; makeup, Alois Strasser, Hela Mertens. Reviewed at the Berlin Forum of the Young Cinema, Feb. 14, 1990. Running time: **88 MIN.**

Olaf	Dieter Mann
Karin	Monika Gabriel
Horst	Kaspar Eichel
Krautmann	Erwin Geschonneck
Hütte	Hanns Hardt-Hardtloff

Also with: Harald Warmbrunn, Kurt Böwe, Jürgen Frohriep, Rudolf Ulrich, Hans-Joachim Hamisch, Achim Schmidtchen.

■ **A very circumspect and carefully worded picture, quite innocent by today's standards, this 1965 production was Gerhard Klein's last feature film, which he never completed or saw on a screen before his death in 1970.**

The film, implying the young generation is misunderstood and deprived because it refuses to comply with elders' conduct, is essentially episodic, revolving around Olaf, a young Berliner who loves his motorcycle and his leather jacket.

He loves even more the pretty nightclub singer who works weekdays in a restaurant and has a shady husband in the background. Meanwhile, Olaf and his friend, Horst, represent the irreverent freshness of youth.

Loosely jointed script doesn't fully develop characters or situations, skipping instead from one to the other and offering a social survey of working class conditions at the time. There is a generally sympathetic look at the characters, including the older ones who may be set in their ways but undoubtedly have good intentions.

Once again, the blame is not put on the system, which everybody is keen on helping to succeed, but rather on individual misconceptions that have to be corrected. The East German censors, evidently, found that even this was too much for them to take.

— *Edna.*

Cry-Baby

Hollywood A Universal Pictures release of an Imagine Entertainment presentation. Produced by Rachel Talalay. Executive producers, Jim Abrahams, Brian Grazer. Written and directed by John Waters. Camera (Deluxe color), David Insley; editor, Janice Hampton; music score, Patrick Williams; music supervision, Becky Mancuso, Tim Sexton; sound (Dolby), Richard Angelella, Dwayne Dell; choreography, Lori Eastside; production design, Vincent Peranio; art direction, Delores Deluxe; costume/makeup design, Van Smith; set decoration, Chester Overlock 3d, Virginia Nichols; unit production manager, Karen Koch; assistant director, Mary Ellen Woods; casting, Paula Herold, Pat Moran. Reviewed at Directors Guild of America, L.A., March 30, 1990. MPAA Rating: PG-13. Running time: **85 MIN.**

Cry-Baby	Johnny Depp
Allison	Amy Locane
Ramona	Susan Tyrrell
Mrs. Vernon-Williams	Polly Bergen
Belvedere	Iggy Pop
Pepper	Ricki Lake
Wanda	Traci Lords
Hatchet Face	Kim McGuire
Milton	Darren E. Burrows

■ With its cult humor likely to elude today's teens and its plot too conventional for in-the-know fans, John Waters' mischievous satire of the teen exploitation genre will have a hard time finding a large enough audience to recoup its cost.

Even so, pic is entertaining as a rude joyride through another era, full of great clothes and hairdos, snappy dialog and the perverse fun of its oddball casting (including Patty Hearst, David Nelson, Troy Donahue and Willem Dafoe).

Pic's sassy score includes clever originals ("Doin' Time For Bein' Young") by L.A. music scenesters Dave Alvin, J.D. Souther and Waddy Wachtel, plus little-known oldies gems like Doc Starkes' "Women In Cadillacs."

Set on Waters' Baltimore turf, "Cry-Baby" returns to the nascent days of rock 'n' roll when teens were king, where the clean-cut "squares" are pitted against the hoodlum "drapes."

Cry-Baby (Johnny Depp), a handsome delinquent with a perpetual tear in his eye (in memory of his criminal parents who died in the electric chair), takes the bait from a pony-tailed blonde from the well-bred set (Amy Locane).

He steals her away from the country club to hear him sing at a redneck rockabilly concert, and the predictable mayhem ensues when the males from her crowd show up to seek vengeance, starting a fight that lands Cry-Baby in reform school.

He then must escape to be reunited with his girl and his gang, but not before he and his cellmates have time for some jailhouse rock.

Once it's clear the plot is just a raucous rebel without a cause with a handful of inspired elements clipped to a wornout "Romeo & Juliet" storyline, a lot of the foolery begins to wear thin. In "Hairspray," Waters' 1988 crossover hit, one could root for such subversively engrossing themes as tv dance show integration or chubbette Ricki Lake's romance.

"Cry-Baby's" gorgeous star Depp is nobody's underdog, not even with an electric chair tattooed on his chest nor with supporting bizarros (including Lake as his "knocked-up" sister, Pepper).

The goofy, pandering gags in pic's second half are like something out of a Chevy Chase movie, particularly when a rat leads Cry-Baby down the wrong tunnel in his attempted prison escape and then laughs at him, and also when Allison's uptight grandmother (Polly Bergen) gets moving in a rock 'n' roll dance number.

That Waters hasn't lost his wicked sense of humor is evident in a scene at an orphanage where the children are displayed, pet-shop style, in glass cages. It's just that his old and new intentions don't always mix comfortably.

There's so much commotion in the pic, with its 11 full-fledged dance numbers and elaborate production values, that one can't help but catch on that a story's missing.

Depp is great as the delinquent juve, delivering the melodramatic lines with straight-faced conviction and putting some Elvis-like snap and wiggle into his moves.

Choreography by Lori Eastside is whimsical and sharp, as are costumes by Van Smith. — Daws.

I Love You To Death

New York A Tri-Star Pictures release of a Chestnut Hill production. Executive producers, Charles Okun, Michael Grillo. Produced by Jeffrey Lurie, Ron Moler. Coproducers, Patrick Wells, Lauren Weissman. Directed by Lawrence Kasdan. Screenplay, John Kostmayer; camera (Technicolor), Owen Roizman; editor, Anne V. Coates; music, James Horner; sound (Dolby), David MacMillan; production design, Lilly Kilvert; art direction, Jon Hutman; set decoration, Cricket Rowland; costume design, Aggie Guerard Rodgers; assistant director, Grillo; production manager, Okun; additional camera, Stephen H. Burum; associate producers, John Marsh, Lori Cristina Weiss, Lynn Isenberg, Kostmayer; casting, Wallis Nicita. Reviewed at Gemini 1 theater, N.Y., March 30, 1990. MPAA Rating: R. Running time: **96 MIN.**

Joey Boca	Kevin Kline
Rosalie Boca	Tracey Ullman
Nadja	Joan Plowright
Devo	River Phoenix
Harlan	William Hurt
Marlon	Keanu Reeves
Lt. Schooner	James Gammon
Lacey	Victoria Jackson
Joey's mother	Miriam Margolyes
Wiley	Jack Kehler
Girl at disco	Phoebe Cates
Dewey Brown	Kathleen York
Bridget	Heather Graham
Lawyer	Lawrence Kasdan

Also with: Alisan Porter, Jon Kasdan, Michelle Joyner, John Kostmayer, Samantha Kostmayer.

■ "I Love You To Death" is a stillborn attempt at black comedy that wastes considerable acting talent. Audiences attracted by the big names will likely feel insulted rather than amused.

Lawrence Kasdan's four previous directorial efforts have successfully tackled genres as diverse as film noir ("Body Heat") and the Western ("Silverado"), but he fails to exert the control necessary to create a dark but humorous tone here. Film plays like one long in-joke reminiscent of the Rat Pack offerings of three decades ago.

Opening credits stress tale is based on a true story, but John Kostmayer's screenplay never makes events remotely interesting. In his third Kasdan outing, Kevin Kline mugs beyond his Oscar-winning "A Fish Called Wanda" assignment to create a stereotypical Italian restaurant owner (complete with Don Novello's Father Guido Sarducci accent) who can't help cheating with scores of women on his frumpish wife, Tracey Ullman.

Awkward script has Ullman discovering Kline at the end of the second reel in a tryst at a library and, after brief consultation with her Yugoslav mom Joan Plowright, resolving to kill him.

Remainder of the film consists of variations on the gag of Kline's invulnerability to bumbling murder attempts by Ullman, Plowright, best friend River Phoenix and hired space cadet hitmen William Hurt & Keanu Reeves. "Harold And Maude" it ain't. Conclusion of Kline & Ullman reconciling after all the mayhem may be true to reality but is pure corn.

Film founders because the cast is out of control. Kasdan allows his American actors (many of them pals or relatives) to ham it up in revue sketch fashion with no consistency.

Chief culprit is Hurt, an actor whose screen career has been linked advantageously to Kasdan since "Body Heat," but who pulls faces embarrassingly here as a retarded hippie. Some of his final shots look like outtakes misguidedly left in the film à la Blake Edwards' trailblazing "Return Of The Pink Panther" inclusion of Catherine Schell breaking up at Peter Sellers' antics. Here a cardinal sin is committed: footage isn't funny.

At the other extreme, the three British actresses here are models of professionalism, reflecting the difference between taking comedy seriously or treating it as a joke. Ullman unfortunately fades into the woodwork by steadfastly adopting a bland speech pattern and looking as homely as possible. Plowright is solid as her mom.

Film's only funny scene takes place the in final reel as Miriam Margolyes ("Little Dorrit") visits the hospital to repeatedly slap her son Kline on his bullet wound-bandaged head in exasperation.

Kline's exaggerated approach works for a while, but he's virtually written out of the middle reels. Ironically, one of the better sequences occurs at a disco when Kline trots out some wild come-on lines in attempting to pick up uncredited guest star Phoebe Cates, his real-life wife. By not being part of the "real film," Cates is allowed to be quite natural and is more appealing than the leads.

Keanu Reeves is pleasantly dippy as Hurt's dimwitted partner, but River Phoenix' heavy method acting is not conducive to comedy.

As a big-budget project, film's technical polish cannot be faulted, including crisp photography by Owen Roizman (his first since Harold Becker's "Taps" and "Vision Quest") and Stephen Burum (who also did the dark comedy "The War Of The Roses").

Unfortunately, Kasdan delivers little action and creates no distinctive atmosphere via the arbitrary Tacoma, Wash. location. Director can't take all the blame, as 10 producers are credited in various capacities. — Lor.

Ernest Goes To Jail

New York A Buena Vista release of a Touchstone Pictures presentation, in association with Silver Screen Partners IV, of an Emshell Producers Group production. Executive producer, Martin Erlichman. Produced by Stacy Williams. Coproducer, Coke Sams. Directed by John Cherry. Screenplay, Charlie Cohen; camera (CFI color, Technicolor prints), Peter Stein; editor, Sharyn L. Ross, Farrel Levy; music, Bruce Arntson, Kirby Shelstad; sound (Dolby), Richard E. Schirmer; production design, Chris August; art direction, Mark Ragland; set decoration, Connie Gray; costume design, Shawn Barry; assistant director, Patrice Leung; production manager, Carol Sue Byron; visual effects supervisor, Tim McHugh; 2d unit director, J. Clarke Gallivan; stunt coordinator, Chuck Waters; special effects coordinator, William H. Schirmer; associate producer, Phil Walden; casting, Ben Rubin. Reviewed at Baronet theater, N.Y., March 31, 1990. MPAA Rating: PG. Running time: **81 MIN.**

Ernest P. Worrell/
Mr. Nash/Auntie Nelda. . . . . .Jim Varney
Chuck. . . . . Gailard Sartain
Bobby. . . . . Bill Byrge
Charlotte Sparrow. . . . . . .Barbara Bush
Rubin Bartlett. . . . . .Barry Scott
Lyle. . . . . .Randall (Tex) Cobb
Oscar Pendlesmythe. . . . . .Dan Leegant
Warden. . . . . .Charles Napier
Eddie. . . . . .Jim Conrad
Judge. . . . . .Jackie Welch

■ **Disney's third "Ernest" picture is a funny low-brow comedy, with enough sight gags and action to amuse the targeted smallfry audience and deliver okay off-season b.o. in a market niche once belonging to Don Knotts.**

Comedian Jim Varney, whose autobiography should be titled "The Importance Of Being Ernest," has the bumbling, cornpone character down to a science. He's no Buster Keaton (who Varney vaguely resembles physically with his ever-present cap on screen), but a rubber-faced creation that is genuinely amusing.

Charlie Cohen's script provides a solid formula basis this time: Bank janitor Ernest P. Worrell (Varney) is trapped in prison while serving on jury duty when the unscrupulous defendant (Barry Scott) accused of murdering a fellow con notices the resemblance between Ernest and powerful inmate Nash (also Varney). Switch is arranged when the judge and jury visit the scene of the crime, the prison yard.

Remainder of "Ernest Goes To Jail" concentrates on Varney's dual portrayals of fishes out of water: Ernest in jail impersonating the King Rat lookalike (giving the comic a chance to trot out cute carbons of Cagney, Bogart and others), while sleazy Nash on the outside plans to rob the bank where Ernest works. Pic relies heavily on well-timed slapstick and interesting special effects, notably Ernest

as a human magnet when electrified.

Varney naturally dominates the picture, getting a chance to show potential as a villain in the Nash footage. His craggy features take on a sinister edge easily. Supporting cast is solid, ranging from the effective team of Gailard Sartain and Bill Byrge as security guards to lovely, tall redhead Barbara Bush (no resemblance to the First Lady) as romantic interest.

As the tough black con, Barry Scott creates a believable character instead of a caricature. Randall (Tex) Cobb is sympathetic as a tender-hearted goon in stir.

Pic provides solid production values on a presumably modest budget, notably Chris August's convincing prison sets that Peter Stein's pastel lighting stylizes for cartoonish effect. — *Lor.*

Cyrano de Bergerac
(FRENCH)

Paris A Hachette Première/UGC release (Orion Classics in U.S.) of a Hachette Première/Caméra One/Films A2/D.D. Productions/UGC coproduction. Produced by René Cleitman, Michel Seydoux. Directed by Jean-Paul Rappeneau. Screenplay, Rappeneau, Jean-Claude Carrière, from the play by Edmond Rostand; camera (color), Pierre Lhomme; editor, Noëlle Boisson; music, Jean-Claude Petit; sound, Pierre Gamet, Dominique Hennequin; art direction, Ezio Frigerio; costumes, Franca Squarciapino; makeup, Jean-Pierre Eychenne; nose creator, Michele Burke; assistant director, Thierry Chabert; production managers, Gérard Gaultier, Patrick Bordier; casting, Romain Brémond. Reviewed at the Gaumont Ambassade theater, Paris, March 28, 1990. Running time: **138 MIN.**
Cyrano de Bergerac. . . .Gérard Depardieu
Roxane. . . . . Anne Brochet
Christian de Neuvillette. . . .Vincent Perez
Count de Guiche. . . . . .Jacques Weber
Rageneau. . . . . Roland Bertin
Le Bret. . . . . . .Philippe Morier-Genoud
Viscount of Valvert. . . . .Philippe Volter
Carbon de Castel-Jaloux. .Pierre Maguelon
The Duenna. . . . . .Josiane Stoleru
Monk. . . . . Jeromé Nicolin
Montfleury. . . . . Gabriel Monnet

■ **A winner by more than a nose, "Cyrano de Bergerac" attains a near-perfect balance of verbal and visual flamboyance. Gérard Depardieu's grand performance as the facially disgraced swordsman-poet sets a new standard with which all future "Cyranos" will have to reckon.**

Jean-Paul Rappeneau's sumptuous ($17-million) screen adaptation of Edmond Rostand's heroic verse play has dash, lyricism, and a superb acting ensemble. Evergreen appeal of the play should

make it a domestic favorite and a strong export item.

Subtitling will be a daunting obstacle in many markets, though producer René Cleitman spared no expense to get Anthony Burgess to personally adapt his own famous translation for the English-subtitled version. Cleitman is courting other literateurs to do likewise in their respective languages.

Rappeneau and screenwriter Jean-Claude Carrière have opened up the play conventionally but intelligently. Their basic concern has been to iron out the stagy kinks in Rostand's fanciful plot and provide for a smooth, purely filmic rhythm.

For example, the first act begins, like the play, inside the Hotel de Bourgogne playhouse, where Cyrano hounds a pompous actor off the stage. The filmmakers invent enough credible business to then move the action out onto the front steps of the theater for the celebrated verse duel.

Rappeneau and Carrière were understandably bothered by the unlikely arrival of Roxane, who managed to pass Spanish blockades with a wagon full of victuals for the starving French. They thus invented a wordless scene in which a band of Gallic soldiers try to penetrate enemy lines and save Roxane (more credibly disguised in boy's clothing).

Rostand's famous Alexandrine rhyming couplets have been preserved as film dialogue. Carrière has done a subtle job of pruning the text, weeding out obscure phrases and windiness that obstruct the film's elegant flow. Writer invented some 100 new verses of his own for transitions, but only a Rostand scholar would detect the tampering.

The play's 17th century Paris settings are opulently reimagined by Italian stage designer Ezio Frigerio (who has worked with Giorgio Strehler). Frigerio strikes a fine balance of preserved historical locations and splendid studio recreations. Franca Squarciapino's costumes are gracious and perfectly embodied, a visual reflection of Rostand's verbal panache.

Pierre Lhomme's lensing is both subtle and sensational. The charming balcony scene and Cyrano's twilight death scene are both exquisite studies in finely graded light and shadow. There is grandeur in the battle of Arras sequences (shot on location in Hungary) with some unforgettable shots

of Spanish lances stabbing up at the French redoubt in a Kurosawa-inspired composition.

All these elements are masterfully drawn together by Rappeneau's direction. He's as comfortable with the story's swashbuckling verve as with its delicate intimacy. His real triumph, without which everything else would be just glossy dressing, is his work with the cast.

In the mouths of lesser actors, Rostand's rhyming couplets (and French verse drama in general) can degenerate easily into an insipid torrent of jingling and jangling sonorities, deprived of sense. But Rappeneau guides his players into finding the right spoken cadences. They transform the highly artificial stage dialog into film dialog that resounds credibly in the more realistic film settings.

Depardieu's Cyrano erupts in the first act as a versifying 17th century raging bull, a man who loves a fight as much as a good rhyme. Then from this monolithic public image, Depardieu evolves with moody sensibility the more complex image of the private Cyrano, a wounded lonely romantic who must use the handsome Christian as an empty human envelope in which to send his expansive love letters to Roxane.

Heroically swathed in cape and a striking wide brimmed plumed felt hat, Depardieu is simply (and sometimes literally) smashing. And that nose designed by Michele Burke is a clever enlargement of Depardieu's own prominent proboscis. The actor wears it as he wears his costumes — as if he were born with it.

Opposite Depardieu is a blue ribbon supporting cast. Roxane is played with finesse and feeling by Anne Brochet, who captures the romantic immaturity and generosity of soul. She swoons graciously every time she reads Cyrano's stirring verses.

Vincent Perez does quite well with the usually dull role of Christian, the young comrade-in-arms in love with and loved by Roxane. Character's the inverse of Cyrano; a beautiful face, but a shallow inexpressive soul. Perez manages the paradoxical feat of giving substance to a personage singularly lacking in it.

Jacques Weber, who was a much admired Cyrano in a recent stage revival, is admirable as De Guiche, who completes Rostand's trio of lovestruck male warriors.

Weber enriches the aristocratic preciosity and vengefulness with a quiet dignity, courage and humor that makes the count's heroic turnabout on the battlefield plausible and touching.

Among the well chosen supporting actors, Roland Bertin deserves special mention as Ragueneau, amateur poet/professional pastry-maker whose shop is the setting for Roxane's first rendezvous with the deceived Cyrano.

Jean-Claude Petit's lush score is good icing on an appetizing theater and cinema confectionery though at moments (notably in the first scenes), it's laid on too thick. Other tech credits are classy.

— *Len.*

In The Spirit

New York A Castle Hill Prods. release of a Julian Schlossberg presentation of a Running River production. Produced by Schlossberg, Beverly Irby. Directed by Sandra Seacat. Screenplay, Jeannie Berlin, Laurie Jones; camera (TVC color), Dick Quinlan; editor, Brad Fuller; music, Patrick Williams; sound, William Sarokin; production design, Michael C. Smith; art direction, Jacqueline Jacobson; costume design, Carrie Robbins; assistant director, Lisa Zimble; production manager, Joseph C. Stillman; 2d unit director-associate producer, Phillip Schopper; casting, Paula Herold. Reviewed at Loews Tower East theater, N.Y., March 29, 1990. MPAA Rating: R. Running time: **93 MIN.**

Marianne Flan	Elaine May
Reva Prosky	Marlo Thomas
Crystal	Jeannie Berlin
Roger Flan	Peter Falk
Lureen	Melanie Griffith
Sue	Olympia Dukakis
Lt. Kelly	Chad Burton
Det. Pete Weber	Thurn Hoffman

Also with: Laurie Jones, Michael Emil, Hope Cameron, Rockets Redglare, Danny Davin, Christopher Durang.

■ **Elaine May and Marlo Thomas make a memorable screen odd couple in "In The Spirit." Kooky black comedy is for specialized tastes but stands a chance to find an appreciative audience among those longing for off-the-wall humor.**

Pic is an unusual case on the current scene of big-name talent gathering with friends to make a low-budget pic freed of mainstream good taste and gloss. Experiment works and plays like a throwback to the looser, madcap '60s.

"Spirit" also harkens back to the black comedy spirit of Jules Feiffer's "Little Murders," as directed for the screen in 1971 by Alan Arkin. Again, New York is a nightmare, with May moving back to Gotham from Beverly Hills with her just-fired hubby Peter Falk. She's thrown together with ditzy mystic Thomas after hiring her to redecorate an apartment.

Almost as goofy as Thomas is Jeannie Berlin, a prostie neighbor. Her matter-of-fact foul-mouthed pronouncements cue Falk's hilarious takes of astonishment. Fact of family resemblance between Berlin and real-life mom May (who directed her in "The Heartbreak Kid") gives a strange, bookends look to these early scenes.

Berlin, coscripter with Laurie Jones, writes herself out of the picture after the second reel and "Spirit" spins off in a different direction. Thomas and May flee the city to hole up at Michael Emil's new age retreat in upstate N.Y., pursued by a murderer. First-time director Sandra Seacat emphasizes slapstick but also female bonding as the gals on the lam reach beyond their wacky survivalist tactics to address feminist issues.

Pic works in fits and starts; its weakest element being a stupid framing device of a mystical narrator telling us about the cosmic links between the characters. Midway change in tone may put off some viewers, but others will likely relish the intensity of the May and Thomas segment.

Script by Berlin and Jones (latter also popping up as a clumsy maid) perceptively mocks trendy attitudes à la Catlin Adams/Melanie Mayron's "Sticky Fingers." In-jokes range from the obvious (mystical Shirley MacLaine) to the obscure (Robin Byrd's local cable access tv show).

In her first screen role since '78 ("California Suite"), May is very funny, giving a lesson in rat-a-tat-tat delivery. Thomas proves a perfect foil, leading to a satisfying role reversal at pic's end.

Besides Falk, who's morose enough here to challenge monologist Brother Theodore (Gottlieb) in the realm of dark humor, guest star Melanie Griffith is perfect as a prostitute interviewed by Thomas and May (both funny in disguise as fellow hookers), who strips down to her black undies in homage to her previous Mike Nichols' "Working Girl" role. Emil and Olympia Dukakis are wasted in brief assignments.

Pic is claustrophobic with its emphasis on closeups, but that's not damaging due to its overall paranoia theme. — *Lor.*

Side Out

Los Angeles A Tri-Star Pictures release of a Jay Weston production, in association with Aurora Prods. and Then Prods. Produced by Gary Foster. Executive producer, Weston. Director, Peter Israelson. Screenplay, David Thoreau; camera (CFI color, Technicolor prints), Ron Garcia; editor, Conrad Buff; music, Jeff Lorber; sound (Dolby), Vince Gutierrez; production design, Dan Lomino; art direction, Bruce Crone; set decoration, Cloudia; assistant director, Marty Eli Schwartz; coproducer, John Zane; associate producer, Russ Krasnoff; casting, Jane Jenkins, Janet Hirshenson, Robin Allan. Reviewed at Cineplex Odeon Fairfax theater, L.A., March 30, 1990. MPAA Rating: PG-13. Running time: **100 MIN.**

Monroe Clark	C. Thomas Howell
Zack Barnes	Peter Horton
Samantha	Courtney Thorne-Smith
Kate Jacobs	Harley Jane Kozak
Wiley Hunter	Christopher Rydell
Uncle Max	Terry Kiser
Rollo Vincent	Randy Stoklos

■ **A hackneyed swipe at capturing the sizzle of beach volleyball with a "Rocky" beat, "Side Out" offers all the trappings of a 100-minute L.A. Gear commercial, providing as much suspense as a California sunset with less substance. Pic should have a tough time clearing the net at the b.o.**

Pic's sparse appeal hinges on spring break elements, having seemingly employed every bikini-clad babe within 20 miles of Hermosa Beach, and leads C. Thomas Howell and Peter Horton, who at least picked up great tans.

Director Peter Israelson makes his feature debut after a career in commercials. More than a film, "Side Out" is a feature-length product-placement opportunity with a sandswept morality twist.

Howell plays a Milwaukee college kid who comes to L.A. to work for his lawyer uncle (Terry Kiser, reprising his creep from "Weekend At Bernie's") and gets a job evicting tenants.

One delinquent renter, Horton, is a 1-time volleyball whiz who's buried himself up to the neck betting on ponies. This, like most other plot points, conveniently washes out to sea along the way.

Howell passes his morality exam about half-way through the pic, giving Kiser the heave-ho. The only question is whether Horton will throw the big tournament match he and Howell enter to appease ex-g.f. Harley Jane Kozak, promoter with nebulous ties to the other team.

The laughably cliched moments could fill a sandbox, beginning with the buxom blond (Courtney Thorne-Smith, recently seen on "L.A. Law") who literally flops out of the surf and into Howell's life.

The most ridiculous part is taken as a given: that Howell, even as a 1-time basketball star, could within weeks hold his own against Olympic-caliber volleyball players, most of whom play themselves. Except for champs Randy Stoklos and Sinjin Smith, who prove that, as actors, they're great volleyball players.

Howell is likable but has no personality in David Thoreau's script, filled with vacuous characters cut from Coppertone billboards. Horton fares better but does it mostly on his own, since there are no clues to his self-destructive streak or why he would change.

Both are reasonably convincing athletically, though Howell's a bit of a runt as volleyball players go. Israelson brings little flair to the action, dragging it out with slow-motion photography until all the flying sand evokes "Lawrence Of Arabia," though that felt shorter.

Fusionist Jeff Lorber scores the film's lone point with his jazzy soundtrack. The editing, however, is at times confusing and the film ends abruptly, as if in a hurry to get somewhere. Most who see it will share the feeling. — *Bril.*

Closer And Closer Apart
(AUSTRALIAN)

Sydney A Rosa Colosimo Films production. Produced by Rosa Colosimo. Directed by Steve Middleton. Screenplay, Angelo Salamanca, inspired by the opera "La Cavalleria Rusticana" by Pietro Mascagni; camera (Eastmancolor), Vladimir Osherov; editor, Catherine Birmingham; music, Joe Dolce; sound, Peter Clancy; production design, Maria Ferro; production manager, Alison Sadler; assistant director, Rick Lappas. Reviewed at Mosman screening room, Sydney, Nov. 6, 1989. Running time: **88 MIN.**

Sam	Steve Bastoni
Lois	Marie-Louise Walker
Angie	Linda Hartley
Alfio	George Harlem
Mrs. Macca	Kate Jason-Omodei
Connie	Yvette Bentata
Mr. Giblisco	Vince D'Amico
Enzo	George Kapiniaris
Mrs. Serini	Bettina Spivakovsky
Mr. Serini	Dino Nicolosi

■ **An appealing tale of friendship and love in Melbourne's Italian community, "Closer And Closer Apart" is the best of three 1989 pics from prolific producer Rosa Colosimo. A modest arthouse run is indi-**

cated, especially in its home-town, while video possibilities are promising.

Inspired by the 1-act opera, "La Cavalleria Rusticana," pic revolves around childhood friends Sam (Steve Bastoni) and Alfio (George Harlem). Alfio works for his fishmonger dad, and Sam is about to join the army. They both have girlfriends: Alfio is dating the flashy, fun-loving Lola (Marie-Louise Walker), while Sam goes out with the quiet, virginal Angie (Linda Hartley) and is a bit jealous of his pal.

Problems arise when Lola decides she prefers Sam to Alfio and seduces him. Soon after, Sam joins the army and Lola marries Alfio. When the army stint is over, Sam returns but spurns the faithful Angie and secretly resumes his liaison with Lola. Angie discovers what's going on and tells Alfio, resulting in a bitter confrontation between the two erstwhile buddies.

Plot matters less than atmosphere and characters. The milieu of Melbourne's mostly Sicilian community is beautifully rendered, evoking memories of "Moving Out," a modest hit from 1982. Performances are all spot on, and Angelo Salamanca's well-written screenplay moves along briskly, helped by first-time director Steve Middleton's firm pacing.

Sex scenes between Sam and Lola are fairly hot. The final confrontation between Sam and Alfio is painful because, despite their flaws, they're likeable. Supporting characters, mostly family members, are beautifully portrayed by an ethnic cast.

Production values are modest. Location shooting is occasionally marred by curious passers-by gazing at the camera. Joe Dolce's music is uninspired. Overall this bright and truthful pic is not a world-beater, but one worth seeking out. — *Strat.*

Think Big

New York A Concorde Pictures release of a Motion Picture Corp. of America presentation of a Brad Krevoy/Steven Stabler production. Produced by Krevoy, Stabler. Directed by Jon Turteltaub. Screenplay, Edward Kovach, David Tausik, Turteltaub, from story by R.J. Robertson, Jim Wynorski; camera (Foto-Kem color), Mark Morris; editor, Jeff Reiner; music, Michael Sembello, Hilary Bercovici; additional music, Stephen Graziano; sound (Ultra-Stereo), Russel Fager; production design, Robert Schullenberg; production manager, Steve Brown; stunt coordinator, Gary

Jensen; coproducer, David Cobb; associate producer, Tausik; casting, Sharon Nederlander; title animation, Carole Holliday. Reviewed at Westside Cinema 2, N.Y., March 31, 1990. MPAA Rating: PG-13. Running time: **86 MIN.**

Vic & Rafe . . . . . Peter Paul, David Paul
Holly Sherwood . . . . Ari Meyers
Dr. Brueckner . . . . .Martin Mull
John Sweeney . . . . . . .David Carradine
Dr. Irene Marsh . . . . .Claudia Christian
Irving . . . . Richard Kiel
Thornton . . . . .Richard Moll
Hap . . . . Michael Winslow

Also with: Thomas Gottschalk, Tony Longo, Peter Lupus, Sal Landi, Tiny Lister Jr., Rafer Johnson, Jimmy Briscoe.

■ **This undemanding physical comedy is obviously aimed at the video fan, but offers okay gags for theatrical audiences waxing nostalgic for the generally unlamented '70s vehicular comedies involving trucks and cars.**

The Barbarian Bros., actually twins Peter Paul and David Paul, topline as a pair of affable but somewhat retarded truckers hauling a load of toxic waste across country. Brainy but beautiful 16-year-old Ari Meyers stows away in their vehicle, as she's on the lam with her secret weapon developed at Martin Mull's think tank for kids.

There's plenty of effective slapstick as cartoonish villains chase after the trio, who are joined later by Meyers' school psychologist, the fast maturing starlet Claudia Christian. David Carradine, in particular, is fun (costumed to resemble his brother Keith) as a nutty repo man.

Meyers, who plays Susan Saint James' daughter on tv's "Kate & Allie" series, is delightful as the precocious heroine and manages to maintain a straight face opposite the cuddly but oversize nonactor Paul brothers. Except for a sex scene with a voluptuous waitress at a diner, the duo remain squeaky clean comic heroes for kids.

Cast's cameos include Richard Kiel gently spoofing his familiar screen heavy image and Olympic great Rafer Johnson cast opposite wrestling star Tiny Lister Jr. (a.k.a. "Zeus") as fellow truckers.

Only thing getting in the way of the decent gags and 1-liners is an unfortunate emphasis on plugola for Coca-Cola products. — *Lor.*

Transylvania Twist
(COLOR/B&W)

New York A Concorde Pictures release. Executive producer, Roger Corman. Produced by Alida Camp. Directed by Jim Wynorski. Screenplay, R.J. Robertson; camera (Foto-Kem color, b&w), Zoran Hochstätter; editor, Nina Gilberti; music, Chuck Cirino; sound, Craig Felberg; production design, Gary Randall; art direction, Beth Elliott; costumes, Jill Conner; production manager, Adam Moos; stunt coordinator, Merritt Yohnka; 2d unit director, Steve Mitchell; 2d unit camera, Steve McNulty. Reviewed at Criterion 5 theater, N.Y., March 31, 1990. MPAA Rating: PG-13. Running time: **82 MIN.**

Lord Byron Orlock . . . . .Robert Vaughn
Marisa Orlock . . . . .Teri Copley
Dexter Ward . . . . .Steve Altman
Prof. Van Helsing . . . . .Ace Mask
Stefan . . . . .Angus Scrimm
Patricia . . . . .Monique Gabrielle
Uncle Ephraim . . . . .Jay Robinson
Hans Upp . . . . .Steve Franken
Marinus Orlock . . . . . .Howard Morris
Rita . . . . .Becky LeBeau
Boris Karloff . . . . .Himself

Also with: Brinke Stevens, Deanna Lund, Kelli Maroney, Toni Naples, Suzanne Hughes, Forrest J. Ackerman.

■ **In regional release sans fanfare since October, "Transylvania Twist" is an occasionally hilarious horror spoof notable for the range of its comical targets. It has definite potential as a cult favorite in upcoming ancillary exposure.**

Filmmaker Jim Wynorski and scripter R.J. Robertson normally take a tongue-in-cheek approach but here let all the stops out in silliness worthy of Mel Brooks (whose regular Howard Morris pops up in an effective supporting role). Their batting average on jokes is low; yet there're enough direct hits to carry the film.

Immediately with the teaser opening of perennial Wynorski starlet Monique Gabrielle (uncredited though in a big role) being stalked through the woods by Jason, Freddy Krueger and Leatherface, pic applies a scattershot approach delving into other genres as well. For example, a Transy cab driver launches into Robert De Niro's classic "You talkin' to me?" bit and a videotaped last will and testament turns into "The Newly Dead Game" spoof of tv.

Robert Vaughn, who got his start starring for producer Roger Corman in "Teenage Caveman" (1958), is delightful as a Dracula-styled vampire pronouncing the end of his last name Orlock with relish. His beautiful niece Teri Copley is an American singing star who travels to his castle in Transylvania upon the death of her father, accompanied by wise-cracking sidekick Steve Altman.

Mixed into the comic stew are many delightful reflexive bits: tracking camera that gets sidetracked on bodacious women passing by;

a black & white sequence when stars visit a set that looks left over from "The Honeymooners," replete with a visit from an actor doing Art Carney as Ed Norton; and a terrifically edited appearance by the late Boris Karloff who interacts with Altman in the manner of Carl Reiner/Steve Martin's "Dead Men Don't Wear Plaid."

Copley is a most alluring, dizzy blond heroine. Altman makes the most of his turn doing impressions and intentionally bad jokes. Hip script makes numerous references to legendary horror writer H.P. Lovecraft. Angus Scrimm of "Phantasm" is cast as Vaughn's butler and effectively spoofs his previous films.

Tech credits are modest, with appropriate emphasis on stock footage taken from earlier Corman efforts. — *Lor.*

Twisted Justice

Los Angeles A Seymour Borde & Associates release of a Hero Films production. Executive producers, Gerald Milton, Arnie Lakeyn, S. Leigh Savidge. Produced, written and directed by David Heavener. Camera (color), David Hue; editor, Gregory Schorer; sound, Rick Waddell; art direction, Dian Skinner; costumer, Kevin Ackerman; stunt coordinator, Warren Stevens; assistant director, Carlton Thomas; associate producer, Tanya York. Reviewed at Beverly Hills Screening Room, L.A., March 28, 1990. MPAA Rating: R. Running time: **90 MIN.**

James Tucker . . . . .David Heavener
Cmdr. Gage . . . . .Erik Estrada
Mrs. Granger . . . . .Karen Black
Hinkle . . . . .Shannon Tweed
Morris . . . . .Jim Brown
Kelsey . . . . .James Van Patten
Luther Pantelli . . . . .Don Stroud

■ **This do-it-yourself futuristic cop actioner by writer-producer-director David Heavener, who also stars, gets an obligatory 50-100 screen theatrical release to fulfill a presales pact with Arena Home Video, which already has the cassette boxes ready.**

Too bad multifaceted Heavener can't also fill theater seats by himself, as he's the only one likely to be interested in what's on-screen.

It's hard to create a futureworld when you've got no budget, so Heavener's angle is to pretend that it's 2020 and violence in L.A. has gotten so bad that guns are outlawed even for cops.

They use plastic tranquilizer guns called "stingers" and wear medieval-style chain mail vests to protect themselves from whatever the baddies come up with.

Heavener plays a scruffy "renegade cop" whose idea of rebellion is to wear dirty clothes and pack a real gun. It comes in handy when a psycho develops a drug that makes thugs superpowerful and immune to the stingers.

Heavener's fellow cops try to take away his illegal weapon even while he's using it to track down the drug-monger, whose sideline is murdering rich women. It won't spoil any suspense to reveal that good old-fashioned hardware saves the day, though one has to wonder what the point is.

More remarkable than the story, which suffers from deadly pacing, dreadful dialog, talkiness and a dearth of logic, are the production values, as pic seems to have been shot in a week, edited with an ax and sound mixed in the bed of a moving truck.

Inadvertent laughs abound, as the psycho bad guy, described by one clever cop as a "turbo-charged fruit loop," chases his prey around like a Frankenstein monster.

Heavener's wiseguy persona occasionally works on a tv series level, but his grungy style holds no appeal. Regrettably, Erik Estrada and Karen Black are also repped here, just as the posters promise. Presence of former Playboy playmate of the year Shannon Tweed, as a cop dispatcher, will also likely move a few extra cassettes. — *Daws.*

Caged Fury

New York A 21st Century Film presentation of a Atlantic Pictures production. Produced by Bill Milling, Bob Gallagher. Written and directed by Milling. Camera (RGB color; TVC prints), Kenneth Wiatrak; editor, Matthew Mallinson; music, Joe Delia; sound, Marty Kasparian; assistant director, Elizabeth Rodeno; martial arts supervisor, George Goldsmith; stunt coordinator, Solly Marx; camera (Mexico), Ken Gibb; line producer, Laura Gherardi; associate producers, Gerry Wolff, Erik Estrada, James Hong, Paul Smith, Michael Parks, Edith Simms. Reviewed on RCA/Columbia Pictures vidcassette, N.Y., March 22, 1990. No MPAA Rating. Running time: **95 MIN.**

Victor.	Erik Estrada
Dirk Ramsey.	Richie Barathy
Kathie Collins.	Roxanna Michaels
Head guard.	Paul Smith
Det. Stoner.	James Hong
Mr. Collins.	Michael Parks
Mr. Castaglia.	Jack Carter
Rhonda Wallace.	April Dawn Dollarhide
Buck Lewis.	Blake Bahner
Det. Elston.	Hugh Farrington
Tracy Collins.	Elena Sahagun
Warden Sybil Thorn.	Ty Randolph
Tony.	Beano
Spyder.	Greg Cummins
Pizzaface.	Ron Jeremy Hyatt

Blond escapee.	Alison LePriol (Kascha)

■ **The first of Menahem Golan's 21st Century pics to go direct-to-video, "Caged Fury" is a haphazardly slapped together but entertaining throwback to the women in prison genre of the early '70s. It's unrelated to a 1984 Filipino-made release of the same name.**

Pic is set in the underbelly of L.A., where unscrupulous Jack Carter and Beano prey on young girls like Utah-born Roxanna Michaels who head to lotus land to become actresses. She goes to an audition, the videotape of which is used by Carter & Beano to frame her for a jail sentence.

It turns out to be a fake prison, run by entertainingly exotic dominatrix "warden" Ty Randolph (in the film's most impressive role). This is a front for white slavery and it takes Michaels' older sister Elena Sahagun and pals Erik Estrada and Richie Barathy to save the heroine and expose the scam.

Fast-paced pic is virtually a catalog of genre cliches, but suffers from poor editing. Several brief scenes seem placed out of order and the finale is loaded with contradictions.

Cast does a good job, particularly Michaels as the heroine and karate expert Barathy kicking every heavy in sight. Porn star Ron Jeremy, previously featured in Golan's "52 Pick-Up," pops up as a prison guard and film opens memorably with statuesque porn actress Kascha (billed here as Alison LePriol) crawling around in her lace undies trying to escape from stir. — *Lor.*

Heaven Tonight
(AUSTRALIAN)

Sydney Boulevard Films production. Executive producer, Peter Boyle. Produced by Frank Howson. Directed by Pino Amenta. Screenplay, Howson, Alister Webb; camera (color), David Connell; editor, Phil Reid; music, John Capek; sound, Andrew Ramage; production design, Jeannie Cameron; coproducer, James Michael Vernon; line producer, Barbi Taylor; production coordinator, Deborah Samuels; assistant director, John Powditch; casting, Greg Apps. Reviewed at Mosman screening room, Sydney, March 29, 1990. Running time: **95 MIN.**

Johnny Dysart.	John Waters
Annie Dysart.	Rebecca Gilling
Baz Schultz.	Kim Gyngell
Tim Robbins.	Sean Scully
Paul Dysart.	Guy Pearce
Robbins' secretary.	Sarah de Teliga

Caretaker.	Ted Hepple
Policeman.	Bruce Venables
Priest.	Syd Conabere
Norm.	Reg Evans
Carl.	Robert Morgan
Stewart.	Bryan Dawe

■ **"Heaven Tonight," starring w.k. Aussie actor (not the U.S. "Cry-Baby" director) John Waters as a showbiz personality facing midlife crisis, is much tighter than filmmakers' previous "Boulevard Of Broken Dreams," and should find an audience in Australia and, possibly, abroad.**

"Heaven Tonight" is from the same team (writer-producer, director, cameraman) and features two of the same actors as "Boulevard Of Broken Dreams," which won 1988 Australian film awards for actor (Waters) and supporting actor (Kim Gyngell) but received less than enthusiastic critical notices.

In the new film, Waters plays a former '60s rock star. Opening black & white newsreel footage intercuts scenes of Martin Luther King and Robert Kennedy with a montage of Waters' group, the Chosen Ones. Seems they went through the usual ups and downs, had one sock hit ("Heaven Tonight"), and then dissolved after one of them, Baz (Gyngell), got heavily into drugs.

Now 40 (and looking older), Waters is still fond of his long-suffering wife, Annie (Rebecca Gilling), and is struggling to make a comeback. At the same time, his 18-year-old son (Guy Pearce) is starting his own musical career, and father-son jealousy becomes a factor.

Matters aren't helped by the return from overseas of Baz, still on heroin and committing robberies to fuel his addiction. Gyngell gives an extremely effective performance as the washed-out, drugged-out musician.

Sean Scully is excellent, too, as he underplays the role of head of a music company who wants to sign Dysart, *fils,* but who won't take a risk on Dysart *père.* Scully does wonders in his relatively short screen time.

Basic story of a once-famous personality desperately trying to start out again in a changed world is a touching one, and Waters makes the most of the character's pain and confusion. Tilt to melodrama in the final reel, when the police close in on Baz for a back-alley shoot-out, is handled well, but seems an unnecessary plot device, given the relative strength of the material.

Boulevard Films' house-style still tends to overemphasize and underline points already made clear, but this, company's best production to date, is less prone to such defects.

Technically, pic is fine, with the musical numbers well recorded. There's also some sharp dialog, with lines like "This is the only business in the world where they penalize you for long service."

With critical support, pic should do good to very good business locally, with popularity of Waters a major factor. — *Strat.*

LATE FILM REVIEW

Impulse

NewYork A Warner Bros. release of a Ruddy Morgan production. Executive producer, Dan Kolsrud. Produced by Albert S. Ruddy, André Morgan. Directed by Sondra Locke. Screenplay, John De Marco, Leigh Chapman, from De Marco's story; camera (Technicolor), Dean Semler; editor, John W. Wheeler; music, Michel Colombier; sound (Dolby), Don H. Matthews; production design, William A. Elliott; set decoration, Tom Bugenhagen; production manager, Kolsrud; assistant director, Doug Metzger; casting, Glenn Daniels. Reviewed at 57th St. Playhouse, N.Y., April 2, 1990. MPAA Rating: R. Running time: **108 MIN.**

Lottie.	Theresa Russell
Stan.	Jeff Fahey
Lt. Joe Morgan.	George Dzundza
Charley Katz.	Alan Rosenberg
Rossi.	Nicholas Mele
Dimarjian.	Eli Danker
Frank Munoff.	Charles McCaughan
Dr. Gardner.	Lynne Thigpen

Tony Peron.	Shawn Elliott

■ **Theresa Russell gives a solid performance in Sondra Locke's well-directed film noir "Impulse," but script deficiencies make this a weak b.o. entry.**

The third major cop film this year with a prominent woman's role (after Jamie Lee Curtis in "Blue Steel" and Laurie Metcalf's supporting part in "Internal Affairs"), "Impulse" continues the prevailing themes (since "Sea Of Love") of paranoia and insecure, self-divided characters among the men and women in blue.

Russell is cast as a beautiful undercover cop whose life is going nowhere, hence the title: She would like to break out of her rut and act on impulse like one of the prostitute or druggie personas she routinely adopts in her work.

Along with her sexist boss George Dzundza, she's assigned to work with young assistant d.a. Jeff Fahey to find missing witness Shawn Elliott in an important gangster case. Elliott has $900,000 stolen in a Colombian drug deal, and there's only three weeks to find him before Fahey begins the trial. Complicating matters is Fahey's other key witness, Eli Danker, who is antsy and afraid to testify without Elliott's corroboration.

Scripters John De Marco and Leigh Chapman keep the pot boiling and flesh out the three main characters adequately until a crucial scene 55 minutes into the pic. On her way home after a tough assignment, Russell gets a flat tire and impulsively goes to a bar and is picked up by none other than Elliott (whose mug she hasn't been shown by her superiors).

Key plot element that she lets herself go with this guy is believable and well-developed, but all other details here ring false. The contrived script has Dzundza pointedly taking away her gun (it's not police issue) in the immediately previous scene since, scripting backwards, she can't have one in the scene that follows. Her not knowing what Elliott looks like is a ridiculous but equally necessary gimmick.

Elliott is murdered while Russell freshens up at his pad. She

covers up the evidence, afraid of being accused of the killing, but phones in a tip that the murder has taken place.

Film never recovers from the rapid piling-on of coincidences here, a basic misunderstanding of the premise that Russell's character is free to act randomly but that her screen universe must remain logical and consistent.

Just like the Kevin Costner thriller "No Way Out" (in which Dzundza also costarred), some suspense is generated by an identikit drawing of the mystery woman who witnessed Elliott's murder — the viewer recognizes it as Russell but Dzundza and Fahey take longer to tumble to the fact.

Next twist is pretty good: Fahey has Russell pose as the mystery witness in order to flush out Elliott's killer, but by this time he knows that she *is* the witness (but didn't see the killer's face, yet

another hokey contrivance). Revelation of the killer's identity is a nice surprise that plays fair with the audience.

Russell and Fahey have some interesting exchanges that expose their characters, but there are too many prefacing sentiments, with "What if I told you that ... " yielding unintentionally risible results. Sharpest writing comes in a scene of Fahey and his partner Alan Rosenberg talking about women and relationships in terms from real estate — "curb appeal" and "depreciating."

Director Locke, in her second feature after "Ratboy," gets high marks for the visceral, swift nature of her violent stagings. She also manages an impressively tactile sex scene that involves Russell and Fahey.

Russell is terrific in suggesting her character's insecurities after several failed romances, and pic benefits from a smooth performance by Lynne Thigpen as her shrink. Fahey, soon to be seen costarring in Clint Eastwood's "White Hunter, Black Heart," is a handsome, effective foil, and Dzundza almost makes one believe his ambiguously corrupt persona.

Aussie lenser Dean Semler maintains a murky look befitting the protagonists' dark motives. Michel Colombier's moody score is a plus. — *Lor.*

Crazy People

New York   A Paramount Pictures release. Executive producer, Robert K. Weiss. Produced by Tom Barad. Directed by Tony Bill. Screenplay, Mitch Markowitz; camera (Technicolor), Victor J. Kemper; editor, Mia Goldman; music, Cliff Eidelman; sound (Dolby), David Ronne; production design, John J. Lloyd; art direction, Steven Schwartz; set decoration, Rick T. Gentz; costume design, Mary E. Vogt; assistant director, Allan Wertheim; associate producer, Markowitz; casting, Lynn Stalmaster. Reviewed at Paramount 29th floor screening room, N.Y., April 2, 1990. MPAA Rating: R. Running time: **90 MIN.**
Emory Leeson. . . . . .Dudley Moore
Kathy Burgess. . . . . . . .Daryl Hannah
Stephen Bachman. . . . . . . .Paul Reiser
Dr. Liz Baylor. . . . . . .Mercedes Ruehl
Charles Drucker. . . . . .J.T. Walsh
Dr. Horace Koch. . . . . . . .Ben Hammer
Mort Powell. . . . . .Dick Cusack
Judge. . . . . Alan North
George Cartelli. . . . . . .David Paymer
Saabs. . . . . Danton Stone
Hsu. . . . . Doug Yasuda
Bruce Concannon. . . . . .Bill Smitrovich
Manuel Robles. . . . . .Paul Bates
Eddie Avis. . . . . .Floyd Vivino
Adam Burgess. . . . . . . .John Terlesky
Mark Olander. . . . . .David Packer
Larry King. . . . . Himself

■ "Crazy People" combines a hilarious dissection of advertising with the warmest view of so-called insanity since "King Of Hearts." Paramount has a potential word-of-mouth goldmine in this clever film, assuming audiences have not overdosed with tv satire of the "SCTV" and "Saturday Night Live" ilk.

Pic had a rocky production history as two weeks into lensing last year star John Malkovich was replaced by Dudley Moore, and screenwriter Mitch Markowitz ceded his directing chair to Tony Bill (accompanied by a new cinematographer). Finished film is a credit to all hands.

Markowitz has trumped a genre dating back to the MGM classic "The Hucksters" by simply using real products as the target of his Madison Avenue satire. With very funny and sometimes vulgar gag lines, he cuts to the heart of what is really being sold to the public and the techniques of obfuscation that keep the consumer society greased.

Paramount, itself the butt of one of the jokes, reportedly did not seek permission from the well-known target manufacturers. The only ringer reflecting creative nervousness is use of a fictional cigarette, Amalfi, instead of any w.k. brand.

Moore, in his best screen acting since Steve Gordon's "Arthur" a

decade ago, toplines as a burnt-out ad man working with fast-talking Paul Reiser (perfect as a type commonplace in business) for a tyrannical boss, J.T. Walsh, who's even better here as an ogre than he was as the heartless studio chief in "The Big Picture."

Under deadline pressure, he turns in campaigns that attempt an honest approach, e.g., selling Volvos as "boxy but good" or promoting Greek vacations with a negative campaign: "Forget France; the French can be annoying." This raises more than eyebrows, but when Moore hands in "Most of our passengers get there alive" to promote United Air Lines, the film jumpcuts emphatically to Bennington Sanitarium, his new home.

As with most so-called controversial films that step on the toes of some special interest group, the supposed bad taste of "Crazy People" regarding the mentally ill is defused by sitting through the picture. Director Bill envisions this looney bin as an idyllic retreat, with a natural, warm and beautiful Daryl Hannah as Moore's nutty playmate there. The visual mismatch (she towers over the diminutive star) pays off.

Hannah, as an emotionally troubled young woman who longs to be reunited with her brother, projects the type of innocence and wonder that made her a star in "Splash."

At the asylum Moore is befriended by a winning group of zanies, mainly depicted by Markowitz as obsessive-compulsives. Notable is the cuddly David Paymer, who punctuates all his speech with "hello," and Bill Smitrovich as a potential go-getter who lacks confidence. Mercedes Ruehl is very sympathetic as the no-nonsense shrink who tries to help Moore out of his funk.

Markowitz' ingenious twists overcome the gag-driven nature of the film. First, Moore's oddball ads accidentally get printed and create a consumer rush to buy the products. Walsh hires Moore back and latter gets his fellow inmates to work on ad copy for him as a form of group therapy. It works and soon the inmates are virtually running the asylum.

Fly in the ointment is Walsh's taking credit on "The Larry King Show" for the phenomenal success of the ads and his imperious firing of Moore and all his helpers when they seek recognition and perks. Script's most perceptive scene comes when Walsh convenes meetings to have his crack staff try out the new honesty concept themselves, but they come up completely dry.

As in Philippe De Broca's cult fave "King Of Hearts," Markowitz convincingly shows how only the so-called nuts are really sane, leading to a delightfully romantic fairy tale ending. Balancing the picture's up - the - establishment populist appeal is the rather touching, old-fashioned Moore/Hannah romance and even a cute bouncing ball singalong during the end credits.

Besides the able principals, pic benefits from a solid ensemble including Ben Hammer as the mean sanitarium chief. Tech credits are clean and simple including Cliff Eidelman's sprightly score. — *Lor.*

Vital Signs

Hollywood A 20th Century Fox release of a Perlman production. Produced by Laurie Perlman, Cathleen Summers. Directed by Marisa Silver. Screenplay, Larry Ketron, Jeb Stuart, based on a story by Ketron; camera (color, Deluxe prints), John Lindley; editor, Robert Brown, Danford B. Greene; music, Miles Goodman; sound, Petur Hliddal; production design, Todd Hallowell; costume design, Deborah Everton; set design, Keith Burns; set decoration, Dan May; unit production manager/associate producer, Tom Joyner; assistant director, Betsy Magruder; casting, Margery Simkin. Reviewed at Century Plaza Theater, L.A., April 5, 1990. MPAA Rating: R. Running time: **103 MIN.**

Michael Chatham.	Adrian Pasdar
Gina Wyler.	Diane Lane
Dr. Redding.	Jimmy Smits
Henrietta.	Norma Aleandro
Kenny Rose.	Jack Gwaltney
Lauren Rose.	Laura San Giacomo
Suzanne Maloney.	Jane Adams
Bobby Hayes.	Tim Ransom
Dr. Ballentine.	Bradley Whitford

■ **"Vital Signs" is a strikingly well-done ensemble piece about a pivotal year in the lives of a group of medical students, with script, direction and performances polished to max potential. Only problem is it's too similar to what's available free of charge on tv.**

Fox should have developed this one as a 2-hour pilot for its network. As is, it's likely to disappear from theaters with barely a ripple.

As a gifted doctor-to-be who oozes charm and good looks, Adrian Pasdar is the focus of this group of serious strivers navigating their tough third year at L. A. Central's med school. Diane Lane is the crisp but compassionate fellow student he falls in love with. Jack

Gwaltney plays the blander, grimmer fellow from a less-advantaged background who's determined not to let Pasdar surpass him in tense competition for internship honors.

Turn of events surrounding the moral dilemma giving Gwaltney an unfair edge over Pasdar affords pic solid substance in the third act, and contributes to some satisfying character development. Everybody-wins ending is a bit too convenient, but fits in with pic's overall glossy but earnest tone.

Interesting subplots are played out in the relationship of Gwaltney and his neglected wife (Laura San Giacomo, in an effective but unexciting plain-jane turn), who's wearing out shoe leather as a waitress to support his studies; and the amusing discomfort of best pals Jane Adams and Tim Ransom after they cross into romantic involvement.

Indeed there are plenty of promising characters here. It seems a shame pic doesn't continue as a series to follow them in their fourth year of school.

Director Marisa Silver does a good job of getting across characters' emotional lives, making these mainstream twenty-something types absorbing, and fashions a crisply moving story. Dramatic camera angles and portentous theme music accompanying doctors as they stride down the halls seem overwrought, but it's understandable that the story must be pumped up to fill the big screen.

Jimmy Smits makes a buoyant contribution as the demanding dean whose respect they all must curry. It's not much of a stretch from his "L.A. Law" role, but still a choice performance, as he displays all the right instincts; formidably brisk at times, unpredictable at others. His casting is certainly more interesting than the standard grey-haired head doc.

Norma Aleandro ("Gaby") also give pic a classy dimension in a winning, fully dimensional performance as a sharp teacher stricken with cancer. — *Daws.*

The First Power

New York An Orion Pictures release of a Nelson Entertainment presentation of an Interscope Communications production. Executive producers, Ted Field, Robert W. Cort, Melinda Jason. Produced by David Madden. Written and directed by Robert Resnikoff. Camera (Deluxe color), Theo van de Sande; editor, Michael Bloecher; music, Stewart

Copeland; sound (Dolby), Hans Roland; production design, Joseph T. Garritz; art direction, Pat Tagliaferro; set decoration, Jerie Kelter; costume design, Tim D'Arcy; wardrobe consultant-associate producer, Marilyn Vance-Straker; production manager, Kelly Van Horn; assistant director, Matt Hinkley; special makeup effects, Edward French; stunt coordinator, John Moio; casting, Mindy Marin. Reviewed at Embassy 2 theater, N.Y., April 7, 1990. MPAA Rating: R. Running time: **98 MIN.**

Det. Russell Logan.	Lou Diamond Phillips
Tess Seaton.	Tracy Griffith
Patrick Channing.	Jeff Kober
Det. Oliver Franklin.	Mykel T. Williamson
Sister Marguerite.	Elizabeth Arlen
Commander Perkins.	Dennis Lipscomb
Lt. Grimes.	Carmen Argenziano
Grandma.	Julianna McCarthy
Bag lady.	Nada Despotovich
Carmen.	Sue Giosa

Also with: Clayton Landey, Hansford Rowe, Philip Abbott, David Gale, J. Patrick McNamara, Grand L. Bush, Melanie Shatner.

■ **"The First Power," previously titled "Pentagram" and "Transit," is a third-rate supernatural horror film due for fast playoff from Orion.**

Cornball storyline, most recently appearing in Wes Craven's "Shocker," has a boring vendetta between L.A. cop Lou Diamond Phillips and a killer granted immortality by Satan, Jeff Kober.

Instead of the more photogenic electrocution gimmick of "Shocker" and countless other fright pics, "Power" sends Kober to the gas chamber, but he won't die. He keeps possessing other bodies until Phillips, his psychic helper Tracy Griffith and a nun by inspired "The Omen," Elizabeth Arlen, stake him through the heart just to set up two false endings.

Debuting filmmaker Robert Resnikoff makes cardinal errors that kill the picture. He never whips up the apocalyptic story details or mood that makes this subgenre from "The Exorcist" to "The Seventh Sign" carry some dread. Also, his episodic, poor continuity structure includes not only supernatural events but dozens of hallucinations by the principals.

As a result, audience is left with a very local mad killer who's overequipped in power and must sit through a score of illogical red herrings to get to the real fantasy. Incest is thrown in as pic's corniest plot cog.

Finale is completely botched by Resnikoff, who makes it utterly confusing whether Kober is possessing other people's bodies (Arlen included) as implied previously, or is still using his own body and merely making people think he

looks like a nun, bag lady, etc. As a result, the final transformation of a corpse in repose is backwards.

Phillips puts his acting on hold in another routine action assignment post-"La Bamba," and Kober has a poorly conceived role. Redhead beauty Tracy Griffith is a sexy heroine who oddly resembles Tippi Hedren, yet she's actually Melanie Griffith's half-sister (same dad), but unrelated to Hedren. Phillips' cop boss Dennis Lipscomb knows the turf; he starred in a film three years earlier with the same premise, "Retribution."

Tech credits are unexceptional, with production entities Interscope and Nelson saving a buck by deemphasizing visual effects. — *Lor.*

Le Royaume ou l'asile
(The Kingdom Or The Asylum)
(CANADIAN)

Berlin A Les Films du Crépuscule presentation of a Les Productions Quatre Vins Neufs film in association with the National Film Board of Canada. Produced by Jean Gagné, Pierre Duceppe. Written and directed by Serge Gagné, Jean Gagné. Camera (color), Michel Le Veaux; music, André Duchesne. Reviewed at the Berlin Film Festival (market), Feb. 12, 1990. Running time: **90 MIN.**

With: Roger Léger, Jocelyn Béubé, Lou Babin, Luc Proulx, Geneviève Rioux, Marthe Tugeon, Claude Gautheir, Paula de Vasconcelos, Bernard Lalonde, Nemo Babin, Claude Demers.

■ **A great title wasted on a collage of unintelligible mumbo jumbo destined for total obscurity in Quebec and abroad. Pic is in release in Montreal.**

It's difficult to decipher why such an experimental piece, with no conventional storyline whatever, was shot on 35m and not on Super 8 for a student-type fest. A microphone floating at the top of the frame on several shots is also amateur.

Early references to 1960s' utopia, heroin, morphine and cocaine are a strong indicator of the blurred vision that follows.

Carol B. (Roger Léger) is a biker who recounts his wicked childhood to a nameless armchair shrink/journalist (Lou Babin) with whom he unsurprisingly winds up in bed. Patched around this sketchy scenario are hundreds of closeups of cut-and-paste collages, including such images of Carol B. as a kid in prisoner's garb. Deep. Very deep.

Other people come and go, appear and disappear without explanation or continuity until Carol B. is in bed with another woman (Paula de Vasconcelos). She leaves for Mexico and he plays pool with egg-shaped balls. Zen. Very zen.

Extracts of the collage-laden sequences might be considered "art" in a video. As a film, it is torture. — *Suze.*

Beyond El Rocco
(AUSTRALIAN-DOCU)

Sydney A Lucas Produkzions film, made with the participation of Sydney Improvised Music Assn., the Professional Musicians Club, the Australian Council, Australian Film Finance Corp., in association with Channel 4 (U.K.). Produced by Kevin Lucas, Aanya Whitehead. Directed by Lucas. Camera (color), Simon Smith; editor, Dany Cooper; musical advisor, Peter Rechniewski; sound, Gary O'Grady; production design, Laurie Faen; production manager, Cindy Watson. Reviewed at Mosman screening room, Sydney, March 25, 1990. Running time: **101 MIN.**
Zoot Finster . . . . .Tony Berry

■ **"Beyond El Rocco," an affectionate docu about modern jazz Down Under, contains valuable material on some of the country's top jazz musicians. Pic is aimed at jazz fans the world over, who will revel in the anecdotes told by the musicians as well as the performances themselves. For non-jazz addicts, pic will have zero appeal.**

Film is bookended by some gimmicky non-docu sequences involving actor Tony Barry as Zoot Finster, a self-confessed "aging hipster" who acts as tour guide and narrator and takes the audience back to the '50s when the El Rocco was Australia's first jazz spot. The fictional trimmings, despite Barry's pro performance, are unnecessary additions to what's otherwise a basic docu filled with interviews, archive footage and musical numbers.

Somewhat overlong at 101 minutes (though that won't worry the fans), "Beyond El Rocco" kicks off with a limited theatrical release in Australia before inevitably becoming a staple item in video stores and on the small screen. From an archival point of view, this putting on record the comments and the music of Australia's modern jazz stars has been an invaluable service. — *Strat.*

Le Champignon des carpathes
(The Carpathian Mushroom)
(FRENCH)

Paris A Films du Losange release of a Films du Trèfle production. Produced by Marie Bodin. Written and directed by Jean-Claude Biette. Camera (color), Denis Morel; editor, Marie-Catherine Miqueau; sound, Martin Boissau, Yann Le Mapihan; assistant director, Jean-Jacques Jauffret. Reviewed at the Luxembourg theater, Paris, April 1, 1990. Running time: **93 MIN.**
With: Tonie Marshall, Valerie Jeannet, Thomas Badek, Laurent Cygler, Howard Vernon, Laura Betti, Patachou.

■ **Despite the exotic title, this mouldy Paris-based auteur film merely has a group of characters floating pointlessly through vague situations.**

Jean-Claude Biette, a Cahiers du Cinema critic with two previous features behind him, wrote and directed, uninterestingly on both counts.

Most of the players are linked in one manner or another to a struggling pocket-sized production of "Hamlet," which Howard Vernon, as a faded Yank legit glory, is trying to mount. Problem is that the actress chosen to play Ophelia has been the victim of a nuclear plant accident in southern France. Vernon is banking on her to recover. This is the basic "suspense" of the story, though little really happens.

There is, in fact, a mushroom in the story, a rare mysterious fungus that grows in the Carpathian mountains and supposedly has extraordinary medicinal powers. No explanation then why a young woman (Valerie Jeannet) finds one at the foot of the Eiffel Tower (at the moment of the nuclear plant accident hundreds of miles away).

Mushroom is coveted by Jeannet's boyfriend, who wants to exploit it commercially. However, her brother, who has landed a job as electrician for Vernon's production, thinks it could be used to heal the distressed "Ophelia." But the no-nonsense clinic head (Patachou) will hear nothing of it.

The acting is somewhat better than the script. Vernon has some pungent moments as the grizzled Shakespearean whom an estranged daughter (Tonie Marshall) seeks out one day. Laura Betti turns up for a pointless cameo. Patachou, the well-known music hall star, proves again that she has a powerful screen personality, but still awaits a genuine role she can sink her teeth into. — *Len.*

Bloodmoon
(AUSTRALIAN)

Sydney A Roadshow release of a Village Roadshow Pictures presentation, in association with Michael Fisher Prods. (Intl. Sales, Carolco.) Executive producers, Graham Burke, Greg Coote. Produced by Stanley O'Toole. Directed by Alec Mills. Screenplay, Robert Brennan; camera (color), John Stokes; editor, David Halliday; music, Brian May; sound, Ian Grant; production design, Philip Warner; production manager, Judy Hamilton; assistant director, Bruce Redman; stunts, Phil Brook; associate producer, David Munro; Village Roadshow executive, Daniel O'Toole. Reviewed at Hoyts 7, Warringah Mall, Sydney, March 25, 1990. Running time: **102 MIN.**
Myles Sheffield . . . . .Leon Lissek
Virginia Sheffield . . . . .Christine Amor
Kevin. . . . . Ian Williams
Mary Huston. . . . . . . .Helen Thomson

■ **An abysmal attempt at an Aussie slasher pic, "Bloodmoon" is so woefully deficient that a gimmicky attempt has been made to scare up business in its splash release (sans press screenings) with a "fright break." But promo gimmicks aren't worth much when the product itself is so poor.**

Tired script by Robert Brennan centers on a private boarding school for young women (looking more mature than the 16-year-olds they're supposed to be). The obligatory nude shower and dorm scenes are included with other topless sequences involving heavy petting with youths from a nearby boys' school.

An unseen killer is garrotting couples as they make out in the woods. The villain, revealed two-thirds into the pic, turns out to be the nerdy spouse of headmistress Christine Amor.

Director Alec Mills tries to whip up audience interest in the fate of lissome heroine Helen Thomson (supposedly from Texas, though she has an Aussie accent) and b.f. Ian Williams, but without much success. Pic suffers from a weak and predictable screenplay, awkward thesping and inert direction. Pacing is far too slow with lotsa dreary padding early on.

So-called "fright break," an idea used with far more imagination by William Castle for his 1961 release "Homicidal," occurs 68 minutes in, interrupting the action mid-scene (just as the killer's identity has been revealed) while an unctuous voice taunts the audience to ankle now and get their money back or remain for the "horrifying conclusion." Teens

at the public screening caught were noisily unimpressed by this exhortation and by the film itself.

Even the moon looks phony in "Bloodmoon," which will undoubtedly appear on video shelves in the very near future. — *Strat.*

Weekend With Kate
(AUSTRALIAN)

Sydney A Phillip Emanuel Production. Produced by Phillip Emanuel. Directed by Arch Nicholson. Screenplay, Henry Tefay, Kee Young; camera (color), Dan Burstall; editor, Rose Evans; music, Bruce Rowland; sound, Tim Lloyd; production design, Larry Eastwood; production manager, Sally Ayre-Smith; assistant director, Bob Donaldson; coproducer, David C. Douglas; casting, Alison Barrett. Reviewed at Film Australia screening room, Lindfield, Sydney, March 23, 1990. Running time: **95 MIN.**
Richard Muir. . . . . .Colin Friels
Kate Muir. . . . .Catherine McClements
Jon Thorne. . . . . .Jerome Ehlers
Carla. . . . . Helen Mutkins
Phoebe. . . . . Kate Sheil
Gus. . . . . Jack Mayers
Ted. . . . . Rick Adams

■ **Sophisticated screwball comedy has been in short supply in Aussie cinema lately, so "Weekend With Kate" comes as a welcome surprise (marred only by director Arch Nicholson's death in February). Though modest in scope, pic should benefit from good reviews locally and do smart cinema biz. With right handling, it has global prospects as well.**

Henry Tefay and Kee Young's well constructed script indicates a knowledge of romantic comedies of another era. Setup has journalist turned rock music promoter Colin Friels torn between beautiful wife Catherine McClements, who wants to have a baby, and his ambitious mistress Helen Mutkins, who wants Friels.

He decides to tell his wife he's leaving her during a weekend they plan to spend alone at her family's beach house. She, in turn, has decided to use the intimacy of the weekend to get pregnant.

Both plans go astray when British rock idol Jerome Ehlers arrives and moves in for a peaceful weekend of fishing. At this point, pic starts to resemble a far less cynical "Kiss Me Stupid," as Ehlers, at first turned off by McClements' obvious distaste at his unwanted presence, is gradually turned on by her beauty, talent (as painter and pianist) and the fact that Friels has secretly revealed to him that the marriage is over.

Friels, meanwhile, tries with little success to make his important guest feel at home, efforts that include a dismal home-cooked dinner and a disastrous fishing expedition. The egotistical Ehlers mellows only when he takes a nude midnight swim with McClements, after which the inevitable occurs.

Next day Friels discovers his wife's infidelity and all efforts to make Ehlers happy go out the window as he jealously determines to win McClements back. Matters are further complicated by the arrival of Mutkins, who's only too happy with the setup.

These sexual adventures are exuberantly captured on screen. Dialog is sharp and witty, direction is brisk and well-timed, and performances are top notch.

Friels is fine as the errant, ambitious husband, and is nicely contrasted with Ehlers as the lanky, self-centered rock star. McClements is a joy as Kate, making the character so appealing and sexy that one wonders how her husband could ever have contemplated leaving her. As mistress Carla, Helen Mutkins is effectively acerbic.

Also worthy of nods are Larry Eastwood for his production design, Dan Burstall for his smart camerawork and Rose Evans for smooth editing.

Technical credits are the more remarkable because of the pic's troubled production history. Principal photography (with the title "Depth Of Feeling") was completed a year ago, with additional shooting taking place several months later to provide a new ending and bridging scenes. At one point in postproduction, a scene involving Friels had to be shot in Paris (where the actor was) with a French crew. Also, Nicholson was terminally ill during the latter stages of postproduction.

Miraculously, none of this is evident in the final film. Though undeniably simple, pic should work theatrically in Australia because of its good humor and top thesping. Abroad, it could go the fest route, where comedy pics are rare, and rack up appreciative notices prior to arthouse release.

Nicholson, whose sparse feature film career embraced the HBO thriller "Fortress" (with Rachel Ward), which played theatrically in Australia, as well as the action-comedy "Buddies" and the rogue-croc thriller "Dark Age," has left

behind a delightful pic. — *Strat.*

Koko Flanel
(BELGIAN-FRENCH)

Brussels An MPG release of a Trampoline Films/CFC coproduction. Executive producer, Maurits de Prins. Produced by Erwin Provoost. Coproducers, Christian Charret, Jean F. de Smedt. Directed by Stijn Coninx. Screenplay, Coninx, Urbanus; camera (color), Willy Stassen; editor, Susana Rossberg; music, Dirk Brosse; art direction, Hubert Pouille. Reviewed at the Eldorado theater, Brussels, March 26, 1990. Running time: **97 MIN.**
With: Urbanus, Bea van Der Mat, Willeke van Ammelroy, Jan Decleir, Herbert Flack, Ann Petersen, Henri Garcin, Koen Krucke.

■ **Flemish funnyman Urbanus broke Belgian b.o. records with his 1988 film debut "Hector," but his second feature, "Koko Flanel," is an inept followup unlikely to climb out of the lowlands.**

Still, "Koko Flanel" has received an unprecedented launch in Belgium for a homegrown picture (80 prints) and promises to rival "Hector," awarded the grand prize at the 1988 Chamrousse Humor Film Festival, for profits.

Urbanus again concocted the puerile, inconsistent script with his titular director, Stijn Coninx. "Hector" introduced the bearded goggle-eyed clown's conventionally enough as the bemused innocent who manages to triumph over adversity and even get the girl in the end. The writers have seen no reason to change the formula.

In "Koko Flanel" he's a sparrow-brained birdhouse vendor who accidentally becomes a top male model. Urbanus is less interested in his new métier than in the pretty production assistant (Bea van der Mat) at the ad/pub agency that has shackled him to a 15-year pact.

The simpleton is anxious to fulfill his father's deathbed wish that he have kids and live up to the example set by his not much brighter policeman brother.

There's plenty of low comedy antics and slapstick shenanigans, climaxing with a parodic fashion show, but helmer Coninx succeeds in flubbing most of the directing opportunities offered by the ragged screenplay.

Urbanus could be a more engaging screen comedian if he'd put himself in the hands of a real comedy screenwriter and director,

but he's obviously satisfied with this profitably mediocre setup.
— *Len.*

T'es Belle Jeanne
(You're Beautiful, Jeanne)
(CANADIAN)

Montreal An Aska Films release of a Productions Vidéofilms production in association with Producteurs TV-Films Associés and the National Film Board of Canada. Produced and directed by Robert Ménard. Screenplay, Claire Wojas; camera (color, 16m), Jean-Charles Tremblay; editor, Hélène Girard; music, Richard Grégoire; art director, François Lamontagne; production director, Michelle Marcil. Reviewed at Famous Players' Le Parisien cinema, March 30, 1990. Running time: **82 MIN.**

Jeanne	Marie Tifo
Paul	Pierre Curzi
Bert	Michel Côté
Loulou	Angele Coutu
Doctor	Claude Maher
Lucie	Marie Michaud

■ **In this yarn best suited to its original target venue, the tube, a vibrant woman adapts to life as a paraplegic when a crippling accident ultimately destroys her marriage and propels her into a romance with a man who is also wheelchair-bound.**

Produced in a 10-part telefilm package by a consortium of Quebec production houses for network Radio Quebec, "T'es Belle Jeanne" is the second pic in the series to make the unusual leap to theatrical. Unlike Michel Brault's "A Paper Wedding" (which was blown up to 35m for the official competition at the Berlin fest), "T'es Belle Jeanne" doesn't qualify as commercially releasable material. But it's primetime tv quality for French-lingo territories.

Marie Tifo (Jeanne) and Pierre Curzi (Paul) are married thesps who bring realistic emotions to the roles of the pic's betrothed. Out of love for Pierre, Jeanne cancels the marriage when she realizes she'll never resume sexual activity, a focal point of the film.

During rehabilitation, she falls in love with another accident victim, played brilliantly by Michel Côté (from producer/director Robert Ménard's "Meet Market"). Unfortunately, there's never any doubt yarn will have a happy ending, which erases the suspense factor and shifts the pic from being a potentially juicy tragedy to a sociological slice-of-life essay.

Tech credits are fine. Homevid is possible for French territories, but tv is pic's best target. — *Suze.*

Ameriikan raitti
(Paradise America)
(FINNISH)

Berlin A White 'n Blue Films presentation of Jorn Donner Film production. Produced by Jorn Donner. Directed by Lauri Toerhoenen. Screenplay, Toerhoenen, as based on a novel by Antti Tuuri; camera (Eastmancolor), Esa Vuorinen; editor, Tuula Mehtonen-Strandberg; music, Pedro Hietanen; sound, Johan Haake; costumes, Minna Uotila; line producer, Chuck Rowley; production manager, Pekka Lehto; assistant directors, Raili Salmi, Kelly Browning. Reviewed at Berlin Film Festival (market), Feb. 13, 1990. Running time: **120 MIN.**
With: Kari Sorvali, Mari Rantasila, Jari Jaervimaa, Ake Lindman, Markku Huhtamo, Markku Toikka, Tor Planting, Kalle Nikila, Rex King, Dwight Sauls, Bradford Devine, William Shook.

■ **Basing his film on a salty novel by Antti Tuuri, Lauri Toerhoenen packs some punch in "Ameriikan raitti," but is too muddled in his story-telling ways to raise hopes of off-shore sales beyond television.**

Running away from tax evasion suits, Errki and Taisto, small-time provincial businessmen, seek their "Paradise Amerika" in Florida exile. They have taken Errki's pregnant wife along, and she is the first to find life in the U.S. less than an Eden.

In Florida, the Finns meet several resident countrymen. The males all seem to be spending their time boozing while their bored wives go shopping. Having brought plenty of dirty dollars with them, Errki and Taisto at first join in the boozing, then shake themselves out of boredom by hiring on illegally as laborers at a construction site, only to run into union trouble and violence.

Errki, essentially the steadier guy but still without a work permit, turns to night-time driving of a lorry carrying live lobsters from the Florida Keys to the north.

Errki has had a quarrel with his wife and is first derouted by an invitation to a whorehouse disguised as a Finnish sauna, then more seriously by the police when bags of heroin are found among the lobsters.

Making his escape from cops and crocs through the swamps, Errki finds his wife gone. He follows her back to Finland in time for a reunion at the maternity ward.

All this and much more is ladled out sloppily in a stew that never gets really steamy. Comedy interchanges with touches of tragedy without too much conviction being put into either.

Kari Sorvali and Mari Rantasila are, however, quietly touching in the husband and wife leads, and Esa Vuorinen's cinematography has a vivid sense of the offbeat whether exploring body movements or exotic locales. — *Kell.*

Les Noces de Papier
(A Paper Wedding)
(CANADIAN)

Berlin A Les Productions du Verseau Inc. production in association with the National Film Board of Canada. Produced by Aimée Danis. Directed by Michel Brault. Screenplay, Jefferson Lewis in collaboration with Andrée Pelletier; camera (color), Sylvain Brault; editor, Jacques Gagné; music editor, Alice Wright; sound, Dominique Chartrand; costumes, Mario Davignon; associate producer, Daniele Bussy. Reviewed at the Berlin Film Festival (competition), Feb. 15, 1990. Running time: **90 MIN.**

Claire.	Geneviève Bujold
Pablo.	Manuel Aranguiz
Annie (lawyer).	Dorothé Berryman
Gaby (mother).	Monique Lepage
Milosh (lover).	Téo Spychalski
Miguel (Pablo's friend).	Jorge Fajardo
Bouchard	Gilbert Sicotte
Theriault	Jean Mathieu
Judge.	Robert Gravel

■ Thrown together by fate and the Canadian immigration system, the tale of unlikely newlyweds becomes a plausible, comic and tender love story of theatrical potential. No matter that it was shot on 16m for television.

Successfully blown up to 35m for the Berlin fest competition, it does justice to helmer Michel Brault's realistic and subtly executed vision of an illegal Latin American immigrant, Pablo, who seeks political refuge via a fake marriage to a Quebec woman, Claire.

The ''paper wedding'' arranged by Claire's lawyer sister affords Pablo Canadian citizenship and gives Claire an unexpected, and eventually welcome, exit from her solitude as a 40-year-old university professor and mistress (to Milosh, slyly played by Téo Spychalski).

It is one of Geneviève Bujold's finest performances. The thesp's strength is matched by that of Manuel Aranguiz, whose personal history as a Chilean-born actor and Canadian citizen adds authen-

ticity to the role.

When immigration officers set out to prove the marriage is fake, Pablo and Claire are forced to share the same dwelling as they prepare to pass an ''interview.'' With a list of intimate details they must learn about one another in order to pass the immigration test, the two finally settle into serious and intimate conversation. In the end, they fall in love.

Shot as if through a wedding veil, much of the pic has a hazy, serene glow. Slightly grainy imagery works well on such unglossy subject matter shot by Brault's son, Sylvain.

Liquid cinematography obviously runs in the family, and with Michel Brault's return to directing they make a good team.

''A Paper Wedding'' is more marketable than Brault's last political feature, ''Les Ordres'' (about martial law in Quebec during the October Crisis) which won him best director at the 1972 Cannes fest.

Delicately handled sexual scenes between Claire and Milosh are non-explicit and clear the path for pic's second life on the tube.
— *Suze.*

Torn Apart

New York A Castle Hill Prods. release of a City Lights production, in association with Jerry Menkin. Executive producer, Peter Arnow. Produced by Danny Fisher, Menkin. Coproducer, Doron Eran. Directed by Jack Fisher. Screenplay, Marc Kristal, based on Chayym Zeldis' novel ''A Forbidden Love;'' camera (Precision color), Barry Markowitz; editor, Michael Garvey; music, Arnow; sound (Dolby), Daniel I. Matalon; art direction, Yoram Shaier; assistant director, Yoram Kislev; associate producer, Tobi Wilson; casting, Lynn Kressel. Reviewed at Magno Preview 4 screening room, N.Y., March 29, 1990. MPAA Rating: R. Running time: **96 MIN.**

Ben Arnon.	Adrian Pasdar
Laila Malek.	Cecilia Peck
Mahmoud Malek.	Machram Huri
Prof. Mansour.	Arnon Zadok
Ilana Arnon.	Margrit Polak
Moustapha.	Michael Morim
Fawzi.	Amos Lavi
Jamilah.	Hanna Azulai
Arie Arnon.	Barry Primus
Laila in '67.	Yaffit Mazar

■ ''Torn Apart'' looks at the Middle East crisis from a different angle, using a ''Romeo And Juliet'' type of love story, but the result is a flat picture. Best chances are in commercial tv use.

Adrian Pasdar, currently starring in Fox' ''Vital Signs,'' toplines as a Jew who is brought by his dad (Barry Primus) to New York from Israel after the 6-day war in 1967. He returns in 1973 to serve in the Israeli army and becomes romantically involved with Laila (Cecilia Peck), an Arab girl he grew up with.

Of course both families are dead set against such a liaison, but matters are made worse when Peck goes to a friendly Arab professor (Arnon Zadok) for advice. He's a liberal who hopes for improved relations between the Palestinians and Israelis, while Peck's family and friends begin to think of her as a traitor. All hell breaks loose in a tragic ending that unfortunately doesn't have the grace of the Shakespeare play.

Debuting director Jack Fisher gets good atmosphere from his location filming in Israel, but pic founders due to an awkward structure built around an undelivered letter and Pasdar's reminiscences. Despite its R rating, film is too bland for its own good and definitely not strong enough to capture the attention of demanding theatrical audiences.

Cast is generally effective, with swarthy Pasdar passing for a sabra, and the graceful Peck, daughter of Gregory Peck in her biggest screen role to date, surprisingly

convincing in an ethnic role. Yaffit Mazar is well-matched to Peck in portraying the same character in the '67 prolog.

Exec producer Peter Arnow contributes an interesting, melancholy musical score. — *Lor.*

Pacific Palisades
(FRENCH)

Paris An AFMD release of a BVF/Sandor/ Antenne 2 coproduction. Produced by Bernard Verley, Lise Fayolle. Directed by Bernard Schmitt. Screenplay, Marion Vernoux, Schmitt; camera (color), Martial Barrault; editor, Gilbert Namiand; music, Jean-Jacques Goldman, Roland Romanetti; sound, Rolly Bellhassen; casting, Michael Lien (U.S.), Shula Siegfried (France). Reviewed at the UGC Biarritz theater, Paris, March 30, 1990. Running time: **94 MIN.**

Bernadette.	Sophie Marceau
Ben.	Adam Coleman Howard
Liza.	Anne Curry
Shirley.	Virginia Capers

Also with: Toni Basil, Virgil Frye, Diana Barton, Sydney Lassick, Andre Weinfeld, Caroline Grimm, Farida Kelfa, Isabelle Mergault.

■ ''Pacific Palisades'' is a transatlantic romance bringing Sophie Marceau to America for a change of climate (physical and emotional). She's in for some surprises, but the audience isn't. First feature by prizewinning vidclip helmer Bernard Schmitt and neophyte scripter Marion Vernoux sinks into the tar pits of culture shock clichés.

Gallic sweetheart Marceau is a dissatisfied Parisian waitress who heads for L.A. on a bum job offer and finds herself living alone in a large modern suburban house. She's quickly exasperated and bored by the shallow amiability of the natives, the nonexistent street life and an assortment of males who are not interested in romance (they're gay, impotent or just plain thick).

Marceau works in a local diner where she gets involved with the Canadian boyfriend (Adam Coleman Howard) of a Yank actress she initially was to have flown in with. After a difficult, mostly 1-way courtship — she chases him, then he chases her — they finally resolve their differences and move into his place.

Despite the platitudes and plot inconsistencies, film is charmingly acted by Marceau in her first (mostly) English-lingo role. Howard is okay as the romantic interest whose idea of a hot date is a group outing to a hockey game. Supporting parts are all colorfully cast and tech credits are professional.

— *Len.*

Wedding Band

Chicago An IRS Media release. Produced by John Schouweiler, Tino Insana. Executive producers, Miles Copeland 3d, Paul Colichman. Directed by Daniel Raskov. Screenplay, Insana; camera (Image Transform color), Christian Sebaldt; editor, Jonas Thaler; music, Steve Hunter; sound (Ultra-Stereo), Douglas Murray; production design, Tori Nourafchan; art direction, Michael Thomas; set decoration, Lucie Munoz; costume design, Rozanne Taucher; assistant director, Thomas A. Keith; associate producers, Steven Reich, Toni Phillips. Reviewed at the Norridge Theater, March 14, 1990. MPAA Rating: R. Running time: **82 MIN.**

Marshall Roman	William Katt
Karla Thompson	Joyce Hyser
Hugh Bowmont	Tino Insana
Ritchie	Lance Kinsey
Max	David Bowe
Nicky	Pauly Shore
Veronica	Fran Drescher
Sloane Vaughn	David Rasche

■ **"Wedding Band" is a mild, good-natured, but ultimately tired comedy about the small-time trials and tribulations of a musical combo that specializes in nuptials. After brief regional release is annulled, pic may settle down to comfortable domesticity in undiscriminating videostores.**

William Katt toplines as leader of the Shakers, an ersatz rock 'n' roll outfit eking out a living at an endless round of wedding receptions. Romantic conflict arises when girlfriend Joyce Hyser pressures him to drop the marriage biz, concentrate on writing his own tunes and tie the knot with her.

That plotline meanders through an episodic series of wedding-related settings: a Mafia ceremony, an Amish ceremony, a Buddhist ceremony, a high-powered shower for bridal consultant Hyser. Gags are plentiful, but most fall flat, either from predictability or overwork.

These scenes are larded with cameos by Joe Flaherty, Tim Kazurinsky, director Penelope Spheeris and Jim Belushi in an uncredited appearance as an Amish minister, but they fail to enliven the proceedings significantly.

Pic is also marred by a flat, lifeless soundtrack; a serious flaw in a film where music is of central importance. Bland covers of bland pop songs like Paul Fishman's "The Politics Of Dancing" (per-

formed by the H Factor and lip-synched by the Shakers) sound as if they are being played back through a high-school p.a. system. That drawback is particularly surprising, given the production company's IRS Records origins.

— *Brin.*

Mr. Hoover & I
(DOCU)

New York A Turin Film release and production, in association with Channel 4 (U.K.). Written and directed by Emile DeAntonio. Camera (Duart color, 16m), Morgan Wesson, Matthew Mindlin; editor, George Spyros. Reviewed at Public Theater, N.Y., March 21, 1990. No MPAA Rating. Running time: **85 MIN.**

With: Emile DeAntonio, John Cage.

■ **Emile DeAntonio's final film is a thought-provoking form of "meta-film," the type of rumination that preoccupied Orson Welles in his later work. It's a must for fans of the late artist and anyone interested in the cutting edge of docus.**

Basically consisting of DeAntonio addressing the camera with a feisty recounting of his memoirs (coming off oddly like another late rebel, I.F. Stone), film moves beyond talking head format into other realms signaled by gueststar John Cage. The avant-garde composer is a close friend of DeAntonio's and he's seen cooking in the kitchen and simultaneously discussing his methods of using random processes in his music.

DeAntonio takes this to heart with editing reminiscent not only of Cage's structuralism but also William Burroughs', as scenes alternate in clockwork yet seemingly random fashion. The director also keeps calling attention to the filmmaking process, and uses the whir of the camera motor as part of his method.

Aim is to debunk myths about FBI major domo J. Edgar Hoover and to fill in, often with rancor, blanks about this shadowy figure. DeAntonio talks with authority, but there is never any pretense about "documentary reality." It's a given this is one man's highly opinionated view of history.

DeAntonio used the Freedom of Information Act to get tons of government files about himself, but points out emphatically that this somewhat useful gimmick has an important loophole: Many key documents are routinely suppressed (by clever misfiling) to circum-

vent the public's right to know. He discusses other cases, particularly the FBI's persecution and dirty tricks against the late Jean Seberg, to make his point. Film, however, is mainly a personal history.

Made last year, much of the film's pronouncements not only ring true but have a prophetic value given subsequent world events. It also has a cutting to the heart of the matter quality, especially when DeAntonio discusses censorship in the land of the free as illustrated with his own works.

— *Lor.*

Blood Red

New York A Hemdale release of a Kettledrum production. Executive producers, John Daly, Derek Gibson. Produced by Judd Bernard, Patricia Casey. Directed by Peter Masterson. Screenplay, Ron Cutler; camera (Monaco color, CFI prints), Toyomichi Kurita; editor, Randy Thornton; music, Carmine Coppola; sound (Ultra-Stereo), Doug Axtell; production design, Bruno Rubeo; costume design, Ruth Myers; assistant director, Stephen M. McEveety; 2d unit camera, Walt Lloyd; casting, Pam Rack. Reviewed on Nelson Entertainment vidcassette, N.Y., April 12, 1990. MPAA Rating: R. Running time: **91 MIN.**

Marco Collogero	Eric Roberts
Sebastian Collogero	Giancarlo Giannini
Berrigan	Dennis Hopper
Andrews	Burt Young
Miss Jeffreys	Carlin Glynn
Angelica	Lara Harris
Rosa Collogero	Francesca de Sapio
Maria Collogero	Julia Roberts
Anna Collogero	Alexandra Masterson
Samuel Joseph	Joseph Running Fox
Antonio Segestra	Al Ruscio
Enziio	Michael Madsen
Silvio	Elias Koteas
Michael Fazio	Marc Lawrence
Dr. Scola	Frank Campanella
Father Stassio	Aldo Ray

Also with: Gary Swanson, Susan Anspach, Charles Dierkop, Horton Foote Jr., Maurine Logan.

■ **"Blood Red," a saga of oppressed Sicilian winegrowers in 19th century California, is an unsuccessful throwback to earlier forms of filmmaking. First-time screen teaming of siblings Eric and Julia Roberts makes this a definite curiosity item.**

Project was announced in 1976 by producer Judd Bernard, filmed in 1986 and given a perfunctory regional release last summer by Hemdale.

Future film historians will ponder why this wasn't a Paramount picture, since it conforms to the themes and mood of "The Godfather," "1900" and Eric Roberts' first starring pic, "The King Of The Gypsies." All that's missing

is the late Sterling Hayden.

A robust Giancarlo Giannini is patriarch of one of two families in Brandon, Calif., and soon is warring with robber baron railroad magnate Dennis Hopper (fitted with an unconvincing Scottish brogue here) determined to get his land for his railroad's right of way.

Giannini's rebellious son, Eric Roberts, is in love with the beautiful daughter (Lara Harris) of another winegrowing clan. Hopper hires Burt Young (miscast) and his gang of mercenaries to convince Giannini and the other growers to clear out, resulting in violence. Pic ends in boring fashion with a whimper.

Ron Cutler's utterly predictable script is mainly to blame for draining "Blood Red" of interest. It emerges as a depiction in black hat/white hat terms of history in the mode of "Heaven's Gate" but without that film's controversial (but awesome) production values. Peter Masterson's direction is flat, and though there are some pretty shots, the love of the land and specifics of winegrowing are not developed.

Eric Roberts is more subdued than usual as the script fails to develop a 3-dimensional character for him. His scenes with real-life sister Julia, cast as his sister, are intriguing because of the visual match. She doesn't get much chance to emote, but that nascent star quality already is evident.

Alexandra Masterson is a good match as the third sibling, while helmer's wife, Carlin Glynn (previously featured in Masterson's "The Trip To Bountiful"), is solid representing the local gentry in supporting the Sicilians' just cause.

Carmine Coppola delivers a romantic musical background that underscores the genre connection. — *Lor.*

Perfect World
(DANISH-B&W)

Berlin A Danish Film Institute presentation of Fortuna Film production with the DFI. Produced by Peter Aalbaek Jensen. DFI consultant producer, Kirsten Bonnen Rask. Directed by Tom Elling. Screenplay, Tomas Gislason, Elling; camera (b&w), Per Dreyer; editor, Jesper Westerlin Nielsen; music, Bjarne Roupe, Svend Hvidtfeldt Nielsen, Christian Skeel; sound, Peter Mogensen. Reviewed at Berlin Film Festival (market), Feb. 11, 1990. Running time: **80 MIN.**

Rita	Anne-Mette Rosenkilde
Lucy	Tabita Vinten

■ Eight months after its delivery, "Perfect World," a first feature by Danish Film School grad and ex-painter Tom Elling, is still looking for a home territory distribution.

This film is the non-story of a dream dreamed, apparently jointly, by two young women. They have salvaged from the harbour an old suitcase (presumably full of more dreams) that they had lost when they were kids, playing with sticks in the raging waters beneath a waterfall.

The women, Rita and Lucy, now travel through the harbor area in an old van during a rain-swept night. They smoke cigarettes and are photographed upside down and downside up in endless frames of evocative cinematography while spouting cascades of words, spoken in a monotone, that constitute some kind of high-falutin' gobble-dygook poetry.

Elling's dream on behalf of the two women is just about as unintelligible as anybody's dreams invariably are to anybody but the dreamer himself and maybe his psychoanalyst. Although the director has Per Dreyer's camera constantly on the move and in exquisite technical control, absolutely nothing happens.

Water (enough to float three Andrei Tarkovsky features, Elling's obvious inspiration) spills over everything, eventually drowning out every last vestige of what might have connected "Perfect World" to even the severest of glutton-for-punishment art cinema audiences. — *Kell.*

Du Elvis, Ich Monroe
(You Elvis, Me Monroe)
(WEST GERMAN)

Berlin A Lothar Lambert production. Produced, written, directed and edited by Lothar Lambert. Camera (b&w, 16m), Albert Kittler. Reviewed at the Berlin Film Festival (Panorama section), Feb. 15, 1990. Running time: **70 MIN.** .
Tarek. . . . . Baduri
Frau Korkmaz. . . . . .Nilgun Taifun
Karin. . . . . .Inga Schrader
Susanne. . . . . .Susanne Gautier
Also with: Erika Rabau, Lothar Lambert, Dagmar Beiersdorf, Robert Cutts.

■ Dedicated to "all the impossible love affairs of the world," Lothar Lambert's 1-man production is one of those wonderfully impossible black & white subversive pics which makes great late-night festival fare. Its life beyond fests and Berlin arthouses is unlikely.

Shots of the Berlin wall with Leonard Cohen's droning voice singing "after 20 years of boredom, or trying to change the system from within, first we take Manhattan, then we take Berlin" is a timely touch. However, pic is mainly about intimacy between neighbors and impossible love.

Tarek is a young Arab who moves into an apartment building where everyone knows everyone or spies through doors left ajar to get to know them. Tarek meets Frau Korkmaz who supplies him with a chair, dishes and "anything else" he wants. He eventually winds up with the daughter Susanne until the blond Monroe-like neighbor, Karin, is invited into erotic scenes which include the women kissing and the daughter peeking from the other room.

When Tarek reprimands the women for their behavior, they warn "You need to be normal. Don't think in categories." Another Cohen song pipes in: "I don't care what the people say: I still carry on in this way."

Such 1960s "carrying on" will never draw a commercial audience in the sanitized '90s, but pic has all the ingredients for underground cinema. — *Suze.*

Tripwire

New York A New Line Cinema release of a Cinetel Films production. Executive producer, Paul Hertzberg. Produced by Lisa M. Hansen. Directed by James Lemmo. Screenplay, B.J. Goldman, from story by William Lustig, Spiro Razatos; camera (Alpha Ciné color), Igor Sunara; editor, Christopher Cibelli; music, Richard Stone; sound, Jonathan Stein; production design, Bill Cornford; art direction, Dian Perryman; assistant director, Whitney Hunter; production manager, John S. Engel; stunt coordinator, Razatos; 2d unit camera, Henning Schellerup; coproducer, Jefferson Richard; casting, Susan Bluestein. Reviewed on RCA/Columbia Pictures vidcassette, N.Y., March 24, 1990. MPAA Rating: R. Running time: **91 MIN.**
Jack DeForest. . . . . .Terence Knox
Josef Szabo. . . . . .David Warner
Annie. . . . . .Isabella Hoffman
Trudy. . . . . .Charlotte Lewis
Rick DeForest. . . . . . . .Andras Jones
Turbo. . . . . .Sy Richardson
El Tigre. . . . . .Marco Rodriguez
Hans. . . . . .Viggo Mortensen
Lee Pitt. . . . . .Yaphet Kotto
Julia. . . . . .Meg Foster
Also with: Tommy Chong, Shelby Chong.

■ A bland lead performance sinks "Tripwire," an unpretentious Cinetel action pic briefly released theatrically in January by New Line ahead of hv.

Terence Knox plays an FBI man who interferes with terrorists, led by David Warner, who are sabotaging a train. He kills Warner's son, starting a vendetta. Warner kills Knox' wife Meg Foster and kidnaps his son.

When Knox is bounced from the federal payroll for not obeying orders he embarks on his 1-man campaign to get Warner, aided from the inside by romantic FBI coworker Isabella Hoffman. Film ends in smug, far too pat fashion.

Biggest problem here is casting of Knox, who's simply too stolid, dead-on as a colorless FBI guy. Casting against type might have worked.

Supporting cast is arresting, including the always dependable Foster, Charlotte Lewis as a very sympathetic terrorist and Yaphet Kotto once again essaying his "Midnight Run" persona as Knox' FBI boss. Tommy Chong and his wife pop up in pointless cameos.
— *Lor.*

Het Sacrament
(The Sacrament)
(BELGIAN)

Brussels A Warner Bros. release of a Silent Sunset production. Produced by Patrick Beuls, Patrick Conrad. Written and directed by Hugo Claus, based on his novel "Omtrent Deedee." Camera (color), Gilberto Azevedo; editor, Menno Boerema; music, Frederic Devreese; sound, Dominique Warnier; art direction, Hubert Pouille; costumes, Suzanne Van Well; production manager, Guy de Lombaert. Reviewed at the Studio Passage theater, Brussels, Jan. 19, 1990. Running time: **90 MIN.**
With: Jan Decleir, Frank Aendenboom Huigo van den Berghe, Carl Ridders, Marc Didden, Chris Lomme, Ann Petersen, An de Donder.

■ "Het Sacrament" is an appealing if theatrical satiric family portrait.

It's the sixth feature by writer-director Hugo Claus, based on his 1963 novel "Omtrent Deedee" (which he first adapted for the stage in 1971 as "Interieurs"). As in the play, Claus creates an impressive Kammerspiel style supported by an extraordinary acting ensemble.

Set in the 1950s, film covers an annual reunion of the Heylen family, in the presence of a priest, to commemorate the death of the clan's matriarch. After the mass, the partying begins. All the characters talk, eat and drink. As they drink, the tensions grate and frustrations erupt. For fun, they disguise themselves for several little theatricals, but the results are not quite what everyone expected.

Film (Belgium's official selection for this year's foreign-language Oscar nominations) is rich in pathos, leavened with humor. Claus creates a vivid personal universe, peopled with men and women in a Catholic environment who expose their feelings freely.

Claus' sense of plotting, with its highly dramatic conclusion, is somewhat old-fashioned but ambiguous. The cast is perfect.
— *John.*

Nightmare At Noon

New York An Omega Pictures production. Produced and directed by Nico Mastorakis. Screenplay, Mastorakis, Kirk Ellis; camera (United color; Technicolor prints), Cliff D. Ralke; editor, George Rosenberg, Mastorakis; music, Stanley Myers, Hans Zimmer; sound (Dolby), Blake Wilcox; production manager, Steve Celniker; assistant director, Perry Husman; aerial photography, Rexford Metz; associate producer, Bob Manning. Reviewed on vidcassette, N.Y., March 24, 1990. MPAA Rating: R. Running time: **96 MIN.**
Ken Griffith. . . . . .Wings Hauser
Riley. . . . . .Bo Hopkins
Sheriff Hanks. . . . . . .George Kennedy
The albino. . . . . .Brion James
Sherry Griffith. . . . . . .Kimberly Beck
Julia. . . . . .Kimberly Ross
Charley. . . . . .Neal Wheeler
Dr. Miller. . . . . . . .David Christiansen
Deputy. . . . . .Mark Haarman
Lori. . . . . .Jean Pflieger
Woman in curlers. . . . . . .Tabi Cooper
Also with: S.A. Griffin, Herman Poppe, Kim Milford, Terry Seago, Larry Campbell.

■ This compact thriller, shot three years ago with moniker "Deathstreet USA," is reviewed here for the record following its homevideo release.

Pic has sci-fi overtones, as heavy Brion James (made up as an albino here) executes a warfare experiment using the people of tiny town of Canyonland as guinea pigs. A chemical is put in their water, driving the folks crazy.

Wings Hauser is vacationing with wife Kimberly Beck. She samples the water and goes nuts (in a hammy, funny scene straight out of acting class). Sheriff George Kennedy locks her up and teams up with Hauser and down-on-his-luck ex-cop Bo Hopkins to find the bad guys and keep the craziness under control. When Kennedy is put out of commission, his pretty daughter (and fellow cop) Kimberly Ross takes over.

Film benefits from excellent stuntwork and a good score by

high-profile team of Stanley Myers ("Deer Hunter") and Hans Zimmer ("Rain Man," "Driving Miss Daisy") who've frequently worked for filmmaker Nico Mastorakis. Weakest element is when Hopkins does a plot recap for the duller members of the audience halfway through the pic. — *Lor.*

Jigsaw
(AUSTRALIAN)

Sydney A Rosa Colosimo Films production. Produced by Colosimo. Directed by Marc Gracie. Screenplay, Gracie, Chris Thompson, from a story by Colosimo; camera (Eastmancolor), James Grant; editor, Nicolas Lee; music, Dalmazio Babare; sound, John McKerrow; production design, Chris Kennedy; production manager, Simon Rosenthal; assistant director, Paul Healey; casting, Angelo Salmanca. Reviewed at Mosman screening room, Sydney, Oct. 31, 1989. Running time: **89 MIN.**
Virginia York. . . . . . . .Rebecca Gibney
Det-Const. Broulle. . . .Dominic Sweeney
Ed Minter. . . . . .Nico Lathouris
Gordon Carroll. . . . . .Gary Day
Jack McClusky. . . . . . .Terence Donovan
Aaron York. . . . . .Michael Coard
Ray Carpenter. . . . . .James Wright
Laura Carpenter. . . . . . . .Peppie D'Or
Ted Lanski. . . . . .Peter Black
Alex York. . . . . . . .David Bradshaw
Oliver Kady. . . . . .John Flaus
Jean. . . . . Brenda Addie

■ **This intriguing thriller, though modest in scale, looms as one of the most successful to date from the Rosa Colosimo stable. Nevertheless, it is better suited to video and the tube than to theatrical release.**

Pic opens with the discovery of the body of Alex York (David Bradshaw) on a rocky beach; seems Alex, a real estate developer, was married for only a day to Virginia (Rebecca Gibney) following a whirlwind relationship — Virginia has never even been to her husband's apartment.

Investigating cop Broulle (Dominic Sweeney) sniffs around and discovers shady development deals involving the local Mayor (Terence Donovan) who is chummy with a nervous politico (Gary Day). Virginia, meanwhile, discovers that Alex had an ex-wife and teen son (Michael Coard) she knew nothing about. She's also being followed by a mean-looking type (Nico Lathouris) who seems to be trying to kill her.

Director Marc Gracie (who helmed the Colosimo production "Blowing Hot And Cold" last year) does an ok job with this material but stages his action scenes without real conviction. A mid-film chase scene through sub-

urban streets passes muster, but the final shootout between Sweeney and Lathouris, both clinging onto the car Gibney is driving at speed, stretches credulity.

Still, scenes such as the one where the bride/widow hears her dead husband's voice on his answering machine, or discovers a tape in which he reveals his love for her, do carry a charge.

Gibney is effective as the frightened woman at the center of the drama and Lathouris could make a career out of sinister villains. Supporting cast is adequate. Technically, pic is fine given its low budget. — *Strat.*

Sirup
(Syrup)
(DANISH)

Copenhagen A Kärne Film release of Per Holst Film production. Produced by Holst. Written and directed by Helle Ryslinge. Camera (Eastmancolor), Dirk Brüel; editor, Birger Möller-Jensen; music, Peer Raben; sound, Niels Arild; production design, Peter de Neergaard; costumes, Malin Birch-Jensen; production management, Gitte Sindlev, Thomas Heinesen. Reviewed at the Scala, Copenhagen, March 16, 1990. Running time: **114 MIN.**
Lasse. . . . . . . .Peter Hesse Overgaard
Ditte. . . . . .Kirsten Lehfeldt
Jesper. . . . . .Steen Svare
The Rack. . . . . .Inger Hovmand
Pia. . . . . . . .Pernille Höjmark-Jensen
Terje. . . . . .Henrik Scheele
Bente. . . . . .Marianne Moritzen
Goldbauer. . . . . .Aage Haugland
Liza Finkelstein. . . . .Karen Claybourn
Mr. Finth. . . . . .Sören Ostergaard
Jesus. . . . . .Nicolai Brüel
Also with: Michael Simpson, Kirsten Peuliche, Lars Ottosen, Lillian Tillegren, Ase Hansen, Lilli Holmer, Cecilia Zwick, Freddy Thornberg.

■ **"Sirup" is comedy satire, poured expertly by writer-helmer Helle Ryslinge in her second feature after "Coeurs Flambés." As her debut, "Syrup" will most likely gain offshore exposure via fest circuits and arthouses.**

Chief target for Ryslinge's venom is handsome young Lasse (Peter Hesse Overgaard), a self-styled video artist/art promoter. Lasse is a sponger on the Greenwich Village-like Copenhagen setting. Taking advantage of Ditte (Kirsten Lehfeldt), a gifted painter who loves him, Lasse moves in with her.

Overlong film has an underdeveloped plot about Lasse's small swindles in connection with the visit of a New York art tycoon (played by international opera ace Aage Haugland). What Ryslinge

is better at is her meticulous depiction of a self-centered man who actually has no center at all. Lasse hides his hollowness for himself and for most everybody else behind bright, excited chatter, while he lies and pulls off all kinds of small and big deceits without really recognizing himself guilty.

NORDIC FILM FESTIVAL REVIEWS

Honungsvargar
(Honey Wolves)
(SWEDISH)

Kristiansand, Norway A Sandrew Film release of Belladonna Film production in association with the Swedish Film Institute, Sandrew Film and SVT-2. Produced by Marianne Persson. Directed by Christina Olofson. Screenplay, based on Sun Axelsson's novel, Olofson; additional dialog, Annika Thor; camera (Eastmancolor), Lisa Hagstrand; editor, Sigurd Hallman; music, Eva Dahlgren, Lars Andersson; sound, Bo Persson; production design, Birgitta Brensen; costumes, Sven Lunden, Kim Aström; production manager, Zoltan Kirs. Reviewed at 8th Nordic Film Festival, Kristiansand, March 29, 1990. Running time: **98 MIN.**
Mignon . . . . Maria Grip
Pär . . . . Johan Rabaeus
Nick . . . . Nicolas Chagrin
Elizabeth . . . . Agneta Ekmanner
Mignon's father . . . . Inger Hirdvall
Also with: Marika Lindström, Douglas Johansson, Hans Lannerstedt, Fredrik Ultvedt.

■ **Some foreign sales might still be seen for "Honey Wolves," since the film has both a provocative title, referring to the story's men, and a lot of fine, imaginative cinematography by Lisa Hagstrand. It also has good acting by bulky Johan Rabaeus.**

Poet-novelist Sun Axelsson relates, with fire, her incendiary life as a writer and lover in several semi-autobiographical books. Christina Olofson, in her feature bow, uses one of them to tell of Mignon. The budding young woman of the 1950s struggles in Stockholm and Paris to find her own voice as a writer while most of the time submitting to the amiable tyranny of two professional men, one of letters, the other of mathematics.

Olofson, who attracted international attention in 1988 with her docu portrayal of famous women orchestra conductors in "A Woman Is A Risky Bet," unfortunately smothers her fiction film in literary dust, especially in long stretches of dialog more or less lifted from the essays of Pär Radström

Ryslinge deftly describes the manners & mores of the bohemian milieu's (mostly) lower strata. All technical credits are first-rate, and Overgaard's performance as a weak man is a strong and convincing one. Lehfeldt supports him with warmth and intelligence. — *Kell.*

(who was novelist Axelsson's real-life lover), Leo Tolstoy and others. What she hopes to emulate with these quotes is the way men of literature are supposed to talk, but hardly do.

Rabaeus, as Pär, takes Mignon to Paris but cannot see the city as anything but a launching pad for lofty reflections on books and cinema. As his successor in Mignon's graces, Chile's Nicolas Chagrin plays the warmly virile but inevitably male chauvinistic Latin lover to the hilt.

Most of the time, however, the sheer radiancy of newcomer Maria Grip's beautifully chiseled face and her way of moving (as if to the rhythm of unheard music) commands attention. But when Grip is meant to act out a writer's torment, her director has her spout empty pieties and resorts to the shopworn device of showing her hand writing lines of empty poetry in calligraphy on sheets of luxurious stationery.

In the role of Mignon's devoted father, Inger Hirdvall adds muted counterpoint to the general portrayal of men as highbrow numbskulls. Agneta Ekmanner displays cool grace and irony as Mignon's mature woman friend. All production credits are first-rate; the '50s city locales and interiors are done without excess of over-researched detail. The music quoted is well-chosen within the dramatic context. — *Kell.*

Til en ukjent
(To A Stranger)
(NORWEGIAN-B&W/ COLOR)

Kristiansand, Norway A KF release of Magdalena Film production for Norsk Film, Norsk Film Studio and Film Teknikk Norge. Produced by Bente Erichsen. Written and directed by Unni Straume. Camera (b&w/Eastmancolor), Harald Paalgard; editor, Trygve Hagen, Unni Straume, Michael Lesczylovski; sound, Sturla Einarson; music, Cecilie Ore; production design, Carle Lange; costumes, Runa Fönne; production manager, Bente Melgaard. Reviewed at 8th Nordic Film Festival, Kristiansand, March 28 1990. Running time: **82 MIN.**

Ane . . . . .Hilde Aarö
The composer. . . . .Harald Heide-Steen Jr.
Ane as child. . . . . .Toril Brevik
Svein. . . . . .Sven Rasmussen
Ane's mother. . . . . . . .Inger Heldal
Ane's father. . . . . .Jan Haarstad
Ane's grandmother. . .Ragnhild Michelsen

■ **Unni Straume's "To A Stranger" (meaning the viewer) is more a tribute to the late Andrei Tarkovsky's style and themes than a personal rendition of a grownup's search for catharsis in reliving childhood events. Because of her fine artistic control and shiny technical credits, film is likely to find offshore fest exposure.**

Straume's bow as a writer-helmer, done 99% in black & white, uses little dialog but a lot of inner-voice poetic-existentialist (or is it Zen?) droning. Ane, a young woman (blond, bland but fresh-faced Hilde Aarö) leaves the big city to take stock. Her quest for what really constitutes her soul takes her to the village-by-the-sea of her childhood.

For a while, she has a middle-aged composer and self-styled "collector of sounds" (Harald Heide-Steen Jr.) as her traveling companion. He more or less orchestrates the mental music that appears to be one of her driving forces.

The woman then visits the small frame house where she was brought up by stern, religious parents. She does not seem to have suffered any injustices, but has been suppressing the memory of a sister who died in a fire. By the sea she found, and has kept, a bottle containing fragments of thoughts penned in Russian "nezna komumu" (to a stranger).

Having relived her past in nonconclusive flashes, Ane now lies down by the sea and gazes peacefully into the sun as the bottle rolls back into the waves, presumably bringing its message forward to other finders and audiences. The message may well be termed pretty empty, but it is delivered with consummate taste.

The rumblings and flashes of a volcano's belly, dramatic highlights of Tarkovsky's mirrored universe, are absent, while the master's obsession with the sounds of water and fire is echoed faithfully by pupil.

Harald Paalgard, a master of action cinematography, works in harmony with the director's subdued moods. His lighting of black & white adds depth and shadings to shots that hold both grace and suspense even when moving at their slowest pace. This goes for a few color takes at film's end, too. On the soundtrack, the footfalls of ants crossing their hill can actually be heard it. — *Kell.*

Bulen
(The Bump)
(SWEDISH)

Kristiansand, Norway A Planborg Film release of Filmstallet production for Exat and the Swedish Film Institute. Produced by Anders Birkeland and Katinka Farago. Written and directed by Karsten Wedel. Camera (Eastmancolor), Mischa Gavrjusjov; editor, Wedel; music, Lars-Eric Brossner; production design, Anders Barreus; costumes, Pia Wahlquist; sound, Christian Gyllensten; production manager, Kaska Petras. Reviewed at 8th Nordic Film Festival, Kristiansand, March 29, 1990. Running time: **97 MIN.**

With: Thomas von Brömssen, Nora Plau, Christina Stenius, Henric Holmberg, Lars Brandeby, Tommy Johnson, Per Oscarsson.

■ **After almost a year on the shelf, "The Bump" has finally found a distributor, but it's likely to find the going tough.**

Item hangs in tatters on all counts, as narrative as well as stylistically and technically.

"The Bump" suffered worse than mild injury during its production run in 1988-89. Producer Anders Birkeland exited when production financier Exat Film collapsed. When Katinka Farago took over for the Swedish Film Institute in a rescue operation, Karsten Wedel's little comedy was actually beyond salvaging.

Without a firm producer's hand to guide him, writer-director Wedel has hardly one of his myriad satiric and romantic ideas sustained long enough to make its point. He flirts with so many cinematic styles that only a hodgepodge of frustrated ambitions remain in evidence.

Wedel's story about a man who quits family and work routines in favor of the freer life of a garbage collector is familiar enough. Even so, Thomas von Brömsen (the nice uncle of Lasse Hallström's "My Life As A Dog") delivers a charmingly befuddled performance as 40ish Nisse, who bumps into a telephone pole while sneaking a look over his shoulder at a pretty passerby.

The bump sparks his mental metamorphosis, and it is clear to see that much fun might have ensued had the production not been allowed to flounder and eventually sink like lead.

"The Bump" contains a lot of music, most of it borrowed but rendered with spirited abandon, especially by the plot's jazz band of garbage collectors emulating Armstrong, the Bob Crosby Bob Cats and what was once the Disney studios' Firehouse Five of near-professional amateurs.
— *Kell.*

Sigurd Drakedreper
(Sigurd The Dragon-Slayer)
(NORWEGIAN)

Kristiansand, Norway A KF release of Mediagjöglerne production in association with Filmeffekt and Norsk Film. Written, produced and directed by Lars Rasmussen, Knut Jorfald, based on novel by Torill Torstadt Hauger; camera (Eastmancolor), Kjell Vassdal; editor, Skule Eriksen; music, Randall Meyers, Stein Berge Svendsen (English-dubbed version); sound, Jan Lindvik; production design, Frode Krogh; costumes, Lisbet Narud. Reviewed at 8th Nordic Film Festival, Kristiansand, March 31, 1990. Running time: **93 MIN.**

Sigurd. . . . . .Kristian Tonby
The earl. . . . . .Terje Strömdal
Orm. . . . . .Per Jansen
Also with: Per Kristian Indrehus, Brit Elsebeth Haagenslie, Rulle Smit, Joachim Calmeyer, Pia Rosenberg.

■ **Kurosawa or George Lucas it isn't, but "Sigurd The Dragon-Slayer" makes the historical adventure grade as smooth and appealing youth entertainment. Item is most likely headed for international tv distribution.**

Sigurd, the 11-year-old son of a Viking earl, must win his father's respect as a swordsman before he can be recognized by the earl's men as heir to throne. He would rule a tiny nation that sends longships abroad to fight and bring home goods and thralls. There is also a neighboring tribe of black-clad warriors who must be fought off constantly.

Blond and frail Sigurd fails at many a test before being accepted as a true Viking and eventually, after his father's death in battle, an earl himself. He gains valuable insights in the life of thralls and banished people living in the mountains above the fjord where lies the Viking village.

Grownups susceptible to movie violence may object to the film's honest look at the occasional brutality inherent to the Viking way of life, but the filmmakers never indulge in wanton displays of bloodshed.

Their story hangs well together, its characters ring true and are well played by good actors. Kjell Vassdal's cinematography has dramatic strength and records spectacular natural scenery. — *Kell.*

ARCHIVE FILM REVIEW

Otets Sergey
(Father Sergius)
(RUSSIAN-B&W)

Brussels A Joseph Ermolieff production (Moscow, 1917), first released in Moscow, May 14, 1918. Preserved and presented by the Gosfilmofond film archive. Directed by Jacob Protazanov. Screenplay, Protazanov, Alexandre Volkov, based on the story by Leo Tolstoy; camera (b&w), Fedot Burgasov, Nikolai Rudakov; sets, Vladimir Balyuzhek, Alexander Lochakov; costumes, V. Vorobyev. Reviewed at the Royal Belgian Film Archive, Brussels, Jan. 14, 1990. Length: 7,144 ft. Running time (at 18 frames per second): **106 MIN.**

Stepan Kasatsky/
Father Sergius. . . . . . .Ivan Mozhukhin
Czar Nicholas I. . . . . .Evgeny Gaidarov
The widow Makovkina. . .Natalia Lissenko
Maria Korotkova. . . . .Vera Dzheneyeva
Countess Korotkova. . . .Olga Kondorova
Merchant. . . . . .Ivan Talanov
Merchant's daughter. . . . . .Vera Orlova

■ **This masterpiece of the early, privately owned Russian film industry turned out to be the swan song of pre-Soviet cinema. Jacob Protazanov's film is a must-see in the currently touring show of pre-revolutionary Russian cinema.**

Made between the February and October revolutions of 1917, "Father Sergius" was held up for release until 1918, when its producer Joseph Ermolieff had already fled south to Yalta with his company to create a new studio (most would emigrate to France in 1920).

"Father Sergius" dominates other landmark films of the 1910s by its lavish production, adult manner, psychological density and the unsurpassed title performance by Russian film star Ivan Mozhukhin. As the late Russian and Soviet film historian Jay Leyda rightly noted, few excuses have to be made for it today for new audiences. Film is one of those classics that everybody knows by reputation but few have seen, despite the fact that it has long been available in the Sovexport catalog.

Story is based on the controversial Leo Tolstoy tale that czarist censors had kept out of the hands of film producers. Protazanov and his screenwriter, Alexandre Volkov (the future emigré director of "Casanova" and other famous Mozhukhin vehicles), made a remarkably faithful adaptation of the material.

They retained the inherent social and political critique and dramatically forthright treatment of such themes as spiritual pride and sexual desire. Yet they happily drew the line at Tolstoy's moralizing tone. The film's final scenes, for instance, are all the more powerful for their ambiguity.

"Father Sergius" is the monastic name of an ambitious young imperial guard officer under Nicholas I who, revolted by the revelation that his fiancée has been the czar's mistress, abandons his commission and aristocratic title to enter a monastery.

His subsequent fame as monk, priest and hermit, however, only fans his pride and enflames his sexual hunger. Fleeing himself and temptation he finishes his life in Siberia, an aged vagabond.

Mozhukhin's performance is a riveting tour de force in which the entire life span of its protagonist is mapped out with dramatic precision, from the callow hotheaded teen cadet who worships the Czar to the burnt-out old holy man condemned to exile and spiritual desolation.

More than a mere virtuoso display of physical transformation and makeup, Mozhukhin's tormented hero burns with a tragic intensity that makes this one of the acting highlights of the silent period.

Protazanov's direction is masterly both in its large-scale stagings (a spectacular ball at the imperial palace) and intimate dramatic scenes.

Rightly famous is the long sequence in a hermit's cell where Sergius chops his finger off with a axe in order to kill the lust incited by a frivolous young widow (played by Mozhukhin's companion and costar Natalia Lissenko) who has asked shelter for the night.

Production dressing was considered sumptuous for the period

and remains impressive. Camera work, sets and costumes are first-rate. A painterly shot of Father Sergius tutoring ignorant peasants is an obvious tribute to the aged Tolstoy, who personally took charge of the education of his peasants. (A frame blowup often is reprinted in film history books on the period.)

Despite its somber dramatic content, pic was one of the rare early Russian films to have a relatively wide international distribution and may have had a real pictorial influence. Could Chaplin and Eisenstein have remembered it when they composed famous shots in "The Gold Rush" (the lonely tramp looking at a dance hall window) and "Ivan the Terrible" (the sculptural silhouette of the long-bearded Czar)?

Despite grading problems in print screened, film has been well restored by the Soviet film archives, Gosfilmofond.

Unlike the other great Protazanov classic of the same period, "The Queen Of Spades," the surviving materials for "Father Sergius" have survived in more complete state. — *Len.*

Q&A

New York   A Tri-Star Pictures release of a Regency Intl. Pictures/Odyssey Distributors Ltd. presentation. Produced by Arnon Milchan, Burtt Harris. Executive producer, Patrick Wachsberger. Directed by Sidney Lumet. Screenplay, Lumet, based on Edwin Torres' novel; camera (Technicolor), Andrzej Bartkowiak; editor, Richard Cirincione; music, Rubén Blades; sound (Dolby), Chris Newman; production design, Philip Rosenberg; art direction, Beth Kuhn; set decoration, Gary Brink; costumes, Ann Roth, Neil Spisak; production manager, John H. Starke; assistant director, Harris, Vincente Juarbe (Puerto Rico); associate producer, Lilith A. Jacobs; casting, Joy Todd. Reviewed at Columbia screening room, N.Y., March 22, 1990. MPAA Rating: R. Running time: **132 MIN.**
Mike Brennan. . . . . .Nick Nolte
Al Reilly. . . . . .Timothy Hutton
Bobby Texador. . . . . .Armand Assante
Kevin Quinn. . . . . . . .Patrick O'Neal
Leo Bloomenfeld. . . . . .Lee Richardson
Luis Valentin. . . . . .Luis Guzman
Sam Chapman. . . . . . .Charles Dutton
Nancy Bosch. . . . . .Jenny Lumet
Roger Montalvo. . . . . .Paul Calderon
Jose Malpica. . . . .International Chrysis
Larry Peach. . . . . . .Dominick Chianese
Nick Petrone. . . . . . .Leonard Cimino
Preston Pearlstein. . . . . .Fyvush Finkel
Lubin. . . . . .Tommy A. Ford
Sylvester/Sophia. . . . . . . .Brian Neill
Flo. . . . . .Susan Mitchell
Agnes Quinn. . . . . . . .Cynthia O'Neal

 Sidney Lumet grabs a tiger by the tail with "Q&A," a hard-hitting thriller that takes on weighty topics of racism and corruption in the New York City justice system. Bravura thesping by Nick Nolte should earn this morbid but riveting film noir a solid audience reception.

For Lumet it's a natural assignment in the same vein as his "Serpico" and "Prince Of The City." Working from Judge Edwin Torres' novel, Lumet has scripted in concise, suspenseful fashion, opening with cop Nolte ruthlessly killing a Latino drug dealer outside an after-hours club and then intimidating witnesses on the scene.

As his first job as a new assistant d.a., Timothy Hutton is summoned by his cooly evil boss Patrick O'Neal (a man with unbridled political ambitions) to do a routine investigation, writing up a q&a with Nolte and other principal players. He's obviously the fall guy, meant to miss the cold-blooded murder and report back Nolte's justifiable homicide and one less villain on the city streets.

Key to film's success is how the case gradually uncovers new layers of corruption and insidious racism, with escalating awareness (and danger) for Hutton. A suspect (Armand Assante) who once

worked with the victim accuses Nolte of wrongdoing and one of Hutton's police assistants, Luis Guzman, also smells a rat.

In short order, Hutton finds out he's been set up in a trail of dirty linen that extends to his much-loved cop father, his ex-girl friend Jenny Lumet (now Assante's main squeeze) and scary revelations linking the dead man to Nolte and O'Neal. Film's chilling finale comes close to nihilism in stating that not only is Hutton powerless to do the right thing in this case but that much bigger corruption has been covered up in the past.

Atmospherically lensed on N.Y. turf by Andrzej Bartkowiak, Lumet's film paints a bleak picture of the Big Apple indeed. Nolte in his first film role as a baddie is outstanding, bringing utter conviction to the stream of racist and sexist epithets that pour from his good ole boy lips.

Lumet has adventurously used the technique of master shots only on Nolte's big acting scenes (ditto for Assante, letter-perfect as the Latin gangster), allowing the thesp to create scenes in a stage manner without interruption and framing the whole body on screen. Rather than a cost-cutting device on this economical indie picture, it works dramatically. The topbilled actor doesn't have a big chunk of screen time but makes every second count.

Hutton is steady in an underplayed central role. Lumet's daughter Jenny (granddaughter of Lena Horne) has the pivotal female part; she's affecting relating the trauma of Hutton's unconscious negative reaction when he met her black father for the first time. This helps add to pic's theme that internalized racism permeates all the main characters and thereby the justice system, but along with the contrivance of putting Hutton at cross-purposes with the investigation of Assante and Lumet puts too much weight on the character to be believable.

Supporting cast is led by perfectly chosen O'Neal, out to protect his own interests and a misguided view of tradition; and Lee Richardson, who makes the most of Lumet's vivid dialog in playing the veteran lawyer who acts as Hutton's guardian angel until things get out of hand.

Not since William Friedkin's "Cruising" has a film dared to expose a dark, twisted underworld with homosexuals and transsexuals integrated into the plot. Nolte's character persecuting minorities is given a universal application as he manhandles the transvestite hooker played by Brian Neill, the gay key witness played by Paul Calderon and Calderon's she-male friend essayed by International Chrysis, all deeply affecting as victims.

Guzman and Charles Dutton give solid characterizations as Hutton's investigative cops and comic relief is delivered in choice ethnic turns by Fyvush Finkel as Assante's mealy-mouthed lawyer and Tommy A. Ford as the wisecracking stenographer taking down the q&a. Leonard Cimino has a delightful scene as a Mafia godfather.

Adding to the film's momentum is a driving vocal "Don't Trouble Cross" by Rubén Blades, used during opening and end credits as well as during a climactic action sequence.

Tech credits are top-drawer, particularly crisp sound recording of dialog in a thriller driven by words, not car chases. — Lor.

Miami Blues

Hollywood An Orion Pictures release of a Tristes Tropiques production. Produced by Jonathan Demme, Gary Goetzman. Directed by George .Armitage. Executive producers, Edward Saxon, Fred Ward. Screenplay, Armitage, based on the novel by Charles Willeford. Camera (color, DeLuxe), Tak Fujimoto; editor, Craig McKay; production design, Maher Ahmad; music, Gary Chang; sound (Dolby), Dan Sable; costume design, Eugenie Bafaloukos; set decoration, Don K. Ivey; assistant directors, Bozman, Kyle McCarthy; coproducers, Kenneth Utt, Ron Bozman; associate producer, William Horberg; casting, Howard Feuer. Reviewed at the UA Coronet Theater. L.A., April 16, 1990. MPAA Rating: R. Running time: 99 MIN.
Frederick J. Frenger Jr. . . . . .Alec Baldwin
Sgt. Hoke Moseley. . . . . . .Fred Ward
Susie Waggoner. . . . .Jennifer Jason Leigh
Ellita Sanchez. . . . . .Nora Dunn
Sgt. Bill Henderson. . . . .Charles Napier
Pablo. . . . . .Jose Perez
Sgt. Frank Lackley. . . . . .Paul Gleason

■ Alec Baldwin's star appeal, buoyed by "The Hunt For Red October," surfaces with his wild-eyed psycho in this quirky and sometimes brutally funny film. But "Miami Blues" is as pointless as an episode of "Miami Vice," and the unsettling blend of violence and humor will limit b.o. firepower.

Based on Charles Willeford's novel, the film strings together terrific moments but never takes a point of view. Junior (Baldwin) blows into town, initiates a crime spree with a homicide detective's stolen badge and settles down with a simple-minded hooker named Susie (Jennifer Jason Leigh).

The sense that Junior can go off at any time, and the explosive and graphic bursts of violence create tension throughout. Baldwin is more than equal to the task, and his intense machismo and make-believe posturing bring to mind some of Robert De Niro's menace in "Taxi Driver."

Leigh also is wondrously odd, her eyebrows knitting in frustration at the simplest of questions, her drawl filled with rapture at the recipes she can concoct for her new beau.

Pic, however, is missing a key ingredient: a discernible plot. If it's the detective (Fred Ward) seeking to reclaim his badge, false teeth and gun, it's a wispy one at best. And the strange romance between Junior and Susie offers chuckles but doesn't connect all the action.

In short, "Miami Blues" presents a series of intriguing moments spiced by overall rebelliousness, beginning with the obscure song "Spirit In The Sky" over the opening credits.

For many, director-scripter George Armitage's stylized tone will be enough to savor, with graphic violence that wouldn't be out of place in a slasher pic with oddball humor. It also has a potentially off-putting effect, however, for those who might be drawn to the performances.

The film's best moments are those between Junior and Susie, as well as Junior's reverse Robin Hood antics of robbing thieves, then keeping the loot. Armitage nonetheless dips into that till a few times too many, and the film starts to sag during its last half-hour.

There's also an unusual dichotomy in that the film's central couple, a hooker and thief-murderer, lead a more conventional existence than its ostensible protagonist, a sleazy, dim cop more adept at exchanging porkchop recipes than nabbing bad guys.

In that respect, the film is nonjudgmental; an appealing twist likely to be lost on the bulk of filmgoers, conditioned to look for heroes, villains and clear delineation between right and wrong.

Technical credits are superb, especially Tak Fujimoto's atmospheric lensing of Miami, from the detective's seedy apartment to Junior's squeaky-clean new house, a subtle illustration of the pic's overall tone. — Bril.

Tatie Danièlle (Auntie Danielle) (FRENCH)

Paris An AMLF release of a Téléma/FR3 Films production/Les Prods. du Champ Poirier coproduction. Produced by Charles Gassot. Directed by Etienne Chatiliez. Screenplay, Florence Quentin; camera (color), Philippe Welt; editor, Catherine Renault; music, Gabriel Yared; sound, Guillaume Sciama, Dominique Dalmasso; art direction, Geoffrey Larcher; assistant directors, Patricia Eberhard, Frédéric Blum; casting, Romain Brémond. Reviewed at the Gaumont Ambassade theater, Paris, April 4, 1990. Running time: 113 MIN.
Auntie Danielle. . . . . . . .Tsilla Chelton
Catherine Billard. . . . .Catherine Jacob
Jean-Pierre Billard. . . . . . . .Eric Prat
Odile. . . . . Neige Dolsky
Sandrine. . . . . Isabelle Nanty
Jeanne Billard. . . . . . .Laurence Fevrier

■ "Tatie Danièlle" is a tart comedy providing welcome Gallic relief to the saccharine Hollywood-endorsed stereotypes of the elderly as armchair dispensers of love and bromides. Pic had a strong Paris bow and stands good chances in foreign markets.

Second film by the click indie producing-writing-directing unit of Charles Gassot-Florence Quentin-Etienne Chatiliez enters more dangerous comic waters than did their smash social farce "Life Is A Long Quiet River," but is kept briskly afloat by its iconoclastic humor, bright direction and malicious title performance.

If the Disney studios, more inclined to Geritol generation sentimentality, put this one through their remake plant, it would be a delicious irony. Quentin and Chatiliez prove that "Life" wasn't a fluke and that good commercial no-star comedies are still possible in France.

Quentin, who never wrote a script before that 1988 sleeper success, is now one of the hot new French screenwriters. Chatiliez, the prize-winning wunderkind of French commercials (with Quentin as his assistant and Gassot as producer) directs with a sure sense of irony and a complete sympathy with his perfect cast.

Danielle is a little old lady who's neither sweet nor helpless. She's spiteful, intolerant and cunning. She enjoys sicking the dog on the mailman and trampling freshly planted petunia patches. She despises kindness in others, especially in her aged long-suffering companion-housekeeper, whom she virtually drives to her death.

Auntie's only confidant is her dead husband, whose cross-eyed military mug hangs in a frame above her dresser. Woe then to her surviving Paris relations, nephew Eric Prat and wife Catherine Jacob, who, out of the goodness of their middle-class hearts, rush to save her from her provincial solitude and distress.

For a while Auntie acts the part of helpless grateful aunt, but then she begins to sabotage the bourgeois well-being and patience of the household, disturbing the couple's privacy and posing as a neglected, incontinent, senile relation for house guests.

One day she meets her match. The family, desperate for a rest, signs up for a vacation in Greece and leaves Auntie at home in the hands of a young companion-nurse (Isabelle Nanty). Unfortunately for the oldtimer, Nanty is every bit as dour and mean, and won't stand for any of her ward's Machiavellian behavior.

Auntie is stunned, then grudgingly admiring. She's found a soul mate in her old age. But Nanty is still a young woman interested in males and that becomes an obstacle to their companionship.

Paris stage veteran Tsilla Chelton (associated in particular with the plays of Eugene Ionesco and Jacques Audiberti) gets her first genuine screen role at age 71. Her Auntie Danielle is an sly, irresistible portrait of mildewed malice, yet the composition is never hateful. She may have a heart of stone, but she has a heart nonetheless, and Chelton allows us to sense it beating without ever begging for sympathy.

One could fault Quentin and Chatiliez for surrounding Chelton with a bunch of guiless ninnies, but the facile social caricatures are charmingly humanized by a talented supporting cast. Prat and Jacob (who won a César for her supporting role in "Life Is a Long Quiet River") are endearing in their charitable foolishness.

Neige Dolsky, another elderly screen newcomer, is marvelous as Chelton's hapless stoic companion. Nanty is crabbily perfect as the caustic young nurse. Rest of the cast is comically right and the tech credits are fine. — Len.

The Guardian

Hollywood A Universal Pictures release of a Joe Wizan production. Produced by Wizan. Directed by William Friedkin. Executive producer, David Salven. Screenplay, Steven Volk, Dan Greenburg, Friedkin, based on Greenburg's story ''The Nanny;'' camera (Technicolor), John A. Alonzo; editor, Seth Flaum; music, Jack Hues; sound (Dolby), James R. Alexander, Tom Causey; production design, Gregg Fonseca; art direction, Bruce Miller; set decoration, Sarah Budick; costume design, Denise Cronenberg; assistant director, Newton Dennis Arnold; coproducers, Todd Black, Mickey Borofsky, Greenburg; casting, Louis DiGiamimo. Reviewed at the Cineplex Odeon Century Plaza Cinemas, L.A., April 19, 1990. MPAA Rating: R. Running time: 98 MIN. Camilla.Jenny
Seagrove
Phil. . . . . .Dwier Brown
Kate. . . . . .Carey Lowell
Ned Runcie. . . . . .Brad Hall
Ralph Hess. . . . . .Miguel Ferrer
Molly Sheridan. . . . . .Natalia Nogulich

■ Despite the credentials of its makers, ''The Guardian'' is an ill-conceived, simple-minded horror flick that won't scare up much of a response in theaters or at the boxoffice. Who knows what possessed William Friedkin to straight-facedly tell this absurd ''tree bites man'' tale, but it's an impulse he should have exorcised.

Wispier horror premises than this one have yielded commercial hits, though they at least found some fright in their absurd situations. ''The Guardian'' isn't even particularly scary, even with Jack Hues' tension-laden score working overtime.

The scant plot involves an attractive yuppie couple (Dwier Brown, Carey Lowell) who hire a live-in nanny to take care of their infant son.

The nanny (Jenny Seagrove) turns out to be some sort of evil spirit that sacrifices newborns to this big, anthropomorphic tree, a species apparently indigenous to the canyon areas of metropolitan Los Angeles.

Trumpeted as Friedkin's first horror film since ''The Exorcist,'' ''The Guardian'' is more likely to make viewers think at best of the wan film adaptation of ''Pet Sematary,'' at worst of the talking trees in ''Thw Wizard Of Oz.'' The design is so shoddy one half expects it to start talking and pitching apples.

Friedkin's goal of creating a gothic atmosphere fails miserably, in part due to the bright California settings (much of the action occurs in broad daylight) and plastic performances.

Seagrove looks properly bewitching but never brings much menace or mystery to her role as, what, a witch, evil spirit or (as intimated by a pre-title scroll) a tree-worshipping druid? It's never remotely explained, although, pardon the expression, she looks wooden, not druidical.

Brown, last seen as Kevin Costner's dad in ''Field Of Dreams,'' has a larger role here but probably a less substantial one. His climactic sequence is ludicrous at best and, without giving too much away, might have been subtitled ''California Chainsaw Massacre.''

Lowell, a former Bond girl, has the least to do as the confused wife. Friedkin can't even elicit much response to the baby's warblings, and cameraman John A. Alonzo's forced-perspective baby's-eye-view shots are technically impressive but utterly pointless.

Friedkin continues to be an inconsistent filmmaker, going from a classic like ''The French Connection'' to the ponderous ''Sorcerer,'' rebounding with the stylish ''To Live And Die In L.A.'' and then following it with ''Rampage'' and this latest pic.

Technical credits are all subpar for a major studio production, starting with the unconvincing special effects and production design. Hues' dissonant soundtrack is effective if not terribly subtle, more than can be said for the baffling screenplay by Friedkin, Dan Greenburg and Steven Volk.
— Bril.

Panama Sugar
(ITALIAN)

Rome A Delta release of a Trinidad Film production. Produced by Italo Zingarelli. Executive producer, Ezio Palaggi. Directed by Marcello Avallone. Screenplay, Avallone, Vincenzo Mannino, Roberto Parpaglioni, Andrea Purgatori; camera (Telecolor), Roberto Benvenuti; editor, Adriano Tagliavia; music, Gabriele Ducros; art direction, Luciano Sagoni; associate producer, Marisa Palaggi. Reviewed at Anica, Rome, April 11, 1990. Running time: 110 MIN.
Panama. . . . . .Scott Plank
The general. . . . . .Oliver Reed
Liza. . . . . . .Lucrezia Lante della Rovere
Lt. Garcia. . . . . .Memé Perlini
Blue Ball. . . . . .Duilio Del Prete
Also with: Tomas Arana, Vittorio Amandola, Pedro Sarubbi Ruzzi, Francesco Scimemi, Nico Davenia, Josette Martial, Franz Di Cioccio.

■ Italo Zingarelli, producer of the highly successful Bud Spencer/Terence Hill films, stands a good chance of duplicating previous successes with ''Panama Sugar,'' another light adventure pic filled with fistfights, pool games and Club Med beaches.

''Panama'' features handsome Yank thesp Scott Plank, who bears more than a little resemblance to a young Terence Hill. This clean, featherweight entertainer should appeal to young auds in particular.

Story is set on a Caribbean island paradise inhabited by fun-loving types who drink all day and dance all night. Local baddie is the general, played by a slumming Oliver Reed. He takes the side of a brash American wheeler-dealer (Vittorio Amandola) who wants to buy the local bar and transform the undiscovered isle into gamblers' heaven.

Panama, the ultimate laid-back hero, wards off various toughs sent to intimidate the bar owner, while romancing a beautiful stranger (Lucrezia Lante Della Rovere) who arrives in her private yacht. With the help of the thieving dog Pirate, they convince the general there is a pirate's treasure hidden on the island, and he sends the Yank realtors packing. Panama even has time to beat the world champion pool player (Franz Di Cioccio), to the locals' delight, before all ends well.

As the happy-go-lucky Panama, Plank never hits a wrong note. He's irresistibly nice whatever he does: making impossible pool shots without looking, or slugging two nasty hombres out the window with one blow. Rovere is mischievously sophisticated as the mysterious, rich stranger.

Reed gets by with his usual Mussolini posturing, jutting jaw and bull neck, though he has a riveting intensity even in this caricatured role. Supporting cast includes some high-class performers (Memé Perlini, Duilio Del Prete).

Helmer Marcello Avallone is a fan of closeups and colorful lensing. All has been cut for a rapid and easy watch. Gabriele Ducros' scores pic with lighthearted Caribbean rhythms that could play on AM radio. Lensing by Roberto Benvenuti is as pro as the rest.
— Yung.

Sher Mountain Killings Mystery
(AUSTRALIAN)

Sydney An Intertropic Films P/L production. Executive producer, Peter Taylor. Produced by Phil Avalon. Directed by Vince Martin. Screenplay, Denis Whitburn; camera (color), Ray Henman; editor, Ted Otton; music, Art Phillips; sound, Bob Clayton; production design, Keith Holloway; production manager, Veronica Sive; assistant director, Robin Newell. Reviewed at Mosman screening room, Sydney, April 9, 1990. Running time: 86 MIN.
Caine Cordeaux. . . . . . . .Phil Avalon
Alex Cordeaux. . . . . . .Tom Richards
Muriel. . . . . Abigail
Conrad. . . . . .Ric Carter
Sole. . . . . .Ron Becks
Dianne Cordeaux. . . . .Elizabeth McIvor
Davey-Joe Cordeaux. . . . .Jeffrey Rhoe
Billy Cordeaux. . . . . . . .Steven Jacobs
The ranger. . . . . .Joe Bugner

■ The exceedingly tame thriller-fantasy ''Sher Mountain Killings Mystery'' will be hard put to find customers, even on video. Theatrical exposure seems out of the question.

After laboriously setting up the theft of a mystical stone by two hoods from a 100-year-old eccentric (only to have the stone accidentally passed on to the retarded brother of the younger hood), early reels lack interest and tension.

The picture plods along until the eight principal characters, including three bad guys, two femmes, a youth, the brother and the nominal hero, find themselves in ''Deliverance''-like country.

The good guys are saved, thanks to the intervention of a ghostly forest ranger with a bow and arrow. He's played by a popular Aussie heavyweight boxing champ Joe Bugner, who definitely should stick to fisticuffs.

Bugner really is no worse than the other castmembers, who include producer Phil Avalon as Caine and Abigail as Avalon's sister. In a nasty piece of ethnic typecasting, black actor Ron Becks plays the lead villain.

The biggest mystery here is the presence of screenwriter Denis Whitburn on the credits. He usually comes up with something better than this collection of trite situations and inane dialog (he's co-scripter of the upcoming Bryan Brown-starrer, ''Blood Oath'').

Technical credits are strictly ho-hum, and the film seems much longer than its 86 minutes. Action scenes are poorly staged and carry little charge.

In production, pic was variously titled ''Sher Mountain Mystery'' and ''Sher Mountain Killings.'' Combination of the two, resulting in the awkward final title, smacks of desperation.
— Strat.

Lisa

Hollywood An MGM/UA release of a United Artists presentation. Produced by Frank Yablans. Directed by Gary Sherman. Screenplay, Sherman, Karen Clark; camera (color, Deluxe), Alex Nepomniaschy; additional photography, Stanley Lazan; editor, Ross Albert; music, Joe Renzetti; sound (Dolby), Maury Harris; production design, Patricia Van Ryker; set design, Nancy Patton; set decoration, Stewart Kane McGuire; costume design, Shari Feldman; assistant director, Tom Davies; associate producers, Karen Lucas Clark, Lucas Foster, Ronald B. Colby; casting, Michael Chinich. Reviewed at AMC Century 14, L.A., April 17, 1990. MPAA rating: PG-13. Running time: 93 MIN.
Katherine . . . . Cheryl Ladd
Richard . . . . D.W. Moffett
Lisa . . . . Staci Keanan
Wendy . . . . Tanya Fenmore
Mr. Marks . . . . Jeffrey Tambor
Ralph . . . . Edan Gross
Mrs. Marks . . . . Julie Cobb

■ Played-out genres eventually slide into self-parody, and that's what happened with MGM/UA's "Lisa," an unintentionally risible women-in-jeopardy film. Modest b.o. may be wrung out of the teen trade for date-night giggling, screaming and boyfriend-clutching.

Teenager Staci Keanan (in the title role) and Cheryl Ladd (as her glamorous mom) are presented by filmmaker Gary Sherman as two of the dumbest screen heroines ever to stumble into the clutches of a psychopath.

Sherman, who made a genuinely chilling low-budgeter of this type called "Vice Squad" (1982), has no excuses for this cheap-looking Frank Yablans production's lack of suspense or originality, since Sherman also scripted with Karen Clark. They leave no cliché unturned in their lifeless and uninvolving replay of the plot about a heavy-breathing phone freak stalking and killing female victims.

The stab at novelty here is that the 14-year-old title character triggers her own victimization by making provocative phone calls to D.W. Moffett, who by a wild coincidence just happens to be "The Candlelight Killer," terrorizing L.A. by breaking into women's apartments and setting out candles and glasses of wine beside their beds before strangling them.

It's impossible to be emotionally involved with the stupefyingly naive Keanan character, who must be the only teenaged girl in the U.S. unaware that it's dangerous to play sexual come-on games with strangers, particularly when she lives in a seamy Venice neighborhood and the papers are full of screaming headlines about a serial killer.

Moffett, who has the bland and surly good looks of a GQ model (he has his own "fashion consultant" credited), is given far too much screen time to be as intriguing and frightening as he needs to be. But then there's not much else going on in the film other than Keanan's squabbling with her stubbornly obtuse mother over not being allowed to go out on dates.

The long winded, overly literal script continually rams home the point that Keanan wouldn't have to indulge in reckless fantasies if the uptight Ladd were more comfortable with her own and her daughter's sexuality.

Given the girl's obsession with Moffett, however, the scripters never credibly motivate the crucial plot shift of Keanan turning the killer's sexual focus toward her mother, which serves only to set up a laughably overdone struggle at the end.

If it served as a coup de grace to a genre that produced a few good films and a great deal of offensive schlock along the way, "Lisa" would be a worthwhile endeavor.

It's more likely, however, to be just a forgettable footnote in the history of women-in-jeopardy pics, the postfeminist era's coarser equivalent of film noir. — Mac.

Damned River

New York An MGM/UA Communications release from United Artists of a Silver Lion Films production. Produced by Lance Hool. Directed by Michael Schroeder. Screenplay, John Crowther, Bayard Johnson; camera (color), George Tirl; editor, Mark Conte; music, James Wesley Stremple; sound (Dolby), Rüdiger Payrhuber; production manager, Ian Ross; coproducer, Conrad Hool; associate producer, Elena Azuola; casting, Penny Perry, Donna Anderson. Reviewed on CBS/Fox vidcassette, N.Y., April 7, 1990. MPAA Rating: R. Running time: 95 MIN.
Ray . . . . Stephen Shellen
Anne . . . . Lisa Aliff
Carl . . . . John Terlesky
Luke . . . . Marc Poppel
Jerry . . . . Bradford Brancroft
Von Hoenigen . . . . . Louis Van Niekerk

■ This United Artists pickup, originally lensed two years ago with moniker "Devil's Odds," tries to be a coed "Deliverance" without much success. Pic had minimal theatrical exposure last fall and is now in videostores courtesy UA's output deal with CBS/Fox.

Four Americans are in Zimbabwe for a white water adventure vacation, with rugged former soldier Stephen Shellen as their guide. After some nicely lensed footage of rafting in treacherous waters, the film disintegrates into a corny battle for survival against Shellen. Climax is set at a dangerous rapids called "Devil's Odds."

A rape scene involving lovely heroine Lisa Aliff is gratuitously graphic. Her presence on the expedition is unconvincingly explained as a substitute for a guy who had to bow out.

Cast is okay: youngsters' camaraderie carries the pic, which would have benefited from more rafting action scenes. Helmer Michael Schroeder, a Paul Bartel protégé who previously directed "Mortuary Academy," doesn't come up with a consistent tone. — Lor.

A Cry In The Wild

Houston A Concorde-New Horizons Corp. release. Produced by Julie Corman. Directed by Mark Griffiths. Screenplay, Gary Paulsen, Catherine Cryan, based on novel "Hatchet" by Paulsen; camera (color), Gregg Heschong; editor, Carol Oblath; music, Arthur Kempel; production design, Michael Clausen; executive in charge of production, Byrdie Lifson; production manager, John (Jake) Jacobson; 2d unit director, Adam Davidson; 2d unit cameraman, Jack Anderson; animal trainers, Nick Toth, Elizabeth Toth, Helena Walsh; animal stunts, Terry Moore. Reviewed at Houston Intl. Film Festival, April 19, 1990. MPAA Rating: PG. Running time: 81 MIN.
Brian . . . . Jared Rushton
Mom . . . . Pamela Sue Martin
Dad . . . . Stephen Meadows
Pilot . . . . Ned Beatty

■ If there's still an audience in smaller markets for outdoor dramas in the "Grizzly Adams" and "Wilderness Family" tradition, Concorde-New Horizons may do respectable business with "A Cry In The Wild," the kind of picture many parents are wishing for when they decry the dearth of "family movies."

The question is whether children — especially boys ages 5-14, the film's obvious target audience — have the patience for something paced more slowly than "Teenage Mutant Ninja Turtles."

Screenwriters Gary Paulsen and Catherine Cryan have adapted Paulsen's prizewinning novel "Hatchet" into a modestly compelling saga of survival in northern California.

While flying to visit his father in Canada following his parents' divorce, 13-year-old Brian (Jared Rushton) is stranded in an isolated, heavily wooded area after the pilot (Ned Beatty) has a fatal heart attack. Brian manages to crash-land the plane in a lake, and he swims to shore as the crippled aircraft sinks to the bottom. Then his real troubles start.

Most of the movie is a 1-man show for Rushton, as he depicts Brian's efforts to secure food and shelter, avoid the threats of bears and inclement weather, and maintain his sanity.

Complicating matters is Brian's free-floating rage, the bitter aftereffect of his parents' break-up, and he must struggle to channel his anger into the task of staying alive. The breakup is depicted in fragmented flashbacks, which indicate the chief problem in the marriage was Mom's adultery.

Even so, Mom (Pamela Sue Martin) isn't the villain of the piece. She's the one who gave Brian the camper's hatchet that turns out to be his chief tool for wilderness survival. Director Mark Griffiths doesn't evidence much visual flair during the film's few action sequences. A hand-to-claw fight with an angry bear looks especially unconvincing. Worse,

he permits the final portion of the film, Brian's rescue and reunion with his parents, to seem anticlimactic.

There's some murky psychology at work here: The movie appears to be saying that there's nothing like being stranded in the wilderness, and nearly getting killed by a bear, to make you less resentful and more tolerant of your parents' failings. Griffiths does vary the mood and pace during the many scenes of Rushton's solo wanderings. The film's chief asset is Rushton's performance.

The young actor deftly balances anger and fear in his running commentary on Brian's predicament, so the character never comes off as a 1-note whiner. It's a difficult role, requiring almost constant on-screen presence, and Rushton pulls it off with a welcome sense of humor.

Martin and Beatty do professional work in cameo roles. Gregg Heschong's color cinematography of the locales in and around Quincy, Calif., is firstrate. Other tech credits are acceptably plain and simple. — Ley.

Barrela
(BRAZILIAN)

Rio de Janeiro An Embrafilme release of an Embrafilme/Nadia Filmes production. Produced by Marcelo Pietsch Franca in association with Armando Conde. Directed by Marco Antonio Cury. Screenplay by Cury, based on a play by Plinio Marcos; camera (Eastmancolor), Antonio Penido; editor, Marilia Alvim; art direction, Marcos Flaksman; music, Zeca Assumpcao; sound, Solon do Valle; costumes, Adrian Leite; associate producers, Invest S.A., Banco Nacional, Blec-Berd Producoes, Cinedia. Reviewed at Estacao Botafogo 1 theater, Rio de Janeiro, March 5, 1990. Running time: **72 MIN.**

Portuga. . . . . .Claudio Mamberti
Bereco. . . . . .Paulo Cesar Pereio
Tirica. . . . . .Marcos Palmeira
Fumaca. . . . . . . .Cosme dos Santos
Bahia. . . . . .Chico Dias
Madman. . . . . . . .Roberto Bomtempo
Boy. . . . . .Marcos Winter

■ The film version of "Barrela," a play written in 1958 by Plinio Marcos and banned in Brazil for 20 years, appears dated and exists more as a document of the raw impact of the original play.

Everything happens in a small cell with six dangerous criminals. A middle-class young man arrested after a bar quarrel is taken to the same cell. The six ultimately rape the boy. ("Barrela" is old slang for sexual violence.)

Story reveals the tension among the six men, who live at the edge of extreme violence. They alternate alliances, attacking the weaknesses of their fellow prisoners. The more they reject and are rejected by society, the more each feels compelled to choose an enemy among his cellmates.

Adaptation by Marco Antonio Cury — a veteran editor and assistant director debuting as a director — fails to achieve the proper atmosphere, and dialog does not seem as strong as in most of Marcos' plays (especially "Doise Perdidos Numa Noite Suja," which Marcos himself adapted for cinema in the '70s). As a result, characters seem half lost.

Film is the first of several low-budget features (costing nearly $70,000 each) undertaken by producer Marcelo Franca and produced under a system in which part of the cast and the technical crew exchange work for a share in the billings. There is basically one location and almost no supporting cast. Everything was shot in less than two weeks to achieve an immediate distribution.

Cast is fine, though technical credits often reveal the conditions under which the film was made.
— Hoin.

Bad Jim

New York A 21st Century Film presentation of a Wouk/Ware production. Produced by Joseph Wouk. Written and directed by Clyde Ware. Camera (Rank color), David Golia; editor, Glenn Garland; music, Jamie Sheriff; sound, Charles Hansen; production design, Michael E. Ferrell; assistant director, Ray Marsh; production manager, Marc S. Fischer; coproducers, Robert Hummel, Les Greene; associate producer, Meir Fenigstein; casting, C.J. Lyons. Reviewed on RCA/Columbia Pictures vidcassette, N.Y., April 14, 1990. MPAA Rating: PG. Running time: **90 MIN.**

B.D.. . . . . .James Brolin
July. . . . . .Richard Roundtree
John T. Coleman. . . . . .John Clark Gable
C.J. Lee. . . . . .Harry Carey Jr.
Sam Harper. . . . . .Rory Calhoun
Tom Jefferd. . . . . .Ty Hardin
Virgilio Segura. . . . . . . .Pepe Serna
Customer. . . . . .Bruce Kirby
Banker. . . . . .Joe George
Elizabeth. . . . . .Suzanne Wouk
Piano man. . . . . .Scotty Wright
Also with: Pierette Grace, Tonya Townsend, Teresa Vander Woude.

■ "Bad Jim" is a good-natured Western about three kindly desperadoes and Billy the Kid's horse. It's a direct-to-video release that should satisfy sagebrush buffs.

Filmmaker Clyde Ware brings authenticity and enthusiasm to the moribund genre. Casting interestingly teams up James Brolin, who played Clark Gable in "Gable And Lombard," with sidekick John Clark Gable, the late star's son and a dead ringer for Kevin Costner. Third member of triumvirate is Richard Roundtree, in good form and overdue for a Western since "Charley One-Eye" 17 years earlier.

The trio is intercepted by Pepe Serna, on the lam from the authorities. He had been riding with the late Billy the Kid and sells them what he claims to be the Kid's horse. Gable renames it Jim and the three ne'er-do-wells begin a series of bank robberies posing as Billy and his gang.

Rather uneventful film is long on atmosphere, with good lensing of Arizona locations and well-researched folklore (notably a primitive form of lacrosse played by a local Indian tribe). Ware avoids racism or condescension, though his script has a little too much hindsight at times, such as Gable lecturing a young woman on tolerance: "Put yourself in the other guy's shoes or moccasins."

Brolin is comfortable in the saddle and Gable shows promise. Supporting cast is peppered with veterans like Ty Hardin and Rory Calhoun who are fun to see again in this context. *— Lor.*

Martians Go Home

Hollywood A Taurus Entertainment release of an Edward R. Pressman production. Produced by Michael D. Pariser. Executive producer, Pressman. Directed by David Odell. Screenplay, Charlie Haas, based on the novel by Frederic Brown; camera, Peter Deming; editor, M. Kathryn Campbell; music, Allan Zavod; sound, David Brownlow; production design, Catherine Hardwicke, Don Day; art direction, Tom Cortese; costume design, Robyn Reichek; set decoration, Gene Serdena; assistant director, Richard Strickland; coproducers, Ted Bafaloukos, Anthony Santa Crose; associate producer, Elon Dershowitz; casting, April Webster. Reviewed at Mann's Fox Theater, L.A., April 20, 1990. MPAA Rating: PG-13. Running time: **85 MIN.**

Mark. . . . . .Randy Quaid
Sara. . . . . .Margaret Colin
Dr. Jane. . . . . .Anita Morris
Donny. . . . . .John Philbin
Stan Garrett. . . . . .Gerrit Graham
Martian No. 1. . . . . .Barry Sobel
Martian No. 2. . . . . .Vic Dunlop

■ Obnoxious Martians with pea-soup complexions invade the earth and torment humans until a Hollywood composer (Randy Quaid) can reverse the musical invitation that lured them. Quaid's delightful, but all else is a bore, meaning the only green this Ed Pressman pic will see already came out of the makeup jars.

Their planet's a dump, so the spacemen come to Earth as jealous tourists, lured by the siren call of a sci-fi tv theme that's accidentally bounced off satellites when Quaid plays it over the phone for his girlfriend (Margaret Colin) who works at a radio station.

All-knowing and able to pop up anywhere, "Bewitched'-style, the visitors disrupt life on earth until everything's a shambles and people sit around and brood about the good old pre-Martian days. Quaid hits on a way to get rid of them, but he's intercepted by the government as a suspected Martian sympathizer and locked in a loony bin.

Script, adapted by Charlie Haas from a 1950s novel by Frederic Brown, has a few genuinely clever lines, but many more bad ones. As presented by first-time director David Odell, pic amounts to a lot of raucous nonsense with some pretty awful passages.

In one seg, a nutso Martian (Vic Dunlop) invades the office of the radio shrink Colin works for and stirs up a kind of symphony of craziness with the other basket cases in the room. It's a piece of extended agony that adds nothing whatsoever to the story, and sends a clear signal that the pic is going nowhere.

With its heavy parody of the cheesy Tinseltown that Quaid toils in (his cop show is called "Transfer To Danger"), "Martians" is actually fairly amusing until the aliens show up, and even then, Quaid and the warm wistful Colin remain appealing enough to make the action almost bearable.

John Philbin is a sweet-natured burglar and Anita Morris as the resourceful radio adviser also earn their laughs and a welcome mat for other pics with distinctive characterizations.

The space invaders, who are about as otherworldly as Catskills comedians in makeup, are nothing but a vehicle for lazy gagwriting, and the concept overall is bottom-of-the-barrel stuff.

Most situations are thinly established, and production looks cheap, despite the indulgence in plenty of "around-the-world" reaction shots as Eskimos, Japanese, Russians, et al., respond to the antics of the green funnymen.

Story's resolution is designed to make viewers take a look around them at life on Earth and notice how sweet it is, after all. Just like being released from the theater that's screening this tormenting pic.

Completed almost two years ago, this "Martians" slips into the soft pre-summer market via limited release by Taurus. *— Daws.*

HONG KONG INTL. FILM FESTIVAL REVIEWS

The Elephant Keeper
(THAI/WEST GERMAN)

Hong Kong A Promitr/Manfred Durniok production. Produced by Kamla Shethi, Manfred Durniok. Written and directed by Chatri Chalerm Yukol. Camera (color), Yukol; editor, Yukol. Reviewed at Hong Kong Intl. Film Festival, April 16, 1990. Running time: **137 MIN.**
   With: Sorapong Chatri, Doungduen Chathaisong, Rhone Rhithchai.

■ "The Elephant Keeper" is a film of commendable purpose existing somewhat awkwardly between documentary and action drama. Based on a reputedly true story about illegal logging in the diminishing teak forests of Thailand, this Thai-West German production lacks focus and structure.

The result is a film with some good moments, but it's too long at over two hours. Ultimately, the primary theme — the awful damage man, through greed, can inflict on the environment — is diluted.

Pic opens with a ranger counseling young trampers about the need to conserve Thailand's forests and about the damage being wrought by illegal loggers.

He then tells the story of a conflict between the illegals and the rangers. The central character is young elephant keeper Boonsong (Sorapong Chatri), who is caught between the worlds of subsistence living and advancing technology.

Boonsong and his elephant, Tangon, save the chief ranger's life, but later are compelled to join the outlaw lumberjacks because elephant power in the legitimate timber trade is being phased out.

Boonsong and his family also are being threatened by a corrupt businessman who is about to take their land if they do not pay a longstanding debt.

Good triumphs but has its price, and a message of constant vigilance against greed and corruption ushers in the fadeout.

While the film's message always is clear, the unraveling of the conflict between rangers, loggers, corrupt entrepreneurs and the peasants has its confusions, particularly when minor characters (like the village police sergeant) abruptly emerge as major items.

The cast contains a mix of professional and amateur Thai actors with Chatri (Thailand's biggest star) most at ease. The elephant scenes, which underscore the main theme, are a delight. — *Nic.*

Black Snow
(CHINESE)

Hong Kong Beijing Youth Film Studios production. Directed by Xie Fei. Screenplay, Liu Heng; camera (color), Xiao Feng; art director, Li Rongxin. Reviewed at Hong Kong Intl. Film Festival, April 15, 1990. Running time: **107 MIN.**
   With: Jiang Wen, Cheng Lin, Cai Hongxiang, Yue Hong.

■ "Black Snow" is one of a number of new Asian titles that are contemporary in story and mood, skillfully made and readily accessible to Western audiences.

Directed by Xie Fei, a former head of the Beijing Film Academy, the pic shuns polemics and propaganda as it explores the bid of an ex-convict ready to settle into life in a city where values no longer are the ones he remembers and lives by.

The pic has humor and tragedy and a strong central character and constantly surprises in the way it handles its theme of an individual dealing with an often-uncaring society.

Li Huiqian (impressively played by Jiang Wen) returns to the home he once shared with his now-deceased mother. He is 24, unmarried and semiliterate. He takes a job selling clothes in a market and becomes infatuated with an aspiring singer (Cheng Lin), whom he meets in a local bar.

He finds readjustment difficult. One of his aunts wants to mother him, the other cuts him off. People have become greedy and self-centered and consider him odd when he shows a natural generosity. In an unexpected and sudden moment of violence, he falls victim to this "naivete."

Xie's handling of these themes and Jiang's thoroughly integrated and detailed performance constantly illuminate the simple plot line. An example is the way the character of the singer moves from innocence to sophistication, placing her further out of reach just when

Li is finding the resolve to confront her with his feelings.

There is a flavor of the Hollywood social realism movies of the '30s and '50s in "Black Snow," but that in no way detracts from the pic's uniqueness and modernity. Given the possibility of such subject matter being delivered in a heavyhanded way, its ease, lightness — and natural elegance — are entertaining and affecting.
— *Nic.*

Highschool Girls
(TAIWANESE)

Hong Kong A Dragons Group Film Co. production. Produced by Tung Chinshu. Directed by Chen Kuofu. Screenplay, Hsiao Yeh; camera (color), He Yungcheng; editor, Huang Chiukuei. Reviewed at Hong Kong Intl. Film Festival, April 14, 1990. Running time: **95 MIN.**
   With: To Tsunghua, Chang Shih, Lu Yuanchi, Chen Teyung.

■ "Highschool Girls" is predictable and surprisingly sluggish from the Taiwan industry, which has begun to show it is creatively and technically one of the most lively and innovative in Asia.

A rare burst of exuberance occurs in the official program of the Hong Kong Film Fest when the debut feature of Taiwanese critic Chen Kuofu is described as putting him in the class of the noted Hou Hsiao Hsien ("City Of Sadness"). On the evidence of "Highschool Girls," a girl buddy movie that confirms classroom discipline and parental indifference can be a problem the world over, he has some way to go.

"Highschool Girls" focuses on best friends Moly (Lu Yuanchi), forced by her boyfriend into prostitution, and Hsio (Chen Teyung), who rescues her. Subplots involve the b.f.'s shady semi-gangster existence, the schoolboy who loves Moly from afar and the teacher who tries to do his best handling an unruly class with other things on his mind.

While most of the ingredients are familiar, the central character and her dilemma offer possibilities of deeper drama before the upbeat ending. That this does not happen is a measure of the distance the debuting helmer has to travel. Not enough of how Moly is affected by her experience comes through, just as her family environment (presumably a negative experience) is cursorily handled.

The director says that although "Highschool Girls" is based on true events, it does not address education issues or the problems of adolescence. The intent is to explore the hidden, suppressed emotions of several characters. He takes audiences only a short step of the way. — *Nic.*

The Guard
(SOVIET-COLOR/B&W)

Hong Kong A Lenfilm Studios production. Directed by Alexander Rogozhkin. Screenplay, Ivan Loschilin; camera (color/b&w), Valeri Martynov; production design, Alexander Zogoskin. Reviewed at Hong Kong Intl. Film Festival, April 14, 1990. Running time: **96 MIN.**
   With: Sergei Kupriyanov, Alexei Buldakov, Alexei Poluyan, Alexander Smirov.

■ "The Guard" is a brilliantly conceived and executed study of male brutality and spiritual suffocation that uses the confines of a train transporting prisoners to forced labor camps in the Soviet Union as the crucible.

The lens, which is on the guards rather than the prisoners, unambiguously tracks the chain of physical and psychological humiliation unleashed in an environment of mindless function and negative purpose.

Allegorical in intent, the story is a *cri de coeur* of the most striking kind. But the graphic bestiality (and the difficulty, no doubt intended, of individualizing members of the guard) may limit exposure to festivals only.

A new recruit, Chlustov, joins the guard of the train bearing prisoners to camps in the far northeast. As the journey progresses, the brutality of the guards toward prisoners, and guards toward each other, ignites in sadistic rituals and demeaning taunts. When a prostitute is hoisted aboard for the guards' drunken pleasures, Chlustov snaps and a blood bath ensues.

Shot mainly in black & white (apart from a surreal sequence near the end and fragmentary scenes earlier), pic's awful realism pervades. The camerawork of Valeri Martynov is impeccable in its unremitting tracking of bleak carriage corridors and quarters. The performances, given the difficulty of distinguishing the players, are raw and convincing.

The only escapes from the claustrophobic power of the piece are a vision of a seeming Christ figure bearing a cross in the snow near the rail tracks, and the discovery (near the end of the film) that there might be ordinary passengers also riding the train.

These images, finally, add to the intensity of the film's message: man's inhumanity to man and therefore to himself. This is a peculiarly masculine dilemma and one not just confined to a pre-glasnost time of Russian angst, as reflected in Soviet social and political history and traditions.

— *Nic.*

Dancing Bull
(HONG KONG)

Hong Kong A Dancing Bull Prod. Co. presentation. Produced by Willy Tsao, Allen Fong. Directed by Fong. Screenplay, Cheung Chi-sing; camera (color), Chang Lok-yee; editor, Kwok Keung. Reviewed at Hong Kong Intl. Film Festival, April 16, 1990. Running time: **120 MIN.**
With: Cora Miao, Lindzay Chan, Anthony Wong.

■ In his new film, "Dancing Bull," Allen Fong shows he has a neat way with sly comedy, but, overall, depth of conception and expression, elements that could have propelled story and characters into another realm, are missing. Stronger actors would have helped.

Pic strikes a blow for the performing artist's right to freedom of expression, no matter how that expression might be subsidized.

Cradled in a story about an artist who breaks under pressure and then recovers, this is a spirited stand to take in an Asian metropolis like Hong Kong, where major support for live theater, dance and music is provided by local government.

That the blow may not register particularly is because of the pic's failing in other important respects. What might have been another involving story about the performing artist's impulse to create is thin and superficial. What is missing in the tale is interior intensity of character and action.

Lisa (Cora Miao) is a dancer who performs for a government-run dance company that also employs her choreographer boyfriend, Ben (Anthony Wong). The conservatism of the dance administrators eventually frustrates them, and they find other money to start a company of their own.

The effort exacts a toll. Ben has

a breakdown, and the pair separates. Lisa's career takes off. Ben finds a new love, and, as a result of events in Tiananmen Square, a new impetus to create.

Some of the film's best moments come from well-observed scenes of artists seeking money from committees and the committees pondering the merits of the artists' product. — *Nic.*

The Ballad Of
Yellow River
(CHINESE/HONG KONG)

Hong Kong A Tian Heo Films Co./Xi'an Film Studio (China)/China Film presentation. Produced by Cheung Tian-heo, Ma Jilong. Directed by Teng Wenji. Screenplay, Lu Wei, Chu Xiaoping; camera (color), Zhi Lei; music, Cheng Zihong. Reviewed at Hong Kong Intl. Film Festival, April 17, 1990. Running time: **113 MIN.**
With: Yu Lin, Duan Xiu, Chi Peng.

■ "The Ballad Of Yellow River" treats the epic landscape of China's most famous river valley as lovingly as John Ford did Death Valley in his best Westerns. This conjunction of East/West genres suggests the pic will win audiences outside its immediate market.

Crumbling cliffs and dry reaches, magnificent in their expanse and desolation, frame a classic tale about adventurers, bandits and the maidens they fight over.

The delights of helmer Teng Wenji's treatment lie as much in his humor and willingness to poke fun at what he is doing as in the breathtaking sweep of the terrain.

There is an almost urbane approach to his handling of characters that removes them from misty legend and places them (almost) in the here and now. He tries for a bit both ways, and for the most part gets away with it.

"The Ballad Of Yellow River" begins when a caravan of porters takes a young girl to a village where she is to be married off. The young porter, Bitter Herb (Yu Lin), falls in love with her, but they are destined never to wed. Bitter Herb tries to kidnap her and is thwarted by his archenemy, the bandit Black Scalper. Years pass.

Bitter Herb loves and loses Black Scalper's young wife, who has fled the tyrant. More years pass. Bitter Herb meets Black Scalper again when they are both old men and their passion for life almost is spent.

The director extracts many

shades from the material and most of the performers. Yu Lin is especially impressive in the lead role, showing a talent for irony as well as action.

Dolby sound amplifies the periodically overemphatic folksong track. Shot for a big screen, pic's technical values are first-class.

— *Nic.*

Song Of The Exile
(HONG KONG/
TAIWANESE)

Hong Kong A Cos Films Co. Ltd. production. Produced by Jessinta Liu. Directed by Ann Hui. Screenplay, Wu Nien-jen; camera (color), Chung Chi-man; editor, Wong Yee-shun. Reviewed at Hong Kong Intl. Film Festival, April 17, 1990. Running time: **98 MIN.**
With: Lu Shao-fen, Maggie Cheung, Waise Lee.

■ Exile and dislocation from homeland are familiar themes in contemporary Asian films. What gives Ann Hui's latest work, "Song Of The Exile," special quality is the way they are woven into a story of conflict between mother and daughter.

Pic's concerns, immediacy and its universality made it an excellent choice to close the 14th Hong Kong Intl. Film Festival. Heavily autobiographical, the Hong Kong/Taiwan production moves about in time as it explores the stormy relationship between a young woman, who returns to Hong Kong with a degree from London, and her Japanese-born mother.

The first half gradually exposes the sources of resentment each harbors: the young woman's childhood attachment to her paternal Chinese grandparents and the mother's frustrations in living in a Chinese community, which she takes out on the daughter.

A modus vivendi develops and the daughter accompanies her widowed mother to Japan on the mother's first visit since her marriage in Manchuria. The experience enables each to see the other more clearly and affirmatively. The relationship assumes new maturity.

Working with Taiwanese writer Wu Nien-jen, Ann Hui has shaped a film that, if not altogether successful, provides many moments of insight and enjoyment. The first and final parts, in which the focus is tight on the two women, register strongly with the admirable Mag-

gie Cheung, playing the daughter, in fine form.

The Japanese section is least successful, allowing too much coincidence (the mother's encounter with her old schoolteacher) and superficial treatment. Several episodes slow the drive toward the final reconciliation of the women.

By and large, little interior intensity is achieved in the acting, outside of Cheung and the small girl who plays the daughter as a child. This dilutes the impact of the piece. As the mother, Lu Shao-fen tends to play off the surface rather than from the depths.

— *Nic.*

Farewell China
(HONG KONG)

Hong Kong A Friend Cheers Ltd. production. Produced by Anthony Chow. Directed by Clara Law. Screenplay, Fong Ling-ching; camera (color), Jingle Ma; editor, Ma Kam; music, Jim Shum. Reviewed at Hong Kong Intl. Film Festival, April 16, 1990. Running time: **115 MIN.**
With: Maggie Cheung, Tony Leung, Hayley Man, Liu Chin.

■ In her third film, "Farewell China," Clara Law has gone for a bold international look, and pic's production values are high. But it lacks a coherent structure and development of the main characters.

Pic commands respect for its all-stops-out approach to a difficult theme of cultural dislocation and individual disintegration. That it gets only part way indicates the ambitious attempt by a helmer not yet in control of storytelling techniques.

"Farewell China" is set in 1988-89. After several rejections, Li (Maggie Cheung) is granted a visa to travel to the U.S. Her husband Zhou (Tony Leung) and their young child will join her when she secures immigration status. Within a year Li writes to Zhou from New York seeking a divorce.

Zhou enters America illegally to find his wife. With the help of a teenage Chinese-American girl (a raving Madonna lookalike), he starts to track down the worlds and people Li has collided with. Only when he has almost given up the search, and begun to make his own life, does he suddenly discover her. But Li has changed, with tragic results for them both.

Pic's opening scenes augur well as Li, ecstatic about everything

American, prepares herself and then undertakes the fateful interview with the U.S. consul. But once the action moves to New York (real locations are used), problems of pace and logic arise. Zhou is thinly developed, and the fashionable '90s model features of Leung aren't appropriate for that Mainland China ancestry.

The New York sequences lapse into cliché instead of that compelling view of city underbelly the story demands.

What cannot be discounted, however, is the mesmerizing performance of Cheung as the split-personality Li. The film's shortcomings in no way detract from her chilling finale. — *Nic.*

La Campagne de Ciceron (Cicero's Country) (FRENCH)

Paris An Amorces Diffusion release of an ACS/Les Films Aramis coproduction. Produced by Guy Cavagnac. Directed by Jacques Davila. Screenplay, Davila, Michel Hairet, Gérard Frot-Coutaz; camera (color), Jean-Bernard Menoud; editor, Christiane Lack; music, Bruno Coulais; sound, Yves Zlotnicka; art direction, Jean-Jacques Gernol-le; production manager, Nicole Azzaro; assistant director, Philippe Lacomblez. Reviewed at the 3 Luxembourg theater, Paris, April 15, 1990. Running time: **110 MIN.**

Nathalie	Tonie Marshall
Françoise	Sabine Haudepin
Hippolyte	Jacques Bonnafé
Christian	Michel Gautier
Hermance	Judith Magre
Simon	Carlo Brandt
Charles-Henry	Jean Roquel
Simone	Antoinette Moya

■ **Some marvelous comic writing and acting buoys "La Campagne de Ciceron," but this talky comedy-drama suffers from nondescript direction and a lack of genuine feeling for its characters. Still, it's the best of the three pics made by Jacques Davila, who's stronger with the pen than the camera.**

There's a pseudo-Eric Rohmer quality to this story of seven Parisians, mostly artist types, in what they think is a relaxing stay at the country home (the "Cicero's Country" of the title) of ex-opera singer Judith Magre, who now runs a classic music festival with critic husband Jean Roquel.

House guests include Tonie Marshall, a neurotic pianist; Jacques Bonnafé, a stuck-up culture ministry music official; Michel Gautier, a passive failed actor; Carlo Brandt, a Don Juan type who has been Magre's lover, and Sabine Haudepin, Gautier's ex-girl friend.

There's no plot to speak of, just a series of crossed romantic wires that provide the fuse to an explosive climax. Marshall is hot for Bonnafé, who doesn't respond to her signals. Magre still pines for Brandt, who gets the hots for sexually available Haudepin, while the somewhat slow-witted Gautier looks on as an observer.

In an unconvincing climax, the insanely jealous Magre mistakenly shoots Gautier when she goes after the 2-timing Brandt, who has taken off with Haudepin.

Best part of this clumsily structured film, cowritten by Gérard Frot-Coutaz and Michel Hairet, comes before the principals wind up at Magre's place. With some marvelously written dialog, scenes at Marshall's own country hideaway depict Marshall's frustrated courtship of the nature-hating, affected Bonnafé.

When the scene changes to "Cicero's Country" the performances remain sharp but the script's comic energy begins to run down before the arbitrarily melodramatic fadeout. — *Len.*

L'Avaro (The Miser) (ITALIAN-FRENCH-SPANISH)

Rome A UIP release of RAI-1/Splendida Film (Rome)/Carthago Film (Paris)/Velarde Film (Madrid) coproduction. Produced and directed by Tonino Cervi. Screenplay, Cervi, Cesare Frugoni, Rodolfo Sonego, Alberto Sordi, based on the play by Molière; camera (color), Armando Nannuzzi; editor, Nino Baragli; music, Piero Piccioni; art direction, Mario Garbuglia. Reviewed at Etoile Cinema, Rome, April 3, 1990. Running time: **119 MIN.**

Arpagone	Alberto Sordi
Frosina	Laura Antonelli
Mother	Lucia Bosè
Cleante	Miguel Bosè

Also with: Christopher Lee, Marie Laforêt, Valerie Allain, Franco Angrisano, Carlo Croccolo, Nicola Farron, Nunzia Fummo, Franco Interlenghi, Anna Kanakis, Adriana Russo, Mattia Sbragia, Jacques Sernas.

■ **"The Miser," a Romanized version of Molière's classic comedy written expressly for comic Alberto Sordi, aims at getting the same warm reception local auds gave "The Imaginary Invalid," also featuring Sordi and Laura Antonelli, several years back.**

Local boxoffice has confirmed the public's undying enthusiasm for the comic, who is nearing 70 but shows no sign of slowing down. Fans of the French playwright will be less delighted to find "The Miser" transformed into just another Italo comedy with high production values. Visually, it's an eye-pleaser.

The action of Tonino Cervi's film takes place in Rome. Playing off Sordi's public image as a miserly scrooge and altar-shy bachelor, pic gives him full rein to ham it up as the rich widower who keeps his gold locked in a chest in his bedroom. He is suspicious of his servants and children alike, imagining they're after his riches. While two Swiss clock-makers prepare the ultimate hiding place for home wealth, Arpagone makes some arbitrary decisions about his family's future.

Cleante (Miguel Bosè) his handsome young son, has fallen in love with impoverished Marianne. Elisa, his daughter, is having a passionate affair with equally impoverished Valerio. There is even someone in love with fat, insensitive Arpagone: Frosina (Laura Antonelli), a lusty wench who runs a brothel for him.

Frosina hopes to get Arpagone to the altar. (Antonelli's one joke is thrusting her main attraction under his nose at every opportunity.) The miser remains unmoved, but a visit to the mercenary cardinal (this is Rome) convinces him he had better get married fast, or be forced to tie the knot with the cardinal's sister, expert poisoner.

He makes Frosina procure possible brides, but they're all so ugly he picks a quiet, modest girl he sees in church (Marianne). Arpagone plans to marry her while his offspring marry suitors of his choice, thereby saving on wedding expenses with three at one go. The last scene unravels the comedy's tangled threads, putting everyone back with their proper partner.

Luscious visuals, the work of cameraman Armando Nannuzzi and production designer Mario Garbuglia, are the classiest thing about this "Miser." The rest is left to audience's goodwill toward Sordi, who gives a dandy performance in his easy, laugh-getting Roman idiom.

Rest of the cast breezes through 1-dimensional parts with little to grab hold of. Scripters have thrown out the play and kept dialog fast and contemporary. What remains of Molière are cumbersome, old-fashioned plot machinations, now little more than the skeleton to which gags are attached. — *Yung.*

Le Silence d'ailleurs (The Silence Of Elsewhere) (FRENCH)

Paris Movie DA/MC4 release of a Films du Rabb production. Written, produced and directed by Guy Mouyal. Camera (color), Alain Choquart; editor, Catherine Dehaut; music, Patrice Pellerin, Olivier Lacan; sound, Jean-Michel Chauvet; art direction, Bernard Vezat. Reviewed at the Pathé Wepler theater, Paris, Feb. 19, 1990. Running time: **94 MIN.**

Jeanne	Clémentine Célarié
Christophe	Grégoire Colin
François	Daniel Olbrychski
Marcel	Jean-Paul Lillienfeld
Henri	Michel Galabru
Mostephe	Smail Mekki

■ **In "Le Silence d'ailleurs," a well-acted but uninvolving first film, newcomer producer/writer/director Guy Moyal gives the film technical polish and** mood, but fails to convince.

Situation set in and around an isolated service station in a desert-like region of southern France (deliberately recalling the American West) concerns Clémentine Célarié. She's a young woman who runs the station in the company of her 12-year-old son and her lover (Jean-Paul Lillienfeld), who's hooked on her, though reverse is not true.

Clémentine and her son anxiously await the return of her husband (Daniel Olbrychski), who two years earlier had upped and left without a word.

Film describes the activities of mother and son as they try to fill the void of long empty days and landscapes. Célarié makes occasional trips to town and allows men to give her a lift back only if they drive a car similar to the one Olbrychski left in.

The boy also makes his escapes to the city where he befriends a young Arab man. In the meantime, Olbrychski lurks on the outskirts, biding his time enigmatically before he returns to claim his family.

Enclosed in their respective shells, the characters fail to move, despite the sincere performances. Worth special mention is Michel Galabru, as Lillienfeld's retired postal worker uncle, the most genuine person in the story. Tech credits are good. — *Len.*

Mister Frost
(FRENCH-BRITISH)

Paris AAA release (SVS Films in U.S.) of a Hugo Films/AAA/OMM coproduction. Executive producers, Stephane Marsil, Claude Ravier, Michael Holzman. Produced by Xavier Gelin. Directed by Philippe Setbon. Screenplay, Setbon, Brad Lynch; camera (color), Dominique Brenguier; editor, Ray Lovejoy; sound, Bernard Rochut; art direction, Max Berto; costumes, Judy Schrewsbury, Steve Levine; coproducer, John Simenon. Reviewed at the Club Gaumont Marignan, Paris, April 3, 1990. Running time: **104 MIN.**
Mr. Frost	Jeff Goldblum
Felix Detweiller	Alan Bates
Sarah Day	Kathy Baker
Dr. Reynhardt	Roland Giraud
Inspector Corelli	Jean-Pierre Cassel
Simon Scolari	Daniel Gélin
Frank Larcher	Maxime Leroux
Christopher Kovac	François Negret
Thief	Charlie Boorman

■ A self-styled "European" coproduction (French and English), "Mister Frost" banks on Anglo-Saxon star casting of Jeff Goldblum, Alan Bates and Kathy Baker, but founders on a weak script and un-goose-pimply direction by Gallic writer-helmer Philippe Setbon. Off-shore potential looks lukewarm.

It's a tepid thriller about a mass murderer who claims to be the devil himself. Goldblum, who has made his last three pics in Europe, is Mister Frost, a seemingly cordial country gentleman (in England, apparently) who casually confesses to police to having tortured and murdered no less than 24 men, women and children, buried on his property.

In first of script's implausible elements, Goldblum is neither imprisoned nor executed, but shipped around Europe to various psychiatric clinics with minimal police escort. Goldblum seems to have no traceable past nor social identity, and his subsequent muteness intrigues the Continent's top shrinks, who all want a crack at deciphering him.

Most of the story is set in a clinic "somewhere in Europe" where Goldblum breaks his silence to communicate with lady psychiatrist Kathy Baker. He makes her his privileged interlocutor. Yes, he's Satan in person, he tells her, and he's fuming mad because modern psychiatry has cheated him out of authorship in 20th century evil.

Now he wants to make a comeback and has chosen Baker as his agent. He wants to prove his power by inducing the shrink to shoot him in cold blood. It's a foregone conclusion that by the end of the film, she comes around to the belief that he is the Prince of Darkness and does shoot him dead, which of course is a vain action.

In the meantime, strange things are happening. A young clinic inmate (François Negret), soon to be released, goes on a shooting spree, potting first his own dad, then local clergymen (mostly Catholic priests, but also a rabbi, for ecumenical relief).

If the ways of God and the devil are mysterious, so too are those of the screenwriter, who allows Negret to run conspicuously around a town where the only policeman seems to be French-accented Jean-Pierre Cassel, who is in no apparent hurry to apprehend the culprit or prevent further mayhem.

None of this is particularly terrifying or gripping, especially since Setbon is incapable of creating any suspenseful doubt about whether Goldblum is indeed Satan, or merely a dangerous schizophrenic with psychic and hypnotic powers. Goldblum is by turns hospitable, sullenly mute or mysteriously threatening, but never suggests cosmic force of evil he is meant to embody.

Bates is relegated to a hardly more convincing part as Goldblum's arresting police officer, a religious man who is the first to realize that this killer is the devil and now devotes his life to trying to convince others. His subsequent romantic entanglement with Baker is poorly handled.

This is Setbon's second writing-directing credit, after a ponderous thriller vehicle for French pop singer Michel Sardou, "Cross." Setbon's direction here is by comparison somewhat more slick, but it's still derivative (the opening credits sequence cribs the helicopter shot opening of Stanley Kubrick's "The Shining").

Supporting cast is mostly French, and mostly (well) dubbed. Roland Giraud plays the clinic's self-important director and Daniel Gélin is Bates' father-in-law. Tech credits are good. — *Len.*

Les 1,001 nuits
(The 1,001 Nights)
(FRENCH-ITALIAN)

Paris A UGC release of a Cinemax/Telemax/Antenne 2/Films A2/RAI 2/Telepool/Club Investissement Media coproduction. Executive producer, Maurice Ilouz. Produced by André Djaoui. Directed by Philippe de Broca. Screenplay, de Broca, Jérôme Tonnerre; camera (color), Jean Tournier; music, Gabriel Yared; sound, Gérard Barra; art direction, François de Lamothe; special effects direction, Christian Guillon; costumes, Jacques Fonteray; makeup, Paul Le Marinel; assistant director, Patrick Jacquillard; line producers, Claudio Mancini, Sarim Fasssi Fihri; production manager, Bernard Farrel; casting, Shula Siegried, Teresa Topolski. Reviewed at the Triomphe theater, Paris, April 20, 1990. Running time: **93 MIN.**
Sheherazade	Catherine Zeta-Jones
Jimmy Genius	Gérard Jugnot
Caliph of Bagdad	Thierry Lhermitte
Aladdin	Stéphane Freiss
Sinbad	Vittorio Gassman
Grand Vizir	Roger Carel

■ "Les 1,001 nuits," yet another spinoff of the "Arabian Nights" fantasy, is a pointless pastiche confected by French comedy specialist Philippe de Broca. Though handsomely mounted and pleasantly acted, pic still couldn't be more out of sync with current trends and tastes.

Sheherazade (Catherine Zeta-Jones) is an ex-slave who has been foisted on the Caliph of Bagdad as wife in lieu of the grand vizir's daughter. This monarch (Thierry Lhermitte) is a monogamous romantic who decides to take a new wife each day and have her executed the morning after in order to insure fidelity.

The wily Sheherazade makes her escape, and the essential of the movie is her flight with various allies, including Aladdin, Sinbad and a magic lamp.

Basic twist in the script by de Broca and Jérôme Tonnerre is that the genie (Gerard Jugnot) of the magic lamp is summoned in from the 20th century, complete with an arsenal of motorcyles, planes and accessories to save Sheherazade from many a fix. This sort of time-tripping anachronistic humor is facile and has been done to death. The idea of the tv set as a magic time/space gateway is another surreal gimmick that has long been recycled by tv and theatrical commercials.

Zeta-Jones (dubbed by Sabine Haudepin) is a tawny, gracile Sheherazade. Lhermitte is an agreeable Prince Charming who dreams of being an acrobat. Jugnot has flustered bonhomie as the genie (in fact a former Bagdad astronomer condemned by Allah to live in the future "Land of Eternal Rain" (London).

Freiss, as a footlose Aladdin, and Vittorio Gassman as an aquaphobic Sinbad the Sailor, are wasted in episodic roles. Roger Carel is amusing as the Machiavellian grand vizir. François de Lamothe's sets and the special effects directed by Christian Guillion give this some fanciful color. Location lensing in southern Morocco is attractive. — *Len.*

Räpsy & Dolly
(FINNISH)

Kristiansand A Finnkino release of Filminor production. Produced by Heikki Takkinen. Directed by Matti Ijäs. Screenplay by Ijäs, Arto Melleri; camera (Eastmancolor) Tahvo Hirvonen; editor, Timo Linnasalo; music, Otto Donner, Tuomari Nurmio; sound, K. J. Koski; production design, Kati Lukka. Reviewed at 8th Nordic Film Festival, Kristiansand, Norway, March 30, 1990. Running time: **90 MIN.**
Räpsy	Matti Pellonpää
Dolly	Raija Paalanen
Karisto	Kari Väänänen
Börje	Pertti Sveholm
Enni	Eeva Litmanen
Venkula	Risto Salmi

■ With "Räpsy & Dolly," a comedy romp about a paroled

jailbird's doomed attempts to walk the straight and narrow, Matti Ijäs could well follow countryman Aki Kaurismäki into solid offshore exposure. All acting and technical credits are firstrate.

In "Räpsy & Dolly," Ijäs follows styles and themes of Kaurismäki's, even using latter's favorite actor, melancholy-faced Matti Pellonpää, in the lead as Räpsy.

Although hardly as slyly subtle in his story-telling technique as his mentor, Ijäs displays the same loyalty to his gallery of seamy characters, i.e., petty criminals, their customers and derelict dancehall and bar help, and cops who are hard to tell from felons.

On the loose, Räpsy owes a debt to porno dealer/fake art smuggler Börje (Pertti Sveholm) and must handle a few jobs for him. Constantly tailed by a tough cop (Kari Väänänen), Räpsy tries to hide by shacking up with Dolly (Raija Paalanen), an old and voluminous former cabaret dancer-singer on the alcoholic skids.

When fate and ill fortune demand it, Räpsy finds another cover and bedfellow in Enni (Eeva Litmanen), a younger beauty who preaches some sectarian gospel from a van out in the sticks.

There are plenty of genuinely human touches in each of the characters. The porno dealer is devoted to his invalid, dying mother. Dolly dresses and makes herself up to radiate a bit of her former glamor. Räpsy really tries to behave as the perfect gentleman even when buried in a dump.

"Räpsy & Dolly" is less successful when opting for straight-out Runyonesque farce than when sticking to compassionate black comedy with people and situations linked with real-enough social drama. — *Kell.*

Daddy's Dyin' . . . Who's Got The Will?

Hollywood An MGM/UA release of a Propaganda Films production. Produced by Sigurjon Sighvatsson, Steve Golin, Monty Montgomery. Executive producers, Bobbie Edrick, Del Shores, Michael Kuhn, Nigel Sinclair. Directed by Jack Fisk. Screenplay, Del Shores, based on his play; camera (Deluxe color), Paul Elliott; editor, Edward Warschilka Jr.; music, David McHugh; sound, Darrell Henke; production design, Michelle Minch; costume design, Elizabeth Warner Nankin; set decoration, Susan Eschelbach; assistant director, Matthew Carlisle; coproducer, Jay Roewe. Reviewed at Filmland screening room, Culver City, Calif., April 26,

1990. MPAA Rating: PG-13. Running time: **95 MIN.**

Orville	Beau Bridges
Evalita	Beverly D'Angelo
Sara Lee	Tess Harper
Harmony	Judge Reinhold
Lurlene	Amy Wright
Marlene	Patrika Darbo
Mama Wheelis	Molly McClure
Daddy	Bert Remsen
Clarence	Keith Carradine

■ A hit at the Dallas Film Fest, where it world-premiered last week, "Daddy's Dyin' . . . Who's Got The Will?" is perfectly scaled to the rhythms and true colors of its beguiling source material. Pic gets limited release in L.A. and several Southwest cities May 4. With careful handling, it should bequeath satisfactory b.o. and vid returns.

Del Shores' hit play about squabbling Texas siblings settling old scores beside their father's deathbed is brought to the screen with panache. Shores' script, delivering a "Steel Magnolias" without the overkill, presents a bittersweet family reunion, as three sisters and a brother who don't like each other convene in tiny Loakie, Texas, to find out who got what in the will.

Since dotty dad, who hasn't quite slipped away yet, can't remember where he put it, they're stuck together to play out their old antagonisms while they ransack the rambling old farmhouse looking for it.

Shore's script delivers ribald, delectable comedy and fresh provincial dialog ("What in the cat hair's goin' on here?") as the sparks fly. These are the kinds of roles in which actors can blossom, and the fine ensemble cast does.

Amy Wright as the pious, mothering sister who became a preacher's wife, Tess Harper as the salty-tongued single gal who wound up taking care of dad, and Molly McClure as righteous and rock-steady Mama Wheelis are all excellent.

Beau Bridges has an uncanny bead on blind, dumb cruelty as Orville, the boorish younger brother, an obstinate redneck garbage collector who keeps his hefty wife Marlene (Partrika Darbo) pinned under his meaty thumb with constant put-downs.

Beverly D'Angelo steals scenes as the spoiled, scattered little run-around sister who's brought home a beatific California hippie-musician (Judge Reinhold) as the latest

in a long line of consorts.

Like Bridges, D'Angelo is caught between a fragile, disastrous attempt at adulthood and the pull of her unfinished childhood, and the struggle is visible in her performance.

It's a theme director Jack Fisk knowingly carries throughout the piece, beginning with sepia-toned visuals of the siblings playing on a merry-go-round swing as children and continuing to the last frame, with dissolves to them as kids again, seen through the eyes of their addled father (Burt Remsen).

Fisk (who helmed "Raggedy Man" and "Violets Are Blue") opens film up gracefully into the country roads and honky-tonk environs of Loakie, particularly when Marlene waits on the steps of a bar while Orville goes inside to wangle a cheap case of beer.

There's also a lovely scene in the kitchen between Darbo and Reinhold as opposites attract after he introduces her to "marijuana cigarets."

A number of themes are left half-resolved, such as Orville's near-dangerous cruelty to his wife, and Keith Carradine seems wasted as the skirt-chasing local Harper pretends she's engaged to, but pic overall sets a naturalistic tone as viewers get the feeling each of these distinctive characters has plenty left to deal with after the credits roll.

D'Angelo gets to stretch her lungs as a country-western chantoosie in a barroom scene and also supplies vocals on pic's lovely theme song, penned by David McHugh.

Production design incorporates plenty of amusing touches, from the reject-model cars everyone drives to the giant plastic cups of iced tea Mama Wheelis serves.

This is filmmaking on a sensible scale that still delivers plenty of entertainment along with its pungent truths. — *Daws.*

Mindfield
(CANADIAN)

Montreal A Cinegem release of an Allegro Films production. Produced by Tom Berry, Franco Battista. Directed by Jean-Claude Lord. Screenplay, William Deverall with the collaboration of Berry, George Mihalka; camera (color), Bertrand Chentrier; editor, Yves Langlois; music, Milan Kymlicka; production designer, Guy LaLande; associate producer,

Tony Duatre. Reviewed at Cineplex Odeon Cinema Le Faubourg, April 7, 1990. MPAA Rating: R. Running time: **92 MIN.**

Kellen O'Reilly	Michael Ironside
Sarah Paradis	Lisa Langlois
Dr. Satorius	Christopher Plummer
Raolo Basutti	Stefan Wodoslawsky

■ After 92 minutes of a mindless exercise about brainwashing experiments by the CIA in the 1970s in Montreal, one needs a good brain wash. Pic is a sad example of Canadian product by any measure, including tech credits. Its only hope is the tube.

The purpose of the film is as confused as the back-to-back fiction-versus-fact info following the opening credits. Initially, "Mindfield" protects itself from possible lawsuits by dismissing all content as pure fiction.

Still, a text extracted from a 1977 New York Time article uncovered a CIA scandal in Montreal where unsuspecting victims purportedly underwent LSD-related brainwashing experiments (loosely linked to the Cold War) and trained killers had top secret missions erased from their memories.

Evidently the audience is supposed to take the film as seriously as readers may have regarded the newspaper article, but it doesn't work.

This detective "thriller" (and here the term is used loosely) focuses on a rebellious cop (a wishy-washy performance by Michael Ironside) who stumbles into a hocus drugstore robbery. Via his instinctive street smarts, he uncovers the CIA ring responsible for the "robbery," the experiments and various mindless murders.

Unsurprisingly, it turns out the cop was one of the brainwashing victims, which partially explains why he's somewhat brain dead himself.

A romantic involvement with a lawyer (Lisa Langlois) who is defending other brainwashing victims in an ongoing court battle, exploits the first element of the tired sex and violence formula. Of course, the cop eventually saves the day (and the girl) after a ridiculous shootout where the ultimate bad guy from the CIA is unceremoniously executed by 1,000 or so other cops. Now that's overkill.

It's no surprise that talented helmer Jean-Claude Lord ("Tadpole And The Whale," "He Shoots, He Scores") publicly divorced himself from "Mindfield" via an editorial in "La Presse."

He said the film "has absolutely nothing to do with my work," and the producers had total "control" over the film after the "first cut."

When film appeared in theaters with no premiere or press screening, pic's publicist said it was because "it's not a critic's film." Fair enough; however, it's not a "public's film" either. — *Suze.*

Enrapture

New York A Platinum Pictures presentation, in association with DB Films. Produced by Kenneth Schwartz, Chip Lambert. Directed by Chuck Vincent. Screenplay, Schwartz, Vincent, from story by Vincent, Kevin Thomsen; camera (color), Larry Revene; editor, "Martha Ubell" (Vincent); music, Joey Mennonna; art direction, Todd Rutt; costumes, Don Newcomb; assistant director and casting, Edd Rockis; associate producers, Vito Di Bari, Riccardo Di Bari. Reviewed on Atlas Entertainment videcassette, N.Y., Feb. 14, 1990. MPAA Rating: R. Running time: **86 MIN.**

Keith	Kevin Thomsen
Chase	Ona Simms
Marshall Webb	Harvey Siegel
Martha	Deborah Blaisdell
Karl	Richard Parnes
Det. Cox	Emilio Cubeirio
Martin	Frank Stewart
Chris	Marcus Allen Cooper
Frank	Alan Naggar
Annie	Jane Hamilton
Star	Jamie Gillis

■ Chuck Vincent's thriller "Enrapture" has several okay audience hooks but peters out in the final reel. Video fans may give it a tumble as a direct-to-video title.

Kevin Thomsen (who also cowrote the story with Vincent) is bland but believable as an aspiring Gotham actor who works as a chauffeur for rich banker Harvey Siegel. Siegel's sexy wife, Ona Simms, is mean to her hireling at first, but comes on to him after he sees her behaving in the backseat like a prostitute with other men.

Midway through the film she's found murdered, setting up some effective plot twists. In short order, Thomsen loses his job, gets fired from an acting assignment, and his girlfriend (Deborah Blaisdell) walks out on him.

Climax involves several duplicitous characters but Vincent piles too many switches into the finale to be believable.

Simms, who uses the moniker Ona Zee in adult videos, is quite effective as the femme fatale, though even she has trouble keeping a straight face when called upon to beat up Thomsen with a baseball bat.

Fans may be surprised to see

Blaisdell nearly 50 pounds heavier than she was in Vincent's other recent release "Wildest Dreams." Billed via her more famous alternate handle Tracey Adams, the actress allows some good-natured kidding of her tons-of-fun new look in her recent adult video release "The Adventures Of Buttman."

Tech credits for the New York- and Toronto-lensed feature are okay, except for the cramped look to studio-lensed interiors. — *Lor.*

Private Collections

Hollywood A Red Wing Prods. production. Produced by David Heisler. Directed by Bruce Williams. Screenplay, Williams, Heisler; camera (Foto-Kem color), Joseph E. Hernandez; editor, Lawrence Maddox; music, Marty Blasick. Reviewed at the American Film Institute, L.A., April 17, 1990. No MPAA rating. Running time: **86 MIN.**

Jake Blue	David Heisler
Helen	Mary Dryden
Claire	Julie Vesselle

■ "Private Collections" is likely to remain private. This shoestring budget AFI workshop project, premiering in the Festival's U.S. indie showcase, lacks the cleverness, style or point of view that sometimes merit attention for pics in this category. It unspools with an aimless and unalleviated ennui.

David Heisler, who also produced and cowrote with director Bruce Williams, plays a drifting lover-boy and would-be actor whose one talent seems to be chumming up to women. He gets involved with a photographer (Mary Dryden), which inspires the jealousy of her agent (Julie Vesselle), who's infatuated with her.

Though script tries to create links to "the art world," pic is mostly about the sordid goings-on in the unhealthy private lives of this flatly rendered trio.

Among its many loose ends is the photographer's penchant for killing off her lovers with a pipe while they perform sexual acts on her, a deed she carries out with no apparent consequences.

Under Williams' direction, whole production seems to suffer from a lack of oxygen as actors go through the motions of their perplexing assignments. Too often pic resorts to softcore porn in an attempt to create some interest

onscreen.

Heisler puts across a degree of screen presence and fleshes out his character a bit with his deliberate style.

In all technical matters, production is barely adequate. — *Daws.*

Vincent And Theo
(BRITISH-FRENCH)

Hollywood A Hemdale release (U.S. and Canada) of a Belbo Films/Central Films/La Sept/Telepool/RAI Uno/Vara/Sofica Valor production. Produced by Ludi Boeken. Executive producer, David Conroy. Directed by Robert Altman. Screenplay, Julian Mitchell; camera (Eastmancolor), Jean Lepine; editor, Françoise Coispeau, Geraldine Peroni; music, Gabriel Yared; sound, Alain Curvelier, Jean-François Auger; production design, Stephen Altman; art direction, Dominique Douret (France), Ben Van, Jan Roelfs (Holland); art coordinator (Holland), Karin Van De Werff; set decoration (France), Pierre Siore; costumes, Scott Bushnell; sketch and reproduction artist, Robin Thiodet; associate producer, Harry Prins; assistant director, Christian Faure; casting, Nathalie Cheron, Françoise Combadiere (France), Hans Kemna (Holland). Reviewed at Sunset Towers screening room, L.A., April 24, 1990. No MPAA Rating. Running time: **138 MIN.**

Vincent van Gogh	Tim Roth
Theo van Gogh	Paul Rhys
Sien Hoornik	Jip Wijngaarden
Jo Bonger	Johanna Ter Steege
Paul Gauguin	Wladimir Yordanoff
Dr. Paul Gachet	Jean-Pierre Cassel
Marguerite Gachet	Bernadette Giraud
Uncle Cent	Adrian Brine
Leon Bouscod	Jean-François Perrier
Rene Valadon	Vincent Vallier
Andries Bonger	Hans Kesting
Marie	Anne Canovas

■ Long in the margins of commercial filmmaking, Robert Altman is poised for a mainstream comeback with his splendid "Vincent And Theo," featuring British actor Tim Roth's staggering performance as van Gogh. The Euro-made English-language film, which has preemed in the Netherlands, should do well with sophisticated U.S. audiences this fall.

A study of van Gogh's last years as seen through his tortured relationship with his brother, "Vincent And Theo" is shrewdly timed to hit screens in the midst of worldwide hoopla surrounding the centenary of van Gogh's death.

Paradoxically this is one of Altman's most cinematically conventional films as well as one of his most deeply personal. As such, it may be the rare Altman film that can satisfy both his coterie of admirers and a wider audience.

Bearing little resemblance to the glamorized, overheated Kirk Douglas-Vincente Minnelli 1956

van Gogh biopic "Lust For Life," this Altman masterwork operates in the intimate, thoughtful vein of the great BBC bios of artistic figures.

Altman's only avant-garde touch is the audaciously witty and apropos opening sequence, in which video footage of the recent auction of a van Gogh painting at Christie's in London for £22.5 million is juxtaposed visually and aurally with the painter lying filthy and wretched in his shabby digs.

Having set the tone, Altman and his incisive scripter Julian Mitchell focus on Vincent's obsessive devotion to his craft and the failure of his financially supportive but overly timid art dealer-brother to win him acceptance in an art world that scorned his idiosyncratic genius.

For "Vincent And Theo," production designer Stephen Altman (director's son) lovingly recreates the tactile textures of life in the Holland and France of 1886-91. Pic didn't have the budget to indulge in extraneous spectacle, a fact that Robert Altman turns to his benefit, keeping the camera on the two brothers' kinship.

They're like two halves of a symbiotic personality, underscored by the title appearing as a joint signature on a painting. Pic provides a provocative examination of the art-commerce clash that has bedeviled Altman's career.

Altman has almost as much sympathy for Theo (Britisher Paul Rhys), the man tormented by his conventionality and vicariously living out his undeveloped artistic instincts, as the director does for the more mercurial and iconoclastic Vincent.

The heart of the film is its exploration of the destructive, unacknowledged but important relationship between artist and patron. Rhys skillfully inhabits a character even more wretchedly unhappy than his brother, who at least has the consolation of his art, and Theo's own incipient madness gives the film much of its unsettling tone.

Seldom has an artist been so convincingly or movingly portrayed on screen. Roth powerfully conveys Vincent's heroic, obsessive concentration on his work, and the resultant loneliness and isolation. His performance brings alive the backbreaking work and discipline required for artistic creation.

With his rotten teeth and paint-smeared face, hands and clothing, he's the artist as peasant workman, a refreshing change from the usual cinematic depictions of painters as Byronic visionaries. Slight, shambling, melancholic, feral, he provides a window onto the internal life of the artist that eluded Douglas' overly extroverted work in "Lust For Life."

Jip Wijngaarden's slyly humorous, subtly touching portrayal of Vincent's earthy prostitute mistress and model is his perfect complement from the other side of the canvas, and Johanna Ter Steege's freshly scrubbed beauty as Theo's wife gives a tantalizing sense of what Vincent is denied.

While avoiding undue histrionics (he's often pensive and removed), Roth makes Vincent's descent into violent insanity as precipitous and appalling as any Altman has evoked in a career often fixated on that theme. Artist's affliction is left somewhat mysterious; his epilepsy unmentioned.

Altman's stately pacing and Jean Lepine's somber, Vermeer-like lighting wisely opt not to emulate van Gogh's style, saving the thunder for two spectacular visual arias. One captures the artist's frenzied creation of his sunflower paintings, and the other a shockingly beautiful suicide scene that evokes van Gogh's eerie painting of a sky full of crows.

Unusual for its genre in that it shows a real interest in the artist's work and the evolution of his artistic consciousness, "Vincent And Theo" also avoids trivializing the torment of madness by explicitly mocking the facile and conventional notion, expressed by smugly patronizing doctor Jean-Pierre Cassel, that Vincent was really sane and "the rest of us are the sick ones."

The respect for the artist and his struggles that suffuse "Vincent And Theo" is an empathy that comes from the depth of the soul and one that shows the brilliantly original but often erratic director at the mature height of his powers. — Mac.

Terminal City Ricochet
(CANADIAN)

Vancouver A Festival Films release of an E. Motion Films production. Executive producer, Dan Howard. Produced by John Conti. Directed by Zale Dalen. Screenplay, Conti, Bill Mullan, Phil Savath, Al Thurgood, Ken Lester; camera (color), Paul Sarossy; editor, Haida Paul; art director, Bill Fleming; assistant art direction, David Webb; set design, Richard Gagne; costumes, Sheila White; props, Ken Hanis. Reviewed at Ridge Theater, Vancouver, April 12, 1990. Running time: 100 MIN.

Ross Glimore	Peter Breck
Bruce Coddle	Jello Biafra
Ace Tomlinson	Germain Houde
Officer Friendly	Joe Keithley
Officer Goodbuddy	Gene Kiniski
Alex Stevens	Mark Bennett
Beatrice Tomlinson	Lisa Brown
Jim Glimore	Gabriel Khouth
Tulip Glimore	Gerri Lee Smith
Chip Ferguson	Shawn Macdonald

■ Cult-video renters would appear to be only realistic potential market for this local low-budgeter. Any theatrical success beyond the local market would probably come from urban repertory houses specializing in low-budget midnight rock pics.

Pic has done well in its home-town theatrical market with three consecutive weeks in downtown venues, a run as long as any recent Canadian film save "Jesus Of Montreal." Local popularity could stem from presence of rocker Jello Biafra and Vancouver band "D.O.A." Also, several local celebs, including "D.O.A.'s" Joe Keithley and wrestler Gene Kiniski, appear.

Storyline is futuristic with a city's mayor (Vancouver acting teacher Peter Breck of '60 tv's "Big Valley" oater) campaigning for votes amidst squalor of a world wrecked by returning space junk. Corrupt police shoot looters on sight with only a handful of citizens standing up to the mayor and his henchmen.

The writing/rewriting credits go to five screenwriters of varying experience. Result is a watered-down final script with few lines taking advantage of the space junk concept. Acting and tech credits are lame, with exception of Breck's somewhat effective hamming and some of Gagne's gothic sets.
— Cadd.

1,700 meter fra fremtiden
(The Future Lies
1,500 Yards Ahead)
(DANISH-DOCU)

Copenhagen A Kommunefilm release of Nordfilm production. (Intl. sales: Statens Filmcentral.) Produced by Andreas Fischer-Hansen. Written and directed by Ulla Boje Rasmussen. Camera (color), Fischer-Hansen, Boje Rasmussen; editor, Janus Billeskov Jansen, Marete Brusendorf; music, Edward Elgar, Harald Säverud, Carl Nielsen, Niels Viggo Bentzon; sound, Per Meinertsen, Erik Jensen; production consultant (Faroe Island), Jóan Pauli Joensen. Reviewed at the Vester VovVov, Copenhagen, April 23, 1990. Running time: 85 MIN.

■ Ulla Boje Rasmussen's "The Future Lies 1,500 Yards Ahead," a calm and sympathetic look at a tiny Faroe Islands community, is hardly going to be a hot item outside educational circuits and tv.

Documentarist Boje Rasmussen meets and talks with each of the 16 (yes, 16) villagers of Gásadalur. The community seemed doomed to extinction until the authorities of Denmark's self-governing North Atlantic province decided to connect the isolated village of Gásadalur with a larger township by blasting a tunnel through the mountain separating the two settlements.

Resident shepherds, cattlemen and birdcatchers combine their chores with maintenance of a landing pad for a helicopter and hauling of mail and goods over the rocky mountain that falls so steeply into the sea. (Boats can unload only rarely at Gásadalur.)

Only a single woman and one child are in evidence among the interviewees, who take their time telling, in interesting detail, about their work life. They reveal facts like why sheep must be shorn even if there is practically no money in selling the wool any longer: Only a new growth of wool will protect the animals when winter sets in.

Things get rough at times. When a man has fallen off the steep face of the mountain, he is located in the ocean (where he is caught face-down between rocks) only by the special coloring of the soles of his shoes.

Interwoven with the interviews and edited with logic and fine rhythm are the director and Andreas Fischer-Hansen's magnificent cinematography that catches the majesty of the mountains, the pastoral calm of the grazing land and the ferocity of the sea. That makes it easy to understand why young folks flee the village and why their elders still cling to it.

What is missing, however, is any attempt at describing, let alone probing, the psychological problems that must inevitably go with life in such isolation. Modesty on the part of filmmakers and interview subjects alike is hardly a virtue in a docu.

While the absence of any "Mondo Cane" approach is commendable, some candid insights, in words or pictures, would have given the film as less mundane feel and shaken it out of its occasional doldrums of politeness.
— Kell.

Frankenhooker

Houston A Shapiro Glickenhaus Entertainment release of an Ievins/Henenlotter production. Executive producer, James Glickenhaus. Produced by Edgar Ievins. Directed by Frank Henenlotter. Screenplay, Robert Martin, Henenlotter; camera (color), Robert M. Baldwin; editor, Kevin Tent; music, Joe Renzetti; special makeup effects, Gabe Bartalos; casting, Caroline Sinclair. Reviewed at the Houston Intl. Film Festival, April 28, 1990. No MPAA Rating. Running time: 90 MIN.

Jeffrey Franken	James Lorinz
Elizabeth	Patty Mullen
Honey	Charlotte Helmkamp
Spike	Shirley Stoler
Jeffrey's mom	Louise Lasser
Zorro	Joseph Gonzalez
Crystal	Lia Chang
Angel	Jennifer Delora
Sugar	Vicki Darnell
Amber	Kimberly Taylor
Chartreuse	Heather Hunter
Monkey	Sandy Colisimo
Anise	Stephanie Ryan
Goldie	Paul Felix Montez

■ Even hardcore devotees of "Basket Case" and "Basket Case 2" may have a hard time with this latest bit of gore-and-grins campiness from cult filmmaker Frank Henenlotter. "Frankenhooker" is a grisly, grotesque horror comedy recommended only for the stout of heart and strong of stomach.

It could catch on as a favorite on the midnight-movie circuit, especially with that easily exploitable title. But it's difficult, if not impossible, to imagine that Shapiro Glickenhaus will get many mainstream bookings for the film.

James Lorinz, who resembles Dana Carvey, plays Jeffrey Franken, a New Jersey Gas & Electric worker who aspires to be a mad scientist. When he isn't blissing out by plunging an electric drill into his brain, Franken labors mightily to restore his pretty girlfriend to something resembling life.

There isn't much left of Elizabeth (Patty Mullen) after her fatal run-in with a remote-control lawn mower. But Franken has preserved her head in his garage laboratory. All he needs is a new body to make the package complete.

Henenlotter and co-scriptwriter Robert Martin spring a modestly clever idea at this point: They have Jeffrey drive across the river to Times Square to find street-walkers more than willing to sell (or at least rent) their bodies.

Merely killing a single hooker or two wouldn't satisfy Henenlotter's taste for gruesome excess. So Jeffrey manufactures a lethal "super-crack," offers the high-octane drug to an entire roomful of prostitutes, and helps himself to the dismembered parts after the girls quite literally explode.

The special effects here are deliberately cheesy — all the "victims" clearly are mannequins — but the scene likely will gross out, and maybe even chase out, a fair share of the audience. Those who stick around may have a few laughs as Elizabeth, newly revived with her head atop a patchwork quilt of hooker parts, returns to 42d Street to work at the oldest profession. Her clients die even messier deaths than the crack-smoking prostitutes.

No one in his right mind would attend a movie called "Frankenhooker" and expect to encounter signs of enlightened thinking. Still, even by genre standards, "Frankenhooker" often is offensive in its repeated reliance on murdering, dismembering and humiliating women for laughs.

At the very end of the film, Jeffrey is revived from death with a woman's body, a fate he clearly feels is much worse than death. That may say a lot about the mentality of the folks on the other side of the cameras.

To give credit where it's due, Lorinz has some inspired moments of self-absorbed craziness as Jeffrey, and Mullen reveals a fine talent for physical comedy when Elizabeth returns as the lumbering, mind-blown Frankenhooker.

When he isn't exploding hookers on the cheap, Gabe Bartalos does some impressive work with special-effects makeup. One memorable scene near the end has mutated hooker body parts crawling about the garage lab, looking like nothing so much as refugees from a Hieronymous Bosch painting. — *Ley.*

Twice Under

Houston Overlook Films Ltd. production. Produced by Maureen Sweeney. Directed by Dean Crow. Screenplay, Charles Joseph; camera (color), Jon Gerard; editor, Chris Hodapp; art direction, Carol Marsh; production design, Jacque Workman; associate producer, Lisa Dashiell. Reviewed at Houston Intl. Film Festival, April 23, 1990. No MPAA Rating. Running time: **90 MIN.**
Rick . . . . Ian Borger
Daggat . . . . Ron Spencer
Cammy . . . . Amy Lacy
Ed . . . . Jack O'Hara

■ **A potentially interesting premise lies at the heart of "Twice Under," but the people who made this amateurish thriller lack the talent and the budget to do much with it. Chalk this one up as fodder for video stores desperate to fill the action-adventure shelves.**

Produced in Indianapolis, the revenge melodrama deals with a crazed Vietnam veteran who makes novel use of his wartime experiences as a "tunnel rat" by using sewer tunnels as his private hunting ground. Daggat (Ron Spencer) vows to keep killing unarmed public works personnel until he's given a crack at supervisor Ed Chambers (Jack O'Hara), who left Daggat for dead in a Viet Cong ambush 17 years ago.

Relatively early in the film, it appears Chambers is killed in a Daggat-triggered booby trap. Rick (Ian Borger), Chambers' Amerasian teenage son, is eager to find Daggat, particularly after the crazed vet kidnaps Rick's girlfriend (Amy Lacy). Long after Daggat starts chasing him through the sewers, Rick discovers his father isn't dead after all, but merely is hiding in wait for Daggat.

Indicative of film's ineptitude is that Dad's sudden reappearance is neither greatly surprising nor particularly interesting. Director Dean Crow pads out Charles Joseph's thin script with some of the slowest, dullest chase sequences in recent memory.

Spencer comes off as a road-company Jack Nicholson as Daggat, hamming up the bug-eyed villainy with all the exuberance of actor intent on making a memorable impression in an inconsequential film. The other performances range from barely adequate to worse. Tech credits are undistinguished. — *Ley.*

Golden Braid
(AUSTRALIAN)

Sydney An Australian Film Commission and Film Victoria presentation in association with Illumination Films. Executive producer, William Marshall. Produced by Paul Cox, Paul Ammitzboll, Santhana K. Naidu. Directed by Cox. Screenplay, Cox, Barry Dickins, based on "La Chevelure" by Guy de Maupassant; camera (Eastmancolor), Nino Martinetti; editor, Russell Hurley; sound, James Currie; production design, Neil Angwin; production manager, Ammitzboll. Reviewed at Hendon Studios screening room, Adelaide, March 8, 1990. Running time: **91 MIN.**
Bernard . . . . Chris Haywood
Terese . . . . Gosia Dobrowolska
Joseph . . . . Paul Chubb
Antique shop owner . . . Monica Maughan
Psychiatrist . . . . Norman Kaye
Housekeeper . . . . Marion Heathfield
Ernst . . . . Robert Menzies
Ernst's wife . . . . Jo Kennedy
Priest . . . . Paul Cox
Hairdresser . . . . Barry Dickins

■ **The latest film from Australia's most interesting auteur, Paul Cox, is one of his best and encompasses the themes and obsessions of his earlier work in an intriguing and sometimes provocative package loosely based on a Guy de Maupassant short story.**

Pic's amusing philosophizing allied to its understated humor, moments of eroticism, plus top-notch performances make this a potential hit on the international art circuit.

Cox has often dealt with obsession in his work, and his protagonist here, Bernard (Chris Haywood) fits well and truly into this obsessive pattern. Of Central European extraction, Bernard lives alone among a world of clocks: he's an expert clock-maker and repairer, and also collects antique clocks and furniture. For him, clocks represent in the most tangible way the passing of time, and he's also haunted by thoughts of aging and death.

Bernard is also, we discover, something of a womanizer, and at present is involved in an affair with Terese (Gosia Dobrowolska), wife of an unsuspecting Salvation Army major (Paul Chubb). The lovers appear happy and enjoy a guilt-free relationship which cools only when Bernard is sidetracked by a new obsession: a braid of hair he discovers in a 100-year-old, supposedly Venetian, cabinet he's purchased from an antique shop.

Following sequences, as Bernard becomes more and more "in love" with the hair, talking to it, sleeping with it and even (in one of the film's most bizarre scenes) making love to it, are genuinely strange. But Terese fights for her man, and, in the last part of the film, succeeds in winning back her errant lover through persistence and the sheer power of her love.

All this is told in measured pacing, interpolated with the usual dream sequences familiar to Cox

aficionados. Also present are all the recurring Cox themes of loneliness, memory, love, trust and the beauty of art objects, plus occasional moments of unexpected humor.

Though the mood of the film is generally somber (a mood accentuated by Chris Haywood's strong performance), it is leavened by the intensity of its love story.

Dobrowolska, in a radiant performance, provides the strongest femme character in any Cox film to date, making Terese a complex woman whose passion for the reclusive Bernard is seen in sharp contrast to her dying marriage to a myopically indifferent husband (who's touchingly enacted by Chubb).

There are also neat cameos from Norman Kaye, as Bernard's world-weary shrink, Marion Heathfield as his disapproving Welsh housekeeper, and Monica Maughan as the antique shopkeeper, still bitter over the infidelities of her late husband.

Robert Menzies (star of Cox' "Cactus") as Bernard's disapproving brother, Jo Kennedy as the brother's slightly spacey wife, and Cox himself as a priest to whom Bernard goes for an unsatisfying confession also stand out.

Technically, "Golden Braid" is very fine, with lovely camerawork by Nino Martinetti (formerly camera operator to Yuri Sokol, who shot several of Cox' earlier films) and exceptional sound recording and mixing by James Currie, who creates a veritable symphony of ticking and chiming clocks.

Russell Hurley's editing allows for some slight slackness in the early scenes, and perhaps a few too many shots of the mechanism of the ever-present clocks.

These are minor blemishes in a film which shows a complete return to form for Cox (whose last, "Island," disappointed some of his followers). Pic was fully funded by the Australian Film Commission and Film Victoria, indicating wise government support for a filmmaker whose body of work is by now as interesting as any to emerge from this country.
— *Strat.*

Evelina e i suoi figli
(Evelina And Her Sons)
(ITALIAN)

Rome A Penta Distribuzione release. Produced by Mario and Vittorio Cecchi Gori for Penta Film; Roberto Cicutto, Vicenzo De Lee for Aura Films. Written and directed by Livia Giampalmo. Camera (Kodak, Cinecittà color), Maurizio Dell'Orca; editor, Claudio Di Mauro; music, Paolo Belli, Enrico Prandi; art direction. Mariangela Capuano. Reviewed at Embassy Cinema, Rome, April 9, 1990. Running time: **84 MIN.**
Evelina. . . . . .Stefania Sandrelli
Nanà. . . . . .Pamela Villoresi
    Also with: Roberto De Francesco, Cochi Ponzoni, Maurizio Donadoni, Flavio Bonacci, Massimo Bellinzoni.

■ **First-time effort by helmer Livia Giampalmo is a respectable job with an authentically female p.o.v. What film lacks in emotional high points, it makes up for in believable characters and a good-humored outlook.**

An original achievement for Italian films, "Evelina And Her Sons" has failed to draw the femme viewers who would most identify with its heroine, and local b.o. has been disappointing. It could be a pick-up for women's fests and other quality outlets.

Stefania Sandrelli glowingly animates "Evelina And Her Sons," the portrait of a divorced mother whose life revolves around her two teenage offspring.

Pic plays on a warm, homey feeling of everyday life in Rome's middle class. Evelina wakes Giulio and Carlo with morning coffee and maternally gets them off to school before trying to get her car started and go to work (she writes fables for children in an office). She's a highly distracted but mightily appealing lady, and attracts the attention of a bachelor neighbor, as well as a coworker, without noticing.

Her best friend Nanà (a plump, comfortable Pamela Villoresi) listens to Evelina's worries about Carlo's report card and Giulio smoking joints, and wails out her own anxieties over an errant husband. They worry about their weight and overeat.

Evelina starts dating their next-door neighbor with a ferocious sense of guilt. When the sons find out, they give her the cold shoulder treatment and almost break up the burgeoning relationship. But a crisis situation brings the neighbor-lover back into the picture as an ideal father figure.

Pic is no "Rocco And His Brothers." Tragedy is far from the film's concerns. Aiming at nothing more than painting a realistic picture of a woman's problems and feelings, "Evelina And Her Sons" holds attention from start to finish.

Much merit goes to Sandrelli's 1-woman show as the over-anxious, over-guilty working mom. Her gifts as a comedienne share time with the strong screen presence of a warm and sexy woman. She deals effectively with over-written dialog, which can become irritatingly nonstop.

Giampaolo overreaches in a few scenes, like the strangely off-screen car accident at the end. Supporting cast is credible enough. Interiors by Mariangela Capuano stand out. — *Yung.*

Without You I'm Nothing

New York An MCEG release of a Jonathan D. Krane/Nicolas Roeg production, in association with Sterling Entertainment. Executive producer, Roeg. Produced by Krane. Directed by John Boskovich. Screenplay, Sandra Bernhard, Boskovich, based on Bernhard's 1-woman show; camera (Foto-Kem color, Technicolor prints), Joseph Yacoe; editor, Pamela Malouf-Cundy; music, Patrice Rushen; sound (Dolby), Mark Sheret; choreography, Karole Armitage; costume design, Raymond Lee; assistant director, Peggy Jacobson; production manager, Krista Montagna; line producer, Jim Czarnecki. Reviewed at Florence Gould Hall, L'Alliance Française, N.Y., April 27, 1990. MPAA Rating: R. Running time: **90 MIN.**
Sandra Bernhard. . . . . .Herself
Steve Antin. . . . . .Himself
Singer. . . . . .John Doe
Ingrid Horn. . . . . .Lu Leonard
Emcee. . . . . .Ken Foree
Roxanne. . . . . .Cynthia Bailey
Shower woman. . . . . . . .Robin Byrd

■ **Sandra Bernhard's screen adaptation of her 1-woman show is a rigorous, experimental examination of performance art that's of interest to film scholars but packs precious little entertainment value for either general audiences or her fans.**

Stepping back from comedy per se, Bernhard and her collaborator, director John Boskovich, have fashioned a remote, self-absorbed and often cryptic picture. Solemn tone and ambiguity as to Bernhard's point-of-view smothers the humor of her often on-target material.

Most ambitious device here is a failure: except for brief interstitial footage of "witnesses" such as Steve Antin (as himself) or Lu Leonard (portraying Bernhard's manager) addressing the camera, film unfolds in performance on stage at a large, ersatz night club before a predominantly black audience. Crowd reacts only with silent, quizzical expressions or files out apparently not enjoying the show.

This gimmick scrupulously avoids the canned "live audience" of performance films or tv specials, but results in distancing Bernhard's act. In turn, she plows through her monologs without any pauses (for laughs) or interaction. Result is an over-rehearsed routine lacking in any spontaneity.

The "You" of the title refers to the audience. The film's in-joke putdown of the audience reverberates all too literally on the performer as the title says.

Irony is that Bernhard has set her film in a quasi-jazz milieu, reinforced by excellent musical accompaniment throughout by jazz pianist Patrice Rushen (an attractive performer who oddly is represented onscreen by a stand-in). Improvisation by the star is nowhere evident, however.

Though she has several white targets for her sarcasm, notably friend Madonna (poorly carboned by a platinum-haired dancer), Andy Warhol, Patti Smith, Barbra Streisand and Jodie Foster (latter's costar in "The Accused" Steve Antin is present for this purpose), Bernhard cryptically emphasizes a black motif throughout the pic.

Though not donning blackface makeup for obvious reasons, she portrays several black characters, starting with Aunt Sarah ("my name is Peaches") in a dashiki; then a composite satire of greats ranging from Sarah Vaughan to Carmen McRae in her mannered rendition of "Me & Mrs. Jones;" and a boring carbon of mid-career Diana Ross, with slicked-down hairdo.

Her lover Joe in a simulated sex scene is black, and most cryptic of all there is a black dream woman, who silently wanders around in random footage outdoors, in a science lab, etc. Film ends with this beautiful woman the only audience member left watching Bernhard's striptease dance.

Pic's highlight underscores the material's emphasis on roleplaying and androgyny: a 1978-set "I Feel Real" monolog/song with Bernhard pretending to be two guys in a disco, one of whom gets turned on by a black man and comes out of the closet. With helmer Boskovich letting loose his camera for once from its slow, monotonous pirouetting, scene is a showstopper. There's also a cute but padded disco number "Do You Wanna Funk With Me?"

Elsewhere, Bernhard's singing is mediocre, and there's far too much of it. Endless finale has her making fun of Prince and his entourage with a tired rendition of "Little Red Corvette," segueing to her exotic dance parodying strippers on N.Y.'s cable tv show "The Robin Byrd Show." Byrd appears nude in a cameo shower scene opposite the covered-up black woman. The quick wit and audience rapport Bernhard displays as a guest on Byrd's show would have been preferable.

Besides Rushen, there are guest spots for talented jazz singer Dianne Reeves and drummer Terri Lyne Carrington. Tech credits are modest for an evidently low budget MCEG production. — *Lor.*

FESTIVAL OF MEXICAN CINEMA FILM REVIEWS

Intimidades en un Cuarto de Baño
(Bathroom Intimacies)
(MEXICAN)

Guadalajara A Profesionales y Sociedad Cooperativa de Producciones-Cinematográfica José Revueltas production. Written and directed by Jaime Humberto Hermosillo. Camera (color), Guillermo Navarro; music, Rockrigo González; sound, Salvador de la Fuente; art direction, Leticia Venzor. Reviewed at the 5th annual Festival of Mexican Cinema, March 30, 1990. Running time: **75 MIN.**

Gabriela . . . . Gabriela Roel
Roberto . . . . Alvaro Guerrero
Bertha . . . . María Navarro
Esperanza . . . . María Rojo
Juan . . . . Emilio Echeverría

■ **Rather than using the camera to open up space, Mexican helmer Jaime Humberto Hermosillo restricts all action into a minimalistic exercise in voyeurism with his latest pic, "Bathroom Intimacies."**

Although the film is an interesting experiment and capable of generating its own quiet sense of tragedy, marketing it may prove difficult due to pic's static approach to narration. Also, its scatological aspects may prove too intimate for some viewers.

With this 16th feature, Hermosillo continues challenging viewers through nonconventional approaches to film. In "Bathroom Intimacies," he utilizes a fixed camera and continuous action (a technique he used in his 1-hour 1989 video "La Tarea") to capture the bathroom habits of four members of a family and a maid.

Functioning as the bathroom mirror (or fourth wall, in legit terms), the candid camera records the movements — in all senses of the word — of a family through a dozen scenes, delineated only by fade-outs and fade-ins.

Naturalistic acting by a core of Mexico's best talent, including Gabriela Roel, María Rojo and María Navarro, underline the basically misogynistic theme of a family in crisis.

The mother, Bertha (Navarro), spends her afternoons with lovers while her husband seeks solace with pornographic magazines in the loo. Because of economic difficulties, daughter Gabriela (Roel) and her husband, Roberto (Alvaro Guerrero) are forced to live with the in-laws. In each case, the husbands haven't lived up to their roles as head of household and chief breadwinner.

Hermosillo shows an able hand in using the restricted set to good effect. The individual frustrations of each member of the ménage emerge within this claustrophobic work.

"Bathroom Intimacies" will likely make the fest circuit and select art screenings, but further appeal may be limited. — *Lent.*

Matan a Chinto
(Kill Chinto)
(MEXICAN)

Guadalajara A Conacine-Estudios Churubusco production. Written and directed by Alberto Isaac. Camera (color), Jorge Stahl; editor, Carlos Savage; music, Lucía Alvarez; sound, Daniel García, René Ruíz Cerón; art direction, Enrique Bernal; costumes, Adán Palacios. Reviewed at the 5th annual Festival of Mexican Cinema, Guadalajara, March 30, 1990. Running time: **90 MIN.**

Chinto . . . . Pedro Armendáriz
Rerré . . . . Gerardo Quiroz
Inés . . . . Héctor Ortega
Palancares . . . . . Eduardo López Rojas
Emma . . . . Patricia Páramo
Consul Kraft . . . . Xavier Masse
Jácome . . . . Alfredo Dávila

■ **"Matan a Chinto," written and helmed by former Mexican Film Institute head Alberto Isaac, is an amusing but flawed black comedy. Despite good intentions, pic loses pace somewhere in the middle and limps to an expected ending.**

Based on a real event that took place at Christmastime 1944 in the port city of Colima, the film relates the story of Chinto, a psychotic hotel manager (Pedro Armendáriz), who one day becomes fed up with everything. He suddenly goes on a shooting spree, holding the town, local police and later the army and navy at bay.

While various bodies pile up, authorities take command and map out plans to disable Chinto. But it's to no avail.

Although much of the humor at the beginning of the film stems from surprise, the repeated confrontations coupled with directorial indifference work to dispel momentum.

And while Isaac's 1987 period pic, "Mariana, Mariana," was distinguished by its admirable attention to detail, "Matan a Chinto" is marred by the inclusion of many anachronistic objects. — *Lent.*

Intimidad
(Intimacy)
(MEXICAN)

Guadalajara A Metropolis production. Produced by León Constantiner. Directed by Dana Rotberg. Screenplay, Leonardo García Tsao, based on a play by Hugo Hiriart; camera (color), Carlos Markowich; editor, Oscar Figueroa; music, Gerardo Batiz; sound, José Antonio García; art direction, Carlos Herrera. Reviewed at the 5th annual Festival of Mexican Cinema, Guadalajara, April 3, 1990. Running time: **100 MIN.**

Julio . . . . Emilio Echevarría
Tere . . . . Liza Owen
Marta . . . . Angeles González
Pedro . . . . Acuaro Guerrero
Tony . . . . Juan José Nebreda
Madre Quintanicca . . . Ana Ofelia Murguía
Margarito . . . . Agustín Silva

■ **"Intimacy," an admirable first feature by Mexican documentary filmmaker Dana Rotberg, is a fresh, well-paced commercial comedy that should garner respectable domestic returns.**

Story involves a middle-aged literature teacher (Emilio Echevarría), who is despised by his wife and grown mama's-boy son. His students likewise ignore him. He spends his evenings working on a novel he will never finish, dreaming of a better life.

One day, by chance, he meets an attractive neighbor (Liza Owen) and his whole life changes. While at first he finds new meaning to his quotidian existence, reality later intrudes with financial and marital obligations and the fantasy falls apart.

Script by Leonard García Tsao, based loosely on the eponymous legit farce by Hugo Hiriart, is well-constructed and lets the comedy emerge through situations and strong characterization. At the same time, the script does not ignore pic's serious intent.

Rotberg maintains a steady hand on the narrative, keeping firm control of the many twists and turns of the plot. Acting and tech credits also are up to par. — *Lent.*

Una Moneda en el Aire
(A Coin In The Air)
(MEXICAN)

Guadalajara A SINC-Cooperativa José Revueltas production. Directed by Ariel Zúñiga, Hugo Bonaldi; camera (color), Guillermo Navarro; editor, Gilberto Macedo; sound, Alejandro Aguilar. Reviewed at the 5th annual Festival of Mexican Cinema, Guadalajara, March 31, 1990. Running time: **90 MIN.**

Conrado . . . . Arturo Beristáin
Isabel . . . . Isabel Benet
Maira . . . . Andrea Ferrari
Also with: Jorge Martínez de Hoyos, Delia Casanova, Carmen Delgado, Rafael Cruz.

■ **Mexican feature "A Coin In The Air" should more aptly be titled "a storyline in the air." This arty treatment of a B movie never touches ground long enough to reveal its plot. Sales potential also will prove "in the air."**

Fourth feature by experimental filmmaker Ariel Zúñiga, this attempted thriller boasts all the elements of an exciting action pic: explosions, murder, shootouts, hidden microfilm and treacherous beauties — everything but plot and characterization.

It seems as if Zúñiga has deliberately snipped away all expository moments from this technically well-made and well-acted film in a pretentious stab at art.

In the end, the viewer gets tired of trying to figure out what's going on, and mere plot conventions and suggestions are not enough to sustain interest. — *Lent.*

HOUSTON INTL. FILM FESTIVAL REVIEWS

Revenge Of The Radioactive Reporter (CANADIAN)

Houston A Pryceless production. Produced and directed by Craig Pryce. Executive producers, Andre Bigio, Howard Goldfarb. Screenplay, David Wiechorek, Pryce; camera (color), Paul Sarossy; editor, Gary Zubeck; music, David Bradstreet; special effects supervisor, John A. Gajdecki. Reviewed at the Houston Intl. Film Festival, April 21, 1990. Running time: **84 MIN.**

Mike R. Wave	David Scammell
Richelle Darlington	Kathryn Boese
Richard Swell	Derrick Strange
Joe Wave Jr.	Randy Pearlstein

■ "Revenge Of The Radioactive Reporter" is a lame sci-fi spoof that's too relentlessly dumb to be funny or frightening. This Canadian production might find some limited pre-video life on the midnight movie circuit.

Trying, and failing, for the tongue-in-cheek, trashy B-movie spirit of "Swamp Thing" and "The Toxic Avenger," pic unleashes a deliberately clichéd plot. Zealous reporter David Scammell investigates radioactive leaks at a Toronto nuclear power plant operated by villain Derrick Strange and his yuppies-from-hell board of directors. To stop the reporter's snooping, Strange pushes Scammell into a vat of radioactive waste. (Actually, it looks like the world's biggest washing machine, on the high-suds cycle.)

The reporter doesn't die. Instead, he emerges from the vat as a horribly disfigured, dangerous contaminated freak whose burning touch brings painful death.

Disguised in trenchcoat and slouch hat, Scammell goes on a systematic rampage, killing members of the power plant board in grisly ways meant to elicit more laughter than shrieks. One victim is scalded by the hero's own radioactive waste when he urinates into her bath water.

That pretty much exemplifies the level of sophistication in the flat screenplay by David Wiechorek and producer-director Craig Pryce. A joking description of solitaire as "playing with yourself" is used twice. The tech credits are no better than they absolutely have to be. The acting isn't even that good. — *Ley.*

A Girl's Guide To Sex

Houston A Six Shooter Films presentation. Produced by Tom G. Gniazdowski. Directed by Tom Rondinella. Screenplay, Rondinella, William Pace; camera (color), Dennis Peters; editor, Rondinella; music, Daniel Licht; production designer, Michael Anderson; costumes, Alexandra Welker; executive producers, Gianfranco Galluzzo, Thomas Gniazdowski, William Gniazdowski, Richard Whitehouse; casting, Adine Durton, Larry Golin. Reviewed at Houston Intl. Film Festival, April 22, 1990. No MPAA rating. Running time: **93 MIN.**

Tracy	Catherine Dent
Jeremy	Tom Gallop
Tory	Maureen Pierson
Bridget	Rachel True
Kyle	Jim Barcena
Clint	Brad Friedman
Finister	John Bigham

■ Despite the salacious come-on in its title, and despite two or three words that might never slip past network tv censors, "A Girl's Guide To Sex" remains as relentlessly perky and squeaky-clean as Archie comic books. It's worth a few laughs, but is better suited for home-vid than theatrical exposure.

Written by William Pace and director Tom Rondinella, the film is an extremely mild romantic comedy about two teams of college students — one male, one female — that compete in a video production contest sponsored by the National Education and Resource Dept. (NERD, get it?). Independently, group leaders Catherine Dent and Tom Gallop hit on the idea of filming, and updating, a 1937 etiquette book for proper young ladies.

Stridently prudish campus administrator John Bigham sees red when he hears of their projects, expecting the worst of anything with "sex" in the title, and plots to sabotage the "dirty movies." Ultimately, the rival student teams decide unity, professional and otherwise, is the best artistic defense against the self-appointed censor.

Very early in the film, a marketing professor tells his class that "The mere mention of [sex] in a title is enough to sell a product." This may be Rondinella's none-too-subtle way of acknowledging that he's using bait-and-switch tactics with his film's moniker.

In any case, hardly anything — certainly not any of the romances that bloom among the video students — ever gets out of hand in "A Girl's Guide To Sex." Chaste good-night kisses are par for the course, leading a viewer to wonder if Rondinella intended this as a date pic for high-schoolers.

Even the tongue-in-cheek segments that each video team shoots ("Saying Goodnight," "How to Overcome Differences") are relatively innocuous. One that involves punkish-looking but charmingly polite teens on a first date is genuinely amusing, though not adequately developed. Anyone expecting a series of "Groove Tube" type blackouts will be bitterly disappointed.

At the very end of the film, all the video students are paired off, and the three couples offer a sweetly sincere introduction to their video, "A Couple's Guide To Sex." One keeps waiting for some kind of punchline, but it never arrives. Neither does the completed video. Rondinella never shows us the final result of the students' collaboration, perhaps figuring that anything he would show at that point would be a letdown.

Maureen Pierson and Rachel True join Dent on the girls' side, while Jim Barcena and Brad Friedman join Gallop on the boys' team. All six players are brightly attractive, and if they haven't been offered lead roles on tv sitcoms yet, they doubtless will be soon.

As the prudish administrator, an uptight guy who keep a photo of Oliver North on his office desk, Bigham overplays his villainy in a fashion that might have been too strenuously silly for a "Beach Party" movie of the 1960s.

Tech credits are fine, especially in producing the "video-on-film" effect needed for the comedy segments. Opening credits are clever variations of the drawings you would expect to find in an old-fashioned "Girl's Guide To Sex" book. — *Ley.*

Red Surf

Houston Arrowhead Entertainment presentation of a Greg H. Sims production. Executive producer, Greg H. Sims. Produced by Richard C. Weinman. Directed by H. Gordon Boos. Screenplay, Vincent Robert, from story by Brian Gamble, Jason Hoffs, Robert, with additional written material by Boos; camera (color), John Schwartzman; editor, Dennis Dolan; music, Sasha Matson; sound (Ultra-Stereo), Eddie Mahler; production design, Lynda Burbank; associate producers, Jacob Wellington, John Thomas, Vincent Sghiatti; coproducer, Jason Hoffs; casting, Ronnie Yeskel. Reviewed at Houston Intl. Film Festival, April 21, 1990. MPAA Rating: R. Running time: **105 MIN.**

Remar	George Clooney
Attila	Doug Savant
Rebecca	Dedee Pfeiffer
Doc	Gene Simmons
True Blue	Philip McKeon
Calavera	Rick Najera

■ "Red Surf" is a slickly produced, casually amoral melodrama about surfers turned drug runners in the seedier environs of San Pedro, Calif. B.o.prospects are, at best, iffy.

H. Gordon Boos, the award-winning assistant director of "Platoon" (and, currently, Francis Coppola's a.d. on "Godfather III"), does a thoroughly professional job in his first effort as helmer. But neither Boos nor his generally fine cast can fully overcome the handicap of a predictable, cliché-stuffed screenplay about partners in crime on the prowl for "one last big score."

The antiheroes of the piece are Remar (George Clooney), an ex-champion surfer gone to pot (and cocaine), and Attila (Doug Savant), a hard-partying biker who dreams of owning a garage "to repair vintage Harleys." Along with their handpicked crew of equally rowdy San Pedro beach dwellers, they ride their wet-bikes out to offshore drug drops, then take their illegal cargo to the L.A. barrio headquarters of gang leader Calavera (Rick Najera). It's a simple life, but a rewarding one.

Remar discovers his live-in girlfriend, Rebecca (Dedee Pfeiffer, Michelle's younger sister) is pregnant, and wants to move to Portland, far away from the L.A. drug scene. The news comes as a shock, but it's not altogether unwelcome. Already, Remar and Attila have been talking about getting out of the drug business, if only to avoid dealing with homicidal psychos like Calavera.

Doc (Gene Simmons), a Vietnam vet who serves as chief sage for the San Pedro group, advises Remar to give even more serious consideration to early retirement.

Unfortunately, things take a potentially tragic turn when Remar's cohort True Blue (Philip McKeon) is arrested for drug peddling. Rather than fink on his friends, True Blue fingers members of Calavera's gang. The drug lord demands "simple justice;" i.e., True Blue's head on a platter. Attila and Remar make the mistake of trying to con Calavera into thinking they have executed True Blue. Then they make an even bigger mistake by attempting one last drug run under Calavera's sponsorship.

Brian Gamble, Jason Hoffs and screenwriter Vincent Robert worked on the story; director Boos provided "additional written material," but all this teamwork resulted in few original ideas.

Calavera, though played with crafty restraint by newcomer Najera, comes off as little more than a stylish grotesque in the familiar "Miami Vice" mode. (He keeps wolves in his basement to gnaw on people who displease him.) The climactic raid on Calavera's headquarters looks and sounds like the ending of dozens of movies and tv shows. And even with the wet bikes, there's nothing terribly innovative about the offshore chase scenes, either.

The closest "Red Surf" comes to finding a new wrinkle for an old story is when it kills off Remar during the ill-fated final drug run, to motivate the shoot-'em-up climax. Clooney (a star of the new ABC series "Sunset Beat") brings some charismatic fire to his performance as the self-indulgent, self-loathing Remar, and his character's death comes as a mild shock.

"Red Surf" works best when it develops some surprisingly effective emotional heat during the give-and-take between Clooney and costar Pfeiffer, who reinvigorate their hackneyed dialog through sheer force of persuasive acting.

Also, the buddy-buddy relationship between Clooney and Savant is somewhat more compelling than is the norm for this kind of movie.

Simmons, the Kiss rock 'n' roller usually cast as Mr. Bad Vibes, is very effective in a relatively sympathetic role, indicating he may be ready for roles of greater complexity. McKeon, all grown up since his days on tv's "Alice," is fine as the doomed True Blue. Boos keeps "Red Surf" humming along at a reasonably brisk pace, but takes just enough time for characterization details that bring welcome depth and texture to a thin plot.

Technically, pic is a textbook example of making the most on a relatively small budget, thanks to impressive contributions from cinematographer John Schwartzman (Vittorio Storaro protégé), editor Dennis Dolan and production designer Lynda Burbank.

Some mainstream critics may complain (not without justification) that "Red Surf" often seems to glamorize drug dealers. At the very end, though, it appears most of the surviving characters have cleaned up their acts. This doesn't stop them from keeping the money from their last drug deal, but at least it gives "Red Surf" some semblance of a happy ending.

— *Ley.*

ARCHIVE FILM REVIEW

Feu Mathias Pascal
(The Late Mathias Pascal)
(FRENCH-B&W/TINTED)

Paris A Cinémathèque Française restoration and presentation of a Films Albatros-Cinégraphic coproduction (1925-26), first released in Paris by Les Films Armor, Feb. 12, 1926. Restoration laboratory, Renov-Film. Produced by Alexandre Kamenka. Written and directed by Marcel L'Herbier, based on the novel by Luigi Pirandello. Camera (b&w), Paul Guichard, Jean Letort, Fedote Bourgassoff, Jimmy Berliet, Nicolas Roudakoff; sets, Alberto Cavalcanti, Lazare Meerson; assistant director, Cavalcanti. Reviewed at Théâtre de la Ville, Paris, March 26, 1990. Length: 11,465 ft. Running time (at 20 frames per second): **153 MIN.**
Mathias Pascal . . . . . . Ivan Mosjoukine
Romilde . . . . Marcelle Pradot
Jerome Pomino . . . . Michel Simon
Adrienne Paleari . . . . Lois Moran
Aunt Scolastica . . . . . . Pauline Carton
Terence Papiano . . . . Jean Hervé
Batta Maldagna . . . . . . Isaure Douvan
The widow Pescatore . . . . Madam Barsacq
Scipion Papiano . . . . . . Pierre Batcheff

■ **Cinémathèque Française has restored Marcel L'Herbier's** enchanting silent adaptation of "The Late Mathias Pascal" to its original length and its pictorial 35m splendor, complete with the lovely tints that firstrun audiences enjoyed at time of pic's release in 1926.

Adapted from Luigi Pirandello's seriocomic novel, pic never has been a lost or forgotten classic, but its reputation has been tarnished by the wretched, frequently incomplete 16m black & white prints that continue to circulate in the nontheatrical market.

L'Herbier already had a place of honor in French avant-garde cinema when he bought the rights to the Pirandello book and signed a copoduction agreement with Films Albatros, the Paris-based emigé Russian film company whose chief asset was actor Ivan Mosjoukine (Ivan Mozhukhin in usual Anglo-Saxon spelling).

Mathias Pascal was Mosjoukine's last role for Albatros before he moved to bigger commercial vehicles such as "Michel Strogoff" and "Casanova."

The unlikely collaboration of coldly intellectual Gallic filmmaker and mercurial Russian star was a gamble that paid off. Pic was a critical and commercial smash, proving L'Herbier could reconcile his own formal preoccupations with the demands of commercial filmmaking. Of all his classics (except his 1928 "L'Argent"), this film has dated the least.

L'Herbier remained largely faithful to the novel's plot about a timid young Italian provincial who adopts a new identity and personality in the big city when family and friends think he has been killed in an accident. A lucky streak at a roulette table in Monte Carlo provides him with the means to start anew.

Money cannot solve personal dilemmas arising when he falls in love with the engaged daughter of his Roman pensione landlord. Without genuine identity papers, he is nothing but a living dead man.

Filmmaker manages to inject many of his personal touches into the story (such as making the henpecked young Mathias a closet intellectual, toiling at a philosophical opus called "Freedom").

L'Herbier also contrives a happy ending that improves on Pirandello's own pessimistic conclusion, though the filmmaker dilutes the effect in an unconvincing climactic digression. Fellow French director Pierre Chenal adapted a similar, more cleverly contrived denouement in his elegant 1936 remake, "The Man From Nowhere."

Mosjoukine's colorful personality gives the film a warmth and humor conspicuously absent from L'Herbier's previous films. Mosjoukine's wide physical and emotional range — he moves with astonishing ease from Buster Keaton-like farce to melodramatic pathos — never received a more worthy showcase.

Marvelous exteriors in the Italo countryside and Rome are balanced by the stylized studio settings by Alberto Cavalcanti and debutant designer Lazare Meerson (who would go on to greater fame with René Clair and Jacques Feyder). L'Herbier enjoyed the luxury of having at least five ace lensers at his command.

Pic, by the way is, also remembered as the first screen appearance of the ineffable Michel Simon, who plays Mosjoukine's timid best friend. At the time, Simon had been noticed for his stage performance in Pirandello's "Six Characters In Search Of An Author."

Occasion for the film's recent Paris revival was a musical presentation by Martial Solal, who provided live piano accompaniment. — *Len.*

Tales From The Darkside: The Movie

New York A Paramount Pictures release of a Richard P. Rubinstein production. Produced by Rubinstein, Mitchell Galin. Directed by John Harrison. Screenplay, "Lot 249" segment: Michael McDowell, from story by Sir Arthur Conan Doyle; "Cat From Hell" segment: George A. Romero, from story by Stephen King; "Lover's Vow" segment: McDowell; camera (Technicolor), Robert Draper; editor, Harry B. Miller 3d; music, "Wraparound story," Donald A. Rubinstein; "Lot 249," Jim Manzie, Pat Regan; "Cat From Hell," Chaz Jankel; "Lover's Vow," Harrison; sound (Dolby), Brit Warner; production design, Ruth Ammon; art direction, Jocelyne Beaudoin; set decoration, Jacqueline Jacobson; costume design, Ida Gearon; assistant director, Mary Beth Hagner; production manager, Victoria Westhead; special makeup effects, KNB Efx Group; Robert Kurtzman, Greg Nicotero, Howard Berger; makeup effects consultant, Dick Smith; "Lover's Vow" visual effects, Ernest Farino; stunt coordinator, Edgard Mourino; coproducer, David R. Kappes; casting, Julie Mossberg, Brian Chavanne. Reviewed at Paramount 29th floor screening room, May 4, 1990. MPAA Rating: R. Running time: **93 MIN.**

Betty . . . . Deborah Harry
Andy . . . . Christian Slater
Halston . . . . David Johansen
Drogan . . . . William Hickey
Preston . . . . James Remar
Carola . . . . Rae Dawn Chong
Wyatt . . . . Robert Klein
Bellingham . . . . Steve Buscemi
Timmy . . . . Matthew Lawrence
Lee . . . . Robert Sedgwick
Susan . . . . Julianne Moore
Mummy . . . . Michael Deak
    Also with: Ashton Wise, Philip Lenkowsky, Alice Drummond, Delores Sutton, Mark Margolis.

■ **Paramount's annual spring horror picture is a well-made anthology, short on scares but long on atmosphere and good performances. It should drum up good boxoffice, perhaps skewed higher than usual in age bracket.**

Following comfortably in the wake of producer Richard P. Rubinstein's "Creepshow" pics, "Tales From The Darkside" is significantly gorier than its namesake tv series, and has better production values.

Anthology format peaked in the '70s with the popular Amicus pictures by Max J. Rosenberg and Milton Subotsky. This one resembles them in emphasizing solid stories, with source material from Stephen King, Sir Arthur Conan Doyle and "Beetlejuice" writer Michael McDowell.

Structure is a lift from Scheherazade in "1,001 Nights," as Deborah Harry prepares to cook little boy Matthew Lawrence she's imprisoned. He delays his fate by telling her a trio of horror stories.

Most ambitious segment,

McDowell's "Lover's Vow" is saved for last: Gotham artist James Remar witnessing a barman's extremely gory murder by a gargoyle come to life. To save his skin he vows to the gargoyle not to tell anyone what happened, but after meeting beautiful Rae Dawn Chong, romancing her and marrying her, 10 years later he spills the beans with tragic results.

Sexy and sinister Chong is a delight in this one, with solid support from Remar and as his wry agent, Robert Klein. Director Harrison also contributes an evocative score and some ambiguous imagery, notably a tender shot of the gargoyle and its offspring.

Other segments are more routine. George A. Romero's adaptation of a Stephen King story is punched up by casting David Johansen as a hit man assigned to kill a black cat by drug tycoon William Hickey. As with the Chong finale, creature makeup effects are outstanding here.

Curtainraiser is a corny but effective tale from the creator of "Sherlock Holmes:" college student Steve Buscemi bringing an ancient mummy back to life for revenge with ironic results. Good twists and another quality Jack Nicholson-esque performance by lead Christian Slater work to advantage.

Tech credits are way above average, with cinematographer Robert Draper (who operated his own camera) sustaining the horror atmosphere with careful lighting. Editor Harry B. Miller 3d's clever use of wipes is another plus.
— Lor.

Short Time

Hollywood A 20th Century Fox release of a Gladden Entertainment presentation. Produced by Todd Black. Executive producers, Joe Wizan, Mickey Borofsky. Directed by Gregg Champion. Screenplay, John Blumenthal, Michael Berry; camera (Gastown color, Deluxe prints), John Connor; editor, Frank Morriss; music, Ira Newborn; sound (Dolby), Larry Sutton; production design, Michael Bolton; art direction, Eric Fraser; set decoration, Peter Hinton; costume design, Christopher Ryan; stunt coordinator, 2d unit director, Conrad Palmisano; 2d unit camera, Curtis Petersen; Canadian stunt coordinator, Jacob Rupp; supervising producer, Malcolm R. Harding; coproducer-assistant director, Rob Cowan; casting, Lynne Carrow. Reviewed at Avco Center Cinema, L.A., April 26, 1990. MPAA Rating: PG-13. Running time: **97 MIN.**

Burt Simpson . . . . . . Dabney Coleman
Ernie Dills . . . . Matt Frewer
Carolyn Simpson . . . . Teri Garr
Captain . . . . Barry Corbin
Scalese . . . . Joe Pantoliano
Stark . . . . Xander Berkeley
Dan Miller . . . . Rob Roy
Dougie Simpson . . . . . Kaj-Erik Eriksen
Spivak . . . . Deejay Jackson
Older Dougie . . . . Shawn Clements

■ **Forgetting that black comedies have to be funny as well as morbid, 20th's "Short Time" in short order turns from being routinely stupid to actively repulsive. A short time is all it'll have at the boxoffice.**

Dabney Coleman works hard but can't redeem this pic, by turns heartless and mechanically sentimental, about a cop nearing retirement who mistakenly thinks he's dying and tries to get killed so his family can collect the insurance.

Anyone trying to make a black comedy should be made to watch the classic "Harold & Maude" about 20 times before venturing into what too often is a sorely misused genre. Walking the line between cruelty and wit, and trying to find some genuine sentiment in between, totally eludes scripters John Blumenthal and Michael Berry and debuting director Gregg Champion.

Champion's extensive work as a second-unit director evidently hasn't prepared him for dealing with the nuances of human emotion. His idea of humor in this uneasy cross between farce and disease-of-the-week melodrama is to pile the desperate Coleman into a police car and have him crash into about half of the vehicles in Seattle before angrily stepping out in one piece, long after the gag ceases to be funny.

Though the stunt work engineered by Conrad Palmisano is technically admirable, the excessive and thoughtless sequence epitomizes what is wrong with the film.

Champion wants to turn Coleman's dilemma from farce into genuine emotion as the film progresses, but the character's callous disregard of other people's lives in his own quest for death makes him impossible to care about when the soapy music begins.

He's otherwise a seemingly decent guy who has alienated wife Teri Garr, typecast as a drab but understanding featherhead.

Scripters think it's hilarious naming Coleman and his laid-back partner (Matt Frewer) Burt and Ernie and having them repeat the pair of "Sesame Street" names

about 50 times in 97 minutes.

Frewer manages a loopy charm despite the dialog and an embarrassing sequence in which he's made to mistake Coleman's newly affectionate manner for a homosexual pass.

The real problem is the subplot about a black bus driver (Deejay Jackson), whose urine sample has been mixed up with Coleman's, and who's really the one dying of a rare blood disorder but doesn't realize it.

It's awful enough not to engineer a farcical twist to make sure Jackson also comes out alive at the end, but the film rubs in its cruelty by trying to wring yocks out of the poor man going blind and running into things with his bus. Unbelievably, the film ends at Jackson's funeral and tries to make light of his death.

Did the filmmakers actually think that casting the character as a black man would take some of the sting out of his predicament and make him an expendable butt of humor? The ploy gives "Short Time" a sour taste of racist insensitivity on top of its other idiocies.

Tech credits are mostly routine on this Gladden Entertainment potboiler, which was lensed in Vancouver but fails to take full advantage of that city's distinctive scenery since it is misguidedly trying to pass it off as Seattle. — Mac.

Class Of 1999

New York A Taurus Entertainment release of a Lightning Pictures (Vestron) presentation of an Original Pictures production. Executive producers, Lawrence Kasanoff, Ellen Steloff. Produced and directed by Mark L. Lester. Screenplay, C. Courtney Joyner, from story by Lester; camera (CFI color), Mark Irwin; editor, Scott Conrad; music, Michael Hoenig; in Dolby stereo; costume design, Leslie Ballard; assistant director, Richard Abramitis; production manager-coproducer, Eugene Mazzola; visual effects supervisor-2d unit director, Eric Allard; special makeup effects, Rick Stratton; stunt coordinator, Paul Baxley; android graphics, R/Greenberg & Associates; associate producer, Stanley Mann. Reviewed at Moviemakers screening room, N.Y., May 2, 1990. MPAA Rating: R. Running time: **98 MIN.**

Cody Culp . . . . Bradley Gregg
Christie Langford . . . . Traci Lind
Dr. Miles Langford . . Malcolm McDowell
Dr. Bob Forrest . . . . Stacy Keach
Mr. Bryles . . . . Patrick Kilpatrick
Ms. Connors . . . . Pam Grier
Mr. Hardin . . . . John P. Ryan
Sonny . . . . Darren E. Burrows
Angel . . . . Joshua Miller
Janice Culp . . . . Sharon Wyatt
Hector . . . . Jimmy Medina Taggert
Flavio . . . . Jason Oliver
Dawn . . . . Jill Gatsby

Reedy . . . . Sean Haggerty
Mohawk . . . . Sean Gregory Sullivan

■ A followup to the 1981 pic "Class Of 1984," this violent exploitation film is too pretentious for its own good. Socko special effects in the final reel will attract genre fans patient enough to sit through the campy buildup.

As he did in the original, director Mark L. Lester takes a cynical, fake-hip view of young people's future, as defined in terms accessible to what used to be the drive-in audience.

C. Courtney Joyner's inconsistent screenplay posits high-schoolers out of control a decade hence. So-called free-fire zones have been set up in urban areas around the schools as no man's land for outsiders, and are literally under the control of youth gangs. Yet Joyner still depicts the kids going to school each day, depositing their guns (including automatic weapons) at the door.

Hamming it up as an albino megalomaniac, Stacy Keach is carrying out an experiment sending three androids reconverted from army surplus to serve as teachers at Kennedy H.S. in Seattle and whip the students into shape. Simultaneously, hero Bradley Gregg has been let out of jail and returned to class at Kennedy in an experimental furlough program.

The gimmick of the androids beating up the kids is funny at first, with most of the laughs generated by the tongue-in-cheek video graphics (done by R/Greenberg & Associates) listing punishment options from the robot point-of-view.

However, lack of script development makes the film tiresome and repetitive. Gregg has endless fights en route to a saver climax in which the warring teen gangs unite against a common enemy, the androids.

John P. Ryan and Pam Grier are loads of fun as the androids, latter mocking her image when not only her breasts but inner workings are revealed for the final reel through hokey makeup effects. Third android, Patrick Kilpatrick, doesn't get into the spirit of the black humor.

Malcolm McDowell is wasted playing the school principal and dad of pretty heroine Traci Lind. Formerly monikered Lin (her cred-

it is incorrect on this 1988 production), she subsequently had a much better role in the quite different sci-fier "The Handmaid's Tale."

Gregg is merely okay; he looks like a teen Kenneth Branagh but acts like rocker Lou Reed. Scene-stealer is Joshua Miller, androgonous young actor who scored in "River's Edge."

Lester tries to inject a message into the "Robocop" action, but film disintegrates into an effects show. In mocking society's slide toward police state tactics, he ends up merely servicing the audience's need for vicarious ultraviolence. McDowell's presence reminds one of Stanley Kubrick's "A Clockwork Orange," a controversial but serious-minded meditation on the subject that opened the floodgates.

Tech credits are good but the overbearing musical score is just noise. — *Lor.*

Spaced Invaders

Hollywood A Buena Vista release of a Touchstone Pictures presentation, in association with Silver Screen Partners IV, of a Smart Egg Pictures-Luigi Cingolani production. Produced by Cingolani. Executive producer, George Zecevic. Directed by Patrick Read Johnson. Screenplay, Johnson, Scott Lawrence Alexander; camera (CFI color), James L. Carter; editor, Seth Gaven, Daniel Gross; music, David Russo; production design, Tony Tremblay; art direction, Alexander; set decoration, Chava Danielson; make-up effects/animatronics, Criswell & Johnson Effects; assistant director, Kelly Van Horn; line producer, John S. Curran; associate producers, Caroline Pham Johnson, Jason Clark; casting, Barbara Remsen, Anne Remsen Manners. Reviewed at AMC Century City Theaters, L.A., April 26, 1990. MPAA Rating: PG. Running time: **100 MIN.**
Sam . . . . Douglas Barr
Wrenchmuller . . . . Royal Dano
Kathy . . . . Ariana Richards
Brian (Duck) . . . . J.J. Anderson
Klembecker . . . . Gregg Berger
Vern . . . . Wayne Alexander
Blaznee . . . . Kevin Thompson

■ Disney figures to cash in briefly on the spillover kid market from Ninja Turtlemania with this timely infestation of a small band of "cute" green aliens, though it's such a simple-minded effort it should play only among the youngest of tykes.

Relentless special effects at least make the pic interesting to look at even if the dim script is rather painful to endure.

The prime appeal will be watching the pint-sized Martians, a visual cross between the alien bounty hunter from the "Star Wars" cantina scene, Ewoks and Oz, the Great and Terrible.

The quintet, part of intergalactic force invading another star system, errantly blasts down on a sleepy Midwestern town after intercepting a Halloween-night radio broadcast of "The War Of The Worlds" saying Martians have invaded Earth. (This moment, while a familiar one, proves the pic's most inspired.)

After that, the film is just a tangled mess of sloppily patched together scenes relying almost entirely on slapstick and the fact that the aliens use quaint Earth colloquialisms like "Let's boogie" and "dude."

The sole discernable personality in the group belongs to Blaznee (also the only character performed and voiced by the same person, Kevin Thompson). He wears dark sunglasses, a flight jacket and Lakers T-shirt while affecting a Jack Nicholson accent throughout. It's an amusing conceit, but one that quickly wears thin, much like the rest of the film.

Director Patrick Read Johnson, previously a special-effects supervisor, makes a less-than-auspicious debut in terms of his handling of actors. The children, in particular, are some of the most grating screen kids in recent memory.

Mercifully, the reliable Royal Dano is on hand as a crusty old codger who first espies the aliens, while Douglas Barr plays the bland lead as the town's sheriff.

David Russo, obviously told to think like John Williams, complies with an appropriate, gale-force score.

The creature design, however, is effective but neither particularly interesting nor impressive, as if someone was mulling what head shape would be the easiest to merchandise as an action figure.

Climax offers a crowd-pleasing turn of events that's extremely predictable but probably won't be to the film's target audience.
— *Bril.*

The Crossing
(AUSTRALIAN)

Sydney A Hoyts (Australia) release of a Beyond Intl. Group production, with the assistance of the Australian Film Finance Corp. Executive producers, Al Clark, Philip Gerlach. Produced by Sue Seeary. Directed by George Ogilvie. Screenplay, Ranald Allan; camera (color), Jeff Darling; editor, Henry Dangar; music, Martin Armiger; sound, David Lee; production design, Igor Nay; costumes, Katie Pye; assistant director, Chris Webb; production manager, Debbie Samuels; associate producer, Jenny Day; casting, Faith Mar-

tin. Reviewed at Hoyts Center 6, Sydney, April 22, 1990. Running time: **94 MIN.**
Meg . . . . Danielle Spencer
Johnny . . . . Russell Crowe
Sam . . . . Robert Mammone
Jean . . . . Daphne Gray
Sid . . . . George Whaley
Marion . . . . Jacqy Phillips
Nev . . . . Patrick Ward
Peg . . . . May Lloyd
Jenny . . . . Emily Lumbers
Shorty . . . . Rodney Bell
Billy . . . . John Blair
Granddad . . . . Les Foxcroft

■ The emotional impact derived from George Ogilvie's first-rate direction, plus the fine thesping of a trio of exciting newcomers, bodes well for the commercial success of "The Crossing" on its home turf, and offshore possibilities are indicated.

"The Crossing," first production from Beyond Intl., is a classically constructed romantic drama about a teenage girl torn between two lovers in an outback town some 30 years ago.

The story takes place within the space of several hours on Anzac Day (the Australian equivalent of Veterans Day), starting with a dawn service of remembrance and ending soon after darkness has fallen. The tale is told from three different viewpoints, allowing conflicting emotions, ambitions, dreams and desires to intersect.

Meg (Danielle Spencer), is a farmer's daughter who had been in love with Sam (Robert Mammone), son of the local hotel-keeper. But Sam, frustrated with the limitations of small-town life, had ankled some 18 months earlier to find work in the city, and he chooses this particular day to return, unannounced, to persuade Meg to join him.

Meg, meanwhile, has become involved with Johnny (Russell Crowe), a clean-cut local boy whose father died of alcoholism (and whose tearful mother looks to be following the same route). When the film begins, Johnny and Meg have spent a night together in a barn and are discovered by Meg's father. It's naturally assumed the couple will marry, but Meg also is chafing at country life and seeking wider horizons.

Sam's return opens up another opportunity for her, and during the course of the day she is forced to decide between the two youths and two different paths into the future.

The fact that there's to be a tragic denouement to the triangular relationship is intimated throughout the film with significant images of heavy freight trains passing through the town and the railway crossing that's the starting point for the drag race held at midday by local rivals.

The three young leads are extremely effective, and their roles here could be significant stepping-stones. Spencer (previously seen in "What The Moon Saw") is a looker who radiates innocence, while Mammone and Crowe expertly depict the characteristics of the rivals, who are also close friends.

The supporting cast also is tops, with George Whaley (as Sam's publican father) and Patrick Ward (as Meg's old-fashioned father) the standouts. However, even the smallest parts in the film are precisely cast and winningly played.

Technical credits are firstrate. Jeff Darling's camerawork beautifully evokes the passing hours. Occasional tricksy moments (an angle shot of a train, speeding clouds) are minor blemishes.

Henry Dangar's editing of the climactic race to the railway crossing is firstrate. Also deserving a nod is Igor Nay's fine production design.

Martin Armiger's robust score is effective, as is the use of several songs whose lyrics take the place of explanatory dialog in some scenes (such as the arrival in town of Sam while "Nature Boy" is heard on the soundtrack).

This is Ogilvie's best film to date, and his sensitivity and command of actors (features of his distinguished stage career) have not been equaled in his previous films. The only quibble here is the tacked-on epilog, which not only removes the film from its 24-hour structure, but also attempts to leaven the tragic ending with some mundane images and alarmingly trite emotions. This scene could easily be excised, however.

The film compares interestingly with another recent Aussie pic about troubled teens from a country town in another era — "The Delinquents." Thanks to the first-rate casting and playing, "The Crossing" looms as a far more successful artistic and, in the end perhaps even commercial, success than the Kylie Minogué effort.

— *Strat.*

Struck By Lightning
(AUSTRALIAN)

Sydney A Dark Horse Pictures production. (Intl. sales, Beyond Films Ltd.) Executive producer, Terry J. Charatsis. Produced by Trevor Farrant. Directed by Jerzy Domaradzki. Screenplay, Farrant; camera (Fujicolor), Yuri Sokol; editor, Simon James; music, Paul Smyth; sound, Toivo Lember; production design, Peta Lawson; assistant director, David Wolfe-Barry; production manager, Lesley Parker; line producer, Su Armstrong; casting, Faith Martin. Reviewed at Colorfilm screening room, Sydney, April 12, 1990. Running time: **109 MIN.**

Ollie Rennie . . . . Garry McDonald
Pat Cannizzaro . . . . Brian Vriends
Jill McHugh . . . . . Catherine McClements
Kevin . . . . Brian Logan
Spencer . . . . Syd Brisbane
Gail . . . . Briony Williams
Noel . . . . Henry Salter
Also with: Denis Moore, Peter Douglas, Jocelyn Betheras, Dick Tomkins, Roger Haddad, Jeremy Anderson, Maria Donato, Vittorio Andreacchio, Judith Stratford, Dennis Olsen, Su Cruickshank, Daphne Grey.

■ **"Struck By Lightning" is a feel-good pic that could do excellent business in Australia and in key territories around the world.**

An inspiring tale, about a school for physically disabled adults, pic avoids mawkishness thanks to large dollops of salty, down-to-earth humor and a standout performance from Garry McDonald as the school's cynical director.

Initially, focus of attention is on Pat Cannizzaro (Brian Vriends), a cheerful physical education teacher (and keen soccer player) who gets fired from his job in a state school when he wrecks the school snack bar in protest against the junk food being sold to the children.

He gets a job at Saltmarsh (motto: "Independence With Dignity"), which is administered by a charitable foundation composed of status-seeking snobs and which is funded by government grants.

Saltmarsh is run by Ollie Rennie (McDonald), a bald, embittered alcoholic failure who calls his students "retards" and lusts vainly after pretty social worker Jill McHugh (Catherine McClements).

Ollie doesn't allow his charges to think for themselves, but Pat quickly discovers that most of the people at the school have lively minds. He encourages them to form a soccer team (male and female) and trains them in the sport to give them some new motivation in life.

That's the basis for an unpatronizing and genuinely human tale of achievement against the odds. The hopelessly inadequate players lose all their matches (one against a team of nurses) until, at the climax, the most advanced of them actually manages to score a single goal in a match against a team of convicts. They lose the match by a mile, but that single goal is a great victory in itself.

This is the first film Jerzy Domaradzki has made outside his native Poland, and he brings it off with great skill, emphasizing the Australian humor of the characters to excellent effect. Domaradzki, best known for his 1984 "The Great Race" (banned for a while by the Polish government), makes a seemingly effortless transition to an English-language picture.

Screenwriter and producer Trevor Farrant has come up with a warm and touching screenplay that more than makes up for his script contribution to the execrable "The Pirate Movie" of a few years back.

In "Struck By Lightning" (known as "Riders On The Storm" during production), Farrant takes a serious theme and gives it the warmth and entertainment values that should make audiences want to see it. A scene in which the prime minister's wife makes an official visit to Saltmarsh and is confronted by the institution's resident "flasher" is a comic highlight.

The large cast is made up of actors and a few genuinely disabled people (such as Jocelyn Betheras, who has Down syndrome and who beautifully plays the affectionate Jodie); the combination works well. Vriends is charismatic as the enthusiastic, good-hearted, but maladroit Pat, and McClements, though not as effective here as she was in Arch Nicholson's "Weekend With Kate," is charming as the love interest.

McDonald steals the film, however, with a droll performance as the self-pitying, sardonic Ollie. This popular comedian never has really scored in his film roles until now, but he could be in the running for a local acting award for his funny, touching portrayal.

Final scene, in which the "retards" rally round to defend him and express their affection for him after he's been fired from his job, is delightfully handled and marred only by a lengthy, and unneces-

sary, speech from Vriends.

Yuri Sokol, best known for his work with Paul Cox, does a very professional lighting job behind the camera, and all other technical credits are very professional. Beyond should rack up some useful sales with this one. — *Strat.*

Def By Temptation

Hollywood A Troma release of a Bonded Filmworks production. Executive producers, Charles Huggins, Kevin Harewood, Nelson George. Produced, written and directed by James Bond 3d. Camera (Technicolor), Ernest Dickerson; editor, Li-Shin Yu; music, Paul Laurence; sound, Ron Kalish; production design, David Carrington; art direction, Marc Henry Johnson; assistant directors, Marcus Turner, Tyrone M. Henderson; coproducers, Kervin Simms, Hajna O. Moss; casting, Bonded Enterprises, Hush Management. Reviewed at Cineplex Odeon Century Plaza Cinemas, L.A., April 27, 1990. Running time: **95 MIN.**

Joel . . . . James Bond 3d
K . . . . Kadeem Hardison
Dougy . . . . Bill Nunn
Temptress . . . . Cynthia Bond
Grandma . . . . Minnie Gentry

■ **Slated to get a gradual U.S. rollout from Troma, this stylish horror film promises to play extremely well both in urban markets and homevid.**

It's buoyed by a blend of knowing humor, genuine tension, eroticism and a terrific all-black cast. Pic is a rousing debut for writer-director-producer-star James Bond 3d.

Bond stars as a divinity student who goes to find himself in New York before entering the ministry and becomes prey to the demon Cynthia Bond, who is hell-bent on leading him astray and sullying his pure ascestral line.

He leaves the audience shaken and stirred with his direction, while Cynthia Bond is stunningly seductive and menacing as the demon. Kadeem Hardison (from tv's "A Different World") and Bill Nunn ("Do The Right Thing") provide comic highlights in fine supporting roles.

This low-budget effort manages to look far more opulent than its means, and features some excellent special effects. It's undoubtedly the best film Troma has released, having cashed in with schlocky cult pics like the "Toxic Avenger" series.

Bond says he plans to follow the pic with another in the same genre. If so, he may carve out a niche among black filmmakers, an area with creative and commercial potential. — *Bril.*

SHOWING AT THE CANNES FILM FESTIVAL

Porte aperte
(Open Doors)
(ITALIAN)

Rome An Istituto Luce/Italnoleggio release of an Erre Produzioni/Istituto Luce/Italnoleggio/ Urania Film production, in association with RAI-TV Channel 2. Produced by Angelo Rizzoli. Executive producers, Conchita Airoldi, Dino Di Dionisio. Directed by Gianni Amelio. Screenplay, Amelio, Vincenzo Cerami, with Alessandro Sermoneta, based on a novel by Leonardo Sciascia; camera (color), Tonino Nardi; editor, Simona Paggi; music, Franco Piersanti; art direction, Franco Velchi. Reviewed at Holiday Cinema, Rome, April 19, 1990. (In Cannes Film Festival, Directors Fortnight.) Running time: **111 MIN.**
Vito Di Francesco . . . Gian Maria Volontè
Consul . . . . Renato Carpentieri
    Also with: Ennio Fantastichini, Renzo Giovanpietro.

■ **A conscientious Sicilian judge saves a half-mad murderer from the death sentence in Gianni Amelio's finely scripted "Open Doors," a moral thriller that keeps viewer on the seat's edge.**

Though it lacked the emotional pitch to score high at Italian wickets, pic should attract audiences abroad and have a lively festival run. It opens the Directors Fortnight at Cannes.

Intelligent without being tearful, "Doors" paints a disturbing picture of Fascist Italy through an apparently nonpolitical trial. It also raises a clear voice against capital punishment.

Tommaso Scalia has confessed to a triple murder: His boss who fired him, the man who took his place and his wife. In 1937, the death sentence recently had been instituted, and the courtroom crowd at Scalia's trial loudly demands it. The 6-man jury includes one professional judge, Vito Di Francesco (Gian Maria Volontè). It is he who starts probing into the murderer's motivations, despite the hostility and derision of the onlookers.

What emerges is a sordid tangle of embezzlement and forced prostitution. With the aid of a simple farmer, Di Francesco swings the jury to a surprise sentence of life imprisonment, even though he knows it will be overturned in the appeals court. He is transferred out of Palermo for his trouble.

The consistently on-target Amelio brings out the darkness of Leonardo Sciascia's novel through slow, patient work. Likewise, Volontè's judge works with stubborn endurance, probing into corners and dragging out ugly conclusions. For a hero, he has a surprisingly sinister intensity.

Title comes from a warning meant to intimidate the judge: "Proper folk need to feel safe, to go to sleep with open doors." Film is full of closing doors, and only at the end does a really open space offer a breather from the oppressive atmosphere.

Cinematographer Tonino Nardi again demonstrates he is one of Italy's finest, giving an air of menace to an otherwise postcard Palermo with velvety blacks and sensuous shadows. Amelio has a taste for elegant, slightly stylized lensing that works well with this story. He wisely keeps his cerebral side in check, except for the closing scenes in the farmer's splendid library, a curious idea that rings a little false. — *Yung.*

La Captive du désert
(Prisoner Of The Desert)
(FRENCH)

Paris A Pari Film release of a Titane/ Double D Copyright coproduction. Executive producers, Pascale Dauman, Jean-Luc Ormière. Producers, Roger Diamantis, Jean-Bernard Feytoux, Jean-Luc Larguier. Written and directed by Raymond Depardon. Camera (color), Depardon; music, Jean-Jacques Lemètre; sound, Claudine Nougaret, Sophie Chiabaut, Gerard Lamps; assistant director, Patrice Martineau; production manager, Baudoin Capet. Reviewed at Gaumont, Neuilly, April 9, 1990. (In Cannes Film Festival, competing.) Running time: **100 MIN.**
    With: Sandrine Bonnaire.

■ **"Prisoner Of The Desert" is a laconic, hypnotically spare film from French photojournalist/documentary filmmaker Raymond Depardon. Repping France in the Cannes competition, pic walks a fine line between fascination and boredom, and probably will divide audiences into two vocal camps.**

"La Captive du désert" records the magnificent and terrifying beauty of the desert as experienced by a young French woman held captive by native rebels. Depardon, who wrote, directed and lensed, based his story on an incident he covered as a reporter in 1975: the capture and detention in Chad, for about 15 months, of a young Gallic researcher by rebel soldiers.

In his second fiction feature endeavor, Depardon isn't interested in historical or political reconstruction. There is no biographical info provided on the protagonist or exposition on the armed revolt of the indigents who took her hostage.

Depardon plunges us into the world of hostage and captors. The film's opening sequence is magnificent: against a vast desert landscape a caravan — camels, men, women and children — files before the stationary camera. Just as the shot begins to try our patience, there suddenly appears the figure of a white woman, flanked by two gun-bearing African escorts. The tone and theme are set.

There is no overt drama or suspense — the woman is under no immediate physical threat from her guardians — only the constant image of a young woman, yanked suddenly from her environment and entourage, fighting heat, physical discomfort, exhaustion, loneliness and despair. After months of captivity, during which she unsuccessfully attempts to escape, the rebels decide to free her.

No doubt Sandrine Bonnaire's performance as the captive will be underrated simply because she submitted to 2¹/₂ months of unsimulated rigors in the torrid heat of the Nigerian desert. But she endows her sketchy characterization with the subtlety and psychological ambiguity that makes this woman's plight all the more intriguing.

Depardon's desert imagery is stunning, alluring and repelling. The high quality of sound work by Claudine Nougaret and Sophie Chiabaut is a major contribution to the film's spell. — *Len.*

Ucho
(The Ear)
(CZECH-B&W)

Berlin A Barrandov Film Studios production. Directed by Karel Kachyna. Screenplay, Jan Prochazka, Kachyna, from a story by Prochazka; camera (b&w), Josef Illik; editor, Miroslav Hanek; music, Svatopluk Havelka; sound, Jiri Lenoch; production design, Ester Krumbachova, Ladislav Winkelhofer. Reviewed at Berlin Film Festival (market), Feb 18, 1990. (In Cannes Film Festival, competing.) Running time: **95 MIN.**
Anna . . . . Jirina Bohdalova
Ludvik . . . . Radoslav Brzobohaty
    With: Gustav Opocensky, Miloslav Holub, Lubor Tokos, Borivoj Navratil, Jiri Cisler.

■ **This nightmarish Czechoslovakian thriller, receiving its first public screening outside its home turf in a competing slot in Cannes, should grab plenty of attention thanks to its taut structure, terse script, stylish direction and lead performances.**

Banned for 20 years, "Ucho" was made at the very beginning of the illustrious new wave of Czechoslovak cinema, a movement that flourished beginning in about 1963.

The drama unfolds during one night, supposedly in the Stalinist '50s (though audiences, if they'd ever had a chance to see it, surely would have identified it with the tensions of the post-'68 period). Ludvik, a high-ranking government official, attends a reception with his wife, Anna. The marriage is obviously on the rocks, and the couple strain to be polite to each other.

At the reception, attended by Soviet military officers, Ludvik discovers that his immediate superior and other key government officials have just been arrested. Ludvik, sobered by uneasiness about his future, and a very drunken Anna arrive back at their suburban home to find things aren't as they should be. They've lost their keys (were they stolen?), but a supposedly locked door turns out to be unlocked.

Once inside, they find they have no power and no phone, but lights are on in the next-door house. There's a sinister-looking car parked down the street and indications that someone might have been searching the house.

In this oppressive situation, the tensions between husband and wife explode into a violent argument, interrupted by the ringing of the doorbell. The latenight visitors are drunken partygoers returning the lost keys. After they leave, Ludvik and Anna discover a number of listening devices ("ears") scattered around the house.

Director Karel Kachyna, a 46-year-old veteran when the film was made, builds the tension brilliantly. The party sequences (shown as flashbacks) are filled with mordant humor: Officials whisper mysteriously to each other, Russians get drunk, women congregate together at one end of the room. Somebody notes that all the waiters must belong to the secret police because they're such lousy waiters.

The increasingly bitter domestic battle reaches a climax just as the husband realizes he may be the next victim of an apparent purge. Thanks to Kachyna's clever direction and Josef Illik's subtle black

& white camerawork, the nightmarish aspects of the situation are powerfully presented. There's a wholly satisfactory conclusion to the drama.

Kachyna and dissident writer Jan Prochazka worked together before ("Carriage To Vienna"), and they make a fine team.

Following the Golden Bear won by Jiri Menzel's long-banned "Larks On A String," made a year before "The Ear," it looks as though 1990 could be the year of rediscovery of the Czech cinema. Kachyna's film is a revelation and a prime example of suspense in the cinema. — Strat.

Przesluchanie
(The Interrogation)
(POLISH)

Berlin A Unit X, Zespoly Filmowe production. Produced by Tadeuz Drewno. Directed by Ryszard Bugajski. Screenplay, Bugajski, in association with Janusz Dymek; camera (color), Jacek Petrycki; editor, Katarzyna Maciejko; sound, Danuta Zankowska; production design, Janusz Sosnowski; assistant director, Hanna Hartowicz. Reviewed at the Berlin Film Festival (market), Feb. 17, 1990. (Competing in Cannes film fest). Running time: **122 MIN.**
Antonia Dziwisz . . . . . . Krystyna Janda
Zawada . . . . Janusz Gajos
Morawsky . . . . Adam Ferency
Witowska . . . . Agnieszka Holland
Also with: Anna Romantowska, Bozena Dykiel, Olgiard Lukaszewicz.

■ **The last banned Polish film to be taken off the shelf and shown to the world, "The Interrogation," which bears a 1982 date, is a devastating and genuinely chilling prison drama graced by an exceptional performance from lead actress Krystyna Janda.**

Selected to compete in the Cannes fest, pic should at least be in the running for an acting prize.

Set in 1951, though with obvious allusions to the imposition of martial law 30 years later, "The Interrogation" is told entirely from the point of view of Antonia Dziwisz, a flighty nightclub singer who, in the opening sequence, quarrels with her husband after she finishes her evening performance, and goes off on a drunken binge with two strangers who turn out to be plainclothes police.

They deliver her, in a drunken stupor, to police headquarters where she's stripped, searched and thrown into a filthy cell with other women. Unable to comprehend what happened to her, and certain, at first, that it must be a mistake,

Tonia tries in vain to reason with the authorities.

A long interrogation begins, with two officers taking turns asking her the most intimate questions that seem to have no purpose. Only gradually does she realize that her "confessions" will be used to frame other, far more important, people in an upcoming political trial.

Tonia endures months of political and physical torture, with the constant fear she will be summarily shot. Her husband is brought to visit her, only to tell her he wants a divorce. She attempts suicide (in an especially rugged scene) by biting her wrists. And, gradually, she finds herself attracted to the the younger, and marginally more sympathetic interrogator, an attraction leaving her in an even worse plight: pregnant.

The film is a showcase for the talent of its leading actress. Janda is extraordinary as the victim of this massive, and for a long time inexplicable, injustice. But there's also a strong supporting cast, which includes film director Agnieszka Holland ("Angry Harvest," "To Kill A Priest") as a woman who's been forced to confess she was a spy for the U.S.

Filmmaker Ryszard Bugajski is to be commended for making this more than just a harrowing exploration of state inhumanity towards the individual. He makes it clear the inquisitors themselves believe in the innocence of their victims, which makes them even more monstrous. In one scene, Tonia calls her persecutor "gestapo," and receives a chilling lecture about how much worse the Nazis were.

The very grim nature of the subject matter will obviously limit wide audience appeal for this powerful film, but there should be worldwide arthouse interest in Janda's performance and in this rigorous, but unquestionably depressing, picture. — Strat.

Benim Sinemelarim
(My Cinemas)
(TURKISH)

Istanbul A Mine Film production. Produced by Kadri Yurdatap. Written and directed by Füruzan, based on her novel of the same name. Camera (color), Ertuno Senkay; editor, Mevlüt Kocak; music, Selim Atakan. Reviewed at Istanbul Film Festival, April 12, 1990. (In Cannes Film Festival, Intl. Critics Week.) Running time: **116 MIN.**
Nesibe . . . . Hulya Avsar
Mother . . . . Sema Aybars
Father . . . . Yaman Okay

Also with: Aysegül Uygurer, Güzin Coragan.

■ **The basic plot of "My Cinemas," a desperate young woman from a poor and unhappy family turning to prostitution, is in the best Turkish melodramatic tradition. Distinguished by skillful handling and good acting, pic should attract notice at fests and specialty screenings.**

Pic's domestic success will be buoyed by presence of striking red-haired, green-eyed favorite Hülya Avsar as Nesibe. Subject is of universal appeal, and reminisces of the glory days of cinema are in vogue, although this version is far more pessimistic.

The film opens and closes with a nostalgic Felliniesque sequence as children chase a wagon displaying a blowup of Sinbad on horseback. To calliope music, a hawker booms out the traveling cinema show's program for the evening. It symbolizes the escape the silver screen provides for Nesibe from an early age.

Clips from '50s and '60s romances and musicals provide charming interludes. A more serious aspect of Nesibe's infatuation with movies is implied when she turns to prostitution, loveless couplings with much older men, to buy new outfits and emulate her role models on screen.

Nesibe's parents are the unemployed father (Yaman Okay) who resorts to blows when his authority is threatened, and the overworked and ineffectual mother (Sema Aybars). They are stereotypes in Turkish cinema, but are given a human dimension here.

Füruzan, who wrote the script from her novel, incorporates insightful details of Nesibe's psychology without sentimentality.

Avsar's range increases as film progresses, and she's especially believable in touching scenes on dates with a young naval officer.

Tech credits are fine. Lensing is conventional but good, and the piano/horn score is suitable but overbearing at times. The pic loses its connection with the cinema in parts and occasionally lags, but on the whole sustains interest.
— Sam.

SAN FRANCISCO FILM FESTIVAL REVIEWS

The Secret Of
The Secret Weapon
(ROMANIAN)

San Francisco An Artexim release, produced by Romaniafilm. Written and directed by Alexander Tatos. Camera (color), Vivi Dragan Vasile; editor, Mircea Ciociltei; music, Horia Moculescu; sound, Tiberiu Borcoman; art direction, Mircea Neagu; costumes, Lia Mantoc. Reviewed at the San Francisco Film Festival, May 1, 1990. No MPAA rating. Running time: **91 MIN.**
With: Victor Rebengiuc, Mircea Diaconu, Manuela Harabor, Adrian Paduraru, Carmen Galin, Mitica Popescu, Horatiu Malaele, Dem Radulescu, Aristide Teica, Emilia Dobrin Besoiu.

■ **Though colorful and expressive, "The Secret Of The Secret Weapon" unfortunately loses its wit in the subtitling.**

Supposedly, this last pic by the late Romanian writer-director Alexander Tatos casts a lot of barbs at a dictatorship he despised, but his best shots aren't evident in the translation.

Set in a mythical kingdom where people talk of discos but dress for the Dark Ages, "Weapon" takes on the mutual, and contradictory, attractions of peace and war, packaged in a contest to marry a beautiful princess. She, naturally enough, is most attracted to the peaceful hero while her father and his council are drawn to warriors and their weaponry.

There are additional subplots with doubtlessly added significance. But on the surface, most is silliness and slapstick with an abundance of fairy-tale touches and some music.

Art director Mircea Neagu and costumer Lia Mantoc both create a splendid background for exuberant performances. Without an underlying message to be grasped, however, attention begins to wander. — Har.

Thousand Pieces Of Gold

San Francisco An American Playhouse/Maverick Films/Kelly/Yamamoto/Film Four Intl. production. Produced by Kenji Yamamoto, Nancy Kelly. Exec producers, Lindsay Law, Sidney Kantor, John Sham. Directed by Kelly. Screenplay, Anne Makepeace, based on novel by Ruthanne Lum McCunn; camera, Bobby Bukowski; editor, Yamamoto; music, Gary Remal Malkin; sound, Judy Karp; production design, Dan Bishop; costume design, Lydia Tanji; assistant director, Eric (Elvis) Heffron; associate producer, Rachel Lyon; coproducer, Sarah Green; casting, Lora Kennedy, Bill McQuillen. Reviewed at the San

Francisco Film Festival, April 30, 1990. No MPAA Rating. Running time: **105 MIN.**

Lalu	Rosalind Chao
Charlie	Chris Cooper
Jim	Dennis Dun
Hong King	Michael Paul Chan

■ **Virtue, hard work and true love triumph over venality, hindrance and lust in "Thousand Pieces Of Gold," an intelligent and capable first feature from documentarian Nancy Kelly.**

Kelly approaches her picture with a minimum of passion, saving herself from the clichés of romantic page-turners and the temptations of beating hearts and throbbing loins.

"Gold's" suffering heroine and handsome hero are so carefully cut from popular historical fiction that it's no small feat for Rosalind Chao and Chris Cooper to stay centered in this gentle little love story.

Though set against a perilous background on the Gold Rush frontier, nothing very terrible ever happens. This probably is a good thing, because the heroine has a tendency toward suicide and the hero responds to crises by getting drunk.

Sold into slavery to feed her starving family in China, Chao ends up on the market in San Francisco's Barbary Coast, where she is purchased by Dennis Dun on behalf of Michael Paul Chan, a saloon-keeping pimp in a small mining settlement.

Chao reluctantly is resigned to becoming Chan's love-slave, but she refuses to service the rest of the boys. She is advised on this by the kindly Cooper, whose role in the community is unclear except that he owns Chan's saloon and is one of it best customers.

The young girl's only prospect for getting home to China seems to be Dun, who's smitten with her on their mule trek north. He is willing to buy her away from Chan as soon as he can save the money from his mule-train business. While Dun's away working, however, Chan decides to raffle off Chao to his regular customers.

Cooper wins her in a poker game, and Dun returns to find the couple cohabiting platonically. But he doesn't know it's platonic, and in one of those wonderful melodramatic scenes in which nobody tells anybody anything, Dun jumps on his conclusions and rides out of town while Chao silently watches her best chance for salvation disappear on the horizon.

Fortunately, the relationship and the performances between Chao and Cooper start to ripen at this point. Given the freedom to prosper, Chao does so with an eye on a ticket home to China. But she also falls in love with Cooper, who wants to build her a little nest in the West.

This obviously is a conflict. But it will be resolved. In the process, Kelly comes up against problems of racism and feminism, but she keeps the love story progressing toward a happy ending. You can hear the audience sigh contentedly when the outcome is revealed in an end-title. — *Har.*

Finzan
(MALIAN)

San Francisco A Kora-Films production. Written and directed by Cheick Oumar Sissoko. Camera (color), Sissoko; editor, Ouoba Motandi; sound, Ibrahim Khalil Thera. Reviewed at the San Francisco Film Festival, May 1, 1990. No MPAA rating. Running time: **107 MIN.**

With: Diarrah Sanogo, Namory Keita, Saidou Toure, Moussa Keita, Helene Diarra.

■ **If widely shown in the West, "Finzan" might evoke furious sympathy for the plight of its African tribal women. Unfortunately, it won't be seen much in the villages where its impact could do the most good.**

In his second feature after "Garbage Boys" in 1987, writer-director-photographer Cheick Oumar Sissoko shows a sure hand. With little tech help in his impoverished surroundings, he mixes concern for a grim and brutal existence with just enough lightheartedness for relief.

Diarrah Sanogo is quietly powerful as a young woman suddenly freed by the death of the old man she was forced to marry as a teen. According to village custom, however, she is now obliged to join the harem of her brother-in-law, an even worse prospect. She refuses, earning the wrath of the village elders and her own family. Though the other women share her contempt for their men, they have little to offer Sanogo in the way of alternatives.

Her problem, however, almost seems slight compared to the plight of a younger friend who has somehow reached maturity without undergoing the tribal rite of female circumcision. Though this amounts to an outrageous sexual mutilation in the name of marital fidelity, the director is honest in demonstrating how the practice is encouraged and maintained by the village women as much as the men. Even Sanogo herself seems surprised at her friend's reluctance.

Sissoko doesn't have to get explicit in handling this uncomfortble subject. Just the sight of a razor against the victim's screams is enough to set audiences squirming.

Not surprisingly, the director has no neat ending for circumstances brought on by centuries of conditioning. But there's always a chance that powerful films like "Finzan" can help bring the centuries to an end. — *Har.*

HOUSTON INTL. FILM FESTIVAL REVIEWS

Just Like In The Movies

Houston An Alon Kasha Prods. presentation. Produced by Alon Kasha. Written and directed by Bram Towbin, Mark Halliday. Camera (color), Peter Fernberger; editor, Jay Keuper; music, John Hill; production design, Marek Dobrowolski; costume design, Linda Fisher; casting, Brian Chavanne. Reviewed at the Houston Intl. Film Festival, April 24, 1990. Running time: **90 MIN.**

Ryan Legrand	Jay O. Sanders
Dean	Alan Ruck
Tura	Katherine Borowitz
Vernon	Michael Jeter
Carter	Alex Vincent

■ **Filmmakers Bram Towbin and Mark Halliday establish themselves as fresh talents worthy of serious attention with "Just Like In The Movies," a small-budget, high-interest comedy-drama that may find a modestly profitable life beyond the festival circuit.**

The codirectors, graduates of the Dartmouth College film program, have drawn on their experience as cinematographers for a private investigator to fashion a screenplay that could be described as a seriocomic cross between "The Conversation" and "Kramer Vs. Kramer." But it plays much better than that sounds.

Jay O. Sanders is exceptionally good as Ryan Legrand, a New York investigator who specializes in matrimonial cases. Legrand takes a dead-serious, just-the-facts approach to gathering evidence of adultery, leaving most of the jokes to his free-spirited cinematographer,

Dean (Alan Ruck).

Even when a wife starts to break down on hearing the messy details of her husband's affair, Legrand remains all business and simply offers to call back at another time.

Legrand has kept a tight leash on his emotions for far too long, a fact that even a control freak such as himself recognizes as unhealthy. So he joins a video dating service, and gets involved with a struggling actress, Tura (Katherine Borowitz), who's incredibly tolerant of, and bemused by, his uptight behavior.

Her tolerance has its limits. When Legrand ruins a weekend with her friends with his moody peevishness, she drifts away from him. Heartbroken, Legrand responds the only way he knows how — he begins a surveillance of her.

During all this, Legrand periodically attempts to re-establish a bond with his pre-teen son, Carter (Alex Vincent), fearing the boy prefers to spend time with his ex-wife's new husband. Trouble is, Legrand is even less temperamentally suited for fatherhood than he is for romantic giving.

Only when it's obvious Tura is a lost cause does Legrand find some partial redemption in becoming a better, more emotionally accessible parent.

Towbin and Halliday do their film a disservice by not having more scenes of Legrand and Carter together, scenes that would help the father-son relationship have more compelling impact. Even so, "Just Like In The Movies" is largely successful in its balance of sensitive drama and oddball humor.

The biggest laughs come from incidental details and loony supporting characters: a passerby plays Mozart on his boom box; a birthday party magician worries about impressing small children, and a zonked-out blind date (a great bit by Margaret Devine) evidences an unhealthy regard for the killer rat from "Willard."

Sanders gives a fearless performance, refusing to soften Legrand's selfishness or emotional bullying in his dealings with Tura and Carter. At the same time, though, he manages to let enough of Legrand's desperate yearning and basic decency shine through.

Ruck provides energetic comic relief with brutally sage wisecracking. "Just Like In The Movies" makes the most of a limited budget, and has a thoroughly professional polish. It has definite sleeper potential. — *Ley.*

Robot Jox

Houston A Triumph release of an Epic Prods. presentation of a Charles Band production. Produced by Albert Band. Executive producer, Charles Band. Directed by Stuart Gordon. Screenplay, Joe Haldeman, from story by Gordon; camera (color), Mac Ahlberg; editor, Ted Nicolaou, Lori Scott Ball; music, Frederic Talgorn; production design, Giovanni Natalucci; visual effects, David Allen. Reviewed at Houston Intl. Film Festival, April 28, 1990. MPAA Rating: PG-13. Running time: **96 MIN.**

Achilles	Gary Graham
Athena	Anne-Marie Johnson
Alexander	Paul Koslo
Commissioner Jameson	Robert Sampson
Dr. Matsumoto	Danny Kamekona
Prof. Laplace	Hilary Mason
Tex Conway	Michael Alldredge

■ **After three years of delays caused by the mid-production collapse of Empire Pictures, Stuart Gordon's "Robot Jox" finally emerges as a disappointingly routine sci-fi adventure.**

Flashy special effects might have made it more impressive, but the $6.5-million budget allows only for painfully obvious miniature work that won't impress the film's target audience. Expect minimal theatrical exposure before a quick homevid release.

Scripted by sci-fi writer Joe Haldeman from Gordon's original story, pic is set 50 years after a nuclear holocaust. War has been abolished, but the Common Market (the U.S. and surviving allies) still competes for territory with the Confederation (the USSR).

The superpowers settle their disputes via 1-on-1 bouts between heavily armed, 120-ft. robots operated by highly trained "robot jox." Achilles (Gary Graham), Common Market champ, hopes to score the 10th and final victory of his career against the sadistic Alexander (Paul Koslo).

During their match, however, Alexander launches an unauthorized projectile at his opponent, and misses. While trying to shield spectators from the weapon, Achilles crashes into the grandstand, killing more than 300 fans.

Seriously spooked, Achilles retires, abandoning the game to a new breed of robot jox: test-tube babies ("tubies"), trained since birth to pilot the robots. Athena (Anne-Marie Johnson), an ambitious tubie, wins the honor of fighting the rematch against Alexander. When she's knocked down for the count, Achilles steps in to fight one last time.

Surprisingly, considering the grisly tongue-in-cheek humor of his "Re-Animator" and "From Beyond," Gordon treats the plot here with a plodding seriousness.

Koslo wins top acting honors (virtually by default) as the gleefully wicked Alexander with a touch of Klaus Maria Brandauer's flamboyance. Other cast members, including Michael Alldredge as a corrupt robot jox trainer, are sincere and colorless. Tech credits reflect a tight budget. The robots appear to be knock-offs of the Transformer toys.

For the record, "Robot Jox" (known as "Robojox" before the "Robocop" producers complained) originally was planned as a Christmas 1987 release. After interiors were shot at the Empire studio in Italy, Empire crumbled, and pic shut down for eight months. Filming resumed in L.A. under the auspices of Trans World (now Epic), and the robot model work (by David Allen) was shot in the Mojave Desert.

Per the director, Triumph plans a late fall U.S. release. — *Ley.*

Chopper Chicks In Zombietown

Houston A Triax Entertainment Group release of a Chelsea Partners presentation. Produced by Maria Snyder. Written and directed by Dan Hoskins. Camera (color), Tom Fraser; editor, W.O. Garrett; music, Daniel May; special effects, Art Brewer; casting, Billy Da Mota; makeup effects, Edward French; associate producer, James Hardy; executive producer, Arthur Sarkissian. Reviewed at the Houston Intl. Film Festival, April 27, 1990. MPAA rating: R. Running time: **89 MIN.**

Dede	Jamie Rose
Rox	Catherine Carlen
Jojo	Kristina Loggia
Mae Clutter	Martha Quinn
Ralph Willum	Don Calfa

■ **"Chopper Chicks in Zombietown" is a surprisingly funny B-movie spoof with a feminist edge and a crafty sense of humor. With the right handling, this occasionally hilarious deadpan farce could break out of the midnight circuit, and attract a crossover audience in mainstream bookings.**

Writer-director Dan Hoskins, another USC film school grad, has a great deal of fun scrambling genres. It's a classic story of bikers invading a secluded town and rattling the suspicious populace.

At the same time, it's another classic story: The local mad scientist is killing off citizens, reviving them as zombie slaves, and generally making the town a miserable place to live.

Among the big differences here, the bikers are leather-and-chain-wearing women. Leader of the pack Rox (Catherine Carlen) is a hard-bitten (but not bad-looking) motorcycle mama who proudly proclaims herself "a big, bad bulldyke." Her gang, the Cycle Sluts, includes an ex-homecoming queen (Jamie Rose), an AWOL demolitions expert (Kristina Loggia) and a sex-crazed "nymfomaniac" (Whitney Reis).

The mad scientist is played by Don Calfa, who is decked out to be a dead ringer for Robert Mitchum in "Night of the Hunter." He admits he's not making zombies for money or for science: "I'm just mean!"

Hoskins isn't able to sustain the level of lunacy throughout "Chopper Chicks," and several scenes suggest the Harley-riding actresses have been asked to vamp until a funny line comes along. Worse, he doesn't always trust his own material. To make sure the audience laughs when the ersatz "Living Dead" zombies run amok, he underscores their approach with Spike Jones-type music.

Still, there is a lot to laugh about, and dialogue that moviegoers will quote for days afterward. The funniest moment comes when zombies surround a stalled bus full of blind orphans, and the most ill-tempered of them cracks: "Blind! No parents! And now this!" Performances are effectively straight-faced, making them very funny indeed in this context.

Carlen goes straight over the top, but remains in character, even when she launches into a rousing, teasing rock 'n' roll number at the local pool hall-cafe. When she sings "Better do what your big mama told ya," she is, quite simply, formidable.

Martha Quinn of MTV (and movie theater blurbs for Sprite) has a clever cameo as a small-town dweller not at all happy to see her late mother come back as a zombie. Tech credits are better than they have to be. — *Ley.*

Nerds Of A Feather

Houston An Intl. Investment Holdings Ltd. presentation of a Romeo production. (Intl. sales, Double Helix Films.) Produced and codirected by Romeo M. (Mario R. Milano). Directed by Gary Graver. Screenplay, Mario R. Milano, based on his original story; camera (color), Richard Aguilar; editor, Terry Anderson; production design, Sterling von Franck; executive producer, Cyris P. Lawson 2d. Reviewed at the Houston Intl. Film Festival, April 27, 1990. Running time: **90 MIN.**

Peter	Mario R. Milano
Jennifer	Kathleen Kichta
Professor	Pat McCormick
Anna	Anya Karin
Granny	Charles Pierce

■ **"Nerds of a Feather" (a.k.a. "Young Hearts, Deadly Spies") is a grotesquely unfunny comedy, painful to watch and probably impossible to market.**

Produced, written and "codirected" as a vanity production by Mario R. Milano, actor and real estate investor, pic plays like a mutant hybrid of juvenile Jerry Lewis farce and '60s-era spy spoof, with some Benny Hill-type pratfalls and vulgar jokes tossed in for bad measure.

Milano plays a chronically unemployable klutz who falls for a pretty coworker (Kathleen Kichta) at a retirement home.

Pat McCormick plays Kichta's uncle, a defecting Soviet scientist who makes his way to his niece in Los Angeles, pursued by a beautiful blond KGB agent (Anya Karin), a dwarf assistant (Peter Risch) and midget Russian commandos.

Nothing that happens to any of these people is the least bit amusing. Most of the cast, including female impersonator Charles Pierce as Kichta's fortune-teller aunt, overact stridently.

Production values are second-rate. One good laugh during the opening credits is shot in the style of a 007 film. It's all downhill after that. — *Ley.*

Bird On A Wire

New York A Universal Pictures release of a Badham-Cohen Entertainment Group/Interscope Communications production. Produced by Rob Cohen. Executive producers, Ted Field, Robert W. Cort. Directed by John Badham. Screenplay, David Seltzer, Louis Venosta, Eric Lerner, from story by Venosta, Lerner; camera (Widescreen, Deluxe color), Robert Primes; editor, Frank Morriss, Dallas Puett; music, Hans Zimmer; sound (Dolby), Rick Patton; production design, Philip Harrison; art direction, Richard Hudolin; set decoration, Rose Marie McSherry; costume design, Wayne Finkelman, Eduardo Castro, Monique Stranan (Vancouver); assistant director, Peter Marshall; production manager, Matthew O'Connor; 2d unit director, Cohen; 2d unit camera, Peter McLennan; aerial unit director, James Gavin; aerial camera, Frank Holgate; stunt coordinators, Mic Rodgers (L.A.), Betty Thomas (Vancouver); special effects coordinator, John Thomas; coproducers, Fitch Cady, Venosta, Lerner; associate producers, Dana Satler, Keith Rubinstein; casting, Mike Fenton, Judy Taylor, Lynda Gordon, Lynne Carrow. Reviewed at Beekman theater, N.Y., May 10, 1990. MPAA Rating: PG-13. Running time: 110 MIN.
Rick Jarmin . . . . Mel Gibson
Marianne Graves . . . . Goldie Hawn
Sorenson . . . . David Carradine
Diggs . . . . Bill Duke
Joe Weyburn . . . . . Stephen Tobolowsky
Rachel Varney . . . . Joan Severance
Marvin . . . . Harry Caesar
Lou Baird . . . . Jeff Corey
Raun . . . . Alex Bruhanski
Jamie . . . . John Pyper-Ferguson
Mr. Takawaki . . . . Clyde Kusatsu

■ "Bird On A Wire" is an overproduced, tedious road movie that's the first of the summer mega-budgeted pics to open. That early-bird timing plus superstar casting should yield a couple of good weeks at the boxoffice, with foreign chances better.

Frank Capra's "It Happened One Night" established the format, but John Badham is stuck with a terrible script on this '90s version. Emphasis for nearly two hours is on the stars of this calculated, topheavy vehicle. Only the chemistry of Goldie Hawn and Mel Gibson makes the film watchable.

Gibson plays a shnook who's been hiding out for 15 years under an FBI witness relocation program. He gave testimony on a drug deal and the man he fingered (David Carradine) is just out of prison. Contrived and thoroughly unconvincing plot cog has Gibson discovered incognito by old flame Hawn at the Detroit gas station where he works just as Carradine and partner Duke catch up with him. Resulting shootout throws Hawn and Carradine together on the lam for the rest of the pic.

Though storyline is simple-minded and without depth, pic nonetheless has tons of verbal exposition. Needless confusion is caused by beginning the film with '60s hit song "Aquarius" from "Hair," followed by several poorly done flashbacks limning Hawn, Gibson and deceased pal John Pyper-Ferguson in '60s antics.

However, the good old days here are closer to 1975, an anachronism apparently caused by casting. Rather than have Hawn and Gibson be 45 (i.e., lovers in the '60s), they're each 35 here. The thesps' 11-year age difference is belied by Hawn's youthful figure and intact beauty, but fans are bound to recall the "Laugh-In" girl's career longevity compared to "Mad Max."

Rekindling of duo's romance is best thing about the repetitive chase format, set in numerous U.S. locations but shot almost entirely in British Columbia. Brightest sequence is enlivened by a brief role for lovely Joan Severance as a veterinarian and romantic rival, but she's written out of the episodic script quickly. Character actors ranging from Carradine and Duke as stock nemeses to Jeff Corey as a senile old pal are given wafer-thin roles.

Both stars show off their naked posteriors (assuming no doubles were on the payroll) as a sort of in-joke that is more cryptic than entertaining. Similarly, a sequence set in Wisconsin reuniting Gibson with several swishy hairdressers who were former coworkers is not funny enough to overcome the antiquated aspects of the material.

Main kudos go to British designer Philip Harrison, who's allowed to run hog wild in a large-scale climax set at a zoo exhibit depicting a Brazilian rain forest. In this final reel Badham turns off the comedy, switching to cliff-hanger suspense and grisly violence (a bad guy eaten by piranhas) that doesn't come off. Elsewhere the roller coaster ride is enlivened by dangerous-looking stuntwork and solid mechanical effects.

Hans Zimmer's perky musical score is a plus. — Lor.

Cadillac Man

Hollywood An Orion Pictures release of a Donaldson/Roven-Cavallo production. Produced by Charles Roven, Roger Donaldson. Directed by Donaldson. Screenplay, Ken Friedman; camera (Deluxe color), David Gribble; editor, Richard Francis-Bruce; music, J. Peter Robinson; sound (Dolby), Jay Bockelheide; production design, Gene Rudolf; art direction, Patricia Woodbridge; set decoration, Justin Scoppa Jr.; assistant directors, Lewis Gould, Gina Randazzo; associate producer, Ted Kurdyla; casting, David Rubin. Reviewed at the UA Coronet Theater, Westwood, May 9, 1990. MPAA Rating: R. Running time: 97 MIN.
Joey O'Brien . . . . Robin Williams
Larry . . . . Tim Robbins
Tina . . . . Pamela Reed
Joy Munchack . . . . Fran Drescher
Harry Munchack . . . . . . Zack Norman
Donna . . . . Annabella Sciorra
Lila . . . . Lori Petty
Little Jack Turgeon . . . . . Paul Guilfoyle

■ This dilapidated Robin Williams vehicle has the distinction of being the loudest film of 1990 and one of the worst. Actor's manic energy and string of recent hits should help it coast to some early b.o. before the flat script and direction bring "Cadillac Man" to a screeching halt.

Denied an opportunity to showcase his deft rapid-fire comic skills, Williams produces few laughs amid wreckage of the screenplay and poorly paced direction.

Only Tim Robbins gets out alive as a crazed, simple-minded, cuckolded husband who ultimately makes hostages of the womanizing Joey (Williams) and everyone else in the car dealership where he works, suspecting correctly that his wife (Annabella Sciorra) is having an affair.

While hardly a stretch for Robbins, who employs many of the puzzled expressions that endeared him to audiences in "Bull Durham," role is at least consistent in its denseness, more than can be said for anything else in the film.

Pic opens with a funeral scene that has car salesman Williams in voiceover pondering whether to pitch a grieving widow. Film later employs direct-to-camera addresses as he drives down the street discussing selling. Puzzlingly, pic abandons both practices.

Donaldson moves leisurely through the first half of the film, introducing the audience to Joey's ex-wife (Pamela Reed) and various mistresses. Joey's spending in relation to women is equally promiscuous, and he's in danger of losing his job.

Boring pic's salvation is supposed to occur when Robbins crashes into the dealership, setting in motion a series of events that will ultimately simplify Joey's life.

Unfortunately, the segment is so shrill, it's almost unwatchable. Customers and dealers respond to the raid with a numbing chorus of shrieks, while Robbins answers with more screams and gunfire.

Joey becomes the point man in defusing the hostage situation, though there's no hint in his character as to why he might sacrifice himself to save his philandering boss (Paul Guilfoyle).

Williams lapses in and out of what seems to be a New York-Italian street accent. Aside from being a smart aleck, however, he's rarely funny and shows little depth until the predictable ending.

Some minor pleasures can be found in smaller roles drawn from the N.Y. street scene, especially Lauren Tom as a pushy and abusive waitress in a neighborhood dim sum restaurant.

Tech credits are ho-hum, and the score over the final scenes is cloying. "Cadillac Man" is a lemon. — Bril.

Any Man's Death

New York An INI Entertainment Group release of a Goldenberg Films presentation of an Intl. Entertainment Corp. production, in association with Independent Networks. Executive producers, Joseph Goldenberg, Sandi Conolly. Produced by John Karie, S.D. Nethersole. Directed by Tom Clegg. Screenplay, Iain Roy, Chris Kelly; camera (Technicolor), Vincent G. Cox; editor, Max Lemon; music, Jeremy Lubbock; sound (Dolby), Philip Key; production design, Robert van de Coolwijk; assistant director, Howard Rennie; production manager, Carol Hickson; casting, Callie Bristow, Kevin Alber. Reviewed at Criterion 6 theater, N.Y., May 11, 1990. MPAA Rating: R. Running time: 110 MIN.
Leon Abrams . . . . John Savage
Schiller/Bauer . . . . William Hickey
Gerlind . . . . Mia Sara
Gantz . . . . Ernest Borgnine
Harvey . . . . Michael Lerner

■ "Any Man's Death" turns out to be a preachy morality play instead of an action pic. Made at the height of the 1988 South African production boom, pic is another video-ready title that doesn't hold up well on the big screen.

John Savage indulges in some laughable tics and method mannerisms as a burnt-out reporter sent by tyrannical editor Michael Lerner to Namibia to get the story behind some mysterious photos.

He ends up discovering Nazi war criminals, contacts the Israelis and comes up against a crisis of conscience.

Iain Roy and Chris Kelly's pretentious screenplay tries to address important issues, but is uncinematic. Helmer Tom Clegg, known for his tv work and features like "McVicar," founders in the final reels, culminating in a 20-minute talking head exchange between Savage and snake researcher William Hickey. Latter plays a Jew who assisted Nazi death camp experiments.

This boring talkathon is followed by an anticlimax of hammy Ernest Borgnine spewing Nazi venom in a role usually essayed by Donald Pleasence. Naturally the Israelis pick up Borgnine for a little glass booth action, but not before Savage is duped into committing himself for once on a moral issue.

Hickey brings conviction to his role, overcoming most of its clichés. Mia Sara handles her accent best and adds diverting beauty to the bleak African expanses.

Fans will chortle over the dubious casting as an Israeli secret agent of South African action star James Ryan (star a decade ago of "Kill Or Be Killed" and other films for Film Ventures Intl., now a subsid of the U.S. backer of "Any Man's Death"). — Lor.

Elliot Fauman, Ph.D.

New York A Taurus Entertainment release of a Ventcap Film Partners production. (Intl. sales, Double Helix Films). Executive producers, Stan Wakefield, Jerry Silva. Produced, written and directed by Ric Klass. Camera (Precision color), Erich Roland; editor, Judith Herbert; music, Roger Trefousse; sound, Jim Gilchrist; production design, Henry Shaffer; art direction, Tony Cisek; costume design, Sheri Dunn; assistant director, Steve Apicella; production manager, Karen Renaudin. Reviewed at UA Eastside theater, N.Y., May 11, 1990. MPAA Rating: PG-13. Running time: 86 MIN.
Elliot Fauman . . . . Randy Dreyfuss
Meredith Dashley . . . . . Jean Kasem
Stella . . . . Tamara Williams
Stromberg . . . . Shelley Berman
Denton . . . . . . Bryan Michael McGuire
Gene . . . . John Canada Terrell

■ This woefully amateurish comedy reps the bottom rung of theatrical release. Padded 1-joke exercise is suited for undemanding video audiences.

Fledgling filmmaker Ric Klass has little cinematic feel for a tale as old as "The Seven Year Itch:" nerdy guy falls for beautiful woman with little girl voice.

Randy Dreyfuss is a psychology prof researching hookers for a breakthrough paper leading to tenure at his Washington, D.C. area college. He's first attracted to brunet streetwalker Tamara Williams, but gets a film-long crush on Jean Kasem, styled to look like Brigitte Nielsen in the unconvincing role of a screen/stage star who pretends to be a prostie once Dreyfuss mistakes her for one.

Film goes nowhere in its lame spoofing of academia and street life. A lengthy sequence of a pimps convention in a laundromat is typical of pic's embarrassingly claustrophobic nature, often looking like a home movie shot in 35m.

Young lead actor unwisely imitates the vocal delivery of his cousin Richard Dreyfuss, whom he slightly resembles. He should find a persona of his own or he'll go the way of Neil Connery. Kasem is unattractively photographed here and slips out of her Jean Hagen ("Singin' In The Rain") accent too often to be convincing.

Newcomer Williams shows promise, but Klass inexplicably writes her out of the romantic triangle early to focus on Kasem/Dreyfuss. Supporting cast, including John Canada Terrell of "She's Gotta Have It," is enthusiastic. Shelley Berman is unfunny as a prof wearing a bad rug, as well as doing a pointless Julia Child imitation in drag. — Lor.

Honeymoon Academy

New York A Triumph release from Trans World Entertainment of a Sarlui/Diamant presentation of a Fidelity Films/Paul Maslansky production. Executive producers, Paul Maslansky, Eric Ellenbogen. Produced by Tony Anthony. Directed by Gene Quintano. Screenplay, Quintano, Jerry Lazarus, from Quintano's story; camera (CFI color), John Cabrera; editor, Hubert C. de la Bouillerie; music, Robert Folk; sound (Ultra-Stereo). Tony Smyles; assistant director, David Ian; stunt director, Alain Petit; 2d unit director-associate producer, David Lipman; postproduction supervisor, Fima Noveck; casting, Ed Mitchell. Reviewed at 23d St. West 1 theater, N.Y., May 11, 1990. MPAA Rating: PG-13. Running time: 94 MIN.
Chris . . . . Kim Cattrall
Sean McDonald . . . . Robert Hays
Doris . . . . Leigh Taylor-Young
Alex . . . . Charles Rocket
Lance . . . . Lance Kinsey
Lazos . . . . Christopher Lee

■ Dumped unceremoniously into the marketplace by Sony's Triumph label, "Honeymoon Academy" is an old-fashioned chase comedy that wastes the talents of Kim Cattrall in her first topbilled role.

Depressing b.o. prospects are reflected in zero paying customers showing up for a 9:30 opening night performance at the Manhattan theater where it was reviewed, following no press screenings.

Pic's inappropriate title is an afterthought based on the success of exec producer Paul Maslansky's "Police Academy" films. Lensed in spring 1988 as "For Better Or For Worse," pic has no school for newlyweds.

Cattrall, styled as a thin blond, is a State Dept. secret agent thrown together with Robert Hays in a library. It's love at first sight and they marry and go off to Madrid for a honeymoon, a gift from her boss Leigh Taylor-Young.

Taylor-Young sends agent Charles Rocket to force Cattrall to work during the holiday as a courier of payoff money for counterfeiter Christopher Lee. Endless slapstick and an unsuccessful detour into "Romancing The Stone" territory pad out pointless footage.

Cattrall projects the appeal of Laraine Day but deserves better pics. Hays is a capable physical comedian, playing straight in the manner of his "Airplane" persona in a role originally cast for Paul Reiser. Supporting cast, notably Rocket, is hammy. Lee brightens up the film very briefly.

Technical credits are acceptable, but for poorly synched dialog set in a forest with waterfalls interfering with direct sound recording. — Lor.

A Show Of Force

Hollywood A Paramount release of a John Strong production in association with Golden Harvest. Produced by Strong. Directed by Bruno Barreto. Executive producer, Raymond Chow. Screenplay, Evan Jones, Strong, based on the book "Murder Under Two Flags" by Anne Nelson; camera (Technicolor), James Glennon; editor, Henry Richardson; music, Georges Delerue; sound (Dolby), William Stevenson; production design, William J. Cassidy, Sonya Polansky; art direction, William J. Durrell Jr.; set decoration, Rob McGraw; costume design, Kathryn Morrison-Pahoa; assistant directors, John O'Connor, Ty Arnold, Luis Rosario Albert, Zachary Weintraub; coproducer, Fred Weintraub; associate producer, Robert E. Warner; casting, Pamela Rack. Reviewed at the Paramount Studio Theater, L.A., May 11, 1990. MPAA Rating: R. Running time: 93 MIN.
Kate . . . . Amy Irving
Luis Angel Mora . . . . Andy Garcia
Jesus Fuentes . . . . Lou Diamond Phillips
Howard . . . . Robert Duvall
Frank Curtin . . . . Kevin Spacey
Machado . . . . Erik Estrada

■ Even with its surprisingly good cast (many in misleadingly small roles), "A Show Of Force" will have a tough time exhibiting any force at the b.o.

Brazilian Bruno Barreto's first U.S. pic could've been dismissed as a tepid political thriller if it didn't degenerate into silliness in the final reel, wildly fictionalizing events on which it's based.

Foremost, pic's a showcase for Amy Irving, as a tv newswoman covering the death in 1978 of two alleged terrorists seeking Puerto Rican independence from the U.S.

Involved none-too-subtly in the deaths are an undercover cop (Lou Diamond Phillips) who framed the pair, and an ever-present FBI agent (Kevin Spacey) who may have his own insidious role.

While listed prominently in the credits, Robert Duvall and especially Andy Garcia appear in little more than cameos as Irving's squeamish boss and an opposition lawyer, respectively.

The film's events are a tired reworking of the Watergate era government-as-bad-guy theme. What ultimately blows the whole thing out of the water is a final scroll admitting that some characters are "wholly fictional," including Spacey's FBI agent, who figures prominently in the crowd-pleasing finale.

Although based on "real" events, pic feels so false that it carries little emotional weight, and it becomes hard not to feel completely jerked around.

Barreto ("Dona Flor And Her Two Husbands," MGM's "Gabriela,") slows the action with short, choppy scenes that add little to the narrative. There are also plenty of slow fade-outs, making one suspect a belated effort in the editing room to put this humpty-dumpty story back together again.

Irving isn't much of a lead, though the newswoman-in-peril setup (done about as convincingly in "Teenage Mutant Ninja Turtles") prevents that from being entirely her fault.

Georges Delerue's score works overtime, rushing to crescendos that far exceed the scope of the action. James Glennon's camera at least provides a pretty postcard for the island. — Bril.

COMPETING AT CANNES

Come See The Paradise

Cannes A 20th Century Fox release. Produced by Robert F. Colesberry. Written and directed by Alan Parker. Camera (Deluxe color), Michael Seresin; editor, Gerry Hambling; music, Randy Edelman; sound (Dolby), Danny Michael; production design, Geoffrey Kirkland; costume design, Molly Maginnis; art direction, John Willett; set decoration, Jim Erickson; assistant director, Aldric La' Auli Porter; casting, Lisa Clarkson. Reviewed at Cannes Intl. Film Festival (competing), May 13, 1990. No MPAA rating. Running time: **138 MIN.**

Jack McGurn . . . . Dennis Quaid
Lily Kawamura . . . . Tamlyn Tomita
Mr. Kawamura . . . . Sab Shimono
Mrs. Kawamura . . . . . . Shizuko Hoshi
Charlie Kawamura . . . . Stan Egi
Harry Kawamura . . . . Ronald Yamamoto
Dulcie Kawamura . . . . . Akemi Nishino
Joyce Kawamura . . . . . Naomi Nakano
Frankie Kawamura . . . Brady Tsurutani
Young Mini . . . . Elizabeth Gilliam
Middle Mini . . . . Shyree Mezick
Older Mini . . . . Caroline Junko
King Augie . . . . Pruitt Taylor
Vince Gerry McGurn . . . . Colm Meaney
Marge McGurn . . . . . Becky Ann Baker

■ In Alan Parker's richly mounted romantic saga of the World War II relocation camps, the Asian-American cast is exemplary and Dennis Quaid has never been better. Lengthy and convoluted script delays the bombing of Pearl Harbor until midpoint, making this less than the definitive story of the camps. Nonetheless, public curiosity should be high and b.o. solid.

Noble if overlong effort from Fox depicts the love affair between an Irish-American labor activist and a woman from a well-established Japanese family ripped from its Los Angeles roots. It's a step in the right direction for American pics in the illumination of a painful chapter that helped form the identity of a major U.S. cultural group.

Quaid plays Jack McGurn, a newcomer to L.A. in 1936 who gets a job as a projectionist in a Little Tokyo theater and falls in love with the boss' daughter (Tamlyn Tomita). After he's fired and forbidden to see her again, they elope to Seattle, where, unlike in California, it was legal for a Japanese-American and a Caucasian to marry.

Quaid creates an engaging character in lively, passionate McGurn, and though his leftist union concerns don't quite mesh with the rest of the story, they establish him as a persistent man who's used to making trouble for what he believes in.

In Seattle, McGurn gets a job in a fish cannery, and soon returns to union-organizing against his wife's wishes. She takes their child and goes back to L.A. just in time to see her father arrested after Pearl Harbor.

Parker lingers long and well on the love story between Jack and Lily, though it's disappointing that Lily seems incapable of relating to Jack's beliefs, or to anything beyond the security of their union.

Likewise, when her family is uprooted in L.A. after the war puts all Japanese "under suspicion," the focus is on the unjust disruption of their lives, but their feelings in relation to the Japanese aggression are never mentioned.

In general, Parker avoids most of the complexities behind the internment in favor of a broad, sentimental tale that emphasizes emotions.

Japanese are portrayed as so full of chatter, cheer, talent and industriousness that by the time one is certain that they are wonderful people, one is also weary of this 1-note portrait. It's not until late in their internment that serious internal divisions emerge, as one radicalized youth, Charlie (Stan Egi), repatriates to Japan (a place he's never been) while his brother Harry joins the U.S. forces.

Left until late in the film, these intriguing conflicts are rushed over. It's as though Parker was seduced by the love story at the expense of the main story. On the other hand, it pays off for mainstream audiences, as McGurn's devotion to the family — he follows them as far as he can to the camps and goes AWOL from the Army to visit them — is truly affecting.

Quaid gives a wonderfully open and unaffected performance, putting across romance, charm and integrity without resorting to any of the gimmicks he's used in earlier films. Tomita is a lovely, if under-nuanced, actress, and Egi as her brother is particularly interesting among the large supporting cast.

Parker's use of a Caucasian lead character in this Japanese-American story has drawn some criticism, but it actually works quite well as a turnaround comment on cultural suspicion. At first it's McGurn who is ostracized by the Japanese, then it's the family that is herded behind barbed wire. In the end, it's clear how superficial such barriers are.

The U.S.-born Japanese in this film, or Nisei, are constantly having to point out that they are Americans, and this film, to its credit, is a further exploration of what that means.

Lensed in Washington, Oregon and California, pic is beautifully photographed by Michael Seresin and lushly designed by Geoffrey Kirkland. Original music by Randy Edelman helps create an epic tone and adds momentum to a film overladen with exposition.

Period music, some of it Japanese, is also well-chosen and memorable. — *Daws.*

CANNES FILM FESTIVAL OFFICIAL SELECTIONS

Dreams
(JAPANESE)

Cannes A Warner Bros. release of a Steven Spielberg presentation of an Akira Kurosawa USA production. Produced by Hisao Kurosawa, Mike Y. Inoue. Written and directed by Akira Kurosawa. Camera (color), Takao Saito, Masaharu Ueda; editor, Tome Minami; music, Shinichiro Ikebe; sound, Kenichi Benitani; art direction, Yoshiro Muraki, Akira Sakuragi; costume design, Emi Wada; assistant director, Takashi Koizumi; visual effects, Industrial Light & Magic; creative consultant, Ishiro Honda; associate producers, Allan H. Liebert, Seikichi Iliizumi. Reviewed at Cannes Intl. Film Festival (noncompeting), May 10, 1990. Running time: **119 MIN.**

I . . . . Akira Terao
I as a Boy . . . . Mitsunori Isaki
Van Gogh . . . . Martin Scorsese
Old Man . . . . Chishu Ryu
Snow Fairy . . . . Mieko Harada
Mother . . . . Mitsuko Baisho
Weeping Ogre . . . . . . Chosuke Ikariya
Power Station Worker . . . . . Hisahi Igawa
I as a Child . . . . Toshihiko Nakano

■ Exquisite craftsmanship and unparalleled visual enchantment make Akira Kurosawa's 28th film a treasure for the ages, but excessive length and some gloom-and-doom nuclear apocalpyse segs erode the buoyant freshness of its sweeter passages.

Pic will be a prestige item on fest circuits, but a tough sell in theaters, even with Warner Bros. marketing and the Steven Spielberg seal of approval luring the adventurous.

"Dreams" takes shape like a concert of eight musical pieces, its lightest themes bookending the *sturm und drang.* Recurring motifs are a nostalgic cry for a way of life that respects nature (particularly resonant in these times) and an emphatic, anguished struggle against death, both of the individual and the planet.

In "Sun Shining Through The Rain," a small Japanese boy ventures into a sun-streaked forest during a rain shower to secretly observe a wedding procession of foxes, which, according to legend, are held only on such days. Appearance of the sly, furtive creatures, walking two by two to a flute and percussion march, is pure magic, aided by extraordinarily imaginative costumes and silver streaks of rain.

Segment ends too abruptly after the boy's mother tells him an angry fox has come looking for him and he must go and make amends. Still, the seg establishes the range of magic possible when one invests fully in the vividness of nature, and theme is carried over into the next "dream," the sublime "Peach Orchard."

In it, a boy chases a girl into a razed peach orchard, where a group of china dolls in exquisite costume come alive and chastise him for letting his family destroy the trees. Arranged on a tiered green hillside in Yokohama, episode again is astonishing in its visual beauty and craftsmanship.

"The Blizzard" uses a team of exhausted, confused and snow-blind travelers as a metaphor for the struggle against death, with a seductive angel visting the near-frozen leader and nearly leading him into sweet oblivion before he summons his will and blasts her away.

As before, scene is shot with extraordinary feel for color and visual expression, even in the subtle blues, greens, purples and golds of the ice world.

Anguish of death, while life enticingly goes on without one, again is explored in "The Tunnel," a mesmerizingly theatrical 1-take scene in which an army commander straggling home is confronted by the ghosts of his entire dead platoon, all wanting his assurance that their demise is not permanent.

Among the most delightful segs,

both for its slapdash humor and delirious pleasure in art, is "Crows," in which an enthusiastic character known as "I" (stand-in for the author) steps into a series of van Gogh canvases and travels through the vivid country scenes to confront the master himself, played by Martin Scorsese speaking in rapid-fire New York patois blithely unaltered for the role.

Though visual effects (created by George Lucas' Industrial Light & Magic) are important throughout, here they truly add magical dimensions as the landscapes take on the vivid, surreal hues of van Gogh's brush.

Crowning effect of a flock of black crows rising above the wheat (staged naturally and captured in a 1-shot, 1-second take) is a marvelous achievement. Pic could have ended here and been sheer delight, but the weight of several more segs takes its toll.

"Mt. Fuji In Red" stages an awesome vision of a nuclear disaster that sends the population of Japan plunging into the sea. But it seems didactic and dated. The mutant hell that awaits the survivors is vividly depicted in "The Weeping Ogre," but it unfolds at a dreary pace.

The uplifting coda of this concert of images, an idyllic sequence in which a happy 103-year-old man instructs the appreciative "I" in the customs and values that make human life a joy, also feels pedantic and unspontaneous when compared with the effervescent, unfettered surprises of the early passages. It is less a dream than a lesson, and feels like one.

Notably, in this extraordinarily visual film, it is the segments with minimal dialog that work magic, and despite the abbreviated length of the seg, they demonstrate the classical storytelling skills Kurosawa is famed for. Framing and direction are exemplary throughout.

Working with many of his longtime creative team, the 81-year-old Kurosawa has created a bold and rejuvenating work. — *Daws*.

White Hunter, Black Heart

Sydney A Warner Bros. release of a Malpaso/Rastar production. Executive producer, David Valdes. Produced and directed by Clint Eastwood. Screenplay, Peter Viertel, James Bridges, Burt Kennedy, from the novel by Viertel; camera (Technicolor), Jack N. Green; editor, Joel Cox; music, Lennie Niehaus; sound, Peter Handford; production design, John Graysmark; costumes, John Mollo; production manager, Roy Button; assistant director, Patrick Clayton; 2d unit director/camera, Simon Trevor; coproducer, Stanley Rubin; casting, Mary Selway. Reviewed at Village Roadshow screening room, Sydney, March 13, 1990. (In Cannes Film Festival, competing.) MPAA Rating: PG. Running time: **110 MIN.**
John Wilson . . . . Clint Eastwood
Pete Verrill . . . . Jeff Fahey
Paul Landers . . . . George Dzundza
Ralph Lockhart . . . . Alun Armstrong
Kay Gibson . . . . Marisa Berenson
Hodkins . . . . Timothy Spall
Mrs. McGregor . . . . Mel Martin
Phil Duncan . . . . Richard Vanstone
Mrs. Duncan . . . . Jamie Koss
Irene Saunders . . . . . Catherine Neilson
Basil Fields . . . . Richard Warwick
Kivu . . . . Boy Mathias Chuma
Alec Laing . . . . Geoffrey Hutchings
Tom Harrison . . . . Christopher Fairbank
George (butler) . . . . . Norman Lumsden
Miss Wilding . . . . . . Charlotte Cornwell

■ **With careful handling, Clint Eastwood's new film should generate strong firstrun business and build by word-of-mouth to successful wider release. It's competing at the Cannes festival.**

The Warners release isn't an African adventure epic, as those unaware of Peter Viertel's 1953 book might have surmised from the title. It's an intelligent, affectionate study of an obsessive American film director who, while working on a British film in colonial Africa, becomes sidetracked by his compulsion to hunt elephants.

Though the end credits note that this is "a work of fiction," and though the director is named John Wilson, this is clearly a story about John Huston and the preproduction period for "The African Queen" (called "The African Trader" here). The Huston classic became basis of an unsold tv pilot, "Safari" starring James Coburn and Glynis Johns, as well as a tv remake featuring Warren Oates and Mariette Hartley.

Eastwood plays the Huston character with obvious appreciation of the man: He wears Huston clothes and hats, assumes Huston mannerisms, smokes Huston cigars and speaks with the characteristic Huston timbre.

This is no nightclub impersonation, however. Eastwood, working with an existing screenplay by Viertel, James Bridges and Burt Kennedy, is concerned about exploring the character of a brilliant and gifted man who behaved with gross irresponsibility, brushing off his personal debts and the real concerns of his producer, a role George Dzundza cleverly models on Sam Spiegel (who produced "The African Queen" under the pseudonym, "S.P. Eagle.").

The first 20 minutes of the pic unfolds in England, where Wilson is living in a splendid old stately home as if he were a country squire, complete with secretary and butler. He even dresses in traditional hunting "pink" to gallop around the countryside.

It's here that Wilson welcomes Pete Verrell (Jeff Fahey), his biographer, and it's from Verrell's perspective that the events unfold. Once the film crew moves to Africa for location scouting and pre-production, it becomes clear that Wilson's interest in making the film takes second place to his impractical passion for big-game hunting. His determination to bag an elephant assumes an importance out of all proportion, and the man's undoubted egocentricity starts to border on insanity.

When Verrill calls killing such a noble animal a crime, Wilson launches into a strange defense of his motives, pointing out that shooting an elephant is *not* a crime, but is, in fact, the only legal sin. And that's why he wants to do it.

"White Hunter, Black Heart" unfolds at a leisurely pace and avoids any action sequences, apart from a downbeat scene in which Wilson, having endured anti-Semitic comments from a colonial housewife and having verbally crushed her, gets soundly beaten in a violent fistfight with a hotel manager.

Wilson suffers a different kind of defeat at the film's climax in a very well staged sequence in which he and his black guide (Boy Mathias Chuma) finally confront elephants; resolution makes for a satisfactory conclusion to a complex, compelling character study.

This is another film in which Eastwood tries to break away from the action roles that made him famous. As director, he has shown ever since "Play Misty For Me" that he is more than just a fine craftsman, and his willingness to tackle difficult, even unfashionable, subjects is commendable. It makes for tricky boxoffice predictions, however.

Working from a well-written screenplay, Eastwood has assembled a fine cast and crew here. Fahey has the rather thankless role of observer, but he does a good job with the character. Among the supporting cast, Alun Armstrong is a standout as the bigoted unit manager whose conservative British background is at odds with the raffish ways of his American employer. Marisa Berenson is convincing as Kay Gibson, the lead actress (based on Katharine Hepburn), while Richard Vanstone is a convincing Bogart lookalike.

Production design (John Graysmark) and costume design (John Mollo) beautifully recreate a world of 40 years ago when the British Empire and its values still held sway over much of Africa. The smallest details are convincing.

Conservationists and animal libbers will be relieved to discover that, in this film about the lure and the myths of big-game hunting, not one animal is killed. — *Strat*.

Korczak
(POLISH-B&W)

Cannes A Filmstudio Perspektywa/Regina Ziegler Filmproduktion/Telmar Film Intl./Erato Films/ZDF/BBC Films coproduction. Produced by Regina Ziegler, Janusz Morgenstern, Daniel Toscan du Plantier. Directed by Andrzej Wajda. Screenplay, Agnieszka Holland; camera (black & white), Robby Muller; editor, Ewa Smal; music, Wojciech Kilar; art direction, Allan Starski. Reviewed at the Cannes Film Festival (noncompeting), May 10, 1990. Running time: **115 MIN.**
Korczak . . . . Wojtek Pszoniak
Stefa . . . . Ewa Dalkowska
Heniek . . . . Piotr Kozlowski
Estera . . . . Marzena Trybala
    Also with: Wojciech Klata, Adam Siemion, Karolina Czernicka, Agnieszka Kruk.

■ **Andrzej Wadja's first time behind the cameras since he became a senator of the new Polish People's Republic, and his first film lensed in Poland in five years, "Korczak" is a surprisingly straightforward bi-opic, one that willfully abstains from stylistic fireworks.**

Lensed in black & white and intercut with grim newsreels of the Warsaw ghetto, pic doesn't make light viewing. Fest screenings are more likely than a commercial run on this one.

With "Korczak," Wajda takes off a pious hat to legendary Polish pedagogue and educator Janusz Korczak and his heroic dedication to protecting Jewish orphans during the war.

Wojtek Pszoniak, one of Wajda's regulars, plays the Jewish doctor Henryk Goldszmit, better known by his pseudonym Janusz Korczak (he also wrote children's books). A man of almost absurdly high principle, he is unafraid of shouting at German officers and frequently has to be persuaded to save his own life. His orphanage, set up in a cramped school after the Nazis created the Warsaw ghetto in 1940, provided asylum to 200 homeless kids.

Agnieszka Holland's script opens with such rapid incident it becomes intelligible only after the pic switches to the orphanage. Putting his experimental educational methods into practice, he installs a kind of children's self-government, whose justice is in sinister contrast to what is happening in the outside world.

Right in front of the school, dozens of other kids are dying or being killed every day. Their naked bodies lie on the street unattended. Though Korczak is assured by the ghetto's Jewish mayor that the city's orphanages will be saved, the threat of death hangs heavy.

One plucky lad keeps slipping into the ghetto to visit his dying mother. Another boy is rebuffed by his non-Jewish girlfriend when the going gets rough.

Korczak maintains saintly integrity till the end, begging for food and money from rich Jews, shown carousing in a wild nightclub in one startling scene. When the final roundup comes, he refuses to accept a Swiss passport, preferring to board the trains to Treblinka with his orphans. All die in the gas chambers, passing into Polish history.

Tale is chilling but morally uplifting. Wajda and Holland are so intent on celebrating their hero they leave little room for complications and doubt. Result is an out-and-out hagiography lacking in character development.

Despite Korczak's unwavering heroism, Pszoniak manages to create a forceful and very human character and gives the film a strong center. Around him, his teachers (no less heroic in their quiet way) and the kids have built-in appeal. Polish censorship has kept Jewish themes and history out of films for decades.

In this context, Wajda's film is hard not to admire, though it may be remembered more as a gesture of solidarity and historical record than as one of his finest imaginative works.

Robby Muller's black & white cinematography bravely avoids the beautiful in favor of harsh realism.

He blends Wajda's lensing with wartime newsreels on several occasions.

A striking touch is the appearance of German officers doubling as newsreel cameramen, who shoot the very footage that has provided a historical record of the ghetto terrors and tragedy. Their cold indifference to the suffering they film puts "Korczak's" fierce commitment in a new light. — *Yung.*

Il sole anche di notte
(The Sun Also Shines At Night)
(ITALIAN-FRENCH-GERMAN)

Rome   A Filmtre/RAI-TV Channel 1 (Rome)/Capoul/Interpool/Sara Film (Paris)/Direkt Film (Munich) coproduction. Produced by Giuliani G. De Negri. Executive producer, Grazia Volpi. Directed by Paolo and Vittorio Taviani. Screenplay, Paolo and Vittorio Taviani, with Tonino Guerra, based on "Father Sergius" by Leo Tolstoy; camera (Cinecittà color), Giuseppe Lanci; art direction, Gianni Sbarra; costumes, Lina Nerli Taviani; editor; Roberto Perpignani; music, Nicola Piovani; production organizer, Claudio Grassetti. Reviewed at Cinecittà lab, April 24, 1990. (In Cannes Film Festival, noncompeting.) Running time: **112 MIN.**
Sergio Giuramondo . . . . . . Julian Sands
Cristina . . . . Nastassja Kinski
Aurelia . . . . Patricia Millardet
Matilda . . . . Charlotte Gainsbourg
Prince Santobuono . . . . Massimo Bonetti
Sergio's mother . . . . . Margarita Lozano
Sergio's sister . . . . . . Pamela Villoresi
King Charles 3d . . . . . . Rüdiger Vogler
   Also with: Geppy Gleijeses, Sonia Gessner, Gaetano Soperandeo, Matilde Piana, Vittorio Capotorto, Riccardo Patrizio Perrotti, Salvatore Rossi, Teresa Brescianini.

■ "The Sun Also Shines At Night" (a.k.a. "Night Sun") is another quintessential Taviani brothers film, a compendium of the very particular style and moral obsessions that have put them among Italy's most individualistic directors. The strong storyline makes film a compelling watch and a good b.o. bet at home and in specialized sites offshore.

With the help of scripter Tonino Guerra, the Tavianis have seamlessly transposed "Father Sergius," Tolstoy's short story about a young nobleman who becomes a monk and saintly hermit, to 19th century southern Italy.

Julian Sands plays the intense Sergio Giuramondo, a small country squire who is one of King Charles 3d's (Rüdiger Vogler) cadets. His strong personality makes the king choose him as his personal aide-de-camp, upstaging young Prince Santobuono (Massimo Bonetti). But when Sergio discovers

the fascinating duchess he is being married off to (Nastassja Kinski) was the king's mistress, he exchanges military garb for the cassock.

Gossipped about and laughed at by the Neapolitan nobility, monk Sergio takes up a lonely hermit's life. On a mountaintop he engages in a spiritual tussle with a second female (Patricia Millardet), a flighty widow bent on seducing him. Sergio avoids temptation by extreme means — he chops off a finger. Horrified and chastened, the adventuress takes the veil.

News that Father Sergio has converted the "city whore" spreads, and, despite himself, Sergio is forced to work another miracle: He gives back speech to a robber's son. Now the hermitage is besieged by pilgrims and decked out with holy pictures like a Christmas tree. Father Sergio's fame extends from Rome to Madrid.

In the lowest moment of his faith, Sergio succumbs to the sexual temptation of a diabolic little girl (Charlotte Gainsbourg). He flees the hermitage in horror at what he's done, and for the rest of his life wanders through the countryside as an unknown beggar.

Religious element may surprise fans of the strongly political filmmakers, but "Sun" is almost as full of ironic ambiguity as Buñuel's "Simon Of The Desert." Focus of attention in this very moral film is the individual's struggle against the temptations of the world in both their broadest senses (fame, glory, riches) and also as personal pride and the longing for absolute perfection.

Sands shows the transformation of Sergio's character from the boy full of faith to a disillusioned man without losing audience sympathy for a moment. He never is more credible than when he explains why he became a hermit: to fight people's indifference toward each other with his own example.

Though all the characters are more or less stylized, cast holds up under the strain better than in other Taviani films. Kinski is a tremulous, lovable bride. Millardet is maliciously sexy as the adventuress out to seduce Father Sergio. Gainsbourg is a chilling seducer, readable as either devil or pitiable human being.

In "Sun," the Tavianis reach a great equilibrium between the direct, head-on lensing they prefer

and their subject.

Breathtaking views of natural settings vie with splendid aristocratic palaces, captured simply by Giuseppe Lanci's camera. Nicola Piovani's soaring, emotional score plays an important role in communicating a sense of spiritual exuberance. — *Yung.*

Abraham's Gold
(WEST GERMAN)

Munich   A Futura/Filmverlag release of an Aviata Film, A.& II. Rimbach, Pro-ject Film im Filmverlag der Autoren, Adanos Film and ZDF. Produced by Alena and Herbert Rimbach. Directed by Jörg Graser. Screenplay, Graser; camera (color), Henning Stegmüller; editor, Helga Borsche; sound, Günter Knon; costumes, Petra Kray. Reviewed at Arri theater, Munich, April 27, 1990. (In Cannes Film Festival, Un Certain Regard section.) Running time: **98 MIN.**
Bärbel . . . . Hanna Schygulla
Karl Lechner . . . . Günther-Maria Halmer
Annamirl . . . . Daniela Schötz
Hunzinger . . . . Robert Dietl
Lechner's mother . . . . Maria Singer
Mayor . . . . Karl Friedrich
Priest . . . . Otto Tausig

■ "Abraham's Gold" is an antifascist heimat (homeland) film, genre dealing with German communal life and patriotic traditions, the main theme of which is a concealed Nazi past and latent anti-Semitism in a rural Bavarian village.

Despite a firstrate cast and excellent script, pic is a downer, with theatrical possibilities limited to the German-lingo territories. Offshore, best bet is tv, the arthouse and fest circuits.

Film begins with the return of an aging hippie, Bärbel (Hanna Schygulla), who left the village to join the flower children movement in the 1960s. Her unconventional appearance and behavior starkly contrasts the staid, pious villagers, and she receives a hostile welcome from her innkeeper father Hunziger, who has raised her 14-year-old daughter Annamirl.

The villagers are unaware that Hunziger, a stern advocate of law and order, was a guard at the Auschwitz death camp in Poland. While Bärbel takes her daughter on excursions nearby trying to explain why she abandoned the village in search of freedom, Hunziger and his friend Karl Lechner, the beer deliverer, drive to Poland, where the innkeeper had years ago buried gold fillings from the teeth of murdered Jews.

Lechner's aged mother discovers some of the gold fillings and suspects they are from the death camp victims. Lechner, saying he was born in 1938, tells his mother Auschwitz means nothing to him, until he learns from her he is a Jew himself. She was not his real mother but a former employee in a Jewish household, who had saved him from the Nazis when the family was deported.

Lechner confronts Hunziger, breaks with him and calls him a murderer. Hunziger, fearing that he will be exposed and prosecuted by the Israelis, launches a tirade against Jews and forces Annamirl to agree to tell police that Lechner had sexually molested her.

Daniela Schötz as the helpless victim of her dominating Nazi grandfather shows impressive talent. In a welcome return to the German screen, Schygulla is convincing in the hippie role. Under Graser's direction, Günther-Maria Halmer gives a superb performance as Karl, the naive friend of the unrepentent Nazi Hunziger, masterfully played by noted stage actor Robert Dietl.

Classic composers Bach, Grieg, Vivaldi, Franck and Johann Strauss supplied the music for the score. Credits, especially Henning Stegmüller's poetic lensing of the Bavarian countryside, are tops.
— *Kind.*

The Reflecting Skin
(BRITISH)

Paris A Fugitive Films production. Executive producer, Jim Beach. Produced by Dominic Anciano, Ray Burdis. Written and directed by Philip Ridley. Camera (color), Dick Pope; editor, Scott Thomas; sound, George Tarrant; art direction, Rick Roberts; assistant director, Don French; casting, Therese Reinsch. Reviewed at the Empire theater, Paris, April 23, 1990. (In Cannes Film Festival, Intl. Critics Week.) Running time: **93 MIN**
Cameron Dove . . . . . . Viggo Mortensen
Dolphin Blue . . . . Lindsay Duncan
Seth Dove . . . . Jeremy Cooper
Ruth Dove . . . . Shelia Moore
Luke Dove . . . . Duncan Fraser
Joshua . . . . David Longworth
Sheriff Ticker . . . . Robert Koons
Deputy . . . . David Bloom

■ **This pretentious essay in the grotesque was an odd choice as curtain raiser for the Intl. Critics Week at Cannes. British newcomer Philip Ridley shows technical ability and a macabre sense of humor, but the script's abnormal situations and morbid characters pall quickly and leave little more than a bad aftertaste.**

Set in grassroots America of the 1950s (film was shot in Canada), story describes how a young boy persecutes and catalyzes the death of a young widow whom he thinks is a vampire with bloodthirsty aims on his older brother.

Nobody in the story is normal. The boy has a penchant for sadistic practical jokes, which include inflating the bellies of frogs with air, then exploding them with a peashooter as curious passersby stop to look. Mom is hysterically obsessed by odors, and dad, a service station operator with a history of pederasty, commits suicide (by gasoline immolation) when accused of sodomy and murder of his son's friend.

Latter crime is the work of a roaming carload of young perverts, who also do in the boy's other playmate and, climactically, the widow.

The lovers (widow and brother) are bent, too. Latter is clearly disturbed by his recent military service in the Pacific, while the widow, a British woman whose rube husband hung himself, is a necrophile fetishist.

Ridley tops things off with some twisted religious symbolism, such as the fossilized fetus the boy finds in a barn and befriends.

Film does offer one memorable line towards the end, when the annoyed brother says to the kid: "Why don't you go play with your friends?" Response: "They're all dead."

Tech credits, notably Dick Pope's striking color images, are fine. — *Len.*

Quiet Days In Clichy
(FRENCH-ITALIAN-WEST GERMAN)

Paris A Pathé-Europa release of an Italfrance/Tvor/Cofimage 2/Cinécitta/AZ Films Production/Direkt Film coproduction. Executive producer, Antonio Passalia. Produced by Pietro Innocenzi. Directed by Claude Chabrol. Screenplay, Chabrol, Ugo Leonzio; camera (Eastmancolor), Jean Rabier; editor, Monique Fardoulis; music, Matthieu Chabrol; sound, Edward Parente, Stanislav Litera, Maurice Gilbert; art direction, Marco Dentici; costumes, Ezio Altieri; assistant director, Alain Wermus; production manager, Jacques Juranville; casting, Carlo Quinterio, Risa Kes. Reviewed at the Marignan Concorde theater, Paris, May 9, 1990. (In Cannes Film Festival Market.) Running time: **122 MIN.**
Henry . . . . Andrew McCarthy
Alfred . . . . Nigel Havers
Colette . . . . Stephanie Cotta
Nys . . . . Barbara de Rossi
Ania . . . . Isolde Barth
Adrienne . . . . Stéphane Audran
Edith . . . . Anna Galiena
Sebastien . . . . Wolfgang Reichman
Regentag . . . . Mario Adorf
(English soundtrack)

■ **Just when it seemed Claude Chabrol was once again a filmmaker to be taken seriously, along comes "Quiet Days In Clichy" to destroy that illusion. Chabrol has allowed himself to get into soulless international coprods before, but this one reaches new depths of trashiness.**

As the title suggests, this softcore, soft-brained period film is inspired by Henry Miller's autobiographical novel of the same name, previously adapted as a Danish film in 1970. Chabrol and his screenwriter, Ugo Leonzio, have gutted the source material so completely that it finally bears no resemblance to its model, either in setting, character, incident or mood.

Miller's book was an often comical, sometimes poignant account

---

Original Version

Quiet Days In Clichy
(DANISH-B&W)

Cannes Grove Press (U.S.) release of S.B.A. (Copenhagen)-A/S Dans-Svensk (Europe) production. Directed by Jens Jörgen Thorsen. Features Louise White, Paul Valjean, Wayne Rodda, Ulla Lemvigh-Mueller. Screenplay, Thorsen, based on Henry Miller's novel, "Quiet Days In Clichy." Camera (black & white), Jesper Hoem; music, Country Joe McDonald, Ben Webster; editor, Anker. No other credits. Reviewed at Cinema Le Star, Cannes Festival (noncompeting), May 8, 1970.

Running time: **100 MIN.**

of erotic episodes during his Paris period in the early '30s, when he struggled to establish himself as a writer. Apart from the exuberant sexual escapades, book was notable for capturing a time, place and expatriate mentality.

None of that remains here, not even Clichy: neither the suburb, where Miller and his colleague boarded, nor the famous Place Clichy, where the writer hung out. Instead we get a hideous studio reconstruction (done in Rome) that makes the most fanciful Hollywoodian Paris-street set look like documentary realism.

Film's most unforgivable sin is that it cynically travesties Miller's experience of Paris, using book's reputation as a front for a puerile cavalcade of '30s decadence, devoid of all eroticism or observation. Rather than a record of a seedy sexual gratification in the midst of poverty, we watch the well-fed, well-dressed protagonist on a tour of garishly baroque bordellos and fashionable cocktail bars.

Andrew McCarthy is too young and fresh-faced to play Miller, but Nigel Havers has some zest as his comrade-in-debauchery. Among the women is Chabrol's ex-wife and ex-leading lady, Stéphane Audran, who maintains an air of being above it all. One understands her. — *Len.*

Sunless Days
(HONG KONG-JAPANESE-DOCU)

Minneapolis An NHK Enterprises production. Executive producers, Takao Kobayashi, Tetsuya Ichinose. Produced by Masami Ogahara. Directed by Shu Kei. Screenplay, Wu Nien-Jen, Kei; camera (color), Wong Chung-Piu; editor, Sammy Chow; music, Danny Chung; sound, Kohnosuke Oda; production manager, Stephen Wong; assistant director, Jaco Li. Reviewed at Rivertown Intl. Film Festival, May 7, 1990. (In Cannes Film Festival Market.) Running time: **90 MIN.**

■ **"Sunless Days," a rambling documentary tracing the reactions of Chinese artists and ex-patriots to last year's Tiananmen Square events, is best suited for arthouses in major** cities and in college towns with large enclaves of Chinese students.

With the 1989 People's Republic pro-democracy movement and ensuing government repression as the subject, Hong Kong director Shu Kei lensed interviews with Chinese poets, journalists, actors and film directors in Hong Kong, Australia, Canada and England. The responses, as might be expected, were unanimously pessimistic, hence the title. Chinese literati living abroad feel they are permanently cut off from their homeland.

Of particular interest is the situation Kei encountered in Hong Kong where sympathetic demonstrations for the pro-democracy movement were silenced by the British government in response to pressure from Beijing. Hong Kong is due to revert to Chinese control in 1997. Chinese residents are already starting to emigrate to the west in the aftermath of the brutality by the Chinese regime.

Originally produced as a 1-hour special for NHK Television in Japan, "Sunless Days" has been expanded to 90 minutes for theatrical release. The tighter version may have been preferable, since the additional footage seems to have slowed the docu's pace.

— *Rees.*

Chicago Joe And The Showgirl (BRITISH)

London A Palace Pictures release (New Line in the U.S.) of a Polygram/Working Title production in association with BSB. Produced by Tim Bevan. Directed by Bernard Rose. Screenplay, David Yallop; editor, Dan Rae; camera, Mike Southon; music, Hans Zimmer, Shirley Walker; production designer, Gemma Jackson; costume designer, Bob Ringwood; sound designer, Nigel Holland; sound editor, Mark Auguste; assistant director, Waldo Roeg; art directors, Peter Russell, Richard Holland; associate producer, Jane Frazer; casting, Leo Davis, John Lyons. Reviewed at the North London screening room, May 6, 1990. (In Cannes Film Festival, market.) Running time: **103 MIN.**
Georgina Grayson . . . . . . Emily Lloyd
Rick Allen . . . . Kiefer Sutherland
Joyce Cook . . . . Patsy Kensit
Lenny Bexley . . . . Keith Allen
Mrs. Evans . . . . Liz Fraser
Violet . . . . Alexandra Pigg
Inspector Tansil . . . . Ralph Nossek
Robert De Mott . . . . Colin Bruce
Inspector Tarr . . . . Roger Ashton-Griffiths
Morry . . . . Harry Fowler
George Heath . . . . John Junkin

■ "Chicago Joe And The Showgirl" closed within a month of release in the U.K., an accurate enough reflection of the quality and appeal of this professed "Bonnie and Clyde"-style pic, and its chances offshore look equally dim.

The British film industry is hoping this pic is only an aberration in the usually canny work of Working Title ("My Beautiful Laundrette," "Wish You Were Here," "Sammy and Rosie Get Laid"). The producers misired this time, although not for lack of juicy material.

Scripter David Yallop was inspired and intrigued by the sensational Hulten/Jones murder case of 1944, which became known as the "Cleft Chin Murder Case" after the disappearance of a London taxi driver. It made household names of American serviceman Karl Hutten and British showgirl Elizabeth Maud Jones, beating war news to the headlines.

Shame is Yallop was unable to ignite anything sensational in the finished product. The trial, which resulted in the hanging of Hulten (the only execution of a Yank by the British) and the reprieve of Jones, is passed up. Yallop instead focuses on duo's 6-day London crime spree, beginning with theft of an army truck and a fur, and finishing with murder of the cabbie.

While supposedly trying to explore the psychological motivations of the two, Yallop and director Bernard Rose end up lost in an unatmospheric mist. Pic plays up Jones' obsession with gangster and moll fantasies, and portrays Hulten as a weak, aimless GI led astray by her powers of seduction and his own desire for kicks. He's been dating a virtuous English rose (Patsy Kensit), and been doted on by her parents.

Meanwhile, it transpires he's left a wife back home in the States. The fact that neither his relationships with Lloyd nor Kensit are sexually consummated adds to a wild frustration that drives him to crime. Problem is that Emily Lloyd totally fails to deliver the necessary allurement, and Kiefer Sutherland is weak in playing a weak character. End result is a pair of languid leads fumbling their way through a passionless picture.

Lloyd, despite her topnotch debut in "Wish You Were Here" and pics in the U.S. since, shows no signs of development and lacks the charm needed to win the audience's sympathy. Her Jones (stage name is Georgina Grayson) is just crude and unfocused. Sutherland's Hulten, who calls himself Ricky Allen, is insipid. It's a relief when they're caught.

Whole pic is shot on sets rather than on location, and despite Gemma Jackson's thoughtful designs, the overall look is cheap. Lensing varies from spot-on to out of focus. Fantasy scenes, where Lloyd imagines herself as moll to Sutherland's gangster, look like children's pantomime. — *Krug.*

Back To The Future, Part III

Hollywood A Universal release of a Steven Spielberg presentation of an Amblin Entertainment production. Executive producers, Spielberg, Frank Marshall, Kathleen Kennedy. Produced by Bob Gale, Neil Canton. Directed by Robert Zemeckis. Screenplay, Gale, from story by Zemeckis, Gale; camera (Deluxe color), Dean Cundey; editor, Arthur Schmidt, Harry Keramidas; music, Alan Silvestri; sound (Dolby) William B. Kaplan; production design, Rick Carter; art direction, Marjorie Stone McShirley, Jim Teegarden; set decoration, Michael Taylor; costume design, Joanna Johnston; special visual effects, Industrial Light & Magic; visual effects supervisors, Ken Ralston, Scott Farrar; mechanical effects supervisor, Michael Lantieri; stunt coordinator, Walter Scott, assistant director, David McGiffert; 2d unit director, Max Kleven; 2d unit camera, Don Burgese; associate producer, Steve Starkey; casting, Mike Fenton, Judy Taylor, Valorie Massalas. Reviewed at Universal Studios, L.A., May 15, 1990. MPAA Rating: PG. Running time: **188 MIN.**
Marty/Seamus McFly . . . . Michael J. Fox
Dr. Emmett Brown . . . . Christopher Lloyd
Clara Clayton . . . . . . Mary Steenburgen
Buford (Mad Dog)Tannen/
Biff Tannen . . . . Thomas F. Wilson
Maggie/Lorraine McFly . . . Lea Thompson
Jennifer . . . . Elisabeth Shue
Bartender . . . . Matt Clark
Barbed wire salesman . . . . Richard Dysart
Marshal Strickland . . . . . . James Tolkan
   Also with: Pat Buttram, Harry Carey Jr., Dub Taylor, Christopher Wynne, Sean Gregory Sullivan, Mike Watson, ZZ Top.

■ **Though probably too much to hope that "Back To The Future, Part III" will resuscitate the Western genre (inevitably, pic's b.o. success will be attributed to sci-fi and sequel elements), this relaxed, affectionate takeoff is an unalloyed delight both for those who love Westerns and those who've never seen one on the big screen.**

After the huge commercial success of the first two parts of the Steven Spielberg/Universal "Back To The Future" trilogy, director Robert Zemeckis and writing partner Bob Gale take a daringly avant-garde step in the context of today's Hollywood. They take their characters back through time into a classically minimalist Western plot.

In the process, they have fun with the conventions of the genre as filtered through the modern perspective of a youthful character whose knowledge of the period is limited to Clint Eastwood spaghetti Westerns, and they recover the style and wit and grandiose fantasy elements that captivated audiences in the original "Back To The Future."

The simplicity of plot, and the wide expansiveness of its use of space, are a refreshing change from the convoluted, visually cramped and cluttered second part of the trilogy, whose plot made sense only to viewers with advanced degrees in metaphysics. If there's any significant b.o. falloff this time, it'll be more a result of lingering disappointment over the last film's quality than a reflection on this one's quality.

Alarmingly, "Future III" starts with another reprise of part I and a long-winded expository sequence in which Christopher Lloyd's Doc Brown compounds the confusion of part II while attempting to recap its plot —How he can simultaneously be present in 1955 and still have to be rescued from 1885? But then, all that becomes irrelevant.

The screen seems to expand before the eyes in a splendid sight gag as Michael J. Fox' Marty McFly in his time-travelling Delorean finds himself in the midst of a band of charging Indians in John Ford country, Monument Valley 1885.

His mission is to bring back Doc before he is shot in the back by Thomas F. Wilson's hilariously unhinged Buford (Mad Dog) Tannen, an ancestor of McFly's 20th century nemesis Biff Tannen, who bears an uncanny resemblance to Ford's most extravagant villain, Lee Marvin's Liberty Valance.

Viewers will recall from the last pic that the idealistic Doc always wanted to live in the old West, yet his desire to stay there puts him at odds with his oft-expressed warnings to Fox about tampering with the "space-time continuum." His reluctance to return is compounded by a refreshing new development in the trilogy. This time when Doc gets that thunderstruck look, it's over a woman, the delectable Mary Steenburgen.

With amiable modesty, Fox, too old to keep playing this eternal teenager, steps into the background of the story and lets Lloyd have the chance to play the romantic lead for a change. Doc's offbeat romance with Steenburegen's Clara Clayton, a spinster schoolmarm who shares his passion for Jules Verne, is funny, touching and exhilarating. Their ultimate journey through time gives the plot trajectory an unexpected and entirely satisfying resolution.

The fun of this meta-Western is partly the recognition of elements familiar from genre classics: the dance from "My Darling Clementine," the sobering-up concoction from "El Dorado," the costume from "A Fistful of Dollars." Fox reexperiences all this, literally flying through the screen (at an incongruous Monument Valley drive-in) into every Western fan's dream of being a character in a "real" Western.

When he enters the saloon standing in the embryonic Hill Valley in the same spot where the malt shop will be in 1955 and the Cafe '80s in 2015, Fox steps into a world reassuringly populated by such familiar Western faces as bartender Matt Clark and the chorus of old geezers played by Pat Buttram, Harry Carey Jr. and Dub Taylor.

When asked his name, Fox identifies himself as Clint Eastwood, leading to such derisive comments as Buttram's cackling, "Everybody, everywhere, will see Clint Eastwood is the biggest yellabelly in the West," and Wilson's snarling, "What kind of stupid name is that?" (Showing himself a remarkably good sport, Eastwood is thanked for his cooperation in the end credits.)

Visually "Future III" is full of thrills: swooping helicopter shots, grandiose crane movements and Zemeckis' typically hyperkinetic action set pieces smoothly edited by Arthur Schmidt and Harry Keramidas.

These elements underscore the larger-than-life, tall-tale quality of the film, satisfyingly enhanced by Alan Silvestri's bombastic score and the bluegrass tune played by the rock band ZZ Top.

Despite the size and enjoyable extravagance of this $40-million film, it's mellower and less frenzied than the director's previous work, luxuriating in the eye-popping scenery captured in the lovely autumnal palette of Dean Cundey's camerawork, in the warmth of Joanna Johnston's costuming and the tintype quality of Rick Carter's production design.

The only regret is that, out of force of habit, the direction still is a bit rushed in spots. But "Future III" has a joyousness seldom seen on the screen these days, a sense of exuberance in the breaking of boundaries of time, space and genre, and in the way a hard-working character actor (Lloyd) finally earns his chance to be a leading man, at the same time as he wins the hand of the actress who spurned him on screen in her film debut and only previous Western, "Goin' South."

Usually it's a relief when filmmakers announce they're tired of making sequels, but this time it's a shame that Zemeckis and Gale want to retire the "Back To The Future" cycle, particularly since the film ends with wonderful Industrial Light & Magic visual effect that suggests a whole new dimension to the adventures of Doc and Clara. — *Mac*.

Fire Birds

New York A Buena Vista release from Touchstone Pictures of a Nova Intl. Films presentation of a Keith Barish/Arnold Kopelson production. (Intl. sales, Inter-Ocean Film Sales.) Produced by William Badalato. Executive producers, Kopelson, Barish. Directed by David Green. Screenplay, Nick Thiel, Paul F. Edwards, from story by Step Tyner, John K. Swensson, Dale Dye; camera (Deluxe color; Technicolor prints), Tony Imi; editor, Jon Poll, Norman Buckley, Dennis O'Connor; music, David Newman; sound (Dolby), Mark Ulano; production design, Joseph T. Garrity; set decoration, Jerie Kelter; costume design, Ellis Cohen; aerial sequences design-2d unit director, Richard T. Stevens; assistant director, Matt Earl Beesley; production manager, Susan Zwerman; stunt coordinator, Dennis (Danger) Madalone; aerial photography, Stan McClain; additional camera, Paul (Doc) Byrd; model unit camera, Rick Fichter; special effects coordinator, Mike Menzel; coproducers, Swensson, Dye; associate producer, Bettina Giloi; casting, Mike Fenton, Judy Taylor, Valorie Massalas. Reviewed at Festival theater, N.Y., May 17, 1990. MPAA Rating: PG-13. Running time: **85 MIN.**
Jack Preston . . . . Nicolas Cage
Brad Little . . . . Tommy Lee Jones
Billie Lee Guthrie . . . . Sean Young
Breaker . . . . Bryan Kestner
A.K. McNeil . . . . Dale Dye
Janet Little . . . . Mary Ellen Trainor
Gen. Olcott . . . . J.A. Preston
Stoller . . . . Bert Rhine

■ **Canny casting against type defuses some of the gung ho militarism of this enjoyable, old-fashioned aerial adventure pic. Indie pickup should provide Disney with good biz for several weeks and has better offshore potential.**

Originally titled "Wings Of The Apache" for the Apache assault helicopters prominently featured, "Fire Birds" resembles a morale booster project leftover from the Reagan era. A paean to Yankee air power, it shows the U.S. Army as a take-charge outfit able to kick the butt of those South American drug cartel jerks.

Not surprisingly, given changing times and politics, "Fire Birds" has a tongue-in-cheek aspect. Camaraderie and rat-a-tat-tat dialog among stars Nicolas Cage, Sean Young and Tommy Lee Jones may have started out as fun à la Howard Hawks' classic "Only Angels Have Wings" but emerges at times as a satire of the genre.

Formula script, which inevitably recalls Tom Cruise's hit "Top Gun," has Cage training to use the army's Apache aircraft while vainly trying to rekindle a romance with old flame Young. Jones is dead-on as the taskmaster instructor who cornily singles out Cage for rough treatment.

After straightening out an eye problem interfering with his sharp-shooting, Cage is ready for aerial dogfights with nemesis Bert Rhine, well-staged and edited by a vast crew of experts. Film's main novelty is having Young also sent into combat instead of being the woman sitting on the sidelines, and she proves instrumental in saving the skin of her macho colleagues.

British helmer David Green brings it in at a trim 85 minutes, main defect of which is the skimpy characterizations afforded the supporting cast. Villain Rhine is a remote menace without dialog or scene of his own.

Cage is fascinating to watch, allowed to explode occasionally from his tightly clamped shell. Young, sporting a new, short haircut, is fully believable as a modern woman who won't take any guff from a man, professionally or in the sack. Duo's sex scene is presented as tame, and no threat to Disney's PG-13.

Tech credits are effective in delivering the vicarious thrills of war action during peacetime.
— *Lor*.

Boys In The Island
(AUSTRALIAN)

Sydney A Great Scott production. Executive producer, Brian Rosen. Produced by Jane Scott. Directed by Geoffrey Bennett. Screenplay, C.J. Koch, Tony Morphett, from the novel by Koch; camera (Eastmancolor), Andrew Lesnie; editor, Suresh Ayyar; music, Sharon Calcroft; sound, Gary Wilkins; production design, Igor Nay; production manager, Fiona McConaghy; assistant director, Steve Andrews; casting, Michael Lynch (Forcast). Reviewed at Film Australia screening room, Sydney, April 12, 1990. Running time: **107 MIN.**

George Farrell . . . . James Fox
Frank . . . . Yves Stening
Keeva . . . . Jane Stephens
Heather . . . . Lexa Murphy
Louis . . . . Joseph Clements
Heather's father . . . . Steve Jacobs

■ **A rites-of-passage pic with a difference, "Boys In The Island" starts slowly, but develops into an intriguing, blackly comic crime film. Popularity of pic's source novel should give it a positive kick-off Down Under, with arthouse expectations in other markets depending on reviews.**

C.J. (Christopher) Koch ("The Year Of Living Dangerously,") wrote the autobiographical book in 1958, but has revised it for its latest publication. "Boys" has been a long-time project for producer Jane Scott, with Carl Schultz originally tagged as director. Schultz, however, dropped out and was replaced by first-timer Geoffrey Bennett, who has music videos and tv drama as credits.

Book wasn't easily transposed to the screen, since it starts off as a traditional, familiar tale of four teenage boys going through adolescent traumas on the island state of Tasmania (south of the Australian mainland) in the '50s.

Focus here is on Frank (newcomer Yves Stening), a dreamer who longs to live on the mainland, preferably in alluring Melbourne. Louis (Joseph Clements), leader of the group, is a youth who dreams, somewhat bizarrely, of a life of crime as the answer to his limited horizons.

Curiously, the parents of the youths are never seen, except for Frank's father who briefly appears to admonish him for failing his exams. Almost total absence of family life places the boys in a strange vacuum. In almost every other respect, the first half of the film is familiar, though more serious than most teen pics.

Frank has spent too much time mooning over Heather (Lexa Murphy), the pretty but flighty girl he met at a dance. One curious scene has Frank witness Heather's father (Steve Jacobs) whip his wife before taking her off to bed; she seems to enjoy it, and Heather in the end prefers a local tough guy to the sensitive Frank.

About halfway through, the action shifts to Melbourne, whence all four friends have finally arrived. Louis does attach himself to a petty criminal, Farrell (British actor James Fox, top-billed but in a small role) and carries out an amusingly botched bank robbery.

Farrell's girl, Keeva (Jane Stephens), is a young siren who plays the boys off against each other, even seducing the shy Frank in one of the film's best scenes.

The switch to off-center film noir in the second half of the film gives "Boys In The Island" a distinctiveness that sets it apart from other pics of this genre. The Melbourne scenes are handled with just the right mixture of menace and comedy, and bring the film to a satisfying conclusion.

However, writers Koch and Morphett, and Bennett, linger too long over the more conventional early scenes; more time spent in the company of the devious Keeva and the cuckolded Farrell might have been time better spent.

Cinematographer Andrew Lesnie creates moments of visual magic. Performances are good, with Stephens stealing the pic as the ambiguous Keeva; Murphy's Heather is a much more conventional female interest. — *Strat.*

Overexposed

Chicago A Concorde Pictures release. Produced by Roger Corman. Directed by Larry Brand. Screenplay, Brand, Rebecca Reynolds; camera (color), David Sperling; editor, Patrick Rand; music, Mark Governor; production design, Robert Franklin; art director, Ella Blakey; set decoration, Tom Margules; assistant director, J.B. Rogers; executive in charge of production, Rodman Flender; casting, Al Guarino. Reviewed at the Chestnut Station Theater, Chicago, May 9, 1990. MPAA rating: R. Running time: **80 MIN.**
Kristen . . . . Catherine Oxenberg
Phillip . . . . David Naughton
Helen . . . . Jennifer Edwards
Hank . . . . William Bumiller
Terrance . . . . John Patrick Reger
Morrison . . . . Larry Brand
Mrs. Towbridge . . . . Karen Black

■ **Basically a yawner, "Overexposed" manages to pique some interest with a grotesque twist ending, but it's not enough to make the preceding 70 minutes worthwhile. Pic's exploitable theme could result in some ancillary business, but b.o. potential is limited to the sleaze circuit.**

Only remarkable aspect of this tame thriller about a tv actress who fears she is being targeted by a homicidal fan is its unpleasant foundation in a real-life problem. Film is a creepy reminder of sitcom actress Rebecca Schaeffer's murder last year, particularly since topliner David Naughton appeared with her in CBS' "My Sister Sam." Plotline is absurd enough to be interesting, even surprising, at times and the scripters have taken the trouble to include a couple of effective red herrings.

Acting throughout is ho-hum, except for Karen Black's entertaining turn as a babbling tv freak who calls the lead character a "whore of the air-waves" and tries to attack her with a TV Guide. Technical credits are lackluster, barring the sound quality, which is worse. — *Brin.*

Point Of View
(ISRAELI)

New York A Contrast Ltd. production. Produced by Noam Yavor, Haim Sharir. Executive producers, Ben Har-El, Michael Segal, Jonathan Siegal, E. Robert Goidkind. Director, Yavor. Screenplay, 20David Aharon Cohen; camera (color), Ilan Rosenberg; editor, Irit Raz, Moshe Avni, Eunice Mountjoy; music, Arik Rudich. Reviewed at Israel Film Festival, Biograph Cinema, N.Y., May 8, 1990. Running time: **90 MIN.**
Amnon Yehoshua . . . . John Savage
Karina . . . . Myriam Cyr
Avi . . . . Fisher Stevens
(English soundtrack)

■ **Set in war-torn Israel, "Point of View" at first appears to be a standard military drama, but it's actually a thoughtful film juxtaposing fiction and reality. Pic's serious, philosophical nature may help it find an arthouse audience.**

Although this is an Israeli production, most of the actors are Americans. The director chose to make the film in English with the goal of broad distribution in mind. His decision could well pay off, and having John Savage in the cast won't hurt either.

Made in 1988, "Point of View" has not yet been released because the director does not want to give the appearance of making a political statement. There should be no question that it is really more of a philosophical one.

Pic opens with three Israeli soldiers conducting a secret mission in the desert. When they happen upon a shepherd boy, they must decide whether to spare him, and jeopardize their own lives, or kill him and live with that decision. After they decide, the setting abruptly shifts to a writer at his desk, and it turns out the preceding scene comes from his story called "War Shepherds."

Eventually, audience learns that the writer, Amnon Yehoshua, actually did face such a difficult decision in wartime, and that his friend, Captain Jacobson, died in combat. Further blurring the borders of fiction and reality, Amnon lets a film class make two different versions of his story.

A sensitive filmmaker, Avi, wants to know how much of the story is true and treats it as a psychological study. An egotistical film student, Daniel, makes a chauvinistic version of the story and casts himself in a lead role. His girlfriend, Karina, works on Avi's film and meets Amnon in an attempt to find out the truth behind the short story.

The film concerns the fighting in Israel, but only within the context of filmmakers trying to make art out of conflict. Avi's army unit is called into action, and he must interrupt his film about war for the real thing. When he returns, having lost one of his soldiers, he says to Karina, "You have no idea how stupid it feels to be making a movie about war."

Nonetheless, he does complete his version, as does Daniel. Amnon attends the screening and pronounces that neither film is the correct one for his story. "The problem with film is it kills the tension between fiction and reality," he says. "Both chose only one reality. In this country we have 4-million different realities."

Savage gives a convincing performance as the tormented writer who tries to exorcise his demons through his work. When the actor depicts the horrors of warfare, his role in "The Deer Hunter" automatically comes to mind.

As the students who track him down, Myriam Cyr and Fisher Stevens are appropriately earnest and well-intentioned. Those attributes apply to the film, as well.
— *Stev.*

Far Out Man

San Francisco A New Line Pictures release of a Cinetel production. Produced by Lisa M. Hansen. Executive producer, Paul Hertzberg. Written and directed by Tommy Chong. Camera (Fotokem color), Greg Gardiner, Eric Woster; editor, Stephen Myer, Gilberto Costa Nunes; music, Jay Chattaway; sound, Michael S. Clark; art direction, David B. Miller; costumes, Dennis Michael Bansmer, James Gutierrez; assistant director, Kelsey T. Howard; coproducer, Howard Brown; associate producer, Eric Woster. Reviewed at the Galaxy Theater, S.F., May 14, 1990. MPAA rating: R. Running time: **91 MIN.**

Far Out Man	Tommy Chong
Tree	Shelby Chong
Kyle	Paris Chong
C. Thomas Howell	Himself
Psychiatrist	Martin Mull
Rae Dawn Chong	Herself
Bobby	Bobby Taylor
Lou	Reynaldo Taylor
Misty	Peggy F. Sands
Detective	Al Mancini
Judd Nelson	Himself
Weebee Cool	Paul Bartel
Cheech Marin	Himself

■ **With a Friday-night opening take of $313, $588 on Saturday and $400 on Sunday, "Far Out Man" might be well on its way to recovering its negative costs in one theater. From the looks of the pic, in fact, that $1,301 should just about pay for the whole thing.**

There's still homevideo ahead, which could create a demand in Congress for an entirely new kind of labeling for consumers. Surely, with all the w.k. names in the cast, people might be led to believe there was a film somewhere in the box.

They would be misled. It's hard to say exactly what "Far Out Man" is beyond an impromptu romp among the Chong family and friends. Tommy Chong takes credit for the writing and directing, but there's not much of either. In the vanity credits at the start, he also labels this a "Tommy Chong Attempt," apparently on the correct presumption he would not achieve anything.

Except for a cameo, Chong is working without Cheech Marin, his old sidekick in previously successful comedies constructed around various chemical adventures. Drugs are still around in "Far Out," but have become villainous, and Chong himself even drops a warning or two. His character, however, is warning enough: A vapid, burned-out aging hippie with a vocabulary largely limited to repeating the title.

For no particularly interesting reason in the story, Chong is in search of his ex-girlfriend (Shelby Chong) and their son (Paris Chong), taking what's left of his '60s sensibilities into various haunts of the '90s, repeating a lot of jokes from the '30s.

Technically, pic is a mess. Two lensers are credited, so it may be possible that one held the camera while the other held the film and the director never came out of character long enough to tell them what to do with either.

As for editing, there is a curiosi-ty: In the middle of the picture, one scene is repeated precisely. There are several explanations possible. It could be a creative cinematic device, but that would suggest a cinematically creative mind not evident anywhere else. It could be the participants liked the scene so much, they just wanted to show it again. It wasn't that good a scene.

Or maybe somebody involved in making the picture would have had to watch the whole thing to notice the repetition. But nobody wanted to watch the whole picture. Understandable. Just say no.
— *Har.*

Letter To The Next Generation
(DOCU)

New York Directed by James Klein. Camera (Du Art color), Don Lenzer; editor, Klein with Paul Barnes, Tony Heriza; sound, J.T. Takagi, John Dildine; coproducer, Susan Wehling. Reviewed at Anthology Film Archives, N.Y., May 20, 1990. No MPAA rating. Running time: **78 MIN.**

■ **Taking the tragic May 4, 1970, incident at Kent State as its starting point, James Klein's highly personal documentary depicts today's self-absorbed college students. The film's the-atrical prospects may be limited, but it should be picked up by PBS eventually.**

Klein, 40, who protested against Vietnam in his student days, perceptively contrasts the politicized atmosphere at schools 20 years ago with the current ethos of pre-professionalism.

A moving film for those who lived through Vietnam, as well as for those too young to recall it, "Letter To The Next Generation" is also scathingly funny. It shifts from old footage of demonstrations to contemporary fraternity parties and tanning salon visits. (A salon manager says he operates 24 hours a day and has a long waiting list prior to spring break).

This is a far cry from the altruistic protesters of the 1960s, four of whom lost their lives when the National Guard fired on the crowd at Kent State.

Docu begins with a typical campus tour, which ends with the complacent guide's mention of the memorial to the slain students: "It is something that we do remember, but it's also something we're trying to move away from." Most of the students interviewed by the filmmaker show a similar disinterest. They are concerned only with having fun, finding a good corporate job and making lots of money.

Klein does interview a cross-section of students and faculty, a few of whom recount the slaying, and concludes that activism is returning to campuses. Although ROTC drills and Greek parties are the norm at Kent State, there is also a guerilla theater company, a black students group and a meeting of young activists.

While the film succeeds in contrasting current collegiate conservatism with 1970 radicalism, it would have been even better if it had more film and tv clips from the Vietnam era. Klein's low budget may have prevented him from acquiring more footage.

At times the film unfairly ridicules contempo college kids. The director has students sing "The Brady Bunch" theme, which naturally they all know by heart. But an ROTC coordinator offers a logical reason for the business orientation of most students at Kent State: Tuition was only $300 a semester in 1970; now students are buried in debt when they graduate.

An absorbing account of two disparate generations, "Letter To The Next Generation" is just what its title says. It's a plea to the next round of college students to try to change the world, as students did 20 years ago, rather than emulate today's materialistic undergraduates. — *Stev.*

CANNES FILM MARKET REVIEWS

Pump Up The Volume
(U.S.-CANADIAN)

Cannes A New Line Cinema release of a New Line production, in association with SC Entertainment. Executive producers, Sara Risher, Nicolas Stiladis, Syd Cappe. Produced by Rupert Harvey, Sandy Stern. Written and directed by Allan Moyle. Camera (color), Walt Lloyd; editor, Wendy Bricmont, Ric Keeley, Kurt Hathaway; music coordinator, Nicole Freegard; production design, Bruce Bolander; costumes, Michael Abbot; first assistant director, Josh McLaglen; executive in charge of production, Deborah Moore; post-production supervisor, Joe Fineman; casting, Judith Holfstra. Reviewed at Cannes Film Festival (market), May 15, 1990. No MPAA Rating. Running time: **105 MIN.**

Mark Hunter	Christian Slater
Nora	Samantha Mathis
Jan Emerson	Ellen Greene
Keith Hunter	Scott Paulin
Paige	Cheryl Pollak
Murdock	Andy Romano
Martha Hunter	Mimi Kennedy
Mrs. Cresswood	Annie Ross

Also: Mark Ballou, Jill Jarres, Lala, Ahmet Zappa, Dan Eisenstein, Nigel Gibbs, Seth Green, James Hampton, Clayton Landey.

■ **"Pump Up The Volume" is a perceptive film with a bracingly uncondescending take on a topic both timeless and contemporary: misunderstood teens. If marketed honestly and aggressively it could appeal not only to '90s teens, but to sympathetic young adults who remember the stormy passage through adolescence.**

Writer-director Allan Moyle's story about a shy high school student who galvanizes an Arizona suburb with a rebellious pirate radio show has rambunctious energy and defiant attitude.

Christian Slater is first-rate as a bright but alienated student who feels trapped and disconnected in a suburban "whitebread land" where "everything is sold out." Everything includes his father (Scott Paulin), a former '60s radical who has bought into the yuppie dream and followed a successful career in education from New York to Arizona, where he's a county schools commissioner.

Slater's personality is split between the bookish, withdrawn persona he presents to the world at large and the caustically funny firebrand who reaches out to his contemporaries in "Paradise Hills" from a low-frequency radio station he's set up in his room.

His "Talk Hard" program offers an improvisational stream of rudely obscene humor, heated jeremiads against a sterile society, savage japes at the high school administration, and a mix of confrontational thrash-rock and rap music.

Unlike the children of the '60s who had great causes and a counterculture to rally around, Slater and his schoolmates at "Hubert Humphrey High" are burdened with suppressed discontent for which there is no outlet. America, says the d.j., has evolved into a smug and "sleazy country — a place you can't trust," and its children have "nothing to do anymore."

Starting his show as a playful experiment, Slater quickly attracts a cult of listeners. They gather in a parking lot where his signal carries clearly and begin spreading bootleg tapes of his broadcasts.

Slater, a new kid in town, shines in the creative writing class taught by teacher Ellen Greene, but has no friends in the large, impersonal school. Greene, who does not overplay her role, is the only adult remotely in touch with the students' feelings. The principal (Annie Ross) is an insensitive martinet who keeps the student body grade point average up by expelling troubled students without just cause.

Slater's rebellious late-night broadcasts soon make him a hero and stir up the dormant anger of other alienated kids. But one night his talk-radio antics go out of control. A desperate phone-in listener threatens to commit suicide and the d.j. is just a little too flip about it.

When the boy goes through with it, Slater is shattered and almost gives up. The authorities turn their attention to the radio rebel. Their concern mounts when a model student (Cheryl Pollak), dominated by a manipulative father, defiantly sets a microwave-triggered explosion in her kitchen.

Slater's parents are oblivious to the goings-on in their own house, and urge their son to see a shrink or get some hobbies and a girlfriend. Nora (Samantha Mathis) falls in love with Slater's disembodied voice and becomes obsessed with learning the identity of the mysterious messenger. When she does he tries to reject her, but eventually discovers a kindred soul.

Other students get swept up in the rebellion. Television and the newspapers make the d.j. a hot story, embarrassing the police and the FCC. The principal cracks down in draconian fashion and fires Greene when the teacher pushes for students' rights.

Moyle resolves things in favor of love and justice, but his ending resolutely refuses to sell out the movie's angry stance against complacency. Slater handles nu-

merous monolog scenes with conviction and charisma. Newcomer Mathis and Paulin show a good grasp of their characters.

While the film's title seems to promise wall-to-wall music, contempo sounds are used mainly to convey the defiant ambience of a pic that presents an unvarnished view of modern teens of the '90s.
— *Rich.*

Una Vita Scellerata
(A Violent Life)
(ITALIAN-FRENCH-GERMAN)

Rome An Artisti Associati Intl. release of a Leader Cinematografica/Cinemax coproduction in association with RAI-TV Channel 2 and Beta Taurus. Produced by Raffaello Monteverde. Directed by Giacomo Battiato. Screenplay, Vittorio Bonicelli, based on Benvenuto Cellini's autobiography; camera (color), Dante Spinotti; editor, Claudio Di Mauro; music, Franco Battiato; art direction, Gianni Quaranta. Reviewed at Europa Cinema, Rome, May 7, 1990. (In Cannes Film Festival Market.) Running time: **103 MIN.**
Benvenuto Cellini . . . . Wadeck Stanczak
Pope Clement VII . . . . . Max Von Sydow
Governor . . . . Ben Kingsley
Servant . . . . Pamela Villoresi
   With: Sophie Ward, Bernard Pierre Donnadieu.

■ Giacomo Battiato's biopic of 16th century goldsmith-sculptor Benvenuto Cellini is a visual banquet and a rousing passionate homage to the artist as tormented human being. Director's previous success abroad (notably with "Blood Ties," which aired for a year on Showtime) could help get the theatrical release onto offshore screens.

"A Violent Life" was inexplicably snubbed in Rome in its opening week theatrically, but may get wider Italian viewing when it airs as a three-part tv miniseries on RAI-TV. The biopic is a long-time RAI-2 project that passed through many hands before Battiato received the green light.

Battiato has never before been taken up by the festival circuit, but a retro of his films would reveal a unique talent eternally struggling to balance his artistic imagination against mainstream filmmaking. There is much in "A Violent Life" to recall Derek Jarman's "Caravaggio," for example.

This $10 million costumer fully exploits one of the most violent and adventurous lives in the history of Italian art, a man completely engaged in the brutal events of his time.

Vittorio Bonicelli's script, based on Cellini's autobiography, takes plenty of imaginative license in reconstructing the Renaissance. Freely ranging back and forth among the artist's memories (which from a 20th century perspective seem far larger than life), film depicts an epic hero.

Cellini was born a Florentine and learned the goldsmith's craft of making beautiful objects. But his model was Michelangelo, and his artistic ambition unlimited.

Acclaimed as a great fabricator of jewelry and ornamental vases, patronized by two popes and the king of France, he never got the commissions he wanted.

The tremendous final scenes, where he casts his great statue Perseus at his own expense, melting down everything in his house and setting the roof on fire, testify to his unflagging faith in himself and rage for creation.

Film ends on this high point, leaving the titles to mention the incredible way Cellini survived another 20 years, as feisty as ever.

Battiato's taste for violence, familiar from the Mafia thriller "Blood Ties," is in full force here. Strong stomachs are required to watch the hand-to-hand combat, scenes of the plague and a spectacular, grisly depiction of the Sack of Rome.

Cinematographer Dante Spinotti's remarkable lighting, playing off various painterly styles, opens with a startling black & white scene of hyper-violence in which young Cellini battles three youths.

In other moments he ferociously stabs someone who slanders him; sews up the mouth of a knight; shoots the Bourbon leader through the head; rapes a compliant gentlewoman, etc.

In spite of his delicate features, Polish actor Wadeck Stanczak creates a coherent figure of the artist as a boastful, lusty, hard-living man who frequently got in hot water for murder and other infractions of 16th century standards.

One unforgettable scene shows his imprisonment in Castel Sant'Angelo, where later, half-mad, he fights the Bourbons at the side or Pope Clement VII (a fine, reflective Max Von Sydow).

Showing the age as a ruthless fight for survival, "A Violent Life" has its moments of humor.

Best is Ben Kingsley's delightful performance as the mad governor who thinks he's a bird and orders Cellini to make him wings,

with disastrous results. Even while he's carousing with wenches and pals, like Rosso Fiorentino and Giulio Romano, Cellini comes across as a heroic figure of giant proportions.

Pamela Villoresi is excellent as the artist's faithful maid, consoling him when all his battles have done him in. Franco Battiato's score, like script and lensing, tends to the avant-garde. Gianni Quaranta also gets free rein for his startling set design, a tribute to the imagination. — *Yung.*

Movie In Your Face
(HONG KONG-U.S.)

Cannes A Northcoast Entertainment production. Executive producer, Michael Courtney. Produced by Joseph Butcher. U.S. footage directed by David Merwin. Screenplay, Tommy Sledge, Tom Sparks, Stan Evans, Scott Silverman, John Content, Mark Richardson, Tony Frankel, Wendy Westerwille, Lee McKay; camera (color), Marty Oppenheimer; editor, Pat Barber; sound, Aaron Sonego; art direction, Terry Tennesen; associate producer, Donna Hines. Reviewed at Cannes Film Festival (market), May 12, 1990. Running time: **86 MIN.**
   With: Tommy Sledge, Kent Cheng, Wong Chin, Wang Yu, Dorothy Yu.

■ This Seattle-produced item attempts to repeat the cult success won by Woody Allen's 1966 "What's Up Tiger Lily?," which redubbed and recut a Japanese spy thriller with hilarious results.

In this case, the production team has made the mistake of using as their basic material not a "serious" film, but a Hong Kong comedy about gangsters. Adding supposedly funny dialog to situations that already are farcical is much less successful.

Undemanding youngsters may go for the raunchy dialog imposed on the original, but most will tire of the joke very quickly. Newly shot footage, involving Tommy Sledge as a private eye, is no bonus.

Cult success is a possibility here, but seems unlikely. — *Strat.*

Schweitzer

Cannes A Concorde Pictures release. (Intl. sales, Sugar Entertainment.) Produced by Ashok Amritraj. Executive producer, Edgar Bold. Directed by Grey Hofmyer. Screenplay, Michel Potts; camera (Agfacolor), Buster Reynolds; editor, Peter Grosett; music, Zane Kronje; costumes, Rui Philips; production design, Michael Phillips; line producer, Michel Games. Reviewed at Cannes Film Festival (market), May 18, 1990. No MPAA

Rating. Running time: **100 MIN.**
Albert Schweitzer . . . . Malcolm McDowell
Mrs. Schweitzer . . . . Susan Strasberg
Amanda Hampton . . . . Helen Jessop
Lionel Curtis . . . . Andrew Davis
Horton Herschel . . . . John Carson

———

■ "Schweitzer" is a fictional episode based on philosopher-musician-doctor Albert Schweitzer's life at work in his French Congo (now Gabon) hospital. Although bursting with production values (location shooting in Zimbabwe and the Ivory Coast), a future on the small screens seems most likely for this one.

Item is the third feature by Gray Hofmeyr whose approach, along with that of the screenplay, is blandly reverent even though the idea is to get to the root of a controversy that was to plague the famous man after World War II.

Schweitzer's "reverence of life" philosophy and insistence on running his jungle hospital in a literally down-to-earth way did not jell with the demands put forward by his various sponsors, especially those from the U.S., that he use more modern methods.

That Schweitzer was also accused of bad racial attitudes also became an issue before he received the Nobel Peace Prize in 1952, but this is hardly touched upon in this film.

The story, which may or may not be based on fact, takes place around 1947. A doctor and former pupil return to Lamberene with a do-gooder lady and a bluff U.S. publisher in tow. Coming back at the same time is Mrs. Schweitzer, who is played by Susan Strasberg with angelic mien throughout.

Neither spiritual confrontations nor narrative action following get much of a chance to bloom as drama. The Americans not only frown at Schweitzer's refusal to turn his hospital into a steel-and-chrome institution, they also threaten to cut off his funds.

The doctor turns his back to them to play Bach on his organ or spouts pious words in defense of his own ways. The Americans verge on gross caricature, while the young doctor is placed in a dilemma of sympathies.

Schweitzer, played as a rather benign old buzzard by Malcolm McDowell, is also followed through his saving of a native woman who gives birth to twins. The local witch doctor insists that one of the babies is given to the gods, but he is defeated by Sch-

weitzer, who also reveals an attempt to poison his patient.

Without too much to connect him to the main story, a French colonial official is seen attacked and bloodied in his bed by a lioness. — *Kell.*

———

Jobman
(SOUTH AFRICAN)

———

Cannes A Blue Rock Films production. Produced by Christopher Coy. Executive producers. Elizabeth Shorten, Patricia Shorten. Directed by Darrell Roodt. Screenplay, Roodt, Gregg Latter, based on a short story by Achmat Dangor; camera (color), Paul White; editor, Shelley Wells; music, Joel Goldsmith; sound, Robin Harris; art direction, Dave Barkham; costume design, Sylvia Van Heerden. Reviewed at Cannes Film Festival (market), May 12, 1990. Running time: **97 MIN.**
Jobman . . . . Kevin Smith
Karel . . . . Tertius Mientjies
Anna . . . . Lynn Gaines

———

■ South African director Darrell Roodt has created a lyrical but violent tale focusing on a black deaf-mute. Visually stunning piece is too spare and slow-moving for general audiences, but could lend itself to specialized theatrical and tv exploitation in certain world markets.

Kevin Smith plays Jobman, a preacher's son born without a tongue whose stubborn spirit and refusal to accept menial labor makes him threatening to blacks and whites alike in his farm community.

Beaten like an animal by thugs in the city, the silent protagonist comes home to fetch his child and common-law wife away from her parents, who despise him. After he's ostracized both at home and in the city, he roams the backcountry as a renegade.

When an armed posse goes after him, Jobman methodically kills them, shooting them in the back as they flee. The locals appeal to Karel (Tertius Mientjies), who's recently inherited the farm Jobman grew up on, to help track and kill him, but the white man fiercely resists being coerced into the murder of his boyhood friend.

A string of violence ensues as others take up their guns and go after the cold-blooded crackshot renegade.

Based on a short story by Achmat Dangor, the film is beautifully framed and photographed but thematically vague, as it's never clear why Karel is so deeply ambivalent

about what Jobman's fate should be.

Bullets and antagonisms fly freely across color lines, and the racial and political conditions that shape Jobman's community are left largely unarticulated, or are taken for granted in a way that world audiences probably will not fathom.

Smith, in a striking and subtle performance as the ragged, wordless pilgrim, clearly communicates the prideful rage that fuels Jobman's decision to make off with the few tender things the world has to offer him and strike down anyone who comes after him.

The moments of intimacy and understanding that pass beween him and his wife (Lynn Gaines) are beautifully handled, and Roodt and cameraman Paul White conjure up many lasting images in this artfully lensed saga.

Result is a simple, poetic tale with a powerful central image that hints at underlying social and political themes but fails to really activate them. One gets the feeling that Roodt, like his protagonist, lacked the ability to express much of what might have been said.

Skillful use is made of black & white photography in flashbacks to Jobman's youth, and Joel Goldsmith's score adds a haunting tone. — *Daws.*

———

Delta Force 2: The
Colombian Connection

———

Cannes A Cannon Intl. release of a Cannon Films production. Produced by Yoram Globus, Christopher Pearce. Directed by Aaron Norris. Screenplay, Lee Reynolds; camera (color), Joao Fernandes; editor, Michael J. Duthie; music, Frederic Talgorn. Reviewed at the Cannes Film Festival (market), May 13, 1990. MPAA Rating: R. Running time: **105 MIN.**
Col. Scott McCoy . . . . Chuck Norris
Ramon Coda . . . . Billy Drago
Paul . . . . Bobby Chavez
Gen. Taylor . . . . John R. Ryan
John Page . . . . Richard Jaeckel
Conquina . . . . Begonia Plaza
Ernesto . . . . Mateo Gomez

———

■ Chuck Norris fans have all they could ask for with Cannon's "Delta Force 2." It looks like a strong entry in the season's action market.

Norris and a dozen U.S. Marines fly into the South American drug capital "San Carlos," destroy half the country's cocaine production, and rub out the land's untouchable drug czar, in a cathartic blaze of exploding missiles and flying fists.

At a time when U.S. military enemies are fast becoming an endangered species, "Delta Force 2" latches onto the year's easiest target, Colombia (modestly veiled as "San Carlos" here) and the head of the drug cartel. History's Escobar is transformed into handsome, hypnotically evil Ramon Coda (Billy Drago).

The underlying fantasy that gives pic its charge is that a handful of American musclemen can lick the Medellin cartel in about two days.

After establishing Norris's good nature and unbeatable brawn, and his partner Bobby Chavez's attachment to wife and home, "Delta" introduces the inhuman ruthlessness of Coda. For a whim, he kills a peasant woman's husband and baby and rapes the lady (Begonia Plaza).

First set piece is an exuberant parachute scene, where Norris and pal arrest Coda on an airplane and jump to a waiting Navy cruiser.

Unfortunately, Coda gets out of jail on $10-million bail, and immediately takes revenge. Chavez comes home to find his family murdered, takes off after Coda and meets his end in a scenographic gas chamber.

Norris invades with a hand-picked team of bull-necked Marines trained for all eventualities, and a general (a lively John R. Ryan) gleeful at the prospect of blasting coke fields out of existence.

The American president is backing the operation, but San Carlos' numero uno creates obstacles. Norris goes in early to climb up a sheer mountain cliff (accomplished effortlessly), while Ryan follows with the Marines.

Payoff is a long sequence of destruction. Norris frees some DEA hostages and goes for Coda, knocking off scores of armed thugs. When he gets his hands on the boss, however, legal scruples spring up. The retreat is considerably complicated by having to drag Coda along for another U.S. trial.

Meanwhile, the Marines lay waste to the drug czar's heavily guarded headquarters, mostly with missiles shot from a helicopter. Norris and Coda get out in a chase scene driving a huge limo, while angry jeeps fire at their heels. To keep things going a little longer, the Marines also blow up a native village (minus the villagers, who are on their side and, in this story at least, happy to get rid of Coda's entourage).

Pic closes with an exciting helicopter lift. Norris makes it through a tremendous bashing without a scratch. Coda is killed in all legality — by accident.

(During the filming, five people were killed in a May 15, 1989, helicopter crash in the Philippines: pilot Jo Jo Imperial, stuntmen Geoffrey Brewer, Mike Graham and Gadi Danzig, and gaffer Don Marshall. Three others were injured.)

Production values are high throughout, with an endless stream of ammunition and extras. Lensing is pro, and score has a tropical flavor that stays pleasantly in the background.

Norris is a minimalist actor, rightly concentrating on the action. As the sadistic Coda, Drago has a Medusa-like presence that produces shivers just from looking at him. Except for Ryan as the general, supporting players are standard types.

Most of the violence can be watched with open eyes. Bullets, stabbings, and some judo throws are the main ingredients, with little gore and no sex to be borne.

— *Yung.*

Shredder Orpheus

New York An Image Network presentation. (Intl. sales, Manley Prods.) Executive producer, Robert McGinley. Produced by Lisanne Dutton. Written and directed by McGinley. Camera (color), Erich Volkstorf; editor, Linda Mitchell, Kathy Schickling; music, Roland Barker; sound, Al Swanson; art direction, Randy Ericksen; production manager, Lora Goncharoff; assistant director, Christine Dickerson; 2d unit camera, Carl Morgan; associate producer, Josh Conescu. Reviewed on AIP vidcassette, N.Y., May 8, 1990. (In Cannes Film Festival Market.) No MPAA Rating. Running time: **88 MIN.**
Axel . . . . Stephen J. Bernstein
Orpheus . . . . Robert McGinley
Eurydice . . . . Megan Murphy
Hades . . . . Gian-Carlo Scandiuzzi
Persephone . . . . Vera McCaughan
Razoreus . . . . Marshall Reid
Scratch . . . . Linda Severt
Linus . . . . John Billingsley
EBN Producer . . . . Brian Faker
Apollo . . . . Whitney Shapiro

■ **The Greek legend that produced arthouse faves "Orpheus" and "Black Orpheus" crashes to earth in the idiotic punk sci-fi feature "Shredder Orpheus." It's for fans of injokes only.**

Helmer Robert McGinley also toplines as Orpheus, a band leader (of the Shredders) in a post-apocalyptic world where hipsters live in shanty towns known as the Grey Zone. McGinley's underdeveloped script posits an easy enemy, the Euthanasia Broadcast Network which involves Cronenberg-style philosophizing (out of his "Videodrome") as weak satire.

Punk tv programmers want Eurydice (Megan Murphy) for their new show. The underworld in this sci-fi universe is a place where people's memories are shredded faster than you can say Oliver North.

Orpheus becomes a tv star playing an electronic lyre instrument supposedly invented by Jimi Hendrix. Heroine disappears after Orpheus violates the "Don't look back" warning and gazes at her; rest of film is him searching for her. Finale involving skateboarders is stupid.

Apparently McGinley didn't watch Jean Cocteau's 1950 classic very closely since he leaves out the poignant role of Heurtebise (played eloquently in "Orphée" by François Périer). He also fails to find any equivalent to Cocteau's inspired anachronisms, and is instead content to littering the dialog with advertising slogans and catch phrases.

Acting is amateurish and technical quality, mixing film and video footage, subpar. — *Lor.*

Book Of Love

Cannes A New Line Cinema release. Produced by Rachel Talalay. Directed by Bob Shaye. Screenplay, William Kotzwinkle, based on his novel, "Jack In The Box;" camera (color), Peter Deming; editor, Terry Stokes; music supervisor, Bonnie Greenburg; sound, James Thornton; production design, C.J. Strawn; costume design, Susie DeSanto; art direction, Timothy Gray; set decoration, James R. Barrows; assistant director, Raymond T. King; casting, Annette Benson. Reviewed at Cannes Film Festival (market), May 14, 1990. No MPAA Rating. Running time: **82 MIN.**
Jack Twiller . . . . Chris Young
Crutch Krane . . . . Keith Coogan
Lily . . . . Josie Bissett
Mrs. Twiller . . . . Jill Jaress
Peanut . . . . Aeryk Egan
Gina Gabooch . . . . . Trisha Leigh Fisher
Floyd . . . . John Cameron Mitchell
Spider . . . . Danny Nucci
Mr. Twiller . . . . John Achorn
Adult Jack Twiller . . . . Michael McKean
Angela . . . . Beau Dremann

■ **This well-paced, skillfully molded nostalgic comedy from New Line has a bright cast and strokes of charm and imagination, but it covers material far too familiar to U.S. audiences to survive more than a brief theatrical release. Video and foreign sales could extend its life.**

New Line founder Bob Shaye directs a 1950s tale of a horny adolescent whose very typical coming-of-age story is somewhat distinguished by amusing opticals in which aspects of his "vivid imagination" come to life. Photographs talk to him, cartoons come alive, movie images affect him absurdly (he does a miserable James Dean imitation).

Aside from that, pic goes through the typical paces, setting up the story of nice but awkward teen, Jack Twiller (Chris Young), a new kid in town who's befriended by geeky Crutch Kane (Keith Coogan) and falls hopelessly in love with a blonde teen princess, Lily (Josie Bissett), who is usually squired by the local ethnic bully, Angelo (Beau Dremann).

Twist is that Jack later ends up in a disastrous marriage to Lily (not shown) and pic takes the form of a flashback in which the newly divorced Jack (Michael McKean) reflects on his folly in not pursuing another girl, Angelo's tough-talking but sincere sister Gina (Trisha Leigh Fisher).

Augmenting the usual plotline about teenage boys scheming hopelessly to get laid, pic rounds the well-trodden bases of nostalgia such as the first car, the wild parties when parents go away and the senior prom.

For the most part it's sweet and funny, but just very familiar. Shaye directs comfortably and with some amusing twitches, such as never showing the face of Jack's father (John Achorn), who issues directions from behind the newspaper.

Young gives an engaging performance as young Jack, displaying a nice, modulated charm in the Ron Howard mode that bodes well for his future. Coogan makes a bright and funny supporting player, and both Danny Nucci and John Cameron Mitchell project noticeable talent as the other members of the misfit gang.

Peter Deming's subdued photography is a big asset, giving pic a subtle glow. C.J. Strawn contributes apropos, unfussy production design. — *Daws.*

A Ay
(TURKISH-B&W)

Istanbul Produced by Metis Film, Images and Cameras Export Agency, Paris. Written and directed by Reha Erdom. Camera (black & white), Ugur Eruzun; editor, Nathalie Le-guay. Reviewed at Istanbul Intl. Film Festival (out of competition), April 13, 1990. (In Cannes Film Festival Market.) Running time: **102 MIN.**
With: Yesim Tozan, Gulsen Tuncer, Nuriniza Yildirim, Munir Ozkul.

■ **The French training and experience of helmer Reha Erdom is evident in this striking luminescent black & white tone poem, a startling departure from traditional Turkish cinema. With proper promo, pic should do well in arthouse release and at fests.**

Yekta (Yesim Tozan) lives with her aunt, grandfather and a lame seagull in an old house on the Bosphorus. Kindly indulged by her elders, she is often on her own and develops a rich imagination, which leads to psychological and mythological interpretation of her dreams, often centering on her dead mother who disappeared in a boat.

When Yekta's mother appears to her, passing by her window on a boat, she brings a playmate over to verify it and take photographs. Yekta begins a spiritual communion with the apparition and refuses to be swayed in her belief.

Her well-meaning aunt is exasperated when Yekta balks at being sent off to school. She assumes Yekta is going through a phase and will soon lose interest in her mystical preoccupation.

Dialog is sparse, a moody atmosphere prevails accented by cello and string quartet music. Pic is an homage to the Ottoman flavor of many streets and the wild beauty of much of the Bosphorus. Tozan is a natural in the role that is made sympathetic without being the slightest bit cloying. — *Sam.*

Après après-demain
(The Day After The Day After Tomorrow)
(FRENCH)

Paris Imperia release of a Pro-Images/La Sept/Planète et cie/Cout de Coeur coproduction. Produced by Calixte Jouon, Loic Haroche. Directed by Gérard Frot-Coutaz. Screenplay, Frot-Coutaz, Jacques Davila; camera (Fujicolor), Jean-Bernard Menoud; editor, Frank Mathieu; music, Roland Vincent; sound, Bernard Rochut; art direction, Jean-Jacques Gernolle; costumes, Nathalie Cercuel; production manager, Eliane Lacroux; casting, Shula Siegfried. Reviewed at the Gaumont Ambassade theater, Paris, May 6, 1990. (In Cannes Film Festival Market.) Running time: **84 MIN.**
Isabelle . . . . Anémone
Paul . . . . Simon de la Brosse
Sophie . . . . Agnès Soral
Alex . . . . Claude Pieplu

Neighbor . . . . Micheline Prèsle
Madam Leguennec . . . . . . Joanna Pavlis

■ Gérard Frot-Coutaz, who coscripted and directed, confirms what his first pic ("Beau temps mais orageux en fin de journée") demonstrated: lack of directorial ability, both with cast and camera. His temperament seems better suited to screenwriting, though script for this film is far from brilliant.

In this soporific, graceless romantic comedy, good-looking Simon de la Brosse falls head-over-heels in love with not-so-good looking Anémone. De la Brosse plays a young gym instructor whose passion for Anémone, a struggling fashion designer, is one of those prerequisites that one must accept for the rest of the story to function.

Anémone, whose unpredictable nature and fear of romance drives de la Brosse to distraction, has rarely been so charmless. Understandably, he never seems at ease in trying to convince us it's Anémone or no one, not even the more appealing but loveless Agnès Soral.

Frot-Coutaz' poor handling of the cast extends to supporting players Claude Pieplu and Micheline Prèsle. Prèsle has a dumb comic role as Anémone's flustered neighbor, who sees in Anémone's rich benefactress (Joanna Pavlis) her own long-lost daughter.

For a comedy, Jean-Bernard Menoud's camerawork is oddly glum. Other credits are so-so.
— *Len.*

Il sole buio
(The Dark Sun)
(ITALIAN)

Cannes   A Penta Distribuzione release of a Cecchi Gori Group Tiger Cinematografica production. Produced by Mario and Vittorio Cecchi. Directed by Damiano Damiani. Screenplay, Damiani, Ennio De Concini; camera (color), Nino Celeste; editor, Enzo Meniconi; music, Riz Ortolani; art direction, Umberto Turco. Reviewed at the Cannes Film Festival (market), May 14, 1990. Running time: **107 MIN.**
Lucia . . . . Jo Champa
Ruggero Brickman . . . . . . Michael Paré
Lawyer . . . . Phyllis Logan
    Also with: Erland Josephson.

■ Damiano Damiani's thriller "The Dark Sun" lacks the dramatic impact of popular series like "The Octopus" and died quickly at local wickets. Though its serious intention to depict contempo Mafia prob-

lem fizzles, it has enough action to do tv and vidcassette biz abroad.

Dramatizing a number of recent headlines that have created a stir, including the "maxi-trial" of multiple mob bosses in Palermo, tale finds young heir Ruggero Brickman (played by Yank thesp Michael Paré) returning from the States to Sicily, where his Italian mother has died.

She was the benefactress of a girls' reformatory, and Ruggero soon takes a special interest in one inmate, Lucia (Jo Champa). The underage drug pusher/ex-hooker is released thanks to Ruggero's intercession with the police. His stepfather (Erland Josephson) is an influential lawyer.

Idealist legal eagle Phyllis Logan, however, casts doubt on Josephson's unimpeachable reputation..

Meanwhile, Lucia's father is gunned down for informing on a killer. Like most of Palermo's citizens, she believes he deserved it because he "squealed." Only Ruggero, in his brash American way, waxes indignant over the killing. When Lucia says she got a look at the guy, and has seen him again, he insists they notify the police.

Pacing speeds up in the second half. The killer is a slick pusher Lucia goes to bed with. Not to avenge her father, but to protect Ruggero from the guy's suspicions, Lucia shoots him. This lands her back in the reformatory until she's released on bail.

Inevitably, romance blooms between Lucia and her protector. At first she has to take the initiative (he's too much the gentleman to take advantage of her generosity). Later he offers to marry her, but Lucia nobly refuses: she doesn't want to be pitied.

Ruggero leaves her marching with a grief-stricken crowd in a funeral procession for her girlfriend's dead lover, a mobster. On the other side of town, a brave cop's funeral is deserted. (This is a real fact of life, much quoted in the newspapers.)

Wide-eyed, overgrown gamine Champa, a talented Yank who has appeared in a number of Italo releases, turns in pic's one redeeming performance. Her unsentimental intensity (and colorful Sicilian accent) give Lucia a realistic foothold even in this slippery plot.

Paré doesn't get beyond an im-

possible role, somewhere between Prince Charming and amateur sleuth. Peripheral characters, from lawyers to cops, are standard.

Technical credits are up to the mark. — *Yung.*

Wings Of Fame
(DUTCH)

Amsterdam   A Cannon Tuschinski release of a First Floor Features production. Produced by Laurens Geels, Dick Maas. Directed by Otakar Votocek. Screenplay, Votocek, Herman Koch; camera (color), Alex Thomson; editor, Hans van Dongen; music, Paul M. van Brugge; art direction, Dick Schillemans; production supervisor, Wim Lehnhausen. Reviewed at the Cinema theater, Amsterdam, March 20, 1990. (In Cannes Film Festival Market.) Running time: **116 MIN.**
Valentin . . . . Peter O'Toole
Smith . . . . Colin Firth
Bianca . . . . Marie Trintignant
Theresa . . . . Andréa Ferréol
Dr. Frisch . . . . Maria Becker
Ziatogorski . . . . Gottfried John
Receptionist . . . . Walter Gotell
    (English soundtrack)

■ Shot in English with a European name cast, "Wings Of Fame" wavers between the superproduction and think-pic, and suggests that maybe first-time director Otakar Votocek might have been better off with a leaner production.

Still, laced with irony and sarcasm, this quirky and imaginative fantasy about the famous dead in the beyond is both compelling and frequently funny.

Screenplay by Votocek and Herman Koch is set on an island with a large hotel where the celebrated dead are ferried and lodged so long as their earthly fame lasts. Once their notoriety fades, they are thrown into the sea to join the ordinary dead, condemned to bob up and down forever.

Peter O'Toole is excellent as a vain over-the-hill matinee movie idol who has been killed by a devil-may-care writer (perfectly played by Colin Firth) because O'Toole had cannibalized Firth's text for his own autobiography. Firth then dies in an accident.

They both arrive together at the island hotel. O'Toole doesn't mind being killed, but wants to know why. Firth delights in withholding the information, especially when both males begin to stalk bewildered young Marie Trintignant, who died in a state of amnesia.

Story premise provides for a good deal of extraneous fun. For instance, it brings in Einstein, the

Lindbergh baby, a mass murderer and even Lassie. But some of the jokes tend to get convoluted and a number of minor roles, thrown in to underline the point that jealousy, malice and gossip thrive after death as well, weigh down the middle of the film.

Votocek's direction of his first-rate cast, elegant matter-of-fact style and ingenious control of pacing create high expectations for his new feature. Ace lenser Alex Thomson does a marvelous job in rendering the hotel as a cold, lifeless sort of railway terminal with furniture. — *Wall.*

Night Club

Cannes   A Crown Intl. Pictures release of an Artists Film Group production. Produced by Mark Headley, Nicolas Hoppe. Directed by Michael Keusch. Screenplay, Deborah Tilton; camera (color), Louis di Cesare; editor, Michael Keusch; music, Dana Walden, Barry Fasman; art director, prop master, Naomi Kaneda. Reviewed at Cannes Film Festival (market), May 13, 1990. MPAA rating: R. Running time: **90 MIN.**
Nick . . . . Nicholas Hoppe
Beth/Liza . . . . Elizabeth Kaitan
Eddie . . . . Ed Trotta
Peter . . . . Peter Jurasik
Debbie . . . . Deborah Tilton
Joe . . . . Joe Morena

■ With a storyline carried by dream sequences and flashbacks, no suspense buildup and lack of audience sympathy with the players, "Night Club's" possibilities are limited to vid at best. Explicit lingo restricts tv; theatrical possibilities nil.

A psychothriller without the thrills, clichéd plot concerns a young married couple who have pumped all their coin into a night club project in an abandoned factory. When the city condemns the property, a mobster demands return of his investment, or else.

Plot proceeds in a series of flashbacks and pseudosurrealistic dream sequences evidently reflecting the non-hero's emerging insanity. Knee-tremblers, sex with clothes on, marital strife, and a stilted dialog merely irritate rather than entertain. A mediocre rock music soundtrack compounds the artistic felony. Consign to electronic limbo. — *Kind.*

CANNES FILM FESTIVAL REVIEWS (COMPETITION)

The King's Whore
(FRENCH-AUSTRIAN-BRITISH-ITALIAN)

Cannes An ASC/FR3 Film Prods./Cinema é Cinema/Umbrella Prods. coproduction. (Intl. sales, J&M Entertainment.) Produced by Maurice Bernart, Wieland Schulz-Keil, Paolo Zaccaria. Directed by Axel Corti. Screenplay, Daniel Vigne, Frederic Raphael, Corti, based on the novel "Jeanne, putain du roi" by Jacques Tournier; additional dialog by Derek Marlowe; camera, Gernot Roll; editor, Joelle Van Effenterre; music, Gabriel Yared; sound, Michele Boehm; production design, Francesco Frigeri; costume design, Carlo Diappi; art direction, Atos Mastrogirolamo, François Marcepoil; set decoration, Lorenzo D'Ambrosio, Jacques Leguillon; stunt coordinator, Neno Zamperla; choreography, Alberto Testa; assistant director, Tony Brandt, Alain Centonze, Michel Ferry. Reviewed at the Cannes Film Festival (competing), May 16, 1990. Running time: **138 MIN.**

King Vittorio Amadeo	Timothy Dalton
Jeanne de Luynes	Valeria Golino
Count di Verua	Stéphane Freiss
Charles	Robin Renucci
Scaglia	Feodor Chaliapin
Queen	Eleanor David
Dowager Countess	Margaret Tyzack
Duke	Paul Crauchet

(English soundtrack)

■ **Exhilarating dimensions of Austrian director Axel Corti's production of "The King's Whore" are seductive indeed, but the 17th century melodrama is less magnificent than it first appears, as it proves to be built around the small and inflexible obsessions of less-than-heroic characters.**

For the actors, however, the film is a triumph. Best prospects lie in arthouse arenas, as pic's tragic arc is likely to turn off mainstream audiences.

Lensed in English, pic appears to spare no expense in recreating the royal court of Piedmont in Northern Italy, where the king (Timothy Dalton) falls violently in love with the young wife of his chamberlain (Stéphane Freiss).

This singularly spirited young woman (Valeria Golino), happily in love with her husband, resists the king's advances, until the entire court, including the church and her husband, is pressuring her to give in. Filled with rage, she submits, but uses her favored position to wreak heavy vengeance on all who've betrayed her, while demanding to be paid as a whore in jewelry and art.

The king's obsession is to make her love him; hers is to escape him. Their relentless private battle soon escalates into a war with France that she persuades the king to take on. Even after she's stricken with smallpox and he abandons his army to minister tirelessly and tenderly to her illness, saving her life and her beauty, she still refuses to love him.

Though the story is merely grand melodrama, the film is made extraordinary by the scale on which Corti renders it. All of his images are vital and sensual, his instinct for dramatic staging approaches the delirious.

The elegant and often brilliant script has Dalton speaking in provocative epigrams, telling her that she and her husband have done the cruelest thing by showing that happiness is possible, and advising her that jealousy can be very destructive as he sends a falcon into the sky to tear out the heart of another.

Corti has a fervent, almost horrifying appetite for contrasts that thicken the drama. In one scene, a priest acts as Dalton's pimp, advising Golino in the confession booth that she must attend to the king's "illness." In another, when he first enters her chambers, she is so frightened she vomits delicately into a flower pot.

While film's first hour is masterful, its rich tapestry begins to unravel as it becomes clear the story will not really develop beyond this tedious clashing of wills. The pair's self-obsessed indifference to the fate of others who depend on them begin to resemble some of history's least-loved despots.

Resolving itself after 2 hours 16 minutes in the romantic-tragic fashion of love realized too late, script sympathizes with their folly, rather than mocking it.

Film grows more and more absurd as it descends into excess, at times putting the actors in ridiculous positions, as when Dalton grovels on the floor making love to his mistress's bodice.

In the end, having destroyed his body in a swordfight, he's shown suspended in a ridiculous, crucifix-like mobile structure that is apparently the 17th century version of a wheelchair. One can't avoid thinking that Corti ends up in the same position, pilloried in this absurd and magnificent structure he's created.

Aside from a few unfortunate scenes, Dalton has never been seen on the screen to better advantage, projecting subtlety, control, virility and vulnerability to mesmerizing effect.

Pic is also a tour-de-force for Golino, and both Freiss as her husband and Eleanor David as the queen are standout in the supporting cast.

Production credits are lush and first-rate on all counts, from Gernot Roll's lensing to Gabriel Yared's score. — *Daws.*

Taxi Blues
(SOVIET-FRENCH)

Cannes An MK2 Diffusion release of a Lenfilm/ASK Eurofilm/MK2 Prods./La Sept coproduction. Produced by Marin Karmitz. Written and directed by Pavel Lounguine. Camera (color), Denis Evstigneev; editor, Elisabeth Guido; music, Vladimir Chekassine; art direction, Valeri Yurkevich; production manager, Vladimir Repnikov. Reviewed at the Cannes Film Festival (competing), May 12, 1990. Running time: **110 MIN.**

Liocha	Piotr Mamonov
Shlikov	Piotr Zaitchenko
Old man	Vladimir Kachpur
Christina	Natalia Koliakanova

Also with: Hal Singer, Elena Safonova, Sergei Gazarov.

■ **This tale of an unlikely friendship between two men is a "Taxi Driver" from the other side, a portrait of today's violent, contradictory USSR. Colorful, lively and a lot of fun, pic ought to appeal to Western audiences who enjoyed the likes of "Little Vera."**

Explosive, sardonic "Taxi Blues" is one of the first of the new East-West coproductions expected to revolutionize Soviet film. Scripter Pavel Lounguine makes his bow behind the camera in a Lenfilm coprod with Marin Karmitz and a French budget.

In a nighttime Moscow lit up like Las Vegas, quiet taxi driver Shlikov (Piotr Zaitchenko) ferries a carload of drunken merrymakers on a vodka bust. The ride ends with the zaniest of the group, Liocha (Piotr Mamonov), skipping out on the fare. When the cabbie catches up to him the next day, he confiscates his saxophone to pay the debt. This starts a long and quite funny love-hate relationship between the stodgy cabbie and the alcoholic Jewish musician.

Realizing the value of the sax, Shlikov decides to return it. He finds Liocha strumming on a guitar for kopecks and begging for a drink. Bachelor Shlikov decides to take his artiste home and "make him a man" — force him to dry out and work for a living. Liocha lets the bath overflow and destroys three apartments as thanks.

Back and forth they go in a bright, disorderly merry-go-round of being best pals and worst enemies. At one point Shlikov puts the sax player in jail but changes his mind a minute later.

A kind of Russian fascist, the childish, muscle-bound taxi driver really believes in justice, love and friendship. By pic's end Liocha has been acclaimed a musical genius. Shlikov's pride swells, but when Liocha fails to return Shlikov's feelings (close to love, but not explicitly labeled homosexual), the cabbie goes berserk. A violent, but not tragic, finale closes the doomed friendship.

Film is studded with tour-de-force scenes, like Shlikov's private party for fun-loving Christina (exuberant Natalia Koliakanova) that turns sour when his music-making slave captures the lady's interest.

"Taxi Blues" also offers surprising backstage views at the microcosm of Moscow cab-driving with its frantic backseat dealing, and a less convincing look at the local music industry. Mamonov, who plays the crazed musician with inimitable glee, is one of Russia's first rock stars.

Zaitchenko, a stage actor, is equally on target as the all-Russian cabbie. As Shlikov's patriotic, anti-Semitic housemate, Vladimir Kachpur shows what has become of all those famous Russian values that could be played straight just a few years ago. American jazz musician Hal Singer cameos in a sax duo.

Whole film is heavily underlined by a modern jazz score composed and performed by Vladimir Chekassine. Denis Evstigneev's eye-catching cinematography is oriented to extremist pop images. "Taxi Blues" is one of the first Soviet films to be shot with live sound, thanks to a French sound crew. — *Yung.*

Shi no Toge
(The Sting Of Death)
(JAPANESE)

Cannes A Shochiku Co. production. Produced by Toru Okuyama. Executive producers, Hiroshi and Yoshiki Nomura. Directed by Kohei Oguri. Screenplay, Oguri, based on a novel by Toshio Shimao; camera (color,

Imagica), Shohei Ando; music, Toshio Hosokawa; sound, Hideo Nishizaki; art direction, Yoshinaga Yokoo; assistant director, Tsukasa Sasaki; line producer, Seiya Araki. Reviewed at Cannes Film Festival (competing), May 15, 1990. Running time: **115 MIN.**

Miho . . . . Keiko Matsuzaka
Toshio . . . . Ittoku Kishibe
Shinichi . . . . Takenori Matsumura
Maya . . . . Yuri Chikamori
Kuniko . . . . Midori Kiuchi
Masagoro . . . . Akira Yamanouchi
Riki . . . . Miyuko Nakamura

■ This superbly photographed recreation of Toshio Shimao's intensely personal novel about a marriage in crisis reinforces a number of unfortunate stereotypes about Japanese cinema. As a result, it's likely to be facilely dismissed as a regional specialty.

It deserves better. No question that "The Sting Of Death" is a tough slog. Director Kohei Oguri has been taken for some time with Shimao's work, set in the 1950s and concerning a thirtysomething couple with two young children coming to grips with the husband's infidelity.

The director has generally used the book's style (a genre called Shishosetsu, an inward, egoistic approach towards the material) that deliberately confines the film's focus almost exclusively to the couple. That presents special risks when the characters turn out to be less than riveting.

Keiko Matsuzaka, a Shochiku studio actress, is the wife. Ittoku Kishibe, a former pop singer, is the husband. He is a schoolteacher of extraordinary passivity. She is an emotional wreck, pained to psychosis by her husband's affair with a rather plain-looking woman, a relationship that ends shortly after "Sting" begins. He is guilty, and vows to restore the marriage.

There is talk of suicide by both wife and husband. Two muddled attempts (one after the husband cries out to relieve his pain, an extraordinarily affecting moment) are played in almost slapstick style, leaving the audience uncomfortably uncertain about how to respond to the material. Spouses gradually cut themselves off from the world, even from their own children, to restore their marriage, a plot solipsism that is tricky to handle.

The inward progression of the pic is accomplished at a snail's pace, relieved by Shohei Ando's excellent photography. His work reflects the mood of each scene,

alternating between claustrophobic grays for interior scenes to controlled splendor for outdoor action. Nature scenes border on the idyllic, nicely offsetting the grim, leisurely pace of the action.

Kishibe can't do much with the underdeveloped role of the husband. Matsuzaka is expert at the emotionally charged delivery often persued by Japanese actresses on tv. The pain and anguish, however, come across as real rather than as easy, lachrymose sentimentality. Director Oguri sees his characters as somehow shaped by momentous events of the Showa era, which ended with Hirohito's death.

All that is interesting, perhaps, except that "Sting" is so hermetically sealed from its surroundings, the period of its setting seems virtually irrelevant.

Oguri, 45, remains one of Japan's most intriguing directors. His moving "Doro No Kawa" (Muddy River), a spare, black & white drama of a young boy and his father, was developed in contained style that nonetheless permitted a strongly emotional conclusion. The pic won a silver medal at the Moscow Film Fest nine years ago and was released in the U.S.

Oguri's "Sting," despite photographer Ando's extraordinarily professional contribution, appears headed for no such fate. — *Sege.*

Matj
(The Mother)
(SOVIET)

Cannes A Sovexport presentation of Mosfilm (Moscow) production in association with Cinecitta and RAI-2 (Rome). Produced by Nello Santi for Cinefin (Italy). Directed by Gleb Panfilov. Screenplay, Panfilov based on novel by Maxim Gorky; camera (color), Mikael Agranovich; editor, E. Galkina; music, Vadim Bibergan; sound, Roland Kazarian; production design, Levan Ladichvili. Reviewed at Cannes Film Festival (competing), May 17 1990. Running time: **200 MIN.**

The Mother . . . . Inna Tchourikova
Pavel Viassov . . . . Viktor Rakov
Pavel as a boy . . . . . Sacha Chichonok
The Father . Lioubomiras Laoutsiavitchous

■ Gleb Panfilov goes thoroughly traditionalist in his rendering of Maxim Gorky's novel "The Mother." Female lead Inna Tchourikova turns in a solid performance, but otherwise pic is too obviously made with television serialization in mind to bring Western audiences to a cinema for three hours.

A coproduction with (among

others) Italy's RAI, the film employs the classical frame size, suitable for the home screen. Clearly divided into four parts (but no intermission indicated for theaters), it is also obvious that most of the violence the original story calls for has been toned down to permit primetime beamings.

The action is set at the turn of the century in Sormovo, a steel mill town where a mother sees her husband turned into a drunken brute by his inhuman work conditions. Mostly she suffers in silence but is defended by her teenage son Pavel until he, after the father's death, reports to the factory and starts drinking himself.

The next episode has Pavel saved in more ways than one. He and a group of friends become underground activists in the Socialist cause. One friend, Klimov, turns informer, and the group finds the going tough. Inspiration, however, seeps in via reports of Ouliamov's early Socialist manifesto. Pavel and his friend create a clandestine pamphlet press. Pavel's mother stays mostly in the background, worried, but angelically patient.

When Pavel finds out about Klimov, he forces him to commit suicide. Pavel is caught by the secret police himself, but his life is spared when he, too, promises to turn informer. At this time, he has already spent time in jail, while his mother has turned activist in her own small way by smuggling pamphlets into the factory via food parcels.

Pavel defeats the police by leading a May 1 protest march, carrying a red flag that his mother has fashioned with lettering denouncing autocracy (which she spells wrong). He is beaten up and goes to court where he makes a speech in defense of all workers.

Meanwhile, the Czarist family is seen posing for a group photo, "far from the madding crowd," and far from understanding what the workers' protests are all about.

Film's final part finds Pavel and his friends on their way to Siberia. Mother makes a brave gesture of distributing a pamphlet of his final speech in a crowded railroad station. She is apprehended by soldiers, but a secret police assassin, also one of Pavel's earlier companions, kills her.

All this is told in meticulous detail to denote time and place, but the narrative pacing is so leisurely that there are stretches when

the production design overpowers the action. Panfilov is good with actors, however, and always knows how to bring out expression via nuance rather than grimace.

Panfilov won a Berlin Film Fest Golden Bear in 1987 for "The Theme." Formerly banned, stylistically daring pic was took a sharp look at anti-Semitism in high USSR places.

With "The Mother," Panfilov has created what is more of a paean to traditional Communist establishment values, complete with the incorporation of a wilfully anachronistic "Long Live Glasnost" shouted along with "Down With The Czar" and "For An Eight-Hour Working Day" in the climactic protest march.

— *Kell.*

Nouvelle Vague
(New Wave)
(SWISS-FRENCH)

Cannes A Vega Film SA production. Produced by Alain Sarde. Written, directed and edited by Jean-Luc Godard. Camera (color), William Lubtchansky; art direction, Anne-Marie Mieville. Reviewed at Cannes Film Festival (competing), May 18, 1990. Running time: **89 MIN.**

With: Alain Delon, Domiziana Giordano.

■ Droll, poetic and resolutely recondite, "Nouvelle Vague" is another allegorical rumination from Jean-Luc Godard on love as the antidote to the spiritual bankruptcy of modern materialism. Given the indifferent reception in the U.S. to Godard's recent work, pic will be a tough sell to American specialty distribs more wary than ever of difficult foreign films.

A sort of lifestyles of the rich and existentially disaffected, "Nouvelle Vague" is set on a lush Swiss estate from which a beautiful, domineering and emotionally remote woman (Domiziana Giordano) commands a far-flung industrial empire. Tooling through the gorgeous countryside one day in her high-priced sportscar, she clips a well-dressed hitchhiker (Alain Delon).

Responding to some atavistic need for emotional connection, she picks up Delon, tends his bruises and sets him up on the estate as a philosophical boy-toy. The mournfully grave and serenely macho Delon and the "unconquerable" queen of capitalism enter into a complex, tension-filled emotional tug-of-war, pushed and pulled by sexual desire, gender antagonism, clashing world views and class division.

The scenario provides an ample platform for Godard's usual grab bag of voiceover aphorisms and fragmented lyrical speculations on the nature of God and humankind and the destiny of civilization. At the heart of it lies the age-old post-Eden rivalry between man and woman: Man, quoth Godard, poses the mystery; woman reveals the secret.

What precisely does this (or any other of the film's similarly opaque declamations) mean? That, as always is the case with Godard, is up to the viewer.

There is much to delight the eye in "Nouvelle Vague." Nature — in marsh, forest, lake and meadow — is celebrated adoringly with dazzlingly crisp photography and an uplifting score. But the rich are indifferent to the landscape they own. The faces of the rapacious corporate types who surround Giordano often are set in half-shadow, as if to suggest their incompleteness.

Giordano summons a coterie of humorless suits to help plan a takeover. The henchmen, preoccupied with greed and power-lust, contemptuously condescend to their beautiful bored wives and mistresses, who languish around the estate. The fat-cats read the New York Times and Business Week and scramble desperately for the latest electronically transmitted updates on the value of the U.S. dollar.

The servant girl reads and quotes Schiller. The industrialists and investors fixate on beating the Japanese in the global corporate jungle. The gardener ruminates on how nature makes its own suggestions for creation.

Godard is thoroughly fed up with a late 20th century economic system he views as barbarically antiquated; preserved only by the desperate siege mentality of the superwealthy. Some day, he ponders, people will recall with astonishment the time when there were still rich and poor. Godard cannot resist japes at current showbiz events. "We've just bought Warner Communications for $5-billion," one of the fat-cats announces. "Now we have to know what a picture is."

A priceless Degas is snared from a hapless Arab trapped in the slaughter of Beirut. The bargain-buyers congratulate themselves,

and spend maybe 10 seconds on a crudely esthetic appreciation of the nude. Meanwhile, Delon and Giordano's relationship unspools in a roundelay of unsmiling anti-chemistry. Giordano, a strawberry blonde, green-eyed beauty obliged to emote deadpan, nicely withstands stonefaced, probing closeups.

Delon, world-weary, sun-wrinkled and magnetically pensive, fills the bill as the wounded, mysterious stranger in town. "Trust," quoth Godard, "reigns over the fate of love." It takes a lot of twisting and turning, but like all great filmmakers, Godard accommodates his audience with a resolution that satisfies. It might even be called a happy ending. — *Rich.*

Hidden Agenda
(BRITISH)

Cannes A Hemdale release and production. Executive producers, John Daly, Derek Gibson. Produced by Eric Fellner. Directed by Ken Loach. Screenplay, Jim Allen; camera (Eastmancolor), Clive Tickner; editor, Jonathan Morris; music, Stewart Copeland; sound, Simon Okin; production design, Martin Johnson; production manager, Ginny Roncoroni; assistant director, Julia Kennedy; coproducer, Rebecca O'Brien; casting, Susie Figgis. Reviewed at Cannes Film Festival (competing), May 16, 1990. No MPAA Rating. Running time: **108 MIN.**

Kerrigan	Brian Cox
Ingrid Jessner	Frances McDormand
Paul Sullivan	Brad Dourif
Moa	Mai Zetterling
Henri	Bernard Bloch
Maxwell	John Benfield
Brodie	Jim Norton
Alec Nevin	Patrick Kavanagh
Sir Robert Neil	Bernard Archard
Teresa Doyle	Michelle Fairley
Harris	Maurice Roeves
Fraser	Oliver Maguire

■ **Ken Loach's new film may spur controversy, but the Hemdale pic will find the boxoffice going more difficult.**

At the very least, "Hidden Agenda" will provoke lotsa controversy because of its hard-hitting attack on allegedly ruthless methods of the British police in Northern Ireland, and of top-level government dirty tricks and coverups.

Pic is set in 1982, and seems inspired by the notorious Stalker case. Stalker was a top-level British police officer sent to Northern Ireland to investigate the Royal Ulster Constabulary. His eventual highly critical report was hushed up, and he resigned and went public.

In "Hidden Agenda," Brian Cox plays the Stalker-like Kerri-

gan, brought to Belfast to investigate the killings of an IRA sympathizer and an American lawyer (Brad Dourif in a tiny role). Kerrigan befriends Dourif's bereaved girlfriend (Frances McDormand, good in a Jane Fonda-type role).

He quickly discovers the men were killed by members of Royal Ulster Constabulary, and exposes a high-level coverup. His subsequent investigations are thwarted when they lead to a senior aide, to Margaret Thatcher and to other pillars of the British establishment.

Jim Allen's provocative screenplay includes references to British secret service and their dirty tricks against the Heath and Wilson governments of the '70s, the aim being to get a far-right-wing government (Thatcher) in power. All of this will set tongues wagging in Britain, where the sometimes thick Irish accents will be more readily decipherable than they will be elsewhere.

Loach is one of Britain's most radical and uncompromising helmers and, for over 20 years, has produced forceful film and tv productions (including "Cathy Come Home" and "Kes"). But as a filmmaker, he's no Costa-Gavras, and "Hidden Agenda," though it attempts to make an acceptable theatrical entertainment out of a complex political saga, lacks big-screen impact.

Talky screenplay is partly to blame for the tv feel of the production. Likewise, Clive Tickner's camerawork is flat and the sound mix occasionally fuzzy. Sometimes the film comes vibrantly to life (as it does in the early scenes and in a sequence in Dublin, where McDormand risks her life for a vital audiocassette).

Cox is solid as the dogged Kerrigan. The film has a very open ending, leaving in question the honest cop's future. Other cast members are strong, though fourth-billed Mai Zetterling merely has a walk-on role.

Loach and his team deserve plaudits for the courage of their convictions, and for bringing to the screen a disturbing and saddening contemporary story.

— *Strat.*

Tilai
(The Law)
(BURKINA FASO)

Cannes A Les Films de l'Avenir presentation of Les Films de l'Avenir (Burkina Faso) production in association with Waka Film (Zurich) and Rhea Film (Paris). Written, produced and directed by Idrissa Ouedraogo. Executive producer, Beatrice Korc. Camera (color), Alix Comte, Dominique Hennequin; editor, Luc Barnier; music, Abdullah Ibrahim (a.k.a. Dollar Brand); associate producer, Sylvia Voser. Reviewed at the Cannes Film Festival (competing), May 17, 1990. Running time: **81 MIN.**

Saga	Rasmane Ouedraogo
Nogma	Ina Cisse
Kuilga	Roukieto Barry
Kougri	Assane Ouedraogo
Poko	Sibidou Sidibe

Also with: Mariam Barry, Seydou Ouedraogo, Mariam Ouedraogo, Daouda Porgo, Kogre Warma, Mamadou Ganame.

■ **With "The Law," Idrissa Ouedraogo confirms the reputation he created for himself last year with "Yaaba" as Africa's most skilled producer, writer and director. He also has a highly personal style and approach.**

"Yaaba" has traveled far and wide since its bow last year in the Cannes Directors Fortnight, and "The Law" is sure to follow even if the initial impact of Ouedraogo's way of seeing things is, quite naturally, less of a happy surprise the second time around.

The themes of Ouedraogo's work are connected to life in his desert village, where he does all his filming, using family and friends in the roles. In "Yaaba" he had a small boy defy village law successfully by befriending an outcast aunt. In this film, however, the law wins out when a father takes a son's fiancée to make her his own second wife.

Saga, the son, becomes a criminal when he sullies his father's honor by taking the woman, Nogma, with him to live in hiding. He then is branded guilty of incest, since Nogma officially is his mother. Most everybody in the village is willing to side with the young couple, but the law obviously is the law.

Saga's brother makes a dangerous sacrifice when he claims to have obeyed an order to kill Saga. He, too, must suffer in the end, when Saga and Nogma's brief life together is ended. Nogma's father commits suicide out of "family shame" and Saga's mother dies, possibly of grief.

Nobody in "The Law" is seen as anything less than deeply human.

Even the unbending father essentially is a well-meaning man. Ouedraogo doesn't denounce the village traditions, but simply records how life must adhere to certain patterns. As he looks at the villagers with compassion and subtle humor, Ouedraogo shows nature's grand, desolate vistas. All his nonprofessional actors respond just as naturally to the camera's and the director's demands.

One other special charm of Ouedraogo's films is repeated in "The Law." He refuses to look at women as victims. All his women walk proud and are as susceptible to foolish pride as any male. In one funny scene, Nogma is bragging about having been nearly raped by a man who actually was only a friendly passing stranger. Saga just smiles at her indulging in this fantasy.

Evocative music, used sparsely, is improvised for the film by a trio led by South African pianist Abdullah Ibrahim (Dollar Brand).
— *Kell.*

Daddy Nostalgie
(FRENCH)

Cannes A Clea Prods.-Little Bear-Solyfic Eurisma Co. production. Produced by Adolphe Viezzi. Directed by Bertrand Tavernier. Screenplay, Colo Tavernier O'Hagan; camera (Widescreen, Eastmancolor), Denis Lenoir; editor, Ariane Boeglin; music, Antoine Duhamel; sound, Michel Desrois; production design, Jean-Louis Poveda; production manager, Yvon Crenn; assistant director, Tristan Ganne. Reviewed at Cannes Film Festival (competing), May 14, 1990. Running time: **106 MIN.**
Daddy . . . . Dirk Bogarde
Caroline . . . . Jane Birkin
Juliette . . . . Emmanuelle Bataille
Barbara . . . . Charlotte Kady
Caroline as a child . . . . . Michele Minns
(English & French soundtrack)

■ Bertrand Tavernier's "Daddy Nostalgie" is a miniature jewel of a film, a delicate piece essentially for three players, and is acted and directed with exceptional subtlety. It should fare well in arthouses around the world.

Dirk Bogarde makes a welcome return to the screen after 12 years (his last appearance was in Rainer Werner Fassbinder's "Despair") as an Englishman married to a Frenchwoman with whom he has retired to a villa in the south of France.

Their daughter, Caroline (Jane Birkin), a screenwriter, lives in Paris. She hasn't been close to her father, who neglected her when she was a child, but she drops everything to come to his hospital sickbed when she hears he's undergone a serious heart operation. He recovers, and Caroline moves into her parents' villa.

The subtle screenplay, by Colo Tavernier O'Hagan, has no big dramatic scenes, but a series of delicate sequences (with dialog shifting between English and French) establishes the growing bond between father and daughter. Avoiding sentimentality, the film builds to a moving climax.

The finesse with which Tavernier treats this delicate material is exceptional, and the film will be especially meaningful for anyone who has elderly or sickly parents.

Bogarde gives a beautifully modulated performance as the weary father, who still enjoys his whiskey and wine and recalls his life with fondness. (In one scene he rails against the middle-class, xenophobic England he left behind, and audience is reminded that the actor himself is an exile from England.)

Birkin gives a sensitive performance as the daughter whose father once ignored her but now "makes me laugh and dream." Also notable is stage actress Odette Laure as the wife, who's both religious and bigoted.

Denis Lenoir's fine Scope camerawork gives the drama depth and space, and the film is of very high technical quality. Commercially, pic will need special handling but could settle in for good runs in major cities. — *Strat.*

Tutti Stanno Bene
(Everybody's Fine)
(ITALIAN-FRENCH)

Cannes A Miramax release (in the U.S.) of an Erre Produzioni (Rome)/Les Films Ariane (Paris) coproduction in association with Silvio Berlusconi Communications. (Intl. distribution, Sovereign Pictures.) Produced by Angelo Rizzoli. Executive producer, Mario Cotone. Directed by Giuseppe Tornatore. Screenplay, Tornatore, with Tonino Guerra; camera (color), Blasco Giurato; editor, Mario Morra; music, Ennio Morricone; art direction, Andrea Crisanti. Reviewed at the Cannes Film Festival (competing), May 20, 1990. Running time: **125 MIN.**
Matteo Scuro . . . . . Marcello Mastroianni
Train lady . . . . Michele Morgan
Canio . . . . Marino Cenna
Guglielmo . . . . Roberto Nobile
Tosca . . . . Valeria Cavali
Norma . . . . Norma Martelli
Also with: Antonella Attili, Giorgio Libassi, Gioacchino Civiletti, Nicola Di Pinto.

■ With "Everybody's Fine," "Cinema Paradiso's" young helmer shows he's not a one-shot director. With a little less weepy emotion but no less enthusiasm, Giuseppe Tornatore's third effort involves audiences in a sentimental film with strong b.o. appeal.

Some critics at Cannes have hung back at film's blatant grab for viewer sympathy, and have taken issue with a few slowdowns that mar the action. Others have greeted it with the same simple enjoyment filmgoers are likely to show, particularly those who relished "Cinema Paradiso," 1989 best foreign film Oscar-winner.

In "Everybody's Fine," Marcello Mastroianni is perfectly in tune with the spirit of the film as lively oldtimer Matteo Scuro, who leaves his native Sicily one day to make a trip around Italy to visit his five grown children.

Peering in excitement through thick glasses, the big-hearted gentleman leaves his wife behind and boards a train for Naples. Matteo's first stop is a failure. His favorite son Alvaro isn't in town. He recalls Alvaro as a grinning little boy (Salvatore Cascio, the waif in "Cinema Paradiso").

In Rome, he gets a warm welcome from Canio (Marino Cenna), a son who has become an important local politician. He's introduced with a good gag, making a pompous speech to an empty room papered with photos of the masses. Only when Matteo leaves is there a clue that appearances aren't quite reality. Canio is really just some deputy's speechwriter.

In Florence, Tosca (the self-possessed Valeria Cavali) has become a fashion model and stage actress. She lives in a big apartment with a breathtaking view.

But she's hiding facts that all she models is lacy underwear, the apartment belongs to an old flame who wants it back, and that baby in the kitchen is hers. Best scene is an irresistible babysitting session in which Matteo discovers the kid just wants to watch tv, though watching the washing machine ˜n does just as well.

In a brief interlude, Matteo lets a dignified lady on the train (a fine Michele Morgan) talk him into accompanying a group of retirees to Rimini. Fellini's hometown sparks a filmic homage or two. Tornatore also takes off his hat to Fellini in the Roman sequence, with its Trevi fountain, marble statue and Japanese tourists.

Ignoring warnings from Morgan not to make surprise visits to grown kids, Matteo is back on the trail. He drops in on Guglielmo (Roberto Nobile), who turns out not to play the violin in a symphony orchestra, but only the bass drum. Embarrassed, Guglielmo pretends to have to leave town.

Settling into a familiar pattern, pic's train trips, during which Matteo always drops a worn photo of the family, and his irritating habit of telling people to ask him questions, begin to get on the nerves.

Luckily, tale is decorated with Matteo's highly visual memories. Most striking is his recurrent nightmare of a big black ball with dangling strings coming down on a beach and carrying his five small kids away to a sinister world. Blasco Giurato's cinematography gives the image a surrealist quality that's quite horrifying.

Last visit is to Turin where his daughter Norma (Norma Martelli) lives. Supposedly a big exec at the phone company, she actually sneaks into the operators' room when Matteo isn't looking and assumes her humble job. That night Matteo overhears her husband wishing he'd leave them in peace, and Matteo spends the night outdoors in a wooden crate with some bums, and sadly starts south the next morning.

In Rome he insists on calling the family together for a patriarchal meal, but only two sons turn up. They confess what they've been principally hiding: Alvaro is dead, a suicide.

Matteo has a heart attack on the next train. The family gathers around his hospital bed, but he feels no joy at seeing them, and they feel only awkwardness at their lies and hiding. Their biggest secret is, simply, they didn't live up to dad's expectations. In a final revelation, Matteo recounts pious lies himself to his wife back home — in the cemetery where she's buried.

Beyond the bare bones of the plot, film connects with an intimate lensing and acting style. Mastroianni deserves much credit, but the supporting roles are filled with solid, unobtrusive performances. Ennio Morricone's score hovers perilously close to the facetious at times, but mainly works.

Unusual in an Italo film, "Everybody" is liberally sprinkled with ideas that provide the viewer with periodic payoffs and laughs, often in the form of sight gags.

Film's philosophy is shallower than its visual savvy, however.

tudes, with his final message something like, "there's no place like home" and "the modern world is a harsh and nasty place." Viewers prone to agree will be glad to take refuge in the old-time entertainment film has to offer. — *Yung*.

Wild At Heart

Cannes   A Samuel Goldwyn Co. release (in the U.S.) of a Polygram/Propaganda production. Produced by Monty Montgomery, Steve Golin, Joni Sighvatsson. Directed by David Lynch. Screenplay, Lynch, based on the novel by Barry Gifford; camera (color), Fred Elmes; editor, Duwayne Dunham; music, Angelo Badalamenti; sound, John Wentworth, John Power; costume design, Patricia Norris; production manager, Kool Marder; 1st assistant directors, Margayx Mackay, Charles Myers; 1st assistant camera, Robert Sweeny; special effects makeup, David B. Miller, Louis Lazzara; special effects pyrotechnics, David Domeyer; casting, Johanna Ray. Reviewed at the Cannes Film Festival (competing), May 19, 1990. No MPAA rating. Running time: **127 MIN.**

Sailor Ripley	Nicolas Cage
Lula Pace Fortune	Laura Dern
Marietta Pace	Diane Ladd
Bobby Peru	Willem Dafoe
Perdita Durango	Isabella Rossellini
Johnnie Farragut	Harry Dean Stanton
Dell	Crispin Glover
Juana	Grace Zabriskie
Marcello Santos	J.E. Freeman
Mr. Reindeer	Morgan Shephard

Also with: Calvin Lockhart, David Patrick Kelly, Bellina Logan, Glenn Walker Harris Jr., Gregg Danddridge, Freddie Jones, Charlie Spradling, Eddie Dixon, Marvin Kaplan, Brent Fraser, John Lurie, Jack Nance, Tommy G. Kendrick, Scott Coffey.

■ **Joltingly violent, wickedly funny and rivetingly erotic, David Lynch's "Wild At Heart" is a rollercoaster ride to redemption through an American gothic heart of darkness.**

Lynch's widely praised tv serial "Twin Peaks" (downright genial by comparison) is certain to augment Lynch cultists with curious new audiences who will discover a thoroughly original American filmmaker.

But the Samuel Goldwyn Co. is certain to face a ratings showdown with the Motion Picture Assn. of America if it attempts to defend the integrity of the director's cut shown at Cannes.

In "Twin Peaks" and his groundbreaking "Blue Velvet," Lynch worked from the premise that unspeakable evil lurks just beneath mainstream America's complacent patina of normalcy. But in "Wild At Heart" there are no boundaries between the everyday and a lurid subterranean netherworld.

Other filmmakers have poked beneath the U.S. underbelly but

rarely has the demimonde of losers, hard-cases, shamans, conmen and crazies been lit up with such incandescent heat. In "Wild At Heart" Lynch controls such extraordinary cinematic power that his most bizzare and incongruous over-reachings mesmerize.

The brutal opening of "Wild At Heart" signals that this film is not for the faint of heart. Sailor (Nicolas Cage), an Elvis-acolyte whose snakeskin jacket proclaims his "duality and individuality," and his seethingly sexy 18-year-old girlfriend Lula (Laura Dern) are waylaid leaving a dance hall somewhere in the Carolinas.

Sailor has spurned the toilet-stall advances of Lula's insanely obsessive mother, Marietta (Dern's real-life mother, Diane Ladd), so she sends an assassin to gut him. Sailor, who backs down to no man, literally cracks open the assassin with his bare hands. He does two years for manslaughter in "Pee Dee" state pen, while Lula waits.

Few actresses could have brought off the insouciant, uninhibited sexual cyclone Lula. Raped at 13, witness to her father's murder, battling the black-magic spell of her witchy mother who planned that murder with her mobster lover, Lula is one screwed up but beautiful gal.

Cage, who has overacted in other roles, can't possibly do so in the anything-goes Lynchian universe. He's born to the roll of the rock 'n roll macho man Sailor, a tough guy with a tender heart "who never had any parental guidance." Together they hit their own "yellow brick road" in a love story unlike any since "Bonnie And Clyde."

Lynch does a lot more than suggest their molten sexual bond. Although life-affirming and crucial to establishing their relationship, it's unlikely that Cage and Dern's transfixing lovemaking scenes will survive the censors' scissors in the climate currently prevailing in the U.S.

When Lula and Sailor are not lovemaking, they are dancing or talking and chain-smoking. The talk ranges from the banal (cigaret brands) to the bizzare. Lulu's flash-backed recollections include the story of a cousin (Crispin Glover) psychotically fixated on Christmas and fond of putting cockroaches in his underwear.

These things seem entirely possible in the context of "Wild At

Heart." Sailor breaks parole and absconds with Lula to New Orleans, pursued by private eye Johnnie Farragut (Harry Dean Stanton) who's hired by Marietta, his sometime lover.

His rival for this psychotic witch's affections are mobster Marcello Santos (J.R. Freeman), also unleashed on the lovers' trail as a precaution by mamma. Santos tabs a bordello-dwelling hit-man to annihilate Stanton in a bayou-style ritual murder. It's not the storyline's first or last doublecross.

Meanwhile the lovers head for California via vast and mysterious Texas. Sailor, who confesses to Lula that he was a driver for mobster Santos and witnessed her father's murder, is heading for the town of Big Tuna. There he hopes ex-girlfriend Perdita (Lynch's wife, Isabella Rossellini) will let him know if a contract is out on him.

The road to Big Tuna turns nightmarish. A bloody nighttime auto wreck is an omen. The barren junkyard town is populated with

human castaways, pornographers and all-around bad characters, principally the malevolent Bobby Peru (Willem Dafoe). Dafoe is malignantly charismatic as the dangerous Peru, the first real challenge to Sailor; psychically and sexually.

Peru (who comes to a shockingly heady demise) is the conduit through which Sailor and the now-pregnant Lula will enter the third and ultimately redeeming act of their love story. This redemption is not totally uplifting after what's come before, but it allies the filmmaker with the forces of light.

"Wild At Heart's" droll, profane, black-humored script labors under a self-imposed metaphorical comparison to "The Wizard Of Oz." A more metaphysical device (or none at all) could have been concocted to rationalize the film's fantastical anti-logic.

Outstanding photography, editing, sound and special effects contribute significantly to this tapestry of human extremity. — *Rich*.

CANNES FILM FESTIVAL (OUT OF COMPETITION)

Umetni Raj
(Artificial Paradise)
(YUGOSLAVIAN)

Cannes   A Viba Film production. Executive producer, Pavle Kogoj. Produced by Josip Kosuta. Directed by Karpo Godina. Screenplay, Branko Vucicevic; camera (Eastmancolor), Tomislav Pinter; editor, Godina; music, Predrag and Mladen Vranesevic; sound, Marjan Horvat; art direction, Janez Kovic; costumes, Alenka Bartl. Reviewed at Cannes Film Festival (noncompeting), May 12, 1990. Running time: **102 MIN.**

Fritz Lang	Jurgen Morche
Karol Gatnik	Vlado Novak
Katarina Gatnik	Dragana Mrkic
Willy	Zeljko Ivanek
Elsa	Marusa Oblak
Countess	Gudrun Gabriel
Rose Schwartz	Nerine Kidd
Blatnik	Peter Bostjancic
Joachim	Marcus Zbonek
Jackson	Michael Gable

■ **First Clint Eastwood's impersonation of John Huston in "White Hunter, Black Heart," and now, in another pic in the official section of the Cannes fest, German thesp Jurgen Morche plays Fritz Lang in a Yugoslavian film made to mark the 100th anni of the celebrated helmer's birth.**

Unfortunately, Karpo Godina's "Artificial Paradise" is altogether too slow and lifeless to find an audience outside hardcore film

buffs who might be interested in this fictionalized depiction of how Lang supposedly first got the filmmaking bug.

The film opens in Hollywood in 1935 as the exiled Lang awaits a call from MGM (to start production of his first Yank film, "Fury"). Talking to an eager young scribe, he recalls the weeks in 1915 when, as a young officer during the war, he was billeted with a Slovene lawyer, Karol Gatnik, in a small Baltic town.

The character of Gatnik is based on Dr. Karol Grossmann, a Slovene nationalist and friend of Lang. During his stay, Lang is introduced to cinematography by his pal, and shoots a scene involving Gatnik's secretary, Elsa, in the nude.

He also becomes involved with Gatnik's neurotic, suicidal wife, Katarina, and a young soldier, Joachim, who, apparently maddened by the war, starts sniping at passers-by on the street and is gunned down.

It all sounds rather more interesting than it actually is, because Godina's treatment is so posed and static. Clips from Lang classics ("Siegfried," "Metropolis" and "Woman Of The Moon") afford some relief.

The film is beautiful, thanks to Tomislav Pinter's camerawork and Janez Kovic's art direction, but Godina (who previously made the far more energetic "Raft Of The Medusa" and "Red Boogie") is unable to make the subject matter come alive for contempo audiences. The climax, again set in Hollywood in 1935, is genuinely bizarre.

All technical credits are very fine. — *Strat.*

Non Ou A Va Gloria De Mandar
(No, Or The Vain Glory Of Command)
(PORTUGUESE-FRENCH)

Cannes A Madragoa Filmes (Lisbon), Tornasol Filmes (Madrid), Gemini Films (Paris), SGGC Films (Paris) coproduction, in association with Radiotelevisao Portuguesa and Radiotelevision Espanola (RTVE). Produced by Paulo Branco. Written and directed by Manoel de Oliveira; camera (Eastmancolor), Elso Roque; editor, Oliveira, Sabine Franel; music, Alejandro Masso; sound, Gita Cerveira; set decoration, Luis Monteiro, Maria Jose Branco; costumes, Isabel Branco; assistant directors, Jaime Silva, Jacques Arhex, Manuel Joao Aguas; production manager, Xavier Decraene, Alexandre Barradas, Graca de Almeida. Reviewed at the Cannes Film Festival (noncompeting), May 14, 1990. Running time: **110 MIN.**
With: Luis Miguel Cintra, Diogo Doria, Miguel Guilherme, Luis Lucas, Carlos Gomes, Antonio S. Lopes, Mateus Lorena, Lola Forner, Raul Freire, Rui de Carvalho, Teresa Meneses, Leonor Silveira.

■ Portugal's oldest and most respected helmer, Manoel de Oliveira, has limned a sweeping, didactic parable about his country. As an interpretive lecture on Portuguese history, item may be of interest to cognoscenti, but as film entertainment, pic falls flat.

Much of "Non" is set on a truck transporting troops into the African hinterland in 1973, just prior to the Portuguese revolution. Pace is set in the opening sequence, as the camera inches along on a road focusing on a tree. The soldiers then engage in philosophical conversation.

One of them is especially knowledgeable on Portuguese history. As he pontificates, various key historical episodes are shown, from the battle against the Moors to the latest colonial wars in Africa.

Most ambitious flashback is the Moors conflict, but the fighting looks more like stylized theater than blood and gore battle, despite a large number of extras charging about on horses and on foot.

Vasco da Gama's voyages and other historical episodes are likewise illustrated.

Pic concludes with the modern-day soldiers being ambushed as they tramp on a detail through the jungle. One of those shot is the lecturing soldier, who also plays parallel parts in other Portuguese military debacles portrayed in the film.

Despite Oliveira's reputation, it seems unlikely item will ever be released commercially. Even for tv, this overlong pic is too overindulgent and hermetic to spark much interest. — *Besa.*

CANNES FILM FESTIVAL REVIEWS
(UN CERTAIN REGARD)

V Gorode Sochi Temnye Nochi
(Dark Are Nights On The Black Sea)
(SOVIET-ITALIAN)

Cannes A Podarok production in association with Excelsior Film TV (Rome) and Zhil Sozbank (Moscow). Produced by Mark Levin with Silvia D'Amico Bendico. Directed by Vasili Pichul. Screenplay, Maria Khmelik; camera (color), Efim Reznikov; music, Vladimir Matevski; art direction, Nicolai Terekhov; costumes, Nina Ermilova. Reviewed at the Cannes Film Festival (Un Certain Regard), May 12, 1990. Running time. **115 MIN.**
Lena . . . . Natalia Negoda
Evgeny Stepanich . . . . . . Alexei Zharkov
With: A. Mironov, A. Sokolov, G. Manukov.

■ Vasili Pichul, Soviet boy wonder who caught on in the West with his hard-hitting "Little Vera," stumbles in a disappointing second effort, "Dark Are Nights On The Black Sea." Even the lure of star Natalia Negoda will have a hard time drawing more than dedicated fans of new Soviet cinema, most of whom will be found in front of fest screens.

In what is little more than a yawning jumble of seemingly random incidents, glamour of Negoda ("Little Vera") is slashed to zero with big glasses and shaggy hair. As the undergraduate Lena, she plays a dull character interrupted by unmotivated screaming bouts.

As pic opens, she becomes hysterical at finding her boyfriend in bed with another girl. Result is a court citation and mild fine, but it's enough to get her kicked out of college. Sent to a small town in the north by her film club to deliver an award to some obscure filmmaker, Lena finds herself being courted by a trio of young men. All are married.

Maria Khmelik's script dawdles over drunken rivalry in a hotel room, absurd and presumably typical Russian ceremonies, and more hysterics. To its credit, "Dark Nights" has a sarcastic sense of humor capable of pulling through long scenes. It pokes fun at a wide range of silly characters in often witty jokes.

Problem is there is no apparent point to anything. Lena's story is intercut with that of Stepanich, a balding con man who pretends to be interested in an apartment switch with Lena's alcoholic mother. He also pretends to be a film director.

When his estranged son Borya wins over a girl he likes, it's the final blow for Stepanich. In an off-season resort on the Black Sea, he bluffs his way into the best hotel and prepares to commit suicide, helped at one point by Lena, who calmly helps him carry butane bottles into the bathroom for another try.

Script takes a few more absurd turns before it reaches a perplexing end. Lena and Stepanich find themselves trapped in the hotel room with a broken door lock as end credits roll.

"Dark Nights" has some funny moments and revealing scenes of the pointless, tasteless lives most people appear to lead. At best, it has an amusingly arch p.o.v. that recalls "Little Vera's" disenchanted outlook. What it lacks is the first film's dramatic force and bitterness. In its place are overlong dialog and interminable scenes of failed seductions.

Negoda fans are likely to be disappointed at her plain-Jane anonymity. As the aging born liar Stepanich, Alexei Zharkov is fine. Lensing is professional throughout. — *Yung.*

Scandalo Segreto
(Secret Scandal)
(ITALIAN)

Cannes An Academy Pictures Italy release of a Komika Film production in association with Reteitalia. Produced by Roberto Russo. Directed by Monica Vitti. Screenplay, Russo, Vitti, Gianfranco Clerici; camera (color), Luigi Kuveiller; editor, Alberto Gallitti; art direction, Luciana Marinucci. Reviewed at the Cannes Film Festival (Un Certain Regard), May 12, 1990. Running time: **85 MIN.**
Margherita Morelli . . . . . . Monica Vitti
Tony . . . . Elliott Gould
Paolo . . . . Gino Pernice
Laura . . . . Catherine Spaak
Nicoletta . . . . Carmen Onorati
Watchman . . . . Pietro De Vico

■ A woman videotapes her marriage breaking up in "Secret Scandal," actress Monica Vitti's first directing effort. Best thing about the film is a vivacious performance by Vitti that keeps things rolling. Local boxoffice in Italy and related markets should bite.

This lively comedy is marred by a gimmick that goes stale: whole film is shot as though it's the videotape itself. Ending is thrown away in a bizarre, illogical plot twist.

For her birthday, Margherita's (Vitti) friend Tony (Elliott Gould), a frustrated director, gives her a funny-looking vidcamera that's remote controlled. She becomes obsessed with talking into it (hubby Gino Pernice has no inclination to listen to her incessant chatter). More or less surreptitiously, she trains the lens on their bedroom, living room, themselves and their friends.

By accident, lens registers a phone call revealing her husband is having an affair with her best friend Laura (Catherine Spaak). Margherita confronts her rival in one of pic's funniest scenes. Far from being penitent, Laura consoles her with the fact the affair's been going on for 10 years. Completely shattered, Margherita throws her husband out and sinks into a deep depression.

After she swallows a bottle of sleeping pills, Tony rushes in to announce he's been in the next room watching everything the camera tapes. There, his editing team is using Margherita's disastrous life to make a "true-to-life" film. She throws the camera out the window.

The premise of the dangerous gift prying into private life and altering reality as it documents it, has possibilities. Pic goes overboard in its case against camcorders, though. Moral of "Secret Scandal" seems to be that film kills.

Is this the accumulated wisdom of an actress who's made some of Italy's legendary pics (her first film, "L'Avventura," was made 30 years ago)? Impression is it's just tongue-in-cheek fun, on the same wavelength as the light comedies Vitti has specialized in for most of her career. Pic is much more convincing in depicting human relations.

Margherita's problems have universal resonance, and they're scripted in an appealing comic key. Vitti is instantly identifiable in the role of the happily married lady who feels lonely and unlistened to. Still as attractive as ever, she has a forgivable tendency to steal scenes in raucous screams and whispers.

Gould is a bubbling presence in a small and ultimately impossible role he waltzes through.

A trick whose novelty soon wears off is having the entire film shot as though through the lens of Margherita's camera, with blackouts every time she turns the thing off. Laughter-getting at first, it soon wears thin as a gag.

Veteran cinematographer Luigi Kuveiller is hand-tied. The device is not even used consistently, because sometimes lens zooms in and out without Margherita touching her remote control. In any case, the effect doesn't justify the trouble. — *Yung.*

Pummarò
(Tomato)
(ITALIAN)

Rome A Filmauro release of a Numero Uno Intl./Cineuropa '92 coproduction, in association with RAI-TV Channel 2. Produced by Claudio Bonivento. Executive producer, Pietro Valsecchi. Directed by Michele Placido. Screenplay, Sandro Petraglia, Stefano Rulli, Placido; camera (Luciano Vittori color), Vilko Filac; editor, Ruggero Mastroianni; music, Lucio Dalla, Mauro Malavasi; art direction, Lorenzo Baraldi. Reviewed at CDS, Rome, May 7, 1990. (In Cannes Film Festival, Un Certain Regard.) Running time: **102 MIN.**
Kwaku . Thywill Abraham Kwaku Amenya
Eleonora . . . . Pamela Villoresi
Nanou . . . . Jacqueline Williams
Professor . . . . Gerardo Scala
  Also with: Franco Interlenghi, Nicola Di Pinto.

■ Popular thesp Michele Placido debuts as a director in "Pummarò," a strongly accented view of black immigrants in Italy. Timeliness of the topic

and curiosity over the director should help pic overcome local audience inertia. After beginning its offshore career at Cannes, pic should go on to specialized playoff.

The first Italo pic to tackle issues of racism and exploitation head-on, "Pummarò" is a courageous shot from the liberal camp. It takes an honorable place alongside Placido starrers "The Octopus" (on the Mafia) and "Forever Mary" (juvenile delinquency) in the recent vein of hard-nosed social fiction with a violent entertainment edge.

Thywill Amenya heads an almost all-black cast as Kwaku, a medical student from Ghana who comes to Italy to find his brother, nicknamed Pummarò (tomato). Pummarò has been working as an underpaid field hand in the south to send Kwaku to Canada, where he can become a surgeon and help his people. But he has crossed the local Camorra, and had to flee north.

Kwaku's search takes him from the violent Neapolitan countryside to Rome's "Valley of Hell," a camp for prostitutes and penniless immigrants on the edge of the city. Nanou (Jacqueline Williams), a tender hooker expecting Pummarò's baby, knows only that he's gone to Verona. Kwaku brawls with Nanou's pimp, delivers a drugged runaway's baby in an abandoned railway car behind the station, and hits the road.

In foggy Verona, Kwaku misses his brother again, but finds a decent job (though paid half union rates) in a steel mill. He also finds romance with Eleonora (Pamela Villoresi), a volunteer teacher. Like Romeo and Juliet, Kwaku and Eleonora are torn apart by their warring "clans" — mainly, the undisguised contempt of well-heeled Verona towards mixed couples.

The journey ends in Frankfurt, where (after humiliating treatment from the German police), Kwaku and Nanou find Pummarrò in a morgue, killed senselessly. A check from his employers will allow them to leave for Canada.

Scripted by Sandro Petraglia, Stefano Rullo and Placido, "Pummarò" balances its rather obvious finger-pointing against fast pacing and violent clashes between the black heroes and white racists.

The handful of sympathetic whites, like field hand Gerardo Scala or love interest Villoresi, end up beaten and fearful.

Assisted by award-winning Yugoslav cinematographer Vilko Filac, Placido proves himself an economical lenser who never forgets an average viewer's attention span. He claims inspiration from Pietro Germi's "The Path Of Hope" (1950), about southern Italians trudging north in search of an improbable paradise.

A big plus is the finely tuneful score, composed by Lucio Dallas and Mauro Malavasi around African rhythms.

Most natural scene has Thywill Amenya, a fine professional drummer on his first round before the cameras, joyfully taking part in a jam session. Amenya is a natural, dignified thesp who doesn't fade out into anonymity.

In contrast, stage thesp Villoresi comes across as well-meaning but strained. More credible is Williams as the gentle Nanou.
— *Yung.*

CANNES FILM FESTIVAL REVIEWS (DIRECTORS FORTNIGHT)

December Bride
(IRISH)

Cannes A Film Four Intl./CTE/British Screen presentation of a Little Bird production. Produced by Jonathan Cavendish. Executive producer, James Mitchell. Directed by Thaddeus O'Sullivan. Screenplay, David Rudkin, from the novel by Sam Hanna Bell; camera, Bruno de Keyzer; editor, Rodney Holland; music, Jürgen Knieper; sound, Peter Lindsay; production design, Adrian Smith; art director, Steve Simmonds; costume design, Consolata Boyle; assistant director, Seamus Byrne; casting, Noala Moiselle, Susie Figgis. Reviewed at the Cannes Film Festival (Directors Fortnight) May 16, 1990. Running time: **90 MIN.**
Hamilton . . . . Donal McCann
Sarah . . . . Saskia Reeves
Frank . . . . Ciaran Hinds
Sorleyson . . . . Patrick Malahide
Martha . . . . Brenda Bruce
Fergus . . . . Michael McKnight
Echlin . . . . Geoffrey Golden
Young Martha . . . . Dervla Kirwan

■ "December Bride" is the story of an unconventional love triangle in the north of Ireland at the turn of the century told by a director too hesitant to let its sensual elements shine through.

Remote, repressed approach may be true to the character of the land,

but it makes the film a slow and somber sit. Not likely to play beyond festivals and certain Euro markets, pic nonetheless drew strong applause in its Cannes Directors Fortnight premiere.

Director Thaddeus O'Sullivan and crew shot on Taggert's Island, a national preserve, as well as in Dublin, for a carefully crafted, very authentic portrayal of a rural community.

Story tells of a strong-willed servant girl, Sarah (Saskia Reeves) who goes to work in the house of two brothers. Free of her mother's influence, she rejects the church and after a long while, begins a sexual relationship with both men.

When she becomes pregnant, unsure which man is the baby's father, the pressure of the community and the Presbyterian parish comes down upon her to marry, but she refuses, voicing a hatred of the church and its compulsion to "smooth things over on the outside, but leave them all botched inside."

The scandal of her position as the child grows becomes more and

more an affront to the community, with the minister Sorleyson (Patrick Malahide) repeatedly pleading with her to choose a husband. Her stinging answers lead him to his own crisis of faith.

When one brother (Ciaran Hinds) makes a play for a local girl, her brothers beat the outcast 'til he's crippled. Still, Sarah doesn't marry until her grown daughter, requiring a name so she can go around in the community, persuades her — thus the title, "December Bride."

The rural Irish portrayed are hard laborers of closed emotions and few words, and O'Sullivan likewise takes a tongue-tied approach to filming, shying away puritanically from the sexual encounters, editing short the few scenes of conflict, and even shooting a jealous fight between the brothers from a silent distance.

Given the beauty of the film's postcard landscapes and careful compositions, which somewhat relieve its somberness, O'Sullivan comes across more like a painter or still photographer than a dramatist.

As Sarah mostly remains at home, achieving some degree of equality with the brothers as a manager of the farm, her conflict with the townsfolk is minimized, and her quarrels with the clergyman take on a one-note tone.

It is only the open face and wide, expressive eyes of the actress, Reeves, that provides some light through the film's dark curtain of muted emotions. Her performance, and that of the brothers played by Hinds and Donal McCann, are exemplary, while the scenes between the minister and his wife ring somewhat false.

Pic attempts a great time leap that doesn't quite come off, with makeup daubed onto the actors to age them 15 or 20 years. David Rudkin's careful screenplay captures the clipped, measured dialect of the region (difficult to make out sometimes), while Jurgen Kneiper's somber, sometimes ponderous score throws another blanket on the whole affair.

— Daws.

Pont De Varsovia
(Warsaw Bridge)
(SPANISH)

Cannes A J.A. Gonzalez i Serrat production for Films 59. Directed by Pere Portabella. Screenplay, Portabella, Octavi Pellissa, Carles Santos; camera (Eastmancolor), Tomas Pladevall; editor, Marisa Aguinaga. Reviewed at Cannes Film Festival (Directors Fortnight), May 16, 1990. Running time: **90 MIN.**
Musician . . . . Paco Guijar
Writer . . . . Jordi Dauder
Professor . . . . Carme Elias
Also with: Ona Planas, Jose Maria Pou, Jaume Comas, Francesc Orella, Pep Ferrer.
(Catalan soundtrack)

■ This talky, highly personal and rather pretentious film is nigh incomprehensible due to a rambling succession of tableaux from a writer's past. The pacing is slow, and no attempt is made to link the elements together into a story. Commercial chances for this murky Catalan exercise in obscurity seem nil.

First half hour of pic unfolds at a reception for the awarding of an important literary prize for a novel called "Warsaw Bridge." After seemingly interminable jejune chit chat among the guests, the author of the book decides to summarize the novel to an admirer, upon which the credits roll, a half hour into the film.

Declining to provide a coherent story, Portabella rambles on in disjointed images and dialogs, delving into the personages' and his own past. These range over scenes in a Berlin subway, a group of fat women singing an aria, a conductor leading a symphony orchestra and endless "deep" conversations about life, love and art, most of them handled in a plodding auteur style.

However, pic does provide a most unusual form of death: As the victim is scuba-diving in a lake, a seaplane scoops him up while loading water and drops him as part of the load on a forest fire. Therewith ends the non-story of "Warsaw Bridge." — *Besa*.

End Of The Night
(B&W)

Cannes An In Absentia production. Produced by Ngoc Ngo. Executive producer, Lynn Wagenknecht. Written and directed by Keith McNally. Camera (black & white), Tom DiCillo; editor, Ila von Hasperg; music, Jurgen Kneiper; costumes, Susan Lyall; assistant director and associate producer, Gary Marcus; sound, Mathew Price; casting, Walken/Jaffe. Reviewed at the Cannes Film Festival (Directors Fortnight), May 18, 1990. Running time: **110 MIN.**
Joe Belinsky . . . . Eric Mitchell
Mary Belinsky . . . . Audrey Matson
French Girl . . . . Nathalie Devaux
Tom . . . . Darroch Greer
Steiner . . . . Sam Bress
Willie . . . . Mark Mikesell

■ Enervating existential pretension and heavy-handed European-influenced black & white photography obscure and distract from the story in the New York-lensed "End Of The Night." It's no great loss, as writer-director Keith McNally begins and ends with nothing compelling to say.

Mundane tale of a middle-class urban drudge who is so disoriented by his wife's pregnancy that he begins a pathetic pursuit of strange young women may find a few arthouse admirers, but prospects are limited in any market.

McNally has enlisted the talents of director of photography Tom DeCillo, who lensed the first Jim Jarmusch film; Ila von Hapsburg, editor of numerous Fassbinder films; and composer Jürgen Kneiper, who scored Wim Wenders' "Wings Of Desire."

Their pedigreed contributions lend the film a heavy veneer of artiness, but it's more oppressive than effective, as McNally's slight script, with its muted noises of existential struggle, is overwhelmed.

Protagonist Joe Belinsky (Eric Mitchell, writer-director of "Underground U.S.A."), after losing his job at an insurance company, impulsively takes work as a counterman at an all-night slophouse frequented by a hip young crowd from a nearby dance club.

He falls for an aloof and nameless young French woman (Nathalie Devaux) and chases her through the streets to her apartment, where they fornicate in the kitchen and he stays the night. He develops an obsession with the girl, and unknown to his blithely supportive wife (Audrey Mason), quits his coffee shop job to spend nights in futile pursuit of her.

Some brief scenes in a mixed-race dance club offer the only real moment of energy in the film, suggesting McNally might do better with music video. Otherwise, script follows a turgid course, with camera lingering annoyingly on such meaningless mundane items as coffee cups, faucets and toilets.

Meanwhile, suspense is provided by the unresolved nature of Joe's ear infection, apparently a metaphor for his inner maladies and loss of balance. When the French girl refuses to see him again, he begins to demand attention from every attractive young woman he sees. They all shun him, but he persists. His wife ends up having their baby without him. Joe ends up very much a lost cause, and the film itself beats him to that conclusion.

At one point Joe drives his father to the airport and the old man says, "What are we doing here?," and Joe says, "I don't know, why don't we go back," and so they go back home. That is the kind of journey this film provides. — *Daws*.

Inimene, Keda Polnud
(The Man Who Never Was)
(ESTONIAN-SOVIET-
COLOR/SEPIA)

Cannes A Sovexport presentation of Tallinnfilm Studios production. No producer's credit. Directed by Peeter Simm. Screenplay, Tomas Raudam; camera (color, sepia), Ago Rous; editor, Sirje Haagel, Helju Soerd; music, Tynou Raadik; sound, Rein Ourm; production design, Ronald Kolmann, Hardi Volmer. Reviewed at Cannes Film Festival (Directors Fortnight), May 11, 1990. Running time: **98 MIN.**
Imbi . . . . Katri Horma
Imbi as child . . . . Mari Simm
Her father . . . . Tynou Kilgas
Her uncle . . . . Youri Krukov
Her aunt . . . . Rita Raave
Hans . . . . Tinou Raadik
Madame Fiche . . . . Raine Loo
Also: Andres Lepik, Soulev, Louik, Maria Kokamiagui, Lillemats, Robert Chestakov.

■ "The Man Who Never Was" is an Estonian comedy-of-terrors. Told as a rather murky allegory that never explains its own title, this film could still appeal to arthouses with its mix of fanciful black comedy dialog and kooky characters with tragic overtones.

Writer Tomas Raudam and director Peeter Simm display their new artistic freedom to tell the story of a taciturn girl who comes of age amid first German occupation, then Russian "liberation" of her country. Taciturn as she is, Imbi finds plenty of occasion to express herself anyway. The child of showbusiness parents, she has developed aptitude for sound imitations stretching from a bird's squeak to an operatic bass.

This helps her when the Germans invade Estonia. She is an avid listener to forbidden radios and has a kind of an affair with a Wehrmacht musician under the sunlamp in his apartment.

When the Russians take over, the 1949 mass deportation of Estonians to Siberia follows. By this time, Imbi has become a radio star specializing in readings of fairy tales (full of allegories). The secret police suspect her of various schemes, but she escapes with her newborn son, who also has a talent for sound imitations.

The absurdist styles of 1960s Czech cinema clearly have inspired Simm. When he gets grim about matters, it is mostly in an offhand way. Since blond Katri Horma in the lead remains deadpan for most of the film, the tragedy of her character never achieves a deeper resonance. The other actors in the cast perform with an obvious gusto that often gives the film a vaudeville flavor.

Color is used only in film's opening and closing sequences. The rest is shot in neatly handled sepia. Whether this was a cost-saving measure or meant to have a deeper meaning remains unclear but doesn't matter much anyway. Music is used inventively throughout to underscore points of wit and irony. — *Kell*.

Halfaouine
(Boy Of The Terraces)
(TUNISIAN-FRENCH)

———

Cannes A Cinetelefilm/RTT Tunisian TV/ France Media/Scarabee Films/La Sept/WDR coproduction. Produced by Ahmed Attia, Eliane Stutterheim. Written and directed by Ferid Boughedir. Camera (color), Georges Barsky; editor, Moufida Tlatli, M. Rougerie; music, Anouar Braham. Reviewed at the Cannes Film Festival (Directors Fortnight), May 12, 1990. Running time: **98 MIN.**
Noura . . . . Selim Boughedir
Latifa . . . . Carolyn Chelby
With: Mohamed Driss, Helene Katzaras, Anouche Setbon, Rabia Ben Abdallah, Fatma Ben Saidane, Mustapha Adouani, Zehira Ben Ammar, Fethi Heddaoui.

———

■ **Ferid Boughedir makes a fine directorial bow in "Halfaouine." Fest outings should help it find takers in specialized art-film markets abroad.**

This tender, relaxed story of a lad's sexual awakening breaks new ground for Tunisian pictures. Its explicit female nudity and inherent sensuality will probably get pic banned in most Arab countries and possibly in liberal Tunisia itself.

Noura (intense newcomer Selim Boughedir) is a 12-year-old curious about the facts of life, and a glimpse of his father's air-brushed men's mags does little to satisfy his curiosity.

Because he's small for his age, his mother still gets him into the ladies' Turkish baths, where huge, Fellini-esque women stroll half-naked through the steam, their thin underclothes clinging to plump flesh.

The young girls he'd most like to see, however, cover their lower regions with a bath glove or, even more incredibly, to unfamiliar eyes, with water.

Noura observes the provocative lady next door who hangs her bras in his courtyard and sneaks afternoon trysts with his friend the shoemaker. (The shoemaker is arrested for writing an anti-government slogan on a wall in one of pic's several blows for local glasnost.)

When pretty young Latifa (Carolyn Chelby) comes to live in the household as a servant, Noura has a chance to experience a gentle sexual initiation, satisfying for both boy and girl.

Childhood and sexuality are not familiar themes in Arab films. "Halfaouine" breaks the taboos, certainly not just filmic, to show naked women in a land of veils.

Further, it insists female sexuality is natural and uninhibited. Beneath the veils are real flesh-and-blood women with an enviably healthy attitude toward their bodies. Boughedir is a director of broad ideas more than a stylist, yet the pic manages to capture and hold viewers from start to finish.

Setting is the old Arab quarter of Tunis called Halfaouine. It presents a new image of Tunisia: more than a Muslim society, it seems to be a free-thinking, laughing Mediterranean country warm with eroticism. Little Selim Boughedir is sober and intelligent as the boy and dozens of peripheral characters color the scenes in tiny parts.

Georges Barsky's lensing captures the flavor of the colorful old Arab city several decades ago. Particularly eye-catching are the Turkish bath scenes, surprising in their frankness. — *Yung.*

HOUSTON INTL. FILM FEST REVIEWS

An American Summer

———

Houston A Boss Entertainment Group presentation. Executive producer, Jane Hamsher. Written, produced and directed by James Slocum. Camera (color), Bruce Dorfman; editor, Ron Rosen; music, Roger Neill; sound (Dolby), Wolf Schmidt; production design, Damon Fortier; costume design, Linda Susan Howell; coproducer, Charles Faithorn; associate producer, Wade W. Danielson. Reviewed at Houston Intl. Film Festival, April 28, 1990. No MPAA Rating. Running time: **99 MIN.**
Tom . . . . Michael Landes
Fin . . . . Brian Austin Green
Aunt Sunny . . . . Joanna Kerns
Traci . . . . Amber Susa
Cari . . . . Sherrie Krenn
Rockman . . . . Wayne Pere

———

■ **"An American Summer" updates Mark Twain's "Tom Sawyer" to 1978 and moves the plot to California surfing country. That may not sound terribly promising, but the movie is surprisingly successful as an entertaining coming-of-age story, and it sustains a fair degree of respect for its source material.**

Freshman filmmaker James Slocum, serving as producer and director for his own screenplay, scores with an agreeable little picture that could have b.o. potential and definitely has prospects for a long homevid afterlife.

Michael Landes, late of tv's "The Wonder Years," plays the 14-year-old lead, Tom Travis, a Chicago hockey fan who's shipped off to an aunt on the West Coast while his parents thrash out their divorce. Tom doesn't like the California town of Oceanhaven, hates being called "dude" and doesn't even seem overly fond of his Aunt Sunny (Joanna Kerns), a 30-ish love child who works as an artist while she raises her infant (and conspicuously fatherless) daughter.

Despite his general surliness, Tom manages to make a new friend, Fin (Brian Austin Green), an enterprising young surfer who cons Tom into helping him sell sunglasses on the beach and deliver newspapers. Tom returns the favor when, taking a page from Mark Twain's classic, he tricks Fin into helping him paint his aunt's fence.

Tom and Fin spend most of their time checking out the babes on the beach, coping with a cocky young lifeguard and planning for the end-of-summer surfing competition.

They witness a murder committed by Rockman (Wayne Pere), a local drug dealer who apparently leaves town after the boys report him to the police. Late in the pic, however, Rockman turns up at an abandoned mine, where he rudely interrupts a romantic encounter between Tom and pretty blond Traci (Amber Susa). What happens next won't surprise anyone who's read the Mark Twain original.

Slocum gets fine performances from his cast. And he goes just far enough in finding modern-day equivalents for key incidents from Twain's novel while vividly recreating the late 1970s ambiance. Aptly chosen period music is used generously, but not overbearingly. A nice gag: In the opening scene, Tom can't find a radio station that isn't playing disco.

Kerns, of tv's "Growing Pains," gets some laughs as a Woodstock era survivor who's shocked to learn Tom doesn't know who Bob Dylan is. Onscreen drug use is limited to a comic-relief sequence in which Tom and Fin get high on Aunt Sunny's marijuana.

The surfing footage is routine, but dramatically effective. Other tech credits are first-rate. Pic was shot in and around Pasadena.
— *Ley.*

———

Geld
(Money)
(WEST GERMAN)

———

Houston An Olga-Film GMBH-Production release. Directed by Doris Dorrie. Screenplay, Dorrie, Michael Juncker; camera (color), Helge Weindler; editor, Raimund Barthelmes, Hana Mullner; music, Phillip Johnston; sound (Dolby), Michael Etz; architecture, Jorg Neumann; costumes, Siegbert Kammerer; makeup, Werner A. Puthe, Udo Riemer; production manager, Gerd Huber. Reviewed at the Houston Intl. Film Festival, April 28, 1990. Running time: **98 MIN.**
Carmen Muller . . . . Billie Zockler
Werner Muller . . . . . Uwe Ochsenknecht
Lothar Fuchs . . . . August Zirner
Gabriele . . . . Sunnyi Melles

———

■ **After her unspectacular made-in-America "Me And Him," West German director Doris Dorrie returned home for "Geld," which isn't likely to crack the international market. Pic lacks a sharp focus, and the actors appear to be trying too hard.**

Oddly enough, this thin comedy about a middle-class suburban housewife who tries bank robbery as a way of alleviating household debts bears more than a superficial resemblance (in satirical tone and at least one major plot development) to "Rosalie Goes Shopping," a recent American-made film by Dorrie's countryman, Percy Adlon.

"Geld" looks and sounds like something that could easily be Americanized for an improved remake with, say, Bette Midler as the gun-toting housewife. Billie Zockler is the leading lady here, playing Carmen Muller as a dowdy, doughy-faced housefrau who's shocked to learn her husband of several years, Werner (Uwe Ochsenknecht), was fired two months ago, and has been unemployed ever since.

Worried about the massive debts facing the family (they have two sullen teen-age children), Carmen disguises herself as a femme fatale and enters the Munich bank operated by her handsome, affluent and somewhat younger neighbor, Lothar Fuchs (August Zirner).

The actual bank robbery is the pic's comic highpoint. Carmen virtually freezes after drawing a toy gun, and must be coached by a customer's precocious youngster. ("Okay, now say, 'Everybody lie down!' ") Carmen takes Lothar as a hostage, brings him home on the bus, and keeps him tied up in the back room. Werner is understandably shocked, but helps his wife hide Lothar until she goes on the lam with her unwilling companion.

During his wife's absence, Werner begins to loosen up to the point of tentatively wooing Lothar's attractive live-in girlfriend, Gabriele (Sunnyi Melles). Meanwhile, in the trailer park where she spent her honeymoon with Werner, Carmen and Lothar begin to warm up to each other.

Neither extramarital romance really blossoms into anything. The same could be said of the movie itself, which gives the feeling of a long setup for a punchline that never arrives.

Like "Rosalie Goes Shopping," "Geld" makes the not-so-novel point that, with corporations wheeling and dealing and mounting huge debts, common folks shouldn't hesitate to steal to improve their own bad credit ratings. Also like "Rosalie," "Geld" relies on computer-hacker trickery to resolve its contrived plot. — *Ley.*

Across The Tracks

Houston A Rosenbloom Entertainment presentation. Produced by Dale Rosenbloom. Written and directed by Sandy Tung. Camera (color), Michael Delahoussaye; editor, Farrel Levy; music, Joel Goldsmith; sound (Ultra Stereo), Tung, Levy; production design, Thomas Meleck; associate producers, Francesca Bill, Robert A. Schacht. Reviewed at the Houston Intl. Film Festival, April 28, 1990. Running time: **100 MIN.**
Billy . . . . Rick Schroder
Joe . . . . Brad Pitt
Louie . . . . David Anthony Marshall
Mom . . . . Carrie Snodgress

■ **Writer-director Sandy Tung won't win any points for originality with "Across the Tracks," but he may win some hearts and minds with a movie that boasts fine performances, persuasive emotional impact and a well-developed sense of life on the lower-middle-class fringes.**

Rick Schroder, completely demolishing his squeaky-clean "Silver Spoons" tv image, gives a strong performance as a recent reform-school graduate who returns to the trailer-park home of his widowed mother Carrie Snodgress and older brother Brad Pitt.

Schroder got caught joyriding in a stolen car (a bad companion actually stole the vehicle), and just about everybody's ready to write off the sullen teen as a career criminal. Pitt seems especially resentful of his brother's return, fearing Schroder will upset their mother and somehow interfere with his college plans.

Pitt is a classic overachiever, having always felt pressed to win at everything to secure his alcoholic father's love. Schroder is a chronic screw-up, and needs the support of his family more than he'll ever admit.

Eventually, the two brothers make peace, and Pitt suggests that Schroder, who's attending another high school across town, join that school's track team. Unfortunately, this places Schroder in direct competition with his brother, who's on the verge of nervous collapse after overtraining for an upcoming meet. Even more unfortunately, it's obvious that Schroder is the better runner.

Tung hits most of the predictable bases, even dragging in a sleazy companion from the bad old days (David Anthony Marshall) to tempt Schroder into backsliding. But Tung also generates a fair degree of interest, and even some genuine suspense, by concentrating on the give and take between the two brothers.

There's an exceptional scene midway through the film that begins with Pitt (excellent in a complex role) and Schroder jokingly debating the relative sex appeal of Jane Pauley and Vanna White. The talk turns more personal, as the brothers reveal their real feelings about their dead father, and about each other. That's when it stops being a scene, and simply is.

Tech credits are pro. — *Ley.*

ISTANBUL INTL. FILM FESTIVAL REVIEWS

Küçük Balıklar Üzerine Bir Masal (A Fable On Little Fishes) (TURKISH)

Istanbul A Kedi Film production (Intl. sales, Warner Bros.) Produced by Baris Pirhasan. Written and directed by Pirhasan. Camera (color), Anton Klima; editor, Mevlüt Koçak; music, Derya Köroglu. Reviewed at Istanbul Intl. Film Festival (competing), April 10, 1990. Running time: **93 MIN.**
Feryal . . . . Hale Soygazi
Sinan . . . . Nihat Ileri
Mesut . . . . Derya Köroglu
Also with: Yasemin Alkaya.

■ **The believable relationship between husband and wife is sustained for a time through a triangle, but as it begins to disintegrate, so does the plot. Motivation is hazy and this "Fable" flounders midway through.**

Feryal (popular actress Hale Soygazi) and her husband Sinan (Nihat Ileri) have an "open" relationship that allows no secrets. When Feryal forms a friendship with Sinan's best friend Mesut and then begins an affair, she discusses the situation with Sinan.

The story is believable in mirroring the plight of modern couples who want to be hip and permissive but can't face the confusion that develops when they become jealous. It is interesting that in this case the woman (and a wife and mother) is the wandering party, a novel concept that will no doubt offend many viewers.

The affection between the married couple is quite touching and in marked contrast to the obvious lack of chemistry between Feryal and Mesut.

By the time Sinan's ex-girlfriend Sedef arrives on the scene to further complicate the situation, most viewers will have lost interest. Tech standards are okay. — *Sam.*

Karartma Geceleri (Blackout Nights) (TURKISH)

Istanbul A Senar Film production. Produced by Senar Turgut. Directed by Yusuf Kurçenli. Screenplay, Kurçenli based on the novel of the same name by Rifat Ilgaz; camera (color), Colin Mounier; editor, Ismail Kalkan. Reviewed at Istanbul Intl. Film Festival, April 10, 1990. Running time: **110 MIN.**
With: Tarik Akan, Nurseli Idiz, Bülent Bilgiç, Deniz Kurtoglu, Omar Colakoglu, Erol Günaydin, Sükrü Türen, Menderas Samancilar.

■ **Winner of the best Turkish film award at the Istanbul Film Fest follows in the familiar mode of the sociopolitical drama but distinguishes itself with maturity and believability. Domestic b.o. will be sparked by its near-banning while subject is handled in a way that should appeal to broad general audiences.**

Handsome one-time matinee idol Tarik Akan, best known to foreign audiences from his lead role in Yilmaz Güney and Serif Gören's "The Road," has developed into a fine actor.

In a story loosely based on the biography of the same name of prolific writer Rifat Ilgaz, Akan is cast as poet Mustapha Ural, whose book is banned at the end of World War II after which he is hunted as a suspected Communist.

Ural goes into hiding and much of the appeal of the story comes from his interaction with those who befriend him during this period. The somber tone is lightened with humorous touches and the cafes and their inhabitants are suitably colorful.

Ural's reunion with his wife (Nurseli Idiz) is genuinely sensuous and her gradual resentment about the restrictions placed on her life is seen as a natural reaction rather than callousness. It is inevitable that Ural will be forced to turn himself in.

Torture in prison is not avoided nor overly emphasized. In a most effective scene, Ural is stripped down and blindfolded, then writhes in agony as he is doused with cold water from all directions.

The story unfolds with a gentle rhythm and makes its point in an understated manner. Although the topic of man's cruelty to man in the struggle for control is played out, the film ultimately is optimistic, a paean to the durability of the human spirit.

Tech credits are good, especially the camerawork. The supporting cast is uniformly solid.
— *Sam.*

Filim Ritti
(The Film Is Over)
(TURKISH)

Istanbul A Z Film Ltd. production. Written and directed by Yavuz Ozkan. Camera (color), Ertunç Senkay. Reviewed at Istanbul Intl. Film Festival April 10, 1990. Running time: **101 MIN.**
  With: Kadir Inanir, Zeliha Berksoy, Halil Ergun, Meral Oguz.

■ A technically adept film-within-a-film, it has its moments of truth, but much of the interaction is contrived. Director often seems more concerned with showing how Westernized modern Turks are than building up a believable love triangle among the leads.

An actor and actress are about to get a divorce but get an offer to star in a movie and accept. The tension that develops during the film, as the wife is confronted by her husband and his new lover, causes her to tell the director that she wants to quit.

The film's plot mirrors what is happening in real life but on-screen, the wife welcomes the other woman and proclaims her husband's happiness is her only concern. The insight given on the making of a film is interesting, but scenes start to drag when allowed to continue to the point of being repetitious.

The women are much more emotive than the modern husband who shifts suddenly from an impassive pose to one of hysterical or murderous rage. Veteran actor Kadir Inanir gives a restrained performance as the director but often looks somewhat confused by the action.

Some humor is provided by the producer who, as is to be expected, is concerned about the budget and is carried raving off the set, or the fantasy fulfillment as the director throws a cake in the face of a harping critic.

Other sequences, as when the cast and crew run out to dance in the rain, look unnatural. — *Sam.*

Bütün Kapilar Kapaliydi
(All The Doors Were Closed)
(TURKISH)

Istanbul An Ugur Film production exported by Mine Film. Produced and directed by Memduh Ün. Screenplay, Sühelya Acar Kalyoncu; camera (color), Orhan Oguz; editor, Ün; music, Önde Focan. Reviewed at Istanbul Intl. Film Festival, April 11, 1990. Running time: **90 MIN.**

Nil . . . . Asli Altan
Ates . . . . Ugur Polat
  Also with: Nalan Orgut, Matin Belgin, Dilek Damlacik, Ali Uyandiran, Sabahat Isik.

■ A psychological drama, winner of the special jury prize at the Istanbul fest, deals with a young woman's attempt to heal her life and regain stability after spending six years in jail. Plot is handled sensitively but may be too unrelentingly somber to appeal to wide audiences.

Nil (appealing newcomer Asli Altan), was sentenced to six years in jail while a political activist in college. Scenes from her past life are seen in flashback as she is finally released and re-enters the outside world.

Nil's attempts to re-establish her old lifestyle are thwarted on every side. Her family feels awkward around her, she has to lie about her record in order to get a job and, worst of all, her mental state is delicate and she often becomes disoriented.

A relationship with a kind and patient architect Ates (sympathetic Ugur Polat) presents a ray of hope. He is supportive about her career and artistic pursuits, and tender when her memories of prison sexual abuse prevent her from responding sexually. Nil's overriding obsession is to gain custody of the daughter she thinks she has left with her ex-husband, and Ates vows to help raise her.

The title is apt on many levels from the actual doors that were locked in jail, to those that are symbolically shut because her past cuts her off from the real world.

Acting is good and the poignancy of Nil's dilemma is touching. Lensing of courtship scenes along the Bosphorus provides a welcome relief to heavier interludes.

The plot's linear progression, without much doubt as to the ultimate outcome, deprive the script of much suspense. The grating electric guitar and organ score was to be changed on producer's orders.
— *Sam.*

Ask Filmlerinin
Unutulmaz Yönatmeni
(The Unforgettable Director
Of Love Movies)
(TURKISH)

Istanbul An Erler Film production. Produced by Türker Inanoglu. Written and directed by Yavuz Turgul. Camera (color), Orhan

Oguz; editor, Mehmet Bozkus; music, Atilla Ozdemiroglu. Reviewed at Istanbul Intl. Film Festival, April 11, 1990. Running time: **100 MIN.**
Director . . . . Sener Sen
Actress . . . . Pitircik Akerman
  Also with: Yavuzer Centinkaya, Gül Onat, Aytacç Yörükaslan.

■ Sener Sen, Turkey's foremost comedian, has perfected the role of the rural aga over the years but displays a new depth as a down-on-his-luck director. His name alone would guarantee its local success, but the delightful rendering of a far from unique plot could give it legs beyond the usual specialty fests.

Excellent photography highlight everyday Istanbul street scenes as "The Unforgettable Director Of Love Movies" is seen involved in his quest to get backing to produce a "serious" film based on a script dealing with social issues.

His attempts are met with skepticism. The producer says growing a beard is not enough while his ex-wife uses the occasion to berate him for past misdeeds.

The flavor of contemporáry Istanbul life is revealed through scenes in bars, card games in cafes and in restaurants. The stunning young actress (Pitircik Akerman) seems fittingly bemused by Sen's awkward advances.

Yet the actress, along with the eclectic cast and crew, begins to believe in the project despite her initial skepticism. Aytac Yörükaslan has a memorable turn as a crusty old character actor whose main companion is a turtle. As Sen approaches him in his cluttered house, he slurps down a concoction of bread soaked in raki (anisette liquor).

Sen is at his most expressive when he woefully ravels one of the reels of his completed film around his neck and tries to light it in order to end it all. His excellent timing and facial expression evoke a perfect blend of black humor and pathos, while the whimsical piano-horn score establish the proper mood. — *Sam.*

Nocturne
(B&W)

New York A Lyric Films Production. Produced and directed by Mark T. Harris. Screenplay, Harris; camera (black & white), Ed Talavera; editor, Harris. Reviewed at the New York Intl. Festival of Lesbian and Gay Film, N.Y., May 1, 1990. No MPAA rating. Running time: **100 MIN.**
Martin . . . . T. Ryder Smith
Gino . . . . Gabriel Amor
Ron . . . . Mark Woodcock
Lisa . . . . Lisa Allyn Worth

■ Despite good intentions, this low-budget first film by Mark T. Harris suffers from poor production values, pretentious dialogue and a surfeit of sentimentality. It will most likely reach only a small audience.

The story of a repressed gay pianist who finally allows himself to fall for a college student, only to be heartbroken in the end, was filmed in New York and makes excellent use of a number of locations.

This "Nocturne" is not to be confused with Joy Chamberlain's British film of the same name, which also debuts in this year's New Festival. This offering by a recent film school grad is too literary and dimly lit reflecting Harris' inexperience. The film's sound is poor: Every shoe creak is audible and conversations are sometimes muffled.

Plot concerns a young pianist named Martin, who is new to the city and is just coming to terms with being gay. In Central Park he meets a leather-jacketed student, Gino, who shares Martin's interest in literature. Although the naive Martin thinks he has found the man of his dreams, his hopes are shattered when Gino ultimately gives him the cold shoulder. After being unceremoniously dumped, Martin becomes closer to his roommate, Ron, who embodies virtually every gay stereotype.

The actors are unable to rise above the script's literary pretentions. In fact, the material would probably make a better short story than a film. Toward the end, Martin turns to Ron and asks, "Do you think life is sacred, or anything else that we do?" T. Ryder Smith manages to deliver such lines with a straight face, but he cannot make them sound convincing.

The story does get more interesting when a traumatic incident from Martin's past is revealed. But the episode is recounted in overly meaningful dreams that Martin relates to his friend Lisa. Harris may aspire to be Ingmar Bergman, but that is a lofty ambition for a first feature.

Besides its technical limitations, pic's main problem is that Martin is not all that likable. He is rather pretentious, repressed and self-pitying. The other characters are also little more than 1-dimensional types: Gino seems sincere, but is really a Don Juan. Ron is the flamboyant, wisecracking sidekick. Lisa is merely a sympathetic friend who listens to Martin's lament. Unfortunately, we have to listen, too.

The film's best aspects are its use of locations and music, the latter consisting primarily of a mournful Chopin nocturne. It complements the film's overall dreary tone. Harris has attempted to depict gay life in New York realistically, but the result is overwritten, overacted and not terribly compelling. — *Stev.*

Fools Of Fortune
(BRITISH)

London A Palace Pictures release (New Line Cinema in U.S.) of a Polygram/Working Title production in association with Film Four Intl. Executive producers, Tim Bevan, Graham Bradstreet. Produced by Sarah Radclyffe. Directed by Pat O'Connor. Screenplay, Michael Hirst, based on the novel by William Trevor; camera, Jerzy Zielinski; editor, Michael Bradsell; music, Hans Zimmer; production design, Jamie Leonard; costume design, Judy Moorcroft; associate producer, Caroline Hewitt; casting, Debbie McWilliams. Reviewed at Mr. Young's Preview Theater, London, May 8, 1990. Running time: **104 MIN.**
Marianne . . . Mary Elizabeth Mastrantonio
Willie . . . . Iain Glen
Mrs. Quinton . . . . Julie Christie
Mr. Quinton . . . . Michael Kitchen
Young Willie . . . . Sean T. McClory
Tim Paddy . . . . Frankie McCafferty
Josephine . . . . Niamii Cusack
Sereant Rudkin . . . . Neil Dudgeon
Imelda . . . . Catherine McFadden

■ "Fools of Fortune" is an historical saga written with lucidity and performed with sensitivity, but tending to melodrama. There's limited appeal in this gentle and unprobing film.

Political angle is present only by implication, and certain characterizations are not fully enough explored, but top quality lensing and thesping should keep most engrossed, if unchallenged.

The Irish war of independence is the starting point for the story of a family's destruction and the survival of an unlikely love. The Quinton family seem sheltered in their grand rural home until one of their workers is murdered by the Republicans on suspicion of spying for the British forces. In retaliation, the British-employed soldiers, the Black and Tans, burn down the Quintons' house, and shoot down Quinton.

The only survivors of the massacre are Quinton's wife (Julie Christie), her son Willie (first, Sean T. McClory, and then as an adult, Iain Glen), and their maid (Niamii Cusack). Willie becomes an introspective and withdrawn young man, while his mother becomes a manic depressive and chronic alcoholic, a role which Christie relishes in.

When Christie finally commits suicide, Willie is comforted by childhood playmate Marianne, who's grown into an exquisitely beautiful woman (Mary Elizabeth Mastrantonio).

Result of this comfort is a child, but by the time Marianne returns to Ireland from her home in England to confront Willie, he's disappeared. Turns out he's sought retribution by murdering the leader of the Black and Tans who murdered his father and sisters, and has gone into self-imposed exile on an island off Wales.

She and the child live with Willie's aunts in the only part of the old Quinton house not devastated by the fire (the ruins of the house are eerily untouched), while Willie agonizes in his ramshackle cabin far away. Finally a message from the dying maid calls him back home, where he's reunited with Marianne and the daughter he's never known.

Glen plays Willie as a profoundly tortured soul, and it's a moving performance. Mastrantonio captures the purity and innocence of Marianne, while at the same time seeming somewhat too beautiful and inherently sexy to be attracted to the boy. Their love is never totally believable. Cusack's maid is a promising character but underwritten, which is frustrating as she seems to have an unexplained hold on Willie.

Pic is technically superior, music is highly atmospheric and the production design is stunning. Real star is the Irish landscape, which alone is enough to captivate.
— *Krug.*

Force Of Circumstance

New York An Upfront Films release. Produced and directed by Liza Bear. Screenplay, Craig Gholson, Bear; camera (Duart color), Zoran Hochstätter; editor, Bear, J.P. Rolandlevy; music, M. Mader; sound, Barbara Becker, Stephanie Cote. Reviewed at Broadway screening room, N.Y., May 15, 1990. No MPAA Rating. Running time: **89 MIN.**
Mouallem . . . . Borbala Major
Katrina . . . . Jessica Stutchbury
Hans . . . . Tom Wright
Envoy . . . . Eric Mitchell
Charles Floris . . . . Glenn O'Brien
Herman . . . . Mark Boone Jr.
Hortensia . . . . Kathleen Anderson
Virgil . . . . Steve Buscemi
Also with: Filip Pagowski, Evan Lurie, Rockets Redglare, Pam Osowski.

■ "Force Of Circumstance" is an unwatchable assemblage of footage shot in 1987 purporting to be a feature film. Definitely derrière garde, interminable exercise inexplicably escaped from the lab and is being released theatrically.

With scenes ending arbitrarily via execrable editing, nonstory never takes root. Borbala Major walks through a lead role (her dialog has been replaced in post-production) of a courier repping Moroccan dissidents who arrives in Washington, D.C. with secret documents.

In one of the worst performances ever committed to celluloid, Tom Wright stumbles through his part as a Virginia mansion owner pondering whether to sell the estate to wooden Eric Mitchell (Gotham filmmaker wearing a fez) as a safe haven for fleeing Moroccan royalty.

There's no evidence of directorial or writing talent in this amateur farrago, made possible by grants from N.Y. State Council on the Arts, NEA and Jerome Foundation. Most prominent thesp on view, Steve Buscemi, looks lost in a nonrole as a pig tender. — *Lor.*

Dédé
(FRENCH)

Paris A Capital-Cinéma release of a Septembre Films/SGGC/Films A2 coproduction. Produced by Jean Nainchrik. Written and directed by Jean-Louis Benoit. Camera (color), Dominique le Rigoleur; editor, Bénédicte Brunet; music, Roland Vincent; art direction, Laurent Tesseyre; assistant director, Antoine Santana; production manager, Philippe Desmoulins. Reviewed at the Georges V cinema, Paris, May 8, 1990. Running time: **79 MIN.**
Dédé . . . . Luc Thuillier
Yvonne . . . . Hélène Vincent
Raymond . . . . Didier Besace
The father . . . . Yves Afonso
Grandmother . . . . Renée Faure
Priest . . . . Jacques Mathou
Monique . . . . Marion Grimault

■ "Dédé" is a well-done but pointless seriocomic rehash of "Hamlet," set in a southern French wine region in 1957, with the Algerian War and the launching of the Russian Sputnik as sociopolitical backdrop. This sort of pastiche isn't new, even for French movies: Claude Chabrol did something similar in his 1962 feature, "Ophelia," which was set among the provincial gentry.

For writer-director Jean-Louis Benoit, Hamlet is a young soldier (Luc Thuillier) about to be shipped off to Algeria, but who's first going home for a few days to attend his mom's remarriage to his uncle. Thuillier thinks it's suspiciously too soon after dad's death: he apparently fell into the well during a drunken stupor. It seems though that his brother (Didier Besace), who's long been hankering after sister-in-law Hélène Vincent, helped him a bit.

The ghost of Thuillier's good-for-nothing dad (Yves Afonso) goads him on to avenge his death, though Thuillier beats around the local bush so long he finally ships out to Algeria without accomplishing his mission. He also fails to kill the Polonius figure, or drive his "Ophelia" to a mad death. A real washout. As reward for his filial services, Afonso haunts him all the way across the Mediterranean.

Pic is entertaining as an ironic portrait of a provincial homestead in the manner of French author Marcel Aymé. Benoit gives film a good feeling of time and place and is admirably served by fine actors who cut crisp portraits: Thuillier, Besace, Vincent, Renée Faure (as the grandmother) and especially the hilarious Afonso, who's first otherworldly command to Thuillier is not for revenge but a glass of red wine.

For all its incidental pleasures, "Dédé" doesn't really add up to much. Still, Benoit is obviously somebody to watch. — *Len.*

CANNES FILM FESTIVAL MARKET REVIEWS

After Dark, My Sweet

Cannes An Avenue Pictures release. (Intl. sales, Samuel Goldwyn Co.) Produced by Ric Kidney, Robert Redlin. Executive producer, Cary Brokaw. Directed by James Foley. Screenplay, Redlin, Foley, based on the novel by Jim Thompson; camera, Mark Plummer; editor, Howard Smith; music, Maurice Jarre; sound, David Brownlow; art direction, Kenneth Hardy; set decoration, Margaret Goldsmith; assistant director, David B. Householter; casting, David Rubin. Reviewed at Cannes Film Festival (market), May 17, 1990. MPAA Rating: R. Running time: **114 MIN.**

Collie . . . . Jason Patric
Fay . . . . Rachel Ward
Uncle Bud . . . . Bruce Dern
Doc Goldman . . . . . . George Dickerson
Charlie . . . . James Cotton
Jack . . . . Corey Carrier

■ **Director-cowriter James Foley has given this near-perfect adaptation of a Jim Thompson novel a contempo setting and emotional realism that make it as potent as a snakebite. Handled savvily, this small-scale jewel should do sharp business in U.S. theaters and have a tenacious life in video and foreign.**

Foley's take on "After Dark, My Sweet" feels right from the first frame, as ex-boxer and nuthouse escapee "Kid" Collins (Jason Patric) shambles into a desert town with a cardboard bundle under his arm, accompanied by his own desultory narration of Thompson's pungent first-person prose.

In a bar he meets Fay Anderson (Rachel Ward), who tortures and tests him with her wit before taking him home. "I'm worried about Mr. Anderson," say Collins before coming inside. "He's dead. He went to hell," says Fay, in one of pic's many examples of tart dialog.

She puts him to work as a handyman on the rambling estate, while both provoking and fending off their sensual attraction. Out for a beer and a dance in a country-western joint, the two are joined by a wily ex-detective (Bruce Dern), who immediately gets designs on Collie, as Fay calls him, as a partner in a kidnaping scheme.

Kid gets sucked into it, but as he keeps telling Fay, he's not stupid. Dern has pegged him as someone with nothing to lose, but the boxer is trained at defending his life, and

soon ends up in control of the other two in a cat-and-mouse game of suspicion and savvy. His love for Fay, finally consummated in a powerful and unrestrained scene, raises the stakes, as Collie more than anything wants someone to trust.

The rattlesnake of a script by Foley and Robert Redlin is full of tight corners and neat surprises, and includes voiceover passages of Thompson's mesmerizing interior prose. The detached point of view in this suspense thriller leaves audience as much twisted by doubt as Collie. One is never sure how much is certain, or what is really going on.

Foley, who demonstrated a talent for making on-the-fringe characters compelling in the Sean Penn and Christopher Walken-starrer "At Close Range," goes a few notches better in this, surely his best picture yet. Framing establishes a sense of menace from the outset, and camera stays right in with the characters until the very last image, offering many an indelible moment.

Ward is at her direct and provocative best as the lonely widow who can never give a straight answer, and Patric is enigmatic and affecting as the bruised drifter. Even in the critical scene where he tells Fay his "mental illness" was all a scam to avoid a rap for murder in the ring, one can't be sure.

Dern has his best role in years as the grasping con-man Uncle Bud, and actually evokes some sympathy for the weasely character, while George Dickerson as Goldman, a doctor who takes rather too personal an interest in Collie's well-being, adds elusively creepy undertones to the role.

Pic's triumph is that it steers clear of genre and period trappings and yet achieves such emotional veracity. Lensed in the arid and existential sun-blasted landscape of Indio, Calif., the pungently seedy film creates a kind of genre unto itself, a film soleil, perhaps.

Oddly, the line "After Dark, My Sweet" is never heard, nor does it evoke the story. — *Daws.*

The Marilyn Diaries

Cannes A Private Screenings presentation. (Intl. sales, Double Helix Films.) Produced by Gary P. Conner. Directed by Eric Drake. Screenplay, Don Shiffrin based on his story; camera (color), Larry Revene; music, Jonathan Hannah, costume design, Cherie Zucker; executive producer, Ernest G. Gauer. Reviewed at the Cannes Film Festival (market), May 17, 1990. MPAA Rating: R. Running time: **91 MIN.**

With: Marilyn Chambers, Tara Buckman, Michael Rose, Sean Westin.

■ **Only excuse for this genially frilly softcore comedy is to witness the grace and good humor with which ex-porn star Marilyn Chambers moves into middle age. She still looks in sufficiently solid shape to survive this inane outing.**

Because its title is likely to generate unfounded anticipation, "The Marilyn Diaries" may have a life on cable tv and video. Theatrical potential is virtually zilch.

Pic is not hardcore. Chambers is cast as the mysterious author of an erotic diary recounting several sexual adventures. (She is referred to, simply, as Marilyn throughout.) The book falls into the hands of a bespectacled reporter for something called "Voyeur Magazine."

The reporter is charged with tracking down the identity of the author in tandem with his estranged, photographer-girlfriend. The sketchy plot is merely a device for recreating the erotic passages of the diary in strictly softcore fashion with Chambers going through her paces handily.

None of this is taken very seriously. There are, for example, at least two cutesy visual references to Chambers' prior stints as an Ivory Snow model and the "Behind The Green Door" hardcore heroine. The proceedings are likely to strike Chambers fans as rather demure, underlining the comedy rather than the heavy breathing. — *Sege.*

Freedom: The Voice Of Ein-Harod
(U.S.-ISRAELI)

Cannes A Sunrise Films production. (Intl. sales, Double Helix Films.) Produced by Doron Eran, Yoram Kislev. Directed by Eran. Screenplay, Rami Na'Aman, based on Amos Kenan's "The Road To Ein-Harod;" camera (color), Avi Karpik; editor, Irit Raz; associate producer, Shimshon Refaeli. Reviewed at the Cannes Film Festival (market), May 17, 1990. Running time: **90 MIN.**

Saul Jordan . . . . Tony Peck
Leora . . . . Alessandra Mussolini
Mahmoud . . . . Arnon Zadok

■ **"Freedom: The Voice Of Ein-Harod" is a standard shoestring adventure film noteworthy for the stance it takes against the military occupation in Israeli. Pic's offshore chances are likely to be mainly in the homevid market.**

If nothing else, "Ein-Harod" will leave a footnote in history for being an Israeli film featuring Mussolini's granddaughter.

Because of a drought, water is being rationed, and the Army has stepped in to quell signs of unrest. Liberal reporter Saul Jordan (Yank thesp Tony Peck) is taken off water rations for signing a petition against the military occupation. When he gets wind they're coming to get him, he escapes with a sadistic Army captain on his heels.

The "voice of freedom" giving Saul a goal is a radio station broadcasting from the community of Ein-Harod, which it calls the last stronghold of democracy. Saul joins forces with a burly Arab on the run, Mahmoud (Arnon Zadok).

They pick up a pair of hostages on the way: a bull-necked colonel and his wide-eyed g.f., Leora (Alessandra Mussolini). Mahmoud is supposed to help the group slip by the Arabs while Rafi helps them get by the Jews. Nobody trusts anybody.

The band struggles through an inhospitable desert with bombs bursting behind them every time their pursuers get close. The whole idea is so unrealistic and prosaically lensed that the freedom-seekers win little sympathy.

All four characters are stereotypes, from Peck's wounded hero unwilling to surrender to the strong, silent Arab through the bare-legged girl who looks on with an expression of mild dismay.

Mussolini is more a curiosity item in the role of a Jew than an acting discovery, and even a nude scene doesn't ignite. When they finally reach Ein-Harod, the land of freedom is just a chimera, as is easily foreseeable.

Jeeps, helicopters and other military artifacts provide most of the scenery. For an adventure pic, action is weak and plotting flaccid. — *Yung.*

Fatal Sky
(U.S.-AUSTRALIAN-YUGOSLAV)

Cannes An ITC Entertainment Group presentation of a Sugar Entertainment (L.A.)-Intl. Film Entertainment (Melbourne)-Jadran Film (Zagreb)-Inconvent (L.A.) production. Executive producers, Larry Sugar, Arnie Fishman, Paul Lichtman. Produced by Antony I. Ginnane, Steven Strick. Directed by Frank Shields. Screenplay, "Anthony Able" (David Webb Peoples); camera (color), Richard Michalak; editor, Leslie Rosenthal; music, Allan Zavod; sound, Bob Allen; production design, Zeljko Senecic; aerial camera, Simon Werry; production manager, Ante Deronja; assistant director, Robert Howard; casting, Vlado Bacic. Reviewed at the Cannes Film Festival (market), May 11, 1990. Running time: **89 MIN.**

Jeff Milker	Michael Nouri
Bird McNamara	Darlanne Fluegel
George Abbott	Maxwell Caulfield
Colonel Clancy	Charles Durning
Beggs	Sebastian Allen
Bergen	Frano Lasic
Corbin	Darren Nesbitt
Sumner	Janez Vajevec
Mrs. Sumner	Ena Begovic
Farmer	Vjenceslav Kapural

■ A promising subject is doomed by an unpolished screenplay (by pseudonymous Anthony Able) and what looks to have been a logistical nightmare — shooting in Yugoslavia when the setting's supposed to be Norway. B.o. prospects are slim, but there could be a useful video career.

Basic story is in the tradition of Howard Hawks pics about friendly male rivals and a strong-willed femme. Michael Nouri plays Yank newspaperman Milker, and Maxwell Caulfield is suave British tv news anchorman Abbott. Both become involved with an apparent UFO landing in a Norwegian forest and a coverup led by a NATO commander (Charles Durning).

Helping them is Bird McNamara (Darlanne Fluegel), an intrepid flyer who's more than a match for the men. Fluegel provides by far the film's best performance as the glamorous femme. The trouble is, not enough is made either of the rivalry between the two journalists, their relationship with Fluegel, or the sci-fi plot itself.

When local farmers, gypsies and anthropologists come down with painful sores, and animals are found mutilated, something's obviously wrong, but the development of the plot is less than enthralling.

This is the more suprising because director Frank Shields has made a couple of decent thrillers ("Hostage" and "The Surfer," latter nabbed for the Cannes Directors Fortnight a couple of years ago). He seems uninvolved with the material, and the mix of action, suspense and comedy remains superficial.

Production designer Zeljko Senecic made a valiant attempt to tranform Zagreb into Trondheim and the Yugoslav countryside into Norwegian vistas. Scandinavians will most definitely not be fooled, and the rest won't much care.

A lot of the film's problem is the underdeveloped screenplay by "Anthony Able." During production, Yank writer-director David Peoples ("Leviathan," "Salute Of The Jugger") was credited with the script. Crucial scenes, like the absurd ease with which the three leads penetrate the secret NATO base, are laughably inept.

During production, "Fatal Sky" was titled "No Cause For Alarm," and that original title is referred to three times in early dialog scenes. Techical credits are passable.
— *Strat.*

The Children
(BRITISH-WEST GERMAN)

Cannes An Isolde Films production in association with Film Four Intl., Arbo Films & Maram GmbH, Bayerliche Landesanstalt, for Ayfbaufinanziereung. (Intl. sales, Gavin Films.) Produced by Andrew Montgomery. Directed by Tony Palmer. Screenplay, Timberlake Wertenbaker, based on the novel by Edith Wharton; camera (color), Nic Knowland; editor, Palmer; sound, John Murphy; production design, Chris Bradley, Paul Templeman; costume design, John Hibbs; coproducer, Harald Albrecht. Reviewed at Cannes Film Festival (market), May 18, 1990. Running time: **115 MIN.**

Martin Boyne	Ben Kingsley
Rose Sellars	Kim Novak
Judith	Siri Neal
Joyce Wheater	Geraldine Chaplin
Cliffe Wheater	Joe Don Baker
Lady Wrench	Britt Ekland
Lord Wrench	Donald Sinden
Sybil Lullmer	Karen Black
Dobree	Robert Stephens
Gerald Ormerod	Rupert Graves
Duke of Mendip	Terence Rigby
Princess Buondelmonte	Marie Helvin
Miss Scope	Rosemary Leach
Terry	Mark Asquith
Blanca	Anouk Fontaine
Bun	Ian Hawkes
Beechy	Elleen Hawkes
Zinnie	Hermione Eyre
Chippo	Edward Michie

■ Previously filmed by Paramount as "The Marriage Playground," Edith Wharton's 1928 novel, "The Children," comes to the screen as a somewhat dated enterprise. Story of a middle-aged man's infatuation for a teenage girl unfolds at a snail's pace, but middle-aged audiences may be willing to go along with the old-fashioned narrative.

Ben Kingsley is Martin Boyne, a middle-aged engineer returning to Europe after years in Brazil. He hopes to marry Rose Sellars (Kim Novak, looking ageless), his lifelong love recently widowed and living in an Alpine village.

On the voyage home, he meets a group of seven children, the oldest of which is the budding Judith (Siri Neal). The children have a rendezvous in Venice with their parents (or, since they come from a variety of broken marriages, stepparents) Geraldine Chaplin and Joe Don Baker appear in the parental roles.

Martin lingers on in Venice with the children, who seem to

1929 version

The Marriage Playground
(B&W)

A Paramount production and release. Cofeaturing Mary Brian and Fredric March. Directed by Lothar Mendes. Based on Edith Wharton's novel, "The Children." Adapted by J. Walter Ruben. Camera (black & white), Victor Milner. Reviewed at Paramount, New York, Dec. 13, 1929. Running time: **70 MIN.**

Judy	Mary Brian
Martin	Fredric March
Cliff Weader	Huntley Gordon
Joyce Weader	Lilyan Tashman
Lady Wrench	Kay Francis
Lord Wrench	William Austin
Terry	Phillip de Lacey
Mrs. Seegar	Seena Owen

---

fascinate him, but eventually heads for the hills and Rose. The children, abandoned again, soon follow. The rest of the film depicts Martin's indecision and his gradual emotional shift away from the demanding Rose to the guileless, appealing Judith, who appears to encourage him. His eventual rejection by her comes as no surprise to the viewer.

Director-editor Tony Palmer ("Testimony") lingers far too long on inessentials throughout "The Children" which cries out for a brisker pace and sharper cutting.

Kingsley gives one of his most affecting performances as the confused protagonist, and young Siri Neal is a find as the child-woman. Novak does a good job as the attractive widow, though the other adult actors have relatively little to do.

Cinematography, by Nic Knowland, of Venice and Alpine scenery, adds a lot to "The Children," though Palmer's fondness for using Steadicam to follow his characters around the Venetian streets becomes wearying.

A beautiful, sad love story might have been made from this material, but "The Children" comes across as uninvolving and dated. It'll be a hard sell, but in territories where English period pieces have a following it could have some chances. Otherwise, television sales are indicated. — *Strat.*

I Bought A Vampire Motorcycle
(BRITISH)

Cannes A Dirk production. (Intl. sales, Majestic Films.) Produced by John Wolskel, Mycal Miller. Directed by Dirk Campbell. Screenplay, Miller, Wolskel; camera (color), Tom Ingle; editor, Miller; music, Dean Friedman. Reviewed at Cannes Film Festival (market), May 16, 1990. Running time: **90 MIN.** With: Neil Morrissey, Amanda Noar, Michael Elphick, Anthony Daniels, Andrew Powell, George Rossi.

■ The best thing about this low-budget British offering is the title. Mixture of low-camp gore and comedy aims for cult success, but misses the mark.

Gimmick here is that, during an affray between satanists and bikers, a vintage motorbike becomes vampirized. From then on, it runs on blood, doesn't function in daylight, recoils from crucifixes, and consumes humans and animals.

The filmmakers rely heavily on simple comedy allied to gore. When hero Neil Morrissey's friend is found dismembered, he remarks: "Not like him to go to pieces." Another running joke is the foul breath emanating from garlic-eating cop Michael Elphick.

Film's low point is a toilet-joke of gratuitous bad taste in every sense.

Undemanding audiences may go for this, and there could be a latenight following, especially in the U.K. But the jokes wear thin very quickly. — *Strat.*

Grim Prairie Tales

Cannes An East/West Film Partners Prods. Produced by Richard Hahn. Executive producers, Rick Blumenthal, Larry Haber. Written and directed by Wayne Coe. Camera, Janusz Minski; editor, Earl Ghaffari; music, Steve Dancz; sound, Beau Franklin; production design, Anthony Zierhut; art direction, Angela Levy; costume design, Ron Tolsky; set decoration, Shirley Starks; coproducer, Andrzej Kamrowski; associate producers, Chet Halperin, Ron Wilton, Evan Brownstein; assistant director, Chris Bongirne; casting, Herb Dufine. Reviewed at the Cannes Film Festival (market), May 19, 1990. MPAA Rating: R. Running time: **94 MIN.**

Morrison	James Earl Jones

Farley	Brad Dourif
Lee	Will Hare
Tom	Marc McClure
Jenny	Michelle Joyner
Arthur	William Atherton
Maureen	Lisa Eichhorn
Eva	Wendy Cooke

■ An anthology pic of creepy tales told by two old West travelers as they sit around the campfire all night isn't a bad idea, but their tales are about as much fun as saddle sores. Cheesy writing and patchy direction give this low-budgeter a ghost of a chance in any market.

James Earl Jones plays an unwashed bounty hunter with bad teeth and an animal skin wardrobe who shares camp with a stranger, a nervous, intellectual clerk from Seattle (Brad Dourif) who's headed East to meet up with his wife.

To pass the time, Jones tells a couple of stories for shock value, one about a cowpoke who's buried alive by Indians as he sleeps, and another about a young traveling man who tries to help a dirty-faced and pregnant woman he finds wandering in the desert. Proving to be not at all what she appears, she seduces him, leading to a vulgar supernatural ending.

Warming to his companion, Dourif works up a long tale about a homesteading family troubled by the father's nighttime activities — he goes out lynching black men. Each tale comes to life on the screen with a different cast and setting, the third and longest being the least successful as it's ill-paced, loosely directed and ends on a flat note.

Not to be outdone, Jones adds another story (probably the best) about a meticulous gunslinger who's plagued by gruesome, bloody consequences after he guns down a grimy Indian in a contest.

The idea has possibilities, but the tone set by director Wayne Coe is one of schlock rather than craft. The film overall is more of a hoot than a horror.

Obviously a very low-budget effort in which the principal actors have nothing more strenuous to do than face off over a campfire, pic suggests that the same sort of material, handled with more care, could transfer well to a cable or television series. — *Daws.*

Grave Secrets

Cannes A Shapiro Glickenhaus presentation of Planet production. Produced by Michael Alan Shores. Directed by Donald P. Borchers. Screenplay, Jeffrey Polman, Lenore Wright; camera (Eastmancolor), Jaie Thompson; music, Jonathan Elias. No further credits available. Reviewed at Cannes Film Festival (market), May 19, 1990. Running time: **89 MIN.**

Iris Norwood	Renée Soutendijk
David Shaw	Paul LeMat
Farnsworth	David Warner

Also with: Lee Wink, Olivia Barash.

■ Donald P. Borchers, producer of "Children Of The Corn" and "Crimes Of Passion," has turned to directing with "Grave Secrets," a modest haunted house psychodrama destined to haunt homevid and television at best.

Renée Soutendijk plays Iris, a young woman scared out of her wits by ghostly disturbances in her house in a small town. She asks David Shaw (Paul LeMat), a young psychic phenomena professor, for help, but then regrets it and asks him to go away.

Shaw sticks around, however, in spite of Iris and of protests from villagers who do not want to see certain recent local events brought up for revision. Especially not the beheading, reportedly in a traffic accident, of an unnamed man.

After recording disturbances (doors opening and closing by themselves, etc.) via his monitors, Shaw calls in Farnsworth, an old friend and a professional transmedium. Farnsworth can cajole spirits to enter and act through his own body.

David Warner lends considerable authority to this role, while real horrors, staged with neat special effects, start escalating. The beheaded man is seen roaming the house, and his head is finally seen taking the place of Farnsworth's own. It is, of course, a murderously growling head.

The prof forces Iris to recall events she has so far hidden even from herself. In grisly detail, she is shown giving birth to the child of a rapist who snatches the baby away to bury it alive.

There is much common psychologizing en route to an ending that has Iris and the professor settling down to shared bedroom comfort. But is there still something lurking under the bed?

Since real chills occur too rarely, it is possible that "Grave Secrets" would have been a better film if done as the comedy its title seemed to promise. — *Kell.*

The Fifth Monkey

Cannes A 21st Century Film production. Produced by Menahem Golan. Directed by Eric Rochat. Screenplay, Rochat, based on a book by Jacques Zibi; camera (Rank color), Gideon Porath; editor, Alain Jakubowicz, Fabien D. Tordjmann; music, Robert O. Ragland; art direction, Pedro Nanni; associate producer, Avram Berman. Reviewed at the Cannes Film Festival (market), May 17, 1990. Running time: **93 MIN.**

Cunda	Ben Kingsley
Octavia	Mika Lins
Mrs. Watts	Vera Fischer
Maria	Silvia De Carvalho

Also with: Carlos Kroeber, Milton Gonzalves, Julio Levy, Rinaldo Rinaldi, Paulo Vinicius.

■ Stunning natural backdrops, lots of animals and winning performances from the human team make "The Fifth Monkey" a natural pickup for general audiences. Eric Rochat's simple and unpretentious pic harbors a serious message of respect for animals — and genuine humans.

Good family adventure toplines Ben Kingsley as an innocent Brazilian snake hunter who treks cross-country with four cute chimpanzees. A simple man living in a remote jungle paradise, Cunda (Kingsley) makes a humble living catching snakes and rare animals, which he sells to a local dealer. He hopes to make enough money to marry Maria (Silvia De Carvalho), a local lady with many admirers.

He sees his chance when one day four chimps appear. Winning the animals' trust, Cunda lures them down the long path to the city, where he intends to sell them.

On his way he stumbles into several adventures. In a rough gold-mining camp, prospectors sell their souls to find a tiny gold nugget in a riverbed. Cunda begins to catch gold fever when a violent robbery convinces him to take his chimps and get a move on.

Next he comes across a peaceful village, whose inhabitants are summarily rounded up by mercenaries to work for big landowners. Cunda and company are nabbed along with an exotic local girl Octavia (a very fresh and appealing Mika Lins). They escape and stay together for rest of pic.

Later, the baby chimp is kidnaped and the rest, along with Cunda, land in front of a comical judge. Rich eccentric Mrs. Watts (Vera Fischer) pays their fine and give Cunda and Octavia a job.

They work as servants in her house, while the chimps are treated as honored guests and dine at the table. Octavia finds the missing chimp in a vivisection lab. They rescue it too late, and it dies in her arms. Cunda sneaks it into a coffin in a funeral home.

Octavia has fallen in love with the gentle Cunda, but because he's many years her senior, he encourages her to look elsewhere. He leaves her and sells all three chimps to a dock worker, who will export them on the next ship out. But he changes his mind in time for a happy fantasy ending in which love wins out.

Director Rochat ("Story of O, Part II") shows Brazil as a natural paradise filled with bright-colored toucans, snakes and other wildlife. He keeps this side of erotica, though Lins adds a sensual presence without false innocence.

Kingsley shines in yet another offbeat role, giving quiet dignity to the poor snake catcher who learns the value of true love and friendship. The adventure music score is a little silly, but exterior lensing lush and inviting. — *Yung.*

Dragon Hunt

Cannes A Shapiro Glickenhaus Entertainment presentation of a Twin Dragon production. Executive producer, Michael McNamara. Written and produced by McNamara. Directed by Charles Wiener. Camera (color), Paul Dunlop; editor, Wiener, McNamara; sound, Kimberley Meadows. Reviewed at Cannes Film Festival (market), May 18, 1990. Running time: **89 MIN.**

With: Michael McNamara, Martin McNamara.

■ This truly awful film is destined for scant attention in any medium, although a narrow homevid niche no doubt lurks in less discerning territories.

Essentially plotless pic sees the nimble McNamara twins, world champion kickboxers, caught in a manhunt engineered by a mad mercenary seeking revenge on his lost hand, which one the twins put an arrow through some years ago.

Pitted against overweight rednecks with names like Red Skull and Beastmaster, all seemingly world's worst shots and clumsiest fighters, the mustached twins nimbly bash, stab and shoot their way out. For some reason they're duped into the manhunt by their girlfriends (one a cop), but why this happens is anybody's guess.

Most of the film comprises endless ground shots of running through the same patch of Canadian forest, punctuated by "get them" and "kill them" dialog. Most of the players are full contact fighters, not actors, and it shows. This wouldn't be so bad if the fisticuffs weren't so repetitive.

Credits note that the pic was in "no way developed" with assistance by Telefilm or the Ontario Film Corp. No wonder. — *Doch.*

The Big Steal
(AUSTRALIAN)

Cannes A Hoyts (Australia) release of a Cascade Films production. (Intl. sales, Overseas Film Group.) Produced by Nadia Tass, David Parker. Directed by Tass. Screenplay, Parker; camera (color), Parker; editor, Peter Carrodus; music coordinator, Chris Gough; sound, John Wilkinson; production design, Paddy Reardon; production manager, Catherine Bishop; assistant director, Tony Mahood; associate producer, Bryce Menzies. Reviewed at Cannes Film Festival (market), May 18, 1990. Running time: **100 MIN.**

Danny Clark	Ben Mendelsohn
Joanna Johnston	Claudia Karvan
Gordon Farkas	Steve Bisley
Mr. Clark	Marshall Napier
Mark Jorgensen	Damon Herriman
Vangoli Petrakis	Angelo D'Angelo
Mr. Johnston	Tim Robertson
Mrs. Clark	Maggie King
Pan Schaeffer	Sheryl Munks
Mrs. Johnston	Lise Rodgers
Frank	Frankie J. Holden

■ Once it hits its stride, "The Big Steal" turns out to be a warm, funny comedy which should find appreciative audiences in Australia and Europe. Domestically, the picture may prove to be too lightweight.

The third feature from husband-and-wife team Nadia Tass (who directs) and David Parker (writer and cinematographer) is an improvement on their last, "Rikky And Pete," but lacks the level of originality of their first, "Malcolm." But it has a low-key charm that's appealing, and a couple of riotously funny scenes.

Ben Mendelsohn is Danny, a shy 18-year-old who wants two things: to own a Jaguar and to date Joanna (Claudia Karvan). Danny's father (Marshall Napier in a rich comic performance) gives him a car for his birthday, but it's a 1963 Nissan Cedric the family has owned for years. Danny decides to trade this in for a 1973 Jag in time for his first date.

Trouble is that car dealer Gordon Farkas (Steve Bisley giving a splendidly sleazy performance) is a crook who's switched engines on Danny. His "new" car conks out as he's driving Joanna home.

He and his mates decide to hit back by lifting the engine from Farkas' own Jag while he's having a drunken time at a sex club. Farkas retaliates by stealing what he thinks is Mr. Clark's car but which, in fact, is a car belonging to Joanna's irate father (Tim Robertson).

Whenever the adult characters are on the screen, "The Big Steal" is on safe ground. Bisley gets laughs as the odious Farkas, especially when picked up by the police, hopelessly drunk, wearing red high-heeled shoes and stockings. Robertson, as a plumber very protective of his teenage daughter, has a dry line in humor (he reveals that he installed the toilets in the disco the youngsters plan to visit. "I'll check them out," says Danny, helpfully).

Tass and Parker also provide a satisfying final scene, which actually interrupts the final credit roll for a further joke or two.

The early scenes establishing the characters and basic plot are plodding. The slight humor in the film's first half hour seems amusing in hindsight, but audiences may get restless waiting for the plot to come to the boil.

Teens here are incredibly unsophisticated compared to 18-year-olds in Hollywood teen comedies, and that's part of the film's charm. Mendelsohn (from "The Year My Voice Broke") and Karvan (who's grown up a lot since playing Judy Davis' daughter in "High Tide") are quite sweet in their roles.

"The Big Steal" is technically slick, with some attractive imagery shot by Parker. At 100 minutes, it's a shade overlong.

Hoyts should do fine with this in Australia, but in other territories, a lot of work will have to be put into promotion to persuade audiences that "The Big Steal" is as enjoyable as it is. — *Strat.*

Mirror, Mirror

Cannes A Shapiro Glickenhaus Entertainment presentation of an Orphan Eyes production. Executive producers, Virginia Perfili, Gary Rasmussen, Michael Mihalich. Produced by Jimmy Lifton. Directed by Marina Sargenti. Written by Yuri Zeltser, Sargenti; screenplay, Annette and Gina Cascone; camera (color), Robert Brinkmann; music, Lifton; casting, Ira Belgrade. Reviewed at Cannes Film Festival (market), May 18, 1990. Running time: **103 MIN.**

Mrs. Gordon	Karen Black
Megan	Rainbow Harvest
Nikki	Kristin Dattilo
Ron	Ricky Paull Goldin
Emelin	Yvonne De Carlo
Mr. Veze	William Sanderson

■ This debut horror pic from music clip and commercial director Marina Sargenti is an above-average Cannes market offering for the genre. Though not strong enough for mainstream theatrical markets, it could play off well in some territories, and has definite hv and cable potential.

Pic uses the premise of a mirror acting as a gateway to a demon netherworld, corrupting and eventually killing Rainbow Harvest after she and her recently widowed mother Karen Black move into a house previously owned by a mad spinster.

Sargenti builds up a strong atmosphere without resorting to undue gore, set against a standard high school backdrop. Pic is sufficiently quirky and well-structured to escape many of the clichés of similar pics, and the presence of vets such as Yvonne De Carlo and Black doesn't hurt.

Pic lags occasionally, yet is compensated for by a neat twist ending, and the semiappearance of the demon through the mirror (a great effect) at the end.

New player Kristin Dattilo, as Harvest's only friend who tries to outfox the demon, is also a solid plus. In all, some good new talent here, and a good addition to Shapiro Glickenhaus' catalog.
— *Doch.*

Tunnelkind
(Tunnel Child)
(AUSTRIAN)

Cannes An Austrian Cinema Film release for Teamfilm Produktion Wien. Directed by Erhard Riedlsperger. Screenplay, Riedlsperger, Peter Zeitlinger; camera (color), Zeitlinger; editor, Veronika Putz; sound, Uwe Kohrs; art direction, Fritz Hollergschwandtner; production manager, Wolfgang Rest. Reviewed at Cannes Film Festival (market), May 14, 1990. Running Time: **89 MIN.**

Julia	Silvia Lang
Roman	Josef Griesser
Alexander	Volker Fuchs
Elisa	Claudia Martini
Herbert	August Schmoelzer
Volek	Christoph Kuenzler
Teacher	Georges Kern

■ Theatrical possibilities for this German-language film are limited to the art and fest circuits in the German lingo territories, television and video. Offshore possibilities are dim.

This tender story of a 13-year-old girl dates back to 1969 at the height of the Cold War when border guards shot to kill trespassers. Plot, topical now that the barriers between East and West have been breached, revolves around her accidental discovery of a tunnel, and her relationship with a Czech surveyer on the other side of the heavily guarded border.

After her father is killed in an accident, Julia (played convincingly by Silvia Lang) takes a subjective vow of silence and attempts to alleviate her grief by letters to her deceased dad. Refusing to speak in school, she becomes further alienated when her mother's lover moves in with them.

Wandering along the wooded border, a group of her schoolmates dare her to cross over into Czechoslovakian territory. Taking the dare, she discovers a tunnel leading to the other side, a breach in the border fortifications.

Julia is discovered, protected from the guards and befriended by Roman (Josef Griesser), a surveyor and a loner like herself. The two develop a father-daughter relationship after Julia thinks she has at last found somebody who understands her.

After discovering that new border fences are to be constructed there, Julia breaks her silence with Griesser just to persuade him to alter the course of the fence so that the tunnel could still be used as an escape.

Speaking again at last, she begins to emerge from her self-imposed isolation from her mother and schoolmates, and even gets to know her first boyfriend. In her last crossing over, Julia finds the building camp empty and her frend Roman gone. But she has learned to overcome her limitations and accept her father's death.

"Tunnelkind," ably directed by Erhard Riedlsperger in his first feature film, was based on a script which was awarded a prize in a screenplay writing contest. Credits are excellent, although print screened at Cannes was grainy in places. — *Kind.*

Perfume Of The Cyclone

Cannes A Movie Group presentation. Produced by Ian Ross. Directed by David Irving. Screenplay, Patrick Lee; camera (Eastmancolor), James Robb. No other credits available. Reviewed at Cannes Film Festival (market), May 17, 1990. Running time: **87 MIN.**

Stan Wozniak . . . . . Kris Kristofferson
Adam Garrison . . . . Jeff Meek
Jorge . . . . Runeke
Venna . . . . Kimb Stark
Françoise . . . . Marisa Berenson
Capt. Reeves . . . . Tony Fredjohn
Teddy Mayder . . . . Michael Brenner

■ **This story about a Chicago cop tracking down his 16-year-old daughter in a Caribbean island is too tame to generate much b.o. interest. The heavies aren't mean enough, the action is anemic and comes too late, and the father/daughter drama is weak.**

After his wife commits suicide (offscreen), Stan Wozniak's (Kris Kristofferson) young, pretty daughter, takes a modeling job for a commercial shoot in a Caribbean island. The young thing falls in love with a local painter, who also captains a fishing boat for tourists.

Artist falls for cop's daughter, but his shady past catches up with him after a clumsily shot sequence in which a native girl is killed by a tourist on the boat. The artist is involved with local mafia. The Chicago cop rescues his daughter, and the others get their desserts. But the script never ignites on screen, despite a cyclone blowing across the sets.

As a cop, Kristofferson just isn't tough enough. The supporting cast is bland and most of the situations seem contrived. A few final action sequences seem an afterthought. Perfume of this pic will not be sweet for theatrical, but item should prove okay for homevid and tv release. — *Besa.*

Meet The Feebles
(NEW ZEALAND)

Cannes A South Gate Entertainment release (U.S.) of a Wingnut Films production. (Intl. sales, Perfect Features, London). Produced by Jim Booth, Peter Jackson. Directed by Jackson. Screenplay, Jackson, Danny Mulheron, Frances Walsh, Stephen Sinclair; camera (color), Murray Milne; editor, Jamie Selkirk; music, Pete Dasent; supervising puppeteers, Jonathan Acorn, Ramon Aguilar. Reviewed at the Cannes Film Festival (market), May 16, 1990. Running time: **96 MIN.**

Voices of: Donna Akersten, Stuart Devenie, Mark Hadlow, Ross Jolly, Brian Sergent, Peter Vere Jones, Mark Wright.

■ **Peter Jackson's adult fantasy pic, "Meet The Feebles," confirms an inventive skill and anarchic ability in handling adult material. His first feature, "Bad Taste," became a minor late night theatrical and video cult pic Down Under and this new dark alley entertainment should achieve similar notoriety.**

Jackson does have a problem, however: overkill. At times he is too determined to splatter the most gross material over the screen without judging ultimate effect. In "Feebles" such indulgence detracts from an singularly dark comic virtuosity and talent.

"Meet The Feebles," titled "Just The Feebles" for the U.S., centers on a tired theater in a sleazy part of town. A company of outrageous people is rehearsing a variety show which it hopes will win a syndicated series on tv.

But sex, drugs and rock 'n' roll threaten to undermine proceedings. And torch singer Heide the Hippo does not intend to sit idly by when her man, producer Bletch the Walrus, gets entangled with a Siamese pussy, Samantha.

Jackson and a trio of writers, Danny Mulheron, Frances Walsh and Stephen Sinclair, have produced a full slate of characters with appetites and excesses that run the gamut from sweet Robert the Hedgehog, fresh out of a method acting school, to the Fly, a muckraker from the gutter press. The pace rarely slackens.

Jackson's prowess is best displayed in the heavy action sequences, including a hilarious parody of the raft of pics that have emerged from the Vietnam War. He is not so successful, given these times of AIDS angst, in achieving laughter with one of his central characters, Harry the Hare, stricken by a fatal sex disease.

The film is too scattershot to ultimately score heavily, but its occasional bulls-eye ensures it cannot be ignored or discounted.
— *Nic.*

The Shrimp On The Barbie
(U.S.-NEW ZEALAND)

Cannes A Vestron release of a Unity Pictures Corp.-Evaux Investments Ltd. production. Executive producer, Jerry Offsay. Produced by R. Ben Efraim. Directed by "Alan Smithee" (Michael Gottlieb). Screenplay, Grant Morris, Ron House; camera (Eastmancolor), James Bartle, Andrew Lesnie; editor, Fred Culack; music, Peter Kaye; production design, Ron Highfield; opening sequence by John Pruno; production manager, Murray Francis; assistant director, Chris Short; casting, Joselyn Morton, Michael Lynch. Reviewed at Cannes Film Festival (market), May 17, 1990. Running time: **87 MIN.**

The American . . . . Cheech Marin
Alexandra Hobart . . . . . . Emma Samms
Bruce Woodley . . . . Vernon Wells
Wayne . . . . Bruce Spence
Dominique . . . . Carole Davis
Sir Ian Hobart . . . . Terence Cooper
Maggie . . . . Jeanette Cronin
Postman . . . . Jonathan Coleman

■ **This primitive comedy aims at a "Crocodile Dundee" in reverse (the title is derived from Paul Hogan's famous blurbs for the Aussie tourist board) but comes up virtually laughless. Prospects are slim, even in Australia and New Zealand.**

One of the film's basic problems is that, apart from a brief prologue in which its American hero (Cheech Marin) arrives in Sydney and is photographed alongside some well-known landmarks, the bulk of the film was shot in Auckland, New Zealand, when Aussie unions balked at the project. Production designer Ron Highfield does his best to hide the fact, but Down Under audiences won't be fooled.

The basic yarn is extremely slim and silly. Marin gets a job in a Mexican restaurant and meets a rich-bitch heiress, Alexandra (Emma Samms) engaged to Bruce (Vernon Wells), an all-Australian ex-football hero who does beer commercials (there are endless plugs in the film for a well known brand of Australian beer). Because Alex' father (Terence Cooper) doesn't approve of her fiancé, she provides an even less likely prospect — Marin. On this thin premise hangs a whole lot of tired jokes and situations.

Needless to say, the millionaire's daughter and the raffish Latino wind up in love, and the picture ends in an airport scene that's the equivalent of the subway sequence in the first "Croc." But comparisons are only invidious for "Shrimp" which fails to register much in the way of humor or charm.

Performances are barely adequate, while script and direction are woeful. This is another pic credited to the pseudonymous Alan Smithee; Michael Gottlieb was listed as director during production. Presence of two cameramen in the credits (one Australian, one New Zealander) also suggests some reshooting.

Pic's low point comes with a female character's impersonation of a lustful horse. The best line comes from Alexandra who says at one point. "Shut up! This isn't funny!" Too true. — *Strat.*

Night Angel

Cannes A Fries Entertainment release through Paragon Arts of a Paragon Arts Intl. production. Produced by Joe Augustyn, Jeff Geoffray. Executive producer, Walter Josten. Directed by Dominique Othenin-Girard. Screenplay, Augustyn, Josten; camera (color), David Lewis; editor, Jerry Brady; music, Cory Lerios; production design, Ken Aichele; costume design, Renee Johnston; special effects, Steve Johnson, XFX Group, K.N.B. EFX Group; stunt coordinator, Shane Dixon; choreographer, Joanne DeVito; associate producers, Michael Josten, Tom Hamilton, Patricia Bando Josten. Reviewed at Cannes Film Festival (market), May 12, 1990. MPAA Rating: R. Running time: **90 MIN.**

Lilith . . . . Isa Anderson
Rita . . . . Karen Black
Craig . . . . Linden Ashby
Kirstie . . . . Debra Feuer
Sadie . . . . Helen Martin
Ken . . . . Doug Jones
Rod . . . . Garry Hudson

■ **A gallery of horrific special effects should offer some shock value to genre fans in this energetic entry from Paragon Arts, which met some success with "Witchboard" and "Night Of The Demons." Otherwise, story is more silly than satisfying.**

Loosely borrowing from the legend of Lilith, a pre-Biblical she-demon who steals the souls of men, filmmakers create a modern-day tale of a primordial creature who takes the shape of a beautiful woman to wreak evil through the power of seduction. Lilith infiltrates a high-profile fashion magazine to persuade the editor (Karen Black) to feature her exotic photo on the cover so she can corrupt the entire world via mass media.

The mag's male employes who fall for Lilith come to violent and shocking ends. Still, everyone is inexplicably slow to catch on, and the vamp soon has Black fawning at her feet in a lustful trance as the dazed art staff works overtime to accommodate Lilith's aims.

True love is the only antidote to the she-devil's nastiness, so it's up to art director Craig (Linden Ashby), who's been bestowed that gift by Black's younger sister Kirstie (Debra Feuer), to kill her off. Meanwhile, Craig is plagued by a hellscape of surreal dreams and visions that offer some of the pic's best sequences, particularly when he stumbles through a vivid tunnel of the damned.

Director Dominique Othenin-Girard has a flair for the horrific, but other scenes have a callow tone that's more vulgar than sympathetic. Supporting players are broadly directed without getting laughs, and all the perfs, including Black's, are unremarkable.

Character played by Helen Martin (a 70-year-old black cab driver/voodoo healer who holds the secret to Lilith's destruction) seems a condescending addition to the script, particularly as performed in a clumsy, semicomic style. Ken Aichele's production design includes some smart touches.
— *Daws.*

Sweethearts
(AUSTRALIAN)

Cannes A Sweethearts Film production. (Intl. sales, Kim Lewis Marketing.) Executive producers, Kim Lewis, Colin Talbot. Produced by Lynda House. Directed by Talbot. Screenplay, Talbot, based on his novel; camera (Eastmancolor), Terry Howells; editor, Christina de Podolinski; music, Paul Grabowsky; sound, Rex Watts, Steve Burgess; production design, Nick van Roosendael; production manager, Fran Lanigan; assistant director, Phil Jones; casting, Talbot. Reviewed at Cannes Film Festival (market), May 20, 1990. Running time: **79 MIN.**
Juliet . . . . Christabel Wigley
Z . . . . John F. Howard
Doug Atom . . . . . Richmond Clendinnen
M.C. at Zero Motel . . . . . . Henry Maas
Laura . . . . Marianne Steele
Davida . . . . Bethany Lee
P.M. . . . . Margot Duell
Raymond . . . . Tim McKew
Ace . . . . Bill Tisdall
Pam . . . . Rhia
Bob . . . . .'. . . . . Freddo Dirk

■ **First-time writer-director Colin Talbot adapted his own novel, "Sweethearts," to the screen, so he presumably did it the way he wanted. Unfortunately, the result is a cultish, "in" picture which only fitfully displays the humor and charm that might have made it accessible to a general audience. Prospects are dim.**

Juliet (Christabel Wigley) and the film's narrator, known as Z (John F. Howard) live together. Z is devoted to Juliet, but she's tiring of him; she keeps the relationship going because Z has money.

Juliet has a steamy affair with a womanizing rock star, Doug Atom (Richmond Clendinnen), who's later announced "missing over the Bermuda Triangle." Eventually, Juliet wins some money and

leaves Z with a broken heart.

"Sweethearts" seems to be made with a specific, but extremely limited, audience in mind. Too much footage of the (commendably brief) running time is taken up with aimless scenes involving Juliet and her girlfriends and the acts at a down-market nightclub called Zero Motel.

An occasional sequence combines pathos and humor well; for example, when Juliet invites Doug Atom to visit and shares a sofa with him and the jealous Z. In another well-handled scene, Z comes home inconveniently when Juliet and Doug are making love and appears to believe her when she tells him she has a fever and he should go for some medicine.

The soundtrack contains a number of songs which could help the film drum up an audience, but the

central character of Juliet, though well played by Wigley, is so unpleasant to poor Z that most audiences are hardly likely to relate to her. Despite fine camerawork (Terry Howells), the film is a sad disappointment.

Put it down to inexperience or self-indulgence, the net result is a pic of limited appeal both for Australia and elsewhere.
— *Strat.*

CANNES FILM FESTIVAL REVIEWS (OFFICIAL SELECTIONS)

Ostatni Prom
(The Last Ferry)
(POLISH)

Cannes A Polish Film Producers Corp.-Film Unit Zodiak film written and directed by Waldemar Krzystek. Camera (Fujicolor), Dariusz Kuc; editor, Krzysztof Osiecki; music, Przemyslaw Gintrowski; sound, Norbert Medlewski; production design, Tadeusz Kosarewicz; production manager, Pawel Rakowski. Reviewed at Cannes Film Festival (Un Certain Regard), May 19, 1990. Running time: **88 MIN.**
Marek . . . . Krzysztof Kolberger
Renata . . . . Agnieszka Kowalska
Kasia . . . . Dorota Segda
Ewa . . . . Ewa Wencel
Rysiek . . . . Artur Barcis
Andrzej . . . . Jerzy Zelnik

■ **Fest directors and distribs seeking films reflecting the new situation in East Europe will want to include this pic, which depicts how desperately many Poles want to flee their country.**

Item is of greater interest as a document reflecting the current situation in Poland than as a sustained drama.

Helmer-writer Krzystek quickly sets the mood in a telling opening sequence where mobs of buyers descend upon an already-depleted supermarket. Time is set in December 1981. Most of pic unfolds on a ship carrying Poles on an excursion. However, almost all of the passengers have already decided to jump ship when the vessel docks in Hamburg.

Interwoven is the story of a dissident high school teacher being sent abroad by Solidarity. His mission is to carry addresses of underground printing offices, contact points, etc. to sympathizers abroad in case the labor org is banned in Poland.

However, he is being sharply watched by the secret police, who are anxious to lay their hands on the info.

Just as the ship is out in the middle of the Baltic, martial law is declared in Poland and the ship is militarized. The captain announces he will turn about and return to home port.

In a startling sequence, many of the anguished passengers, life vests over their heads, jump into the sea, where they are picked up by two German ships.

The teacher, however, decides to return to Poland to carry on the struggle for freedom. Scripting tends to be loose, so that the drama is diluted and the threat to the teacher not delineated strongly enough.

Cinematography is fuzzy, but acting is okay.

Pic probably will be limited to the fest circuit and film programs specializing on East European developments. — *Besa.*

Plein fer
(Full Steel)
(FRENCH)

Paris A Chrysalide Films/La Cinq coproduction. Produced by Monique Annaud. Directed by Josée Dayan. Screenplay, Vincent Lambert, Bernard Stora, based on the novel by Serge Martinat. Camera (color), André Domage; editor, Anne Boissel; music, Roland Romanelli; sound, Jean-Paul Mugel; art direction, Michele Susini; production manager, Hughes Nonn. Reviewed at the Centre National du Cinema, Paris, April 27, 1990. (In Cannes Film Festival, Perspectives on French Cinema.) Running time: **93 MIN.**
Emilio . . . . Serge Reggiani
Jean . . . . François Negret
Sara . . . . Aurélie Gibert
Pascal . . . . Olivier Martinez
Casino . . . . Jean-Pierre Bisson
Sabatier . . . . Patrick Bouchitey
Fabiani . . . . Julien Guoimar
Napoleon . . . . Jean-Paul Roussillon

■ **Josée Dayan's feature doesn't get high grades for plot originality or breath-bating sus-**

pense, but the milieu it documents and the fine performances make it a neat little entertainment for tv, if not for theatrical exposure.

Sports and gangsterism have been violent bedfellows in countless movie thrillers, but "Plein fer" relocates the genre conventions to a game never highlighted on the screen: "boules," the Gallic bowls.

"Boules" are steel balls that players toss on a hard dirt court. Aim of the game is to land one's boule closest to a target ball, and usually involves displacing the opponent's own well-aimed shots. Sport, popular in southern France, is usually seen in Marcel Pagnol films.

Exploding the quaint, folkloric reputation of the sport, screenplay by Vincent Lambert and Bernard Stora presents the game as an unromantic sport involving high stakes and professinal bookies, ruthless politico sponsors and violent penalties for those who don't play by rules.

Plot revolves around a Marseilles youth (François Negret), whose father, a boules champion, was "suicided" years earlier by the thugs of corrupt local politician, Julien Guiomar.

Negret subsequently was brought up by granddad Serge Reggiani, a revered boules referee, who secretly has been training the boy (ignorant of the fact that his dad was murdered) to follow in his father's footsteps.

When he feels Negret is ready, he manipulates Guiomar and his champion player, Jean-Pierre Bisson, into a high-stakes playoff.

Though the plot mechanism may seem convoluted, the action and atmosphere are dexterously handled by Dayan and her actors, who give local color and relief to familiar characters.

Reggiani is marvelous as the granddad, patiently plotting his longterm revenge with paternal, almost mystical confidence.

Guiomar limns a potent silhouette as a sort of regional godfather, trying to impose his "sponsorship" on Negret as he'd failed to do with latter's father.

Bisson is fine as the weary champ who meets defeat with a sense of release.

Patrick Bouchitey brings a note of bemused menace as Guiomar's secretary and Jean-Paul Roussillon is Reggiani's sidekick.

Young Negret does well enough as the future champ. — *Len.*

Innisfree
(SPANISH-DOCU)

Cannes A Paco Poch A.V. and Virginia Films production, in association with Television Espanola (RTVE), Le Sept, P.C Guerin and Samson Films Ltd. Written, directed and edited by Jose Luis Guerin. Camera (Eastmancolor), Gerardo Gormezano; music, Victor M. Young; art direction, Sindria Segura; consultant, Lord Killanin. Reviewed at Cannes Film Festival (Un Certain Regard), May 19, 1990. Running time: **110 MIN.**
(English soundtrack)

■ **Innisfree is the village in Ireland where John Ford shot "The Quiet Man" in 1951. However, this docu only marginally touches upon the making of the film. Instead, it concentrates mostly on the daily life of the present-day village.**

Using a slow, rambling style, Guerin shoots unrelated and seemingly pointless snippets: an interview with a hitchhiker, scenes of fishermen, a group of small children telling the plot of the Ford film, old-timers in a pub reminiscing about the IRA, long static shots of a train station, a wall, the ocean. These are mixed together with occasional clips from "The Quiet Man," but not following any kind of logical order.

Result is a rather pointless exercise in arbitrariness, striving for auteur images rather than elucidation. Sales, if any, will at best be limited to tv. — *Besa.*

Chernaya Roza . . .
Krasnaja Roza
(Black Rose . . . Red Rose)
(SOVIET-COLOR-B&W)

Cannes A Mosfilm Studios production. Written and directed by Sergei Soloviov. Camera (color, black & white), Yuri Klimenko; editor, Vera Kruglova; music, Boris Grebenchikov, Minna Black. Reviewed at the Cannes Film Festival (Un Certain Regard), May 20, 1990. Running time: **110 MIN.**

Alessandra	Tatiana Drubich
Vladimir	Alexander Abdulov
Mitya	Michael Rosanov

Also with: Alexander Bashirov, Ilya Ivanov.

■ **Facetiously called the second part of the triology "Kitsch And Perestroika," "Black Rose . . . Red Rose" by Mosfilm helmer Sergei Soloviov is a forced, occasionally successful attempt to construct a Russian cult movie.**

To Western eyes, the overall effect appears close to a chaotic, out-of-control videomusic clip. Pic could make a nice late-night surprise at film fests abroad, for viewers willing to jump over the culture gap.

In the USSR, "Rose" has turned a nice profit for director Soloviov (head of Mosfilm's Krug studio). He bought domestic rights from producer Mosfilm after pic was finished, and has released it himself onshore (in its original 2-hour-30-minute version) with an energetic publicity campaign. Local auds obviously have more chance than others to catch the hundreds of jokes and references littering pic's flimsy plot.

In a fast opening, Alessandra (Tatiana Drubich), a trendy 20-year-old spoiled brat, is locked in a tiny apartment by her father, trying to get her to study for exams. She escapes from her prison by climbing over rooftops and calls her playboy boyfriend Vladimir (Alexander Abdulov) from an empty apartment.

The second apartment is inhabited by sweet 15-year-old Mitya (Michael Rosanov), whose uncle has just died in Cannes, France, leaving him millions. His flatmate Tolyk is a crazy Abyssinian punk fixated on Stalin. He brews vicious alcoholic beverages in the kitchen.

Alessandra and Vladimir make love on the floor. They're carefree and liberated children of Gorbachev's '90s, but when she tells him she's pregnant, he backs off. Dreamy Mitya offers to marry her. Her nutty middle-class parents are delighted because he's rich. There is an interminable wild party. Tolyk dies. The baby is born. Mitya is baptized.

Switching back and forth between color and black & white, film strains after novelty. It courts its audience with tongue in cheek. Much of "Rose" is talky nonsense aimed at young sophisticates who like Russian pop (the forgettable soundtrack is by Boris Grebenchikov, billed as "the new Bob Dylan"). So much passes over the head that it takes a lot of good will to believe anything but teenage fun is intended.

Though film is clearly on the side of "kitsch and perestroika," it casts an ironic eye on the newly emerging bourgeoisie, represented by the lovely Tatiana Drubich, a versatile actress with true star quality, and her big blond hunk in his ski gear.

On another level, film turns its wildness around to raise questions about the hysterical kind of freedom it depicts as reigning, if only as a fantasy, in the USSR today. It breaks every taboo from gratuitous female nudity to a sarcastic playback of Brezhnev's funeral, as viewed on tv in a home for the mentally retarded. The effect is both amusing and unsettling.

Film gets some of its best laughs from off-the-wall intertitles, advising viewers to brace themselves for what's coming. A recurring image out of Russian films from the 1920s, the battleship Aurora, returns at the end as a part of "Black Rose" — Mitya is one of the revolutionary sailors.
— *Yung.*

Ju Dou
(CHINESE-JAPANESE)

Cannes A China Film, Tokuma Shoten Publishing, Tokuma Communications, China Film Export & Import Corp. coproduction, in association with Xi-An Film Studio. Executive producers, Tatsumi Yamashita, Shigemi Suzuki. Produced by Zhang Wen-ze, Yasuyoshi Tokuma, Hu Jian. Directed by Zhang Yi-mou, in collaboration with Yang Feng-liang. Screenplay, Lui Heng; camera (color), Gu Chang-wei, Yang Lun; editor, Du Yuan; music, Zhao Ji-pin; sound, Li Lan-hua; production design, Cao Jiu-ping, Zia Rujin;costumes, Zhang Zhi-an; assistant director, Zhou You-zhao. Reviewed at Cannes Film Festival (competition), May 19, 1990. Running time: **95 MIN.**

Ju Dou	Gong Li
Yang Tian-qing	Li Bao-tian
Yang Jin-shan	Li Wei
Yang Tian-bai (child)	Zhang Yi
Yang Tian-bai (youth)	Zhen Ji-an

■ **With the Japanese resources available through this Chinese-Japanese coproduction, director Zhang Yi-mou has come up with a stunning film. The rich colors, used for dramatic effect, are a major element in this romantic tragedy set in a mountain village in the '20s. Arthouse prospects around the world are good.**

The story centers on the house and factory of dye-maker Yang Jin-Shan. Lengths of brightly colored cloths hang to dry from poles which extend above the roof. Large tanks of dye cover the floor, and complex wheels and pullies roll the cloth when it's ready to be baled.

Yang Tian-qing works for his uncle, and becomes fascinated by a pretty young woman, Ju Dou, the old man has bought for a bride. From the cries of distress he hears at night, he realizes the impotent old man is beating and torturing the girl, who appears every morning with fresh bruises on her face and body. Tian-qing spies on her as she bathes, and she becomes aware of this.

One night, when the old man's out, the pair become lovers. A son is eventually born. Soon after the old man is crippled from the waist down in an accident. The lovers blatantly display their relationship in front of him, as he lies helpless. But they can never bring themselves to kill him.

As time goes by, the child acknowledges the old man as his father. Family and village pressure takes its toll on the adulterous couple, even more so when the old man is accidentally drowned in a vat of red dye by the child.

As can be seen from the above, the plot has all the elements of a Hollywood melodrama of the '40s (both "The Postman Always Rings Twice" and "Leave Her To Heaven" come to mind), and the picture is, indeed, as deliriously enjoyable as it sounds, but with the added dimension of age-old tradition forcing the characters into roles they don't want to play.

Visually, the picture is extraordinary, with the splendid set of the dye factory impressively used. Director Zhang Yi-mou, Golden Bear-winner at Berlin a while back with "Red Sorghum," is obviously fascinated with the color red, which dominates in his new film, too.

Incidentally, the subtitled credits list Yang Fen-liang as codirector, while the press book lists Zhang as sole director and Yang as his "collaborator."

Performances are full-blooded. Gong Li (the femme lead in "Red

Sorghum'' also) is superb as the lustful wife, while Li Bao-tian is dogged as the ardent lover. Li Wei, as the vicious old husband who gets his comeuppance and spends much of the film in a wheelchair made from a barrel, is also fine, and both actors who play the avenging son bring an edge to the role.

With this picture it seems that Chinese cinema, with Japanese assistance, has recovered from the traumas of last year and is back in line to make an impact on the international arthouse market.

— *Strat.*

The Comfort Of Strangers
(ITALIAN-U.S.)

Cannes An Erre Produzioni/Sovereign Pictures production is association with Reteitalia. Executive producer, Mario Contone. Produced by Angelo Rizzoli. Directed by Paul Schrader. Screenplay, Harold Pinter, based on the novel by Ian McEwan; camera (color), Dante Spinotti; editor, Bill Pankow; music, Angelo Badalamenti; sound, Drew Kunin; production design, Gianni Quaranta; set decoration, Stefano Paltrinieri; costume design, Mariolina Bono; production supervisor, Fabrizio Castellani; 1st assistant director, Giacomo Lesina; production manager, Adriano Di Lorenzo; associate producers, Linda Reisman, John Thompson; casting, Mary Selway. Reviewed at Cannes Film Festival (out of competition), May 20, 1990. Running time: **107 MIN.**
Robert . . . . Christopher Walken
Colin . . . . Rupert Everett
Mary . . . . Natasha Richardson
Caroline . . . . Helen Mirren
   Also with: Manfredi Aliquo, Giancarlo Previati, Antonio Serrano, Mario Cotone.

■ **Neither the beguiling romance of Venice nor the undraped bodies of Natasha Richardson and Rupert Everett can disguise the hollowness of "The Comfort Of Strangers." This pointless psychological melodrama, about a troubled English couple's encounter with the unexpected on a holiday, has the trappings to open at the boxoffice, but lacks the substance to last.**

Mary (Richardson) and Colin (Everett) are an unmarried, live-apart couple who have returned to Venice in an attempt to rekindle their romance and assess their relationship. They do a lot of balcony gazing, day-tripping, lolling and dining while trying to bridge the gap that's grown between them.

These handsome, bright media types spar with one another in a tense, if affectionate, coded dialog in which each tries to grasp the high ground of emotional control.

He's cool, stolid, ambivalent. She's simmery, restless, probing. Eventually, Venice's ravishing charms — photographed languorously in various permutations of light, shadow and hue — cast their spell. The couple abandon narrow twin beds for wild abandon.

While both actors are paradigms of beauty, Harold Pinter's labored scenario would have us believe that all of Venice is transfixed by the heart-stopping magnificence of — Everett. The camera complies with an adoration that's embarrassing. This may be the first and last time that Richardson in dishabille (or even in Armani wardrobe) is treated as an afterthought.

Among the many Venetian souls smitten by Everett's Apollonian magnetism is a man in an ice-cream suit whose curious personal history has been related in voice-over from the opening credits.

Robert (Christopher Walken) is the grave, courtly son of an Italian diplomat. Apparently his father was so tyrannical that his son was forever warped and wounded. But Walken did learn to speak English

with a ludicrous Italianate accent, and did marry the emotionally fragile daughter of a Canadian diplomat, Caroline (Helen Mirren).

Unbeknownst to the English tourists, Walken has been photographing Everett obsessively since their arrival. At loose ends in a Venice they've visited before, the couple are easy prey for Walken's blandishments. So smarmily sauve is his seduction, that one assumes either a kinky-sex or vampire story is unfolding.

The couple visit Walken's backstreet bar, accept an invitation to sleep in his house and join him and Mirren for dinner. A stupefying search for their laundered clothes gives Everett and Richardson the liberating opportunity to wander semi-nude among richly appointed surroundings.

There's also a peculiar bit of character-shaping byplay when Walken sucker-punches Everett in the gut for the offhanded remark that his apartment is a museum dedicated to preserving the past.

Wisely, the couple duck out before coffee.

Unwisely, they wind up back at the Walken household just when it seems they've rekindled their love. By this time it's Everett who wants to marry and Richardson who's backing away from commitment. The whole relationship in any case becomes moot when Richardson and Everett take a tea from which one of them will never return.

Director Paul Schrader and Pinter wrap the whole thing up in the cinematic equivalent of a shaggy dog story.

The women outperform the men in this hapless scenario, but nobody comes off very well. There isn't much charm in the Richardson-Everett relationship or in the perverse union between Walken and Mirren (seems she suffered a permanent injury as the result of rough sex).

Undermined by the script, the actors are also constantly upstaged by the timeless glories of Venice and their meticulously designed surroundings. — *Rich.*

CANNES FILM FESTIVAL REVIEWS (INTL. CRITICS WEEK)

Outremer
(Overseas)
(FRENCH)

Paris A Europex presentation of a Paradise Prods./Lira Films coproduction. Produced by Serge Cohen-Solal. Directed by Brigitte Roüan. Screenplay, Roüan, Philippe Le Guay, Christian Rullier, Cédric Kahn; camera (color), Dominique Chapuis; editor, Yann Dedet; music, Glück, Pierre and Mathieu Foldes; sound, Dominique Vieillard, Dominique Hennequin; art direction, Roland Deville; technical advisor, Jacques Fansten; production manager, Daniel Champignon. Reviewed at the Empire theater, Paris, April 22, 1990. (In Cannes Film Festival, Intl. Critics Week.) Running time: **98 MIN.**
Zon . . . . Nicole Garcia
Malene . . . . Brigitte Roüan
Gritte . . . . Marianne Basler
Paul . . . . Philippe Galland
Gildas . . . . Yann Dedet
Maxime . . . . Bruno Tedeschini
Uncle Alban . . . . Pierre Doris
Aunt Leonie . . . . . . Monique Mélinand

■ **For her first feature, actress Brigitte Roüan conceived the story, cowrote the screenplay, directed and played one of the lead roles; admirably in each instance. Pic shimmers with life, love of life, humor and tragedy. "Overseas" could make it overseas in specialized situations and festivals.**

Roüan, who has been acting in film, theater and television since 1971 and won a César award in 1985 for a short film she directed and starred in, is a thesp and director of temperament. She's one of the bright new hopes of the 1990s.

This richly detailed, moving colonial family account about three sisters during the Algerian War also is outstanding as one of the rare French films to cogently represent French colonial life in that country during its bloody bid for independence.

Though not overtly political, pic captures the mentality of the French inhabitants and deftly suggests the sociopolitical realities and human contradictions that encroach dramatically on the charmed lives of its protagonists.

Story's three sisters are played with marvelous deep feeling by Nicole Garcia, Roüan and Marianne Basler. Garcia, the eldest, marries a French naval officer and has a brood of kids. Couple's passionately romantic domestic bliss ends when the husband is reported missing in action. In despair, Garcia contracts stomach cancer and dies.

Roüan is the second sister, also a wife and mother, but with a rather passive bookworm of a husband. Unlike the superficially mannered Garcia, Roüan is more nervous and pragmatic. She's administrator of the family wine-producing concern and must deal with the crises arising from the deteriorating political situation. She meets a violent death in a terrorist ambush.

The only survivor is the kid sister (Basler), an adorable, but no less willful nurse who refuses the seductions of married life, and despite the presence of a charming, attractive suitor, carries on a

clandestine affair with an Arab freedom fighter. When latter is killed, Basler returns to France, where in the ironic coda, she is led to the altar, but cannot be made to pronounce "I do."

Rather than intercut three destinies in the usual narrative manner, Roüan chooses a triptych approach, following each sister separately. When Garcia dies, the film rolls back to the first images and follows the adventures of Roüan, then Basler.

Several key sequences, notably a ball, are replayed three times, but always from a different point of view that divulges new information that retroactively colors what has already been seen.

This construction, à la "Rashomon," is never pretentious or mannered, thanks first of all to the psychological authenticity of the characters and the complexity of the events. (It evolved at the script level by Roüan and her three coscreenwriters.) As director, Roüan understands and "sees" each section and each sister with a subtly contrasting vision and sense of ellipse.

Shot on location in Tunisia, film owes much to a superb supporting cast, Dominique Chapuis' versatile lensing and Yann Dedet's densely textured editing. Moonlighting here, Dedet also plays Roüan's bookish, chair-bound spouse. (Wife's exasperation with him provides one of the film's funniest outbursts.)

Other tech credits are solid.
— *Len.*

Cas Sluhu
(Flunkey Time)
(CZECHOSLOVAKIAN)

Paris A Barrandov Film Studios production. Written and directed by Irena Pavlaskova. Camera (color), S.A. Brabec; editor, Jan Svoboda; music, Jiri Chlumecky, Jiri Vesely; sound, Vaclav Vondracek; art direction, Boris Halmi; production manager, Vaclav Eisenhamer. Reviewed at the Empire theater, Paris, April 22, 1990. (In Cannes Film Festival, Intl. Critics Week.) Running time: **115 MIN.**

Dana . . . . Ivana Chylkova
Milan . . . . Karel Roden
Lenka . . . . Jitka Asterova
Marek . . . . Miroslav Etzler
Lubos . . . . Libor Zidek
Bohunka . . . . Eva Holubova
Hanka . . . . Vilma Cibulkova
Jarsa . . . . Petr Cepicky
Prazak . . . . Jiri Brozek

■ **Debutant helmer Irena Pavlaskova wrote and directed "Cas Sluhu" before last winter's pro-democracy revolution, so pic now has extra value as a document. Overlong and sometimes redundant, it nevertheless has sharp satiric point and a fine double-edged performance by Ivana Chylkova.**

A mordant look at opportunism and treachery in Communist Czech society, film is a portrait of a wallflower who becomes a flytrap. Chylkova plays a timid, withdrawn young medical student who is so droopy and asexual that boyfriend Miroslav Etzler leaves her.

She seeks solace with her friends, Jitka Asterova and Karel Roden, a seemingly solid young couple. Through emotional blackmail, she manages to convince Roden to marry her, just for a few weeks she says, long enough to avenge herself on her former beau.

Chylkova succeeds not in winning Etzler back but in seducing Roden into real wedded life. She squeezes hubby's parents out of the family flat so that the couple can move in. It's the beginning of her ascension as matriarch and predator. Her growing self-confidence is matched by her maturing physical attractiveness. She helps Roden rise through the ranks of the diplomatic service at the foreign trade ministry by conniving and manipulating others.

Her egotism extends to taking a lover, but she overreaches herself when she allows the relationship to go as far as a tentative engagement. Comeuppance comes when the future hick in-laws show up one day on her doorstep, ready to move in. She must turn for help to a husband she despises and resume the role of housewife. The film ends on a final ironic twist during a ministry reception when she runs into her old boyfriend.

Pavlaskova, 30, who's been an assistant director at the Barrandov Studios, is worth watching as a figure in the new Czech cinema.
— *Len.*

Beyond The Ocean
(ITALIAN)

Cannes An Augusto Caminito and Reteitalia presentation of a Scena Intl. and Reteitalia production. Directed by Ben Gazzara. Screenplay, Gazzara, Anthony Foutz; camera, Franco Di Giacomo; editor, Nino Baragli; sound, Carlo Palmieri; production design, Gianni Giovagnoni; costume design, Raffaella Fantasia. Reviewed at Cannes Film Festival (Intl. Critics Week), May 17, 1990. Running time: **110 MIN.**

John . . . . Ben Gazzara
Laidlaw . . . . Treat Williams
Eric . . . . Peter Riegert
Ellen . . . . Jill Clayburgh
Marissa . . . . Rebecca Glenn
Wayan . . . . Gito Rollies
Jenny . . . . Helena Michell
(English soundtrack)

■ **This unusual Italian-financed production of a film shot in English with an American story and actors is made even more unusual by the fact that it's unlikely to see U.S. distribution.**

In his debut as director, Ben Gazzara delivers a poorly paced and flatly visualized story of a successful man in crisis with his identity. Production values and level of inspiration are very low, and the Berlusconi-financed pic is unlikely to be seen outside of fests.

Gazzara stars as a 50ish U.S. businessman who escapes from the rat race for some soul-searching in Bali just as his company is about to go public, causing no end of frenzied phone calls from his colleagues in Manhattan.

He arrives in the tropical paradise world-weary and fatigued, and in terms of range of emotion, the character develops only a few degrees throughout the picture. He falls for a beautiful model (Rebecca Glenn). Of her performance, it can best be said that she's very convincing in the role.

Gazzara pursues her around the island, in between tasting a few tropical pleasures and unwinding in his suite, where he dictates his thoughts on his own internal crisis into a video recorder.

These comments are addressed to "John," which is the character's name, though film buffs will no doubt read into it a conversation with the late John Cassavetes, influential colleague of Gazzara's to whom the film is dedicated. It's worth noting that stylistically, the formally composed film bears none of Cassavetes' influence.

Gazzara is "tired of the dog and pony show" and determined to take some time to sort things out, he tells his Manhattan colleagues, who insist everything is going to hell without him. Photography as Gazzara samples the island's pleasures with Glenn is flat and underlit, roughly on par with a video travelogue. Camera is usually in a disadvantaged position, and a minimum of angles betray a very low budget.

Others in the cast, including Jill Clayburgh and Peter Riegert as Gazzara's wife and brother who show up at his hotel to try to bring him to his senses, were apparently not averse to spending a little work time in Bali. The still-supple Clayburgh is fine, but the others, including Treat Williams as a fellow burnout, mostly draw heavy sighs and shuffle through their marks, the weight of the world on their shoulders.

The dilemmas of John's paradoxically unhappy character are well-worth mulling and, script, cowritten by Gazzara with Anthony Foutz, has some good lines, but it can't be said that the film brings its subject to life.

Making matters worse is a melancholy, reflective saxophone score that would be more apropos in an urban setting. — *Daws.*

Queen Of Temple Street
(HONG KONG)

Cannes A Sil-Metropole release of a Filmways Production Co. production. Produced by William Tam, Wong Yat-ping. Directed by Lawrence Ah Mon. Screenplay, Chan Man-keung; camera (color), Chan Ying-kit; editor, Yu Shun, Kwong Chi-leung; art direction, Yank Wong; sound, Wong Kwansai; assistant director, Bill Yip, Wong Yat-ping, Joey Shum. Reviewed at the Cannes Intl. Film Festival (Intl. Critics Week), May 18, 1990. Running time: **110 MIN.**

Big Sis Wah . . . . Sylvia Chang
Yan . . . . Rain Lau
Connie . . . . Alice Lau
Elvis . . . . Lo Lieh
Mabel . . . . Ha Ping
Simon . . . . Wang Wai-tak
Octopussy . . . . Sandy Chan
Candy . . . . Yuen King
Dan Venus . . . . Josephine
Ku Swallow . . . . Lo Koon Lan
Mandy . . . . Lee Ming
Chu Shu . . . . Tsang
Yiu Ming Uncle Luke . . . . Kwan Hoi Sun

■ **This is director Lawrence Ah Mon's first feature since his debut four years ago with "Gangs." The South African-born, U.S.-educated helmer has a genuine feel for gritty realism, but needs work in structuring a straight-ahead meller at a pace and rhythm more leisurely than full-out hysteria.**

"Temple Street" is set in a red light district deep in the highly populated Mong Kok section on Hong Kong's Kowloon side. The film captures the flavor of the area with detailed accuracy, a testament to the director's keen and welcome eye for the specific.

Protagonist is a madam of a cut-rate brothel, a veteran of two marriages to a pair of deadbeats and the mother of a rebellious, self-destructive teenage girl. The story centers on the quotidian details of brothel life and on the mother-daughter feud and final reconciliation.

Details of daily life in the whorehouse are uncompromisingly clinical and unglamorous, as keenly observed as the madame's domestic vicissitudes. As nicely portrayed by Sylvia Chang, the woman is a strong, sad woman who manages to fashion a decent family environment against great odds.

"Temple Street" is a bit long on the melodrama, especially in a series of scenes with Rain Lau as the rebellious daughter. But both Lau and Chang are performers of such strength that they make their scene transcend commonplace, tv-style sentimentality.

Some may see the film as some sort of metaphor of Hong Kongers forced to make tough compromises in the face of approaching China takeover of the colony in 1997. That's to saddle the film with more political-social baggage than it can probably stand.

"Temple Street" is a generally strong drama, describing a peculiar milieu in terms that warrant attention in world film fests.

— *Sege.*

RIVERTOWN INTL. FILM FESTIVAL REVIEWS

L'ange
(FRENCH)

St. Paul Produced and directed by Patrick Bokanowski. Camera, Phillippe Lavalette; editor, Bokanowski; music, Michele Bokanowski; special effects, Patrick Bokanowski; set design, Christian Daninos; costume design, Domenika. Reviewed at Rivertown Intl. Film Festival, Minneapolis, May 10, 1990. Running time: **70 MIN.**

First Librarian . . . . Maurice Baquet
Man in a Bath . . . . Jean-Marie Bon
Servant . . . . Martine Couture
Swordsman/
Man without hands . . . . . Jacques Faure
Apprentice . . . . Mario Gonzales
Artist . . . . Rene Patignani
Woman . . . . Rita Renoir
Also with: Max Guy Cravagnac, Denis, Abby Patrix, Alain Salomon, Dominique Serrand, Nicolas Serreau, Patricia Peretti, Netra.

■ **It might be art, but "L'ange" is definitely not entertainment. If there's a place for this mishmash of surrealistic optical views, it's probably the archives of a museum or library.**

Pic is a series of seemingly unrelated scenes in which various characters go through motions which are repeated over and over ad nauseum. There's no dialog, no plot, no continuity and, to most filmgoers, no sense to these goings on. Apparently director Patrick Bokanowski spent five years putting this oeuvre together. The running time of 70 minutes seems to take a few eons longer than that.

As confounding as the visual is Michele Bokanowski's background music, which endlessly repeats discordant tones. The resulting jumble of sight and sound is puzzling, aggravating and, ultimately, tedious. — *Rees.*

Lines Of Fire
(DOCU)

Minneapolis A First Run Features release of an Oasis Pictures production. Written, produced and directed by Brian Beker. Camera (color), Marcus Birsel; editor, Joanna Kirnan; assistant editor, Claire Bush. Reviewed at the Rivertown Intl. Film Festival, Minneapolis, May 6, 1990. Running time: **62 MIN.**

■ **Because of its grim subject matter, "Lines Of Fire" is a better bet for cable or public tv shows than it is for commercial filmhouses. But young (31) filmmaker Brian Beker has done an admirable job on this docu about the civil war in Burma.**

The fighting in Burma is like similar wars in Cambodia, El Salvador and Ethiopia. Unlike the others, it has been largely ignored by the world media. It has also been going on for 40 years, pitting the military dictatorship of Gen. Ne Win against most of Burma's rural population. As in China, the government has cracked down on dissidents, imprisoning 10,000 indefinitely and killing an estimated 40,000.

The "good guys," however, are not all on one side. Gen. Khun Sa, a rebel warlord, has profited from a thriving heroin trade. In a senseless effort to halt the drug traffic, the U.S. gave Ne Win's government crop dusting planes to spray the opium fields with an Agent Orange-like herbicide. The planes were employed indiscriminately against other crops, farm animals and unsuspecting civilians. The long-range toll will be devastating.

At considerable danger to himself and his film crew, Beker (who also narrates his docu) visited various jungle locations to show Burma's genuine freedom fighters are attempting to counteract the military regime. The Burmese people are attractive and articulate, and Beker's interviews with some of them are touching. He also included video footage of student demonstrators being fired upon by the army in Rangoon.

Beker's outlook of looming tragedy needed to be communicated. Sadly, it will probably be disregarded by a world that seems insensitive to genocide. — *Rees.*

Porno
(POLISH)

Minneapolis A Zebra Film Group production. Written and directed by Marek Koterski. Camera (color), Jacek Blawut; editor, Teresa Miziolek; music, Bernard Kafka; sound, Miroslaw Dobek; production design, Borzyslawa Chomnicka; production manager, Marek Wolski. Reviewed at the Rivertown Intl. Film Festival, Minneapolis, May 15, 1990. Running time: **82 MIN.**

With: Zbigniew Rola, Agnieszka Wojcik, Iwona Kasia Pawlak, Ewa Grabarczyk, Katarzyna Figura, Anna Gronostaj, Henryk Bista, Zbigniew Buczkowski, Miroslawa Dubrawska, Boguslaw Linda.

■ **"Porno" may be the ultimate example of the new freedom eastern European filmmakers are testing in bringing intimacies to the screen. By western standards, it's not pornographic, but some of its content is erotic and nudity abounds.**

Thin storyline has a middle-aged man lying sleeplessly in bed, recalling his many sexual encounters. The various couplings are haphazard, loveless affairs in which most of the women are as anxious to find sexual release as is the man. Director/writer Marek Koterski's theme appears to be that pornography is the true definition of promiscuity. His character fails to find fulfillment and is left with feelings of despair and hopelessness.

The film is dated by today's AIDS epidemic. However, the affairs portrayed preceded the AIDS outbreak. The leading man does make repeated visits to a public clinic for venereal disease treatment.

Zbigniew Rola as the shallow lothario is okay, as are his conquests, mostly attractive Polish models with little acting experience. Technical credits are satisfactory.

The film was subsidized by the pre-Solidarity Communist government which tried to dissuade Koterski from making it but declined to suppress it. It was not condemned by the Polish Catholic church, but drew scathing criticism in the Catholic press. It ran nine weeks in Poland and will find audiences in the U.S. because of its titillating subject matter.

— *Rees.*

The Drayman And The King
(SOVIET)

Minneapolis A Central Gorky Studios of Children and Youth Film production. Produced by Mark Ruzansky. Directed by Vladimir Alenikov. Screenplay, Asar Eppel, Alenikov; music, Alexander Vhurbin; lyrics, Eppel; camera (color), Anatoly Grishko; production design, Mark Gorelik; costume design, Olga Akil, Julia Belomlinskaya, Lyubov Popkova. Reviewed at Rivertown Intl. Film Festival, Minneapolis, May 14, 1990. Running time: **160 MIN.**

With: Armen Jigarkhanyan, Zinovy Gerdt, Irina Rozanova, Raisa Nedashkovskaya, Tatyana Vasilyeva, Maxim Leonidov.

■ **Tevya has moved from the country to the city in the 1920s and has turned into Mack the Knife in this overlong Soviet musical. It's a production of epic proportions but considerably less than epic stature, and it's far too slow moving to appeal to U.S. audiences.**

The drayman of the title is a wealthy, elderly owner of a livery stable who lords it over his family, neighbors and workers. No shining example to others, he indulges in excesses, cheats on his wife and browbeats his grown, shiftless sons, planning to disinherit them.

The elder son, known as "the king," eventually wrests control of the business from his father. Few of the characters offer any redeeming virtues. There are occasional touches of humor, but the mood throughout is generally somber.

Like "Fiddler On The Roof," "Drayman" limns the autocracy of a Russian Jewish father. There the similarity ends. The village of "Fiddler" and the Odessa setting of "Drayman" are worlds apart. "Drayman" lacks the charm and uplift that made "Fiddler" such a hit. The musical score and lyrics, reportedly due to be transplanted to Broadway next fall, are bleak, giving the film a Bertolt Brecht feeling.

Director Vladimir Alenikov's cast of hundreds includes some of the top Russian actors. Armen Jigarkhanyan as Mendel Krik, the drayman, and Zinowy Gerdt as Benya Krik, the king, are splendid, and acting by both principals and bit players is topnotch. Technical credits are firstrate as well.

Where the production lags is in Alenikov's failure to evoke any feelings of sympathy for the characters and in the film's torpid pace.

"Drayman" was adapted from Isaac Babel's "Odessa Tales" and his play "Sunset." Babel was a victim of Stalin's purges some 40 years ago. — *Rees.*

Seman
(A Lost Hero)
(MALAYSIAN)

Minneapolis An Until Films presentation. Written, produced and directed by Mansor bin Puteh. Camera (color), bin Puteh; editor, bin Puteh. Sound, Rosli Othman; production team, Badaruddin Azmi, Ahmas Bahiki Selamat, Shambokhari Longche, Abdul Shukor, Abdullah. Reviewed at Rivertown Intl. Film Festival, Minneapolis, May 12, 1990. Running time: **83 MIN.**
With: Nordin Kardi, Shamsidar Omar, Amran Karim, Ahmad Tajuddin, Fatimah Hamid, Rosnani Shahrom.

■ **The good news is there's a film industry in Malaysia. The not-so-good news is it has a long way to go to compete with product of most other countries, judging from this pic by first-time filmmaker Mansor bin Puteh.**

It's probably unfair to correlate Malaysian film capability with this one-man effort. Bin Puteh is not only a novice but appears to be a maverick. In his heavily autobiographical script, a young ad exec is aligned against higher-ups in attempting to mount an ad campaign for a new client. Part of the narrative is stream of consciousness, and transitions between mental fingerpainting and reality are difficult to follow.

Direction also leaves much to be desired. Thesping by lead actor Nordin Kardi and others is generally uninspired. Bin Puteh made the film on a shoestring budget of $120,000, which shows in the end product. It was filmed in 16m and transferred to 35m. Subtitles that are often largely illegible make the film unsuitable for export.
— *Rees.*

Kelid
(The Key)
(IRANIAN)

Minneapolis An Institute for the Intellectual Development of Children and Young Adults production. Directed by Ebrahim Forouzesh. Screenplay, Abbas Kiarostami; camera (color), Mohammad Aladpoush; editor, Kiarostami. Reviewed at Rivertown Intl. Film Festival,

Minneapolis, May 12, 1990. Running time: **76 MIN.**
With: Mahnas Ansarian, Fatemah Asar, Amir Poorhassan, Emad Taheri.

■ **A 4-year-old boy is the star of "The Key," a stunning Iranian film that packs humor, pathos and suspense into its 76 minutes. Pic is a good bet for arthouses and public tv.**

At the pic's outset, a mother sets out on shopping errands, leaving her small son and his baby brother alone in the family's apartment. She instructs the boy to feed the baby a bottle of milk she has prepared. The youngster, however, has his own priorities, drinking part of the bottle himself, feeding some to the pet bird and spilling the rest when he gives it to the infant.

The baby's crying attracts a worried neighbor who is unable to gain access to the locked apartment. Minor crisis piles on crisis, culminating in the threat of disaster when a pot of food, cooking on the gas range, boils over, dousing the fire. Frantic neighbors and the boys' grandmother yell advice to the youngster who displays remarkable resourcefulness. As tension mounts, the suspense is electrifying, and the relief at the conclusion is palpable.

Ebrahim Forouzesh's direction of his young charge is marvelous, as is Mohammed Aladpoush's photography, turning an apartment into a potential house of horrors. Mahnas Ansarian as the 4-year-old is a knockout. The picture was named "Best Children's Film" at the '89 Berlin Film Fest. — *Rees.*

CANNES FILM FESTIVAL REVIEWS (DIRECTORS FORTNIGHT)

Paper Mask
(BRITISH)

Cannes A Film Four Intl., Granada and British Screen presentation. Produced and directed by Christopher Morahan. Screenplay, John Collee, based on his novel; camera, Nat Crosby; editor, Peter Coulson; music, Richard Harvey; sound, Hugh Strain; production design, Caroline Hanania; art direction, Andrew Rothschild; costume design, Amy Roberts; assistant director, Gary White; coproducer, Sue Austen; casting, Doreen Jones. Reviewed at Cannes Film Festival (Directors Fortnight), May 20, 1990. Running time: **118 MIN.**

Matthew Harris	Paul McGann
Christine Taylor	Amanda Donohoe
Dr. Mumford	Frederick Treves
Dr. Thorn	Tom Wilkinson
Celia Mumford	Barbara Leigh-Hunt
Alec Moran	Jimmy Yuill

■ **With excellent performances by Paul McGann and Amanda Donohue, Christopher Morahan's taut suspense thriller should do some smart theatrical business and has excellent worldwide television potential.**

From John Collee's script about a young man who gets away with posing as an emergency room doctor in a British hospital, pic raises provocative questions about human pretense and the ruses of professional survival.

Morahan demonstrates impressive directorial control in a tightly paced work laced with touches of visual humor and chilling irony.

Pic focuses on a dissatisfied hospital worker, Matthew (McGann), who seizes the chance to assume the identity of a promising young doctor after the other man dies in a car crash and his papers fall into Matthew's hands.

After winning a hospital post in another town as Dr. Simon Hennessey, McGann goes through a nightmarish initiation in the gory and panic-filled emergency room as it seems his incompetence will be found out at every turn. But strange quirks of human behavior save him, as does his discovery of various forms of duplicity among others.

Befriended by a competent and sympathetic nurse (Donahoe), he survives day by day. But the stakes are dramatically raised when he accidentally kills a doctor's wife with an overdose of anesthesia. To his astonishment, the hospital protects him, and in turn, itself.

The self-critical Donohoe wrongly takes the blame, and he lets her, knowing that there's no turning back from his ruse. Meanwhile, a friend of his from his former life turns up as a strong threat to blow his cover. With blood already on his hands, Matthew proves capable of anything to protect himself. Pic piles up irony and suspense in a fascinating web of entrapment and escape.

Highly entertaining as a thriller-chiller, film is equally engrossing on a psychological level as it is always some aspect of the typically self-absorbed beings surrounding him that allows Matthew to pull off his deception. Characters are thereby illuminated in a much more sophisticated way than is usually seen onscreen, and acting all around is excellent.

Pic's least convincing aspect is willingness of forthright Donohoe to remain sympathetic to McGann after she finds him out. One can only surmise she is lonely and needs him, but script scarcely makes that clear enough.

Photography by Nat Crosby and editing by Peter Coulson are fluid and appropriate and production values overall are high. — *Daws.*

Shimaguni Konjo
(Homemade Movie)
(JAPANESE)

Cannes A Malpaso Prods. presentation. Produced, directed and edited by Fumiki Watanabe. No screenplay credit. Camera (color), Shinji Tomita; music, Watanabe; sound, Akira Sawahata. No other credits provided. Reviewed at Cannes Film Festival (Directors Fortnight), May 17, 1990. Running time: **110 MIN.**

Watanabe family	
Fumiki (father)	Fumiki Watanabe
Tsugiko (mother)	Tsugiko Watanabe
Butaro (son)	Hidefumi Mimura
Ichihara family	
Zenkichi (father)	Isamu Shigihara
Yumiko (mother)	Naoko Kubo
Nobuko (daughter)	Yoko Shikami

■ **This thoroughly unpredictable, surprisingly affecting piece of personal cinema transcends its apparent amateurism in quirky and unexpected ways. That said, it should be underscored that "Homemade Movie" is only for the most patient audiences willing to go with totally unpackaged films without advance credentials.**

Fumiki Watanabe is a 37-year-old junior high school tutor who has been making films on his own since he was 18. This is his first 35m feature, and he employs before the camera himself, his wife, various friends and passersby to recreate a loosely constructed story about an amorous tutor and the familial misadventures of infidelity.

"Homemade" is the second Japanese-made feature (after "The Sting Of Death" in the main competition) to play the Cannes fest this year using infidelity as a point of departure. Happily, the pic lacks "Sting's" somber sense of *sturm und drang*. It is at heart a cinematic lark that provides Westerners an unusually detailed and penetrating look into daily life in provincial Japan.

Watanabe plays himself as a no-nonsense tutor who prepares his pupils for high school entrance examinations in rigorous fashion. He is not above using force to make a point, and there's a surprising amount of minor fisticuffs in the film.

Bored by his wife, the tutor takes up with the mother of one of his female students (nicely played by Yoko Shikami) not knowing that the student is dating his own son (Hidefumi Mimura). Much of "Homemade" dotes on the emotionally messy consequences of parental dalliance for both students and parents.

No moralism crops up, and the families at film's end realign themselves slightly with only minor psychic abrasions. The film does not present itself as fully professional fruits of Japan's sophisticated film industry. Instead, it brandishes its roughhewn look (there are, for example, a profusion of hand-held camera shots of people running) with the dialogue appearing to be largely improvised.

Graceful surprises crop up, making pic's relatively shapeless look worth tolerating. In all, an adventurous pie of uncompromisingly uncommercial filmmaking that justifiably deserves broad look-sees on the festival circuit. — *Sege.*

Lebedyne Ozero — Zona
(Swan Lake — The Zone)
(UKRAINIAN-SOVIET)

Cannes A Kobza Intl. (Kiev/Toronto) presentation of Video Ukraine and Kobza Intl. production in association with Swe Sov Consult (Stockholm) and Dovzhenko Film Studio (Kiev). Produced by Virko Baley, Yuri Illienko. Executive producers, Mykola Moros (Canada), Robert Gardine (Sweden). Directed by Illienko. Screenplay, Illienko, based on three short stories by Sergei Paradjanov; camera (Technicolor), Illienko; editor, Eleanora Summovska; music, Baley, Illienko; sound, Bokdan Mikhnevych; production design, Oleksandr Danylenko; costume design, Nadia Sovtus; animation, Oleksandr Mukhin. Reviewed at Cannes Film Festival (Directors Fortnight), May 13, 1990. Running time: **96 MIN.**

The Man . . . . Victor Solovyov
The Woman . . . . . Liudmyla Yefymenko
The Boy . . . . Pylyp Illienko
The Morgue Attendant . . Maya Bulhakova
The Prison Guard . . . . . Victor Demertash
Also: M. Tzuzura, V. Tzybenko, O. Danylenko, S. Povarov, V. Kotko, A. Kuzmenko, O. Nikel-Shyskin, I. Demianov,

A. Nykyforov, S. Kharun.

———

■ The art circuit may welcome "Swan Lake — The Zone." Yuri Illienko's retelling of Sergei Paradjanov's short stories about his life in a prison camp has highly inventive cinematography at the service of grim realism alternating with fantastic episodes and macabre humor.

Ukraine's internationally known cinematographer-director Illienko ("A White Bird With A Black Spot," "Straw Bells") shares coproducer credits for "Swan Lake — The Zone" with his countryman, Las Vegas Symphony conductor Virko Baley. The film has considerable Canadian and Swedish involvement, too, and may thus get more offshore exposure than such a grim prison film otherwise would.

Tall, gaunt Victor Solovyov, eyes shining with controlled madness, plays the man who escapes from prison just three days before his scheduled release.

A beautiful woman (Liudmyla Yefymenko), who lives alone with her 12-year-old son in a desolate wasteland, finds her dreams of love fulfilled when she helps the starving man. But the boy is jealous of her mother's new lover and turns him in. Back in prison, the man sets about killing himself by drinking paint.

So far, the story has been told mostly as stark realism, interspersed with a few flashes of dream imagery or animated sequences of swans flying majestically before tumbling into a poisonous pool of industrial waste.

Film then changes tone with a long sequence of morbid and absurdist comedy with a prison guard, the man and a woman morgue keeper, involving a blood transfusion from prison guard to corpse.

Pic then shifts back to mostly realism in prison, where the other prisoners swear to kill the man since he has betrayed their brotherhood by accepting blood from a guard.

A Calvary symbolism is invoked here, along with hints of male bonding and a profusion of red herrings, all grist for the inevitable audience interpretation mill.

The playing in all roles is mostly taciturn and film has virtually no dialog.

The production dress is spare but always to the point. When Illienko indulges in stylistic imagery at the cost of the film's narrative logic, it's possible to forgive him, since he is so brilliantly creative as a cinematographer. — *Kell.*

Laguerat
(The Camp)
(BULGARIAN)

Cannes A Bulgarian Cinematography production. Directed by Georgy Dyulgerov. Screenplay, Dyulgerov, Georgy Danialov; camera (color), Radoslav Spassov; editor, Nikolina Momchilova, Christina Milva; music, Bozhidar Pektov; sound, Margarita Marinova; production design, Boriana Semerdjeva. Reviewed at Cannes Film Festival (Directors Fortnight), May 18, 1990. Running time: **90 MIN.**
With: Samuel Fintsi, Dessislava Karoushkova, Radena Vulkanova, Iliana Doichinova, Eugeni Djourov.

———

■ The idea of a Young Pioneer (Communist) camp of the 1950s as a microcosm for Stalinism has been tried before in Eastern European cinema (the 1981 Polish "Shivers," a Silver Bear winner at the Berlin fest). Director Georgy Dyulgerov adds nothing basically new to the theme in "The Camp," well-made but predictable.

Early sequences take place in the '50s at a seaside camp, and the action then shifts forward 10 years to a "voluntary labor" camp.

In either setting, the message is the same: The Communist system molds impressionable young people, discouraging individuality. With a little nudity and sex thrown in, "The Camp" still emerges as a surface look at totalitarianism.

The young actors are fine, and the film is technically an improvement on the average Bulgaro film of the past. But more original scripts will be needed if Bulgarian cinema is to make its mark on world cinema in the present climate. — *Strat.*

———

Pervii Etage
(Ground Floor)
(SOVIET-B&W)

Cannes An Odessa Film Studios production. (Intl. sales, Primodessa Film.) Directed by Igor Minaev. Screenplay, Olga Michailov; camera (black & white), Vladimir Pankov; editor, Polina Roudikh; music, Anatoli Dergachev; sound, Iasnikova Riabinin; production design, Anatoli Naoumov. Reviewed at Cannes Film Festival (Directors Fortnight), May 16, 1990. Running time: **70 MIN.**
Nadia . . . . Eugenia Dobrovolskaia
Sergei . . . . Maxim Kisilev
Also with: Nicolai Tokar, Svetlana Kruchkova, Ludmila Davidova.

———

■ A simple story of a doomed love affair between a shy 18-year-old youth and a worldly 20-year-old woman, "Ground Floor," doesn't aim high, but director Igor Minaev (in his second feature) does what he does with feeling.

The film will be too modest for the international arthouse market, but fests and specialized tv programs could be interested in this gentle, sad love story.

Enhanced by beautiful black & white photography, the film is familiar in theme: The youth loves the woman far more than she loves him, and after they move in together she gets more and more irritated with him. It ends in her death at his hands.

Eugenia Dobrovolskaia is lovely as the teasing, sophisticated girl first seen under police arrest after a roundup. Maxim Kisilev is just right as her awkward lover.

Scenes involving their respective mothers bring further insight into the characters.

Director Minaev evokes "Carmen" in this straightforward tragedy, which is interrupted by intertitles which regularly remind us of the season and the month.
— *Strat.*

Margarit i Margarita
(Margarit And Margarita)
(BULGARIAN)

Cannes A Bulgarian Film production. Written and directed by Nikolai Volev. Camera (color), Krassimir Kostov; editor, Polia Sharalieva; art direction, Ivan Andreev. Reviewed at the Cannes Film Festival (Directors Fortnight). Running time: **90 MIN.**
Margarit . . . . Hristo Shopov
Rita . . . . Irini Zhambona
Nerizanov . . . . Vassil Mihailov
Julian . . . . Rashko Mladenov
Also with: Ilia Raev, Maya Tomova.

———

■ Bulgaria's big domestic hit of the season is "Margarit and Margarite," tragic tale of two teenage lovers whose school rebellion ends in prostitution, violence and death. Pic looks more geared to Eastern European viewers than foreign arthouse fans.

Director Nikolai Volev ("All For Love") builds interest around a lively script full of incident. Western audiences could find the hero and heroine's preoccupations, beginning with whether the boys can wear long hair to school, out of date.

In class, pretty Margarita, known

as Rita (fresh newcomer Irini Andonis), is in love with tall, quiet Margarit (Hristo Shopov). His troubles begin when he fights a boy who plays a practical joke on her.

The school principal is an old guard authoritarian who (unjustly, it's implied) thinks all kids are bound for alcohol, abortion, theft and violence. He demands the boy shave his head as punishment. With Rita's encouragement, Margarit refuses, and both are thrown out of school.

They break with their families and go to live in a shack. They get a job washing dishes in a nightclub, but all Rita does is stand around watching the floor show. For a joke she jumps onstage and dances up a storm, attracting the attention of Julian (Rashko Mladenov), a gay dance instructor.

Julian takes a serious interest in training Rita to dance in his folk dance company. Margarit is jealous, but Rita sticks to her guns. She also has an abortion and refuses to marry him.

The girl's brave stance turns out to be the first step on the road to disaster, however. Julian gets her arrested for passing a bag of money to a bartender, and Rita convinces Margarit to take the rap. He gets a suspended sentence.

Next Rita attracts the eye of lustful party boss Nerizanov (Vassil Mihailov), who offers to get her an apartment if she sleeps with him. She becomes his paid mistress and, sure enough, turns to alcohol.

Final disaster is not long in coming. After raping Rita on her wedding day, Nerizanov tries to stage an orgy with Julian and Margarit. Margarit kills him, is convicted of murder, and commits suicide. Rita apparently does the same.

Obviously there's a lot here that couldn't be said just a few pre-glasnost years ago. Subjects like official corruption, prostitution and homosexuality are much more openly shown than before, though "Margarit" has no earth-shaking revelations to make. Westerners will be more bemused at how the young people decorate their room with magazine illustrations of flashy cars and apartments.

There is a fair amount of tension to keep action moving along swiftly. But film's message is ambiguous. Though it appears to be on the side of the high school rebels, it shows all the principal's most clichéd fears coming true the

minute parental guidance is sidestepped.

It also depicts pink-cheeked Rita as one of the most lethal femme fatales on the screen. Lensing is on the murky side. Thesping is up to standard. — *Yung.*

Hardware
(BRITISH-U.S.)

Cannes A Miramax Films release (in the U.S.) of a Palace/Miramax Films presentation, in association with British Screen and BSB. A Wicked Films production. Executive producers, Harvey Weinstein, Bob Weinstein, Nik Powell, Stephen Woolley, Trix Worrell. Produced by Joanne Sellar, Paul Trybits. Written and directed by Richard Stanley. Camera (color), Steven Chivers; editor, Derek Trigg; music, Simon Boswell; production design, Joseph Bennett; special makeup effects and robotics, Image Animation. Reviewed at the Cannes Film Festival (market), May 13, 1990. No MPAA Rating. Running time: **92 MIN.**

Mo	Dylan McDermott
Jill	Stacey Travis
Shades	John Lynch
Lincoln	William Hootkins
Angry Bob	Iggy Pop

■ **A cacophonic, nightmarish variation on the postapocalyptic cautionary genre, "Hardware" has the makings of a punk-sensibility cult film and quintessential midnight movie. Richard Stanley's run-amok sci-fi/horror fantasy will need calculated promotion, keyed to its trendy environmental paranoia, to maximize potential as an underground event item.**

After the nuclear holocaust, vast reaches of incinerated North America have been reduced to an infrared desert ravaged by guerrilla warfare and littered with cybernetic scrapheaps. Moses (Dylan McDermott) and Shades (John Lynch) are "zone tripper" soldiers of fortune who scavenge the corpse-strewn, irradiated wasteland for techno-detritus to black market in the big city.

Mission completed, they return to New York, N.Y., where freelance anarchy and dog-eat-dog survivalism prevail among the skyscraper shanties. Mutation, insanity and slow death fester under boiling poison skies. Disk jockey Angry Bob (Iggy Pop) wakes up Gotham every morning with the admonition that "there is no ----ing good news." All this, to a relentless thrash-metal beat.

Moses and Shades ponder a new life in the space colonies, but Moses, wasting away from radiation cancer, wants to return to his woman, Julie. She's a fiercely cynical techno-alchemist, fond of smoking packaged dope, who keeps a fortress workshop in a blasted downtown apartment block.

Reunited in a frenzied sexual collision of pulse-pounding eroticism, the couple ponder their outer-limits relationship of love in the

ruins. Julie is skeptical of Moses' appropriately messianic belief in an unattainable better future. They veer between need and alienation, hope and utter despair.

Stanley's dialog is a fragmented pastiche of existential and religious epigrams, invoking Darwin, the Bible and Hindu transcendentalism. Post-apoco spirituality surfaces in the person of Kali, goddess of creation and destruction, and the grim injunctions of Mark 13: "No flesh shall be spared." Mark 13 is also the name of a new death-dealing cyborg, designed by the government to implement its emergency population control bill.

The law is touted to the masses as "clean break with procreation" by a retro-Orwellian propagandistic tv that also offers rock and rolling mutants, radiation-free reindeer meat, and a stream of alarming bulletins about enemies within and without. There are also Afro-American freelance security patrols, a video-phone peeper-breather who lusts for Julie and a mutated dwarf who middlemans for Moses and Shades in the junk metal market.

Stanley, who might have done better to elaborate on his wicked satirical futuristic motifs, plummets the pic headlong into horror. Moses has brought Julie a gift from the desert: a robotic helmet that mystifies both of them. This is the head of a Mark 13, which remorselessly regenerates itself in Julie's workshop and launches into a death-dealing rampage of mutilation and destruction.

"Hardware" veers loonily out of control and becomes a black comic exercise in F/X tour-de-force. There's nothing subtle about "Hardware," and its intended audience probably wouldn't have it any other way.

For a low-budget film the production design and special effects harrowingly evoke a ruined world in which the remains of late 20th century technology are given over to survivalist improvisation. Performances are solid and believable in the context of a frenetic movie that's ceaselessly pushing itself over the top. — *Rich.*

Red Blooded American Girl
(CANADIAN)

Cannes An SC Entertainment presentation. Executive producer, Syd Cappe. Produced by

Nicolas Stiliadis, Paco Alvarez. Directed by David Blyth. Screenplay, Allan Moyle; camera (color), Ludek Bogner; editor, Nick Rotundo; music, Jim Manzie; production design, Ian Brock; line producer, Edgar Egger; casting, Adriana Michel. Reviewed at the Cannes Film Festival (market), May 15, 1990. Running time: **87 MIN.**

Owen Urban	Andrew Stevens
Paula	Heather Thomas
Dr. John Alcore	Christopher Plummer
Dennis	Kim Coates

■ **Although technically solid, storyline is dull and devoid of thrills. With its connotations of eroticism and horror — although neither is present — it'll probably find okay home-vid success.**

Confused story sees scientist Andrew Stevens sign on to work for Christopher Plummer, who runs a viral blood disorder laboratory. problem is that he's stumbled on a virus that engenders symptoms similar to vampirism, and has infected himself and some staff.

Unbeknownst to Stevens, his brief is to find a cure. With clinic volunteer Heather Thomas, he starts sensing something is amiss when they find a near dead staff member on the premises. Thomas gets infected though, thus Stevens has a race against time (which seems interminable) to find a cure. Perhaps the original script had promise, but the on-screen result from Kiwi helmer David Blyth is dreary and far from suspenseful.

Actors do what they can. Plummer seems like he's well and truly thinking of his next film by pic's limp ending. Mark this one down for the video shelves. — *Doch.*

Men Of Respect

Cannes A Central City Film Co./Arthur Goldblatt production. (Intl. sales, Sugar Entertainment.) Produced by Ephraim Horowitz. Executive producers, Arthur Goldblatt, Eric Kitain. Written and directed by William Reilly. Camera (color), Bobby Bukowski; editor, Elizabeth Kling; music, Misha Segal; art direction, William Barclay; line producer, Gary Mehlman. Reviewed at the Cannes Film Festival (market), May 16, 1990. Running time: **107 MIN.**

Mike Battaglia	John Turturro
Ruthie	Katherine Borowitz
Bankie Como	Dennis Farina
Duffy	Peter Boyle
Charlie D'Amico	Rod Steiger
Also with: Steven Wright.	

■ **"Men Of Respect" is a tight, taut action thriller poised to go down in history as the first Mafia tale to be based on "Macbeth." Writer-director William Reilly does a first-class job, working with a par-**

ticularly fine cast. Pic certainly should do action market biz, but could enjoy much wider release.

The gamble of scripting a Godfather story around an unrelated Shakespeare plot works out as more of an in-joke than anything else, but it's fun to recognize the elements. (Similarly, "Joe Macbeth," a 1950s British gangster pic, also borrowed from the Bard. — *Ed.*)

The New York crime syndicate is at war. In a blood-drenched opening, a lone and half-crazed gunman, Mike Battaglia (John Turturro), knocks off a whole restaurant full of rival mafiosi. He reports back to the padrino, Charlie D'Amico (Rod Steiger), and is richly praised for his loyalty.

On the way home, Mike and buddy Bankie Como (Dennis Farina) stop to have their fortunes told by a batty old spiritualist who predicts Mike will become capo regime and, in time, padrino. Bankie will die and his son rise to the top. Bankie scoffs (his son just graduated from business school). Mike is impressed.

At home, Mike's young wife Ruthie (Katherine Borowitz) ambitiously urges him to go for it: to kill D'Amico and take his place. At first repulsed, Mike-Macbeth soon comes round and, with his lady's help, bumps off the trusting padrino, asleep in the next room. Ruthie calms her husband's nerves while she washes his bloody clothes.

At the funeral, the family pays its respects to Mike, assumed to become the new padrino. The most suspicious is the Irish Duffy (Peter Boyle), capo of an allied family. The rest let Mike take over. But his conscience won't rest easy. At first Ruthie tries to assuage his guilt, but soon she starts losing her sense of reality and worrying about that damned spot that won't come out — of the bathtub.

Tormented by bad dreams, Mike returns to the spiritualist. She predicts no mother's son can kill him. In a final, tense shootout, it turns out Duffy's mother was dead when he was born — and that's the end of Macbeth.

It's still a great plot, filled with greed, ambition, murder, guilt and retribution. Reilly rarely lets his model get the upper hand, however. Thesps talk in natural street jargon, and the action owes more to Coppola than the Bard. An

unwary viewer could miss the reference altogether.

Turturro is a tough desperado with a lot of extraordinary personality facets. Completely believable as a mobster (he resembles a young Robert De Niro more than a little), he builds the character of Mike into a complex figure.

Equally out of the norm is Borowitz as his Lady Macbeth, a handsome woman with unlimited ambitions for her gangster husband. Boyle and Farina contribute more realism in supporting roles.

Production values are high throughout, beginning with Bobby Bukowski's eerie nighttime cinematography. — *Yung.*

Wahre Libe
(True Love)
(AUSTRIAN)

Cannes A Telepool/Cinepool presentation of Wega Film (Vienna) production in association with Julian R. Film (Munich). Produced by Veit Heiduschka. Directed by Kitty Kino. Screenplay, Kino, Reinhard Meirer, with Juergen Haake, Paul Stein; camera (Eastmancolor), Walter Kindler; editor, Ingrid Koller; music, Freddy (Redlock) Gigele; sound, Heinz Ebner; production design, Tommy Voegel; costume design, Gera Graf, Clarisse Praun; production manager, Gebhard Zupan. Reviewed at the Cannes Film Festival (market), May 11, 1990. Running time: **98 MIN.**

Roxanne	Wookie Mayer
Karl	August Zirner
Erwin	Helmuth Zierl
Barbara	Sabine Berg
Terry	Anita Kolbert

Also with: Rainer Anders, Oliver Karbus, Lotte Loebenstein, Donata Margiol.

■ **"True Love," Austrian helmer Kitty Kino's third feature, is repetitious and often contrived in the plot twist department. Pic runs out of steam soon after starting, and is headed for little exposure outside German-speaking territories.**

From a screenplay by Kino and regular associate Reinhard Meirer, item continues her stylish comic investigations of sexual confusion among 30ish smart-set protagonists in internationalized Vienna.

Everybody in "True Love" appears to be out of the pages of a fashion magazine. Roxanne (blond, energetic Wookie Mayer) runs a rock music management business as a real boss. At home, she cannot stand her live-in lover's stubborn insistence that he is essentially a loner.

When she bumps into Karl (bland, mild-mannered August Zirner), then loses sight of him again,

she feels that true love may finally have struck.

Trying to find Karl again proves difficult, however, even though they walk in and out of the same offices, beauty parlors and rock concerts. Karl, a computer whiz with a major company, also feels that the woman he met so briefly may be his destiny. Karl is married to the beautiful but dissatisfied mother of their little girl. He is the more caring parent.

Point of the film is that everybody longs for an ideal beyond a reality they cannot adopt. They would probably not be able to live with true love if they ever got the chance. Roxanne and Karl don't. They never actually find each other again, as a lot of office intrigue, rock racket exposure and fine rock performances go on around them.

There is no trace of sexist preaching in Kitty Kino's film. Actually, the men are generally seen as more sympathetic than the women, but that is hardly meant to be a point. Nobody is really knocked, not even a pathetic and silly-looking rock singer, who is performing Kino's own alternately raucous punk rock and romantic lyrics.

All production credits have fine professional gloss. — *Kell.*

Dick Tracy

Hollywood A Buena Vista release of a Touchstone Pictures presentation in association with Silver Screen Partners IV. Executive producers, Barrie M. Osborne, Art Linson, Floyd Mutrux. Produced and directed by Warren Beatty. Screenplay, Jim Cash, Jack Epps Jr., based on characters created by Chester Gould for the "Dick Tracy" comic strip; camera (Technicolor), Vittorio Storaro; editor, Richard Marks; music, Danny Elfman; songs, Stephen Sondheim; sound (Dolby), Thomas Causey; production design, Richard Sylbert; art direction, Harold Michelson; set decoration, Rick Simpson; costume design, Milena Canonero; visual effects, Buena Vista Visual Effects Group; special character make-up, John Caglione Jr., Doug Drexler; music numbers staged by Jeffrey Hornaday; assistant director-associate producer, Jim Van Wyck; 2d unit directors, Billy Burton, Marks, Osborne; 2d unit camera, James M. Anderson; coproducer, Jon Landau; casting, Jackie Burch. Reviewed at Walt Disney Studios, Burbank, Calif., May 31, 1990. MPAA Rating: PG. Running time: **103 MIN.**

Dick Tracy	Warren Beatty
Kid	Charlie Korsmo
Tess Trueheart	Glenne Headly
Breathless Mahoney	Madonna
Big Boy Caprice	Al Pacino
Mumbles	Dustin Hoffman
Flattop	William Forsythe
Chief Brandon	Charles Durning
88 Keys	Mandy Patinkin
Lips Manlis	Paul Sorvino
Pruneface	R.G. Armstrong
D.A. Fletcher	Dick Van Dyke

Also with: Seymour Cassel, James Keane, Allen Garfield, John Schuck, Charles Fleischer, James Tolkan, Kathy Bates, Catherine O'Hara, Henry Silva, James Caan, Bert Remsen, Frank Campanella, Michael J. Pollard, Estelle Parsons, Mary Woronov, Henry Jones, Mike Mazurki.

■ "Dick Tracy" is a major disappointment. Though it looks ravishing, Warren Beatty's longtime pet project is a curiously remote, uninvolving film. Touchstone pic will have a splashy bow, but probably won't reach the megahit level promised by advance hype.

Film's look never disappoints. The true stars are production designer Richard Sylbert and lenser Vittorio Storaro. Producer-director Beatty and his well-chosen collaborators have created a boldly stylized 1930s urban milieu that captures the comic strip's quirky, angled mood, while dazzling the eye with deep primary colors and most alluring miniature and matte work.

All dressed up with nowhere to go, "Dick Tracy" is stymied by a leaden script credited to Jim Cash and Jack Epps Jr. (Bo Goldman is mentioned as "special consultant"), Beatty's low emotional wattage in scenes with Madonna and Glenne Headly, fragmented misuse of unmemorable Stephen Sondheim songs, and a lurching plot line letting the grotesque secondary characters run the show.

Beatty — ultrastylish in yellow raincoat and snap-brim hat, black suit, red tie and crisp white shirts — is so cool he appears frozen. He never seems to get a handle on the character, coming off as passive and listless. Only occasionally he finds humor in the role.

Provocative casting of Beatty's real-life g.f. Madonna as an underworld siren is one of the film's potent selling tools, especially for younger viewers who don't know or care much about Beatty.

The casting seems perverse, however, since there's little sexual chemistry in their scenes together. Though Beatty's camera is voyeuristic, his Tracy barely responds to the fervent come-ons of Madonna's Breathless Mahoney, who's given consistently heavy-handed double entendres by the miscast "Top Gun" scripters.

Torn between Madonna's allure — she's costumed in black & white by Milena Canonero and lit by Storaro to look like a steamy low-rent version of Josef von Sternberg's Marlene Dietrich — and the more low-key beauty and sweetness of Headly's redhead Tess Trueheart, Beatty simply sits there and mopes, occasionally rousing himself into bursts of action.

As an actor, Beatty has often played against his sybaritic off-screen image, emphasizing emotional tentativeness and maladjustment.

Here, however, his inertia works against the film, leaving a void where there should be a fiery young Cagney rather than an overoccupied producer-director beginning to show "some mileage" (as Madonna fondly puts it).

Not the most interesting of comic heroes, Dick Tracy hardly allows the kind of complexity Beatty found in John Reed ("Reds") and presumably will find in Howard Hughes when he makes his other long-cherished project.

Chester Gould's gallery of grotesques always seemed more intriguing than his square-jawed detective. The cartoonist's equation of moral and physical ugliness made for a truly disturbing nightmare world in which Tracy's clean-cut personality (accentuated here by the even more handsome Beatty's lack of character makeup) seemed flat and wooden by comparison.

A large part of what fun there is in the pic comes from the inventive character makeup by John Caglione Jr. and Doug Drexler, who mostly succeed in the difficult task of creating live-action cartoon figures.

Dustin Hoffman takes an eerie turn as Mumbles, R.G. Armstrong is chilling as Pruneface, Paul Sorvino hilariously disgusting as Lips, William Forsythe spooky as Flattop, and a host of other notables appearing under varying degrees of face-distorting goo (too bad Mucus-Face is missing).

Beatty and his writers, however, never find enough for most of these characters to do, letting them remain one-note visual jokes like the madeup stars in John Huston's "The List Of Adrian Messenger."

Major exception is Al Pacino, who virtually runs away with the show in a sizable role as Tracy's nemesis, the Richard III-like hunchbacked villain Big Boy Caprice. His manic energy lifts the overall torpor, and his ranting pretensions to erudition and sensitivity suggest a comic complexity the film otherwise misses.

Equally fine is young Charlie Korsmo, who made a striking screen debut earlier this year in "Men Don't Leave" and, together with the lovely Headly, who resembles a young Maggie Smith, gives the film a necessary counterbalance of normality.

The street urchin's courageous efforts in rescuing Tracy time and again from the villains, in gratitude for his tentative adoption by the detective, are never cloying, and Korsmo's clear-eyed maturity of emotion stands in contrast to Beatty/Tracy's reluctance to commit himself, even in the painfully drawn-out ending.

This expensive mounting of "Dick Tracy" is worth seeing for the lacquered brilliance of its art deco sets, the fantastically intricate cityscapes, the subtlety with which the film integrates miniatures and live action, and the richness of the palette with which it paints its imaginary world.

All the visual beauty in the world isn't enough to rescue a screenplay that doesn't justify the time and expense that went into its production. Nor can the brassy score by Danny Elfman, overheated editing by Richard Marks and flamboyant sound effects by various hands camouflage that fact.

— *Mac.*

Gremlins 2: The New Batch

New York A Warner Bros. release of an Amblin Entertainment presentation of a Michael Finnell production. Produced by Finnell. Executive producers, Steven Spielberg, Frank Marshall, Kathleen Kennedy. Directed by Joe Dante. Screenplay, Charlie Haas, based on characters created by Chris Columbus; camera (Technicolor), John Hora; editor, Kent Beyda; music, Jerry Goldsmith; source music, Alexander Courage; cartoon music, Fred Steiner; sound (Dolby), Ken King, Douglas Vaughan; sound effects, Mark Mangini, David Stone; production design-2d unit director, James Spencer; art direction, Joe Lucky, Rick Butler (N.Y.); set decoration, John Anderson; costume design, Rosanna Norton; assistant director, Victor Hsu; production manager, Phil Rawlins, Lee Haas (N.Y.); Gremlin & Mogwai effects supervisor-coproducer, Rick Baker; Bugs Bunny & Daffy Duck animation written and directed by Chuck Jones; visual effects supervisor, Dennis Michelson; visual effects camera, Bill Neil; stopmotion animation, Doug Beswick; Bluemax photography, Apogee Prods.; visual effects animation, VCE/Peter Kuran; special effects supervisor, Ken Pepiot; stunt coordinator, Mike McGaughy; casting, Marion Dougherty, Glenn Daniels. Reviewed at Loews 84th St. 3 theater, N.Y., June 2, 1990. MPAA Rating: PG-13. Running time: **105 MIN.**

Billy Peltzer	Zach Galligan
Kate Beringer	Phoebe Cates
Daniel Clamp	John Glover
Grandpa Fred	Robert Prosky
Forster	Robert Picardo
Dr. Catheter	Christopher Lee
Marla Bloodstone	Haviland Morris
Murray Futterman	Dick Miller
Sheila Futterman	Jackie Joseph
Katsuji	Gedde Watanabe
Mr. Wing	Keye Luke
Microwave Marge	Kathleen Freeman
Voice of Gizmo	Howie Mandel
Voice of Brain Gremlin	Tony Randall
Voices of Bugs & Daffy	Jeff Bergman

Also with: Don Stanton, Dan Stanton, Shawn Nelson, Raymond Cruz, Hulk Hogan, Paul Bartel, Rick Docommun, John Astin, Henry Gibson, Kenneth Tobey, Page Hannah, Jason Presson, Leonard Maltin, Dick Butkus, Bubba Smith, Jerry Goldsmith, Charlie Haas.

■ Joe Dante & co. have concocted an hilarious sequel featuring equal parts creature slapstick for the small fry and satirical barbs for adults. "Gremlins 2" looms as the top family audience draw this summer.

Film is nearly "Chris-less" this time, with the 1984 original's screenwriter Chris Columbus (who created the characters) and creatures designer Chris Walas absent, having both become film directors since "Gremlins." Addition of Christopher Lee to the cast as a mad genetics engineering scientist is a perfect touch, however.

Charlie Haas' serviceable script targets popular culture, a subject dear to director Dante's mission. Film opens with a premise familiar from Amblin Entertainment's "Batteries Not Included:" the wrecking ball demolishing Keye Luke's old curiousity shop in downtown Manhattan to make way for another development project by megalomaniac Daniel Clamp, played with relish but no mimicry by John Glover as equal parts Donald Trump and Ted Turner.

The cuddly Mogwai creature Gizmo (wonderfully voiced by Howie Mandel) escapes but is immediately captured by twins Don & Dan Stanton as a research subject for Lee's science lab Splice of Life Inc. The lab is located in the new Clamp Center office building and, when Gizmo gets loose and exposed to water, the first of hundreds of horrific gremlins are unleashed to wreak mayhem.

Encoring from the first film are Zach Galligan, now a designer for Clamp, and girlfriend Phoebe Cates, sporting a silly hat as a Clamp Center tour guide. Also returning is Dick Miller as the number one gremlins hunter. The three team up to try and contain the critters before they infest Gotham.

Boasting a $50-million negative cost, about double that of the original, "Gremlins 2" is the only megabuck film this year sans star-power, but its creatures more than make up for the lack of marquee lure. As realized by Rick Baker, the innumerable creations are quite an eyeful. Perfect voice casting has Tony Randall doing a quasi-William F. Buckley Jr. turn as the brainy gremlin who leads his confreres in a rousing rendition of Kander & Ebb's "New York, New York."

Dante's subversive approach makes fun of the enterprise at hand (Leonard Maltin cameos to pan the original, while a Times Square theater advertises "The Howling XI") and regularly interrupts the action. A literal showstopper (recalling Mel Brooks' "Blazing Saddles") transfers the action to a movie theater showing "Gremlins 2." In fact, it takes no less than guest star Hulk Hogan to put things right!

The barbs at Turner and Trump are dead-on, with frequent mocking of tycoon Clamp's cable network CCN, including a promo for "Casablanca" ("now in color and with a happier ending") and Clamp's grandiose schemes (he authored "I Took Manhattan").

Surprising bit, considering the pic was shot last summer long before the Marla Maples scandal broke, has Clamp falling in love with a major character named Marla, memorably essayed as Galligan's mean boss by Haviland Morris. It must have taken ingenious reshooting to adapt her name after the fact, but tastefully Clamp has no wife in the picture.

Robert Picardo is also excellent as Clamp's officious assistant and Kathleen Freeman is delightful as a heavy-drinking tv chef. Glaring lapse in taste is casting of Robert Prosky as Grandpa Fred, a frustrated tv horror movie host for kiddies who gets his chance to be a cable newscaster when the gremlins take over the building. Prosky's persona is shamelessly ripped off from comic Al Lewis' well-remembered Grandpa character on tv's "The Munsters."

Otherwise, the referential gags are effective, ranging from a gremlin crashing through a wall to leave a hole in the shape of WB's "Batman" logo to Bugs Bunny & Daffy Duck bookending the feature in new footage directed by Chuck Jones. Even WB's upcoming film of Andrew Lloyd Webber's "The Phantom Of The Opera" gets several sight gags.

Visuals by Dante's usual team of cinematographer John Hora and designer James Spencer are impressive, as is returning composer Jerry Goldsmith's musical score. (The maestro, who appears in a cameo at an ice cream counter, resists the temptation to spoof his own "Rambo" films' theme music when Gizmo heroically imitates Stallone in a key subplot.)

For Dante and longtime partner/producer Michael Finnell "Gremlins 2" represents a return to Eden. After five years of commercial disappointments ("Explorers," "Innerspace" and "The 'Burbs"), they're clearly headed for hitsville this time out. — Lor.

Total Recall

Hollywood A Tri-Star (U.S.) and Carolco Intl. (foreign) release of a Carolco Pictures production. Produced by Buzz Feitshans, Ronald Shusett. Executive producers, Mario Kassar, Andrew Vajna. Directed by Paul Verhoeven. Screenplay, Shusett, Dan O'Bannon, Gary Goldman, from a story by Shusett, O'Bannon, Jon Povill, inspired by short story "We Can Remember It For You Wholesale" by Phillip K. Dick; camera (Technicolor), Jost Vacano; editor, Frank J. Urioste; music, Jerry Goldsmith; sound (Dolby), Nelson Stoll, Fred Runner; production design, William Sandell; conceptual artist, Ron Cobb; art direction, James Tocci, Jose Rodriguez Granada; set decoration, Robert Gould; costume design, Erica Edell Phillips; special makeup effects-character visual effects, Rob Bottin; visual effects supervisor, Eric Brevig; special effects supervisor, Thomas L. Fisher; special visual effects, Dream Quest Images; visual effects camera, Rexford Metz; additional optical effects, Industrial Light & Magic (visual effects supervisor, Dave Carson); stunt coordinator, Vic Armstrong, Joel Kramer; assistant directors, Juan Carlos (Kuki) Lopez, Miguel Lima; 2d unit director, Armstrong; 2d unit camera, Alex Phillips; associate producers, Elliot Schick, Robert Fentress; casting, Mike Fenton, Judy Taylor, Valorie Massalas (U.S.), Claudia Becker (Mexico). Reviewed at Cineplex Odeon Century Plaza Cinemas, L.A., May 30, 1990. MPAA Rating: R. Running time: **109 MIN.**

Quaid/Hauser . . . Arnold Schwarzenegger
Melina . . . . Rachel Ticotin
Lori . . . . Sharon Stone
Cohaagen . . . . Ronny Cox
Richter . . . . Michael Ironside
George/Kuato . . . . Marshall Bell
Benny . . . . Mel Johnson, Jr.
Helm . . . . Michael Champion
Dr. Edgemar . . . . Roy Brocksmith
McClane . . . . Ray Baker
Dr. Lull . . . . Rosemary Dunsmore
Fat Lady . . . . Priscilla Allen

■ **"Total Recall" deserves high praise for its craftsmanship and profit potential and a generally good score for imagination, but a poor grade for civic responsibility. Troubling questions about the film's ultraviolence recede in the harsh light of the product's unmistakable salability — Arnold Schwarzenegger on Mars.**

Estimates of the production cost of this Paul Verhoeven futuristic extravaganza, filmed in 22 weeks at Churubusco Studios in Mexico City, range from $60-70-million, making it one of the most expensive pics ever made. The credits list in the pressbook goes on for 16 pages.

There are gargantuan sets repping Mars and a futuristic Earth society, grotesque creatures galore, genuinely weird and mostly seamless visual effects, and enough gunshots, grunts and explosions to keep anyone in a high state of nervous exhiliration.

The story is actually a good one. Ronald Shusett, Dan O'Bannon and Gary Goldman have based their screenplay on an adaptation by Shusett, O'Bannon and Jon Povill (everything in this film takes a lot of hands) taking off from Phillip K. Dick's celebrated sci-fi tale "We Can Remember It For You Wholesale."

It took Schwarzenegger's clout to rescue this off-the-wall script resembling a "Twilight Zone" episode conceived on an acid trip from years of development hell.

Sylvester Stallone or Chuck Norris, to Schwarzenegger's credit, wouldn't be caught dead in the middle of a paranoiac dream-or-reality game that somehow brings to mind "Last Year At Marienbad" even while horrific mutants provide much of the visual interest and Schwarzenegger makes his entrance into Mars society bursting out of a disintegrating fat woman's body.

With his urbane demeanor in the midst of chaos, his physical grace, his ability to combine superhuman strength with a nonchalant lack of offensive muscle-preening, Schwarzenegger is the Cary Grant of the Hollywood Ubermensch set.

The cryptic plot, which keeps teasing the viewer with the possibility of an alternate interpretation in which Schwarzenegger is the villain, capitalizes on the star's intelligence and gives more sophisticated viewers (however few there may be) a second level of interest beyond the slam-bang pyrotechnics.

Schwarzenegger's character, a working stiff in the year 2084, keeps having these strange nightmares about living on Mars, and it transpires that he once worked in the colony as an intelligence agent before rebelling against dictator Ronny Cox.

When he learns the secret behind Cox' control of the planet by hoarding its air supply and dribbling it out to the drones in his sleazy kingdom, Schwarzenegger has most, but not quite all, of his bad memories erased and is sent to Earth to work on a construction crew, with a sexy but treacherous wife (Sharon Stone) supplied by Cox to keep him under submission.

A visit to a mind-altering travel agency named Rekall Inc. alerts Schwarzenegger to the truth, setting him off on an energetic rampage through Earth and Mars en route to confronting Cox and liberating the red planet with the help of equally tough female sidekick Rachel Ticotin.

The fierce and unrelenting pace set by director Verhoeven and editor Frank J. Urioste, accompanied by a tongue-in-cheek strain of humor in the roughhouse screenplay, keeps the film moving like a juggernaut.

Production designer William Sandell, conceptual artist Ron Cobb, special makeup effects and character visual effects creator Rob Bottin, lenser Jost Vacano and composer Jerry Goldsmith help conjure up a ghastly and fascistic future owing a lot to Fritz Lang's "Metropolis."

The most disturbing thing about the morally schizoid, simultaneously sophisticated and crude "Total Recall" is the thin line — all but invisible — between Schwarzenegger's "heroism" and the villainy of Cox and his minions.

Though Schwarzenegger is given the film's few fleeting gestures of compassion, he keeps adding to the body count throughout with robotlike brutality, cracking little jokes to keep the audience anesthetized.

While Schwarzenegger's sympathies, once he's seen the light, ostensibly are on the side of the enslaved, there's more than a hint of the Nietzschean superman in his character, and it isn't just because of his Austrian accent. The quasimystical mountaintop ending with Schwarzenegger as savior amid streaming sunbeams inescapably recalls Leni Riefenstahl.

The moral ambiguities that run under the surface of "Total Recall" (and undoubtedly stimulated Verhoeven's creative energies) will go over the heads of many viewers, who will enjoy the visceral kicks, outlandish gore and callously jocular touches of a film that pushes the boundaries of the R rating to a dubious extreme.

The Motion Picture Assn. of America Classification & Rating Administration's leniency toward "Total Recall" is sure to intensify the debate about whether the ratings system is biased in favor of big-budget productions.

While the temptation is just to shrug off "Total Recall" as an excessive but exciting "no-brainer," enough intelligence and artistry lie behind the numbing spectacle to also make one regret its heedless contribution to the accelerating brutality of its time.

— *Mac.*

Curse Of The Blue Lights

New York   A Tamarack Corp./Blue Lights Partners production. Produced and directed by John Henry Johnson. Screenplay, Johnson, from story by Bryan Sisson, Johnson; camera (Western Cine color), Johnson; editor, Johnson; music, Randall Crissman; art direction, Robert Balazs, Catherine Alber; costume design, Carol Cartmell; assistant director, Sisson; special makeup effects, Sisson, David Romero, Mark Sisson. Reviewed on Magnum Entertainment videocassette, N.Y., April 18, 1990. No MPAA Rating. Running time: **96 MIN.**

Louth	Brent Ritter
Witch	Bettina Julius
Ken	Patrick Keller
Sandy	Deborah DeVencenty
Paul	Clayton A. McCaw
Alice	Becky Golladay
Officer Fox	Marty Bechina
Sam	James Asbury
Bob	Kent E. Fritzell
Scarecrow	Willard Hall
Muldoon Man	George Schanze

■ **Nice special effects highlight this regional horror pic, a one-man effort made in Colorado by John Henry Johnson three years ago and currently in vidstores.**

Title refers to a remote weekend hangout, reportedly haunted, on the outskirts of the small town of Dudley, where teens congregate. Unfortunately for Patrick Keller and his chums, three ghouls in a crypt led by Brent Ritter are conjuring up the dreaded Muldoon Man, a missing link of sorts, to take over Earth.

The kids go to witch Bettina Julius for help. They ultimately defeat the baddies, including the Muldoon Man, who blows up real good at the cemetery climax.

Naive pic is fun to watch and could have been a sleeper success if Johnson had built his story around something less clichéd than the old "teens on an outing" standby. Acting is weak, but makeup effects are interesting.

Johnson has done his homework, even coming up with a nice Jean Cocteau-invented mirror-to-another-dimension gimmick. — *Lor.*

Coming Out
(EAST GERMAN)

Berlin   A DEFA-Studio fuer Spielfilme presentation of DEFA-Studio, Group Babelsberg production. Produced by Horst Hartwig. Directed by Heiner Carow. Screenplay, Wolfram Witt; camera (Orwocolor), Martin Schlesinger; editor, Evelyn Carow; music, Stefan Carow; production design, Georg Wratsch; costumes, Regina Viertel; assistant director, Hanna Seydel. Reviewed at the Berlin Film Festival, Feb. 11, 1990. (In N.Y. Intl. Festival of Lesbian and Gay Films.) Running time: **109 MIN.**

Philip	Mathias Freihof
Tanja	Dagmar Manzel
Matthias	Dirk Kummer
Achim	Michael Gwisdek
The older man	Werner Dissel
Frau Moellemann	Gudrun Ritt

Also with: Walfriede Schmitt, Axel Wandtke, Pierre Bliss, Thomas Gumbert, Robert Hummel, Gertrud Kreissig, Gudrun Okras, Joachim Pape.

■ **East German helmer Heiner Carow, who has explored the agonies of heterosexual love successfully in two earlier films, has turned to Wolfram Witt's original screenplay for "Coming Out," which treats male homosexual love with tact and sensitivity.**

Overlong and, at times, nearly at a standstill, the fact the film was made in East Germany before the walls literally came tumbling down, should create some interest.

Philip, a young high school teacher, is torn between inclinations towards romancing male friends and a wish to comply with society's standards. When he bumps into Tanja, a colleague, hard enough to give her a nosebleed, the two characters establish instant intimacy.

Philip moves in with Tanja but is haunted by other feelings, which lead to an affair with Matthias whom he meets at a transvestite ball. Philip does not tell Matthias about Tanja nor Tanja about Matthias, a dilemma of telling proportions.

Storytelling may be slow-stop stuff but no false notes are struck and characters are treated loyally. The descriptions of East Berlin's gay scene are revelations in themselves. — *Kell.*

Ach, Boris
(Oh, Boris)
(AUSTRIAN)

Cannes   A Telepool/Cinepool presentation of Wega Film production (Vienna). Produced by Veit Heiduschka. Directed by Niki List. Screenplay, List, Werner E. Sallmeier, Peter Berenc; camera, (Eastmancolor), Hanus Polak; editor, Edith Koller; music, Franz Liszt, Freddy Gigele, Harald Kloser; production design, Manfred Ebner; costume design, Martina List; production manager, Michael Katz. Reviewed at the Cannes Film Festival (market), May 12, 1990. Running time: **85 MIN.**

Clara	Jutta Hoffmann
Sophie	Anne Mertin
Margaretha	Hilde Weinberger
Paul	Gerd Kunath
Boris Kaminsky	Ulrich Wildgruber

Also with: Susanne Altschul, Dominik Kaschke, Andreas Steppan, Fredl Schauer.

■ **With "Oh, Boris," Austria's Niki List comes up with a black comedy that is such an accomplishment in pure style, it may forfeit audience sympathy.**

Pic's bleak, morbid style and the gruesome comedy is underscored by Hanus Polak's cinematography. He enlarges detail to the point of the grotesque while moving vividly with the action in frames of larger scope. Action is such that it would have packed a wallop even if seen only at a distance.

Three sisters, old Margaretha, middle-aged Sophie and youngish Clara, tyrannize each other in their old suburban villa in the middle of a large garden.

Margaretha steals the monthly installments on their joint inheritance. Sophie is reduced to the role of housekeeper and cook.

Clara, who once had an affair with now-famous concert pianist Boris, plays Liszt at full blast on her record player while the sisters allow her 30 minutes (no more, no less) with Paul, the mailman and neighbor who brings the inheritance payments around.

The morbidity of all this is explored and added to by character delineations that could be inspired either by Arthur Kopit's "Oh, Dad, Poor Dad, Mama's Hung You In The Closet And I'm Feeling So Bad" or by Robert Aldrich's "Whatever Happened To Baby Jane?" as the story proceeds to have the two older sisters kill off each other. Or are the deaths suicides out of spite?

The mailman buries the first body in the garden, then moves in to take over the oldest sister's role as family tyrant. He even spends most of his time in her wheelchair.

This literally brings about the demise of sister No. 2.

When Boris (whose letters to Clara over the years were hidden by the sisters) finally turns up, Clara is in the midst of a murderous demolition spree of her own. There is a certain logic to the action, but it is hard to attach much sympathy to any single member of his macabre household. So "Oh, Boris" stays relentlessly ghastly and ghoulish.

It's acted with talent and fervor by its small German and Austrian cast, and its fine rhythmic storytelling pacing never lets up. All the while, however, the film lacks the elements of madcap slapstick and human compassion that could have made it all really palatable.

(List bowed in 1982 with "Malaria," a fine exercise in pop art stylistics, and went on to a modicum of international fest praise and some sales for "Miller's Office" and "Sternberg — A Shooting Star.") — *Kell.*

Jezebel's Kiss

Cannes   A Shapiro Glickenhaus Entertainment presentation of a Film Warriors production. Executive producer, Seth M. Willenson. Produced by Eric F. Sheffer. Written and directed by Harvey Keith. Camera (color), Brian Reynolds; editor, Mort Fallick; music, Mitchel Forman; art director, Alan Baron; production manager, Alain Siller; assistant director, Tom Archuleta; casting, Cathy Henderson, Michael Cutler. No MPAA Rating. Reviewed at the Cannes Film Festival (market), May 11, 1990. Running time: **97 MIN.**

Jezebel	Katherine Barrese
Ben Faberson	Malcolm McDowell
Virginia De Leo	Meredith Baxter-Birney
Amanda Faberson	Meg Foster
Dan Riley	Everett McGill
Margie De Leo	Elizabeth Ruscio
Hunt Faberson	Brent Fraser
Dr. Whatley	Bert Remsen

■ **"Jezebel's Kiss" is a contrived revenge tale entirely built around the buxom charms of Katherine Barrese. The teasing ad campaign may pull in a few customers, but video is the natural place for this indifferently made effort.**

To begin with, Harvey Keith's screenplay makes little sense. Barrese plays Jezebel (she refuses ever to give her last name), who arrives at a beachside community after a car driven by Hunt (Brent Fraser), drunken son of real-estate developer Faberson (Malcolm McDowell) knocks her off her motorbike.

Apparently unscathed, she settles into the Faberson home and proceeds to have sex with the three most significant men in the neighborhood: the sheriff (Everett McGill) and the Fabersons, father and son.

Throughout, black & white flashbacks refer to 8-year-old Jezebel witnessing the death of her beloved Granpa, who owned a beach hut coveted by Faberson for an ambitious development project. It seems Faberson and the sheriff were responsible for the old man's demise.

Why then, should Jezebel give each of them, plus Faberson Jr., the pleasure of a sexual encounter with her? What kind of vengeance is this? It makes no sense, of course, except in the context of showing as much of Barrese as often as possible.

Barrese isn't called upon to act a great deal, and nor is McDowell (in one of his most thankless roles). Other thesps, among them Meg Foster as McDowell's hysterical wife, tend to overemote.

Pic does deliver the requisite number of sex scenes, but without any coherent context. Editing (Mort Fallick) is scrappy and camerawork (Brian Reynolds) uneven. Strictly for undemanding, unrequited male chauvinists. — *Strat.*

Flex

Cannes A Triax Entertainment release of a North Star Entertainment Group production. (Intl. sales, Double Helix Films.) Executive producer, Jack Munari. Written, produced and directed by Harry Grant. Camera (color), Dan Swietlik; editor, Skip Williams, Steve Denicola; music, Harry Manfredini; in Ultra-Stereo; production design, Gary Randall; codirectors, Pat Domenico, Sally Marshall. Reviewed at the Cannes Film Festival (market), May 11, 1990. MPAA Rating: R. Running time: **87 MIN.**
Vince DeCola . . . . Harry Grant
Kim . . . . Lorin Jean Vail
Gina Carlino . . . . Wendy Fraser
Ken Waller . . . . Ken Waller
Tom Steele . . . . Tom Platz
Stevie . . . . Dale Levine

 A gallon of sweat glistens and drips off bulging biceps and thigh muscles in an appropriately billed "steamy drama set in the world of gyms, athletes and bodybuilding." Plot line is thin in this low-budget effort headed straight for video, and interest is probably limited to curiosity seekers.

First-time helmer Harry Grant (Mr. Los Angeles and Mr. Southern California) doubles as lead Vince DeCola, a gym trainer at an upscale hotel in San Diego. In

film's beginning, Vince is taking melancholy walks by the sea at sunset in an attempt to overcome the loss of his g.f. Kim, a vacuous blonde whose great smile and body ensure her popularity.

Vince's obsession with owning his own gym lead him to dally with wealthy Gina Carlino, who tries to convince her father to back Vince. Dad's a tough cookie who sees through Vince and sets him up in a tryst with his secretary. Inadvertently both Gina and Kim crash in on the entwined lovers and afterwards, Vince is worked over by some thugs.

A phony psychological motivation for Vince's behavior comes in his short talk with Kim about his dysfunctional background. Boss Ken Waller delivers the "message" of the film to down-and-out Vince: "You lack commitment to anything."

Vince finds some meaning to life by helping Stevie, a handicapped boy train for the Special Olympics and presumably reassesses his priorities. Meanwhile, Kim has become involved with Tom Steele (Tom Platz, Mr. Universe), a musclebound superstar.

The inane dialog and amateurish handling of the actors deprives them of much sympathy. The mostly hostile exchanges between Kim and Vince are followed by fairly tame marathon lovemaking. Much of the last quarter of the flick is close-quarter scrutiny of grunting and groaning bodybuilding sessions. Sequence's essentially a promo that might appeal to exercise enthusiasts.

Harry Manfredini's blaring rock score with puerile lyrics seems somehow appropriate for this abrasive view of a subculture. — *Sam.*

Diving In

Cannes A Maurer/Shaw Prods. presentation of a Creative Edge Films production. (Intl. sales, Skouras Pictures.) Executive producers, Michael Maurer, Mark Shaw. Produced by Martin Wiley. Directed by Strathford Hamilton. Screenplay, Eric Edson; camera (color), Hanania Baer; editor, Marcy Hamilton. Reviewed at the Cannes Film Festival (market), May 11, 1990. No MPAA Rating. Running time: **88 MIN.**
Wayne . . . . Matt Adler
Coach . . . . Burt Young
Jerome . . . . Matt Lattanzi
Terry . . . . Kristy Swanson
Amanda . . . . Yolanda Jilot

■ **A competent but strictly formula teen pic destined for small screen life, "Diving In" is the standard story of winning against the odds, peopled by stock characters of bullies, bimbos and burdensome adults.**

Scenario this time is set against a struggle to succeed in diving, with tentative teen Matt Adler trying to make the Olympic team. Along the way he has to trounce Matt Lattanzi, state champion diver, girl-getting leader of the pack, and erstwhile boyfriend of Adler's sister, Kristy Swanson.

Jaded coach Burt Young won't help him, so counterpart Yolanda Jilot, who just happens to be an Olympic diver, comes to his aid. She of course not only teaches him how to dive, but gets involved romantically, although that's made none too clear at the time.

Sugar-sweet ending is in keeping with the strictly black & white elements. The diving angle is an interesting backdrop, and the pic's well-made by music clipper Strathford Hamilton, but it's a small film, made before in many forms. — *Doch.*

Weiningers Nacht
(Weininger's Last Night)
(AUSTRIAN)

Cannes A Wega Film Prods. Vienna, Camera-Film Berlin production. Produced by Veit Heiduschka. Directed by Paulus Manker. Screenplay, Manker based on the stage play "Weiningers Nacht" by Joshua Sobol; camera (color), Walter Kindler; editor, Ingrid Koller, Marie Homolkova; music, Hansgeorg Koch; sound, Walter Ammann, Karl Schlifelner; set decoration, Birgit Voss; costumes, Voss, Erika Navas; production manager, Michael Katz, Gebhard Zupan. Reviewed at the Cannes Film Festival (market). Running time: **100 MIN.**
Otto Weininger . . . . . . Paulus Manker
Adelaide Weininger/Adele . . Hilde Sochor
Double . . . . Josefin Platt
Leopold Weininger/
Sigmund Freud . . . . . . Sieghardt Rupp
Clara . . . . Andrea Eckert
Berger . . . . Peter Faerber
August Strindberg/
Paul Julius Moebius . . . Hermann Schmid

■ **"Weiningers Nacht" is an excellent lensing of a play at the Vienna Volkstheater. Subtitled "The Soul Of A Jew," the heavy going, intellectual German-lingo pic's only chance for theatrical distribution is in the arthouse and fest circuits. Public tv is possible; homevid nil.**

Otto Weininger was a 23-year-old doctor of philosophy who, driven by his inexplicable homosexuality and loathing of his Jewish extraction, committed suicide in Beethoven's death chamber.

Through the night of Oct. 3, 1903, Weininger's life unfolds in a series of flashbacks revealing the reasons for the tortured intellectual's total self-abnegation. Set during a time when anti-Semitism was developing in Austria, Weininger denounces his faith and has himself baptized as a Protestant, unlike other Viennese Jewish converts, who turned to Catholicism.

After completing his masterpiece, "Geschlecht und Charakter" (Sex and Character), Weininger meets Sigmund Freud, who accuses him of plagiarism and fails to recommend the text to a publisher. The book contains Weininger's ideas on women and Judaism, revealed by such statements as "The absolute Jew is without a soul" and "The lowest of men is still infinitely higher than the highest of women."

The German writer, Paul Julius Moebius, author of "On the Physiological Deficiency of Women," also attacks Weininger, saying the ideas were his.

The intellectual ferment in Vienna at the fin-de-siècle, ideologically marked by Marxism, Christian socialism, German nationalism, political anti-Semitism and Zionism, forms the background to the film, which was shot in 16m and blown up to 35m.

Despite the excellent cast and a superb performance by Paulus Manker as Weininger, the film's intellectual structure limits audience possibilities. — *Kind.*

Viva Villaveien!
(Crazy Neighbors)
(NORWEGIAN)

Cannes A KF release of Team Film production with NRK/TV. Produced by Mattis Mathiesen. Directed by Tor M. Törstad. Screenplay, Lennart Lidström; camera (Eastmancolor), Bengt Kristiansen; editor, Robert Rolén; music, Geir Böhren. Bent Aserud; sound, Stein ödegaard, Tom Matsen; production management, Anne Birte Brunvold. Reviewed at Cannes Film Festival (market), May 19, 1990. Running time: **92 MIN.**
Reidar Frank/Preben . . Brasse Brännström
Sigurd Vatne/Torben . . . . Sverre Hansen
Mrs. Lindeberg . . . . Elsa Lystad
Tourist Guide Kleveland . . . . Karl Sundby

■ **"Crazy Neighbors" takes the characters of a popular Nor-**

wegian sitcom called "Long Live Suburbia!" and leaves them to sink or swim in a full-length feature.

They mostly sink as writer Lennart Lidström and helmer Tor M. Törstad bring them, unbeknownst to each other, on a holiday to the Canary Islands. Having kept up fighting all through the tv series, the characters are not about to suddenly make peace just because they are away from home. After getting lost in the desert, thrown in jail and driving a Norse tourist guide stark staring mad, they all return to Oslo on stretchers.

Sverre Hansen and Swedish guest star Brasse Brannström, both in double roles to create mistaken identity plot twists, supply nimble farcical comedy. Karl Sundby as the guide goes gloriously mad, too. Visual farce mechanics are handled reasonably well by helmer Törstad.

What is missing is a resemblance between any of the characters and ordinary human beings. Familiar to home audiences via their tv exposure, they will probably have domestic audiences cheering them once more, but the English subtitling would seem an expense unlikely to pay off. — *Kell.*

Circuitry Man

Cannes A Skouras Pictures release of an IRS Media presentation. Produced by Steven Reich, John Schouweiler. Executive producers, Miles A. Copeland III, Paul Colichman. Directed by Steven Lovy. Screenplay, Steven and Robert Lovy; camera (Foto-Kem color), Jamie Thompson; editor, Jonas Thaler; music, Deborah Holland; production designer, Robert Lovy. Reviewed at Cannes Film Festival (market), May 15, 1990. Running time. **87 MIN.**

Danner . . . . Jim Metzler
Lori . . . . Dana Wheeler-Nicholson
Juice . . . . Lu Leonard
Plughead . . . . Vernon Wells
Yoyo . . . . Barbara Alyn Woods
Also with: Dennis Christopher.

■ **This high-tech action-adventure set in the near future borrows a bit from past hits of the genre ("Bladerunner," "Mad Max"). Appealing leads, a believable romantic twist, okay tech credits and a tongue-in-cheek humor add up to escapist fun with an underlying ecological message that should win over general audiences.**

Los Angeles is depicted as having poisonous air unfit to breath. The city moves underground where greed is the primary motivator and unsavory violent types roam the streets. The only truly futuristic aspect is the move underground.

Luscious blonde Lori (Dana Wheeler of "Fletch") has been working as a bodyguard for Juice (Lu Leonard), a female gangleader. Lori wants to clean up her act and go straight but has one last assignment, delivering computer microchips to New York. The chips are electronic narcotics that deliver an exhilarating high when plugged into a user's brain.

Lori meets Juice in an underworld nightclub to make the connection, but police arrive on the scene. When a shootout begins, the lights go out and Lori escapes with the chips, pursued by the police and Juice's gang.

Leading the pack is Plughead (Vernon Wells), a sadistic addict whose bald head is equipped with a convenient array of receptacles allowing him to get a buzz off chips or better yet tap directly into others' brain waves and his attractive but sour companion, Yoyo (Barbara Alyn Woods).

Lori pairs up with Danner (Jim Metzler of "Old Gringo," "The River's Edge"), a sexy and sympathetic biosynthetic android who still clings to the old-fashioned notion of finding and maintaining true love. Leech (Dennis Christopher), a twisted character who imparts his favorite recipe for cooking the slimy creatures that gave him his name, convinces Lori and Danner to take him to New York by the dangerously polluted "topside," in exchange for use of some oxygen.

Lori and Danner are doublecrossed by Leech and left stranded at "The Last Gasp Cafe," an oxygen station, in which they have a humorous run-in with the locals. They develop a hankering for each other as they vow to reach New York, struggling against oxygen shortages, kinky adversaries and the police.

The leads are likable and generate some chemistry in love scenes, and the supporting cast provides as much humor as suspense. Tech credits are fine with good lensing, the bluesy country-western score a standout, and sci-fi effects are modest but effective.

Pic holds up well enough on the widescreen, but its proper niche will be carved in video action.
— *Sam.*

Werther
(SWEDISH)

Cannes A Swedish Film Institute presentation of Meyerateljeerna/Alexandersson/de Geer production. Produced by Freddy Olsson, Lisbeth Gabrielsson. Directed by Hakan Alexandersson. Screenplay, Alexandersson with Johann P. Eckermann, Tomas Norstroem, as based on Goethe's "The Suffering On The Young Werther;" camera (Eastmancolor), Christer Strandell; editor, Tomas Taeng; music, Kjell Westling; production design, Carl Johan de Geer. Reviewed at Cannes Film Festival (market), May 16, 1990. Running time: **92 MIN.**

Lessing . . . . Gert Fylking
Lotte/Lotta . . . . Ulrika Hansson
Walther . . . . Peter Kneip
Emilia . . . . Ellen Lamm
Ossian . . . . Jon Mellquist
Max Karlsson . . . . . . Tomas Norstroem
Also with: Peter Sjoequist, Lena Stroemdahl, Goeran Thorell, Pernilla Glaser.

■ **The cast has a fine time mugging lightly through their roles in "Werther," which may be very much an inside joke in Swedish film circles. Offshore, the world in general could share in its fun, but pic will probably be restricted to minor fests or the elitist art circuit.**

"Werther" is a spoof feature about the making of a film based on Goethe's romantic 18th century novel "The Sufferings Of Young Werther," which literally inspired hosts of young readers to emulate the hero and shoot themselves.

Director Hakan Alexandersson and production designer Carl Johan de Geer have been working together for years outside the system, making films that few ever saw. They work on broader comedy turf here with a story that has a tough producer (Gert Fylking) harassing his director (Tomas Norstroem) throughout a shooting doomed to end up in a ditch.

The fictional writer-director is a hapless fellow but also a strong dreamer. When he finally succeeds in getting the producer to stay out of his way (if only very temporarily) and his actress-wife to give up getting a part in the film, he promptly falls in love with his debutante leading lady.

He also falls in love with Goethe's novel to a degree where he, at the end, lifts a pistol to his own temple. This happens, as film's lead actors roar off together on a motorbike. All this comes out fairly funny and looks good.

The producer did not yell in vain, "Remember production values!" from his position in a helicopter hovering above the location. — *Kell.*

Simadia Tis Nichtes
(Scars Of The Night)
(GREEK)

Cannes A Panos Kokkinopoulos/Greek Film Center/ET 1 coproduction. Executive producer, Bessie Voudouri. Written and directed by Panos Kokkinopoulos; editor, Dimitri Papacostandis; editor, Takis Yannopoulos; music, Eleni Karaindrou; art direction, Dora Lelouda. Reviewed at the Cannes Film Festival (market), May 14, 1990. Running time: **94 MIN.**

Maria . . . . Katerina Lehou
Kosmas . . . . Antonis Katsaris
Also with: Dimitri Katalifos.

■ **Good production values, an attractive cast and a promising storyline are not enough to save this routine thriller with folkloric overtones. The plot wanders in many directions and viewers might be tempted to do the same.**

The atmospheric introduction begins with a recitation, in classic Greek dramatic fashion, of the legend of Maria, a mysterious sorceress who was in possession of a talisman that protected an island from pestilence and destruction. Consequently, she became regarded as a saint.

Alkis (Stratos Tzortzoglou, appealing lead of "Striker With The No. 9") is released from prison and begins a search for his friend Vassilis who owes him money and presumably an apology for sticking him with a five-year rap.

He arrives on the same Greek island described in the introduction just before its yearly feast day and to his surprise is led to Vassilis' funeral. As he opens the coffin, he notices large gouges and strange markings on his chest. The ominous silence of the crowd is broken by an excited blind man who shouts warnings and urges Alkis to leave. He catches the penetrating gaze of Maria (Katerina Lehou), a sultry local beauty.

A tip from a local worker leads him to the unsympathetic baker Kosmas, Vassilis' uncle (established character actor Antonis Katsaris). He also warns Alkis about continuing his quest and attributes Vassilis' demise to the acting out of old "fairy tales," in which he thought he could walk on air and plunged to his death from his roof.

Alkis encounters Maria later in the evening and she makes insinuating remarks. Despite more warnings from her to drop his pursuit, Alkis persists. Because of a yearning for Maria, Alkis volunteers to help her find the talisman left in her grandmother's possession to ensure the safety of the island.

Much of pic's latter section is devoted to this quest. Alkis witnesses confusing primitive rituals administered by Kosmos, is pursued by a small whirlwind that sounds like a rabid dog and has weird erotic dreams that end with Maria gouging his chest.

After falling down a well, this Alkis in Wonderland clambers through a cave and encounters various difficulties before emerging on the port. The villagers are preparing for their lumbering ritual dance around an elevated straw and wooden symbol that is ignited. Maria seems completely possessed and under the control of Kosmos, an inpassive angel of death.

The lensing is of high quality and shows off the quaint architecture of medieval villages but the special effects are feeble and unconvincing.

The haunting score of Eleni Karaindrou, emerging as Greece's finest movie composer, strives to establish a supernatural aura but muddled plot and wooden acting deprive the film of any real suspense. More animation is present in the everyday settling of a bill in a tavern than is evident in any key scenes.

Veteran tv director Kokkinopoulos' first feature is unlikely to attract much interest in theatrical release at home or abroad. A four-part miniseries or video version could get some action by capitalizing on eye and ethnic appeal.
— *Sam.*

Future Zone

Cannes An Action Intl. Studios production in association with David Carradine Entertainment. Produced by Kimberly Casey. Executive producers, David Winters, Bruce Lewin. Written and directed by David A. Prior. Camera (color), Voya Mikulic; music, William T. Stromberg; associate producers, Gail Jensen, Regina Salszberg Hulkower, Mandi Perekh. Reviewed at Cannes Film Festival (market), May 17, 1990. Running time: **80 MIN.**
John Tucker . . . . David Carradine
Billy . . . . Ted Prior
Marion . . . . Gail Jensen
Hoffman . . . . Patrick Culliton
Also with: Ron Taft, Renee Cline, Charles Napier.

■ **Low-budget action adventure flick probably will not sustain a theatrical engagement, even if capitalizing on presence of lead David Carradine, and**

video appeal is limited to the bloodthirsty. Gratuitous violence, blatant sexism and foul language combine to create a jaundiced view of a Southern town that's both distasteful and boring.

Carradine is John Tucker, a tough cop who's the fastest gun in Alabama, perhaps the entire South. He has not endeared himself to the underworld, nonchalantly picking off drug pushers, snarling mobsters and smalltime thugs more quickly than they can extinguish one another.

In true Western tradition, Tucker is challenged by Billy (Ted Prior), a muscular upstart, a New Age cowboy who wears shimmering seethrough tee shirts and a rhinestone stud in his ear. From Tucker and Billy's first conversation in a shooting contest, their real relationship is quite obvious and deprives the script of any suspense.

Billy wants to follow in Tucker's footsteps and manages to convince Tucker to show him the ropes. They survive shootouts, car crashes, explosions and fist fights between them.

All the time, Tucker's long-suffering wife Marion (badly miscast Gail Jensen), prepares elaborate dinners, garbs herself in revealing lingerie and finally threatens to leave Tucker when none of these ploys succeed in getting him to stay in for an evening so that she can tell him she is pregnant.

Eventually it is revealed that Billy has come back from 30 years in the future via a time machine in order to change Tucker's destiny.

Billy has a crude charm. Carradine rarely varies his pained expression. It is interesting to note that Carradine also is featured in ''Bird On The Wire,'' a recently released megabudget road movie topling Goldie Hawn and Mel Gibson. His indiscriminate choice of films results in another tasteless endeavor.

Camerawork is uneven, often sloppy. Score is tedious and supporting cast does little more than walk through their roles before being blown away. — *Sam.*

Porttikielto taivaasen
(Banned From Heaven)
(FINNISH)

Cannes A Finnkino presentation of National Filmi production. Produced by Marko Roehr. Directed by Tapio Suominen. Screenplay by

Suominen, Jorma Kalliokoski; camera (Eastmancolor), Timo Heinaenen; editor, Suominen; music, Johnny Lee Michaels; sound, Camus-Vargas; production design-costume design, Pertti Hilkamo; assistant director, Nadja Pyykkoe. Reviewed at Cannes Film Festival (market), May 18, 1990. Running time: **96 MIN.**
With: Kari Sara, Satu Silva, Nina Nurminen, Minna Aaltonen, Riikka Suikkari.

■ **Offshore homevid sales are in the cards for "Banned From Heaven," a glossy-looking production of Tapio Suominen's relentlessly grim look at high-class prostitution in Helsinki. It's fiction using a lot of researched facts.**

Although certain sequences have the look of soft-core porn, Suominen intends to scare rather than charm when he describes the constant fear in which his group of girls for hire in a luxury hotel live.

The hotel manager, the girls' pimp, is as relentless in his demands on performance from his girls as he is of the members of an ice-hockey team he also owns.

The girls are all described as rather feeble-minded sentimental fools, so it is hard to attach much sympathy even when they are harrassed and beaten.

Cuddling their frilly dolls are the only consolation in the poor girls' sordid lives. Some start popping pills or hitting the bottle.

Nothing new in ''Banned From Heaven,'' no social outcast depths or psychologies explored. The playing by all thesps is convincing. The film moves well and has excellent cinematography along with a fine modern jazz score. — *Kell.*

Father
(AUSTRALIAN)

Sydney A Barron Films-Latin Quarter production (Intl. sales: Latin Quarter Films.) Executive producer, Paul Barron. Produced by Damien Parer, Tony Cavanaugh, Graham Hartley. Directed by John Power. Screenplay, Cavanaugh, Hartley; camera (Eastmancolor), Dan Burstall; editor, Kerry Regan; music, Peter Best; sound, Andrew Ramage; production design, Phil Peters; production manager, John Wild; assistant director, Stuart Wood. Reviewed at Greater Union screening room, Sydney, April 30, 1990. Running time: **100 MIN.**
Joe Mueller . . . . Max Von Sydow
Anne Winton . . . . Carol Drinkwater
Iya Zetnick . . . . Julia Blake
Bobby Winton . . . . Steve Jacobs
George Coleman . . . . . . Tim Robertson

■ **In an unfortunate coincidence, "Father" is strikingly similar to Costa-Gavras' "Music Box," but the Aussie**

film stands a chance at the international wickets as a variation on the theme. "Father" boasts a good screenplay, firm direction and a couple of very strong performances.

The story unfolds in Melbourne where German-born Joe Mueller (Max Von Sydow) has lived since the war. Since his wife's death, and his retirement, he's lived with his devoted daughter, Anne (Carol Drinkwater), son-in-law Bobby (Steve Jacobs) and two granddaughters in a comfortable apartment above a bar Bobby owns.

Their peaceful lifestyle is disrupted by a television program in which an old woman, Iya Zetnick (Julia Blake) accuses Mueller of wartime atrocities. Mueller vigorously denies the charges, but winds up in an Australian court.

He's acquitted, however, after a journalist informs his daughter that Zetnick had previously laid similar charges in Britain and has a history of mental illness. This is not the end of the story, however, and the fadeout is very similar to that of ''Music Box.''

Writers Tony Cavanaugh and Graham Hartley introduce an extra element into the drama, however: a more general war guilt. Son-in-law is a Vietnam vet and admits that he knows all about making war against civilians. ''It's in all of us,'' he says. Steve Jacobs gives an impressive performance.

Von Sydow is a tower of strength as the accused German who may, or may not, be guilty, while Blake is extremely touching as the accusing survivor of Nazi atrocities. Her climactic scene in the picture, in which she breaks into the family's apartment at night, is extremely powerful.

A few improbabilities lie in the script, such as why a tv program would broadcast accusations against a man without attempting to contact him beforehand for his response. But on the whole, this is a well-constructed drama.

Steve Jodrell (director of producer Paul Barron's earlier, critically successful ''Shame'') was originally to have helmed ''Father,'' but ankled during preproduction.

He was replaced by John Power, who returns to the cinema screen for the first time since ''The Picture Show Man'' (1977) (he's slaved away in tv drama in the interval). Power brings intelligence and strength to the material.

Technical credits, starting with

Dan Burstall's very professional camerawork, are all firstrate.

The bottom line is that there's no escaping comparisons with the Costa-Gavras film, and it remains to be seen how distribs, critics and the public will respond to this Australian variation on the topical subject of war guilt. — *Strat.*

Blood Oath
(AUSTRALIAN)

Sydney A Greater Union (Australia) release (Sovereign Pictures-intl. distribution) of a Village Roadshow Pictures presentation of a Blood Oath production, with the participation of the Australian Film Finance Corp. Executive producers, Graham Burke, Greg Coote, John Tarnoff. Produced by Charles Waterstreet, Denis Whitburn, Brian Williams. Directed by Stephen Wallace. Screenplay, Whitburn, Williams; camera (Eastmancolor), Russell Boyd; editor, Nicholas Beauman; music, David McHugh, Stewart D'Arrietta, Don Miller-Robinson; sound, Ben Osmo; production design, Bernard Hides; costumes, Roger Kirk; production manager, Helen Watts; assistant director, Chris Webb; coproducer, Annie Bleakley; line producer, Richard Brennan; casting, Alison Barrett, Nobuaki Murooka. Reviewed at Village-Roadshow screening room, Sydney, May 1, 1990. Running time: **105 MIN.**

Capt. Robert Cooper . . . . . Bryan Brown
Vice-Admiral Baron Takahashi . George Takei
Major Tom Beckett . . . . . Terry O'Quinn
Major Frank Roberts . . . . John Bach
Lt. Hideo Tanaka . . . . Toshi Shioya
Mike Sheedy . . . . John Clarke
Sister Carol Littell . . . . . . Deborah Unger
Pvt. Jimmy Fenton . . . . John Polson
Lt. Jack Corbett . . . . Russell Crowe
Sgt. Keenan . . . . Nicholas Eadie
Capt. Wadami Ikeuchi . . . Tetsu Watanabe
Shinji Matsugae . . . . Sokyu Fujita
Lt. Col. Johnson . . . . Ray Barrett
Lt. Noboru Kamura . . Kazuhiro Muroyama
Pvt. Talbot . . . . Jason Donovan
Flt-Lt. Eddy Fenton . . . . . . David Argue

■ **"Blood Oath" is a courtroom drama that raises questions about wartime crime and punishment. A forceful performance from Bryan Brown as the prosecuting officer should attract discriminating audiences worldwide, though the film is more arthouse than mainstream material.**

The drama, based on actual incidents, takes place on the Indonesian island of Ambon in late 1945. Ambon, site of a Japanese POW camp for Australian prisoners, was under the command of aristocratic, Oxford-educated Vice-Admiral Baron Takahashi (George Takei). Pic opens with the discovery of more than 300 bodies of Aussie soldiers in a shallow grave.

Brown plays Capt. Cooper, Aussie officer assigned to prosecute Takahashi and his men for war crimes. He finds his hands tied at every turn, mainly because an American "observer" at the trial, Major Beckett (Terry O'Quinn), doesn't want Takahashi found guilty, figuring he'll be more useful in reconstructed postwar Japan.

Cooper doggedly tries to prove that Takahashi ordered the execution of the 300 Aussies, but the Japanese officer is found not guilty. (His men remain tight-lipped and there's no proof of the crime.)

Cooper next tries to fix the blame for the murder of four RAAF airmen who crashed near Ambon. But the officer in command of that execution (Tetsu Watanabe) commits hara-kari. The ultimate irony is that a Christian, English-speaking Japanese signals officer, who has voluntarily given himself up and who shows considerable integrity throughout, is the only Japanese to face a firing squad at the film's conclusion.

At least half the film takes place in the courtroom, and director Stephen Wallace stages these surefire scenes with maximum tension, helped by a fine gallery of Australian and Japanese actors.

This is Brown's strongest performance to date. He brings sardonic humor and a wholly convincing feeling of frustration to the tenacious character of Cooper (who is actually based on the father of coscripter/coproducer Brian A. Williams).

Also worthy of note are John Bach as the devious judge advocate; John Clarke as a battered journalist covering the trial, and John Polson as a beaten and tortured survivor who gives damning evidence against the Japanese.

Newcomer Deborah Unger makes an impression in her few scenes as a sympathetic nurse (romance is kept firmly at bay, however). Teen fave Jason Donovan (costar of the "Neighbors" tv series, a hit in several territories) seems to have succumbed to the editor's scissors, since he has only one line of dialog and a few meaningful looks to contribute.

Among the many talented Japanese actors on display, "Star Trek" vet Takei is a knockout as the arrogant Takahashi; Toshi Shioya is very moving as the ultimate scapegoat; Watanabe is commanding as the brutal camp sadist, and Sokyu Fujita is effective as the defense counsel.

With budget reported at $10-million, "Blood Oath" is expensive by Aussie standards, especially since so much of it is interiors. Even the jungle appears to be studio-located (great production design by Bernard Hides). Russell Boyd did his usual pro job of cinematography.

Screenplay by Williams and Denis Whitburn is on the wordy side, but manages to keep the complex narrative clear. Wallace also deserves credit for lucidity. More might have been made of the bombing of Hiroshima and Nagasaki (Shioya's family was killed in the blast) and that extra level of guilt and responsibility.

As a dramatized conflict between the extremes of political expediency and legal certainty, however, "Blood Oath" makes for a satisfying drama.

Interestingly, Brown's first major role was in Bruce Beresford's "Breaker Morant," also a courtroom drama exploring similar themes. In the earlier pic, Brown was a victim of injustice at fadeout, and the finger was pointed at the British. Here, postwar U.S. policy comes in for criticism, and O'Quinn perfectly delineates the ugly American.

"Blood Oath" may be seen in some quarters as anti-Japanese, but it's clearly a serious attempt to shed new light on a 45-year-old tragedy. The result is a film of considerable power. — *Strat.*

ARCHIVE FILM REVIEWS

L'Atalante
(FRENCH-B&W)

Paris A Gaumont restoration and release of a Jacques Louis-Nounez production, first released in Paris by Gaumont-Franco Film-Aubert Sept. 13, 1934 as "Le Chaland qui passe." Restoration supervisors, Pierre Philippe, Jean-Louis Bompoint. Restoration labs, Dames (image), Lobster Film/Ramses (sound), Exposure (special effects). Directed by Jean Vigo. Screenplay, Vigo, Albert Riéra, from an original scenario by Jean Guinée; camera (black & white), Boris Kaufman; editor, Louis Chavance; music, Maurice Jaubert; songs, Jaubert, Charles Goldblatt (lyrics); sound, Marcel Royné, Lucien Baujard; set design, Francis Jourdain; makeup, Acho Chakatouny; assistant directors, Riéra, Goldblatt, Pierre Merle. Reviewed at Gaumont, Neuilly, May 11, 1990. (In Cannes Film Festival, special presentation.) Running time: **89 MIN.**

Jean . . . . Jean Dasté
Juliette . . . . Dita Parlo
Pères Jules . . . . Michel Simon
Cabin boy . . . . Louis Lefèbvre
Peddler . . . . Gilles Margaritis

■ **Jean Vigo's "L'Atalante," one of the most magical (and most mangled) of French film masterpieces, has been restored in a new version which may cause some controversy among critics and archivists, but most certainly will provide a good deal more in cinematic pleasure and sense of rediscovery.**

Restoration world-preemed May 13 at the Cannes fest, where it introed a series of events devoted to film preservation. That was prior to its theatrical rerelease May 16 throughout France. The Cannes screening was apt, too, because one of the earliest champions of Vigo's artistic rehabilitation after World War II was Gilles Jacob, current fest general delegate.

"L'Atalante," an audaciously lyrical exploration of life and love aboard a Seine river barge, was butchered by its distrib, Gaumont, for its original 1934 release. Since then it has been seen (and admired) in various incomplete prints, though there were several attempts to restore cut material.

What that "original" version was may remain moot, since Vigo himself was too ill to edit the film (though he supervised from his sickbed). His death at age 29, just weeks after pic's catastrophic release, cut short a most promising incandescent career.

Now, 55 years later, Gaumont has made amends by investing some $250,000 in the reconstruction of "L'Atalante" to a form as close as possible to that trade-screened for an icy audience of distribs and exhibs in April 1934. Running time is now 89 minutes, apparent length of Vigo's definitive cut. There are some 10 minutes of restored footage, much of it lovely, all of it welcome.

Filmmakers Pierre Philippe and Jean-Louis Bompoint are responsible for the restoration, admirable in most respects, though certain editorial prerogatives are likely to reopen the debate on ethics of film reconstruction. Restorers worked with Vigo's personal shooting script and several hours of rushes deposited at the Cinemathèque Française, plus the memories of the production's surviving participants.

Most important (and discovered only early this year) was an

excellent nitrate print shown in Britain and preserved by the British National Film Archive. Copy clearly was prepared before the mutilation began, and, astonishingly, probably before the film was fully completed, since it's missing the breathtaking final shot (taken some time after filming ended officially): an aerial view of the barge, the "Atalante," plowing up the Seine to the accompaniment of Maurice Jaubert's unforgettable music.

Philippe and Bompoint effected some 40 editorial interventions. They range from the insertion of single shots and of entire scenes and bits of dramatic business to the technical execution of effects Vigo intended, but, probably due to his health and existing lab constraints, did not carry out.

Many of the additions are isolated shots of wistful beauty, such as fleeting images added to the opening sequence of the village wedding, where the principals, the barge captain and his young peasant wife, lovingly embodied by Jean Dasté and Dita Parlo (later to play the lonely German war widow in "The Grand Illusion"), are introduced.

Michel Simon, in one of his most beloved roles as the bizarre, tattooed, cat-loving mate, Père Jules, benefits from other insertions, such as a legendary shot (known from surviving photos) in which he sticks a lighted cigarette in his navel.

Then there is the restorers' most surprising interpolation: a short series of dissolves highlighting Simon's comical demonstration of Greek wrestling on the barge deck.

Vigo's script is precise in this effect, but it was never executed. Is there justification for doing what remained a written intention? The debate is open, but the result delightful.

The scene in the riverside cabaret, famous in good part for Jaubert's jaunty java, is more complete and more enchanting. Restored are the entirety of the witty sales pitch song by the itinerant peddler played with ethereal charm by Gilles Margaritis, who whets the young bride's desire to see Paris. Her unauthorized departure to the city triggers the couple's climactic crisis.

Parlo's near-tragic excursion is announced by another sequence (never entirely filmed) found among the rushes and reinstated, which shows an early runaway

attempt in a fogbound dock.

Philippe and Bompoint were also faced with the enigma of the stunning surreal shot of Dasté licking a block of ice. Taking a clue from matching shot numbers, they inserted it in the famous gramophone scene in which Simon and the cabin boy try to boost the spirits of Dasté, after he abandoned his wife in Paris.

Assembled from the surviving rushes, the new negative does full justice to Boris Kaufman's sublimely melancholy images of river and city life, not to mention the powerful erotic charge that characterizes the Dasté/Parlo relationship.

Though early French talkies were notorious for their scratchy, defective sound recording, the renovation of pic's soundtrack is frequently sensational. Not only can one fully savor the pleasures of Jaubert's score, but Simon's inimitable diction (a sound man's nightmare) is no longer a barrier to understanding some of the script's most quirky bits of dialog. — *Len.*

Der Lebende Leichman/ Zhivoi Trup
(The Living Corpse)
(GERMAN-SOVIET-B&W)

Berlin Stiftung Deutsche Kinematek (Berlin) restoration and presentation of a Mezhrapomfilm, Moscow/Prometheus-Film, Berlin/Landerfilm, Berlin, coproduction (1928). First released in Berlin by Prometheus-Film, Feb. 29, 1929. Restoration supervisor, Martin Koerber. Directed by Fedor Ozep. Screenplay, B. Gussman, Anatoly Marienhof, based on the play by Leo Tolstoy; camera (b&w), Anatoly Golovnya, Piel Jutzi, editor, Ozep, Vsevolod Pudovkin; music, Werner Schmidt-Boelcke; set design, Sergei Koslovski, Victor Simov; assistant director, Marc Sorkin, Georges Freedland. Length: 9,853 ft. Reviewed at the Stiftung Deutsche Kinematek, Berlin, April 1, 1990. Running time: **120 MIN.** (at 22 frames per second); **132 MIN.** (at 20 frames per second).
Fedya Protassov . . . . Vsevolod Pudovkin
Lisa Protassov . . . . Maria Jacobini
Sasha . . . . Viola Garden
Anna Pavlova . . . . Julie Serda
Masha . . . . Natasha Watznadze
Victor Karenin . . . . Gustav Diessl
The "Lady" . . . . Vera Mareskaya
Artemjev . . . . D. Wedensky
Petushkov . . . . Sergei Uralsky

■ "The Living Corpse" survived as little more than a historical footnote as the first official coproduction between Germany and the Soviet Union, and as acting vehicle for Vsevolod Pudovkin, better known as the director of such Soviet masterpieces as "Mother" and "Arsenal."

Imaginatively directed by Fedor Ozep, an underestimated pioneer of the Russian and Soviet film industry, pic is outstanding. Ozep took advantage of this coprod to continue his career in Germany (where he made the highly lauded early talkie, "The Murderer Dimitri Karamazov") and France, where he was largely consigned to routine commercial features.

He fled to North America in 1940, and finished his filmmaking days in Canada. The anonymity of his later films has unjustly obscured his genuine achievements in Russia and Germany as screenwriter and director.

"The Living Corpse" is one of the many adaptations made of Tolstoy's moral drama about a wayward husband whose efforts to free his unhappy spouse from conjugal bondage so that she can remarry are tragically obstructed by the religious fetters of Russian Orthodox society.

Pudovkin gives an immensely introverted performance that is a high watermark of silent thesping, even in the reductive sanitized screenplay, which transformed Tolstoy's debauched but sympathetic protagonist into a pure-hearted social rebel.

There is imaginative and narrative vigor in Ozep's direction, which vividly blends German and Soviet film aesthetics. The startling montage effects (such as the opening collage of church spires) liken this to Eisenstein. The many elaborately staged atmospheric setpieces (i.e. the tavern and flophouse sequences) establish a kinship to the German street films of the time. That Pudovkin participated in the preparation and editing of the film does not detract from Ozep's unmistakable contributions.

So much virtuosity takes a toll on the overall rhythm, and as a result the pacing suffers. But the cumulative effect, culminating in Pudovkin's suicide in an empty courtroom, is one of brooding poignancy and force.

West Berlin's Stiftung Deutsche Kinematek is behind the restoration, which involved a complex collation of extant prints conserved by several continental archives. Editorial continuity and image quality are admirable. Film preemed in Berlin last year and also opened the Pordenone Silent Film Festival.

Original score for pic's 1928 Berlin premiere has also been salvaged. Music is effective but the projection speed it imposes (22 frames per second) is too fast.
— *Len.*

Another 48 HRS.

Hollywood A Paramount Pictures release of a Lawrence Gordon production in association with Eddie Murphy Prods. Produced by Gordon, Robert D. Wachs. Directed by Walter Hill. Executive producers, Mark Lipsky, Ralph S. Singleton. Screenplay, John Fasano, Jeb Stuart, Larry Gross; story, Fred Braughton; camera (Technicolor), Matthew F. Leonetti; editor, Freeman Davies, Carmel Davies, Donn Aron; music, James Horner; sound (Dolby), Jerry Ross; production design, Joseph C. Nemec III; costume design, Dan Moore; art direction, Gary Wissner; set decoration, George R. Nelson; assistant directors, James R. Dyer, Barry K. Thomas; coproducer, D. Constantine Conte; associate producers, Raymond L. Murphy Jr., Kenneth H. Frith Jr.; casting, Jackie Burch. Reviewed at the Mann Village Theater, Westwood, June 4, 1990. MPAA Rating: R. Running time: **95 MIN.**

Reggie Hammond . . . . . . Eddie Murphy
Jack Cates . . . . Nick Nolte
Ben Kehoe . . . . Brion James
Blake Wilson . . . . Kevin Tighe
Frank Cruise . . . . Ed O'Ross
Willy Hickok . . . David Anthony Marshall
Cherry Ganz . . . . Andrew Divoff
Kirkland Smith . . . . Bernie Casey
Burroughs . . . . Brent Jennings
Malcolm Price . . . . Ted Markland
Amy Smith . . . . Tisha Campbell

■ Less a sequel than a remake, "Another 48 HRS." should cash in on its format and stars (who are both far bigger b.o. draws today than before), but pic disappoints in its failure, after eight years, to introduce even the faintest wrinkle of something new.

Pic's really misnamed, since it's not "Another 48 HRS." but the same "48 HRS.," the 1982 mismatched buddy action pic that helped launch a durable genre and the film career of Eddie Murphy.

The filmmakers have gone the calculated and crowd-pleasing route. They trace the path of the original almost step by step, down to Murphy belting out "Roxanne," kicking tail in a biker bar and finding himself in a precarious position in the final shootout. The warmth in the recognition factor is cooled by a sense of utter creative bankruptcy.

Director Walter Hill, reprising those chores along with most of the behind-the-scenes crew, knows the terrain and tills it with all the familiar elements: bawdy humor, cannon-loud gunplay, hissable bad guys and plenty of action.

Murphy and Nick Nolte manage to recapture some of their initial chemistry, but for the most part the film is curiously flat — in part due to a jumbled plot that's so quickly tied up at the end it seems everyone was in a hurry to get their checks and get out of town.

In fact, at 95 minutes the film feels as if it's been sliced to the bone, leaving in action and scenes showcasing Murphy's comedic talents while excising any connective material that wasn't deemed essential.

There's also a disturbing side to the initial setup, which has cop Jack Cates (Nolte) on the verge of losing his badge and Reggie Hammond (Murphy) still in prison, finishing a five-year stint after having been framed shortly after the events of the original film.

Those who remember the first "48 HRS." will recall that Reggie was due out of stir shortly and on the road to redemption. Depressingly, audience discovers he's been in prison this whole time and that Cates has ignored his plight —the better to let them remake the first pic, as the two again dislike each other and develop a grudging friendship.

The plot even hinges on the first film, as two hit men are dispatched to kill Murphy, one the brother of the lead baddie offed in "48 HRS."

Cates, meanwhile, has spent the past four years chasing a faceless drug kingpin called the Iceman, who paid for the hit on Reggie. He's been thwarted at every turn, however, leading Reggie to suspect corruption within the police department.

Hill and his trio of screenwriters choose the stale and predictable route at almost every turn, the plot being strictly a slender means of allowing Murphy and Nolte to strut their stuff.

In that respect, at least, the film doesn't disappoint, since the Reggie Hammond character is more perfectly suited to Murphy's talents than any role he's had since. It allows him to be snide and funny, yet tough and self-assured in a manner that doesn't come off as smugness.

Nolte looks much trimmer but still plays Cates as a growling bear, with a strong sense of right and John Wayne swagger. His character, too, has grown little since the first pic, having squandered his relationship with his girlfriend-turned-wife.

Hill, with his clenched-teeth direction, brings a lot of flair to action sequences. Most of the second-unit and stunt work is superb, including a terrific scene that culminates with a bus flipping over.

The conclusion, however, is an utter mess, with wanton gunplay and slow-motion shots that rob it of any suspense, until it's hard to ascertain or even care who's doing the shooting.

James Horner's score is again first-rate, while lenser Matthew F. Leonetti brings the same gritty look to the film he instilled in Hill's "Johnny Handsome."

Supporting players suffer in the stripped-down plot, even if Ted Markland, David Anthony Marshall and Andrew Divoff cut striking figures as the villains, a cross between a Hell's Angels nightmare and Charles Manson.

Brion James, Bernie Casey and Ed O'Ross are largely wasted in ill-defined roles, while Kevin Tighe is a mere caricature as the internal affairs officer after Cates.

It would be easier to forgive "Another 48 HRS." were the layoff not so long, or if there weren't films like "Lethal Weapon 2" that actually improved on their originals. As it is, chalk this one up to laziness as a belated effort to capitalize on its top-notch forebearer. — *Bril.*

Ghosts Can't Do It

San Francisco A Triumph release of an Epic Prods. picture. Produced by Bo Derek. Written and directed by John Derek. Camera (color), Derek; music, Junior Homrich, Randy Tico. No other credits available from distributor or production company. Reviewed at the Alexandria Theater, June 2, 1990. MPAA rating: R. Running time: **95 MIN.**

Kate . . . . Bo Derek
Scott . . . . Anthony Quinn
Winston . . . . Don Murray
Fausto . . . . Leo Damian
Angel . . . . Julie Newmar
Donald Trump . . . . Himself

■ A virile older man in "Ghosts Can't Do It" leaves a beautiful young widow so obsessively in love with him that she can't wait for her "great one" to get back from beyond the grave so she won't have to take up with handsome young men. The film was written and directed by virile older John Derek and stars his beautiful young wife, Bo Derek.

In concept and execution, there's enough Ernest Hemingway here for an Old Man and the CPR, a Farewell to Garments and a lifetime of entries in the dialog contests at Harry's Bar. "He has my heart!" Bo cries. "How can I live without my heart?"

Unfortunately for the husband, Anthony Quinn, his own heart is giving out as "Ghosts" gets under way, interrupting Bo's opening horseback ride in the Wyoming snows. He's very rich and they have this big mansion where she stores a lot of cute outfits and an endless supply of head coverings.

Quinn's days are clearly numbered. After a few final nibbles on Bo's lower lip, a loud noise thunders from upstairs, and before you know it, she's wearing a black fur hood with a veil and fussing at Quinn's ghost, "Damn you and your shotgun!"

In mourning, Bo journeys to their favorite South Seas island, where she can get naked on the beach and ponder Quinn's plan to find another body for himself. "You would take another body and make love to me," she exclaims. "I don't know, it sounds kinky."

Kinky or not, there's also business to tend to because raiders are swooping down on the $2-billion business Bo must now run. So it's off to Hong Kong and into the shower and out of the shower and into the pool, losing her towel and all the other usual stuff a beautiful young executive has to do before sitting down to negotiate with Donald Trump.

Of course, she's just mouthing the words that ghost Quinn whispers through the ether, but they defeat Trump, who retreats with gracious stares into those big blue eyes and assures her, "You're too pretty to be bad."

Anyway, it's back to the island and time to give some serious consideration to finding Quinn a corpus. The obvious choice is hunky Leo Damian, who has a terrific smile, an incredible body and such a lousy personality that nobody will moan his loss.

Quinn can take possession of the property only at the moment Damian dies, which sets up the need for a murder Bo doesn't want to do. The anxiety is awful and right in the middle of one emotional moment, she just dumps her head into the hot tub. Yes, she does, and it helps.

Working it all out, she gets naked some more, flies a plane, drives a train and dances barefoot while the men drool until a fire-and-brimstone preacher suddenly appears and she has to dump another bucket of water on her head, leaving her wet clothes clinging to her bosom.

Fortunately, Damian goes diving and caught in the nets. Bo has to bring him to the surface for mouth-to-mouth. It's a tense moment: If Damian is dead already, he's a wasted vessel. But if she can breathe life into him for just a second before he dies again . . .

Back at the ranch, Bo has a new husband who looks like Damian but talks like Quinn. Bo, however, still talks like Bo. "Did I make bells ring for you?" she coos from the pillow. "You make the whole world ring for me," he answers, suggesting that some conversational skill must be sacrificed in spiritual adventures.

Technical achievements — as usual when John photographs Bo — consist of a lot of tight closeups from chin to hat. These are very good tight closeups. And great hats. — *Har.*

Passport
(FRENCH-SOVIET-
ISRAELI)

Cannes A Passport Prods. production. Produced by Constantin Alexandrov, Phillipe Ratton. Directed by Guerogui Danelia. Screenplay, Danelia, Revaz Gabriadze, Arkady Hait, Constantin Alexandrov, Philippe Ratton; additional dialog by Jean-Pierre Carrasso; camera (color), Vadim Youssov; editor, Catherine Kelber, Tatiana Egoritcheva; music, Guya Kantcheli; production design, Dimitri Takaishvili. Reviewed at the Cannes Intl. Film Festival (in Perspectives on French Cinema), May 16, 1990. Running time: 105 MIN.
Yasha/Merab . . . . Gerard Darmon
Also with: Oleg Iankovski, Nathalia Goundareva, Armen Djigarkhanian, Mamouka Kikaleishvili, Christian Fellat, Sharon Hacohen-Brandon and Albert Nirschl.
(In French with English subtitles)

■ Notable as the first French-Soviet-Israeli coproduction and yet another demonstration of Mikhail Gorbachev's liberation of Soviet filmmaking, "Passport" is also timely in light of the international controversy over the emigration of Soviet Jews to Israel.

A wry comic performance by Gerard Darmon (who plays two brothers) and impressive use of locations in the USSR, Austria and Israel could be exploited by a specialty distributor familiar with launching unusual foreign films in major markets like New York, Los Angeles and Chicago.

Yasha and Merab are half brothers who live in ruggedly beautiful Tblissi, Soviet Georgia. Merab and his stern patriarchal father are Russian nationalists. Yasha, a dead-ringer for his younger brother, had a Jewish mother and is taking advantage of Gorbachev's open-door policy to emigrate to Israel.

Initially outraged, Yasha's father relents and instructs Merab to accompany his brother, sister-in-law and niece to Moscow for their flight. In a comedy-of-errors airport vignette that barbs the pass-the-buck Soviet bureaucracy, Merab winds up with his brother's passport and ticket when buying duty-free champagne for a farewell celebration.

Penniless and without luggage, Merab takes off for Vienna, where his brother's family was to connect for Tel Aviv. On the plane he encounters Boris, an emigré and black marketeer who plans to skip the connecting flight and head for "Hawaii — paradise on Earth" after a stopover in the casinos of Monte Carlo.

Merab heads to the Soviet embassy to repatriate himself, but is cruelly rebuffed and arrested for trespassing when he presses his case. Released, he runs into Boris, who has lost all his smuggled U.S. dollars at a Viennese casino.

In Tel Aviv, Merab's Israeli half-uncle Issy is skeptical about the fate of Yasha and his family. He concludes that Merab is a KGB agent and banishes him.

Merab is cheated in the bazaar, denounced by Issy when he tries to crash an elite Soviet emigré wedding, ignored by Boris and booted by the Soviet embassy when he claims himself a spy and demands urgent repatriation. No lie is too big, no improvisation too ridiculous for the hapless hang-dog hustler.

Eventually he falls in with an embittered Jewish Soviet WWII hero, who promises to smuggle him across the border to Jordan. From there Merab will cross into Turkey and then Soviet Georgia.

Naturally things go awry. An ambitious U.S. photojournalist grants Merab unwanted celebrity in a magazine piece on emigrés. An African businessman tries and fails to swap him for a countryman imprisoned on espionage charges in Russia. Finally, Merab and the war hero are arrested and imprisoned for hijacking a truck and kidnapping its crew.

Back in Georgia, Merab's father makes a friendly hostage out of a cooperative American tourist in an attempt to force the Israelis to return his son. When Merab finally crosses the border, he's imprisoned by the Jordanians. Back in the USSR, brother Yasha curses the man who first invented borders.

Darman renders the indomita-ble Merab and his sheepish half-brother Yasha in a skillful, ironic performance.

Director Gueorgui Daniela, takes full advantage of the shifting locations to fashion a clever satire on the whole notion of national identity in a transient world.

Crisp cinematography by Vadim Youssov and an evocative folkloric score by Guya Kantcheli nicely augment the filmmaker's style.
— *Rich.*

Desire: Sexuality In
Germany 1910-1945
(BRITISH-DOCU)

New York A Mayavision Production for Channel Four Television. Produced by Rebecca Dobbs. Directed by Stuart Marshall. Camera (color, black & white), Anne Cottringer; editor, Joy Chamberlain. Reviewed at the Anthology Film Archives, N.Y., May 31, 1990. No MPAA rating. Running time: 87 MIN.

■ In "Desire: Sexuality In Germany 1910-1945," British documentarian Stuart Marshall recounts an age of sexual liberation that ended abruptly and tragically with the Nazi persecution of gays and lesbians. The importance of that often-neglected history (and its relevance in the AIDS era) pushes this striking film beyond its flaws.

Pic opens with an intriguing, if not completely satisfying, account of Germany's naturist, or body culture, movement in the years preceding World War I. Wonderful photographs and sometimes hilarious archival film footage illustrate the artistic posing (think Isadora Duncan) and pseudo-classical pretentions of the German youths who took to the woods. Rejecting civilization (and clothing), the naturists, as one historian notes, sought "wholeness as an idea and as a desire."

While the naturists were frolicking in the countryside, Berlin's Dr. Magnus Hirschfeld, founder of the ground-breaking Institute for Sexual Research, championed the theory that homosexuality was biological in cause and that homosexuals should be accorded the rights of a legitimate minority. With the naturists in the forests and Hirschfeld in the city, Germany was primed for an era of social experimentation.

Unfortunately, Germany also was primed for a movement of an entirely different sort. In one of the pic's most unsettling moments, Hilde Radmusch, a lesbian and communist, recalls hearing that Hitler had taken power. "I knew," she says, "that I could count on being arrested."

"Desire" draws much of its strength from the oral histories of Radmusch and a few (too few) others. Notable is Michael Ritterman's chilling account of his brutal interrogation by Nazis, in which various officers took turns beating him as he refused to inform on other homosexuals.

Disappointingly, other elements of the film fall short of achieving the power of the eyewitness accounts. Marshall relies much too heavily on visual stylization, favoring frequent (and lengthy) shots of lush German countryside.

Set to the strains of Mahler and Schubert, Anne Cottringer's distinctive yet repetitious cinematography slides rather quickly from beauty to tedium. Even the telling juxtaposition of Germany's natural wonders with the brazen homo-eroticism of fascist art and architecture grows wearisome as Marshall pummels the metaphor into place.

Most regrettable about Marshall's decision to devote so many of the film's 87 minutes to mood-setting is his slighting of crucial information. At no point does the film offer a convincing social or political context, much less historical sweep, in which to place the naturists, Hirschfeld or the gay movement that sprang from both.

Viewer can only speculate how a specific culture at a specific time could produce two men as disparate as Hitler and Hirschfeld.

Despite its flaws, "Desire," which debuted in shorter form on British tv last year, strikes a note that resonates all too clearly with contemporary audiences. The final shots of an Amsterdam monument bearing the familiar pink triangle could easily be mistaken for an AIDS memorial, were it not for the inscription reading "Gay Victims of Facism."

One historian offers an epitaph for the early gay movement that could just as easily be taken as a warning: It wasn't so much the use of laws that destroyed Germany's gay culture, he says. It was the use of fear. — *Evan.*

San Ge Nu: Ren
(A Story Of Women)
(CHINESE)

Paris A Shanghai Film studio production. Directed by Peng Xiao Lian. Screenplay, Xiao Mao; camera (color), Liu Li Hua; music, Yan Mao. Reviewed at the Creteil Women's Film Festival, Creteil, France, April 1, 1990. Running time: **90 MIN.**

With: Zhang Wen Rong, Zhang Min, Shong Ru Hui.

■ This gently observed, wistfully affecting drama by one of China's few women filmmakers won a deserved special mention at this year's Women's Film Festival in Creteil. Pic deserves wide festival exposure.

Peng Xiao Lian made this film (her second) in 1988 and now studies at New York U. She has a clear-eyed sensibility and technical sureness. Script by Xiao Mao tells of a trip to the big city by three women from a village perched in the shadow of the Great Wall. The women hope to sell their homemade darning wool in the city's street marts.

Though the trio obviously is meant to represent the experience of the contemporary peasant woman, each is warmly fleshed out by the actresses and the sympathetic direction.

Through their encounters with people in the city (among them a lonely young construction worker from the provinces, who briefly romances one of the women), film achieves a vivid cross-section of society. Neither script nor direction succumbs to the facile country-city opposition.

Though the women have their share of misadventures (a conman robs one quite early on; a sudden downpour in an open-air market ruins much of the remaining wool), the city is viewed as a place of wonder, rich with human possibilities.

It reinforces the friendship and solidarity of the three peasants, who return home with a stronger sense of self and a readiness to confront their domestic tribulations.

Tech credits are fine. — *Len.*

Deep Sleep
(CANADIAN)

Vancouver A Corifest Inc., Festival Films (Canada only) release of a Deep Sleep production. Produced by Michael Lebowitz, John

M. Eckert. Written and directed by Patricia Gruben. Camera (color), Rene Ohashi; editor, Lara Mazur; music, Martin Gotfrit; art director, Marian Wihak; set decorator, Ane Christensen; costume design, Patricia Flynn; assistant director, Michael Zenon; production manager, Eckert; stunt coordinator, Bill Stewart; casting, Stuart Aikins. Reviewed at Starlight Theater, Vancouver, May 22, 1990. Running time: **85 MIN.**
Shelley McBride . . . . . . Megan Follows
Bob Bolden . . . . Stuart Margolin
Barbara McBride . . . . . . Patricia Collins
Terry McBride . . . . David Hewlett
Angel . . . . Damon D'Oliveira
Dr. Cole . . . . Deanne Henry
Lyman McBride . . . . Rob Roy
Matina . . . . Margot Kane
Hugh McBride . . . . Ken Camroux

■ Patricia Gruben's first directorial outing is a strong effort weakened by a mediocre script filled with too much clichéd dialog to appeal to theatrical audiences. Video success is possible although pic's greatest assets, Marian Wihak's art direction and Rene Ohashi's cinematography, would lose effect on the small screen.

Also watchable is Megan Follows (from Canadian tv's "Anne Of Green Gables") as a young woman obsessed with the death of her father. Follows is particularly powerful in several no-dialog dream sequences, which tie together the events leading to her nervous breakdown and the relationship between her dead father and her mother's fiancé.

The dream sequences are pic's most intriguing component, each installment heightening the drama. Unfortunately, Gruben never really takes advantage of the dreams' foreshadowing and is unable to sustain the dramatic levels when Follows eventually wakes up and attempts to find the cause of her father's mysterious death.

Supporting cast, including Stuart Margolin (tv's "The Rockford Files") as the fiancé, Patricia Collins as Follows' mother and Damon D'Oliveira as a Filipino man with ties to Margolin, flesh out thinly drawn characters.

Tech credits are exceptional, particularly considering the challenge of the dream sequences and the size of the budget, reported to be less than $C3-million. — *Cadd.*

Babylone
(CANADIAN-BELGIAN)

Montreal A Prima Film release of a Les Prods. du Regard and Azimut Prods. Belgique coproduction in association with RTFB Belgique. Produced by Maguerite Bavaud,

Jean-Roch Marcotte. Directed by Manu Bonmariage. Screenplay, Luc Jabon, Marcotte; camera (color), Eric Cayla; editor, Denise Vindevogel; music, Yves Laferriere; sound, Patrick Van Loo; costumes, Lolly Joukowski. Reviewed at Cineplex Odeon Complexe Desjardins Cinema 2, Montreal, May 24, 1990. Running time: **90 MIN.**
Anna . . . . Marie Tifo
Nadine . . . . Charlotte Laurier
Bruno . . . . Frederic Deban
Marco . . . . Rafael Sanchez
D'Alemberg . . . . Christian Crahay
Luigi . . . . Pierre Curzi
Mr. Michiels . . . . Dirk Buyse
Madame Michiels . . . . . Netty Vangheel
Jacques . . . . Georges Siatidis
Eddy . . . . François Sikivie
Robert . . . . Jacques de Bock
Vincent . . . . Marc Fege

■ A weird cross between "Time Of The Gypsies" (minus the magic) and "Paris Texas" (minus the intensity), this Quebec/Belgian coprod is a cultural melting pot that lacks punch. French-lingo tv is pic's best venue.

Yarn revolves around the fate of young Marco (Rafael Sanchez) after his gypsy mother (Marie Tifo) shoots the boy's father and puts Marco up for adoption. The older brother Bruno (Frederic Deban) takes the murder rap and eventually becomes obsessed with reuniting mother and son once released from prison.

Quebec starlet Charlotte Laurier dons an international French accent to play Bruno's love interest Nadine. First two reels are plodding and intro a flimsy script, obviously written to meet coprod terms.

When Bruno's search for Marco is finally underway, Nadine, who always pops up at the right time in the right place with no consideration for story continuity, becomes his accomplice.

Like Travis in "Paris Texas," Bruno eventually resorts to kidnaping the child from the adoptive parents. Unlike Travis, Bruno is an insensitive brute (badgering both girlfriend and mother), a thief (he steals a car to search for Marco) and an idiot (he gives chocolate to a diabetic).

When Marco has a diabetic seizure during the kidnaping scene, Bruno's hopeless quest comes to a screeching halt, as does the film, when the boy is taken away in an ambulance.

Quebec's Pierre Curzi adds a special touch with a credible Ital-

ian accent in the role of Luigi, the mother's boyfriend.

Pic has its moments, but too many coprod compromises have been made for it to be a real French "oeuvre d'art." Tech credits and thesping are fine. — *Suze.*

Alligator Eyes

Cannes A Laughing Man Partnership production. (Intl. sales: J&M Entertainment.) Executive producer, David Marlow. Produced by John Feldman, Ken Schwenker. Written and directed by Feldman. Camera (Eastmancolor), Todd Crockett; editor, Cynthia Rogers; music, Sheila Silver; sound, Antonio Arrogo; production manager, Bill Burke; co-executive producer, Jo Manuel; casting, Susan Shopmaker. Reviewed at the Cannes Film Festival (market), May 14, 1990. Running time: **101 MIN.**
Pauline . . . . Annabelle Larsen
Robbie . . . . Roger Kabler
Lance . . . . Allen McCullough
Marjorie . . . . Mary McLain
Peterson . . . . John Mackay

■ With this low-budget feature, first-time writer-director John Feldman could launch an interesting career since he's created some unusually strong characters and situations out of what could have been a routine road movie. "Alligator Eyes" has already been invited to some fests, and could get modest commercial attention.

The film opens with a sequence in which 2-year-old Pauline witnesses her mother and the mother's lover gunned down by a jealous man who then strikes the child, apparently blinding her. Years later, Pauline is hitchhiking alone when picked up by a trio of friends from New York who take her along for the ride, not knowing at first that she's blind.

Robbie (Roger Kabler) is a wisecracking type on the rebound after a failed relationship. He immediately latches on to the pretty Pauline, and sleeps with her. Marjorie (Mary McLain) is recently divorced and trying to renew a relationship with former boyfriend Lance (Allen McCullough). She keeps writing letters to her child back home. The trio originally planned a vacation in North Carolina, but find that Pauline is directing their movements.

As played by Annabelle Larsen, Pauline is a genuinely enigmatic character. She brazenly pries Lance away from Marjorie, even though she seems to prefer Robbie, and yet elicits Marjorie's sympathy for her plight.

As a road movie, this one's unusually well-written, directed and acted. The characters are multidimensional, and Feldman shows a relaxed style while all the time piling up details of information and suspense with skill.

The ending comes as a disappointment after the subtle buildup, and a more ingenious conclusion might have been devised. But it's not in any way a disaster, even though the rendezvous Pauline is heading for ends the picture on a puzzling note.

The film is beautifully shot (Todd Crockett) and evocatively scored (Sheila Silver). It also introduces four promising new actors, each one showing range and skill with these well-rounded roles.

It's only when it attempts to become a thriller in the final reel that "Alligator Eyes" starts to falter; all the mythic details brought into the film (Pauline's fascination for the alligators that lurk in the Carolina swamps, and her fixation with the legend of Atlantis) prepare the way for something more intriguing as a resolution.

But Feldman shows he has an unusual talent here, and his next pic will be awaited with interest.
— *Strat.*

Megaville

Cannes   A Heritage Entertainment presentation of a White Noise production. (Intl. sales: Amazing Movies.) Executive producers Robert M. Steloff, Peter Lehner. Produced by Christina Schmidlin, Andres Pfaeffli. Written and directed by Peter Lehner. Camera (Foto-Kem color), Zoltan David; editor, Pietro Scalia; music, Stacy Widelitz; sound, Leonard Marcel; production design, Milo; associate producer/production manager, Cynthia Hill; assistant director, Marshall Crosby; casting, Michael Cutler. Reviewed at the Cannes Film Festival (market), May 13, 1990. Running time: **95 MIN.**
Panilov/Jensen . . . . Billy Zane
Newman . . . . J.C. Quinn
Mrs. Panilov . . . . Grace Zabriskie
Christine . . . . Kristen Cloke
Duprell . . . . Daniel J. Travanti
Dr. Vogel . . . . Stefan Gierasch
Heller . . . . John Lantz

■ A commendable attempt to make a sci-fi thriller without special effects or big action scenes, "Megaville" falls between the stools of mainstream and arthouse, but should be sought out by buffs for whom the references to the Jean-Luc Godard classic, "Alphaville,"

are there for the taking.

Billy Zane, confirming the talent he displayed in "Dead Calm," plays a member of the police force of the Hemisphere, a puritanical fascist state of the future where all forms of entertainment have been abolished. He's sent to the sin city of Megaville, where films and television are still legal. He has to pose as his double, a criminal, and on his arrival is quickly taken up by the double's girlfriend.

Just as Godard used contemporary Paris for his city of the future, so writer-director Peter Lehner has Los Angeles stand in for Megaville. The film develops into a steely drama about mind control and the evils of science, but the tone is too low-key and the plot probably a bit too convoluted for the film to be entirely successful.

Still, it's a brave attempt to do a different kind of sci-fi picture, and it's technically sleek. The cast is generally solid, with newcomer Kristen Cloke appealing as the femme interest. The final image, of death and desolation in a vast desert, evokes, of all films, Erich Von Stroheim's "Greed." — *Strat.*

Sweet Revenge
(U.S.-FRENCH)

Cannes   A The Movie Group presentation of Chrysalide Film with Canal Plus production (premiering on cable via TNT in U.S.). Produced by Monique Annaud. Executive producer, Daniel Marquet. Directed by Charlotte Brandstrom. Screenplay, Janet Brownell; camera (Eastmancolor), Olivier Gueneau; editor, Marie-Sophie Gally; music, Didier Vasseur; production design, Françoise Benoit-Fresco; costume design, Patricia Saalburg; assistant director. Patrick Delabriere; production manager, Daniel Delume; line producer, Françoise Leherissey; casting, Françoise Menidrey. Reviewed at the Cannes Film Festival (market), May 14, 1990. Running time: **93 MIN.**
Kate . . . . Rosanna Arquette
Linda . . . . Carrie Fisher
John . . . . John Sessions
Frank . . . . François Eric Gendron
Ruth . . . . Myriam Moszko
Jim Harris . . . . John Hargreaves
   Also with: Bruno Madinier, Consuelo de Haviland, Carina Barone, Van Doude, Yves Brainville, Jerome Natali, Dominique Macavoy, Susan Carlson, Claire Mardsen, Andrea Schieffer, Anny Romand.

■ "Sweet Revenge" is a stab at old-fashioned screwball romantic comedy that comes off only half-heartedly because Americanized Swedish-French helmer Charlotte Brandstrom works from a screenplay that relies on squeaky contrivances in every twist of its convoluted

plot.

The presence of Rosanna Arquette and Carrie Fisher, both in fine, charming shape, weren't enough to generate theatrical business (film has been bought for TNT premiere in July). Homevid and television (French movie channel Canal Plus is a coproducer) should welcome the item.

Fisher plays Linda Michaels, a Paris-based corporation lawyer, who pays out-of-work actress Kate Williams (Rosanna Arquette) to trap her ex-husband John (England's dark and curly-headed John Sessions), a struggling writer, into a mock marriage so that Linda can get out of paying him the alimony awarded him because he originally footed the costs of sending Linda to law school.

The actress and the writer, of course, fall in real love right away and, after an ultra-brief tiff that creates no suspense whatsoever, forgive and forget Linda's ploy. Linda, her loyalties divided between her law career and various men, has a harder time of it, but comes through with her icy facade thoroughly melted.

"Sweet Revenge" has a neat production dress but uses the attractions of its Paris locations in a distracted way. Romance, in other words, is served up pretty cold throughout although Arquette and Sessions do kindle a flickering flame convincingly for a few moments.

The fun is handled best by John Hargreaves as a womanizing executive. — *Kell.*

Modern Love

Cannes   A Triumph Releasing release of an SVS presentation in association with Michael Holzman and Jeffrey Ringler of a Lyric Films and Soisson/Murphey production. Executive producers, Michael S. Murphey, Joel Soisson. Written, produced and directed by Robby Benson. Camera (color), Christopher G. Tufty; editor, Gib Jaffe; music, Don Peake; sound, Russell C. Fager; production design, Carl E. Copeland; costume design, Robin Lewis; art direction, Nancy Harvin; associate producers, Jane Rayleigh, Robert P. Cohen. Reviewed at the Cannes Film Festival (market), May 16,1990. MPAA Rating: R. Running time: **109 MIN.**
Greg . . . . Robby Benson
Billie . . . . Karla DeVito
Evelyn . . . . Rue McClanahan
Col. Parker . . . . Burt Reynolds
Mr. Hoskins . . . . Frankie Valli
Greg's Mom . . . . Louise Lasser
Receptionist . . . . Kaye Ballard
Greg's Dad . . . . Lou Kaplan
Dirk . . . . Cliff Bemis
Chloe . . . . Lyric Benson

■ This modest romantic comedy, struggling by on an ordinary story about young married life and punctuated by unfunny attempts at bizarre comedy, is likely to move briskly out of theaters and into video.

Written, produced and directed by Robby Benson, shot in South Carolina and starring Benson and his family and friends, "Modern Love" was actually put together as part of a state university media class he was teaching in Columbia, S.C., where some scenes were lensed.

It follows the adventures of Greg and a ditzy urologist named Billie (Benson and wife Karla DeVito) who "meet cute" when she examines him in her office. Their whirlwind courtship consists of dozens of shots of them kissing against pretty backdrops, followed by telling each other lame jokes and then giggling and saying "I'm sorry." It may be charming in life, but not to paying customers.

Pic improves as it moves into their family years, with Benson's frustrated attempts to be a hands-on father giving things an interesting twist and DeVito getting a more substantial role as a capable mom, peacemaker and would-be nightclub comic.

Benson, a fairly capable director, works hard at pumping energy and humor into a flat script, succeeding about as often as it falls flat. But the convenient casting gives pic a community theater feel, and it's overall too undistinquished to do business in cinemas.

Burt Reynolds, a longtime friend with whom Benson worked in "The End" and "Lucky Lady," plays Billie's threatening father. Daughter Lyric Benson makes her debut as their 5-year-old.

Kaye Ballard, with whom Benson and DeVito appeared on Broadway in "The Pirates Of Penzance," plays an intimidating receptionist in Billie's office, and Rue McClanahan does a good job as Billie's mother, who comes to take care of the baby, typically getting in the way.

Actors worked for scale, and cast and crew included all the members of Benson's filmmaking course. — *Daws.*

On The Block

Cannes A Snakeskin Pictures production. Produced and directed by Steve Yeager. Screenplay, Linda Chambers, Yeager; camera (Eastmancolor), Erich Roland; editor, Yeager; music, Charles Barnett; sound, William Kaplan; production design, Barbara Jalhott; costume design, Van Smith; associate producer, Chambers. Reviewed at Cannes Film Festival (market), May 18, 1990. Running time: **95 MIN.**

Libby	Marilyn Jones
Lt. Rucci	Jerry Whiddon
Hugo	Michael Gabel
Mimi	Erika Bogren
Clay Beasley	Howard Rollins
Blaze Starr	Herself

■ Baltimore filmmaker Steve Yeager makes an unremarkable debut with "On The Block," an explicit look at life among the strippers of Baltimore's red-light district that's unredeemed by any particular style or vision. Softcore porn elements could make it commercial in some fringe markets.

Though the seamy side of life has been exposed slews of times in books and film, usually with a lot more style, this may be the first pic that tries to make a moral crusade out of preserving the illicit sex and drug trade.

Denizens of the Block, as the area is known, are portrayed compassionately as outcast souls who've at least found acceptance somewhere, while the villain is a developer (Howard Rollins, in a cardboard portrayal) who wants to raze the block for urban renewal.

Full nudity, language and graphic portrayal of drug use abound, while filmmakers, taking themselves seriously, try to insert a meaningful story via the upward curve of newcomer Marilyn Jones, a motivated but down-on-her-luck dancer who's just kicked junk and is trying to stay clean and get it back together.

She crosses paths with a love-sick vice cop, who, unfortunately for all concerned, especially the audience, turns out to be a borderline psycho killer nursing a ton of guilt left over from his years in the seminary.

He goes nuts when she rejects him, and pic incorporates some violent thriller aspects as he chases her down. Lead perfs are unremarkable, though Erika Bogren shows some promise as a doomed teenage junkie, and Michael Gabel is convincing as a sweet but slow-witted janitor.

Stripper Blaze Starr, whose relationship with Louisiana guv Earl Long was the basis of last year's "Blaze," was apparently the owner of Baltimore's 2 O'Clock Club, where story is centered, and she makes a brief appearance as herself (fully clothed), lamenting the days when stripteasing was an art form.

"This is Blaze Starr's club. There's no place like it in the world," says one character, but you wouldn't know it from this generic-looking pic. Production values are okay, though the flat, neon-toned photography of Erich Roland doesn't add much atmosphere. — Daws.

Il gèle en enfer
(It's Freezing In Hell)
(FRENCH)

Paris A Koala Films production and release. Coproduced by SGGC. Produced and directed by Jean-Pierre Mocky. Screenplay, Mocky, Andre Ruellan, based on the novel "Black Wings Has My Angel" by Elliot Chaze. Camera (color), Raoul Coutard; music, Vladimir Cosma; sound, Denis Tribalet; art direction, Etienne Mery; assistant director, Jean-Philippe Bonnet. Reviewed at the Georges V cinema, Paris, May 8, 1990. Running time: **85 MIN.**

Tim	Jean-Pierre Mocky
Georgia	Laura Grandt

■ Jean-Pierre Mocky's 30th film in 30 years is a thriller in helmer's typically sloppy manner. Mocky, 60, is an "enfant terrible" with a small critical following at home and limited export potential. "Il gèle en enfer" isn't likely to change his status.

Plot is a mixture of caper suspense and sexy love story. It's based on an American novel by Elliot Chaze about an escaped con and a hooker planning a heist in a small town. Mocky himself plays the male lead, a seedy fugitive dreaming of the ultimate heist. To pull off the job he falls in with an independent-minded call girl (lustily played by newcomer Laura Grandt).

Neither aspect works. The caper is old hat (it involves hijacking an armored van during a bank stop in an Alpine border town) and the torrid romancing is tepid, neither erotic nor touching. Mocky, usually a good offbeat actor, has miscast himself disastrously.

As director, Mocky is still Mocky: no style, a haphazard concern for production dressing, and a supporting cast that includes many cretinous looking individuals. If it looks somewhat less shabby than previous Mocky efforts, it's because helmer has treated himself to Raoul Coutard, though the ace lenser is working at far beneath his usually classy norm. Mainstream composer Vladimir Cosma did the score, but only underlines Mocky's monotonous sense of film music. — Len.

Bingo
(SWISS-GERMAN)

Zurich An Elite Film release of a Vega Film (Zurich), Agora Film (Munich) and Swiss tv DRS Zurich coproduction. Executive producer, Ruth Waldburger. Directed by Markus Imboden. Screenplay, Philipp Engelmann, Thomas Turner, Imboden; camera (color), Martin Führer; editor, Rainer Maria Trinkler; music, Benedict Jeger; sound, Ruedi Guyer; art direction, Hanspeter Remund; costume design, Claudia Flütsch. Reviewed at Corso 3, Zurich, May 17, 1990. Running time: **85 MIN.**

Sturzi	Ruedi Walter
Bingo	Mathias Gnädinger
Schorschi	Robert Hunger-Bühler
Erika	Teresa Harder
Chouchou	Immy Schell

■ Swiss stage and screen thesps Ruedi Walter and Mathias Gnädinger are the main assets of "Bingo," a comedy meller in Swiss dialect by Markus Imboden, his first feature film. Otherwise, it is an average effort with mostly local appeal.

Sturzi, over 70, and Bingo, near 50, are petty criminals who met in jail where they planned to head for Brazil after their release, using Sturzi's savings. But the plan misfires when the old man is forced to use his saved money to pay off his debts.

In order to realize their dream, Bingo coaxes his buddy into a bank holdup scheme, together with a third partner. Sturzi reluctantly agrees.

Against all odds, the holdup succeeds, but Bingo is killed. By a trick, the old man escapes under a false name and is last seen boarding a plane to Rio — with the money.

If it weren't for Walter and Gnädinger, both experienced pros and immensely popular, charismatic players, the film would have little to recommend it. The former is a softspoken, everyday Swiss type, and Gnädinger, a massive man with a salty vocabulary, provides the necessary contrast. Supporting players are below par.

Imboden's direction fails to make up for the script's loopholes. Lensing by Martin Führer is okay, though sometimes too low-key. — Mezo.

In Too Deep
(AUSTRALIAN)

Sydney A Skouras Pictures release of a Media World production. Produced by Colin South, John Tatoulis. Directed by South, Tatoulis. Screenplay, Deborah Parsons; camera (color), Mark Gilfedder, Peter Zakharov; editor, Michael Collins, Nicolas Lee; music, Tassos Ioannides; sound, John Wilkinson; production design, Phil Chambers; production manager, Yvonne Collins; assistant director, Stephen Saks. Reviewed at Mosman screening room, Jan 20, 1990. Running time: **106 MIN.**

Mack	Hugo Race
Wendy	Santha Press
JoJo	Rebekah Elmaloglou
Miles	John Flaus
Dinny	Dominic Sweeney
Ivan	Craig Alexander
Henry	Richard Aspel
Margaret	Helen Rollinson
Mrs. Lyall	Gerda Nicolson
Mrs. Lyall	Robert Essex

■ This moody, erotic thriller from two first-time directors overcomes its slight narrative with its confident, bravura direction and cinematography. Good returns are indicated in selected cinemas, with a long video shelf life also in the cards.

Pic has the look and feel of a French film, in that atmosphere and sexual tension take pride of place over a slender plotline involving an affair between a femme jazz singer, Wendy, and Mack, a knife-wielding young hood. Also involved is Wendy's young sister, JoJo, a 15-year-old who gets turned on by her sister's sexual activities.

Tale takes place in an Australian city (Melbourne) in the middle of summer; heat is a factor in every sense of the word. Characters perspire a lot, and no wonder, given the energy of the numerous sex scenes.

Mack is an antisocial young gangster who plots a bank holdup. He is also in possession of an incriminating tape, sought after by both police and rival mobsters. His steamy liaison with Wendy for a while interrupts his criminal activities, though the law is hot on his trail.

Hugo Race, an Aussie rock singer, gives Mack a sinister persona. He never tries for audience sympathy, but is a powerful presence nonetheless. Newcomer Santha Press is a knockout as the sensual Wendy. She not only gets to warble a number of classic jazz standards ("Tenderly," "Fever,"

"Love For Sale"), but she's also convincing as a woman who throws caution to the wind in her very physical relationship with Mack.

Third corner of the triangle is the kid sister, played by Rebekah Elmaloglou, who is touching as the aroused teen whose attraction for her sister's dangerous boyfriend nearly ends in tragedy.

Also on hand is John Flaus, excellent as a world-weary cop out to nab Mack. Flaus, respected film academic and buff who occasionally appears in pics, gives his finest performance to date here, modeling his character after classic film noir lawmen from Hollywood's past.

Some may wish for rather more plotline than screenwriter Deborah Parsons provides, but "In Too Deep" gives the viewer plenty of other things to enjoy, including the fine music, stylish direction and impressive camerawork.

With fresh faces before and behind the camera, the film promises a lively future for all concerned. Some may wince at scenes in which the self-absorbed Mack slaps his lovely mistress around, but all of this is in keeping with the gallic mood created and well sustained.

Video career looks very strong, with theatrical success dependent to a large degree on critical reaction and marketing. This is a low-budgeter which deserves to find an audience. — *Strat.*

Herzlich Willkommen (WEST GERMAN)

Berlin A Filmverlag der Autoren release of a ZDF-TV and Hamburger Kinokompanie production. Directed by Hark Bohm. Screenplay, Bohm with Dorothée Schön from the novel by Walter Kempowski; camera, Hermann Fahr; music, Jens Peter Ostendorf; sound, Richard Burowski; art direction, Christian Bussmann; costumes, Birgit Missal. Reviewed at Berlin Film Festival, Zoo Palast, Feb. 16, 1990. Running time: 123 MIN.
Friedrich . . . . Uwe Bohm
Elke Kramer . . . . Barbara Auer
Fritz . . . . David Bohm
Direktor . . . . Hark Bohm
Iris . . . . Anna Thalbach
Secretary . . . . Eva-Maria Hagen
Superintendent . . . . . Michael Gwisdek
Forester . . . . Peter Franke
Iris' father . . . . Heinz Hoenig
Counselor . . . . Claus Rathjens
Refugee . . . . Peter Hick
Girl . . . . Simone Guillaumon

■ With this stark portrayal of postwar Germany, Hark Bohm puts himself at the lead of a new breed of West German directors trying to shake intellectual dust off filmmaking here and produce old-fashioned human-interest pics.

This latest film may not prove as popular at the b.o. as his 1987 "Romeo And Juliet" takeoff, "Yasemin," because it offers less sheer entertainment. But it is easily his most well-rounded film, and could travel well on the festival and specialty house circuit.

"Herzlich Willkommen" (cordially welcome) are the words that greet pic's protagonist (helmer's thesp son Uwe Bohm) as he arrives in West Germany after fleeing the East in the mid-1950s. A former political prisoner in East Germany, the new arrival's first job is at a home for wayward children in a converted castle.

The welcome is anything but cordial from the teenage thugs and the holdover Nazi who runs the joint. Our hero's efforts to save a difficult young boy from succumbing to the system, and a budding love affair with an attractive teacher, form the fulcrum for the plot.

On a deeper level, of course, West Germany itself is the bratty youth who secretly wants to be loved and to amount to something. Bohm skillfully develops this metaphor toward a baptism under fire — gunfire — along a river dividing the two Germanys.

The elements of humor which brightened "Yasemin" do not work this time around, and the occasional slapstick bit is distracting. The love interest and the relationship between the child and the young man are handled well.

Kudos to musical soundtrack by Jens Peter Ostendorf. It gives the pic just the right touch for period and mood.

Special kudos to the other Bohm son, young David, as the lovable brat. He's the best of a strong crew of young thesps in challenging roles.

Tech credits give the pic polish beyond its limited budget. — *Gill.*

Spur der Steine (Traces Of The Stones) (EAST GERMAN)

Berlin A DEFA Studio for Films production. Directed by Frank Beyer. Screenplay, Karl Georg Egel, Beyer, from the novel by Erik Heutsch; camera (black & white), Gunter Marczinskowsky; editor, Hildegard Conrad; music, Wolfram Heicking; sound, Werner Dibowski; production design, Harald Horn; production manager, Dieter Dormeier. Reviewed at the Berlin Film Festival, Feb. 15, 1990. Running time: 134 MIN.
Hannes Balla . . . . Manfred Krug
Kati Klee . . . . . . Krystyna Stypulkowska
Werner Horrath . . . . . . Eberhard Esche
Also with: Johannes Wieke, Walter Richter-Reinick, Hans-Peter Minetti, Walter Jupe, Ingeborg Schumacher, Brigitte Herwig, Gertrud Brendler, Helga Goring, Erich Mireck, Gunter Meier, Karl Brenk.

■ On the shelf for over 20 years, "Traces Of The Stones" (1966) emerges as a witty, probing exploration of the way the Communist system worked at grassroots level. Interest in the black & white picture will be limited to fests and retros, and to students of Communist cinema.

The drama set on a construction site centers around the disgrace of a Communist party secretary (Eberhard Esche) accused of "immoral behavior, careerism and political and ideological failure." His chief crime was that, as a married man with a small child, he had a secret affair with a young technologist (Krystyna Stypulkowska), who got pregnant as a result.

Also involved is Manfred Krug, who plays a charismatic worker who leads a "brigade." They dress like cowboys and go on drunken binges, but deliver the goods on the building site. Krug is also in love with Stypulkowska, and his cynical attitude towards the system results in some humorous barbs at the party's role in the workplace.

Though it's fairly esoteric material for outsiders, "Traces Of The Stones" proved too critical for the East German authorities of the mid-'60s. Not only was it banned, but director Beyer was unable to make another film for nearly 10 years.

Seen now, it's a well made, classical piece of filmmaking, about 20 minutes too long, but beautifully acted and wittily scripted. Sarcastic comments about life in West Germany seem even more pertinent in light of current events.

Manfred Krug is excellent as the sardonic working class hero, and the film is technically slick.
— *Strat.*

Il Segreto (The Secret) (ITALIAN)

Berlin A C.G. Group Cinematografica, Rete Italia presentation of a Cinelife production. Produced by Mario and Vittorio Cecchi Gori, Giuseppe Giovanni. Written and directed by Francesco Maselli. Camera (Eastmancolor), Pierluigi Santi; editor, Carla Simoncelli; music, Giovanna Marini; sound, Edwin R. Forrest; set designer, Marco Dentici; costumes, Lina Nerli Taviani. Reviewed at the Berlin Film Festival, Feb. 15, 1990. Running time: 109 MIN.
Lucia . . . . Nastassja Kinski
Carlo . . . . Stefano Dionisi
Franco . . . . Franco Citti
Lilli . . . . Chiara Caselli
Also with: Alesandra Marson, Franca Scagnetti, Raffaella Davi, Enzo Saturni, Antonio de Giorgi, Michela Bruni, Luigi Diberti.

■ Even the staunchest supporters of helmer Francesco Maselli will have a hard time finding something nice to say about this effort.

A subproletarian love story that degenerates, by the second half, into a dubious romantic triangle, the film desperately drags on for almost two hours on a plot that could barely survive a short.

Nastassja Kinski plays a waitress plagued by serious emotional problems who involves herself with Stefano Dionisi, a timid and emotionally raw messenger boy. There is also an older man, Franco Citti, who was a friend of Kinski's father and who befriends Dionisi.

That's about all there is in this movie, except for the numerous closeups of the lovers despondently clinging to each other.

Murky photography is evidently intended to lend the film a drab look suitable to the social status of its heroes.

After this film, Kinski may regret allowing Maselli to mess up her looks, but she's not the only one whose reputation is on the line. Cameraman Santi couldn't have obtained a flatter image had he worked blindfolded, and editor Simoncelli must have taken a nap, to allow the picture to proceed in such a lazy fashion. — *Edna.*

Strangers (AUSTRALIAN)

Cannes A Genesis Films production. (Intl. sales: Beyond Films Ltd.) Produced by Wayne Gross, Craig Lahiff. Directed by Lahiff. Screenplay, John Emery, from a story by Emery, Lahiff; additional dialog, Bob Ellis; camera (color), Steve Arnold; editor, Denise Haratzis; music, Frank Strangio; sound, Mike Piper; production design, Derek Mills; production manager, Ron Stigwood; assistant director, Soren Jenson; casting, Anne Peters, Jan Killen. Reviewed at the Cannes Film Festival (market), May 12, 1990. Running time: 88 MIN.
Anna . . . . Anne Looby
Gary . . . . James Healey

Rebecca . . . . Melissa Docker
Anna's father . . . . Tim Robertson
Sergeant . . . . Paul Mason
Joanne . . . . Mary Regan
Graham . . . . Jim Holt
Frank . . . . Geoff Morell
Agent . . . . John Clayton

■ "Strangers On A Train" (actually Plane in this case) meets "Fatal Attraction" in this extremely derivative, but entertaining, thriller. The Beyond Group should rack up video sales, and theatrical possibilities also exist with the target of undemanding audiences.

Gary (James Healey), a yuppie stockbroker separated from his grasping wife Joanne (Mary Regan) and involved with sympathetic Rebecca (Melissa Docker), meets Anna (Anne Looby) on a plane and is soon having a fling with her in his hotel room. Trouble is, the mentally unstable Anna is playing, she thinks, for keeps and, when rejected, starts killing people with the luckless Joanne the first victim.

Joanne is killed at a fair, and the Hitchcock references come thick and fast, to be augmented by the notion (borrowed from "Play Misty For Me" as well as "Fatal Attraction") that a sexually active woman is probably also a dangerous psychopath. Anna's daddy (Tim Robertson) gets the chop because he wants to put her in a mental home, and then Anna takes a pair of lethal garden shears to poor Rebecca.

Despite the by-the-numbers script (augmented by some occasionally witty dialog by Bob Ellis), "Strangers" isn't hard to endure because Craig Lahiff ("Coda," "Fever") is a skilled director who knows how to manipulate an audience. Thanks to Lahiff, "Strangers" packs a few visceral thrills.

The film is technically good, with Steve Arnold's camerawork taking some trouble to create a distinctive, burnished look. Looby, as the vengeful villainess, is an unusual personality who could make an impact in subsequent, more ambitious pictures. — *Strat.*

Jipangu
(Zipang)
(JAPANESE)

New York   An EXE and Tokyo Broadcasting System presentation, in cooperation with Daio Paper Corp., Kanematsu Corp. and Seiyou Kankyokaihatsu. Produced by Kouji Tsutsumi, Kosuke Kuri. Directed by Kaizo Hayashi. Screenplay, Noriyuki Kurita, Hayashi; camera (color), Masaki Tamura; editor, Osamu Inoue; music, Hidehiko Urayama, Yoko Kumagaya; sound (Dolby), Hisayuki Miyamoto; art direction, Takeo Kimura; costume design, Sachiko Ito; fighting instructor, Kanta Ina; assistant director, Masayuki Taniguchi. Reviewed at Japan House, N.Y., June 2, 1990. Running time (intl. version): **100 MIN.**
With: Masahiro Takashima, Narumi Yasuda, Haruko Wanibuchi, Mikijiro Hira, Yukio Yamato, Chiyonosuke Azuma.

■ "Zipang" is a tongue-in-cheek samurai fantasy whose best U.S. chances would come in a dubbed version for action audiences.

Director Kaizo Hayashi scored with art film enthusiasts via his "To Sleep So As To Dream" (1986), followed by "Circus Boys," but this time has adopted too cutesy an approach to appeal to serious-minded Japanese film buffs. It's analogous to Joseph Losey's comic strip film "Modesty Blaise" as applied to the revered tradition of period samurai epics.

Already trimmed from its Japanese release version of 118 minutes to a better-paced 100-minute cut for international distribution, pic is ripe for dubbing in its unusual use of flippant English subtitles: Characters are translated with vulgarisms and anachronistic hip expressions that lampoon the action.

Film proper includes anachronisms as well: infrared binoculars, mortar shells and even a slide projector figure into the action set several centuries ago as a shogun seeks a legendary island kingdom of gold known as "Zipang" (which turns out to be Japan after all).

Hokey group of characters makes Kenneth Robeson's "Doc Savage" troupe look serious by comparison. Handsome swordsman Masahiro Takashima is painfully hip in his styling, with an okay gag (suitable for ripoff by "Saturday Night Live" or Mel Brooks) of him using numbered swords like golf clubs: In battle, he calls out to his squire (or caddie) for "number 7" and the appropriate club is soon skewering hundreds of baddies one by one.

This comical mayhem creates an anticlimax early in the film in a bravura single-take overhead shot of him decimating over 50 warriors merely to cross a bridge.

Overload of subplots feature a shogun questing not only for gold but the meaning of love; a ridiculously modern girl (replete with Louise Brooks hairdo) named Yuri the Pistol who spars with but soon becomes enamored of Takashima, a ghostly ancient warrior helped by the heroes to finally unite with his lost love, a queen, and a silly pâpier-maché type baby elephant.

The specter of Steven Spielberg hangs heavily over the proceedings, ranging from a "Raiders Of The Lost Ark" sequence in a cave to a final gag lameduckedly spoofing the music and sharkfin image of "Jaws."

En route Hayashi provides entertainment via speeded up camera action, nimble ninja cavortings (led by the comical Yukio Yamato) and some interesting special effects. The musical score, which owes more to Ennio Morricone than traditional Japanese samurai pics, is sprightly and effective.

Acting is over the top and won't be seriously impeded by dubbing, especially the unconvincingly sentimental "timeless" love story.

Art director Takeo Kimura, in whose honor Japan Society hosted this U.S. preem in Gotham, has used Aztec and Incan monuments as his design inspiration to impressive effect. — *Lor.*

Hunting
(AUSTRALIAN)

Sydney   A Boulevard Films production. (Intl. sales, J&M Entertainment.) Executive producer, Peter Boyle. Written, produced and directed by Frank Howson. Camera (Panavision, color), David Connell, Dan Burstall; editor, Philip Reid; music, John French, David Herzog; sound, John Rowley; production design, Jon Dowding; production manager, Lesley Parker; assistant director, John Powditch; costume design, Aphrodite Kondos; casting, Greg Apps; coproducer, James Michael Vernon; line producer, Barbi Taylor. Reviewed at Film Australia screening room, Sydney, May 31, 1990. Running time: **97 MIN.**
Michael Bergman . . . . John Savage
Michelle Harris . . . . . . Kerry Armstrong
Larry Harris . . . . Jeffrey Thomas
Sharp . . . . Guy Pearce
Debbie McCormick . . . . . . Rebecca Rigg
Bill Stockton . . . . . . Rhys McConnochie
Piggott . . . . Nicholas Bell
Holmes . . . . Ian Scott
Roberts . . . . Stephen Whittaker

■ With "Hunting," Boulevard Films moves away from somber midlife crisis pics ("Boulevard Of Broken Dreams," "Heaven Tonight"). New pic, the first directed by Frank Howson (scripter and producer of the other films), is an extravagant, mostly enjoyable widescreen melodrama.

Pic starts off realistically but gets crazier as it goes along, although the basic plot is unexceptional. Michelle Harris (Kerry Armstrong) is a private secretary for the boss of a large financial company. Her husband, Larry (Jeffrey Thomas), an adman, is unemployed and bitter about it. Their marriage is suffering as a result.

Enter wealthy Michael Bergman (John Savage). Michelle is almost literally swept off her feet, and a torrid affair begins. Larry quickly cottons on, and discovers the identity of his wife's lover. He unwisely threatens Bergman, who is secretly involved in money laundering and drug dealing. Bergman's goons eliminate Larry, making it look like suicide.

Michelle shacks up with Bergman in his palatial mansion, where video cameras record their passionate coupling for the benefit of the servants. But Bergman's business dealings run into trouble, he dallies with Michelle's best friend (Rebecca Rigg), and she discovers the truth about Larry's death. The stage is set for a violent finale.

After a relatively sober first reel, Howson turns up the heat until the wild climactic scenes which include a memorably dizzy sequence in which poor Michelle is sexually humiliated during a formal banquet, on a dining table laden with evil-looking fish.

It's hard to tell how audiences (and critics) will respond to this. Howson seems to be aiming at David Lynch territory, and he makes a good stab at it, but is let down to a degree by his actors, especially Armstrong, who isn't up to the demands of playing the passionate, ultimately vengeful, Michelle.

More in tune with the writer-producer-director is Kiwi actor Thomas, who makes an impression as the unfortunate husband, nursing his jealousy as he watches daytime tv. Guy Pearce (the young Errol in Boulevard's upcoming "Flynn"), is effectively malevolent as Bergman's bodyguard and hitman. Savage is an acceptable heavy.

"Hunting" looks and sounds great. The Panavision camerawork is seamless despite the fact that the original director of photography, David Connell, ankled during production (to shoot "Neverending Story 2" in Germany). Dan Burstall effectively took over, and emulated Connell's style.

Howson walks a fine line between the enjoyably melodramatic and the daft. Audiences who go along with his approach should enjoy the picture. Those who find most Aussie films irritatingly safe and serious may welcome this walk on the wilder side. — *Strat.*

Master Of Dragonard Hill

New York A Cannon Intl. presentation. Executive producer, Avi Lerner. Produced by Harry Alan Towers. Directed by Gerard Kikoïne. Screenplay, Rick Marx, "Peter Welbeck" (H.A. Towers), based on Rupert Gilchrist's novel; camera (color), Gerard Loubeau; editor, Caroline Gombergh; music, uncredited; sound, Colin McFarlane; production design, Leonardo Coen Cagli; assistant director, Dominique Comb, K.C. Jones; production manager, Peter Warnaby; associate producer, John Stodel; casting, Don Pembrick, Gianna Pisanello & Associates. Reviewed on Media Home Entertainment vidcassette, N.Y., June 4, 1990. MPAA Rating: R. Running time: **91 MIN.**
Capt. Shanks . . . . Oliver Reed
Naomi . . . . Eartha Kitt
Gastone Le Farge . . . . . . Herbert Lom
Jane Abdee . . . . Kimberly Sissons
Arabella . . . . Claudia Udy
Richard Abdee . . . . . Patarick Warburton
Gov. Warburton . . . . . . Dennis Folbigge
Sergeant . . . . Ron Smerczak
Calabar . . . . Martin Dewee

■ **This enjoyably trashy film in the "Mandingo" genre is a followup to Cannon's 1987 pic "Dragonard," reviewed here for the record after its direct-to-video release last year.**

South African-lensed effort is set in St. Kitts, picking up the action after a slave revolt led by white former slave Patrick Warburton. Now he's happily married (to cute blond Kimberly Sissons) and everything looks peachy at their inherited plantation, Dragonard Hill.

Hell breaks loose when local slut Arabella (played with wonderfully campy relish by Claudia Udy) is caught by her father making love to black slave Martin Dewee and daddy ends up dead. Dewee is blamed and Warburton's family gets in trouble when they give him refuge on the lam.

Evil Oliver Reed is appointed the new governor and brings back the use of the whip (called a "dragonard") on slaves. There's plenty of mayhem before the good guys revolt and put things right.

Besides Udy's fun turn, there's a guest role for Herbert Lom as a friendly smuggler. Both he and Eartha Kitt (cast here as a brothel madam) previously appeared in the West German film of "Uncle Tom's Cabin."

Helmer Gerard Kikoïne, whose output ranges from hardcore porn to Tony Perkins' "Edge Of Sanity," pours on the sleaze. Funniest twist is final reel changeover in which nasty Udy suddenly sees the error of her ways and becomes a nice person in time for a rushed happy ending. — *Lor.*

SEATTLE INTL. FILM FESTIVAL REVIEWS

The Man Inside

Seattle A New Line Cinema presentation of a Philippe Diaz production. Directed by Bobby Roth. Screenplay, Roth, based on writings of Gunter Wallraff; camera (color), Ricardo Aronovitch; editor, Luce Grunewaldt; music, Tangerine Dream; art direction, Didier Naert; executive producer, Roth; assistant producer, Oliver Loiseau. Reviewed at Seattle Intl. Film Festival, June 5, 1990. Running time: **101 MIN.**
Gunter Wallraff . . . . . Jurgen Prochnow
Henry Tobel . . . . Peter Coyote
Christiane . . . . Nathalie Baye

■ **"The Man Inside" is a fast-moving political thriller based upon the real-life experiences of a West German investigative reporter. Film should play well in European markets, and has definite U.S. arthouse potential.**

Gunter Wallraff is best known for his political exposés, one of which is the basis for this startling story proving once again fact can be stranger than fiction.

Story opens with Wallraff (Jurgen Prochnow) posing as an arms trader to uncover ties between a highly placed West German official and a foreign general planning a right-wing military coup. Revelation causes a scandal and provokes a secret meeting of a select group of West German political and business leaders, headed by the chief editor of the Standard, most widely read newspaper in Germany.

During the meeting, it's decided to "neutralize" Wallraff's influence by intimidation, and an immediate campaign to discredit him in the Standard is begun.

When physical threats against him and those closest to him mount, Wallraff goes on the run and changes identities with the help of a friend, transforming himself physically and mentally. Thus disguised, Wallraff infiltrates the Standard.

Wallraff is teamed with reporter Henry Tobel (Peter Coyote), who shows Wallraff how to twist facts and invent interviews in order to write the Standard's kind of truth. Wallraff begins to suffer emotionally from his participation in these vicious campaigns.

He forces himself to stay until he can uncover the newspaper's purpose in publishing the lies. Wallraff later learns major politico Hermes Brauner's direct role in determining what is published as truth in the Standard to support his own personal aims.

The state security force eventually discovers that Wallraff has infiltrated the newspaper, and the journalist narrowly escapes capture on espionage charges. He then goes on to write a book exposing Brauner and his influence over the paper, but the book's publication is stalled in court by Wallraff's powerful adversaries.

It isn't until Tobel brings Wallraff a secret dossier that Wallraff is able to prove the truth of his information, and the book is published and becomes a bestseller in West Germany.

The movie's weakest point is also its strongest: It's almost impossible to believe that such a corrupt newspaper could be a respected publication in a free world country. The knowledge that this was based upon actual experience, and that the real Wallraff continues his journalistic exploits, certainly add a sharper edge to the film.

Prochnow turns in a very convincing performance as Wallraff, both as a brave, crusading reporter and a frightened, tormented man.

The film speeds along under the capable direction of Bobby Roth, who has crafted a tense, revealing drama. The moody music of Tangerine Dream adds to the almost-surreal quality of the film.

Poor sound and print quality, however, detract from the film's otherwise high standards. — *Magg.*

Stages

Seattle A Paul-Thompson Films production. Produced and directed by Randy Thompson. Screenplay, Thompson, Ron Reid, Dan Lishner; camera (color), Wm. Brooks Baum; music, Randy Thompson. Reviewed at the Seattle Intl. Film Festival, May 29, 1990. Running time: **114 MIN.**
Doug Atkin . . . . Ron Reid
Brock Mason . . . . Dan Lishner
Andy Miller . . . . Randy Thompson

Charlie McKnight . Mayme Paul-Thompson

■ **Seattle filmmaker Randy Thompson draws upon his own experience as a comedian to make his feature debut which gives a humorous yet realistic view of the not-always-so-funny life on the road as a nightclub comic.**

This low-budget venture represents a good first-start for Thompson, but uneven pacing prevents the film from gaining the necessary momentum to reach its potential as a really funny movie. Distribution for a general audience seems doubtful, although it played well to the hometown audience.

"Stages" looks at the story of three comedians and a "cut-rate" agent/producer through a series of four one-night comedy shows over a period of five days. It focuses not on the on-stage part of the trip, but on the kinds of bad accommodations, unusual performance situations, the audiences, and the relationships between these comics. Not knowing each other at the start, they must deal with each other's egos, spend long hours traveling together and performing.

There are some genuinely funny one-liners, sight gags and story-telling during the film, but all too often they are left hanging in the air so that the story lacks a sense of comedic continuity. The film is troubled by a slow start and further weakened by an ending which tries to neatly wrap up everything without providing a basis for these actions to occur.

For instance, Andy, the trip's headliner (Thompson), becomes increasingly hostile and disgusted with Brock (Dan Lishner), an unprofessional and not very talented comedian. Yet, in the end, Andy tries to help out Brock by giving him the names of some possible agents to help him get work.

Acting is generally amateurish, although Lishner turns in a capable performance as Brock, a disgusting comedian who thrives on raunchy, sexist jokes and never breaks character throughout the film.

Filmed in 35m for about $200,000, the film was shown at the Seattle Intl. Film Fest in 16m since the film production couldn't afford the 35m. — *Magg.*

Julia Has Two Lovers

Seattle A South Gate Entertainment release of an Oneira Pictures Intl. production. Produced and directed by Bashar Shbib. Screenplay, Daphna Kastner, Shbib; camera (color), Stephen Reizes; editor, Dan Foegelle, Shbib; music, Emilio Kauderer; original songs, Tim Ray; sound, Al Samuels; executive producers, Christoph Henkel, Randy Davis; associate producer, Janet Cunningham. Reviewed at the Seattle Intl. Film Festival, June 3, 1990. Running time: **85 MIN.**

Julia . . . . Daphna Kastner
Daniel . . . . David Duchoveny
Jack . . . . David Charles

■ While this tale of romance on the telephone has an interesting story concept, the conversation itself drags on for too long, leading to the film's uneven and frequently too-slow pace. Tighter editing could produce a snappier version while omitting little content. Boxoffice outlook is dim.

Julia (Daphna Kastner), an attractive but somewhat frustrated woman, has lived with her lover Jack (David Charles) for two years. When he unexpectedly asks her to marry him, she stalls, feeling uneasy about the prospect of making their arrangement permanent. The next morning, Jack, irritated by her lack of commitment, pursues the issue, precipitating a crisis in their relationship.

As he leaves for work, Julia answers the phone and encounters an amicable young man, Daniel (capably played by David Duchoveny, who resembles a young Richard Gere). Julia soon finds herself drawn to Daniel, who apparently has dialed the wrong number. Neither of them wants to hang up. Both on portable phones, they spend the morning together following their daily routines, telling each other about themselves.

Almost all of the stories are sexual in nature, and tend to become repetitious and a bit boring as the conversation stretches itself through morning shaves, showers and baths (with just enough gratuitous nudity).

Jack comes home unexpectedly, quickly makes love to Julia in the kitchen and then stalks out when she still refuses to say "yes" to his proposal — all the while Daniel listens in.

The pace really becomes bogged down when the writers (Bashar Shbib, who altered the spelling of his name from Bachar Chbib, and Kastner) throw in some unexpected guests for Julia and Daniel: a quarreling couple and Daniel's landlord and wife. These confusing scenes are prime candidates for cutting.

Julia is bright and creative, but afraid of both being alone and being with the wrong person. Daniel portrays himself as understanding, sensitive and romantic, the very image of Julia's passionate fantasies. Inevitably (and finally), she invites Daniel over for lunch the next day.

The pace pics up considerably once they put down the phones and Daniel arrives at Julia's (although the anticipated love scene could easily have been edited down). At this point (nearly two-thirds into the film), the story begins to take new twists, adding considerably more interest.

This isn't the first time Daniel has dialed the "wrong" number, for instance. And Julia, who is not an entirely sympathetic character, develops more self-determination as the plot unfolds, giving her an added depth and interest.

Like "Shirley Valentine," "Julia Has Two Lovers" deals with a woman realizing she does not need to define herself in terms of a relationship with a man. Unlike "Shirley," however, in "Julia" the realization is a bit trite because the characters never seem fully developed.

Production values are mediocre, with too many blurred images. — *Magg.*

Enid Is Sleeping

Seattle A Vestron Pictures presentation of a Davis Entertainment Co. production. Produced by John A. Davis, Howard Malin. Executive producers, Mitchell Cannold, Dori Berinstein, Adam Platnick. Directed by Maurice Phillips. Screenplay, A.J. Tipping, James Whaley, Phillips; camera (color), Affonso Beato; editor, Malcolm Campbell; music, Craig Safan; costume design, Lisa Jensen; art direction, Gershon Ginsburg; production design, Paul Peters; line producer, Susan Vogelfang; executive in charge of production, Scott Kramer; associate producers, Robert Anderson, Darlene K. Chan; coproducer, Bill Brigode; casting, Janet Hirshenson, Jane Jenkins. Reviewed at the Seattle Intl. Film Festival, May 27, 1990. No MPAA rating. Running time: **100 MIN.**

June . . . . Elizabeth Perkins
Harry . . . . Judge Reinhold
Floyd . . . . Jeffrey Jones
Enid . . . . Maureen Mueller
Mavis . . . . Rhea Perlman

■ The original director's cut of "Enid Is Sleeping" is a funny, fast-paced film that does not deserve to die with Vestron Pictures, which bought original rights and unsuccessfully tried to peddle its own edited version. Correctly handled, this offbeat black comedy shows potential to become an arthouse winner.

During two showings at the Seattle Intl. Film Fest of the original cut by director Maurice Phillips, the macabre but humorous film drew strong, favorable audience reaction.

The story centers on the botched attempts of June (Elizabeth Perkins) to dispose of the body of her much-despised older sister, Enid. June accidentally kills Enid after Enid comes home and catches June in bed with her husband Harry (Judge Reinhold). Although a police officer in the small New Mexico town, Harry tells June to get Enid's body out of town and make it look like she died in a car accident.

What follows is a series of hilarious, rapid-fire scenes — including a satisfying twist ending — deftly directed by Phillips, who only occasionally slips in his timing. The fast pace combined with the comedic talents of Perkins, Reinhold and Jeffrey Jones, who plays Harry's partner Floyd, turn an unbelievable plot into solid entertainment.

Perkins gives a particularly fine performance as a small-town, dizzy blond with big city angst. As the younger sister who grew up being tormented by her mean older sister, her monologs directed at her dead sister provide some of the movie's best scenes.

Part of the film's success lies in its ability to reflect a very real state-of-mind of life in a small town where everyone knows everyone else, and no one's going anywhere. The town is surrounded by vast expanses of absolutely spectacular scenery, yet the characters are frequently at home, frustrated and bored, blankly staring at their tvs.

Tech credits are fine. — *Magg.*

ARCHIVE REVIEW

Don't Play Us Cheap

New York A Movin On Distribution presentation of a Yeah production. Produced and directed by Melvin Van Peebles. Screenplay, Van Peebles, based on his play; camera (CFI color), Bob Maxwell; editor, Van Peebles; music, Van Peebles; musical supervision, Harold Wheeler; sound, Tom Scott; costume design, Bernard Johnson; production manager, Ernest Murray; 2d unit director, Jim Hinton; associate producers, Jerry Weissman, Charles Blackwell. Reviewed at Museum of Modern Art 5th floor screening room, N.Y., June 6, 1990. No MPAA Rating. Running time: **104 MIN.**

Miss Maybell . . . . Esther Rolle
David . . . . Avon Long
Earnestine . . . . Rhetta Hughes
Mrs. Bowser . . . . Mabel King
Mr. Bowser . . . . Robert Dunn
Mrs. Washington . . . Joshie Jo Armstead
Mr. Washington . George (Ooppee) McCurn
Trinity . . . . Joseph Keyes
Mr. Percy . . . . Thomas Anderson
Mrs. Johnson . . . . Jay Vanleer
Mr. Johnson/cockroach . . . . . Frank Carey
Harold Johnson/rat . . . . . . Nate Barnett

■ Melvin Van Peebles' film of his play "Don't Play Us Cheap" is an entertaining artifact made 18 years ago. Put on the shelf after having only benefit screenings in 1973, pic offers some terrific musical numbers and an ebullient look at black culture of a generation back.

Utilizing the same cast that he directed on Broadway, Van Peebles creates the atmosphere of a house party in Harlem that's a direct forerunner of the Hudlin Bros.' recent hit "House Party."

His fantasy premise of an imp and little devil crashing the party to spoil it out of pure meanness allows the filmmaker's militant themes to be expressed in humor and whimsy.

Among the dozen tunes composed by Van Peebles is a show-stopping number "Quittin' Time" sung by lanky George (Ooppee) McCurn. It's a sterling example of the power of recording musical numbers in direct sound, a technique revived for the occasion (two years before Peter Bogdanovich's similarly inclined "At Long Last Love") by Van Peebles, who went to the trouble of building sets in New Mexico and using mobile sound trucks for that purpose.

There's also an extremely complex roundelay of four songs sung together which comes off impressively. Hurting the film's overall

Original Play
Don't Play Us Cheap

A Melvin Van Peebles presentation of a musical comedy in two acts (14 numbers), with book, music and lyrics by Melvin Van Peebles. Staged by Melvin Van Peebles; scenery, Kurt Lundell; costumes, Bernard Johnson; lighting, Martin Aronstein; musical supervision, Harold Wheeler. General managers, Eugene Wolsk, Emanuel Azenberg; company manager, David Payne; publicity, Michael Alpert, Arthur Rubine; stage managers, Charles Blackwell, Charles Briggs; assistant, Jerry Lawes; advertising, Blaine-Thompson (Michael De Louise). Opened May 16, '72, at the Ethel Barrymore Theater, N.Y.; $10 top.

Rat, Harold Johnson	Nate Barnett
Roach, Mr. Johnson	Frank Carey
Mr. Percy	Thomas Anderson
Mrs. Washington	Joshie Jo Armstead
Mr. Bowsey	Robert Dunn
Earnestine	Rhetta Hughes
Trinity	Joe Keyes Jr.
Mrs. Bowser	Mabel King
David	Avon Long
Mr. Washington	George (Ooppee) McCurn
Miss Maybell	Esther Rolle
Mrs. Johnson	Jay Vanieer

Musicals numbers: "Some Days It Seems That It Just Don't Even Pay To Get Out Of Bed," "Break That Party," "8 Day Week," "Saturday Night," "I'm A Bad Character," "You Cut Up The Clothes In My Closet Full Of Dreams," "It Makes No Difference," "Quittin' Time," "Ain't Love Grand," "The Book Of Life," Counterpart Quartet ("Ain't Love Grand," "Know Your Business," "Big Future," "Break That Party"), "Feast On Me," "The Phoney Game," "Smash Him."

impact is Van Peebles' use of visual tricks left over from the '60s, particularly superimpositions, that stunt the live performance feel. In particular, coloratura Rhetta Hughes' big number is ruined by the disconcerting multiple images of her overlaid on screen.

Fantasy elements climax with black comedy of topliner Esther Rolle smashing the little devil in the form of a cockroach with a rolled up newspaper. Rolle is in great form as the party hostess, ably supported by an ensemble cast.

Tech credits range from top-notch sound recording to shaky camerawork. Most setups are filmed using the multiple camera method and both focus and framing are too loose at times. Editing, credited to the filmmaker, is haphazard where a seamless approach would have benefited the "live" feel.

Pic deserves a second round of look-sees by potential distributors, as it shares the same time capsule qualities that finally earned "The Plot Against Harry" a latter-day release. — *Lor.*

The Punisher

London A Castle Premier release (in the U.K.) of a New World Intl. presentation of a Robert Kamen production. Produced by Kamen. Executive producer, Robert Guralnick. Directed by Mark Goldblatt. Screenplay, Boaz Yakin; camera (Eastmancolor), Ian Baker; editor, Tim Wellburn; music, Dennis Dreith; sound (Dolby), David Lee; production design, Norma Moriceau; art direction, Peta Lawson; assistant director, Philip Hearnshaw; coproducer, Su Armstrong; casting, Faith Martin (Australia), Melissa Skoff. Reviewed at the Cannon Oxford Street Theater, London, June 5, 1990. MPAA Rating: R. Running time: **90 MIN.**

Frank Castle	Dolph Lundgren
Jake Berkowitz	Louis Gossett Jr.
Gianni France	Jeroen Krabbe
Lady Tanaka	Bryan Marshall
Dino Moretti	Nancy Everhard
Shake	Barry Otto
Tommy Franco	Brian Rooney
Tanaka's daughter	Zoshka Mizak
Tarrone	Todd Boyce

■ **With origins in a Marvel Comics character, "The Punisher" is, as might be expected, two-dimensional. Headliner Dolph Lundgren and the promise of Rambo-style weaponry will attract the usual schlock-action audience in theatrical and video.**

The over-the-top violence in this comic-strip come to life, however, has ensured its classification (in the U.K.) will exclude the vital teen market. The Punisher has killed 125 people before the film even begins, and the ensuing 90 minutes are crammed with slaughters of every conceivable kind.

Pic was the only product of the now-defunct New World offshoot Down Under. It's amusing to see a large proportion of the Aussie thesping industry shot, stabbed, hanged, poisoned and generally mutilated, but it won't draw any raves for the dramatic talents of the antipodes.

Lundgren looks just as if he's stepped out of a comic book. All that's missing from his actions is the "pow!" "bam!" or "wham!" Thankfully, he breezes through the B-grade plot with tongue firmly placed in cheek, and the script allows him some nice one-liners that indicate no one is really taking this caper seriously.

Louis Gossett Jr. is far too good for the material, and Bryan Marshall is killed off in the first five minutes.

Story involves an ex-cop whose wife and children were murdered by the mafia in New York. He hides from civilization in the city's sewers, having one-way conversations with God in which he vocalizes the torture of his soul. For five years he's been killing the various heads of the mob families in non-stop vengeance.

Another party comes to play; the Japanese mafia headed by the glamorous, stony cold Lady Tanaka. She launches a takeover bid for the depleted and weakened New York mafia, which is, of course, rejected, and the two teams are promptly at war.

The Punisher is quite content to see his enemies slaughter each other until the Japanese kidnap the locals' children. Kids are a soft spot for the antihero, so he intervenes, and a predictable bloodbath ensues.

Technically, the film is fine, but not as slick as it could have been, and authenticity takes a beating, with New York looking decidedly like North Sydney. — *Krug.*

The Gumshoe Kid

New York A Skouras Pictures release of an Argus Entertainment production. Executive producer, Victor Bardack. Produced and directed by Joseph Manduke. Screenplay, Bardack; camera (Image Transform color), Harvey Genkins; editor, Richard G. Haines; music, Peter Matz; sound (Ultra-Stereo), Garry Cunningham; production design, Batia Grafka; costume design, Ron Talsky; production manager-coproducer, Larry Kostroff; assistant director, Jim Behnke; additional editor, Robert Ross; stunt coordinator, Spiro Razatos; casting, Barbara Remsen, Ann Remsen Manners. Reviewed on Academy vidcassette, N.Y., June 11, 1990. MPAA Rating: R. Running time: **98 MIN.**

Jeff Sherman	Jay Underwood
Rita Benson	Tracy Scoggins
Ben Sherman	Vince Edwards
Gracie Sherman	Arlene Golonka
Mona	Pamela Springsteen
Emily Sherman	Amy Lynne
Capt. Billings	Biff Yeager
Monty	Xander Berkeley
Meester	Gino Conforti

Also with: Miguel Sandoval, Tim Halderman, David Dunard, Michael Alaimo, Stephen Young.

■ **"The Gumshoe Kid," alternately titled "The Detective Kid," is a charming little comedy that pays homage to the private eye genre.**

Currently available in vidstores, film had a brief theatrical run in Albuquerque in February.

Jay Underwood, performing with the self-assurance of a younger Tom Hanks, carries the picture as a guy obsessed with Bogart who gets a job in Vince Edwards' agency through the efforts of his mom, Arlene Golonka. Finally assigned to a field case in surveillance, he's thrown together with femme fatale Tracy Scoggins.

The two of them are on the lam for the rest of the film after Scoggins' boyfriend is nabbed by persons unknown. Helmer Joe Manduke maintains a lighthearted mood, giving both principal players a chance to let their hair down engagingly en route to a friendly finish.

This is breezy, light entertainment that seems out of step in today's cinema but enjoyable nonetheless. Solid supporting turns, notably by Gino Conforti as an uppity sign painter and cute Pamela Springsteen as Edwards' ditzy secretary, make for a winning package. — *Lor.*

False Identity

Hollywood An RKO Pictures release. Produced by James Shavick. Executive producers, Ted Hartley, Gerald Offsay, Daniel Sarnoff. Directed by James Keach. Screenplay, Sandra Bailey; camera, Bernard Aurox; sound, Gerald B. Wolfe; production design, Kevin Ryan; art direction, Trey Scott; set decoration, Ron Lombard; associate producers, Bailey, Rachel Shavick. Reviewed at Samuel Goldwyn Pavilion Theater, June 7, 1990. MPAA Rating: PG-13. Running time: **92 MIN.**

Rachel	Genevieve Bujold
Ben	Stacy Keach
Marshall	Tobin Bell
Luther	Mike Champion
Vera	Veronica Cartwright

■ **This low-energy murder mystery, destined for quick video release through Prism Entertainment, is unlikely to find theatrical exposure beyond its single-screen L.A. playoff.**

Slow-moving and seamily produced pic casts Stacy Keach as a man presumed dead who returns to his hometown after 17 years in prison. He tries to piece together his identity, but he's hampered by the fact that his face was carved up in a murder attempt. He also has a steel plate in his head.

Genevieve Bujold reprises her "Choose Me" assignment as a radio personality, but this time she's a terrier-like reporter who's gotten hold of a dirty bone involving the murder, some 20 ago, of a local Vietnam vet.

Keach shows up trying to figure out why he remembers the place right about the time she launches a radio program prodding the townspeople to give up their secrets about the fallen local hero.

After much stonewalled detective work and random violence on the part of someone who's trying to suppress the ugly past, the truth comes out in an avalanche of dirty laundry typical of a bad novel. The town baddie is arrested, and Keach is restored to his rightful place in the bosom of a wealthy family.

Plot is as complicated as it sounds, and strains credibility both logically and medically.

Keach's role requires him to lurch around with a numbed brain in a project that has no discernible aspirations beyond its dubious entertainment value.

Bujold, too, suffers some diminishment in these dim surroundings, although her performance surpasses the requirements.

Other casting is very uneven, as is pic's overall tone under Jim Keach's direction. — *Daws*.

Raspad
(U.S.-UKRAINIAN)

Cannes A Dovzhenko Studios (Kiev)/Peter O. Almond Prods./Pacific Film Fund (San Francisco) coproduction. Executive producer, Mikhail Kistikowski. Directed by Mikhail Belikov. Screenplay, Belikov, Oleg Pridhodko; camera (color, black & white), Alexander Shagayev, Piotr Trashevski; sound (Dolby), Tom Johnson, Skywalker Sound Lucas Arts Entertainment Co. Reviewed at the Cannes Film Festival (market), May 17, 1990. Running time: **95 MIN.**
Zhuralev . . . . Sergei Shakurov

■ "Raspad" has a subject bound to stir up interest: It's a dramatized tale of the aftereffects of the Chernobyl disaster told from a Ukrainian p.o.v. Pic should find wider audiences than the usual arthouse release, especially on tv.

Begun by the Dovzhenko Film Studios in Kiev, pic was completed with additional postproduction funding (used mostly for Dolby sound and film stock) by San Francisco-based producers Peter O. Almond and Susan O'Connell of the Pacific Film Fund.

Veteran helmer Mikhail Belikov weaves the highly dramatic story elements taking place before, during and after the Chernobyl nuclear power plant accident into a fairly routine film. Though it lacks stylistic tension, pic's sincerity gives it some emotional payoff.

Events revolve around Zhuralev (played by the handsome, strong-jawed Sergei Shakurov), whose wife has taken up with a rich young Party official. He swallows his pride to keep the family together.

Meanwhile, April 25, 1986, rolls around. Script throws away the main event when the reactor blows up. (Too hard for the special-effects department?) All that's shown is firefighters rushing in just after the explosion.

One of Zhuralev's pals, a medic, is there. Horrified by what he's seen, he returns to the nearby inhabited center, Energotechnicians City, and begins a hopeless, hysterical attempt to persuade people to get their kids off the street "so they won't die." No one listens, but before pic can wring this reaction for its full tragic irony, they are evacuating apartment buildings and piling people into buses.

One cute little boy gets separated from his mother. They put him on a bus that passes her (with baby) on a bridge, but the driver won't stop because he's been warned the bridge is highly radioactive.

A pair of newlyweds leave their wedding banquet with the unfortunate idea of spending their honeymoon camping in the woods near Chernobyl. Belikov has a heavy hand in contrasting their carefree loving on the grass with the appearance, a few seconds later, of a squad of men in rubber suits and face masks, planting nuke warnings everywhere.

The couple ends up in a church begging the priest to marry them, but he's too busy saving radioactive icons. Meanwhile, Zhuralev's wife decides to catch the last ride out of Kiev before the authorities close the city. She and son leave with the Party official.

Zhuralev decides on suicide by volunteering to return to Chernobyl with a hand-picked cleanup squad. There they find the cute tyke alone in a completely deserted city, waiting for his mother to come back for him.

"Raspad" goes for a number of easy effects and pathetic situations. In spite of its obvious plotting, however, the weight of the tragedy comes through with surprising force. Not as clever as "The Day After," and much less believable, the film draws its strength from viewer's morbid curiosity to see the worst visualized and the knowledge it really happened.

More than doomed children and newlyweds, it is random images that hit home in "Raspad." One is an awesome aerial shot of an infinite column of buses threading its way out of Energotechnicians City, a re-created scene that looks like newsreel.

In another memorable image, a fleet of sinister black limos pulls up on the airport runway, and out pour the families of Party VIPs, flying out of Kiev while officials are caught between claiming there's no danger and being unable to evacuate the city.

Another shocker is a railway station scene jammed with desperate refugees trying to get an impossible train ticket. In an overflowing hospital, doctors perform assembly line abortions while announcing the health minister has suspended its ban of the operation under the circumstances.

Obviously there's a lot to stare at, and a lot of food for thought. As sobering an antinuclear film as has been made East or West, "Raspad" is an example of the new Soviet glasnost in action, as well as an early look at what U.S. aid can do to help get worthy projects finished and into circulation.

An interesting footnote is how the film crew faced unknown risks in going back to Chernobyl and the still-deserted city to film the final scenes. — *Yung*.

Robocop 2

New York An Orion Pictures release of a Jon Davison production. Executive producer, Patrick Crowley. Produced by Davison. Directed by Irvin Kershner. Screenplay, Frank Miller, Walon Green, from story by Miller, based on characters created by Edward Neumeier, Michael Miner; camera (Duart color; Deluxe prints), Mark Irwin; editor, William Anderson; music, Leonard Rosenman; sound (Dolby), Edward Tise; sound effects, Stephen Hunter Flick; production design, Peter Jamison; art direction, Pam Marcotte; set decoration, Ronald R. Reiss; costume design, Rosanna Norton; assistant director, Tom Davies; production manager, Patrick Crowley; special effects supervisors, Dale Martin, William Greg Curtis; animation sequences, Phil Tippett; Robocop designed and created by Rob Bottin; Robocop costumes, Bottin; special photographic effects, Peter Kuran/VCE; matte paintings, Rocco Gioffre; digital character performance, de Graf/Wharman; stunt coordinator-2d unit director, Conrad E. Palmisano; 2d unit camera, Jamie Anderson; associate producers, Jane Bartelme, Tippett; casting, Sally Dennison, Julie Selzer, Justine Jacoby. Reviewed at Festival theater, N.Y., June 18, 1990. MPAA Rating: R. Running time: **118 MIN.**
Robocop . . . . Peter Weller
Anne Lewis . . . . Nancy Allen
Old man . . . . Daniel O'Herlihy
Juliette Faxx . . . . Belinda Bauer
Cain . . . . Tom Noonan
Hob . . . . Gabriel Damon
Donald Johnson . . . . Felton Perry
Sgt. Reed . . . . Robert Do'Qui
Angie . . . . Galyn Görg
Duffy . . . . Stephen Lee
Mayor Kuzak . . . . Willard Pugh
Whittaker . . . . Roger Aaron Brown
Lab technician Garcia . Patricia Charbonneau
Holzgang . . . . Jeff McCarthy
Estevez . . . . Wanda De Jesus
Schenk . . . . John Doolittle
Delaney . . . . Ken Lerner
Tzi Ma . . . . Tak Akita
Sunblock woman . . . . . Fabiana Udenio
Whittaker . . . . Roger Aaron Brown
Also with: John Glover, Mario Machado, Leeza Gibbons, Yogi Baird.

■ This ultraviolent, nihilistic sequel has enough technical dazzle to impress hardware fans, but it's a punishing film unlikely to attract or entertain crossover audiences.

Obviously no one in the Orion front office told filmmakers Jon Davison and Irvin Kershner that less is more. Pic climaxes at roughly the 90-minute mark, with a half hour of pummeling tacked on.

Estimated $30-million budget is more than double that of Paul Verhoeven's breakthrough film three years earlier and is Orion's largest commitment for a production (second in overall cost to Orion's pickup "Valmont").

"Robocop 2" is a textbook example of what writer Umberto Eco ("The Name Of The Rose") described a decade ago in his "Superman theory," to explain the lure of popular entertainment ranging from soap operas and comic strips to pabulum movies (as well as predicting today's sequelitis). Robocop is a mythic figure who is never consumed, never ages or experiences anything beyond the ephemeral job at hand.

In fact, at film's end, the main heroes (Peter Weller and Nancy Allen) and villains (corporate leader and corrupt mayor) are still in place with only hundreds of lowly druggies and innocent people left dead. The society has not changed a bit and protagonists are ready to repeat the process.

As Eco pointed out, to keep an audience interested in an adventure where nothing *really* happens (that goes for Verhoeven's current opus "Total Recall" as well), increasingly decadent and outré details are needed for diversion. Here the level of constant violence, with noisy sound effects, explosions and hundreds of thousands of rounds fired by automatic weaponry, is at first arresting but ultimately numbing and boring.

Social satire provided here by writers Walon Green (whose "The Hellstrom Chronicle" for David Wolper was a sci-fi classic) and

Frank Miller (who helped revivify a comic book hero by writing "Batman: The Dark Knight Returns") is stale. The future is represented by a crumbling Detroit (actually filmed like the original in Texas, however), dominated by Dan O'Herlihy's Omni Consumer Products company. He's set to foreclose on loans and literally take possession of Motown.

Standing in his way is a loose cannon, drug magnate/user Tom Noonan, whose goal is to flood society with designer versions of his drug Nuke. Weller as Robocop must defeat both factions while effeminate mayor Willard Pugh (in a campy comic relief turn) gets in the way.

Director Kershner fails to make this interesting due to repetition. Robocop and even Noonan's character are literally destroyed several times only to come back again for redundant, showy battles. Latter is reconstituted as Robocop 2 by O'Herlihy's sexy assistant Belinda Bauer, providing the film's final half hour of spectacular stop-motion animation by Phil Tippett. It's a pure display of great special effects as an end in themselves.

Film logically ends when Robocop wipes out the druggies, notably Gabriel Damon as a 12-year-old gangster whose precocious performance is the best thing in the picture. Amount of swearing and violence meted out by Damon and other children on screen is the film's most antisocial and controversial aspect, especially given its youthful target audience.

Though purportedly a critical, antiestablishment message, film's script becomes confused in a lengthy segment of O'Herlihy having Robocop reprogrammed as Mr. Nice Guy. For purposes of eliciting cheap laughs, film whips up the audience to root for his inevitable return to normal, i.e., ruthless, vigilante behavior.

Fans are left with black humor to enjoy, notably a tv commercials featuring John Glover (of "Gremlins 2") as a futuristic car hawker and ultra-sexy Fabiana Udenio peddling suntan oil after the ozone layer has been destroyed.

Acting is variable, with Noonan and Weller workmanlike, while Bauer and dancer Galyn Görg provide earthy beauty. Leonard Rosenman's old-fashioned score is weak and inappropriate. — *Lor.*

Turné
(On Tour)
(ITALIAN)

Rome A Penta Distribuzione release. Produced by Gianni Minervini for AMA Film and Mario and Vittorio Cecchi Gori for C.G. Tiger Group Cinematografica and Reteitalia. Directed by Gabriele Salvatores. Screenplay, Francesca Marciano, Fabrizio Bentivoglio, Salvatores; camera (color), Italo Petruccione; editor, Nino Baragli; music, Roberto Ciotti; art direction, Marco Dentici. Reviewed at Eden Cinema, Rome, May 8, 1990. Running time: **88 MIN.**
Dario . . . . Diego Abatantuono
Vittoria . . . . Laura Morante
Federico . . . . Fabrizio Bentivoglio
Also with: Luigi Montini, Barbara Scoppa.

■ After "Marrakech Express," helmer Gabriele Salvatores again demonstrates his penchant for offbeat road movies in "On Tour." Though good-humored to the point of being a comedy, film has done just so-so business onshore.

A trio of thesps, led by the fine Diego Abatantuono, buoys the one-note plot of a stage group touring Italy as a hidden love triangle is revealed gradually.

Actor Dario (the burly, effervescent Abatantuono) has just stolen Vittoria (Laura Morante) away from his best friend, Federico (Fabrizio Bentivoglio). All the slight, scraggly haired Federico knows is she didn't sleep at home the night before. Guilty but protective, Dario gets him a gig in "The Cherry Orchard" and forces him to go on tour in his beaten-up Mercedes.

Every night, Federico bombs and Dario tries to cover up for him. Between cooing telephone calls to Vittoria, Dario consoles his pal. But the truth will out (in an obvious scene in which Federico overhears a revealing phone call).

In Rome, during a three-way confrontation, the lady decides she loves them both, but fails to impose a workable ménàge à trois. Seething rivalry persists as all three hit the road. By pic's end, Vittoria leaves, but it looks like Dario and Federico's friendship might survive.

Thin story was penned by the director and two actors (Bentivoglio and Francesca Marciano). Except in the case of Abatantuono, who keeps pic alive through what seems to be improvised dialog, thesping isn't up to the challenge.

The elegant, normally rational Morante is motiveless as a timid seductress unable to let go of one boyfriend. Bentivoglio is stuck in a part that calls for show-stopping brilliance that doesn't come across. When a Yank director prefers him to Abatantuono, the explanation is more in the script than on film.

To its credit, pic shows backstage life for the tiring grind it is, without diminishing the magic tension of actors entering into other lives. Especially good are two old-time troupers in the play's cast.

Foreign audiences will appreciate the magnificent views of rural Italy that sparkle throughout. Photography (by Italo Petruccione) is a pleasure, and music (Roberto Ciotti) lively and insistent. Pic unspooled in this year's Cannes Film Festival Un Certain Regard section. — *Yung.*

Rockula

New York A Cannon release. Executive producers, Yoram Globus, Christopher Pearce. Produced by Jefery Levy. Directed by Luca Bercovici. Screenplay, Levy, Christopher Verwiel; camera (TVC color), John Schwartzman; editor, Maureen O'Connell; music, Hilary Bercovici; music supervisor, Joachim H. Hansch; sound (Ultra-Stereo), Greg Choa; production design, Jane Ann Stewart; costume design, Pamela Sydney Skaist, Claire Louise Joseph; choreography, Russell Clark, Toni Basil; production manager, Ernest Johnson; assistant director, Richard Wells; special makeup effects, Tony Gardner, Larry Hamlin; casting, Nancy Lara-Hansch. Reviewed on Warner Home Video/Cannon vidcassette, N.Y., June 12, 1990. MPAA Rating: PG-13. Running time: **91 MIN.**
Ralph . . . . Dean Cameron
Phoebe . . . . Toni Basil
Mona . . . . Tawny Feré
Stanley . . . . Thomas Dolby
Chuck . . . . Susan Tyrrell
Also with: Bo Diddley, Nancye Ferguson, Kevin Hunter, Rick Zumwalt, Tamara De-Treaux, Visiting Kids.

■ Music is welded to the horror genre for the umpteenth time with poor results in "Rockula," a marginal Cannon picture that went into release in February and recently played briefly on 42d Street in Manhattan.

More likely to find its audience among video fans, pic limns the uninteresting story of 400-year-old virgin vampire Dean Cameron, who every 22 years has been fated to meet his dream girl (Tawny Feré), only to lose her sans consummation when an evil pirate kills her each time on Halloween.

Numerous rock songs and music video-styled interludes pad the running time of this innocuous exercise, which could have used a much stronger storyline.

Several music industry personalities pop up, notably Toni Basil as Cameron's sexy vampire mother and Thomas Dolby as an English twit. Feré, previously unveiled in "Angel III," is most alluring as the heroine and belts a rock song well. — *Lor.*

Peacemaker

Chicago A Fries Entertainment release through Paragon Arts of a Gibraltar Releasing Organization and Mentone Pictures production. Executive producer, Charles Fries. Produced by Andrew Lane, Wayne Crawford. Written and directed by Kevin S. Tenney. Camera (color), Thomas Jewett; editor, Dan Duncin; music, Dennis Michael Tenney; sound, George Alch; stunt coordinator, B.J. Davis; makeup, John Blake; production design, Rob Sissman; art direction, Tucker Johnston; costume design, Lennie Barin; assistant director, David Cobbs; co-executive producer, Joel Levine; coproducer, Cary Glieberman; casting, Maira Suro Castles. Reviewed at the Chestnut Station Theater, Chicago, May 24, 1990. MPAA Rating: R. Running time: **90 MIN.**
Yates . . . . Robert Forster
Townsend . . . . Lance Edwards
Dori Caisson . . . . Hilary Shepard
Sgt. Frank Ramos . . . . Robert Davi
Doc . . . . Bert Remsen

■ Kevin S. Tenney's "Peacemaker" is an unexpected gem, a sci-fi action thriller that really delivers the goods despite an apparent low budget. Pic suffered from underexposure during its brief theatrical run, but will most likely satisfy anyone who stumbles upon it on cable or video.

Inventive plot is a tale of two humanoid aliens who crash-land on Earth. One is an intergalactic serial killer, the other a police officer, or peacemaker.

A simple set-up, except for one complication: Both claim to be the cop. Since each is equally violent and intent on killing the other, it becomes difficult to decide which one is actually the good guy.

Both aliens attempt to enlist the aid of assistant medical examiner Hilary Shepard, hoping she can help them find the key to the one functional space rover that survived their crash landing. Shepard is drawn into the conflict after watching one of them regenerate on a morgue slab after being shot about 400 times by overzealous L.A. police.

The aliens, it seems, can be destroyed only by massive damage to the brain, a quirk that provides the opportunity for some spectacular mayhem. These boys absorb shotgun blasts, sever their own limbs to escape handcuffs, even crash into a dynamite shack and blow themselves sky-high without slowing down.

"Peacemaker" is a stunt extravaganza, a nonstop, fast-paced assemblage of chases, shootouts and explosions building to an impressive climax. It also boasts surprisingly effective makeup and special effects.

Pic has a big-budget look throughout, boosted by the rich, nighttime cinematography of Thomas Jewett. Production's lack of resources is betrayed only by the occasional continuity error and a few poorly timed chase sequences that clearly could have used another take.

Tenney's screenplay holds interest by weaving elements of romance and humor into the story and putting an intriguing spin on conventions lifted from innumerable standard-issue police yarns.

Acting throughout is above par. Robert Forster is especially effective as the older, more taciturn alien and newcomer Lance Edwards more than holds his own as Forster's foil. — *Brin.*

A Time To Remember

New York A Filmworld Distributors release of a Tra/Zan Group presentation of a Miam production. Executive producer, John Zandt. Produced by Thomas Travers, Randy Jurgensen, Terence O'Leary. Directed by Travers. Screenplay, Travers; camera (TVC color), Rich Lee; editor, Lorenzo Marinelli; music, Bill Grabowski; sound, Dan Kennedy; art direction, Miko Vejzovic; production manager, Paula Connelly; assistant director, Hugh Rawson; casting, Navarro Bertoni. Reviewed on Studio Entertainment vidcassette, N.Y., June 11, 1990. MPAA Rating: G. Running time: **72 MIN.**
Father Walsh . . . . Donald O'Connor
Mama Theresa . . . . Morgana King
Frank Villano . . . . Raymond Serra
Angelo Villano . . . . Ruben Gomez
Father Halloran . . . . Tommy Makem
  Also with: Suzanne Gardner, Paris Dimoleon, Mark Mensch, Alison Case, Joseph Kakuk, Joseph D'Orio, Anthony Russ.

■ **Old-fashioned sentimentality is overdone in "A Time To Remember," reviewed here for the record after nominal release two years ago.**

Pic was shot five years back as "Miracle In A Manger" in upstate N.Y. Its abbreviated running time indicates some problems along the way, but filmmaker Thomas Travers simply doesn't demonstrate the chops needed to singlehandedly bring back a genre (associated with Bing Crosby) popular over four decades ago.

Donald O'Connor brings sincerity to his role as a priest who encourages young Ruben Gomez in his choral work. The kid wants to be the next Lanza or Caruso and is encouraged by mamma Morgana King (excellent in a more ethnic approach than her "Godfather" role) but opposed vehemently by daddy Raymond Serra.

Told awkwardly in a flashback structure from the vantage point of hero's concert hall success as an adult, pic lumbers along with an unconvincing central motif of the kid losing his voice temporarily after a fight. Other attempts at pathos fall flat and cast's singing is mediocre.

Give Travers credit for good intentions, but his film falls wide of the mark. — *Lor.*

Keaton's Cop

New York A Cannon release of a Third Coast production. Executive producer, Maurice Duke. Produced and directed by Bob Burge. Screenplay, Michael B. Druxman; camera (Film Service color), Ozzie Smith; editor, Terry Chambers; music, Kevin Barnes, David Connor; sound (Ultra-Stereo), Mike Hall; production design, John Iacovelli; assistant director, Bonnie Kate Brown; production manager-associate producer, Peggy Slater; stunt coordinator, Marvin Walters; special effects, Michael Thompson; casting, Tony Roberts, Janice Head (Texas). Reviewed on Warner Home Video/Cannon vidcassette. N.Y., June 15, 1990. MPAA Rating: R. Running time: **95 MIN.**
Mike Gable . . . . Lee Majors
Louie Keaton . . . . Abe Vigoda
Susan Watson . . . . . Tracy Brooks Swope
Jake Barber . . . . Don Rickles
Archie (Big Mama) . . . . . June Wilkinson
Det. Hayes . . . . Art LaFleur
Lt. Spence . . . . Robert Hilliard
Jimmy Gable . . . . Clinton (Austin) Shirley
Blue the dog . . . . Himself
Marsha . . . . Fredrika Duke

■ **Abe Vigoda's flavorful turn as a crusty gangster enlivens the uneventful cop thriller "Keaton's Cop." Released regionally by Cannon in March, pic recently played 42d Street.**

Vigoda is the Keaton of the title, paired with cop Lee Majors after Majors' partner Don Rickles is murdered. They're out to unravel who put the hit on Vigoda and ended up wasting Rickles.

Trail laboriously leads to Big Mama, a well-cast, well-endowed and well-preserved June Wilkinson who's now running a gang in Galveston. Unfortunately, the former pinup and dinner theater ("Pajama Tops") star is off-screen for most of the picture and not well utilized by director Bob Burge, who previously cast her in other

films like "Vasectomy." Tracy Brooks Swope has a better role as Vigoda's nurse who, natch, falls in love with the one-time $6-million guy.

Majors and Vigoda make an okay team, with latter getting in some bon mots and fun physical shtick. It's sort of a geriatric version of "48 HRS."

Low-budget lensing in Galveston is unspectacular and film almost sinks under the turgid weight of a subplot focusing on Majors' cute son. — *Lor.*

Boca de Ouro
(Golden Mouth)
(BRAZILIAN)

Rio de Janeiro An Art Films/Columbia Pictures release of a JN Filmes production. Produced by Jofre Rodrigues. Directed by Walter Avancini. Screenplay, Avancini, based on the play by Nelson Rodrigues; camera (color), Carlos Egberto; music, Edu Lobo; executive producers, Jofre Rodrigues, Fernando Silva; associate producers, Jose C. Padilha, Adalberto M. Calabria, Nelson Rodrigues Filho. Reviewed at Art Fashion Mall 2 theater, Rio de Janeiro, May 16, 1990. Running time: **95 MIN.**
Boca de Ouro . . . . Tarcisio Meira
Guigui . . . . Claudia Raia
Celeste . . . . Luma de Oliveira
Caveirinha . . . . Hugo Carvana
Maria Luiza . . . . Maria Padilha
Leleco . . . . Ricardo Petraglia
  Also with: Grande Otelo, Osmar Prado, Joao Signorelli, Betty Gofman, Marcia Couto, Nelson Sacha Rodrigues, Tarcisio Filho.

■ **In this new version of the 1959 play by Nelson Rodrigues, director Walter Avancini attempts to interfere in fundamental aspects of the action in search for what he believes to be a strict cinematic approach. Result is far from faithful to the brightness of the play.**

Avancini, a well-known director of novellas and series for tv, is making his feature debut in the project produced by Nelson Rodrigues' son Jofre (who last year won the race for the movie rights to the life of ecologist Chico Mendes). Pic was originally to be directed by Nelson Pereira dos Santos, who directed the first version of the same play in 1962.

When Avancini took over, following disagreements between Santos and Jofre Rodrigues, he prepared a screenplay less committed to the interpretation of Nelson's work than to the idea of making it commercial.

Leading tv stars, such as Tarcisio Meira and Claudia Raia, were cast, and the deep psychological approach of the play to its main

character, a Brazilian mafia godfather, was nearly forgotten.

"Boca de Ouro," the criminal who took out all his teeth to replace them with golden ones in a statement of power, tends to loose contact with the social reality, which is the stage of his action. As this happens, the rich character turns out to be a caricature.

Boca's lover Guigui (Raia) seems to be acting in a sophisticated light comedy, not in the strong drama by Rodrigues. She and Celeste (top model Luma de Oliveira), a character who's sold to "Boca de Ouro" by her own husband, found it difficult to approach their roles in a meaningful way.

Rodrigues' characters are known by a subtle ambiguity which reveal them from outside to inside. In "Boca de Ouro," they are instruments framed by a system of corruption of the political class, and the power of a world of outsiders legitimized by society. Fundamentally, however, Rodrigues deals with the pathetic universe inside the human being.

These elements are minimized as helmer builds his idea of cinematic form, far from the strength of the material he is working with. This is a classic tramp to most stagers and filmmakers dealing with Rodrigues' material because the dramatic elements are to be found in the characters rather than the plot. — *Hoin.*

SYDNEY FILM FESTIVAL REVIEWS

An Angel At My Table
(NEW ZEALAND-AUSTRALIAN)

Sydney A Hibiscus Films production in association with the New Zealand Film Commission, Television New Zealand, Australian Broadcasting Corp. Produced by Bridget Ikin. Directed by Jane Campion. Screenplay, Laura Jones, based on the autobiographies of Janet Frame; camera (color), Stuart Dryburgh; editor, Veronica Haussler; music, Don McGlashan; sound, John Dennison; production design, Grant Major; costume design, Glenys Jackson; production manager, Owen Hughes; assistant director, Corrie Soeterboek; coproducer, John Maynard; casting, Diana Rowan. Reviewed at the Sydney Film Festival, June 10, 1990. Running time: **156 MIN.**

Janet Frame	Kerry Fox
Young Janet	Alexia Keogh
Teenage Janet	Karen Fergusson
Mum	Iris Churn
Dad	K.J. Wilson
Myrtle	Melina Bernecker
Isabel	Glynis Angell
June	Sarah Smuts-Kennedy
John Forrest	Colin McColl
Frank Sargeson	Martyn Sanderson
Patrick	David Letch
Bernard	William Brandt
Mark Goulden	Peter Dennett

Also with: David McKenzie, Paula Sanchez, Peter Needham, Natalie Ellis, Eddie Hegan, Andrew Binns, Melanie Reid, Willa O'Neill, Karla Smith, Edith Campion.

■ Following the international critical success of "Sweetie," Jane Campion has come up with a touching and memorable biography of New Zealand author Janet Frame. Though originally made as a three-part tv miniseries (each part 52 minutes), "An Angel At My Table" could easily find global fest and arthouse success.

Pic's top-quality 16m lensing would suitably blow up to 35m. In a theatrical version, minimal editing would be necessary because the film, though long, is totally absorbing.

In the 1950s, Frame spent eight years in a mental home undergoing shock treatment for wrongly diagnosed schizophrenia. Far from being a downer, Campion and screenwriter Laura Jones have come up with a life-affirming celebration of the world of an eccentric, but obviously talented, woman.

Part one, "To The Island," deals with the writer's childhood in a rural community in the country's South Island. One of a large family (a twin sister died soon after birth), Janet is seen as a plump, curly-haired redhead with an inquiring mind who becomes fascinated by poetry at an early age.

Young Alexia Keogh is a charmer as the precocious child, whose father (K.J. Wilson) is extremely strict. Tragedy strikes early when Janet's beloved older sister, Myrtle (Melina Bernecker) drowns in a swimming accident.

As a teen (played by Karen Fergusson), Janet undergoes a painful puberty and becomes exceptionally shy. Finding it hard to deal with strangers, she obviously makes a wrong career choice when she decides to become a teacher.

In part two, "An Angel At My Table," Janet (Kerry Fox) goes to university but is unable to cope with practical teaching. Further tragedy enters her life when, in a bizarre coincidence, her younger sister and best friend, Isabel (Glynis Angell), also drowns.

Soon after, a friendly lecturer suggests she "take a little rest" to get over her shyness and isolation. She spends the next eight years in shock treatment, during which time she's saved from a lobotomy only because a book of her poems is published.

With her first novel also published, Janet, in part three ("The Envoy From Mirror City"), travels on a literary grant to London and then Spain. She rents a room in a fishing village and has her first (and only?) love affair with a young poet (William Brandt). When he inevitably leaves her, she deals with the disappointment with fortitude.

The film ends with her return to New Zealand following the death of her father, and the continuation of her career as a writer.

One of the many remarkable elements of this beautiful film is the way the characters, though all based on real people (and approved by Frame herself, who still lives and works in a small New Zealand town) seem to have stepped from other Campion pics. They have the same sweet eccentricities and sexual and emotional hangups as the characters in "Sweetie" and the director's short films. Family scenes are also instantly recognizable as Campion's work.

Above all, a potentially painful and harrowing film is imbued with gentle humor and great compassion, which makes every character (even the unappealing ones) come vividly alive. With no less than 140 speaking parts, the film is perfectly cast, with Fox giving a quite remarkable performance as the adult Janet.

Campion constructs the film in a series of short, sometimes elliptical scenes, establishing a situation and then moving briskly on to the next sequence, sometimes skipping over considerable periods of time, but always keeping the narrative lucid.

The transitions involving the three actresses playing Janet at different ages are handled very matter-of-factly. There are also some magical moments, such as a suggestion of premonition when, just before the doomed Myrtle is drowned, her image is mysteriously erased from a family photo.

Visually, the film lacks the striking images of "Sweetie" and the short films. Camerawork here is more functional, but is often still extremely beautiful. Other technical credits are of the highest order.

Whether it screens theatrically or on television, "An Angel At My Table" is bound to appeal to audiences seeking an intelligent and compassionate study of a troubled but gifted woman. Campion demonstrates, once again, that she has a special vision of the world.

— *Strat.*

The Street Of Dreams
(AUSTRALIAN-DOCU)

Sydney A Street of Dreams P/L production. Executive producer, Jo Sharp. Produced and directed by Martin Sharp. Camera (color), Geoff Burton, Russell Boyd, Tom Cowan, Michael Edols, Mike Glasheen; editor, Sharp, Marsha Bennett, Haydn Keenan; sound, Jef Doring, Bill Hicks; production coordinator (New York), Susan Ray. Reviewed at the Sydney Film Festival, June 9, 1990. Running time: **108 MIN.**

With: Tiny Tim.

■ "The Street Of Dreams," in production off and on since 1976, is partly a tribute to the eccentric, falsetto-voiced American warbler, Tiny Tim, and partly a valentine to Luna Park, Sydney's Coney Island. Both themes have obsessed artist Martin Sharp for years, and the film is akin to a personal exorcism.

Finding an audience (outside of a small cult following) for the film will pose a problem because people fascinated by Tiny Tim's persona and career won't necessarily appreciate the lengthy footage given to the accident-prone amusement park, site of Tim's first attempt (1979) to break the world nonstop singing record.

Sharp structures his film around that marathon, which lasted 2¼ hours. Tim has a pleasant singing voice and a formidable memory for the lyrics of popular songs. He has since broken the Luna Park record with a 3-hour-10-minute marathon stint.

Frustratingly, Sharp seems uninterested in telling Tim's bio, instead showing random scenes of the singer at different stages over a decade. He is in New York with his seemingly disapproving mother, on various talkshows and at several performances, "discovering" a voluptuous transvestite stripper in Australia.

The apparently ultrareligious man, who stated many times that "s-e-x" was only for procreation, also is incongruously seen in a New York hotel room sharing a bed with a voluptuous, near-naked woman.

These scenes, and others' (including old footage of the famous television wedding to Miss Vicky), give a surface impression of a seemingly eccentric entertainer. It would have been useful if Sharp had been willing to dig deeper and tell us more. But his intention seems to have been more a celebration of Tiny Tim than a critical analysis of the man.

Sharp is equally interested in Luna Park, which for years was one of the most perfectly situated (on Sydney Harbor) amusement parks in the world. Soon after Tiny Tim's marathon, however, two fatal accidents occurred which the filmmaker believes were acts of deliberate sabotage perpetrated on behalf of those interested in developing the valuable real estate.

Newsreel footage of the fire on the ghost train attraction that killed a man and his two sons is a grim reminder of the background of the park's closure some time ago. Sharp, who painted the giant clown's face at the entrance to the park over 20 years ago, is leading a fight to have the place reopened.

There are really two films in one here, and they have only a tenuous connection. But, against the odds, Sharp, who describes his pic as "a magical horror maze," has come up with an attractive, if formless, document. An imposing team of Australian cameramen (including Russell Boyd) worked on the pic through the years.

Sharp claims "The Street Of Dreams" is still unfinished, and that the print unspooled at the Sydney fest is a "work in progress." This version was first shown at the Brighton (England) Film Festival in 1988, and at Montreal's World Film Festival last August. — *Strat.*

Cartel

New York A Shapiro Glickenhaus release of a Cobra Entertainment presentation of a Promark production. Executive producer, Carol M. Rossi. Produced by Ronnie Hadar. Directed by John Stewart. Screenplay, Moshe Hadar; camera (Foto-Kem color), Thomas L. Callaway; editor, Terry J. Chiappe; music, Rick Krizman; sound (Ultra-Stereo), Tony Smyles; production design, Yuda Ako; costume design, Frank Billecci; assistant director, Richard Oswald; production manager-associate producer, Jonathan Tzachor; stunt coordinator, Gunter Simon; casting, Ann Bell. Reviewed on Shapiro Glickenhaus vidcassette, N.Y., June 14, 1990. MPAA Rating: R. Running time: 99 MIN.

Chuck Taylor . . . . Miles O'Keeffe
Tony King . . . . Don Stroud
Donna Grey . . . . Crystal Carson
Nancy . . . . Suzanne Slater
Rivera . . . . Gregory Scott Cummins
Mason . . . . William Smith
Camarillo . . . . Marco Fiorini
Baker . . . . Jack West
Clark . . . . Gary Littlejohn
Steve/Bill . . . . Sal Lopez

■ **Good stunts and pyrotechnics are the draw of the direct-to-video feature "Cartel," recently screened to foreign buyers at the Cannes market.**

Miles O'Keeffe adopts an Elvis accent for his role as a charter pilot arrested in a frameup of drug runners. He escapes from prison after a run-in there with gangster Don Stroud and sets about avenging the murder of his beautiful sister Suzanne Slater.

Plot runs out of steam in a hurry due to overemphasis on the action scenes. Film's ruthless, cynical ending is just another paean to vigilantism.

O'Keeffe is too low-key to arouse sympathy while Stroud has fun with his scenery-chewing villain. Beautiful Suzanne Slater is arresting as the blond heroine (not to be confused with similar blond B-movie bombshell Suzanne Snyder). — *Lor.*

Days Of Thunder

Hollywood A Paramount release of a Don Simpson and Jerry Bruckheimer production. Produced by Simpson, Bruckheimer. Executive producer, Gerald R. Molen. Directed by Tony Scott. Screenplay, Robert Towne, from a story by Towne, Tom Cruise; camera (Panavision, Technicolor), Ward Russell; additional camera, Charles Mills; editor, Billy Weber, Chris Lebenzon; music, Hans Zimmer; guitar solos, Jeff Beck; sound (Dolby), Charles Wilborn; art direction, Benjamin Fernandez, Thomas E. Sanders; set decoration, Thomas L. Roysden; costume design, Susan Becker; stunt coordinator, Gary McCarty; assistant director, James W. Skotchdopole; production manager, Molen; casting, David Rubin. Reviewed at Mann National Theater, West L.A., June 25, 1990. MPAA Rating: PG-13. Running time: 107 MIN.

Cole Trickle . . . . Tom Cruise
Harry Hogge . . . . Robert Duvall
Dr. Claire Lewicki . . . . . Nicole Kidman
Tim Daland . . . . Randy Quaid
Rowdy Burns . . . . Michael Rooker
Russ Wheeler . . . . Cary Elwes
Big John . . . . . . Fred Dalton Thompson
Buck Bretherton . . . . John C. Reilly
Waddell . . . . J.C. Quinn
Aldo Bennedetti . . . . Don Simpson

■ **Though this expensive genre film about stock car racing is a comedown for Tom Cruise after his "Born On The Fourth Of July" triumph, "Days Of Thunder" has all the elements of a can't-miss summer b.o. firecracker: thrilling racing footage, as many Cruise closeups as any starstruck fan could want, canny Robert Towne dialog for adult viewers and another indelible Robert Duvall performance.**

The Don Simpson-Jerry Bruckheimer production has many of the elements that made their "Top Gun" a blockbuster, but the producers this time have recruited Towne to make more out of the story than junk food. Though credited to Cruise, a racetrack aficionado, and Towne, it's basically the same old plot sports pics have always used, for better or worse.

There's the cocky but insecure young challenger (Cruise) breaking into the big time, the hardened champion he's trying to unseat (Michael Rooker), the grizzled manager who dispenses fatherly wisdom (Duvall), the crass promoter (Randy Quaid), and the sexy lady from outside (Nicole Kidman) who questions the point of it all.

The audience probably won't have much trouble predicting the curve of events, but that doesn't matter as the film unfolds, given its state-of-the-art camerawork in the Nascar circuit racing sequences, and the grease-stained authenticity Towne brings to the milieu

and characters.

(Greg Sacks is Cruise's racing double and advisor. Pic's racing consultant is Dan Greenwood; technical advisors are Rick Hendrick, Jimmy Johnson, Harry Hyde and Dr. Jerry Punch.)

Director Tony Scott and debuting feature lenser Ward Russell plunge the viewer into the maelstrom of stock car racing. A highly effective blending of car-mounted camerawork (for subjective effects) and long lenses (to capture the intensity of high-speed pack racing) imparts documentary credibility and impact, along with all the spectacle the wide Panavision screen supplies.

Viewers who aren't hardcore stock racing fans should find the action scenes irresistible. Filmmakers, differentiating each race visually and dramatically, avoid indulgent bloodlust that too often accompanies the sport yet bring out the slam-bang excitement.

Editing by Billy Weber and Chris Lebenzon (under pressure to make the summer release date) grabs the viewer, while Hans Zimmer's pulsating score and virtuoso sound mixing help keep the film in a high state of tension.

It's too much to expect Cruise to top his heartrending performance in "Born On The Fourth Of July," but if he keeps reprising the kind of uninteresting callow-but-cocky kid he plays here, "Born" may come to be regarded as a premature career peak.

Cruise's Cole Trickle (one of Towne's many whimsical character names, evidently borrowed from that of Nascar driver Dick Trickle) is a prime example of what the more high-toned Kidman scorns as "infantile egomaniacs," bad-ole-boy race-car drivers who also drive crazily on city streets because, per Cruise, "I'm more afraid of bein' nothing than I am of bein' hurt."

"Days Of Thunder" constantly zigzags between exploiting his likable grin and charming vulnerability and portraying him as an emotional loser. It's an uncertain and unsatisfying mix.

When he's up against the wily old pro Duvall, or Rooker, who is superb as doomed driver Rowdy Burns, Cruise comes alive, but otherwise the actor (who seemed to mature by a quantum jump as Ron Kovic in "Born") doesn't demand enough of himself here.

In an inauspicious U.S. film debut, the lissome redheaded Aussie actress Kidman (of "Dead

Calm") is shoehorned into the story as Cruise's love interest, an improbably gorgeous and vapid brain surgeon who somehow made it through med school without it leaving a single line on her face.

She and Cruise, who meet too cutely and conveniently when his brains are temporarily scrambled in a crash, make a handsome but dull screen couple. When it seems as if they're about to strike some real sparks in the film's only bedroom scene, pic cuts prudishly away, overly anxious to keep its PG-13 rating and to get back to the safer racetrack action.

The film's real glory is Duvall. Drawn back into the racing world from his farm by the smalltime hustler Quaid, Duvall's character has a cloud hanging over him, the legacy of his unresolved conflict between caring for his drivers and pushing them and their cars beyond reasonable limits.

Though his role fills the pedagogic function such characters have in sports films and Westerns, Duvall is not a lovable cliché, despite his downhome manner. His duplicitous, ruthless streak hovers just below the surface, giving a sense of inner danger to the racing scenes in which he coaches the untrusting Cruise by radio from trackside, wheedling him into risk.

Superstar Cruise and the racing scenes may be credited with making "Days Of Thunder" must-see summer fare, but it's Duvall's magisterial performance that will be remembered for years. — *Mac.*

Ghost Dad

Hollywood A Universal Pictures presentation of an SAH Enterprises production. Produced by Terry Nelson. Executive producer, Stan Robertson. Directed by Sidney Poitier. Screenplay, Chris Reese, Brent Maddock, S.S. Wilson, based on a story by Maddock, Wilson; camera (Deluxe color), Andrew Laszlo; editor, Pembroke Herring; music, Henry Mancini; sound (Dolby), Michael Evje, Joe Kenworthy; production design, Henry Bumstead; art direction, Bernie Cutler; set design, John Cartwright; set decoration, Richard Goddard; costume supervisor, Winnie D. Brown; visual effects, Apogee Prods., the Chandler Group; optical stretch effects, R/Greenburg Associates; assistant director, Candace Allen; 2d unit director, Fred M. Waugh; 2d unit camera, David Nowell; casting, Nancy Nayor. Reviewed at Universal Studios lot, L.A., June 21, 1990. MPAA Rating: PG. Running time: 84 MIN.

Elliot . . . . Bill Cosby
Diane . . . . Kimberly Russell
Joan . . . . Denise Nicholas
Sir Edith Moser . . . . Ian Bannen
Danny . . . . Salim Grant
Amanda . . . . Brooke Fontaine
Tony Ricker . . . . Dana Ashbrook
Stuart . . . . Omar Gooding

Carol . . . . .Christine Ebersole

■ **Cartoonish antics and ghostly special effects will entertain the kiddies, but like Bill Cosby's ghostly incarnation, this pic disappears when the lights come on. Expect a fast fade from theaters, but on Cosby's appeal, this one could haunt video shelves for awhile.**

In many ways "Ghost Dad" serves Cosby well. He plays a growly, funny, animated and lovable dad with lots of opportunities for physical, facial and vocal comedy. Cosby dies and turns into a ghost 10 minutes into this picture; the story outlives him, but not by much.

Under director Sidney Poitier (who reteams with Cosby as director for the third time), pic opens at a very promising clip. Cosby teems with charm and vitality as he deals with his family, a neighbor and a high-pressure corporate job, all on his way to a date with disaster in the form of an insane cab driver who takes him on a hellish, fatal ride.

This astounding sequence is the best part of the film, hair-raising and full of surprises. As Cosby crawls out of the water after the car has gone off a bridge, he discovers he's invisible. He's a ghost, as he sadly reports to his children after trudging home, visible only when the lights are dimmed, and solid only when he concentrates. Otherwise he falls through floors.

Premise offers plenty of opportunity for optical illusions and gags, and they're abundant, but once the novelty of Cosby's plight wears off, it's the script that does the disappearing act. Penned by Chris Reese, Brent Maddock and S.S. Wilson, it has Cosby keep trying to close one last business deal, ostensibly to provide for his family, amid situations that grow pretty hard to swallow.

Meanwhile his kids are demanding attention and being bratty about it, particularly his teen daughter, Diane (Kimberly Russell), who turns sulky over a disagreement about the school creep (Dana Ashbrook) in one of the film's several bizarre and unresolved situations.

Overall thrust is that dad will learn it's more important to spend time with the kids (he's got only three days left before he'll be whisked off earth forever), but the

ending feels forced and saccharine after the way they've acted.

Still, there's some fun in the opticals, as Cosby flies through the air, moves things invisibly, passes through walls and has things pass right through him in a mix of effects including split screen, front-lit bluescreen, stop motion, plate photography, traveling matte and motion control photography. In the best scene, Cosby is "hit" by a speeding bus and passes right through the bus floor and pops out the back of it.

Poitier, who previously collaborated with Cosby on "Uptown Saturday Night," "Let's Do It Again" and "A Piece Of The Action," directs with vitality and punch, but when the script deserts him, things grow tedious. Frames are designed for the younger set, having a simple, cartoonish look with no frills.

Henry Mancini score is undistinguished, other tech credits are fine. — *Daws.*

Betsy's Wedding

Hollywood A Touchstone Pictures release in association with Silver Screen Partners IV. Produced by Martin Bregman, Louis A. Stroller. Written and directed by Alan Alda. Camera (Technicolor), Kelvin Pike; editor, Michael Polakow; music, Bruce Broughton; sound (Dolby), John Pritchett, Frank Haber; production design, John Jay Moore; costume design, Mary Malin; set decoration, Barbara Kahn; assistant director, Yudi Bennett; casting, Mary Colquhoun. Reviewed at Avco Cinemas, L.A.; June 18, 1990. MPAA Rating: R. Running time: **98 MIN.**

Eddie Hopper . . . . Alan Alda
Lola Hopper . . . . Madeline Kahn
Betsy Hopper . . . . Molly Ringwald
Connie Hopper . . . . Ally Sheedy
Stevie Dee . . . . Anthony LaPaglia
Oscar Henner . . . . Joe Pesci
Eddie's father . . . . Joey Bishop
Jake Lovell . . . . Dylan Walsh
Gloria Henner . . . . Catherine O'Hara
Georgie . . . . Burt Young
Grandma . . . . Julie Bavasso
Henry Lovell . . . . Nicolas Coster
Nancy Lovell . . . . Bibi Besch

■ **From a bolt of ordinary cloth Alan Alda has fashioned a thoroughly engaging matrimonial romp in "Betsy's Wedding." The lively ensemble comedy should do smart business for Touchstone in theaters, and should become a popular video title.**

Most of the action comes from the clash of personalities and wills as unconventional daughter Betsy (Molly Ringwald) announces her plans to wed boyfriend Jake (Dylan Walsh), and everyone jumps into the act.

Overreaching dad (Alda) wants a big, wonderful Italian Jewish wedding, and plans accelerate into a one-upmanship contest when Jake's wealthy WASP parents try to take the reins.

The trodden-on couple just wants it simple, with "a few friends and no religion," but it's not to be.

To finance the bash, Alda, a contractor, unwittingly throws in with some funny-money Italian business partners, as arranged by his double-dealing brother-in-law (Joe Pesci), and soon finds his Long Island construction site occupied by high-paid layabouts who are helping their employer "move some money."

Meanwhile the crime boss' young lieutenant, a preening odd duck named Stevie Dee (Anthony LaPaglia), takes a shine to Alda's other daughter, Connie (Ally Sheedy), who's a cop.

Three-tiered plot propels Alda's whimsical confection toward some delicious comedic peaks, as payoffs come from all directions.

Setting a buoyant, anything-could-happen tone from the outset, Alda as director creates what he's striving for: a feeling of being caught up in the warm craziness of this family, as all its vivid characters push and tug to impose their will on the proceedings.

His punchy, impertinent script is equally good, delivering many a zinger and setting a tone of contagious madness.

Romance between LaPaglia and Sheedy threatens to steal the picture. LaPaglia's fastidious Stevie Dee is quite a creation; a gallant and ludicrous old world prince of the streets who has Sheedy squinting to figure out what to make of him. His mannerisms come from De Niro, his manners from another century.

Madeline Kahn is also excellent as Alda's wife, a seasoned observer trying to exercise her tenuous control over her husband, the circus ringleader. Kahn's balance of centeredness and wackiness serves her well as she sizes up the WASP-y new in-laws: "We're going to have correct, invisible grandchildren," she fears. "We won't even know they visited us until they send a thank-you note."

Ringwald moves smoothly toward adulthood in this role, creating a calm but ticking center for the pic as the bride-to-be whose cool is sorely tested by the antics of her elders.

Pesci as Alda's blithely unscrupulous brother-in-law triggers much of the comic momentum. Joey Bishop fittingly extends the Alda character's sensibilities in ghostly drop-ins as his dead father, still there for advice.

Shot in North Carolina and New York, pic is first-rate on all technical counts. Mary Malin's costume designs, particularly Ringwald's unique garb, play a starring role, and Bruce Broughton contribs a breezy, buoyant score. — *Daws.*

Simon Les Nuages
(Simon The Dreamer)
(CANADIAN)

Montreal A Cinema Plus presentation a Les Films Vision 4 production in association with the National Film Board of Canada. Produced by Claude Bonin, Ian Boyd. Written and directed by Roger Cantin. Camera (color), Michel Caron; editor, Yves Chaput; sound, Dominique Chartrand; art director, Vianney Gauthier; set designer, Claudine Charbonneau; associate producers, Doris Girard, Monique Letourneau. Reviewed at Famous Players Cinema Parisien, June 21, 1990. Running time: **82 MIN.**

Simon . . . . Hugolin Chevrette-Landesque
Pierre-Alexandre . . . . . Patrick St-Pierre
Picard . . . . Benoit Robitaille
Laperle . . . . Naad Joseph
Carole . . . . Jessica Barker
Helen . . . . Isabelle Lapointe

■ **A tribute to the wonderful powers of a child's imagination, this charming but sometimes corny tale is perfect summer fare for kids aged 5-12 and their parents. No violence. No computers. Just imagination.**

Set in a charming village near an ancient forest, pic revolves around a young dreamer who convinces other youngsters that believing in make-believe holds strange and exciting adventures. Simon is the new kid in town, visiting his sheltered, spoiled cousin, Pierre-Alexandre, for the summer. Pic begins (and ends) with Simon's dreams of paradise where dinosaurs and pirates roam the wilds.

Night after night the dreams recur until Simon is convinced it's a real place to be found through a series of clues and checkpoints much like a treasure hunt. The catch is that the kids can't be seen by an adult during the hunt or the paradise will burst like a bubble.

Thanks to the blabbermouth cousin, Simon reluctantly winds up with a whole gang of followers who don't really believe they'll find the ocean and prehistoric creatures on the other side of the woods. A few failed attempts later, Simon successfully leads them to the "sea" and dives headlong into the "ocean," which becomes a bathtub when a dreaded adult arrives on the scene.

They take up their adventure again that night and find themselves in the midst of "megacuriosaurs" (a type of dinosaur). That's when pic gets corny, and low-budget effects look cheap, pic's major flaw. But the film makes it's point: Children need to exercise their limitless imaginations and allow themselves to be absorbed by the world of make-believe.

Tech credits are fine, except for the special effects. Stunning images of nature are a plus. Thesping is okay. Pic has a good chance theatrically in French-lingo territories, and is a natural for tv and homevid. — *Suze.*

The Invisible Maniac

New York A Smoking Gun Pictures presentation of an Anthony Markes production. Produced by Markes. Directed by Rif Coogan. Screenplay, Coogan, from story by Coogan, Matt Devlen; camera (color), James Bay; editor, Ron Resnick; music, Marc David Decker; sound, Jan Brodin; production design, Holly MacConkey; assistant director, Pierre Lorillard; production manger, Sonya Burres; special effects, Carlo Cuccelleli; stunt coordinator, Jon Pochron; coproducer, Devlen. Reviewed on Republic Pictures vidcassette, N.Y., June 21, 1990. MPAA Rating: R. Running time: **85 MIN.**

Kevin Dornwinkle	Noel Peters
Vicky	Shannon Wilsey
Bunny	Melissa Moore
Chet	Robert R. Ross Jr.
Gordon	Rod Sweitzer
Bubba	Eric Champnella
Joan	Kalei Shellabarger
April	Gail Lyon
Betty	Debra Lamb
Mrs. Cello	Stella Blalack
Dr. McWaters	Clement von Franckenstein
Newscaster	Dana Bentley
Telescope gal	Tracy Walker
Scientist	Cindy Pamplin

■ **The sex tease genre introed nearly a decade ago with "Zapped" and recently sequelized as "Zapped Again" is streamlined via the top-heavy video "The Invisible Maniac." Voyeurs will dig this one.**

Harking back in many ways to the original voyeur films of 30 years back, "The Immoral Mr. Teas" and "Paradiso," "Maniac" is chock full of characters given to peeping. Principal among these is Noel Peters as a boy treated cruelly by his mom who grows up to become a nutty physicist. He develops an invisibility

formula and, before you can say Claude Rains, develops megalomania.

Escaping from an insane asylum after he has killed four scientists at a conference, he finds employment as a substitute physics teacher for high school physics students. However, instead of nerds these are oversexed coeds, led by beautiful blond Shannon Wilsey and statuesque Melissa Moore, latter a young vet of horror pics like "Scream Dream."

Pic uses invisibility for the standard shower room scenes and magical clothes removal, but, unlike its forebears, emphasizes a horror format of Peters killing the youngsters.

Its low budget is a major drawback as the invisibility effects are so poorly done that some scenes consist largely of a crew member throwing things in the frame from behind the camera.

Saving grace is copious amounts of topless footage featuring attractive young women. Nudity should keep undiscriminating homevid and pay-cable fans happy, but its removal for tv grindslots (such as Gilbert Gottfried's USA cable gig) would effectively kill this feature.

Peters overacts while using a voice reminiscent of Adam West. He would have done much better to match West's straight ahead "Batman" approach. Moore and Gail Lyon literally stick out among the actresses on view.—*Lor.*

Happily Ever After
(ANIMATED)

New York A Kel-Air Entertainment release from First National Film of a Filmation presentation of a Lou Scheimer production. Produced by Scheimer. Directed by John Howley. Sequence directors: Gian Celestri, Kamoon Song, Larry White. Screenplay, Robby London, Martha Moran; camera (CFI color), Fred Ziegler; editor, Jeffrey C. Patch, Joe Gall; music, Frank W. Becker; songs, John Lewis Parker, Richard Kerr, Stephanie Tyrell, Ashley Hall, Barry Mann; sound (Dolby), Steve Pickard, Louie Montoya; art direction, John Grusd; special effects animation supervisor, Bruce Heller; production manager, Bob Pope, Chuck Mitman; associate producers, Erika Scheimer, London, Grusd; casting, Cheryl Bascom. Reviewed on First National vidcassette, N.Y., June 16, 1990. MPAA Rating: G. Running time: **74 MIN.**

Voices of:

Snow White	Irene Cara
Scowl	Edward Asner
Muddy	Carol Channing
Looking Glass	Dom DeLuise
Mother Nature	Phyllis Diller
Blossom	Zsa Zsa Gabor
Critterina/Marina	Linda Gary
Sunflower	Jonathan Harris
Prince	Michael Horton
Sunburn	Sally Kellerman

Lord Maliss	Malcolm McDowell
Moonbeam/Thunderella	Tracey Ullman
Batso	Frank Welker

■ **An unauthorized sequel to the Walt Disney classic "Snow White," "Happily Ever After" is a well-crafted but uninspired animated fantasy that should entertain small fry in video form. Its theatrical chances this summer are slim.**

Lou Scheimer's Filmation banner began work on the pic in 1986 simultaneously with another unauthorized sequel to a Disney masterpiece, "Pinocchio And The Emperor Of The Night," which flopped in theaters as a Christmas 1987 release from New World.

Action picks up here with the evil queen's brother Lord Maliss (drawn to resemble Basil Rathbone and voiced with gusto by Malcolm McDowell) in a vendetta to avenge sis' death by zonking Snow White and her handsome Prince. Snowy takes refuge in the seven dwarfs' cottage when the Prince is captured.

The little fellows are away slaving in the mines, but their femme cousins, the seven dwarfelles, entertain Snowy with their fantastic control of natural phenomena. Climax has Mother Nature (Phyllis Diller) testing the dwarfelles on a mission to help Snowy rescue the Prince in the realm of doom.

As a sequel, film relies quite heavily on inversions of familiar fairy tales, e.g., the prince is charmed and has to be released from his spell as Shadowman by Snow White; the gender change in most of the main roles.

Voice casting, including Ed Asner, Linda Gary and Jonathan Harris from Filmation's "Pinocchio" followup, is pic's big plus. Irene Cara warbles a catchy, uptempo song "Love Is The Reason" by John Lewis Parker to bookend the film, but unfortunately for a musical it's not integrated with the action. Three other songs spotlight Asner, Diller and a very effective vocal from Tracey Ullman simulating a little girl's voice. Animated format allows for non-stereotyped, undistracting casting of Cara. Prince as the Prince would have been a clever if costly elaboration of this approach.

Attractive backgrounds and okay character animation suffice, but lack the sparkle of bigger-budget efforts from Disney or Don Bluth. Film's emphasis on horror content is handled tastefully within the

confines of a G rating. — *Lor.*

Vincent et Moi
(Vincent And Me)
(CANADIAN)

Cannes An Astral release (in Canada) of a Les Prods. La Fete production. Produced by Rock Demers. Written and directed by Michael Rubbo; camera (color), Andreas Poulsson; editor, Andre Corriveau; music, Pierick Houdy; sound, Yvon Benoit; art director, Violette Daneau; costume design, Hughette Gagne; coproducer (France), Claude Nedjar; associate producer (Holland), Nico Crama. Reviewed at the Cannes Film Festival (market), May 18, 1990. Running time: **100 MIN.**

Jo	Nina Petronzio
Felix	Christopher Forrest
Joris	Paul Klerk
Tom Mainfield	Matthew Mabe
Gran	Anna-Maria Giannotti
Dr. Winkler	Alexandre Vernon Dobtcheff
Mrs. Wallis	Andree Pelletier
Burt	Wally Martin
Mr. Caruthers	Michel Maillot
Silva	Tamara Witcher
Frank Purvis	Charles Pitts
Jo's mother	Dora Petronzio
Jo's father	Vittorio Rossi
Madame Calmant	Madame Calmant
Vincent Van Gogh	Tcheky Karyo

■ **The 11th film in Rock Demers' long-running and valuable family series, "Tales For All," is a thoroughly likable story concerning a young art student's admiration for the work of Van Gogh, skillfully told with genuine charm and good humor.**

Thirteen-year-old Josephine (Nina Petronzio) goes to Montreal from Western Canada to study art. Inspired by the paintings of Van Gogh, she learns everything she can about the artist, painting and sketching in his style, talking to him on occasion while she works, and imagining him painting in the fields.

One day she meets a mysterious stranger from Holland who asks her to draw some farm animals. Later she learns that a Japanese businessman has paid $1-million for some "newly discovered childhood sketches" by Van Gogh, which of course, are her drawings. Together with her two friends, Jo goes to Amsterdam where, after exciting adventures on the canals, the villain is confronted and a den of forgers is brought to light.

The film moves easily and lightly through the story and its highlights are Jo's meeting with a lively 115-year-old lady, Madame Calmant, still living in Arles, who met Van Gogh when she was 13 and remembers that he "was very rude to me."

That leads to a wonderfully charming time-travel sequence, in which Jo dreams of meeting Van Gogh (nicely played by French actor Tcheky Karyo). He is highly amused when she tells him he is famous, and highly disbelieving when he hears that his paintings (he only sold one in his lifetime) are selling for millions of dollars.

The performances of all the young players, Petronzio as Jo in particular, cannot be faulted. The supporting characters are amusingly larger than life.

Pic, cleverly written and directed by Michael Rubbo, who also painted and drew the Van Goghs shown, has a clearly defined Canadian identity which blends smoothly with the magical, moral moments of good fairy tales.

Pic is a creative and enjoyable introduction for young people to the world of art and artists. All technical credits are first rate. Van Gogh would be pleased. — *Prat.*

Watchers II

New York A Concorde Pictures presentation of a Concorde-Centaur production. Produced by Roger Corman. Directed by Thierry Notz. Screenplay, Henry Dominic, based on Dean R. Koontz' novel "Watchers;" camera (Foto-Kem color), Edward Pei; editor, Adam Wolfe, Diane Fingado; music, Rick Conrad; sound (Ultra-Stereo), Bill Robbins; production design, Gary Randall; assistant director, Chris Edmonds; special makeup effects, Joe Rodner, John Criswell; Outsider created by Dean Jones, William Starr Jones; stunt coordinator, Patrick J. Statham; 2d unit director, Louis Morneau; 2d unit camera, Janusz Kaminski; additional camera, Jurgen Baum, Dick Buckley; coproducer, Rodman Flender; associate producer, Joel DeLoach; casting, Kevin Reidy. Reviewed on IVE vidcassette, N.Y., June 16, 1990. MPAA Rating: R. Running time: **97 MIN.**
Paul Ferguson . . . . Marc Singer
Barbara White . . . . Tracy Scoggins
Steve . . . . Jonathan Farwell
Sarah . . . . Irene Miracle
Dr. Glatman . . . . Mary Woronov
Outsider . . . . Tom Poster
Einstein . . . . Dakai the dog
   Also with: Donald Pugsley, Joseph Hardin, Diana James, John Lafayette, Kip Addota, Raquel Rios, Daryl Haney.

■ **Roger Corman's second try at adapting Dean R. Koontz' bestseller is a marked improvement, yielding a suspenseful thriller. The first pic, Canadianmade, got a spotty release by Universal while the remake is headed straight for video.**

Once again a government project developing weaponry for the next war has created two genetically linked superbeings: AE74, a Gill-man type of monster known

as the Outsider, and AE73, a beautiful golden retriever named Einstein with amazing intelligence.

The Natl. Security Agency orders this Aesop project terminated, but good-bad guy Jonathan Farwell in charge feels sorry for his critters so he has animal rights advocates steal away the lab animals. Outsider kills a few of the do-gooders and escapes as well.

Unlike the 1988 film which cornily emphasized youngster Corey Haim in the lead role, this version is blissfully free of pandering to kids/teens. Marc Singer plays a marine on the way to the stockade for punching a superior officer. Einstein helps him escape from custody. In a clever scene reminiscent of charades, the dog communicates to Singer that he must phone Barbara White (played by Tracy Scoggins), who was his animal psychologist during the project.

Scoggins, Singer and Einstein team up to foil the government heavies, leading to a nice moment of pathos at the climax when Outsider meets his destiny.

Scoggins and Singer make an attractive, personable team. They've already made another video together, "The Raven Red Kiss-Off." Though the Outsider's bodysuit is a bit fake looking, pic's effects are adequate. Director Thierry Notz keeps the pace crackling and there are several fun scenes of Einstein demonstrating his intelligence.

As Singer's sympathetic ex-wife, Irene Miracle delivers an alluring bubble bath scene that brings back fond memories of her initial exposure in "Midnight Express." Further pulchritude is provided by buxom Raquel Rios, a dead ringer for porn star Keisha.
— *Lor.*

Pas de repit pour Melanie (The Case Of The Witch Who Wasn't) (CANADIAN)

Cannes An Astral release (in Canada) of a Les Prods. La Fete production. Produced by Rock Demers. Directed by Jean Beaudry. Screenplay, Stella Goulet, Beaudry; camera (color), Eric Cayla; editor, Helene Girard; music, Jean Corriveau; sound, Serge Beauchemin; art director, Vianney Gautheir; costume design, Hughette Gagne. Reviewed at the Cannes Film Festival (market), May 19, 1990. Running time: **95 MIN.**
(English soundtrack)
Melanie . . . . Marie-Stefane Gaudry
Florence . . . . Kesnamelly Neff

Benjamin . . . . Vincent Bolduc
Mrs. Labbé . . . . Madeleine Langlois
Louis . . . . Alexandre Neszvecsko
Gaston Dupuis . . . . Paul Dion
Melanie's father . . . . . . Clement Cazelais
Melanie's mother . Johanne-Marie Tremblay
Sarah . . . . Camille Cyr-Desmarais
Alexis . . . . Ellery Picard
Mr. Hootch . . . . Ghyslain Tremblay
Chief of Police . . . . Jocelyn Berube
Doctor . . . . Claire Pimpare
Julie . . . . Capucine Powers
Freddy . . . . Marc Desourdy

■ **Another winning tale (the 10th) in the library of Les Prods. La Fete telling of two young girls, one white, one black, on holiday in Calixa-Lavallee, Quebec, and of their determination to put the words of the fox in Saint-Exupery's "Little Prince" to good effect: "One becomes responsible for everything one establishes ties with."**

Pen pals Melanie and Florence, both 12, expect an uneventful summer holiday. They decide to help out a lonely and eccentric old lady locked behind the closed shutters of her big house. The children of the village have labelled her a wicked witch.

After several attempts they become friends with Mrs. Labbé,

only to find their efforts ruined when burglars tie her up, ransack her home and steal her jewels and pet pig.

The girls become detectives and track down the rascals, but are then faced with the task of rescuing their new friend from, for her, a fate worse than death — being confined to an old people's home.

Stella Goulet's responsible screenplay combines a good story with some quiet observations on race relations, the love of animals and the meaning of friendship, all sympathetically directed by Jean Beaudry. The performances of the young cast are natural, with children's quarrels and upsets taking place in the natural course of daily life.

The rest of the cast enter into the spirit of the whole and, as with all the films in this admirable family series, the events are seen and described from the children's point-of-view without being patronizing or preachy. All technical credits are fine. "The Case Of The Witch Who Wasn't" is the title of the dubbed-into-English track version, which looks and sounds quite convincing. — *Prat.*

SYDNEY FILM FESTIVAL REVIEWS

Nirvana Street Murder (AUSTRALIAN)

Sydney A Vellis/Cochrane production, assisted by the Australian Film Commission (creative development branch). Produced by Fiona Cochrane. Directed by Aleksi Vellis. Screenplay, Vellis; camera (color), Mark Lane; editor, Vellis; music, John Clifford White; sound, Mark Atkin; production design, Lisa Thompson; production manager, Wendy Clarke; assistant director, Peter Jordan. Reviewed at the Sydney Film Festival, June 20, 1990. Running time: **72 MIN.**
Luke O'Hagan . . . . Ben Mendelsohn
Boady O'Hagan . . . . Mark Little
Helen . . . . Mary Coustas
Penny . . . . Tamara Saulwick
Molly . . . . Sheila Florance
Smeg . . . . Yiorgo
Hector . . . . Roberto Micale
Boss . . . . Russell Gilbert
Newsreader . . . . Paul Harris
Cop . . . . John Flaus

■ **First-time writer-director Aleksi Vellis shows plenty of promise with this ultra-low-budget comedy-thriller that successfully preemed at both the Melbourne and Sydney film fests. Limited domestic theatrical release, however, is indicated prior to video, with overseas prospects problematic.**

The pic, funded by a division of the Australian Film Commission which gives cash to short films, was completed with the help of a private commercial sponsor.

Although the ending is truncated (subsequent action is described in a title card), the picture plays smoothly enough and is well-acted by a small but willing cast. Focus is on two brothers who share an apartment in inner-suburban Melbourne.

One brother, Luke (Ben Mendelsohn), is a law-abiding citizen involved in a passionate romance with a Greek-Australian teacher (Mary Coustas) whose conservative Greek-speaking parents are unaware of the liaison.

Boady (Mark Little), on the other hand, is a manic type into unsuccessful dope deals. A confrontation with the police forces them, plus Penny (Tamara Saulwick), Boady's pregnant girlfriend, to hide out in the spacious house occupied by a bedridden old woman (Sheila Florance) Luke has befriended.

Vellis seems to be aiming for

the mood of a Melbourne "Mean Streets," with a mixture of comedy and drama culminating in the death of one of the principal characters.

The strong ethnic element adds richness to the story. Dialog is spare but often amusing. Thesping is the film's major asset, with Mendelsohn (a busy young actor who toplined in three features unspooled in the Melbourne fest) very appealing as the "good" brother and Little making the "bad" Boady likable though dangerously off the wall.

Among the supporting players are Sydney radio critics John Flaus and Paul Harris playing, respectively, a cop and a tv newsreader.

"Nirvana Street Murder" is modest fare which won't set the world on fire, but could become a cult item at rep cinemas in Australia and possibly find small-screen and vid distribution elsewhere. It's made with feeling and indicates that, with a bigger budget, Vellis could come up with an impressive, more mainstream pic next time around. — *Strat.*

Mana Waka
(NEW ZEALAND-DOCU-B&W)

Sydney   A Te Puea Estate-Turangawaewae Marae production. Produced by Ngaruawahai. Directed by Merata Mita. Camera (black & white), R.G.H. Manley; editor, Annie Collins; music, Turangawaewae Marae; sound, Mita. Reviewed at the Sydney Film Festival, June 17, 1990. Running time: **82 MIN.**

■ "Mana Waka" is a film of considerable archival, anthropological and festival interest, but its specialized material makes it an unlikely bet in theatrical and even video.

Basically, the film is a record of the construction of a number of Maori *waka* (canoes) during the late '30s. In 1937, the Maori queen, Princess Te Puea Herangi, initiated a project to build a fleet of canoes to be used at the 1940 ceremonies to celebrate the 100th anniversary of the signing of the Treaty of Waitangi (which brought peace between the Maoris and European settlers in New Zealand).

R.G.H. (Jim) Manley photographed the construction of the canoes over a three-year period (1937-40). He shot on 35m, but without sound, and covered the felling of the great kauri trees, the

process of hollowing out, the trek to the sea (in which teams of bullocks were used), the intricate wood carving which embellished the craft and the commemorative ceremony.

Manley's footage was never edited into a film, and the material languished for years until it was handed to the New Zealand Film Archive for restoration. Now, Maori filmmaker Merata Mita has supervised the editing of the footage and the construction of a very effective soundtrack, incorporating authentic Maori songs.

Seeing these great trees slowly transformed into magnificent vessels makes for a surprisingly gripping experience. The original footage was expertly shot, and the soundtrack has been faithfully constructed for this new release.

Naturally, material of this sort will be of limited interest, but the footage casts its spell over the viewer and the Sydney fest audience appeared enthralled.

Special permission had to be obtained from the current Maori queen, Dame Atairangikahu, for this rare and sensitive material to be publicly screened at the fest.
— *Strat.*

Die Hard 2

Hollywood   A 20th Century Fox release of a Gordon Co./Silver Pictures production. Produced by Lawrence Gordon, Joel Silver, Charles Gordon. Executive producers, Lloyd Levin, Michael Levy. Directed by Renny Harlin. Screenplay, Steven E. de Souza, Doug Richardson, based on the novel "58 Minutes" by Walter Wager; certain original characters by Roderick Thorpe; camera (Panavision, Deluxe color), Oliver Wood; editor, Stuart Baird, Robert A. Ferretti; music, Michael Kamen; sound (Dolby), Robert G. Henderson, Alan Robert Murray; production design, John Vallone; art direction, Christiaan Wagener; set decoration, Robert Gould; costume design, Marilyn Vance-Straker; special makeup effects, Thomas R. Burman, Bari Dreiband-Burman; assistant directors, Terry Miller, Michael Alan Kahn, Todd Grodnick; production manager/line supervisor, James Herbert; visual effects, Industrial Light & Magic; supervisor of visual effects, Michael J. McAlister; additional visual effects sequences, Apogee; visual effects supervisor, Peter Donen; stunt coordinator/2d unit director, Charles Picerni; 2d unit camera, Frank Holgate; coproducer, Steve Perry; associate producer, Suzanne Todd; casting, Jackie Burch. Reviewed at 20th Century Fox, L.A., June 22, 1990. MPAA Rating: R. Running time: **124 MIN.**

John McClane	Bruce Willis
Holly McClane	Bonnie Bedelia
Thornberg	William Atherton
Al Powell	Reginald VelJohnson
Esperanza	Franco Nero
Stuart	William Sadler
Grant	John Amos
Carmine Lorenzo	Dennis Franz
Barnes	Art Evans
Trudeau	Fred Dalton Thompson
Marvin	Tom Bower
Samantha Copeland	Sheila McCarthy
Garber	Don Harvey

Also with: Tony Ganios, Peter Nelson, Robert Patrick, Michael Cunningham, John Leguizamo, Tom Verica, John Costelloe, Michael Francis Clarke, Steve Pershing, Tom Everett, Sherry Bilsing, Karla Tamburrelli, Jeanne Bates, Colm Meaney, Steffen Gregory Foster, James Lancaster.

■ Fox' "Die Hard 2" lacks the inventiveness of the original but compensates with relentless action, looking as overbudget as it's reputed to be. Still, boxoffice should far exceed the negative cost, likely placing it high on the list of summer 1990's borderline blockbusters.

"Die Hard," with John McTiernan's throat-clutching direction and its wrong-guy-in-the-right-place scenario, emerged as the most enjoyable action film of 1988. Bruce Willis exhibited big-screen star quality for the first time as John McClane, a likable protagonist who, while resourceful and brave, was shaken by grim circumstances.

That chemistry obviously is hard to reconstitute, so, rather than try, McClane has been turned into a cross between Indiana Jones and Rambo.

Nevertheless, the film works

for the most part as sheer entertainment, a full-color comic book with shootouts, brutal fistfights and bloodletting aplenty, as well as "Die Hard's" cable and home-vid exposure as a "Harder" selling point.

Minding his own business, McClane is in D.C.'s Dulles Airport to pick up wife Holly (Bonnie Bedelia) to spend Christmas with her folks. They've reconciled since the events in "Die Hard" and the Gotham cop has joined the LAPD.

Unlike most domestic flights, the story takes off immediately, as terrorists seize control of the airport to free a Manuel Noriega-esque foreign dictator (Franco Nero) being transported to the U.S. The band is led by a ruthless loose cannon Marine-type, played with convincing menace by William Sadler.

McClane stumbles on the plot and, despite his hostage-rescue rep, is promptly ignored by dim-witted airport officials, especially the security chief (Dennis Franz, in the pic's worst-written role).

Fortunately, such weaknesses are easy to overlook, thanks to the frenetic pace. Director Renny Harlin, whose only major credits are the fourth "A Nightmare On Elm Street" and Fox' upcoming "The Adventures Of Ford Fairlane," does a creditable job with such a daunting large-scale action assignment.

That's not to say the film is without shortcomings. Harlin lacks McTiernan's vicelike grip on action and strays into areas that derail certain scenes, using slow-motion in early sequences and sapping their energy.

It's also less appealing to have McClane be such a self-assured good guy in contrast to his panting, rather refreshing state of confusion during the first film.

Willis has become a convincing action star but often flounders in the film's softer moments. When he bellows his wife's name near the end it sounds like a bad parody of "A Streetcar Named Desire," producing one of the film's few unintentional chuckles.

Its most grating element, however, is "Hard" holdover William Atherton's amoral tv newsman, as preposterous as he is cartoonish, and on hand only to showcase the Bedelia character's own Rambo streak.

If it's not quite "Die Hard," it is good fun, with a requisite amount of humor, such as McClane's astonishment that such a horrendous series of events could happen to the same person twice. (News flash: If all goes well, get ready for a third time.)

More important, the action is generally well-conceived and executed, with big, splashy effects, and one fabulous blue-screen shot that has Willis ejecting from a grounded plane as it explodes beneath him.

The drama also possesses an epic quality: a high-stakes, against-the-clock game with plenty of techno-babble to keep the audience off-balance, courtesy of writers Doug Richardson and Steven E. de Souza, the latter a veteran of clock-ticking action pics, having penned the original "48 HRS."

Technical aspects of the film are superb, from Stuart Baird's editing to Oliver Wood's nighttime cinematography — including, among other things, a gun-battle joust aboard snowmobiles. Michael Kamen's score is bombastic in quieter scenes but usually dovetails with the onscreen pyrotechnics.

It's also noteworthy that the filmmakers again have assembled an ethnically mixed company, frequently casting blacks in roles that don't necessarily call for minority characters.

The other notable color is blood red, and "Die Hard 2," like most of the summer's major releases, seems to revel in it. The high level of gore may put off the squeamish but doubtless won't hurt the film's b.o. body count. — *Bril.*

Jetsons: The Movie
(ANIMATED)

Hollywood A Universal release of a Hanna-Barbera Studios production in association with Wang Film Prods. and Cuckoos Nest Studios. Produced and directed by William Hanna, Joseph Barbera. Supervising producer, Bruce David Johnson. Supervising animation director, David Michener. Animation director, Ray Patterson. Supervising director, Iwao Takamoto. Screenplay, Dennis Marks, based on "The Jetsons" tv series; additional dialog, Carl Sautter; in CFI color; supervising film editor, Pat Foley, Terry W. Moore, Larry C. Cowan; music, John Debney; sound recording director (Dolby), Gordon Hunt; production design, Al Gmuer; layout director, Deane Taylor; computer animation, deGraf/Wahrman Inc.; vehicle animation, Kroyer Films; optical effects, Perpetual Motion Pictures, Howard Anderson Co.; film sequence for "You And Me" song, Kurtz and Friends; associate producer, James Wang. Reviewed at Cineplex Odeon Universal City Cinemas,

L.A., June 30, 1990. MPAA Rating: G. Running time: **82 MIN.**

Voices of:
George Jetson	George O'Hanlon
Mr. Spacely	Mel Blanc
Jane Jetson	Penny Singleton
Judy Jetson	Tiffany
Elroy Jetson	Patric Zimmerman
Astro	Don Messick
Rosie the Robot	Jean VanderPyl
Rudy 2	Ronnie Schell
Lucy 2	Patti Deutsch
Teddy 2	Dana Hill
Fergie Furbelow	Russi Taylor
Apollo Blue	Paul Kreppel
Rocket Rick	Rick Dees

■ **Here's George Jetson. On the big screen. It's not a tv show, but it sure feels like one. William Hanna and Joseph Barbera's "Jetsons: The Movie" (delayed from a previously slated Christmas slot) is bland but serviceable G-rated animated fare in a summer dominated by bloody action pics.**

There's an undeniable showmanship that has kept the minimal Hanna-Barbera Saturday ayem animation style commercially viable on the airwaves for kiddie audiences who, sadly, don't have many other options, but the limitations of the style are even more glaringly apparent on the theater screen. Characters, whose liveliest facial expression is lip flap, are magnified to enormous proportions.

If the endearingly chuckleheaded Jetsons family had been brought to the screen with the classical full-animation style as it is still being practiced by Disney or Don Bluth, a "Jetsons" film might have managed to transcend its origins. But this film differs from a tv rerun mostly by being 82 minutes long rather than 30. The viewer can almost sense subliminal commercial breaks in Dennis Marks' shambling plot.

There's a deja vu quality to this pic, whose ambiance has been only marginally updated to reflect changes in the culture since "The Jetsons" first aired in space-crazy 1962. George, Jane, Judy and Elroy Jetson, along with their dog Astro and housekeeper Rosie the Robot, still seem like Kennedy era suburbanites caught in the time warp of a mildly satirical space-age lifestyle, oblivious to SDI, Challenger and the Hubble space telescope.

This time around, rock star Tiffany does the voice of teenybopper Judy. She croons some easy-to-take bubblegum music in an interracial romance with a two-toned alien named Apollo Blue.

The colors are a bit prettier, the pace more kinetic and the music

(by John Debney) louder and sprightlier than on the series. But most of the running time is still taken up with stale (especially for adults) sitcom-style domestic gags.

The mood of innocuous escapism starts to become mind-numbing as the plot seems to have nothing more on its mind than George's promotion by Mr. Spacely from his earthly job to a vice-presidency of a mining and manufacturing operation on a remote asteroid. Then comes a plot twist too late to redeem the film entirely, but enough to awaken adults dozing over their watches.

Spacely Sprockets' asteroid proves to be populated by sweet-natured subterranean furry creatures called Grungies, whose Lucas-like civilization is being destroyed (unbeknown to Jetson) by the unscrupulous Spacely's mining. Elroy, the Grungy Squeak, a little robot and a hairy turquoise creature called Fergie Furbelow join forces with Judy, Apollo and Jane to drum some environmental consciousness into George's thick skull.

Confronting the blustering Spacely, George transforms the asteroid into an ecologically sound, non-exploitive operation run in partnership with the Grungies, while sacrificing his own promotion. The message is a simple but timely one, and parents will find it preferable to the message of death and destruction sold by some of the summer's big action pics.

Pic is dedicated to the memory of George O'Hanlon and Mel Blanc, original voices of George and Mr. Spacely, who died last year after completing their roles.

Penny Singleton as Jane, Jean VanderPyl as Rosie and Don Messick as Astro pleasingly encore their tv characterizations as well. Patric Zimmerman subs for the late Daws Butler as Elroy and Tiffany for Janet Waldo, who is credited for other voice work.
— *Mac.*

Private War

New York A Smart Egg Pictures presentation of a Luigi Cingolani production. Produced by Cingolani. Executive producer, George Zecevic. Directed by Frank De Palma. Screenplay, Terry Borst, Björn Carlström, De Palma, from Jan Guillou's story; camera (Avala color), Karpo Godina; editor, Seth Gaven; music, Harry Manfredini, Arlon Ober; sound (Dolby), Svetislav Ristic; art direction, Niemanja Petrovic; production manager, Dusko Markovic; assistant director, Goran Radova-

novic; special makeup effects, Dusan Mihajlovic; stunt coordinator, Slavoljub Plavsic; coproducers, Alexander Strojanovic, Hans Iveberg; casting, Barbara Remsen & Associates. Reviewed on Republic Pictures vidcassette, N.Y., June 27, 1990. MPAA Rating: R. Running time: **94 MIN.**
Phil Cooper	Martin Hewitt
Sg. Vincent Rayker	Joe Dallesandro
Kim	Kimberly Beck
Cal Liston	Reggie Johnson
Major Donnerman	George Shannon
Joe Bates	Sam Hennings
Roland Caldwell	B.J. Turner
Angelo Rossi	Robert J. Bennett
Paul De Vries	Curt Lowens
Col. Peterson	David Clover

■ **Joe Dallesandro gives an effective character performance in the above-average action drama "Private War." Completed 18 months ago, pic comes off the shelf to become a direct-to-video title.**

Known from his stardom 20 years ago in Andy Warhol/Paul Morrissey hits like "Flesh" and "Trash," Dallesandro is cast against type as a very tough special forces sergeant who's gone off the deep end. Early in the film he's relieved of his command due to physically terrorizing his soldiers, stationed at an Army Airborne infantry unit in Northern Italy.

Notable target for his venom is Martin Hewitt, whose dad served with Dallesandro in Vietnam and is still listed as missing in action. Actually, he died when Dallesandro left him behind in combat to save his own skin, guilt for which has turned him latterly into a psycho.

Though dwelling on a corny subplot of corrupt military brass and self-styled patriots on a hunting expedition (with Kimberly Beck along as the tight-sweatered investigative reporter trying to expose them), film develops panache in the final reels.

Filmed atmospherically in Yugoslavia on actual sites of World War II battles, the payoff of Dallesandro having trained Hewitt to be his executioner is thematically resonant and well played. Cruel finish takes an overly despairing view of humanity.

Spitting out colorful, unexpurgated dialog and looking the part with a butch military haircut, Dallesandro is surprisingly convincing in an acting stretch. Frank De Palma's direction is well-paced and photography by Karpo Godina (a director in his own right, repped at the Cannes fest by "Artificial Paradise") is firstrate.
— *Lor.*

Boom Boom
(SPANISH)

Madrid An Arsenal Films (Spain), Lamy Films (Brussels) coproduction. Exec producers, Rosa Romero, Benoit Lamy. Directed by Rosa Vergés. Screenplay, Vergés, Jordi Beltrán; camera (Agfa), Josep M. Civit; editor, Susana Rossberg; sound, Miguel Rejas; set design, Rosa Ros. Reviewed at Cine Proyecciones, Madrid, June 23, 1990. Running time: **92 MIN.**

Sofía . . . . Viktor Lazlo
Tristán . . . . Sergi Mateu
Angel . . . . Fernando Guillén
Eva . . . . Angels Gonyalons
    Also with: Pepe Rubianes, Pepa López, Inés Navarro, Benadette Lafont, Gemma Cuervo, Ann Petersen, Conrado San Martín, Félix Rotaeta, Angel Jové.

■ **Directorial bow for Catalan femme helmer Rosa Vergés shows considerable promise in this romantic comedy about two singles who live in the same building. However, weak spots in the script and a bland performance by Viktor Lazlo as Sofía in the lead undermine this youth pic.**

Story revolves around Sofía and Tristán, each of whom has sworn off relations with the opposite sex after disastrous amorous relations. Though Sofía's apartment is right above Tristán's, they have never met. Tristán owns a shoe shop, Sofía works as a dental assistant.

After a kind of comedy of errors involving an attractive bartender, a dentist and a girl who runs a newsstand, Sofía and Tristán finally meet near the end of the film, though their romance has been cooking all through the pic.

Some droll situations give ''Boom Boom'' (the sound of heartthrobs) an occasional lift, but the story is too rambling to score solidly. Best thesping is by Sergi Mateu as the shoe salesman. Production design and direction are good, as are most technical credits.

Pic did some biz in its Barcelona release, but bombed in Madrid. World sales being handled by French banner, Europex. — *Besa.*

King Kung Fu

New York A King Gemini presentation of a Walterscheid production. Produced by Bob Walerscheid. Executive producers, Ken Welk, Danny Zeck. Written and directed by Lance D. Hayes. Camera (United color), Hayes; editor, Hayes; music, Michael Linn, Alan Oldfield; sound (Ultra-Stereo), Dwight Pennebaker; production design, Hayes; production manager-associate producer, Pat Hayes; postproduction supervisor, Herbert L. Strock. Reviewed on King Gemini videcassette, N.Y.,

June 23, 1990. MPAA Rating: G. Running time: **95 MIN.**

King Kung Fu . . . . John Balée
Rae Fey . . . . Maxine Gray
Captain Duke . . . . Tom Leahy
Herman . . . . Tim McGill
Bo Burgess . . . . Billy Schwartz
Officer Pilgrim . . . . Steve Sisley
    Also with: Jim Erickson, Robert Carroll, Lois Ayers, Lance D. Hayes, Stephen Young, Pat Hayes, Bob Walterscheid.

■ **This Wichita-made oddity is an old-fashioned spoof recommended to fans of cornpone humor. G-rated opus was completed in 1987 and is awaiting distribution.**

Filmmaker Lance Hayes shows a genuine affection for old movies, his main homage here being to the 1933 classic ''King Kong.'' Strained storyline has China sending to America a gorilla trained in the martial arts as part of a cultural exchange program. He escapes from captivity, takes a liking to pretty blond Maxine Gray (as ''Rae Fey'') and ascends the town's tallest building, a Holiday Inn.

This puerile entertainment is easy to watch though out of step with today's sensational approach. Targets of satire range from the David Carradine ''Kung Fu'' tv series (the ape is called Jungle Jumper instead of Weed Hopper), tv newscasts and John Wayne movies. Tom Leahy does an okay Duke impression, but looks more like Leo V. Gordon than the targeted superstar.

Bumbling comedy team of Tim McGill and Billy Schwartz gets some laughs, though their costuming and styling makes film look like an early '70s production. Gray manages to provide some alluring pulchritude without threatening pic's G tag.

Finale features extremely poor stop-motion animation to simulate the gorilla's fall from the roof onto a helicopter. John Balée wearing the apesuit is unimpressive.

— *Lor.*

ARCHIVE FILM REVIEW

Stop

New York A Warner Bros. presentation of a Paul M. Heller production. Produced by Heller. Written and directed by Bill Gunn. Camera (Duart color), Owen Roizman; editor, Sam Ornstein; music, Fred Myrow; guitar solos, Ry Cooder; sound, Paul Jaeger; consultant art director, Gene Callahan; set design, Nina; assistant director, Alan Hopkins. Reviewed at Whitney Museum of American Art, N.Y., June 30, 1990. MPAA Rating: X. Running time: **92 MIN.**

Lee Berger . . . . Linda Marsh
Michael Berger . . . . Edward Bell
Marlene Matheson . . . . . Marlene Clark
Richard Matheson . . . . . . Richard Dow
John . . . . John Hoffmeister
Ellen . . . . Anne Marie Aries
Whore . . . . Vicky Hernandez
Mr. Dome . . . . Michael Peters
Mrs. Dome . . . . Miki Jaeger
    Also with: Nydia Caro, Angel Rigau, Benito Alvarez, Charlie Gibbs.

■ **''Stop'' is an ambitious but unsuccessful dissection of empty people in an arid marriage. X-rated feature was permanently shelved by Warner Bros. in 1970 and is reviewed here for the record.**

It's easy to see why WB rejected this uncommercial effort. Obscure narrative is tedious to the point of an audience almost sharing the suicidal tendencies of the unsympathetic protagonists. Film nonetheless has several sharp scenes and would be of retrospective interest to European film fest

programmers.

Writer-director Bill Gunn, who died last year, made a noteworthy breakthrough here as a black helmer not restricted to a black-themed picture. (Only Sidney Poitier's ''Hanky Panky'' vehicle for Gene Wilder and Gilda Radner, Michael Schultz' ''Sgt. Pepper's'' or Asian American director Wayne Wang's nonethnic ''Slamdance'' since have escaped that sort of typecasting.)

Opening scene, reminiscent of the classic breakfast sequence in Orson Welles' ''Citizen Kane,'' establishes whitebread, yuppie couple Edward Bell (a writer-translator) and Linda Marsh already at the end of their tether, barely able to talk to each other without sarcasm. They fly to San Juan, Puerto Rico to take up residence at an inherited mansion, Bell's brother having just murdered *his* wife and committed suicide.

With Bell haunted by nightmarish fantasy-memories of that incident (he obviously wasn't present but imagines the details), film immediately suggests potential as a gothic horror pic, like Gunn's well-regarded next feature ''Ganja And Hess.'' Since film's structure and subplot suggest WB's Stanley Kubrick adaptation of ''The Shining'' a decade hence (writer in a

remote mansion going crazy), that's a missed opportunity.

Instead, ''Stop'' disintegrates into a series of '60s semi-obligatory lyrical interludes. Always artfully photographed, these sequences of sex, brooding or just wandering are dullsville.

Final half of the picture degenerates into the then-hot topic of spouse swapping (e.g., ''Bob And Carol And Ted And Alice,'' ''All The Loving Couples'') when old pal Richard Dow (named Richard Matheson in the script as an apparent in-joke) pops up with his beautiful black wife Marlene Clark.

Sex scenes are rather tame (no full nudity), but a homosexual tryst plus strong language probably earned the X tag. Low point here is a gauche dinner party scene using a Screw Magazine story on masturbation as a starting point for a vulgar discussion.

Gunn's best footage is a stark confrontation between Marsh and a Puerto Rican prostitute (Vicky Hernandez in pic's best performance) after she catches Bell in bed with the working girl. Another setpiece has camera mounted overhead in the bedroom from a Godlike point-of-view to record a take of Bell and Marsh screaming at each other and almost coming to blows. It lasts a couple minutes but is too shrill to be effective.

Heroine Marsh, who looks somewhat like Gayle Hunnicutt and Barbara Harris, played Ophelia to Richard Burton's ''Hamlet'' in WB's 1964 Electronovision feature, but has little characterization to chew on here. Bell is a blank. When the two are locked together in a ''No Exit'' finale, the viewer still doesn't know what makes them tick.

Gunn reportedly was unhappy with the studio's final version of the film. A cryptic penultimate scene and heavy use of voiceover exposition indicate some postproduction second thoughts.

For a color-blind feature, it is perhaps not surprising that the one black role, played by Marlene Clark (later to star in ''Ganja And Hess''), is presented as merely an exotic, erotic cipher rather than given an independent voice.

Pic notably represents the first feature for Owen Roizman, soon to lense William Friedkin's landmark ''The French Connection'' and ''The Exorcist.'' Roizman's compositions are unusual as is Fred Myrow's eclectic musical score, featuring guitarwork by Ry Cooder. — *Lor.*

Ghost

Hollywood A Paramount Pictures presentation of a Howard W. Koch production. Produced by Lisa Weinstein. Executive producer, Steven-Charles Jaffe. Directed by Jerry Zucker. Screenplay, Bruce Joel Rubin; camera (Technicolor), Adam Greenberg; editor, Walter Murch; music, Maurice Jarre; sound (Dolby), Jeff Wexler; production design, Jane Musky; art direction, Mark Mansbridge; set decoration, Joe D. Mitchell; costume design, Ruth Morley; special visual effects, Industrial Light & Magic — supervisor, Bruce Nicholson; good spirits, dark spirits visual effects supervisors, John van Vliet, Katherine Kean; end sequence visual effects supervisor, Richard Edlund; associate producer, Rubin; casting, Jane Jenkins, Janet Hirshenson. Reviewed at Paramount Studio Theater, L.A., July 6, 1990. MPAA Rating: PG-13. Running time: **127 MIN.**

Sam Wheat	Patrick Swayze
Molly Jensen	Demi Moore
Oda Mae Brown	Whoopi Goldberg
Carl Brunner	Tony Goldwyn
Willie Lopez	Rick Aviles
Louise	Gail Boggs
Clara	Armelia McQueen
Subway ghost	Vincent Schiavelli

■ **An unlikely grab bag of styles that teeters, spiritlike, between life and death, "Ghost" could nonetheless be a hit for Paramount and star Patrick Swayze.**

This lightweight romantic fantasy delivers the elements a "Dirty Dancing" audience presumably hungers for, down to the romantic/nostalgic Righteous Bros.-performed tune that laces the soundtrack. Shimmering special effects are also likely to satisfy customers, but this farfetched effort is purely for escapists, as demanding filmgoers won't buy it.

Swayze and Demi Moore play Sam and Molly, a have-it-all Manhattan couple (he's a banker, she's an artist) who have just happily renovated their new Tribeca loft when he's shot and killed by a street thug.

Unknown to her, he's walking around as a ghost, desperate to communicate with her because she's still in danger. He stumbles upon a spirit-world medium (Whoopi Goldberg) who can hear him and drags her in to help him as a money-laundering and murder plot unfolds around them.

As the first dramatic film directed by Jerry Zucker (who collaborated on "Airplane!" "Ruthless People" and "The Naked Gun" with David Zucker and Jim Abrahams), "Ghost" is an odd creation — at times nearly smothering in arty somberness, at others veering into good, wacky fun.

Film opens with fog-filtered images of sweating, muscular figures bashing away at barriers (renovating a loft, as it turns out). Later a wooden angel is hoisted through the air. Then there's an arty-erotic clay-making scene that borders on ludicrous.

Two-hour-plus film really takes its time unfolding, and it's not until Goldberg is brought in that the first laughs occur, but things do get wilder as Swayze explores his ghostly powers, especially when he encounters a violent fellow spirit (Vincent Schiavelli) who throws him off a subway and teaches him how to make things move.

Like Universal's current release "Ghost Dad," this film gains a lot of interest from visual effects, particularly pass-through effects as Swayze swats at people he can't touch.

Effects sometimes do suggest an interesting spirit world. When bad guys die, they get dragged away by little black banshees. When good guys die, they're beknighted with sparkling light and get to stick around and be heroes.

"Ghost" pushes Swayze through all kinds of emotional paces, requiring him to look anguished, horrified, appalled and enraged one after another. It's a by-the-numbers perf, but he does fine with the tumbling, stumbling ghostly business and in romantic clinches.

Sporting a boyish haircut and her usual husky voice, Moore mostly has to spout tears and look vulnerable as she mourns Swayze and tries to avoid Goldberg, who she's convinced is a con artist.

Goldberg, as the irritable psychic, registers the most convincing presence on screen. She ignites her scenes with the spunky comedic elements Zucker seems most adept with.

Though it's all over the map stylistically, "Ghost" becomes absorbing as its thriller elements click in, and romantic momentum, aided by Maurice Jarre's lush orchestrations of the "Unchained Melody" theme, will pull most viewers along.

Production design, particularly of the sumptuous loft, seems way out of proportion for this pic's true dimensions but in line with Zucker's elaborate ambitions for it.

— *Daws.*

Quick Change

Hollywood A Warner Bros. release of a Devoted production. Produced by Robert Greenhut, Bill Murray. Executive producer, Frederic Golchan. Directed by Howard Franklin, Murray. Screenplay, Franklin, based on the book by Jay Cronley; camera (Duart color), Michael Chapman; editor, Alan Heim; music, Randy Edelman; sound (Dolby), Les Lazarowitz; production design, David Gropman; art direction, Speed Hopkins; costume design, Jeffrey Kurland; set decoration, Susan Bode; assistant director, Thomas Reilly. Reviewed at Raleigh Studios, L.A., July 2, 1990. MPAA rating: R. Running time: **88 MIN.**

Grimm	Bill Murray
Phyllis	Geena Davis
Loomis	Randy Quaid
Chief Rotzinger	Jason Robards
Bank guard	Bob Elliott
Bus driver	Phillip Bosco
Cabbie	Tony Shalhoub

■ **Bill Murray delivers a smart, sardonic and very funny valentine to the rotten Apple in "Quick Change," a potential fast money-maker for Warner Bros., given the dearth of summer comedies.**

Winning mix of lunacy and integrity in this New York-lensed crime caper could overcome audience resistance to what initially seems like a dismissible effort. Combined with WB's intriguing marketing campaign, pic could bring in both a general following and a hip urban crowd.

Pic became Murray's directing debut (he shares the chores with screenwriter Howard Franklin) after he and Franklin became too attached to the project to bring anyone else in. Their instincts pay off, as the film comes off as cannily true to itself and refreshingly different.

Material, based on Jay Cronley's book, is neither ambitious nor particularly memorable, but it's brought off with a sly flair that makes it most enjoyable.

Murray plays a fed-up New Yorker who enlists his girlfriend (Geena Davis) and lifelong pal (Randy Quaid) in a bank heist so they can get outta town.

Murray dresses up as a balloon-carrying clown, riding the crowded subway to the bank, and sliding in just before closing time after a hassle with an eager-to-knock-off guard (Bob Elliott of comedy team Bob and Ray).

Hold-up, which nets a million dollars and a very nice watch, sets off a carnival of police and crowd reaction in the New York streets, but none of it flaps the dynamite-rigged Murray, who under the clown makeup is so droll, world-weary and unperturbable that audiences will be leaning forward to catch his every ripe, sarcastic barb.

Route of escape for him and his cohorts is too clever to give away, but it proves to be no escape at all, as after one little screw-up, bizarro New York closes in on the fleeing felons, hitting them with every conceivable obstacle in an "After Hours"-style nightmare as they try to make it to the airport.

With Jason Robards as a crusty police inspector who's as crazily sharp as "Twin Peaks'" agent Cooper and not about to be humiliated by a clown, pic offers some crazy little setpieces in a manic game of chase.

Murray and Franklin always seem to be daring the material and the cast to see how much suspense can be wrung from a common situation, like a guy sweating it out in line at a corner grocery to get correct change in time to catch a bus.

Never mind that he has stolen money taped to his shins, two irritable cops behind him in line and a mad-dog mobster across the street looking to break his head open.

With Robert Greenhut's production and Michael Chapman's camerawork, pic is so thick with gritty, tired, scuzzy N.Y. atmosphere viewer wants to scrape it off the skin.

Even better, everyone is involved in working out their personal stands in the midst of chaos. Davis, in a sumptuous turn as Murray's uncertain partner in love and crime, and Quaid as the big loyal galoot they take care of, are particularly winning in the way they keep getting absorbed in personal discussions.

Only in the final reel do things feel broadly contrived, concurrent with pic's move from N.Y. locations to a Florida soundstage for airport shooting.

Among the excellent supporting cast, Elliott is a real stitch as the bank guard, and Tony Shalhoub is a scene-stealer as a cabbie who speaks no English. — *Daws.*

The Adventures Of Ford Fairlane

Hollywood   A 20th Century Fox release of a Silver Pictures production. Produced by Joel Silver, Steve Perry. Directed by Renny Harlin. Executive producer, Michael Levy. Screenplay, Daniel Waters, James Cappe, David Arnott, based on a story by Cappe, Arnott; characters created by Rex Weiner; camera (Panavision, Deluxe color), Oliver Wood; editor, Michael Tronick; music, Yello; sound (Dolby), John Dunn, Stephen Flick; production design, John Vallone; art direction, Christiaan Wagener; set decoration, Linda Spheeris; costume design, Marilyn Vance-Straker; assistant director, Terry Miller, Michael Alan Kahn, Albert Cho; associate producer, Suzanne Todd; casting, Jackie Burch. Reviewed at the Cineplex Odeon Theater, Westwood, Calif., July 5, 1990. MPAA Rating: R. Running time: **104 MIN.**

Ford Fairlane . . . . . . Andrew Dice Clay
Julian Grendel . . . . Wayne Newton
Colleen Sutton . . . . Priscilla Presley
Don Cleveland . . . . Morris Day
Jazz . . . . Lauren Holly
Zuzu Petals . . . . Maddie Corman
Johnny Crunch . . . . . . Gilbert Gottfried
Sam . . . . David Patrick Kelly
The Kid . . . . Brandon Call
Smiley . . . . Robert Englund
Lt. Amos . . . . Ed O'Neill

■ **Surprisingly funny and expectedly rude, Andrew Dice Clay's first starring vehicle promises to track down a solid boxoffice bounty and pave the way for more big-screen feats — in part, no doubt, because of the furor surrounding him.**

Groups offended by Clay's standup act will have a bit less to complain about in this Fox release, except that it should expose the U.S.' most vilified comic to plenty of new eyeballs.

The film's decidedly lowbrow humor is a sort of modern equivalent of that of the Three Stooges, with jokes that leave men laughing even as they shoot sheepish glances at female companions who may be left scratching their heads.

Still, even some women will find the title character plucked closely from Clay's standup act amusingly dim, and the bonehead's gallery of camp supporting players is equally diverting.

Clay plays Ford Fairlane, a private eye specializing in cases involving rock acts (hence his overused nickname, "the rock & roll detective"). He gets drawn into a murder mystery linked to a shock-radio deejay (Gilbert Gottfried, in a hilarious cameo), and a sleazy record executive (Wayne Newton) and his ex-wife (Priscilla Presley).

Adept with a gun, Fairlane isn't much for brains or business. Most of the clients pay him with odd artifacts. That explains his nifty guitar and the live koala bear (actually, a rather lame puppet) in his living room; supposedly a payment from the Aussie band INXS.

While it's hard at times not to cringe at some of the dialog (credited to Daniel Waters, James Cappe and David Arnott), there are plenty of knowing in-jokes thrown in, including a reference to Clay's banishment from MTV.

In fact, with its heavy rock bent and the direction of Renny Harlin, already a hot property thanks to Fox' "Die Hard 2," much of the film resembles a musicvideo, including its opening scene and perhaps its most offensive one, in a college sorority that's part health club, part Sodom and Gomorrah.

Still, Harlin brings a certain energy to the film, and while it's at times both inane and grating, it's certainly never boring. Clay, who's acted before in supporting roles, is provided with a perfect showcase, and the story moves along at a pace that masks the patchwork plot's thinness.

What may be lost amid all the controversy is that those who don't appreciate Clay's material, at least here, can laugh at his character instead of with him.

Indeed, aside from his appeal to rednecks and high-school boys overly impressed by certain four-letter words, Clay's chain-smoking goombah in many ways self-parodies the macho ethic that prize rock 'n' roll, fast cars and cheap bimbos above all else.

There's also a more than passing effort to soften the "Dice" persona around the edges and give Fairlane some redeeming qualities, most notably through his interplay with set-upon assistant Jazz (Lauren Holly) and an unwashed waif (Brandon Call) who follows him around.

The film's most significant find, undoubtedly, is Holly (former "All My Children" regular and absolute knockout) who brings a lot of flash and charisma to a difficult role as Fairlane's longing girl Friday. Better roles and skimpier outfits no doubt await.

For the music-minded, Morris Day and rapper Tone Loc appear. Also, Robert Englund (aka Freddy Krueger) plays a sadistic killer, sans makeup.

Cameraman Oliver Wood brings a sleek look to the Los Angeles locations and other tech credits are fine, from Fairlane's vintage wheels to John Vallone's production design and Marilyn Vance-Straker's outlandish costumes. — *Bril.*

Witchcraft Part II: The Temptress

New York   A Vista Street Entertainment presentation of a Feifer/Miller production. Executive producers, Jerry Feifer, Tony Miller. Supervising producer, James R. Hanson. Produced by Megan Barnett, Reza Mizbani. Directed by Mark Woods. Screenplay, Sal Manna, Hanson; camera (color), Jens Stürup; editor, Miller; music, Mirium Cutler; sound, Mike Draghi; production design, Cragi R. Voigt; art direction, Suzanne Gibson; assistant director-casting, Gabriela Bacher; stunt coordinator, Tony Snegoff; associate producer, Joseph Barmettler. Reviewed on Academy videcassette, N.Y., June 23, 1990. MPAA Rating: R. Running time: **87 MIN.**

William Adams . . . . . . Charles Solomon
Dolores, temptress . . . . . Delia Sheppard
Boomer . . . . David L. Homb
Michelle . . . . Mia Ruiz
Mr. Adams . . . . Jay Richardson
Mrs. Adams . . . . Cheryl Janecky
Audrey . . . . Kirsten Wagner
Rev. Cross . . . . Frank Woods

■ **This sequel to the 1988 video pic is an effective showcase for the charms of newcomer Delia Sheppard. This is another direct-to-vid release, but Sheppard will be featured on the bigscreen in "Rocky V."**

She plays a temptress, out to charm young hero Charles Solomon who's being groomed (unknown to him) as the supreme warlock to take over the world. As detailed in the first film (flashbacks of which are presented here), Solomon's parents and foster parents all practiced witchcraft.

Opposing Sheppard are the local reverend (Frank Woods), whose daughter Mia Ruiz is Solomon's girlfriend. One cute gag has Woods complaining about exorcism that "Catholics are so much better than Methodists at this."

Direction by Mark Woods is okay, though the climax is directed too much like a heavy metal musicvid. Center of attention is Sheppard, previously seen in the barely released "Sexbomb." She's severely styled as a dominating blond hellcat in trashy, revealing costumes. Her campy performance tags Sheppard as the '90s answer to Mamie Van Doren.

Tech credits, especially the optical effects, are chintzy. — *Lor.*

Arachnophobia

Hollywood A Buena Vista release of a Hollywood Pictures/Amblin Entertainment presentation of a Tangled Web Prods./Amblin production. Produced by Kathleen Kennedy, Richard Vane. Executive producers, Steven Spielberg, Frank Marshall. Coexecutive producers, Ted Field, Robert W. Cort. Directed by Marshall. Screenplay, Jakoby, Wesley Strick, from a story by Jakoby, Al Williams; camera (Deluxe color), Mikael Salomon; editor, Michael Kahn; music, Trevor Jones; sound (Dolby), Ronald Judkins; production design, James Bissell; art direction, Christopher Burian-Mohr; costume design, Jennifer L. Parsons; special effects supervisor, Matt Sweeney; visual effects supervisor, David Sosalla; creature effects supervisor, Chris Walas; assistant directors, Bruce Cohen, Luisa De La Ville (Venezuela); coproducer, Don Jakoby; associate producer, William S. Beasley; casting, Mike Fenton, Judy Taylor, Valorie Massalas. Reviewed at Century 7 Theaters, North Hollywood, Calif., July 11, 1990. MPAA Rating: PG-13. Running time: 109 MIN.
Dr. Ross Jennings . . . . Jeff Daniels
Molly Jennings . . . . . Harley Jane Kozak
Delbert McClintock . . . . . John Goodman
Dr. James Atherton . . . . . . Julian Sands
Sheriff Parsons . . . . Stuart Pankin
Chris Collins . . . . . . Brian McNamara
Jerry Manley . . . . Mark L. Taylor
Dr. Sam Metcalf . . . . Henry Jones
Henry Beechwood . . . . Peter Jason
Milton Briggs . . . . James Handy
Irv Kendall . . . . Roy Brocksmith
Blaire Kendall . . . . Kathy Kinney
Margaret Hollins . . . . . . Mary Carver

■ "Arachnophobia" (meaning "fear of spiders") has all the symptoms of a monster hit.

The first release of Disney's Hollywood Pictures expertly blends horror and tongue-in-cheek comedy in the tale of a small California coastal town overrun by Venezuelan killer spiders. Frank Marshall's sophisticated feature directing debut for Amblin Entertainment probably will be the summer's top-grossing film.

Having learned his lessons well from both longtime associate Steven Spielberg and from Alfred Hitchcock — whose "The Birds" this film most closely resembles — Marshall adroitly controls the audience's reaction in a thrill ride that always knows how far to push the shock effects and how to balance them with giggles.

Not since "Jaws" has a film come along to make audiences jump in their seats so regularly and enjoyably. Some moviegoers will find the vicious, bloodsucking arachnids too unsettling to watch, but "Arachnophobia" never indulges in ultimate gross-out effects and carefully chooses both its victims and its means of depicting their dispatch.

Beginning like an "Indiana Jones" film with an 18-minute prolog of British entomologist Julian Sands' expedition in the Venezuelan jungle, "Arachnophobia" cleverly follows the route of a prehistoric male spider hitching a ride to California in the coffin of expedition photographer Mark L. Taylor and escaping to the farm of newly arrived town doctor Jeff Daniels.

Although the tv ads make it seem that John Goodman is the star of "Arachnophobia" (and that the film is an out-and-out farce, which it isn't), the droll Goodman actually has a relatively small part as the town's magnificently slobby and incompetent exterminator, while the debonair Daniels has the more low-key lead role.

Daniels is the one with the arachnophobia, which, like James Stewart's trauma in Hitchcock's "Vertigo," must be agonizingly overcome in the spectacular climax, as he vanquishes both the spiders and the town's hysterical accusations that he is to blame for the mysterious deaths caused by the infestation.

Marshall has the directorial confidence to allow scripters Don Jakoby and Wesley Strick (working from a story by Jakoby and Al Williams) plenty of screen time to develop characters more fully than usual in a horror film. That pays off in greater audience empathy when action intensifies.

The yuppieish Daniels, fleeing S.F. with wife Harley Jane Kozak and kids to live out his dream of a quieter, rustic existence, finds a nightmare instead. Crotchety old sawbones Henry Jones has reneged on his promise to retire and the picturesque farmhouse they've bought is full of termites.

Then Daniels' patients start dropping dead, and after Jones also expires, the locals begin referring to the stranger in their midst as "Dr. Death."

No one listens to him when he begins piecing together evidence indicating that a rare breed of spiders might be responsible, a theory even Goodman refuses to believe until it's almost too late to stop them.

With a variety of versatile spider performers including live South American tarantulas (Steven Kutcher was supervising entomologist and Jim Kundig the live spider coordinator) and more than 40 mechanical creatures devised by Chris Walas, Marshall is able to do just about anything he wants in terms of creepy-crawly effects.

And since spiders can appear in silence from anywhere in the frame at any time, they're hard to top as objects of fright.

The rot in the farmhouse and the infestation in Daniels' barn, where the Venezuelan spider builds its nest, set the tone for the film's Hitchcockian depiction of a seemingly placid normality underpinned by a secret menace unleashed by willful complacency.

While "The Birds" anticipated the ecological movement by showing nature striking back against human cruelty, "Arachnophobia" shows unscrupulous science, in the person of Sands, indulging in exploration without regard for the horrors it may unleash, a theme well suited to current anxieties.

The townsfolks' smug unawareness of the ubiquitous menace provides a welcome interlacing of humor, such as Goodman's swaggering stupidity, the black-humored nonchalance of undertaker Roy Brocksmith or the film's brilliant twist on the "Psycho" shower scene, substituting spiders for Norman Bates' mother.

Mikael Salomon's lensing combines suitably idyllic views of the natural beauty of Cambria in San Luis Obispo County, Calif. (here called Canaima, after the place in Venezuela where the jungle scenes were shot), with eerily lit and bizarrely angled scenes of arachnid life.

All other tech credits are top-notch, including Michael Kahn's editing, James Bissell's production design and Trevor Jones' music, and all hands avoid the crude and obvious effects that could have made this an exploitation pic rather than a subtly constructed crowd-pleasing triumph. — Mac.

Navy Seals

Hollywood An Orion Pictures release of a Brenda Feigen production. Produced by Feigen, Bernard Williams. Directed by Lewis Teague. Screenplay, Chuck Pfarrer, Gary Goldman; camera (Technicolor color, DeLuxe prints), John A. Alonzo; production design, Guy J. Comtois, Veronica Hadfield; editor, Don Zimmerman; music, Sylvester LeVay; sound (Dolby), Martin Maryska; set decoration, Malcolm Stone, Debra Schutt; costume design, Brad Loman; special-effects supervisor, John Stears; assistant directors, Jose Kuki Lopez Rodero, Frank Capra III; 2d-unit directors, Bud Davis, Bob Carmichael; casting, Sally Dennison, Julie Selzer. Reviewed at the UA Coronet Theater, Westwood, Calif., July 11, 1990. MPAA Rating: R. Running time: 113 MIN.
Hawkins . . . . Charlie Sheen
Curran . . . . Michael Biehn
Claire . . . . Joanne Whalley-Kilmer
Leary . . . . Rick Rossovich
Rexer . . . . Cyril O'Reilly
Graham . . . . Bill Paxton
Ramos . . . . Paul Sanchez
Ben Shaheed . . . . Nicholas Kadi
Captain Dunne . . . . Ron Joseph

■ Nifty performances make this routine action flick better than it probably has a right to be, but the formula (more "The Green Berets" than "Top Gun") may have a tough time blasting through the ranks of higher-profile summer fare. B.o. prospects seem marginal, though "Navy Seals" could wash up as a hot homevideo item.

Playing to the "Rambo" mentality by focusing on an elite naval-attack group kicking tail around the globe, the film won't be a favorite of peaceniks or any Arab anti-defamation leagues.

Its main purpose seems to be to provide a cathartic thrill in seeing the U.S. throttle terrorist groups and free hostages, rather ironic since real Western hostages have remained in captivity so long. Someone should tell the government how easy it is to fly into Beirut and extricate these people.

Then again, suspending disbelief is a necessity in a film where a country that spends billions on defense seems to have only seven guys available to handle all its covert operations. If they lose a man in combat, they don't even replace him on the next mission.

That's because these are the Navy Seals, a unit that doesn't officially exist, trained in sea, air and land operations. In their off time they pal around like fraternity boys, swilling beer and savaging golf courses.

Fortunately, the script and Lewis Teague's direction allow for very little off time. The film begins with a full-blown assignment and repeatedly sends the group out on elaborate suicide missions, showcasing plenty of gee-whiz gimmickry in the process.

That first mission involves freeing U.S. personnel from terrorists who, it turns out, have access to handheld stinger missiles. The Navy Seals must subsequently locate the missiles and then eliminate them, aided (preposterously) by a beautiful tv reporter (Joanne Whalley-Kilmer).

As lame as the description may sound, "Navy Seals" is a clear case of style triumphing over substance, combining firstrate effects and well-choreographed stunts with a workable old storyline about duty, honor and grit under fire.

Principally, it helps having fine actors, namely Michael Biehn and Charlie Sheen, in such thinly written roles to raise the pic somewhat above its shallow ambitions.

Biehn has emerged as one of the more watchable actors around and displays plenty of quiet determination, while Sheen cuts loose as a borderline psycho whose maverick style and cat-and-mouse games with death occasionally endanger fellow team members.

The one overlooked presence is Whalley-Kilmer, relegated to the role of pretty window-dressing even as her character badly compromises her journalistic integrity by becoming a government shill, despite her protestations to the contrary.

Teague brings a real flair to much of the action, though the messy, overlong finale — set, no less, in the ravaged streets of Beirut — gets way out of hand.

The climax nonetheless proves a showcase for production designers Guy Comtois and Veronica Hadfield, who do a splendid job with the international locations, shot primarily in Spain. Cameraman John A. Alonzo also deserves kudos for his night battle and underwater sequences, and other tech credits are equally gung-ho.
— *Bril.*

Fatal Mission

New York A Funahara production. Executive producers, Takahide Kawakami, Yutaka Oe. Produced by Chosei Funahara. Directed by George Rowe. Screenplay, Anthony Gentile, John Gentile, Rowe, Funahara, Peter Fonda, from story by Erlinda Quiaoit Rowe; camera (Technicolor), Phil Parmet; editor, Branka Mrkic, Jay Freund, Gervacio Santos; music, Mark Winner; sound, Michael Jordan, Michel Carton; production design, Helene Guetary; production manager, George Rosales; stunt coordinator, Gilar Ceo; associate producer, Franz Harland. Reviewed on Media Home Entertainment vidcassette, N.Y., July 11, 1990. MPAA Rating: R. Running time: **84 MIN.**

Ken Andrews . . . . Peter Fonda
Mai Chong . . . . Tia Carrere
Trang . . . . Mako
CIA man . . . . Ted Markland
Capt. Bauer . . . . Jim Mitchum
NVA Sgt. Tuong . . . . . . Felind Obach
NVA Capt. Hao . . . . . . Joonce Gamboa
Vietnam general . . . . Joe Mari

■ **A few more rewrites might have saved "Fatal Mission," an interesting two-character war film that self-destructs in the final reel.**

Six scripters are credited already on this 1988 Filipino-lo-

caled production originally titled "Enemy." Protagonists are Peter Fonda, a CIA hireling in Vietnam in the '60s who assassinates a North Vietnamese general, and Tia Carrere, a beautiful agent from China on a similar mission who captures Fonda.

Like dozens of similar films, notably the Peter Strauss-Candice Bergen trekker "Soldier Blue," pic revolves around the love-hate relationship of the duo. They traipse southward and begin to treat each other as equals since both must kill various enemies to survive. Climax is very disappointing, as Fonda escapes in a stolen plane with Carrere written out of the script, making Fonda's fate soon after.

Up until that stinko fadeout, helmer George Rowe does a decent job whipping up atmosphere. It's still tough to accept "Easy Rider" Fonda as a gung-ho war hero, but the romantic chemistry between him and the too-pretty Carrere (she looks more like a Miss Philippines finalist than secret agent in black pajamas) works. Name talent like Mako and Jim Mitchum have only brief roles.

As is often the case in these pictures, Filipino thesps in supporting roles do not look convincing as Vietnamese. — *Lor.*

Hang Tough

New York A Moviestore Entertainment presentation of an Astral Bellevue Pathé and Joe Wizan production. Executive producers, Harold Greenberg, Joyce Lukow. Produced by Greenberg. Directed by Daryl Duke. Screenplay, W.D. Richter, John Herzfeld, from Don Bredes' novel; camera (Astral Bellevue Pathé color, Harry Makin; editor, Tony Lower; music, Micky Erbe, Maribeth Solomon; sound, Richard Lightstone; production design, Douglas Higgins; art direction, Guy Tuttle; assistant director, Bill Corcoran; production manager, David Earl Pamplin. Reviewed on Monarch vidcassette, N.Y., July 14, 1990. MPAA Rating: R. Running time: **106 MIN.**

Bernie . . . . Carl Marotte
Wilnona Lockhart . . . Charlaine Woodard
Latham Lockhart . . . . Grand Bush
Linwood . . . . Vincent Bufano
Barbara . . . . Lisa Langlois
Leo . . . . Allan Katz
Leslie Wolstein . . . . . Stephanie Miller
Mother . . . . Sylvia Llewellyn
Father . . . . Michael Donaghue
Holland . . . . Vlasta Vrana

■ **A lightweight precursor of the '80s teen rites of passage comedy genre, "Hang Tough" was filmed in 1980 but only now released as a direct-to-video title.**

Film, previously titled "Hard Feelings" and "Sneakers," could

be thought of as part of a parallel world of 20th Century Fox. Though eventually acquired for distribution by Moviestore, the Daryl Duke picture was made for "Porky's" banner Astral Bellevue Pathé and Joe Wizan, latter becoming Fox topper soon after. Its scripters W.D. Richter and John Herzfeld both helmed features for at Sherwood and Fox in 1983 that were released by Fox.

Result here is in the same genre popularized by Bob Clark in "Porky's" but far too tame. Carl Marotte heads a mixed Canadian and U.S. cast as a teen growing up in Long Island who longs to score, but his sex scenes with fast girl Stephanie Miller and good girl Lisa Langlois are a study in *coitus interruptus*: Adults always arrive home early with unfunny results.

Overlong pic has two key subplots which are handled arbitrarily. Marotte is victimized by the school bully Vincent Bufano and even flees for Atlanta after Bufano kills his dog. There he strikes up a romance with free-spirited black student Charlaine Woodard but soon returns home to pick up the makeout with Langlois. When Woodard visits relatives in Harlem, Marotte falls in love with her in earnest and even gets her brother Grand Bush to teach him how to handle the bully. Ending is pat and corny.

Black cast members Woodard and Bush sympathetically make the best impression as their white-bread counterparts led by Marotte are given paper-thin roles. Some vulgar dialog presages "Porky's" but is extremely mild by comparison. — *Lor.*

Double Revenge

New York A Smart Egg Pictures release of a Luigi Cingolani production. Executive producers, Cingolani, George Zecevic. Produced

by T.J. Castronovo, John S. Curran. Directed by Armand Mastroianni. Screenplay, Brian Tobin, John Sharkey, from Tobin's story; camera (United color), Arnie Sirlin; editor, Seth Gaven; music, Harry Manfredini; sound (Ultra-Stereo), Stu Fox; production design, Gene Abel; assistant director, Kelly Van Horn; production manager, Jason Clark; stunt coordinator-2d unit director, Spiro Razatos. Reviewed on Republic Pictures vidcassette, N.Y., June 30, 1990. MPAA Rating: R. Running time: **96 MIN.**

Nick Taylor . . . . Leigh McCloskey
Joe Hulsey . . . . Joe Dallesandro
Angie Corello . . . . . . Theresa Saldana
Susie Taylor . . . . Nancy Everhard
Sheriff Blanchfield . . . . . . Richard Rust
Ray Hulsey . . . . Chris Nash
Burt . . . . Bobby DiCicco

■ **This unconvincing action picture was released on a regional basis in the south in 1988 and belatedly pops up in vidstores.**

The first of two back-to-back assignments for Joe Dallesandro for the indie Smart Egg Pictures, "Double Revenge" casts the former Warhol star as an unredeeming critter. Named Joe (so he can show off his real-life tattoo left over from the '60s), he's just out of prison and drags his young brother Chris Nash along on a savings & loan robbery.

During their escape, Nash is killed when innocent bystander Leigh McCloskey intervenes. McCloskey's wife is killed by Dallesandro; latter is apprehended and gets off on a technicality.

This begins a vendetta between McCloskey and Dallesandro, directed in heavyhanded fashion by horror specialist Armand Mastroianni to be a commentary on the legal system. Far too many U.S. flag shots and a phony ending hammer home film's cynical theme.

Acting is okay, but Dallesandro was better in the more challenging Smart Egg's "Blood Lesson." Composer Harry Manfredini gives his "Friday The 13th" music a rest, but unwisely copies Ennio Morricone soundtracks. — *Lor.*

LATE FILM REVIEW

The Freshman

New York A Tri-Star Pictures release of a Lobell/Bergman production. Produced by Mike Lobell. Written and directed by Andrew Bergman. Camera (Technicolor), William A. Fraker; editor, Barry Malkin; music, David Newman; sound (Dolby), Richard Lightstone; production design, Ken Adam; art direction, Alicia Keywan, Dan Davis (N.Y.); set decoration, Gordon Sim, Gary J. Brink (N.Y.); costume design, Julie Weiss; Marlon Brando's hair and makeup, Philip Rhodes; assistant director, Louis D'Esposito; casting, Mike

Fenton, Judy Taylor, Lynda Gordon (U.S.), Karen Hazzard (Canada). Reviewed at Magno Review 2 screening room, N.Y., July 16, 1990. MPAA Rating: PG. Running time: **102 MIN.**

Carmine Sabatini . . . . . . Marlon Brando
Clark Kellogg . . . . . . Matthew Broderick
Victor Ray . . . . Bruno Kirby
Tina Sabatini . . . . . Penelope Ann Miller
Steve Bushak . . . . Frank Whaley
Chuck Greenwald . . . . Jon Polito
Arthur Fleeber . . . . Paul Benedict
Lloyd Simpson . . . . Richard Gant
Dwight Armstrong . . . . . . Kenneth Welsh
Liz Armstrong . . . . Pamela Payton-Wright
Edward . . . . B.D. Wong

Larry London/Hans . . . Maximilian Schell
Social club barkeep . . . . Leonardo Cimino
Bert Parks . . . . Himself
Maitre d' . . . . Gianni Russo

■ **Marlon Brando's sublime comedy performance elevates "The Freshman" from screwball comedy to a quirky niche in film history — among films that comment on cult movies. Critical kudos and potential upbeat word of mouth could extend its audience from film buffs to wider acceptance.**

The picture was a brief cause célèbre last year when Brando trashed it at the end of shooting, then quickly recanted. His performance is strictly professional, bound to delight his fans, and amounts to his most screen time in at least a decade.

Screenwriter-director Andrew Bergman bounces back creatively after the debacle of his previous assignment, "Big Trouble," an homage/imitation re: Billy Wilder's "Double Indemnity" on which Bergman ceded the director's chair to John Cassavetes during shooting in 1984.

This time Mario Puzo and Francis Coppola's "The Godfather" is Bergman's starting point. Incoming NYU film student Matthew Broderick is exposed not only to that Paramount film (and its sequel) in pretentious prof Paul Benedict's classroom but meets up with a virtual doppelganger for Don Vito Corleone in the form of mobster Carmine Sabatini (Brando).

The ornate and intentionally screwy plotline has Brando making an irresistible offer to Broderick to work for him part-time as a delivery boy. Broderick's first assignment is transporting a huge (but real) lizard from the airport, cueing effective slapstick when it gets loose in a shopping mall creating the sort of panic associated with its distant rubbery relative "Godzilla."

Broderick quickly tumbles to the criminality of Brando and his nutty partner Maximilian Schell, but is unable to extricate himself. By the picture's climax at a movable feast held by the Gourmet Club — with a decadent set of jetsetters paying six figures to dine on endangered species — its screwy plotline is all tied together too neatly.

From the initial lizard reference to the centerpiece of the definitive screwball comedy, Howard Hawks' "Bringing Up Baby," Bergman remains confident and straightfaced in his approach to increasingly outlandish situations.

Previous homage films ranging from David Giler's "The Black Bird" (taking off on "The Maltese Falcon") and Charles Winkler's "You Talking To Me?" ("Taxi Driver" riffs) to Carl Reiner's "Dead Men Don't Wear Plaid" have erred on the side of quickie pastiche. Here Brando takes an instantly recognizable spoof (his makeup by Philip Rhodes recalls Dick Smith's Don Vito makeup for him 18 years earlier and he's photographed at first in looming shadows à la Gordon Willis) and invests the throwaway lines with panache. This full-bodied role extends to physical activity including a cute ice skating routine.

Pic's weakest element is the recurring satire of film studies. Although Benedict is droll as an academic poseur, the mocking of film analysis is puerile and obvious. The best gag is a subtle one: Amidst the huge blowups of filmmakers adorning his classroom walls ranging from Stanley Kubrick to Martin Scorsese, a dramatic scene is framed with a glowering Brian DePalma poster backing Broderick, while opposite wall frames Alfred Hitchcock, out-of-focus, in the reverse shot.

Finale spotlights the inspired gag of Bert Parks singing at the dinner, including a pastiche version of Bernie Wayne's anthem "There She Is (Miss America)" sung to the lizard about to be eaten. More subtle is the same scene's gag of Gianni Russo popping up as maitre d' and old chum of Brando; the actor memorably portrayed Brando's wifebeating son-in-law Carlo in "The Godfather."

For his third Tri-Star film in a row, Broderick again is the underplaying spine around which the picture is built. He's ably abetted by two previous costars: Penelope Anne Miller ("Biloxi Blues"), winning as an offbeat form of mafia princess; and "M. Butterfly's" B.D. Wong (who popped up in "Family Business") as Schell's goofy partner in culinary crime.

As pal and nemesis, respectively, Frank Whaley (styled here to look like River Phoenix in "Jimmy Reardon") and Bruno Kirby (who appeared in "The Godfather, Part II") also are solid.

Tech credits on the mixed New York and Toronto shoot are good, capturing the right amount of Greenwich Village ambience. Ken Adam provides an interesting art deco set for the prefab tent housing the gourmets' final-reel bash.

— *Lor.*

Presumed Innocent

Hollywood A Warner Bros. release of a Mirage production. Executive producer, Susan Solt. Produced by Sydney Pollack, Mark Rosenberg. Directed by Alan J. Pakula. Screenplay, Frank Pierson, Pakula, based on Scott Turow's novel; camera (Duart color; Technicolor prints), Gordon Willis; editor, Evan Lottman; music, John Williams; sound (Dolby), James Sabat; production design, George Jenkins; art direction, Bob Guerra; set decoration, Carol Joffe; costume design, John Boxer; assistant director, Alex Hapsas; production manager, David Starke; casting, Alixe Gordin. Reviewed at Warner Bros. Studios, Burbank, Calif., July 18, 1990. MPAA Rating: R. Running time: **127 MIN.**
Rusty Sabich . . . . Harrison Ford
Raymond Horgan . . . . . . Brian Dennehy
Alejandro (Sandy) Stern . . . . . Raul Julia
Barbara Sabich . . . . Bonnie Bedelia
Judge Larren Lyttle . . . . . . Paul Winfield
Carolyn Polhemus . . . . . Greta Scaacchi
Det. Lipranzer . . . . John Spencer
Tommy Molto . . . . Joe Grifasi
"Painless" Kumagai . . . . . Sab Shimono
Nat Sabich . . . . Jesse Bradford

■ **Honed to a riveting intensity by director Alan Pakula and featuring the tightest script imaginable, "Presumed Innocent" is a demanding, disturbing javelin of a courtroom murder mystery that will have audiences vigorously debating its plausibility and the U.S. legal system's merits. Justice should prevail at the b.o. with high receipts for Warner Bros.**

Hewing closely to Scott Turow's bestselling 1987 novel, "Presumed Innocent" begins with the book's grave "I am a prosecutor . . ." opening, quoted in voiceover by Harrison Ford, whetting appetites for an ironic dissection of our system of justice.

The harrowing tale that follows unfolds with nary a wasted step, as deputy prosecutor and family man Rusty Sabich (Ford) arrives at work to learn his beautiful colleague Carolyn Polhemus (Greta Scacchi) has been brutally murdered.

Forced to lead the investigation by his longtime boss Raymond Horgan (Brian Dennehy), who's in a deep sweat over his re-election campaign, Sabich can scarcely admit he'd had an affair and an unfinished sexual obsession with the dead attorney.

But his pained, steely cool wife (Bonnie Bedelia) knows, and she's none too sypathetic or forgiving about it. Sabich has scarcely begun the messy job of covering his own tracks en route to finding a suspect when he's confronted by rat-like ex-colleague Tommy Molto (Joe Grifasi), who's part of an opposing campaign for the chief prosecutor's office and has jumped on the investigation as a political tool.

Molto swears Sabich was at Carolyn's apartment the night of the murder and has a beer glass with his prints on it to prove it. Sabich is charged and arrested, and before long is embroiled in a grand jury investigation that spurs his politically frightened boss to turn on him.

With a sly, magnetic Raul Julia brought in as Sabich's crafty defense lawyer, the struggle to build a case is dramatic enough, but for newcomers to Turow's story, the real fascination is that one never knows, until pic's astonishing denouement, whether Sabich did the deed or not.

Ford, in a very mature, subtle, lowkey performance, pulls off the difficult feat of making it impossible to be sure. Moving under a cloud of grief, guilt and strain like a man underwater, he's so bottled up, so grim, that one can imagine him blowing up — and then again not. The adolescent pain that registers on his face when Polhemus rejects him (shown in flashback) is so apart from his normal ramrod character, it's believable he might have acted in violent rage.

Likewise, Pakula, in his most riveting work since "All The President's Men," works so precisely and specifically that every detail is heavy with possibilities.

Script by Frank Pierson and Pakula is a triumph of craft, so completely fat-free that one cannot afford to miss a word and still hope to keep up. The American system of justice, as shown here, is tragically vulnerable to the private agendas of those who best know how to manipulate it. With characters as reprehensible as all these running the show, it's a frightening situation.

At the same time, script hews so relentlessly to its purpose of moving the story forward, and pic's overall tone is so somber, grim and demanding, that some audiences may find "Presumed Innocent" just too joyless of a ride.

Minus the perilous suspense scenes (outside the trial's parameters) that would mark it as a thriller, "Innocent" is a chess-like game of possibility and doubt that engages intellectually more than emotionally. One scarcely knows either Sabich or Carolyn outside this situation, and pic indulges very little in what made it so hard for him to forget her.

Nonetheless pic offers a vivid gallery of performances to savor. Bedelia is wondrously controlled as Ford's intelligent but wounded wife, struggling with her self-esteem but still in love with him, and Scacchi, sans any hint of a European accent, is convincing and seductive as the enigmatic, ambitious Carolyn.

Paul Winfield gives a bursting, larger-than-life perf as the judge; Dennehy is powerful as the turncoat D.A., and Sab Shimono runs away with the coroner's role in his irreverent take on it.

Dark, somber photography by Gordon Willis and realistic production design by George Jenkins create a claustrophobic atmosphere that expands on Sabich's rattled state of mind, while editing by Evan Lottman deftly aids the film's back-and-forth time changes.

— *Daws.*

Men In Love

New York A Tantric Films production. Produced by Scott Catamas. Executive producers, Richard Babson, David Charry. Directed by Marc Huestis. Screenplay, Catamas, Emerald Starr; camera (color), Fawn Yacker, Marsha Kahm; editor, Frank Christopher; music, Donald James Regal; sound, Lauretta Molitor; art direction, Vola Ruben; production manager, Wendy Dallas; lighting director, Alan Steinheimer; video engineers, Larry Jandro, Chris Coughlin, Louis Block; assistant director, Alan Steinfeld. Reviewed at Liaison Group screening room, N.Y., July 17, 1990. No MPAA rating. Running time: **87 MIN.**

Steven . . . . Doug Self
Peter . . . . Joe Tolbe
Robert . . . . Emerald Starr
Christiana . . . . Kutira Decosterd
B.S. . . . . Vincent Schwickert
Jonathan . . . . James A. Taylor
Rocco . . . . Carlo Incerto
Jaiia . . . . Jaiia
Victor . . . . Scott Catamas
Laurel . . . . Renee De Palma
Lulu . . . . Lulu
Also with: Steve Warren, Maura Nolan, Joe Capetta, Lily Gurk, Toni Maher.

■ **At times resembling nothing so much as an instructional video on new age meditation techniques, "Men In Love" should appeal only to those who don't snicker when characters join hands to "gather energies."**

With a budget of $300,000, San Francisco producer Scott Catamas and director Marc Huestis have created an all-too-earnest pic about the grief of AIDS and the emotional healing powers of new age spirituality. Audiences should have little difficulty relating to the grief part, but the pat answers offered through the pseudo-spiritualism

will leave many chuckling or rolling their eyes.

Plot centers on Steven, a young San Franciscan whose lover, Victor, recently has died of AIDS. Honoring Victor's final wishes, Steven heads to Hawaii to scatter Victor's ashes near the Eden-like home of Victor's former lover, Robert. Upon arriving in Maui, Steven meets Robert and his community of new age-enthusiast friends.

Steven's reaction to the spiritualists is, like that of the audience, one of skepticism and anger. When he castigates Robert for not visiting Victor during the final stages of illness, Robert explains that he did indeed visit Victor — spiritually, through a "vision quest." Both Robert and the film take this babble seriously.

Before he can say "tantric rituals," Steven has joined the new age. The audience should be so lucky. Without Steven's healthy, and arguably well-founded, skepticism, the film surrenders much too easily and completely to the hokum.

As Steven, Doug Self (cast's only professional actor) shows moments of tenderness, although his emoting often gets the best of him. When Steven runs off to a cave for a bit of isolated self-discovery, Self screams, pounds walls, asks "Why? Why? Why?" He emerges from the cave muddy but healed, overacting apparently good for the soul.

Still, Self's acting is topnotch compared with that of others in the cast. Emerald Starr as Robert would deserve pity for the stilted lines he's forced to say ("The new moon is a time of letting go and planting seeds," etc.) were he not given a story credit.

Other cast members, particularly at a full-moon memorial ceremony, look as though they've just graduated from the hippie school in "Billy Jack."

Although "Men In Love" is both compassionate and well-intentioned (the film promotes safe sex as well as spirituality), pic rarely rises above sappiness. Huestis can't resist a sentimental opportunity. When two characters make love, the camera cuts to two kittens frolicking nearby. When Steven makes his spiritual breakthrough, a flower blossoms. Seriously.

Pic's only innovation came with its filming. Shot in Beta SP, the

video was mastered in D-1 digital component tape and blown up to 35m film. The result is better than might be expected, although even the lush Hawaiian backgrounds have a dull flatness. That could explain Huestis' reliance on closeups, including an unfortunate number of unnecessary establishing shots. The "baggage claim" sign at the airport hardly merits the attention it receives. — *Evan.*

Ruby And Rata
(NEW ZEALAND)

Wellington A Preston/Laing production in association with the New Zealand Film Commission. Produced by Robin Laing. Directed by Gaylene Preston. Screenplay, Graeme Tetley; camera (color), Leon Narbey; editor, Paul Sutorius; music, Jonathan Crayford. Reviewed at the Wellington Film Festival, Wellington, July 14, 1990. Running time: **105 MIN.**

Ruby . . . . Yvonne Lawley
Rata . . . . Vanessa Rare
Willie . . . . Lee Mete-Kingi
Buckle . . . . Simon Barnett

■ **Gaylene Preston's second feature, "Ruby And Rata," is a good-natured neighborhood pic that gently unfolds a tale of loneliness, humor and mutual dependence in the suburbs. This pic should be attractive for niche theatrical and most tv and video markets.**

Story centers on fiercely independent 83-year-old Ruby (Yvonne Lawley), who is determined to live her own life in her own home. She will not be interned in Sunset Village, even though nephew Buckle (Simon Barnett) seeks to convince her of the benefits. With Buckle's reluctant help, she rents her basement apartment to single mother Rata (Vanessa Rare) and 8-year-old Willie (Lee Mete-Kingi).

Ruby soon discovers Rata is not quite the person she thought she was, and she learns that Willie has "taking ways" at the corner store. Both women are strong-willed and unprepared to concede they might need each other's friendship. To gain the upper hand, Ruby "kidnaps" Willie. But it will be the boy who brings them together.

Helmer Preston's "Mr. Wrong" (released in the U.S. as "Dark Of The Night") was a quirky femme thriller that showed the helmer's ability to draw antipodean flavor from the Ealing Studios' comedy tradition. Here, the story seems slight and its handling too matter-of-fact.

However, once Ruby and Willie make contact (she entices him upstairs by baiting chocolate fish on a rod and playing out the line to the garden below), the richness of the material is evident. The finale is upbeat, and writer Graeme Tetley conjures a sweet twist at fadeout.

Lawley, a thesp of formidable ability, excels. Thin as a reed and stooped, she plays Ruby with shrewd acuity. She provides a sure focus for the film, and her scenes with first-timer Mete-Kingi are particularly affecting.

Rare, another newcomer, has the looks and strength for Rata, if not the craft that would allow her to give the character more dimension. But she has an enviable ease before the camera that guarantees more work — and the experience that comes from that. — *Nic.*

Romeo
(DUTCH)

Amsterdam A Concorde Film release of a Horizon/NOS coproduction. Produced by Frans Rasker. Written and directed by Rita Horst. Camera (Eastmancolor), Theo Bierkens; editor, Ot Louw; music, Boudewijn Tarenkseen; sound, Hugo de Vries, Ot Louw; art direction, Philippe Graff; assistant director, Oline Engelvaart; casting, Jeanette Snik. Reviewed at the Cinema theater, Amsterdam, March 27, 1990. Running time: **91 MIN.**
Anne . . . . Monique van de Ven
Matthijs . . . . Johan Leysen
Nel . . . . Ottolien Boeschoten
Doctor . . . . Hans Croiset
Anne's mother . . . . Coby Timp
Anne's father . . . . . . Bob van den Berg
Director . . . . Wick Ederveen
Chiel . . . . Peter Bolhuis

■ **A strong script, fine performances and assured direction from a feature newcomer with vast tv experience makes "Romeo" moving drama with offshore possibilities.**

Johan Leysen and Monique van de Ven are a well-married couple, awaiting their first child, when the doctor informs them that it can't live, and an abortion is induced. Leysen doesn't want to talk about it; van de Ven can talk of nothing else.

The emotional strain takes its toll. Leysen concentrates on getting on with living. Van de Ven is obsessed with the "Why?" Why her, why this child? When the marriage is nearly on the rocks, he has a breakdown, and van de Ven

realizes that he has suffered as deeply as she has. This brings them closer together again, no longer two people in love, but a loving couple.

Writer-director Rita Horst based her script on her own personal tragedy, which began as an article and gradually developed into a film story. Leysen, the male star, is Horst's real-life mate. Her direction is both daring and restrained, using subplots to keep the film moving along. In addition to the perfect central performances, the supporting parts are solid. — *Wall.*

Bashu, The Little Stranger
(IRANIAN)

Hollywood An Intl. Home Cinema release. Produced by Ali Reza Zarrin. Written and directed by Bahram Beizai. Camera (color), Firooz Malekzadeh; editor, Beizai; sound, Jahangir Mirshekari, Asghar Shahverdi, Behrooz Moavenian. Reviewed at AMC Theaters, Santa Monica, Calif., July 16, 1990. No MPAA Rating. Running time: **120 MIN.**
Nai . . . . Susan Taslimi
Bashu . . . . Aduan Afravian
Nai's husband . . . . . Parvis Pourhosseini

 A slow-moving allegorical tale about an Iranian war orphan who awakens compassion in a defiant peasant woman, the underdeveloped "Bashu, The Little Stranger" is likely to leave Westerners and other outsiders more baffled than engaged.

Pic has scant commercial prospects outside areas with significant Iranian populations.

Director Bahram Beizai begins the tale vividly, with explosions decimating a Persian Gulf village and killing the family of 10-year-old Bashu (Aduan Afravian).

The boy flees the harsh desert in the back of a northbound truck and wakes in an entirely new land, the lush, pastoral area near the Caspian sea, where his dark skin and Arabic dialect make him an object of derision.

Nai (the magnificent Susan Taslimi) takes in the shell-shocked waif, despite the open hostility of her neighbors, who can't understand why she would burden herself with a stranger.

No one seems to have a clue about where Bashu is from (as if they'd never heard the language of their southern countrymen), and all are horrifyingly racist (the learned man, or "doctor," ignores a gravely ill Bashu because he doesn't treat "black people").

The pic founders as its thin setup leaves it with nowhere to go. Will Bashu ever be accepted by the villagers and the family's absent father? Will he cease being homesick and stay? There is little else to wonder about, except why the film is two hours long when 88 minutes would have done the job nicely.

What "Bashu" does have to offer are beautiful, fluid, startling images of rural Iranian life (Beizai and cinematographer Firooz Malekzadeh certainly are talented picturemakers) and a fiery, earthy performance by Taslimi as the isolated earth mother who'd rather communicate with wild things (birds, boars and children) than with her petty neighbors.

Pic occasionally flashes a social message, as when Bashu and the neighbor boys come together as "children of Iran" despite the bickering of their elders.

But mostly the film is about a maternal love that overcomes all external obstacles. Theme could have been overly sentimental, but Beizai is too subtle to go that route.

The problem is he's too subtle all the way around. For offshore audiences hungry for cross-cultural understanding, "Bashu" is only a shadow of what it could have been. — *Daws.*

Istanbul:
Keep Your Eyes Open
(SWEDISH)

New York A Cori Films Intl. presentation of an Omegafilm production. Produced by Peter Kropénin. Directed by Mats Arehn. Screenplay, Bo Sigvard Nilsson, Thomas Samuelson, Arehn; camera (Film Labor color), Erling Thurmann-Anderson; editor, Samuelson; music, Tomas Ledin; sound, Mats Lindskog; production design, Eric Johnson; costume design, Hedvig Ander; assistant director, Sarl Sahbaz; production manager, Zafer Dogan; associate producer, Cemal Sener. Reviewed on Magnum Entertainment vidcassette, N.Y., July 7, 1990. MPAA Rating: PG-13. Running time: **85 MIN.**
Frank Collins . . . . . . Timothy Bottoms
Maud . . . . Twiggy
Atkins . . . . Robert Morley
Mia . . . . Emma Kihlberg
Ingrid . . . . Lena Endre
Consul . . . . Sverre Anker Ousdal
Uncle . . . . Engin Inal
(English soundtrack)

■ **"Istanbul" is a low-energy, mindless thriller made by Swedes for the international market.**

Best thing here is the theme song accounting for its subtitle "Keep Your Eyes Open."

Timothy Bottoms, soon to be seen back in A moviedom in "Texasville," walks through his role as a New York Times correspondent based in Sweden who travels to Istanbul with his preteen daughter (Emma Kihlberg) on a secret mission.

Having received a videotape from the boy's father, he's seeking mysterious information about his stepson of half-Turkish descent (mama is Swede Lena Endre). Preposterous plot gimmick kills the film early on, as Bottoms on his wife's advice takes Kihlberg with him rather than his son, and the young girl is the victim of endless kidnaping attempts.

Equally unbelievable is the appearance in Istanbul of Twiggy with her own daughter. She befriends Bottoms and manipulates him as part of a murky plot. Robert Morley is also along for a brief cameo to deliver pointless exposition about illegal arms trading.

With this unpromising material, director Mats Arehn bungles the climax which makes no sense as presented.

Acting is weak and film is further sabotaged by variable sound recording which creates a synthesizer distortion in dialog scenes that is annoying. — *Lor.*

Laura Adler's Last
Love Affair
(ISRAELI)

Jerusalem A Paralax Prods. Ltd. production. Produced by Marek Rozenbaum. Written and directed by Avram Heffner. Camera, David Gurfinkel; editor, Lina Kadish; music, Shem Tov Levy; production design, Ariel Kadish. Reviewed at the Jerusalem Film Festival, July 18, 1990. Running time: **96 MIN.**
Laura . . . . Rita Zohar
Becky . . . . Shulamit Adar
Sawitch . . . . Menashe Warshavski
Menashe . . . . Avram Moor
Palevitz . . . . Yacov Shapiro

■ **Despite some touching and amusing moments in this comedy-drama set in Israel's fading Yiddish-theater scene, a sketchy "Laura Adler's Last Love Affair" hardly scratches the potential of its setting. Pic may have some interest for Jewish audiences abroad.**

The story is set among aging thespians of an amateurish Yiddish theater troupe in Tel Aviv. The star of the group is middle-aged beauty Laura Adler, worshipped by her quiet dressmaker Becky, loved by her buffoonish co-actor Sawitch, adored by the small, elderly crowds who continue to attend the performances.

Out of the blue, Laura is given a last chance for personal and professional renewal. She is offered the starring role in an American film production based on an Isaac Bashevis Singer story, and she has a passionate, brief romance with a mysterious and handsome younger man. But her dreams are dashed after she learns she has terminal cancer, and Laura decides to leave life as she lived it — onstage.

First half of film is best, as the troupe rehearses for a performance of a typically corny Yiddish melodrama. Unfortunately, story becomes overly predictable towards the tragic finish, with intriguing plot lines and characters left undeveloped.

Laura is clearly meant to symbolize the Yiddish theater as a whole, doomed to eventual oblivion despite occasional comebacks and a gallant dedication to a fading art. That idea is fine; writer-director Heffner errs in failing to give Laura the depth necessary to make her a believable, three-dimensional personality.

Though Rita Zohar, a child star of the Israeli Yiddish theater working in Hollywood for the past decade, is an attractive and capable performer, she is never given the crucial scenes needed to build her character.

The rest of a cast comprising other Yiddish theater veterans does well, particularly Shulamit Adar as the adoring Becky. Only false note among the performances is due to the inexplicable casting of a South African actress as the U.S. film director who gives Laura her final big break.

Technical credits are superior for an Israeli production, particularly David Gurfinkel's moody, shadow-drenched lighting. — *Cbd*.

Mo' Better Blues

New York A Universal Pictures release of a 40 Acres And A Mule Filmworks production. Produced, written and directed by Spike Lee. Camera (Duart color; Deluxe prints), Ernest Dickerson; editor, Sam Pollard; music, Bill Lee, performed by Branford Marsalis Quartet featuring Terence Blanchard; sound (Dolby), Skip Lievsay; production design, Wynn Thomas; costume design, Ruth E. Carter; assistant director, Randy Fletcher; line producer, Jon Kilik; coproducer, Monty Ross; casting, Robi Reed. Reviewed at Universal Studios Alfred Hitchcock Theater, Hollywood, July 18, 1990. MPAA Rating: R. Running time: **127 MIN.**

Bleek Gilliam	Denzel Washington
Giant	Spike Lee
Shadow Henderson	Wesley Snipes
Indigo Downes	Joie Lee
Clarke Bentancourt	Cynda Williams
Left Hand Lacey	Giancarlo Esposito
Butterbean Jones	Robin Harris
Bottom Hammer	Bill Nunn
Big Stop Gilliam	Dick Anthony Williams
Moe Flatbush	John Turturro
Petey	Rubén Blades
Rhythm Jones	Jeff (Tain) Watts
Josh Flatbush	Nicholas Turturro
Lillian Gilliam	Abbey Lincoln
Jeanne	Linda Hawkins
Young Bleek/Miles	Zakee L. Howze
Father of the bride	Bill Lee
Branford Marsalis	Himself

Also with: Samuel L. Jackson, Leonard Thomas, Charles Q. Murphy, Steve White, Joe Seneca, Tracy Camilla Johns, John Canada Terrell, Monty Ross.

■ **Personal rather than social issues come to the fore in "Mo' Better Blues," a Spike Lee personality piece dressed in jazz trappings that puffs itself up like "Bird" but doesn't really fly.**

More focused on the sexual dilemmas of its main character than on musical themes, pic might well be subtitled "He's Gotta Have It." Universal should take in substantial door money for early shows, but anyone expecting director-producer-writer Lee to blow the room away will be disappointed.

Pic's fabulous opening sequence, in which the camera does a sensual pan of jazz images — a horn, a man's ear, his mouth — raises expectations for a definitive film on jazz and an ambitious step forward for Lee. But the script unfolds to notes from a different scale: basically the same unique but limited range Lee has drawn on before.

Contempo tale stars Denzel Washington as Bleek Gilliam, a self-absorbed New York horn player who leads a jazz quintet on a roll at a trendy Manhattan club called Beneath the Underdog. The diminutive Lee plays Giant (as in "giant pain in the ass," one character observes), Bleek's ne'er-do-well friend who's found a precarious niche as the band's manager.

Joie Lee (Lee's sister) and Cynda Williams play the women who compete for Bleek's attention, although he sees them as nothing but distractions.

Also overlooked by the self-centered trumpeter is his sax player, Shadow (Wesley Snipes, in a standout perf), a restless and ambitious showman who's frustrated by Bleek's domineering style.

The cool, aloof Bleek, declaring music his first priority, tunes everyone else out so he can accomplish things in the precise, controlled style that suits him.

Even as played by the subtle, smoldering Washington, who triumphed last year with his Oscar-winning role in "Glory," Bleek is not a particularly interesting character. As a performer, he's polished but not exciting; as a lover, his action's all on the surface.

Pic's frothy, enticing and fluidly filmed love scenes are high on its list of attractions, but Bleek is so emotionally frozen that when his women press him to choose, he can only invite them to leave if they can't "hang."

But if "Mo' Better" is soft in the center, the characters in and around the band and the nightclub provide winning entertainment. Like the residents of the overheated Bed-Stuy block in "Do The Right Thing," they're a riotous ensemble, spewing out the raps Lee writes and directs so well.

Pic's virtuosity is the jazzlike way the ensemble scenes are conducted, as one character (often Giant) moves into a group spouting his nervy solo and then beats a graceful retreat.

Giancarlo Esposito adds one of the funniest bits as floundering piano player Left Hand Lacey, who shows up late every night with an ersatz French girlfriend.

Lee, essentially reprising his role as fast-talking Mookie from "Do The Right Thing," is a comic delight, particularly in the nonsensical routines with his Spanish-speaking bookie (Rubén Blades).

In these dense ensemble sequences and in the offhand character bits, Lee finds his surest footing and most uproarious moments. But for the most part, the film isn't convincing.

Bleek eventually gets his comeuppance, but it occurs so late in this 127-minute piece that one has stopped expecting a traditional conclusion. And the frenzied cutting between Bleek's playing onstage and the back-alley violence dealt to Giant at the film's turning point feels like an attempt to force a connection that isn't there.

The heavily melodramatic tone of the third act is unconvincing. When Lee turns up the sound of applause as Bleek takes the stage for a comeback attempt, it's the sound of a filmmaker trying to fake last-minute impact.

At one point, Shadow tries to buy a stack of John Coltrane CDs with an American Express Gold Card, only to have the card rejected. It's a worthwhile metaphor for the film, as all the resources at Lee's disposal don't make this rich, glossy production a significant film about jazz. When Coltrane's spiritual "A Love Supreme" enters the soundtrack, that fact is particularly clear.

Production values are firstrate. Characters inhabit a clean, stylish realm noticeably different from other music films. Ernest Dickerson, who photographed Lee's three previous pics, brings imagination and flair to the rich, colorful lensing and lighting, and Ruth Carter comes up with a sharp scheme for the bebop-influenced costumes.

Composer and bassist Bill Lee (Lee's father) created the stylish middleweight score, and soundtrack features Branford Marsalis, Terence Blanchard, Miles Davis, Charles Mingus, Coltrane and the full arrangements of Bill Lee's 100-piece Natural Spiritual Orchestra.

The late Robin Harris ("Do The Right Thing," "House Party"), makes his final screen appearance doing a blue comedy routine at the club. — *Daws*.

Young Guns II

Hollywood A 20th Century Fox release of a James G. Robinson presentation of a Morgan Creek production. Produced by Paul Schiff, Irby Smith. Executive producers, Robinson, Joe Roth, John Fusco. Coexecutive producers, David Nicksay, Gary Barber. Directed by Geoff Murphy. Screenplay, Fusco; camera (Deluxe color), Dean Semler; editor, Bruce Green; music, Alan Silvestri; songs, Jon Bon Jovi; sound (Dolby), Louis L. Edemann, Donald J. Malouf; production design, Gene Rudolf; art direction, Christa Munro; set decoration, Andy Bernard; costume design, Judy Ruskin; assistant directors, Scott Javine, Thomas Schellenberg, Irby Jay Smith Jr.; associate producer, Dixie J. Capp; casting, Michael Chinich. Reviewed at the Century Plaza Cinemas, Hollywood, July 26, 1990. MPAA Rating: PG. Running time: **103 MIN.**

William H. Bonney	Emilio Estevez
Doc Scurlock	Kiefer Sutherland
Chavez Y Chavez	Lou Diamond Phillips
Arkansas Dave Rudabaugh	Christian Slater
Pat Garrett	William Petersen

Hendry French	Alan Ruck
D.A. Rynerson	R.D. Call
John Chisum	James Coburn
Tom O'Folliard	Balthazar Getty
Ashmun Upson	Jack Kehoe

■ **Although it's more ambitious than most sequels, "Young Guns II" exhausts its most inspired moment during the opening credits and fades into a copy of its 1988 predecessor — a slick, glossy MTV-style Western.**

Bratpack appeal should help the film at the starting gate, but it seems sure to falter in the home stretch. Even the film's one surprise — a wizened horseman emerging from the desert, circa 1950, to recount the tale of Billy the Kid — feels lifted from Arthur Penn's 1970 classic "Little Big Man," all the way down to Emilio Estevez' hoarse, whispering narration.

The producers seem to be counting on the fact that the target audience either never saw "Little Big Man" or wasn't alive when it was released, emphasizing the teen appeal of its stars and songs by Jon Bon Jovi. The story also is derived from a Western that predates the MTV set: Sam Peckinpah's 1973 "Pat Garrett & Billy The Kid." To blast home the point, there's even a cameo by James Coburn, Garrett in the earlier film.

Still, the questioning of right and wrong in the Old West undertaken by both those films is absent from this oater, which follows a stripped-to-the-bone storyline that picks up the adventures of Billy Bonney's Lincoln County gang a few years after the events in 1988's "Young Guns." Told in flashback, the story essentially involves the gang's hell-bent rush toward the perceived safety of Mexico with a band of government men — headed by ally-turned-adversary Pat Garrett (William Petersen) — in hot pursuit.

Estevez, Kiefer Sutherland and Lou Diamond Phillips are back, but the rest of the gang is new, and the other characterizations prove disappointingly thin. Christian Slater has a nice recurring bit as a Gun with an inferiority complex over his lack of notoriety (it seems Arkansas Dave Rudabaugh wasn't exactly a household name), but he's generally underemployed. Petersen cuts a striking figure as Garrett without providing much insight into his motives or suggested ambivalence.

As in the first film, Estevez' performance as the wild-eyed Billy the Kid is uneven. Although he leans toward portraying him as slightly psychotic, his Billy seems more like an eccentric punk than an outlaw. Still, posturing and attitude was what "Young Guns" was all about.

Director Geoff Murphy paces the sequel a little better than the original, which lagged painfully in its final act. Some of the editing in the latest ride is sloppy, however, and the second-unit work is generally undistinguished.

A what-happened-to device at the end — meant to bring some weight to the events that preceded it — also misfires.

Even with all the stress on Bon Jovi's songs, it would be a crime to overlook Alan Silvestri's brilliant, hypnotic score, the film's one shining achievement. Pic was lensed at a number of stunning locations in New Mexico and Arizona. — *Bril.*

Problem Child

Hollywood A Universal release of an Imagine Entertainment production. Produced by Robert Simonds. Directed by Dennis Dugan. Executive producer, James D. Brubaker. Screenplay, Scott Alexander, Larry Karaszewski; camera (Deluxe color), Peter Lyons Collister; editor, Daniel Hanley, Michael Hill; music, Miles Goodman; sound (Dolby), Larry Mann; production design, George Costello; art direction, Michael Bingham; set decoration, Denise Pizzini; costume design, Eileen Kennedy; assistant directors, James S. Simons, Steven Hirsch, George Fortmuller; associate producer, Michael Torres; casting, Nancy Nayor, Valerie McCaffrey. Reviewed at the Beverly Center Cineplex, L.A., July 27, 1990. MPAA Rating: PG. Running time: **81 MIN.**

Ben	John Ritter
Big Ben	Jack Warden
Junior	Michael Oliver
Mr. Peabody	Gilbert Gottfried
Flo	Amy Yasbeck
Martin Beck	Michael Richards
Roy	Peter Jurasik

■ **All of "Problem Child's" problems should be solved by a very, very quick exit from theaters.**

Universal took a step in the right direction by whittling it down to just 81 minutes but didn't go far enough. The studio should have excised another 75 minutes and released this unbelievable mess as a short.

(Several characters listed in the credits never show up onscreen, and a scene used in the film's billboard ads, with a kitten in a washing machine, is not in the final cut.)

John Ritter and Amy Yasbeck play a yuppie couple determined to have a child, primarily so they can be invited to the neighbors' birthday parties for their own kids.

Unable to conceive themselves, they get suckered into adopting round-faced Junior (Michael Oliver), a child repulsive enough to make nuns cheer when he's taken from their care.

The major subplot has Junior becoming pen pals with a serial killer (Michael Richards) who busts out of prison to see him, leading to a kidnaping and chase that makes "Smokey And The Bandit" look like "Citizen Kane."

Oliver bears a slight resemblance to Opie from "The Andy Griffith Show," though it would be hard to imagine a more annoying child actor, and he's allowed to mug shamelessly. If there's supposed to be a bond developing between Ritter and his son, only maudlin piano music on the score indicates it.

The film marks an atrocious bigscreen debut for actor and episodic tv director Dennis Dugan. Every time it seeks to flesh out a character, it quickly retreats into bad lowbrow farce.

Similarly, the story oscillates between scenes of Junior as little monster and those designed, completely in vain, to make the audience feel sympathy for him.

The most offensive character, however, is Yasbeck's shrill, status-conscious wife.

Tech credits match the script and direction, from the overbearing score to unimpressive stuntwork. — *Bril.*

Farlig leg
(Games)
(DANISH)

Copenhagen A Warner & Metronome release of a Metronome production with Panorama Film Intl. and Urkbar Film. Produced by Mads Egmont Christensen. Executive producers, Bent Fabricius-Bjerre, Just Betzer, Pernille Siesbye. Written and directed by Preben Österfelt; camera (Eastmancolor), Erik Zappon, editor, Jesper W. Nielsen; music, Kim Menzer, Lars Trier; theme song "I Wanna Make Love To You" by J. L. Williams; sound, Jan Juhler, Lars Lund; production design, Sven Wickman; costume design, Kristian Vang Rasmussen; production manager, Henrik Möller-Sörensen, Ida Zerureith; associate producer, Bent Christensen. Reviewed at Warner & Metronome screening room, Copenhagen, July 23, 1990. Running time: **87 MIN.**

Pia	Charlotte Sieling
Michael	Michael Caröe
Simon	Torben Jensen

Also with: Dhami Anne Panjwani, Lisbeth Gajhede, Anthony Michael, Ilse Rande, Elna Brodthagen, Henning Jensen, Guri Richter, Pia Österfelt Hanne Boel.

■ **"Games" is first-time writer-director Preben Österfelt's attempt to get close to the hearts and minds of a trio of lovers. A modest homevid future is its best bet, although it will see initial theatrical exposure in Denmark. Item started its international marketing at Cannes in May.**

The lovers are Michael, a normal-enough yuppie; Simon, a millionaire with sexual bondage fetishes, and Pia, the young woman who cannot make up her mind about which of the two men she wants to settle down with.

Österfelt gets plenty close to the nude body of ample-bosomed but otherwise elegantly slim Pia (brunette Charlotte Sieling) but not to anything or anybody else.

Pia appears happy with live-in lover Michael (curly-haired, boyish Michael Caröe). They share tub and bed with lusty old-fashioned abandon until Pia's former friend Simon (Torben Jensen, who exudes equal measures of bonhomie and menace) turns up to claim her presence in his hunting-lodge, latter complete with fireplace and brass-bed and handcuffs.

Pia flitters from domestic sexual pursuits to tied-up flings and appears to be miserably unhappy in both situations. No wonder. Young Michael is a roll-over-and-light-cigarettes kind of lover, and Simon is never seen getting beyond an embarrassed spectator stage while Pia tugs at her cuffs and moans absentmindedly.

In short, "Games" (original Danish title even means "Dangerous Games") cannot make up its mind whether to go all-out in the softcore skin-flick genre or to opt for psycho sex and thrills with a bit of Hitchcockian suspense thrown in. Trying both gets it nowhere.

At one point, Michael arms himself with a gun to go after Simon when latter has just put his small daughter on a merry-go-round horse. Pale shades of "Strangers On A Train" here, but typically, the gun never gets fired.

Whatever happens or, rather, does not happen, all three main characters are left completely unexplained as to who or what they really are. They remain wooden pawns throughout set pieces and cliché games, further constrained by stilted dialogue and dull cinematography. — *Kell.*

Challenge The Wind

New York A Sell Entertainment presentation of a Vidark Films production. Produced by Ken Howard, Bill Martin, William Blackburn, John Bateman. Directed by Blackburn. Screenplay, Howard, Marla Young, Blackburn; camera (color), Bateman; editor, Ann Trucke; music, Jeff Rhoades; sound, John Paul Bateman. Reviewed on Sell vidcassette, N.Y., July 4, 1990. No MPAA Rating. Running time: **91 MIN.**
Matthew Harding . . . . Mark Whittington
Maryanne . . . . Katy Dickson
Billy Dale . . . . James Collins
Grandma . . . . Norma Smith
Grandpa . . . . Jay Jones
Robert . . . . Jack Shamblin
Emily . . . . Leigh Smith
    Also with: Bill Dickson, Paula Baxter, Orin Frank, John Bateman, William Blackburn, Ken Howard.

■ "Challenge The Wind" commits the cardinal error of well-meaning family films: It's deadly dull. Best chances are in markets seeking squeaky-clean product.

Heavy regional accents punctuate the cast of the this Arkansas-lensed effort, headed by young Mark Whittington who returns to his hometown to live with his grandparents. He wants to follow in his late dad's footsteps as a track star and gets added impetus when kindly grandpa (Jay Jones) cornily keels over with a fatal heart attack.

Clichéd dialog often sounds like a recruiting poster. Absurd climax has Whittington forced to run to a track meet when his car breaks down and then he wins one for the gipper by delivering a speedy final leg to the team's mile relay race.

Flat, amateurish line readings hamper this modest effort. — *Lor.*

Ninja Academy

New York An Omega Pictures presentation. Produced and directed by Nico Mastorakis. Screenplay, Jonathan Gift; camera (Technicolor), William Steven Shaw; editor, Barry Zetlin; music, Jerry J. Grant; sound (Ultra-Stereo), David Yaffe; production design, Gary New; assistant director, Mike Snyder; production manager, Harlan Freedman; stunt coordinator, James Lew; additional camera, Paul Pollard. Reviewed on Quest Entertainment vidcassette, N.Y., July 21, 1990. No MPAA Rating. Running time: **93 MIN.**
Josh . . . . Will Egan
Gayle . . . . Kelly Randall
Chiba . . . . Gerald Okamura
Phillip . . . . Michael David
George . . . . Robert Factor
The mime . . . . Jeff Robinson
Suzy . . . . Kathleen Stevens
Lynn . . . . Lisa LeCover
Claude . . . . John Freiberger
Addleman . . . . Seth Foster
Gonzales . . . . Art Cammacho
    Also with: Deena Driskill, Orly Benyar, Patti Negri, Dee Copolla, Fiama Fricano,
Becky LeBeau, Kerry O'Brien, Bonnie Paine, Michelle Burger, Anna Kim, Shari Blum.

■ A mild entry in the ongoing trainee film sweepstakes (e.g., "Police Academy"), this direct-to-video feature includes enough gags and pretty girls to prove diverting.

Motley cast members assemble at Gerald Okamura's martial arts academy to gain toughness, an update of traditional military academy films. Modern version features a coed dorm, featuring sexy blond Kathleen Stevens, her pal Lisa LeCover and especially the bodacious instructor (Okamura's daughter) Kelly Randall. En route to a climactic battle with a rival school (just like in every Hong Kong kung fu film), the goofballs run through the usual antics, including spying on a neighboring nudist camp and mocking the obstacle course. Running gag has a James Bond type (he's named 007-11, working for M&M) who plays the entire film in his tuxedo as well as a mime who's consistently out of place.

Cast is enthusiastic in what amounts to an audition for bigger features. End credits reflect filmmaker Nico Mastorakis' fondness for in-jokes but are pretty lame.
— *Lor.*

Flatliners

Hollywood A Columbia Pictures release of a Stonebridge Entertainment production. Produced by Michael Douglas, Rick Bieber. Executive producers, Scott Rudin, Michael Rachmil, Peter Filardi. Directed by Joel Schumacher. Screenplay, Filardi; camera (Deluxe color), Jan De Bont; editor, Robert Brown; music, James Newton Howard; sound (Dolby), David MacMillan; production design, Eugenio Zanetti; art direction, Jim Dultz; costume design, Susan Becker; set design, Stephen Homsy, Paul M. Sonski; set decoration, Anne L. Dulgian; stunt coordination, Bill Erickson; special effects, Philip Cory, Hans Metz; assistant directors, Jeff Rafner, John Kretchmer; casting, Mali Finn. Reviewed at Columbia Studios, Culver City, Calif., July 30, 1990. MPAA Rating: R. Running time: **111 MIN.**
Nelson . . . . Kiefer Sutherland
Rachel . . . . Julia Roberts
Labraccio . . . . Kevin Bacon
Joe . . . . William Baldwin
Steckle . . . . Oliver Platt
Winnie Hicks . . . . Kimberly Scott
Billy Mahoney . . . . Joshua Rudoy

■ "Flatliners" is a provocative and original enough pic to score big b.o. for Columbia, drawing both mainstream and cult audiences.

Death, the ultimate rush, is the target experience for a group of daring young medical students who break on through to the other side —and live to tell about it.

A cautionary tale that ends along fairly traditional horror-sci-fi lines, "Flatliners" is a strikingly original, often brilliantly visualized film from director Joel Schumacher ("The Lost Boys") and writer Peter Filardi.

Decision to cast the "scientists" as attractive young mavericks was sharp. Kiefer Sutherland, Julia Roberts and Kevin Bacon give the film immediacy for the young viewers most likely to turn out for it, and hot newcomer William Baldwin (younger brother of Alec) and Oliver Platt both make strong contributions.

Ditto the writer's contention that going after the answers about death makes sense for explorers of the current generation, having seen the west, space, drugs and the inner world explored before them. Premise is that daring doctor-in-training Nelson (Sutherland) decides to make his mark on medicine by stopping his heart and brain ("flatlining," as the lack of vital signs produces a flat line on the EKG and EEG monitors) and then having himself brought back by the gifted medical students he recruits to help him.

Initially angry and reluctant, the others end up totally seduced by the excitement of what they've done, vying with each other for the chance to go next by offering to flatline the longest.

Experiments, conducted nightly in the coven-like atmosphere or a gothic university lab building, take on an intoxicating urgency parallel to drug experiments or satanic rituals, and director Schumacher, working with cinematographer Jan De Bont and production designer Eugenio Zanetti, pushes the connection with wild, hallucinogenic scenes of Halloween rituals going on outside.

Problem is, as Nelson discovers, that the curtain of death, once penetrated, doesn't close behind you, and Nelson finds himself haunted by an aggressive demon from another world. Before he can bring himself to admit that his idea wasn't such a good one, all the others but one have gone over.

Once beyond the setup, "Flatliners" becomes a tad disappointing, as the dimensions of its "answers" about the experience beyond life are rather small. Film becomes mostly a cautionary horror tale, as Nelson is pursued by vicious Billy Mahoney, a demon from his past. Pic's comforting ending is not only a cop-out but probably scientifically impossible.

What remains impressive is the skill with which Schumacher brings his visions of "the beyond" to the screen. Each time someone "dies," the screen tips over into an entirely new experience so mesmerizing viewers can feel the powerful tug-of-war between temptation of death and struggles of the young doctors to shock the patient back to life.

"Flatliners" keeps things mostly on a secular plane, though there are religious overtones.

Filardi's script so interested exec producer Scott Rudin that he set off fireworks by bidding against Columbia (where he had an exclusive pact) for the rights. Rudin winds up sharing exec producer credit with Filardi and Michael Rachmil, while Michael Douglas and Rick Bieber, for whom Col originally wanted it.

Script shapes up as not only a high-concept coup but a smart, smoothly crafted entertainment with plenty of sharp dialog.

Schumacher not only does a masterful job of orchestrating the atmospherics of the spiritual and horror elements, but also draws compelling performances.

Sutherland, as always, registers real presence and pulls off a wildly demanding role, but the remarkably gifted Roberts is the film's true grace note as the low-key, private and intensely focused Rachel. "See you soon," she says softly each time a "flatliner" goes under. No doubt about it.

James Newton Howard's orchestral and choral score emphasizes spiritual and classical dimensions of story's quest for knowledge, and is a classier choice than the rock 'n' roll soundtrack that might have sufficed. — *Daws.*

Duck Tales: The Movie — Treasure Of The Lost Lamp

Hollywood A Buena Vista release of a Disney Movietoons presentation of a Walt Disney Animation (France) S.A. production. Produced and directed by Bob Hathcock. Screenplay, Alan Burnett; camera (Technicolor), uncredited; editor, Charles King. Keith Holden (London); music, David Newman; sound (Dolby), uncredited; production design, Skip Morgan; sequence directors, Paul Brizzi, Gaetan Brizzi, Clive Pallant, Mattias Marcos Rodric, Vincent Woodcock; coproducers, Jean-Pierre Quenet, Robert Taylor; associate producer, Liza-Ann Warren. Reviewed at Avco Cinema Center, L.A., July 28, 1990. MPAA Rating: G. Running time: **73 MIN.**

Voices of:
Scrooge . . . . Alan Young
Huey, Dewey, Louie
    & Webby . . . . Russi Taylor
Genie . . . . Rip Taylor
Merlock . . . . Christopher Lloyd
Dijon . . . . Richard Libertini
Mrs. Featherby . . . . June Foray
Mrs. Beakley . . . . Joan Gerber
Duckworth . . . . Chuck McCann
Launchpad . . . . Terence McGovern
   Also with the voices of: Charlie Adler, Jack Angel, Steve Bulen, Sherry Lynn, Mickie T. McGowan, Patrick Pinney, Frank Welker.

■ **Disney's new Movietoons label for animated films makes a splashy debut with "Duck Tales: The Movie," a lushly animated, smartly scripted, wise-quacking adventure cartoon that should bring satisfying returns to the studio.**

Built-in audience for the pic, which is based on Disney's three-year-old syndicated daytime cartoon series, should be pleased with its stretch to the bigscreen.

Disney appears to have spared no expense, recruiting more than 500 artists and technicians to work on the film at Disney's new animation studios in France and England as well as in Los Angeles.

Animation veteran Bob Hathcock, who produced nearly one-third of the "Duck Tales" tv episodes, produced and directed the film, and staff writer Alan Burnett scripted.

Resulting crisply paced 73-minute film is a visual delight, with richly painted backgrounds, elaborate action-adventure sequences and dazzling multiplane and computer-assisted effects.

Effort to impress makes the film seem too complex and overloaded throughout first act, but as story settles down into a simpler mode, scripter Burnett sounds the true notes that will hook young viewers.

Tale centers on a magic lamp found by jillionaire Scrooge McDuck (Alan Young) and his nephews Huey, Dewey and Louie and their female friend Webby (each voiced by Russi Taylor) when they fly off to find buried treasure in an Indiana Jones-style adventure.

Once back in the Duckberg mansion, Webby discovers there's a genie in the lamp, and the ducklings begin a wishing spree that brings them giant ice cream sundaes, live toys and dolls, hangliders, etc.

The fun is interrupted by arrival of lamp's former owner, Merlock, a villain who changes shapes as he travels, becoming a cougar, a bird, a rat and a cockroach during his quest to recover the lamp.

Once he wrests the lamp away from the ducks, evil Merlock (Christopher Lloyd) uses it to seize Scrooge's wealth and turn Duckberg upside down.

The outcast ducks must find a way to get it back, with the help of their new friend Genie (Rip Taylor), who has a wish of his own — to be turned into a real boy.

Third act is quite impressive, with elaborate multiplane effects as Merlock transforms Scrooge's money bin into a fortress, and an imaginative closing sequence.

Burnett's script turns on tried-and-true kid's themes but has a wacky tone and enough sharp, irreverent dialog to entertain adult viewers.

Pic's scenic frames, with their startling depth, detail and rich color sense are a treat to behold. Voice actors all hit their marks, particularly Taylor as the zesty genie and Young doing the warm Scottish burr of grumpy but kindly Uncle Scrooge.

Ninety percent of animation was done at Walt Disney Animation France by a team of 110 mostly European artists under the direction of Paul and Gaetan Brizzi. Opening and closing sequences were created by 80 artists at Walt Disney Animation U.K., under direction of Clive Pallant and Vincent Woodcock.

Film was written, storyboarded, laid out and color keyed in L.A., and camerawork and cel painting were done in China. — *Daws*.

Kaj's fødselsdag (Kaj's Birthday) (DANISH)

Copenhagen A Regner Grasten Film release of a Danish Film Studio, Regner Grasten production in association with Sata Film (Warsaw) and Trade Recording Corp. Produced by Regner Grasten. Directed by Lone Scherfig. Screenplay by Peter Bay Clausen and Krzystof (Kris) Kolodziejski; camera (Eastmancolor), Kim Hattensen; editor, Leif Kjeldsen; music, Anders Koppel, Michael Boesen; sound, Morten Degnböl; production design, Claus Bjerre; costume design, Margrethe Rasmussen; production manager, Per Arman, Janne Find; assistant directors, Ib Tardini, Ali Rizvi. Reviewed at the Palads, Copenhagen, Aug. 1 1990. Running time: **89 MIN.**

Kaj . . . . Steen Svare
Magdalena . . . . Dorota Pomykala
Benny . . . . Bertel Abildgard
Kuno . . . . Ivan Horn
Krisser . . . . Peter Bay Clausen
Basse . . . . Michael Boesen
Alslev . . . . Peter Gantzler
   Also with: Dorota Kaminska, Emilian Kaminski, Boguslaw Linda, Kamila Sammler, Tomasz Zaliwski, Torben Zeller, Raimo Bärlund, Peter Aude, Peter Esterhaz.

■ **"Kaj's Birthday," a neat helmer bow for Lone Scherfig, combines sentiment and satire in a low-key telling of a story that would have tempted others towards outright farce.**

Offshore prospects, especially in newly opened Eastern markets, loom as particularly good considering item's subject matter and its partly Polish cast.

Scherfig and writers Peter Bay Clausen and Poland's Kris Kolodziejski have been inspired by the boat outings popular among hard currency-carrying Danes looking for cheap booze and easy lays across the Baltic Sea in the Polish port city of Swinoujscie.

Here an impoverished population has its dance hall operators, restaurateurs, black marketeers and prostitutes standing ready to serve and be humiliated by their 24-hour visitors, reciprocating by gypping them.

When his four boisterous male friends invite shy Kaj, a reluctant bachelor and owner-operator of a sidewalk hot dog stand, to celebrate his 40th anniversary on a trip to Swinoujscie, it is mostly to see Kaj bedded down for a quickie with any female.

In a case of mistaken identities, Kaj winds up with a nice Polish family who thinks he has come to marry their spinster daughter and take her (and maybe all of them) back to milk and honey land — Denmark. During the night, true love is sparked between chubby Kaj and no less amply endowed Magdalena.

Back at the dance hall-restaurant, Kaj's pals drink themselves silly and get in all kinds of trouble with nice and not-so-nice Poles. Instead of having their pants unbuttoned by willing women, they all wind up in a Russian Army prison cell. In the morning, they re-unite with Kaj and go back to Denmark, poorer and certainly not happier for their experiences.

There is no silver lining to any of this except for a sweet smile in the corner of Kaj's eye as he pursues his hot dog stand life back home. What is nice and different about the film is that it is never condescending even when it shows its Danes to be gross and piggish, and its Poles to be mercenary and exploitative.

Everything and everybody have a human edge and an individual touch (one of the Danes is a closet gay). Truly drunken people are never nice to look at or listen to, and neither are the people who are reduced to taking advantage of them. There is no glamour to prostitution, but none to starvation either.

Scherfig does not use her film to preach. She just keeps a watchful and sympathetic eye on proceedings, tempering their sordidness with understated humor.

Film's narrative structure is faltering here and there, and tempos are often lagging, but the cast's Danes and Poles all perform with intelligence and nuance. In the lead, Denmark's Steen Svare and Poland's Dorota Pomykala are totally convincing as well-intentioned people doomed by nature and circumstance never to see their dreams come true. — *Kell*.

The Two Jakes

Hollywood A Paramount release of a Robert Evans, Harold Schneider production. Produced by Evans, Schneider. Directed by Jack Nicholson. Screenplay, Robert Towne; camera (Technicolor), Vilmos Zsigmond; editor, Anne Goursaud; music, Van Dyke Parks; sound (Dolby), Julia Evershade; production design, Jeremy Railton, Richard Sawyer; art decoration, Richard Schreiber; set decoration, Jerry Wunderlich; costume design, Wayne Finkelman; 1st assistant director, Michael Daves; 2d assistant director, Linda Wilder Rockstroh, Michael Kennedy; associate producer, Alan Finkelstein; unit production manager, Max A. Stein; casting, Terry Liebling. Reviewed at Mann National Theater, Westwood, Calif., Aug. 6, 1990. MPAA Rating: R. Running time: **138 MIN.**

Jake Gittes . . . . Jack Nicholson

Jake Berman . . . . Harvey Keitel
Kitty Berman . . . . Meg Tilly
Lillian Bodine . . . . . . Madeleine Stowe
Cotton Weinberger . . . . Eli Wallach
Mickey Nice . . . . Rubén Blades
Newty . . . . Frederic Forrest
Loach . . . . David Keith
Earl Rawley . . . . ⌣. Richard Farnsworth
Tyrone Otley . . . . Tracey Walter
Walsh . . . . Joe Mantell
Khan . . . . James Hong
Capt. Escobar . . . . Perry Lopez
Tilton . . . . Jeff Morris
    Also with: Rebecca Broussard, Paul A.
DiCocco Jr., John Hackett, Rosie Vela, Allan
Warnick, Susan Forristal, Will Tynan, Van
Dyke Parks, William Duffy, Sue Carlton.

■ Following a trek to the bigscreen almost as convoluted as its plot, this oft-delayed sequel proves a jumbled, obtuse yet not entirely unsatisfying follow-up to "Chinatown," rightly considered one of the best films of the '70s.

Once initial curiosity from film buffs subsides, however, Paramount will find luring younger filmgoers to theaters difficult, even with Jack Nicholson's marquee value as director and star.

That may leave many to wait for the film on homevideo, where its ample length and tangled web of plot twists should seem less oppressive, though whatever its shortcomings "The Two Jakes" isn't exactly boring.

Like much of the film noir of the 1940s, "Jakes" simply spins a web of intrigue so thick its origins become imperceptible, at which point the inherent pleasure came in just watching the star — be it Bogart, Dick Powell or Alan Ladd — wading through smoke-filled clubs and a parade of mysterious characters.

In that respect, no living actor is more equal to the task than Nicholson, who brings charisma and world-weariness to his reprise of Jake Gittes despite carrying a paunch and all the 16 years since "Chinatown."

There's also a stellar cast down to the smallest roles, with Meg Tilly and Madeleine Stowe radiating some of the same shrouded femme fatale qualities found in films like "The Big Sleep," which "The Two Jakes," at its confounding and unfortunately rare best, most closely recalls.

The pic works modestly at least in creating a certain atmosphere, from its post-World War II look and sumptuous costumes to the bluesy, sullen aura surrounding the narrative, augmented by a Nicholson voiceover added long after the film was shot that, albeit heavy-handed, helps a bit in trying to sort

out the story.

Where the film stumbles, however, is in its lack of great moments to spice the long and winding storyline.

Picking up in 1948, 11 years after the events in "Chinatown," Gittes has become a prosperous and respected private investigator, though he still makes his living spying on an unfaithful wife (Tilly) for her suspicious husband, Jake Berman (Harvey Keitel).

Berman seems to be enforcing the oldest law when he murders the man he's caught in bed with his spouse, until it turns out the deceased is his partner, from whom Berman will inherit all profits of their joint real-estate venture.

When the name of Katherine Mulwray turns up on an audiotape of the couple in bed together, it revives Gittes' ghosts of events that occurred in "Chinatown," linking sex, murder and deceit to the role of precious resources — "Chinatown," water; here, oil — in a developing Southern California.

The film then takes on a dual structure, with Gittes in the eye of the hurricane as holder of the incriminating tape while seeking to unravel its connection to Katherine Mulwray, the memorable product of the coupling of father and daughter in Roman Polanski's earlier film.

Those who haven't seen "Chinatown" or don't remember it would probably be hard-pressed to follow "The Two Jakes." Those familiar can initially savor sighting returning characters, from Joe Mantell as Gittes' sidekick to Perry Lopez as hardened police captain Lou Escobar.

While it may be unfair to put "Jakes" alongside its predecessor, film's deficiencies are more striking by comparison. Especially the frequent feeling that the plot isn't going anywhere, that peripheral characters and scenes aren't advancing the action.

A few scenes do carry tremendous power, especially Gittes' confrontation with detective Loach (David Keith) and, from a comic standpoint, his encounter with the murdered man's not-so-grieving widow Lillian (Stowe).

Still, Nicholson the director (working from Robert Towne's script) provides too few moments of that stripe for Nicholson the star, and the finale seems trifling in light of the ordeal that led to it, a perception that starts to build naggingly

about two-thirds of the way into the film.

Of the cast, Tilly, from her downcast eyes to her halting, self-possessed intonation, shines brightest as she has often before, while Richard Farnsworth has a scene-stealing turn as a smooth-talking oilman. There are several notable cameos, including Tom Waits as one of the cops.

Technically, the women's costumes recall the glamour of the '40s. Van Dyke Parks delivers a nicely evocative score, and period songs are put to good use. Vilmos Zsigmond's camera brings the right look to the film, recapturing a long-gone Southern California as vintage cars cruise dirt lanes that lead to open spaces and oil fields.

"The Two Jakes," its few pleasures notwithstanding, might have done well to heed the advice given Gittes at the end of "Chinatown": Leave it alone. — *Bril.*

Act Of Piracy

New York A Blossom Pictures release of a Marton Holdings presentation of a Major Arts production. Executive producers, Edgar Bold, Franklin B. Lieberman. Produced by Igo Kantor, Hal Reed. Directed by John (Bud) Cardos. Screenplay, Reed; camera (color), Vincent G. Cox; editor, Ettie Feldman; music, Morton Stevens; additional orchestrations, Ken Thorne; sound, Philip Key; production design, Peter Williams; art direction, Graeme Orwin; production manager, Debi Nethersole; stunt coordinator, Scott Ateah; associate producer, Robert Lewis. Reviewed on Warner (Lorimar) vidcassette, N.Y., Aug. 2, 1990. MPAA Rating: R. Running time: **101 MIN.**
Ted Andrews . . . . Gary Busey
Sandy Andrews . . . . Belinda Bauer
Jack Wilcox . . . . Ray Sharkey
Laura . . . . Nancy Mulford
Sean . . . . Arnold Vosloo
Dennis . . . . Dennis Casey Park
Herb . . . . Ken Gampu
    Also with: Anthony Fridjhon, Mathew Stewardson, Candice Hillebrand, Nadia Bilchik, Joe Stewardson, Brian O'Shaugnessy, Melody O'Brian, John (Bud) Cardos.

■ Standard action pic teaming Gary Busey and Ray Sharkey had a curious production and release history, and is finally arriving in vidstores via Warner Home Video.

Filmed independently in South Africa and Greece in fall 1987, picture was acquired for homevid by Lorimar and duly inherited by WB when it swallowed Lor. Film was finally released theatrically in March in Miami by N.Y.-based indie Blossom Pictures.

Feature isn't of much interest, as Busey (introed in opening scene riding his motorcycle sans hel-

met!) portrays a guy taking his yacht to Australia to sell it and who's victimized when mercenary Sharkey hijacks the boat.

Story, set in Zimbabwe and Greece, doesn't make much sense and is merely an excuse for exploitation footage. Notable is Sharkey's unmotivated killing of lovely Nancy Mulford: He throws her off a skyscraper balcony for no reason, cueing a vivid stunt. Maybe he just saw Busey's WB hit "Lethal Weapon," aping the opener.

Helmer John (Bud) Cardos, who also filmed "Skeleton Coast" and "Outlaw Of Gor" in southern Africa, emphasizes stuntwork to the detriment of his acting contingent. Belinda Bauer, as Busey's estranged wife, is particularly shrill. Supporting cast includes many South African character actors including Joe Stewardson and Arnold Vosloo. — *Lor.*

Wendy Cracked A Walnut
(AUSTRALIAN)

Sydney A Rosen, Harper, Mortlock Entertainment presentation of a Classic Films P/L production, in association with the Australian Broadcasting Corp. Executive producers, Brian Rosen, Sandra Levy. Produced by John Edwards. Directed by Michael Pattinson. Screenplay, Suzanne Hawley; camera (color), Jeffrey Malouf; editor, Michael Honey; music, Bruce Smeaton; sound, Nick Wood; production design, Leigh Tierney; associate producer, Ray Brown; production manager, Susan Wild; assistant director, Scott Hartford-Davis; casting, Liz Mullinar. Reviewed at Film Australia screening room, Sydney, March 18, 1990. Running time: **87 MIN.**
Wendy . . . . Rosanna Arquette
Ronnie . . . . Bruce Spence
Jake . . . . Hugo Weaving
Deidre . . . . Kerry Walker
Elsie . . . . Doreen Warburton
Cynthia . . . . Desiree Smith
Caroline . . . . Susan Lyons
Mrs. Taggart . . . . Betty Lucas
Sonny Taggart . . . . Dennis Hoey
Mr. Leveredge . . . . Douglas Hedge
Pierre . . . . Barry Jenkins

■ Rosanna Arquette fans will wonder if her trip Down Under was worth the effort if they ever get to see "Wendy Cracked A Walnut," limply executed romantic fantasy/comedy.

Nobody emerges from the pic with much credit, and boxoffice prospects look grim.

It's hard to figure out what audience the film was aimed at, but it's safe to say it will have difficulty attracting paying cinema customers. It may have a life on video, but seems bound to disappoint even there. (In the U.S., Magnum Entertainment will release the pic on video in December under the title "Almost.")

On paper, it might have seemed a good idea to cast Arquette as a Sydney housewife (her Yank accent unexplained) who, stuck with a preoccupied husband and boring job, drifts off into a world of fantasy triggered by her devotion to Mills and Boon tomes. The result, however, is a listless, laughless affair which suffers from dire miscasting and awkward direction.

As Ronnie, Wendy's inept salesman husband, lanky comic actor Bruce Spence is surprisingly unsympathetic. Hugo Weaving, cast as Wendy's idealized dream lover, isn't any better. The talented actor is encouraged to imbue the role of Jake with such sleaziness that it's incomprehensible someone as lively as Wendy would fall for him for a second, even in her dreams.

If good comedy is based on a bedrock of reality, "Wendy" never gets to first base because nothing about the characters or their situation convinces from the outset. Wendy works a computer at a city factory, but despite the couple's two incomes, and lack of children, they live in miserable circumstances in a rundown, noisy apartment. This is obviously meant to accentuate Wendy's plight, but it simply doesn't work.

Equally unconvincing are Ronnie's laborious misadventures in the bush, where car breakdowns, grasping gas station owners and a (well-staged) tempest prevent him from being home in time to celebrate his wedding anniversary. His hare-brained idea to build a diner for Wendy out of a ramshackle edifice located in a swamp is a plot contrivance which should never have got past first draft.

Director Michael Pattinson, whose last film was the suspense thriller "Ground Zero," fumbles badly this time around, and stages his comedy without flair. Wendy's hallucinations are basically rather grim and sad, something the filmmakers seem not to have thought through when prepping this so-called comedy.

Bruce Smeaton's music strives to jolly things along, but there's too much of it, and it succeeds only in deadening the pic with aural overkill. Technically, pic is otherwise acceptable. — Strat.

The American Angels: Baptism Of Blood

New York   A Paramount Pictures presentation of a Sebastian Intl. Pictures production. Produced and written by Ferd Sebastian, Beverly Sebastian, Ben Sebastian. Directed by Ferd & Beverly Sebastian. Camera (color) & editor, Ferd Sebastian; music, George Hovis Hamilton; sound, George Hamilton; production design, Beverly Sebastian; costume design, Cathy Ehlers, production manager, Jim Rossi; casting, Terence Harris. Reviewed on Paramount vidcassette, N.Y., July 24, 1990. MPAA Rating: R. Running time: **99 MIN.**

Lisa Kane . . . . Jan MacKenzie
Dazzling Dave . . . . Tray Loren
Magnificent Mimi . . . . . . Mimi Lesseos
Paml . . . . Trudy Adams
Marita . . . . Patricia Cavoti
Pattie . . . . Sue Sexton
Black Venus . . . . Jean Kirkland
Samson . . . . Jeff Lundy
Announcer . . . . Lee Marshall
Killer Kane . . . . Robert D. Bergen
Malibu . . . . Jayne Hamlin
Big Mama . . . . Lynn Baxton
   Also with: Jan Flame, Amy Barcroft, Debbie Gordon, Nadia Sammons, Michelle Delia, Julia Tavella, Regina Ansley.

■ **Women's wrestling is entertainingly depicted in "The American Angels," a direct-to-video feature release backed by Paramount. Future installments seem likely.**

Filmmakers Beverly and Ferd Sebastian bring back their leading actors Jan MacKenzie and Tray Loren from a previous Paramount release, "Gator Bait II," to mix convincingly with real-life femme wrestlers here.

Emphasis on depicting highly physical training sessions pays off in defusing the disappointing nature of previous wrestling pics where the fakeness of the matches is crystal clear. In fact, lovely redhead MacKenzie looks to be really taking some bumps and bruises as the pro grapplers toss her around like a sack of potatoes.

Conventional storyline has go-go dancer MacKenzie, Trudy Adams (herself a pro familiar from the "Glow" tv series) and Patricia Cavoti trying out to become the newest members of promoter Tray Loren's American Angels wrestling league. The veterans pick on them unmercifully, building to the effective promotion of a grudge match between mean but beautiful champ Mimi Lesseos and Mac-Kenzie.

There's a melodramatic subplot involving a drug dealer who's unwilling to let Adams start a new life, but pic is mostly a fun romp which refreshingly concedes the amount of training and team effort that goes into wrestlers putting on a show (rather than the usual pretense that it's "real").

With Sue Sexton as the gals' trainer, the grueling warmup sessions are impressive. Final match in which MacKenzie trots out her finishing hold "The Snap" (taught to her by her legendary grandpa Killer Kane) is okay with Lesseos not killed as expected but recuperating for a happy ending pointing towards a rematch sequel.

MacKenzie, whose short stature has the other wrestlers making fun of her but whose full figure is well-displayed in shower and sex scenes, continues to impress as an effervescent B-movie starlet.

Lesseos, who wrestles under the moniker Magnificent Mimi, shows nascent acting ability and the other grapplers escape embarrassment. It's not a picture to rank with Robert Aldrich's A-movie version "All The Marbles," but still is an affectionate tribute to a much-maligned area of show business. — Lor.

The Spring

New York   A Quest Entertainment presentation, with Orlando Film Partners II, of a Hugh Parks production. Produced by Parks. Directed by John D. Patterson. Screenplay, Parks; camera (TVC color), Greg Patterson; editor, Mike Palma; music, Don Hughes; sound, Chuck Buchanan; art direction, David Meo; assistant director, Wally Parks; production manager, Michael Rapley; underwater camera, Jordan Klein Jr.; casting, Paul Bengston, David Cohn. Reviewed on Quest Entertainment vidcassette, N.Y., July 19, 1990. No MPAA Rating. Running time: **100 MIN.**

Andy Peterson . . . . Dack Rambo
Dianne Windsor . . . . Shari Shattuck
Matty . . . . Gedde Watanabe
Mark . . . . Steven Keats
Palinya . . . . Virginia Watson

■ **"The Spring" is an oddball romance about Ponce De Leon's fabled fountain of youth. Florida-made feature went direct to video for the voyeur trade.**

Filmmaker Hugh Parks (who produced and scripted) seems obsessed with the old Cecil B. DeMille formula of pulchritude, flashbacks and spirituality. Like his previous film "Before God" (released as "After School"), "Spring" mixes contemporary footage with topless flashbacks of Indian girls at the magical spring when the Spanish explorer arrived 400 years ago.

Main tale deals with museum researcher Dack Rambo and his assistant Gedde Watanabe heading for Florida with evidence as to the whereabouts of the Fountain of Youth. They arrive coincidentally with a cosmetics confab where venal industrialist Steven Keats is out to exploit the find.

Rambo falls in love with blond beauty Shari Shattuck, who turns out to be an 87-year-old woman preserved by the magic waters guarded by an ancient Indian chief (Robert V. Barron). Aided by a voodoo priestess (Virginia Watson), the heroes make it through a phony happy ending.

Main draw here is Shattuck. Tech credits are fine, especially Jordan Klein Jr.'s underwater photography. —Lor.

Taking Care Of Business

San Francisco A Buena Vista Pictures release of a Hollywood Pictures production in association with Silver Screen Partners IV. Executive producer, Paul Mazursky. Produced by Geoffrey Taylor. Directed by Arthur Hiller. Screenplay, Jill Mazursky, Jeffrey Abrams; camera (Technicolor), David M. Walsh; editor, William Reynolds; music, Stewart Copeland; sound (Dolby), Jerry Jost; production design, Jon Hutman; costume design, Marilyn Matthews; set decoration, Donald Krafft, Linda Spheeris; assistant director, Alan B. Curtiss; coproducer, Duncan Henderson; associate producer, Elizabeth Sayre; casting, Lynn Stalmaster. Reviewed at Regency II Theater, San Francisco, Aug. 9, 1990. MPAA rating: R. Running time: **103 MIN.**

Jimmy . . . . James Belushi
Spencer . . . . Charles Grodin
Debbie . . . . Anne DeSalvo
Jewel . . . . Loryn Locklin
Walter . . . . Stephen Elliott
Warden . . . . Hector Elizondo
Elizabeth . . . . Veronica Hamel
Sakamoto . . . . Mako
Diane . . . . Gates McFadden

■ **Charles Grodin and James Belushi come together too late in the plot to prevent a poky start for "Taking Care Of Business," but their mutual chemistry eventually kicks in some jovial jousting; not enough, however, to take care of the outlook for "Business" business.**

Brash Belushi and befuddled Grodin were perfect casting for a yarn about a likable escaped con who assumes the identity of a stuffy, overworked ad agency exec.

Script by Jill Mazursky and Jeffrey Abrams, however, holds no surprises beyond what the pair can pull off on their own with the help of director Arthur Hiller. At the start, Belushi is still in county jail, and there's some fun as he high-fives it with fellow inmates and torments warden Hector Elizondo. Mostly familiar schtick.

Ditto Grodin's intro as he fusses with his workload and neglects wife Victoria Hamel. Though Belushi is set for release in days, he can't wait to see the World Series so he escapes just as Grodin arrives in L.A. to pitch his agency to a Japanese tycoon.

At the airport, Grodin loses his time-planning book — "Business" is one long commercial itself for a particular brand (Filofax, as pic was once titled) — and Belushi finds it. For Grodin, loss of the book and his credit cards is a total loss of his identity, casting him into a series of misadventures.

Setting himself up in a Malibu mansion, Belushi proceeds to live Grodin's life just the opposite of how the businessman would do it,

romancing the boss' daughter (played with sexy feistiness by Loryn Locklin), beating the potential client (Mako) at tennis, criticizing his products and making sexist remarks to fierce, feminist exec (Gates McFadden.)

Meanwhile, Grodin has been mugged, lost his luggage and fallen into the lovestruck clutches of Anne DeSalvo, whose vulnerable, cross-eyed wackiness is one of the best things about the picture. Inevitably, Grodin catches up with Belushi and the farcical convolutions multiply with the arrival of Hamel. As the action picks up, so does the dialog.

Struggling with Hamel to iron out the confusion of who's been bedding whom, Locklin says, "You don't look like the type to be married to a man with a tattoo."

Hiller and cast are hitting their stride here, but too much time has been wasted before, and they have to rush through a lot of potentially hilarious but underdeveloped situations in order to get Belushi back into jail so he can get out legally. Too bad they couldn't have anticipated that from the script before they started shooting. — *Har.*

Air America

Hollywood A Tri-Star (U.S.) and Carolco Intl. (foreign) release of a Mario Kassar, Andrew Vajna/Carolco Pictures presentation of a Daniel Melnick/Indieprod production. Produced by Melnick. Executive producers, Kassar, Vajna. Directed by Roger Spottiswoode. Screenplay, John Eskow, Richard Rush, based on the book by Christopher Robbins; camera (Rank color, Deluxe prints), Roger Deakins; editor, John Bloom, Lois Freeman-Fox; music, Charles Gross; sound (Dolby), Simon Kaye, Tommy Causey (L.A.), John Reitz, David Campbell, Gregg Rudloff; production design, Allan Cameron; art direction, Steve Spence, Tony Reading, Cate Bangs (L.A.); set decoration, Fred Carter, Cricket Rowland (L.A.); costume design, John Mollo; stunt coordinator-3d unit director, Vic Armstrong; special effects supervisor, George Gibbs; assistant director, Albert Shapiro; 2d unit director, Garth Craven; 2d unit camera, Robin Browne; aerial unit director, Marc Wolff; aerial camera, Adam Dale, David Nowell (U.S.); line producer, Michael J. Kagan; coproducers, Allen Shapiro, Eskow; casting, Janet Hirshenson, Jane Jenkins; casting (Thailand), Patsy Pollock, Kate Kagan, Rassami Paoluengthong. Reviewed at UA Coronet, West L.A., Aug. 8, 1990. MPAA Rating: R. Running time: **112 MIN.**

Gene Ryack . . . . Mel Gibson
Billy Covington . . . . . Robert Downey Jr.
Corinne Landreaux . . . . . . Nancy Travis
Maj. Donald Lemond . . . . . . Ken Jenkins
Rob Diehl . . . . . . David Marshall Grant
Sen. Davenport . . . . Lane Smith
Jack Neely . . . . Art La Fleur
Pirelli . . . . Ned Eisenberg
O.V. . . . . Marshall Bell
Saunders . . . . David Bowe
Gen. Lu Soong . . . . Burt Kwouk
Babo . . . . Tim Thomerson

■ **Spectacular action sequences and engaging perfs by Mel Gibson and Robert Downey Jr. should make the dark aspects of "Air America" palatable to a wide audience. The Tri-Star release should carry heavy b.o. cargo.**

Navigating with ease through treacherous thematic terrain, the Carolco big-budgeter is entertaining and provocative.

Though it backs off from exploring some of the deeper causes of the unholy alliance between the U.S. government and Laotian opium growers and traffickers during the "secret" war in that country, "Air America" goes surprisingly far for a mass-market pic in exploring themes generally neglected by all but left-wing journalists and docu filmmakers.

It's probably news to most of the audience even at this late date that the CIA, through its proprietary Air America, was using drug money to finance the war in Southeast Asia and condoning the refining and exportation of heroin both to GIs in that part of the world and to the American public.

Air America became known as "a dope airline," as Christopher Robbins' 1979 source book puts it, and the filmmakers here don't shrink from showing Gibson knowingly flying opium and cynically justifying it as essential to the U.S. war effort. The exploration of such a taboo subject lifts the film above jokey actioner.

Using plot conventions familiar from old Bogart pics and the "Terry And The Pirates" comic strip, scripters John Eskow and Richard Rush develop Gibson as a sardonic, war-weary pro finally lifted out of his moral lethargy for one decent humanitarian gesture, under prodding from earnest younger flyer Downey.

Starting off as a reckless radio station helicopter pilot in a wild stunt sequence on an L.A. freeway in 1969, Downey is recruited by the CIA to perform his hair-raising flying feats for Uncle Sam in Laos, where oxymoronic military intelligence officer David Marshall Grant insists, "We're not actually here."

The Alice-in-Wonderland quality of the Air America operations is depicted with an enjoyable sense of absurdism, though the film never quite takes off into the outer levels of satire it might have achieved had Rush, who developed the project for several years, directed instead of the more literal-minded Roger Spottiswoode.

But with his reported $35 million budget and a vast army of tech assistants to help carry out the stunt flying and crashes on the atmospheric Thailand locations (there's not only an aerial unit but a second unit and a third unit), Spottiswoode does an efficient job in marshaling his forces and walking the thin line required to keep a black comedy from becoming gruesome or flippant.

The film takes a tunnel-vision look at the war in Southeast Asia, seeing the events from the perspective of the jaded pilots and only peripherally suggesting the toll of human suffering inflicted on the populace. While it lacks profundity of a "Dr. Strangelove" or inspired zaniness of "Mash," "Air America" mostly succeeds in its narrower take on the immoral conjunction of war, diplomacy and international corporations.

Ken Jenkins is right on target as the creepy "retired" U.S. major running Air America's operations. He coordinates refining and drug dealing with U.S. puppet Laotian general Burt Kwouk out of an "abandoned" Pepsi-Cola bottling plant on the outskirts of Vientiane. Elements are drawn from reality, if somewhat softened by the filmmakers.

Jenkins not only must fend off Downey's sabotage efforts but also the troublesome inquiries of visiting U.S. senator Lane Smith, whose marvelous recent role as Richard Nixon in "The Final Days" mini-series adds ironic humor to the casting.

The film vacillates between mocking Smith and taking him seriously. Using him as an investigative looking-glass gives Congress far too much credit for caring about what went on with the Laotian drug operation.

The somewhat thinly developed script also falters in not fully exploring the relationship between Gibson and Downey (Gibson seems underused on screen for a star of his magnitude), and in paying scant attention to women's roles. Female lead Nancy Travis is hardly in the film as an unambiguously presented U.S. government do-gooder aiding refugees.

But the filmmakers mine satiric gold in this hitherto neglected ground. An epilog linking the characters to the Iran/contra scandal, Gen. Manuel Noriega and the savings and loan ripoff cleverly reminds the audience of the subject's continuing relevance.

— *Mac.*

My Blue Heaven

Hollywood A Warner Bros. presentation of a Hawn/Sylbert production. Produced by Herbert Ross, Anthea Sylbert. Executive producers, Goldie Hawn, Nora Ephron, Andrew Stone. Directed by Ross. Screenplay, Ephron; camera (Technicolor), John Bailey; editor, Stephen A. Rotter; music, Ira Newborn; sound (Dolby), Al Overton; production designer, Charles Rosen; art direction, Richard Berger; set design, Jim Bayliss, Robert Maddy, Nick Navarro; costume design, Joseph G. Aulisi; choreographer, Lynne Taylor-Corbett; assistant director, Ariel Levy; coproducer, Joseph Carraciolo; casting, Hank McCann. Reviewed at Mann's National Theater, Ł.A., Aug. 17, 1990. MPAA rating: R. Running time: **95 MIN.**
Vinnie . . . . Steve Martin
Barney Coopersmith . . . . . Rick Moranis
Hannah Stubbs . . . . Joan Cusack
Crystal . . . . Melanie Mayron
Shaldeen . . . . Carol Kane
Kirby . . . . Bill Irwin

■ **Steve Martin and Rick Moranis do the mismatched pair o' guys shtick in "My Blue Heaven," a lighthearted fairy tale. Boxoffice prospects look mild, as scripter Nora Ephron's fish-out-of-water premise isn't funny enough to sustain a whole picture.**

Martin plays Vinnie, an incorrigible Italian-American criminal who teaches the white-bread citizens of a suburban town how to loosen up and have fun. Moranis plays Barney Coopersmith, a stiff-necked FBI agent who's assigned to settle mobster Martin into a new life "somewhere in America" as part of a government witness-protection program.

Life in a brand-new subdivision is too placid for Vinnie, who immediately starts getting involved in illegal mischief that brings him into the jurisdiction of the ultra-straight district attorney Hannah Stubbs (Joan Cusack).

It's a mess for Moranis, who has to keep getting Vinnie out of the d.a.'s clutches so that he can testify in a New York mob murder trial.

Moranis hates the frosty, zealous prosecutor, but Martin thinks she's cute and bird-dogs her around town. It's one of the running diversions in a picture in which there isn't enough going on once the setup is established.

Pic takes some satirical potshots at life in the have-a-nice-day suburban bubble, but beyond that it twiddles its thumbs waiting for the mob trial, which comes and goes without incident, except that nerdy law enforcer Coopersmith has a great time in New York, where he learns to dress sharp and

dance the merengue under Vinnie's tutelage.

Plot turns this way and that, finally pairing Moranis and Cusack in a not-too-credible romance.

Bouyant, talkative Vinnie's a charmer, but the way Moranis goes soft for him is hard to swallow, no matter how boring the bureau man's life is.

Martin's characterization of Vinnie as exuberant and dapper but a little dumb will be the film's drawing card, as there are quite a few laughs in watching straight-arrows like Stubbs, when she's still unwise to this totally screwy character, attempt to take him at face value.

His slightly off-speed delivery sounds like it was spawned from his old "wild and crazy guy" tv character.

Cusack ("Working Girl") comes on strong in the comic and romantic modes when she's playing across from Martin, but her role deteriorates in the weak pairing with Moranis.

There's a nice use of title cards for a tongue-in-cheek storybook feel between sequences, and director Herb Ross keeps things bouncing along enjoyably for at least as long as it takes to figure out the story isn't going anywhere. Pic's ending is way too big, but then, what's a Ross film anymore without an overwrought ending?

Tech credits are fine, and Ira Newborn's bouyant and appealing score makes a considerable contribution to maintaining the idea that a lot of fun is being had here.

— *Daws.*

Darkman

Hollywood A Universal Pictures release of a Darkman production. Produced by Robert Tapert. Directed by Sam Raimi. Screenplay, Chuck Pfarrer, Raimi, Ivan Raimi, Daniel Goldline, Joshua Goldin, based on a story by Sam Raimi; camera (Deluxe color), Bill Pope; supervising editors, Bud Smith, Scott Smith; editor, David Stiven; music, Danny Elfman; sound (Dolby), Don Summer; production design, Randy Ser; art direction, Phil Dagort; set design, George Suhayda, Ginni Barr; costume design, Grania Preston; makeup effects, Tony Gardner, Larry Hamlin; optical effects, VCE/Peter Kuran; special visual effects, Introvision Systems Intl.; visual effects miniature sequences, 4-Ward Prods.; stunt coordinator, Chris Doyle; 2d unit camera, Peter Deming; aerial camera, the Flying Camera Co., Frank Holgate; assistant director, Scott Javine; line producer, Daryl Kass. Reviewed at Directors Guild of America Theater, L.A., Aug. 17, 1990. MPAA Rating: R. Running time: **95 MIN.**
Peyton Westlake/
Darkman . . . . Liam Neeson
Julie Hastings . . . . . Frances McDormand
Louis Strack Jr. . . . . Colin Friels
Robert G. Durant . . . . Larry Drake
Yakitito . . . . Nelson Mashita
Eddie Black . . . . Jesse Lawrence Ferguson
Rudy Guzman . . . . . . Rafael H. Robledo
Skip . . . . Danny Hicks
Rick . . . . Theodore Raimi
Smiley . . . . Dan Bell
Pauly . . . . Nicholas Worth
Final shemp . . . . Bruce Campbell
Doctor . . . . Jenny Agutter

■ **Despite occasional silliness, Sam Raimi's "Darkman" has more wit, pathos and visual flamboyance than is usual in contemporary shockers. This imaginative piece of Grand Guignol could be a b.o. sleeper, particularly with teens.**

Universal, studio that first brought the Phantom of the Opera to the screen, returns to its hallowed horror-film traditions with this tale of a hideously disfigured scientist (Liam Neeson) seeking revenge on L.A. mobsters.

Raimi's gripping story (unevenly scripted by the director and others) more closely echoes the 1941 Peter Lorre chiller "The Face Behind The Mask" in its nightmarish tale of a man whose burned face makes him a social pariah and brutal criminal. The idea resonates with primal terror.

Providing more entertainment on its limited budget than some of the bigger-buck entries in the summer marketplace, "Darkman" moves quickly from one outrageous scene to another. Tongue-in-cheek pic creates a title character with the kind of emotional complexity that used to drive horror films before special effects took over.

Neeson, working on a holographic technique to synthetically re-create damaged skin and body parts, is the innocent victim of sadistic thug Larry Drake, who likes to snip people's fingers off with his cigar cutter. He orders his minions to dip Neeson's head into an acid vat before blowing up his lab.

Drake's expertly vicious and campy villain is a striking about-face from his mentally retarded Benny in tv's "L.A. Law." He's after an incriminating document left in Neeson's lab by the scientist's lawyer/g.f., Frances McDormand, who has caught a client, real estate developer Colin Friels, in corrupt practices.

Rather incredibly, she begins dating the oily Friels after the acid attack, thinking Neeson is dead and unaware Friels was behind it.

"Darkman" falters in not sufficiently delving into Neeson's ambivalent feelings toward his shallow and disloyal object of affection, who at first recoils from his true appearance, forcing him to fabricate a lifelike face mask in order to resume their courtship.

Each mask lasts only for 100 minutes before turning into glop, so he has to keep slipping away from her for what he calls "therapy" sessions, and she doesn't catch on until the story is almost over.

The strange romance lacks the poetic quality it might have attained (as in Georges Franju's "Eyes Without A Face"). While Neeson's final judgment on McDormand is satisfying, it doesn't pack the emotional punch it should have had. The most intriguing and original parts of "Darkman" are the title character's revenge forays against the gangsters, in which he wears a succession of masks that counterfeit their faces.

In one bravura sequence, Neeson masquerades as Drake, confronting the bewildered hood in a Chinatown chase and shootout. In other scenes, it's tantalizingly unclear just who's playing whom.

There's welcome wit and intelligence in the character's revenge, a sophisticated manipulation of his victim's psychological quirks, that helps draw the viewer into Neeson's p.o.v. even as his trail of violence gets increasingly revolting and desperate.

Neeson's sympathetic performance never lets the film become entirely facetious, despite its over-the-top quality, sometimes laughable dialog and occasionally ludicrous directorial concepts, such as staging Neeson's climactic confrontation with Friels on the exposed girders high atop his "City Of The Future" construction site.

Director Raimi, lenser Bill Pope and production designer Randy Ser conjure up a flamboyantly expressionistic world out of downtown L.A.'s bizarre architectural mix of gleaming skyscrapers and decaying warehouses. Viewer also is periodically plunged into Neeson's twisted mind and body with an effective array of weird visual effects.

After some ragged editing in the plotty early sections of the film, the rhythm becomes suitably frenzied and dreamlike in its visual and emotional pirouettes. Danny

Elfman's score provides a suitable sense of melodrama and dread, but far too much of it is blaring wall-to-wall music, aping his recent and familiar scores for "Batman" and "Dick Tracy." — *Mac.*

Cold Dog Soup
(AUSTRALIAN)

Syndey A Hoyts (Australia) release of a Handmade Films, Aspen Film Society production. Executive producers, George Harrison, Denis O'Brien. Produced by Richard E. Abramson, William E. McEuen, Thomas Pope. Directed by Alex Metter. Screenplay, Pope, from a novel by Stephen Dobyns; camera (Technicolor), Frederick Elmes; editor, Kaja Fehr; music, Michael Kamen; sound, Robert Anderson Jr.; production design-associate producer, David L. Snyder; production manager, Claude Binyon Jr.; assistant director, Josh McLaglen; casting, Marcia Shulman. Reviewed at Mosman screening room, Sydney, Aug. 2, 1990. Running time: **89 MIN.**

Jack Cloud	Randy Quaid
Michael Latchmer	Frank Whaley
Sarah Hughes	Christine Harnos
Mrs. Hughes	Sheree North
Mme. Chang	Nancy Kwan
JoJo	Seymour Cassel
Marty	Pierre Epstein
Benny	Brent Hinkley
Gang leader	Michael De Lorenzo
The Boker	Nick Latour

■ **For about half its length, "Cold Dog Soup" shapes up as an enjoyably weird variation on "After Hours," but inspiration flags in the second half, making pic a dubious commercial proposition.**

As in "After Hours," "Cold Dog Soup" has a naive but lustful innocent who finds himself involved with strange characters in unpleasant situations.

Here, Michael Latchmer (Frank Whaley) dreams of an intimate liaison with seductive Sarah Hughes (Christine Harnos). It soon becomes obvious that he's not going to make it, however. The couple meet at a sports club, with the lovely Sarah explaining she has only one hand because an office copier fell in love with her and "sucked her in." The hand was never found, and she wears a glove constantly.

She invites the infatuated Michael home for dinner with her mother (Sheree North). Dinner is delayed when Jasper, the Hughes' dog, which has shown an alarming interest in Michael's private parts, suddenly expires after drinking the guest's cocktail. Though he reluctantly agrees to perform the kiss of life on the hound, it's of no use.

Michael is dispatched to bury Jasper, with the promise of sexual favors ("the pressure cooker is ready") on his return. That's when he meets eccentric cab driver Jack Cloud (Randy Quaid in an ebullient turn), who insists the dead dog could be sold and drags the reluctant Michael all over New York in the vain hope of finding a buyer.

Eventually Sarah joins the pair in their increasingly bizarre adventures, including a visit to the h.q. of gangsters, a Chinese restaurant, a hot dog joint, a voodoo club and a back alley controlled by a gang of bikers.

Director Alex Metter isn't able to prevent interest flagging as the long night wears on, and it quickly becomes clear Michael won't wind up in the sack with Sarah, and he'll have little luck disposing of his "doggie bag." Consequently the enjoyable and offbeat early scenes give way to tedium. Only Quaid's energetic performance keeps the viewer intrigued.

Technically "Cold Dog Soup" is fine, but the picture (dated 1989) will have difficulty finding a significant audience. Theatrically, the late night/cult route is the best way to go. It could have a long life on video once word gets around as to the pic's bizarre nature. It opens for a limited run in a Sydney arthouse Sept. 1. — *Strat.*

Blood Salvage

Chicago A Paragon Arts Intl. release of a Ken C. Sanders production in association with High Five Prods. Executive producers, Ken Sanders, Evander Holyfield. Produced by Martin J. Fischer, Sanders. Directed by Tucker Johnston. Screenplay, Johnston, Sanders; camera (color), Michael Karp; editor, Jacquie Freeman Ross; music, Tim Temple; sound (Ultra Stereo), Alan Selk; production design, Robert Sissman; art director, Sissman; special makeup effects, Bill Johnson; costume design, D. Jean Hester; assistant director, Don Simmons; Dan Coffie; associate producer, Brett Wolcott; production manager, Wolcott; casting, Annette Stilwell & Associates, Amanda Karr (Los Angeles). Reviewed on Magnum Entertainment vidcassette, Chicago, Aug. 16, 1990. MPAA Rating: R. Running time: **98 MIN.**

Jake Pruitt	Danny Nelson
April Evans	Lori Birdsong
Clifford Evans	John Saxon
Mr. Stone	Ray Walston
Hiram Pruitt	Christian Hesler
Roy Pruitt	Ralph Pruitt Vaughn
Pat Evans	Laura Whyte
Bobby Evans	Andy Greenway
Boxer	Evander Holyfield

■ **Gorehounds who like a little levity with their splatter will**

appreciate the humorous approach in "Blood Salvage," another down-home tale about a band of backwoods psychos preying on stray city slickers.

Film rates a respectable position in its subgenre: It's not "The Texas Chainsaw Massacre," but it's not "Barn Of The Naked Dead" either.

Setting for the mayhem in this entry is a chop shop (in more than one sense of the word) run by good-old-boy Jake Pruitt and his two sons. Jake and his boys run tourists off the road and steal their parts — both automotive and anatomical — for resale.

Jake is not only a master mechanic and a religious nut, but a medical genius as well. Using only a few second-hand textbooks and some pumps and tubes that happen to be lying around in the yard, he keeps his moaning victims alive long enough to sell their vitals, piece by piece, to a traveling organ broker (Ray Walston).

Trouble starts when Jake develops a crush on a wheelchair-bound teen competing in a nearby beauty contest.

Determined to cure the girl and marry her, Jake arranges for her family's RV to crash down the road from his garage. Mom, Dad and baby brother quickly wind up in the spare parts department, but little April is not so easy to handle.

The decision to up the emotional ante in this film by placing the standard-issue, endangered bimbette in a wheelchair is a risky one, resulting in several queasy scenes, particularly when the paraplegic girl comes close to being sexually molested twice.

However, it does provide "Blood Salvage" with an unusual touch of irony. Jake destroys April's family, but he also heals her injury. Also, her physical handicap is offset by her intelligence and craftiness. When the rest of her family goes wandering around the grounds in case there are any wackos around that might like to attack them, April locks herself in the RV with a shotgun.

Even more unusual for a film of this type, the girl is not depicted as a helpless potential victim. In fact, she has a genuine mean streak, refreshingly portrayed by newcomer Lori Birdsong.

Danny Nelson, best known in the Atlanta area as a tv pitchman for Cates Pickles, is more than adequate as Jake, clearly enjoying the chance to spout Old Testament-style phraseology while poking his patients with a power drill. Christian Hesler provides the most effective comic moments as his son Hiram, a whining, bile-filled, redneck par excellence.

John Saxon as April's dad has little to do beyond peering over reading glasses and becoming an unwilling liver donor. Also, heavyweight boxer Evander Holyfield, who served as co-executive producer, has a cameo. Tech credits are fine, and first-time director Tucker Johnston keeps things rolling along admirably toward a semi-exciting climax. — *Brin*.

Gentile Alouette (CHILEAN-FRENCH)

New York A Three Oceans production. Written, produced and directed by Sergio Castilla. Camera (color), Patricio Castilla; editor, Christine Pansu; music, Gustav Mahler; sound, Serge Deraison, Dennis Tribalat. Reviewed at the Public Theater, N.Y., July 20, 1990. (In Festival Latino, N.Y.). Running time: **105 MIN.**
Colonel . . . . Hector Alterio
Angela Duverger . . . . . Geraldine Chaplin
Ortiz . . . . John Leguizamo
Inspector Durel . . . . Alain Ollivier
Sounkalou . . . . Mamdou Traore

■ **A broad farce that simultaneously wants to be a suspense film and a serious look at insanity, this 1985 Chilean-French coproduction (in French, Spanish and English) fails on all counts.**

Its title taken from the familiar children's song, "Gentile Alouette" is notable primarily for its pretty Paris locations and the presence of Geraldine Chaplin, who strives in vain to lend credibility to an outlandish plot.

The bizarre story concerns a colonel (Hector Alterio) who runs the secret police force for an unnamed Latin American country in Paris. He is obsessed by a former love, the actress Angela Duverger (Chaplin), and becomes convinced that she is plotting against his government.

She is actually in Paris simply to shoot a film (an excuse for a scene at Versailles) and work on a script. But the colonel sends his assistant, Ortiz (John Leguizamo), to spy on her and eventually to try to kill her by pushing her in front of a subway train.

What could have been a fairly entertaining thriller degenerates into a humorless comedy when Leguizamo hams it up as the dim underling. He dresses up as a geisha girl to spy on Chaplin and later puts fish fins up his nose to create a mock moustache.

Unfortunately, his mugging is not funny, but merely irritating. There are equally few laughs when the colonel kicks his servant in the groin for failing to kill Chaplin, and when he smears mashed potatoes on his face.

Even Chaplin is obliged to act foolish at times. In a scene that demonstrates the film's baffling logic, she dances the Charleston on a table in order to get a photograph of her assailant.

At one point her boyfriend, a film producer, says to her, "If you didn't waste your time on bad scripts you'd be a great actress." The same goes for Chaplin, who has been touching in "Cria" and amusing in "Nashville." In this idiotic caper she is truly wasting her time, as is Alterio, an Argentine actor best known for "The Official Story."

If the movie fails as a thriller/comedy, it falls just as flat as a portrait of a madman. When Chaplin tries to persuade Leguizamo that the colonel is actually just an actor gone mad, her captor replies, "Everybody's sick, but we must go on."

The movie becomes distinctly unfunny when she is tied to a bed and raped by the colonel. As if to justify the abrupt change of tone, somber Mahler music takes over the soundtrack. (At least it's an improvement on the insipid pop version of "Gentile Alouette," which is played a few times).

In the film's sour conclusion, the colonel goes on a delirious shooting spree. The audience is meant to sympathize with him, as though he were merely a victim of his own delusions. But it is far too late to take "Gentile Alouette" seriously.

After being subjected to inane slapstick and various far-fetched plot twists, viewers may choose to focus on the Parisian scenery rather than the buffoons in the foreground. — *Stev*.

The Exorcist III

San Francisco A 20th Century Fox release of a Morgan Creek production. Produced by Carter DeHaven. Executive producers, James G. Robinson, Joe Roth. Written and directed by William Peter Blatty, based on his novel, "Legion." Camera (Deluxe color), Gerry Fisher; editor, Todd Ramsay, Peter Lee-Thompson; music, Barry Devorzon; sound (Dolby), Richard Van Dyke; production design, Leslie Dilley; art direction, Robert Goldstein, Henry Shaffer; costume design, Dana Lyman; assistant director, Richard Abramitis; special effects coordinator, Bill Purcell; stunt coordinator-2d unit director, Paul Baxley. Reviewed at the Alexandria Theater, San Francisco, Aug. 17, 1990. MPAA rating: R. Running time: **110 MIN.**
Kinderman . . . . George C. Scott
Father Dyer . . . . Ed Flanders
Gemini Killer . . . . Brad Dourif
Patient X . . . . Jason Miller
Father Morning . . . . . . Nicol Williamson
Dr. Temple . . . . Scott Wilson
Nurse Allerton . . . . Nancy Fish
Stedman . . . . George DiCenzo
Nurse X . . . . Viveca Lindfors

■ **Since "The Exorcist" was one of the most frightening films ever and "Exorcist II" one of the goofiest, chances favored "The Exorcist III" to fall somewhere in between, though not nearly far enough up the scale to rival the original. So Fox can brag that it doesn't have the worst "Exorcist" ever done, but that's not much of a marketing hook.**

As directed by William Friedkin from William Peter Blatty's riveting bestseller, the initial "Exorcist" was a rare combination of intelligence, compelling characters and (for its time) astonishing effects.

Ironically, "III" might have slipped by years ago as a reasonably harmless first sequel since Blatty (who contributed nothing to "II") at least shares his own sensibilities for the material, though Blatty as director can't match Friedkin, even with the advantage of more modern technical effects.

The Devil and the Church have clashed in too many other pics since with increasingly ingenious ways to burst bodies, leaving Blatty with all mood and no meat.

Much too often, he lingers under flickering lights in dark corridors where nothing happens. At least twice after a big buildup, a character is startled by something harmless. When that proves to be more frightening than anything else that happens to that character, the picture is in trouble.

It's been 15 years since Father Karras battled the Devil for the little girl and ended up dead at the bottom of the stairway. Now his old policeman friend (George C. Scott) is confronted with a series of sacrilegious murders bearing the trademarks of a killer executed about the same time the priest died.

This is puzzling, indeed, and Scott is grandly awful as he goes about lifting sheets off mutilated bodies and cursing God for such a world, especially when one of the new victims is another friend and priest (Ed Flanders).

At the peak of his ranting and screaming, it's a wonder nobody calls in an exorcist for the actor.

Anyway, there's a guy in chains over at the nuthouse who sometimes appears to Scott as Karras (Jason Miller) and sometimes as the executed killer (Brad Dourif), and it's all very confusing.

It would be downright incomprehensible, in fact, if Dourif didn't do such a dandy job in explaining things in a couple of long, madman monologs.

Though Scott can bellow back at the demons, he's not much of a match. The actual exorcist of this chapter is Nicol Williamson in a minor part, which says a lot about the film's dramatic structure.

Eventually, as expected, good will triumph over evil. Unfortunately, good will not triumph over director Blatty and the unleashed furies of George C. Scott. — *Har*.

MEN AT WORK

HOLLYWOOD A Triumph Releasing Corp. release of an Epic Prods. presentation of an Epic/Elwes/Euphoria production. Produced by Cassian Elwes. Executive producers, Irwin Yablans, Moshe Diamant. Written and directed by Emilio Estevez. Co-producer, Barbara Stordahl. Camera (Deluxe color), Tim Suhrstedt; editor, Craig Bassett; music, Stewart Copeland; sound (Ultra-Stereo), Craig S. Clark; production design, Dins Danielsen; art direction, Patty Klawonn; set decoration, Kathy Curtis Cahill; costume design, Keith Lewis; assistant directors, Mark A. Radcliffe, George Parra, Geoff Hansen; associate producer, Frances Fleming; casting, Marci Liroff. Reviewed at the GCC Beverly Connection Theaters, Aug. 24, 1990. MPAA Rating: PG-13. Running time: **99 MIN.**

Carl Taylor	Charlie Sheen
James St. James	Emilio Estevez
Susan Wilkins	Leslie Hope
Louis Fedders	Keith David
Pizza man	Dean Cameron
Maxwell Potterdam 3d	John Getz
Biff	Hawk Wolinski
Mario	John Lavachielli

Emilio Estevez and Charlie Sheen appropriately spend a lot of time scrounging around in garbage in this inane comedy. The real-life brothers appear to be having fun together, but audiences won't. Emilio & Charlie's idiotic adventure seems a longshot to haul away more than minimal boxoffice and homevideo.

Actually, the none-too-bright pair are reminiscent of Orion's Bill & Ted, finishing each other's sentences and clowning their way through dire situations. It's just that Estevez' dreadful garbagemen-in-danger script makes any decent screwball farce smell like a rose.

Estevez directed the disappointing 1986 drama "Wisdom," and he fares little better with comedy. The film teems with cartoonish characters, and its few laughs come from recurring gags that rely on excrement and Sheen's perplexed double takes.

Sheen and Estevez play garbagemen who discover the body of a political candidate stashed in a can on their route. It seems the candidate (Darrell Larson) was involved in a toxic-waste dumping scheme and sought to cross the honcho behind it (John Getz), the personification of corporate callousness.

For a while it seems the main gag will be what to do with the body. Since no one will go to the police, the pair plots with their new supervisor Louis (Keith David), a wigged-out veteran eager to throttle just about anybody.

But strategy is abandoned for chases with the goofy mobsters and a battle royale that seems designed to amuse only the World Wrestling Federation audience.

None of the characters makes much sense, especially Leslie Hope as the deceased politico's campaign manager. She romps with Sheen on the beach about 15 minutes after meeting him.

The film also introduces a number of minor plot points that aren't raised again or resolved. Will these guys ever junk their garbage jobs and open that surf shop? Who knows, though it's doubtful many will hang around long enough to find out.

Sheen exhibits the best flair for comedy with his arched-eyebrow stupidity, while Estevez simply extends his impish punk persona from the "Young Guns" pics. Getz, normally a fine actor, has little to do but sputter the limp dialog.

Estevez seems to toy with delivering an environmental message but mercifully stops short. Tech credits are generally poor, although the reliable Stewart Copeland turns in a bouncy, fun-loving score that captures what "Men At Work" no doubt aspired to deliver. — *Bril.*

DEN HEMLIGA VÄNNEN
(THE SECRET FRIEND)
(SWEDISH)

STOCKHOLM A Sonet Film release of a Paris Förlag production. Written, produced and directed by Marie-Louise Ekman. Camera (Eastmancolor), Tomas Boman; editor, uncredited; music, Benny Andersson; sound, Per Boström, Richard Loman; production design, Peder Freiij; costume design, Marie Olsson, Birgitta Johansson, Lotta Lindahl-Danfors. Reviewed at Sonet Film screening room, Bromma, Stockholm, Aug. 16, 1990. Running time: **90 MIN.**

Bertil	Ernst-Hugo Järegard
His wife	Margaretha Krook
Jerkerz	Gösta Ekman
Albert Hansson	Carl Billquist

"The Secret Friend," by multimedia artist Marie-Louise Ekman, formerly working under the surname of de Geer Bergenstrahle, is an absurdist romp through equal parts of Strindbergian marital hell and Beckett-inspired high-level clowning behind masks of outright tragedy.

Thanks to the local popularity of its quartet of superior actors, "The Secret Friend" has done better at Swedish theaters than similar experimental fare usually could expect. Offshore opportunities are not unlikely, although specialized situations would be required. The film has crazy wit as well as tragic wisdom.

During one long evening at a luxurious Stockholm apartment building, the marriage of a middle-aged couple is seen entering its final stage of damnation as the wife ties up her patiently consenting husband after making him drink medicine that contains poison. She tells him that she is leaving him to look for pleasure elsewhere.

As soon as the wife leaves, the husband, who only pretended to drink the medicine, has a friend come in to commiserate with him. The friend is an innocent type who goes along when the husband encourages him to put on the wife's underwear and to play her part in an improvised retelling of the low points of their marriage.

As director and co-actor of this "play," the husband must teach his friend to play a woman, so he changes into drag himself. The wife returns with her pickup, a clinical psychiatrist who soon is persuaded to change into female flimsies, too. The wife again slams the door disgustedly behind her.

The three men now act out, physically and verbally, what they consider the agonies of women's demands on men and vice-versa. They look ridiculous, of course, but what they do and say appear brutally sad and true.

There is no superficial intellectual banter in Ekman's film. Everything is from the gut, but she keeps it under her stern artistic control. Although gross clowning meets sliding-down-the-roof suspense here, "The Secret Friend" is mostly a straight stage play that has been made to move in cinematic rhythms.

All four actors put in performances that are joyous to watch. Margaretha Krook is both hilarious and gross as the wife, but her inner pain is apparent even as she roughs up everything and everybody around her. Ernst-Hugo Järegard as her husband is a self-pitying blubberer with a core of iron-willed egotism to survive on. Gösta Ekman plays the friend with angelic but sly patience and a mien that is only superficially innocent. Carl Billquist as the doctor is a marvel of academic wisdom mired in human ignorance.

The secret friend of the film's title is never seen or mentioned. Most likely, he is a kind of special Godot that all married people are waiting for to get them out of their earthly mess. Since the quartet's wild romping is, at the end, replaced by a muted conversational duet, Ekman seems, after all, to believe in the possibility of a happy ending. — *Kell.*

NEW YORK FEST
MILLER'S CROSSING

HOLLYWOOD A Twentieth Century Fox release of a Circle Films presentation of a Jim Pedas/Ben Barenhotz/Bill Durkin production. Produced by Ethan Coen. Executive producer, Ben Barenhotz. Co-producer, Mark Silverman. Directed by Joel Coen. Screenplay, Joel Coen and Ethan Coen; camera (Duart color), Barry Sonnenfeld; editor, Michael Miller; music, Carter Burwell; sound, Allan Byer; production design, Dennis Gassner; art direction, Leslie McDonald; set design, Kathleen McKernin; set decoration, Nancy Haigh; costume design, Richard Hornung; assistant director, Gary Marcus; casting, Donna Isaacson, John Lyons. Reviewed at Twentieth Century Fox screening room, Los Angeles, Aug. 15, 1990. MPAA Rating R. Running time: **114 MIN.**

Tom	Gabriel Byrne
Leo	Albert Finney
Verna	Marcia Gay Harden
Johnny Caspar	Jon Polito
Bernie Bernbaum	John Turturro
The Dane	J.E. Freeman

It'll be "Miller's Crossing," not "Dick Tracy," that's remembered as the standout 1930s gangster film of the year. For substance — the missing ingredient in so many of the year's flashy filmic exercises — is here in spades, along with the twisted, brilliantly controlled style on which filmmakers Joel and Ethan Coen made a name.

Classic-quality outing surely will put Fox square at the boxoffice if the studio's marketers can mount a campaign as good as this film.

Formal constraints of a richly composed genre piece are apparent in "Miller's Crossing," but bumping around beneath them are the same wild-at-heart impulses that made the Coens' Texas film noir thriller "Blood Simple" so nervily compelling. Result: One never knows what's going to pop.

Story unspools in an unnamed Eastern city where dim but ambitious Italian gangster Johnny Caspar (Jon Polito) has a problem named Bernie Bernbaum (John Turturro). Seems Bernie is angling in on his angle so he can't fix a fight anymore without somebody riding his hip for a chunk of the profit.

"If you can't trust a fix what can you trust?" complains Caspar.

He wants approval from the city's Irish political boss, Leo (Albert Finney), to rub out the cause of his complaint, but Leo's not giving in. He's fallen in love with Bernie's sister, Verna (Marcia Gay Harden), who wants Bernie protected.

Leo's cool, brainy aide-de-camp Tom (Gabriel Byrne) sees that Leo is making a big mistake, and it's up to Tom to save him as his empire begins to crumble.

The complication is that Tom also is in love with Verna, though he's loath to admit it, making it tough for him to get a clear fix even on his own motives.

The pic is about character, friendship and ethics in the grayest of contexts — Caspar as much as says so in the marvelously twisted opening scene. But it's mainly about heart. According to Verna, Leo has one but Tom doesn't. Irony is that Tom's heart is bigger than anyone's, and that, along with gambling, is both his downfall and his redemption.

Rarely does a screen hero of Tom's gritty dimensions come along, and Irishman Byrne ("Julia And Julia," "A Soldier's Tale"), who's destined to earn widespread recognition with this performance, brings him gracefully and profoundly to life.

Like Verna, he's a tough loner who trusts nobody and nothing, least of all sentiment. Everything he does, he does for Leo — not that anyone would know it. Like Verna says, he always takes the long way around.

Tom figures Verna's taking Leo for a ride, and he despises her but he still can't stay away from her. As portrayed by screen newcomer Harden, Verna has the verve and flintiness of a glory-days Bette Davis or Barbara Stanwyck.

Tom and Verna have some great scenes together. "Intimidating helpless women is part of my job," he tells her after hunting her down in a women's room. "Then why don't you find one and intimidate her," she snaps.

Also outstanding is Finney as the big-hearted political fixer who usually has the mayor and the police chief seated happily across his desk. He's as cool in a spray of bullets as he is vulnerable in affairs of the heart.

But it's not as if the urge to create full-fleshed characters has taken the fun out of the Coens' game. There's still Polito as the apoplectic Caspar, twisting the tough ethical questions around his thick tongue and thick brain, and the hysterically rude portrayals of his wife and kid.

There's still his human watchdog, The Dane (as in Great Dane, it seems), played by J.E. Freeman, plus a gallery of leeringly satirical fringe characters.

Not at all least, there's Turturro as the weasly Bernie, marvelously despicable with his wheezing laugh and fidgety shrug ("Someone gives me an angle, I play it. Does that mean I should die?").

Animating these characters is a script chock-full of lovingly resurrected period dialog, phrases like "What's the rumpus?" and lines like "We're a coupla heels, Tom, you 'n' me."

Graphic violence and vivid spectacle abound here, but in this case, as in few other recent pics, they add up to something.

The Coens have brought along a number of their "Blood Simple" and "Raising Arizona" mates, including Carter Burwell, whose subtle, lilting Irish score offers a wry contrast to the action.

Cinematographer Barry Sonnenfeld, who went wild in "Raising Arizona," bows artfully to convention in this dark-hued, richly composed film, though at least once he jerks his leash.

Buffs will note cameos by director Sam Raimi, with whom the Coens collaborated on his "Evil Dead," and Frances McDormand, who made her indelible debut in "Blood Simple."

Pic's rather bland title refers to a lonely spot in the woods where a certain corpse is destined to fall. The thickly twisted script — likely to be deemed one of the best blueprints of the year — was written by the Coen brothers. — *Daws.*

LISTEN UP
(DOCU)

NEW YORK Warner Bros. release of a Courtney Sale Ross production. Produced by Ross. Directed by Ellen Weissbrod. Camera (Foto-Kem, Duart, Image Transform-for video transfer color; Technicolor prints), Stephen Kazmierski; editor, Milton Moses Ginsberg, Pierre Kahn, Andrew Morreale, Laure Sullivan, Paul Zehrer; music, Quincy Jones; music supervisor, Arthur Baker; sound (Dolby), Petur Hliddal, others; additional camera, Craig Spirko, Weissbrod, others; line producer-production manager, Melissa Powell. Reviewed at WB screening room, N.Y., Aug. 21, 1990. (In Edinburgh, Toronto, New York film festivals.) MPAA Rating: PG-13. Running time: 114 MIN.

With: Quincy Jones, Clarence Avant, George Benson, Richard Brooks, Tevin Campbell, Ray Charles, Miles Davis, El DeBarge, Kool Moe Dee, Sheila E., Billy Eckstine, Ahmet Ertegun, Ella Fitzgerald, Flavor Flav, Siedah Garrett, Dizzy Gillespie, Irvin Green, Alex Haley, Lionel Hampton, Herbie Hancock, Ice-T, James Ingram, Jesse Jackson, Lucy Jackson Rembert, Lloyd Jones, Jolie Jones, Big Daddy Kane, Michel Legrand, Morris Levy, Harry Lokofsky, Sidney Lumet, Bobby McFerrin, Benny Medina, Melle Mel, Chan Parker, Greg Philingaines, Ian Prince, Frank Sinatra, Steven Spielberg, Barbra Streisand, Al B. Sure!, Clark Terry, Bobby Tucker, Sarah Vaughan, Oprah Winfrey and voice of Michael Jackson.

Warner Bros. continues its recent preeminence among the majors in the music documentary field with "Listen Up" (subtitled "The Lives Of Quincy Jones"), an informative and invigorating portrait of an unusual American success story.

Pic is going the film fest route before opening domestically in the fall. Like "Imagine" and "Straight No Chaser," its primary audience will be found in ancillary markets.

Filmmakers Courtney Sale Ross and Ellen Weissbrod adapt a kaleidoscopic editing approach that is disconcerting at first but (aided by the exciting underscore) eventually makes sense. It dovetails with their subject and prime interviewee Jones' statement late in the film that a biographical question raises a host of associations, "like 17 tributaries of a river."

Basic facts about Jones' singular life are imparted: his traumatic childhood; the big break of joining Lionel Hampton's touring big band while still a teen; his being hired at Mercury Records and producing his first pop hits for Lesley Gore there. He arranged music for Count Basie and Frank Sinatra; scored over 30 motion pictures; co-produced Michael Jackson's breakthrough albums, including "Thriller"; and supervised such ambitious projects as "We Are The World."

Through dozens of interviews and archive footage, a complex individual emerges. As is common with portrait films, there's little critical material, but Jones' flaw of being a workaholic is illuminated by perceptive comments from his daughter, Jolie. His three marriages, last to actress Peggy Lipton, ended in divorce. And his nearly nonstop career fixation was sidelined only momentarily by an aneurysm.

Celebrity interviewees ranging from Steven Spielberg and Frank Sinatra to rappers like Ice-T and Big Daddy Kane offer convincing testimony to Jones' creative contributions and ability to inspire performers. Putting his career in context are nononsense comments from Miles Davis and Dizzy Gillespie, as well as mentors Lionel Hampton and Billy Eckstine, whose collective oral history complements that of WB's "Straight No Chaser" docu on Thelonious Monk.

Though many subjects, particularly Ella Fitzgerald, are reticent, film accurately zeroes in on the racism that confronts black artists in America. Most telling are anecdotes by Gillespie, Jones himself and Kane that counterpoint the traditional horror stories of decades past with very recent discriminatory incidents.

On a lighter note, the filmmakers' frenetic cutting technique cutely matches and contrasts comments on Jones' trumpet playing ability from folks like Eckstine and Davis.

His contributions to film are attested to by interviews with Oprah Winfrey (hired by Jones for "The Color Purple"), as well as Sidney Lumet and Richard Brooks, who cite the fresh approach of Jones' scores for their films, such as "The Pawnbroker" and "In Cold Blood" (demonstrated by filmclips and sound excerpts). Musical high points of the film include performances by greats like Fitzgerald, the late Sarah Vaughan and youngsters Sideah Garrett and Tevin Campbell in the studio for Jones' "Back On The Block."

Though there are extensive identifying end credits, the filmmakers take the novel approach of avoiding superimposed titles by having each interviewee announce his own name. This leads to amusing results, especially for Ray Charles and Frank Sinatra. Michael Jackson is interviewed, but refuses to be photographed.

Tech credits are good, with okay transfer to film of videotaped material by Image Transform lab. — *Lor.*

TORONTO FEST

TUNE IN TOMORROW

TORONTO Cinecom release of a Polar Films production. Produced by John Fiedler, Mark Tarlov. Executive producer, Joe Caracciolo Jr. Directed by Jon Amiel. Screenplay, William Boyd based on the novel "Aunt Julia And The Scriptwriter" by Mario Vargas Llosa; camera (color), Robert Stevens; editor, Peter Boyle; music, Wynton Marsalis; production design, Jim Clay; costume design, Betsy Heiman; choreography, Quinny Sacks; casting, Billy Hopkins. Reviewed at Cineplex Odeon screening room, Toronto, Aug. 29, 1990. Running time: **102 MIN.**

Aunt Julia	Barbara Hershey
Martin Loader	Keanu Reeves
Pedro Carmichael	Peter Falk
Puddler	Bill McCutcheon
Aunt Olga	Patricia Clarkson
Sam & Sid	Jerome Dempsey
Richard Quince	Peter Gallagher
Robert Quince	Dan Hedaya
Father Serafim	Buck Henry
Margaret Quince	Hope Lange
Dr. Albert Quince	John Larroquette
Elena Quince	Elizabeth McGovern
Elmore Dubuque	Robert Sedgwick
Big John Coot	Henry Gibson

"**T**une In Tomorrow," Jon Amiel's screen version of Mario Vargas Llosa's acclaimed novel "Aunt Julia And The Scriptwriter," is lusty and full of zany characters, but it's so cluttered and overdone that theatrical possibilities are muted.

Aunt Julia (Barbara Hershey), a double divorcée, returns to New Orleans in 1951 at age 36 to find a rich third husband. Instead, she finds her 21-year-old nephew by marriage (Keanu Reeves), a local radio station newswriter, who falls in love with her. The aunt succumbs, incurring her family's anger. On top of that plot is the more complicated story of a disheveled writer (Peter Falk), who's new in town.

Falk's Pedro Carmichael creates a successful radio soap opera laced with incest and anti-Albanian sentiment. While actors read their lines on the air, different ones, including John Larroquette, Hope Lange, Peter Gallagher and Elizabeth McGovern, act out the scenes in dramatic soap style.

Falk manipulates the nephew-aunt relationship, and, to Reeves' anger, reproduces the couple's arguments in his soap. Falk, a self-declared artist, decides to get out of the radio business when he is told to toe the line, and he plans to bomb the studios. But the protesting Albanians torch the place before he gets to it.

There's enough in William Boyd's sprawling script for three films. And while the action is fun for much of the first half, the storylines ultimately smother each other.

Hershey and Reeves are outstanding and Falk is delightfully melodramatic. And the soap opera players are terrific as well. Music by Wynton Marsalis and brief appearances by jazzmen Jimmy McGriff and Howard Johnson are excellent. Robert Stevens' camerawork is zesty throughout, especially robust in scenes at New Orleans jazz clubs. — *Adil.*

MONTREAL FEST

SANDINO
(SPANISH-CHILEAN)

MONTREAL An RTVE-Miguel Littin Prods. co-production in association with TVE, Umanzor, Beta Films, Reteitalia, Granada TV. Produced by Francisco Ariza. Directed by Miguel Littin. Screenplay, Littin, Leo Benvenutti, Tomas Perez Turrent, Giovana Koch, John Briley; camera (color), Hans Burmann; editor, Pedro del Rey; music, Joakin Bello; production design, Enrique Estevez; sound, Bernardo Menz; casting, Jesus G. Ciordia; production manager, Francisco Lopez; assistant director, Walter Prieto. Reviewed at Montreal World Film Festival (competing), Aug. 27, 1990. Running time: **136 MIN.**

Tom Holte	Kris Kristofferson
Augusto C. Sandino	Joaquim de Almeida
Hatfield	Dean Stockwell
Teresa Villator	Angela Molina
Blanca Arruz	Victoria Abril
Don Gregorio	Omero Antonutti
Rosanna	Blanca Guerra
Anastasio Somoza	Jose Alonso

A reverential biopic about legendary Latin American guerrilla leader Augusto C. Sandino (after whom Nicaragua's Sandinistas were named), Miguel Littin's "Sandino" is an often spectacular but rarely subtle production aimed at a wide international audience.

As charismatically played by Joaquim de Almeida, the revolutionary leader is a dashing, handsome hero whose only flaws are a lust for beautiful women and a tendency to trust politicians. The latter proved to be his downfall in 1933, when he was betrayed by Anastasio Somoza. Sandino's body never has been found; in Littin's film, Sandino and his aides are murdered and buried in unmarked graves.

Kris Kristofferson plays, somewhat incongruously, a sympathetic Yank journalist who befriends Sandino.

"Sandino" explores American policies toward Nicaragua since 1912 (when U.S. forces invaded the country); Dean Stockwell, playing a belligerent American officer, is simply a caricature of the despised Yankee. Most of the film is taken up with lavishly staged jungle battles, with a bit of intrigue and sex thrown in.

Sandino had a wife (Victoria Abril) who didn't join him in his jungle hideout, where he had a mistress, played by the fiery, gun-toting Angela Molina. The scene in which he delivers his dying wife's baby, after the doctors and midwives have given up, is one of the picture's less convincing moments.

Still, "Sandino" looms as a popular item in Latin American territories, and there will be American audiences that will want to learn more about Latin America's most revered revolutionary. The picture, shot entirely in Nicaragua, is lavishly produced.
— *Strat.*

THE BIG MAN
(BRITISH)

MONTREAL A Miramax release (in U.S.) of a Palace Prods. picture, in association with Miramax Film Corp., British Satellite Broadcasting and British Screen. Executive producer, Nik Powell. Produced by Stephen Wooley. Directed by David Leland. Screenplay, Don MacPherson, from the book by William McIlvanney; camera (color), Ian Wilson; editor, George Akers; music, Ennio Morricone; production design, Caroline Amies; sound, Colin Nicolson; co-executive producers, Harvey Weinstein, Bob Weinstein; associate producer, Redmond Morris; casting, Susie Figgis; production manager/assistant director, David Brown. Reviewed at Montreal World Film Festival (competing), Aug. 25, 1990. Running time: **115 MIN.**

Danny Scoular	Liam Neeson
Beth Scoular	Joanne Whalley-Kilmer
Matt Mason	Ian Bannen
Frankie	Billy Connolly
Cam Colvin	Maurice Roeves
Gordon	Hugh Grant
Fiona Mason	Carla Cannn
Margaret Mason	Juliet Cadzow
Cutty Dawson	Rab Affleck
Tommy Brogan	Tom Watson
Melanie	Julie Graham
Billy	Pat Roach

Though unquestionably well-intentioned and determined not to pull any punches, "The Big Man" may have miscalculated the effects of its depressing theme and ultra-violent conclusion. Tough times loom theatrically for this Miramax release that, though not without merits, is severely flawed.

The early scenes, set in a depressed Scottish village where an abandoned coal mine and mass unemployment reflect the aftermath of Britain's crippling miners' strike, look promising. Liam Neeson comes on strong as the unemployed Danny, who was imprisoned during the strike for hitting a policeman and now has a middle-class wife (Joanne Whalley-Kilmer) and two bright children to support.

His best friend, Frankie (an engaging "straight" turn from Scottish comedian Billy Connolly), acts as a runner for Mason (Ian Bannen), a corrupt businessman who needs Danny to fight for him. Motives for the fight, a bare-knuckle affair with no rules, are obscure, as are frequent cuts to a Spanish poolside where an overweight character is sunning himself.

Danny leaves home to train, and his wife responds by dating a man she feels is closer to her own status. Anguished by her behavior, and by the uncertainty of the ordeal ahead, Danny is a troubled man.

The fight, when it comes, is one of the most grueling ever caught on film. Top marks go to the makeup team, which provided the battered and bloodied faces for the actors. But audiences, even strong-hearted ones, may not easily endure such an extended bout of brutality and cruelty. Many may lose interest in the film at this point, since motivation remains obscure, and Neeson, for all his acting ability, never makes Danny a very likable character.

The revelation that the fight was an elaborate wager and that the outcome will affect an assassination to take place in Spain only adds to the confusion. Film's final scenes evoke a populist message in which good more or less triumphs over evil, but many may miss the point.

For U.S. audiences, there may be problems with the Scottish accents many of the characters employ; at the Montreal fest screening, many (non-French) viewers were puzzling over bits of dialog.

David Leland, whose first feature was the exceptionally charming "Wish You Were Here," and who stumbled with his Yank effort, "Checking Out," may have made a bad move by going for explicit and bloody violence in the final reels. Technically, the film is good, if overlong, and Enno Morricone's score is too insistent at times.

Neeson heads a strong cast, with Bannen providing some charming villainy. Whalley-Kilmer makes the most of her underwritten role. And Connolly, in perhaps the film's best performance, shows there's a career for him outside the stand-up comic circuits.

But "The Big Man" doesn't deliver as entertainment, and it makes its serious theme unpalatable for many "serious" filmgoers who might have taken the message if it were not coated with so much gut-wrenching blood and gore. — *Strat.*

BRIGHT ANGEL

MONTREAL A Hemdale release of a Hemdale-Northwood/Bright Angel production. Executive producers, John Daly, Derek Gibson. Produced by Paige Simpson, Robert MacLean. Directed by Michael Fields. Screenplay, Richard Ford, from his short stories "Children" and "Great Falls"; camera (CFI color), Elliott Davis; editor, Melody London, Clement Barclay; music, Christopher Young; sound, Ed White; production design, Marcia Hinds Johnson; supervising producer, Sue Baden-Powell; casting, Risa Braman, Billy Hopkins; production manager, Cathy Michel Gibson; assistant director, Josh King; associate producer, Stuart Regan. Reviewed at Montreal World Film Festival (Cinema of Today & Tomorrow), Aug. 25, 1990. MPAA Rating: R. Running time: **94 MIN.**
George Russell . . . Dermot Mulroney
Lucy . . . . Lili Taylor
Jack Russell . . . . Sam Shepard
Aileen Russell . . . . . Valerie Perrine
Bob . . . . Bill Pullman
Art Falcone . . . . Burt Young
Nina Bennett . . . . . Sheila McCarthy
Judy . . . . Mary Kay Place
Billy . . . . Kevin Tighe
Harley . . . . Delroy Lindo
Claude . . . . Benjamin Bratt

"Bright Angel" is one of those films that breathe freshness and life into familiar genres. Basically a road movie about a pair of young lovers who become involved in crime, Michael Fields' first feature as a director boasts a full cast-list of near-perfect performances. With proper handling, this could attain critical kudos and respectful audiences, though it'll never be a big commercial success.

The intelligent and spare screenplay is by Richard Ford, who based it on two of his short sto-

ries.

The setting is Montana, "where the Great Plains begin." George Russell (Dermot Mulroney), 18, lives with his parents (Sam Shepard and Valerie Perrine) who separate violently when his father finds his mother with another man (though it could have been an innocent encounter). George is attracted to Lucy (Lili Taylor), who has spent an afternoon in a motel with the father of his best friend, an Indian. She needs to get to the Wyoming town where her brother's in prison, and George offers to drive her.

Much of the film is taken up with the relationship between the naive and good-hearted George and the old-beyond-her-years Lucy as they journey to their destination, and with the characters they become involved with, including George's too-affectionate aunt (Mary Kay Place), her crippled, bitter husband (Delroy Lindo), and a mysterious cowboy (Kevin Tighe) who offers George a job.

Journey's end brings a tragic resolution when George reluctantly goes along with Lucy's plan to bribe a couple of witnesses who could testify against her brother. Bill Pullman as the manic Bob and Burt Young as the quieter, but far more dangerous Art, push the story into a starkly dramatic direction, though it's leavened with grim humor by Nina (Sheila McCarthy), Art's chattering, motherly mistress.

Fields and Ford are dealing with a familiar genre here, but they avoid clichés: no sex scenes (but a great deal of sexual tension); no shootouts (but an agonizing sequence of suspense); no neat ending. In fact, after the film apparently has concluded, with the death of one of the leading characters, it continues with a simple but effective coda that provides a most satisfying conclusion.

The cast is firstrate down the line, though Shepard and (especially) Perrine are in for only brief scenes near the beginning. Mulroney will certainly add to his reputation with his subtle underplaying of George, while Lili Taylor (memorable in "Mystic Pizza") is a knockout as Lucy, a child-woman who, though not conventionally beautiful, radiates sensuality. Supporting characters are all well played.

"Bright Angel" is technically

proficient and edited to the point that not a frame is wasted. It's an intelligent and stimulating debut picture. — *Strat.*

NUIT D'ETE EN VILLE
(SUMMER NIGHT IN TOWN)
(FRENCH)

MONTREAL An AAA release of an Elefilm-AAA Prods.-TSR Prods. picture. Produced and written by Rosalinde Deville. Directed by Michel Deville. Camera (Eastmancolor), Bernard Lutic; editor, Raymonde Guyot; music, Camille Saint-Saens; sound, Philippe Lioret; production design, Thierry Leproust; production manager, Franz Damamme; assistant director, Thierry Petit. Reviewed at Montreal World Film Festival (competing), Aug. 26, 1990. Running time: **85 MIN.**
Louis . . . . . . Jean-Hugues Anglade
Emilie . . . . Marie Trintignant

Michel Deville's first feature since "La Lectrice," which won the top prize at the Montreal fest two years ago, is played out in the confined setting of an apartment between two characters over a single night. From these limited resources, the director attempts, with mixed success, to chart the beginning of a relationship.

The film opens with the couple, Emilie and Louis, naked in her bed after making love for the first time. They met earlier that evening, and she brought him home, something she says she doesn't usually do (preferring to go the man's apartment in such circumstances).

For the first half-hour of the film, both Jean-Hugues Anglade and Marie Trintignant play their roles completely naked, as the lovers engage in post-coital chit-chat and then share a bath together. Later they wear minimal clothing.

As the summer night wears on, they talk about past lovers, first sexual encounters, their jobs (she's a teacher, he grows plants) and their hopes and fears for this new relationship. They play games, touch and feel each other, listen to music (Saint-Saens), argue and make up.

The dialog is extremely frank at times, and the film, without ever showing the couple making love, involves enough foreplay to qualify for an X rating.

Nevertheless, there's a beauty and frank innocence about the way these young people explore and relate to each other that almost belongs to another time,

perhaps the '60s, when casual sexual encounters were more common than today. AIDS never is discussed in this film.

The dialog often is witty, as in most Deville pictures, but it's asking a lot of audiences to accept this long night of small-talk. Both thesps deserve commendation for willingly entering into the frank nature of the film, and both give touching and convincing performances, neatly capturing the weaknesses and vulnerabilities of their characters.

"Summer Night In Town" could attract an arthouse crowd, but this will not be counted among Deville's best efforts. — *Strat.*

FARENDJ
(FRENCH)

MONTREAL A Vidmark Entertainment presentation of a River Films production with Joe Sheridan, Negatwa Kelkai, Benjamin Zephaniah. Executive producers, Bruno Held, Reza Lari, Mark Amin. Produced by Held. Directed by Sabine Prenczina. Screenplay by Prenczina, Barbara Jago; camera (Eastmancolor), Elisabeth Prouvost; editor, Genevieve Letellier; music, Mino Cinelu; sound, Philippe Senechal, François Groult; production designer, Oliver Raoux; production manager, Jean de Tregoman; assistant director, Vincent Canaple. Reviewed at Montreal World Film Festival (Cinema of Today & Tomorrow), Aug. 27, 1990. Running time: **103 MIN.**
Anton . . . . Tim Roth
Julie . . . . Marie Matheron
Bruno . . . . Mathias Habich
Yssa . . . . Hodan Siad
Zeleka . . . . Negana Kelaki
Bob . . . . Jo Sheridan
Moses . . . . . . Benjamin Zephaniah
(In English)

A somber tale of a dissolute English writer going to seed in Ethiopia, "Farendj" is beautifully shot on little-seen locations, but the story is an unappealing downer. Auds will find the going tough, despite its qualities.

British thesp Tim Roth plays an odious character here. Anton travels with French g.f. Julie, who works for a humanitarian group, to Ethiopia. While there he discovers a house in which Rimbaud once lived, and becomes obsessed with finding out more about the French poet. He leaves the distraught Julie and shacks up with a local girl, Yssa, granddaughter of Zeleka, the old woman who owns the house.

The film suggests that Zeleka exerts some kind of mystical domination on Anton, who eventually gives up the trappings of his Western background and heads for the desert, with Julie and a German friend following him in a vain search.

But Anton is so obnoxious, few will care very much what happens to him. Roth makes the most of the role, but he's hard to take. Supporting characters add a certain amount of flavor.

The film's main asset is director Sabine Prenczina's evident feel for the country and people, which are lovingly filmed. There's also an attractive score. Technically, "Farendj" is first class.

— *Strat.*

FESTIVAL LATINO

MARIA CANO
(COLOMBIAN)

NEW YORK A Focine production. Directed by Camila Loboguerrero. Screenplay, Loboguerrero, Luis Gonzalez, Felipe Aljure; camera, Carlos Sanchez; editors, Luis Alberto Restrepo, Gabriel Gonzalez; music, Santiago Lanz K. Reviewed at Cineplex Odeon Worldwide Cinemas, N.Y., Aug. 19, 1990. (In Festival Latino.) Running time: **104 MIN.**
Maria Cano . . . Maria Eugenia Davila
Ignacio Torres Giraldo . Frank Ramirez
Carmen Lucia Cano . . . . . . Maguzo
Tomas . . . . Diego Velez
Meleche . . . . Jorge Herrera
Ezequiel . . . . German Escallon

Thirty-three years after her death in obscurity, the charismatic Colombian labor leader Maria Cano is given a compassionate if superficial eulogy in the form of this biographical film.

"Maria Cano" is bookended with brief scenes of Cano's embittered final years. Reduced to ineffectuality and eccentric reclusion, the elderly Cano watches helplessly as her ailing sister dies. Her three-year career as a much-loved labor organizer in the 1920s in shown in flashback, outlining the momentary glory that brought on ultimate dissipation.

Starting with Cano's recruitment by her cousin into the radical labor movement in 1925, the film bounces from highlight to highlight as Cano takes on ever greater importance in the struggle against oppression and horrendous working conditions. With her fiery style and common-woman approach, Cano soon becomes a leader to the movement and a folk hero to Colombia's

poor.

But Cano's work is to be short-lived. Jailed by the corrupt military government, she emerges five years later to find that former friends and comrades have either been killed, deported or co-opted into the system they once fought. The revolution (or lack thereof) has passed her by.

Although the film's episodic structure keeps things moving, it provides little insight into the disillusionment portrayed in the final scene. Character developments seem to happen without precedent, as when the young Cano much too quickly casts aside her fears and joins the movement. When the elderly Cano angrily lashes out at her longtime lover (and former fellow labor leader) Ignacio, both Ignacio and the viewer can only surmise her motivations.

Fortunately, Maria Eugenia Davila's razor-sharp performance in the title role provides a continuity Camila Loboguerrero's sometimes stilted direction lacks. The passion with which Davila recites one of Cano's romantic poems suggests more about the character's idealism than much of the script is able to convey.

Even a scene as contrived as the one in which Cano expresses her insecurities to her sister is given dignity and poignance by the smart, dead-on performance. Davila's is matched by another fine performance, that of Maguzo as Cano's sister, Carmen. But it is Davila's final, freeze-framed expression that captures the futility of Cano's life.

Not that Loboguerrero's direction is entirely without inspiration. The dingy, claustrophobic house in which the elderly Cano lives with her sister and Ignacio becomes an airy, brightly painted home in the flashback scenes. In depicting the 1928 massacre of thousands of banana pickers, Loboguerrero fades to black with the first shots and resumes several seconds later to show the brutal aftermath of the slaughter. Even if the choice to forgo a costly battle scene was prompted by budget limitations, the result is no less effective.

A low budget also may have contributed to the grainy, out-of-focus look of the film, and the "elderly" make-up worn by the actors in the opening and closing scenes is ludicrously bad (the characters appear to be suffering more from some tropical skin disease than old age).

Despite its flaws, though, "Maria Cano" should appeal to anyone interested in either the films or history of South America. A wider audience would simply do well to catch Davila's lovely performance. — *Evan.*

A HUNDRED TIMES, NO
(ARGENTINIAN)

NEW YORK A Rosafrey, S.R.L. production. Directed by Alejandro Doria. Screenplay, Doria, Ricardo Talesnik; camera (color), Miguel Rodriguez; editor, Silvia Ripoll; music, Leo Sujatovich; sound, Gabriel Coll. Reviewed at Worldwide Cinema, N.Y., Aug. 19, 1990. (In Festival Latino.) Running time: **92 MIN.**
Mother . . . . Norma Aleandro
Father . . . . Luis Brandoni
Daughter . . . . Andrea del Boca

This 1989 farce concerns the frantic efforts of social-climbing parents to find a husband for their pregnant daughter. Thanks to appropriately broad performances, "A Hundred Times, No" adroitly satirizes a bourgeois Argentine family and its attempts to maintain respectability.

Norma Aleandro is particularly amusing as the overbearing, oversexed mother. Nominated for an Academy Award for "The Official Story," Aleandro's presence could help secure a distributor for this sharp comedy.

The seemingly devoted parents quickly turn on their daughter (Andrea del Boca) when her pregnancy is revealed. Because she does not know who the baby's father is, her parents desperately try to arrange a marriage with one of her many suitors.

The family patriarch (Luis Brandoni) goes from fawning to fuming over his sexually active teenage daughter. He is hilarious as he screams with rage upon hearing the news. "She's got a cake in the oven," he yells out the door. "She's inflated." He then destroys a tree, decorated with everything from the daughter's baby shoes to diplomas, that was the parents' shrine to her.

When the daughter's respectable boyfriend shows up, the parents immediately hide their anger and pretend to be a model family again. Brandoni asks how much the man makes — in dollars, of course. Although largely indifferent to this boyfriend, the daughter feigns passionate interest in him to secure a marriage proposal.

After that attempt falls

through, the parents meet another potential husband, even though this one has no desire to marry the daughter or get a job. He calls himself a psycho-anarchist. "Is that left or right?" Aleandro wonders.

Aleandro is at her funniest when trying to lure a wealthy, older boyfriend by serving tea and speaking (halting, mispronounced) English. Her expressive face and wide eyes are as well suited to comedy as they are to drama. In the same scene, Brandoni is convincingly furious when he throws a fit about having to speak English; his major regret in life was deciding not to open a laundromat in America.

As their sexpot of a daughter, del Boca also earns frequent laughs. She uses babytalk to charm her parents and steamy language to seduce her suitors. In this story, the parents are not the only hypocrites.

The director and co-writer, Alejandro Doria, keeps the action moving along at a brisk pace. Although it never becomes boring, the film takes place almost entirely inside the family's house. Perhaps it is the director's intent to make the audience feel trapped in this madhouse, just as the daughter does.

Doria debuted "Waiting For The Pallbearers" at the Festival Latino in 1987. He deserves to attract wider exposure with this enjoyable domestic farce. — *Stev.*

HAUGESUND FEST

HERMAN
(NORWEGIAN)

HAUGESUND, NORWAY A KF release of Filmeffekt production. Produced by Petter J. Borgli. Directed by Erik Gustavson. Screenplay, Lars Saabye Christensen, based on his novel; camera (Eastmancolor), Kjell Vassdal; editor, Martin Asphaug; music, Randall Meyers; sound, Kari Nytrö; production design, Frode Krohg; costume design, Inger Derlick; production manager, Jeanette Sundby. Reviewed at Norwegian Film Festival, Haugesund, Aug. 19, 1990. Running time: **106 MIN.**
Herman . . . . . Anders Danielsen Lie
His mother . . . . Elisabeth Sand
His father . . . . Björn Floberg
Rudy . . . . Linn Aaronsen
Panten . . . . Jarl Kulle
Tjukken . . . . Harald Heide-Steen Jr.
Also with: Frank Robert, Per Jansen, Kim Haugen, Joachim Calmeyer, Kjersti Holmen, Tor Stokke, Philip Borgli, Sossen Krohg, Erlend Sandem, Anne Marit Jacobsen, Sverre Bentzen, Oeyvind Blunck.

"**H**erman" is a sweet film about an 11-year-old boy who starts losing his hair. Based on Lars Saabye Christensen's screenplay from his own best-selling novel, Erik Gustavson's film is headed for major domestic boxoffice and might fare neatly in international sales as well.

The time is 1961, and detailed period atmosphere is evoked in a blend of what was typically Norwegian as well as internationally trendy. The place is Frogner, a district of Oslo where children from social extremes went to the same schools. Herman's father is a crane operator; his mother helps out at a greengrocer's. They are loving parents, but they have a hard time understanding their son's moods and imaginative intellect.

Herman is a silent sufferer despite the mobbing at school. When he does speak, it's in a curious language of his own that sounds like that of a pedantic adult.

As his hair disappears, Herman hides under a variety of hats. At night, he dreams of Zorro coming to his rescue, but even Zorro admits to being stumped on the boy's particular problem.

But some real friends stick around to help him. His parents do their good-humored best, and Herman reaps wisdom from his dying grandfather and other insights from an elderly drunk. The baldness they cannot cure, but the drunk says beer makes hair grow, so Herman acts on the tip with not-too-disastrous results.

As Herman, Anders Danielsen Lie has obvious kiddie star presence. He looks sad, wise, mischievous, angry and joyful with equal ease and conviction. As his ersatz girlfriend, Linn Aaronsen is a match for him all the way.

"Herman" is family entertainment that displays an honest respect for an audience's intelligence. All production values have a handsome gloss. The running time occasions some dry stretches, but 10 minutes sheared from its 106 minutes could do wonders. — *Kell.*

SMYKKETYVEN
(TWICE UPON A TIME)
(NORWEGIAN)

HAUGESUND, NORWAY A Norsk Film Distribusjon release of a Norsk Film production in association with the Swedish Film Institute, the Danish Film Institute and Nordisk Film (Denmark). Produced by Gunnar Svensrud. Directed by Anja Breien. Screenplay by Breien and Carl Martin Borgen; camera (Eastmancolor), Philip Oengard; editor, Einarr Egeland; music, Jan Gabarek; sound, Kari Nytrö, Conrad Weyns; production design, Anne Siri Bryhni; costume design, Eirin Osen; production management, Peter Böe, Hilde Berg, Christian Heian. Reviewed at Haugesund Norwegian Film Festival (competing), Aug. 21, 1990. Running time: **91 MIN.**
Stig Ström . . . . Sven Wollter
Lillian . . . . Kjersti Holmen
Rut . . . . Ghita Nörby
Hilde . . . . Lene Bragli
Ida . . . . Gisken Armand

A veteran explorer of the sexual-psychological manners and morals of Nordic men and women, helmer Anja Breien this time turns her sights on a middle-aged Don Juan who's mired in despair as his many women go briskly about their life.

The dust of 1930s psychological love stories lies heavily on "Twice Upon A Time," smothering its offshore chances beyond Denmark and Sweden, contributors of production coin and a few thesps.

The weary, ailing and slightly boozy Stig Ström (Sweden's able Sven Wollter looking suitably lost) is a stage designer seeking out some of the women he used to have at his feet. But none are the least bit interested.

Stig, feeling the sting of the jealousy he once despised in others, proceeds to lay siege to his ex-wife, Lillian (Kjersti Holmen). He moves into a turret across from her new boyfriend's apartment so he can bombard her with flowers and phone calls. He also has a shotgun at the ready.

Lillian once expressed a wish to have a certain necklace as a token of Stig's love. So now, in white tie and tails and stage-prop raven's head, Stig breaks into the Egyptian embassy after a party to steal the necklace from the ambassador's wife. (Film's original title, "Smykketyven," means "The Jewel Thief.")

When redemption through the love of a young woman also eludes Stig, the film resorts to epigrammatic literature for a final frame, which tells us that change can come to a lost soul only through madness or love.

"Twice" has neat production values and sweeping, imaginative cinematography. The actors are mostly puppets, except for Wollter, who seems inclined to doze off most of the time. Denmark's Ghita Nörby (the title role of this year's Oscar-nominated "Waltzing Regitze") shines in a cameo that is wrongly credited as a lead. — *Kell.*

DÖDEN PA OSLO S
(DEATH AT OSLO C)
(NORWEGIAN)

HAUGESUND, NORWAY A Norsk Film Distribusjon release of Norsk Film production. Produced by Harald Ohrvik. Executive producer, Gunnar Svensrud. Directed by Eva Isaksen. Screenplay, Axel Hellstanius, based on Ingvar Ambjörnsen's novel; camera (Eastmancolor), Philip Oegard; editor, Pal Gengenbach; music, Kjartan Kristiansen; sound, Are Kalmar; production design, Hege Palm; costume design, Tone Skjelfjord; production management, Jan Olav Brynjulfsen; assistant directors, Anne Siri Bryhni, Sirin Eide. Reviewed at Norwegian Film Festival, Haugesund (competing), Aug. 23, 1990. Running time: **100 MIN.**
Pelle . . . . Havard Bakke
Proffen . . . . Tommy Karlsen
Lena . . . . Helle Figenschow
Mother . . . . Brit Elisabeth Haagensli
Father . . . . Viggo Jönsberg
Skanseth . . . . Björn Sundquist
Leffy . . . . Roy A. Hansen
Stein . . . . Pepito Gutierrez
  Also with: Henning Syverud, Pal Obrestad, Monica Rue, Mia Norum Robsahm, Stein Winge, Tien Ton-That, Geir Kvarme.

"**D**eath At Oslo C," a youth meller about Big City teenagers and drugs, has all the technical shine of a U.S. tv movie, but helmer Eva Isaksen delivers a fine emotional wallop and captures neon glitter and sidewalk despair to boot.

Her film would be an obvious pick for homevid and tv exposure everywhere and could have a limited future in offshore theaters as well.

Isaksen's variation on this often-told story has two 15-year-old boys chasing a reform school principal who not only sells drugs, but abuses teenage girls sexually. One of the boys falls in love with a nice and proper girl who turns out to be one of the villain's victims.

Combining the thriller element with character probing sometimes detracts from the film's narrative flow. Still, Isaksen is canny at juxtaposing shots and composing frames that create immediacy. She also works in fine rhythm with cinematographer Philip Oegard and editor Pal Gengenbach.

A troupe of teenaged amateur thesps, notably Havard Bakke, Tommy Karisen and Helle Figenschow in the three leads, exude natural grace and, when required, agony. All the characters, including the adults, are sharply defined as individuals. As a straight-arrow boy's "retired hippies" parents, Viggo Jönsberg and Brit Elisabeth Haagensli are appealing.

Technical credits are of a high order, and Kjarten Kristiansen's music is mood-enhancing but never intrusive. — *Kell.*

MONTREAL FEST

STATE OF GRACE

An Orion Pictures release of a Cinehaus production. Produced by Ned Dowd, Randy Ostrow, Ron Rotholz. Directed by Phil Joanou. Screenplay, Dennis McIntyre; camera (De Luxe color), Jordan Cronenweth; editor, Claire Simpson; music, Ennio Morricone; sound, Peter A. Ilardi; production design, Patrizia von Brandenstein, Doug Kraner; production manager, Michael Hausman; assistant director, Thomas Mack; casting, Bonnie Timmermann. Reviewed at Montreal World Film Festival, Aug. 30, 1990. MPAA Rating: R. Running time: **134 MIN.**

Terry	Sean Penn
Frankie	Ed Harris
Jackie	Gary Oldman
Kathleen	Robin Wright
Nick	John Turturro
Stevie	John C. Reilly
Nicholson	R.D. Call
Borelli	Joe Viterelli
Finn	Burgess Meredith
Irene	Deidre O'Connell
Cavello	Marco St. John

World preemed in a sneak at the Montreal World Film Festival, Orion's "State Of Grace" is a handsomely produced, mostly riveting, but ultimately overlong and overindulgent gangster picture. It could open to decent figures, but looks to have short legs because of its grimly downbeat plot and languorous pacing.

In one of his best performances to date in the lead, Sean Penn plays Terry, one of New York's Irish residents who grew up in Hell's Kitchen with his friends, brothers Frankie (Ed Harris) and Jackie (Gary Oldman) and their sister, Kathleen (Robin Wright), with whom he was once in love.

Terry's been away from New York for 12 years, but now he returns and signs up with the Irish mob headed by the ruthless Frankie. He also resumes his passionate relationship with Kathleen.

An early sequence has alerted audiences to the fact that Terry isn't all he seems, and in fact he's an undercover cop assigned to get the goods on Frankie. He has to convince the brothers that he's a hardened gunman, which he does by faking the death of cop John Turturro, who acts as his liaison with the police department.

Penn is excellent as Terry, who drinks too much and who ultimately gets too personally involved with his mission. Harris is a malevolent Frankie, who carries out his executions personally. He makes the character wonderfully crafty, devious and smooth.

Oldman is suitably manic as the unstable younger brother, whose personal crusade against the Italian mobsters with whom Frankie has become involved leads to the film's ultra-violent climax.

Wright, though she gives a glowing performance as Kathleen, who has moved as far as she can uptown to get away from her brothers, seems to belong to an altogether different movie.

Director Phil Joanou ("U2 — Rattle And Hum") shows he has a talent for establishing and maintaining suspense, but relies too heavily on the legacy of Sam Peckinpah. The final shoot-out, in a smoky bar between Terry and Frankie and his hoods, is a lengthy, blood-spattered, hymn to violence. It's extremely well-handled, but it smacks of overkill.

It's a pity, too, Joanou couldn't have tightened his pacing. At 134 minutes "State Of Grace" is certainly half an hour too long. A cameo from Burgess Meredith, who has one scene as an old-timer who owes Frankie money, seems unnecessary in the overall scheme of things.

Yet the young director shows a command of his craft, and is helped by a grimly witty screenplay by Dennis McIntyre, which emphasizes ethnic Irish and Catholic elements in the drama.

Also outstanding is the cinematography of Jordan Cronenweth, turning in some of his best work. The main streets, back alleys, little bars and restaurants and grimy apartments of Hell's Kitchen are beautifully lit and shot.

With a string of hard-boiled gangster films about to open, leading up to "The Godfather Part III" at the end of the year, "State Of Grace" runs the risk of being overlooked. Orion will have to hope that word-of-mouth about the ultra-violence will pay off in boxoffice dollars. — *Strat.*

BETHUNE:
THE MAKING OF A HERO
(CANADIAN-CHINESE-FRENCH)

A Filmline Intl., August 1st Film Studio and Parmentier/Belstar presentation of a Pieter Kroonenburg and Nicolas Clermont production. Produced by Kroonenburg and Clermont (Filmline), Wang Xingang, Jacques Dorfmann. Directed by Phillip Borsos. Screenplay, Ted Allan; camera (color), Mike Molloy, Raoul Coutard; editor, Yves Langlois, Angelo Corrao; music, Alan Reeves. Reviewed at Montreal World Film Festival, Aug. 27, 1990. Running time: **115 MIN.**

Dr. Norman Bethune	Donald Sutherland
Frances Penny Bethune	Helen Mirren
Mrs. Dowd	Helen Shaver
Chester Rice	Colm Feore
Mr. Tung	James Pax
Dr. Chian	Guo Da
Dr. Fong	Harrison Liu
Marie-France Coudaire	Anouk Aimee
Alan Coleman	Ronald Pickup

Canada's $C18 million political saga has hit the screen at long last. Neither a masterpiece nor a disaster, it's a thorough documenting of the life of Canadian doctor Norman Bethune, a hero in China for his medical input during the long march in Mao Tse-tung's revolution.

The film belongs to Donald Sutherland, who delivers a stunning performance as the complex and controversial surgeon.

Bethune, a man virtually unknown to Canadians, is honored in China's Red Book for his selfless and tireless commitment to Mao's army.

This psychological portrait is intended to make Bethune as famous in Canada and the rest of the world as he is in China, which is why the pic seems more like a documentary than a fiction feature — its major flaw.

Editing is patchy. Cross-cutting hopscotches among several decades as a journalist interviews Bethune's friends and family. Flashback sequences — the guts of the story — are misused as filler.

Harrison Liu delivers a fine performance as Bethune's protégé, Dr. Fong, but Helen Shaver (as a missionary in China) and Helen Mirren (as Bethune's wife) pale beside Sutherland.

His intense personal commitment to the role fuels his performance as he "becomes" Bethune, the perfect showcase for his vast range as an actor.

Bethune was at once a boozing womanizer, a loving husband, a revolutionary surgeon and an ardently committed antifascist. He often had more enemies than allies due to his fast temper, arrogance and general intolerance of "greed and hypocrisy" in the medical profession.

Bethune unsuccessfully attempted to convince the Canadian government to deprivatize the medical industry (which ironically was done years after his death).

He made a slew of enemies among colleagues and government officials before he declared himself a "red" and headed first to Spain and then to China (the latter of which provides magnificent scenery in the film).

Pic should not encounter difficulties as a procommunist doctrine. It isn't. Via script and acting, pic argues that Bethune was an idealist who believed every human, rich or poor, is entitled to medical attention. Humanistic appeal outweighs the story's political bent.

"Bethune: The Making Of A Hero" has limited theatrical potential due to a general lack of action, music, rhythm and passion.

As a miniseries (for which another version of "Bethune" is being edited), however, it should be brilliant. Its thorough and intense dramatic elements are perfect for the small screen. As a document, it's a valuable tool for history teachers.

After several years of financial problems from both coprod partners (China and Canada), it's a relief that the film is better than expected and a disappointment that it is not as good as hoped. It's also a genuine treat thanks to Sutherland at his finest. — *Suze.*

DER ACHTE TAG
(THE EIGHTH DAY)
(W. GERMAN)

A Von Vietinghoff Filmproduktion. (World sales: Metropolis Film, Berlin.) Produced by Joachim von Vietinghoff. Written and directed by Reinhard Munster. Camera (color), Axel Block; editor, Raimund Barthlemes; sound, Hardy Hardt; production manager, Gudrun Ruzickova-Steiner. Reviewed at Montreal World Film Festival (competing), Aug. 30, 1990. Running time: **102 MIN.**

Vera Pukall	Katharina Thalbach
Dr. Svoboda	Hans-Chrisian Blech

Also with: Heinz Honig, Hannelore Elsner, Heinz Weerner Kraehkamp, Fritz Schediwy, Lukas Aman, Peter Simonischek, Ulrich Pleitgen.

A thriller about an investigating journalist who unravels a nasty case of illegal genetic engineering, "The Eighth Day" tells a tall story with a certain amount of conviction. But commercial possibilities outside German-speaking territories don't look promising.

Katharina Thalbach is the journalist, who is called out to meet a mystery phone caller with a big story only to discover that (a) he's a very famous scientist and (b) he's very dead. The police say it was suicide. She, naturally, thinks he was murdered.

Against the wishes of her editor (presented as being a decidedly obtuse character) she probes into the affair, and eventually discovers that science and commerce have allied to start cloning people in a way Frankenstein never dreamed of. In fact, the dead man's widow has been impregnated with an embryo taken from her own father's cells.

Now that she knows too much, Thalbach finds herself menaced by steely-eyed killers, but she knows how to look after herself and stages one incredible escape while driving in a fast-moving car. The film's climax involves amazing revelations and suicide on live television.

First-time writer-director Reinhard Munster manages to make the scientific details here more convincing than the thriller elements. But he's come up with a sufficiently intriguing notion to attract audiences on his home turf. As a competing film in an international festival, however, "The Eighth Day" looked slim.

Thalbach is in fine form as the determined journalist who finds her own life in danger, and technically the film is first-rate in every department. — *Strat.*

RAFALES
(BLIZZARD)
(CANADIAN)

An Aska Film production, in association with the National Film Board of Canada and with support of Telefilm Canada. Produced by Yuri Yoshimura-Gagnon, Claude Gagnon. Directed by André Melançon. Screenplay, Melançon, Marcel Leboeuf, Denis Bouchard; camera (Eastmancolor), Pierre Mignot; editor, André Corriveau; music, Osvaldo Montes; production design, Michel Proulx, André Chamberland; special effects, Louis Craig; assistant director, Frank Ruszczynski. Reviewed at Montreal World Film Festival (competing), Aug. 31, 1990. Running time: **87 MIN.**
Louis-Philippe Trepanier . . . . Denis Bouchard
Gerard Crepeau . . . . Marcel Leboeuf
Normand Crepeau . . . Guy Thauvette
Pouliot . . . . Claude Blanchard
Nicole . . . . Sylvie Ferlatte
Radio station manager . . Remy Girard
Also with: Monique Spaziani, Serge Theriault, Raymond Legault, Kim Yaroshevskaya, Pipo Gagnon.

"**B**lizzard" is a very well-staged thriller with something to say about the media. It should perform well in French Canada, with crossover potential less likely, as foreign language genre pictures always have trouble finding space in the crowded international marketplace.

This drama takes place during a few hours on Christmas Eve. Three men plan to rob a department store, but one (Claude Blanchard) opts out at the last minute, leaving brothers Normand (Guy Thauvette) and Gerard (Marcel Leboeuf) to cope with the situation. During their panicky exit with the loot, someone is killed. Normand is nabbed by the police. Gerard gets away with the money.

Unknown to him, he's followed by a headline-grabbing radio journalist, Trepanier (Denis Boucheard), who witnessed the robbery and smells a scoop. He latches on to the terrified Gerard and proposes that he, Trepanier, be taken hostage by the reluctant gunman inside his radio station.

Thus the film develops into a different kind of drama, one that points a finger at the media's insatiable thirst for the sensational story — and the greed of the sponsors who call up to demand that their ads interrupt the real-life drama going on at gunpoint in the studio.

Director André Melançon, who dedicates the film to John Cassavetes, skillfully stages the street scenes with a fierce blizzard raging. He is also adept at building up tension and irony into the second half of the film. Result is a modest but striking pic that deserves a wider release than it will probably get.

It also boasts a number of excellent performances, notably Leboeuf as the frightened and confused gunman. — *Strat.*

NAPLO APAMNAK, ANYAMMNAK
(DIARY FOR MY FATHER AND MOTHER)
(HUNGARIAN)

A Budapest Studio, Mafilm production. (World sales: Cine Magyar, Budapest.) Produced by Gabor Hanak. Directed by Márta Mészáros. Screenplay, Mészáros, Eva Pataki; camera (Eastmancolor and b&w), Nyika Jancso; editor, Eva Karmento; music, Zsolt Dome; sound, Istvan Sipos; production design, Eva Martin. Reviewed at Montreal World Film Festival (competing), Sept. 1, 1990. Running time: **115 MIN.**
Juli . . . . Zsuzsa Czinkoczi
Janos . . . . Jan Nowicki
Vera . . . . Mari Torocsik
Ildi . . . . Ildiko Bansagi
Magda . . . . Anna Polony
Also with: Lajos Balazsovits, Jolan Jaszai, Irina Kouberskaya, Erzsebet Kutvolgyi, Lili Monori, Miklos B. Szekeley, Istvan Hirtling, Eva Szabo.

The third and final episode in Marta Mészáros' "Diary" trilogy is less successful than the earlier films. However, distribs in territories in which the first two films were screened will doubtless want to round out the story. The three films together provide a fascinating look at recent Hungarian history.

Mészáros made the first film, originally called "Diary" (later "Diary For My Children") in 1982. It was banned by nervous Hungarian authorities because of perceived anti-Soviet content, but released a few years later. Then came "Diary For My Loves" in '87.

The first two films told the story of young Juli (the Mészáros character, since these are autobiographies) whose father, a Communist artist, took his family to Moscow in the '30s and died there, a victim of Stalin's purges. Juli returned to Budapest in part 1 to stay with Magda, her aunt, a Communist official whose lover, Janos, looked very much like Juli's dead father. (Both are played by Jan Nowicki.)

The story continued in part 2, which ended in 1956 with Juli in the Moscow film school when the so-called "counterrevolution," in which Janos played a major role, occurred back home.

The new film makes no attempt to explain the principal characters to audiences that might not have seen the earlier segments of the trilogy. As a result, pic will be nearly incomprehensible to some viewers. This could be rectified by a reprise of scenes from the earlier films at the start of this one.

Part 3 is almost entirely concerned with the events of 1956, and one of Mészáros' great strengths is to integrate newsreel and archive footage with new, re-enacted material. A good example of this is the scene in which a giant statue of Stalin is toppled by an angry crowd.

Mészáros is less successful, however, in clarifying the different roles and motives of the principal characters. Her touch is heavy at times. A lengthy New Year's Eve party, in which people with opposing political viewpoints are gathered together for a night of celebration and grief (the revolution has by now been violently crushed by Soviet tanks) is too obvious a symbol of the turbulent times.

One of the film's most effective scenes comes near the end when actual color newsreel footage of the 1957 May Day Parade in Budapest indicates that, only a few months after the traumatic events of October and November, thousands of Hungarians packed the city's vast square to celebrate the Communist Party. This footage is an eye-opener.

Mészáros also points the finger at the way some of her fellow countrymen succeeded in shifting their position with each change in the political climate. When Janos is brought to trial, he cries out that the "traitors" (in this case Communists, but in another era they were Fascists) who try to control Hungary will be active long into the future — not only in 1958, but in '68 and even 1998. The line may ring bells in former Communist countries where the film is seen.

Certainly this is as anti-Communist a film as has ever been made in Central Europe, but it also puts some blame on the U.S., pushing the point that the small countries of Central Europe were betrayed after the war by America so that the status quo could be maintained. All this is solid stuff, but unfortunately the film is also frequently confusing and unsubtle.

Now that she has these personal memories exorcised, it's to be hoped that Mészáros may find a niche in post-Communist Hungarian cinema making the films she makes best — intimate dramas about relationships between men and women. — *Strat.*

TEN TO CHI TO
(HEAVEN AND EARTH)
(JAPANESE)

A Triton Pictures release of a Haruki Kadokawa Films production. Executive producer, Haruki Kadokawa. Produced by Yutaka Okada. Directed by Kadokawa. Screenplay, Kadokawa, Toshio Kamata, Isao Yoshihara, from the novel by Chogoro Kaionjii; camera (color), Yonezo Maeda; editor, Akira Suzuki, Robert C. Jones (U.S. version); music, Tetsuya Komuro; sound, Tetsuo Segawa; production design, Hiroshi Tokuda; costume design, Yoko Tashiro; associate producer, Hisao Maru; line producer, Yutaka Shimomura; assistant director, Mitsuyuki Yakushiji; production supervisor (Canada), Douglas MacLeod; production manager (Canada), Tom Dent-Cox; assistant director (Canada), Bill Bannerman; stunt supervisor (Canada), John Scott; fight coordinator (Canada), Jean Pierre Fournier. Reviewed at Montreal World Film Festival (noncompeting), Sept. 3, 1990. Running time: **106 MIN.; 119 MIN.** (Japanese version).

Kagetora	Takaaki Enoki
Takeda	Masahiko Tsugawa
Usami	Tsunehiko Watase
Nami	Atsuko Asano
Yae	Naomi Zaizen
Kakizaki	Binpachi Ito
Kansuke	Isao Natsuyagi
Naoe	Akira Hamada
Okuma	Masataka Naruse
Irobe	Osamu Yayama
Murakami	Takeshi Obayashi
Narrator	Stuart Whitman

At a reputed $33 million, "Heaven And Earth" ranks as one of Japan's most expensive epics, and initial b.o. this summer suggests the gamble of exec producer/director Haruki Kadokawa has paid off. However, sketchy plotting and oppressive English narration dilute the impact of the spacious battle scenes in the international version reviewed here.

The story itself is a simple one. In the 16th century, when rival warloads fought battles all over the country, the young Shinto nobleman Kagetora finds himself opposed to the ruthless Takeda for control of a united Japan.

In this version of the film (about 13 minutes shorter than the Japanese release version), plotting and characterization are pared to the bone. As much running time as possible is given over to the lavishly staged battle scenes shot on location in Alberta, Canada, where the required number of horses and vast, unspoiled landscapes were available.

The battle scenes, shot by a crew of 400 with more than 2,800 extras, are undeniably well-staged. Vast numbers of fighting men, many of them on horseback, with brilliantly colored costumes and banners charge and counter-charge with spectacular precision. Scenes of hand-to-hand combat are often thrilling, and there is fine stuntwork from horses and riders alike.

But almost nonstop battle sequences get tedious after a while, and there's very little else to be found in this version of the film. Most of the plot is contained in a narration spoken in husky, avuncular tones by Stuart Whitman. The narration appears to fill in the gaps left by the cutting, and also to repeat and re-emphasize events already depicted on the screen. Many audiences will find this voiceover maddeningly intrusive. The production company should revise it, and, in versions of the film shown in other countries, such as Britain, provide a more neutral voice.

There was potential drama to be had from the relationship between the hero, Kagetora, and his friend and adviser, Usami. Kagetori falls in love with Usami's daughter, Nami, but later, for reasons unclear, Usami betrays a friend, who is forced to kill him in a hand-to-hand struggle on the battlefield. This should have come as a tragic moment, but goes for little. The love story peters out before it's even begun.

Nor is there much impact when Takeda's warrior mistress, Yae, is shot by Kagetora. She has had almost no screen time to establish herself as a character. The result of this lack of plot is that the battles are everything, and that may not be enough for international audiences.

Production of "Heaven And Earth" was severely disrupted when the actor originally cast as Kagetora, Ken Watanabe, was taken ill on the Canadian location and had to be replaced by Takaaki Enoki. This is said to have added about $2 million to the pic's cost.

The actors have almost no chance to make an impression here; what counts is the spectacle and stuntwork. These are top quality, but without more substantial drama, "Heaven And Earth" is far less dramatically satisfying than were such Akira Kurosawa samurai epics as "Kagemusha" or "Ran." — *Strat.*

PRIMO BABY
(CANADIAN)

A Victory Film production. Produced by Nives Lever, Eric James. Directed by Eda Lever Lishman. Screenplay, A.A. Lever; camera (color), David Herrington; editor, Rick Benwick; music, Amin Bhatia, Luciano Giachetta; sound, George Tarrant; set design, Rick Roberts. Reviewed at Montreal World Film Festival, Aug. 26, 1990. Running time: **110 MIN.**
With: Duncan Regehr, Janet-Laine Green, Esther Purves-Smith, Tim Battle, Jackson Cole.

In the longest 110 minutes in the history of Canadian cinema, a teenage foster child is adopted by a rich rancher and turns a glue horse into a champion racer. There is never a doubt from frame one that Primo Baby will end up being a winner. The rest of the pic is a test of endurance. The acting is bad. The script is transparent and painfully earnest.

Fifteen-year-old Paschal is a streetwise kid whose father is in jail. She's taken into the Armstrong family to essentially babysit a teenage boy, Clancy, who is in a wheelchair due to a car accident in which his mother was killed. Clancy's dad, Charles, blames the boy for the death of the mother. Primo Baby is going blind despite meticulous breeding planned by Clancy and his computer. Trainer, a perfect blond woman who is the ranch trainer, rounds out the "family."

There is zip happening between Trainer and Charles although they live on the same ranch and are both single. The kids fight and finally make up when Primo Baby wins a race. The evil neighbors, also horse racers, get their just desserts. All ends happily ever after.

There is no tension, action or twist in the plot. This is about as bad as an earnest Canadian can get. — *Suze.*

UNE HISTOIRE INVENTEE
(AN IMAGINARY TALE)
(CANADIAN)

An Astral Films (Canada) release of a Groupe Film Téléscene/Les Prods. C.M. Luca production, in collaboration with the National Film Board of Canada, Téléfilm Canada, La Société Générale des Industries Culturelles-Quebec, Super Ecran and Radio-Québec. (World sales: Film Transit, Montreal.) Executive producers, Jamie Brown, Claudio Luca. Produced by Robin Spry, Luca. Directed by André Forcier. Screenplay, Forcier, Jacques Marcotte; camera (color), Georges Dufaux; editor, Francois Gill; music, Serge Fiori; sound, Marcel Pothier; production design, Réal Oulette; line producer, Lise Abastado; production manager, Jean-Marie Comeau; assistant director, Anne Murphy. Reviewed at Montreal World Film Festival (competing), Aug. 28, 1990. Running time: **91 MIN.**

Gaston Turcotte	Jean Lapointe
Florence	Louise Marleau
Soledad	Charlotte Laurier
Richard Lentaignes	Marc Messier
Tibo	Jean-François Pichette
Alys	France Castel
Toni	Tony Nardi
Gros Pierre	Marc Gelinas
Alfredo	Louis De Santis
Slim	Warren (Slim) Williams
Rolland	Donald Pilon
Nicole	Leo Munger
Arlette	Louise Gagnon
Theodule	Angelo Cadet

Quebec director André Forcier generally makes raucous comedies that involve groups of exuberantly off-the-wall Montrealers, and "An Imaginary Tale" is his most successful effort to date.

Pic looms as a hit in French Canada, and could be picked up for selected international arthouses, perhaps after successful fest outings, where the crazy characters and colorful milieu should make a pleasant change from more somber offerings.

There's nothing realistic about Forcier's picture, yet the characters all have a basis in reality, which makes them all the more appealing. Focus of attention is on Gaston, known around the area as the "Don Juan of the trumpet." Played somewhat in the style of the older Jean Gabin by Jean Lapointe, Gaston is a world-weary figure who returns with the two other members of his trio to Montreal and the Black Butter club after some unsuccessful gigs in Cleveland.

This is good news for Florence Desruisseaux (Louise Marleau), a youthful-looking middle-aged woman who has always loved Gaston. But he's the only man who rejected her favors.

Florence is followed everywhere by a clutch of adoring males of all ages and backgrounds, and seems to love the presence of her fans.

Florence has a daughter, Soledad (Charlotte Laurier), an actress appearing in a slapdash stage production of "Othello" produced by Toni (Tony Nardi), a flamboyant director whose Mafia-connected uncle is paying for a rundown theater to be used for the play. Soledad is Desdemona, and her lover, Tibo, is playing Othello.

On opening night she catches Tibo and the play's dresser having a quickie before curtain. She takes her revenge on Tibo by making a play for Gaston, who falls for the beautiful young girl, but Florence is naturally put off that the man of her dreams prefers her daughter.

This is just the bare bones of a plot filled with incidents and characters, including a permanently drunken cop, his homely girlfriend, a black cab driver who's another of Florence's loyal fans and a gay critic who nonetheless falls for Florence's charms. There's also an unrequited affair between the other members of Gaston's trio — Alys (who's eager) and the religious Slim (who isn't).

Some of the jokes cheerfully lampoon racist attitudes in Montreal, with sniping at special treatment for ethnics. Some might take offense at these barbs. The film reaches its absurd apogee when Gaston, handcuffed to Soledad, is forced to go on stage for her death scene — and is a hit with the jaded audience, all of whom have been paid by the director's uncle to watch the show night after night.

In the last reel, Forcier attempts to nudge the film to a tragicomedy conclusion, involving an on-stage murder-suicide, but the smiles come out again for the film's final scene, a raucous funeral.

"An Imaginary Tale" seems in tune with a Quebec audience, and the hard-to-answer question now is, Will the film travel? If it does, global audiences are in for some fun. Pic is technically tops and boasts a sharp music score that is in itself a major asset. Actors give enjoyable performances. — *Strat.*

WUMUK BAEMEE UI SARANG
(THE LOVERS OF WUMUK BAEMEE)
(S. KOREAN)

A Morgard Korea production. Produced by Suh Byung-ki. Directed by Chang Sun-woo. Screenplay, Sun-woo, Im Jong-jae, from a story by Park Young-hen; camera (color), Yoo Young-gil; editor, Kim Hyon; music, Lee Jong-gu; sound, Kim Kyung-il; production design, Cho Yung-sam. Reviewed at Montreal World Film Festival (noncompeting), Aug. 28, 1990. Running time: **116 MIN.**
With: Park Jong-hoon, Choi Myong-gil, Yoo Hen-ri, Lee Dae-kun.

This turgid tale of an adulterous love affair is unlikely to travel outside Asian markets. By Western standards, the characters are too unappealing to be of interest, and the direction is merely adequate.

Set in the suburbs, pic tells of Pae Il-do, married with a baby, who treats his wife shamefully. He starts an affair with Kong-reh, a married woman, but the intrigue is eventually discovered.

He's disgraced in front of his family, and Kong-reh is forced to leave the area, leaving her sympathetic husband and child behind.

Pae's behavior is outrageously chauvinistic and unfeeling, and yet the film seems to identify with his position (he's described as "naive" in the pressbook).

The film has the feeling of an average commercial production, and certainly lacks the poetry and style of the best films from South Korea shown from time to time at international festivals.

The English subtitles on the print unspooled at Montreal were written by someone with a minimal knowlege of the English language. — *Strat.*

VENICE FEST
GOODFELLAS

A Warner Bros. release of an Irwin Winkler production. Produced by Winkler. Executive producer, Barbara De Fina. Directed by Martin Scorsese. Screenplay, Nicholas Pileggi, Scorsese, based on Pileggi's book "Wiseguy"; camera (Technicolor), Michael Ballhaus; editor, Thelma Schoonmaker; sound (Dolby), James Sabat, Tom Fleischman; production design, Kristi Zea; art direction, Maher Ahmad; set decoration, Les Bloom; costume design, Richard Bruno; stunt coordinator, Michael Russo; assistant director-2d unit director, Joseph Reidy; associate producer, Bruce Pustin; casting, Ellen Lewis. Reviewed at Raleigh Studios, Los Angeles, Aug. 30, 1990. (In Venice Film Festival, competing.) MPAA Rating: R. Running time: **146 MIN.**
James Conway . . . . . Robert De Niro
Henry Hill . . . . Ray Liotta
Tommy DeVito . . . . Joe Pesci
Karen Hill . . . . Lorraine Bracco
Paul Cicero . . . . Paul Sorvino
Frankie Carbone . . . . . Frank Sivero
Sonny Bunz . . . . Tony Darrow
Frenchy . . . . Mike Starr
Billy Batts . . . . Frank Vincent
Morris Kessler . . . . Chuck Low
Tuddy Cicero . . . . Frank DiLeo
Young Henry . . Christopher Serrone
   Also with: Henny Youngman, Jerry Vale.

Simultaneously fascinating and repellent, "Goodfellas" is Martin Scorsese's colorful but dramatically unsatisfying inside look at Mafia life in 1955-80 New York City. Commercial prospects for the overlong release appear relatively modest, and noisy bloodletting is likely to take place between warring critical camps.

Scorsese's intent here, to show how a life of brutal crime could look compelling to an Irish-Italian kid whose sordid upbringing hasn't prepared him for anything better, is undercut by the offputting, opaque characterization of Ray Liotta. Sympathy is not the issue here; empathy is.

First half of the film, introing Liotta and viewer to the Mafia milieu, is wonderful. Scorsese's perfectly cast friezes of grotesque hoodlum types are caricatures in the best sense of the word. There's a giddy sense of exploring a forbidden world with conventional blinders removed.

The second half, however, doesn't develop the dramatic conflicts between the character and the milieu that are hinted at earlier. The effect is simply to keep piling on and intensifying Liotta's horrific and ultimately numbing descent into depravity.

Working from the nonfiction book "Wiseguy" by Nicholas Pileggi, who collaborated with him on the screenplay, Scorsese returns to the subject matter of his 1973 "Mean Streets" but from a more distanced, older, wiser and subtler perspective.

Liotta starts as a gofer for laconic neighborhood godfather Paul Sorvino, gradually coming under the tutelage of Robert De Niro, cast as a middle-aged Irish hood of considerable ruthlessness and repute.

The often misplaced dramatic thread is the question of whether Liotta will adhere to his mentor's early lesson of never ratting on his fellow mobsters.

The character's split ethnic identity never comes clearly into focus, whether as a tragic figure like Al Pacino in "The Godfather" or as an unabashed psychopath like the title characters in "The Krays," recent Brit pic.

"Being somebody in a neighborhood of nobodies" in "Goodfellas" means going along with whatever brutalities are required. This is made clear right from the credit sequence, in which Liotta queasily watches De Niro and Joe Pesci perform a coldblooded execution. Scorsese never spares the viewer the heinousness of the murders regularly punctuating the story.

The skewed concept of loyalty involved is intertwined with an adolescent obsession with machismo, most memorably captured in Pesci's short-statured, short-fused psycho.

Liotta develops a flashy, pretty-boy persona that overcomes the inadequately dramatized misgivings of Lorraine Bracco, who plays a Jewish girl drawn into the life of a Mafia wife. "I gotta admit the truth — it turned me on," she tells the audience after Liotta viciously beats up someone who made a pass at her.

"Goodfellas" seems to be building up to a change of heart by Liotta about what he's becoming, and to a violent break with Bracco. But both options are bypassed as the pic shows Liotta emerging from jail in 1974 to become a cocaine dealer with Bracco's enthusiastic help and against the orders of the old-fashioned Sorvino.

Sorvino's scruples recall those of Marlon Brando in "The Godfather," but since "Goodfellas" doesn't share the "Godfather" films' examination of the Mafia's evolution in reaction to social injustice, the conflict has no weight and Scorsese misguidedly abandons his focus on the mob community to tell the unrewarding story of a lone wolf.

The film's style in the second half turns into a frenetic, feverish mimicry of the wasted-looking Liotta's coked-up mental state. De Niro, who's in the process of sealing his own destruction by eliminating fellow participants in a big heist, goes along with the new economics of crime, and Liotta winds up having to choose in a pinch between freedom and loyalty.

One of the film's major flaws is that De Niro, with his menacing charm, always seems more interesting than Liotta, but he isn't given enough screen time to explore the relationship fully in his top-billed supporting role.

All tech contributions are first-rate, particularly the lensing by Michael Ballhaus and production design by Kristi Zea, who manage to make the film look bright and alluring while still capturing the slimy bad taste of the milieu.

Thelma Schoonmaker's always masterful editing is taut in the first half, but the film rambles seriously after that, wearing out its interest at least half an hour before it's over. — *Mac.*

MR. & MRS. BRIDGE

A Miramax Films release of a Cineplex Odeon presentation (in association with Miramax) of a Merchant Ivory/Robert Halmi production. (Intl. sales, Cineplex Odeon Films Intl.) Executive producer, Robert Halmi. Produced by Ismail Merchant. Directed by James Ivory. Screenplay, Ruth Prawer Jhabvala, based on Evan S. Connell's novels "Mrs. Bridge" and "Mr. Bridge"; camera (Technicolor), Tony Pierce-Roberts; editor, Humphrey Dixon; music, Richard Robbins; sound (Dolby), Ed Novick; production design, David Gropman; costume design, Carol Ramsey;

assistant director, David Sardi; additional camera (Canada), Larry Pizer; associate producer, Mary Kane, Humbert Balsan (France); casting, Joanna Merlin. Reviewed at Tribeca Film Center, N.Y., Aug. 29, 1990. (In Venice Film Festival, competing.) No MPAA Rating. Running time: **124 MIN.**

Walter Bridge	Paul Newman
India Bridge	Joanne Woodward
Douglas Bridge	Robert Sean Leonard
Carolyn Bridge	Margaret Welsh
Ruth Bridge	Kyra Sedgwick
Grace	Blythe Danner
Dr. Sauer	Simon Callow
Dr. Forster	Malachy McCourt
Mr. Gadbury	Austin Pendleton
Julia	Diane Kagan
Harriet	Saundra McClain
Mabel Ong	Gale Garnett
Gil Davis	Marcus Giamatti
Virgil Barron	Remak Ramsey

Paul Newman & Joanne Woodward plus the Merchant Ivory Prods. team are in top form for "Mr. & Mrs. Bridge," an affecting study of an upper-crust Midwestern family 50 years ago. Obvious contender for Venice Film Fest prizes shapes up as a potent arthouse entry this winter.

Merchant Ivory collaborator Ruth Prawer Jhabvala has adapted two Evan S. Connell novels into a taut script. Books "Mrs. Bridge" (1959) and "Mr. Bridge" (1969) painted (from each spouse's point of view) a portrait of stuffy Kansas City lawyer Walter Bridge and his stifled wife, India, by a steady accretion of anecdotal detail.

The screenplay presents a series of highly dramatic scenes in their lives, the payoffs among the novels' hundreds of brief chapters. Vignette structure is retained, but pic's two hours breeze by thanks to director James Ivory's concise approach and crisp editing (including careful wipes) by Humphrey Dixon.

Central theme of India Bridge's gradual realization that her life has been crushed in her husband's shadow is strongly conveyed by Woodward in the role.

Physically resembling the late Geraldine Page, she should be in the Oscar running this year for a nuanced, often funny portrayal of a multidimensional woman whose options have gradually been snuffed out.

Casting of hubby Newman as her husband resonates in their intimate scenes, particularly a 1939 vacation to Paris when the Bridges briefly rekindle their romance, only to have it cut short by the onset of World War II.

Newman's controlled performance as the iron-willed conservative is both a career change of

pace and highlight.

While India becomes increastrated with being a housewife and country club member, and a change is in the wind: Best friend Grace (Blythe Danner perky in film's showiest role) is a kook and free spirit. Their mutual pal Grace Ong (singer Gale Garnett in an arresting brief turn) boasts of the values of psychoanalysis. All three Bridge offspring are in open rebellion against their parents and conservative society.

Kyra Sedgwick, recently Tom Cruise's g.f. in "Born On The Fourth Of July," is smashing as the Bridges' bohemian daughter who takes off for New York and an arts career. Feisty Margaret Welsh has a showstopping scene telling her mom off after her defiant marriage to a boy from across the tracks ends up on the rocks. Robert Sean Leonard as duo's son is solid in key emotional scenes with Woodward and Newman.

Pic's climax retains the shattering finale of "Mrs. Bridge," but presents it in a different context. Careful selection of supporting players pays off: Stage thesp Diane Kagan is a powerhouse as Newman's secretary, expressing her pain at having been equally neglected by him over 20 years. Saundra McClain is a tower of strength as the family's maid, and Austin Pendleton and Simon Callow provide comic relief.

Producer Ismail Merchant has arranged for impressive period detail including setpieces such as a tornado while Newman calmly dines with his wife at the country club and an evocative trip to Paris. Tech credits by MIP regulars are of a high standard, notably Tony Pierce-Roberts' sharp focus photography and Richard Robbins' spare, threatening musical score.

An amusing end credit reads: "Shakespearean tutor to Mr. Newman: Sen. Bob Dole," referring to the Kansas politician's reading of "Romeo And Juliet" to help the star develop his flinty characterization. — *Lor.*

LA LUNA EN EL ESPEJO
(THE MOON IN THE MIRROR)
(CHILEAN)

Produced and directed by Silvio Caiozzi. Executive producer, Andrés Silva. Screenplay, José Donoso, Caiozzi, based on an idea by Donoso; camera,

Nelson Fuentes; editor, Alvaro Ramirez, Caiozzi; production design, Laura Gubelic, Guadalupe Bornand. Reviewed at Cine Ducal, Santiago, Aug. 10, 1990. (In Venice Film Festival, competing.) Running time: **75 MIN.**

Lucrecia	Gloria Munchmeyer
Don Arnaldo	Rafael Benavente
Gordo	Ernesto Beadle
Neighbor	María Castiglione
Gordo's voice	Roberto Poblete
Neighbor's voice	Loreto Valenzuela

Also with: Mónica Echeverría.

"The Moon In The Mirror's" downbeat feel and slowish pace make for so-so local boxoffice, but it's a natural for international fests.

Pic was shot in 1985, intended as part of a trilogy based on stories by Latin American writers. The plan fell through, so director Silvio Caiozzi decided to go it alone. And now "La Luna en el Espejo" is the first Chilean film to compete in Venice.

W.k. novelist José Donoso provided the idea for the film and wrote the screenplay with the director.

The housebound Don Arnaldo (Rafael Benavente) is a retired navy man whose meager pension does not allow him to rent a house with a view of the sea, which he loves. He lives in the hills surrounding Valparaiso with his adult son, Gordo, who is at his father's beck and call.

An attractive older widow next door could brighten the son's future, but not under the eyes of the old man, who uses mirrors to keep a stern watch on goings-on in the house. A walk by the sea may symbolize hope, but these three characters are trapped in a world from which there is no escape.

Caiozzi, a solid craftsman, creates a typical Donoso atmosphere of slow decay that is contrasted with views of the beautiful outside world.

Despite its tight 75 minutes, is sometimes seems as if the short story were being drawn out into a novel. But the acting is good, and it is unlikely that anyone would guess that Ernesto Beadle (Gordo) never had acted before. — *Amig.*

THE COMPANY OF STRANGERS
(CANADIAN)

A National Film Board of Canada production. Executive producers, Colin Neale, Rina Fraticelli, Peter Katadotis. Produced by David Wilson. Directed by Cynthia Scott. Written by Gloria De-

mers with Scott, David Wilson, Sally Bochner; camera (color), David de Volpi; editor, David Wilson; music, Marie Bernard; sound, Jacques Drouin. Reviewed at the National Film Board of Canada Studio 3, May 16, 1990. (In Venice Film Festival, noncompeting.) Running time: **100 MIN.**

With: Alice Diabo, Constance Garneau, Winifred Holden, Cissy Meddings, Mary Meigs, Catherine Roche, Michelle Sweeney, Beth Webber.

A feminist cross between "On Golden Pond" and "Gilligan's Island," Oscar-winning helmer Cynthia Scott's debut feature is original, quirky and touching. Pic is a senior citizen's delight with little boxoffice appeal beyond the golden agers' group. Tv is the perfect venue for this alternative drama.

The seventh in the NFB series where non-actors play themselves in a fictitious setting, "The Company Of Strangers" features seven elderly women marooned in an abandoned country house near an idyllic lake after their bus breaks down. A safe quiet journey becomes an adventure in survival, and in their quest for food they rediscover the hunger of youth.

These seven perfect strangers and their younger bus driver (a lively Montreal jazz singer, Michelle Sweeney) become fast friends through lengthy conversations, many of which shot in real time.

Pacing is slow and Hollywood-style action nonexistent. Entire story revolves around the women's lives, secrets, fears and joys.

The Mohawk woman (Alice Diabo) teaches them about fishing with pantyhose. A nun (Catherine Roche) in jeans manages to catch a pail full of frogs for dinner and is the self-appointed saviour who walks 20 miles for help.

Mary Meigs is an artist and lesbian who publishes books. Winnie Holden does great bird imitations. Constance Garneau seems to regret most of her 88 years. Beth Webber is an 80-year-old woman who looks 50 and never stops worrying about looking old. Cissy Medding steals the show with her sense of humor and indifference to life's perils.

Much of the film sounds like grandmothers talking about bygone eras, faded dreams and the inconvenience of growing old when still feeling young.

Stylistically, pic breaks every

rule in the book, but the honesty and vulnerability of the characters make it work on its own terms. It's great family viewing for the tube. — *Suze.*

POSTCARDS FROM THE EDGE

A Columbia Pictures release. Produced by Mike Nichols, John Calley. Executive producers, Neil Machlis, Robert Greenhut. Directed by Nichols. Screenplay, Carrie Fisher, based on her novel; camera (Technicolor), Michael Ballhaus; editor, Sam O'Steen; music, Carly Simon; musical numbers supervisor, Howard Shore; sound (Dolby), Gene S. Cantamessa, Lee Dichter; production design, Patrizia Von Brandenstein; art direction, Kandy Stern; set decoration, Chris A. Butler; costume design, Ann Roth; associate producer, Sue MacNair; assistant director, Michael Haley; casting, Juliet Taylor, Ellen Lewis. Reviewed at Cineplex Odeon Century Plaza Cinemas, Los Angeles, Sept. 5, 1990. MPAA Rating: R. Running time: **101 MIN.**

Suzanne Vale	Meryl Streep
Doris Mann	Shirley MacLaine
Jack Falkner	Dennis Quaid
Lowell	Gene Hackman
Dr. Frankenthal	Richard Dreyfuss
Joe Pierce	Rob Reiner
Grandma	Mary Wickes
Grandpa	Conrad Bain
Evelyn Ames	Annette Bening
Simon Asquith	Simon Callow
Marty Wiener	Gary Morton
Wardrobe mistress	Dana Ivey

Mike Nichols' film of Carrie Fisher's novel "Postcards From The Edge" packs a fair amount of emotional wallop in its dark-hued comic take on a chemically dependent Hollywood mother and daughter (Shirley MacLaine and Meryl Streep). Pic looks like a hot b.o. performer.

Cautionary tale of a "spoiled, selfish, coked-up little actress" trying to find meaning in her robotic existence by rekindling her relationship with her overbearing actress mother is one Fisher tells with ample inside knowledge, though for the most part too shallowly and glibly.

Streep's tour through Hollywood hell is signposted with many recognizable, on-target types: predatory macho creep (Randy Quaid), sleazy business manager (Gary Morton), oafish producer (Rob Reiner), airheaded and roundheeled actress (Annette Bening) and sternly paternalistic director (Gene Hackman).

Fisher's screen dialog and situations suggest the daydreams of a smart-alecky Hollywood kid doing a bitchy camp on old pics about the industry with a drug

era update. Still, her two central characters are endearingly vulnerable, and the plot is as compelling to watch as a car crash.

Refreshingly guileless in a role requiring casual clothing and no accent, Streep plays an overgrown child who's spent her life in her mother's shadow and has resorted to drugs to blunt her pain and boredom.

"Postcards" frequently echoes archetypal Hollywood tragedy "A Star Is Born," but it stays on the edge and never quite descends into the abyss, going instead for brittle humor about brittle people.

Fisher deftly mocks the pomposities of a detox center and the smarmy hypocrisies of the Hollywood establishment toward drugs. But in dealing with the mother-daughter relationship the writer tends to crack wise rather than be wise.

While having fun with the MacLaine character and her flamboyant evocation of the old studio system's absurd aspects, film takes quite a while to get beyond her familiar scatterbrained mannerisms and get down to the dramatic nitty-gritty.

(Nichols insists, for the record, that the character isn't based on Fisher's mom, Debbie Reynolds, even though MacLaine's wickedly salacious memories of life at Louis B. Mayer's MGM might suggest otherwise.)

While casting of MacLaine in the role of an arch, ditzy, impossible stage mother is somewhat predictable, the actress gradually makes it her own until, stripped of her glamour in the climactic scene, she abandons the rampant egotism of the character to reveal the frightened creature underneath.

The central comic situation is that after being rescued from a near-fatal overdose by kindly doctor Richard Dreyfuss (an injoke, given his own publicized drug problems some years back), Streep is ordered by the insurers of her next film to live with a responsible party during shooting. That means moving back in with mother, who, as an unemployed boozehound, hardly fits the bill.

MacLaine sees no symmetry between her surreptitious drinking and her daughter's drugtaking. Newly sober Streep's attempts to force her mother to face her own failings are funny and touching, even if they don't blow the audience's socks off.

MacLaine's jealousy forbids her to pull for her daughter's success. Then a drunken car accident puts MacLaine in hospital and exposes her pretense of sobriety and superiority.

The hospital reunion scene between mother and daughter lifts the film to unexpected heights. MacLaine allows herself to be filmed without wig, makeup or eyebrows. She looks much older and more frail than the audience has ever seen her, until Streep tenderly reapplies her public face.

MacLaine's desolation captures the emptiness with which the film biz leaves many people, even the most successful, as they age. Her physical and emotional nakedness finally allows her to make that long-severed connection with daughter.

The Burbank-Malibu-Holmby Hills atmosphere is attractively and knowingly captured by lenser Michael Ballhaus and production designer Patrizia Von Brandenstein. Editor Sam O'Steen helps the actors by letting many two-shots play uncut at considerable length, and Carly Simon contributed an unobtrusively moving score.

Nichols uses an old but effective device to stop the audience exodus from the theater before the end credits stop rolling. He lets the finale, Streep's rousing film-within-a-film C&W number, continue underneath. — *Mac.*

MEMPHIS BELLE
(BRITISH)

A Warner Bros. release of an Enigma production. Produced by David Puttnam, Catherine Wyler. Directed by Michael Caton-Jones. Screenplay, Monte Merrick; camera, David Watkin; editor, Jim Clark; music, George Fenton; production design, Stuart Craig; costume design, Jane Robinson; associate producer, Eric Rattray; special effects supervisor/model unit director, Richard Conway; casting, Marion Dougherty, Juliet Taylor. Reviewed at Warner West End, London, July 15, 1990. Running time: **106 MIN.**

Dennis	Matthew Modine
Danny	Eric Stoltz
Luke	Tate Donovan
Phil	D.B. Sweeney
Val	Billy Zane
Rascal	Sean Astin
Clay	Harry Connick Jr.
Virge	Reed Diamond
Eugene	Courtney Gains
Jack	Neil Giuntoli
Commanding officer	David Strathairn
Col. Bruce Derringer	John Lithgow

Offering a romanticized view of heroism drawn from the Hollywood war epic, "Memphis Belle" is unashamedly com-

mercial. Its moral fabric is thinner than that of other David Puttnam productions, but it's still likely to be a classy draw this fall.

As with Puttnam's "Chariots Of Fire," "The Killing Fields" and "The Mission," there is a grandness about "Memphis Belle." The sweeping landscapes are stunningly photographed, and the score is emphatically emotional.

Director Michael Caton-Jones, following his theatrical debut on "Scandal," choreographed a cast of 10 distinctive young men and a host of original World War II fighter planes. He handles with equal flair the emotional exchanges on the ground and action sequences in the air.

Pic's subject is the 25th and final mission of the Memphis Belle, the most celebrated of the U.S. Air Force B-17 bombers. The plane flew 24 perfect missions, and its 25th became part of a massive p.r. drive to boost warbond sales and morale.

The plane and its team are sent to Germany to drop one last load, setting the scene for suspense, tension, terror and a fitting celebration when all return safe and (almost) sound.

Large chunk of the film is set on the ground, providing adequate exposition of events and character to involve the audience in the mission. Played up is the fact that these 10 guys are barely out of their teens and don't see themselves as heroes. They're just doing their job for Uncle Sam (a cliché actually used by Dennis, Matthew Modine's character, at the end).

It's easy to be cynical about the subject matter, especially considering the post-Vietnam view of war. But war is not the central issue in this film; it's friendship, idealism and good old-fashioned bravado.

Performances are all keen. Dennis is the quiet, understated leader. The romantic Danny is played expressively by Eric Stoltz. Billy Zane's suave Val, medico for the troupe, reveals himself as a fake when Danny's life is in danger. Tate Donovan's ambitious copilot, Luke, unwittingly causes the death of the crew in a companion plane, a breathtaking and horrific scene.

By the end of the mission the audience should feel as relieved as the Memphis Belle's mascot dog, which lies in wait by the airstrip as the other planes return. The dog may seem like over-the-top schmaltz, but it really existed.

Original footage from the 1944 documentary "Memphis Belle" by William Wyler, father of co-producer Catherine Wyler, is used for the guaranteed tear-jerking scene, with letters from parents of dead soldiers read over it by the commanding officer, thoughtfully played by David Strathairn.

Action scene camerawork is superb, and Caton-Jones' depiction of the claustrophobic conditions inside the plane is vivid. Use of five original B-17s, three ME-109s and eight Mustangs adds to the feel of authenticity. On a 70m screen, the flying sequences are outstanding.

"Memphis Belle" makes for a thoroughly entertaining night at the cinema, which is all Puttnam and Caton-Jones say they set out to achieve. — *Krug.*

MINDWALK

A Mindwalk Prods. and Atlas Co. presentation. Produced by Adrianna A.J. Cohen. Executive producer, Klaus Lintschinger. Directed by Bernt Capra. Screenplay, Floyd Byars, Fritjof Capra from a story by Bernt Capra based on the "The Turning Point" by Fritjof Capra; camera, Karl Kases; editor, Jean Claude Piroue; music, Philip Glass; sound, Rainer Wiehr; costume design, Bambi Breakstone; associate producer, Robin Holding; casting, Rick Montgomery, Dan Parada. Reviewed at Samuel Goldwyn Pavilion Cinemas, Los Angeles, June 26, 1990. No MPAA Rating. Running time: **112 MIN.**

Sonia	Liv Ullmann
Jack	Sam Waterston
Thomas	John Heard
Kit	Ione Skye
Romain	Emmanuel Montes

Characters in this extraordinary piece of renegade filmmaking declare the world to be sorely lacking in vision and perspective, commodities "Mindwalk" is out to provide. Given careful handling in the vein of "My Dinner With Andre," pic could gain a following in exclusive urban settings, with further potential in public tv and video.

This keenly timed conversation/story offers an approach for healing the planet via an "ecological" view based on modern science and the theory of living systems. Filmed on the medieval French island of Mont St. Michel, "Mindwalk" stars Liv Ullmann, John Heard and Sam Waterston as a physicist, poet and politician who

wrangle over the world's problems as if their lives depended on the outcome.

Essence of the film is that their conversation truly is that important, for it involves forming a new approach to world crises by mending the way the universe is perceived.

As the characters explore the medieval island, their dialog carefully explains the evolution of thought from the mechanistic world view of the Middle Ages to a holistic and ecological view.

Latter idea comes from the teachings of scientist, author and Green Party activist Fritjof Capra, who wrote the book "The Turning Point," on which "Mindwalk" is based.

The book's slant is cunningly explained in the film via physicist Ullmann, who illustrates the startling essential similarities of all matter, from subatomic particles to human beings.

Talk-heavy as the film may be, it actually lays out its themes as gracefully as many a fine dramatic feature, with the progression, surprises and epiphanies coming from the astonishment and revelation within the scientific concepts.

Pic's content definitely flies in the face of what today's audiences are accustomed to, and that will be its biggest hurdle, as many viewers will reject its dialog as too dense and demanding.

But setting the pic in Mont St. Michel, which is flooded daily by the tides, invites a slowed-down state of mind appropriate to absorbing the pic's ideas, and viewers who can stop racing their engines long enough to take it in will find themselves rewarded.

A light dramatic story has been provided by the scripters, involving the personal crises of Waterston, a practical former U.S. presidential candidate struggling to find new inspiration and problem-solving approaches, and Ullman, a scientist who has exiled herself on the island until she can clarify her ideas into a coherent message.

While Ullmann is the surrogate for author Capra, Waterston is the audience surrogate, demanding to know what use her ideas are in the practical world.

Heard, playing a cynical American living in Paris as a poet, injects the wry humor and puckish charm needed to lighten their dilemmas. The three share a rath-

er magical day of discovery and intense conversation during their encounter on the island.

Audiences should approach this film prepared for an intellectual journey, or they may be left quickly behind. Director Bernt Capra, brother of the scientist, finds a lovely, meditative tone that ties the natural features of the island and the weather to the emerging dialog. The production designer of such pics as "Bagdad Cafe" and "This Is Spinal Tap," Capra also wrote the story for the script penned by Floyd Byars and Fritjof Capra.

Ione Skye has a small role as Ullmann's teenage daughter with whom she has a failing relationship. Philip Glass wrote the haunting cello score. — *Daws.*

NARROW MARGIN

A Tri-Star Pictures release of a Carolco Pictures production. Produced by Jonathan A. Zimbert. Executive producers, Mario Kassar, Andrew Vajna. Directed by Peter Hyams. Screenplay, Hyams, inspired by the 1952 screenplay "The Narrow Margin" by Earl Felton from story by Martin Goldsmith, Jack Leonard; camera (Panavision, Technicolor), Hyams; editor, James Mitchell; music, Bruce Broughton; sound (Dolby), Ralph Parker; production design, Joel Schiller; supervising art direction, David Willson; art direction, Kim Mooney, Eric Orbom; set decoration, Kim MacKenzie; assistant director, Jack Frost Sanders; production manager-associate producer, Mary Eilts; stunt coordinator, Glenn Wilder; coproducer, Jerry Offsay; casting, Lynne Carrow. Reviewed at Columbia screening room, N.Y., Aug. 30, 1990. MPAA Rating: R. Running time: **97 MIN.**

Robert Caulfield	Gene Hackman
Carol Hunnicut	Anne Archer
Nelson	James B. Sikking
Michael Tarlow	J.T. Walsh
Sgt. Benti	M. Emmet Walsh
Kathryn Weller	Susan Hogan
Jack Wootton	Nigel Bennett
Martin Larner	J.A. Preston
Leo Watts	Harris Yulin

Spectacular stunt work and Canadian locations punch up the train thriller "Narrow Margin," but feature remake is too cool and remote to grab the viewer. Boxoffice outlook is weak for the technically well-made Carolco picture.

As a sign of Hollywood inflation, Richard Fleischer's trim 1952 classic for RKO had a nega-

Original film

HOLLYWOOD An RKO release of a Stanley Rubin production. Directed by Richard Fleischer. Screenplay, Earl Felton; story, Martin Goldsmith, Jack Leonard; camera (black & white), George E. Diskant; editor, Robert Swink. Previewed March 24, 1952. Running time: **71 MIN.**

Walter Brown	Charles McGraw
Mrs. Neil	Marie Windsor
Ann Sinclair	Jacqueline White
Tommy Sinclair	Gordon Gebert
Mrs. Troll	Queenie Leonard
Kemp	David Clarke
Densel	Peter Virgo
Gus Forbes	Don Beddoe
Jennings	Paul Maxey
Train conductor	Harry Harvey

tive cost of only $230,000, while the remake logged in at $21 million, a nearly 100 times increase. That extra bread shows up on screen in impressive production values but filmmaker Peter Hyams fails to make his story involving.

Basic plotline is retained in the new version. In the Charles McGraw role, Gene Hackman plays a deputy d.a. delivering key witness Anne Archer to testify against gangster Harris Yulin. Rather unconvincing first reel has her unwittingly witness (from the next room) Yulin having his henchmen kill her blind date J.T. Walsh. In the original the situation was more clearcut: It was a gangster's widow en route to testify against the mob.

Hackman's teammate, cop M. Emmet Walsh, is killed leaving Hackman and Archer to escape from a helicopter of armed heavies. They flee to a train headed across remote stretches of Canada and have to play cat and mouse with the thugs (led by evil James B. Sikking) who've boarded the train to eliminate them.

Both versions of the story rely heavily on the plot device of the woman's identity being unknown, and Hyams satisfyingly switches the key twist involving her. With brief, vivid violence punctuating the film, suspense is generated. Yet, it isn't until the final reel that nailbiting is encouraged.

Stunt coordinator Glenn Wilder finally pulls out the stops with stuntmen dangling from the side of the speeding train, photographed in dangerous terrain. The principal actors, including stars Hackman and Archer, also appear in numerous unfaked shots on the train's roof, thereby adding to the fright of the finale.

Hackman adds panache to a one-dimensional role which logically might have gone to Charles Bronson (especially given the physical resemblance to original topliner McGraw). Archer is stuck with a nothing part, proving she's a good trouper in scenes involving physical danger but given barely one monolog to express her character's feelings.

Curiously there is no sex or suggestion of romance in the film. Hackman's character is presented as incorruptible, but his stoicism is overdone.

Virtually the only Hollywood director since Josef von Sternberg who doubles as his own cinematographer, Hyams uses widescreen lensing to offer unusual vistas inside the train, a rare environment for anamorphic photography. For exteriors, the Panavision aerial shots of Canadian forests and lakes during the journey are breathtaking, as is the realism of the stunts. As scripter, Hyams is less successful in whipping up the banter that was *de rigueur* in '40s and '50s films noirs.

In support, Canadian thesp Susan Hogan is very convincing as a lonely but attractive woman who chats up Hackman on the train with surprising results. Cast is thin, however, with a noticeable absence of memorable villains or helpmates to share Hackman's burden. Tech credits are uniformly impressive. — *Lor.*

SOLAR CRISIS
(JAPANESE)

A Shochiku-Fuji release of a Gakken Publishing-NHK Enterprises production. (Intl. sales, Inter-Ocean Films.) Produced by Tsuneyuki Morishima, James Nelson. Executive producers, Takehito Sadamura, Takeshi Kawata. Directed by Richard C. Sarafian. Screenplay, Joe Gannon, Ted Sarafian, based on a novel by Kawata; camera (color), Russ Carpenter; music, Maurice Jarre; production design, George Jenson; art direction, John Bruce; costume design, Robert Turturice; special visual effects, Richard Edlund. Reviewed at the Shochiku Marion Theater, Tokyo, Aug. 11, 1990. MPAA Rating: PG-13. Running time: **118 MIN.**

Steve Kelso . . . . Tim Matheson
Skeet Kelso . . . . . . Charlton Heston
Teague . . . . Peter Boyle
Alex . . . . Annabel Schofield
Ken Minami . . . . . . Tetsuya Bessho
Mike Kelso . . . . Corky Nemec
Travis . . . . Jack Palance
Gurney . . . . Sandy McPeak
Dr. Hass . . . . Paul Koslow
McBride . . . . . Scott Alan Campbell
Lamare . . . . Fritz Turner
T.C. . . . . Silvana Gallardo
Harvard . . . . Dan Shor
Claire Beeson . . . . . . Brenda Bakke
Berg . . . . Dorian Harewood
Meeks . . . . Richard Scott

As the latest example of '90s-style international film finance, "Solar Crisis" is exceptionally interesting. As a movie, it's an unmitigated stiff. B.o. will depend largely on how well this clunky, overproduced sci-fi outing is promoted in each territory.

In Japan, where advance ticket sales are the order of the day, pic's principal backers — publishing company Gakken and NHK Enterprises — have flogged "Crisis" into a moderate hit. In markets where advance sales don't prevail, the pic will be forced to win an audience on its own dubious merit.

Based on a Takeshi Kawata novel, Joe Gannon and Ted Sarafian's not especially coherent script has a crew putting out on a mission to the sun. The year is 2050, and the sun's been threatening to fry the planet. The mission is to correct the hotspot and save Earth.

Within this straightforward premise are subplots involving the son of the spaceship's captain (Corky Nemec is the son; Tim Matheson is the captain) lost in a plane crash in the Nevada desert; an evil conglomerateur (amusingly played by Peter Boyle) intent on cornering the world market in somethingorother by sabotaging the space mission; and the peregrinations of a grizzled eccentric (Jack Palance), who lives in a shack and befriends the missing youth, whose grandfather (Charlton Heston) is a stalwart Navy admiral.

There's more, but it's too silly to go into. As directed by Richard Sarafian in confusingly eclectic style, "Crisis" borrows openly from a range of relatively recent pics, from "Star Wars"-type spaceships to "Mad Max"-type desert inhabitants to a cut-rate "2001: A Space Odyssey" finale.

The background noise generated in production designer George Jenson's elaborately technological sets is overmiked, drowning chunks of the dialog. What does come through convinces that the clutter is just as well.

This is NHK Enterprises' first film production, paid for largely by an industrial group assembled by the profit-making arm of pubcaster NHK and by Gakken.

Although the original story is Japanese in origin and Japanese-American actor Tetsuya Bessho is cast in a prominent role as a spaceship member, the production, shot in English in the U.S. and played off here with Japanese subtitles, has the feel of those geographically amorphous pan-European outings that Lew Grade came up with in the 1970s. — *Sege.*

TORONTO FEST

REVERSAL OF FORTUNE

A Warner Bros. release of an Edward R. Pressman production in association with Shochiku Fuji and Sovereign Pictures. Produced by Pressman and Oliver Stone. Executive producer, Michael Rauch. Directed by Barbet Schroeder. Screenplay, Nicholas Kazan, based on the book by Alan Dershowitz; camera (color), Luciano Tovoli; editor, Lee Percy; music, Mark Isham; production design, Mel Bourne; costume design, Judianna Makovsky, Milena Canonero; coproducers, Elon Dershowitz, Kazan. Reviewed at the Toronto Festival of Festivals, Sept. 12, 1990. MPAA Rating: R. Running time: **120 MIN.**

Sunny von Bulow . . . . . Glenn Close
Claus von Bulow . . . . . Jeremy Irons
Alan Dershowitz . . . . . . Ron Silver
Carol . . . . Anabella Sciorra
Maria . . . . Uta Hagen
David Marriott . . . . . Fisher Stevens
Andrea Reynolds . Christine Baranski
Also with: Mano Singh, Felicity Huffman, Alan Pottinger, Julie Haggerty, Sarah Fearon, Jad Mager.

Reversal Of Fortune" turns the sensational Claus von Bulow case into a riveting film with outstanding potential for worldwide boxoffice. The story of the Newport society figure's trial, conviction and acquittal on appeal for the attempted murder of his wealthy wife is presented here in an absorbing, complex mosaic.

Jeremy Irons gives a memorable performance as the inscrutable European blueblood emigré Claus von Bulow. Cast in perfect apposition is Ron Silver, seizing with dynamic gusto the role of a career as von Bulow's passionately idealistic but streetwise defense attorney, Harvard law professor Alan M. Dershowitz.

Glenn Close is typically excellent in the smaller but pivotal role of Sunny von Bulow, who narrates the story and appears in flashbacks.

On one level, "Reversal Of Fortune" deals with the impossibility of knowing the truth about the unknowable. Was von Bulow guilty of injecting his wife with a near-fatal dose of insulin? Was he framed by Sunny's maid (Uta Hagen) or family? Or did the profoundly unhappy woman attempt suicide?

The filmmakers' decision to address these questions through a time-shifting narrative with multiple points-of-view enhances their tantalizing ambiguity.

On other levels, "Reversal Of Fortune" is a finely detailed manners study of the superwealthy, a drama of conflicting principles and values and an engrossing legal detective story.

In 1980, von Bulow is found guilty of attempted murder and sentenced to a long prison term. Physical evidence of an insulin-encrusted hypodermic needle and circumstantial evidence of a murky past, marital infidelity and a huge prospective inheritance from his wife are good enough for the Rhode Island court — and the court of public opinion, which widely despises him. But the frosty von Bulow steadfastly maintains his innocence, and at the urging of his latest upper-crust girlfriend hires the brilliant and renowned "Jewish lawyer" Dershowitz.

Dershowitz, a Brooklyn boy made good in big-time academic law, agrees to take von Bulow's appeal for the money and because of a hunch that the haughty millionaire, guilty or not, might have been railroaded.

He assembles a team of the best and brightest students and young attorneys, including his reluctant former flame (Anabella Sciorra), to search for a salient appealable issue by dissecting the prosecution's case.

Not convinced of his client's innocence, Dershowitz initially resists von Bulow's desire to tell his side of the story. But as procedural flaws and evidentiary inconsistencies in the trial are gradually unearthed, the lawyer solicits his client's testimony.

Von Bulow dispassionately recounts a marriage in which passion had long since evaporated into convenience, a relationship codified by the rarefied rules of the super-rich.

One of the film's achievements is its balance between opposing views of von Bulow as calculating opportunist or hapless victim. Even as he appeals for empathy, the ultrareserved von Bulow never permits himself to be a sympathetic figure. Obliquely, he explains his detachment as a matter of cultural conditioning.

Irons renders von Bulow's droll, arrogant self-righteousness with masterful subtlety. His is the rich man's *droit du signeur*, a world view despised by the intensely democratic Dershowitz.

When the attorney's dogged persistence and sheer legal brilliance finally pay off in acquittal, the two men part ways without bridging the enormous class differences between them. Justice in this case, Dershowitz tells his assistants, is enigmatic, and "Reversal Of Fortune" does not pretend to offer a final judgment.

Director Barbet Schroeder explores the psychological dimension of the von Bulow affair but never permits it to overwhelm the narrative momentum. The legal maneuverings by Dershowitz and his strategists have an impeccably researched authenticity, even though some incidents and dialog were invented for the script.

The von Bulows' stormy married life is seen through beautifully mounted flashbacks in which rich production design gives fresh meaning to the notion that money cannot buy happiness.

Except for one brief scene of flowering love, Close is obliged to play Sunny as a haggard, emotionally damaged woman whose fate may or may not have been the outcome of an impulse toward self-destruction.

Seamless editing, handsome cinematography and top-line makeup and costumes contribute greatly to a classy piece of filmmaking. — *Rich.*

MOTION & EMOTION
(BRITISH-DOCU)

A Lucida Prods. film. Produced by Chris Rodley. Directed by Paul Joyce. Camera (color), Ken Morse; editor, Tony Lawson; sound, Jim Corcoran, Jim Hilton. Reviewed at Toronto Festival of Festivals, Sept. 8, 1990. Running time: **90 MIN.**
With: Wim Wenders, Harry Dean Stanton, Peter Falk, Dennis Hopper, Ry Cooder, Sam Fuller.

Chockablock with info, Paul Joyce's crisp, delightful documentary about the films of Wim Wenders is a must for fest and arthouse audiences, both already and soon-to-be fans of one of the New German Cinema darlings.

Using mostly talking heads of Wenders' collaborators, clips from his films and interviews with Wenders himself, Joyce juxtaposes both hosannas and discerning criticisms. His editing technique provides warmth and humor, leading to new insights about Wenders' body of work and his style of directing.

Sitting at his editing desk, Wenders recalled that as a postwar German growing up in an environment of national denial, he found his identity in rock 'n' roll. Later, as a filmmaker, he sought the right images for the sound, as shown in clips from "Summer In The City," with the Kinks on the soundtrack. Dennis Hopper, who toplined in "The American Friend," swoons over Wenders' record collection.

Wenders loved the American road, which resulted in "Kings Of The Road." Featured player Hanns Zischler comments that European roads are not as wide as those in "Easy Rider," and that Wenders' strength as a filmmaker comes from being a boy looking out the window.

Longtime Wenders cinematographer Robby Müller shares his thoughts on working in both black & white and color with Wenders. Sam Fuller pays the highest compliment: He can recognize any Wenders shot. Harry Dean Stan-

ton talks about acting with a child on a set of "Paris, Texas," and Ry Cooder recalls Wenders' tersely soliciting by phone his services as musician.

With the ever-prevalent effect of U.S. culture on European cinema as a constant theme, Wenders had to do his Hollywood gig, which ended in a disastrous experience on "Hammett." Maybe he discovered America has a bad side, he muses. The clips from "The State Of Things," an exorcism of his "Hammett" experience, are hilariously malicious.

Critic Kraft Wetzel provides fascinating, critical insights into Wenders' inability to deal with female sexuality in any of his films, and his cinematic problems of fathers and sons as well.

Docu traces Wenders' development as an alienated filmmaker from "The Goalie's Anxiety At The Penalty Kick" to his return to the real Germany of his collective memory in "Wings Of Desire" (for which he selected Peter Falk to star because "he was an actor who was a former angel").

Pic establishes his place with Fassbinder, Herzog, Schlöndorff and Kluge in the New German Cinema of the '70s — Wenders is utterly charming and otherworldly in his descriptions about his place — and also confirms his position as leader of contempo German cinema.

Wenders' filmmaking secrets are laid bare in Joyce's docu. He can come up with 10 beginnings, but never has an ending in his films.

Critic Wetzel crystallizes the enigma of Wenders' films: "Women are strange, children are good. Let's listen to another record." — *Devo.*

MUSICIANS IN EXILE
(CANADIAN-DOCU-B&W)

A Nemesis Prods. production. Produced by Jacques Holender. Camera (black & white), Robert Fresco. No other credits available. Reviewed at the Toronto Festival of Festivals, Sept. 9, 1990. Running time: **75 MIN.**

"Musicians In Exile," a dandy, spirited 75-minute docu well-suited to tv, is themed to musicians in either political or voluntary exile.

Pic features South African trumpeter Hugh Masekela, Chilean folk group Quilapayun and others in concert and talking about their reasonably cheerful life in

exile.

All share a profound love of their native countries, be it South Africa, Chile or Cuba, and talk about returning someday. Robert Fresco's camerawork is effectively tight, but docu needs further editing. — *Adil.*

THE HOT SPOT

An Orion Pictures release. Produced by Paul Lewis. Executive producers, Bill Gavin, Derek Power, Stephen Ujlaki. Directed by Dennis Hopper. Screenplay, Nona Tyson, Charles Williams, based on Williams' novel "Hell Hath No Fury"; camera (Panavision color), Ueli Steiger; editor, Wende Phifer Mate; music, Jack Nitzsche; production design, Cary White; costume design, Mary Kay Stolz; stunt coordinator, Eddy Donno; assistant directors, Frank Bueno, Wendy Yorkshire; associate producer, Valerie Tyson; unit production manager, Paul Lewis; coproducer, Deborah Capogrosso; casting, Lauren Lloyd, Gail Levin. Reviewed at the Toronto Festival of Festivals, Sept. 5, 1990. MPAA Rating R. Running time: **120 MIN.**

Harry Madox	Don Johnson
Dolly Harshaw	Virginia Madsen
Gloria Harper	Jennifer Connelly
Lon Gulik	Charles Martin Smith
Frank Sutton	William Sadler
George Harshaw	Jerry Hardin
Sheriff	Bary Corbin
Julian Ward	Jack Nance

Also with: Leon Rippy, Virgil Frye, John Hawker.

Director Dennis Hopper just won't say no to kinky amorality, and that's all to the good in this twisting, languorous and very sexy thriller. If "The Hot Spot" is marketed to exploit its seductive appeal, it could draw audiences seeking something other than by-the-numbers entertainment.

Hopper has revived Don Johnson's floundering big-screen career by eliciting a sharp, understated performance from the former "Miami Vice" star, who's neither a cop nor a good guy here. As the low-key, manipulative drifter Harry Madox, Johnson shakes things up in a godforsaken Texas town, where his job at a used car lot involves him with two restless women yearning to beat the heat.

Gloria Harper (Jennifer Connelly) is the sweetly stunning office girl; Dolly Harshaw (Virginia Madsen) is the irresistibly tempting boss' wife. This is the type of town, says Madsen, where there are "only two things to do," and one of them is watching tv. Johnson charts a sexual collision course with both women. But he has another agenda.

Once he's insinuated himself

into the town, Johnson aims to con the yokels. He's contemptuous of his crotchety cuckold boss (Jerry Hardin), tolerant of his car lot sidekick (Charles Martin Smith) and suspicious of a degenerate loner (William Sadler) who has some strange power over Connelly.

Johnson unwinds in the town's topless joint (the "Hot Spot") habituated by the lecherous local banker (Jack Nance). Johnson pulls off a neat fail-safe bank heist, but he's jailed anyway until Madsen concocts an alibi to set him free. By this time, Johnson has fallen for Connelly, but Madsen's voracious desire for him will not be denied.

Hopper clearly was impressed by what he learned from working with David Lynch on "Blue Velvet." "The Hot Spot" seeps with atmosphere, unfolds at a deceptively relaxed pace, steadily accumulates noirish grit, then dizzily plunges into a Lynch-like plumbing of the dark passions and nasty secrets at the heart of Main Street, USA.

Defying current standards of sanitized movie morality, Hopper loads up on nudity and dangerous sex, taking the MPAA's R rating to its erotic outer limits. Even more refreshing is an ironic denouement that leaves the conventional notion of a happy ending with just rewards twisting in the Texas dust.

Johnson's cynical and charismatic lone wolf is splendidly baited by Madsen, who inhabits the wicked seductress Dolly with relish. Connelly is a believable eyeful in her role as the tarnished innocent, Gloria. Sadler, as Gloria's evil tormentor, and Hardin as Madsen's hapless husband are both very good.

And if the script by Nona Tyson and Charles Williams has its share of dangling threads, it ultimately ties them up with a gleeful malevolence. Ueli Steiger's lensing and Jack Nitzche's bare blues score enhance the film's murky, rootless mood.
— *Rich.*

THE GOLDEN BOAT
(COLOR-B&W-16m)

A Duende Picures/Symbolic Exchange production. Produced by Jordi Torrent, James Schamus. Written and directed by Raul Ruiz. Camera (color/ black & white-16m), Maryse Alberti; editor, Sylvia Wallga; music, John Zorn; sound, Piero Mura. Reviewed at the Toronto Festival of Festivals, Sept. 9, 1990. (Also in New York Film Festival.)

Running time: **88 MIN.**
With: Michael Kirby, Jim Jarmusch, Vito Acconci, Kathy Acker, Ruth Malezchech, Peyton Smith.

Working for the first time in English, surrealist Raul Ruiz has fashioned a helter-skelter metaphysical parody of film noir and B detective conventions. Somewhat more plotted than the standard Ruiz pastiche, "The Golden Boat" nevertheless stands narrative logic on its head and blithely defies deconstruction.

Obviously a commercial leper, "The Golden Boat" is an art-cult item that should delight cineastes. It deserves a niche in festival programs everywhere.

A giant-size, articulate and insane assassin wanders the garbage-strewn streets of Manhattan's Lower East Side. He enjoys knifing his victims in the gut, and to demonstrate his empathy and existential pain, self-inflicts similar wounds.

Although "always on the verge of death," the assassin is apparently invulnerable. This "lost" black angel "from Los Angeles" encounters a young rock critic/ musician/philosopher. They embark on a series of hallucinatory adventures that stand as a metaphor for the search for God. In the Ruizian universe, this search appears to be superfluous. "God," says one character, "speaks through the newspapers."

Killer and disciple fall in with various existential weirdos: flophouse nightclerk, Mexican soap opera star, her doctor husband (who may or may not be the assassin's son) and the rock critic's neighbor/girlfriend.

Reality, dream and time merge in a vertiginous warped continuum. Ruiz seems to be suggesting that human redemption and spiritual resurrection are possible in the most benighted landscapes. None of this is meant to be taken too seriously. Film invites audiences to either lie back and enjoy it, or, as did some at its Toronto fest world preem, take a hike.

Ruiz, a Paris-based Chilean, benefits from working in English and on location in New York. Although unmistakably a Ruiz concoction, "The Golden Boat" has a punchy contemporary atmosphere lacking in his French-language museum pieces. Bizarre editing and no-frills cinematography make for arrestingly disconcerting images that evoke a cockeyed alternative universe.
— *Rich.*

TRUST

A True Fiction Pictures/Zenith Prods. production. (Domestic sales, Republic Pictures; foreign sales, the Sales Co.) Produced by Bruce Weiss. Executive producer, Jerome Brownstein. Written and directed by Hal Hartley. Camera (color), Mark Spiller; music, Phil Reed; sound, Jeff Pullman; production design, Daniel Ouellette; costume design, Claudia Brown; production manager, Ann Ruark; assistant directors, Ted Hope, Eddie Rosenstein. Reviewed at the Toronto Festival of Festivals, Sept. 7, 1990. Running time: **90 MIN.**
Maria Coughlin . . . . Adrienne Shelly
Matthew Slaughter . . Martin Donovan
Jean Coughlin . . . . . Merritt Nelson
Jim Slaughter . . . . . . John MacKay
Peg Coughlin . . . . Edie Falco
John Coughlin . . . . Marko Hunt

Long Island filmmaker Hal Hartley progresses from his debut feature, "The Unbelievable Truth," in this bleak, off-center comedy about dysfunctional families in working class suburbia. This distinctive low-budget film could draw alternative-minded audiences, but it will require a dedicated distrib prepared for a challenging sell.

When Maria (Adrienne Shelly) gets pregnant by the high school quarterback, she's dropped by her boyfriend, drops out of school and her father drops dead of a heart attack. Maria's hard-bitten mother treats her like a pariah.

Meanwhile, Matthew (Martin Donovan), an intellectually inclined reform school graduate with a talent for fixing things, quits his mind-numbing job assembling computers. His abusive father is obsessed with order but, like Maria's mother, his inner life is ruled by raging psychic disorder.

Following a showdown with this harsh taskmaster, Matthew wanders the streets, encounters Maria and takes the shattered girl to his home. When this arrangement is terminated by Matthew's father, the outcast pair go back to Maria's house, where her mother makes them only slightly more welcome. This sets the stage for a tale of uneasy love and spiritual anomie in the sterile precincts of middle America.

Lonely, unhappy characters grope for communication in fragmentary deadpan exchanges dripping with corrosive irony. Hartley's mordant script skews the banalities of everyday life, casting barbs at marriage, the abortion debate, tv addiction and free enterprise.

Still, Hartley shows compassion for his damaged characters. "Trust" offers a despairing view of the American dream. When Matthew refuses to compromise, he and Maria pay a price for trying to be different.

The film could use some editing as it builds toward its denouement, but "Trust" largely succeeds in revealing a world of painfully funny emotional chaos under the peeled-back patina of suburban normalcy.

Donovan is excellent as the brooding misfit, and Shelly is tangibly right as the suburban brat. Also very good are Merritt Nelson as Maria's emotionally alienated mother and John MacKay as Matthew's bullying father.

Actors in smaller supporting roles are also well-chosen and directed. Lensing and design help to establish a consistently realistic milieu. — *Rich.*

UCHCHI VEYIL
(HIGH NOON)
(INDIAN-TAMIL)

A T.M. Sundaram M.A. film presentation of a Jwala Film production. Produced by T.M. Sundaram. Directed by Jayaabharathy. Screenplay, Ravindran Ramamurthy; camera (color), Ramesh Vyas; editor, Babu Shankar; music, L. Vaidyanathan; sound, Raja Ram; art direction, V. Kalai. Reviewed at the Toronto Festival of Festivals, Sept. 7, 1990. Running time: **105 MIN.**
With: Delhi Ganesh, Sri Vidya, Uma Kuppuswamy, Vijai.

This fictional study of poverty, family structure and elderly respect in India is shot in real time. Pic's gentle rythmn mutes foreign possibilities although it should do well at fests.

At dawn in a small village, a grandfather goes out to fetch the morning newspaper. The paper boy says his family can't afford the subscription. Cut off from the town's only media, he retires to the kitchen. A loud clock ticks incessantly throughout the film.

The supportive old man, an ex-freedom fighter (a Ghandist) living with his insolvent son and in-laws, convinces the family to take in a boarder, cousin Shankar. Grandfather falls ill, but sets out for a distant town with granddaughter and Shankar to be honored (at long last) for his service to Ghandi's cause.

This is the kind of no-sex-or-violence pic people could screen to gain a better understanding of foreign cultures, but one mainstream America would refuse at the b.o. — *Suze.*

FREEZE—DIE—COME TO LIFE
(ZAMRI OUMI VOSKRESNI)
(SOVIET-B&W)

An Intl. Film Exchange release of a Lenfilm Studio production. Written and directed by Vitali Kanévski. Camera (black & white), Vladimir Bryliakov; music, Sergei Banevich. Reviewed at the Toronto Festival of Festivals, Sept. 8, 1990. (Also in New York Film Festival.) Running time: **105 MIN.**
With: Dinara Droukarova, Pavel Nazarov, Eléna Popova.

Winner of the Gold Camera for best first feature at Cannes, "Freeze — Die — Come To Life," is a stark, transfixing tale of two children adrift in the harsh postwar world of an isolated mining town in Soviet Asia. This demanding film probably will be best appreciated by fest audiences and those with a special interest in the latest developments in glasnost-era Soviet cinema.

Valerka, a 12-year-old boy whose mother survives by prostitution, supports himself as a tea-bearer in the town flea market. There, he competes with Galiya, a spunky girl his own age, whose friendship he reluctantly reciprocates. These urchins dwell in a gloomy subarctic landscape.

The coal miners intermingle with the slave laborers and Japanese prisoners of war interned in an adjacent work camp. Life in the Stalin-era outpost is one of grim discipline and crushing routine, a Darwinist jungle where people do what they must to exist. Valerka's mother has ambitions for her son, but he already is an incorrigible rebel.

Filmmaker Vitali Kanévski unfolds his story with unadorned documentary detachment, employing techniques of neorealism and cinéma vérité. Like François Truffaut's indomitable child heroes, Valerka and Galiya improvise rules for dealing with an arbitrary adult world.

Valerka's rebellious impulse for self-expression leads him to acts of devious sabatoge and a life on the run. He travels to his grandmother's town, where he falls in with thieves and witnesses a murder. When the plucky Galiya arrives to coax him home, the child pals are pursued by the hardened criminals with tragic consequences.

On one level, the film celebrates the resilient Russian soul, reflected in folk songs with plaintive lyrics about love and faraway places. Black & white photography enhances the sense of hellish reality where hope is exiled but routine cruelties are redeemed by small kindnesses.

Set against a startling tableau of human grotesquerie, the child actors play their parts with an unstudied naturalness. In its unflinching depiction of the Soviet past, "Freeze — Die — Come To Life" stands as a cautionary tale for the present. — *Rich.*

VENICE FEST

MARTHA UND ICH
(MARTHA AND I)
(W. GERMAN-FRENCH)

An Iduna Film (Kirch Gruppe)-Progefi-TF1 Films co-production in collaboration with ZDF, ORF, Canal Plus and Raidue. (Intl. sales: Sacis, Rome.) Produced by Sabine Tettenborn, Marius Schwarz. Written and directed by Jiri Weiss. Camera (color), Viktor Ruzicka; editor, Gisela Haller; music, Jiri Stivin; production design, Karel Vacek; costume design, Maria Frankova; production managers, Jan Kladec, Susanne Schlaepfer, Philippe Verro. Reviewed at Venice Film Festival (competing), Sept. 7, 1990. Running time: **106 MIN.**
Martha . . . . . . Marianne Sägebrecht
Dr. Ernst Fuchs . . . . . Michel Piccoli
Emil (teenager) . . . . Vaclav Chalupa
Emil (adult) . . . . Ondrej Vetchy
Rosa Kluge . . . Bozidara Turzonvova
Ida Fuchs . . . . Jana Brezinova
Elsa Fuchs . . . . . . Sona Valentova
Kamila Fuchs . . . . . Jana Altmanova
Ilona . . . . Zuzana Kocurikova
Bertl . . . . Klaus Grunberg
Werner . . . . Michael Kausch
Dr. Benda . . . . Jiri Menzel

Marianne Sägebrecht gives another winning performance in a non-comic role in "Martha And I," a film which marks a comeback, after 20 years, for Czech director Jiri Weiss. Despite serious flaws, the film deserves to be seen for its warm-hearted treatment of a familiar theme.

In Weiss' semiautobiographical story, a kindly Jewish doctor (Michel Piccoli) in prewar Prague divorces his faithless wife and marries his loyal maid. The first half of the film, which works better than the second half, has young Emil (engagingly played by Vaclav Chalupa) sent to live with his uncle Ernst.

That was after his mother caught him in a compromising situation with a family servant. Ernst encourages the boy in every way, and becomes his role model. Emil also responds warmly to Martha (Sägebrecht), who becomes a mother to him.

Unfortunately, pic's second part isn't as convincing, partly because Ondrej Vetchy, who plays the older Emil, doesn't look at all like Chalupa, and is a far less endearing character. The abrupt change of actors is a dislocation many will find hard to take.

An equally serious problem, particularly for international audiences, is the language. Emil and his uncle (and the uncle's disapproving sisters) are Czech, whereas Martha and her pro-Nazi brothers are German-Czechs. It would be logical to have the Czech characters speak Czech, and, indeed, essential to make the points so crucial to the second half of the film when the Jewish Czechs are rounded up by Nazis.

Since everyone speaks German throughout, however, audiences outside Germany (where dubbing is the norm) are likely to be hopelessly confused. A more palatable international version, using multiple languages, should be produced.

Still, Weiss, whose most famous films "Wolf Trap" and "Romeo, Juliet And Darkness" predated the Czech new wave of the late '60s, is telling a touching story here. Piccoli and Sägebrecht ("Bagdad Cafe," "Rosalie Goes Shopping") are both excellent, the latter never falling into the trap of playing for comedy. Indeed, her final scene is extremely moving.

Location work in Prague ensures the film's splendid look. Czech director Jiri Menzel makes an amusing cameo as a dentist who is bribed to fix Martha's teeth before she marries her doctor. — *Strat.*

BASTA! CI FACCIO UN FILM
(THAT'S ENOUGH! LET'S MAKE A FILM)
(ITALIAN)

An Emmer Production S.a.s. Produced by Gino Usai. Directed by Luciano Emmer. Screenplay, Luciano Emmer, David Emmer, Paolo Taggi; camera (color), Elio Bisignani; editor, Adriano Tagliavia; music, Antonello Venditti. Reviewed at Venice Film Festival (out of competition), Sept. 6, 1990. Running time: **100 MIN.**
Dadi . . . . David Emmer
Andrea . . . . Gianluca Angelini
Luisa . . . . Verde Visconti di Modrone
Claudio . . . . Claudio De Rossi
Carlo . . . . Carlo Marino
Michela . . . . Barbara Troiani
Frederica . . . . . . Martina Fiorentino

Director Luciano Emmer, 72, returns with his first feature film in 30 years, and has a go at updating one of his past successes from the '50s. As is often the case when a veteran tries to make a film about youth, however, the result is more academic than convincing.

In the '40s, Emmer was one of Italy's top documentary directors. His most famous feature film "Sunday In August" (1950), was widely shown internationally. His new film begins with the opening sequence of another Emmer, "Terza Licio" (1954), which was about students.

Modern-day students watch the vintage classics, and they derisively throw tomatos at the screen. As unseen man (presumably Emmer himself) approaches them, and they rough him up and throw him in the harbor, but he perseveres, suggesting they join forces to make a new film about high school life.

Most of the ensuing pic actually takes place during summer vacation. The youngsters are mostly from unhappy homes, form various romantic attachments and face inevitable separations.

All of this is fairly predictable, with the wild member of the bunch (Claudio De Rossi) becoming more stable, a rather snobbish girl (Verde Visconti di Modrone) opting for a yuppie lifestyle, and another youth (Carlo Marino) deciding to enter the workforce rather than go to the university. In the central role, co-scripter David Emmer plays perhaps the most conventional character of the lot.

The final result is a lightweight offering, not without moments of charm, but one that's unlikely to fare well in the tough international marketplace. — *Strat.*

HENRY AND JUNE

A Universal Pictures release of a Walrus & Associates Ltd. production. Produced by Peter Kaufman. Directed by Philip Kaufman. Screenplay, Rose and Philip Kaufman, based on the book by Anais Nin; camera (Deluxe color), Philippe Rousselot; editor, Vivien Hillgrove, William S. Scharf, Dede Allen; production design, Guy-Claude François; sound, Alan Solet; costume design, Yvonne Sassinot de Nesle; production manager, Claude Albouze; assistant director, Eric Bartonio; associate producer, Yannoulla Wakefield; casting, Margot Capelier (France), Donna Isaacson (U.S.), John Lyons. Reviewed at the Venice Film Festival (out of competition), Sept. 14, 1990. MPAA rating: X. Running time: **136 MIN.**

Henry Miller	Fred Ward
June Miller	Uma Thurman
Anais Nin	Maria de Medeiros
Hugo	Richard E. Grant
Osborn	Kevin Spacey
Eduardo	Jean-Philippe Ecoffey
Jack	Bruce Myers
Publisher/editor	Jean-Louis Bunuel
Spanish dance instructor	Feodor Atkine
Emilia	Sylvie Huguel
Brassai	Artus de Penguern
Friend	Pierre Etaix
Magician No. 1	Pierre Edernac
Magician No. 2	Gaetan Bloom
Clown	Alexandra de Gall
Henry's whore	Brigitte Lahaie
Frail prostitute	Maite Maille

"**H**enry And June" will be considered liberating by some and obscene by others. Its credentials as a serious, non-pornographic, treatment of the subject are unquestionable, but its length and subject matter may make it difficult commercially, especially outside big-city runs. Television looks out of the question in most countries, but video sales should be lively.

The lovemaking scenes in his previous film, "The Unbearable Lightness Of Being," proved that director Philip Kaufman was perhaps the best director to handle the story of the long-secret, passionate affair between writers Henry Miller and Anais Nin in Paris in 1931-32. Kaufman has achieved the near-impossible by depicting several intricate love scenes without even a glimpse of frontal nudity. The sex scenes are surprisingly unerotic.

Pic's title, also the title of the Nin book, is actually a misnomer. This is the story of Henry and Anais; June, playing a marginal role, is offscreen much of the time. The film opens with Anais (who has published a defense of the "notorious" British author, D.H. Lawrence) and her banker husband, Hugo, establishing themselves in Paris.

It quickly becomes clear that, although fond of the rather stuffy Hugo, Anais, who keeps a secret diary, isn't telling him everything, and is eager to experience the kind of things she imagines in her erotic dreams. Miller's arrival is the catalyst. Anais immediately sees in him someone with similar ideas and desires, and before long they embark on a passionate love affair. Anais is also attracted to Miller's wife, June, who visits occasionally from America, and dreams of erotic experiences in which June assumes the male role.

During this period, Anais still has relations with Hugo. On one occasion, after Miller has been impotent with her, she returns home to make love to her husband. Then, in one of the film's most provocative scenes, she takes him to a brothel (one Miller frequents) and hires his favorite whore, and another woman, to perform sexual acts.

In its depiction of Depression Paris and sexual candor, "Henry And June" succeeds. The central performances of Fred Ward, as the cynical, life-loving Miller, and Maria de Medeiros, as the beautiful, insatiable Anais, splendidly fulfill the director's vision.

Pic is less successful in gaining audience sympathy for these hedonists. The scenes in which the two literary giants write and read from their works are no better than similar scenes in lesser Hollywood biopics. Screenplay by Kaufman and wife Rose straddles the fence on Anais. For many, she could be a monstrous character, for others a liberated feminist of another era.

Also, the character of June (Uma Thurman) is ill-defined. She herself claims, "I've done the vilest things, but I've done them superbly." She seems at first to be even more attuned to exotic sexual experiences than Anais. Yet, when she and Anais are sharing a bed together, and she discovers that Henry and Anais are lovers, she reacts as a conventionally jealous woman.

These are relatively minor flaws, however, in a generally impressive film. The production design is modest, but Philippe Rousselot's splendid camerawork more than makes up for that.

Domestic commercial prospects for "Henry And June" will hinge largely on whether the current Motion Picture Assn of America X rating stands. Outside the U.S., where the version at Venice will be shown without modifications, the film stands a good chance to do solid, if not sensational business. — *Strat.*

MONTREAL FEST

ARCHANGEL
(CANADIAN)

A Greg Klymkiw production. Executive producer, Andre Bennett. Produced by Klymkiw. Directed by Guy Maddin. Screenplay, Maddin, George Toles; camera (black & white), Maddin; editor, Maddin; sound, Maddin; art director, Maddin, Jeff Solylo. Reviewed at the Montreal World Film Festival, Sept. 1, 1990. (Also in Telluride Film Fest.) Running time: **90 MIN.**

Lt. John Boles	Kyle McCulloch
Veronkha	Kathy Marykuca
Philbin	Ari Cohen
Danchuk	Sarah Neville
Jannings	Michael Gottli
Geza	David Falkenberg
Doctor	Michael O'Sullivan
Baba	Margaret Anne Macleod
Captain	Victor Cowie
Monk	Ihor Procak
Kaiser Wilhelm	Professor Steve Snyder

Destined to become a monumental cult classic, Guy Maddin's wickedly perverted love story delves into previously uncharted realms of the macabre. His brilliant script will be insulting to most commercial audiences; his images offensive to the uninitiated. But if targeted properly, pic will delight "Eraserhead" fans.

Similarities between "Archangel" and David Lynch's black & white classic end in the fact that both are bizarre, mindboggling works of art. Maddin does not copy Lynch's style; his film is original.

Set during the Bolshevik revolution in Archangel in the Russian Arctic, plot revolves around a group of men and women who have been exposed to mustard gas. They have severe memory disorders and are consequently confused about whom they love.

Lt. Boles (played dashingly by Kyle McCulloch) is a Canadian soldier in love with Iris, who's dead. When he meets beautiful Russian nurse Veronkha, he thinks she is Iris. Unfortunately, Veronkha is married to a Belgian aviator, Philbin, who always forgets he's married (even on his wedding night, "the happiest day of his vague life").

Veronkha eventually believes Boles is Philbin and marries him too. The Russian soldier, Danchuk, is married to Jannings, who also loves Boles. Around and around it goes, which is undoubtedly the point. It makes no sense, and it makes perfect sense. Maddin is one very twisted director.

The first clue that this pic is something completely different is Maddin's absurd tongue-in-cheek definition of love at pic's beginning. Up and running, director introduces the contradiction that war poses to love. The line "A crime against humanity is a crime against God. We must restore peace to this earthly garden" is accompanied by a shot of a soldier eating his victim's throat. From that linear point on, anything goes.

Rabbits stand in as a metaphor for Bolsheviks who are "half man, half beast, with great big ears, great big eyes and great big claws." At which point, rabbits hop into the trenches.

The script defies logic. One of the best lines in the film (which could be aptly applied to hundreds of other love stories) comes from Veronkha's hypnotist when she confesses that Philbin slept with the chambermaid on their wedding night, "Your husband has no memory of her so there's no infidelity."

The gore also is plenty wacko. When Jannings is knifed by a Bolshevik and his guts of link sausage spill onto the floor, he picks them up and uses one to strangle the killer. "Strangled by an intestine," reads one of the many titles Maddin uses for comic relief and to strengthen the silent film noir flavor.

Overall, "Archangel" is a smashing follow-up to Maddin's first non-budget feature, "Tales From The Gimli Hospital," and proof that he is destined for a weird, wonderful cinematic career. This $C500,000 pic should never be shown on television. — *Suze.*

CINE ARE DREPTATE?
(WHO'S RIGHT?)
(ROMANIAN)

A Romaniafilm presentation of a Maison 4 Film production. Directed by Alexandru Tatos. Screenplay, Paul Everac; camera (color), Vivi Dragan Vasile; sound, Horea Murgu, Mihai Popescu; set design, Dudus Neagu Mircea. Reviewed at Montreal World Film Festival, Aug. 25, 1990. Running time: **90 MIN.**

With: Andrei Ralea, Oana Pellea, Andrei Finti, Zoltan Vadasz, Maria Munteanu, Ovidiu Ghinita, Valeriu Preda.

Bathed in suspicion and misdirected espionage, "Who's Right?" is exactly what one would expect out of Romania given this year's past events, but pic has few prospects abroad.

Innocent people are blamed for crimes of others. Officials are corrupt. Confusion dominates a probe of damages in a big factory. Inspector Nedelcu falls in love with his prime suspect, Lidia. His investigation — along with the film — becomes as complicated as a Chinese puzzle.

An hour into the film it becomes apparent that Lidia's former lover is the real suspect, although he too is supposedly innocent. Perhaps intentionally, it is never made clear if any crime was committed at all. One thing is certain, it wasn't Lidia's fault, and the inspector imagines a true love affair. But her mistrust of officials leads them both to an inevitable unhappy ending.

Heavy-handed shots in the factory recall Fritz Lang's "Metropolis." Dominating structures, ugly buildings and horribly functional furniture provide a bleak surrounding. A lakefront is a visual haven for both Lidia and the audience. It is the only place where things are clear and unmuddled, even if only temporarily.— *Suze.*

NEL GIARDINO DELLE ROSE
(AGE OF DISCRETION)
(ITALIAN)

A Surf Film, Dania Film (in collaboration with Reteitalia) presentation. Executive producer, Pietro Innocenzi. Directed by Luciano Martino. Screenplay, Martino, Sauro Scavolini; camera (color), Luigi Kuweiller; editor, Amedeo Salfa; sound, Raffaele de Luca; set design, Giuseppe Pirrotta. Reviewed at the Montreal World Film Festival, Aug. 29, 1990. Running time: 94 MIN.
With: Ottavia Piccolo, Massimo Ghini, Barbara de Rossi, Gioia Scola, Rossy de Palma, Gianfranco Manfredi, Leo Gullotta, Giancarlo Giannini, Galeazzo Benti, Remo Girone, Alessandro Borrelli, Angelo Barnabacci.

This is the stuff great soap operas are made of. Sad, tender, weepy scenes about a tragic mother/son relationship left few dry eyes at its world preem. Television is the only foreign window for this type of tragedy, which middle-class America re-

lentlessly devours.

It could never be argued that this is a great film, but its meticulous development and prolonged suspense begot a strong emotional reaction from the audience. The story builds slowly until the source of misunderstanding between them is finally revealed.

It begins in a rose garden (literal translation of the title: "in the rose garden") where the young mother recites poetry to her boy, Claudio. "Footsteps echo in memory along the corridor we didn't take to the door we never opened. . ." The film subtly details which footsteps echo in her memory, along the unexplored corridor to a door she locked many years ago.

Years later, Claudio is a successful yuppie living in Milan with his girlfriend. His mother is a lonely, debt-ridden widow who lives in a dreamworld in Naples with her dog. They never see each other. He never calls.

Claudio has never confronted his mother about a scene which changed both their lives. When he was young, he once saw her with her fellow schoolteacher Tramontano (a character never developed in the film, but played sentimentally by Giancarlo Giannini) in a tender embrace.

Assuming she had betrayed his drunken father, Claudio began a lifelong resentment of his beloved mother. Even though he was taunted by his classmates, who also assumed she was having an affair, he chose to assume she was guilty rather than express his feelings and ask her what happened.

Claudio became incapable of developing any positive relationship with a woman, as evidenced by his girlfriend who accuses him of "sleeping with women only to collect scalps." He is a tragic figure, preoccupied by memories of his lost mother. Freud would have loved this script.

He is forced to confront his feelings only when he receives a call that his mother is on her deathbed. An airplane strike prevents him from flying to Naples, and the last third of the pic is his road trip to see her one last time. By the time he arrives, she's dead and Tramontano, her last friend in the world, gives him a letter.

Per the letter, she never slept with the man she loved (Tramontano) but could never tell Claudio that because he never asked. By the time he reads her side of

the story, it's too late, but he's supposed to go on living with the knowledge of that rose garden poem about unopened doors and echoing corridors. Sob.

This pic is seriously sentimental, but it works. Well-acted and edited, it builds at a soap-opera snail's pace until the tragedy is revealed. — *Suze.*

CITY OF CHAMPIONS
(CANADIAN)

A Champions Films production. Produced by Norm Fassbender and Joseph Viszmeg. Written and directed by Joseph Viszmeg. Camera (color), Peter Wunstorf; editor, Dominique Fortin; music, John Millard; sound, John Clough. Reviewed at the Montreal World Film Festival, Aug. 31, 1990. Running time: 70 MIN.
West . . . . Phil Zyp
Moochie . . . . Marie Dame
Dixie/Yolanda . . . . . Kathryn Fraser
Gabrielle . . . . Geraldine Carr

This tongue-in-cheek comedy about four losers in the "city of champions" is too dry to command much respect at the box office. Pic's best suited for Canadian tv where nets can use it in their Canadian content quotas required by the federal government.

Gabrielle is the bank robber who picks up two hitchhikers, Dixie and West. Dixie is a spoiled rich kid looking for thrills. West is fleeing his insipid girlfriend, Moochie (who works as a sales clerk and has only one ambition, to have a "real" family and a "real" apartment).

Debutant helmer Joseph Viszmeg paints a grim and comical picture of life in a western Canadian town known only for it's elaborate shopping center, the Edmonton Mall. These teens shop 'til they drop with money they robbed from a bank.

Viszmeg's witty script and exploitation of a miniscule production budget ($C40,000) indicate the man has potential.

The characters are intentionally two-dimensional, and the lack of action typifies their angst. They spend 24 hours together, drinking, dancing, shopping and eventually in bed.

After their night on the tear, Yolanda returns home (to go shopping with her mother), Gabrielle disappears with the money, West is leaving town to see the world, and Moochie is going to kill herself. Comic ships that pass in the night.

It's a very simple story relying entirely on the characters. Budget constraints eliminated any possible effects or locations (a drawback). The acting doesn't measure up to the script, but pic should draw a respectable audience on Canadian tv. — *Suze.*

ALBERTO EXPRESS
(FRENCH)

A Malofilm (Canada)/UGC (France) presentation of a Mainstream film production. Executive producer, Alain Centonze. Produced by Maurice Bernart. Directed by Arthur Joffe. Screenplay, Joffe, Jean-Louis Benoit; camera (color), Philippe West; editor, Marie Castro-Brechignac; sound, Jean-Paul Mugel; set design, Bernard Vezat. Reviewed at the Montreal World Film Festival, Aug. 29, 1990. Running time: 98 MIN.
Alberto . . . . Sergio Castellitto
Alberto's father . . . . . Nino Manfredi
Clara . . . . Marie Trintignant
The controller . . . . . . Marco Messeri
The baroness . . . . . . Jeanne Moreau
Juliette . . . . Eugenia Marruzzo
Diamond tooth man . . Dennis Goldson
Waiter . . . . Roland Amstutz
Train conductor . . . Dominique Pinon
The grandfather . . . . . Nanni Tamma

There's never a dull moment in this absurd action-packed comedy, which has terrific potential, especially in French and Italian territories (dialog is in both languages). It is well-acted, edited and guarantees a good laugh.

Pic begins when Alberto is 15 and leaving home. His father takes him aside for a man-to-man talk, hauls out an adding machine and a stack of receipts (of all the money he spent raising Alberto). He makes the boy add them up: He owes his father 30,250,000 lire, which must be repaid before Alberto's first child is born.

Cut to Alberto lying in bed 15 years later with his very pregnant wife. The race is on for him to get from Paris to Rome to settle his debt by morning. Now a penniless thief, Alberto hops the train running faster than the locomotive at a speed which sets the pace for bizarre adventure.

Every quirky character on the train becomes involved (and robbed), loading the story with endless scenarios. One constantly wonders "what on earth can happen next?" as the camera hops from one bit of insanity to the next.

As it turns out, the train controller is an old friend and lends him 50,000 lire (leaving only 30,200,000 lire to go) instead of tossing him off the express train. Alberto meets a wild variety of wierdos, including a black homosexual with a diamond tooth, his ex-girlfriend, and a child who seduces him to rob his father, who in turns offers Alberto larger rewards if Alberto will make love to his sexy young wife in front of him. Everyone on the train is thoroughly strange. Each situation is light and comical.

Two thirds into the pic, script enters the realm of bizarre but saves itself in the last 10 minutes with an unexpected happy ending which tightly ties all loose ends together.

Pic is helmer Arthur Joffe's second feature, one which will put him on the map as solid comedy director. "Alberto Express" is hilarious entertainment which will find a natural second life in homevid and tv. — *Suze.*

ATTO DI DOLORE
(ACT OF PAIN)
(ITALIAN)

An Istituto Luce-RAI-Rete 2 production. Directed by Pasquale Squitieri. Screenplay, Squitieri, Sergio Bianchi, Nanni Balestrini; camera (color), Romano Albani; editor, Florenza Muller; music, Rossini; production design, Massimo Carubelli; production manager, Bruno Cardinale. Reviewed at Montreal World Film Festival (competing), Aug. 30, 1990. Running time: **110 MIN.**
Elena Basile . . . . . Claudia Cardinale
Sandro . . . . Karl Zinny
Martina . . . . Giulia Boschi
Also with: Bruno Cremer.

Pasquale Squitieri, whose last outing was Tri-Star's little-seen international thriller "Russicum," bounces back with this contemporary drama about a mother whose teenage son becomes a heroin addict. Unfortunately, a strong subject is defeated by the director's tendency towards overkill and melodrama.

Claudia Cardinale gives a sterling performance as Elena, a widow who sells old wares in a street market and lives with daughter Martina and son Bruno. One night she awakens to find Bruno in agony undergoing drug withdrawal. She had been unaware he was an addict.

Soon, Bruno is sending his mother out to the local bar to buy him a fix. He keeps promising to kick the habit, but never does, and gets involved with robbery and

violence. He disappears for a long period, and is found in a coma.

Treatment in a rural commune doesn't help, and he returns to the city (Milan) to terrorize his mother, stealing her money and jewelry and frequently beating her. She finally takes violent action to rid herself of her terrifying offspring.

No doubting Squitieri and his writing team set out to make a grim picture of the drug scene, the inability of the police and social workers to deal with junkies and the degrading effects of the habit. It's all been done before, however, in films from different countries, and usually with more thoughtful treatment than it gets here.

The Rossini choral music over the most dramatic scenes — especially the hysterical, almost comic climax — adds nothing to the drama. But there are creditable performances from the players. Cardinale enters into her role with relish in the sort of part that wins awards, but she has actually done better work in less showy circumstances.

Theatrical chances outside Italy appear to be limited for this basically familiar material.
— *Strat.*

GUA FU CUN
(THE VILLAGE OF WIDOWS)
(CHINESE)

A Pearl River Film Studio production. Directed by Wang Jin. Screenplay, Chen Luzhou, Wang Yen; camera (Scope, color), Zhao Xiaoshi; music, Cheng Dazhao; production design, He Qun. Reviewed at Montreal World Film Festival (Chinese Cinema of Today section), Aug. 28, 1990. Running time: **95 MIN.**
With: Liang Yujin, Yu Li, Hao Jialing, Tao Zeru, Xie Yuan.

This pictorially magnificent Chinese production's chief asset is its beautiful Scope camerawork by Zhao Xiaoshi. Dramatically, however, pic is rather thin.

Pic is set in 1949 in a small fishing village still recovering from the effects of a big storm some years earlier in which many of the men died. Regeneration is made more difficult by the bizarre customs of the place, which decree that young people marry early, but that wives are only allowed to see their husbands three times a year. Pregnancy is forbidden.

Consequently, there's a fair number of secret liaisons, resulting in strict punishment. Violators are drowned.

It's never very clear exactly why such customs are still in place in 1949 (the time Communism came to China), but "The Village Of Widows" certainly presents a bizarre situation. — *Strat.*

RIO NEGRO
(VENEZUELAN-FRENCH)

A Yavita Film (Venezuela) and Flach Film (France) production. Produced by Jean-François Lepetit. Directed by Atahualpa Lichy. Screenplay, Lichy, Antonio Larreta, Manuel Matji, Eduardo de Gregorio, Joaquin Gonzalez, Diana Lichy; camera (color), Mario Garcia Joya; editor, Jacqueline Meppiel; music, Jose Mario Vitier, Rafael Salazar; sound, Jean-Louis Ughetto, Jean-Paul Loublier. Reviewed at Montreal World Film Festival, Aug. 27, 1990. Running time: **116 MIN.**
With: Angela Molina, Marie-Jose Nat, Nathalie Nell, Fanny Bastien, Frank Ramirez, Daniel Alvareado, Javier Zapata.

In 1912, political strife, revolution and power struggles plagued Rio Negro and established the roots of unrest in that remote South American region where power-hungry men rise and fall like the sun.

Marking his directorial debut, Atahualpa Lichy has an obvious flare for miniseries. This pic would make good tv fare.

Pic begins when Osuna, a bull-headed governor, arrives with his wife (who hates "the jungle") and two small children to break Carerra's reign of terror. Accomplishing his task on day 1, Osuna then finds his real rival, Funes, rearing his ugly head. Funes plays the power game with more tact, and their struggle for leadership becomes the pic's focal point.

Women and roosters are treated equally poorly by these macho men. Prostitutes and cockfights further establish the power structure. When Osuna allows a large ferry to dock and become the town brothel, Funes is disgusted by their drinking and carousing (despite the fact that he leaves lash marks on his partner's back).

Osuna and Funes inevitably reach a turning point when Funes' cock defeats Osuna's in front of the entire town, and Osuna winds up dead. His abuse of power is replaced by Funes' abuse of power. In the end, another cycle begins when Funes

is shot by another power-hungry stranger.

Script is predictable, but Lichy's flare for miniseries pacing would make for good small screen fare. Tech credits are fine. Colors are vibrant. Thesping is average. — *Suze.*

FALLING OVER BACKWARDS
(CANADIAN)

An Astral Films presentation of a Ranfilm Prods. film. Produced by Mort Ransen, Stewart Harding. Written and directed by Ransen. Camera (color), Savas Kalogeras; editor, Rita Roy; music, Milan Kymlicka; sound, Jacques Drouin; set design, Claude Pare. Reviewed at Montreal World Film Festival, Aug. 25, 1990. Running time: **104 MIN.**
Mel . . . . Saul Rubinek
Harvey . . . . Paul Soles
Jackie . . . . Julie St-Pierre
Rose . . . . Helen Hughes
Marilyn . . . . Carolyn Scott
Walter . . . . Montie Stethem
Arthur . . . . Barry Stethem
Evangeline . . . Rose-Andree Michaud

After two jolly hours, "Falling Over Backwards" stumbles headlong into a controversial ending: abortion. This film did not need an issue. It's a cleverly scripted, terrifically acted, sometimes dumb romantic comedy perfect for all forms of tv.

The young woman who initially wants the abortion, Jackie, is depicted as a happy cross between a "good girl," a stripper, a singer and a landlord, whose boyfriend busts up her furniture. She becomes quick pals with a tenant, Harvey, a wheelchair-ridden old man who moves in with his son, Mel (Saul Rubinek), a pudgy guy terrified of women.

Harvey's only disappointment is that Jackie isn't Jewish (there are tons of Jewish jokes in the pic that make light fun of racist tendencies). Jackie's bouncer boyfriend, Walter, eventually hits her and gets thrown out, at which point she finds out she's pregnant.

Predictably, she ends up with Mel, and he and Harvey convince her to have the baby. Harvey's ex-wife, Rose, moves in with the family after her hubby, Jerry, died doing push-ups (a fact that almost kills Harvey with laughter). Their relationship is a great source of humor.

Tech credits are good. Thesping is A-1 on all fronts, and Rubinek remains one of the joys of Canadian cinema.
— *Suze.*

MOODY BEACH
(CANADIAN)

A Max Films production in association with the National Film Board of Canada. Produced by Pierre Gendron. Written and directed by Richard Roy. Camera (color), Guy Dufaux; editor, Michel Arcand; music, Yves Laferriere; sound, Richard Besse, Marcel Pothier; set design, Frances Calder. Reviewed at Montreal World Film Festival, Aug. 28, 1990. Running time: **90 MIN.**
Simon . . . . Michel Cote
Laurence . . . . Claire Nebout
Lawyer . . . . Philip Spensley
Antique dealer . . . Andree Lachapelle
Simon's ex-girlfriend . . Johanne-Marie Tremblay
Waitress . . . . Stephanie Morgenstern
Car salesman . . . . . . Griffin Brewer

This film works more as a nostalgic glance into a bygone era than it does as a contemporary flick. It's unpretentious, often funny and entertaining. Outside of its native Quebec, where audiences will throng to see thesp Michel Cote in anything, pic will wind up on the small screen.

Simon (Michel Cote), a 40-year-old angst-ridden bailiff, doesn't want to get a life; he's trying to get rid of one. He leaves his woman, takes his $38,550, buys a red convertible and drives to Florida where he plans to sell his deceased mother's house for more cash.

When he gets to the house on Moody Beach, he falls in lust with a complementary desperado, Laurence (Claire Nebout), a liar, squatter and thief. Living aimlessly in the abandoned beach house, she's also in serious need of a life.

Together they frolic in the sun and surf, indulge in sex and don't have a care in the world. This '70s theme is both the strength and weakness of the pic. It looks like fun, but it's not terribly believable in the hard-boiled '90s.

Slick images (once again by Guy Dufaux of "Jesus Of Montreal" calibre) and a terrific music score help Richard Roy make a respectable directorial debut. His casting is also superb.

Cote delivers another topnotch performance as the antithesis of a yuppie, and Nebout is ideal as the pouting brat. There is more anger than electricity between them as they work through their personal dilemmas and inevitably fall in love.

In one of pic's better scenes, they wind into a tender, crazy and improbable dialog of limited words. Trying to express themselves first in five-word phrases and then in three-word snippets, they slide into one- and two-word definitions of how they feel. Dufaux captures tight and claustrophic images of their faces which aptly communicate their alienation from the world.

In some of the pic's worst scenes, they break windows, hurl rocks and direct pent-up anger at each other as if they've invented the mid-life crisis.

In the predictable finale, they overcome their hang-ups: they're two of a kind. They can't live together, but they can't live without each other. They finally find out each other's names. Now they've just got to get a job. Welcome to 1990. — *Suze.*

CAIDOS DEL CIELO
(FALLEN FROM THE SKY)
(PERUVIAN-SPANISH)

An Inca Films SA-Tornasol Films SA coproduction with TVE. Produced by Gerardo Herrero. Directed by Francisco Lombardi. Screenplay, Lombardi, G. Pollarolo, A. Cabada, Herrero; camera (color), Jose Luis Lopez Linares; editor, Alberto Arevalo; music, Alejandro Masso; sound, Daniel Padilla; production design, Marta Mendez Iturriaga; production manager, Emilio Moscoso; casting, Monica Dominguez. Reviewed at Montreal World Film Festival (competing), Aug. 28, 1990. Running time: **127 MIN.**
With: Gustavo Bueno, Diana Quijano, Leontina Antonina, Carlos Gassols, David Zuniga, Edward Centeno, Delfina Paredes, Oscar Vega.

A grim reflection of life in inflation-ridden Lima, "Fallen From The Sky" interlocks three stories involving characters of different ages and backgrounds. Overlong but handled with feeling, pic might attract some international attention.

An elderly, well-to-do couple are so determined to build themselves a magnificent tomb that they sell their furniture and even their home, winding up in an old people's hospital.

Meanwhile, an impoverished, blind old woman, who lives in a shack with her grandsons, is given a pig which must be fattened to be valuable. She's so intent on getting the porker fed that she neglects the boys, even when one becomes dangerously ill. Her fate is a frightful one.

The third story deals with a lonely, facially scarred radio announcer who saves a pretty girl from suicide and gives her shelter. He falls for her, but at first she rejects him. This story, too, ends in tragedy.

Indeed, there's not much humor in the film, except of the very grim kind. But the performances are firstrate down the line, and director Francisco Lombardi (whose "The City Of The Dogs" went the festival route a while back) shows plenty of sympathy for his oddball characters.

Slow pacing is likely to diminish the film's international arthouse chances, however, though there should be interest in Spanish territories for this quality effort. — *Strat.*

TEXASVILLE

A Columbia Pictures release of a Nelson Entertainment presentation, in association with Cine-Source. Executive producers, Jake Eberts, William Peiffer. Produced by Barry Spikings, Peter Bogdanovich. Directed by Bogdanovich. Screenplay, Bogdanovich, based on Larry McMurtry's novel; camera (Deluxe color), Nicholas von Sternberg; editor, Richard Fields; sound, Kirk Francis, Michael Haines; production design, Phedon Papamichael; set decoration, Daniel Boxer; costume design, Rita Riggs; production manager-coproducer, Al Ruban; assistant director, John S. Curran; supervising producers, Henry T. Weinstein, Robert W. Whitmore; associate producers, Steve Foley, Neil Koenigsberg; casting, Gary Chason, Ross Brown. Reviewed at Sutton theater, N.Y., Sept. 17, 1990. MPAA Rating: R. Running time: **123 MIN.**
Duane Jackson . . . . . . Jeff Bridges
Jacy Farrow . . . . . . Cybill Shepherd
Karla Jackson . . . . Annie Potts
Sonny Crawford . . . Timothy Bottoms
Ruth Popper . . . . . Cloris Leachman
Lester Marlow . . . . . . Randy Quaid
Genevieve . . . . Eileen Brennan
Dickie Jackson . . . William McNamara
Also with: Angie Bolling, Su Hyatt, Earl Poole Ball, Katherine Bongfeldt, Allison Marich, Lavelle Bates, Romy Snyder, Jimmy Howell, Loyd Catlett, Pearl Jones, Harvey Christiansen, Leiland Jaynes, Sharon Ullrick, Barclay Doyle, Gordon Hurst.

Peter Bogdanovich's sequel to "The Last Picture Show" is long on folksy humor and short on plot. Several fine performances can't hide the pointless nature of "Texasville," due for mild results at the b.o.

In adapting Larry McMurtry's 1987 followup novel (predecessor "The Last Picture Show" was penned in 1965, filmed in 1971), Bogdanovich uses an impending county centennial celebration as the weak spine for this slice of small-town Texas life.

Set in 1984 and already dated by endless references to local problems caused by falling oil prices, film revolves around the nonadventures of oil tycoon Jeff Bridges. He's $12 million in debt and his loyal assistant, Cloris Leachman, is ready to quit.

Bogdanovich has rounded up many of the first film's players (notably absent are Oscar-winner Ben Johnson, whose character died, Ellen Burstyn, Clu Gulager, Sam Bottoms and John Hillerman), but the plum role goes to Annie Potts as Bridges' domineering wife. Given the best lines (which she delivers in perfect deadpan fashion) and looking marvelous, Potts walks off with the film.

Less successful is Cybill Shepherd, whose career was

launched with the 1971 pic. Making a delayed entrance as Bridges' old flame who's brooding over the death of her son, Shepherd adopts a no-makeup look and is unflatteringly photographed. This does not produce the desired effect of aging her (the "Last" teen characters are all pushing 50 here), but merely makes her look weatherbeaten, especially opposite the vivacious Potts.

Apart from a few set pieces involving the Archer County pageant parade celebrating Texasville, pic is static and poorly lensed by Nicholas von Sternberg (his first major assignment). Endless closeups in bland color make one yearn for the elegiac style of the late Robert Surtees' black & white cinematography for Bogdanovich last time out.

The subject matter is radically different, however. In place of the nostalgic early '50s is a crass '80s community of good ole boys & girls with sex on their mind. Bridges, sporting a spare tire and greying hair, is feeling old since his rambunctious son William McNamara has bedded down most of his girlfriends. He rekindles his high school romance with Shepherd, but soon she has taken away his dog, his family and even his wife (with comical implication of a lesbian relationship) to live with her.

Timothy Bottoms, topbilled in "Picture Show," is stuck with the unplayable role of town mayor/simpleton. His unspecified mental illness causes him to hallucinate, thinking he's seeing movies in the sky.

Other returnees get only one or two good scenes each: Randy Quaid as the corrupt town banker wallowing in self-pity; Leachman pouring her heart out as Bridges' conscience; Eileen Brennan simulating Marie Dressler gone fishing. Pic would have benefited from more ensemble work and less emphasis on its topliners.

The writer-director scores highest marks for milking a scene's laughs, especially some uproarious groupings featuring Potts, her quirky offspring and various firearms. McNamara is fine as Potts and Bridges' gallavanting son, while daughter-in-law Allison Marich and buxom daughter Katherine Bongfeldt make good impressions. Pearl Jones as the family housekeeper gets off several funny wisecracks, mainly at Bridges' expense.

Tech credits are on the chintzy side. Bogdanovich has again eschewed a background score to rely on source music (mainly on the radio) to good advantage, ranging from Willie Nelson to Bruce Springsteen. — *Lor.*

REPOSSESSED

A Seven Arts release through New Line Cinema. Produced by Steven Wizan. Written and directed by Bob Logan. Camera (CFI color), Michael Margulies; editor, Jeff Freeman; music, Charles Fox, production design, Shay Austin; art direction, Gae Buckley; set decoration, Lee Cunningham; costume design, Timothy D'Arcy; assistant director, Bill Berry; co-producer, Jean Higgins; casting, Adriana Michel. Reviewed at General Cinema's Beverly Connection Theater, L.A., Sept. 14, 1990. MPAA Rating: PG-13. Running time: **84 MIN.**
Nancy Aglet . . . . Linda Blair
Ernest Weller . . . . Ned Beatty
Father Mayii . . . . Leslie Nielsen
Father Brophy . . . . Anthony Starke
Also with: Lana Schwab, Thom J. Sharp.

Nonstop silliness keeps this frightless spoof of "The Exorcist" entertaining enough to keep an undemanding audience happy, and it's probably more fun than the alternative — the currently playing "The Exorcist III." Pic will possess theater screens only briefly, but video prospects look strong.

Linda Blair, her teeth and face encrusted with green gunk, once again plays the devil's host. Leslie Nielsen plays the priest pulled out of retirement to battle Satan, making the pic's giddy lowbrow satire resemble "Airplane!".

It's "pukeface" vs. "the collar jockey," only this time, the rematch is staged on national tv.

Blair is a housewife who prepares (what else?) split-pea soup for her suburban family until Satan flies out of the television during an evangelist show and takes possession of her soul.

Earnest young priest Anthony Starke is called in to help, but he's no match for swivel-neck, so Nielsen has to be persuaded. Meanwhile, the church condones the exorcism, but only if evangelist Ned Beatty and his Tammy Faye Bakker-style wife (Lana Schwab) can televise it. (The clash of faiths is passed over.)

No joke is too tasteless, no gag too weak, as the script romps along trying to pad its thin premise out to feature-length. Still, there's a certain amount of fun in watching Nielsen and the smart-mouthed she-demon go at it, wrestling match-style, while Mean Gene Okerlund and Jesse Ventura provide commentary.

Helmer Bob Logan's script doesn't make much sense (since when does the devil hate rock 'n' roll?), and the televised climax is a bust, but pic's irreverent tone carries the day, and the endless array of gags, costume changes, special effects and distractions should mollify the target audience. A little less green vomit, however, would have gone a long way in critical circles.

Starke more than holds up his end as the timid clergyman, and Beatty and Schwab are a hoot as the evangelists.

Production values are fairly generous, with special effects by Sam Nicholson ("Ghostbusters II") and makeup by Steve LaPorte ("Beetlejuice").

Cameo performers include Jack LaLanne, Wally George, bodybuilder Jake Steinfeld and VARIETY's Army Archerd, who spoofs his duties as red-carpet emcee of the Oscars in a scene where celebs arrive to catch the live taping of "Exorcism Tonight."

— *Daws.*

FUNNY ABOUT LOVE

A Paramount Pictures release of a Jon Avnet/Jordan Kerner production. Produced by Avnet, Kerner. Directed by Leonard Nimoy. Screenplay, Norman Steinberg, David Frankel, based on Bob Greene's article "Convention Of The Love Goddesses"; camera (Technicolor), Fred Murphy; editor, Peter E. Berger; music, Miles Goodman, featuring Toots Thielemans (harmonica) and Oscar Castro-Neves (guitar); sound (Dolby), Gene S. Cantamessa; production design, Stephen Storer; art direction, Nathan Haas, Robert Guerra (N.Y.); production manager, Lynn Morgan, Roger Paradiso (N.Y.); assistant director, Douglas E. Wise; associate producer, Martin Huberty; casting, Amanda Mackey. Reviewed at Paramount 29th Floor screening room, N.Y., Sept. 18, 1990. MPAA Rating: PG-13. Running time: **101 MIN.**
Duffy Bergman . . . . . . Gene Wilder
Meg . . . . Christine Lahti
Daphne . . . . Mary Stuart Masterson
E.T. . . . . Robert Prosky
Hugo . . . . Stephen Tobolowsky
Adele . . . . Anne Jackson
Claire . . . . Susan Ruttan
Vivian . . . . Jean De Baer
Dr. Benjamin . . . . . David Margulies
Redhead . . . . Tara Shannon

"Funny About Love" is a not-so-funny Gene Wilder vehicle. Sappy combination of smiles and sentimentality marks an off-day for the talented comic.

Tale of the biological clock regarding procreation is told from a male point of view here, with director Leonard Nimoy doing a good job of making palatable the more vulgar aspects of the script. However, Wilder's problems as a would-be daddy aren't interesting or compelling.

Cast as a sort of Garry Trudeau political cartoonist, Wilder bumps into Christine Lahti in a "meet cute" situation. She's working for the caterer at a book signing event, and Wilder complains about her cappuccino preparation. In a well-paced and well-edited opening reel, the divorcées strike up a romance and get married.

Inability to conceive bogs the film down in almost clinical detail. Funniest bit has Wilder sticking ice cubes in his jockey shorts on doctor's advice to get his sperm temperature down.

Film takes an absurd turn in the third reel when Wilder's child bride of a mother, Anne Jackson, is killed by a falling stove (meant to be black humor). Pic hardly recovers from this failed bit of whimsy.

While the viewer may be thinking of Irene Dunne and Cary Grant in a similar baby-less situation in the classic "Penny Serenade," duo breaks up so that Lahti can fulfill herself in a career as restaurateur.

Co-star Mary Stuart Masterson doesn't enter the scene until a full hour has elapsed, and one is likely to wonder if she's going to reprise her baby maker role from "Immediate Family" with Lahti in the Glenn Close slot. Instead, Masterson is a modern young woman whose lingo pushes the limits of the film's PG-13 rating.

Wilder meets her at a convention of beautiful sorority girls where he's guest speaker. Another whirlwind romance ensues, and Masterson is pregnant. Silly touch has no less than basketball star Patrick Ewing cameoing to announce the impending blessed event to Wilder in the Knicks' locker room.

Masterson's miscarriage and breakup with Wilder are poorly scripted en route to the predictable reconciliation with Lahti. Like "Penny Serenade," story resolution is in adoption, but the finale is padded and tedious.

Wilder has his moments in a role that overdoes the crying jags and self-pity. Both Lahti and Masterson remain most appealing actresses in search of challenging roles, not provided here. Jackson and Robert Prosky are wasted as Wilder's unlikely parents, while Susan Ruttan overdoes the ditzy routine as Prosky's next wife.

Miles Goodman's jaunty musical score and Fred Murphy's loverly views of the Big Apple make this pill easy to swallow, but it's not Mr. Spock's (or even Dr. Spock's) finest hour. — *Lor.*

VENICE FEST

ROSENCRANTZ AND GUILDENSTERN ARE DEAD
(BRITISH)

A Cinecom Entertainment Group release of a Brandenberg Intl. production. Executive producers, Louise Stephens, Thomas J. Rizzo. Produced by Michael Brandman, Emanuel Azenberg. Written and directed by Tom Stoppard, based on his play. Camera (color), Peter Biziou; editor, Nicolas Gaster; music, Stanley Myers; sound, Louis Kramer; production design, Vaughan Edwards; costume design, Andreane Neofitou; mime choreographer, Ivica Boban; production manager, Boris Dmitrovic; co-producers, Iris Merlis, Patrick Whitley; assistant director, Bill Westley; casting, Doreen Jones. Reviewed at Venice Film Festival (competing), Sept. 9, 1990. (In Mill Valley Film Festival, Calif.) MPAA Rating: PG. Running time: **118 MIN.**
Rosencrantz . . . . Gary Oldman
Guildenstern . . . . Tim Roth
The Player . . . . . Richard Dreyfuss
Hamlet . . . . Iain Glen
Ophelia . . . . Joanna Roth
Claudius . . . . Donald Sumpter
Gertrude . . . . Joanna Miles
Osric . . . . Ljubo Zecevic
Polonius . . . . Ian Richardson
Laertes . . . . Sven Medvesck
Horatio . . . . Vili Matula
English ambassador . . . John Burgess
Also with: Livio Badurina, Tomislav Maretic, Mare Mlacnik, Srdjan Soric.

Twenty-three years after it was first produced on the London stage, "Rosencrantz And Guildenstern Are Dead" comes to the screen in a cleverly acted and staged production. Pic has quality written all over it, and should perform well in major city arthouses, especially in English territories where the sublime dialog will be fully appreciated.

Marking his debut as director, playwright Tom Stoppard takes two marginal characters from Shakespeare's "Hamlet," and places them at the center of a comedy-drama, while the major characters of the play — Hamlet, Ophelia, Claudius and the rest — are only part of the background.

Rosencrantz and Guildenstern are never certain about what's going on in Elsinore. They overhear crucial conversations and encounters, they talk briefly to the King and to Hamlet, and, in the end, they accompany Hamlet on a voyage to England, but they're never a part of the central drama.

Stoppard is a genius with words, and words are crucially important here, which is why great care will have to be taken in subtitling or dubbing the film for foreign territories.

The play has been seen as a mixture of Samuel Beckett and Shakespeare, but on film, Stoppard adds cinematic references so that the two protagonists, with their endless word games, come across as a mixture of Abbott and Costello (the "Who's On First" routine) and Laurel and Hardy (with the clumsy Rosencrantz forever annoying and frustrating the superior Guildenstern). There's also a touch of Monty Python in the zaniness of the characters and their verbal and visual antics.

Gary Oldman and Tim Roth are splendid in their roles. Oldman plays his character as a shrewd simpleton, and Roth plays his as a man who thinks he's clever, but really isn't. These two consummate performers handle the intricate dialog with seemingly effortless skill, and a sequence in which they play a game of verbal tennis is a knockout.

Also giving a formidable performance is Richard Dreyfuss as the leader of a band of strolling players. Dreyfuss, long-haired, charming and powerful, is a delight as he describes his art ("We do on-stage what's supposed to happen off") and his style ("The Love, Blood and Rhetoric School of acting").

By its very nature, this is a film in which words are all-important, but Stoppard hasn't come up with a literal version of a filmed play. Pic was shot in Yugoslavia, and is handsomely mounted, with plenty of visual as well as aural humor. Especially impressive are the various

Original Play

LONDON National Theater presentation of comedy-drama in three acts by Tom Stoppard. Staged by Derek Goldby; sets, Desmond Heeley; lighting, Richard Pilbrow; music and sound effects, Marc Wikinson; mime, Claude Chagrin. Opened April 11, '67, at the Old Vic, London, $4.55 top.

Rosencrantz . . . . John Stride
Guildenstern . . Edward Petherbridge
Player . . . . Graham Crowden
Players . . . . . . Alan Adams, Oliver Cotton, Neil Fitzpatrick, Luke Hardy, Roger Kemp
Hamlet . . . . John McEnery
Ophelia . . . . Caroline John
Claudius . . . . . Kenneth Mackintosh
Gertrude . . . . Mary Griffins
Polonius . . . . Peter Cellier
Fortinbras . . . . David Bailie
Horatio . . . . . . David Hargreaves
Ambassador . . . . David Ryall
Courtiers and attendants . David Bailie, Petronelia Barker, David Belcher, Margo Cunningham, Denis de Marne, Kay Gallie, Reginald Green, David Hargreaves, William Hobbs, Richard Kay, Lee Menzies, Lennard Pearce, Ron Pember, Frederick Pyne, Maggie Riley, David Ryall, Christopher Timothy
Player-Musicians . Lawrence Kennedy (flute), Laurie Morgan (drums), Stephen Nagy (oboe)
Offstage Musicians . . . . Malcolm Hall, Edward Wilson

plays performed by Dreyfuss and his troupe, including a performance of "Hamlet" itself, staged for the castle's kitchen staff.

Back in the '70s, "Rosencrantz And Guildenstern" was a film project for John Boorman that never materialized. The author himself is responsible for the screen version, and a better translation could not be imagined.

This film for a specialized audience should garner positive reviews and perform exceedingly well in arthouse venues. It also will have a very long life on video and tv. — *Strat.*

S'EN FOUT LA MORT
(NO FEAR, NO DIE)
(FRENCH-WEST GERMAN)

A Cinea-Pyramide-Les Films de Mindif-Camera One-NEF Produktion-La Sept co-production. (Intl. sales: Pyramide Intl., Paris.) Produced by Francis Boespflug, Philippe Carcassone. Directed by Claire Denis. Screenplay, Denis, Jean-Pol Fargeau; camera (color), Pascal Marti; editor, Dominique Auvray; music, Abdullah Ibrahim; sound, Jean-Paul Mugel; production design, Jean-Jacques Caziot; production manager, Nicolas Daguet, Brigitte Faure; assistant director, Gabriel Julien Laferriere. Reviewed at Venice Film Festival (competing), Sept. 10, 1990. Running time: **92 MIN.**
Dah . . . . Isaach de Bankole
Jocelyn . . . . Alex Descas
Pierre Ardennes . . Jean-Claude Brialy
Toni . . . . Solveig Dommartin
Michel . . . . . Christopher Buchholz
Ti Emile . . . . Gilbert Felmar
Henri . . . . Daniel Bellus
François . . . . . François Oloa Biloa
Toni's mother . . . . . . Christa Lang

Unfortunately, director Claire Denis, whose "Chocolat" made a mark at Cannes two years ago and has enjoyed some success on the international arthouse circuit since, opts to set her new drama in the ugly milieu of cockfighting. Film has opened softly in France, and international chances look to be negligible also.

This downbeat drama concerns two black friends, one from Africa and the other from the West Indies, who are involved in illegal activities on the fringes of French society. Premise might have sounded promising, but pic, with its deliberately ungrammatical title, becomes almost a documentary on training fighting cocks and the rituals of the illegal "sport."

Some scenes, in which Dah (Isaach de Bankole, the lead actor from "Chocolat"), and Jocelyn (Alex Descas) lovingly train their birds are quite beautiful. But despite a closing title asserting no birds were hurt during filming, the numerous cockfights come across as utterly disgusting. In some countries, censor boards may even prohibit the film for these scenes alone.

Denis is a talented filmmaker. She makes the most of her dank settings in the outer suburbs, with their dismal gas stations and dingy apartments. Jean-Claude Brialy gives an effective performance as the cockfight organizer. Solveig Dommartin (the memorable lead of Wim Wenders' "Wings Of Desire") has little to do but look alluring as Brialy's barmaid wife.

De Bankole and Descas make their friendship a tangible one, so the final tragedy is quite moving. It's just a pity Denis couldn't have come up with a less socially unacceptable game for these characters to play. — *Strat.*

EDINSTVENIJAT SVIDETEL
(THE SOLE WITNESS)
(BULGARIAN)

A Studio Boyana production. Produced by Boris Chadziev. Directed by Mikhail Pandurski. Screenplay, Nikolai Nikiforov; camera (color), Ivo Furnadziev; editor, Madlena Djakova; music, Valeri Milovansky; sound, Svetlozar Georgiev; production design, Neli Pekareva; production manager, Mirco Borisow; assistant director, Doco Cvetkovski. Reviewed at Venice Film Festival (competing), Sept. 12, 1990. Running time: **61 MIN.**
Christo Panov . . . . . . Oleg Borisov
The bus driver . . . . . . Kiril Varijcki
Georginova . . . . Irin Krivosieva
Vladimir Panov . . . . Ljuben Catalov

Christo's wife . . . . . . Katja Cukova
Bus driver's wife . . . Saska Bratanova

An extremely modest drama, centering around a moral problem, "The Sole Witness" is more suited to tv than the bigscreen, but the 1988 pic still found its way into the Venice competition, where it won prizes for best actor (Oleg Borisov) and for its pleasant but unremarkable music score.

A humble, tired factory worker, effectively played by Russian actor Borisov, is traveling home one night and gets involved in a fracas with a bus driver, who threatens him with an iron bar. A woman passenger on the bus is so angered she files an official complaint.

The chastened bus driver comes to Borisov to apologize, and later his wife and three children show up, begging him not to testify. He agrees, but then the woman who filed the complaint in the first place finds herself accused of slandering the bus driver.

It's a no-win situation, and the film has no resolution. Along the way there's the usual grim depiction of working class life. The protagonist lives in a small, cramped apartment with his nagging wife and middle-aged son, a functionary at the factory, who has a number of girlfriends and wants his father's help to get an apartment of his own.

With a running time of barely an hour, "The Sole Witness" seems unlikely to make its mark internationally. The story is really no more than an anecdote padded with long, lingering shots of the hero's mournful face. A more ambitious treatment was needed here. — *Strat.*

I HIRED A CONTRACT KILLER
(FINNISH-SWEDISH)

A Villealfa Filmprods.-Swedish Film Institute co-production, in association with Finnkino, Esselte Video, Megamania, Pandora Film, Pyramide Films, Channel 4. (Intl. sales: Christa Saredi Sales, Zurich.) Produced, written and directed by Aki Kaurismäki. Camera (Metrocolor), Timo Salminen; editor, Kaurismäki; production design, John Ebden; sound, Timo Linnasalo; production manager, Klaus Heydemann; assistant director, Pauli Pentti. Reviewed at Venice Film

Festival (competing), Sept. 13, 1990. (Also in New York Film Festival.) Running time: **79 MIN.**
Henri Boulanger . . Jean-Pierre Léaud
Margaret . . . . Margi Clarke
Harry (the killer) . . . Kenneth Colley
Vic . . . . Serge Reggiani
Department head . . . . Trevor Bowen
Secretary . . . . Imogen Clare
Landlady . . . . Angela Walsh
Pete . . . . Nicky Tesco
Al . . . . Charles Cork
Miller's boss . . . . . Michael O'Hagan
Receptionist . . . . . . Walter Sparrow
Guitarist . . . . Joe Strummer
Harry's daughter . . . . . . Ette Eliot
(In English)

In his second feature this year, an English-language pic set in London and topling Truffaut actor Jean-Pierre Léaud, prolific Finn director Aki Kaurismäki cheerfully pokes fun at cinematic clichés. Results are mixed, at best, as the director doesn't come up with dialog or situations quite funny enough.

Kaurismäki fans (who seem to be growing in numbers) will be pleased if not overwhelmed by this new effort, which, if not one of his best films, is still good enough to warrant international exposure in specialized venues.

Following up this year's "The Match Factory Girl," "I Hired A Contract Killer" has a plot that has seen service in Hollywood pics of the past. Solitary type Léaud has worked for 15 years as a clerk at the office of Her Majesty's Waterworks until he's dismissed (and given a gold watch that doesn't work) because the public facility has been privatized.

With no one to turn to, Léaud attempts suicide, but when he sticks his head in a gas oven, a gas strike commences. So he withdraws his life savings and gets a cab driver to take him to a seedy bar where he announces he needs to hire a killer, and arranges to have himself bumped off.

Not surprisingly, immediately after the contract is signed, his life changes. He starts to drink and smoke, and he meets a girl who sells roses in pubs. Now he's in love and wants to live, but the h.q. of the hired killer's boss has been demolished, and the killer, himself dying of cancer, is hot on his trail.

The plot has no surprises, but the film is tolerably amusing because of Kaurismäki's offhand sense of humor and taste for bizarre characters. The oddest of those is Serge Reggiani, who runs a French-style hamburger stand apparently in the middle

of a famous London cemetery.

The early scenes are funny, too, with Léaud well cast as the somewhat strange loner whose phone book contains only two numbers (the company that fired him and a deceased aunt).

But the level of invention isn't fully maintained, and pic remains spasmodically amusing rather than captivating. Though obviously shot quickly and economically, it looks very good, with fine use of London locations.

Margi Clarke ("Letter To Brezhnev") is adequate as the flower-seller. Kenneth Colley is quite memorable as the dogged, terminally ill contract killer who reads the Financial Times. There's also an in-joke reference to Turkish film director Ali Ozgentürk. — *Strat.*

DOCTEUR PETIOT
(DR. PETIOT)
(FRENCH-COLOR/B&W)

An AAA release (Aries Film Releasing in U.S.) of an M.S. Prods.-Sara Films-Cine 5 coproduction, in association with Canal Plus. Produced by Michel Serrault, Alain Sarde, Philippe Chapelier-Dehesdin. Directed by Christian de Chalonge. Screenplay, Dominique Garnier, de Chalonge; camera (Eclair color, black & white), Patrick Blossier; editor, Anita Fernandez; music, Michel Portal; sound, Marie-Jeanne Wyckmans; sets, Yves Brover; costume design, Corinne Jorry; assistant director, Jacques Royer; production manager, François Menny; associate producer, Christine Gozlan. Reviewed at N.Y. Film Festival, Sept. 20, 1990. Running time: **102 MIN.**
Dr. Petiot . . . . Michel Serrault
Drezner . . . . Pierre Romans
Nathan Guzik . . . . Zbigniew Horoks
Georgette Petiot . Berangere Bonvoisin
Celestin Nivelon . . . André Chaumeau
Madame Guzik . . . . . . Aurore Prieto
Louis Rossignol . . Axel Bogousslavski
Gérard Petiot . . . . . Maxime Coillion
Forestier . . . . André Julien
Collard . . . . Nini Crepon
Madame Kern . . . . Nita Klein
Cecile Drezner . Martine Mongermont
Vampire . . . . Jean Lio

Michel Serrault's tour-de-force performance as "Dr. Petiot" illuminates a sordid episode in a dark chapter of French history: the German Occupation during World War II. Film's stylish approach overcomes the morbid nature of its subject matter and makes for a potent arthouse attraction via Aries release.

On pic's home turf, Serrault and ongoing interest in this period (Claude Chabrol hit with "Story Of Women") should attract attention and boxoffice.

The venal and negative aspects of behavior of many Parisians during the Occupation was brilliantly captured in Claude Autant-Lara's 1956 classic "Four Bags Full," in which Jean Gabin and Bourvil portrayed two contrasting types involved in the black market.

In "Dr. Petiot," Serrault and his director Christian de Chalonge tackle the difficult matter of a physician who was secretly a serial killer. Under the pretext of assisting Jews in fleeing the country (supposedly headed for Argentina), he killed them with lethal injections he claimed were vaccinations, stole their valuables and disposed of the corpses in a homemade crematorium.

Petiot's crimes were not discovered until 1944 when a fire in his furnace got out of control and attracted the gendarmes and fire brigade. He escaped apprehension, found new identities including an interrogator of suspected collaborationists and was finally caught and guillotined on 27 counts of murder in 1946.

This grisly subject matter recalls Richard Fleischer's fine film "10 Rillington Place" about the fake doctor Christie's London murders during the '40s. Unlike that film's realism, de Chalonge adopts a fantastic, almost expressionistic approach, beginning with Serrault literally jumping into a movie screen showing a vampire film.

What follows are stylized episodes noted by color drained visuals, exotic makeup (Petiot's heavy eye liner suggests screen heavies of yore). Serrault's flamboyant performance, constantly on the move and even dancing around the room as he ransacks his victims' belongings, is outstanding and cleverly leavened with moments of black humor.

Graphic depiction of his deeds are wisely left to the imagination, yet the horrendous nature of this parallel episode to the contemporaneous Nazi death camps comes through forcefully. Also notable is de Chalonge's inclusion of the anti-Semitic newsreel propaganda projected before the feature at the local Parisian cinema, documenting a 1942 exhibition on "Jewish traits."

Petiot is apprehended in a movie theater after writing an open letter on his deeds to the newspaper, which matches up with his own handwriting. Crashing through a movie screen the second time, he doesn't escape into fantasy but into the hands of the police.

Serrault dominates the film, with supporting cast of unfamiliar thesps well-matched to their roles. Patrick Blossier's deep focus photography is arresting, including several scenes in a vast arcade where Petiot lives that recall Orson Welles' setting for "The Trial."

Michel Portal contributes bandoneon music for the ironic scenes of Serrault serenading his duped victims "headed for Argentina." Elsewhere, a saw played by an old man at the arcade adds to the film's eerie mood. — *Lor.*

TORONTO FEST

THE LONG WALK HOME

A Miramax Films release of a New Visions Pictures production. Produced by Howard W. Koch Jr., Dave Bell. Executive producers, Taylor Hackford, Stuart A. Benjamin. Directed by Richard Pearce. Screenplay, John Cork; camera (color), Roger Deakins; editor, Bill Yahraus; music, George Fenton; production design, Blake Russell; costume design, Shay Cunliffe; assistant directors, Victoria E. Rhodes, Randy Fletcher; unit production manager, Lyda Blank; associate producer, Edwin C. Atkins; casting, Shari Rhodes, Jo Doster. Reviewed at the Toronto Festival Of Festivals, Sept. 10, 1990. MPAA Rating: PG. Running time: **97 MIN.**

Miriam Thompson . . . . Sissy Spacek
Odessa Cotter . . . . Whoopi Goldberg
Norman Thompson . . Dwight Schultz
Herbert Cotter . . . . . . Ving Rhames
Tunker Thompson . . . . Dylan Baker
Selma Cotter . . . . . Erika Alexander
Mary Catherine . . Lexi Faith Randall
Theodore Cotter . Richard Habersham
Franklin Cotter . . . . . Jason Weaver
Narrator . . . . . . Mary Steenburgen
   Also with: Crystal Thompson, Cherene Snow, Chelcie Ross, Dan E. Butler, Phil Sterling, Haynes Brooke, Stacy Fleming, Jeff Taffet, Jay Reed, Afemo Omilami, Norman Matlock.

Set in Montgomery, Ala., during the 1955 civil rights bus boycott, "The Long Walk Home" is an effectively mounted drama about the human impact of changing times on two families. Its major selling points are the sturdy performances by Sissy Spacek as an uppercrust white housewife and Whoopi Goldberg as her maid.

Pic's historical sensibility, while relevant, may be too remote for wide audiences, but this modest, worthwhile film is well-suited for video, cable and foreign ancillary playoff.

Narrated in the present from the point of view of Spacek's young daughter Mary Catherine, "The Long Walk Home" quickly establishes the uneasy symbiosis between blacks and whites during the last decade of the segregated South. Spacek's Miriam Thompson is a prim model of upper-middle-class Southern womanhood who cannot run her household without her indispensable maid Odessa.

Goldberg limns the dignified, hard-working maid with conviction and control. Obviously familiar with women like Miriam, Spacek fills out the character with subtlety and insight. Although casually solicitous of Goldberg's welfare, Spacek's world view is blurred by deep-seated blindspots.

Her eyes begin to open when Goldberg takes Spacek's daughter and two white girls to picnic in a segregated park, where she's humiliated by a policeman. The well-connected housewife calls the police chief and forces a formal apology from the cop. This incident, however, doesn't materially change the relationship between maid and mistress or liberate Spacek from her cultural inculcation.

Racist jokes are commonplace during cocktail parties and family dinners, where Spacek's brother-in-law (Dylan Baker) espouses hard-line segregationist attitudes. When Spacek's mother makes a crude racial remark in Goldberg's presence, the housewife is embarassed, but does nothing. Neither does Goldberg, whose overriding concern is providing for her family.

Goldberg's hard-working husband (Ving Rhames) and three well- mannered kids make a loving family, but the household's mood is tense because of external events. Local black leaders call for a bus boycott to end segregated seating, and Goldberg is honor-bound to trek to work on foot.

Initally more concerned about the disruption of the household schedule than her maid's new hardship, Spacek offers to drive Goldberg on those days when other business takes her near the maid's neighborhood. She keeps this secret from her husband, drawing her daughter into a conspiracy of silence.

As the black boycott stiffens, so does white resistance, which turns ugly with the bombing of Martin Luther King's house. Afraid of change, the town establishment refuses to compromise. Spacek's realtor husband (Dwight Schultz) joins the local Citizens' Council in a show of solidarity with other pillars of the community, taking comfort in the fact that he hasn't joined the Ku Klux Klan.

The screenplay makes effective use of such contradictions in probing the psychology of segregation. This is a world, after all, in which advantaged Southern whites spent a good part of their childhoods in the care of black nannies. Still, Spacek's husband sincerely declares that Goldberg, belongs "to a different species — she can never be like us."

Although the role of the black church in the civil rights movement has been extensively depicted on film, director Richard Pearce evokes the spiritual milieu of gospel-inspired rallies with economy and strength.

He also stages powerful but controlled scenes of inevitable racist violence. When Spacek's husband learns that his wife has been chauffeuring the maid, he forces her to take a stand. Barely able to articulate her reasons, she throws in with the boycott organizers. Spacek's pivotal change of mindset becomes an emblem for the onset of profound social upheaval, reflected in a wrenching climactic scene.

Some critics may take "The Long Walk Home" to task for a "lest-we-forget" tone that suggests America has put the worst of its racial problems behind it. But the film resists the temptation to succumb to sentimentality and offers believable characterizations in the context of its time and place. Period production design is firstrate. — *Rich.*

THE GRIFTERS

A Miramax Films release of a Cineplex Odeon Films presentation of a Martin Scorsese production. Produced by Scorsese, Robert Harris, James Painten. Executive producer, Barbara De Fina. Directed by Stephen Frears. Screenplay, Donald Westlake, based on the novel by Jim Thompson; camera (color), Oliver Stapleton; editor, Mick Audsley; music, Elmer Bernstein; sound, John Sutton; art director, Leslie McDonald; co-producer, Peggy Rajski. Reviewed at the Toronto Festival Of Festivals. MPAA rating: R. Running time: **113 MIN.**

Roy Dillon . . . . John Cusack
Lilly Dillon . . . . Anjelica Huston
Myra Langtry . . . . . Annette Bening
   Also with: Pat Hingle, J.T. Walsh.

Two prominent filmmakers have taken Jim Thompson's intriguing novel about the subculture of small-time hustlers and fashioned a curiously uneven movie in "The Grifters."

Producer Martin Scorsese and director Stephen Frears may have had the ideal sensibilities for this quirky tale of of deception and erotic gamesmanship, but the film lacks the edgy nuance and emotional punch needed to hook an audience. Boxoffice prospects seem iffy.

Donald Westlake's screenplay sticks to the form and spirit of Thompson's underworld narrative. John Cusack plays Roy Dillon, a Los Angeles con man whose salesman's job is a cover for his real vocation.

Roy's mother, Lilly (Anjelica Huston), gave birth at the tender age of 14, then fashioned a lucrative career as a roving racetrack bag lady, putting down bets for the Baltimore mob.

Roy left home as a teen and learned the tricks of the grifter's trade on the road. One of his favorite scams is to order a beer, flashing a $20 bill at the bartender. When his drink arrives he palms over a $10 note and, if he's lucky, gets change for $20. One day his luck turns bad and a bartender busts him full force in the gut with a baseball bat. This run-in lays him low with some nasty internal bleeding.

Roy is ministered to by his sexy girlfriend Myra (Annette Bening), who lives by her wits and her tightly wrapped body. When Roy's mother turns up out of the blue in "Los Angle-ees," the hardened moll's maternal instincts take over. While Roy recovers in the hospital at Lilly's expense, his mother tries to scotch his affair with Myra and browbeats him to reveal the truth about his life.

But the cynical grifter keeps his mother at emotional arm's length and intensifies his relationship with the seductive Myra.

Meanwhile, the mob boss travels west to teach Lilly a painful lesson for skimming mob money at the track. Clearly these characters share a proclivity for risk, and Frears unfolds the story with shadowy overtones of inevitable big trouble.

Roy believes he's safe from danger as he long as he sticks to the "short con," nickel-and-diming local suckers for easy scores. When Roy and Myra take a holiday in La Jolla, she reveals her true colors. Myra, is an expert at the "big con," elaborate swindles like phony investment setups, geared to netting five- and six-figure scores.

In a bizarre flashback, she tells Roy about her life with a master con artist. Myra correctly suspects Roy's little secret: a large horde of hidden cash accumulated from years of grifting.

When he spurns her proposal for a big-con partnership leading to a life of ease, Myra lashes out by accusing him of harboring incestuous desires for Lilly. Enraged, Roy throws her out, setting in motion an accelerating train of events from which only one player in the triangle will survive.

The crucial flaws in "The Grifters" are as slippery to divine as a fast-moving shell game. Westlake takes chunks of prime dialog from the novel, and Frears is comfortable enough in the story's sordid milieu. But the pivotal sexual tension between Roy and his mother is muted until the very last minute.

Myra's manipulative nature is so sugar-coated by a bubbly exterior that her true nature seems startlingly schizophrenic when finally revealed. Cusack underplays Roy, making him an unbelievable wiseguy, a colorless cipher too akin to the saps he loves to fleece. When its shattering endgame finally kicks in, "The Grifters" has largely exhausted its suspense and is tilting toward claustrophobia.

Production exigencies probably accounted for setting the film in an undefined present, rather than the novel's more innocent early '60's context. Although Frears' previous films have been brilliantly in touch with both contemporary and period settings, "The Grifters" suffers from an unsettling dislocation from its time and place. — *Rich*.

WHERE
(U.S.-B&W)

A Where Film production. Written, produced and directed by Gabor Szabo. Camera (black & white), Nyika Jancso; sound, George Pinter; art direction, Attila Kovacs. Reviewed at Toronto Festival of Festivals, Sept. 14, 1990. Running time: **96 MIN.**
With: Miklos Ace, Renata Satler, Dennis Cornell.

 abor Szabo's first feature deals with the murky subject of sexual degradation.

Bleakly shot and badly acted, "Where" depicts a man forcing a woman to commit repeated sexual acts with and on him without her enjoying or objecting or saying much at all. He then treats a male college student like a slave, without touching him, to the same nonreaction.

Pic was filmed in an unidentified U.S. city and the question is not where but why. — *Adil*.

RESIDENT ALIEN
(U.S.-DOCU)

A Films Around the World presentation. Produced and directed by Jonathan Nossiter. Camera (color), Frank Prinzi, John Foster; editor, Nossiter. Reviewed at the Toronto Festival of Festivals, Sept. 16, 1990. Running time: **85 MIN.**
With: Quentin Crisp, John Hurt, Sting, Holly Woodlawn, Fran Lebowitz, Emile de Antonio, Paul Morrissey.

This is fun festival fare that will find its niche in metropolitan underground circuits, as did its subject, gay rights activist Quentin Crisp. In addition to adventurous arthouses, pic has a shot on tv outlets prepared to take a risk.

For those hip to the gay scene's perils and triumphs, this is a terrifically funny film. The dry-witted, tragicomic Crisp epitomizes the fear, bravery and alienation of honest gays. Helmer Jonathan Nossiter weaves nostalgic and cunning footage into a clever package.

It quietly introduces the 81-year-old Crisp as a New York "resident alien" from the U.K. who moved to the U.S. in 1973 riding the crest of publicity on the pic, "The Naked Civil Servant," a fictional account of his life starring John Hurt (as Crisp).

This docu picks up where the fiction film left off. New footage captures Crisp's unfailing wit. Old footage testifies to the endurance of his struggle.

In one sequence, Nossiter utilizes footage of Crisp on the Sally Jessy Raphael talk show to garner a hearty laugh and expose middle class American attitudes about gays. In the clip, Crisp is being lampooned by "straight" guests and told "Homosexuality and lesbianism is just plain perversion."

In another scene, Crisp is sitting around a dimly lit table with old pals reminiscing about the Andy Warhol years.

Crisp's crowd (old and young) have all taken a walk on the wilder side. Nossiter manages to capture the highs and lows of the gay scene via their personal stories. Likewise, most of the pic has an upbeat, comic tone, but Nossiter also unveils the darker side of life on the outskirts.

He films Crisp eating a can of pork and beans for dinner as readily as he depicts his showbiz flare. One of Crisp's colleagues points out that his autobiography ends with the desperate plea: "I stumble to my grave confused and hurt and hungry," a line which resonates long after the laughs have subsided. — *Suze*.

MONTREAL FEST

DON JUAN, MI QUERIDO FANTASMA
(DON JUAN, MY DEAR GHOST)
(SPANISH)

A UIP (Spain) release of a BMG production in collaboration with TVE and Productora Andaluza de Programas. (Intl. sales: RTVE, Madrid.) Produced by Jose Maria Calleja. Directed by Antonio Mercero. Screenplay, Mercero, Joaquin Oristrell; camera (Eastmancolor), Carlos Suarez; editor, Rosa Graceli-Salgado; music, Bernardo Bonezzi; sound, Miguel A. Polo; production design, Rafael Palmero; choreography, Paco Romero; production manager, Francisco Beilot; assistant director, Euschio Graziani. Reviewed at Montreal World Film Festival (competing), Sept. 2, 1990. Running time: **103 MIN.**
Don Juan/
Juan Marquina . Juan Luis Galiardo
Dona Ines . . . . . . Maria Barranco
Sra. de Marquina . . . Veronica Forque
Ana . . . . Loles Leon
Widow Prodini . . . . . Rossy de Palma
Commissioner
Ulloa . . . . . Jose (Saza) Sazatornil
Monreal . . . . Luis Escobar
Mendez . . . . Rafael Alvarez
Ciutti . . . . Vicente Diez
Ruben . . . . Pedro Reyes

A spirited, briskly paced comedy involving a ghost and mistaken identity, this looks like a money-spinner in Latin territories, with wider international possibilities also. Pic could cash in on the current genre of ghostly movies.

The plot is simple enough, and variations of it have been played out in Hollywood comedies in the past. The setting is Seville on the Day of the Dead (Nov. 1). The ghost of Don Juan emerges from his tomb, as he does for 24 hours every year, hoping to escape purgatory by doing something worthwhile.

Meanwhile, hammy actor Juan Marquina (Juan Luis Galiardo) is appearing in a local theater production as Don Juan. (His costume is identical to that of the ghost.) Marquina is involved in drug dealing, and the police are watching him. He also has a frustrated wife, and a number of mistresses on the side.

Before long, actor and ghost have exchanged places. Don Juan is accepted as the actor, while Marquina, through a series of unfortunate incidents, has been arrested for public nudity.

The rest of the film explores all the possibilities of the basic mistaken identity plot. Marquina's women respond ecstatically to Don Juan's lovemaking, and the increasingly hysterical actor is unable to convince anyone who he really is.

Matters are complicated by the presence of two incompetent cops who have established themselves in Marquina's hotel to try to record on video the drug deal.

Since the ghost, though tangible in every other way, doesn't appear on film or video, these maladroit law enforcers become increasingly perplexed and confused. Director Antonio Mercero directs with a brisk pace and a fine feeling for farce, and is well-served by his cast.

Galiardo is fine as both the ghost and the actor, and manages the differences in the two characters well. But the film is stolen by vet comedian Jose (Saza) Sazatornil in a fine comic turn as the befuddled police commissioner.

Mércero uses a few modest special effects (the ghost passing through walls, for example), but he concentrates on basic slapstick situations, proving that plenty of fun can still be had from the oldest jokes in the world.

An added attraction is that the opening credits are entirely sung. Another good idea is that one female character speaks only through the sound of her castanets, which are subtitled.

Festivals looking for comic relief should be interested in this one, and so should distributors after a good old-fashioned comedy. The picture is handsomely produced, with a robust music score. — *Strat*.

REYHANEH
(IRANIAN)

An Erfani Farabi Cinema Foundation production. Written, produced and

directed by Alireza Raiessian. Camera (color), Mahmod Kalari; editor, Abbas Ganjavi; music, Kambiz Roshanravan; sound, Eshagh Khan; production design, Iraj Raminfar. Reviewed at Montreal World Film Festival (Cinema of Today & Tomorrow), Aug. 26, 1990. Running time: **83 MIN.**
Reyhaneh . . . Fatemah Motamed Aria
Heydar . . . . Majid Mozafari
Eskandar . . . . . . Hossein Mahjub
Also with: Sorur Nejatollahi, Akbar Abdi, Hamid Jebeli.

Although a fascinating portrait of a divorced woman in contemporary Iran, "Reyhaneh" is less successful than some of the other Iranian pics on the fest circuit these days.

In the opening sequence of black & white stills with voice-over, the title character is divorced from her husband, who treated her brutally. She travels to the country to stay with her older brother, but he's not pleased to see her, not only because, as a divorcée, she's a disgrace, but also because he's bankrupt. Before long, he winds up in prison for nonpayment of debts.

Reyhaneh goes to live with an aunt, who encourages her to meet a new man, but happiness seems likely to elude the long-suffering heroine.

All this is rather stolidly handled by writer-producer-director Alireza Raiessian. In the leading role, Fatemah Motamed Aria is called upon to do little apart from suffer nobly.

The background, a provincial town with ancient houses, is always worth watching, and the film will interest anyone fascinated by the role of women in contemporary Iran. The English subtitles on the print that unspooled in Montreal were woefully inadequate. — *Strat.*

ALL THE VERMEERS IN NEW YORK

An American Playhouse Theatrical Films production. Executive producer, Lindsay Law. Produced by Henry S. Rosenthal. Conceived and directed by Jon Jost. Camera (color), Jost; editor, Jost; music, Jon A. English; sound, John Murphy; production manager, Molly Bradford. Reviewed at Montreal World Film Festival (competing), Aug. 27, 1990. (In Mill Valley Film Festival, Calif.) Running time: **87 MIN.**
Anna . . . . Emmanuelle Chaulet
Mark . . . . Stephen Lack
Felicity . . . . Grace Phillips
Gracie Mansion . . . . Herself
Gordon . . . . . Gordon Joseph Weiss
Ariel . . . . Laurel Kiefer
Max . . . . Roger Ruffin
Nicole . . . . Katherine Bean

This film from established U.S. independent Jon Jost is one of his best. Scheduled to air on PBS in the fall, "All The Vermeers" should play the international festival route, and it also deserves theatrical outings in specialized situations.

Jost takes a simple idea here, but by combining exciting images, effective casting and a luxurious jazz score (played by the Bay Area Jazz Composers Orchestra) he comes up with a haunting picture.

The principal characters are Anna, a would-be actress from France living in New York with her friend, Felicity, and a girl who practices voice training at all hours; and Mark, a hardworking, burned-out Wall Street broker. Anna and Mark meet at an exhibition of paintings by Jan Vermeer, the 17th century Dutch master.

The storyline itself could be written on the head of a pin, but Jost is more interested in creating a beguiling mood and in giving the film the look of a Vermeer. In this he succeeds admirably, having photographed the material himself using new Kodak fine-grain, high-speed stock. It looks sublime, with its soft lighting and elegant camera moves.

The actors serve the director well. Emmanuelle Chaulet, who rose to fame in Eric Rohmer's "Boyfriends And Girlfriends," is charming as Anna, while Stephen Lack, a veteran of Canadian cinema, brings a world-weary quality to the role of Mark. Some improvisational acting is apparent.

Supporting roles are also well played, with Grace Phillips especially good as Anna's friend. A scene in which Anna pretends she can't speak English and uses Felicity to interpret during her first date with Mark is a gem.

Pacing is slow, as befits the mood, and the film builds to a touching climax. Jost's comments on art and commerce in today's world are well taken, and he says the pic is, in some ways, "an elegy for the '80s."

Jost presented his subsequent film, "Sure Fire," at the Toronto film fest. — *Strat.*

SHIKIBU MONOGATARI (MT. ASO'S PASSIONS) (JAPANESE)

A Seiyu Ltd. production. (Intl. sales, except Asia: Metropolis Film, Zurich.) Produced by Kazunobu Yamaguchi. Written and directed by Kei Kumai, based on the play by Matsuyo Akimoto. Camera (color), Masao Tochizawa; editor, Osamu Inoue; music, Teizo Matsumura; sound, Yukio Kubota; production design, Takeo Kimura; production manager, Masahiro Oba; assistant director, Kazuo Hara. Reviewed at Montreal World Film Festival (competing), Aug. 29, 1990. Running time: **112 MIN.**
Toyoichi Otomo . . . . . . Eiji Okuda
Priestess Chisu . . . . . . Keiko Kishi
Terue Otomo . . . . . . Mieko Harada
Isa Otomo . . . . Kyoko Kagawa
Ume . . . . Taiko Shinbashi
Uchiko . . . . Rika Abiko
Yumenosuke . . . . . . Tetta Sugimoto

Religious fanaticism in contemporary Japan is tackled with uneven results in the latest film from writer-director Kei Kumai. For non-Japanese, it's a subject not fully comprehensible, which will make the handsomely produced pic difficult to market outside Asian territories.

The original Japanese title literally means "Tales Of Shikibu." Shikibu was an 11th century poetess who traveled the country preaching Buddhism and cured the sick and crippled by taking on their illnesses herself. Legend has it that Shikibu is reincarnated regularly, with her powers of healing intact.

This background (not really explained in the film) is essential to comprehend the characters' motivations. Toyichi (Eiji Okuda) is a young man suffering severe mental illness after an accident in the factory where he worked. He lives at the foot of Mt. Aso with his wife, who is having an affair with another man, and his protective mother.

He's befriended by two members of a religious sect, and when he goes to their headquarters becomes infatuated by the sect's chief priestess, Chishu, believing her to be Buddha himself. Chishu, supposedly the 68th reincarnation of Shikibu, seems more interested in manipulating the deranged young man and, in the end, using him for sexual gratification.

Japanese film buffs will be intrigued by the casting of Keiko Kishi as Chishu. The actress worked with Japanese masters Ozu ("Early Spring"), Kobayashi ("Kwaidan") and Ichikawa ("Her

Brother") several decades ago, but here plays a role in which she must be sexually alluring to a fanatical young man.

Writer-director Kumai has always tended to be literal in his approach to his subjects, and that's the case here. It's difficult to establish his approach to the religious fanatics. Chishu's disciples are a noisy lot, forever weeping and wailing in the background.

The locations are handsomely used. One magnificent moment has a man falling from a high cliff, but the effect of the stunt is diminished by the revelation that he somehow survives the fall.

The acting style is, to put it mildly, full-blooded. There's no room for subtleties in this frenetic look at religious extremism. The character of the mentally ill hero is, however, sketchily defined.

This beautiful but ultimately unsatisfactory film, despite its visual qualities, seems to miss the marks the director aimed for. — *Strat.*

DARK RIVER (BRITISH)

A Driftwood Films production. Produced by Shellie Smith, Malcolm Taylor. Written and directed by Taylor. Camera (Technicolor), Colin Clarke; editor, Stuart Taylor; music, Keith Miller; sound, Trevor Barber; production manager, Tom Mattinson; assistant director, Isaac Mabikwa. Reviewed at Montreal World Film Festival (Cinema of Today & Tomorrow), Aug. 24, 1990. Running time: **100 MIN.**
Johnny Deacon . . . . Tom Bell
Lydia Priestley . . . . . Kate Buffery
Mrs. Blessington . . . . . Sian Phillips
The official . . . . Freddie Jones
Shrike . . . . Ian McNeice
Oliver Priestley . . . . Michael Denison
Also with: Tony Haygarth, Frank Middlemass, Rosemary Leach, Bryan Pringle, Alex Tetteh-Lartey.

First-time writer-director Malcolm Taylor's look at the British colonialists of Central Africa explores no new ground, but it attempts an original structure. B.o. prospects are limited, with tv outings a better bet.

The picture is bookended by a trip down an African river by Johnny Deacon (Tom Bell), who's leaving the community of tired English men and women. It's suggested he's meeting with an existential death on a remote riverbank.

Meanwhile, Deacon's encounters with his fellow Brits are seen only as monologs, with each character delivering a speech to the camera. A film that consists of speeches like these had better be pretty well written and acted to work, and "Dark River" is below par.

Characters include Kate Buffery as the girl Deacon impregnated and who married another man; Michael Denison (in a rare screen appearance these days) as her world-weary, alcoholic father; Sian Phillips as a garrulous woman who drinks nothing but iced chocolate; and others of even less interest.

Apart from Denison, who does sterling work, the actors seem constrained by the director's limitations, and audiences are likely to get fidgety at all the talk, which resurrects every cliché of colonial life in Africa. Prospects are slim for this one. — *Strat.*

NGON DEN TRONG MO
(THE LIGHT AT THE END OF THE DREAM)
(VIETNAMESE-B&W)

A Studio for Children's Films production. Produced by Nguyen Thu. Directed by Do Minh Tuan. Screenplay, Le Ngoc Minh; camera (black & white), Pham Ngoc Lan; sound, Ta Quoc Khanh; production design, Nguyen Van Vy. Reviewed at Montreal World Film Festival (Cinema of Today & Tomorrow), Aug. 26, 1990. Running time: **100 MIN.**
Trang . . . . Tuan Dung

n inspirational film aimed at young teens, "The Light At The End Of The Dream" is a useful, if not outstanding, addition to Asian sections in international festivals, or for showing in expatriate Vietnamese communities.

The hero is a 13-year-old whose parents have divorced and abandoned him. He tries to look after himself and at the same time do well in his studies. He becomes a model young citizen, but he comes up against prejudice when the parents of his young girlfriend refuse to let her see him because he's "not from a good family."

Opening with a quote from Ho Chi Minh, pic is simple fare handled in a straightforward style

with sharp black & white camerawork (marred by overuse of the zoom lens) and a cheerful score.
— *Strat.*

PENNY ANTE— THE MOTION PICTURE

A Penny Ante production. Produced by Allan Nadohl, Marc Sachnoff. Directed by Gavin Wilding. Screenplay, Sachnoff; camera (color), Jacob Eleasari; editor, Adam Wolfe; music, Gene Page; sound, Jay Patterson; production design, Kevin Constant; production manager, Bill Rice; assistant director, Mark Oppenheimer; casting, Elza Bergeron. Reviewed at Montreal World Film Festival (Cinema of Today & Tomorrow), Aug. 24, 1990. Running time: **93 MIN.**
Isadore (Izzy) Perlman . Jack Kruschen
R.J. Wallis . . . . Don Fullilove
Dale Martinez . . . . Erica Gimpel
Mom . . . . Roxie Roker
Aunt . . . . Ja'net DuBois
The deacon . . . . Ted Lange
Davidson . . . . . . Vincent Schiavelli
Roy . . . . Bruce Glover
Willie . . . . Teddy Wilsin

Hardly different from the mainstream, "Penny Ante — The Motion Picture," is basically a buddy movie involving missing dope. The filmmakers didn't have the resources, or the invention, to do much with the tired premise.

Jack Kruschen is in good form as an elderly gumball machine vendor who discovers his just-deceased partner was using the machines to distribute crack. The old man teams up with R.J. (Don Fullilove), an engaging and streetwise black man, and the two set about smashing a couple of rival dope rings.

With more resources, first-time director Gavin Wilding might have come up with a better film, but he still would have faced the glut of black & white partner pictures on the market. "Penny Ante" actually starts off as if it might be interesting, with an unexpected musical number in a diner, but music is dropped for slowly paced dialog and low-voltage action scenes.

As a comedy, the film is marginally more successful, but here, too, the laughs are on the thin side, despite valiant performances. The 1989 picture will have to battle to find an audience.
— *Strat.*

LA LIBERTE D'UNE STATUE
(THE MOVING STATUE)

(CANADIAN-B&W)

A Max Films presentation of an Amerique Film production. Produced by Martin Paul-Hus. Written and directed by Olivier Asselin. Camera (black & white), Asselin; editor, Asselin, Claude Palardy; sound, Christian Fortin; set design, Asselin. Reviewed at Montreal World Film Festival, Aug. 24, 1990. Running time: **90 MIN.**
Anne . . . . Lucille Fluet
Hilarion . . . . Ronald Houle
P.T. Robertson . Serge Christaenssens
E.J. Cantarel . . . . Roch Aubert

This concept pic would make a terrific short or a unique musicvideo, but it's seriously lacking in content as a feature.

The concept: Vintage black & white silent footage is "discovered" in Egypt and spliced together in contemporary times. A voiceover makes the silent movie a talkie in which a gifted woman, Anne, wanders in a desert. She meets a strange man, and they discover she creates miracles when she sneezes.

Her first miracle is the resurrection of a dead woman. She later turns a water tower into a crude spaceship. Her powers are appreciated by scientific-minded men who see the potential of her magic. Together, this unusual group discovers the phonograph and photographic reproduction.

Pic's only English character, who speaks French with a horrendous accent, immediately exploits the venture by selling snapshots of Anne. He also sells her life insurance.

Comic touches are occasionally provided by a narrator, although they're difficult to hear. Sound is pic's weakest tech aspect and music is nonexistent. Debutant helmer Olivier Asselin took his "silent movie" theme a little too literally.

Other technical elements, handled almost exclusively by Asselin, are well manipulated to capture the vintage feel. The 16m print blown up to 35m adds a grainy texture that works to pic's advantage. A curious and innovative camera adds authenticity to the home movie effect.

Pic's lack of rhythm will make it difficult to find an audience even on home turf, but Asselin deserves kudos for originality.
— *Suze.*

SMUTECNI SLAVNOST
(FUNERAL CEREMONY)
(CZECH-B&W)

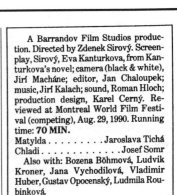

A Barrandov Film Studios production. Directed by Zdenek Sirový. Screenplay, Sirový, Eva Kanturkova, from Kanturkova's novel; camera (black & white), Jiří Macháne; editor, Jan Chaloupek; music, Jiří Kalach; sound, Roman Hloch; production design, Karel Cerný. Reviewed at Montreal World Film Festival (competing), Aug. 29, 1990. Running time: **70 MIN.**
Matylda . . . . Jaroslava Tichá
Chladi . . . . Josef Somr
Also with: Bozena Böhmová, Ludvik Kroner, Jana Vychodilová, Vladimir Huber, Gustav Opocenský, Ludmila Roubinková.

Another long-banned Czech film surfaces with "Funeral Ceremony," made in 1969. This grim picture of the effects of the Communist farm policies of the '50s is given telling treatment, though some of the details may be lost on audiences who never lived through such a period.

The film is divided into three parts. The rather confusing second part is a long flashback to the period when farms were taken from individual owners and delivered to the state. Many of the valuables and personal possessions of these once-affluent farmers were literally stolen by Party officials.

The film begins with the death of Chladi (Josef Somr, remembered from "Shop On The Main Street," made four years before this). He was a landowner who bitterly attacked the collectivization policy and was stripped of all his belongings. His widow (Jaroslava Tichá) decides he must be given a proper funeral and be buried in a crypt that belonged to his family.

The dogged Matylda refuses to take no for an answer, and reluctant Communist officials give in to her request. But the incident opens up old wounds, and the resulting funeral escalates into a large demonstration against the Party.

When the screenplay for the film was being written, early in 1968, "Funeral Ceremony" must have seemed just right for the changing, more liberal times, Long before the picture was completed, however, the times had changed again, and the picture was undoubtedly seen as an attack on the Communist system, which it is. Hence the long ban.

Director Zdenek Sirový handles his somber subject in low-key fashion. The drama's set in winter, with a blanket of snow covering everything, adding to the oppressive feel of the story.

For the uninitiated, however, the arguments and debates between the uncertain Communist officials, one of whom had a personal hand in the dead man's original misfortune, aren't always clear.

Sirový had made two little-known features before this one, and has made several, none of them world-beaters, since. An exceptionally strong performance from Ticha as the determined widow is the centerpiece of this solid, serious picture. — *Strat.*

PRINCES IN EXILE
(CANADIAN)

A Cinepix-National Film Board of Canada production. Executive producers, Andre Link, Colin Neale. Produced by John Dunning, producer, Marrin Canell (NFB). Directed by Giles Walker. Screenplay, Joe Wiesenfeld, from the novel by Mark Schreiber; camera (color), Savas Kalogeras; editor, Richard Todd; music, Normand Corbeil; production manager, Irene Litinsky; associate producer, Jeffrey Barmash. Reviewed at Montreal World Film Festival (competing), Aug. 30, 1990. (In Independent Feature Film Market, N.Y.) Running time: **104 MIN.**

Ryan Rafferty	Zachary Ansley
Holly	Stacie Mistysyn
Robert	Nicholas Shields
Dr. Merritt	Chuck Shamata
Gabriel	Alexander Chapman
Marlene Lancaster	Andrea Roth

Director Giles Walker, known for amusing insights into masculinity, tackles completely different material in this low-key drama about teens and children suffering from cancer. B.o. prognosis is iffy for such a downbeat subject, though Walker and writer Joe Wisenfeld try their best to make this a positive, life-affirming experience.

At a summer camp for cancer victims, Ryan (well-played by Zachary Ansley) is suffering from a brain tumor, and has two ambitions — to have his journal published and to get laid.

His eye first falls on pretty intern Marlene (Andrea Roth), who rejects him, and then on a fellow patient, Holly (Stacy Mistysyn), who has had a leg amputated because of bone cancer. The couple's plans to make out on the last night of camp are frustrated.

The other major character is Robert (Nicholas Shields), a self-confident daredevil nicknamed "The Stuntman." He has leukemia and succumbs before the summer is over.

Walker ("The Masculine Mystique," "90 Days") faced a challenge here to present his grim subject in an entertaining fashion without getting mawkish. He's only partially successful, since the script falls into a few clichés along the way. Also, once the word gets around as to the subject matter, there may no lines forming around the block.

This is acknowledged in one of the film's best scenes, where the kids put on a comic sketch, lambasting their doctors, their parents and themselves. It brings an acerbic humor to the film which otherwise tends to wallow in self-pity, like Ryan himself is accused of doing.

This was obviously a low-budget item, so it stands a reasonable chance of recovering its costs in the long haul. It's a pity that this subject couldn't have been handled with a touch more inspiration. — *Strat.*

CINETEX FEST

DEAD MEN DON'T DIE

A Trans Atlantic Pictures release (overseas) of a Waymar Prods. film. Produced by Wayne Marmorstein. Written and directed by Malcolm Marmorstein. Camera, Tom Fraser; editor, Michael Ornstein; music, David Williams; sound, Clark Will; production design, Phillip Vasels, Diane Hughes; art direction, Michael L. Strawn; makeup, Byrd Holland, Isabbelle Csaki; assistant director, Adam Alexander; associate producers, Hubie Kerns, Stan Foster; casting, Joe Reich. Reviewed at Cinetex Intl. Comedy Film Festival, Las Vegas, Sept. 8, 1990. No MPAA rating. Running time: **94 MIN.**

Barry	Elliott Gould
Dulcie	Melissa Anderson
Jordan	Mark Moses
Chafuka	Mabel King
Nolan	Philip Bruns
Cavanaugh	Jack Betts
Mungo	Robert Dryer
Carlos	Robert Covarrubias
Frank	Phil Shipko
Neal	Jerome Guardino
Archie	Stanley Kamel
Isadora	Andee Gray
Floor manager	Eric Lawrence
Margo	Judy Kain
Director	Charlie Brill

If there's word-of-mouth for satisfying silliness on the homevideo circuit, then "Dead Men Don't Die" should ultimately do fine as a bit of harmless fun for families to watch together.

Given a chance to let loose as an ashen, red-eyed resurrected corpse, Elliott Gould has a grand time. Even when nothing else is happening to hold adult interest, it's fun to watch him enjoy himself.

Suffice to say, this is not Gould's most subtle performance. Writer-director Malcolm Marmorstein has constructed a simple plot even the youngest kids can follow with no trouble: News-anchor Gould stumbles across a drug deal going down at the station where he works and gets himself murdered.

Finding the body, rival anchorlady Melissa Anderson is more interested in the story possibilities than grieving. But before she can get back with a camera, a voodoo cleaning lady (Mabel King) brings him back from the dead.

In addition to his sudden loss of suntan, Gould has a bullet hole in his forehead that causes problems for the makeup woman. He can no longer talk except for words prompted voodooishly by King, who's not exactly accomplished at rip-and-read. Even while noting the changes, nobody suspects Gould is actually dead, including the hopeless young detective (neatly played by Mark Moses) assigned to investigate Anderson's claim that she had found his body.

Seeing him on the air, the murderers return to finish the job and, one by one, they manage to get themselves dead, too. This keeps King busy and before long the station is buzzing with zombies, confounding Moses' already inept investigation and crimping Anderson's efforts to get at least one murder story on the air before the corpse comes back to life and disappears. Oh, yes, and at least once Gould gets to wear a dress. — *Har.*

LOVE HURTS

A Vestron Pictures production. Produced by Bud Yorkin, Doro Bachrach. Directed by Bud Yorkin. Screenplay, Ron Nyswaner; camera (CFI color), Adam Greenberg; editor, John C. Horger; music, Burt Bacharach; production design, Armin Ganz; assistant director, Robert Girolami; casting, Deborah Lucchesi. Reviewed at Cinetex Intl. Comedy Film Festival, Las Vegas, Sept. 8, 1990. MPAA rating: R. Running time: **106 MIN.**

Paul	Jeff Daniels
Susan	Judith Ivey
Nancy	Cynthia Sikes
Mom	Cloris Leachman
Karen	Amy Wright
Dad	John Mahoney
Sarah	Mary Griffin
David	Thomas Allen

Indeed, "Love Hurts," but director Bud Yorkin and a splendid cast make the pain bearable in this bittersweet little comedy-drama about a fractured family whose cracks can never be repaired but can be patched.

Caught philandering once too often, Jeff Daniels hasn't quite owned up to his responsibility for the divorce decree he's just received from Cynthia Sikes. Still, he's grieving for the loss of his high-school sweetheart and their two kids as he heads home for the wedding of his sister (Amy Wright). Unexpectedly, Sikes and the children are also there, reopening Daniels' wounds.

Old habits die hard, and Daniels is soon in pursuit of one of the bridesmaids, Judith Ivey, nervously ready to venture out of her own unhappy marriage for the first time. Yorkin and writer Ron Nyswaner construct an absolutely perfect no-tell-motel scene where Ivey finally decides to make the plunge — with heated enthusiasm — just as Daniels comes to the realization of how self-destructive his manipulation of women is.

As a man divided against himself, Daniels is superb, assisted in every scene by the ensemble of Cloris Leachman as his sweet mother trying to see the best in her family, his alcoholic father (John Mahoney) struggling to express his own love, and Wright, delightful as a doubting bride.

Clearly outstanding are the two youngsters, Thomas Allen as the teen son who understands what's happened to his parents better than his resentful little sister, Mary Griffin, definitely a promising child star who handles a difficult part with maturity and dexterity.

All of this, however, is far from grim. Yorkin extracts a lot of laughs with an eye for the absurd, including a wonderful scene where Leachman seeks to shelter the bride from a wedding-day downpour by shrouding her in Saran Wrap.

Clearly, laughter helps when love hurts. Even when there's no chance of living happily ever after, the stricken can still survive on a smile. (Film was not released last year due to Vestron's financial difficulties.)
— *Har.*

BOSTON FEST

NEVER LEAVE NEVADA
(B&W)

A Cabriolet Films presentation of a South of Canada production. Produced by Diane Campbell. Written and directed by Steve Swartz. Camera (black & white), Lee Daniel; editor, Gordon A. Thomas; music, Ray Benson; sound, Randy Burk, Dee Montgomery; production managers, Cynthia Malley, Kate Bennett; assistant director, Ed Fuentes. Reviewed at the Boston Film Festival, Aug. 29, 1990. Running time: **88 MIN.**

Sean Kaplan	Steve Swartz
Luis Ramirez	Rodney Rincon
Bettie Gurling	Janelle Buchanan
Lou Ann Pearlstein	Katherine Catmull

"**N**ever Leave Nevada" has the look and feel of early '60s indie productions combining "New Wave" techniques with American themes. Most of them didn't get anywhere and neither does this one. Shot on a shoestring in 1987, commercial prospects for this quirky, idiosyncratic film are difficult to see.

Sean Kaplan (filmmaker Steve Swartz) and Luis Ramirez (Rodney Rincon) head to a nuclear testing site in Nevada to sell tube socks and t-shirts to the protestors there. From there they hope to hit other anti-nuke rallies in the southwest. Instead they become involved with Bettie Gurling (Janelle Buchanan), a doctor whose clients include the women at the local bordello, and her roommate Lou Ann Pearlstein (Katherine Catmull).

Pic lacks narrative drive and a sense of who these people are. Much is made, for example, of Bettie being a sensitive doctor to whom the local hookers can open up (she treats one for a sexually transmitted ailment). Yet when Sean shows up in her office late at night after wrenching his back at the bordello, it is only a matter of moments before they are in bed together.

Some attempt is made to show how short-sighted the women are, but it never really gels. They resent the protestors because "they're disrupting a lifestyle we've gotten used to." It doesn't help that Swartz plays Sean as an incredibly annoying personality. Even his onscreen business partner gets fed up with him. Swartz never gives us any reason to care about what happens to him or anyone else in the film.

Tech credits are of the earnest, low-budget school, which is to say as professional as can be expected under the circumstances without ever approaching Hollywood slickness. This is festival fodder, and perhaps an audition film for Swartz. It's hard to see why anyone would want to sit through it. — *Kimm*.

THEY CALL ME MACHO WOMAN

A Troma Team release of a Lloyd Kaufman-Michael Herz presentation and New Gold Prods. production. Executive producers, Newman Goldstein, Dee Donahue. Written, produced and directed by Patrick G. Donahue. Camera (color), Mike Pierce; sound, Tom Pinney; art director, Lee Mason; assistant directors, Reonne Haslett, Oscar Briones. Reviewed at the Allied Advertising screening room, Sept. 11, 1990. (In Boston Film Festival.) Running time: **82 MIN.**

Susan	Debra Sweaney
Mongo	Brian Oldfield
Terk	Sean P. Donahue
Frankie	Mike Donahue
Georgie	Jerry Johnson

Part of the "Aroma du Troma" sidebar at the Boston Film Festival, this revenge flick was shot in 1989 under the title "Edge of Fear." Film has high camp value, but otherwise is strictly for undemanding action audiences.

Susan (Debra Sweaney) is a young widow looking to buy a home in the country. Prancing about in a long aquamarine sweater, she looks like a junior leaguer spending the day with the local realtor. Unfortunately for her, she accidentally witnesses the drug smuggling operation headed up by Mongo (Olympic medalist Brian Oldfield).

The realtor is quickly killed off, but Mongo's gang can't seem to figure out to do with Susan. Every time they're set to engage in rape and murder, she escapes, killing or maiming a few in the process. Finally she repairs to an old tool shed where she becomes the "Macho Woman" of the title, and counterattacks with axes and steel spikes.

How this helpless suburbanite became an expert in the martial arts is not really explained, but then neither is anything else in the film. These characters exist only to be pushed around by the plot. If Susan is picked up by three young men they will not only ignore her pleas for help, they will stop the car and threaten to rape her.

This would be tasteless except that no sooner is the car stopped than all three men are killed (by Mongo's gang), and yet Susan is again allowed to escape. Logic is not the film's long suit.

Tech credits fit right in with campy goings-on from a visible microphone popping out of the bushes to actors obviously pulling their punches so that no one will be really injured.

Thesping is on the same level, with most of the cast having their hands full simply remembering their lines. Only Oldfield is credible as the chief baddie.
— *Kimm*.

PACIFIC HEIGHTS

A 20th Century Fox release of a Morgan Creek production. Produced by Scott Rudin, William Sackheim. Executive producers, James G. Robinson, Joe Roth. Coexecutive producers, Gary Barber, David Nicksay. Directed by John Schlesinger. Screenplay, Daniel Pyne; camera, Dennis E. Jones; editor, Mark Warner; music, Hans Zimmer; production design, Neil Spisak; art direction, Gershon Ginsburg, Sharon Seymour; costume design, Ann Roth, Bridget Kelly; set decoration, Clay A. Griffith, Debra Shutt; assistant director, Herb Gains; coproducer, Dennis Jones; casting, Mali Finn. Reviewed at 20th Century Fox, Los Angeles, Sept. 18, 1990. MPAA rating: PG-13. Running time: **102 MIN.**

Patty Palmer	Melanie Griffith
Drake Goodman	Matthew Modine
Carter Hayes	Michael Keaton
Toshio Watanabe	Mako
Mira Watanabe	Nobu McCarthy
Stephanie MacDonald	Laurie Metcalf
Lou Baker	Carl Lumbly

Nightmare landscape of landlord-tenant relations is ripe for thriller exploitation, but one can't help but prefer to see it from the populist side. In "Pacific Heights," deedholders Melanie Griffith and Matthew Modine go through hell with tenant Michael Keaton. Fox can count on about six weeks' reasonable rent from theaters before pic gets evicted.

Set against the stressful high-stakes world of California real estate investing, an area with which film execs are no doubt familiar, pic might have been a hotter commodity before the market declined and the subject became less appealing.

Still, the specter of a menace who invades one's home turf and can't be ousted is universally disturbing, and director John Schlesinger goes all out to make this creepy thriller-chiller as unsettling as it needs to be.

Story has babes-in-the-woods home buyers Patty (Griffith) and Drake (Modine) spending their every dime to restore an 1883 Victorian house in San Francisco, counting on the income from two downstairs apartments to meet the mortgage.

A nice Asian couple takes the one-bedroom, but the studio falls to reptilian Michael Keaton, who smoothtalks Modine into handing over a key without money up front.

After he "takes possession," it becomes clear they'll never see a dollar from this unnerving man. They encounter the shock of a legal system that's always on the renter's side; at least it is in this bizarre universe of cops who won't listen, judges who don't care, and nervous, impersonal lawyers whose hands are tied.

"Pacific Heights" rides pretty high for at least an hour. It's enjoyable watching the cute-as-a-button couple bring their dream to life, and engrossing watching the ways Keaton goes about destroying it.

First-time film scripter Daniel Pyne sets up a menacing cat-and-mouse game as sociopath Keaton plays the system to his advantage, finally provoking Modine into attacking him so he can go after his assets with a lawsuit.

Pic loses its grip when it tips over into psycho-chiller territory. There's something laughable about the discovery that Keaton is breeding cockroaches in his apartment as a means of warfare, and something Huck Finnish about the way Modine crawls under the house to eavesdrop on Keaton's angry latenight arguments with his shady co-conspirators.

Schlesinger never manages to convincingly meld pic's schizophrenic halves of sweet normality and bizarre menace. Keaton is a fine actor whose take on his character is elusive and unsettling, but he comes off as almost a parody of a creep, the way he sits around twisting razor blades in the dark.

When this tenant gets evicted, he has nowhere to go, and neither does the film.

Griffith, in her first role since "Working Girl," lights up the screen as the kittenish but incontrol Patty who lets her instincts be her guide. But it's hard to figure out her plan when she takes off after Keaton on a one-woman crusade for justice.

Her meeting in the desert with Keaton's gin-soaked former girlfriend (Beverly D'Angelo, as "Anne from the desert") is the film's nonsensical nadir.

Ultimately, pic's thriller aspects are a bust, but this "Fatal Attraction" for yuppie landlords is still a film about the fear of people who believe the system was designed to prevent them from prospering, and that there are People Out There who want to take what they have. Lock the doors and raise the security deposits.

On the plus side, one has to admire pic's nonracist, nonsexist casting. — *Daws.*

ETERNITY

A Paul Entertainment release and production. Executive producers, Hank Paul, Dorothy Koster Paul. Directed by Steven Paul. Screenplay, Jon Voight, Steven Paul, Dorothy Koster Paul; camera (Crest color), John Lambert; editor, Christopher Greenbury, Peter Zinner, Michael Sheridan; music, Michel Legrand; sound (Ultra-Stereo), George Alch; production design, Martin Zboril; art direction, Robert Farthing; production manager, Eric M. Breiman; coproducer, Stuart Paul; casting, Dorothy Koster Paul. Reviewed on Academy Entertainment vidcassette, N.Y., Sept. 25, 1990. MPAA Rating: R. Running time: **125 MIN.**
James/Edward . . . . Jon Voight
Sean/Roni . . . . . . Armand Assante
Valerie/Dahlia . . . . Eileen Davidson
Eric/King . . . . Wilford Brimley
Selma/Sabrina . . . . . . Kaye Ballard
Spinelli/Jester . . . . Joey Villa
Harold/Tax collector . . . Steven Keats
Bernice/Mother . . . . . Lainie Kazan
Governor/Ridley . . . . Eugene Roche
Domingo/Grandpa . . Robert Carricart
Judge/Tax collector . . Charles Knapp
Guido/Taxpayer . . . . . Frankie Valli
Prosecutor/Thomas . . . John P. Ryan
Video editor . . . . . . Charles Dierkop
Stage manager . . . . Steven Paul
Also with: Perri Lister, Jilly Rizzo.

Jon Voight's first feature film in five years is an entertaining but overly preachy personal effort. Basic tale of good vs. evil has slim theatrical chances but should attract a devoted following via its November home-video release.

"Eternity" has a close precedent in theme and structure in Irwin Allen's 1957 film adaptation of Hendrik Willem Van Loon's "The Story Of Mankind." Forgotten now, that Ronald Colman-starrer earned a camp reputation due to its weird all-star cast including Harpo Marx as Isaac Newton, Dennis Hopper as Napoleon and Marie Wilson as Marie Antoinette.

Written in collaboration with director Steven Paul and his mother Dorothy Koster Paul, Voight's vision of mankind's dilemma revolves around mystical notions of reincarnation. Opening reel is a medieval prolog in which Voight wars with his brother Armand Assante over a kingdom, resulting in the death of his beloved Eileen Davidson.

Voight wakes up and, in true "Wizard Of Oz" style, recognizes all the people in his life as reincarnations of relatives and other folks from the dream. Assante is now a megalomaniacal, right-wing industrialist out to control the media, the U.S. presidency (earmarked for his governor stooge, Eugene Roche) and push

a vast weapons project he believes will deter war through strength and preparedness.

Voight is a self-professed do-gooder, who opposes Assante's militaristic approach and in particular his scheme to push through a pipeline for his Wesco Oil Co. Voight's tv documentary show investigates some Indians' problems and his alter ego from the past tells him that Assante is clandestinely drilling for uranium on the Indians' land.

Assante attempts to buy out Voight's show to silence him and then co-opts his girlfriend (Davidson again) by making her a tv star on his network. When Voight broadcasts his own protest tirade against Assante, the villain sues for libel, cueing a hearing of the case on Assante's "Judgment Day" tv show.

Director Paul takes a controversial tack by filming the climax of the film (the televised kangaroo court trial) as a burlesque, even casting himself as the stage manager who manipulates the audience's applause and booing. This sugarcoats the pill of listening to Voight's heart-on-sleeve, populist summation for the jury. Romantic happy ending that follows is equally hokey.

Like the current hit "Ghost," "Eternity" is designed for people who want to believe. Others will reject it out of hand.

Voight invests equal measures of naturalism and quirks in his messianic role which goes over the top occasionally. Davidson stands out in the supporting cast, possessing an unusual beauty reminiscent of Polish star Joanna Pacula. Wilford Brimley is convincing both as Voight's no-nonsense boss and as his father.

Tech credits are acceptable, though film's ambitious theme would have benefited from a big-budget, worldwide scale presentation. — *Lor.*

BERKELEY IN THE SIXTIES
(DOCU-COLOR/B&W-16m)

A Mark Kitchell production in association with P.O.V. Theatrical Films, a division of PBS. Produced and directed by Kitchell. Camera (color, black & white), Stephen Lighthill; editor, Veronica Selver. Reviewed at the Nuart Theater, Los Angeles, Sept. 25, 1990.

Running time: **117 MIN.**
With: Mario Savio, Clark Kerr, Joan Baez, Allen Ginsberg, the Grateful Dead, Huey Newton, Jack Weinberg, Jentri Anders, John Gage, Frank Bardacke, Jackie Goldberg, Michael Rossman, John Searle, Suzy Nelson, Ruth Rosen, Bobby Seale, David Hilliard, Hardy Frye, Barry Melton, Mike Miller, Susan Griffin.

Rise and fall of the Berkeley, Calif.-based student protest movement is vividly and thoroughly explored in Mark Kitchell's excellent docu. Subject is of keen interest to many, giving pic strong b.o. potential in specialized settings.

Unspooling in Los Angeles at roughly the same time as Ken Burns' PBS epic "The Civil War" (reviewed on page 89), "Berkeley" makes a startling counterpart, for no two periods in U.S. history have been as divisive.

Docu, which won the audience award at the 1990 Sundance U.S. Film Festival, begins in 1960 with a student demonstration against the House Un-American Activities Committee. HUAC made a propaganda film about the incident called "Operation Abolition" that backfired, inspiring countless students to head for UC-Berkeley to demonstrate.

Pic points out that the civil rights and free speech movements, not the Vietnam War, seeded the tumult, which grew to encompass the antiwar protest, growth of the counterculture, the women's movement and Black Panthers before activity declined in 1970.

Six years in the making, project benefits from strikingly immediate footage culled from Bay Area tv station archives, intercut with present day interviews with 15 activists, some of it cleverly matched with old clips showing them at the height of their student involvement.

Long list of potent clips catches the violence and hysteria of the demonstrations in Oakland and on campus in 1969, when then-Gov. Ronald Reagan sent troops to surround the demonstrators and a helicopter dropped nausea gas.

Also memorable is footage of Reagan chiding university faculty for allowing the campus ruffians to gain any ground. Another choice clip shows busloads of young draftees reporting to an induction center surrounded by protesters. A young male activist urges them to change their minds. (None do.)

Pic lags a bit in showing how strongly the student views, especially early on, clashed with the outside world, but images of ultra-straight administrators like UC president Clark Kerr trying to address the unruly student body go a long way.

Effect of drug use on student attitudes seems unrealistically downplayed, but music tracks, limited to well-chosen protest tunes rather than an onslaught of nostalgic '60s sounds, are highly effective.

Kitchell's well-sequenced, highly informative work benefits from a remarkably balanced historical perspective, given the scant 20 years since pic's events. Docu doesn't make many claims for the movement's accomplishments, save one activist's assertion that it limited U.S. ability to wage war. Perhaps Kitchell's most effective touch is the epilog telling how each of the activist/interviewees have continued to work for social change.

Production involved getting contributions of $300,000 from more than 1,000 people. More than 100 worked on the project, many as volunteers, with production beginning in the fall of 1985 and editing begun a year later.

Bay Area tv stations KRON, KPIX and KQED donated the use of their archives for $1, the filmmakers report, while independent and amateur footage was tracked down from as far away as Finland. — Daws.

DEATH WARRANT

An MGM/UA release of a Mark DiSalle production. Produced by DiSalle. Directed by Deran Sarafian. Screenplay, David S. Goyer; camera (Deluxe color), Russell Carpenter; editor, G. Gregg McLaughlin, John A. Barton; music, Gary Chang; sound (Dolby), Mike LeMare; production design, Curtis Schnell; art direction, Robert E. Lee; set decoration, Richard Hummel; costume design, Joseph Porro; assistant directors, Chase Newhart, David Kelley; associate producer, Andrew G. La Marca; casting, Cathy Henderson, Michael Cutler. Reviewed at the Filmland Corporate Center, Culver City, Calif., Sept. 14, 1990. MPAA Rating: R. Running time: **88 MIN.**
Louis Burke . Jean-Claude Van Damme
Hawkins . . . . Robert Guillaume
Amanda Beckett . . . . . Cynthia Gibb
Tom Vogler . . . . . George Dickerson
Sergeant DeGraf . . . . . Art LaFleur
The Sandman . . . . Patrick Kilpatrick
Douglas Tisdale . . . . . Joshua Miller
Romaker . . . . Hank Woessner
Konefke . . . . George Jenesky
Ben Keane . . . . Jack Bannon
Priest . . . . . Abdul Salaam El Razzac

Unusually sadistic even by genre standards, this well-made exploitation yarn unravels under the weight of its dim-witted carnage. Relentless pace and Jean-Claude Van Damme's fancy footwork provide a brief stay of execution at the b.o., but pic otherwise should be sentenced to a quick trip to homevideo.

In a sense, pic marks a slight reach for Van Damme: Instead of playing a kickboxer, he gets to branch out as an undercover cop who knows how to kickbox.

That's apparently supposed to be a career breakthrough (à la Chuck Norris moving beyond a karate champ in "Code Of Silence"), but the distinction gets lost in the final reel, an overlong melee featuring more spinning kicks than a chorus line.

Tyro screenwriter David S. Goyer starts with clichés from the first scene, as officer Louis Burke (Van Damme) single-footedly confronts a psychopath (Patrick Kilpatrick) who did in his partner (partners being an expendable commodity in such films).

Goyer has also provided the skimpiest of setups, placing Van Damme undercover in a penal facility where, for unexplained reasons, prisoners keep dying. Getting the protagonist into stir quickly moves the narrative into an action mode, which is, after all, the whole point.

Director Deran Sarafian and cameraman Russell Carpenter have put in their time creating a gritty atmosphere, down to the racial rifts between inmates and constant threat of violence. They also throw in weird nuances, such as the Sodom-like prison area draped in veils or the eerie purple-blue light bathing some scenes.

The investigation into the convict killings is predictable but at least provides a hook to pull the story along. Unfortunately, it's ultimately dispatched to make way for an extended, bloodthirsty finale.

Sarafian is more successful at establishing mood than in pulling off the blandly choreographed action scenes.

The final battle, in fact, is unusually brutal and moronic, with Van Damme emerging as the first monkey-wrench-proof hero, one who can plummet several stories onto concrete and still struggle to his feet to exchange head kicks with a psycho behemoth.

The cast is probably better than it has a right to be under the circumstances, with Robert Guillaume firstrate as a hardened one-eyed convict, Cynthia Gibb as the perky attorney masquerading as Burke's wife, and a scene-stealing turn by Joshua Miller ("The River's Edge") as a horny teenage computer hacker.

Their presence provides a major boost, since Van Damme looks great posturing and punching but risks guffaws every time he mouths the sort of dialog written. Unlike fellow muscleman Arnold Schwarzenegger, he seems to take himself far too seriously.

Tech credits are generally top-drawer, from Gary Chang's score to the weird art direction, which rivals recent higher-budgeted prison sequences in films like "An Innocent Man" or "Tango & Cash." — Bril.

I COME IN PEACE

A Triumph Releasing Corp. release of a Vision presentation of a Damon/Saunders production. Produced by Jeff Young. Directed by Craig R. Baxley. Executive producers, Mark Damon, David Saunders. Screenplay, Jonathan Tydor, Leonard Maas Jr.; camera (Deluxe color), Mark Irwin; editor, Mark Helfrich; music, Jan Hammer; sound (Ultra-Stereo), Richard Shorr, Michael Redbourn; production design-set decoration, Phillip M. Leonard; art direction, Nino Candido; costume design, Joseph Porro; assistant directors, Craig R. West, Thomas Zapata; associate producer, Ron Fury; coproducers, Jon Turtle, Rafael Eisenman; casting, Karen Rea. Reviewed at the Mann Criterion Theaters, Santa Monica, Calif., Sept. 24, 1990. MPAA Rating: R. Running time: **93 MIN.**
Caine . . . . Dolph Lundgren
Smith . . . . Brian Benben
Diane . . . . Betsy Brantley
Bad Alien . . . . Matthias Hues
Good Alien . . . . Jay Bilas
Malone . . . . Jim Haynie
Switzer . . . . David Ackroyd
Victor Manning . . . Sherman Howard
Warren . . . . Sam Anderson

Dolph Lundgren makes a bid to join the elite Arnold-Sly-Chuck group of musclebound leading men in this better-than-average sci-fi thriller. It's well-paced and possesses a much-appreciated sense of humor.

Pic should make an okay b.o. showing thanks to genre fans, but, as a late fall release, it seems best-suited to do most of its damage in homevideo.

Similar in plot to "The Hidden," an underappreciated 1987 pic starring Kyle MacLachlan, pic deals with an intergalactic fugitive leaving bodies strewn around downtown Houston. He's pursued by an equally matched alien-cop (Dolph Lundgren) and FBI agent (Brian Benben).

While "The Hidden" dealt with small creatures invading human hosts, the E.T.'s in this case are seven-foot-tall, white-eyed behemoths that shake off shotgun blasts and sever the throats of human prey with wafer-thin projectiles.

Putting an interesting twist on the "Just say no" campaign, the evil alien (Matthias Hues) keeps offing drug dealers to obtain heroin and then kills people with it, siphoning off the endorphins it produces in the human brain, substance viewed as an illegal narcotic on his planet.

That's about all the explanation director Craig R. Baxley allows, though it's an intriguing enough framework for the action. The script also fails to address the alien's extremely limited if ironic vocabulary, which serves as the film's title.

Perhaps it's just as well. The plot is perfectly serviceable to show off Lundgren, who's surprisingly engaging as the befuddled cop who stumbles onto the extraterrestrial drug dealer while pursuing those of the earthbound variety.

Aside from occasionally gargling his dialog, only drawback to Lundgren's casting is that he's so big himself, the towering alien seems less imposing.

After his other stoic film roles, Lundgren surprises by exhibiting a nice sense of humor, at one point threatening to hit his partner . . . hard. (Too bad that his best line is given away in the film's trailer.)

Benben is also fine as the officious by-the-book sidekick, while Mark Lowenthal has a small but extremely amusing role as an over-caffeinated scientist.

The aliens' look is fairly conventional but nonetheless striking, while Phillip M. Leonard's production design surpasses an otherwise modest budget. Jan Hammer also chips in with a firstrate synthesized score.

Baxley, who made his feature debut with "Action Jackson," does a solid job barring a few excesses. He goes overboard, for example, in repeatedly showing the same gruesome, yet rather mundane effect: The alien taps a victim's chest with a long cord, then buries a spike into his forehead. The scenes aren't particularly compelling and should appeal only to rabid gore fans.

Otherwise, this undemanding cinematic comic book may come in peace but doesn't seem likely to go all that quietly. — *Bril.*

MAN WITHOUT PIGS
(DOCU)

An Institute of Papua New Guinea Studies film in association with Research School of Pacific Studies, Australian National U. Produced and directed by Chris Owen. Camera (Eastmancolor, 16m), Owen; editor, Owen; sound, Andrew Pike; associate producers, Pike, John Waiko, Hank Nelson, Gavan Daws; postproduction consultant, Les McLaren. Reviewed at Margaret Mead Film Festival, New York, Sept. 25, 1990. No MPAA rating. Running time: **60 MIN.**

At the time of its Margaret Mead film fest screening, "Man Without Pigs" had not secured a U.S. distributor. Although the film deserves to be made available, its shortcomings could keep audiences either confused or simply away.

Anyone who's ever planned a large family get-together knows the fear of transgressing protocol, of offending some branch of the clan with an unintended breach in etiquette. John Waiko, subject of Australian filmmaker Chris Owen's uneven new documentary, is a study in that fear.

Waiko is the titular "Man Without Pigs," and as the title suggests, his dilemma has nothing to do with who sits next to whom at the table of honor. Waiko, a Papua New Guinean, is faced with the problem of distributing pig parts.

After becoming the first member of his village to get a Western education, Waiko returns to his birthplace (camera crew in tow) to organize a celebration. His doctoral degree in anthropology does not fully prepare him for the antagonism that results when he fails to observe the strict rituals in planning for the feast.

In particular, Waiko has neglected to prepare for the distribution of gifts (especially pigs and pieces thereof) to important villagers.

As "Man Without Pigs" details the complexities of ritual, Owen attempts to explore class divisions, community allegiance and conflict between Western thought and ancient village customs. His results are unsatisfying.

Although the docu offers a fascinating glimpse into a little-seen world, and the intricacies of family ties are both intriguing and universal, too many ques-

tions remain unanswered. Most important, was Waiko's return staged for the benefit of the cameras, and why was he so ill-prepared?

Waiko himself comes off as dull compared to his colorful relatives, surely the filmmaker's fault. No attempt is made to illustrate the internal drive that took him from isolated Tabara to the Australian National U. Nor are his feelings as a man caught between two cultures made clear.

What exposition there is comes from Hank Nelson, Waiko's academic mentor. The information is usually relayed via tedious talking head shots, a technique doubly unfortunate since it steals time from the film's greatest asset: its depiction of the New Guineans as they prepare for (and argue about) the feast.
— *Evan.*

EATING

An Intl. Rainbow Pictures release. Produced by Judith Wolinsky. Written and directed by Henry Jaglom. Camera (Deluxe color), Hanania Baer; sound, Sunny Meyer. Reviewed at Cinetex Intl. Comedy Film Festival, Las Vegas, Sept. 6. No MPAA rating. Running time: **110 MIN.**

Helene	Lisa Richards
Kate	Mary Crosby
Sophie	Gwen Welles
Martine	Nelly Alard
Whitney	Frances Bergen
Nancy	Elizabeth Kemp
Sadie	Marlena Giovi
Jennifer	Daphna Kastner
Lydia	Marina Gregory

With: Beth Grant, Tony Basil, Savannah Boucher, Claudia Brown, Rachelle Carson, Anne E. Curry, Donna Germain, Aloma Ichinose, Taryn Power, Jacquelin Woolsey.

The ladies who lunch — and munch, breakfast, binge, dine, diet, starve and sample — are delicious in "Eating," but writer-director Henry Jaglom labors over the stove too long, harming a tasty soufflé. Public appetite seems limited.

Jaglom clearly succeeds in making the film he intended to make, and he's a genuinely fine observer of contemporary angst who extracts wonderful moments from a large ensemble of fine actresses.

An almost nonexistent plot, however, allows the self-obsessions of "Eating" to lapse into so many declarations about the therapeutic comforts and betrayals in food that the picture begins to resemble a meeting of Overeaters Anonymous.

Convening a large collection of

diverse friends to celebrate a three-tiered birthday party, Lisa Richards is observing her 40th, Mary Crosby her 30th and Marlena Giovi her 50th.

There's plenty of savvy conversation marking each passage, but mainly the birthday girls and their friends reveal how so much of their lives have been dominated by food, either as a substitute for affection or a form of self-destruction.

Richards, Crosby and Giovi are splendid, as is Frances Bergen as Richards' mother, at first taking a lofty older-generation view of the talk but ultimately shedding her own covers. At the other end of the age scale, Daphna Kastner is also captivating as Giovi's dominated daughter, plumping herself in defense.

Gwen Welles stands out as a bitchy, back-biting bulemic. Nelly Alard is also good as a visiting French filmmaker making a docu about American women. But this device, reflected throughout in Jaglom's own camera, ill serves the picture with repetitive closeups, though many of them are individually amusing and touching.

Visually, Jaglom crafts many neat touches, particularly when the three big birthday cakes are cut and the plates go round and round the party from hand to hand with nobody taking a piece to eat.

Subplots abound, but there's no main plot and no involving developments, just a bite here and a bite there, with nary a place to sit down and have a meal. — *Har.*

DON'T TELL HER IT'S ME

A Hemdale release. Produced by George G. Braunstein, Ron Hamady. Executive producers, John Daly, Derek Gibson. Directed by Malcolm Mowbray. Screenplay, Sarah Bird, based on her novel, "The Boyfriend School"; camera (Cine Film processing, CFI color), Reed Smoot; editor, Marshall Harvey; music, Michael Gore; sound (Ultra-Sound Stereo), Douglas Axtell, Andy D'Addario, Jim Bolt; production design, Linda Pearl; set decoration, Debra Schutt; costume design, Carol Wood; associate producer, Chris Coles; assistant director, Scott Easton; casting, Karen Rea. Reviewed at Cineplex Odeon Beverly Center, Los Angeles, Sept. 18, 1990. MPAA Rating: PG-13. Running time: **101 MIN.**

Gus Kubicek	Steve Guttenberg
Emily Pear	Jami Gertz
Lizzie Potts	Shelley Long
Trout	Kyle MacLachlan
Mitchell Potts	Kevin Scannell
Mandy	Madchen Amick
Babette	Beth Grant

Annabelle Potts	Caroline Lund, Sally Lund

"**D**on't Tell Her It's Me" starts with an awkward, impossible-to-remember title and goes downhill from there. This grotesquely unfunny comedy, with Shelley Long as a romance novelist transforming shy brother Steve Guttenberg into a swaggering stud, should escape quickly from theaters.

Writer Sarah Bird, who adapted her novel "The Boyfriend School" (film's more attractive production title), started with a premise that might have been an amusing sendup of what Long calls "porn for housewives."

Bird, romance novelist under the pseudonym of Tory Cates, has a usable base of inside knowledge of the genre. But the lameness of the first-time scripter's dialog is exceeded only by the incredible miscalculations in her characterization and plotting. Director Malcolm Mowbray's clumsy staging and Reed Smoot's wobbly camerawork don't help.

The usually reliable Guttenberg is virtually unrecognizable at the onset as a cartoonist who has gone bald and bloated because of chemotherapy for Hodgkin's disease. This is not exactly the stuff of hilarity, but the film seems to think so, regularly attempting humor at the expense of his pathetic appearance.

The usually adorable Long, dithering terribly here, makes it her mission to rescue Guttenberg from his reclusive self-pity and immerse him in "the whirling vortex of desire."

Her first attempt is an excruciating disaster. Mag writer Jami Gertz visits Long's home to do a mocking article for zany magazine editor Kyle MacLachlan, throwing up the revolting dinner offered by Long's oafish husband Kevin Scannell.

Worse, Gertz is also revolted by Guttenberg's appearance and his introverted manner, and coldly rebuffs him, forcing Long to transform her brother into a sort of Mad Max clone, a long-maned New Zealander called "Lobo," the kind of doltish muscleman doted over by readers of her bodice-rippers.

Guttenberg finds a few agreeable wisps of humor in his feigned studliness, but the film makes Gertz, a likable actress, seem offensive and idiotic with her superficial standards of romantic preference. Her only caveats about Lobo are whether he's gay or "free of disease."

The script could have made a sharp satiric thrust by having Guttenberg dump her after realizing how shallow she is when she falls in love with his phony macho persona rather than with his sensitive everyday self, but instead he becomes more infatuated with Gertz en route to a soppy finale.

The film's essential callousness is underscored by a running gag about Long's little daughter sticking dangerous things in her mouth and putting her tongue into electric sockets. This cruel strain of antichild humor, unfortunately common in contemporary films, would be considered unacceptable if directed at minority groups.

Another symptom of pic's ineptitude is its failure to take advantage of the antebellum beauty of its Charleston, S.C., locations, where filming was mostly completed before Hurricane Hugo swept through the area.
— *Mac.*

UN WEEKEND SUR DEUX
(EVERY OTHER WEEKEND)
(FRENCH)

An MK2 release (MK2 Prods. USA in U.S.) of a Sara Film production. (Intl. sales: World Marketing Film, Paris.) Produced by Alain Sarde. Directed by Nicole Garcia. Screenplay, Garcia, Jacques Fieschi, Anne-Marie Etienne, Philippe Le Guay; camera (color), William Lubtchansky; editor, Agnes Guillemot; music, Oswald d'Andrea; sound, Jean-Pierre Duret; production design, Jean-Baptiste Poirot; assistant director, Radu Mihaileanu; casting, Frederique Moidon. Reviewed at Venice Film Festival (out of competition), Sept. 12, 1990. (In San Sebastian Film Festival.) Running time: **100 MIN.**
Camille Valmont . . . . Nathalie Baye
Vincent . . . . Joachim Serreau
Gaelle . . . . Felicie Pasotti
Adrian . . . . Miki Manojlovic
Camille's agent . . . . . . Henri Garcin
Stephane . . . . Gilles Treton
Graziella . . . . Marie Daems
Marie-Ange . . . . . . Michelle Goddet
Martha . . . . Susan Carlson
Jacquet . . . . Jacques Boudet
Lombard . . . . Jacques Vincey

The first film directed by actress Nicole Garcia is a sure-footed contemporary drama about a woman and her estranged children. With a strong central performance from Nathalie Baye, the film stands a chance in the international arthouse market.

Baye plays Camille Valmont, an actress whose profession has caused the breakup of her marriage. Her ex-husband has custody of their two children, Vincent, 10, and Gaelle, 5. One weekend, Camille has the youngsters with her and takes them to Vichy, where she is emceeing a Rotary benefit night at a swank hotel.

Alarmed by a phone call from her ex, in which he protests about taking the children on this trip, she walks out on the benefit and drives south in a rented car, taking the youngsters with her.

Her flight also develops into an attempt to break through to the seriously troubled Vincent, who is hostile to her. His passion for astronomy and for a predicted meteor spectacular a few days away proves to be the point of contact, and Camille heads for a Spanish mountain from where the shooting stars can best be seen.

Baye gives a beautiful performance in which she subtly changes from a busy, self-centered career woman to a mother who puts her children first. She is ably assisted by the child actors, especially soulful Joachim Serrault as the neglected son.

The film also works as a road movie, in which the characters journey from Paris to central France and then to the coast, and on across the border into Spain. Excellent lensing by William Lubtchansky adds to the success of the picture.

Garcia, whose credits include Alain Resnais' "My American Uncle" and Michel Deville's "Death In A French Garden," makes a confident directorial debut. Her pacing is a little slow at times, but she clearly has a precise vision and (not surprisingly) knows how to work with actors.

"Every Other Weekend" could find an appreciative audience in major cities, and is a natural for women's film fests. Technically, pic is very good, and the climactic meteor sequence very effective. — *Strat.*

VREMA CUDA
(TIME OF MIRACLES)
(YUGOSLAVIAN)

A Singidunum Film Prods.-Televizija Belgrade production in association with Channel 4 and Metropolitan Pictures. (Intl. sales: Capitol Films, London.) Executive producer, Dragana Ilic. Produced and directed by Goran Paskaljevic. Screenplay, Paskaljevic, Borislav Pekic, from the novel by Pekic; camera (color), Radoslav Vladic; editor, Olga Obradov; music, Zoran Simjanovic; sound, Sinisa Jovanovic Singer; production design, Miodrag Nikolic; coproducer, George Weiss. Reviewed at Montreal World Film Festival (out of competition), Aug. 29, 1990. (In San Sebastian Film Festival.) Running time: **100 MIN.**
Nicodemus . . Predag Miki Manojlovic
Lazarus . . . . . Dragan Maksimovic
The young man . . Svetozar Cvetkovic
Martha . . . . Mirjana Karanovic
John . . . . Danilo Bata Stojkovic
Maria . . . . Mirjana Jokovic
Pope Luke . . . . Ljuba Tadic
Ozren . . . . Slobodan Ninkovic
Pope Luke's wife . . . . . Neda Arneric

Handsomely lensed, "Time Of Miracles" has already attracted festival interest, and, even though it's rare to find space given to Yugoslav productions, arthouse distribution in key cities isn't out of the question. It's one of Goran Paskaljevic's best films.

This thoughtful look at the coming of Communism to a small Yugoslav village in 1945 already unspooled in the Cannes Directors' Fortnight and is competing at the San Sebastian film fest.

As the names of the characters suggest, Paskaljevic is telling a parable. Nicodemus, the local Communist leader, takes over the village church when the school burns down, and insists that the ancient icons painted on the church walls be covered with white paint. Lazarus, the village teacher injured in the fire, assists in the conversion of the church, while the priest and his congregation fulminate outside.

The miracles begin. The icons reappear through the paint. Lazarus apparently dies, but comes to life after a visit from a mysterious, deaf-mute stranger. For Nicodemus, the resulting religious fervor is anathema.

Paskaljevic tells his story with bold strokes, helped by a fine cast. Director's ironic sense of humor is never far away, as he presents a timeless clash between two dogmas and, as a result, tackles a far wider political and religious theme in microcosm.

This is certainly one of the better pics to come from Yugoslavia in recent years. — *Strat.*

RAGAZZI FUORI
BOYS ON THE OUTSIDE
(ITALIAN)

A Filmauro release (Italy) of a Numero Uno Intl. production, in association with RAI-TV Channel 2. Produced by Claudio Bonivento. Directed by Marco Risi. Screenplay, Aurelio Grimaldi, Risi; camera (color), Mauro Marchetti; editor, Franco Fraticelli; music, Giancarlo Bigazzi; in Dolby stereo; art direction, Massimo Spano; production manager, Massimo Ferrero. Reviewed at the Venice Film Festival (competing), Sept. 5, 1990. Running time: **116 MIN.**
Natale . . . . Francesco Benigno
Mery . . . . Alessandro Di Sanzo
Antonio . . . . Roberto Mariano
Carmelo . . . . Alfredo Li Bassi
Claudio . . . . Maurizio Prollo
Matteo . . . . Filippo Genzardi
King Kong . . . . . . Salvatore Termini
Marcello . . . . Giuseppe Pierico
Tomasso . . . . . . Alessandro Calamia
Salvo . . . . Carlo Berretta
Also with: Antonino Marino, Benza Attardo, Santi Bellina, Tatu La Vecchia, Aurora Quattrocchi, Guia Jelo.

Director Marco Risi's heartrending portrait of Palermo street kids is so relentlessly bleak, it may turn off some viewers. But the film has good prospects for the same specialized play and film fest showings as its predecessor, "Forever Mery."

As moving as its forerunner and using the same cast of nonpros, "Boys On The Outside" continues where "Mery" left off, showing what happens on the outside of reform school to kids forced into juvenile delinquency by a hostile environment.

Belonging to the long tradition of Italo social protest films, "Boys" has a crude realism that brings its subject seething to the surface. At the same time, Risi's years of experience making popular films aimed at teen audiences serve him well when it comes to making the story watchable.

His dynamic, American-style lensing enlivens a weak script, but pic's real strength lies in the believability of the cast, who act out their own lives and speak a local dialect almost incomprehensible to other Italians.

The boys' stories alternate in a series of disastrous, heartbreaking (and predictable) encounters with a world of cruelty and violence. Lacking a central character to bring the threads together, "Boys" tends to fly off in all directions. The only progression is in the horrible end the characters meet.

Mery (Alessandro Di Sanzo), the seductive young transvestite jailed in the first film for fighting with a client, here is found on parole, living peacefully with a friend. When the case comes up in court, Mery gets an outrageously stiff sentence.

Gentle Antonio (Roberto Mariano) has two little kids to support. He tries selling potatoes on the street, but the police, who are never around when they're needed, confiscate his three-wheeled truck because he doesn't have a license. He turns to selling drugs, gets caught, ferociously beaten, and sent back to jail.

In Natale's (Francesco Benigno) excessively graphic visit to a prostitute as soon as he gets out of jail, vulgarity overflows. In other moments, viewers are made to wallow in squalor seen very much from the outside, unrelieved by any ray of dignity.

The one exception is a touching scene between young Claudio (Maurizio Prollo) and his street urchin-girlfriend, who make love (each for the first time) in an abandoned railway car. It makes Claudio's revenge murder by an old cellmate (Alfredo Li Bassi) all the more shattering.

Pic's high point is a breathtaking chase sequence, shot like a "French Connection" on foot. A policeman runs up and down the streets of Palermo after the likable King Kong (Salvatore Termini) steals a car radio. The exciting race comes to a chilling end, however, when the cop catches the boy and shoots him in the head in a moment of rage.

A loud, pulsating score with strains of Arabic music (composed by Giancarlo Bigazzi) gives scenes like this a harsh excitement. Street noise, shouting, blaring horns create a feeling of uneasiness. Mauro Marchetti's camerawork won the film its only prize at Venice.

The tragic chase (and presumably the whole film) is based on a real event. Pic stresses its connection to reality in an epilog in which the young cast gives a brief rundown of their own lives — underprivileged homes, reform school, poignant hopes for the future.

"Boy On The Outside" stirred up controversy at its first public screening at Venice, where co-producer RAI-2 partially disowned the film, condemning its depiction of violence and police brutality. They also tried to ex-

cise pic's dedication to the former mayor of Palermo, Leoluca Orlando, but had to back-pedal after a public outcry at the fest.

Film buffs will pick up blatant citations from famous films, such as the fountain sequence in "La Dolce Vita" and the end of "Los Olvidados." — Yung.

TRACCE DI UNA VITA AMOROSA
(TRACES OF AMOROUS LIFE)
(ITALIAN)

A Mikado Film release of an Aura Film production, in association with RAI-TV Channel 1. Produced by Roberto Cicutto, Vincenzo De Leo, Peter Del Monte. Directed by Del Monte. Screenplay, Del Monte, Giuseppe Manfridi, Alessandra Vanzi; camera (color), Alessandro Pesci; editor, Simona Paggi; music, Nicola Piovani; art direction, Beatrice Scarpato, Carla Volpato. Reviewed at Venice Film Festival (competing), Sept. 11, 1990. Running time: **105 MIN.**
With: Luciano Bartoli, Giorgio Biavati, Giovanna Bozzolo, Simona Caramelli, Chiara Caselli, Walter Chiari, Georges Claisse, Massimo Dapporto, Roberto De Francesco, Stefano Dionisi, Gioele Dix, Valeria Golino, Angela Goodwin.

Boxoffice outlook is definitely not bright for "Traces Of Amorous Life." Nor did its outing at the Venice film fest garner critical support.

Pic's bold concept of stringing together fragments of people's love lives without exploring any of the characters in depth fails to ignite any feelings in the viewer other than puzzlement and frustration. "Traces" doesn't amount to much more than a screening of inconclusive shorts.

Director Peter Del Monte's ("Julia And Julia") opening episode (of 14) is one of the best: A little boy jealous over the birth of a baby brother hides in the yard and watches his parents' discomfort. The last is one of the head-scratchers: A very sick man (Walter Chiari), lovingly if excessively tended by his wife, leaves the clinic to stroll naked into the freedom of the night.

Between the alpha and omega fall mixed snippets. A few of them are curiously touching, others are banal, anecdotal or downright silly. All are distinguished by a poetic sensibility that comes across mostly as forced and stilted. Adding to this is the irritation of having the good, potentially interesting, stories truncated before they have a chance to get started.

Result is that film loses viewer's good will early on, and audience's mounting hostility leads to derisive laughter at the many unprofessional thesps who stumble through their skits.

Still, Del Monte can be a stylish filmmaker with enough aplomb to turn some flimsy stories around. Among the better ones is Laura Morante's episode, in which she struggles to break up with bitter mate Massimo Dapporto.

In general, the best sequences are those sustained by strong actors. Valeria Golino almost makes the outlandish premise of her story work: A girl follows a man who has had a heart transplant from her dead boyfriend. Similarly, Stefania Sandrelli makes a malicious and delicious rich lady who helps a young shoplifter get away from department store detectives.

Nicola Piovani's heavy musical comment is dragged out in continuation to lend drama and mystery to stories that have neither. Alessandro Pesci's cinematography adds an elegant patina.

"Traces" was made using a curious production formula. The actors, both famous names and newcomers, skipped a fee for percentage points. Given film's episodic structure, the sacrifice wasn't great, but their reward looks distant. — Yung.

REQUIEM FUR DOMINIC
(REQUIEM FOR DOMINIC)
(AUSTRIAN)

A Terra Film production in association with OFF and ORF. Produced by Norbert Blecha. Directed by Robert Dornhelm. Screenplay, Michael Kohlmeier, Felix Mitterer; camera (color), Hans Selikovsky; editor, Ingrid Koller, Barbara Heraut; music, Harald Kloser; sound, Helmut Junker, Michael Kranz; production manager, Carl Ludwig; assistant director, Werner Boote. Reviewed at Venice Film Festival (out of competition), Sept. 7, 1990. Running time: **90 MIN.**
Paul . . . . Felix Mitterer
Clara . . . . Viktoria Schubert
Dominic . . . . . . August Schmolzer
Codrata . . . . . . Angelica Schutz
Antonia . . . . Antonia Rados
Nick . . . . Nikolas Vogel
Ostenhof . Georg Hoffmann-Ostenhorf
Doctor . . . . Werner Prinz
Priest . . . . Georg Metzenrad

Director Robert Dornhelm has made the most remarkable political thriller since "Z," though "Requiem For Dom-

inic" is even more startling because of its immediacy. Despite some grueling material, pic should spark a lot of international attention, with strong arthouse possibilities.

Dornhelm ("She Dances Alone," "Echo Park") was born in Timisoara, provincial Romanian city where the anti-Communist movement began last December. Shot there last May, "Requiem" was inspired by Dornhelm's childhood friendship with Dominic Paraschiv, who, in the frantic drama of the violent pre-Christian revolution, was accused of being "the butcher of Timisoara" and responsible for 80 murders.

Paraschiv was seen on news reports all over the world lying wounded and enveloped in a kind of net. He subsequently died, but a few weeks later was rehabilitated by the new Romanian government since his innocence was belatedly discovered.

Dornhelm and an Austrian crew, with co-screenwriter and lead actor Felix Mitterer in the front line, filmed on the streets where the real-life drama had taken place only a few months before. In the face of deep-seated local suspicions about the dreaded secret police, the filmmaking itself looks to have been dangerous.

Dornhelm seamlessly integrates footage of original demonstrations and street fighting (with extremely rugged shots of naked corpses piled into hospitals) and recreated material. Mitterer plays Paul, a Romanian-born Austrian who comes to Timisoara in December to meet his friend Dominic, only to be told the man is a mass-murderer. Horrified at first, then disbelieving, Paul sets out to find out the truth at the risk of his own life.

As a political thriller, "Requiem" is nail-biting cinema. But it's more than that because of a reality even the best thrillers lack. This amazing true story was shot where it happened with maximum authenticity.

Pic looms as a best foreign film Oscar contender next year unless there's a technicality about the soundtrack: Of necessity, some of the dialog is in Romanian, with some French, though it's mostly in German. — Strat.

LA DISCRÈTE
(THE DISCREET)
(FRENCH)

A Pan European/President Films release of a Les Prods. Lazennec production. Directed by Christian Vincent. Screenplay, Vincent, Jean-Pierre Roussin; camera (color), Romain Winding; editor, François Ceppi; music, Jay Gottlieb; associate producer, Adeline Lescallier. Reviewed at Venice Film Festival (critics week section), Sept. 4, 1990. Running time: **94 MIN.**

Antoine	Fabrice Luchini
Catherine	Judith Henry
Jean	Maurice Garrel
Solange	Marje Bunel
Manu	François Toumarkine

"The Discreet," a curious tale of seduction, marks the bow of a notable filming talent, Christian Vincent. Clearly a pupil of Eric Rohmer, the 35-year-old director describes the sentimental relationship between a young man and a girl who's "not his type" with wit, brio and insight.

Praised on its first fest outing at Venice's Critics Week, film should find an appreciative audience at specialized houses and other film festivals.

The neo-libertine Antoine (played by Rohmer actor Fabrice Luchini), a writer and heartless seducer of women, is set up by his friend Jean (equally fine Maurice Garrel), a small-time publisher, to carry out a "literary" experiment.

Antoine is to avenge himself on a girlfriend (Marie Bunel) who walked out on him by seducing a stranger and immediately abandoning her. The results will furnish material for an erotic diary Jean wants to publish.

Antoine, a compulsive talker full of the philosophical citations and paradoxes dear to the French, at last agrees. His victim is to be a poor typist, Catherine (Judith Henry), but when he meets her he finds her too ugly to sleep with. At Jean's insistence he perseveres, only to find his plans upset when he accidentally falls in love. But it is too late: Catherine discovers what's been going on, and leaves him with a dignified letter.

Halfway between "Dangerous Liaisons" and "The Lacemaker," "The Discreet" explores the more delicate zone of romantic feeling with mature wisdom. Filled with clever dialog and monologs by Antoine, script by Vincent and Jean-Pierre Roussin is talky in the best sense.

Luchini, whose role seems to have been sewed on him, turns in a sparkling performance. Judith Henry is no less extraordinary, transforming herself from a mousy, banal typist to a feminine woman whose inner strength and simplicity disarm the narcissistic, mean-spirited intellectual.

There is much to smile at in "The Discreet" (title comes from the tiny pieces of taffeta women used to glue to their faces to hide blemishes). The premise is clever, and the storytelling, though without much variation in tone, proceeds smoothly. Beyond that, film furnishes food for thought on modern morals, sexual and otherwise.

Technical work is professional. — *Yung.*

ROMEO–JULIET
(BELGIAN)

A PH Consulting production. (Intl. sales, Loeb & Loeb, N.Y.) Produced by Paul Hespel. Directed by Armando Acosta. Screenplay, Acosta, Koen van Brabant, Victor Spinetti, from the play by William Shakespeare; camera (color), Acosta; editor, Acosta, Jan Reniers; music, Sergei Prokofiev, Emanuel Verdi, Acosta; sound, Stephane Clement. Reviewed at Venice Film Festival (out of competition), Sept. 6, 1990. Running time: **130 MIN.**

With: John Hurt; voices of: Robert Powell, Francesca Annis, Ben Kingsley, Vanessa Redgrave, Maggie Smith, John Hurt, Victor Spinetti.

(In English)

"Romeo-Juliet" is likely to go down in film history as one of the strangest ever Shakespeare adaptations. Director, co-writer and cinematographer Armando Acosta has cast all the famous characters with cats. The gimmick probably won't attract too many Shakespeare lovers, though cat fans will be tempted.

Juliet is a white Turkish Angora, and Romeo a long-haired grey. Unfortunately, these felines aren't particularly good actors, even when voiced by some of the top names in British theater. The backgrounds (Venice, Ghent and New York, with the balcony scene taking place at Coney Island) are as strange as the concept.

Perhaps the oddest element is casting of John Hurt as a Venetian bag lady, which, next to the Elephant Man, must be the actor's weirdest role.

Photography is grainy with an overuse of slow motion, but the soundtrack is lovely, with Prokofiev's "Romeo And Juliet" used, as well as a theme specially composed for the film. And then there are those wonderful voices. — *Strat.*

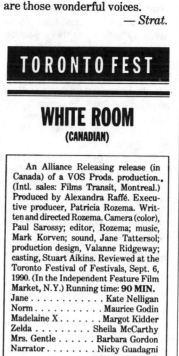

WHITE ROOM
(CANADIAN)

An Alliance Releasing release (in Canada) of a VOS Prods. production. (Intl. sales: Films Transit, Montreal.) Produced by Alexandra Raffé. Executive producer, Patricia Rozema. Written and directed Rozema. Camera (color), Paul Sarossy; editor, Rozema; music, Mark Korven; sound, Jane Tattersol; production design, Valanne Ridgeway; casting, Stuart Aikins. Reviewed at the Toronto Festival of Festivals, Sept. 6, 1990. (In the Independent Feature Film Market, N.Y.) Running time: **90 MIN.**

Jane	Kate Nelligan
Norm	Maurice Godin
Madelaine X	Margot Kidder
Zelda	Sheila McCarthy
Mrs. Gentle	Barbara Gordon
Narrator	Nicky Guadagni

In her previous film, "I've Heard The Mermaids Singing," Patricia Rozema explored the fantasy world of a lonely urban outcast. In the fabulistic, somewhat precious "White Room," the Canadian filmmaker expands upon this theme with mixed results. U.S. theatrical prospects appear limited.

Norm (Maurice Godin) is a young, would-be writer who lives with his parents and dwells in his imagination. His sexual repression and religious indoctrination are suggested through nebulous dream images of milky water, splashing blood and the angelic voices of a church choir.

Breaking out, he roams Toronto by night and begins to spy on a beautiful woman. One night, "Rear Window"-style, he witnesses her brutal rape and murder. Horrified, Norm rushes home and flagellates himself with a thorn bush.

Following this traumatic epiphany, Norm renounces voyeurism and leaves home in search of "honor, action and love." He finds Zelda, a hippie-dippy "environmental artist" (Sheila McCarthy), who recruits him to share her newsstand job and invites him to move into her hut, which stands in the middle of a bleak landfill.

Zelda fails to seduce Norm, who is preoccupied with the discovery that the murdered woman was the enormously popular reclusive rock star Madelaine X (Margot Kidder in a flashback cameo).

Attending the funeral Norm meets a grief-stricken, enigmatic woman in black. When he encounters her again Norm follows the mystery lady to a secluded shabby cottage in a woodsy suburb and offers his services as a gardener.

Predictably, Jane (Kate Nelligan) and Norm fall in love, but the brooding woman is guarding a deep secret that keeps her at an emotional distance. Love liberates the smitten Norm from writer's block, but his flowerly prose tribute to Jane infuriates the spurned schemer Zelda. Norm and Zelda arrive at the none too surprising conclusion that Jane's secret concerns Madelaine X.

As it turns out, the dead pop icon and the moody hermit shared the persona of Madeleine X. Jane gives Norm the details during a climactic scene of prolonged confessional coitus that's discomfiting to watch. When the vengeful Zelda unleashes the media hoards on Jane's pastoral retreat, the shattered genius takes the only way out. Norm is left with memories, apparently a better man for them.

Visually, "White Room" is effective in evoking a corroded urban landscape where relationships and values are doomed to wilt. But the film is burdened with cinematic affectations such as unedifying interiorized flashbacks, a storybook narrator and a pointlessly energetic New Age score.

McCarthy and Nelligan do a good job with their peculiar characters, and Godin is adequate enough as the relentless naif. But "White Room" ultimately calls too much attention to itself while offering too little in return. — *Rich.*

MR. JOHNSON

An Avenue Pictures release of a Michael and Kathy Fitzgerald production. Produced by Michael Fitzgerald. Directed by Bruce Beresford. Executive producer, Bill Benenson. Screenplay, William Boyd, based on the novel by Joyce Carey. Camera (Kodak color), Peter James; editor, Humphrey Dixon; music, Georges Delerue; sound (Dolby), Leslie Hodgson; production design, Herbert Pinter; art direction, Fabian Adibe; set decoration, Graham Sumner; costume design, Rosemary Burrows; assistant directors, Guy Travers, Nick Laws, Adam Sidy; coproducer, Penelope Glass; casting, Susie Bruffin. Reviewed at the Filmland Corporate Center, Culver City, Calif., Sept. 7, 1990. Running time: **103 MIN.**

Mister Johnson	Maynard Eziashi
Harry Rudbeck	Pierce Brosnan

Sargy Gollup . . .	Edward Woodward
Celia Rudbeck	Beatie Edney
Bulteen	Denis Quilley
Tring	Nick Reding
Bamu	Bella Enahoro
Waziri	Femi Fatoba

Capitalism and colonialism intertwine like a two-headed snake in this ponderous but well-made film. Director Bruce Beresford's modestly scaled followup to Oscar winner "Driving Miss Daisy" suffers from a slow, marginally involving storyline that should keep b.o. prospects equally modest.

Premiering at the Toronto Film Festival, pic's foremost discovery is Nigerian actor Maynard Eziashi in the title role as a young African obsessed with British mores, resourcefully working outside the rigid limits of his colonial clerkship.

Johnson uses that knack to help his boss Rudbeck (Pierce Brosnan) build a road connecting their small outpost to the outside world, though his consistent circumvention of proper channels eventually catches up with him and proves his downfall.

Johnson has come to identify so strongly with English customs that he considers himself an Englishman, though it's an image skewed by conspicuous consumption and a burning desire to amass wealth.

Working from a 1939 novel by Joyce Carey set in the 1920s, Beresford and writer William Boyd have delivered a film strangely devoid of emotion and lacking a clear point of view.

While the film uses the road as a symbol of progress the natives hadn't particularly sought, the formal relationship between Rudbeck and Johnson in the latter's puppy-dog panting for acceptance still has a paternalistic quality.

The cherub-faced Eziashi brings charisma to a role so thinly delineated that his achievement is all the more impressive. He's mostly left to prattle on cheerfully about his adoration for his wife (Bella Enahoro) and for England, with little evidence of the former and no reason given for the latter.

Brosnan's cardboard performance provides even less insight. His straight-legged bureaucrat proves so stiff and lifeless there's no sense of caring in any direction, toward either his wife (Beatie Edney) or Johns· n.

By keeping the characters at arm's distance, pic fails to draw in the audience, leaving behind lovingly photographed scenes that connect only sparingly.

Edward Woodward injects much-needed life into the staid proceedings as a vulgar expatriate English shop owner, a boozy bigot who voices the worst of colonial impulses toward their subjugated wards.

Even with first-rate tech credits and its snail's pace, "Mr. Johnson" finally suffers the same fate as its title character, never coming close to being as important as it desperately wants to be. — *Bril.*

H
(CANADIAN)

An ARTO-pelli production. Produced by Stavros C. Stavrides and Darrell Wasyk. Written and directed by Wasyk. Camera (color), Gerald Packer; editor, Tom McMurtry; music, Rob Carroll; sound, McMurtry; set decoration, Mya Ishiura; costume design, Lisa Rankine. Reviewed at the Toronto Festival of Festivals, Sept. 11, 1990. (In Independent Feature Film Market, N.Y.) Running time: **90 MIN.**
Snake . . . . Martin Neufeld
Michelle . . . . Pascale Montpetit

This blatantly honest story about two junkies kicking the "H" habit won't cause a b.o. stampede even though it's beautifully shot, the music is ideal, the lighting extraordinary and the research thorough. Already a critical favorite, it marks an impressive debut for helmer Darrell Wasyk.

Heroin withdrawal is a sordid, messy affair, but for the viewer willing to ride it out with this pic's two lovers, the rewards are great. Insights into the complex seduction of heroin addiction are abundant in "H." Addicts who have screened the film reportedly call it accurate. There's no sensationalism or happy illusions presented here. Just the scummy facts in a fictional setting.

Snake, the macho "hero" with a giant cobra tattoo, decides to "kick" while his lover Michelle is sleeping.

As the credits roll, lucid extreme closeups of a needle on skin, a hammer pounding a nail and a toilet flushing syringes are elegantly cross-cut with bright blue titles. Edith Piaf's blue tune "La Vie En Rose" fits the bill perfectly.

Snake has imprisoned them, painted the windows black, boarded up the doors and flushed the drugs. When Michelle awakens, she freaks. She needs a "hit." The conflict is set.

First third of the pic is spent establishing their bondage to drugs and each other, and mapping out heroin withdrawal symptoms. Unlike "Christiane F.," where 20 minutes is spent in a room and the rest of the film is in the streets, Snake and Michelle are prisoners of their addiction, their pasts, their overdosed friends, and now, their dingy apartment (whose textured stone walls are a visual plus).

Shot entirely on a set, claustrophobia is rampant. Scenes of withdrawal sickness are mercifully short as pic focuses more on psychological aspects. An unusually erotic sex scene is presented as a triumph in the withdrawal process (he was incapable of making love as a junkie).

It moves into the realm of bizarre when Snake shaves his head, makes a cross of forks and spoons, and moves into the closet for "rituals." It's all believable in context.

Pic's turning point comes when he discovers a hit of dope hidden in a book. He immediately shoots up and accidentally drowns himself in the bathtub. Her future ends on an intentionally ambiguous note as she flees the apartment. A nice, realistic ending: one winner, one loser. No false pretense that all H junkies have the strength to kick the habit.

Pic is not a downer, but a fair portrait of a growing addiction and the complexities which surround the drug and accompanying lifestyle. Rehabilitation centers need such films.

Pascale Montpetit (as Michelle) upstages Martin Neufeld (as Snake) with a gripping performance as a woman addicted to a man and a drug and the ability to face them both.

The fairly explicit sex scene presents a problem for public tv in North America but not in Europe, the pic's target audience. Wasyk didn't compromise the grim reality of addiction to boost foreign sales. He avoids the pitfall of sanitizing "dirty" stories (typical of many Canadian pics), which is perhaps why he received zero government funding. With a tiny budget, he tells a painful story exceedingly well. — *Suze.*

PRIVILEGE

A Zeitgeist Films release. Written, produced and directed by Yvonne Rainer; camera (color, 16m), Mark Daniels; editor, Rainer; sound, Antonio Arroyo; art directors, Anne Stuhler, Michael Selditch. Reviewed at Toronto Festival of Festivals, Sept. 10, 1990. (Also in New York Film Festival and Independent Feature Film Market, N.Y.). No MPAA Rating. Running time: **103 MIN.**
With: Alice Spivak, Novella Nelson, Blaire Baron, Rico Elias, Gabriella Farrar, Tyrone Wilson, Yvonne Rainer, Dan Berkey, Claudia Gregory, Mark Niebuhr, Minnette Lehmann, Faith Ringgold, Shirley Triest, Helene Moglen, Catherine English Robinson, Evelyn Cunningham, Gloria Sparrow, Audrey Goodfriend, Vivian Bonnano.

Yvonne Rainer's quasi-documentary about women and menopause strives to be entertaining but fails. Grindingly didactic, "Privilege" is best suited for feminist and other politically oriented festivals.

The filmmaker flaunts her artiness, styling "Privilege" as a collage of ruminative talking heads, snippets of risable '50's-era sex education films, scrolled computer data and encounter-style interviews between the filmmaker and friends.

Rainer makes extensive use of unsuccessfully realized, fiction-like "hot flashbacks," in which one subject re-enacts scenes from her life before menopause. These somewhat fantastical sequences restate familiar observations about stereotypes and the linkage of race, class, sex and economic discrimination in America.

An African-American filmmaker who refuses to limit herself to racial issues, Rainer also touches upon the problems of the handicapped. But for all its thematic hopscotching, "Privilege" invariably returns to the life crises of women over 40.

The filmmaker does not let her sisters off the hook: After years of feminist consciousness-raising, women "have achieved nothing," she declares. Through their submission to male-engendered self-images of post-menopausal worthlessness, women have succumbed to precisely the type of "pathetic" self-loathing expected of them, she argues.

Instead of resorting to estrogen therapy or submitting to

self-abnegation, women must embrace menopause as a liberating life phase, say Rainer and her subjects.

Regrettably, the viewer must slog through a good deal of preachiness while "Privilege" makes its point. — *Rich.*

BLOOD CLAN
(CANADIAN)

A Festival Films presentation. Produced by Glynis Whiting. Directed by Charles Wilkinsen. Screenplay, Whiting; camera (color), Ken Hewlett; editor, Allan Lee; sound, George Tarrant; set design, Rick Roberts. Reviewed at the Montreal World Film Festival, Aug. 30, 1990. Running time: **87 MIN.**
With: Michelle Little, Gordon Pinsent, Robert Wisden, Anne Mansfield, Jacqueline Dandeneauo.

A mild horror pic with latenight tv potential, this film centers on a teenage girl, Katie, whose murderous, cannibalistic, incestuous family is hanged while the credits roll.

For the most part, "Blood Clan" resembles "Little House On The Prairie" until mysterious murders claim the lives of neighboring farm children and Katie's heritage is in thrown into question.

Presumed innocent, she's adopted by the judge who sentenced her clan to death. He and his family move from Scotland to western Canada to forge a new life.

A handsome law clerk from Scotland (and the judge's business partner) turns out to be the sole survivor of the Bean clan as well as the local murderer.

In the end, the judge's conniving wife and promiscuous daughter are slaughtered, but Katie saves the day by shooting her "cousin" to save her adopted father.

The moral of the story is clear on the nature/nurture front: Bad blood is not all in the genes.

Tech credits are good. Violence takes place offscreen.
— *Suze.*

AU CHIC RESTO POP
(CANADIAN-DOCU)

A National Film Board of Canada production. Produced by Eric Michel. Written and directed by Tahani Richard. Camera (color), Jacques Leduc; editor, Monique Fortier; editor, Monique Fortier; sound, Esther Auger, Claude Beaugrand. Reviewed at Montreal World Film Festival, Aug. 29, 1990. Running time: **84 MIN.**

Chic Resto Pop is the name of a funky soup kitchen in Montreal's east end. In this docu, the Resto Pop employees use six original tunes to sing about poverty and the hope which fuels them. Unfortunately, they don't sing too well: pic's weakest element.

Minus most of the melodies, the pic would score as a good tv docu on quality nets.

Pic's strength lies in its original subject matter (a happy soup kitchen) and its explanation of restaurant workings. The people behind this remarkable effort bare all secrets so the docu could essentially be used as a how-to for other groups in need of a model.

The concept is based on the fact that tons of perfectly edible food are scrapped daily because of minor imperfections. Resto Pop employees get as much as they can for free, and turn it into healthy, cheap meals for an entire neighborhood.

Docu is perfect fare for tv because viewers can feel comfortable knowing someone out there is doing something to help the needy. It poses no questions and offers no challenges about the roots of poverty. It simply accepts it as a part of life which must be dealt with as best as possible.

It's a safe record about an innovative group of people who have clear consciences and wobbly voices. — *Suze.*

AVALON

A Tri-Star Pictures release of a Baltimore Pictures production. Produced by Mark Johnson, Barry Levinson. Written and directed by Levinson. Camera (Technicolor), Allen Daviau; editor, Stu Linder; music, Randy Newman; sound (Dolby), Gloria S. Borders; production design, Norman Reynolds; costume design, Gloria Gresham; art direction, Fred Hole, Edward Richardson; set decoration, Linda DeScenna; assistant directors, Peter Giuliano, Christine Larson; associate producers, Marie Rowe, Charles J. Newirth; casting, Ellen Chenoweth. Reviewed at the Columbia Studios, Culver City, Sept. 28, 1990. MPAA Rating: PG. Running time: **126 MIN.**
Hymie Krichinsky . . . . . . Leo Fuchs
Dottie Kirk . . . . Eve Gordon
Gabriel Krichinsky . . . . . Lou Jacobi
Sam Krichinsky . Armin Mueller-Stahl
Ann Kaye . . . . . . Elizabeth Perkins
Eva Krichinsky . . . . Joan Plowright
Izzy Kirk . . . . Kevin Pollak
Jules Kaye . . . . Aidan Quinn
Nathan Krichinsky . . . Israel Rubinek
Michael Kaye . . . . Elijah Wood
Teddy Kirk . . . . Grant Gelt

A beautifully shot look at America's immigrant experience through one multigenerational family, "Avalon" proves a lifeless experience devoid of a central conflict or purpose. Despite inherent warmth and terrific lead performance by Armin Mueller-Stahl, film's slow pace and European sensibility make it ideal for limited arthouse release but should blunt any wider b.o. prospects.

Barry Levinson, in his first directorial outing since the Oscar-winning "Rain Man," returns to the city that provided his backdrop for both "Diner" and "Tin Men": Baltimore. "Avalon" is named for the first location in which the story's four brothers resided.

Dealing with an extended Jewish family headed by brothers who came from Europe in the early 20th century, the director seeks to recapture both a period (the post-World War II era, as television became king) and the essence of family life, with all its feuding, pettiness and tumult.

In that respect, the film is largely successful. The huge, raucous and often shrill family gatherings possess a wry ring of truth as the characters interact in often-infuriating ways, just like a real family.

The patriarch of the central nuclear family is Sam Krichinsky (Mueller-Stahl), who arrives wide-eyed in the U.S. on the Fourth of July. His reminiscences to his grandchildren introduce us to the extended clan and come closest to giving the film meaning, namely how one family survives the assimilation process and maintains a hold on its past.

Still, beyond the beautiful photography by Allen Daviau, spotless classic cars and slavishly detailed sets, the film lacks focus or a real reason for being.

Ultimately, Levinson takes a series of cinematic snapshots of the Kruchinsky family album without punctuating them with enough dramatic moments to sustain a two-hour-plus film. It's as if the writer-director couldn't settle on any one story to pursue, finally offering a potpourri of scenes that generally work but never entirely come together.

With Randy Newman's glorious score and Daviau's filtered images, the film at times feels like Levinson's "The Natural," but without any grand-slam emotional crescendos to tie the story together.

The film is essentially an ensemble piece, but Mueller-Stahl, West German actor recently seen in "Music Box," delivers a towering performance as Sam, demanding that the family history be told and retold to each new generation.

Son Jules (Aidan Quinn) changes his name and goes into business selling tv sets. Emerging role of tv in 1950s family life serves as an amusing and understated subtext to the family wrangling.

Jules marries and has his own son (Elijah Wood), who becomes close to Sam, while Jules' wife (Elizabeth Perkins) chafes under the intrusiveness of his mother (Joan Plowright).

There's less to distinguish Sam as the central figure in the script than in Mueller-Stahl's presence, from his quaint and chronic bickering with his wife to his petty feud with his elder brother (Lou Jacobi).

After meandering through the family life for nearly two hours, Levinson rushes to what proves a moving conclusion, one that seeks to connect all that proceeded it on some higher level.

Still, the film is mostly a celebration of the mundane, and, while watching grandma and grandpa bicker at the dinner table may spur a fond glimmer of recognition, it's a wispy premise on which to hang this sort of lavish undertaking.

There is much to laud in Levinson's keen ear and warm recollections, but "Avalon," when all's said and done, demonstrates good filmmaking but not a very good film. — *Bril.*

BACKSTREET DREAMS

A Vidmark Entertainment release of an O'Malley Film production. Produced by Jason O'Malley, Lance H. Robbins. Directed by Rupert Hitzig. Screenplay, O'Malley; camera (Deluxe color), Stephen M. Katz; editor, Robert Gordon; music, Bill Conti; sound (Dolby), George Alch; production design, George Costello; costume design, Elisabeth Scott; assistant director, Jack Breschard; production manager, Cary Glieberman, Michael P. Petrone (N.J.); stunt coordinator-2nd unit director, B.J. Davis; line producer, Glieberman; casting, Michael Cutler. Reviewed at 23rd St. West 2 theater, N.Y., Sept. 28, 1990. MPAA Rating: R. Running time: **104 MIN.**
Stephanie Bloom . . . . Brooke Shields
Dean Costello . . . . . . Jason O'Malley
Lucy Costello . . . . . . Sherilyn Fenn
Manny . . . . Tony Fields
Luca . . . . Burt Young
Angelo Carnivale . Anthony Franciosa
Mikey . . . . Nick Cassavetes
Also with: Joe Pantoliano, Ray (Boom Boom) Mancini, Meg Register, John & Joseph Viezzi.

"**B**ackstreet Dreams" is a vanity production unsuccessfully mixing exploitation film clichés with fake uplift of a tv disease-of-the-week pic. Theatrical chances are slim; Brooke Shields name should arouse homevid rental interest.

Writer-co-producer-star Jason O'Malley assiduously imitates Sylvester Stallone's "Rocky" showbiz formula: starring in a film from his own script as a *lumpen* guy (from New Jersey) working on the fringe of crime as a loan collector, and commandeering "Rocky" stalwarts Burt Young and composer Bill Conti.

Fitting uncomfortably into a stew including scenes straight out of blaxploitation films of 20 years ago is a central plot involving O'Malley's three-year-old autistic son (played by brothers John & Joseph Viezzi). O'Malley is juggling his criminal activities with raising the intractable kid. Wife (Sherilyn Fenn) has run out on them.

Shields, still beautiful and much taller after being absent from leading roles in cinema for several years, plays the do-gooder, an NYU grad student who tries to bring the child out of its shell and cornily falls in love with O'Malley. She encourages him to get out of his rut and after a melodramatic climax involving the death of O'Malley's no-good partner (Tony Fields), a saccharine happy ending is fabricated.

Despite usual quota of swearing and violence, pic's gangster segments involving minor boss Young and big shot Joe Pantoliano (uncredited in a small role) carry little impact and suffer mightily from comparison with the various big-budget mobster pics currently in release.

O'Malley's earnest performance can't carry the film, and Shields is unsure where to go with her part — at times sexy and in other scenes asexually pure and boring. Net result is a secular kin to dated religioso films, e.g., Don Murray's "The Cross And The Switchblade."

Costar Sherilyn Fenn, pre-"Twin Peaks," is wasted. She goes topless during the opening credits and is soon written out of the script. Best thesping is by Tony Franciosa, making the most of a cornball role as ex-boxer/wrestler who helps the protagonists. — *Lor.*

NEW YORK FEST

AMERICAN DREAM
(DOCU)

A Cabin Creek Films production. Produced by Barbara Kopple, Arthur Cohn. Directed by Kopple. Camera (color), Peter Gilbert, Kevin Keating, Hart Perry, Mark Petersson, Mathieu Roberts; editor-co-directors, Cathy Caplan, Tom Haneke, Lawrence Silk; associate editor, Robert McFalls; music, Michael Small; coordinating producers, Peter Miller, Esther B. Cassidy; associate producers, Ernest Hood, Jonathan House, Molly Ornati, Gail Rosenschein, William Susman. Reviewed at New York Film Festival, Oct. 4, 1990. (In Independent Feature Film Market.) Running time: **100 MIN.**

Academy Award-winning documentary filmmaker Barbara Kopple has made a stirring film about one union's fight against wage cuts. Although its serious tone may preclude significant business, "American Dream" is an important docu for audiences interested in the state of U.S. unions.

Set in the mid-1980s, pic tells an emotional story in a balanced, engaging way. Beginning with a montage of television news stories from the early 1980s, it skips ahead to a scene of Jesse Jackson speaking to workers in 1986 and then moves back to 1984 when the action really begins. This initial jumping around is unnecessary, and some of the clips give away the outcome of the union's struggle.

Once Kopple ("Harlan County U.S.A.") returns to the beginning, her film becomes an absorbing drama instead of just a depressing labor story. When Hormel, a profitable corporation, cuts wages in its Austin, Minn., plant, the union members call in labor consultant Ray Rogers, who grabs the media's attention and exhorts the workers to turn down the pay cut.

The national union leadership, headed by Lewie Anderson, disagrees with Rogers' confrontational tactics and warns the workers they may lose their jobs. The local union supports Rogers, however, and refuses to accept Hormel's offer. The impasse eventually leads to a strike. When management calls in replacement workers, union members must decide whether or not to cross the picket line.

"American Dream" reaches an emotional climax as the workers struggle over loyalty to families, jobs and union. The outcome is a disappointment not only for the union members, but also for the labor movement nationally.

Although Kopple's film is sympathetic to the workers, she does not choose sides between the local and national union leaders, or between the union and the company management. To her credit, she gives Hormel reps opportunities to give their side of the issue.

Result is a fair view of a complicated subject. As a record of the decline of unions during the Reagan era, "American Dream" may one day be studied in history classes. For the present, it sounds an alarm that a profitable company can underpay its workers, freeze them out and then hire permanent replacement workers at lower salaries.

"American Dream" may not be as entertaining as "Roger & Me," nor does it stand to make as much money, but it's equally involving. Showing far less corporate bias than "Roger," Kopple does not blame any one person or group. Indeed, she shows that the union leaders made tactical mistakes and engaged in excessive amounts of infighting.

Using traditional documentary techniques, she recounts both one example of a union's struggle and the larger picture of American labor movement setbacks in the '80s. — *Stev.*

SAN SEBASTIAN

MOTIVSUCHE
(LOCATION RESEARCH)
(EAST GERMAN)

A DEFA Studio Für Spielfilme, Gruppe Johannisthal production. Directed by Dietmar Hochmuth. Screenplay, Henry Schneider from a story by Andreas Scheinert; camera (color), Dieter Chill. Reviewed at San Sebastian Film Festival, Sept. 25, 1990. Running time: **110 MIN.**
With: Peter Zimmermann, Arianne Gorbach, Mario Klaszynski, Dorothea Rohde, Florian Martens, Lothar Bisky.

Future trivia buffs may want to remember "Motivsuche" was the last film made in East Germany before the DDR became part of the West. Otherwise, there is little memorable in this tedious film about a filmmaker who feels, at age 37, he has to make a pic about "living people" after having made only documentaries.

Unfortunately, the real-life subject he chooses is a young couple he meets in a welfare office. The director starts to shoot the film, but the youths bicker and are less interested in cinema than the helmer.

When the kid's father dies, the director takes him into the bosom of his family, while the boy's sidekick gives birth to an illegitimate baby. The director's own family breaks up, and he winds up as a drifter, a development that pleases him.

The young couple is a singularly unattractive and boring pair, the filmmaker's midlife crisis is not very interesting, and the technical level of the film is pretty basic. — *Besa.*

LA SETTIMANA DELLA SFINGE
(THE WEEK OF THE SPHINX)
(ITALIAN)

An Angelo Rizzoli presentation of an Erre Produzioni-Silvio Berlusconi Communications production. Executive producer, Mario Cotone. Directed by Daniele Luchetti. Screenplay, Luchetti, Franco Bernini, Agnelo Pasquini; camera (color), Tonino Nardi; editor, Angelo Nicolini; music, Dario Lucantoni; sound, Franco Borni; sets, Giancarlo Basili, Leonardo Scarpa; costume design, Paola Bonucci. Reviewed at San Sebastian Film Festival, Sept. 22, 1990. Running time: **100 MIN.**
Gloria . . . . Margherita Buy

Eolo . . . . Paolo Hendel
Ministro . . . . Silvio Orlando
Ferruccio . . . . Isaac George
   Also with: Delia Boccardo, Gigi Gaspari, Silvia Mocci.

Daniele Luchetti's second film is a disappointment. The brilliance and zaniness of his first pic ("Domani Accadra") here degenerates into aimless buffoonery. Repeated irony and attempted humor never hit their mark. The loosely structured script invites only tedium.

Yarn revolves around a simpleminded waitress working in a restaurant in the Appennines who falls in love with a tv repairman. She likes puzzles and enigmas and dreams of some day going to Egypt to see the Sphinx.

After a one-night stand with the repairman, she quits her job and pursues her male prey. But he fails to take interest in her, despite her persistence.

Throughout pic, Luchetti strives for humorous situations, but neither Margherita Buy's ebullience nor Paolo Hendel's deadpan style can save this floundering script. Item is probably destined to be tv fodder. — *Besa.*

AVA & GABRIEL, UN HISTORIA DI AMOR
(AVA & GABRIEL, A LOVE STORY)
(CURAÇAOAN)

A Hungry Eye Pictures presentation of a Cosmic Illusion production. Produced by Norman de Palm. Directed by Felix de Rooy. Screenplay, de Palm, from a story by de Rooy; camera (Agfacolor), Ernest Dickerson; editor, Ton de Graaf; sound, Peter Flamman; music, Roy Louis; production design, de Rooy; costume design, Ellen van der Wiel. Reviewed at San Sebastian Film Festival, Sept. 25, 1990. Running time: 100 MIN.
Ava Recordina . . Nashaira Desbarida
Gabriel Goedbloed . . Cliff San-A-Jong
Carlos Zarius . . . Carol Brown Winkel
Father Fidelius . . . . Theu Boermans
Bishop Hildebrand . . . . Dolf de Vries
   Also with: Geert de Jong, Edmond Classen, Frederick de Groot, Janine Veeren, Serge Ubrette, Rina Penso, Norman de Palm, Burny Every, Ana Muskus, Helen Kamperveen.

As an offbeat, exotic film, at times whimsical but also critical of racism and colonialism, "Ava & Gabriel" is a good bet. This strange item from Caraçao, spoken in Dutch and the local Papiamentu dialect, is colorful, light and gay and could appeal to specialized audiences in many climes.

Felix de Rooy's film, set in 1948, concerns a black painter from Surinam commissioned to do a mural of the Virgin Mary for the local church. Naturally the local burghers are alarmed when the Virgin is depicted as having Negroid traits.

The painter, meanwhile, falls for a local mixed-blood schoolteacher, whom he uses as a model for the painting. She, in turn, is engaged to a white police major. Fuel is added when the governor's Dutch wife takes a fancy to the painter.

Helmer handles the diverse strands of the story deftly, at times building up the dramatic situations, at other times contenting himself with wry sarcasm. The island background is presented in vivid colors and particular care is taken in lighting, sets, costumes and camerawork, all of the highest quality.

"Ava & Gabriel" is a delightful romp, with asides on more serious subjects. Fine thesping by Nashaira Desbarida and Cliff San-A-Jong as the two lovers.
   — *Besa.*

LUBA
(DUTCH)

An Allarts Prods. production. Produced by Kees Kassander, Denis Wigman. (Intl. sales: the Sales Co.) Written and directed by Alejandro Agresti. Camera (color), Miguel Rodriguez; editor, Rene Wiegmans; music, Paul van Bruggen; sound, Mark Glynne; art director, Dorine de Vos. Reviewed at the Toronto Festival of Festivals, Sept. 6, 1990. (Also in San Sebastian Film Festival.) Running time: **90 MIN.**
Roberto . . . . Elio Marchi
Luba . . . . Bozena Lasota
Madame . . . . Viveca Lindfors
   Also with: Adrian Brine, Alex van der Wyck, Michael Matthews.

Visual style fails to compensate for muddied thematic substance in this English-language Dutch production by Argentinian Alejandro Agresti. A dense and talky parable about improbable lovers in Nazi-occupied Holland, "Luba" is unlikely to meet the commercial criteria of American artfilm distributors.

Roberto (Elio Marchi), a writer and intellectual with a bizarre fetish for prosthetic devices, is on the run from the secret police in Rotterdam, circa 1941. He takes sanctuary in a cabaret/brothel operated by a salty madame (Viveca Lindfors in a quirky turn) who's preoccupied with surviving in cataclysmic times. He pays for a luxury suite and the company of the beautiful but cynical prostitute Luba (Bozena Lasota), a refugee from Poland.

The narrative unfolds during the long hours the pair spend indulging in merciless verbal combat. Roberto is an idealist who believes that artists are meant "to unveil mysteries." Luba, scarred by experience, is a deeply skeptical pragmatist who's convinced that ideas are pathetically futile weapons against tyranny.

The self-absorbed free-thinker and the worldly wise tart-tongued tart pass the time absorbed in an escalating confrontational relationship, fueled by unconsummated sexual tension. Agresti is concerned with the indomitability of the human spirit in the face of man-made horrors. Indulgently, he smothers these noble impulses with surreal trappings that have the beguiling but impenetrable quality of hallucinations. There's some rarefied comic relief in the presence of two foul-mouthed gestapo types and assorted bordello-dwellers.

The gossamer nature of time is celebrated by Roberto's old professor, who warns him that survival demands obliteration of the past. An Argentinian chanteuse, who may or may not be a figment of Roberto's memory, celebrates the glories of pre-war Buenos Aires in lyrically unfettered flights of fancy. When one old reprobate drinks a toast to the heroism of misfits, Agresti's film has made its point.

Lasota is commanding as the strong-willed whore, and Marchi credibly conveys the jumbled insecurities of the hunted intellectual. Both actors are fluent in English but their accents, while tolerable, become wearisome with the relentless drone of Agresti's leaden dialog.

Art direction and design are elegant, but on their own are unlikely to satisfy any but the most dedicated cineastes.
   — *Rich.*

SANTA CRUZ, EL CURO GUERRILLERO
(SANTA CRUZ, THE WARRIOR PRIEST)
(SPANISH)

A Zauli Films S.A. production. Executive producer, Angel Amigo. Directed by José María Tuduri. Screenplay, Mitxel Gaztambide, José A. Vitoria, Tuduri, based on a story by Tuduri; camera (Eastmancolor), Gonzalo F. Berridi; editor, Ivan Aldeo; music, Amaia Zubiria, Pascal Gaigne; costume design, Eli Ilizondo. Reviewed at San Sebastian Film Festival, Sept. 26, 1990. Running time: **97 MIN.**
Azurmendi . . . . Carlos Zabala
Santa Cruz . . . . Ramón Barea
Jabonero . . . . Ramón Agirre
La Vinatera . . . . . . Aitzpea Goenaga
   Also with: Joseba Aierbe, Mikel Laskurain, Agustin Arrazola, Patxi Santamaria, Paco Sagarzazu, Juani Mendiola, Daniel Trepiana.

Even Spaniards will be hard-pressed to make sense of "Santa Cruz, The Warrior Priest," based on a historical footnote about a 1860s conflict in the Basque region, the Second Carlist War.

Though over $1 million was spent in making this item about a guerrilla priest who goes about butchering civilians he considers his enemies, pic's only action scene looks like it was filmed with 30 extras, instead of the 200 that "Santa Cruz" supposedly had.

Woven into the yarn, which is shot mostly in the woods, is a slim love story about a boy who flees a seminary and wants to take a ship to America. He doesn't get far before being pressed into the service of the bearded priest, and not before striking up a flirtation with a plain village girl. She reappears periodically throughout the film, and the happy couple are reunited at the end, as Santa Cruz escapes over the border to France.

Though thesping by Ramón Barea as the warrior priest and Carlos Zabala are fine, and cinematography and direction are professional, there's little to hold audience interest, except perhaps in the Basque provinces (where film was financed).

Somehow, pic strives to present the priest in a favorable light, which can hardly be justified since he was a religious fanatic, illiterate, cruel and bigoted. — *Besa.*

HISTORIA NIEMORALNA
(AN IMMORAL STORY)
(POLISH)

A Film Studio KADR production. Written and directed by Barbara Sass. Camera (color), Wieslaw Zdort; editor, Maria Orlowska; music, Michal Lorenc, Marcin Pospieszalski; sound, Krzysztof Grabowski; art direction, Anna Bohdziewicz-Jastrzebska; production manager, Tadeusz Lampka. Reviewed at San Sebastian Film Festival, Sept. 29, 1990. Running time: **108 MIN.**
Ewa . . . . Dorota Stalinska
Magda.Teresa Budzisz-Krzyzanowska
Also with: Michal Bajor, Marek Lewandowski, Olaf Lubaszenko, Henryk Bista, Stanislawa Celinska.

Told as a film within a film, "An Immoral Story" is about an aging actress on the skids might have proved a little more effective without the interruptions of editing room scenes when the director is supervising and rearranging the cutting.

Ewa is a flamboyant, pushy actress whose career and love life have come to a dead end. She lives in a faceless housing development and is alternately prone to tantrums and tenderness. She is totally engrossed in herself, is soused much of the time and still dreams of making a comeback as a singer. But her overbearing personality time after time sets her at loggerheads with those she tries to work with in the theater and in her bedroom.

Though well acted by Dorota Stalinska, storyline is too thin to sustain pic's overlong running time. The plight of a washed-up Polish actress, interrupted by the musings of a femme director, will not likely interest many, at least not the way helmer Barbara Sass presents it. — *Besa.*

LAS CARTAS DE ALOU
(LETTERS FROM ALOU)
(SPANISH)

An Elías Querejeta production with Television Española. Written and directed by Montxo Armendáriz; camera (Agfa color), Alfredo F. Mayo; editor, Rori Sainz de Rozas; music, L. Mendo, L. Fuster; sound, Pierre Lorraine; production manager, Primitivo Alvaro; sets, Llorenc Miguel; costume design, Maiki Marin. Reviewed at Cine Renoir, Madrid, Aug. 28, 1990. (In San Sebastian Film Festival.) Running time: **92 MIN.**
Alou . . . . Mulie Jarju
Carmen . . . : . . . . Eulalia Ramón
Moncef . . . . Ahmed El-Maaroufi
Mulie . . . . Akonio Dolo
Jorge . . . . Albert Vidal
Also with: Rosa Morata, Mamaadou Lamine, Ly Babali, M'Barick Guisse, Joaquín Notario, Margarita Calahorra, Fredy Rippers.

Montxo Armendáriz' "Letters From Alou" eloquently illustrates the poignant plight of Africans trying to make a go of it in Spain. Film should arouse interest on fest circuits and could garner commercial nibbles at arthouses.

Alou, a Senegalese, is smuggled into Spain with a group of other blacks and Arabs and left on an abandoned beach. Penniless and unable to understand Spanish, Alou drifts from one menial job to another, occasionally befriending other illegals and even beginning a romance with a bartender.

The Spaniards that Alou and his brethren encounter are for the most part tolerant and decent. But Alou has a lively temper and takes offense quickly at their slights. As he gets into trouble, he is obliged to pull up stakes repeatedly.

Helmer/scripter Armendáriz avoids overdramatizing the story. Memorable vignettes include Alou touching snowflakes for the first time and learning the intricacies of checkers.

Pic boasts a good performance by Mulie Jarju as Alou, topnotch production credits and fine lensing by Alfredo Mayo. — *Besa.*

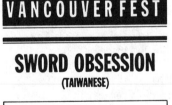

SWORD OBSESSION
(TAIWANESE)

A Central Motion Picture production. Produced by Kuo Mu Sheng. Directed by Yeh Hung Wei. Screenplay, Hsiao Yeah; camera (color), Yan Weh Hann; editor, Chern Bor Wean; music, Chiou Jiuan Jiuan; sound, Liu Der Kuang; art direction, Chiou Lie Kawn. Reviewed at Toronto Festival of Festivals, Sept. 10, 1990. (In Vancouver Intl. Film Festival.) Running time: **100 MIN.**
With: Tao Chong Hwa, Ye Chong Cheng, Chao Hseng Li, Wei Hsao Peng, Chiang Ching Hsin, Mei Fang, Ling Yang, Wu Min.

Theatrical potential is grim for this Taiwanese Romeo and Juliet, in which lovers are thwarted by family politics, and their arranged marriage eventually erupts in violence.

Excessive blood and vomit closeups will disgust North American audiences, but, in pic's context, will be overlooked by Asian film specialists. There is little to distinguish this pic from other violent Asian films.

This one begins and ends in a cemetery where a photog shoots a family portrait. (Family is smaller after all the killings which take place in between.)

Like his murdered father once was, young Hue becomes a gang leader. He runs away with a powerful politician's daughter whom he is forbidden to see by both his own family and hers. Unforeseen circumstances and several killings later, the girl is at the arranged wedding. Hue arrives to shoot her father.

Titled "Sword Obsession" presumably because of the young hero's dreams of sword fighting (although he uses a gun), this incongruous pic will be difficult for many to grasp, even if it does mirror directionless youth in Taiwan. — *Suze.*

LONELY IN AMERICA

An Arista Films presentation of an Apple Prods. film. Produced by Tirlok Malik, Phil Katzman. Directed by Barry Alexander Brown. Screenplay, Satyajit Joy Palit, Brown, based on a story by Malik; camera (color), Katzman; editor, Tula Goenka; music, Gregory Arnold; sound, Chris Tergesen; art direction, Eduardo Capilla; costume design, Mary Marsicano; assistant director, Nesya Blue; casting, Sue Crystal. Reviewed at Vancouver Intl. Film Festival, Sept. 30, 1990. No MPAA Rating. Running time: **96 MIN.**
Arun . . . . Ranjit Chowdry
Max . . . . Tirlok Malik
Faye . . . . Adelaide Miller
Jim . . . . Robert Kessler
Duncan . . . . David Toney
Becky . . . . Melissa Christopher
Carlos . . . . Franke Hughes
Also with: Tanya Soler, Richard Raphael, Cee-Cee Rider.

This exceedingly witty cross-cultural romantic comedy is a guaranteed crowd-pleaser with terrific commercial potential if targeted properly.

This warm and funny film marks a smashing directorial debut for Barry Alexander Brown, editor of pics by Spike Lee (who's in a cameo as "Lonely In America" credits roll).

Pic makes as many poignant cultural jokes as U.K. hit, "My Beautiful Laundrette." Here, the hero, Arun, is a New Delhi lone ranger who heads to New York in search of the American dream. He's unwillingly steeped in Indian tradition via relatives already established in N.Y.

His own humble crusade is to submerge into America's vast cultural melting pot, which he eventually does with comic bravado, and skip the whole prearranged marriage and imported family structure.

Pic's quality is foreshadowed in the credits. Hawking papers in the family-run newsstand, Arun plunks down a magazine on the counter. The mag's headline bears a credit. Other credits follow on other mags, a subscription card, a scratch 'n' win lottery ticket and, for the director credit, a trashy tabloid. (This may be the first time a non-industry audience applauded each credit.)

This seductive intro hooks the audience instantly. It delivers the goods (the titles), sets the stage (immigrant enters the family biz) and establishes all the main characters (everyone buying or selling a paper stops at the newsstand on their way to work).

Arun's not satisfied to eke out a meager living selling mags for his uncle. He takes night courses and accidentally lands a computer job. He meets a wild array of N.Y. characters that speaks volumes about America itself.

Co-worker Jim offers Arun a free apartment in return for a little computer help. The pad is Jim's "temple of love" and his advice to Arun on American women is: ". . . never tell them the truth." When trying to pick up a couple of girls, he leans on "his" Mercedes and the car starts yelling, "Help, help! Thief!"

When he finally gets a chance with Faye, another co-worker, Arun can't get his pants off. He's defeated. He's lonely. He writes to his mother: "I don't want to depress you, so I just won't describe my life at present."

Later, Arun calls off the prearranged wedding, and he eventually gets hooked up with Faye and writes his mother: "I've finally melted into the pot."

This very simple story is tightly scripted and perfectly cast. A kind of Robin Williams on tranquilizers, Ranjit Chowdry is brilliant as the modest maverick. His understated screen presence is electrified by crackerjack delivery.

Tirlok Malik, who dreamed up the story and co-produced the pic, brings his own New Delhi/New York authenticity to the role of immigrant monarch Max.

Ultimately, this is one of those tiny-budget indie sleepers which should get a lot of mileage out of small-town word-of-mouth and critics who cater to consumers, not other critics. Homevid is a natural for round two. — *Suze.*

THE GARDEN
(BRITISH)

> A Bazilisk Prods., Channel 4, British Screen, ZDF, Uplink production. Produced by James McKay. Written and directed by Derek Jarman. Camera (color), Christopher Hughes; editor, Peter Cartwright; music, Simon Fisher Turner. Reviewed Sept. 4, 1990, at Toronto Festival of Festivals. (In Vancouver Intl. Film Festival.) Running time: **90 MIN.**
> With: Kevin Collins, Roger Cook, Jody Graber, Pete Lee-Wilson, Philip Macdonald, Johnny Mills, Tilda Swinton.

Derek Jarman's dense "The Garden," a graphic look at homosexual discrimination laden with campy gestures, music and religious dream sequences, will prove disconcerting to mainstream audiences.

As in "Caravaggio" and "The Last Of England," Jarman forfeits the standard storyline for a panoply of images. The walkouts during this screening indicate that many viewers won't be able to transcend the tedium.

Michael Gough's gently resonant voiceover laments, "My friends went so silently," and the legacy of AIDS is alluded to powerfully. Jarman combines camera images and backdrops to juxtapose contempo England with the Passion of Christ.

It's a journey without direction, starting with images of a black & white Jesus on the cross, a drunken writer at his desk and a color scene of 12 women sitting at a Last Supper table.

A gay male couple make recurring appearances. They are arrested and persecuted, culminating in an ugly tar-and-feathering session. Mary floats in and out. The gay couple wind up on the cross. Jesus walks under power lines near a nuclear plant.

Simon Turner's score is excellent, but often out of sync with the self-conscious, symbolic action on the screen.

Jarman is an acquired taste, and while his individual shots can be stunning, his ambiguous references coupled with the grand personal scheme of this film make it tough going. — *Devo.*

MAGICIANS OF THE EARTH
(U.S.-DOCU)

> A Fernando Treuba production. Produced by Trueba. Directed and narrated by Philip Haas. Camera (color), Tony Wilson; editor, Belinda Cowdy; music, David Byrne; sound, Graham Wyse. Reviewed at Vancouver Intl. Film Festival, Oct. 1, 1990. Running time: **120 MIN.**

Helmer Philip Haas is pioneering uncharted territory with docu footage of aboriginal Australians in spiritual "ground painting" ceremonies, but a serious lack of narration often leaves the viewer baffled about the significance of events.

A docu in such a remote place conducting ancient rituals in a language foreign to 99% of the planet requires much more context and detail. If the narrator shed more light on these fascinating artistic customs, pic would be great fare for educational tv.

"The Giant Woman And The Lightning Man" is the first of four "Magicians Of The Earth" film episodes, essentially shot for Euro tv. Commissioned by the Centre Georges Pompidou to direct four one-hour shows on the "living arts," Haas first trekked to Yuendumu, Australia and filmed aboriginal men creating a ground painting called "The Giant Woman Dreaming."

Shot in real time with the camera as passive observer, the artists prepare their materials and make the sculpture/painting long before the narrator indicates what's happening and what it means. He finally explains (as did Werner Herzog in "Where The Green Ants Dream") that the basis of all aboriginal beliefs is "dreaming," including language, spirituality, earthly objects and art.

In the second half hour, Haas heads to Maningrida (in Northern Australia) where an aboriginal tribe renowned for its paintings on tree bark paints "The Lightning Man."

Haas has some unique footage here. His minimalist narration and sound is pure, but it lacks detail and rhythm. Without more sound and info, the silent world of the aboriginal artists doesn't stand much of a chance in a world full of channel zappers. With a little more of David Byrne's music track, it would be ideal for the tube.

Much like the first episode, part two of "Magicians Of The Earth" is a visually stunning docu about ancient art forms in remote places. Narration her far outshines the first.

As in the first 60-minute episode, this show covers two distinct regions so each hour could be split to create a series of half-hour shows. Both are suitable for quality tv outlets worldwide.

In the "Young Man's Dream" segment, Haas goes to southern Madagascar to explore hand-carved wooden tomb sculptures that supposedly serve as a messenger between the living world and ancestral spirits.

In the "Woman's Secret" segment, Haas introduces the painter Nera Jambruko of Papua New Guinea whose house decorating combines ancient beliefs and modern commerce.

Haas' narration in this segment contextualizes and entertains at the same time. If he could liven up the previous segments to match this one, the series would be a dynamite number for the PBS outlets of the world. — *Suze.*

THE FAMINE WITHIN
(CANADIAN-DOCU)

> A Kandor Prods. Ltd. production. Executive producer, Paul Jay, High Road Prods. Written, produced and directed by Katherine Gilday. Camera (color), Joan Hutton, Barry Stone; editor, Petra Valier; music, Russell Walker; sound, Penny Hazy. Reviewed at Bloor Cinema, Toronto, Aug. 31, 1990. (In Vancouver and Toronto film festivals.) Running time: **120 MIN.**

Young girls in North America have been subscribing to the media message to be thin, often with devastating results, says first-time helmer Katherine Gilday in "The Famine Within," a slickly packed docu whose excessive length and lack of conclusive remedies diminishes the subject's punch.

This hot topic will fare well with pubbroadcasters and educators, who can address both girls and boys about the problems of early cultural imposition of body types. (Pic was produced in association with the National Film Board of Canada's Studio D.)

Pic gives an overview of eating disorders via a series of talking heads: Anorexic and bulimic girls say they're afraid of food but totally obsessed with it.

Leading feminist anthropologists and therapists voice their concerns with urgency that to be a woman now means worrying about weight. Model agents describe their ideal body type, and Gilday intercuts these interviews with modern businesswomen in corporate suits undressing to reveal ultrathin bodies in neon exercise gear.

Gilday gives historical perspective to the centuries of socialization that define girls in terms of beauty. Teens on camera reveal personal dieting histories that have led to hospitalization. Kindergarten girls already discuss their fear of flab.

Psychotherapists such as Susie Ohrbach ("Fat Is A Feminist Issue") find it ironic that in the 1990s, feminism finds women making cosmic strides in professional fulfillment, but there's a renewed emphasis on beauty and weight, supported by heavily publicized fitness and diet crazes.

Gilday presents scores of information throughout, although the references to surveys about body images and weight gain need more solid documentation.

Fat women here have lots to say about their diet-induced obesity as well as their experiences of being taunted. Anorexic girls share their feelings of low self-worth and starvation for love. Some men's p.o.v. would have been useful, too.

Gilday has assembled an articulate bunch of lay and professional people, who are clearly made to feel comfortable in front of her camera. But a solid half hour needs to be clipped. — *Devo.*

CHICAGO FEST

YO, LA PEOR DE TODAS
(I, THE WORST OF THEM ALL)
(ARGENTINE)

> A GEA Cinematografica production. Executive producer, Gilbert Marouani. Produced by Lita Stantic. Directed by Maria Luisa Bemberg. Screenplay, Bemberg, Antonio Larreta, based on a book by Octavio Paz; camera (color), Felix Monti; music, Luis Maria Serra; production design, Voytek; costume design, Graciela Galan. Reviewed at Venice Film Festival (out of competition), Sept. 10, 1990. (In Chicago Intl. Film Festival.) Running time: **109 MIN.**
> Sister Juana . . . . . . Assumpta Serna
> Viceroy's wife . . . . Dominique Sanda
> Viceroy . . . . Hector Alterio
> Archbishop . . . . Lautaro Murua

Thanks to a splendid central performance from Assumpta Serna as a gentle, gifted nun who becomes the enemy of the country's woman-hating archbishop, this new film from Argentine director Maria Luisa Bemberg harbors strong possibilities for international arthouse release.

Set in 17th century Mexico, this grim tale of religious and sexual persecution during the Inquisition starts out with Sister Juana, a noted poet and writer, under the protection of Mexico's cultured viceroy (Hector Alterio). His wife (Dominique Sanda) spends as much time as possible with the young nun, giving her support and even a kind of love.

It's clear from the start the church hierarchy will crush this rebellious nun who admits she's not very pious. The archbishop's hatred for women is so great he won't even sit at a table with a woman. The film suggests that his hatred may, in fact, be masking his lust. There's even a suggestion he might be Juana's unknown father.

Once the viceroy and his wife are recalled to Spain, Juana's position becomes grim. The film's title is taken from the text of her final confession of her sins.

Serna, the Spanish actress who was memorable in Pedro Almodóvar's "Matador," gives an extremely intelligent and moving performance as the nun whose passion for knowledge and literature are her eventual undoing. She's backed by a strong supporting cast.

Though slowly paced, the film is visually elegant thanks to fine lensing by Felix Monti (who also shot "Old Gringo").

With careful handling, pic by Bemberg ("Camila," "Miss Mary") could find appreciative audiences outside Spanish-speaking territories. It's also likely to interest festivals of women's films.
— Strat.

IL Y A DES JOURS...
ET DES LUNES
(THERE WERE DAYS
AND MOONS)
(FRENCH)

A Films 13-TF1 Films production, in association with Sofica Valor. Produced and directed by Claude Lelouch. Screenplay, Lelouch, Valerie Bonnier, Marc Rosenbaum; camera (Widescreen, East-

mancolor), Jean-Yves Le Mener; editor, Sophie Bhaud, Helene de Luze; music, Francis Lai, Erik Berchot; sound, Dominique Levert; production manager, Tania Zazulinsky; assistant director, Paul Gueu; casting, Arlette Gordon. Reviewed at Venice Film Festival (out of competition), Sept. 7, 1990. (In Chicago Intl. Film Festival.) Running time: **130 MIN.**
Truckdriver . . . . Gérard Lanvin
Doctor . . . . Patrick Chesnais
"Heads or tails" man . Vincent Lindon
Priest . . . . Francis Huster
Woman alone . . . . . Annie Girardot
Naive woman . . . . Marie Sophie L.
Singer . . . . Philippe Léotard
Motorcyclist . . . . . Gérard Darmon
    Also with: Paul Preboist, Christine Boisson, Serge Reggiani, Caroline Miola, Jacques Gamblin, Charles Gerard.

"There Were Days And Moons" demonstrates the best and worst of Claude Lelouch's style: a great idea, a fine cast, interesting locations, some brilliant filmmaking. Yet, it's often pretentious, overlong and overempathetic, and with another all-enveloping music score.

None of Lelouch's many features has achieved the success of his international hit "A Man And A Woman." The 1966 pic's popularity may even have harmed his career as critics worldwide reacted against the tv commercial style in his direction and the schmaltzy music score.

New film's idea is that daylight saving, with clocks going forward an hour, coincides with a full moon, when instabilities supposedly surface. Lelouch takes a clutch of characters with various personal and emotional problems and throws them together on a collision course. One of them is doomed to die at fadeout.

The characters include a quick-tempered trucker, a philandering doctor, a too-handsome priest, a lonely woman who hasn't seen her daughter in six years, a bride and groom who split up on their wedding night, a sweet young Air France hostess and a couple of garrulous old men.

Lelouch opens the film with a 13-minute homage to the Brittany coast, including a famous scene from "A Man And A Woman" as well as the ill-fated wedding of the young couple. When the film proper begins, other weddings follow before a "Several Years Later" title.

Rest of the pic unfolds within a space of a few hours as daylight saving results in missed planes, excessive speed to make up for the lost hour and tension. In addition, the full moon brings out the worst in people.

All of this could have been

fascinating, but Lelouch smothers the drama with deafening music and intrusive camerawork. Swinging back and forth between two people having a conversation is surely old hat by now. There are moments of charm, with the women characters faring better than the mostly unattractive males, but in the end, it's a deadening experience.

There's no doubt Lelouch is prodigious with his ideas and his obvious love of cinema, but "There Were Days And Moons" seems unlikely to provoke new interest in Lelouch's career Stateside. — Strat.

L'AMOUR
(LOVE)
(FRENCH)

A Paris Classics production. (Intl. sales: Les Films du Volcan, Paris.) Produced by Humbert Balsan. Written and directed by Philippe Faucon. Camera (Eastmancolor), Bernard Tiphine; editor, Christian Dior; music, Benoit Schlosberg; sound, Francesco Veloso; production design, Marie-Françoise Argentino; assistant director, Christian Argentino. Reviewed at Montreal World Film Festival (Cinema of Today & Tomorrow section), Sept. 1, 1990. (In Chicago Intl. Film Festival.) Running time: **80 MIN.**
Sandrine . . . . . Laurence Kertekian
Martine . . . . Julie Japhet
Joel . . . . Nicolas Porte
Riri . . . . Mathieu Bauer
Alex . . . . Sylvain Cartigny
Perrine . . . . Marina Golovine
Sophie . . . . Judith Henry
    Also with: Guillaume Briat, Cedric Dumont, Emmanuel Mauro.

"L' Amour," already a prizewinner in France, is an excellent example of a genre of French cinema which, when sensitively handled, can attract audiences worldwide. This modest debut from writer-director Philippe Faucon is a gem.

Setting is a Paris suburb in late summer, and the focus is on a group of teens with sex on their minds. Some are better at handling relationships than others, and the girls seem to make the running in this society.

Sandrine is going out with Didier, but is a bit bored with him (and with having to pay for the hotel room they rent from time to time). She decides she likes Joel, a gangly youth who's also attracted to her, and before long they're spending a night at the home of Sandrine's friend, Martine, whose parents are conveniently away.

Eventually Sandrine's father discovers the couple together, and there's a bitter row, but

daughter and father make up in time to dance together at Martine's wedding.

The other stand-out character in a flawless ensemble is Riri, a shy, eager youth who fancies Valerie even though she already has an English boyfriend (who doesn't speak French). He tags along after the lovers, but looks as if he's a born loser and never gets anywhere. The other characters looking for love include the attractive sisters, Perrine and Sophie, both of whom like the popular Joel.

What's attractive about the film is that the teenagers are sympathetically and naturally depicted. Young cast is composed of nonpro actors, and they're all excellent, especially Mathieu Bauer as the lovesick Riri.

There isn't much of a plot here, but there is a fond feeling for young people groping, sometimes agonizingly, for love and affection in a difficult world. The settings in cafés, bars, a disco, a laundromat and the various homes of the youngsters are all lovingly observed. (A little nudity accompanies the youths' exploration of sexual urgings.)

Given the right handling, "L'Amour" should charm selected audiences. Though small-scale, it's filled with delicacy and humor. Faucon is a young director whose next film will be awaited with anticipation. — Strat.

DESPUES DE LA
TORMENTA
(AFTER THE STORM)
(ARGENTINE)

A Killarney Films production in association with TVE. Produced by Edgardo Pallero. Directed by Tristan Bauer. Screenplay, Bauer, Ruben Alvarez, Graciela Maglie; camera (color), Richardo de Angelis; editor, Cesar D'Angiolillo; music, Rodolfo Mederos; sound, Abelardo Kuschnir; art direction, Abel Facello. Reviewed at Toronto Festival of Festivals, Sept. 12, 1990. (In Chicago Intl. Film Festival.) Running time: **120 MIN.**
With: Lorenzo Quinteros, Patricio Contreras, Ana Maria Picchio, Eva Hernandez, Jofre Soares.

"After The Storm" is a sweeping tale of the deterioriation of a laborer's family that, by extension, reps the declining economic and political climate of contempo Argentina. Pic's a natural for Latin American audiences, and it might also find success on pubbroadcasting film series.

Factory worker Ramon Decima loses his job when his plant closes down. With a wife and two children to look after, he is desperate for work. He doesn't pass a physical for a new job, and is forced to move from his meager house to a slum on the outskirts of Buenos Aires.

Ramon is humiliated and disgraced by his bad luck. His wife Norita must go to work as a housemaid. His son Andres starts hanging out with local thieves and gets arrested for participating in a drug deal.

Hopeless at finding work in the city, Ramon goes back to the country where his brother and father are still living. Dad lost his memory; brother Santos recalls that their father took the profits from the harvest years back to buy a car, which now sits as a chicken nest in the garage.

Unfortunately Ramon brings bad fortune to the country, too. He and his brother are responsible for the death of the rich landowner's mare. Ramon's father finally dies while plowing in the field, and the sons are forced to tear wood from their shack on the farm to build his coffin.

Making a confident directorial debut, Tristan Bauer infuses the story with striking, magical images that touch on the reality of poverty and the loss of spirit in Argentina. Heavy mists sit over the festering garbage dump in Ramon's slum neighborhood, as local people pick through the scraps to find food to eat and metal to sell.

A solid cast is led by Lorenzo Quinteros and Ana Maria Picchio, who bring empathy and strength to their roles.

Bauer's $400,000 budget is put to effective use in the rich camerawork and moving score. The director's docu experience shines in this indictment of his impoverished nation. — *Devo.*

WELCOME HOME, ROXY CARMICHAEL

A Paramount Pictures presentation of an ITC Entertainment Group production. Executive producer, Karen Leigh Hopkins. Produced by Penney Finkelman Cox. Directed by Jim Abrahams. Screenplay, Hopkins; camera (Deluxe color), Paul Elliott; editor, Bruce Green; music, Thomas Newman; sound, David Kelson; production design, Dena Roth; art direction, John Myhre, Rosemary Brandenburg; art direction - Ohio, Nina Ruscio; set design, Richard G. Huston; set design - Ohio, James A. Gelarden; set decoration, Tom Talbert; set decoration - Ohio, Maria Nay; costumes, Betsy Heimann; assistant director, John T. Kretchmer; casting, Mali Finn. Reviewed at Paramount Studios, L.A., Oct. 8, 1990. MPAA Rating: PG-13. Running time: **98 MIN.**

Dinky Bossetti . . . . . Winona Ryder
Denton Webb . . . . .Jeff Daniels
Elizabeth Zaks . . . . . . Laila Robins
Gerald Howells . Thomas Wilson Brown
Barbara Webb . . . . Joan McMurtrey
Les Bossetti . . . . . . Graham Beckel
Rochelle Bossetti . . . Frances Fisher
Beannie . . . . Robby Kiger
Evelyn Whittacher . . . Dinah Manoff
Libby . . . . Sachi Parker
Bill Klepler . . . . Stephen Tobolowski

Fans of rising young star Winona Ryder will definitely want to catch her in an offbeat role as the town rebel in this teen-oriented smalltown saga; unfortunately, the rest of the production doesn't quite match up. Paramount can look forward to a few bright weekends before "Roxy" hitchhikes outta town.

"Welcome Back Roxy Carmichael" scripted and executive produced by Karen Leigh Hopkins, has a charmingly imaginative tone and premise that doesn't quite pay off. It's promising, rife with influences and quirky humor, but not quite there yet. Beth Henley, in her "Miss Firecracker" screenplay, did this kind of comedy a whole lot better.

Ryder plays 15-year-old Dinky Bossetti, a moody, glowering misfit who scribbles poetry, wears baggy black clothes and doesn't comb her hair. Her nowhereville hometown of Clyde, Ohio, is all in a dither about the impending return of legendary local Roxy Carmichael, and Dinky, being adopted, decides that Roxy must have been her real mother.

Roxy was a rebel, Roxy had guts, Roxy went off 15 years ago and proved how special she was by getting famous, and Dinky identifies completely. As obsessed with Roxy as the rest of the town, she starts preparing herself to be reclaimed.

Also certain that Roxy is coming back for him is Jeff Daniels as Denton, formerly the teenaged boyfriend with whom she had a baby, now a married man with a family. As all gossip turns to Roxy and her precocious local deeds, Denton's wife (Joan McMurtrey) gets fed up with the situation and leaves him.

Meanwhile the socially reviled Dinky is being pursued by a nerdy guidance counselor who wants to put her in a school for misfits, and a rather blank-slated surfer-looking dude (Thomas Wilson Brown) who wants to be her boyfriend.

None of the subplots is very convincing; least true of all is the hokey way Roxy's memory has been enshrined by the entire population of the town. Just as one is prepared to learn she is the femme equivalent of Elvis Presley, it turns out she hasn't done much at all to deserve this adulation.

As entire pic builds to the occasion of Roxy's homecoming, it's difficult to comment without revealing the outcome; suffice it to say that viewers will wind up feeling as deflated as the townsfolk.

The only part of the story that rings true is Dinky's passionate fantasy about her connection to Roxy; it's a perceptive comment on how celebrity fills the empty places, particularly in smalltown or disconnected lives.

Director Jim Abrahams ("Big Business") of the David Zucker-Jim Abrahams-Jerry Zucker team fares best with scenes showcasing Dinky's offbeat personality — like the one where she recites her apocalyptic poetry to a nervous class. Not so good are the caricatures that fill out the picture. Parody like this is done best when the characters seem crazy from deep inside, as in "Miss Firecracker" or Del Shores' hilarious "Daddy's Dyin' . . . Who's Got The Will?" Here, the quirks seem daubed on for effect by a condescending artist.

Also perplexing is the director's portrayal of Roxy, via teasing inserts, as a lingerie-clad Hollywood glamor goddess. Who is she, Kathleen Turner, one wonders? It's a fantasy that's neither anchored nor paid off in the script.

Casting of ozoner Brown as Ryder's romantic admirer also makes no sense; he adds no interest at all apart from his looks.

Ryder's performance, on the other hand, has a subtle glow and maturity that mesmerizes. Her keenly observed creation of the spooky, androgynous Dinky, with her low voice and deadpan delivery, injects her scenes with a natural comedy far more satisfying than the more hysterical efforts being made around her.

Daniels does a serviceable turn as Denton; more interesting is Laila Robins as a sympathetic guidance counselor who befriends Dinky.

Dena Roth's production design, particularly in the historical Roxy Carmichael house, does much to create a stylish, audacious presence for the mostly offscreen character. Gutsy soundtrack songs by Melissa Etheridge are a strong asset. — *Daws.*

QUIGLEY DOWN UNDER

An MGM/UA Communications release from MGM of a Pathé Entertainment presentation. Produced by Stanley O'Toole, Alexandra Rose. Directed by Simon Wincer. Screenplay, John Hill; camera (Panavision, Colorfilm color), David Eggby; supervising editor-2nd unit director, Adrian Carr; editor, Peter Burgess; music, Basil Poledouris; sound (Dolby), Lloyd Carrick; production design-additional costume design, Ross Major; art direction, Ian Gracie; costume design (for Selleck, San Giacomo), Wayne Finkelman; assistant director, Robert Donaldson; production manager, Stephen Jones; stunt coordinator, Guy Norris; 2d unit camera, Ross Berryman; coproducer, Megan Rose; casting, Michael Lynch, Rae Davidson. Reviewed at MGM screening room, N.Y., Sept. 27, 1990. MPAA Rating: PG-13. Running time: **119 MIN.**

Matthew Quigley . . . . . Tom Selleck
Crazy Cora . . . . . Laura San Giacomo
Elliott Marston . . . . . Alan Rickman
Major Pitt . . . . Chris Haywood
Grimmelman . . . . Ron Haddrick
Dobkin . . . . Tony Bonner
Coogan . . . . Jerome Ehlers
Hobb . . . . Conor McDermottroe
Brophy . . . . Roger Ward
O'Flynn . . . . Ben Mendelsohn

"Quigley Down Under" is an exquisitely crafted, rousing Western made in Oz. The Tom Selleck-starrer is likely to be a worldwide hit with definite repeat business prospects.

For Alan Ladd Jr. at Pathé Entertainment, the pic reps a solidly commercial work that bears comparison to the quality sagebrushers his dad starred in.

If the MGM/UA release performs up to its potential at the boxoffice, it also will represent a lost opportunity for Warner Bros., which had three chances to handle the film. John Hill's script was written for Steve McQueen in the '70s, then developed in 1984 by CBS Theatrical for WB release, Rick Rosenthal to helm; project was reactivated in 1986 for WB and the Aussie UAA banner with Lewis Gilbert scheduled to direct.

Ultimately, the project moved to Pathé with Simon Wincer (Aussie director of tv's acclaimed oater "Lonesome Dove") helming last year. WB picked up distribution rights and was ready to launch the film this summer when that deal fell through and MGM/UA inherited the Pathé product line.

Selleck is in the title role as a sharpshooter from the American West who answers villain Alan Rickman's ad and heads to Fremantle in Western Australia. Quigley is informed that he's been hired to kill aborigines with his longrange, custom-made rifle as part of Rickman's campaign of genocide, encouraged by the local authorities.

Selleck's violent response to the request begins a vendetta in which Rickman has him left for dead in the middle of nowhere. Along for the ensuing survival trek is Laura San Giacomo, a fellow American haunted by the death of her child in a Commanche raid, who Selleck befriended. Bulk of the film consists of Selleck convincingly wiping out any and all henchmen Rickman sends against him.

Though basically a lighthearted popcorn picture, "Quigley" gains surprising depth from its aboriginal theme. The natives spontaneously respond to the tall American as a magic spirit sent to aid them and, sure enough, he is an able protector. In return, they appear at crucial moments to help Selleck and San Giacomo survive against terrible odds.

Selleck has his best bigscreen casting so far here (not counting the missed opportunity to be Indiana Jones a decade ago). Already tall in the saddle from his tv movies in Louis L'Amour adaptations, he's thoroughly convincing with his custom-made rifle and low-key manner.

Following her effective turns in "Sex, Lies & Videotape" and "Pretty Woman," Laura San Giacomo comes into her own as the feisty heroine. Her earthy per-

formance ranges from craziness (she insists on calling Matthew Quigley "Roy" after her husband in an effective running motif) to a beautifully underplayed scene recounting how she accidentally smothered her child while hiding from the Indians.

Rickman is a perfectly hissable villain. After this film and "Die Hard," he's fast replacing Steven Berkoff as the screen's personification of evil.

Superior stuntwork (including some hair-raising falls of aborigines and horses over a cliffside) and spectacular Panavision vistas of unusual locations photographed by David Eggby distinguish "Quigley" from the run of action programmers. Credit director Wincer for solid pacing of this two-hour adventure.

Basil Poledouris' score is a big plus, capturing the energy of Western tracks from Elmer Bernstein's "The Magnificent Seven." Though once planned as part of the last Western "comeback" (same period as "Pale Rider" and "Silverado"), "Quigley" arrives in time with Kevin Costner's "Dances With Wolves" to, one hopes, revive the genre.

— *Lor.*

MR. DESTINY

A Buena Vista release of a Touchstone Pictures presentation in association with Silver Screen Partners IV. Executive producer, Laurence Mark. Written and produced by James Orr, Jim Cruickshank. Co-producer, Susan B. Landau. Directed by Orr. Camera, Alex Thomson; editor, Michael R. Miller; music, David Newman; production design; Michael Seymour; art direction, Catherine Hardwicke; set design, Kathleen McKernin; set decoration, Naomi Shohan; costume design, Jane Greenwood; sound, Lee Orloff; assistant director, Craig Huston; casting, Risa Bramon, Billy Hopkins, Heidi Levitt. Reviewed at Avco Cinema Center, Los Angeles, Ca., Oct. 4, 1990. MPAA rating: PG-13. Running time: **105 MIN.**
Larry Burrows . . . . . James Belushi
Ellen Burrows . . . . Linda Hamilton
Mike . . . . Michael Caine
Clip Metzler . . . . Jon Lovitz
Niles Pender . . . . . . Hart Bochner
Leo Hansen . . . . . . Bill McCutcheon
Cindy Jo . . . . Rene Russo

Producer-writers James Orr and Jim Cruickshank have delivered a heavy-handed, by-the-numbers fantasy about an ordinary Joe who thinks his life would have been different if he'd connected with that all-important pitch in a high school baseball game. Pic might connect with the blue-collar

masses it panders to and spin turnstiles for a few weeks, but if the filmmakers were batting for another home run like their "Three Men And A Baby," also for Touchstone, they've swung too low.

One of the most dispiriting aspects of "Mr. Destiny" is its overproduction; all the top-drawer resources piled onto this ill-thunk concept don't give it any more charm.

Also annoying is the voiceover narrative by Belushi that spoonfeeds the already simple plotline to the audience.

Belushi plays smalltown white-collar working stiff Larry Burrows, who on his depressing 35th birthday stumbles into a bar where a mysterious, twinkly-eyed barman (Michael Caine) serves him up a "spilt milk" elixir that sends him spinning back in time to take another swat at that baseball. He hits a home run, and his whole life turns out differently, just as he expected.

But guess what?

He's not any happier than he was before.

So what if he's married to the dishy prom queen (Rene Russo) and has become the absurdly wealthy president of a sports equipment company — the same one he slaved for in his other life. He misses his original wife (Linda Hamilton) and their unpretentious lifestyle, and whether it makes sense or not, he sets out to win her back.

His efforts to convince her that he, now her rich and hated boss, was her husband in another life have a "Ghost"-like sentimental appeal that provides the only interest in this otherwise snore-worthy vehicle.

Much of the plot is involves machinations at the sporting goods company, where slickly sinister Niles Pender (Hart Bochner, in a cartoon role) is trying to engineer a hostile takeover by the Japanese.

Belushi gets to play the hero, punching Pender out in front of the board of directors.

Pic want us to reach the conclusion that in spite of his newfound power, Belushi was better off before, and the way director Orr steers us through every heavily exaggerated situation, there's little else we can do.

On the subject of destiny, the filmmakers prove to be bland theorists, offering up the comforting notion that things turn

out as they do for a good reason, that the grass isn't always greener, etc.

Everyman role of Larry is another high-paid cakewalk for Belushi, doing nothing to expand his gifts. Michael Caine is appealing, but Jon Lovitz tries too hard for laughs and attention in his offbeat role as the geeky high school friend who still clings close to Belushi, and becomes annoyingly distracting.

Soundtrack songs "Gimme Some Lovin," and "I Got You (I Feel Good)" sound too familiar, but are likely to appeal to the same people that appreciate this film's status quo philosophy.

Mansion used as the L.J. Burroughs home is the same Asheville, N.C. estate seen in Peter Sellars' "Being There."

— *Dows.*

GODA MÄNNISKOR
(GOOD PEOPLE)
(SWEDISH-COLOR/B&W)

A Folkets Bio release of Stefan Jarl Film production with the Swedish Film Institute, Filmteknik, Filmfotograferna, LO, LRF. Produced by Staffan Hedqvist. Written and directed by Stefan Jarl. Camera (color, black & white), Per Källberg, Stefan Hencz; editor, Anette Lykke Lundberg; music, Ulf Dageby, Gustav Sjöquist; sound, Bengt Andersson; production design, Staffan Hedquist; costume design, Tina Johansson; assistant director, Henrik Georgsson. Reviewed at the Victoria, Malmö, Sweden, Sept. 12, 1990. Running time: **107 MIN.**
Daddy . . . . Ernst Günther
Viggo . . . . Viggo Lundberg
The Dane . . . Peter Hesse-Overgaard
Acke . . . . Axel Danielsson
Schoolmarm . . . . . Karin Nordström
Also with: Sindi Stalhammar, Arne Magnusson, Johan Hald, Johannes Fjällström.

The visually striking documentaries of Stefan Jarl, controversial and idiosyncratic creator of "The Threat" and "Time Has No Name," have traveled far, but none as far as "Good People," his belated bow as feature film writer-helmer, is likely to go.

In "Good People," Jarl matches countryman Lasse Hallström's "My Life As A Dog" in the realistic and artistic, tender and funny look at the childhood of a boy who will not run with the crowd.

Daddy (Ernst Günther), an elderly service station caretaker and mechanic, has left the big city for undisclosed reasons and moved to a village in southern Sweden, where he lives with his 7-year-old son, Viggo, who feels estranged in the new environment. He is an introvert anyway, and is happiest alone outdoors.

When Viggo finds a wounded falcon, he nurses it back to health but keeps it his secret prisoner in his hidden treehouse. Opposite the falcon's perch, he has built a shrine to the late Olaf Palme, alleged by his father to have been a personal acquaintance.

Daddy, burly and hearty enough, loves his son but does not understand his taciturn ways. Daddy goes to dances and bingos with the local folks. Viggo allows only a slightly older boy near his treehouse until one day an intruder arrives.

It's the Dane, the village looney. The young man wears a foundry worker's dark glasses, even at night, because, he says, Queen Sylvia was blind when she came to Sweden, so she stole his beautiful eyes and gave him those of a dog instead.

The Dane promises not to tell anybody about the falcon and the treehouse if Viggo will come and listen to him playing the organ next morning in the otherwise empty church. Viggo complies but soon runs away even though the Dane does play nicely. The Dane is now released from his pledge of secrecy.

Toward the end Viggo must, of course, let the falcon free. He howls miserably: "I don't want to grow up." There is nothing further in way of plot. Emotion and the social and psychological aspects of village life fill out the film as it moves along leisurely.

Having a fine way with amateur actors, Jarl is also helped grandly by veteran character actor Günther, who exudes quiet worry under a surface of unbreakable strength. As his son, Viggo Lundberg is all-Swedish blond innocence with the strength of the born loner. As his mock mirror image as an adult, Peter Hesse Overgaard's morose Dane puts in a neatly modulated performance.

Documentarist Jarl works his poignant observations of everyday village life into his story without missing a narrative beat: Three identical dogs stare mutely out of a window; elderly villagers talk small at a bingo-dance. Snippets could easily be edited out, however. A running time of 107 minutes is overlong for what is essentially a minimalist film.

Sweeping landscape cinema-tography by regular Jarl cohort Per Källberg works to stunning effect, especially when it serves to cushion the lonely boy's running through the fields. Black & white is used in an intro and in a coda as a purely esthetic conceit. Ulf Dageby's music score is subtly supportive of the film's interspersed moments of suspense.
— *Kell.*

ZENA S KRAJOLIKOM
(LANDSCAPE WITH A WOMAN)
(YUGOSLAVIAN)

A Centar (Belgrade) production in association with TV Sarajevo. Written and directed by Ivica Matic. Camera (color), Karpo Acimovic Godina; production design, Ljiljana Pejcinovic. Reviewed at Montreal World Film Festival (competition), Aug. 25, 1990. Running time: **70 MIN.**
With: Stole Aranddelovic, Bozidarka Frait, Uros Kravliaca, Zaim Muzaferija, Jadranka Matkovic, Spela Rozin, Miodrag Brezo.

"**L**andscape With A Woman" is an enormously appealing film about a native painter who finds his subjects in a small Bosnian village. While it's a must for any film series about art and artists, pic also could find a wider public if a loving distributor is willing to take a chance.

Sadly, pic was the only feature made by Ivica Matic (1948-76), who died of a heart attack at the end of shooting. His footage was untouched for years, but recently it was assembled by some of his crew members and friends. The material was well worth resurrecting, because this film, though extremely simple, is a touching tribute to an obsessive artist whose life, like that of the filmmaker, was tragically cut short.

Stole Arandelovic plays an employee of the forestry department who arrives in a small village and amazes the locals with his dedication to art. He asks women to pose nude for him, paints landscapes, houses, animals. The villagers are at first suspicious; they spy on him, and even break into his home and urinate on his canvases.

But he perseveres, and eventially marries a local woman before his untimely and unexpected death.

Images of village life are lovingly detailed in Matic's film, which is marred visually only by the grainy quality of the 16m blowup. Local songs and music provide an exhilarating soundtrack.

Pic, shot for standard ratio, was shown on a wide screen at the festival screening caught, which ruined its careful compositions and decapitated characters in many scenes. — *Strat.*

CHURAGHANUN GOSUN NALGAEGA ISSDA
(ALL THAT FALLS HAS WINGS)
(SOUTH KOREAN)

A Danam Enterprise production. Produced by Lee Ji-ryong. Directed by Chang Kil-su. Screenplay, Yoon Daesung, Lee Chong-hwak, Chang Kil-su, from a novel by Lee Mun-yal; camera (color), Lee Seok-ki; editor, Kim Heesoo; music, Shin Byung-ha; sound, Kim Byung-soo. Reviewed at Montreal World Film Festival (Cinema of Today & Tomorrow section), Aug. 24, 1990. Running time: **120 MIN.**
With: Son Chang-min, Kang Sooyeon.

Though director Chang Kil-su and his writers seem to be trying to say something serious about a certain kind of expatriate Korean, "All That Falls Has Wings" emerges as a trite romance taking place on three continents over 20 years.

It kicks off in Seoul, where Hyung-bin falls in love with fellow student Yoon-ju until he discovers that she's not a virgin and that she frequents bars where Americans hang out. Despite these blots on her reputation, he's willing to marry her, but she ankles for the U.S. and marriage with a Yank.

Years pass and our hero, a failed marriage behind him, is in L.A. working for a multinational company and unable to forget his lost love. Imagine his joy when he sees her, by chance, in a Las Vegas nightclub.

The resume their affair, and marry but Yoon is used to spending big, and soon Hyung has money troubles — he even embezzles from his company. When his wife takes off for Europe with another man, he follows with murder on his mind.

Yoon is a genuinely ugly character, and it's hard to feel any sympathy for Hyung and his endless devotion to her. She hates blacks and Hispanics and considers most Koreans "swine." And she certainly doesn't want to live in Seoul after tasting the high life in the U.S. of A.

It's good material for a tale of mad love, but Chang makes little of it. He isn't helped by the atrocious English subtitles ("I couldn't control over me," says Hyung when he makes sexual advances on Yoon). Technically, the film's fine, but it will be of little international interest outside Asian markets. — *Strat.*

WINCKELMANNS REISEN
(WINCKELMANN'S TRAVELS)
(GERMAN-B&W)

A Novoskop Film production, with Pandora Film and WDR. (Intl. sales: Pyramide Films, Paris.) Executive producer, Eric Nellessen. Directed by Jan Schütte. Screenplay, Schütte, Thomas Strittmatter; camera (black & white), Sophie Maintigneux; editor, Renate Merck; music, Claus Bantzer; sound, Wolfgang Schukrafft; production design, Katharina Woppermann; assistant director, Regina Gmeiner. Reviewed at Venice Film Festival (out of competition), Sept. 11, 1990. Running time: **81 MIN.**
Ernst Winckelmann . . . Wolf-Dietrich Sprenger
Aline . . . . Susanne Lothar
Aline's father . . . . . Traugott Bühre
Rudiger . . . . Udo Samel
Rosa . . . . Mine-Marei Wiegandt
Berner . . . . Mathais Gnadinger

This small-scale, black & white feature about lost and lonely characters could play the festival route, but theatrical possibilities outside German territories are slight.

Jan Schütte's new film isn't as appealing as his first feature, the amiable "Dragon Chow," which won some prizes on the fest circuit three years ago, but "Winckelmann's Travels" shows a director with a special, sensitive talent.

Ernst Winckelmann is a traveling salesman, but not a very good one. He travels around northern Germany, flogging Swiss shampoo to pharmacies and hairdressing salons, but doesn't make many sales.

His personal life also is a mess. He still cares about his ex-wife, who's remarried and has a daughter. But he also likes his increasingly bored girlfriend who works in her father's pub but would like to accept a job offer in Belgium. The father, meanwhile, is nostalgic about the time he spent in Miami, which remains his ideal city.

Nothing much happens in the film. Winckelmann spends some time with his ex-wife's child (in scenes reminiscent of Wim Wenders' classic "Alice In The Cities") and manages to change his conservative image into something a bit more "with it." This seems to help with his sales, but it doesn't stop his girl from going to Ostend.

"Winckelmann's Travels" has a modest charm, but it's pretty slight material. The black & white camerawork by Sophie Maintigneux is beautiful, and the performers are all perfectly adequate. As with his previous film, Schütte's only use of color is in the opening and closing credits, which this time are printed in green. — *Strat.*

CURSED
(CANADIAN)

A Pax film production. Produced by Jean-Marc Felio. Directed by Mychel Arsenault. Screenplay; Felio, Pierre Dalpe; camera (color), John Berrie; editor, Martial Ethier; sound, Gabor Vadny; set design, John Meigen. Reviewed at the Montreal World Film Festival, Sept. 3, 1990. Running time: **87 MIN.**
With: Ron Lea, Catherine Colvey, Tom Rack, Kirsty MacEachern, Joy Boushel, Claire Riley, Michael Sinelnikiff.

In Italy, critics have invented a new category for film, per one Italian journalist. After "excellent, good, fair and poor, there is now "not even with a gun to my head." "Cursed" fits into this latter classification. Perhaps the title cursed the film.

An exceptionally bad schlock horror pic, the story is about cursed gargoyles. During a storm, one falls from a church and kills a priest. A chemist and his girlfriend see the accident. He takes a piece of the statue to his lab and she (an art restorer) winds up hired by church officials to put the gargoyle back together.

It turns out the gargoyle possesses demonic powers that apply to the chemist's genetics research. Meanwhile, as he's experimenting, mysterious deaths occur in the neighborhood, leaving each victim full of a strange green fluid.

Tech credits are good but wasted on this suspenseless, senseless tale. Helmer Mychel Arsenault should stick to directing corporate videos and advertisements. — *Suze.*

PENSION SONNENSCHEIN
(PENSION SUNSHINE)
(GERMAN)

A Manfred Durniok production in association with ZDF. Produced by Durniok. Written and directed by Filip Bajon. Camera (color), Piotr Sobocinski; editor, Wanda Zemen; music, Michael Lorenc; sound, Jerry Blaszynski; production manager, Rainer Shulte; assistant director, Jerzy Moniak. Reviewed at Montreal World Film Festival (Cinema of Today & Tomorrow), Aug. 25, 1990. Running time: **108 MIN.**
Herrmann Moberg . . Ernst Stankovski
Elisabeth Moberg . . . Nicole Heesters
Gustaw . . . . Tadeusz Lomnicki
Slawa . . . . Slawa Kwasniewska
Andras . . . . Michael Kausch

"Pension Sunshine" is a timely drama that will be of considerable interest to audiences in central Europe but will remain confined to the festival route elsewhere.

Polish director Filip Bajon ("Aria For An Athlete," "Children On Strike") has come up with a contempo tale of an elderly Berlin architect who, en route to a lecture date in Kiev, stops over with his younger wife to visit the Polish village where he grew up. Before the war, this village was part of Germany, and the area has been worried that a united Germany might one day reclaim it.

The visit sparks the inevitable memories, mostly about the wartime betrayal of the local pharmacist, who was suspected (incorrectly) of being a Jew. But this isn't a flashback picture, it's a modern, moral story, and rather talky, which may limit its theatrical possibilities.

Despite this drawback, the subject is sufficiently fascinating and the theme sufficiently momentous to make the film very acceptable in those territories. Performances are solid, with vet Polish actor Tadeusz Lomnicki making his usual mark as the current occupant of the "pension" (guesthouse) where the architect once lived.

A quiet but effective score by Michael Lorenc is an asset to the picture, which tells its story in a matter-of-fact style that's exactly right for this subject. — *Strat.*

SU TAG
(THE ROOSTER)
(SOUTH KOREAN)

A Dae Dong Heung Up Co. Ltd. production. Produced by Do Dong Hwan. Directed by Shin Seung-soo. Screenplay, Kwon Jae-woo, Nah Han-bong; camera (color), Jin Young-ho; editor, Kim Hyun; sound, Kim Byung-soo, Lee Seong-keun; production design, Stephen Do. Reviewed at Montreal World Film Festival (competition), Sept. 1, 1990. Running time: **111 MIN.**
Chang Doo-chil . . . . . Kim In-moon
Shim Ok-ja . . . . Choe Yoo-ra
Mrs. Chang . . . . Kim Ae-kyung
Ttuk dae . . . . Kim Hui-ra
Mother-in-law . . . . Yoon In-ja
Ilan . . . . Chon Hae-sung

Korean films have rarely caught on in the international arthouse market in the way other films from Asia have, and "The Rooster," which won the best-film prize at the Korean Film Awards in March, seems unlikely to redress the balance.

This is a contemporary story about an adulterous relationship, a seemingly popular theme as all three Korean pics unspooled at the Montreal film fest dealt with the subject.

Chang is a middle-aged man who runs a chicken farm. He has lost his sexual desire, to the annoyance of his frustrated wife, but he soon recovers when he meets Ok-ja, a young woman who works in an egg-purchasing office. They embark on a joyous relationship which ends when Mrs. Chang and her daughter go to see Ok-ja, and she agrees to fade out of the picture.

One of the problems with a film like this is the acting style, which, by Western standards, is flamboyant and unrestrained. Maybe this is why Korean period pictures, where such acting appears to be more fitting, have usually been more successful than contemporary subjects with the international festival audiences.

Also, the macho attitudes of the male characters are very alien by contemporary Western standards, though the films tend to endorse them.

This said, it's clear that director Shin Seung-soo has talent. He stages scenes among the chickens with some flair, and from time to time brings off a piece of action that works well.

But generally speaking, "The Rooster" seems unlikely to reach an audience outside Asia, whatever its domestic success might have been. — *Strat.*

SOBACHI PIRE
(DOG'S FEAST)
(SOVIET)

A Lenfilm production. Directed by Leonid Menaker. Screenplay, Victor Merejko; camera (Sovcolor), Vladimir Kovzel; editor, Igor Rudenko; music, Andrei Petrov, Alexander Sisolatine; production design, Yuri Pougatch. Reviewed at Montreal World Film Festival (competition), Aug. 26, 1990. Running time: **100 MIN.**
Jeanne . . . . Natalia Goundareva
Arkady Petrovich . Sergei Chakourov
Alexandra . . . Larissa Oudovitchenko
Natasha . . . . Anna Polikospova

"Dog's Feast," depicting wretched people living in appalling conditions, is a solid pic unlikely to go the international arthouse route.

This forthright drama focusing on alcoholism in the Soviet Union is set during a bitter winter in a small town near Leningrad. At a railway station, cleaning woman Jeanne drunkenly picks up a stranger on New Year's Eve and takes him back to her squalid, dirty apartment.

Since he has just completed an enforced stay in a hospital for alcoholics and has, as a result, lost his wife and children (who now live with another man), Arkady is in no mood to put up with Jeanne's boozy binge.

But he takes pity on her, and the next day misses his train to do her work for her when she's incapable of doing it herself. He then stays on in her apartment, but he sleeps on the floor because he's attracted to Alexandra, single mother next door.

Structured around a strong performance from Natalia Goundareva as the unfortunate Jeanne, "Dog's Feast" doesn't flinch from showing what alcohol has wrought on its characters. While Arkady tries desperately to stay off the booze, Jeanne and a teenage visitor, Natasha, exist in a perpetually drunken haze.

The grim, freezing apartment, with its unpainted walls, meager facilities and tatty, minimal furniture (black & white tv plays musical programs continually) becomes a dank metaphor for wasted, hopeless lives.

There's also a lot of bitter talk about perestroika and democracy, grand concepts that mean little to these ravaged, hopeless characters.

"Dog's Feast" is distinguished by sharp camerawork and solid thesping. — *Strat.*

THE END OF INNOCENCE

A Skouras Pictures release. Produced by Thom Tyson, Vince Cannon. Executive producers, Leonard Rabinowitz, Stanley Fimberg. Written and directed by Dyan Cannon. Camera (color), Alex Nepomniaschy; editor, Bruce Cannon; music, Michael Convertinio; production design, Paul Eads; costume design, Carol Little; production supervisor, Helen Pollack; assistant directors, Craig Beaudine, Joan Van Horn. Reviewed at the Toronto Festival of Festivals, Sept. 7, 1990. No MPAA Rating. Running time: 102 MIN.
Stephanie . . . . Dyan Cannon
Dean . . . . John Heard
Dad . . . . George Coe
Mom . . . . Lola Mason
Stephanie at 18 . . . Rebecca Schaeffer
Michael . . . . Steve Meadows
Also with: Billie Bird, Dennis Burkley, Viveka Davis, Eric Harrison, Stoney Jackson, Paul Lieber, Michael Madsen, Madge Sinclair, Renee Taylor.

A moralistic drama about a woman's struggle for self-determination, "The End Of Innocence" is a well-intentioned vehicle for writer-director-star Dyan Cannon. But pic's sincerity will not help at the b.o., where it should be hobbled by a dulling clinical tone better suited for cable playoff.

In its peppy opening, Cannon time-telescopes the childhood, adolescence (played by the late Rebecca Schaeffer) and young womanhood of Stephanie Lewis, a lovely if malleable only child of querulous middle-class Jewish parents. Through a rapidly unfolding montage of set-piece scenes, Cannon traces Stephanie's passage through schoolgirl romances, a failed marriage and a dating phase that peaks with the arrival of Mr. Right.

Predictably enough, selfish struggling writer Michael (Steve Meadows), turns out to be not much different than the boorish cad who deflowered Stephanie on her prom night long ago.

Desperate to validate her life through this imbalanced relationship, she refuses to face facts. She's impervious to the hectoring of her neurotic, nosy mother ("How's the sex?" mom wants to know) and insensitive father.

A caring platonic male friend, lost in the narrative shuffle, tries to warn her off Michael to no avail. Drifting through life with no real career or focus, Stephanie deals with her deep unhappiness with junk food, mood pills and marijuana.

American women, Cannon suggests, have entered the post-feminist era essentially unliberated from the dominance of lovers, parents and the overbearing cultural pressure to conform to gender roles. This theme is presented convincingly enough, but when Stephanie's relationship with Michael finally sends her off the deep end, Cannon's film tends to follow.

Michael's infidelity triggers a shattering nervous breakdown that lands Stephanie in a pricey rehabilitation clinic. The miserable heroine casts herself as a prisoner in a nuthouse, ministered to by psychiatrists, nurses and a dedicated encounter group leader in the person of John Heard. Director Cannon stumbles as the film bogs down interminably in Stephanie's tortuous rehab.

At this critical juncture, "The End Of Innocence" is marred by maudlin, movie-of-the-week hysterics that should be edited way down before the film is released. Slowly and reluctantly, Stephanie begins to bond with her pathetic fellow patients and drops her resistance to treatment. Surviving one reefer-induced lapse, she finally comes to grips with the fact that Michael was a creep.

This long-overdue insight frees Stephanie to begin life anew in the outside world. The new Stephanie takes no guff from men, no manipulation from her parents and settles on an appropriately healthy career as an exercise instructor.

Cannon, looking remarkably good, has a field day dominating the film. Studios are not greenlighting many meaty star parts for women, and this is by no means the worst type of vanity project. But the auteur/star gets too carried away with a sense of mission here, hammering with grim preachiness at a theme that breaks no new ground.

Appropriately, in the none too subtle context of the script, George Coe and Lola Mason lay on the histrionics as the hapless, blameworthy parents. — *Rich.*

PICTURES AT THE BEACH
(CANADIAN)

A Fountainhead Pictures production. Written, produced and directed by Aaron J. Shuster. Camera (color), Martin McInnaly; editor, Shuster; music, Richard Nimmo; sound, Michael Katz; set design, Guylaine Beauchemin. Reviewed at the Montreal World Film Festival, Aug. 30, 1990. Running time: 70 MIN.
With: Paul Babiak, Catherine Kuhn, Benson Simmonds, Christopher Crumb, Tamara Guner, Robert Bidamman, Ann Curran.

"Pictures At The Beach" is painfully nice Canadian pic about angst-ridden yuppies reuniting for a day at the beach. Their problems are common: not enough sex, money or time.

Edited like a home movie, each of the six friends confesses his fears or desires to another, sequences that work fairly well. Pic's problem is that it trivializes Torontonians. One guy's biggest problem is a scratched sportscar.

Pic is pleasant but dull: Nothing really happens at the beach. They take pictures. They go home. It would be better in a photo album where stills are appreciated. — *Suze.*

I TARASSACHI
(THE DANDELIONS)
(ITALIAN)

A Cooperativa Nuovo Film production. Produced by Laurentina Guidotti. Written and directed by Francesco Ranieri Martinotti, Rocco Mortelliti, Fulvio Ottaviano. Camera (color), Giuseppe Lanci; editor, Annalisa Forgione; music, Fiorenzo Carpi; art direction, Luca Donnini. Reviewed at Venice Film Festival, Sept. 8, 1990. Running time: 65 MIN.
With: Athina Cenci, Sergio Castellitto, Cochi Ponzoni, Laurentina Guidotti, Nini Salerno, Adriano Giacchetti, Matteo Chioatto, Enrico Lo Verso, Miscia Maser, Scilla Ficcadenti, Cristina Pellegrini, Ilaria Borrelli.

"The Dandelions" explores the drug problem in 10 sketches lensed with seriousness and sensitivity. The 65-minute docudrama was produced on a shoestring by a film co-op involving some of Italy's top technicians, including cameraman Giuseppe Lanci. Euro tv is pic's most likely outlet.

Young writer-directors Francesco Ranieri Martinotti, Rocco Mortelliti (who have each made a film previously), and Fulvio Ottaviano (in his debut) make a basic decision to de-sensationalize their material and show the normal, everyday faces of those tragically involved with drugs.

Depicting addicts neither as victims of society, nor as criminal monsters roaming the streets, "Dandelions" manages to bring the audience close up to the problem.

Stories range from the physical suffering of an infant born to a drug-dependent mother to the loneliness of an old man living alone with his dog and popping presciption pills at bedtime.

The most involving scenes feature professional actors. Athina Cenci plays a pharmacist working the night shift who helps a boy cope with withdrawal by keeping him company until morning. Sergio Castellitto is featured in a therapy session in which he violently acts out his anger at his father.

Other episodes are so touchingly simple they don't require acting. Three friends watch mutely from a parked car as a family buries a child dead from an overdose. A girl who has broken the habit receives the gift of coral earrings her mother had hidden from her when she took drugs.

Pic's youthful producer Laurentina Guidotti also appears in the film as a middle-class student who tries to tempt her roommate back into heroin.

Film takes its title from the garish yellow dandelions that look strong but are soon reduced to gossamer seeds that spread easily. The young filmmakers capture the immediacy of the drug problem, showing the depths to which addicts can sink, but suggest there's hope for those who want to come out of the dark.
— *Yung.*

ECHOS AUS EINEM DÜSTEREN REICH
(ECHOES FROM A SOMBER EMPIRE)
(GERMAN-FRENCH-DOCU)

A Sera Film Prods.-Werner Herzog Filmproduktion-Films Sans Frontières co-production. Executive producer, Walter Saxer. Produced by Galeshka Moravioff, Werner Herzog. Directed by Herzog. Camera (color), Jorg Schmidt-Reitwein, Martin Manz; editor, Rainer Standke, Thomas Balkenhohl; sound, Harald Maury. Reviewed at Venice Film Festival (out of competition), Sept. 11, 1990. Running time: 91 MIN.
With: Michael Goldsmith.

Werner Herzog's docu is

about the former dictator of the Central African Republic, who was accused, among other things, of cannibalism. It's a good subject for Herzog, and he turns it into a grimly fascinating and informative film.

As his focal point, the filmmaker uses Michael Goldsmith, a journalist accused by Jean Bedel Bokassa of spying for South Africa. Goldsmith was beaten by the "emperor" himself and spent time in prison because, as he relates, a telexed story to his paper got garbled and Bokassa's secret police assumed it must be in code.

Bokassa seized power in 1966 in a coup aided by the French, appointed himself president for life six years later and, in 1977, crowned himself emperor in an extraordinarily lavish ceremony financed by the French government.

Less than two years later, following a massacre of a hundred children, he was deposed while on a visit to Libya. He was sentenced to death in his absence, but then, amazingly, returned voluntarily to his country where he was tried, found guilty and sentenced to death once again. (The sentence was commuted to life imprisonment.)

Goldsmith interviews his wife and some of his children in France, and also talks to a French lawyer, to the man who deposed Bokassa and who was imprisoned by him, and to several of the women the "emperor" took as his mistresses. He was, apparently, sexually insatiable and had a vast number of children by different women, including two Vietnamese and a Romanian.

Goldsmith also returns to the Central African Republic and tours Bokassa's gutted palace, where huge freezers once stored bodies before they were cooked and eaten. There's also a rundown private zoo, where Bokassa threw victims to lions and crocodiles.

Along with the interviews, there is footage of Bokassa's reign that includes extensive coverage of the coronation, with Bokassa crowning himself and sitting **on a giant throne shaped like a golden eagle; his small son sits nearby, unable to stop yawning. Herzog cuts brutally from Bokassa in coronation robes to Bokassa on trial, sending personal messages to members of the French**

government via the tv news cameras.

Though tv is the most obvious outlet for "Echoes," the film could well enjoy limited theatrical runs in major cities, especially where Herzog has a reputation.

Though the director sticks to the docu format most of the time, occasional moments go beyond documentary, such as the bizarre opening sequence of thousands of crabs coming up on shore and the strangely sad ending in which a monkey in Bokassa's zoo puffs away on a cigaret. — *Strat.*

BLANKT VAPEN
(AT SWORDS' POINTS)
(SWEDISH)

A Svensk Filmindustri release of Filmhuset production for the Swedish Film Institute, Svensk Filmindustri, SVT-1, Film Teknik. Produced by Katinka Farago. Executive producer, Waldemar Bergendahl. Directed by Carl-Gustav Nykvist. Screenplay, Nykvist, Lasse Summanen; camera (Eastmancolor), Ulf Brantas; editor, Summanen; music, Johan Zachrisson; sound, Bengt Säll; production design, Birgitta Brensén; costume design, Malin Bergendal; production management, Malte Forssell, Serina Björnbom; assistant director, Henrik von Sydow. Reviewed at the Palladium, Malmö, Sweden, Aug. 29, 1990. Running time: **110 MIN.**

Richard . . . . Boman Oscarsson
Bruno . . . . Reine Brynnolfsson
Anita . . . . Maria Grip
Mama . . . . Harriet Andersson
Harald . . . . Linus Tunström
Also with: Ing-Marie Carlsson, Ulrika Hansson, Leif André, Rickard Wolff, Anette Reimers.

This second entry in a proposed trilogy introduced with "The Women On The Roof" is helmer-writer Carl-Gustav Nykvist's look at the psychosexual drives that lead some to inner torment. Though "Women" competed in Cannes 1989, "At Swords' Points" will find offshore fencing much harder.

"Women" had lyrical, exquisitely lit cinematography by Ulf Brantas and a gripping screenplay by the helmer and Lasse Summanen. "Swords," made by the same trio, has clogged plotlines and often unintelligible dialog, and the lighting occasionally fails.

Worse, this pic's action is so heavy it tends to overpower itself. However, audiences should not overlook the fact that extraordinary, if overly ambitious, talent is at work.

"At Swords' Points" mixes elements of "Alice In Wonderland" (Nykvist once did a docu on Lewis Carroll) with Hitchcockian psychology and shock tactics and an abundance of red herrings. Even though it's obscure, this film might well end up a cult favorite.

The story: Richard, 28, helps Bruno smuggle a medieval icon out of Germany. Back home, Richard becomes obsessed with the symbolism of the characters in the icon: mother and baby, holy men with swords, etc.

He gets involved in shady dealings with a middleman as his messy private life catches up to him. He moves into the apartment of an absconded half brother and has unfortunate encounters with an ex-girlfriend and with his hospitalized mother.

The apartment turns out to be a kind of haunted house in which strange people, and phantom visions, keep turning up. In the basement, Richard finds his childhood photos with the heads cut out. Through a positioned spy telescope he sees, or thinks he sees, a neighboring couple making violent love to the point where one partner pushes a knife into the back of the other.

Richard decides he must find his cartoonist brother before he can find himself. The quest has a gruesome ending but maybe a helpful one.

Acting is mostly stylized. Boman Oscarsson, son of Sweden's great actor Per Oscarsson, gives an essentially stodgy performance. As his friend, Reine Brynulfsson adds irony and fun to the goings-on. Other actors, including Ingmar Bergman veteran Harriet Andersson, look like borrowed display items from some thespian museum. — *Kell.*

DELTA FORCE COMMANDO
(ITALIAN)

A Realtà Cinematografica production. Produced by Alfred Nicolaj. Directed by "Frank Valenti" (Pierluigi Ciriaci). Screenplay, David Parker Jr.; camera (Luciano Vittori color), Al Bartholomew; editor, Fiorenza Muller; music, Elio Polizzi; sound, Marco De Biase; production manager, Michele Germano; stunt coordinator, Mario Novelli. Reviewed on HBO, Boca Raton, Fla., Aug. 17, 1990. No MPAA Rating. Running time: **93 MIN.**

Tony Turner . . . . Brett Clark
Capt. Beck . . . . . . Fred Williamson
Col. Keitel . . . . Bo Svenson

Also with: Mark Gregory, Divana Maria Brandão, Emy Valentino.

War, Italian style, is given an entertaining if pointless workout in "Delta Force Commando." The 1987 production debuted directly on paycable in the U.S., an unusual case of playing without an MPAA rating.

A sequel reportedly has been lensed with Glenn Ford and Fred Williamson.

Brett Clark toplines (in a role originally targeted for Nicholas Clay or Reb Brown) as an ex-Delta Force member whose pregnant wife is murdered before his eyes by terrorists stealing a nuclear weapon from a Puerto Rican military base.

Film dwells on the uneasy camaraderie between Clark and Williamson, a pilot Clark shanghais to assist on his mission of vengeance. Pursuit of the nasty bad guys takes them to Nicaragua, but Brazil actually fills in for all locations.

Corny finale, after the heroes pull a what-do-we-do-now scene out of "Butch Cassidy," imitates the second Rambo film in making the whole mission regarding the terrorists turn out to be a fake maneuver dreamed up by top brass.

Muscular thesp Clark makes a convincing hero. Williamson is reliable in a sidekick assignment. Williamson's frequent screen teammate Bo Svenson pops up briefly as a fellow officer, but his dialog is disconcertingly postsynched by someone else. Supporting cast is adequately dubbed.

Thank-you credit to the Brazilian navy is well-earned, as film projects a scale well beyond its modest budget. — *Lor.*

UTOLI MOI PECHALI
(ASSUAGE MY SORROW)
(SOVIET)

A Mosfilm production. Directed by Viktor Prokhorov, Alexander Alexandrov. Screenplay, Alexandrov; camera (Sovcolor), Yevgeny Korzhenkov; music, Alexei Rybnikov; sound, A. Bubrevsky; production design, Tatiana Lapshina, Alexander Myagkov. Reviewed at Pitt Cinema 3, Sydney, July 28, 1990. Running time: **92 MIN.**

Boris . . . . Sergei Koltakov
Lyuba . . . . Yelena Safonova
Also with: Varvara Soshalskaya, Artyom Mironov, Konstantin Voinov, Andrei Boltnev, Galina Samoilova.

relentlessly grim picture of life in a present-day apartment block in Moscow, "Assuage My Sorrow" is a depressing experience. With its unpleasant characters, film is unlikely to make much of an international mark.

Focus is on a couple, Boris and Lyuba, whose marriage has broken down. Boris, who regularly stays out all night, is looking for a new apartment to move into, which is no easy task.

He locates a place in his own building occupied by an old lady scheduled to move to a retirement home. The old woman is unhappy with the arrangement and invites a young woman, the girlfriend of a singer, to share her apartment. In one quite graphic scene, Boris virtually rapes the protesting girl, but she accepts the situation, and at the end of the film they've become a couple. Thus they are entitled to the apartment.

Pic ends with Lyuba causing a bitter scene at a housewarming party. All this is seen through the eyes of the couple's intelligent young son.

As with most contemporary Russian films (this one bears a 1989 date), there's a fair amount of sex and nudity, as well as an apparent eagerness to depict the grimness of everyday life without pulling punches. — *Strat.*

MASTERS OF MENACE

A New Line release of a Cinetel Films production. Produced by Lisa M. Hansen, Tino Insana. Directed by Daniel Raskov. Screenplay, Insana; camera (Foto-Kem color), Edward J. Pei; editor, Stephen Myers; sound, Beau Franklin; production design, Richard Hummel; art direction, Douglas Leonard; associate producer, Catalaine Knell; assistant director, Steve Love. Reviewed at Cinetex Intl. Comedy Film Festival, Las Vegas, Sept. 7, 1990. MPAA Rating: PG-13. Running time: 97 MIN.
Buddy . . . . David Rasche
Kitty . . . . Catherine Bach
Wallace . . . . Lance Kinsey
Sunny . . . . Teri Copley
Hoover . . . . Ray Baker
Schouweiller . . . . . . Malcolm Smith
Sheriff Julip . . George (Buck) Flower
Horny Hank . . . . Tino Insana
Roy Boy . . . . Lee (Ving) James
Sloppy Joe . . . . David Bowe
Fat Frank . . . . . . Lonnie Parkinson
Also with: Dan Aykroyd, Jim Belushi, John Candy, George Wendt, Carol Ann Susi, John Hazelwood, David L. Lander.

"**M**asters Of Menace" starts on a middle finger, quickly followed by a crotch gag and two guys relieving themselves on a bush, and ends with the villain face down in a tub of manure. So it goes for the contender in the Cinetex Intl. Film Festival and Comedy Competition, where original humor obviously was not required.

Giving them the benefit of considerable doubt, writer Tino Insana and director Daniel Raskov may have set out to satirize those old biker pics in which gangs of ruffians try so hard to be socially unacceptable. Exploring the bodily functions of the already socially unacceptable is not a great step forward, however, and hardly inspiration for whimsy.

As often happens, the gang of hairy fat guys on Harleys has a clean-shaven, semi-sensitive leader (David Rasche) whose major character defect is the company he keeps.

Rasche has a wife (Catherine Bach) who wants a house and a baby, and a lawyer (Lance Kinsey) who wants to keep the gang out of jail by keeping them on probation inside the county line.

In a cameo, however, biker Jim Belushi gets himself killed in an accident, and the gang becomes determined to hit the road so he can get a proper burial with his kinfolk.

Presumably, the corpse they drag around is a dummy, not Belushi, but it's hard to tell because some cameos last longer than others and his performance as the live biker would be hard to distinguish from one of a dead biker.

Dan Aykroyd is no better as a former gang member who's now a stunt rider with loudly creaking joints. Nor is John Candy as the driver of a beer truck prominently plugging a w.k. brand.

Why these actors would appear in this film is really no mystery, since actors do strange things. But one would think a major brewery would care more about its reputation. — *Har.*

IO, PETER PAN
ME, PETER PAN
(ITALIAN)

An August Entertainment release (U.S.) of a Prisma Seven production. Directed by Enzo Decaro. Screenplay, Decaro, Francesco Asioli, Giangiacomo Nasi; camera, Carlo Cerchio; editor, Filippo Bussi; art direction, Valeria Tiberi, Asioli; costume design, Angela Beale. Reviewed at Cinema Eden, Rome, Aug. 10, 1990. Running time: 92 MIN.
Fabio . . . . Roberto Citran
Giulia . . . . Violaine Ledoux
Luisa . . . . Mariella Valentini
Daniela . . . . Angela Finocchiaro

Though dotted with touching moments, "Io, Peter Pan" is sabotaged by a flat, unimaginative script with one-dimensional characters. But pic could have found a sympathetic audience if it had not been released during the summer doldrums.

Neapolitan helmer Enzo Decaro's second film takes a bittersweet look at how a thirtysomething father-to-be tries to dodge his responsibilities.

Giulia (Violaine Ledoux) eagerly anticipates the couple's first child. Fabio (Roberto Citran) would rather play soccer with kids in the street than take his wife to the doctor for her checkups. He takes refuge from the pressures of daily life in the silence of the zoo's reptile house. As played by Citran, Fabio's unrealistic approach to life and desire to remain a child come across more spineless than endearing.

Crisis looms when Fabio quits his job to open a travel agency with an unreliable friend. Giulia explodes when he suggests the couple take a vacation in the Maldive Islands. A confrontation sends him into the arms of sexy neighbor Luisa, who makes him face up to his fears just in time to take Giulia to the hospital.

Action lags in several scenes. Main characters often fail to engage audience sympathy or even attention. Young character actress Angela Finocchiaro stands out as a neurotic career woman.

Pic was produced with a subsidy from the entertainment ministry. Rome locations look anonymous and accurately reflect suburban middle-class life. Technical credits are adequate. — *Clrk.*

THIS IS NO
WAY TO LIVE
(SOVIET-DOCU)

A Mosfilm, the Circle and Filmverlag der Autoren presentation of a FTPO Mosfilm production. Directed by Stanislas Govoroukhin. Written by Govoroukhin. Camera (color), G. Engstrem; editor, N. Vasilieva; music, V. Vysotsky; sound, I. Mayorov. Reviewed at Montreal World Film Festival, Aug. 30, 1990. Running time: 109 MIN.

This hard-hitting documentary pulls no punches in its condemnation of Soviet society from Lenin to Gorbachev.

Authoritative BBC-type narration, crackerjack editing and relentless images of crime, alcoholism and poverty make this a powerful docu.

Pic is guaranteed to shock Westerners who believe things have improved since perestroika, and it undoubtedly will arouse sympathy from viewers. It's very solid fare for tv, where the docu format is often perceived as "truth." If carefully handled, it should draw a solid audience.

Docu's manipulative structure makes it a Soviet "Roger & Me," minus the humor and entertainment qualities, which will limit its appeal. However, it's bound to be just as controversial if it finds the right audience.

Pic's politics are difficult to decipher. At a glance, it appears anti-communist. It makes "Red Nightmare" look like child's play. It condemns perestroika with equal vengeance. In one strategically placed scene, a 70-year-old farm woman says of the situation since Gorbachev took the helm, "It couldn't get any worse."

Numerous statistics without an identified source flash across the screen stating that crime has risen dramatically since 1988.

Early in the pic, director Stanislas Govoroukhin cross-cuts between police incidents in New York and Moscow. In New York, he interviews two cops who, on request, produce revolvers with lightning speed. In Moscow, he interviews a cop walking his beat; the billy club strapped to his wrist impedes his ability to quickly draw his gun. The comparison is clear: New York cops are better prepared to deal with crime.

In another N.Y. scene, the narrator explains that a small crime — in which "a prostitute is pushed into a car perhaps to extract a ransom from her pimp" — produces quick results from the police. "Look how many policemen showed up," says the voice, noting that "the papers and tv covered the incident" as well.

These are just two examples of Govoroukhin's anti-crime message, but never at any point does the docu acknowledge that New York has difficulty controlling its own crime rate. Presentation is very one-sided.

Govoroukhin makes no bones about his belief that the current social and economic climate in Moscow and numerous other Russian cities and villages is "no way to live." It shows images of what Westerners have suspected for years: Life behind the iron curtain is no picnic. — *Suze.*

THE FIELD
(BRITISH)

An Avenue Pictures release of a Granada Film production. Produced by Noel Pearson. Executive producer, Steve Morrison. Directed by Jim Sheridan. Screenplay, Sheridan, based on the play by John B. Keane; camera (color), Jack Conroy; editor, J. Patrick Duffner; sound, Kieran Horgan; production design, Frank Conway; art direction, Frank Hallinan Flood; costume design, Joan Bergin; makeup, Tommie Manderson; production manager, Mary Alleguen; line producer, Arthur Lappin; production executive, Pippa Gross; casting, Nuala Moiselle. Reviewed at Toronto Festival Of Festivals, Sept. 12, 1990. No MPAA Rating. Running time: **110 MIN.**
Bull McCabe . . . . . . Richard Harris
Bird O'Donnell . . . . John Hurt
The American . . . . . . Tom Berenger
Tadgh McCabe . . . . Sean Bean
Young widow . . . . . Frances Tomelty
Maggie . . . . Brenda Fricker

uperb acting and austere visual beauty are offset by a somewhat overheated screenplay in this tragic tale about an indomitable Irish peasant's blood ties to the land.

With careful handling, "The Field" could enjoy a respectable arthouse run. It opens in New York and Los Angeles in December.

Richard Harris returns to the screen in the larger-than-life role of a patriarchal Irish tenant farmer with a ferocious temperment and blazing charisma. The time is the 1930s, when the memory of the great famine was fresh and feudal ways held sway in the Irish countryside.

For most of his life, Bull McCabe has farmed a field belonging to a wealthy widow (Frances Tomelty), who one day decides to sell the plot. Bull is outraged. Having transformed the field from a rocky lot to a lush emerald swath, he believes the field is his, in accordance with tribal codes that predate modern law.

Respected and feared throughout the countryside, Bull gets no argument from villagers when he announces his intention to claim the field in a public auction. But the widowed landlady, who depises Bull, declares she will never sell to him. This sets the stage for an inexorable conflict.

Bull's wild white hair and beard and ever-present walking stick give him the look of a biblical prophet crossed with King Lear. He's an unpredictable force, capable of volcanic rage one minute and roistering bonhomie the next.

He holds in thrall his slow-witted son Tadgh (Sean Bean) and even slower-witted crony Bird O'Donnell (John Hurt). The suicide of another son during the famine still haunts Bull, and his wife Maggie (Brenda Fricker) has not spoken to him in the 20 years since.

Neither the local police chief nor the young, upright village priest (well played by Sean McGinley) can sway Bull from his obsession. "Who would insult me by bidding for my field?" he demands at the local pub.

No one but an Irish-American from Boston (Tom Berenger), who has returned to his ancestral village with a plan to pave Bull's field for an access road to lucrative limestone deposits.

Bull rails against the Yank as the latest in a series of outsiders — the British, the priests, the rich, the widowed landlady and the emigrés — who have flourished or fled while his kinsmen endured war, starvation and lives of back-breaking labor. When the American refuses to give way, Bull enlists Tadgh in a plan to drive him off. This has fatal consequences and leads to the destruction of everything Bull holds dear.

Harris gives a resonant, domineering performance as the prideful peasant, casting him as a pagan throwback who views God and nature as one. Incredibly disguised, Hurt is remarkable as the pathetic village idiot who lives for the reflected glory of the most fearsome man in town. Bean brings a rough-hewn sensitivity to the son's gradual rebellion against his father's tyranny. Fricker, silent for most of the film, emerges during a small powerful scene when she bolsters her man in a time of awful moral anguish.

Power of "The Field" derives from the wonderful compositions of cinematographer Jack Conroy, who frames the brown-green countryside and mud-paved village in tableaux of startling clarity. The weather-beaten faces, homespun clothes and the village's clannish folkways are rendered with stark believability.

But the film is undermined by the script's tendency to delineate the causes of Bull's grief and outrage in blustery, repetitive speeches echoing familiar themes of classic Irish literature. Sheridan's scipt is based on a play by John B. Keane, who undoubtedly was influenced by the plays of J.M. Synge. Like Synge's fishermen, these hard-scrabble villagers lead a life of unrelenting grimness.

"The Field," unlike Sheridan's previous film, "My Left Foot," ultimately fails to elevate this grimness with the uplifting possibility of hope. — *Rich.*

DANCE OF THE DUCK
(SPANISH)

A United Intl. Pictures release of an El Catalejo production. Written and directed by Manuel Iborra. Camera (color), Carles Gusi; editor, Miguel Angel Santamaria; music, Santi Arisa; sound, Miguel Polo. Reviewed at Worldwide Cinemas, N.Y., Aug. 24, 1990. (In Festival Latino.) Running time: **85 MIN.**
With: Antonio Resines, Verónica Forqué, Carlos Velat, Enrique San Francisco, Angie Gray.

Inspired no doubt by Pedro Almodóvar's funky portraits of contempo Spanish life, Manuel Iborra depicts the fast-paced, fast-track Madrid lifestyle in "Dance Of The Duck."

Pic is livened by upbeat music, colorful characters and amusing incidents, but it's too episodic to sustain interest.

Journalist Carlos (Antonio Resines) has just separated from wife Bea (Verónica Forqué), and joins the frenzied nightlife by drinking, dancing, using cocaine and sleeping around.

At work, he talks on three phones at once and has to alter his writing style to please an egomaniacal editor. His home is largely taken over by his libidinous younger brother.

Carlos checks out the latest in experimental theater, as well as an s&m club, where he encounters his boss in Western attire. At a trendy restaurant, a waitress puts an hourglass on the table. "This place is for eunuchs," he says. "Everyone's castrated."

Other characters include fellow reporter Lorenzo (Carlos Velat). He's in love with temperamental model Lala (Angie Gray), who refers to herself in the third person. Dish designer Roberto (Enrique San Francisco) is a druggie. Carlos' secretary keeps prophylactic reminders of bed mates.

Although there are a number of funny moments, the film is too self-consciously wild and crazy. Madrid is no doubt a fun town, with New York's kind of energy, but the nonstop partying gets a bit tiring, even on film.

In the end, the audience may not care if Carlos reunites with Bea, who isn't the most sympathetic character. After all, she dates a man named Achilles simply because he appeared in a Fassbinder film. The rather pat ending rings false, as do the clichéd Polaroid updates on the characters.

The final scene takes place in the same airport that witnessed the shootout in Almodévar's "Women On The Verge Of A Nervous Breakdown." Iborra offers the same frenetic pace and offbeat individuals that "Women" did, but his storyline is weak.

Like the characters' decadent lifestyles, the film is superficially enjoyable but fundamentally insubstantial. — *Stev.*

HET PHOENIX MYSTERIE
(THE PHOENIX MYSTERY)
(DUTCH)

An NFM/IAF release of a Phoenix Films production. Produced by Fransjoris de Graaf. Written and directed by Leonard Reterl Helmrich. Camera (color, 16m), Jan Wich; editor, Marc Nolens; music, Lauran van der Sanden; sound, Kees Linthorst; art direction, Rebecca Geskus; production manager, Mariet Bakker. Reviewed at the Nederlands Filmmuseum, Amsterdam, June 14, 1990. Running time: **90 MIN.**
Albakry . . . . Luc Boyer
Natasha . . . . Liz Snoyink
Malou . . . . . Manouk van der Meulen

"The Phoenix Mystery," Leonard Helmrich's low-budget ($125,000) debut may not rise far beyond its Tilburg, Holland, home turf but the writer-director shows promise.

Tilburg helped fund its native son's pic, and it contributed cameos and extras, including the city mayor, aldermen and council. The droves of town officials and other bit players unfortunately give film an amateurish feel.

Film falls into the category of "minimal movies," a tag dreamed up by the prolific Pim de la Parra for those low- to no-budget films he makes and the method he recommends to aspiring directors who fail to get government production coin.

With unpaid crew and actors and daily improvised story and dialog, the results usually are questionable, as this film shows.

Film's satire on life in an ambitious middle-size city segues into a lofty melodrama about a dark stranger, an Egyptian architect who comes to the city to design a prestigious new office building. His ideas, nurtured by the mystique and style of an ancient civilization, clash with the modern monotony of glass and concrete the municipality banks on as it bulldozes old Tilburg.

It's all highly symbolic, right down to the climactic hallucinations of its melancholy protagonist. The screenplay is weak; the pic's considerable surprises are mostly visual.

Lenser Jan Wich catches the banality of the city as sharply as the mysteries of its death-minded hero. Unfortunately, minimal moviemaking is increasingly popular in Holland these days.
— *Ewa.*

DANGER ZONE III: STEEL HORSE WAR

A Danger Zone Co. release of a Jason Williams production. Produced by Williams. Executive producer, Bernard Subkoski. Directed by Douglas Bronco. Screenplay, Gregory Poirier, Williams; camera (Crest color), Daniel Yarussi; editor, Bob Murawski; music, Robert Etoll; sound, Brent Beckett; art direction, Brian McCabe; assistant director-associate producer, Todd King; stunt coordinator, Mike Tino. Reviewed on vidcassette, N.Y., Aug. 22, 1990. No MPAA Rating. Running time: **91 MIN.**
Wade Olsen . . . . . . Jason Williams
Grim Reaper . . . . . . Robert Random
Rainmaker . . . . . . Barne Subkoski
Skin . . . . Juanita Ranney
Tester . . . . Rusty Cooper
Buford . . . . Giles Ashford
Also with: Andres Carranza, Roger Gutierrez, Denise Ames, Kari French, Susan Para, Julie Hunter, Kendra Tucker, Scott Brown, Cole McKay.

The '60s biker film and traditional loner Western are ably updated in "Danger Zone III," indie picture from filmmaker Jason Williams that has opened theatrically in northern California.

Previous two films in the series, dating from 1987 and 1989, went direct to video and featured many of the same characters. Williams' point of departure here is to frame pic in terms of a young boy (Scott Brown) reading a comic book of the story à la "Creepshow."

Williams reprises his lead role as Wade Olsen, an ex-cop whose girlfriend was murdered by the Reaper, a malevolent biker who's just escaped from police custody while being transported from prison. Williams sets out on his chopper to track down the Reaper (the authorities haven't a clue how to catch him), who's taken his gang of bikers on a search for a buried cache of gold.

With stark vistas of the open road and desert photographed by Daniel Yarussi, film looks like the drive-in biker films of yore. Plot mirrors a Western, although nearly all the characters, good and bad, ride motorcycles rather than horses. The fact that the search leads them to gold hidden during the Civil War by Quantrill's Raiders cements the period-film connection.

Williams is effective as a loner good guy who's befriended by a stray dog (whose injured paw he treats) in traditional fashion. Robert Random's controlled portrayal of unredeeming cruelty marks him as a perfect choice for playing an unclichéd Charles Manson on screen.

Violence here is brief but vivid. — *Lor.*

DE GULLE MINNAAR
(THE GENEROUS LOVER)
(DUTCH)

A Motion Picture Group release of a Verenigde Nederlandsche Filmcompagnie production. Produced by Rob Houwer. Directed by Mady Saks. Screenplay, uncredited, based on two novels by Marjan Berk; camera (Eastmancolor, widescreen), Frans Bromet; music, Hennie Vrienten. Reviewed at the Tuschinski theater, Amsterdam, July 6, 1990.
Peter . . . . Peter Faber
Mascha . . . . . . Mariska van Kolck
Also with: Sylvia Millecam, Maarten Spanjer, Rick Launspach, Ella van Drumpt, Lieneke Le Roux, Ian Smith, Christiana Ramseyer, Rob Veldhuijsen, Jan Lenferink, Adele Bloemendaal.

Universal critical drubbing greeted this new film from producer Rob Houwer. Youthful audiences eager for sexual enlightenment or expecting titillating novelties might be attracted. Only that and perhaps curiosity generated by its lengthy angry reviews can save "The Generous Lover" from flopping.

Houwer ("Turkish Delight," "Soldier of Orange," "The Fourth Man") clearly was banking on the regular audience of tv-oriented youth. The film unfolds like a string of vidclips. It may be assumed that the (uncredited) choppy editing and the final version of the (equally uncredited) script were the work of the producer.

Story, or what there is of it, consists of minor variations on one simple idea: the irresistible attraction of sex for Peter (Peter Faber, popular on Dutch stage and screen), and his adventures with all the youngish compliant ladies of the neighborhood and beyond. To Faber's credit, he goes through the romantic and sexual motions with surprising good humor.

A vengeful discarded mistress (Sylvia Millecam) uses her ex, a press photographer (Maarten Spanjer), to publicize Peter's prowess in a gossipy weekly. This temporarily separates the hero from the true love he at last finds, radio announcer and would-be-pop singer Mascha (Mariska van Kolck, a singer-dancer and radio announcer in her spirited screen debut).

One pities the struggling performers, tried and untried, as well as helmer Mady Saks, who displayed skill and sympathy for women's problems in the realistic dramatic features "Breathless" and "Iris." Music by Hennie Vrienten is a happy plus.
— *Ewa.*

KINDERGARTEN
(ARGENTINE)

An Argentina Sono Film. Produced by Salvador d'Antonio, Carlos L. Mentasti. Directed by Jorge Polaco. Screenplay, Polaco, Daniel Gonzalez Valtuena, based on the novel by Asher Benatar; camera (color), Jose Trela; editor, Oscar Gomez; music, Hector Magni; sound, Eusebio Aguilera; art direction, Polaco. Reviewed at Cineplex Odeon Worldwide Cinemas, N.Y., Aug. 23, 1990. (In Festival Latino, N.Y.) Running time: **83 MIN.**
Graciela . . . . Graciela Borges
Arturo . . . . Arturo Puig
Grandmother . . . . Luisa Vehil
Elvira . . . . Elvira Romei
Luciano . . . . Luciano Sanguineri
Silvia . . . . Cecilia Etchegaray
Popcorn seller . Alejandro Urdapilleta

Had the Argentine government not confiscated this pretentious and annoying film as pornography, its 15 minutes of fame might have been reduced to 4$^1/_2$ or so. Yet another argument against censorship.

"Kindergarten," Jorge Polaco's first film since 1988's "In The Name Of The Son," is an incomprehensible, tedious challenge to audience perseverance.

Perhaps this was Polaco's intention. Talk about hollow victories.

The wafer-thin plot concerns a middle-aged couple, Graciela and Arturo, struggling to keep their relationship alive amid such complications as aging (or dead) parents and Arturo's young son from a previous marriage.

Arturo's first, and dead, wife makes periodic ghostly visits to stir things up, as does his young mistress. Latter's role as a sex kitten is blatantly illustrated by her alternately lime-green and mauve pubic hair. The Horse of a Different Color was used to better effect in "The Wizard Of Oz."

Less a narrative than a mishmash of scenes apparently designed to show the complexities of house, home, marriage and love, "Kindergarten" employs a bizarre, pseudo-surrealistic style in which dreams and fantasies coexist with (for lack of a better term) reality. Strange characters wander in and out, none stranger than a popcorn vender whose mugging would embarrass Pinky Lee.

Directing with what may be the heaviest hand in South America, Polaco shoots not one, but three frenzied scenes with a circling, dizzying camera. He requires the same over-the-top approach from his cast.

Arturo Puig is especially adept at overacting, and Luciano Sanguineri as the young son gives the most obnoxious performance by a juvenile since the monster-baby in "Eraserhead."

Technically, the film is adequate, although a 10-minute segment ran without subtitles (the audience didn't seem to notice or care).

As for the charges of pornography, "Kindergarten" does include male and female nudity and one or two brief sex scenes. They're not exactly shocking, but then nothing in this wearisome film attains its desperate desire to outrage. — *Evan.*

SWORDSMAN
(CHINESE)

A Long Shong Pictures-Golden Princess Film Prods. presentation of a Film Workshop production. Produced by Tsui Hark. Directed by King Hu. Screenplay adapted from a novel by Louis Cha; camera (color), Ardy Lam, Peter Pau; music, James Wong, Romeo Diaz; art direction, James Leung; stunt directors, Ching Siu-Tung, Lau Chi-Ho; co-directors, Tsui Hark, Ching Siu-Tung, Raymond Lee. Reviewed at Toronto Festival of Festivals, Sept. 7, 1990. Run-

ning time: **110 MIN.**
With: Sam Hui, Jacky Cheung, Cicilia Yip, Chang Man, Fennie Yeun, Lau Siu-Ying, Yuen Wah, Liu Suen.

Action-packed, zany, comical and violent, this black magic pic is set during the mid-Ming Dynasty when the royal court was ruled by a eunuch. Pic is total nonsense but prime material for those who devour unusual variations on the kung fu pics.

Pic stabs at tradition with an utterly confusing plot about rival parties after the Sacred Scroll — pic's proverbial MacGuffin — is stolen from the Forbidden City.

Plenty of blood is spilled onscreen as heads are lopped off with huge swords or carelessly exploded with the sweep of a hand. There's no primitive kung fu stuff for these flying swordsmen and their magical powers.

The swordsman is a young buck and part of the Sun Wah sect that fights against the rival, rough 'n' tough Chief Zhor and his clan. The swordsman has learned secret tactics from an old man, one of the great sword masters.

After slicing and dicing a small army (single-handedly, of course), he says, "We are all made of flesh and blood, so why do we make such a mess of this world?" A good question aptly buried for such a wonderfully frivolous film.

Several beautiful young women, who summon snakes with a whistle to battle their foe, also help the swordsman find the Sacred Scroll. — *Suze.*

SILENT SCREAM
(BRITISH)

A British Film Institute and Film Four Intl. presentation in association with the Scottish Film Prod. Fund of an Antonine production. (Intl. sales, BFI.) Executive producers, Alan Fountain, Colin McCabe, Ben Gibson. Produced by Paddy Higson. Directed by David Hayman. Screenplay, Bill Beech; camera (color), Denis Crossan; editor, Justin Krish; music, Bob Last, Calum McNair; production design, Andy Harris; sound, Cameron Crosby; associate producer, Alan J. Wands; production manager, Christine MacLean; assistant director, Wands; casting, Anne Henderson. Reviewed at Berlin Film Festival (competition), Feb. 13, 1990. Running time: **86 MIN.**
Larry Winters . . . . Iain Glen
Mary Winters . . . . . . Anne Kristen
Don Winters . . . . Alexander Morton
Frank Witers . . . . Harry Jones
Shuggie . . . . Andy Barr
Rab . . . . Kenneth Glenaan
Mo . . . . Steve Hotchkiss
Ken Murray . . . . John Murtagh

Alice/Betty . . . . Julie Graham
Young Larry . . . Michael MacDonald

A knockout performance from Iain Glen in the leading role is the peg on which to hang this demanding, difficult drama based on the grim life of Larry Winters, a murderer who found fame as a writer and poet in his prison cell.

First-time director David Hayman has made a challenging pic that needs critical raves to overcome b.o. resistance.

Glen, who won kudos for his role in Bob Rafelson's "Mountains Of The Moon," is impressive as Larry Winters, whose grim experiences behind bars are alleviated by flights of fantasy about his happy youth in the Highlands of Scotland.

While he's onscreen, which he is for much of the time, pic grabs attention. But Hayman doesn't make it easy on the audience as he jumbles memories, fantasies and reality. Audiences may find this style unsettling, and pic may suffer commercially as a result.

Still, when the device works, it works brilliantly, as in scenes that move from past to present without a cut. Fact that it's a true story is a plus.

Winters was convicted for shooting a London barkeep with a gun he'd picked up during his time as a paratrooper. In prison, his wild behavior got him placed in a drug program, and he became an addict.

This is not the stuff for a relaxing night at the movies, but if the critics respond, "Silent Scream" could find a niche in arthouses. Crossover looks unlikely, however, because of the subject matter and Hayman's style.

Anne Kristen makes a big impression as Winters' long-suffering mother, and supporting roles all are expertly filled. Pic is technically good in every department.

Glen's strong performance is the lasting impression of this impressive, troubling pic. — *Strat.*

PARIS IS BURNING
(DOCU)

An Off White Prods. release. Produced by Jennie Livingston, Barry Swimar. Directed by Livingston. Camera (color), Paul Gibson, Maryse Alberti. Reviewed at Margaret Mead Film

Festival, New York, Sept. 26, 1990. Running time: **71 MIN.**

Jennie Livingston's documentary is a fascinating study of the world of drag balls where gay men, mostly black, realize their dreams by dressing up and posing like models. Although the terrain will be quite foreign to most viewers, the film makes it vivid and immediate.

No doubt made on a shoestring, "Paris Is Burning" is a compelling docu that deserves theatrical release. It may not go over in middle America, but it should appeal to anyone who wants a closeup view of a subculture where freedom of expression is not just condoned, but encouraged.

Long before Madonna discovered vogueing, it was being practiced at the Paris Ballroom in the Bronx. (Contrary to pic's title, it's not set in Paris, and no one is on fire.) Besides vogueing, contestants may enter competitions for weightlifters, would-be executives, cadets, aspiring models and butch queens.

The object, according to the many memorable personalities interviewed, is to be a legend. As one contestant puts it, balls are "as close as we're going to get to fame and fortune and spotlight."

Being black, male and gay, these fame seekers already have three strikes against them in the real world. Here they do not have to blend in with straight society — unless they want to enter the category for "realness," which judges how well contestants pass for straight men and women.

The highly competitive balls allow participants to escape from their ordinary lives. Beneath the humor and beauty at the balls lies an undertone of sadness. Many of the regulars come from broken homes, or have been thrown out by their parents.

The the final image is of Corey applying makeup and talking about his diminished expectations. "Everybody wants to leave something behind them, some impression, some mark on the world," he says. "Then you think you leave a mark on the world if you just get through it." Above all, the people interviewed are survivors.

Film's only fault is its failure to provide background information on the ballroom. It's never

revealed whether the competitors pay to attend and who pays for the trophies. And it wouldn't hurt to explain the title. — *Stev.*

KNOCKOUT
(JAPANESE)

A Genjiro Arato Jimusho production. (Intl. sales, Gaga Communications.) Executive produced by Genjiro Arato. Written and directed by Junji Sakamoto. Camera (color), Norimichi Kasamatsu; editor, Kenichi Yakashima; music, Kazuhiro Hara; sound, Masatoshi Yokomizo; art direction, Tomoyuki Maruo; assistant director, Hiromitsu Yamanaka. Reviewed at Japan Society, N.Y., Sept. 17, 1990. Running time: **102 MIN.**
Eiji Adachi . . . . Hidekazu Akai
Takako Kamoi . . . . . Haruko Sagara
Daisuke Kamoi . . . . Akaji Maro
Makio Sajima . . . . . . Yoshio Harada
Jiro Kitayama . . . . . Kenichi Mikawa
Satoru Kiyota . . . . . Takeshi Yamato
Eagle Tomoda . . . . Masaharu Owada

"Knockout," a 1989 independent production from Japan, is based on a true story, beginning with a boxer's bloody defeat and ending with his comeback attempt. Unlike the "Rocky" series, this is not a heroic look at the sport, but a gritty, downbeat portrayal.

It is stylishly filmed by first-time director Junji Sakamoto, and the performances are fine. But the film could use some editing; it gets bogged down in one long training scene after another. A hit in Japan, "Knockout" is not likely to repeat its success beyond those shores.

The fairly routine story involves the comeback attempt of Eiji Adachi, a boxer who is badly beaten, undergoes brain surgery and is warned by doctors not to return to the ring. Naturally, that's exactly what Adachi decides to do.

The story is based on the life of a former boxer, Hidekazu Akai, who more or less plays himself as Adachi. Akai, who did suffer a devastating defeat but did not risk a comeback, gives a compelling performance as the temperamental boxer. Equally good is Yoshio Harada as a trainer and former champion.

Unfortunately, the film is marred by the portrayal of Adachi's business partner (Kenichi Mikawa) as a stereotypically effeminate homosexual who becomes an object of ridicule.

On the positive side, "Knockout" has a distinctive look, and Sakamoto moves his camera elegantly. Two of the best scenes are set in an elevator that rises high above Osaka, providing an eerie view of the city. And in scenes set in housing projects, Sakamoto shows Osaka to be much less glitzy than Tokyo.

Less inventive is the frequent use of slow motion during fight sequences. For anyone who is not a boxing fan, these scenes go on too long. The many training episodes should have been edited, too.

The problem with "Knockout" is that it's *only* about boxing and nothing else. Akai makes the boxer real — after all, he lived most of the film — but Adachi is so obsessed with the sport that he is not very likable. At least Rocky had a life outside the ring. Adachi seldom leaves it, and the film might be more entertaining if he did. — *Stev.*

CHICAGO FEST

ISKINDIRIAH KAMAN OUE KAMAN
(ALEXANDRIA, AGAIN AND ALWAYS)
(EQYPTIAN-FRENCH)

A Misr Intl./Paris Classics production in association with La Sept. Written and directed by Youssef Chahine. Camera (color), Ramses Marzouk; editor, Rachida Abdelsalam; music, Mohamed Nouh; sound, Olivier Schwob, Dominique Hennequin; set design, Onsi Abou Seif. Reviewed at the Montreal World Film Festival, Aug. 30, 1990. (In Chicago Intl. Film Festival.) Running time: **108 MIN.**
With: Yousra, Youssef Chahine, Hussein Fahmy, Amr Abdel Gelil, Hicham Selim, Tahia Carioca, Hoda Sultan.

This pic is an insider's revelation on the life and films of Arab helmer, Youssef Chahine.

Chock-full of references to his various pics, including "La Terre," "Alexandria, Again And Always" focuses on Chahine (played by Chahine himself) winning Berlin's Golden Bear for "Alexandrie Pourquoi?" the first Arab film to win an international prize, according to the pic.

An intimate, behind-the-scenes exposé on the life of an internationally renowned director, pic should delight fest regulars everywhere. — *Suze.*

FLOP
(ARGENTINE)

A Faro Films production. Produced by Cipe Fridman. Directed by Eduardo Mignogna. Screenplay, Mignogna and Graciela Maglie; camera (color), Richard de Angelis; editor, Cesar D'Angiolillio; music, Litto Nebbia; art direction, Jorge Ferrari. Reviewed at the Toronto Festival of Festivals, Sept. 15, 1990. (In Chicago Intl. Film Festival.) Running time: **98 MIN.**
With: Victor Laplace, Inda Ledesma, Leonor Manso, Enrique Pinti, Federico Luppi.

This film's title sums up its foreign sales potential in one word: flop. Starring Flop the comedian, pic is about the life of a magician/stage actor, loosely based on the life of Argentine showman Florencio Parravicini. As such, it should work on home turf, but it's antiquated theatrics and old magic tricks won't cut it elsewhere.

Pic begins with Flop on stage wearing a black top hat and carrying a magic wand. He gets his show rolling with the announcement: "Pay attention to rogues and tidy ass-kissers . . . " Backstage is the "real" Flop being interviewed about his life. Past and present are then crosscut throughout. Flop says he started "rehearsing the role of Casanova" in his mother's womb. Interview cuts to a pregnant woman being led by her fetus: every time an attractive woman passes, the pregnant woman swings about face to follow her.

This and other such scenes are cute but awfully corny. When Flop was 7, his father was appointed prison director, and the whole family was moved into a house within the prison walls, the set for most offstage flashbacks thereafter.

Some of pic's most interesting dialog takes place between a young Flop and a prisoner, Grimlat, who warns that "happiness isn't a matter of doing what you like but to enjoy what you're doing."

Pic is overlong, and editing is patchy. And the music is awful. Other tech credits are fine, but this old tale of days gone by is not one of the more impressive Argentine films to surface in recent years. — *Suze.*

SIBLING RIVALRY

A Columbia Pictures release of a Castle Rock Entertainment presentation in association with Nelson Entertainment. Executive producers, George Shapiro, Howard West. Produced by David V. Lester, Don Miller, Liz Glotzer. Directed by Carl Reiner. Screenplay, Martha Goldhirsh; camera (color), Reynaldo Villalobos; editor, Bud Molin; music, Jack Elliott; sound (Dolby), Richard Bryce Goodman; production design, Jeannine Claudia Oppewall; set decoration, Lisa Fischer; costume design, Durinda Wood; assistant director, Marty Ewing; production manager, Lester; casting, Marci Liroff. Reviewed at Magno Preview 9 screening room, N.Y., Sept. 12, 1990. MPAA Rating: PG-13. Running time: **88 MIN.**

Marjorie Turner	Kirstie Alley
Nick	Bill Pullman
Iris	Carrie Fisher
Jeanine	Jami Gertz
Harry Turner	Scott Bakula
Charles Turner	Sam Elliott
Wilbur	Ed O'Neill
Mrs. Turner	Frances Sternhagen
Mr. Turner	John Randolph
Pat	Bill Macy
Mr. Hunter	Matthew Laurance
Dr. Plotner	Paul Benedict

"Sibling Rivalry," an amusing black comedy by Carl Reiner, has strong sleeper potential, though it is not for all tastes and probably won't achieve the megahit status of Castle Rock's previous entry, "When Harry Met Sally."

First-time screenwriter Martha Goldhirsh has fashioned an elegant structure for farce with the unusual side benefit of sympathetic characters instead of archetypes. None of what happens is believable, but the clockwork-like construction of coincidences and wrong-headed behavior develops an engrossing modern equivalent to Restoration Comedy.

In her first solo-starring vehicle, Kirstie Alley — who plays the creatively stifled wife of a stuffy young doctor, played by Scott Bakula — comes into her own with a flamboyant, highly physical performance. Film's trailer gives away the first key plot twist: Her adulterous hop in the sack with mystery hunk Sam Elliott results in his death by heart attack after strenuous love-making.

What follows involves three sets of siblings: Alley and her slightly ditzy younger sister and rival, Jami Gertz; weird vertical blinds salesman Bill Pullman as the black sheep younger brother of upwardly mobile cop Ed O'Neill; and the massive clan of doctors comprising Bakula, his

sister (Carrie Fisher) and brother, Elliott.

The surprise that Elliott turns out to be Alley's brother-in-law is effectively developed and launches several hilarious setpieces. Pullman and Alley are united in crime after Pullman thinks **he** accidentally killed Elliott with his vertical blinds equipment. Both he and Alley attempt to cover up the fatality as a suicide. Alley's pride in authorship of the suicide note — before settling down she had planned to be a novelist — is milked for plenty of humor and thematic relevance.

Among the other complications are Gertz and O'Neill falling in love, and Pullman's potential manslaughter rap for a crime he didn't commit, threatening O'Neill's impending appointment as police chief.

Though the rushed happy ending doesn't ring true, "Sibling Rivalry" creates a cheerful mood from morbid material. Reiner directs swiftly and efficiently, getting maximum yocks out of borderline vulgar content.

Pullman and Gertz are terrific in creating slow-witted characters who are still interesting. Bakula and O'Neill are solid in less showy roles, as are Frances Sternhagen and John Randolph as Bakula's parents. Elliott is a casting coup: sexy alive and a droll corpse. — *Lor.*

WHITE PALACE

A Universal Pictures release of a Mirage/Double Play production. Produced by Mark Rosenberg, Amy Robinson, Griffin Dunne. Executive producer, Sydney Pollack. Co-producer, Bill Finnegan. Directed by Luis Mandoki. Screenplay, Ted Tally, Alvin Sargent, based on Glenn Savan's novel; camera (Deluxe color), Lajos Koltai; editor, Carol Littleton; music, George Fenton; sound (Dolby), Bob Grieve; production design, Jeannine C. Oppewall; art direction, John Wright Stevens; set decoration, Lisa Fischer; costume design, Lisa Jenson; associate producer, Robin Forman; assistant director, Chris Soldo; casting, Nancy Nayor. Reviewed at the Cineplex Odeon Universal City Cinemas, L.A., Oct. 15, 1990. MPAA Rating: R. Running time: **104 MIN.**

Nora Baker	Susan Sarandon
Max Baron	James Spader
Neil	Jason Alexander
Rosemary	Kathy Bates
Judy	Eileen Brennan
Sol Horowitz	Steven Hill
Rachel	Rachel Levin
Larry Klugman	Corey Parker
Edith Baron	Renee Taylor
Mary Miller	Jonathan Penner
Sherri Klugman	Barbara Howard

Outstanding performances by **Susan Sarandon** and

James Spader, working from a relentlessly witty script, make "White Palace" one of the best films of its kind since "The Graduate." Rave word-of-mouth should help warm up the boxoffice grill, but it will take careful handling by Universal to cook this exceptionally smart romance to its full sizzling potential.

That could mean a major Oscar push for Sarandon, clearly a serious contender in this meaty role as Nora, a 43-year-old fast-food worker who gets involved with a 27-year-old advertising exec — the same sort of character Spader played in "Pretty In Pink," now mellowed and matured.

Both have experienced terrible loss — Max (Spader) is a widower; Nora's child has died — and they share a magnetic sexual attraction.

Their "Odd Couple" differences, however, include class, religion and hygiene (he's a buttoned-down neat freak; she's a gregarious slob) in addition to the Mrs. Robinson-esque age discrepancy.

The ferocity that director Luis Mandoki brings to the pair's early love scenes helps establish how two people can fall into lust and worry about love later.

The torrid nature of those scenes also will require deft marketing, since "Palace" runs several degrees hotter than tepid romances like "Ghost" and "Pretty Woman," which have exhibited huge appeal among romance-starved audiences.

Still, the film unpretentiously builds its case toward a rather mushy conclusion: No one knows why anyone loves anyone, and it's perhaps best to just follow one's heart.

Mandoki and writers Ted Tally and Alvin Sargent, working from Glenn Savan's novel, don't really know how to end the film, it doesn't seem to matter. (Savan provides his apparent blessing by appearing as an extra in the burger joint where the two meet.)

Tally and Sargent's script is peppered with comic gems. When Max relents and takes Nora to a Thanksgiving gathering, brilliant lines follow at an assembly-line rate, and laughs nearly drown the dialog.

Impressively, a number of those moments emanate from smaller players, who possess distinct personalities despite their scant screen time. Rachel Levin, for example, is delightfully chipper as the wife of Max' best

friend.

Bravely allowing herself to look the character's age, Sarandon brings uncommon sensuality to the part of Nora, equaling, if not surpassing, her own standard in films like "Bull Durham" and "Atlantic City."

Raunchy yet vulnerable, Sarandon carefully avoids the clichés that might have been associated with Nora. For an actress who's excelled in exuding sex appeal, this could be the part of a lifetime.

Spader continues to establish himself as star material, especially when it comes to playing self-conscious yuppies. Like his character in "Sex, Lies And Videotape," Max is a damaged soul who isn't beyond salvation.

Tech credits are flawless. George Fenton's jazzy score ranges from unshackled sexuality to understated longing.

For Mandoki, a Mexican national who drew international attention with "Gaby — A True Story," "White Palace" is a regal U.S. debut, and a morsel likely to linger on more than a few palates come Oscar time. — *Bril.*

NIGHT OF THE LIVING DEAD

A Columbia Pictures release of a 21st Century Film and George A. Romero presentation of a Menahem Golan production. Produced by John A. Russo, Russ Steiner. Executive producers, Golan, Romero. Co-exec producer, Ami Artzi. Directed by Tom Savani. Screenplay, Romero, based on Russo and Romero's 1968 screenplay; camera (TVC color), Frank Prinzi; editor, Tom Dubensky; music, Paul McCollough; sound (Ultra-Stereo), Thomas Pettinato; art direction, James Feng; set decoration, Brian J. Stonestreet; costume design, Barbara Anderson; special makeup effects, John Vulich, Everett Burrell; production manager, Marc S. Fischer; associate producer, Christine Romero. Reviewed at Columbia Studios, Culver City, Calif., Oct. 17, 1990. MPAA Rating: R. Running time: **89 MIN.**
Ben . . . . .Tony Wood
Barbara . . . . Patricia Tallman
Harry . . . . Tom Towles
Helen . . . . McKee Anderson
Tom . . . . William Butler
Judy Rose . . . . . . Katie Finnerman
Johnnie . . . . Bill Mosley
Sarah . . . . Heather Mazur

The original producers of "Night Of The Living Dead" have remade their own cult classic in a crass bit of cinematic grave-robbing. Columbia won't have much to chew on after this slapdash pic's first sitting at the boxoffice banquet-table.

The only legitimate reason to

remake the 1968 film would have been to improve its effects and sub-$200,000 budget, although the dimly shot black & white images were far creepier than any of its color progeny.

Under the direction of Tom Savini — a special-effects goremeister making his feature debut — the new "Dead" is surprisingly low on gore, lame in the effects department and actually less frightening than the original.

The story faithfully follows the original except for the bonehead decision to replace the ending with a "meaningful" twist that reeks of pretentiousness.

The plot still involves seven people trapped in a farmhouse fending off hordes of walking corpses intent on devouring them. Never explained is what animated the bodies in the first place, although a solid bash to the brain deanimates them.

The hero still is Ben (Tony Wood), and the bad guy still is a middle-aged businessman named

Original Film

Continental (Walter Reade) release of Image Ten (Russell Streiner-Karl Hardman) production. Directed by George A. Romero. Screenplay, Romero, John A. Russo; camera, Romero; sound, Gary Streiner. Previewed in screening room, N.Y., Oct. 10, 1968. Running time: **90 MIN.**
Barbara . . . . Judith O'Dea
Johnny . . . . Russell Streiner
Ben . . . . Duane Jones
Harry . . . . Karl Hardman
Tom . . . . Keith Wayne
Judy . . . . Judith Ridley
Helen . . . . Marilyn Eastman
Karen . . . . Kyra Schon

Harry (Tom Towles) who holes up in the basement with his wife and daughter. The one beefed-up role is that of the female lead (Patricia Tallman), who reveals a Rambo-esque bent.

At least Romero can't blame anyone else for raiding his (literally) groundbreaking work, since he did it himself, exec producing and rewriting the screenplay he wrote with John A. Russo.

Savini doesn't show himself to be much of a director, and the performances are about as bad as they were the first time around, though it all seemed more forgivable in the dank light of the first "Dead's" constraints.

No effort has been made to update or even establish the context of the film. The '90s, after all, represent a slightly different mindset than the cultish paranoia that permeated the original.

This remake, like those corpses, has no discernable reason for being, except perhaps as a belated effort by the makers of the first "Living Dead" to cash in on their labors. If that's all there is left to do, then perhaps it's time to let the dead rest, once and for all. — *Bril.*

MARKED FOR DEATH

A 20th Century Fox release of a Victor & Grais production in association with Steamroller Prods. Produced by Michael Grais, Mark Victor, Steven Seagal. Co-producer, Peter MacGregor-Scott. Directed by Dwight H. Little. Screenplay, Grais, Victor; camera (Deluxe color), Ric Waite; editor, O. Nicholas Brown; music, James Newton Howard; sound (Dolby), Rick Franklin, Fred Judkins; production design, Robb Wilson King; art direction, James Burkhart; set decoration, Robert Kensinger; costume design, Isabella Von Soest Chubb; associate producers, John Todgya, Julius R. Nasso; stunt director, 2nd unit director, Conrad E. Palmisano; assistant directors, Jerry Ziesmer, Michael-McCloud Thompson; casting, Fred Champion, Pamela Basker, Sue Swan. Reviewed at the Beverly Connection Theaters, L.A., Oct. 5, 1990. MPAA Rating: R. Running time: **94 MIN.**
Hatcher . . . . Steven Seagal
Screwface . . . . Basil Wallace
Max . . . . Keith David
Charles . . . . Tom Wright
Leslie . . . . Joanna Pacula
Melissa . . . . Elizabeth Gracen
Kate Hatcher . . . . Bette Ford
Also with: Kevin Dunn, Arlen Dean Snyder, Danielle Harris, Jimmy Cliff.

Steven Seagal has demonstrated considerable cinematic talent in terms of breaking bones and snapping up boxoffice. He certainly does a lot of the former and seems destined to do more of the latter with this dim-witted revenge yarn.

It would be hard to imagine a more straightforward plot: Former Drug Enforcement Agency troubleshooter Hatcher (Seagal) quits his job and goes home to visit his family. At the local tavern, he crosses a group of Jamaican drug dealers who mark him and his family for death. Naturally, he has to kill the leader to protect his loved ones.

The leader of the drug "posse," Screwface (Basil Wallace), practices voodoo and sports braids. Because of this, the filmmakers apparently felt compelled to shift the scene briefly to Jamaica and throw in a speech about how not all Jamaicans are drug dealers — a message soon forgotten as the film gets back to the business of killing as many Jamaicans as possible.

(The end credits also carry a

disclaimer saying the "posse phenomenon" should not detract from the Jamaican people, though it's hard to believe that will mollify anybody.)

This is the simplest of showcases for Seagal — an extremely compelling action presence with his brutal martial arts fighting style, imposing size and nasty demeanor.

Still, he's hardly branching out from his earlier shoot-'em-ups, content to keep playing some sort of cop forced to turn to vigilante justice.

The twist in Seagal's pics is that there's usually some sort of liberal bent — here Hatcher's statement that the drug war has been for naught — in contrast to the right-wing leanings of many other films in the genre.

He also has a penchant for black sidekicks, here a former Army buddy (Keith David) who seemingly abandons his job as a high school football coach to run around the city and then the Carribean firing automatic weapons.

But Seagal fans aren't likely to be disappointed, since director Dwight H. Little keeps the pedal to the metal.

Mercifully little is made of the pic's voodoo element, and a twist regarding the bad guy is interesting but badly telegraphed. At least the script by producers Michael Grais and Mark Victor includes a few snappy throwaway lines.

Beyond the incumbent violence there's a fair amount of nudity in the film. Alas, that's about all female characters are allowed to show off, as Joanna Pacula turns in little more than a cameo as an expert on voodoo and Elizabeth Gracen gets strictly damsel-in-distress treatment as Seagal's sister.

Production values are generally sound, with a Jimmy Cliff song cameo augmenting James Newton Howard's score. — *Bril.*

HAKON HAKONSEN
(SHIPWRECKED)
(NORWEGIAN)

A Syncron/SF Norway release of Filmkammeraterne production in association with Svensk Filmindustri (Stockholm) and Buena Vista. Produced by John M. Jacobsen. Executive producer, Nigel Wool. Directed by Nils Gaup. Screenplay, Gaup, Bob Foss, Greg Dinner, Nick Thiel, from O.V. Falck-Ytter's novel; camera (Panavision color), Erling Thurmann-Andersen; editor, Niels Pagh Andersen; music, Patrick Doyle; sound (Dolby), Jan Lindvik; production design, Harald Egede-Nisssen, Roger Cain; costumes, Lotte Dandanell, Bente Winther-Larsen; special visual effects, Richard Conway; assistant director, Steve St. Peter; casting, Jeremy Zimmerman, Torill Ek. Reviewed at the Colosseum, Oslo, Oct. 4 1990. Running time: **91 MIN.**
Hakon . . . . Stian Smedstad
Lt. Merrick . . . . Gabriel Byrne
Mary . . . . Louisa Haigh
Jens . . . . Trond Peter Stamsö Munch
Hakon's father . . . . Björn Sundquist
The captain . . . . Kjell Stormoen
Also with: Eva von Hanno, Frank Krog, Karl Sundby, Guy Fithen, Ian Mackenzie, William Ilkley, Terry Duran, Knut Walle, Joachim Rafaelsen, Jon Sigurd Kristensen.

With historical adventure film "The Pathfinder," the Norwegian team of producer John M. Jacobsen and writer-helmer Nils Gaup won a best foreign-language-film Oscar nomination in 1988. With straight-out family-oriented swashbuckler "Hakon Hakonsen," the duo has entered the Disney realm and added some Spielberg dash.

"Hakon Hakonsen" was produced with the aid of some Disney know-how, and a substantial part of its $10 million budget was supplied by Buena Vista. English-language version of the film is scheduled to open in the U.S. next February with the title "Shipwrecked."

Based on a classical juvenile novel, "Hakon Hakonsen" tells the story of 13-year-old Hakon (Stian Smedstad) who, in 1850, becomes a deck hand on an ocean-going ship to make money to save his crippled father's farm. The seasick Hakon soon comes to fear the cat-o'-nine-tails more than the waves.

During the voyage, the boy learns about shipboard life the hard way. He makes friends with everyone but a fake British navy lieutenant (Gabriel Byrne), whom the boy discovers is smuggling arms to fellow pirates in the South Seas.

The film is chock-full of an ocean adventure's proper ingredients, including a stowaway, played by 13-year-old Louisa Haigh with an all-knowing mien. The character is a wonderful counterpoint to Smedstad's fresh-faced Hakon. With Jens, a straight-arrow sailor, they overcome every danger.

When the ship goes down in a storm, the friends separately find safety on neighboring islands. Hakon's island is deserted, but footprints soon lead him to a buried treasure, which he expects the pirates soon will come to collect. He builds a series of jungle traps around the treasure and has a friendly gorilla try them out.

The pirates don't arrive until the three friends have reunited. Lots of chasing, teeth-gnashing, hokum and hilarity, along with some genuine suspense, ensue.

Cinematography, editing, sound, music and neatly controlled acting (even Byrne's scoundrel avoids gross stereotyping) all add up to a high-profile professional achievement. — *Kell.*

STEEL & LACE

A Fries Distribution release through Paragon Arts of a Cinema Home Video production. Produced by John Schouweiler, David DeCoteau. Directed by Ernest Farino. Screenplay, Joseph Dougherty, Dave Edison; camera (Foto-Kem color), Thomas L. Callaway; editor, Chris Roth; music, John Massari; sound, D.J. Ritchie; production design, Blair Martin; costume design, Maria Aguilar; assistant director, Keith Carpenter; production manager, J.B. Rogers; special makeup effects, S.O.T.A. F/X — supervisors, Jerry Macaluso, Roy Knyrim; stunt coordinator, Chuck Borden; 2nd unit camera, Michael Michaud; additional camera, Howard Wexler. Reviewed at Magno Review 2 screening room, N.Y., Oct. 10, 1990. No MPAA Rating. Running time: **93 MIN.**
Gaily . . . . Clare Wren
Albert . . . . Bruce Davison
Alison . . . . Stacy Haiduk
Det. Dunn . . . . David Naughton
Daniel . . . . Michael Cerveris
Tobby . . . . Scott Burkholder
Oscar . . . . Paul Lieber
Norman . . . . Brian Backer
Craig . . . . John J. York
Duncan . . . . Nick Tate
Schumann . . . . David L. Lander
Also with: John DeMita, Brenda Swanson, Cindy Brooks, Hank Garrett, Beverly Mickins, William Prince, Mary Boucher, Dave Edison.

"Steel & Lace" is an entertaining new take on horror and revenge pictures, well-timed for some Halloween business. Above-average cast and execution should help in home-video as well.

Horror buffs say you can't kill off a good monster. "Lace" manages to re-create interest in a female Frankenstein's monster after "Frankenhooker" threatened to close the book on that concept through satire.

Clare Wren plays the cyborg with panache, having been re-animated by her ex-NASA scientist brother (Bruce Davison) after her opening-reel suicide. She was driven to suicide after a trial in which Michael Cerveris gets off scot-free after raping her.

Five years later she's back, donning various disguises, to avenge herself on Cerveris' friends, who lied in court. She saves Mike for last.

Standard revenge format is heightened by imaginative makeup effects and a romantic subtext, ably delivered by Bruce Davison (in a solid bigscreen followup to his excellent turn in "Longtime Companion"). Also making a good impression as the investigative protagonist is Stacy Haiduk, a young Kathleen Turner type with eerie blue eyes.

Grisly murder scenes are loaded with blood, yet one segment of Wren exacting her revenge on a conspirator while making love to him is effectively depicted with grotesque sound effects only.

First-time director Ernest Farino does a good job keeping the film's tongue-in-cheek elements in check, making the picture accessible to fans who like their horror straight as well as the camp followers. — *Lor.*

STREET HUNTER

A DGP release of a 21st Century Film presentation of a Street Hunter production. Produced by David Gil. Directed by John A. Gallagher. Screenplay, Gallagher, Steve James; camera (TVC color), Phil Parmet; editor, Mary Hickey; music, Dana Walden, Barry Fasman; sound, Melanie Johnson; production design, John Paino; costumes, Jane Tabachnik; assistant director, Sam Sarowitz; production manager, David Fitzgerald; stunt coordinator, Phil Neilson; special effects, Matt Vogel; casting, Judy Henderson, Alycia Aumuller. Reviewed at Movie Makers screening room, N.Y., July 18, 1990. MPAA Rating: R. Running time: **94 MIN.**
Logan Blade . . . . Steve James
Col. Walsh . . . . Reb Brown
Angel . . . . John Leguizamo
Denise . . . . Valarie Pettiford
Don Mario Romano . . . Frank Vincent
Riley . . . . Tom Wright
Daze . . . . Richie Havens
Louis Romano . . Richard Panebianco
Jannelli . . . . Sam Coppola
Wellman . . . . Thom Christopher
Rivera . . . . Emilio Del Pozo
Mustache Diablo . . . Victor Colicchio

Several Cannon Group alumni unite for "Street Hunter," an effective actioner made in New York that has okay urban theatrical prospects beyond its video value.

Steve James, erstwhile sidekick in numerous Cannon war pictures, co-wrote and toplines as Logan Blade, a Gotham bounty hunter — dressed in slicker, wide-brim hat and other Western garb — who's accompanied by his partner, a Doberman. A streamlined "action man," Blade has a girlfriend (vocalist Valarie

Pettiford), but lives in his van and significantly rides off at pic's end with his four-legged friend rather than his main squeeze.

Story, obviously designed as the prototype for a series of films, has James getting embroiled in a turf war between two rival drug gangs, the Diablos (led by baby-faced John Leguizamo in a fun performance) and Frank Vincent's mafia family. Interesting wrinkle has mercenary Reb Brown, an ex-CIA operative, spouting Nietzschean philosophy as he counsels Leguizamo on battle tactics.

Satisfying climax pits the muscular Brown and James in a martial arts battle. The fact that Brown usually is cast as a monosyllabic hero like "Yor, The Hunter From The Future," adds humor to his frequent quotations from philosophers.

James' cool, authoritative manner dominates the picture and bodes well for future toplining adventures for the former second banana.

John Gallagher's direction is well-paced, with time out for dramatic outbursts from the cast, including hot-headed policeman Thom Christopher. David Gil, who produced the 1970 Peter Boyle hit "Joe" for Cannon, gets the most out of the modest budget and New York locations.

Phil Parmet's mostly night-time lensing is sharp, and Dana Walden and Barry Fasman have contributed an invigorating score, reminiscent of Roy Budd's catchy music-box tones for the *film noir* classic, "Get Carter."

The Blade moniker for a street-savvy hero was used for the title character of an unrelated 1973 John Marley cop vehicle. — *Lor.*

DESPERATE HOURS

An MGM/UA release of a Dino De Laurentiis Communications production. Produced by De Laurentiis, Michael Cimino. Line producer, Mel Dellar. Executive producer, Martha Schumacher. Directed by Cimino. Screenplay, Lawrence Konner, Mark Rosenthal, Joseph Hayes, based on Hayes' novel and play "The Desperate Hours." Camera (Technicolor), Doug Milsome; supervising editor, Peter Hunt; music, David Mansfield; sound (Dolby), Keith A. Wester, Jay Harding, Bill Benton; production design, Victoria Paul; art direction, Patricia Klawonn; set design, Tom Lindblom; costume design, Charles De Caro; assistant director, Brian Cook; casting, Mary Colquhoun, Cate Praggastis (Salt Lake City). Reviewed at Columbia Studios, L.A., Sept. 30, 1990. MPAA Rating: R. Running time: **105 MIN.**

Michael Bosworth	Mickey Rourke
Tim Cornell	Anthony Hopkins
Nora Cornell	Mimi Rogers
Chandler	Lindsay Crouse
Nancy Breyers	Kelly Lynch
Wally Bosworth	Elias Koteas
Albert	David Morse
May Cornell	Shawnee Smith
Zack Cornell	Danny Gerard
Ed Tallent	Gerry Bamman
Kyle	Matt McGrath

Out to demonstrate that they're good boys now and can bring in a film economically, Michael Cimino and Dino De Laurentiis unfortunately have neglected the other side of the filmmaking equation — quality. "Desperate Hours" is a coldly mechanical and uninvolving remake of the 1955 Bogart pic "The Desperate Hours," with Mickey Rourke as the hood terrorizing a suburban family. The MGM/UA release looks like a middling performer.

Ever since "Heaven's Gate," his wildly expensive, hugely ambitious and reviled 1980 Western masterwork, director Cimino has been trying to live down his rep-

Original Film

Paramount release of William Wyler production. Stars Humphrey Bogart, Fredric March; features Arthur Kennedy, Martha Scott, Dewey Martin, Gig Young, Mary Murphy. Directed by Wyler. Screenplay, Joseph Hayes, based on hos own novel; camera (Vista Vision), Lee Garmes; editor, Robert Swink; music, Gail Kubic. Previewed Criterion Theater, N.Y., Sept. 8, '55. Running time: **112 MIN.**

Glenn	Humphrey Bogart
Dan Hilliard	Frederic March
Jesse Bard	Arthur Kennedy
Eleanor Hilliard	Martha Scott
Hal	Dewey Martin
Chuck	Gig Young
Cindy	Mary Murphy
Ralphie	Richard Eyer
Kobish	Robert Middleton
Detective	Alan Reed
Winston	Bert Freed
Masters	Ray Collins
Carson	Whit Bissell
Fredericks	Ray Teal
Detective	Michael Moore
Detective	Don Haggerty
Sal	Ric Roman
Dutch	Pat Flaherty
Miss Swift	Beverly Garland
Bucky Walling	Louis Lettieri
Mrs. Walling	Ann Doran

Stage Version

Howard Erskine & Joseph Hayes production of melodrama in three acts by Hayes, based on his own novel. Stars Karl Malden, Nancy Coleman; features Paul Newman, James Gregory, George Mathews, Kendall Clark, Patricia Peardon, Rusty Lane. Direction, Robert Montgomery; scenery and lighting, Howard Day; costumes, Robert Randolph. At Ethel Barrymore, N.Y., Feb. 10, '55; $5.75 top ($7.50 opening).

Tim Winston	Judson Pratt
Jesse Bard	James Gregory
Harry Carson	Kendall Clark
Eleanor Hilliard	Nancy Coleman
Ralphie Hilliard	Malcolm Brodrick
Dan Hilliard	Karl Malden
Cindy Hilliard	Patricia Peardon
Glenn Griffin	Paul Newman
Hank Griffin	George Grizzard
Robish	George Mathews
Chuck Wright	Fred Eisley
Mr. Patterson	Wyrley Biren
Lt. Carl Fredericks	Rusty Lone
Miss Swift	Mary Orr

Tv Version

THE DESPERATE HOURS

An ABC-TV presentation. Produced by Daniel Melnick. Directed by Ted Kotcheff. Written by Clive Exton. **120 MIN.**

With: George Segal, Teresa Wright, Arthur Hill, Yvette Mimieux, Barry Primus, Michael Conrad, Michael Kearney, Dolph Sweet, Ralph Waite, Graham Jarvis, Martin Hulswit.

utation for profligacy.

With "Desperate Hours," he may succeed in remaining bankable, but in giving Hollywood the kind of impersonal pic he thinks it wants, he's undercutting his own talent.

De Laurentiis, coming off the collapse of his now-bankrupt company with this production for his new Dino De Laurentiis Communications, has slickly packaged a property that seems old-hat in a contemporary setting and is markedly inferior to the not-great William Wyler original.

Joseph Hayes' plot (first written as a novel, then as a play) is pure 1950s paranoia about three scruffy guys who invade the sanctity of the home, mocking a family's helplessness until Dad reasserts his control.

Despite being minimally updated with intensified blood and brutality on the part of the hoods and the authorities, "Desperate Hours" seems as familiar as the hostage situations that serve as ratings fodder on nightly newscasts, but with no new insights to offer.

The clunky script — credited to Lawrence Konner, Mark Rosenthal and Hayes — doesn't permit any vestige of humanity to Rourke, who's portrayed as a simple psycho with a low flash point, viciously brutalizing his improbably gorgeous pro-bono lawyer (Kelly Lynch) even as she helps him escape from prison.

Rourke, though bringing some leavening jocularity to the role, has to work against his typecasting as a scuz, and he can't begin to compare with memories of Humphrey Bogart.

Something's badly awry when Rourke's two henchmen (David Morse and Elias Koteas) seem much more complex than his character does.

Anthony Hopkins, in the Fredric March role of the initially weak-seeming father, brings his formidable skills to the task of involving the audience in the family's terror, but he seems mismatched with his estranged wife Mimi Rogers and implausibly reckless in his defiance of Rourke.

Rather than focusing the drama on the Hopkins (a highly successful criminal lawyer) outwitting the slower-witted thugs, the film makes him into a suburban Rambo.

In place of the original film's sheriff (Arthur Kennedy), who made it a priority to avoid endangering the lives of the hostages, the Cimino version has a demented FBI agent (Lindsay Crouse).

Doug Milsome's handsome lensing of the autumnal locations of the Colorado wilderness and suburban Salt Lake City (substituting for the Indianapolis setting of the original) is complemented by Victoria Paul's elegant production design of the Hopkins home. David Mansfield contributed a subtly creepy score.

— *Mac.*

MILL VALLEY

TOO MUCH SUN

A New Line Cinema release of a Cinetel Films production. Produced by Lisa M. Hansen. Directed by Robert Downey Sr. Exec producers, Seymour Morgenstern, Paul Hertzberg, Al Schwartz. Screenplay, Downey, Laura Ernst, Schwartz. Camera (Fotokem color), Robert Yeoman; editor, Joe D'Augustine; music, David Robbins; sound, Charles Kelly, David Brownlow; production design, Shawn Hausman; co-producers, John V. Stuckmeyer, Joe Bilella; associate producer, Catalaine Knell; assistant director, David Householter. Reviewed at Mill Valley (Calif.) Film Festival, Oct. 10, 1990. MPAA Rating: R. Running time: **110 MIN.**

Reed	Robert Downey Jr.
Sonny	Eric Idle
Bitsy	Andrea Martin
Father Kelly	Jim Haynie
Susan	Laura Ernst
George	Leo Rossi
Frank Jr.	Ralph Macchio
O. M.	Howard Duff
Gracia	Jennifer Rubin
Sister Ursula	Lara Harris
Frank Sr.	James Hong
Nurse	Melissa Jenkins

There's too little fun in "Too Much Sun," which is a shame because it has a promising premise and a great cast that turns on the heat but gets lost in the mirages of a wandering script.

Director Robert Downey Sr. has an eye for satire, and he's obviously set out to be outrageous with a story about two homosexual couples — male and female — trying to achieve parenthood before a Catholic priest steals the inheritance from the two siblings' father he more-or-less murdered.

Downey sets this up with Howard Duff as the dying dad, persuaded on his death bed by priest Jim Haynie to leave his millions to the church unless Eric Idle or Andrea Martin come up with a naturally conceived grandchild within a year.

Idle, however, is romantically paired with Leo Rossi, and Martin is wooing Laura Ernst. Any effort to change partners long enough to conceive might have been enough to make the picture work.

Downey starts in this direction, finding considerable amusement in the jealous bickering between the males over Idle's decision to impregnate Ernst. Initially, the romantic moment is laughable, too, with Ernst dressed as a boy to interest him and Idle wearing ladies' undies to get her aroused.

The director quickly loses interest in this course, however, and shifts to Martin's memory that she once had a baby out of wedlock many years earlier. He proves to be Ralph Macchio, partnered in a boiler-room operation with Robert Downey Jr.

The plot starts to thin as Downey struggles to bring Macchio and Downey Jr. into the story, relying on a farcical mistake by an increasingly crazy Martin that never jells. Even worse, the demands placed on Haynie and his nuns to remain menacingly present become increasingly cartoonish instead of clever.

Jennifer Rubin is good as a hooker hanging around the action, but by this point her part never pays off either. And James Hong is funny to watch as Martin's seedy, long-lost heterosexual interest. But he's excess baggage, too.

Whether it would be the way "Sun" satirizes priests or the way it ridicules homosexuals, there is certainly enough insult here for amusing irritation. Without more amusement, however, the waste of talent is just plain irritating.

— *Har.*

THE NEVERENDING STORY II: THE NEXT CHAPTER
(GERMAN)

A Warner Bros. release of a Time Warner Co. presentation of a Dieter Geissler production. Produced by Geissler. Executive producer, Tim Hampton. Directed by George Miller. Screenplay, Karin Howard, based on Michael Ende's novel "The Neverending Story"; camera (Panavision, Eastman color), Dave Connell; editor, Peter Hollywood, Chris Blunden; music, Robert Folk; songs, Giorgio Moroder; sound (Dolby), Chris Price; production design, Bob Laing, Götz Weidner; conceptual art, Ludwig Angerer; costume design, Heidi Weber; assistant director, Bert Batt; production manager, Norbert Preuss; special visual effects, Derek Meddings; creature effects, Colin Arthur; mattes supervisor, Albert T. Whitlock; stunt coordinator, Martin Grace; visual effects camera, Paul Wilson; coproducer, Bodo Scriba; associate producer, Klaus Kahler; casting, Hank McCann. Reviewed at Warner screening room, N.Y., Oct. 15, 1990. No MPAA Rating. Running time: **89 MIN.**
Bastian Bux . . . . . Jonathan Brandis
Atreyu . . . . Kenny Morrison
Xayide . . . . Clarissa Burt
Childlike empress . . Alexandra Johnes
Nimbly . . . . Martin Umbach
Barney Bux . . . . . John Wesley Shiff
Mrs. Bux . . . . Helena Michell
Tri Face . . . . Chris Burton
Koreander . . . . Thomas Hill
(English soundtrack)

This lavish sequel to the **1984 fantasy hit should score with international audiences (it bowed in Germany Oct. 26). Domestic b.o. will probably be mild, geared toward younger audiences.**

Followup, produced by Germans based in Munich with location filming in Canada, Argentina, Australia, France and Italy, is a natural, since first film directed by Wolfgang Petersen only covered half of Michael Ende's classic novel.

Part II utilizes a whole new cast (except for Thomas Hill, reprising as Koreander the bookseller) to depict adventures in the imaginary world of Fantasia. Main innovation is that young hero Bastian joins his fantasy counterpart Atreyu in a heroic trek in search of the childlike empress locked in her Ivory Tower in Fantasia, rather than just reading about him. Bastian's father (John Wesley Shipp, tv's "The Flash," taking over for Gerald McRaney this time) is back home in Washington state reading the tale in "The Neverending Story" book and rooting his offspring on.

Another improvement is the inclusion of a delicious villainess, dark beauty Clarissa Burt as Xayide, who suckers Bastian into making numerous wishes, each time losing a bit of his memory in return. This develops picture's main theme, how the basic human traits of memory and imagination gradually are being lost. As with Part I, a creeping emptiness gradually is overtaking the world of dreams, Fantasia, which needs Bastian's love and courage to fill its void.

Climax recalls elements of "The Wizard Of Oz," with Bastian outsmarting Xayide, who wants him to use his final wish merely to go home. Father-son bonding of the ending is also well-realized and will help the film in many territories such as the Far East where such themes are popular.

Film is effective in its own right, but as with most sequels, it lacks freshness. Since its subject matter is the power of imagination, this "one more time" aspect is a crucial flaw that should prevent its popularity from exceeding the original's.

American actress Burt is any adolescent boy's fantasy seductress. Rest of the cast is adequate, but a letdown compared with the original's. In particular, enthusiastic Jonathan Brandis as Bastian lacks the panache of Petersen's hero Barret Oliver, while Kenny Morrison has the right American Indian look but is stiff in Noah Hathaway's warrior role.

Young Alexandra Johnes, who made a good impression starring in "Zelly & Me" opposite Isabella Rossellini, has little to do here as the empress.

Colin Arthur's creatures encored from Part I are fun, including the doggy dragon Falkor and chummy monster Rock Biter, who gets a cute little kid this time. Globehopping locations and excellent matte shots create the most impressive fantasy world since Ridley Scott's "Legend." Aussie director George Miller does a good job of maintaining a serious tone and sprightly pace. He is the director of "The Man From Snowy River" and new to the WB family, not the George Miller who made "The Road Warrior," "The Witches Of Eastwick" and several other WB pics. Fellow Aussie Dave Connell has done an exemplary job of widescreen lensing and Robert Folk's romantic musical score is a plus.

— *Lor.*

THE SPIRIT OF '76

A Columbia release of a Black Diamond production for Commercial Pictures. Executive producers, Roman Coppola, Fred Fuchs. Producers, Susie Landau, Simon Edery. Written and directed by Lucas Reiner, based on a story by Coppola and Reiner. Camera (Deluxe color), Stephen Lighthill; editor, Glen Scantlebury; music, David Nichtern; production design, Daniel Talpers; costume design, Sofia Coppola; art direction, Isabella Kirkland; set decoration, Thomas Weigand, Victoria Ruskin; casting, Susie Landau. Reviewed at Warner Hollywood studio theater, Los Angeles, Oct. 18, 1990. MPAA Rating: PG-13. Running time: **82 MIN.**
Adam-11 . . . . David Cassidy
Chanel-6 . . . . Olivia D'Abo
Heinz 57 . . . . Geoff Hoyle
Chris . . . . Jeff McDonald
Tommy . . . . Steve McDonald
Rodney . . . . Liam O'Brien
Eddie . . . . Leif Garrett
Dr. Von Mobil . . . . Carl Reiner
Dr. Cash . . . . Rob Reiner

Which American decade would you least want to spend the price of a cinema ticket to revisit in a time machine? If you said the '70s, this appropriately tacky low-budget comedy from Commercial Pictures is likely to disappear a lot faster than disco.

Pic's frazzled time-travel plot mimics "Bill & Ted's Excellent Adventure," but while those dudes went spinning through history from one bodacious century to another, this film is mostly stuck in 1976 — one very bad fashion year.

Brothers Jeff and Steve McDonald (of '70s retro-rock group Red Kross) do a modified "Bill & Ted" routine, but they're not time travelers, they're teenagers stuck living in the '70s and dumbfounded why anyone would want to come back from the future to record it (viewers will be too — was it really this bad?).

With their waist-length hair, striped bellbottoms and dizzy-sweet attitudes, this pair is a lot more fun than the pic's real protaganists — ex-Partridge David Cassidy, prissy Newton-John clone Olivia d'Abo and clownish Geoff Hoyle — who've come back from the future searching for "the birth of the nation" in the year 1776 but missed it by 200 years.

You can't blame them for being confused, the filmmakers might posit, what with the Bicentennial celebration going on and mementos of '76 being exploited by merchants and the media all over the place.

But viewers will blame them for being unbearably dimwitted, for being horribly dressed, for being in this movie.

Comedic flogging is provided by Liam O'Brien as hyperactive nerd Rodney Snodgrass, a kind of overemotional Pee-wee Herman, who wants to steal the time machine's battery so he can win the school science fair. A thirty-something Leif Garrett (that's two '70s teen idols in one movie) is squeezed into white bellbottoms, a polyester patterned shirt and puka beads to play Rodney's disco dancin' older brother.

Responsible for all this are the sons and daughters of some of Hollywood's finest — writer and director Lucas Reiner, son of Carl, who's in the movie, and brother of Rob, who's also in the movie; exec producer and co-writer Roman Coppola, son of Francis; producer Susie Landau, daughter of Martin; and more assorted relatives.

Pic is not without laughs, and Reiner achieves a kind of lackadaisical, trash-as-art amusement factor that earns some points in the guilty pleasures department.

Soundtrack songs play a major role, but this isn't about nostalgia. With tunes like "Midnight At The Oasis" and "Kung Fu Fighting," it's obvious the filmmakers are trying to like rully rully gross us out.

Kudos to the design team for a perversely loving re-creation of the era, from cars to furniture to consumer products, and to Cassidy for not aging a bit (he looks a mature 21).

Columbia is test-marketing the film in Austin, Texas, and Seattle, where it opened Oct. 12.
— *Daws.*

NEUROTIC CABARET

A Kipp Prods. presentation. Executive producer, Tammy Stones. Written and produced by John Woodward, Stones. Directed by Woodward. Camera (color), Danny Anaya; editor, Woodward; music, John Mills; sound, Scott Szabo; production design, John Perdichi; costume design, Angela Keen; associate producer, Pamela Lane. Reviewed at Bel Air theater, Houston, Texas, Sept. 1, 1990. No MPAA rating. Running time: **85 MIN.**
Terri . . . . Tammy Stones
Nolan . . . . Edwin Neal
Nick . . . . Dennis Worthington
Annette . . . . Colleen Keegan
Pat . . . . Pat Kelly
Cheo . . . . Paul Vasquez

Art imitates life, but to no great effect, in "Neurotic Caba-

ret," a vanity production that will be hard-pressed to attract an audience beyond the Houston topless-bar scene it so leeringly glamorizes. Even as exploitation fodder, it fails miserably: There's too little sex and too much silliness.

Pic's all about a would-be actress who raises money for her director-boyfriend's first film (and her first starring vehicle) by dancing at an exotic nightclub. Tammy Stones, the star, exec producer and co-scripter of the piece, reportedly researched her role by dancing topless at Rick's, a notorious Houston nitery where much of the film was shot.

Rank has its privileges: Stones never strips beyond her lacy bra and panties. But a few of her co-stars are not so modest.

Director and co-writer John Woodward, Stones' real-life significant other, tries to play the situation for broad laughs. Most of the gags are of the wink-wink, nudge-nudge variety. There is some mildly offensive stereotyping in the pic's mocking depictions of Hispanic and gay characters. But, then again, they seem no more thick-witted than the straight WASP types on view.

The filmmakers have difficulty maintaining the light, bright tone when Terri (Stones) graduates from stripping and vamping for tips to setting up a slick Mexican high roller (Paul Vasquez) for a shakedown.

While she distracts the fellow in a hotel bed, her director boyfriend (Edwin Neal) tries to break into his money-stuffed briefcase. Terri has to do a lot of distracting, which doesn't seem to upset her. That's when a dumb movie begins to turn downright sleazy.

Only Colleen Keegan makes much of an impression, playing a topless dancer with the voice, and feistiness, of Holly Hunter. The other performances range from barely adequate to embarrassing.

Technical credits are no better than they absolutely have to be. The title, incidentally, has nothing whatsoever to do with the film. — *Ley.*

THE APPLEGATES

A Roadshow release (Australia) of a New World Intl. presentation in association with Cinemarque Entertainment. Executive producer, Christopher Webster. Produced by Denise Di Novi. Directed by Michael Lehmann. Screen-

play, Redbeard Simmons, Lehmann; camera (color), Mitchell Dubin; associate producer, Iya Labunka. Reviewed at Village Roadshow theater, Sydney, Oct. 16, 1990. Running time: **82 MIN.**
Dick Applegate . . . . . Ed Begley Jr.
Jane Applegate . . Stockard Channing
Sally Applegate . . . . . Cami Cooper
Johnny Applegate . . . . Bobby Jacoby
Aunt Bea . . . . Dabney Coleman
Greg Samson . . . . . . Glenn Shaddix
Vince Samson . . . . Adam Biesk
Sheriff Heidegger . Roger Aaron Brown
Dottie . . . . Savannah Smith Boucher
Kevin . . . . Philip Arthur Ross
Kenny . . . . Steven Robert Ross

Can a family of giant Brazilian cockroaches impersonate a typical American family? They can and do in Michael Lehmann's "The Applegates," an off-the-wall but very funny followup to his weird 1988 debut "Heathers" that has definite cult potential.

Film — also titled "Meet The Applegates" — is being released in the U.S. early next year. In Oz, Roadshow is releasing via indie screens, which are promoting the film as an "eco-comedy."

In "Heathers," Lehmann gave a bizarre twist to the usual portrayal of U.S. teen life. In this pic he takes an even more extreme approach to sending up American family life. In a bid to save the Brazilian rain forest from development, a family of giant beetles is sent to infiltrate American society and blow up a nuclear power station as a warning.

Chameleon-like, they assume the form of humans, and, learning from a "Fun With Dick And Jane" reader, become the average American family. Scope for satire here certainly presents new opportunities, to say the least: surrounded by temptations in a community-minded town in Ohio, the family soon degenerates, with Dick having an affair, Jane becoming obsessed with credit and alcohol (grasshoppers are a favorite), Johnny turning into a dope dealer, Sally becoming pregnant and Spot the dog (a baby bug) falling prey to their neighbor, an exterminator played by Glenn Shaddix.

Such a wacky premise could derail easily, but Lehmann handles it with humor and paces it well. Begley and company play it for all it's worth, and seem to be having a ball. Cami Cooper is particularly good as the girl next door who turns rotten, and scenes of the Applegates becoming bugs (usually with disastrous consequences) are cleverly done.

However, pic's ending, with the redoubtable Dabney Coleman as the beetle queen taking over the planned sabotage, borders on tiresome, and any intended environmental message comes across as trite given the screwball tone of the pic.

Nevertheless, word of mouth among those who like offbeat humor could create added interest in "The Applegates." Essentially it's a lot of fun, and that's never been bad for business.
— *Doch.*

CHINA CRY

A Penland release of a TBN Films presentation of a Parakletos production. Produced by Don LeRoy Parker. Executive producer, Paul F. Crouch. Written and directed by James F. Collier, based on the book by Nora Lam and Irene Burke. Camera (CFI color), David Worth; editor, Duane Hartzell; music, Al Kasha, Joel Hirschhorn; sound, Michael Strong; production design, Norman Baron; art director, Jonathan Cheung; set decoration, Linda Allen; costume design, Gigi Choa; associate producers, Ele Parker & Matt Crouch; assistant director, Larry Lipton. Reviewed at CFI Film Labs screening room, Los Angeles, Oct. 23, 1990. MPAA Rating: PG-13. Running time: **107 MIN.**
Sung Neng Yee . . . Julia Nickson-Soul
Lam Cheng Shen . . . . Russell Wong
Dr. Sung . . . . James Shigeta
Mrs. Sung . . . . France Nuyen
Col. Cheng . . . . Philip Tan

First film production from Trinity Broadcasting Network, a Christian media organization, boasts a stirring character portrait and sparkling performance by Julia Nickson-Soul, but is marred by a tedious second half. Despite the pic's handsomely mounted material, a true story of escape from communist China in the '50s, the result is too uneven to sweep general audiences.

Based on the book by Nora Lam, who escaped from China in 1958, and Irene Burke, pic is a striking portrait of Lam as a vigorously self-determined young woman who took control of her destiny down to pursuing her husband-to-be.

The privileged daughter of a doctor who loses everything when the Japanese invade Shanghai in 1941, Lam, known then as Sung Neng Yee, emerges as a gifted and confident university student eager to play a part in the Communists' "new society."

She's soon disillusioned when the party accuses her father of a "crime against the people" and humiliates him, then begins to persecute her for a youthful flirtation with Christianity.

She's tortured, and then sent before a firing squad. But in a vaguely explained sequence, she miraculously survives when a lightning flash temporarily blinds the gunmen, an event that solidifies her growing Christian faith. Later she's sentenced to work in a labor camp.

Lam arranges for her husband's escape to Hong Kong with a temporary exit visa, and eventually she gets her own visa and follows him.

Nickson-Soul, who appeared in the NBC-TV miniseries "Noble House" and "Around The World In Eighty Days," carries the picture squarely on her young shoulders, exuding a fearlessness and fineness that seem bred in her.

Pic's early reels ride on her romance with aloof law student Lam Cheng Shen (Russell Wong), whom she marries, but the momentum created by this attractive young couple winds down as pic proceeds.

Rather than making Lam's escape from China a turning point, filmmakers save it for the very end, dwelling way too long on repetitive abuses and bureaucratic frustrations that precede it.

Though "Cry" initially seems a strong bet for family entertainment, younger children are likely to be bored to death in second hour.

Production is lavish in some respects, vividly depicting daily life in newly communist China. But it demonstrates admirable economy in some key scenes, including the wedding and a waterfront sendoff.

Director James F. Collier, who also scripted, begins the pic on a stagy note with a melodramatic depiction of the Japanese invasion. He finds an effective rhythm in middle scenes involving Nickson-Soul, but he loses it again in later reels involving the labor camps.

Vivid lensing was achieved by director of photography David Worth, a veteran of such mainstream commercial pics as "Any Which Way You Can."

About $5.5 million of pic's $6.6 million budget was raised via nonreturnable donations from TBN viewers, based on exec producer and TBN founder Paul Crouch's avowed desire to return inspiring family fare to cinemas.

Pic is opening at 200 sites in 25 U.S. cities Nov. 2. — *Daws.*

ANTIGONE/RITES FOR THE DEAD

An ASA Communications release of an Eclipse production. Produced and directed by Amy Greenfield. Screenplay, Greenfield, based on Sophocles' plays "Antigone" and "Oedipus At Colonus"; camera (Duart & TVC color, 16m), Hilary Harris, Judy Irola; editor, Greenfield, Bernard Hajdenberg; music, Glenn Branca, Diamanda Galas, Paul Lemos, Elliott Sharp, David Van Tieghem; sound, Hajdenberg; costume design, Betty Howard, Jane Townsend; choreography, Greenfield; assistant directors, Barbara Fisher, Allessandra Ross; associate producer, Robert Haller. Reviewed at Museum of Modern Art, N.Y., Oct. 16, 1990. No MPAA Rating. Running time: **85 MIN.**
Antigone . . . . Amy Greenfield
Oedipus/Creon . . . . . Bertram Ross
Ismene . . . . Janet Eilber
Haemon . . . . Sean McElory
Polynices . . . . Henry Montes
Eteocles . . . . Silvio Facchin

Director Amy Greenfield's ambition far exceeds her technical grasp in "Antigone/Rites For The Dead." Silent film version of two Sophocles plays is of academic interest, though ASA Communications is staging a theatrical release.

Starring herself as "Antigone," Greenfield interprets the tragic saga of Oedipus' daughter in terms of dance and movement. Imagery resembles that of the climax of Ken Russell's innovative (and silent) rock opera film "Tommy," with opening reel of rock climbing and final shot of Antigone's sister Ismene reaching for the heavens.

Though her ensemble of dancers, including Bertram Ross and Janet Eilber, excel at the living-theater contortions, Greenfield errs in overuse of closeup photography, inimical to capturing performance on film. Her occasional long shots (filmed in Massachusetts, New Hampshire and New York) are impressive in the manner of Pier Paolo Pasolini's Greek tragedies, and the film would have benefited from a more austere approach.

Ross stands out among the performers, playing both Oedipus and his successor Creon in radically different personas. Adopting modern dress as Creon, he strides around imperiously with the severe mien of Alain Cuny.

Greenfield and Eilber overdo the thrashing about but each has her moments. Filmmaker has little use for language, reducing the text to spoon-fed voiceover

exposition that sounds like telegram writing. An overbearing musical score branded "modern" drones incessantly; it might have been more interesting to go against the grain and use a jazz score. — *Lor.*

OLD EXPLORERS

A Taurus Entertainment release of a River Road Prods. films. Produced by David Herbert, William Pohlad, Tom Jenz. Directed and written by Pohlad, based on the play by James Cada and Mark Keller. Camera (Technicolor), Jeffrey Laszlo; editor, Miroslav Janek; music, Billy Barber; sound (Dolby), Matt Quast; production designer, Peter Stolz; costume design, Tessie Bundick; production manager, Sherry Virsen; co-producer, Robert Schwartz; assistant director, Eric Heffron; casting, Riki Wuolle. Reviewed at Centennial Lakes Cinema, Edina, Minn., Oct. 10, 1990. MPAA Rating: PG. Running time: **91 MIN.**
Warner Watney . . . . . . Jose Ferrer
Leinen Roth . . . . . James Whitmore
Alex Watney . . . . . Jeffrey Gadbois
Leslie Watney . . . . . Caroline Kaiser
Tugboat captain . . . William Warfield
Billy Watney . . . Christopher Pohlad
Scott Watney . . . . Storm Richardson
Lafitte . . . . Dominique Berrand
Nurse . . . . Molly Atwood
Watch commander . . . James Cada
Waiter . . . . Marn Evan Jacobs
Priest . . . . Peter Stolz
City bartender . . . Kristen Andersen
Mongol warrior . . . . . . Peter Moore
Soho harlot . . . . Mary Rehbein
Woman with dog . . . . Tessie Bundick
First policeman . . . . Tom Jenz
Second policeman . . . . David Herbert
Sailor . . . . Clark Sanford
Soccer team . . . . . . Jeffrey Smalley,
Patrick Stolz, Shawn Trusten

"Old Explorers" is an agonizingly slow-moving character study with no appreciable audience. Given its two w.k. stars, unknown to today's young filmgoers, its best outlets may be cable and video.

Title roles refer to a pair of aging Indiana Joneses who get their kicks from imaginary adventures. As explorer Henry Stanley and archaeologist Heinrich Schliemann, they get together once a week to play mind games, searching for the lost city of Atlantis and other fabled treasures.

The script is talky and ponderous, and humor is lacking. The picture says something about the pain of growing old but never really comes to grips with the problem. "Old Explorers," adapted for the screen from a play by James Cada and Mark Keller, worked better on the stage than it does, augmented by special effects, on the screen.

Jose Ferrer and James Whitmore do the best they can with the soggy material. In the only supporting roles of note, Jeffrey Gadbois and Caroline Kaiser are okay as Ferrer's son and daughter-in-law. Cinematography is so-so. Best of the technical credits is Billy Barber's original score.

The film preemed in Minneapolis where much of it was lensed. Subsequent fall openings in New York, Los Angeles, Seattle and Miami are tentative.

— *Rees.*

NAKED TANGO

A Scotia Intl. release (in Germany) of a Sugarloaf/Gotan production in association with Towa Prod. Co., Praesens-Film, Grupo Baires. Produced by David Weisman. Written and directed by Leonard Schrader. Camera, Juan Ruiz-Anchia; editor, Lee Percy, Debra McDermott; music, Thomas Newman; sound, Jose Luis Diaz; production design, Anthony Pratt; costume design, Patricio Bisso; art direction, Tom Sanders; set decoration, Coca Oderigo; choreography, Carlos Rivarola; associate producers, James W. Skotchdopole, Tony Payne; co-producers, Milena Canonero, Michael Maiello; assistant director, Fernando Bassi, casting, David Rubin, Laura Kennedy. Reviewed at Big Time Studios, Los Angeles, Calif., Oct. 10, 1990. No MPAA Rating. Running time: **93 MIN.**
Cholo . . . . Vincent D'Onofrio
Stephanie/Alba . . . . . . Mathilda May
Zico Borenstein . . . . . . Esai Morales
Judge Torres . . . . . . Fernando Rey
Mama . . . . Cipe Lincovsky
Bertoni the jeweler . . . . Josh Mostel
Gaston the hairdresser . Patricio Bisso

Tango equals sex equals death in writer-director Leonard Schrader's fatally dark exploration of the 1920s tango underworld. **Too morbid and narrowly conceived to interest mainstream audiences, this highly stylized pic, now playing in Germany, is likely to pass its theatrical life in the shadows.**

"Tango" was created by Schrader and producer David Weisman, who also collaborated on the breakthrough indie hit "Kiss Of The Spider Woman."

Schrader scripted "Kiss" from Argentine writer Manuel Puig's play; the genesis for "Tango" was found among Puig's unpublished manuscripts about the Buenos Aires underworld of the '20s. The film is credited onscreen as "inspired by" the late playwright.

Production casts French actress Mathilda May as Stephanie, restless new bride of a wealthy, elderly Argentine judge (Fernando Rey). She slips her leash while on board a ship bound for Buenos Aires and trades identities with a waif who has just

hurled herself overboard.

From the other miss' diary, May learns she is now Alma, a Polish mail-order bride bound for a rendezvous with her future husband on the docks.

He proves to be handsome young Zico (Esai Morales), part of a wealthy Jewish household, and the future looks pleasant.

But nothing is what it seems — a basic tenet of "Tango." Zico is actually a gangster and a pimp who runs a tango bordello with his mercenary, cold-hearted mother (Cipe Lincovsky) and aloof, brutal "tango king" brother, Cholo (Vincent D'Onofrio).

Alma murders the first john they send her; after that the pic becomes a sort of underlit gangster chase thriller as the local mafia, known as the Black Hand, demands a sacrifice for the killing.

Alma knows she's protected if she can get Cholo on her side, so she goes after the unattainable Hun. Resulting scenes of arrogant tango and degrading sex are likely to appeal only to a fringe element.

This romanceless pic hasn't much driving it other than its narcotic decadence and its conceits about the nature of intense sexual passion (a hurtling toward death) versus real love.

Unfortunately, there is none of the latter on the screen.

But first-time director Schrader (brother of director-screenwriter Paul) has put a vivid and specific vision on the screen. His bordello world crawls with menace, brutal deception and the poetry of the afflicted. His boldness with high melodrama is somewhat diminished by the sometimes-clumsy gangster action scenes.

In fact, if a vision of hell were required, this place would fill the bill, with Zico an apt tour guide.

Pic's performances are nothing to compare with the depth of those in "Spider Woman." Here, the characters' complexities are all in what they stand for, not in who they are. D'Onofrio radiates dangerous presence, sexuality and physical style, but the role is limiting.

Morales, so potent in "La Bamba," never seems at ease in the unflattering role of Zico and gives a pallid portrayal. May has the spirit and looks for her part, but adds nothing to the role's cardboard outlines.

Choreography by Carlos Rivarola is surprisingly sparse. Pho-

tography by Juan Ruiz-Anchia cloaks the film in dramatic darkness appropriate to its vision. Lush, imaginative production design by Anthony Pratt and all art-related work are firstrate.

— *Daws.*

A.W.O.L.
(LIONHEART)

An Imperial Entertainment presentation and production. (Universal release in U.S.) Produced by Ash R. Shah, Eric Karson. Executive producers, Sunil R. Shah, Anders P. Jensen, Sundip R. Shah. Directed by Sheldon Lettich. Screenplay, Lettich, Jean-Claude van Damme; camera (color), Robert New; editor, Mark Conte; music, John Scott; production design, Gregory Pickerell. Reviewed at Cannes Film Festival (market), May 18, 1990. Running time: **105 MIN.**
Lyon . . . . . Jean-Claude van Damme
Cynthia . . . . . . Deborah Rennard
Joshua . . . . Harrison Page
Helene . . . . Lisa Pelikan
Nicole . . . . Ashley Johnson
Russell . . . . Brian Thompson

A primitive, clichéd film set in the New York and Los Angeles bare-knuckles fight circuit, "A.W.O.L." is also known as "Wrong Bet" and will be labeled "Lionheart" for its U.S. release. Good initial business at action houses can be expected ahead of surefire homevid sales.

Director Sheldon Lettich and co-writing star Jean-Claude van Damme move their film forward at a fast clip. The well-staged and violent fights occur at five-minute intervals.

Plot has van Damme deserting the French Foreign Legion to rescue a brother involved with L.A. drug dealers. He arrives to find his brother dead. The young widow and small daughter left behind turn their backs on the legionnaire, thinking he caused it all.

In the U.S., the deserter also has to fight the lady crook who runs the fights and two thugs sent by the Foreign Legion to bring him back. There is fun in the way Deborah Rennard plays the lady, and she is well supported by Brian Thompson as her bodyguard. Harrison Page is fast-talking and witty as the ex-streetfighter who chaperones van Damme through violence and romance.

The punching is relieved by romantic, sentimental interludes involving the widow and child. Van Damme moves with near-balletic grace and is handsome in

an old-fashioned hero way.

— *Kell.*

GOD AFTON, HERR WALLENBERG
(GOOD EVENING, MR. WALLENBERG)
(SWEDISH)

A Sandrew Film release of Sandrew Film production with Scansat/TV3, the Swedish Film Institute, Filmhuset and Film Teknik in association with Hunnia Film Studios (Budapest). Produced by Katinka Faragó. Executive producer, Klas Olofsson. Written and directed by Kjell Grede. Camera (color), Esa Vuorinen; editor, Darek Hodor; music, János Solyom, Frans Helmersson; sound, Björn Gunnarsson; production design, László Gardonyi; costume design, Inger Pehrsson; production management, Thomas Nilsson, Lajos Ovari; assistant director, Zsuzsa Gurban. Reviewed at the Astoria, Stockholm, Oct. 5, 1990. Running time: **115 MIN.**
Raoul Wallenberg . Stellan Skarsgard
Marja . . . . Katharina Thalbach
Szamosi . . . . Károly Eperjes
Ferenc Moser . . . . Miklós B. Szekely
Stockholm rabbi . . . Erland Josephson
Marja's Papa . . . . Franciszek Pieczka
Officer . . . . Jesper Christensen
Eichmann . . . . László Soós

"Good Evening, Mr. Wallenberg" is a somber exploration of one man's venture into the heart of Nazi darkness to save 65,000 Jews from death in the Budapest ghetto in January 1945, the eve of the victorious USSR army's arrival. The film has unique cinematic atmosphere and will find a place in arthouses everywhere.

The man, Swedish diplomat Raoul Wallenberg, was whisked away by the Russians and never see again. The film shows him waving goodbye to some Jewish friends he has saved but does not speculate on his fate.

Veteran writer-helmer Kjell Grede's film has the clear ring of truth, but this truth does not include conventional heroics, and the thriller element is limited to the feelings evoked by watching ordinary men (German troopers and Hungarian Nyilas collaborators) wantonly and willfully kill ordinary men and women (the many Jews that Wallenberg did not get to rescue after all).

Wallenberg (portrayed by Stellan Skarsgard), is a former small-scale international businessman who has been sheltered by his family wealth. Inspired by "The Scarlet Pimpernel," he becomes a man with a mission, an artist who has finally found his true skill.

Sent to Budapest in December 1944 and semi-attached to the Swedish Embassy, Wallenberg uses the embassy's immunity status to shelter hundreds of Jews sought by Eichmann's Sonderkommando. He issues Swedish passports to others or hides them from the Nazis and Hungarian Nyilas.

Grede focuses on 20 Jews, captured and left under guard in the back of a broken-down truck. Wallenberg visits them constantly, waving papers and threats at the guards. He also visits a trio of Jews in an apartment overlooking the street on which the truck is stalled.

"Good Evening, Mr. Wallenberg" strictly adheres to historically recorded names and deeds, but Grede's storytelling challenges the meaning of truth and reality. Grede is clearly indebted to Kafka for much inspiration.

Finnish cinematographer Esa Vuorinen's work is intimate even when calling for large-scale frames and action. Production credits are of the highest order, and the bits of classical music and piano improvisations enhance the overall glum mood while reminding audiences of beauty lost.

Skarsgard, whose international career began with roles in "The Unbearable Lightness Of Being" and "The Hunt For Red October," acts with quiet desperation throughout. He is well supported, particularly by Erland Josephson as a skeptical Stockholm rabbi, Katharina Thalbach as a Jewish woman and Jesper Christensen as a German officer in charge of a morbidly conducted art auction in a bombed-out site. — *Kell.*

MILL VALLEY

HARD ACT TO FOLLOW

A Green Line production. Produced by Terry Eubanks. Directed by Issam B. Makdissy. Screenplay, Eubanks; camera (color), Emiko Omori; editor, John Nutt, Makdissy; music, Todd Boekelheide; sound, Dan Gleish; art direction, Bruce Mink; assistant director, Kristine Peterson. Reviewed at Mill Valley (Calif.) Film Festival, Oct. 8, 1990. No MPAA rating. Running time: 99 MIN.
Sami . . . . Mark Taylor
Curt . . . . Kent Minault
Rachel . . . . Deborah Mosca
Jihad . . . . Rafik Assad
Rubadub . . . . J.J. Johnson
Debbie . . . . Shanda Sawyer
Tony . . . . David Martin
Joan . . . . Lori Beth Holden
Jimmy . . . . Durand Garcia
Koko . . . . Rick Bruno
Mother . . . . Pamela Marsh
Marty . . . . Jackson
Frankie . . . . Frank Ergus
Paul . . . . Doug Ferrari

Times always are tough for any little independent picture like "Hard Act To Follow," with no stars and a gritty story about a suicidal central character. Times are doubly tough when the film seeks sympathy for Arab-Americans.

That's not to say they don't deserve it and "Act" is hardly a political picture, anyway. Still, director Issam B. Makdissy draws his conflict from the civil war in Beirut and its impact on a second-generation Lebanese in the U.S. and his family.

Carrying most of the dramatic load, Mark Taylor is excellent as a standup comic whose greatest ambition is to be the second-best-known American Lebanese after Danny Thomas. On a visit to the old country, however, he's briefly drawn into the war and returns to the U.S. haunted by what he saw and took part in.

It's grim going as Taylor's nightmares worsen and his personality deteriorates, lightened only a little by his new friendship with J.J. Johnson and a couple of other winos. Unfortunately, Makdissy and writer-producer Terry Eubanks don't reveal until the very end what torments Taylor so.

But "Act" seems to be a thoroughly honest picture, and it's certainly different. — *Har.*

THE MONEY TREE

A Black Sheet Film, produced by Christopher Dienstag. Directed by Alan Dienstag. Dialog improvised from story by Alan and Christopher Dienstag; camera, Don Bonato; editor, Susan Crutcher; music, Lorin Rowan. Reviewed at Mill Valley (Calif.) Film Festival, Oct. 7, 1990. No MPAA rating. Running time: 94 MIN.
David . . . . . . Christopher Dienstag
Erica . . . . Monica T. Caldwell
Chad . . . . Nik Martin
Girlfriend . . . . . Kathrine Schutzman
Vincent . . . . Malcolm Cohen
Charly . . . . . Richard Roughgarden
Pasquel . . . . Carlos Deloche
Rusty . . . . Gregory Wilker

Normally, nothing but horror could be expected from "The Money Tree," which stars the producer, is directed by his father and is a totally ad-libbed outing with a local Marin County cast. But the finished product is actually quite good.

Relaxed and casual all the way, producer-star Christopher Dienstag is on-camera most of the time as a rather agreeable young man trying to get his marijuana crop to market despite the ravages of weather, wild pigs and pestilence, plus patrolling police officers and rip-off artists.

Success, of course, is not going to get this aspiring entrepreneur into the 4-H Club. But the weed remains a good cash crop, and Dienstag prefers it to a regular job in the family business of his insistent girlfriend (Monica T. Caldwell.)

In addition to bucolic shots of beautiful woods and enough plant pampering for an agricultural documentary, director Alan Dienstag mainly advances the plot through a series of simple scenes with friends and enemies.

Though each scene could be labeled "now here is where the girlfriend gets mad" and "here is where the bad guys try to steal the dope," the cast makes the encounters convincing (except where wide shots reveal the nervous actors' stiff and fluttering fingers) and the story becomes involving.

A couple of terrific scenes, in fact, probably could not have been improved upon with pages of script, particularly Dienstag's barroom discussion of love with Kathrine Schutzman and his talks about responsiblity with Nik Martin.

"The Money Tree" amounts to a good feature to be dubbed to videotape — the kind you take around looking for more work. — *Har.*

TERMINAL BLISS

A Distant Horizon production. Produced by Brian Cox. Executive producer, Anant Singh. Written and directed by Jordan Alan. Camera (Technicolor), Gregory Smith; editor, Bruce Sinofsky; music, Frank W. Becker; sound, Pawel Wdowczak; production design, Catherine Tirr; art direction, David Poses; associate producers, Paul Janssen, Sudhir Pragjee, Sanjeev Singh, Mickey Nivelli; assistant director, Tom Willey; casting, Linda Phillips Palo. Reviewed at Mill Valley (Calif.) Film Festival, Oct. 6, 1990. No MPAA rating. Running time: 91 MIN.
Alex . . . . Tim Owen
John . . . . Luke Perry
Stevie . . . . Estee Chandler
Kirsten . . . . Sonia Curtis
Bucky . . . . Micah Grant
Craig . . . . Alexis Arquette
Tanya . . . . Heather Jones Challenge
Judy . . . . Susan Nichols
Jack . . . . Bruce Taylor

Definitely a fine first feature for 21-year-old writer-director Jordan Alan, "Terminal Bliss" shows just enough overwriting and underdirecting to miss its mark. Presumably, though, Alan will progress with both crafts, especially if he's able as a writer to work with a seasoned director or able to direct a more experienced writer.

Still, it's a pleasure to find a picture about teenagers who talk instead of toss food at each other. Even better, when they do talk, Alan's teens generally take an honest look at their contributions to their own problems.

Unfortunately, many of the conversational exchanges would have been worthy of philosophers in ancient Athens. That's not to say that today's young people aren't capable of that or even that they don't reach such heights of insight at moments; but it's doubtful they talk as grandly as the characters so often do in "Terminal Bliss."

Otherwise, Alan has a keen eye for the problems of his peers, and his young cast is splendid, especially the three leads (Tim Owen, Luke Perry and Estee Chandler) caught in a delusional love triangle, plus a superb supporting turn by Alexis Arquette as their Deadhead pal.

The setting is familiar: The suburbs and second homes of the young and beautiful who can find no purpose for their lives beyond fast cars, quick sex and lots and lots of drugs.

Owen stops to think about what that all means while his friend Perry rushes toward destruction and Chandler vacillates between them. If not exactly fresh, it's still real.

There isn't, of course, one single admirable adult in the whole picture. That's neither fresh nor real. But maybe the adults will appear as Alan grows older. — *Har.*

HISTORIAS DE LARGATOS
(LIZARDS' TALES)
(CHILEAN)

A Third World Newsreel release of a Producciones Bustamante production. Produced by Silvia Camposano. Written and directed by Juan Carlos Bustamante. Camera (color), Toño Farías, Juan Osvaldo Claramount; editor, Bustamante, Pedro Chaskel; music, Jaime de Aguirre; sound, Miguel Hormazábel. Reviewed at Chicago Latino Film Festival, Sept. 29, 1990. Running time: **80 MIN.**
With: José Soza, Roberto Espina, Gloria Barrera, María de los Angeles Lazo, Oscar Zimmerman, Gonzalo Febres, Alvaro Sepúlveda, Alejandro Trejo, Pamela Estay, Juan Muhr, Mariana Prat, Mario Peña.

Chilean helmer Juan Carlos Bustamante's second directorial effort, "Lizards' Tales," is an anthology pic of three dense, imagistic incidences in northern Chile's barren countryside. Film is finding select screenings at arthouses and festivals and seems best fitted to the nontheatrical market.

Chile's vast countryside, inhabited by shepherds and poor country folk, is the principal character in Bustamante's abstract vision. In the end, the landscape controls the lives of those who live there.

Initial story, "The Skies," concerns the flight of two men across this broad terrain, wandering by truck, by horse, on foot and eventually by boat. One of the men is wounded, which gives the tale urgency. Are they criminals? Are they political prisoners? Where are they going? The story picks them up mid-journey and deposits them still on the trail as they row into the distance. Scenes are punctuated by images of flags waving in silhouette.

"The Son" deals with a drifter who is persuaded to play the part of a prodigal son who left his father alone many years earlier.

The final story, "Antón," is a fragmented portrait of a man who destroys everything he comes into contact with: a woman who comes to visit, farm animals and the lizards of the title. He sees himself as a lizard, alone, staring at the road endlessly waiting for something, anything.

Story fragments are well paced, while tech credits are strictly low budget: 16m lensing is uneven and synchronization of minimal dialog is awkward.
— *Lent.*

O CIRCULO DE FOGO
(FIRE CIRCLE)
(BRAZILIAN)

An Aquarela Produções production in association with Embrafilme. Written and directed by Geraldo Rocha Moraes. Camera (color), Walter Carvalho; editor, Walter Goulart; art direction, Malú Moraes; set decoration, Rachel Arruda. Reviewed at Chicago Latino Film Festival, Sept. 29, 1990. Running time: **100 MIN.**
Luciana . . . . Cristina Prochaska
Alfonso . . . . Tonico Pereira
Mayor . . . . Ednei Giovenazzi
Tapuio . . . . Roberto Bomfim
Das Doresz . . . . Malú Moraes
Father Ernesto . . Venarando Ribeiro

Second feature by Brasilia-based filmmaker Geraldo Rocha Moraes, "Fire Circle," won't set any blazes internationally with its muddled recounting of a power struggle in the Brazilian outback.

Full of local color, drama is sparked by the murder of a rural worker over a land dispute. When village priest Father Ernesto (Venarando Ribeiro) demands an investigation, he ruffles the feathers of the local strong-arm mayor (Ednei Giovenazzi), a wealthy landowner who ordered the crime.

In an effort to pressure the priest, the mayor hikes taxes at the town market where the priest runs a pottery store, forcing the store to close its doors.

The mayor is not without repentance. He has been a bad boy and his maid, Das Doresz, a candomblé priestess, dresses as the mayor's stern mother and whips him for his vile deeds.

Such repentance is not enough for the priest, leading the mayor to pressure the bishop to have the priest transferred to another town.

In a parallel story, Luciana (Cristina Prochaska), a potter rumored to be a witch, is tricked by her tv-watching brother Alfonso, the mayor's right-hand man, into taking over the store. He nurses incestuous feelings for her and is furious because she has taken up with a former ally of the priest and an instigator of revolt at the market.

With all of these plot elements, Rocha Moraes loses control over the meandering storyline. Basic conflict falls apart when the priest is transferred and the central struggle averted. The opposing role shifts to Luciana, but this conflict is also avoided when the mayor suddenly gives in and resigns. The story once again shifts focus, to the less-interesting tale of Luciana's attempt to break free of her brother.

Theme is not without interest, yet stylistic devices inserted into the story also tend to diffuse the narrative. Magical elements, such as miraculous healing and bursts of flame, come off as confusing, obfuscating the filmmaker's intentions.

Also interesting is the use of the women at the pottery shop, who function as a type of Greek chorus, gossiping about town events and offering expository reflections on the story.

Walter Carvalho's lean lensing strives for tone that is often lost within the shifting narration and "Fire Circle" leaves the viewer with only smoke in the place of fire. — *Lent.*

LA LEYENDA DEL CURA DE BARGOTA
(THE LEGEND OF THE PRIEST FROM BARGOTA)
(SPANISH)

An Origen P.C. production in association with Televisión Española (TVE), Reteitalia, Telecip, RTP and Taurus Films. Directed by Pedro Olea. Screenplay, Olea, Juan Antonio Porto; camera (color), Hans Surmann; music, Carmelo Bernaola. Reviewed at Chicago Latino Film Festival, Sept. 29, 1990. Running time: **88 MIN.**
Father Juan . Fernando Guillén Cuervo
Dona Beatríz . . . . Lola Forner
Also with: Jaume Valls, Mabel Ordóñez, Encarna Paso, Raf Vallone.

The Legend Of The Priest From Bargota," by Spanish helmer Pedro Olea, is anything but legendary. Pic's potentially dramatic theme receives only routine handling here, and b.o. interest appears limited.

Second part of a six-pic package exploring historical cases of witchcraft, the film recounts a 16th-century legend about a handsome young priest from Spain's Rioja Baja region, Juan de Irusta (Fernando Guillén Cuergo), who discovers at his dying mother's bedside that he is the son of the devil.

"Now, go to your father," she mutters, and he does.

Episode is not Juan's first encounter with the Prince of Darkness. Early in the story, while still a student at the seminary in Salamanca, a classmate invited him to witness a blood pact with the devil in exchange for unlimited power. In fact, it seems that the devil is cavorting with almost everyone.

It is Juan's lust for dark-eyed Doña Beatríz (Lola Fornar) that causes him to falter from his vow of chastity and brings him into league with Lucifer. Devilish doings soon have him drenched in water during the middle of a drought or covered with snow in the middle of summer. His parishioners begin to suspect the good father is not what he seems.

Story is told in flashback as the priest is interrogated by the Holy Office. Suspense is kept to a minimum and evil is reduced to a couple of orgy scenes. Special effects consist of a few atmospheric lighting cues, a couple of fades and a ghastly soundtrack, while the devil is depicted only as a crude stone carving with a bad voiceover. — *Lent.*

A-GE-MAN: TALES OF A GOLDEN GEISHA

An Itami Films production. Executive producers, Yukuo Takenaka, Nigel Sinclair, Paul L. Sandberg. Produced by Yasushi Tamaoki, Juzo Itami. Written and directed by Itami. Camera (Fuji color), Zenko Yamazaki; editor, Akira Suzuki; music, Toshiyuki Honda; sound, Osamu Onodera; set design, Shuji Nakamura; lighting, Matsusaku Kato; set decorator, Teru Yamazaki; costume design, Emiko Koai; assistant director, Hisashi Toma; production manager, Takashi Kawasaki; co-producer, Seigo Hosogoe. Reviewed at the Chicago Intl. Film Festival, Oct. 10, 1990. No MPAA rating. Running time: **118 MIN.**
Nayoko . . . . Nobuko Miyamoto
Mondo Suzuki . . . Masahiko Tsugawa
Zenbo Okura . . . . . . Shogo Shimada
Chijiwa . . . . Hideji Otaki

Having tackled the other big topics — death, money and food — in his previous films, Juzo Itami turns his attention to love in this charmer, an offbeat tale blending the traditional world of the geisha with modern Japanese politics and finance.

The earthy humor, raw sexuality and gusto that distinguish Itami's earlier efforts still are in evidence in "A-Ge-Man," though in a more restrained form. Here, the emphasis is on the heart, the longing of an idealized Japanese woman for an ideal man.

Nobuko Miyamoto, Itami's wife and perennial star, again turns in a rich, emotionally textured performance as Nayoko, an abandoned waif who grows up to be a geisha girl and the personification of the Japanese ideal of womanly virtue.

Nayoko is attractive, intelligent, strong, resourceful, morally pure, graceful, loving, completely self-effacing and dedicated to her man. Above all, she is considered to be an A-Ge-Man, a human good-luck charm, a woman whose love — according to tradition — brings automatic success to her mate.

Nayoko passes from one man to another like Aladdin's lamp, to a 62-year-old Buddhist bishop who officially deflowers her at age 18, a philandering bank executive, a political fixer and a scheming candidate for the premiership.

All of them profit from the good fortune she brings and trade her away like a blue-chip stock except for the banker, Nayoko's true love. He cheats on her, but he doesn't sell her. For that dubious virtue, he is rewarded in the end.

Itami, aided by Zenko Yamazaki's lush color photography, has completely romanticized Tokyo, transforming it into a fairytale locale. The city that seemed almost frenzied in "A Taxing Woman" and its sequel now seems picturesque and intimate — a suitably lovely setting for a love story. — *Brin.*

FRANKENSTEIN UNBOUND

A 20th Century Fox release of a Mount Co. production. Produced by Roger Corman, Thom Mount, Kabi Jaeger. Directed by Corman. Screenplay, Corman, F.X. Feeney, based on Brian W. Aldiss' novel; camera (Deluxe color), Armando Nannuzzi, Michael Scott; editor, Jay Cassidy, Mary Bauer; music, Carl Davis; sound (Ultra-Stereo), Gary Alper; production design, Enrico Tovaglieri; set decoration, Ennio Michettoni; costume design, Franca Zuchelli; assistant director, Tony Brandt; special visual effects, Illusion Arts, Syd Dutton, Bill Taylor; additional special visual effects, Gene Warren Jr.; special makeup effects & monster design, Nick Dudman; 2nd unit director, Thierry Notz; stunt coordinator, Paul Weston; associate producers, Laura Medina, Cassidy; casting, Caro Jones. Reviewed at 20th Century Fox screening room, N.Y., Oct. 30, 1990. MPAA Rating: R. Running time: **85 MIN.**

Dr. Joe Buchanan	John Hurt
Dr. Frankenstein	Raul Julia
Mary Godwin	Bridget Fonda
Frankenstein monster	Nick Brimble
Elizabeth	Catherine Rabett
Lord Byron	Jason Patric
Percy Shelley	Michael Hutchence
Justine	Catherine Corman
General	Mickey Knox
Voice of car	Terri Treas

Roger Corman's "Frankenstein Unbound" is a competent but uninspired riff on the venerable legend. Delayed from spring until November debut, 20th Fox release has weak chances.

Fans of the famous filmmaker will want to check out his first directorial effort since United Artists' "Von Richtofen And Brown" in 1971. He's produced hundreds of pictures for his New World and Concorde banners since then.

For Corman, it's also a return trip to modern British sci-fi, adapting, with F.X. Feeney, a Brian W. Aldiss novel (co-scripter Ed Neumeir is uncredited, but gets a thank-you nod). In 1974 Corman released a British adaptation of Michael Moorcock's "The Final Programme," a more adventurous, pop art pic trimmed and retitled "Last Days Of Man On Earth" for U.S. consumption.

John Hurt toplines as a mad scientist in New Los Angeles of 2031, trying to develop a laser weapon that causes objects to implode. His goal is to concoct something that, unlike nuclear bombs, would not threaten to destroy the entire world. Unfortunately, his experiments are causing time slips, violent dislocations including one that sudden-

ly transports Hurt to Switzerland in 1817.

Hurt chances upon Dr. Frankenstein in a local pub and faster than you can say "Rowing To The Wind" or "Haunted Summer," he's visiting gothic folk Mary Godwin (soon to be Shelley), Lord Byron and Percy Shelley.

Tough to swallow is Hurt's belief that the Frankenstein legend is real, though he gives a copy of her famous "novel" to a very surprised Mary, who's just started writing it. It's one thing for time travel films to visit historical personages but quite another to meet up with fictional characters, though Sherlock Holmes has had his "Time After Time" entry. Out on the rampage is Frankenstein's monster, killing people until his creator fabricates a mate for him.

Film relies heavily on Hurt's modern car (a robot contraption à la tv's "Knight Rider," with Concorde regular Terri Treas providing its female voice) having been transported to the past along with him. It's used as a power source in Frankenstein's lightning experiments as well as an incongruous sight motoring along untouched 19th century Swiss landscapes.

While warring with Frankenstein and his monster, Hurt ultimately identifies with them, leading to an interesting, somber climax set in icy wastes as in Shelley's original novel.

Though some of the dialog is clutzy, acting is generally good with top honors to Raul Julia as a thoughtful Frankenstein. More single-minded is Hurt's sketchy role, not properly motivated beyond an overweening desire to destroy.

Bridget Fonda is attractive and remarkably similar to Laura Dern (of "Haunted Summer") in the Mary Godwin role, overshadowed by British actress Catherine Rabett (more famous for her liaison with Prince Andrew as publicized in the British tabloids than her thesping), who brings panache to the role of Frankenstein's fiancée, later resurrected as bride for the monster.

Both Jason Patric (young star of "After Dark, My Sweet") and Michael Hutchence (of Aussie band INXS) are miscast in brief appearances as Lord Byron and Percy Shelley.

Monster design by Nick Dudman is closer to Swamp Thing than the familiar '30s Karloff ma-

keup, but is interesting, and Nick Brimble is okay underneath. There's enough gore to keep modern audiences contented.

While lots of laser lights and optical effects keep things alive, Corman fails to keep the narrative advancing in riveting fashion. Hopefully he will continue to direct films and find his stride again.

Carl Davis' musical score keeps a straight face no matter how improbable the action gets.

— *Lor.*

JACOB'S LADDER

A Tri-Star release of a Carolco Pictures production. Produced by Alan Marshall. Executive producers, Mario Kassar, Andrew Vajna. Directed by Adrian Lyne. Screenplay, Bruce Joel Rubin; camera (Technicolor), Jeffrey L. Kimball; editor, Tom Rolf; additional editing, Peter Amundsun, B.J. Sears; music, Maurice Jarre; sound (Dolby), Tod A. Maitland, Andy Nelson, Steve Pederson, Michael Getlin; production design, Brian Morris; principal art direction, Jeremy Conway; art direction, Wray Steven Graham; set decoration, Kathleen Dolan, Leticia Stella-Serra (Puerto Rico); costume design, Ellen Mirojnick; special prosthetic effects design, Gordon J. Smith; associate producer, Rubin; assistant director, Joseph Reidy; casting, Risa Bramon, Billy Hopkins, Heidi Levitt. Reviewed at UA Coronet, L.A., Oct. 24, 1990. MPAA Rating: R. Running time: **113 MIN.**

Jacob Singer	Tim Robbins
Jezzie	Elizabeth Pena
Louis	Danny Aiello
Michael	Matt Craven
Paul	Pruitt Taylor Vince
Geary	Jason Alexander
Sarah	Patricia Kalember
Frank	Eriq La Salle
George	Ving Rhames
Doug	Brian Tarantina
Rod	Anthony Alessandro
Jerry	Brett Hinkley
Gabe	Macaulay Culkin

Adrian Lyne's "Jacob's Ladder" means to be a harrowing thriller about a Vietnam vet (Tim Robbins) bedeviled by strange visions, but it's dull, unimaginative and pretentious. The $40 million Carolco production probably will surrender quickly at the boxoffice.

Writer Bruce Joel Rubin ("Ghost") telegraphs his plot developments and can't resist throwing in supernatural elements that prompt giggles at the most unfortunate moments. Right from the battlefield prolog in Vietnam, where members of Robbins' battalion act strangely and throw fits, it's clear that somebody messed with their brains.

It comes as no surprise when Rubin gradually doles out his big plot revelation that the battalion was being used by the army for secret chemical warfare experiments. Robbins, whose earnest and touching performance belongs in a better film, spends most of the story struggling to understand the "demons" pursuing him back home in N.Y.

Audience, however, is allowed to keep miles ahead of him, so the film lacks suspense and emotional punch.

Lyne's laborious flashbacks to Vietnam and his supposedly hellish images of Gotham street life add nothing fresh visually or dramatically to previous film and tv depictions of troubled Viet vets' psyches.

Nor does Jeffrey L. Kimball's lensing attempt anything original in its hazy, monotonous look, concentrating on dark, smudgy colors and recycling nightmarish images recalling such pics as "Hour Of The Wolf" and "The Devils."

Living in a dim, dingy apartment and working in a dronelike postal service job, Robbins was wrongly told by the army that he was discharged on psychological grounds. His very existence denied by the Veterans Administration, he thinks he's possessed, but eventually pieces together the truth with the help of his battalion buddies.

In a plot device borrowed from "The Manchurian Candidate," it turns out they're all having the same hallucinations, based on a common experience the army wants to keep under wraps.

Adding to Robbins' troubles are memories of his dead son Macaulay Culkin. Culkin appears in visions and flashbacks so often that his climactic reunion with Robbins in the afterlife, which should be deeply moving, is only mildly affecting. The use of Al Jolson's "Sonny Boy" as a musical motif also misfires.

Elizabeth Pena, as Robbins' drab and whiny live-in lover, isn't much help to the poor guy, complaining about how he's bothering her with his mental problems and demanding, after one of his worst traumatic experiences, "Are you okay?"

The revelation that Robbins is a ghost comes as no shock, considering that the scripter unwisely had a fortuneteller spill the beans early in the story. How a hallucinogenic drug turned the soldier into a supernatural being isn't explained, however, and the dramatic purpose of the gimmick is also unclear.

Any would-be thriller that, for reasons best known to its makers, has Danny Aiello giving the hero not one but two lengthy chiropractic treatments remains hopelessly mired in the mundane. — *Mac.*

SONNY BOY

A Triumph Films release of a Trans World Entertainment production. Produced by Ovidio G. Assonitis. Directed by Robert Martin Carroll. Screenplay, Graeme Whifler; camera (Panavision, Luciano Vittori color), Roberto D'Ettore Piazzoli; editor, Claudio Cutry; music, Carlo Mario Cordio; theme song, David Carradine; sound (Dolby), David Waelder; production design, Mario Molli; assistant director, Matthew Clark; casting, Ed Mitchell. Reviewed at 23rd St. West 1 theater, N.Y., Oct. 26, 1990. MPAA Rating: R. Running time: **98 MIN.**
Pearl . . . . David Carradine
Slue . . . . Paul L. Smith
Weasel . . . . Brad Dourif
Dr. Bender . . . . Conrad Janis
Charlie . . . . Sydney Lassick
Sandy . . . . Savina Gersak
Rose . . . . Alexandra Powers
Sheriff . . . . Steve Carlisle
Sonny Boy . . . . Michael Griffin

They don't get much worse than "Sonny Boy," an inept adventure film about child abuse that inexplicably received a major theatrical release via Columbia Pictures Entertainment's Triumph Films label.

Italian producer Ovidio Assonitis, whose career peaked 16 years ago with "Beyond The Door" and "Last Snow Of Springtime," made this nonsense three years ago in New Mexico for video company TWE. The script, credited to Graeme Whifler, is about as unappetizing as any in memory.

David Carradine camps it up in drag for the entire picture, playing the wife of burly psychotic Paul L. Smith (the sadistic prison guard of "Midnight Express," typecast as a monster). Prolog set in 1970 shows their nutcase stooge Brad Dourif (also typecast) kidnaping a baby boy, causing instant maternal bonding for Carradine.

Film's laughably haphazard structure has brief vignettes showing the boy growing up wild, with Smith torturing the child to toughen him up. What emerges at age 17 is a scarred and scraggly Michael Griffin, his tongue cut out by Smith and used as a brutal monster to kill the ogre's enemies (and drink their blood).

Smith rules a small town until, of course, Sonny Boy rebels and with the aid of a fantasy blond Alexandra Powers (who rides into the film on a motorcycle, a riff stolen from the drive-in classic "Vanishing Point"), he starts a local revolution. The townsfolk form a lynch mob to kill the young monster, and a fake happy ending is tacked on.

Sole point of interest in this farrago is Carradine. With tattoos and plenty of body hair showing, he remains in character throughout as a woman with cryptic results. Film's stance toward homosexuality is never spelled out, and thankfully there are no bed scenes of Smith and Carradine, who are introduced in the terminally bickering stage of their "marriage."

Griffin as the wild child strikes poses of a dyspeptic James Dean until local doctor Conrad Janis sews a monkey tongue into the boy's mouth and he starts chattering away. Powers is pretty, and film's villainess is European starlet Savina Gersak who has makeup to suggest rotted teeth so we'll know she's bad.

Technical credits are erratic, especially the widescreen photography. — *Lor.*

CONTRA EL VIENTO
(AGAINST THE WIND)
(SPANISH)

A Francisco Periñán and Maestranza Films production, in association with Productora Andaluza de Programes S.A. and Cartel. Written and directed by Paco Periñán; camera (Eastmancolor), Gerard de Battista; editor, Carmen Frias; music, Ramón Ferran; sound, Eduardo Fernandez; sets, Javier Fernandez. Reviewed at San Sebastian Film Festival, Sept. 24, 1990. Running time: **95 MIN.**
Juan . . . . Antonio Banderas
Ana . . . . Emma Suarez
Petersen . . . . Bruce McGuire
Rosario . . . . Rosario Flores
    Also with: Francisco Guijar, Rafael Diaz, Germán Cobos, Patricia Palacios, Queta Claver, Carmen Balague, Estanislao Gonzalez.

This contrived film, stiffly acted and poorly directed, will be relegated to the ample limbo of Spanish films that open and close in a trice. Even Antonio Banderas' angry stares and a story involving incest and a nuclear waste-disposal plant aren't enough to arouse a spark of interest.

Pic revolves around an incestuous relationship between a brother and sister. He has fled from her to work as a welder in the nuclear plant, but she tracks him down and they renew their affair.

Thickening the plot are two poorly acted characters, a gypsy girl who also loves the brother and an English engineer.

The Brit romances the sister when she's on the rebound from her brother. What could have been a tragic denouement never materializes, and the siblings drift apart at the end in supremely undramatic fashion.

Some of the dialog is so clumsy it had audiences here squirming in their seats. — *Besa.*

GRAVEYARD SHIFT

A Paramount Pictures release of a Larry Sugar production. Produced by William J. Dunn, Ralph S. Singleton. Directed by Singleton. Executive producers, Bonnie Sugar, Larry Sugar. Screenplay, John Esposito, based on the short story by Stephen King; camera, Peter Stein; editor, Jim Gross, Randy Jon Morgan; music, Anthony Marinelli, Brian Banks; in Dolby Stereo; production design, Gary Wissner; costume design, Sarah Lemire; second unit director-effects supervisor, Peter Chesney; associate producers, Joan V. Singleton, Anthony Labonte. Reviewed at the Mann Chinese Theaters, Hollywood, Oct. 26, 1990. MPAA Rating: R. Running time: **87 MIN.**
John Hall . . . . David Andrews
Jane Wisconsky . . . . Kelly Wolf
Warwick . . . . Stephen Macht
The exterminator . . . . . Brad Dourif
Danson . . . . Andrew Divoff
Brogon . . . . Vic Polizos
Nardello . . . . Ilona Margolis
Carmichael . . . . . . Jimmy Woodard

Paramount discovered with "Pet Sematary" it could cash in at the b.o. on even a bad Stephen King adaptation, but that theory is pushed well beyond the limit with "Graveyard Shift." Pic may squeeze in an okay opening weekend on the strength of the horrormeister's name but should be buried quickly by word of mouth, even from genre fans.

"Graveyard Shift" is the 19th adaptation for tv or film of a King novel or short story, with two more on the way in 1990. It may be the worst of the lot, a rather dubious accomplishment.

Aside from being so dark and murky as to be almost unwatchable, the pic's sole distinction is that it employs more rats — largely of the puppy-sized variety — than perhaps any film since "Ben."

The rats are actually far scarier than the film's monster, which is never entirely seen. Only occasional glimpses of slime-laden parts are provided, no doubt intended to resemble "Alien," which can only be reminisced about fondly by comparison.

Ralph S. Singleton, making his directing debut, was an associate producer on "Pet Sematary" and learned all the wrong lessons a little too well.

Working from John Esposito's confounding adaptation of a King short story, Singleton continually returns to the clichés of eerie music and jump-out gimmicks, generating more boredom than suspense or fright.

The only real shock to be found here stems from pic's relentlessly poor technical quality, including cheesy-looking special effects, shoddy camerawork and uneven sound quality that at times (perhaps mercifully) renders the dialog inaudible.

The story centers on a small-town mill run by a nasty boss (Stephen Macht) determined to clean out its rat-laden bottom level. No one seems to wonder why employes keep disappearing, and the film's lone amusing gag involves its ever-in-use "now hiring" sign.

Along comes a drifter (David Andrews) who takes over the graveyard shift. His background is as nebulous as everything else in the limited storyline, such as what made the monster and why Warwick (Macht) needs the bottom level so badly.

The cast is uniformly bland, with Macht affecting a strange sort of South African accent and Andrews completely stoic in the lead. Brad Dourif has the only moments that indicate any thought went into the screenplay at all as a wigged-out exterminator, though the character's demise, unlike that of the film, comes far too quickly.

Despite various credits to effects advisors and consultants (including veterans Harold Michelson and Albert J. Whitlock), the film proves a mess visually, concluding with a series of dankly lit sequences in underground caverns that prove extremely difficult to follow — assuming, of course, that by then anyone is still around to try. — Bril.

SOULTAKER

An Action Intl. Pictures release of a Pacific West Entertainment Group production, in association with Victory Pictures. Produced by Eric Parkinson, Connie Kingrey. Executive producers, Den-

nis J. Carlo, Charles Luria, Ivor Royston. Directed by Michael Rissi. Screenplay, Vivian Schilling, based on story by Schilling, Parkinson; camera (Image Transform & Crest color), James A. Rosenthal; editor, Jason Coleman, Rissi; music, Jon McCallum; sound, Bob Grant; art direction, Thad Carr; stunt coordinator, Bob Ivy; coproducers, Anthony Dalesandro, John Scherer; casting, Mary Gaffney. Reviewed on AIP vidcassette, N.Y., Sept. 23, 1990. No MPAA Rating. Running time: **95 MIN.**
Soultaker . . . . Joe Estevez
Natalie . . . . Vivian Schilling
Zach Taylor . . . . . . Gregg Thomsen
Angel of Death . . . . . . Robert Z'dar
Brad . . . . David Shark
Tommy . . . . Chuck Williams
Also with: Jean Reiner, David Fawcett, Gary Kohler, Dave Scott.

A very intriguing premise distinguishes the horror thriller "Soultaker," due for theatrical release ahead of AIP homevid exposure. Young starscripter Vivian Schilling earns high marks for this effort.

Her innovation for horror/fantasy fans dovetails nicely with current hit "Ghost" in creating a new myth about potential afterlife. (Pic opened theatrically Oct. 26 in Wichita and Tucson.)

Schilling and three young friends are involved in a car crash, but wake up thrown from the car apparently unhurt. It seems a "displacement" has occurred: Angel of Death (massive heavy Robert Z'dar in a blond wig) sends his undead minion Soultaker (Joe Estevez, Martin Sheen's brother) to fetch the four teens' souls pronto.

Well-paced direction by Michael Rissi develops the undead teens' predicament suspensefully. They first realize something is seriously wrong when a shopkeeper acts like they're invisible, and the operator can't hear them on the phone.

Another plus is introduced in the form of a dark strain of romanticism as Estevez, himself a soul caught in limbo, attempts to unite with Schilling (whom he believes is a reincarnated old flame) for eternity. Film's shooting title was "The Kiss Of Death," referring to the smooch Estevez tries to apply to seal Schilling's fate.

Minor special effects are used for the moment of "soultaking." Pic's weakest moments come in the final reel when a race against the clock is staged in anticlimactic fashion. All told, the mechanics of the afterlife are more consistently presented here than in "Ghost," where Patrick Swayze could learn to punch villains but couldn't "touch" Demi Moore.

Schilling is an attractive, forceful heroine who's written herself a fine showcase. Estevez brings panache to his role. — Lor.

MANDEN, DER VILLE VAERE SKYLDIG
(THE MAN WHO WOULD BE GUILTY)
(DANISH-FRENCH)

A Pathé-Nordisk Film (Denmark) release of Nordisk Film & TV (Denmark) and PCA/Michèle Dimitri (France) production in association with the Danish Film Institute. Produced by Bo Christensen, Michèle Dimitri. Directed by Ole Roos. Screenplay, Roos, based on Henrik Stangerup's novel; camera (Eastmancolor), Peter Roos; editor, Jörgen Kastrup; music, Ib Glindemann; sound, Dominique Duchatelle, Jacques Ballay; production design, Palle Arestrup; costume design, Annelise Hauberg; production manager, Thomas Lydholm, Amer Ghandour; casting, Pascale Beraud, Jette Terman. Reviewed at the Palads, Copenhagen, Sept. 4, 1990. Running time: **91 MIN.**
Adam . . . . Jesper Klein
Edith . . . . Anna Karina
Jesper . . . . . . Claes Rose Mikkelsen
Eva/FBS 2 . . . . Kirsten Norholt
FBS 1 . . . . Bent Christensen
Kaminsky . . . . Sam Besekow
Psychiatrist . . . . . . Poul Bundgaard

Ole Roos' adaptation of Danish author Henrik Stangerup's futuristic novel "The Man Who Would Be Guilty" boasts technical gloss and fine acting but little suspense.

Book had fine runs in England, France and Germany, so the film, a Danish-French coproduction, should find distribution in the same territories. The French contributions are restricted to exteriors in Paris' La Défence area and a brief but strong performance by Anna Karina.

Jesper Klein is convincing as Adam, the novelist whose life and art are threatened by bookburning authorities who reject literature with any adventure and imagination.

Beginning to suspect that his own wife, Edith (Karina), has submitted to the teachings of the power elite, Adam gets drunk and flies into a rage that leads to fatal violence.

Convinced he's a murderer, Adam is bewildered when he is released from a mental institution and told to pick up his life, although his son has been removed from his care, and no trace of Edith survives.

Adam plays around with the idea of guilt, a phenomenon supposedly abolished in this new society. He tries to find his son, but is stonewalled and kept under close guard.

What everybody actually wants from Adam is a clue to his publisher's hiding place. Adam, in a continuing daze of bewilderment, leads the agents to the publisher, who's suspected of encouraging underground literature.

Adam is reunited with his son and Edith, who survived after all. It is vaguely indicated that the obvious happiness of the family reunion somehow puts the trio beyond all evil.

The shiny emptiness surrounding Adam and Edith is threatening, as are the blank faces of the psychiatrists, security agents and bureaucrats who gang up on them.

Missing are real chill and thrill, fantasy and imagination. Adam is just a fumbler, and it is hard to see how he could be dangerous to even the most intolerant of mind-bending authorities. And the old publisher comes on as more of a romantic dodderer than as a wielder of subversive strength. — Kell.

ZEIT DER RACHE
(TIME OF VENGEANCE)
(AUSTRIAN)

A DOR Filmproduktion production. Produced by Danny Krausz, Milan Dor. Directed by Anton Peschke. Screenplay, Peschke, Dor, Gebhard Birnbaumer; camera (Fujicolor), Michael Riebl; editor, Ulli Schwarzenberger; music, Willi Resetarits, Schurli Herrnstadt; sound, Michael Etz; art direction, Christoph Kanter; costume design, Susanne Heger. Reviewed at San Sebastian Film Festival, Sept. 27, 1990. (Also at Chicago Intl. Film Festival.) Running time: **93 MIN.**
Orhan . . . . Cumhur Vural
Robert . . . . Otto Sander
Werner . . . . Dominic Raacke
Sylvie . . . . Anette Uhlen
Grandfather . . . . Tuncel Kurtiz

"Time Of Vengeance" is a drawn-out film that could have been told in a half-hour.

A Turkish shepherd boy, about 10, manages to stow away on a truck bound for Vienna, where he somehow finds (by himself) the man who killed his father in a hit-and-run accident. At the end of the film, another truck materializes as if by magic and safely returns him to his village.

What the boy does in Vienna isn't really very much. He musters hardly a word throughout since he speaks only Turkish.

He does, however, strike up a friendship with an Austrian kid and hang out in the kitchen of a night club called 1,001 Nights, where he meets the man who killed his father.

No one ever discovers the boy is carrying a pistol, even after he fires off a few shots. The subplot of a love triangle never gets off the ground. — Besa.

THE RAINBOW THIEF
(BRITISH)

A Timothy Burrill production. (Intl. sales: Europex, Paris.) Executive producer, Johannes Weineck. Produced by Vincent Winter. Directed by Alexandro Jodorowsky. Screenplay, Berta Dominguez D.; camera (color), Ronnie Taylor; editor, Mauro Ronaoni; music, Jean Musy; production design, Alexander Trauner, Didier Naert. Reviewed at Venice Film Festival (out of competition), Sept. 8, 1990. Running time: **91 MIN.**
Prince Meleagre . . . . . Peter O'Toole
Dima . . . . Omar Sharif
Uncle Rudolf . . . . . Christopher Lee
Tiger Lily . . . . . Berta Dominguez D.
Lady Jane . . . . Jane Chaplin

Alexandro Jodorowsky, flamboyant director of "El Topo" and "The Holy Mountain," was absent from films for most of the '80s, but he made a startling comeback last year at Cannes with "Santa Sangre." His fans will be less delighted with his latest film. It'll be a tough sell, despite name actors involved.

A surprisingly conventional and even sentimental effort distinguished by handsome and inventive visuals, film is set in an unnamed city (exteriors were shot in Gdansk, Poland) where Dima (Omar Sharif) is a down-and-outer who scavenges food on the streets by the harbor.

Peter O'Toole plays Prince Meleagre, a reclusive eccentric whose family considers him insane. He retreats to the sewers of the city where he establishes himself in a reasonably comfortable abode with Dima as servant.

Meleagre's millionaire uncle (Christopher Lee) is another eccentric who prefers dogs to people. When entertaining, he feeds his guests bones and his dogs caviar. It's thought he'll leave his fortune to Meleagre, but when he suffers a stroke during an orgy with brothel prosties and later dies, the dogs and the whores get the loot.

The disillusioned Dima, realizing his loyalty to Meleagre won't be repaid in hard cash, decides to ankle, but a deus ex machina arrives in the form of a flood. Dima returns to rescue his friend who's trapped in the sewers by the rising floodwaters.

Those who've come to expect hard-edged, surreal black fantasy from Jodorowsky will find "The Rainbow Thief" excessively whimsical. The atmosphere is cloying rather than acerbic, a mood closer to "Mary Poppins" than to "El Topo."

Nevertheless the film is magnificent to look at. Veteran Alexander Trauner and his adopted son, Didier Naert, have created some wonderful sets on soundstages at Shepperton, and cinematographer Ronnie Taylor has filmed them lovingly. The Polish exteriors also are fascinating.

Handsome visuals don't sell tickets, however, and there may be disappointing reactions to the film as a whole. O'Toole and Sharif are reunited ("Lawrence Of Arabia"), but the former gives another standard interpretation of a lordly eccentric, while Sharif overdoes the sentimentality.

Lee is more successful in his brief appearance as the uncle, and his character is closer to the usual inhabitant of a Jodorowsky film.

Not strong enough for a mainstream audience, too conventional for a cult audience, "The Rainbow Thief" looks like it will face a rocky road at the boxoffice, though it could have a longer life in ancillary media. — Strat.

FUGA DAL PARADISO
(ESCAPE FROM PARADISE)
(ITALIAN)

A Titanus release of an Azzurra Film/RAI-2 co-production, in association with Cinemax (Paris) and Iduna Film (Munich). Produced by Luciano Luna, Claudia Mori. Directed by Ettore Pasculli. Screenplay, Pasculli, Lucio Mandarà; camera (color), Alfio Contini; editor, Ruggero Mastroianni; music, Michel Legrand; art direction, Giorgio and Marco Luppi. Reviewed at Venice Film Festival, Sept. 13, 1990. Running time: **111 MIN.**
Teo . . . . Fabrice Josso
Beatrice . . . . Ines Sastre
Thor . . . . Horst Buchholz
Sara . . . . Aurore Clement
Eliseo . . . . Jacques Perrin
Also with: Paolo Bonacelli, Barbara Cupisti, Lou Castel (Ulv Quarzel), Olivia Toscani Anker, Van Johnson.

"Escape From Paradise" is a bizarre, incoherent sci-fi yard spun by Ettore Pasculli, a Cinecittà exec making his directorial bow.

Set in a post-ecological-disaster future, pic is decipherable mainly because of its similarity to other tales. What remains unclear is what audience it could be destined for. At first glance a film for kids, "Escape" has many scenes of ugly violence seemingly geared to adult viewers.

But adults may be irritated at the elementary setup. Old hermit-narrator Van Johnson tells the story to a cute little boy on the beach. This clumsy device repeatedly interrupts the story, which gets rolling occasionally, to give irrelevant particulars none of the characters could know.

Story (told as a half-narrated flashback) has good-looking teen Teo (Fabrice Josso) living in a futuristic cave with his parents (Aurore Clement and Jacques Perrin). Dad is a member of the ruling council and wears a special medallion around his neck.

Teo has secretly fallen in love with pretty teen Beatrice (Ines Sastre) via a huge video screen. Nobody outside the family is allowed to meet in the subterranean city, and all contacts are electronic. But through his father's medallion, Teo learns not only that there's a big world upstairs, but that he and Beatrice can meet by sneaking out the conduit pipes.

This leads them into a neat adventure and a miraculous exit into the outside world (an empty desert). Thor (Horst Buchholz) is sent to round them up. By the time his men find the youngsters, they have stumbled onto the ruins of a city and the rat-like mutants who live there.

With blowtorches, Thor's men go on a rampage exterminating the mutants (not a sight for weak stomachs). Beatrice, separated from Teo, is whisked to a mutant village by writhing mute ("Ulv Quarzell alias Lou Castel" in the credits).

Teo turns mean after he sees his parents burned to death on tv. After a few more senseless adventures, the mutants escape aboard an old steamer led, for no particular reason, by Teo, while Beatrice looks on admiringly. The narrator turns out to be Teo as a melancholy oldtimer.

Film is enlivened by special effects, which combine with Giorgio and Marco Luppi's detailed sets to give a suitable gloss to the visuals. Performances are walked through, except for the good/bad Buchholz, a relatively complex character for this film. The two young leads are attractive. — Yung.

COLD LIGHT OF DAY
(BRITISH)

A Creative Artists production. Produced by Richard Driscoll. Written and directed by Fhiona Louise. Camera (color), Nigel Axworthy; editor, Leroy Stamps; music, sound, Paul Stuart Davies; production design, Ski Newton; production manager, Richard Bilu. Reviewed at Venice Film Festival (out of competition), Sept. 8, 1990. Running time: **76 MIN.**
Jordan March . . . . Bob Flag
Inspector Simmons . Geoffrey Greenhill
Joe . . . . Martin Byrne-Quinn
Stephen . . . . Andrew Edmans
Albert Green . . . . Bill Merrow
Prostitute . . . . Clare King
The poor boy . . . . Mark Hawkins
Julie Stay . . . . Jackie Cox

Obviously made on a tiny budget, this film by a 23-year-old woman director is an extraordinarily grim case history of a mass murderer. Though the treatment is matter-of-fact, the crimes committed are so hideous, commercial possibilities (including tv) are extremely limited.

An opening title says the film is "based on actual events but not on an account." The criminal is a homosexual employment officer who lives alone in a tatty London apartment. One night he brings home a young man and kills him, using his corpse for sex after death.

Eventual 15 victims all are carefully dissected with body parts hidden in drains and under floorboards. One grisly moment shows the murderer boiling the head of one victim on a kitchen stove.

Pic is constructed around an angry and disgusted policeman's interrogation of the murderer, with flashbacks to the crimes. Although many of the supporting players give self-conscious and awkward performances, Bob Flag is thoroughly convincing as the killer, a mild-mannered, bespectacled man whose motivation, pic suggests, stems from childhood when he witnessed the sudden death of his grandfather on a beach.

This is pretty simplistic psychology, and the film is on stronger ground when it depicts the horrendously routine life of the killer whose banal looks conceal his terrible crimes.

Helmer Fhiona Louise dedicates the film to "those too sensitive for this world." It's safe to say few will be sufficiently strong-stomached to endure her all-too-powerful film without feeling queasy. — *Strat.*

L'AFRICANA
(THE WOMAN FROM AFRICA)
(ITALIAN-GERMAN-FRENCH)

An Artisti Associati release of a Scena Group (Rome)/Bioskop Film (Munich)/Rachel Prods. (Paris) co-production in association with RAI-2. Produced by Augusto Caminito. Written and directed by Margarethe von Trotta. Camera (color), Tonino Delli Colli; editor, Nino Baragli; music, Eleni Karaindrou; art direction, Antonello Geleng; executive producer, Giuseppe Auriemma; production director, Angelo Zamella. Reviewed at Venice Film Festival (competition), Sept. 4, 1990. Running time: **104 MIN.**
Martha . . . . Barbara Sukowa
Anna . . . . Stefania Sandrelli
Victor . . . . Sami Frey
Swirnarsky . . . . Jan Biczycki
Andrej . . . . . Alexandre Mnouchine
Also with: Jacques Sernas, Kadidia Diarra, Pierre Deny, Bernard Tachl.

Can two women remain friends when they love the same man? Margarethe von Trotta is determined to demonstrate they can in "The Woman From Africa," a Franco-Italo-German co-prod she wrote and directed. Pic is too intent on proving its thesis to ignite on an emotional level.

Though a sensitive, probing pic graced with fine performances by Stefania Sandrelli and Barbara Sukowa, prospects are for a dignified but quiet arthouse run in Europe and America.

The whole story is summarized in an opening dream sequence in which German doctor Martha (Sukowa) and Italian Anna (Sandrelli) exchange places in bed after a struggle. The object of both their longing is *homme fatal* Victor (Sami Frey), a handsome and successful political journalist.

Originally Martha's partner, he left her to marry her best friend, Anna. When Anna falls seriously ill, she imagines Martha has cast a spell on her from Africa, where the rejected woman has fled like a Foreign Legionnaire. She begs Victor to write to Martha and bring her back to Paris, in the hope this will break the spell and cure her.

The three-way love ties that come out of Martha's return are tense but predictable. More affecting and real is the love-hate relationship between the two women, which von Trotta describes with a rare degree of sympathy and understanding. Sukowa's tough, intellectually rig-

orous Martha, ever bitter and unsmiling, stands in sharp contrast to Sandrelli's soft, superstitious Anna, ridden with guilt over having stolen Victor away.

Both actresses brave most of the film without flattering make-up, adding a realistic, down-to-earth touch that brings the audience closer to them. Their eventual reconciliation may be a foregone conclusion, but it's pic's one really convincing emotional exchange.

Film is strong when it explores the substratum of interpersonal feelings and relations. It stumbles when it tries to force situations into intellectual schemes and coy ideas. It's particularly hard to believe Anna really thinks that giving Martha back to Victor could be her salvation.

Another weird touch is a pair of mysterious old men who spy benignly on the trio through a Hitchcockian rear window, and keep butting into their lives. And what to think of the teasing finale, in which Africa appears as a paradise of emotional liberation (bigamy)?

Notable is Eleni Karaindrou's heavily atmospheric score, complementing Tonino Delli Colli's dark and brooding cinematography. In contract, Victor and Anna's beautiful designer apartment bears little resemblance to its occupants. — *Yung.*

SPIELER
(GAMBLERS)
(GERMAN)

A Bavaria Film production. Produced by Michael Hild. Directed by Dominik Graf. Screenplay, Christoph Fromm; camera (color), Klaus Eichhammer; editor, Christel Suckow; music, Ottorino Respighi, Samuel Barber, Andreas Kobner, Graf; production design, Sherry Hermann; production manager, Kirsten Hager. Reviewed at Venice Film Festival (competition), Sept. 9, 1990. Running time: **111 MIN.**
Jojo . . . . Peter Lohmeyer
Kathrin . . . . Anica Dobra
Tom . . . . Hansa Czypionka
Strobek . . . . Joachim Kemmer
Hugo . . . . Claus Dieter Reents
Roy . . . . Anthony Dawson

This lightweight entry is a cheerful but overlong romantic comedy seemingly influenced by early Truffaut and German cinema of the '60s. With its freewheeling style and attractive heroine, "Spieler" might perform on its home territory, but seems too insubstantial to travel.

Jojo (Peter Lohmeyer), bespectacled and unhandsome, is a compulsive gambler who's forever broke. He anticipates a legacy from a rich relative, but winds up inheriting only a large dog. His pretty country cousin, convent-educated Kathrin (charmingly played by Yugoslav actress Anica Dobra), gets all the loot. Jojo sets about half-heartedly seducing Kathrin and pockets her money, but then finds himself falling in love with her.

After its promising start, film develops into a kind of road movie/romantic thriller. The couple, together with Jojo's friend Tom, travel to the South of France for more gambling and lovemaking. They meet a corrupt cop, who is shot by Kathrin, and at fadeout only she is a survivor, and also the mother of Jojo's child.

None of this is meant to be taken seriously, and director Dominik Graf displays a light touch most of the time. Much sharper editing would have improved the picture a lot.

A voiceover narration is one of the many references to an earlier, '60s style of cinema. Location camerawork is a plus, and Dobra, who could easily have a stellar career ahead of her, has the kind of personality that overwhelms her rather pallid co-stars.
— *Strat.*

HE'S STILL THERE

A Fulquest Films production. Executive producer, Robert Gray. Produced by Kathleen J. Powell, Halfdan Hussie. Written and directed by Hussie. Camera (black & white, 16m), Tom DeFore; editor, Hussie; music, Noel B. Flatt; associate producers, Bruce Hallmark, Terri Evans; assistant director, Fady Trad; casting, Powell, Jens M. Hussie. Reviewed at Venice Film Festival (out of competition), Sept. 9, 1990. Running time: **76 MIN.**
Boston . . . . Michael McNeill
Adrael Walker . . . Stacy Huntington
Phil . . . . Christopher Briante
Nancy . . . . Suzanne Fountain
Pam . . . . Katie Johnson
Becky . . . . Ann Kellogg
Mary . . . . Satir DeMarco
Jamie . . . . Sheila Traister
Jeff . . . . Joel Nagle

Dated 1987, this black & white low-budgeter ambitiously attempts to explore a number of relationships involving a self-centered youth. It's a laudable effort, but is unlikely to make it into cinemas, outside the fest circuit, since it's simply too small and marginal.

The young protagonist (Michael McNeill) tries to date several different women, but none of them turn out satisfactorily. One is a single mother of two with a bruised past, another is a coke addict and yet another (in a surprising twist) is a lonely middle-aged woman.

But McNeill's dream girl, played by Stacy Huntington, stays tantalizingly out of his reach and, in the end, suicides over another, unhappy, relationship.

It doesn't take much to work out that the problem with all these relationships is McNeill himself, but the young filmmakers are rather earnest about this revelation. The pic, lensed in 16m, has all the hallmarks of a student production, made with lots of love, but without much thought as to where it will ever find an audience.

At the Venice film fest, reactions were respectful if unenthusiastic. — *Strat.*

DOVIDENIA V PEKLE, PRIATELIA
(SEE YOU IN HELL, MY FRIENDS)
(CZECHOSLOVAKIAN-ITALIAN)

A Slovenska Filmova Tvorba-RAI-2 co-production. Produced by Jan Svikruha, Viliam Canky. Directed by Juraj Jakubisko. Screenplay, Jakubisko, Karel Sidon; camera (color), Jakubisko; editor, Patrik Pass; music, Fiorenzo Capri; sound, Alexander Pallos, Stefan Svana; production design, Milos Kalina, Slavo Procházka. Reviewed at Venice Film Festival (out of competition), Sept. 12, 1990. Running time: **75 MIN.**
Rita . . . . Olinka Berova
Petras . . . . Jan Melkovic
Colonel . . . . Nino Besozzi
Old man . . . . Mila Beran
Hermit . . . . . . Carlo Campannelle
Postman . . . . August Kuban
First witch . . . . . . Jana Brezinova
Second witch . . . . . Jana Stehnova
Postman's assistant . . . Zdenek Dusak

Theatrical possibilities are dubious for this strange, alienating picture, but fests around the world will be interested in this famous "unfinished" pic from the golden days of Czechoslovakian cinema.

One after another, banned Czech films of the late '60s and early '70s tumble from the shelves, but Juraj Jakubisko's "See You In Hell My Friends" was not only banned — production was stopped before shooting had finished. Twenty years later, Jakubisko has managed to complete his film, though presumably it now has a rather different form from what originally was intended.

Unfortunately, the material seems to have dated badly, because, like much of the late '60s cinema, the frenetic style hasn't stood the test of time. Jakubisko was always working in a kind of Fellini-ish world of colorful characters and bizarre situations, but here the film is incoherent. The hand-held camerawork, choppy editing and a totally postsynced soundtrack, in which lip movements rarely matched voices, are no help.

Some of these problems can be explained by the film's 20-year production history, but Jakubisko's previous pic, "Birds, Orphans And Fools," showed signs of frantic form at the expense of content and wound up far below the standard set by his 1968 masterpiece, "The Deserter And The Nomads."

"See You In Hell" is a heavy-handed allegory based on Noah's Ark, with allusions to Communism thrown in. It centers on a ménage à trois of lovely Olinka Berova and two men, the ardent Jan Melkovic and the elderly Nino Besozzi. They frolic happily together in a farmhouse, and Rita has a daughter. All goes well until a couple of strange women arrive, bringing along the disapproval of the outside world.

All this is framed by a story (presumably filmed over the last year) in which the principal actors are visibly much older: a vintage car crash in the snow, and Melkovic, thrown from the wreck, having dreams of his happy past life.

There's some black satire here, but many of the film's barbs at Czech communism will be obscure to non-Czechs. The noisy soundtrack and flashy visuals don't make for a comfortable viewing experience. There's plenty of nudity, but also a rather nasty scene in which pigs and geese are slaughtered.

Jakubisko seems to be saying that all Czechs (and Slovaks, for this is actually a Slovak film) were to blame for what happened to their country, and that only children are really innocent. He has dedicated the pic "to all collaborators and actors who didn't live to see the first screening of the film in freedom."

— *Strat.*

BLACKJACK
(SWEDISH)

An SF release of a Svensk Filmindustri production with FilmTeknik. Produced by Waldemar Bergendahl. Directed by Colin Nutley. Screenplay, Nutley, Johanna Hald, Catti Edfeldt; camera (Fujicolor), Jörgen Persson; editor, Perry Schaffer; music, Lasse Holm, Bert Mansson, Peter Grundström, Magnus Persson, Björn Isfält; sound, Eddie Axberg, Lasse Liljeholm; production design, Lasse Westfelt; costume design, Inger Pehrsson; production manager, Ann Collenberg. Reviewed at the Palladium, Malmö, Sweden, Oct. 9, 1990. Running time: **91 MIN.**
Inger . . . . Helena Bergström
Kaj . . . . Jan Mybrand
Tommy . . . . Carl Kjellgren
Robert . . . . Reine Brynolfsson
Lennart . . . . Johannes Brost
Anja . . . . Ing-Marie Carlsson

"**B**lackjack," Colin Nutley's second Swedish feature, is a charming slice-of-life pic about a provincial dance band that's the chief attraction for a small group of twentysomething friends. Pic should earn offshore sales and friends.

The divorced Inger (Helena Bergström) returns to her hometown from Stockholm with her young son just as her widowed father is about to pull up roots. Restless, Inger goes to the local dance hall for companionship.

Inger becomes infatuated with Tommy (Carl Kjellgren), the drummer of the dance hall band, Blackjack. She keeps nice and cleancut Kaj (Jan Mybrand) waiting on the sidelines. To Tommy, Inger obviously is just another affair, but it takes her a long time to realize that.

Film ends sadly and wistfully as Inger heads back for Stockholm, alone again, and the friends and bandmembers appear to realize that an epoch in their lives has ended.

Nutley, who's resided in Sweden for a decade, has a keen eye for the essential Swedishness of the dance halls and the role they play in the social life of young adults. He deftly paints minuscule character delineations and minimal subplots.

Not much happens in the pic, besides flirting and a few pranks, but acting is excellent, and behavior and dialog are well-observed. The music primarily is what such dance hall bands play: buoyantly corny stuff. — *Kell.*

LA STAZIONE
(THE STATION)
(ITALIAN)

An Academy release of a Fandango production. Produced by Domenico Procacci. Directed by Sergio Rubini. Screenplay, Umberto Marino, Filippo Ascione, Rubini, based on Marino's play; camera (color), Alessio Gelsini; editor, Angelo Nicolini; art direction, Carolina Ferrara, Luca Gobbi. Reviewed at Venice Film Festival (Critics Week section), Sept. 11, 1990. Running time: **92 MIN.**
Domenico . . . . Sergio Rubini
Flavia . . . . Margherita Buy
Danilo . . . . . . Ennio Fantastichini

Unapologetically indebted to its stage origins, "The Station" turns a three-actor drama into an involving film with plenty of laughs thrown in. Pic was a hit at the Venice fest's Critics Week, and should do brisk business with Academy releasing domestically. It could be a sleeper offshore with the right handling.

Stage thesp and director Sergio Rubini makes an eye-catching debut as helmer. Domenico (Rubini) is stationmaster of a sleeping train stop. On one cold and rainy night, he passes the long hours comically timing everything he can think of with his chronometer, from when the trains pass to how long it takes the coffee to perk.

At a fancy party in a villa, rich girl Flavia (the sparkling Margherita Buy) quarrels with her overbearing lover Danilo (Ennio Fantastichini). She impetuously runs off to catch the next train for Rome, while he furiously watches a contract go up in smoke without her backing.

Opposites Domenico and Flavia get acquainted during a long night of waiting for the 6 a.m. train. Their budding friendship, told with humor and tenderness, is abruptly interrupted by Danilo's drunken return. He goes on a rampage and wrecks the station, while Domenico and Flavia barricade themselves inside.

Alessio Gelsini's cinematography perfectly communicates a feeling of cold warmth in the little station lost in the great, stormy night. Director Rubini goes beyond conveying the tragicomic relationships among the trio, creating a charming fable poised between drama and hyperrealism. Gulf between the poor Southern provincial and rich city girl gently touches on a social theme without exaggerating.

All three principals know their characters inside out, having played them for three years on the stage. Buy shines as the sophisticated but vulnerable blond heiress. Rubini is a naive and tender stationmaster, recalling the hero of "Closely Watched Trains" as much as one of Ermanno Olmi's pure, country hermits.

Fantastichini, the arrogant, violent fiancé, is enjoyable as an over-the-top villain, even if a touch too theatrical compared to the other two. In "The Station," many will find the fresh new Italian film they've been waiting for. — *Yung.*

KAWASHIMA YOSHIKO
(THE LAST PRINCESS OF MANCHURIA)
(CHINESE)

A Golden Harvest presentation of a Friend Cheers Ltd. production. Executive producer, Teddy Robin. Produced by Anthony Chow, Erix Tsang. Directed by Eddie Fong (Fong Ling-ching). Screenplay, Li Pak-wah; camera (color), Jingle Ma; editor, Henry Chang; music, Jim Shum; production design, Eddy Mok, Fong Ying; costumes, John Hau; production manager, Janet Lam; assistant director, Eddy Yeung. Reviewed at Venice Film Festival (out of competition), Sept. 9, 1990. Running time: **109 MIN.**
Yoshiko Kawashima . . . . . Anita Mui
Ah Fook . . . . Andy Lau
Tanaka . . . . Patrick Tse
Amakasu . . . . Yee Tung-sing

In the wake of "The Last Emperor," a number of films based on real-life Chinese royalty emerge from China and Hong Kong. "Kawashima Yoshiko" is based on the character who was depicted in the Bernardo Bertolucci film in a lesbian relationship with Joan Chen. There are arthouse possibilities here, outside of the usual Chinatown circuit around the world.

Although the name is Japanese, Yoshiko Kawashima actually was an imperial princess of China who, in 1913 at the age of 6, was sent to Japan to be raised there, the idea being to provide a future link between the Chinese and Japanese empires.

Eddie Fong's handsome film purports to be a faithful biopic of this rather mysterious woman, who, at age 17, was married off to a Mongolian crown prince she didn't love. Soon after, she started wearing men's clothes and later became an army officer. In the film, she falls for a Japanese army captain, attempts suicide, shoots a lover as he's embracing her, uses drugs and overdrinks, smokes cigars and has affairs with men and women.

In the leading role, Anita Mui (memorable from "Rouge") is outstanding as this assertive woman who could also be exceedingly feminine. Her eventual downfall after the war, when she was brought to trial and executed for being a traitor to her native China, is given added irony by the fact that she never considered herself Chinese.

With location work in both Japan and mainland China, "The Last Princess Of Manchuria" looks suitably sumptuous. Occasionally interspersed newsreel footage emphasizes the basis on real-life characters, though with bits of kung fu and oodles of glamor thrown in, pic obviously takes liberties with history.

Nonetheless, it's an elegantly made and enjoyable saga, and is ultimately quite moving. — *Strat.*

DENVER FEST

CADENCE

A New Line Cinema release of a Republic Pictures and Intl. Movie Group presentation, in association with Northern Lights Entertainment. Produced by Richard Davis. Executive producers, Peter E. Strauss, Frank Giustra, Timothy Gamble. Directed by Martin Sheen. Screenplay, Dennis Shryack, Sheen, based on Gordon Weaver's novel, "Count A Lonely Cadence"; camera (color), Richard Leiterman; editor, Martin Hunter; music, George Delerue; production design, Ian Thomas; co-producer, Glennis Liberty. Reviewed at Denver Intl. Film Festival, Oct. 17, 1990. MPAA Rating: PG-13. Running time: **90 MIN.**

Bean	Charlie Sheen
Sgt. McKinney	Martin Sheen
Garcia	F. Murray Abraham
Stokes	Larry Fishburne
Spoonman	Blu Mankuma
Webb	Michael Beach
Sweetbread	Harry Stewart
Lawrence	John Toles-Bey
Lamar	James Marshall
Gerald	Ramon Estevez

There's a surefire cadence to the Stockade Shuffle, a winning putdown of chain gang group singing, but that's not the rhythm this ill-fitted film succeeds in maintaining, although that is its most memorable sequence.

Martin Sheen's directorial debut fails to reveal a talent at the helm corresponding to his acting ability. His film vacillates between a lonely guy film, a psychopathic bully film, a film about a social group finding strength in unity and a film about racism. These disparate elements make the film abrupt in its opening scenes, confusing and only intermittently on target.

Pic treads on the familiar ground of "From Here To Eternity," which set the standard for films about high-minded loners in conflict with the brutal military mind. A shapeless, meandering script combined with stale elements results in divided directorial energies.

Charlie Sheen plays an introverted soldier from Montana in conflict with his father, a relationship not shown but indicated very abruptly. He gets roaring drunk when his father dies, and ends up in the stockade where he joins five blacks in the usual jockeying for position.

The elaborate Stockade Shuffle this quintet executes with great style gives them the fortitude to withstand the taunts of Sgt. McKinney (Martin Sheen).

Martin Sheen runs the stockade by sudden feints to catch the prisoners off guard, but fails to win respect. A brief phone call to his wife is considered sufficient explanation of his woeful tyranny, but, like the film, it is a superficial element. Sheen lacks cogency in a role which fails to earn compassion.

Pic's climax is a midnight patrol to the work farm in a rainstorm where the over-the-cliff sergeant shoots one of the men.

The most involving sequences have to do with Sheen's efforts to restore a dilapidated windmill, and the excitement when it pumps out water. This lift is too quickly over.

Charlie Sheen's inability to project emotion makes him withdrawn from the action and turns him into a zero. There are animated performances by fellow prisoners Larry Fishburne, Blu Mankuma, Michael Beach, Harry Stewart and John Toles-Bey. F. Murray Abraham in several brief scenes shows his usual competence as an army legal eagle.

Richard Leiterman's camerawork is always good, making the Vancouver locations do for Germany's Black Forest region. No dramatic use is made of the encampment being in Germany, another instance of muddled filmmaking. — *Alyo.*

THE CHEATER
(SOVIET)

A Mosfilm Studios release. Directed by Sergei Bodrov. Screenplay, Valery Barakin, Bodrov; camera (color), Sergei Taraskin. Reviewed at Denver Intl. Film Festival, Oct. 15, 1990. Running time: **98 MIN.**
With: Valeria Garkavian, Yelena Safonova, Nodar Mgaloblishvili, Viktor Pavlov, Luisa Mosends.

Russian director Sergei Bodrov holds the heat to the seat of this intensely filmed thriller. His technical mastery and the care with which he draws the viewer into his web show the director's acknowledged debt to such directors as John Huston and Carol Reed.

"The Cheater," also known as "The Card Sharp," is the story of Greek, a handsome fellow whose life is divided between running excursion boats and playing cards for money. When his associate in the boating business loses heavily in cards to a man of mystery known as "the director" and is killed, Greek vows vengeance and determines to find the large cache of his associate's money.

Tracking down the director leads Greek into a corrupt world where everything has a price. He passes through varied segments of Russian society which seem sunny but quickly turn dark. One seeming friend is suspected of treachery, and from then on the film takes an increasingly dramatic vision, with Greek's life on the edge.

Bodrov has a great gift for casting to further a sense of reality. Valeria Garkavian plays Greek with disarming flair and acute dramatic skills. All the playing is uniformly firstrate.

Bodrov stages the cardplaying scenes ably, and in several scenes of violence shows a force and directness that chills. In every scene the filming by Sergei Taraskin is superbly evident. — *Alyo.*

THESSALONIKI

EROTIS STI XOURMADIA
(LOVE UNDER THE DATE TREE)
(GREEK)

An Alekos Papageorgiou, Stavros Tsiolis, Greek Film Center production. Written and directed by Tsiolis. Camera (color), Vassilis Kapsouros; editor, Costas Iordanidis; music, Pavlos Papadopoulos, Stamatis Spanoudakis; sound, Thanassis Arvanitis; sound recording, Costas Poulentzas. Reviewed at the Thessaloniki Greek Film Festival, Oct. 6, 1990. Running time: **84 MIN.**

Panayotis	Argyris Bakirtzis
Yanis (the maestro)	Lazaros Andreou
Anna	Dora Masklavanou
Filites	Vina Asiki

"Love Under The Date Tree," best film awardwinner at the Thessaloniki fest, is a magnificently shot, cleverly cast and well-scripted comedy about two mismatched friends who roam the Greek countryside searching for a significant date tree. Admissions for domestic films are down, but pic should travel well.

Shortly after his wife's funeral, Panayotis (superbly played by Argyris Bakirtzis, dynamic lead singer of a popular musical group), confronts close friend Yannis (Lazaros Andreou), the maestro with a photo he found of Yannis and his late wife Maria, taken under a date tree.

Yannis, practicing the violin he used to play during duets with pianist Maria, is dumbstruck. Panayotis is certain the photo proves Maria's infidelity, and he knows of no date trees in Greece.

The maestro, shielded by his violin case, explains his side of the story in one of the film's most memorable episodes. A brilliantly paced rapid-fire exchange ensues as the maestro spills his story in bits and pieces to the skeptical Panayotis. The fest audience roared and burst into applause.

The maestro insists the photo was taken on an innocent outing on a seashore in the Peloponnese, but he can't recall exactly where. So they set off to find it.

The rugged mountainous terrain and sea views are breathtaking. The interiors and exteriors of the traditional stone houses in villages recall a more hospitable era.

The pace seems to lag midway through, and the enticing premise of the search for the date tree seems extraneous. Panayotis cuts a wide swath across the Peloponnese, renewing old flames and adding new conquests including Anna (Dora Masklanou), a sympathetic bartender.

Pic's main virtue, ultimately, is in sketching the characters of this odd couple. The maestro, in a subtle sweet-natured performance that won Andreou the best actor award in Thessaloniki, is a short, unimposing figure most often with a lachrymose expression, a perfect foil for his tall, elegantly bearded sidekick.

Their physical contrast and interaction, with the gentle maestro always accommodating his self-centered obsessive friend, is reminiscent of Peter Cook and Dudley Moore.

The musical score, from bouzouki to violin, is cleverly integrated. Especially memorable is the scene in which the two perform a choreographed version of the Everly Bros.' "Bye, Bye Love."

Pic ends as it began, with a funeral, and it is apparent the hunt for the date tree was more or less a MacGuffin. But this doesn't hinder its appeal as a well-crafted and humorous view of a relationship. — *Sam.*

SINGAPORE SLING
(GREEK-B&W)

A Greek Film Center-Marni Film-Cinekip production. Produced by Maria-Louise Bartholomew. Written and directed by Nicos Nicolaidis. Camera (black & white), Aris Stavrou; editor, Andreas Andreadakis; sound, Argyris Lazarides; mixing, Sound Studio/Nikos Despotidis; art director, Marie-Louise Bartholomew. Reviewed at the Thessaloniki Greek Film Festival, Oct. 6, 1990. Running time: **114 MIN.**
Daughter/Laura . . . Meredyth Herold
Mother . . . . Michele Valley
Singapore Sling . . Panos Thanassoulis
(English soundtrack)

Nicos Nicolaidis' violent black & white shocker "Singapore Sling" is a film noir view of a bawdy "Psycho" with campy overtones of "The Rocky Horror Picture Show."

Pic, definitely unsuitable for general audiences, should aim for a cult niche on the midnight show and specialty tracks. It could run into a rating problem, especially in countries that enforce restrictions on theatrical and vid release of violent pics.

"Singapore Sling" opens with mom (German-Swiss actress Michele Valley) and daughter (Meredyth Herold) in mud-splattered rain gear and goggles, digging the grave for the not-quite-dead chauffeur.

A flashback establishes that Laura (also Herold), an innocent secretary, applied for work at the mansion where mom and

daughter live. After engaging in a weird sexual parody recalling Zap comic books during the interview, she is stabbed to death in the kitchen. Mom, decked out like Theda Bara, and daughter grin ghoulishly as they plop the bloody, throbbing viscera on the table, giving viewers a clue this is not a movie for the squeamish.

Singapore Sling arrives during a thunderstorm (that continues until pic's end) and is desperate and wounded. After daughter knocks him out, she and mom find out from a note he carries he is searching for his vanished lover Laura.

A "film noir" atmosphere is established by the use of total night scenes, the frequent refrain of Otto Preminger's "Laura" theme and a voiceover in Greek explaining Singapore Sling's search. Aris Stavrou won the best cinematography award at Thessaloniki for his luminescent, ominous black & white lensing.

"Singapore Sling" fails to hold an audience's attention by a solid scenario or underlying social comment, so is forced to rely on voyeuristic kicks. Ultimately, it's a highly stylized exercise in kinky sex and violence.

American model Herold got the best actress nod in Thessaloniki for her convincing bow as the nubile and decidedly deft daughter. Mom is strictly highcamp in standard vampiress tradition. Singapore Sling is silent and semicomatose. This crew makes it difficult to create any audience identification.

Although it would seem the viewers would be completely densensitized by the time the literal and figurative climax unfolds in a vicious ultra-Freudian version of "Psycho," its total effect is unrelentingly savage.

Final scenes, accompanied by Rachmaninoff's "Rhapsody On The Theme Of Paganini" reveal helmer's fascination with the apotheosis of death, which loomed so large in previous features "The Sweet Bunch" and "Morning Patrol." It doesn't look as pretty here.

Nicolaidis insists pic is a black comedy, but the Thessaloniki SRO crowd did not laugh. Still, the screening caused a sensation and he captured the fest's best director award. — *Sam.*

KUKOLKA
(THE DOLL)
(SOVIET)

A Mosfilm production. Directed by Isaac Fridberg. Screenplay, Igor Agheev; camera (Sovcolor), Vladimir Nakhabtsev; music, David Tukhmanov; sound, Oleg Burkova; production design, Tatyana Lapshina. Reviewed at Pitt Center 3, Sydney, Aug. 4, 1990. Running time: **131 MIN.**
With: Svetlana Zasypkina, Irina Metlitskaya, Vladimir Menshov.

"The Doll" is an uncompromising critique of the effects of rigorous athletic training on youths in the USSR and, presumably, in other countries.

Pic's likely to grab the attention of arthouse audiences and could have a successful international career.

Pic opens with a semi-documentary sequence depicting an audition among 6-year-old girls for future training as gymnasts. One, Tania, is chosen and undergoes years of solid coaching. She emerges with a massive ego and a narrow outlook on the world outside sports.

For a while, she successfully represents the USSR in world competition, but, during a meet in Britain, she injures her back. No longer of use to the sporting world, she is forced to enter normal life. At 16, she attends a public school for the first time.

Not surprisingly, she has an attitude problem, and the bulk of the film depicts her pathetic attempts to assert herself in the classroom now that her glory days are over. Her determination to be No. 1. is frustrated by a young schoolteacher, Elena, who sympathizes and tries to help but finds the devious, scheming teenager a formidable opponent.

All this is quite an eye-opener, and there's more: In one quite tender sequence, the lonely teacher sleeps with a student who has a crush on her.

This scene apparently caused a stir in Moscow two years ago (the film is dated 1988). Actor Rolan Bykov (best known for his lead role in "The Commissar"), artistic director of the newly formed youth unit at Mosfilm (which produced "The Doll") strongly objected to the scene. The matter had to be arbitrated by the filmmakers union, which found in favor of director Isaac

Fridberg.

The focus of attention in this powerful pic is a thoroughly convincing performance from young Svetlana Zasypkina as the odious, bullying and yet pathetic former athlete.

Zasypkina, obviously trained as a gymnast herself, is chillingly convincing as the self-important youngster who, despite her size, sets out quite deliberately to disrupt and control her fellow students. Her performance certainly deserves international attention, and so does this solidly made pic with its revealing ideas about sporting heroes. — *Strat.*

NOUVEAU CINEMA

LE DIABLE D'AMERIQUE
(THE DEVIL OF AMERICA)
(CANADIAN-DOCU)

A National Film Board of Canada production in association with P.A.F. Produced by Yvon Provost, Eric Michel, Muriel Rose. Directed by Gilles Carle. Camera (color, 16mm), Jean-Pierre Lachapelle; editor, Christian Marcotte; music, Dr. John; sound, Richard Besse. Reviewed at the Festival Intl. du Nouveau Cinema et de la Video Montreal, Oct. 23, 1990. Running time: **73 MIN.**

Trying to define the "devil" is the subject of this chatty docu, which is more like radio with illustrations than film with narration. Dozens of talking heads provide wall-to-wall dialogue in rapid succession as helmer Gilles Carle attempts to explain the roots of North America's belief in Satan.

Carle's research includes documentation from Jesuit priests in 1637 to present-day voodoo rituals in the Louisiana bayou, to modern-day priests in rural Quebec townships. "The Devil In America" may be informative, but it's also exhausting. Outside its native Quebec, pic's only venue is tv. (Ranging in length from 51 to 74 minutes, however, they will be difficult to program as a package.)

Docu is part of a National Film Board of Canada four-part "collection" of films titled "Parler D'Amerique" (Talking About America). In "The Devil In America" numerous authorities are interviewed from Quebec and the U.S., explaining "what" the devil is and where the concept originated.

One religious historian, Benoit Lacroix, argued the devil was "inspired by popular imagination." Another said, "all we're trying to do is control sex." Pic touches on many points without drawing any distinct conclusions.

Anything negative can be blamed on the devil, per this docu, including the atom bomb, shopping malls, pollution and computer technology. The last talking head argues that the devil is a manmade creation, an interesting conclusion in itself.

A terrific soundtrack (by Dr. John) is underused and could have provided some welcome breathing space. Footage of people in devilish costumes riding horses on misty beaches provided pretty punctuation throughout, but were also undermined by the incessant narration. (Pic would have to be dubbed or screened only for speed readers with subtitles).

Carle, who made his reputation directing thesp Carole Laure in a slew of fiction films including "Marie Chapdeleine," fails to bring his refined talent for fiction to the docu genre. — *Suze.*

CARGO
(CANADIAN)

A Prima Film presentation of a Velvet Camera and Cleo 24 production. Produced by Bruno Jobin, Francine Forest. Directed by François Girard. Screenplay, Michel Langlois, Girard, Marcel Beaulieu; camera (color), Daniel Jobin; editor, Gaétan Gravel; music, Bill Vorn, Gaétan Gravel; sound, Artefact; assistant director, Jacques Laberge. Reviewed at the Festival Intl. du Nouveau Cinema et de la Video Montreal, Oct. 24, 1990. Running time: **90 MIN.**
Marcel . . . . Michel Dumont
Alice . . . . Geneviève Rioux
Philippe (papa) . . . . . Guy Thauvette

This capricious debut film won't establish François Girard as a serious director even on home turf. Only thing making "Cargo" watchable is Daniel Jobin's postcard-perfect cinematography. Pic's sole venue is local tv.

It takes Girard 90 minutes to make one simple point: Throw caution to the wind, "just do it." There is never a moment's doubt from reel one that Girard was leading up to this message.

This profundity takes place on a sailboat. The spokesperson is a young woman, Alice, advising her workaholic father to lighten up and have fun. He just wants to get off the boat (smart man).

When a savage storm interrupts their dinner and advice session, Alice is pitched overboard. Her lover Marcel, also on the trip, foolishly dives in to rescue her. In one of the two scenarios Girard pursues, they both drown. In the other, the father is rescued by a cargo ship mysteriously carrying Alice and Marcel, who have survived.

Although it's never clear which is the "real" story, in the end the two have vanished and the father, as predicted, throws caution to the wind by staying on the cargo ship. — *Suze.*

SATURDAY, SUNDAY AND MONDAY
(ITALIAN)

A Silvio Berlusconi Communications production in conjunction with Reteitalia and Carlo Ponti. Produced by Alex Ponti. Directed by Lina Wertmuller. Screenplay, Wertmuller, Raffaele La Capria, based on the play by Eduardo de Filippo; camera (color) Carlo Tapani; set design, Enrico Job; costumes, Benito Persico; associate producer, Thierry Caillon. Reviewed at the Chicago Intl. Film Festival, Oct. 25, 1990. No MPAA Rating. Running time: **119 MIN.**
Rosa . . . . Sophia Loren
Don Peppino . . . . . Luca de Filippo
Guililannela . . . Alessandra Mussolini

"Saturday, Sunday And Monday" is a surprisingly low-key effort by director Lina Wertmuller.

Wertmuller, whose best-known films are cursed and blessed by outrageous excess, does a capable job with this pleasant domestic comedy, but it's sober and even-handed to the point of somnolence.

Boxoffice potential is limited to the drawing power of topliner Sophia Loren. She's fine as Rosa, an aging Italian matriarch who fears she is losing her husband's affections.

Eduardo de Filippo's stage play of the same title, a big international success in the '50s, was reportedly written with her in mind, and it's easy to see why. As an icon of Italian femininity, an almost-mythical representation of the Great Mother (a term that manages to work its way into virtually every scene), she's a natural.

Maybe a bit too natural. It's clear Loren felt no need to stretch for this role, and she seems to be going through the motions for most of the film. Of course, Loren going through the motions can be more enjoyable than many actresses working at full-tilt.

As Don Peppino, Rosa's foolishly jealous husband, Luca de Filippo acquits himself well, but mainly seems to be serving as a mournful-eyed stand-in for Wertmuller's erstwhile leading man, Giancarlo Giannini.

The story itself, about a marital crisis that resolves itself over a three-day period, is entertaining enough, though a bit overlong. Lots of colorful character roles offer earthy respite from the ersatz sophistication of Rosa and Peppino's battle of the sexes. — *Brin.*

KONECHNAYA OSTANOVKA
(THE LAST STOP)
(SOVIET)

A Sovexportfilm presentation of a Kazakhfilm Studios production. Written and directed by Serik Aprimov. Camera (color), Murat Nugmanov. Reviewed at Toronto Festival of Festivals, Sept. 13, 1990. (In Chicago Intl. Film Festival.) Running time: **77 MIN.**
With: Sabil Kurmanbekov, Murat Ajmetov, Nuguimbek Samaev.

Serik Aprimov's first feature is a slice of life in the barren, shabby landscape of Aksuat, Kazakhstan, that will appeal to curiosity seekers. But with its weak storyline, shaky tech credits and amateur thesping, "The Last Stop" has little else to offer audiences.

Erken returns home to Aksuat after an army stint, only to find his world greatly changed. His fiancée married someone else six months after he left, and he can't find a job.

After attending a local wedding, Erken and his buddies wind up drinking, and a brawl ensues. Erken convinces his ex-fiancée to have a sexual liaison with him in a spare room of his friend's house, and he despairingly realizes the futility of the relationship. He finally decides to leave town forever.

Aprimov uses nonprofessional townspeople as actors and portrays them as lazy and unmotivated. But he captures the lives of these people in their mud-built homes on the desolate plains of Kazakh as they eke out a living.

At screening caught, audience was laughing throughout and could not produce the proper compassion for the lead character. Pic does work as a travelog of an obscure part of the Soviet Union. — *Devo.*

LA MUERTE INUTIL DE MI SOCIO MANOLO
(THE USELESS DEATH OF MY PAL MANOLO)
(CUBAN-COLOR/B&W)

An Instituto Cubano de Artes e Industiras cinematográficos (ICAIC) production. Produced by Muguel Mendoza. Directed by Julio García Espinosa. Screenplay, García Espinosa, based on the play "Mi Socio Manolo," by Eugenio Hernández; camera (color, black & white), Livio Delgado; editor, Justo Vega; music, Juan Blanco; song, Pablo Milanes. Reviewed at II Festival CineSan Juan, Puerto Rico, Oct. 13, 1990. Running time: **84 MIN.**
Manolo . . . . Mario Balmaseda
Cheo . . . . Pedro Rentería

Never one to refrain from experimentation, Cuban Film Institute chief Julio García Espinosa has brushed up on deconstruction theories for this quirky big-screen version of Eugenio Hernández' play "My Pal Manolo." Outside select fest and arthouse screenings, international distrib possibilities seem extremely limited.

Emphasizing the artifice of the theatrical text, pic moves in and out of legit setting and is rife with directorial devices inserted to distance the viewer.

Story begins with a visit Cheo (Pedro Rentería) pays to old friend Manolo (Mario Balmaseda), whom he had not seen in many years. Out comes the alcohol and in comes the polemic as they both deliver a series of charged monologues about life and their opposing interpretations of the revolution, in which they both had fought.

That this highly hermetic work should be produced at this time seems appropriate, since it mirrors Cuba's resistance to the democratic movements throughout the socialist world.

Acting is larger than life, and Balmaseda's frenetic thesping is effective for the stage but overwhelms his screen presence.

Text abounds with local Cuban

expressions and concerns that find little in common with other Spanish-speaking countries, limiting any popular success in Latino markets.

Livio Delgado's rich lensing, full of long takes and disturbing closeups, only underlines pic's essential coldness of tone. Final third of the film is shot in black & white for no obvious reason except to once again call attention to the fact that this is only a film. Unfortunately though, this is not a very interesting one. — *Lent.*

LOS CUENTOS DE ABELARDO
(ABELARDO'S TALES)
(PUERTO RICAN)

A Corporación de Producciones Culturales production. Produced and directed by Luis Molina Casanova. Screenplay, Gilda Galán, based on the works of Albelardo Díaz Alfaro; camera (color), Milton Graña; editor, Alfonso Borrell; music, Javier Hernández; sound, Antonio Betancourt. Reviewed at II Festival CineSan Juan, Puerto Rico, Oct. 14, 1990. Running time: **82 MIN.**
Don Teyo Gracia . . Juan Ortíz Jiménez
"DON PROCOPIO EL DESPEDIDOR DE DUELOS"
Don Procopio . . . . José Luis Marrero
Juana Tiburcio . . . . Gilda Galán
"PEYO MERCÉ ENSEÑA INGLÉS"
Peyo Mercés . . . . . Jacobo Morales
Peyo's wife . . . . . Gladys Rodríguez
"BAGAZO"
Domingo . . . . . . Orlando Rodríguez
Wife . . . . . Luz Minerva Rodríguez
Mayordomo . . . . Jaime Ruiz Capataz

"Abelardo's Tales," docu-maker Luis Molina Casanova's first feature, is an anthology pic incorporating three tales into an uneven folksy venture that may attract fans of an old radio show based on same source material, but is unlikely to draw today's filmgoers.

Puerto Rican writer Abelardo Díaz Alfaro's stories of simple folk living in rural towns entertained radio listeners in the '40s. His narratives were portraits of neighbors and friends related through the fictional character of Don Teyo Gracia, who never missed an opportunity to bend someone's ear.

First story, "Don Procopio el Despedidor de Duelos," is the most successful in its whimsical portrayal of a gleeful undertaker, always ready with a few words and an outstretched hand. His happiness is haunted by his awareness that one day he also will be in need of these services.

The more political "Peyo Mercé Enseña Inglés" revolves around

a country teacher forced to teach English to rural children at the expense of their Spanish.

"Bagazo," is a manipulative account that bogs down in facile clichés. Closest to a traditional story, episode concerns an aging canecutter fired by a new field boss, who turns an unhearing ear to the man's plight.

Cameraman Milton Graña opts for a static lensing infused with a rich patina, leaving the viewer a cinematic impression of a Maxfield Parrish painting.

Thesping is fine, especially Juan Ortiz Jiménez as Don Teyo, a potential bore who everyone seems to tolerate.

Use of local expressions and obscure *jibaro* proper names is amusing, as is the tone of the first two stories. But overall effect is marred by uneven selection of material and an effort to be too literal to the text. — *Lent.*

DANCES WITH WOLVES

An Orion Pictures release of a Tig production. (Intl. sales: Majestic Films Intl.) Produced by Jim Wilson, Kevin Costner. Executive producer, Jake Eberts. Directed by Costner. Screenplay, Michael Blake, based on his novel; camera (Panavision, Deluxe color), Dean Semler; editor, Neil Travis; music, John Barry; sound (Dolby), Russell Williams, Mary Jo Devenney; production design, Jeffrey Beecroft; costume design, Elsa Zamparelli; art direction, Wm Ladd Skinner; set decoration, Lisa Dean; associate producer, Bonnie Arnold; assistant director, Douglas C. Metzger; 2nd unit director, John Huneck, Philip C. Pfeiffer; 2nd unit camera, Huneck, Pfeiffer; casting, Elisabeth Leustig. Reviewed at Orion Pictures screening room, L.A., Oct. 25, 1990. MPAA Rating: PG-13. Running time: **183 MIN.**
Lt. Dunbar . . . . Kevin Costner
Stands With A Fist . Mary McDonnell
Kicking Bird . . . . . . Graham Greene
Wind In His Hair . . Rodney A. Grant
Ten Bears . . . . . . Floyd Red Crow Westerman
Black Shawl . . . . . Tantoo Cardinal
Timmons . . . . . . Robert Pastorelli
Lt. Elgin . . . . Charles Rocket
Maj. Fambrough . . . . Maury Chaykin
Stone Calf . . . . Jimmy Herman
Smiles A Lot . . . . Nathan Lee Chasing His Horse

In his directorial debut, Kevin Costner brings a rare degree of grace and feeling to this elegiac tale of a hero's adventure of discovery among the Sioux Indians on the pristine Dakota plains of the 1860s. Despite its three-hour length, pic stands a good chance of being a word-of-mouth hit and one of the season's most widely popular pics.

Costner stars as Lt. John Dunbar, a Union officer in the Civil War invited to choose his own post after an act of heroism. Opting for the farthest reaches of the frontier because he "wants to see it before it disappears," he transplants himself from a weary and cynical war culture to the windswept clarity of the Dakota plains.

Arriving at the remote outpost assigned him by an insane major (Maury Chaykin), Dunbar finds it deserted and, to the disbelief of his wagon driver (Robert Pastorelli), opts to unload his provisions and stay.

His only company as he passes the days are his horse, a gangling wolf who keeps a nervous distance, and, finally, a Sioux Indian who tries to steal the horse and is frightened off by Dunbar.

Because whites and Indians automatically killed each other upon meeting, each party lived in ignorance of the other. Dun-

bar's virtue is that he resists violence, putting himself at risk with the Sioux until they trust him and accept him.

Dunbar keeps a journal, hoping to create "a trail for others to follow." He discovers a culture so deeply refreshing to his spirit, compared with the detritus he's left behind, that, by the time the U.S. Army bothers to look for him, he has become a Sioux and his name is Dances With Wolves.

Of course, the Union soldiers completely misunderstand his purposes, giving pic the tragic cast this saga historically deserves.

Script by Michael Blake portrays the Sioux culture with appreciation, establishing within it characters of winning individuality and humor. Design team accents the diverse beauty of the actors (all Native Americans) with striking combinations of paint, feathers and deerskin in costuming.

Unfortunately, the script seems to have run out of understanding by the time the Union soldiers arrive to do a job on the "traitor" Dunbar, and portrayal of this loutish and brutal mob, who refuse so much as to hear him out, is pic's weakest and most manipulative passage.

Still, it makes effective drama and, if interpreted metaphorically, the scene conveys the spirit of rape and plunder that had vanquished the Sioux culture within a mere 13 years of this story's unfolding, according to the screen epilog.

Lensed on location in South Dakota over 17 weeks, pic is infused with the natural grandeur of the plains and sky, captured in all their variance by cinematographer Dean Semler.

Score by John Barry makes a major contribution, varying from the elegiac tone of the main theme to the spirited adventure of classic Westerns, to the heart-racing primal rhythms of the buffalo and scalp dances.

Costner's directing style is fresh and assured. A sense of surprise and humor accompany Dunbar's adventures at every turn, twisting the narrative gently this way and that and making the journey a real pleasure.

Perhaps he is a bit precious with himself as star. One wonders how many times he's going to tip over backward in mock defeat to show us he's a playful guy, or how much masochism he'll indulge in when Dunbar is imperiled.

But making up for it are scenes of mystical power and beauty, such as Dunbar's first earth-shaking nighttime encounter with the buffalo as they hurtle past him through the fog.

Contrasting the gentle Sioux with the savage and aggressive Pawnee who made war on them, pic lends a sense of history to their ultimate vanquishment.

Project, first from Costner and co-producer Jim Wilson's Tig Prods., reps a teaming of three longtime friends — Costner, Wilson and writer Blake, who first collaborated in 1981 on "Stacy's Knights," Costner's first starring pic.

From its three-hour length, which amazingly does not become tiresome, to its bold use of subtitled Lakota language (the Sioux tongue) for at least a third of the dialog, it's clear the filmmakers were proceeding without regard for the rules. Their audacity in doing so, because they knew what they had, is as inspiring as the film itself.

Mary McDonnell ("Matewan") is impressive as Stands With A Fist, an emotionally traumatized white woman adopted by the Sioux who helps Dunbar communicate with them. Her perf is particularly notable for the technical accomplishment of her tremulous, flat-sounding delivery of English, a language she hasn't heard since early childhood.

Native American actors Graham Greene (as the holy man Kicking Bear) and Rodney Grant (as the warrior Wind In His Hair) give vivid, transfixing performances, bringing much spirit and skill to Orion's early entry in the Christmas derby. — *Daws.*

CHILD'S PLAY 2

A Universal Pictures release of a David Kirschner production. Produced by Kirschner. Directed by John Lafia. Executive producer, Robert Latham Brown. Screenplay, Don Mancini, based on characters he created; camera (Deluxe color), Stefan Czapsky; editor, Edward Warschilka; music, Graeme Revell; sound (Dolby), John M. Stacy; production design, Ivo Cristante; art direction, Donald Maskovich; set decoration, Debra Combs; costume design, Pamela Skaist; Chucky design-engineering-2nd unit director, Kevin Yagher; 2nd unit camera, Max Pomerleau; co-producer, Laura Moskowitz; casting, Karen Rea. Reviewed at the Universal Studios screening room, Nov. 5, 1990. MPAA Rating: R. Running time: **85 MIN.**

Andy Barclay . . . . . . Alex Vincent
Joanne Simpson . . . . . Jenny Agutter
Phil Simpson . . . . . . Gerrit Graham
Kyle . . . . Christine Elise
Voice of Chucky . . . . . Brad Dourif
Grace Poole . . . . . . Grace Zabriskie
Also with: Peter Haskell, Beth Grant, Greg Germann, Raymond Singer, Charles C. Meshack, Stuart Mabray.

"**C**hild's Play 2" is another case of rehashing the few novel elements of an original to the point of utter numbness.

Sadistic and mercifully brief, this cloddish sequel can score big initially with the audience that made its predecessor a hit. But it doesn't appear to have the legs to sustain further Chucky incarnations.

Universal actually came on board the Chucky bandwagon one film too late, having picked up rights to "Play 2" after MGM/UA, under Qintex' short-lived management, opted not to go ahead with it on moral grounds.

While this marketing-driven horrorfest is certainly no worse than conventional slasher fare, there is a troubling side to its manipulative reliance on having this homicidal doll repeatedly torment the same little boy (Alex Vincent), returning castmember from the first pic.

The novelty of a smiling doll spouting expletives and crinkling his nose has also long since worn off, so the filmmakers simply hammer away at walk-down-the-hallway clichés in an effort to provide the cheapest thrills.

Failure to satisfactorily explain what brought back Chucky — especially after the doll was thoroughly and deservingly mangled at the end of the first film — demonstrates a disdain for the audience.

The original "Child's Play" involved a serial killer/Satan worshiper who, before his death, transferred his consciousness into an oversized doll. He then spent the rest of the film trying to get out of the doll and into the body of the little boy who owned it, while the boy's mother and a slow-to-convince detective sought to thwart his plans.

Here, little Andy (Vincent) has been separated from his mother, temporarily institutionalized after the ordeal. He is placed in a foster home with two drab parents (Jenny Agutter, Gerrit Graham) and a rebellious teen (Christine Elise), ultimately the only person to believe him.

With Chucky (again voiced by Brad Dourif) doing mischief, poor little Andy is blamed for every bad thing that occurs. It's less amusing to note that Andy, this time, is practically the sole focus of Chucky's homicidal rage, sending a delightful message to children about dolls coming to life and seeking to kill them. That should save everyone some bucks on Christmas presents.

Director John Lafia and writer Don Mancini, who shared writing credit on the original with its director, Tom Holland, milk each situation far beyond its interest level. Chucky's dialog, as plastic as the character himself, relys on the fact that a toy mouthing four-letter words is somehow titillating.

The puppet techniques are finely executed, but it's difficult after awhile to take this 3-foot-high version of the Terminator seriously.

Barclay is two years older but still cute as a button, but when he pulls a Rambo and arms himself with an electric carving knife, unintentional laughter is hard to suppress.

No other living character is equally animated, as the adults are essentially pincushions, with about as much personality.

Tech credits are adequate, though the film's climactic sequence in a toy factory is both predictable and choppily edited. If only Chucky could have possessed that sequence and given it a few well-deserved whacks as well. — *Bril.*

GUNS

A Malibu Bay Films release and production. Produced by Arlene Sidaris. Written and directed by Andy Sidaris. Camera (Filmservice color), Howard Wexler; editor, Michael Haight; music, Richard Lyons; sound (Ultra-Stereo), Jon M. Hall; production design, Cherie Day Ledwith; art direction, William Pryor; costume design, Rina Eliashiv; assistant director, Mike Freedman; stunt coordinator, James Lew. Reviewed at Magno Review 2 screening room, N.Y., Nov. 8, 1990. MPAA Rating: R. Running time: **95 MIN.**

Jack of Diamonds . . . . . Erik Estrada
Donna Hamilton . . . . . . Dona Speir
Nicole Justin . . . . . Roberta Vasquez
Bruce Christian . . . . . Bruce Penhall
Edy Stark . . . . . . Cynthia Brimhall
Lucas . . . . William Bumiller
Cash . . . . Devin Devasquez
Shane Abilene . . . . . Michael Shane
Kathryn Hamilton . . . . Phyllis Davis
Abe . . . . Chuck McCann
Also with: Chu Chu Malave, Richard Cansino, George Kee Cheung, Danny Trejo, Rodrigo Obregon, John Brown, Kym Malin, Liv Lindeland.

"**G**uns" is the fifth and campiest film in the "Malibu Express" adventure series. Combo of bullets and bosoms is out of step with current theatrical tastes but shapes up as a potent video title for RCA/Columbia next year.

Erik Estrada joins the cast of regulars as an evil gunrunner using Hawaii (homebase of the Malibu team) to ship modern weaponry from China to South America. He's also carrying out a vendetta against Dona Speir, undercover agent whose cover is an air cargo service based in Molokai.

Years back Estrada killed Speir's dad and is now having her associates murdered, with his trademark Jack of Diamonds playing card left on the corpses. William Bumiller rounds up the usual team of government spooks to protect Speir and put Estrada out of business.

Filmmaker Andy Sidaris includes his usual quota of well-staged explosions and action scenes, including a nifty plane chasing motorcycle sequence.

Though the film is played ostensibly straight, several scenes and the cast of beauties' stilted acting quickly provoke unintentional hilarity. By having Estrada's two hitmen henchmen (Chu Chu Malave, Richard Cansino) dressed in drag most of the time, as well as regular Rodrigo Obregon also dressing up in high heels, Sidaris poaches on Pedro Almodóvar territory with funny results.

Estrada, comic relief magician/undercover man Chuck McCann and "Vegas" tv veteran Phyllis Davis (as Speir's mother, who is the attorney general of Nevada) give pro performances but the rest of the cast of mainly Playboy magazine models, pinups and male musclebuilders needs intensive remedial training with Stella Adler.

Speir's new teammate Roberta Vasquez (soon to be seen in Clint Eastwood's "The Rookie") is physically adept in the action as well as the frequent disrobing segments. She takes the place of Speir's partner in three previous films, Hope Marie Carlton, but no explanation is offered for the brunette for blond replacement.

Another statuesque Playboy alumna, Cynthia Brimhall, is literally thrust forward in a major role as a Vegas nightclub singer who warbles the title theme. Villainess Devin Devasquez gets some laughs due to pouting and her intentionally trashy outfits courtesy of designer Rina Eliashiv. — *Lor.*

LA TIGRA
(THE TIGRESS)
(ECUADORAN)

A Grupo Cine Production. Produced by Lilia Lemos. Directed by Camilo Luzuriaga. Screenplay, Luzuriaga, from the novel by Jose de la Cuadra; camera (color), Rogrigo Cueva, Diego Falconi; editor, Pocho Alvarez; music, Sebastian Cardemil, Diego Lazuriaga; sound, Carlos Naranjo; production design, Socrates Ulloa. Reviewed at Montreal World Film Festival, Aug. 29, 1990. Running time: **80 MIN.**
With: Lissette Cabrera, Rossana Iturralde, Veronica Garcia, Aristides Vargas, Virgilio Valero.

Said to be the first feature produced in Ecuador since 1980, "The Tigress" won't be a commercial bet outside Latin America, but a curiosity item.

Two older, sexually active sisters have been warned by a medicine man that their younger sister must remain a virgin forever to pay for the sins of the village. The pair do everything to keep men away from her.

Writer-director Camilo Luzuriaga has made a tentative and plodding picture. However, given the evident lack of a regular filmmaking base, this one-off production is to be commended. More films from Ecuador will be awaited on the fest circuit.

The three actresses enter into the pic's spirit with gusto. Male characters are far less convincingly written and played. Technically, "The Tigress" is perfectly adequate. — *Strat.*

BULLET IN THE HEAD
(HONG KONG)

A Milestone Entertainment presentation of a John Woo Film production. Produced and directed by Woo. Screenplay, Woo, Patrick Leung, Janet Chun; camera (color), Ardy Lam, Wilson Chan, Somchai Kittikun, Wong Wing-Hang; editor, Woo; music, James Wong, Romeo Diaz; art direction, James Leung; action coordinator, Lau Chi-Ho. Reviewed at the Toronto Festival of Festivals, Sept. 10, 1990. (In Vancouver Intl. Film Festival.) Running time: **100 MIN.**
Ben . . . . Tony Leung
Frank . . . . Jacky Cheung
Paul . . . . Waise Lee
Luke . . . . Simon Yam
Jane . . . . Fennie Yuen
Sally . . . . Yolinda Yan

In the wildest Vietman film to date, helmer John Woo ("The Killer") spares no blood in this graphically violent, vile and thoroughly disturbing depiction of war. A must-see for cinephiles, it's likely to be a homevid hit among specialists, but much too intense for commercial audiences.

Machine-gun editing sets a relentless pace. Lush cinematography heightens the wicked realism. Casting is superb, but this is not a pretty picture. Gallons of blood and brains are splattered across the screen during a gut-wrenching 100 minutes. Comic and romantic touches provide occasional breathers.

Pic begins in Hong Kong slums in 1967 where gang wars ruled the streets and demonstrations were commonplace. Three inseparable teens with Ninja warrior potential — Ben, Frank and Paul — are quickly established as vicious survivors.

On Ben's wedding night, Frank is mangled by a rival gang leader when fetching funds to pay the caterer. The war is on. The rival leader is ruthlessly murdered and the boys flee the country.

A scene in which Ben bids farewell to his new bride is a harbinger of the violence to come. During a demonstration, a bomb expert errs and, screaming and armless, staggers into the street. There's a tender moment in which Jane advises Ben to forget her.

With a suitcase full of pharmaceutical drugs to deliver in Saigon for quick cash, the boys' hopes are dashed again when another bomb accidentally blows their car (and drugs) sky high during a military assassination.

A handsome Rambo-like Eurasian rebel with a heart of gold, Luke, becomes mentor and savior to Ben, Frank and Paul. With a pocketful of explosive cigars and an arsenal of guns at his disposal, Luke engineers a gold heist which leads to a bloodbath and introduces the next love interest, Sally (who dies during their semi-successful escape).

The boys wind up in a prison camp where G.I.'s pleading for their lives are blown away in closeup. But Rambo-Luke arrives with the U.S. "cavalry" in the nick of time.

Woo avoids a happy ending. Paul, overcome with greed and still lugging the chest of gold secured during the heist, shoots Frank in the head because his wounded body is too heavy to carry. Ben is shot in action but rescued by monks. Luke is helicoptered to safety with Frank's half-dead body by the U.S. army. Yet another grim and graphic end awaits the trio back in Hong Kong.

A heroin addict with a bullet still lodged in his head, Frank is mercifully shot by Ben as scarfaced Luke gazes on.

This pic is absolutely relentless. Its ultra-anti-romantic view of war offers no hope and little breathing space. As vile as Norman Mailer's "The Naked And The Dead" and as riveting as "The Deer Hunter," this repulsive portrait of war will undoubtedly encounter barriers in North America for its extreme violence. — *Suze.*

BAKENBARDY
(SIDEBURNS)
(SOVIET)

A Lenfilms Studio production. Directed by Yuri Mamin. Screenplay, V. Leikin; camera (color), S. Nekrasov; editor, O. Adrianova; music, A. Zalivalov, L. Gavrichenko; sets, P. Parkhomenco. Reviewed at San Sebastian Film Festival, Sept. 27, 1990. Running time: **102 MIN.**
With: A. Vakha, O. Alabysheva, A. Lykov, O. Samarina, A. Shuravliov, V. Mikhailov.

Interest in this whimsical pic will be limited mostly to students of perestroika and lovers of Pushkin, who also may chuckle at some of the outlandish farce.

Pic opens with a Russian youth organization scandalizing its small town with its unruly behavior. Dressed like punks, the group, called "The Chapel," races about dancing, singing and shouting.

Enter two men dressed in 19th-century garb who espouse the patriotic and liberalizing ideas of the Russian poet Pushkin. They convert a clay bust of Lenin into one of Pushkin and form a club named after him to bring back nationalist Russian culture and dignity.

Gradually new members join the Pushkin group. They dress in black, wear derbies and ride about stiffly on bicycles. With the consent of the authorities, they take on the punks, first restoring order to the town and then gradually seizing political power. (The antics are often seen through a fish-eye lens.)

Just when peace seems to have been reestablished, Pushkin's old followers reappear, only now they sport yellow jackets and recite poems by Mayakovsky.

Overwrought and purposely overacted, pic has a kind of bizarre charm and qualifies as a curiosity in Russo cinema.

— *Besa.*

LA FRACTURE DU MYOCARDE
(CROSS MY HEART)
(FRENCH)

A Belbo Films production. (Intl. sales: Transit Film, Montreal.) Produced by Ludi Boeken, Jacques Fansten. Written and directed by Fansten. Camera (color), Jean-Claude Saillier; editor, Colette Farruggia; music, Jean-Marie Senia; sound, Jules Dantan; production design, Gilbert Gagneux; production manager, Eric Dussart. Reviewed at Montreal World Film Festival (Cinema of Today & Tomorrow section), Sept. 1, 1990. Running time: **105 MIN.**
Martin Gaudinier . . . Sylvain Copans
Jerome . . . . Nicolas Parodi
Marianne . . . . Cecilia Rouaud
Claire . . . . Lucie Blossier
Helene . . . . Delphine Gouttman
Also with: Kaldi El Hadj, Mathieu Poissin, Wilfried Flandrin, Romauld Jarny, Benoit Gautier, Wilfird Blin.

A film about a 12-year-old boy's reactions to the unexpected death of his mother, "Cross My Heart" is given light and charming treatment. Arthouse possibilities are good for this delightfully offbeat first feature from an established tv director.

At first appearing to be unduly morbid, pic starts out with young Martin finding his mother, a cleaning woman, dead on her bed. Because he never knew his father, he's terrified of being sent to an orphanage, and doesn't know what to do.

His schoolmates rally 'round when they discover his plight. They help him conceal the fact that his mother is dead. An old grandfather clock becomes a coffin, a hated stepmother's car becomes a hearse and wasteland outside town becomes a graveyard.

But burying the body is only the beginning of the problem. They have to organize to feed Martin and tutor him so teachers won't suspect anything. Even more complicated, Martin discovers that his next-door neighbor, a married man, was having an affair with the mother and wants to know her whereabouts.

When the authorities catch on near the end, an orphanage scene indicates the children were right to fight such a fate. The place seems determined to crush any individuality.

Writer-director Jacques Fansten has made a loving film about the world of children. The youngsters are so determined to help and protect their bereaved friend that they all achieve goals they might never have even attempted if the crisis hadn't occurred.

Fansten doesn't neglect humor, either. Some scenes are wickedly funny, others delicately touching. There's also a fair amount of suspense ("Like a Hitchcock film," says one of the boys).

Above all, the young and enthusiastic cast gives delightfully natural performances, headed by Sylvain Copans as the orphan who touchingly talks to his mother's photo and makes a heartbreaking speech at her "funeral."

Though it lacks stellar names and a name director, "Cross My Heart" (the French title refers to the dead mother's heart condition) is a winner, and, with loving distribution, could find success in almost any territory. Few will remain unmoved by the resourceful Martin and his loyal friends. — *Strat.*

ZVLASTNI BYTOSTI
(STRANGE BEINGS)
(CZECHOSLOVAKIAN)

A Barrandov Film Studios production. Directed by Fero Fenic. Screenplay, Fenic, Evzen Pltek; camera (color), Jaroslav Drabek; editor, Jiri Matoln; music, Jiri Dulis. Reviewed at the Vancouver Intl. Film Festival, Oct. 9, 1990. Running time: **78 MIN.**
With: Jan Tesarz, Ewa Zukowska, Jiri Babek, Vaclav Babka, Miroslav Suchy.

Laden with metaphors and heavy-handed symbols of decadence, decline and death, "Strange Beings" is very theatrical but lacks the cinematic punch needed for Western territories.

Zdenek, a political bureaucrat in serious personal decline and a symbol of decadent state bureaucracy, is the target of this political satire, which will be better received in former Eastern Bloc countries than in the West.

As the title suggests, each character is a "strange being," a symbol within a system seriously run amok. (Pic was shot just before last year's "Velvet Revolution" in Prague.)

Zdenek was losing it when his secretary/mistress decided to get him out of town before anyone noticed. Throughout the film, she comes to represent the victim, a repentant woman who questions why she always bowed to the whim of every bureaucrat. They are driven by a chauffeur, who eventually becomes the symbol of disillusioned youth, to his aunt's funeral, but it's the wrong funeral in the wrong town.

Finally reaching his hometown, he finds more strange beings roaming the streets and pubs. Raising a toast to expatriate Czech writer Milan Kundera, Zdenek finds himself being drawn into somewhat of an orgy (naked and semiclad youngsters watching a live sex act). Further confused, he winds up among old co-workers and eventually in the street after a stranger has slashed his tires.

When he and his mistress finally find the right funeral, the dead person turns out to be his own son. Zdenek is scolded by other family members who tell him: "You didn't care about him all these years: all you cared about was getting to the top." Zdenek has hit rock bottom.

Many scenes are bathed in red light, which casts an eerie glow on the whole film. — *Suze.*

NIE IM LEBEN
(NEVER EVER)
(AUSTRIAN-WEST GERMAN)

A Marwo Film (Vienna)-Voiss Film (Munich) co-production. Executive producer, Monika Maruschko. Written and directed by Helmut Berger, Nina Grosse. Camera (color), Han Günther Bücking; editor, Eliska Stribrova; music, Flora St. Loup, Lothar Scherpe; sound, Günther Knon; art direction, Angela Hareiter; costume design, Erika Navas. Reviewed at San Sebastian Film Festival, Sept. 23, 1990. Running time: **90 MIN.**
Scheiner . . . . Peter Hallwachs
Minski . . . . Helmut Berger
Mimi . . . . Anica Dobra

Never ever are the commercial prospects for "Never Ever," a turgid, tedious and self-indulgent film.

Pic lurches in its non-story from surreal imagery to humorless sight gags, and sometimes it

comes to a virtual stop as it seemingly improvises the next scene or dialog.

Item loosely revolves around a man trying to commit suicide, a girl who has just arrived in Vienna and a supposed bank robber. This unattractive threesome aimlessly mopes around in a story that has no beginning, middle or end. — *Besa.*

JITENSHA TOIKA
(BICYCLE SIGHS)
(JAPANESE-COLOR/B&W)

A PFF presentation of a Pia Co. production. Produced by Takashi Nishimura, Yutaka Suzuki. Directed by Sion Sono. Screenplay, Sono, assisted by Hishashi Saito; camera (black & white, color), Hiroyuki Kitazawa; editor, Hajime Ishihara; music, Great Riches/Bobo Brazil; sound, Yoshiaki Kitahara, Taku Iwasa; assistant director, Hisashi Saito, Takaaki Takeuchi. Reviewed at the Vancouver Intl. Film Festival, Oct. 9, 1990. Running time: **93 MIN.**
Shiro Kita . . . . Sion Sono
Katako Kita . . . . . Hiromi Kawanishi
Keita Tamura . . . Masahiro Sugiyama
Kyoko . . . . Hiroko Yamamoto
Nonomura . . . . Ryosuke Yamamichi
Kyoko's mother . . . . . . Yoko Takagi
Katako's mother . . . . . Izumi Sono

An amateur and jumbled feature debut, "Bicycle Sighs" is as vague as its title, and it's laden with narrative and technical difficulties.

Pic revolves around a group of teens who ride bicycles and want to make a Super 8 film about baseball. Billed as a film about "adolescent growing pains and frustrations," it perhaps manifests the director's own frustrations with filmmaking, resulting in a lot of navel-gazing.

Helmer Sion Sono plays Shiro Kita, who tries unsuccessfully to direct the Super 8 film himself. Black & white film within the film turns out far more interesting than the final product.

A dinosaur (a fellow student wearing a trenchcoat and a dinosaur mask) is an "invisible," imaginary baseball player. Fed up with the rigid structure of the game (three bases and homeplate), he disappears with first base, leaving a long trail of white baseline powder for the others to follow. As the teens desperately search for him, they begin to see other "invisible" characters because they are becoming invisible themselves.

Meanwhile, in the "real" film, Shiro Kita is thwarted by an ever-changing world where his

friends grow up and leave town, with his film unfinished. Several factors introduced in the last half hour, including two boys who douse themselves in gasoline and later appear unscathed, are never explained or resolved.

The crosscutting between the color and black & white sequences is choppy. The soundtrack is shrill. Other tech credits are average. — *Suze.*

MANKURTS
(SOVIET-TURKISH)

A Turkmenia Studios production in association with Tugra Film (Turkey). Directed by Hodzhakull Narliev. Screenplay, M. Urmyatov, based on the novel "The Day Lasts More Than A Hundred Years" by Chinghiz Aitmatov; camera (color), Nurtay Borviev; editor, Narliev. Reviewed at the Vancouver Intl. Film Festival, Oct. 4, 1990. Running time: **96 MIN.**
With: Artyk Dzhalliyev, Maygozel Aimedova, Yilmazy Duru.

Consequences of war have been depicted on film many times before this pic, but tech credits and action choreography in "Mankurts" surpass its country's usual standards.

Ancient Turkmenia's motto was: "Cowards run: men fight." So fight they did, riding camels and horses, flailing swords, resisting fascists, protecting the homeland and suffering torture.

Battle scene in which the hero Yoloman is captured is beautifully shot and slickly edited. Visual violence is kept to a minimum in torture scenes. Pic is set in numerous Asian locations.

Once captured, Yoloman is one of many prisoners subjected to a ritual whereby they lose their memories. (Their heads are shaved and tightly wrapped with the skin and fur of a freshly killed camel.) Tied to a stake and left to wither in the desert sun, most prisoners perish.

The survivors, including Yoloman, become slaves (mankurts) to a vicious totalitarian regime. Yoloman's blind devotion eventually leads him to shoot his own mother who has come to rescue him.

Narliev has directed a beautiful antitotalitarian metaphor which could be adapted to any war in any country. He avoids a sappy ending but unfortunately uses the tired slow-motion, freeze-frame finale.

Pic isn't destined for boffo b.o.

anywhere; it doesn't shock. However, translation is excellent and may help to find the pic a place on tv or homevid. — *Suze.*

AYA
(AUSTRALIAN)

A Ronin Films (Australia) release of a Goshu Films P/L production, with the assistance of Film Victoria and the Australian Film Finance Corp. (Intl. sales, Kim Lewis Marketing.) Produced by Denise Patience, Solrun Hoaas. Written and directed by Hoass. Camera (Fujicolor), Geoff Burton; editor, Stewart Young; music, Roger Mason; sound, Ben Osmo; production design, Jennie Tate; production manager, Robert Kewley; assistant director, Euan Keddie; associate producer, Katsuhiro Maeda; casting, Hoaas. Reviewed at Montreal World Film Festival (Cinema of Today & Tomorrow section), Aug. 30, 1990. Running time: **96 MIN.**

Aya	Eri Ishida
Frank	Nicholas Eadie
Mac	Chris Haywood
Junko	Micki Oikawa
Inoue	Takahito Masuda
Kato	John O'Brien
Nancy	Mayumi Hoskin
Barry	DJ Foster
Frank's mother	Marion Heathfield
Doctor	Tim Robertson
Ken, age 5	Christopher Parker
Ken, age 12	Jed Chedwiggen

A well-meaning picture about a Japanese war bride in postwar Australia, "Aya" has considerable qualities but ultimately fails because of a thin and disconnected screenplay. Theatrical possibilities loom difficult; perhaps video is a better bet.

Writer-director Solrun Hoaas is a Norwegian-born Australian who lived for several years in Japan and speaks the language fluently. She previously made a documentary, "Green Tea And Cherry Ripe," on the same subject as her feature debut. Docu seems to have been a dress rehearsal for the film.

Hoaas depicts the uneasy relationship between a typical Australian man and a sensitive, displaced Japanese woman. Unfortunately, director Hoaas is ill-served by writer Hoaas' screenplay, which too often smacks of first-draft material. Viewers are never told enough about the characters, and have to fill in too many gaps the filmmaker left wide open.

The film begins soon after the war, with Aya and Frank already married. Apart from one scene of awkward lovemaking, they never seem to be very happy. Frank dislikes Japanese food, hides Aya away from his mother and mistreats her. Nicho-las Eadie brings little depth to this boorish character.

Potentially more interesting is family friend Mac, who speaks Japanese and seems much closer to Aya than her husband. But, as played by Chris Haywood, Mac remains an elusive character. Why didn't he marry Aya himself, as he seems so fond of her? It's hinted he's gay, but the character remains frustrating.

So does the all-important background. Presumably Aya and Frank met when he was a soldier in defeated Japan, but little is known of her background apart from hearing the letters she writes back to her sister.

Proceeding in fits and starts and with little rhythm, great holes appear in the narrative as time passes. Offscreen, Frank has an accident and is consequently unable to work. Offscreen Aya (presumably) has an affair with a Japanese-Australian man, and gets pregnant.

In the film's most awkward sequence, Aya goes to see a lecherous doctor (overplayed by Tim Robertson) recommended by Mac. It doesn't ring true that a friend would recommend such a despicable doctor.

As Aya, the popular Japanese actress Eri Ishida is the pic's strongest point. With little material to work on, she manages to make Aya a touching, vulnerable, yet tenacious character.

Cinematographer Geoff Burton does a fine job, sometimes staging setups reminiscent of Japanese films. Other technical credits are good.

"Aya," though it has charming and touching moments, is ultimately frustrating because, given pic's story and resources, Hoaas could surely have made something more cohesive and substantial. — *Strat.*

CONNECTING LINES
(CANADIAN)

Produced by Dave Wilson, Mary Daniel. Written and directed by Daniel. Camera (color), William Evans; editor, Daniel; music, David Kershaw. Reviewed at the Vancouver Intl. Film Festival, Oct. 8, 1990. Running time: **108 MIN.**
With: David Brass, M. J. Daniel, Don DeMille, Guy Evans, Bee Farquhar.

An academic study of film structure and narrative directed for cinema intelligentsia, "Connecting Lines" has fine thesping and tech credits, but no future off campus.

Set in one boxcar on a four-day train ride, pic goes from Seattle to Los Angeles to New Orleans to Chicago and finally, back to Seattle. The only set is a booth where numerous passengers swap stories with the director (who plays a woman in limbo). Miles of boring scenery unspool in the window behind the table.

As the train pulls out of the station, the helmer confesses she "lost a love for my own anecdotes." She subsequently buries the viewer in an avalanche of anecdotes.

"When I started out I was just a little housewife and now I'm a full-fledged feminist: all in less than a month," explains one elderly woman.

Most folks on this train ride should be dealt with by advice from "The Accidental Tourist": Always carry a book. But the obnoxiously talkative passengers in this film are unavoidable, and for the most part, boring.

This Canadian pic probably was shot in the U.S. because Canada's VIArail coast-to-coast line has been eliminated, as have any long circular routes. The archetypical characters could be Canadian as easily as American.
— *Suze.*

GRAFFITI BRIDGE

A Warner Bros. presentation of a Paisley Park production. Executive producer, Peter MacDonald. Produced by Arnold Stiefel, Randy Phillips. Written and directed by Prince. Camera, Bill Butler; editor, Rebecca Ross; music, Prince; sound (Dolby), Matthew Quast; production design, Vance Lorenzini; costume design, Helen Hiatt, Jim Shearon; choreography, Otis Sallid; assistant directors, Kelly Schroeder, Jack Gallagher; associate producer, Simon Edery; coproducer, Craig Rice. Reviewed at UA Coronet Theater, L.A., Nov. 2, 1990. MPAA Rating: PG-13. Running time: **95 MIN.**

The Kid	Prince
Aura	Ingrid Chavez
Morris Day	Himself
Jerome	Jerome Benton
Melody Cool	Mavis Staples
George Clinton	Himself

Also with: Rosie Gaines, Miko Weaver, Levi Seacer, Michael Bland, Jimmy Jam, Terry Lewis, Jessie Johnson, Jellybean Johnson, Monte Moir.

Six years have passed since Prince's hit "Purple Rain" fell on filmgoers, and nothing so provocative has grown in the popstar's garden since. Warner Bros. will have a tough time recouping on this $7.5 million indulgence, even with the Warner Records sound-track.

Reviving the characters from the 1984 pic, including a reunited Morris Day and the Time, "Graffiti Bridge" amounts to a half-baked retread of tired MTV imagery and childish themes that will have even fans of the music eyeing the exit signs.

Plot revolves around rivalry between the Kid (Prince) and Day for control of a club they co-own. Day wants to play the songs the people want to hear; the Kid wants to focus on the music he's hearing from a higher power. They duel it out in various musical showdowns.

Chief embarrassment is the spotlight on Ingrid Chavez, latest of Prince's femme discoveries, as the cooingly coy love child with a direct line to the Maker.

"Mine?" the Kid (Prince) asks her as they lay cuddling in bed. "His," she says, pointing portentously at the ceiling. Either there's a richer guy upstairs, or she's trying to bring the Kid a Message.

Featured as a vocalist on one song, "Seven Corners," on which she shares writing credit with Prince, Chavez mostly whiles away her time at the park writing gooey poetry under Graffiti Bridge, a cute little archway symbolizing a pathway to a better place.

In one snippet of verse she sums up the plot and her place in it: "Seven corners/Two souls fight/One wants money/One wants light/Child of the spirit/Neither one can ignore/Has to show them/Heaven's door."

She wears no makeup when she writes, so it's clear she's an angel, and her bridge scenes are shot in soft focus.

That Prince wrote and directed this homage to his own creative process is evident. No idea is pursued for more than a few cartoonish minutes. What sustains a five-minute song doesn't sustain a bigscreen feature, as has been demonstrated too many times before by rockers-turned-filmmakers.

Mostly this amounts to a cinematic sandbox in which the Mascaraed One can play, pose and change costumes, inviting most of his gang to join in.

Most of the artists from Prince's Paisley Park record label show up in the film, including Mavis Staples, George Clinton, T.C. Ellis, Robin Power, Jerome Benton and the Time.

Sugar-voiced 13-year-old Tevin Campbell nearly steals the film with his brightly choreographed street performance. — *Daws*.

DICEMBRE
(DECEMBER)
(ITALIAN)

An Istituto Luce/Italnoleggio Cinematografica release of an Ager 3 producer, in association with RAI-1, Istituto Luce/Italnoleggio Cinematografica. Produced by Giuliani G. De Negri, Grazia Volpi. Written and directed by Antonio Monda. Camera (color), Tonino Nardi; editor, Roberto Perpignani; music, Gianluca Podio; art direction, Luciana Vedovelli Levi. Reviewed at Venice Film Festival (Critics Week section), Sept. 6, 1990. Running time: **90 MIN.**
Aunt Gianna . . . . . . Pamela Villoresi
Andrea . . . . Leonardo Trame
Federico . . . . Alessandro Haber
Alberto/Eduardo . . . . . . Pino Colizzi
Ida . . . . Susanna Marcomeni
Don Luigi . . . . Mattia Sbragia
Also with: Norma Martelli, Pierluigi Misasi, Salvatore Puntill, Elena Croce, Amelia Del Frate.

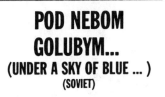

Antonio Monda overreaches in his ambitious directorial debut, "December," which probably won't make it far beyond a short arthouse run. The young helmer, however, shows enough talent and drive to be heard from again.

Film is interesting, especially during the first half, in its comparison of the viewpoints of a child and an adult in a story where little happens.

Andrea (Leonardo Trame) is at the center of a family drama taking place one December. His nonconformist aunt Gianna (Pamela Villoresi), a painter, suddenly loses her husband. After the funeral ceremony, beautifully depicted in all the baroque splendor of Catholic ritual, Gianna urges Andrea to stay in her magnificent Roman apartment and keep her company. The boy is eager for the chance to be with the aunt he has always admired. Out of compassion, his parents (Alessandro Haber and Susanna Marcomeni) let him stay through New Year's.

Andrea and his eccentric aunt share an enthusiasm for the cinema, fairy tales and the world of the imagination; Andrea because he's a child, Gianna in order to escape from reality. Eventually she drags the boy into what seems a paranoiac fantasy that she is being watched and stalked.

In a facile conclusion, it turns out Gianna was right all along, and Andrea plays a hero's role in trapping the burglar.

Monda, who worked with the Taviani brothers and dedicated an earlier docu to Michael Cimino, assigns himself the difficult task of telling the tale through the eyes of a child unable to grasp the real significance of what he sees. He finds his aunt beautiful, extraordinary and strong, whereas the viewer is clued in about her emotional fragility and loneliness. In the end, unluckily, pic becomes more academic in carrying out its project than emotional and involving.

Pic is strongest in drawing a portrait of the large, well-to-do family that is settled in Rome from Calabria. The Christmas scenes are full of atmosphere and warmth; the church visits are shown with unusual realism for an Italo film.

For a first film, "December" (title seems to echo Woody Allen's "September") is very accomplished visually. Tonino Nardi does a superb job of lighting Luciana Vedovelli Levi's ravishing sets. The aunt's apartment is a real delight.

Acting also is on a surprisingly high level. If Villoresi is too strong a taste for some palates, here she at least has a 3-D role to fill. Little Trame is an appealing eyewitness to the adult drama. Haber stands out in the semi-comic role of his father. — *Yung*.

POD NEBOM GOLUBYM...
(UNDER A SKY OF BLUE ...)
(SOVIET)

A Kinostudia-Belarus Film Studio production. Directed by Vitali Dudin. Screenplay, Viktor Merezko; camera (Sovcolor), Vladimir Kalasnikov; editor, Oleg Resetnikovoj; music, Vladimir Rjabov; sound, Vladimir Demkin; production design, Evgeni Ignatev; production manager, Rubim Sapiro. Reviewed at Venice Film Festival (out of competition), Sept. 13, 1990. Running time: **87 MIN.**
Alexei . . . . Igor Furmanjuk
Lena . . . . Anna Janovskaya
Kostyrina . . . . Nina Usatova
Sobolev . . . . Juozas Budrajtis

Yet another grim depiction of social ills in the Soviet Union, this ironically titled picture is about drug addicts and their effect on friends and family. "Under A Sky Of Blue ... " won't have much of a chance theatrically, but it could well feature in fests and film weeks.

Pic is well made, and has moments of fine direction, but it also raises the question of whether the endless stream of downbeat pictures emanating from Soviet studios are turning cinemagoers away.

Alexei and his girlfriend, Lena, are heroin addicts. Alexei's father, Sobolev, has bankrupted himself trying to pay for his son's habit, and is first seen vainly trying to sell a valueless icon to a gallery. Lena's father, who is an important state functionary and lives in a posh apartment guarded by KGB officers, has rejected his daughter and refuses even to see or talk to her.

Alexei, Lena and some of their more aggressive friends have taken over Sobolev's apartment. With nowhere to go, he seeks help from an acquaintance, Kostyrina, a plump, kindly, practical woman. She decides to sort things out herself, but gets more than she bargained for when she discovers that Lena is being held for ransom by Alexei's friends.

Nina Usatova makes the well-meaning Kostyrina the film's most interesting character. Her efforts to mediate between Lena and her unrelenting father are completely misunderstood (the bitter father assumes that Kostyrina is one of the people holding his daughter a virtual prisoner). Anna Janovskaya is appealing as the tragic Lena who, cut off from parental love and help, finally takes a drastic way out of her troubled life.

Director Vitali Dudin, in his first feature, paints an unrelentingly grim picture of contemporary Soviet life, with ugly, grimy apartments and little contact between the generations. He also brings off a number of outstanding moments and insights into his characters and their plight.

Only the ending lets him down, with a melodramatic and unconvincing conclusion. Nevertheless, he is clearly a director to watch in the future. — *Strat*.

ROJO AMANECER
(RED DAYBREAK)
(MEXICAN)

A Cinematográfica Sol production. Produced by Valentín Trujillo, Héctor Bonilla. Directed by Jorge Fons. Screenplay, Xavier Robles, Guadalupe Ortega Varges; camera (color), Miguel Garzón; editor, Sigfrido García; music, Karen, Eduardo Roel; sets, Helmut Greiser. Reviewed at San Sebastian Film Festival, Sept. 23, 1990. Running time: **97 MIN.**
With: María Rojo, Demián Bichir, Eduardo Palomo, Bruno Sichir, Héctor Bonilla, Jorge Fegan, Ademar Arau, Carlos Cardán, Martha Aura.

Set in 1968 during Mexico's brutal suppression of the student uprising, "Rojo Amanecer," shot entirely in one interior, chronicles the events of two days as they affected a middle-class family with two sons involved in the uprising.

Though pic has some good thesping and a slam-bang finale, its poor technical quality detracts greatly from its effect. The direction, dubbed sound, lighting and music are substandard.

Before rioting breaks out, the family is introduced: a grandfather who is an ex-military man; a a father who is a government functionary; a conciliatory mother; and two rebellious sons with posters of Che Guevara and the Beatles in their room.

Drama builds nicely as the sons leave the house, despite their parents' warnings, to join a street "meeting." Little by little, the violent events outside unfold. All that's seen, however, is the family looking out the window and gasping. Even a bit of stock footage would have been better than this total disregard of the deeds in the streets.

Director Jorge Fons and his scripters build the story to a contrived but emotive end. But the one-set ploy doesn't allow the pic to unfold properly.

Item might cull some interest for its outspoken condemnation of the Mexican government, still ruled by the same PRI party.
— *Besa*.

THIS IS NO WAY TO LIVE
(SOVIET-DOCU)

A Mosfilm, the Circle and Filmverlag Autoren presentation of a FTPO Mosfilm production. Directed by Stanislas Govoroukhin. Written by Govoroukhin. Camera (color), G. Engstrem; editor, N. Vasilieva; music, V. Vysotsky; sound, I. Mayorov. Reviewed at Montreal World Film Festival, Aug. 30, 1990. Running time: **109 MIN.**

This hard-hitting documentary pulls no punches in its condemnation of Soviet society from Lenin to Gorbachev. Authoritative BBC-type narration, crackerjack editing and relentless images of crime, alcoholism and poverty make this a very powerful docu.

Pic is guaranteed to shock westerners who believe things have improved since perestroika. It will undoubtedly arouse sympathy from its viewers. It's very solid fare for tv where the docu format is often perceived as "truth." If carefully handled, it should draw a solid audience.

Docu's manipulative structure makes it a Soviet "Roger And Me," minus the humor and entertainment qualities, which will limit its appeal. However, it's bound to be just as controversial if it finds the right audience.

Pic's politics are difficult to decipher. At a glance, it appears anti-communist. It makes "Red Nightmare" look like child's play. It condemns perestroika with equal vengeance. In one strategically placed scene, a 70-year-old farm woman says of the situation since Gorbachev took the helm, "It couldn't get any worse."

Numerous statistics without an identified source flash across the screen stating that crime has risen dramatically since 1988.

Early in the pic, Govoroukhin crosscuts between police incidents in New York and Moscow. In New York, he interviews two cops who, upon request, produce revolvers with lightning speed. In Moscow, he interviews a cop walking his beat; the billy club strapped to his wrist impeding his ability to quickly draw his gun. The comparison is clear: New York cops are better prepared to deal with crime.

In another NYC scene, narrator explains that a small crime — where "a prostitute is pushed into a car perhaps to extract a ransom from her pimp" — produces quick results from the police force. "Look how many policemen showed up," says the voice, noting that "the papers and tv covered the incident" as well.

These are just two examples of Govoroukhin's anti-crime message, but never at any point does the docu acknowledge that New York has difficulty controlling its own crime rate. Presentation is very one-sided.

Govoroukhin makes no bones about his belief that the current social and economic climate in Moscow and numerous other Russian cities and villages is "no way to live." It shows images of what westerners have suspected for years: Life behind the iron curtain is no picnic. — *Suze.*

LUISA, CARLA, LORENZA E... LE AFFETTUOSE LONTANANZE
(LUISA, CARLA, LORENZA AND... AFFECTIONATE DISTANCES)
(ITALIAN)

A Chance Film/RAI-3 release. A Maestranze e Tecnici del Cinema with Ciak Selezione Immagine production. Produced by Beppe Scavuzzo. Directed by Sergio Rossi. Screenplay by Age, Sergio Rossi; camera (color), Franco Lecca; editor, Massimo Palumbo Cardella; music, Maurizio Abeni, Anna Karin Klockar; art direction, Maria Silvana Farci. Reviewed at Fiamma Cinema, Rome, Aug. 6, 1990. Running time: **94 MIN.**
Luisa . . . . Lina Sastri
Carla . . . . . . Fiorenza Marchegiani
Lorenza . . . . . . Angela Finocchiaro
Also with: Giampiero Bianchi, Massimo De Rossi, Paco Reconti, Gisella Burinato.

Sergio Rossi's "Luisa, Carla, Lorenza And . . . Affectionate Distances" is an experimental portrait of three Italian women in their 40s. Pic often looks too much like intellectual entertainment for large audiences. It could have more fest runs.

Luisa, Carla and Lorenza are close friends who are professionally satisfied but living in deep solitude. Carla (Fiorenza Marchegiani) is a single mother who has had a longstanding love affair with a married man; Lorenza (Angela Finocchiaro) is believable as a ready-to-fall-in-love gynecologist.

The plot focuses on divorced art history prof Luisa (a smiling, self-consciously captivating Liná Sastri) and her encounter with a cautious cartoonist. He is divorced too, and their romance is precarious. Situations that seem headed toward psychodrama get lost in banal, predictable dialog.

Nothing really happens to the heroines, and they end up alone together. Despite its lack of dramatic dimension, "Distances" holds the attention, perhaps because of the agile editing.

This pic is representative of a new wave that examines the female universe, but its p.o.v. is unconvincing.

Soft lighting serves the general tone of the feature, but sometimes shots are out of focus or not balanced. — *Dani.*

ROCKY V

An MGM/UA release of a United Artists presentation of a Robert Chartoff-Irwin Winkler production. Produced by Winkler, Chartoff. Directed by John G. Avildsen. Executive producer-unit production manager, Michael S. Glick. Screenplay, Sylvester Stallone; camera (Deluxe color), Steven Poster; additional photography, Victor Hammer; editor, Avildsen, Michael N. Knue; music, Bill Conti; sound (Dolby), David B. Cohn; production design, William J. Cassidy; art direction, William Durrell Jr.; set decoration, John Dwyer; special makeup, Michael Westmore; assistant directors, Clifford C. Coleman, Hope R. Goodwin, Richard (Dub) Wright; associate producer, Tony Munafo; casting, Caro Jones. Reviewed at Columbia Studios' Cary Grant Theater, L.A., Nov. 11, 1990. MPAA Rating: PG-13. Running time: **104 MIN.**
Rocky . . . . Sylvester Stallone
Adrian . . . . Talia Shire
Paulie . . . . Burt Young
Rocky Jr . . . . Sage Stallone
Mickey . . . . Burgess Meredith
Tommy . . . . Tommy Morrison
George W. Duke . . . . . Richard Gant
Tony . . . . Tony Burton
Jimmy . . . . James Gambina
Karen . . . . Delia Sheppard
Merlin Sheets . . . . . Michael Sheehan
Union Cane . . . . . . Micheal Williams

Production notes and press interviews indicate Sylvester Stallone has rung the final bell on his Philly boxer series. That would be nice since "Rocky V" is the most dimwitted of the sequels. Still, MGM/UA should enjoy strong early rounds at the ticket window, even if this latest bout's slow pace ultimately mutes its trumpets.

It's hard to resist milking a fatted calf so "Rocky VI" doesn't appear to be such a long shot, despite the fact that its protagonist is now older than George Foreman. If film watchers have learned anything, it's to not count out Rocky prematurely.

John G. Avildsen, original "Rocky" director who's been off doing his own miniversions of the film ("The Karate Kid" pics) while Stallone was directing sequels II through IV, has returned.

Each series has pounded away at the original spirit of "Rocky" until all that remains of it is Bill Conti's score, which still brings a chill when it strikes up its fanfare.

Still, when the underdog always wins he's not much of an underdog anymore, and the narrative cartwheels Stallone has turned over the years to put Rocky in that position have peeled away the novelty — except, admittedly, to the hordes who willingly suspend disbelief to hoot and holler for each new "miraculous" comeback.

So it is with "Rocky V." Stallone again scripted and continues to evince a thudding lack of storytelling subtlety, sinking to a new low with the ending, which seems inspired by championship wrestling.

Stallone has never shied away from clichés in his "Rocky" sequels, but he positively goes wild with them here: Rocky left broke by mismanagement of his fortune, a Don King-like promoter (Richard Gant) pressuring Rocky to fight again, strained relations between Rocky and his son (real-life son Sage) because of Rocky's tutelage of a young boxer (Tommy Morrison) who ultimately turns on him.

The central problem is that Rocky suffers brain damage from his various beatings in the ring, making it risky for him ever to fight again. This point doesn't stretch reality much because Rocky hasn't blocked or dodged a punch since some time early in "Rocky II." It becomes ridiculous only when that threat is conveniently ignored so that Rocky can give his brawny protegé his comeuppance — this time in a bare-knuckled street brawl.

The film reaches absurd extremes all over the place, from the press corps lambasting and insulting interviewees (a real Nixon's-eye-view of the media) to the promoter allowing his mega-million-dollar dreams to be squandered during a live, televised street fight.

Burt Young has his moments as the slobbish Paulie. Talia Shire has become shrill and annoying as Adrian, more a symbol of Rocky's goodness in his unwavering devotion to her than an individual character in her own right.

Gant is perfectly hissable as Duke. Boxer-turned-actor Morrison (unlikely to launch a solo career as Mr. T, Hulk Hogan and Dolph Lundgren have off their "Rocky" roles) is serviceable as the ham-fisted heavy.

Flashy editing and long fight montages can't offset the film's sluggish pace, which lacks the sort of climactic high found in previous sequels. Conti's score remains the series' greatest asset, while its fight choreography has long since become a joke to anyone who's ever watched a real boxing match.

Rocky remains Stallone's most enduring, likable and unintelligible character, free of the stoicism and baggage of Rambo, his other franchise character. It's no wonder he keeps returning to it, like going home to a place where one can be genuinely loved.

Still photos over the closing credits seek to reinforce that this, indeed, will be the final "Rocky." Perhaps, but as long as audiences are punchy enough to keep coming back, don't count on it.
— *Bril.*

HOME ALONE

A 20th Century Fox release of a John Hughes production. Written and produced by John Hughes. Executive producers, Mark Levinson, Scott Rosenfelt. Directed by Chris Columbus. Camera (Deluxe color), Julio Macat; editor, Raja Gosnell; music, John Williams; sound, Jim Alexander; production design, John Muto; costume design, Jay Hurley; art direction, Dan Webster; set design, Bill Fosser, Karen Fletcher-Trujillo; set decoration, Eve Cauley, Dan Clancy; assistant director-associate producer, Mark Radcliffe; casting, Janet Hirshenson, Jane Jenkins. Reviewed at Avco Cinema, L.A., Nov. 8, 1990. MPAA rating: PG-13. Running time: **102 MIN.**

Kevin . . . . Macauley Culkin
Harry . . . . .Joe Pesci
Marv . . . . Daniel Stern
Kate . . . . Catherine O'Hara
Peter . . . . .John Heard
Marley . . . . Roberts Blossom
Gus Polinski . . . . .John Candy

Can writer-producer John Hughes and director Chris Columbus pull off an elaborate Christmas comedy with nothing in the center but an endangered eight-year-old kid? As the juvie protagonist cries every time he zaps a bad guy, Yes! And will Fox make money on it? Yes!

In standard Hughes style, tale spins from simplest premise. The family of poor little dumped-upon Kevin (Macauley Culkin) has rushed off to catch their holiday plane and accidentally left him behind.

Now they're in Paris, frantically trying to reach him, and he's home alone, where a storm has knocked out the telephones, the neighbors are away for the holiday and the houses on the street are being systematically cleaned out by a team of burglars.

Generally perceived by his family as a helpless, hopeless little geek, Kevin is at first delighted to be rid of them, gorging on forbidden pleasures like junk food and violent videos, but when the bandits (Joe Pesci, Daniel Stern) begin circling his house, he realizes he's on his own to defend the place.

Imaginative schemes he cooks up to baffle or foil them will delight kid viewers, while parents may be concerned about the level of violence. Columbus, working with virtuoso fluidity and bull's-eye instincts, plays the brutal gags cartoon-style, like a Roadrunner-Wile E. Coyote routine, a technique that lets the gags make their impact without really hurting.

Declining to seek outside help (for a reason that's never explained), Kevin proves he's not such a loser by defending the fort with wits and daring (his triumphant "Yes!" punctuating his every victory) and by the time Mom (Catherine O'Hara) comes rushing back from Europe, everything's in order.

Did it really happen? That's a question pic leaves up to the viewer, with a touch of magic that makes this entertainment just right for the holiday season.

Pic's psychology of comfort and abundance — Kevin's house is a roomy showplace stocked with all the good stuff and money never seems to be an obstacle to anyone's actions — may not ring true for much of the audience, but it's probably a welcome Christmas fantasy.

A firstrate production in which every element contributes to the overall smartly realized tone, pic boasts wonderful casting, with Culkin a delight as funny, resilient Kevin, and O'Hara bringing a snappy, zesty energy to the role of Mom.

Pesci, playing not quite as bad a fella as in "Goodfellas," is aces in the role of slippery housebreaker Harry, who does a Two Stooges routine with lanky sidekick Stern, and their stunt scenes offer plenty of laughs.

Hughes, whose formula falters from time to time, is in peak form here, and Columbus, the "Adventures In Babysitting" tyro who fell flat with Touchstone's tuneless Elvis fantasy "Heartbreak Hotel," has regained pro standing here.

John Williams' score is exceptionally apt, supporting the mood without prescribing it. Julio Macat's cinematography is impressive.

John Candy, with a wink and a nod to his role in a previous Hughes Yule Christmas entry "Planes, Trains And Automobiles," plays a traveling polka band leader who offers Kevin's mom a cross-country lift in a brief screen appearance sure to push buttons with the mainstream audience. — *Daws.*

THE NUTCRACKER PRINCE
(CANADIAN-ANIMATED)

A Warner Bros. release in the U.S. (Cineplex Odeon Films in Canada) of a Lacewood Prods. production. Produced by Kevin Gillis. Executive producer, Sheldon S. Wiseman. Directed by Paul Schibli. Screenplay, Patricia Watson, based on the book, "The Nutcracker And The Mouseking," by E.T.A. Hoffman; sequence directors, Chris Schouten, Shivan Ramsaran, Bill Speers, Zdenko Gasparovich; in color; music, Victor Davies; songs, Kevin Gillis, Jack Lenz; art director, Peter Moehrle; background-layout design, Sue Butterworth, Michel Guerin. Reviewed at Cineplex Odeon screening room, Toronto, Nov. 5, 1990. Running time: **75 MIN.**

Voices of: Kiefer Sutherland, Megan Follows, Peter O'Toole, Mike MacDonald, Phyllis Diller, Peter Boretski, Noam Zylberman, Diane Stapley, George Merner, Lynne Gorman, Stephanie Morgenstern, Christopher Owens, Mona Wasserman, Teresa Sears.

Animated feature, "The Nutcracker Prince," retells "The Nutcracker" in high style. Strong theatrical business with annual holiday season runs and enduring afterlife is predicted. It's not the ballet, but it's still a wonderfully romantic, rich adventure for kids and adults.

Faithful to the evergreen original, the story concentrates on 11-year-old Clara and her dreams. At her parents' Christmas party, magician-clockmaker Uncle Drosselmeir tells her the story of a young clockmaker assistant's transformation by a wicked mouse queen into a handsome nutcracker.

Story is dramatized vividly with much action, particularly from playfully arch mouse queen Phyllis Diller who, alas, gets killed off too quickly. At night, Clara creeps back to the living room where the toy soldiers and her nutcracker come alive to battle the roaring mouse king.

The next night the dolls come alive and, reduced to their size, Clara is transported to a magical land where the Nutcracker Prince proposes. She politely refuses, wanting to go back to her world, where she recognizes her prince in Drosselmeir's young nephew.

Animation work is high class, except for the few dull exterior scenes mainly at the beginning. Peter O'Toole, as wheezy, bumbling calvary leader Pantaloon, is fun. Toronto standup comic Mike MacDonald is deliciously menacing as the throughly wicked mouse king seeking revenge.

Vet Toronto actor Peter Boretski is pure magic as Drosselmeir. Megan Follows (Clara) carries the plot with style and grace. But Kiefer Sutherland comes off flat and lacks princely force. All other voices strongly match their character.

The London Philharmonic, conducted by Boris Brott, plays the Tchaikovsky score effectively, seemlessly blending with the plot. The two original songs, one of them, "Save This Dance" played over end credits, are okay but jar with the timeless score. Tech credits are excellent. This "Nutcracker" is a keeper. — Adil.

THE RETURN OF SUPERFLY

A Triton Pictures release of a Crash Pictures production. Produced by Sig Shore, Anthony Wisdom. Executive producers, Jon Goldwater, Rudy Cohen. Directed by Shore. Screenplay, Wisdom; camera, Anghel Decca, editor, John Mullen; music, Curtis Mayfield; sound, Jack Cooley; production design, Jeremie Frank; art direction, Charlotte Snyder; costume design, Ida Gearon, Varcra Russal; set decoration, Robert Covelman; assistant director, R.W. Dixon; coproducers, Robert Freibrun, Tom Gruenberg, Hank Blumenthal, Ray Bernstein; casting, Sarah Hyde-Hamlet. Reviewed at the Hollywood Pacific Theater, L.A., Nov. 9, 1990. MPAA Rating: R. Running time: **95 MIN.**
Priest	Nathan Purdee
Francine	Margaret Avery
Joey	Leonard Thomas
Tom Perkins	Christopher Curry
Hector	Carlos Carrasco
Nate	Sam Jackson
Wolinski	David Groh

Laconic direction and routine production make it unlikely anyone — even target black urban audience — will care about "The Return Of Superfly."

This time Eddie's dead, not Freddie, and Priest messes up pushers in a half-hearted turnaround from his drug-dealing days in the original "Superfly."

Nathan Purdee plays ex-pusher Priest (the Ron O'Neal role in the 1972 hit film), who returns from exile in Paris and is immediately detained by feds who want him to infiltrate his old gang and break it up. He's not interested, but after the old gang crosses him one too many times he sets

out to put them out of business.

Pic starts off with a rush in a suitably gritty, sleazy, ultraviolent seg in which the crack lords make a hit on rival pushers and wipe them out, ending with the execution of Priest's old pal Eddie.

Producer Sig Shore, directing for the first time since 1986 ("The Survivalist"), shows the right feel for a pulpy, degenerate joyride, with the action set to rhythm by Curtis Mayfield's funky-primal Afro-Caribbean score.

But the pace quickly dissipates after Purdee appears, slowing to a near-crawl for much of the film as script goes through its pointless, overfamiliar motions.

Purdee has the cool and authority for the role but the character's a bore, with not much on his mind. He's still "one cool sheet of ice," audience is told, and that's about it.

Writer Anthony Wisdom avoids giving Priest an antidrug mission — perhaps to avoid turning off pic's potential audience — but result is that he has no purpose or passion.

Other characters are sketched in so lightly and bumped off so fast they barely matter.

Shore brings no style or humor to a routine portrayal of New York's drug undergound. Pic's constant, predictable violence becomes dull, and Anghel Decca's underlit photography offers little to engage the eye.

Soundtrack is a plus, with Mayfield's update of his classic "Superfly" theme subtly put over. Tone-Loc and other rappers are heavily featured. Original plan to open film on the heels of the Capitol soundtrack's late summer release was flubbed, meaning that it's unlikely to fuel the picture. — Daws.

THE RESCUERS DOWN UNDER

A Buena Vista release of a Walt Disney Pictures production in association with Silver Screen Partners IV. Produced by Thomas Schumacher. Directed by Hendel Butoy, Mike Gabriel. Screenplay, Jim Cox, Karey Kirkpatrick, Byron Simpson, Joe Ranft, suggested by characters created by Margery Sharp; story supervisor, Ranft; camera (Technicolor), John Aardal, Chris Beck, Mary E. Lescher, Gary W. Smith, Chuck Warren; editor, Michael Kelly; music, Bruce Broughton; sound (Dolby), Louis L. Edemann, Paul Timothy Carden; art direction, Maurice Hunt; supervising animators, Glen Keane, Mark Henn, Russ Edmonds, David Cutler, Ruben A. Aquino, Nik Ranieri, Ed Gombert, Anthony De Rosa, Kathy Zielinski, Duncan Marjoribanks; layout supervisor, Dan Hansen; background supervisor, Lisa Keene; effects supervisor, Randy Fullmer; supervising character leads, Bill Berg, Brian Clift, Renee Holt, Emily Juliano, Marty Korth, Vera Lanpher; computer animation, Tina Price, Andrew Schmidt; casting, Mary V. Buck, Susan Edelman. Reviewed at the Mann National Theater, L.A., Nov. 10, 1990. MPAA Rating: G. Running time: **74 MIN.**
  Voices of: Bob Newhart, Eva Gabor, John Candy, Tristan Rogers, Adam Ryen, George C. Scott, Wayne Robson, Douglas Seale, Frank Welker.

This sort-of sequel to the 1977 hit "The Rescuers" boasts reasonably solid production values and fine character voices. Too bad they're set against such a mediocre story that adults may duck. Still, the inoffensive pic may be well-timed to cash in with youngsters during the holiday film crush.

Unlike Disney's better animated films, including recent entries like "The Little Mermaid" and "The Great Mouse Detective," this film doesn't achieve that highest level of appeal to "children of all ages" and may even bore a few 10-year-olds who've just sat through a 25-minute featurette and intermission.

The bare-bones storyline hinges on a little boy who inexplicably cavorts with animals in Dolittle-esque fashion, including a huge golden eagle, a species apparently indigenous to the Aussie Outback.

The bird is the prey of an evil hunter, McLeach (voiced by George C. Scott), who kidnaps the boy, resulting in a round-the-world call for those fearless mice of the Rescue Aid Society to come a-runnin'.

The film opens with its strongest sequence, as the boy frees the great eagle and then romps through the clouds aboard him. From there, however, it's a simple quest pic, as mice Bernard (Bob Newhart), Miss Bianca (Eva Gabor) and guide Jake (Tristan Rogers) fumble their way through the jungle, with Bernard poised to pop the question to his rodent love only to be interrupted by one threat after another.

Unlike most recent animated features, the film is not a musical. Instead, the producers have gone the action-adventure route, adding comic relief based largely on the simpleminded villains and the mice's transportation, an awkward albatross named Wilbur (John Candy).

Bruce Broughton augments the action immeasurably with his strongest score since "Silverado," providing soaring accompaniment to the film's opening credits and flight scenes.

The animation is fluid and sporadically beautiful, making clever use of computer animation to give devices like McLeach's tank-like vehicle a three-dimensional quality.

The character design, however, is bland, and too much of the film plays it cute, aiming below adult tastes. Younger children should be more impressed, at least by some of the visuals.

Scott seems to have fun with McLeach but he's hardly one of the memorable Disney villains. Newhart and Gabor, meanwhile, are given little material to chew on as the two mice.

While well-crafted technically, this story wouldn't be out of place airing at 3 p.m. on some independent tv station. With the labor that goes into an animated feature, the studio would be well advised to make sure the words soar before taking flight with its next animated sojourn.

"The Rescuers Down Under," however, has nowhere to go but up, following "The Prince And The Pauper," unimpressive 25-minute "featurette" and first Mickey Mouse vehicle since "Mickey's Christmas Carol" in '83.

The layouts are gorgeous, but Disney squanders the rich Mark Twain subject matter with a poorly assembled story and marginal animation. After the initial thrill of seeing Mickey onscreen, even children may be bored by the plodding pace.

Emphasis is on slapstick, but the pic isn't all that funny, generating a few chuckles with an underused Donald Duck and the incompetent weasel guards.

One nice twist to the Dan Rounds production directed by George Scribner involves some precredit tomfoolery and a Mickey hand counting down the intermission until "The Rescuers." — Bril.

DISTURBED

A Live Entertainment/Odyssey Distributors release. Produced by Brad Wyman. Directed by Charles Winkler. Screenplay, Emerson Bixby, Winkler; camera (color), Bernd Heinl; editor, David Handman, music, Steven Scott Smalley; sound, Dennis Carr; production design, Marek Dobrowolski; costume design, Pia Dominguez; art direction, Anna Ritti Raineri; stunt coordinator, Rawn Hutchinson; assistant director, Tommy Burns; coproducer, Patricia Foulkrod; casting, Tony Markes. Reviewed at Carolco screening room, L.A., Nov. 6, 1990. MPAA Rating: R. Running time: **96 MIN.**

Dr. Russell	Malcolm McDowell
Micheal	Geoffrey Lewis
Nurse Francine	Priscilla Pointer
Sandy Ramirez	Pamela Gidley
Pat Tuel	Irwin Keyes
Brian	Clint Howard

"**D**isturbed" is what film-goers will be if they plunk down admission price to this woeful exercise, but since the pic hasn't a chance of struggling through more than a week's booking, the general public will remain unharmed. Video distrib Live Entertainment self-booked a two-screen L.A. exposure started Nov. 16.

Lending his credibility to a project of truly dispiriting standards, Malcolm McDowell plays the chief psychiatrist (actually, the only one, owing to pic's low budget) at a secluded loonie hutch called Bergen Field. There he preys on female patients. In pic's charming opening sequence, he drugs and rapes one, leading to her suicide.

Years later, along comes a particularly feisty and bewitching wench (Pamela Gidley) who suffers more or less the same fate at his hands. Only she won't stay dead, which eventually drives him bonkers.

McDowell is enough of an actor to keep things watchable, while poor Gidley, lovely as she is, seems to think she's Jessica Lange in "Frances," and who can blame her, given the way pic borrows liberally from that and other nutso sagas. Is it "One Flew Over The Cuckoo's Nest?" one may think. Is it "Animal House"? Is it over yet?

Pic's creators, producer Brad Wyman and born-to-the-biz director Charles Winkler (son of Irwin) must have been as deluded as the inmates of Bergen Field when they told their unit publicist about the pic's stylistic references to Hitchcock and Carol Reed ("The Third Man").

Lenser Bernd Heinl ("Bagdad Cafe"), taking project and reputation a lot less seriously, kept amused during the shoot with wacko and genre-mocking camera angles. — *Daws.*

THE RAIN KILLER

A Concorde release of a Califilm production. Produced by Rodman Flender. Executive produced and directed by Ken Stein. Screenplay, Ray Cunneff; camera (Foto-Kem Laboratories color), Janusz Kaminski; editor, Patrick Rand; music, Terry Plumeri; sound (Ultra-Stereo), Bill Robbins; art director, Johan LeTenoux; set director, Colin de Rouin; costume design, Greg LaVoi; associate producer, Jonathan Winfrey. Reviewed at AMC Town & Country 10, Houston, Tex., Sept. 22, 1990. MPAA Rating: R. Running time: **93 MIN.**

Capra	Ray Sharkey
Dalton	David Beecroft
Adele	Tania Coleridge
Reese	Michael Chiklis
Hacket	Bill LaVallee
Rosewall	Woody Brown

Ray Sharkey and Michael Chiklis, survivors of "Wired," have a new film to live down. "The Rain Killer."

This limp, by-the-numbers thriller is in for a short, dry spell at the boxoffice during its current regional release. Vid forecast: brief flurry of interest, followed by arid stretch of obscurity.

Sharkey plays a hardboiled, heavy-drinking Los Angeles cop on the trail of a serial killer with an offbeat m.o. During those rare nights of L.A. rainfall, the villain stalks the streets, slashing attractive, wealthy and dripping wet women.

It turns out that each of the women is a recovering substance abuser from the same support group. This is a potentially interesting idea, but neither first-time director Ken Stein nor screenwriter Ray Cunneff can do anything interesting with it.

Take away the four-letter words and the laughably gratuitous nudity, and "The Rain Killer" resembles nothing so much as a tv pilot for a series few would bother to watch.

Sharkey glowers a lot, and gives the pic much more than it ever gives him. Chiklis, cast as his partner, wears a Boston Celtics cap most of the time. In one scene, however, he switches to a Cincinnati Reds cap. That passes for character development.

David Beecroft is the FBI agent assigned to work with Sharkey. Tania Coleridge is the agent's ex-wife, a wealthy recovering drug addict (uh-oh!) who falls for Sharkey. Coleridge looks so muscular — indeed, so androgynous — that, for a few moments, "Rain Killer" threatens to pull off a surprise twist.

But no: Beecroft spends most of the pic walking around with an expression that screams, "I'm the mad killer! I'm the mad killer!" After a while, Sharkey begins to notice.

Tech credits are mediocre. Several interiors are lit and photographed in a failed attempt at film noir. Quite often, it looks like "The Rain Killer" was shot in a low-lying cloud bank, or on a set where most of the crew were chain-smokers. — *Ley.*

A BULLET IN THE HEAD
(CANADIAN)

A Creon Prod. film in association with Mainfilm Independent Filmmakers Cooperative Montreal. Written, produced and directed by Attila Bertalan. Camera (color), Michel Lamothe; editor, Bertalan; music, Janet Lumb, Lorenzo Katona; sound, Martin Belanger; art direction, Kathleen Horner; set decoration, Jonathan Sommer; assistant director, Helene Tremblay. Reviewed at the Vancouver Intl. Film Festival, Oct. 2, 1990. Running time: **90 MIN.**

Dudka	David Garfinkle
Vida	Attila Bertalan
Mari	Andrea Sadler
Woodcutter	Jack Spinner
Gypsy woman	Victoria Sands
Wagon Driver	Claude Forget
Witch	Kathleen Horner
Verina	Susan Eyton-Jones
Katya	Rebecca Posner
Old enemy soldier	Jan Stychalsky
Young enemy soldier	
	Andrew Campbell

Audacious, modest and poignant, Attila Bertalan's "languageless" debut feature is a simple allegory about war and friendship. Its originality won't compensate on the commercial circuit for lack of action. Pic's outlets will be arthouses and tv.

The "no language" factor also means no dubbing or subtitles for any territory. Not to be confused with John Woo's "Bullet In The Head," Bertalan's film is slow-paced and essentially non-violent.

Intentionally universal in its statement, "A Bullet In The Head" is far from being silent. A terrific music score is used to communicate emotions and intro events.

The extremely limited dialog is gobbledygook, but one can easily imagine what the characters would be saying ("hello," "help," "money," etc.). Each character is a variation on Mr. Everyman, saying things which are said the world over. The setting is also intentionally fictitious: European country "X" around 1900.

In the first five minutes, a green-coated soldier named Vida (played by the director himself) loses his comrades and gets a tiny bullet lodged on the front of his skull, and spends the rest of the film trying not to get shot.

Elsewhere, a civilian named Dudka sets out to find medicine for his dying wife and is captured by blue-coated "enemies." Vida rescues Dudka, although the two don't become companions until close to the end of the pic when Dudka rescues Vida.

His clothing stolen by gypsies, Vida takes a blue coat off a dead soldier, and is mistaken by his green-coated comrades for the enemy. Having joined the green coats at random (after his wife died), Dudka must save his enemy/friend from torture.

Neither group of soldiers is depicted as right or wrong, good or bad. Aside from these two, the heroes and villains are interchangeable. Both sides commit atrocious crimes. Humanitarian qualities such as sympathy or compassion have no place in war.

Bertalan has managed to create an antiwar film where most violence happens offscreen, language is a virus and respect is a triumph. With a miniscule budget, this message is conveyed with surprisingly good production credits. Thesping, too, is good.
— *Suze.*

THE SECOND CIRCLE
(SOVIET)

A Lenfilm Studios production. Directed by Aleksandr Sokhurov. Screenplay, Yuri Arabov; camera (black & white, color), Alexander Burov; editor, R. Lissova; music, Olivier Nussio; sound, Vladimir Persov. Reviewed at the Toronto Festival of Festivals, Sept. 14, 1990. Running time: **92 MIN.**
With: Piotr Alexandrov.

A haunting masterpiece about death in, and of, the Soviet Union but a totally uncommercial film, "The Second Circle" is a jewel for scholars and specialists.

Minimalist sound, dialogue, editing, action and set design hinder any chance of b.o. in Western countries, although intellectuals will analyze these elements for their artistic and metaphorical contributions. Intentional mix of color and black & white footage is manipulated to perfection.

Sokhurov has made an intensely personal film which speaks volumes about contemporary Russia. Death lingers in the back room, with only a ray of hope for the future.

An impoverished young man's father dies on the weekend when funeral parlors are closed. The entire film takes place in his apartment with the dead man in the back room. Not much happens as the young man tries to come to terms with the death and his own future.

One of many austere images to unveil the son's emotional state is a two-minute closeup of the dead man's face from the son's perspective. The camera swings around to the dead man's point-of-view, focusing long and hard on the son's grim face. This chilling, highly stylized visual metaphor is structured by light, editing and absence of movement or sound.

Sokhurov makes a point of the dire Soviet economy as the son has trouble finding 200 rubles to pay for the burial. Monday finally arrives. The son helps an undertaker wrap his father's body in a white sheet, put it in the coffin and try to get it out of the apartment. It's a very hands-on process in stark contrast to Western funeral procedures.

After finally ridding himself of death in the apartment and in his life, light comes pouring through the windows.

An extremely slow-moving, sometimes still portrait of Soviet poverty and despair, it only offers a ray of hope in the final frame. No illusions, tricks or special effects are used. Such a vision is as pure as cinema gets. It will make a refreshing addition to archives and cinematheques.
— *Suze.*

BIOTEXNIA ONEIRON
(DREAM FACTORY)
(GREEK-COLOR/B&W)

A Tassos Boulmetis-Greek Film Center-ET 1 production. Written and directed by Tassos Boulmetis. Camera (color, black & white), Lefteris Pavlopoulos; editor, Giorgos Triantafyllou; music, Thimios Papadopoulos; sound, Marinos Athanassopoulos; costumes, Calliope Kopanitsa; sets, Michalis Sdougos; production manager, Mantis Voyatzidis; special effects, Christos Mangos. Reviewed at Thessaloniki Greek Film Festival, Oct. 1, 1990. Running time: **101 MIN.**
Dreamer/Jason . . . . Giorgos Constas
Athena/Underground leader. . . . . .
Filareti Comninou
Also with: Ilias Logothetis, Manos Vamvakoussis.

"The Dream Factory" has an interesting but improperly developed premise that leads its visual technique to override plot. The futuristic drama is best suited for arthouse release or fantasy fests.

Helmer Boulmetis, educated in film and video at UCLA, won best first feature award at the Thessaloniki fest. Film was blown up from video to 35m at great expense.

Action begins in sepia-toned scenes in an underground factory, sometime in the future after the "epidemic." The dream factory setting is strongly influenced by German expressionism, especially Fritz Lang's "Metropolis."

The Master Dreamer (Giorgos Constas) listens to clients who describe their dreams in great detail, especially the colors. Then he lies down and sleeps, and the dreams are re-enacted on a large screen, much to the delight of the clients. This seems to be a method to control individual innovation or any collective action, for not more than one person is allowed to have the same dream.

The setting changes to contemporary Athens. Lonely archaeologist Athena (Filareti Comninou) lectures a group while an unseen observer takes photographs in the bushes.

The focus is on a budding romance between Athena and her neighbor Jason, an actor, and a parallel relationship between the dreamer and a mysterious woman who becomes a member of an underground group aimed at changing Athens back to its old ways.

Little of the decaying metropolis' ugliness is shown. Athena works at the ancient Agora, a site of breathtaking beauty, and she and Jason live in a charming elegant older building, instead of one of the characterless concrete blocks of flats that congest the cityscape.

Too many tantalizing hints are thrown out and never expanded upon. Jason belongs to a strange, outcast theatrical company and has phone conversations with the director Yuri, who encourages him to report on Athena. The purpose of this group is not revealed and the "epidemic" never explained.

The love affairs never blossom, and the few intimate scenes between Athena and Jason are cut short. She relates her dream about two young girls, which

becomes an obsession with the dreamer: He keeps seeing the dream instead of those of his clients, which enrages both them and his supervisor.

"The Dream Factory" follows in a long tradition of surrealistic explorations from Luis Buñuel's "Un Chien Andalou" to Akira Kurosawa's "Dreams." It invites Freudian and Jungian interpretations, and is bound to appeal to viewers in analysis.

Technical credits are topnotch. Pic carried off the best makeup, sets and editing awards at the Thessaloniki fest.

Foremost Greek actor Constas (Jason, the dreamer) gives a polished performance in his two roles. Rest of cast is good, especially Manos Vamvakoussis, who won a special award for supporting actor as a dream client and an actor. — *Sam.*

AENIGMA EST
(GREEK-DOCU)

An ET 2 production. Written and directed by Dimitris Mavrikios. Camera (color), Lefteris Pavlopoulos; editor, Mavrikios, Christos Voupouras; music, Nicos Kipourgos; sound, Dimitris Athenesopoulos; production manager, Giovanna Ilis Tempou; science advisor, Wieland Schmied; narrators, Dimitris Maronitis, Yannis Mavrikios. Reviewed at Thessaloniki Greek Film Festival, Oct. 3, 1990. Running time: **72 MIN.**

A tasteful and uplifting docu, "Aenigma Est" explores the life, art and philosophical writings of Greek artist Giorgio De Chirico. It should revive interest at home in this respected but often overlooked painter, and it's an eminently watchable candidate for offshore docu fests and tv.

Title refers to a De Chirico saying ("And what if I should love not the enigma?") that comprises a focal point of his philosophy and art. Pic won best documentary feature prize at Thessaloniki.

Born in Greece, De Chirico (Kirikos, in Greek), had a restless nature that led him to seven cities outside his homeland during his 90-year life span, including Rome, Turin, Milan and Paris.

De Chirico's devotion to architectural details are lovingly incorporated into his art. Finely lensed views of actual settings are alternated with his rich, earth-toned paintings, providing an interesting comparison. Combined with voiceover revealing biograph-

ical info on the artist, an engrossing spiritual and visual travelog of picturesque cities unfolds.

Judging from his writings and the anxious look of his self-portraits, De Chirico wrestled with the enigmatic nature of life. Emphasizing this quality, the moody score accented by haunting cello music won the award for best score for Nicos Kipourgos at the Thessaloniki fest.

The study of this intense artist is not strictly chronological. Old photos are incorporated to provide bridges between different time periods.

De Chirico, despite his peripatetic nature, was still a native son. On departure from the small city of Volos, he recalls, "Volos was the departure for the Argonauts; yet Ariadne reminds us that all journeys end finally in a labyrinth." This hints at his growing realization that one cannot escape from personal difficulties via wandering.

Fest audience was respectfully attentive and soundly applauded at the finish. — *Sam.*

NORDIC FEST

IEVAS PARADIZES DARZS
(EVA'S GARDEN OF EDEN)
(LATVIAN)

A Riga Film Studios presentation and production. Directed by Arvids Krievs. Screenplay, Krievs, David Simanis, based on Arvid Grigula's novel "Fateful Secrets"; camera (Eastmancolor), Simanis; editor, Liene Balina; music, Martins Brauns. Reviewed at Nordic Film Days (competition), Lübeck, Germany, Nov. 4, 1990. Running time: **93 MIN.**
Eva . . . . Dita Krenberga
Dr. Duburs . . . . Valentin Maculevics
Tom . . . . Alvis Hermanis
Also with: Saulus Balandis, Karlis Teihmanis.

Limited festival exposure is the likely fate of "Eva's Garden Of Eden," elegant and visually fanciful film which had no public showings before its acceptance in Lübeck's Nordic Film Days.

Latvian writer-helmer Arvids Krievs has nursed this project for more than a decade, getting the go-ahead only when Moscow censorship at the project stage was lifted.

Although based on a 1936 novel,

"Eva's Garden Of Eden" is actually a semisurrealistic rendering of Latvia at the time of the Nazi Germany-USSR nonaggression pact signing in 1940. As Latvia was more or less traded over to the Russians, the tiny Baltic republic's tradition for untroubled multiracial coexistence was shattered.

Rapid emergence of spying and counterspying, accommodation with the new powers and attempts to escape the country are now mirrored in a opulent mixture of symbolic narrative involving circus artists and members of the upper classes. Latter indulges in love-games, alcoholic beverages and dancing aboard luxury cruise ships when not cavorting about in foreign sports cars.

The titular Garden of Eden belongs to a mysterious Dr. Duburs. He lends his place to a couple of young lovers, a blond magician and a blonde girl. The magician has just left his former mistress, a married Jewish woman. Duburs has designs of his own on the girl.

Sundry other characters, more or less shady, are trying to frame Duburs as either a criminal or a traitor. At one point, the girl gets abducted by hooded men but doesn't seem to mind much.

Practically everything in the narrative is obscure. Not a single character seems real; they're all puppets of symbolism.

"Eva's Garden Of Eden" is full of double-exposure cinematography, beautifully lit and framed, alternating with newsreel shots of political deeds of the time and funny quotes from Alexander Rusteika's 1930 Latvian epic film "Lac Plesis" (Hero Of The Nation).

The acting is as stilted as in "Lac Plesis," which had the excuse of being a silent. While an audience's guessing game will hardly be rewarded, there is plenty of visual fun and beauty for the eye. — *Kell.*

LUCIFER—SENSOMMER: GUL OG SORT
(LUCIFER—INDIAN SUMMER: YELLOW AND BLACK)
(NORWEGIAN)

A UIP release (Norway) of Atom Film production. Produced by Odd G. Iversen. Written and directed by Roar Skolmen. Camera (Eastmancolor), Svein Krövel; editor, Skolmen, Roy Fenstad; music (piano improvisations), Nils Ökland; sound, Fenstad; production design, Dagfinn Kleppan; costumes, Ingrid Wiese; production manager, Trond Gaute Lockertsen, Ivar Köhn. Reviewed at Nordic Film Days (competition), Lübeck, Germany, Nov. 4, 1990. Running time: **94 MIN.**
The young man . . . . Björn Andresen
The teenage girl . . Anniken Krogstad
Also with: Jan Clementz, Astrid Folstad.

Writer-helmer Roar Skolmen's "Lucifer — Indian Summer: Yellow And Black" opened to disastrous reviews at home and was placed into the competition program of the Lübeck fest as a last-minute entry. Item is warmed-over teenage flirting with erotic philosophizing.

Offshore, film's only attraction would be Luchino Visconti's "Death In Venice" thesp Björn Andresen in the lead as a young roamer who puts his small boat ashore on a sunlit rocky coast to hire on as a day laborer at a small farmstead.

The young man, blond and handsome in a vague way, meets a 15-year-old girl who lives with an uncle and her grandmother. The girl taunts the youngster sexually but is all moves with no intent. She is a narcissist who also likes to pose as a pagan environmentalist.

He, on the contrary, is somehow identifying himself with a Jesus Christ doubtful of his own godliness.

Late in the film, the girl's uncle emerges as a murderous homosexual maniac out of his closet to rape the young man (everybody in the film remains nameless throughout) after a lethal weapons duel. Both are naked, and both spill some blood.

After that, the young man sets sail again as the girl dispatches a boy her own age to the grocery store to buy condoms.

The filmmaker's own synopsis would be needed to make any sense of all the Lucifer/Jesus Christ symbolism, and even with that, the going is tough. Only Svein Krövel's cinematography brings relief as it sums up the natural beauties of the Norse coast. — *Kell.*

ZUVIES DIENA
(FISH DAY)
(LITHUANIAN)

A Lithuanian Film Studio presentation and production. Produced and directed by Algimantas Puipa. Screenplay, Puipa, Regina Vosiliute based on stories by Liuejta Armanoité; camera (Fujicolor), Rimantas Juodvalkis; editor, Puipa; music, Juozas Sirvinskas; production design, A. Bruzas, L. Krisciunas. Reviewed at Nordic Film Days, Lübeck, Germany, Nov. 4, 1990. Running time: **90 MIN.**
Veronica . . . . Daiva Stubraité
Todas . . . . Sakalas Uzdavinys
Clarissa . . . . Irena Zitkuté
The neighbor . . . . Antan Mackevicius
Also with: Pranas Stankus, V. Kelmyté, V. Petrevicius, K. Smoriginas, O. Dautartaité.

Since Moscow has freed Baltic filmmakers from preproduction censorship, they have indulged in stylistic experimentation, often without substance. With "Fish Day," Lithuania's Algimentas Puipa has produced such a pic that's unlikely to make it except as another bit of fest esoterica.

The film has opulent looks and high technical credits. It is also visually imaginative in its portrayal of Veronica, a woman author whose mind switches back and forth between characters in her real life and characters and situations in her stories. Audiences are left without a clue as to why they should be interested in this self-obsessed woman.

In the lead, Daiva Stubraité has brooding good looks, high cheekbones, a full mouth and wide-set eyes plus a keenly handled acting talent to make up for the non-story's lack of deeper psychological insights. Occasionally, she is seen boarding airplanes, presumably taking her to Paris to buy all her stylish clothes, which she changes about every two minutes.

All secondary characters, including a flock of sheep, a shepherd, a neighbor with his finger stuck in a mailbox and woman friend with menstrual problems, are all too flimsily sketched to make much difference.

Sumptuous looks and too many presumptions make "Fish Day" imitation Alain Resnais, about 20 years out of date. — *Kell.*

LONDON FEST

102 BOULEVARD HAUSSMANN
(BRITISH)

A BBC-TV production in association with La Sept. Executive producer, Mark Shivas. Produced by Innes Lloyd. Directed by Udayan Prasad. Screenplay, Alan Bennett; camera (Eastmancolor), John Hooper; editor, Ken Pearce; music, George Fenton; sound, Mike Spencer; production design, Jan Spoczynski; costume design, Michael Burdle; assistant director, Christine McMurrich; production associate, Ralph Wilton. Reviewed at 34th London Film Festival (British Cinema), Nov. 9, 1990. Running time: **75 MIN.**
Marcel Proust . . . . Alan Bates
Celeste . . . . Janet McTeer
Odilon . . . . Jonathan Coy
Concierge . . . . Gillian Martell
Gaston Poulet . . . . Philip Rham
Victor Gentil . . . . . Michael Wilcox
Amable Massis . . . . Paul Rhys
Louis Ruyssen . . . . . . Peter Geeves
Dr. Bize . . . . Philip McGough
Mme Massis . . . . Celia Imrie
Paul Morand . . . . Michael Grandage
Princess Soutzo . . Lesley Nightingale
Head waiter . . . . Richard Syms
Pétain . . . . Benjamin Buckton

With Alan Bennett providing the words and Alan Bates in eye-rolling form, this vignette from the life of French writer Marcel Proust is never less than solid, intelligent fare. Talky tone and unadventurous direction, however, make it strictly a pubcaster item.

BBC-TV production in association with France's La Sept is slated to go out in British web's Screen Two series in January.

Slim story comes from an incident in Proust's later years. In 1916, the asthmatic scribe hired a group of musicians to play Franck's Quartet in D for his personal delectation in his chambers. Also stirring the reclusive writer's creative juices is Massis (Paul Rhys), the group's handsome young viola-player, whom he later invites back for some solo performances.

Pic develops Proust's fascination for the youth alongside his ongoing chore of penning the mammoth masterwork, "Remembrance Of Things Past," all under the watchful eye of his devoted housekeeper, Celeste (Janet McTeer). As such, it's less a biopic than a three-way character study, interspersed with the novelist's voiceover thoughts on the creative process.

Material is slightly familiar with Percy Adlon's 1981 West German pic, "Celeste," which draws on the housekeeper's own account of the period. But "102 Boulevard Haussmann" is more about the dying writer's obsession with Massis, a "Death In Venice"-like relationship in which Proust ends up the loser.

McTeer is firstrate as the protestive Celeste, performing miracles with a few lines and plenty of looks. Rhys is okay as the wan youth. But it's Bates' performance that keeps the movie ticking, tossing off bon mots and hinting at darker passions with lovelorn gazes.

Scotland's Perth and Glasgow double capably for Paris in the few exteriors. Jan Spoczynski's realistic sets are a big plus in such an interior movie. — *Drek*.

THEY NEVER SLEPT
(BRITISH)

A BBC-TV production. Produced by Kenith Trodd. Directed by Udayan Prasad. Screenplay, Simon Gray; camera (Eastmancolor), Chris Seager; editor, Ken Pearce; music, Carl Davis; sound, Jim Greenhorn; production design, Bruce Macadie; costume design, Anna Buruma; assistant director, Mervyn Dougherty; production associate, Geoffrey Paget. Reviewed at 34th London Film Festival (British Cinema), Nov. 11, 1990. Running time: **74 MIN.**
Monk . . . . Edward Fox
Corporal Merriman . . . Emily Morgan
Bob . . . . James Fleet
Petunia . . . . Patricia Lawrence
Panter . . . . Pete Postlethwaite
Producer . . . . Imelda Staunton
Admiral . . . . . . François Chaumette
Ninette . . . . Maria Laborit
Maurice . . . . Maurice Risch
Henri. . . . . Patrick Fierry
Cat Lady . . . . Harriet Walter
Sally . . . . Elaine Ford

This zany send-up of British stiff-upper-lippery during World War II could have turned a theatrical penny or two with a proper budget and bigscreen direction.

Despite working miracles on a measly £800,000 ($1.5 million) budget, however, the Simon Gray-scripted romp for the BBC Screen Two series won't stiffen many wallets in 35m blowups because of its constricted tv look. But "They Never Slept" should garner major plaudits on fest and broadcast outings.

Star of the show is Gray's irreverent script, initially based on an unnamed novel acquired by producer Kenith Trodd and developed into something completely his own. Gray even kills off the novel's heroine, Sally, in the opening minutes. Thereafter it's a rollercoaster ride of undercover antics, secret agents dropping like flies and dirty deeds on the upper floor of BBC Radio's Broadcasting House.

Pic kicks off with a witty spoof on wartime broadcasts and segues to the story of good-girl Merriman (Emily Morgan) recruited into the Secret Service run from Clapham Psychiatric Hospital by the loony Monk (Edward Fox). She's almost a female

Candide figure, and soon finds herself caught up in shenanigans involving the London-based Free French network, a deadly German spy called Cat Lady (Harriet Walter) and Operation Fattypuff & Thinnifer.

After unmasking Cat Lady as the BBC's patriotic spieler sending coded messages, pic climaxes with Monk's team in a nighttime drop into occupied France on a do-or-die mission. They do, and they don't die.

Gray's well-practiced skill at spoofing British manners gets a full workout as Fox gives his best performance in years. Morgan, as the wide-eyed heroine, is immensely assured in pic's key role, more than holding her own among the high-powered histrionics on all sides, including deliciously nasty playing by Walter as Cat Lady and Maria Laborit as a French spy.

Wartime depiction design and costumes are tops, and even more of Carl Davis' insouciant score would not have gone amiss.
— *Drek*.

EL ANONIMO
(THE ANONYMOUS LETTER)
(SPANISH)

A Sagutxo production. Executive producers, José Maria Lara, Iñaki Ros. Produced and directed by Alfonso Arandia. Screenplay, José Antonio Gómez, Arandia, from an idea by Gómez; camera (Eastmancolor), Gonzalo F. Berridi; editor, Juan I. Sanmateo; music, Mikel Erentxum; sound, Alfonso Pina. Reviewed at 34th London Film Festival (World Panorama), Nov. 9, 1990. Running time: **87 MIN.**
Charly . . . . Miguel Molina
Yon . . . . Jorge de Juan
Juanjo . . . . Martxelo Rudio
Peio . . . . Carlos Zabala
Don Manuel . . . . . . Nacho Martínez
Manoli . . . . Rosa Maria Sardá
Charo . . . . Alejandra Greppi
Evaristo . . . . Alex Angulo
Fernando . . . . Mikel Erentxun
Yoli . . . . Nuria Gallardo
Pili . . . . Maite Diaz

Salty dialog and good ensemble performances should give "El Anonimo" a following in Hispanic markets, but so-so English subtitles and uncertain pacing will limit it mostly to fest bookings elsewhere. Pic runs out of puff long before the players.

This breezy Spanish comedy about four guys who try to rescue an embarrassing letter from a mailbox is a likable enough debut for young helmer Alfonso Arandia. Given the shortage of

good Spanish comedies, and film's bright, poster-color look, comparisons with the movies of Pedro Almodóvar will be inevitable, if unfair.

Arandia's not in that league yet. Plot gathers together a large collection of zany characters, but that's it. He and co-scripter José Antonio Gómez seem uncertain what to do with everyone.

Pic kicks off with a funny sequence of one of the four friends cheating in his exam through a remote-controlled transmitter hidden under fake head bandages. But when Yon (Jorge de Juan) learns he's flunked his finals, he pens an anonymous letter to his professor. Only problem is that he mistakenly includes his results notice in the envelope.

Plot then becomes a shaggy-dog story of Yon and his mates trying quietly to get rid of the big yellow mailbox they've hijacked to their apartment. Further problems: their two g.f.s get suspicious of what they're up to, and a joke hood, Don Manuel (nicely played by Nacho Martínez), is after the package of cocaine that the mailbox was used as a drop for.

Most of the action takes place in and near the friend's apartment block. Assortment of other characters includes a luscious hooker on the floor below, a paranoid postman, a feisty janitress and a leather-clad safecracker.

Ensemble playing is up to scratch, even if actors lack real star clout. Given script's one-joke premise, tighter editing would have helped, but other tech credits are good, with Gonzalo F. Berridi's bright, sharp lensing standing out.

Pic was shot entirely in city of San Sebastián, with everyone chipping in half their pay on a cooperative basis. — *Drek*.

CELLO
(BRITISH)

A BBC-TV production. Produced by Robert Cooper. Executive producer, Mark Shivas. Written and directed by Anthony Minghella. Camera (Eastmancolor), Remi Adefarasian; editor, John Stothart; music, Barrington Pheloung; sound, Jim Greenhorn; production design, Barbara Gosnold; costume design, James Keast. Reviewed at 34th London Film Festival (British Cinema), Nov. 10, 1990. Running time: **105 MIN.**
Nina . . . . Juliet Stevenson
Jamie . . . . Alan Rickman
Sandy . . . . Bill Paterson
Mark . . . . Michael Maloney
Burge . . . . Jenny Howe

Titus . . . . . . Christopher Rozycki
George . . . . David Ryall
Maura . . . . Stella Maris
Plumber . . . . Keith Bartlett
Claire . . . . Deborah Findlay

A BBC-TV production shooting for theatrical dates in a 35m blowup prior to broadcast, "Cello" boasts strong performances by a name cast, but won't make much music beyond the box. There's a fatal lack of bigscreen oomph to draw paying customers.

This sharply scripted study of a bereaved woman who literally wishes her partner back from the grave, "Cello" is an impressive directorial bow by British playwright Anthony Minghella. Despite surface similarities with "Ghost," pic has a different feel and theme.

As pic opens, Nina (Juliet Stevenson) is still cut up about losing her longtime partner, virtuoso cellist Jamie (Alan Rickman). Despite her caring friends and co-workers, she still feels his presence in her tiny London flat, where plumbing's gone bananas and rats are moving in.

One day, while she's doodling at the piano, Jamie literally reappears and thereon it's a matter of reliving their idyllic relationship until it's time for both to move on — he to a higher plane, she to a growing friendship with young social worker Mark (Michael Maloney) who can give her the child Jamie never wanted.

Downbeat sound of plot never transpires. Scenes with Jamie alternate between moments of lyrical romance and high-spirited humor, as when Jamie invites some of his spirit buddies back to watch videos. Sans special effects, pic manages to suspend belief through fine ensemble playing and sheer strength of the main performances.

It's Stevenson's movie through and through (project was in the works for some years and was penned for her), and although she sometimes overdoes the histrionics, as in scenes with her shrink, it's a tour de force of sustained playing.

Rickman, in a very different role to his villain in "Die Hard," gives subtle support, with a nice line in poe-faced comedy. Bill Paterson, as Stevenson's boss, and Stella Maris as a Latino woman friend, are standout among supporting thesps, and Maloney impresses as her zany young suitor.

Tech credits are all fine, with special bouquets for Remi Adefarasian's crisp 16m lensing and Barrington Pheloung's evocative music. — *Drek.*

THE SHELTERING SKY

A Warner Bros. release. Produced by Jeremy Thomas. Executive producer, William Aldrich. Directed by Bernardo Bertolucci. Screenplay, Mark Peploe, Bertolucci, based on the book by Paul Bowles; camera, Vittorio Storaro; editor, Gabriella Cristiani; music, Ryuichi Sakamoto; original North African music by Richard Horowitz; sound (Dolby), Ivan Sharrock; production design, Gianni Silvestri; costume design, James Acheson; art direction, Andrew Sanders; set decoration, Cynthia Sleiter; assistant director, Serena Canevari; casting, Juliet Taylor. Reviewed at the Directors Guild of America theater, L.A., Nov. 19, 1990. MPAA Rating: R. Running time: **137 MIN.**

Port . . . . John Malkovich
Kit . . . . Debra Winger
Tunner . . . . Campbell Scott
Mrs. Lyle . . . . Jill Bennett
Eric Lyle . . . . Timothy Spall
Balqassim . . . . Eric Vu-An

Paul Bowles' classic 1949 novel of a journey into emptiness has been visualized with intense beauty by the creative team of "The Last Emperor." But those who haven't read the book (vast majority of filmgoers) will be left bewildered, as Bowles' delicate achievement has not managed the transfer to celluloid. This trek will find few ticket-buyers.

John Malkovich and Debra Winger play Port and Kit Moresby, Americans traveling without destination or itinerary in postwar North Africa. Their 10-year marriage is unraveling while their opportunistic companion, Tunner (Campbell Scott), looks on.

They press on through Tangiers, Niger and Algeria, moving with a perverse sense of purpose further from comfort, ego and the signposts of the familiar. Tunner grows exasperated with their style of travel, and so will most viewers.

Nothing much happens as the first hour ticks by, and while director Bernardo Bertolucci may think that these characters' interior lives are unspooling in the big silent spaces he leaves for them, they aren't.

Pic boils down to the existential love story between Kit and Port, who are groping through the ruins of their infidelities toward whatever is left between them when all is lost.

What, if anything, lies behind the sheltering sky is the larger question for these idle, suffering seekers, but whether this is an appropriate target for a major budget, mainstream studio film is an even better one.

Those who have read the book and know what is supposedly going on can get a certain number of thrills from this production, in which everyone seemed to be straining their creative powers to capture this thing that so tantalized but eluded them.

What could be better than to see that painter with light, cinematographer Vittorio Storaro, unleashed between the spellbinding clarity of the North African sky and the golden sensuality of the sands to make images with his cousin in poetry, Bertolucci?

The costumes are richly detailed, locations reverently chosen and original North African music bewitching. Everything is infused with fineness and feeling by a crew that, according to advance publicity, kept reading copies of Bowles' novel throughout the shoot, probably as a much-needed map.

In a marvelous directorial conceit, Bowles himself, 80 years old and projecting a quiet repose, watches his characters from a seat in a Tangiers cafe, acting as occasional narrator and silent witness.

Malkovich is an excellent choice as Port, his shifting, centaur-like physicality — sometimes fey and graceful, sometimes rooted and intransigent — filling in for the interior life the screen can't provide.

Both he and Winger are capable of suggesting, like true intellectuals, that the worlds they carry inside them and between them are more important than their surroundings.

But as camp follower to Port, Winger has less to play and a tougher time of it. Aside from her resemblance to writer Jane Bowles, who inspired Kit, she is less interesting to watch. Like Kit in the screenplay, she seems to be struggling to keep up with the program, and the contemporary rhythms she brings to the role are distracting.

When Port dies of typhoid, it is a relief that Winger can stop incessantly punctuating the air with his name. In fact, familiar language completely disappears, as shell-shocked Kit wanders into the desert and becomes a sex slave to the wandering Taureg leader Belqassim (played by Eric Vu-An of the Paris Ballet).

Subtitles replace English, and Kit, subsisting on food and sex alone in an alien culture, slowly goes mad.

The book is read by some as a metaphor for Port's struggle to deny his supposed homosexuality in a repressive 1940s culture.

The repulsive sissy Eric Lyle (British stage actor Timothy Spall), a fellow traveler who turns up everywhere with his beastly mother (Jill Bennett), can be viewed in a macabre comic light as Port's worst fears pursuing him through the desert. Spall and Bennett, in the John Huston tradition of bizarre supporting players, make an indelible impression.

Glimpses of odd, provocative sexuality are very much a part of the film's tone, and the several explicit scenes make pic's R rating (rather than NC-17) a bit of a surprise, given the recent flap over "Henry & June."

Pic comes closest to achieving something equal to the book in scenes of Port's fatal illness, when rhythms of the music, editing, and images combine with Malkovich's gift for delirium to become the cacophony of confusion created by the fevers consuming him.

Still, in some cases there is no substitute for the art of prose, and "The Sheltering Sky" is one of them.

"Champagne, yes, philosophy, no," Kit tells her adulterous suitor, Tunner. That's just what Bertolucci's beautiful but unsatisfying companion piece to the novel delivers. Having drunk of it, viewers are likely to come away with muddled memories and a slight headache. — *Daws.*

MISERY

A Columbia Pictures release of a Castle Rock Entertainment production, in association with Nelson Entertainment. Produced by Andrew Scheinman, Rob Reiner. Directed by Reiner. Screenplay, William Goldman, based on Stephen King's novel; camera (color; CFI prints), Barry Sonnenfeld; editor, Robert Leighton; music, Marc Shaiman; sound (Dolby), Robert Eber; production design, Norman Garwood; costume design, Gloria Gresham; assistant director, Dennis Maguire; special makeup effects, KNB EFX; 2nd unit director, Sonnenfeld; co-producers, Steve Nicolaides, Jeffrey Stott; casting, Jane Jenkins, Janet Hirshenson. Reviewed at Coronet theater, N.Y., Nov. 15, 1990. MPAA Rating: R. Running time: **107 MIN.**

Paul Sheldon . . . . James Caan
Annie Wilks . . . . Kathy Bates
Virginia . . . . . . Frances Sternhagen
Buster . . . . . . Richard Farnsworth
Marcia Sindell . . . . . Lauren Bacall
Libby . . . . Graham Jarvis
Chief Sherman Douglas . . . J.T. Walsh

Rob Reiner pushes the right buttons in "Misery," a very obvious and very commercial gothic thriller. Tongue-in-cheek sadistic exercise should be a counterprogramming hit for the holiday season.

In William Goldman's functional adaptation of the Stephen King bestseller, James Caan's film career comes full circle. His first major role on screen 26 years ago was terrorizing an immobile Olivia De Havilland in "Lady In A Cage." Now he's a bestselling novelist flat on his back after a car accident and tormented by his obsessed "No. 1 fan" Kathy Bates.

With Lauren Bacall cast in the small role of Caan's literary agent, one immediately recalls that topical but unsuccessful pic "The Fan" of a decade ago. However, Reiner wisely provides enough cuteness and "just kidding" dimension beneath the surface scares to keep the material palatable. It's the same ploy that put over the early James Bond films, criticized in some quarters for their sadistic content.

Basically a two-hander dealing with King themes touched upon in Stanley Kubrick's adaptation of "The Shining," "Misery" is the name of the 19th century heroine of a series of gothic romances penned by Caan. During the opening credits his car crashes on slippery Colorado roads and Bates digs him out of the snow and wreckage.

A plump former nurse, she fixes up his severely injured legs and virtually holds him prisoner, incommunicado, for the rest of the film. As in the classic Robert Aldrich gothics like "Whatever Happened To Baby Jane?" the fun comes from the ebb and flow nastiness of the two characters in a love/hate (often hate/hate) relationship.

There are several "money" scenes, the kind of shockers that guarantee a critical mass of audience to jump out of their seats. For example, whenever Robert Leighton's crisp editing causes Bates to suddenly appear in the frame menacingly or the late-in-film "hobbling" scene where she graphically smashes Caan's feet with a sledgehammer.

On a more serious note, Reiner gets across King's concerns in a vivid portrayal of Bates forcing Caan to burn the only manuscript of his just-completed novel since she doesn't approve of its profanity, as well as Caan's turn of the screw taunting her with his written-under-duress "Misery" tome.

Key plot gimmick is that he's killed off the profitable but hackwork Misery character, an act that turns adoring fan Bates against him and sets in motion her obsession that he resurrect the fictional character.

Sexual connotations of the central relationship are not explored here, probably a wise decision given the b.o. failure of similar "The Beguiled" (adapted from Thomas Cullinan's novel).

In that 1971 pic Clint Eastwood departed from his screen image by playing a wounded Union soldier preyed upon by sexually repressed southerners Geraldine Page and Elizabeth Hartman. Instead of Bates' foot-smashing scene, director Don Siegel staged a symbolic castration when the women amputated Eastwood's leg, which severely disturbed preview audiences and was later edited down.

In "Misery," Bates' paroxysms of emotion are cued by literary matters solely or playing her Liberace records. Pic's misogynistic content, culminating in Caan literally bashing Bates with a series of blunt objects, is its most controversial aspect but like the ending of "Fatal Attraction" is a proven crowd-pleaser.

Casting of Caan is effective, as his snide remarks and grumpy attitude are backed up by a physical dimension that makes believable his inevitable fighting back. Bates has a field day with her role, creating a quirky, memorable object of hate. The story's several inversions, both in gender reversal and contempt for the "little person"/sympathy for the celebrity, work well.

Excellent makeup effects for Caan's maimed legs by the KNB team help the thesp convincingly portray the pain of his condition and thereby build audience sympathy.

Richard Farnsworth as an alternately shrewd and slow-witted local sheriff and Frances Sternhagen as his flinty wife offer relief from the two-character duel.

Wheeze of a coda, in which Caan has one last fake encounter with Bates, is poor, the type of "Carrie"-induced tag that horror films can't seem to resist. Reportedly this wasted scene had to be reshot because preview audiences didn't buy Caan back on his feet again sans limp after the mayhem endured 18 months earlier.

Tech credits on this $21 million pic are very good, including Reno-area location shots. — *Lor.*

COMPLEX WORLD

A Heartbreak Hits presentation. Produced by Geoff Adams, Rich Lupo, Dennis Maloney. Executive producer, Lupo. Written and directed by James Wolpaw. Camera (color, black & white), Maloney; editor, Steven Gentile; music, Stephen Snyder; sound, Tom Payne; assistant director, Adams; associate producer, Charles Thompson, Ed Lupo; casting, Carol Larkin. Reviewed at the Somerville Theater, Mass., Nov. 18, 1990. No MPAA rating. Running time: **81 MIN.**

Morris Brock	Stanley Matis
Jeff Burgess	Dan Welch
Gilda	Margot Dionne
Malcolm	Daniel von Bargen
Robert Burgess	Bob Owczarek
Boris Lee	Captain Lou Albano

Also with: Andrew Mutnick, the Young Adults, NRBQ, Roomful of Blues.

"**C**omplex World" is a showcase for some fresh talent as it sets off a madcap tale of a rock club facing a terrorist bombing and a biker gang attack same evening. Irreverent humor mixed with some solid musical talent suggests b.o. potential in urban and collegiate situations.

Jeff Burgess (Dan Welch) is proprietor of Heartbreak Hotel, a nitespot lusted after by local developers who want to tear it down and convert it into a shopping mall. An aide to the mayor hires a local biker gang (headed up by pro wrestler Captain Lou Albano) to trash the place so it can be shut down.

Meanwhile, Burgess's father (Bob Owczarek), a right-wing presidential candidate, hires a terrorist group to blow up the place so that he can get rid of his embarrassing son while making himself look tough on terrorism.

Younger Burgess is so laidback he refuses to believe either threat is real, laughing off repeated calls by the terrorist leader (Daniel von Bargen) about the bomb in his basement.

Writer-director James Wolpaw shows a steady hand for pacing as the various elements of the script come together for the inevitable explosion. While the writing lacks polish, it shows a strong structure with gags paying off in unexpected ways.

Film is helped immeasurably by musical numbers, both the mock folk songs from Morris (Stanley Matis) on such themes as Nikita Khruschev not having any friends, to the real, and often comic, rock of the Young Adults, which includes the title song and a dance number called "Do The Heimlich."

Production values are solid, if low-budget, with editor Steven Gentile and cinematographer Dennis Maloney due special praise for making pic look tight and slick. The film relies too much on a tv style; lots of closeups and few, if any, long shots, but in the long run that may help in the homevid market.

Shot in Providence, R.I., last year, "Complex World" is on the verge of being picked up for national distribution, after engagements in Providence and greater Boston. Pitched to college age crowds it should prove worth the investment. — *Kimm.*

LITTLE VEGAS

An IRS Releasing release of a Maclang production. Produced by Peter Macgregor-Scott. Executive producer, Harold Welb. Written and directed by Perry Lang. Camera (Deluxe color), King Baggot; editor, John Tintori; music, Mason Daring; sound, Rocco Moriana; production design, Michael Hartog; art direction, Daniel Brewer; costume design, Cynthia Flint; casting, Junie Lowry. Reviewed at the Filmland Corporate Center, L.A., Nov. 12, 1990. MPAA Rating: R. Running time: **92 MIN.**

Carmine	Anthony John Denison
Lexie	Catherine O'Hara
Martha	Anne Francis
Frank	Michael Nouri
Steve	Perry Lang

Also with: P.J. Ochlan, John Sayles, Bruce McGill, Jay Thomas, Michael Talbot, Jerry Stiller, Bob Goldthwait.

Apparently unsure what he wants this film to be, first-time director Perry Lang ends up wandering aimlessly through this sort-of comedy. Despite an intriguing cast, pic should leave IRS equally thirsty at the b.o.

Most of the film plays like a bad episode of an ensemble tv drama. Characters glide in and out for brief scenes that never seem to connect. Lang pulls a few of them together at the end, but by then it's too late.

Carmine (Anthony John Denison), a trailer-park gigolo and one-time mafioso, seeks to escape his past and reclaim his future. Big event in his life was his relationship with the much older Martha (Anne Francis), since deceased, who counsels him on life through gauzy flashbacks.

As his mobster brother (Michael Nouri) presses him to return to the family fold, Carmine gets another chance for redemption in the form of Martha's daughter (Catherine O'Hara).

Denison (tv's "Crime Story,"

"Wiseguy") is an interesting actor given too ill-defined a role. His direct-to-camera remarks shed little light on motivation while contributing to an inconsistency plaguing the whole pic.

Lang, a John Sayles protégé (per production notes), employs cute little camera tricks adding nothing to the story.

Familiar faces pop up in peripheral roles, only adding to the impression that this is little more than a low-budget homevideo.

Aside from Denison, lone bright spot is Francis as the warmhearted Martha, though even her dreamy monologs are as unfocused as the lens that shoots them.

Mason Daring's melancholy score dovetails with the film's almost soporific pace. — *Bril.*

TAKESHI
(JAPANESE)

A Hyogensha production. Executive producer, Fujio Fujiko. Directed by Masahiro Shinoda. Screenplay, Taichi Yamada, based on original stories by Hyozo Kashiwabara ("The Long Road") and Fujiko ("Shonen Jidai"); camera (color), Tatsuo Suzuki; art director, Takeo Kimura; musical director, Shinichiro Ikebe. Reviewed on videcassette during the Chicago Intl. Film Festival, Nov. 2, 1990. No MPAA rating. Running time: **117 MIN.**
Shinji Kazama . . . . . Tetsuya Fujita
Takeshi Ohara . . . . Yuji Horioka
Futoshi Tanabe . Katsuhisa Yamazaki
Kensuke Sudo . . . Noritake Kohinata
Minako Saeki . . . . . Atsuko Koyama

An engrossing but slow-moving tale of childhood trials and tribulations, "Takeshi" scores points for universality of theme and depth of characterization, but is too sober and serious to make much of a boxoffice impression, even on the arthouse circuit.

Film deals with a major event in the life of many Japanese during the final years of World War II: Evacuation of children from the cities to the countryside to avoid U.S. bombing.

Tokyo harbormaster son Shinji (Tetsuya Fujita) is farmed out to a country uncle. At his new school, he quickly falls under the influence of Takeshi (Yuji Horioka), president of the fifth-grade class and self-imposed student-body dictator.

Far from being a standard-issue thug, Takeshi is one of the smartest students at the school, with a penchant for art and literature. Nonetheless, he has a sav-

age temper and a need to dominate that even he does not understand. It possibly stems from the fact that as the poor son of a fisherman, he will be unable to continue his studies beyond elementary school.

At first, Shinji enjoys Takeshi's protection. The two boys strike up a genuine friendship, based on Takeshi's admiration of Shinji's book collection and storytelling ability.

Soon, however, Takeshi begins to treat Shinji as just another minion, beating him and essentially relegating him to the role of his court jester.

Unable to accept Takeshi's brutality and stung by the teasing of a girl who accuses him of knowing how to get along in the world, Shinji drops out of Takeshi's gang. Soon after, he is involved in a miniature *coup d'etat*, which unseats Takeshi and places another junior tyrant in his place.

"Takeshi" attempts to depict the schoolyard as a microcosm of the adult world, complete with master-slave relationships, crises of conscience, power struggles and tumultuous shifts in fortune. It succeeds, to a large extent, thanks to to the thoughtfulness of the scenario and director Masahiro Shinoda's meticulous work with his young actors.

The formal and elaborate plot to undo Takeshi, which gradually evolves from clandestine meetings to open, organized revolt, is particularly fascinating. Even so, the pace of the action is too slow for much emotional involvement.

Other high points of the film include Tatsuo Suzuki's picturesque cinematography and unsettling scenes of the schoolyard boys preparing to become soldiers. They mock-bayonet caricatures of Churchill and Roosevelt and extend their arms in Nazi salutes while watching newsreel footage of Adolf Hitler. — *Brin.*

1871
(BRITISH)

A Norstar presentation of a Film Four Intl. production in association with La Sept (France). Produced by Stewart Richards. Directed by Ken McMullen. Screenplay, Terry James, James Leahy, McMullen; camera (color), Elso Roque; editor, William Diver; music, Barrie Guard; sound, Carlos Pinto; art direction, Paul Cheetham; associate producer, Olivia Stewart. Reviewed at Toronto Festival of Festivals, Sept. 16, 1990. Running time: **100 MIN.**
Severine . . . . Ana Padrao
Grafton . . . . Roshan Seth
O'Brien . . . . John Lynch

Cluseret . . . . Jack Klaff
Ramborde . . . . Timothy Spall
Maria . . . . Maria De Medeiros
Street Singer . Jacqueline Dankworth
Prince of Wales . . . . . Ian McNeice
Napoleon III . . . . Dominique Pinon
Karl Marx . . . . Med Hondo

This lavish period piece about the rise and fall of the Paris commune in 1871 has all the elements of terrific television: romance, revolution, murder, a good cast and topnotch production values.

Helmer Ken McMullen has crafted a well-researched, intriguing portrait of a rarely depicted period in French history. During Napoleon III's reign, trade unions and proletarian parties were forbidden. The commune rose and fell, claiming some 30,000 lives in under a month.

To emphasize the theatrics of the time, McMullen uses the stage as a character (as in Volker Schlöndorff's "Death Of A Salesman"), with revolutionary actors and political patrons as vehicles between sets. The format will work on tv, but it's too static for the bigscreen.

The life of Severine, beautiful stage actress-prostitute-revolutionary, is the key to the play within the film and the film itself. Heralded as "the toast of Paris," she does a sex nymph number in a theater reputed to be a part-time brothel. There she falls in love with revolutionary O'Brien and becomes a prostitute for English spy Grafton.

As turmoil rises and the theater is temporarily closed, Severine becomes an ardent revolutionary committed to the commune and her lover, but remains at the financial mercy of Grafton, who is powerless to save her from a firing squad.

During the various acts leading to the commune's defeat, the theater remains the pinnacle of events. In several sequences, the camera swings like a slow-moving pendulum past the walls of the set — a technique adding to the theatrical aspect — eavesdropping on various conversations exposing the hypocrisy and corruption of the day.

McMullen also has utilized a unique script touch to his advantage. The French-speaking characters speak French while English-speaking characters answer in English. They understand each other yet speak in their own tongues. This technique enriches the film and sheds light on the

era, but may prove difficult subtitling for the tube.

Many of the script's lines are terribly cliché, but one line spoken by revolutionary leader Cluseret rings true: "This battle we are fighting . . . will be fought again and again until true democracy is achieved."

Pic is chockful of interesting historical tidbits, lavish costumes and good thesping. The set is innovatively manipulated, and the roving camera is a big plus.
— *Suze.*

HUANG XUE
(SNOWY WILDERNESS)
(CHINESE)

A Shanghai Film Studio production. Executive director, Tang Xiaodan. Directed by Bao Zhifang. Screenplay, Xu Yali; camera (color), Luo Zhengshenh; music, Liu Yanxi; production design, Chen Fuxing. Reviewed at Montreal World Film Festival (Chinese Cinema of Today section), Sept. 3, 1990. Running time: **100 MIN.**
With: Lu Xiaohe, Xu Songzi, Yuan Zhiqiang, Yin Wen.

A melodrama about a drunkard who rapes a widow and then tries to make amends, "Snowy Wilderness" is chiefly of interest for its landscapes and setting. The plotting leaves something to be desired.

The film does depict the impact of recent economic reforms on life in a remote village, where the protagonist is able to become rich by setting up a prosperous flour mill. He then tries to woo the woman he previously violated, and she's torn between him and another man.

This is standard fare competently, but not exceptionally, executed. — *Strat.*

XTRO II
(CANADIAN)

A North American Releasing release of a North American Pictures-Excaliber Pictures production. Executive producers, Lloyd A. Simandl, John A. Curtis. Produced by Simandl, Curtis. Directed by Harry Bromley-Davenport. Screenplay, Curtis; camera (color), Nathaniel Massey; editor, Derek Whelen; music, Braun Farnon, Robert Smart; production design, Glenn Patterson; associate producers, A. William Smyth, James Westwell, John Smith, John Proust; line producer, Michael Mazo; creative design, Charlie Grant; visual effects, Cyberflex Films. Reviewed at Robson Communications Center, Vancouver, Oct. 30, 1990. No MPAA Rating. Running time: **92 MIN.**

Dr. Ron Shepherd . . . .
.... Jan-Michael Vincent
Dr. Alex Summerfield . . . Paul Koslo
Dr. Julie Casserly . . . . Tara Buckman
McShane . . . . Jano Frandsen
Baines . . . . Nicholas Lea
Jedburg . . . . W.F. Wadden
Zunoski . . . . Rolf Reynolds
Mancini . . . . Nic Amoroso

"**X**tro II" looks to be an easy sell to most foreign territories if only because the look of this low-budget pic is decidedly upscale. The in-studio special effects are imperfect, but few sci-fi fans will suspect that this Vancouver-lensed film cost less than $1 million.

Storyline has scientists trying to send three explorers to a parallel world, against the wishes of the U.S. government which recalls the failure of this "Nexus" project in "Xtro." The one man who made it to the other side and returned in the first Nexus attempt (Jan Michael-Vincent) is called back to the project when the three go missing.

He steps back in as a consultant and love interest to project manager Tara Buckman but tries to derail the project when he thinks there is nothing to be gained by bringing back the trio. One member of the threesome appears to have survived, but she is hiding a monster inside, one that gets out and threatens to destroy Nexus and the scientific team.

Problems here include the fact that the monster tends to grow by eating human flesh, à la "Alien," with lots of other gory details that resemble that pic. Script is no great shakes either with most of the dialog clichéd and the characters, except for Buckman, getting no help from the actors.

But North American Pictures/Releasing has never pitched screenplay or performance quality. This pic has tech credits comparable to special effects five or six times its budget and should do well in most foreign markets. — *Cadd.*

SANGEN OM KIRSEBAERTID
(THE CHERRY BLOSSOM BALLAD)
(DANISH)

A Dan-Ina Film release of Hanne Höyberg Film production with the Danish Film Institute. Produced by Hanne Höyberg. Written and directed by Irene Werner Stage. Camera (color), Henning Bendtsen; editor, Kasper Schyberg; music, Karsten Vogel; sound, Niels Arild; production design, Per Flink Basse; costume design, Annette Hage. Reviewed at the Delta Bio, Copenhagen, Sept. 7, 1990. Running time: **96 MIN.**
The woman . . . . Lea Brögger
Young meterman . . . .
.... Kenneth Kreutzmann
Stage director/actress . . . Maria Kulle
The husband . . . . . Henrik Jandorff
The German soldier . . . .
.... Lars Guldberg Bang
The father . . . . John Lambreth

Tedium threatens throughout "The Cherry Blossom Ballad," writer-helmer Irene Werner Stage's recounting of the daydreams and reminiscences of a woman married to a tightlipped tyrant.

The woman sits forlornly in her kitchen, rolls cigarets and drinks coffee as she recalls her girlhood at her father's home, where wine flowed, lilting music was played and suitors flocked to drawing room and garden.

Unfortunately, most of the guests were Germans who stayed on in uniforms even after World War II broke out and Denmark was occupied by the Nazis. But what is a young girl to do when her only local suitor is a rapist and a handsome Hun, all sweetness and romance?

The girl pays the price when the Resistance comes to power, and obviously she has been paying through her miserable marriage ever since. Her daydreams and a visit from a mooning meterman are her only consolations. What separates dreams from reality, however, is unclear.

Even if murkiness is Stage's aim, it will be hard for audiences to care. Snippets of an experimental theater group's staging of an anti-fascist cabaret are the only relief in an endless flashing between now and then.

Dreams can be told in energetic cinematic terms, but in this film, narration is vapid and the story is told through a hazy filter.

Worse, Lea Brögger, who plays the woman both as maiden and matron, comes across as a dimwit. She hasn't got an iota of fight to make her appealing.

In spite of everything, "The Cherry Blossom Ballad" looks terrific. Production values are impeccable, and cinematography is masterly. No wonder, since it is handled by Henning Bendtsen, still-active veteran of Carl Th. Dreyer's "Ordet." Of subdued poignancy is Karsten Vogel's score. — *Kell.*

KRACHT
(STRENGTH)
(DUTCH)

A The Movies Filmdistribution release of a Sigma Filmproductions production in association with Trust Toneel. Produced by Matthijs van Heijningen. Executive producer, Guurtje Buddenberg. Written and directed by Frouke Fokkema. Camera (Eastmancolor), Theo Bierkens; editor, Wim Louwrier; music, Lodewijk de Boer; sound, Marcel de Hoogd; art direction, Roel Schneeman; production manager, Patricia McMahon. Reviewed at the Movies Theater, Amsterdam, Sept. 21, 1990. Running time: **100 MIN.**
Bert . . . . Theu Boermans
Roos . . . . Anneke Blok
Thomas . . . . Dave van Dinther

Frouke Fokkema makes an astonishing film debut with "Strength" because of the way she masters cinematic problems with the ease and grace of an old hand.

Pic's strong points are manifold: the atmosphere of rural life, the empty landscapes, uninhibited sex scenes, words remaining unsaid, speeches tumbling out, unfinished gestures. Trouble is, however, the film has no definite attitude towards its content.

Despite its long period of gestation, basic blemishes were allowed to stay in this film about how a small farmer lives and a tiny community bristles against anything foreign and unusual.

Pic, which opened the 10th Netherland Film Days and won the Golden Calf for best direction, begins excellently on a note of farce and then changes moods. An ordinary tale follows, punctuated by lighthearted interludes and somber undercurrents. Tragedy builds fiercely and grimly to an horrific sequence and an ironic coda.

Bert (Theu Boermans) and his wife worked hard for 15 years building their farm. The wife suddenly dies of a brain tumor, leaving Bert shattered and disoriented and his 9-year-old boy without a mother.

At a big city agricultural exhibition, a woman painter photographs the farmer. They dine together, and she arranges a hotel room for him, and they share it. He goes home, and she comes to stay as an honored guest. They have a passionate affair. The village marvels. She gets pregnant. There's a violent quarrel and a shockingly tragic ending to the affair.

Boermans' phenomenal acting won him a Golden Calf nomination. His farmer is strong, proud, dead-honest, and keeps to himself and within himself. Anneke Blok as the painter does her considerable best, but her character, torn between country and city and between farm life's romantic aspects and its stark brutality, never becomes clear or identifiable.

Young Dave van Dinther is excellent as the son. Most smaller parts are very well acted and directed. Cameraman Theo Bierkens' lighting and photography also are excellent.

Fokkema, 38, herself experienced the dilemma between country and city life. Daughter of an actress and a sailor, she started at a drama academy, switched to an agricultural school, worked on farms in the Netherlands, Norway, Israel and the Pyrénées. She returned to the theater and became an acclaimed playwright. — *Wall.*

JAG SKALL BLI SVERIGES REMBRANDT ELLER DÖ
(I SHALL BECOME SWEDEN'S REMBRANDT OR DIE)
(SWEDISH-DOCU)

An Athena Film production in association with the Swedish Film Institute and SVT-2. Produced by Göran Gunér. Executive producers, Katinka Faragó, Oloph Hansson. Written and directed by Gunér; camera (color), Bengt Danneborn; editor, Lena Dahlberg-Runge; music, Ernst Josephson, J.A. Hägg; sound, Jan Alvermark; production design-costume design, Gunér; casting, Olle Westholm. Reviewed at the Fagel Bla, Stockholm, Oct. 5, 1990. Running time: **90 MIN.**
Ernst Josephson . . . Magnus Nilsson
Allan Österlind . . Kenneth Söderman
Anna . . . . . Sanna Danneborn-Spjuth
Christian Skredsvisk . . . Kim Hauken
The critic . . . . Thomas Roos
The river god . . . . . . Mikael Säflund
Also with: Mikael Andersson, Göran Engman, Marianne Ahrne, Emilie Gunér, Anders Malmberg.

Art historian-filmmaker Göran Gunér's "I Shall Become Sweden's Rembrandt Or Die" styles itself a docu, but the drama in the story of Swedish painter Ernst Josephson makes this film a choice morsel for art museum showings and tv.

Gunér's ploy is to portray the painter, who died in 1906, in voice only. Magnus Nilsson somberly reads aloud from Josephson's letters as viewers are led through stagings of key events in the painter's ill-starred life. (He rarely was recognized by critics of his time and went insane after contracting syphilis.)

Josephson's paintings assume extraordinary life as scrutinized by cinematographer Bengt Danneborn. Sound and other production credits work to perfection, especially in the approach to light and sound lent to Josephson's most famous painting, "Strömkarlen" (The River God).

Josephson also was a composer, and his music, played on piano and guitar, has lively, dramatic qualities that go well with the visuals. — *Kell.*

FULL FATHOM FIVE

A Concorde Pictures release. Produced by Luis Llosa. Executive producer, Rodman Flender. Directed by Carl Franklin. Screenplay, Bart Davis, based on his novel. Camera (Foto-Kem color), Pili Flores Guerra; editor, Karen Horn; music, Allan Zavod; sound (Ultra-Stereo), Edgar Lostanau; production design, Fernando Vasques de Velasco; assistant director, Ramsay Ross; special visual effects, Mark Williams Effects, Bryan Moore, Larry Smith; stunt coordinator, Jose Luy; 2d unit director, Louis Morneau. Reviewed at Criterion 4, N.Y., Sept. 9, 1990. MPAA Rating: PG. Running time: **78 MIN.**
Capt. Peter McKenzie . . . .
　　　　　　　　　　Michael Moriarty
Justine . . . . Maria Rangel
Garvin . . . . Michael Cavanaugh
Labovic . . . . John LaFayette
Johnson . . . . Todd Field
Santillo . . . . Daniel Faraldo
Mishkin . . . . Ramsay Ross
Ambassador Fletcher . . Carl Franklin

Boredom sets in early during "Full Fathom Five," cheapjack variation on "The Hunt For Red October."

Made by Roger Corman's Concorde outfit and a MGM/UA's video release, threadbare effort is set in December 1989, just before the U.S. invasion of Panama. A Panamanian officer captures the Soviet submarine Kirov (far too easily) at gunpoint and holds the U.S. ransom via the cruise missiles aboard.

U.S. sub captain Michael Moriarty has to do away with the Kirov so America can protect its strategic interests.

Film dwells on preposterous gimmicks, such as a Cuban jailbird made captain of the stolen Soviet sub, who rebels against the Panamanians and sets himself up as a one-man nuclear power. Moments away from bombing Houston, he and his ship are blasted out of the water by Mori-

arty with no explanation of what happens to the armed cruise missiles.

Closest thing to topicality is that the Cuban's first demo target to prove he means business is sinking a Saudi Arabian oil tanker.

For PG-rated love interest, sexy Maria Rangel as a Panamanian rebel unconvincingly throws away her dislike for Americans and beds down discreetly with Moriarty.

Acting is particularly bad, with the cast's listlessness contagious for the viewer. Director Carl Franklin doubles in a support role as the U.S. ambassador. Model shots of the subs are okay, but desultory action scenes are cheaply shot in closeup. Production was reportedly lensed in Peru. — *Lor.*

NO APOLOGIES
(CANADIAN)

A Filmline Intl. presentation of a b.i.g. Films Ltd. production. Produced by Terry Greenlaw. Executive producer, William D. MacGillivray. Written and directed by Ken Pittman. Camera (color), Lionel Simmons; editor, William D. MacGillivray, John Harris; music, Alexander Tilley; sound, John Rillie; art direction, Keith Curry. Reviewed at the Toronto Festival of Festivals, Sept. 20, 1990. Running time: **90 MIN.**
Mark . . . . Barrie Dunn
Matthew . . . . Bryan Hennessey
Mattie . . . . Maisie Rillie
Tim . . . . Tony Quinn
Peter . . . . Ken Mercer
Genny . . . . Mary Lewis
Anna . . . . Frances Knickle
Martha . . . . . . Frankie O'Flaherty
Simon . . . . Rick Mercer

Made unapologetically depressing and intentionally drab, "No Apologies" has no commercial future.

Newfoundland writer/helmer Pittman is obviously a man with a mission. He's telling the world that the island on Canada's east coast is an economic disaster, and families who live there are paying the price. Unfortunately, the way Pittman choses to tell his sad family drama will interest no one except Newfoundlanders.

Story revolves around a father dying of an industrial disease. His adult children reunite at the family home in Newfoundland during his final days. A major problem is that the father's disease is never identified

so the theme becomes a heavy-handed anti-industrial statement: big corporate villain vs. sincere individual.

The siblings have all left the province except for Mark, a documentary filmmaker. Once reunited for the death of the father (symbol for the death of the province), they bicker constantly about local politics. Even during a baseball game, Pittman drags a potentially fun scene into the doldrums with another family feud. There's no relief in this pic.

The Newfoundland region has many examples of industrial exploitation, but Pittman's unable to pinpoint one of them. Unlike films from politically repressed countries, which often suggest a triumph of will on the part of the individual, there is no light at the end of the picture.

Perhaps it's a realistic portrayal of life in Canada's poorest province, but Pittman, who based this story on personal experiences, has seriously overlooked fundamental filmmaking principles. Even the music is a downer.

Exec producer William D. MacGillivray, who directed a riveting statement about life in eastern Canada called "Life Classes," should have given Pittman a few pointers on cinema. — *Suze.*

THREE MEN AND A LITTLE LADY

A Buena Vista release of a Touchstone Pictures presentation of a Jean François LePetit-Interscope Communications production. Produced by Ted Field, Robert W. Cort. Executive producer, Jean François Lepetit. Directed by Emile Ardolino. Screenplay, Charlie Peters, based on a story by Sara Parriott, Josann McGibbon, based on the film "Trois Hommes Et Un Coiffin," written by Coline Serreau; camera, Adam Greenberg; editor, Michael A. Stevenson; music, James Newton Howard; sound (Dolby), C. Darin Knight; production design, Stuart Wurtzel; costume design, Louise Frogley; art direction, David M. Haber; set design, Mark Poll, Sig Tinglof; set decoration, Ethel Richards; assistant director, Yudi Bennett; coproducer, Neil Machlis; casting, Ilene Starger, Mary Selway. Reviewed at Avco Cinema Center, L.A., Nov. 15, 1990. MPAA Rating: PG. Running time: **100 MIN.**
Peter . . . . Tom Selleck
Michael . . . . Steve Guttenberg
Jack . . . . Ted Danson
Sylvia . . . . Nancy Travis
Mary . . . . Robin Weisman
Edward . . . . . Christopher Cazenove
Vera . . . . Sheila Hancock
Miss Lomax . . . . Fiona Shaw
Also with: John Boswall, Jonathan Lynn, Sydney Walsh, Lynne Marta, Everett Wong, Edwina Moore.

Baby grows up. Disney cleans up. It's really that simple as the studio trots out this two-dimensional sequel to its 1987 hit, "Three Men And A Baby." Project proffers old-fashioned romance and family values while ticking along with all the machine-like calculation of a modern-day presidential campaign.

Thinking people will be hard-pressed to find a single interesting moment in this relentlessly predictable fantasy, but then, at the boxoffice as at the polls, they are reliably in the minority.

Back in their places for the sequel are the three bachelor dads of the waif who landed on their doorstep in part one: vain actor Ted Danson and biological dad, and architect Tom Selleck and illustrator Steve Guttenberg, the honorary dads.

What's new is that Selleck has fallen in love with the baby's mom, Sylvia (Nancy Travis), the actress who shares their new apartment, though he hasn't admitted it to her or himself.

Crisis occurs when baby turns 5 and enrolls in preschool, thereby encountering other children. Concerned heads decide it won't do for her to remain in an unconventional home environment (thereby doing away with pic's fleeting nod to present-day social reality), so Mom decides she must marry.

She accepts a proposal from her director friend, Edward (Christopher Cazenove), and plans to move to England with little Mary (Robin Weisman), all because bachelor No. 2 (Selleck) is too confused to pop the question.

Rest of the pic is standard romantic comedy in a race to the altar as Selleck, moping around about the end of his improvised family, realizes he must face his feelings and ask for her hand. But will he make it to the church in time?

Piling convention upon convention, pic makes a beeline for a happy ending, tying things up so patly that a second sequel is unlikely. Unless Sylvia runs off, making way for "Three Men And A Third Grader." Let's hope not.

Scripter Charlie Peters spoon-feeds the audience with a plodding script that seems based more on demographic research about middle-American emotional/sentimental triggers than on any wisp of a creative impulse. Emile Ardolino directs with the same degree of competent but calculated nonrisk.

As for the actors, they have nothing to play. Selleck is a tongue-tied lug, Guttenberg is a sweet, brotherly guy, and Travis is sweet, radiant, and still a little ditzy. Only Danson seems unable to play it straight-faced. Flashes of mischief and mockery light up the edges of his delivery.

Pic perhaps has no truer moment than the absurd scene in which the three men, slow-tongued and not at all of the street, perform a little "rap lullaby" for their adored Mary, looking like trained dogs performing for their dinner. No doubt they'll be well-fed. — *Daws.*

PREDATOR 2

A 20th Century Fox release of a Gordon/Silver/Davis production. Produced by Lawrence Gordon, Joel Silver, John Davis. Executive producers, Michael Levy, Lloyd Levin. Directed by Stephen Hopkins. Screenplay, Jim Thomas, John Thomas, based on characters they created; camera (Deluxe color), Peter Levy; editor, Mark Goldblatt; music, Alan Silvestri; sound (Dolby), Richard Raguse; production design, Lawrence G. Paull; art direction, Geoff Hubbard; set decoration, Rick Simpson; costume design, Marilyn Vance-Straker; creature created by Stan Winston; makeup designed and created by Scott H. Eddo; visual effects coordinator, J.W. Kompare; visual effects supervisor, Joel Hynek; assistant director, Josh McLaglen; coproducers, Tom Joyner, Terry Carr; associate producer, Suzanne Todd; casting, Jackie Burch, Ferne Cassel. Reviewed at 20th Century Fox' Darryl F. Zanuck Theater, L.A., Nov. 19, 1990. MPAA Rating: R. Running time: **108 MIN.**
Harrigan . . . . Danny Glover
Keyes . . . . Gary Busey
Danny . . . . Ruben Blades
Leona . . . . . Maria Conchita Alonso
Jerry . . . . Bill Paxton
The Predator . . . . . Kevin Peter Hall
Also with: Robert Davi, Adam Baldwin, Kent McCord, Morton Downey Jr., Calvin Lockhart.

This overproduced sequel's relentless pace makes it extremely entertaining despite shortcomings. Studio may have blundered with its flippant ad campaign, but "Predator 2" still seems well positioned to chop the legs out from under holiday b.o. competition and take away a sizable trophy.

Following the "Die Hard 2" formula for sequel success, producer Joel Silver amplifies the original's action points to balletic, gory extremes. While the film doesn't achieve the same thrills of the final 45 minutes of "Predator" in terms of overall excitement, it outdoes its first safari in start-to-finish hysteria.

The real star is the pic's design, and production designer Lawrence G. Paull almost deserves to have his name above the title. Granted, the look is derivative of "Blade Runner" (earlier Paull credit), while the story takes pieces from just about every recent sci-fi film ("Robocop," "Aliens," "Alien," "Predator").

Writers Jim and John Thomas (who also wrote the original) don't waste much time on character development. Still, there are plenty of solid performers here, all heavily armed but with no place to go. For such a good cast, this isn't exactly an actors' showcase.

The setting is Los Angeles, 1997, where outgunned cops face hordes of Jamaican, Colombian and other assorted drug dealers who rule the streets.

It's a balmy 109 degrees in the globally warmed basin, where Glover heads a dedicated, ethnically mixed group of cops who are more than a little confused as the drug dealers start turning up dead in droves. The plot thickens when a fed (Gary Busey) comes in to take charge of the investigation.

Centerpiece is, again, a massive alien gifted with the strange weaponry and camouflage abilities like his kinsman that, it's told, had visited the planet 10 years earlier.

Director Stephen Hopkins' action scenes work fitfully, partly because only glimpses of the alien are provided through the pic's first half. Since the original "Predator" played the same game, it seems unnecessary to be coy about the creature's appearance this time around.

Squeaky clean L.A. subway looks suspiciously like San Francisco's BART system. A climactic battle in a warehouse is eerily bathed in pastel tones.

The pace of the film is absolutely frenetic, at times oppressively so. Still, its high points are impressive, and the look of the production is spectacular. An awe-inspiring set in the closing sequence recalls the climactic moment in "Aliens."

Stripped-to-the-bones script provides the right sort of revenge incentives and science-fiction elements, though there are unfortunately few surprises.

Then again, nothing is subtle about this pic, from the unimaginative dialog to Alan Silvestri's pounding score. Even the humor is crude and bathroom-oriented, but it fits easily into the general tenor of the whole production.

Despite all that the cast is generally fine, with Glover convincing enough as the determined hero, and Maria Conchita Alonso and Bill Paxton providing solid support. Seven-footer Kevin Peter Hall again gets the unenviable task of playing the alien, brought ably to life by an army of tech wizards.

With the not-so friendly skies apparently full of alien hunters, the idea of "Predator 3" isn't all that farfetched. Ending hints at another followup. — *Bril.*

SHAKING THE TREE

A Magnificent Mile Prods. presentation of an Anthony J. Tomaska/Robert J. Wilson production. Produced by Wilson. Executive producers, Tomaska, Richard Wagstaff. Directed by Duane Clark. Screenplay, Clark, Steven Wilde; camera (color), Ronn Schmidt; editor, Martin L. Bernstein; music, David E. Russo; sound (Ultra-stereo), Hans Roland; production design, Sean Mannion; costumes, Susan Michel Kaufman; casting, Eddie Foy III. Reviewed at the Chicago Intl. Film Festival, Oct. 24, 1990. No MPAA rating. Running time: **107 MIN.**
With: Arye Gross, Gale Hansen, Doug Savant, Steven Wilde.

This lackluster tale of four childhood buddies generates little interest despite competent technical credits all-around and some nice acting turns. The who-cares factor is simply too high.

"Shaking The Tree" documents the growing pains of an aspiring novelist, a rich ne'er-do-well, a rising young exec and a bartender, all of whom are confronted with major personal dilemmas as they approach serious adulthood.

Pic is probably a bit too serious for its own commercial good. Laughs are not plentiful, despite a good deal of horsing around by the young bucks. Romance, though emphasized as a prime source of angst, is viewed from such a one-sided (male) angle that it offers little relief.

Most of the time, the characters wallow in one kind of emotional trauma or another, including one purely gratuitous near-suicide scene.

Pic is bolstered by some attractive low-budget cinematography (film was reportedly made for less than $800,000) by Ronn Schmidt. — *Brin.*

EMINENT DOMAIN
(CANADIAN-ISRAELI-FRENCH)

A Vestron U.K. (in U.K.) release of an Arama Entertainment-Alan Neuman, SVS presentation of a Harlech Films-Shimon Arama production, in association with AFP-Eminent Domain Prods.-Stephan Films-UGC Images. Produced by Shimon Arama. Executive producer, Patrick Dromgoole, Paul Sarony. Directed by John Irvin. Screenplay, Andrzej Krakowski, Richard Gregson, from a story by Krakowski; camera (Eastmancolor), Witold Adamek; editor, Peter Tanner; music, Zbigniew Preisner; sound, Dani Natovich; production design, Allan Starski; art director, David Gauher, Ewa Braun, Barbara Nowak; costume design, Dorota Roqueplo; assistant director, Miguel Gil; co-producer, Claude Leger, Vera Belmont; associate producer, Elaine Ford Arama; line producer, Rony Yacov. Reviewed at 34th London Film Festival (Festival on the Square), Nov. 11, 1990. Running time: **107 MIN.**
Josef Borski . . . . Donald Sutherland
Mira . . . . Anne Archer
Ewa . . . . Johdi May
Ben . . . . Paul Freeman
Kowal . . . . Anthony Bate
Anton . . . . Pip Torrens
Slowak . . . . Bernard Hepton
Nicole . . . . Françoise Michaud
Roger . . . . Yves Beneyton

Only the gum on Donald Sutherland's mustache holds this clinker together. Preglasnost (1979) yarn about a humbled Polish politico and his eventual revenge lacks both tension and a decent script. Fast playoff in undiscriminating markets is indicated, before word-of-mouth closes the theatrical file for good.

Multinational co-production is officially billed as Canadian-Israeli-French, which helps to sort out the slew of producer credits. But pic draws heavily on British and Yank talent on both sides of the camera, as well as Polish expertise. Film bills itself as the first western production to be made in Poland since Solidarity came to power, and was lensed entirely in Warsaw and the port of Gdánsk.

Sutherland is the loyal politburo member whose talent for letting his superiors win at poker has given him a comfy flat, Swiss schooling for his daughter, dollars in his pockets and no need for his beautiful wife (Anne Archer) to queue for groceries.

Then one day it all disappears: His job is put on hold, he's trailed everywhere and, after his daughter is accidentally knocked down by a car, his wife ends up in the funny farm.

After 75 minutes, it's revealed it was all a loyalty test, which party boss Slowak (Bernard Hepton) tells him he's passed with flying colors. But Sutherland sets to engineering a quick exit with his wife and two friends.

Aside from the bland script, which squanders the talents of a largely British supporting cast, there's no real sense of Sutherland's growing nightmare and of the walls closing in on his privileged life.

Archer spends most of the pic looking pained, and there's some truly appalling dialog put into the daughter's mouth (Johdi May, sounding revoiced). Only thesps to emerge without scars are Sutherland, who looks great with an overcoat over his shoulders, and Paul Freeman as his best friend.

Pic's real star is the beautifully lit photography by Poland's Witold Adamek. Sound dub and music score are as subtle as sledgehammers. — *Drek.*

BAT LEUNG GAM
(EIGHT TAELS OF GOLD)
(HONG KONG)

A Golden Harvest presentation of a Maverick Films production. Produced by John Sham, John K.C. Chan. Executive producer, Sham. Directed by Mabel Cheung. Screenplay, Alex Law, Cheung; camera (color), Bill Wong, Tony Ducchiari (U.S.); editor, Yu Shun, Kwong Chi-leung; music, Lo Ta-yu, Richard Lo; production design, Law; art director, Rebecca Li; costume design, Lam Ngan; assistant director, Mark Ying, Tam Wai-keung; associate producer, Law. Reviewed at 34th London Film Festival (Hong Kong Focus), Nov. 17, 1990. Running time: **119 MIN.**
Slim Cheng . . . . Sammo Hung
Jenny . . . . Sylvia Chang
Also with: Gu Hui, Liu Guoping, He Dexiong, Chen Minquan, Danny Chu, Danny Wong.

One of the best pics exploring Hong Kong's edgy relationship with mainland China in the run-up to the 1997 handover, "Eight Taels Of Gold" is a bittersweet comedy romance with definite broad appeal. Picturesque locations in Canton and accessible playing by two leads could mean paydirt with specialist handling.

New York cabbie Slim Cheng (Sammo Hung) journeys back to his native village in mainland China after 16 years. He meets and falls for distant cousin Jenny (Sylvia Chang), nicknamed "Odds And Ends." Problem is she's about to get hooked to another overseas Chinese.

First half of film is played mostly for laughs, with Slim, worldly-wise and laden with gifts, running up against country yokels, chaotic transport system (one funny sequence has everyone on the plane writing out their wills when they hit turbulence) and grasping relatives.

Second half movingly traces his growing affection for the ambitious but naive Jenny, climaxing in a will-they-won't-they finale at her wedding ceremony.

Hung, better known for chopsocky pics, makes a touching figure of the brash, podgy prodigal-made-good. Taiwan actress Chang convincingly plays down her sophisticated looks as the femme mainlander, although Mandarin-speakers will notice she still has a Taiwanese accent.

Direction by New York-trained Mabel Cheung (in her third feature) is smooth, and location lensing by Bill Wong nice to behold. Pic's title refers to Slim's saying, "a man is not a man without eight taels (400 grams) of gold." — *Drek.*

FAUX ET USAGE
DE FAUX
(FORGERY AND THE USE
OF FORGERIES)
(FRENCH)

A UGC release (in France) of a PCC-Cine 5-Messine production. Produced by Alain Terzain. Directed by Laurent Heynemann. Screenplay, Jean-Marc Roberts, Christel Egal, Heynemann, from the book "L'homme que l'on croyait" by Paul Pavlowitch; camera (color), Robert Alazraki; editor, Armand Psenny; music, Philippe Sarde; sound, Michel Desrois; production design, Valérie Graal; costume design, Catherine Leterrier, Charlotte David; assistant director, Tristan Ganne. Reviewed at 34th London Film Festival (Panorama: France), Nov. 10, 1990. (Also in Sarasota French Film Festival.) Running time: **99 MIN.**
Anatole Hirsch . . . . . Philippe Noiret
Martin . . . . Robin Renucci
Sylvie . . . . Laure Killing
Gisèle Laumière . Monique Chaumette
Charles Laumière . Jean-Claude Brialy
Daniel Laumière . . . François Perrot
Jacqueline Ségur . . . . Caroline Sihol

Despite a provocative screenplay and Napoleonic playing by the ever-dependable Philippe Noiret, this acid look at the French literati scene won't produce much black ink outside the local market. References are too in-grown, and the clumsy title is no help.

Opening title points out that, although plot is based on the famous "affaire Ajar," the central figure "merely evokes" author Romain Gary (onetime spouse of Jean Seberg). It's all about an esteemed novelist, Anatole Hirsch (Noiret), who, partly from inner rage, partly from boredom, pens a shocker under a pseudonym and walks off with the Prix Goncourt.

Meanwhile, his young cousin Martin (Robin Renucci), whom Hirsch uses to front as his "Emile Arthus," gets used to the acclaim and tries to break free of his puppet role. When Hirsch tries the same trick again, and deliberately bombs, the joke turns sour.

Pic has plenty to say about "respectability" in France's lit world, but it's more about one man directing another man's life.

The role is tailor-made for Noiret, and he gives it his imperious, cigar-chomping best. He's also good in quieter scenes. He gets considerable support from Renucci (in one of his meatiest parts to date), who turns a potentially second-league role into a co-starrer. Both switch easily between the pic's lighter and darker moments.

Strong down-the-line casting gives film a solid feel. Caroline Sihol impresses as a femme journalist who eventually susses the truth. Only weak link is Laure Killing, in an underwritten role as Renucci's wife who ups and leaves as the joke takes over their life.

Tech credits are up to scratch, and Philippe Sarde's melodious, chamber-like score helps to keep things following. — *Drek.*

MING-YÜEH CHI-SHIH
YÜAN
(AUTUMN MOON)
(TAIWANESE)

A United Communications Group production, in association with KCI Prods. Produced by Yeh Wen-li. Executive producer, Chester C.Y. Koo. Directed by Richard Chen. Screenplay, Hua Yen, Ko Pi, from the novel by Hua Yen; camera (Eastmancolor), Kuo Musheng; editor, Ch'en Po-wen; music, Peter Chang Hung-yi; lyrics, Yao Ch'ien; sound, Hsian Chiang-sheng, Hu Ting-yi; production design, Li T'ung; costume design, Rosalie Huang; assistant director, Chou Hsing-min; associate producers, Yüan Pin, Wang Ming-ts'an; line producers, C.Y. Chen, Richard Chen. Reviewed at 34th London Film Festival (Three Continents: Asia), Nov. 13, 1990. Running time: **137 MIN.**
With: Cora Miao, Lu Hsiao-fen, Chang Fu-chien, Tuan Ching-yi, K'o Yi-cheng, Chou Shao-tung.

"Autumn Moon," an immensely stylish and beautifully lensed drama about the breakup of a novelist's marriage and her spiritual rebirth, is talky but rewarding, thanks to fine acting. Fest outings should spur debate, but offshore commercial chances rate slim.

Co-written by director Richard Chen (under the pseudonym Ko Pi) from a 1985 novel by local authoress Hua Yen, story follows reaction of sophisticated, prizewinning Wan To-hung (Cora Miao) to sudden news that her hubby (Chang Fu-chien) fathered a child years ago in the U.S.

For the first time she has to cope with a melodrama in her own life, rather than on the printed page, and she's not up to it. Pic shows her gradually coming to terms with the values she's espoused in her novels (especially one called "Love And Forgiveness").

She finally takes a recuperative trip from Taiwan to rural mainland China with her sister (Lu Hsiao-fen), a looser cannon involved with a married man.

Soap-opera plot is deliberately reined back by stylized, formal images, low-key playing, and use of "literary" dialog. It's a film of interior rather than exterior emotions.

Miao (familiar from "Dim Sum" and other pics by husband Wayne Wang) is tops as the novelist, in a luminous performance. Lu Hsiao-fen (from Chen's previous "Spring Swallow") is excellent in the smaller role as the sister.

Postproduction was done in Japan. Color grading is immaculate, and use of direct sound (still rare in Taiwan pics) a major bonus. Following world preem at London fest, Taiwan-made pic, with locations also in Singapore and mainland China (near Yan'an), is slated for spring release back home. — *Drek.*

FORGET ABOUT ME
(BRITISH-HUNGARIAN)

A Thames TV-Magyar Televizió production. Produced by Richard Handford. Executive producers, Alan Horrox, Mihály Gál. Directed by Michael Winterbottom. Screenplay, Frank Cottrell Boyce; camera (Eastmancolor, 16m), Ray Orton; editor, Trevor Waite, Olivia Hetreed; music, Simple Minds; sound, Jeff Matthews, Tim Partridge; production design, Katalin Kalmár; assistant director, Ian Ferguson, Mihály Farkas Csapó; co-producer, György Müller. Reviewed at 34th London Film Festival (British Cinema), Nov. 10, 1990. Running time: **72 MIN.**

Broke . . . . Ewen Bremner
Bunny . . . . Brian McCardie
Csilla . . . . Zsuzsanna Várkonyi
Atila . . . . Atilla Grandpierre
Anna . . . . Katalin Pataki

Unlike most Brit tv pics, this comedy romance shows a feature film struggling to get out. Great all-around playing and slick look adds up to an impressive debut by helmer Michael Winterbottom, 29. Specialized dates are a possibility.

Project started out under title "The Snow Queen" as a 52-minute film for educational tv. Finished version was shot on same budget, with U.K. commercial web Thames providing all production coin and Hungarian tv extra crew and facilities.

Story follows a pair of Scots on leave from their West German army base for a bit of Hungarian Hogmanay. On the road they pick up looker Csilla, who gives them a taste of Budapest's party life and finally falls for the sensitive one of the duo.

Ewen Bremner is fine as the quiet, perceptive Broke, and Brian McCardie handles the wisecracking, cocky part of Bunny with aplomb. But the real scenestealer is young Magyar thesp Zsuzsanna Várkonyi as the capricious Csilla, switching from Hungarian to English with ease and equally convincing in both.

Script and 16m lensing are crisp and colorful. Chunks of Hungarian dialog are sans subtitles, which helps to stress the boys' isolation. It's their thick Scottish accents that could prove a bigger problem for North American viewers. — *Drek.*

IL VIAGGIO DI CAPITAN FRACASSA
(CAPTAIN FRACASSA'S JOURNEY)
(ITALIAN-FRENCH)

A Penta release. Produced by Mario and Vittorio Cecchi Gori for Penta Film-Gaumont, in association with Studio E.L.-Mass Film. Directed by Ettore Scola. Screenplay, Scola, Furio Scarpelli, based on Theophile Gautier's novel; camera (color), Luciano Tovoli; editor, Raimondo Crociani, Francesco Malvestito; music, Armando Trovajoli; art direction, Luciano Ricceri, Paolo Biagetti; costumes, Odette Nicoletti. Reviewed at the Barberini Cinema, Rome, Nov. 16, 1990. Running time: **135 MIN.**
Pulcinella . . . . Massimo Troisi
Serafina . . . . Ornella Muti
Baron of Sigognac . . . . Vincent Perez
Isabella . . . . Emmanuelle Béart
Matamoro . . . . Jean-François Perrier
Servant . . . . Ciccio Ingrassia
Also with: Renato Nicolini, Remo Girone, Tosca D'Aquino, Marco Messeri, Maria Angela Giordano, Claudio Amendola, Patrizia Sacchi, Giuseppe Cederna, Lauretta Masiero, Massimo Wertmuller, Toni Ucci.

Penta-Gaumont coprod "Captain Fracassa's Journey" is the biggest, longest and classiest product of the Italo season so far. Ettore Scola has realized his long-cherished dream of bringing Theophile Gautier's novel to the screen.

A visually lavish, very theatrical costumer in the style of Jean Renoir's "The Golden Coach," "Captain Fracassa" is a celebration of the European theater tradition. It may not have blockbuster stuff, but the film pleases

CAPT. FRACASSE
(FRENCH MADE)

Theophile Gautier's well-known book of adventure, "Le Capitaine Fracasse," has been screened [directed and cowritten] by Alberto Cavalcanti and converted into a good French picture for P.J. de Venloo and the Lutece Corp. This is the production Maurice Tourneur was to have adopted for pictures.... Picture constitutes a creditable release for native fans liking adventure of the middle ages. Pierre Blanchar is the hero, and a fine actor if a bit out of place here. Lien Deyers, blonde heroine, makes a delicious comedienne, but her Isabella is not her best effort. [Also features Charles Boyer, Daniel Mendaille. Reviewed Feb. 25, 1929.]

the eyes and should appeal to the arthouse crowd offshore.

The Scola pic is doing fair business in limited Italian release, though recouping the costs of its $15 million budget will be tricky. (Between the adaptations of the novel produced in the late '20s and in the early '60s, Abel Gance's "Capitaine Fracasse"

came out in 1943 and never received a VARIETY review apparently due to the Nazi Occupation of France.)

Set in the early 17th century, pic follows the adventures of an amiable group of traveling players wending their way to Paris. Ornella Muti and Massimo Troisi headline as two colorful thespians. Serafina (Muti) is a 35-year-old aging beauty adept at seducing men, but too pensively pessimistic to find a steady mate.

When the company stumbles onto an old castle one rainy night, flea-ridden young Baron of Sigognac (Vincent Perez) falls for Serafina and travels along with the company. Gentlemanly old actor Matamoro (Jean-François Perrier) dies, leaving his young blonde protégé Isabella (Emmanuelle Béart) alone.

Serafina pushes the baron into her arms, mostly to spite herself. Another unlucky couple is Pulcinella (Troisi) and Zerbina (Tosca D'Aquino).

Performing before an audience of nobles, the company's three young actresses each attract the attention of a potential rich protector. Out of love for Zerbina,

LE CAPITAINE FRACASSE
(FRENCH-DYALISCOPE)

Unidex release of Plazza-Metzger & Woog-Paris Elysees Films-Hoche-Documento production. Directed by Pierre Gaspard-Huit. Screenplay, Albert Vidalie, Gaspard-Huit from novel by Theophile Gautier; camera (Eastmancolor), Marcel Grignon; editor, Luisette Hautecoeur. Reviewed at Normandie, Paris, May 30, 1961. Running time: **105 MIN.**
De Sigognac . . . . Jean Marais
Isabelle . . . . Genevieve Grad
Vallombreuse . . . . . . Gerard Barray
Scapin . . . . Louis De Funes
Marquise . . . . . Anna-Maria Ferrero
Sophie . . . . Daniele Godet

Pulcinella makes her accept the offer so she can lead a life of ease.

Serafina refuses an outrageously candid offer by another blueblood (rakish Renato Nicolini, a w.k. member of parliament and Rome's former cultural alderman).

Isabella repulses the marquis of Vallombrosa (the somberly dignified Remo Girone, villain from "The Octopus" series) so gracelessly that her paramour, Sigognac, has to challenge him to a ruinous duel. To save Sigognac's life, she agrees to go off with Vallombrosa. This brings Sigognac back to Serafina's arms.

Between love for the theater and affairs of the heart, "Captain Fracassa" charts a lighthearted course. Scola delights in under-

lining the theatricality of the film with Luciano Ricceri and Paolo Biagetti's marvelous backdrops and Odette Nicoletti's costumes. Film draws much of its strength from Troisi's warm, funny performance as Pulcinella, a famed character from the *commedia dell'arte* tradition. The inventive young comic is right on-target in a role that exploits his natural gift for surrealistic monologs within the part's bounds.

— *Yung.*

BANANEN — SKRÄL DEN FÖR DIN NABO
(BANANA BUSTERS)
(DANISH)

A Regner Grasten Film release and production. Produced by Sven Methling Jr. Executive producer, Kimi Christensen. Directed by Regner Grasten. Screenplay, Grasten, Michael Hardinger; camera (Eastmancolor)-stunt director, Lasse Spang Olsen; editor, Mette Schramm, Sven Methling; music, Michael Hardinger, Rasmus Swenege; sound, Jörgen (Lyd) Nielsen; production design, Hummer Höimark; costumes, Merete Engbäk. Reviewed at the Palads, Copenhagen, Nov. 9, 1990. Running time: **82 MIN.**
Mortensen . . . . Dick Kaysö
Police chief . . . . Ole Ernst
Ms. Hansen . . . . Katrine Stenz
Also with: Brian Patterson, Helle Michaelsen, Thomas Höeg, Lasse Aagard, Sune Svanekier, Thomas Eje (voice).

Nobody slips on a banana peel in "Banana Busters," but every other imaginable farcical device from Mack Sennett to National Lampoon is tried and falls flat. Regner Grasten produced, directed and co-wrote this demolition derby.

Since no big-name actors are involved, "Banana Busters" will have to rely on fast playoff in home territory to make it commercially. Several offshore presales, however, were made at Mifed, and an English-dubbed version is in the works.

Grasten is only nominally pic's helmer since about 95% of the action is devoted to car chases, explosions, and violent banging, bashing and smashing of things and bodies. All of this is handled, along with camera chores, by stunt director Lasse Spang Olsen.

Acting is confined to grimacing and yelling. Streams of obscene language from a ventriloquist's dummy and a talking dog supposedly make up for the dialog's lack of wit.

Thin plot tells of a dumb detective's attempt to break up a gang of heroin smugglers. Loud pop rock music accompanies all the desperate cavorting but cannot drown out the fact that farce cannot be made to work without the semblance of structure.

— *Kell.*

HAVANA
(BRITISH-DOCU)

> A BBC production. Produced and directed by Jana Bokova. Camera (color), Jose Riera, Ramon Suarez; editor, Yves Deschamps; sound, Jose Borras, Henri Lopez. Reviewed at Toronto Festival of Festivals, Sept. 8, 1990. Running time: **105 MIN.**

Filmmaker Jana Bokova has crafted a sharp view of the Cuban capital in "Havana," a clearly biased anti-Castro documentary which will find homes on the fest circuit and risk-taking pubbroadcasting webs.

Bokova, who left her native Czechoslovakia for the U.S. and France in 1968, pans her camera over the once majestic buildings of Havana and into the slums of crumbling ex-convent halls. Most of her subjects (ranging from illiterate peasants to articulate artists) seem willing to talk honestly about events since Castro took over in 1959.

An old woman in a tarpaper shack sticks to the credo, "God in his heaven and Fidel on earth." This is juxtaposed with Cuban poet and playwright Pablo Armando Fernandez, who lives in a luxurious home, reading a poem he wrote about his own identity.

Bokova catches the spontaneity of street festival dancing, pick-up jazz bands jamming in courtyards and couples doing the rumba outside their homes.

Bokova also finds expatriate Cuban artists in the U.S. revealing horror stories about their arrests and persecutions. One homosexual writer in Miami says the government found no place for "negative pessimism" in Cuban society.

The director allows her floating camera and lingering closeups on people in their decrepit surroundings to talk to her. There's no flip side viewpoint at all; that's simply not Bokova's agenda. — *Devo.*

FLEISCHWOLF
(THE MEAT GRINDER)
(AUSTRIAN)

> An EPO Film production. Produced by Bertram Hubner. Directed by Houchang Allahyari. Screenplay, Allahyari, Tom D. Allahyari; camera (color), Herbert Tucmandi, Udo Maurer; editor, Charlotte Mullrer, Michaela Mullner; music, Thomas Morris; sound, Harald Hennings. Reviewed at Toronto Festival of Festivals, Sept. 14, 1990. Running time: **75 MIN.**
> Jorg . . . . Hanno Poschi
> Mother . . . . Cecile Nordegg
> Mario . . . . Maximilian Mullner

Director Houchang Allahyari's training as a psychiatrist comes to the fore in "The Meat Grinder," gutsy drama about life in prison. Graphic subject matter will make it a tough sell commercially, but pic may find takers on the fest circuit.

Pic says nothing new about the psychological breakdown of prisoners, but Allahyari extracts potent performances from his cast of nonprofessional thesps.

Story focuses on three young men in an Austrian prison. Mario is plagued by horrific images of his mother, who hung out with degenerate men and who may have abused him.

Ritchie is the father of a new baby. Angelic-looking Karl is an easy target for the macho prison honcho, Jorg.

After the kitchen staff rapes the boy, there seems to be no choice for Karl but suicide, and the act is sparingly and dramatically filmed.

Black market cigaret deals, weekly church services, the buddy system and the constant threat of violence are all smoothly delineated. — *Devo.*

LACENAIRE
(FRENCH)

> A Partner's Prods.-UGC production in association with Hachette Premiere and La Cinque Prods. (Intl. sales: World Marketing Film, Paris.) Produced by Ariel Zeitoun. Directed by Francis Girod. Screenplay, Georges Conchon, Girod. Camera (color), Bruno de Keyzer; music, Laurent Petitgirard; sound, Andre Hervee; assistant directors, Olivier Horlait, Jerome Navarro; costume design, Yvonne Sassinot De Nesle. Reviewed at the Sarasota (Fla.) French Film Festival, Nov. 17, 1990. Running time: **122 MIN.**
> Lacenaire . . . . Daniel Auteuil
> Allard . . . . Jean Poiret
> Princess Ida . . Marie-Armelle Deguy
> Hermine . . . . . Maiwenn Le Besco
> Arago . . . . Jacques Weber
> Avril . . . . Patrick Pineau
> Lusignan . . . . Samuel Labarthe
> Lacenaire's father . . . François Perier
> Lacenaire's mother . Genevieve Casile

"Lacenaire," Francis Girod's stylistically audacious and savagely witty drama based on the life of the gentleman murderer who scandalized (and entertained) 19th-century France, is the next masterwork of French cinema.

With the right handling, this lavishly produced pic could score a major success in the U.S. arthouse market, and might even pick up a few Oscar nominations in acting and tech categories.

Certainly, Daniel Auteuil deserves a fistful of international awards for his portrayal of Pierre-François Lacenaire (1800-36), the self-dramatizing rogue and indefatigable seducer who has long been a darkly mythic figure in French history.

Film buffs will recall Lacenaire as a supporting character, memorably played by Marcel Herrand, in Marcel Carné's "Children Of Paradise." Here, however, he is the star, and Auteuil plays him accordingly.

Failed playwright, petty thief, artful con man, brutal killer — Lacenaire played a variety of roles, sometimes two or more simultaneously, during a brief but colorful career that ended in his "suicide by guillotine."

Girod and co-scriptwriter Georges Conchon begin their account with Lacenaire's final days in his sumptuous prison cell, where he entertains assorted guests and completes an image-enhancing autobiography. After the execution, the film interweaves flashbacks of Lacenaire confidantes reading about him, and themselves, in his last testament.

What emerges is an enthralling portrait of a willfully self-destructive man in lifelong rebellion against the proprieties and hypocrisies of his time. The smug, conservative family scion, after killing a gambler who cheated him at cards, devotes himself to low crimes and high life, usually achieving his goals by smooth talk, not violence.

Lacenaire says "the only talent nature has given me" is his style of seduction, which is at once intensely intimate and clinically detached — with men as well as women. But he's impotent when he tries to bed down an aristocrat (Marie-Armelle Deguy) he truly cares about.

The charmer really hits his stride after his arrest for the clumsy murders of a crooked pawn-broker and the villain's mother. At his highly publicized trial, Lacenaire becomes a showman extraordinaire, dazzling spectators and even bowling over the judges as he turns the legal proceedings into a hand-tooled star vehicle.

Throughout, but most impressively during the trial sequences, Auteuil plays Lacenaire with a mesmerizing mixture of grandstanding flamboyance, sardonic humor and aggressive intelligence. Ultimately, Lacenaire uses the trial to condemn the very society that created him. By that time, however, it's clear that he wants his audience to think the worst of him: Only by proving himself worthy of the death penalty, he figures, can he attain his goal of immortality.

As the police chief who brings Lacenaire to justice and the celebrity author who takes notice of the criminal, Jean Poiret and Jacques Weber are excellent as intelligent, self-assured men who cannot help falling under Lacenaire's spell. Patrick Pineau is very good as Avril, Lacenaire's ill-fated partner in crime.

Still, Auteuil's is the only face most audiences will remember seeing, his voice the only one they will remember hearing, when they think of "Lacenaire." Lacenaire himself would have wanted it that way. — *Ley.*

TROIS ANNÉES
(THREE YEARS)
(FRENCH)

An AAA Classic release of a Mod Films-TF1 Films production. Produced by Jacques Kirsner. Directed by Fabrice Cazeneuve. Screenplay, Jacques Tournier, based on the novella by Anton Chekhov. Camera (color), Pierre-Laurent Chenieux; editor, Yann Dedet; music, Michel Portal; sound, Dominique Viellard; set design, Jimmy Vanstenkiste; costumes, Cécile Balme; executive producer, Patrick Grandperret. Reviewed at the Sarasota (Fla.) French Film Festival, Nov. 17, 1990. Running time: **92 MIN.**

Julia	Sabine Azema
Alexandre	Jacques Villeret
Constantin	Philippe Volter
Pilou	Lucas Belvaux
Nina	Zouc
Gregoire	Jean-Marie Winling

Jacques Villeret, usually cast as a chubby buffoon in French comedies, gives a performance of unexpected delicacy and affecting poignance in "Three Years," director Fabrice Cazeneuve's version of a classic Chekhov novella.

Pic itself is an intelligent and subtle work, but it lacks the necessary spark needed to find theatrical life beyond the international film festival circuit.

Scriptwriter Jacques Tournier has transferred the storyline to 1870 France. Villeret plays a good-hearted, well-to-do fellow in his mid-30s who fears his likely future as a lonely bachelor. He's in love with the beautiful, somewhat younger daughter (Sabine Azema) of the village's aging doctor (Claude Bouchery).

Much to his amazement, she accepts his clumsy but heartfelt proposal. Much to his frustration, he realizes she married him primarily for security and not for love. She, too, feared life as an unmarried loner.

In a series of richly detailed, deliberately paced episodes, Cazeneuve and Tournier follow the first three years of the couple's marriage, counterpointing Villeret's growing disenchantment with Azema's gradual realization of just how much she really loves her husband.

Villeret takes over, and saves, the family business after his senile father nearly bankrupts them. He gets so wrapped up in financial affairs, however, that he fails to recognize wife's change of heart.

"Trois Années" certainly isn't lacking in incident. Births, deaths, mental breakdowns and assorted other complications emerge. Even so, the drama remains muted, sometimes too much for pic's own good.

Still, Villeret is quite moving in his not-so-quiet desperation, particularly in the film's first half. Azema (late of Bertrand Tavernier's "Life and Nothing But") manages the difficult task of breaking her co-star's heart without losing audience sympathy.

Fine support is offered by Philippe Volter and Lucas Belvaux as cheerfully freeloading friends, and Bouchery as the cantankerous father. Pierre-Laurent Chenieux' cinematography, Jimmy Vanstenkiste's sets and Cécile Balme's costumes greatly enhance the period flavor. — *Ley.*

DANCING MACHINE
(FRENCH)

A Leda Prods.-TF1 Films production. (Intl. sales: Roissy Films, Paris.) Produced by Sophie Gueronik. Directed by Gilles Behat. Executive producer, Alain Delon. Screenplay, Paul-Loup Sulitzer, Loup Durand, Jean-Marc Cerrone; camera (color), José-Luis Alcaine; music, Jean-Marc Cerrone; sound (Dolby), Paul Laine; costumes, Marie-Françoise Perochon. Reviewed at the Sarasota (Fla.) French Film Festival, Nov. 16, 1990. Running time: **105 MIN.**

Alan Wolf	Alain Delon
Inspector Eparvier	Claude Brasseur
Chico	Patrick Dupond
Daphne	Tonya Kinzinger
Ella	Marina Saura
Moreno	Inaki Aierra
Le Guellec	Etienne Chicot
Liselotte Wagner	Consuelo De Havilland

"Dancing Machine" is nonsense served up with enough verve, visual flair and star power to make it more entertaining than it has a right to be. Properly promoted, this slick French thriller might find a cult audience in urban U.S. centers. An English-dubbed version could gain acceptance on video and cable.

Alain Delon, sporting a Don Johnson stubble and a Lord Byron limp, toplines as the brooding, autocratic manager of a Paris dance studio where professionals train and wanna-bes learn. The former ballet superstar's career ended after being injured in a motorcycle mishap that killed his lover, another great dancer.

Bitterness has made Delon a cruel taskmaster: Through his choreographer-instructor (Patrice Dupond), he runs the studio as brutal monarchy. Apparently, most of the female students are madly in love with the dictatorial dance master. And for a few of them, dismissal from the studio is sufficient grounds for suicide.

Enter Claude Brasseur as a hardboiled cop called in by Delon's ex-wife when ex-students start turning up dead. The inspector's suspicions are aroused when a woman literally dances herself to death outside Delon's window after being told to clean out her locker.

The dance-of-death sequence is a showstopper, one of several that suggest director Gilles Behat prepared by screening "Flashdance" and "All That Jazz" several times. Almost all of the dance sequences, which are cleverly integrated into the naturalistic narrative, have the Bob Fosse touch.

A particularly impressive sequence, set in an underground garage, features Tonya Kinzinger as a beautiful young dancer (and sister of the ballet teacher's late paramour) who falls under teacher's fatal charm. While the sister dances, Delon provides the lighting with his headlights, driving closer, ever closer, to his student.

If anyone in the cast ever winked at the camera, "Dancing Machine" would collapse into hopeless silliness. But the actors and dancers perform in dead earnest, even during the shamelessly corny climax.

Delon, listed as executive producer, plays with just the right amount of intensity, giving the cold-blooded character unexpected poignance. Brasseur makes a worthy foil, as a crude but cunning antagonist with a hidden agenda. Dupond is a flamboyant choreographer and a credible red herring. Dancer-actress Kinzinger rates a 10 for looks, eight for dancing, six for acting.

Tech credits, particularly Jose-Luis Alcaine's evocative cinematography, are firstrate. — *Ley.*

LONDON FEST

SHAKHA PROSHAKHA
(BRANCHES OF THE TREE)
(INDIAN-FRENCH)

A Satyajit Ray Prods. (India)-Erato Films-DD Prods. (France) production, in association with Distri Films (U.K.)-Sopro Films (France). (Intl. sales: Erato Films, Paris.) Produced by Gérard Depardieu, Daniel Toscan du Plantier. Written and directed by Satyajit Ray. Camera (color), Barun Raha; editor, Dulal Dutt; music, Ray; sound, Pierre Lenoir, Denis Carquin; art director, Ashok Bose. Reviewed at 34th London Film Festival (Three Continents: Asia), Nov. 23, 1990. Running time: **120 MIN.**

Ananda Majunda	Ajit Banerjee
Probodh	Maradan Banerjee
Proshanto	Soumitra Chatterjee
Probir	Deepankar De
Protap	Ranjit Mallik
Uma	Lily Charraborty
Tapati	Mamata Shankar

Satyajit Ray's "Branches Of The Tree" is a talky family drama about four sons (plus spouses) who gather at their father's country home after he has a heart attack. Slow, boxily shot pic will garner fest invites on strength of Ray's name, but it's tough going for all but total devotees.

Film is Indian helmer's second since his heart troubles of the mid-1980s, and an improvement on his previous "An Enemy Of The People" (1989). Story was actually penned 25 years ago, and is said to contain no autobiog elements, but there's no mistaking its flavor: autumnal, retrospective, Chekhovian.

Ajit Banerjee portrays a respected, hard-working, principled man who lives with his aged father and second son (Soumitra Chatterjee), both of whom are slightly out to lunch. When Banerjee collapses during a 70th birthday tribute in a village in North Bengal, the rest of the family come in from Calcutta.

It's not often they're all together, and soon the tensions start to show. Eldest son (Maradan Banerjee) is a general manager who's fleecing his company; third son (Deepankar De) likes the horses; and youngest son (Ranjit Mallik) has just chucked his job on a point of principle and wants to become a thesp.

While father lies unconscious, each of the sextet plays off against the others in a series of interior scenes, with Chatterjee, who only has flashes of lucidity, in a seer-like role.

Pic climaxes in the only major exterior, a picnic in a forest. After father recovers (and accidentally learns some home truths about his brood), life returns to the menage of the start.

Potentially there's a lot going on here: the mixture of four generations under one roof, the clash of values between father and sons, the creeping effect of everyday corruption. But a stagy script with yards of expository dialog and static direction make most of the drama stillborn.

Thesping also has a legit feel, with only Banerjee as the father and Mamata Shankar as third son's wife really convincing.

Pic was shot in same Calcutta studio as "Enemy Of The People," with French production coin from Ray admirers Gérard Depardieu and Daniel Toscan du Plantier. Tech credits are average. Ray, busy on a new pic, was unable to attend world preem at the London film fest. — *Drek.*

BUN NGO TSONG TINNGAI
(WILD SEARCH)
(HONG KONG)

A Silver Medal Prods. presentation of a Born Top production. Produced and directed by Ringo Lam. Executive producer, Tony Chow. Screenplay, Nam Yin; camera (color), Lau Wai-keung; editor, Tony Chow; music, Lowell Lo; production design, Luk Tze-fung; costume design, Thomas Chong; assistant director, Ko Mun-wing, To Yun-ha. Reviewed at 34th London Film Festival (Hong Kong Focus), Nov. 17, 1990. Running time: **95 MIN.**

Mickey Lau . . . . Chow Yun-fat
Cher . . . . Cherie Chung
Hung . . . . Paul Chin
Ka-ka . . . . Chan Cheuk-yan
Leung . . . . Lau Kong
Lam . . . . Tommy Wong
Tiger . . . . Roy Cheung
Grandpa . . . . Ku Feng

Several notches above the usual Hong Kong crime actioner, "Wild Search" is more a gentle love story between a disillusioned cop and a naive country girl. Shootouts remain, but pic has more substance than recent slambangers like "The Killer." Beyond fest outings and buff audiences, though, it may fall between two stools.

Pic marks a softening of style for helmer Ringo Lam after three iron-jawed thrillers, "City On Fire," "Prison On Fire" and "School On Fire."

Bleary-eyed cop Lau (Chow Yun-fat) is hunting some Triad arms dealers when, during a bungled setup, a femme intermediary gets blown away. Her young daughter is taken in care by sister Cher (Cherie Chung), who lives quietly in Hong Kong's New Territories. Between hunting his prey, Lau falls for the simple country girl.

It's virtually a two-hander be-

tween local superstars Chow and Chung, with each showing greater depth than in most of their commercial chores. The climax, when it comes, is suitably cathartic, and directed with confidence by Lam.

Pic's look is slick without being overglossy, with sharp stabs of violence and no flashy effects for their own sake. There's also that rarity for a film of this kind — a script. Result generated tasty returns of $HK16 million on local release last year. — *Drek.*

LE BAL DU GOUVERNEUR
(THE GOVERNOR'S PARTY)
(FRENCH)

A Cinéa-FR3 production. (Intl. sales: Président Films, Paris.) Produced by Philippe Carcassonne. Executive producer, Philippe Lauro-Baranes. Written and directed by Marie-France Pisier. Camera (Agfacolor), Denis Lenoir; editor, Claudine Merlin; music, Khalil Chahine; sound, Pierre Lenoir; art director, Michel Barthelemy; costume design, Christian Gasc; assistant director, Marie Beauchaud. Reviewed at 34th London Film Festival (Panorama: France), Nov. 20, 1990. Running time: **100 MIN.**

Marie Forestier . Kristin Scott-Thomas
Charles Forestier . . . Didier Flamand
Dr. Royan . . . . . . Laurent Grevill
Governor . . . . Jacques Sereys
Théa Forestier . . . . Vanessa Wagner
Isabelle Demur . . . . Edwige Navarro
Benoit Forestier . . . Renaud Menager
Jean-Baptiste . . . . . Julien Kouchner

A comely coming-of-age pic in a French colonial setting, "The Governor's Party" tries to pack too much into a slim bottle. Presence of Anglo thesp Kristin Scott-Thomas could attract offshore interest, but tube sales look more likely.

Pic started life some 10 years ago as a script by w.k. French actress Marie-France Pisier who, on advice of François Truffaut, turned it into a bestselling 1984 novel. But story's anticolonial tone (setting is 1957) still made it a long haul to raise production coin.

Though not strictly an autobiog, plot draws on elements of Pisier's childhood. Like her 11-year-old heroine, she spent time in the Pacific colony of New Caledonia, was the daughter of a senior civil servant and witnessed a stormy marriage.

Pic opens with a preteen Théa (Vanessa Wagner) experiencing first flushes of womanhood with best pal (Edwige Navarro). Mum

(Scott-Thomas) is a flighty blond given to early-morning riding jaunts on the seashore. Dad (Didier Flamand) is a boring career solon who plays jazz piano.

When mum comes to breakfast one morning with her jodhpurs torn, rumors start spreading of hanky-panky with a young doctor (Laurent Grevill). Climax is a stiff-collar bash thrown by the island's governor for a visiting minister.

In her directorial bow, Pisier is remarkably assured. She knows where to put the camera, makes striking use of color in interiors, and pic has an easy flow. Only problem is the switching back and forth from moppets to adults to colonial unrest; final product ending up unconvincing.

Scott-Thomas seems mannered compared with other thesps, but she's clearly done her French homework. Flamand adds layers to his part as it progresses. Best is young Wagner in what should have been the central role: her Théa is more spiteful tease than peaches and cream.

Tech credits are handsome, especially Denis Lenoir's lensing. Pic lensed for five weeks in New Caledonia, with well-matched segs back in France (Antibes and just outside Paris). — *Drek.*

VRAT SE DO HROBU
(READY FOR THE GRAVE)
(CZECHOSLOVAKIAN)

A Barrandov Film Studios production. Directed by Milan Steindler. Screenplay, Halina Pawlowská, Steindler; camera (color), Miroslav Cvorsjuk; editor, Vera Flaková; music, Miloslav Halík; sound, Tomás Janecek; art director, Jindrich Goetz; assistant director, Roman Fara. Reviewed at 34th London Film Festival (World Panorama), Nov. 21, 1990. Running time: **101 MIN.**

With: Milan Steindler, Dana Batulková, Klára Pollertová, Krystof Kolácek, Jan Trávnícek, Ales Machalícek.

An easygoing Czech comedy about a henpecked thirtysomething who decides to swing before it's too late, "Ready For The Grave" is largely familiar fare, thin on real yocks. Some tv outings could be in order before nailing down the coffin lid.

Pic's original title literally means "Back To The Grave," which gives a better idea of the tone. First-time helmer Milan Steindler plays (like a scalded puppy) a researcher in an obscure sociological department. He's sent to do a report on the

social responsibility of young people, and goes undercover in a high school class.

He soon finds that kids just wanna have fun. Before long he's getting moony looks from mini-skirted Klára Pollertová. Back home, wife Dana Batulková and two kids start to feel left out.

Czech cinema is not short of comedies like this, and performances are good all round, especially from the three leads.

But pic could do with some tightening, especially in the first half, and script dissipates the real message of how functionaries, who've never given a real opinion in their lives, can adjust to the growing openness. (Pic was made in 1989, before the latest developments.)

Tech credits are up to scratch, marred only by occasionally sloppy postsynching. A final vertiginous crane shot shows Steindler can tweak an audience when he wants to. — *Drek.*

GUNGUN HONGCHEN
(RED DUST)
(HONG KONG)

A Tomson (HK) Films presentation of a Pineast Pictures production. Produced by Tang Chün-nien. Executive producer, Hsu Feng. Directed by Yim Ho. Screenplay, Echo Chen De Quero, Yim; camera (color), Poon Hang-seng; editor, Sammy Chow; music, Shih Chieh-yung, Lo Ta-yu; design consultant, William Cheung; art directors, Jessinta Lau, Edith Cheung; costume design, Cheung; associate producer, Jessinta Lau. Reviewed at 34th London Film Festival (Hong Kong Focus), Nov. 22, 1990. Running time: **94 MIN.**

With: Lin Ching-hsia, Chin Han, Maggie Cheung, Richard Ng, Josephine Koo, Yim Ho.

A strikingly lensed meller played out against the turbulent backdrop of 20th century China, "Red Dust" could stir up interest beyond the Asian circuit with extra-special handling. Topnotch femme leads and intelligent direction put this in a different league from other Asian historicial sudsers.

Opening in 1938, pic follows the love affair between an independent young femme writer (Lin Ching-hsia) and a cultural officer (Chin Han) who's collaborating with the Japanese. Despite warnings from her best pal (Maggie Cheung), Lin won't give him up. Even after being separated during the post-World War II civil war, the couple are fated to meet one more time. Story ends with a coda in 1989.

There's a touch of "Doctor Zhivago" in the love-across-chaos story. Asian buffs will spot canny casting of Lin and Chin, who made their reps in flossy Taiwan mellers of the 1970s. Helmer Yim Ho has put a favorite Asian genre through the mincer and produced a tour de force.

Major plaudits go to Lin and Cheung, especially in their scenes of sisterly friendship. Chin lacks depth as the object of Lin's desire but he's well-covered by the direction.

Tech credits are impeccable. Lensing by Hong Kong's Poon Hang-seng catches the cold winter light of northern China in the exteriors and warmer glow of the relationships in the interiors.

Musical score by Taiwan's Shih Chieh-yung, of which there's plenty, is up-front but attentive.

Pic was financed by Hong Kong arm of Taiwan's Tomson Films, and shot entirely in mainland China (Harbin and Changchun) last winter for just over $1 million. Film bowed in Cantonese dub Nov. 23 in Hong Kong.
— *Drek.*

UNA MITRAN DI YAAD PYAARI
(IN MEMORY OF FRIENDS)
(INDIAN-DOCU-16m)

> Produced and directed by Anand Patwardhan. (Intl. sales: Jane Belfour Films, London.) Camera (color), Patwardhan; editor, Patwardhan; music, Jaimal Singh Padda, Navnirman, Amritsar Kala Kendra; sound, Parvez Merwanji, Narinder Singh. Reviewed at 34th London Film Festival (Three Continents: Asia), Nov. 21, 1990. Running time: **65 MIN.**

A strong docu on the Sikh fundamentalist problem in the Indian state of Punjab, "In Memory Of Friends" is natural fest material and a strong candidate for specialist webs.

Pic's springboard is the legacy of young socialist Bhagat Singh, hanged at age 23 by the Brits in 1931. Born a Sikh but later an atheist, Singh preached Hindu-Sikh unity but his message has since been twisted.

The state government hails him as a patriot but forgets his socialism. Sikh separatists claim him as an early militant. The leftists see him as a man of the people. Pic takes a hard look at this exploitation of a legend, with a prolog sketching the historical background and plenty of face-to-face material with politicos.

By default, government side (blamed by many for Sikh militancy) gets off the hook lightly; director Anand Patwardhan didn't get access to the big boys. Sikh militants come over as hooked on an endless cycle of retaliation. Patwardhan's sympathies (well-disguised) seem more with the leftists.

Already known on the fest circuit for his '85 docu "Bombay — Our City," helmer plans a companion pic on Hindu fundamentalism. About 100 videcassettes of "In Memory Of Friends" circulate in Punjab, but pic hasn't been shown theatrically.

Technically, 16m pic is okay, with astute subtitling. Lensed from 1987 to 1989, pic cost around $110,000. — *Drek.*

LE TRÉSOR DES ILES CHIENNES
(LAND OF THE DEAD)
(FRENCH-PORTUGUESE)

> A Gemini Films-Trois Lumières Prods.-La Sept (France)-Filmargem (Portugal) production. Produced by Paulo Branco, Oskar Leventon. Written and directed by F.J. Ossang. Camera (black & white, Cinemascope), Darius Khondji; editor, Natalie Perrey; music, Messageros Killers Boys; sound (Dolby), Gita Cerveira; art director, Jean-Vincent Puzos; costume design, Robert Nardonne; assistant director, Philippe Heumann. Reviewed at 34th London Film Festival (Panorama: France), Nov. 16, 1990. Running time: **105 MIN.**
> With: Stéphane Ferrara, Diogo Doria, José Wallenstein, Mapi Galan.

Despite striking scope lensing in high-contrast black & white, this post-punk apocalyptic low-budgeter is strictly late-night fest material. Gobbledygook script puts "Land Of The Dead's" commercial chances six feet under.

Plot and look recall Luc Besson's "The Last Combat," but this one's closer to the edge. A group of druggies, murderers, plus a mute femme returns from an obscure mission to the devastated Bitch Islands. When the group isn't mainlining, screaming at each other or throwing up, island's mad genius is given to heartfelt soliloquies. Everyone ends up dead. Pic ends.

Helmer F.J. Ossang, 34, a rock musician and poet, keeps things moving with iris effects and deafening music. Portuguese and Azores locations are suitably nightmarish thanks to Darius Khondji's skillful camerawork. — *Drek.*

ARCHIVE

PEPI, LUCI, BOM Y OTRAS CHICAS DEL MONTON
(PEPI, LUCI, BOM AND THE OTHER GIRLS)
(SPANISH)

> A Pepon Corominas-Figaro Films production (1980). Written and directed by Pedro Almodóvar. Camera (color), Paco Femenia. Reviewed at the Vancouver Intl. Film Festival, Oct. 11, 1990. Running time: **80 MIN.**
> With: Carmen Maura, Eva Siva, Alaska, Felix Rotaeta, Concha.

In his first feature, Pedro Almodóvar delivers what has come to be expected of him: masochism and macho men in sexploitation parodies. This raw formative film, by far his most blatant pic, contains material that could handicap distribs in many territories. Still, it's a collector's item.

The roots of Almodóvar's down-and-dirty, intentionally amoral and often disgusting films are abundant in "Pepi, Luci, Bom And Other Girls."

While not as slick or sophisticated as "Tie Me Up, Tie Me Down!", it nonetheless addresses some of Almodóvar's favorite topics, including consenting rape and sadism.

In "Pepi," Almodóvar also challenges conventional definitions of perversion (in one scene, Bom urinates on Luci's face as Pepi watches) and heterosexuality.

Luci, who enjoys being beaten by her psychocop husband, temporarily leaves him for a lesbian relationship with Bom, a funky punk rock singer. They hook up with sex kitten Pepi after she's raped by Luci's husband. The three share wild adventures.

In a nightclub scene, some men agree to a genital competition. Luci, the chosen one, performs for the crowd.

Other unique Almodóvarisms include advertisements for Pick Knickers (innovative underwear), a campaign for menstruating dolls and "the tallest transvestite in Europe."

But never fear, "everything in cinema is fake," per this script. The line is spoken by Pepi when the girls are planning to make their own little film (a nice cinematic subplot later addressed in "Tie Me Up!" via that film director's obsessions).

The framing leaves much to the viewer's imagination, and the soundtrack is explicit. All tech credits are amateur by current standards, a flaw which will likely be overlooked by archivists, cinephiles and hardcore Almodóvar fans, the only ones likely to ever see the pic. — *Suze.*

LA VIRGEN DE LA CARIDAD
(THE VIRGIN OF CHARITY)
(CUBAN-B&W)

> A BPP Pictures release (1930). Executive producers, Francisco (Baby) Dell Barrio, Max Tos Quella. Directed by Ramon Peon. Screenplay, Enrique Agüero Hidalgo; camera (black & white), Ricardo Delgado; art direction, Ernesto Caparrós. Reviewed at the Festival Latino, N.Y., Aug. 22, 1990. Running time (at 24 frames per second): **71 MIN.**
> With: Diana V. Marde, Miguel Santos, Roberto Navarro, Estelita Echazabal, Mario Nasseur, Juan Antonio Lopez, Sergio Muro, Julio-Galle, Ramon Peon.

A 1930 Cuban silent that received a belated Yank premiere at the Public Theater's 1990 Festival Latino, the creaky melodrama of "The Virgin Of Charity" manages to pass muster on sheer conviction.

The simple story is not without its ideological ramifications. Small landowner Yeyo (Miguel Santos) is in love with Trina (Diana V. Marde), the daughter of a wealthy rancher. The father regards Yeyo as too insignificant to be his daughter's groom.

The more formidable obstacle is a returning expatriate. Now awash in wealth, he enters into a cabal to dispossess Yeyo of his land and lover. In the absence of any documentary proof, he casts doubt on whether Yeyo's father (seen in flashbacks dying in Cuba's War of Independence) ever really purchased his land. In the process the interloper wins the consent of Trina's father to marry his daughter.

If the plotline fits in with Cuba's current national politics, the climax clearly does not. In desperation over his plight Yeyo seeks divine help. He kneels before a picture of the Virgin Mary, and a workman's accident on the other side of the wall causes the painting to fall apart, revealing the deed hidden for years.

Armed with this evidence, Yeyo rushes to thwart the civil ceremony and win Trina for himself, presumably, with a church wedding.

Director Ramon Peon infused this dated (even then) material with the naturalism of the Cuban countryside and a straight-faced approach that is never condescending.

Acting and tech credits are competent. —*Lomb.*

THE LOVE TEST
(BRITISH-B&W)

A Fox British production (1935). Produced by Leslie L. Landau. Directed by Michael Powell. Screenplay, Selwyn Jepson, from a story by Jack Celestin; camera (black & white), Arthur Crabtree. Reviewed at 34th London Film Festival (New National Film Archive Restorations), Nov. 14, 1990. Running time: **63 MIN.**

Mary	Judy Gunn
John	Louis Hayward
Thompson	Dave Hutcheson
Minnie	Googie Withers
Company president	Morris Harvey
Vice-president	Aubrey Dexter
Kathleen	Eve Turner
Allan	Bernard Miles
Managing director	Jack Knight
H. Smith	Gilbert Davies

"The Love Test" is a solid British programmer from the 1930s that would hardly rate a mention if the director's name wasn't Michael Powell. (It didn't even rate that in helmer's autobiog.) It's a light, bright romantic comedy set in a research lab.

Pic was one of a string of "quota-quickies," generally financed with U.S. coin at the rate of £1 a foot, to fulfill British quota restrictions on the lower half of double bills so Yank distribs could unload major features. Original bow was in July 1935.

Plot is strictly back-of-a-napkin fluff. A group of lab technicians, working on a formula for fireproofing celluloid, hatch a plot to deflect a straitlaced femme colleague's ambitions by making her fall in love. That way, they reckon, they won't have a woman as head of the department.

Apart from a long opening tracking shot through the lab, there's little here for Powell buffs to get excited about. But it's ably put together, lensed in glistening style by future director Arthur Crabtree, and vigorously played by an ensemble cast.

Judy Gunn is good as the bluestocking who swaps sweaters for cocktail gowns; ditto a pre-Hollywood Louis Hayward as her initially unwilling beau.

Notable supports are Googie Withers as a gum-chewing secretary-vamp who crank-starts Hayward's engine; Dave Hutcheson as the office smart-ass who dreams up the idea, and Morris Harvey as the company's joke prez.

Restored print by U.K.'s National Film Archive is topnotch in all respects.

Pic, previously thought lost, re-preemed at London fest with another NFA-restored Powell quota-quickie, "The Night Of The Party" (reviewed in VARIETY Feb. 13, 1934.) — *Drek.*

HAVANA

A Universal release of a Mirage production. Produced by Sydney Pollack. Executive producer, Ronald L. Schwary. Directed by Pollack. Screenplay, Judith Rascoe, David Rayfiel, based on a story by Rascoe; camera (Deluxe color), Owen Roizman; editor, Fredric Steinkamp, William Steinkamp; music, Dave Grusin; sound (Dolby), Peter Handford; production design, Terence Marsh; art direction, George Richardson; set decoration, Michael Seirton; costume design, Bernie Pollack; assistant director, David Tomblin; 2nd unit camera, Richard Bowen; casting, Lynn Stalmaster. Reviewed at Worldwide Cinemas 1, N.Y., Dec. 6, 1990. MPAA Rating: R. Running time: **145 MIN.**

Jack Weil	Robert Redford
Bobby Duran	Lena Olin
Joe Volpi	Alan Arkin
Menocal	Tomas Milian
Arturo Duran	Raul Julia
Marion Chigwell	Daniel Davis
Julio Ramos	Tony Plana
Diane	Betsy Brantley
Patty	Lise Cutter
Professor	Richard Farnsworth
Meyer Lansky	Mark Rydell
Willy	Vasek Simek
Baby Hernandez	Fred Asparagus
Mike MacClaney	Richard Portnow
Roy Forbes	Dion Anderson
Captain Potts	Carmine Caridi
Corporal	James Medina

Much as the filmmakers would like to get there, "Havana" remains a long way from "Casablanca." In their seventh outing over a 25-year period, director Sydney Pollack and star Robert Redford have lost their normally dependable quality touch as they slog through a notably uncompelling tale of a gringo caught up in the Cuban revolution.

Redford's return after a four-year acting hiatus and a heavy sell for this $45 million-plus production will guarantee some initial b.o., but this clunky vehicle will run out of gas as quickly as the 1950s Cadillac Redford drives in it.

Behind the camera for the first time since winning multiple Oscars for "Out Of Africa" five years ago, Pollack returns to his favorite format, that of a bittersweet romance set in a colorful historical-political context. But as the budget has ballooned, his storytelling snap and knack for fostering star chemistry has faltered, resulting in a leaden concoction that never convinces or excites.

In a 12-minute precredit shipboard prolog, Redford's rogue gambler character, Jack Weil, strikes a few sparks with Lena Olin's mysterious Bobby Duran and agrees to smuggle into Havana a radio that will help Castro spread his word in the capital in the waning days of 1958.

Although the city is astir with rumors concerning the rebel leader's activities in the mountains, it's still business as usual under the Batista dictatorship, with Havana reigning as the primo fleshpot and gambling center of the Western world.

As was Bogart in some of his most famous 1940s roles, Redford here is a seemingly rootless, amoral loner with no declared sympathies, a middle-aged operator out for one big score at the high-stakes poker table before clearing out. However, his eye for Olin leads him into dangerous political territory involving her wealthy left-wing husband Arturo (played suavely by an uncredited Raul Julia), a CIA spook posing as a food critic and various military toughs.

Action meanders between two fronts. Professionally, Redford chases financial backing for his bigtime poker game from mob boss Meyer Lansky through world-weary casino operator Alan Arkin. Personally, he becomes increasingly absorbed in Olin's problems after her husband is apparently murdered and she is tortured for her affiliations.

Unfortunately, the tentative romance between the two is never really credible. As usual, Redford is cool, reserved and a bit bemused, while the striking Olin, so outstanding in "The Unbearable Lightness Of Being" and "Enemies, A Love Story," is mercurial and intense. The combination doesn't take, and any anticipated heat is negated by the pair's lackluster, abbreviated sex scenes.

With the film already well over two hours long, even the inevitable climax on New Year's Eve, 1958-1959, when Batista fled and Castro triumphed, fails to quicken the pulse or stir the imagination. Once again, the forces of history serve to pull two lovers apart, but the fates of a Yankee gambler and dilettantish revolutionary seem of marginal interest in this convulsive context.

Judith Rascoe's original script was written in the mid-1970s. As rewritten by David Rayfiel, yarn is a mishmash of old-hat Hollywood conventions, political pussyfooting and loads of bad dialog. Character motivation remains a notably weak point, as it is hard to swallow Redford's quick conversion to altruism.

Even in the absence of a topnotch story, one would have expected, given the budget and collaborators' previous credits, a picture swimming in overripe, sexy atmosphere. To the contrary, production has a rather dry, claustrophobic feel.

Much of the running time is spent with two characters in small, dark rooms, and even the vast re-creation of central Havana (built in the Dominican Republic) has a backlot feel. Pic looks rich and thoroughly professional all the way down the line, but all hands have done more impressive work in the past. Verisimilitude is given a nice boost by some presumably "stolen" second unit shots of the real Havana, which remains off limits to American companies.

Despite his seedier-than-usual character, Redford still looks as healthy and clean as ever, with costuming that recalls "Gatsby" or "The Sting." He looks a bit older now, and opinion will probably be divided between those struck by his rugged, weatherbeaten appeal, and those who note the encroachment of time. His easygoing charm remains, but script here gives him virtually no background and little subtext to play with.

Olin acts on a smoldering, feverish plane that would no doubt be effective in many other situations, but exists in a different world from that of the other actors here. Such pros as Arkin, Julia and Tomas Milian bring effortless authority to one-note roles, while Richard Farnsworth, as an old gambler, and director Mark Rydell, as a furious Meyer Lansky, have but one scene apiece.

Dave Grusin's nice score, which does what it can to prop up a love story that just doesn't click, is fleshed out by a couple of dozen vintage tunes. — *Cart.*

ALICE

An Orion Pictures release of a Jack Rollins and Charles H. Joffe production. Produced by Robert Greenhut. Executive producers, Jack Rollins, Charles H. Joffe. Written and directed by Woody Allen. Camera (Duart color, Deluxe prints), Carlo Di Palma; editor, Susan E. Morse; sound, James Sabat; production design, Santo Loquasto; art direction, Speed Hopkins; set decoration, Susan Bode; costumes, Jeffrey Kurland; associate producers, Thomas Reilly, Jane Read Martin; assistant directors, Reilly, Richard Patrick; casting, Juliet Taylor. Reviewed at the Orion Screening Room, Century City, Nov. 28, 1990. MPAA Rating: PG-13. Running time: **106 MIN.**

Alice	Mia Farrow
Joe	Joe Mantegna
Ed	Alec Baldwin
Dorothy	Blythe Danner
Vicki	Judy Davis
Doug	William Hurt
Dr. Yang	Keye Luke
Muse	Bernadette Peters
Nancy Brill	Cybill Shepherd
Alice's mother	Gwen Verdon

Also with: Julie Kavner, Holland Taylor, Robin Bartlett, Patrick O'Neal, Caroline Aaron, James Toback, David Spielberg, Bob Balaban, Elle Macpherson.

Woody Allen once again combines serious themes with comic observations in "Alice," a likable little pic that will please his fans but probably won't win him any new converts. While film has many virtues, it faces an uphill struggle at the boxoffice amid the avalanche of holiday offerings.

If "Stardust Memories" was Allen's "8½" and "Radio Days" his "Amarcord," then "Alice" is his "Juliet Of The Spirits." It's a subtler, gentler retelling of Federico Fellini's tale of a pampered but unappreciated housewife who learns to shed her illusions by giving in to her fantasies.

In quick, hilarious strokes, Allen introduces Alice (Mia Farrow), who's been married 16 years to ultrasuccessful businessman William Hurt.

Though her deepest daily concerns are gossip, decorators, fitness trainers, Bergdorf Goodman and pedicures, she feels a kinship with Mother Theresa and, like many of Allen's past characters, is sure she has untapped talent — she's just not sure for what.

But sudden fantasies about a divorced father (Joe Mantegna) at her kids' school and a trip to an unorthodox herbalist-acupuncturist (Keye Luke) set off a chain of sexual, mystical, frequently comic events. Telling more would spoil the fun because of the unexpected and improbable form in which Alice's adventures take shape.

"Alice" offers variations on the usual Allen topics: passion vs. restraint, infidelity, self-doubt, the yearning underneath the chic Manhattan lifestyle and religious questioning. Alice is a lapsed Catholic, and filmmaker bypasses Jewish jokes to make some pointed Catholic gags.

Pic's conclusion that happiness comes from shedding externals and getting in touch with one's true self may seem disappointingly simplistic to some, but others will find the sweetness and warmth a big relief after the bleakness of "Crimes And Misdemeanors."

Performances are strong all around, with a succession of top actors making the most of their brief turns.

Standouts in smaller roles include Alec Baldwin as Farrow's first love, who turns up in a surprising way; Bernadette Peters, who does some of her best film work in about two minutes on screen; Luke as the gruff-voiced, chain-smoking healer, and Gwen Verdon and Blythe Danner as Farrow's mom and sister, respectively.

Mantegna is offbeat and appealing as the love interest, displaying a welcome vulnerability. But the center of the pic is Farrow, who's funny and touching as she conveys the dichotomy between the polite product of Catholic schooling and the growing awareness of the mature woman inside.

Farrow has a rare gift for making acting look easy. She's become such an inevitability in Allen's pics that it's easy to overlook her contributions to his work. In nearly every frame of "Alice," she's subtly spectacular.

Carlo Di Palma's cinematography, in burnished, autumnal colors, is gorgeous, as is Santo Loquasto's production design. Soundtrack, as usual, features an oddball assortment of tunes — including "Limehouse Blues," "La Cumparsita" and "I Remember You" — that are just right. All other tech credits are great.
— *Gray.*

EDWARD SCISSORHANDS

A 20th Century Fox release. Produced by Denise De Novi, Tim Burton. Executive producer, Richard Hashimoto. Directed by Burton. Screenplay, Caroline Thompson, from a story by Burton, Thompson; camera (color), Stefan Czapsky; editor, Richard Halsey; music, Danny Elfman; sound (Dolby), Peter Hliddal; production designer, Bo Welsh; art direction, Tom Duffield; set design, Rick Heinrichs, Paul Sonkski, Ann Harris; set decoration, Cheryl Carasik; costume design, Colleen Atwood; special makeup-effects, Stan Winston; associate producer, Thompson; assistant director, Jerry Fleck; casting, Victoria Thomas. Reviewed at Avco Cinema Center, L.A., Nov. 29, 1990. MPAA Rating: PG-13. Running time: **98 MIN.**

Edward Scissorhands	Johnny Depp
Kim	Winona Ryder
Peg	Dianne Wiest
Jim	Anthony Michael Hall
Bill	Alan Arkin
Joyce	Kathy Baker
Kevin	Robert Oliver
Helen	Conchata Ferrell
The inventor	Vincent Price

Director Tim Burton's audacity and originality continue to impress in this post-"Batman" effort in which he takes a character as wildly unlikely as a boy whose arms end in pruning shears, and makes him the center of a delightful and delicate comic fable.

"Edward Scissorhands" will clip out a sizable b.o. reward if Fox marketers can convince the public this pic isn't too strange.

Half the fun is seeing how long Burton and screenwriter Caroline Thompson can sustain their outrageous concept, and the answer is, almost long enough.

Conventional melodrama in pic's last reels shows less imagination than the premise, causing pic to sag a bit, but a final fairy tale flourish more or less restores pic's charm.

Fablelike tale follows the scattered tradition of the lonely and "deformed" outsider who is brought into a community where his differences will be either appreciated or rejected.

Johnny Depp plays Edward, who lives in isolation in a gloomy mansion on the hill until a sunny Avon lady (Dianne Wiest) discovers him and takes him into her suburbia home and mothers him like a crippled bird.

The creation of an inventor (Vincent Price) who died and left him unfinished, Edward sports an astonishing pair of hands — five-fingered, footlong blades that render him either lethal, with every gesture a dangerous slash or stab, or extraordinarily skillful, as he proves when he goes to work on the shrubbery.

For the bevy of bored housewives in the pastel-colored nabe, gentle and exotic Edward becomes an instant celeb who amuses them by artistically pruning their hedges, their dogs and their coiffures. With his pale, scarred face, wild raven hair and smudge of purple lipstick, the weirdest sex symbol yet snips away at his creations with mad concentration and grace while the middle-aged femmes compete for his attention.

But when he's wrongly accused in a burglary, his star falls and they turn on him, eventually driving him out of the community.

Meanwhile his wistful and impossible attraction to Kim (Winona Ryder), the Avon lady's teenage daughter, adds another level of tension.

What makes "Edward Scissorhands" remarkable is Burton's brilliance as a visual storyteller. Every element in this seamlessly produced work gels to create an entrancing, slyly comic vision.

Production design, costumes and performances combine to paint a deliciously funny ultrasuburbia stuck stylistically in the early '60s, where women subsist on voracious gossip and men return from work en masse, sweeping nightly into the culs-de-sac in a parade of headlights.

Problem is, once this magically funny world is established, story hasn't much of anywhere to go. Edward doesn't have to save the world or even the neighborhood. He has only to maintain his delicate perch in the community, increasingly hard because of his growing attraction to Kim (Ryder), who's closely guarded by her thuggish boyfriend (Anthony Michael Hall).

Commenting on both celebrity and tolerance, Burton has the same people who embraced Edward's differences as fashionable eventually turn on him. But mostly Burton's out to create a fairy tale (as pic's storybook beginning and ending attest), but it's a tale with edges.

Depp, former tv teen idol in his second starring screen role (after "Cry-Baby"), gives a sensitive reading of Edward as a sad, funny clown with a Chaplinesque shuffle. Acting under whiteface and with elaborate footlong blades rigged to his arms, he's left to express himself with his eyes and bizarre movements, and does a deft and affecting job.

With Ryder kept mostly in the background, Wiest's mother figure shares the screen with Depp, and she's a smash. Her outpouring of cheery tenderness is absolutely the right balance for Edward's ghoulish uniqueness.

Also a hoot is Alan Arkin as her unexcitable husband, who consistently underreacts to Edward's bizarreness, and Kathy Baker as a sex-starved vixen.

Edward's twitching, insectlike pincers are an inspired effort by designer Stan Winston. Pic's extraordinary design scheme, for which 44 houses in a Florida suburb were repainted in pastels, is likely to be vying with "Dick Tracy" for honors at Oscar time. — *Daws.*

THE ROOKIE

A Warner Bros. release of a Malpaso production. Produced by Howard Kazanjian, Steven Siebert, David Valdes. Directed by Clint Eastwood. Screenplay, Boaz Yakin, Scott Spiegel. Camera (Technicolor), Jack N. Green; editor, Joel Cox; music, Lennie Niehaus; sound (Dolby), Alan Robert Murray, Robert G. Henderson; production design, Judy Cammer; art direction, Ed Verreaux; set decoration, Dan May; special effects supervisor, John Frazier; assistant directors, Matt Earl Beesley, Frank Capra III, Jeffrey Wetzel; casting, Phyllis Huffman. Reviewed at the Warner Bros. Studios Screening Room, Burbank, Calif., Dec. 3, 1990. MPAA Rating: R. Running time: **121 MIN.**
Nick Pulovski . . . . . Clint Eastwood
David Ackerman . . . . Charlie Sheen
Strom . . . . Raul Julia
Liesl . . . . Sonia Braga
Eugene Ackerman . . . . Tom Skerritt
Sarah . . . . Lara Flynn Boyle
Lt. Ray Garcia . . . . . . Pepe Serna
Loco . . . . Marco Rodriguez
Cruz . . . . Pete Randall

Overlong, sadistic and stale even by the conventions of the buddy pic genre, Clint Eastwood's "The Rookie" may fill the cupboard with some early b.o. coin but won't survive long in the big leagues. Toe-tag this as one of the season's major holiday turkeys.

Eastwood has always repaid Warner Bros. for underwriting his artistic aspirations with breadwinning action fare but never with anything as relentlessly dimwitted as this. And normally, the actor-director brings a twist to his non-"Dirty Harry" action pics, either in a comedic vein ("Bronco Billy") or with a troubled character ("Tightrope") who breaks the standard Eastwood mold.

Not so here. Eastwood seems to be doing a bad impersonation of his own tough-guy image, which would be forgivable if costar Charlie Sheen wasn't doing his own poor parody of it as well.

"The Rookie" is actually "Dirty Harry 5½" since Eastwood's tough-as-nails cop Nick Pulovski could just as easily be named Harry Callahan, and his penchant for breaking in partners (and getting them killed) is a holdover from "Harry's" first three patrols.

This time, however, the troubles lie in partner Sheen, a rich kid working out childhood guilt and hostility against his parents by playing policeman.

Pair pursues a stolen-car ring operated by ruthless thief Raul Julia and sweaty henchwoman Sonia Braga (in a nearly nonverbal role). Pulovski is taken hos-

tage, and Sheen's character has to find himself by, essentially, disregarding all conventional legal channels and destroying as much property as possible.

The formula would be easier to bear if it were handled with any flair or subtlety, but Eastwood's direction of Boaz Yakin and Scott Spiegel's flat script proves utterly devoid of both. With little chemistry between the stars, pic turns into a flabby two-hour rollercoaster ride.

After a spark-flying opening night chase on the Hollywood Freeway, film offers only one memorable action shot (a car crashing out of an exploding building) that's been completely overexposed in the film's ad campaign.

The normally brilliant Julia lapses into and out of a bad German accent like something out of "Hogan's Heroes," Braga has just a window-dressing bad-girl role, and "Twin Peaks' " Lara Flynn Boyle is Sheen's blandly drawn girlfriend.

Eastwood the actor seems rightfully bored with the material, while Sheen continues to hammer away at his own tough-guy rep with only marginal success. He was more convincing in "Navy Seals."

Most surprising in light of Eastwood's normally superb craftsmanship is the shoddy technical quality; choppy editing, murky camerawork and dull music droning the same three notes over and over.

The scene in which Braga seduces the trussed-up Eastwood is so incongruous with the pic's general tone that one wonders if the wrong reel got slipped in by accident.

The only other kink in this straight-arrow storyline stems from the heroes' utter contempt for legal parameters. When good guys murder (the word isn't used lightly) bad guys so brazenly, it's as if the leads' marquee value establishes their goodness and that no moral differentiation need be made.

A key point in the story derives from the disparaging power of the word "amateur." For "The Rookie," ironically, it's about the only term that fits. — *Bril.*

LIVING TO DIE

A PM Entertainment release of a Richard Pepin/Joseph Merhi production. Produced by Pepin, Merhi. Directed by Wings Hauser. Screenplay, Stephen Smoke; camera (Foto-Kem color), Pepin; editor, Geraint Bell; additional editor,

Paul Volk; music, John Gonzalez, Lon Price; sound, Mike Hall; art direction, MaryBeth Horiari; production manager, John Ross; assistant director-associate producer, Charla Driver. Reviewed on PM vidcassette, N.Y., Dec. 3, 1990. MPAA Rating: R. Running time: **84 MIN.**
Nick Carpenter . . . . . Wings Hauser
Maggie . . . . Darcy DeMoss
Eddie . . . . Asher Brauner
Jimmy . . . . Arnold Vosloo
Lt. Howard . . . . R.J. Walker
Jasmine . . . . Minnie Madden
Also with: Wendy MacDonald, Rebecca Barrington, John Ross, Janice Carter, Raymond Martino, Carol Hooper, Cheryl Nishi, Denise Lash.

"Living To Die" is a mishmash of an action film, notable mainly for its unusual ending. Currently in regional theatrical release it is due to hit vidstores in February.

The second feature as director for thesp Wings Hauser (after 1989 production "Coldfire"), pic plays like a debut in its incoherent mix of conflicting elements.

Slow start is an irrelevant precredits sequence of Hauser as a police detective showing rookie cop Wendy MacDonald the ropes. Without adequate explanation, he's no longer a cop but a private eye type in film proper.

Old pal Asher Brauner hires Hauser to clean up a sticky business for him: femme fatale hooker Darcy DeMoss dies of a drug overdose in Brauner's presence and her b.f. Arnold Vosloo is blackmailing him.

Tortured plot twist has DeMoss turning up alive and soon taking up with Hauser who tries to play both ends against the middle. Romantic interludes and night club scenes fail to advance the plot.

Surprise ending turns the picture into film noir but is hard to swallow.

DeMoss, a familiar face from action and horror pics, is impressive here either in or out of costume, and Hauser remains comfortable with tough guy roles. Brauner is effective in a change-of-pace, purely villainous assignment. South African thesp Arnold Vosloo, his accent aside, is a good choice as the slimy blackmailer whose main job is taking dirty photographs.

Technical credits including on-location filming in Las Vegas mark a step up for the PM Entertainment outfit. — *Lor.*

STEP ACROSS THE BORDER
(GERMAN-SWISS-DOCU-B&W)

A Cine Nomades Filmproduction-Res Balzli & Cie production. Written and directed by Nicolas Humbert and Werner Penzel. Camera (black & white), Oscar Saigodo; editor, Gisela Castronari; music, Fred Frith, Joey Baron, Ciro Batista, Iva Bitova; sound, Jean Vapeur. Reviewed at Toronto Festival of Festivals, Sept. 11, 1990. Running time: **90 MIN.**
With: Robert Frank, Jolia Judge, Jonas Mekas, Ted Milton.

"Step Across The Border," an unconventional, energetic and intense documentary about British blues composer and performer Fred Frith, can be assured of a wild reception by avant-garde music fans, but it's a bit inaccessible for mainstream audiences.

In grainy, nervous black & white, filmmakers Nicolas Humbert and Werner Penzel provide Frith a platform to free-float about his musical style and intention (without much biographical data).

Then the two Munich film school grads and former collaborators transpose musician's broad range of fresh sounds to jumpy visual images of cityscapes, street people and randomly found musical instruments.

Pic takes place in European, U.S. and Japanese cities, where Frith and his band members improvise, rehearse, give formal concerts and chat about their spontaneous jamming.

The band experiments with standard guitars, saxophones and drums, and then concocts inventive percussion and string instruments. For example, they use bowls of dried beans and nori perched on a quasi-guitar to come up with innovative sounds.

Sitting in a smoke-filled sukiyaki house in Japan, the classically trained musician reveals his amazement at hearing blues for the first time.

"It was like hearing the guitar being a human voice," he recalls, and has never looked back. He knows his bracing musical sound is not commercial, but is pleased if one person comes away perplexed or in some kind of changed state.

The weird sounds and non sequitur images hanging on the screen can either irritate or excite.

Film is sprinkled with other "Dada" bits: Jonas Mekas explains that a butterfly's flapping wings affects everything else in the world, five band members disjointedly tell the Zen story of the sound of one hand clapping, Robert Frank rides a train, and a violinist plays bird songs on a promontory fully of swooping seagulls.

Frith and the band members are not identified by name, and there's no traditional narration. But "Step Across The Border" has a big payoff in experiencing the original edge of its music in film. — *Devo.*

REISE DER HOFFNUNG
(JOURNEY OF HOPE)
(SWISS)

A Columbus Film Zurich release of a Catpics AG (Alfi Sinniger) and Condor Features (Peter-Christian Fueter) production in association with Enzo Porcelli, Antea (Rome), Bernd Hellthaler, Dewe Hellthaler Intl. (Stuttgart), Peter Hürlimann, Cinerent, Zollikon (Zurich), SRG/RTSI, Zurich/Lugano, and Film Four Intl. (London). (Intl. sales: Catpics, Condor Features.) Produced by Mandred Eicher. Directed by Xavier Koller. Screenplay, Koller, Feride Çiçekoglu; camera (color), Elemer Ragalyi; editor, Galip Iyitanir; music, Jan Garbarek, Terje Rypdal, Arild Andersen; sound, Pavol Jasovsky, Remo Belli; production manager, Peter Spörri (Switzerland), Turgay Aksoy, Penta Film (Turkey), Stefano Alleva (Italy); art direction, Kathrin Brunner (Switzerland), Luigi Pelizzo (Italy); assistant director, Konstantin Schmidt, Martin Steiner, Nello Correale. Reviewed at Studio Nord-Süd, Zurich, Oct. 5, 1990. Running time: **110 MIN.**

Haydar	Necmettin Çobanoglu
Meryem	Nur Sürer
Mehmet Ali	Emin Sivas
Adana	Erdinç Akbas
Türkmen	Yaman Okay
Haci Baba	Yasar Güner
Selçuk	Hüseyin Mete
Ilyas	Yaman Tarcan

(Turkish and German soundtrack)

Acute problem of asylum seekers from third world countries is a hot topic in Switzerland, and "Journey Of Hope" is a compassionate plea for humanity and tolerance, bound to stir up emotions. Director Xavier Koller wisely avoids one-sided polemics, but never leaves any doubt on which side he stands.

Koller, who directed the successful Swiss pics "Das gefrorene Herz" (The Frozen Heart) and "Der schwarze Tanner" (Black Tanner), was inspired to write "Reise der Hoffnung" by a tragic event in the Swiss Alps two years ago: A seven-year-old Turkish boy froze to death during the family's attempt to cross the border illegally.

Resulting fact-based fiction pic was filmed on location in Turkey, Italy and Switzerland. A couple from southeast Turkey decides to emigrate to the "land of milk and honey," Switzerland, with the brightest of their seven children.

Having sold all their belongings, they embark on a freighter to Naples as stowaways. A Swiss truck driver takes them to the Swiss border, but they are refused and sent back to Milan.

Professional immigrant smugglers send them, and several others, over the mountains into Switzerland, despite disastrous weather. After a harrowing crossing the group finally arrives, but the peasant boy has died in his father's arms from cold and exhaustion.

Turkish actors Necmettin Çobanoglu as the father, Nur Sürer as his wife and Emin Sivas as the doomed child are perfectly cast, making it hard to believe they are professional actors.

Among the few Swiss in the cast, Mathias Gnädinger stands out in the relatively small part of the friendly truck driver.

Technical credits are all firstrate, from Elemer Ragalyi's sensitive atmospheric lensing to Pavol Jasovsky and Remo Belli's realistic sound.

Using music from existing soundtracks of ECM Munich (Manfred Eicher) musicians Jan Garbarek, Terje Rypdal, Arlid Andersen and Egberto Gismonti was a good idea. Pic was awarded a bronze leopard at this year's Locarno Film Festival. — *Mezo.*

LONDON FEST

DEATH IN BRUNSWICK
(AUSTRALIAN)

A Roadshow (Australia) release of a Meridian Films production, in association with Film Victoria and Australian Film Finance Corp. Executive producer, Bryce Menzies. Produced by Timothy White. Directed by John Ruane. Screenplay, Ruane, Boyd Oxlade, based on Oxlade's novel; camera (Eastmancolor), Ellery Ryan; editor, Neil Thumpston; music, Philip Judd; sound, Lloyd Carrick; production design, Chris Kennedy; assistant director, John Wild; associate producer, Lynda House; casting, Greg Apps. Reviewed at Village Roadshow screening room, Sydney, Nov. 19, 1990. (In London Film Festival.) Running time: **109 MIN.**

Carl Fitzgerald	Sam Neill
Sophie Papafagos	Zoe Carides
Dave	John Clarke
Mrs. Fitzgerald	Yvonne Lawley
June	Deborah Kennedy
Mustafa	Nico Lathouris
Laurie	Boris Brkic
Yanni	Nicholas Papademetriou
Carmel	Doris Younane

Structured around a winning performance from Sam Neill, "Death In Brunswick" is an unusual, intelligent black comedy. Some will find the film outrageous, but word-of-mouth should give the pic legs on the international arthouse circuit, as well as prestige success on home turf.

In Brunswick, Melbourne inner suburb with a large Greek community, Carl Fitzgerald (Neill), about 40, apparently hails from a well-to-do background but, with a failed marriage behind him, is living in a cheap house and can't even afford the rent.

He gets a job as cook in a roach-infested kitchen in a nightclub owned and operated by Greek entrepreneur Yannis. Carl's assistant is Mustafa, a drug-dealing Turk. Carl quickly (too quickly for the film's credibility) becomes involved with Sophie (Zoe Carides), a voluptuous teen waitress.

The day after they meet, Carl and Sophie bed down on the family couch while mum and dad are out. Carl's problems escalate when he accidentally kills Mustafa because the latter, drunk and recovering from a beating, attacked him.

He seeks help from old buddy Dave (John Clarke), who works in a cemetery, to hide the body. The hilarious but disgusting sequence in which Dave deposits Mustafa's corpse in the coffin of a long-dead Italian woman is likely to test audiences.

Much of the fun stems from Neill playing effectively against type. He's a wimpy character manipulated by just about everyone in his life. His mother (Kiwi actress Yvonne Lawley) nags him, Sophie seduces him, Dave orders him about and Dave's disapproving wife (Deborah Kennedy), humiliates him. Despite all these confrontations, Carl emerges as an interesting and amusing character.

World-preemed at the London film fest, "Death In Brunswick" is the feature debut of Melbourne director John Ruane, who scored with the medium-length "Feathers" a while back.

Although early scenes appear

to be unduly rushed, and pic veers alarmingly from one mood to another, Ruane provides offbeat and frequently funny fare, though he tends to stereotype some of the Greek characters.

Neill is excellent in a role he clearly revelled in, and he's ably backed by a strong supporting cast. John Clarke provides hilarious deadpan humor as Dave, and Carides is exactly right as the sexy teen who's old beyond her years.

Cinematographer Ellery Ryan gives this low-budgeter a handsome feel and is ably backed by Chris Kennedy's creative production design. Philip Judd provides a sprightly music score. — *Strat.*

DIE DEUTSCHEN UND IHRE MÄNNER
(THE GERMANS AND THEIR MEN)
(GERMAN-DOCU-16M)

A Helke Sander Filmproduktion-Bremer Institut Film-Fernsehen for ZDF production. Produced by Claudia Richarz, Sara Schilling. Written and directed by Helke Sander. Camera (color), Lilly Grote; editor, Claudia Vogeler, Sander, Wolfgang Heine; music, Mia Schmidt; sound, Volker Zeigerman, Kurt Eggmann, Csaba Kulcsar. Reviewed at 34th London Film Festival (World Panorama), Nov. 20, 1990. Running time: **103 MIN.**
Elisabeth Müller . . . . . Renée Felden

Change the copyright date on this to 1969 and it would have some archival interest. As it stands, this 1989 feminist docu looks as dinosaurlike as some of the menschen it tries to take to the floor. This is strictly a converts-only item.

Subtitled "Bericht aus Bonn" (Report From Bonn), it features actress Renée Felden as an Austrian journalist on a hubby-hunting expedition in the German capital. To make sure she doesn't land up with a porker, she decides to ask some key questions of the local manhood, armed with a copy of "Who's Who" and a fistful of statistics.

After quizzing travelers at the airport on why they wear ties, she gradually zeroes in on assorted solons, with key questions like, "Have you ever felt ashamed to be a man?" and "Do you feel responsible as a man for the high number of rapes?" The answers are as boring as the questions.

There's a funny little 10-minute film hiding in here somewhere, and a few well-aimed barbs at stonewalling politicos. Lensing looks more like a Super-8 blowup than 16m. London fest screening saw a high number of walkouts. — *Drek.*

HALLELUJAH ANYHOW
(BRITISH)

A BBC Television production. (Intl. sales: BBC Enterprises.) Executive producers, Mark Shivas, Colin McCabe. Produced by David Stacey. Directed by Matthew Jacobs. Screenplay, Jean (Binta) Breeze, Jacobs; camera (Rank color), Remi Adefarasin; editor, Sue Wyatt; music, Rev. Basil Meade; sound, Colin Marsh; production design, Rochelle Selwyn; costume design, Pat Godfrey. Reviewed at 34th London Film Festival, Nov. 15, 1990. Running time: **90 MIN.**
Adlyn . . . . Dona Croll
Will . . . . Keith David
Sonny . . . . George Harris
Ray . . . . Maynard Eziashi
Opal . . . . Clare Perkins
Paul . . . . Sylvester Williams
Cynthia . . . . Valerie Buchanan
Also with: Corinne Skinner-Carter, Ram John Holder, Joan Hooley, Ellen Thomas, Marsha Millar, T-Bone Wilson, Tony Hippolyte, Kamilla Blanche.

Though made by a white filmmaker, this collaboration for the BBC between black poet Jean (Binta) Breeze and first-time director Matthew Jacobs is an important step forward for Britain's black cinema. Accorded a centerpiece slot at London's film fest, "Hallelujah Anyhow" pleased a packed audience.

Still, it's doubtful whether this examination of evangelical religion and sexual politics in London's West Indian community has the legs for a theatrical as well as tv release, except on a small scale. Despite wholehearted performances, pic has rough edges and ponderous moments. Production values, however, are by no means negligible.

A strong-willed woman preacher, married to an ambitious pastor, has a guilty secret. Her son is the result of an earlier liaison. When a prosperous stranger from the U.S. appears at the funeral of an elder, it looks as if the game is up. He wants to see his son, but will they confront the past?

Dona Croll as Adlyn, the central character, and Keith David as the boy's real father merit high praise, and the contribution of members of an actual London church and the London Community Choir infuse this emotional struggle with authenticity.

The pressures on individuals, families and a community struggling to keep its identity, but still react to changing times, are also well-marked out.

The film, though, takes a bit of time to get going. The scene is set too long before the drama's real thrust appears. Breeze's screenplay doesn't succeed in giving its chief characters enough depth. Neither direction nor writing are fluent enough to be truly cinematic.

But a lot can be forgiven by audiences who are grateful British cinema is dealing with such aspects of contemporary British life with understanding. Black writers and actors get few chances to express themselves.

The British cinema has yet to learn that small budgets, whether financed by television or not, in the end frequently mean small films. Still, this is a praiseworthy and encouraging attempt to put the strength and vitality of the U.K.'s Afro-Caribbean community on the screen. Better films may follow. — *Malc.*

DREAMING
(BRITISH)

A BBC Scotland production. Produced by Andy Park. Directed by Mike Alexander. Screenplay, William McIlvanney, from a short story in his book "Walking Wounded"; camera (color, 16m), Stuart Wyld; editor, Dave Harvie; music, Deacon Blue; lyrics, McIlvanney; sound, Alan Cooper; production design, David McKenzie; costume design, Brenda Brown. Reviewed at 34th London Film Festival (British Cinema section), Nov. 19, 1990. Running time: **89 MIN.**
With: Ewen Bremner, Mary McCusker, Michael Carter, Shirley Henderson, Billy Connolly, Robert Carr.

A nice idea hamstrung by flat direction and iffy script, "Dreaming" can do just that about its chances beyond tv. Comedy about a day in the life of a gawky Walter McMitty is thin fare even as fest fodder.

BBC Scotland production, part of the pubcaster's '91 Screen Two series, is set in Kilmarnock. A beardless 17-year-old (Ewen Bremner) wanders around the Scottish town worrying about job projects and whether he'll make it that night with his g.f. (Shirley Henderson).

Witty dream sequences include a "Guys And Dolls" song-and-dance parody (lacking pizzazz) and a banjo number with Scottish comedian Billy Connolly (better). Youth's close encounter with the girl starts as a French movie with Scottish subtitles and segues to a black & white Keystone Kops bit (best).

But it's not enough. Mike Alexander's direction is routine and McIlvanney's script lacks bite and focus. Story's thin, and jibes at Thatcherite Britain are scattergun rather than integrated.

Bremner, so good in Thames TV's slick "Forget About Me," is okay within pic's limitations. Editing could be tighter and 16m lensing is so-so. Production came in for around £250,000 ($480,000). — *Drek.*

MORPHINE AND DOLLY MIXTURES
(BRITISH)

A BBC Television production. (Intl. sales: BBC Television.) Produced by Ruth Kenley Letts. Executive producer, Ruth Caleb. Directed by Karl Francis. Screenplay, Francis, from the book by Carol-Ann Courtney; camera (Kodacolor), Russ Walker; editor, Roy Sharman; music, John E.R. Hardy; sound, Jeffrey North; production design, Ray Price; costumes, Michael Taylor. Reviewed at 34th London Film Festival, Nov. 9, 1990. Running time: **92 MIN.**
With: Patrick Bergin, Sue Roderick, Joanna Griffiths, Sian Merrick.

"Morphine And Dolly Mixtures" is yet another small but worthwhile British pic which, despite its quality, does not warrant much theatrical exposure. Television sales will be a different matter.

Based on Carol-Ann Courtney's moving book about her own childhood, pic looks good cinematically and well recalls its time and place, a small Welsh town some 40 years ago.

Well-made and finely acted throughout, "Morphine And Dolly Mixtures" is an affecting tale of a 12-year-old girl who, upon her mother's death, is faced with looking after the family's younger brood as her father declines into alcoholism.

The girl both loves and fears her father, whose moods vary from affectionate to brutal. Her only real friend is her maternal grandmother whom dad eventually bans from the home.

Everything ultimately depends upon the two central performances. Patrick Bergin as the guilty father and young Joanna

Griffiths as daughter, give performances of great truth and honesty.

Welsh director Karl Francis' depicts childhood fears and the terrors of alcoholism with restrained power. Time is found for humor as well as drama in the telling of a story which never seems overly downbeat and depressing. — *Malc.*

SAN BUNGAN BATLEUNG
(FRONT PAGE)
(HONG KONG)

A Hui's Film production. Executive producer, Michael Hui. Directed by Philip Chan. Screenplay, Hui, Chan; camera (color), Lam Kwok-wah; editor, Ma Chung-yiu, Tsu San-kit; music, Chau Kai-sang; lyrics, Samuel Hui; sound, Chan Wai-hung; production design, David Chan; costume design, Gemma To; assistant director, Wong Fun-wa; associate producer, Chan Yat-ming. Reviewed at 34th London Film Festival (Hong Kong Focus), Nov. 14, 1990. Running time: **93 MIN.**

With: Michael Hui, Samuel Hui, Ricky Hui, Catherine Hung, Li Sze-kei, Mao Shun-kuen, Lau Siu-ming.

This latest outing by Hong Kong's Hui Bros. won't chalk up many headlines outside Asian circuits, despite socko local rentals of $HK26 million this autumn. Episodic comedy-satire on the colony's paparazzi needs less pratfalls and more bits for Western readers.

Pic's Chinese title refers to "The Private Eyes" (1976), one of several breakthrough comedies Michael Hui made for Golden Harvest. But Hong Kong movies have moved on since then, and even by local comparisons "Front Page" lacks originality. Appeal is in the reteaming of the famous brothers.

Though actor-director Philip Chan is at the helm this time, it's still a Michael Hui showcase all the way. He plays the ruthless editor of struggling blat "Truth Weekly" who decides to give the public what it wants to boost circulation — inventing a secret lover for a starlet (Catherine Hung) in the shape of his own reporter (Samuel Hui).

This entails a lot of dressing up, hiding between bushes, mistaken identity and the rest. It's all done neatly enough, and Hui is as good as ever as the Machiavellian boss. But the script lacks sharpness of distinguished recent Cantonese comedies like

Clifton Ko's "Chicken And Duck Talk," also a Hui-starrer.

Tech credits are adequate. — *Drek.*

SINNUI YAUMAN II YANGAN DOU
(A CHINESE GHOST STORY II)
(HONG KONG)

A Golden Princess presentation of a Film Workshop production. Executive producer, Tsui Hark. Directed by Ching Siu-tung. Screenplay, Lau Tai-mok, Lam Kei-to, Leung Yiu-ming, from a story by Tsui, Yuen Kai-chi; camera (color), Arthur Wong; editor, Mak Chi-seen; music, James Wong, Romeo Diaz; costume design, William Cheung; martial arts directors, Kwok Tsu, Wu Chi-long; special effects, Cinefex Workshop, Dave Watkins, Nick Allder. Reviewed at 34th London Film Festival (Hong Kong Focus), Nov. 20, 1990. Running time: **103 MIN.**

With: Leslie Cheung, Joey Wang, Michelle Li, Wu Ma, Jacky Cheung, Waise Lee, Lau Siu-ming, Liu Shun, Ku Feng.

There's no lack of stamina in this slambang followup to 1987's "A Chinese Ghost Story." Monsters, martial arts, giant centipedes and razzle-dazzle effects should ensure regular hauntings in the same mansions.

Opening reprises original's love story between poor scholar (Leslie Cheung) and beautiful ghost Sian. Then, after the caption "The story continues...," it's time to fasten seatbelts.

Complex yarn, again set in ancient China, is basically about the scholar escaping from prison and meeting a swordswoman (Joey Wang) who happens to look exactly like love-of-his-life Sian. With his buddy (Jacky Cheung), who's a human tunneling machine, and her sister (Michelle Li), who's also got eyes for Ying, a motley group sets off to do battle with a wicked high priest.

Gore and flying limbs are plentiful, but it's all cartoon stuff, handled with pace and glee. Standout segs include a stop-start battle with a lovesick monster, and the whirlwind finale with flying swords and centipede.

Former stunt director Ching Siu-tung, who helmed original (plus recent "A Terra-Cotta Warrior"), spends less time on romance and more on his forte.

Cheung and Wang topline again with ease, and technically it's fine all round, with inventive sfx by Cinefex Workshop. Pic was nine months in the works, for a reported $HK26 million.

Hong Kong outing alone scooped a hunky $HK21 million in the summer. — *Drek.*

THE GODFATHER PART III

A Paramount release from Zoetrope Studios. Produced and directed by Francis Ford Coppola. Executive producers, Fred Fuchs, Nicholas Gage. Screenplay, Mario Puzo, Coppola. Camera (Technicolor), Gordon Willis; editor, Barry Malkin, Lisa Fruchtman, Walter Murch; music, Carmine Coppola; additional music and themes, Nino Rota; sound (Dolby), Clive Winter; sound design, Richard Beggs; production design, Dean Tavoularis; supervising art director, Alex Tavoularis; set design (Italy), Maria Teresa Barbasso, Nazzareno Piana; supervising set decorator, Gary Fettis; set decorator (Italy), Franco Fumagalli; costume design, Milena Canonero; associate producer, Marina Gefter; coproducers, Fred Roos, Gray Frederickson, Charles Mulvehill; assistant directors, H. Gordon Boos, Gianni Arduini-Plaisant (Italy); casting, Janet Hirshenson, Jane Jenkins, Roger Mussenden. Reviewed at the Loews Astor Plaza, N.Y., Dec. 12, 1990. MPAA Rating: R. Running time: **161 MIN.**

Michael Corleone . . . . Al Pacino
Kay Adams . . . . Diane Keaton
Connie Corleone Rizzi . . . Talia Shire
Vincent Mancini . . . . . . Andy Garcia
Don Altobello . . . . Eli Wallach
Joey Zasa . . . . Joe Mantegna
B.J. Harrison . . . . . George Hamilton
Grace Hamilton . . . . . Bridget Fonda
Mary Corleone . . . . . . Sofia Coppola
Cardinal Lamberto . . . . Raf Vallone
Anthony Corleone . Franc D'Ambrosio
Archbishop Gilday . . . Donal Donnelly
Al Neri . . . . Richard Bright
Frederick Keinszig . . Helmut Berger
Dominic Abbandando . . . Don Novello
Also with: John Savage, Franco Citti, Mario Donatone, Vittorio Duse, Enzo Robutti, Michele Russo, Al Martino, Robert Cicchini, Rogerio Miranda.

Faced with the extraordinary task of recapturing magic he created 16 and 18 years ago, Francis Ford Coppola has come very close to completely succeeding with "The Godfather Part III."

While certain flaws may prevent it from being regarded as the full equal of its predecessors, which are generally ranked among the greatest modern American films, it nonetheless matches them in narrative intensity, epic scope, sociopolitical analysis, physical beauty and deep feeling for its characters and milieu. In addition, it is certainly the most personal of the three for the director.

It is impossible to know if Paramount's $55 million-plus production investment will yield huge profits, but it should stand as a major b.o. attraction.

Dragged back into bloody gangland activities after laboriously enshrouding himself in the trappings of respectability, Al Pacino's Michael Corleone laments,

"Just when I thought I was out, they pull me back in." This could be read as Coppola's comment upon his own involvement in this celebrated trilogy.

Once again, Coppola has managed to fuse matters of close concern to him with the stuff of richly satisfying commercial entertainment. Preoccupations with aging, diminished power, family, passing the mantle, sin and redemption are easily combined with dramatic familial and political intrigue, violent power plays, international high finance and corruption in the Vatican. Most of it plays beautifully.

Reminders of the earlier pictures are present both explicitly, via brief clips, and implicitly, through the repetition of storytelling motifs. Like the original, Part III opens with a lengthy festival celebration punctuated by backroom dealings. It is 1979, and Michael Corleone, having divested himself of his illegal operations, is being honored by the Catholic Church for his abundant charitable activities.

The party at the family's lavish New York apartment introduces characters both familiar and new. Michael's ex-wife Kay (Diane Keaton), now remarried, comes to see him for the first time in eight years, principally to support the desire of the couple's son Anthony (Franc D'Ambrosio) to quit law school and become an opera singer. Unmarried and without a romantic attachment, Michael receives his emotional support from his sister Connie (Talia Shire).

Hopeful of bringing his family closer together, Michael dotes on his daughter Mary (Sofia Coppola), and understandably becomes perturbed by her affair with cousin Vincent (Andy Garcia), hotheaded, violence-prone illegitimate son of Michael's late brother Sonny. Vincent has been unhappily working for slumlord and old-style thug Joey Zasa (Joe Mantegna), who has taken on Michael's less savory holdings.

Also on the scene are friendly rival Don Altobello (Eli Wallach), new counsel B.J. Harrison (George Hamilton), replacing the absent Robert Duvall's Tom Hagen, Hagen's priest son Andrew (John Savage), singer Johnny Fontane (Al Martino), the highly placed Archbishop Gilday (Donal Donnelly) and a journalist (Bridget Fonda) who seeks an interview with Don Corleone but happily settles for a roll in the hay with Vincent.

Bad blood between the ruthless Zasa and the Corleone family mounts just as Michael tries, with $600 million, to buy a controlling interest in the European conglomerate Immobiliare, a move that would cement his business legitimacy and financial future. The company is owned by venerable European families presented as being even more corrupt than the Mafia, and both sides lobby for the favor of the Vatican, which must ratify the Corleone takeover.

But old ways die hard, as Zasa, feeling slighted, spectacularly massacres most of the old dons at an Atlantic City conclave. Michael and Altobello escape with their lives, whereupon the irrepressible Vincent undertakes a personal vendetta against his impudent former boss.

After exactly midpoint, 80 minutes, the action switches to Italy, where it remains for the duration. Ostensibly, the family is gathering in Sicily to attend the operatic debut of Anthony, but there is much business to look after. Pacino and Wallach's old dons can't help begin scheming against one another, much as they profess to want to live out their remaining days quietly.

In one extremely potent scene, Michael begins confessing his countless sins to a cardinal (Raf Vallone), which forces him to confront his most heinous crime, the murder of his brother Fredo. Even more powerful is the sequence in which Michael officially anoints his bastard nephew as a Corleone, giving him the power of a don.

But the best is still yet to come. In one of the most masterful examples of sustained intercutting in cinema, Anthony's performance on opening night in "Cavalleria Rusticana" serves as the backdrop for several murderous missions.

Both Michael and Altobello are targets at the opera house, two financial kingpins are victimized, a bishop is pursued and the Pope himself (the actual John Paul I, who died mysteriously after a very short reign) falls under an assassin's hand. Suspense generated here is genuine and considerable, and is topped off by a rather shocking denouement that, given the death of one of Coppola's sons a few years ago, could not be more deeply felt.

With one glaring exception, which may unfortunately become the subject of an inordinate amount of criticism, casting and acting is exemplary down the line. For the third time out in his career role, Pacino is magnificent. With his character trying to take the initiative in reconciling his family and pushing through new business deals, Pacino is more animated and varied than he was going into his deep freeze in Part II. He manages to generate considerable sympathy despite his venal history, and injects a measure of rueful humor as well.

Andy Garcia brings much-needed youth and juice to the ballsy Vincent, heir apparent to the Corleone tradition, much as James Caan sparked the first film and Robert De Niro invigorated the second.

Looking and acting better than she has before as Kay (hardly her most memorable role), Diane Keaton proves a welcome, if brief, presence in warming the film, and Talia Shire seems pleased with the opportunity to do some dirty work at long last. Wallach, Mantegna, Vallone, Donnelly and Fonda are all impressive, while Hamilton has very little to do but stand behind Pacino.

Film's main flaw, unavoidably, is Sofia Coppola in the important, but not critical, role of Michael's daughter. Ungainly, afflicted with a valley girl accent and not an actress who can hold her own in this august company, the director's daughter simply doesn't cut it. This renders pic's main romantic element uncompelling and essentially unbelievable, and undercuts the force of the ending.

Unfortunate casting decision was made after original actress Winona Ryder had to bow out at the start of production, and created a furor within the company. Sad to say, the naysayers were correct.

A few awkward lines of dialog pop up here and there, and finale feels too abrupt, as Coppola seems to put too quick a capper on his great saga. But these are the only notable drawbacks in a mostly outstanding work.

As before, production values are spectacular. Myriad settings created by Dean Tavoularis and countless costumes fashioned by Milena Canonero provide a constant visual delight. Gordon Willis' cinematography, dark as before, gloriously matches his supreme accomplishments on the preceding films.

Carmine Coppola's score artfully incorporates the late Nino Rota's themes into outstanding new musical backgrounding, and editing by Barry Malkin, Lisa Fruchtman and Walter Murch keeps the disparate elements in balance while shining in individual setpieces.

Like Michael Corleone, Coppola seems to have been looking for a certain absolution with this film and, in exploring his major themes here so richly, with the maturity and resignation gained with age, he has arguably achieved it.

He has also created a dramatic and commercial powerhouse that can stand easily on its own and as the conclusion of a remarkable trilogy. — *Cart.*

MANIAC COP 2

A Movie House Sales Co. Ltd. and Fadd Enterprises presentation of a Larry Cohen production. Produced by Cohen. Directed by William Lustig. Screenplay, Cohen; camera (Foto-Kem), James Lemmo; editor, David Kern; music, Jay Chattaway; sound (Dolby), Craig Felburg; production design, Gene Abel, Charles LaGola; assistant director, John Cameron (L.A.), Gary Sales (N.Y.); stunt coordinator-2nd unit director, Spiro Razatos; special effects supervisor, John Carter; special effects coordinator, Matt Vogel; special makeup effects, Dean Gates; co-producer, John S. Engel; associate producer, Anthony DeFelice; casting, LDG & Associates, Ira Belgrade. Reviewed at TVC Moviemakers screening room, N.Y., Dec. 11, 1990. MPAA Rating: R. Running time: **88 MIN.**

Sean McKinney . . . . Robert Davi
Susan Riley . . . . . Claudia Christian
Edward Doyle . . . . . Michael Lerner
Jack Forrest . . . . . . Bruce Campbell
Teresa Mallory . . . . Laurene Landon
Matt Cordell . . . . . . Robert Z'Dar
Blum . . . . Clarence Williams III
Turkell . . . . Leo Rossi
Det. Lovejoy . . . . Lou Bonacki
Also with: Paula Trickey, Charles Napier, Claude Earl Jones.

"**M**aniac Cop 2" is a thinking man's exploitation film. Improving on the 1988 original, followup opened in France this summer and still awaits domestic release.

That earlier picture made by the same creative team was a theatrical flop but reportedly generated brisk homevideo sales. The sequel could attract some attention in the action market if it's properly handled.

This time out the title character Cordell, a framed cop killed in prison three years ago, is resurrected as a disfigured supernatural character stalking the streets of Manhattan. Writer Larry Cohen's premise is that the tall, burly, backlit monster in blue is a figure of fear rather than protection for Gotham citizens already frightened by crime.

With director William Lustig creating a brooding, morbid atmosphere akin to classical film noir, pic benefits from Cohen's extremely dark humor. Time and again the cop-monster shows up at a crime scene and violently aids the criminal rather than the victim.

Most outlandish conceit mocks the genre's most overused subject matter: a serial killer (Leo Rossi) of strippers in the Times Square district is about to be apprehended when the maniac cop comes in and rescues him.

The two killers become friends, and guest star Rossi, almost unrecognizable with long hair and a bushy beard, is terrific as the nut with a gift of gab. Film climaxes in prison where the maniac cop's revenge quest comes to an end in spectacular stunts by Spiro Razatos, including lengthy man-aflame footage that is quite eerie.

Hero Robert Davi in slouch hat as the sympathetic but unyielding detective on the case is most persuasive, styled as if auditioning to become Sam Raimi's "Darkman." Ironically, the Raimi regular actor who briefly plays "Darkman" at the end of that Liam Neeson pic, Bruce Campbell, co-stars as the cop who dealt with monster Z'Dar in the first "Maniac Cop." Cohen and Lustig gleefully off Campbell and other major cast members without warning here.

Claudia Christian also impresses as the no-nonsense police psychologist treating Davi, Campbell and frightened police woman Laurene Landon. — *Lor.*

AWAKENINGS

A Columbia Pictures release. Produced by Walter F. Parkes and Lawrence Lasker. Executive producers, Penny Marshall, Arne Schmidt, Elliot Abbott. Directed by Marshall. Screenplay, Steven Zillian, based on the book by Oliver Sacks; camera (Technicolor), Miroslav Ondricek; editor, Jerry Greenberg, Battle Davis; music, Randy Newman; sound (Dolby), Les Lazarowitz; production design, Anton Furst; costume design, Cynthia Flynt; art direction, Bill Groom; set decoration, George DeTitta Jr.; assistant director, Tony Gittelson; associate producer, Amy Lemisch; casting, Bonnie Timmerman. Reviewed at Mann Westwood Theater, L.A., Dec. 10, 1990. MPAA Rating: PG-13. Running time: **121 MIN.**
Dr. Malcolm Sayer . . . Robin Williams
Leonard Lowe . . . . . Robert De Niro
Eleanor Costello . . . . . Julie Kavner
Mrs. Lowe . . . . Ruth Nelson
Dr. Kaufman . . . . John Heard
Paula . . . . . . Penelope Ann Miller
Lucy . . . . Alice Drummond

Robin Williams finds another role well-suited to his gifts in "Awakenings," and the moving drama benefits beautifully. But this true tale's medical specifics make it less universally appealing than "Dead Poets Society," and, despite shared quality and inspiring themes, b.o. for "Awakenings" is likely to be more confined.

Here, Williams stirs the life force in invalids who decades ago turned to stone much like Williams the teacher awakened a passion for self-expression in students in the earlier pic. He joins Robert De Niro and director Penny Marshall in enacting the story of neurologist Oliver Sacks, who in 1966 encountered a group of statuelike paralytics in a Bronx hospital and insisted something could be done for them.

Doggedly pursuing clues to their affliction, Sacks/Sayer discovers they were stricken with encephalitis, which claimed many victims in the 1920s. Damage to their nervous systems had eventually rendered them motionless, a condition in which they survived for decades.

Certain they are still alive inside, Sayer wins permission to test L-DOPA, a new drug then being used to combat Parkinson's disease, and is able to "awaken" Leonard Lowe (De Niro), frozen since contracting the sleeping sickness 30 years before.

Extraordinary effect of Leonard's full-blown personality on those who'd considered him more or less dead inspires donations, and soon Sayer is able to awaken a whole tribe of these time-warp individuals, who head out for sightseeing and dancing.

But the miracle cure proves temporary, and Leonard begins a poignant process of deterioration from which Sayer is powerless to rescue him.

Rendered broadly and brightly accessible in the hands of director Marshall and screenwriter Steven Zallian, who adapted Sacks' book, "Awakenings" dwells predictably on the picture's upbeat themes: the miracle of health taken for granted, and the joy and meaning in life's simple things.

But its more compelling subthemes give the pic ballast. Who was right, Sacks or the cynical hospital establishment that told

him his experiment would fail? Indeed, all but one of the patients die. And why is happiness fleeting? The joyful Leonard quickly falls prey to frustration, anger and violence in his quest for more of life.

Marshall infuses this audience-pleasing project, which Columbia picked up in turnaround from Fox, with a sense of dedication, miracle and wonder. Unexpected comedy abounds, such as a scene in which the so-called statues, all lined up, play catch with each other, its bizarreness tempered by comic relief.

Scenes of the "awakenings" are choreographed with graceful restraint. At times, though, film caters more to smooth pacing than to believability. No sooner are the statues stirred than they're out painting the town.

Enacting the shy, fidgety doctor, Williams extends the extraordinary dramatic gifts he displayed in "Dead Poets Society." Sympathy and tenderness shine from his bright blue eyes. He's also very funny, as when he describes his earthworm experiment while applying for the staff position.

De Niro, far more effective here than in his portrayal of an illiterate man in "Stanley & Iris," has this visceral, demanding role by the tail. Watching this sweet firebrand of a man struggling through a blizzard of tics to stay engaged in life is miraculous and heartbreaking.

Photography by Miroslav Ondricek brings a quality of expansiveness and possibility to the hallways of Brooklyn's Kingsboro Psychiatric Center, particularly in artfully lit night scenes.

Sixties street environs are also aptly re-created, with the era suggested but not permitted to distract. — *Daws.*

THE RUSSIA HOUSE

An MGM/UA release of a Pathé Entertainment presentation. Produced by Paul Maslansky, Fred Schepisi. Directed by Schepisi. Screenplay, Tom Stoppard, based on the novel by John le Carré; camera (Technicolor, Technovision widescreen), Ian Baker; editor, Peter Honess; music, Jerry Goldsmith, featuring Branford Marsalis; sound (Dolby), Chris Munro; production design, Richard MacDonald; costume design, Ruth Myers; supervising art direction, Roger Cain; set decoration, Simon Wakefield; casting, Mary Selway. Reviewed at the Loews 84th Street Sixplex, N.Y., Dec. 10, 1990. MPAA Rating: R. Running time: **123 MIN.**
Barley Blair . . . . Sean Connery
Katya . . . . Michelle Pfeiffer
Russell . . . . Roy Scheider
Ned . . . . James Fox
Brady . . . . John Mahoney
Clive . . . . Michael Kitchen
Quinn . . . . J.T. Walsh
Walter . . . . Ken Russell
Wicklow . . . . David Threlfall
Dante . . . . . Klaus Maria Brandauer

The Soviet Union makes a spectacular Hollywood debut in "The Russia House." Attractive as they are, Sean Connery and Michelle Pfeiffer are constantly upstaged by the fresh and arresting settings in which the stars play out an absorbing but muted yarn of romance and political intrigue.

John le Carré's glasnost-era espionage novel has been turned into intelligent adult entertainment, but somber tone, utter lack of action and sex, and complexity of plot will tilt this mainly to upscale audiences, giving it only a moderate b.o. outlook.

Regardless of its dramatic qualities, the film has already earned a historical niche as the first U.S. non-coproduction to be shot substantially in the USSR. The opportunity has not been lost on director Fred Schepisi and his longtime lenser Ian Baker, who feast on the Moscow-area and Leningrad locations in a way that fills the widescreen with continual riches and will no doubt thrill Soviet tourism entities.

Although the tale holds the interest, thrilling is not the word for this story of a reluctant spy exploring the hazy political frontiers of the new Russia. Schepisi's physicalization of Tom Stoppard's tight, sometimes structurally playful script is confident and convincing. But such close attention must be paid to follow the subtle twists in plot and motivation that some viewers will inevitably be lost along the way.

Sean Connery plays Barley Blair, a boozy, iconoclastic London publisher to whom a highly sensitive manuscript is sent via a Moscow book editor named Katya (Michelle Pfeiffer). Intercepted by British authorities, the text, authored by a leading physicist, purports to lay out the facts about Soviet nuclear capabilities in devastating detail, revealing the country's military weakness and disarray once and for all.

Over his protestations, Blair is sent to Moscow in his role as prospective publisher to meet the writer, the mysterious Dante, determine his reliability and put more questions to him. His intermediary for this operation is the beautiful Katya, whom he spends considerable time courting, both personally and professionally. Understandably, he falls in love with her, and affairs of state are soon compromised by an affair of the heart.

During his meetings with Katya, when he is trying to insinuate himself into her life as well as do his job as a spy, Blair wears a hidden microphone so his masters back at the office can keep up with every development. While provoking some amusement, this technique most effectively clarifies Blair's position as a pawn in the hands of professional Cold Warriors, whose mindsets were formed in the frozen tundra of the 1950s and '60s and who count on the perpetuation of hostilities to keep their jobs.

Opening reels roll along nicely, as quick flashbacks fill in necessary background, colorful British intelligence characters quiz Blair at length and dazzling Russian locations provide a constant source of fascination as Katya gives Blair a travelog tour of her hometown.

Although Blair's declaration of love for Katya comes as no surprise, her immediate acceptance of him into her family unit, and her aligning her fate with his, feels abrupt and unearned.

From this point on, the traditional plot machinations of Cold War thrillers, from le Carré back to Graham Greene, are rather too noticeable. The politics have changed, but the dramatic clichés have not, resulting in a climax and conclusion of only mild impact.

As the flawed, unreliable publisher who plays saxophone for recreation and is reintroduced to life's possibilities by his rendezvous in Moscow, Connery is in top form. Gruff, stubborn, sensitive to gifted, interesting people and deeply fond of Russia, Blair is a rich character marvelously realized by the actor.

Pfeiffer's Katya is a much more guarded figure, a woman whose sympathies are clear but who has clearly been raised to watch what she says, and to whom she says it. Pfeiffer's Russian accent proves very believable, and one is drawn to the lovely actress, but she has limited notes to play.

Most of the supporting roles are one-dimensional British or U.S. intelligence types, but such thesps as James Fox, Roy Scheider, John Mahoney and Michael Kitchen embody them solidly and with wit when possible. Director

Ken Russell amusingly hams it up as an impishly aggressive spy master. Brandauer is strong as always in his brief appearance as the charismatic Dante.

Baker's camera is almost constantly on the prowl, providing countless beautifully shaded perspectives of the unique locations and offering a visual correlative for the uncertain ground the characters occupy. However, the widescreen Technovision format creates some problems, as there are apparent difficulties with distortion and focus.

All behind-the-scenes contributions are outstanding. Richard MacDonald's superior production design makes it impossible to tell location shots from built sets. Peter Honess' editing keeps the action clear if one pays close attention, and Jerry Goldsmith moody jazz-oriented score expertly lends an understated urgency to the proceedings.

"The Russia House" would be a creditable addition to any distributor's release slate, but isn't the type of picture upon which MGM/UA and Pathé should pin major financial hopes. — *Cart.*

MERMAIDS

An Orion Pictures release of a Nicita/Lloyd/Palmer production. Produced by Lauren Lloyd, Wallis Nicita, Patrick Palmer. Directed by Richard Benjamin. Screenplay, June Roberts, based on the novel by Patty Dann; camera (Technicolor, Deluxe prints), Howard Atherton; editor, Jacqueline Cambas; music, Jack Nitzsche; sound (Dolby), Richard Lightstone; production design, Stuart Wurtzel; art direction, Steve Saklad, Evelyn Sakash; set decoration, Hilton Rosemarin; costume design, Marit Allen; assistant directors, Jim Van Wyck, Princess McLean; associate producer, Suzanne Rothbaum; casting, Margery Simkin. Reviewed at the UA Coronet Theater, Westwood, Calif., Dec. 5, 1990. MPAA Rating: PG13. Running time: **111 MIN.**
Mrs. Flax . . . . Cher
Lou Landsky . . . . Bob Hoskins
Charlotte Flax . . . . . Winona Ryder
Joe . . . . Michael Schoeffling
Kate Flax . . . . Christina Ricci
Carrie . . . . . . Caroline McWilliams
Mother Superior . . . . Jan Miner

Aside from its star leads, "Mermaids" presents an imposing marketing problem — confusingly titled, slowly paced and dramatically unfocused. With crowded holiday waters to navigate, this genial period piece looks to have limited boxoffice potential.

As eccentric mother-daughter films go, this one falls into the

same category as "Terms Of Endearment," with many of the same comedic pleasures and dramatic pitfalls. Set in the early '60s, "Mermaids" begins rousingly, introducing flamboyant Mrs. Flax (Cher) and her two daughters: confused, Charlotte (Winona Ryder), 15, who is obsessed with Catholicism, and Kate (Christina Ricci), 9, who's obsessed with swimming.

Constantly on the move due to mother's vagabond ways, they soon relocate to a small New England town that brings with it new romantic entanglements. Mrs. Flax takes up with a lovelorn shoe salesman (Bob Hoskins), while Charlotte becomes enamored with a dreamy groundskeeper (Michael Schoeffling) from the local nunnery, conveniently situated just down the road.

Since she's unable to communicate with her wanton mother, Ryder's dialog is largely limited to voiceover confessions and pleas to God, often while staring intently, wordless and wide-eyed, at her mother or Joe (Schoeffling), the unsuspecting object of her near-crazed lust.

Screenwriter June Roberts' adaptation is peppered with comic gems, and director Richard Benjamin makes a strong comeback after a couple of disappointing efforts.

Unfortunately, like the mythological characters of the title, the film ultimately proves caught between worlds, oscillating between broad comic strokes and tired familial melodrama.

Storyline progresses languidly, and the denouement has the ring of desperation, resulting in an emotional outpouring that fails to add meaning to what's otherwise merely a pleasant, albeit overlong, coming-of-age comedy.

Comparison to "Terms Of Endearment" is unavoidable, from the shaky mother-daughter relationship calling into question who takes care of whom, to Hoskins' amusing, steadying presence as the new man in mom's life.

The film's foremost charms, however, stem from a quirky sensibility attributable almost wholly to Roberts' crisp dialog and the delightful Ryder, who, billing notwithstanding, is really the star.

With roles in "Welcome Home, Roxy Carmichael" and "Edward Scissorhands," Ryder has practically cornered the market on angst-ridden teens. She's adept at projecting an appealing com-

bination of beauty and vulnerability. The role here is her best since her career-making performance in "Heathers."

Cher is also fine as the cavalier, self-centered mom, an equally amusing if less sympathetic character. Ricci is perhaps the most adorable and engaging child actress since "Miracle On 34th Street's" 9-year-old Natalie Wood, whom she resembles.

Too bad the structure of the film isn't equal to the individual parts. With too few crescendos in the story, all that's left is to savor its better moments, ranging from Hoskins' magical means of winning the girls over to Ryder and Cher's joyous warbling of period '60s tunes.

The era is splendidly captured in the hairdos, sets and costume designer Marit Allen's brassy colors and styles. Jack Nitzsche has delivered an uncharacteristically restrained score, in keeping with the film's melancholy tone.
— *Bril.*

ALMOST AN ANGEL

A Paramount Pictures release of an Ironbark Films production. Executive producer, Paul Hogan. Produced and directed by John Cornell. Screenplay, Hogan; camera (Deluxe color; Technicolor prints), Russell Boyd; editor, David Stiven; music, Maurice Jarre; sound (Dolby), Tom Brandau; production design, Henry Bumstead; costume design, April Ferry; assistant director-associate producer, Mark Turnbull; production manager-line producer-2nd unit director, Kelly Van Horn; stunt coordinator, Spike Silver; 2nd unit camera, Richard Yuricich; casting, Dianne Crittenden. Reviewed at Paramount 29th Floor screening room, N.Y., Dec. 13, 1990. MPAA Rating: PG. Running time: 95 MIN.
Terry Dean . . . . Paul Hogan
Steve . . . . Elias Koteas
Rose . . . . Linda Kozlowski
God . . . . Charlton Heston
Mrs. Garner . . . . Doreen Lang
Thief . . . . Joe Dallesandro
Also with: Robert Sutton, Sammy Lee Allen, Douglas Seale, Ruth Warshawsky, Parley Baer, Ben Slack, David Alan Grier, Larry Miller, Hank Worden.

Paul Hogan delivers the season's slightest entry, "Almost An Angel," an innocuous inspirational comedy that is unlikely to play beyond the holidays.

Given the star's 2 for 2 winning streak at the boxoffice with his "Crocodile Dundee" features, "Angel" will serve as a litmus test of his draw. It's simply a no-effort vanity project with only Hogan's easygoing charm to fill the space between the sprocket holes.

Instead of stretching his acting muscles, Hogan (who scripted and also served as executive producer) assigns himself the comfortable role of an electronics expert/cracksman just released from prison who turns into an inveterate do-gooder.

Hogan, in between bank heists, instinctively saves a guy from a traffic accident and is himself run down. Hospital scene has him dreaming of (or actually) floating to the clouds where uncredited guest star Charlton Heston as God reads him the riot act. Typical of the film as a whole, the casting of Heston is cute but remains undeveloped, as he sends Hogan back to Earth for a second chance as an angel of mercy on probation.

At first Hogan disbelieves and continues robbing banks, but when bullets don't harm him during an abortive holdup (they're blanks) he's convinced the dream is true.

Trekking to the small town of Fillmore, Calif., he sets about being kind to people. Chief recipients of his largesse are Elias Koteas, a bitter young man suffering from a terminal illness confining him to a wheelchair, and his self-sacrificing sister, Hogan's real-life wife and inevitable co-star Linda Kozlowski.

As scripter Hogan tips his hand early on with a clip on tv from Michael Landon's "Highway To Heaven" series, "Almost An Angel" plays like a subpar segment from that show, pouring on the religious message with a trowel. Paramount made a mint this year with its "you must believe" hit "Ghost," but Hogan's well-meaning faith in an afterlife here is way too cornily presented.

As if hedging its bets, "Angel" shamelessly crossplugs Paramount's other Christmas release "The Godfather Part III" on several occasions: a poster, verbal reference and pastiche of Nino Rota's theme. Film's best scenes stress Hogan's strong suit for mimicry (as displayed in his syndicated Aussie tv show) when he impersonates Willie Nelson and Rod Stewart during holdups.

Elsewhere Koteas is affecting as the cripple with a chip on his shoulder. Kozlowski, styled plain with dark hair, is wasted as the mildest of romantic interests.

Direction by Hogan's partner John Cornell is sluggish, with uneventful scenes allowed to run on endlessly. Production values are quite modest and the special effects to suggest fantasy content are meager. — *Lor.*

LOOK WHO'S TALKING TOO

A Tri-Star Pictures release of a Jonathan D. Krane production. Produced by Krane. Directed by Amy Heckerling. Screenplay, Heckerling, Neal Israel; camera (Alpha Ciné color; Technicolor prints), Thomas Del Ruth; editor, Debra Chiate; music, David Kitay; music supervision, Maureen Crowe; sound (Dolby), Ralph Parker; production design, Reuben Freed; costume design, Molly Maginnis; assistant director, Bill Mizel; production manager-co-producer, Bob Gray; special character effects, Chris Walas Inc.; title sequence visual effects, JEX Efx – supervisor, Gary Platek; casting, Stuart Aikins. Reviewed at Gemini theater, N.Y., Dec. 8, 1990. MPAA Rating: PG-13. Running time: **81 MIN.**
James . . . . .John Travolta
Mollie . . . . .Kirstie Alley
Rosie . . . . .Olympia Dukakis
Stuart . . . . .Elias Koteas
Rona . . . . Twink Caplan
Also with: Gilbert Gottfried, Lorne Sussman, Megan Milner, Georgia Keithley, Nikki Graham, Danny Pringle, Neal Israel, Paul Shaffer, and voices of Bruce Willis (Mikey), Roseanne Barr (Julie), Damon Wayans (Eddie), Mel Brooks (Mr. Toilet Man).

This vulgar sequel to 1989's longest-running sleeper hit is assured of big openings due to predecessor's familiarity but bad word of mouth should guarantee weak legs.

Few predicted the success of same team's "Look Who's Talking," launched after delays in October 1989 to enjoy an unusually long 30-week U.S. run en route to ranking among the '89-'90 international b.o. leaders.

Credit Tri-Star with getting a followup into theaters in timely fashion to maximize its b.o. potential, but the resulting mishmash looks like a rush job.

Joined by her husband Neal Israel (who also appears as star Kirstie Alley's mean boss) in the scripting, filmmaker Amy Heckerling overemphasizes toilet humor and expletives — none deleted — to make the film appealing mainly to adolescents rather than an across-the-board family audience.

Unwed mom Alley and cabbie John Travolta are married for the sequel, with her cute son metamorphosed into Lorne Sussman, still voiceovered as precociously by Bruce Willis. First mutual arrival is conceived during a clever title sequence in which some sperm (also getting comical voiceovers) manage to find a way around Alley's diaphragm and fertilize an egg.

What hatches is undeniably cute Megan Milner (at 1 year old, after infants Nikki Graham and Georgia Keithley personify baby Julie), unfortunately voiced over by Roseanne Barr. Comedienne gets a couple of laughs but is generally dull, leaving Willis to again carry the load in the gag department with well-read quips.

Lack of an interesting plotline is evident throughout the sequel's abbreviated 81-minute running time. Ostensibly it revolves around the bickering of Alley and Travolta whose jobs (accountant and would-be airline pilot) and personalities clash, as well as the rites of passage of the two kids. New characters, notably Alley's obnoxious brother Elias Koteas, are added to ill effect.

An unconscionable amount of footage is devoted to the issue of potty training. Mel Brooks is enlisted to voiceover Mr. Toilet Man, a fantasy bathroom bowl come to life, spitting blue water and anxious to bite off Mikey's privates. Family's ecstatic reaction to Mikey finally learning toiletiquette is pure corn.

Alley and Travolta are a likable team that play off each other well. Too bad Hollywood doesn't take a leaf from its Golden Age and find *new* material for such romantic combos (à la '30s Fred MacMurray/Carole Lombard or '40s Tracy/Hepburn teamings) rather than merely recycle them in the sequel craze.

Both youngsters are cute enough to please an undemanding audience, and with an eye towards the cash register a third infant, lovable black tot Danny Pringle, is added in a few scenes as a precociously streetwise playmate for Mikey.

Richard Pryor originally was signed to voiceover Pringle's wisecracks but was inexplicably replaced by Damon Wayans who does a good job in delivering knowing but young-sounding jive. All three kids articulate while the voicing occurs in a non-match that resembles the visual effect of a dubbed-in-English Japanese horror movie.

One cute gag involves the playing of the Tri-Star logo musical theme (by Dave Grusin) to climax a scene where Richard Strauss' "Thus Sprach Zarathustra" from "2001: A Space Odyssey" is traditionally employed. Elsewhere there's plenty of paid-for plugola.

With Koteas a gun-toting babysitter who abandons the kids to an accidental fire in their apartment, film strays far from good taste and good sense in a desperate search for gags. Various creature effects, notably Julie growing in mom's womb, are well executed by Chris Walas' organization and New York locale for this Vancouver-lensed effort is adequately faked by some second unit shots.

Conspicuous sequel "beefing up" is most evident in pointless inclusion of many golden oldies on the soundtrack, ranging from expensive Elvis Presley tracks (allowing Travolta to throw in one of his trademark dance numbers) to John Lennon and George Harrison. — *Lor.*

SPRINGFLOD
(SPRING TIDE)
(DANISH)

A Warner & Metronome release of Nina Crone Film production in association with the Danish Film Institute and DR/FI. Produced by Nina Crone. Written and directed by Eddie Thomas Petersen. Camera (color), Dirk Brüel; editor, Leif Axel Kjeldsen; music, Fini Höstrup; sound, Johan Carlsen; production design, Sören Kragh Sörensen; production manager, Nico; assistant director, Marianne Moritzen. Reviewed at the Scala, Copenhagen, Sept. 27, 1990. Running time: **95 MIN.**
Franco . . . . . .Jesper Gredeli Jensen
Pauline . . . . .Trine Dyrholm
Pauline's father . . . .Peter Schröder
Pauline's mother . . . .Kirsten Olesen
Franco's mother . . .Jannie Faurschou

Making a conspicuous feature bow, writer-director Eddie Thomas Petersen demonstrates fine control of technical aspects and his new and veteran cast members. A neat future in arthouses, before television stations start vying for "Spring Tide," seems a safe bet.

Real life fills every frame of the softspoken and original young love story, said to be borrowed from actual events. Still, a fairytale tone is evident.

Franco, a Copenhagen nearslum teen in trouble with the law, has been shipped to volunteer foster parents in the remote Jutland marshes near the German border. Dreaming of becoming a bullfighter, he would rather have gone to Spain to join his long-gone father.

The foster parents' daughter Pauline tends sheep to save

enough money for a trip to the U.S. after graduation. She also plays trombone in the high school band — and to her sheep. Her dreams are old-fashioned romantic ones.

Pauline's father is a border patrolman who doesn't have his heart in keeping aliens from entering the Danish haven illegally. Soon, Franco begins to feel at ease in his new surroundings. Inevitably, the two young hearts meet and sweet music flows.

Caught in the rising waters of a full moon spring tide, the youngsters barely make it to safety in a remote beach house, where their love is consummated. However, they also run into an illegal entrant and a gun-toting informer. To help the foreigner, Franco has to steal a car for a getaway.

Add to this that Pauline soon finds herself with child and that her mother hurriedly packs Franco off to Copenhagen, where the authorities have him earmarked for a reform school. Meller conventionalism is indicated, but all melodramatics are cut off briskly at the root.

Sticking to a sedate but rhythmically pulsating tempo throughout, helmer Petersen illuminates every take and sequence with warm and witty touches and viewpoints that take characters and developments refreshingly off the beaten track.

Finally, "Spring Tide" allows itself a happy ending that would be preposterous if it had not happened to characters that really appear to have true love and *joie de vivre* in their hearts. All roles, big and small, are full-bodied and played with natural grace.

A jazz score played by Palle Mikkelborg, Niels Henning Örsted Pedersen, Bjarne Roupé and Niels Ratzer melts with the landscapes of vast horizons and surprising colors, caught stunningly by Dirk Brüel's beautifully lighted and sweeping cinematography. — *Kell.*

YSTÄVÄT, TOVERIT
(FRIENDS, COMRADES)
(FINNISH)

A Finnkino release of Filmi-Molle production in association with Finnkino, the Finnish Film Foundation, YLE-2 and the Swedish Film Institute. Produced and directed by Rauni Mollberg. Screenplay, Mollberg, Joni Skiftesvik,

Raija Kouri; camera (Eastmancolor), Kjell Lagerroos; editor, Kaieene Rääk; music, Kari Rydman; sound (Dolby), Oskari Viskari, Johan Hake; production design, Tom Hamberg; costumes, Salme Lahtinen; special effects, Lasse Sorsa; associate producer, Katinka Faragó; production manager, Arja Nurmi. Reviewed at the Bristol, Helsinki, Nov. 15, 1990. Running time: **127 MIN.**
Jurmala . . . . Mikk Mikiver
Lisa . . . . Stina Ekblad
Jaunhahns . . . . Hannu Lauri
Kaakamo . . . . Paavo Liski
Ulla . . . . Tuire Salenius
Jopi . . . . Ilkka Rosma
Lisma . . . . Tapio Aarre-Ahtio
Igumeni . . . . Rein Aren
Also with: Oto Sevcik, Ain Lutsepp, Elle Kull, Janus Orgulas, Güran Schauman, Joone Nurminen, Walter Bacon.

International business intrigue and high drama merge in "Friends, Comrades" by Finnish filmmaker Rauni Mollberg. Ambitious and dynamic control of cinematic narrative techniques are likely to reward the picture with all-media offshore sales.

Mollberg first achieved worldwide acclaim in 1973 with "Earth Is A Sinful Song," a robust outdoors meller pitting nature against man's abuse of it. He has enlarged the same theme to epic scale in his new film.

Mollberg's film reads like fundamentalist preaching and depicts men and nations exploiting and destroying nature as well as human beings strictly for profit. Fortunately, helmer's grandiose filmmaking skills make lapses into message-mongering easily forgiven.

Much of "Friends, Comrades" is centered on nickel mine owner Jurmala's gala 50th anniversary party, which takes place on the eve of World War II. Government emissaries scheme against each other while Orthodox masses are held, children's choirs sing, mine workers perform witchcraft dances, all to praise Jurmala and please the guests, who are supplied with women commanded to sleep with them.

The party is over when war breaks out between Finns, Russians and Nazi occupiers of Norway. The second part of the film records gory battles, more business conniving and bawdy whorehouse cavortings set alternately to Cossack and German beer hall music.

In between, Lisa is done away with and replaced by someone richly productive. Jurmela travels indiscriminately to Berlin and to Moscow to receive honorary medals. No sooner has WW2 come to and end than he is busy

greeting new shoppers for his wares.

With nary a wrinkle added to his brow, he greets them all with his familiar "Friends, Comrades" speech. All this would be preposterously simpleminded if it had not been served up with superior acting in all parts, smooth-paced story telling and sumptuous technical credits.

Estonian actor Mikk Mikiver, a Sean Connery look-alike, plays Jurmela with gentility disguising a tyrannical will. With grace and ease, the Finn proposes a toast to one side and orders an assassination to the other.

Played with exquisite control by Sweden's gauntly beautiful Stina Ekblad, wife Lisa once believed, as did Jurmala, in the true romance of her marriage. But the union has produced no heir, and passion is rekindled only with the aid of morphine.

The editing is seamless, and young Swede Kjell Lagerroos' stunning cinematography captures both natural beauty and gory battle. Abundant facial closeups are fine-tuned to the narrative pulse.

Kari Rydman's music subtly underlines moods of irony and pity. When needed, it is brash and brassy, but it is never obtrusive. — *Kell.*

DEFY GRAVITY
(CANADIAN)

A Creative Exposure release of a Castalian Films and P.S. Production Services presentation of a Shifting Weight production. (Intl. sales agent: Film Transit.) Produced by Douglas Dales, Michael Gibson. Executive producer, Don Haig. Written and directed by Gibson. Camera (color), Douglas Koch; editor, Darryl Cornford; music, Mark Gane, Martha Johnson; sound, Allan Scarth; production design, Linda Del Rosario. Reviewed at Toronto Festival of Festivals, Aug. 31, 1990. Running time: **90 MIN.**
Bill Fiddich . . . . R.H. Thomson
Patrick . . . . Simon Reynolds
Mary Fiddich . . . . . . Chapelle Jaffe
Miss McInnis . . . . Tracey Moore
Debbie . . . . Karen Saunders
Sandra . . . . Juno Mills Cockell

First time director Michael Gibson is on unsteady ground in "Defy Gravity," a quirky but dark coming-of-age story presenting a teen's need to let go of paternal adulation and deal with domestic violence. Pic will have difficulty finding a sizable theatrical audience but will play much better on tv.

Solid lead performance by consistently energized R.H. Thom-

son, as a frustrated inventor with an oddball world view and a habit of physically abusing his wife and daughter, fails to redeem the other gaps in the pic.

Simon Reynolds plays an unstable 15-year-old struggling to come to terms with peer pressure, potential girlfriends and a slouching commitment to academics. His history teacher (Tracey Moore) sees glimpses of wisdom in her student, and invites him into her confidence.

It's not exactly the Cleaver family on the home front. Reynolds has to deal with dad's chaotic outbursts and skewed reasoning until finally confronted with the need to take responsibility for the eroding family structure. Son calls the police to take father away.

Gibson's lame dream cycles showing the son's escape from the abusive family atmosphere rarely work. Script tries to make father an empathetic and charming character, but it's difficult to transcend the modus operandi of a wife beater.

Reynolds, sensitive and enthusiastic in a teen angst role, handles his conflict with father worship well, but is called upon to do too many forced wacky stunts to be believed.

Tech credits are okay, but pic's $C1 million budget shows as it plays like a made-for-tv'er.
— *Devo.*

EL MEJOR DE LOS TIEMPOS
(THE BEST OF TIMES)
(SPANISH)

An Arenal Productores Asociados S.A. production. Produced by Manuel Grosso, Juan A. Pedrosa, Juan A. Mendoza. Directed by Felipe Vega. Screenplay, Vega, Igancio Gutierez Solana; camera (color), Jose Luis Lopez-Linares; editor, Ivan Aledo; music, Bernardo Bonezzi; sound, Daniel Goldstein, Ricardo Steinberg; art direction, Josean Gomez. Reviewed at the Toronto Festival of Festivals, Sept. 16, 1990. Running time: **109 MIN.**
Daniel . . . . .Jorge de Juan
Maria . . . . Iciar Bollain
Sara . . . . Rosario Flores
Carmen . . . . Carmen Bullejos
Teo . . . . Rafael Diaz
Luis . . . . .Gracian Quero

One essential element is missing in "The Best Of Times": a story. Two or three different plots are meticulously set up, but none are ever resolved. The only links between the various scenarios are the characters.

On a train from Spain, Daniel heads to a small town to deliver a briefcase. Upon arrival, a police raid prevents him from delivering the goods. Briefcase contents (drugs or money?) are never revealed, making the setup pointless.

In scenario two, Daniel meets his love interest, Maria. She initially detests him (understandable since he follows her everywhere despite her protests), but Maria inevitably falls for his macho charms.

In scenario three, Maria works in a greenhouse which uses untested (and purportedly dangerous) chemicals to preserve fruit for shipping. Her pregnant friend and roommate, Carmen, is hospitalized due to the chemical's side effects.

Maria and her alcoholic boss, Teo, decide to terrorize the plant and save the workers, which never pans out. One hour into the film, the story still has no obvious focus and, unfortunately, never gets one.

What could be a hip "save the planet" theme, is washed out to sea with the love story. The romance temporarily congeals as Maria convinces Daniel to help the environmental cause, but Daniel is mysteriously arrested before they can sabotage the plant.

While Daniel is in jail playing soccer, Teo tells Maria she can't help the cause because she's a woman. The credits roll quoting Dickens' "A Tale Of Two Cities" at the end ("It was the best of times, it was the worst of times . . .").

Presumably, the quote is meant to explain pic's title, but in this case, could be the "most obscure of times." — *Suze*.

CUCHILLOS DE FUEGO
(FLAMING KNIVES)
(VENEZUELAN-SPANISH)

A Gente de Cine-Foncine-Televisión Española (TVE) co-production. Produced by Miguel Angel Landa. Directed by Román Chalbaud. Screenplay, David Suárez, Chalbaud, based on Chalbaud's play "Todo Bicho de Uña"; camera, José María Hermo; editor, Sergio Curiel; music, Federico Ruíz. Reviewed at II Festival Cine San Juan, Puerto Rico, Oct. 18, 1990. Running time: **110 MIN.**
With: Miguel Angel Landa, Marisela Berti, Javier Zapata, Charlis Barri, Natia Martínez, Gabriel Fernández, Pedro Landere, William Moreno, Raúl Medina.

A tale of revenge with a bit of magic realism thrown in, "Flaming Knives" presents an obvious exercise in facile psychology that will burn itself out without sparking much international interest other than diehard followers of Venezuelan filmmaker Román Chalbaud.

Script boasts some interesting elements that might have been cleaned up in a rewrite. Unfortunately, directorial laziness bogs the story in Freudian clichés that make it appear like a case study gone haywire.

Based on Chalbaud's play "Todo Bicho du Uña," "Flaming Knives" recounts the sufferings of a boy who, along with his saintly mother, is rejected by a macho father. His mother is soon the victim of a savage rape and murder that takes place before the boy's horrified eyes.

He is taken in by a traveling circus troupe, and as the years go by, he gradually assumes the job as assistant to the knife-thrower, who teaches the boy his craft. The boy's hatred ignites the blades, directing them to their targets in flashes of flame.

While traveling, he searches for his mother's murderer and, as fate would have it, he finds him. The two form an odd bond bordering on the homoerotic as the boy entraps the killer into an ardorous web while retracing all the phases of his early life.

"Flaming Knives" brims with colorful circus elements that, while delightful, can't distract from the film's obvious failings, notably its awkward and facile ending. Superimposed images of the mother that appear from time to time to haunt the boy are clichéd and clumsy, while the overacted death scenes are strictly amateur. — *Lent*.

FUGLEKRIGEN I KANOFLESHOVEN
(WAR OF THE BIRDS)
(DANISH-ANIMATED)

A Kärne Film release of Per Holst Film production in association with Dansk Tegnefilm, the Danish Film Institute and the Swedish Film Institute. Produced by Per Holst. Directed by Jannik Hastrup. Screenplay, Bent Haller, Hastrup. Camera (color) Jacob Koch; editor, Holst; music, Sören Kragh-Jacobsen; sound (Dolby), Niels Arild; directing animators, Nancy Carrig, Michael Helmuth Hansen, Walter Lehman, Harry Rasmussen, Asta Sigurdardottir,

Georges Stoyanoff; color styler, Tine Karrebäk; graphics, Bigita Faber; production manager, Marie Bro. Reviewed at the Palads, Copenhagen, Sept. 29 1990. Running time: **65 MIN.**
Voices of: Tommy Kentner, Lisbeth Dahl, Emil Tarding, Lasse Jonsson, Sofie Bredesen, Barbara Rothenborg Topsöe, Vigga Bro, Claus Ryskjär, Per Pallesen, Helle Ryslinge, Anne Marie Helger, Pernille Hansen, Ove Sprogö.

A good story is chopped to pieces in veteran animator Jannik Hastrup's "War Of The Birds," but it has enough cute fun, baroque character delineations and rollicking music to mildly amuse kids and adults. That should help usher in offshore distribution via video and broadcast.

Pic's fun is both verbal and visual, so outside Denmark, local voices must be lent to characters such as the W. C. Fields-ish owl, two multicolored sparrows, cowardly dove and the two would-be aviator mice who find it hard to unite efficiently against Fagin, a ferocious bird of prey who threatens the peace in a never-never-land forest.

Adept at outsmarting a cat in the nearby Big City, teen sparrow Ophelia falls in love with Oliver, her less amorously inclined adolescent male counterpart, who is bent on waging war on Fagin. Together they build various traps for the big-beaked tyrant. (Names notwithstanding, story is totally unrelated to Charles Dickens.)

In brief interludes, the winged protagonists break into song and dance routines. This is where adult audiences will have the best fun, especially in a dive-by-the-seaside sequence where a piano-playing seagull leads all the boozers, cardplayers and one very naughty hen into an all-out dance extravaganza.

Drawing style comes closer to Ralph Bakshi than to Disney, but Hastrup has his own way of combining the cute with the robust. He works with more limited production means, but that would hardly matter if his storytelling had not been less jerky. Much dramatic punch potential is lost in non sequiturs.

True suspense is lagging, and the menace of Fagin negligible. Although the evil bird meets a violent death by fire, little in the film will bring a 5-year-old, who may be puzzled about what's what, to the edge of his seat.
— *Kell*.

GREEN CARD
(AUSTRALIAN-FRENCH)

A Buena Vista release of a Touchstone presentation. Written, produced and directed by Peter Weir. Executive producer, Edward S. Feldman. Camera (Technicolor), Geoffrey Simpson; editor, William Anderson; music, Hans Zimmer; sound (Dolby), Pierre Gamet; production design, Wendy Stites; art direction, Christopher Nowak; set decoration, John Anderson, Ted Glass; assistant director, Alan B. Curtiss; associate producer, Ira Halberstadt; coproducers, Jean Gontier, Duncan Henderson; casting, Dianne Crittenden. Reviewed at the Magno Preview 9 screening room, N.Y., Dec. 13, 1990. MPAA Rating: PG-13. Running time: **108 MIN.**

George Faure	Gérard Depardieu
Bronte Parrish	Andie MacDowell
Lauren	Bebe Neuwirth
Phil	Gregg Edelman
Bronte's lawyer	Robert Prosky
Mrs. Bird	Jessie Keosian
Gorsky	Ethan Phillips
Mrs. Sheehan	Mary Louise Wilson
Bronte's parents	Lois Smith, Conrad McLaren
Anton	Ronald Guttman
Oscar	Danny Dennis
Mr. Adler	Stephen Pearlman
Mrs. Adler	Victoria Boothby

Also with: Ann Wedgeworth, Stefan Schnabel, Anne Shropshire, Simon Jones.

Although a thin premise endangers its credibility at times, "Green Card" is a genial, nicely played romance that will please upscale urban audiences and could parlay its charm into wider playoff if marketing and word-of-mouth combine fortuitously.

Gérard Depardieu makes a winning major American film debut in the tailor-made role of a French alien who pairs up with New Yorker Andie MacDowell in a marriage of convenience in order to remain legally in the United States.

An Australian-French co-production shot in Gotham and completed Down Under, modest pic is essentially a two-character piece and looks to have been made on a very low budget, which translates into a decent gamble for Disney.

Writer-director-producer Peter Weir's plot, which is no more expansive than that of many an Off-Broadway play, is an inversion of the 1930s screwball comedies in which a divorcing couple spend the entire running time getting back together.

"Green Card" begins with Depardieu and MacDowell, who have scarcely been introduced, getting married, then charts the tricky weekend the two tempermental opposites spend getting to know each other in a hurry when faced with a government probe of their relationship.

Such a setup almost inevitably calls for a happy ending in which love triumphs over all manner of obstacles, but Weir skirts around the looming clichés with intelligence and stops short of any cloying sentimentality.

Trifle gets started in leisurely fashion, as the two go their separate ways after a perfunctory ceremony. Playing a socially conscious horticulturist who seems more comfortable around plants than people, MacDowell uses her new married status to land her dream apartment, complete with ornate greenhouse.

When the INS begins looking into the status of the marriage, MacDowell is forced to find Depardieu, whom she claims is a composer away in Africa doing research, and embark with him upon a crash course of mutual knowledge that will enable them to survive a thorough quiz by the authorities.

Elements that might look hokey on paper — he's a freewheeling bohemian, she's an uptight prude; he's a smoker and enthusiastic carnivore, she practically faints upon exposure to a cigarette or a piece of meat — go down easily because the two leads incorporate these attitudes believably into generally well-rounded characters.

Given the simple framework, behavioral niceties are crucial to the film's success, and the two actors provide many. Speaking hesitant but charming English, Depardieu, who acted in the language once before in Marco Ferreri's little-seen "Bye Bye Monkey" (1978), projects his usual charisma, and ideally personifies a man whose casualness and overbearing physicality could be offputting at first but ultimately carries the day against the forces of repression and denial embodied by MacDowell.

Latter's character is sometimes irritating in her unwillingness to compromise her earnest beliefs on behalf of the necessities of getting along with the Frenchman. After all, she's an equal partner in this ruse, and should be willing to shoulder some of the responsibilities.

But any realistic probing into the storyline would turn up other problems. If the INS were so intent on nailing Depardieu, for instance, it might check his passport to determine if he's really been to Africa.

Or, more centrally, why does MacDowell marry the man at all? Obtaining a nice apartment seems like a flimsy excuse for entering into a deceitful marriage. And why does she feel compelled to hide her action from even her closest female friend, as well as her family and so-called boyfriend? For comic and melodramatic reasons only.

But Weir choreographs the ostensible mismatch nicely, and the little tale becomes gradually sweeter and more engaging as it moves along toward its upbeat but restrained conclusion. Comic highlight comes during a dinner party at which Depardieu is obliged to show his stuff as an alleged avantgarde composer and pianist, a moment the actor puts over with tremendous brio.

For her part, MacDowell acts within a limited range between skittishness and exasperation, but does so with appealing flair, and late-blooms touchingly. Other performers, mostly N.Y. stage thesps, are in just briefly for telling sketch work.

To give this duet a little breathing room, Weir lets Manhattan provide all the local color it can, bringing in various ethnic sights and sounds appropriate to the subject. Tech contributions, as usual with the director, are solid, with special attention warranted by William Anderson's zippy editing. — *Cart.*

THE BONFIRE OF THE VANITIES

A Warner Bros. release. Produced and directed by Brian De Palma. Executive producers, Peter Guber, Jon Peters. Screenplay, Michael Cristofer, based on the novel by Tom Wolfe; camera (Technicolor), Vilmos Zsigmond; editor, David Ray, Bill Pankow; music, Dave Grusin; sound (Dolby), Les Lazarowitz, James Tanenbaum; production design, Richard Sylbert; art direction, Peter Lansdown Smith, Greg Bolton; set design, Richard Berger, Robert Maddy, Nick Navarro; set decoration, Joe Mitchell, Justin Scoppa; costume design, Ann Roth; coproducer, Fred Caruso; associate producer, Monica Goldstein; assistant director, Chris Soldo; casting, Lynn Stalmaster. Reviewed at the Warner screening room, N.Y., Dec. 13, 1990. MPAA Rating: R. Running time: **125 MIN.**

Sherman McCoy . . . . . . Tom Hanks
Peter Fallow . . . . Bruce Willis
Maria Ruskin . . . . . Melanie Griffith
Judy McCoy . . . . Kim Cattrall
Jed Kramer . . . . Saul Rubinek
Judge White . . . . . Morgan Freeman
Weiss . . . . . . F. Murray Abraham
Reverend Bacon . . . . . John Hancock
Tom Killian . . . . Kevin Dunn
Albert Fox . . . . Clifton James
Ray Andruitti . . . . Louis Giambalvo
Det. Martin . . . . . Barton Heyman
Det. Goldberg . . . . . Norman Parker
Mr. McCoy . . . . Donald Moffat
Arthur Ruskin . . . . Alan King
Also with: Beth Broderick, Kurt Fuller, Adam LeFevre, Richard Libertini, Andre Gregory, Rita Wilson.

Brian De Palma's take on Tom Wolfe's "The Bonfire Of The Vanities" is a misfire of inanities. A strained social farce in which the gap between intent and achievement is yawningly apparent, ultralavish production has the money cast and bestseller name value to pull an initial public, but downbeat reviews and word-of-mouth will surely prevent recoupment of WB's $45 million-plus ante.

One of the most famous books of recent years, Wolfe's first novel boasted rich characters and teeming incident that proved highly alluring to filmmakers. Unfortunately, De Palma was not the man for the job, as he constantly aims for broad comic effects that inevitably come off as labored and heavy-handed. It doesn't take long to turn off and tune out on this glitzy dud.

De Palma is on record as having been inspired in this instance by Stanley Kubrick's mordant satiric works "Lolita" and "Dr. Strangelove," and the influence is apparent in the exaggerated performances and wide, often distorted camera angles. But the approach just doesn't take, and fans of the book will come away disappointed.

Tireless in his search for spectacular shots, helmer comes up with two stunners to open the film. First is a time-lapse skyline vista picturing weather cascading over NYC until nightfall and bright lights arrive.

Second is five minutes of Steadicam virtuosity, beginning with a drunken Bruce Willis arriving by limo in an underground garage and continuing as he is escorted through corridors and into an enormous, glittering lobby filled with extras.

Dozens, if not hundreds, of people appear in the take, loaded with props, dialog and bits of business. As an eye-popping, if utterly gratuitous, example of technologically induced camera wizardry, it leaves the similar shot in "Goodfellas" in the dust.

But early sequences of marital discord between Wall Street maestro Sherman McCoy (Tom Hanks) and wife Judy (Kim Cattral) possess a grating, uncertain quality, and film never manages to locate a consistent tone.

The "Master of the Universe" due to his impeccable breeding, social standing and dizzying financial acumen, McCoy is having an affair with Southern bombshell Maria Ruskin (Melanie Griffith), and clearly stands as a symbol for Success, 1980s style. Monkeywrench arrives in the form of an automobile mishap one night in deepest Bronx.

Seemingly threatened by two black youths, Maria backs Sherman's Mercedes into one of them, slightly injuring him. The couple takes off, and while Sherman's conscience bothers him and they debate informing the police, they ultimately figure the incident can never catch up with them.

When the kid falls into a coma, the machinery of law, politics and journalism begins grinding, and soon traps Sherman. The rich man's status as one of society's privileged and allegedly untouchable figureheads makes him an ideal scapegoat for multifarious social ills, as well for as the personal agendas of the city's most shameless operators.

Among them are district attorney Weiss (an unbilled F. Murray Abraham), whose mayoral candidacy will be helped if he can "nail the WASP to the wall"; assistant d.a. Jed Kramer (Saul Rubinek), who can reverse a bumbling career with a conviction; Rev. Bacon (John Hancock), a politicized Harlem preacher who cries "racist" as quickly as the boy cried wolf, and, most prominently, Peter Fallow, a down-and-out alcoholic reporter who parlays the McCoy story into fame and fortune.

Once McCoy is arrested, his life turns into a media circus. At a black tie party that absurdly takes place at his home on the evening of his arraignment, he is informed that he is out of a job and a wife. Bereft, he decides he must turn the tables on his duplicitous mistress, whom he has protected up until now.

In the calamitous trial's aftermath, audience is treated to a sanctimonious sermon about the need for "decency" from the presiding judge (Morgan Freeman). As a commentary on greed and lack of caring in the decade just past, it's pretty feeble.

De Palma and screenwriter Michael Cristofer are attempting to expose the unthinking avariciousness of all the characters. Unfortunately, the caricatures are so crude and the "revelations" so unenlightening of the human condition, that the satire is about as socially incisive as a "Police Academy" entry.

All those onscreen are good actors, but are generally victims of miscasting and misguided trust in their director. Too young for the part as conceived by Wolfe, Hanks bears the burden of an uptight, unsympathetic character and appears stiff and strained most of the time.

The journalist Fallow slides through the story in a desensitized, bemused state, sometimes due to his inebriation and otherwise because he can barely believe his good luck in latching onto such a huge story. Willis has little trouble conveying this, but there is no depth required by the role, and none given.

Griffith is every inch the jet-set sexpot who could make many men lose their right minds, and her running malapropisms are lightly amusing. Also on the upside is John Hancock's dead-perfect impersonation of a self-righteous Rev. Al Sharpton type.

But in general, the people here are ugly and obnoxious, just as the film itself is arch and brittle. Visually, De Palma and lenser Vilmos Zsigmond pull every trick in the book and invent some new ones, but to deadening effect.

Undoubtedly with Kubrick and Welles in mind, they move the camera almost incessantly. When it remains stationary, compositions are generally in glaringly deep focus with lots of distortion.

Production opulence is evident in nearly every scene, with the film exposing and exemplifying an era of excess. "Bonfire" is a far cry from De Palma's start on New York streets with "Greetings" and "Hi, Mom!," which both could have been filmed on this pic's lunch budget. — *Cart.*

HAMLET

A Warner Bros. release of a WB and Nelson Entertainment presentation of an Icon production. Produced by Dyson Lovell. Executive producer, Bruce Davey. Directed by Franco Zeffirelli. Screenplay, Christopher De Vore, Zeffirelli, adapted from the play by William Shakespeare; camera (Rank Film Labs color), David Watkin; editor, Richard Marden; music, Ennio Morricone; sound (Dolby), David Stephenson; production design, Dante Ferretti; supervising art director, Michael Lamont; art direction, James Morahan, Franco Ceraolo, Antonio Tarolla, Alan Tomkins; set decoration, Francesca Lo Schiavo; costume design, Maurizio Millenotti; assistant director, Michael Murray; casting, Joyce Nettles. Reviewed at the Warner screen-

ing room, N.Y., Dec. 11, 1990. MPAA Rating: PG. Running time: **135 MIN.**
Hamlet . . . . Mel Gibson
Gertrude . . . . Glenn Close
Claudius . . . . Alan Bates
The Ghost . . . . Paul Scofield
Polonius . . . . Ian Holm
Ophelia . . . . Helena Bonham-Carter
Horatio . . . . Stephen Dillane
Laertes . . . . Nathaniel Parker
Guildenstern . . . . Sean Murray
Rosencrantz . . . . . Michael Maloney
The Gravedigger . . . Trevor Peacock
Osric . . . . John McEnery
Also with: Richard Warwick, Christien Anholt, Dave Duffy, Vernon Dobtcheff, Pete Postlethwaite, Christopher Fairbank.

In one of those artistic moves that popular actors sometimes make to confer ostensible seriousness upon themselves, Mel Gibson has taken on Shakespeare's most famous character after achieving stardom in the action arena. Unsurprisingly, his best moments come in the highly physical duelling scene that climaxes the play. Otherwise, Mel's Hamlet is blond, Franco Zeffirelli's "Hamlet" is bland and b.o. prospects are bad.

As can be expected from the director, the production is physically handsome and has a pleasing rambunctiousness to it. Although the performances from an illustrious cast are solid, an arresting interpretation, a *raison d'etre* to justify one more return to Elsinore, is lacking here.

Having brought Shakespeare to the masses so successfully with "Romeo And Juliet" 22 years ago and, to a lesser extent, with "The Taming Of The Shrew" before that, Zeffirelli seems to have been motivated by similar impulses this time out. By slicing the text virtually in half, down to a shade over two hours, and casting a matinee idol in the lead, the director clearly hoped to engage viewers who might otherwise never give the time of day and $7 to the Prince of Denmark.

Unfortunately, this Hamlet seems no more modern or pertinent to contemporary concerns than any other on stage, screen or tube in recent decades (and pales by comparison to Kevin Kline's recent outing). Nor does it possess the rugged freshness of the last Shakespearean film to draw a significant public, Kenneth Branagh's "Henry V."

Strategy of Zeffirelli and fellow adaptor Christopher De Vore has been to cut for plot with the idea of creating a tight dramatic flow. In the process, however, the immortal play has become a

jagged, deficiently nuanced drama lacking in depth or enveloping rhythm.

Familiar story unfolds in and around a formidable fortress that is actually a combination of three ancient structures in the British Isles. Deeply aggrieved by the death of his father, Hamlet is commanded by his father to avenge his murder at the hands of his brother Claudius, who has since become king and married Hamlet's mother, Gertrude.

This rendition's contributions to "Hamlet" lore are minor, but include a heavy eroticization of Gertrude's character. Not only is she mightily aroused by Claudius, but she indulges in incestuous tendencies in another direction by taking every opportunity to kiss her son fully, and sometimes lingeringly, on the lips.

Performances all fall in a middle range between the competent and the lackluster. Gibson gets the dialog and soliloquies out decently, but rolls and bugs his eyes a lot and tends to keep his mouth agape. It's not a bad or embarrassing job, just an uninteresting one that will neither excite his usual fans nor win plaudits from the highbrows.

Best is probably Paul Scofield as the ghost, although Zeffirelli irritatingly cuts or pulls away from him midstream. Alan Bates is a solid Claudius, nicely conveying the man's misguided belief in his own blamelessness, while Helena Bonham-Carter turns in a serviceable Ophelia.

Glenn Close brings a juicy vigor to Gertrude, but at times the actress verges on getting carried away with the histrionic opportunities. Nathaniel Parker is a spirited Laertes, and Trevor Peacock shines as the gravedigger, but Ian Holm, normally a most dependable actor, overdoes it as the ill-fated Polonius.

Working on a no doubt limited budget, production designer Dante Ferretti and costume designer Maurizio Millenotti have coordinated a look resplendent in earth tones with dashes of red. As photographed by David Watkin, picture looks great, even if the direction itself rides roughshod over subtleties and psychology. Ennio Morricone's score is one of his most atypical, as it backdrops the action in surprisingly conventional fashion.

Duelling scene was a highlight in Zeffirelli's "Romeo And Juliet," and so the climactic fight between Hamlet and Laertes is

here. Gibson seems to suddenly come alive upon being handed a sword, goofing off and fooling around in combat before becoming serious. Deaths of the leading characters come suddenly and shockingly, and helps send the film off with some power.

Nevertheless, this is a generally flat-footed production, an illustrated gloss on the full Shakespearean text. — *Cart.*

KINDERGARTEN COP

A Universal Pictures release. Produced by Ivan Reitman, Brian Grazer. Executive producers, Joe Medjuck, Michael C. Gross. Directed by Reitman. Screenplay, Murray Salem, Herschel Weingrod, Timothy Harris, based on a story by Salem; camera, Michael Chapman; editor, Sheldon Kahn, Wendy Bricmont; music, Randy Edelman; sound (Dolby), Gene S. Cantamessa; production design, Bruno Rubeo; costumes, Gloria Gresham; set design, Joseph B. Pacelli, Jr., Beverli Eagan, Larry Hubbs; assistant director, Peter Guilano; associate producers, Kahn, Gordon Webb; 2d unit director, Michael C. Gross; casting, Michael Chinich. Reviewed at the Directors Guild of America, L.A., Dec. 13, 1990. MPAA Rating: PG-13. Running time: **110 MIN.**
Kimble . . . . Arnold Schwarzenegger
Joyce . . . . Penelope Ann Miller
Phoebe . . . . Pamela Reed
Miss Schlowski . . . . . . Linda Hunt
Cullen Crisp . . . . Richard Tyson
Mrs. Crisp . . . . Carroll Baker
Dominic . . . . Joseph Cousins, Christian Cousins

Big, scary Arnold Schwarzenegger playing an uptight cop in a classroom full of chaotic kindergartners who want to run him over: Is that funny or what? Hardly ever, even with Ivan Reitman ("Twins," "Ghostbusters") at the helm. Therein lies the end of MCA's hopes for a big Christmas.

With the bright (if disappointing) concept going for it and Universal's typically savvy mainstream marketing campaign at work, pic should attract flocks of family filmgoers in the initial weeks, but b.o. will likely dry up same time Christmas trees do.

The polished comic vision that gave "Twins," Schwarzenegger's comedy breakthrough, a storybook shine completely eludes Reitman here. Result is a mishmash of violence, pyschodrama and lukewarm kiddie comedy that stands to gain nothing from word of mouth.

Problem is this isn't a kid's-eye-view story, as audiences might expect. It's an adult world story shot through with violence and the pain of sick or broken families. Pic's PG-13 rating is a clue that it's not exactly child's fare.

Schwarzenegger plays a stoic, unfriendly and ultradedicated L.A. cop obsessed with putting away a murderous drug dealer (Richard Tyson). He needs the testimony of Tyson's ex-wife, who's supposedly living in Oregon on piles of drug money she stole from Tyson.

Cock-eyed premise has Schwarzenegger going off to Oregon with his only lead to the wife being the name of the school her son attends.

Plan is for Schwarzenegger's goofy gal-pal partner (Pamela Reed) to infiltrate the kindergarten as a teacher and figure out which kid is Tyson's, but when Reed gets a bad stomach flu Schwarzenegger has to report for the job.

It's supposed to be wildly funny to have this grim, musclebound control freak confronted with 5-year-olds he can't intimidate, but it isn't. Reitman and pic's passel of scripters (including "Twins" scribes Herschel Weingrod and Timothy Harris) don't get inside the kids.

The moppets are not mean or devious, just clumsy, disorganized and a little dumb. Result is a bland pairing, and though Schwarzenegger struggles to put some life into the role, it's one of his least effective.

Unlike in "Twins," where he played his slow sweetness off the manic, despicable Danny DeVito, here Schwarzenegger has to carry the pic alone. He never finds his focus.

Neither does Reitman, who veers away from comedy into disturbingly graphic scenes of violence and psychosis. Pic's climax involves a bloody shootout at the school, while would-be kidnapper Tyson, who's just set the place on fire, begs for his son's trust.

Along with a scene where Schwarzenegger roughs up a child abuser, pic has a lot of ugliness that audiences probably aren't bargaining for, and it makes one wonder who it's aimed at.

The picture's undercurrent of sadness about the epidemic of broken families might have had substance in another, more serious film. Here, it's just a miscalculation.

There's plenty of cute kid stuff as Schwarzenegger marches his charges around the schoolyard like a drill sergeant, but, unlike in current boxoffice pacesetter "Home Alone," the scenes lack inspiration.

Reed takes a good, feisty stab at holding up her corner of the pic as Schwarzenegger's food-obsessed and lovewise partner, and Penelope Ann Miller is fittingly sweet and vulnerable as the single mother who romances Schwarzenegger, but Schwarzenegger's still pretty much on his own.

Location lensing in Astoria, northwest Oregon, with views of the Columbia River, gives pic's smalltown scenes a refreshing look, but Randy Edelman's bland but obtrusive score is obnoxiously manipulative. — *Daws.*

CORPORATE AFFAIRS

A Concorde-New Horizons release. Produced by Julie Corman. Directed by Terence H. Winkless. Screenplay, Winkless, Geoffrey Baere; camera, Ricardo Jacques Gale; editor, Karen Horn; music, Jeff Winkless; sound, Bill Robbins, D.J. Richie; art direction, Johan LeTenoux; assistant director, Gregory Stone; casting, Steve Rabiner. Reviewed at Cinetex '90, Las Vegas, Sept. 9, 1990. No MPAA rating. Running time: **85 MIN.**
Tanner . . . . Peter Scolari
Jessica . . . . Mary Crosby
Ginny . . . . Kim Gillingham
Strickland . . . . Ken Kercheval
Doug . . . . Chris Lemmon
Carolyn . . . . Lisa Moncure
Peter . . . . Charlie Stratton
Kindred . . . . Richard Herd
Buster . . . . Frank Roman
Astrid . . . . Sharon McNight
Sandy . . . . Jeanne Sal
Darren . . . . Bryan Cranston

This super-softcore "Corporate Affairs" should not be confused with the hardcore release with the same title a few years back. For one thing, the porno pic was much better acted and certainly made more sense.

Filmmakers who aim no higher than to concoct an elaborate excuse to stage a wild party scene should never attempt to use the world of high finance as a backdrop. Inevitably, this will require performers to explain the plot at least once or twice, requiring dialog that stretches to three sentences or more. This is not a task the cast of "Corporate Affairs" is prepared for.

When that glazed look passes over the faces of otherwise capable performers like Peter Scolari, Mary Crosby, Chris Lemmon, Ken Kercheval and Richard Herd, there's a hint they're just doing their best to get the lines out without having to hang around for a second take.

It makes no difference, of course, since in films like this those who keep their clothes on are just there to provide a reason for others to take their clothes off.

As the pages of the script pass mindlessly through the actors' heads to their microphones, the stars are also filmed by director Terence H. Winkless scurrying about the office in confusion over whether Kercheval is dead and whether they killed him.

If nothing else, this device provides a constant excuse to encounter various participants in the orgy going on throughout the premises.

Why an orgy is going on throughout the premises is not necessary for the audience to know or understand. Even worse, given the mild titillation aimed for, it's a very bad orgy. — *Har.*

INSTANT KARMA

An MGM release of a Rosenbloom Entertainment presentation of a Desert Wind Films production. Produced by Dale Rosenbloom, Bruce A. Taylor, George Edwards. Executive producers, Steven J. Bratter, Craig Sheffer. Directed by Roderick Taylor. Screenplay, Taylor, Rosenbloom; camera (CFI color), Thomas Jewitt; editor, Frank Mazzola; music, Joel Goldsmith; sound, Mary Jo Devenney; production design, Edwards, Michele Seffman; assistant director, Jeffrey B. Mallian; casting, Barbara Remsen, Ann Remsen Manners. Reviewed at Filmland screening room, Culver City, Calif., Dec. 3, 1990. MPAA Rating: R. Running time: **95 MIN.**
Zane . . . . Craig Sheffer
Penelope . . . . Chelsea Noble
Reno . . . . David Cassidy
David . . . . Glenn Hirsch
Jerry . . . . James Gallery
Oscar Meyer . . . . . Alan Blumenfeld
Pop . . . . William Smith
Dr. Berlin . . . . Orson Bean

"Instant Karma," a gleeful parody of life in the tv production grind, should win a few admirers in the trade, but narrow focus and quick disintegration will deter filmgoers. Playoff will be fleeting.

Craig Sheffer, also one of film's exec producers, plays the young writer-producer of a tv cop show called "Rock 'N' Roll P.I." He looks successful but is really lonely and miserable.

Standup comic Glenn Hirsch plays the cynical writing partner who can't understand Sheffer's maladies. Chelsea Noble plays the luscious blond actress who shows him the way out of his doldrums with positive vibes.

David Cassidy is perfect as the arrogant star of the "P.I." show, in which he plays a cop by day, rock 'n' roller by night, partnered on motorcycles with his dad (William Smith), the veteran cop who adopted him.

Created by young veterans of the industry's inside grind, "Instant Karma" has a deliciously wicked edge when depicting the self-deluding ways and wiles of the well-paid denizens of hack television, but pic goes soft when dealing with life issues.

Sheffer's search for an escape from a life he despises is resolved as facilely as it would have been on one of the shows this pic parodies. The writing disintegrates and so do the visuals, with romantic montages and dream scenes among the offenses.

First-time feature director Roderick Taylor sustains a nice tongue-in-cheek tone as long as pic is grounded in real settings but loses it when things enter a fantasy realm. Unreal black backdrop for Sheffer's sessions with his therapist (Orson Bean) is a misstep.

Though it doesn't add up overall, the picture has some choice lines of dialog and flashes of humor, including an offbeat scene at Venice Beach in which a homeless lunatic offers to marry Sheffer and Nobel. Tech credits are mostly fine, with a few uneven patches. — *Daws.*

GENUINE RISK

An IRS release. Produced by Larry J. Rattner, Guy J. Louthan, William Ewart. Executive producers, Miles A. Copeland III, Paul Colichman. Written and directed by Kurt Voss. Camera (color), Dean Lent; editor, Christopher Koefoed; music, Deborah Holland; production design, Elisabeth A. Scott; costumes, Angela Balogh-Calin; art direction, Christopher Neely; casting, Don Pemrick, Jeff Gerrard. Reviewed at Raleigh Studios, Hollywood, Nov. 20, 1990. MPAA Rating: R. Running time: **89 MIN.**
Hellwart . . . . Terence Stamp
Henry . . . . Peter Berg
Girl . . . . Michelle Johnson
Cowboy Jack . . . . M.K. Harris
Chris . . . . Max Perlich
Billy . . . . Teddy Wilson
Curly . . . . Sid Haig

Genuine Risk" is for the pic's backers, who took an ill-advised gamble, as pic (recently opened in L.A.) is unlikely to run more than once around the seven-day theatrical track.

Filmmaker Kurt Voss continues his downhill slump from "Border Radio" with this lazily uninspired and derivative scenario of an unlucky horseplayer who gets sucked into two-bit crimes.

Resemblance to his second film, "The Horseplayer," acquired by Greycat Entertainment but still unreleased in the U.S., illustrates the limited range flattening this effort. Peter Berg plays a young downward-spiral type who turns to debt-collecting for a racketeer (Terence Stamp) after a run of sour luck at the track.

M.K. Harris is the self-styled operator who tries to control Henry. There's also a girl (Michelle Johnson), who slides into Berg's apartment and turns out to be working for Stamp.

Voss, who has a thing about low-life milieus, seems to want to do a film noir about the loser but displays no first-hand insight into the world he's depicting. He should check out "The Grifters." Direction veers aimlessly out of control. A bungled hit on some crooked bookies turns into lame farce, much to the detriment of actor Harris, whose one-note cardboard shark routine collapses when he tries to be either wild or funny.

Later, pic rambles off onto a losers on the lam path, as Berg and the increasingly "comical" Harris head into the desert. It doesn't take binoculars to see where this cliché-ridden film is headed, and, with characters as empty as these, it's an aimless ride.

Berg, a puppyish Tom Cruise lookalike whose appearance and screen presence bespeak future roles, apparently got no good direction from Voss, who let him drag along a heavy-handed Mickey Rourke imitation.

Harris is getting better at the low-life predator character he did in "The Horseplayer," but the thin role gets way too much screen time here.

Voss' talented cinematographer, Dean Lent, is back at work, adding extra depth and interest to the frames, but the effort falls by the wayside in such a listless tale. — *Daws.*

LE MARI DE LA COIFFEUSE
(THE HAIRDRESSER'S HUSBAND)
(FRENCH)

A Lambart Prods.-TF1 Films production. (Intl. sales: President Films, Paris.) Executive producer, Monique Guerrier. Produced by Thierry de Ganay. Directed by Patrice Leconte. Screenplay, Leconte, Claude Kotz; camera (color), Edouardo Serra; editor, Joelle Hache; music, Mikael Nyman; sound, Pierre Lenoir; art direction, Yvan Maussion. Reviewed at Toronto Festival of Festivals, Sept. 14, 1990. Running time: **90 MIN.**
Anthony . . . . .Jean Rochefort
Matilda . . . . Ana Galiena
Also with: Henri Hocking, Maurice Cehvit, Roland Bertin, Philippe Clevenot, Ticky Holgado.

"The Hairdresser's Husband," another of director Patrice Leconte's original, hypnotic efforts about sexual longing and romantic obsession, is certain to find a welcome arthouse run.

Delicate and stylish, it's the story of a man who fulfills his childhood dream of marrying a lady hairdresser. Intercut childhood scenes depict a 12-year-old with an aching crush on a plump hairdresser whose breast he spies through her clothes. Days later he finds her dead on the shop floor from a barbituate overdose.

At age 50, still transfixed by her and by wildly dancing to Arabic music, he wanders into a barbershop and immediately proposes to its lovely owner, who accepts as quickly.

Both are loners. They live above the shop, which he, apparently jobless, inhabits all day while she works. In a madcap scene they get drunk on cologne and shaving lotion.

Passionately in love, the lady barber frequently questions how long love will last. After 10 years, she drowns herself while the romance remains in full bloom because she fears it might die as they age. Left alone in the shop, the man is taught proper steps to the Arabic music by a customer.

Jean Rochefort is outstanding as the man obsessed. Ana Galiena, who has a beautiful model-type presence, is a dream come true as his lovely wife whose past never gets revealed.

Excellent script by Leconte and Claude Kotz leaves many details unexplained, such as Rochefort's adult background. But in this case, that just heightens the pic's dramatic punch. — *Adil.*

LIFE IS SWEET
(BRITISH)

A Thin Man Films production. Produced by Simon Channing-Williams. Written and directed by Mike Leigh. Camera (color), Dick Pope; editor, John Gregory; music, Rachel Portman; sound, Malcolm Hirst; production design, Alison Chitty; art direction, Sophie Becher; assistant director, Gus Maclean; costume design, Lindy Hemming. Reviewed at 34th London Film Festival, Nov. 15, 1990. Running time: **102 MIN.**
Wendy . . . . Alison Steadman
Andy . . . . Jim Broadbent
Aubrey . . . . Timothy Spall
Natalie . . . . Claire Skinner
Nicola . . . . Jane Horrocks
Nicola's lover . . . . . David Thewlis
Paula . . . . Moya Brady
Patsy . . . . Stephen Rea
Steve . . . . David Neilson
Nigel . . . . Jack Thorpe Baker

Few recent low-budget British films have better fest and arthouse prospects than "Life Is Sweet," Mike Leigh's third pic after "Bleak Moments" and "High Hopes." This highly sympathetic comedy, embroidered by a superb performance from helmer's wife Alison Steadman, is perhaps the most universal of the three, though still wholly British in tone.

Steadman, one of Britain's finest actresses, is ideally cast as a suburban housewife and mother who sells baby clothes, supports her husband (Jim Broadbent), and attempts to look after her twin teen daughters (one a plumber, the other an anorexic rebel).

She is the heart and soul of the family which, without her, might fall apart. She still finds time to help a friend (Tim Spall) open a new restaurant, acting as a waitress on his disastrous opening night when nobody comes.

Her husband falls at work, arriving home in plaster. Her rebel daughter veers towards breakdown, and almost everything that could go wrong does. But she is a survivor, who helps others survive too.

That's the moral of the comedy, which is made funnier and, in the end, more moving because of its serious core. Her final encounter with her difficult daughter, which gives the unhappy girl new hope, is perhaps the pic's fulcrum.

As a precise observation of British types and a virtuoso piece of carefully observed ensemble playing, the film would be hard to beat. With Steadman in the lead, "Life Is Sweet" seems certain to gather awards.

Production values are good, if not lavish, and Leigh's direction is enhanced by Dick Pope's color photography and by production design that scarcely misses a trick. Although the film is well set within a certain class and setting, its appeal should be wider.

Few comedies have as much truth in them, and few directors have Leigh's capacity to provoke laughter and thought at the same time. It is difficult to imagine any audience disliking or being bored by this pic. — *Malc.*

WERNER—BEINHART
(GERMAN)

A Neue Constantin Film release. Produced by Bernd Eichinger. Live action segments directed by Niki List. Animation segments directed by Gerhard Hahn, Michael Schaack. Screenplay, Ernst Kahl based on a character created by Rötger Feldmann; camera (color), Egon Werdin; editor, Ingrid Koller; music, Jörg Evers; sound, Frank Jahn. Reviewed at Kino Center Cinema in Hamburg, Germany, Dec. 8, 1990. Running time: **85 MIN.**
Brösel . . . . Rötger Feldmann
Pastor Amen . . . . . . .Ludger Pistor
Rumpelstiltskin . . . . . Meret Becker

"Werner – Beinhart," an ambitious mixture of animation and live action in the "Roger Rabbit" tradition, promises boffo biz at German hardtops if only because of the lack of German-made animated features. Offshore prospects are dimmed by the pic's focus on a comic book figure popular in Germany in the 1980s but unknown elsewhere.

Setting and humor are strictly regional in nature, and even folks in the German-lingo market could have a hard time understanding some of the northern German coastal dialect.

Live action is helmed by Austrian wunderkind Niki List, whose "Müller's Büro" proved a boxoffice hit with laugh-hungry German audiences in 1986. He is a master of the belch-and-barf brand of humor, mainstay of this picture.

"Werner" is an inarticulate inner-city layabout whose chief occupation is to outwit traffic cops as he roars along the autobahn on his souped-up motorcycle in search of the next case of beer.

He is the antithesis of the stereotypical German workaholic and, as such, is a cult hero among young Germans who bought millions of "Werner" comics, calendars, plastic figures and other merchandising items over the past decade.

This pic has nothing new to offer, but Werner fans will hoot and howl just the same. Animation is adequate and in keeping with the sparse style of the original comics, most of which were published without color. — *Gill.*

DING ET DONG: LE FILM
(DING AND DONG: THE FILM)
(CANADIAN)

A Max Films presentation of a Max Films production. Produced by Roger Frappier. Executive producer, Frappier, Pierre Gendron. Directed by Alain Chartrand. Screenplay, Claude Meunier; camera (color), Karol Ike; editor, Francois Gill; music, Jean-Marie Benoit, Yves Lapierre; sound, Dominique Chartrand, Marcel Pothier; production direction, Richard Lalonde; art direction, Louise Jobin; costume design, Suzanne Harel; associate producer, Suzanne Dussault; casting, Lucie Robitaille. Reviewed at the Cineplex Odeon Cinema Dauphin, Dec. 7, 1990. Running time: **90 MIN.**
Ding . . . . Serge Theriault
Dong . . . . Claude Meunier
Guetan . . . . . . Raymond Bouchard
Sarah . . . . Sophie Faucher
Jipi . . . . Yves Jacques
Leboeuf . . . . Denis Bouchard

"**D**ing And Dong: The Film" marks the eighth anni of a standup duo who are virtually household names in Quebec. But this quasi "behind-the-scenes" film about two raving imbeciles will never travel beyond provincial borders.

Making Quebec slang close to incomprehensible, pic would need subtitles in other French territories, but titles would ultimately render the jokes meaningless.

Comedy that plays on language simply does not translate, and this is a prime example. In English it would be hopeless. Serge Theriault and Claude Meunier are in character as Ding and Dong during the entire pic, a problem for a supposed "behind-the-scenes" structure.

Their calamities begin in a shabby apartment with D&D waiting for work to arrive via the phone, which it does. Hired to do a show in a seedy club in a rural town, the act is a disaster when a fight breaks out in the audience.

For the first hour of the film, the two hapless comedians bumble through one catastrophic situation after another, trying to

make ends meet. Strung together like a series of standup shows, pic lacks continuity.

They eventually inherit $30 million (Canadian, unfortunately, per their lawyer) and buy their own stage, Theatre De La Nouvelle Tragedie (Theater of New Tragedy). This is when the film picks up.

They happily massacre classic plays, scenes which deftly capture the duo's idiotic nature, and reaffirm that their natural place is on stage, not celluloid.

Pic is a radical departure for producer Roger Frappier ("Jesus Of Montreal") and a big step for helmer Alain Chartrand, assistant director on over 20 films including "Les Ordres."

Tech credits are fine, except for a troubled soundtrack, which is a problem in a film with wall-to-wall slang. Quebeckers will no doubt be forgiving during the holiday season. — *Suze.*

ALISSA IN CONCERT
(DUTCH-B&W)

A Melior Films release of an Allarts, Kees Kasander, Denis Wigman production. Written and directed by Erik van Zuylen. Camera (black & white), Alejandro Agresti; editor, Lin Friedman; music, Frances-Marie Uitti; sound, Erik Langhout, Jan van Sandwijk; art direction, Jan Roelfs, Ben van Os. Reviewed at the Movies, Amsterdam, Sept. 4, 1990. Running time: **75 MIN.**
With: Frances-Marie Uitti, Michael Matthews, Pim Lambeau, Johan Leysen.

Backed by a dedicated and experienced cast and an extraordinary crew, Erik van Zuylen has made "Alissa In Concert" an absorbing exercise in cinema. It should grace fests and arthouses worldwide.

In the faint outline of a story, Alissa searches everywhere, even in the hereafter, for her lover, Justice, who may have just left or he may have died. Alissa, a concert cellist who always carries her instrument with her, is played by Frances Marie Uitti, a w.k. cellist raised in the U.S. and living in the Netherlands. She also wrote and played the music.

Harlem, N.Y.-born Michael Matthews, who now lives in Haarlem, Holland, plays Justice as someone who wants no stress and no problems. He plays four small parts as well.

Belgian actor Johan Leysen plays three bit parts most efficiently; his compatriot Pim Lambeau, two larger ones.

Alejandro Agrestis' camera gracefully crosses the border between ordinariness and fantasy, between tragedy and stylized farce. South African-born Lin Friedman's editing and Jan Roelfs and Ben van Os' ("The Cook, The Thief, His Wife, Her Lover") art direction add flair.

Uitti's original music serves as captivating leitmotif, but the ultimate credit is due van Zuylen. His virtuoso rhythm changes are as exciting as his transformation of a "Brief Encounter" into an act of fate.
— *Wall.*

THE AMBULANCE

A Triumph Films release of an Epic Prods. and Sarlui/Diamant presentation of an Esparza/Katz production. Produced by Moctesuma Esparza, Robert Katz. Written and directed by Larry Cohen. Camera (color), Jacques Haitkin; editor, Armond Lebowitz, Claudia Finkle; music, Jay Chattaway; production design, Lester Cohen; costume design, Sylvia Vega-Vasquez; production manager, Chris Bright; assistant director, Ken Ornstein; stunt coordinator, Spiro Razatos; special makeup effects, Rob Benevides; associate producer, Barbara Zitwer. Reviewed at Broadway screening room, N.Y., Dec. 27, 1990. MPAA Rating: R. Running time: **95 MIN.**
Josh Baker . . . . Eric Roberts
Lt. Spencer . . . . . .James Earl Jones
Elias . . . . Red Buttons
Sandy Malloy . . . . . Megan Gallagher
Cheryl . . . . Janine Turner
Doctor . . . . Eric Braeden
Jerilyn . . . . Jill Gatsby
Detective . . . . Richard Bright
Also with: Stan Lee, Nicholas Chinlund, Jim Dixon, Laurene Landon, Jacqueline Webb.

"**T**he Ambulance" is a wild thriller laced with black humor. Entertaining exercise in urban paranoia will be shown at the Avoriaz fantasy film fest in France and gives Triumph Films a genuine sleeper for 1991 domestic release.

As with his recent "Maniac Cop" horror pics, filmmaker Larry Cohen works with the inversion principle: taking a symbol of rescue, a vintage red ambulance, and making its appearance and siren fearful. Here he tilts the balance toward humor, though hair-raising stunts and sudden moments of violence teem.

Eric Roberts introduces the film as sort of a day in the life of James Toback ("The Pick-Up Artist" helmer). In telephoto shots on Manhattan streets (apparently using real-life people as extras), he tries to pick up beautiful Janine Turner.

As she valiantly gives him the brush-off, she suddenly faints, and a sinister ambulance, controlled by heavy Eric Braeden, whisks the diabetic girl to a hospital. After work, Roberts tries to find her and, as the film's shooting title suggested, she's vanished "Into Thin Air."

With fast repartee and a gallery of quirky characters spurring the tale along, Roberts continues his search but finds little help from disbelieving police inspector James Earl Jones. His paranoia increases by quantum leaps as mad scientist Braeden's henchmen start eliminating people around him and give Roberts a frightening ambulance ride.

Help finally surfaces in unlikely sidekick Red Buttons, an aging N.Y. Post reporter Roberts rooms with at the hospital. Jones' pretty assistant on the force, Megan Gallagher, is another kindred spirit leading to an exciting climax at a downtown dance club where Braeden keeps his kidnap victims upstairs as medical experiments.

With unpredictable plot twists coming fast and furious, this fresh approach to the thriller format is especially of interest to genre fans. Real-life Marvel Comics exec Stan Lee has a nice guest role playing himself as Roberts' boss, and the comic book backdrop is used effectively as Roberts draws large panels of Turner and the ambulance to aid his investigation.

Cohen puts a sting in this tale with a delightful false ending that trumps the "Carrie" finish tacked onto nearly every horror film of recent vintage.

Reteamed here with Jones shortly after they filmed "Best Of The Best" two years ago, Roberts is perfectly cast. His familiar abrasiveness ("Star 80," "The Pope Of Greenwich Village") is used to good advantage.

Jones is a hoot as the gum-chewing cop whose know-it-all attitude gets him in trouble. Buttons steals his scenes in his best film assignment since "The Poseidon Adventure."

Following up on her tv policewoman duty on the defunct series "Hill Street Blues," Gallagher is a bigscreen find as the tough cop who believes in Roberts. Turner, adopting a different look with long, dark hair here, develops considerable sympathy in her brief assignment. Supporting cast is solid, including Richard Bright (of "The Godfather Part III") as a no-nonsense cop and Braeden, inverting his messianic scientist role of Dr. Forbin, memorable to genre fans in the classic "Colossus: The Forbin Project."

Tech credits exploit the NYC terrain well, especially Spiro Razatos' unusual chases and stuntwork. — *Lor.*

THE FOOL
(BRITISH)

A Sands Films-Film Four Intl.-British Screen-John Tyler presentation of a Sands Films production. Produced by Richard Goodwin, Christine Edzard. Directed by Edzard. Screenplay, Edzard, Olivier Stockman, from interviews in "London Labour & The London Pour" (1851) by Henry Mayhew; camera (Technicolor), Robin Vidgeon; editor, Stockman; music, Michel Sanvoisin; sound (Dolby), Paul Carr, Brian Paxton; production design, Sands Films. Reviewed at Museum of London, Dec. 14, 1990. Running time: **135 MIN.**

Sir John/Mr. Frederick	Derek Jacobi
The ballad seller	Cyril Cusack
The girl	Ruth Mitchell
Lord Paramount	Paul Brooke
Sir Thomas	Corin Redgrave
The marquess	Alec Wallis
Sir Martin Locket	Jonathan Cecil
Mr. Blackthorn	Jim Carter
Mr. Maclean	John McEnery
Mr. Simkins	Frederick Treves
The blind man	Don Henderson
Mr. Tatham	Michael Hordern

Also with: Maria Aitken, Irina Brook, James Cosmo, Rosalie Crutchley.

Three years after their marathon, "Little Dorrit," husband-and-wife producers Richard Goodwin and Christine Edzard tread the same streets and salons to lesser effect in "The Fool." Pic's look and casting are suited for specialized dates, while flat helming and Dickens-less script add up to small expectations for more general b.o.

In 1857, an obscure theater clerk (Derek Jacobi) engineers a financial scam to show up the monied classes. Problems start when, posing as the carefree Sir John, he's recognized by some theater folk, and he starts taking his alter ego too seriously.

Later scenes, with their "Wall Street" lingo and Jacobi's crisis of conscience, are an obvious allegory of the me-too 1980s. But there're a long time coming, and the thrill of the paper chase is lacking.

Without a strong central yarn like Dickens' "Dorrit," pic becomes a series of one-off routines by w.k. Brit thesps.

First real conflict is some 90 minutes in when a girl (Ruth Mitchell) tells Jacobi he's turning into the kind he most despises. He gives her a five-minute monolog that would be fine in legit theater. Pic climaxes with showy scenes of his two characters clashing and a society bash where he berates his "victims" holding his £1 million pile in a brown paper package.

Helmer and co-scripter Edzard shows off her research and topnotch design with street characters based on interviews by 19th century social journalist Henry Mayhew. They're fine on their own terms, right down to the dirt under their fingernails, but Edzard needs to make up her mind whether she's building a museum or making a movie.

Thesping throughout is reliable. Jacobi's campy clerk and urbane pretender carry the pic in style. Cyril Cusack is genial as the ballad seller, Mitchell firm as the girl, Paul Brooke oily as the chief mark and Alec Wallis smooth as a sickly marquis. John McEnery struts his stuff as a Victorian thespian.

Robin Vidgeon's okay lensing has a natural-light look, and co-scripter Olivier Stockman's restless editing makes up for the static, tv-style camerawork. Pic could have benefited from more of Michel Sanvoisin's 19th century music.

In print caught, dialog was badly out of synch in many sequences in the latter half. Like "Dorrit," pic was lensed at the producers' Thames-side studio in Rotherhithe in 17 weeks (as opposed to nine months for "Dorrit"). — *Drek.*

WAITING
(AUSTRALIAN)

A Ronin Films release (Australia and New Zealand) of a Filmside production for the Australian Broadcasting Corp., in association with Film Four Intl. Executive producer, Penny Chapman. Produced by Ross Matthews. Written and directed by Jackie McKimmie. Camera (color), Steve Mason; editor, Mike Honey; sound, Nick Wood; production design, Murray Picknett; associate producer, Wayne Barry; production manager, Carol Chirlian; assistant director, Tony Tilse; casting, Liz Mullinar. Reviewed at Walker Street Cinema, North Sydney, Dec. 21, 1990. Running time: **90 MIN.**

Clare	Noni Hazlehurst
Diane	Deborra-Lee Furness
Michael	Frank Whitten
Sandy	Helen Jones
Therese	Fiona Press
Frank	Ray Barrett
Bill	Denis Moore

"Waiting," a warmhearted and likable film with a strong feminist theme, should do modest-to-good business on the international arthouse circuit. Festival exposure also is indicated.

Writer-director Jackie McKimmie's second feature (after "Australian Dream") also toplines Noni Hazlehurst as a surrogate mother awaiting delivery of her child in an isolated farmhouse surrounded by girlfriends and various hangers-on.

McKimmie explores familiar but pertinent points about pregnancy, the medical profession and postfeminism. Dramatic comedy opens charmingly with a scene of a woman swimming naked in a country river. She emerges from the water to reveal she's nine months pregnant.

Hazlehurst was game to agree to appear in this and other swimming scenes later in the film, and her beauty and unselfconsciousness are appealing. Her friends are a good cross-section of the post-'60s generation.

Helen Jones, playing the woman for whom Hazlehurst's baby is intended, is married to Frank Whitten, who had sex with Hazlehurst to father the child. Jones can't have children of her own and has two adopted boys, one Asian, one aboriginal.

Whitten is an academic who combines causes (he's currently on a fast and looks very skinny) with womanizing; the marriage is going through a bad phase.

Fiona Press, as an overweight single mother and radical filmmaker, has a poster over her workbench proclaiming "Dead Men Don't Rape." She's making a film attacking doctors for their attitude toward women, and Hazlehurst's natural birth is to be the film's conclusion.

A smart, elegant fashion magazine editor (Deborra Lee Furness, the lead from "Shame") differs from the others. Just back from Europe, she has her latest man (Denis Moore) in tow. Hazlehurst herself is an artist who plans to leave for Paris after the baby is born. She misses her ex-lover, who might also be the baby's father.

The friends talk and drink and smoke as they await the birth. They also discover that Whitten has slept with Furness and Jones knows about it, and, eventually, that Hazlehurst is having second thoughts about giving up her baby. Pic's mood is gently amusing, but thinking audiences, especially women, should get a lot out of these human characters.

The dialog could have been sharper and wittier, but the film works as a slice of comic realism, not as a fictional confection. Performances are good down the line, with the four women especially notable. Fun, too, is Ray Barrett, a local farmer full of dire predictions and tall stories. He plays a major role in the birth.

Technically, "Waiting" is fine. Though tending to glide the camera across the outside walls of the farmhouse once too often, Steve Mason's attractive camerawork is a big step up from his work on "Luigi's Ladies." Exterior vistas are beautiful, but not the sundrenched Australia most people know. It seems to be raining most of the time.

Pic should find appreciative audiences happy to accept its calm mood and flashes of quiet humor. — *Strat.*

LAS EDADES DE LULÚ
(THE AGES OF LULU)
(SPANISH)

An Iberoamericana Films and Apricot co-production. Produced by Andrés Vicente Gómez. Directed by Bigas Luna. Screenplay, Luna, Almudena Grandes, based on novel by Grandes; camera (Eastmancolor), Fernando Arribas; editor, Pablo G. del Amo; music, Carlos Segarra; sound, Goldstein and Steinberg S.A.; line producer, José G. Lacoste; production manager, Rafael Fernández; sets, Miguel Chicharro; costume design, Antonio Alvarado; associate producer, Santiago Ganuza. Reviewed at Cine Proyecciones, Madrid, Dec. 6, 1990. Running time: **99 MIN.**
Lulu . . . . Francesca Neri
Pablo . . . . Oscar Ladoire
Ely . . . . Maria Barranco
Marcelo . . . . Fernando Guillén
Also with: Rosana Pastor, Javier Bardem, J.A. Navarro.

The pre-opening word-of-mouth that "The Ages Of Lulu" would prove the year's erotic Spanish bombshell has been borne out after thesp Angela Molina's much-publicized refusal to do the lead. Item could rack up nifty bucks, but playoffs will be sharply limited by the X rating pic surely will be given. It may be banned altogether in some countries.

Almost from the opening to the closing frame, "Lulu" consists of a virtually uninterrupted succession of potent erotic imagery running the gamut of sexual variations, including sadomasochism, voyeurism, multiple sex with gays, masturbation, transvestites and a long etc.

Though presented as a first-person confession (in an offscreen voice), pic doesn't have much of a story. The few dialogs that do crop up are stilted and unconvincing. Story starts with Lulu as an adolescent. She meets a mature friend of her brother's who one day takes her to a rock concert.

After the show, in Pablo's car, the friend initiates Lulu into oral sex. Speedily following are other variations. Some time later, after Pablo, who is a professor, returns from the States, the two get hitched, and Lulu even has a baby girl between sex scenes.

Ultimately tired of her life with Pablo (though no convincing reason is given why), she leaves home and starts to hang out in shady bars where she seeks offbeat sex thrills. All are explicitly chronicled.

Pic is well-lensed, mostly in interiors. Oscar Ladoire, often cast in comic parts, is his usual deadpan self. Italo thesp Francesca Neri makes an alluring Lulu, though the part doesn't call for any thesping ability.

Bigas Luna's direction is suitably kinky, with plenty of anatomical closeups. — *Besa.*

SMALL TIME
(B&W)

A Norman Loftis production (Intl. sales, Grokenberger Film, N.Y., Munich). Written and directed by Loftis. Camera (black & white), Michael C. Miller; editor, Marc Cohen, Loftis; music, Arnold Bieber; sound, Phillipe Saint-Gilles; art director, Nancy Evangelista. Reviewed at the Toronto Festival of Festivals, Sept. 8, 1990. No MPAA Rating. Running time: **88 MIN.**
Vince Williams . . . . Richard Barboza
Vicki . . . . Carolyn Kinebrew
Also with: Scott Ferguson, Keith Allen, Jane Williams.

With public outrage over urban crime at a fever pitch, Norman Loftis' unadorned portrait of a Harlem street thug is undeniably relevant. "Small Time" is too rough for commercial tastes, but could appeal to foreign tv buyers' fascination with the underside of U.S. life.

Uneasily straddling a fine line between apology and case study, Loftis frames the narrative as the confessional reflections of small time mugger Vince (Richard Barboza). Plaintively addressing the audience from the cell where he's imprisoned for murder, he laments that his whole life was like a jail which he could

never escape.

As the film states Vince's case, poverty and a broken home set the odds against him from the get-go. "I just tried to even things out a little," he says.

Employing documentary realism and appropriately gritty black & white photography, Loftis depicts Vince as a pragmatic survivalist, who keeps things going for his mother and kid brother by "getting paid" from purse snatching and other scams.

Somewhat redeemingly, Vince draws the line at drug dealing and discourages his brother from emulating him. At one point he's arrested and roughed up at the local precinct, but released when his victim declines to get further involved. Vince's tragic lack of self-control puts him under the spell of some bad characters, drawing him deeper into a life of crime.

The film suggests that Vince and his cohorts may have untapped potential. One of his gang, for example, is a skilled rapper lacking the ambition to develop his talent.

Loftis' keen ear for street argot is the best thing about a screenplay that's often weighed down with sociological clichés. "Small Time" comes alive in the tense, self-aggrandizing patter of its subjects. Two of the best moments occur when Vince and two cohorts in the "posse" plan a big job over lunch in a yuppie restaurant and in a schoolyard.

In both instances the filmmaker casts a harsh light on the psychological one-upmanship with which his subjects mask their wretched self-images.

Vince vents his insecurity-fed fury on his girlfriend (Carolyn Kinebrew) whom he treats with animal-like brutality in one wrenching, if overlong, sequence. The death of a buddy during a botched holdup disturbs him, but he lacks the will to take a new direction. Vince's involvement in a graphically rendered, senseless murder occurs with a grim inevitability.

"Small Time" is often performed too close to the edge of hysteria, and while Loftis' raw technique pays off in powerful moments it also produces disjointed awkward stretches. Cumulatively it's a pessimistic view of blighted lives in the inner city. — *Rich.*

CALUGA O MENTA
(TOFFEE OR MINT)
(CHILEAN)

An Arca-Filmcentro co-production with Spanish Television (TVE S.A.). Executive producer, Luis Justiniano. Directed by Gonzalo Justiniano. Screenplay, G. Justiniano with Gustavo Frías, Juan Andrés Peña; camera, Gastón Roca; editor, Claudio Martinez; music, Jaime de Aguirre; sound, Eugenio Gutierrez; production design, Hernán Cox; art direction, Francisco Cañete; associate producer, Carlos Tironi. Reviewed at the Rex II, Santiago, Dec. 12, 1990. Running time: **100 MIN.**
Niki . . . . Mauricio Vega
Nacho . . . . Aldo Parodi
Manuela . . . . . . Patricia Rivadeneira
Also with: Cecilia Godoy, Miriam Palacios, Luis Alarcón, Mauricio Pesutic.

Gonzalo Justiniano's "Caluga O Menta," one of the best of the year's seven Chilean features, is grabbing both good local b.o. and international fest exposure.

Pic returns to the subject of "Children Of The Cold War," one of the director's two previous films dealing with the frustration of young people in a grey environment. Focus was on the middle class last time; now it's on squalid tenement blocks.

Niki, Nacho and their friends have little to look forward to in the way of work or family life. Boredom has become a way of life, and petty crime is the only alternative. Their activities escalate to drug running.

In the last third of the pic, with the appearance of Manuela, the film abandons its tone of gritty realism and tends toward abstraction and metaphor that don't quite blend. A game of toffee or mint (life or death, heaven or earth) implies a choice, but in reality there is none. Justiniano does not attenuate his pessimism.

Technical credits are okay, and acting, partly by nonprofessionals, is mostly good. — *Amig.*

LA TAREA
(HOMEWORK)
(MEXICAN)

A Clasa Films Mundiales production. Executive producer, Lourdes Rivera. Produced by Pablo and Francisco Barbachano. Directed by Jaime Humberto Hermosillo. Screenplay, Hermosillo; camera (color), Tony Kuhn; songs, Luis Arcaraz, Los Hermanos Martínez Gil; sound, Nerio Barberis; art direction, Laura Santa Cruz. Reviewed at

the Museum of Modern Art, N.Y., Dec. 8, 1990. Running time: **121 MIN.**
Virginia . . . . María Rojo
Marcelo . . . . José Alonso

Filmed in just four days on one set, "Homework" is a clever exercise in filming from one perspective. Like Hitchcock's "Rope," it was made in long takes interrupted only by film changes, but this item's so risqué it may not find a distrib.

For her film class assignment, a student (María Rojo) decides to secretly film her ex-husband (José Alonso) making love to her. She invites him to her apartment and, with the camera hidden under a chair, she turns it on and the audience shares its point of view.

Hermosillo manages to keep things interesting despite the lack of camera movement. At one point, the ex-husband hangs his coat on the chair and the screen becomes black. Later, he tries to take her into the bedroom and she pushes him back into range.

Device becomes tiring occasionally, but Hermosillo adds some comic twists, including Alonso's growing suspicion ("I feel like someone is watching us").

Finally, he discovers the camera and is understandably upset. Rojo admits she thought of him partly because he doesn't turn off the lights during sex. Alonso's eventually forgives her and even manages to plug his burial business in her film.

Toward the end, the student filmmaker makes a speech about seeking revenge "using men as an object." Her motives didn't need to be spelled out so explicitly. Most of the time, though, Hermosillo keeps the tone light.

In a variation on "Sex, Lies And Videotape," the woman in "Homework" is the filmmaker and the man is the sex object. Hermosillo (director of "Doña Herlina And Her Son") first made a video of a man filming a woman. His low-budget film is more intriguing because of the role reversal.

Pic's nudity and sexual content will deter domestic distribs. It may be an experimental film, but many will consider it merely pornographic.

One of Mexico's leading filmmakers, Hermosillo prefers daring subject matter and is clearly unafraid of offending people. (Some walked out of the MoMA screening.) "Homework" may never reach a large audience,

but it's further proof of the director's ability to shock and amuse.
— *Stev.*

SURE FIRE

A Complex Corp. production. Produced by Henry S. Rosenthal. Written, directed and edited by Jon Jost. Camera (color), Jost; music, Erling Wold; sound, Alenka Sunday Pavlin. Reviewed at Toronto Festival of Festivals, Sept. 12, 1990. Running time: **86 MIN.**
Wes . . . . Tom Blair
Larry . . . . Robert Ernst
Bobbi . . . . Kristi Hager
Ellen . . . . Kate Dezina

Spare and disturbing, but with dark comic touches, "Sure Fire" will get a welcome reception on the fest scene, and, with proper handling, could break out to larger theatrical audiences.

Director Jon Jost's tale of a truculent patriarch businessman who brings disaster to his small world in rural Utah opens with a shot of two men sitting at a diner counter. The sequence starts with the camera at the base of their boots, gradually working up their backs, and then picks up their conversation as the sounds around them get louder.

It's as if the audience is intruding on a long chat between two townspeople. There's a feeling of spontaneity to the sparseness of the words and action, and most of the script, as such, was improvised.

The two men are local entrepreneur Wes (Tom Blair) and rancher-in-debt Larry (Robert Ernst). Wes is trying to cash in on the purity of air and land in Utah and sell houses to Californians fed up with their polluted lifestyles. Larry resists Wes' attempts to hoodwink him into his real estate schemes.

Characters unfold gradually, and Jost indulges in long takes of conversation.

There's not much of a plot, except in Wes' plans. Blair, with his shocking white blond hair, plays him as an autocratic, magnetic guy who gets entirely miffed when things don't go exactly as he planned.

Wes initiates his son into the rites of manhood by taking him on his first hunt. They go into the woods to shoot dear with Larry and another buddy. In a droll encounter before the hunt, Wes tries to seize the moment to tell the 16-year-old about sex, but he tells his dad he's learned it all at

school. In the next instant they have a terrible altercation, and on the hunt Wes cracks, resulting in stunning family tragedy.

Jost's camera embraces the gorgeous Utah countryside, but he uses the scenery in an unsettling way. The family discords underscore the country & western music, which swells to eerie tones. Jost runs quotations from Mormon texts across the screen in blood red at opportune times.

Acting by the core cast of four is solid and economical. Blair is appropriately on target as the charming authoritarian figure, using annoying clichés to make Wes funny, irritating and devoid of irony. He and Ernst take full advantage of the long takes to get into the rhythm of their characters.

"Sure Fire" is tough going at the start before the pace and tone are established, with many scenes changing hues and attitudes midway through them. But Jost gives the pic a lean and hungry look, and, like the work of David Lynch, taps into the noxious underbelly of the picturesque American landscape.
— *Devo.*

SLUMBER PARTY MASSACRE 3

A Concorde Pictures release. Produced by Catherine Cyran. Directed by Sally Mattison. Screenplay, Cyran; camera (Foto-Kem color), Jürgen Baum; editor, Tim Amyx; music, Jamie Sheriff; sound (Ultra-Stereo), Bill Robbins; production design, Stephanie Lytar; costume design, Sandra Araya Jensen; assistant director, Michele Weisler; production manager, Dean Jones, Starr Jones. Reviewed on Concorde vidcassette, N.Y., Dec. 27, 1990. MPAA Rating: R. Running time: **77 MIN.**
Jackie . . . . Keely Christian
Ken . . . . Brittain Frye
Morgan . . . . M.K. Harris
Duncan . . . . David Greenlee
Juliette . . . . Lulu Wilson
Maria . . . . Maria Ford
Diane . . . . Brandi Burkett
Janine . . . . Hope Marie Carlton
Sonia . . . . Maria Claire
  Also with: David Lawrence, Garon Grigsby, Devon Jenkin, Wayne Grace, Marta Kober.

Third entry in this slasher film series eschews the role reversal aspects of Amy Jones' superior 1982 original to focus repetitively on a driller killer. Pic has played theatrically since September.

Debuting helmer Sally Mat-

tison proves once again one doesn't have to be male to execute a sexist horror pic. By the final reel, when five full-bodied females are scurrying helplessly as the man wielding the phallic drill skewers them, even die-hard genre fans will be groaning in dismay.

Poorly scripted by producer Catherine Cyran, pic has almost no subtext to divert one's attention. After a beach volleyball intro, six young women (several played by older actresses) go to Keely Christian's house for a slumber party while her parents are away. Among the boys and men who arrive to pester them, killer Ken (Brittain Frye) is a handsome nutcase with a drill, apparently deranged due to child abuse at the hands of his cop uncle.

Except for t&a interludes in which Maria Ford and voluptuous Lulu Wilson (or perhaps her body double) strip for the other girls and camera, pic consists of the women running around the house being killed. Gore is plentiful but unimaginative.

Worse yet, drill-as-phallus image dating back to the original's infamous 1982 poster is overemphasized: Ken is impotent but has his handy drill.

Christian does her best with the inevitable worm-turns central role but the rest of the cast is wasted. Technical support is meager. — *Lor.*

SHAKMA

A Quest Entertainment release of a Hugh Parks production. Produced and directed by Parks. Co-director, Tom Logan. Screenplay, Roger Engle; camera (TVC color), Andrew Bieber; editor, Mike Palma; music, David C. Williams; sound (Ultra-Stereo), Carl Carden; art direction, Edward Bennett; costume design, Leslie Gilbertson; production manager-assistant director, Wally Parks; special makeup effects, Rick Gonzales; casting, Ashley Dane-Michael. Reviewed on Quest vidcassette, N.Y., Dec. 27, 1990. MPAA Rating: R. Running time: **101 MIN.**
Sam . . . . Christopher Atkins
Tracy . . . . Amanda Wyss
Kim . . . . Ari Meyers
Prof. Sorenson . . . . Roddy McDowall
Gary . . . . Robb Morris
Richard . . . . Greg Flowers
Bradley . . . . Tre Laughlin
Laura . . . . Ann Kymberlie
Brenda . . . . Donna Jarrett
Shakma the baboon . . . . . . Typhoon

Though overlong, "Shakma" is an effective horror pic about a killer baboon terrorizing youngsters during an acted-out "Dungeon & Dragons" type game. In regional release since

October it should satisfy genre vid fans.

Claustrophobic lensing at Universal Studios Florida fits the piece as Christopher Atkins and other budding doctors are trapped with experimental baboon Shakma (played by talented animal actor Typhoon) after hours in their research building. Meanwhile, their prof/gamemaster Roddy McDowall communicates with players via walkie talkies.

Bulk of film is the "Andromeda Strain" type suspense and horror as the players discover (some too late) that real-life violence has been substituted for the clues-and-moves game of trying to rescue the princess (beautiful co-worker Ari Meyers) from the sixth floor.

With agile physical stunts performed by Typhoon, the danger is made real, and directors Hugh Parks and Tom Logan keep the pic moving. Games with the baboon eventually become repetitious, however, and about a reel of cutting would have helped.

Script is surprisingly ruthless in killing off characters that normally would be saved at the last minute in a horror opus. Downbeat ending is heavy in irony.

Though characterization is kept to a minimum in favor of action/peril, cast does a good job with attractive youngsters like Atkins, Amanda Wyss and Meyers in the leads. Tech credits are serviceable on this modest-budgeted effort. — *Lor.*

REN, GUI, QING
(WOMAN, DEMON, HUMAN)
(CHINESE)

A Shanghai Film Studio production. Directed by Huang Shuqin. Screenplay, Huang, Li Ziyu, Song Guoxun; camera (color), Xia Lixing, Ji Hongsheng; music, Yang Mao, conducted by Wang Yongji; art director, Zheng Changfu. Reviewed at National Film Theater, London, Dec. 4, 1990. Running time: **104 MIN.**
With: Xu Shouli, Li Baotian, Pei Yanling, Gong Lin, Wang Feifei, Ji Qilin.

A Chinese backstage drama with a difference, "Woman, Demon, Human" is well-suited to Western palates. Flashback look at the lonely life of a Soochow Opera star is good fodder for specialist programs and tube outings, with sidebar feminist appeal.

Pic, shot in 1987 and released locally in spring 1988, has already had some fest slots but missed wider attention due to flashier "Red Sorghum," released at same time.

Abstract opening shows mature Qiu Yun (Xu Shouli) applying face paint for her most famous role, male demon Zhong Kui. Film then retraces her life through three periods — as a stagestruck moppet (played by Wang Feifei), feisty teenager (Gong Lin) and present-day star. Timespan is 1950s to '80s.

Sensitive script sidesteps most meller clichés, and matching of the three femmes in main role is spot on, physically and dramatically. Li Baotian stands out as the peasant dad who sacrifices himself for her first big break.

Middle-aged helmer Huang Shuqin, in her sixth pic, shows good visual control, especially in fantasy sequences with the Zhong Kui character. Music is neatly placed, and sharp color lensing tops. — *Drek.*

BLACKEYES
(BRITISH)

A Paravision Production in association with BBC. Produced by Rick McCallum. Written and directed by Dennis Potter. Camera (color), Andrew Duncan; editor, Clare Douglas, Michael Parker; music, Max Harris; production design, Geoff Powell; casting, Michele Guish. Reviewed at Toronto Festival of Festivals, Sept. 12, 1990. Running time: **98 MIN.**
Morris Kingsley . . . . Michael Gough
Shelly . . . . Carol Royle
Blackeyes . . . . Gina Bellman
Jeff . . . . Nigel Planer

Cryptic and elliptical as always, scriptwriter Dennis Potter delivers another stylish puzzler in "Blackeyes," his feature directing debut. Though there's much to admire, pic has limited arthouse possibilities and would work best on tv.

The film opens with a mystery: Who is the woman found dead near a pond? Writer Potter ("Pennies From Heaven") plays an intriguing game, mixing the lives of a fictional character, a model named Blackeyes (Gina Bellman), with an angry real-life woman (Carol Royle) whose life she claims an aging writer has based on hers.

That writer (Michael Gough) was her guardian from childhood and, she says quietly to the camera, he sexually abused her.

Blackeyes leads her own life, saying little, bedding down with an advertising exec after landing the poster job and keeping an interested neighbor (Nigel Planer) at a distance.

Her own feelings rarely come across, except during a country weekend when she is wrongly and laughingly blamed by the rich host and other models for leading on a man who is trying to bed her.

In several sequences, Gough reads the Blackeyes novel to an appreciative audience. He also appears in flashbacks as the guardian.

The picture is composed of layers of dizzying plot, abruptly punctuated by standard American pop tunes, all part of Potter's script trademark. Present, too, are naked mannequins in various apartments and rooms, inhabited or walked through by Blackeyes.

"Get me out of this story," Blackeyes cries a few times to the real-life woman who does not otherwise feature in her part of the story. Audiences will echo that remark as Potter fails to resolve his elaborate but ultimately noninvolving jigsaw, returning only to more mystery at the end.

Blackeyes and the real-life woman separately walk into the pond, yet only the real-life one is found dead, the latter one after killing the writer-guardian.

Director Potter's work is tight. Andrew Duncan's camerawork is stylish as are other production values. — *Adil.*

PANZIR
(SHELL)
(SOVIET-B&W)

A Sovexportfilm presentation of a Lenfilm Studios production. Produced by Mixhail Wawilow. Directed by Igor Alimpijev. Screenplay, Alimpijev, Piotr Koschewnikov; camera (black & white), Wladimir Iljin; sound, Artur Schichow. Reviewed at Toronto Festival of Festivals, Sept. 14, 1990. Running time: **90 MIN.**
With: Piotr Koschwnikow, Alexander Sporykin, Anna Bytschkowa.

In "Shell," a Soviet "thirty-something," a group of friends in Leningrad are trying to deal with life under perestroika and glasnost. But it's a somber, muddled time for both the young cast as well as the audience, who may not care enough about these people to flock to the wickets.

It's the first feature for Moscow Film School grad Igor Alimpijev, who uses his past docu film training here in counterpoint to the personal stories.

Wild seed Sanjan likes the Rolling Stones and Olya, sometime girlfriend of militiaman Oleg. Sanjan's father is drunk and dying, and the son has to deal with his paternal relationship in addition to trying to establish a substantive romantic tie.

The gang hangs out at Yasha's house, where all the old schoolmates drink, do drugs, listen to rock 'n' roll and sing political tunes. Beatles posters fill the room. A guitarist and violinist perform an inspired "Stairway To Heaven." The guys have chicken fights in the courtyard. Some members are working, some are contemplating careers, some are doing nothing.

It's the same crises younger people in Western countries had in the 1960s and 1970s, only this group is experiencing it in an environment topsy-turvy with liberal thinking. Alimpijev interjects docu interviews with people on the street to find out if they prefer life after glasnost.

The director uses no formal plot, just a series of individual and group portraits interspersed with surreal images and camerawork, some of which don't work: Men jump off a roof in angels' wings, vacant-looking people ride on interminable subway escalators, a turtle's face in closeup.

Cast works well as an ensemble, simultaneously conveying a feeling of disorientation, depression and hope. They want change, but don't have a clue as to the responsibilities of freedom. Sanjan and Oleg have a final personal confrontation, which also represents the clash between old and new Soviet values.

Alimpijev combines too many variant film techniques to give a solid base to his contemporary chronicle of confusion in his native country. — *Devo.*

A FLOR DE PIEL
(SKIN DEEP)
(PUERTO RICAN)

A Comisión Para los Asuntos de la Mujer-Zaga Films production. Executive producer, Roberto Gándara. Directed by Marcos Zúriñaga. Screenplay, Magaly Gracia Ramis; camera (color), Zúriñaga; editor, Gándara; music, Angel Cuco Peña; art direction, Julio Biaggi; production manager, Luis Collazo. Reviewed at IV Americas Festival, Washington, D.C., Oct. 28, 1990. Running time: **75 MIN.**
Cecilia Balseiro . . . Cordelia González
Alfredo . . . . Pablo Alarcon
Also with: Elia Enid Cadilla, Claribel Medina, René Monclova, Tony Chiroldes, Cladyo Aguayo.

Originally filmed in 35m for Puerto Rican tv and a few theatrical venues, Marcos Zúriñaga's third feature "A Flor de Piel" is an upbeat, well-paced quasidrama/in-house docu designed to inform viewers of the Puerto Rican Women's Commssion, pic's financier. Film may find offshore special interest following, especially among women's groups.

Eschewing a hard-line approach, pic is structured around the character of Cecilia Balseiro (Cordelia González), a p.r. rep hired by the commission to work on a docu to toast its 10th anni.

While the story revolves around Cecilia's professional and private life, especially her romantic interest with Alfredo (played by Argentine actor Pablo Alarcón), pic is interspersed with scenes of the women discussing possible themes for the documentary project.

Episode dealing with the battery of a neighbor has a quiet power, as does the subsequent discovery that it had been documented by an amateur video buff, complete with its suggestion of kinky peeping-Tom aspects.

Although pic's positive reinforcements tend to get gushy, overall softsell tone and decision to focus on fictional characterization maintain interest, and keep the film from straying into cliché territory. — *Lent.*

ON THE WIRE
(BRITISH-16M)

A National Film and Television School production. Produced by Laurie Borg. Written and directed by Elaine Proctor. Camera (Technicolor, 16m), Yoshi Tezuka; editor, David Freeman; music, Lucien Windrich, Eric Windrich; sound, Ben Young; production design-costume design, Carmel Collins; art direction, Ian White; assistant directors, Brett Turnbull, Tony Clarkson. Reviewed at 34th London Film Festival, Nov. 25, 1990. Running time: **85 MIN.**
Wouter Fourie . . . . . Michael O'Brien
Aletta Fourie . . Aletta Bezuidenhout
Lizzie . . . . Valerie Gozo
Dominee . . . . Laurens Seliye
Piet . . . . Gys de Villiers
Hannie . . . . Marie Human

This impressive first feature by South African-born writer-director Elaine Proctor may be low-budget and made by semi-professionals, but it beats many more expensive features both in form and content.

Production values are excellent with 16m photography that could be easily blown up to 35m. Television sales and festival screenings are likely and specialized theatrical exhibition is a maybe.

An Africaaner on the South African Defense Force and his wife live in a strict Calvinist community where sexual repression, tacit racism and religious fervor are commonplace. He is a good soldier who wants to turn his back on the ceaseless war against insurgency and start a family. He has also been implicated in the rape of a young black woman captured during a skirmish.

What he wants from his wife is not what she can naturally give him. But, throwing caution to the wind, she finally embarks with him upon a half-guilty sexual adventure. He is, however, fatally scarred by his experiences as a soldier and by his strict upbringing, and their newfound physical relationship turns horrifyingly sour.

Pic's message is that apartheid bites into the soul and destroys everything it touches, even their sexual freedom. The result is psychosis.

Such a film could have become hopelessly melodramatic or pretentious, but Proctor's handling of a difficult subject persuades otherwise. Both script and direction are sure, and the two central performances, particularly that of Aletta Bezuidenhout as the wife, are totally convincing. So is the atmosphere of the stifling community in which both are fatally enmeshed.

The film's purposes are not erotic, but the sex scenes are honest and give the film an emotional charge. "On The Wire" slowly but surely makes its point while also leaving some hope at the end.

Proctor had a good team around her, despite its lack of experience, and she is a new director of note. — *Malc.*

KANINMANNEN
(THE RABBIT MAN)
(SWEDISH)

A Sandrew Film release of Omega Film & Television AB production. Produced by Peter Kropeénin. Written and directed by Stig Larsson; camera (Eastmancolor), Andra Lasmanis; editor, Bengt Johansen; music, Dror Feiler; sound, Mats Lindskog; production design, Elsa Angeberg, Martin Jonsson; costume design, Nina Sandström; production manager, Maritha Norstedt. Reviewed at the Palladium, Malmö, Sweden, Aug. 30, 1930. Running time: **100 MIN.**
With: Börje Ahlfeldt, Leif Andrée, Stina Ekblad, Björn Gedda, Eva Engström, Domenika Posserén, Erika Ullenius, Krister Henrikson, Tomas Pontén, Sven Holm.

Stig Larsson's "The Rabbit Man" is a frugally produced but absorbing and intelligent closeup of a rapist, his wife and his father. Human insight and subtle performances will secure sales of this one worldwide, theatrically maybe, television definitely.

Paced with precision and a special kind of unhurried urgency, pic has a secondary suspense element to support an almost non-plot. The wife (Stina Ekblad) may have suspected that hubby (Leif Andrée) was seeking refuge or even revenge away from home for his humiliations as a teacher. At school he is regularly and physically mobbed by his pupils.

The teacher's father (Börje Ahlfeldt), a robust tv crime news anchorman with no close ties to his own family, stumbles on to the possibility of his son's double life by accident.

Clinging to their newborn baby, Ekblad locks her suspicions inside herself, but Ahlfeldt confronts his son. He is, of course, lied to, but the father cannot bring himself to go to the police. Still, he pursues the case, while Andrée goes on committing more crimes.

There is a subplot about the short shrift given some staffers when two tv services are forced to merge. This serves mostly to underline the newsman's insensitivity. When, in the end, he has to turn over his son to the cops, his hard shell has been softened.

In his second feature, young writer-helmer Larsson focuses on the agonies at work inside the three lead characters. In this he gets next to sublime support by Ahlstedt as the father, André as the son and Ekblad as wife, each one conveying minimalist expression to maximum effect.

A kind of happy ending with wife and dad visiting the rapist in an institution feels like a paste-on job. Moreover, suddenly blaming everything on the father is sociopsychological manipulation out of place in a film that otherwise lets art supply the truths. — *Kèll.*

CASANOVA
(DANISH)

A Kärne Film release of Per Holst Film Production in association with the Danish Film Institute. Produced by Per Holst. Directed by Morten Lorentzen. Screenplay, Bjarne Reuter, Lorentzen based on Reuter's novel; camera (Eastmancolor), Jan Richter-Friis; editor, Finn Henriksen, Kenneth Kainz, Morten Lorentzen; music, Frans Bak, Mek Pek & the All Rights; sound, Henrik (Gugge) Garnov; production design, Palle (Lunte) Arestrup; costumes, Pia Myrdal; production manager, Henriette Sörensen, Tatjana Kolvig. Reviewed at the Palads, Copenhagen, Dec. 5 1990. Running time: **75 MIN.**
Bertil . . . . Mek Pek
Hugo . . . . Allan Olsen
Uncle Albin . . . . Paul Hagen
Don Fefe . . . . Erik Paaske
Dr. Zulo . . . . Ole Fick
Fatman . . . . Steen Svare
Also with: Poul Bundgaard, Jörgen Kiil, Jesper Klein, Trine Dyrholm, Anja Jensen.

Although handsomely produced and rich in chuckle-raising asides, "Casanova" lacks originality in its plot maneuvering of high and low thieving among a Runyonesque cast of characters. **Fair domestic boxoffice is likely to be followed by steady ancillary business. Foreign audiences are less likely to be seduced.**

In "Casanova," producer Per Holst, enlisting screenwriter Bjarne Reuter (novelist of wit and high sales) and director Morten Lorentzen, clearly envisions the birth of a series to match Nordisk Film and Erik Balling's "Olsen Gang" concept, which led to 13 comedies topping Danish b.o. in 13 years and to successful cover versions in Sweden and Norway.

Repeat success is not assured. This film's title is the name of a huge diamond hidden in a wine bottle in a beauty box innocently lifted by two youngsters who know nothing of its contents. An Arab sheik, an Italian mafioso and a nice retired circus artist uncle take turns chasing (by car, balloon, etc.), stealing and losing bag, bottle and gem.

The uncle lives in a therapy room-speakeasy in an old people's home. This place is sketched in with fine baroque drollery.

Otherwise, run-of-mill devices of hit-and-run farce are delivered in mild-mannered and predictable ways without true snap and crackle. Jesper Klein has a fine cameo as an Indian taxi driver. — *Kell.*

BATTUTMATDIK YAN
(A FISHY STORY)
(HONG KONG)

A Golden Harvest release of a Bo Ho Films-Mobile Film production. Produced by Leonard Ho. Executive producer, Chan Puiwah. Directed by Antony Chan. Screenplay, Lo Wing-keung, Eddie Fong, Chan; camera (color), Peter Pao; editor, Yee Chun, Kwong Chi-leong; music, Richard Yuen; production design, William Szeto; costume design, Shirley Chan; associate producer, Alfred Cheung. Reviewed at 34th London Film Festival (Hong Kong Focus), Nov. 12, 1990. Running time: **99 MIN.**
Ah-chung . . . . Kenny Bee
Ah-chu . . . . Maggie Cheung
Mrs. Koo . . . . Josephine Koo
Paul Chen . . . . Antony Chan
Also with: Carrie Ng, Season Ma.

Miles removed from the normal run of Cantonese comedies, "A Fishy Story" is a slick period romance with a screwball flavor. Careful handling could build this into a cult item among offshore Asian buffs.

Pic is set in Hong Kong, 1967, but its retro look and style of playing has a '30s, Runyonesque feel to Yank eyes. He (Kenny Bee) is a hard-up cabbie with occasional toyboy biz from a rich socialite (Josephine Koo). She (Maggie Cheung) is a golddigging bimbo who can spot a diamond at 30 paces.

He's trying to buy his own cab, and she's trying to make it in the movies. They meet, spat and starve together. Meanwhile, the colony's in chaos from political demos overspilling from mainland China's cultural revolution.

Some of the funniest bits are parodies of commercial filmmaking of the time, including a show-stopping number that's a cross between "Big Spender" and "Irma La Douce."

Actor-director Antony Chan, a former drummer with local pop group the Wynners, knows his music. Use of Jerome Kern's "Smoke Gets In Your Eyes" and other numbers almost makes this a de facto musical sans words.

Playing and tech credits are high-style throughout, with special bows due to Cheung's Kowloon Baby and Peter Pao's atmospheric lensing. Film only did so-so biz ($HK7 million) on local release in 1989. — *Drek.*

JIT
(ZIMBABWEAN)

A Film Africa-Mukuvisi Film production. (Intl. sales: Gavin Film, London.) Produced by Rory Kilalea. Written and directed by Michael Raeburn. Camera (Fujicolor), Joao (Funcho) Costa; editor, Justin Krish; sound, Meskola; production design, Lindie Pankiv; assistant directors, Joel Phiri, Farai Sevenso. Reviewed at 34th London Film Festival, Nov. 16, 1090. Running time: **92 MIN.**
With: Dominic Makuvachuma, Sibongile Nene, Farai Sevenzo, Oliver Mtukudzi, Winnie Ndemera, Lawrence Simbarashe, Kathy Kuleya, Jackie Eeson.

Few films shot in Africa with a black cast and a white director have come so near to the traditional African-style comedy as "Jit," a lively and charming story that should appeal to audiences intrigued by African life and seeking something defiantly different.

Set in Zimbabwe (where the helmer Michael Raeburn was brought up), "Jit" concerns a country boy who seeks his fortune in Nairobi, falls in love with a beautiful but probably unobtainable girl and hurls himself into the task of raising the high bride-price her greedy father demands.

Preferring a rich suitor, she is at first uninterested in the poor young man, but gradually he convinces her that anyone with his tenacity just might make a good husband. Besides, her original boyfriend turns out to be a crook.

The comedy's fantasy edge is supplied by the boy's traditional Jukwa or guiding spirit, an old woman who appears and disappears throughout the film, either chiding or helping him. The Jukwa wants him to send money home to his village, return there and forget his romance. But if he supplies her with liberal doses of the local beer, she may help him get his girl first.

The film has its rough edges, but lensing is generally professional, with a fast and furious pace developing as the boy's various strategems succeed or fail.

One of the film's bull points is its catchy and authentic music by some of Zimbabwe's foremost bands. The title is taken from the Shona words "jiti" and "jikiti," meaning to dance and jump up and down.

"Jit" has been satisfactorily blown up from 16m to 35m and looks as colorful as its story, the moral of which is that the traditional African lifestyle allows for more rule-breaking than some suspect.

It is difficult to believe that the cast is all amateurs. The acting is natural, particularly from Dominic Makuvachuma as the youth and Sibongile Nene, who makes a strikingly beautiful heroine. Winnie Ndemera, a retired teacher, is the jukwa, clad in animal skins and beads.

Pic may have limited ambitions, and sometimes Raeburn's direction unnecessarily camps things up with quick-motion and similar devices. But it's great fun, matching the spirit of its catchy music and an entertaining effort all around. — *Malc.*

LET THE MUSIC DANCE
(DUTCH)

A Concorde Film release of a Minimal Movies Europe production. Executive producer, Sherman de Jesus. Directed by Pim de la Parra. Screenplay, de la Parra, Paul Ruven; camera (color, Fuji), Tom Erisman; editor, Marc Nolens; music, Ake Danielson; sound, Ed van Baaren; production design, de la Parra; assistant director, Ruven. Reviewed at the Movies, Amsterdam, Sept. 4, 1990. Running time: **93 MIN.**
Adam Adamus . . Boudewijn de Groot
Alexandra Kuipers . Eugenie Schellen
Dana Steele . . . . . Bonnie Williams
Maurits Dahlberg . . Marc Hazewinkel
Bijou . . . . Ingrid Willemse
Zep Friday . . . . . . Pim de la Parra
Hannah Friday . . . . . Hedda Oledsky

Another minimal film by Pim de la Parra, "Let The Music Dance" is a good-humored opus with plenty of gags, characters in various stages of undress, zany music and sex. Pic could fare well at the Dutch b.o. and wherever people will pay to see onscreen romps from bed to bed and song to song.

The European Commission commissions a European hymn from pop and ballad musician (well played by former Dutch ballad king Boudewijn de Groot). He has a deadline, but no team, no singer and no idea. What he does have is too many women.

With just a five-day shooting sked, film's improvised throughout. De la Parra also performs in the pic, so assistant director Paul Ruven came in for much work.

The cast, not always knowing what to do next, acts well. The camera adapts with gusto to the mixture of styles and to the different lighting.

Pic has so many gags and good ideas that they sometimes jostle each other off the screen. De la Parra's concentration on male sex organs and the roofs of Amsterdam (both seen from above) has not diminished. — *Wall.*

FEIYUT WONGFAN
(BEYOND THE SUNSET)
(CHINESE)

A Sil-Metropole Organization presentation of a Dream Factory production. Executive producer, Kenny Fan. Directed by Jacob C.L. Cheung. Screenplay, Cheung, Chan Kam-cheung; camera (color), Lei Kin-keung; editor, Cheung Siu-hung; music, Chan Wing-leung; production design, Yank Wong; assistant director, Terrence Fok, Lo Kit-yin; associate producer, Barry M.K. Chung. Reviewed at 34th London Film Festival (Hong Kong Focus), Nov. 22, 1990. Running time: **115 MIN.**
Pearl . . . . Cecilia Yip
Her mother . . . . Fong Bo-bo
Wong . . . . Richard Ng
Allen, Pearl's husband . . . Lowell Lo
Derek . . . . Alexander Roels

This quiet study of the strained relationship between a middle-aged widow and her prodigal daughter is a welcome relief from most Hong Kong actioners. Despite a melodramatic finale, it could fit snugly into fest slots or specialist webs.

Story follows westernized Pearl

(Cecilia Yip) as she returns from California with young son Derek to visit the mom (Fong Bo-bo) she left years earlier. After patching things up, Pearl sets about engineering a romance between mom and Wong (Richard Ng), a swimming coach who's an old friend.

It's a character piece first and foremost, with a gentle line in comedy to lard the more serious stuff. Tone recalls Cantonese dramas of the 1950s, with the added clash of generational values and, until the end, emotions aren't allowed to run amok.

With a solid script to work from, young helmer Jacob C.L. Cheung (31) gives plenty of rein to his experienced cast. Former juve Yip gives evidence of a relaxed, maturing talent in the role of the daughter, and w.k. vets Fong and Ng are cleverly cast to play off against her.

Tech credits are solid all around. It's only Cheung's second pic, after striking gold with the Sammo Hung-starrer, "Lai Shi, China's Last Eunuch," finally released in 1988. "Beyond The Sunset" sank like a stone ($HK4.3 million) on local release in mid-1989, but garnered good reviews on the way down. — *Drek.*

ODORE DI PIOGGIA
(THE SCENT OF RAIN)
(ITALIAN)

A DAC release of a Mediterranea film production. Produced and directed by Nico Cirasola. Screenplay, Cirasola, Tommaso Di Ciaula; camera (color), Lorenzo Fiore; editor, Alessandra Consoli; music, Nino Lepore; art direction, Elia Canestrari. Reviewed at the Brazilian Study Center, Rome, Dec. 10, 1990. Running time: **92 MIN.**
Toto . . . . Toto Onnis
The American woman . . . .
. . . . Agnete Vossgard
Toto's father . . . . . . Mario Mancini
Toto's mother . . . . . Grazia Daddario
   Also with: Frank Lino, Claudia Criesmayer, Renzo Arbore, Gianni Colaiemma, Mino Barbarese, Teodosio Barresi, Ferdinando Nictoera, Digeo Verdegiglio, Gianni Pellegrino, Elia Canestrari, Clelia Logoluso, Nico Cirasola, Vito Riviello.

Filmmaker Nico Cirasola has taken a lighthearted, satirical look at a provincial poet's daily doings and dreams, but the pace is slow and the humor heavy-handed. Released in 1989, pic has thus far been confined to small festivals and is not likely to go beyond.

A plotless series of disjointed comic vignettes of small town life in the south of Italy serves as backdrop to the yearnings of an unemployed, enthusiastic young poet (Toto Onnis).

Son of the local station master (Mario Mancini), Toto lives near the railroad tracks where the clatter of trains and his parents' nagging interfere with sleeping late.

When not napping, Toto tools about the countryside on a motorcycle and visits with village characters, including the town barber (Italy's top tv satirist Renzo Arbore, in a cameo bit).

He fantasizes about a blonde angel/muse (Claudia Criesmayer), and dallies with the dissatisfied spouse (Agnete Vossgard) of an U.S. serviceman. He also expounds his poetry and longs for a place where his talents would be appreciated.

To helmer Cirasola's credit, he pokes fun at his poet-protagonist and doesn't take Toto much more seriously than do the despairing father and mocking townfolk.

Lead actor Onnis also seems to have his tongue firmly in cheek, but Cirasola is basically sympathetic to his hero's poetic and romantic aspirations and grants him a happy ending: Toto heads off by train for the north — with the pretty muse aboard — to receive a literary prize.

Pic's lackadaisical pace might mean to convey the boredom and banality of a provincial backwater, but more likely reflects lack of comic and cinematic inspiration on Cirasola's part.

The strong regional dialect spoken by the characters, although a possible humorous plus for Italo audiences, will be lost on foreign viewers. — *Led.*

ARCHIVE REVIEW

LE JOUEUR D'ECHECS
(THE CHESS PLAYER)
(FRENCH)

A La Société des Films Historiques production (1926). Directed by Raymond Bernard. Screenplay, Bernard, Jean-José Frappa, from a novel by Henry Dupuy-Mazuel; camera (black & white), Joseph-Louis Mundviller, Marc Bujard, Willy Faktorovitch; music, Henri Rabaud; art direction, Jean Perrier, Eugene Carré; costume design, Eugène Lourié, René Decrais; assistant directors, Jean Hemard, Lily Jumel; special effects, W. Percy Day. Reviewed at Dominion theater, London, Dec. 7, 1990. Running time: **133 MIN.**
Boleslas Vorowski . . Pierre Blanchar
Baron von Kempelen . . Charles Dullin
Sophie Novinska . . . . Edith Jehanne
Major Nicolaieff . . . . . Camille Bert
Prince Oblomoff . . . . Pierre Batcheff
Catherine II . .Marcelle Charles-Dullin
   Also with: Jacky Monnier, Armand Bernard, Alexiane, Pierre Hot, James Devesa, Fridette Fatton, Albert Préjean, Pierre de Canolle, Boris de Fast, Laurent Morlas, Pierre Mindaist.

Lauded locally at the time, Raymond Bernard's "The Chess Player" (1926) dusts off as an interesting example of Gallic megabuck productions of the time. It's no "Napoleon" and script and thesping are mostly routine, but offbeat elements and a strong score make this item worthwhile.

Pic was the second outing for indie La Société des Films Historiques, set up in 1923 with the aim of mapping French history in a series of big productions. "The Chess Player" (nothing to do with French history) was lensed from March to October 1926 on a budget of 6 million francs. The film preemed on Jan. 6, 1927, at Salle Marivaux, Paris, for a three-month run.

This sabre-and-breeches yarn opens in Vilnius, 1776, with Poles under the Russo yoke. First seg, "The Song Of Independence" (69 minutes), shows local patriot Boleslas crippled in an abortive uprising. Second part, "The Great Deception" (64 minutes), has him hiding inside a mechanical chess-playing automaton invented by crafty Baron von Kempelen, and carted off to the court of Catherine II in St. Petersburg.

Story (refilmed in 1938 with Conrad Veidt as von Kempelen) can also be read as an allegory for Jewish oppression. Original camera neg was confiscated by Nazis during World War II, and Bernard, a Jew, spent the war in hiding. He died in Paris in 1977.

Script, from a novel by Henry Dupuy-Mazuel (1885-1962), is based on events and characters of the time: The baron and his automaton actually existed, the latter later revealed as a hoax. Theme gives rise to pic's best moments, with von Kempelen a cross between the loony robot-inventor of "Metropolis" (in production at same time) and the cobbler from Grimms' fairy tales.

Scenes in his studio, controlling life-size automata, have a ghostly feel, heightened by Henri Rabaud's music. A later climax has a squad of robot soldiers hacking a traitor to death, shot and scored like a jerky, horror *ballet mécanique.*

Script's problem is there's too much going on and no sense of overall dramatic line. Continuity is jumpy, with the automaton stuff taking precedence in part two over the various political and romantic subplots. Courtly comic bits leaven the drama, but ultimately get in the way.

Other setpieces still impress, notably the battle climaxing part one, re-imagined by heroine Sophie as a victory for the Poles. Lensing here and in later snow scenes in snappy. But apart from a long opening track through nighttime Vilnius, the rest is mostly fixed-tripod stuff.

Top of the thesp stakes is legit star Charles Dullin as the baron, with a nice line in wily comedy. Pierre Blanchar is okay as the gaunt patriot Boleslas, though he has little to do in part two. Edith Jehanne is soupy-eyed as Sophie.

Restoration by the U.K.'s National Film Archive from three nitrate sources is fine, with two-tone tinting (ochre and blue) throughout. Print preemed in London Dec. 7 under the Thames Silents banner, with Carl Davis conducting Rabaud's original score played by a 40-piece orchestra and with newly translated Anglo intertitles.

Further shows are skedded in Luxembourg and Paris for the centenary of Bernard's birth in 1991. — *Drek.*

INDEX

A

B

Back to the Future, Part III 5-23-90
Backstreet Dreams 10-8-90
Bad Blood 5-10-89
Bad Influence 3-14-90
Bad Jim 4-25-90
Bail Jumper 3-7-90
Baisers de secours, Les (Emergency Kisses) 9-6-89
Bakenbardy (Sideburns) 11-12-90
Bal du Governeur, Le (The Governor's Party) 12-3-90
Bal poussiere (Dusty Ball) 8-16-89
Ballad of Yellow River, The 4-25-90
Ban (The House) 3-15-89
Banana Shoot 3-15-89
Bananen - Skral Den For Din Nabo (Banana Busters)
 12-3-90
Bande des quatre, La (Band of Four) 3-1-89
Bankomatt 3-15-89
Bapteme (Baptism) 9-13-89
Barbare, La (The Savage) 7-26-89
Barrela 4-25-90
Barroco (Baroque) 5-24-89
Bashu, the Little Stranger 7-25-90
Basket Case 2 3-7-90
Basta! Ci Faccio un Film (That's Enough! Let's Make a
 Film) 9-17-90
Bat Leung Gam (Eight Taels of Gold) 11-26-90
Batman 6-14-89
Battutmatdik Yan (A Fishy Story) 12-31-90
Baxter 4-5-89
Bearskin: An Urban Fairytale 12-20-89
Beautiful Dreamers 3-28-90
Because of That War 11-1-89
Beeld van een kind (Image of a Child) 6-21-89
Beiquing Chengshi (A City of Sadness) 9-20-89
Bella de La Alhambra, La (The Belle of the Alhambra)
 3-7-90
Benim Sinemelarim (My Cinemas) 5-9-90
Berkeley in the Sixties 10-1-90
Berlin Jerusalem 9-13-89
Berlin um die Ecke (Berlin Around the Corner) 3-28-90
Bert Rigby, You're a Fool 3-1-89
Best of the Best 11-8-89
Bethune: The Making of a Hero 9-10-90
Betsy's Wedding 6-27-90
Beverly Hill Brats 10-11-89
Beverly Hills Vamp 11-8-89
Beyond El Rocco 4-11-90
Beyond the Doors 11-22-89
Beyond the Ocean 5-30-90
Big Bang, The 9-20-89
Big Dis, The 2-15-89
Big Man on Campus 5-17-89
Big Man, The 9-3-90
Big Picure, The 2-8-89
Big Steal, The 5-30-90
Bill & Ted's Excellent Adventure 2-22-89
Bille en tete (Headstrong) 7-26-89
Bingo 6-13-90
Biotexnia Oneiron (Dream Factory) 11-19-90
Bird on a Wire 5-16-90
Black Eagle 1-18-89
Black Lights, White Shadows 9-13-89
Black Rain 9-20-89
Black Roses 1-18-89
Black Snow 4-25-90
Blackeyes 12-31-90
Blackjack 11-5-90
Blankt Vapen (At Swords' Points) 10-15-90
Blauaugig (Blue Eyes) 9-20-89
Blaze 12-13-89
Blind Fear 11-29-89
Blind Fury 7-26-89

Blinde Ohr der oper, Das (The Blind Ear of Opera) 3-7-90
Blood & Sand 5-24-89
Blood Clan 10-1-90
Blood Oath 6-6-90
Blood Red 4-11-90
Blood Reincarnation 4-12-89
Blood Salvage 8-22-90
Bloodfist 10-18-89
Bloodhounds of Broadway 6-7-89
Bloodmoon 4-11-90
Bloodstone 5-10-89
Blowing Hot & Cold 5-31-89
Blueberry Hill 4-5-89
Boca de Oro (Golden Mouth) 6-20-90
Boda Secreta (Secret Wedding) 9-27-89
Body Chemistry 3-14-90
Bois noirs, Les (Dark Woods) 9-6-89
Bonfire of the Vanities, The 12-24-90
Book of Love 5-23-90
Boom Boom 7-4-90
Boris Godunov 12-6-89
Born on the Fourth of July 12-20-89
Botta di vita, Una (A Taste of Life) 1-18-89
Boulevards d'Afrique 3-15-89
Bounty Hunter, The 11-8-89
Boys in the Island 5-23-90
Breaking In 5-24-89
Brenda Starr 5-17-89
Bright Angel 9-3-90
Brothers in Arms 4-12-89
Brown Bread Sandwiches 9-27-89
Bruch, Der (The Break) 3-1-89
Bruch, Der (The Break) 9-6-89
Brun Bitter (Hair of the Dog) 3-8-89
Bryllupsfesten (The Wedding Party) 8-30-89
Bulen (The Bump) 4-18-90
Bullet in the Head 11-12-90
Bullet in the Head, A 11-19-90
Bumashnyie Glasa Prischvina (Prischvin's Paper Eyes)
 3-21-90
Bumerang - Bumerang (Boomerang Boomerang) 3-7-90
Bun Ngo Tsong Tinngai (Wild Search) 12-3-90
Bunker Palace Hotel 6-28-89
Buon Natale, Buon Anno/Joyeux Noel, Bonne Annee
 (Merry Christmas, Happy New Year) 3-7-90
Burbs, The 2-22-89
Butter brot (Bread & Butter) 3-14-90
Butun Kapilar Kapaliydi (All the Doors Were Closed)
 5-23-90
Buying Time 5-24-89
Bye Bye Baby 7-26-89
Bye Bye Blues 9-6-89

C

Cadence 11-5-90
Cadillac Man 5-16-90
Cafe des Jules, Le (The Guys in the Cafe) 8-2-89
Cage 9-13-89
Caged Fury 4-4-90
Caidos del Cielo (Fallen from the Sky) 9-17-90
Caluga o Menta (Toffee or Mint) 12-31-90
Cameron's Closet 4-12-89
Camille Claudel 1-4-89
Camino Largo a Tijuana, El (The Long Road to Tijuana)
 8-30-89
Campagne de Ciceron, La (Cicero's Country) 5-2-90
Cannibal Women in the Avocado Jungle of Death 2-22-89

D

E

G

H

K

L

M

Mielott befejezi roptet a denever (Before the Bat's Flight Is Done) 2-22-89
Mighty Quinn, The 2-15-89
Mijn vader woont in Rio (My Father Lives in Rio) 6-21-89
Milagro en Roma (Miracle in Rome) 1-18-89
Milan noir (Black Milan) 1-18-89
Mille et un nuits, Les (The 1,001 Nights) 5-2-90
Millenium 8-23-89
Miller's Crossing 9-3-90
Mind Games 8-23-89
Mindfield 5-2-90
Mindwalk 9-10-90
Ming-Yueh Chi-Shih Yuan (Autumn Moon) 11-26-90
Ministry of Vengeance 11-15-89
Miraklet i Valby (Miracle in Valby) 8-30-89
Mirror, Mirror 5-30-90
Miserables, Les 7-26-89
Misery 11-26-90
Misplaced 4-26-89
Miss Firecracker 4-19-89
Miss Right 1-4-89
Missing Link 7-19-89
Mister Frost 5-2-90
Mixwix 3-7-90
Mo' Better Blues 8-1-90
Mob Story 10-25-89
Modern Love 6-13-90
Moitie-moitie (Fifty-Fifty) 4-5-89
Mona et Moi (Mona & I) 9-6-89
Monde Sans Pitie, Un (A World Without Pity) 9-27-89
Money Tree, The 10-29-90
Mono Loco, El (The Mad Monkey) 9-13-89
Montalvo et l'enfant (Montalvo & the Child) 5-24-89
Montoyas y Tarantos 7-26-89
Moody Beach 9-17-90
Morgan's Cake 2-8-89
Morphine & Dolly Mixtures 12-10-90
Mortal Passions 10-18-89
Motel 2-1-89
Motion & Emotion 9-17-90
Motivsuche (Location Research) 10-8-90
Movie in Your Face 5-23-90
Moya Babushka (My Grandmother) 4-26-89
Mr. & Mrs. Bridge 9-10-90
Mr. Destiny 10-15-90
Mr. Hoover & I 4-18-90
Mr. Johnson 10-1-90
Muerte Inutil de Mi Socio Manolo (The Useless Death of My Pal Manolo) 11-5-90
Murder Story 8-9-89
Murphy's Fault 1-18-89
Music for Old Animals 10-25-89
Musicians in Exile 9-17-90
Mutant on the Bounty 9-27-89
Mutants in Paradise 12-20-89
Muzh i doch Tamari Alexandrovni (Tamara Alexandrovna's Husband & Daughter) 9-27-89
My Blue Heaven 8-22-90
My Left Foot 8-23-89
My Mom's a Werewolf 5-17-89
My Name Is Bertolt Brecht - Exile in U. S. A. 3-29-89
Mystery Train 5-17-89

N

Nacion Clandestina, La (The Secret Nation) 10-11-89
Naga Bonar 2-22-89

Naked Tango 10-29-90
Nam Angels 7-19-89
Nama-ye Nazdik (Close-Up) 3-7-90
Naplo Apamnak, Anyammnak (Diary for My Father and Mother) 9-10-90
Narrow Margin 9-17-90
Nash Dvor (Our Courtyard) 4-29-89
Natalia 6-21-89
National Lampoon's Christmas Vacation 12-6-89
Navy Seals 7-18-90
Nayakan (Hero) 2-22-89
Ne reveillez pas un flic qui dort (Let Sleeping Cops Lie) 1-18-89
Near Death 10-11-89
Necromancer 4-12-89
Nel Giardino delle Rose (Age of Discretion) 9-17-90
Nerds of a Feather 5-9-90
Neurotic Cabaret 10-29-90
Never Leave Nevada 9-24-90
Never on Tuesday 8-2-89
Neverending Story, The II: The Next Chapter 10-29-90
New Year's Day 5-3-89
New York Stories (includes Life Lessons, Life Without Zoe & Oedipus Wrecks) 3-1-89
Next of Kin 10-25-89
Nezna revoluce (The Gentle Revolution) 3-7-90
Ngon Den Trong Mo (The Light at the End of the Dream) 9-24-90
Nie im Leben (Never Ever) 11-12-90
Night Angel 5-30-90
Night Club 5-23-90
Night Game 9-20-89
Night Life 5-31-89
Night of the Living Dead 10-22-90
Night Visitor (Never Cry Devil) 5-24-89
Nightmare at Noon 4-18-90
Nightmare on Elm Street 5, A: The Dream Child 8-9-89
Nightmare Sisters 8-30-89
Nijusseiki Shonen Dokuhon (Circus Boys) 9-13-89
Nikita 3-21-90
Nine-Seven-Six EVIL 3-29-89
Nineteen Ninety-nine - Nen No Natsu Yasumi (Summer Vacation: 1999) 3-22-89
Ninja Academy 8-1-90
Nino de la Luna, El (The Moon Child) 5-10-89
Nirvana Street Murder 6-27-90
No Apologies 11-26-90
No Daireikai II (Big Spirit World II) 3-28-90
No Holds Barred 5-24-89
No Justice 11-8-89
No Matsuri, Ume (A Festival of Dreams) 10-4-89
No More Boomerang 1-18-89
No Retreat, No Surrender II 2-1-89
No Safe Haven 10-4-89
Nobody's Perfect 5-24-89
Noce blanche (White Wedding) 12-20-89
Noces de papier, Les (A Paper Wedding) 4-11-90
Noch Ein Wunch (One More Wish) 8-30-89)
Noche Oscura, La (The Dark night) 3-1-89
Nocturne 5-30-90
Nocturne indien (Indian Nocturnal) 8-23-89
Noiembrie, Ultimul Bal (November, The Last Ball) 10-4-89
Non Ou a Va Gloria de Mandar (No, or the Vain Glory of Command) 5-23-90
Norman's Awesome Experience 11-1-89
Notater om Korlighedon (Notes on Love) 10-4-89
Nouvelle Vague (New Wave) 5-23-90
Nowhere to Run 9-27-89
Nuit d'Ete en Ville (Summer Night in Town) 9-3-90
Nuit de l'eclusier, La (The Night of the Sluice Guard) 3-29-89

Nunca Estuve en Viena (I've Never Been to Vienna) 8-2-89
Nuns on the Run 3-14-90
Nutcracker Prince, The 11-19-90

O

O Grande Mentecapto (The Blissful Misfit) 5-31-89
O Re (The King of Naples) 3-15-89
O Sangue (The Blood) 9-20-89
Obsession: A Taste for Fear 4-12-89
Occultist, The 10-18-89
Ochlim Lokshim 4-5-89
Odore di Pioggia (The Scent of Rain) 12-31-90
Odpadnik (Maverick) 3-1-89
Of Men & Angels 2-8-89
Offerings 6-28-89
Office Party 1-4-89
Oh Babylon 3-29-89
Oiji (Mr. Canton & Lady Rose) 12-13-89
Old Explorers 10-29-90
Old Gringo 5-24-89
Olga Robards 11-29-89
On the Block 6-13-90
On the Make 6-28-89
On the Wire 12-31-90
Onde Bate o Sol (Where the Sun Beats Down) 9-27-89
One Hundred Two Boulevard Haussmann 11-19-90
One Man Force 8-9-89
Ongedaan gedaan (Deed Undone) 6-21-89
Ongeshreven geshiedenis, Een (An Unwritten History)
    1-18-89
Opportunity Knocks 3-28-90
Opstand in Sobibor (Revolt in Sobibor) 10-11-89
Options 5-10-89
Orchestre rouge, L' (The Red Orchestra) 11-29-89
Order of the Eagle 7-5-89
Ori 12-13-89
Ostatni Prom (The Last Ferry) 5-30-90
Otets Sergey (Father Sergius) 4-18-90
Othello 5-31-89
Otokowa Tsuraiyo Torajiro Sarada Kinenki (Tora-San's
    Salad-Day Memorial) 12-6-89
Otokowa Tsuraiyoo Toraijiro Kokoro no Tabiji (Tora-san
    Goes to Vienna) 11-15-89
Otto - Der Ausserfriesische 10-11-89
Out Cold 2-15-89
Out of the Dark 5-3-89
Out of Time 5-31-89
Out on Bail 8-30-89
Outback 6-14-89
Outlaw of Gor 4-12-89
Outremer (Overseas) 5-30-90
Overexposed 4-23-90

P

Pacific Heights 10-1-90
Pacific Palisades 4-18-90
Package, The 8-23-89
Paganini 5-17-89
Palanquin des larmes, Le (The Palanquin of Tears) 1-4-89
Palombella Rossa (Red Lob) 9-27-89

Panama Sugar 4-25-90
Panzir (Shell) 12-31-90
Papa est parti, maman aussi (Daddy's Gone, & Mom, Too)
    3-29-89
Papeles Secundarios (Supporting Roles) 10-11-89
Paper Mask 5-30-90
Paperitahti (Paper Star) 3-7-90
Parenthood 8-2-89
Parents 1-25-89
Paris by Night 3-1-89
Paris Is Burning 10-15-90
Party Incorporated (Party Girls) 5-10-89
Pas de repit pour Melanie (The Case of the Witch Who
    Wasn't) 6-27-90
Pasion de Hombre (A Man of Passion) 5-31-89
Passport 6-13-90
Peacemaker 6-20-90
Peaux de Vaches (Thick Skinned) 10-4-89
Pekin Teki Suikaz (Beijing Watermelon) 3-28-90
Penn & Teller Get Killed 9-13-89
Penny Ante - The Motion Picture 9-24-90
Pension Sonnenschein (Pension Sunshine) 10-15-90
Pepi, Luci, Bom y Otras Chicas del Montan (Pepi, Luci,
    Bom & the Other Girls) 12-3-90
Pere et passe, Un (Fathers) 9-27-89
Perfect Model, The 4-12-89
Perfect World 4-18-90
Perfume of the Cyclone 5-30-90
Perigord noir (Black Perigord) 7-26-89
Periodes met zon (Sunny Spells) 10-11-89
Personal Choice 5-31-89
Pervii Etage (Ground Floor) 5-30-90
Pestalozzis Berg (Pestalozzi's Mountain) 3-1-89
Pet Sematary 4-19-89
Petite voleuse, La (The Little Thief) 1-25-89
Peuple singe, Le (The Ape People) 5-10-89
Phantom Empire, The 8-9-89
Phantom of Death 1-18-89
Phantom of the Mall 5-31-89
Phantom of the Opera, The 11-8-89
Philippines, My Philippines 1-4-89
Philosoph, Der (The Philosopher) 3-15-89
Phoenix Mysterie, Het (The Phoenix Mystery) 10-15-90
Physical Evidence 1-25-89
Piano Panier 8-16-89
Piccoli equivoci (Little Misunderstandings) 5-31-89
Pictures at the Beach 10-15-90
Pikovaya dama (The Queen of Spades) 3-21-90
Pink Cadillac 5-31-89
Piravi (Birth) 8-16-89
Piravi 2-8-89
Piroska es a farkas (Bye Bye Red Riding Hood) 2-22-89
Plaff 1-4-89
Plan Delta 3-22-89
Play Me Something 3-22-89
Plein fer (Full Steel) 5-30-90
Pleure pas My Love (Don't Cry, My Love) 1-18-89
Plot Against Harry, The 9-13-89
Pod Nebom Golubym... (Under a Sky of Blue...) 11-12-90
Point of View 5-23-90
Pol 3-8-89
Police Academy 6: City under Siege 3-15-89
Polizei 3-15-89
Ponedelnik Soutrin (Monday Morning) 3-22-89
Pont de Varsovia (Warsaw Bridge) 5-23-90
Porno 5-30-90
Porte aperte (Open Doors) 5-9-90
Portion d'eternite (Looking for Eternity) 9-13-89
Porttikielto taivaasen (Banned from Heaven) 6-6-90
Posed for Murder 5-31-89
Posetitel Muzeia (Visitor to a Museum) 8-2-89
Positiv (Positive) 3-14-90

T

U

V

W

X

Y

Z

Zabij Mnie, Glino (Kill Me, Cop) 3-22-89
Zadar! Cow from Hell 2-8-89
Zaman-e az Dast rafteh (Last Time) 3-7-90
Zanzibar 5-24-89
Zazie 9-20-89
Zeit der Rache (Time of Vengeance) 11-5-90
Zena s Krajolikom (Landscape with a Woman) 10-15-90

Zengin Mutfagi (The Kitchen of the Rich) 5-17-89
Zilch 5-24-89
Zui Hou De Feng Kuang (Desperation: The Last Frenzy) 5-31-89
Zuvies Diena (Fish Day) 11-19-90
Zvlastni Bytosti (Strange Beings) 11-12-90
Zwerfsters (Wayfarers) 6-21-89